COMICS VALUES ANNUAL

2000 EDITION

THE COMIC BOOK PRICE GUIDE

by Alex G. MALLOY

edited by Stuart W. Wells III
features editor: Robert J. Sodaro

© 2000 by

Alex G. Malloy & Stuart W. Wells III

Published by

Antique Trader Books, a division of

700 E. State Street • Iola, WI 54990-0001
Telephone: 715/445-2214

Please call or write for our free catalog of publications.
Our toll-free number to place an order or obtain a free catalog is 800-258-0929 or please use
our regular business telephone 715-445-2214 for editorial comment and further information.

Designed by Stuart W. Wells III
Cover art by Mike Mignola

ISBN: 1-58221-020-9

Printed in the United States of America

CONTENTS

The Continuing Saga:
FORWARD TO THE MILLENNIUM

By Alex Malloy

Ah here we are, chasing down the end of the second millennium.

Now, before any of you get your shorts in a knot, let's review a little bit of math. You have 1,000 coins when? Of course, when you have 1,000 of them, not 999. So, as this book is shipping in the year 2000, this book is, not the first CVA of the new millennium (the 21st century), but rather the final CVA book of the 20th century. This is why the classic science fiction movie was titled *2001: A Space Odyssey*, not 2000—because it occurred in the 21st not the 20th century.

So, to all of you who think that the new millennium began on Jan 1, 2000, that's fine, but I'll be stopping by each of your houses to collect the 12th egg from every dozen, and the 6th can from every six-pack, because you don't want a little thing like math confusing you during your every-day life.

To celebrate our millennium-ending issue (our eighth consecutive issue), I'd like to do something a little bit different. This time out, instead of our crack team of writers telling you about what their impression of the events of the past year, we decided to let a number of very knowledgeable industry insiders talk directly to you themselves. That is why this year we are delivering to you an all-interview CVA. The three individuals we've lined up include a noted retailer (Mike Raub, owner of Flamingo Street Comics in Norwalk, CT.); Jim Valentino, creator of Shadowhawk, and the newly-installed publisher of Image; and Randy Stradly, the editor-in-chief of maverick publisher, Dark Horse Comics.

As an aside, last year's e-mail interview with Warren Ellis proved to be so successful, that we're doing another round of e-mail interviews this year, with both Jim and Randy. We learned that while e-mail does cut into an interview's spontaneity, it does allow our subject the ability to reflect at length on his answers and offers a greater depth to the interview. Further, it not only allows us (greater), access to people to whom we love to speak, but are exceptionally busy, it affords us the opportunity to actually corral them into granting an interview.

As for our subjects, Mike Raub has been a successful comicbook retailer for some 15 years, and offers us some clear, insights into the business end of this industry, which has been admittedly lacking from CVA's pages for a couple of years. Jim Valentino, comes to us not only as an artist and writer, but someone who has produced some very intensively personal comics, as well as some very spectacularly popular and flamboyant comics. He is truly one of the few professionals in this field who possesses the unique and uncanny ability to be both an independent cartoonists, as well as a mainstream, fan favorite—not to mention the publisher of one of the most innovative, and ground-breaking publishers of the last half century. It is fair to say that Image Comics helped to forever changed the face of comics.

And, last, but certainly not least, Randy Stradly, the VP of publishing of Dark Horse. When Dark Horse began publishing, it was just another Left Coast publisher doing odd-ball comics. Only it never really were. These guys had a plan, and a stable of top-flight cartoonists working with them. They, perhaps more successfully than any other publisher larger or smaller have consistently proven that they have the ability to not only translate their creator's concepts into other media, but so in reverse as well. Look at the movies that have had solid runs at Dark Horse; Star Wars, Alien, Terminator, Predator, Robocop, and Starship Trooper, just to name a few. On the other side of the coin, there's been The Mask, and last year's wonderful Mystery Men (feature editor Bob Sodaro's personal choice of best-ever comicbook movie).

And speaking of our staff, we never got around to mentioning it last year, but with our '99 issue, Bob—who has been with us since the '93-'94 issue—was officially made our features editor. Bob was a reporter for our old Comics Values Monthly, and has been providing us with themed issues, celebrity interviews, and market updates, as well as acquiring covers for us since '96. Bob works under editor Stuart W. Wells, III who has been compiling our listing from the very beginning. And if you think that CVA is just dropping a bunch of lists into a page template, then you have another thing coming. CVA is hundreds of man-hours of work, and that's just between the production end (Stuart), and the pricing (myself), of literally thousands of comicbook titles and hundreds of publishers. Which is not to say that we don't have fun doing this.

For, while collecting comics may not be as popular, or as cool as they were just a few short years ago, all of us here at CVA truly love this colorful and exciting medium, and couldn't think of anything else we'd rather be doing. So here is to all the wonderful years that comics provided to us during the old millennium, and to all of the exciting years ahead of us in the next millennium.

Oh yes, and one last thing. As we close out this millennium, and open another, we'd like to state for the record what we read, collect, and archive are "comicbooks" not "comic books" Our reasoning for this is simple, in the intro to Les Daniels' 1993 book Marvel: Five Fabulous Decades of the World's Greatest Comics Stan Lee explains his use of the word "comicbooks" over the more generally used "comic books." We at CVA wholeheartedly subscribe to Stan's theory, and thus have determined to utilize "comicbook" as one word rather than two, for—as Stan stated—comicbooks have become a legitimate medium unto them themselves, and are not merely "books" that are "comical." Besides, if it's good enough for Stan, then it's good enough for us.

At this time, we' like to take the opportunity to thank all of our special guests (in this, and previous years), and staff (including publisher Allan W. Miller), for their efforts, indulgence, and assistance in getting this issue (and previous), published. We'd also like to thank Mike Raub for allowing us to photograph items from his store for this issue, as well as his assistance in the past. However, most of all, we'd like to thank all of the creators who have worked so diligently during the past millennium to make our comicbook reading so entertaining, and we look forward to a new millennium where comics will be every bit as exciting.

That should be it for now boys, girls, superheroes, and other sentient creatures. See you all next century! We've had fun for our parts of this past one, and we honestly think the next one is gonna be a four-color (interactive), blast!

Interview with Mike Raub

Conducted by Robert J. Sodaro

While the name Mike Raub might not be familiar to the rank-and-file of comicdom he has been an active participant in the industry for several years, as a fan, store owner, and art dealer. Over the past decade-and-a-half, he has—from his own little corner of the Omniverse—done whatever he could to promote the comicbook medium. In fact; for a while there in the mid-'90s, he was poised right on the edge of breaking new ground. His smallish chain of Connecticut-based comicbook shops (Dream Factory), was all set to go national, and nearly made it.

What brought the dream crashing down was no small amount of boardroom politics, and subterfuge from smoke-filled rooms. His chain of some 12 stores merged with the Chicago-based Moondog's comics via a circuitous route that involved the long-defunct First comics, and Classics Illustrated. While far too much to go into here, when the dust settled Mike, his wife and Dream Factory co-owner Lori Raub, as well as partners Mike Gold and Dom Corbo, along with other key personnel were out.

After a protracted lawsuit, Moondog's (the newly-renamed chain), went belly up, and the Raubs eventually returned to comicbook retailing. Operating now as Flamingo Street Comics (ironically enough, in the original location of the first Dream Factory), Mike is happy to be once again owning and operating a comicbook retail store, even if the landscape of the industry has been radically (and perhaps irrevocably), altered since he was last here.

While it is tough to blame the comicbook crash that followed on the type of corporate in-fighting that occurred when Dream Factory and Moondog's merged, it certainly couldn't have helped an already fractured, and fragmented industry.

From his location at 130 New Canaan Avenue in Norwalk, CT (HYPER-LINK http://www.flamingoStret.com) www.flamingoStreet.com), Mike took time out his day to chat amicably about comics, retailing, and life in general.

Bob Sodaro: How long have you been in the comicbook business?

Mike Raub: I had my first store in 1977 with three guys in Columbus, Ohio. Dream Factory opened up here in Sept. 1985, so I guess that makes it 14 years almost to the day we're doing this.

Bob: What was the name of the original store?

Mike: Funnybooks. It lasted about six months. It was way before the direct market, almost before Phil Seuling. There wasn't enough material then to make it happen.

Bob: When I was a kid I had an idea for a what is essentially today's comicbook specialty shop. I envisioned that it would carry all of the really cool stuff that I liked to buy.

Mike: That was probably would have been a great idea, but the problem is that there wasn't enough material, there to sell to pay for rent, even in our case we're talking (in our case), about it was 1977 and there just wasn't enough. Comics, per se were, I think, at that point, 35¢ for standard issues, maybe some things were 50¢, but that was about it. We weren't near having anything a dollar I think DC created the dollar comic about a year later. There wasn't enough stuff to make a business worthwhile.

Bob: So, when did comics become a viable way to make a living as a retailer? Or, was it ever?

Mike: Well that's a double-sided question, first of all, it depends on the area. I think there are some people in New York that have made a living at it for a long time. Joe Lieack, Village Comics (located in NYC's Greenwich Village). I was shopping with Joe back in 1980, '81. His store was there then, it's there now. I'm pretty sure that's how Joe makes his living. However I'm sure that you weren't able to do that in, I don't know, Southbend, Indiana in the early '80s or, Kentucky, or…

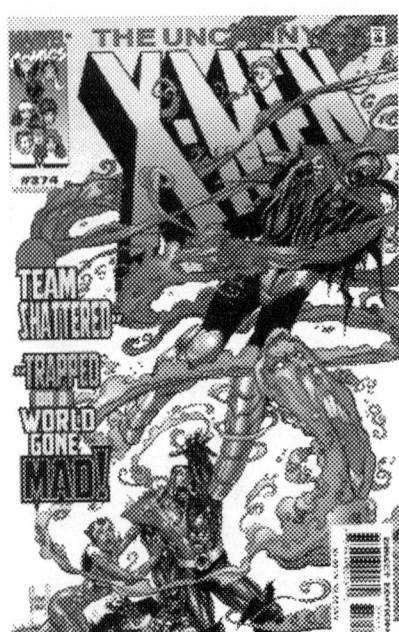

The Uncanny X-Men #374
© Marvel Entertainment Group

Bob: In Norwalk, CT.…

Mike: …In Norwalk, CT. Absolutely true. It changed a lot over the years. The market changed, more people became interested in things. You had a distribution system that was set up and, at one time consisted of at least three distributors at any given time. There was Capital, Diamond, and Heroes' World., later on, or, in the beginning when it was Capital, Russ Ernst deal I forget the name of that thing he had out there from out there that famous one that went under. (FIX) Big Rapids, all those different guys. There were a number of different places to go. There was a lot more going on. Somebody asked me the other day why nobody at the comics company had or at the distribution end had started a comicbook store starter pack. I guess this was in Diamond's hand if they decided to do it, but somebody suggested that they actively go out and seek new accounts, and teach people to open stores, and have a starter order form that you could go out that would be the standard to do and generally just try and grow the industry, because nobody's really trying to do that at all anymore. It just isn't happening, there's no growth in this industry at all. Anybody with any money has pretty much pulled out, and looks at us almost as they did in the early '80s—as the little red-headed step-child that didn't quite reach potential.

Bob: I don't know, I kind of like it, because all of the speculators are gone, all the nonsense is gone, and perhaps we can get back to making real comics again.

Mike: There's a lot more than that out there. There are manufacturers that aren't looking at us anymore, there are major companies that aren't looking at us anymore. Two days ago Marvel announced this new Internet deal they have where they've hired a major company to take over their Internet business for them. Their Internet business isn't going to be based on helping the comic-book stores, their internet business isn't going to be based on growing the market per se, by having cool samples of Marvel comics that—once you see 'em you're directed to a store—not at all. They're going to be selling product on-line, they're going to be creating product for on-line, and they're going to be their own business. It's going to be nothing to do with the comics store per se.

Bob: I can see where that's a bad thing from your aspect, but is that a bad thing from the industry aspect?

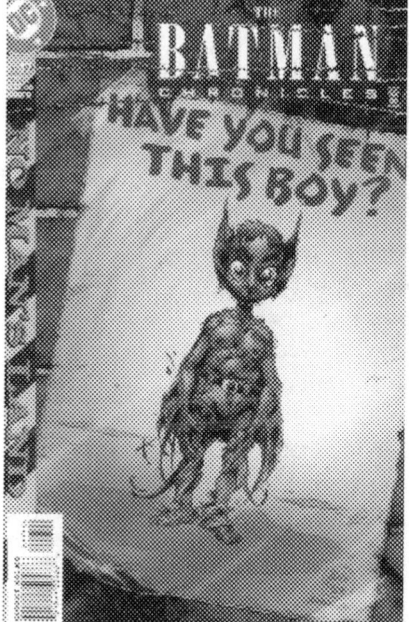

The Batman Chronicles #17
© DC Comics

Mike: From the industry aspect…yes, I think so, because you become very cyclical at that point. I think that everybody creates their own little market, and their own little universe, and none of those universes grow together to become one large universe, and they come and go at will, they can die off, and nothing really grows. There's no real massive growth. There's a lot of little villages, but no big city.

Bob: It seemed to me over the years that back during the industry's heyday, when there were new superhero universes popping up all over the place (Malibu, Milestone, Dark Horse's Comics Greatest World, the various Image studio universes, Valiant, and everybody and their brother constructing whole universes), each company seemed to be intent on developing their piece of the comicbook audience pie by cut-

Daredevil Vol 2, #6
© *Marvel Comics Group*

ting into someone else's portion of the pie, and not by going out and attempting to attract a new audience into our marketplace.

Mike: Well, there was always talk about advertising, there was talk about tie-ins, and industry ad campaigns, but none of that stuff ever happened. We never did any of it.

Bob: Why didn't it ever happen?

Mike: I don't know why, it just never came together.

Bob: it seems as if we cut our own throat when we started doing variant issues, gold leaf, and day-glo covers, and all that other crap. Printing up a bazillion copies of X-Men when everybody knew that there were really only 100,000 people actually reading comics. Did we do that? Did we basically erode our own market?

Mike: I'm not sure that I'm comfortable with the word "we" there, because I don't think that you had anything to do with it, and I didn't have anything to do with that, and the people who had something to do with that are long gone. They're long gone. I don't think that had a lot to do with it. I think that major money came into this industry in the '90s, and I don't mean speculators, I mean major outside people, who looked at the comicbook companies. They looked at the Malibus they looked at the Marvels, they looked at the DCs—maybe as an example, not as something they could purchase—and they said, "Okay, this is a viable industry, let's see what we can do with it." And in turn, inside, we really didn't perform for them. We never got together and got a national chain together. We never got together and got a national organization together, compared to the video industry or compared to several other types of industries. We never really showed we knew where it was at, or that we could even find it. Pretty soon they just moved away, and in turn, after they turned away, a lot of people who came from our industry. Case in point is Todd McFarlane. McFarlane's toy products right now are going to other outlets way before they come to the comicbook market. And these are comic-book-based toys. The Movie Maniac 2 series that he just put out that's got Crow—and some movie characters as well in it—is certainly based towards the comicbook industry at some point, yet those figures are in small retail outlets, that aren't comicbook stores. They are available to them now (Sept. 1999), and then in two weeks, and our industry won't see those toys until the early part of October.

Bob: Is this because he feels that he can make more money doing it that way?

Danger Girl #5
© Wildstorm

Mike: I don't know, I don't think so. I think that they think that in the long run we're just a bunch of guys that just couldn't get it together.

Bob: Are we still in this drought period that has been plaguing us for the past couple of years? For a time comics were a big booming industry and there were a dozen support publications out there about comics, and now there's what...two, there maybe?

Mike: Well there's a few, you've got your older stuff, there's Alter Ego, and Comic Marketplace, You've got the Comics Buyer's Guide, and Wizard. And again, it wasn't the industry that killed that, it was the advertising money. Nobody wanted to advertise. Nobody had the money, to get it rolling. That was the big problem there.

Bob: How do you think that the product stacks up now, as to a few years ago? Is it better? Is it the same?

Mike: A lot of product is good, but a lot of product isn't coming out on time. Everybody wants to see Daredevil, and never saw it for a certain number of times. Unlike in years past, when they stood patiently by the shelf and wait- ed for it to come out, they now walked away. Daredevil failed, it dropped pre- cipitously this year. Battle Chasers and Danger Girl sales have dropped as much if not more than Daredevil has. People are really saying that they don't want to pay a lot of money for a comic. And they don't want to wait for them. They don't care how good they are. There's too much other entertainment out there. Product may look good, but to be real honest, the competition also looks real good.

Bob: So what's the deal then? What's keeping these people from getting this stuff out on time then? Is it really that difficult or are we just dealing with amateurs?

Mike: I don't know the answer for that. There's a number of folks that will shake their head and go, "Gee, I wish I knew that too." I don't think there's any- thing...I, I can't tell you. I never wrote into a comic so I guess anything I would guess would be kind of silly. However, it doesn't make any difference, what the cause is, it's just happening. Nobody's producing comics at a rate anywhere near where they were in the past. We had a guy like Jack Kirby that was drawing five comics a month, 12 times a year. Now you got guys like...the most prolific guy in the business doing a monthly comic seven times a year. Which...it ain't working.

Action Comics #759
© *DC Comics*

Bob: I always remember something that Jim Shooter said. His comment was that, yes, this is a creative industry, and you're dealing with creative people; but the bottom line is that you have to buy it for five and sell it for 10, and you have to get it there by Tuesday, because that's the ship date. Actually, I believe that he was quoting some old movie mogul who was asked, "Do you want it good, or do you want it Tuesday." And his answer was, "I want it Tuesday!" And, according to Shooter, the real challenge was the balance between getting there Tuesday and getting it right, because if getting it there right meant getting it there a year from Tuesday, then you're going to lose your audience, as you said.

Mike: The problem is that Daredevil and books like it, have lost their audience. they've lost a major part of their audience.

Bob: From your end, you used to have eight or 12 stores, now you just have the one. Do you miss having more stores? Would you ever consider opening more stores again? Or is it just not feasible any more?

Mike: Well, that's three different questions, and I'm going to answer them in order for you. Do I miss it? Considering where I am in my life right now; no. Would I consider doing more of them; In the marketplace the way it is right now, not necessarily. Do I think it's feasible to happen in this industry? Yeah I know there are people who are doing it very very well. Jamie Graham in Chicago has at least eight stores, and I think that at this point in time he may have opened his ninth in the past couple of weeks. He's doing great. He's doing wonderful. He's put together a mix of stuff in the store and his business that allows cash flow to fly in from a number of different sources—not just strictly selling new comics off the rack—and he's doing very very well with that. So do I think the industry can support it? Yeah, I do.

Bob: You have a Web site (HYPERLINK http://www.flamingostreet.com www.flamingostreet.com), do you do much business off your Web site, or is that just there because you're in business, and you need to have a Web site?

Mike: We do good business on our Web site, and we do a lot of good business with on-line auctions, obviously with Ebay, with Yahoo, and whatever. The only thing that stops us from doing more is the old time factor, but there is a tremendous amount of business, but there's a tremendous amount of business going on out there being done on the Web, and as the year comes to an end,

Sailor Moon #8 © Mixx

and more and more people like less and less human contact in the new millennium, I think that that sort of business is going to increase for everybody. There's business on the Web whether your selling comicbooks or lawnmowers.

Bob: Unless of course we all crash in Y2K.

Mike: There'll be something out there...Macs will work, so we'll be fine.

Bob: So how do you personally feel about the industry? Are you upbeat or ambivalent? Or what? What's your take on what's happening?

Mike: I guess the industry itself is a double-sided coin. Right now, comic books in our store that is, new comics, our third-best selling item. Japanese anime is very strong right now, and toys are very strong right now.

Bob: When you say toys, do you mean specifically action figures or all toy types?

Mike: I'm talking about action figures, models, statues, everything that we personally categorize that way. That stuff is very big, and now we run into the Christmas season. On the whole, I'm very pleased with my business. If I had nothing in there except a rack of new comics, and some back issues, would I be as pleased, probably not. So if you're asking me if I'm pleased with the comicbook industry—not, necessarily.

Bob: But your business as a whole is doing fine?

Mike: Yes, I'm very happy with our business.

Bob: Pokémon seems to be all the rage right now.

Mike: It is, and it's brought a lot of people in, whether we've managed to capitalize on them and turn them into reading Batman or not, has yet to be determined. We'd all like to see that happen, unfortunately I'm not sure that's going to happen.

Bob: The kids who come in to buy the Pokémon-related cards and items, do they buy the Pokémon comics as well?

Mike: Some do. Some are unfamiliar with the comicbook form, which is pretty frightening. There are six and seven-year-olds that don't understand what that is, and a number of them are uninterested in the comicbook form. A number of them would prefer to read prose than to read comics, it's really

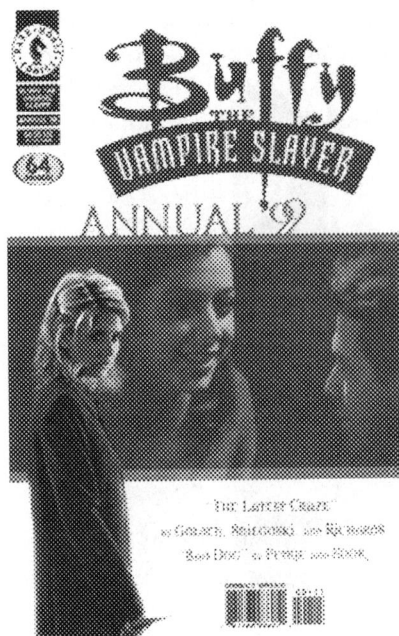

Buffy the Vampire Slayer, Annual '99
© *Dark Horse Comics*

amazing. There are Pokémon novels out right now that are easy to read, kid's novels that are squarebound. I've seen them pick those up in lieu of picking up a handful of comics.

Bob: We were talking about the Web, how do you operate off the Web? Can they come on-line and have stuff mailed to them…?

Mike: They can buy stuff. We have a section of overstock that and they are able to order that. We also tie our Web page directly into our Ebay auction site, which means that we have a potential viewership of the Web page of any given moment of zillions of people.

Bob: When you say you do Ebay, how are you doing this? What kinds of things are you auctioning off?

Mike: Everything. Anything that we get in that I don't think we can sell in the store, or anything that we have excess of, or any oddball items, or usually Golden and Silver Age comics…

Bob: Do you sell off autographed stuff?

Mike: Yeah, sure. Anything like that.

Bob: Do you feel that when comics end up in the mainstream in movies or on TV it helps to bring people in to comic shops? We were talking about the upcoming X-Men movie that's due out at the end of this year. Do you think that will bring people into your shop looking for X-Men stuff?

Mike: Maybe, but you have to understand that there's a whole generation of people who's only exposure to X-Men was a very popular Fox-TV show.

Bob: How about something like last year's Mystery Men. Dark Horse seems to be the only comicbook company that has a serious understanding of translating their product into other media; and has been very successful in transforming other media into comics. With the Terminator, Aliens, Star Wars, and other movie properties.

Mike: I think it's great. It's very admirable. I think their Buffy the Vampire Slayer comic and their Xenia Warrior Princess comic are tremendous for that type of thing—bringing people in. On the other hand I haven't had a legion of people knocking down my door to get Mystery Men stuff. There have been a couple of people who want to see a Janeane Garofalo action figure (laughter)…

Bob Burden's Original Mysterymen #2 ©
Dark Horse Comics

Mystery Men: Mr. Furious action figure
Toy Fair prototype

Bob: (laughter), …Yeah, me too!

Mike: Well it's out there, but that's pretty much been it. I hasn't really turned the world on. I think that there is a great lesson to be learned in Pokémon, and rather than for people to sit around and go, "this is a fad, it's like Beanie Babies." It's not, it really isn't.

Bob: What makes it different?

Mike: I don't know. But I think that someone who really has a vested interest, in expanding their universe, should really take the time and the money and research this. There's a lesson to be learned here. It's not easily found on the surface, and its going to take some time and some research money to do so, but if I had a comic company and the sales of my books are right where everybody is these days compared to where they were five years ago, I'd be doing some research.

Bob: Do you mean to translate Pokémon into comicbook form, or to develop something similar to it?

Mike: What is it that caused this product—and let's not even call it Pokémon, let's call it Product A—What caused Product A to be dropped in the laps of America, and caused it to be accepted so rapidly and in such great quantities? What is it? What did it? Was it a certain type of cartoon? Was it a certain way it was marketed? Do we need to have a legion of people to go to the junior highs and the middle schools and talk about how cool Batman Beyond is, and get the movers and shakers in the schools behind you?

Pokemon, The Electric Tale of Pikachu
#1 © Viz Comics

Bob: I know that the Pokémon stuff is banned in some schools because they don't want the kids trading the cards there.

Mike: That's an whole 'nother thing, but what I'm saying is, that's the market we have to reach. We have to reach those kids. Does a Marvel Comics—and I know the answer to this already—or does a DC rather than spend some time on some projects, do they ever do focus groups? And if they do, do they ever bring in of eight or ten 8-11 year-olds, and ask them what's going on? Are you reading comics? Why? Look at this, what do you think's wrong with it? They're very honest, they'll tell you what it is, what's wrong with it.

Bob: I think that part of that is when you and I first got into comics there were kid comics. First of all, there's the whole Archie comics and the Hot Stuff, and the Dells and Gold Keys. There were these comics that were specifically kid comics. As we got older, and more sophisticated we all grew up, and the comics grew up with us, and nothing filled in at the entry level. When I started reading comics, Peter Parker was older than I was, I've long since caught up, and passed him. For a while it looked as if they were trying to re-create kid comics, because someone apparently finally realized that you need to hook kids at a young age, or they'll grow up never finding and not needing comicbooks, which is ultimately bad for the continued growth of the industry. Somehow or another it seems as if they've dropped the ball on this.

Mike: That's because they didn't have any properties that the kids were interested in. They had nothing out there. The reason that Disney continues to be somewhat successful with kids is that they were successful with parents and the parents force the kids into Disney.

Bob: It's safe.

Mike: What we need to find out, we don't need another Disney, we need to find out where the next Pokémon is coming from Dragonball Z is a great example. Kids love Dragonball Z its usually a fairly safe leap from a six or eight year-olds into Pokémon once he discovers Dragonball Z then they get into that, or Sailor Moon, or whatever else. They've accepted a lot of this stuff in great quantities. Much more than the younger kids have accepted Spider-Man. We need to find out why. Putting out a line of kids comics with unrecognizable characters doesn't necessarily work. Which Marvel tried with it's

Star line of comics tried about 10 years ago. Putting them out with characters which we think is cool but aren't really cool to kids, and that may include Looney Tunes, or Popeye, or Little Lulu, or any of those things, is all just a vanity act and a waste of time.

Bob: With the end of the millennium approaching do you think that comics can make the leap to the 21st century?

Mike: I hope so, I truly hope so, but it's going to take a lot more than a bunch of people trying to hang onto their youth. It's going to take a lot more than that.

Bob: I once had this conversation with (former DC editor), Mike Gold, back when Marvel was first entering bankruptcy, I can't imagine a world without Spider-Man or the X-Men. How is it possible to lose characters that are so

Dragonball Z, Part 2, #10
© *Viz Comics*

ingrained in the public psyche. His response was, how did we lose Doc Savage, The Shadow, The Lone Ranger, and Zorro? In today's world those characters—while they all may enjoy some niche markets—are essentially dead, and no where near as popular as they were 40 or 50 years ago. To which I then agreed, we could possibly lose Spidey, Superman, and all of the rest, and a whole new generation of characters could emerge over the next generation. Do you agree that we actually could lose these great icons of our youth?

Mike: Oh, absolutely. Unless something happens to make them interesting. Absolutely. A movie may do that. It may help out a lot. A TV show may do it and help out a lot.

Bob: Wasn't there a lot of interest when Superman was on TV; the Lois and Clark show, then the Batman movies always seem to spark some kind of interest. Of course the last Batman movie turned into such a farce there probably will never be another one; and the fallout probably killed the Superman movie as well.

Mike: There are bigger problems at this moment in time to worry about with Superman than a movie, and that would be who owns it.

Bob: (laughter), Yeah, there is that. That decision could certainly turn this entire industry around.

Mike: It could really turn it around.

Bob: To backtrack for a moment, when Star Wars the Phantom Menace came out, did that bring a lot of new people into your store?

Mike: Absolutely, they're a lot of Star Wars people out there, but their not comicbook people.

Bob: Do they come in and buy the Star Wars comics that Dark Horse does?

Mike: They bought some of them, but again, it's unfortunate because it was, and this isn't Dark Horse's fault at all, but they wanted a Darth Maul comicbook. There was no Darth Maul comicbook.

Bob: Do you think that's Lucas, because Lucas doesn't want information about Darth Maul out there, or because he hasn't figured out anything about him either?

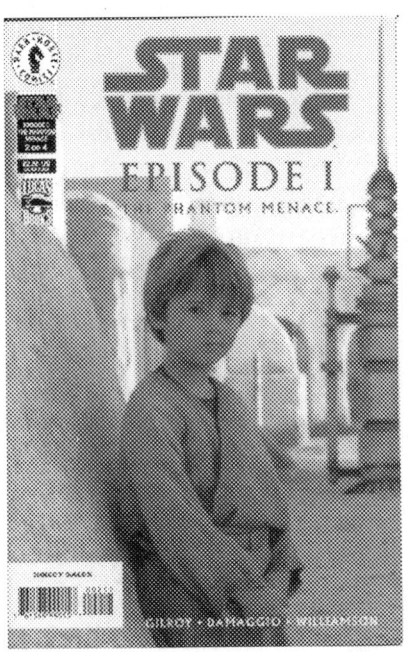

Star Wars, The Phantom Menace #2
© Lucas Arts

Mike: I don't know who's fault that is, but I'm sure that Dark Horse would love to add a Darth Maul comic. I know those guys, and I think that they're all very smart and astute to what's going on, but there are reasons why it didn't happen. That doesn't mean that that it worked, that the kids came in and they wanted Dark Horse comics. But they wanted that, and we didn't have anything to offer them, so they moved on.

Bob: Is there anything else that you want to say, or observations that you'd like to make before we wrap this up?

Mike: Not really, other than to say that there's going to have to be some real working together in a lot of different areas to make this work; to make this thing continue into the new millennium, and to make us not talk about this as a thing of the past in another five years. I want to continue to sell comics, and I will sell anything else I can find to pay the rent so I can continue to sell comics. If that makes me a bad person, then it makes me a bad person, but my rent's paid and I'm happy and my family's fed and everything's fine in that respect. I would love to sell more comics, and I would love to do anything I could to do so, to sell more comics. I can't do it alone.

Bob: No. No you can't. We seem to be so fractured, even when everything was going good for us as an industry, everyone seemed to be pulling in a different direction. Do you think its possible to get enough people to pull the same way for us to actually go someplace?

Star Wars, The Phantom Menace #3
© Lucas Arts

Mike: I would like to see that, but to be real honest I don't see anybody stepping out of the crowd. I would love to see that, but I don't see it happening at this point in time. Rising Star, the J. Michael Straczynski comic from Top Cow is a perfect example. Everybody was looking forward to it, and he had the chance to turn all of the people in Babylon 5 towards his new thing, which was this comicbook company. They put out one issue and the second issue is three months late, and nobody cares.

Bob: So what happened to getting three issues in the can before soliciting for a comic?

Mike: Nobody does that. Now, you don't even start a comic. You do a cover. You send it to Diamond; Diamond puts it in the catalogue; they solicit for it, and if it doesn't look like it's a good deal, you bail out of it. Nobody wants to roll the dice.

Bob: Yeah, that makes it difficult for us here at CVA to do our listings, because it's then tough to find out if solicited comics actually ever came out.

Mike: The only way for you to know, rather than do the Diamond solicitation is to download—and you can do it from the regular Diamond page—is a list of what ships every week, and you can use that, otherwise you're going to be doing what Maggie Thompson (of Comics Buyers' Guide) does, and Maggie's constantly going, "Did Wolfenberg #92 ship? Did all this other stuff ever happen? By the time you chase it down you've got a guide that's not cost-effective to publish.

Interview with Randy Stradley

(V.P. of Publishing, Dark Horse Comics)

Conducted by Robert J. Sodaro

In some respects, Dark Horse Comics is like the Marvel Comics of the 1960s, in others it is like Eclipse of the '80s. With respect to both companies, it publishes a wealth of material across all genres. It is a "House of Ideas" if you will, for just as Marvel of the '60s sparked a revolution, and Eclipse of the '80s had that raw, energetic feel to it, so too does Dark Horse, save that Dark Horse has not only feel of an underdog, it has a willingness to play with the genre as well.

More so than any other contemporary comicbook company, Dark Horse has somehow managed to straddle the line as to what a comicbook company is. It has both successful comics based on popular movies, and made successful movies based on its creator's popular comics. It has both creator-owned comics as well as company-owned comics. Known for its devotion to the non-superhero form, it nonetheless dove head-first into the long underwear set in the '90s along with everyone else, and had a critical, if not financial success with the form.

Mystery, Sci-fi, adaptations, original material, B&W, color, series, stand-alones, anthologies, western, European, Asian—it doesn't seem to matter to Dark Horse, the company will try it all. To talk about the company and its prolific output, V.P. of Publishing Randy Stradley agreed to be interviewed, and as virtually everyone else this year, he did it by e-mail.

Bob Sodaro: Unlike many of your contemporary comicbook companies Dark Horse seems to run the gamut of this industry in the kinds of comics you publish. These include anthologies, horror, mystery, creator-owned, company owned, superheroes, funny animals, Manga, and (for lack of a better term), Ground level comics. How is it that you seem so successful with such a broad appeal while others can't seem to (and haven't), made the grade?

Randy Stradley: Part of it, I have to believe, has to do with taste. Publisher Mike Richardson, myself, and all of the

Aliens Apocalypse, The Destroying Angles #3 © Dark Horse Comics

editors at Dark Horse, have eclectic tastes. None of us could survive on a steady diet of any one genre. So we go after a wide variety of projects. But we are also careful to pick projects that we feel have a broad appeal. Occasionally we'll go after something that we know has a limited audience, but we never forget that we want to stay in business.

Bob: You've published at least two lines of "imprint" comics (Legend and Maverick). Why didn't the first one succeed, and—given that it didn't succeed—why try it again?

Randy: First of all, you have to define success. The Legend books, overall, sold quite well. What didn't succeed was the imprint. Legend was set up as an exclusive club, run by creators for creators. Dark Horse was the publisher, but Legend made its own rules. From what I can tell, what happened was that every member had a different idea of what the club/imprint was supposed to be, supposed to accomplish, and what members were supposed to do. Eventually, it just fell apart. Maverick, on the other hand, really is an imprint—one that is owned and operated by Dark Horse. We have criteria for which books bear the imprint, but none of the Maverick creators involved is beholden to any of the other Maverick creators. All any creator has to be concerned with is his or her own project.

Bob: How have you managed to successfully and consistently attract such top-flight talent like Frank Miller, Mike Mignola, Paul Chadwick, John Byrne, Mike Allred, and all of the others?

Nexus Vol. 2, #96
© Dark Horse Comics

Sock Monkey Vol 2, #2
© Dark Horse Comics

Randy: Originally it was because we were the only publisher in the business who offered real creators' rights deals, and in the late-eighties and early-nineties, creator rights was a rallying cry for much of the industry's top talent. We were lucky enough to be there when guys like Paul and Frank and Mike were looking for an alternative to work-for-hire. Now that other companies are offering similar deals, we try to hang on to creators by keeping them involved in all aspects of production and by maintaining a commitment to quality.

Bob: Dark Horse has been around for over 13 years, ever since Dark Horse Presents debuted in summer of '86. So many other comic companies have come and gone in those years, How have you managed to have survived?

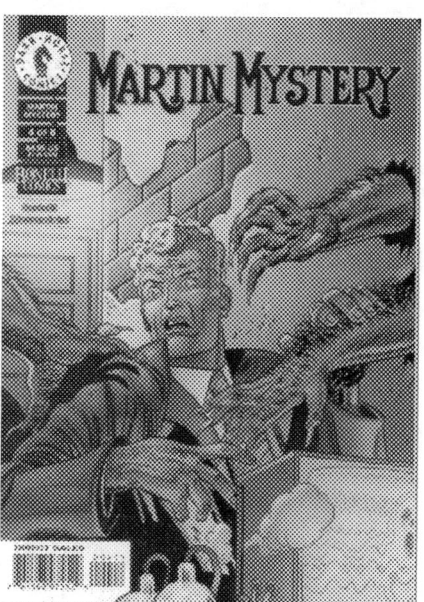

Martin Mystery #4
© Bonelli-Dark Horse Comics

Randy: We're too ornery to die? I think our survival has a lot to do with the fact that Dark Horse isn't owned by a larger company. We sink or swim on our own merits. It keeps us hungry and on the look out for new, interesting projects and new opportunities—and it prevents us from blowing our profits like drunken sailors during times of plenty so that we have resources to carry us through times like the present.

Bob: Dark Horse also has an impressive run of adaptations of movies (not just movies translated into comics, but "continued adventures of..." series), which includes Star Wars, Terminator, Predator, RoboCop, Aliens, Starship Troopers, and others. How is it that you've managed to get such solid hooks into Hollywood?

Randy: By trying as hard as we can to make each movie-related project a good comics project. It doesn't always work, though. Sometimes we're at the mercy of licensing departments that know nothing of (and care nothing for) comics, and whose only concern is the slavish adherence to the source material. However, we have been very successful in educating the folks at many of the studios as to what works best in comics, and once they see that we're not out to trample their properties, they give us pretty much free reign.

Bob: Are you planning to continue any of these series (Star Wars, Aliens, Terminator, and Predator all currently have on-going comics), will some of the others return?

Randy: Except for some special projects, Aliens, Predator, and The Terminator

Dark Horse Presents Annual '99
© Dark Horse Comics

are going on hiatus in 2000. We of course have new properties coming in to fill those voids in the schedule. Unfortunately, I'm not currently at liberty to say what they are.

Bob: You have also have had successful translations of your comics into movies (The Mask, Mystery Men). How is it that you have been so successful in getting your comics made (and made well into movies)?

Randy: In the early '90s, studios began to realize the wealth of story (and franchise) material that was available in comics. Many people in comics fell all over themselves accepting the first offer they got. A lot of our success—or at least opportunities for success—originally grew from the fact that Mike Richardson wasn't afraid to tell the studios "no." That drove the folks in Hollywood crazy; made them want the property even more. Mike held out—not necessarily for more money, but for more control. Wherever possible, creators have been involved in the film projects based on their characters, and Dark Horse has tried (though not always successfully) to shape the movies into what we want them to be.

Bob: Given the above, is there some trick to getting comics successfully made into movies?

Randy: See the answer to the above question

Bob: I read in one of your anthology books (Dark Horse Presents, I believe), that you are actively looking for new stories and concepts for the anthology. Could you (briefly), outline what kinds of stuff you are looking for, and how someone who submits work can "rise to the top of the heap" as it were?

Randy: Well, I always tell people that if I knew what I was looking for, I'd just call the writers and artists I know and tell them what to do. Primarily, I'm looking for good, solid storytelling—both in the writing and the art. In terms of genre, DHP skews toward action-adventure, but any long-time reader will tell you that there's also room for slice-of-life stories, humor, sci-fi, and superheroesque stories. Getting published in DHP is no guarantee of long-term success (most series are allowed three 8-page installments at most), but it'll get your foot in the door. The thing that seems to trip most people up is telling an interesting story in a limited number of pages. In many ways, short stories are harder to write and construct than four-issue arcs.

Bob: With your Comics' Greatest World imprint, you attempted to launch a holistic superhero world. Unfortunately, it didn't take (only Ghost survives), why do you think the others didn't fly?

Randy: There were a number of factors—both internally at Dark Horse, and externally in the market—that contributed to the dissolution of Comics' Greatest World. Conceptually, I think we had something that could have been a huge success, but in hindsight we perhaps tried to take too big a step at the outset.

Bob: I personally thought that X was the hottest book in that series, and am quite upset that there is no on-going X series. Is there any chance of a revival?

Randy: Everybody has a different favorite. I'd love to see King Tiger get a shot, and with some re-tooling Vortex could be really cool. X gets asked about a lot,

Mask: Toys in the Attic #4
© Dark Horse Comics

though. I'm about 80% certain that X will return. We're just trying to find the right way to bring him back so that he can have a long, healthy run and not just a four-issue stint.

Bob: Could you talk a little about the digest-size Bonelli Comics? a) How did you get the rights to re-publish them? b) When were they originally published? c) Will there be more of them (either from Bonelli or other foreign publishers)?

Randy: Bonelli is a huge comics publisher based in Italy, where they sell more Martin Mystery, Nathan Never, etc., than Marvel sells X-Men over here. All of those series have been running for years (decades) in Europe, and we thought it'd be interesting to get them into the hands of American readers. Whether or not Dark Horse will publish more is still up in the air, but Bonelli continues to publish them in Europe.

Bob: Of all the types of books that you guys produce, which is your favorite genre? (And why?)

Randy: I guess it would depend upon when you ask me. A few months ago I would have said horror is my favorite genre. Lately, though, I've been getting really excited about the kinds of things that can be done with superheroes. Like I said at the outset, I have eclectic tastes.

Bob: Do you feel that DH's eclectic publishing lineup is one of the things that keeps the company going? (Since no one comic nor genre can support the

Cud Comics #5
© Dark Horse Comics

entire company, your diversity will keep all sorts of people coming in.)

Randy: I think it keeps the editors and creators fresh. Nobody gets pigeonholed doing just one thing. Even within something like the Star Wars line there's room for a wide range of stories. While I'm sure that there are a number of genre-specific fans among our readership, I think that most Dark Horse readers are people who enjoy the storytelling medium of comics. Just like television viewers don't just watch sitcoms or medical dramas, comics fans don't just read superheroes or sci-fi.

Bob: Do you see Dark Horse as an industry rebel, or has your longevity made you part of the "establishment."

Randy: Shortly after we had our first success, somebody asked me if Dark Horse was going to change its name once it was no longer a "dark horse." I told them that we'd leave the name and just let it be ironic. However, after all these years, I still don't feel like an industry insider. It still surprises me when creators or retailers know who I am.

Bob: Was your path (from where DH started to where it is now), an organic evolvement?

Randy: Totally. When we started, Mike and I jokingly put together a pie-in-the-sky plan of where we wanted the company to be 10 years down the road. By the end of our second year so many things had happened and so many new opportunities had opened to us that our plan looked pathetically short-sighted.

Bob: Where do you see DH going?

Randy: Everywhere. Our goal is to become a full-service entertainment company. Personally, I can't wait for more toys.

Bob: Where (given the recent ups and downs of the marketplace), do you see the industry going?

Randy: The other day, senior editor Diana Schutz was talking with Too Much Coffee Man creator Shannon Wheeler when she made a comment about the industry going "to hell in a handbasket." Shannon's response was, "There's a handbasket?" Seriously, I expect things to get even worse before they get better, but that's my own pessimistic outlook. Industry-wide, about the same total number of comics are being sold today as when Dark Horse started. The only problem is there are three times as many titles. It seems obvious to me that this is not a state which the market can sustain.

Bob: Do you think that our "Glory Days" are over, or are there better days ahead?

Randy: Dark Horse has lived through two runs of "Glory Days"—the black-and-white boom of the late '80s and the industry-wide boom of the early '90s. No doubt we'll hit some high points again in the future. The mistake many people have made is fooling themselves into believing that those peaks were the norm and that the "valley" that we're currently in is the aberration. It's just the opposite.

Masakazu Katsura's Shadow Lady #8
© Dark Horse Comics

Bob: Given all problems that the entire industry has suffered over the past few years (the boom and bust of so many companies during the '90s Marvel's Bankruptcy, the loss of some of your partners), are you still as upbeat as you were when the industry was riding high on the hog?

Randy: There's a handbasket?

Bob: Do you think there is a future out there for us still?

Randy: There's always a future, unless you give up. The question nobody can answer is what will that future be like? What form will comics take?

Bob: Do you think that we "shot ourselves in the foot" so to speak with all of the variant, special edition and gold leaf covers of that era?

Randy: The industry didn't just shoot itself in the foot, it blew both of its legs (and its balls) off at the waist. At Dark Horse we fought those trends and fads as much as we could. We tried to take the high road. We preached that the real value of a comic book was the story it told. We pushed reading over collecting. But we lost to short-term greed. Cynically, if I had to do it over again, I'd put out variants of everything and squeeze all the dough I could out of those people who were, ultimately, going to leave the market anyway when they discovered that they couldn't turn a profit on their "investments."

Bob: Do you think comicbooks will ever move into an interactive, (CD or on-line based), medium?

Randy: They are already, and I'm sure that will expand in the future. (I recently

Blade of the Immortal #36
© *Dark Horse Comics*

Ghost, Vol. 2, #11
© *Dark Horse Comics*

read about a still-experimental information-transfer system for the Internet called the Abilene Network that's supposed to be 47,000 times as fast as a 56K modem. At that point switching locations on the Internet will be as fast as changing channels on a TV, and there'll be no more waiting for images to load.) Still, a moving image with sound is not the same thing as a comic book. To me, the beauty of the comics medium is that it's already interactive—the interaction takes place in the reader's mind, between panels.

Bob: Getting back to movies for a second, do you think that there has ever been a faithful translation of a comicbook character to TV or the movies (I don't mean one that has made money, but one that has been faithful to the source material—as an aside, I don't blame George Clooney for the disappointing showing of Batman and Robin, but director/producer Joel Shumacher. I believe that he looked at his source material and said, "Hey it's a comicbook! I can do whatever I want." and then proceeded to make not a movie based on a comicbook, but a movie based on what his perception of what a comicbook superhero was. For my money, the first Darkman, and Mystery Men were closer to what a comicbook movie should be than all of the movies based on comics thus far produced.)

Randy: I love Darkman. Sam Raimi's genius. I just saw (on a bootleg video tape!) the movie Storm Riders, which is based on a comic book published in China. I haven't seen the comic, but the movie certainly stretched the envelope of the kinds of images that can be put on the screen. The Matrix was good, too. But I think we're talking genre here, not comics.

Bob: Stepping back for a moment, these days it seems that comics sole justification for existence is that they are breading grounds for potential movie or TV deals. Do you feel that comics can (or should), be more than just an "intellectual medium"

Randy: It's a balancing act. Publishers have to stay in business, so at least some of what they publish has to make money somewhere. Comics that aspire to be capital "A" art are great, but if a publisher goes broke publishing them, nothing else gets published. Dark Horse does way more than our share of books that lose money—because we think they're worth publishing for reasons other than financial ones.

Tarzan #9
© *Edgar Rice Burroughs, Inc.*

Bob: What kind of comics attract you as a reader?

Randy: As stated previously, I like good storytelling—the kind of work that engages my brain and my emotions and makes me forget that I'm reading a comic.

Bob: What comics (other than comics that Dark Horse publishes), do you read?

Randy: Sadly, I no longer read much for pleasure. Editing has ruined it for me. I'm always aware that I'm reading a comic and either noticing things that could be done to make it better, or seeing the construction of the story and realizing where it's going. I'm the same way with movies, too. (Am I the only one who wasn't surprised by the ending of The Sixth Sense?)

Bob: Do you see yourself staying with DH for the long haul? In the comicbook industry?

Randy: I've managed to reach the position where I can't be fired, but they won't let me quit.

Bob: Any question that I (or other interviewers), haven't (ever), asked that you that you wish they would?

Randy: "Did you know that Catherine Zeta-Jones thinks you're cute?"

Interview with Jim Valentino

(Publisher, Image Comics)

Conducted by Robert J. Sodaro

More so than any other creator, Jim Valentino has run the gamut of this industry. He started out writing and drawing some very personal underground (or ground level), B&W comics, worked at Marvel both writing and writing/drawing mainstream comics as work-for-hire, that were owned by a corporation. He's acted as his own studio head (of Shadowline), again producing mainstream superhero comics (this time ones that he owned). From there he went to "discovering" and "brokering" (if you will), several independent comics and gaining (or attempting to gain), them mainstream acceptance by publishing them under the auspices of Shadowline under the Image banner; and now he's the publisher of Image, succeeding Larry Marder in this position

As with all of the interviews this year, this interview was conducted by e-mail. Jim proved himself to be a serious net-addict (given by this interviewer's ability to not only catch him on-line, but by Jim's swift response to e-mail, and how his e-interview was peppered with on-lineisms (i.e., shorthand tricks that net-heads use in ordinary "speech"). In the interests of both accuracy in reporting, and to preserve the unique flavor of the inter-view, we've decided to leave them in. In deference to any readers who are not as familiar with these "isms", a brief guide of terms used in the interview is presented here:

[:)] = Smily face (something funny was said)

(g) =Grin (something mildly amusing was said/occurred)

LOL = Laugh out Loud (Something so very funny occurred as to cause laughter)

Bob Sodaro: Given your unique—and twisty—career path (see intro), could you give us your overview of the industry? Yeah, yeah, I like to start with the easy ones first :).

Jim Valentino: I would hope that my experience in the various strata of the indus-

Shadowhawk #3
© Jim Valentino

try; in retail, in distribution, as a creator, as a publisher would help me be more sensitive to the concerns of each. From a freelancer's point of view I understand how nerve-wracking it is to send in a proposal and not hear back from a publisher. On the publisher's side I know what it means to try and second guess what will or will not sell. On the editor's side I know about dealing with late freelancers and from the retailer's side I understand how late books impact cash flow and one's ability to do business. Being sensitive to all of these concerns will, hopefully, allow me to communicate with each in a way all can hear—and, hopefully, solve some of the on-going concerns we all have.

Ascension #19 © Top Cow

Bob: Of all the roles you've held (given the above), if you had to choose one to do either over again, or for the rest of your career, which would it be, and why?

Jim: I have found enjoyment and fulfillment in each at different points in my life. So I could see myself doing any or all of them in the future depending on how I feel. I've always followed my instincts on what I should do next…of course, all things considered I guess I should rethink that strategy a bit (g).

Bob: Do you see yourself as an industry rebel (again, given the above), or was your "path" an organic evolvement?

Jim: I've never given it any thought at all, to be honest with you. I see everything I've done to this point as being more organic, a natural extension of my eclectic interests both as a creator and a fan.

Bob: Are you interested in being a rebel?

Jim: LOL—I don't believe that I have any choice in the matter. I try not to be, but no one buys it.

Bob: Could you talk briefly about how you came to be involved with the other Image co-founders, and what lead to your breaking away as a group.

Jim: Rob Liefeld and I were friends and studio mates—he initiated Image between the people he most trusted in the industry—Todd, Erik and I. So, I was there from the very start. The rest, as they say, is history.

Bob: I had heard that you never really meant to form a new publishing company, that your original vision of Image was to be a sub-imprint or universe within the Marvel line where the characters were wholly owned by yourselves.

Jim: That's totally false. The fact is that Terry Stewart offered the Epic imprint to us and Todd told him where he could shove it in no uncertain terms. There was never any discussion about being a part of Marvel. We were breaking away from Marvel not negotiating with them.

Bob: If you had the ability to found Image all over again, what would you do differently, and what would you do the same?

Jim: I note a lot of your questions are speculative in nature, as odd as this may seem for someone who writes fiction I never deal in speculation about what might have

Darkness #27 © Top Cow

been in real life.

Bob: It is now some five or six years later, and while many at the time thought Image wouldn't last the year, you obviously did, and did so quite successfully, anything you'd like to say to those people now?

Jim: Actually, on February 1 it will be 8 years. I have nothing to say to any of them. I believe our still being here is comment enough. We've already proven we were right and they were wrong. What more need be said? After all, actions always speak louder than words.

Bob: Given all problems that the entire industry has suffered over the past few years (the boom and bust of so many companies during the '90s Marvel's Bankruptcy, the loss of some of your partners), are you still as upbeat as you were when the industry was riding high on the hog?

Jim: I am, yes. I believe that there are more interesting and diverse comics out there now than at any other time in our history. I believe that this will directly translate into a revitalization of the industry as we become more palatable to a wider audience.

Bob: Do you think there is a future out there for us still?

Jim: Yes, I really do. I believe that there are new opportunities open to us and that so long as we are willing to change and adapt with the times we will always have a future. The question before us is whether or not we have the courage and the fortitude to embrace those changes and, again, my answer is yes, I believe we do.

Bob: Do you think that we "shot our-selves in the foot" so to speak with all of the variant, special edition and gold leaf covers of that era?

Jim: No. I believe that was an era of unprecedented speculation that was destined to burn itself out regardless what we did or didn't do. I point to Beanie Babies and Pokéman as recent proof of this argument. Just like "fuzzy covers" (as I always called them) they are collectible commodities with a short term life-span. This happens over and over again and no one ever seems to learn their lesson from it as we search endlessly for the next hot item and short term gain.

Deity: Revelations Vol. 3, #2
©Karl Altstaetler & Robert Napton

Bob: Do you think that those boom years are gone for good or are we—as an industry—can regain some of our lus-ter?

Jim: I think I would argue whether or not one should equate that era with any "luster". I would suggest that our true value is in the ideas that we gener-ate…but, no doubt, that's the artist in me speaking.

Bob: Given all the competition for the consumer's entertainment dollar (videogames, movies, etc.), do you think that an outdated medium such as print comicbooks can survive?

Jim: Yes, but I think we have to accept the notion that we are not rock and roll. It occurs to me that for a while there our conventions looked more like boat shows than comic cons. We have to accept the fact that we are closer to club jazz, a small sub-niche market. And, more, that there is nothing wrong with that.

Bob: Do you think comicbooks will ever move into an interactive, (CD or on-line based), medium?

Jim: Yes. These are some of the new vistas that have been opened to us. But, I also believe that it will be the next generation to come, the kids who have never known a world without the Internet who will be able to fully capitalize artistically in this new medium. For us in this generation it would behoove us to explore and experiment and not be afraid of the potential for both business and creativity it offers. We should never be afraid of the future.

Forever Amber #3, © Donald Hudson & Hudson International

Bob: Do you think that there has ever been a successful translation of a comicbook character to TV or the movies (and by successful, I don't mean one that has made money, but one that has been faithful to the source material—as an aside, I don't blame George Clooney for the disappointing showing of Batman and Robin, but director/producer Joel Shumacher. I believe that he looked at his source material and said, "Hey it's a comicbook! I can do whatever I want," and then proceeded to make not a movie based on a comicbook, but a movie based on what his perception of what a comicbook superhero was. For my money, the first Darkman, and last year's Mystery Men were closer to what a comicbook movie should be than all of the movies based on comics thus far produced.)

Jim: I guess it's all a matter of opinion. I enjoyed a lot of the first Superman and Batman movies myself. And there have been several movies like The Terminator and Star Wars that are, in my opinion, comic books on film.

Bob: Stepping back for a moment, these days it seems that comics sole justification for existence is that they are breeding grounds for potential movie or TV deals. Do you feel that comics can (or should), be more than just an "intellectual medium"

Jim: I don't think that there is necessarily a conflict of interest there, so again, it all depends on where an individual stands. My belief is that if a creator wants to exploit his property through any other medium, this is a good thing and does nothing to lessen the original work. I just don't understand the criticism here at all and find it to be indicative extremely myopic world-view. In terms of business it is a criticism without merit.

Bob: Can Image survive the loss of both Rob Liefeld's Extreme Studio and Jim Lee's Wildstorm?

Jim: We already have. It has been nearly three years since Rob has been gone, over a year for Jim. We are still here.

Bob: I realize that the departure of Jim was far different that that of Rob, and animosity aside, were the remaining partners surprised by Jim's sale of Wildstorm last year to Warner Bros.?

Jim: No. We all knew that Jim had been shopping his company around for

Lady Rawhide, Other Peoples Blood #3
© Zorro Productions, Inc.

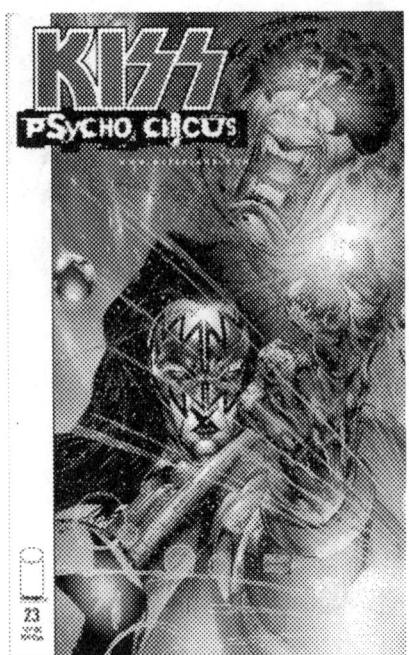

Kiss, Psycho Circus #23
© Kiss Catalog, Inc.

quite a while.

Bob: Is this (save for the loss of two studios), where you expected Image to be?

Jim: I had no expectations on where Image would be. I think I was just hopeful that Image would still be in existence and believed it would be obviously or I wouldn't have tossed in with them. What form that would take was anybody's guess and I was too busy at the time to engage in the idle speculation that seemed to consume those who had no interest in the company and only third hand information about it.

Bob: What's next for Image?

Jim: Image will continue to look forward, not behind us. We will continue to champion creator's rights here at Image Central and continue to present as wide a diversity of comics to the public as possible. We will attempt to constantly improve our relations with retailers, fans and creators…we want to get better—and, I believe, we have.

Bob: You told me that you are looking for new talent and/or new comics. What specifically are you looking for in these new comics (besides superheroes).

Jim: Actually, if you look at our output, with the possible exception of The Savage Dragon, we don't publish any superheroes at all anymore. There are no panties and capes punching one another over Metropolis in our entire line. I'm looking for good books. Books that are well written, well drawn. Books that the creator believes in. Genre, subject, style and format are truly not relevant—commitment and excellence are.

Bob: Do you think that any other original members will jump ship? And if so, could Image survive the loss of another original partner?

Jim: As far as I know no partner is contemplating leaving at this time. It would be incredibly foolish if one did. The Diamond contract in and of itself makes that a very unwise move. Image has shown an amazing resiliency and adaptability thus far. I wouldn't count us out until we say it's over, our demise has been predicted too often to be anything but embarrassed by the prediction.

Bob: It has been stated (see Mike Raub interview, elsewhere in this volume), that Todd seems to be catering more to the non-comicbook market (not only issuing more toys than comics, but by releasing those toys to mainstream shops weeks before comic shops get them.) Could you respond to this?

Jim: I am not certain what there is for me to respond TO here. Todd is a businessman how he conducts his business is his deal, not mine and not yours or anyone else's. Apparently this comes as a shock to some but the purpose of being in business is to make money. That Todd realizes a positive revenue stream from other segments of his empire has nothing to do with his comics. And, in point of fact, he has increased his comics output in the last year, an obvious display of his loyalty to this industry and to this marketplace. I would hope that his success in these other venues would serve to call national attention to comics…and the downside of this is what? If there is a nega-

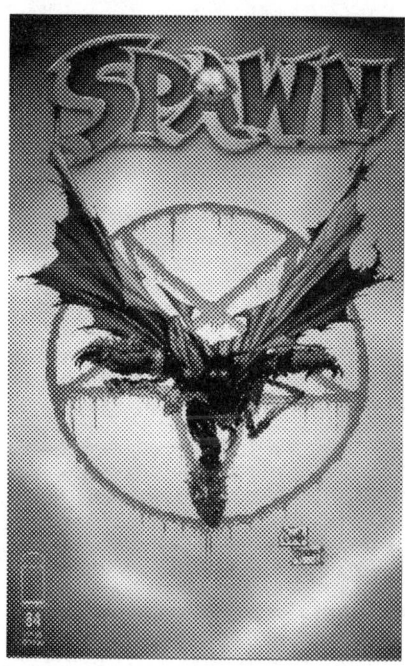

Spawn #84
© *Todd McFarlane Productions*

Witchblade # 32
© *Top Cow*

tive impact on this industry I'm just too dumb to see it, but then I have never understood why any individual would begrudge another his success. I say God Bless him and anyone who manages to do what he has done.

Bob: It is safe to say that Image and the original seven partners not only redefined comics in the '90s, but reinvented (and reinvigorated), the market through their approach to storytelling, art, and marketing. Do you think that it is possible for Image to remain on the leading edge of the market?

Jim: I would feel uncomfortable commenting on the former part of the question, on the later I would say, yes, so long as we are willing to provide a haven for young, forward thinking creators willing to experiment with new ideas and new media.

Mage #13 © Matt Wagner

Bob: Do you see yourself staying with Image for the long haul? In the comic-book industry?

Jim: Yes to both. I'm a cartoonist, comics are my medium. I have never had any desire to do anything else and I am eternally grateful that I have been able to earn my living for the last twenty years in the industry I love.

Bob: Given all you have already done in this industry, is there anything you haven't yet done that you'd still like to do?

Jim: Yes, putting on my fanboy hat for a moment here—I'd love the opportunity to play in DC's sandbox for a little while. I've never been able to and theirs are the characters of my youth.

Bob: Anything you'd like to do again?

Jim: Probably, but not in the same way I did it before. I have no interest in endlessly repeating myself.

Bob: Anything you'd like to do over (differently)?

Jim: No, I've learned from every mistake, every pratfall. I tend to believe that everything happens for a reason, even if we can't figure out why at the time.

Bob: Are there any Image comics headed for either TV or movies (live action or animation)?

Jim: I don't know. Image does not own any properties, unlike Marvel, DC or

Savage Dragon #66
© Erik Larsen

Dark Horse and, as such, we do not involve ourselves in a creator's business. We pretty much hear about it at the same time the public does, it's really just none of our business. Our business is comics.

Bob: Can you tell us about any upcoming Image comics?

Jim: There are so many coming that I'm afraid I'll be leaving someone out—if I do, I apologize. We have books as diverse as new titles from WildStorm expatriates Mat Broome and Brett Booth, to Wahoo Morris, Geeksville, Pakkins Land, Astounding Space Thrills, Tony Daniel's new title F-5, Trina Robbins' Go-Girl, so many more and I'm closing deals with even more major players every day. Some of which I am just not at liberty to discuss.

Bob: Are there any that will cause us to camp out in front of our local comicbook shop to get?

Jim: The politically correct answer, of course, is all of them! But I think the ones to watch out for would be Dan Fraga's The Gear Station, which is using 3-D modeling in new and revolutionary ways, Greg Horn's JUDGE which is utilizing Photoshop and Paintshop in a manner that is nothing short of revolutionary and a new book from Digital Broome that is utilizing some of the most unique special effects I've ever seen. Completely state-of-the-art. I realize that I've only mentioned art here, But, despite all criticisms to the contrary, we are concerned with story and we are addressing that aspect of the creative process as well.

Bob: And (finally), given all the ups and downs we've already been through in this industry, do you think it is possible for us (or those that follow), to get that excited about comics again? (And if so, will we have to wait 20 or 30 years for it to happen?

Jim: If you are not excited about the diversity of material out there right now, the problem is yours and not the industry's. Every single publisher is putting out great stuff by some of the best artists and writers to ever work in this medium. We are in one of the most creative and inventive periods of our history—now is the time to be excited!!

GCVA GRADING GUIDE

In David Brin's science fiction–fantasy novel, *The Practice Effect*, things improve with use. You start with a crudely made tool and keep using it until it becomes a fine instrument. If our world worked that way, you could read your Golden Age comics as often as you liked and they would just get better looking each time. Unfortunately, our world does not work that way, and reading your comics (along with just about everything else) causes comics to deteriorate.

Even if you could protect your comics from external light, heat, cold, moisture, pressure and everything else, you couldn't protect them from their own paper. Most comic books were printed on pulp paper, which has a high acid content. This means that the paper slowly turns brittle with age, no matter what you do to it, short of special museum-style preservation.

Very old, well-preserved comics are coveted collector's items. In most cases, people did not save their comic books for future generations. They read them and discarded them. Comic books were considered harmless ephemera for children. When these children outgrew their comics, their parents often threw them away. If everybody kept all of their comics, comics would not be valuable because everybody would have them scattered about the house!

The value of any comic depends on scarcity, popularity and condition. Scarcity increases with age and popularity depends on the whim of the public — only condition automatically decreases with age. Newer comics are generally available in near-mint condition, so newer comics in lesser condition have little collector potential. However, older comics are scarce, so they are still collectible in less than near-mint condition, but the value is obviously less. This is a basic tenet of all collectibles. A car is more valuable with its original paint. A baseball card is more valuable if it has not been marred by bicycle spokes. Coke bottles, stamps, coins, and toys in good condition are all more valuable than their abused counterparts. Comic books are no exception.

New comic book collectors should learn how to assess the prospective value of a comic in order to protect themselves from being fleeced by unscrupulous dealers or hucksters. Yet, a majority of dealers, especially store owners, can be considered reliable judges of comic grade. Because comic retail may be their primary source of income, certain dealers are particularly adept at noticing comic book imperfections, especially in issues they intend to purchase. As such, hobbyists and collectors must understand that dealers need to make a minimum profit on their investments. Buying collectible comics entails certain risks. Therefore, dealers must scrutinize a comic to determine if the particular book will stand a chance of resale. Well-preserved comics are invariably more desirable to dealers because they are more desirable to collectors.

There are eight standard comic grades: mint, near mint, very fine, fine, very good, good, fair, and poor. Clearly, these eight grades could be split into even finer categories when haggling over an exceptionally rare or coveted Golden Age comic. In most cases, however, comic books can be evaluated using these eight standard grades. The values listed in *Comics Values Annual* are all for comics in "Near Mint" condition. The grading/price chart given at the back of this book should be used to adjust this price for comics in different grades.

Mint

Finding new comics in true mint condition can be difficult. Finding old comics in mint condition is almost impossible. Mint condition comics usually fetch prices higher than price guide listings. Mint comics can sell for 120% or more of *Comics Values Annual* listed prices. The reason for this is the strict criteria reserved for mint comics.

Mint comics are perfect comics and allow no room for imperfections. Pages and covers must be free of discoloration, wear, and wrinkles. A mint comic is one that looks like it just rolled off the press. Staples and spine must meet perfectly without cover "rollover." The cover must be crisp, bright, and trimmed perfectly. The staples must not be rusted and the cover should not have any visible creases.

The interior pages of a mint comic are equally crisp and new. A mint comic must not show any signs of age or decay. Because of the paper stock used on many older comics, acid and oxygen cause interior pages to yellow and flake. It is much harder to find pre-1970 mint comics because of inferior storage techniques and materials. In the early days of collecting, few people anticipated that the very boxes and bags in which they stored their comics were contributing to decay. Acid from bags, backing boards, and boxes ate away at many comics.

Near Mint

A near mint comic and a mint comic are close siblings, with their differences slight, even to an experienced eye. Most of the new comics on the shelf of the local comic shop are in near mint condition. These are comics that have been handled gingerly to preserve the original luster of the book.

Near mint comics are bright, clean copies with no major or minor defects. Slight stress lines near the staples and perhaps a very minor printing defect are permissible. Corners must still be sharp and devoid of creases. Interior pages of newsprint stock should show almost no discernible yellowing. Near mint comics usually trade for 100% of the suggested *Comics Values Annual* listed prices.

Very Fine

A very fine comic is one that is routinely found on the shelves and back issue bins of most good direct market comic shops. This grade comic has few defects, none of them major. Stress around the staples of a very fine comic are visible but not yet radical enough to create wrinkles. Both the cover and interior pages should still be crisp and sharp, devoid of flaking and creases. Interior pages may be slightly yellowed from age.

Most high-quality older comics graded as very fine can obtain 80-90% of *Comics Values Annual* listed prices. Newer comics graded as very fine get about 70-85% because many near mint copies probably exist. Despite that, very fine comics are desirable for most collectors.

Fine

Fine comics are often issues that may have been stored carefully under a bed or on a shelf by a meticulous collector. This grade of comic is also very desirable because it shows little wear and retains much of its original sharpness. The cover may be slightly off center from rollover. The cover retains less of its original gloss and may even possess a chip or wrinkle. The comers should be sharp but may also have a slight crease. Yellowing begins to creep into the interior pages of a comic graded as fine.

Fine comics are respectable additions to collections and sell for about 40-60% of the listed prices.

Very Good

A very good comic may have been an issue passed around or read frequently. This grade is the common condition of older books. Its cover will probably have lost some luster and may have two or three creases around the staples or edges. The corners of the book may begin to show the beginnings of minor rounding and chipping, but it is by no means a damaged or defaced comic. Comics in very good condition sell for about 30-40% of *Comics Values Annual* listed prices.

Good

A good comic is one that has been well read and is beginning to show its age. Although both front and back covers are still attached, a good grade comic may have a number of serious wrinkles and chips. The corners and edges of this grade comic may show clear signs of rounding and flaking. There should be no major tears in a good comic nor should any pages be clipped out or missing. Interior pages may be fairly yellowed and brittle. Good comics sell for about 15-25% of the *Comics Values Annual* listed prices.

Fair

A fair comic is one that has definitely seen better days and has considerably limited resale value for most collectors. This comic may be soiled and damaged on the cover and interior. Fair comics should be completely intact and may only be useful as a comic to lend to friends. Fair comics sell for about 10-20% of the *Comics Values Annual* listed prices.

Poor

Comics in poor condition are generally unsuitable for collecting or reading because they range from damaged to unrecognizable. Poor comics may have been water damaged, attacked by a small child, or worse, perhaps, gnawed on by the family pet! Interior and exterior pages may be cut apart or missing entirely. A poor comic sells for about 5-15% of the *Comics Values Annual* listed price.

Sniffing Out Grades

Despite everything that is mentioned about comic grading, the process remains relative to the situation. A comic that seems to be in very good condition may actually be a restored copy. A restored copy is generally considered to be in between the grade it was previous to restoration and the grade it has become. Many collectors avoid restored comics entirely.

Each collector builds his collection around what he believes is important. Some want every issue of a particular series or company. Others want every issue of a favorite artist or writer. Because of this, many collectors will purchase lower-grade comics to fill out a series or to try out a new series. Mint and near mint comics are usually much more desirable to hard-core collectors. Hobbyists and readers may find the effort and cost of collecting only high-grade comics financially prohibitive.

Getting artists or writers to autograph comics has also become a source of major dispute. Some collectors enjoy signed comics and others consider those very comics defaced! The current trends indicate that most collectors do enjoy signed comics. A signature does not usually change the grade of the comic.

As mentioned, comic grading is a subjective process that must be agreed upon by the buyer and seller. Buyers will often be quick to note minor defects in order to negotiate a better price. Sellers are sometimes selectively blind to their comic's defects. *Comics Values Annual:2000* provides this grading guide as a protection for both parties.

Name	Abbr.
Abel, Jack	**JA**
Abell, Dusty	DAb
Abnett, Dan	DAn
Abrams, Paul.	PlA
Adams, Art	AAd
Adams, Neal	NA
Addeo, Stephen	StA
Adkins, Dan	DA
Adlard, Charlie	CAd
Albano, John	JAo
Albrecht, Jeff	JAl
Alcala, Alfredo	AA
Alcazar, Vincent	VAz
Alexander, Chris	CAx
Alibaster, Jo	JoA
Allred, Michael	MiA
Alstaetter, Karl	KIA
Althorp, Brian	BAp
Amaro, Gary	GyA
Amendola, Sal	Sal
Ammerman, David	DvA
Anderson, Bill	BAn
Anderson, Brent	BA
Anderson, Murphy	MA
Andriola, Alfred	AIA
Andru, Ross	RA
Aparo, Jim	JAp
Aragones, Sergio	SA
Arcudi, John	JAr
Artis, Tom	TAr
Ashe, Edd	EA
Augustyn, Brian	BAu
Austin, Terry	TA
Avison, Al	AAv
Ayers, Dick	DAy
Bachalo, Chris	**CBa**
Badger, Mark	MBg
Bagley, Mark	MBa
Baikie, Jim	JBa
Bailey, Bernard	BBa
Bair, Michael	MlB
Baker, Kyle	KB
Baker, Matt	MB
Balent, Jim	JBa
Banks, Darryl	DBk
Barks, Carl	CB
Baron, Mike	MBn
Barr, Mike	MiB
Barras, John	DBs
Barreiro, Mike	MkB
Barreto, Ed.	EB
Barry, Dan	DBa
Batista, Chris	CsB
Battlefield, D.	DB
Beatty, John	JhB
Beatty, Terry	TBe
Beauvais, Denis	DB
Beeston, John	JBe
Belardinelli, M.	MBe
Bell, Bob Boze	BBB
Bell, George	GBl
Bell, Julie	JuB
Benefiel, Scott	ScB
Benes, Ed	EBe
Benitez, Joe	JBz
Benjamin, Ryan	RBn
Bennett, Joe	JoB
Bennett, Richard	RiB
Benson, Scott	StB
Berger, Charles	ChB
Bernado, Ramon	RBe
Bernstein, Robert	RbB
Bierbaum, Mary	MBm
Bierbaum, Tom	TBm
Biggs, Geoffrey	GB
Binder, Jack	JaB
Bingham, Jerry	JBi
Birch, JJ	JJB
Biro, Charles	CBi
Bisley, Simon	SBs
Bissette, Stephen	SBi
Blaisdell, Tex.	TeB
Blasco, Jesus.	JBl
Blevins, Bret	BBl
Blum, Alex	AB
Bode, Vaughn.	VB
Bogdanove, Jon	JBg
Bolland, Brian.	BB
Bolle, Frank	FBe
Boller, David.	DdB
Bolton, John	JBo
Bond, Philip	PBd
Booth, Brett	BBh
Boring, Wayne.	WB
Bossart, William	WmB
Boxell, Tim	TB
Bradstreet, Tim	TBd
Braithwaite, Doug	DBw
Brasfield, Craig	CrB
Braun, Russell	RsB
Breeding, Brett	BBr
Brereton, Daniel	DlB
Brewster, Ann	ABr
Breyfogle, Norm	NBy
Bridwell, E. Nelson	ENB
Briefer, Dick	DBr
Bright, Mark	MBr
Brigman, June	JBr
Broderick, Pat	PB
Brodsky, Allyn	AyB
Broom, John	JBm
Broome, Matt	MtB
Brothers, Hernandez	HB
Brown, Bob	BbB
Browne, Dick	DkB
Brunner, Frank	FB
Bryant, Rick	RkB
Buckingham, Mark	MBu
Buckler, Rich	RB
Budget, Greg	GBu
Bugro, Carl.	CBu
Bulanadi, Danny	DBl
Burchett, Rick	RBr
Burgard, Tim	TmB
Burke, Fred.	FBk
Burns, John	JBn
Burns, Robert.	RBu
Burroughs, W.	WBu
Buscema, John	JB
Buscema, Sal.	SB
Busiek, Kurt	KBk
Butler, Jeff	JBt
Butler, Steve	SBt
Buzz	Buzz
Byrd, Mitch.	MBy
Byrne, John.	JBy
Calafiore, Jim.	**JCf**
Caldes, Charles	CCa
Callahan, Jim.	JiC
Calnan, John	JCa
Cameron, Don	DCn
Cameron, Lou	LC
Campbell, Eddie.	ECa
Campbell, J. Scott	JSC
Campbell, Stan	StC
Campenella, Robert	RbC
Campos, Marc.	MCa
Capullo, Greg	GCa
Cardy, Nick	NC
Carey, Mike	MCy
Cariello, Sergio	SCi
Carlin, Mike	MCr
Carpenter, Brent D.	BDC
Carralero, Ricky	RCl
Carrasco, Dario	DoC
Carter, Joe.	JCt
Case, Richard	RCa
Casey, Joe	JoC
Castellaneta, Dan	DaC
Castellini, Claudio	CCt
Castrillo, Anthony	ACa
Chadwick, Paul	PC
Chan, Ernie	ECh
Chang, Bernard	BCh
Charest, Travis.	TC
Chase, Bobbie	BCe
Chaykin, Howard	HC
Check, Sid	SC
Chen, Mike	MCh
Chen, Sean	SCh
Chestney, Lillian	LCh
Chiarello, Mark	MCo
Chichester, D.G.	DGC
Chiodo, Joe	JCh
Choi, Brandon	BCi
Chriscross.	Ccs
Christopher, Tom	TmC
Chua, Ernie	Chu
Chun, Anthony	ACh
Churchill, Ian	IaC
Cirocco, Frank	FC
Citron, Sam.	SmC
Claremont, Chris	CCl
Clark, Mike	MCl
Clark, Scott	ScC
Cockrum, Dave	DC
Cohn, Gary	GCh
Coker, Tomm	TCk
Colan, Gene	GC
Colby, Simon	SCy
Cole, Jack	JCo
Cole, Leonard B.	LbC
Colletta, Vince	ViC
Collins, Max Allan	MCn
Collins, Mike	MC
Collins, Nancy	NyC
Colon, Ernie	EC
Conner, Amanda	ACo
Conway, Gerry	GyC
Cooper, Dave	DvC
Cooper, John	JCp
Corben, Richard.	RCo
Costanza, Peter	PrC
Cowan, Denys.	DCw
Cox, Jeromy	JCx
Craig, Johnny	JCr
Crandall, Reed.	RC
Crespo, Steve	SCr
Crilley, Mark	MCi
Crumb, Robert	RCr
Cruz, E. R.	ERC
Cruz, Jerry	JCz
Cruz, Roger	RCz
Culdera, Chuck	CCu
Cullins, Paris	PCu
Currie, Andrew	ACe
Damaggio, Rodolfo	RDm
Daniel, Tony	**TnD**
Danner, Paul	PuD
Darrow, Geof	GfD
David, Peter.	PDd
Davis, Alan	AD
Davis, Dan	DDv
Davis, Guy	GyD
Davis, Jack	JDa
Davis, Malcolm	MDa
Davison, Al	ADv
Day, Dan	Day
Day, Gene	GD
DeFalco, Tom.	TDF
Deitch, Kim	KDe
Delano, Jamie.	JaD
DeLaRosa, Sam	SDR
Delgado, Richard	DRd
Dell, John	JhD
DeMatteis, J. M.	JMD
DeMulder, Kim	KDM
Deodato, Jr., Mike	MD2
Derenick, Tom.	TDr
DeZago, Todd.	TDz
DeZuniga, M.	MDb
DeZuniga, Tony	TD
Diaz, Paco	PaD
Dillin, Dick	DD
Dillon, Glyn	GlD
Dillon, Steve	SDi
Dini, Paul	PDi
Ditko, Steve	SD
Dixon, Chuck	CDi
Dixon, John.	JDx
Dobbyn, Nigel	ND
Dodson, Terry	TyD
Doherty, Peter	PD
Dominguez, Luis.	LDz
Doran, Colleen	CDo
Dorey, Mike	MDo
Dorkin, Evan	EDo
Dorman, Dave	DvD
Doucet, Julie.	JDo
Drake, Stan.	SDr
Dresser, Larry	LDr
Dringenberg, Mike	MDr
Drucker, Mort.	MD
DuBerkr, Randy	RDB
Duffy, Jo	JDy
Dumm, Gary	GDu
Dunn, Ben	BDn
Duranona, Leo	LDu
Duursema, Jan	JD
Dwyer, Kieron	KD
Eastman, Kevin	**KEa**
Eaton, Scott	SEa

Name	Abbr.
Edginton, Ian	IEd
Edlund, Ben	BEd
Egeland, Marty	MEg
Eisner, Will	WE
Elder, Bill	BE
Eldred, Tim	TEl
Elias, Lee	LE
Elliot, D.	DE
Ellis, Warren	WEl
Ellison, Harlan	HaE
Emberlin, Randy	RyE
Englehart, Steve	SEt
Ennis, Garth	GEn
Epting, Steve	SEp
Erskine, Gary	GEr
Erwin, Steve	StE
Esposito, Mike	ME
Estes, John	JEs
Estrada, Ric	RE
Evans, George	GE
Everett, Bill	BEv
Ewins, Brett	BEw
Ezquerra, Carlos	CE
Fabry, Glenn	**GF**
Fago, Al	AFa
Farmer, Mark	MFm
Fegredo, Duncan	DFg
Feldstein, Al	AF
Ferry, Pascual	PFe
Fine, Lou	LF
Fingeroth, Danny	DFr
Finnocchiaro, Sal	SF
Fleisher, Michael	MFl
Fleming, Robert	RFl
Flemming, Homer	HFl
Foreman, Dick	DiF
Forte, John	JF
Forton, Gerald	GFo
Fosco, Frank	FFo
Foster, Alan Dean	ADF
Fox, Gardner	GaF
Fox, Gill	GFx
Fox, Matt	MF
Fraga, Dan	DaF
Franchesco	Fso
Frank, Gary	GFr
Frazetta, Frank	FF
Freeman, John	JFr
Freeman, Simon	SFr
Frenz, Ron	RF
Friedman, Michael Jan	MFr
Friedrich, Mike	MkF
Frolechlich, A.	AgF
Fry III, James	JFy
Fujitani(Fuje), Bob	BF
Furman, Simon	SFu
Gaiman, Neil	**NGa**
Galan, Manny	MaG
Gallant, Shannon	ShG
Gammill, Kerry	KGa
Garcia, Dave	DaG
Garner, Alex	AGo
Garney, Ron	RG
Garzon, Carlos	CG
Gascoine, Phil	PGa
Gaughan, Jack	JGa
Gecko, Gabe	GG
Geggan	Ggn
Gerard, Ruben	RGd
Gerber, Steve	SvG
Giacoia, Frank	FrG
Giarrano, Vince	VGi
Gibbons, Dave	DGb
Gibson, Ian	IG
Giella, Joe	JoG
Giffen, Keith	KG
Gilbert, Michael T.	MGi
Giordano, Dick	DG
Glanzman, Sam	SG
Golden, Michael	MGo
Gonzalez, Jorge	JGz
Goodman, Till	TGo
Goodwin, Archie	AGw
Gordon, Al	AG
Gottfredson, Floyd	FG
Gould, Chester	ChG
Grant, Alan	AlG
Grant, Steve	StG
Grau, Peter	PGr
Gray, Mick	MGy
Green, Dan	DGr
Green, Randy	RGr
Greene, Sid	SGe
Grell, Mike	MGr
Griffith, Bill	BG
Griffiths, Martin	MGs
Grindberg, Tom	TGb
Gross, Daerick	DkG
Gross, Peter	PrG
Grossman, R.	RGs
Gruenwald, Mark	MGu
Grummett, Tom	TG
Guardineer, Frank	FG
Guay, Rebecca	RGu
Guice, Jackson	JG
Guichet, Yvel	YG
Guinan, Paul	PGn
Gulacy, Paul	PG
Gustovich, Mike	MG
Ha, Gene	**GeH**
Haley, Matt	MHy
Hall, Bob	BH
Halsted, Ted	TeH
Hama, Larry	LHa
Hamilton, Tim	TH
Hamner, Cully	CHm
Hampton, Bo	BHa
Hampton, Scott	SHp
Hanna, Scott	SHa
Hannigan, Ed	EH
Hanson, Neil	NHa
Harras, Bob	BHs
Harris, N. Steven	NSH
Harris, Tim	THa
Harris, Tony	TyH
Harrison, Lou	LuH
Harrison, Simon	SHn
Hart, Ernest	EhH
Hartsoe, Everette	EHr
Hathaway, Kurt	KtH
Hawkins, Matt	MHw
Hayes, Drew	DHa
Haynes, Hugh	HH
Hazlewood, Douglas	DHz
Heath, Russ	RH
Hebbard, Robert	RtH
Heck, Don	DH
Heisler, Mike	MHs
Hempel, Mark	MaH
Henry, Flint	FH
Herman, Jack	JH
Hernandez, Gilbert	GHe
Hernandez, Jaime	JHr
Herrera, Ben	BHr
Hester, Phil	PhH
Hewlett, Jamie	JHw
Hibbard, E.E.	EHi
Hicklenton, John	JHk
Higgins, Graham	GHi
Higgins, John	JHi
Higgins, Michael	MHi
Hitch, Bryan	BHi
Hobbs, Bill	BlH
Hoberg, Rick	RHo
Hoffer, Mike	MkH
Hogarth, Burne	BHg
Holcomb, Art	AHo
Holdredge, John	JHo
Hoover, Dave	DHv
Hopgood, Kevin	KHd
Horie, Richard	RHe
Hotz, Kyle	KHt
Howarth, Matt	MHo
Howell, Rich	RHo
Hudnall, James	JHl
Hughes, Adam	AH
Hund, Dave	DeH
Hunt, Chad	CH
Immonen, Stuart	**SI**
Infantino, Carmine	CI
Ingles, Graham	GrI
Iorio, Medio	MI
Isherwood, Geoff	GI
Ivie, Larry	LI
Ivy, Chris	CIv
Jackson, Julius	JJn
Janke, Dennis	DJa
Janson, Klaus	KJ
Javinen, Kirk	KJa
Jenkins, Paul	PJe
Jenney, Robert	RJ
Jensen, Dennis	DJ
Jimenez, Leonardo	LJi
Jimminiz, Phil	PJ
Johnson, Dave	DvJ
Johnson, Jeff	JJ
Johnson, Paul	PuJ
Johnson, Todd	TJn
Jones, Casey	CJ
Jones, Gerard	GJ
Jones, J.B.	JJo
Jones, Jeff	JeJ
Jones, Kelley	KJo
Jones, Malcolm	MJ
Jones, R.A.	RAJ
Jones, Robert	RJn
Jurgens, Dan	DJu
Jusko, Joe	JJu
Kaluta, Mike	**MK**
Kamen, Jack	JKa
Kaminski, Len	LKa
Kane & Romita	K&R
Kane, Bob	Bka
Kane, Gil	GK
Kanigher, Bob	BbK
Kaniuga, Trent	TKn
Karounos, Paris T.	PaK
Katz, Jack	JKz
Kavanagh, Terry	TKa
Kelly, Walt	WK
Kennedy, Cam	CK
Keown, Dale	DK
Kerschl, Karl	KlK
Kesel, Babara	BKs
Kesel, Karl	KK
Kieth, Sam	SK
King, Hannibal	HbK
Kinsler, Everett R.	EK
Kirby, Jack	JK
Kisniro, Yukito	YuK
Kitson, Barry	BKi
Kobasic, Kevin	KoK
Kolins, Scott	ScK
Krause, Peter	PKr
Krenkel, Roy	RKu
Krigstein, Bernie	BK
Kristiansen, Teddy H.	TKr
Kruse, Brandon	BKr
Kubert, Adam	AKu
Kubert, Andy	NKu
Kubert, Joe	JKu
Kupperberg, Paul	PuK
Kurtzman, Harvey	HK
Kwitney, Alisa	AaK
LaBan, Terry	TLa
Lago, Ray	**RyL**
Laird, Peter	PLa
Lanning, Andy	ALa
Lansdale, Joe	JLd
Lapham, Dave	DL
Lark, Michael	MLr
Larkin, Bob	BLr
LaRocque, Greg	GrL
Larroca, Salvador	SvL
Larsen, Erik	EL
Lash, Batton	BLs
Lashley, Ken	KeL
Lavery, Jim	JLv
Lawlis, Dan	DLw
Lawrence, Terral	TLw
Lawson, Jim	JmL
Layton, Bob	BL
Leach, Garry	GL
Leach, Rick	RkL
Lee, Elaine	ELe
Lee, Jae	JaL
Lee, Jim	JLe
Lee, Patrick	PtL
Lee, Scott	ScL
Lee, Stan	StL
Leeke, Mike	MLe
Leialoha, Steve	SL
Leon, John Paul	JPL
Leonardi, Rick	RL
Levins, Rik	RLe
Lieber, Larry	LLi
Liefeld, Rob	RLd
Lightle, Steve	SLi
Lim, Ron	RLm
Linsner, Joseph M.	JLi
Livingstone, R.	RLv
Lloyd, David	DvL
Lobdell, Scott	SLo
Locke, Vince	VcL
Loeb, Jeph	JLb
Lopez, Jose	JL

Lopez, Jose . . . . JL	. . . . HMo	Olivetti, Ariel . . . . AOl	Raboy, Mac . . . . MRa
Lopresti, Aaron . . . . . . AaL	Meskin, Mort . . . . MMe	Olliffe, Patrick. . . . . PO	Ramos, Humberto . . . HuR
Louapre, Dave . . . . . DLp	Messner-Loebs, Bill . . BML	One, Dark . . . . DOe	Ramos, Rodney . . . . . RyR
Lowe, John. . . . . Low	Michelinie, David . . . . DvM	Ordway, Jerry . . . . . . JOy	Randall, Ron . . . . RoR
Lubbers, Bob . . . . BLb	Miehm, Grant . . . . GtM	Orlando, Joe. . . . . JO	Raney, Tom . . . . TR
Lustbader, Eric Van. . ELu	Mighten, Duke . . . . . . DMn	Ortiz, Jose. . . . . JOt	Rankin, Rich . . . . RRa
Luzniak, Greg. . . . . . . GLz	Mignola, Michael . . . . MMi	Oskner, Bob. . . . . BO	Rapmund, Norm. . . . . NRd
Lyle, Tom . . . . TL	Miki, Danny . . . . DaM	Ostrander, John . . . . . JOs	Raymond, Alex. . . . . . AR
Macchio, Ralph . . . . RMc	Milgrom, Al . . . . AM	Owen, James . . . . . . JOn	Redondo, Nestor . . . . NR
Mack, David. . . . . DMk	Millar, Mark . . . . MMr	Ozkan, Tayyar . . . . . . TOz	Reed, David. . . . . DvR
Mackie, Howard. . . . . HMe	Miller, Frank. . . . . FM	Pace, Richard. . . . . . . RPc	Reeves-Stevens, Judith
Madan, Dev. . . . . DeM	Miller, Mike S. . . . . . . MsM	**Pacella, Mark . . . . . . MPa**	. . . . JRv
Madureira, Joe . . . . . . JMd	Miller, Steve. . . . . SM	Pacheco, Carlos. . . . . CPa	Reinhold, Bill . . . . BR
Maggin, Elliot S. . . . . ESM	Milligan, Peter. . . . . . PrM	Palais, Rudy. . . . . RP	Richards, Ted . . . . TR
Maguire, Kevin. . . . . . . KM	Mills, Pat . . . . PMs	Palmer, Tom . . . . TP	Richardson, Mike . . . MRi
Magyar, Rick . . . . RM	Minor, Jason. . . . . JnM	Palmiotti, Jimmy . . . . . JP	Ricketts, Mark . . . . . . MRc
Mahlstedt, Larry . . . . . LMa	Mitchel, Barry . . . . . . BM	Pamai, Gene. . . . . GPi	Rico, Don . . . . DRi
Mahnke, Doug. . . . . . DoM	Moder, Lee. . . . . LMd	Panalign, Noly. . . . . . . NPl	Ridgeway, John. . . . . . JRy
Mandrake, Tom . . . . . TMd	Moebius. . . . . Moe	Paniccia, Mark . . . . . . MPc	Rieber, John Ney . . . . JNR
Maneely, Joe . . . . JMn	Moeller, Chris. . . . . . . CsM	Panosian, Dan . . . . . . DPs	Riley, John . . . . JnR
Manley, Mike. . . . . MM	Moench, Doug. . . . . . DgM	Parkhouse, Annie. . . . APh	Riply . . . . Rip
Mann, Roland . . . . . . RMn	Montano, Steve . . . . . SeM	Parkhouse, Steve . . . . SvP	Robbins, Frank. . . . . . . FR
Mann, Roland. . . . . . . Man	Mooney, Jim. . . . . JM	Parobeck, Mike . . . . . MeP	Robbins, Trina. . . . . . . TrR
Manning, Russ. . . . . . RsM	Moore, Alan . . . . AMo	Pascoe, James . . . . . JmP	Robertson, Darrick. . . DaR
Marais, Raymond . . . RdM	Moore, Jeff . . . . JMr	Pasko, Martin. . . . . . . MPk	Robinson, James . . . . JeR
Mariotte, Jeff . . . . JMi	Moore, Jerome . . . . . JeM	Patterson, Bruce . . . . BrP	Rodier, Denis . . . . DRo
Maroto, Esteban . . . . . EM	Moore, John Francis. . JFM	Pearson, Jason . . . . . JPn	Rogers, Marshall . . . . . MR
Marrinan, Chris . . . . ChM	Moore, Terry . . . . TMr	Pelletier, Paul. . . . . . . PaP	Romita, John . . . . JR
Marrs, Lee . . . . LMr	Morales, Rags . . . . . . RgM	Pence, Eric. . . . . ErP	Romita, John Jr. JR2
Martin, Gary . . . . GyM	Moretti, Mark. . . . . . . MMo	Pennington, Mark. . . . MPn	Rosenberger, J. . . . . . JRo
Martin, Joe . . . . JMt	Morgan, Tom . . . . TMo	Pensa, Shea Anton . . SAP	Ross, Alex . . . . AxR
Martinbrough, Shawn. SMa	Morisi, Pete . . . . PMo	Perez, George . . . . GP	Ross, David . . . . DR
Martinez, Henry . . . . . HMz	Morosco, Vincent. . . . VMo	Perham, James. . . . . . JPh	Ross, John . . . . JRs
Martinez, Roy Allan . . RMr	Morrison, Grant . . . . . GMo	Perlin, Don. . . . . DP	Ross, Luke . . . . LRs
Marz, Ron . . . . RMz	Morrow, Gray . . . . GM	Perryman, Edmund . . . EP	Roth, Werner. . . . . WR
Marzan, Jose . . . . JMz	Mortimer, Win . . . . . . WMo	Peterson, Brandon . . . BPe	Royle, Jim . . . . JRl
Mason, Tom . . . . TMs	Motter, Dean. . . . . DMt	Peterson, Jonathan. . . JPe	Royle, John . . . . JRe
Massengill, Nathan . NMa	Moy, Jeffrey . . . . JMy	Petrucha, Stefan . . . . SPr	Rozum, John . . . . JRz
Matsuda, Jeff . . . . JMs	Murray, Brian . . . . . . BrM	Peyer, Tom . . . . TPe	Rubi, Melvin. . . . . MvR
Mattsson, Steve . . . . . SMt	Musial, Joe. . . . . JoM	Phillips, Joe . . . . JoP	Rubinstein, Joe. . . . . . JRu
Maus, Bill. . . . . BMs	Muth, Jon J. . . . . JMu	Phillips, Scott. . . . . . . SPl	Rude, Steve . . . . SR
Mayer, Sheldon . . . . . ShM	Mychaels, Marat . . . . MMy	Phillips, Sean . . . . SeP	Ruffner, Sean . . . . SRf
Mayerik, Val . . . . VMk	Naifeh, Ted . . . . TNa	Pini, Richard . . . . RPi	Russell, P. Craig . . . . . CR
Mazzucchelli, David. . . DM	Napolitano, Nick. . . . . NNa	Pini, Wendy . . . . WP	Russell, Vince . . . . . . VRu
McCarthy, Brendon . . BMy	Napton, Bob. . . . . BNa	Platt, Stephen. . . . . . . SPa	Ryan, Matt . . . . MRy
McCloud, Scott . . . . . SMl	Nauck, Todd. . . . . TNu	Pleece, Warren . . . . . WaP	Ryan, Paul. . . . . PR
McCorkindale, B . . . . BMC	Neary, Paul . . . . PNe	Ploog, Mike . . . . MP	Ryder, Tom . . . . TmR
McCraw, Tom . . . . . . TMw	Nebres, Rudy. . . . . RN	Plunkett, Kilian. . . . . . . KPl	Sakai, Stan . . . . SS
McCrea, John . . . . . . JMC	Nelson. . . . . Nel	Pollack, Rachel . . . . . RaP	Sale, Tim . . . . TSe
McDaniel, Scott . . . . . SMc	Netzer, Mike . . . . MN	Pollard, Keith . . . . KP	Salmons, Tony . . . . . . TSa
McDaniel, Walter. . . . WMc	Newton, Don . . . . DN	Pollina, Adam. . . . . . . AdP	Saltares, Javier. . . . . . . JS
McDonnell, Luke. . . . . LMc	Nguyen, Hoang . . . . . HNg	Pope, Paul. . . . . PPo	Sanders, Jim III. JS3
McDuffie, Dwayne. . . DMD	Nichols, Art . . . . ANi	Porch, David . . . . DPo	Sasso, Mark . . . . MSo
McFarlane, Todd . . . . . TM	Nicieza, Fabian . . . . . FaN	Portacio, Whilce . . . . . WPo	Saviuk, Alex. . . . . AS
McGregor, Don . . . . . DMG	Nino, Alex . . . . AN	Porter, Howard. . . . . . HPo	Schaffenberger, Kurt. . . KS
McKean, Dave . . . . . . DMc	Nocenti, Ann . . . . ANo	Post, Howard. . . . . . . HwP	Schane, Tristan . . . . . TnS
McKeever, Ted. . . . . . TMK	Nocon, Cedric . . . . . CNn	Potts, Carl . . . . CP	Schiller, Fred . . . . FdS
McKenna, Mike . . . . . MkK	Nodell, Martin . . . . . . MnN	Powell, Bob . . . . BP	Schmitz, Mark . . . . . . MaS
McKie, Angus . . . . . . AMK	Nolan, Graham . . . . . . GN	Power, Dermot. . . . . . DPw	Schultz, Mark. . . . . . . MSh
McKone, Mike. . . . . . MMK	Nord, Cary . . . . CNr	Pratt, George. . . . . . . GgP	Scoffield, Sean . . . . . SSc
McLaughlin, Frank . . . FMc	Norem, Earl . . . . EN	Priest, Christopher . . . CPr	Scott, Jeffery. . . . . JSc
McLaughlin, Sean . . . SML	Nostrand, Howard . . . . HN	Prosser, Jerry . . . . . . JeP	Scott, Trevor. . . . . TvS
McLeod, Bob . . . . BMc	Novick, Irv. . . . . IN	Pugh, Steve . . . . StP	Seagle, Steven T. . . . . SSe
McMahon, M. . . . . . . MMc	Nowlan, Kevin . . . . KN	Pulido, Brian. . . . . BnP	Sears, Bart. . . . . BS
McManus, Shawn . . . SwM	Nutman, Philip . . . . . . PNu	Queen, Randy . . . . . . RQu	Sekowsky, Mike . . . . . MSy
McWilliams, Al . . . . . AMc	O'Barr, James. . . . . . . JOb	Quesada, Joe . . . . JQ	Semeiks, Val . . . . VS
Medina, Angel . . . . . . AMe	O'Neil, Denny . . . . . . DON	Quinn, David . . . . DQ	Senior, Geoff. . . . . GSr
Medley, Linda . . . . LiM	O'Neill, Kevin. . . . . . . KON	Quinones, Peter. . . . . . PQ	Serpe, Jerry . . . . JyS
Mercadoocasio, Harvey	**Olbrich, Dave . . . . . . DO**	**Raab, Ben. . . . . BRa**	Severin, John . . . . JSe

Shanower, Eric . . . . . . EiS	Steacy, Ken . . . . KSy	Tucci, Bill. . . . . BiT	Wildey, Doug. . . . . DW
Sharp, Liam . . . . LSh	Steffan, Dan. . . . . . . DnS	Turner, Dwayne . . . . . . DT	Wildman, Andrew . . . . Wld
Shaw, Sean . . . . SSh	Stelfreeze, Brian . . . . . BSf	Tuska, George . . . . GT	Williams, Anthony . . . . AWi
Sherman, Jim . . . . JSh	Stephenson, Eric. . . . . ErS	**Ulm, Chris . . . . CU**	Williams, David . . . . . DdW
Shoemaker, Terry . . . . TSr	Steranko, Jim . . . . JSo	**Vachss, Andrew . . . . AVs**	Williams, J.H. . . . . JWi
Shooter, Jim. . . . . JiS	Stern, Roger . . . . RSt	Vado, Dan . . . . DVa	Williams, Keith . . . . . . KWi
Shum, Howard . . . . . HSm	Stern, Steve . . . . SSt	Valentino, Jim . . . . JV	Williams, Kent . . . . KW
Shuster, Joe . . . . JoS	Stevens, Dave. . . . . . . DSt	Vallejo, Boris . . . . BV	Williams, Scott. . . . . . . SW
Sibal, Jonathan . . . . . . JSb	Stiles, Steve . . . . SvS	Van Fleet, John. . . . . . JVF	Williamson, Al . . . . AW
Siegel & Shuster . . . . S&S	Story, Karl . . . . KIS	Vancata, Brad. . . . . . . BVa	Williamson, Skip . . . . . SWi
Sienkiewicz, Bill . . . . . BSz	Stout, William . . . . WiS	Vance, Steve . . . . SVa	Wingham, Bill . . . . . . BWg
Silvestri, Eric . . . . EcS	Stradley, Randy . . . . . RSd	VanHook, Kevin . . . . . KVH	Willis, Damon . . . . DaW
Silvestri, Mark . . . . MS	Strazewski, Len . . . . . . LeS	Vargas, Vagner. VV	Wilshire, Mary. . . . . . . MW
Sim, Dave . . . . DS	Stroman, Larry . . . . . . LSn	Veitch, Rick . . . . RV	Wilson, Colin . . . . CWi
Simon & Kirby . . . . . . S&K	Sullivan, Lee. . . . . LS	Velez, Ivan, Jr. IV	Wilson, Gahan . . . . GW
Simon, Joe. . . . . JSm	Sutton, Tom . . . . TS	Velluto, Sal . . . . SaV	Wilson, Keith S. . . . . . KSW
Simonson, Louise . . . . LSi	Swan, Curt. . . . . CS	Vess, Charles. CV	Woch, Stan . . . . SnW
Simonson, Walt. . . . . . WS	Sweetman, Dan. . . . . DSw	Vey, Al . . . . AV	Woggin, Bill. . . . . BWo
Simpson, Don. . . . . . . DSs	**Taggart, Tom . . . . TTg**	Vigil, Tim . . . . TV	Wojtkiewicz, Chuck . . . Woj
Simpson, Howard. . . . HSn	Takenaga, Francis. . . . FTa	Vokes, Neil. . . . . NV	Wolf, Chance . . . . CWf
Simpson, Will . . . . . . WSm	Takezaki, Tony . . . . . . ToT	Von Eeden, Trevor . . . TVE	Wolfe, Joseph. . . . . . . JWf
Sinnott, Joe . . . . JSt	Talbot, Bryan . . . . BT	Vosburg, Mike . . . . MV	Wolfman, Marv . . . . . MWn
Skroce, Steve . . . . . . SSr	Tallarico, Tony . . . . TyT	**Wagner, Matt. . . . . . . MWg**	Wolverton, Basil . . . . . . WB
Smith, Andy. . . . . ASm	Tan, Billy. . . . . BTn	Wagner,Ron . . . . RoW	Wood, Bob . . . . BoW
Smith, Barry W. . . . . . BWS	Tanaka, Masashi . . . . MTk	Waid, Mark . . . . MWa	Wood, Teri Sue . . . . . TWo
Smith, Beau . . . . BSt	Tanghal, Romeo. . . . . . RT	Walker, Kevin . . . . KeW	Wood, Wally. . . . . WW
Smith, Cam . . . . CaS	Tappin, Steve . . . . SeT	Waltrip, Jason . . . . . . JWp	Woodring, Jim . . . . . . JWo
Smith, Jeff . . . . JSi	Taylor, David. . . . . DTy	Waltrip, John. . . . . JWt	Wormer, Kirk Van. . . . KWo
Smith, John. . . . . JnS	Taylor, R.G. . . . . RGT	Ward, Bill. . . . . BWa	Wright, Greg . . . . GWt
Smith, Malcolm. . . . . . MSt	Templeton, Ty . . . . TTn	Warner, Chris . . . . CW	Wrightson, Berni. . . . . BWr
Smith, Paul . . . . PS	Teney, Tom . . . . TmT	Warren, Adam . . . . . . AWa	Wyman, M.C. . . . . . . MCW
Smith, Robin . . . . RSm	Tenney, Mark . . . . MaT	Washington 3, Robert 3RW	**Yaep, Chap . . . . CYp**
Smith, Ron. . . . . RS	Texeira, Mark . . . . MT	Watkiss, John. . . . . . . JWk	Yeates, Tom . . . . TY
Snejbjerg, Peter. . . . . PSj	Thibert, Art. . . . . ATi	Weeks, Lee . . . . LW	Yeowell, Steve . . . . SY
Sniegoski, Tom. . . . . . TSg	Thomas, Dann . . . . . . DTs	Wein, Len . . . . LWn	**Zabel, Joe . . . . JZe**
Spark . . . . Spk	Thomas, Roy . . . . RTs	Weinstein, Howard . . HWe	Zachary, Dean . . . . DZ
Sparling, Jack . . . . . . JkS	Thomason, Derek. . . . DeT	Welch, Larry. . . . . LyW	Zaffino, Jorge . . . . JZ
Spiegelman, Art . . . . . ASp	Thompson, Jill . . . . JIT	Wendel, Andrew . . . . AdW	Zeck, Mike. . . . . MZ
Spiegle, Dan . . . . DSp	Thorne, Frank. . . . . FT	Wenzel, David. . . . . . DWe	Zick, Bruce. . . . . BZ
Spinks, Frank . . . . FrS	Tinker, Ron. . . . . RnT	Weringo, Mike. . . . . . MeW	Zulli, Michael. . . . . MZi
Springer, Frank. . . . . . . FS	Torres, Angelo . . . . AT	West, Kevin. . . . . KWe	Zyskowski, Joseph . . . JZy
Sprouse, Chris . . . . . CSp	Toth, Alex . . . . ATh	Weston, Chris . . . . . . CWn	Zyskowski, Steven . . . . SZ
St.Pierre, Joe . . . . JPi	Totleben, John. . . . . . . JTo	Wheatley, Mark . . . . . MkW	
Starlin, Jim . . . . JSn	Trimpe, Herb . . . . HT	Whitney, Ogden . . . . . OW	
Starr, Leonard . . . . . . LSt	Truman, Timothy. . . . . . TT	Wiacek, Bob. . . . . BWi	
Staton, Joe . . . . JSon	Truog, Chas . . . . ChT	Wiesenfeld, Aron . . . . AWs	

GENERAL ABBREVIATIONS FOR COMICS LISTINGS

Adaptation. . . . . Adapt.	Giant Size. . . . . G-Size	Plotted by. . . . . (pl)
Appearance of . . . . A:	Golden Age . . . . G.A.	Prestige Format . . . . PF
Anniversary . . . . Anniv.	Graphic Album. . . . . GAm	Preview. . . . . Prev.
Annual . . . . Ann.#	Graphic Novel . . . . GN or GNv	Reprinted issue . . . . rep.
Art & Plot . . . . (a&pl)	Hardcover. . . . . HC	Retold . . . . rtd.
Art & Script . . . . (a&s)	Identity Revealed . . . . IR:	Return/Revival of . . . . R:
Artist . . . . (a)	Inks by . . . . (i)	Scripted/Written by . . . . . . (s)
Back-Up Story . . . . BU:	Introduction of . . . . I:	Scripts & inks . . . . (s&i)
Beginning of. . . . . B:	Joins of. . . . . J:	Silver Age. . . . . S.A.
Birth of . . . . b:	King Size. . . . . K-Size	Softcover . . . . SC
Cameo Appearance . . . . . . C:	Leaving of . . . . L:	Special . . . . Spec.
Cover . . . . (c)	New Costume . . . . N:	Team-up . . . . T.U.
Cover and Script . . . . (c&s)	No Issue Number . . . . N#	Trade Paperback . . . . . . TPB
Crossover with. . . . . . . x-over	Origin of. . . . . O:	Versus . . . . V: or vs.
Death/Destruction of. . . . . . D:	Painted Cover . . . . P(c)	Wedding of . . . . W:
Edition . . . . Ed.	Part . . . . pt. or Pt.	With . . . . w/
Ending of. . . . . E:	Pencils by . . . . (p)	Without . . . . w/o
Features. . . . . F:	Photographic cover . . . . . Ph(c)	

3RW . Robert Washington 3	BDC . . . Brent D Carpenter	CCu . . . . . . Chuck Culdera	DgM . . . . . . Doug Moench
AA . . . . Alfredo Alcala	BDn . . . . Ben Dunn	CDi . . . . Chuck Dixon	DGr . . . . Dan Green
AAd . . . . Art Adams	BE . . . . Bill Elder	CDo . . . . . Colleen Doran	DH . . . . Don Heck
AaK . . . . . . Alisa Kwitney	BEd . . . . Ben Edlund	CE . . . . . Carlos Ezquerra	DHa . . . . . . Drew Hayes
AaL . . . . . Aaron Lopresti	BEv . . . . Bill Everett	CG . . . . . . Carlos Garzon	DHv . . . . . Dave Hoover
AAv . . . . Al Avison	BEw . . . . Brett Ewins	CH . . . . Chad Hunt	DHz . . Douglas Hazlewood
AB . . . . Alex Blum	BF . . . . Bob Fujitani(Fuje)	ChB . . . . . Charles Berger	DiF . . . . . . Dick Foreman
ABr . . . . Ann Brewster	BG . . . . Bill Griffith	ChG . . . . . . Chester Gould	DJ . . . . . Dennis Jensen
ACa . . . . Anthony Castrillo	BH . . . . Bob Hall	ChM . . . . Chris Marrinan	DJa . . . . . Dennis Janke
ACe . . . . . . Andrew Currie	BHa . . . . Bo Hampton	CHm . . . . Cully Hamner	DJu . . . . . Dan Jurgens
ACh . . . . . Anthony Chun	BHg . . . . . Burne Hogarth	ChT . . . . . . Chas Truog	DK . . . . . . Dale Keown
ACo . . . . . Amanda Conner	BHi . . . . Bryan Hitch	Chu . . . . . . Ernie Chua	DkB . . . . . Dick Browne
AD . . . . Alan Davis	BHr . . . . . Ben Herrera	CI . . . . Carmine Infantino	DkG . . . . Daerick Gross
ADF . . . . Alan Dean Foster	BHs . . . . Bob Harras	CIv . . . . Chris Ivy	DL . . . . Dave Lapham
AdP . . . . . . Adam Pollina	BiT . . . . Bill Tucci	CJ . . . . Casey Jones	DlB . . . . . Daniel Brereton
ADv . . . . Al Davison	BK . . . . . Bernie Krigstein	CK . . . . Cam Kennedy	DLp . . . . Dave Louapre
AdW . . . . Andrew Wendel	Bka . . . . Bob Kane	CNn . . . . . Cedric Nocon	DLw . . . . . Dan Lawlis
AF . . . . Al Feldstein	BKi . . . . . . Barry Kitson	CNr . . . . Cary Nord	DM . . David Mazzucchelli
AFa . . . . Al Fago	BKr . . . . Brandon Kruse	CP . . . . Carl Potts	DMc . . . . Dave McKean
AG . . . . Al Gordon	BKs . . . . . Babara Kesel	CPa . . . Carlos Pacheco	DMD . . Dwayne McDuffie
AgF . . . . . A. Frolechlich	BL . . . . Bob Layton	CPr . . . Christopher Priest	DMG . . . Don McGregor
AGo . . . . . . Alex Garner	BLb . . . . Bob Lubbers	CR . . . . . P. Craig Russell	DMk . . . . . . David Mack
AGw . . . . Archie Goodwin	BlH . . . . Bill Hobbs	CrB . . . . Craig Brasfield	DMn . . . . . Duke Mighten
AH . . . . . . Adam Hughes	BLr . . . . . . Bob Larkin	CS . . . . Curt Swan	DMt . . . . . Dean Motter
AHo . . . . Art Holcomb	BLs . . . . . . Batton Lash	CsB . . . . . . Chris Batista	DN . . . . Don Newton
AlA . . . . . . Alfred Andriola	BM . . . . Barry Mitchel	CsM . . . . . Chris Moeller	DnS . . . . Dan Steffan
AKu . . . . . . Adam Kubert	BMc . . . . Bob McLeod	CSp . . . . . Chris Sprouse	DO . . . . . Dave Olbrich
ALa . . . . Andy Lanning	BMC . . B. McCorkindale	CU . . . . Chris Ulm	DoC . . . . Dario Carrasco
AlG . . . . . . Alan Grant	BML . . Bill Messner-Loebs	CV . . . . . . Charles Vess	DOe . . . . . . Dark One
AM . . . . Al Milgrom	BMs . . . . Bill Maus	CW . . . . . Chris Warner	DoM . . . . Doug Mahnke
AMc . . . Al McWilliams	BMy . . Brendon McCarthy	CWf . . . . . . Chance Wolf	DON . . . O'Neil, Denny
AMe . . . . . Angel Medina	BNa . . . . . . Bob Napton	CWi . . . . . Colin Wilson	DP . . . . . . Don Perlin
AMK . . . . . Angus McKie	BnP . . . . . Brian Pulido	CWn . . . . Chris Weston	DPo . . . . . Porch, David
AMo . . . . . Alan Moore	BO . . . . . . Bob Oskner	CYp . . . . . Chap Yaep	DPs . . . Dan Panosian
AN . . . . Alex Nino	BoW . . . . Bob Wood	**DA . . . . Dan Adkins**	DPw . . . . Power, Dermot
ANi . . . . Art Nichols	BP . . . . Bob Powell	DAb . . . . . Dusty Abell	DQ . . . . . . David Quinn
ANo . . . . . . Ann Nocenti	BPe . . . Brandon Peterson	DaC . . . . Dan Castellaneta	DR . . . . . . Ross, David
AOl . . . . Ariel Olivetti	BR . . . . Bill Reinhold	DaF . . . . . . Dan Fraga	DRd . . . Richard Delgado
APh . . . . Annie Parkhouse	BRa . . . . Ben Raab	DaG . . . . . Dave Garcia	DRi . . . . Don Rico
AR . . . . . . Alex Raymond	BrM . . . . . . Brian Murray	DaM . . . . . Danny Miki	DRo . . . . . Denis Rodier
AS . . . . Alex Saviuk	BrP . . . . . Bruce Patterson	DAn . . . . . . Dan Abnett	DS . . . . Dave Sim
ASm . . . . . Andy Smith	BS . . . . Bart Sears	DaR . . . Darrick Robertson	DSp . . . . . Dan Spiegle
ASp . . . . . Art Spiegelman	BSf . . . . . Brian Stelfreeze	DaW . . . . Damon Willis	DSs . . . . . Don Simpson
AT . . . . . . Angelo Torres	BSt . . . . . . Beau Smith	Day . . . . . . Dan Day	DSt . . . . . Dave Stevens
ATh . . . . Alex Toth	BSz . . . . . Bill Sienkiewicz	DAy . . . . . . Dick Ayers	DSw . . . Dan Sweetman
ATi . . . . Art Thibert	BT . . . . Bryan Talbot	DB . . . . . . D. Battlefield	DT . . . . . . Dwayne Turner
AV . . . . Al Vey	BTn . . . . . . Billy Tan	DB . . . . . Denis Beauvais	DTs . . . . . Dann Thomas
AVs . . . . . . Andrew Vachss	Buzz . . . . Buzz	DBa . . . . . . Dan Barry	DTy . . . . . . David Taylor
AW . . . . Al Williamson	BV . . . . Boris Vallejo	DBk . . . . . Darryl Banks	DvA . . . David Ammerman
AWa . . . . . Adam Warren	BVa . . . . . . Brad Vancata	DBl . . . . . Danny Bulanadi	DVa . . . . Dan Vado
AWi . . . . Anthony Williams	BW . . . . . Basil Wolverton	DBr . . . . . Dick Briefer	DvC . . . . . Dave Cooper
AWs . . . . Aron Wiesenfeld	BWa . . . . Bill Ward	DBs . . . . . John Barras	DvD . . . . . Dave Dorman
AxR . . . . Alex Ross	BWg . . . . . Bill Willingham	DBw . . . . Doug Braithwaite	DvJ . . . . . Dave Johnson
AyB . . . . . . Allyn Brodsky	BWi . . . . . . Bob Wiacek	DC . . . . . Dave Cockrum	DvL . . . . . . David Lloyd
BA . . . . . Brent Anderson	BWo . . . . . . Bill Woggin	DCn . . . . . Don Cameron	DvM . . . . David Micheline
BAn . . . . . . Bill Anderson	BWr . . . . . Berni Wrightson	DCw . . . . . Denys Cowan	DvR . . . . . . David Reed
BAp . . . . . . Brian Althorp	BWS . Barry Windsor-Smith	DD . . . . Dick Dillin	DW . . . . . . Doug Wildey
BAu . . . . Brian Augustyn	BZ . . . . Bruce Zick	DdB . . . . . David Boller	DWe . . . . David Wenzel
BB . . . . Brian Bolland	**CAd . . . . . Charlie Adlard**	DDv . . . . . Dan Davis	DZ . . . . . Dean Zachary
BBa . . . . . Bernard Bailey	CaS . . . . . Cam Smith	DdW . . . . David Williams	**EA . . . . Edd Ashe**
BbB . . . . Bob Brown	CAx . . . . Chris Alexander	DE . . . . D. Elliot	EB . . . . Ed Barreto
BBB . . . . . Bob Boze Bell	CB . . . . Carl Barks	DeH . . . . . Dave Hunt	EBe . . . . Ed Benes
BBh . . . . Brett Booth	CBa . . . . . Chris Bachalo	DeM . . . . Dev Madan	EC . . . . . . Ernie Colon
BbK . . . . . . Bob Kanigher	CBi . . . . . . Charles Biro	DeT . . . Derek Thomason	ECa . . . . Eddie Campbell
BBl . . . . Bret Blevins	CBu . . . . . . Carl Bugro	DFg . . . . Duncan Fegredo	ECh . . . . . . Ernie Chan
BBr . . . . . . Brett Breeding	CCa . . . . Charles Caldes	DFr . . . . Danny Fingeroth	EcS . . . . . Eric Silvestri
BCe . . . . . . Bobbie Chase	CCl . . . . Chris Claremont	DG . . . . . Dick Giordano	EDo . . . . . Evan Dorkin
BCh . . . . . Bernard Chang	Ccs . . . . Chriscross	DGb . . . . Dave Gibbons	EH . . . . . . Ed Hannigan
BCi . . . . . . Brandon Choi	CCt . . . . Claudio Castellini	DGC . . . . D.G. Chichester	EhH . . . . Ernest Hart

EHi . . . . E.E. Hibbard	GrI . . . . . . Graham Ingles	JDa . . . . Jack Davis	JOn . . . . . . James Owen
EHr. . . . . Everette Hartsoe	GrL. . . . . . Greg LaRocque	JDo . . . . Julie Doucet	JoP . . . . Joe Phillips
EiS. . . . . . Eric Shanower	GSh . . . Gerry Shamray	JDx . . . . John Dixon	JoS . . . . Joe Shuster
EK . . . . Everett R. Kinsler	GSr . . . . Geoff Senior	JDy . . . . Jo Duffy	JOs . . . . . John Ostrander
EL. . . . . Erik Larsen	GT . . . . . . George Tuska	JeJ . . . . Jeff Jones	JOt . . . . Jose Ortiz
ELe . . . . Elaine Lee	GtM . . . . . . Grant Miehm	JeM . . . . . Jerome Moore	JOy . . . . . . Jerry Ordway
ELu . . . Eric Van Lustbader	GW. . . . . . Gahan Wilson	JeP . . . . Jerry Prosser	JP. . . . . . . Jimmy Palmiotti
EM . . . . . Esteban Maroto	GWt . . . . Greg Wright	JeR. . . . . James Robinson	JPe . . . Jonathan Peterson
EN . . . . Earl Norem	GyA . . . . . . Gary Amaro	JEs . . . . John Estes	JPh . . . . . James Perham
ENB . . . E. Nelson Bridwell	GyC . . . . . Gerry Conway	JF . . . . John Forte	JPi . . . . . . Joe St.Pierre
EP . . . . Edmund Perryman	GyD . . . . Guy Davis	JFM . . John Francis Moore	JPL. . . . . . John Paul Leon
ERC . . . . E.R. Cruz	GyM . . . . . . Gary Martin	JFr . . . . . . John Freeman	JPn . . . . . . Jason Pearson
ErP . . . . Eric Pence	**HaE. . . . . . Harlan Ellison**	JFy . . . . James Fry III	JQ . . . . Joe Quesada
ErS . . . . . Eric Stephenson	HB . . . Hernandez Brothers	JG . . . . Jackson Guice	JR . . . . John Romita
ESM . . . . . Elliot S. Maggin	HbK. . . . . . Hannibal King	JGa . . . . . Jack Gaughan	JR2 . . . . . John Romita, Jr.
FaN . . . . . Fabian Nicieza	HC . . . . . Howard Chaykin	JGz . . . . Jorge Gonzalez	JRe . . . . John Royle
FB . . . . . . Frank Brunner	HFI . . . . Homer Flemming	JH . . . . . . Jack Herman	JRl. . . . . Jim Royle
FBe. . . . . . . Frank Bolle	HH. . . . . . . Hugh Haynes	JhB. . . . . John Beatty	JRo . . . . . . J. Rosenberger
FBk . . . . . . Fred Burke	HK . . . . Harvey Kurtzman	JhD . . . . John Dell	JRs . . . . John Ross
FC. . . . . . Frank Cirocco	HMe . . . . Howard Mackie	JHi . . . . . . John Higgins	JRu . . . . . Joe Rubinstein
FdS . . . . . . Fred Schiller	HMo . . . . Howard Porter	JHk . . . . John Hicklenton	JRv Judith Reeves-Stevens
FF . . . . . . Frank Frazetta	Harvey Mercadoocasio	JHl. . . . . . James Hudnall	JRy . . . . . John Ridgeway
FFo . . . . . . Frank Fosco	HMz . . . . . Henry Martinez	JHo . . . . . John Holdredge	JRz . . . . . . John Rozum
FG. . . . Frank Guardineer	HN. . . . . Howard Nostrand	JHr . . . . Jaime Hernandez	JS . . . . . Javier Saltares
FG. . . . Floyd Gottfredson	HNg. . . . . Hoang Nguyen	JHw . . . . Jamie Hewlett	JS3 . . . . . Jim Sanders III
FH . . . . Flint Henry	HPo . . . . . Howard Porter	JiC . . . . . Jim Callahan	JSb . . . . . Jonathan Sibal
FM . . . . Frank Miller	HSm . . . . . Howard Shum	JiS . . . . . . Jim Shooter	JSc . . . . . Jeffery Scott
FMc. . . . Frank McLaughlin	HSn . . . . Howard Simpson	JJ . . . . Jeff Johnson	JSC . . . . J. Scott Campbell
FR . . . . . . Frank Robbins	HT. . . . . Herb Trimpe	JJB. . . . . JJ Birch	JSe. . . . . . John Severin
FrG . . . . . . Frank Giacoia	HuR. . . . Humberto Ramos	JJn . . . . . Julius Jackson	JSh . . . . . Jim Sherman
FrS. . . . . . Frank Spinks	HWe . . . Howard Weinstein	JJo . . . . J.B. Jones	JSi. . . . . . . Jeff Smith
FS . . . . . Frank Springer	HwP . . . . . Howard Post	JJu . . . . . Joe Jusko	JSm . . . . . . Joe Simon
Fso . . . . Francesco	**IaC . . . . . . Ian Churchhill**	JK . . . . Jack Kirby	JSn. . . . . . Jim Starlin
FT . . . . . . Frank Thorne	IEd . . . . . . Ian Edginton	JKa . . . . . Jack Kamen	JSo. . . . . Jim Steranko
FTa . . . . Francis Takenaga	IG . . . . Ian Gibson	JkS . . . . . Jack Sparling	JSon . . . . . . Joe Staton
GaF . . . . . . Gardner Fox	IN . . . . Irv Novick	JKu . . . . . Joe Kubert	JSt . . . . . . Joe Sinnott
GB. . . . . . Geoffrey Biggs	IV . . . . . . Ivan Velez, Jr.	JKz . . . . . . Jack Katz	JTo . . . . . John Totleben
GBl. . . . . . . George Bell	**JA . . . . Jack Abel**	JL. . . . . . . Jose Lopez	JuB. . . . . Julie Bell
GBu . . . . . Greg Budget	JaB. . . . . . . Jack Binder	JLb . . . . Jeph Loeb	JV . . . . . Jim Valentino
GC. . . . . . . Gene Colan	JaD . . . . . Jamie Delano	JLd. . . . . Joe Lansdale	JVF . . . . John Van Fleet
GCa . . . . . Greg Capullo	JaL. . . . . Jae Lee	JLe . . . . Jim Lee	JWf . . . . . Joseph Wolfe
GCh. . . . . . Gary Cohn	JAl. . . . . . Jeff Albrecht	JLi . . . Joseph M. Linsner	JWi . . . . . J.H. Williams
GD . . . . Gene Day	JAo . . . . . John Albano	JlT. . . . . . . Jill Thompson	JWk . . . . . John Watkiss
GDu . . . . . Gary Dumm	JAp . . . . . . Jim Aparo	JLv. . . . . . Jim Lavery	JWo. . . . . Jim Woodring
GE . . . . . George Evans	JAr . . . . . . John Arcudi	JM . . . . . . Jim Mooney	JWp . . . . . Jason Waltrip
GeH . . . . Gene Ha	JB . . . . . John Buscema	JMC . . . . John McCrea	JWt . . . . . John Waltrip
GEn . . . . . Garth Ennis	JBa . . . . . . Jim Baikie	JMd . . . Joe Madureira	JyS . . . . . . Jerry Serpe
GEr. . . . . . Gary Erskine	JBa . . . . . . Jim Balent	JMD . . . J.M. DeMatteis	JZ. . . . . . . Jorge Zaffino
GF. . . . . . . Glenn Fabry	JBe . . . . . John Beeston	JMi . . . . . . Jeff Mariotte	JZe . . . . Joe Zabel
GfD . . . . . . Geof Darrow	JBg. . . . . Jon Bogdanove	JmL . . . . . Jim Lawson	JZy . . . . Joseph Zyskowski
GFo. . . . . Gerald Forton	JBi . . . . . . Jerry Bingham	JMn. . . . . Joe Maneely	**K&R. . . . . Kane & Romita**
GFr . . . . . . Gary Frank	JBl . . . . . . Jesus Blasco	JmP . . . . James Pascoe	KB . . . . Kyle Baker
GFx . . . . Gill Fox	JBm . . . . . John Broom	JMr. . . . . . Jeff Moore	KBk. . . . . . . Kurt Busiek
GG . . . . . . Gabe Gecko	JBn . . . . . John Burns	JMs. . . . . Jeff Matsuda	KD . . . . . . Kieron Dwyer
Ggn . . . . Geggan	JBo. . . . . . John Bolton	JMt. . . . . . Joe Martin	KDe . . . . Kim Deitch
GgP . . . . . George Pratt	JBr . . . . . . June Brigman	JMu . . . . . Jon J. Muth	KDM . . . . Kim DeMulder
GHe . . . Gilbert Hernandez	JBt . . . . Jeff Butler	JMy. . . . . . Jeffrey Moy	KEa. . . . . Kevin Eastman
GHi . . . . . Graham Higgins	JBy . . . . . . John Byrne	JMz. . . . . Jose Marzan	KeL . . . . . Ken Lashley
Gl . . . . . . Geoff Isherwood	JBz. . . . . . Joe Benitez	JnM . . . . . Jason Minor	KeW . . . . Kevin Walker
GJ . . . . . . Gerard Jones	JCa . . . . . John Calnan	JnR . . . . . . John Riley	KG . . . . . . Keith Giffen
GK . . . . Gil Kane	JCf . . . . . . Jim Calafiore	JNR . . . John Ney Rieber	KGa . . . . . Kerry Gammill
GL. . . . . Garry Leach	JCh . . . . . . Joe Chiodo	JnS . . . . . John Smith	KHd . . . . Kevin Hopgood
GlD . . . . Glyn Dillon	JCo . . . . Jack Cole	JO . . . . . . Joe Orlando	KHt . . . . Kyle Hotz
GLz . . . . . Greg Luzniak	JCp . . . . . John Cooper	JoA. . . . . . Jo Alibaster	KJ . . . . . . Klaus Janson
GM . . . . . . Gray Morrow	JCr. . . . . . Johnny Craig	JoB . . . . . Joe Bennett	KJa . . . . . . Kirk Javinen
GMo . . . . Grant Morrison	JCt . . . . Joe Carter	JoC . . . . . . Joe Casey	KJo . . . . . Kelley Jones
GN. . . . . . Graham Nolan	JCx . . . . . Jeromy Cox	JOb . . . . James O'Barr	KK . . . . . . Karl Kesel
GP . . . . . . George Perez	JCz. . . . . . . Jerry Cruz	JoG . . . . . Joe Giella	KIA . . . . Karl Alstaetter
GPi . . . . . . Gene Pamai	JD . . . . . . Jan Duursema	JoM . . . . . Joe Musial	KIK. . . . . Karl Kerschl

Abbr.	Name	Abbr.	Name	Abbr.	Name	Abbr.	Name
KIS	Karl Story	MCr	Mike Carlin	MSy	Mike Sekowsky	RAJ	R.A. Jones
KM	Kevin Maguire	MCW	M.C. Wyman	MT	Mark Texeira	RaP	Rachel Pollack
KN	Kevin Nowlan	MCy	Mike Carey	MtB	Matt Broome	RB	Rich Buckler
KoK	Kevin Kobasic	MD	Mort Drucker	MTk	Masashi Tanaka	RbB	Robert Bernstein
KON	Kevin O'Neill	MD2	Mike Deodato, Jr.	MV	Mike Vosburg	RbC	Robert Campenella
KP	Keith Pollard	MDa	Malcolm Davis	MvR	Melvin Rubi	RBe	Ramon Bernado
KPl	Kilian Plunkett	MDb	M. DeZuniga	MW	Mary Wilshire	RBn	Ryan Benjamin
KS	Kurt Schaffenberger	MDo	Mike Dorey	MWa	Mark Waid	RBr	Rick Burchett
KSW	Keith S. Wilson	MDr	Mike Dringenberg	MWg	Matt Wagner	RBu	Robert Burns
KSy	Ken Steacy	ME	Mike Esposito	MWn	Marv Wolfman	RC	Reed Crandall
KtH	Kurt Hathaway	MEg	Marty Egeland	MZ	Mike Zeck	RCa	Richard Case
KVH	Kevin VanHook	MeP	Mike Parobeck	MZi	Michael Zulli	RCl	Ricky Carralero
KW	Kent Williams	MeW	Mike Weringo	**NA**	**Neal Adams**	RCo	Richard Corben
KWe	Kevin West	MF	Matt Fox	NBy	Norm Breyfogle	RCr	Robert Crumb
KWi	Keith Williams	MFl	Michael Fleisher	NC	Nick Cardy	RCz	Roger Cruz
KWo	Kirk Van Wormer	MFm	Mark Farmer	ND	Nigel Dobbyn	RDB	Randy DuBerkr
LbC	**Leonard B. Cole**	MFr.	Michael Jan Friedman	Nel	Nelson	RdM	Raymond Marais
LC	Lou Cameron	MG	Mike Gustovich	NGa	Neil Gaiman	RDm	Rodolfo Damaggio
LCh	Lillian Chestney	MGi	Michael T. Gilbert	NHa	Neil Hanson	RE	Ric Estrada
LDr	Larry Dresser	MGo	Michael Golden	NKu	Andy Kubert	RF	Ron Frenz
LDu	Leo Duranona	MGr	Mike Grell	NMa	Nathan Massengill	RFl	Robert Fleming
LDz	Luis Dominguez	MGs	Martin Griffiths	NNa	Nick Napolitano	RG	Ron Garney
LE	Lee Elias	MGu	Mark Gruenwald	NPl	Noly Panalign	RGd	Ruben Gerard
LeS	Len Strazewski	MGy	Mick Gray	NR	Nestor Redondo	RgM	Rags Morales
LF	Lou Fine	MHi	Michael Higgins	NRd	Norm Rapmund	RGr	Randy Green
LHa	Larry Hama	MHo	Matt Howarth	NSH	N. Steven Harris	RGs	R. Grossman
LI	Larry Ivie	MHs	Mike Heisler	NV	Neil Vokes	RGT	R.G. Taylor
LiM	Linda Medley	MHw	Matt Hawkins	NyC	Nancy Collins	RGu	Rebecca Guay
LJi	Leonardo Jimenez	MHy	Matt Haley	**OW**	**Ogden Whitney**	RH	Russ Heath
LKa	Len Kaminski	MI	Medio Iorio	**PaD**	**Paco Diaz**	RHe	Richard Horie
LLi	Larry Lieber	MiA	Michael Allred	PaK	Paris T. Karounos	RHo	Rick Hoberg
LMa	Larry Mahlstedt	MiB	Mike Barr	PaP	Paul Pelletier	RHo	Rich Howell
LMc	Luke McDonnell	MJ	Malcolm Jones	PB	Pat Broderick	RiB	Richard Bennett
LMd	Lee Moder	MK	Mike Kaluta	PBd	Philip Bond	Rip	Riply
LMr	Lee Marrs	MkB	Mike Barreiro	PC	Paul Chadwick	RJ	Robert Jenney
Low	John Lowe	MkF	Mike Friedrich	PCu	Paris Cullins	RJn	Robert Jones
LRs	Luke Ross	MkH	Mike Hoffer	PD	Peter Doherty	RkB	Rick Bryant
LS	Lee Sullivan	MkK	Mike McKenna	PDd	Peter David	RkL	Rick Leach
LSh	Liam Sharp	MkW	Mark Wheatley	PDi	Paul Dini	RKu	Roy Krenkel
LSi	Louise Simonson	MlB	Michael Bair	PFe	Pascual Ferry	RL	Rick Leonardi
LSn	Larry Stroman	MLe	Mike Leeke	PG	Paul Gulacy	RLd	Rob Liefeld
LSt	Leonard Starr	MLr	Michael Lark	PGa	Phil Gascoine	RLe	Rik Levins
LuH	Lou Harrison	MM	Mike Manley	PGn	Paul Guinan	RLm	Ron Lim
LW	Lee Weeks	MMc	M. McMahon	PGr	Peter Grau	RLv	R. Livingstone
LWn	Len Wein	MMe	Mort Meskin	PhH	Phil Hester	RM	Rick Magyar
LyW	Larry Welch	MMi	Michael Mignola	PJ	Phil Jimminiz	RMc	Ralph Macchio
MA	**Murphy Anderson**	MMK	Mike McKone	PJe	Paul Jenkins	RMn	Roland Mann
MaG	Manny Galan	MMo	Mark Moretti	PKr	Peter Krause	RMr	Roy Allan Martinez
MaH	Mark Hempel	MMr	Mark Millar	PlA	Paul Abrams	RMz	Ron Marz
Man	Roland Mann	MMy	Marat Mychaels	PLa	Peter Laird	RN	Rudy Nebres
MaS	Mark Schmitz	MN	Mike Netzer	PMo	Pete Morisi	RnT	Ron Tinker
MaT	Mark Tenney	MnN	Martin Nodell	PMs	Pat Mills	RoR	Ron Randall
MB	Matt Baker	Moe	Moebius	PNe	Paul Neary	RoW	on Wagner
MBa	Mark Bagley	MP	Mike Ploog	PNu	Philip Nutman	RP	Rudy Palais
MBe	M. Belardinelli	MPa	Mark Pacella	PO	Patrick Olliffe	RPc	Richard Pace
MBg	Mark Badger	MPc	Mark Paniccia	PPo	Paul Pope	RPi	Richard Pini
MBm	Mary Bierbaum	MPk	Martin Pasko	PQ	Peter Quinones	RQu	Randy Queen
MBn	Mike Baron	MPn	Mark Pennington	PR	Paul Ryan	RRa	Rich Rankin
MBr	Mark Bright	MR	Marshall Rogers	PrC	Peter Costanza	RS	Ron Smith
MBu	Mark Buckingham	MRa	Mac Raboy	PrG	Peter Gross	RsB	Russell Braun
MBy	Mitch Byrd	MRc	Mark Ricketts	PrM	Peter Milligan	RSd	Randy Stradley
MC	Mike Collins	MRi	Mike Richardson	PS	Paul Smith	RsM	Russ Manning
MCa	Marc Campos	MRy	Matt Ryan	PSj	Peter Snejbjerg	RSm	Robin Smith
MCh	Mike Chen	MS	Mark Silvestri	PtL	Patrick Lee	RSt	Roger Stern
MCi	Mark Crilley	MSh	Mark Schultz	PuD	Paul Danner	RT	Romeo Tanghal
MCl	Mike Clark	MsM	Mike S. Miller	PuJ	Paul Johnson	RtH	Robert Hebbard
MCn	Max Allan Collins	MSo	Mark Sasso	PuK	Paul Kupperberg	RTs	Roy Thomas
MCo	Mark Chiarello	MSt	Malcolm Smith	**RA**	**Ross Andru**	RV	Rick Veitch

RyE . . . . . Randy Emberlin
RyL . . . . Ray Lago
RyR . . . . . Rodney Ramos
S&K . . . . . Simon & Kirby
S&S . . . . . Siegel & Shuster
SA . . . . . Sergio Aragones
Sal . . . . Sal Amendola
SAP . . Shea Anton Pensa
SaV . . . . Sal Velluto
SB . . . . Sal Buscema
SBi . . . . . Stephen Bissette
SBs . . . . . . Simon Bisley
SBt . . . . Steve Butler
SC . . . . Sid Check
ScB . . . . . . Scott Benefiel
ScC . . . . Scott Clark
SCh . . . . Sean Chen
SCi. . . . . Sergio Cariello
ScK . . . . Scott Kolins
ScL . . . . Scott Lee
SCr . . . . . . Steve Crespo
SCy. . . . . . . Simon Colby
SD . . . . Steve Ditko
SDi. . . . . . . Steve Dillon
SDr . . . . Stan Drake
SDR . . . . Sam DeLaRosa
SEa . . . . Scott Eaton
SeM . . . . . Steve Montano
SeP . . . . . . Sean Phillips
SEp. . . . . . Steve Epting
SeT . . . . . . Steve Tappin
SEt. . . . . Steve Englehart
SF. . . . . . Sal Finnocchiaro
SFr. . . . . Simon Freeman
SFu . . . . . Simon Furman
SG . . . . . Sam Glanzman
SGe . . . . Sid Greene
SHa. . . . . . . Scott Hanna
ShG . . Shannon Gallant
ShM . . . . Sheldon Mayer
SHn . . . . Simon Harrison
SHp . . . . . Scott Hampton
SI. . . . . . Stuart Immonen
SK . . . . Sam Kieth
SL . . . . . . Steve Leialoha
SLi . . . . . . Steve Lightle

SLo. . . . . . . Scott Lobdell
SM . . . . Steve Miller
SMa . Shawn Martinbrough
SmC . . . . Sam Citron
SMc. . . . . Scott McDaniel
SMl . . . . . Scott McCloud
SML . . . Sean McLaughlin
SMt. . . . . Steve Mattsson
SnW . . . . . . Stan Woch
SPa . . . . . . Stephen Platt
Spk . . . . Spark
SPl . . . . . . Scott Phillips
SPr . . . . Stefan Petrucha
SR . . . . Steve Rude
SRf. . . . . . Sean Ruffner
SS . . . . . . Stan Sakai
SSc . . . . . Sean Scoffield
SSe . . . . Steven T. Seagle
SSh. . . . . . . Sean Shaw
SSr . . . . . Steve Skroce
SSt . . . . . . Steve Stern
StA . . . . . Stephen Addeo
StB. . . . . Scott Benson
StC . . . . . Stan Campbell
StE. . . . . . Steve Erwin
StG . . . . . . Steve Grant
StL . . . . Stan Lee
StP . . . . . . Steve Pugh
SVa . . . . . . Steve Vance
SvG . . . . . Steve Gerber
SvL . . . . Salvador Larroca
SvP . . . . Steve Parkhouse
SvS . . . . . . Steve Stiles
SW . . . . . Scott Williams
SWi . . . . Skip Williamson
SwM. . . . Shawn McManus
SY. . . . . . Steve Yeowell
SZ. . . . Steven Zyskowski
TA . . . . Terry Austin
TAr. . . . . . . Tom Artis
TB . . . . Tim Boxell
TBd . . . Tim Bradstreet
TBe . . . . . Terry Beatty
TBm . . . . . Tom Bierbaum
TC . . . . . . Travis Charest
TCk. . . . . . . Tomm Coker

TD. . . . . . Tony DeZuniga
TDF . . . . . . Tom DeFalco
TDr . . . . . Tom Derenick
TDz . . . . . Todd DeZago
TeB . . . . . Tex Blaisdell
TeH . . . . . . Ted Halsted
TEl. . . . . . . Tim Eldred
TG. . . . . . Tom Grummett
TGb . . . . Tom Grindberg
TGo . . . . . Till Goodman
TH . . . . . . Tim Hamilton
THa . . . . . . Tim Harris
TJn . . . . . Todd Johnson
TKa . . . . Terry Kavanagh
TKn. . . . . Trent Kaniuga
TKr . . Teddy H. Kristiansen
TL. . . . . Tom Lyle
TLa . . . . . . Terry LaBan
TLw . . . . Terral Lawrence
TM . . . . . Todd McFarlane
TmB. . . . . Tim Burgard
TmC . . . . Tom Christopher
TMd. . . . . Tom Mandrake
TMK . . . Ted McKeever
TMo. . . . . . Tom Morgan
TmR. . . . . . Tom Ryder
TMr . . . . . Terry Moore
TMs . . . . . Tom Mason
TmT. . . . . . Tom Teney
TMw . . . . . Tom McCraw
TNa . . . . . . Ted Naifeh
TnD . . . . . Tony Daniel
TnS . . . . . Tristan Schane
TNu . . . . . Todd Nauck
ToT . . . . . Tony Takezaki
TOz . . . . . Tayyar Ozkan
TP . . . . . . Tom Palmer
TPe . . . . . . Tom Peyer
TR. . . . . . . Tom Raney
TR . . . . . Ted Richards
TrR . . . . . Trina Robbins
TS. . . . . . Tom Sutton
TSa. . . . . Tony Salmons
TSe . . . . . . Tim Sale
TSg . . . . . Tom Sniegoski
TSr. . . . Terry Shoemaker

TT . . . . . Timothy Truman
TTg . . . . Tom Taggart
TTn . . . . . . Ty Templeton
TV . . . . Tim Vigil
TVE . . . Trevor Von Eeden
TvS . . . . Trevor Scott
TWo. . . . . Teri Sue Wood
TY . . . . Tom Yeates
TyD . . . . . Terry Dodson
TyH. . . . . . . Tony Harris
TyT . . . . . Tony Tallarico
VAz. . . . . Vincent Alcazar
VB . . . . . . Vaughn Bode
VcL . . . . . . Vince Locke
VGi . . . . . Vince Giarrano
ViC . . . . . Vince Colletta
VMk . . . . . Val Mayerik
VMo . . . . Vincent Morosco
VRu. . . . . . Vince Russell
VS . . . . . . Val Semeiks
VV . . . . . . Vagner Vargas
WaP . . . . . Warren Pleece
WB . . . . . Wayne Boring
WBu . . . . . W. Burroughs
WE. . . . . . . Will Eisner
WEl . . . . . . Warren Ellis
WiS . . . . . William Stout
WK . . . . . . Walt Kelly
Wld. . . . . Andrew Wildman
WmB. . . . William Bossart
WMc . . . . Walter McDaniel
WMo . . . . Win Mortimer
Woj . . . Chuck Wojtkiewicz
WP . . . . Wendy Pini
WPo . . . . Whilce Portacio
WR . . . . . . Werner Roth
WS . . . . . Walt Simonson
WSm . . . . . Will Simpson
WW . . . . . Wally Wood
YG. . . . . . . Yvel Guichet
YuK . . . . . Yukito Kisniro

GENERAL ABBREVIATIONS FOR COMICS LISTINGS

A: . . . . Appearance of	GAm. . . . . Graphic Album	Prev. . . . . Preview
(a) . . . . Artist	GN or GNv . . . . Graphic Novel	pt. or Pt. . . . . Part
Adapt. . . . . Adaptation	G-Size. . . . . Giant Size	rep. . . . . Reprinted issue
Anniv. . . . . Anniversary	HC. . . . . Hardcover	R: . . . . Return/Revival of
Ann.# . . . . Annual	I: . . . . Introduction of	rtd. . . . . Retold
(a&pl) . . . . Art & Plot	(i) . . . . Inks by	(s) . . . . Scripted/Written by
(a&s) . . . . Art & Script	IR: . . . . Identity Revealed	S.A. . . . . Silver Age
B:. . . . . Beginning of	J: . . . . Joins of	SC . . . . Softcover
b: . . . . Birth of	K-Size. . . . . King Size	(s&i) . . . . Scripts & inks
BU: . . . . Back-Up Story	L: . . . . Leaving of	Spec. . . . . Special
C: . . . . . . Cameo Appearance	N: . . . . New Costume	TPB . . . . . . Trade Paperback
(c) . . . . Cover	N# . . . . . No Issue Number	T.U. . . . . Team-up
(c&s) . . . . . . Cover and Script	O: . . . . Origin of	V: or vs. . . . . Versus
D:. . . . . . Death/Destruction of	P(c) . . . . Painted Cover	W: . . . . Wedding of
Ed. . . . . Edition	(p) . . . . Pencils by	w/ . . . . With
E: . . . . Ending of	PF . . . . Prestige Format	w/o . . . . Without
F:. . . . . Features	Ph(c) . . . . . Photographic cover	x-over. . . . . Crossover with
G.A. . . . . Golden Age	(pl) . . . . Plotted by	

DC COMICS

A. BIZARRO
1999
1 (of 4) SvG,MBr,F:Al Bizarro 2.50
2 SvG,MBr,A:Superman. 2.50
3 SvG,MBr, ... 2.50
4 SvG,MBr, Viva Bizarro 2.50

ABSOLUTE VERTIGO
1995
Ashcan: Invisibles, other samples . . 6.00

ACTION
June, 1938
1 JoS,I&O:Superman;Rescues Evelyn
  Curry from electric chair. 185,000.00
2 JoS,V:Emil Norvell 22,000.00
3 JoS,V:Thorton Blakely 15,000.00
4 JoS,V:Coach Randall 8,500.00
5 JoS,Emergency of
  Vallegho Dam 8,000.00
6 JoS,I:Jimmy Olsen,
  V:Nick Williams 8,000.00
7 JoS,V:Derek Niles 14,000.00
8 JoS,V:Gimpy 6,500.00
9 JoS,A:Det.Captain Reilly . . 6,200.00
10 JoS,Superman fights
  for prison reform 10,000.00
11 JoS,Disguised as
  Homer Ramsey 3,300.00
12 JoS,Crusade against
  reckless drivers 3,300.00
13 JoS,I:Ultra Humanite 5,500.00
14 JoS,BKa,V:Ultra Humanite,
  B:Clip Carson 3,200.00
15 JoS,BKa,Superman in
  Kidtown 4,500.00
16 JoS,BKa,Crusade against
  Gambling. 2,500.00
17 JoS,BKa,V:Ultra Humanite . 3,500.00
18 JoS,BKa,V:Mr.Hamilton
  O:Three Aces 2,400.00
19 JoS,BKa,V:Ultra Humanite
  B:Superman (c) 3,200.00
20 JoS,BKa,V:Ultra Humanite . 3,000.00
21 JoS,BKa,V:Ultra Humanite . 2,000.00
22 JoS,BKa,War between Toran
  and Galonia. 1,900.00
23 JoS,BKa,SMo,I:Lex Luthor . 6,000.00
24 JoS,BKa,BBa,SMo,FG,Meets
  Peter Carnahan 2,000.00
25 JoS,BKa,BBa,SMo,V:Medini 2,000.00
26 JoS,BKa,V:Clarence Cobalt. 2,000.00
27 JoS,BKa,V:Mr & Mrs.Tweed 1,600.00
28 JoS,BKa,JBu,V:Strongarm
  Bandit 1,600.00
29 JoS,BKa,V:Martin 2,000.00
30 JoS,BKa,V:Zolar 1,600.00
31 JoS,BKa,JBu,V:Baron
  Munsdorf 1,000.00
32 JoS,BKa,JBu,I:Krypto Ray Gun
  V:Mr.Preston 1,100.00
33 JoS,BKa,JBu,V:Brett Hall,
  O:Mr. America 1,100.00
34 JoS,BKa,V:Jim Laurg 1,000.00
35 JoS,BKa,V:Brock Walter . . . 1,000.00
36 JoS,BKa,V:StuartPemberton 1,000.00
37 JoS,BKa,V:Commissioner
  Kennedy, O:Congo Bill. . . . 1,100.00
38 JoS,BKa,V:Harold Morton . . 1,000.00
39 JoS,BKa,Meets Britt Bryson 1,000.00
40 JoS,BKa,Meets Nancy
  Thorgenson 1,000.00
41 JoS,BKa,V:Ralph Cowan,

E:Clip Carson 900.00
42 V:Lex Luthor,I&O:Vigilante. . 1,400.00
43 V:Dutch O'Leary,Nazi(c) 900.00
44 V:Prof. Steffens,Nazi(c) 900.00
45 V:Count Von Henzel,
  I:Stuff,Nazi(c) 900.00
46 V:The Domino 850.00
47 V:Lex Luthor—1st app. w/super
  powers,I:Powerstone 1,400.00
48 V:The Top 900.00
49 I:Puzzler 950.00
50 Meets Stan Doborak 900.00
51 I:Prankster. 950.00
52 V:Emperor of America. 1,000.00
53 JBu,V:Night-Owl. 700.00
54 JBu,Meets Stanley
  Finchcomb 600.00
55 JBu,V:Cartoonist Al Hatt. 600.00
56 V:Emil Loring 600.00
57 V:Prankster 600.00
58 JBu,V:Adonis 600.00
59 I:Susie Thompkins,Lois
  Lane's niece 550.00
60 JBu,Lois Lane-Superwoman! . 600.00
61 JBu,Meets Craig Shaw. 550.00
62 JBu,V:Admiral Von Storff 550.00
63 JBu,V:Professor Praline 550.00
64 I:Toyman 650.00
65 JBu,V:Truman Treadwell 525.00
66 JBu,V:Mr.Annister 525.00
67 JBu,Superman School for
  Officer's Training. 525.00
68 A:Susie Thompkins 525.00
69 V:Prankster 525.00
70 JBu,V:Thinker 525.00
71 Superman Valentine's
  Day Special 500.00
72 V:Mr. Sniggle. 500.00
73 V:Lucius Spruce. 500.00
74 Meets Adelbert Dribble. 500.00
75 V:Johnny Aesop. 500.00
76 A Voyage with Destiny 500.00
77 V:Prankster 500.00
78 The Chef of Bohemia 500.00
79 JBu,A:J. Wilbur Wolfingham. . 500.00
80 A:Mr. Mxyzptlk (2nd App) 800.00
81 Meets John Nicholas 550.00
82 JBu,V:Water Sprite. 500.00
83 I:Hocus and Pocus. 500.00
84 JBu,V:Dapper Gang. 500.00
85 JBu,V:Toyman 500.00
86 JBu,V:Wizard of Wokit 500.00
87 V:Truck Hijackers. 500.00
88 A:Hocus and Pocus 500.00
89 V:Slippery Andy 500.00
90 JBu,V:Horace Rikker and the
  Amphi-Bandits 500.00
91 JBu,V:Davey Jones 475.00
92 JBu,V:Nowmie Norman 475.00
93 Superman Christmas story . . . 475.00
94 JBu,V:Bullwer `Bull' Rylie 475.00
95 V:Prankster 475.00
96 V:Mr. Twister 475.00
97 A:Hocus and Pocus 475.00
98 V:Mr. Mxyzptlk, A:Susie
  Thompkins 475.00
99 V:Keith Langwell 475.00
100 I:InspectorErskineHawkins 1,050.00
101 V:Specs Dour,A-Bomb(c). . 1,000.00
102 V:Mr. Mxyzptlk 450.00
103 V:Emperor Quexo 450.00
104 V:Prankster 450.00
105 Superman Christmas story . . 450.00
106 Clark Kent becomes Baron
  Edgestream 450.00

Action #29 © DC Comics, Inc.

107 JBu,A:J.Wilbur Wolfingham . 450.00
108 JBu,V:Vince Vincent. 450.00
109 V:Prankster 450.00
110 A:Susie Thompkins 450.00
111 Cameras in the Clouds 450.00
112 V:Mr. Mxyzptlk 450.00
113 Just an Ordinary Guy 450.00
114 V:Mike Chesney. 450.00
115 Meets Arthur Parrish 450.00
116 A:J. Wilbur Wolfingham 450.00
117 Superman Christmas story . 450.00
118 The Execution of Clark Kent. 450.00
119 Meets Jim Banning. 450.00
120 V:Mike Foss. 450.00
121 V:William Sharp 450.00
122 V:Charley Carson. 450.00
123 V:Skid Russell 450.00
124 Superman becomes
  radioactive 475.00
125 V:Lex Luthor 475.00
126 V:Chameleon 450.00
127 JKu,Superman on Truth or
  Consequences 500.00
128 V:`Aces' Deucey 425.00
129 Meets Gob-Gob 425.00
130 V:Captain Kidder 425.00
131 V:Lex Luthor 425.00
132 Superman meets George
  Washington 425.00
133 V:Emma Blotz 425.00
134 V:Paul Strong. 425.00
135 V:John Morton 425.00
136 Superman Show-Off! 425.00
137 Meets Percival Winter 425.00
138 Meets Herbert Hinkle 425.00
139 Clark Kent...Daredevil! 425.00
140 Superman becomes Hermit . 425.00
141 V:Lex Luthor 425.00
142 V:Dan the Dip 425.00
143 Dates Nikki Larve. 425.00
144 O:Clark Kent reporting for
  Daily Planet 450.00
145 Meets Merton Gloop 425.00
146 V:Luthor. 425.00
147 V:`Cheeks' Ross 425.00
148 Superman, Indian Chief 425.00
149 The Courtship on Krypton! . . 425.00
150 V:Morko. 425.00
151 V:Mr.Mxyzptlk,Lex Luthor
  and Prankster. 425.00
152 I:Metropolis Shutterbug

All comics prices listed are for *Near Mint* condition.

Action Comics #250 © DC Comics, Inc.

Society	425.00
153 V:Kingpin	425.00
154 V:Harry Reed	425.00
155 V:Andrew Arvin	425.00
156 Lois Lane becomes Super-woman,V:Lex Luthor	425.00
157 V:Joe Striker	425.00
158 V:Kane Korrell O:Superman (retold)	1,000.00
159 Meets Oswald Whimple	400.00
160 I:Minerva Kent	400.00
161 Meets Antara	400.00
162 V:`IT!'	350.00
163 Meets Susan Semple	350.00
164 Meets Stefan Andriessen	350.00
165 V:Crime Czar	350.00
166 V:Lex Luthor	350.00
167 V:Prof. Nero	350.00
168 O:Olaf	350.00
169 Caveman Clark Kent!	350.00
170 V:Mad Artist of Metropolis	350.00
171 The Secrets of Superman	350.00
172 Lois Lane..Witch!	350.00
173 V:Dragon Lang	350.00
174 V:Miracle Twine Gang	350.00
175 V:John Vinden	350.00
176 V:Billion Dollar Marvin Gang	350.00
177 V:General	350.00
178 V:Prof. Sands	350.00
179 Superman in Mapleville	350.00
180 V:Syndicate of Five	350.00
181 V:Diamond Dave Delaney	325.00
182 The Return from Planet Krypton	325.00
183 V:Lex Luthor	325.00
184 Meets Donald Whitmore	325.00
185 V:Issah Pendleton	325.00
186 The Haunted Superman	325.00
187 V:Silver	325.00
188 V:Cushions Raymond gang	325.00
189 Meets Mr.&Mrs. John Vandeveir	325.00
190 V:Mr. Mxyzptlk	325.00
191 V:Vic Vordan	325.00
192 Meets Vic Vordan	325.00
193 V:Beetles Brogan	325.00
194 V:Maln	325.00
195 V:Tiger Woman	325.00
196 Superman becomes Mental Man	325.00
197 V:Stanley Stark	325.00
198 The Six Lives of Lois Lane	325.00
199 V:Lex Luthor	325.00
200 V:Morwatha	325.00

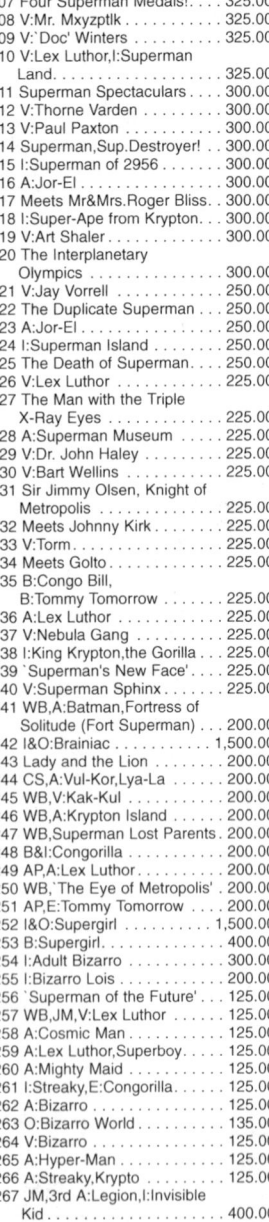

201 V:Benny the Brute	325.00
202 Lois Lane's X-Ray Vision	325.00
203 Meets Pietro Paresca	325.00
204 Meets Sam Spulby	325.00
205 Sergeant Superman	325.00
206 Imaginary story featuring Lois Lane	325.00
207 Four Superman Medals!	325.00
208 V:Mr. Mxyzptlk	325.00
209 V:`Doc' Winters	325.00
210 V:Lex Luthor,I:Superman Land	325.00
211 Superman Spectaculars	300.00
212 V:Thorne Varden	300.00
213 V:Paul Paxton	300.00
214 Superman,Sup.Destroyer!	300.00
215 I:Superman of 2956	300.00
216 A:Jor-El	300.00
217 Meets Mr&Mrs.Roger Bliss	300.00
218 I:Super-Ape from Krypton	300.00
219 V:Art Shaler	300.00
220 The Interplanetary Olympics	300.00
221 V:Jay Vorrell	250.00
222 The Duplicate Superman	250.00
223 A:Jor-El	250.00
224 I:Superman Island	250.00
225 The Death of Superman	250.00
226 V:Lex Luthor	225.00
227 The Man with the Triple X-Ray Eyes	225.00
228 A:Superman Museum	225.00
229 V:Dr. John Haley	225.00
230 V:Bart Wellins	225.00
231 Sir Jimmy Olsen, Knight of Metropolis	225.00
232 Meets Johnny Kirk	225.00
233 V:Torm	225.00
234 Meets Golto	225.00
235 B:Congo Bill, B:Tommy Tomorrow	225.00
236 A:Lex Luthor	225.00
237 V:Nebula Gang	225.00
238 I:King Krypton,the Gorilla	225.00
239 `Superman's New Face'	225.00
240 V:Superman Sphinx	225.00
241 WB,A:Batman,Fortress of Solitude (Fort Superman)	200.00
242 I&O:Brainiac	1,500.00
243 Lady and the Lion	200.00
244 CS,A:Vul-Kor,Lya-La	200.00
245 WB,V:Kak-Kul	200.00
246 WB,A:Krypton Island	200.00
247 WB,Superman Lost Parents	200.00
248 I&I:Congorilla	200.00
249 AP,A:Lex Luthor	200.00
250 WB,`The Eye of Metropolis'	200.00
251 AP,E:Tommy Tomorrow	200.00
252 I&O:Supergirl	1,500.00
253 B:Supergirl	400.00
254 I:Adult Bizarro	300.00
255 I:Bizarro Lois	200.00
256 `Superman of the Future'	125.00
257 WB,JM,V:Lex Luthor	125.00
258 A:Cosmic Man	125.00
259 A:Lex Luthor,Superboy	125.00
260 A:Mighty Maid	125.00
261 I:Streaky,E:Congorilla	125.00
262 A:Bizarro	125.00
263 O:Bizarro World	135.00
264 V:Bizarro	125.00
265 A:Hyper-Man	125.00
266 A:Streaky,Krypto	125.00
267 JM,3rd A:Legion,I:Invisible Kid	400.00
268 WB,A:Hercules	125.00
269 A:Jerro	125.00
270 CS,JM,A:Batman	135.00
271 A:Lex Luthor	125.00
272 A:Aquaman	125.00
273 A:Mr.Mxyzptlk	125.00

Action Comics #275 © DC Comics, Inc.

274 A:Superwoman	125.00
275 WB,JM,V:Braimiac	125.00
276 JM,6th A:Legion,I:Brainiac 5, Triplicate Girl,Bouncing Boy	175.00
277 CS,JM,V:Lex Luthor	100.00
278 CS,Perry White Becomes Master Man	100.00
279 JM,V:Hercules,Samson	100.00
280 CS,JM,V:Braniac, A:Congorilla	100.00
281 JM,A:Krypto	100.00
282 JM,V:Mxyzptlk	100.00
283 CS,JM,A:Legion of Super Outlaws	125.00
284 A:Krypto,Jerro	100.00
285 JM,Supergirl Existence Revealed, C:Legion (12th app.)	125.00
286 CS,JM,V:Lex Luthor	75.00
287 JM,A:Legion	75.00
288 JM,A:Mon-El	75.00
289 JM,A:Adult Legion	75.00
290 JM,C:Phantom Girl	75.00
291 JM,V:Mxyzptlk	75.00
292 JM,I:Superhorse	75.00
293 JM,O:Comet-Superhorse	100.00
294 JM,V:Lex Luthor	75.00
295 CS,JM,O:Lex Luthor	75.00
296 V:Super Ants	75.00
297 CS,JM,A:Mon-El	75.00
298 CS,JM,V:Lex Luthor	75.00
299 O:Superman Robots	75.00
300 JM,A:Mxyzptlk	75.00
301 CS(c),JM,O:Superhorse	40.00
302 CS(c),JM,O:Superhorse	40.00
303 CS(c),Red Kryptonite story	40.00
304 CS,JM,I&O:Black Flame	50.00
305 CS(c),O:Supergirl	40.00
306 JM,C:Mon-El,Brainiac 5	40.00
307 CS,JM,A:Saturn Girl	40.00
308 CS(c),V:Hercules	40.00
309 CS,A:Batman,JFK,Legion	50.00
310 CS,JM,I:Jewel Kryptonite	35.00
311 CS,JM,O:Superhorse	35.00
312 CS,JM,V:Metallo-Superman	35.00
313 JM,A:Supergirl,Lex Luthor, Batman	35.00
314 JM,A:Justice League	35.00
315 JM,V:Zigi,Zag	35.00
316 JM,A:Zigi,Zag,Zyra	35.00
317 JM,V:Lex Luthor	35.00
318 CS,JM,A:Brainiac	35.00
319 CS,JM,A:Legion,V:L.Luthor	35.00
320 CS,JM,V:Atlas,Hercules	35.00
321 CS,JM,A:Superhorse	35.00
322 JM,`Coward of Steel'	35.00

323 JM,A:Superhorse 35.00	398 NA(c),CS,MA,I:Morgan Edge . 15.00	450 MGr,Green Arrow. 5.50
324 JM,A:Abdul 35.00	399 NA(c),CS,MA,A:Superbaby . . 15.00	451 MGr,Green Arrow. 5.50
325 CS,JM,SkyscraperSuperman . 35.00	400 NA(c),CS,MA,Kandor Story . . 20.00	452 CS,MGr,Green Arrow. 5.50
326 CS,JM,V:Legion of Super	401 CS,MA,V:Indians 12.00	453 CS,Atom 4.50
Creatures. 35.00	402 NA(c),CS,MA,V:Indians 15.00	454 CS,E:Atom. 4.50
327 CS,JM,C:Brainiac. 35.00	403 CS,MA,Vigilante rep. 15.00	455 CS,Green Arrow 5.50
328 JM,Hands of Doom 35.00	404 CS,MA,Aquaman rep. 15.00	456 CS,MGr,Green Arrow. 5.50
329 JM,V:Drang 35.00	405 CS,MA,Vigilante rep. 15.00	457 CS,MGr,Green Arrow. 5.50
330 CS,JM,Krypto 35.00	406 CS,MA,Atom & Flash rep. . . . 15.00	458 CS,MGr,I:Black Rock 5.50
331 CS,V:Dr.Supernatural. 35.00	407 CS,MA,V:Lex Luthor 15.00	459 CS,BO,Blackrock. 4.50
332 CS,A:Brainiac 35.00	408 CS,MA,Atom rep. 15.00	460 CS,I:Karb-Brak 4.50
333 CS(c),A:Lex Luthor 35.00	409 CS,MA,T.Tommorrow rep. . . . 15.00	461 CS,V:Karb-Brak 4.50
334 JM(c),A:Lex Luthor,80pgs . . . 60.00	410 CS,MA,T.Tommorrow rep. . . . 15.00	462 CS,V:Karb-Brak 4.50
335 CS,V:Lex Luthor 30.00	411 CS,MA,O:Eclipso rep. 15.00	463 CS,V:Karb-Brak 4.50
336 CS,O:Akvar 30.00	412 CS,MA,Eclipso rep. 15.00	464 CS,KS,V:Pile-Driver 4.50
337 CS,V:Tiger Gang 30.00	413 CS,MA,V:Brainiac 15.00	465 CS,FMc,Luthor 4.50
338 CS,JM,V:Muto 30.00	414 CS,MA,B:Metamorpho 10.00	466 NA(c),CS,V:Luthor 4.50
339 CS,V:Muto,Brainiac 30.00	415 CS,MA,V:Metroplis Monster . . 10.00	467 CS,V:Mzyzptlk 4.50
340 JM,I:Parasite 30.00	416 CS,MA. 10.00	468 NA(c),CS,FMc,V:Terra-Man . . . 4.50
341 CS,V:Vakox,A:Batman 20.00	417 CS,MA,V:Luthor. 10.00	469 CS,TerraMan 4.50
342 WB,JM,V:Brainiac 20.00	418 CS,MA,V:Luthor,	470 CS,Flash Green Lantern 4.50
343 WB,V:Eterno 20.00	E:Metamorpho 10.00	471 CS,V:Phantom Zone Female . . 4.50
344 WB,JM,A:Batman. 20.00	419 CS,MA,CI,DG,I:HumanTarget . 11.00	472 CS,V:Faora Hu-Ul 4.50
345 CS(c),A:Allen Funt 20.00	420 CS,MA,DG,V:Towbee. 9.00	473 NA(c),CS,Phantom Zone
346 WB,JM. 20.00	421 CS,MA,B:Green Arrow. 10.00	Villians 4.50
347 CS(c),A:Supergirl, 80pgs. . . . 45.00	422 CS,DG,O:Human Target 9.00	474 KS,V:Doctor Light 4.50
348 WB,JM,V:Acid Master 20.00	423 CS,MA,DG,A:Lex Luthor 9.00	475 KS,V:Karb-Brak,A:Vartox 4.50
349 WB,JM,V:Dr.Kryptonite. 20.00	424 CS,MA,Green Arrow 10.00	476 KS,V:Vartox 4.50
350 A:JLA 20.00	425 CS,DD,NA,DG,B:Atom. 17.00	477 CS,DD,Land Lords of Earth . . . 4.50
351 WB,I:Zha-Vam 20.00	426 CS,MA,Green Arrow 7.00	478 CS,Earth's Last 4.50
352 WB,V:Zha-Vam 20.00	427 CS,MA,DD,DG,Atom 7.00	479 CS. 4.50
353 WB,JM,V:Zha-Vam. 20.00	428 CS,MA,DG,Luthor 7.00	480 CS,A:JLA,V:Amazo 4.50
354 JM,A:Captain Incredible 20.00	429 CS,BO,DG,C:JLA 7.00	481 CS,A:JLA,V:Amazo 4.50
355 WB,JM,V:Lex Luthor 20.00	430 CS,MA,DD,DG,Atom 7.00	482 CS,Amazo 4.50
356 WB,JM,V:Jr. Annihilitor. 20.00	431 CS,MA,Green Arrow 7.00	483 CS,Amazo,JLA 4.50
357 WB,JM,V:Annihilitor 20.00	432 CS,MA,DG,Toyman 7.00	484 CS,W:Earth 2 Superman
358 NA(c),CS,JM,A:Superboy. . . . 20.00	433 CS,BO,DD,DG,A:Atom. 7.00	& Lois Lane 5.00
359 NA(c),CS,KS,C:Batman 20.00	434 CS,DD,Green Arrow 7.00	485 NA(c),CS,rep.Superman#233. . 6.00
360 CS(c),A:Supergirl, 80pgs. . . . 45.00	435 FM(c),CS,DD,DG,Atom 7.00	486 GT,KS,V:Lex Luthor 5.00
361 NA(c),A:Parasite 17.00	436 CS,DD,Green Arrow 7.00	487 CS,AS,O:Atom. 5.00
362 RA,KS,V:Lex Luthor. 17.00	437 CS,DG,Green Arrow	488 CS,AS,A:Air Wave 4.50
363 RA,KS,V:Lex Luthor. 17.00	(100 page giant) 20.00	489 CS,AS,A:JLA,Atom 4.50
364 RA,KS,V:Lex Luthor. 17.00	438 CS,BO,DD,Atom 7.00	490 CS,Brainiac 4.50
365 A:Legion & J.L.A. 17.00	439 CS,BO,DD,Atom 7.00	491 CS,A:Hawkman 4.50
366 RA,KS,A:J.L.A. 17.00	440 1st MGr Green Arrow. 11.00	492 CS,'Superman's After Life'. . . . 4.50
367 NA(c),CS,KS,A:Supergirl 17.00	441 CS,BO,MGr,A:Green Arrow,	493 CS,A:UFO. 4.50
368 CS,KS,V:Mxyzptlk 17.00	Flash,R:Krypto 6.00	494 CS. 4.50
369 CS,KS,Superman's Greatest	442 CS,MS,MGr,Atom 5.00	495 CS. 4.50
Blunder 17.00	443 CS,A:JLA(100 pg.giant). 15.00	496 CS,A:Kandor 4.50
370 NA(c),CS,KS 17.00	444 MGr,Green Arrow. 6.00	497 CS. 4.50
371 NA(c),CS,KS 17.00	445 MGr,Green Arrow. 6.00	498 CS,Vartox 4.50
372 NA(c),CS,KS 17.00	446 MGr,Green Arrow. 6.00	499 CS,Vartox 4.50
373 A:Supergirl,(giant size). 35.00	447 CS,BO,RB,KJ,Atom. 5.00	500 CS,Superman's Life Story
374 NA(c),CS,KS,V:Super Thief . . 15.00	448 CS,BO,DD,JL,Atom 5.00	A:Legion. 6.00
375 CS,KS,The Big Forget 15.00	449 CS,BO. 5.00	501 KS. 2.50
376 CS,KS,E:Supergirl 15.00		502 CS,A:Supergirl,Gal.Golem . . . 2.50
377 CS,KS,B:Legion. 15.00		503 CS,'A Save in Time'. 2.50
378 CS,KS,V:Marauder. 15.00		504 CS,'The Power and Choice'. . . 2.50
379 CS,JA,MA,V:Eliminator 15.00		505 CS. 2.50
380 KS,Confessions of Superman 15.00		506 CS. 2.50
381 CS,Dictators of Earth 15.00		507 CS,A:Jonathan Kent 2.50
382 CS,Clark Kent-Magician. 15.00		508 CS,A:Jonathan Kent 2.50
383 CS,The Killer Costume. 15.00		509 CS,JSn,DG 2.75
384 CS,The Forbidden Costume. . 15.00		510 CS,Luthor 2.50
385 CS,The Mortal Superman. . . . 15.00		511 CS,AS,V:Terraman,
386 CS,Home For Old Supermen . 15.00		A:Air Wave 2.50
387 CS,A:Legion,Even		512 CS,RT,V:Luthor,A:Air Wave . . . 2.50
Supermen Die 15.00		513 CS,RT,V:Krell,A:Air Wave. 2.50
388 CS,A:Legion,Puzzle of		514 CS,RT,V:Brainiac,A:Atom. 2.50
The Wild Word 15.00		515 CS,AS,A:Atom. 2.50
389 A:Legion,The Kid Who		516 CS,AS,V:Luthor,A:Atom 2.50
Struck Out Superman 15.00		517 CS,DH,A:Aquaman 2.50
390 CS,'Self-Destruct Superman' . 15.00		518 CS,DH,A:Aquaman 2.50
391 CS,Punishment of		519 CS,DH,A:Aquaman 2.50
Superman's Son. 15.00		520 CS,DH,A:Aquaman 2.50
392 CS,E:Legion 15.00		521 CS,AS,I:Vixen,A:Atom 2.50
393 CS,MA,RA,A:Super Houdini . 15.00		522 CS,AS,A:Atom. 2.50
394 CS,MA. 15.00		523 CS,AS,A:Atom 2.50
395 CS,MA,A:Althera 15.00		524 CS,AS,A:Atom. 2.50
396 CS,MA. 15.00		525 JSon,FMc,AS,I:Neutron
397 CS,MA,Imaginary Story 15.00		A:Air Wave 2.50

Action Comics #308 © DC Comics Inc.

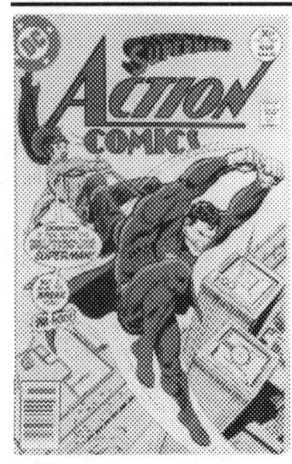

Action Comics #469 © DC Comics, Inc.

526 JSon,AS,V:Neutron 2.50
527 CS,AS,I:Satanis,A:Aquaman . . 3.00
528 CS,AS,V:Brainiac,A:Aq'man . . . 2.50
529 GP(c),CS,DA,AS,A:Aquaman,
    V:Brainiac. 2.50
530 CS,DA,Brainiac 2.50
531 JSon,FMc,AS,A:Atom 2.50
532 CS,C:New Teen Titans. 2.50
533 CS,V:The. 2.50
534 CS,AS,V:Satanis,A:Air Wave . . 2.50
535 GK(c),JSon,AS,
    A:Omega Men 2.50
536 JSon,AS,FMc,A:Omega Men . . 2.50
537 IN,CS,AS,V:Satanis
    A:Aquaman 2.50
538 IN,AS,FMc,V:Satanis,
    A:Aquaman 2.50
539 KG(c),GK,AS,DA,A:Flash,
    Atom,Aquaman 2.50
540 GK,AS,V:Satanis 2.50
541 GK,V:Satanis 2.50
542 AS,V:Vandal Savage 2.50
543 CS,V:Vandal Savage 2.50
544 CS,MA,GK,GP,45th Anniv.
    D:Ardora,Lexor 3.50
545 GK,Brainiac 2.50
546 GK,A:JLA,New Teen Titans . . . 2.50
547 GK(c),CS. 2.50
548 GK(c),AS,Phantom Zone 2.50
549 GK(c),AS 2.50
550 AS(c),GT 2.50
551 GK,Starfire becomes
    Red Star 2.50
552 GK,Forgotten Heroes
    (inc.Animal Man) 6.00
553 GK,Forgotten Heroes(inc.
    Animal Man). 6.00
554 GK(a&c) 2.50
555 CS,A:Parasite (X-over
    Supergirl #20) 2.50
556 CS,KS,C:Batman 2.50
557 KS,Terra-man 2.50
558 KS 2.50
559 KS,AS 2.50
560 AS,KG,BO,A:Ambush Bug. . . . 2.50
561 KS,WB,Toyman 2.50
562 KS,Queen Bee. 2.50
563 AS,KG,BO,A:Ambush Bug . . . 2.50
564 AS,V:Master Jailer 2.50
565 KG,KS,BO,A:Ambush Bug . . . 2.50
566 BO(i),MR 2.50
567 KS,AS,PB 2.50
568 CS,AW,AN. 2.50
569 IN 2.50
570 KS 2.50

571 BB(c),AS,A:Thresh 222 . . . . . . 2.50
572 WB,BO 2.50
573 KS,BO,AS 2.50
574 KS 2.50
575 KS,V:Intellax 2.50
576 KS,Earth's Sister Planet. 2.50
577 KG,BO,V:Caitiff 2.50
578 KS,Parasite 2.50
579 KG,BO,Asterix Parody 2.50
580 GK(c),KS,Superman's Failure . 2.50
581 DCw(c),KS,Superman
    Requires Legal aid 2.50
582 AS,KS,Superman's Parents
    Alive. 2.50
583 CS,KS,AMo(s),Last Pre
    Crisis Superman. 7.00
584 JBy,DG,A:NewTeenTitans,
    I:Modern Age Superman. 3.00
585 JBy,DG,Phantom Stranger. . . . 2.50
586 JBy,DG,Legends,V:New
    Gods,Darkseid 2.50
587 JBy,DG,Demon 2.50
588 JBy,DG,Hawkman 2.50
589 JBy,DG,Gr.Lant.Corp. 2.50
590 JBy,DG,Metal Men. 2.50
591 JBy,V:Superboy,A:Legion 2.50
592 JBy,Big Barda 2.50
593 JBy,Mr. Miracle 2.50
594 JBy,A:Booster Gold 2.50
595 JBy,A:M.Manhunter,
    I:Silver Banshee. 2.50
596 JBy,A:Spectre,Millenium. 2.50
597 JBy,L.Starr(i),Lois V:Lana. . . . 2.50
598 JBy,TyT,I:Checkmate 3.50
599 RA,JBy(i),A:MetalMen,
    BonusBook. 2.50
600 JBy,GP,KS,JOy,DG,CS,MA,
    MMi,A:Wonder Woman;
    Man-Bat,V:Darkseid 6.00
Becomes:

ACTION WEEKLY
1988–89
601 GK,DSp,CS,DJu,TD,
    B:Superman,Gr.Lantern,
    Blackhawk,Deadman,Secret
    Six,Wilddog 2.00
602 GP(c),GK,DSp,CS,DJu,TD. . . . 2.00
603 GK,CS,DsP,DJu,TD 2.00
604 GK,DSp,CS,DJu,TD. 2.00
605 NKu/AKu(c),GK,DSp,CS,
    DJu,TD 2.00
606 DSp,CS,DJu,TD. 2.00
607 SLi(c),TD,DSp,CS,DJu. 2.00
608 DSp,CS,DJu,TD,E:Blackhawk . 2.00
609 BB(c),DSp,DJu,TD,CS,
    E:Wild Dog,B:Black Canary . . . 2.00
610 KB,DJu,CS,DSp,TD,CS
    A:Phantom Stranger. 2.00
611 AN(c),DJu,DSp,CS,BKi,TD,
    BKi,B:Catwoman 3.00
612 PG(c),DSp,CS,BKi,TD,
    E:Secret Six,Deadman 2.50
613 MK(c),BKi,CS,MA,TGr,
    Nightwing,B:Phantom Stranger. 2.50
614 TG,CS,Phantom Stranger
    E:Catwoman 2.50
615 MMi(c),CS,MA,BKi,TGr,
    Blackhawk,B:Wild Dog 2.00
616 ATh(c),CS,MA,E:Bl.Canary . . . 2.00
617 CS,MA,JO,A:Ph.Stranger. 2.00
618 JBg(c),CS,MA,JKo,TD,
    B:Deadman,E:Nightwing. 2.00
619 CS,MA,FS,FMc,KJo,TD,FMc,
    B:Sinister Six. 2.00
620 CS,MA,FS,FMc,KJo,TD 2.00
621 JO(c),CS,MA,FS,FMc,KJo,
    TD,MBr,E:Deadman 2.00
622 RF(c),MBr,TL,CS,MA,FS,
    FMc,A:Starman,E:Wild
    Dog,Blackhawk 2.00

Action Comics #601 © DC Comics, Inc.

623 MBr,TD,CS,MA,FS,FMc,JL,
    JKo,A:Ph.Stranger,
    B:Deadman,Shazam 2.00
624 AD(c),MBr,FS,FMc,CS,MA,
    TD,B:Black Canary. 2.00
625 MBr,FS,FMc,CS,MA,
    TD,FMc 2.00
626 MBr,FS,FMc,CS,MA,JKo,TD,
    E:Shazam,Deadman 2.00
627 GK(c),MBr,RT,FS,FMc,CS,
    MA,TMd,B:Nightwing,Speedy . . 2.00
628 TY(c),MBr,RT,TMd,CS,MA,
    FS,FMc,B:Blackhawk 2.00
629 CS,MA,MBr,RT,FS,FMc,TMd . . 2.00
630 CS,MA,MBr,RT,FS,FMc,TMd,
    E:Secret Six 2.00
631 JS(c),CS,MA,MBr,RT,TMd,
    B:Phantom Stranger. 2.00
632 TGr(c),CS,MA,MBr,RT,TMd . . . 2.00
633 CS,MA,MBr,RT,TMd. 2.00
634 CS,MA,MBr,RT,TMd,E:Ph.Stranger,
    Nightwing/Speedy,Bl.hawk 2.00
635 CS,MA,MBr,RT,EB,E:Black
    Canary,Green Lantern 2.00
636 DG(c),CS,MA,NKu,MPa,FMc,
    B:Demon,Wild Dog,Ph.Lady,
    Speedy,A:Phantom Stranger. . . 2.00
637 CS,MA,KS,FMc,MPa,
    B:Hero Hotline 2.00
638 JK(c),CS,MA,KS,FMc,MPa. . . . 2.00
639 CS,MA,KS,FMc,MPa 2.00
640 CS,MA,FS,FMc,MPa,
    E:Speedy,Hero Hotline 2.00
641 CS,MA,JL,DG,MPa,E:Demon,
    Phant.Lady,Superman,Wild Dog,
    A:Ph.Stranger,Hum.Target 2.00
642 GK,SD,ATi,CS,JAp,JM,CI,KN,
    Green Lantern,Superman 2.00
Becomes:

ACTION COMICS
1989–97
643 B:RSt(s),GP,BBr,V:Intergang . . 2.50
644 GP,BBr,V:Matrix. 2.00
645 GP,BBr,I:Maxima 2.00
646 KG,V:Alien Creature,
    A:Brainiac. 2.50
647 GP,KGa,BBr,V:Brainiac 2.00
648 GP,KGa,BBr,V:Brainiac 2.00
649 GP,KGa,BBr,V:Brainiac 2.00
650 JOy,BBr,CS,BMc,GP,KGa,
    ATi,DJu,A:JLA,C:Lobo 4.50
651 GP,KGa,BBr,Day of Krypton
    Man #3,V:Maxima 3.00
652 GP,KGa,BBr,Day of Krypton

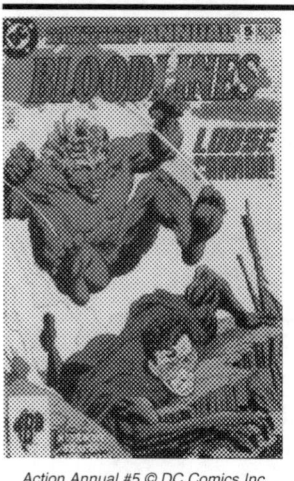

Action Annual #5 © DC Comics Inc.

Man #6,V:Eradicator 3.00
653 BMc,BBr,D:Amanda 2.00
654 BMc,BBr,A:Batman Pt.3 . . . . . . 2.50
655 BMc,BBr,V:Morrisson,Ma
  Kent's Photo Album 2.00
656 BMc,BBr,Soul Search #1,
  V:Blaze 2.00
657 KGa,BBr,V:Toyman 2.00
658 CS,Sinbad Contract #3 . . . . . . 2.00
659 BMc,BBr,K.Krimson
  Kryptonite #3 . . . . 3.50
660 BMc,BBr,D:Lex Luthor 3.00
661 BMc,BBr,A:Plastic Man 2.00
662 JOy,JM,TG,BMc,V:Silver
  Banshee,Clark tells
  Lois his identity 4.00
662a 2nd printing 2.00
663 BMc,Time & Time Again,pt.2,
  A:JSA,Legion 2.00
664 BMc,Time & Time Again,pt.5 . . 2.00
665 TG,V:Baron Sunday 2.00
666 EH,Red Glass Trilogy,pt.3 . . . . 2.00
667 JOy,JM,TG,ATi,DJu,Revenge
  of the Krypton Man,pt.4 . . . . . 2.25
668 BMc,Luthor confirmed dead . . . 2.00
669 BMc,V:Intergang,A:Thorn 2.00
670 BMc,A:Waverider,JLA,JLE 2.00
671 KD,Blackout,pt.2 . . . . 2.00
672 BMc,Superman Meets Lex
  Luthor II 2.00
673 BMc,V:Hellgramite 2.00
674 BMc,Panic in the Sky (Prologue)
  R:Supergirl(Matrix) 6.00
675 BMc,Panic in the Sky #4,
  V:Brainiac. 3.00
676 B:KK(s),JG,A:Supergirl,Lex
  Luthor II 2.00
677 JG,Supergirl V:Superman 2.00
678 JG,O:Lex Luthor II 2.00
679 JG,I:Shellshock 2.00
680 JG,Blaze/Satanus War,pt.2 . . 2.00
681 JG,V:Hellgramite 2.00
682 DAb,TA,V:Hi-Tech 2.00
683 JG,I:Jackal,C:Doomsday 3.00
683a 2nd printing 1.50
684 JG,Doomsday Pt.4. . . . . 4.00
684a 2nd printing 2.00
685 JG,Funeral for a Friend#2 . . . . 3.00
686 JG,Funeral for a Friend#6 . . . . 3.00
687 JG,Reign of Superman #1,Direct
  Sales,Die-Cut(c),Mini-Poster,
  F:Last Son of Krypton. 2.50
687a newsstand Ed. 2.00
688 JG,V:Guy Gardner. 3.00
689 JG,V:Man of Steel,A:Superboy,

Supergirl,R:Real Superman . . . 3.50
690 JG,Cyborg Vs. Superboy 2.50
691 JG,A:All Supermen,V:Cyborg
  Superman,Mongul 3.00
692 JG,A:Superboy,Man of Steel . . 2.00
693 JG,A:Last Son of Krypton. 2.00
694 JG,Spilled Blood#2,V:Hi-Tech. . 2.00
695 JG,Foil(c),I:Cauldron,A:Lobo . . 3.00
695a Newsstand Ed. 2.00
696 JG,V:Alien,C:Doomsday. 2.50
697 JG,Bizarro's World#3,
  V:Bizarro 2.00
698 JG,A:Lex Luthor. 2.00
699 JG,A:Project Cadmus 2.00
700 JG,Fall of Metropolis#1 . . . . . . 3.00
700a Platinum Edition. 15.00
701 JG,Fall of Metropolis#5,
  V:Luthor. 2.00
702 JG,DvM,B:DyM(s),R:Bloodsport 2.00
703 JG,DvM,Zero Hour. 2.00
704 JG,DvM,Eradicator. 2.00
705 JG,DvM,Supes real? 2.00
706 JG,DvM,A:Supergirl 2.00
707 JG,DvM,V:Shado Dragon. 2.00
708 JG,DvM,R:Deathtrap 2.00
709 JG,DvM,A:Guy Gardner,
  Warrior. 2.00
710 JG,DvM,Death of Clark Kent,pt.3
  [new Miraweb format begins] . . 2.25
711 JG,DvM,Death of Clark
  Kent,pt.7 . . . . 2.25
712 Rescue Jimmy Olsen. 2.25
713 . . . . 2.25
714 R:The Joker. 2.25
715 DvM,DaR,V:Parasite 2.25
716 DvM,DaR,Trial of Superman . . 2.25
717 DvM,DaR,Trial of Superman . . 2.25
718 DvM,DRo,mystery of Demolitia 2.25
719 DvM,DRo. 2.25
720 DvM,DRo,Lois ends
  engagement 3.00
721 DvM,DRo,lottery fever 2.25
722 DvM,DaR,Tornados in
  Smallville 2.25
723 V:Brainiac 2.25
724 V:S.T.A.R.labs monster 2.25
725 Tolos 2.25
726 DvM(s),TMo,DRo,Krisis of the
  Krimson Kryptonite follow-up . . 2.25
727 DvM(s),TMo,DRo,brutal weather
  in Metropolis, Final Night tie-in . 2.50
728 DvM(s),TG,DRo, Some
  Honeymoon!. 2.50
729 DvM(s),TG,DRo, in Fortress of
  Solitude 2.50
730 DvM(s),TG,Ro, ... 2.50
731 DvM(s),TG,DRo, R:Cauldron . . 2.50
732 DvM(s),TG,DRo, Atomic Skull
  rampages through Metropolis . . 2.25
733 DvM(s),TG,DRo, V:Matallo,
  A:Ray. 2.25
734 DvM(s),TG,DRo, Superman &
  Atom in Kandor 2.25
735 DvM(s),TG,DRo, V:Savior 2.25
736 DvM(s),TG,DRo. 2.25
737 MWa(s),TG,DRo, Luthor gets
  day in court 2.00
738 SI,JMz,Lois sent to Australia . . 2.00
739 SI,JMz,Superman imprisoned . 2.00
740 SI,JMz,Lucy Lane disappears . 2.00
741 SI,JMz,V:C.O.M.P.U.T.O. 2.00
742 SI,JMz, ... 2.00
743 SI,JMz,F:Slam Bradley. 2.00
744 SI,JMz,Millennium Giants
  x-over. 2.00
745 SI,JMz,The Prankster 2.00
746 SI,JMz,The Prankster,pt.2 . . . . 2.00
747 SI,JMz,The Prankster,pt.3 . . . . 2.00
748 SI,JMz,Dominus Theory. 2.00
749 RMz(s),TGb,TP,City of the
  Future, pt.1 x-over 2.00

750 SI,JMz,I:Crazytop, 48-page . . . 3.00
751 SI,JMz,A:Geo-Force 2.00
752 SI,JMz,Supermen of
  America x-over. 2.00
753 SI,JMz,A:JLA. 2.00
754 SI,JMz,R:Dominus,
  A:Wonder Woman 2.00
755 SI&MMr(s),King of the
  World aftermath 2.00
756 VGi,old villain is back. 2.00
757 TPe(s),TGb,Hawkworld,pt.3 . . 2.00
758 SI,JMz,V:Boss Moxie 2.00
Ann.#1 AAd,DG,A:Batman 8.00
Ann.#2 MMi,CS,GP,JOy,DJu,BBr,
  V:Mongul 4.00
Ann.#3 TG,Armageddon X-over . . . 3.00
Ann.#4 Eclipso,A:Captain
  Marvel 3.00
Ann.#5 MZ(c),Bloodlines, I:Loose
  Cannon 3.00
Ann.#6 Elseworlds,JBy(a&S) 3.00
Ann.#7 Year One Annual 4.00
Ann.#8 DvM,"Legends of the Dead
  Earth" 3.00
Ann.#9 DvM,VGi,BBr,Pulp Heroes . 4.00
Archives, Vol. 1 S&S rep. 50.00
Archives, Vol. 2 S&S rep. 50.00
Gold.Ann.rep.#1 . . . . 1.50
#0 Peer Pressure,pt.4 (1994) 2.00
Spec.#1,000,000 MSh(s),RLm,JMz. 2.00

ADAM STRANGE
1990
1 NKu,A.Strange on Rann 5.00
2 NKu,Wanted:Adam Strange 4.50
3 NKu,final issue 4.50

ADVANCED
DUNGEONS & DRAGONS
1988–91
1 JD,I:Onyx,Priam,Timoth,
  Cybriana,Vajra,Luna 5.00
2 JD,V:Imgig Zu,I:Conner 4.00
3 JD,V:Imgig Zu. 4.00
4 JD,V:Imgig Zu,I:Kyriani 3.00
5 JD,Spirit of Myrrth I. 3.00
6 JD,Spirit of Myrrth II 3.00
7 JD,Spirit of Myrrth III. 2.50
8 JD,Spirit of Myrrth IV 2.50
9 JD,Catspawn Quartet I 2.50
10 JD,Catspawn Quartet II 2.50

Advanced Dungeons & Dragons #25
© DC Comics, Inc.

DC COMICS

11 JD,Catspawn Quartet III	2.50
12 JD,Catspawn Quartet IV	2.50
13 JD,Spell Games I	2.50
14 JD,Spell Games II	2.50
15 JD,Spell Games III	2.50
16 JD,Spell Games IV	2.50
17 JD,RM,Kyriani's Story I	2.50
18 JD,RM,Kyriani's Story II	2.50
19 JD,RM,Luna I	2.50
20 JD,RM,Luna II	2.50
21 JD,RM,Luna III	2.50
22 JD,RM,Luna IV	2.50
23 TMd,RM,Siege Dragons I	2.50
24 Scavengers	2.50
25 JD,RM,Centaur Village	2.00
26 JD,Timoth the Centaur	2.00
27 JD,Kyriani,Dragons Eye #1	2.00
28 JD,Dragons Eye #2	2.00
29 JD,RM,Dragons Eye #3	2.00
30 JD,RM,Carril's Killer Revealed	2.00
31 TMd,Onyx'Father,pt.1	2.00
32 TMd,Onyx'Father,pt.2	2.00
33 JD,Waterdeep,pt.1	2.00
34 JD,Waterdeep,pt.2	2.00
35 JD,RM,Waterdeep,pt.3	2.00
36 JD,RM,final issue	2.00
Ann.#1 JD,RM,Tmd	4.00

ADVENTURE COMICS
Nov. 1938–83
[Prev: New Comics]

32 CF(c)	3,200.00
33	1,500.00
34 FG(c)	1,500.00
35 FG(c)	1,500.00
36 Giant Snake(c)	1,500.00
37 Rampaging Elephant(c)	1,500.00
38 Tiger(c)	1,500.00
39 Male Bondage(c)	1,600.00
40 CF(c),1st app. Sandman	35,000.00
41 Killer Shark(c)	4,500.00
42 CF,Sandman(c)	5,500.00
43 CF(c)	2,500.00
44 CF,Sandman(c)	5,500.00
45 FG(c)	2,500.00
46 CF,Sandman(c)	3,800.00
47 Sandman (c)	3,600.00
48 1st app.& B:Hourman	22,000.00
49	2,000.00
50 Hourman(c)	1,900.00
51 BBa(c),Sandman(c)	2,500.00
52 BBa(c),Hourman(c)	1,800.00
53 BBa(c),1st app. Minuteman	1,600.00
54 BBa(c),Hourman(c)	1,600.00
55 BBa(c),same	1,600.00
56 BBa(c),same	1,600.00
57 BBa(c),same	1,600.00
58 BBa(c),same	1,600.00
59 BBa(c),same	1,600.00
60 Sandman(c)	2,500.00
61 CF(c),JBu,Starman(c)	12,000.00
62 JBu(c),JBu,Starman(c)	1,400.00
63 JBu(c),JBu,same	1,400.00
64 JBu(c),JBu,same	1,400.00
65 JBu(c),JBu,same	1,400.00
66 JBu(c),JBu,O:Shining Knight, Starman(c)	2,000.00
67 JBu(c),JBu,O:Mist	1,500.00
68 JBu(c),JBu,same	1,500.00
69 JBu(c),JBu,1st app. Sandy, Superman(c)	1,600.00
70 JBu(c),JBu,Starman(c)	1,500.00
71 JBu(c),JBu,same	1,400.00
72 JBu(c),S&K,JBu,Sandman	11,000.00
73 S&K(c),S&K,I:Manhunter	12,000.00
74 S&K(c),S&K,You can't Escape your Fate-The Sandman	1,500.00
75 S&K(c),S&K,Sandman and Sandy Battle Thor in	

`Villian from Valhalla'	1,500.00
76 S&K(c),Sandman(c),S&K	1,500.00
77 S&K,(c),S&K,same	1,500.00
78 S&K(c),S&K,same	1,500.00
79 S&K(c),S&K,Manhunter in `Cobras of the Deep'	1,600.00
80 S&K(c),Sandman(c),S&K	1,500.00
81 S&K(c),MMe,S&K,same	1,000.00
82 S&K(c),S&K,Sandman X-Mas story	1,000.00
83 S&K(c),S&K,Sandman Boxing(c),E:Hourman	1,000.00
84 S&K(c),S&K	1,000.00
85 S&K(c),S&K,Sandman in `The Amazing Dreams of Gentleman Jack'	1,000.00
86 S&K(c),Sandman(c)	1,000.00
87 S&K(c),same	1,000.00
88 S&K(c),same	1,000.00
89 S&K(c),same	1,000.00
90 S&K(c),same	1,000.00
91 S&K(c),JK	850.00
92 S&K(c)	750.00
93 S&K(c),Sandman in `Sleep for Sale'	750.00
94 S&K(c),Sandman(c)	750.00
95 S&K(c),same	750.00
96 S&K(c),same	750.00
97 S&K(c),same	750.00
98 JK(c),Sandman in `Hero of Dreams'	750.00
99 JK(c)	750.00
100	1,000.00
101 S&K(c)	750.00
102 S&K(c)	750.00
103 B:Superboy stories,(c),BU: Johnny Quick,Aquaman,Shining Knight,Green Arrow	2,500.00
104 S&S,ToyTown USA	800.00
105 S&S,Palace of Fantasy	550.00
106 S&S,Weather Hurricane	550.00
107 S&S,The Sky is the Limit	550.00
108 S&S,Proof of the Proverbs	550.00
109 S&S,You Can't Lose	550.00
110 S&S,The Farmer Takes it Easy	550.00
111 S&S,The Whiz Quiz Club	550.00
112 S&S,Super Safety First	550.00
113 S&S,The 33rd Christmas	500.00
114 S&S,Superboy Spells Danger	500.00
115 S&S,The Adventure of Jaguar Boy	500.00
116 S&S,JBu,Superboy Toy Tester	500.00
117 S&S,JBu,Miracle Plane	500.00
118 S&S,JBu,The Quiz Biz Broadcast	500.00
119 WMo,JBu,Superboy Meets Girls	500.00
120 S&S,JBu,A:Perry White; I:Ringmaster	525.00
121 S&S,Great Hobby Contest	450.00
122 S&S,Superboy-Super- Magician	450.00
123 S&S,Lesson For a Bully	450.00
124 S&S,Barbed Wire Boys Town	450.00
125 S&S,The Weight Before Christmas	450.00
126 S&S,Superboy:Crime Fighting Poet	450.00
127 MMe,O:Shining Knight; Super Bellboy	450.00
128 WMo,How Clark Kent Met Lois Lane'	450.00
129 WMo,Pupils of the Past	450.00
130 WMo,Superboy Super Salesman	450.00
131 WMo,The Million Dollar Athlete	400.00

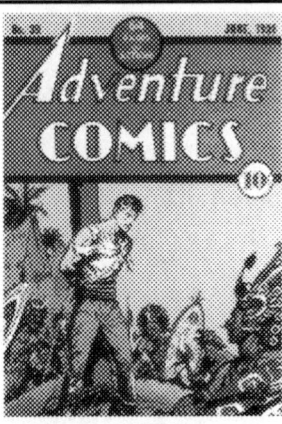

Adventure Comics #39
© DC Comics, Inc.

132 WMo,Superboy Super Cowboy	400.00
133 WMo,Superboy's Report Card	400.00
134 WMo,Silver Gloves Sellout	400.00
135 WMo,The Most Amazing of All Boys	400.00
136 WMo,My Pal Superboy	400.00
137 WMo,Treasure of Tondimo	400.00
138 WMo,Around the World in Eighty Minutes	400.00
139 WMo,Telegraph Boy	400.00
140 Journey to the Moon	400.00
141 WMo,When Superboy Lost His Powers	400.00
142 WMo,The Man Who Walked With Trouble	450.00
143 WMo,The Superboy Savings Bank,A:Wooden Head Jones	450.00
144 WMo,The Way to Stop Superboy	450.00
145 WMo,Holiday Hijackers	450.00
146 The Substitute Superboy	450.00
147 Clark Kent,Orphan	450.00
148 Superboy Meets Mummies	450.00
149 Fake Superboys	450.00
150 FF,Superboy's Initiation	500.00
151 FF,No Hunting(c)	500.00
152 Superboy Hunts For a Job	425.00
153 FF,Clark Kent,Boy Hobo	500.00
154 The Carnival Boat Crimes	325.00
155 FF,Superboy-Hollywood Actor	425.00
156 The Flying Peril	325.00
157 FF,The Worst Boy in Smallville	400.00
158 The Impossible Task	325.00
159 FF,Superboy Millionaire?	400.00
160 Superboy's Phoney Father	325.00
161 FF	400.00
162 `The Super-Coach of Smallville High!'	325.00
163 FF,`Superboy's Phoney Father'	400.00
164 Discovers the Secret of a Lost Indian Tribe!	325.00
165 `Superboy's School for Stunt Men!'	325.00
166 `The Town That Stole Superboy'	325.00
167 `Lana Lang, Super-Girl!'	325.00
168 `The Boy Who Out Smarted Superboy'	325.00
169 `Clark Kent's Private Butler'	325.00

170 `Lana Lang's Big Crush'. . . . 310.00
171 `Superboy's Toughest
     Tasks!' 310.00
172 `Laws that Backfired' 310.00
173 `Superboy's School of
     Hard Knocks' 310.00
174 `The New Lana Lang!' 310.00
175 `Duel of the Superboys' 310.00
176 `Superboy's New Parents!' . . 310.00
177 `Hot-Rod Chariot Race!' 310.00
178 `Boy in the Lead Mask'. 310.00
179 `The World's Whackiest
     Inventors' 310.00
180 Grand Prize o/t Underworld . 310.00
181 `Mask for a Hero' 310.00
182 The Super Hick from
     Smallville'. 300.00
183 `Superboy and Cleopatra'. . . 300.00
184 `The Shutterbugs of
     Smallville'. 300.00
185 `The Mythical Monster'. 300.00
186. . . . . 300.00
187 `25th Century Superboy' . . . 300.00
188 `The Bull Fighter from
     Smallville'. 300.00
189 Girl of Steel(Lana Lang). . . . 300.00
190 The Two Clark Kents 300.00
191 . . . . 300.00
192 `The Coronation of
     Queen Lana Lang' 300.00
193 `Superboy's Lost Costume'. . 300.00
194 `Super-Charged Superboy'. . 300.00
195 `Lana Lang's Romance
     on Mars!' 300.00
196 `Superboy vs. King Gorilla'. . 300.00
197 V:Juvenile Gangs. 300.00
198 `The Super-Carnival
     from Space' 300.00
199 `Superboy meets Superlad' . 300.00
200 `Superboy and the Apes!'. . . 450.00
201 `Safari in Smallville!'. 300.00
202 `Superboy City, U.S.A.'. 300.00
203 `Uncle Superboy!' 325.00
204 `The Super-Brat of
     Smallville'. 300.00
205 `The Journey of the
     Second Superboy!' 300.00
206 `The Impossible Creatures' . 300.00
207 `Smallville's Worst
     Athlete'. 300.00
208 `Rip Van Winkle of
     Smallville?' 300.00
209 `Superboy Week!' 300.00
210 I:Krypto,`The Superdog
     from Krypton'. 3,200.00
211 `Superboy's Most
     Amazing Dream!' 250.00
212 `Superboy's Robot Twin'. . . . 250.00
213 `The Junior Jury of
     Smallville!' 250.00
214 A:Krypto. 500.00
215 `The Super-Hobby of
     Superboy' 250.00
216 `The Wizard City' 250.00
217 `Superboy's Farewell
     to Smallville' 250.00
218 `The Two World's of
     Superboy' 250.00
219 The Rip Van Wrinkle of
     Smallville 250.00
220 The Greatest Show on Earth
     A:Krypto 250.00
221 `The Babe of Steel' 225.00
222 `Superboy's Repeat
     Performance' 225.00
223 `Hercules Junior' 225.00
224 `Pa Kent Superman'. 225.00
225 `The Bird with
     Super-Powers' 225.00

Adventure Comics #293
© DC Comics Inc.

226 `Superboy's Super Rival!'. . . 225.00
227 `Good Samaritan of
     Smallville'. 225.00
228 `Clark Kent's Body Guard' . . 225.00
229 . . . . 225.00
230 `The Secret of the
     Flying Horse' 225.00
231 `The Super-Feats of
     Super-Baby!'. 225.00
232 `The House where
     Superboy was Born' 225.00
233 `Joe Smith, Man of Steel!' . . 225.00
234 `The 1,001 Rides of
     Superboy!' 225.00
235 `The Confessions of
     Superboy!' 225.00
236 `Clark Kent's Super-Dad!'. . . 225.00
237 Robot War of Smallville!. . . . 225.00
238 `The Secret Past of
     Superboy's Father' 225.00
239 `The Super-Tricks of
     the Dog of Steel'. 225.00
240 `The Super Teacher
     From Krypton'. 225.00
241 `The Super-Outlaw of
     Smallville'. 225.00
242 `The Kid From Krypton' 225.00
243 `The Super Toys From
     Krypton'. 225.00
244 `The Poorest Family in
     Smallville'. 225.00
245 `The Mystery of Monster X' . 225.00
246 `The Girl Who Trapped
     Superboy!' 225.00
247 I&O:Legion 5,000.00
248 Green Arrow 175.00
249 CS,Green Arrow 175.00
250 JK,Green Arrow. 175.00
251 JK,Green Arrow. 175.00
252 JK,Green Arrow. 175.00
253 JK,1st Superboy &
     Robin T.U 250.00
254 JK,Green Arrow. 185.00
255 JK,Green Arrow. 185.00
256 JK,O:Green Arrow 600.00
257 CS,LE,A:Hercules,Samson. . 150.00
258 LE,Aquaman,Superboy 150.00
259 I:Crimson Archer 150.00
260 1st S.A. O:Aquaman 650.00
261 GA,A:Lois Lane 125.00
262 O:Speedy 125.00
263 GA,Aquaman,Superboy 125.00

264 GA,A:Robin Hood 125.00
265 GA,Aquaman,Superboy 125.00
266 GA,I:Aquagirl 125.00
267 N:Legion(2nd app.) 800.00
268 I:Aquaboy 125.00
269 I:Aqualad,E:Green Arrow . . . 225.00
270 2nd A:Aqualad,B:Congorilla . 125.00
271 O:Lex Luthor rtd. 250.00
272 I:Human Flying Fish. 125.00
273 Aquaman,Superboy 125.00
274 Aquaman,Superboy 125.00
275 O:Superman/Batman
     T.U. rtd. 200.00
276 Superboy,3rd A:Metallo 110.00
277 Aquaman,Superboy 110.00
278 Aquaman,Superboy 110.00
279 CS,Aquaman,Superboy 110.00
280 CS,A:Lori Lemaris 110.00
281 Aquaman,Superboy
     E:Congorilla 110.00
282 5th A:Legion,I:Starboy 200.00
283 I:Phantom Zone 175.00
284 CS,JM,Aquaman,Superboy . 110.00
285 WB,B:Bizarro World 150.00
286 I:Bizarro Mxyzptlk. 150.00
287 I:Dev-Em,Bizarro Perry White,
     Jimmy Olsen 100.00
288 A:Dev-Em 100.00
289 Superboy 100.00
290 8th A:Legion,O&J:Sunboy,
     I:Brainiac 5. . . . . 175.00
291 A:Lex Luthor 75.00
292 Superboy,I:Bizarro Lucy Lane,
     Lana Lang 75.00
293 CS,O&I:Marv-El,I:Bizarro
     Luthor. 125.00
294 I:Bizarro M.Monroe,JFK 125.00
295 I:Bizarro Titano 75.00
296 A:Ben Franklin,George
     Washington 75.00
297 Lana Lang Superboy Sister . . 75.00
298 The Fat Superboy 75.00
299 I:Gold Kryptonite 75.00
300 B:Legion,J:Mon-El,
     E:Bizarro World 400.00
301 CS,O:Bouncing Boy 125.00
302 CS,Legion 90.00
303 I:Matter Eater Lad 90.00
304 D:Lightning Lad 90.00
305 A:Chameleon Boy 90.00
306 I:Legion of Sub.Heroes 80.00
307 I:Element Lad 90.00
308 I:Light Lass 90.00
309 I:Legion of Super Monsters . . 80.00
310 A:Mxyzptlk. 80.00
311 CS,V:Legion of Substitue
     Heroes 70.00
312 R:Lightning Lad 80.00
313 CS,J:Supergirl 70.00
314 A:Hitler 70.00
315 A:Legion of Substitute
     Heroes 70.00
316 O:Legion 60.00
317 I&J:Dreamgirl. 60.00
318 Legion 60.00
319 Legion 60.00
320 A:Dev-Em 60.00
321 I:Time Trapper 75.00
322 JF,A:Legion of Super Pets . . 50.00
323 JF,BU:Kypto. 50.00
324 JF,I:Legion of
     Super Outlaws 50.00
325 JF,V:Lex Luthor 50.00
326 BU:Superboy 50.00
327 I&J:Timber Wolf 50.00
328 Legion 50.00
329 I:Legion of Super Bizarros . . . 50.00
330 Legion 50.00
331 Legion 35.00

DC COMICS

Adventure Comics #326
© DC Comics, Inc.

332 Legion 35.00
333 Legion 35.00
334 Legion 35.00
335 Legion 35.00
336 Legion 35.00
337 Legion 35.00
338 Legion 35.00
339 Legion 35.00
340 I:Computo 35.00
341 CS,D:Triplicate Girl (becomes
    Duo Damsel) 26.00
342 CS,Star Boy expelled. 25.00
343 CS,V:Lords of Luck 25.00
344 CS,Super Stalag,pt.1. . . . . . 25.00
345 CS,Super Stalag,pt.2 . . . . . 25.00
346 CS,I&J:Karate Kid,Princess
    Projectra,I:Nemesis Kid 25.00
347 CS,Legion 15.00
348 I:Dr.Regulus. 18.00
349 CS,I:Rond Vidar. 15.00
350 CS,I:White Witch 18.00
351 CS,R:Star Boy 15.00
352 CS,I:Fatal Fire 15.00
353 CS,D:Ferro Lad 20.00
354 CS,Adult Legion. 15.00
355 CS,J:Insect Queen. 15.00
356 CS,Five Legion Orphans 15.00
357 CS,I:Controller. 15.00
358 I:Hunter 15.00
359 CS,Outlawed Legion,pt.1 . . . 15.00
360 CS,Outlawed Legion,pt.2 . . . 15.00
361 I:Dominators (30th century) . . 15.00
362 I:Dr.Mantis Morto 15.00
363 V:Dr.Mantis Morlo 15.00
364 A:Legion of Super Pets 15.00
365 CS,I:Shadow Lass,
    V:Fatal Five 15.00
366 CS,J:Shadow Lass. 15.00
367 N:Legion H.Q.,I:Dark Circle . . 15.00
368 CS. 15.00
369 CS,JAb,I:Mordru 15.00
370 CS,JAb,V:Mordru. 15.00
371 CS,JAb,I:Chemical King. 15.00
372 CS,JAb,J:Timber Wolf,
    Chemical King 15.00
373 I:Tornado Twins 15.00
374 WM,I:Black Mace. 15.00
375 I:Wanderers 15.00
376 Execution of Cham.Boy 15.00
377 Heroes for Hire 15.00
378 Twelve Hours to Live 15.00
379 Burial In Space 15.00
380 The Amazing Space Odyssey
    of the Legion,E:Legion 15.00

381 The Supergirl Gang
    C:Batgirl,B:Supergirl 60.00
382 NA(c),The Superteams Split
    Up,A:Superman 15.00
383 NA(c),Please Stop my Funeral,
    A:Superman,Comet,Streaky . . 15.00
384 KS,The Heroine Haters,
    A:Superman 15.00
385 Supergirl's Big Sister 15.00
386 The Beast That Loved
    Supergirl 15.00
387 Wolfgirl of Stanhope;
    A:Superman;V:Lex Luthor. . . . 15.00
388 Kindergarten Criminal;
    V:Luthor,Brainiac 15.00
389 A:Supergirl's Parents,
    V:Brainiac. 15.00
390 Linda Danvers Superstar
    (80 page giant). 30.00
391 The Super Cheat;A:Comet. . . 15.00
392 Supergirls Lost Costume 15.00
393 KS,Unwanted Supergirl 15.00
394 KS,Heartbreak Prison 15.00
395 Heroine in Haunted House . . . 15.00
396 Mystery o/t Super Orphan . . . 15.00
397 Now Comes Zod,N:Supergirl,
    V:Luthor. 15.00
398 Maid of Doom,A:Superman,
    Streaky,Krypto,Comet 15.00
399 CI,Johnny Dee,Hero Bum . . . 30.00
400 MSy,35th Anniv.,Return of the
    Black Flame 25.00
401 MSy,JAb,The Frightened
    Supergirl,V:Lex Luthor 12.00
402 MSy,JAb,TD,I:Starfire,
    Dr.Kangle. 15.00
403 68 page giant. 30.00
404 MSy,JAb,V:Starfire. 12.00
405 V:Starfire,Dr.Kangle 12.00
406 MSy,JAb,Suspicion 12.00
407 MSy,JAb,Suspicion Confirmed
    N:Supergirl 12.00
408 The Face at the Window 12.00
409 MSy,DG,Legion rep. 15.00
410 N:Supergirl 15.00
411 CI,N:Supergirl 15.00
412 rep.Strange Adventures #180
    (I:Animal Man). 18.00
413 GM,JKu,rep.Hawkman 15.00
414 Animal Man rep. 15.00
415 BO,GM,CI,Animal Man rep. . . 15.00
416 CI,All women issue,giantsize . 15.00
417 GM,inc.rep.Adventure #161,
    Frazetta art. 16.00
418 ATh,Black Canary 35.00
419 ATh,Black Canary 15.00
420 Animal Man rep. 15.50
421 MSy,Supergirl 10.00
422 MSy,Supergirl 10.00
423 MSy,Supergirl 10.00
424 MSy,E:Supergirl,A:JLA. 10.00
425 AN,ATh,I:Captain Fear. 20.00
426 MSy,DG,JAp,Vigilante 10.00
427 TD. 10.00
428 TD,I:Black Orchid. 25.00
429 TD,AN,Black Orchid. 15.00
430 A:Black Orchid. 15.00
431 JAp,ATh,B:Spectre. 30.00
432 JAp,AN,A:Spectre,Capt.Fear . 18.00
433 JAp,AN 18.00
434 JAp 18.00
435 MGr(1st work),JAp,Aquaman . 18.00
436 JAp,MGr,Aquaman. 18.00
437 JAp,MGr,Aquaman. 18.00
438 JAp,HC,DD,7 Soldiers 18.00
439 JAp 18.00
440 JAp,O:New Spectre 25.00
441 JAp,B:Aquaman. 4.00
442 JAp,A:Aquaman. 4.00
443 JAp 7.00
444 JAp 4.00

Adventure Comics #426
© DC Comics, Inc.

445 JAp,RE,JSon,Creeper 4.00
446 JAp,RE,JSon,Creeper 7.00
447 JAp,RE,JSon,Creeper 7.00
448 JAp,Aquaman 4.00
449 JAp,MN,TA,Jonn J'onz 4.00
450 JAp,MN,TA,Supergirl 4.00
451 JAp,MN,TA,Hawkman 4.00
452 JAp,Aquaman 4.00
453 MA,CP,JRu,B:Superboy
    & Aqualad 4.00
454 CP,DG,A:Kryptonite Kid 4.00
455 CP,DG,A:Kryptonite Kid
    E:Aqualad 4.00
456 JSon,JA. 4.00
457 JSon,JA,JO,B:Eclipso 5.00
458 JSon,JAp,JO,BL,E:Superboy
    & Eclipso 4.00
459 IN,FMc,JAp,JSon,DN,JA,A:Wond.
    Woman,New Gods,Green Lantern,
    Flash,Deadman,(giant size) . . 12.00
460 IN,FMc,JAp,DN,DA,JSon,JA,
    D:Darkseid 12.00
461 IN,FMc,JAp,JSon,DN,JA,
    B:JSA & Aquaman 12.00
462 IN,FMc,DH,JL,DG,JA,
    D:Earth 2,Batman. 12.00
463 DH,JL,JSon,FMc 8.00
464 DH,JAp,JSon,DN,DA,
    Deadman. 8.00
465 DN,JSon,DG,JL 8.00
466 MN,JL,JSon,DN,DA 8.00
467 JSon,SD,RT,I:Starman
    B:Plastic Man 10.00
468 SD,JSon 4.00
469 SD,JSon,O:Starman 4.00
470 SD,JSon,O:Starman 4.00
471 SD,JSon,I:Brickface. 4.00
472 SD,RT,JSon. 4.00
473 SD,RT,JSon. 4.00
474 SD,RT,JSon. 4.00
475 BB(c),SD,RT,JSon,DG,
    B:Aquaman 4.00
476 SD,RT,JSon,DG. 4.00
477 SD,RT,JSon,DG. 4.00
478 SD,RT,JSon,DG. 4.00
479 CI,DG,JSon,Dial H For Hero,
    E:Starman and Aquaman 4.00
480 CI,DJ,B:Dial H for Hero 4.00
481 CI,DJ. 4.00
482 CI,DJ,DH 4.00
483 CI,DJ,DH 4.00
485 GP(c),CI,DJ,DH 4.00
485 GP(c),CI,DJ. 4.00
486 GP(c),DH,RT,TVE 4.00

487 CI,DJ,DH 4.00
488 CI,DJ,TVE 4.00
489 CI,FMc,TVE 4.00
490 GP(c),CI,E:Dial H for Hero 4.00
491 KG(c),DigestSize,DN,
    Shazam,rep.other material . . . 12.00
492 KG(c),DN,E:Shazam 12.00
493 KG(c),GT,B:Challengers of
    the Unknown,reprints 12.00
494 KG(c),GT,Challengers,
    reprints. 12.00
495 ATh,reprints,Challengers 12.00
496 GK(c),ATh,reprints,
    Challengers 12.00
497 ATh,DA,reps.,E:Challengers. . 12.00
498 GK(c),reprints,Rep.Legion . . . 12.00
499 GK(c),reprints,Rep 12.00
500 KG(c),Legion reprints,Rep . . . 12.00
501 reprints,Rep. 12.00
502 reprints,Rep. 12.00
503 reprints,final issue 12.00
Giant #1, 80 page, 7 tales (1998) . . 5.00

Adventures in the DC Universe #15
© DC Comics Inc.

ADVENTURE COMICS
1999
1 JeR,PSj,F:Starman & The Atom . 2.00

ADVENTURES IN THE DC UNIVERSE
1997–98
1 F:New JLA 4.00
2 F:The Flash,Catwoman. 2.00
3 Wonder Woman vs. Cheetah;
  Poison Ivy vs. Batman 2.00
4 F:Green Lantern vs. Glorious
  Godfrey; Mister Miracle 2.00
5 F:Martian Manhunter, all alien
  issue 2.00
6 F:Ocean Master, Power Girl 2.00
7 SVa(s),F:Shazam Family 2.00
8 SVa(s),F:Blue Beetle &
  Booster Gold 2.00
9 SVa(s),F:Flash,V:Grodd,Cipher. . 2.00
10 SVa(s),Legion month 2.00
11 SVa(s),F:Green Lantern &
   Wonder Woman 2.00
12 SVa(s) 2.75
13 SVa(s),A:Martian Manhunter . . . 2.00
14 SVa(s),Flash races Superboy. . . 2.00

15 SVa(s),Shazam,Aquaman 2.00
16 SVa(s),F:Green Lantern. 2.00
17 SVa(s),F:Batman, Creeper. 2.00
18 SVa(s),F:JLA 2.75
19 F:Catwoman, Wonder Woman . . 2.00
Ann.#1 magic amulets,5 stories . . . 4.00

ADVENTURES OF ALAN LADD
1949–51
1 Ph(c) 750.00
2 Ph(c) 400.00
3 Ph(c) 300.00
4 Ph(c) 300.00
5 Ph(c),inc.Destination Danger. . 225.00
6 Ph(c) 225.00
7 . . . . 225.00
8 Grand Duchess takes over . . . 225.00
9 Deadlien in Rapula 225.00

ADVENTURES OF BOB HOPE
1951–68
1 Ph(c). 1,200.00
2 Ph(c) 600.00
3 Ph(c) 350.00
4 Ph(c) 325.00
5 thru 10 . . . . @300.00
11 thru 20 . . . . @150.00
21 thru 40 . . . . @100.00
41 thru 90 . . . . @75.00
91 thru 93 . . . . @30.00
94 C:Aquaman 35.00
95 thru 105 . . . . @30.00
106 thru 109 NA . . . . @45.00

ADVENTURES OF DEAN MARTIN AND JERRY LEWIS
1952–57
1 . . . . 650.00
2 . . . . 325.00
3 thru 10 . . . . @150.00
11 thru 20 . . . . @100.00
21 thru 40 . . . . @75.00
Becomes:

ADVENTURES OF JERRY LEWIS
1957–71
41 thru 55 . . . . @55.00
56 thru 69 . . . . @40.00
70 thru 87 . . . . @35.00
88 A:Bob Hope. 40.00
89 thru 91 . . . . @30.00
92 C:Superman 35.00
93 thru 96 . . . . @25.00
97 A:Batman & Joker 45.00
98 thru 100 . . . . @30.00
101 thru 104 NA . . . . @45.00
105 A:Superman. 35.00
106 thru 111 . . . . @20.00
112 A:Flash 30.00
113 thru 116 . . . . @20.00
117 A:Wonder Woman 25.00
118 thru 124 . . . . @15.00

ADVENTURES OF FORD FAIRLANE
1990
1 DH,DG 1.50
2 thru 4 DH . . . . @1.50

ADVENTURES OF THE OUTSIDERS
(see BATMAN & THE OUTSIDERS)

ADVENTURES OF OZZIE AND HARRIET
1949–50
1 Ph(c) 650.00
2 . . . . 350.00
3 thru 5 . . . . @300.00

ADVENTURES OF REX, THE WONDERDOG
1952–59
1 ATh 800.00
2 ATh 400.00
3 ATh 300.00
4 . . . . 250.00
5 . . . . 250.00
6 thru 11 . . . . @150.00
12 thru 20 . . . . @100.00
21 thru 46 . . . . @75.00

ADVENTURES OF SUPERBOY
(See: SUPERBOY)

ADVENTURES OF SUPERMAN
(See: SUPERMAN)

AGENT LIBERTY SPECIAL
1992
1 DAb,O:Agent Liberty. 2.00

ALIEN NATION
1988
1 JBi,movie adaption 2.50

ALL-AMERICAN COMICS
1939–48
1 B:Hop Harrigan,Scribbly,Mutt&Jeff,
  Red,White&Blue,Bobby Thatcher,
  Skippy,Daiseybelle,Mystery Men
  of Mars,Toonerville. 5,800.00
2 B:Ripley's Believe It or Not. . 1,700.00
3 Hop Harrigan (c) 1,200.00
4 Flag(c). 1,200.00
5 B:The American Way 1,200.00
6 ShM(c),Fredric Marchin in
  `The American Way' 1,000.00
7 E:Bobby Thatcher,C.H.
  Claudy's `A Thousand Years
  in a Minute' 1,000.00
8 B:Ultra Man 1,400.00
9 . . . . 950.00
10 ShM(c),E:The American Way,
   Santa-X-Mas(c) 900.00
11 Ultra Man(c). 850.00
12 E:Toonerville Folks. 850.00
13 `The Infra Red Des'Royers' . . 850.00
14. . . . . 850.00
15 E:Tippie and Reg'lar Fellars . . 850.00
16 O&1st App:Green Lantern,
   B:Lantern(c). 68,000.00
17 SMo(c) 13,000.00
18 SMo(c) 8,500.00
19 SMo(c),O&I: Atom, E:Ultra
   Man. 13,000.00

All-American Comics #26
© DC Comics, Inc.

20 I:Atom's costume,Hunkle
  becomes Red Tornado. . . . 3,500.00
21 E:Wiley of West Point
  & Skippy 2,100.00
22 . . . . 2,000.00
23 E:Daieybelle 2,000.00
24 E:Ripley's Believe It or Not . 2,700.00
25 O&I:Dr. Mid-Nite 8,400.00
26 O&I:Sargon the Sorcerer. . . 3,200.00
27 I:Doiby Dickles 3,500.00
28 . . . . 1,300.00
29 ShM(c) 1,300.00
30 ShM(c) 1,300.00
31 Adventures of the underfed
  orphans. 1,300.00
32 . . . . 1,000.00
33 . . . . 1,000.00
34 . . . . 1,000.00
35 Doiby discovers Lantern's ID 1,000.00
36 . . . . 1,000.00
37 . . . . 1,000.00
38 . . . . 1,000.00
39 . . . . 1,000.00
40 . . . . 1,000.00
41 . . . . 800.00
42 . . . . 800.00
43 . . . . 800.00
44 `I Accuse the Green Lantern!'. 800.00
45 . . . . 800.00
46 . . . . 800.00
47 Hop Harrigan meets the
  Enemy,(c). 800.00
48 . . . . 800.00
49 . . . . 800.00
50 E:Sargon 800.00
51 `Murder Under the Stars' . . . 700.00
52 . . . . 700.00
53 Green Lantern delivers
  the Mail 700.00
54 . . . . 700.00
55 `The Riddle of the
  Runaway Trolley' 700.00
56 V:Elegant Esmond. 700.00
57 V:The Melancholy Men 700.00
58 . . . . 700.00
59 `The Story of the Man Who
  Couldn't Tell The Truth' 700.00
60 . . . . 700.00
61 O:Soloman Grundy,`Fighters
  Never Quit' 4,000.00
62 `Da Distrik Attorney' 650.00
63. . . . . 650.00
64 `A Bag of Assorted Nuts!'. . . . 650.00
65 `The Man Who Lost
  Wednesday' 650.00

66 `The Soles of Manhattan!' . . . 650.00
67 V:King Shark 650.00
68 Meets Napoleon&Joe Safeen. 650.00
69 `Backwards Man!' 650.00
70 JKu,I:Maximillian O'Leary,
  V:Colley, the Leprechaun . . 650.00
71 E:Red,White&Blue,`The
  Human Bomb'. 550.00
72 B:Black Pirate 550.00
73 B:Winkey,Blinky&Noddy,
  `Mountain Music Mayhem' . . 550.00
74. . . . . 550.00
75. . . . . 550.00
76 `Spring Time for Doiby' 550.00
77 Hop Harrigan(c) 550.00
78 . . . . 550.00
79 Mutt & Jeff 550.00
80 . . . . 550.00
81 . . . . 550.00
82 . . . . 550.00
83 Mutt & Jeff 550.00
84 `The Adventure of the Man
  with Two Faces' 550.00
85. . . . . 550.00
86 V:Crime of the Month Club. . . 550.00
87 `The Strange Case of
  Professor Nobody' 550.00
88 `Canvas of Crime' 550.00
89 O:Harlequin 800.00
90 O:Icicle 700.00
91 `Wedding of the Harlequin' . . . 700.00
92 `The Icicle goes South'. 700.00
93 `The Double Crossing Decoy'. 700.00
94 A:Harlequin 700.00
95 `The Unmasking of the
  Harlequin'. 700.00
96 ATh(c),`Solve the Mystery
  of the Emerald Necklaces!'. . 700.00
97 ATh(c),`The Country Fair
  Crimes'. 700.00
98 ATh,ATh(c),`End of Sports!' . . 700.00
99 ATh,ATh(c),E:Hop Harrigan . . 700.00
100 ATh,I:Johnny Thunder. . . . 1,500.00
101 ATh,ATh(c),E:Mutt & Jeff . . 1,000.00
102 ATh,ATh(c),E:GrnLantern . 2,000.00
Becomes:

ALL-AMERICAN
WESTERN
1948–52
103 A:Johnny Thunder,`The City
  Without Guns,'All Johnny
  Thunder stories 350.00
104 ATh(c),`Unseen Allies' 250.00
105 ATh(c),`Hidden Guns'. 225.00
106 ATh(c),`Snow Mountain
  Ambush'. 150.00
107 ATh(c),`Cheyenne Justice' . . 225.00
108 ATh(c),`Vengeance of
  the Silver Bullet' 150.00
109 ATh(c),`Secret of
  Crazy River' 150.00
110 ATh(c),`Ambush at
  Scarecrow Hills' 150.00
111 ATh(c),`Gun-Shy Sheriff'. . . . 150.00
112 ATh(c),`Double Danger' 150.00
113 ATh(c),`Johnny Thunder
  Indian Chief' 175.00
114 ATh(c),`The End of
  Johnny Thunder'. 150.00
115 ATh(c),`Cheyenne Mystery' . 150.00
116 ATh(c),`Buffalo Raiders
  of the Mesa'. 150.00
117 ATh(c),V:Black Lightnin 125.00
118 ATh(c),`Challenge of
  the Aztecs' 125.00
119 GK(c),`The Vanishing
  Gold Mine' 125.00
120 GK(c),`Ambush at
  Painted Mountain'. 125.00
121 ATh(c),`The Unmasking of

All-American Western #116
© DC Comics, Inc.

  Johnny Thunder'. 125.00
122 ATh(c),`The Real
  Johnny Thunder'. 125.00
123 GK(c),`Johnny Thunder's
  Strange Rival'. 125.00
124 ATh(c),`The Iron Horse's
  Last Run' 125.00
125 ATh(c),`Johnny Thunder's
  Last Roundup' 125.00
126 ATh(c),`Phantoms of the
  Desert' 125.00
Becomes:

ALL-AMERICAN
MEN OF WAR
1952–66
127 (0) 750.00
128 (1) 500.00
2 JGr(c),Killer Bait. 400.00
3 Pied Piper of Pyong-Yang. . . . 400.00
4 JGr(c),The Hills of Hate 400.00
5 One Second to Zero 300.00
6 IN(c),Jungle Killers 300.00
7 IN(c),Beach to Hold 300.00
8 IN(c),Sgt. Storm Cloud 300.00
9 . . . . 300.00
10. . . . . 300.00
11 JGr(c),Dragon's Teeth 300.00
12. . . . . 250.00
13 JGr(c),Lost Patrol. 250.00
14 IN(c),Pigeon Boss 250.00
15 JGr(c),Flying Roadblock. 250.00
16 JGr(c),The Flying Jeep. 250.00
17 JGr(c),Booby Trap Ridge 250.00
18 JKu(c),The Ballad of
  Battling Bells 250.00
19 JGr(c),IN,Torpedo Track. 175.00
20 JGr(c),JKu,Lifenet to
  Beach Road. 175.00
21 JGr(c),IN,RH,The
  Coldest War 175.00
22 JGr(c),IN,JKu,Snipers Nest . . 175.00
23 JGr(c),The Silent War 175.00
24 JGr(c),The Thin Line 175.00
25 JGr(c),IN,For Rent-One
  Foxhole 175.00
26. . . . . 175.00
27 JGr(c),RH,Fighting Pigeon . . . 175.00
28 JGr(c),RA,JKu,Medal
  for A Dog 175.00
29 IN(c),JKu,Battle Bridges. 200.00
30 JGr(c),RH,Frogman Hunt 175.00
31 JGr(c),Battle Seat 200.00
32 JGr(c),RH,Battle Station. 200.00

33 JGr(c),IN,Sky Ambush 175.00
34 JGr(c),JKu,No Man's Alley . . . 175.00
35 JGr(c),IN, Battle Call 150.00
36 JGr(c),JKu,Battle Window . . 150.00
37 JGr(c),JKu,The Big Stretch . . 150.00
38 JGr(c),RH,JKu,The
  Floating Sentinel. 150.00
39 JGr(c),JKu,The Four Faces
  of Sgt. Fay 150.00
40 JGr(c),IN,Walking Helmet. . . . 150.00
41 JKu(c),RH,JKu, The 50-50 War 100.00
42 JGr(c),JKu,Battle Arm 100.00
43 JGr(c),JKu,Command Post. . . 100.00
44 JKu(c),The Flying Frogman . . 100.00
45 JGr(c),RH,Combat Waterboy . 100.00
46 JGr(c),IN,RH,Tank Busters. . . 100.00
47 JGr(c),JKu,MD,Battle Freight . 100.00
48 JGr(c),JKu,MD,Roadblock . . . 100.00
49 JGr(c),Walking Target 100.00
50 IN,RH,Bodyguard For A Sub . 100.00
51 JGr(c),RH,Bomber's Moon 75.00
52 JKu(c),RH,MD,Back
  Seat Driver. 75.00
53 JGr(c),JKu,Night Attack 75.00
54 JKu(c),IN,Diary of a
  Fighter Pilot 75.00
55 JKu(c),RH,Split-Second Target. 75.00
56 JKu,IN,RH,Frogman Jinx 75.00
57 Pick-Up for Easy Co. 75.00
58 JKu(c),RH,MD,A Piece of Sky . 75.00
59 JGr(c),JKu,The Hand of War . . 75.00
60 JGr(c),The Time Table 75.00
61 JGr(c),IN,MD,Blind Target 75.00
62 JGr(c),RH,RA,No(c) 75.00
63 JGr(c),JKu,Frogman Carrier . . 75.00
64 JKu(c),JKu,RH,The Other
  Man's War 75.00
65 JGr(c),JKu,MD,Same
  Old Sarge. 75.00
66 JGr(c),The Walking Fort. 75.00
67 JGr(c),RH,A:Gunner&Sarge,
  The Cover Man 250.00
68 JKu(c),Gunner&Sarge,
  The Man & The Gun. 75.00
69 JKu(c),A:Tank Killer,
  Bazooka Hill. 75.00
70 JKu(c),IN,Pigeon
  Without Wings 75.00
71 JGr(c),A:Tank Killer,Target
  For An Ammo Boy 75.00
72 JGr(c),A:Tank Killer,T.N.T.
  Broom 75.00
73 JGr(c),JKu,No Detour 75.00
74 The Minute Commandos 75.00
75 JKu(c),Sink That Flattop. 75.00
76 JKu(c),A:Tank Killer,
  Just One More Tank 75.00
77 JKu(c),IN,MD,Big Fish-
  little Fish. 75.00
78 JGr(c),Tin Hat for an
  Iron Man. 75.00
79 JGr(c),RA,Showdown Soldier . 75.00
80 JGr(c),RA,The Medal Men 75.00
81 JGr(c),IN,Ghost Ship of
  Two Wars. 60.00
82 IN(c),B:Johnny Cloud,
  The Flying Chief. 60.00
83 IN(c),Fighting Blind 60.00
84 IN(c),Death Dive 60.00
85 RH(c),Battle Eagle. 60.00
86 JGr(c),Top-Gun Ace. 60.00
87 JGr(c),Broken Ace 60.00
88 JGr(c),The Ace of Vengeance . 60.00
89 JGr(c),The Star Jockey 60.00
90 JGr(c),Wingmate of Doom 60.00
91 RH(c),Two Missions To Doom . 60.00
92 JGr(c),The Battle Hawk 60.00
93 RH(c),The Silent Rider. 60.00
94 RH(c),Be Brave-Be Silent 60.00
95 RH(c),Second Sight
  For a Pilot 60.00

96 RH(c),The Last Flight
  of Lt. Moon. 60.00
97 IN(c),A 'Target' Called
  Johnny. 60.00
98 The Time-Bomb Ace 60.00
99 IN(c),The Empty Cockpit 60.00
100 RH(c),Battle o/t Sky Chiefs. . . 60.00
101 RH(c),Death Ship of
  Three Wars 30.00
102 JKu(c),Blind Eagle-Hungry
  Hawk 30.00
103 IN(c),Battle Ship-
  Battle Heart 30.00
104 JKu(c),The Last Target. 30.00
105 IN(c),Killer Horse-Ship 30.00
106 IN(c),Death Song For
  A Battle Hawk 30.00
107 IN(c),Flame in the Sky 30.00
108 IN(c),Death-Dive of the Aces . 30.00
109 IN(c),The Killer Slot 30.00
110 RH(c),The Co-Pilot was
  Death. 30.00
111 RH(c),E:Johnny Cloud, Tag–
  You're Dead 30.00
112 RH(c),B:Balloon Buster,Lt.
  Steve Savage-Balloon Buster . 30.00
113 JKu(c),The Ace of
  Sudden Death 30.00
114 JKu(c),The Ace Who
  Died Twice. 30.00
115 IN(c),A:Johnny Cloud,
  Deliver One Enemy Ace-
  Handle With Care. 30.00
116 JKu(c),A:Baloon Buster,
  Circle of Death 30.00
117 Sept.–Oct., 1966 . . . . 30.00

ALL-AMERICAN COMICS
1999
1 RMz(s),F:Green Lantern &
  Johnny Thunder. 2.00

ALL-FLASH
1941–47
1 EHi,O:Flash,I:The Monocle 13,000.00
2 EHi,The Adventure of Roy
  Revenge 2,500.00
3 EHi,The Adventure of
  Misplaced Faces 1,300.00
4 EHi,Tale of the Time
  Capsule. 1,200.00
5 EHi,The Case of the Patsy

All-Flash #7 © DC Comics Inc.

  Colt! Last Quarterly 1,000.00
6 EHi,The Ray that Changed
  Men's Souls 800.00
7 EHi,Adventures of a Writers
  Fantasy, House of Horrors . . 800.00
8 EHi,Formula to Fairyland! 800.00
9 EHi,Adventure of the Stolen
  Telescope. 800.00
10 EHi,Case of the Curious Cat . 800.00
11 EHi,Troubles come
  in Doubles 700.00
12 EHi,Tumble INN to Trouble,
  Becomes Quarterly on orders
  from War Production Board
  O:The Thinker 700.00
13 EHi,I:The King. 700.00
14 EHi,I:Winky,Blinky & Noddy
  Green Lantern (c). 800.00
15 EHi,Secrets of a Stranger . . . 600.00
16 EHi,A:The Sinister 600.00
17 Tales of the Three Wishes . . . 550.00
18 A:Winlky,Blinky&Noddy
  B:Mutt & Jeff reprints 550.00
19 No Rest at the Rest Home . . . 550.00
20 A:Winky, Blinky & Noddy 550.00
21 I:Turtle. 500.00
22 The Money Doubler,E:Mutt
  & Jeff reprints. 500.00
23 The Bad Men of Bar Nothing . 500.00
24 I:Worry Wart,3 Court
  Clowns Get Caught 500.00
25 I:Slapsy Simmons,
  Flash Jitterbugs 500.00
26 I:The Chef,The Boss,Shrimp
  Coogan,A:Winky, Blinky &
  Noddy 550.00
27 A:The Thinker,Gangplank
  Gus story 500.00
28 A:Shrimp Coogan,Winky,
  Blinky & Noddy. 500.00
29 The Thousand-Year Old Terror,
  A:Winky,Blinky & Noddy 500.00
30 The Vanishing Snowman 500.00
31 A:Black Hat,The Planet
  of Sport 500.00
32 I:Fiddler,A:Thinker 800.00

ALL FUNNY COMICS
1943–48
1 Genius Jones 400.00
2 same 150.00
3 same 100.00
4 same 100.00
5 thru 10 . . . . @100.00
11 Genius Jones. 75.00
12 same. 50.00
13 same 75.00
14. . . . . 60.00
15. . . . . 75.00
16 A:DC Superheroes. 250.00
17 thru 23 . . . . @75.00

ALL-STAR COMICS
Summer, 1940–51
1 B:Flash,Hawkman,Hourman,
  Sandman,Spectre,Red White
  & Blue 12,000.00
2 B:Green Lantern and Johnny
  Thunder. 5,000.00
3 First meeting of Justice Society
  with Flash as Chairman . . 35,000.00
4 First mission of JSA 4,500.00
5 V:Mr. X,I:Hawkgirl 4,000.00
6 Flash leaves 2,900.00
7 Green Lantern becomes Chairman,
  L:Hourman, C:Superman,
  Batman & Flash. 3,000.00
8 I:Wonder Women;Starman and
  Dr. Mid-Nite join,Hawkman

All-Star Comics #42 © DC Comics, Inc.

becomes chairman 26,000.00
9 JSA in Latin America 2,400.00
10 C:Flash & Green Lantern,
    JSA Time Travel story 2,400.00
11 Wonder Women joins;
    I:Justice Battalion 2,200.00
12 V:Black Dragon society 2,200.00
13 V:Hitler 2,000.00
14 JSA in occupied Europe . . . 2,000.00
15 I:Brain Wave,A:JSA's
    Girl Friends 2,000.00
16 Propaganda/relevance issue 1,600.00
17 V:Brain Wave 1,600.00
18 I:King Bee. 1,700.00
19 Hunt for Hawkman 1,600.00
20 I:Monster 1,600.00
21 Time travel story 1,500.00
22 Sandman and Dr. Fate leave,
    I:Conscience, Good Fairy. . 1,500.00
23 I:Psycho-Pirate 1,500.00
24 Propaganda/relevance issue,
    A:Conscience&Wildcat,Mr.Terrific;
    L:Starman & Spectre; Flash
    & Green Lantern return . . . 1,500.00
25 JSA whodunit issue. 1,300.00
26 V:Metal Men from Jupiter . . 1,300.00
27 Handicap issue,A:Wildcat . . 1,300.00
28 Ancient curse comes to life . 1,100.00
29 I:Landor from 25th century . 1,100.00
30 V:Brain Wave 1,100.00
31 V:Zor 1,100.00
32 V:Psycho-Pirate 1,100.00
33 V:Soloman Grundy,A:Doiby
    Dickles, Last appearance
    Thunderbolt. 2,400.00
34 I:Wizard 1,000.00
35 I:Per Degaton 1,000.00
36 A:Superman and Batman . . 2,300.00
37 I:Injustice Society of
    the World. 1,300.00
38 V:Villians of History,
    A:Black Canary 1,500.00
39 JSA in magic world,
    Johnny Thunder leaves . . . 1,000.00
40 A:Black Canary,Junior Justice
    Society of America. 1,000.00
41 Black Canary joins,A:Harlequin,
    V:Injustice Society
    of the World. 1,000.00
42 I:Alchemist. 950.00
43 V:Interdimensional gold men . 950.00
44 I:Evil Star. 950.00
45 Crooks develop stellar
    JSA powers 900.00
46 Comedy issue 900.00
47 V:Billy the Kid 900.00

48 Time Travel story 900.00
49 V:Comet-being invaders. 900.00
50 V:College classmate of Flash . 950.00
51 V:Diamond men from center
    of the Earth 900.00
52 JSA disappears from
    Earth for years 900.00
53 Time Travel issue. 900.00
54 Circus issue. 900.00
55 JSA fly to Jupiter 900.00
56 V:Chameleons from
    31st Century. 900.00
57 I:Key. 1,300.00
Becomes:

ALL STAR WESTERN
April-May 1951
58 Trigger Twins. 300.00
59 . . . . 150.00
60 . . . . 150.00
61 thru 64 ATh 125.00
65 . . . . 125.00
66. . . . . 125.00
67 GK,B:Johnny Thunder 150.00
68 thru 81 . . . . @75.00
82 thru 98 . . . . @60.00
99 FF. 75.00
100 . . . . 60.00
101 thru 104 . . . . @45.00
105 O:JSA, March, 1987. . . . . . . 45.00
106 and 107 . . . . @45.00
108 O:Johnny Thunder 125.00
109 thru 116 . . . . @45.00
117 CI,O:Super-Chief 60.00
118 . . . . 45.00
119 . . . . 40.00

ALL-STAR COMICS
1976–78
58 RE,WW,R:JSA,I:Power Girl 9.00
59 RE,WW,Brain Wave. 6.00
60 KG,WW,I:Vulcan. 6.00
61 KG,WW,V:Vulcan. 6.00
62 KG,WW,A:E-2 Superman. 6.00
63 KG,WW,A:E-2 Superman,
    Solomon Grundy 6.00
64 WW,Shining Knight 6.00
65 KG,WW,E-2 Superman,
    Vandal Savage. 6.00
66 JSon,BL,Injustice Society. 6.00
67 JSon,BL 6.00
68 JSon,BL 6.00
69 JSon,BL,A:E-2 Superman,
    Starman,Dr.Mid-Nite 12.00
70 JSon,BL,Huntress 6.00
71 JSon,BL 5.00
72 JSon,A:Golden.Age Huntress. . . 5.00
73 JSon 5.00
74 JSon 5.00

ALL STAR COMICS
1999
1 JeR(s),F:Justice Society
    of America, V:Stalker's Seven. . 3.00
2 JeR(s) conclusion. 3.00
Giant #1 80-page 5.00

ALL STAR SQUADRON
1981–87
1 RB,JOy,JSa,I:Degaton 3.50
2 RB,JOy,Robotman 2.00
3 RB,JOy,Robotman 2.00
4 RB,JOy,Robotman 2.00
5 RB/JOy,I:Firebrand(Dannette). . . 2.00
6 JOy,Hawkgirl 2.00
7 JOy,Hawkgirl 2.00
8 DH/JOy,A:Steel 2.00
9 DH/JOy,A:Steel 2.00
10 JOy,V:Binary Brotherhood 2.00

All Star Squadron #4 © DC Comics, Inc.

11 JOy,V:Binary Brotherhood 2.00
12 JOy,R:Dr.Hastor O:Hawkman. . . 2.00
13 JOy,photo(c) 2.00
14 JOy,JLA crossover. 2.00
15 JOy,JLA crossover. 2.00
16 I&D:Nuclear. 2.00
17 Trial of Robotman 2.00
18 V:Thor. 2.00
19 V:Brainwave 2.00
20 JOy,V:Brainwave 2.00
21 JOy,I:Cyclotron (1st JOy
    Superman) 2.50
22 JOy,V:Deathbolt,Cyclotron 2.00
23 JOy,I:Amazing-Man 2.00
24 JOy,I:Brainwave,Jr.. . . . . 2.50
25 JOy,I:Infinity Inc. 2.50
26 JOy,Infinity Inc. 2.50
27 Spectre 2.00
28 JOy,Spectre. 2.00
29 JOy,retold story 2.00
30 V:Black Dragons 2.00
31 All-Star gathering. 2.00
32 O:Freedom Fighters. 2.00
33 Freedom Fighters,I:Tsunami. . . . 2.00
34 Freedom Fighters 2.00
35 RB,Shazam family 2.00
36 Shazam family 2.00
37 A:Shazam Family 2.00
38 V:The Real American. 2.00
39 V:The Real American. 2.00
40 D:The Real American 2.00
41 O:Starman 2.00
42 V:Tsunami,Kung. 2.00
43 V:Tsunami,Kung. 2.00
44 I:Night & Fog 2.00
45 I:Zyklon 2.00
46 V:Baron Blitzkrieg 2.00
47 TM,O:Dr.Fate. 3.50
48 A:Blackhawk 2.00
49 A:Dr.Occult 2.00
50 Crisis. 2.50
51 AA,Crisis 2.00
52 Crisis. 2.00
53 Crisis,A:The Dummy 2.00
54 Crisis,V:The Dummy 2.00
55 Crisis,V:Anti-Monitor 2.00
56 Crisis. 2.00
57 A:Dr.Occult 2.00
58 I:Mekanique. 2.00
59 A:Mekanique,Spectre. 2.00
60 Crisis 1942, conclusion 2.00
61 O:Liberty Belle. 2.00
62 O:The Shining Knight. 2.00
63 O:Robotman 2.00
64 WB/TD,V:Funny Face 2.00

DC COMICS

65 DH/TD,O:Johnny Quick 2.00
66 TD,O:Tarantula 2.00
67 TD,Last Issue,O:JSA 2.00
Ann.#1 JOy,O:G.A.,Atom 2.00
Ann.#2 JOy,Infinity Inc. 2.00
Ann.#3 WB,JOy,KG,GP,DN. 2.00

ALL STAR WESTERN
(see WEIRD WESTERN TALES)

ALPHA CENTURION
1996
Spec.#1 . . . . 3.00

AMBER:
THE GUNS OF AVALON
Aug. 1996
1 (of 3) adapt. of Roger Zelazny
  classic 6.95
2 and 3 conclusion . . . . @6.95

AMBUSH BUG
1985
1 KG,I:Cheeks. 1.25
2 KG thru 4 . . . . @1.00

AMBUSH BUG:
STOCKING STUFFER 1986
1 KG,R:Cheeks. 1.25

AMBUSH BUG:
NOTHING SPECIAL 1992
1 KG,A:Sandman,Death 2.50

AMERICA vs.
JUSTICE SOCIETY
Jan.–April, 1985
1 AA,R,Thomas Script 2.00
2 AA 1.50
3 AA 1.50
4 AA, ... 1.50

AMERICAN FREAK: A
TALE OF THE UN-MEN
Vertigo 1994
1 B:DLp,(s),VcL,R:Un-Men 2.25
2 VcL,A:Crassus 2.25
3 VcL,A:Scylla 2.25
4 VcL,A:Scylla 2.25
5 VcL,Final Issue. 2.25

AMETHYST
[Limited Series] 1983–84
[PRINCESS OF GEMWORLD]
1 Origin. 1.25
2 thru 7 EC . . . . @1.00
8 EC,O:Gemworld 1.00
9 thru 12 EC . . . . @1.00
Spec.#1 KG 1.25
[Regular Series]
1985–86
1 thru 12 EC . . . . @1.00
13 EC,Crisis,A:Dr.Fate 1.00
14 EC. 1.00
15 EC,Castle Amethyst Destroyed . 1.00
16 EC. 1.00
Spec.#1 EM 1.25
[Mini-Series]
1987–88
1 EM. 1.25
2 EM. 1.25
3 EM. 1.25

4 EM,O:Mordru 1.25

ANARKY
March 1997
1 AIG(s),NBy,JRu,Anarky vs.
  Etrigan. 2.50
2 AIG(s),NBy,JRu,V:Darkseid. 2.50
3 AIG(s),NBy,JRu,A:Batman 2.50
4 AIG(s),NBy,JRu,A:Batman,concl. 2.50

ANARKY
1999
1 AIG(s),NBy,JRu,F:JLA 2.50
2 AIG(s),NBy,JRu,F:GreenLantern . 2.50
3 AIG(s),NBy,JRu,F:GreenLantern . 2.50
4 AIG(s),NBy,JRu,V:Ra's al Ghul . . 2.50
5 AIG(s),NBy,JRu,V:Ra's
  al Ghul,pt.2 . . . . 2.50
6 AIG(s),NBy,JRu,F:Ra's
  al Ghul,pt.3 . . . . 2.50

ANGEL & THE APE
1991
1 Apes of Wrath,pt.1 . . . . 1.00
2 Apes of Wrath,pt.2,
  A:G.Gardner. 1.00
3 Apes of Wrath,pt.3,
  A: Inferior Five 1.00
4 Apes of Wrath,pt.4,
  A: Inferior Five, final issue 1.00

ANIMA
Vertigo 1994–95
1 R:Anima. 2.00
2 V:Scarecrow 2.00
3 V:Scarecrow 2.00
4 A:Nameless one 2.00
5 CI,V:Arkana 2.00
6 CI,V:Arkana 2.00
7 Zero Hour. 2.00
8 Nameless One 2.00
9 Superboy & Nameless One 2.00
10 A:Superboy 2.00
11 V:Nameless One 2.00
12 A:Hawkman,V:Shrike 2.00
13 A:Hawkman,Shrike 2.00
14 Return to Gotham City 2.00
15 V:Psychic Vampire, final issue . . 2.25

ANIMAL ANTICS
1946–49
1 . . . . 275.00
2 . . . . 150.00
3 thru 10 . . . . @90.00
11 thru 23 . . . . @65.00

ANIMAL-MAN
1988–95
1 BB(c),B:GMo(s),ChT,DHz,
  B:Animal Rights,I:Dr.Myers 7.00
2 BB(c),ChT,DHz,A:Superman . . . 5.00
3 BB(c),ChT,DHz,A:B'wana Beast . 3.00
4 BB(c),ChT,DHz,V:B'wana Beast,
  E:Animal Rights 3.00
5 BB(c),ChT,DHz,
  I&D:Crafty Coyote 3.50
6 BB(c),ChT,DHz,A:Hawkman 3.00
7 BB(c),ChT,DHz,D:Red Mask 3.00
8 BB(c),ChT,DHz,V:Mirror Master . 3.00
9 BB(c),DHz,TG,A:Martian
  Manhunter 3.00
10 BB(c),ChT,DHz,A:Vixen,
  B:O:Animal Man 3.00
11 BB(c),ChT,DHz,I:Hamed Ali,
  Tabu,A:Vixen 3.00
12 BB(c),D:Hamed Ali,A:Vixen,

B'wanaBeast 3.00
13 BB(c),I:Dominic Mndawe,R:B'wana
  Beast,Apartheid 3.00
14 BB(c),TG,SeM,A:Future Animal
  Man,I:Lennox 3.00
15 BB(c),ChT,DHz,A:Dolphin 3.00
16 BB(c),ChT,DHz,A:JLA. 3.00
17 BB(c),ChT,DHz,A:Mirr.Master. . . 3.00
18 BB(c),ChT,DHz,A:Lennox. 3.00
19 BB(c),ChT,DHz,D:Ellen,
  Cliff,Maxine 3.00
20 BB(c),ChT,DHz,I:Bug-Man 3.00
21 BB(c),ChT,DHz,N&V:Bug-Man . . 3.00
22 BB(c),PCu,SeM,A:Rip Hunter. . . 3.00
23 BB(c),A:Phantom Stranger. 2.50
24 BB(c),V:Psycho Pirate 2.50
25 BB(c),ChT,MFm,I:Comic
  Book Limbo 2.50
26 BB(c),E:GMo(s),ChT,MFm,
  A:Grant Morrison 2.50
27 BB(c),B:PMi(s),ChT,MFm 2.50
28 BB(c),ChT,MFm,I:Nowhere Man,
  I&D:Front Page 2.50
29 ChT,SDi,V:National Man 2.50
30 BB(c),ChT,MFm,V:Angel Mob . . 2.50
31 BB(c),ChT,MFm. 2.50
32 BB(c),E:PMi(s),ChT,MFm. 2.50
33 BB(c),B:TV(s),SDi,A:Travis
  Cody 2.50
34 BB(c),SDi,Requiem 2.50
35 BB(c),SDi,V:Radioactive Dogs . . 2.50
36 BB(c),SDi,A:Mr.Rainbow 2.50
37 BB(c),SDi,Animal/Lizard Man . . . 2.50
38 BB(c),SDi,A:Mr.Rainbow 2.00
39 BB(c),TMd,SDi,Wolfpack in
  San Diego 2.00
40 BB(c),SDi,War of the Gods
  x-over. 2.00
41 BB(c),SDi,V:Star Labs
  Renegades,I:Winky 2.00
42 BB(c),SDi,V:Star Labs
  Renegades. 2.00
43 BB(c),SDi,I:Tristess,A:Vixen. . . . 2.00
44 BB(c),SDi,A:Vixen. 2.00
45 BB(c),StP,SDi,I:L.Decker 2.00
46 BB(c),SDi,I:Frank Baker. 2.00
47 BB(c),SDi,I:Shining Man,
  (B'wana Beast). 2.00
48 BB(c),SDi,V:Antagon 2.00
49 BB(c),SDi,V:Antagon 2.00
50 BB(c),E:TV(s),SDi,I:Metaman. . . 3.50
51 BB(c),B:JaD(s),StP,B:Flesh
  and Blood. 2.50
52 BB(c),StP,Homecoming 2.50

Animal Man #37 © DC Comics Inc.

Animal Man #60 © DC Comics, Inc.

53 BB(c),StP,Flesh and Blood..... 2.50
54 BB(c),StP,Flesh and Blood..... 2.50
55 BB(c),StP,Flesh and Blood..... 2.50
56 BB(c),StP,E:Flesh and Blood,
    Double-sized 3.00

Vertigo
57 BB(c),StP,B:Recreation,
    Ellen in NY............. 2.50
58 BB(c),StP,Wild Side 2.50
59 BB(c),RsB,GHi(i),Wild Town.... 2.50
60 RsB,GHi(i),Wild life 2.50
61 BB(c),StP,Tooth and Claw#1 ... 2.50
62 BB(c),StP,Tooth and Claw#2 ... 2.50
63 BB(c),V:Leviathan 2.50
64 DIB(c),WSm,DnS(i),
    Breath of God............. 2.50
65 RDB(c),WSm,
    Perfumed Garden.......... 2.25
66 A:Kindred Spirit 2.25
67 StP,Mysterious Ways #1 ..... 2.25
68 StP,Mysterious Ways #2 ..... 2.25
69 Animal Man's Family 2.25
70 GgP(c),StP 2.25
71 GgP(c),StP,Maxine Alive? 2.25
72 StP 2.25
73 StP,Power Life Church....... 2.25
74 StP,Power Life Church....... 2.25
75 StP,Power Life Church....... 2.25
76 StP,Pilgrimage problems 2.00
77 Cliff shot 2.00
78 StP,Animal Man poisoned 2.00
79 New Direction 2.00
80 New Direction 2.00
81 Wild Type,pt.1 .... 2.00
82 Wild Type,pt.2 .... 2.00
83 Wild Type,pt.3 .... 2.00
84 F:Maxine,SupernaturalDreams.. 2.00
85 Animal Mundi,pt.1 .... 2.25
86 Animal Mundi,pt.2 .... 2.25
87 Animal Mundi,pt.3 .... 2.25
88 Morphogenetic Fields........ 2.25
89 final issue 2.25
Ann.#1 BB(c),JaD,TS(i),RIB(i),
    Children Crusade,F:Maxine ... 4.25
TPB Rep.#1 thru #10 .... 19.95

ANIMANIACS
Warner Bros./DC May 1995
1 F:Yakko,Wakko,Dot 1.50
2 Health Spa............... 1.50
3 Travel back in time 1.50
4 .... 1.50
5 .... 1.50

6 V:Cleopatra 1.50
7 Scratchinsniff Replaced 1.50
8 Disputin win Newton.......... 1.50
9 thru 12 .... @1.50
13 thru 17................ @1.75
18 visit to France 1.75
19 "The Y Files" 1.75
20 "Rebels Just Because"........ 1.75
21 x-mas issue,A:Santa 1.75
22 .... 1.75
23 F:Hellow Nurse 1.75
24 F:The Goodfeathers,A:Pinky and
    the Brain 1.75
25 F:Slappy Squirrel........... 1.75
26 "Haunted House of Pancakes".. 1.75
27 "Plane for Keeps"........... 1.75
28 "Science Issue" 1.75
29 "The Return of Hello Nurse,
    Agent of H.U.B.B.A." 1.75
30 "Electro-Walter and
    Dyna-Squirrel" 1.75
31 Nastina LeCreep 2.00
32 "Lifestiles of the Old & Cranky" . 2.00
33 "The Long Lost Warner"....... 2.00
34 Minerxa, Warrior Princess 2.00
35 .... 2.00
36 Generation Gap............ 2.00
37 F:Brain 2.00
38 special all-cute issue 2.00
39 Arnold Nobel 2.00
40 Slappy Squirrel 2.00
41 Slappy's Mother Goose 2.00
42 Stepford Warner 2.00
43 F:Pinky & The Brain.......... 2.00
44 F:Pinky & The Brain.......... 2.00
45 Brain Loses his Mind 2.00
46 F:Lobel Ebrain............. 2.00
47 Brainita 2.00
48 Brain Takes over world 2.00
49 Shakespeare, Jane Austen 2.00
50 Hello Nurse 2.00
51 Away With Wurds 2.00
52 I Never Promised You
    a Kindergarten 2.00
53 F:Pinky and the Brain 2.00
Christmas Spec................. 1.50

ANTHRO
1968–69
1 HwP..................... 40.00
2 HwP..................... 28.00
3 thru 5 HwP .... @28.00
6 HwP,WW(c&a) 28.00

AQUAMAN
[1st Regular Series] 1962–78
1 NC,I:Quisp 700.00
2 NC,V:Captain Sykes........ 300.00
3 NC,Aquaman from Atlantis ... 175.00
4 NC,A:Quisp 150.00
5 NC,The Haunted Sea 150.00
6 NC,A:Quisp 125.00
7 NC,Sea Beasts of Atlantis.... 125.00
8 NC,Plot to Steal the Seas.... 125.00
9 NC,V:King Neptune........ 125.00
10 NC,A:Quisp 125.00
11 I: Mera 100.00
12 NC,The Cosmic Gladiators... 100.00
13 NC,Invasion of the Giant
    Reptiles 100.00
14 NC,AquamanSecretPowers .. 100.00
15 NC,Menace of the Man-Fish . 100.00
16 NC,Duel of the Sea Queens.. 100.00
17 NC,Man Who Vanquished
    Aquaman 100.00
18 W:Aquaman & Mera....... 100.00
19 NC,Atlanteans for Sale...... 100.00
20 NC,Sea King's DoubleDoom . 100.00
21 NC,I:Fisherman........... 60.00

22 NC,The Trap of the Sinister
    Sea Nymphs 60.00
23 NC,I:Aquababy........... 60.00
24 NC,O:Black Manta......... 60.00
25 NC,Revolt of Aquaboy 60.00
26 NC,I:O.G.R.E............. 60.00
27 NC,Battle of the Rival
    Aquamen'................ 60.00
28 NC,Hail Aquababy,King of
    Atlantis................ 60.00
29 I:Ocean Master........... 50.00
30 NC,C:JLA............... 50.00
31 NC,V:O.G.R.E............. 50.00
32 NC,V:Tryton............. 50.00
33 NC,I:Aquagirl 60.00
34 NC,I:Aquabeast........... 35.00
35 I:Black Manta............ 35.00
36 NC,What Seeks the
    Awesome Threesome?...... 35.00
37 I:Scavenger 35.00
38 NC,I:Liquidator............ 35.00
39 NC,How to Kill a Sea King.... 35.00
40 JAp,Sorcerers from the Sea... 35.00
41 JAp,Quest for Mera,pt.1...... 20.00
42 JAp,Quest for Mera,pt.2...... 20.00
43 JAp,Quest for Mera,pt.3...... 20.00
44 JAp,Quest for Mera,pt.4...... 20.00
45 JAp,Quest for Mera,pt.5...... 20.00
46 JAp,Quest for Mera concl..... 20.00
47 JAp,Revolution in Atlantis #1
    rep.Adventure #268 .... 20.00
48 JAp,Revolution in Atlantis #2
    rep.Adventure #260 .... 25.00
49 JAp,As the Seas Die 20.00
50 JAp,NA,A:Deadman........ 50.00
51 JAp,NA,A:Deadman........ 50.00
52 JAp,NA,A:Deadman........ 50.00
53 JAp,Is California Sinking? 8.00
54 JAp,Crime Wave 8.00
55 JAp,Return of the Alien 8.00
56 JAp,I&O:Crusader (1970).... 8.00
57 JAp,V:Black Manta (1977).... 8.00
58 JAp,O:Aquaman rtd 9.00
59 JAp,V:Scavenger........... 8.00
60 DN,V:Scavenger 8.00
61 DN,BMc,A:Batman......... 8.00
62 DN,A:Ocean Master......... 7.00
63 DN,V:Ocean Master,
    final issue................ 7.00

[2nd Regular Series] 1991–92
1 Poseidonis Under Attack,
    C:J'onn J'onzz,Blue Beetle 2.25
2 V:Ournland 2.00

Aquaman 2nd Series #9
© DC Comics, Inc.

3 I:Iqula. 2.00
4 V:Iqula,A:Queequeg 1.50
5 A:Aqualad,Titans,M.Manhunter,
   R:Manta. 1.50
6 V: Manta. 1.50
7 R:Mera. 1.50
8 A:Batman,V:NKV Demon 1.50
9 Eco-Wars#1,A:Sea Devils. 1.50
10 Eco-Wars#2,A:Sea Devils 1.50
11 V:Gigantic Dinosaur 1.50
12 A:Iaula. 1.50
13 V:The Scavenger. 1.50
14 V:The Scavenger. 1.50

[3rd Regular Series] 1994–97
0 B:PDd(s),Paternal secret 7.50
1 PDd(s),R:Aqualad,I:Charybdis . . 6.00
2 V:Charybdis 7.00
3 B:PDd(s),Superboy. 4.00
4 B:PDd(s),Lobo 4.00
5 New Costume. 4.00
6 V:The Deep Six 3.00
7 Kako's Metamorphosis 3.00
8 V:Corona and Naiad 3.00
9 JPi(c&a),V:Deadline,A:Koryak. . 2.00
10 A:Green Lantern,Koryak 2.00
11 R:Mera 2.00
12 F:Mera. 2.00
13 V:Thanatos 2.00
14 PDd,V:Major Disaster,Underworld
   Unleashed tie-in 2.00
15 PDd,V:Tiamat 2.00
16 PDd,A:Justice League 2.00
17 PDd,V:underwater gargoyles . . . 2.00
18 . . . . 2.00
19 PDd,V:Ocean Master. 2.00
20 PDd,V:Ocean Master. 2.00
21 PDd,JCf,A:Dolphin,
   V:ThiernaNaOge 2.00
22 PDd(s). 2.00
23 PDd(s),I:Deep Blue (Neptune
   Perkins) 2.00
24 PDd(s),A:Neptune Perkins 2.00
25 PDd(s),MEg,HSm,Atlantis united,
   Aquaman king? 2.00
26 PDd(s),MEg,HSm,Oceans
   threatened, Final Night tie-in. . . 2.00
27 PDd(s),MEg,HSm,V:Demon
   Gate, dolphin killer 2.00
28 PDd(s),JCf,JP,A:J'Onn J'Onzz . . 2.00
29 PDd(s),MEg,HSm, ... 2.00
30 PDd(s),MEg,HSm,"The Pit" . . . 2.00
31 PDd(s),V:The Shark, mind-
   controlled aquatic army 2.00
32 PDd(s),A:Swamp Thing 2.00
33 PDd(s),Aquaman's dark powers
   affect him physically 2.00
34 PDd(s),V:Triton 2.00
35 PDd(s),JCf,I:Gamesman,
   A:Animal Man. 2.00
36 PDd(s),JCf,R:Poseidonis,
   Tempest,Vulko 2.00
37 PDd,JCf,Genesis,V:Darkseid . . . 2.00
38 PDd,JCf,capitalism 2.00
39 PDd,JCf,Perkins Family Reunion 2.00
40 PDd(s),JCf,Dr. Polaris 2.00
41 PDd,JCf,BSf,F:Power Girl 2.00
42 PDd,JCf. 2.00
43 PDd,JCf,Millennium Giants,
   pt.2 x-over, A:Superman Red . . 2.00
44 PDd,JCf,F:Golden Age Flash,
   Sentinel 2.00
45 PDd,JCf,V:Triton 2.00
46 PDd,JCf,news of Mera. 2.00
47 DAn,Shadows on Water,pt.1 . . . 2.00
48 DAn,Shadows on Water,pt.2 . . . 2.00
49 DAn,ALa,JCf,V:Tempest. 2.00
50 EL,NRd,New Costume. 2.00
51 EL,NRd,V:King Noble 2.00
52 EL,V:Fire Trolls 2.00
53 EL,A:Superman 2.00
54 EL,A:Landlovers 2.00

55 EL,wooing Mera. 2.00
56 EL,V:Piranha Man,pt.1 . . . . 2.00
57 EL,V:Piranha Man,pt.2 . . . . 2.00
58 EL,V:DemonGate & BlackManta 2.00
59 EL,drugs in Atlantis 2.00
60 NRd,W:Tempest & Dolphin . . . 2.00
Ann.#1 Year One Annual, V:Triton,
   A:Superman,Mera 4.00
Ann.#2 Legends o/t Dead Earth . . 3.50
Ann.#3 Pulp Heroes (Hard Boiled) . 4.50
Ann.#4 PDa, Ghosts. 3.50
Ann.#5 JOs(s),MBr,DG, JLApe
   Gorilla Warfare 3.00
Spec.#1,000,000 DAn&ALa(s),TGb,
   BAn, King of Waterworld. 2.00
Secret Files #1 EL 5.00
TPB Time and Tide. 10.00

AQUAMAN
[1st Limited Series] 1986
1 V:Ocean Master 5.00
2 V:Ocean Master 3.00
3 V:Ocean Master 3.00
4 V:Ocean Master 3.00

[2nd Limited Series] 1989
1 CS,Atlantis Under Siege 3.00
2 CS,V:Invaders 1.75
3 CS,Mera turned Psychotic 1.50
4 CS,Poseidonis Under Siege 1.50
5 CS,Last Stand,final issue 1.50
Spec#1 MPa,Legend o/Aquaman . . 2.00

AQUAMAN: TIME & TIDE
1993–94
1 PDd(s),O:Aquaman 3.00
2 and 3 PDd(s),O:Aquaman
   contd. . . . . @2.00
4 PDd(s),O:Aquaman,final issue. . 2.00
TPB rep.#1–4 . . . . 10.00

ARAK
1981–85
1 EC,O:Ara 1.50
2 EC 1.00
3 EC,I:Valda 1.00
4 thru 10 EC . . . . @1.00
11 EC,AA 1.00
12 EC,AA,I:Satyricus 1.00
13 thru 19 AA . . . . @1.00
20 AA,O:Angelica 1.00
21 thru 23 AA 1.00
24 Double size 1.50
25 thru 30 . . . . @1.00
31 D Arak,becomes shaman. 1.00
32 thru 48 . . . . @1.00
49 CI/TD 1.00
50 TD 1.25
Ann.#1 . . . . 1.00

ARCANA: THE BOOKS OF MAGIC
Vertigo 1994
Ann.#1 JBo(c),JNR(s),PrG,Children's
   Crusade,R:Tim Hunter,
   A:Free Country. 5.00

ARGUS
[Mini-Series] 1995
1 R:Argus,I:Raver 1.50
2 Blinded by metahuman hitmen . . 1.75
3 Spy Satellite 1.75
4 The Watcher. 1.75
5 Data Highways 1.75
6 Restored Sight 1.75

Arion Lord of Atlantis, #7
© DC Comics Inc.

ARION, LORD OF ATLANTIS
1982–85
1 JDu 1.50
2 JDu 1.00
3 JDu 1.00
4 JDu,O:Arion 1.00
5 JDu 1.00
6 JDu 1.00
7 thru 12 . . . . @1.00
13 JDu 1.00
14 JDu 1.00
15 JDu 1.00
16 thru 35. . . . . @1.00
Spec. 1.25

ARION THE IMMORTAL
1 RWi,R:Arion 1.75
2 RWi,V:Garffon 1.50
3 RWi,V:Garn Daanuth 1.50
4 RWi,V:Garn Daanuth 1.50
5 RWi,Darkworlet. 1.50
6 RWi,MG,A:Power Girl 1.50

ARMAGEDDON 2001
May 1991
1 DJu,DG,I&O:Waverider. 4.00
1a 2nd printing 2.00
1b 3rd printing (silver) 1.75
2 DJu,ATi,Monarch revealed as Hawk,
   D:Dove,L:Capt Atom(JLE) 2.00
Spec.#1 MR 1.75

ARMAGEDDON 2001
ARMAGEDDON: THE ALIEN AGENDA
1991–92
1 DJu,JOy,A:Monarch,Capt.Atom. . 1.75
2 V:Ancient Romans 1.25
3 JRu(i),The Old West 1.25
4 DG,GP,V:Nazi's,last issue 1.25

ARMAGEDDON: INFERNO
1992
1 TMd,LMc,A:Creeper,Batman,
   Firestorm 1.75

DC COMICS

Armageddon The Alien Agenda #1
© DC Comics, Inc.

2 AAd,LMc,WS,I:Abraxis,A:Lobo . . 1.50
3 AAd,WS,LMc,TMd,MN,R:Justice
    Society 1.50
4 AAd,WS,LMc,TMd,MN,DG,
    V:Abraxis,A:Justice Society . . . 1.50

ARSENAL
Aug., 1998
1 (of 4) F:Black Canary 2.50
2 F:Green Arrow 2.50
3 F:Vandal Savage 2.50
4 conclusion 2.50

ARTEMIS: REQUIEM
1996
1 BML(s) (of 6) 1.75
2 thru 6 BML(s),EBe, ... @1.75

ATARI FORCE
1984–85
1 JL,I:TempestDart 1.50
2 JL. 1.00
3 JL. 1.00
4 RA/JL/JO 1.00
5 RA/JL/JO 1.00
6 thru 12 JL . . . . @1.00
13 KG 1.00
14 thru 21 EB . . . . @1.00

ATLANTIS CHRONICLES
1990
1 EM,Atlantis 50,000 years ago . . . 3.50
2 EM,Atlantis Sunk 3.25
3 EM,Twin Cities of Poseidonis
    & Tritonis 3.25
4 EM,King Orin's Daughter
    Cora Assumes Throne 3.25
5 EM,Orin vs. Shalako. 3.25
6 EM,Contact with Surface
    Dwellers. 3.25
7 EM,Queen Atlanna gives Birth to
    son(Aquaman)48 pg.final issue. 3.25

ATOM, THE
1962–68
1 MA,GK,I:Plant Master 775.00
2 MA,GK,V:Plant Master 325.00
3 MA,GK,I:Chronos 225.00
4 MA,GK,Snapper Carr 150.00

5 MA,GK 150.00
6 MA,GK 150.00
7 MA,GK,1st Atom & Hawkman
    team-up 250.00
8 MA,GK,A:JLA,V:Doctor Light. . 125.00
9 MA,GK 125.00
10 MA,GK. 125.00
11 MA,GK. 100.00
12 MA,GK. 100.00
13 MA,GK. 100.00
14 MA,GK. 100.00
15 MA,GK. 100.00
16 MA,GK. 75.00
17 MA,GK. 75.00
18 MA,GK. 75.00
19 MA,GK,A:Zatanna 75.00
20 MA,GK. 75.00
21 MA,GK. 50.00
22 MA,GK. 50.00
23 MA,GK. 50.00
24 MA,GK,V:Jason Woodrue 50.00
25 MA,GK 50.00
26 GK. 45.00
27 GK. 45.00
28 GK. 45.00
29 GK,A:E-2 Atom,Thinker. 150.00
30 GK. 50.00
31 GK,A:Hawkman 45.00
32 GK. 45.00
33 GK. 45.00
34 GK,V:Big Head 45.00
35 GK. 45.00
36 GK,A:Golden Age Atom 65.00
37 GK,I:Major Mynah 45.00
38 "Sinister stopover Earth" 45.00
Becomes:

ATOM & HAWKMAN
1968–69
39 MA, V:Tekla 50.00
40 DD,JKu,MA 40.00
41 DD,JKu,MA 40.00
42 MA,V:Brama 40.00
43 MA,I:Gentleman Ghost. 40.00
44 DD. 40.00
45 DD. 40.00

ATOM SPECIAL
1 SDi,V:Chronos (1993). 3.00
2 Zero Hour Atom (1994). 3.00

AVATAR
1991
1 A:Midnight & Allies 8.00
2 Search for Tablets 6.00
3 V:Cyric, Myrkul, final issue 6.00

AZRAEL
1994
1 I:New Azrael,Brian Bryan 6.00
2 A:Batman,New Azreal. 4.50
3 V:Order of St. Dumas 3.50
4 The System 3.00
5 BKi(c&a),R:Ra's al Ghul,Talia
    [new Miraweb format begins] . . 3.00
6 BKi(c&a),Ra's al Ghul,Talia 2.50
7 Sister Lily's Transformation 2.50
8 System Secret 2.25
9 Jean Paul Vanishes 2.25
10 DON,BKi,JmP,F:Neron,
    Underworld Unleashed tie-in. . 2.00
11 DON,BKi,JmP,A:Batman 2.00
12 DON,BKi,JmP,Azrael looks
    for Shondra 2.00
13 DON,BKi,Demon Time,pt.1 . . . . 2.00
14 DON,BKi,Demon Time,pt.2 . . . . 2.00
15 DON,BKi,Contagion,pt.5 . . . . . . 2.50
16 DON,BKi,Contagion,pt.10 . . . . . 2.00
17 DON,BKi,JmP,A:Dr.Orchid 2.00

Azrael #47 © DC Comics, Inc.

18 DON,BKi,JmP,A:Dr.Orchid 2.00
19 DON(s) 2.00
20 DON(s) 2.00
21 DON(s) 2.00
22 DON(s),BKi,JmP,"Angel in
    Hiding," pt.2 (of 3) 2.00
23 DON(s),BKi,JmP,"Angel in
    Hiding," pt.3 . . . . 2.00
24 DON(s),BKi,JmP,The Order's
    return. 2.00
25 DON(s),BKi,JmP,V:Brother
    Rollo 2.00
26 . . . . 2.00
27 DON(s),BKi,JmP,"Angel Insane,
    "pt.1 . . . . 2.00
28 DON(s),BKi,JmP,Joker, Riddler
    & Two-Face escape from
    Arkham Asylum 2.00
29 DON(s),DBw,JmP, F:Ra's Al
    Ghul, pt.1 . . . . 2.00
30 DON(s),DBw,JmP, F:Ra's Al
    Ghul, pt.2 . . . . 2.00
31 DON(s),JmP "Angel and the
    Monster Maker" pt.1 (of 3) 2.00
32 DON(s),JmP "Angel and the
    Monster Maker" pt.2 . . . . 2.00
33 DON(s),JmP "Angel and the
    Monster Maker" pt.3 concl. 2.00
34 DON(s),JmP,Genesis,
    a parademon 2.00
35 DON(s),JmP,F:Hitman 2.00
36 DON,JmP,Return of Bane,pt.1 . . 2.00
37 DON,JmP,Return of Bane,pt.2 . . 2.00
38 DON,JmP,Return of Bane,pt.3 . . 2.00
39 DON,JmP 2.00
40 DON,JmP,Cataclysm,pt.4,x-over 4.50
41 DON,JmP,A:Devil Latour 2.00
42 DON,JmP,Madame Kalypso 2.00
43 DON,JmP,Lilhy,Brian Bryan 2.00
44 DON,JmP,Luc & Lilhy disappear 2.00
45 DON,JmP,V:Deathstroke,
    A:Calibax 2.00
46 DON(s),JmP,V:Calibax. 2.25
47 Road to No Man's Land, flip-book
    Batman:Shadow of the Bat 4.00
48 DON(s),JmP,No Man's Land . . . 2.25
49 DON(s),JmP,New Costume 2.25
50 DON(s),JmP,New Costume 2.25
51 DON(s),JmP,V:Demonic Trio . . . 2.25
52 DON(s),JmP,No Man's Land . . . 2.25
53 DON(s),JmP,V:Calibax. 2.25
54 DON(s),JmP,V:Death Dancer . . 2.25
55 DON(s),JmP,V:Death Dancer. . . 2.25
56 DON(s),JmP,A:Batgirl 2.25
57 DON(s),JmP,No Man's Land . . . 2.25

Ann.#1 Year One Annual 4.00
Ann.#2 Legends o/t Dead Earth . . . 3.00
Ann.#3 Pulp Heroes (Hard Boiled) . 4.00
Spec.#1,000,000 DON(s),VGi,JmP
  F:Green Arrow,Robin,Hawkman 2.00
GN Azrael/Ash 5.00

AZRAEL/ASH
March 1997
1 one-shot DON(s),JQ,V:Surtr,
  A:Batman, x-over 5.00

AZRAEL PLUS
Oct. 1996
1 one-shot, DON(s),VGi,F:Vic
  Sage, The Question 3.00

AZTEK:
THE ULTIMATE MAN
1996–97
1 GMo&MMr(s),NSH,I:Aztek &
  Synth 4.00
2 GMo&MMr(s),NSH,A:Green
  Lantern 2.00
3 GMo&MMr(s),NSH,V:Doll-Face. . 2.00
4 GMo&MMr(s),NSH,I:Lizard King,
  Vanity. 2.00
5 GMo&MMr(s),NSH,O:Aztek,
  V:Lizard King 2.00
6 GMo&MMr(s),NSH,V:Vanity,
  A: Joker 2.00
7 GMo&MMr(s),NSH,A:Batman . . . 2.00
8 GMo&MMr(s),NSH,return to Brotherhood of Zuetzatcoatl,A:Raptor . 2.00
9 GMo&MMr(s),NSH,V:Parasite,
  A:Superman. 2.00
10 GMo&MMr(s),NSH,A:Justice
  League, final issue 5.00

BABYLON 5
1995
1 From TV series 16.00
2 From TV series. 11.00
3 Mysterious Assassin. 8.00
4 V:Mysterious Assassin 8.00
5 Shadows of the Present,pt.1 . . . 8.00
6 Shadows of the Present,pt.2 . . . 8.00
7 Shadows of the Present,pt.3. . . 7.00
8 Laser-Mirror Starweb,pt.1 . . . . . 7.00

Babylon 5, In Valen's Name #1
© DC Comics Inc.

9 Laser-Mirror Starweb,pt.2 . . . . . 7.00
10 Laser-Mirror-Starweb,pt.3 . . . . 7.00
11 final issue 7.00
TPB The Price of Peace 10.00

BABYLON 5:
IN VALEN'S NAME
Jan., 1998
1 (of 3) PDd, from TV series 3.00
2 PDd 3.00
3 PDd 3.00

BATGIRL
1988
Spec.#1 V: Cormorant,I:Slash. 8.00

BATGIRL ADVENTURES
Dec. 1997
1-shot RBr,V:Poison Ivy,A:Harley
  Quinn. 4.00

BATMAN
Spring, 1940
1 I:Joker,Cat(Catwoman),
  V:Hugo Strange . . . 65,000.00
2 V:Joker/Catwoman team . . 12,000.00
3 V:Catwoman 7,500.00
4 V:Joker 6,000.00
5 V:Joker 4,500.00
6 V:`Clock Maker' 3,700.00
7 V:Joker 3,500.00
8 V:Joker 3,500.00
9 V:Joker 3,500.00
10 V:Catwoman 3,500.00
11 V:Joker,Penguin 5,500.00
12 V:Joker. 2,200.00
13 V:Joker. 2,300.00
14 V:Penguin;Propaganda sty . 2,500.00
15 V:Catwoman 2,200.00
16 I:Alfred,V:Joker 4,500.00
17 V:Penguin. 1,500.00
18 V:Tweedledum &
  Tweedledee. 2,000.00
19 V:Joker 1,500.00
20 V:Joker 1,500.00
21 V:Penguin. 1,100.00
22 V:Catwoman,Cavalier 1,100.00
23 V:Joker 1,600.00
24 I:Carter Nichols, V:Tweedledum
  & Tweedledee 1,200.00
25 V:Joker/Penguin team 1,600.00
26 V:Cavalier. 1,100.00
27 V:Penguin. 1,100.00
28 V:Joker 1,200.00
29 V:Scuttler 1,100.00
30 V:Penguin,I:Ally Babble. . . . 1,100.00
31 I:Punch and Judy. 900.00
32 O:Robin,V:Joker. 950.00
33 V:Penguin,Jackall 1,000.00
34 A:Ally Babble. 900.00
35 V:Catwoman 900.00
36 V:Penguin,A:King Arthur 900.00
37 V:Joker. 1,000.00
38 V:Penguin 900.00
39 V:Catwoman,Christmas Story. 900.00
40 V:Joker. 1,100.00
41 V:Penguin 700.00
42 V:Catwoman 700.00
43 V:Penguin 700.00
44 V:Joker,A:Carter Nichols,Meets
  ancester Silas Wayne 1,100.00
45 V:Catwoman 700.00
46 V:Joker,A:Carter Nichols,
  Leonardo Da Vinci 650.00
47 O:Batman,V:Catwoman. . . . 2,800.00
48 V:Penguin, Bat-Cave story . . 800.00
49 I:Mad Hatter & Vicki Vale. . . 1,300.00

50 V:Two-Face,A:Vicki Vale 700.00
51 V:Penguin 650.00
52 V:Joker 700.00
53 V:Joker 700.00
54 V:`The Treasure Hunter'. 650.00
55 V:Joker 700.00
56 V:Penguin 650.00
57 V:Joker 700.00
58 V:Penguin 650.00
59 I:Deadshot. 650.00
60 V:`Shark' Marlin 650.00
61 V:Penguin. 800.00
62 O:Catwoman,I:Knight
  & Squire. 900.00
63 V:Joker 600.00
64 V:Killer Moth 600.00
65 I:Wingman,V:Catwoman. 625.00
66 V:Joker 625.00
67 V:Joker 625.00
68 V:Two-Face,Alfred story 550.00
69 I:King of the Cats,
  A:Catwoman. 600.00
70 V:Penguin 550.00
71 V:Mr. Cipher. 550.00
72 `The Jungle Batman' 550.00
73 V:Joker,A:Vicki Vale 650.00
74 V:Joker 550.00
75 I:The Gorilla Boss 550.00
76 V:Penguin 550.00
77 `The Crime Predictor'. 550.00
78 `The Manhunter from Mars' . . . 650.00
79 A:Vicki Vale 550.00
80 V:Joker 550.00
81 V:Two-Face 550.00
82 `The Flying Batman'. 450.00
83 V:`Fish' Frye 450.00
84 V:Catwoman 500.00
85 V:Joker 450.00
86 V:Joker 450.00
87 V:Joker 450.00
88 V:Mr. Mystery. 450.00
89 I:Aunt Agatha. 450.00
90 I:Batboy. 375.00
91 V:Blinky Grosset 375.00
92 I:Ace, the Bat-Hound 375.00
93 `The Caveman Batman'. 500.00
94 Alfred has Amnesia 375.00
95 `The Bat-Train'. 375.00
96 `Batman's College Days' 375.00
97 V:Joker. 375.00
98 A:Carter Nichols,Jules Verne . 375.00
99 V:Penguin,A:Carter Nichols,
  Bat Masterson 375.00
100 `Great Batman Contest'. . . 2,200.00
101 `The Great Bat-Cape Hunt'. . 450.00
102 V:Mayne Mallok 400.00
103 A:Ace, the Bat-Hound 400.00
104 V:Devoe. 400.00
105 A:Batwoman 450.00
106 V:Keene Harper gang 375.00
107 V:Daredevils 375.00
108 Bat-cave story 375.00
109 `The 1,000 Inventions
  of Batman' 375.00
110 V:Joker 375.00
111 . . . . 300.00
112 I:Signalman 300.00
113 I:Fatman 300.00
114 . . . . 300.00
115 . . . . 300.00
116 . . . . 300.00
117 . . . . 300.00
118 . . . . 300.00
119 . . . . 300.00
120 . . . . 300.00
121 I:Mr.Freeze 350.00
122. . . . . 210.00
123 A:Joker 200.00
124 "Mystery Seed from Space" . 200.00
125. . . . . 200.00
126. . . . . 200.00

Batman #34 © DC Comics, Inc.

Batman #39 © DC Comics, Inc.

127 A:Superman & Joker	225.00
128	200.00
129 O:Robin(Retold)	265.00
130	200.00
131 I:2nd Batman	175.00
132 `Lair of the Sea-Fox'	175.00
133	175.00
134	175.00
135	175.00
136 A:Joker,Bat-Mite.	200.00
137 V:Mr.Marvel,The Brand	175.00
138 A:Bat-Mite	175.00
139 I:Old Batgirl	200.00
140 A:Joker	200.00
141 V:Clockmaster	175.00
142 Batman robot story.	175.00
143 A:Bathound	175.00
144 A:Joker,Bat-Mite,Bat-Girl	175.00
145 V:Mr.50,Joker.	185.00
146 A:Bat-Mite,Joker	125.00
147 Batman becomes Bat-Baby	125.00
148 A:Joker	150.00
149 V:Maestro	125.00
150 V:Biff Warner,Jack Pine	125.00
151 V:Harris Boys	100.00
152 A:Joker	110.00
153 Other Dimension story	100.00
154 V:Dr. Dorn	100.00
155 1st S.A. Penguin	450.00
156 V:Gorilla Gang	110.00
157 V:Mirror Man	110.00
158 A:Bathound,Bat-Mite	110.00
159 A:Joker,Clayface	125.00
160 V:Bart Cullen	110.00
161 A:Bat-Mite	110.00
162 F:Robin	110.00
163 A:Joker	110.00
164 CI,A:Mystery Analysts,new Batmobile	100.00
165 V:The Mutated Man	100.00
166 Escape story	100.00
167 V:Karabi & Hydra, the Crime Cartel	100.00
168 V:Mr. Mammoth	100.00
169 A:Penguin	125.00
170 V:Getaway Genius	100.00
171 CI,1st S.A. Riddler	450.00
172 V:Flower Gang.	65.00
173 V:Elwood Pearson	65.00
174 V:Big Game Hunter	65.00
175 V:Eddie Repp	65.00
176 Giant rep.A:Joker,Catwom..	75.00
177 BK,A:Elongated Man,Atom.	65.00
178 CI	65.00
179 CI,2nd Riddler(Silver)	135.00
180 BK,A:Death-Man	65.00
181 CI,I:Poison Ivy	150.00

182 A:Joker,(giant size rep)	70.00
183 CI,A:Poison Ivy	100.00
184 CI,Mystery of the Missing Manhunters	60.00
185 Giant rep.	65.00
186 A:Joker	50.00
187 Giant rep.A:Joker.	65.00
188 CI,A:Eraser	35.00
189 CI,A:Scarecrow	55.00
190 CI,A:Penguin	45.00
191 CI,The Day Batman Soldout.	35.00
192 CI,The Crystal ball that betrayed Batman	35.00
193 Giant rep.	45.00
194 MSy,BK,A:Blockbuster,Mystery Analysts of Gotham City	35.00
195 CI	35.00
196 BK,Psychic Super-Sleuth	35.00
197 MSy,A:Bat Girl,Catwoman	75.00
198 A:Joker,Penguin,Catwoman, O:Batman rtd,(G-Size rep)	75.00
199 CI,`Peril o/t Poison Rings'	35.00
200 NA(c),O:rtd,A:Joker,Penguin, Scarecrow	150.00
201 A:Batman Villians.	40.00
202 BU:Robin	25.00
203 NA(c),(giant size)	45.00
204 FR(s),IN,JG	25.00
205 FR(s),IN,JG	25.00
206 FR(s),IN,JG	25.00
207 FR(s),IN,JG	25.00
208 GK,new O:Batman, A:Catwoman	50.00
209 FR(s),IN,JG	25.00
210 A:Catwoman	27.00
211 FR(s),IN,JG	22.00
212 FR(s),IN,JG	22.00
213 RA,30th Anniv.Batman,new O: Robin,rep.O:Alfred,Joker	65.00
214 IN,A:Batgirl	22.00
215 IN,DG	22.00
216 IN,DG,I:DaphnePennyworth	22.00
217 NA(c)	24.00
218 NA(c),giant	45.00
219 NA,IN,DG,Batman Xmas	45.00
220 NA(c),IN	20.00
221 IN,DG	20.00
222 IN,Rock'n Roll story	35.00
223 NA(c),giant	35.00
224 NA(c)	20.00
225 NA(c),IN,DG	20.00
226 IN,DG I:10-Eyed Man.	20.00
227 IN,DG,A:Daphne Pennyworth	20.00
228 giant Deadly Traps rep.	35.00
229 IN	20.00
230 NA(c),Robin	20.00
231 F:Ten-Eyed Man	20.00
232 DON(s),NA,DG, I:Ras al Ghul	100.00
233 giant Bruce Wayne iss.	35.00
234 NA,DG,IN,1stS.A.Two-Face	125.00
235 CI,V:Spook	25.00
236 NA	30.00
237 NA	50.00
238 NA,JC,JKu,giant	35.00
239 NA,RB	22.00
240 NA(c),RB,giant,R-Ghul	22.00
241 IN,DG,RB,A:Kid Flash	22.00
242 RB,MK	22.00
243 NA,DG,Ras al Ghul	35.00
244 NA,Ras al Ghul	35.00
245 NA,IN,DG,FMc,Ras al Ghul	35.00
246	22.00
247 Deadly New Year	22.00
248	22.00
249 `Citadel of Crime'	22.00
250 IN,DG	22.00
251 NA,V:Joker	60.00
252	22.00
253 AN,DG,A:Shadow	22.00

254 NA,GK,B:100 page issues	30.00
255 GK,CI,NA,DG,I:CrazyQuilt	45.00
256 Catwoman	25.00
257 IN,DG,V:Penguin	25.00
258 IN,DG	25.00
259 GK,IN,DG,A:Shadow	25.00
260 IN,DG,Joker.	45.00
261 CI,GK,E:100 page issues.	25.00
262 A:Scarecrow	22.00
263 DG(i),A:Riddler	15.00
264 DON(s),DG,A:Devil Dayre	12.00
265 RB,BWr	13.00
266 DG,Catwoman(old Costume)	15.00
267 DG	12.00
268 DON(s),IN,TeB,V:Sheikh	12.00
269 A:Riddler	12.00
270 B:DvR(s)	12.00
271 IN,FMc.	12.00
272 JL	12.00
273 V:Underworld Olympics/76	12.00
274	12.00
275	12.00
276	12.00
277	12.00
278	12.00
279 A:Riddler	14.00
280	12.00
281	12.00
282	12.00
283 V:Camouflage	12.00
284 JA,R:Dr.Tzin Tzin.	12.00
285	12.00
286 V:Joker	15.00
287 BWi,MGr,Penguin	12.00
288 BWi,MGr,Penguin	12.00
289 MGr, V:Skull.	12.00
290 MGr,V:Skull Dagger	12.00
291 B:Underworld Olympics #1, A:Catwoman	12.00
292 A:Riddler	12.00
293 A:Superman & Luthor	12.00
294 E:DvR(s),E:Underworld Olympics,A:Joker	14.00
295 GyC(s),MGo,JyS,V:Hamton	12.00
296 B:DvR(s),V:Scarecrow	12.00
297 RB,Mad Hatter.	12.00
298 JCA,DG,V:Baxter Bains	12.00
299 DG	12.00
300 WS,DG,A:Batman E-2, Robin E-2	22.00
301 JCa,TeB	10.00
302 JCa,DG,V:Human Dynamo	10.00
303 JCa,DG	10.00
304 E:DvR(s),V:Spook	10.00
305 GyC,JCa,DeH,V:Thanatos	11.00
306 JCa,DeH,DN,V:Black Spider.	11.00

307 B:LWn(s),JCa,DG,
  I:Limehouse Jack 11.00
308 JCa,DG,V:Mr.Freeze 11.00
309 E:LWn(s),JCa,FMc,
  V:Blockbuster. 11.00
310 IN,DG,A:Gentleman Ghost . . . 11.00
311 SEt,FMc,IN,Batgirl,
  V:Dr.Phosphorus. 11.00
312 WS,DG,Calenderman. 11.00
313 IN,FMc,VTwo-Face 11.00
314 IN,FMc,V:Two-Face 11.00
315 IN,FMc,V:Kiteman 11.00
316 IN,FMc,F:Robin,
  V:Crazy Quilt 11.00
317 IN,FMc,V:Riddler 12.00
318 IN,I:Fire Bug 11.00
319 JKu(c),IN,DG,A:Gentleman
  Ghost,E:Catwoman. 11.00
320 BWr(c). 11.00
321 DG,WS,A:Joker,Catwoman . . . 12.00
322 V:Cap.Boomerang,Catwoman 11.00
323 IN,A:Catwoman 11.00
324 IN,A:Catwoman 11.00
325. . . . . 11.00
326 A:Catwoman 11.00
327 IN,A:Proffessor.Milo 11.00
328 A:Two-Face 11.00
329 IN,A:Two-Face 11.00
330. . . . . 11.00
331 DN,FMc,V:Electrocutioner . . . 11.00
332 IN,DN,Ras al Ghul.1st solo
  Catwoman story 12.00
333 IN,DN,A:Catwoman,
  Ras al Ghul 10.00
334 FMc,Ras al Ghul,Catwoman. . 10.00
335 FMc,Ras al Ghul,Catwoman,Ras al
  Ghul 10.00
336 JL,FMc,Loser Villains. 10.00
337 DN,V:Snow Man 10.00
338 DN,Deathsport. 10.00
339 A:Poison Ivy 10.00
340 GC,A:Mole. 10.00
341 A:Man Bat 10.00
342 V:Man Bat 10.00
343 GC,KJ,I:The Dagger 10.00
344 GC,KJ,Poison Ivy. 10.00
345 I:New Dr.Death,A:Catwoman . 10.00
346 DN,V:Two Face 10.00
347 A:Alfred 10.00
348 GC,KJ,Man-Bat,A:Catwoman . 10.00
349 GC,AA,A:Catwoman 10.00
350 GC,TD,A:Catwoman 10.00
351 GC,TD,A:Catwoman 10.00
352 Col Blimp. 10.00
353 JL,DN,DA,A:Joker 11.00
354 DN,AA,V:HugoStrange,A:
  Catwoman 10.00
355 DN,AA:A:Catwoman. 10.00
356 DG,DN,Hugo Strange 10.00
357 DN,AA,I:Jason Todd. 11.00
358 A:King Croc 10.00
359 DG,O:King Croc,Joker 11.00
360 I:Savage Skull 10.00
361 DN,Man-Bat,I:Harvey Bullock. 10.00
362 V:Riddler 10.00
363 V:Nocturna. 10.00
364 DN,AA,J.Todd 1st full solo
  story (cont'd Detective #531) . 10.00
365 DN,AA,C:Joker 10.00
366 DN,AA,Joker,J.Todd in
  Robin Costume 15.00
367 DN,AA,PoisonIvy 9.00
368 DN,AA,I:2nd Robin
  (Jason Todd) 12.00
369 DN,AA,I:Dr.Fang,V:Deadshot . 7.00
370 DN,AA. 7.00
371 DN,AA,V:Catman 4.50
372 DN,AA,A:Dr.Fang. 4.00
373 DN,AA,V:Scarecrow. 4.00
374 GC,AA,V:Penguin 5.00
375 GC,AA,V:Dr.Freeze 4.00

Batman #480 © DC Comics Inc.

376 DN,Halloween issue. 4.00
377 DN,AA,V:Nocturna. 4.00
378 V:Mad Hatter. 4.00
379 V:Mad Hatter 4.00
380 AA,V:Nocturna. 4.00
381 V:Batman. 4.00
382 A:Catwoman 4.50
383 GC 4.00
384 V:Calender Man. 4.00
385 V:Calender Man. 4.00
386 I:Black Mask. 4.00
387 V:Black Mask. 4.00
388 V:Capt.Boomerang & Mirror
  Master 4.00
389 V:Nocturna,Catwoman 4.50
390 V:Nocturna,Catwoman 4.50
391 V:Nocturna,Catwoman 4.50
392 A:Catwoman 4.50
393 PG,V:Cossack 3.50
394 PG,V:Cossack 3.50
395 V:Film Freak 3.50
396 V:Film Freak 3.50
397 V:Two-Face,Catwoman 4.00
398 V:Two-Face,Catwoman 4.00
399 HaE(s),Two-Face. 3.50
400 BSz,AAd,GP,BB,A:Joker 20.00
401 JBy(c),TVE,Legends,
  A:Magpie 3.50
402 JSn,Fake Batman 3.50
403 DCw,Batcave discovered 3.50
404 DM,FM(s),B:Year 1,I:Modern
  Age Catwoman. 12.00
405 FM,DM,Year 1 . . . . 8.00
406 FM,DM,Year 1 . . . . 8.00
407 FM,DM,E:Year 1 . . . . 8.00
408 CW,V:Joker,
  new O:Jason Todd 5.00
408a 2nd printing 1.00
409 DG,RA,V:Crime School 4.00
409a 2nd printing 1.00
410 DC,Jason Todd 4.00
411 DC,DH,V:Two Face 3.00
412 DC,DH,I:Mime 3.00
413 DC,DH. 3.00
414 JAp,Slasher. 3.00
415 JAp,Millenium Week #2 . . . . . 3.00
416 JAp,1st Batman/Nightwing
  T.U. 3.00
417 JAp,B:10 Nights,I:KGBeast . . . 9.00
418 JAp,V:KGBeast 8.00
419 JAp,V:KGBeast 8.00
420 JAp,E:10 Nights,D:KGBeast. . . 8.00
421 DG 3.50
422 MBr,V:Dumpster Slayer 3.00

423 TM(c),DC,Who is Batman 4.00
424 MBr,Robin 3.00
425 MBr,Gordon Kidnapped 3.00
426 JAp,B:Death in the Family,
  V:Joker. 9.00
427 JAp,V:Joker. 9.00
428 JAp,D:2nd Robin 7.00
429 JAp,A:Superman,
  E:Death in the Family. 5.00
430 JAp,JSn,V:Madman 4.00
431 JAp,Murder Investigation 2.75
432 JAp 2.75
433 JBy,JAp,Many Deaths of the
  Batman #1 . . . . 4.00
434 JBy,JAp,Many Deaths #2 . . . . 3.00
435 JBy,Many Deaths #3 . . . . 3.00
436 PB,B:Year#3,A:Nightwing,I:Tim
  Drake as child 5.00
436a 2ndPrint(green DC logo) 2.00
437 PB,year#3 . . . . 3.00
438 PB,year#3 . . . . 2.50
439 PB,year#3 . . . . 2.50
440 JAp,Lonely Place of Dying #1,
  A:Tim Drake (face not shown) . 3.00
441 JAp,Lonely Place Dying 3.00
442 JAp,I:3rd Robin(Tim Drake) . . . 5.00
443 JAp,I:Crimesmith 2.00
444 JAp,V:Crimesmith 2.00
445 JAp,I:K.G.Beast Demon. 2.00
446 JAp,V:K.G.Beast Demon 2.00
447 JAp,D:K.G.Beast Demon 2.00
448 JAp,A:Penguin#1. . . . . 2.50
449 MBr,A:Penguin#3 . . . . 2.50
450 JAp,I:Joker II 2.00
451 JAp,V:Joker II 2.00
452 KD,Dark Knight Dark City#1. . . 2.00
453 KD,Dark Knight Dark City#2. . . 2.00
454 KD,Dark Knight Dark City#3. . . 2.00
455 Identity Crisis#1,
  A:Scarecrow. 2.50
456 IdentityCrisis#2 . . . . 3.00
457 V:Scarecrow,A:Robin,
  New Costume 5.00
457a 2nd printing 2.00
458 R:Sarah Essen 2.00
459 A:Sarah Essen 2.00
460 Sisters in Arms,pt.1
  A:Catwoman 3.00
461 Sisters in Arms,pt.2
  Catwoman V:Sarah.Essen 3.00
462 Batman in San Francisco. 2.00
463 Death Valley 2.00
464 V:Two-Hearts. 2.00
465 Batman/Robin T.U.. . . . . 3.00
466 Robin Trapped. 2.00
467 Shadowbox #1(sequel to
  Robin Mini-Series) 2.50
468 Shadowbox #2. . . . . 2.00
469 Shadowbox #3. . . . . 2.00
470 War of the Gods x-over 1.75
471 V:Killer Croc 1.75
472 The Idiot Root,pt.1 . . . . 1.75
473 The Idiot Root,pt.3. . . . . 1.75
474 Destroyer,pt.1 (LOTDK#27) . . . 2.25
475 R:Scarface,A:VickiVale. 1.75
476 A:Scarface. 1.75
477 Ph(c),Gotham Tale,pt.1 . . . . . 1.75
478 Ph(c),Gotham Tale,pt.2 . . . . . 1.75
479 TMd,I:Pagan 1.75
480 JAp,To the father I never
  knew 1.75
481 JAp,V:Maxie Zeus 1.75
482 JAp,V:Maxie Zeus 1.75
483 JAp,I:Crash & Burn 1.75
484 JAp,R:Black Mask 1.75
485 TGr,V:Black Mask 1.75
486 JAp,I:Metalhead. 1.75
487 JAp,V:Headhunter. 1.75
488 JAp,N:Azrael 7.00
489 JAp,Bane vs Killer Croc,
  I:Azrael as Batman. 6.00

Batman #497 © DC Comics, Inc.

489a 2nd Printing 2.00
490 JAp,Bane vs.Riddler 7.00
490a 2nd Printing 1.75
490b 3rd Printing 1.50
491 JAp,V:Joker,A:Bane 4.00
491a 2nd Printing 1.50
492 B:DgM(s),NB,Knightfall#1,
   V:Mad Hatter,A:Bane 5.00
492a Platinum Ed. 7.00
492b 2nd Printing 1.50
493 NB,Knightfall,#3,Mr.Zsasz 3.00
494 JAp,TMd,Knightfall #5,A:Bane,
   V:Cornelius,Stirk,Joker 2.50
495 NB,Knightfall#7,V:Poison
   Ivy,A:Bane 2.50
496 JAp,JRu,Knightfall#9,V:Joker,
   Scarecrow,A:Bane 2.50
497 JAp,DG,Knightfall#11,V:Bane,
   Batman gets back broken 4.00
497a 2nd Printing 1.75
498 JAp,JRu,Knightfall#15,A:Bane,
   Catwoman,Azrael Becomes
   Batman 2.50
499 JAp,SHa,Knightfall#17,
   A:Bane,Catwoman 2.50
500 JQ(c),JAp,MM,Die Cut(c),
   Direct Market,Knightfall#19,
   V:Bane,N:Batman. 3.00
500a KJo(c),Newstand Ed. 2.50
501 MM,I:Mekros 2.00
502 MM,V:Mekros 2.00
503 MM,V:Catwoman 2.00
504 MM,V:Catwoman 2.00
505 MM,V:Canibal 2.00
506 KJo(c),MM,A:Ballistic 2.00
507 KJo(c),MM,A:Ballistic 2.00
508 KJo(c),MM,V:Abattior 2.00
509 KJo(c),MM,KnightsEnd#1,
   A:Shiva 3.00
510 KJo(c),MM,Knights End #7,
   V:Azrael 2.00
511 Zero Hour, A:Batgirl 2.00
512 Killer Croc sewer battles 2.00
513 Two-Face and convicts 2.00
514 Identity Crisis 2.00
515 KJo,Return of Bruce Wayne,
   Troika,pt.1 . . . . 2.00
515 Collector's Edition 3.50
516 V:The Sleeper 2.00
517 V:The Sleeper 2.00
518 V:The Black Spider 2.00
519 KJo,V:The Black Spider
   [new Miraweb format begins] . . 2.00
520 EB,A:James Gordon 2.00
521 R:Killer Croc 2.00

522 R:Scarecrow 2.00
523 V:Scarecrow 2.00
524 DgM,KJo,V:Scarecrow 2.00
525 DgM,KJo,Underworld
   Unleashed tie-in 2.00
526 DgM,A:Alfred,Nightwing,Robin . 2.00
527 DgM,V:Two-Face,I:Schism 2.00
528 . . . . 2.00
529 DgM,KJo,Contagion,pt.6 . . . . . 2.50
530 DgM,KJo,The Aztec
   Connection,pt.1 . . . . 2.50
530a collector's edition 2.50
531 DgM,KJo,The Aztec
   Connection,pt.2 . . . . 2.00
531a collectors edition 2.50
532 DgM(s),KJo,"The Aztec Connec-
   tion," pt.3, A:Deadman 2.00
532a card stock cover 2.50
533 DgM(s),KJo,Legacy prelude. . . 2.00
534 DgM(s),KJo,Legacy, pt.5 . . . . . 2.00
535 DgM(s),KJo,JhB,I:The Ogre,
   double size. 3.50
535a Collector's edition,
   gatefold cover 4.00
536 DgM(s),KJo,JhB,V:Man-Bat,
   Final Night tie-in 2.00
537 DgM(s),KJo,JhB,A:Man-Bat,
   pt.2 . . . . 2.00
538 DgM(s),KJo,JhB,A:Man-Bat,
   pt.3 . . . . 2.00
539 . . . . 2.00
540 DgM(s),KJo,JhB,Spectre,pt.1 . . 2.00
541 DgM(s),KJo,JhB,Spectre,pt.2 . . 2.00
542 DgM(s),KJo,JhB,V:Faceless,
   pt. 1 . . . . 2.00
543 DgM(s),KJo,JhB,pt. 2 . . . . 2.00
544 DgM(s),KJo,JhB, F:Joker,pt.1 . . 2.00
545 DgM(s),KJo, F:Joker, Demon,
   pt.2 . . . . 2.00
546 DgM(s),KJo,JhB,F:Joker,
   Demon, pt.3 concl. 2.00
547 DgM,KJo,JhB,Genesis tie-in . . . 2.00
548 DgM,KJo,JhB,V:Penguin pt.1 . . 2.00
549 DgM,KJo,JhB,V:Penguin, pt.2 . . 2.00
550 DgM,KJo,JhB,I:Chase 3.50
550a deluxe, with file card inserts . . 3.50
551 DgM,KJo,JhB,F:Ragman 2.00
552 DgM, ... 2.00
553 DgM,KJo,SB,Cataclysm
   x-over, pt.3. . . . . 3.00
554 DgM,KJo,SB,Cataclysm, ... 3.00
555 DGm,JhB,SB,BSf,Aftershock . . 2.00
556 DGm,NBy,BSf,Aftershock. 2.00
557 DGm,VGi,SB,BSf,F:Ballistic . . . 2.00
558 DGm,JAp,SB,doubts 2.00
559 DgM(s),BH,SB,Aftershock 2.00
560 CDi,SB,A:Nightwing & Robin . . 2.00
561 CDi(s),JAp, No Man's Land . . . 2.00
562 CDi(s),JAp, No Man's Land . . . 2.00
563 No Law and A New Order, pt.3 2.00
564 F:Batgirl, Mosaic,pt.1 . . . . 2.00
565 F:Batgirl, Mosaic,pt.3 . . . . 2.00
566 JBg,A:Superman 2.00
567 SCi,F:Batgirl, pt.1,x-over 2.00
568 DJu,BSz,Fruit of the
   Earth, pt.2 . . . . 2.00
569 F:Batgirl. 2.00
570 MD2,No Man's Land, The
   Code, pt.1 . . . . 2.00
Ann.#1 CS 700.00
Ann.#2 . . . . 300.00
Ann.#3 A:Joker. 300.00
Ann.#4 . . . . 150.00
Ann.#5 . . . . 150.00
Ann.#6 . . . . 125.00
Ann.#7 . . . . 125.00
Ann.#8 TVE,A:Ras al Ghul 8.00
Ann.#9 JOy,AN,PS 7.00
Ann.#10 DCw,DG,V:HugoStrange. . 7.00
Ann.#11 JBy(c),AMo(s),V:Penguin . 8.00
Ann.#12 RA,V:Killer 5.00

Ann.#13 A:Two-Face 6.00
Ann.#14 O:Two-Face 4.00
Ann.#15 Armageddon,pt.3 . . . . 6.00
Ann.#15a 2nd printing(silver) 2.50
Ann.#16 SK(c),Eclipso,V:Joker 3.00
Ann.#17 EB,Bloodline#8,
   I:Decimator. 3.00
Ann.#18 Elseworld Story. 3.50
Ann.#19 Year One, O:Scarecrow . . 4.00
Ann.#20 Legends o/t Dead Earth . . 2.95
Ann.#21 Pulp Heroes (Weird
   Mystery) DgM(s). 3.95
Ann.#22 BWr(c) Ghosts 3.00
Ann.#23 CDi(s),GN,MPn, JLApe
   Gorilla Warfare 3.00
Specials & 1-shots
Giant Ann.#1 Facsimile edition 5.00
Spec.#0 (1994). 3.00
Spec.#1 MGo,I:Wrath 4.00
Spec.#1,000,000 DgM(s),SB,
   F:Toy Wonder. 2.00
Giant #1, seven tales, 80pg (1998) . 5.00
Giant#2, 80-page 4.95
Batman: Arkham Asylum — Tales
   of Madness, AIG, Cataclysm
   tie-in (1998) 3.00
Batman: Batgirl, JBa,RBr,
   Girlfrenzy (1998) 2.00
Batman: Blackgate, CDi(s), JSon,
   in Blackgate prison (1996) 4.50
Batman: Blackgate — Isle of Men,
   DgM, JAp,BSf,BSz,
   Cataclysm (1998) 3.00
Batman Dark Knight Gallery (1995). 3.50
Batman: Death of Innocents, DON(s),
   JSt, BSz, Land mine victims
   (1996) 4.00
Batman Gallery,collection of past
   (c),posters,pin-ups,JQ(c) (1992) 4.00
Batman: Gotham By Gaslight,MMi,
   V:Jack the Ripper. 6.00
Batman: Joker's Apprentice 4.00
Batman: The Killing Joke,BB,
   AMo(s),O:Joker,Batgirl
   paralyzed (1988) 18.00
   2nd thru 6th Printings . . . . . . @5.00
Batman: Mitefall, V:Bane
   Mite (1995). 4.95
Batman: Penguin Triumphant
   (1992) 5.00
Batman: Plus (1997). 3.00
Batman Record Comic (1996) 1.00
Batman/Riddler: The Riddle
   Factory (1995) 4.95
Secret Files #1 SMc(c) inc.
   O:Batman (1997) 6.00
Batman: Seduction of the Gun,
   V:Illegal Gun Control (1992) . . . 3.00
3-D Batman:Scarecrow. 4.00
Batman/Two-Face: Crime and
   Punishment (1995) 4.95
   2nd printing (1998) 5.00
Two-Face Strikes Twice #1. . . . . . . 5.25
Two-Face Strikes Twice #2. . . . . . . 5.25
Batman: Vengeance of Bane,
   GN,I:Bane (1992) 30.00
   2nd Printing 5.00
Batman: Vengeance of Bane II
   (1995) 3.95
Batman Villains Secret Files,
   AIG,CDi,RMz,BB,F:Greatest Foes
   (1998) 5.00
Elseworld 1-shots
Batman: The Blue, The Grey, and
   The Bat, JL (1992) 5.95
Batman: Brotherhood of the Bat
   (1995) 5.95
Batman: Castle of the Bat. 5.95
Batman: Dark Allegiances (1996) . . 5.95
Batman: Holy Terror (1991). 6.50
Batman: I, Joker, BH, in

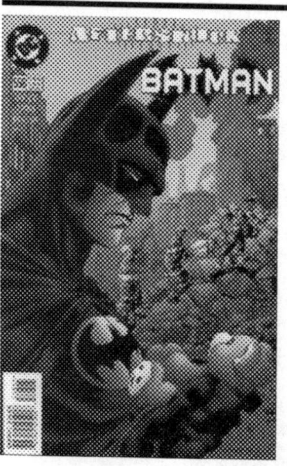

Batman #558 © DC Comics, Inc.

2083 (1998) 4.95
Batman: In Darkest Knight
　MiB(s),JBi (1994) 5.50
Batman Knightgallery (1995). 3.50
Batman: Masque, MGr, in turn of
　the century Gotham 7.00
Batman: Master of the Future,EB,
　Sequel to Goth.by Gaslight
　(1991) 6.00
Batman: Scar of the Bat (1996). . . . 5.00
Batman: Two Faces (1998). 4.95
Batman: Master of the Future(1998) 5.95
Graphic Novels
The Abduction 6.00
Batman A Lonely Place of Dying
　(1990) rep. Batman #440–442
　& New Titans #60–61 . . . . 4.00
Batman: Blind Justice, rep. Detective
　Comics #598–600 (1992) 7.50
Batman: Bloodstorm 13.00
Batman: Bullock's Law 5.00
The Book of Shadows 6.00
Batman: Dark Joker, KJo 12.00
Many Deaths of the Batman;
　rep. #433-#435 (1992) 3.95
Batman: Full Circle AD,
　A:Reaper (1992). 7.00
Batman: Harley Quinn (1998) 5.95
Batman: Mr. Freeze 5.00
No Man's Land, 48-page No Law
　and a New Order, pt.1 . . . . . . 3.00
No Man's Land, lenticular (c) 4.00
No Man's Land Gallery 4.00
Nosferatu 6.00
Batman: Poison Ivy. 5.00
Reign of Terror 5.00
Batman: Scar of the Bat 5.00
The Scottish Connection 6.00
Batman: Ten Knights of the Beast,
　rep. #417–#420 (1994) 5.95
Batman: Two Faces 5.00
Batman: The Ultimate Evil:
　1 Novel adaptation (of 2) 5.95
　2 Novel adaptation, finale 5.95
Hard Covers & Trade Paperbacks
The Batman Adventures 8.00
Batman Archives Vol.3 . . . . 39.95
HC Archives, Vol. 4, rep. 50.00
Batman: Anarky 13.00
Batman: Arkham Asylum,DMc
　HC (1989) 28.00
　TPB 15.00
Birth of the Demon, O:Ras al
　Ghul (1992)

HC 25.00
TPB (1993). 13.00
Batman: Bloodstorm,KJo,V:Joker,
　Vampires, (sequel to Red Rain)
　HC 24.95
　TPB 12.95
Bride of the Demon, TGr,
　V:Ra's al Ghul
　HC 21.00
　TPB 13.00
Cataclysm 18.00
Contagion. 13.00
Crimson Mist
　HC 25.00
The Dark Knight Adventures 8.00
Batman: Dark Knight Dynasty,
　three elseworlds stories
　HC (1998) 25.00
Batman: A Death in the Family,
　rep. Batman #426-429 (1988)
　TPB 8.00
　2nd printing 5.00
　3rd printing. 4.00
Batman: Digital Justice (1990)
　HC 26.00
Batman: Faces (1995)
　TPB 10.00
Batman: Gothic, rept. Legends of
　the Dark Knight #6–#10 (1992)
　TPB 13.00
　New printing 13.00
Greatest Batman Stories
　HC 35.00
　TPB 16.00
Greatest Batman Stories, Vol. 2
　TPB 17.00
Greatest Joker Stories
　HC 20.00
　TPB 15.00
Batman: Knight's End, rep. Batman
　#509–#510, Shadow of the Bat
　#29–#30, Detective #676–#677,
　Legends #62–#63, Catwoman
　#12, Robin #8–#9
　TPB 14.95
Knightfall rep. #1–#11
　TPB 12.95
Knightfall rep. #12-#19
　TPB 12.95
Batman: The Last Angel, F:Catwoman
　V:Aztec bat-god (1994)
　TPB 12.95
Batman: The Last Arkham
　TPB 12.95
Legacy, sequel to Contagion, rep. (1996)
　TPB 18.00
Batman: Night Cries,SHa 30.00
　TPB 13.00
Batman: Prodigal, rep,
　TPB 15.00
Batman: Son of the Demon,JBi (1987)
　HC 55.00
　TPB 17.00
　2nd thru 4th printings 8.95
Batman: Tales of the Demon (1991)
　TPB 20.00
Batman: Thrillkiller 13.00
Batman: Year One Rep. Batman
　#404-#407 (1998)
　HC 16.00
　TPB 14.00
　2nd Printing 10.00
　3rd Printing. 10.00
Batman: Four of a Kind, from
　Year One annuals (1998)
　TPB 15.00
Year Two (1990) rep. Detective
　Comics #575–#578
　TPB 10.00
Movies
TPB The Movies, (all 4) (1997) . . . 20.00

HC 25.00
Batman, JOy, Movie adaptation . . . 3.00
　Perfect Bound 6.00
Batman Returns, SE,JL Movie
　Adaption, ... 6.00
　Newsstand Format 4.00
Batman: Mask of the Phantasm,
　animated movie adapt. 5.25
　Newstand Ed. 3.25
Batman Forever, Movie Adaptation . 5.95
　Newsstand version 3.95
Batman and Robin, DON(s), Movie
　Adaptation (1997) 3.95
　Collector's edition, ... 5.95
GN Batman: Bane, BSz(c) movie
　tie-in (1997) 4.95
GN Batman: Batgirl, BSz(c) movie
　tie-in (1997) 4.95
GN Batman: Mr. Freeze, BSz(c)
　movie tie-in (1997) 4.95
GN Batman: Poison Ivy, BSz(c)
　movie tie-in (1997) 4.95
X-overs
GN Batman & Superman Adventures:
　World's Finest (1997) adaptation
　of animated adventures, 64pg . 7.00
Batman/Captain America (DC/Marvel
　1996) Elseworlds 6.00
Batman/Deadman, Death and
　Glory, JeR(s),JEs (1996)
　HC 25.00
　TPB 12.95
Batman/Demon (1996) 5.00
Batman/Dracula:Red Rain KJo,MJ,
　Batman becomes Vampire,
　HC Elseworlds Story (1991) . . 35.00
　SC (1992) 12.00
Batman/Green Arrow: The Poison
　Tomorrow,MN,JRu,V:Poison
　Ivy (1992) 6.25
Batman/Houdini: The Devil's
　Workshop (1993) 6.50
Batman: Huntress/Spoiler—Blunt
　Trauma, CDi,Cataclysm (1988). 3.00
Batman/Judge Dredd: Judgement on
　Gotham,SBs,V:Scarecrow, Judge
　Death (1991) 9.00
Batman/Judge Dredd: Vendetta in
　Gotham, AIG(s),V:Ventriliquist
　(1993) 5.25
Batman/Judge Dredd: The Ultimate
　Riddle (1995) 5.00
Batman/Phantom Stranger, AIG(s),
　Lemurian artifact (1997) 5.00
Batman/Punisher: Lake of Fire,
　DON(s),BKi,A:Punisher,V:Jigsaw
　(DC/Marvel 1994). 5.25
Batman/Spawn: War Devil, DgM,CDi,
　AIG(s), KJ,V:Croatoan (1994) . . 6.00
Batman/Spider-Man (1997). 5.00
Batman vs. The Incredible Hulk
　(DC/Marvel 1995). 4.00

BATMAN ADVENTURES
1992–95
(Based on TV cartoon series)
1 MeP,V:Penguin 5.00
2 MeP,V:Catwoman 4.00
3 MeP,V:Joker 3.00
4 MeP,V:Scarecrow 3.00
5 MeP,V:Scarecrow 3.00
6 MeP,A:Robin 3.00
7 MeP,V:Killer Croc,w/card. 6.00
8 MeP,Larceny my Sweet 2.50
9 MeP,V:Two Face. 2.50
10 MeP,V:Riddler 3.00
11 MeP,V:Man-Bat 2.00
12 MeP,F:Batgirl 2.00
13 MeP,V:Talia 2.00
14 MeP,F:Robin 2.00
15 MeP,F:Commissioner Gordon . . 2.00

Batman Adventures #25
© DC Comics, Inc.

16 MeP,V:Joker	2.00
17 MeP,V:Talia	2.00
18 MeP,R:Batgirl	1.75
19 MeP,V:Scarecrow	1.75
20 MeP,V:Mastermind,Mr.Nice, Perfessor	1.75
21 MeP,V:Man-Bat,Tygrus	1.75
22 MeP,V:Two-Face	1.75
23 MEP,V:Poison Ivy	1.75
24 MeP,I:Kyodi Ken	1.75
25 MeP,dbl.size,Superman	2.50
26 MeP,A:Robin,Batgirl	1.75
27 MeP,I:Doppleganger	1.75
28 Joker	1.75
29 A:Talia	1.50
30 O:Mastermind, Mr. Nice	1.50
31 I:Anarcky	1.50
32 Criminals dressed as Napoleonic Soldiers	1.75
33 Bruce and date mugged	1.75
34 V:Dr. Hugo Strange	1.75
35 A:Catwoman	1.75
36 V:Joker, Final issue	1.75
Ann.#1 Roxy Rocket	3.00
Ann.#2 JBa,BBI,DG,TG,SHa,BKi,MM, GN,JRu,V:Demon,Ra's al Ghul,Etrigan	3.50
Holiday Special	2.95
Spec. Mad Love	3.95
TPB Collected Adventures #1	6.00
TPB Collected Adventures #2	6.00

BATMAN ADVENTURES: THE LOST YEARS
Nov. 1997
1 (of 5) BHa,TBe,Batgirl	2.00
2 BHa,TBe,Dick Grayson quits	2.00
3	2.00
4 BHa,TBe,F:Tim Drake	2.00
5 BHa,TBe,Tim Drake new Robin	2.00

BATMAN ADVENTURES: THE LOST YEARS
1999
1 (of 6) TBe	2.00
2 thru 6	@2.00

BATMAN AND THE OUTSIDERS
Aug., 1983
1 B:MiB(s),JAp,O:Outsiders, O:Geo Force	3.00
2 JAp,V:Baron Bedlam	2.50
3 JAp,V:Agent Orange	2.00
4 JAp,V:Fearsome Five	2.00
5 JAp,A:New Teen Titans	2.50
6 JAp,V:Cryonic Man	1.50
7 JAp,V:Cryonic Man	1.50
8 JAp,A:Phantom Stranger	1.50
9 JAp,I:Master of Disaster	1.50
10 JAp,A:Master of Disaster	1.50
11 JAp,V:Takeo	1.50
12 JAp,DG,O:Katana	1.50
13 JAp,Day,O:Batman	1.50
14 BWg,Olympics,V:Maxi Zeus	1.50
15 TVE,Olympics,V:Maxi Zeus	1.50
16 JAp,L:Halo	1.50
17 JAp,V:Ahk-Ton	1.50
18 JAp,V:Ahk-Ton	1.50
19 JAp,A:Superman	1.50
20 JAp,V:Syonide,R:Halo	1.50
21 TVE,JeM,Solo Stories	1.50
22 AD,O:Halo,I:Aurakles	1.50
23 AD,O:Halo,V:Aurakles	1.50
24 AD,C:Kobra	1.50
25 AD,V:Kobra	1.50
26 AD	1.50
27 AD,V:Kobra	1.50
28 AD,I:Lia Briggs(Looker)	1.50
29 AD,V:Metamorpho	1.50
30 AD,C:Looker	1.50
31 AD,I&J:Looker	1.50
32 AD,L:Batman	1.50
Ann.#1 JA N:Geo-Force, I:Force of July	1.75
Ann.#2 V:Tremayne,W:Metamorpho & Sapphire Stagg	1.50

Becomes:
ADVENTURES OF THE OUTSIDERS
May, 1986
33 AD,V:Baron Bedlam	1.50
34 AD,Masters of Disaster	1.50
35 AD,V:Adolph Hitler	1.50
36 AD,A:Masters of Disaster	1.50
37	1.50
38	1.50
39 thru 47 JAp,reprints Outsiders #1-#9	@1.50

BATMAN AND ROBIN ADVENTURES, THE
Nov. 1995
1 TTn	2.00
2 TTn,V:Two-Face	1.75
3 TTn,V:The Riddler	1.75
4 TTn,V:The Penguin	1.75
5 TTn	1.75
6 TTn,Robin Fired?	1.75
7 TTn,V:Scarface	1.75
8 TTn(s)	1.75
9 TTn(s),F:Batgirl & Talia	1.75
10 TTn(s),F:Ra's Al Ghul	1.75
11 TTn(s),Alfred & Robin look for monster in Batcave	1.75
12 TTn(s),BKr,RBr, sequel to "Bane" TV episode	1.75
13 TTn(s),BKr,RBr,V:Scarecrow	1.75
14 TTn(s),BKr,RBr,young criminal turns to Batman for help	1.75
15 TTn(s)	1.75
16 TTn(s),V:Catman,A:Catwoman	1.75
17 PDi&TTn(s),JSon,RBr,Mad Hatter dies in Arkham	1.75

Batman and Robin Adventures #24
© DC Comics, Inc.

18 TTn(s),BKr,TBe,A:Joker, Harley Quinn	1.75
19 TTn(s),BKr,TBe,The Huntress	1.75
20 TTn(s),BKr,TBe, office pool	1.75
21 TTn(s),JSon,Riddler kidnaps Commissioner Gordon	1.75
22 TTn(s),BKr,TBe,V:Two-Face	1.75
23 TTn(s),TBe,V:Killer Croc	1.75
24 TTn(c),F:Poison Ivy	1.75
25 TTn,TBe,final issue, 48pg	3.00
Ann.#1 PDi(s),TTn, sequel to Batman: Mask of the Phantasm	3.00
Ann.#2 JSon,TBe,V:Hypnotist	4.00
Sub-Zero one-shot, F:Mr. Freeze, Nora, 64pg	3.95

BATMAN & SUPERMAN: WORLD'S FINEST
1999
1 (of 10) KK(s),DTy,RbC,48-page	5.00
2 KK(s),DTy,RbC	2.00
3 KK(s),DTy,RbC,Arkham Asylum	2.00
4 KK(s),DTy,RbC,Metropolis	2.00
5 KK(s),DTy,RbC,Batgirl	2.00
6 KK(s),DTy,RbC,trade identities	2.00
7 KK(s),PD,RbC	2.00

BATMAN: BANE OF THE DEMON
Feb., 1998
1 (of 4) CDi,GN,TP, Bane & Ra's al Ghul	2.00
2 CDi,GN,TP,Talia	2.00
3 CDi,GN,TP,the Lazarus Pit	2.00
4 CDi,GN,TP,Bane imprisoned	2.00

BATMAN BEYOND
1999
1 (of 6) RBr,TBe,Rebirth	2.00
2 RBr,TBe,Rebirth,pt.2	2.00
3 RBr,TBe,V:Blight	2.00
4 JSon,TBe,F:Demon Etrigan	2.00
5 JSon,TBe,V:Mummy	2.00
6 JSon,TBe,V:Inque	2.00

BATMAN BLACK & WHITE
1996
1 JLe(c) numerous artists (of 4)	6.00

2 thru 4 . . . . @5.00
HC 40.00

BATMAN:
BOOK OF THE DEAD
1999
1 (of 2) DgM(s),BKi,Elseworlds . . . 5.00
2 DgM(s),BKi,Conclusion. 5.00

BATMAN CHRONICLES
1995
1 CDi,LW,BSz, multiple stories. . . . 3.50
2 V:Feedback 3.00
3 All villains issue 3.00
4 F:Hitman 10.00
5 Oracle, Year One story 3.00
6 Ra's Al Ghul. 3.00
7 JOy,LW, woman on death row. . . 3.00
8 Talia goes to Gotham to
    eliminate Batman 3.00
9 CDi(s),F:Batgirl, Mr. Freeze,
    Poison Ivy 3.00
10 BSn, anthology 3.00
11 CDi,JFM, Elseworlds stories. . . . 3.00
12 Cataclysm x-over. 3.00
13 F:GCPD 3.00
14 SB(c),F:Alfred,Huntress. 3.00
15 Road to No Man's Land 3.00
16 F:Batgirl,No Man's Land tie-in . . 3.00
17 V:Penguin,No Man's Land 3.00
18 No Man's Land 3.00
Gallery #1, Pin-ups. 3.50
GN The Gauntlet 4.95

BATMAN: THE CULT
1988
1 JSn,BWr,V:Deacon Blackfire. . . . 9.00
2 JSn,BWr,V:Deacon Blackfire. . . . 7.00
3 JSn,BWr,V:Deacon Blackfire. . . . 7.00
4 JSn,BWr,V:Deacon Blackfire. . . . 6.00
TPB Rep.#1-#4. . . . . 14.95

BATMAN:
DARK KNIGHT
OF THE ROUND TABLE
1998
1 (of 2) BL,DG,Elseworlds,48pg. . . 5.00
2 BL,DG, conclusion 5.00

BATMAN: THE DARK
KNIGHT RETURNS
1986
1 FM,KJ,V:Two-Face 20.00
1a 2nd printing 5.00
1b 3rd printing 3.00
2 FM,KJ,V:Sons of the Batman . . . 9.00
2a 2nd printing 3.00
2b 3rd printing 2.50
3 FM,KJ,D:Joker 7.00
3a 2nd printing 3.00
4 FM,KJ,Batman vs.Superman,
    A:Green Arrow,D:Alfred 5.00
HC 50.00
Paperback book 20.00
Warner paperback 17.00
HC,sign/num. 270.00
    2nd-8th printing 12.95
TPB 10th Anniv. Spec, 224 pg. . . . 14.95

BATMAN FAMILY
Sept.–Oct., 1975
1 MGr,NA(rep.) Batgirl &
    Robin begins,giant 15.00
2 V:Clue Master. 10.00

3 Batgirl & Robin reveal ID 10.00
4 . . . . 10.00
5 . . . . 10.00
6 Joker Daughter. 15.00
7 CS,A:Sportsmaster,
    G.A.Huntress. 9.00
8 First solo Robin story,
    C:Joker's Daughter. 9.00
9 Joker's Daughter 15.00
10 R:B'woman,1st solo Batgirl sty. 15.00
11 MR,Man-Bat begins 12.00
12 MR 12.00
13 MR,DN,BWi. 12.00
14 HC/JRu,Man-Bat 9.00
15 MGo,Man-Bat 9.00
16 MGo,Man-Bat 9.00
17 JA,DH,MG,Batman, B:Huntress
    A:Demon,MK(c),A:Catwoman . 12.00
18 MGo,JSon,BL,Huntress,BM . . . 12.00
19 MGo,JSon,BL,Huntress,BM . . . 12.00
20 MGo,JSon,DH,A:Ragman,
    ElongatedMan, Oct.–Nov.,1978. 12.00

BATMAN: GCPD
[Mini-Series] Aug. 1996
1 CDi(s),JAp,BSz 2.25
2 CDi(s),JAp,BSz 2.25

Batman GDPD #2 © DC Comics Inc.

3 CDi(s), JAp,BSz,F:Montoya,
    Kitch & Bullock. 2.25
4 CDi(s), JAp,BSz, finale 2.25

BATMAN:
GORDON'S LAW
October 1996
1 CDi(s),KJ,Gordon looks for
    bad cops 2.00
2 CDi(s),KJ,Gordon combats
    corruption. 2.00
3 CDi(s),KJ,. 2.00
4 (of 4) CDi(s),KJ, concl. 2.00

BATMAN:
GORDON OF GOTHAM
April 1998
1 (of 4) DON,DG,KJ,F:Jim Gordon. 2.00
2 DON,DG,KJ,Cuchulain 2.00
3 DON,DG,KJ,break-in 2.00
4 DON,DG,KJ,past revealed 2.00

BATMAN:
GOTHAM ADVENTURES
April 1998
1 TTn,RBr,TBe,F:Joker 3.00
2 TTn,RBr,TBe,F:Two-Face 2.00
3 TTn,RBr,TBe,V:Scarecrow 2.00
4 TTn,RBr,TBe,A:Catwoman 2.00
5 RBr,TBe,TTn,A:Mr.Freeze. 2.00
6 TTn,RBr,TBe,O:Deadman. 2.00
7 TTn,RBe,TBe,V:Danger Dixon . . 2.00
8 TTn,RBe,TBe,Batgirl. 2.00
9 TTn,RBe,TBe,V:League
    of Assassins. 2.00
10 TTn,RBe,TBe,F:Nightwing
    & Robin, A:Harley Quinn 2.00
11 TTn,RBe,TBe,V:Riddler 2.00
12 TTn,RBe,TBe,V:Two-Face 2.00
13 RBe,TBe,V:Mastermind 2.00
14 TTn(s),TBe,V:Harley Quinn 2.00
15 V:Bane 2.00
16 TBe,Alfred Kidnapped 2.00
17 TBe. 2.00

BATMAN:
GOTHAM NIGHTS
1 Gotham City Mini-series 2.00
2 Lives of Gotham Citizens 2.00
3 Lives of Gotham Citizens 2.00
4 Lives of Gotham Citizens 2.00

BATMAN:
GOTHAM NIGHTS II
1995
1 Sequel to Gotham Nights 2.00
2 F:Carmine Sansone 2.00
3 Fire 2.00
4 JQ(c) Decisions 2.00

BATMAN/HELLBOY/
STARMAN
DC/Dark Horse 1998
1 JeR(s),MMi, x-over. 2.50
2 JeR(s),MMi, conclusion. 2.50

BATMAN: JAZZ
[Mini-Series] 1995
1 I:Blue Byrd 2.50
2 V:Brotherhood of Bop 2.50
3 F:Blue Byrd 2.50

BATMAN/JUDGE DREDD:
DIE LAUGHING
1998
1 (of 2) AlG(s),GF 48-pg. 5.00
2 AlG(s),GF conclusion 5.00

BATMAN: LEGENDS OF
THE DARK KNIGHT
1989
1 EH,Shaman of Gotham,pt.1,
    Yellow(c) 4.00
1a Blue,Orange or Pink(c) 4.00
2 EH,Shaman of Gotham,pt.2 . . . . 3.00
3 EH,Shaman of Gotham,pt.3 . . . . 3.00
4 EH,Shaman of Gotham,pt.4 . . . . 3.00
5 EH,Shaman of Gotham,pt.5 . . . . 3.00
6 KJ,Gothic,pt.1. . . . . 3.00
7 KJ,Gothic,pt.2. . . . . 2.50
8 KJ,Gothic,pt.3. . . . . 2.50
9 KJ,Gothic,pt.4. . . . . 2.50
10 KJ,Gothic,pt.5 . . . . 2.50
11 PG,TA,Prey,pt.1 . . . . 6.00

Batman/Judge Dredd: Die Laughing #2
© DC Comics, Inc.

12 PG,TA,Prey,pt.2	5.00
13 PG,TA,Prey,pt.3	5.00
14 PG,TA,Prey,pt.4	5.00
15 PG,TA,Prey,pt.5	4.00
16 TVE,Venom,pt.1	5.00
17 TVE,JL,Venom,pt.2	5.00
18 TVE,JL,Venom,pt.3	5.00
19 TVE,JL,Venom,pt.4	5.00
20 TVE,JL,Venom,pt.5	5.00
21 BS,Faith,pt.1	2.50
22 BS,Faith,pt.2	2.50
23 BS,Faith,pt.3	2.50
24 GK,Flyer,pt.1	2.50
25 GK,Flyer,pt.2	2.50
26 GK,Flyer,pt.3	2.50
27 Destroyer,pt.2 (Batman#474)	3.00
28 MWg,Faces,pt.1,V:Two-Face	4.00
29 MWg,Faces,pt.2,V:Two-Face	4.00
30 MWg,Faces,pt.3,V:Two-Face	4.00
31 BA,Family	2.50
32 Blades,pt.1	2.50
33 Blades,pt.2	2.50
34 Blades,pt.3	2.50
35 BHa,Destiny Pt.1	2.50
36 BHa,Destiny Pt.2	2.50
37 I:Mercy,V:The Cossack	2.50
38 KON,R:Bat-Mite	2.50
39 BT,Mask#1	2.50
40 BT,Mask#2	2.50
41 Sunset	2.25
42 CR,Hothouse #1	2.25
43 CR,Hothouse #2,V:Poison Ivy	2.25
44 SMc,Turf #1	2.25
45 Turf#2	2.25
46 RH,A:Catwoman,V:Catman	2.50
47 RH,A:Catwoman,V:Catman	2.50
48 RH,A:Catwoman,V:Catman	2.50
49 RH,A:Catwoman,V:Catman	2.50
50 BBl,JLe,KN,KM,WS,MZ,BB, V:Joker	6.00
51 JKu,A:Ragman	2.25
52 Tao #1,V:Dragon	2.25
53 Tao #2,V:Dragon	2.25
54 MMi	2.00
55 B:Watchtower	2.00
56 CDi(s),V:Battle Guards	2.00
57 CDi(s),E:Watchtower	2.00
58 Storm	2.50
59 DON(s),RoW,B:Qarry	2.50
60 RoW,V:Asp	2.50
61 RoW,V:Asp	2.50
62 RoW,KnightsEnd#4,A:Shiva, Nightwing	3.50
63 Knights End #10,V:Azrael	2.00

64 CBa	2.00
65 Joker	2.00
66 Joker	2.00
67 Going Sane,pt.3	2.00
68 Going Sane,pt.4	2.00
69 Criminals,pt.1	2.00
70 Criminals,pt.2	2.00
71 Werewolf,pt.1	2.00
72 JWk(c&a),Werewolf,pt.2 [new Miraweb format begins]	2.00
73 JWk(c&a),Werewolf,pt.3	2.00
74 Engins,pt.1	2.00
75 Engins,pt.2	2.00
76 The Sleeping,pt.1	2.00
77 The Sleeping,pt.2	2.00
78 The Sleeping,pt.3	2.00
79 Favorite Things	2.00
80 Idols,pt.1	2.00
81 Idols,pt.2	2.00
82 Idols, climax	2.00
83 new villain	2.00
84 WEI(s)	2.00
85 JeR(s)	2.00
86 DgM,JWi,MGy,Conspiracy,pt.1	2.00
87 DgM,JWi,MGy,Conspiracy,pt.2	2.00
88 DgM,JWi,MGy,Conspiracy,pt.3	2.00
89 AIG(s),"Clay," pt. 1	2.00
90 AIG(s),"Clay," pt. 2	2.00
91 "Freakout," pt.1	2.00
92 GEn(s),WSm,"Freakout," pt.2	2.00
93 GEn(s),WSm,"Freakout," pt.3	2.00
94 MGi(s),Saul Fisher's story	2.00
95 DAn&ALa(s),AWi,ALa,"Dirty Tricks" pt.1	2.00
96 DAn&ALa(s),AWi,ALa,"Dirty Tricks" pt.2	2.00
97 DAn&ALa(s),AWi,ALa,"Dirty Tricks" concl.	2.00
98 PJe(s),SeP,"Steps," pt.1	2.00
99 PJe(s),SeP,"Steps," pt.2	2.00
100 DON,JRo,F:Robin, 64pg.	4.00
101 CE,KN(c)100 years in future	2.00
102 JRo,PuJ,"Spook," pt.1	2.00
103 JRo,PuJ,"Spook," pt.2	2.00
104 JRo,PuJ,"Spook," pt.3	2.00
105 TVE,JRu,"Duty," pt.1	2.00
106 TVE,JRu,"Duty," pt.2	2.00
107 LMr,"Stalking," pt.1	2.00
108 LMr,"Stalking," pt.2	2.00
109 SEt,DAb,Primal Riddle,pt.1	2.00
110 SEt,DAb,Primal Riddle,pt.2	2.00
111 SEt,DAb,Primal Riddle,pt.3	2.00
112 DVa,FC,V:Lord Demise,pt.1	2.00
113 DVa,FC,V:Lord Demise,pt.2	2.00
114 JeR(s),DIB,TBd	2.00
115 LMc,DIB(c)	2.00
116 IEd,Bread and Circuses,pt.1	2.00
117 IEd,Bread and Circuses,pt.2	2.00
118 JPn,Alfred in No Man's Land	2.00
119 MD2,Claim Jumping,pt.1	2.00
120 MD2,Assembly	2.00
121 RBr,V:Mr.Freeze	2.00
122 LHa(s),PG, Low Road to Golden Mountain,pt.1	2.00
Ann.#1 JAp,KG,DSp,TL,JRu, MGo,JQ,`Duel",C:Joker	5.50
Ann.#2 MN,LMc,W:Gordn&Essen	4.00
Ann.#3 MM,I:Cardinal Sin	3.75
Ann.#4 JSon(s),Elseworlds Story	3.75
Ann.#5 CDi(s)Year One Annuals, O:Man-Bat	3.95
Ann.#6 Legends o/t Dead Earth	2.95
Ann.#7 Pulp Heroes (War)	3.95
Halloween Spec.I	6.95
Halloween Spec.II	4.95
Ghosts, Halloween Special	4.95
TPB Shaman rep.#1–#5 (1993)	12.95
TPB Batman: Gothic, rep. #6–#10 (1992)	12.95
TPB Prey, rep.Legends of the Dark Knight #11–#15 (1992)	12.95

Batman: Legends of the Dark Knight Annual #7 © DC Comics, Inc.

TPB Batman: Venom, TVE, rep. #16–#20 (1993)	9.95
TPB Collected Legends of the Dark Knight,BB(c),rep.#32-#34,#38, #42-#43 (1994)	12.95
TPB Other Realms	13.00

BATMAN: THE LONG HALLOWEEN
October 1996

1 (of 13) JLb,TSe,Who is Holiday? F: usual suspects	11.00
2 JLb(s),TSe,V:Holiday,A:Solomon Grundy	8.00
3 JLb,TSe,	9.00
4 JLb(s),TSe,"New Year's Eve"	9.00
5 JLb(s),TSe,F:Poison Ivy, Search for Holiday	5.00
6 JLb(s),TSe,F:Poison Ivy, Catwoman	5.00
7 JLb(s),TSe,V:The Riddler	4.00
8 JLb(s),TSe,V:Scarecrow	4.00
9 JLb(s),TSe,A:Holiday,Scarecrow	4.00
10 JLb(s),TSe,V:Scarecrow,Mad Hatter	4.00
11 JLb(s),TSe,V:Holiday	3.50
12 JLb(s),TSe,Harvey Dent	3.50
13 JLb(s),TSe,concl.,48pg.	5.00
TPB Haunted Knight, rep. Fears, Madness & Ghosts	12.95

BATMAN: MAN-BAT
1995

1 R:Man-Bat, painted series	5.00
2 F:Marilyn Muno.	5.00
3 JBo,Elseworlds story, concl.	5.00
TPB rep. mini-series	14.95

BATMAN: RUN, RIDDLER RUN
1992

1 MBg,Batman V:Riddler	5.50
2 MBg,Batman V:Riddler	5.25
3 MBg,V:Perfect Securities	5.25

BATMAN/SPIDER-MAN
Aug., 1997

GN JMD,GN,KK,V:Kingpin & Ra's al Ghul	5.00

BATMAN: SHADOW OF THE BAT
1992–97

1 NB,Last Arkham Pt.1	3.50
1a Collector set,w/posters,pop-up	5.50
2 NB,Last Arkham Pt.2	3.00
3 NB,Last Arkham Pt.3	3.00
4 NB,Last Arkham Pt.4	3.00
5 NB,A:Black Spider	2.50
6 NB,I:Chancer	2.50
7 Misfits Pt.1	2.50
8 Misfits Pt.2	2.50
9 Misfits Pt.3	2.50
10 MC,V:Mad Thane of Gotham	2.00
11 V:Kadaver	2.00
12 V:Kadaver,A:Human Flea	2.00
13 NB,`The Nobody'	2.00
14 NB,Gotham Freaks#1	2.00
15 NB,Gotham Freaks#2	2.00
16 BBI,MM,A:Anarchy,Scarecrow	2.00
17 BBI,V:Scarecrow	2.00
18 BBI,A:Anarchy,Scarecrow	2.00
19 BBI,Knightquest:The Crusade,pt.2, V:Gotham criminals	2.00
20 VGi,Knightquest:The Crusade, V:Tally Man	2.00
21 BBI,Knightquest:The Search, V:Mr.Asp	2.00
22 BBI,Knightquest:The Search, In London.	2.00
23 BBI,Knightquest:The Search	2.00
24 BBI,Knightquest:The Crusade	2.00
25 BSf(c),BBI,Knightquest: Crusade, A:Joe Public,V:Corrosive Man	2.00
26 BSf(c),BBI,Knightquest: Crusade, V:Clayface	2.00
27 BSf(c),BBI,Knightquest: Crusade, I:Clayface Baby	2.00
28 BSf(c),BBI	2.00
29 BSf(c),BBI,KnightsEnd#2, A:Nightwing	3.50
30 BSf(c),BBI,KnightsEnd#8, V:Azrael	2.25
31 Zero Hour, V:Butler	2.00
32 Ventriloquist,Two-Face	2.00
33 Two-Face	2.00
34 V:Tally Man	2.00
35 BKi,Return of Bruce Wayne, Troika,pt.2	2.00
35a Collectors Edition	2.95
36 Black Canary	2.00
37 Joker Hunt	2.00

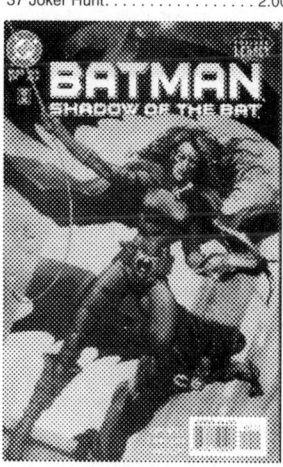

Batman Shadow of the Bat #53
© DC Comics Inc.

38 V:The Joker	2.00
39 BSf(c),R:Solomon Grundy [new Miraweb format begins]	2.00
40 BSf(c), F:Anarky	2.00
41 Explosive Dirigible	2.00
42	2.00
43 Secret of the Universe,pt1	2.00
44 AIG,BSz(c) Secret of the Universe,pt.3	2.00
45 AIG,BSz(c) 100 year old corpse.	2.00
46 AIG,BSz(c) V:Cornelius Stirk	2.00
47 AIG,BSz(c) V:Cornelius Stirk	2.00
48 AIG	2.00
49 AIG,Contagion,pt.7	2.00
50 AIG,Nightmare on Gotham,pt.1	2.00
51 AIG,DTy, Nightmare on Gotham,pt.2 (of 3)	2.00
52 AIG(s),"Nightmare on Gotham," pt.3	2.00
53 AIG(s),Legacy, prelude	2.00
54 AIG(s),Legacy, pt. 4, x-over	2.00
55 AIG(s),RBr,KJ,Bruce Wayne a murderer? A:Nightwing	2.00
56 AIG(s),DTy,SnW,"Leaves of Grass,pt.1,V:Poison Ivy	2.00
57 AIG(s),DTy,SnW,"Leaves of Grass,pt.2	2.00
58 AIG(s),DTy,SnW,"Leaves of Grass,pt.3	2.00
59 AIG(s),DTy,SnW,"Killer, Killer," pt.1	2.00
60 AIG(s),DTy,SnW,"Killer, Killer," pt.2	2.00
61 AIG(s),JAp,SnW,night of second chances	2.00
62 AIG(s),DTy,SnW,Two-Face,pt.1	2.00
63 AIG(s),DTy,SnW,Two-Face,pt.2	2.00
64 AIG(s),DTy,SnW,A:Jason Blood	2.00
65 AIG(s),NBy,JRu, A:Oracle, pt.1	2.00
66 AIG(s),NBy,JRu, V:Thinker, Cheat, pt.2	2.00
67 AIG(s),NBy,SnW,CsM,V:Thinker, Cheat, pt.3, concl.	2.00
68 AIG(s),JAp,SnW,annual killer	2.00
69 AIG(s),MBu,WF,CsM, The Spirit of 2000, pt. 1	2.00
70 AIG(s),MBu,WF,CsM, pt.2	2.00
71 AIG(s),MBu,WF,CsM,detective	2.00
72 AIG(s),MBu,WF	2.00
73 AIG(s),MBu,WF,Cataclysm x-over,pt.1	3.00
74 AIG(s),MBu,WF,Cataclysm cont.	2.00
75 AIG(s),MBu,WF,Aftershock	3.00
76 AIG(s),MBu,WF,Aftershock	2.00
77 AIG(s),MBu,WF,quake-torn	2.00
78 AIG(s),MBu,Aftershock	2.00
79 AIG(s),MBu,V:Mad Hatter, Narcosis	2.00
80 Road to No Man's Land, flip-book Azrael:Agent of the Bat #47	4.00
81 AIG(s),MBu,No Man's Land	2.00
82 AIG(s),MBu,No Man's Land	2.00
83 No Law and a New Order, pt.2.	2.00
84 IEd,Bread and Circuses, pt.2	2.00
85 IEd(s),Bread & Circuses,concl.	2.00
86 GyD,No Man's Land	2.00
87 MD2, Claim Jumping, pt.2	2.00
88 DJu,BSz,Fruit of the Earth,pt.1	2.00
89 IEd(s),SB,No Man's Land.	2.00
90 LHa(s),PG,No Man's Land	2.00
Ann.#1 TVE,DG,Bloodlines#3, I:Joe Public	3.75
Ann.#2 Elseworlds story	3.95
Ann.#3 Year One Annual	3.95
Ann.#4 Legends of the Dead Earth	2.95
Ann.#5 AIG(s), Pulp Heroes	2.00
Spec.#1,000,000 AIG(s),MBu, Origin of 853rd-century Dark Knight	2.00

BATMAN: SWORD OF AZRAEL
1992–93

1 JQ,KN,I:Azrael	10.00
2 JQ,KN,A:Azrael	7.00
3 JQ,KN,V:Biis,A:Azrael.	5.00
4 JQ,KN,V:Biis,A:Azrael.	5.00
TPB rep.#1-#4	11.00
TPB Platinum	25.00

BATMAN/GRENDEL: DEVIL'S MASQUE & DEVIL'S RIDDLE

1 MWg,Batman meets Grendel	5.25
2 MWg,Batman Vs. Grendel	5.25

BATMAN: TOYMAN
1998

1 (of 4) LHa(s),AWi,KJ	2.25
2 LHa(s),AWi,KJ	2.25
3 LHa(s),AWi,KJ	2.25
4 LHa(s),AWi,KJ conclusion.	2.25

BATMAN vs. PREDATOR
DC/Dark Horse 1991–92

1 NKu,AKu,inc.8 trading cards bound in (Prestige)	5.00
1a Newsstand	4.00
2 NKu,AKu,Inc. pinups (prestige)	4.00
2a Newsstand	3.00
3 NKu,AKu,conclusion,inc. 8 trading cards (Prestige)	4.00
3a Newsstand	3.00
TPB,rep.#1-#3	5.95

BATMAN vs. PREDATOR II BLOODMATCH
1994–95

1 R:Predators	2.75
2 A:Huntress	2.50
3 Assassins	2.50
4 V:Head Hunters	2.50
TPB Rep.#1-#4.	6.95

BATMAN/PREDATOR III: BLOOD TIES
DC/Dark Horse 1997

1 (of 4) CDi,RDm,RbC, vs. pair of Predators	2.00

Batman/Wildcat #2 © DC Comics, Inc.

DC COMICS

2 CDi,RDm,RbC, pt.2 . . . . 2.00
3 CDi,RDm,RbC, pt.3 . . . . 2.00
4 CDi,RDm,RbC, concl.. . . . . 2.00
TPB rep.. . . . . 8.00

BATMAN/WILDCAT
Feb. 1997
1 (of 3) CDi&BSt(s),SCi,ATi,
  Batman and Robin discover
  Secret Ring of combat 2.25
2 CDi&BSt(s),SCi,V:KGBeast,
  Willis Danko. 2.25
3 CDi&BSt(s),SCi, Batman vs.
  Wildcat, concl. 2.25

BATTLE CLASSICS
Sept.–Oct., 1978
1 JKu, reprints. 1.50

BEAUTIFUL STORIES FOR UGLY CHILDREN
Piranha Press 1989–91
1 thru 11 . . . . @2.00
12 thru 14 . . . . @2.50
15 Blood Day 2.50
16 thru 23. . . . . @2.50

BEOWOLF
April-May, 1975
1 thru 5 . . . . @1.00
6 Feb.–March, 1976 . . . . 1.00

BEST OF THE BRAVE & THE BOLD
1 JL(c),NA,rep.B&B #85. . . . . . . 2.50
2 JL(c),NA,rep.B&B #81 . . . . 2.50
3 JL(c),NA,rep.B&B #82 . . . . 2.50
4 JL(c),NA,rep.B&B #80 . . . . 2.50
5 JL(c),NA,rep.B&B #93 . . . . 2.50
6 JL(c),NA,rep.B&B #83 . . . . 2.50

BEWARE THE CREEPER
1968–69
1 . . . . 12.00
2 thru 6 . . . . @7.50

BIG ALL-AMERICAN COMIC BOOK
Dec., 1944
1 JKu 11,000.00

BIG BOOK OF FUN COMICS
Spring, 1936
1 . . . . 12,000.00

BIG BOOK OF CONSPIRACIES, THE
DC/Paradox Press B&W 1995
TPB 12.95

BIG BOOK OF DEATH, THE
DC/Paradox Press B&W 1994
TPB 12.95

BIG BOOK OF HOAXES, THE
DC/Paradox Press B&W 1996
TPB 14.95

BIG BOOK OF LITTLE CRIMINALS, THE
DC/Paradox Press B&W 1996
TPB 14.95

BIG BOOK OF LOSERS, THE
DC/Paradox Press B&W
TPB by Paul Kirchner 14.95

BIG BOOK OF MARTYRS
DC/Paradox Aug., 1997
TPB 15.00

BIG BOOK OF SCANDAL
Oct., 1997
TPB 15.00

BIG BOOK OF THUGS, THE
DC/Paradox B&W Oct. 1996
TPB 14.95

BIG BOOK OF THE UNEXPLAINED
DC/Paradox B&W April 1997
GN DgM(s),strange phenomena . . 14.95

BIG BOOK OF URBAN LEGENDS, THE
DC/Paradox B&W 1994
TPB 12.95

BIG BOOK OF WEIRDOS, THE
DC/Paradox Press B&W 1995
TPB 12.95

BIG BOOK OF THE WEIRD WILD WEST
July 1998
TPB 15.00

BIRDS OF PREY: BATGIRL
Dec., 1997
1 CDi,Batgirl & Black Canary 3.00

BIRDS OF PREY: MANHUNT
1996
1 CDi(s),MHy,F:Black Canary,
  Oracle 2.00
2 CDi(s),MHy,V,Archer Braun,
  A:Catwoman 2.00
3 CDi(s),MHy,V:Catwoman,
  Huntress 2.00
4 CDi(s),MHy,V:Lady Shiva 2.00

Birds of Prey/Batgirl 1
© DC Comics, Inc.

BIRDS OF PREY: REVOLUTION
one-shot CDi(s),BMc 2.95

BIRDS OF PREY: THE RAVENS
May 1998
1-shot, CDi,Girlfrenzy 2.00

BIRDS OF PREY: WOLVES
Aug., 1997
1-shot CDi,DG,F:Oracle & Black
  Canary. 3.00

BIRDS OF PREY
1998
1 CDi(s),Black Canary & Oracle. . . 2.00
2 CDi(s),V:Jackie Pajamas 2.00
3 CDi(s),V:Hellbound 2.00
4 CDi(s),V:Ravens. 2.00
5 CDi(s),V:Ravens,pt.2 . . . . 2.00
6 CDi(s),V:Ravens,pt.3 . . . . 2.00
7 CDi(s),PKr, ... 2.00
8 CDi(s),F:Nightwing 2.00
9 CDi(s),V:Iron Brigade 2.00
10 CDi(s),DG,V:Dr.Pop 2.00
TPB Birds of Prey. 18.00

BLACK CANARY
[Limited Series] 1991–92
1 TVE/DG,New Wings,pt.1 . . . . . . 2.25
2 TVE/DG,New Wings,pt.2 . . . . . . 2.00
3 TVE/DG,New Wings,pt.3 . . . . . . 2.00
4 TVE/DG,New Wings,pt.4,Conc . . 2.00

[Regular Series] 1993
1 TVE,Hero Worship,pt.1 . . . . 2.25
2 TVE,Hero Worship,pt.2. . . . . . . 2.00
3 TVE,Hero Worship,pt.3. . . . . . . 2.00
4 TVE,V:Whorrsman 2.00
5 . . . . 2.00
6 Blynde Woman's Bluff. 2.00
7 TVE,V:Maniacal Killer. 2.00
8 . . . . 1.75
9 A:Huntress 1.75
10 TVE,A:Nightwing,Huntress. . . . 1.75
11 TVE,A:Nightwing 1.75
12 final issue 1.75

BLACK CANARY/ORACLE: BIRDS OF PREY
1996
1-shot DDi, double size. 3.95

BLACK CONDOR
1992–93
1 I&O:Black Condor. 1.25
2 V:Sky Pirate 1.25
3 V:Sky Pirate 1.25
4 V:The Shark 1.25
5 V:Mind Force 1.25
6 V:Mind Force 1.25
7 Forest Fire 1.25
8 MG,In Jail. 1.25
9 A:The Ray 1.25
10 . . . . 1.25
11 O:Black Condor 1.25

BLACKHAWK
Prev: Golden Age
1957–1984
108 DD,CCu,DD&CCu(c),The Threat from the Abyss A:Blaisie. 450.00
109 DD,CCu,DD&CCu(c),The Avalance Kid 150.00
110 DD,CCu,DD&CCu(c),Mystery of Tigress Island. 150.00
111 DD,CCu,DD&CCu(c),Menace of the Machines 150.00
112 DD,CCu,DD(c),The Doomed Dog Fight 150.00
113 DD,CCu,CCu(c),Volunteers of Doom 150.00
114 DD,CCu,DD&CCu(c),Gladiators of Blackhawk Island 150.00
115 DD,CCu,DD&CCu(c),The Tyrant's Return. 150.00
116 DD,CCu,DD&CCu(c),Prisoners of the Black Island 140.00
117 DD,CCu,DD&CCu(c),Menace of the Dragon Boat 140.00
118 DD,CCu,DD&SMo(c),FF,The Bandit With 1,000 Nets 150.00
119 DD,CCu,DD&SMo(c), V:Chief Blackhawk 100.00
120 DD,CCu,DD&SMo(c),The Challenge of the Wizard 100.00
121 DD,CCu,DD&CCu(c),Secret Weapon of the Archer. 100.00
122 DD,CCu,DD&CCu(c),The Movie That Backfired 100.00
123 DD,CCu,DD&CCu(c),The Underseas Gold Fort 100.00
124 DD,CCu,DD&CCu(c),Thieves With A Thousand Faces 100.00
125 DD,CCu,DD&CCu(c),Secrets o/t Blackhawk Time Capsule. 100.00
126 DD,CCu,DD&CCu(c),Secret of the Glass Fort. 100.00
127 DD,CCu,DD&CCu(c),Blackie-The Winged Sky Fighter 100.00
128 DD,CCu,DD&CCu(c),The Vengeful Bowman. 100.00
129 DD,CCu,DD&CCu(c),The Cavemen From 3,000 B.C. . . 100.00
130 DD,CCu,DD&SMo(c),The Mystery Missle From Space . 100.00
131 DD,CCu,DD&CCu(c),The Return of the Rocketeers 75.00
132 DD,CCu,DD&CCu(c),Raid of the Rocketeers. 75.00
133 DD,CCu,DD&CCu(c),Human Dynamo 75.00
134 DD,CC,DD&CC(c),The Sinister Snowman 75.00
135 DD,CCu,DD&CCu(c),The

Blackhawk #247 © DC Comics Inc.

Underworld Supermarket 75.00
136 DD,CCu,DD&CCu(c),The Menace of the Smoke-Master. 75.00
137 DD,CCu,DD&CCu(c),The Weapons That Backfired. 75.00
138 DD,CCu,DD&SMo(c),The Menace of the Blob 75.00
139 DD,CCu,DD&CCu(c),The Secret Blackhawk. 75.00
140 DD,CCu,DD&CCu(c),The Space Age Marauders 75.00
141 DD,CCu,DD&CCu(c),Crimes of the Captive Masterminds . . 60.00
142 DD,CCu,DD&CCu(c),Alien Blackhawk Chief. 60.00
143 DD,SMo,DD&CCu(c),Lady Blackhawk's Rival. 60.00
144 DD,CCu,DD&CCu(c),The Underworld Sportsmen. 60.00
145 DD,CCu,DD&CCu(c),The Deadly Lensman 60.00
146 DD,CCu,DD&CCu(c),The Fantastic Fables of Blackhawk 60.00
147 DD,SMo,DD&CCu(c),The Blackhawk Movie Queen 60.00
148 DD,CCu,DD&CCu(c),Four Dooms For The Blackhawks. . 60.00
149 DD,CCu,DD&CCu(c),Masks of Doom 60.00
150 DD,CCu,DD&SMo(c), Blackhawk Mascot from Space 50.00
151 DD,CCu,DD&CCu(c),Lost City 50.00
152 DD,CCu,DD&SMo(c),Noah's Ark From Space. 50.00
153 DD,CCu,DD&SMo(c), Boomerang Master. 50.00
154 DD,CCu,DD&SMo(c),The Beast Time Forgot 50.00
155 DD,CCu,DD&CCu(c),Killer Shark's Land Armada. 50.00
156 DD,CCu,DD&SMo(c),Peril of the Plutonian Raider. 50.00
157 DD,CCu,DD&SMo(c),Secret of the Blackhawk Sphinx. 50.00
158 DD,CCu,DD&SMo(c),Bandit Birds From Space. 50.00
159 DD,CCu,DD&SMo(c),Master of the Puppet Men 50.00
160 DD,CCu,DD&CCu(c),The Phantom Spy 50.00
161 DD,SMo,DD&SMo(c),Lady Blackhawk's Crime Chief 50.00
162 DD,CCu,DD&CCu(c),The Invisible Blackhawk 50.00
163 DD,CCu,DD&SMo(c),

Fisherman of Crime 50.00
164 DD,O:Blackhawk retold 75.00
165 DD,V:League of Anti Blackhawks 30.00
166 DD,A:Lady Blackhawk 30.00
167 DD,The Blackhawk Bandits . . 30.00
168 DD,Blackhawk Time Travelers 25.00
169 DD,Sinister Hunts of Mr. Safari. 25.00
170 DD,A:Lady Blackhawk,V:Killer Shark. 25.00
171 DD,Secret of Alien Island. . . . 25.00
172 DD,Challenge of the GasMaster 20.00
173 DD,The Super Jungle Man. . . 20.00
174 DD,Andre's Impossible World 20.00
175 DD,The Creature with Blackhawk's Brain 20.00
176 DD,Stone Age Blackhawks . . 18.00
177 DD,Town that time Forgot . . . 18.00
178 DD,Return of the Scorpions . . 18.00
179 DD,Invisible Dr.Dunbar. 18.00
180 DD,Son of Blackhawk 18.00
181 DD,I:Tom Thumb Blackhawk . 20.00
182 DD,A:Lady Blackhawk 20.00
183 DD,V:Killer Shark. 20.00
184 DD,Island of Super Monkeys 20.00
185 DD,Last 7 days of the Blackhawks 20.00
186 DD,A:Lady Blackhawk 20.00
187 DD,V:Porcupine 20.00
188 DD,A:Lady Blackhawk 20.00
189 DD:O:rtd 20.00
190 DD,FantasticHumanStarfish . . 20.00
191 DD,A:Lady Blackhawk 20.00
192 DD,V:King Condor 15.00
193 DD,The Jailer's Revenge 15.00
194 DD,The Outlaw Blackhawk. . . 15.00
195 DD,A:Tom Thumb Blackhawk. 15.00
196 DD,Blackhawk WWII Combat Diary story 15.00
197 DD:new look 15.00
198 DD:O:rtd 20.00
199 DD,Attack with the Mummy Insects. 20.00
200 DD,A:Lady Blackhawk, I:Queen Killer Shark 20.00
201 DD,Blackhawk Detached Diary Story,F:Hendrickson 20.00
202 DD,Combat Diary,F:Andre . . . 20.00
203 DD:O:Chop-Chop. 20.00
204 DD,A:Queen Killer Shark 20.00
205 DD,Combat Diary story 20.00
206 DD,Combat Diary, F:Olaf 20.00
207 DD,Blackhawk Devil Dolls . . . 20.00
208 DD,Detached service diary F:Chuck. 20.00
209 DD,V:King Condor 20.00
210 DD,Danger..Blackhawk Bait rep.Blackhawk #139. . . . . 15.00
211 DD,GC,Detached service diary. 15.00
212 DD,Combat Diary, F:Chop-Chop 15.00
213 DD,Blackhawk goes Hollywood 15.00
214 DD,Team of Traitors. 15.00
215 DD,Detached service diary F:Olaf. 15.00
216 DD,A:Queen Killer Shark 15.00
217 DD,Detached service diary F:Stanislaus 15.00
218 DD,7 against Planet Peril. . . . 15.00
219 DD,El Blackhawk Peligroso . . 15.00
220 DD,The Revolt of the Assembled Man 15.00
221 DD,Detach service diary F:Hendrickson 15.00

Blackhawk 3rd Series
#11 © DC Comics, Inc.

222 DD,The Man from E=MC2 . . . 15.00
223 DD,V:Mr.Quick CHange 15.00
224 DD,Combat Diary,
   F:Stanislaus 15.00
225 DD,A:Queen Killer Shark 15.00
226 DD,Secret Monster of
   Blackhawk Island 15.00
227 DD,Detached Service diary
   F:Chop-Chop 15.00
228 DD (1st art on JLA characters)
   Blackhawks become super-heroes,
   Junk-Heap heroes #1(C:JLA) . . 18.00
229 DD,Junk-Heap Heroes #2
   (C:JLA). 15.00
230 DD,Junk-Heap Heroes concl.
   (C:JLA). 15.00
231 DD,A:Lady Blackhawk 15.00
232 DD,A:Lady Blackhawk 15.00
233 DD,Too Late,The Leaper 15.00
234 DD,The Terrible Twins 15.00
235 DD,A Coffin for
   a Blackhawk. 15.00
236 DD,Melt,Mutant, Melt 15.00
237 DD,Magnificent 7 Assassins. . 15.00
238 DD,Walking Booby-Traps. . . . 15.00
239 DD,The Killer That Time
   Forgot 15.00
240 DD,He Who Must Die. 15.00
241 DD,A Blackhawk a Day 15.00
242 Blackhawks back in blue &
   black costumes 15.00
243 Mission Incredible (1968) 15.00
244 GE,new costumes,Blackhawks
   become mercenaries (1976). . . 3.00
245 GE,Death's Double Deal 3.00
246 RE,GE,Death's Deadly Dawn. . 3.00
247 RE,AM,Operation:Over Kill. . . . 3.00
248 JSh,Vengeance is Mine!..
   Sayeth the Cyborg 3.00
249 RE,GE,V:Sky-Skull 3.00
250 RE,GE,FS,D:Chuck(1977) . . . 3.00
251 DSp,Back to WWII(1982). 3.00
252 thru 258 DSp . . . . @3.00
259 . . . . 3.00
260 HC,ATh 3.00
261 thru 271 DSp . . . . @3.00
272. . . . . 3.00
273 DSp. 3.00
274 DSp. 3.00

[2nd Series]
1 HC Mini-series,Blackhawk accused
   of communism 3.50
2 HC,visits Soviet Union 3.00

3 HC,Atom Bomb threat to N.Y. . . . 3.00
[3rd Series]
1 All in color for a Crime,pt.1
   I:The Real Lady Blackhawk . . . 1.50
2 All in color for a Crime,pt.2 . . . . . 1.50
3 Agent Rescue Attempt in Rome . 1.50
4 Blackhawk's girlfriend murdered . 1.50
5 I:Circus Organization 1.50
6 Blackhawks on false mission . . . 1.50
7 V:Circus,A:Suicide Squad, rep.
   1st Blackhawk story 2.50
8 Project: Assimilation 1.50
9 V:Grundfest 1.50
10 Blackhawks Attacked. 1.50
11 Master plan revealed 1.50
12 Raid on BlackhawkAirwaysHQ. . 1.75
13 Team Member Accused of 1.75
14 Blackhawk test pilots 1.75
15 Plans for independence 1.75
16 Independence, final issue 1.75
Ann.#1 Hawks in Albania 2.95
Spec.#1 Assassination of JFK
   to Saigon,1975. . . . . 3.50

BLACK HOOD
Impact 1991–92
1 O:Black Hood. 1.25
2 Nick Cray becomes Black Hood . 1.00
3 New Year's Eve,A:Creeptures. . . 1.00
4 Nate Cray become Black Hood,
   Dr.M.Harvey becomes Ozone. . 1.00
5 E:Nate Cray as Black Hood
   V:Ozone. 1.00
6 New Black Hood. 1.00
7 History of Seaside City 1.25
8 V:Hit Coffee 1.25
9 V:Hit Coffee 1.25
10 Slime of Your Life #1 . . . . 1.25
11 Slime of Your Life #2 . . . . 1.25
12 Final Issue. 1.25
Ann#1 Earthquest,w/trading card . 2.50

BLACK LAMB, THE
DC/Helix Sept. 1996
1 TT,Vampire saga 2.50
2 TT,war between werewolf clans . 2.50
3 TT,O:Black Lamb,V:Lykaon. 2.50
4 TT thru 6. . . . . @2.50

BLACK LIGHTNING
1977–78
1 TVE/FS,I&O:Black Lightning. . . . 3.50
2 TVE/FS,A:Talia. 2.50
3 TVE,I:Tobias Whale 2.50
4 TVE,A:Jimmy Olsen 2.50
5 TVE,A:Superman 2.50
6 TVE,I:Syonide 2.50
7 TVE,V:Syonide 2.50
8 TVE,V:Tobias Whale. 2.50
9 TVE,V:Annihilist 2.50
10 TVE,V:Trickster 2.50
11 TVE,BU:The Ray 3.00

[2nd Series] 1995–96
1 He's Back. 2.00
2 V:Painkiller. 2.00
3 V:Painkiller. 2.00
4 V:Painkiller,Royal Family. 2.00
5 Flashbacks of Past. 2.00
6 V:Gangbuster. 2.25
7 V:Gangbuster 2.25
8 V:Tobias Whale 2.25
9 I&V:Demolition 2.25
10 Jefferson Pierce becomes Black
   Lightning full time 2.25
11 Hunt for Sick Nick 2.25
12 V:Sick Nick's death squad 2.25
13 final issue 2.25

BLACK MASK
1993–94
1 I:Black Mask. 5.00
2 V:Underworld 5.00
3 V:Valentine 5.00

BLACK ORCHID
1993–95
1 DMc,O:Black Orchid,
   A:Batman,Luthor,Poison Ivy . . . 6.00
2 DMc,O:cont,Arkham Asylum. . . . 7.00
3 DMc,A:SwampThing,conc. 6.00
TPB rep. #1 thru #3 . . . . 20.00
Vertigo
1 DMc(c),B:DiF(s),JIT,SnW,I:Sherilyn
   Somers,I:Logos,F:Walt Brody . . 2.50
1a Platinum Ed. 12.00
2 JIT,SnW,Uprooting,V:Logos. . . . 2.25
3 JIT,SnW,Tainted Zone,
   V:Fungus 2.25
4 JIT,SnW,I:Nick & Orthia. 2.25
5 DMc(c),JIT,SnW,
   A:Swamp Thing 2.25
6 JIT,BMc(i),God in the Cage. 2.25
7 JIT,RGu,SnW,
   Upon the Threshold 2.25
8 DMc(c),RGu,A:Silent People. . . . 2.25
9 DMc(c),RGu 2.25
10 DMc(c),RGu 2.25
11 DMc(c),RGu,In Tennessee 2.25
12 DMc(c),RGu 2.25
13 DMc(c),RGu,F:Walt Brody 2.25
14 DMc(c),RGu,Black Annis 2.00
15 DMc(c),RGu,Kobolds. 2.00
16 DMc(c),RGu,Suzy,Junkin 2.00
17 Twisted Season,pt.1 . . . . 2.00
18 Twisted Season,pt.2 . . . . 2.00
19 Twisted Season,pt.3 . . . . 2.00
20 Twisted Season,pt.4 . . . . 2.00
21 Twisted Season,pt.5 . . . . 2.00
22 Twisted Season,pt.6, final iss. . . 2.25
Ann.#1 DMc(c),DiF(s),GyA,JnM,F:Suzy,
   Childrens Crusade,BU:retells
   Adventure Comics#430 . . . . . . 4.25

BLASTERS SPECIAL
1989
1 A:Snapper Carr, Spider Guild . . . 2.00

Black Orchid #1 © DC Comics, Inc.

BLOOD: A TALE
DC/Vertigo Sept. 1996
[Mini-series, re-release of Marvel Epic]
1 JMD(s),KW, quest for truth begins 3.00
2 JMD(s),KW, Blood falls in love . . 3.00
3 JMD(s),KW, companion dies. . . . 3.00
4 JMD(s),KW, finale. 3.00

BLOOD & SHADOWS
(Vertigo) 1996
1 . . . . 6.00
2 Journal of Justice Jones 6.00
3 Chet Daley flung into 21st century 6.00
4 V:God of the Razor, finale. 6.00

BLOODBATH
1993
1 A:Superman. 3.75
2 A:New Heroes 3.75

BLOODPACK
[Mini-Series] 1995
1 I:Blood Pack, V:Demolition 1.50
2 A:Superboy 1.50
3 Loira's Corpse 1.50
4 Real Heroes Final Issue 1.50

BLOOD SYNDICATE
(Milestone) 1993–96
1 I:Blood Syndicate,Rob Chaplick, Dir.Mark.Ed.,w/B puzzle piece, Skybox card,Poster 3.50
1a Newstand Ed. 2.00
2 I:Boogieman,Tech-9 Vs. Holocaust. 1.75
3 V:S.Y.S.T.E.M.,I:Mom,D:Tech-9 . . 1.75
4 V:S.Y.S.T.E.M. 1.75
5 I:John Wing,Kwai,Demon Fox. . . 1.75
6 V:John Wing. 1.75
7 I:Edmund,Cornelia 1.75
8 V:Demon Fox 1.75
9 O:Blood Syndicate,I:Templo 1.75
10 WS(c),Ccs,Shadow War,I:Iota, Sideshow,Rainsaw,Slag,Ash, Bad Betty,Oro. 2.25
11 IV(s),Ccs,A:Aquamaria. 1.75
12 IV(s),Ccs,V:Dinosaur 1.75
13 IV(s),Ccs,B:Roach War 1.75
14 IV(s),Ccs,V:Roaches 1.75
15 IV(s),Ccs,E:Roach War 1.75
16 IV(s),Ccs,Worlds Collide#6, A:Superman. 1.75
17 Ccs,Worlds Collide#13,V:Rift . . . 1.75
18 Ccs,V:S.Y.S.T.E.M. 1.75
19 . . . . 1.75
20 . . . . 1.75
21 . . . . 1.75
22 . . . . 1.75
23 F:Boogieman. 1.75
24 L:Third Rail,Brickhouse 1.75
25 R:Tech-9 . . . . 2.95
26 Return of the Dead 1.75
27 R:Masquerade. 1.75
28 Tech-9 takes control. 2.50
29 Reader's Choice 1.00
30 Long Hot Summer 2.50
31 V:New Threat 2.50
32 MC(c),V:Soulbreaker 2.50
33 Kwai returns to paris Island 1.00
34 Visit to Kwen Lun 2.50
35 final issue 3.50

BLOODY MARY
DC/Helix Aug. 1996
1 (of 4) GEn(s),CE, near-future war. 2.25
2 thru 4 GEn(s),CE, near-future war, concl. . . . . @2.25

BLOODY MARY: LADY LIBERTY
DC/Helix July 1996
1 (of 4) GEn(s),CE, ... 2.50
2 GEn(s),CE,V:Achilles Seagal . . . 2.50
3 GEn(s),CE,V:Vatman 2.50
4 GEn(s),CE,V:Vatman, concl. 2.50

Blue Beetle #14 © DC Comics Inc.

BLUE BEETLE
1986–88
1 O:Blue Beetle 1.50
2 V:Fire Fist. 1.00
3 V:Madmen 1.00
4 V:Doctor Alchemy. 1.00
5 A:Question 1.00
6 V:Question 1.00
7 A:Question 1.00
8 A:Chronos 1.00
9 A:Chronos 1.00
10 Legends, V:Chronos 1.00
11 A:New Teen Titans. 1.00
12 A:New Teen Titans. 1.00
13 A:New Teen Titans. 1.00
14 Pago Island,I:Catalyst 1.00
15 RA:V:Carapax 1.00
16 RA,Chicago Murders 1.00
17 R:Dan Garrett/Blue Beetle 1.00
18 D:Dan Garrett 1.00
19 RA,R:Dr. Cyber 1.00
20 RA,Millennium,A:JLI. 1.00
21 RA,A:Mr.Miracle, Millennium tie in 1.00
22 RA,Prehistoric Chicago 1.00
23 DH,V:The Madmen 1.00
24 DH,final issue 1.00

BLUE DEVIL
1984–86
1 O:Blue Devil 2.00
2 . . . . 1.50
3 A:Superman. 1.50
4 A:JLA. 1.50

5 . . . . 1.50
6 EC,I:Bolt. 1.00
7 KG 1.00
8 GV 1.00
9 thru 16 . . . . @1.00
17 Crisis. 1.25
18 Crisis. 1.25
19 . . . . 1.00
20 RM,Halloween. 1.00
21 RM,I:Roadmaster. 1.00
22 RM,A:Jorj & Lehni 1.00
23 A:Jorj & Lehni 1.00
24 V:Blue Devil Toys. 1.00
25 Mary Frances Cassidy 1.00
26 Special Baseball issue. 1.00
27 Godfrey Goose 1.00
28 real live fan guest star 1.00
29 . . . . 1.00
30 Double sized 1.25
31 BSz,V:Seraph 1.25
Ann.#1 . . . . 1.50

BOB, THE GALACTIC BUM
[Mini-Series] 1995
1 A:Lobo 2.00
2 Planet Gnulp,A:Lobo. 2.00
3 V:Khunds 2.00
4 Rando's Coronation 2.00

BOGIE MAN, THE
DC/Paradox/Pocket (April 1998)
TPB 6"x8" AIG,b&w 14.00

BOMBA, THE JUNGLE BOY
1967–68
1 CI,MA,I:Bomba 15.00
2 thru 7 . . . . @10.00

BOOK OF FATE, THE
1 KG(s),RoW,BR, ... 2.25
2 KG(s),RoW,BR,"The Chaos-Order War," pt.1 (of 4) 2.25
3 KG(s),RoW,BR,"The Chaos-Order War," pt.2 . . . . 2.25
4 KG(s),RoW,BR,"The Chaos-Order War," pt.3, A:Two-Face . . 2.25
5 KG(s),RoW,BR,"The Chaos-Order War," pt.4 . . . . 2.25
6 KG(s),RoW,BR,Convergence," pt.1 x-over 2.25
7 KG(s),RoW,BR, Signs, pt.1 . . . . . 2.25
8 KG(s),RoW,BR, Signs, pt.2 . . . . . 2.25
9 KG,AIG,BR,Signs, pt.3 . . . . 2.50
10 KG,AIG,BR,Signs,pt.4 . . . . 2.50
11 KG,AIG, in a Swiss Jail 2.50
12 AIG,KG,F:Lobo, final issue. 2.50

BOOKS OF FAERIE, THE
DC/Vertigo Jan. 1997
1 PrG,F:Titania and Auberon 2.50
2 PrG, ... 2.50
3 (of 3) PrG 2.50
TPB 15.00

BOOKS OF FAERIE, THE: AUBERON'S TALE
DC/Vertigo June 1998
1 (of 3) PrG,VcL,F:Early life of King Auberon 2.50
2 PrG,VcL, early life 2.50
3 PrG,VcL, early life, concl. 2.50
TPB Books of Faerie 15.00

DC COMICS

BOOKS OF FAERIE, THE: MOLLY'S STORY
DC/Vertigo 1999
1 (of 4) JNR(s) 2.50
2 CV(c) 2.50

BOOKS OF MAGIC
[Limited Series] 1990–91
1 B:NGa(s),JBo,F:Phantom Stranger,
  A:J.Constantine,Tim Hunter,
  Doctor Occult,Mister E 10.00
2 SHp,F:J.Constantine,A:Spectre,
  Dr.Fate,Demon,Zatanna 10.00
3 CV,F:Doctor Occult,
  A:Sandman 9.00
4 E:NGa(s),PuJ,F:Mr.E,A:Death . . . 9.00
TPB rep.#1-#4 . . . . 20.00

[Regular Series]
Vertigo 1994–97
1 MkB,B:Bindings,R:Tim Hunter . . . 5.00
1a Platinum Edition 9.00
2 CV(c),MkB,V:Manticore 4.00
3 CV(c),MkB,E:Bindings 4.00
4 CV(c),MkB,A:Death 5.00
5 CV(c),I:Khara 3.00
6 Sacrifices,pt.I 3.00
7 Sacrifices,pt.II 3.00
8 Tim vs. evil Tim 3.00
9 Artificial Heart,pt.1 . . . . 2.50
10 Artificial Heart,pt.2 . . . . 2.50
11 Artificial Heart,pt.3 . . . . 2.50
12 Small Glass Worlds,pt.1 . . . . . . 2.50
13 Small Glass Worlds,pt.2 . . . . . . 2.50
14 CV(c),A:The Wobbly 2.50
15 Hell and Back,pt.1 . . . . 2.50
16 Hall and Back,pt.2 . . . . 2.50
17 Playgrounds,pt.1 . . . . 2.50
18 JNR,PrG,Playgrounds,cont. 2.50
19 JNR,PrG,Playgrounds,concl. . . . 2.50
20 Barabatos gives the orders 2.50
21 JNR,PrG,Molly seeks Mayra . . . 2.50
22 . . . . 2.50
23 JNR,V:Margraves Strafenkinder . 2.50
24 JNR,PrG,F:Molly vs. Amadan . . 2.50
25 JNR,PrG,Death and the Endless 2.50
26 JNR,PrG,Rites of Passage, pt.1 . 2.50
27 JNR,PrG,Rites of Passage, pt.2 . 2.50
28 JNR,PrG,Rites of Passage, pt.3,
  Cupid & Psyche 2.50
29 JNR,PrG,"Rite of Passage" 2.50
30 JNR,PrG,"Rite of Passage" 2.50
31 JNR,PrG,"Rite of Passage" 2.50
32 JNR(s),PSj,"Rites of Passage" . . 2.50
33 JNR(s),PSj,"Rites of Passage" . . 2.50
34 JNR(s),PSj,"Rites of Passage" . . 2.50
35 JNR(s),PrG,"Rites of Passage" . . 2.50
36 JNR,"Rites of Passage" cont . . . 2.50
37 JNR, "Rites of Passage" cont. . . 2.50
38 JNR,"Rites of Passage" concl. . . 2.50
39 PrG, at Sphinx casino 2.50
40 JNR(s),F:Tim & Molly 2.50
41 JNR(s),V:Gargoyles 2.50
42 JNR(s),JIT,magical havok. 2.50
43 JNR(s),PrG,F:The Wobbly 2.50
44 JNR(s),goodbye to Zatanna 2.50
45 JNR(s) Slave of Heavens, pt.1 . . 2.50
46 JNR(s) Slave of Heavens, pt.2 . . 2.50
47 JNR(s) Slave of Heavens, pt.3 . . 2.50
48 JNR(s) Slave of Heavens, pt.4 . . 2.50
49 JNR(s) Slave of Heavens, pt.5 . . 2.50
50 JNR(s) Slave of Heavens, pt.6 . . 2.50
51 PrG,MK,an Opener 2.50
52 PrG,MK,Homecoming 2.50
54 PrG,MK,V:Thomas. 2.50
55 PrG,MK,Coming of the Other . . . 2.50
56 PrG,MK,Last Molly Story 2.50
57 PrG,MK,after car crash 2.50
58 PrG,MK,The Other. 2.50

59 PrG,MK,The Other. 2.50
60 PrG,MK,The Other. 2.50
61 PrG,MK(c),The Other, concl. . . . 2.50
62 PrG,MK(c),crossroads 2.50
63 GyA,MK(c), ... 2.50
64 PrG,MK(c),Wild Hunt 2.50
65 PrG,MK,new life cont. 2.50
Ann.#2 JNR(s) Minotaur 4.00
Ann.#3 PrG 4.00
TPB Rep. #5-#13 & Rave #1 . . . 12.95
TPB Reckonings, 192pg.
  rep. #14–#20 . . . . 12.95
TPB rep mini-series 20.00
TPB Bindings, GyA,PrG,WK 13.00
TPB Transformations PrG,MK. . . . 13.00
TPB The Books of Magic 20.00
TPB Girl in the Box 15.00

Booster Gold #24 © DC Comics, Inc.

BOOSTER GOLD
1986–88
1 DJ,V:Blackguard 2.00
2 DJ,V:Minddancer 1.50
3 DJ,V:Minddancer 1.50
4 DJ,V:Minddancer 1.50
5 DJ,V:Fascinator 1.50
6 DJ,A:Superman 1.00
7 DJ,A:Superman 1.00
8 DJ,A:Braniac 5,Cham.Boy,
  Ultra Boy,pt.1 . . . . 1.25
9 DJ,A:Braniac 5,Cham.Boy,
  Ultra Boy,pt.2 . . . . 1.25
10 DJ,V:1000 . . . . 1.00
11 DJ,V:Shockwave 1.00
12 DJ,Booster Weakening 1.00
13 DJ,I:Rip Hunter(modern) 1.00
14 DJ,Rip Hunter 1.00
15 DJ,Rip Hunter 1.00
16 DJ,Boosters new company 1.00
17 DJ,A:Cheshire & Hawk 1.00
18 DJ,V:Broderick. 1.00
19 DJ,V:Rainbow Raider. 1.00
20 DJ,V:Rainbow Raider. 1.00
21 DJ,Goldstar captured by aliens . 1.00
22 DJ,A:J.L.I.,D:Goldstar 1.00
23 DJ,A:Superman & Luthor 1.25
24 DJ,Millenium 1.00
25 DJ,last issue 1.00

BOY COMMANDOS
Winter, 1942–43
1 S&K,O:Liberty Belle;Sandman
  & Newsboy Legion 4,500.00
2 S&K. 1,200.00

3 S&K 800.00
4 . . . . 600.00
5 . . . . 600.00
6 S&K 550.00
7 S&K 400.00
8 S&K 400.00
9 . . . . 400.00
10 S&K. 400.00
11 Infinity(c) 400.00
12 thru 16 . . . . @200.00
17 Science Fiction(c) 225.00
18 . . . . 200.00
19 . . . . 200.00
20. . . . . 225.00
21 . . . . 150.00
22 . . . . 150.00
23 S&K,S&K,(c) 175.00
24 . . . . 160.00
25 . . . . 160.00
26 Science Fiction(c) 200.00
27 . . . . 150.00
28 . . . . 150.00
29 S&K story 160.00
30 Baseball Storm 160.00
31 . . . . 150.00
32 A:Dale Evans(c). 160.00
33 . . . . 150.00
34 I:Wolf. 150.00
35 . . . . 150.00
36 Nov.–Dec., 1949 . . . . 225.00

BRAVE AND THE BOLD
Aug.–Sept., 1955
1 JKu,RH,IN,I:VikingPrince,Golden
  Gladiator,Silent Knight 2,800.00
2 F:Viking Prince 1,200.00
3 F:Viking Prince 650.00
4 F:Viking Prince 650.00
5 B:Robin Hood 700.00
6 JKu,F:Robin Hood,E:Golden
  Gladiator 450.00
7 JKu,F:Robin Hood 450.00
8 JKu,F:Robin Hood 450.00
9 JKu,F:Robin Hood 450.00
10 JKu,F:Robin Hood 450.00
11 JKu,F:Viking Prince 350.00
12 JKu,F:Viking Prince 350.00
13 JKu,F:Viking Prince 350.00
14 JKu,F:Viking Prince 325.00
15 JKu,F:Viking Prince 325.00
16 JKu,F:Viking Prince 325.00
17 JKu,F:Viking Prince 325.00
18 JKu,F:Viking Prince 325.00

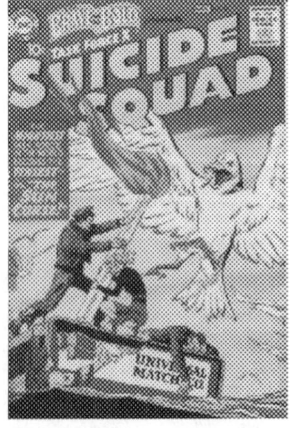

Brave and the Bold #26
© DC Comics, Inc.

19 JKu,F:Viking Prince 325.00	
20 JKu,F:Viking Prince 325.00	
21 JKu,F:Viking Prince 325.00	
22 JKu,F:Viking Prince 325.00	
23 JKu,O:Viking Prince 450.00	
24 JKu,E:Viking Prince,Silent	
Knight. 325.00	
25 RA,I&B:Suicide Squad 400.00	
26 F:Suicide Squad 350.00	
27 Creature of Ghost Lake 325.00	
28 I:Justice League of	
America,O:Snapper Carr . . 5,500.00	
29 F:Justice League. 2,400.00	
30 F:Justice League. 2,000.00	
31 F:Cave Carson 350.00	
32 F:Cave Carson 250.00	
33 F:Cave Carson 250.00	
34 JKu,I&O:S.A. Hawkman . . . 2,000.00	
35 JKu:F:Hawkman 500.00	
36 JKu:F:Hawkman 500.00	
37 F:Suicide Squad 400.00	
38 F:Suicide Squad 225.00	
39 F:Suicide Squad 225.00	
40 JKu,F:Cave Carson 150.00	
41 F:Cave Carson 150.00	
42 JKu,F:Hawkman 300.00	
43 JKu,O:Hawkman 350.00	
44 JKu,F:Hawkman 250.00	
45 CI,F:Strange Sports 75.00	
46 CI,F:Strange Sports 75.00	
47 CI,F:Strange Sports 75.00	
48 CI,F:Strange Sports 75.00	
49 CI,F:Strange Sports 75.00	
50 F:GreenArrow & JonnJ'onzz. . 175.00	
51 F:Aquaman & Hawkman 250.00	
52 JKu,F:Sgt.Rock 150.00	
53 ATh,F:Atom & Flash. 75.00	
54 I&O:Teen Titans. 275.00	
55 F:Metal Man & Atom 50.00	
56 F:Flash & J'onn J'onzz. 50.00	
57 I&O:Metamorpho 150.00	
58 F:Metamorpho 75.00	
59 F:Batman & Green Lantern . . 100.00	
60 A:Teen Titans,I:Wonder Girl . . 100.00	
61 MA,O:Starman,BlackCanary. . 125.00	
62 MA,O:Starman,BlackCanary. . 125.00	
63 F:Supergirl&WonderWoman. . . 40.00	
64 F:Batman,V:Eclipso 60.00	
65 DG,FMc,F:Flash & Doom	
Patrol. 25.00	
66 F:Metamorpho & Metal Men. . . 25.00	
67 CI,F:Batman & Flash 50.00	
68 F:Batman,Metamorpho,Joker,	
Riddler,Penguin 65.00	
69 F:Batman & Green Lantern . . . 32.00	
70 F:Batman & Hawkman. 32.00	
71 F:Batman & Green Arrow. 32.00	
72 CI,F:Spectre & Flash 40.00	
73 F:Aquaman & Atom 30.00	
74 B:Batman T.U.,A:Metal Men. . . 30.00	
75 F:Spectre. 30.00	
76 F:Plastic Man. 30.00	
77 F:Atom 30.00	
78 F:Wonder Woman 30.00	
79 NA,F:Deadman 60.00	
80 NA,DG,F:Creeper 45.00	
81 NA,F:Flash 45.00	
82 NA,F:Aquaman,O:Ocean	
Master 45.00	
83 NA,F:Teen Titans. 50.00	
84 NA,F:Sgt.Rock. 45.00	
85 NA,F:Green Arrow 45.00	
86 NA,F:Deadman 45.00	
87 F:Wonder Woman 25.00	
88 F:Wildcat 25.00	
89 RA,F:Phantom Stranger. 25.00	
90 F:Adam Strange 25.00	
91 F:Black Canary 25.00	
92 F:Bat Squad 25.00	
93 NA,House of Mystery. 45.00	
94 NC,F:Teen Titans. 18.00	

Brave and the Bold #149
© DC Comics Inc.

95 F:Plastic Man. 15.00	
96 F:Sgt.Rock. 15.00	
97 NC(i),F:Wildcat 15.00	
98 JAp,F:Phantom Stranger 15.00	
99 NC,F:Flash 15.00	
100 NA,F:Green Arrow. 40.00	
101 JA,F:Metamorpho 10.00	
102 NA,JA,F:Teen Titans 12.00	
103 FMc,F:Metal Men. 7.00	
104 JAp,F:Deadman. 7.00	
105 JAp,F:Wonder Woman 7.00	
106 JAp,F:Green Arrow 7.00	
107 JAp,F:Black Canary 7.00	
108 JAp,F:Sgt.Rock 7.00	
109 JAp,F:Demon. 7.00	
110 JAp,F:Wildcat. 7.00	
111 JAp,F:Joker 12.50	
112 JAp,F:Mr.Miracle. 15.00	
113 JAp,F:Metal Men 15.00	
114 JAp,F:Aquaman 15.00	
115 JAp,O:Viking Prince 15.00	
116 JAp,F:Spectre 15.00	
117 JAp,F:Sgt.Rock 15.00	
118 JAp,F:Wildcat,V:Joker 16.00	
119 JAp,F:Man-Bat. 6.00	
120 JAp,F:Kamandi 6.00	
121 JAp,F:Metal Men 6.00	
122 JAp,F:Swamp Thing. 6.00	
123 JAp,F:Plastic Man. 6.00	
124 JAp,F:Sgt.Rock 6.00	
125 JAp,F:Flash 6.00	
126 JAp,F:Aquaman 6.00	
127 JAp,F:Wildcat 6.00	
128 JAp,F:Mr.Miracle 6.00	
129 F:Green Arrow,V:Joker 13.00	
130 F:Green Arrow,V:Joker 13.00	
131 JAp,F:WonderWoman,	
A:Catwoman 8.00	
132 JAp,F:King Fu Foom 5.00	
133 JAp,F:Deadman. 5.00	
134 JAp,F:Green Lantern 5.00	
135 JAp,F:Metal Men 5.00	
136 JAp,F:Metal Men,Green Arr.. . . 5.00	
137 F:Demon 5.00	
138 JAp,F:Mr.Miracle 5.00	
139 JAp,F:Hawkman 5.00	
140 JAp,F:Wonder Woman. 5.00	
141 JAp,F:Bl.Canary,A:Joker . . . 12.00	
142 JAp,F:Aquaman 4.00	
143 O:Human Target 4.00	
144 JAp,F:Green Arrow 4.00	
145 JAp,F:Phantom Stranger 4.00	
146 JAp,F:E-2 Batman 4.00	

147 JAp,A:Supergirl 4.00	
148 JSon,JAp,F:Plastic Man. 4.00	
149 JAp,F:Teen Titans 4.50	
150 JAp,F:Superman 4.00	
151 JAp,F:Flash 4.50	
152 JAp,F:Atom 4.00	
153 DN,F:Red Tornado. 4.00	
154 JAp,F:Metamorpho 4.00	
155 JAp,F:Green Lantern 4.00	
156 DN,F:Dr.Fate 4.00	
157 JAp,F:Kamandi 4.00	
158 JAp,F:Wonder Woman. 4.00	
159 JAp,A:Ras al Ghul 4.00	
160 JAp,F:Supergirl 4.00	
161 JAp,F:Adam Strange 4.00	
162 JAp,F:Sgt.Rock 4.00	
163 DG,F:Black Lightning 4.00	
164 JL,F:Hawkman. 4.00	
165 DN,F:Man-bat 4.00	
166 DG,TA,DSp,F:Black Canary	
A:Penguin,I:Nemesis 4.00	
167 DC,DA,F:Blackhawk 4.00	
168 JAp,DSp,F:Green Arrow 4.25	
169 JAp,DSp,F:Zatanna 4.00	
170 JA,F:Nemesis 4.00	
171 JL,DSp,V:Scalphunter 4.00	
172 CI,F:Firestorm 4.00	
173 JAp,F:Guardians 4.00	
174 JAp,F:Green Lantern 4.00	
175 JAp,A:Lois Lane 4.00	
176 JAp,F:Swamp Thing. 4.00	
177 JAp,F:Elongated Man 4.00	
178 JAp,F:Creeper 4.00	
179 EC,F:Legion o/Superheroes. . . 4.00	
180 JAp,F:Spectre,Nemesis 4.00	
181 JAp,F:Hawk & Dove. 4.00	
182 JAp,F:E-2 Robin 4.00	
183 CI,V:Riddler. 4.50	
184 JAp,A:Catwoman. 5.00	
185 F:Green Arrow. 4.25	
186 JAp,F:Hawkman 4.00	
187 JAp,F:Metal Men 4.00	
188 JAp,F:Rose & Thorn 4.00	
189 JAp,A:Thorn 4.00	
190 JAp,F:Adam Strange 4.00	
191 JAp,V:Joker,Penguin 9.00	
192 JAp,F:Superboy. 4.00	
193 JAp,D:Nemesis 4.00	
194 CI,F:Flash 4.00	
195 JA,I:Vampire 4.00	
196 JAp,F:Ragman. 4.00	
197 JSon,W:Earth II Batman &	
Catwoman 5.00	
198 F:Karate Kid 4.00	
199 RA,F:Spectre. 4.00	
200 DGb,JAp,A:Earth-2 Batman,I:	
Outsiders (GeoForce,Katana,Halo),	
E:Batman T.U.,final issue 12.00	

[Limited Series]

1 SAP,Green Arrow/Butcher T.U. . . 2.00	
2 SAP,A:Black Canary,Question. . . 2.00	
3 SAP,Green Arrow/Butcher. 2.00	
4 SAP,GA on Trial;A:Black	
Canary 2.00	
5 SAP,V:Native Canadians,I.R.A.. . 2.00	

BREATHTAKER
1990

1 I:Breathtaker(Chase Darrow) . . . 6.00	
2 Chase Darrow captured 6.00	
3 O:Breathtaker. 6.00	
4 V:The Man, final issue 4.95	
TPB Breathtaker. 15.00	

BRAINBANX
DC/Helix Jan. 1997

1 ELe(s),"Down Upon the	
Darkness" 2.50	
2 ELe(s),Anna flees to the Sheol . . 2.50	

All comics prices listed are for *Near Mint* condition.

3 Ele(s),Anna stranded 2.50
4 ELe(s),Anna & Logan 2.50
5 ELe(s),"To Enter the Kingdom" . . 2.50
6 (of 6) 2.50

BROTHER POWER, THE GEEK
Sept.–Oct., 1968

1 . . . . 45.00
2 Nov.–Dec., 1968 . . . . 25.00

BUGS BUNNY
1990

1 A:Bugs,Daffy,Search for Fudd
　Statues 1.00
2 Search for Statues cont.
　V:WitchHazel 1.00
3 Bugs&Co.in outer space, final . . . 1.50

Butcher #1 © DC Comics, Inc.

BUTCHER, THE
[Limited Series] 1990

1 MB,I:John Butcher 3.50
2 MB,in San Francisco 3.00
3 MB,V:Corporation 3.00
4 MB,A:Green Arrow 2.50
5 MB,A:Corvus,final issue 2.25

BUZZY
1944–58

1 . . . . 165.00
2 . . . . 75.00
3 thru 5 . . . . @40.00
6 thru 10 . . . . @35.00
11 thru 15 . . . . @25.00
16 thru 25 . . . . @25.00
26 thru 35 . . . . @20.00
36 thru 45 . . . . @15.00
46 thru 77 . . . . @15.00

CAMELOT 3000
Dec., 1982

1 BB,O:Arthur,Merlin 3.50
2 BB,A:Morgan LeFay 3.00
3 BB,J:New Knights 3.00
4 BB,V:McAllister 3.00
5 BB,O:Morgan Le Fay 3.00
6 BB,TA,W:Arthur 3.00
7 BB,TA,R:Isolde 3.00

8 BB,TA,D:Sir Kay 3.00
9 BB,TA,L:Sir Percival 3.00
10 BB,TA,V:Morgan Le Fay 3.00
11 BB,TA,V:Morgan Le Fay 3.00
12 BB,TA,D:Arthur 3.00

CAPTAIN ACTION
[Based on toy] Oct.–Nov., 1968

1 WW,I:Captain Action,Action
　Boy,A:Superman 90.00
2 GK,WW, V:Krellik 40.00
3 GK,I:Dr.Evil 40.00
4 GK,A:Dr.Evil 40.00
5 GK,WW,A:Matthew Blackwell,
　last issue 40.00

CAPTAIN ATOM
March, 1987

1 PB,O:Captain Atom 2.50
2 PB,C:Batman 2.00
3 PB,O:Captain Atom 1.75
4 PB,A:Firestorm 1.75
5 PB,A:Firestorm 1.75
6 PB,Dr.Spectro 1.75
7 R:Plastique 1.75
8 PB,Capt.Atom/Plastique 1.75
9 V:Bolt 1.75
10 PB,A:JLI 2.00
11 PB,A:Firestorm 1.50
12 PB,I:Major Force 1.50
13 PB,Christmas issue 1.50
14 PB,A:Nightshade 1.50
15 PB,Dr.Spectro, Major Force . . . 1.50
16 PB,A:JLI,V:Red Tornado 1.75
17 V:Red Tornado;A:Swamp
　Thing,JLI 1.75
18 PB,A:Major Force 1.50
19 PB,Drug War 1.50
20 FMc,BlueBeetle 1.50
21 PB,A:Plastique,Nightshade . . . 1.50
22 PB,A:MaxLord,Nightshade,
　Plastique 1.50
23 PB,V:The Ghost 1.50
24 PB,Invasion X-over 1.50
25 PB,Invvasion X-over 1.50
26 A:JLA,Top Secret,pt.1 . . . . 1.75
27 A:JLA,Top Secret,pt.2 . . . . 1.75
28 V:Ghost, Top Secret,pt.3 . . . . . 1.50
29 RT,Captain Atom cleared
　(new direction) 1.50
30 Janus Directive #11,V:Black
　Manta 1.50
31 RT,Capt.Atom's Powers,
　A:Rocket Red 1.50
32 Loses Powers 1.50
33 A:Batman 2.00
34 C:JLE 1.50
35 RT,Secret o/t Silver Shield,
　A:Major Force 1.50
36 RT,Las Vegas Battle,A:Major
　Force 1.50
37 I:New Atomic Skull 1.25
38 RT,A:Red Tornado,
　Black Racer 1.25
39 RT,A:Red Tornado 1.25
40 RT,V:Kobra 1.25
41 RT,A:Black Racer,
　Red Tornado 1.25
42 RT,A:Phantom Stranger,Red
　Tornado,Black Racer,
　Death from Sandman 1.25
43 RT,V:Nekron 1.25
44 RT,V:Plastique 1.25
45 RT,A:The Ghost,I:Ironfire 1.25
46 RT,A:Superman 1.25
47 RT,A:SupermanV:Ghost 1.25
48 RT,R:Red Tornado 1.25
49 RT,Plastique on trial 1.25
50 RT,V:The Ghost,DoubleSize . . . 2.50

Caption Atom #41 © DC Comics, Inc.

51 RT 1.25
52 RT,Terror on RTE.91' 1.25
53 RT,A:Aquaman 1.25
54 RT,A:Rasputin,Shadowstorm . . . 1.25
55 RT,Inside Quantum Field 1.25
56 RT,Quantum Field cont. 1.25
57 RT,V:ShadowStorm,
　Quantum.Field 1.25
Ann.#1 I:Maj.Force 1.50
Ann.#2 A:RocketRed,Maj.Force . . . 1.50

CAPTAIN CARROT
March, 1982

1 RA,A:Superman,Starro 1.25
2 AA 1.00
3 thru 19 . . . . @1.00
20 A:Changeling,Nov., 1983 . . . . . 1.00

CAPTAIN STORM
May-June, 1964

1 IN(c),Killer Hunt 35.00
2 IN(c),First Shot-Last Shot 20.00
3 JKu,Death of a PT Boat 20.00
4 IN(c),First Command-Last
　Command 20.00
5 IN(c), Killer Torpedo 20.00
6 JKu,IN(c),Medals For An Ocean 20.00
7 IN(c),A Bullet For The General . 20.00
8 IN(c),Death of A Sub 20.00
9 IN(c),Sink That Flattop 20.00
10 IN(c),Only The Last Man Lives. 20.00
11 IN(c),Ride a Hot Torpedo 20.00
12 JKu(c),T.N.T. Tea Party Abroad
　PT 47 . . . . 20.00
13 JKu,Yankee Banzai 20.00
14 RH(c),Sink Capt. Storm 20.00
15 IN(c),My Enemy-My Friend . . . 20.00
16 IN(c),Battle of the Stinging
　Mosquito 20.00
17 IN(c),First Shot for a
　Dead Man 20.00
18 March-April, 1967 . . . . 20.00

CARTOON NETWORK PRESENTS
Warner Bros./DC June 1997

1: Dexter's Laboratory 1.75
2: Space Ghost coast-to-coast . . . 1.75
3 Cartoon All-Stars 2.00
4 Dial `M' for Monkey 2.00
5 Birdman 2.00

6 Cow and Chicken 2.00
7 Wacky Racers 2.00
8 . . . . 2.00
9 Toonami 2.00
10 Cow and Chicken 2.00
11 Wacky Races. 2.00
12 Cartoon All-Stars 2.00
13 Toonami 2.00
14 Cow and Chicken 2.00
15 Wacky Races 2.00
16 Top Cat 2.00
17 Toonami 2.00
18 Cartoon All-Stars 2.00
19 Cow & Chicken 2.00
20 Secret Squirrel, Atom Ant 2.00
21 Toonami 2.00
22 Quick Draw McGraw 2.00
23 Jabberjaws 2.00
24 Scrappy Doo, final issue 2.00

CARTOON NETWORK STARRING
Warner Bros./DC 1999
1 F:Powerpuff Girls 2.00
2 F:Jonny Bravo 2.00

CATWOMAN
[Limited Series] 1989
1 O:Catwoman 6.00
2 Catwoman'sSister kidnapped . . . 5.00
3 Battle 3.00
4 Final,V:Batman 3.00
[Regular Series] 1993–97
0 JBa,O:Catwoman 1.50
1 B:JDy(s),JBa,DG,A:Bane 5.00
2 JBa,DG,A:Bane 3.00
3 JBa,DG,at Santa Prisca 2.75
4 JBa,DG,Bane's Secret 2.50
5 JBa,V:Ninjas. 2.25
6 JBa,A:Batman 2.25
7 JBa,A:Batman 2.25
8 JBa,V:Zephyr 2.25
9 JBa,V:Zephyr 2.25
10 JBa,V:Arms Dealer 2.25
11 JBa 2.25
12 JBa,Knights End #6,A:Batman. . 5.00
13 JBa,Knights End,Aftermath#2 . . 2.00
14 JBa,Zero Hour 2.00
15 JBa,new path. 2.00
16 JBa,Island forterss. 2.00
17 . . . . 2.00
18 . . . . 2.00
19 Amazonia 2.00
20 Hollywood 2.00
21 JBa(c&a)V:Movie Monster
   [new Miraweb format begins] . . 2.00
22 JBa(c&a) Family Ties,pt.1 . . . . . 2.00
23 Family Ties,pt.2 . . . . 2.00
24 . . . . 2.00
25 A:Robin,Psyba-Rats. 2.50
26 AIG,JBa,The Secret of the
   Universe,pt.2 (of 3). 2.00
27 CDi,Underworld Unleashed tie-in 2.00
28 CDi,Catwoman enlists help 2.00
29 CDi,A:Penguin. 2.00
30 . . . . 2.00
31 . . . . 3.00
32 CDi,JBa,Contagion,pt.9 . . . . . . 3.00
33 CDi,JBa,Hellhound,pt.1 . . . . . . 2.00
34 CDi,JBa,Hellhound,pt.2 (of 3). . 2.00
35 CDi,JBa. 2.50
36 CDi,JBa, Legacy, pt.2 x-over . . . 2.00
37 CDi,JBa, Panara, the Leopard
   Woman 2.00
38 DgM(s),JBa,MPn,"Catwoman,
   Year One," pt.1 (of 3) 2.00
39 DgM(s),JBa,MPn,"Catwoman,
   Year One," pt. 2 . . . . 2.00

40 DgM(s), JBa,MPn,"Catwoman,
   Year One," pt. 3 . . . . 2.00
41 DgM(s),JBa,I:MorelandMcShane 2.00
42 DgM(s),JBa,"Red Fang and
   Claw," pt.1 . . . . 2.00
43 DgM(s),JBa,"Red Fang and
   Claw," pt.2 . . . . 2.00
44 DgM(s),JBa,"Red Fang and
   Claw," pt.3 . . . . 2.00
45 DgM(s),JBa,"Nine Deaths of
   the Cat" 2.00
46 DgM(s),JBa,F:Two Face, pt.1. . . 2.00
47 DgM(s),JBa,F:Two Face, pt.2. . . 2.00
48 DgM(s),JBa,V:Morella, pt.1 . . . . 2.00
49 DgM(s),JBa,V:Morella, pt. 2 . . . 2.00
50 DgM(s),JBa,V:Cybercat 3.00
50a metallic cover, collectors ed. . . 3.00
51 DgM(s),JBa,F:Huntress,pt.1 . . . 2.00
52 DgM(s),JBa,F:Huntress,pt.2. . . . 2.00
53 DgM(s),JBa,F:identity learned . . 2.00
54 JBa,improving security. 2.00
55 JBa,. 2.00
56 JBa,Cataclysm x-over,pt.6 . . . . . 2.00
57 JBa,Cataclysm, V:Poison Ivy . . . 2.00
58 JBa,F:Scarecrow, pt.1 . . . . 2.00
59 JBa,F:Scarecrow, pt.2 . . . . 2.00
60 JBa,F:Scarecrow, pt.3 . . . . 2.00
61 JBa,Bank robbery 2.00
62 JBa,A:Nemesis 2.00
63 JBa,A:Batman & Joker, pt.1. . . . 2.00
64 JBa,A:Batman & Joker, pt.2. . . . 2.00
65 JBa,A:Batman & Joker, pt.3 . . . . 2.00
66 JBa,I'll Take Manhattan,pt.1 . . . . 2.00
67 JBa,I'll Take Manhattan,pt.2 . . . . 2.00
68 JBa,I'll Take Manhattan,pt.3 . . . . 2.00
69 JBa,I'll Take Manhattan,pt.4 . . . . 2.00
70 JBa,I'll Take Manhattan,pt.5 . . . . 2.00
71 JBa,I'll Take Manhattan,pt.6 . . . . 2.00
72 JOs(s),JBa,A:Batman 2.00
73 JOs(s),JBa,No Man's Land 2.00
Ann.#1 Elseworlds Story,A:Ra's Al
   Ghul. 2.95
Ann.#2 JBa(c&a) Year One Annuals,
   Young Selina Kyle 3.95
Ann.#3 Legends o/t Dead Earth . . . 2.95
Ann.#4 Pulp Heroes (Macabre). . . . 3.95
Spec. Catwoman Defiant,TGr,DG,
   V:Mr.Handsome 6.00
Spec. Catwoman Plus, LKa,AWi,
   ALa, F:Screamqueen (1997). . . 3.00
Spec.#1,000,000 JBa, on prison
   planet of Pluto 2.00
TPB The Catfile, rep.#15–#19. . . . 10.00

Catwoman #2 © DC Comics Inc.

CATWOMAN: GUARDIAN OF GOTHAM
1999
1 (of 2) Elseworlds,V:Bat-Man 5.95

CATWOMAN/WILDCAT
June 1998
1 (of 4) CDi,TP,SCi,BSf,
   V:Claw Hammer. 2.50
2 CDi,BSt,TP,SCi,BSf 2.50
3 CDi,BSt,TP,SCi,BSf 2.50
4 CDi,BSt,TP,SCi,BSf 2.50

CENTURIONS
June, 1987
1 DH,V:Doc Terror 1.00
2 DH,O:Centurions 1.00
3 DH,V:Doc Terror 1.00
4 DH,Sept., 1987. . . . . 1.00

CHAIN GANG WAR
1993–94
1 I:Chain Gang 2.50
2 V:8-Ball 1.75
3 C:Deathstroke 1.75
4 C:Deathstroke 1.75
5 Embossed(c),A:Deathstroke . . . 2.50
6 A:Deathstroke,Batman 1.75
7 V:Crooked Man 1.75
8 B:Crooked Man 1.75
9 V:Crooked Man 1.75
10 A:Deathstroke,C:Batman 1.75
1꠸ A:Batman. 1.75
12 E:Crooked Man,D:Chain Gang,
   Final Issue 1.75

CHALLENGERS OF THE UNKNOWN
1958–78
1 JK&JK(c),The Man Who
   Tampered With Infinity 2,200.00
2 JK&JK(c),The Monster Maker . 800.00
3 JK&JK(c),The Secret of the
   Sorcerer's Mirror. 700.00
4 JK,WW,JK(c),The Wizard of
   Time 550.00
5 JK,WW&JK(c),The Riddle of
   the Star-Stone 550.00
6 JK,WW,JK(c),Captives of
   the Space Circus 550.00
7 JK,WW,JK(c),The Isle of
   No Return 550.00
8 JK,WW,JK&WW(c),The
   Prisoners of the Robot Planet 550.00
9 The Plot To Destroy Earth. . . . 250.00
10 The Four Faces of Doom. . . . 250.00
11 The Creatures From The
   Forbidden World 175.00
12 The Three Clues To Sorcery . 175.00
13 The Prisoner of the
   Tiny Space Ball 175.00
14 O: Multi Man 175.00
15 Lady Giant and the Beast. . . . 175.00
16 Prisoners of the Mirage World 150.00
17 The Secret of the
   Space Capsules 150.00
18 Menace of Mystery Island . . . 150.00
19 The Alien Who Stole a Planet 150.00
20 Multi-Man Strikes Back 150.00
21 Weird World That Didn't Exist. 150.00
22 The Thing In
   Challenger Mountain. 150.00
23 The Island In The Sky 90.00
24 The Challengers Die At Dawn . 90.00
25 Captives of the Alien Hunter . . 90.00
26 Death Crowns The

Challengers of the Unknown #52
© DC Comics, Inc.

Challenge King. 90.00
27 Master of the Volcano Men . . . 90.00
28 The Riddle of the
Faceless Man. 90.00
29 Four Roads to Doomsday 90.00
30 Multi-Man...Villain Turned
Hero. 90.00
31 O:Challengers 90.00
32 One Challenger Must Die. 40.00
33 Challengers Meet Their Master 40.00
34 Beachhead, USA. 40.00
35 War Against The Moon Beast . 40.00
36 Giant In Challenger Mountain. . 40.00
37 Triple Terror of Mr. Dimension . 40.00
38 Menace the Challengers Made. 40.00
39 Phantom of the Fair. 40.00
40 Super-Powers of the
Challengers 40.00
41 The Challenger Who Quit. 20.00
42 The League of
Challenger-Haters 20.00
43 New look begins 20.00
44 The Curse of the Evil Eye 20.00
45 Queen of the
Challenger-Haters 20.00
46 Strange Schemes of the
Gargoyle 20.00
47 The Sinister Sponge 20.00
48 A:Doom Patrol. 20.00
49 Tyrant Who Owned the World . 20.00
50 Final Hours for the
Challengers 20.00
51 A:Sea Devil 20.00
52 Two Are Dead - Two To Go . . 20.00
53 Who is the Traitor Among Us?. 20.00
54 War of the Sub-Humans. 20.00
55 D:Red Ryan. 20.00
56 License To Kill 20.00
57 Kook And The Kilowatt Killer . . 20.00
58 Live Till Tomorrow 20.00
59 Seekeenakee - The Petrified
Giant 20.00
60 R:Red Ryan. 20.00
61 Robot Hounds of Chang 20.00
62 Legion of the Weird 20.00
63 None Shall Escape the
Walking Evil 20.00
64 JKu(c),Invitation to a Hanging . 20.00
65 The Devil's Circus 10.00
66 JKu(c),Rendezvous With
Revenge 10.00
67 NA(c),The Dream Killers 10.00
68 NA(c),One of Us is a Madman . 10.00
69 JKu(c),I:Corinna. 10.00

70 NA(c),Scream of Yesterdays . . 10.00
71 NC(c),When Evil Calls 10.00
72 NA(c),A Plague of Darkness . . 10.00
73 NC(c),Curse of the Killer
Time Forgot 10.00
74 GT&NA(c),A:Deadman. 20.00
75 JK(c),Ultivac Is Loose 7.00
76 JKu(c),The Traitorous
Challenger 7.00
77 JK(c),Menace of the
Ancient Vials 7.00
78 JK(c),The Island of No Return . . 5.00
79 JKu(c),The Monster Maker. 5.00
80 NC(c),The Day The Earth
Blew Up. 5.00
81 MN&NA(c),Multi-Man's
Master Plan 5.00
82 MN&NA(c),Swamp Thing. 5.00
83 Seven Doorways to Destiny. . . . 5.00
84 To Save A Monster 5.00
85 The Creature From The End
Of Time 5.00
86 The War At Time's End 5.00
87 final issue, July, 1978. . . . . 5.00

CHALLENGERS OF
THE UNKNOWN
1991

1 BB(c) In The Spotlight 1.75
2 . . . . 1.75
3 Challengers `Split Up'. 1.75
4 `Separate Ways'. 1.75
5 Moffet. 1.75
6 GK(c),Challengers reunited. 1.75
7 AAd(c),June pregnant. 1.75
8 final issue 1.75

CHALLENGERS OF
THE UNKNOWN

1 StG(s),JPL 2.25
2 StG(s),LKa,JPL,SMa,Zombies . . 2.25
3 StG(s),JPL,death of Challenger . 2.25
4 StG&LKa(s),JPL,SMa,
O:Challengers 2.25
5 StG&LKa(s)JPL,SMa, V:The
Fearslayer 2.25
6 StG(s),JPL,SMa,"Convergence"
pt. 3 x-over. 2.25
7 StG(s),JPL,"Past Perfect"
pt.1 (of 3) 2.25
8 StG(s),JPL,"Past Perfect" pt.2. . 2.25
9 StG(s),JPL,"Past Perfect"pt.3 . . 2.25
10 StG(s),JIT,F:Brenda Ruskin 2.25
11 StG(s),JPL,in Gothan,pt.1 . . . . . 2.25
12 StG(s),JPL,in Gothan, pt.2. . . . . 2.25
13 StG(s),F:Marlon Corbett. 2.25
14 . . . . 2.25
15 StG(s),JPL,Millennium Giants
pt. 3, x-over. 2.50
16 StG(s),JPL,MZ, original Chalis . . 2.50
17 StG(s),JPL,disappearances 2.50
18 StG(s),DRo,MZ, final issue 2.50

CHASE
Dec., 1997

1 JWi,MGy,from Batman #550 . . . . 2.50
2 JWi,MGy 2.50
3 JWi,MGy,Rocket Reds 2.50
4 JWi,MGy,F:Teen Titans. 2.50
5 JWi,MGy,flashback story. 2.50
6 JWi,MGy,Chase's past 2.50
7 JWi,Shadowing the Bat,pt.1 . . . . 2.50
8 JWi,Shadowing the Bat,pt.2 . . . . 2.50
9 JWi,MBr,MGy,A:Green Lantern . . 2.50
Spec.#1,000,000 Final Issue. 2.50

Checkmate #3 © DC Comics, Inc.

CHECKMATE
April, 1988

1 From Vigilante & Action Comics . 3.00
2 Chicago Bombings cont. 2.00
3 V:Terrorist Right 1.50
4 V:Crime Lords Abroad,B.U.Story
`Training of a Knight' begins . . . 1.50
5 Renegade nation of Quarac 1.50
6 Secret Arms Deal 1.50
7 Checkmate Invades Quarac 1.50
8 Consequences-Quarac Invasion . 1.50
9 Checkmate's security in doubt . . 1.50
10 V:Counterfeiting Ring. 1.50
11 Invasion X-over 1.50
12 Invasion Aftermath extra 1.50
13 CommanderH.Stein's vacation . . 1.50
14 R:Blackthorn 1.50
15 Janus Directive #1. . . . . 1.50
16 Janus Directive #3. . . . . 1.50
17 Janus Directive #6. . . . . 1.50
18 Janus Directive #9. . . . . 1.50
19 Reorganization of Group 1.50
20 `Shadow of Bishop'
A:Peacemaker,pt.1 . . . . 1.50
21 Peacemaker behind Iron
Curtain,pt.2 . . . . 1.50
22 Mystery of Bishop Cont.,pt.3 . . 1.50
23 European Scientists
Suicides,pt.4 . . . . 1.50
24 Bishop Mystery cont.,pt.5. . . . . . 1.50
25 Bishop's Identity Revealed. 1.50
26 Mazarin kidnaps H.Stein's kids. . 1.50
27 Stein rescue attempt,I:Cypher . . 1.50
28 A:Cypher, Bishop-Robots. 1.50
29 A:Cypher,Blackthorn 1.50
30 Irish Knight W.O'Donnell/British
Knight L.Hawkins team-up . . . 1.50
31 V:Cypher International 2.00
32 V:Cypher International 2.00
33 final issue (32 pages). 2.00

CHIAROSCURO: THE
PRIVATE LIVES OF
LEONARDO DaVINCI
Vertigo 1995–96

1 Biographical, Adult 2.50
2 Two of Da Vinci Sisters. 2.50
3 . . . . 2.50
4 F:Salari 2.95
5 Crazy Leonardo 2.95
6 Salai schemes,O:Mona Lisa 2.95
7 V:Borgia & Machiavelli 2.95

8 daVinci returns to Florence 2.95
9 . . . . 2.95
10 finale 2.95

CHILDREN'S CRUSADE
Vertigo 1993–94
1 NGa(s),CBa,MkB(i),F:Rowland,
  Payne (From Sandman) 4.75
2 NGa(s),AaK(s),JaD(s),PSj,A:Tim
  Hunter,Suzy,Maxine,final issue . 4.50

CHRISTMAS WITH
THE SUPER-HEROES
1988–89
1 JBy(c). 2.95
2 PC,GM,JBy,NKu,DG A:Batman
  Superman,Deadman,(last
  Supergirl appearance) 2.95

CHRONOS
Jan., 1998
1 JFM,PGn,SL,Time Travel 2.50
2 JFM,PGn,SL. 2.50
3 JFM,PGn,SL, in 1873 . . . . 2.50
4 JFM,PGn,SL,in Chronopolis 2.50
5 JFM,PGn,DHz,SL,WalkerGabriel 2.50
6 JFM,PGn,Tattooed man 2.50
7 JFM,PGn,DRo,SL,Star City. 2.50
8 JFM,PGn,DRo,SL,
  V:Metrognomes 2.50
9 JFM(s),PGn,SL, The Man
  Who Chose Not to Exist 2.50
10 JFM(s),PGn,SL,Forever Engin . . 2.50
11 JFM(s),PGn,SL final issue 2.50
Spec.#1,000,000 JFM(s) Steals
  time gauntlets. 2.50

CINDER & ASHE
March, 1988
1 JL,I:Cinder & Ashe 2.00
2 JL,Viet Nam Flashbacks 2.00
3 JL,Truth About Lacey revealed . . 2.00
4 JL,final issue, June, 1988 . . . . . 2.00

CLASH
1991
1 AKu,I:Joe McLash(b/w). 4.95
2 AKu,Panja-Rise to Power 4.95
3 AKu,V:Archons,conclusion 4.95

CLAW THE
UNCONQUERED
May-June, 1975
1 . . . . 3.50
2 . . . . 2.50
3 Nudity panel. 2.50
4 . . . . 3.00
5 . . . . 2.50
6 . . . . 2.50
7 . . . . 2.50
8 KG 2.50
9 KG/BL,Origin 2.50
10 KG 2.50
11 KG 2.50
12 KG/BL,Aug.–Sept., 1978. . . . . . 2.50

COMET, THE
Impact 1991–92
1 TL,I&O:Comet I:Applejack, Victoria
  Johnson, Ben Lee 1.50
2 TL,A:Applejack,Lance Perry 1.25
3 TL,V:Anti-nuclear terrorists 1.25
4 TL,I&V:Black Hood,I:Inferno 1.25
5 V:Cyborg Soldier 1.25

6 TL,I:The Hangman 1.25
7 `Press Problems' 1.25
8 TL,Comet ID discovered 1.25
9 TL,`Bad Judgment'. 1.25
10 Fly/Comet T.U.,V:Dolphus 1.25
11 V:Inferno 1.25
12 V:Inferno 1.25
13 O:Comet's Powers. 1.25
14 O:Comet's Powers Pt.2 . . . . . . 1.25
15 Rob finds his mother 1.25
16 V:Aliens. 1.25
17 "Shocking Truth" 1.25
18 Last Issue 1.25
Ann.#1 Earthquest,w/trading card . . 1.75

COMIC CAVALCADE
1942–43
1 Green Lantern, Flash,
  Wildcat, Wonder Woman,
  Black Pirate. 8,500.00
2 ShM,B:Mutt & Jeff 1,800.00
3 ShM,B:HotHarrigan,Sorcerer 1,300.00
4 Gay Ghost, A:Scribby,
  A:Red Tornado 1,200.00
5 Green Lantern, Flash
  Wonder Woman. 1,100.00
6 Flash, Wonder Woman
  Green Lantern 900.00
7 A:Red Tornado, E:Scribby. . . . 900.00
8 Flash, Wonder Woman
  Green Lantern. 900.00
9 Flash, Wonder Woman
  Green Lantern 900.00
10 Flash, Wonder Woman
  Green Lantern 900.00
11 Flash, Wonder Woman
  Green Lantern 750.00
12 E:Red, White & Blue 750.00
13 A:Solomon Grundy 1,100.00
14 Flash, Wonder Woman,
  Green Lantern 750.00
15 B:Johnny Peril 750.00
16 Flash, Wonder Woman,
  Green Lantern 750.00
17 Flash, Wonder Woman,
  Green Lantern 750.00
18 Flash, Wonder Woman,
  Green Lantern 750.00
19 Flash, Wonder Woman,
  Green Lantern 750.00
20 Flash, Wonder Woman,
  Green Lantern 750.00
21 Flash, Wonder Woman,
  Green Lantern 750.00
22 A:Atom 750.00

Comic Cavalcade #6 © DC Comics Inc.

23 A:Atom 750.00
24 A:Solomon Grundy. 850.00
25 A:Black Canary 600.00
26 ATh, E:Mutt & Jeff 600.00
27 ATh,ATh(c). 600.00
28 ATh E:Flash, Wonder Woman
  Green Lantern 600.00
29 E:Johnny Peril 700.00
30 RG,B:Fox & Crow 350.00
31 thru 39 RG . . . . @175.00
40 RG,ShM 150.00
41 thru 49 RG,ShM. . . . . @125.00
50 thru 62 RG,ShM. . . . . @150.00
63 RG,ShM, July 1954 . . . . 250.00

CONGO BILL
Aug.–Sept., 1954
1 . . . . 700.00
2 . . . . 550.00
3 thru 6 . . . . 500.00
7 Aug.–Sept.,1955 . . . . @500.00

CONGO BILL
Vertigo 1999
1 (of 4) RCo(c) 3.00

CONGORILLA
1992–93
1 R:Congo Bill 2.00
2 BB(c),V:Congo Bill 1.75
3 BB(c),V:Congo Bill 1.75
4 BB(c),V:Congo Bill 1.75

CONJURORS
1999
1 (of 3) CDi(s),EB, Elseworlds 3.00
2 CDi(s),EB. 3.00
3 CDi(s),EB, concl. 3.00

CONQUEROR OF
THE BARREN EARTH
1985
1 thru 4 . . . . @1.00

COOL WORLD
1992
1 Prequel to Movie 1.75
2 Movie Adapt. 1.75
3 Movie Adapt. 1.75
4 . . . . 1.75

COPS
1988–89
1 PB,O:Cops,double-size. 2.00
2 PB,V:Big Boss 1.50
3 PB,RT,V:Dr.Bad Vibes 1.25
4 BS,A:Sheriff Sundown 1.25
5 PB,Blitz the Robo-Dog 1.25
6 PB,A:Ms.Demeaner 1.25
7 PB,A:Tramplor 1.25
8 PB,V:BigBoss & Ally 1.25
9 PB,Cops Trapped 1.25
10 PB,Dr.Bad Vibes becomes
  Dr.Goodvibes 1.25
11 PB,V:Big Boss 1.25
12 PB,V:Dr.Badvibe's T.H.U.G.S . . 1.25
13 Berserko/Ms.Demeanor
  marriage proposal 1.25
14 A:Buttons McBoom-Boom 1.25
15 Cops vs. Crooks, final issue. . . . 1.25

DC COMICS

COSMIC BOY
Dec., 1986
1 KG,EC,Legends tie-in 2.00
2 KG,EC,`Is History Destiny' 1.25
3 KG,EC,`Past,Present,Future' . . . 1.25
4 KG,EC,Legends 1.25

COSMIC ODYSSEY
1988
1 MMi,A:Superman,Batman,John
   Stewart,Starfire,J'onnJ'onzz,
   NewGods,Demon,JSn story . . . 4.00
2 MMi,`Disaster'(low dist). 5.00
3 MMi,Return to New Genesis. . . . 3.00
4 MMi,A:Dr.Fate, final 3.00

CREEPER, THE
Oct., 1997
1 LKa,SMa,SB,R:Creeper 2.50
2 LKa,SMa,SB,A:Dr. Skolos. 2.50
3 LKa,SMa,SB,V:Proteus. 2.50
4 LKa,SMa,SB. 2.50
5 LKa,SMa,SB, new job. 2.50
6 LKa,SMa,SB, strange meals. . . . 2.50
7 LKa,SMa,SB,F:Joker, pt.1. . . . . . 2.50
8 LKa,SMa,SB,F:Joker, pt.2. . . . . . 2.50
9 DAn,ALa,All-star issue 2.50
10 LKa,SB,Jack Ryder 2.50
11 LKa,SB,SMa,Creeper splits
   again 2.50
Spec.#1,000,000 LKa,SB,final issue 2.50

CRIMSON AVENGER
1988
1 Mini-series 1.00
2 V:Black Cross. 1.00
3 `V:Killers of the Dark Cross' 1.00
4 `V:Dark Cross,final issue 1.00

CRISIS ON
INFINITE EARTHS
April, 1985
1 B:MWn(s),GP,DG,I:Pariah,I&O:Alex
   Luthor,D:Crime Syndicate. 7.00
2 GP,DG,V:Psycho Pirate,
   A:Joker,Batman 6.00
3 GP,DG,D:Losers. 5.00
4 GP,D:Monitor,I:2nd Dr.Light. . . . 5.00
5 GP,JOy,I:Anti-Monitor 5.00

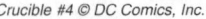

Crucible #4 © DC Comics, Inc.

6 GP,JOy,I:2nd Wildcat,A:Fawcett,
   Quality & Charlton heroes. 5.00
7 GP,JOy,DG,D:Supergirl. 7.00
8 GP,JOy,D:1st Flash. 9.00
9 GP,JOy,D:Aquagirl 4.00
10 GP,JOy,D:Psimon,A:Spectre . . . 4.00
11 GP,JOy,D:Angle Man 5.00
12 E:MWn(s),GP,JOy,D:Huntress,Kole,
   Kid Flash becomes 2nd Flash,
   D:Earth 2 . . . . 5.00

CRUCIBLE
Impact 1993
1 JQ,F:The Comet. 1.25
2 JQ,A:Black Hood,Comet. 1.50
3 JQ,Comet Vs.Black Hood 1.50
4 JQ,V:Tomorrow Men. 1.50
5 JQ,Black Hod vs Shield 1.25
6 JQ,V:The Crucible 1.25

CRUEL AND UNUSUAL
Vertigo 1999
1 (of 4) JaD&TPe(s),JMC,satire . . . 3.00
2 thru 4 JaD&TPe(s),JMC . . . . . @3.00

CRUSADERS
Impact May, 1992
1 DJu(c),I:Crusaders,inc Trading
   cards 1.25
2 V:Kalathar 1.00
3 V:Kalathar 1.00
4 Crusaders form as group 1.00
5 V:Cyber-Punks 1.25
6 V:Cyborg Villains 1.25
7 Woj,Low,F:Fireball 1.25
8 Last Issue. 1.25

CYBERELLA
DC/Helix Sept. 1996
1 HC(s),DCn,. 2.25
2 HC(s),DCn,Secret history
   revealed. 2.25
3 HC(s),DCn,Sunny goes on
   rampage. 2.25
4 HC(s),DCn,Attack on MacroCorp 2.25
5 HC(s),DCn,V:Army of
   Necronauts. 2.25
6 HC(s),DCn,. 2.25
7 HC(s),DCn,Trip to Hell 2.25
8 HC(s),DCn,V:BTIII, concl. 2.25
9 DCn, The Informers 2.25
10 HC(s),DCn,Wuvzums,
   Digitina,pt.1 . . . . 2.25
11 HC(s),DCn,Wuvzums,pt.2 . . . . . 2.25
12 HC(s),final issue 2.50

DALE EVANS COMICS
1948–52
1 Ph(c),ATh,B:Sierra Smith 800.00
2 Ph(c),ATh. 400.00
3 ATh 225.00
4 thru 11 . . . . @200.00
12 thru 24 . . . . @100.00

DAMAGE
1994–96
1 I:Damage,V:Metallo 2.00
2 V:Symbolix. 2.00
3 V:Troll 2.00
4 V:Troll. 2.00
5 A:New Titans,V:Baron. 2.25
6 Zero Hour,A:New Titans 2.25
7 Trial 2.00
8 Fragments,pt.1 . . . . 2.00
9 Fragments,pt.2 . . . . 2.00
10 Fragments,pt.3 . . . . 2.00

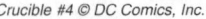

Damage #6 © DC Comics, Inc.

11 Fragments,pt.4. . . . . 2.00
12 Fragments,pt.5 . . . . 2.00
13 Picking Up The Pieces,pt.1 . . . . 2.25
14 Picking Up The Pieces,pt.2
   A:The Ray 2.25
15 Picking Up the Pieces,pt.3 . . . . . 2.25
16 . . . . 2.25
17 V:Bounty 2.25
18 Underworld Unleashed tie-in . . . 2.25
19 Underworld Unleashed tie-in . . . 2.25
20 final issue 2.25

DANGER TRAIL
July-Aug., 1950
1 CI,Ath,I:King For A Day. 850.00
2 ATh 600.00
3 ATh 900.00
4 ATh 500.00
5 March-April, 1951 . . . . 500.00

DANGER TRAIL
1 thru 4 CI,FMc,F:King Faraday
   V:Cobra 2.00

DARK MANSION OF
FORBIDDEN LOVE, THE
Sept.–Oct., 1971
1 . . . . 6.00
2 and 4 March-April, 1972 . . . . @3.50

DARKSEID VS.
GALACTUS THE HUNGER
1 Orion vs. Silver Surfer 4.95
GN JBy,in Apokolips. 6.00

DARKSTARS
1992–96
0 History 2.00
1 TC(c),LSn,I:Darkstars. 3.50
2 TC(c),LSn,F:Ferin Colos. 2.50
3 LSn,J:Mo,Flint,V:Evil Star 2.00
4 TC,V:Evilstar 3.00
5 TC,A:Hawkman,Hawkwoman . . . 3.00
6 TC,A:Hawkman 2.50
7 TC,V:K'llash 2.00
8 F:Ferris Colos. 2.00
9 Colos vs K'lassh 2.00
10 V:Con Artists 2.00
11 TC,Trinity#4,A:Green Lantern,
   L.E.G.I.O.N. 2.00

12 TC(c),Trinity#7,A:Green Lantern, L.E.G.I.O.N.		2.00
13 TC(c),V:Alien Underworld.		2.00
14 I:Annihilator		2.00
15 V:Annihilator		2.00
16 V:Annihilator		2.00
17 Murders.		2.00
18 B:Eve of Destruction		2.00
19 A:Flash		2.00
20 E:Eve of Destruction		2.00
21 A:John Stewart,Donna Troy		2.00
22 A:Controllers		2.25
23 Donna Troy is new Darkstar.		2.25
24 Zero Hour,V:HalJordan,Entropy		2.25
25 Stewart		2.25
26 Alien criminals		2.25
27 and 28		@2.00
29 V:Alien Syndicate.		2.00
30 A:Green Lantern		2.00
31 V:Darkseid.		2.25
32 Crimelord/Syndicate War,pt.3, A:New Titans,Supergirl, Deathstroke		2.25
33 V:Jeddigan		2.25
34		2.25
35 A:Flash		2.25
36 MkF,MC,A:Flash		2.25
37 MkF,MC,Colos vs. Warrior		2.25
38 final issue		2.25

DC CHALLENGE
Nov., 1985

1 GC,Batman		2.50
2 Superman		1.50
3 CI,Adam Strange		1.50
4 GK/KJ,Aquaman.		1.50
5 DGb,Dr.Fate,Capt.Marvel		1.50
6 Dr. 13.		1.50
7 Gorilla Grodd.		1.50
8 DG,Outsiders, New Gods		1.50
9 New Teen Titans,JLA		1.50
10 CS,New Teen Titans,JLA		1.50
11 KG,Outsiders		1.50
12 DCw,TMd,DSp,New Teen Titans, Oct., 1986		2.50

DC COMICS PRESENTS
July-Aug., 1978
[all have Superman]

1 JL,DA,F:Flash.		5.00
2 JL,DA,F:Flash.		4.00
3 JL,F:Adam Strange.		4.00
4 JL,F:Metal Men,A:Mr.IQ		4.00
5 MA,F:Aquaman		4.00
6 CS,F:Green Lantern		4.00
7 DD,F:Red Tornado		4.00
8 MA,F:Swamp Thing		4.00
9 JSon,JA,RH,F:Wonder Woman.		4.00
10 JSon,JA,F:Sgt.Rock.		4.00
11 JSon,F:Hawkman.		3.00
12 RB,DG,F:Mr.Miracle.		4.00
13 DD,DG,F:Legion		4.00
14 DD,DG,F:Superboy		3.00
15 JSon,F:Atom,C:Batman		3.00
16 JSon,F:Black Lightning		3.00
17 JL,F:Firestorm		3.00
18 DD,F:Zatanna		3.00
19 JSon,F:Batgirl		3.50
20 JL,F:Green Arrow		2.50
21 JSon,JSa,F:Elongated Man		2.50
22 DD,FMc,F:Captain Comet		2.50
23 JSon,F:Dr.Fate		2.50
24 JL,F:Deadman		2.50
25 DD,FMc,F:Phantom Stranger.		2.50
26 GP,DG,JSn,I:New Teen Titans, Cyborg,Raven,Starfire A:Green Lantern.		12.00
27 JSn,RT,I:Mongul		4.00
28 JSn,RT,GK,F:Mongul		3.50

29 JSn,RT,AS,F:Spectre		3.50
30 CS,AS,F:Black Canary.		3.00
31 JL,DG,AS,F:Robin.		3.00
32 KS,AS,F:Wonder Woman.		3.00
33 RB,DG,AS,F:Captain Marvel		3.00
34 RB,DG,F:Marvel Family.		3.00
35 CS,GK,F:Man-bat		3.00
36 JSn,F:Starman.		3.50
37 JSn,AS,F:Hawkgirl.		3.00
38 GP(c),DH,AS,DG,D:Crimson Avenger,F:Flash		3.00
39 JSon,AS,F:PlasticMan,Toyman		3.00
40 IN,FMc,AS,F:Metamorpho		3.00
41 JL,FMc,GC,RT,I:New Wonder Woman,A:Joker		8.00
42 IN,FMc,F:Unknown Soldier		3.00
43 BB(c),CS,F:Legion.		3.00
44 IN,FMc,F:Dial H for Hero		3.50
45 RB,F:Firestorm		3.00
46 AS,I:Global Guardians		3.00
47 CS,I:Masters of Universe.		3.00
48 GK(c),AA,IN,FMc,F:Aquaman		3.00
49 RB,F:Shazam!,V:Black Adam.		3.00
50 KS,CS,F:Clark Kent.		3.00
51 AS,FMc,CS,F:Atom,Masters of the Universe.		3.00
52 KG,F:Doom Patrol, I:Ambush Bug		3.00
53 CS,TD,RA,DG,I:Atari Force		3.00
54 DN,DA,F:Gr.Arrow,Bl.Canary		3.00
55 AS,F:Air Wave,A:Superboy		3.00
56 GK(c),F:Power Girl		3.00
57 AS,FMc,F:Atomic Knights		3.00
58 GK(c),AS,F:Robin,Elongated Man		3.00
59 KG,KS,F:Ambush Bug.		3.00
60 GK(c),IN,TD,F:Guardians.		3.00
61 GP,F:Omac		3.00
62 GK(c),IN,F:Freedom Fighters.		3.00
63 AS,EC,F:Amethyst.		3.00
64 GK(c),AS,FMc,F:Kamandi.		3.00
65 GM,F:Madame Xanadu		3.00
66 JKu,F:Demon		3.00
67 CS,MA,F:Santa Claus		3.00
68 GK(c),CS,MA,F:Vixen		3.00
69 IN,DJ,F:Blackhawk		3.00
70 AS,TD,F:Metal Men		3.00
71 CS,F:Bizarro		3.00
72 AS,DG,F:Phant.Stranger,Joker.		5.00
73 CI,F:Flash		3.00
74 AS,RT,F:Hawkman		3.00
75 TMd,F:Arion.		3.00
76 EB,F:Wonder Woman		3.00

DC Comics Presents #35
© DC Comics Inc.

77 CS,F:Forgotten Heroes		5.00
78 CS,F:Forgotten Villains		5.00
79 CS,AW,F:Legion		3.00
80 CS,F:Clark Kent.		3.00
81 KG,BO,F:Ambush Bug.		3.00
82 KJ,F:Adam Strange		3.00
83 IN,F:Batman/Outsiders.		3.00
84 JK,ATh,MA,F:Challengers		3.00
85 RV,AW,AMo(s), F:Swamp Thing		7.00
86 Crisis,F:Supergirl		3.00
87 CS,AW,Crisis,I:Earth Prime Superboy		3.00
88 KG,Crisis,F:Creeper.		3.00
89 MMi(c),AS,F:Omega Men		3.00
90 DCw,F:Firestorm,Capt.Atom.		3.00
91 CS,F:Captain Comet		3.00
92 CS,F:Vigilante		3.00
93 JSn(c),AS,KS,F:Elastic Four		3.00
94 GP(c),TMd,DH,Crisis,F:Lady Quark,Pariah,Harbinger		3.00
95 MA(i),F:Hawkman		3.00
96 JSon,KS,F:Blue Devil.		3.00
97 RV,F:Phantom Zone Villians, final issue,double-sized		3.00
Ann.#1,RB,F:Earth 2 Superman		3.00
Ann.#2 GK(c),KP,I:Superwoman		2.00
Ann.#3 GK,F:Captain Marvel		2.00
Ann.#4 EB,JOy,F:Superwoman.		2.00

DC/MARVEL: ALL ACCESS
October 1996
sequel to DC Versus Marvel

1 (of 4) RMz(s),JG,JRu, crossover crisis again, 48pg		4.00
2 RMz(s),JG,JRu,F:Jubilee,Robin, Daredevil,Two-Face		3.00
3 RMz(s),JG,JRu,F:Doctor Strange, X-Men		3.00
4 RMz(s),JG,JRu,48pg		3.50

DC/MARVEL CROSSOVER CLASSICS

TPB, rep. all x-overs	17.95

DC GRAPHIC NOVEL
Nov., 1983

1 JL,Star Raiders.		8.00
2 Warlords.		8.00
3 EC,Medusa Chain		8.00
4 JK,Hunger Dogs.		15.00
5 Me and Joe Priest		8.00
6 Space Clusters.		8.00

DC ONE MILLION
1998

1 GMo(s),VS,in 853rd-century		3.00
2 GMo(s),VS,V:Hourman Virus		2.00
3 GMo(s),VS,V:Solaris.		2.00
4 GMo(s),VS,finale		2.00

DC SCIENCE FICTION GRAPHIC NOVEL
1985–87

1 KG,Hell on Earth		7.00
2 Nightwings		7.00
3 Frost and Fire.		7.00
4 Merchants of Venus		7.00
5 Metalzoic		7.00
6 MR,Demon-Glass Hand		7.00
7 Sandkings		7.00

DC SPECIAL
Oct.–Dec., 1968
[All reprint]
1 CI,F:Flash,Batman,Adam Strange,
  (#1 thru #21 reps)........ 35.00
2 F:Teen Titans 50.00
3 GA,F:Black Canary......... 35.00
4 Mystery 25.00
5 JKu,F:Viking Prince/Sgt.Rock . 25.00
6 Wild Frontier.............. 25.00
7 F:Strange Sports 25.00
8 Wanted................... 25.00
9 .... 25.00
10 LAW 25.00
11 NA,BWr,F:Monsters 25.00
12 JKu,F:Viking Prince 25.00
13 F:Strange Sports 25.00
14 Wanted,F:Penguin/Joker 27.00
15 GA,F:Plastic Man.......... 27.00
16 F:Super Heroes & Gorillas 10.00
17 F:Green Lantern 10.00
18 Earth Shaking Stories 10.00
19 F:War Against Gianta........ 10.00
20 Green Lantern 10.00
21 F:War Against Monsters..... 10.00
22 Three Musketeers 10.00
23 Three Musketeers 10.00
24 Three Musketeers 10.00
25 Three Musketeers 10.00
26 F:Enemy Ace(rep) 10.00
27 RB,JR,F:Captain Comet...... 10.00
28 DN,DA,Earth disasters....... 10.00
29 JSon,BL,O:JSA 10.00

DC SPECIAL SERIES
Sept., 1977
1 MN,DD,IN,FMc,JSon,JA,BMc,
  JRu,F:Batman,Flash,Green
  Lantern,Atom,Aquaman 9.00
2 BWr(c),BWr,F:Swamp Thing rep. 6.00
3 JKu(c),F:Sgt.Rock 7.00
4 AN,RT,Unexpected Annual 7.00
5 CS,F:Superman 7.00
6 BMc(i),Secret Society Vs.JLA ... 7.00
7 AN,F:Ghosts.............. 7.00
8 RE,DG,F:Brave&Bold,Deadman . 7.00
9 SD,RH,DAy,F:Wonder Woman .. 7.00
10 JSon,MN,DN,TA,Secret Origins,
  O:Dr.Fate................. 7.00
11 JL,KS,MA,IN,WW,AS,F:Flash... 7.00
12 MK(c),RT,RH,TS,Secrets of
  Haunted House 7.00
13 JKu(c),RT,SBi,RE,F:Sgt.Rock .. 7.00

DC Super-Stars #12 © DC Comics, Inc.

14 BWr(c),F:Swamp Thing rep.... 7.00
15 MN,JRu,MR,DG,MGo,
  F:Batman................. 9.00
16 RH,D:Jonah Hex 28.00
17 F:Swamp Thing rep. 7.00
18 JK(c),digest,F:Sgt.Rock rep. ... 7.00
19 digest,Secret Origins
  O:Wonder Woman 7.00
20 BWr(c),F:Swamp Thing rep.... 7.00
21 FM,JL,DG,RT,DA,F:Batman,
  Legion 15.00
22 JKu(c),F:G.I.Combat 7.00
23 digest size,F:Flash.......... 7.00
24 F:Worlds Finest 7.00
25 F:Superman II,Photo Album.... 7.00
26 RA,F:Superman's Fortress..... 10.00
27 JL,DG,F:Batman vs.Hulk 20.00

DC SUPER-STARS
1976–78
1 F:Teen Titans rep........... 10.00
2 F:DC Super-Stars of Space 7.00
3 CS,F:Superman,Legion 7.00
4 DC,MA,F:Super-Stars of Space . 7.00
5 CI,F:Flash rep.............. 7.00
6 MA,F:Super-Stars of Space 7.00
7 F:Aquaman rep............. 7.00
8 CI,MA,F:Adam Strange....... 10.00
9 F:Superman rep............ 7.00
10 DD,FMc,F:Superhero Baseball
  Special,A:Joker 10.00
11 GM,Super-Stars of Magic...... 7.00
12 CS,MA,F:Superboy 7.00
13 SA...................... 15.00
14 RB,BL,JA,JRu,Secret Origins... 7.00
15 JKu(c),RB,RT(i),War Heroes ... 7.00
16 DN,BL,I:Star Hunters 7.00
17 JSon,MGr,BL,I&O:Huntress,O:Gr.
  Arrow,D:EarthII Catwoman ... 10.00
18 RT,DG,BL,F:Deadman,Phantom
  Stranger................. 10.00

DC UNIVERSE HEROES
1998
Secret Files #1............. 5.00

DC UNIVERSE HOLIDAY BASH
1-shot, yuletide tales 3.95
3 64-pg 5.00
Holiday Bash II, GN stories, 64pg. . 4.00

DC UNIVERSE: TRINITY
1993
1 TC,GeH,BKi,F:Darkstars,Green
  Lantern,L.E.G.I.O.N.,V:Triarch . 3.50
2 BKi,SHa,F:Darkstars,Green Lantern,
  L.E.G.I.O.N.,V:Triarch........ 3.50

DC UNIVERSE VILLAINS
1999
Secret Files #1.............. 5.00

DC VS. MARVEL
1996
1 RMz..................... 5.50
1 2nd printing 4.00
2 & 3 see Marvel
4 PDa 5.00

DEAD CORPS(E)
DC/Helix (July 1998)
1 StP, C.J.Rataan 2.50
2 StP, CJ becomes an expired.... 2.50
3 StP,Death is not the end....... 2.50

Deadman #3 © DC Comics, Inc.

4 StP, conclusion............. 2.50

DEADMAN
May, 1985
1 CI,NA,rep................. 3.00
2 NA,rep................... 3.00
3 NA,rep................... 2.50
4 NA,rep................... 2.50
5 NA,rep................... 2.50
6 NA,rep................... 2.50
7 NA,rep.Nov., 1985.......... 2.50
[Mini-Series] 1986
1 JL,A:Batman............... 2.50
2 JL,V:Sensei,A:Batman 2.00
3 JL,D:Sensei 2.00
4 JL,V:Jonah, final issue 2.00

DEADMAN: EXORCISM
[Limited-Series] 1992
1 KJo,A:Phantom Stranger 5.25
2 KJo,A:Phantom Stranger 5.25

DEADMAN: LOST SOULS
TPB Mike Baron, Kelly Jones 19.95

DEADMAN: LOVE AFTER DEATH
1989–90
1 KJo,Circus of Monsters........ 4.25
2 KJo,Circus of Monsters........ 4.25

DEADSHOT
1988–89
1 LMc,From Suicide Squad 2.00
2 LMc,Search for Son 2.00
3 LMc,V:Pantha.............. 1.50
4 LMc,final issue 1.50

DEATH GALLERY
Vertigo
1 DMc(c),NGa Death Sketch
  Various Pinups............. 3.50

DEATH: THE HIGH COST OF LIVING
Vertigo 1993
1 B:NGa(s),CBa,MBu(i),Death
  becomes Human,A:Hettie 9.00
1a Platinum Ed 18.00
2 CBa,MBu(i),V:Eremite,A:Hettie . . 4.50
3 E:NGa(s),CBa,MBu(i),V:Eremite,
  A:Hettie 3.50
3a Error Copy 7.00
HC 19.95
TPB w/Tori Amos Intro 12.95

DEATH: THE TIME OF YOUR LIFE
Vertigo 1995
1 NGa,MBu,four-issue miniseries . . 2.95
2 NGa,MBu,F:Foxglove 2.95
3 NGa,MBu,conclusion 2.95
HC NGa(s),rep. #1–#4 . . . . 19.95

DEATHSTROKE: THE TERMINATOR
1991–94
1 MZ(c),(from New Teen Titans)
  SE,I:2nd Ravager 4.00
1a Second Printing,Gold 3.00
2 MZ(c),SE,Quraci Agents 3.50
3 SE,V:Ravager 3.00
4 SE,D:2ndRavager(Jackel) 3.00
5 Winter Green Rescue Attempt . . 3.00
6 MZ(c),SE,B:City of Assassins,
  A:Batman 3.00
7 MZ(c),SE,A:Batman 2.50
8 MZ(c),SE,A:Batman 2.00
9 MZ(c),SE,E:City of Assassins,
  A:Batman;I:2nd Vigilante 2.00
10 MZ(c),ANi,GP,A:2nd Vigilante . 2.00
11 MZ(c),ANi,GP,A:2nd Vigilante. . 2.00
12 MGo,Short Stories re:Slade 2.00
13 SE,V:Gr.Lant.,Flash,Aquaman . . 2.00
14 ANi,Total Chaos#1,A:New Titans,
  Team Titans,V:Nightwing 2.00
15 ANi,Total Chaos#4,A:New Titans,
  Team Titans,I:Sweet Lili 2.00
16 ANi,Total Chaos#7 . . . . 2.00
17 SE,Titans Sell-Out #2
  A:Brotherhood of Evil 2.00
18 SE,V:Cheshire,R:Speedy 2.00
19 SE,V:Broth.of Evil,A:Speedy . . . 2.00
20 SE,MZ(c),V:Checkmate 2.00
21 SE,MZ(c),A:Checkmate 2.00
22 MZ(c),Quality of Mercy#1 . . . . . 2.00
23 MZ(c),Quality of Mercy#2 . . . . . 2.00
24 MZ(c),V:The Black Dome 2.00
25 MZ(c),V:The Black Dome 2.00
26 MZ(c),SE,in Kenya 2.00
27 MZ(c),SE,B:World Tour,
  in Germany 2.00
28 MZ(c),SE,in France 2.00
29 KM(c),SE,in Hong Kong 2.00
30 SE,A:Vigilante 2.00
31 SE,in Milwaukie 2.00
32 SE,in Africa 2.00
33 SE,I:Fleur de Lis 2.00
34 SE,E:World Tour 2.00
35 V:Mercenaries 2.00
36 V:British General 2.00
37 V:Assassin 2.00
38 A:Vigilante 2.25
39 A:Vigilante 2.25
40 Wedding in Red 2.25
Ann.#1 Eclipso,A:Vigilante 3.75
Ann.#2 SE,I:Gunfire 4.00
Ann.#3 Elseworlds Story 4.25
TPB Full Circle rep#1–#4,
  New Titans#70 . . . . 12.95

Becomes:
DEATHSTROKE: THE HUNTED
1994–95
0 Slade 2.50
41 Bronze Tiger 2.25
42 Wounded 2.25
43 . . . . 2.00
44 . . . . 2.00
45 A:New Titans 2.00
Becomes:
DEATHSTROKE
1995–96
46 Checkmate,Wintergreen 2.00
47 I:New Vigilante 2.00
48 Crimelord/Syndicate War,pt.1 . . . 2.25
49 Crimelord/Syndicate War,pt.4
  A:Supergirl, New Titans, Hawkman
  Blood Pack 2.25
50 A:Titans,Outsiders,Steel 3.50
51 No Fate or Future,pt.1 . . . . 2.25
52 No Fate or Future,pt.2 . . . . 2.25
53 The Borgia Plague,pt.1 . . . . 2.25
54 The Borgia Plague,pt.2 . . . . 2.25
55 MWn,Rebirth? 2.25
56 MWn,Night of the Karrion,pt.2 . . 2.25
57 . . . . 2.25
58 MWn,V:The Joker 2.25
59 MWn,F:Hellriders 2.25
60 MWn,final issue 2.25

DEATHWISH
1994–95
1 New mini-series 1.75
2 F:Rahme 2.50
3 . . . . 2.50
4 V:Boots 2.50

DEMOLITION MAN
1993–94
1 thru 4 Movie Adapt 1.75

DEMON
[1st Regular Series] 1972–74
1 JK,I:Demon 15.00
2 JK 7.00
3 JK 6.00
4 JK 6.00

The Demon 2nd Series #53
© DC Comics Inc.

5 JK 6.00
6 JK 5.00
7 JK 5.00
8 JK 5.00
9 JK 5.00
10 JK 5.00
11 JK 5.00
12 JK 5.00
13 JK 5.00
14 JK 5.00
15 JK 5.00
16 JK 5.00
[Limited Series] 1987
1 MWg,B:Jason Blood's Case 2.00
2 MWg,Fight to Save Gotham 2.00
3 MWg,Fight to Save Gotham 2.00
4 MWg,final issue 2.00
[2nd Regular Series] 1990–95
0 Relationships 2.00
1 VS,A:Etrigan (32 pages) 3.00
2 VS,V:TheCrone 2.50
3 VS,A:Batman 2.25
4 VS,A:Batman 2.25
5 VS,ThePit 2.25
6 VS,In Hell 2.25
7 VS,Etrigan-King of Hell 2.25
8 VS,Klarion the Witch Boy 2.25
9 VS,Jason Leaves Gotham 2.25
10 VS,A:PhantomStranger 2.25
11 VS,A:Klarion,C:Lobo 2.50
12 VS,Etrigan Vs. Lobo 2.50
13 VS,Etrigan Vs. Lobo 2.50
14 VS,V:Odd Squad,A:Lobo 2.50
15 VS,Etrigan Vs.Lobo 2.50
16 VS,Etrigan & Jason Blood
  switch bodies 2.00
17 VS, War of the Gods x-over 2.00
18 VS,V:Wotan,A:Scape Goat 2.00
19 VS,O:Demon,Demon/Lobo
  pin-up 3.00
20 VS,V:Golden Knight 2.00
21 VS,Etrigan/Jason,
  A:Lobo,Glenda 2.00
22 MWg,V:Mojo & Hayden 2.25
23 VS,A:Robin 2.00
24 VS,A:Robin 2.00
25 VS,V:Gideon Ryme 2.00
26 VS,B:America Rules 2.00
27 VS,A:Superman 2.00
28 VS,A:Superman 2.00
29 VS,E:America Rules 2.00
30 R:Asteroth 2.00
31 VS(c),A:Lobo 2.00
32 VS(c),A:Lobo,W.Woman 2.00
33 VS(c),A:Lobo,V:Asteroth 2.00
34 A:Lobo 2.00
35 A:Lobo,V:Belial 2.00
36 A:Lobo,V:Belial 2.00
37 A:Lobo,Morax 2.00
38 A:Lobo,Morax 2.00
39 A:Lobo 2.00
40 New Direction,B:GEn(s) 3.50
41 V:Mad Bishop 2.50
42 V:Demons 2.25
43 A:Hitman 10.00
44 V:Gotho-Demon,A:Hitman . . . 15.00
45 V:Gotho-Demon,A:Hitman . . . 15.00
46 R:Haunted Tank 2.50
47 V:Zombie Nazis 2.00
48 A:Haunted Tank,V:Zombie
  Nazis 2.00
49 b:Demon's Son,A:Joe Gun 2.00
50 GEn(s) 3.00
51 GEn(s),Son & Lovers 2.25
52 Etrigan & son–Hitman 4.00
53 Glenda & child–Hitman 4.00
54 Suffer the Children 2.00
55 Rebellion 2.00
56 F:Etrigan 2.00
57 Last Stand 2.00

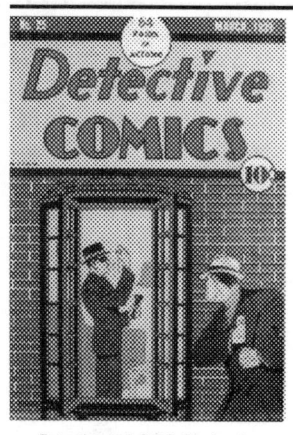

Detective #25 © DC Comics, Inc.

58 Last issue	2.00
Ann.#1 Eclipso,V:Klarion	3.25
Ann.#2 I:Hitman	15.00

DESTINY: A CHRONICLE OF DEATHS FORETOLD
DC/Vertigo (Sept. 1997)

1 (of 3) F:Destiny of the Endless	6.00
2 Destiny of the Endless, pt.2	6.00
3 Destiny of the Endless, pt.3	6.00

DETECTIVE COMICS
March, 1937

1 I:Slam Bradley	65,000.00
2 JoS	15,000.00
3 JoS	10,000.00
4 JoS	6,500.00
5 JoS	6,000.00
6 JoS	4,500.00
7 JoS	4,500.00
8 JoS,Mr. Chang(c)	7,000.00
9 JoS	4,500.00
10	4,500.00
11	3,500.00
12	3,500.00
13	3,500.00
14	3,500.00
15	3,500.00
16	3,500.00
17 I:Fu Manchu	3,500.00
18 Fu Manchu(c)	5,000.00
19	3,000.00
20 I:Crimson Avenger	5,500.00
21	3,000.00
22	3,500.00
23	3,000.00
24	3,000.00
25	3,000.00
26	3,000.00
27 BK,I:Batman	165,000.00
28 BK,V:Frenchy Blake	15,000.00
29 BK,I:Doctor Death	25,000.00
30 BK,V:Dr. Death	6,000.00
31 BK,I:Monk	25,000.00
32 BK,V:Monk	5,500.00
33 O:Batman,V:Scarlet Horde	36,000.00
34 V:Due D'Orterre	4,500.00
35 V:Sheldon Lenox	7,500.00
36 I:Hugo Strange	5,800.00
37 V:Count Grutt, last Batman solo	5,500.00
38 I:Robin, the Boy Wonder	30,000.00
39 V:Green Dragon	5,500.00
40 I:Clayface (Basil Karlo)	6,000.00

41 V:Graves	2,800.00
42 V:Pierre Antal	1,800.00
43 V:Harliss Greer	1,800.00
44 Robin Dream Story	1,800.00
45 V:Joker	2,800.00
46 V:Hugo Strange	1,600.00
47 Meets Harvey Midas	1,600.00
48 Meets Henry Lewis	1,600.00
49 V:Clayface	1,600.00
50 V:Three Devils	1,600.00
51 V:Mindy Gang	1,200.00
52 V:Loo Chung	1,200.00
53 V:Toothy Hare gang	1,200.00
54 V:Hook Morgan	1,200.00
55 V:Dr. Death	1,200.00
56 V:Mad Mack	1,200.00
57 Meet Richard Sneed	1,200.00
58 I:Penguin	3,300.00
59 V:Penguin	1,400.00
60 V:Joker,I:Air Wave	1,400.00
61 The Three Racketeers	1,200.00
62 V:Joker	1,800.00
63 I:Mr. Baffle	1,200.00
64 I:Boy Commandos,V:Joker	3,500.00
65 Meet Tom Bolton	2,500.00
66 I:Two-Face	3,000.00
67 V:Penguin	1,700.00
68 V:Two-Face	1,400.00
69 V:Joker	1,400.00
70 Meet the Amazing Carlo	900.00
71 V:Joker	1,000.00
72 V:Larry the Judge	800.00
73 V:Scarecrow	950.00
74 I:Tweedledum & Tweedledee	800.00
75 V:Robber Baron	800.00
76 V:Joker	1,300.00
77 V:Dr. Matthew Thorne	900.00
78 V:Baron Von Luger	900.00
79 `Destiny's' Auction	900.00
80 V:Two-Face	1,000.00
81 I:Cavalier	750.00
82 V:Blackee Blondeen	750.00
83 V:Dr. Goodwin	775.00
84 V:Ivan Krafft	750.00
85 V:Joker	900.00
86 V:Gentleman Jim Jewell	700.00
87 V:Penguin	750.00
88 V:Big Hearted John	700.00
89 V:Cavalier	700.00
90 V:Capt. Ben	700.00
91 V:Joker	900.00
92 V:Braing Bulow	600.00
93 V:`Tiger' Ragland	600.00
94 V:Lefty Goran	600.00
95 V:The Blaze	600.00
96 F:Alfred	600.00
97 V:Nick Petri	600.00
98 Meets Casper Thurbridge	600.00
99 V:Penguin	900.00
100 V:Digger	1,000.00
101 V:Joe Bart	600.00
102 V:Joker	850.00
103 Meet Dean Gray	600.00
104 V:Fat Frank gang	600.00
105 V:Simon Gurlan	600.00
106 V:Todd Torrey	600.00
107 V:Bugs Scarpis	600.00
108 Meet Ed Gregory	600.00
109 V:Joker	750.00
110 V:Prof. Moriarty	600.00
111 `Coaltown, USA'	600.00
112 `Case Without A Crime'	600.00
113 V:Blackhand	600.00
114 V:Joker	750.00
115 V:Basil Grimes	600.00
116 A:Carter Nichols, Robin Hood	600.00
117 `Steeplejack's Slowdown'	600.00
118 V:Joker	750.00
119 V:Wiley Derek	600.00
120 V:Penguin	1,500.00

Detective #81 © DC Comics, Inc.

121 F:Commissioner Gordon	600.00
122 V:Catwoman	1,000.00
123 V:Shiner	600.00
124 V:Joker	750.00
125 V:Thinker	575.00
126 V:Penguin	575.00
127 V:Dr. Agar	575.00
128 V:Joker	750.00
129 V:Diamond Dan mob	575.00
130	575.00
131 V:`Trigger Joe'	450.00
132 V:Human Key	450.00
133 Meets Arthur Loom	450.00
134 V:Penguin	475.00
135 A:Baron Frankenstein, Carter Nichols	450.00
136 A:Carter Nichols	450.00
137 V:Joker	550.00
138 V:Joker,O:Robotman	900.00
139 V:Nick Bailey	450.00
140 I:Riddler	4,000.00
141 V:`Blackie' Nason	500.00
142 V:Riddler	900.00
143 V:Pied Piper	525.00
144 A:Kay Kyser (radio personality)	525.00
145 V:Yellow Mask mob	525.00
146 V:J.J. Jason	525.00
147 V:Tiger Shark	525.00
148 V:Prof. Zero	525.00
149 V:Joker	800.00
150 V:Dr. Paul Visio	525.00
151 I&O:Pow Wow Smith	550.00
152 V:Goblin	550.00
153 V:Slits Danton	550.00
154 V:Hatch Marlin	550.00
155 A:Vicki Vale	550.00
156 `The Batmobile of 1950'	550.00
157 V:Bart Gillis	500.00
158 V:Dr. Doom	500.00
159 V:T. Worthington Chubb	500.00
160 V:Globe-Trotter	500.00
161 V:Bill Waters	525.00
162 Batman on railroad	525.00
163 V:Slippery Jim Elgin	525.00
164 Bat-signal story	525.00
165 `The Strange Costumes of Batman'	525.00
166 Meets John Gillen	525.00
167 A:Carter Nichols, Cleopatra	525.00
168 O:Joker	3,200.00
169 V:`Squint' Tolmar	525.00
170 Batman teams with Navy and Coast Guard	525.00
171 V:Penguin	700.00
172 V:Paul Gregorian	500.00
173 V:Killer Moth	500.00

DC COMICS

174 V:Dagger	500.00
175 V:Kangaroo Kiley	500.00
176 V:Mr. Velvet	500.00
177 Bat-Cave story	400.00
178 V:Baron Swane	400.00
179 `Mayor Bruce Wayne'	400.00
180 V:Joker	425.00
181 V:Human Magnet	400.00
182 V:Maestro Dorn	400.00
183 V:John Cook	400.00
184 I:Firefly(Garfield Lynns)	400.00
185 `Secret's of Batman's Utility Belt'	400.00
186 `The Flying Bat-Cave'	400.00
187 V:Two-Face	425.00
188 V:William Milden	400.00
189 V:Styx	400.00
190 Meets Dr. Sampson, O:Batman	575.00
191 V:Executioner	375.00
192 V: Nails Riley	375.00
193 V:Joker	425.00
194 V:Sammy Sabre	375.00
195 Meets Hugo Marmon	375.00
196 V:Frank Lumardi	375.00
197 V:Wrecker	375.00
198 Batman in Scotland	375.00
199 V:Jack Baker	375.00
200 V:Brand Keldon	500.00
201 Meet Human Target	375.00
202 V:Jolly Roger	375.00
203 V:Catwoman	400.00
204 V:Odo Neral	375.00
205 O:Bat-Cave	525.00
206 V:Trapper	375.00
207 Meets Merko the Great	375.00
208 V:Groff	375.00
209 V:Inventor	375.00
210 V:`Brain' Hobson	375.00
211 V:Catwoman	375.00
212 Meets Jonathan Bard	375.00
213 V:Mirror-Man	450.00
214 'The Batman Encyclopedia'	350.00
215 I:Ranger, Legionairy, Gaucho & Musketeer,A:Knight & Squire (See World's Finest 89)	350.00
216 A:Brane Taylor	350.00
217 Meets Barney Barrows	350.00
218 V:Dr. Richard Marston	350.00
219 V:Marty Mantee	350.00
220 A:Roger Bacon, historical scientist/philosopher	350.00
221 V:Paul King	350.00
222 V:`Big Jim' Jarrell	350.00
223 V:`Blast' Varren	350.00
224.	350.00
225 I&O:Martian Manhunter (J'onn J'onzz)	6,000.00
226 O:Robin's costume, A:J'onn J'onzz	1,400.00
227 A:Roy Raymond, J'onn J'onzz	500.00
228 A:Roy Raymond, J'onnJ'onz	500.00
229 A:Roy Raymond, J'onnJ'onz	500.00
230 A:Martian Manhunter,I:Mad Hatter	525.00
231 A:Batman,Jr.,Roy Raymond J'onn J'onzz	325.00
232 A:J'onn J'onzz	300.00
233 I&O:Batwoman	1,300.00
234 V:Jay Caird	300.00
235 O:Batman's Costume	600.00
236 V:Wallace Walby	400.00
237 F:Robin	325.00
238 V:Checkmate(villain)	325.00
239 Batman robot story	325.00
240 V:Burt Weaver	325.00
241 The Rainbow Batman	325.00
242 Batcave story	275.00

243 V:Jay Vanney	275.00
244 O:Batarang	275.00
245 F:Comm.Gordon	275.00
246.	275.00
247 I:Professor Milo	275.00
248.	275.00
249 V:Collector	275.00
250 V:John Stannor	275.00
251 V:Brand Ballard	225.00
252 Batman in a movie	225.00
253 I:Terrible Trio	225.00
254 A:Bathound	225.00
255 V:Fingers Nolan	225.00
256 Batman outer-space story	225.00
257 Batman sci-fi story	225.00
258 Batman robot story	225.00
259 I:Calendar Man	225.00
260 Batman outer space story	225.00
261 I:Dr. Double X	200.00
262 V:Jackal-Head	200.00
263 V:The Professor	200.00
264.	200.00
265 O:Batman retold	300.00
266 V:Astro	200.00
267 I&O:Bat-Mite	250.00
268 V:"Big Joe" Foster	200.00
269 V:Director	200.00
270 Batman sci-fi story	210.00
271 V:Crimson Knight,O:Martian Manhunter(retold)	210.00
272 V:Crystal Creature	210.00
273 A:Dragon Society	150.00
274 V:Nails Lewin	150.00
275 A:Zebra-Man	150.00
276 A:Batmite	150.00
277 Batman Monster story	150.00
278 A:Professor Simms	150.00
279 Batman robot story	150.00
280 A:Atomic Man	150.00
281 Batman robot story	125.00
282 Batman sci-fi story	125.00
283 V:Phantom of Gotham City	125.00
284 V:Hal Durgan	125.00
285 V:Harbin	125.00
286 A:Batwoman	125.00
287 A:Bathound	125.00
288 V:Multicreature	125.00
289 A:Bat-Mite	125.00
290 Batman's robot story	125.00
291 Batman sci-fi story	125.00
292 Last Roy Raymond	125.00
293 A:Aquaman,J'onnJ'onzz	125.00
294 V:Elemental Men, A:Aquaman	125.00
295 A:Aquaman	125.00
296 A:Aquaman	125.00

Detective #258 © DC Comics Inc.

297 A:Aquaman	125.00
298 I:Clayface(Matt Hagen)	250.00
299 Batman sci-fi stories	90.00
300 I:Mr.Polka-dot,E:Aquaman	100.00
301 A:J'onnJ'onzz	90.00
302 A:J'onnJ'onnz	80.00
303 A:J'onnJ'onnz	80.00
304 A:Clayface,J'onnJ'onz	80.00
305 Batman sci-fi story	80.00
306 A:J'onnJ'onnz	80.00
307 A:J'onnJ'onnz	80.00
308 A:J'onnJ'onnz	80.00
309 A:J'onnJ'onnz	80.00
310 A:Bat-Mite,J'onnJ'onnz	80.00
311 I:Cat-Man,Zook	90.00
312 A:Clayface,J'onnJ'onnz	70.00
313 A:J'onnJ'onnz	70.00
314 A:J'onnJ'onnz	70.00
315 I:Jungle Man	70.00
316 A:Dr.DoubleX,J'onnJ'onz	70.00
317 A:J'onnJ'onnz	70.00
318 A:Cat-Man,J'onnJ'onnz	70.00
319 A:J'onnJ'onnz	70.00
320 A:Vicki Vale	70.00
321 I:Terrible Trio	75.00
322 A:J'onnJ'onnz	65.00
323 I:Zodiac Master, A:J'onn J'onnz	65.00
324 A:Mad Hatter,J'onnJ'onnz.	65.00
325 A:Cat-Man,J'onnJ'onnz	65.00
326 Batman sci-fi story	65.00
327 CI,25th ann,symbol change	125.00
328 D:Alfred,I:WayneFoundation	125.00
329 A:Elongated Man	65.00
330 "Fallen Idol of Gotham"	65.00
331 A:Elongated Man	65.00
332 A:Joker	50.00
333 A:Gorla	50.00
334	50.00
335	50.00
336	50.00
337 "Deep Freeze Menace	50.00
338	50.00
339	50.00
340	50.00
341 A:Joker	60.00
342	50.00
343 BK,CI,Elongated Man	50.00
344.	50.00
345 CI,I:Blockbuster	50.00
346.	50.00
347 CI,Elongated Man	50.00
348 Elongated Man	50.00
349 BK(c),CI,Blockbuster	50.00
350 Elongated Man	50.00
351 CI,A:Elongated Man, I:Cluemaster	50.00
352 BK,Elongated Man	50.00
353.	50.00
354 BK,Elongated Man,I:Dr. Tzin-Tzin	50.00
355 CI,Elongated Man	50.00
356 BK,Outsider,Alfred	50.00
357.	50.00
358 BK,Elongated Man	50.00
359 I:new Batgirl	135.00
360.	50.00
361 CI	50.00
362 CI,Elongated Man	50.00
363 CI,Elongated Man	50.00
364 BK,Elongated Man	50.00
365 A:Joker	60.00
366 Elongated Man	50.00
367 Elongated Man	50.00
368 BK,Elongated Man	50.00
369 CA,Elongated Man, Catwoman	60.00
370 BK,Elongated Man	55.00
371 BK,Elongated Man	50.00
372 BK,Elongated Man	40.00
373 BK,Elongated Man	40.00

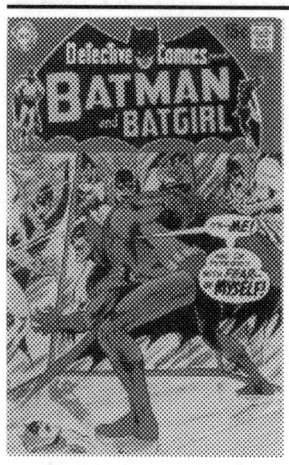

Detective #389 © DC Comics, Inc.

374 BK,Elongated Man........ 40.00
375 CI,Elongated Man 40.00
376.......................... 40.00
377 MA,Elongated Man,
     V:Riddler 40.00
378 Elongated Man 40.00
379 CI,Elongated Man 40.00
380 Elongated Man 40.00
381 GaF,Marital Bliss Miss 40.00
382 FR(s),BbB,JoG,GaF(s),SGe. . 40.00
383 FR(s),BbB,JoG,GaF(s),SGe.. 40.00
384 FR(s),BbB,JoG,GaF(s),SGe,
     BU:Batgirl................ 40.00
385 E:FR(s),BbB,JoG,NA(c),GK,MA,
     MkF,BU:Batgirl............ 40.00
386 BbK,MkF,BbB,JoG,
     BU:Batgirl................ 40.00
387 RA,rep.Detective #27....... 75.00
388 JBr(s),BbB,JoG,
     GK,MA,FR(s) 50.00
389 FR(s),BbB,JoG,GK,MA 40.00
390 FR(s),BbB,JoG,GK,MA,
     A:Masquerader............ 40.00
391 FR(s),NA(c),BbB,
     JoG,GK,MA 28.00
392 FR(s),BbB,JoG,I:Jason Bard . 28.00
393 FR(s),BbB,JoG,GK,MA 28.00
394 FR(s),BbB,JoG,GK,MA 20.00
395 FR(s),NA,DG,GK,MA 35.00
396 FR(s),BbB,JoG,GK,MA 28.00
397 DON(s),NA,DG,GK,MA 35.00
398 FR(s),BbB,JoG,GK,ViC 28.00
399 NA(c),DON(s),BbB,JoG,
     GK,ViC,Robin.............. 30.00
400 NA(c),NA,DG,GK,I:Man-Bat . . 60.00
401 NA(c),FR(s),JoG,
     BbB,JoG,GK,ViC 25.00
402 FR(s),NA,DG,V:Man-Bat 30.00
403 FR(s),BbB,JoG,NA(c),GK,ViC,
     BU:Robin................. 28.00
404 NA,GC,GK,A:Enemy Ace..... 35.00
405 IN,GK,I:League of Assassins . 28.00
406 DON(s),BbB,FrG 28.00
407 FR(s),NA,DG,V:Man-bat..... 35.00
408 MWn(s),LWn(s),NA,DG,
     V:DrTzin Tzin 35.00
409 B:FR(s),BbB,FrG,DH,DG 28.00
410 DON(s),FR(s),NA,DG,DH 35.00
411 NA(c),DON(s),BbB,DG,DH .. 22.00
412 NA(c),BbB,DG,DH 22.00
413 NA(c),BbB,DG,DH 22.00
414 DON(s),IN,DG,DH 22.00
415 BbB,DG,DH 22.00
416 DH...................... 22.00
417 BbB,DG,DH,BU:Batgirl..... 22.00

418 DON(s),DH,IN,DG,A:Creeper. 22.00
419 DON(s),DH 22.00
420 DH...................... 22.00
421 DON(s),BbB,DG,DH,A:Batgirl. 15.00
422 BbB,DG,DH,Batgirl 15.00
423 BbB,DG,DH 15.00
424 BbB,DG,DH,Batgirl 15.00
425 BWr(c),DON(s),IN,DG,DH ... 15.00
426 LWn(s),DG,A:Elongated Man . 15.00
427 IN,DG,DH,BU:Batgirl....... 15.00
428 BbB,DG,ENB(s),DD,JoG,
     BU:Hawkman............. 15.00
429 DG,JoG,V:Man-Bat 15.00
430 BbB,NC,ENS(s),DG,
     A:Elongated Man 15.00
431 DON(s),IN,MA 15.00
432 MA,A:Atom 15.00
433 DD,DG,MA 15.00
434 IN,DG,ENB(s),RB,DG 15.00
435 E:FR(s),DG,IN 15.00
436 MA,(i),DG,A:Elongated Man .. 15.00
437 JA,WS,I:Manhunter 20.00
438 JA,WS,Manhunter 35.00
439 DG,WS,O:Manhunter,Kid
     Eternity rep.............. 35.00
440 JAp,WS 35.00
441 HC,WS 32.00
442 ATh,WS 35.00
443 WS,D:Manhunter 35.00
444 JAp,B:Bat-Murderer,
     A:Ra's Al Ghul 35.00
445 JAp,MGr,A:Talia........... 35.00
446 JAp,last giant........... 11.00
447 DG(i),A:Creeper........... 11.00
448 DG(i),E:Bat-Murderer,
     A:Creeper,Ra's Al Ghul...... 11.00
449 `Midnight Rustler in Gotham' . 11.00
450 WS 12.00
451........................ 11.00
452........................ 11.00
453........................ 11.00
454........................ 11.00
455 MGr,A:Hawkman,V:Vampire . . 10.00
456 V:Ulysses Vulcan.......... 10.00
457 O:Batman rtd............. 12.00
458 A:Man Bat 10.00
459 A:Man Bat 10.00
460........................ 10.00
461 V:Capt.Stingaree 9.00
462 V:Capt.Stingaree,A:Flash.... 9.00
463 MGr,Atom,I:Calc.,Bl.Spider.... 9.00
464 MGr,TA,BlackCanary 9.00
465 TA,Elongated Man 9.00
466 MR,TA,V:Signalman....... 18.00
467 MR,TA 18.00
468 MR,TA,A:JLA............. 18.00
469 WS,I:Dr.Phosphorus 9.00
470 WS,AM,V:Dr.Phosphorus..... 9.00
471 MR,TA,A:Hugo Strange 18.00
472 MR,TA,A:Hugo Strange 18.00
473 MR,TA,R:Deadshot 18.00
474 MR,TA,A:Penguin,
     N:Deadshot 20.00
475 MR,TA,A:Joker............ 25.00
476 MR,TA,A:Joker............ 25.00
477 MR,DG,rep.NA. 20.00
478 MR,DG,I:3rd Clayface...... 15.00
479 MR,DG,A:3rd Clayface...... 15.00
480 DN,MA 7.00
481 JSt,CR,DN,DA,MR,
     A:ManBat............... 15.00
482 HC,MGo,DG,A:Demon...... 8.00
483 DN,DA,SD,A:Demon,
     40 Anniv. 12.00
484 DN,DA,Demon,O:1st Robin ... 6.00
485 DN,DA,D:Batwoman,A:Demon
     A:Ras al Ghul............. 5.00
486 DN,DA,DG,I:Odd Man,
     V:Scarecrow.............. 5.00
487 DN,DA,A:Ras Al Ghul 5.00
488 DN,V:Spook,Catwoman..... 6.50

Detective #468 © DC Comics, Inc.

489 IN,DH,DN,DA,Ras Al Ghul 5.00
490 DN,DA,PB,FMc,A:Black
     Lightning;A:Ras Al Ghul 5.00
491 DN,DA,PB,FMc,A:Black
     Lightning;V:Maxie Zeus 5.00
492 DN,DA,A:Penguin 6.50
493 DN,DA,A:Riddler 6.00
494 DN,DA,V:Crime Doctor 5.00
495 DN,DA,V:Crime Doctor 5.00
496 DN,DA,A:Clayface I 5.00
497 DN,DA.................. 5.00
498 DN,DA,V:Blockbuster....... 5.00
499 DN,DA,V:Blockbuster....... 5.00
500 DG,CI,WS,TY,JKu,Dead-
     man,Hawkman,Robin........ 12.00
501 DN,DA................. 5.00
502 DN,DA................. 5.00
503 DN,DA,Batgirl,Robin,
     V:Scarecrow.............. 5.00
504 DN,DA,Joker............. 7.00
505 DN,DA................. 5.00
506 DN,DA................. 5.00
507 DN,DA................. 5.00
508 DN,DA,V:Catwoman 7.00
509 DN,DA,V:Catman,Catwoma .. 7.00
510 DN,DA,V:Madhatter........ 5.00
511 DN,DA,I:Mirage 5.00
512 GC,45th Anniv............ 5.00
513 V:Two-Face.............. 6.50
514 .... 5.00
515 .... 5.00
516 .... 5.00
517 .... 5.00
518 V:Deadshot 5.00
519 .... 5.00
520 A:Hugo Strange,Catwoman ... 6.00
521 IN,TVE,A:Catwoman,B:BU:Green
     Arrow................... 6.50
522 D:Snowman.............. 5.00
523 V:Solomon Grundy......... 5.00
524 2nd A:J.Todd............. 6.00
525 J.Todd.................. 5.00
526 DN,AA,A:Joker,Catwoman
     500th A:Batman 15.00
527 V:Man Bat 4.00
528 Green Arrow,Ozone........ 4.00
529 I:Night Slayer,Nocturna 4.00
530 V:Nocturna 4.00
531 GC,AA,Chimera,J.Todd (see
     Batman #364)............ 4.00
532 GC,Joker................ 7.00
533...................... 4.00
534 GC,A:Gr.Arrow,V:PoisonIvy ... 4.00
535 GC,A:Gr.Arrow,V:Crazy Quitt
     2nd A:New Robin 6.00

536 GC,A:Gr.Arrow,V:Deadshot . . . 4.00
537 GC,A:Gr.Arrow. 4.00
538 GC,A:Gr.Arrow,V:Catman. 4.00
539 GC,A:Gr.Arrow. 4.00
540 GC,A:Gr.Arrow,V:Scarecrow. . . 4.00
541 GC,A:Gr.Arrow,V:Penguin 5.50
542 GC,A:Gr.Arrow. 4.00
543 GC,A:Gr.Arrow,V:Nightslayer . . 4.00
544 GC,A:Gr.Arrow,V:Nightslayer
   Nocturna 4.00
545. . . . . 4.00
546. . . . . 4.00
547. . . . . 4.00
548 PB. 4.00
549 PB,KJ,AMo(s),Gr.Arrow 4.50
550 KJ,AMo(s),Gr.Arrow 4.50
551 PB,V:Calendar Man 4.00
552 V:Black Mask. 4.00
553 V:Black Mask. 4.00
554 KJ,N:Black Canary. 4.00
555 GC,DD,GreenArrow 4.00
556 GC,Gr.Arrow,V:Nightslayer. . . 4.00
557 V:Nightslayer 4.00
558 GC,Green Arrow 4.00
559 GC,Green Arrow 4.00
560 GC,A:Green Arrow. 4.00
561. . . . . 4.00
562 GC,V:Film Freak 4.00
563 V:Two Face 4.00
564 V:Two Face 4.00
565 GC,A:Catwoman 5.50
566 GC,Joker. 6.00
567 GC,HarlanEllison 5.00
568 KJ,Legends tie-in,A:Penguin . 5.50
569 AD,V:Joker 7.00
570 AD,EvilCatwoman,A:Joker . . . 7.00
571 AD,V:Scarecrow 4.00
572 AD,CI,A:Elongated Man,Sherlock
   Holmes,SlamBradley,50thAnn. . 4.00
573 AD,V:Mad Hatter 4.00
574 AD,End old J.Todd/Robin sty . . 4.00
575 AD,Year 2,pt.1,I:Reaper 8.00
576 TM,AA,Year 2,pt.2,
   R:Joe Chill 6.00
577 TM,AA,Year 2,pt.3,V:Reaper . . 6.00
578 TM,AA,Year 2,pt.4,
   D:Joe Chill 6.00
579 I:NewCrimeDoctor 3.00
580 V:Two Face 3.00
581 V:Two Face 3.00
582 Millenium X-over 3.00
583 I:Ventriloquist. 3.00
584 V:Ventriloquist 3.00
585 I:Rat Catcher 3.00
586 V:Rat Catcher 3.00
587 NB,V:Corrosive Man 3.00
588 NB,V:Corrosive Man 3.00
589 Bonus Book #5 . . . . 4.00
590 NB,V:Hassan 3.00
591 NB,V:Rollo. 3.00
592 V:Psychic Vampire. 3.00
593 NB,V:Stirh 3.00
594 NB,A:Mr.Potato 3.00
595 IN,bonus book #11. . . . . 3.00
596 V:Sladek 3.00
597 V:Sladek 3.00
598 DCw,BSz,Blind Justice #1 . . . 5.00
599 DCw,BSz,Blind Justice #2 . . . 4.00
600 DCw,BSz,Blind Justice #3,
   50th Anniv.(double size) 5.00
601 NB,I:Tulpa 3.00
602 NB,A:Jason Blood 2.50
603 NB,A:Demon 2.50
604 NB,MudPack #1,V:Clayface,
   poster insert 2.50
605 NB,MudPack #2,V:Clayface . . 2.50
606 NB,MudPack #3,V:Clayface . . 2.50
607 NB,MudPack #4,V:Clayface,
   poster insert 2.50
608 NB,I:Anarky 2.00
609 NB,V:Anarky 2.00

610 NB,V:Penguin 3.00
611 NB,V:Catwoman,Catman 3.00
612 NB,A:Vicki Vale 1.75
613 Search for Poisoner. 1.75
614 V:Street Demons 1.75
615 NB,Return Penguin #2 (see
   Batman #448-#449) 2.75
616 NB. 1.75
617 A:Joker 1.75
618 NB,DG,A:Tim Drake. 1.75
619 NB,V:Moneyspider. 1.75
620 NB,V:Obeah,Man. 1.75
621 NB,SM,Obeah,Man 1.75
622 Demon Within,pt.1 . . . . 2.00
623 Demon Within,pt.2 . . . . 2.00
624 Demon Within,pt.3 . . . . 2.00
625 JAp,I:Abattior. 1.75
626 JAp,A:Electrocutioner. 1.75
627 600th issue w/Batman,rep.
   Detective #27. . . . . 4.00
628 JAp,A:Abattoir 1.75
629 JAp,`The Hungry Grass'. 1.75
630 JAp,I:Stiletto 1.75
631 JAp,V:Neo-Nazi Gangs 1.75
632 JAp,V:Creature 1.75
633 TMd,Fake Batman? 1.75
634 `The Third Man' 1.75
635 Video Game,pt.1 . . . . 1.75
636 Video Game,pt.2 . . . . 1.75
637 Video Game,pt.3 . . . . 1.75
638 JAp,Walking Time Bomb 1.75
639 JAp,The Idiot Root,pt.1 . . . . . 1.75
640 JAp,The Idiot Root,pt.4 . . . . . 1.75
641 JAp,Destroyer,pt.3
   (see LOTDK#27) 2.00
642 JAp,Faces,pt.2 . . . . 1.75
643 JAp,`Librarian of Souls' 1.75
644 TL,Electric City,pt.1
   A:Electrocutioner 1.75
645 TL,Electric City,pt.2 . . . . 1.75
646 TL,Electric City,pt.3 . . . . 1.75
647 TL,V:Cluemaster 1.75
648 MWg(c),TL,V:Cluemaster. . . . 1.75
649 MWg(c),TL,V:Cluemaster. . . . 1.75
650 TL,A:Harold,Ace 1.75
651 TL,`A Bullet for Bullock' 1.75
652 GN,R:Huntress 1.75
653 GN,A:Huntress 1.75
654 MN,The General,pt.1 . . . . 1.75
655 MN,The General,pt.2 . . . . 2.00
656 MN,The General,pt.3,C:Bane. . 4.00
657 MN,A:Azrael,I:Cypher 5.00
658 MN,A:Azrael 3.00
659 MN,Knightfall#2,

Detective #658 © DC Comics Inc.

   V:Ventriloquist,A:Bane 3.00
660 Knightfall#4,Bane Vs.
   Killer Croc 2.50
661 GN,Knightfall#6,V:Firefly,
   Joker,A:Bane 2.50
662 GN,Knightfall#8,V:Firefly,
   Joker,A:Huntress,Bane 2.50
663 GN,Knightfall#10,V:Trogg,
   Zombie,Bird,A:Bane 2.50
664 GN,Knightfall#12,A:Azrael 2.50
665 GN,Knightfall#16,A:Azrael 2.50
666 GN,SHa,A:Azrael,Trogg,
   Zombie,Bird 2.25
667 GN,SHa,Knightquest:Crusade,
   V:Trigger Twins 2.00
668 GN,SHa,Knightquest:Crusade,
   Robin locked out of Batcave . . 2.00
669 GN,SHa,Knightquest:Crusade,
   V:Trigger Twins 2.00
670 GN,SHa,Knightquest:Crusade,
   F:Rene Montoya. 2.00
671 GN,SHa,V:Joker. 2.00
672 KJ(c),GN,SHa,Knightquest:
   Crusade,V:Joker. 2.00
673 KJ(c),GN,SHa,Knightquest:
   Crusade,V:Joker. 2.00
674 KJ(c),GN,SHa,Knightquest:
   Crusade. 2.00
675 Foil(c),KJ(c),GN,SHa,Knightquest:
   Crusade,V:Gunhawk,foil(c) . . . 3.25
675a Newsstand ed. 1.75
675b Platinum edition 5.00
676 KJ(c),GN,SHa,Knights End #3,
   A:Nightwing 3.00
677 KJ(c),GN,SHa,Knights End #9
   V:Azrael 3.00
678 GN,SHa,Zero Hour 2.00
679 Ratcatcher. 2.00
680 Batman,Two-Face. 1.75
681 CDi,GN,KJ,Jean-Paul Valley . . 1.75
682 CDi,GN,SHa,Return of Bruce
   Wayne,Troika,pt.3. . . . . 1.75
682a Collector's Edition 2.50
683 R:Penguin,I:Actuary. 1.75
684 Daylight Heist 1.75
685 Chinatown War 1.75
686 V:King Snake,Lynx. 2.00
687 CDi,SHa,V:River Pirate 2.00
688 V:Captian Fear 2.00
689 F:Black Mask,Firefly. 2.00
690 F:Black Mask,Firefly. 2.00
691 V:Spellbinder 2.00
692 CDi,SHa,Underworld
   Unleashed tie-in 2.00
693 CDi,SHa,V:Poison Ivy
   & Agent Orange 2.00
694 CDi,find plant-killer. 2.00
695 CDi 3.00
696 CDi,GN,SHa,Contagion,pt.8. . . 3.00
697 CDi,GN,SHa,pt.1 (of 3)
   V:Lock-up. 2.00
698 CDi(s),A:Two-Face. 2.00
699 CDi(s), ... 2.00
700 double size, Legacy, pt.1
   x-over, R:Bane 3.50
700a cardstock cover 5.00
701 Legacy, pt. 6 x-over, V:Bane . . 2.00
702 CDi(s),GN,SHa,Legacy
   aftermath 2.00
703 CDi(s),GN,SHa, riots in Gotham
   City, Final Night tie-in 2.00
704 CDi(s),GN,TP,V:Al Gabone . . . 2.00
705 CDi(s),GN,Riddler & Cluemaster
   clash 2.00
706 CDi(s),GN. 2.00
707 CDi(s),GN,Riddler/Cluemaster
   concl. 2.00
708 CDi(s),GN,BSz,F:Deathstroke,
   R:Gunhawk, pt.1 (of 3) 2.00
709 CDi(s),GN,BSz,F:Deathstroke,
   Gunhawk,pt.2. . . . . 2.00

Detective #675 © DC Comics, Inc.

710 CDi(s),GN,BSz,F:Deathstroke,
　Gunhawk,pt.3 . . . . 2.00
711 CDi(s),GN,CaS,Bruce Wayne
　fights crime 2.00
712 CDi(s),GN,I:Gearhead 2.00
713 CDi(s),GN,V:Gearhead,pt.2 . . . 2.00
714 CDi(s),GN,F:Martian Manhunter2.00
715 CDi(s),GN,F:Martian Manhunter
　pt.2 . . . . 2.00
716 CDi,JAp,SNw,BSf, ... 2.00
717 CDi,GN,BSf,V:Gearhead,pt.1 . . 2.00
718 CDi,GN,BSf,V:Gearhead,pt.2 . . 2.00
719 . . . . 2.00
720 CDi,GN,KJ,Cataclysm
　x-over,pt.5 . . . . 2.00
721 CDi,GN,KJ,Cataclysm 2.00
722 CDi,JAp,BSf,Aftershock 2.00
723 CDi,BSz,Brotherhood of
　the Fist x-over, pt.2 . . . . 2.00
724 CDi,JAp,BSf,F:Nightwing 2.00
725 CDi,TP,BSf,Aftershock 2.00
726 CDi(s),BSf,V:Joker. 2.00
727 . . . . 2.00
728 CDi(s),BSf,SB,No Man's Land . 2.00
729 CDi(s),SB,No Man's Land 2.00
730 No Law and a New Order,
　concl. 2.00
731 F:Batgirl, Mosaic, pt.2 . . . . 2.00
732 F:Batgirl, Mosaic, pt.4 . . . . 2.00
733 SB,Alfreds advice 2.00
734 F:Batgirl,pt.2 x-over 2.00
735 DJu,BSz,Fruit of
　the Earth,pt.3 . . . . 3.95
736 LHa(s),MD2,V:Bane. 2.00
737 TMo, No Man's Land,
　The Code, concl. 2.00
Ann.#1 KJ,TD,A:Question,Talia,
　V:Penguin 6.00
Ann.#2 VS,A:Harvey Harris. 6.00
Ann.#3 DJu,DG,Batman in Japan . . 2.50
Ann.#4 Armageddon,pt.10 . . . . 3.00
Ann.#5 SK(c),TMd,Eclipso,V:The
　Ventriloquist,Joker 3.00
Ann.#6 JBa,I:Geist 2.75
Ann.#7 CDi,Elseworlds Story 3.25
Ann.#8 CDi,KD(c) Year One Annual
　O:The Riddler. 3.95
Ann.#9 Legends o/t Dead Earth . . . 2.95
Ann.#10 Pulp Heroes (War) CDi(s),
　SB,KJ. 3.95
Spec.#1,000,000 CDi(s) 2.00
TPB Manhunter AGw,WS 10.00

DETENTION COMICS
Aug. 1996
one-shot DON(s) 64pg, 3 stories. . . 3.50

DEXTER'S LABORATORY
Warner Bros./DC 1999
1 Kirbytron 6000 . . . . 2.00
2 Let's Save the World, You Jerk . . 2.00

DHAMPIRE: STILLBORN
DC/Vertigo Sept. 1996
GN Nancy A. Collins adaptation . . . 5.95

DOC SAVAGE
1987–88
1 AKu/NKu,D:Orig. Doc Savage. . . 2.50
2 AKu/NKu,V:Nazi's. 2.50
3 AKu/NKu,V:Nazi's. 2.50
4 AKu/NKu,V:Heinz. 2.50

[2nd Series] 1988–90
1 `Five in the Sky'(painted cov.) . . . 3.00
2 Chip Lost in Himalayas. 2.25
3 Doc declares war on USSR 2.25
4 DocSavage/Russian team-up . . . 2.25
5 V:The Erisians 2.25
6 U.S.,USSR,China Alliance
　vs. Erisians 2.25
7 Mind Molder,pt.1, I:Pat Savage . . 2.25
8 . . . . 2.25
9 In Hidalgo. 2.25
10 V:Forces of the Golden God . . . 2.25
11 Sunlight Rising,pt.1 . . . . 2.25
12 Sunlight Rising,pt.2 . . . . 2.25
13 Sunlight Rising,pt.3 . . . . 2.25
14 Sunlight Rising,pt.4 . . . . 2.25
15 SeaBaron #1 . . . . 2.25
16 EB,Shadow & Doc Savage 2.25
17 EB,Shadow & Doc Savage 2.25
18 EB,Shadow/DocSavage conc. . . 2.25
19 All new 1930's story. 2.25
20 V:Airlord & his Black Zepplin . . . 2.25
21 Airlord (30's story conc.) 2.25
22 Doc Savages Past,pt.1 . . . . 2.25
23 Doc Savages Past,pt.2 . . . . 2.25
24 Doc Savages Past,pt.3 (final). . . 2.25
Ann.#1 1956 Olympic Games 4.50

DOCTOR FATE
July, 1987
1 KG,V:Lords of Chaos 2.50
2 KG,New Dr. Fate 2.50
3 KG,A:JLI. 2.50
4 KG,V:Lords of Chaos Champion . 2.50

[2nd Series] 1988–92
1 New Dr.Fate,V:Demons 2.50
2 A:Andrew Bennett(I,Vampire) . . . 2.00
3 A:Andrew Bennett(I,Vampire) . . . 2.00
4 V:I,Vampire. 2.00
5 Dr.Fate & I,Vampire in Europe . . 2.00
6 A:Petey 2.00
7 Petey returns home dimension . . 2.00
8 Linda become Dr.Fate again. . . . 2.00
9 Eric's Mother's Ghost,
　A:Deadman 2.00
10 Death of Innocence,pt.1 . . . . . . 2.00
11 Return of Darkseid, Death of
　Innocence,pt.2 . . . . 2.00
12 Two Dr.Fates Vs.Darkseid,
　Death of Innocence,pt.3 . . . . . . 2.00
13 Linda in the Astral Realm,
　Death of Innocence,pt.4 . . . . . . 2.00
14 Kent & Petey vs. Wotan 2.00
15 V:Wotan,A:JLI 2.00
16 Flashback-novice Dr.Fate 1.75
17 Eric's Journey thru afterlife. 1.75
18 Search for Eric. 1.75

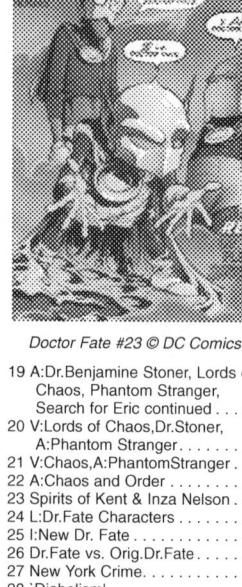

Doctor Fate #23 © DC Comics, Inc.

19 A:Dr.Benjamine Stoner, Lords of
　Chaos, Phantom Stranger,
　Search for Eric continued 1.75
20 V:Lords of Chaos,Dr.Stoner,
　A:Phantom Stranger. 1.75
21 V:Chaos,A:PhantomStranger . . . 1.75
22 A:Chaos and Order 1.75
23 Spirits of Kent & Inza Nelson . . . 1.75
24 L:Dr.Fate Characters 1.75
25 I:New Dr. Fate 1.75
26 Dr.Fate vs. Orig.Dr.Fate 1.75
27 New York Crime. 1.75
28 `Diabolism'. 1.75
29 Kent Nelson. 1.75
30 `Resurrection' 1.75
31 `Resurrection' contd. 1.75
32 War of the Gods x-over 1.75
33 War of the Gods x-over 1.75
34 A:T'Gilian. 1.75
35 Kent Nelson in N.Y. 1.75
36 Search For Inza,A:Shat-Ru 1.75
37 Fate Helmet Powers revealed . . 1.75
38 `The Spirit Motor,'Flashback. . . . 1.75
39 U.S.Senate Hearing. 1.75
40 A:Wonder Woman 1.75
41 O:Chaos and Order,last issue . . 1.75
Ann.#1 TS,R:Eric's dead mother . . . 2.95

DOCTOR MID-NITE
1999
1 (of 3) MWg,F:Dr. Piter Cross. . . . 6.00
2 MWg 6.00
3 MWg, conclusion 6.00

DOME, THE:
GROUND ZERO
DC/Helix (July 1998)
1-shot DGb,AMK 8.00

DOOM FORCE
Spec.#1 MMi(c),RCa,WS,PCu,KSy,
　I:Doom Force. 2.75

DOOM PATROL
[1st series]
(see MY GREATEST
ADVENTURE)

DOOM PATROL
[2nd Regular Series]
Oct., 1987

1 SLi,R:Doom Patrol,plus Who's Who
  background of team, I:Kalki . . . 2.50
2 SLi,V:Kalki 1.75
3 SLi,I:Lodestone 1.75
4 SLi,I:Karma 1.75
5 SLi,R:Chief 1.75
6 B:PuK(s),EL,GyM(i),
  I:Scott Fischer 2.00
7 EL,GyM(i),V:Shrapnel 1.75
8 EL,GyM(i),V:Shrapnel 1.75
9 E:PuK(s),EL,GyM(i),V:Garguax,
  & Bonus Book 1.75
10 EL,A:Superman 2.00
11 EL,R:Garguax 1.75
12 EL,A:Garguax 1.75
13 EL,A:Power Girl 1.75
14 EL,A:Power Girl 1.75
15 EL,Animal-Veg-.Mineral Man . . 1.75
16 V:GenImmotus,Animal-Veg.-
  Mineral Man 1.75
17 D:Celsius,A:Aquaman & Sea
  Devils, Invasion tie-in 3.00
18 Invasion 1.50
19 B:GMo(s),New Direction,
  I:Crazy Jane 5.00
20 I:Rebis(new Negative-Being),
  A:CrazyJane,Scissormen 4.00
21 V:Scissormen 3.50
22 City of Bone,V:Scissormen 3.50
23 A:RedJack,Lodestone kidnap . . . 3.50
24 V:Red Jack 3.50
25 Secrets of New Doom Patrol . . . 3.50
26 I:Brotherhood of Dada 3.00
27 V:Brotherhood of Dada 3.00
28 Trapped in nightmare,V:Dada . . 3.00
29 Trapped in painting,
  A:Superman 3.00
30 SBs(c),V:Brotherhood of Dada . . 3.00
31 SBs(c),A:The Pale Police 3.00
32 SBs(c),V:Cult of
  Unwritten Book 3.00
33 SBs(c),V:Cult,A:Anti-God
  the DeCreator 3.00
34 SBs(c),Robotman vs. his brain,
  R:The Brain & Mr.Mallah 3.00
35 SBs(c),A:Men from
  N.O.W.H.E.R.E. 3.00
36 SBs(c),V:Men from
  N.O.W.H.E.R.E. 3.25
37 SBs(c),Rhea Jones Story 2.50
38 SBs(c),V:Aliens 2.50
39 SBs(c),V:Aliens 2.50
40 SBs(c),Aliens 2.50
41 SBs(c),Aliens 2.50
42 O:Flex Mentallo 2.50
43 SBs(c),V:N.O.W.H.E.R.E. 2.50
44 SBs(c),V:N.O.W.H.E.R.E. 2.50
45 . . . . 2.50
46 SBs(c),RCa,MkK,A:Crazy Jane,
  Dr.Silence 2.50
47 Scarlet Harlot (Crazy Jane) 2.50
48 V:Mr.Evans 2.50
49 TTg(c),RCa,MGb,I:Mr.Nobody . . 2.50
50 SBs(c),V:Brotherhood of Dada
  & bonus artists portfolio 3.00
51 SBs(c),Mr.Nobody Runs for
  President 2.50
52 SBs(c),Mr.Nobody saga conc . . . 2.50
53 SBs(c),Parody Issue,A:Phantom
  Stranger,Hellblazer,Mr.E 2.50
54 Rebis'Transformation 2.50
55 SBs(c),V:Crazy Jane,
  Candle Maker 2.50
56 SBs(c),V:Candle Maker 2.50
57 SBs(c),RCa,V:Candle Maker,
  O:Team,Double-sized 3.00
58 SBs(c),V:Candle Maker 2.25

Doom Patrol #9 © DC Comics Inc.

59 TTg(c),RCa,SnW(i),A:Candlemaker
  D:Larry Trainor 2.25
60 JHw(c),RCa,SnW(i),
  V:Candlemaker,A:Magnus 2.25
61 TTg(c),RCa,SnW(i),A:Magnus
  D:Candlemaker 2.25
62 DFg(c),RCa,SnW(i),
  V:Nanomachines 2.25
63 E:GMo(s),RCa,R:Crazy Jane,
  V:Keysmiths,BU:Sliding from the
  Wreckage 2.25

Vertigo 1993

64 BB(c),B:RaP(s),RCa,SnW(i),
  B:Sliding from the Wreckage,
  R:Niles Caulder 2.25
65 TTg(c),RCa,SnW(i),Nannos 2.25
66 RCa,E:Sliding from the
  Wreckage 2.25
67 TTg(c),LiM,GHi(i),New HQ,I:Charlie,
  George,Marion,V:Wild Girl 2.25
68 TTg(c),LiM,GHi(i),I:Indentity
  Addict 2.25
69 TTg(c),LiM,GHi(i),V:Identity
  Addict 2.25
70 TTg(c),SEa,TS(i),I:Coagula,
  V:Codpiece 2.25
71 TTg(c),LiM,TS(i),Fox & Crow . . . 2.25
72 TTg(c),LiM,TS(i),Fox vs Crow . . 2.25
73 LiM,GPi(i),Head's Nightmare . . . 2.25
74 LiM,TS(i),Bootleg Steele 2.25
75 BB(c),TMK,Teiresias Wars#1,
  Double size 2.25
76 Teiresias Wars#2 . . . . 2.25
77 BB(c),TMK,N:Cliff 2.25
78 BB(c),V:Tower of Babel 2.25
79 BB(c),E:Teiresias Wars 2.25
80 V:Yapping Dogs 2.25
81 B:Masquerade 2.25
82 E:Masquerade 2.25
83 False Memory 2.00
84 The Healers 2.00
85 Charlie the Doll 2.00
86 Imagine Ari's Friends 2.00
87 KB(c),Imagine Ari's
  Friends,pt.4,final issue 2.00
Ann.#1 A:Lex Luthor 2.00
Ann.#2 RaP(s),MkW,Children's
  Crusade,F:Dorothy,A:Maxine . . 4.25
Doom Patrol/Suicide Squad #1 EL,
  D:Mr.104,Thinker,Psi,Weasel . . 2.50
TPB Crawling From the Wreckage,
  SBs(c),rep.#19-#25 . . . . 19.95

DOOMSDAY

Ann.#1 Year One annuals 3.95

DOORWAY TO NIGHTMARE
1978

1 I:Madame Xanadu 1.00
2 . . . . 1.00
3 . . . . 1.00
4 JCr 1.00
5 . . . . 1.00

DOUBLE ACTION COMICS
Jan., 1940

2 Pre-Hero DC 12,500.00

DRAGONLANCE
1988–91

1 Krynn's Companion's advent 3.50
2 Vandar&Riva vs.Riba's brother . . 3.50
3 V:Takhesis,Queen of Darkness . . 3.00
4 V:Lord Soth & Kitiara 3.00
5 V:Queen of Darkness 3.00
6 Gnatch vs. Kalthanan 3.00
7 Raistlin's Evil contd. 3.00
8 Raistlin's Evil concl. 2.00
9 Journey to land o/t Minotaurs
  A:Tanis, Kitiara 2.00
10 Blood Sea,`Arena of Istar' 2.00
11 Cataclysm of Krynn Revealed
  `Arena of Istar' contd. 2.00
12 Horak vs.Koraf, Arena contd. . . . 2.00
13 Test of High Sorcery #1 . . . . 2.00
14 Test of High Sorcery #2 . . . . 2.00
15 Test of High Sorcery #3 . . . . 2.00
16 Test of High Sorcery #4 . . . . 2.00
17 Winter'sKnight:DragonkillPt.1 . . 2.00
18 Winter'sKnight:DragonkillPt.1 . . 2.00
19 Winter'sKnight:DragonkillPt.1 . . 2.00
20 Winter'sKnight:DragonkillPt.1 . . 2.00
21 Move to New World 2.00
22 Taladas,pt.1,A:Myrella 2.00
23 Taladas,pt.2,Riva vs. Dragon . . 2.00
24 Taladas,pt.3,V:Minotaur Lord . . . 2.00
25 Taladas,pt.4,V:Axantheas 2.00
26 Rune Discovery,V:Agents
  of Eristem 2.00
27 V:Agents of Eristem 2.00
28 Riva continued 2.00
29 Riva continued 2.00
30 Dwarf War,pt.1 . . . . 1.75
31 Dwarf War,pt.2 . . . . 1.75
32 Dwarf War,pt.3 . . . . 1.75
33 Dwarf War,pt.4 . . . . 1.75
34 conc., last issue 1.75
Ann.#1 Myrella of the Robed
  Wizards 2.95

DREAMING, THE
DC/Vertigo June 1996

1 TLa(s),PSj,"The Goldie
  Factor,"pt.1 . . . . 2.50
2 TLa(s),PSj,"The Goldie
  Factor,"pt.2 . . . . 2.50
3 TLa(s),PSj,"The Goldie
  Factor,"pt.3 . . . . 2.50
4 SvP,"The Lost Boy", pt.1 (of 4) . . 2.50
5 SvP,"The Lost Boy", pt.2 . . . . . . 2.50
6 SvP,"The Lost Boy", pt.3 . . . . . . 2.50
7 SvP,"The Lost Boy", pt.4 . . . . . . 2.50
8 AaK(s),MZi, visitor from Cain's
  past 2.50
9 BT(s),PD,TOz,"Weird Romance,"
  pt.1 (of 4) 2.50
10 BT(s),PD,TOz,"Weird Romance,"

DC COMICS

pt.2 . . . . 2.50
11 BT(s),PD,TOz,"Weird Romance,"
   pt.3 . . . . 2.50
12 BT(s),PD,TOz,"Weird Romance,"
   pt.4 . . . . 2.50
13 TLa,JIT,"Coyote's Kiss," pt. 1 . . . 2.50
14 TLa,JIT,"Coyote's Kiss," pt. 2 . . . 2.50
15 . . . . 2.50
16 GyA,F:Nuala 2.50
17 PD,DMc,Souvenirs, pt.1. . . . . . . 2.50
18 PD,DMc,Souvenirs, pt.2. . . . . . . 2.50
19 PD,DMc,Souvenirs, pt.3. . . . . . . 2.50
20 ADv, The Dark Rose, pt.1 . . . . . 2.50
21 ADv, The Dark Rose, pt.2 . . . . . 2.50
22 The Unkindness of One, pt.1 . . . 2.50
23 The Unkindness of One, pt.2 . . . 2.50
24 The Unkindness of One, pt.3 . . . 2.50
25 My Life as a Man. 2.50
26 Restitution. 2.50
27 Caretaker Cain 2.50
28 victims of famous fires 2.50
29 PSj,DMc,Abel'sHouse ofSecrets 2.50
30 DMc(c),Lucien's mysteries 2.50
31 House of Secrets, 48-pg. 4.00
32 DG,SvP 2.50
33 The Little Mermaid. 2.50
34 MaH, Cave of Nightmares 2.50
35 DMc(c),Kaleidoscope. 2.50
36 DMc(c),The Gyres, pt.1 . . . . 2.50
37 DMc(c),The Gyres, pt.2 . . . . 2.50
38 DMc(c),The Gyres, pt.3 . . . . 2.50
39 DMc(c),Lost Language
   of Flowers 2.50
40 DMc(c),Foxes & Hounds,pt.1 . . . 2.50
41 DMc(c),Foxes & Hounds,pt.2 . . . 2.50
TPB Beyond the Shores of Night . 20.00
TPB Through the Gates of
   Horn & Ivory. 20.00
GN Trial and Error 6.00

DYNAMIC CLASSICS
Sept.-Oct. 1978
1 Rep. Detective 395 & 438. . . . . . 3.00

ECLIPSO
1992–94
1 BS,MPn,V:South American
   Drug Dealers 2.50
2 BS,MPn,A:Bruce Gordon 2.00
3 BS,MPn,R:Amanda Waller 2.00
4 BS,A:Creeper,Cave Carson 2.00
5 A:Creeper,Cave Carson 2.00

6 LMc,V:Bruce Gordon 2.00
7 London,1891 . . . . 2.00
8 A:Sherlock Holmes. 1.50
9 I:Johnny Peril 1.50
10 CDo,V:Darkseid. 1.50
11 A:Creeper,Peacemaker,Steel . . . 1.50
12 V:Shadow Fighters 1.50
13 D:Manhunter,Commander Steel,
   Major Victory,Peacemaker,
   Wildcat,Dr.Midnight,Creeper . . . 1.50
14 A:JLA 1.50
15 A:Amanda Waller. 1.50
16 V:US Army 1.50
17 A:Amanda Waller,Martian
   Manhunter,Wonder Woman,Flash,
   Bloodwynd,Booster Gold 1.75
18 A:Spectre,JLA,final issue 2.00
Ann.#1 I:Prism 2.50

ECLIPSO: THE DARKNESS WITHIN
1992
1 BS,Direct w/purple diamond,
   A:Superman,Creeper 4.00
1a BS,Newstand w/out diamond . . 3.00
2 BS,MPn,DC heroes V:Eclipso,
   D:Starman 3.00

EGYPT
1995–96
1 College Experiments. 2.50
2 College Experiments. 2.50
3 New York Haunt 2.50
4 V:Seth,Isis 2.50
5 V: The Priests. 2.50
6 . . . . 2.50
7 finale 2.50

80 PAGE GIANTS
Aug., 1964
1 Superman. 500.00
2 Jimmy Olsen. 300.00
3 Lois Lane 200.00
4 Golden Age-Flash. 225.00
5 Batman. 225.00
6 Superman. 200.00
7 JKu&JKu(c),Sgt. Rock's Prize
   Battle Tales 200.00
8 Secret Origins,O:JLA,Aquaman,
   Robin,Atom, Superman 400.00
9 Flash 175.00
10 Superboy. 175.00
11 Superman,A:Lex Luthor 175.00
12 Batman 175.00
13 Jimmy Olsen 175.00
14 Lois Lane. 175.00
15 Superman & Batman 175.00
16 JLA #39. . . . . 75.00
17 Batman #176. . . . . 40.00
18 Superman #183. . . . . 18.00
19 Our Army at War #164. . . . . . 10.00
20 Action #334. . . . . 16.00
21 Flash #160 . . . . 30.00
22 Superboy #129 . . . . 7.00
23 Superman #187. . . . . 13.00
24 Batman #182. . . . . 26.00
25 Jimmy Olsen #95. . . . . 10.00
26 Lois Lane #68. . . . . 10.00
27 Batman #185. . . . . 35.00
28 World's Finest #161 . . . . 11.00
29 JLA #48. . . . . 16.00
30 Batman #187. . . . . 35.00
31 Superman #193. . . . . 13.00
32 Our Army at War #177. . . . . . . 8.00
33 Action #347 . . . . 11.00
34 Flash #169. . . . . 30.00
35 Superboy #138 . . . . 6.00
36 Superman #197. . . . . 12.00

37 Batman #193. . . . . 16.00
38 Jimmy Olsen #104. . . . . 5.00
39 Lois Lane #77 . . . . 6.00
40 World's Finest #170 . . . . 10.00
41 JLA #58. . . . . 12.00
42 Superman #202. . . . . 12.00
43 Batman #198. . . . . 24.00
44 Our Army at War #190. . . . . . . 5.00
45 Action #360 . . . . 8.00
46 Flash #178. . . . . 18.00
47 Superboy #147 . . . . 7.00
48 Superman #207. . . . . 12.00
49 Batman #203. . . . . 14.00
50 Jimmy Olsen #113. . . . . 5.00
51 Lois Lane #86 . . . . 6.00
52 World's Finest #179. . . . . 6.00
53 JLA #67. . . . . 8.00
54 Superman #212. . . . . 12.00
55 Batman #208. . . . . 13.00
56 Our Army at War #203. . . . . . . 5.00
57 Action #373. . . . . 8.00
58 Flash #187. . . . . 13.00
59 Superboy #156 . . . . 6.00
60 Superman #217. . . . . 10.00
61 Batman #213. . . . . 35.00
62 Jimmy Olsen #122. . . . . 5.00
63 Lois Lane #95 . . . . 5.00
64 World's Finest #188. . . . . 6.00
65 JLA #76. . . . . 7.00
66 Superman #222. . . . . 10.00
67 Batman #218. . . . . 13.00
68 Our Army at War #216. . . . . . . 5.00
69 Adventure #390. . . . . 10.00
70 Flash #196. . . . . 12.00
71 Superboy #165 . . . . 6.00
72 Superman #227. . . . . 10.00
73 Batman #223. . . . . 14.00
74 Jimmy Olsen #131. . . . . 5.00
75 Lois Lane #104 . . . . 4.00
76 World's Finest #197. . . . . 5.00
77 JLA #85. . . . . 6.00
78 Superman #232. . . . . 10.00
79 Batman #228. . . . . 12.00
80 Our Army at War #229. . . . . . . 5.00
81 Adventure #403. . . . . 6.00
82 Flash #205 . . . . 9.00
83 Superboy #174 . . . . 6.00
84 Superman #239. . . . . 10.00
85 Batman #233. . . . . 12.00
86 Jimmy Olsen #140. . . . . 5.00
87 Lois Lane #113 . . . . 4.00
88 World's Finest #206. . . . . 5.00
89 JLA #93. . . . . 6.00

Eclipso #5 © DC Comics, Inc.

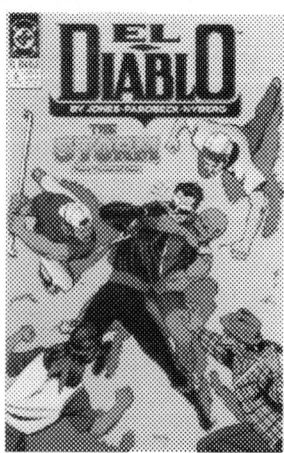
El Diablo #6 © DC Comics, Inc.

All comics prices listed are for *Near Mint* condition.

EL DIABLO
1989–91
1 I:El Diablo, double-size 2.50
2 V:Crime Lord Benny Contreras . . 2.00
3 `Day of the Dead' Celebration. . . 2.00
4 Storm #1 . . . . 2.25
5 Storm #2 . . . . 2.25
6 Storm #3 . . . . 2.25
7 Storm #4 . . . . 2.25
8 V:Car-Theft Ring. 2.00
9 V:Crime Lord of Dos Rios 2.00
10 The Franchise #1. . . . . 2.00
11 The Franchise #2. . . . . 2.00
12 A:Greg Sanders (golden age) . . 2.00
13 The River #1 . . . . 2.00
14 The River #2 . . . . 2.00
15 The River #3 . . . . 2.00
16 Final Issue. 2.00

ELECTRIC WARRIOR
1986–87
1 SF series,I:Electric Warriors 2.50
2 `Bloodstalker Mode' 2.00
3 Rogue Warrior vs. Z-Primes 2.00
4 Primmies vs. Electric Warriors . . 2.00
5 Lek 0-03 Rebels 2.00
6 Lek 0-03 vs. Masters 1.75
7 Lek'sFate,Derek Two-Shadows . . 1.75
8 Derek Two-Shadows Betrayed . . 1.75
9 Fate of Derek Two-Shadows. . . . 1.75
10 Two-Shadows as one 1.75
11 Rebellion 1.75
12 Rebellion continued 1.75
13 V:Prime One 1.75
14 Mutants Join Rebellion. 1.75
15 Invaders Arrival 1.75
16 Unified Warriors vs. Invaders . . . 1.75
17 V:Terrans, O:Electric Warriors . . 1.75
18 Origin continued, final issue 1.75

ELONGATED MAN
1992
1 A:Copperhead 1.00
2 Modora,A:Flash,I:Sonar 1.00
3 A:Flash,V:Wurst Gang 1.00

ELSEWORLD'S FINEST
DC/Elseworlds 1998
1 (of 2) JFM,KD,F:Bruce Wayne
   and Clark Kent, ... 5.00
2 JFM,KD,concl. 5.00
GN Supergirl & Batgirl 6.00

ELVIRA
1986–87
1 DSp,BB(c) 3.25
2 thru 9 . . . . @1.00
10 . . . . 2.00
11 DSt(c)Find Cain 2.50

ENIGMA
Vertigo 1993
1 B:PrM(s),DFg,I:Enigma,Michael
   Smith,V:The Head 3.00
2 DFg,I:The Truth 3.00
3 DFg,V:The Truth,I:Envelope Girl,
   Titus Bird 3.00
4 DFg,D:The Truth,I:Interior
   League. 3.00
5 DFg,I:Enigma's Mother 3.00
6 DFg,V:Envelope Girl 3.00
7 DFg,V:Enigma's Mother,D:Envelope
   Girl,O:Enigma. 3.00
8 E:PrM(s),DFg,final issue 3.00
TPB Rep. #1-#8 . . . . 19.95

ERADICATOR
1996
1 IV,Low, ... 1.75
2 IV,Low, ... 1.75
3 IV,Low,"Reign of the Superman"
   concl.A:Superboy 1.75

ESSENTIAL VERTIGO:
SWAMP THING
DC/Vertigo Sept. 1996
B&W reprints
1 AMo(s), rep. Saga of
   the Swamp Thing #21. . . . . . . 2.50
2 thru 11 AMo(s), rep. Saga of
   the Swamp Thing #22–#31. . @2.00
12 AMo(s) rep. Saga Ann. #2 . . . . 2.00
13 AMo(s) rep. Saga #32–#42 . . @2.00
24 AMo,Windfall, final issue 2.25

ESSENTIAL VERTIGO:
THE SANDMAN
DC/Vertigo 1996
3 NGa(s),SK,MDr,rep. 2.00
4 NGa(s),SK,MDr,rep. F:Etrigan
   the Demon 2.00
5 NGa(s),SK,MJ,F:Morpheus,
   John Dee 2.00
6 NGa(s),SK,MJ,V:Dr. Destiny 2.00
7 . . . . 2.00
8 NGa(s),MDr,MJ,"The Sound
   of Her Wings" 2.00
9 NGa(s),MDr,MJ,"The Doll's
   House" F:Nada. 2.00
10 NGa(s),MDr,MJ,"The Doll's
   House" 2.00
11 NGa(s),MDr,RT 2.00
12 NGa(s),CBa,MJ,"The Doll's
   House," pt.3 . . . . 2.00
13 NGa,rep. "Doll's House," pt.4 . . 2.00
14 NGa,rep. "Doll's House," pt.5 . . 2.00
15 NGa,rep. "Doll's House," pt.6 . . 2.00
16 NGa,rep. "Lost Hearts". 2.00
17 NGa,rep. "Dream Country". 2.00
18 NGa,"Dream of a Thousand
   Cats" 2.00
19 NGa,rep.Sandman #19 . . . . 2.00
20 NGa,rep.Sandman #20 . . . . 2.00
21 NGa,rep.Sandman #21 . . . . 2.00
22 NGa,rep.Season of Mists pt.1 . . 2.00
23 NGa,rep.Season of Mists pt.2 . . 2.00
24 NGa,rep.Season of Mists pt.3 . . 2.00
25 NGa,rep.Season of Mists pt.4 . . 2.00
26 NGa,rep.Season of Mists pt.5 . . 2.00
27 NGa,rep.Season of Mists,pt.6 . . 2.25
28 NGa,rep.Season of Mists,epilog. 2.25
29 NGa,rep.Thermidor 2.25
30 NGa,rep.August. 2.25
31 NGa,rep.Three Septembers
   and a January 2.25
32 NGa,rep. Sandman Special #1
   final issue. 4.50

EXTREME JUSTICE
1995–96
0 New Group 1.50
1 V:Captain Atom 1.50
2 V:War Cyborgs 1.50
3 V:Synge 1.50
4 R:Firestorm the Nuclear Man . . . 1.50
5 Firestorm & Elementals 1.75
6 Monarch,Captain Atom, Booster
   Gold, Maxima. 1.75
7 F:Monarch,Captain Atom 1.75
8 . . . . 1.75
9 F:Firestorm 1.75
10 Underworld Unleashed tie-in . . . 1.75

11 Underworld Unleashed tie-in . . 1.75
12 Monarch's scheme revealed . . . 1.75
13 Monarch vs. Captain Atom. 1.75
14 . . . . 1.75
15 TMo,V:The Slavemaster from
   the Stars 1.75
16 TMo,V:Legion of Doom 1.75
17 TMo,V:Legion of Doom 1.75

EXTREMIST
Vertigo 1993
1 B:PrM(s),TMK,I:The Order,
   Extremist(Judy Tanner) 2.50
1a Platinum Ed. 8.00
2 TMK,D:Extremist(Jack Tanner) . . 2.25
3 TMK,V:Patrick 2.25
4 E:PrM(s),TMK,D:Tony Murphy . . 2.25

FACE, THE
GN DFg,PrM 4.95

FAMILY MAN
Paradox 1995
1 I:Family Man. 4.95
2 V:Brother Charles 4.95
3 Escape. 4.95

FANBOY
1999
1 (of 6) SA, various artists 2.50
2 . . . . 2.50
3 A:JLA 2.50
4 SA, A:Sgt. Rock 2.50
5 SA, A:Batman. 2.50
6 SA, A:Wonder Woman, concl. . . 2.50

FAREWELL
MOONSHADOW
DC/Vertigo
GN JMD(s),JMu, prose & pictures. . 7.95

FATE
1994–96
1 Dr. Fate 2.50
2 Nabu,Astral plane 2.25
3 Bloodstain 2.00
4 Decisions 2.00
5 Judged by Enclave 2.00
6 V:Grimoire 2.00

Fate #4 © DC Comics Inc.

DC COMICS

7 V:Dark Agent 2.00
8 V:Dark Agent 2.25
9 Tries to change his destiny 2.25
10 A:Zatanna 2.25
11 . . . . 2.25
12 A:Sentinel 2.25
13 V:Blaze 2.25
14 LKa,ALa,AWi,Underworld
   Unleashed tie-in 2.25
15 LKa,ALa,AWi,V:Charnelle 2.25
16 LKa,ALa,AWi,canibal drug-cult . . 2.25
17 LKa,ALa,AWi 2.25
18 LKa,ALa,AWi,V:Charnelle 2.25
19 LKa,ALa,AWi,V:men in black . . . 2.25

FAULT LINES
DC/Vertigo March 1997
Mini-series
1 LMr(s),F:Tracey Farrand 2.50
2 LMr(s) 2.50
3 LMr(s) 2.50
4 LMr(s) 2.50
5 (of 6) LMr(s) 2.50
6 LMrs(s) concl. 2.00

Fighting American #6
© DC Comics, Inc.

FIGHTING AMERICAN
1994
1 GrL,R:Fighting American 1.75
2 GrL,Media Circus 1.75
3 GrL,I&V:Gross Nation Product,
   Def Iffit 1.75
4 GrL,V:Gross Nation Product,
   Def Iffit 1.75
5 GrL,PhorOptor 1.75
6 Final Issue 1.75

FINAL NIGHT, THE
Sept. 1996
[Cross-Over Series]
1 KK(s),SI,JMz, Alien crash lands
   on Earth 2.00
2 KK(s),SI,JMz, Earth's sun
   extinguished 2.00
3 KK(s),SI,JMz, Attempts to stave
   off inevitable 2.00
4 KK(s),SI,JMz, Can they save the
   world, and at what price? 2.00
TPB rep. 13.00

FINALS
DC/Vertigo 1999
1 (of 4) College satire 3.00
2 JIT,pt.2 . . . . 3.00

FIREBRAND
1995
1 SaV,Alex Sanchez becomes
   Firebrand 1.75
2 SaV 1.75
3 SaV,Generation Prime case
   climax 1.75
4 SaV,Young gang member 1.75
5 SaV,V;serial killer(s) 1.75
6 BAu,SaV 1.75
7 . . . . 1.75
8 . . . . 1.75
9 final issue 1.75

FIRESTORM
March, 1978
1 AM,JRu,I&O:Firestorm 4.00
2 AM,BMc,A:Superman 3.00
3 AM,I:Killer Froat 3.00
4 AM,BMc,I:Hyena 3.00
5 AM,BMc,Hyena 3.00

FIRESTORM, THE
NUCLEAR MAN
(see FURY OF FIRESTORM)

FIRST ISSUE SPECIAL
April, 1975
1 JK,Atlas 6.00
2 Green Team 7.00
3 Metamorpho 5.00
4 Lady Cop 5.00
5 JK,Manhunter 6.00
6 JK,Dingbats 5.00
7 SD,Creeper 5.00
8 MGr,Warlord 15.00
9 WS,Dr.Fate 7.00
10 Outsiders(not Batman team) . . . 5.00
11 NR,AM Code:Assassin 5.00
12 new Starman 5.00
13 return of New Gods 8.00

First Issue Special #1
© DC Comics, Inc.

FLASH COMICS
Jan., 1940
1 SMo,SMo(c),O:Flash,Hawkman,The
   Whip & Johnny Thunder,B:Cliff
   Cornwall,Minute Movies . . 60,000.00
2 B:Rod Rain 6,500.00
3 SMo,SMo(c),B:The King 4,800.00
4 SMo,SMo(c),F:The Whip 4,000.00
5 SMo,SMo(c),F:The King 3,200.00
6 F:Flash 4,500.00
7 Hawkman(c) 3,800.00
8 Male bondage(c) 2,500.00
9 Hawkman(c) 3,000.00
10 SMo,SMo(c),Flash(c) 3,000.00
11 SMo,SMo(c) 1,600.00
12 SMo,SMo(c),B:Les Watts . . 1,600.00
13 SMo,SMo(c) 1,500.00
14 SMo,SMo(c) 1,600.00
15 SMo,SMo(c) 1,500.00
16 SMo,SMo(c) 1,500.00
17 SMo,SMo(c),E:CliffCornwall 1,500.00
18 SMo,SMo(c) 1,500.00
19 SMo,SMo(c) 1,500.00
20 SMo,SMo(c) 1,500.00
21 SMo(c) 1,400.00
22 SMo,SMo(c) 1,400.00
23 SMo,SMo(c) 1,400.00
24 SMo,SMo(c),Flash V:Spider-
   Men of Mars,A:Hawkgirl . . . 1,500.00
25 SMo,SMo(c). 950.00
26 SMo,SMo(c). 950.00
27 SMo,SMo(c). 950.00
28 SMo,SMo(c),Flash goes
   to Hollywood 950.00
29 SMo,SMo(c) 1,000.00
30 SMo,SMo(c),Flash in`Adventure
   of the Curiosity Ray!' 950.00
31 SMo,SMo(c),Hawkman(c) . . . 900.00
32 SMo,SM(c),Flash in`Adventure
   of the Fictious Villians' 900.00
33 SMo,SMo(c). 900.00
34 SMo,SMo(c),Flash in `The
   Robbers of the Round Table'. 900.00
35 SMo,SMo(c). 900.00
36 SMo,SMo(c),F:Flash, The Mystery
   of the Doll Who Walks Like
   a Man' 900.00
37 SMo,SMo(c). 900.00
38 SMo,SMo(c). 900.00
39 SMo,SMo(c). 900.00
40 SMo,SMo(c),F:Flash, Man Who
   Could Read Man's Souls! . . . 900.00
41 SMo,SMo(c). 800.00
42 SMo,SMo(c),Flash V:The
   Gangsters Baby!. 800.00
43 SMo,SMo(c). 800.00
44 SMo,SMo(c),Flash V:The
   Liars Club. 800.00
45 SMo,SMo(c),F:Hawkman,Big
   Butch Makes Hall of Fame . . 800.00
46 SMo,SMo(c). 800.00
47 SMo,SMo(c),Hawkman in Crime
   Canned for the Duration 800.00
48 SMo,SMo(c). 800.00
49 SMo,SMo(c). 800.00
50 SMo,SMo(c),Hawkman, Tale
   of the 1,000 Dollar Bill 800.00
51 SMo,SMo(c). 700.00
52 SMo,SMo(c),Flash, Machine
   that Thinks Like a Man 700.00
53 SMo,SMo(c),Hawkman, Simple
   Simon Met the Hawkman . . . 700.00
54 SMo,SMo(c),Flash, Mysterious
   Bottle from the Sea. 700.00
55 SMo,SMo(c),Hawkman, Riddle of
   the Stolen Statuette! 700.00
56 SMo,SMo(c). 700.00
57 SMo,SMo(c),Hawkman, Adventure
   of the Gangster & the Ghost . 700.00
58 SMo,SMo(c),`Merman meets
   the Flash' 700.00

59 SMo,SMo(c),Hawkman
  V:Pied Piper 700.00
60 SMo,SMo(c),Flash
  V:The Wind Master 700.00
61 SMo,SMo(c),Hawkman
  V:The Beanstalk 700.00
62 JKu,Flash in `High Jinks
  on the Rinks' 750.00
63 JKu(c),Hawkman in `The
  Tale of the Mystic Urn' 600.00
64 . . . . 600.00
65 JKu(c),Hawkman in `Return
  of the Simple Simon'. 600.00
66 . . . . 600.00
67 JKu(c) 600.00
68 Flash in `The Radio that
  Ran Wild' 600.00
69 . . . . 600.00
70 JKu(c) 600.00
71 JKu(c),Hawkman in `Battle
  of the Birdmen' 600.00
72 JKu 600.00
73 JKu(c) 600.00
74 JKu(c) 600.00
75 JKu(c),Hawkman in `Magic
  at the Mardi Gras'. 600.00
76 A:Worry Wart 600.00
77 Hawkman in `The Case of
  the Curious Casket' 600.00
78 . . . . 600.00
79 Hawkman in `The Battle
  of the Birds' 600.00
80 Flash in `The Story of
  the Boy Genius' 600.00
81 JKu(c),Hawkman's Voyage
  to Venus 600.00
82 A:Walter Jordan 600.00
83 JKu,JKu(c),Hawkman in
  `Destined for Disaster' 600.00
84 Flash V:`The Changeling'. . . . 600.00
85 JKu,JKu(c),Hawkman in
  Hollywood 600.00
86 JKu,1st Black Canary,Flash
  V:Stone Age Menace 2,000.00
87 Hawkman meets the Foil 900.00
88 JKu,Flash in `The Case
  of the Vanished Year!' 900.00
89 I:The Thorn 900.00
90 Flash in `Nine Empty
  Uniforms' 900.00
91 Hawkman V:The Phantom
  Menace 1,000.00
92 1st full-length Black
  Canary story 2,800.00
93 Flash V:Violin of Villainy . . . 1,000.00
94 JKu(c). 1,000.00
95 . . . . 1,000.00
96 . . . . 1,000.00
97 Flash in `The Dream
  that Didn't Vanish' 1,000.00
98 JKu(c),Hawkman in
  `Crime Costume!'. 1,000.00
99 Flash in `The Star Prize
  of the Year' 1,000.00
100 Hawkman in `The Human
  -Fly Bandits!' 2,400.00
101 . . . . 2,000.00
102 Hawkman in `The Flying
  Darkness' 2,000.00
103 . . . . 2,400.00
104 JKu,Hawkman in `Flaming
  Darkness' Feb., 1949. . . . . 6,000.00

FLASH
Feb.–March, 1959

105 CI,O:Flash,I:Mirror
  Master. 5,500.00
106 CI,I&O:Gorilla Grodd,
  O:Pied Piper 1,500.00
107 CI,A:Grodd. 800.00

108 CI,A:Grodd. 700.00
109 CI,A:Mirror Master 500.00
110 CI,MA,I:Kid Flash,
  Weather Wizard. 1,350.00
111 CI,A:Kid Flash,The Invasion
  Of the Cloud Creatures. . . . 375.00
112 CI,I&O:Elongated Man,
  A:Kid Flash. 450.00
113 CI,I&O:Trickster 375.00
114 CI,A:Captain Cold 275.00
115 CI,A:Grodd. 250.00
116 CI,A:Kid Flash,The Man
  Who Stole Central City 250.00
117 CI,MA,I:Capt.Boomerang . . . 300.00
118 CI,MA 225.00
119 CI,W:Elongated Man 225.00
120 CI,A:Kid Flash,Land of
  Golden Giants 225.00
121 CI,A:Trickster 175.00
122 CI,I&O:The Top 175.00
123 I:Earth 2,R:G.A.Flash 1,300.00
124 CI,A:Capt.Boomerang 150.00
125 CI,A:Kid Flash,The
  Conquerors of Time 135.00
126 CI,A:Mirror Master 135.00
127 CI,A:Grodd. 135.00
128 CI,O:Abra Kadabra 135.00
129 CI,A:Capt.Cold,Trickster,A:Gold.
  Age Flash,C:JLA (flashback). 300.00
130 CI,A:Mirror Master,
  Weather Wizard 135.00
131 CI,A:Green Lantern 125.00
132 CI,A:Daphne Dean. 125.00
133 CI,A:Abra Kadabra. 125.00
134 CI,A:Captain Cold 125.00
135 CI,N:Kid Flash 125.00
136 CI,A:Mirror Master 125.00
137 CI,Vandal Savage,R:JSA,
  A:G.A.Flash 450.00
138 CI,A:Pied Piper 125.00
139 CI,I&O:Prof.Zoom(Reverse
  Flash). 150.00
140 CI,O:Heat Wave. 120.00
141 CI,A:Top. 100.00
142 CI,A:Trickster. 100.00
143 CI,A:Green Lantern 100.00
144 CI,A:Man Missile,Kid Flash. . 100.00
145 CI,A:Weather Wizard 100.00
146 CI,A:Mirror Master 100.00
147 CI,A:Mr.Element,A:Reverse
  Flash 100.00
148 CI,A:Capt.Boomerang 100.00
149 CI,A:Abra Kadabra. 100.00
150 CI,A:Captain Cold 100.00

Flash #185 © DC Comics Inc.

151 CI,A:Earth II Flash,
  The Shade 125.00
152 CI,V:Trickster. 75.00
153 CI,A:Mr.Element,Rev.Flash . . 75.00
154 CI,The Day Flash Ran Away
  with Himself 75.00
155 CI,A:MirrorMaster,Capt.Cold,Top
  Capt. Boomerang,Grodd. 75.00
156 CI,A:Kid Flash,The Super Hero
  who Betrayed the World 75.00
157 CI,A:Doralla Kon,The Top. . . . 75.00
158 CI,V:The Breakaway Bandit
  A:The Justice League. 75.00
159 CI,A:Kid Flash 75.00
160 CI,giant 100.00
161 CI,A:Mirror Master 65.00
162 CI,Who Haunts the Corridor
  of Chills 65.00
163 CI,A:Abra kadabra 65.00
164 CI,V:Pied Piper,A:KidFLash . . 65.00
165 CI,W:Flash,Iris West 70.00
166 CI,A:Captain Cold 65.00
167 CI,O:Flash,I:Mopee 65.00
168 CI,A:Green Lantern 65.00
169 CI,O:Flash rtd,giant 100.00
170 CI,A:Abra Kadabra,
  G.A.Flash 65.00
171 CI,A:Dexter Myles,Justice
  League,Atom;V:Dr Light 60.00
172 CI,A:Grodd 60.00
173 CI,A:Kid Flash,EarthII Flash
  V:Golden Man 60.00
174 CI,A:Mirror Master,Top
  Captain Cold 60.00
175 2nd Superman/Flash race,
  C:Justice League o/America . 150.00
176 giant-size. 60.00
177 RA,V:The Trickster. 60.00
178 CI,(giant size) 80.00
179 RA,Fact or Fiction 60.00
180 RA,V:Baron Katana 60.00
181 RA,V:Baron Katana 40.00
182 A:Abra Kadabra 40.00
183 RA,V:The Frog. 40.00
184 RA,V:Dr Yom 40.00
185 RA,Threat of the High Rise
  Buildings 40.00
186 RA,A:Sargon 40.00
187 CI,AbraKadabra,giant. 60.00
188 A:Mirror Master 40.00
189 JKu(c),RA,A:Kid Flash 40.00
190 JKu(c),RA,A:Dexter Myles . . . 40.00
191 JKu(c),RA,A:Green Lantern . . 40.00
192 RA;V:Captain Vulcan 40.00
193 A:Captain Cold 40.00
194. . . . . 40.00
195 GK,MA. 40.00
196 CI,giant 60.00
197 GK. 40.00
198 GK. 40.00
199 GK. 40.00
200 IN,MA 40.00
201 IN,MA,A:G.A. Flash 20.00
202 IN,MA,A:Kid Flash 20.00
203 IN 20.00
204. . . . . 20.00
205 giant 40.00
206 A:Mirror Master 20.00
207. . . . . 20.00
208. . . . . 20.00
209 A:Capt.Boomerang,Grodd
  Trickster 20.00
210 CI 20.00
211 O:Flash 20.00
212 A:Abra Kadabra 20.00
213 CI 20.00
214 CI,rep.Showcase #37
  (O:Metal Men),giant size. 25.00
215 IN,FMc,rep.Showcase #14 . . . 25.00
216 A:Mr.Element. 20.00
217 NA,A:Gr.Lant,Gr.Arrow 22.00

Flash #192 © DC Comics, Inc.

218 NA,A:Gr.Lant,Gr.Arrow	22.00
219 NA,L:Greeen Arrow	22.00
220 IN,DG,A:KidFlash,Gr.Lantern	15.00
221 IN	15.00
222 IN	15.00
223 DG,Green Lantern	15.00
224 IN,DG,A:Green Lantern	15.00
225 IN,DG,A:Gr.Lant,Rev.Flash	11.00
226 NA,A:Capt. Cold	15.00
227 IN,FMc,DG,Capt.Boomerang,	
Green Lantern	11.00
228 IN	11.00
229 IN,FMc,A:Green Arrow,	
V:Rag Doll (giant size)	20.00
230 A:VandalSavage,Dr.Alchemy	11.00
231 FMc	11.00
232 giant	20.00
233 giant	20.00
234 V:Reverse Flash	8.00
235.	7.00
236 MGr.	7.00
237 IN,FMc,MGr,A:Prof Zoom,	
Green Lantern	8.00
238 MGr.	7.00
239	7.00
240 MGr.	7.00
241 A:Mirror Master	7.00
242 MGr,D:Top	7.00
243 IN,FMc,MGr,TA,O:Top,	
A:Green Lantern.	7.00
244 IN,FMc,A:Rogue's Gallery	7.00
245 IN,FMc,DD,TA,I:PlantMaster	7.00
246 IN,FMc,DD,TA,I:PlantMaster	7.00
247.	7.00
248 FMc,IN,I:Master.	7.00
249 FMc,IN,V:Master	7.00
250 IN,FMc,I:Golden Glider	7.00
251 FMc,IN,V:Golden Glider	6.00
252 FMc,IN,I:Molder	6.00
253 FMc,IN,V:Molder	6.00
254 FMc.	6.00
255 FMc,A:MirrorMaster	6.00
256 FMc,V:Top	6.00
257 FMc,A:Green Glider.	6.00
258 FMc,A:Black Hand.	6.00
259 FMc,IN	6.00
260 FMc,IN	6.00
261 FMc,IN,V:Golden Glider	6.00
262 FMc,IN,V:Golden Glider	6.00
263 FMc,IN,V:Golden Glider	6.00
264 FMc,IN,V:Golden Glider	6.00
265 FMc,IN	6.00
266 FMc,IN,V:Heat Wave	6.00
267 FMc,IN,V:Heat Wave	6.00
268 FMc,IN,A:E2 Flash.	6.00

269 FMc,IN,A:Kid Flash	6.00
270 FMc,IN,V:Clown	6.00
271 RB,V:Clown	6.00
272 RB,V:Clown	6.00
273 RB.	6.00
274 RB.	6.00
275 AS,D:Iris West,PCP story.	7.00
276 AS,A:JLA.	6.00
277 AS,FMc,A:JLA,	
V:MirrorMaster	6.00
278 A:Captain.Boomerang	
& Heatwave	6.00
279 A:Captain.Boomerang	
& Heatwave	6.00
280 DH.	6.00
281 DH,V:Reverse Flash	7.00
282 DH,V:Reverse Flash	7.00
283 DH,V:Reverse Flash	7.00
284 DH,Flash's life story	
I:Limbo Lord.	6.00
285 DH,V:Trickster.	6.00
286 DH,I:Rainbow Raider.	6.00
287 DH,V:Dr.Alchemy.	6.00
288 DH,V:Dr.Alchemy.	6.00
289 DH,GP,1st GP DC art; V:Dr.	
Alchemy;B:B.U.Firestorm	8.00
290 GP.	5.00
291 GP,DH,V:Sabretooth	5.00
292 GP,DH,V:Mirror Master.	5.00
293 GP,DH,V:Pied Piper.	5.00
294 GP,DH,V:Grodd.	5.00
295 CI,JSn,V:Grodd.	5.00
296 JSn,A:Elongated Man	5.00
297 CI,A:Captain Cold	5.00
298 CI,V:Shade,Rainbowraider.	5.00
299 CI,V:Shade,Rainbowraider	5.00
300 A:New Teen Titans.	6.00
301 CI,A:Firestorm	5.00
302 CI,V:Golden Glider	5.00
303 CI,V:Golden Glider.	5.00
304 CI,PB,I:Col.Computron;E:B.U.	
Firestorm	5.00
305 KG,CI,A:G.A.Flash,B:Dr.Fate.	4.00
306 CI,KG,V:Mirror Master	4.00
307 CI,KG,V:Pied Piper.	3.00
308 CI,KG	4.00
309 CI,KG	4.00
310 CI,KG,V:Capt.Boomerang	3.00
311 CI,KG,V:Capt.Boomerang	3.00
312 CI,A:Heatwave.	3.00
313 KG,A:Psylon,E:Dr.Fate.	3.00
314 CI,I:Eradicator	3.00
315 CI,V:Gold Face	3.00
316 CI,V:Gold Face	3.00
317 CI,V:Gold Face	3.00
318 CI,DGb,V:Eradicator;B:	
B.U.Creeper.	3.00
319 CI,DGb,V:Eradicator	3.00
320 CI,V:Eradicator	3.00
321 CI,D:Eradicator	3.00
322 CI,V:Reverse Flash	3.00
323 CI,V:Reverse Flash;E:	
B.U.Creeper	3.00
324 CI,D:Reverse Flash	4.00
325 CI,A:Rogues Gallery	3.00
326 CI,A:Weather Wizard	3.00
327 CI,A:JLA,G.Grodd	3.00
328 CI	3.00
329 CI,A:J.L.A.,G.Grodd.	3.00
330 CI,FMc,V:G.Grodd	3.00
331 CI,FMc,V:G.Grodd	3.00
332 CI,FMc,V:Rainbow Raider	3.00
333 CI,FMc,V:Pied Piper	3.00
334 CI,FMc,V:Pied Piper	3.00
335 CI,FMc,V:Pied Piper	3.00
336 CI,FMc,V:Pied Piper	3.00
337 CI,FMc,V:Pied Piper	3.00
338 CI,FMc,I:Big Sir.	3.00
339 CI,FMc,A:Big Sir	3.00
340 CI,FMc,Trial,A:Big Sir.	3.00
341 CI,FMc,Trial,A:Big Sir.	3.00

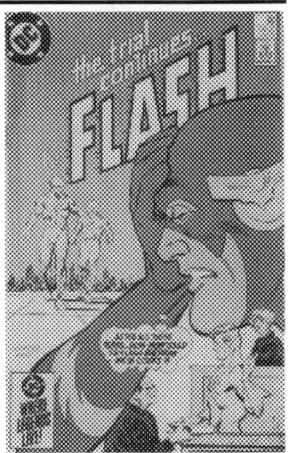

Flash #344 © DC Comics, Inc.

342 CI,FMc,Trial,V:RogueGallery	3.00
343 CI,FMc,Trial,A:GoldFace	3.00
344 CI,O:Kid Flash,Trial	3.00
345 CI,A:Kid Flash,Trial	3.00
346 CI,FMc,Trial,V:AbraKadabra.	3.00
347 CI,FMc,Trial,V:AbraKadabra.	3.00
348 CI,FMc,Trial,V:AbraKadabra.	3.00
349 CI,FMc,Trial,V:AbraKadabra.	3.00
350 CI,FMc,Trial,V:AbraKadabra.	7.00
Ann.#1 O:ElongatedMan,	
G.Grodd.	325.00

FLASH
[2nd Series] Oct., 1985

1 JG,Legends,C:Vandal Savage	6.00
2 JG,V:Vandal Savage.	4.00
3 JG,I:Kilgore	3.00
4 JG,A:Cyborg.	3.00
5 JG,V:Speed Demon	3.00
6 JG,V:Speed Demon	3.00
7 JG,V:Red Trinity	3.00
8 JG,V:BlueTrinity,Millenium.	3.00
9 JG,I:Chunk,Millenium	3.00
10 V:Chunk,Chunks World	2.50
11 Return to Earth	2.50
12 Velocity 9.	2.50
13 Vandal Savage,V:Velocity 9	
Adicts.	2.50
14 V:Vandal Savage.	2.50
15 A:Velocity 9 Junkies.	2.50
16 C:V.Savage,SpeedMcGeePt.1	2.50
17 GLa,Speed McGee,pt.2	2.50
18 GLa,SpeedMcGeePt.3,	
V:V.Savage	2.25
19 JM:+bonus book,R:Rogue	
Gallery,O:Blue/Red Trinity.	2.25
20 A:Durlan	2.25
21 A:Manhunter,Invasion x-over	2.25
22 A:Manhunter,Invasion x-over	2.25
23 V:Abrakadabra.	2.25
24 GLa,FlashRegainsSpeed,	
A:L.Lane	2.25
25 GLa,Search for Flash.	2.25
26 GLa,I:Porcupine Man.	2.25
27 GLa,Porcupine Man as Flash.	2.25
28 GLa,A:Golden Glider,	
Capt.Cold.	2.25
29 A:New Phantom Lady	2.25
30 GLa,Turtle Saga,pt.1	2.25
31 GLa,Turtle Saga,pt.2	2.00
32 GLa,Turtle Saga,pt.3,	
R:G.A.Turtle.	2.00
33 GLa,Turtle Saga,pt.4	2.00
34 GLa,Turtle Saga,pt.5	2.00

35 GLa,Turtle Saga,pt.6,
    D:G.A.Turtle............. 2.00
36 GLa,V:Cult................ 2.00
37 GLa,V:Cult................ 2.00
38 GLa,V:Cult................ 2.00
39 GLa,V:Cult................ 2.00
40 GLa,A:Dr.Alchemy........... 2.00
41 GLa,A:Dr.Alchemy........... 2.00
42 GLa,MechanicalTroubles...... 2.00
43 GLa,V:Kilgore.............. 2.00
44 GLa,V:Velocity............. 2.00
45 V:Gorilla Grod............. 2.00
46 V:Gorilla Grod............. 2.00
47 V:Gorilla Grod............. 2.00
48 .... 2.00
49 A:Vandal Savage........... 2.00
50 N:Flash (double sz)V:Savage... 5.00
51 I:Proletariat.............. 2.00
52 I.R.S. Mission............ 2.00
53 A:Superman,Race to Save
    Jimmy Olsen............. 2.00
54 Terrorist Airline Attack....... 2.00
55 War of the Gods x-over...... 2.00
56 The Way of a Will,pt.1...... 2.00
57 The Way of a Will,pt.2...... 2.00
58 Meta Gene-activated Homeless. 2.00
59 The Last Resort........... 2.00
60 Love Song of the Chunk..... 2.00
61 Wally's Mother's Wedding Day.. 2.00
62 GLa,Year 1,pt.1.......... 2.25
63 GLa,Year 1,pt.2.......... 2.00
64 GLa,Year 1,pt.3.......... 2.00
65 GLa,Year 1,pt.4.......... 2.00
66 A:Aq'man,V:Marine Marauder.. 2.00
67 GLa,V:Abra Kadabra........ 2.00
68 GLa,V:Abra Kadabra........ 2.00
69 GLa,Gorilla Warfare#2...... 2.00
70 Gorilla Warfare#4.......... 2.00
71 GLa,V:Dr.Alchemy.......... 2.00
72 GLa,V:Dr.Alchemy,C:Barry
    Allen.................. 2.50
73 GLa,Xmas Issue,R:Barry Allen. 4.50
74 GLa,A:Barry Allen?......... 3.00
75 GLa,A:Reverse Flash,V:Mob
    Violence................ 3.50
76 GLa,A:Reverse Flash........ 2.25
77 GLa,G.A.Flash vs
    Reverse Flash........... 2.25
78 GLa,V:Reverse Flash........ 2.25
79 GLa,V:Reverse Flash,48 pgs... 3.25
80 AD(c),V:Frances Kane....... 3.00
80a Newstand Ed.............. 2.00
81 AD(c)................... 2.00
82 AD(c),A:Nightwing.......... 2.00
83 AD(c),A:Nightwing,Starfire.... 2.00
84 AD(c),I:Razer............. 2.00
85 AD(c),V:Razer............. 2.00
86 AD(c),A:Argus............ 2.00
86 V:Santa Claus............. 2.00
87 Chrismas issue............ 2.00
88 .... 2.00
89 On Trial................. 2.00
90 On Trial#2............... 2.00
91 Out of Time.............. 5.00
92 I:3rd Flash.............. 12.00
93 A:Impulse............... 5.00
94 Zero Hour............... 5.00
95 Terminal Velocity,pt.1....... 4.00
96 Terminal Velocity,pt.2....... 4.00
97 Terminal Velocity,pt.3....... 2.00
98 Terminal Velocity,pt.4....... 2.00
99 Terminal Velocity,pt.5....... 2.00
100 I:New Flash............. 5.00
100a Collector's Edition........ 2.50
101 Velocity Aftermath......... 2.00
102 V:Mongul............... 2.00
103 Supernatural threat from
    Linda's Past Secret....... 2.00
104 Exorcise Demons.......... 2.00
105 .... 2.00
106 R:Magenta.............. 2.00

107 MWa,Underworld Unleashed
    tie-in................... 2.00
108 MWa,Dead Heat,pt.1....... 2.00
109 MWa,Dead Heat,pt.2....... 2.00
110 MWa,Dead Heat,pt.4....... 2.00
111 MWa,Dead Heat,pt.6....... 2.00
112 MWa,New Flash in town...... 2.00
113 MWa,F:Linda.............. 2.00
114 MWa,V:Chillblaine.......... 2.00
115 thru 117.............. @2.00
118 MWa&BAu(s),Flash returns
    from the future........... 2.00
119 MWa&BAu(s),PR,Final Night
    tie-in................... 2.00
120 MWa&BAu(s),PR,"Presidential
    Race," pt.1.............. 2.00
121 MWa&BAu(s),PR,"Presidential
    Race," pt.2.............. 2.00
122 MWa&BAu(s),PR,.......... 2.00
123 MWa&BAu(s),PR,Flash moves
    to Santa Marta........... 2.00
124 MWa&BAu(s),PR,Wally doesn't
    know reality from illusion..... 2.00
125 MWa&BAu(s),PR,California,
    V:Major Disaster.......... 2.00
126 MWa&BAu(s),PR,V:Major
    Disaster................ 2.00
127 MWa&Bau(s),PR,"Hell to Pay,"
    pt. 1 (of 3)............. 2.00
128 MWa&BAu(s),PR,"Hell to Pay"
    pt. 2, A:JLA............ 2.00
129 MWa&BAu(s),PR,"Hell to Pay"
    pt. 3, concl............. 2.00
130 GMo&MMr(s),PR,new menace. 2.50
131 GMo&MMr(s),PR,V:The Suit.. 2.50
132 GMo&MMr(s),PR,V:The Suit.. 2.00
133 GMo&MMr(s),PR,V:Mirror
    Master................. 2.00
134 GMo&MMr(s),PR,V:Weather
    Wizard & Captain Cold...... 2.00
135 GMo&MMr(s),.............. 2.00
136 GMo&MMr(s),PR,Human
    Race,pt.1............... 2.00
137 GMo&MMr(s),PR,Human
    Race,pt.2............... 2.00
138 GMo&MMr(s),PR,Human
    Race,pt.3............... 2.00
139 MMr(s),Clv,Black Flash,pt.1... 2.00
140 MMr(s),Clv,Black Flash,pt.2... 2.00
141 MMr(s),Clv,Black Flash,pt.3... 2.00
142 MWa&BAu(s),Clv,SLi,wedding of
    Wally West & Linda Park..... 2.00
143 MWa&BAu(s),Clv,V:CobaltBlue 2.00
144 MWa&BAu(s),Clv,O:CobaltBlue 2.00

Flash 2nd Series #80 © DC Comics Inc.

145 MWa&BAu(s),PaP,VRu,
    Chain Lightning, pt.1........ 2.00
146 MWa&BAu(s),PaP,VRu,
    Chain Lightning, pt.2........ 2.00
147 MWa&BAu(s),PaP,VRu,
    Chain Lightning, pt.3........ 2.00
148 MWa&BAu(s),PaP,VRu,
    Chain Lightning, pt.4........ 2.00
149 MWa&BAu(s),PaP,VRu,
    Chain Lightning, pt.5........ 2.00
150 MWa&BAu(s),PaP,VRu, Chain
    Lightning, pt.6, 48-page..... 3.00
151 MWa&BAu(s),PaP,A:Robin
    & Aqualad, flashback issue.... 2.00
152 MWa&BAu(s),PaP,VRu,
    new costume............. 2.00
153 MWa&BAu(s),PaP,JMz,
    V:Folded Man............ 2.00
Ann.#1 JG,The Deathtouch....... 4.00
Ann.#2 A:Wally's Father......... 3.00
Ann.#3 Roots................ 2.50
Ann.#4 Armageddon,pt7......... 2.50
Ann.#5 TC(1st Full Work),Eclipso,
    V:Rogue's Gallery.......... 8.00
Ann.#6 Bloodlines#4,I:Argus...... 2.75
Ann.#7 Elseworlds story........ 2.95
Ann.#8 Year One story......... 3.00
Ann.#9 Legends o/t Dead Earth... 2.95
Ann.#10 Pulp Heroes (Romance).. 3.95
Ann.#11 BAu,BWr, Ghosts...... 3.00
Ann.#12 DBw,AAd(c),JLApe: Gorilla
    Warfare................ 2.95
Spec #1,IN,DG,Cl,50th Anniv.,
    Three Flash's............ 4.50
Spec.#1,000,000 MWa(s),JMz,A:Captain
    Marvel of 853rd-century..... 2.00
T.V. Spec.#1,JS,w/episode guide.. 4.25
TPB Terminal Velocity........... 12.95
TPB The Life Story of the Flash... 13.00
TPB The Return of Barry Allen... 13.00
TPB Born to Run............. 13.00
Spec #1 GN Secret Files........ 5.00
Archives #1 Hardcover......... 50.00
Giant #1 MWa,80-page (1998)... 5.00
Giant #2 80-page............ 5.00
Secret Files #1 MWa,BAu,PRy,
    O:Flash family........... 5.00

FLASH & GREEN LANTREN: THE BRAVE & THE BOLD
1999
1 (of 6) MWa&TPe(s),BKi....... 2.50

THE FLASH PLUS
Nov. 1996
1 MWa(s),F:Wally West, Dick
    Grayson................. 2.95

FLASH GORDON
1988
1 DJu,I:New Flash Gordon....... 2.00
2 DJu,A:Lion-Men,Shark-Men.... 1.75
3 DJu,V:Shark-Men............ 1.50
4 DJu,Dale Kidnapped by Voltan.. 1.50
5 DJu,Alliance Against Ming..... 1.50
6 DJu,Arctic City............. 1.50
7 DJu,Alliance vs. Ming........ 1.50
8 DJu,Alliance vs. Ming........ 1.50
9 DJu,V:Ming, final issue....... 1.50

FLINCH
DC/Vertigo 1999
1 JLe,RCo,horror anthology...... 2.50
2 BSz,RCo(c),3 horror tales..... 2.50
3 KJo,3 horror tales........... 2.50

4 TTn,PGu,3 horror tales 2.50
5 JLd(s),RBr,3 horror tales 2.50

FLINTSTONES AND THE JETSONS, THE
Warner Bros./DC
1 Ancestors and Descendents meet 1.75
2 Dino wins a contest, Bay
 Watchdog 1.75
3 Mr. Spacely a baby 2.00
4 cavewomen 2.00
5 21st century house party 2.00
6 Thanksgiving Feast 2.00
7 CDi, Spy Who Grounded Me . . . 2.00
8 . . . . 2.00
9 I, Rosey 2.00
10 Beast of Bedrock 2.00
11 Mr. Spacely, time travel 2.00
12 Animal appliances on strike 2.00
13 F:Astro 2.00
14 Flintstone Files, UFOs 2.00
15 Mr. Spacely, most powerful being
 in the universe 2.00
16 The Yelling Man 2.00
17 Scooba Dabba Doo 2.00
18 holiday special 2.00
19 bizarre world 2.00
20 Sherock Holmes 2.00
21 final issue 2.00

FLY, THE
Impact 1991–92
1 I&O:Fly I:Arachnix,Chromium . . . 1.50
2 V:Chromium 1.25
3 O:Arachnix, I:Lt.Walker Odell . . . 1.00
4 A:Black Hood, V:Arachnus 1.00
5 V:Arachnus 1.00
6 I:Blackjack 1.00
7 Oceanworld,V:Dolphus 1.00
8 A:Comet,Dolphus 1.00
9 F:Fireball, with trading card 1.00
10 V:General Mechanix 1.00
11 Suicide Issue 1.25
12 V:Agent from WEB 1.25
13 I:Tremor 1.25
14 and 15 V:Domino . . . . @1.25
16 V:Arachnus 1.25
17 Final Issue 1.25
Ann.#1 Earthquest,pt.4,w/card . . . 2.25

The Fly #12 © DC Comics, Inc.

FORBIDDEN TALES OF DARK MANSION
May-June, 1972
5 thru 15 Feb.–March, 1974 . . . . @1.50

FOREVER PEOPLE, THE
1971–72
1 I:Forever People,A:Superman,
 A:Darkseid 50.00
2 A:Darkseid 30.00
3 A:Darkseid 30.00
4 A:Darkseid 30.00
5 . . . . 25.00
6 thru 11 . . . . @12.50

FOREVER PEOPLE
1988
1 Return of Forever People 1.50
2 `Return of Earth of Yesterday' . . . 1.25
3 A:Mark Moonrider 1.25
4 The Dark controlls M.Moonrider . 1.25
5 R:MotherBox,Infinity Man 1.25
6 Donny's Fate, final issue 1.25

FORGOTTEN REALMS
1989–91
1 A:RealmsMaster,PriamAgrivar . . 4.00
2 Mystic Hand of Vaprak,
 A:Ogre Mage 3.00
3 Mystic Hand of Vaprak contd. . . . 2.75
4 Ogre Mage vs.Omen the Wizard. 2.75
5 Dragon Reach #1 . . . . 2.75
6 Dragon Reach #2 . . . . 2.50
7 Dragon Reach #3 . . . . 2.50
8 Dragon Reach #4 . . . . 2.50
9 V:Giant Squid 2.50
10 `Head Cheese'. 2.50
11 Triangles #1 . . . . 2.50
12 Triangles #2 . . . . 2.50
13 Triangles #3 . . . . 2.50
14 A:Lich Viranton the Mage 2.00
15 Avatar Comics tie-in 2.00
16 Mad Gods and Paladins,pt.1 . . 2.00
17 Mad Gods and Paladins,pt.2 . . . 2.00
18 Mad Gods and Paladins,pt.3 . . . 2.00
19 Mad Gods and Paladins,pt.4 . . . 2.00
20 Realms Master Crew captured. . 2.00
21 Catewere Tribe 2.00
22 V:The Akri 1.75
23 A:Sandusk the Leprechaun 1.75
24 `Everybody wants to rule
 the realms' 1.75
25 The Wake, final issue 1.75
Ann.#1 V:Advanced D&D crew . . . 2.95

FOUR STAR BATTLETALES
1973
1 thru 5 . . . . @1.50

FOUR STAR SPECTACULAR
March-April, 1976
1 . . . . 1.50
2 thru 6 . . . . @1.25

FOURTH WORLD GALLERY
1-shot pin-up collection (1996) 3.50

FOX AND THE CROW
Dec.–Jan., 1951
1 . . . . 800.00

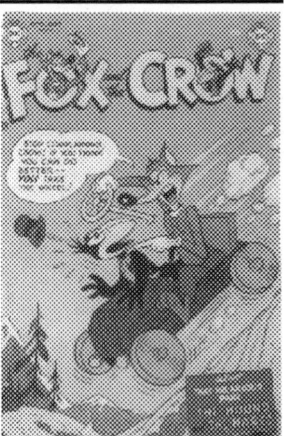

Fox and the Crow #4
© DC Comics, Inc.

2 . . . . 400.00
3 . . . . 250.00
4 . . . . 250.00
5 . . . . 250.00
6 thru 10 . . . . @175.00
11 thru 20 . . . . @125.00
21 thru 40 . . . . @125.00
41 thru 60 . . . . @50.00
61 thru 80 . . . . @35.00
81 thru 94 . . . . @25.00
95 . . . . 30.00
96 thru 99 . . . . @15.00
100 . . . . 18.00
101 thru 108 . . . . @15.00
Becomes:
STANLEY & HIS MONSTER
109 thru 112 Oct.Nov.,1968 . . . . @10.00

FREEDOM FIGHTERS
March-April, 1976
1 Freedom Fighters go to Earth 1 . 1.50
2 . . . . 1.25
3 . . . . 1.25
4 . . . . 1.25
5 A:Wonder Woman 1.25
6 . . . . 1.25
7 . . . . 1.25
8 . . . . 1.25
9 . . . . 1.25
10 O:Doll Man 1.25
11 O:Ray 1.25
12 O:Firebrand 1.25
13 O:Black Condor 1.25
14 A:Batgirl 1.25
15 O:Phantom Lady 1.25

FROM BEYOND THE UNKNOWN
Oct.–Nov., 1969
1 JKu,CI 50.00
2 MA(c),CI,ATh 18.00
3 NA(c),CI 15.00
4 MA(c),CI 15.00
5 MA(c),CI 15.00
6 NA(c),I:Glen Merrit 18.00
7 CI,JKu(c) 15.00
8 NA(c),CI 18.00
9 NA(c),CI 15.00
10 MA(c),CI 15.00
11 MA(c),CI 12.00

12 JKu(c),CI 15.00
13 JKu(c),CI,WW 20.00
14 JKu(c),CI 15.00
15 MA(c),CI 12.00
16 MA(c),CI 12.00
17 MA(c),CI 12.00
18 MK(c),CI 10.00
19 MK(c),CI 10.00
20. . . . . 10.00
21. . . . . 10.00
22 MA(c) 12.00
23 CI,Space Museum 10.00
24 CI 10.00

FUNNY STOCKING STUFFER
March, 1985
1 . . . . 1.00

FUNNY STUFF
Summer, 1944
1 B:3 Mousketeer Terrific
   Whatzit. 650.00
2 . . . . 350.00
3 . . . . 200.00
4 . . . . 175.00
5 . . . . 175.00
6 thru 10 . . . . @150.00
11 thru 20 . . . . @125.00
21 . . . . 75.00
22 C:Superman 300.00
23 thru 30 . . . . @75.00
31 thru 78 . . . . @50.00
79 July-Aug., 1954 . . . . 50.00

FURY OF FIRESTORM
June, 1982
1 PB,I:Black Bison. 3.00
2 PB,V:Black Bison 2.00
3 PB,V:Pied Piper, Killer Frost 2.00
4 PB,A:JLA,Killer Frost 2.00
5 PB,V:Pied Piper 2.00
6 V:Pied Piper 2.00
7 I:Plastique 2.00
8 V:Typhoon 2.00
9 V:Typhoon 2.00
10 V:Hyena 2.00
11 V:Hyena. 2.00
12 PB,V:Hyena. 2.00
13 . . . . 2.00
14 PB,I:Enforcer,A:Multiplex 2.00
15 V:Multiplex. 2.00
16 V:Multiplex. 2.00
17 I:2000 Committee,Firehawk 2.00
18 I:Tokamak,A:Multiplex 2.00
19 GC,V:Goldenrod 2.00
20 A:Killer Frost 2.00
21 D:Killer Frost 2.50
22 O:Firestorm 2.50
23 I:Bug & Byte 2.00
24 I:Blue Devil,Bug & Byte 2.50
25 I:Silver Deer 2.00
26 V:Black Bison 2.00
27 V:Black Bison 2.00
28 I:Slipknot 2.00
29 I:2000 C'tee,I:Breathtaker 2.00
30 V:2000 Committee. 2.00
31 V:2000 Committee 2.00
32 Phantom Stranger 2.00
33 A:Plastique 2.00
34 I:Killer Frost 2 . . . . 2.00
35 V:K.Frost/Plastique,I:Weasel . . . 2.00
36 V:Killer Frost & Plastique 2.00
37 . . . . 2.00
38 V:Weasel. 2.00
39 V:Weasel. 2.00
40 . . . . 2.00
41 Crisis. 2.00

42 Crisis,A:Firehawk. 2.00
43 V:Typhoon 2.00
44 V:Typhoon 2.00
45 V:Multiplex. 2.00
46 A:Blue Devil. 2.00
47 A:Blue Devil. 2.00
48 I:Moonbow. 2.00
49 V:Moonbow. 2.00
50 W:Ed Raymond 2.00
51 A:King Crusher 2.00
52 A:King Crusher 2.00
53 V:Steel Shadow 2.00
54 I:Lava 2.00
55 Legends,V:World's
   Luckiest Man 2.00
56 Legends,A:Hawk 2.00
57 . . . . 2.00
58 I:Parasite II 2.00
59 . . . . 2.00
60 Secret behind Hugo's accident. . 2.00
61 V:Typhoon 2.00
61a Superman Logo 55.00
62 A:Russian `Firestorm' 2.00
63 A:Capt.Atom 2.00
64 A:Suicide Squad 2.00
Ann.#1 EC,A:Firehawk,
   V:Tokamak 2.25
Ann.#2 . . . . 2.25
Ann.#3 . . . . 2.25
Ann.#4 KG,CS,GC,DG 2.25
Becomes:

FIRESTORM, THE NUCLEAR MAN
Nov., 1987
65 A:New Firestorm 2.00
66 A:Green Lantern 2.00
67 Millenium, Week 1 . . . . 2.00
68 Millenium 2.00
69 V:Zuggernaut,Stalnivolk USA . . . 2.00
70 V:Flying Dutchman 2.00
71 Trapped in the Timestream 2.00
72 V:Zuggernaut. 2.00
73 V:Stalnivolk & Zuggernaut 2.00
74 Quest for Martin Stein 2.00
75 Return of Martin Stein 2.00
76 Firestorm & Firehawk
   vs Brimstone 2.00
77 Firestorm & Firehawk in Africa . . 2.00
78 `Exile From Eden',pt.1 . . . . 2.00
79 `Exile From Eden',pt.2 . . . . 2.00
80 A:Power Girl,Starman,Invasion
   x-over. 2.00

Fury of Firestorm, Ann #3
© DC Comics Inc.

81 A:Soyuz,Invasion aftermath 2.00
82 Invasion Aftermath. 2.00
83 V:Svarozhich 2.00
84 . . . . 2.00
85 Soul of Fire,N:Firestorm. 2.00
86 TMd,Janus Directive #7 . . . . 2.00
87 TMd. 2.00
88 TMd,E:Air Wave B:Maser. 2.00
89 TMd,V:Firehawk,Vandermeer
   Steel 2.00
90 TMd,Elemental War #1 . . . . 2.00
91 TMd,Elemental War #2 . . . . 2.00
92 TMd,Elemental War #3 . . . . 2.00
93 TMd,Elemental War concl. 2.00
94 TMd,A:Killer Frost 2.00
95 TMd,V:Captains of Industry . . . 2.00
96 TMd,A:Shango,African God &
   Obatala,Lord o/t White Cloth. . . 2.00
97 TMd,A:Obatala,V:Shango 2.00
98 TMd,A:Masar. 2.00
99 TMd,A:Brimstone,PlasmaGiant . 2.00
100 TMd,AM,V:Brimstone (Firestorm
   back-up story) final issue 3.00
Ann.#5 JLI,Suicide Squad
   I:New Firestorm 2.50

GAMMARAUDERS
1989
1 I:Animal-Warrior Bioborgs 2.00
2 V:The Slugnoids 2.00
3 V:Slugnoids,I:Squawk the
   Penguinoid. 2.00
4 V:Slugnoids 1.50
5 V:Bioborg/Podnoid 1.50
6 Slash vs.Sassin,A:RadicalDebs . 1.50
7 Jok findsSword that was broken . 2.00
8 Jok's search for KirkwardDerby. . 2.00
9 Jok the Congressman. 2.00
10 The Big Nada, final issue. 2.00

GANG BUSTERS
1947–58
1 . . . . 650.00
2 . . . . 300.00
3 . . . . 200.00
4 . . . . 200.00
5 . . . . 200.00
6 . . . . 200.00
7 . . . . 200.00
8 . . . . 200.00
9 Ph(c) 150.00
10 Ph(c) 150.00
11 Ph(c) 125.00
12 Ph(c) 125.00
13 Ph(c) 125.00
14 Ph(c),FF 275.00
15 . . . . 100.00
16 . . . . 100.00
17. . . . . 275.00
18 . . . . 100.00
19 . . . . 100.00
20 . . . . 100.00
21 thru 25 . . . . @90.00
26 JK 90.00
27 thru 40 . . . . @75.00
41 thru 44 . . . . @60.00
45 Comics Code. 60.00
46 thru 50. . . . . 60.00
51 MD 60.00
52 thru 67 . . . . @60.00

GANGLAND
April 1998
1 (of 4) crime anthology. 3.00
2 Platinum Nights 3.00
3 Gang Buff. 3.00
4 conclusion 3.00

GEMINI BLOOD
DC/Helix

1 .... 2.25
2 .... 2.25
3 Royal Caste 2.50
4 V:Shraddhan 2.25
5 WSi(c),V:Rolk 2.25
6 .... 2.50
7 BSz, Gillian's secret revealed ... 2.50
8 Loothka 2.50
9 Nick captured by Loothka,
   final issue. 2.50

GENESIS
Aug., 1997

1 (of 4) JBy,RoW,JRu,AD,MFm,
  Marvel x-over 2.00
2 JBy,RoW,JRu,AD,MFm,x-over . . 2.00
3 JBy,RoW,JRu,AD,MFm,x-over . . 2.00
4 JBy,RoW,JRu,AD,MFm,concl.... 2.00

GHOSTDANCING
Vertigo 1995
[Mini-Series]

1 I:Snake,Ghost Dancing 2.00
2 Secrets. 2.00
3 I:Father Craft 2.50
4 Coyote prisoner 2.50
5 F:Snot Boy 2.50

GHOSTS
Sept.–Oct., 1971

1 JAp,NC(c),Death's Bride-
  groom! 100.00
2 WW,NC(c),Mission
  Supernatural. 50.00
3 TD,NC(c),Death is my Mother.. 40.00
4 GT,NC(c),The Crimson Claw... 40.00
5 NC(c),Death, The Pale
  Horseman 40.00
6 NC(c),A Specter Poured
  The Potion 20.00
7 MK(c),Death's Finger Points ... 20.00
8 NC(c),The Cadaver In
  The Clock. 20.00
9 AA,NC(c),The Last Ride
  Of Rosie The Wrecker 20.00
10 NC(c),A Specter Stalks Saigon 20.00
11 NC(c),The Devils Lake 15.00
12 NC(c),The Macabre Mummy
  Of Takhem-Ahtem 15.00

Ghosts #75 © DC Comics, Inc.

13 NC(c),Hell Is One Mile High . . . 15.00
14 NC(c),The Bride Wore
  A Shroud 15.00
15 AA,NC(c),The Ghost That
  Wouldn't Die. 15.00
16 NC(c),Death's Grinning Face .. 15.00
17 NC(c),Death Held the
  Lantern High 15.00
18 AA,NC(c),Graveyard of
  Vengeance. 15.00
19 AA,NC(c),The Dead Live On .. 15.00
20 NC(c),The Haunting Hussar
  Of West Point. 15.00
21 NC(c),The Ghost In The
  Devil's Chair. 10.00
22 NC(c),The Haunted Horns
  Of Death 10.00
23 NC(c),Dead Is My Darling! 10.00
24 AA,NC(c),You Too, Will Die ... 10.00
25 AA,NC(c),Three Skulls On
  The Zambezi 10.00
26 DP,NC(c),The Freaky Phantom
  Of Watkins Glen 10.00
27 NC(c),Conversation With
  A Corpse 10.00
28 DP,NC(c),Flight Of The
  Lost Phantom. 10.00
29 NC(c),The Haunted Lady
  Of Death 10.00
30 NC(c),The Fangs of
  the Phantom. 10.00
31 NC(c),Blood On The Moon.... 10.00
32 NC(c),Phantom Laughed Last . 10.00
33 NC(c),The Hangman of
  Haunted Island. 10.00
34 NC(c),Wrath of the Ghost Apes 10.00
35 NC(c),Feud with a Phantom ... 10.00
36 NC(c),The Boy Who Returned
  From The Gave 10.00
37 LD(c),Fear On Ice 10.00
38 LD(c),Specter In The Surf 10.00
39 LD(c),The Haunting Hitchhiker 10.00
40 LD(c),The Nightmare That
  Haunted The World 18.00
41 LD(c),Ship of Specters....... 15.00
42 LD(c),The Spectral Sentries... 15.00
43 LD(c),3 Corpses On A Rope .. 15.00
44 LD(c),The Case of the
  Murdering Specters 15.00
45 LD(c),Bray of the
  Phantom Beast. 15.00
46 LD(c),The World's Most
  Famous Phantom........... 15.00
47 LD(c),Wrath of the
  Restless Specters 15.00
48 DP,LD(c),The Phantom Head.. 15.00
49 The Ghost in the Cellar 15.00
50 Home Is Where The Grave Is . 15.00
51 The Ghost Who Would Not Die 15.00
52 LD(c),The Thunderhead
  Phantom 15.00
53 LD(c),Whose Spirit Invades Me 15.00
54 LD(c),The Deadly Dreams
  Of Ernie Caruso. 15.00
55 LD(c),The House That Was
  Built For Haunting. 15.00
56 LD(c),The Triumph Of The
  Teen-Age Phantom. 15.00
57 LD(c),The Flaming Phantoms
  of Oradour 15.00
58 LD(c),The Corpse in the Closet 15.00
59 LD(c),That Demon Within Me.. 15.00
60 LD(c),The Spectral Smile
  of Death. 8.00
61 LD(c),When Will I Die Again. ... 8.00
62 LD(c),The Phantom Hoaxer! ... 8.00
63 LD(c),The Burning Bride 8.00
64 LD(c),Dead Men Do Tell Tales . 8.00
65 LD(c),The Imprisoned Phantom . 8.00
66 LD(c),Conversation With A
  Corpse. 8.00

Ghosts #97 © DC Comics, Inc.

67 LD(c),The Spectral Sword 8.00
68 LD(c),The Phantom of the
  Class of '76 .... 5.00
69 LD(c),The Haunted Gondola ... 5.00
70 LD(c),Haunted Honeymoon 5.00
71 LD(c),The Ghost Nobody Knew . 5.00
72 LD(c),The Ghost of
  Washington Monument....... 5.00
73 LD(c),The Specter Of The
  Haunted Highway. 5.00
74 LD(c),The Gem That Haunted
  the World! 5.00
75 LD(c),The Legend Of The
  Lottie Lowry 5.00
76 LD(c),Two Ghosts of
  Death Row. 5.00
77 LD(c),Ghost, Where Do
  You Hide? 5.00
78 LD(c),The World's Most
  Famous Phantom........... 5.00
79 LD(c),Lure of the Specter...... 5.00
80 JO(c),The Winged Specter..... 5.00
81 LD(c),Unburied Phantom 5.00
82 LD(c),The Ghost Who
  Wouldn't Die. 5.00
83 LD(c),Escape From the Haunt
  of the Amazon Specter....... 5.00
84 LD(c),Torment of the
  Phantom Face 5.00
85 LD(c),The Fiery Phantom
  of Faracutin 5.00
86 LD(c),The Ghostly Garden..... 5.00
87 LD(c),The Phantom Freak 5.00
88 LD(c),Harem In Hell. 5.00
89 JKu(c),Came The Specter
  Shrouded In Seaweed 5.00
90 The Ghost Galleon 5.00
91 LD(c),The Haunted Wheelchair . 5.00
92 DH(c),Double Vision 5.00
93 MK(c),The Flaming Phantoms
  of Nightmare Alley 5.00
94 LD(c),Great Caesar's Ghost.... 5.00
95 All The Stage Is A Haunt 5.00
96 DH(c),Dread of the
  Deadly Domestic 5.00
97 JAp(c),A Very Special Spirit
  A:Spectre. 10.00
98 JAp(c),The Death of a Ghost
  A:Spectre. 10.00
99 EC(c),Till Death Do Us Join
  A:Spectre. 10.00
100 EC&DG(c),The Phantom's
  Final Debt 5.00
101 MK(c),The Haunted Hospital .. 3.00
102 RB&DG(c),The Fine Art

Of Haunting 3.00
103 RB&DG(c),Visions and
    Vengeance. 3.00
104 LD(c),The First Ghost 3.00
105 JKu(c) 3.00
106 JKu(c) 3.00
107 JKu(c) 3.00
108 JKu(c) 3.00
109 EC(c). 3.00
110 EC&DG(c) 3.00
111 JKu(c) 3.00
112 May, 1982 . . . . 3.00

GIANTKILLER
1999
1 (of 6) 2.50
2 DIB. 2.50
3 DIB. 2.50

G.I. COMBAT
Jan., 1957
Prev: Golden Age
44 RH,JKu,The Eagle and
    the Wolves 450.00
45 RH,JKu,Fireworks Hill 250.00
46 JKu,The Long Walk
    To Wansan 200.00
47 RH, The Walking Weapon . . . 200.00
48 No Fence For A Jet 200.00
49 Frying Pan Seat. 200.00
50 Foxhole Pilot 200.00
51 RH,The Walking Grenade . . . 175.00
52 JKu,JKu(c),Call For A Tank. . . 175.00
53 JKu,The Paper Trap. 175.00
54 RH,JKu,Sky Tank. 175.00
55 Call For A Gunner 150.00
56 JKu,JKu(c),The D.I.-And the
    Sand Fleas. 150.00
57 RH,Live Wire For Easy 150.00
58 JKu(c),Flying Saddle 150.00
59 JKu,Hot Corner 175.00
60 RH,Bazooka Crossroads 175.00
61 JKu(c),The Big Run 125.00
62 RH,JKu,Drop An Inch. 125.00
63 MD,JKu(c),Last Stand 125.00
64 MD,RH,JKu,JKu(c),The
    Silent Jet 125.00
65 JKu,Battle Parade 125.00
66 MD,The Eagle of Easy
    Company 125.00
67 JKu(c),I:Tank Killer. 150.00
68 JKu,RH,The Rock 125.00
69 JKu,RH,The Steel Ribbon . . . 125.00
70 JKu,Bull's-Eye Bridge. 125.00
71 MD,JKu(c),Last Stand 100.00
72 MD,JKu(c),Ground Fire 100.00
73 RH,JKu(c),Window War 100.00
74 RH,A Flag For Joey 100.00
75 RH,Dogtag Hill. 100.00
76 MD,RH,JKu,Bazooka For
    A Mouse. 100.00
77 RH,JKu,H-Hour For A Gunner 100.00
78 MD,RH,JKu(c),Who Cares
    About The Infantry 100.00
79 JKu,RH,Big Gun-Little Gun . . 100.00
80 JKu,RH(c),Flying Horsemen. . 100.00
81 Jump For Glory 90.00
82 IN,Get Off My Back 90.00
83 Too Tired To Fight 90.00
84 JKu(c),Dog Company
    Is Holding. 80.00
85 IN,JKu(c),The T.N.T. Trio 80.00
86 JKu,RH(c),Not Return 80.00
87 RH(c),I:Haunted Tank. 500.00
88 RH,JKu(c),Haunted Tank Vs.
    Ghost Tank. 90.00
89 JA,RH,IN,Tank With Wings. . . . 90.00
90 JA,IN,RH,Tank Raiders 90.00
91 IN,RH,The Tank and the Turtle. 90.00

92 JA,IN,The Tank of Doom 90.00
93 RH(c),JA,No-Return Mission . . 90.00
94 IN,RH(c),Haunted Tank Vs.
    The Killer Tank 90.00
95 JA,RH(c),The Ghost of
    the Haunted Tank 90.00
96 JA,RH(c),The Lonesome Tank . 90.00
97 IN,RH(c),The Decoy Tank 90.00
98 JA,RH(c),Trap of Dragon's
    Teeth 90.00
99 JA,JKu,RH(c),Battle of the
    Thirsty Tanks 90.00
100 JA,JKu,Return of the
    Ghost Tank. 90.00
101 JA,The Haunted Tank Vs.
    Attila's Battle Tiger 60.00
102 JKu(c),Haunted Tank
    Battle Window 60.00
103 JKu,JA,RH(c),Rabbit Punch
    For A Tiger. 60.00
104 JA,JKu,RH(c),Blind
    Man's Radar. 60.00
105 JA,JKu(c),Time Bomb Tank . . 60.00
106 JA,JKu(c),Two-Sided War . . . 60.00
107 JKu(c),The Ghost Pipers 60.00
108 JKu(c),The Wounded
    Won't Wait,I:Sgt.Rock. 60.00
109 JKu(c),Battle of the Tank
    Graveyard 60.00
110 IN,JKu(c),Choose Your War . . 60.00
111 JA,JKu(c),Death Trap 60.00
112 JA,JKu(c),Ghost Ace 50.00
113 JKu,RH(c),Tank Fight In
    Death Town 50.00
114 JA,RH(c),O:Haunted Tank . . 125.00
115 JA,RH(c),MedalsForMayhem . 50.00
116 IN,JA,JKu(c),Battle Cry
    For A Dead Man. 50.00
117 JA,RH,JKu(c),Tank In
    The Ice Box 50.00
118 IN,JA,RH(c),My Buddy-
    My Enemy 50.00
119 IN,RH(c),Target For
    A Firing Squad 50.00
120 IN,JA,RH(c),Pull ATiger'sTail . 50.00
121 RH(c),Battle of Two Wars. . . . 30.00
122 JA,JKu(c),Who Dies Next?. . . 30.00
123 IN,RH(c),The Target of Terro . 30.00
124 IN,RH(c),Scratch That Tank . . 30.00
125 RH(c),Stay Alive-Until Dark . . 30.00
126 JA,RH(c),Tank Umbrella. 30.00
127 JA,JKu(c),Mission-Sudden
    Death. 30.00
128 RH(c),The Ghost of
    the Haunted Tank 30.00

G.I. Combat #164 © DC Comics Inc.

129 JA,RH(c),Hold That Town
    For A Dead Man. 30.00
130 RH(c),Battle of the Generals . 30.00
131 JKu&RH(c),Devil For Dinner. . 30.00
132 JA,JKu(c),The Executioner. . . 30.00
133 JKu(c),Operation:Death Trap . 30.00
134 MD,JKu(c),Desert Holocaust . 30.00
135 GE,JKu(c),Death is the Joker. 30.00
136 JKu(c),Kill Now-Pay Later . . . 30.00
137 JKu(c),We Can't See 30.00
138 JKu(c),I:The Losers 75.00
139 JKu(c),Corner of Hell 30.00
140 RH,MD,JKu(c),The LastTank . 30.00
141 MD,JKu(c),Let Me Live..
    Let Me Die 15.00
142 RH,JKu(c),Checkpoint-Death . 15.00
143 RH,JKu(c),The Iron Horseman 15.00
144 RH,MD,JKu(c),Every
    Man A Fort. 18.00
145 MD,JKu(c),Sand,Sun
    and Death 18.00
146 JKu(c),Move the World. 18.00
147 JKu(c),Rebel Tank 18.00
148 IN,JKu(c),The Gold-Plated
    General 18.00
149 JKu(c),Leave The
    Fighting To Us 12.00
150 JKu(c),The Death of the
    Haunted Tank. 12.00
151 JKu(c),A Strong Right Arm. . . 12.00
152 JKu(c),Decoy Tank. 12.00
153 JKu(c),The Armored Ark 12.00
154 JKu(c),Battle Prize 12.00
155 JKu(c),The Long Journey 10.00
156 JKu(c),Beyond Hell 10.00
157 JKu(c),The Fountain 10.00
158 What Price War 10.00
159 JKu(c),Mission Dead End. . . . 10.00
160 JKu(c),Battle Ghost 10.00
161 JKu(c),The Day of the Goth . . 10.00
162 JKu(c),The Final Victor. 10.00
163 A Crew Divided 10.00
164 Siren Song. 10.00
165 JKu(c),Truce,Pathfinder 10.00
166 Enemy From Yesterday 10.00
167 JKu(c),The Finish Line 10.00
168 NA(c),The Breaking Point. . . . 10.00
169 WS(c),The Death of the
    Haunted Tank. 10.00
170 Chain of Vengeance. 10.00
171 JKu(c),The Man Who
    Killed Jeb Stuart. 8.00
172 RH(c),At The Mercy of
    My Foes. 8.00
173 JKu(c),The Final Crash 8.00
174 JKu(c),Vow To A Dead Foe . . . 8.00
175 JKu(c),The Captive Tank 8.00
176 JKu(c),A Star Can Cry 8.00
177 JKu(c),The Tank That
    Missed D-Day 8.00
178 JKu(c),A Tank Is Born 8.00
179 JKu(c),One Last Charge 8.00
180 JKu(c),The Saints Go
    Riding On. 8.00
181 JKu(c),The Kidnapped Tank. . . 8.00
182 JKu(c),Combat Clock. 8.00
183 JKu(c),6 Stallions To
    Hell- And Back 8.00
184 JKu(c),Battlefield Bundle 8.00
185 JKu(c),No Taps For A Tank . . . 8.00
186 JKu(c),Souvenir
    From A Headhunter 8.00
187 JKu(c),The General
    Died Twice 8.00
188 The Devil's Pipers 8.00
189 The Gunner is a Gorilla 8.00
190 The Tiger and The Terrier 8.00
191 Decoy For Death 8.00
192 The General Has Two Faces . . 8.00
193 JKu(c),The War That
    Had To Wait 8.00

G.I. Combat #288 © DC Comics, Inc.

194 GE(c),Blitzkrieg Brain. 8.00
195 JKu(c),The War That
Time Forgot 8.00
196 JKu(c),Dead Men Patrol. 8.00
197 JKu(c),Battle Ark 8.00
198 JKu(c),The Devil
Rides A Panzer 8.00
199 JKu(c),A Medal From A Ghost . 8.00
200 JKu(c),The Tank That Died. . . 10.00
201 NA&RH(c),The Rocking
Chair Soldiers 9.00
202 NA&RH(c),Walking Wounded
Don't Cry 9.00
203 JKu(c),To Trap A Tiger. 9.00
204 JKu(c),A Winter In Hell. 9.00
205 JKu(c),A Gift From
The Emperor 9.00
206 JKu(c),A Tomb For A Tank 9.00
207 JKu(c),Foxhole for a Sherman . 9.00
208 JKu(c),Sink That Tank 9.00
209 JKu(c),Ring Of Blood 9.00
210 JKu(c),Tankers Also Bleed 9.00
211 JKu(c),A Nice Day For Killing . . 6.00
212 JKu(c),Clay Pigeon Crew 6.00
213 JKu(c),Back Door To War. 6.00
214 JKu(c),The Tanker Who
Couldn't Die 6.00
215 JKu(c),Last Stand For Losers. . 6.00
216 JKu(c),Ghost Squadron 6.00
217 JKu(c), The Pigeon Spies 6.00
218 JKu(c), 48 Hours to Die 6.00
219 thru 230 . . . . @6.00
231 thru 288 . . . . @5.00

GIFTS OF THE NIGHT
DC/Vertigo 1999
1 (of 4) PC,JBo 3.00
2 PC,JBo. 3.00
3 PC,JBo. 3.00
4 PC,JBo, conclusion 3.00

GILGAMESH II
1989
1 JSn,O:Gilgamesh 5.00
2 JSn,V:Nightshadow 4.50
3 JSn,V:Robotic Ninja 4.50
4 JSn,final issue 4.00

GIRL WHO WOULD

BE DEATH, THE
DC/Vertigo 1998
1 (of 4) F:Plath 2.50
2 . . . . 2.50
3 . . . . 2.50
4 . . . . 2.50

GODDESS
Vertigo 1995–96
Mini-Series]
1 I:Rosie Nolan 4.00
2 Rosie arrested 4.00
3 I:Jenny 4.00
4 CIA Chase 4.00
5 V:Agent Hooks 4.00
6 V:Harry Hooks 4.00
7 Mudhawks Past 4.00
8 finale 4.00

GOLDEN AGE
Elseworld 1993–94
1 PS,F:JSA,All-Star Squadron 8.00
2 PS,I:Dynaman 7.00
3 PS,IR:Mr. Terrific is
Ultra-Humanite. 7.00
4 PS,D:Dynaman,Mr. Terrific 6.00

GON
DC/Paradox 1996
Book 1 . . . . 6.00
Book 2 Gon Again! 6.00
Book 3 Here Today,Gon Tomorrow . 6.00
Book 4 Going, Going, Gon 6.00
TPB Gon Swimmin' 7.00
TPB Color Spectacular 6.00
TPB Gon Wild rep. books 3 & 4 . . 10.00

GREATEST STORIES
EVER TOLD
Greatest Superman Stories Ever Told:
HC 75.00
SC 15.95
Greatest Batman Stories Ever Told:
HC 60.00
SC 16.00
Vol.#2 Catwoman & Penguin 16.95
Greatest Joker Stories Ever Told:
HC 45.00
SC BBo(c) 15.00
Greatest Flash Stories Ever Told:
HC 30.00
SC 15.00
Greatest Golden Age Stories Ever Told:
HC 25.00
SC 15.00
Greatest Fifties Stories Ever Told:
HC 30.00
SC 15.00
Greatest Team-Up Stories Ever Told:
HC 25.00
SC 15.00

GREEN ARROW
[Limited Series] 1983
1 TVE,DG,O:Green Arrow 5.00
2 TVE,DG,A:Vertigo 3.50
3 TVE,DG,A:Vertigo. 3.50
4 TVE,DG,A:Black Canary. 3.50
[Regular Series] 1988–97
1 EH,DG,V:Muncie 5.00
2 EH,DG,V:Muncie 4.00
3 EH,DG,FMc,V:Fryes 4.00
4 EH,DG,FMc,V:Fryes 4.00
5 EH,DG,FMc,Gauntlet 4.00
6 EH,DG,FMc,Gauntlet 4.00

Green Arrow #81 © DC Comics, Inc.

7 EB,DG,A:Black Canary. 4.00
8 DG,Alaska 3.50
9 EH,DG,FMc,R:Shado 3.50
10 EH,DG,FMc,A:Shado. 3.50
11 EH,DG,FMc,A:Shado. 3.50
12 EH,DG,FMc,A:Shado. 3.00
13 DJu,DG,FMc,Moving Target. . . . 3.00
14 EH,DG,FMc. 3.00
15 EH,DG,FMc,Seattle And Die . . . 3.00
16 EH,DG,FMc,Seattle And Die . . . 3.00
17 DJu,DG,FMc,The Horse Man . . . 2.50
18 DJu,DG,FMc,The Horse Man . . . 2.50
19 EH,DG,FMc,A:Hal Jordan 2.50
20 EH,DG,FMc,A:Hal Jordan 2.50
21 DJu,DG,B:Blood of Dragon,
A:Shado. 2.50
22 DJu,DG,A:Shado 2.50
23 DJu,DG,A:Shado. 2.50
24 DJu,DG,E:Blood of Dragon 2.50
25 TVE,Witch Hunt #1 . . . . 2.25
26 Witch Hunt #2 . . . . 2.25
27 DJu,DG,FMc,R:Warlord 2.25
28 DJu,DG,FMc,A:Warlord 2.25
29 DJu,DG,FMc,Coyote Tears 2.25
30 DJu,DG,FMc,Coyote Tears 2.25
31 FMc,V:Drug Dealers 2.25
32 FMc,V:Drug Dealers 2.25
33 DJu,FMc,Psychology Issue 2.25
34 DJu,DG,A:Fryes,Arrested. 2.25
35 B:Black Arrow Saga,A:Shade. . . 2.25
36 Black Arrow Saga,A:Shade 2.25
37 Black Arrow Saga,A:Shade 2.25
38 E:Black Arrow Saga,A:Shade. . . 2.25
39 DCw,Leaves Seattle 2.25
40 MGr,Spirit Quest,A:
Indian Shaman. 2.25
41 DCw,I.R.A. 2.25
42 DCw,I.R.A 2.25
43 DCw,I.R.A. 2.25
44 DCw,Rock'n'Runes,pt.1 . . . . 2.25
45 Rock'n'Runes,pt.2 . . . . 2.25
46 DCw,Africa 2.25
47 DCw,V:Trappers 2.25
48 DCw,V:Trappers 2.25
49 V:Trappers. 2.25
50 MGr(c),50th Anniv.,R:Seattle . . . 3.00
51 Tanetti's Murder,pt.1. . . . . 2.00
52 Tanetti's Murder,pt.2. . . . . 2.00
53 The List,pt.1,A:Fyres 2.00
54 The List,pt.2,A:Fyres 2.00
55 Longbow Hunters tie-in 2.00
56 A:Lt. Cameron. 2.00
57 And Not A Drop to Drink,pt.1 . . . 2.00
58 And Not A Drop to Drink,pt.2 . . . 2.00
59 Predator,pt.1 . . . . 2.00

All comics prices listed are for *Near Mint* condition.

60 Predator,pt.2 . . . . 2.00
61 FS,F:Draft Dodgers 2.00
62 FS. 2.00
63 FS,B:Hunt for Red Dragon. 2.00
64 FS,Hunt for Red Dragon 2.00
65 MGr(c),Hunt for Red Dragon . . . 2.00
66 MGr(c),E:Hunt for Red Dragon. . 2.00
67 MGr(c),FS,V:Rockband Killer . . . 2.00
68 MGr(c),FS,BumRap 2.00
69 MGr(c),Reunion Tour #1 . . . . . . 2.00
70 Reunion Tour #2 . . . . 2.00
71 Wild in the Streets #1 . . . . 2.00
72 MGr(c),Wild in the Streets#2 . . . 2.00
73 MGr(c),F:Vietnam Vet 2.00
74 SAP,MGr(c),V:Sniper 2.00
75 MGr(c),A:Speedy Shado,
Black Canary 3.00
76 MGr(c),R:Eddie Fyers 2.00
77 MGr(c),A:Eddie Fyers 2.00
78 MGr(c),V:CIA 2.00
79 MGr(c),V:CIA 2.00
80 MGr(c),E:MGr(s),V:CIA 2.00
81 B:CDi(s),JAp,V:Shrapnel,
Nuklon 2.00
82 JAp,I:Rival 2.00
83 JAp,V:Yakuza 2.00
84 E:CDi(s),JAp,In Las Vegas. 2.00
85 AIG(s),JAp,A:Deathstroke 2.00
86 DgM(s),JAp,A:Catwoman. 2.00
87 JAp,V:Factory Owner. 2.00
88 JAp,A:M.Manhunter,Bl.Beetle. . . 2.00
89 JAp,A:Anarky. 2.25
90 Zero Hour 2.25
91 Hitman. 2.25
92 Partner attacked 2.25
93 Secrets of Red File 2.25
94 I:Camo Rouge 2.25
95 V:Camo Rouge 2.25
96 I:Slyfox,A:Hal Jordan 2.00
97 Where Angels Fear to
Tread,pt.2. . . . . 2.25
98 Where Angels Fear to
Tread,pt.3, A:Arsenal 2.25
99 Where Angels Fear to Tread . . . 2.25
100 . . . . 7.00
101 A:Superman,Black Canary . . . 25.00
102 CDi,RbC,Underworld
Unleashed tie-in 3.00
103 CDi,RbC,Underworld
Unleashed tie-in 3.00
104 CDi,RbC,A:Green Lantern 3.00
105 CDi,RbC,A:Robin. 3.00
106 . . . . 2.25
107 CDi,RbC,protects child-king . . . 2.25

108 CDi,A:Thorn. 2.25
109 CDi,JAp,BSz,in Metropolis. . . . 2.25
110 CDi(s),RbC,I:Hatchet, Green
Lantern x-over 3.50
111 CDi(s), RbC,I:Hatchet, Green
Lantern x-over 3.50
112 CDi(s),RbC, ... 2.25
113 CDi(s),RbC,In the Mongolian
wastes 2.25
114 CDi(s) RbC,airplane downed,
Final Night tie-in 2.25
115 CDi(s),RbC,"The Iron Death,"
pt.1 . . . . 2.25
116 CDi(s),RbC,"The Iron Death,"
pt.2 . . . . 2.25
117 CDi(s),RbC,"The Iron Death,"
pt.3, concl. 2.25
118 CDi(s),DBw,RbC,"Endangered
Species" pt.1 . . . . 2.25
119 CDi(s),DBw,RbC,"Endangered
Species" pt.2 . . . . 2.25
120 CDi(s),RbC,at grandfather's
ranch 2.25
121 CDi(s),RbC,V:The Silver
Monkey 2.25
122 CDi(s),RbC, at Idaho ranch . . . 2.25
123 CDi(s),JAp,KJ,"The
Stormbringers" concl. 2.25
124 CDi(s),RbC,V:Milo Armitage. . . 2.25
125 CDi(s),DBw,Green Lantern
x-over,pt.1, 48pg 3.50
126 CDi(s),DBw,x-over, pt.3 . . . . . 2.50
127 CDi(s),DBw,to San Francisco. . 2.50
128 CDi(s),DWb,Russian Mob 2.50
129 CDi,DBw,Jansen prisoner,pt.2 . 2.50
130 CDi,DBw,. 2.50
131 CDi,DBw,F:Crackshot 2.50
132 CDi,DBw,Eddie Fyers returns. . 2.50
133 CDi,DBw,Eddie Fyers pt.2 . . . . 2.50
134 CDi,DBw,Brotherhood of
the Fist x-over,pt.1 . . . . 2.50
135 CDi,DBw,Brotherhood of the
Fist x-over, concl. 2.50
136 CDi,DBw,Green Pastures,pt.1 . 2.50
137 CDi(s),A:Superman 2.50
Ann.#1 A:Question,FablesII 3.50
Ann.#2 EH,DG,FMc,A:Question . . . 3.00
Ann.#3 A:Question 2.50
Ann.#4 `The Black Alchemist' 3.25
Ann.#5 TVE,FS,Eclipso,Batman . . . 3.25
Ann.#6 JBa(c),I:Hook 3.50
Ann.#7 CDi, Year One 3.95
Spec. #0 Return 2.00
Spec.#1,000,000 CDi(s), A:Superman
final issue. 2.00

GREEN ARROW
LONGBOW HUNTERS
Aug., 1987
1 MGr,N:GreenArrow,I:Shado 4.00
1a 2nd printing 2.50
2 MGr,`Shadow' Revealed. 4.00
2a 2nd printing 2.50
3 MGr,Tracking Snow 4.00
TPB, rep. #1-#3 . . . . 12.95

GREEN ARROW:
THE WONDER YEARS
1993
1 MGr,GM,B:New O:Green Arrow . 2.50
2 MGr,GM,I:Brianna Stone. 2.00
3 MGr,GM,A:Brianna Stone 2.00
4 MGr,GM,Conclusion 2.00

GREEN CANDLES
1995
1 Paradox Mystery,F:John Halting 5.95

2 F:John Halting 5.95
3 finale 5.95
TPB B&W rep. #1–#3 . . . . 9.95

GREEN LANTERN
Autumn, 1941
1 O:Green Lantern, V:Master of
Light, Arson in the Slums . 28,000.00
2 V:Baldy,Tycoon's Legacy . . . 6,000.00
3 War cover 4,400.00
4 Doiby and Green Lantern
join the Army 3,200.00
5 V:Nazis and Black
Prophet,A:General Prophet 2,000.00
6 V:Nordo & Hordes of War Hungy
Henchmen,Exhile of Exiles,
A:Shiloh. 1,700.00
7 The Wizard of Odds. 2,000.00
8 The Lady and Her Jewels,
A:Hop Harrigan 1,700.00
9 V:The Whistler, The School
for Vandals 1,500.00
10 V:Vandal Savage,The Man Who
Wanted the World,O:Vandal
Savage 1,500.00
11 The Distardly Designs of
Doiby Dickles' Pals 1,100.00
12 O:The Gambler. 1,100.00
13 A:Angela Van Enters. 1,100.00
14 Case of the Crooked Cook . 1,100.00
15 V:Albert Zero, One...Two...
Three...Stop Thinking. 1,100.00
16 V:The Lizard 1,100.00
17 V:Kid Triangle, Reward for
Green Lantern 1,100.00
18 V:The Dandy,The Connoisseur of
crime,X-mas(c) 1,200.00
19 V:Harpies, Sing a Song of
Disaster A:Fate 1,100.00
20 A:Gambler 1,100.00
21 V:The Woodman,The Good
Humor Man 1,000.00
22 A:Dapper Dan Crocker 1,000.00
23 Doiby Dickles Movie
Ajax Pictures 1,000.00
24 A:Mike Mattson,OnceA Cop 1,000.00
25 The Diamond Magnet 1,000.00
26 The Scourge of the Sea . . . 1,000.00
27 V:Sky Pirate 1,100.00
28 The Tricks of the
Sports Master 1,000.00
29 Meets the Challange of
the Harlequin 1,000.00
30 I:Streak the Wonder Dog. . . 1,000.00
31 The Terror of the Talismans . . 900.00

Green Arrow #110 © DC Comics Inc.   *Green Lantern #25 © DC Comics, Inc.*

32 The Case of the
  Astonishing Juggler 900.00
33 Crime goes West 900.00
34 Streak meets the Princess . . . 900.00
35 V:The Three-in-One Criminal . 900.00
36 The Mystery of the
  Missing Messanger 1,000.00
37 A:Sargon 1,000.00
38 DoublePlay,May-June,1949. 1,000.00

GREEN LANTERN
1960–72, 1976–86

1 GK,O:Green Lantern 2,800.00
2 GK,I:Qward,Pieface 800.00
3 GK,V:Qward 450.00
4 GK,Secret of GL Mask 350.00
5 GK,I:Hector Hammond 350.00
6 GK,I:Tomar-Re 350.00
7 GK,I&O:Sinestro 300.00
8 GK,1st Story in 5700 A.D. . . . 300.00
9 GK,A:Sinestro 300.00
10 GK,O:Green Lantern's Oath . . 300.00
11 GK,V:Sinestro 200.00
12 GK,Sinestro,I:Dr.Polaris 200.00
13 GK,A:Flash,Sinestro 225.00
14 GK,I&O:Sonar,1st Jordan
  Brothers story 175.00
15 GK,Zero Hour story 165.00
16 GK,MA,I:Star Saphire,
  O:Abin Sur 175.00
17 GK,V:Sinestro 165.00
18 GK 165.00
19 GK,A:Sonar 165.00
20 GK,A:Flash 175.00
21 GK,O:Dr.Polaris 150.00
22 GK,A:Hector Hammond,Jordan
  Brothers story 150.00
23 GK,I:Tattooed Man 150.00
24 GK,O:Shark 150.00
25 GK,V:Sonar,HectorHammond. 150.00
26 GK,A:Star Sapphire 150.00
27 GK 150.00
28 GK,I:Goldface 150.00
29 GK,I:Black Hand 160.00
30 GK,I:Katma Tui 150.00
31 GK,Jordan brothers story 120.00
32 GK 120.00
33 GK,V:Dr. Light 120.00
34 GK,V:Hector Hammond 120.00
35 GK,I:Aerialist 120.00
36 GK 120.00
37 GK,I:Evil Star 120.00
38 GK,A:Tomar-Re 120.00
39 GK,V:Black Hand 120.00
40 GK,O:Guardians,A:Golden
  Age Green Lantern 550.00
41 GK,A:Star Sapphire 75.00
42 GK,A:Zatanna 75.00
43 GK,A:Major Disaster 75.00
44 GK,A:Evil Star 75.00
45 GK,I:Prince Peril,A:Golden
  Age Green Lantern 125.00
46 GK,V:Dr.Polaris 75.00
47 GK,5700 A.D. V:Dr.Polaris . . . 75.00
48 GK,I:Goldface 75.00
49 GK,I:Dazzler 75.00
50 GK,V:Thraxon the Powerful . . . 75.00
51 GK,Green Lantern's Evil
  Alter-ego 55.00
52 GK,A:Golden Age Green
  Lantern Sinestro 100.00
53 GK,CI,Jordon brothers story . . 55.00
54 GK,Menace in the Iron Lung . . 55.00
55 GK,Cosmic Enemy #1 . . . . . . 55.00
56 GK 55.00
57 GK,V:Major Disaster 55.00
58 GK,Perils of the Powerless
  Green Lantern 55.00
59 GK,I:Guy Gardner(imaginary
  story) 225.00

Green Lantern #1 © DC Comics, Inc.

60 GK,I:Lamplighter 50.00
61 GK,A:Gold.Age Gr.Lantern. . . 55.00
62 Steel Small,Rob Big 50.00
63 NA(c),This is the Way the
  World Ends 50.00
64 MSy,We Vow Death to Green
  Lantern. 50.00
65 MSy,Dry up and Die. 50.00
66 MSy,5700 AD story 50.00
67 DD,The First Green Lantern . . 50.00
68 GK,I Wonder where the
  Yellow Went? 50.00
69 GK,WW,If Earth Fails the
  Test.. It Means War 50.00
70 GK,A Funny Thing Happened
  on the way to Earth 50.00
71 GK,DD,MA,Jordan brothers . . 25.00
72 GK,Phantom o/t SpaceOpera . 25.00
73 GK,MA,A:Star Sapphire,
  Sinestro 25.00
74 GK,MA,A:Star Sapphire,
  Sinestro 25.00
75 GK,Qward 25.00
76 NA,Gr.Lantern & Gr.Arrow
  team-up begins. 200.00
77 NA,Journey to Desolation . . . 60.00
78 NA,A:Black Canary,A Kind of
  Loving..A Way to Death 60.00
79 NA,DA,A:Black Canary,Ulysses
  Star is Still Alive 50.00
80 NA,DG,Even an Immortal
  can die 50.00
81 NA,DG,A:Black Canary,Death
  be my Destiny 40.00
82 NA,DG,A:Black Canary,
  V:Sinestro,(BWr 1 page) 40.00
83 NA,DG,A:BlackCanary,Gr.Lantern
  reveals I.D. to Carol Ferris . . . 40.00
84 NA,BWr,V:Black Hand 40.00
85 NA,Speedy on Drugs,pt.1,
  rep.Green Lantern #1 . . . . . . 60.00
86 NA,DG,Speedy on Drugs,pt.2,
  ATh(rep)Golden Age G.L. 60.00
87 NA,DG,I:John Stewart,
  2nd Guy Gardner app. 35.00
88 all reprints. 10.00
89 NA,And Through Him Save
  the World 27.00
90 MGr,New Gr.Lantern rings . . . 12.00
91 MGr,V:Sinestro 7.00
92 MGr,V:Sinestro 7.00
93 MGr,TA,War Against the
  World Builders 7.00
94 MGr,TA,DG,Green Arrow
  Assassin,pt.1 . . . . 7.00
95 MGr,Gr.Arrow Assassin,pt.2 . . . 7.00

96 MGr,A:Katma Tui 7.00
97 MGr,V:Mocker 7.00
98 MGr,V:Mocker 7.00
99 MGr,V:Mocker 7.00
100 MGr,AS,I:Air Wave 15.00
101 MGr,A:Green Arrow 6.00
102 AS,A:Green Arrow 5.00
103 AS,Earth-Asylum for an Alien. . 5.00
104 AS,A:Air Wave. 6.00
105 AS,Thunder Doom 6.00
106 MGr,Panic..In High Places
  & Low 6.00
107 AS,Green Lantern Corp.story . . 6.00
108 MGr,BU:G.A.Green Lantern,
  V:Replikon 7.00
109 MGr,Replicon#2,GA.GL.#2. . . . 6.00
110 MGr,GA.GL.#3 . . . . 6.00
111 AS,O:Green Lantern,
  A:G.A.Green Lantern 7.00
112 AS,O&A:G.A. Green Lantern . 12.00
113 AS,Christmas story 5.00
114 AS,I:Crumbler 5.00
115 AS,V:Crumbler. 5.00
116 Guy Gardner as Gr.Lantern . . 30.00
117 JSon,I:KariLimbo,V:Prof.Ojo . . 5.00
118 AS,V:Prof.Ojo. 5.00
119 AS,G.L.& G.A.solo storys . . . 5.00
120 DH,A:Kari,V:El Espectro. 3.50
121 DH,V:El Espectro. 3.50
122 DH,A:Guy Gardner,Superman . 6.00
123 JSon,DG,E:Green Lantern/Green
  Arrow T.U.,A:G.Gardner,
  V:Sinestro 7.00
124 JSon,V:Sinestro 3.50
125 JSon,FMc,V:Sinestro 3.50
126 JSon,FMc,V:Shark 3.50
127 JSon,FMc,V:Goldface 3.50
128 JSon,V:Goldface 3.50
129 JSon,V:Star Sapphire. 3.50
130 JSon,FMc,A:Sonar,B:Tales of the
  Green Lantern Corps 3.00
131 JSon,AS,V:Evil Star 3.00
132 JSon,AS,E:Tales of GL Corps
  B:B.U.Adam Strange 3.00
133 JSon,V:Dr.Polaris. 2.50
134 JSon,V:Dr.Polaris. 2.50
135 JSon,V:Dr.Polaris. 2.50
136 JSon,A:Space Ranger,
  Adam Strange 2.50
137 JSon,CI,MA,I:Citadel,A:Space
  Ranger,A.Strange. 2.50
138 JSon,A&O:Eclipso 4.00
139 JSon,V:Eclipso. 3.00
140 JSon,I:Congressman Block
  Adam Strange 2.50
141 JSon,I:OmegaMen. 6.00
142 JSon,A:OmegaMen 4.00
143 JSon,A:OmegaMen 4.00
144 JSon,D:Tattooed Man,Adam
  Strange 2.50
145 JSon,V:Goldface 2.50
146 JSon,CI,V:Goldface
  E:B.U.Adam Strange 2.50
147 JSon,CI,V:Goldface 2.50
148 JSon,DN,DA,V:Quardians . . . 2.50
149 JSon,A:GL.Corps. 2.50
150 JSon,anniversary 3.50
151 JSon,GL.Exiled in space 2.50
152 JSon,CI,GL Exile #2 . . . . 2.50
153 JSon,CI,Gr.Lantern Exile #3. . . 2.50
154 JSon,Gr.Lantern Exile #4 . . . . 2.50
155 JSon,Gr.Lantern Exile #5 . . . . 2.50
156 GK,Gr.Lantern Exile #6 . . . . . 2.50
157 KP,IN,Gr.Lantern Exile #7 . . . 2.50
158 KP,IN,Gr.Lantern Exile #8 . . . 2.50
159 KP,Gr.Lantern Exile #9. . . . . . 2.50
160 KP,Gr.Lantern Exile #10. . . . . 2.50
161 KP,A:Omega Men,Exile #11 . . 2.50
162 KP,Gr.Lantern Exile #12. . . . . 2.50
163 KP,Gr.Lantern Exile #13. . . . . 2.50
164 KP,A:Myrwhidden,Exile #14 . . 2.50

165 KP,A:John Stewart & Gr.Arrow
Green Lantern Exile #15. . . . . . 2.00
166 GT,FMc,DGi,Exile #16 . . . . 2.00
167 GT,FMc,G.L.Exile #17 . . . . . . 2.00
168 GT,FMc,G.L. Exile #18. . . . . . 2.00
169 Green Lantern Exile #19 . . . . . 2.00
170 GT,MSy,GreenLanternCorps . . 2.00
171 ATh,TA,DGb,Green Lantern
Exile #20 . . . . 2.00
172 DGb,E:Gr.Lant.Exile. 2.00
173 DGb,I:Javelin,A:Congressman
Bloch 2.00
174 DGb,V:Javelin 2.00
175 DGb,A:Flash 2.25
176 DGb,V:The Shark 2.00
177 DGb,rep. Gr.Lant #128. . . . . . 2.00
178 DGb,A:Monitor,V:Demolition
Team 2.00
179 DGb,I:Predator 2.00
180 DGb,A:JLA 2.00
181 DGi,Hal Jordan quits as GL . . . 2.75
182 DGi,John Stewart taks over
V:Major Disaster. 2.50
183 DGi,V:Major Disaster 2.50
184 DGb,Rep. Gr.Lant. #59 . . . . . 3.50
185 DGi,DH,V:Eclipso. 4.00
186 DGi,V:Eclipso 4.00
187 BWi,John Stewart meets
Katma Tui 2.25
188 JSon,C:GrArrow,V:Sonar,John
Stewart reveals I.D. to world. . . 3.50
189 JSon,V:Sonar 2.00
190 JSon,A:Green Arrow/Black
Canary,Guy Gardner 2.00
191 JSon,IR:Predator is Star
Sapphire 2.00
192 JSon,O:Star Sapphire 2.00
193 JSon,V:Replikon,
A:G.Gardner. 2.50
194 JSon,Crisis,R:G.Gardner 5.00
195 JSon,Guy Gardner as Green
Lantern,develops attitude 9.00
196 JSon,V:Shark,Hal Jordan
regains ring 3.00
197 JSon,V:Shark,Sonar,
Goldface 3.00
198 JSon,D:Tomar-Re,Hal returns as
Green Lantern,(double size) . . . 3.00
199 JSon,V:Star Sapphire. 2.00
200 JSon,final Gr.Lantern issue . . . 2.50
Becomes:

GREEN LANTERN CORPS

1986–88

201 JSon,I:NewGr.LantCorps,V:Star
Sapphire, Sonar, Dr.Polaris. . . 2.00
202 JSon,set up headquarters 2.00
203 JSon,tribute to Disney 2.00
204 JSon,Arisia reaches puberty . . 2.00
205 JSon,V:Black Hand 2.00
206 JSon,V:Black Hand 2.00
207 JSon, Legneds crossover. 2.00
208 JSon,I:Rocket Red Brigade,
Green Lanterns in Russia#1 . . . 2.00
209 JSon,In Russia #2 . . . . 2.00
210 JSon,In Russia #3 . . . . 2.00
211 JSon,John Stewart proposes
to Katma Tui. 1.75
212 JSon,W:J.Stewart&KatmaTui . . 1.75
213 Json,For Want of a Male 1.75
214 IG,5700 A.D. Story. 1.75
215 IG,Salaak and Chip quit. 1.75
216 IG,V:Carl 1.75
217 JSon,V:Sinestro 1.75
218 BWg,V:Sinestro 1.75
219 BWg,V:Sinestro 1.75
220 JSon,Millenium,pt.3 . . . . 1.75
221 JSon,Millenium 1.75
222 JSon,V:Sinestro 1.75
223 GK,V:Sinestro 1.75

224 GK,V:Sinestro 2.00
Ann.#1 GK 2.00
Ann.#2 JSa,BWg,S:AnM. 2.50
Ann.#3 JBy,JL,JR 2.00
Spec.#1 A:Superman 2.00
Spec.#2 MBr,RT,V:Seeker. 2.00
TPB rep.#84-#87,#89,Flash
#217-#219 . . . . 12.95
TPB rep. reprints of #1-#7 . . . . . . 8.95

GREEN LANTERN

[2nd Regular Series] 1990–97

1 PB,A:Hal Jordan,John Stuart,
Guy Gardner 5.00
2 PB,A:Tattooed Man. 3.00
3 PB,Jordan vs.Gardner 4.00
4 PB,Vanishing Cities 2.00
5 PB Return to OA 2.00
6 PB 3GL'sCaptive 2.00
7 PB R:Guardians 2.00
8 PB R:Guardians 2.00
9 JSon,G.Gardner,pt.1 . . . . 3.00
10 JSon,G.Gardner,pt.2 . . . . 3.00
11 JSon,G.Gardner,pt.3 . . . . 3.00
12 JSon,G.Gardner,pt.4 . . . . 3.00
13 Jordan,Gardner,Stuart(giant) . . . 2.50
14 PB,Mosaic,pt.1 . . . . 2.00
15 RT,Mosaic,pt.2. . . . . 2.00
16 MBr,RT,Mosaic,pt.3 . . . . 2.00
17 MBr,RT,Mosaic,pt.4 . . . . 2.00
18 JSon,JRu,G.Gardner,
A:Goldface 2.00
19 MBr,PB,JSon,A:All Four G.L.'s,
O:Alan Scott,A:Doiby Dickles
(D.Size-50th Ann.Iss.) 3.00
20 PB,RT,Hal Jordan G.L. Corp
story begins, A:Flicker 1.75
21 PB,RT,G.L. Corp.,pt.2,
V:Flicker. 1.75
22 PB,RT,G.L. Corp.,pt.3,
R:Star Sapphire 1.75
23 PB,RT,V:Star Sapphire,
A:John Stuart 1.75
24 PB,RT,V:Star Sapphire. 1.75
25 MBr,JSon,RT,Hal Vs.Guy,
A:JLA. 2.75
26 MBr,V:Evil Star,Starlings 1.50
27 MBr,V:Evil Star,Starlings 1.50
28 MBr,V:Evil Star,Starlings 1.50
29 MBr,RT,R:Olivia Reynolds 1.50
30 MBr,RT,Gorilla Warfare#1 . . . . 1.50
31 MBr,RT,Gorilla Warfare#3 . . . . 1.50
32 RT(i),A:Floro,Arisia 1.50

Green Lantern #3 © DC Comics Inc.

33 MBr,RT,Third Law#1,
A;New Guardians 1.50
34 MBr,RT,Third Law#2,I:Entropy . . 1.50
35 MBr,RT,Third Law#3,V:Entropy . 1.50
36 V:Dr.Light 1.50
37 MBg,RT,A:Guy Gardner 1.50
38 MBr,RT,A:Adam Strange 1.50
39 MBr,RT,A:Adam Strange 1.50
40 RT(i),A:Darkstar,
V:Reverse Flash. 1.75
41 MBr,RT,V:Predator,
C:Deathstroke 1.50
42 MBr,RT,V:Predator,
Deathstroke 1.50
43 RT(i),A:Itty 1.50
44 RT(i),Trinity#2,A:L.E.G.I.O.N . . . 1.75
45 GeH,Trinity#5,A:L.E.G.I.O.N.,
Darkstars 1.75
46 MBr,A:All Supermen,
V:Mongul 8.00
47 A:Green Arrow. 6.00
48 KM(c),B:Emerald Twilight,I:Kyle
Rayner (Last Green Lantern) . . 7.00
49 KM(c),GJ(s),A:Sinestro 6.00
50 KM(c),GJ(s),D:Sinestro,Kiliwog,
Guardians,I:Last Green
Lantern (in Costume) 8.00
51 V:Ohm,A:Mongul 4.00
52 V:Mongul 2.00
53 A:Superman,V:Mongul 2.00
54 D:Alex,V:Major Force 2.00
55 Zero Hour,A:Alan Scott,
V:Major Force. 2.25
56 Green Lantern and ring 2.00
57 Psimon 2.00
58 Donna Troy,Felix Faust 2.00
59 V:Dr. Polaris 2.00
60 Capital Punishment,pt.3. . . . . . 2.00
61 V:Kalibak,A:Darkstar 2.00
62 V:Duality,R:Ganthet 2.00
63 Parallax View: The Resurrection
of Hal Jordan,pt.1 . . . . 2.00
64 Parallax View,pt.2,A:Superman,
Flash,V:Parallax 2.00
65 Siege of ZiCharan,pt.2 . . . . 2.00
66 V:Sonar 2.00
67 A:Flash,V:Sonar. 2.00
68 RMz,RT,Underworld
Unleashed tie-in 2.00
69 RMz,RT,Underworld
Unleashed tie-in 2.00
70 RMz,RT,A:Supergirl 2.00
71 RMz,RT,Hero Quest,pt.1 . . . . . 2.00
72 RMz,RT,Hero Quest,pt.2 . . . . . 2.00
73 RMz,RT,Hero Quest,pt.3 . . . . . 2.00
74 RMz,RT,A:Adam Strange,
V:Grayven 2.00
75 A:Adam Strange 2.00
76 Green Arrow x-over 2.00
77 Green Arrow x-over 2.00
78 . . . . 2.00
79 V:Sonar 2.00
80 RMz(s),JWi,MGy,V:Dr. Light,
Final Night tie-in 2.00
81 RMz(s),DBk,RT,Memorial for
Hal Jordan 4.00
81a deluxe edition + extra stories,
foil cover on cardstock 6.00
82 RMz(s),TGb,RT,F:Kyle Rayner,
Alan Scott, Guy Gardner &
John Stewart 1.75
83 . . . . 1.75
84 "Retribution," pt.2. . . . . 1.75
85 "Retribution," concl. 1.75
86 RMz,JJ,RT,A:Jade, V:Obsidian. . 1.75
87 RMz,TGb,RT,A:Martian
Manhunter, vs. alien invasion . . 1.75
88 RMz(s),DBk,TA,A:Donna Troy,
visit Kyle's mom 1.75
89 RM(s),TA,V:Machine Messiah . . 1.75
90 RM(s),Why did Kyle Rayner

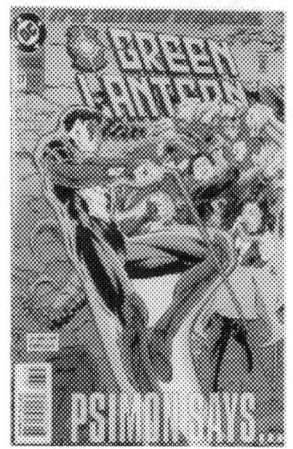

Green Lantern #57 © DC Comics, Inc.

become Green Lantern. 1.75
91 RMz(s),DBk,TA,V:Desaad 2.00
92 RMz(s),DBk,TA,A:Green Arrow,
   x-over. 2.00
93 RMz(s),DBk,TA,F:Deadman . . 2.00
94 RMz(s),PaP,TA,F:Superboy 2.00
95 RMz(s),JSn,TA, deep space. . . . 2.00
96 RMz(s) 2.00
97 RMz(s),MMK,TA,V:Grayven 2.00
98 RMz,DBk,TA,Future Shock,pt.1 . 2.00
99 RMz,DBk,TA,Future Shock,pt.2 . 2.00
100 RMz,DBk,AT,Kyle Rayner and
   Hal Jordan,V:Sinestro, 48pg . . . 3.00
100a deluxe edition 3.00
101 RMz(s),JJ,BWi,Emerald
   Knights,pt.1, bi-weekly 2.00
102 RMz(s),PaP,TA,Emerald
   Knights,pt.2, bi-weekly 2.00
103 RMz(s),JJ,BWi,Emerald
   Knights,pt.3, bi-weekly 2.00
104 RMz(s),JJ,BWi,Greener Pastures
   x-over, concl., Emerald
   Knights,pt.4, bi-weekly 2.00
105 RMz(s),JJ,SEa,BWi,Emerald
   Knights,pt.5, bi-weekly 2.00
106 RMz(s),PaP,TA,Emerald
   Knights,concl.. . . . . 2.00
107 RMz(s),TA,Emerald Knights
   aftermath 2.00
108 DBk,TA,A:Wonder Woman 2.00
109 RMz(s),PaP,TA 2.00
110 RMz(s),TA,A:Green Arrow 2.00
111 RMz(s),TA,DBk,V:Fatality 2.00
112 RMz(s),TA,DBk,back to Earth. . 2.00
113 RMz(s),TA,DBk,Burning
   in Effigy,pt.1 . . . . 2.00
114 RMz(s),TA,DBk,Burning
   in Effigy,pt.2 . . . . 2.00
115 DJu(s),A:Plastic Man &
   Booster Gold, pt.1 . . . . 2.00
116 DJu(s),A:Plastic Man &
   Booster Gold, pt.1 . . . . 2.00
117 RMz(s),DBk,TA,R:Donna Troy . 2.00
Ann.#1 Eclipso,V:Star Sapphire . . . 2.75
Ann.#1 80pg, rep.. . . . . 5.00
Ann.#2 Bloodlines#7,I:Nightblade . . 2.50
Ann.#3 Elseworlds Story. 3.00
Ann.#4 Year One story 3.00
Ann.#5 Legends o/t Dead Earth . . . 3.00
Ann.#6 RMz(s),JJ,Low,Pulp
   Heroes, 64pg. 4.00
Ann.#7 SV,RLm,Clv,BWr,Ghosts. . . 3.00
Ann.#8 MCa,AAd(c),JLApe:Gorilla
   Warfare 2.95
Spec.#1,000,000 RMz(s),BHi,PNe . 2.00

Spec. 3-D #1 V:Dr. Light. 4.00
Secret Files #1 . . . . 5.00
Secret Files Spec.#2 . . . . 5.00
Green Lantern Plus, 1-shot RMz(s),
   F:The Ray,V:Dr. Polaris 3.00
Green Lantern/Silver Surfer, 1-shot
   DC/Marvel RMz,TA A:Thanos
   vs. Parallax 5.00
Green Lantern Gallery, 1 one-shot
   life in pictures 3.50
Green Lantern: Ganthet's Tale,
   1-shot, JBy,O:Guardians. 7.00
Giant #1 80-page 5.00
Giant #2 80-page 5.00
GN Ganthet's Tale, JBy 6.00
Archives, Vol.1, 2nd print 50.00
TPB A New Dawn. 10.00
TPB Emerald Twilight 6.25
TPB Emerald Knights 13.00
TPB A New Dawn. 10.00
TPB Baptism of Fire 13.00

GREEN LANTERN & SENTINEL: HEART OF DARKNESS
Feb. 1998
1 (of 3) RMz(s),PaP,DDv 3.00
2 RMz(s),PaP,DDv. 3.00
3 RMz(s),PaP,DDv. 3.00

GREEN LANTERN CORPS QUARTERLY
1992–94
1 DAb,JSon,FH,PG,MBr,F:Alan
   Scott G'nort 3.00
2 DAb,JSon,PG,AG,Alan Scott 2.75
3 DAb,RT,F:Alan Scott,G'Nort 2.75
4 TA,AG(i),F:H.Jordan,G'Nort. 2.75
5 F:Alan Scott,I:Adam 2.75
6 JBa,TC,F:Alan Scott. 3.25
7 Halloween Issue 3.25
8 GeH,SHa,final issue 3.25

GREEN LANTERN: EMERALD DAWN
[1st Limited Series] 1989–90
1 MBr,RT,I:Mod.Age.Gr.Lantern . . . 5.00
2 MBr,RT,I:Legion (not group) 4.00
3 MBr,RT,V:Legion. 3.00
4 MBr,RT,A:Green Lantern Corps . 3.00
5 MBr,RT,V:Legion. 3.00
6 MBr,RT,V:Legion. 3.00
TPB rep#1–#6. . . . . 5.50

[2nd Limited Series] 1991
1 MBr,A:Sinestro,Guy Gardner. . . . 2.00
2 MBr,RT,V:Alien Aliance 1.75
3 MBr,RT,Sinestro's Home Planet . 1.75
4 MBr,RT,Korugar Revolt 1.75
5 MBr,RT,A:G.Gardner. 1.75
6 MBr,RT,Trial of Sinestro 1.75

GREEN LANTERN/ GREEN ARROW
1983–84
1 NA rep.. 5.00
2 NA,DG rep. 4.00
3 NA,DG rep. 4.00
4 NA,DG rep. 4.00
5 NA,DG rep. 4.00
6 NA,DG rep. 4.00
7 NA,DG rep. 4.00
TPB Roadback 8.95
TPB Traveling Heroes, Vol.1 . . . . 12.95
TPB Traveling Heroes, Vol.2 . . . . 12.95

*Green Lantern: Mosaic #13
© DC Comics, Inc.*

GREEN LANTERN: MOSAIC
1992–93
1 F:John Stewart 2.00
2 D:Ch'p 1.75
3 V:Sinestro. 1.50
4 F:The Children on Oa 1.50
5 V:Hal Jordan 1.50
6 A:Kilowog. 1.50
7 V:Alien Faction 1.50
8 V:Ethereal Creatures 1.50
9 Christmas issue 1.50
10 V:Guardians 1.50
11 R:Ch'p 1.50
12 V:KKK 1.50
13 V:KKK,Racism 1.50
14 A:Salaak,Ch'p 1.50
15 A:Katma Tui,Ch'p. 1.50
16 LMc,A:JLA,Green Lantern 1.50
17 A:JLA 1.50
18 final issue 1.50

GREEN LANTERN: THE NEW CORPS
1999
1 (of 2) CDi(s),SEa 5.00
2 CDi(s),SEa, concl. 5.00

GREGORY III
Bookshelf Ed.. . . . . 5.00
Platinum Ed.. . . . . 8.00

GRIFFIN
1991–92
1 I:Matt Williams as Griffin 5.50
2 V:Carson 5.25
3 A:Mary Wayne 5.25
4 A:Mary Wayne 5.25
5 Face to Face with Himself 5.25
6 Final Issue 5.25

GROSS POINT
July 1997
1 MWa&BAu(s) parody 2.50
2 Independence Day picnic 2.50
3 Ed Gein High School 2.50
4 paranoid driving instructor. 2.50
5 Halloween 2.50
6 trip to Chicago 2.50

7 stuck in Gross Point 2.50
8 Dru Hardly & Nancy Boys 2.50
9 . . . . 2.50
10 Businessman of the Year 2.50
11 Mystery Meat 2.50
12 Cold Hands, Still Heart 2.50
13 terminal illness 2.50
14 The Aisle of Doctor Morose 2.50

GUARDIANS
OF METROPOLIS
Nov. 1994
1 Kirby characters 1.50
2 Donovan's creations 1.50
3 . . . . 1.50
4 Female Furies 1.50

GUNFIRE
1994–95
1 B:LWn(s),StE,I:Ricochet 2.00
2 StE,V:Ricochet 2.00
3 StE,I:Purge 2.00
4 StE,V:Maraud 3 . . . . 2.00
5 StE,I:Exomorphic Man 2.00
6 New costume 2.00
7 Ragnarok 2.00
8 V:Tattoo 2.00
9 V:Ragnarock 2.00
10 V:Yakuza 2.00
11 V:Yakuza 2.00
12 I:New Weapon 2.00
13 A:JLA,V:Ragnarok, final issue . . 2.25

GUNS OF THE DRAGON
Aug., 1998
1 (of 4) TT, set in 1920s 2.50
2 TT 2.50
3 TT 2.50
4 TT conclusion 2.50

GUY GARDNER
1992–94
1 JSon,A:JLA,JLE 2.00
2 JSon,A:Kilowog 1.50
3 JSon,V:Big,Ugly Alien 1.50
4 JSon,G.Gardner vs Ice 1.50
5 JSon,A:Hal Jordan,V:Goldface . . 1.50
6 JSon,A:Hal Jordan,V:Goldface . . 1.50
7 JSon,V:Goldface 1.50
8 JSon,V:Lobo 1.50
9 JSon,Boodikka 1.50
10 JSon,V:Boodikka 1.50
11 JSon,B:Year One 1.50
12 JSon,V:Batman,Flash,Green
  Lantern 1.50
13 JSon,Year One#3 . . . . 1.50
14 JSon,E:Year One 1.50
15 V:Bad Guy Gardner 1.50
16 B:CDi(s),MaT,V:Guy's Brother . . 1.75
Becomes:

GUY GARDNER:
WARRIOR
1994–96
17 V:Militia 2.00
18 B:Emerald Fallout,N:Guy Gardner,
  V:Militia 4.00
19 A:G.A.Green Lantern,V:Militia . . 4.00
20 A:JLA,Darkstars 2.00
21 E:Emerald Fallout,V:H.Jordan . . 2.00
22 I:Dementor 1.75
23 A:Buck Wargo 1.75
24 Zero Hour 1.50
25 A:Buck Wargo 2.50
26 Zero Hour 1.50
27 Capital Punishment 1.50
28 Capital Punishment,pt.2 . . . . 1.50

29 I:Warriors Bar 1.50
29a Collector's Edition 2.95
30 V:Superman,Supergirl 1.50
31 A:Sentinel,Supergirl,
  V:Dementor 1.75
32 Way of the Warrior,pt.1,A:JLA . . 1.75
33 Way of the Warrior,pt.4 . . . . 1.75
34 . . . . 1.75
35 Return of an Old Foe 1.75
36 Underworld Unleashed tie-in . . . 1.75
37 Underworld Unleashed tie-in . . . 1.75
38 A new woman 1.75
39 guest stars galore 1.75
40 . . . . 1.75
41 V:Dungeon 1.75
42 Martika revealed as Seductress . 1.75
43 V:5 foes 1.75
Ann.#1 Year One Annual, Leechun
  vs. Vuldarians 3.50

GUY GARDNER: REBORN
1992
1 JSon,JRu,V:Goldface,C:Lobo . . . 6.00
2 JSon,JRu,A:Lobo,V:Weaponers
  of Qward 5.50
3 JSon,JRu,A:Lobo,N:G.Gardner
  V:Qwardians 5.50

HACKER FILES
1992–93
1 TS,Soft Wars#1,I:Jack Marshall . 2.25
2 TS,Soft Wars#2 . . . . 2.00
3 TS,Soft Wars#3 . . . . 2.00
4 TS,Soft Wars#4 . . . . 2.00
5 TS,A:Oracle(Batgirl) 2.00
6 TS,A:Oracle,Green Lantern 2.00
7 TS,V:Digitronix 2.00
8 TS,V:Digitronix 2.00
9 TS,V:Digitronix 1.75
10 V:Digitronix 2.00
11 TS,A:JLE 2.00
12 TS,V:Digitronix,final issue 2.00

HAMMER LOCKE
1992–93
1 I:Hammerlocke 2.50
2 V:Tharn the Iron Spider 1.75
3 V:Tharn the Iron Spider 1.75
4 O:Hammerlocke 1.75
5 V:Sahara Skyhawk 1.75
6 V:Tharn the Iron Spider 1.75

Hammer Locke #3 © DC Comics Inc.

7 V:Tharn 1.75
8 CSp,V:Iron Spider 1.75

HARDCORE STATION
May, 1998
1 (of 6) JSn,JRu,F:Maximillian 2.50
2 JSn,JRu,V:Synnar 2.50
3 JSn,JRu,F:Kyle Rayner 2.50
4 JSn,JRu,V:Synnar 2.50
5 JSn,JRu,F:JLA 2.50
6 JSn,JRu,conclusion 2.50

HARDWARE
(Milestone) 1993–96
1 DCw,I:Hardware,Edwin Alva,Reprise,
  Dir.Mark.Ed.,w/A puzzle piece,
  Skybox Card,Poster 4.00
1a NewsstandEd. 2.00
1b Platinum Ed. 6.00
2 DCw,V:Repirise,I:Barraki Young . 2.00
3 DCw,O:Edwin Alva,
  I:S.Y.S.T.E.M. 2.00
4 DCw,V.S.Y.S.T.E.M. 2.00
5 DCw,I:Deathwish 2.00
6 DCw,V:Deathwish 1.75
7 DCw,O:Deathwish 1.75
8 DCw(c),O:Hardware 1.75
9 DCw(c),I:Technique 1.75
10 DCw(c),I:Harm,Transit 1.75
11 WS(c),DCw,Shadow War,
  I:Iron Butterfly,Dharma 1.75
12 RB,V:Harm 1.75
13 DCw,A:Reprise 1.75
14 DCw 1.75
15 DCw(c),HuR,V:Alva 1.75
16 Die-Cut(c),JBy(c),DCw,
  N:Hardware 4.25
16a Newsstand ED. 2.25
17 Worlds Collide,pt.2,A:Steel. 1.75
18 Worlds Collide,pt.9,V:Rift 2.00
19 I:Evan,Tetras 1.75
20 . . . . 1.75
21 Arcana,Helga. 1.75
22 Curt & Assistant. 1.75
23 . . . . 1.75
24 . . . . 1.75
25 V:Death Row, Sanction 2.95
26 Hunt For Deathwish,pt.1 . . . . . . 1.75
27 Hunt For Deathwish,pt.2 . . . . . . 1.75
28 Hunt For Deathwish,pt.3 . . . . . . 1.75
29 Long Hot Summer, A:The Blood
  Syndicate, spec.low price 1.00
30 Long Hot Summer 2.50
31 . . . . 2.50
32 Control of Alva. 2.50
33 HC(c), Cyborg 2.50
34 V:Huaca Aires 2.50
35 A:Sanction. 2.50
36 A:Sanction. 2.50
37 . . . . 2.50
38 V:Malleus, without armor 2.50
39 F:Sabrina Alva. 2.50
40 F:Top Dog 2.50
41 . . . . 2.50
42 . . . . 2.50
43 . . . . 2.50
44 A:Heroes 2.50
45 DGC(s),Hardware & Hard
  Company go back to basics . . . 2.50
46 DGC(s),discovery of Edwin
  Alva's artificial intelligence . . . 2.50
47 DGC(s),the truth behind a
  brutal murder 2.50
48 . . . . 2.50
49 DGC(s),Moe(c),V:Tyrant. 2.50
50 DGC(s), 48pg. anniversary issue 3.95
51 DMc(s) final issue 2.50

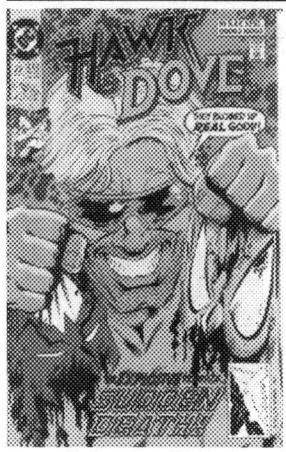

Hawk & Dove #22 © DC Comics, Inc.

HAWK & DOVE
[1st Regular Series] 1968–69
1 SD 50.00
2 SD 40.00
3 GK 35.00
4 GK 35.00
5 GK,C:Teen Titans 40.00
6 GK 35.00

[Limited Series] 1988–89
1 RLd,I:New Dove 5.00
2 RLd,V:Kestrel 4.50
3 RLd,V:Kestrel 4.50
4 RLd,V:Kestrel 4.50
5 RLd,V:Kestrel,O:New Dove 4.50
TPB rep. #1-#5 . . . . 9.95

[2nd Regular Series] 1989–91
1 A:Superman,Green Lantern
  Hawkman 2.00
2 V:Aztec Goddess 1.75
3 V:Aztec Goddess 1.75
4 I:The Untouchables 1.50
5 I:Sudden Death, A:1st Dove's
  Ghost 1.50
6 A:Barter,Secrets o/Hawk&Dove . . 1.50
7 A:Barter,V:Count St.Germain . . . 1.50
8 V:Count St.Germain 1.50
9 A:Copperhead 1.50
10 V:Gauntlet & Andromeda 1.50
11 A:New Titans,V:M.A.C.,
  Andromeda Gauntlet 1.50
12 A:New Titans,V:Scarab 1.50
13 1960's,I:Shellshock 1.50
14 Prelue to O:Hawk & Dove,
  V:Kestrel 1.50
15 O:Hawk & Dove begins 1.50
16 HawkV:Dove,V:Lord of Chaos . . . 1.50
17 V:Lords-Order & Chaos 1.50
18 The Creeper #1 . . . . 1.50
19 The Creeper #2 . . . . 1.50
20 KM,DG,Christmas Story 1.50
21 Dove 1.50
22 V:Sudden Death 1.50
23 A:Velv.Tiger,SuddenDeath 1.50
24 A:Velv.Tiger,SuddenDeath 1.50
25 Recap 1st 2 yrs.(48 pg) 2.00
26 Dove's past 1.50
27 The Hunt for Hawk 1.50
28 War of the Gods,A:Wildebeest
  A:Uncle Sam,final issue,
  double size 2.00
Ann.#1 In Hell 2.00
Ann.#2 CS,KGa,ArmageddonPt.5 . . 2.00
TPB RLd 9.95

HAWK & DOVE
Sept., 1997
1 (of 5) MBn,DZ,DG,Sasha Martens
  & Wiley Wolverman 2.50
2 MBn,DZ,DG,Vixen & Vigilante . . . 2.50
3 MBn,DZ,DG,grave desecrations . 2.50
4 MBn,DZ,DG,V:Suicide Squad . . . 2.50

HAWKMAN
[1st Regular Series]1964–68
1 MA,V:Chac 550.00
2 MA,V:Tralls 200.00
3 MA,V:Sky Raiders 135.00
4 MA,I&O:Zatanna 150.00
5 MA 135.00
6 MA 125.00
7 MA,V:I.Q. 125.00
8 MA 125.00
9 MA,V:Matter Master 125.00
10 MA,V:Caw 125.00
11 MA 75.00
12 MA 75.00
13 MA 75.00
14 GaF,MA,V:Caw 75.00
15 GaF,MA,V:Makkar 75.00
16 GaF,MA,V:Ruthvol 75.00
17 GaF,MA,V:Raven 75.00
18 GaF,MA,A:Adam Strange 50.00
19 GaF,MA,A:Adam Strange 50.00
20 GaF,MA,V:Lionmane 45.00
21 GaF,MA,V:Lionmane 45.00
22 V:Falcon 45.00
23 V:Dr.Malevolo 45.00
24 Robot Raiders from
  Planet Midnight 45.00
25 DD,V:Medusa,G.A.Hawkman . . 45.00
26 RdM,CCu,DD 45.00
27 DD,JKu(c),V:Yeti 45.00

[2nd Regular Series] 1986–87
1 DH,A:Shadow Thief 3.00
2 DH,V:Shadow Thief 2.00
3 DH,V:Shadow Thief 1.50
4 DH A:Zatanna 1.50
5 DH,V:Lionmane 1.50
6 DH,V:Gentleman Ghost,
  Lionmane 1.50
7 DH,Honor Wings 1.50
8 DH,Shadow War contd 1.50
9 DH,Shadow War contd 1.50
10 JBy(c),D:Hyatis Corp 1.50
11 End of Shadow War 1.50
12 Hawks on Thanagar 1.50
13 DH,Murder Case 1.50
14 DH,Mystery o/Haunted Masks . . 1.50
15 DH,Murderer Revealed 1.50
16 DH,Hawkwoman lost 1.50
17 EH,DH,final issue 1.50
TPB rep.Brave & Bold apps 19.95

[3rd Regular Series] 1993–96
1 B:JOs(s),JD,R:Hawkman,
  V:Deadline 4.00
2 JD,A:Gr.Lantern,V:Meta-Tech . . . 2.50
3 JD,I:Airstryke 2.25
4 JD,RM 2.00
5 JD(c),V:Count Viper 2.00
6 JD(c),A:Eradicator 2.00
7 JD(c),PuK(s),LMc,B:King of the
  Netherworld 2.00
8 LMc,E:King of the Netherworld . . 2.00
9 BML(s) 2.00
10 I:Badblood 2.00
11 V:Badblood 2.00
12 V:Hawkgod 2.25
13 V:Hawkgod 2.25
14 New abilities,pt.1 . . . . 2.00
15 New abilities,pt.2 . . . . 2.00
16 Eyes of the Hawk,pt.3 . . . . 2.00
17 Eyes of the Hawk,pt.4 . . . . 2.00
18 Seagle,Ellis, Pepoy 2.00

*Hawkman 2nd Series #1
© DC Comics, Inc.*

19 F:Hawkman 2.00
21 RLm,V:Shadow Thief,
  Gentleman Ghost 2.25
22 Way of the Warrior,pt.3
  A:Warrior,JLA 2.25
23 Way of the Warrior,pt.6 . . . . . . 2.25
24 . . . . 2.25
25 V:Lionmane,painted(c) 2.25
26 WML,Underworld
  Unleashed tie-in 2.25
27 WML,Underworld
  Unleashed tie-in 2.25
28 WML,V:Doctor Polaris 2.25
29 HC(c),V:Vandal Savage 2.25
30 . . . . 2.25
31 serial killer has Tangarian
  technology 2.25
32 MC,Search for serial killer 2.25
Ann.#1 JD,I:Mongrel 3.75
Ann.#2 Year One Annual 3.95

HAWKWORLD
1989
1 TT,Hawkman, Origin retold 5.00
2 TT,Katar tried for treason 4.00
3 TT,Hawkgirl's debut 4.00

[1st Regular Series] 1990–93
1 GN,Byth on Earth,R:Kanjar Ro . . 3.00
2 GN,Katar & Shayera in Chicago . 2.50
3 GN,V:Chicago Crime 2.00
4 GN,Byth's Control Tightens 2.00
5 GN,Return of Shadow Thief 2.00
6 GN,Stolen Thanagarian Ship . . . 2.00
7 GN,V:Byth 2.00
8 GN,Hawkman vs. Hawkwoman . . 2.00
9 GN,Hawkwoman in Prison 2.00
10 Shayera returns to Thanagar . . . 2.00
11 GN,Blackhawk,Express 2.00
12 GN,Princess Treska 2.00
13 TMd,A:Firehawk,V:Marauder . . . 2.00
14 GN,Shayera's Father 2.00
15 GN,War of the Gods X-over 2.00
16 GN War of the Gods X-over 2.00
17 GN,Train Terrorists 2.00
18 GN,V:Atilla 2.00
19 GN,V:Atilla 2.00
20 V:Smir'Beau 2.00
21 GN,Thanagar Pt.1,
  A:J.S.A. Hawkman 2.00
22 GN,Thanagar Pt.2 . . . . 2.00
23 GN,Thanagar Pt.3 . . . . 2.00
24 GN,Thanagar Pt.4 . . . . 2.00
25 GN,Thanagar Pt.5 . . . . 2.00

26 GN,V:Attilla battle armor 2.00
27 JD,B:Flight's End 2.00
28 JD,Flight's End #2 . . . . 2.00
29 TT(c),JDu,Flight's End #3 . . . . . . 2.00
30 TT,Flight's End #4 . . . . 2.00
31 TT,Flight's End #5 . . . . 2.00
32 TT,V:Count Viper,final issue 2.50
Ann.#1 A:Flash. 4.50
Ann.#2 Armageddon,pt.6 . . . . 4.00
Ann.#2a reprint (Silver). 3.50
Ann.#3 Eclipso tie-in. 3.25

HAYWIRE
1988–89
1 . . . . 1.50
2 . . . . 1.25
3 thru 13 . . . . 1.00

HEARTLAND
DC/Vertigo Jan. 1997
1 GEn(s),SDi,Kit faces childhood
    memories 4.95

HEART OF THE BEAST
GNv SeP 19.95

HEART THROBS
DC/Vertigo 1998
1 (of 4) anthology 3.00
2 modern romance 3.00
3 . . . . 3.00
4 . . . . 3.00

HEAVY LIQUID
DC/Vertigo 1999
1 PPo,pt 1 of 5 . . . . 6.00

HECKLER, THE
1992–93
1 KG,MJ,I:The Heckler 1.25
2 KG,MJ,V:The Generic Man 1.25
3 KG,MJ,V:Cosmic Clown 1.25
4 KG,V:Bushwacker. 1.25
5 KG,Theater Date 1.25
6 KG,I:Lex Concord 1.25
7 KG,V:Cuttin'Edge 1.25

HELLBLAZER
Jan., 1988
1 B:JaD(s),JRy,F:John
    Constantine 20.00
2 JRy,I:Papa Midnight 10.00
3 JRy,I:Blathoxi 9.00
4 JRy,I:Resurrection Crusade,
    Gemma 9.00
5 JRy,F:Pyramid of Fear 9.00
6 JRy,V:Resurrection Crusade,
    I:Nergal 6.00
7 JRy,V:Resurrection Crusade,
    I:Richie Simpson 6.00
8 JRy,AA,Constantine receives
    demon blood,V:Nergal 6.00
9 JRy,A:Swamp Thing 6.00
10 JRy,V:Nergal 6.00
11 MBu,Newcastle Incident,pt.1 . . . 5.00
12 JRy,D:Nergal 5.00
13 JRy,John has a Nightmare 4.00
14 JRy,B:The Fear Machine,
    I:Mercury,Marj,Eddie. 4.00
15 JRy,Shepard's Warning. 4.00
16 JRy,Rough Justice 4.00
17 MkH,I:Mr. Wester. 4.00
18 JRy,R:Zed 4.00
19 JRy,I:Simon Hughes 7.00
20 JRy,F:Mr.Webster 5.00

21 JRy,I:Jallakuntilliokan. 5.00
22 JRy,E:The Fear Machine. 5.00
23 I&D:Jerry O'Flynn 4.00
24 E:JaD(s),I:Sammy Morris 4.00
25 GMo(s),DvL,Early Warning 4.00
26 GMo(s) 4.00
27 NGa(s),DMc,Hold Me. 10.00
28 B:JaD(s),RnT,KeW,F:S.Morris . . 4.00
29 RnT,KeW,V:Sammy Morris. 4.00
30 RnT,KeW,D:Sammy Morris. 4.00
31 E:JaD(s),SeP,Constantine's
    Father's Funeral 4.00
32 DiF(s),StP,I&D:Drummond 3.50
33 B:JaD(s),MPn,I:Pat McDonell. . . 3.50
34 SeP,R:Mercury,Marj 3.50
35 SeP,Constantine's Past 3.50
36 Future Death,(preview of
    World Without End) 3.50
37 Journey to England's Secret
    Mystics. 3.50
38 Constantine's Journey contd. . . . 3.50
39 Journey to Discovery 3.50
40 DMc,I:2nd Kid Eternity 4.00
41 B:GEn(s),WSm,MPn,Dangerous
    Habits 6.00
42 Dangerous Habits 4.50
43 I:Chantinelle 4.50
44 Dangerous Habits 4.50
45 Dangerous Habits 4.50
46 Dangerous Habits epilogue,
    I:Kit(John's girlfriend) 4.50
47 SnW(i),Pub Where I Was Born. . 4.00
48 Love Kills. 4.00
49 X-mas issue,Lord o/t Dance 4.00
50 WSm,Remarkable Lives,A:Lord
    of Vampires (48pgs) 6.00
51 JnS,SeP,Laundromat-
    Possession. 5.00
52 GF(c),WSm, Royal Blood. 5.00
53 GF(c),WSm, Royal Blood. 5.00
54 GF(c),WSm, Royal Blood. 5.00
55 GF(c),WSm, Royal Blood. 5.00
56 GF(c),B:GEn(s),DvL,
    V:Danny Drake. 5.00
57 GF(c),SDi,Mortal Clay#1,
    V:Dr. Amis 5.00
58 GF(c),SDi,Mortal Clay#2,
    V:Dr. Amis 5.00
59 GF(c),WSm,MkB(i),KDM,B:Guys
    & Dolls. 5.00
60 GF(c),WSm,MkB(i),F:Tali,
    Chantinelle. 5.00
61 GF(c),WSm,MkB(i),E:Guys &
    Dolls, V:First of the Fallen. 5.00

Hellblazer #2 © DC Comics Inc.

62 GF(c),SDi,End of the Line,I:Gemma,
    AIDS storyline insert w/Death . . 5.00
Vertigo
63 GF(c),SDi,C:Swamp Thing,Zatanna
    Phantom Stranger 5.00
64 GF(c),SDi,B:Fear & Loathing,
    A:Gabriel (Racism). 4.00
65 GF(c),SDi,D:Dez 4.00
66 GF(c),SDi,E:Fear and Loathing . 4.00
67 GF(c),SDi,Kit leaves John 4.00
68 GF(c),SDi,F:Lord of Vampires,
    Darius,Mary 4.00
69 GF(c),SDi,D:Lord of Vampires . . 4.00
70 GF(c),SDi,Kit in Ireland 4.00
71 GF(c),SDi,A:WWII Fighter Pilot . 4.00
72 GF(c),SDi,B:Damnation's
    Flame,A:Papa Midnight 4.00
73 GF(c),SDi,Nightmare NY,
    A:JFK. 4.00
74 GF(c),SDi,I:Cedella,A:JFK 4.00
75 GF(c),SDi,E:Damnation'sFlame . 4.00
76 GF(c),SDi,R:Brendan 4.00
77 Returns to England 4.00
78 GF(c),SDi,B:Rake at the
    Gates of Hell 4.00
79 GF(c),SDi,In Hell 4.00
80 GF(c),SDi,In London 4.00
81 GF(c),SDi 4.00
82 Kit . . . . , ... 4.00
83 Rake,Gates of Hell 4.00
84 John's past 4.00
85 Warped Notions,pt.1 . . . . 4.00
86 Warped Notions,pt.2 . . . . 4.00
87 Warped Notions,pt.3 . . . . 4.00
88 Warped Notions,pt.4 . . . . 4.00
89 Dreamtime. 4.00
90 Dreamtime,pt.2 . . . . 4.00
91 Visits Battlefield 4.00
92 Critical Mass,pt.1 . . . . 4.00
93 Critical Mass,pt.2 . . . . 4.00
94 Critical Mass,pt.3 . . . . 4.00
95 SeP,Critical Mass,pt.4 . . . . 4.00
96 SeP,Critical Mass,pt.5 . . . . 4.00
97 SeP,Critical Mass epilogue. 4.00
98 SeP, helps neighbor. 4.00
99 SeP. 4.00
100 SeP, In a coma 5.00
101 SeP,deal with a demon 3.50
102 SeP,Difficult Beginnings,
    pt.1 (of 3) 3.50
103 SeP,"Difficult Beginnings, pt.2" . 3.50
104 SeP,"Difficult Beginnings, pt.3" . 3.50
105 . . . . 3.50
106 PJe(s),SEp,"In the Line of
    Fire," pt.1 (of 2) 3.50
107 PJe(s),SEp,"In the Line of
    Fire," pt. 2 . . . . 3.50
108 PJe(s),SeP,a Bacchic
    celebration 3.50
109 PJe(s),SeP,cattle mutilations
    in Northern England 3.50
110 PJe(s),SeP,"Last Man
    Standing," pt.1 . . . . 3.50
111 PJe(s),SeP,"Last Man
    Standing," pt.2 . . . . 3.50
112 PJe(s),SeP,"Last Man
    Standing," pt.3 . . . . 3.50
113 PJe(s),SeP,"Last Man
    Standing," pt.4 . . . . 3.50
114 PJe(s),SeP,"Last Man
    Standing," pt.5 . . . . 3.50
115 PJe(s),SeP(s),Dani's ex-
    boyfriend 3.50
116 SeP, "Widdershins" pt.1 (of 2). . 3.50
117 SeP, "Widdershins" pt.2 . . . . . . 3.50
118 PJe(s),SeP,John's a Godfather. 4.00
119 PJe(s),SeP,disasters 3.50
120 PJe(s),SeP,10th anniv. 48pg . . 3.00
121 PJe(s),SeP, Up the Down
    Staircase pt.1 . . . . 3.00
122 PJe(s),SeP, Up the Down

Hellblazer #4 © DC Comics, Inc.

Staircase pt.2	3.00
123 PJe(s),SeP, Up the Down	
Staircase pt.3	3.00
124 PJe(s),SeP, Up the Down	
Staircase pt.4	3.00
125 PJe(s),SeP, How to Play	
with Fire, pt.1	3.00
126 PJe(s),SeP,Play/Fire,pt.2	3.00
127 PJe(s),SeP,Play/Fire,pt.3	3.00
128 PJe(s),SeP,Play/Fire,pt.4	3.00
129	3.00
130 GEn,JHi,GF,Son of Man,pt.2	3.00
131 GEn,JHi,GF,Son of Man,pt.3	2.50
132 GEn,JHi,GF,Son of Man,pt.4	2.50
133 GEn,JHi,GF,Son of Man,pt.5	2.50
134 WEl(s),JHi,Haunted,pt.1	2.50
135 WEl(s),JHi,Haunted,pt.2	2.50
136 WEl(s),JHi,Haunted,pt.3	2.50
137 WEl(s),JHi,Haunted,pt.4	2.50
138 WEl(s),JHi,Haunted,pt.5	2.50
139 WEl(s),JHi,Haunted,pt.6	2.50
140 WEl(s),Locked	2.50
141 WEl(s),ALa	2.50
142 WEI,TBd,The Crib	2.50
Ann.#1 JaD(s),BT,Raven Scar	7.00
Spec.#1 GF(c),GEn(s),SDi,John	
Constantine's teenage years.	4.50
TPB Original Sins,rep.#1–#9	19.95
TPB Dangerous Habits,	
rep.#41–#46	14.95
TPB Fear and Loathing	14.95
TPB Damnation's Flame	17.00

HELLBLAZER/
THE BOOKS OF MAGIC
Oct., 1997

1 (of 2) PJe,JNR	2.50
2 PJe,JNR	2.50

HERCULES UNBOUND
Oct.–Nov., 1975

1 thru 11	@1.25
12 Aug.–Sept., 1977	1.25

HEROES
Milestone 1996

1 Six heroes join	2.50
2 battle royale	2.50
3	2.50
4	2.50
5	2.50

6 final issue	2.50

HEROES AGAINST
HUNGER

1 NA,DG,JBy,CS,AA,BWr,BS,	
Superman,Batman	3.50

HERO HOTLINE

1 thru 6, Mini-series	@1.75

HEX
Sept., 1985

1 MT,I:Hex	2.50
2 MT	2.00
3 MT,V:Conglomerate	2.00
4 MT,V:Conglomerate	2.00
5 MT,A:Chainsaw Killer	2.00
6 MT,V:Conglomerate	2.00
7 MT,Tries to Return to own era.	2.00
8 MT,The Future	2.50
9 MT,Future Killer Cyborgs	1.50
10 MT,V:Death Cult	1.50
11 MT,V:The Batman	3.00
12 MT,A:Batman,V:Terminators	3.00
13 MT,I:New Supergroup	2.50
14 MT,A:The Dogs of War	1.50
15 KG,V:Chainsaw Killer	1.50
16 KG,V:Dogs of War	1.50
17 KG,Hex/Dogs of War T.U.	
V:XXGG	1.50
18 KGr,Confronting the Past,final	
Issue	1.50

HISTORY OF
DC UNIVERSE
Sept., 1986

1 GP, From start to WWII	5.00
2 GP, From WWII to present	5.00

A HISTORY OF VIOLENCE
DC/Paradox Press March 1997

GN B&W	9.95

HITCHHIKER'S GUIDE TO

THE GALAXY

1 Based on the book	7.00
2 Based on the book	6.50
3 Based on the book	6.50
GN from Douglas Adams book	14.95

HITMAN
1996–97

1 GEn, F:Tommy Monaghan	11.00
2 GEn, Attempt to kill Joker	8.00
3 GEn(s),JMC, Mawzin & The	
Arkanonne	4.50
4 GEn(s),JMC,	3.00
5 GEn(s),JMC,	3.00
6 GEn(s),JMC,A:Johnny Navarone,	
Natt the Hatt	3.00
7 GEn(s),JMC, Pat's dead, Hitman	
wants revenge	3.00
8 GEn(s),JMC,barricaded in	
Noonan's Bar, Final Night tie-in.	3.00
9 GEn(s),JMC,A:Six-Pack	3.00
10 GEn(s),JMC,A:Green Lantern	3.00
11	2.25
12 GEn(s),JMC,"Local Heroes,	
"A:Green Lantern	2.25
13	2.25
14 GEn(s),JMC, "Zombie Night at	
the Aquarium," concl.	2.25
15 GEn(s),JMC,"Ace of	

Killers," pt.1, V:Mawzir	2.25
16 GEn(s),JMC, "Ace of	
Killers," pt.2	2.25
17 GEn(s),JMC, "Ace of Killers,"	
pt.3,A:Catwoman, Demon	
Etrigan	2.25
18 GEn(s),JMC, "Ace of Killers,"	
pt.4,A:Demon Etrigan, Baytor	2.25
19 GEn(s),JMC,Ace/Killers,pt.5,	2.25
20 GEn(s),JMC,Ace/Killers,concl.	2.50
21 GEn(s),JMC,Romeo & Juliet	2.50
22 GEn(s),JMC,holiday special	2.25
23 GEn(s),JMc,"Who Dares Wins,"	
pt.1	2.50
24 GEn(s),JMc,Dares/Wins,pt.2	2.50
25 GEn(s),JMc,Dares/Wins,pt.3	2.50
26 GEn(s),JMc,Dares/Wins,pt.4	2.50
27 GEn(s),JMc,Dares/Wins,pt.5	2.50
28 GEn(s),JMC,aftermath	2.50
29 GEn(s),JMC,Tommy's	
Heroes, pt.1	2.50
30 GEn(s),JMC,Heroes, pt.2	2.50
31 GEn(s),JMC,Heroes, pt.3	2.50
32 GEn(s),JMC,Heroes, pt.4	2.50
33 GEn(s),JMC,Heroes, pt.5	2.50
34 GEn(s),A:Superman	2.50
35 GEn(s),Frances Monaghan	2.50
36 GEn(s),	2.50
37 GEn(s).	2.50
38 GEn(s),Dead Man's Land, concl.	2.50
39 GEn(s),JMC,A:RingoChen,pt.1.	2.50
40 GEn(s),JMC,A:RingoChen,pt.2.	2.50
41 GEn(s),JMC,A:RingoChen,pt.3.	2.50
42 GEn(s),JMC,A:RingoChen,pt.4.	2.50
Ann.#1 Pulp Heroes (Western)	3.95
Spec.#1,000,000 GEn(s),JMC	2.50
TPB rep. Demon Annual #2, Batman	
Chronicles #4, Hitman #1–#3	10.00
TPB Ten Thousand Bullets,	
rep. #4–#8	10.00
TPB Hitman: Ten Thousand Bullets	10.00
TPB Hitman: Local Heroes	18.00
TPB Hitman	10.00

HOPALONG CASSIDY
Feb., 1954

86 GC,Ph(c):William Boyd & Topper,	
`The Secret of the Tattooed	
Burro'	250.00
87 GC,Ph(c),`The Tenderfoot	
Outlaw'	135.00
88 Ph(c),GC, `15 Robbers of Rimfire	
Ridge'	100.00
89 GC,Ph(c),`One-Day	

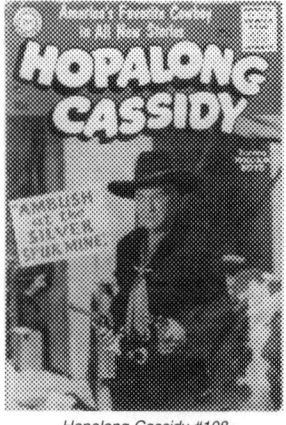

Hopalong Cassidy #108
© DC Comics, Inc.

All comics prices listed are for *Near Mint* condition.

Boom Town' 100.00
90 GC,Ph(c),`Cowboy Clown
   Robberies' 75.00
91 GC,Ph(c),`The Riddle of
   the Roaring R Ranch' 85.00
92 GC,Ph(c),`The Sky-Riding
   Outlaws' 85.00
93 GC,Ph(c),`The Silver Badge
   of Courage' 85.00
94 GC,Ph(c),`Mystery of the
   Masquerading Lion' 85.00
95 GC,Ph(c),`Showdown at the
   Post-Hole Bank' 85.00
96 GC,Ph(c),`Knights of
   the Range' 85.00
97 GC,Ph(c),`The Mystery of
   the Three-Eyed Cowboy' 85.00
98 GC,Ph(c),`Hopalong's
   Unlucky Day' 85.00
99 GC,Ph(c),`Partners in Peril' . . . 85.00
100 GC,Ph(c),`The Secrets
   of a Sheriff' 100.00
101 GC,Ph(c),`Way Out West
   Where The East Begins' 60.00
102 GC,Ph(c),`Secret of the
   Buffalo Hat'. 60.00
103 GC,Ph(c),`The Train-Rustlers
   of Avalance Valley' 60.00
104 GC,Ph(c),`Secret of the
   Surrendering Outlaws' 60.00
105 GC,Ph(c),`Three Signs
   to Danger' 60.00
106 GC,Ph(c),`The Secret of
   the Stolen Signature' 60.00
107 GC,Ph(c),`The Mystery Trail
   to Stagecoach Town' 60.00
108 GC,Ph(c),`The Mystery
   Stage From Burro Bend' 60.00
109 GC,`The Big Gun on Saddletop
   Mountain' 60.00
110 GC,`The Dangerous Stunts
   of Hopalong Cassidy' 50.00
111 GC,`Sheriff Cassidy's
   Mystery Clue' 50.00
112 GC,`Treasure Trail to
   Thunderbolt Ridge 50.00
113 GC,`The Shadow of the
   Toy Soldier' 50.00
114 GC,`Ambush at
   Natural Bridge' 50.00
115 GC,`The Empty-Handed
   Robberies' 50.00
116 GC,`Mystery of the
   Vanishing Cabin' 50.00
117 GC,`School for Sheriffs' 50.00
118 GC,`The Hero of
   Comanche Ridge' 50.00
119 GC,`The Dream Sheriff of
   Twin Rivers' 50.00
120 GC,`Salute to a Star-Wearer' . 50.00
121 GC,`The Secret of the
   Golden Caravan' 50.00
122 GC,`The Rocking
   Horse Bandits' 50.00
123 GK,`Mystery of the
   One-Dollar Bank Robbery' . . . 50.00
124 GK,`Mystery of the
   Double-X Brand'. 50.00
125 GK,`Hopalong Cassidy's
   Secret Brother' 50.00
126 GK,`Trail of the
   Telltale Clues'. 50.00
127 GK,`Hopalong Cassidy's
   Golden Riddle' 50.00
128 GK,`The House That
   Hated Outlaws'. 50.00
129 GK,`Hopalong Cassidy's
   Indian Sign' 50.00
130 GK,`The Return of the
   Canine Sheriff' 50.00
131 GK&GK(c),`The Amazing

Sheriff of Double Creek' 50.00
132 GK,`Track of the
   Invisible Indians'. 50.00
133 GK,`The Golden Trail
   to Danger' 50.00
134 GK,`Case of the
   Three Crack-Shots'. 50.00
135 GK,May-June, 1959. . . . . . . 50.00

HORRORIST
(Vertigo) 1995
1 I:Horrorist. 5.95
2 conclusion 5.95

HOT WHEELS
March-April, 1970
1 ATh 25.00
2 thru 5 ATh. . . . . @20.00
6 NA 30.00

HOURMAN
1999
1 TPe,RgM,A:JLA 2.50
2 TPe(s),RgM,F:Tomorrow Woman 2.50
3 TPe(s),RgM,Timepoint,pt.1 . . . . 2.50
4 TPe(s),RgM,Timepoint,pt.2 . . . . 2.50
5 TPe(s),RgM,Rex Tyler's life 2.50
6 TPe,RgM,JLAndroids,pt.1 . . . . . 2.50
7 TPe,RgM,JLAndroids,pt.2. . . . . 2.50

HOUSE OF MYSTERY
Dec.–Jan., 1952
1 I Fell In LoveWithA Monster . 1,700.00
2 The Mark of X. 750.00
3 . . . . 600.00
4 The Man With the Evil Eye . . . 450.00
5 The Man With the Strangler
   Hands! 450.00
6 The Monster in Clay!. 350.00
7 Nine Lives of Alger Denham! . 350.00
8 . . . . 350.00
9 . . . . 350.00
10 The Wishes of Doom 350.00
11 Deadly Game of G-H-O-S-T . . 275.00
12 The Devil's Chessboard 275.00
13 The Theater Of A
   Thousand Thrills! 275.00
14 . . . . 275.00
15 The Man Who Could Change
   the World 275.00

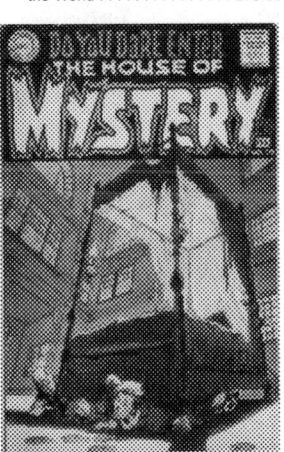

House of Mystery #178
© *DC Comics Inc.*

16 Dead Men Tell No Tales! 225.00
17 . . . . 200.00
18 . . . . 200.00
19 . . . . 200.00
20 The Beast Of Bristol. 200.00
21 Man Who Could See Death . . 200.00
22 The Phantom's Return 200.00
23 . . . . 200.00
24 Kill The Black Cat 200.00
25 The Man With Three Eyes! . . 200.00
26 . . . . 175.00
27 Fate Held Four Aces!. 175.00
28 The Wings Of Mr. Milo! 175.00
29 . . . . 175.00
30 . . . . 175.00
31 The Incredible Illusions! 175.00
32 Pied Piper of the Sea. 175.00
33 Mr. Misfortune!. 175.00
34 The Hundred Year Duel 175.00
35 . . . . 175.00
36 The Treasure of Montezuma! . 150.00
37 MD,The Statue That
   Came to Life. 150.00
38 The Voyage Of No Return . . . 150.00
39 . . . . 150.00
40 The Coins That Came To Life. 150.00
41 The Impossible Tricks! 150.00
42 The Stranger From Out There 150.00
43 . . . . 150.00
44 The Secret Of Hill 14 . . . . . . 150.00
45 . . . . 150.00
46 The Bird of Fate. 150.00
47 The Robot Named Think 150.00
48 The Man Marooned On Earth. 150.00
49 The Mysterious Mr. Omen . . . 150.00
50 . . . . 160.00
51 Man Who Stole Teardrops . . . 125.00
52 The Man With The Golden
   Shoes. 125.00
53 The Man Who Hated Mirrors . 125.00
54 The Woman Who Lived Twice 125.00
55 I Turned Back Time 125.00
56 The Thing In The Black Box. . 125.00
57 The Untamed. 125.00
58 . . . . 125.00
59 The Tomb Of Ramfis 125.00
60 The Prisoner On Canvas 125.00
61 JK,Superstition Day 125.00
62 The Haunting Scarecrow 90.00
63 JK,The Lady & The Creature . 125.00
64 The Golden Doom 90.00
65 JK,The Magic Lantern 125.00
66 JK,Sinister Shadow 125.00
67 The Wizard of Water 90.00
68 The Book That Bewitched . . . 90.00
69 The Miniature Disasters 90.00
70 JK,The Man With Nine Lives . 100.00
71 Menace of the Mole Man 100.00
72 JK,Dark Journey 100.00
73 Museum That Came to Life . . 90.00
74 Museum That Came To Life. . . 90.00
75 Assignment Unknown! 90.00
76 JK,Prisoners Of The Tiny
   Universe. 90.00
77 The Eyes That Went Berserk . . 85.00
78 JK(c),The 13th Hour 90.00
79 JK(c),The Fantastic Sky
   Puzzle 90.00
80 Man With Countless Faces! . . . 85.00
81 The Man Who Made Utopia . . . 85.00
82 The Riddle of the Earth's
   Second Moon. 85.00
83 The Mystery of the
   Martian Eye 85.00
84 JK,BK,The 100-Century Doom 135.00
85 JK(c),Earth's Strangest
   Salesman. 85.00
86 The Baffling Bargains. 80.00
87 The Human Diamond. 80.00
88 Return of the Animal Man 85.00
89 The Cosmic Plant! 85.00

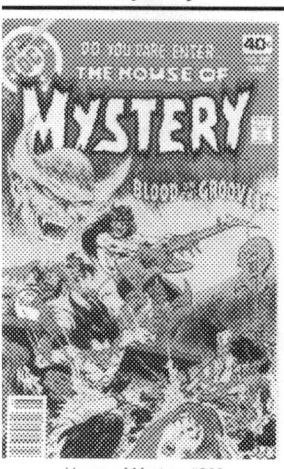

House of Mystery #269
© DC Comics, Inc.

90 The Invasion Of the Energy
Creatures! 85.00
91 DD&SMo(c),The Riddle of the
Alien Satellite 85.00
92 DD(c),Menace of the
Golden Globule 85.00
93 NC(c),I Fought The
Molten Monster 85.00
94 DD&SMo(c),The Creature
In Echo Lake 85.00
95 The Wizard's Gift. 85.00
96 The Amazing 70-Ton Man 85.00
97 The Alien Who Change
History 85.00
98 DD&SMo(c),The Midnight
Creature. 85.00
99 The Secret of the
Leopard God 85.00
100 The Beast Beneath Earth. . . 100.00
101 The Magnificent Monster 75.00
102 Cellmate to a Monster 75.00
103 Hail the Conquering Aliens. . . . 75.00
104 I was the Seeing-Eye Man . . . 75.00
105 Case of the Creature X-14 . . . 75.00
106 Invaders from the Doomed
Dimension 75.00
107 Captives o/t Alien
Fisherman 75.00
108 RMo,Four Faces of Frank
Forbes 75.00
109 ATh,JKu,Secret of the Hybrid
Creatures. 75.00
110 Beast Who Stalked Through
Time. 75.00
111 Operation Beast Slayer 75.00
112 Menace of Craven's
Creatures 75.00
113 RMo,Prisoners of Beast
Asteroid 75.00
114 The Movies from Nowhere . . . 75.00
115 Prisoner o/t Golden Mask. . . . 75.00
116 RMo,Return of the
Barsfo Beast 75.00
117 Menace of the Fire Furies 70.00
118 RMo,Secret o/SuperGorillas . . 70.00
119 Deadly Gift from the Stars . . . 70.00
120 ATh,Catman of KarynPeale . . 70.00
121 RMo,Beam that Transformed
Men 70.00
122 Menace fo the Alien Hero. . . . 70.00
123 RMo,Lure o/t Decoy
Creature. 70.00
124 Secret of Mr. Doom 70.00
125 Fantastic Camera Creature . . 70.00

126 The Human Totem Poles 70.00
127 RMo,Cosmic Game o/Doom. . 70.00
128 NC,The Sorcerer's Snares . . . 70.00
129 Man in the Nuclear Trap. 70.00
130 The Alien Creature Hunt 70.00
131 Vengeance o/t GeyserGod. . . 60.00
132 MMe,Beware My Invisible
Master 60.00
133 MMe,Captive Queen of
Beast Island 60.00
134 MMe,Secret Prisoner of
Darkmore Dungeon 60.00
135 MMe,Alien Body Thief 60.00
136 MMe,Secret o/t StolenFace . . 60.00
137 MMe,Tunnel to Disaster. 60.00
138 MMe,Creature Must Die. 60.00
139 MMe,Creatures of
Vengeful Eye 60.00
140 I&Only app.:Astro. 60.00
141 MMe,The Alien Gladiator 60.00
142 MMe,The Wax Demons 60.00
143 J'onn J'onzz begins 250.00
144 J'onn J'onzz on Weird
World of Gilgana. 150.00
145 J'onn J'onzz app 100.00
146 BP,J'onn J'onzz 100.00
147 J'onn J'onzz. 100.00
148 J'onn J'onzz 100.00
149 ATh,J'onn J'onzz 100.00
150 MMe,J'onn J'onzz 100.00
151 J'onn J'onzz. 100.00
152 MMe,J'onn J'onzz 100.00
153 J'onn J'onzz. 100.00
154 J'onn J'onzz. 100.00
155 J'onn J'onzz. 100.00
156 JM,I:Dial H for Hero (Giantboy
Cometeer,Mole)J.J'onzz sty . 125.00
157 JM,Dial H for Hero (Human
Bullet,Super Charge,Radar
Sonar Man) J'onn J'onnzz sty 100.00
158 JM,Dial H for Hero (Quake
MasterSquid)J'onn J'onzz sty . 90.00
159 JM,Dial H for Hero (Human
Starfish,Hypno Man,Mighty
Moppet) J'onn J'onzz sty . . . 90.00
160 JM,Dial H for Hero (King Kandy
A:Plastic Man,I:Marco Xavier (J'onn
J'onzz new secret I.D.) 150.00
161 JM,Dial H for Hero (Magneto,
Hornet Man,Shadow Man) . . . 75.00
162 JM,Dial H for Hero (Mr.Echo,
Future Man) J'onnJ'onzz sty . . 75.00
163 JM,Dial H for Hero(Castor&Pollux,
King Coil) J'onnJ'onzz sty 75.00
164 JM,Dial H for Hero (Super Nova
Zip Tide) J'onnJ'onzz sty. 75.00
165 JM,Dial H for Hero (Whoozis,
Whatsis,Howzis) J'onn J'onzz
story. 75.00
166 JM,Dial H for Hero (Yankee
Doodle Kid,Chief Mighty Arrow)
J'onn J'onzz sty 75.00
167 JM,Dial H for Hero (Balloon Boy,
Muscle Man,Radar Sonar Man)
J'onn J'onzz sty 75.00
168 JM,Dial H for Hero (Thunderbolt,
Mole,Cometeer,Hoopster)
J'onn J'onzz sty 75.00
169 JM,I:Gem Girl in Dial H for
Hero,J'onnJ'onzz sty. 75.00
170 JM,Dial H for Hero (Baron
BuzzSaw,Don Juan,Sphinx
Man) J'onn J'onzz sty 75.00
171 JM,Dial H for Hero (King Viking
Whirl-I-Gig) J'onnJ'onzz sty . . 65.00
172 JM,Dial H for Hero 65.00
173 E:Dial H for Hero,F:J'onn
Jonzz. 65.00
174 New direction,SA pg.13 . . . . . 50.00
175 I:Cain. 30.00
176 SA,Cain's Game Room 30.00

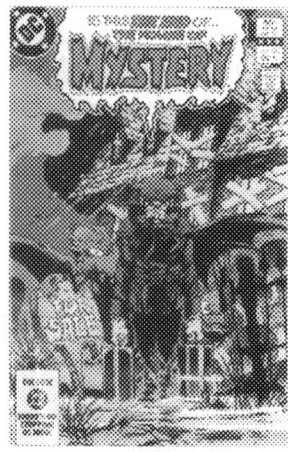

House of Mystery #321
© DC Comics, Inc.

177 Curse of the Car 30.00
178 NA,The Game 40.00
179 BWr,NA,JO,Widow'sWalk 75.00
180 GK,WW,BWr,SA,Room 13 . . . 30.00
181 BWr,The Siren of Satan 30.00
182 ATh,The Devil's Doorway 30.00
183 BWr,WW(i),DeadCanKill. 30.00
184 ATh,GK,WW,Eye o/Basilisk . . 25.00
185 AW,The Beautiful Beast 30.00
186 BWr,NA,Nightmare. 35.00
187 ATh,Mask of the Red Fox. . . . 18.00
188 TD,BWr,House of Madness . . . 30.00
189 WW(i),Eyes of the Cat 18.00
190 ATh,Fright 18.00
191 BWr,TD,Christmas Story,. . . . 18.00
192 JAp,GM,DH,Garnener
of Eden 18.00
193 BWr. 20.00
194 ATh,NR,RH(rep),JK(rep)
Born Loser 25.00
195 NR,BWr,ThingsOld..Things
Forgotten 30.00
196 GM,GK,ATh(rep)A Girl &
Her Dog. 20.00
197 DD,NR,House of Horrors 18.00
198 MSy,NC,Day of the Demon . . 20.00
199 WW,RB,Sno'Fun 25.00
200 MK,TD,The Beast's Revenge. 25.00
201 JAp,The Demon Within 18.00
202 MSy,GC(rep),SA,The Poster
Plague,John Prentice? 18.00
203 NR,Tower of Prey. 18.00
204 BWr,AN,All in the Family 20.00
205 The Coffin Creature 10.00
206 MSy,TP,The Burning 10.00
207 JSn,The Spell 15.00
208 Creator of Evil 10.00
209 AA,JAp,Tomorrow I Hang. . . . 15.00
210 The Immortal. 10.00
211 NR,Deliver Us From Evil 15.00
212 MA,AN,Ever After 10.00
213 AN,Back from the Realm of
15e Damned 15.00
214 NR,The Shaggy Dog 10.00
215 The Man Who Wanted Power
over Women. 10.00
216 TD,Look into My Eyes & Kill. . 10.00
217 NR,AA,Swamp God 15.00
218 FT,An Ice Place to Visit 10.00
219 AA,NR,Pledge to Satan 10.00
220 AA,AN,They Hunt Butterflies
Don't They? 10.00
221 FT,BWr,MK,He Who Laughs
Last 15.00

222 AA,Night of the Teddy Bear . . 10.00
223 Demon From the Deep 10.00
224 FR,AA,SheerFear,B:100pg. . . 35.00
225 AA,FT,AN,See No Evil 35.00
226 AA,FR,NR,SA,Monster in House
    Tour of House of Mystery 35.00
227 NR,AA,The Carriage Man . . . 35.00
228 FR,NA(i),The Rebel 35.00
229 NR,Nightmare Castle,
    last 100 page 35.00
230 Experiment In Fear 8.00
231 Cold,Cold Heart. 8.00
232 Last Tango in Hell 8.00
233 FR,Cake! 8.00
234 AM,Lafferty's Luck 8.00
235 NR,Wings of Black Death. 8.00
236 SD,NA(i)Death Played a
    Sideshow 10.00
237 FT,Night of the Chameleon . . . 8.00
238. . . . . 8.00
239 Day of the Witch 8.00
240 The Murderer. 8.00
241 FR,NR,DeathPulls theStrings. . 8.00
242 FR,The Balloon Vendor 8.00
243 Brother Bear 8.00
244 FT,Kronos..Zagros-Eborak . . . 8.00
245 AN,Check the J.C.Demon
    Catalogue Under...Death 8.00
246 DeathVault of Eskimo Kings. . . 8.00
247 SD,Death Rides the Waves . . . 8.00
248 NightJamieGaveUp theGhost. . 8.00
249 Hit Parade of Death 8.00
250 AN,Voyage to Hell 8.00
251 WW,AA,theCollector,68 pgs . . 10.00
252 DP,RT,AA,FR,AN,ManKillers . 10.00
253 TD,AN,GK,KJ,Beware the
    Demon Child 7.00
254 SD,AN,MR,TheDevil's Place . . 8.00
255 RE,GM,SometimesLeopards . 10.00
256 DAy,AN,Museum of Murders . 10.00
257 RE,MGo,TD(i),MBr,Xmas iss.. . 8.00
258 SD,RB,BMc,DG(i),The Demon
    and His Boy 8.00
259 RE,RT,MGo,DN,BL,`Hair Today,
    Gone Tomorrow,last giant 9.00
260 Go to Hades 8.00
261 The Husker 8.00
262 FreedFrom Infernos of Hell . . . 8.00
263 JCr,Is There Vengeance
    After Death?. 8.00
264 Halloween Issue 8.00
265 The Perfect Host 8.00
266 The Demon Blade 8.00
267 A Strange Way to Die 8.00
269 Blood on the Grooves 8.00
270 JSh,JRu,JBi,Black Moss 8.00
271 TS,HellHound of
    Brackenmoor 8.00
272 DN,DA,theSorcerer's Castle. . . 8.00
273 The Rites of Inheritance. 8.00
274 MR,JBi,Hell Park 8.00
275 JCr,`Final Installment'. 8.00
276 SD,MN,`Epode' 8.00
277 HC,AMi,`LimitedEngagement' . 8.00
278 `TV or Not TV'. 8.00
279 AS,Trial by Fury. 8.00
280 VMK,DAy,Hungry Jaws
    of Death. 8.00
281 Now Dying in this Corner. 8.00
282 JSw,DG,Superman/Radio
    Shack ins 8.00
283 RT,AN`Kill Me Gently'. 8.00
284 KG,King and the Dragon 8.00
285 Cold Storage 8.00
286 Long Arm of the Law 8.00
287 NR,AS,BL,Legend o/t Lost. . . . 8.00
288 DSp,Piper at Gates of Hell . . . 8.00
289 Brother Bobby's Home for
    Wayward Girls & Boys 8.00
290 TS,I:I..Vampire. 8.00
291 TS,DAy,I..Vampire #2. . . . . . . 8.00

292 TS,MS,TD,RE,DSp,Wendigo . . 8.00
293 GT,TS,A:I..Vampire #3 . . . . . . 8.00
294 CI,TY,GT,TD,The Darkness . . . 8.00
295 TS,TVE,JCr,I..Vampire #4 . . . . 8.00
296 CI,BH,Night Women. 8.00
297 TS,DCw,TD,I..Vampire #5 . . . . 8.00
298 TS,`Stalker on a Starless
    Night' 8.00
299 TS,DSp,I..Vampire #6 . . . . . . 8.00
300 GK,DA,JSon,JCr,DSp,Anniv. . . 8.00
301 JDu,TVE,KG,TY `...Virginia' . . 8.00
302 TS,NR,DSp,I..Vampire #7 . . . . 8.00
303 TS,DSp,I..Vampire #8 . . . . 8.00
304 EC,RE,I..Vampire #9 . . . . 8.00
305 TVE,EC,I..Vampire #10 . . . . . 8.00
306 TS,TD,I..Vampire #11,
    A:Jack the Ripper. 8.00
307 TS,I..Vampire #12 . . . . 8.00
308 TS,MT,NR,I..Vampire #13. . . . . 8.00
309 TS,I..Vampire #14 . . . . 8.00
310 TS(i),I..Vampire #15. . . . . 8.00
311 I..Vampire #16 . . . . 8.00
312 TS(i),I..Vampire #17. . . . . 8.00
313 TS(i),CI,I..Vampire #18. . . . . . 8.00
314 TS,I..Vampire #19 . . . . 8.00
315 TS(i),TY,I..Vampire #20 . . . . . 8.00
316 TS(i),GT,TVE,I..Vampire #21 . . 8.00
317 TS(i),I..Vampire #22. . . . . 8.00
318 TS(i),I..Vampire #23. . . . . 8.00
319 TS,JOy,I..Vampire conc.. . . . . . 8.00
320 GM,Project: Inferior 8.00
321 final issue 8.00
Welcome Back to the House of Mystery
    GN BWr(c) horror stories rep. . . 6.00

HOUSE OF SECRETS
Nov.–Dec., 1956
1 MD,JM,The Hand of Doom. . 1,300.00
2 JPr,RMo,NC,Mask of Fear . . . 500.00
3 JM,JK,MMe,The Three
    Prophecies 375.00
4 JM,JK,MMe,Master of
    Unknown 300.00
5 MMe,The Man Who
    Hated Fear. 200.00
6 NC,MMe,Experiment 1000 . . . 200.00
7 RMo,Island o/t Enchantress . . 200.00
8 JK,RMo,The Electrified Man . . 225.00
9 JM,JSt,The Jigsaw Creatures . 175.00
10 JSt,NC,I was a Prisoner
    of the Sea 175.00
11 KJ(c),NC,The Man who
    couldn't stop growing 175.00
12 JK,The Hole in the Sky 200.00

House of Secrets #7 © DC Comics Inc.

13 The Face in the Mist 150.00
14 MMe,The Man who Stole Air . 150.00
15 The Creature in the Camera. . 150.00
16 NC,We matched wits with a
    Gorilla genius 125.00
17 DW,Lady in the Moon. 125.00
18 MMe,The Fantastic
    Typewriter 125.00
19 MMe,NC,Lair of the
    Dragonfly 125.00
20 Incredible FireballCreatures . . 125.00
21 Girl from 50,000 Fathoms . . . 125.00
22 MMe,Thing from Beyond 125.00
23 MMe,I&O:Mark Merlin 135.00
24 NC,Mark Merlin story 125.00
25 MMe,Mark Merlin story. 100.00
26 NC,MMe, Mark Merlin story . 100.00
27 MMe,Mark Merlin. 100.00
28 MME,Mark Merlin. 100.00
29 NC,MMe,Mark Merlin. 100.00
30 JKu,MMe,Mark Merlin 100.00
31 DD,MMe,RH,Mark Merlin 80.00
32 MMe,Mark Merlin. 80.00
33 MMe,Mark Merlin. 80.00
34 MMe,Mark Merlin. 80.00
35 MMe,Mark Merlin. 80.00
36 MMe,Mark Merlin. 80.00
37 MMe,Mark Merlin. 80.00
38 MMe,Mark Merlin. 80.00
39 JKu,MMe,Mark Merlin 80.00
40 NC,MMe,Mark Merlin 80.00
41 MMe,Mark Merlin. 80.00
42 MMe,Mark Merlin. 80.00
43 RMo,MMe,CI,Mark Merlin 80.00
44 MMe,Mark Merlin. 80.00
45 MMe,Mark Merlin. 80.00
46 MMe,Mark Merlin. 80.00
47 MMe,Mark Merlin. 80.00
48 ATh,MMe,Mark Merlin 80.00
49 MMe,Mark Merlin. 80.00
50 MMe,Mark Merlin. 80.00
51 MMe,Mark Merlin. 75.00
52 MMe,Mark Merlin. 75.00
53 CI,Mark Merlin. 75.00
54 RMo,MMe,Mark Merlin. 75.00
55 MMe,Mark Merlin. 75.00
56 MMe,Mark Merlin. 75.00
57 MMe,Mark Merlin. 75.00
58 MMe,O:Mark Merlin 75.00
59 MMe,Mark Merlin. 75.00
60 MMe,Mark Merlin. 75.00
61 I:Eclipso,A:Mark Merlin 175.00
62 MMe,Eclipso,Mark Merlin. . . . 100.00
63 GC,ATh,Eclipso,Mark Merlin . . 75.00
64 MMe,ATh,M Merlin,Eclipso. . . 75.00
65 MMe,ATh,M Merlin,Eclipso. . . 75.00
66 MMe,ATh,M Merlin,Eclipso. . . 110.00
67 MMe,ATh,M Merlin,Eclipso. . . 75.00
68 MMe,Mark Merlin,Eclipso. . . . 70.00
69 MMe,Mark Merlin,Eclipso 70.00
70 MMe,Mark Merlin,Eclipso 70.00
71 MMe,Mark Merlin,Eclipso 70.00
72 MMe,Mark Merlin,Eclipso 70.00
73 MMe,D:Mark Merlin,I:Prince
    Ra-Man; Eclipso. 70.00
74 MMe,Prince Ra-Man,Eclipso . . 70.00
75 MMe,Prince Ra-Man,Eclipso . . 70.00
76 MMe,Prince Ra-Man,Eclipso . . 70.00
77 MMe,Prince Ra-Man,Eclipso . . 70.00
78 MMe,Prince Ra-Man,Eclipso . . 70.00
79 MMe,Prince Ra-Man,Eclipso . . 70.00
80 MMe,Prince Ra-Man,Eclipso . . 70.00
81 I:Abel, new mystery format
    Don't Move It 50.00
82 DD,NA,One & only, fully guaran
    teed super-permanent 100%. . 30.00
83 ATh,The Stuff that Dreams
    are Made of 30.00
84 DD,If I had but world enough
    and time. 30.00
85 DH,GK,NA,Second Chance . . . 40.00

House of Secrets #13
© DC Comics, Inc.

86 GT,GM,Strain. 20.00
87 DD,DG,RA,MK,The Coming
    of Ghaglan 40.00
88 DD,The Morning Ghost 30.00
89 GM,DH,Where Dead MenWalk. 30.00
90 GT,RB,NA,GM,The Symbionts . 35.00
91 WW,MA,The Eagle's Talon. . . . 35.00
92 BWr,TD(i),I:Swamp Thing
    (Alex Olson) 500.00
93 JAp,TD,ATh(rep.)Lonely in
    Death 20.00
94 TD,ATh(rep.)Hyde.and
    go Seek 20.00
95 DH,NR,The Bride of Death. . . . 18.00
96 DD,JAb,WW, the Monster 22.00
97 JAp,Divide and Murder 20.00
98 MK,ATh(rep),Born Losers. 20.00
99 NR,TD(i),Beyond His
    Imagination 20.00
100 TP,TD,AA,Rest in Peace 25.00
101 AN,Small Invasion 20.00
102 NR,A Lonely Monstrosity 20.00
103 AN,Village on Edge o/Forever 15.00
104 NR,AA,GT,Ghosts Don't
    Bother Me...But. 12.00
105 JAp,AA,An Axe to Grind. 12.00
106 AN,AA,This Will Kill You. 15.00
107 AA,The Night of the Nebbish . 15.00
108 A New Kid on the Block 12.00
109 AA,AN...And in Death, there
    is no Escape 12.00
110 Safes Have Secrets, Too 10.00
111 TD,Hair-I-Kari. 10.00
112 Case of the Demon Spawn . . 10.00
113 MSy,NC,NR,Spawns
    of Satan 10.00
114 FBe,Night Game 10.00
115 AA,AN,Nobody Hurts My
    Brother. 10.00
116 NR,Like Father,Like Son 10.00
117 AA,AN,Revenge for the Deadly
    Dummy 10.00
118 GE,Very Last Picture Show . . 10.00
119 A Carnival of Dwarves 10.00
120 TD,AA,The Lion's Share. 10.00
121 Ms.Vampire Killer. 10.00
122 AA,Requiem for Igor 7.00
123 ATh,A Connecticut Ice Cream
    Man in King Arthur's Court 8.00
124 Last of the Frankensteins. 7.00
125 AA,FR,Instant Re-Kill. 7.00
126 AN,On Borrowed Time. 7.00
127 MSy,A Test of Innocence 7.00
128 AN,Freak Out!. 7.00
129 Almost Human. 7.00

130 All Dolled Up!. 7.00
131 AN,Point of No Return 7.00
132 Killer Instinct 7.00
133 Portraits of Death. 7.00
134 NR,Inheritance of Blood. 7.00
135 The Vegitable Garden 7.00
136 Last Voyage of Lady Luck 7.00
137 The Harder They Fall. 7.00
138 Where Dreams are Born 10.00
139 SD,NR,A Real Crazy Kid 10.00
140 NR,O:Patchwork Man 20.00
141 You Can't Beat the Devil 6.00
142 Playmate. 6.00
143 The Evil Side 6.00
144 The Vampire of Broadway 6.00
145 Operation wasSuccessful,But. . 6.00
146 Snake's Alive 6.00
147 AN,The See-Through Thief . . . 6.00
148 SD,Sorcerer's Apprentice. 6.00
149 The Evil One 6.00
150 A:PhantomStranger & Dr.13. . . 6.00
151 MGo,Nightmare 6.00
152 Sister Witch 6.00
153 VM,AN,Don't Look Now 6.00
154 JL,Last issue 6.00

HOUSE OF SECRETS
DC/Vertigo Aug. 1996
1 SSe(s),TKr, judgments on your
    darkest secrets. 3.50
2 SSe(s),TKr, F:Rain 2.50
3 SSe(s),TKr,Seattle's citizens
    secrets. 2.50
4 SSe(s),TKr,Eric's secrets
    exposed. 2.50
5 . . . . 2.50
6 SSe(s),DFg,Other rooms:
    "Meeting" 2.50
7 SSe(s),TKr,"Blueprint:
    Elevation A" 2.50
8 SSe(s),TKr,"The Road to
    You," pt.1 . . . . 2.50
9 SSe(s),TKr,"The Road to
    You," pt.2 . . . . 2.50
10 SSe(s),TKr,"The Road to
    You," pt.3, concl 2.50
11 "The Book of Law" pt.1 (of 5) . . 2.50
12 "The Book of Law" pt.2 . . . . . . 2.50
13 SSe,The Book of Law, pt.3 . . . . 2.50
14 SSe,The Book of Law, pt.4 . . . . 2.50
15 SSe,The Book of Law, pt.5 . . . . 2.50
16 SSe,Book of Law, epilogue 2.50
17 SSe,The Road to You, pt.1 . . . . 2.50
18 SSe,The Road to You, pt.2 . . . . 2.50
19 SSe,The Road to You, pt.3 . . . . 2.50
20 SSe,Other Rooms story. 2.50
21 SSe,Basement, pt.1. . . . . 2.50
22 SSe,Basement, pt.2. . . . . 2.50
23 SSe,Basement, pt.3. . . . . 2.50
24 SSe,TKr,"Attic". 2.50
25 SSe,TKr, final issue 2.50
TPB Foundation, rep.#1–#5 . . . . . 14.95

HUMAN TARGET
SPECIAL
1 DG(i),Prequel to T.V. Series 2.00

HUMAN TARGET
DC/Vertigo 1999
1 (of 4) PrM(s). 3.00
2 PrM(s) 3.00
3 PrM(s) 3.00
4 PrM(s), concl. 3.00

HUNTER'S HEART
1995
1 Cops vs. Serial Killer 4.95

2 . . . . 4.95
3 F:Lieutenant Slidell. 4.95

HUNTRESS, THE
1989–90
1 JSon/DG 2.00
2 JSon,Search for Family's
    Murderer 2.00
3 JSon,A:La Bruja 1.50
4 JSon,Little Italy/Chinatown
    Gangs 1.50
5 JSon,V:Doctor Mandragora. . . . 1.50
6 JSon,Huntress'secrets revealed . 1.50
7 JSon,V:Serial Killer. 1.50
8 JSon,V:Serial Killer. 1.50
9 JSon,V:Serial Killer. 1.50
10 JSon,Nuclear Terrorists in NY . . 1.50
11 JSon,V:Wyvern,Nuclear
    Terrorists contd. 1.50
12 JSon,V:Nuclear Terrorists cont. . 1.50
13 JSon,Violence in NY 1.50
14 JSon,Violence contd.,New
    Mob boss. 1.50
15 JSon,I:Waterfront Warrior. 1.50
16 JSon,Secret of Waterfront

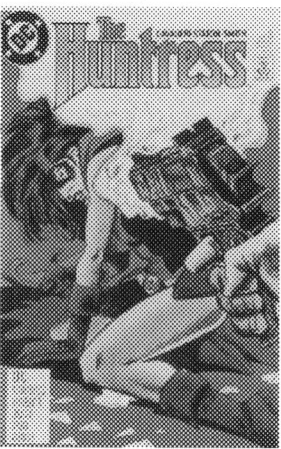

Huntress #6 © DC Comics, Inc.

    Warrior revealed. 1.50
17 JSon,Batman+Huntress#1 . . . . 1.25
18 JSon,Batman+Huntress#2 . . . . 1.25
19 JSon,Batman+Huntress#3,final
    issue 1.25

HUNTRESS
[Limited Series] 1994
1 CDi(s),MN,V:Redzone 1.75
2 MN,V:Redzone 1.50
3 MN,V:Redzone. 1.75
4 MN,V:Spano,Redzone 1.50

ICON
Milestone 1993–96
1 Direct Market Ed.,MBr,MG,I:Icon,
    Rocket,S.H.R.E.D.,w/poster,
    card,C puzzle piece 3.25
1a Newsstand Ed. 2.00
2 MBr,MG,I:Payback 1.75
3 MBr,MG,V:Payback 1.75
4 MBr,MG,Teen Pregnancy Issue. . 1.75
5 MBr,MG,V:Blood Syndicate. . . . 1.75
6 MBr,MG,V:Blood Syndicate. . . . 1.75
7 MBr,MG 1.75

8 MBr,MG,O:Icon. 1.75
9 WS(c),MBr,MG,Shadow War,
   I:Donner,Blitzen1.75
10 MBr,MG,V:Holocaust 1.75
11 MBr,Hero Worship 1.75
12 Sanctimony 1.75
13 MBr,Rocket & Static T.U. 1.75
14 JBy(c) 1.75
15 Worlds Collide,pt.4,A:Superboy . 1.75
16 Worlds Collide,pt.11,
   V:Superman,Rift. 1.75
17 Mothership Connection 1.75
18 Mothership Connection,pt.2 . . . . 1.75
19 Mothership Connection,pt.3 . . . . 1.75
20 Rocket. 1.75
21 . . . . 1.75
22 . . . . 1.75
23 New Rocket. 1.75
24 F:Buck Wild. 1.75
25 V:Oblivion 3.00
26 V:Oblivion 1.75
27 Move to Paris Island projects. . . 2.50
28 Long Hot Summer 2.50
29 Long Hot Summer 2.50
30 Icon Leaves Earth 2.50
31 HC(c) Readers Choice comic. . . 1.00
32 Rocket, Galactic Corporate 2.50
33 V:Rocket 2.50
34 V:Cooperative 2.50
35 . . . . 2.50
36 Rocket returns to Earth 2.50
37 MBr,RT,F:Rocket 2.50
38 DMD(s),RT 2.50
39 DMD(s),RT,V:Holocaust & Blood
   Syndicate 2.50
40 DMD(s),RT, V:Holocaust 2.50
41 DMD(s),RT, V:Blood Syndicate. . 2.50
42 DMD(s),RT 2.50
43 DMD(s),RT,"Blood Reign" concl. 2.50
44 DMD(s),RT,V:Smurphs. 2.50
45 DMD(s),RT, final issue 2.50
TPB A Hero's Welcome 12.95

IMMORTAL DR. FATE
1995
1 WS,KG,rep. 1.75
2 and 3 KG,rep. . . . . @1.25

IMPACT WINTER SPECIAL
Impact 1991
1 CI/MR/TL,A:All Impact Heros,
   President Kidnapped 2.50

IMPULSE
1995–98
1 Young Flash Adventures. 7.00
2 V:Terrorists. 3.50
3 In School 3.00
4 V:White Lightning 3.00
5 V:White Lightning 1.75
6 . . . . 1.75
7 V:Gridlock. 1.75
8 MWa,Underworld
   Unleashed tie-in 1.75
9 MWa,F:XS,. 1.75
10 MWa,Dead Heat,pt.3 . . . . 1.75
11 MWa,Dead Heat,pt.5 . . . . 1.75
12 . . . . 1.75
13 MWa,new daredevil in town 1.75
14 AWi,A:White Lightning 1.75
15 . . . . 1.75
16 . . . . 1.75
17 . . . . 1.75
18 MPk(s),AWi,Virtual reality
   nightmare. 1.75
19 MWa(s),HuR, Bart's dreams. . . . 1.75
20 MWa(s),HuR, baseball. 1.75

Impulse #36 © DC Comics Inc.

21 MWa(s),F:Legion of Super-
   Heroes. 1.75
22 MWa(s). 1.75
23 MWa(s),HuR,Mercury at a
   crossroads 1.75
24 MWa(s),HuR,Impulse's mother
   comes from the future 1.75
25 MWa(s),HuR,Impulse & his mom
   in 30th century 1.75
26 MWa(s),Bart Allen back in the
   20th century. 1.75
27 MWa(s) 1.75
28 . . . . 1.75
29 BML,Bart searches for Max
   Mercury 1.75
30 BML, pt.2, Genesis tie-in 2.00
31 BML, pt.3,V:Dr. Morlo. 2.00
32 BML,Max is home 2.00
33 BML,White Lightning 2.00
34 BML,Devonian Age, pt.1 . . . . . . 2.00
35 BML 2.00
36 BML,Court Dates. 2.00
37 BML,Dr. Morlo 2.00
38 BML,freak snow storm. 2.00
39 BML,V:Trickster. 2.00
40 BML,WF, kid picnic 2.00
41 Return of Arrowette 2.00
42 BML(s),virtual monsters 2.25
43 BML(s),F:Jamal. 2.25
44 BML(s),V:Evil Eye 2.25
45 BML(s),Christmas 2.25
46 BML(s),Chain Lightning x-over. . 2.25
47 BML(s),A:Superman 2.25
48 BML(s),A:Riddler. 2.25
49 BML(s),C:Flash 2.25
50 TDz(s),A:Batman, Joker. 2.25
51 TDz(s),V:Frog Prince 2.25
52 TDz(s),WS,F:Kalibak,pt.1. . . . . . 2.25
53 TDz(s),WS,F:Kalibak,pt.2. . . . . . 2.25
Ann.#2 Pulp Heroes (Western) 3.95
Spec.#1,000,000 BML(s) 2.25
GN Bart Saves the Universe. 6.00
TPB Reckless Youth MWa(s) rep.
   Flash #92–#94 . . . . 14.95
Spec. Impulse/Atom Double-Shot
   DJu, x-over concl. (1997) 3.00
Spec. Impulse Plus 48pg.
   with Grossout (1997) 2.95

INDUSTRIAL GOTHIC
Vertigo 1995
1 Jail Break Plans 2.50
2 thru 5 Jail Break Plans . . . . . . @2.50

INFERIOR FIVE
March-April, 1967
1 MSy 35.00
2 MSy,A:Plastic Man 20.00
3 . . . . 15.00
4 . . . . 15.00
5 . . . . 15.00
6 . . . . 15.00
7 . . . . 15.00
8 . . . . 15.00
9 . . . . 15.00
10 A:Superman 15.00
11 JO(c&a) 15.00
12 JO(c&a) 15.00

INFERNO
Aug., 1997
1 (of 4) SI, from Legion 2.50
2 SI,mall grrls 2.50
3 SI,Legion Month tie-in. 2.50
4 SI, concl. 2.50

INFINITY, INC.
March, 1984
1 JOy,O:Infinity Inc. 3.00
2 JOy,End of Origin 2.50
3 JOy,O:Jade 2.25
4 JOy,V:JSA 2.25
5 JOy,V:JSA 2.25
6 JOy,V:JSA 2.25
7 JOy,V:JSA 2.25
8 JOy, V:Ultra Humanite 2.25
9 JOy,V:Ultra Humanite 2.25
10 JOy,V:Ultra Humanite. 2.00
11 DN,GT,O:Infinity Inc. 2.00
12 Infinity Unmasks,I:Yolanda
   Montez (New Wildcat) 2.00
13 DN,V:Rose & Thorn. 2.00
14 1st TM DC art,V:Chroma 9.00
15 TM,V:Chroma 3.00
16 TM,I:Helix (Mr. Bones) 3.00
17 TM,V:Helix. 3.00
18 TM,Crisis. 3.00
19 TM,JSA,JLA x-over,
   I:Mekanique 3.00
20 TM,Crisis. 3.00
21 TM,Crisis,I:Hourmanll,
   Dr.Midnight. 3.00
22 TM,Crisis. 3.00
23 TM,Crisis. 3.00
24 TM,Crisis. 3.00
25 TM,Crisis,JSA 3.00
26 TM,V:Carcharo 3.00
27 TM,V:Carcharo 3.00
28 TM,V:Carcharo 3.00
29 TM,V:Helix. 3.00
30 TM,Mourning of JSA 3.00
31 TM,V:Psycho Pirate. 3.00
32 TM,V:Psycho Pirate. 3.00
33 TM,O:Obsidian 3.00
34 TM,A: Global Guardians 3.00
35 TM,V:Infinitors 3.00
36 TM,V:Injustice Unl.. . . . . 3.00
37 TM,TD,O:Northwind. 3.00
38 Helix on Trial 1.75
39 O:Solomon Grundy 1.75
40 V:Thunderbolt 1.75
41 Jonni Thunder 1.75
42 TD,V:Hastor,L:Fury 1.75
43 TD,V:Hastor,Silver Scarab 1.75
44 TD,D:Silver Scarab 1.75
45 MGu,A:New Teen Titans,
   V:Ultra-Humanite 1.75
46 TD,Millenium,V:Floronic Man . . . 1.75
47 TD,Millenium,V:Harlequin. 1.75
48 TD,O:Nuklon 1.75
49 Silver Scarab becomes
   Sandman 2.00
50 TD,V:The Wizard,O:Sandman . . 2.50

Infinity #47 © DC Comics, Inc.

51 W:Fury & Sandman,D:Skyman.	1.75
52 V:Helix.	1.75
53 V:Justice Unlimited,last issue	1.75
Ann.#1 TM,V:Thorn	4.00
Ann.#2 V:Degaton,x-over Young All-Stars Annual #1.	2.00
Spec.#1 TD,A:Outsiders,V:Psycho Pirate	1.75

INVASION!
1988–89

1 TM,I:Vril Dox,Dominators (20th century)	4.00
2 TM,KG,DG,I:L.E.G.I.O.N.	3.00
3 BS,DG,I:Blasters	3.00
Daily Planet-Invasion! 16p	2.00

INVISIBLES
Vertigo 1994–96

1 GMo(s).	3.50
2 GMo(s),Down & Out,pt.1.	2.50
3 GMo(s),Down & Out,pt.2.	2.50
4 GMo(s),Down & Out,pt.3.	2.50
5 Arcadia,pt.1	2.25
6 Arcadia,pt.2	2.25
7 Arcadia,pt.3	2.25
8 Arcadia,pt.4	2.25
9 SeP(c),L:Dane	2.50
10 SeP(c),CWn,Jim Crow v. Zombies	2.50
11 V:New Breed of Hunter	2.50
12	2.50
13 GMO,Sheman,pt.1.	2.50
14 GMo,SeP,Sheman,pt.2.	2.50
15 GMo,Sheman,pt.3	2.50
16 GMo,An offer from Sir Miles.	4.00
17 GMo,Entropy in the U.K.,pt.1	4.00
18 GMo,Entropy in the U.K.,pt.2	4.00
19 GMo,Entropy in the U.K.,pt.3	5.00
20 GMo,F:RaggedRobin,Dane,Boy.	7.50
21 GMo,PuJ,F:Dane.	7.50
22 GMo(s),MBu,MPn	7.50
23 GMo(s),MBu,MPn	7.50
24 GMo(s),MBu,MPn	7.50
25 GMo(s),MBu,MPn,final issue Aug. 1996.	11.00

[Volume 2]
DC/Vertigo 1996

1 GMo(s),PJ,"Black Science," pt.1	6.00
2 GMo(s),PJ,"Black Science," pt.2	5.00
3 GMo(s),PJ,"Black Science," pt.3	5.00
4 GMo(s),PJ,"Black Science," pt.4	4.00

5 GMo(s),PJ,In SanFrancisco,pt.1	4.00
6 GMo(s),PJ,In SanFrancisco,pt.2	3.00
7 GMo(s),PJ,BB(c) "Time Machine Go" concl.	3.00
8 GMo(s),PJ,BB(c) "Sensitive Criminals," pt.1.	3.00
9 GMo(s),PJ,BB(c) "Sensitive Criminals," pt.2	3.00
10 GMo(s),PJ,Sensitive Criminals pt.3, concl.	3.00
11 GMo(s),PJ,BB(c),Hand of Glory pt.1	3.00
12 GMo(s),PJ,BB(c),Glory, pt.2	3.00
13 GMo(s),PJ,BB(c),Glory concl.	3.00
14 GMo(s),BB(c),Archons aftermath	3.00
15 GMo(s),BB(c), The Philadelphia Experiment, pt.1	3.00
16 GMo(s),BB(c),Experiment,pt.2	3.00
17 GMo,CWn,BB,Black Science II pt.1	3.00
18 GMo,CWn,BB,Science,pt.2	3.00
19 GMo,CWn,BB,Science,pt.3	3.00
20 GMo,CWn,BB(c),Science,pt.4	2.50
21 GMo,CWn,BB(c),King Mob	2.50
22 GMo,CWn,BB(c) The Tower.	2.50
TPB Counting to None	20.00
TPB Say You Want a Revolution.	20.00
TPB Bloody Hell in America	13.00

VOLUME 3
DC/Vertigo 1999

12 GMo,Satanstorm,pt.1.	3.00
11 GMo,Satanstorm,pt.2.	3.00
10 GMo,Satanstorm,pt.3.	3.00
9 GMo,Satanstorm,pt.4	3.00
8 GMo,Karmageddon,pt.1	3.00
7 GMo,Karmageddon,pt.2	3.00

IRONWOLF
1986

1 HC,rep.	2.00

IRONWOLF: FIRES OF THE REVOLUTION
1992

Hardcov.GN MMi,CR,R:Ironwolf	29.95
TPB Fires of the Revolution	15.00

ISIS
Oct.–Nov., 1976

1 RE/WW	5.00
2 MN.	1.25
3	1.25
4	1.25
5	1.25
6	1.25
7 O:Isis	1.25
8 Dec.–Jan., 1977–78	1.25

IT'S GAMETIME
Sept.–Oct., 1955

1	550.00
2	400.00
3	400.00
4 March-April, 1956	400.00

JACKIE GLEASON AND THE HONEYMOONERS
June-July, 1956

1 Based on TV show	650.00
2	450.00
3	350.00
4	350.00
5	350.00
6	350.00
7	350.00

Jack Kirby's Fourth World #14 © DC Comics, Inc.

8	350.00
9	350.00
10	350.00
11	350.00
12 April-May, 1958	400.00

JACK KIRBY'S FOURTH WORLD
Jan. 1997

1 JBy,Worlds of New Genesis & Apokolips become one	2.00
2 JBy,F:Big Barda vs. Thor	2.00
3 JBy,at Wall of the Source	2.00
4 JBy,Can Highfather save his son	2.00
5 JBy,conflict between the gods.	2.00
6 JBy,Cause of Orion's transformation	2.00
7 JBy,Orion taught lesson	2.00
8 JBy,WS,Genesis tie-in	2.00
9 JBy,WS(c),Genesis aftermath	2.00
10 JBy,WS,	2.00
11 JBy,WS,F:Orion	2.00
12 JBy,WS,F:Mister Miracle	2.00
13 JBy,WS	2.00
14 JBy,WS,Promethean Giant.	2.00
15 JBy,WS,Armaghetto.	2.00
16 JBy,WS,Kalibak vs. Darkseid	2.00
17 JBy,WS,Darkseid	2.00
18 JBy,WS,Darkseid freed	2.00
19 JBy,WS,two stories	2.00
20 JBy,WS,A:Superman,final issue.	2.25

JAGUAR
Impact

1 I&O:Jaguar I: Timon De Guzman, Maxx 13,Prof.Ruiz, Luiza Timmerman	1.25
2 Development of Powers	1.25
3 A:Maxx-13	1.25
4 A:Black Hood	1.25
5 `Void,The Living Black Hole	1.25
6 `The Doomster,'A:Maxx-13	1.25
7 Jaguar Secret Discovered, V:Void	1.25
8 V:Aryan League	1.25
9 I:Moonlighter(w/trading cards).	1.25
10 V:Invisible Terror	1.25
11 Defending Comedienne	1.25
12 V:The Bodyguard.	1.25
13 V:Purge.	1.25
14 'Frightmare in Rio',last iss.	1.25
Ann.#1 Earthquest,w/trading card	2.50

Jemm, Son of Saturn #5
© DC Comics Inc.

JEMM, SON OF SATURN
Sept., 1984

1 GC/KJ mini-series.	1.50
2 GC.	1.25
3 GC,Origin.	1.25
4 A:Superman.	1.25
5 Kin.	1.25
6 thru 12 GC, Aug. 1985	@1.25

JIMMY WAKELY
Sept.–Oct., 1949

1 Ph(c),ATh,The Cowboy Swordsman	900.00
2 Ph(c),ATh,The Prize Pony.	400.00
3 Ph(c),ATh,The Return of Tulsa Tom	400.00
4 Ph(c),ATh,FF,HK,Where's There'sSmokeThere'sGunfire	425.00
5 ATh,The Return of the Conquistadores	275.00
6 ATh,Two Lives of Jimmy Wakely	275.00
7 The Secret of Hairpin Canyon.	275.00
8 ATh,The Lost City of Blue Valley	275.00
9 ATh,The Return of the Western Firebrands	250.00
10 ATh,Secret of Lantikin'sLight	250.00
11 ATh,Trail o/a Thousand Hoofs	250.00
12 ATh,JKU,The King of Sierra Valley	250.00
13 ATh,The Raiders of Treasure Mountain	250.00
14 ATh(c),JKu,The Badmen of Roaring Flame Valley	250.00
15 GK(c),Tommyguns on the Range	250.00
16 GK(c),The Bad Luck Boots.	225.00
17 GK(c),Terror atThunderBasin	225.00
18 July-Aug., 1952	250.00

JLA
Nov. 1996

1 GMo(s),HPo,JhD,V:Hyperclan.	20.00
2	15.00
3 GMo(s),HPo,JhD,"War of the Worlds"	10.00
4 GMo(s),HPo,JhD,battle of the super-heroes, conc.	10.00
5 GMo(s),HPo,JhD "Woman of Tomorrow"	6.00
6 GMo(s),HPo,JhD,"Fire in theSky"	5.00
7 GMo(s),HPo,JhD,"Heaven on Earth".	5.00
8 GMo(s),HPo,JhD,"Imaginary Stories" F:Green Arrow.	5.00
9 GMo(s),V:The Key	5.00
10 GMo(s),HPo,JhD,R:Injustice Gang, pt.1 (of 6).	3.00
11 GMo(s),HPo,JhD,Rock of Ages, pt.2	3.00
12 GMo(s),HPo,JhD,Rock of Ages, pt.3, A:Hourman	3.00
13 GMo(s),HPo,JhD,Rock of Ages, pt.4	3.00
14 GMo(s),HPo,JhD,Rock of Ages, pt.5	3.00
15 GMo(s),HPo,JhD,Rock of Ages pt.6, concl, 48 pg.	3.00
16 GMo(s),HPo,JhD, new member	2.00
17 GMo(s),HPo,JhD, V:Prometheus	2.00
18 MWa,Engine of Chance, pt.1	2.00
19 MWa,Engine of Chance, pt.2	2.00
20 MWa,F:Adam Strange,pt.1	2.00
21 MWa,F:Adam Strange,pt.2	2.00
22 GMo(s),The Star Conquerer.	2.00
23 GMo,V:Star Conquerer, A:Sandman	2.00
24 GMo,HPo,Ultra-Marines,pt.1	2.00
25 GMo,HPo,Ultra-Marines,pt.2	2.00
26 GMo,HPo,Ultra-Marines,pt.3	2.00
27 GMo,HPo,CrisisTimesFive,pt.1	2.00
28 GMo,HPo,CrisisTimesFive,pt.2	2.00
29 GMo,HPo,CrisisTimesFive,pt.3	2.00
30 GMo,HPo,CrisisTimesFive,pt.4	2.00
31 GMo,HPo,CrisisTimes Five,concl.	2.00
32 MWa(s),No Man's Land	2.00
33 MWa(s),No Man's Land	2.00
34 GMo,Super-villains riot.	2.00
Ann.#1 Pulp Heroes (Hard Boiled)	3.95
Ann. #2 TTn,BWr,Ghosts	3.00
Ann.#3 JLApe Gorilla Warfare.	3.00
Spec.#1,000,000 GMo(s),HPo, V:Justice Legion A	2.00
SuperSpec.#1 Justice League of America	6.00
Giant #1, 7 new stories, 80 pg.	5.00
JLA: Tomorrow Woman, 1-shot TPe,Girlfrenzy (1998)	2.00
GN New World Order GMo(s),HPo, JhD, rep. #1–#4	5.95
GN American Dreams rep.#5–#9	8.00
GN Secret Files	4.00
GN Secret Files deluxe.	5.00
GN Secret Files #2.	4.00
GN Foreign Bodies.	6.00
GN JLA/WildC.A.T.S, GMo(s), VS,x-over.	6.00
TPB JLA:Rock of Ages	10.00
TPB Strength in Numbers.	13.00
TPB World Without Grown-Ups.	10.00
TPB Justice League of America: The Nail, Elseworlds.	13.00
TPB Secret Origins Featuring JLA	15.00

JLA: PARADISE LOST
Nov., 1997

1 (of 3) MMr,AOI,F:Zauriel	2.00
2 MMr,AOI,F:Zauriel,Martian Manhunter	2.00

JLA/TITANS
1998

1 (of 3) JLA vs. Teen Titans	3.00
2	3.00
3 conclusion, New Titans	3.00

JLA: WORLD WITHOUT GROWN-UPS
June 1998

1 (of 2) I:Young Justice 48pg	5.00
2 Young Justice, concl.	5.00

JLA: YEAR ONE
Nov., 1997

1 (of 12) MWa,BAu,BKi,48pg.	3.00
2 MWa,BAu,BKi,V:Vandal Savage	2.00
3 MWa,BAu,BKi.	2.00
4 MWa,BAu,BKi,V:Locus	2.00
5 MWa,BAu,BKi,F:Doom Patrol	2.00
6 MWa,BAu,BKi,V:Doom Patrol	2.00
7 MWa,BAu,BKi,V:Weapon Master	2.00
8 MWa,BAu,BKi,MIB,V:Locus.	2.00
9 MWa,BAu,BKi,MIB,V:Locus.	2.00
10 MWa,BAu,BKi,MIB,V:Locus	2.00
11 MWa,BAu,BKi,MIB.	2.00
12 MWa,BAu,BKi,MIB, concl.	3.00
TPB Year One	20.00

JOHNNY THUNDER
Feb.–March, 1973

1 ATh	5.00
2 GK,MD.	4.00
3 ATh,GK,MD,July-Aug., 1973.	4.00

JOKER, THE
1975–76

1 IN,DG,A:TwoFace.	25.00
2 IN,JL WillieTheWeeper	13.00
3 JL,A:Creeper	12.00
4 JL,A:GreenArrow	10.00
5	10.00
6 V:Sherlock Holmes	10.00
7 IN,A:Luthor.	10.00
8	10.00
9 A:Catwoman.	12.00
Greatest Joker Stories Ever Told:	
1 HC	45.00
1a SC	16.00
The Devil's Advocate HC GN	24.95
GN.	12.95

JONAH HEX
1977–85

1 `Vengeance For A Fallen Gladiator'	45.00
2 `The Lair of the Parrot'	20.00
3 `The Fugitive'	14.00
4 `The Day of Chameleon'	14.00
5 `Welcome to Paradise'	14.00
6 `The Lawman'.	10.00
7 `Son of the Apache'	10.00
8 O:Jonah Hex	9.00
9 BWr(c)	9.00
10 GM(c),`Violence at Vera Cruz'	9.00
11 `The Holdout'	7.00
12 JS(c)	7.00
13 `The Railroad Blaster'	7.00
14 `The Sin Killer'	7.00
15 `Saw Dust and Slow Death'	7.00
16 `The Wyandott Verdict!'	5.00
17	5.00
18	5.00
19 `The Duke of Zarkania!'	5.00
20 `Phantom Stage to William Bend'	5.00
21 `The Buryin'!'	5.00
22 `Requiem For A Pack Rat'	5.00
23 `The Massacre of the Celestials!'	5.00
24 `Minister of the Lord'	5.00
25 `The Widow Maker'	5.00
26 `Death Race to Cholera Bend!'	4.00

Jonah Hex: Riders of the Worm and Such #4 © DC Comics, Inc.

27 'The Wooden Six Gun!' 4.00
28 'Night of the Savage' 4.00
29 'The Innocent' 4.00
30 O:Jonah Hex 4.50
31 A:Arbee Stoneham 4.00
32 A:Arbee Stoneham 4.00
33 'The Crusador'. 4.00
34 'Christmas in an Outlaw Town'. . 4.00
35 'The Fort Charlotte Brigade'. . . . 4.00
36 'Return to Fort Charlotte'. 4.00
37 DAy,A:Stonewall Jackson. 4.00
38 . . . . 4.00
39 'The Vow of a Samurai!'. 4.00
40 DAy 4.00
41 DAy,'Two for the Hangman!' . . . 4.00
42 'Wanted for Murder'. 4.00
43 JKu(c) 4.00
44 JKu(c),DAy 4.00
45 DAy,Jonah gets married. 4.00
46 JKu(c),DAy 4.00
47 DAy,'Doom Rides the Sundown
    Town' 4.00
48 DAy,A:El Diablo 4.00
49 DAy 4.00
50 DAy,'The Hunter' 4.00
51 DAy,'The Comforter' 3.50
52 DAy,'Rescue!' 3.50
53 DAy 3.50
54 . . . . 3.50
55 'Trail of Blood' 3.50
56 DAy,'The Asylum' 3.50
57 B:El Diablo backup story 3.50
58 DAy,'The Treasure of Catfish
    Pond' 3.50
59 DAy,'Night of the White Lotus' . . 3.50
60 DAy,'Domain of the Warlord' . . . 3.50
61 DAy,'In the Lair of the Manchus!' 3.50
62 DAy,'The Belly of the Malay
    Tiger!'. 3.50
63 DAy 3.50
64 DAy,'The Pearl!'. 3.50
65 DAy,'The Vendetta!' 3.50
66 DAy'Requiem for a Coward'. . . . 3.50
67 DAy,'Deadman's Hand!' 3.50
68 DAy,'Gunfight at Gravesboro!' . . 3.50
69 DAy,'The Gauntlet!' 3.50
70 DAy 3.50
71 DAy,'The Masquerades'. 3.50
72 DAy,'Tarantula' 3.50
73 DAy,Jonah in a wheel chair 3.50
74 DAy,A:Railroad Bill. 3.50
75 DAy,JAp,A:Railroad Bill 3.50
76 DAy,Jonah goes to Jail 3.00
77 DAy,'Over the Wall' 3.00

78 DAy,Me Ling returns 3.00
79 DAy,'Duel in the Sand'. 3.00
80 A:Turnbull 3.00
81 thru 89 DAy . . . . @3.00
90 thru 92 . . . . @3.00

JONAH HEX AND OTHER WESTERN TALES
Sept.–Oct., 1979
1 . . . . 2.00
2 NA,ATh,SA,GK 3.00
3 Jan.–Feb., 1980 . . . . 1.75

JONAH HEX: RIDERS OF THE WORM AND SUCH
Vertigo 1995
Mini-Series]
1 R:Ronah Hex 2.95
2 At Wildes West Ranch 2.95
3 History Lesson 2.95
4 I:Autumn Brothers. 2.95
5 V:Big worm, final issue 2.95

JONAH HEX: SHADOWS WEST
Vertigo 1998
1 (of 3) JLd(s),TTn. 3.00
2 JLd(s),TTn 3.00
3 JLd(s),TTn concl. 3.00

JONAH HEX: TWO-GUN MOJO
Vertigo 1993
1 B:JLd(s),TT,SG(i),R:Jonah Hex,
    I:Slow Go Smith 8.00
1a Platinum Ed. 20.00
2 TT,SG(i),D:Slow Go Smith,I:Doc
    Williams,Wild Bill Hickok. 6.00
3 TT,SG(i),Jonah captured. 5.00
4 TT,SG(i),O:Doc Williams. 5.00
5 TT,SG(i),V::Doc Williams. 5.00

JONNI THUNDER
Feb., 1985
1 DG,origin issue. 1.25
2 DG. 1.25
3 DG 1.25

JONNY DOUBLE
DC/Vertigo (July, 1998)
1 . . . . 3.00
2 MCo(c) detective 3.00
3 . . . . 3.00
4 . . . . 3.00

JSA
1999
1 JeR,V:Dark Lord 2.50
2 JeR,AD&Mfm(c),A:Hawkgirl 2.50
3 JeR,AD&MFm(c),V:Dark Lord . . . 2.50
Secret Files #1 . . . . 5.00

JUDGE DREDD
1994–96
1 R:Judge Dredd. 2.50
2 Silicon Dreams. 2.25
3 Terrorists 2.50
4 Mega-City One crisis 2.25
5 Solitary Dredd 2.25
6 V:Richard Magg 2.25
7 . . . . 2.25
8 V:Ministry of Fear 2.25

9 V:Mister Synn. 2.25
10 D:Judge Dredd 2.25
11 Mega-City One Chaos 2.25
12 V:Wally Squad 2.25
13 Block Wars,pt.1 . . . . 2.25
14 Block Wars,pt.2 . . . . 2.25
15 Block Wars,pt.3 . . . . 2.25
16 R:Judge with a Grudge 2.25
17 F:Judge Cadet Lewis,
    Nova Scotia 2.25
18 final issue 2.25
Movie Adaptation 5.95

JUDGE DREDD: LEGENDS OF THE LAW
1994–95
1 Organ Donor,pt.1 . . . . 2.50
2 Organ Donor,pt.2 . . . . 2.25
3 Organ Donor,pt.3 . . . . 2.25
4 Organ Donor,pt.4 . . . . 2.25
5 Trial By Gunfire,pt.1 . . . . 2.25
6 Trial By Gunfire,pt.2 . . . . 2.25
7 JHi(c),Trial By Gunfire,pt.3 . . . . 2.25
8 JBy(s),Fall From Grace,pt.1 . . . . 2.25
9 Fall From Grace,pt.2. . . . . 2.25
10 Fall From Grace,pt.3 . . . . 2.25
11 Dredd of Night,pt.1. . . . . 2.25
12 Dredd of Night,pt.2 . . . . 2.25
13 Dredd of Night,pt.3,final issue . . 2.25

JUNK CULTURE
DC/Vertigo May 1997
1 (of 2) TMK 2.50
2 (of 2) TMK "Deuces Wild" 2.50

Justice, Inc. #1 © DC Comics, Inc.

JUSTICE, INC.
May-June, 1975
1 AMc,JKu(c),O:Avenger 3.00
2 JK 1.25
3 JK 1.25
4 JK,JKu(c),Nov.–Dec.,
    1975 . . . . 1.25

[Mini-Series] 1989
1 PerfectBound 'Trust & Betrayal' . 3.95
2 PerfectBound 3.95

JUSTICE LEAGUE AMERICA
(see JUSTICE LEAGUE INTERNATIONAL)

JUSTICE LEAGUE EUROPE
1989–93
1 BS,A:Wonder Woman 4.00
2 BS,Search for Nazi-Killer 3.00
3 BS,A:Jack O'Lantern,
   Queen Bee 2.50
4 BS,V:Queen Bee 2.50
5 JRu,BS,Metamorpho's Baby,
   A:Sapphire Starr 2.50
6 BS,V:Injustice League 2.00
7 BS,Teasdale Imperative#2,
   A:JLA 2.00
8 BS,Teasdale Imperative#4,
   A:JLA 2.00
9 BS,ANi,A:Superman 2.00
10 BS,V:Crimson Fox 2.00
11 BS,C:DocMagnus&Metal Men . . 2.00
12 BS,A:Metal Men. 2.00
13 BS,V:One-Eyed Cat, contd
   from JLA #37 . . . . 2.00
14 I:VCR 2.00
15 BS,B:Extremists Vector saga,
   V:One-Eyed Cat,A:BlueJay. . . . 2.00
16 BS,A:Rocket Reds, Blue Jay . . . 2.25
17 BS,JLI in Another Dimension . . . 2.25
18 BS,Extremists Homeworld 2.25
19 BS,E:Extremist Vector Saga. . . . 2.25
20 MR,I:Beefeater,V:Kilowog 1.75
21 MR,JRu,New JLE embassy in
   London,A:Kilowog 1.50
22 MR,JLE's Cat stolen 1.50
23 BS,O:Crimson Fox. 1.50
24 BS,Worms in London. 1.50
25 BS,V:Worms 1.50
26 BS,V:Starro 1.50
27 BS,JLE V:JLE,A:JLA,V:Starro . . 1.50
28 BS, JLE V:JLE,A:J'onnJ'onzz,
   V:Starro 1.50
29 BS,Breakdowns #2,V:Global
   Guardians 1.75
30 Breakdowns#4,V:J.O'Lantern. . . 1.50
31 Breakdowns #6,War of the
   Gods tie-in 1.50
32 Breakdowns #8,A:Chief(Doom
   Patrol) 1.50
33 Breakdowns #10,Lobo vs.
   Despero. 1.50
34 Breakdowns #12,Lobo
   vs.Despero. 1.50
35 Breakdowns #14,V:Extremists,
   D:Silver Sorceress 1.50
36 Breakdowns #16,All Quit 1.50
37 B:New JLE,I:Deconstructo 1.75
38 V:Deconstructo,A:Batman 1.50
39 V:Deconstructo,A:Batman 1.50
40 J:Hal Jordan,A:Metamorpho. . . . 1.50
41 A:Metamorpho,Wond.Woman . . . 1.50
42 A:Wonder Woman,V:Echidna . . . 1.50
43 V:Amos Fortune. 1.50
44 V:Amos Fortune. 1.50
45 Red Winter#1,V:Rocket Reds. . . 1.50
46 Red Winter#2 . . . . 1.50
47 Red Winter#3,V:Sonar. 1.50
48 Red Winter#4,V:Sonar. 1.50
49 Red Winter #5,V:Sonar 1.50
50 Red Winter#6,Double-sized,
   V:Sonar,J:Metamorpho 3.25
Ann.#1 A:Global Guardians 2.00
Ann.#2 MR,CS,ArmageddonPt.7. . . 3.00
Ann.#3 RT(i),Eclipso tie-in 2.75
Justice League Spectacular JLE(c)
   New Direction. 1.50

Becomes:
Justice League International
[2nd Series]

JUSTICE LEAGUE [INTERNATIONAL]
[1st Series] 1987
1 KM,TA,New Team,I:Max. Lord. . . 6.00
2 KM,AG,A:BlueJay & Silver
   Sorceress. 4.00
3 KM,AG,J:Booster Gold, V:Rocket
   Lords 3.00
3a Superman Logo 60.00
4 KM,AG,V:Royal Flush. 3.00
5 KM,AG,A:The Creeper 3.00
6 KM,AG,A:The Creeper 3.00
Becomes:
JUSTICE LEAGUE INTERNATIONAL
1988–89
7 KM,AG,L:Dr.Fate,Capt.Marvel,
   J:Rocket Red,Capt.Atom
   (Double size) 3.00
8 KM,AG,KG,Move to Paris Embassy,
   I:C.Cobert,B.U.Glob.Guardians. 2.50
9 KM,AG,KG,Millenium,Rocket
   Red-Traitor. 2.50
10 KG,KM,AG,A:G.L.Corps,
   Superman,I:G'Nort 2.50
11 KM,AG,V:Construct,C:Metron. . . 2.50
12 KG,KM,AG,O:Max Lord 2.50
13 KG,AG,A:Suicide Squad 2.50
14 SL,AG,J:Fire&Ice,L:Ron,
   I:Manga Kahn. 2.50
15 SL,AG,V:Magna Kahn 2.00
16 KM,AG,I:Queen Bee 2.00
17 KM,AG,V:Queen Bee. 2.00
18 KM,AG,MPn,A:Lobo,Guy Gardner
   (bonus book) 3.00
19 KM,JRu,A:Lobo vs.Guy Gardner,
   J:Hawkman & Hawkwoman . . . 3.00
20 KM,JRu(i),A:Lobo,G.Gardner . . . 2.00
21 KM,JRu(i),A:Lobo vs.Guy
   Gardner 2.00
22 KM,JRu,Imskian Soldiers. 2.00
23 KM,JRu,I:Injustice League 2.00
24 KM,JRu,DoubleSize + Bonus
   Bk#13,I:JusticeLeagueEurope . 4.00

Justice League International #11
© DC Comics Inc.

25 KM(c),JRu(i),Vampire story 2.00
Ann.#1 BWg,DG,CR. 2.00
Ann.#2 BWg,JRu,A:Joker. 3.00
Ann.#3 KM(c),JRu,JLI Embassies. . 2.50
Spec.#1 Mr.Miracle. 2.00
Spec.#2,The Huntress 2.95
TPB new beginning,rep.#1-#7. . . . 12.95
TPB The Secret Gospel of Maxwell
   Lord Rep. #8-#12, Ann.#1 . . 12.95
Becomes:
JUSTICE LEAGUE AMERICA
1989–96
26 KM(c),JRu(i),Possessed Blue
   Beetle 2.50
27 KM(c),JRu,DG(i),'Exorcist',
   (c)tribute. 2.00
28 KM(c),JRu(i), A:Black Hand 2.00
29 KM(c),JRu(i),V:Mega-Death 2.00
30 KM(c),BWg,JRu,J:Huntress,
   D:Mega-Death 2.00
31 ANi,AH,JRu,Teasdale Imperative
   #1,N:Fire,Ice,A:JLE 3.00
32 ANi,AH,Teasdale Imperative
   #3, A:JLE 3.00
33 ANi,AH,GuyGardner vs.Kilowog. 2.50
34 ANi,AH,`Club JLI','A:Aquaman . . 2.50
35 ANi,JRu,AH,A:Aquaman 2.50
36 Gnort vs. Scarlet Skier. 2.00
37 ANi,AH,L:Booster Gold 2.00
38 JRu,AH,R:Desparo,D:Steel 2.00
39 JRu,AH,V:Desparo,D:Mr.Miracle,
   Robot. 2.00
40 AH,Mr.Miracle Funeral 2.00
41 MMc,MaxForce 2.00
42 MMc,J:L-Ron. 2.00
43 AH,KG,The Man Who Knew Too
   Much #1. . . . . 2.00
44 AH,Man Knew Too Much #2. . . 2.00
45 AH,MJ,JRu,Guy & Ice's 2nd
   date 2.00
46 Glory Bound #1,I:Gen.Glory. . . . 2.00
47 Glory Bound #2,J:Gen.Glory . . . 2.00
48 Glory Bound #3,V:DosUberbot. . 2.00
49 Glory Bound #4 . . . . 2.00
50 Glory Bound #5 (double size). . . 2.50
51 JRu,AH,V:BlackHand,
   R:Booster Gold. 2.00
52 TVE,Blue Beetle Vs. Guy Gardner
   A:Batman 2.00
53 Breakdowns #1, A:JLE. 2.00
54 Breakdowns #3, A:JLE. 2.00
55 Breakdowns #5,V:Global
   Guardians 2.00
56 Breakdowns #7, U.N. revokes
   JLA charter 2.00
57 Breakdowns #9,A:Lobo,
   V:Despero 2.00
58 BS,Breakdowns #11,Lobo
   Vs.Despero. 2.00
59 BS,Breakdowns #13,
   V:Extremists. 2.00
60 KM,TA,Breakdowns #15,
   End of J.L.A.. . . . . 2.00
61 DJu,I:Weapons Master,B:New
   JLA Line-up,I:Bloodwynd 3.00
62 DJu,V:Weapons Master 2.00
63 DJu,V:Starbreaker 2.00
64 DJu,V:Starbreaker 2.00
65 DJu,V:Starbreaker 2.00
66 DJu,Superman V:Guy Gardner . 2.00
67 DJu,Bloodwynd mystery. 2.00
68 DJu,V:Alien Land Baron. 2.00
69 DJu, Doomsday Pt.1-A 10.00
69a 2nd printing 2.00
70 DJu,Funeral for a Friend#1 . . . . 6.00
70a 2nd printing 2.00
71 DJu,J:Agent Liberty,Black Condor,
   The Ray, Wonder Woman 5.00
71a Newsstand ed. 2.00

DC COMICS

Justice League America #42
© DC Comics, Inc.

71b 2nd Printing 1.50
72 DJu,A:Green Arrow,Black
Canary,Atom,B:Destiny's Hand . 4.00
73 DJu,Destiny's Hand #2 . . . . . . 3.00
74 DJu,Destiny's Hand #3 . . . . . . 2.00
75 DJu,E:Destiny's Hand #4,Martian
Manhunter as Bloodwynd 2.00
76 DJu,Blood Secrets#1,
V:Weaponmaster 1.50
77 DJu,Blood Secrets#2,
V:Weaponmaster 1.50
78 MC,V:The Extremists 1.50
79 MC,V:The Extremists 1.50
80 KWe,N:Booster Gold 1.50
81 KWe,A:Captain Atom 1.50
82 KWe,A:Captain Atom 1.50
83 KWe,V:Guy Gardner 1.50
84 KWe,A:Ice 1.75
85 KWe,V:Frost Giants 1.75
86 B:Cults of the Machine. 1.75
87 N:Booster Gold 1.75
88 E:Cults of the Machine. 1.75
89 Judgement Day#1,
V:Overmaster. 1.75
90 Judgement Day#4 . . . . 1.50
91 Aftershocks #1. . . . . 1.75
92 Zero Hour,I:Triumph. 1.75
93 Power Girl and child 1.50
94 Scarabus. 1.50
95 . . . . 1.50
96 Funeral 1.50
97 I:Judgment 1.50
98 J:Blue Devil, Ice Maiden 1.50
99 V:New Metahumes 1.50
100 GJ,Woj,V:Lord Havok,dbl.size . 3.00
100a Collector's Edition 4.00
101 GJ,Woj,Way of the
Warrior,pt.2 . . . . 1.75
102 Way of the Warrior,pt.5 . . . . . . 1.75
103 . . . . 1.75
104 F:Metamorpho 1.75
105 GJ,Woj,Underworld
Unleashed tie-in 1.75
106 GJ,Woj,Underworld
Unleashed tie-in 1.75
107 GJ,Woj,secret of Power
Girl's son 1.75
108 GJ,Woj,The Arcana revealed . . 1.75
109. . . . . 1.75
110 GJ,Woj,V:El Diablo. 1.75
111 GJ,Woj,The Purge,pt.1 (of 3) . . 1.75
112 GJ,Woj,The Purge,pt.2 (of 3) . . 1.75
113 GJ,Woj,The Purge,pt.3 (of 3) . . 1.75
Ann.#4 KM(c),I:JL Antartica 3.00

Ann.#5 MR,KM,DJu,Armageddon . 3.00
Ann.#5a 2nd Printing,silver. 2.00
Ann.#6 DC,Eclipso 2.75
Ann.#7 I:Terrorsmith 2.75
Ann.#8 Elseworlds Story. 3.25
Ann.#9 Year One Annual 3.50
Ann.#10 CPr(s),SCi,NNa,"Legends
of the Dead Earth" 2.95
Justice League Spectacular DJu,
JLA(c) New Direction 2.00
Archives Vol. 4 . . . . 50.00

JUSTICE LEAGUE OF AMERICA: THE NAIL
June 1998
Elseworlds
1 world without a Superman 5.00
2 AID,MFm,Robin & Batgirl dead . . 5.00
3 AID,MFm,concl. 5.00

JUSTICE LEAGUE INTERNATIONAL
[2nd Regular Series] 1993–94
Prev: Justice League Europe
51 Aztec Cult 1.50
52 V:Aztec Cult. 1.50
53 R:Fox's Husband 1.50
54 RoR,I:Creator 1.50
55 RoR,A:Creator. 1.50
56 RoR,V:Terrorists 1.50
57 RoR,V:Terrorists 1.50
58 RoR,V:Aliens 1.50
59 RoR,A:Guy Gardner 1.50
60 GJ(s),RoR 1.75
61 GJ(s),V:Godfrey. 1.75
62 GJ(s),N:Metamorpho,V:Godfrey . 1.75
63 GJ(s),In Africa 1.75
64 GJ(s),V:Cadre 1.75
65 JudgmentDay#3,V:Overmaster . 1.75
66 JudgmentDay#6,V:Overmaster . 1.75
67 Aftershock #3 . . . . 1.75
68 Zero Hour, Final Issue 1.50
Ann.#4 Bloodlines#9,I:Lionheart . . 2.75
Ann.#5 . . . . 3.25
Ann.#6 Elseworlds Story. 2.95

JUSTICE LEAGUE [INTERNATIONAL] QUARTERLY
1990–94
1 I:Conglomerate. 4.00
2 MJ(i),R:Mr.Nebula. 3.50
3 V:Extremists,C:Original JLA 3.50
4 KM(c),MR,CR,A:Injustice
League. 3.00
5 KM(c),Superhero Attacks 3.00
6 EB,Elongated Man,B.U.Global
Guardians,Powergirl,B.Beetle . . 3.00
7 EB,DH,MR.Global Guardians . . . 3.00
8 . . . . 3.00
9 DC,F:Power Girl,Booster Gold . . 3.50
10 F:Flash,Fire & Ice 3.50
11 F:JL Women 3.50
12 F:Conglomerate. 3.50
13 V:Ultraa 7.00
14 MMi(c),PuK(s),F:Captain Atom,Blue
Beetle,Nightshade,Thunderbolt. 3.75
15 F:Praxis. 3.50
16 F:Gen Glory. 3.50
17 Final Issue. 3.50

JUSTICE LEAGUE: A MIDSUMMER'S NIGHTMARE
1996
1 (of 3) MWa(s),FaN,JJ,DaR, ... 5.00
2 MWa(s),FaN,JJ,DaR,Batman &
Superman attempt to free
other heroes. 4.00
3 MWa&FaN(s), Know-Man's plot
revealed, finale . . . . @4.00
TPB Rep. 3 issues 8.95

JUSTICE LEAGUE OF AMERICA
Oct.–Nov., 1960
1 MSy,I&O:Despero 3,200.00
2 MSy,A:Merlin 750.00
3 MSy,I&O:Kanjar Ro. 650.00
4 MSy,J:Green Arrow. 450.00
5 MSy,I&O:Dr.Destiny 400.00
6 MSy,Prof. Fortune. 350.00
7 MSy,Cosmic Fun-House 350.00
8 MSy,For Sale-Justice League . 350.00
9 MSy,O:JLA 450.00
10 MSy,I:Felix Faust 300.00
11 MSy,A:Felix Faust 225.00
12 MSy,I&O:Dr Light. 225.00
13 MSy,A:Speedy. 225.00
14 MSy,J:Atom 225.00
15 MSy,V:Untouchable Aliens . . . 200.00
16 MSy,I:Maestro 175.00
17 MSy,A:Tornado Tyrant 175.00
18 MSy,V:Terrane,Ocana 175.00
19 MSy,A:Dr.Destiny. 175.00
20 MSy,V:Metal Being. 175.00
21 MSy,R:JSA,1st S.A Hourman,
Dr.Fate 350.00
22 MSy,R:JSA 325.00
23 MSy,I:Queen Bee. 100.00
24 MSy,A:Adam Strange 100.00
25 MSy,I:Draad,the Conqueror . . 100.00
26 MSy,A:Despero 100.00
27 MSy,V:I,A:Amazo. 100.00
28 MSy,I:Headmaster Mind,
A:Robin 100.00
29 MSy,I:Crime Syndicate,A:JSA,
1st S.A. Starman 150.00
30 MSy,V:Crime Syndicate,
A:JSA. 125.00
31 MSy,J:Hawkman 100.00
32 MSy,I&O:Brain Storm. 75.00
33 MSy,I:Endless One 60.00

Justice League of America #15
© DC Comics, Inc.

34 MSy,A:Dr.Destiny,Joker 65.00	
35 MSy,A:Three Demons 60.00	
36 MSy,A:Brain Storm,	
Handicap story 60.00	
37 MSy,A:JSA,x-over,	
1st S.A.Mr.Terrific 100.00	
38 MSy,A:JSA,Mr.Terrific. 100.00	
39 Giant 110.00	
40 MSy,A:Shark,Penguin 60.00	
41 MSy,I:Key 60.00	
42 MSy,A:Metamorpho 50.00	
43 MSy,I:Royal Flush Gang 50.00	
44 MSy,A:Unimaginable 50.00	
45 MSy,I:Shaggy Man. 50.00	
46 MSy,A:JSA,Blockbuster,Solomon	
Grundy,1st S.A.Sandman . . . 110.00	
47 MSy,A:JSA,Blockbuster,	
Solomon Grundy 50.00	
48 Giant. 60.00	
49 MSy,A:Felix Faust 40.00	
50 MSy,A:Robin 40.00	
51 MSy,A:Zatanna,Elong.Man. . . . 40.00	
52 MSy,A:Robin,Lord of Time . . . 40.00	
53 MSy,A:Hawkgirl 40.00	
54 MSy,A:Royal Flush Gang 40.00	
55 MSy,A:JSA,E-2 Robin 60.00	
56 MSy,A:JSA,E-2 Robin 45.00	
57 MSy,Brotherhood 40.00	
58 Reprint(giant size). 45.00	
59 MSy,V:Impossibles. 40.00	
60 MSy,A:Queen Bee,Batgirl. . . . 40.00	
61 MSy,A:Lex Luthor,Penguin . . . 40.00	
62 MSy,V:Bulleters 30.00	
63 MSy,A:Key. 30.00	
64 DD,I:Red Tornado,A:JSA 32.00	
65 DD,A:JSA 32.00	
66 DD,A:Demmy Gog. 30.00	
67 MSy,Giant reprints. 45.00	
68 DD,V:Choas Maker 30.00	
69 DD,L:Wonder Woman 28.00	
70 DD,A:Creeper 25.00	
71 DD,L:J'onn J'onnz 25.00	
72 DD,A:Hawkgirl 25.00	
73 DD,A:JSA 25.00	
74 DD,D:Larry Lance,A:JSA 25.00	
75 DD,J:Black Canary 25.00	
76 Giant,MA,two page pin-up 25.00	
77 DD,A:Joker,L:Snapper Carr . . . 22.00	
78 DD,R:Vigilante 22.00	
79 DD,A:Vigilante 22.00	
80 DD,A:Tomar-Re,Guardians. . . . 22.00	
81 DD,V:Jest-Master. 22.00	
82 DD,A:JSA 20.00	
83 DD,A:JSA,Spectre 20.00	
84 DD,Devil in Paradise 20.00	
85 Giant reprint. 30.00	
86 DD,V:Zapper 20.00	
87 DD,A:Zatanna,I:Silver	
Sorceress,Blue Jay. 22.00	
88 DD,A:Mera. 22.00	
89 DD,A:Harlequin Ellis,	
(i.e. Harlan Ellison) 22.00	
90 Cl(c),MA(ci),DD,V:Pale People. 22.00	
91 DD,A:JSA,V:Solomon Grundy . 22.00	
92 DD,A:JSA,V:Solomon Grundy . 20.00	
93 DD:A:JSA,(giant size) 25.00	
94 DD,NA,O:Sandman,rep.	
Adventure #40 . . . . 90.00	
95 DD,rep.More Fun Comics #67,	
All American Comics #25 . . . . 30.00	
96 DD,I:Starbreaker 28.00	
97 DD,MS,O:JLA 25.00	
98 DD,A:Sargon,Gold.Age reps . . 22.00	
99 DD,G.A. reps. 22.00	
100 DD,A:JSA,Metamorpho,	
R:7 Soldiers of Victory 35.00	
101 DD,A:JSA,7 Soldiers 17.00	
102 DD,DG,A:JSA,7 Soldiers	
D:Red Tornado. 17.00	
103 DD,DG,Halloween issue,	
A:Phantom Stranger. 12.00	

104 DD,DG,A:Shaggy Man,	
Hector Hammond 12.00	
105 DD,DG,J:ElongatedMan. 12.00	
106 DD,DG,J:RedTornado 12.00	
107 DD,DG,I:Freedom Fighters,	
A:JSA. 15.00	
108 DD,DG,A:JSA,	
Freedom Fighters 15.00	
109 DD,DG,L:Hawkman 12.00	
110 DD,DG,A:John Stewart,	
Phantom Stranger 25.00	
111 DD,DG,I:Injustice Gang 25.00	
112 DD,DG,A:Amazo 25.00	
113 DD,DG,A:JSA 25.00	
114 DD,DG,A:SnapperCarr. 25.00	
115 DD,FMc,A:J'onnJ'onnz 25.00	
116 DD,FMc,I:Golden Eagle 25.00	
117 DD,FMc,R:Hawkman 6.00	
118 DD,FMc. 6.00	
119 DD,FMc,A:Hawkgirl 6.00	
120 DD,FMc,A:Adam Strange. . . . 6.00	
121 DD,FMc,W:Adam Strange . . . 6.00	
122 DD,FMc,JLA casebook story	
V:Dr.Light. 6.00	
123 DD,FMc,A:JSA 7.00	
124 DD,FMc,A: JSA 7.00	
125 DD,FMc,A:Two-Face 6.00	
126 DD,FMc,A:Two-Face 6.00	
127 DD,FMc,V:Anarchist. 6.00	
128 DD,FMc,J:W.Woman 6.00	
129 DD,FMC,D:RedTornado. 6.00	
130 DD,FMc,O:JLASatellite 5.00	
131 DD,FMc,V:Queen Bee,Sonar . 5.00	
132 DD,FMc,A:Supergirl. 5.00	
133 DD,FMc,A:Supergirl. 5.00	
134 DD,FMc,A:Supergirl. 5.00	
135 DD,FMc,A:Squad.of Justice . . 5.00	
136 DD,FMc,A:E-2Joker. 9.00	
137 DD,FMc,Superman vs.	
Capt. Marvel. 12.00	
138 NA(c),DD,FMc,A:Adam	
Strange 5.00	
139 NA(c),DD,FMc,A:AdamStrange,	
Phantom Stranger,doub.size. . . 7.00	
140 DD,FMc,Manhunters 7.00	
141 DD,FMc,Manhunters 7.00	
142 DD,FMc,F:Aquaman,Atom,	
Elongated Man. 7.00	
143 DD,FMc,V:Injustice Gang. . . . 7.00	
144 DD,FMc,O:JLA 7.00	
145 DD,FMc,A:Phant.Stranger . . . 7.00	
146 J:Red Tornado,Hawkgirl. 7.00	
147 DD,FMc,A:Legion 7.00	
148 DD,FMc,A:Legion 7.00	

Justice League of America #90
© DC Comics Inc.

149 DD,FMc,A:Dr.Light. 7.00	
150 DD,FMc,A:Dr.Light. 7.00	
151 DD,FMc,A:Amos Fortune 6.00	
152 DD,FMc. 6.00	
153 GT,FMc,I:Ultraa 6.00	
154 MK(c),DD,FMc. 6.00	
155 DD,FMc. 6.00	
156 DD,FMc. 6.00	
157 DD,FMc,W:Atom 6.00	
158 DD,FMc,A:Ultraa 6.00	
159 DD,FMc,A:JSA,Jonah Hex,	
Enemy Ace 5.00	
160 DD,FMc,A:JSA,Jonah Hex,	
Enemy Ace 5.00	
161 DD,FMc,J:Zatanna. 5.00	
162 DD,FMc. 5.00	
163 DD,FMc,V:Mad Maestro. 5.00	
164 DD,FMc,V:Mad Maestro. 5.00	
165 DD,FMc. 5.00	
166 DD,FMc,V:Secret Society. . . . 5.00	
167 DD,FMc,V:Secret Society. . . . 5.00	
168 DD,FMc,V:Secret Society. . . . 5.00	
169 DD,FMc,A:Ultraa 5.00	
170 DD,FMc,A:Ultraa 5.00	
171 DD,FMc,A:JSA,D:Mr.Terrific . . 5.00	
172 DD,FMc,A:JSA,D:Mr.Terrific . . 5.00	
173 DD,FMc,A:Black Lightning . . . 5.00	
174 DD,FMc,A:Black Lightning . . . 5.00	
175 DD,FMc,V:Dr.Destiny 5.00	
176 DD,FMc,V:Dr.Destiny 4.00	
177 DD,FMc,V:Desparo 4.00	
178 JSn(c),DD,FMc,V:Desparo 4.00	
179 JSn(c),DD,FMc,J:Firestorm . . . 4.00	
180 JSn(c),DD,FMc,V:Satin Satan . 4.00	
181 DD,FMc,L:Gr.Arrow,V:Star 5.00	
182 DD,FMc,A:Green Arrow,	
V:Felix Faust 5.00	
183 JSn(c),DD,FMc,A:JSA,	
NewGods. 5.00	
184 GP,FMc,A:JSA,NewGods. 5.00	
185 JSn(c),GP,FMc,A:JSA,	
New Gods 5.00	
186 FMc,GP,V:Shaggy Man 4.00	
187 DH,FMc,N:Zatanna. 4.00	
188 DH,FMc,V:Proteus. 4.00	
189 BB(c),RB,FMc,V:Starro 4.00	
190 BB(c),RB,LMa,V:Starro 4.00	
191 RB,V:Amazo 4.00	
192 GP,O:Red Tornado. 4.00	
193 GP,RB,JOy,I:AllStarSquad 4.00	
194 GP,V:Amos Fortune 3.00	
195 GP,A:JSA,V:Secret Society . . . 3.00	
196 GP,RT,A:JSA,V:Secret Soc. . . . 3.00	
197 GP,RT,KP,A:JSA,V:Secret	
Society 3.00	
198 DH,BBr,A:J.Hex,BatLash 3.00	
199 GP(c),DH,BBr,A:Jonah Hex,	
BatLash 3.00	
200 GP,DG,BB (1st Batman),PB,TA,	
BBr,GK,CI,JAp,JKu,Anniv.,A:Adam	
Strange,Phantom Stranger,	
J:Green Arrow 5.00	
201 GP(c),DH,A:Ultraa 2.00	
202 GP(c),DH,BBr,JLA in Space. . . 2.00	
203 GP(c),DH,RT,V:Royal	
Flush Gang 2.00	
204 GP(c),DH,RT,V:R.FlushGang . . 2.00	
205 GP(c),DH,RT,V:R.FlushGang . . 2.00	
206 DH,RT,A:Demons 3 . . . . 2.00	
207 GP(c),DH,RT,A:All Star	
Squadron,JSA 2.50	
208 GP(c),DH,RT,A:All Star	
Squadron,JSA 2.50	
209 GP(c),DH,RT,A:All Star	
Squadron,JSA 2.50	
210 RB,RT,JLA casebook #1 . . . . . 2.00	
211 RB,RT,JLA casebook #2 . . . . . 2.00	
212 GP(c),RB,PCu,RT,c.book #3 . . 2.00	
213 GP(c),DH,RT 2.00	
214 GP(c),DH,RT,I:Siren Sist.h'd . . 2.00	
215 GP(c),DH,RT 2.00	

Justice League of America #242
© DC Comics, Inc.

216 DH. 2.00
217 GP(c),RT(i) 2.00
218 RT(i),A:Prof.Ivo 2.00
219 GP(c),RT(i),A:JSA 2.25
220 GP(c),RT,O:Bl.Canary,A:JSA . . 2.25
221 Beasts #1 . . . . 2.00
222 RT(i),Beasts #2 . . . . 2.00
223 RT(i),Beasts #3 . . . . 2.00
224 DG(i),V:Paragon 2.00
225 V:Hellrazor. 2.00
226 FMc(i),V:Hellrazor 2.00
227 V:Hellrazor,I:Lord Claw 2.00
228 GT,AN,R:J'onnJonzz,War of
   the Worlds,pt.1 . . . . 2.00
229 War of the Worlds,pt.2 . . . . . . 2.00
230 War of the Worlds conc.. . . . . 2.00
231 RB(i),A:JSA,Supergirl. 2.25
232 A:JSA Supergirl 2.25
233 New JLA takes over book,
   B:Rebirth,F:Vibe. 2.00
234 F:Vixen 2.00
235 F:Steel. 2.00
236 E:Rebirth,F:Gypsy 2.00
237 A:Superman,Flash,WWoman . . 2.00
238 A:Superman,Flash,WWoman . . 2.00
239 V:Ox 2.00
240 MSy,TMd 2.00
241 GT,V:Amazo 2.00
242 GT,V:Amazo,Mask(Toy tie-in)
   insert 2.00
243 GT,L:Aquaman,V:Amazo 2.00
244 JSon,Crisis,A:InfinityInc,JSA . . 2.00
245 LMc,Crisis,N:Steel 2.00
246 LMc,JLA leaves Detroit 2.00
247 LMc,JLA returns to old HQ. . . . 2.00
248 LMc,F:J'onn J'onzz 2.00
249 LMc,Lead-in to Anniv. 2.00
250 LMc,Anniv.,A:Superman,
   Green Lantern,Green Arrow,
   Black Canary,R:Batman 2.75
251 LMc,V:Despero 1.75
252 LMc,V:Despero,N:Elongated
   Man 1.75
253 LMc,V:Despero 1.75
254 LMc,V:Despero 1.75
255 LMc,O:Gypsy. 1.75
256 LMc,Gypsy. 1.75
257 LMc,A:Adam,L:Zatanna 1.75
258 LMc,Legends x-over,D:Vibe . . 1.75
259 LMc,Legends x-over 1.75
260 LMc,Legends x-over,D:Steel . . 1.75
261 LMc,Legends,final issue. 4.00
Ann.#1 DG(i),A:Sandman 3.00
Ann.#2 I:NewJLA 2.00
Ann.#3 MG(i),Crisis 2.00

JUSTICE LEAGUE
TASK FORCE
1993–96
1 F:Mart.Manhunter,Nightwing,
   Aquaman,Flash,Gr.Lantern. . . . 2.00
2 V:Count Glass,Blitz. 1.75
3 V:Blitz,Count Glass. 1.75
4 DG,F:Gypsy,A:Lady Shiva 1.75
5 JAl,Knightquest:Crusade,F:Bronze
   Tiger,Green Arrow,Gypsy 2.00
6 JAl,Knightquest:Search,F:Bronze
   Tiger,Green Arrow,Gypsy 1.75
7 PDd(s),F:Maxima,Wonder Woman,
   Dolphin,Gypsy,Vixen,V:Luta . . . 1.75
8 PDd(s),SaV,V:Amazons 1.75
9 GrL,V:Wildman. 1.75
10 Purification Plague#1. . . . . 1.75
11 Purification Plague#2. . . . . 1.75
12 Purification Plague#3. . . . . 1.75
13 Jugdement Day#2,
   V:Overmaster. 1.75
14 Jugdement Day#5,
   V:Overmaster. 1.75
15 Aftershocks #2. . . . . 1.75
16 Zero Hour,A:Triumph 1.75
17 Savage 1.50
18 Savage 1.50
19 Martian Manhunter. 1.50
20 Savage Legacy,pt.4 . . . . 1.50
21 F:Martian Manhunter 1.50
22 F:Triumph 1.50
23 V:Vampire 1.50
24 F:Von Mauler, Gypsy 1.50
25 A:Impulse & Damage, V:Mystek. . 1.75
26 Cut Day 1.75
27 F:L-Ron. 1.75
28 Triumph vs. Manhunter 1.75
29 A:Glenn Gammeron. 1.75
30 Underworld Unleashed tie-in . . . 1.75
31 Despero on trial 1.75
32 Despero vs. terrorists. 1.75
33 . . . . 1.75
34 On Earth, or Skartaris? 1.75
35 A:Warlord Travis Morgan 1.75

JUSTICE RIDERS
1999
1-shot, Elseworlds 6.00

JUSTICE SOCIETY
OF AMERICA
[Limited Series]
April–Nov., 1991
1 B:Veng.From Stars,A:Flash. 2.00
2 A:BlackCanary,V:Solomon Grundy,
   C:G.A.Green Lantern. 1.75
3 A:G.A.Green Lantern,Black Canary,
   V:Sol.Grundy 1.75
4 A:G.A.Hawkman,C:G.A.Flash . . . 1.75
5 A:G.A.Hawkman,Flash 1.75
6 FMc(i),A:Bl.Canary,G.A.Gr.Lantern,
   V:Sol.Grundy,V.Savage. 1.75
7 JSA united,V:Vandal Savage . . . 1.75
8 E:Veng.FromStar,V:V.Savage,
   Solomon Grundy 1.75
Spec.#1 DR,MG,End of JSA. 2.00

[Regular Series] 1992–93
1 V:The New Order. 1.75
2 V:Ultra Gen 1.50
3 R:Ultra-Humanite 1.50
4 V:Ultra-Humanite 1.50
5 V:Ultra-Humanite 1.50
6 F:Johnny Thunderbolt. 1.50
7 ..Or give me Liberty 1.50
8 Pyramid Scheme 1.50
9 V:Kulak. 1.50
10 V:Kulak,final issue 1.50

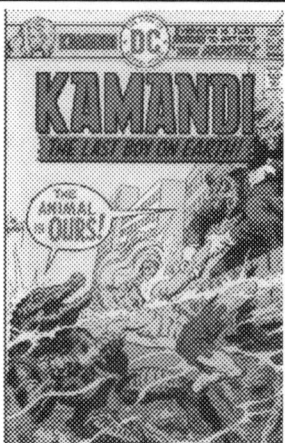

Kamandi, The Last Boy on Earth #36
© DC Comics, Inc.

KAMANDI, THE LAST
BOY ON EARTH
Oct.–Nov., 1972
1 JK,O:Kamandi 30.00
2 JK 20.00
3 JK 8.00
4 JK,I:Prince Tuftan. 8.00
5 JK 8.00
6 JK 8.00
7 JK 7.00
8 JK 7.00
9 JK 7.00
10 JK 7.00
11 JK 7.00
12 JK 7.00
13 thru 24 JK . . . . @6.00
25 thru 28 JK . . . . @3.00
29 A:Superman 3.00
30 JK 3.00
31 . . . . 3.00
32 Double size 4.00
33 thru 57 . . . . @3.00
58 A:Karate Kid 3.00
59 JSn,A:Omac, Sept.–Oct,1978 . . 5.00

KAMANDI: AT
EARTH'S END
[Mini-Series] 1993
1 R:Kamandi 2.00
2 V:Kingpin,Big Q 2.00
3 A:Sleeper Zom,Saphira. 2.00
4 A:Superman 2.00
5 A:Superman,V:Ben Boxer. 2.00
6 final issue 2.00

KARATE KID
March-April, 1976
1 I:Iris Jacobs,A:Legion 4.00
2 A:Major Disaster. 3.00
3 thru 10 . . . . @3.00
11 A:Superboy/Legion 3.00
12 A:Superboy/Legion 3.00
13 A:Superboy/Legion 3.00
14 A:Robin. 3.00
15 July-Aug., 1978 . . . . 3.00

KENTS, THE
1997
1 (of 12) JOs(s),TT,MiB 2.50
2 JOs(s),TT,MiB, tragedy strikes . . 2.50

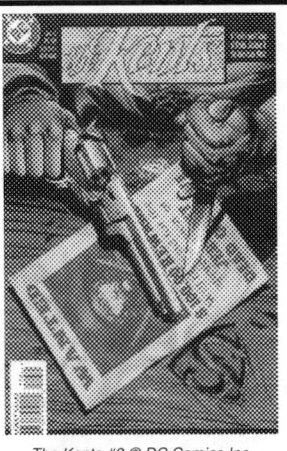

The Kents #9 © DC Comics Inc.

3 JOs,TT,MiB,Jed & Nate Kent . . . 2.50
4 JOs,TT,MiB,Bleeding Kansas,
concl. 2.50
5 JOs,TT,Brother vs.Brother pt.1 . 2.50
6 JOs,TT,Brother vs.Brother pt.2 . 2.50
7 JOs,TT,MiB,Quantrill, Wild
Bill Hickock. 2.50
8 JOs, ... 2.50
9 JOs,TMd,To the Stars
by Hard Ways,pt.1 . . . . 2.50
10 JOs,TMd,To the Stars,pt.2 . . . . 2.50
11 JOs,TMd,To the Stars,pt.3 . . . . 2.50
12 JOs,TMd,To the Stars,pt.4 . . . . 2.50

KID ETERNITY
1991
1 GMo(s),DFg,O:Kid Eternity 5.50
2 GMo(s),DFg,A:Mr.Keeper 5.50
3 GMo(s),DFg,True Origin revealed,
final issue. 5.50

KID ETERNITY
Vertigo 1993–94
1 B:ANo(s),SeP,R:Kid Eternity,
A:Mdm.Blavatsky,Hemlock 2.75
2 SeP,A:Sigmund Freud,Carl Jung,
A:Malocchio 2.50
3 SeP,A:Malocchio,I:Dr.Pathos. . . . 2.25
4 SeP,A:Neal Cassady. 2.25
5 SeP,In Cyberspace. 2.25
6 SeP,A:Dr.Pathos,Marilyn
Monroe 2.25
7 SeP,I:Infinity 2.25
8 SeP,In Insane Asylum. 2.25
9 SeP,Asylum,A:Dr.Pathos. 2.25
10 SeP,Small Wages 2.25
11 ANi(s),I:Slap 2.25
12 SeP,A:Slap 2.25
13 SeP,Date in Hell,pt.1 . . . . 2.25
14 SeP,Date in Hell,pt.2 . . . . 2.25
15 SeP,Date in Hell,pt.3 . . . . 2.25
16 SeP,The Zone 2.25

KILL YOUR BOYFRIEND
Vertigo 1995, 1999
GNv PBd(c) (1995). 4.95
1-shot GMo (1999) 6.00

KINGDOM, THE
1998
1 (of 2) MWa,AOl. 3.00
2 MWa,MZ,JhB,V:Gog. 3.00

Spec.#1 Kid Flash 2.00
Spec.#1 Offspring. 2.00
Spec.#1 Nightstar. 2.00
Spec.#1 Planet Krypton. 2.00
Spec.#1 Son of the Bat. 2.00
DirectCurrents Spec. . . . . free

KINGDOM COME
Elseworlds 1996
1 MWa,AxR. 9.00
2 MWa,AxR,R:JLA. 8.00
3 MWa,AxR,A:Capt. Marvel. 8.00
4 MWa,AxR, final issue 8.00
HC Elseworlds rep. 29.95
TPB MWa,AxR, rep. 15.00

KISSYFUR
1989
1 . . . . 2.00

KOBALT
Milestone 1994–95
1 JBy(c),I:Kobalt,Richard Page . . . 2.25
2 . . . . 2.00
3 I:Slick,Volt,Red Light. 2.00
4 I:Slick,Volt,Red Light. 2.00
5 Richard Page 1.75
6 Volt. 1.75
7 Static 1.75
8 A:Hardward 1.75
9 . . . . 1.75
10 A:Harvest 1.75
11 V:St.Cloud 1.75
12 V:Rabid 1.75
13 V:Harvester 1.75
14 Long Hot Summer, V:Harvester . 2.50
15 Long Hot Summer 2.50

KOBRA
1976–77
1 JK,I:Kobra & Jason Burr. 4.00
2 I:Solaris 2.50
3 KG/DG,TA,V:Solaris 2.50
4 V:Servitor 2.50
5 RB/FMc,A:Jonny Double. 2.50
6 MN/JRu,A:Jonny Double. 2.50
7 MN/JRu,A:Jonny Double last iss . 2.50

KONG THE UNTAMED
June-July, 1975
1 thru 4 . . . . @1.25
5 Feb.–March, 1976 . . . . 1.25

KORAK,
SON OF TARZAN
1975
(Prev. published by Gold Key)
46 B:Carson of Venus, 1972. . . . . 4.00
47 . . . . 3.50
48 thru 59, 1975. . . . . 3.00
Becomes: TARZAN FAMILY

KRYPTON CHRONICLES
1981
1 CS,A:Superman 1.50
2 CS,A:Black Flame 1.25
3 CS,O:Name of Kal-El 1.25

LAST DAYS OF THE
JUSTICE SOCIETY
1986
1 . . . . 3.00

LAST ONE
Vertigo 1993
1 B:JMD(s),DSw,I:Myrwann,Patrick
Maguire's Story 3.25
2 DSw,Pat's Addiction to Drugs . . . 3.00
3 DSw,Pat goes into Coma 3.00
4 DSw,In Victorian age 3.00
5 DSw,Myrwann Memories 3.00
6 E:JMD(s),DSw,final Issue 3.00

L.A.W.
1999
1 (of 6) BL,DG,Living Assault
Weapons 2.50
2 BL,DG 2.50

LEADING COMICS
Winter, 1941–42
1 O:Seven Soldiers of Victory,
B:Crimson Avenger,Green Arrow
& Speedy,Shining Knight,
A:The Dummy 3,300.00
2 MMe,V:Black Star 1,200.00
3 V:Dr. Doome 1,000.00
4 `Seven Steps to Conquest',
V:The Sixth Sense 700.00
5 `The Miracles that Money
Couldn't Buy' 700.00
6 `The Treasure that Time
Forgot' 600.00
7 The Wizard of Wisstark. 600.00
8 Seven Soldiers Go back
through the Centuries. 600.00
9 V:Mr. X,`Chameleon of Crime'. 600.00
10 King of the Hundred Isles. . . . 600.00
11 `The Hard Luck Hat!' 450.00
12 `The Million Dollar
Challenge!' 450.00
13 `The Trophies of Crime' 450.00
14 Bandits from the Book'. 450.00
15 (fa) 200.00
16 thru 22 (fa) . . . . @80.00
23 (fa),I:Peter Porkchops 200.00
24 thru 30 (fa). . . . . @65.00
31 (fa) 50.00
32 (fa) 50.00
33 (fa) 60.00
34 thru 40 (fa). . . . . @50.00
41 (fa),Feb.–March, 1950 . . . . . . 50.00

LEAGUE OF JUSTICE
1996
1 (of 2) Elseworlds. 5.95
2 (of 2) Elseworlds. 5.95

LEAVE IT TO BINKY
Feb.–March, 1948
1 . . . . 175.00
2 . . . . 70.00
3 . . . . 60.00
4 . . . . 60.00
5 thru 14 . . . . @30.00
15 SM,Scribbly 40.00
16 thru 60 . . . . @15.00
61 thru 71. . . . . @7.50

LEGEND OF
THE SHIELD
Impact 1991–92
1 I:Shield,V:Mann-X,I:Big Daddy,
Lt.Devon Hall,Arvell Hauser,Mary
Masterson-Higgins 1.50
2 Shield in Middle East 1.25
3 Shield Goes A.W.O.L. 1.25
4 Hunt for Shield 1.25

5 A:Shield's Partner Dusty 1.25
6 O:Shield, V:The Jewels. 1.25
7 Shield/Fly team-up 1.25
8 V:Weapon 1.25
9 Father Vs. Son 1.25
10 Arvell Hauser 1.25
11 inc,Trading cards 1.25
12 . . . . 1.25
13 Shield court martialed 1.25
14 Mike Barnes becomes Shield . . . 1.25
15 Shield becomes a Crusader. . . . 1.25
16 V:Soviets,final issue. 1.25
Ann.#1 Earthquest,w/trading card . . 2.25

LEGEND OF
WONDER WOMAN
1986
1 Return of Atomia 1.25
2 A:Queens Solalia & Leila 1.25
3 Escape from Atomia 1.25
4 conclusion 1.25

Legends #6 © DC Comics, Inc.

LEGENDS
1986–87
1 JBy,V:Darkseid 3.00
2 JBy,A:Superman 2.00
3 JBy,I:Suicide Squad 2.00
4 JBy,V:Darkseid 2.00
5 JBy,A:Dr. Fate 2.00
6 JBy,I:Justice League. 5.00
TPB rep.#1-#6 JBy(c) 9.95

LEGENDS OF
DANIEL BOONE, THE
Oct., 1955–Jan., 1957
1 . . . . 500.00
2 . . . . 350.00
3 thru 8 . . . . 300.00

LEGENDS OF
THE DARK KNIGHT
(see BATMAN)

LEGENDS OF
THE DC UNIVERSE
Dec., 1997
1 JeR,VS,PNe,A:Superman, pt.1 . . 2.00
2 JeR,VS,PNe,A:Superman, pt.2 . . 2.00

3 JeR,VS,PNe,A:Superman, pt.3 . . 2.00
4 BML,MD2,VRu,Moments, pt.1 . . . 2.00
5 BML,MD2,VRu,Moments, pt.2 . . . 2.00
6 DTy,KN,Robin meets Superman . 2.00
7 DON,DG,Peacemakers, pt.1 . . . . 2.00
8 DON,DG,Peacemakers, pt.2 . . . . 2.00
9 DON,DG,Peacemakers, pt.3 . . . . 2.00
10 TyD,KN,F:Batman & Batgirl,pt.1 2.00
11 KN,TyD,F:Batman & Batgirl,pt.2 . 2.00
12 CPr(s),Critical Mass,pt.1 . . . . . . 2.00
13 CPr(s),Critical Mass,pt.2 . . . . . . 2.00
14 JK,BR,SR,64-page 4.00
15 RCa,Dark Matters, pt.1 . . . . 2.00
16 RCa,Dark Matters, pt.2 . . . . 2.00
17 RCa,Dark Matters, pt.3 . . . . 2.00
18 MWn(s),JG,F:New Teen Titans . 2.00
19 RT,F:Impulse 2.00
20 StG(s),MZ,KJ,Trail of the
   Traitor, pt.1. . . . . 2.00
21 StG(s),MZ,KJ,Trail of the
   Traitor, pt.2. . . . . 2.00
Giant #1 JKu(c), 80 pg.. . . . . 5.00
Spec 3-D Gallery #1. . . . . 3.00
GN Crisis on Infinite Earths. 5.00

LEGENDS OF
THE LEGION
Dec., 1997
1 (of 4) BKi,TPe,TNu,O:Ultra Boy . 2.25
2 . . . . 2.25
3 BKi,TPe,O:Umbra. 2.25
4 BKi,TPe,O:Star Boy 2.25

LEGENDS OF THE
WORLD FINEST
1994
1 WS(s),DIB,V:Silver Banshee,Blaze,
   Tullus,Foil(c). 5.25
2 WS(s),DIB,V:Silver Banshee,Blaze,
   Tullus,Foil(c). 5.25
3 WS(s),DIB,V:Silver Banshee,Blaze,
   Tullus,Foil(c). 5.25
TPB 14.95

L.E.G.I.O.N. '89-94
1989–94
1 BKi,V:Computer Tyrants 3.50
2 BKi,V:Computer Tyrants 3.00
3 BKi,V:Computer Tyrants,
   A:Lobo 3.00
4 BKi,V: Lobo 3.00
5 BKi,J:Lobo(in the rest of the
   series),V:Konis-Biz 3.00
6 BKi,V:Konis-Biz. 3.00
7 BKi,Stealth vs. Dox. 3.00
8 BKi,R:Dox 3.00
9 BKi,J:Phase (Phantom Girl) 2.50
10 BKi,Stealth vs Lobo 2.50
11 BKi,V:Mr.Stoorr 2.50
12 BKi,V:Emerald Eye 2.50
13 BKi,V:Emerald Eye 2.50
14 BKi,V:Pirates 2.50
15 BKi,V:Emerald Eye 2.50
16 BKi,J:LarGand. 2.50
17 BKi,V:Dragon-Ro 2.50
18 BKi,V:Dragon-Ro 2.50
19 V:Lydea,L:Stealth. 2.50
20 Aftermath. 2.50
21 D:Lyrissa Mallor,V:Mr.Starr. 2.50
22 V:Mr.Starr 2.50
23 O:R.J.Brande(double sized) 3.50
24 BKi,V:Khunds 2.50
25 BKi,V:Khunds 2.50
26 BKi,V:Khunds 2.50
27 BKi,J:Lydea Mallor. 2.50
28 KG,Birth of Stealth's Babies. . . . 2.50
29 BKi,J:Capt.Comet,Marij'n Bek . . 2.50

L.E.G.I.O.N. '93 #48 © DC Comics, Inc.

30 BKi,R:Stealth 2.50
31 Lobo vs.Capt.Marvel 3.50
32 V:Space Biker Gang 2.00
33 A:Ice-Man 2.00
34 MPn,V:Ice Man 2.00
35 Legion Disbanded 2.00
36 Dox proposes to Ignea. 2.00
37 V:Intergalactic Ninjas 2.00
38 BKi,Lobo V:Ice Man 2.00
39 BKi,D:G'odd,V:G'oddSquad 2.00
40 BKi,V:Kyaltic Space Station 2.00
41 BKi,A:Stealth'sBaby 2.00
42 BKi,V:Yeltsin-Beta 2.00
43 BKi,V:Yeltsin-Beta 2.00
44 V:Yeltsin-Beta,C:Gr.Lantern 2.00
45 . . . . 2.00
46 BKi,A:Hal Jordan 2.00
47 BKi,Lobo vs Hal Jordan 2.00
48 BKi,R:Ig'nea 2.00
49 BKi,V:Ig'nea. 2.00
50 BKi,V:Ig'nea,A:Legion'67 . . . . . 3.75
51 F:Lobo,Telepath. 2.00
52 BKi,V:Cyborg Skull of Darius . . . 2.00
53 BKi,V:Shadow Creature 2.00
54 BKi,V:Shadow Creature 2.00
55 BKi,V:Shadow Beast 2.00
56 BKi,A:Masked Avenger 2.00
57 BKi,Trinity,V:Green Lantern 2.00
58 BKi,Trinity#6,A:Green Lantern,
   Darkstar. 2.00
59 F:Phase. 2.00
60 V:Phantom Riders 2.00
61 Little Party 2.00
62 A:R.E.C.R.U.I.T.S. 2.00
63 A:Superman 2.00
64 BKi(c),V:Mr.B. 2.00
65 BKi(c),V:Brain Bandit 2.00
66 Stealth and Dox name child 2.00
67 F:Telepath 2.00
68 . . . . 1.75
69 . . . . 2.00
70 Zero Hour, last issue 2.50
Ann.#1 A:Superman,V:Brainiac. . . 5.50
Ann.#2 Armageddon 2001 . . . . 3.50
Ann.#3 Eclipso tie-in. 3.25
Ann.#4 SHa(i),I:Pax 3.75
Ann.#5 Elseworlds story 3.50

LEGION OF
SUBSTITUTE HEROES
1985
Spec.#1 KG 1.50

LEGION OF SUPER-HEROES
[Reprint Series] 1973
1 rep. Tommy Tomorrow 11.00
2 rep. Tommy Tomorrow 7.00
3 rep. Tommy Tomorrow 7.00
4 rep. Tommy Tomorrow 7.00

[1st Regular Series] 1980–84
Prev: SUPERBOY (& LEGION)
259 JSon,L:Superboy 5.00
260 RE,I:Circus of Death 3.50
261 RE,V:Circus of Death 3.50
262 JSh,V:Engineer 3.50
263 V:Dagon the Avenger 3.50
264 V:Dagon the Avenger 3.50
265 JSn,DG,Superman/Radio Shack
   insert 3.50
266 R:Bouncing Boy,Duo Damsel . . 3.00
267 SD,V:Kantuu 3.00
268 SD,BWi,V:Dr.Mayavale 3.00
269 V:Fatal Five 3.00
270 V:Fatal Five 3.00
271 V:Tharok (Dark Man) 2.50
272 CI,SD,O:J:Blok, I:New
   Dial `H' for Hero 2.50
273 V:Stargrave 2.50
274 SD,V:Captain Frake 2.50
275 V:Captain Frake 2.50
276 SD,V:Mordru 2.50
277 A:Reflecto(Superboy) 2.50
278 A:Reflecto(Superboy) 2.50
279 A:Reflecto(Superboy) 2.50
280 R:Superboy 2.50
281 SD,V:Time Trapper 2.50
282 V:Time Trapper 2.50
283 O:Wildfire 2.50
284 PB,V:Organleggor 2.50
285 PB,KG(1st Legion)V:Khunds . . 3.00
286 PB,KG,V:Khunds 3.00
287 KG,V:Kharlak 4.00
288 KG,V:Kharlak 3.00
289 KG,Stranded 3.00
290 KG,B:Great Darkness Saga,
   J:Invisible Kid II 3.00
291 KG,V:Darkseid's Minions 2.00
292 KG,V:Darkseid's Minions 2.00
293 KG,Daxam destroyed. 2.00
294 KG,E:Great Darkness Saga,
   V:Darkseid,A:Auron,Superboy . 2.00
295 KG,A:Green Lantern Corps . . . 1.75
296 KG,D:Cosmic Boys family 1.75
297 KG,O:Legion,A:Cosmic Boy . . . 1.75

Legion of Super-Heroes #270
© *DC Comics Inc.*

298 KG,EC,I:Amethyst 1.75
299 KG,R:Invisible Kid I 1.75
300 KG,CS,JSon,DC,KS,DG. 2.00
301 KG,R:Chameleon Boy 1.75
302 KG,A:Chameleon Boy 1.75
303 KG,V:Fatal Five 1.75
304 KG,V:Fatal Five 1.75
305 KG,V:Micro Lad 1.75
306 KG,CS,RT,O:Star Boy 1.75
307 KG,GT,Omen 1.75
308 KG,V:Omen 1.75
309 KG,V:Omen 1.75
310 KG,V:Omen 1.75
311 KG,GC,New Headquarters 1.75
312 KG,V:Khunds. 1.75
313 KG,V:Khunds. 1.75
Ann.#1 IT,KG,I:Invisible Kid. 3.50
Ann.#2 DGb,W:Karate Kid and
   Princess Projectra 2.00
Ann.#3 CS,RT,A:Darkseid. 2.00
Ann.#4 reprint. 2.00
Ann.#5 reprint. 1.75
Legion Archives Vol 1 HC. 39.95
Legion Archives Vol 2 HC. 39.95
Legion Archives Vol 3 HC. 39.95
Legion Archives Vol 4 HC. 39.95
Becomes:

TALES OF LEGION OF SUPER HEROES

LEGION OF SUPER-HEROES
[3rd Regular Series] 1984–89
1 KG,V:Legion of Super-Villians . . . 3.00
2 KG,V:Legion of Super-Villians . . . 2.50
3 KG,V:Legion of Super-Villians . . . 2.50
4 KG,D:Karate Kid. 2.50
5 KG,D:Nemesis Kid 2.50
6 JO,F:Lightning Lass 2.25
7 SLi,A:Controller 2.25
8 SLi,V:Controller 2.25
9 SLi,V:Sklarians 2.25
10 V:Khunds. 2.25
11 EC,KG,L:Orig 3 members 2.00
12 SLi,EC,A:Superboy 2.00
13 SLi,V:Lythyls,F:TimberWolf 2.00
14 SLi,J:Sensor Girl (Princess
   Projectra),Quislet,Tellus,Polar
   Boy,Magnetic Kid 2.00
15 GLa,V:Dr. Regulus. 2.00
16 SLi,Crisis tie-in,F:Braniac5 . . . . 2.00
17 GLa,O:Legion 2.00
18 GLa,Crisis tie-in,V:InfiniteMan . . 2.00
19 GLa,V:Controller 2.00
20 GLa,V:Tyr 2.00
21 GLa,V:Emerald Empress 1.75
22 GLa,V:Restorer,A:Universo 1.75
23 SLi,GLa,A:Superboy,
   Jonah Hex 1.75
24 GLa,NBi,A:Fatal Five 1.75
25 GLa,V:FatalFive 1.75
26 GLa,V:FatalFive,O:SensorGirl . . 1.75
27 GLa,GC,A:Mordru 1.75
28 GLa,L:StarBoy. 1.75
29 GLa,V:Starfinger 1.75
30 GLa,A:Universo 1.75
31 GLa,A:Ferro Lad,Karate Kid. . . . 1.75
32 GLa,V:Universo,I:Atmos. 1.75
33 GLa,V:Universo 1.75
34 GLa,V:Universo 1.75
35 GLa,V:Universo,R:Saturn Girl . . 1.75
36 GLa,R:Cosmic Boy 1.75
37 GLa,V:Universo,I:Superboy
   (Earth Prime) 5.00
38 GLa,V:TimeTrapper,
   D:Superboy 9.00
39 CS,RT,O:Colossal Boy 1.75
40 GLa,I:New Starfinger 1.75

41 GLa,V:Starfinger 1.75
42 GLa,Millenium,V:Laurel Kent . . . 1.75
43 GLa,Millenium,V:Laurel Kent . . . 1.75
44 GLa,O:Quislet 1.75
45 GLa,CS,MGr,DC,30th Ann. 3.00
46 GLa,Conspiracy. 1.75
47 GLa,PB,V:Starfinger 1.75
48 GLa,Conspiracy,A:Starfinger . . . 1.75
49 PB,Conspiracy,A:Starfinger 1.75
50 KG,V:Time Trapper,A:Infinite
   Man,E:Conspiracy 3.00
51 KG,V:Gorak,L:Brainiac5 . . . . . . 1.75
52 KG,V:Gil'Dishpan 1.75
53 KG,V:Gil'Dishpan. 1.75
54 KG,V:Gorak 1.75
55 KG,EC,JL,EL,N:Legion 1.75
56 EB,V:Inquisitor. 1.75
57 KG,V:Emerald Empress 1.75
58 KG,V:Emerald Empress 1.75
59 KG,MBr,F:Invisible Kid 1.75
60 KG,B:Magic Wars 1.75
61 KG,Magic Wars 1.75
62 KG,D:Magnetic Lad 1.75
63 KG,E:Magic Wars #4,final iss. . . 1.75
Ann.#1 KG,Murder Mystery. 2.50
Ann.#2 KG,CS,O:Validus,
   A:Darkseid 3.00
Ann.#3 GLa,I:2nd Karate Kid 2.50
Ann.#4 BKi,V:Starfinger 2.50
Ann #5 I:2nd Legion Sub.Heroes . . 2.50

[4th Regular Series] 1989–97
1 KG,R:Cosmic Boy, Chameleon . . 3.00
2 KG,R:Ultra Boy,I:Kono 2.50
3 KG,D:Block,V:Roxxas 2.50
4 KG,V:Time Trapper. 2.50
5 KG,V:Mordru,A:Glorith 2.50
6 KG,I:Laurel Gand 2.50
7 KG,V:Mordru 2.25
8 KG,O:Legion 2.25
9 KG,O:Laurel Gand 2.25
10 KG,V:Roxxas 2.25
11 KG,V:Roxxas 2.00
12 KG,I:Kent Shakespeare 2.00
13 KG,V:Dominators,posters. 2.00
14 KG,J:Tenzil Kem 2.00
15 KG,Khund Invasion 2.00
16 KG,V:Khunds. 2.00
17 KG,V:Khunds. 2.00
18 KG,V:Khunds. 2.00
19 KG,cont.from Adv.of Superman
   #478,A:Original Dr. Fate 2.25
20 KG,V:Dominators 2.00
21 KG,B:Quiet Darkness,
   A:Lobo,Darkseid. 3.00
22 KG,A:Lobo,Darkseid 2.50
23 KG,A:Lobo,Darkseid 2.50
24 KG,E:Quiet Darkness,A:Lobo,
   Darkseid,C:Legionairres 2.75
25 DAb,I:Legionairres 3.00
26 JPn,B:Terra Mosaic,V:B.I.O.N . . 2.00
27 JPn,V:B.I.O.N. 2.00
28 JPn,O:Sun Boy 2.00
29 JPn,I:Monica Sade. 2.00
30 JPn,V:Dominators 2.00
31 CS,AG,F:Shvaughn as man. . . . 2.00
32 JPn,D:Karate Kid,Prin.Projectra,
   Chameleon Boy(Legionaires) . . 2.00
33 R:Kid Quantum 2.00
34 R:Sun Boy. 2.00
35 JPN,V:Dominators 2.00
36 JPn,E:Terra Mosaic 2.00
37 JBr,R:Star Boy,Dream Girl 2.00
38 JPn,Earth is destroyed. 5.00
39 SI,A:Legionnaires 2.00
40 SI,Legion meets Legionnaires . . 2.00
41 SI,F:The Legionnaires 2.25
42 SI,V:Glorith 2.00
43 SI,B:Mordru Arises 2.00
44 SI,R:Karate Kid 2.00
45 SI,R:Roxxas 2.00
46 SI, ... 2.00

Legion of Super-Heroes, 4th Series #65
© DC Comics, Inc.

47 SI, ... 2.00
48 SI,E:Mordru Arises. 2.00
49 F:Matter Eater Lad. 2.00
50 W:Tenzil & Saturn Queen,
R:Wildfire,V:B.I.O.N 3.75
51 R:Kent,Celeste,Ivy,V:Grimbor. . . 2.00
52 F:Timber Wolf 2.00
53 SI,V:Glorith 2.25
54 SI,Foil,Die-Cut(c),
N:L.E.G.I.O.N. 3.25
55 SI,On Rimbor. 2.50
56 SI,R:Espionage Squad. 2.00
57 SI,R:Khund Legionnaires 2.00
58 SI,D:Laurel Gand. 2.00
59 SI,R:Valor,Dawnstar. 2.25
60 SI,End of an Era#3 . . . . 2.25
61 SI,End of an Era#6 . . . . 2.25
62 I:New Team 2.00
63 Alien Attack 2.00
64 . . . . 2.00
65 . . . . 2.00
66 I:New Team Members 2.00
67 F:Leviathan 2.00
68 F:Leviathan 2.00
69 V:Durlan 2.25
70 A:Andromeda, Brainiac 5. . . . . 2.25
71 Planet Trom. 2.25
72 . . . . 2.25
73 Sibling Rivalry,pt.1 . . . . 2.25
74 Future Tense,pt2 . . . . 2.25
75 Two Timer,pt.1 (of 2) 2.25
76 F:Valor & Triad. 2.25
77 F:Brainiac 5 . . . . 2.25
78 . . . . 2.25
79 Fatal Five attacks 2.25
80 V:Fatal Five 2.25
81 R:Dirk Morgna 2.25
82 . . . . 2.25
83 . . . . 2.25
84 . . . . 2.25
85 TPe&TMw(s),LMd,A:Superman,
back in 20th century 2.25
86 TPe&TMw(s),LMd,Final Night
tie-in. 2.25
87 TPe&TMw(s),LMd,F:Deadman . . 2.25
88 TPe&TMw(s),LMd,A:Impulse . . . 2.25
89 TPe&TMw(s),LMd,. 2.25
90 TPe&TMw(s),LMd,V:Dr. Psycho. 2.25
91 TPe&TMw(s),LMd,Legion back
together, but trapped in
timestream 2.25
92 TPe&TMs(s),LMd,"Displaced
in Time" 2.25
93 TPe&TMw(s),MC, All-tragedy

issue 2.25
94 TPe&TMw(s),LMd,"22 short
pages about the Legion of
Super-Heroes" 2.25
95 MFm,F:Brainiac 5 . . . . 2.25
96 MFm,wedding 2.25
97 TPe,LMd,Genesis tie-in 2.50
98 TPe&TMC,LMd,C.O.M.P.U.T.O.
the Conqueror, pt.1. . . . . 2.50
99 TPe&TMw,LMd,Computo, pt.2 . . 2.50
100 TPe&TMw, LMd,Computo, pt.3 . 6.00
101 TPe&TMw(s),AD&MFm(c),
F:Sparks 2.50
102 . . . . 2.50
103 TPe&TMw,AD&MFm(c),Star
Boy 2.50
104 TPe&TMw,AD&MFm(c),
changes. 2.50
105 TPe&TMw,AD&MFm(c),
Adventures in Action x-over . . . 2.50
106 TPe&TMw,AD&MFm(c),Dark
Circle Rising, x-over pt.2 . . . . . 2.50
107 TPe&TMw,AD&MFm(c),Dark
Circle Rising, x-over pt.4 . . . . . 2.50
108 TPe&TMw,AD&MFm(c),Dark
Circle Rising, x-over pt.6 . . . . . 2.50
109 DDv,AD,MFm,F:Violet 2.50
110 TPe,V:Thunder. 2.50
111 TPe&TMw(s),V:Daxamite 2.50
112 TPe&TMw(s),In Space 2.50
113 TPe&TMw(s),Kinetix 2.50
114 TPe&TMw(s),Bizarro
Legion,pt.1 . . . . 2.50
115 TPe&TMw(s),Bizarro
Legion, pt.2 . . . . 2.50
116 TPe&TMw(s),V:Pernisius,pt.1 . . 2.50
117 TPe&TMw(s),V:Pernisius,pt.2 . . 2.50
118 TPe&TMw(s),V:Pernisius,pt.3 . . 2.50
119 TPe&TMw(s),A:Valor & Phase . 2.50
120 TPe,TMw,V:Fatal Four,pt.1. . . . 2.50
Ann.#1 O:Ultra Boy,V:Glorith. 3.50
Ann.#2 O:Valor. 3.50
Ann.#3 N:Timberwolf 4.00
Ann.#4 I:Jamm 3.50
Ann.#5 SI(c),CDo,MFm,TMc,
Elseworlds Story 3.75
Ann.#6 Year One Annual + pin-ups. 3.95
Ann.#7 TPe(s),MC,MFm,"Legends
of the Dead Earth" 3.50
Spec.#1,000,000 TPe(s),KG,AG . . 2.50
TPB Great Darkness Saga 17.95
TPB Legion Archives, rep.#1-#3 . . 39.95
TPB Legion Archives, rep.#4 . . . . 49.95
TPB The Beginnings of Tomorrow. 17.95
HC Archives, Vol. 6 rep.Adventure
#350–358. . . . . 49.95
HC Archives, Vol. 7. . . . . 50.00
GN Secret Files, inc.O:Legion. . . . 5.00
Secret Files #2 . . . . 5.00

LEGIONNAIRES
1992–97

1 CSp,V:Mano and the Hand,Bagged
w/SkyBox promo card. 3.50
1a w/out card 2.50
2 CSp,V:Mano. 2.00
3 CSp,I:2nd Emerald Empress. . . . 2.00
4 CSp,R:Fatal Five 2.00
5 CSp,V:Fatal Five 2.00
6 CSp,V:Fatal Five 1.75
7 AH,V:Devil Fish 1.75
8 CDo,F:Brainiac 5 . . . . 1.75
9 CSp,A:Kid Quantum 1.75
10 CSp,A:Kono,I:2nd Kid Psycho . . 1.75
11 CSp,J:2nd Kid Pyscho 1.75
12 CSp,A:2nd Kid Pyscho. 1.75
13 FFo,V:Grimbor. 1.75
14 V:Grimbor 1.75
15 V:Grimbor 1.75
16 In Time 1.75

Legionnaires #1 © DC Comics, Inc.

17 End of An Era #1. . . . . 1.75
18 Zero Hour, LSH 1.75
19 Problems. 1.50
20 Moon Battle 1.50
21 and 22 . . . . @1.50
23 Saturday Night. 1.50
24 F:Triad. 1.50
25 F:Chameleon. 1.50
26 F:Apparition, Ultra Boy. 1.75
27 V:The Daxamites 2.25
28 V:Daxamites 2.25
29 . . . . 2.25
30 Silbing Rivalry,pt.2 . . . . 2.25
31 Future Tense,pt.3. . . . . 2.25
32 Two Timer, pt.2 . . . . 2.25
33 deadly new villain 2.25
34 Shrinking Violet killed?. 2.25
35 . . . . 2.25
36 RSt,V:Fatal Five 2.25
37 RSt,A:Kinetix,The Empress 2.25
38 . . . . 2.25
39 . . . . 2.25
40 . . . . 2.25
41 RSt&TMw(s),JMy,Legion of
Super-Heroes #84 aftermath . . 2.25
42 RSt&TMw(s),JMy,Mysa vs.
Kinetix 2.25
43 RSt&TMw(s),JMy,Legionnaire
try-outs. 2.25
44 TPe&TMw(s),JMy,revenge by
rejected applicants 2.25
45 . . . . 2.25
46 RSt&TMw(s),JMy,M'Onel's life
hangs by a thread 2.25
47 TPe&TMw(s),JMy,Brainiac 5 has
plan to return Legionnaires to
the future 2.25
48 RSt&TMw(s),JMy,"Dawn of the
Dark Lord," pt.1 . . . . 2.25
49 RSt&TMw(s),JMy,"Dawn of the
Dark Lord," pt.2 . . . . 2.25
50 RSt&TMw(s),JMy,"The Bride of
Mordru" 48pg, with poster. . . . 3.95
51 "Picking Up the Pieces" 2.25
52 RSt&TMw(s),JMy,"LeVlathan" . . 2.25
53 RSt&TMw(s),JMy,F:Monstress . . 2.25
54 TPe&TMw(s),JMy,F:G.A. Legion . 2.25
55 RSt&TMw(s),JMy,V:Composite
Man 2.25
56 RSt&TMw(s),JMy,F:M'Onel 2.25
57 RSt&TMw(s),JMy,V:Khunds 2.25
58 . . . . 2.25
59 RSt&TMw(s),JMy,date night. . . . 2.50
60 RSt&TMw(s),JMy,2 join, 2 leave. 2.50
61 RSt&TMw(s),JMy,Adventures

DC COMICS

in Action x-over 2.50	
62 RSt&TMw(s),JMy,Dark	
Circle Rising x-over, pt.1 . . . . . . 2.50	
63 RSt&TMw(s),JMy,Dark Circle	
Rising, x-over, pt.3 . . . . 2.50	
64 RSt&TMw(s),JMy, Dark Circle	
Rising, x-over pt.5 . . . . 2.50	
65 RSt&TMw(s),JMy,aftermath 2.50	
66 F:Invisible Kid 2.50	
67 RSt&TMw(s),JMy,Star Boy 2.50	
68 RSt&TMw(s),JMy,Cosmic Boy . . 2.50	
69 RSt&TMw(s),JMy,Lori Morning . . 2.50	
70 RSt&TMw(s),JMy,Alux Cuspin . . 2.50	
71 RSt&TMw(s),JMy,Dragonmage . 2.50	
72 RSt&TMw(s),JMy,V:Mordru 2.50	
73 RSt&TMw(s),JMy,V:Mordru 2.50	
74 RSt&TMw(s),JMy,V:Elements	
of Disaster 2.50	
75 TPe(s),JMy, ... 2.50	
76 RSt&TMw(s),JMy 2.50	
Ann.#1 Elseworlds Story 2.95	
Ann.#2 Year One Story 3.00	
Ann.#3 RSt&TMw(s) Legends of the	
Dead Earth 3.50	
Spec.#1,000,000 TPe(s),SeP, Justice	
Legion L 2.50	

LEGIONAIRRES THREE
1986

1 EC,Saturn Girl,Cosmic Boy 4.00
2 EC,V:Time Trapper,pt.1 . . . . 3.00
3 EC,V:Time Trapper,pt.2 . . . . 3.00
4 EC,V:Time Trapper,pt.3 . . . . 2.75

LEGION: SCIENCE POLICE
June 1998

1 (of 4) DvM,PR,JRu,set in	
30th century 2.50
2 DvM,PR,JRu,Jarik Shadder 2.50
3 DvM,PR,JRu, ... 2.50
4 DvM,PR,JRu 2.25

LIFE, THE UNIVERSE AND EVERYTHING
1996

1 thru 3 Doug Adams adapt. . . . @6.95

LIMITED COLLECTORS EDITION
Summer, 1973

21 Shazam 20.00
22 Tarzan 15.00
23 House of Mystery 25.00
24 Rudolph, the Red-nosed	
Reindeer 30.00
25 NA,NA(c),Batman 35.00
27 Shazam 15.00
29 Tarzan 12.00
31 NA,O:Superman 20.00
32 Ghosts 22.00
33 Rudolph 20.00
34 X-Mas with Superheroes 15.00
35 Shazam 20.00
36 The Bible 10.00
37 Batman 20.00
38 Superman 15.00
39 Secret Origins 15.00
40 Dick Tracy 12.00
41 ATh,Super Friends 15.00
42 Rudolph 15.00
43 X-mas with Super-Heroes 15.00
44 NA,Batman 15.00
45 Secret Origins-Super Villians . . 12.00
46 ATh,JLA 15.00
47 Superman 12.00

48 Superman-Flash Race 12.00
49 Superboy & Legion of	
Super-Heroes 10.00
50 Rudolph 10.00
51 NA,NA(c),Batman 15.00
52 NA,NA(c),The Best of DC 15.00
57 Welcome Back Kotter 10.00
59 NA,BWr,Batman,1978 . . . . 20.00

LITTLE SHOP OF HORRORS

1 GC 2.50

LOBO
[1st Limited Series] 1990–91

1 SBs,Last Czarnian #1 . . . . 4.00
1a 2nd Printing 2.00
2 SBs,Last Czarnian #2 . . . . 3.00
3 SBs,Last Czarnian #3 . . . . 3.00
4 SBs,Last Czarnian #4 . . . . 3.00
Ann.#1 Bloodlines#1,I:Layla 3.75
Lobo Paramilitary X-Mas SBs 5.50
Lobo:Blazing Chain of Love,DCw . . 1.50
TPB Last Czarnian,rep.#1-#4 . . . . 9.95
TPB Lobo's Greatest Hits 12.95

[Regular Series] 1993–97

1 VS,Foil(c),V:Dead Boys 3.25
2 VS 3.00
3 VS 2.75
4 VS,Quigly Affair 2.75
5 V:Bludhound 2.00
6 I:Bim Simms 2.00
7 A:Losers 2.00
8 A:Losers 2.25
9 V:Lobo 2.25
10 Preacher 2.00
11 Goldstar vs. Rev.Bo 2.00
12 . . . . 2.00
13 . . . . 2.00
14 Lobo, P.I. 2.00
15 Lobo, P.I.,pt.2 . . . . 2.00
16 Lobo, P.I.,pt.3 . . . . 2.00
17 Lobo, P.I.,pt.4 . . . . 2.25
18 Lobo, P.I.,pt.5 . . . . 2.25
19 . . . . 2.25
20 Toilot Fight 2.25
21 AIG,KON,R:Space Cabby 2.25
22 AIG,UnderworldUnleashed tie-in 2.25
23 AIG,Stargaze Rally,pt.1 . . . . . . 2.25
24 AIG,Stargaze Rally,pt.2 . . . . . . 2.25
25 AIG 2.25
26 AIG,V:Erik the Khund 2.25

Lobo #4 © DC Comics Inc.

27 AIG,V:Billy Krono 2.25
28 AIG,A:Great Big Fat Bastiches . . 2.25
29 . . . . 2.25
30 . . . . 2.25
31 . . . . 2.25
32 AIG(s),Lobo attends a seance,	
frags himself 2.25
33 AIG(s),Lobo returns from spirit	
world 2.25
34 AIG(s),vs. Japan, whaling, ... 2.25
35 AIG(s) "Deathtrek" 2.25
36 . . . . 2.25
37 AIG(s),BKi,Lobo's Guide to Girls 2.25
38 AIG(s),Bomandi The Last Boy	
on Earth 2.25
39 AIG(s),"In the Belly of the	
Behemoth,"pt. 1 . . . . 2.25
40 AIG(s),"In the Belly of the	
Behemoth,"pt. 2 . . . . 2.25
41 AIG(s),roommates 2.25
42 AIG(s),A:Perfidia 2.25
43 AIG(s),A:Jonas 2.25
44 AIG(s),Genesis tie-in 2.25
45 AIG(s),battle royale 2.25
46 AIG(s),Jackie Chin 2.25
47 AIG(s),V:Kiljoy Riggs 2.25
48 AIG(s),F:the penguins 2.25
49 AIG(s) 2.25
50 AIG(s),war on DC universe 2.25
51 AIG(s),Slater and Candy 2.25
52 AIG(s),Goldstar funeral 2.25
53 AIG(s),disrupted ceremony 2.50
54 AIG(s),Good Vibes machine 2.50
55 AIG(s),Sheepworld 2.50
56 AIG(s),MPn,GLz,the wedding . . 2.50
57 AIG(s),MPn,GLz, Intergalactic	
Police convention 2.50
58 KG&AIG(s) 2.50
59 AIG(s),V:Bad Wee Bastards 2.50
60 AIG(s),All-New, Nonviolent	
Adventures of Superbo, pt.1 . . 2.50
61 AIG(s),Superbo, pt.2 . . . . 2.50
62 AiG(s),Superbo, pt.3 . . . . 2.50
63 AIG(s),Soul Brothers,pt.1 . . . . . 2.50
64 AIG(s),Soul Brothers,pt.2	
final issue 2.50
Ann.#1 Bloodlines 4.00
Ann.#2 Elseworlds Story 3.50
Ann.#3 AIG Year One 4.95
Spec.#1,000,000 AIG(s),GLz 2.50
Spec. Lobo's Big Babe Spring Break,	
Miss Voluptuous Contest 2.00
Spec. Blazing Chains of Love 2.00
Spec. Bounty Hunting for Fun	
and Profit, F:Fanboy 4.95
Spec. Lobo: Chained AIG(s),	
Lobo in prison 2.00
Spec. Lobo/Demon: Hellowe'en,	
AIG(s),VGi 2.25
Spec. Lobo In the Chair, AIG(s) . . . 2.25
Spec. Lobo:I Quit,AIG,	
nicotine withdrawal 2.25
Spec. Lobo/Judge Dredd: Psycho	
Bikers vs. Mutants From Hell . . 4.95
Spec. Lobo: Portrait of a Victim	
VS,I:John Doe 2.00
GN Fragtastic Voyage AGr,	
miniaturized 6.00
TPB Lobo's Back's Back 10.00
TPB Lobo's Greatest Hits 13.00
Convention Special, comic con 2.00

LOBO: A CONTRACT ON GAWD
1994

1 AIG(s),KD 2.00
2 AIG(s),KD,A:Dave 2.00
3 AIG(s),KD 1.75
4 AIG(s),KD,Final Issue 1.75

Lobo's Back #4 © DC Comics, Inc.

LOBO'S BACK
1992

1 SBs,w/3(c) inside,V:Loo	2.50
1a 2nd printing	1.50
2 SBs,Lobo becomes a woman	2.50
3 SBs,V:Heaven	2.50
4 SBs,V:Heaven	2.50
TPB GF(c),rep.#1-#4	9.95

LOBO: DEATH & TAXES
Aug. 1996
[Mini-series]

1 (of 4) KG&AlG(s)	2.25
2 KG&AlG(s),Interstellar Revenue learns Lobo doesn't pay taxes	2.25
3 KG&AlG(s),Lobo walks into IRS trap	2.25
4 KG&AlG(s),Lobo destroys IRS	2.25

LOBO: INFANTICIDE
1992–93

1 KG,V:Su,Lobo Bastards	2.00
2 Lobo at Boot Camp	1.75
3 KG,Lobo Vs.his offspring	1.75
4 KG,V:Lobo Bastards	1.75

LOBO/MASK

1 AlG&JAr(s),DoM,Kwi, humorous x-over.	5.95
2 AlG&JAr(s),DoM,Kwi, concl.	5.95

LOBO: UNAMERICAN GLADIATORS
1993

1 CK,V:Satan's Brothers	2.00
2 CK,V:Jonny Caesar	2.00
3 CK,MMi(c),V:Satan Brothers	2.00
4 CK,MMi(c),V:Jonny Caeser	2.00

LOBOCOP

1 StG(s)	2.25

LOIS AND CLARK: THE NEW ADVENTURES OF SUPERMAN

TPB	9.95
TPB stories that became episodes	10.00

LOIS LANE
Aug., 1986

1 and 2 GM	@1.50

LONG HOT SUMMER, THE
Milestone 1995
[Mini-Series]

1 Blood Syndicate v. G.R.I.N.D.	2.95
2 A:Icon,Xombi,Hardware	2.50

LOONEY TUNES MAG.

1 thru 6	@2.00

LOONEY TUNES
1994

1 thru 6 Warner Bros. cartoons.	@1.75
7 thru 11 Warner Bros.	@1.75
12 The Cotton Tail Club	1.50
13 F:Tasmanian Devil	1.50
14 Football Season.	1.50
15 Jewel Thief	1.50
16 F:Yosemite Sam,Speedy Gonzales	1.50
17 F:Sylvester	1.50
18	1.50
19 Ben Hur Spoof.	1.50
20 F:Sylvester	1.50
21 thru 23	@1.50
24 thru 32	@1.75
33 F:Tasmanian Devil	2.00
34 F:Daffy	2.00
35 F:Daffy DangerDuck	2.00
36 F:Tweety	2.00
37 F:Crusher, Bugs.	2.00
38	2.00
39 F:Miss Prissy, Foghorn	2.00
40 F:Sylvester and Tweety	2.00
41 F:Porky, Sylvester	2.00
42 F:Sylvester,Pepe	2.00
43 F:Bugs, Sylvester	2.00
44 Frankentweety.	2.00
45 Bad Hare Day	2.00
46 Le Cage Aux Pew	2.00
47 Snow Way Out	2.00
48 Rocky Road.	2.00
49 F:Pepe Le Pew	2.00
50 The Gangs all here	2.00
51 Daffy	2.00
52 Bugs, Sam.	2.00
53 Postman Always Brings Mice.	2.00
54 Marvin & Taz	2.00
55 Twuce or Consequences	2.00
56 Foghorn & Henry Hawk	2.00
57 Claws & Effect.	2.00

LOOSE CANNON
[Mini-Series] 1995

1 AdP,V:Bounty Hunters	1.75
2 V:Bounty Hunters & The Eradicator	1.75
3 A:Eradicator	1.75

LORDS OF THE ULTRAREALM
1986

1 PB	3.50
2 PB	2.00
3 thru 6 PB	@1.50
Spec.#1 PB,DG,Oneshot	2.25

LOSERS SPECIAL
1985

1 Crisis,D:Losers	1.25

MADAME XANADU
1981

1 MR/BB	2.00

MAJOR BUMMER
June 1997

1 JAr(s),DoM,I:Major Bummer	2.50
2 JAr(s),DoM,Major Bummer gets new costume	2.50
3 JAr(s),DoM,bad guys arrive	2.50
4 JAr(s),DoM,alien germs	2.50
5 JAr(s),DoM,dinosaurs, Nazis.	2.50
6 JAr(s),DoM,Mutant bully	2.50
7 JAr(s),DoM.	2.50
8	2.50
9 JAr(s),DoM,epic fight	2.50
10 JAr(s),DoM,Nunzio dead?	2.50
11 JAr(s),DoM,everyone dies?	2.50
12 JAr(s),DoM,Lou Martin dead	2.50
13 JAr(s),DoM,Lauren	2.50
14 JAr(s),DoM,tells the future off.	2.50
15 JAr(s),DoM, final issue.	2.50

MAN-BAT
1975–76

1 SD,AM,A:Batman	20.00
2 V:The Ten-Eyed Man	15.00
Reprint NA(c)	10.00

Man-Bat #1 © DC Comics, Inc.

MAN-BAT
1996

1 CDi,terrorizes city	2.25
2	2.25
3 CDi,V:Steeljacket, finale	2.25

MAN-BAT vs. BATMAN

1 NA,DG,reprint.	4.00

A MAN CALLED AX
Aug. 1997

1 MWn(s),SwM, part rep.	2.50
2 MWn(s),SwM.	2.50
3 MWn(s),SwM, vs. DC universe	2.50
4 MWn(s),SwM,killer cyborg	2.50
5 MWn(s),SwM,R-Mor.	2.50
6 MWn(s),SwM.	2.50
7 MWn(s),SwM,battle in Bedlam	2.50
8 MWn(s),SwM,final issue	2.50

MANHUNTER
1988–90
1 from Millenium-Suicide Squad. . . 1.50
2 in Tokyo,A:Dumas. 1.25
3 The Yakuza,V:Dumas 1.25
4 Secrets Revealed-Manhunter,
Dumas & Olivia 1.25
5 A:Silvia Kandery. 1.25
6 A:Argent,contd.Suicide Squad
Annual #1. . . . . 1.25
7 Vlatavia, V:Count Vertigo 1.25
8 FS,A:Flash,Invasion x-over. 1.25
9 FS,Invasion Aftermath extra
(contd from Flash #22) 1.25
10 Salvage,pt.1 . . . . 1.25
11 Salvage,pt.2. . . . . 1.25
12 . . . . 1.25
13 V:Catman 1.25
14 Janus Directive #5 . . . . 1.25
15 I:Mirage 1.25
16 V:Outlaw 1.25
17 In Gotham,A:Batman 1.50
18 Saints & Sinners,pt.1,R:Dumas . 1.25
19 Saints & Sinners,pt.2,V:Dumas . 1.25
20 Saints & Sinners,pt.3,V:Dumas . 1.25
21 Saints & Sinners,pt.4,
A:Manhunter Grandmaster 1.25
22 Saints & Sinners,pt.5,
A:Manhunter Grandmaster 1.25
23 Saints & Sinners,pt.6,V:Dumas . 1.25
24 DG,Showdown, final issue 1.25

[2nd Series] 1994–95
0 . . . . 2.00
1 . . . . 2.00
2 N:Wild Huntsman 2.00
3 V:Malig. 2.00
4 Necrodyne 2.00
5 V:Skin Walker. 2.00
6 V:Barbarian,Incarnate 2.00
7 V:Incarnate,A:White Lotus
& Capt. Atom 2.25
8 V:Butcher Boys. 2.25
9 V:Butcher Boys. 2.25
10 V:Necrodyne 2.25
11 Return of Old Enemy 2.25
12 Underworld Unleashed, finale . . 2.25

MAN OF STEEL
1986
1 JBy,DG,I:Modern Superman 5.00
1a 2nd edition 3.00
2 JBy,DG,R:Lois Lane 3.50
3 JBy,DG,A:Batman. 3.00
4 JBy,DG,V:Lex Luther 3.00
5 JBy,DG,I:Modern Bizarro 3.00
6 JBy,DG,A:Lana Lang 3.00
TPB rep. Man of Steel #1–#6 . . . . 12.95
TPBa 2nd printing. 7.95

MANY LOVES OF
DOBIE GILLIS
May-June, 1960
1 . . . . 150.00
2 . . . . 75.00
3 . . . . 65.00
4 . . . . 65.00
5 thru 9 . . . . @40.00
10 thru 25 . . . . @28.00
26 Oct., 1964 . . . . 28.00

MARTIAN MANHUNTER
1988
1 A:JLI 1.75
2 A:JLI,V:Death God 1.50
3 V:Death God,A:Dr.Erdel 1.50
4 A:JLI,final issue 1.50

[Mini-Series]
1 EB,American Secrets #1. . . . . . . 5.25
2 EB,American Secrets #2. . . . . . . 4.95
3 EB,American Secrets #3. . . . . . . 4.95

MARTIAN MANHUNTER
Aug. 1998
0 JOs,TMd,A:Batman,Superman . . 2.00
1 JOs,TMd,V:Headman 2.00
2 JOs,TMd,V:Antares 2.00
3 JOs,TMd,V:Bette Noir 2.00
4 JOs,TMd,J'emm, Son of Saturn . 2.00
5 JAr,JD,A:Chase 2.00
6 JOs,TMd,A:JLA,pt.1 . . . . 2.00
7 JOs(s),TMd,A:JLA,pt.2 . . . . 2.00
8 JOs(s),TMd,A:JLA,pt.3 . . . . 2.00
9 JOs(s),TMd,A:JLA,pt.4 . . . . 2.00
10 JOs(s),A:Fire 2.00
11 JOs,PNe,BHi, ... 2.00
Ann. #1 TT,AOI,BWr,Ghosts x-over . 3.00
Ann.#2 AAd(c),JLApe:Gorilla
Warfare 2.95
Spec.#1,000,000 JOs,TMd 2.00

MASK
Dec., 1985
1 HC(c),TV tie-in,I:Mask Team 2.00
2 HC(c),In Egypt,V:Venom. 1.75
3 HC(c),`Anarchy in the U.K.'. 1.75
4 HC(c),V:Venom, final issue,
March, 1986. . . . . 1.00

[2nd Series] Feb., 1987
1 CS/KS,reg.series 1.25
2 CS/KS,V:Venom 1.00
3 CS/KS,V:Venom 1.00
4 CS/KS,V:Venom 1.00
5 CS/KS,Mask operatives hostage. 1.00
6 CS/KS,I:Jacana 1.00
7 CS/KS,Mask gone bad? 1.00
8 CS/KS,Matt Trakker,V:Venom . . . 1.00
9 CS/KS,V:Venom, last issue,
Oct., 1987 . . . . 1.00

MASTERS OF
THE UNIVERSE
May, 1986
1 GT,AA,O:He-Man 1.50
2 GT,AA, V:Skeletor 1.25
3 GT,V:Skeletor 1.25

Masters of the Universe #1
© DC Comics Inc.

MASTERWORKS SERIES
OF GREAT
COMIC BOOK ARTISTS
May, 1983
1 . . . . 2.50
2 . . . . 2.50
3 Dec., 1983 . . . . 2.50

'MAZING MAN
Jan., 1986
1 I:Maze 1.00
2 . . . . 1.00
3 . . . . 1.00
4 . . . . 1.00
5 . . . . 1.00
6 Shea Stadium. 1.00
7 Shea Stadium. 1.00
8 Cat-Sitting 1.00
9 Bank Hold-up 1.00
10 . . . . 1.00
11 Jones Beach 1.00
12 FM(c),last issue, Dec., 1986 . . 1.00
Spec.#1 . . . . 2.25
Spec.#2 . . . . 2.25
Spec.#3 KB/TM 2.25

MEN OF WAR
Aug., 1977
1 I:Gravedigger,Code Name:
Gravedigger,I:Enemy Ace. 1.50
2 JKu(c),The Five-Walled War 1.25
3 JKu(c),The Suicide Strategem . . 1.25
4 JKu(c),Trail by Fire 1.25
5 JKu(c),Valley of the Shadow 1.25
6 JKu(c),A Choice of Deaths 1.25
7 JKu(c),Milkrun 1.25
8 JKu(c),Death-Stroke 1.25
9 JKu(c),Gravedigger-R.I.P. 1.25
10 JKu(c),Crossroads 1.25
11 JKu(c),Berkstaten 1.25
12 JKu(c),Where Is Gravedigger? . . 1.25
13 JKu(c),Project Gravedigger -
Plus One 1.25
14 JKu(c),The Swirling
Sands of Death 1.25
15 JKu(c),The Man With the
Opened Eye. 1.25
16 JKu(c),Hide and Seek The Spy . 1.25
17 JKu(c),The River of Death 1.25
18 JKu(c),The Amiens Assault 1.25
19 JKu(c),An Angel Named Marie. . 1.25
20 JKu(c),Cry:Jerico 1.25
21 JKu(c),Home-Is Where
The Hell Is 1.25
22 JKu(c),Blackout On
The Boardwalk 1.25
23 JKu(c),Mission: Six Feet Under . 1.25
24 JKu&DG(c),The Presidential
Peril 1.25
25 GE(c),Save the President 1.25
26 March, 1980 . . . . 1.25

MENZ INSANA
DC/Vertigo 1998
GN JBo 7.95

MERCY
Vertigo
Graphic Novel I:Mercy 8.00

METAL MEN
1965–78
[1st Regular Series]
1 RA,I:Missile Men. 475.00
2 RA,Robot of Terror 185.00

Metal Men #15 © DC Comics, Inc.

3 RA,Moon's Invisible Army 100.00
4 RA,Bracelet of Doomed Hero . 100.00
5 RA,Menace of the Mammoth
Robots 100.00
6 RA,I:Gas Gang 85.00
7 RA,V:Solar Brain 55.00
8 RA,Playground of Terror 55.00
9 RA,A:Billy 55.00
10 RA,A:Gas Gang 55.00
11 RA,The Floating Furies 55.00
12 RA,A:Missle Men 50.00
13 RA,I:Nameless 50.00
14 RA,A:Chemo 50.00
15 RA,V:B.O.L.T.S. 50.00
16 RA,Robots for Sale 50.00
17 JKu(c),RA,V:Bl.Widow Robot . . 50.00
18 JKu(c),RA 50.00
19 RA,V:Man-Horse of Hades . . . 50.00
20 RA,V:Dr.Yes. 50.00
21 RA,C:Batman & Robin,Flash
Wonder Woman 35.00
22 RA,A:Chemo 35.00
23 RA,A:Sizzler 35.00
24 RA,V:Balloonman 35.00
25 RA,V:Chemo 35.00
26 RA,V:Metal Mods 35.00
27 RA,O:Metal Men,rtd 45.00
28 RA 35.00
29 RA,V:Robot Eater 35.00
30 RA,GK,in the Forbidden Zone . 35.00
31 RA,GK 25.00
32 RA,Robot Amazon Blues 20.00
33 MS,The Hunted Metal Men . . . 20.00
34 MS 20.00
35 MS 20.00
36 MS,The Cruel Clowns 20.00
37 MS,To walk among Men 20.00
38 MS 20.00
39 MS,Beauty of the Beast 20.00
40 MS 20.00
41 MS 20.00
42 RA,reprint 12.00
43 RA,reprint 12.00
44 RA,reprint,V:Missile Men 12.00
45 WS 12.00
46 WS,V:Chemo 12.00
47 WS,V:Plutonium Man 12.00
48 WS,A:Eclipso 15.00
49 WS,A:Eclipso 15.00
50 WS,JSa 10.00
51 JSn,V:Vox 10.00
52 JSn,V:Brain Children 10.00
53 JA(c),V:Brain Children 10.00
54 JSn,A:Green Lantern 10.00
55 JSn,A:Green Lantern 10.00

56 JSn,V:Inheritor 10.00
[Limited Series] 1993–94
1 DJu,BBr,Foil(c) 5.00
2 DJu,BBr,O:Metal Men 3.00
3 DJu,BBr,V:Missile Men 3.00
4 DJu,BBr,final issue 3.00

METAMORPHO
July-Aug., 1965
[Regular Series]
1 A:Kurt Vornok 100.00
2 Terror from the Telstar 60.00
3 Who stole the USA 60.00
4 V:Cha-Cha Chaves 40.00
5 V:Bulark 40.00
6 . . . . 40.00
7 thru 9 . . . . @35.00
10 I:Element Girl 45.00
11 thru 17 March-April, 1968 . . . @20.00
[Limited Series]
1 GN,V:The Orb of Ra 1.75
2 GN,A:Metamorpho's Son 1.75
3 GN,V:Elemental Man 1.75
4 GN,final Issue 1.75

METROPOLIS S.C.U.
Nov. 1994
1 Special Police unit 1.50
2 Eco-terror in Metropolis 1.50
3 Superman 1.50
4 final issue 1.50

MICHAEL MOORCOCK'S MULTIVERSE
DC/Helix (Sept., 1997)
1 WS,three stories, inc. Eternal
Champion adapt. 2.50
2 WS,Eternal Champion 2.50
3 WS,Moonbeams & Roses 2.50
4 WS,Moonbeams & Roses 2.50
5 . . . . 2.50
6 Duke Elric 2.50
7 Metatemporal Detective 2.50
8 Castle Silverskin 2.50
9 Duke Elric 2.50
10 Eternal Champion 2.50
11 WS, Silverskin 2.50
12 WS, concl 2.50

MILLENIUM
Jan., 1988
1 JSa,SEt, The Plan 1.75
2 JSa,SEt, The Chosen 1.75
3 JSa,SEt, Reagen/Manhunters . . 1.75
4 JSa,SEt, Mark Shaw/Batman . . . 1.75
5 JSa,SEt, The CHosen 1.75
6 JSa,SEt, Superman 1.75
7 JSa,SEt, Boster Gold 1.75
8 JSa,SEt,I:New Guardians 1.75

MILLENNIUM FEVER
1995–96
1 Young Love 2.50
2 Nightmares Worsen 2.50
3 Worst Nightmare 2.50
4 . . . . 2.50

MINX, THE
DC/Vertigo (Aug., 1998)
1 PrM,SeP,The Chosen, pt.1 . . . . 2.50
2 PrM,SeP,The Chosen, pt.2 . . . . 2.50
3 PrM,SeP,The Chosen, pt.3 . . . . 2.50
4 PrM,SeP,Monkey Quartet,pt.1 . . 2.50
5 PrM,SeP,Monkey Quartet,pt.2 . . 2.50

6 PrM,SeP,Monkey Quartet,pt.3 . . . 2.50
7 PrM,SeP,Monkey Quartet,pt.4 . . . 2.50
8 PrM,SeP,final issue 2.50

MISTER E
1991
1 (From Books of Magic) 1.75
2 A:The Shadower 1.75
3 A:The Shadower 1.75
4 A:Tim Hunter, Dr. Fate, Phantom
Stranger, final issue 1.75

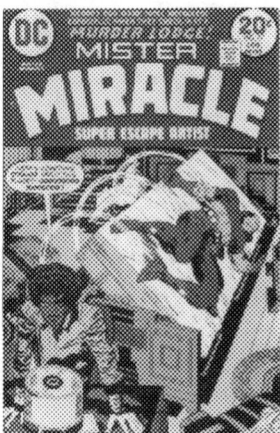

Mister Miracle #17 © DC Comics, Inc.

MISTER MIRACLE
1971–78
1 JK,I:Mr.Miracle 30.00
2 JK,I:Granny Goodness 15.00
3 JK,`Paraniod Pill'. 11.00
4 JK,I:Barda 10.00
5 JK,I:Vermin Vundabar 10.00
6 JK,I:Female Furies 10.00
7 JK,V:Kanto 10.00
8 JK,V:Lump 10.00
9 JK,O:Mr.Miracle,C:Darkseid 8.00
10 JK,A:Female Furies 6.00
11 JK,V:Doctor Bedlum 6.00
12 JK 6.00
13 JK 6.00
14 JK 6.00
15 JK,O:Shilo Norman 6.00
16 JK 6.00
17 JK 6.00
18 JK,W:Mr.Miracle & Barda 6.00
19 MR,NA,DG,TA,JRu,AM 6.00
20 MR 4.00
21 MR 4.00
22 MR 4.00
23 MG 4.00
24 MG,RH 4.00
25 MG,RH 4.00
Spec.#1 SR 2.50
[2nd Series] 1989–91
1 IG 2.00
2 IG 1.50
3 IG,A:Highfather,Forever People . 1.50
4 IG,A:The Dark,Forever People . . 1.50
5 IG,V:TheDark,A:ForeverPeople . . 1.50
6 A:G.L. Gnort 1.25
7 A:Blue Beetle,Booster Gold 1.25
8 RM,A:Blue Beetle,Booster Gold . 1.25
9 I:Maxi-Man 1.25
10 V:Maxi-Man 1.25

11	1.25
12	1.25
13 Manga Khan Saga begins, A:L-Ron,A:Lobo	2.50
14 A:Lobo	2.00
15 Manga Khan contd	1.25
16 MangaKhan cont.,JLA#39tie-in	1.25
17 On Apokolips,A:Darkseid	1.25
18 On Apokolips	1.25
19 Return to Earth, contd from JLA#42	1.25
20 IG,Oberon	1.25
21 Return of Shilo	1.25
22 New Mr.Miracle revealed	1.25
23 Secrets of the 2 Mr. Miracles revealed, A:Mother Box	1.25
24	1.25
25	1.25
26 Monster Party,pt.1	1.25
27 Monster Party,pt.2, A:Justice League	1.25
28 final issue	1.25

MISTER MIRACLE
1996

1 JK, new mythology	2.00
2 V:Justice League	2.00
3 How can Scott Free save Big Barda	2.00
3 accepts his powers	2.00
4 corruption throughout the cosmos	2.00
5 SCr	2.00
6 SCr	2.00
7 final issue	2.00

MR. DISTRICT ATTORNEY
Jan.–Feb., 1948

1 The Innocent Forger	800.00
2 The Richest Man In Prison	350.00
3 The Honest Convicts	250.00
4 The Merchant of Death	250.00
5 The Booby-Trap Killer	250.00
6 The D.A. Meets Scotland Yard	200.00
7 The People vs. Killer Kane	200.00
8 The Rise and Fall of 'Lucky' Lynn	200.00
9 The Case of the Living Counterfeit	200.00
10 The D.A. Takes a Vacation	150.00
11 The Game That Has No Winners	150.00
12 Fake Accident Racket	150.00
13 The Execution of Caesar Larsen	150.00
14 The Innocent Man In Murderers' Row	150.00
15 Prison Train	150.00
16 The Wire Tap Crimes	150.00
17 The Bachelor of Crime	150.00
18 The Case of the Twelve O'Clock Killer	150.00
19 The Four King's Of Crime	150.00
20 You Catch a Killer	150.00
21 I Was A Killer's Bodyguard	100.00
22 The Marksman of Crime	100.00
23 Diary of a Criminal	100.00
24 The Killer In The Iron Mask	100.00
25 I Hired My Killer	100.00
26 The Case of the Wanted Criminals	100.00
27 The Case of the Secret Six	100.00
28 Beware the Bogus Beggars	100.00
29 The Crimes of Mr. Jumbo	100.00
30 Man of a Thousand Faces	100.00
31 The Hot Money Gang	100.00
32 The Case o/t Bad Luck Clues	100.00
33 A Crime Is Born	100.00

Mr. District Attorney #42
© DC Comics Inc.

34 The Amazing Crimes of Mr. X	100.00
35 This Crime For Hire	100.00
36 The Chameleon of Crime	100.00
37 Miss Miller's Big Case	100.00
38 The Puzzle Shop For Crime	100.00
39 Man Who Killed Daredevils	100.00
40 The Human Vultures	100.00
41 The Great Token Take	100.00
42 Super-Market Sleuth	100.00
43 Hotel Detective	100.00
44 S.S. Justice,B:Comics Code	75.00
45 Miss Miller, Widow	75.00
46 Mr. District Attorney, Public Defender	75.00
47 The Missing Persons Racket	75.00
48 Manhunt With the Mounties	75.00
49 The TV Dragnet	75.00
50 The Case of Frank Bragan, Little Shot	75.00
51 The Big Heist	75.00
52 Crooked Wheels of Fortune	75.00
53 The Courtroom Patrol	75.00
54 The Underworld Spy Squad	75.00
55 The Flying Saucer Mystery	75.00
56 The Underworld Oracle	75.00
57 The Underworld Employment Agency	75.00
58 The Great Bomb Scare	75.00
59 Great Underworld Spy Plot	75.00
60 The D.A.'s TV Rival	75.00
61 SMo(c),Architect of Crime	75.00
62 A-Bombs For Sale	75.00
63 The Flying Prison	75.00
64 SMo(c),The Underworld Treasure Hunt	75.00
65 SMo(c),World Wide Dragnet	75.00
66 SMo(c),The Secret of the D.A.'s Diary	75.00
67 Jan.–Feb., 1959	75.00

MR. PUNCH

HC DMc,NGa,Nightmarish tale, 1994	24.95

MOBFIRE
1994–95

1 WaP,Gangsters in London	2.50
2 WaP,	2.50
3 WaP,The Bocor	2.50
4 WaP,V:Bocor	2.50
5 WaP,Voice in My Head	2.50
6 WaP,Genetic Babies, final issue	2.50

MODESTY BLAISE

1 DG,V:Gabriel	4.95
2 DG,V:Gabriel	4.95
GN Spy Thriller	19.95

MOONSHADOW
Vertigo 1994–95

1 JMD(s),JMu,rep	2.25
2 thru 4 JMD	@2.25
5 fully painted	2.25
6	2.25
7 F:Shady Lady	2.25
8 Rep. Search for Ira	2.25
9 JMD,JMu,A:Tittletat Twins	2.25
10 JMD,JMu,Interplanetary Prostitutes	2.25
11 JMu,Ira's life story	2.25
12 Rep. w/6pg new material	2.95

MORE FUN COMICS
(See: NEW FUN COMICS)

MOVIE COMICS
April, 1939

1 `Gunga Din'	3,000.00
2 Stagecoach	1,800.00
3 East Side of Heaven	1,400.00
4 Captain Fury,B:Oregon Trail.	1,100.00
5 Man in the Iron Mask	1,100.00
6 Sept., 1939	1,500.00

MS. TREE QUARTERLY

1 MGr,A:Batman	3.50
2 A:Butcher	2.95
3 A:Butcher	2.95
4 `Paper Midnight'	3.95
5 Murder/Rape Investigation	3.95
6 Gothic House	3.95
7	3.95
8 CI,FMc,Ms Tree Pregnant(c), B.U. King Faraday	3.95
9 Child Kidnapped	3.95
10 V:International Mob	3.50

MUKTUK WOLFSBREATH: HARD-BOILED SHAMAN
DC/Vertigo (June 1998)

1 (of 3) TLa,SvP,lady shaman	2.50
2	2.50
3 TLa,SvP, concl	2.50

MUTT AND JEFF
1939

1	1,200.00
2	650.00
3	500.00
4 and 5	@450.00
6 thru 10	@200.00
11 thru 20	@125.00
21 thru 30	@100.00
31 thru 50	@70.00
51 thru 70	@50.00
71 thru 80	@40.00
81 thru 99	@35.00
100	40.00
101 thru 103	@35.00
104 thru 148	@25.00

MY GREATEST ADVENTURE
Jan.–Feb., 1955

1 LSt,I Was King Of Danger Island	1,300.00
2 My Million Dollar Dive	600.00

DC COMICS

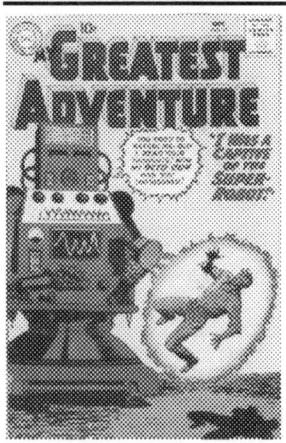

My Greatest Adventure #35
© DC Comics, Inc.

3 I Found Captain
  Kidd's Treasure 375.00
4 I Had A Date With Doom 375.00
5 I Escaped From Castle Morte . 350.00
6 I Had To Spend A Million 350.00
7 I Was A Prisoner On Island X . 325.00
8 The Day They Stole My Face . 325.00
9 I Walked Through The Doors
  of Destiny. 325.00
10 We Found A World Of
  Tiny Cavemen 325.00
11 LSt(c),My Friend, Madcap
  Manning. 250.00
12 MMe(c),I Hunted Big Game
  in Outer Space 250.00
13 LSt(c),I Hunted Goliath
  The Robot 250.00
14 LSt,I Had the Midas
  Touch of Gold. 250.00
15 JK, I Hunted the Worlds
  Wildest Animals 250.00
16 JK,I Died a Thousand Times . 250.00
17 JK,I Doomed the World 250.00
18 JK(c),We Discovered The
  Edge of the World. 250.00
19 I Caught Earth's
  Strangest Criminal 250.00
20 JK,I Was Big-Game
  on Neptune 250.00
21 JK,We Were Doomed By
  The Metal-Eating Monster. . . 250.00
22 I Was Trapped In The
  Magic Mountains 200.00
23 I Was A Captive In
  Space Prison 200.00
24 NC(c),I Was The Robinson
  Crusoe of Space. 200.00
25 I Led Earth's Strangest
  Safari! 200.00
26 NC(c),We Battled The
  Sand Creature 200.00
27 I Was the Earth's First Exile . . 200.00
28 I Stalked the Camouflage
  Creatures. 250.00
29 I Tracked the
  Forbidden Powers 150.00
30 We Cruised Into the
  Supernatural! 150.00
31 I Was A Modern Hercules . . . 125.00
32 We Were Trapped In A Freak
  Valley! 125.00
33 I Was Pursued by
  the Elements 125.00
34 DD,We Unleashed The Cloud
  Creatures. 125.00

35 I Solved the Mystery of
  Volcano Valley 125.00
36 I Was Bewitched
  By Lady Doom 125.00
37 DD&SMo(c),I Hunted the
  Legendary Creatures! 125.00
38 DD&SMo(c),I Was the Slave
  of the Dream-Master. 125.00
39 DD&SMo(c),We were Trapped
  in the Valley of no Return . . . 125.00
40 WeBattled the StormCreature 125.00
41 DD&SMo(c),I Was Tried
  by a Robot Court 100.00
42 DD&SMo(c),My Brother
  Was a Robot 100.00
43 DD&SMo(c),I Fought the
  Sonar Creatures 100.00
44 DD&SMo(c),We Fought the
  Beasts of Petrified Island . . . 100.00
45 DD&SMo(c),We Battled the
  Black Narwahl 100.00
46 DD&SMo(c),We Were Prisoners
  of the Sundial of Doom. 100.00
47 We Became Partners of the
  Beast Brigade. 100.00
48 DD&SMo(c),I Was Marooned
  On Earth 100.00
49 DD&SMo(c),I Was An Ally
  Of A Criminal Creature 100.00
50 DD&SMo(c),I Fought the
  Idol King. 100.00
51 DD&SMo(c),We Unleashed
  the Demon of the Dungeon. . . 85.00
52 DD&SMo(c),I Was A
  Stand-In For an Alien 85.00
53 DD&SMo(c),I, Creature Slayer. 85.00
54 I Was Cursed With
  an Alien Pal 85.00
55 DD&SMo(c),I Beacame The
  Wonder-Man of Space 85.00
56 DD&SMo(c),My Brother-The
  Alien. 85.00
57 DD&SMo(c),Don't Touch Me
  Or You'll Die 85.00
58 DD&SMo(c),ATh,I was Trapped
  in the Land of L'Oz 100.00
59 DD&SMo(c),Listen Earth-I
  Am Still Alive 100.00
60 DD&SMo(c),ATh,I Lived in
  Two Worlds 100.00
61 DD&SMo(c),ATh,I Battled For
  the Doom-Stone 100.00
62 DD&SMo(c),I Fought For
  An Alien Enemy 50.00
63 DD&SMo(c),We Braved the
  Trail of the Ancient Warrior . . . 50.00
64 DD&SMo(c),They Crowned My
  Fiance Their King! 50.00
65 DD&SMo(c),I Lost the Life
  or Death Secret 50.00
66 DD&SMo(c),I Dueled with
  the Super Spirits. 50.00
67 I Protected the Idols
  of Idoro! 50.00
68 DD&SMo(c),My Deadly Island
  of Space. 50.00
69 DD&SMo(c),I Was A Courier
  From the Past 50.00
70 DD&SMo(c),We Tracked the
  Fabled Fish-Man! 50.00
71 We Dared to open the Door
  of Danger Dungeon 50.00
72 The Haunted Beach. 50.00
73 I Defeiller Mountain 50.00
74 GC(c),We Were Challenged
  By The River Spirit 50.00
75 GC(c),Castaway Cave-Men
  of 1950. . . . . 50.00
76 MMe(c),We Battled the
  Micro-Monster 50.00
77 ATh,We Found the Super-

My Greatest Adventure #40
© DC Comics, Inc.

  Tribes of Tomorrow. 55.00
78 Destination-'Dead Man's Alley'. 50.00
79 Countdown in Dinosaur Valley . 50.00
80 BP,I:Doom Patrol 400.00
81 BP,ATh,I:Dr. Janus 160.00
82 BP,F:Doom Patrol 150.00
83 BP,F:Doom Patrol 150.00
84 BP,V:General Immortus 150.00
85 BP,ATh,F:Doom Patrol 150.00
Becomes:

DOOM PATROL
March, 1964

86 BP,I:Brogherhood of Evil 100.00
87 BP,O:Negative Man 80.00
88 BP,O:Chief. 75.00
89 BP,I:Animal-Veg.-MineralMan . . 75.00
90 BP,A:Brotherhood of Evil 75.00
91 BP,I:Manto, Gargvax 75.00
92 BP,I:Dr.Tyme, A:Mento. 75.00
93 BP,A:Brotherhood of Evil 75.00
94 BP,I:Dr.Radich, The Claw. 75.00
95 BP,A:Animal-Vegetable
  -Mineral Man 75.00
96 BP,A:General Immortus,
  Brotherhood of Evil. 70.00
97 BP,A:General Immortus,
  Brotherhood of Evil. 70.00
98 BP,I:Mr.103 . . . . 70.00
99 I:Beast Boy 80.00
100 BP,O:Beast Boy,Robotman. . 100.00
101 BP,A:Beast Boy 50.00
102 BP,A:Beast Boy,Challengers
  of the Unknown 45.00
103 BP,A:Beast Boy 45.00
104 BP,W:Elasti-Girl,Mento,
  C:JLA,Teen Titans 45.00
105 BP,A:Beast Boy 45.00
106 BP,O:Negative Man 45.00
107 BP,A:Beast Boy, I:Dr.Death . . 45.00
108 BP,A:Brotherhood of Evil 45.00
109 BP,I:Mandred. 45.00
110 BP,A:Garguax,Mandred,
  Brotherhood of Evil. 40.00
111 BP,I:Zarox-13,A:Brotherhood
  of Evil. 40.00
112 BP,O:Beast Boy,Madame
  Rouge 40.00
113 BP,A:Beast Boy,Mento 40.00
114 BP,A:Beast Boy 40.00
115 BP,A:Beast Boy 40.00
116 BP,A:Madame Rouge 40.00
117 BP,I:Black Vulture. 40.00
118 BP,A:Beast Boy 40.00
119 BP,A:Madam Rouge. 40.00

120 I:Wrecker. 40.00
121 JO,D:Doom Patrol 100.00
122 rep.Doom Patrol #89 . . . . 5.00
123 rep.Doom Patrol #95 . . . . 5.00
124 rep.Doom Patrol #90 . . . . 5.00

[2nd Series]
See: DOOM PATROL

MY NAME IS CHAOS
1992
1 JRy,Song Laid Waste to Earth . . 4.95
2 JRy,Colonization of Mars 4.95
3 JRy,Search for Eternal Beings . . 4.95
4 JRy,final issue 4.95

MY NAME IS HOLOCAUST
Milestone 1995
[Mini-Series]
1 F:Holocaust (Blood Syndicate) . . 1.75
2 V:Cantano 1.75
3 A:Blood Syndicate 1.75

MYSTERY IN SPACE
April-May, 1951
1 CI&FrG(c),FF,B:Knights of the
  Galaxy,Nine Worlds to
  Conquer 2,800.00
2 CI(c),MA,A:Knights of the
  Galaxy, Jesse James-
  Highwayman of Space. . . . 1,100.00
3 CI(c),A:Knights of the
  Galaxy, Duel of the Planets. . 850.00
4 CI(c),S&K,A:Knights of the
  Galaxy, Master of Doom 750.00
5 CI(c),A:Knights of the Galaxy,
  Outcast of the Lost World . . . 750.00
6 CI(c),A:Knights of the Galaxy,
  The Day the World Melted . . 550.00
7 GK(c),ATh,A:Knights of the Galaxy,
  Challenge o/t Robot Knight . . 550.00
8 MA,It's a Women's World 550.00
9 MA(c),The Seven Wonders
  of Space. 550.00
10 MA(c),The Last Time I
  Saw Earth 550.00
11 GK(c),Unknown Spaceman . . 400.00
12 MA,The Sword in the Sky. . . . 400.00
13 MA(c),MD,Signboard
  in Space. 400.00
14 MA,GK(c),Hollywood
  in Space. 400.00
15 MA(c),Doom from Station X . . 400.00
16 MA(c),Honeymoon in Space. . 400.00
17 MA(c),The Last Mile of Space 400.00
18 MA(c),GK,Chain Gang
  of Space. 400.00
19 MA(c),The Great
  Space-Train Robbery 375.00
20 MA(c),The Man in the
  Martian Mask 350.00
21 MA(c),Interplanetary
  Merry- Go-Round 350.00
22 MA(c),The Square Earth 350.00
23 MA(c),Monkey-Rocket
  to Mars. 350.00
24 MA(c),A:Space Cabby,
  Hitchhiker of Space 350.00
25 MA(c),Station Mars on the Air 325.00
26 GK(c),Earth is the Target 325.00
27 The Human Fishbowl. 325.00
28 The Radio Planet. 325.00
29 GK(c),Space-Enemy
  Number One. 325.00
30 GK(c),The Impossible
  World Named Earth 325.00
31 GK(c),The Day the Earth
  Split in Two. 300.00

32 GK(c),Riddle of the
  Vanishing Earthmen 300.00
33 The Wooden World War. 300.00
34 GK(c),The Man Who
  Moved the World 300.00
35 The Counterfeit Earth. 300.00
36 GK(c),Secret of the
  Moon Sphinx 300.00
37 GK(c),Secret of the
  Masked Martians 300.00
38 GK(c),The Canals of Earth. . . 300.00
39 GK(c),Sorcerers of Space . . . 300.00
40 GK(c),Riddle of the
  Runaway Earth. 300.00
41 GK(c),The Miser of Space . . . 250.00
42 GK(c),The Secret of the
  Skyscraper Spaceship 250.00
43 GK(c),Invaders From the
  Space Satellites 250.00
44 GK(c),Amazing Space Flight
  of North America 250.00
45 GK(c),MA,Flying Saucers
  Over Mars 250.00
46 GK(c),MA,Mystery of the
  Moon Sniper. 250.00
47 GK(c),MA,Interplanetary Tug
  of War 250.00
48 GK(c),MA,Secret of the
  Scarecrow World 250.00
49 GK(c),The Sky-High Man 250.00
50 GK(c),The Runaway
  Space-Train 250.00
51 GK(c),MA,Battle of the
  Moon Monsters. 250.00
52 GK(c),MSy,Mirror Menace
  of Mars. 250.00
53 GK(c),B:Adam Strange stories,
  Menace o/t Robot Raiders . 1,700.00
54 GK(c),Invaders of the
  Underground World 400.00
55 GK(c),The Beast From
  the Runaway World 300.00
56 GK(c),The Menace of
  the Super-Atom 200.00
57 GK(c),Mystery of the
  Giant Footsteps 200.00
58 GK(c),Chariot in in the Sky. . . 200.00
59 GK(c),The Duel of the
  Two Adam Stranges 200.00
60 GK(c),The Attack of the
  Tentacle World 200.00
61 CI&MA(c),Threat of the
  Tornado Tyrant. 175.00
62 CI&MA(c),The Beast with
  the Sizzling Blue Eyes 175.00

Mystery in Space #51
© DC Comics Inc.

63 The Weapon that
  Swallowed Men 175.00
64 The Radioactive Menace 175.00
65 Mechanical Masters of Rann . 175.00
66 Space-Island of Peril 175.00
67 Challenge of the
  Giant Fireflies. 175.00
68 CI&MA(c),Fadeaway Doom . . 175.00
69 CI&MA(c),Menace of the
  Aqua-Ray Weapon 175.00
70 CI&MA(c),Vengeance of
  the Dust Devil. 175.00
71 CI&MA(c),The Challenge of
  the Crystal Conquerors. 175.00
72 The Multiple Menace Weapon 125.00
73 CI&MA(c),The Invisible
  Invaders of Rann 125.00
74 CI&MA(c),The Spaceman
  Who Fought Himself. 125.00
75 CI&MA(c),The Planet That
  Came to a Standstill. 250.00
76 CI&MA(c),Challenge of
  the Rival Starman. 125.00
77 CI&MA(c),Ray-Gun in the Sky 125.00
78 CI&MA(c),Shadow People
  of the Eclipse 125.00
79 CI&MA(c),The Metal
  Conqueror of Rann. 125.00
80 CI&MA(c),The Deadly
  Shadows of Adam Strange . . 125.00
81 CI&MA(c),The Cloud-Creature
  That Menaced Two Worlds . . . 90.00
82 CI&MA(c),World War on
  Earth and Rann 90.00
83 CI&MA(c),The Emotion-Master
  of Space. 90.00
84 CI&MA(c),The Powerless
  Weapons of Adam Strange. . . 90.00
85 CI&MA(c),Riddle of the
  Runaway Rockets 90.00
86 CI&MA(c),Attack of the
  Underworld Giants 90.00
87 MA(c),The Super-Brain of
  Adam Strange,B:Hawkman. . 200.00
88 CI&MA(c),The Robot Wraith
  of Rann 175.00
89 MA(c),Siren o/t Space Ark . . . 175.00
90 CI&MA(c),Planets and
  Peril, E:Hawkman. 175.00
91 CI&MA(c),Puzzle of
  the Perilous Prisons 40.00
92 DD&SMo(c),The Alien Invasion
  From Earth,B:Space Ranger. . 45.00
93 DD&SMo(c),The Convict
  Twins of Space. 45.00
94 DD&SMo(c),The Adam
  Strange Story. 45.00
95 The Hydra-Head From
  Outer Space. 45.00
96 The Coins That Doomed
  Two Planets 45.00
97 The Day Adam Strange
  Vanished 45.00
98 The Wizard of the Cosmos. . . . 45.00
99 DD&SMo(c),The World-
  Destroyer From Space 45.00
100 DD&SMo(c),GK,The Death
  of Alanna 45.00
101 GK(c),The Valley of
  1,000 Dooms 45.00
102 GK,The Robot World of Rann 45.00
103 The Billion-Dollar Time-
  Capsule(Space Ranger),I:Ultra
  the Multi-Agent. 45.00
104 thru 109 . . . . @25.00
110 Sept. 1966. . . . . 25.00
111 JAp,SD,MR,DSp,Sept. 1980. . 25.00
112 JAp,TS,JKu(c) 25.00
113 JKu(c),MGo 25.00
114 JKu(c),JCr,SD,DSp 25.00
115 JKu(c),SD,GT,BB 25.00

116 JSn(c),JCr,SD 25.00
117 DN,GT,March, 1981 .... 25.00

MYSTERY PLAY
Vertigo
HC GMo(s),JMu 19.95

MYTHOS:
THE FINAL TOUR
DC/Vertigo Oct. 1996
1 JNR(s),GyA,PrG,F:Rock Star
    Adam Case 5.95
2 JNR(s),PSj,F:Rock Star Adam
    Case 5.95
3 JNR(s), finale 5.95

NATHANIEL DUSK
Feb., 1984
1 GC(p)..................... 1.50
2 GC(p)..................... 1.25
3 GC(p)..................... 1.25
4 GC(p), May 1984 .... 1.25

NATHANIEL DUSK II
Oct., 1985
1 thru 4 GC,Jan., 1986........ @2.00

NATIONAL COMICS
1999
1 MWa(s),AAl,F:Flash &
    Mr. Terrific 2.00

NAZZ, THE
1990–91
1 Michael'sBook 5.50
2 Johnny'sBook................ 5.00
3 Search for Michael Nazareth. ... 5.00
4 V:Retaliators,final issue 5.00

NEVADA
DC/Vertigo (March, 1998)
1 (of 6) SvG,SL,show girl....... 2.50
2 SvG,SL,dismembered corpse ... 2.50
3 SvG,SL,stabbed an inhuman ... 2.50
4 SvG,SL,another dimension..... 2.50
5 SvG,SL 2.50
6 SvG,SL,Big Bang, concl....... 2.50
TPB Nevada, rep............... 15.00

NEW ADVENTURES
OF SUPERBOY
(See: SUPERBOY)

NEW BOOK OF COMICS
1937
1 Dr.Occult 15,000.00
2 Dr.Occult 7,000.00

NEW COMICS
1935
1 .... 18,000.00
2 .... 7,000.00
3 thru 6 .... @5,000.00
7 thru 11 .... @4,000.00
Becomes:
NEW ADVENTURE
COMICS
Jan., 1937
12 S&S 4,000.00

13 thru 20 .... @3,000.00
21 .... 2,600.00
22 thru 31 .... @2,200.00
Becomes:
ADVENTURE COMICS

NEW FUN COMICS
Feb., 1935
1 B:Oswald the Rabbit,
    Jack Woods........... 40,000.00
2 .... 17,000.00
3 .... 8,000.00
4 .... 8,000.00
5 .... 8,000.00
6 S&S,B:Dr.Occult,
    Henri Duval 20,000.00
Becomes:
MORE FUN COMICS
7 S&S,WK 5,200.00
8 S&S,WK 5,000.00
9 S&S,E:Henri Duval....... 6,000.00
10 S&S 3,500.00
11 S&S,B:Calling all Girls ... 3,200.00
12 S&S 2,800.00
13 S&S 2,800.00
14 S&S,Color,Dr.Occult 13,000.00
15 S&S 4,800.00
16 S&S,Christmas(c) 4,800.00
17 S&S 4,500.00
18 S&S 2,000.00
19 S&S 2,000.00
20 HcK,S&S 2,000.00
21 S&S 1,900.00
22 S&S 1,900.00
23 S&S 1,900.00
24 S&S 1,900.00
25 S&S 1,700.00
26 S&S 1,700.00
27 S&S 1,700.00
28 S&S 1,700.00
29 S&S 1,700.00
30 S&S 1,700.00
31 S&S 1,700.00
32 S&S,E:Dr. Occult........ 1,700.00
33 .... 1,700.00
34 .... 1,700.00
35 .... 1,700.00
36 B:Masked Ranger 1,700.00
37 thru 40 .... @1,700.00
41 E:Masked Ranger 1,300.00
42 thru 50 .... @1,300.00
51 I:The Spectre 5,000.00
52 O:The Spectre,pt.1,
    E:Wing Brady 50,000.00
53 O:The Spectre,pt.2,
    B:Capt.Desmo 35,000.00
54 E:King Carter,Spectre(c) ... 9,000.00
55 I:Dr.Fate,E:Bulldog Martin,
    Spectre(c) 12,000.00
56 B:Congo Bill,Dr.Fate(c) 4,500.00
57 Spectre(c)............. 3,000.00
58 Spectre(c)............. 3,000.00
59 A:Spectre 2,800.00
60 Spectre(c)............. 3,000.00
61 Spectre(c)............. 2,800.00
62 Spectre(c)............. 2,700.00
63 Spectre(c),E:St.Bob Neal .. 2,700.00
64 Spectre(c),B:Lance Larkin .. 2,700.00
65 Spectre(c)............. 2,700.00
66 Spectre(c)............. 2,700.00
67 Spectre(c),O:Dr. Fate,
    E:Congo Bill,Biff Bronson.. 6,500.00
68 Dr.Fate(c),B:Clip Carson ... 2,000.00
69 Dr.Fate(c).............. 2,000.00
70 Dr.Fate(c),E:Lance Larkin .. 2,000.00
71 Dr.Fate(c),I:Johnny Quick .. 5,000.00
72 Dr. Fate has Smaller Helmet,
    E:Sgt. Carey,Sgt.O'Malley . 1,600.00
73 Dr.Fate(c),I:Aquaman,Green

More Fun #41 © DC Comics, Inc.

    Arrow,Speedy 12,000.00
74 Dr.Fate(c),A:Aquaman..... 2,000.00
75 Dr.Fate(c) 1,800.00
76 Dr.Fate(c),MMe,E:Clip Carson,
    B:Johnny Quick 1,800.00
77 MMe,Green Arrow(c)...... 1,800.00
78 MMe,Green Arrow(c)...... 1,800.00
79 MMe,Green Arrow(c)...... 1,800.00
80 MMe,Green Arrow(c)...... 1,800.00
81 MMe,Green Arrow(c)...... 1,000.00
82 MMe,Green Arrow(c)...... 1,000.00
83 MMe,Green Arrow(c)...... 1,000.00
84 MMe,Green Arrow(c)...... 1,000.00
85 MMe,Green Arrow(c)...... 1,000.00
86 MMe 1,000.00
87 MMe,E:Radio Squad...... 1,000.00
88 MMe,Green Arrow(c)...... 1,000.00
89 MMe,O:Gr.Arrow&Speedy .. 1,200.00
90 MMe,Green Arrow(c)...... 1,000.00
91 MMe,Green Arrow(c) 750.00
92 MMe,Green Arrow(c) 750.00
93 MMe,B:Dover & Clover 750.00
94 MMe,Green Arrow(c) 750.00
95 MMe,Green Arrow(c) 750.00
96 MMe,Green Arrow(c) 750.00
97 MMe,JKu,E:Johnny Quick ... 750.00
98 E:Dr. Fate 750.00
99 Green Arrow(c) 750.00
100 Anniversary Issue 1,000.00
101 O&I:Superboy,
    E:The Spectre 7,500.00
102 A:Superboy 1,000.00
103 A:Superboy 800.00
104 Superboy(c)............ 650.00
105 Superboy(c)............ 650.00
106 .... 650.00
107 E:Superboy 650.00
108 A:Genius Jones,´Genius
    Meets Genius' 150.00
109 A:Genius Jones, The
    Disappearing Deposits 150.00
110 A:Genius Jones, Birds,
    Brains and Burglary 150.00
111 A:Genius Jones, Jeepers
    Creepers 150.00
112 A:Genius Jones, The
    Tell-Tale Tornado 150.00
113 A:Genius Jones, Clocks
    and Shocks 150.00
114 A:Genius Jones, The
    Milky Way.............. 150.00
115 A:Genius Jones,Foolish
    Questions.............. 150.00
116 A:Genius Jones,Palette
    For Plunder 150.00
117 A:Genius Jones,Battle of

the Pretzel Benders 150.00
118 A:Genius Jones,The
     Sinister Siren 150.00
119 A:Genius Jones,A
     Perpetual Jackpot. 150.00
120 A:Genius Jones,The Man
     in the Moon 150.00
121 A:Genius Jones,The
     Mayor Goes Haywire 125.00
122 A:Genius Jones,When Thug-
     Hood Was In Floor 125.00
123 A:Genius Jones,Hi Diddle
     Diddle, the Cat & the Fiddle . 125.00
124 A:Genius Jones,
     The Zany Zoo. 125.00
125 Genius Jones,
     Impossible But True 575.00
126 A:Genius Jones,The Case
     of the Gravy Spots 125.00
127 Nov.–Dec., 1947 . . . . 225.00

NEW GODS, THE
Feb.–March, 1971
1 JK,I:Orion 60.00
2 JK 30.00
3 JK 25.00
4 JK,O:Manhunter, rep. 16.00
5 JK,I:Fastbak & Black Racer . . 16.00
6 JK 16.00
7 JK,O:Orion 16.00
8 JK 16.00
9 JK,I:Forager 16.00
10 JK 16.00
11 JK 16.00
12 DN,DA,R:New Gods 6.00
13 DN,DA. 6.00
14 DN,DA. 6.00
15 RB,BMc. 6.00
16 DN,DA. 6.00
17 DN,DA. 6.00
18 DN,DA. 6.00
19 DN,DA. 6.00

NEW GODS
(Reprints) 1984
1 JK reprint 2.25
2 JK reprint 2.00
3 JK reprint 2.00
4 JK reprint 2.00
5 JK reprint 2.00
6 JK rep.+NewMaterial 2.00

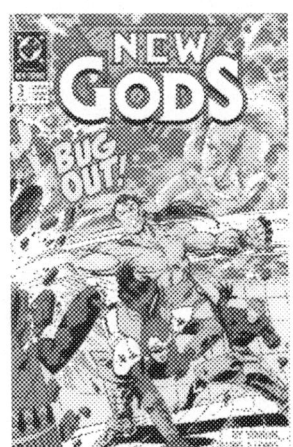

New Gods #3 © DC Comics, Inc.

NEW GODS
[2nd Series] 1989
1 From Cosmic Odyssey 2.00
2 A:Orion of New Genesis 1.50
3 A:Orion. 1.50
4 Renegade Apokolyptian Insect
     Colony 1.50
5 Orion vs. Forager 1.50
6 A:Eve Donner, Darkseid 1.50
7 Bloodline #1 . . . . 1.50
8 Bloodline #2 . . . . 1.50
9 Bloodline #3 . . . . 1.50
10 Bloodline #4 . . . . 1.50
11 Bloodline #5. . . . . 1.50
12 Bloodlines #6. . . . . 1.50
13 Back on Earth 1.50
14 I:Reflektor 1.50
15 V:Serial Killer. 1.50
16 A:Fastbak & Metron 1.50
17 A:Darkseid, Metron 1.50
18 A:YugaKhan,Darkseid,
     Moniters. 1.50
19 V:Yuga Khan 1.50
20 Darkseid Dethroned,
     V:Yuga Khan 1.50
21 A:Orion 1.50
22 A:Metron 1.50
23 A:Forever People. 1.50
24 A:Forever People. 1.50
25 The Pact #1,R:Infinity Man. . . . 1.50
26 The Pact #2. . . . . 1.50
27 Asault on Apokolips,Pact#3 . . . 1.50
28 Pact #4, final issue 1.50

[3rd Series] 1995–97
1 F:Orion vs. Darkseid. 2.00
2 RaP,Underworld Unleashed tie-in 2.00
3 RaP,Darkseid destroyed 2.00
4 RaP,F:Lightray 2.00
5 RaP,F:Orion 2.00
6 . . . . 2.00
7 RaP,R:Darkseid 2.00
8 RaP,DZ,F:Highfather,Darkseid . . 2.00
9 thru 11 . . . . @2.00
12 JBy,BWi,F:Metron 1.00
13 JBy,BWi,Orion reappears
     on Earth 2.00
14 JBy,BWi,A:Forever People,
     Lightray 2.00
TPB rep. #1–#11,b&w. 12.00
Secret Files #1 KK,JBy. 5.00

NEW GUARDIANS
1988–89
1 JSon,from Millenium series. . . . 2.50
2 JSon,Colombian Drug Cartel . . . 1.75
3 JSon,in South Africa,
     V:Janwillem's Army. 1.25
4 JSon,V:Neo-Nazi Skinheads
     in California 1.25
5 JSon,Tegra Kidnapped 1.25
6 JSon, In China, Invasion x-over . 1.25
7 JSon, Guardians Return Home . . 1.25
8 JSon, V:Janwillem 1.25
9 JSon, A:Tome Kalmaku,
     V:Janwillem 1.25
10 JSon, A:Tome Kalmaku 1.25
11 PB,Janwillem's secret 1.25
12 PB,New Guardians Future
     revealed, final issue 1.25

NEW TEEN TITANS
Nov., 1980
1 GP,RT,V:Gordanians (see DC
     Comics Presents #26 . . . . . . 12.00
2 GP,RT,I:Deathstroke the
     Terminator, I&D:Ravager. 12.00

3 GP,I:Fearsome Five 4.00
4 GP,RT,A:JLA,O:Starfire. 5.00
5 CS,RT,O:Raven,I:Trigon 5.00
6 GP,V:Trigon,O:Raven 3.00
7 GP,RT,O:Cyborg. 4.00
8 GP,RT,A Day in the Life 3.00
9 GP,RT,A:Terminator,
     V:Puppeteer. 4.00
10 GP,RT,A:Terminator 5.00
11 GP,RT,V:Hyperion 3.00
12 GP,RT,V:Titans of Myth 3.00
13 GP,RT,R:Robotman 3.00
14 GP,RT,I:New Brotherhood of
     Evil,V:Zahl and Rouge 3.00
15 GP,RT,D:Madame Rouge. 3.00
16 GP,RT,I:Captain Carrot. 3.00
17 GP,RT,I:Frances Kane 3.00
18 GP,RT,A:Orig.Starfire 3.00
19 GP,RT,A:Hawkman 3.00
20 GP,RT,V:Disruptor 3.00
21 GP,RT,GC,I:Brother Blood,
     Night Force 3.00
22 GP,RT,V:Brother Blood. 2.50
23 GP,RT,I:Blackfire 2.50
24 GP,RT,A:Omega Men,I:X-hal . . 2.50
25 GP,RT,A:Omega Men. 2.50
26 GP,RT,I:Terra,Runaway #1 . . . . 2.50
27 GP,RT,A:Speedy,Runaway #2 . . 2.50
28 GP,RT,V:Terra 3.00
29 GP,RT,V:Broth.of Evil 2.00
30 GP,RT,V:Broth.of Evil,J:Terra . . 2.00
31 GP,RT,V:Broth.of Evil 1.50
32 GP,RT,I:Thunder & Lightning . . 1.50
33 GP,I:Trident 1.50
34 GP,V:The Terminator 3.00
35 KP,RT,V:Mark Wright 1.50
36 KP,RT,A:Thunder & Lightning. . . 1.50
37 GP,RT,A:Batman/Outsiders(x-over
     BATO#5),V:Fearsome Five . . . 2.00
38 GP,O:Wonder Girl 1.50
39 GP,Grayson quits as Robin . . . 5.00
40 GP,A:Brother Blood 1.50
Ann.#1 GP,RT,Blackfire. 3.50
Ann.#2 GP,I:Vigilante 3.00
Ann.#3 GP,DG,D:Terra,A:Deathstroke
     V:The H.I.V.E. 3.50
Ann.#4 rep.Direct Ann.#1 . . . . . . 1.25
TPB Judas Contract rep.#39-#44,
     Ann.#3,new GP(c) 14.95

[Special Issues]
Keebler:GP,DG,Drugs. 2.50
Beverage:Drugs,RA 2.50
IBM:Drugs 3.00

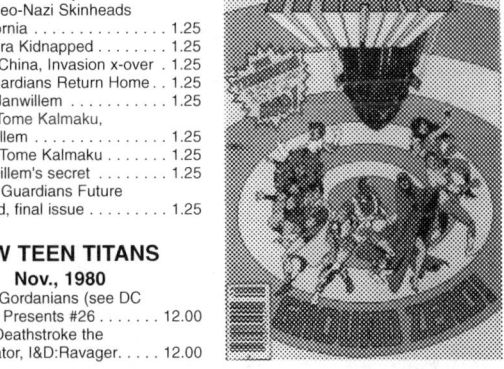

New Teen Titans #10 © DC Comics Inc.

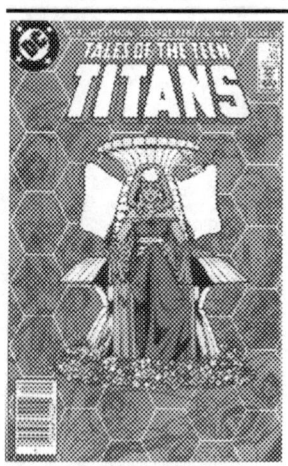

Tales of the Teen Titans #46
© DC Comics, Inc.

Becomes:

TALES OF THE
TEEN TITANS
1984–88

41 GP,A:Brother Blood 2.00
42 GP,DG,V:Deathstroke 5.00
43 GP,DG,V:Deathstroke 5.00
44 GP,DG,I:Nightwing,O:Deathstroke
    Joe Wilson becomes Jericho . 10.00
45 GP,A:Aqualad,V:The H.I.V.E. . . . 2.00
46 GP,A:Aqualad,V:The H.I.V.E. . . . 2.00
47 GP,A:Aqualad,V:The H.I.V.E. . . . 2.00
48 SR,V:The Recombatants 2.00
49 GP,Cl,V:Dr.Light,A:Flash 2.00
50 GP/DG W:Wonder Girl &
    Terry Long,C:Batman,
    Wonder Woman 2.50
51 RB,A:Cheshire 2.00
52 RB,A:Cheshire. 2.00
53 RB,I:Ariel,A:Terminator. 2.50
54 RB,A:Terminator 2.50
55 A:Terminator 2.50
56 A:Fearsome Five 1.75
57 A:Fearsome Five 1.75
58 E:MWn(s),A:Fearsome Five. . . . 1.75
59 rep. DC presennts #26. . . . . . . 1.50
60 thru 91 rep. . . . . @1.50

[Limited Series]

1 GP,O:Cyborg 2.00
2 GP,O:Raven 2.00
3 GD,O:Changling 2.00
4 GP/EC,O:Starfire 2.00

NEW TEEN TITANS
[Direct sales series]
Aug., 1984

1 B:MWn(s),GP,L:Raven 4.00
2 GP,D:Azareth,A:Trigon 3.00
3 GP,V:Raven 3.00
4 GP,V:Trigon,Raven 3.00
5 GP,D:Trigon,Raven disappears . . 3.00
6 GP,A:Superman,Batman. 2.50
7 JL,V:Titans of Myth. 2.50
8 JL,V:Titans of Myth. 2.50
9 JL,V:Titans of Myth,I:Kole 2.50
10 JL,O:Kole 2.50
11 JL,O:Kole. 2.50
12 JL,Ghost story 2.50
13 EB,Crisis 2.25
14 EB,Crisis 2.25
15 EB,A:Raven. 2.25

16 EB,A:OmegaMen. 2.25
17 EB,V:Blackfire 2.25
18 E:MWn(s),EB,V:Blackfire 2.25
19 EB,V:Mento 2.25
20 GP(c),EB,V:Cheshire,J.Todd . . 2.25
21 GP(c),EB,V:Cheshire,J.Todd . . 2.25
22 GP(c),EB,V:Blackfire,Mento,
    Brother Blood 2.25
23 GP(c),V:Blackfire 2.25
24 CB,V:Hybrid. 2.25
25 EB,RT,V:Hybrid,Mento,A:Flash. . 2.25
26 KGa,V:Mento. 2.25
27 KGa,Church of Br.Blood. 2.00
28 EB,RT,V:BrotherBlood,A:Flash . . 2.00
29 EB,RT,V:Brother Blood,
    A:Flash,Robin. 2.00
30 EB,Batman,Superman 2.25
31 EB,RT,V:Brother Blood,A:Flash
    Batman,Robin,Gr.Lantern Corps
    Superman 2.00
32 EB,RT,Murder Weekend 2.00
33 EB,V:Terrorists. 2.00
34 EB,RT,V:Mento,Hybird 2.00
35 PB,RT,V:Arthur & Eve 2.00
36 EB,RT,I:Wildebeest 2.50
37 EB,RT,V:Wildebeest. 2.00
38 EB,RT,A:Infinity 2.00
39 EB,RT,F:Raven 2.00
40 EB,RT,V:Gentleman Ghost. 2.00
41 EB,V:Wildebeest,A:Puppeteer,
    Trident,Wildebeest 2.00
42 EB,RT,V:Puppeteer,Gizmo,
    Trident,Wildebeest 2.00
43 CS,RT,V:Phobia. 2.00
44 RT,V:Godiva 2.00
45 EB,RT,A:Dial H for Hero. 2.00
46 EB,RT,A:Dial H for Hero. 2.00
47 O:Titans,C:Wildebeest 2.00
48 EB,RT,A:Red Star 2.00
49 EB,RT,A:Red Star 2.00
Ann.#1 A:Superman,V:Brainiac. . . 2.50
Ann.#2 JBy,JL,O:Brother Blood. . . . 3.00
Ann.#3 I:Danny Chase 2.50
Ann.#4 V:Godiva 2.50

Becomes:

NEW TITANS
1988–96

50 B:MWn(s),GP,BMc,B:Who is
    Wonder Girl? 4.00
51 GP,BMc 3.00
52 GP,BMc 3.00
53 GP,RT 3.00
54 GP,RT,E:Who is Wonder Girl? . . 3.00
55 GP,RT,I:Troia 3.00
56 MBr,RT,Tale of Middle Titans . . 2.50
57 GP,BMc,V:Wildebeast 2.50
58 GP,TG,BMc,V:Wildebeast 2.50
59 GP,TG,BMc,V:Wildebeast 2.50
60 GP,TG,BMc,3rd A:Tim Drake
    (Face Revealed),Batman 5.00
61 GP,TG,BMc,A:Tim Drake,
    Batman 5.00
62 TG,AV,A:Deathstroke 3.00
63 TG,AV,A:Deathstroke 3.00
64 TG,AV,A:Deathstroke 3.00
65 TG,AV,A:Deathstroke,Tim Drake,
    Batman 3.00
66 TG,AV,V:Eric Forrester. 2.50
67 TG,AV,V:Eric Forrester. 2.50
68 SE,V:Royal Flush Gang 2.50
69 SE,V:Royal Flush Gang 2.50
70 SE,A:Deathstroke 3.00
71 TG,AV,B:Deathstroke,
    B:Titans Hunt 5.00
72 TG,AV,D:Golden Eagle 4.00
73 TG,AV,I:Phantasm 4.00
74 TG,AV,I:Pantha 3.00
75 TG,AV,IR:Jericho/Wildebeest . . . 3.00
76 TG,AV,V:Wildebeests. 2.50
77 TG,AV,A:Red Star,N:Cyborg. . . . 2.50

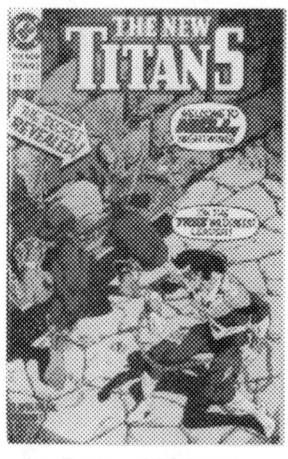

New Titans #82 © DC Comics, Inc.

78 TG,AV,V:Cyborg. 2.50
79 TG,AV,I:Team Titans 3.00
80 KGa,PC,A:Team Titans 2.50
81 CS,AV,War of the Gods 2.50
82 TG,AV,V:Wildebeests. 2.50
83 TG,AV,D:Jericho 3.00
84 TG,AV,E:Titans Hunt 2.50
85 TG,AV,I:Baby Wildebeest 2.50
86 CS,AV,E:Deathstroke. 2.50
87 TG,AV,A:Team Titans 2.50
88 TG,AV,CS,V:Team Titans 2.50
89 JBr,I:Lord Chaos 2.50
90 TG,AV,Total Chaos#2,A:Team
    Titans,D'stroke,V:Lord Chaos . . 2.00
91 TG,AV,Total Chaos#5,A:Team
    Titans,D'stroke,V:Lord Chaos . . 2.00
92 E:MWn(s),TG,AV,Total Chaos#8,
    A:Team Titans,V:Lord Chaos . . 2.00
93 TG,AV,Titans Sell-Out#3 . . . . . . 2.00
94 PJ,F:Red Star & Cyborg 2.00
95 PJ,Red Star gains new powers . 2.00
96 PJ,I:Solar Flare,
    V:Konstantine. 2.00
97 TG,AV,B:The Darkening,R:Speedy
    V:Brotherhood of Evil 2.00
98 TG,AV,V:Brotherhood of Evil . . . 2.00
99 TG,AV,I:Arsenal (Speedy) 2.00
100 TG,AV,W:Nightwing&Starfire,
    V:Deathwing,Raven,A:Flash,Team
    Titans,Hologram(c) 4.00
101 AV(i),L:Nightwing 2.00
102 AV(i),A:Prester John 2.00
103 AV(i),V:Bro. of Evil 2.00
104 Terminus #1. . . . . 2.00
105 Terminus #2. . . . . 2.00
106 Terminus #3. . . . . 2.00
107 Terminus #4. . . . . 2.00
108 A:Supergirl,Flash 2.00
109 F:Starfire 2.00
110 A:Flash,Serg.Steele. 2.00
111 A:Checkmate 2.00
112 A:Checkmate 2.00
113 F:Nightwing 2.25
114 L:Starfire, Nightwing,Panthra,
    Wildebeest. 2.00
115 A:Trigon. 2.00
116 Changling 2.00
117 V:Psimon. 2.00
118 V:Raven + Brotherhood 2.00
119 Suffer the Children,pt.1 . . . . . . 2.00
120 Forever Evil,pt.2 . . . . 2.00
121 Forever Evil,pt.3 . . . . 2.00
122 Crimelord/Syndicate War,pt.2
    J:Supergirl 2.25
123 MWn(s),RRa,O:Minion 2.25

124 The Siege of Zi Charan 2.25
125 The Siege of Zi Charan 3.00
126 Meltdown,pt.1 . . . . 2.25
127 MWn,Meltdown, cont. 2.25
128 MWn,Meltdown, cont. 2.25
129 MWn,Meltdown, cont. 2.25
130 MWn,Meltdown,final issue 2.25
Ann.#5 V:Children of the Sun 3.00
Ann.#6 CS,F:Starfire. 3.00
Ann.#7 Armageddon 2001,I:Future
   Teen Titans 4.00
Ann.#8 PJ,Eclipso,V:Deathstroke . . 3.75
Ann.#9 Bloodlines#5,I:Anima 3.75
Ann.#10 Elseworlds story 3.75
Ann.#11 Year One Annual. 3.95
#0 Spec. Zero Hour,new team 2.00

NEW TITANS
SELL-OUT SPECIAL
1 SE,AV,AH,I:Teeny Titans,
   w/Nightwing poster. 3.75

NEW YEAR'S EVIL:
Dec., 1997
Body Doubles #1 DAn,ALa,JoP,
   JPn(c) 2.00
Dark Nemesis #1 DJu,Ccs,JPn(c). . 2.00
Darkseid #1 JBy,SB,JPn(c). 2.00
Gog #1 MWa,JOy,DJa,JPn(c) 2.00
Mr. Mxyzptlk #1 TMo,JPn(c). 2.00
Prometheus #1 AIG,TMo,JPn(c) . . . 2.00
Scarecrow #1 PrM,DFg,JPn(c) 2.00
The Rogues #1 BAu,RoW,JPn(c) . . 2.00

NEW YORK
WORLD'S FAIR
1 1939 . . . . 25,000.00
2 1940 . . . . 14,000.00

NIGHT FORCE
Aug., 1982
1 GC,1:Night Force 1.25
2 thru 13 GC . . . . @1.25
14 GC,Sept.,1983. . . . . 1.25

NIGHT FORCE
Oct. 1996
1 MWn(s),BA,Baron Winters leads. 2.25
2 MWn(s) 2.25
3 MWn(s) 2.25
4 MWn(s),EB,"Hell Seems a
   Heaven". 2.25
5 MWn(s),Low,SMa,"Dreamers of
   Dreams" pt.1 . . . . 2.25
6 MWn(s),Low,SMa,"Dreamers of
   Dreams" pt.2 . . . . 2.25
7 MWn(s),Low,SMa,"Dreamers of
   Dreams" pt.3 . . . . 2.25
8 MWn(s),"Convergence," x-over. . 2.25
9 MWn(s),Low,Sma,"The Eleventh
   Man" pt.1 (of 3) 2.25
10 MWn(s),"Eleventh Man" pt.2 . . . 2.50
11 MWn(s),"Eleventh Man" pt.3. . . . 2.50
12 MWn(s),Lady of the Leopard
   final issue,Sept. 1997 . . . . 2.50

NIGHTWING
1995
1 R:Nightwing 3.50
2 N:Nightwing 3.00
3 visit to Kravia (of 4). 3.00
4 conclusion 3.00

NIGHTWING
Aug. 1996
1 CDi(s),SMc,KIS,Nightwing goes
   to Bl haven. 4.00
2 CDi(s),SMc,KIS,V:smugglers. . . . 2.50
3 CDi(s),SMc,KIS,run-down bank
   "held up" 2.25
4 CDi(s),SMc,KIS,V:Lady Vick 2.25
5 CDi(s),SMc,KIS,. 2.25
6 CDi(s),SMc,KIS,A:Tim Drake . . . 2.25
7 CDi(s),SMc,KIS,"Rough Justice" . 2.25
8 CDi(s),SMc,KIS,V: the kingpin
   of Bl haven 2.00
9 CDi(s),SMc,KIS,kidnapping, pt.1 . 2.00
10 CDi(s),SMc,KIS,nightmare
   or dream? 2.00
11 CDi(s),SMc,V:Soames,
   Blockbuster 2.00
12 CDi(s),SMc,Mutt 2.00
13 CDi(s),SMc,KIS,A:Batman 2.00
14 CDi(s),SMc,KIS,A:Batman,pt.2. . 2.00
15 CDi(s),SMc,KIS,A:Batman,pt.3. . 2.00
16 CDi(s),SMc,KIS,Nightwingmobile 2.00
17 CDi(s),SMc,KIS,V:Man-Bat. 2.00
18 CDi(s),SMc,KIS 2.00
19 CDi(s),SMc,KIS,Cataclysm
   x-over, pt.2 . . . . 2.00
20 CDi(s),SMc,KIS,Cataclysm. 2.00
21 CDi(s),SMc,KIS,post Cataclysm 2.00
22 CDi(s),SMc,KIS,V:Lady Vic 2.00
23 Brotherhood of
   the Fist x-over, pt.4. . . . . 2.00
24 CDi(s),SMc,KIS,cop story. 2.00
25 CDi(s),SMc,KIS,A:Robin 2.00
26 CDi(s),SMc,KIS,A;Huntress 2.00
27 CDi(s),SMc,KIS,V:Torque 2.00
28 CDi(s),SMc,KIS,V:Torque 2.00
29 CDi(s),SMc,KIS,A:Huntress 2.00
30 CDi(s),SMc,KIS,A:Superman . . . 2.00
31 CDi(s),SMc,KIS,A:Nite-Wing . . . 2.00
32 CDi(s),SMc,KIS,V:DoubleDare . . 2.00
33 CDi(s),SMc,KIS,
   V:Electrocutioner 2.00
34 CDi(s),SMc,KIS,x-over. 2.00
35 CDi(s),SMc,KIS,No
   Man's Land,pt.1 . . . . 2.00
36 CDi(s),SMc,No
   Man's Land,pt.2 . . . . 2.00
Ann.#1 Pulp Heroes (Romance) . . 3.95
Spec.#1,000,000 CDi(s),SMc,KIS . 2.00
Secret Files #1 64-page 4.95
TPB A Knight in Bludhaven,CDi,
   SMc,KIS, rep. #1–#8. . . . . . . 15.00
TPB Ties That Bind, DON,AIG,
   DG,KIS,rep. 13.00
TPB Rough Justice 18.00

NIGHTWING:
ALFRED'S RETURN
1 . . . . 3.50

NIGHTWING
AND HUNTRESS
March, 1998
1 (of 4) BSz,conflict. 2.00
2 BSz,good cop, bad cop. 2.00
3 BSz,Malfatti 2.00
4 BSz,concl. 2.00

NUTSY SQUIRREL
Sept.–Oct., 1954
61 SM 40.00
62 thru 71 . . . . @25.00
72 Nov., 1957. . . . . 25.00

OMAC
Sept.–Oct., 1974
1 JK,I&O:Omac 10.00
2 JK,I:Mr.Big 6.00
3 JK,100,000 foes 6.00
4 JK,V:Kafka 6.00
5 JK,New Bodies for Old 6.00
6 JK,The Body Bank 6.00
7 JK,The Ocean Stealers 6.00
8 JK,Last issue 6.00

[2nd Series] 1991
1 JBy,B&W prestige. 5.00
2 JBy,The Great Depression era . . 4.50
3 JBy,'To Kill Adolf Hitler'. 4.50
4 JBy,D:Mr.Big. 4.50

OMEGA MEN
Dec., 1982
1 KG,V:Citadel. 2.50
2 KG,O:Broot. 2.00
3 KG,I:Lobo. 4.00
4 KG,D:Demonia,I:Felicity 1.50
5 KG,V:Lobo 3.00
6 KG,V:Citadel,D:Gepsen 2.00
7 O:Citadel,L:Auron 2.00
8 R:Nimbus,I:H.Hokum 2.00
9 V:HarryHokum,A:Lobo 2.00
10 A:Lobo (First Full Story) 3.00
11 V:Blackfire. 1.50
12 R:Broots Wife 1.50
13 A:Broots Wife 1.50
14 Karna 1.50
15 Primus Goes Mad 1.50
16 Spotlight Issue. 1.50
17 V:Psions 1.50
18 V:Psions 1.50
19 V:Psions,C:Lobo 1.75
20 V:Psions,A:Lobo 2.00
21 Spotlight Issue. 1.50
22 Nimbus 1.50
23 Nimbus 1.50
24 Okaara 1.50
25 Kalista 1.50
26 V:Spiderguild 1.50
27 V:Psions 1.50
28 V:Psions 1.50
29 V:Psions 1.50
30 R:Primus,I:Artin 1.50
31 Crisis tie-in 1.50
32 Felicity. 1.50
33 Regufe World 1.50
34 A:New Teen Titans. 1.50

Omega Men #1 © DC Comics Inc.

---

35 A:New Teen Titans. 1.50
36 Last Days of Broot. 1.50
37 V:Spiderguild,A:Lobo. 2.00
38 A:Tweener Network 1.25
Ann.#1 KG,R:Harpis. 2.25
Ann.#2 KG,O:Primus 2.25

100 BULLETS
DC/Vertigo 1999
1 F:Dizzy Cordova & Agent Graves 2.50
2 . . . . 2.50
3 F:Mr.Shepard 2.50

100% TRUE?
DC/Paradox Press B&W 1996
1 rep. from Paradox Press books. . 3.50

OUR ARMY AT WAR
Aug., 1952
1 Cl(c),Dig Your FoxholeDeep. 1,500.00
2 Cl(c),Champ. 650.00
3 GK(c),No Exit 500.00
4 IN(c),Last Man 450.00
5 IN(c),T.N.T. Bouquet 400.00
6 IN(c),Battle Flag 400.00
7 IN(c),Dive Bomber 400.00
8 IN(c),One Man Army. 400.00
9 GC(c),Undersea Raider 400.00
10 IN(c),Soldiers on the
   High Wire. 400.00
11 IN(c),Scratch One Meatball . . 400.00
12 IN(c),The Big Drop. 300.00
13 BK(c),Ghost Ace 300.00
14 Drummer of Waterloo. 300.00
15 IN(c),Thunder in the Skies . . . 300.00
16 IN(c),A Million To One Shot . . 300.00
17 IN(c),The White Death 300.00
18 IN(c),Frontier Fighter 300.00
19 IN(c),The Big Ditch 300.00
20 IN(c),Abandon Ship 300.00
21 IN(c),Dairy of a Flattop. 200.00
22 JGr(c),Ranger Raid 200.00
23 IN(c),Jungle Navy 200.00
24 IN(c),Suprise Landing 200.00
25 JGr(c),Take 'Er Down. 200.00
26 JGr(c),Sky Duel. 200.00
27 IN(c),Diary of a Frogman 200.00
28 JGr(c),Detour-War 200.00
29 IN(c),Grounded Fighter 200.00
30 JGr(c),Torpedo Raft 200.00
31 IN(c),Howitzer Hill 200.00
32 JGr(c),Battle Mirror 175.00

33 JGr(c),Fighting Gunner 175.00
34 JGr(c),Point-Blank War 175.00
35 JGr(c),Frontline Tackle 175.00
36 JGr(c),Foxhole Mascot. 175.00
37 JGr(c),Walking Battle Pin 175.00
38 JGr(c),Floating Pillbox 175.00
39 JGr(c),Trench Trap. 175.00
40 RH(c),Tank Hunter 175.00
41 JGr(c),Jungle Target 175.00
42 IN(c),Shadow Targets. 150.00
43 JGr(c),A Bridge For Billy 150.00
44 JGr(c),Thunder In The Desert 150.00
45 JGr(c),Diary of a Fighter Pilot. 150.00
46 JGr(c),Prize Package. 150.00
47 JGr(c),Flying Jeep 150.00
48 JGr(c),Front Seat. 150.00
49 JKu(c),Landing Postponed . . . 150.00
50 JGr(c),Mop-Up Squad 150.00
51 JGr(c),Battle Tag 125.00
52 JGr(c),Pony Express Pilot . . . 125.00
53 JGr(c),One Ringside-For War. 125.00
54 JKu(c),No-Man Secret 125.00
55 JGr(c),No Rest For A Raider . 125.00
56 JKu(c),You're Next 125.00
57 JGr(c),Ten-Minute Break 125.00
58 JKu(c),The Fighting SnowBird 125.00
59 JGr(c),The Mustang Had
   My Number 125.00
60 JGr(c),Ranger Raid 125.00
61 JGr(c),A Pigeon For Easy Co. 110.00
62 JKu(c),Trigger Man. 110.00
63 JGr(c),The Big Toss 110.00
64 JKu(c),Tank Rider 110.00
65 JGr(c),Scramble-War Upstairs 110.00
66 RH(c),Gunner Wanted 110.00
67 JKu(c),Boiling Point 110.00
68 JKu(c),End of the Line 110.00
69 JGr(c),Combat Cage 110.00
70 JGr(c),Torpedo Tank. 110.00
71 JGr(c),Flying Mosquitoes 110.00
72 JGr(c),No. 1 Pigeon 110.00
73 JKu(c),Shooting Gallery 110.00
74 JGr(c),Ace Without Guns 110.00
75 JGr(c),Blind Night Fighter 110.00
76 JKu(c),Clipped Hellcat 110.00
77 JGr(c),Jets Don't Dream. 110.00
78 IN(c),Battle Nurse 110.00
79 JGr(c),What's the Price
   of a B-17?. 110.00
80 JGr(c),The Sparrow And
   The...Hawk 110.00
81 JGr(c),Sgt. Rock in The
   Rock of Easy Co. 2,400.00
82 JGr(c),Gun Jockey. 550.00
83 JGr(c),B:Sgt.Rock Stories,
   The Rock and the Wall . . . 1,000.00
84 JKu(c),Laughter On
   Snakehead Hill. 250.00
85 JGr(c),Ice Cream Soldier 300.00
86 RH(c),Tank 711 . . . . 200.00
87 RH(c),Calling Easy Co. 200.00
88 JKu(c),The Hard Way. 200.00
89 RH(c),No Shoot From Easy . . 200.00
90 JKu(c),3 Stripes Hill 200.00
91 JKu(c),No Answer from Sarge 200.00
92 JGr(c),Luck of Easy 150.00
93 JGr(c),Deliver One Airfield . . . 150.00
94 JKu(c),Target-Easy Company. 150.00
95 JKu(c),Battle Of The Stripes. . 150.00
96 JGr(c),Last Stand For Easy . . 150.00
97 JKu(c),What Makes A
   Sergeant Run?. 150.00
98 JKu(c),Soldiers Never Die . . . 150.00
99 JKu(c),Easy's Hardest Battle . 150.00
100 JKu(c),No Exit For Easy. 150.00
101 JKu(c),End Of Easy 100.00
102 JKu(c),The Big Star 100.00
103 RH(c),Easy's Had It 100.00
104 JKu(c),A New Kind Of War. . 100.00
105 JKu(c),T.N.T. Birthday 100.00
106 JKu(c),Meet Lt. Rock 100.00

107 JKu(c),Doom Over Easy. . . . 100.00
108 JGr(c),Unknown Sergeant . . 100.00
109 JKu(c),Roll Call For Heroes . 100.00
110 JKu(c),That's An Order. 100.00
111 JKu(c),What's The Price
   Of A Dog Tag 100.00
112 JKu(c),Battle Shadow. 100.00
113 JKu(c),Eyes Of A
   Blind Gunner 100.00
114 JKu(c),Killer Sergeant 100.00
115 JKu(c),Rock's Battle Family . 100.00
116 JKu(c),S.O.S. Sgt. Rock. . . . 100.00
117 JKu(c),Snafu Squad. 75.00
118 RH(c),The Tank Vs. The
   Tin Soldier 75.00
119 JKu(c),A Bazooka For
   Babyface 75.00
120 JGr(c),Battle Tags
   For Easy Co. 65.00
121 JKu(c),New Boy In Easy 65.00
122 JKu(c),Battle of the
   Pajama Commandoes 65.00
123 JGr(c),Battle Brass Ring 65.00
124 JKu(c),Target-Sgt. Rock. 65.00
125 JKu(c),Hold-At All Costs. 65.00
126 RH(c),The End Of
   Easy Company. 65.00
127 JKu(c),4 Faces of Sgt. Rock. . 65.00
128 JKu(c),O:Sgt. Rock 225.00
129 JKu(c),Heroes Need Cowards 65.00
130 JKu(c),No Hill For Easy 65.00
131 JKu(c),One Pair of
   Dogtags For Sale. 65.00
132 JKu(c),Young Soldiers
   Never Cry. 65.00
133 JKu(c),Yesterday's Hero 65.00
134 JKu(c),The T.N.T. Book 65.00
135 JKu(c),Battlefield Double 65.00
136 JKu(c),Make Me A Hero. 65.00
137 JKu(c),Too Many Sergeants . . 65.00
138 JKu(c),Easy's Lost Sparrow . . 65.00
139 JKu(c),A Firing Squad
   For Easy 65.00
140 JKu(c),Brass Sergeant. 65.00
141 JKu(c),Dead Man's Trigger. . . 65.00
142 JKu(c),Easy's New Topkick . . 65.00
143 JKu(c),Easy's T.N.T. Crop . . . 65.00
144 JKu(c),The Sparrow And
   The Tiger 65.00
145 JKu(c),A Feather For
   Little Sure Shot. 65.00
146 JKu(c),The Fighting Guns
   For Easy 65.00
147 JKu(c),Book One:Generals
   Don't Die 65.00

148 JKu(c),Book Two:Generals
Don't Die:Generals Are
Sergeants With Stars 65.00
149 JKu(c),Surrender Ticket 65.00
150 JKu(c),Flytrap Hill 65.00
151 JKu(c),War Party,
I:Enemy Ace 300.00
152 Jku(c),Last Man-Last Shot . . 100.00
153 JKu(c),Easy's Last Stand . . . 150.00
154 JKu(c),Boobytrap Mascot 50.00
155 JKu(c),No Stripes For Me. . . . 65.00
156 JKu(c),The Human Tank Trap 50.00
157 JKu(c),Nothin's Ever
Lost In War. 50.00
158 JKu(c),Iron Major-Rock
Sergeant 50.00
159 JKu(c),The Blind Gun. 50.00
160 JKu(c),What's The Color
Of Your Blood. 50.00
161 JKu(c),Dead End
For A Dogface 50.00
162 JKu(c),The Price and
The Sergeant 50.00
163 JKu(c),Kill Me-Kill Me. 50.00
164 JKu(c),No Exit For Easy,
reprint from #100 . . . . 70.00
165 JKu(c),The Return of the
Iron Major. 40.00
166 JKu(c),Half A Sergeant 40.00
167 JKu(c),Kill One-Save One . . . 40.00
168 JKu(c),I Knew The
Unknown Soldier 75.00
169 JKu(c),Nazi On My Back 40.00
170 JKu(c),Buzzard Bait Hill 40.00
171 JKu(c),The Sergeant MustDie 35.00
172 JKu(c),A Slug for a Sergeant . 35.00
173 JKu(c),Easy's Hardest Battle,
reprint from #99 . . . . 35.00
174 JKu(c),One Kill Too Many. . . . 35.00
175 JKu(c),T.N.T. Letter 35.00
176 JKu(c),Give Me Your Stripes . 35.00
177 JKu(c),Target-Easy Company,
reprint from #94 . . . . 35.00
178 JKu(c),Only One Medal
For Easy 35.00
179 JKu(c),A Penny Jackie
Johnson 35.00
180 JKu(c),You Can't
Kill A General 35.00
181 RH(c),Monday's Coward-
Tuesday's Hero 35.00
182 NA,RH(c),The Desert Rats
of Easy. 40.00
183 NA,JKu(c),Sergeants Don't
Stay Dead 40.00
184 JKu(c),Candidate For A
Firing Squad. 30.00
185 JKu(c),Battle Flag For A G.I. . 30.00
186 NA,JKu(c),3 Stripes Hill
reprint from #90 . . . . 40.00
187 JKu(c),Shadow of a Sergeant. 30.00
188 JKu(c),Death Comes for Easy 30.00
189 JKu(c),The Mission Was
Murder 30.00
190 JKu(c),What Make's A
Sergeant Run?, reprint
from #97. . . . . 30.00
191 JKu(c),Death Flies High,
A:Johnny Cloud 30.00
192 JKu(c),A Firing Squad
For A Sergeant. 30.00
193 JKu(c),Blood In the Desert . . . 30.00
194 JKu(c),Time For Vengeance . . 30.00
195 JKu(c),Dead Town 30.00
196 JKu(c),Stop The War-I Want
To Get Off 30.00
197 JKu(c),Last Exit For Easy. . . . 30.00
198 JKu(c),Plugged Nickel 30.00
199 JKu(c),Nazi Ghost Wolf 30.00
200 JKu(c),The Troubadour 35.00
201 JKu(c),The Graffiti Writer 25.00

202 JKu(c),The Sarge Is Dead . . . 20.00
203 JKu(c),Easy's Had It,
reprint from # 103. . . . . 25.00
204 JKu(c) 20.00
205 JKu(c) 20.00
206 JKu(c),There's A War On 20.00
207 JKu(c),A Sparrow's Prayer . . . 20.00
208 JKu(c),A Piece of Rag...And
A Hank of Hair 20.00
209 JKu(c),I'm Still Alive 20.00
210 JKu(c),I'm Kilroy. 20.00
211 JKu(c),The Treasure of
St. Daniel 20.00
212 JKu(c),The Quiet War 20.00
213 JKu(c),A Letter For Bulldozer. 20.00
214 JKu(c),Where Are You? 20.00
215 JKu(c),Pied Piper of Peril 20.00
216 JKu(c),Doom Over Easy,
reprint from # 107. . . . . 25.00
217 JKu(c),Surprise Party. 15.00
218 JKu(c),Medic!. 15.00
219 JKu(c),Yesterday's Hero 15.00
220 JKu(c),Stone-Age War 15.00
221 JKu(c),Hang-Up 15.00
222 JKu(c),Dig In, Easy 15.00
223 JKu(c),On Time 15.00
224 JKu(c),One For The Money . . 15.00
225 JKu(c),Face Front 15.00
226 JKu(c),Death Stop 15.00
227 JKu(c),Traitor's Blood. 15.00
228 JKu(c),It's A Dirty War 15.00
229 JKu(c),The Battle of the
Sergeants, reprint from #128 . 35.00
230 JKu(c),Home Is The Hunter . 15.00
231 JKu(c),My Brother's Keeper . 15.00
232 JKu(c),3 Men In A Tub 15.00
233 JKu(c),Head Count 15.00
234 JKu(c),Summer In Salerno . . . 15.00
235 JKu(c),Pressure Point 15.00
236 JKu(c),Face The Devil 15.00
237 JKu(c),Nobody Cares. 15.00
238 JKu(c),I Kid You Not. 15.00
239 JKu(c),The Soldier 15.00
240 JKu(c),NA 25.00
241 JKu(c),War Story 20.00
242 JKu(c),Infantry 20.00
243 JKu(c),24 Hour Pass 15.00
244 JKu(c),Easy's First Tiger 15.00
245 JKu(c),The Prisoner 15.00
246 JKu(c),Naked Combat 15.00
247 JKu(c),The Vision 12.00
248 JKu(c),The Firing Squad 12.00
249 JKu(c),The Luck of Easy,WW. 15.00
250 JKu(c),90 Day Wonder. 12.00
251 JKu(c),The Iron Major 12.00

Our Army at War #9
© DC Comics Inc.

252 JKu(c),The Iron Hand. 12.00
253 JKu(c),Rock and Iron 12.00
254 JKu(c),The Town 12.00
255 JKu(c),What's It Like 12.00
256 JKu(c),School For Sergeants . 12.00
257 JKu(c),The Castaway. 12.00
258 JKu(c),The Survivors 12.00
259 JKu(c),Lost Paradise 12.00
260 JKu(c),Hell's Island 12.00
261 JKu(c),The Medal That
Nobody Wanted 12.00
262 JKu(c),The Return 12.00
263 JKu(c),The Cage 12.00
264 JKu(c),The Hunt. 12.00
265 JKu(c),The Brother. 12.00
266 JKu(c),The Evacuees. 12.00
267 JKu(c),A Bakers Dozen 12.00
268 JKu(c),The Elite. 12.00
269 JKu(c) 12.00
270 JKu(c),Spawn of the Devil . . . 12.00
271 JKu(c),Brittle Harvest. 12.00
272 JKu(c),The Bloody Flag 12.00
273 JKu(c),The Arena. 12.00
274 JKu(c),Home Is The Hero . . . 12.00
275 JKu(c),Graveyard Battlefield. . 12.00
276 JKu(c),A Bullet For Rock 12.00
277 JKu(c),Gashouse Gang 12.00
278 JKu(c),Rearguard Action 12.00
279 JKu(c),Mined City 12.00
280 JKu(c),Mercy Mission. 12.00
281 JKu(c),Dead Man's Eyes 12.00
282 JKu(c),Pieces of Time 12.00
283 JKu(c),Dropouts. 12.00
284 JKu(c),Linkup. 12.00
285 JKu(c),Bring Him Back. 12.00
286 JKu(c),Firebird 12.00
287 JKu(c),The Fifth Dimension . . 12.00
288 JKu(c),Defend-Or Destroy . . . 12.00
289 JKu(c),The Line 12.00
290 JKu(c),Super-Soldiers 12.00
291 JKu(c),Death Squad. 12.00
292 JKu(c),A Lesson In Blood. . . . 12.00
293 JKu(c),It Figures 12.00
294 JKu(c),Coffin For Easy 12.00
295 JKu(c),The Devil in Paradise . 12.00
296 JKu(c),Combat Soldier 12.00
297 JKu(c),Percentages 12.00
298 JKu(c),Return to Chartres . . . 12.00
299 JKu(c),Three Soldiers 12.00
300 JKu(c),300th Hill 12.00
301 JKu(c),The Farm 12.00
Becomes:

SGT. ROCK
1977–88
302 JKu(c),Anzio-The Bloodbath,
part I 8.00
303 JKu(c),Anzio, part II 6.00
304 JKu(c),Anzio, part III 6.00
305 JKu(c),Dead Man's Trigger,
reprint from #141 . . . . 6.00
306 JKu(c),The Last Soldier 6.00
307 JKu(c),I'm Easy 6.00
308 JKu(c),One Short Step. 6.00
309 JKu(c),Battle Clowns 6.00
310 JKu(c),Hitler's Wolf Children. . . 6.00
311 JKu(c),The Sergeant and
the Lady. 6.00
312 JKu(c),No Name Hill 6.00
313 JKu(c),A Jeep For Joey 6.00
314 JKu(c),Gimme Sky. 6.00
315 JKu(c),Combat Antenna. 6.00
316 JKu(c),Another Hill... . . . . 6.00
317 JKu(c),Hell's Oven 6.00
318 JKu(c),Stone-Age War 6.00
319 JKu(c),To Kill a Sergeant 6.00
320 JKu(c),Never Salute a
Sergeant 6.00
321 JKu(c),It's Murder Out Here . . . 5.00
322 JKu(c),The Killer 5.00
323 JKu(c),Monday's Hero 5.00

DC COMICS

324 JKu(c),Ghost of a Tank 5.00	22 JKu,RA,JGr(c),3 Doorways
325 JKu(c),Future Kill, part I 5.00	To War 100.00
326 JKu(c),Future Kill, part II 5.00	23 RA,IN,JA,JGr(c),Tin Fish Pilot 100.00
327 JKu(c),Death Express 5.00	24 RA,RH,JGr(c),Frogman Duel . 100.00
328 JKu(c),Waiting For Rock 5.00	25 RA,JKu(c),Dead End 100.00
329 JKu(c),Dead Heat 5.00	26 IN,RH,JKu(c),Tag Day 100.00
330 JKu(c),G.I. Trophy 5.00	27 MD,RA,JKu(c),TNT Escort . . . 100.00
331 JKu(c),The Sons of War. 5.00	28 RH,MD,JKu(c),AllQuiet atC.P. 100.00
332 JKu(c),Pyramid of Death 5.00	29 JKu,JKu(c),Listen To A Jet . . . 100.00
333 JKu(c),Ask The Dead. 5.00	30 IN,RA,JKu(c),Fort
334 JKu(c),What's Holding Up	For A Gunner 100.00
The War. 5.00	31 MD,RA,JKu(c),Silent Sub 90.00
335 JKu(c),Killer Compass 5.00	32 RH,MD,RH(c),PaperWorkWar . 90.00
336 JKu(c),The Red Maple Leaf . . . 5.00	33 RH,JKu,JKu(c),Frogman
337 JKu(c),A Bridge Called Charlie. 5.00	In A Net 90.00
338 JKu(c),No Escape From	34 JA,JGr,JKu(c),Calling U-217. . . 90.00
the Front 5.00	35 JA,JGr,JKu(c),Mask of
339 JKu(c),I Was Here Before 5.00	a Frogman 90.00
340 JKu(c),How To Win A War 5.00	36 MD,JA,JKu(c),Steel Soldier . . . 90.00
341 JKu(c),High-Flyer. 5.00	37 JA,JGr,JGr(c),Frogman
342 JKu(c),The 6 sides of	In A Bottle 90.00
Sgt. Rock 5.00	38 RH,RA,JA,JGr(c),Sub Sinker . . 90.00
343 thru 350 . . . . @5.00	39 JA,RH,RH(c),Last Torpedo. . . . 90.00
351 thru 422 . . . . @2.00	40 JGr,JA,JKu,JKu(c),The
	Silent Ones 90.00
OUR FIGHTING FORCES	41 JGr,RH,JA,JKu(c),Battle
Oct.–Nov., 1954	Mustang 125.00
1 IN,JGr(c),Human Booby Trap . 750.00	42 RH,MD,JGr(c),Sorry-
2 RH,IN,IN(c),Mile-Long Step. . . 350.00	Wrong Hill 75.00
3 RA,JKu(c),Winter Ambush . . . 300.00	43 MD,JKu,JGr(c),Inside Battle . . 75.00
4 RA,JGr(c),The Hot Seat 250.00	44 MD,RH,RA,JGr(c),Big Job
5 IN,RA,JGr(c),The Iron Punch . 250.00	For Baker. 75.00
6 IN,RA,JGr(c),The Sitting Tank . 200.00	45 RH,RA,JGr(c),B:Gunner and
7 RA,JKu,JGr(c),Battle Fist 200.00	Sarge, Mop-Up Squad 275.00
8 IN,RA,JGr(c),No War	46 RH,RA,JGr(c),Gunner'sSquad 125.00
For A Gunner 200.00	47 RH,JKu(c),TNT Birthday 75.00
9 JKu,RH,JGr(c),Crash-	48 JA,RH,JGr(c),A Statue
Landing At Dawn 200.00	For Sarge. 60.00
10 WW,RA,JGr(c),Grenade	49 MD,RH,JGr(c),Blind Gunner . . 80.00
Pitcher 225.00	50 JA,RH,JGr(c),I:Pooch,My
11 JKu,JGr(c),Diary of a Sub . . . 150.00	Pal, The Pooch. 60.00
12 IN,JKu,JGr(c),Jump Seat 150.00	51 RA,JA,RH(c),Underwater
13 RA,JGr(c),Beach Party. 150.00	Gunner. 50.00
14 JA,RA,IN,JGr(c),Unseen War . 150.00	52 MD,JKu,JKu(c),The Gunner
15 RH,JKu,JGr(c),Target For	and the Nurse 50.00
A Lame Duck 150.00	53 JA,RA,JGr(c),An Egg
16 RH,JGr(c),Night Fighter 150.00	For Sarge. 50.00
17 RA,JGr(c),Anchored Frogman 150.00	54 . . . . 50.00
18 RH,JKu,JGr(c),Cockpit Seat. . 150.00	55 MD,RH,JGr(c),The Last Patrol . 50.00
19 RA,JKu(c),Straighten ThatLine 150.00	56 RH,RA,JGr(c),Bridge of Bullets 50.00
20 RA,MD,JGr(c),The	57 JA,IN,JGr(c),A Tank For Sarge. 50.00
Floating Pilot 150.00	58 JA,JGr(c),Return of the Pooch . 50.00
21 RA,JKu(c),The Bouncing	59 RH,JA,JGr(c),Pooch-Patrol
Baby of Company B 100.00	Leader 50.00
	60 RH,JA,JGr(c),Tank Target 50.00
	61 JA,JGr(c),Pass to Peril. 50.00
	62 JA,JGr(c),The Flying Pooch . . 50.00
	63 JA,RH,JGr(c),Pooch-Tank
	Hunter 50.00
	64 JK,RH,JGr(c),A Lifeline
	For Sarge. 50.00
	65 IN,JA,JGr(c),Dogtag Patrol. . . 50.00
	66 JKu,JA,JGr(c),Trail of the
	Ghost Bomber 50.00
	67 IN,JA,JGr(c),Purple Heart
	For Pooch 50.00
	68 JA,JGr(c),Col. Hakawa's
	Birthday Party. 50.00
	69 JA,JKu,JGr(c),
	Destination Doom. 50.00
	70 JA,JKu(c),The Last Holdout . . . 50.00
	71 JA,JGr(c),End of the Marines. . 22.00
	72 JA,JGr(c),Four-Footed Spy . . . 18.00
	73 IN,JGr(c),The Hero Maker 18.00
	74 JA,JGr(c),Three On A T.N.T.
	Bull's-Eye 18.00
	75 JKu(c),Purple Heart Patrol 18.00
	76 JKu(c),The T.N.T. Seat. 18.00
	77 JKu(c),No Foxhole-No Home . . 18.00
	78 JGr(c),The Last Medal 18.00
	79 JA,JGr(c),Backs to the Sea . . . 18.00

Our Fighting Forces #7
© DC Comics, Inc.

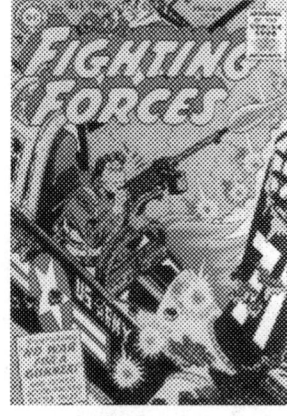

Our Fighting Forces #8
© DC Comics, Inc.

80 JA,JGr(c),Don't Come Back . . . 18.00
81 JA,JGr(c),Battle of
the Mud Marines 18.00
82 JA,JGr(c),Battle of the
Empty Helmets. 18.00
83 RA,JKu(c),Any Marine
Can Do It 18.00
84 JA,JKu(c),The Gun of Shame . 18.00
85 JA,JKu(c),The TNT Pin-Points . 18.00
86 JKu(c),3 Faces of Combat 18.00
87 JKu(c),Battle o/t Boobytraps. . . 18.00
88 GC,JKu(c),Devil Dog Patrol . . . 18.00
89 JKu(c),TNT Toothache 18.00
90 JKu(c),Stop the War. 18.00
91 JKu(c),The Human Shooting
Gallery 15.00
92 JA,JKu(c),The Bomb That
Stopped The War 15.00
93 IN,JKu(c),The Human Sharks. . 15.00
94 RH(c),E:Gunner,Sarge & Pooch,
The Human Blockbusters 15.00
95 GC,RH(c),B:The Fighting Devil
Dog, Lt. Rock, The
Fighting Devil Dog 15.00
96 JA,RH(c),Battle of Fire 15.00
97 IN(c),Invitation To A
Firing Squad. 15.00
98 IN(c),E:The Fighting Devil
Dog, Death Wore A Grin. 15.00
99 JA,JKu(c),B:Capt. Hunter,
No Mercy in Vietnam 20.00
100 GC,IN(c),Death Also
Stalks the Hunter 10.00
101 JA,RH(c),Killer of Vietnam . . . 10.00
102 RH,JKu(c),Cold Steel
For A Hot War 10.00
103 JKu(c),The Tunnels of Death . 10.00
104 JKu(c),Night Raid In Vietnam . 10.00
105 JKu(c),Blood Loyality 10.00
106 IN(c),Trail By Fury 10.00
107 IN(c),Raid Of The Hellcats . . . 10.00
108 IN(c),Kill The Wolf Pack 10.00
109 IN(c),Burn, Raiders, Burn. . . . 10.00
110 IN(c),Mountains Full of Death. 10.00
111 IN(c),Train of Terror 10.00
112 IN(c),What's In It For
The Hellcats? 10.00
113 IN(c),Operation-Survival 10.00
114 JKu(c),No Loot For The
Hellcats 10.00
115 JKu(c),Death In The Desert . . 10.00
116 JKu(c),Peril From the Casbah 10.00
117 JKu(c),Colder Than Death . . . 10.00
118 JKu(c),Hell Underwater 10.00
119 JKu(c),Bedlam In Berlin 10.00
120 JKu(c),Devil In The Dark 10.00

121 JKu(c),Take My Place 10.00
122 JKu(c),24 Hours To Die 10.00
123 JKu(c),B:Born Losers,No
     Medals No Graves 25.00
124 JKu(c),Losers Take All 10.00
125 Daughters of Death 10.00
126 JKu(c),Lost Town 10.00
127 JKu(c),Angels Over Hell's
     Corner 10.00
128 JKu(c),7 11 War. 10.00
129 JKu(c),Ride The Nightmare . . 10.00
130 JKu(c),Nameless Target. 10.00
131 JKu(c),Half A Man 10.00
132 JKu(c),Pooch, The Winner . . . 10.00
133 JKu(c),Heads or Tails. 10.00
134 JKu(c),The Real Losers 10.00
135 JKu(c),Death Picks A Loser . . 10.00
136 JKu(c),Decoy For Death. 10.00
137 JKu(c),God Of The Losers . . . 10.00
138 JKu(c),The Targets. 10.00
139 JKu(c),The Pirate. 10.00
140 JKu(c),Lost...One Loser 10.00
141 JKu(c),Bad Penny, The 10.00
142 JKu(c), 1/2 A Man 10.00
143 JKu(c),Diamonds Are
     For Never. 10.00
144 JKu(c),The Lost Mission. 10.00
145 JKu(c),A Flag For Losers 10.00
146 JKu(c),The Forever Walk 10.00
147 NA(c),The Glory Road 10.00
148 JKu(c),The Last Charge. 10.00
149 FT(c),A Bullet For
     A Traitor. 10.00
150 JKu(c),Mark Our Graves 10.00
151 JKu(c),Kill Me With Wagner. . 10.00
152 JK(c),A Small Place In Hell . . 10.00
153 JK(c),Big Max 10.00
154 JKu(c),Bushido,Live By The
     Code, Die By The Code 10.00
155 JK(c),The Partisans 10.00
156 JK(c),Good-Bye Broadway. . . 10.00
157 JK(c),Panama Fattie 10.00
158 JK(c),Bombing Out On
     The Panama Canal 10.00
159 JK(c),Mile-A-Minute Jones . . . 10.00
160 JKu(c),Ivan 10.00
161 JKu(c),The Major's Dream . . . 10.00
162 Gung-Ho 10.00
163 JKu(c),The Unmarked Graves 10.00
164 JKu(c),A Town Full Of Losers. 10.00
165 LD(c),The Rowboat Fleet 10.00
166 LD(c),Sword of Flame 10.00
167 LD(c),A Front Seat In Hell . . . 10.00
168 LD(c),A Cold Day To Die 10.00
169 JKu(c),Welcome Home-And
     Die. 10.00
170 JKu(c),A Bullet For
     The General. 10.00
171 JKu(c),A Long Day...
     A Long War 10.00
172 JKu(c),The Two-Headed Spy . 10.00
173 JKu(c),An Appointment
     With A Direct Hit. 10.00
174 JKu(c),Winner Takes-Death . . 10.00
175 JKu(c),Death Warrant 10.00
176 JKu(c),The Loser Is A
     Teen-Ager 10.00
177 JKu(c),This Loser Must Die . . 10.00
178 JKu(c),Last Drop For Losers . 10.00
179 JKu(c),The Last Loser 10.00
180 JKu(c),Hot Seat In A
     Cold War 10.00
181 JKu(c),Sept.–Oct., 1978. . . . . 10.00

OUTCASTS
Oct., 1987

1 . . . . 2.00
2 thru 11 . . . . @1.75

OUTLAWS
1991

1 LMc,I:Hood. 2.00
2 LMc,O:Hood. 2.00
3 LMc,V:Evil King 2.00
4 LMc,V:Lord Conductor 2.00
5 LMc,Archery contest. 2.00
6 LMc,Raid on King's Castle 2.00
7 LMc,Refuge, V:Lord Conductor. . 2.00

OUTSIDERS, THE
Nov., 1985
[1st Regular Series]

1 JAp,I:Looker. 3.00
2 JAp,V:Nuclear Family 2.50
3 JAp,V:Force of July 2.00
4 JAp,V:Force of July 2.00
5 JAp,Christmas Issue. 2.00
6 JAp,V:Duke of Oil 2.00
7 JAp,V:Duke of Oil 2.00
8 JAp,Japan 2.00
9 JAp,SD/JOp,Bik Lightning. 2.00
10 JAp,I:Peoples Heroes 2.00
11 JAp,Imprisoned in death camp . . 1.75
12 JAp,Imprisoned in death camp . . 1.75
13 JAp,desert island. 1.75
14 JAp,Looker/murder story 1.75
15 DJu,V:Bio-hazard. 1.75
16 Halo vs.Firefly 1.75
17 JAp,J:Batman 1.75
18 JAp,BB,V:Eclipso. 2.00
19 JAp,V:Windfall 1.75
20 JAp,Masters of Disaster. 1.75
21 JAp,V:Kobra,I:Clayface IV 1.75
22 JAp,V:Strike Force Kobra. 1.75
23 Return of People's Heroes 1.75
24 TVE,JAp,V:Skull,A:Duke of Oil . . 1.75
25 JAp,V:Skull 1.75
26 JAp,in Markovia. 1.75
27 EL,Millenium 1.75
28 EL,Millenium,final issue 1.75
Ann.#1,KN,V:Skull,A:Batman . . . 2.50
Spec.#1,A:Infinity,Inc 1.75

[2nd Regular Series] 1993–95

1 Alpha,TC(c),B:MiB(s),PaP,
     I:Technocrat,Faust,Wylde 3.00
1a Omega,TC(c),PaP,V:Vampires . 3.00
2 PaP,V:Sanction. 2.00
3 PaP,V:Eradicator. 2.00
4 PaP,A:Eradicator 2.00
5 PaP,V:Atomic Knight,A:Jihad. . . . 2.00
6 PaP,V:Jihad 2.00

Outsiders #16 © DC Comics Inc.

7 PaP,C:Batman 2.00
8 PaP,V:Batman,I:Halo 2.00
9 PaP,V:Batman 2.00
10 PaP,B:Final Blood, R:Looker . . . 2.25
11 PaP,Zero Hour,E:Final Blood . . . 2.00
12 PaP. 2.00
13 New base 2.00
14 Martial Arts Spectacular. 2.00
15 V:New Year's Evil. 2.00
16 R:Windfall 2.00
17 A:Green Lantern 2.00
18 Sins of the Father 2.00
19 Sins of the Father, pt.2. . . . . . . 2.25
20 DvA,V:Metamorpho 2.25
21 A:Apokolips 2.25
22 Alien Assassin 2.25
23 V:Defilers. 2.25
24 finale 2.25

PARALLAX:
EMERALD NIGHT

1 RMz(s),MMK,MkK, pivotal tie-in
     to Final Night 4.50

PEACEMAKER
Jan., 1988

1 A:Dr.Tzin-Tzin. 1.25
2 The Wages of Tzin 1.25
3 and 4 . . . . @1.25

PENGUIN
TRIUMPHANT

1 JSon,A:Batman,Wall Street. 6.00

PETER CANNON:
THUNDERBOLT
1992–93

1 thru 6 MC . . . . @1.50
7 MC,'Battleground'. 1.50
8 MC,Cairo Kidnapped 1.50
9 MC. 1.50
10 MC,A:JLA 1.50
11 MC,V:Havoc,A:Checkmate. 1.50
12 MC,final Issue 1.25

PETER PANDA
Aug.–Sept., 1953

1 . . . . 165.00
2 . . . . 95.00
3 thru 9 . . . . @60.00
10 Aug.–Sept., 1958. . . . . 60.00

PETER PORKCHOPS
Nov.–Dec., 1949

1 . . . . 250.00
2 . . . . 125.00
3 thru 10 . . . . @100.00
11 thru 30 . . . . @75.00
31 thru 61 . . . . @50.00
62 Oct.–Dec., 1960. . . . . 50.00

PHANTOM, THE
Oct., 1987

1 JO,A:Modern Phantom,13th
     Phantom 2.00
2 JO,Murder Trial in Manhattan . . . 1.50
3 JO,A:Chessman 1.50
4 JO,V:Chessman,final issue 1.50

PHANTOM, THE
1989–90

1 LMc,V:Gun Runners 2.50
2 LMc,V:Gun Runners 2.00

---

3 LMc,V:Drug Smugglers	1.75
4 LMc,In America,A:Diana Palner	1.75
5 LMc,Racial Riots	1.50
6 LMc,in Africa,Toxic Waste Problem	1.50
7 LMc,'Gold Rush'	1.50
8 LMc,'Train Surfing'	1.50
9 LMc,'The Slave Trade'	1.50
10 LMc,Famine in Khagana	1.50
11 LMc,Phantom/Diana Wedding proposal	1.50
12 LMc,Phantom framed for murder	1.50
13 W:Phantom & Diana Palner C:Mandrake last issue	1.50

PHANTOM STRANGER
Aug.–Sept., 1952

1	1,500.00
2	900.00
3	750.00
4	750.00
5	750.00
6, June-July, 1953	750.00

PHANTOM STRANGER
May-June, 1969

1 CI rep.&new material	85.00
2 CI rep.&new material	35.00
3 CI rep.&new material	35.00
4 NA,I:Tala,1st All-new issue	40.00
5 MSy,MA,A:Dr.13	25.00
6 MSy,A:Dr.13	25.00
7 JAp,V:Tala	25.00
8 JAp,A:Dr.13	25.00
9 JAp,A:Dr.13	25.00
10 JAp,I:Tannarak	25.00
11 JAp,V:Tannarak	20.00
12 JAp,TD,Dr.13 solo story	20.00
13 JAp,TD,Dr.13 solo	20.00
14 JAp,TD,Dr.13 solo	20.00
15 JAp,ATh(rep),TD,Iron Messiah	15.00
16 JAp,TD,MMes(rep)Dr.13 solo	15.00
17 JAp,I:Cassandra Craft	15.00
18 TD,Dr.13 solo	15.00
19 JAp,TD,Dr.13 solo	15.00
20 JAp,'And A Child Shall Lead Them'	15.00
21 JAp,TD,Dr.13 solo	12.00
22 JAp,TD,I:Dark Circle	12.00
23 JAp,MK,I:Spawn-Frankenstein	12.00
24 JAp,MA,Spawn Frankenstein	20.00

Phantom Stranger #9
© DC Comics, Inc.

25 JAp,MA,Spawn Frankenstein	20.00
26 JAp,A:Frankenstein	20.00
27 V:Dr. Zorn	20.00
28 BU:Spawn of Frankenstein	20.00
29 V:Dr.Zorn,BU:Frankenstein	20.00
30 E:Spawn of Frankenstein	20.00
31 B:BU:Black Orchid	20.00
32 NR,BU:Black Orchid	20.00
33 MGr,A:Deadman	12.00
34 BU:Black Orchid	20.00
35 BU:Black Orchid	20.00
36 BU:Black Orchid	20.00
37 "Crimson Gold,"BU:BlackOrchid	20.00
38 "Images of the Dead"	20.00
39 A:Deadman	15.00
40 A:Deadman	15.00
41 A:Deadman	15.00

PHANTOM STRANGER
Oct., 1987–Jan. 1988

1 MMi,CR,V:Eclipso	3.00
2 and 4 MMi,CR,V:Eclipso	@2.25

The Phantom Zone #1
© DC Comics, Inc.

PHANTOM ZONE, THE
Jan., 1982

1 GD/TD,A:Jax-Ur	1.25
2 GC/TD,A:JLA	1.25
3 GC/TD,A:Mon-El	1.25
4 GC/TD	1.25

PICTURE STORIES FROM THE BIBLE
Autumn, 1942–43

1 thru 4 Old Testament	@150.00
1 thru 3 New Testament	@175.00

PINKY AND THE BRAIN
Warner Bros./DC

1 thru 4	@1.75
5 Oklahoma crud	1.75
6 "Plan Brain From Outer Space"	1.75
7 Yuletide tale	1.75
8	1.75
9 SML(s) back to school	1.75
10 V:Melmouse	1.75
11 "Narftasia"	1.75
12 "Beach Blanket Brain"	1.75
13 "Ali Brain and the Forty Thieves"	1.75
14 "Brainlet"	1.75
15 "Biker Mamas from Heck"	1.75

16 "Verminator II:Judgment Night"	2.00
17 Halloween	2.00
18 "Braintech," Manga-style issue	2.00
19 "Anti-Claus"	2.00
20 "The Mice in Pink"	2.00
21	2.00
22 "The Mouse in the Iron Mask"	2.00
23 King of the Sea Monkeys	2.00
24 Love with Cupcake	2.00
25 Dark Pinky	2.00
26 G.I. Brain	2.00
27 Final Issue	2.00

PLASTIC MAN
[1st Series]
Nov.–Dec., 1966

1 GK,I:Dr.Drome (1966 series begins)	60.00
2 V:The Spider	20.00
3 V:Whed	20.00
4 V:Dr.Dome	20.00
5 1,001 Plassassins	20.00
6 V:Dr.Dome	20.00
7 O:Plastic Man Jr.,A:Original Plastic Man,Woozy Winks	20.00
8 V:The Weasel	12.00
9 V:Joe the Killer Pro	12.00
10 V:Doll Maker(series ends)	12.00
11 (1976 series begins)	6.00
12 I:Carrot-Man	6.00
13 A:Robby Reed	6.00
14 V:Meat By-Product & Sludge	6.00
15 I:Snuffer,V:Carrot-Man	6.00
16 V:Kolonel Kool	6.00
17 O:Plastic Man	6.00
18 V:Professor Klean	6.00
19 I&Only App.Marty Meeker	6.00
20 V:Snooping Sneetches Oct.–Nov., 1977	6.00

PLASTIC MAN
1988–89

1 Mini-series,Origin retold	1.25
2 V:The Ooze Brothers	1.25
3 In Los Angeles	1.25
4 End-series,A:Superman	1.25

PLASTIC MAN
1999

Spec.#1 TTn(s),ALo,RBr,48-page	4.00

PLOP!
Sept.–Oct., 1973

1 SA-AA,GE,ShM	5.00
2 AA,SA	4.00
3 AA,SA	4.00
4 BW,SA	4.00
5 MA,MSy,SA	4.00
6 MSy,SA	4.00
7 SA	3.50
8 SA	3.50
9 SA	3.50
10 SA	3.50
11 ATh,SA	4.00
12 SA	3.50
13 WW(c),SA	5.00
14 WW,SA	5.00
15 WW(c),SA	5.00
16 SD,WW,SA	5.00
17 SA	3.50
18 SD,WW,SA	5.00
19 WW,SA	5.00
20 SA,WW	5.00
21 JO,WW	5.00
22 JO,WW,BW	5.00
23 BW,WW	3.00
24 SA,WW,Nov.–Dec., 1976	2.00

POWER GIRL
[Mini-Series] 1988

1	1.00
2 A:The Weaver, mongo Krebs	1.00
3 V:The Weaver	1.00
4 V:Weaver, final issue	1.00

POWER OF SHAZAM!
1995–97

1 R:Captain Marvel	2.00
2 V:Arson Fiend	1.50
3 V:Ibac	1.50
4 JOy,R:Mary Marvel,Tawky, Tawny	1.75
5 JOy(c&a),F:Mary Marvel, V:Black Adam	1.75
6 R:Captain Marvel	1.75
7 V:Captain Nazi	1.75
8 R:Captain Marvel,Jr.	1.75
9 JOy,MM,V:Black Adam	1.75
10 JOy,MM,V:Seven Deadly Enemies of Man	1.75
11 JOy,MM,R:Ibis as Captain Marvel	1.75
12 JOy,MM,How Billy Batson's father met Shazam	1.75
13 JOy,MM	1.75
14 JOy,GK,MM,F:CaptainMarvelJr	1.75
15 JOy,MM,V:Mr.Mind	1.75
16 thru 18	@1.75
19 JOy(s),GK,MM,Captain Marvel Jr. V:Captain Nazi	1.75
20 JOy(s),PKr,MM,A:Superman	1.75
21 JOy(s),PKr,MM,V:Liquidator	1.75
22 JOy(s),PKr,MM,A:Batman	1.75
23 JOy(s),PKr,MM	1.75
24 JOy(s),PKr,MM,V:Baron Blitz-krieg, prelude to new family	1.75
25 JOy(s),PKr,MM,The Marvel Family '97	1.75
26 JOy(s),PKr,MM,new Capt. Marvel framed for murder	1.75
27 JOy(s),PKr,MM,D:Captain Marvel	1.75
28 JOy(s),DG, V:Patty Patty Bang Bang	1.75
29 JOy(c),DG,F:Hoppy	1.75
30 JOy(c),PKr,DG,V:Mr. Finish	1.75
31 JOy,PKr,DG,Genesis x-over	2.00
32 JOy,PKr,DG,Genesis aftermath	2.00
33 JOy,PKr,DG,Madam M, Sin	2.00
34 JOy,PKr,DG,F:Gangbuster	2.00
35 JOy,PKr,DG,Lightning &	

The Power of Shazam #22
© DC Comics Inc.

Stars, pt.2 x-over	2.00
36 JOy	2.00
37 JOy,MM,DG,F:Capt.Marvel Jr.	2.00
38 JOy,PKr,DG,Monster Society of Evil, pt.1	2.00
39 JOy,PKr,DG,Monster, pt.2	2.00
40 JOy,PKr,DG,Monster, pt.3	2.00
41 JOy,PKr,DG,Monster, pt.4	2.00
42 JOy,DG,new logo & design	2.00
43 JOy,DG,I:Bulletgirl	2.50
44 JOy,DG,V:Chain Lightning	2.50
45 JOy,DG,A:JLA	2.50
46 JOy,DG,A:Superman	2.50
47 JOy,V:Black Adam, final issue	2.50
Ann.#1 JOy(s),MM,"Legends of the Dead Earth"	2.95
Spec.#1,000,000 JOy,DG	2.50
GN Power of Shazam	7.50
HC JOy(a&s),O:Captain Marvel	22.00
GNv JOy(a&s),O:Captain Marvel	9.95
TPB JOy, reoffer	7.50

POWER OF THE ATOM
1988–89

1 1st Issue, Origin retold	1.25
2 Return of Powers	1.25
3 I:Strobe	1.25
4 A:Hawkman+bonus book #8	1.25
5 DT,A:Elongated Man	1.25
6 JBy,V:Chronos	1.25
7 GN,Invasion,V:Khunds,Chronos	1.25
8 GN,Invasion,V:Chronos	1.25
9 GN,A:Justice League	1.25
10 GN,I:Humbug	1.25
11 GN,V:Paul Hoben	1.25
12 GN,V:Edg the Destroyer	1.25
13 GN,Blood Stream Journey	1.25
14 GN,V:Humbug	1.25
15 GN,V:Humbug	1.25
16 GN,V:The CIA	1.25
17 GN,V:The Sting	1.25
18 GN,V:The CIA, last issue	1.25

PREACHER
Vertigo 1995–97

1 I:Jesse Custer, Genesis	20.00
2 Saint of Killers	18.00
3 GF(c),I:Angels	15.00
4 GF(c),V:Saint of Killers	10.00
5 Naked City,pt.1	10.00
6 Naked City,pt.2	10.00
7 Naked City,pt.3	8.00
8 GEn,SDi,All in the Family,pt.1	5.00
9 GEn,SDi,All in the Family,pt.2	5.00
10 GEn,SDi,All in the Family,pt.3	5.00
11 GEn,SDi,All in the Family,pt.4	5.00
12 GEn,SDi,All in the Family,pt.5	6.00
13 GEn,SDi,Hunters,pt.1	5.00
14 GEn,SDi,Hunters,pt.2 (of 4)	4.00
15 and 16	@4.00
17 Star captures Cassidy	3.00
18 GEn(s),SDi,secret of Jesse Custer's cigarette lighter	3.00
19 GEn(s),SDi,"Crusaders," pt.1	3.00
20 GEn(s),SDi,"Crusaders," pt.2	3.00
21 GEn(s),SDi,"Crusaders," pt.3	3.00
22 GEn(s),SDi,"Crusaders," pt.4	3.00
23 GEn(s),SDi,"Crusaders," pt.5	3.00
24 GEn(s),SDi,"Crusaders" concl.	3.00
25 GEn(s),SDi,"Cry Blood, Cry Erin"	3.00
26 GEn(s),SDi,"To the Streets of Manhattan I Wandered Away"	2.50
27 GEn(s),SDi, Jessie & Tulip in New York, pt.1	2.50
28 GEn(s),SDi, Jessie & Tulip in New York, pt.2	2.50
29 GEn(s),SDi, south to New Orleans	2.50

30 GEn,SDi,in New Orleans	2.50
31 GEn,SDi,in New Orleans	2.50
32 GEn,SDi,in New Orleans	2.50
33 GEn,SDi,in New Orleans,concl.	2.50
34 GEn,SDi,War in the Sun,pt.1	2.50
35 GEn,SDi,War in the Sun,pt.2	2.50
36 GEn,SDi,War in the Sun,pt.3	2.50
37 GEn,SDi,War in the Sun,pt.4	2.50
38 GEn,SDi,GF,Utah radioactive	2.50
39 GEn,SDi,GF,out of the desert.	2.50
40 GEn,SDi,GF,Arsefaced World	2.50
41	2.50
42 GEn(s),SDi,GF,V:Meatman	2.50
43 GEn(s),SDi,GF,V:Meat Man	2.50
44 GEn(s),SDi,GF,Gunther Hahn	2.50
45 GEn(s),SDi,GF,V:Meat Man	2.50
46 GEn(s),SDi,GF,Miss Oatlash	2.50
47 GEn(s),SDi,GF,Salvation	2.50
48 GEn(s),SDi,GF,Salvation	2.50
49 GEn(s),SDi,GF,First Contact	2.50
50 GEn(s),SDi,GF,48-page	3.75
51 GEn(s),SDi,GF,Tulip's past,pt.1	2.50
52 GEn(s),SDi,GF,Tulip's past,pt.2	2.50
53 GEn(s),SDi,GF,road trip story.	2.50
54 GEn(s),SDi,GF,Jesse & Tulip	2.50
TPB Gone to Texas, rep.#1–#7.	15.00
TPB Proud Americans GEn(s)	15.00
TPB Until the End of the World	15.00
TPB Ancient History	15.00
TPB War in the Sun	15.00
GN Preacher Spec. Cassidy: Blood and Whisky, GEn(s) (1997)	6.00
Spec. The Good Old Boys, parody	5.50
Spec. The Story of You-Know-Who GEn(s),RCa,O:Arseface (1996)	5.00

PREACHER SPECIAL: SAINT OF KILLERS
DC/Vertigo 1996

1 GEn(s),StP	6.00
2 GEn(s),StP	4.50
3 GEn(s),StP	3.50
4 GEn(s),StP	3.00

PREZ
Aug.–Sept., 1973

1 I:Prez (from Sandman #54)	12.00
2 thru 4 F:Prez	8.00

PRIDE & JOY
DC/Vertigo May 1997
[Mini-series]

1 (of 4) GEn(s),JHi	2.50
2 GEn(s),JHi	2.50
3 GEn(s),JHi	2.50
4 GEn(s),JHi,concl.	2.50

PRIMAL FORCE
1994–95

O New Team	2.00
1 Claw	2.00
2 Cataclysm	2.00
3	2.00
4 Claw	2.00
5 V:Demons	2.00
6 V:The Four Beasts	2.00
7 Trip to the Past	2.00
8 N.Choles(p),I:New Team	2.25
9 Maltis worsens, Tornado speaks	2.25
10 V:August	2.25
11	2.25
12 Black Condor vs. August	2.25
13 Underworld Unleashed tie-in	2.25
14 final issue	2.25

Primal Force #3 © DC Comics, Inc.

PRINCE
Piranha Press
1 DCw,KW,based on rock star . . . 10.00
1a Second printing 2.50
1b 3rd printing 2.00

PRISONER, THE
1988–89
1 Based on TV series 5.00
2 'By Hook or by Crook' 5.00
3 'Confrontation' 5.00
4 'Departure' final issue 5.00

PSYBA-RATS, THE
[Mini-Series] 1995
1 CDi,A:Robin 2.50
2 CDi,A:Robin 1.50
3 CDi,F:Razorsharp,final issue . . . 1.50

PSYCHO
1 I:Psycho 12.00
2 Sonya Rescue 10.00
3 'Psycho against the World' 7.00

QUEST FOR CAMELOT
June 1998
1-shot movie adaptation 5.00

QUESTION, THE
Feb., 1987
1 DCw,R:Question,I:Myra,A:Shiva . 3.00
2 DCw,A:Batman,Shiva 2.00
3 DCw,I:Mayor Firman 2.00
4 DCw,V:Hatch 2.00
5 DCw,Hub City fall Apart 2.00
6 DCw,Abuse story 2.00
7 DCw,V:Mr.Volk 2.00
8 DCw,I:Mikado 2.00
9 DCw,O:Rodor 2.00
10 DCw,O:Rodor cont. 2.00
11 DCw,Transformation. 2.00
12 DCw,Poisoned Ground 2.00
13 DCw,V:The Spartans 2.00
14 DCw,V:The Spartans 2.00
15 DCw,The Klan in Hub City 2.00
16 DCw,'Butch Cassidy &
   Sundance Kid' 2.00
17 DCw,A:Green Arrow 2.50
18 DCw,A:Green Arrow 2.50
19 DCw,V:Terrorists 2.00

20 DCw,Travelling Circus 2.00
21 DCw,V:Junior Musto 2.00
22 DCw,Election Night 2.00
23 DCw,Election Night contd. 2.00
24 DCw,Election Night contd. 2.00
25 DCw,Myra Critically Ill 2.00
26 A:Riddler 2.00
27 DCw 2.00
28 DCw,A:Lady Shiva 2.00
29 DCw,V:Lady Shiva 2.00
30 DCw,V:Lady Shiva 2.00
31 DCw,Hub City Chaos contd . . . 2.00
32 DCw,Identity Crisis. 2.00
33 DCw,Identity Crisis contd 2.00
34 DCw,Identity Crisis contd 2.00
35 DCw,Fate of Hub City 2.00
36 DCw,final issue (contd.G.A.Ann#3
   Question Quarterly #1) 2.00
Ann.#1 DCw,A:Batman,G.A. 3.00
Ann.#2 A:Green Arrow 4.00

QUESTION QUARTERLY
1 DCw 4.50
2 DCw 3.95
3 DCw(c) Film 2.95
4 DCw,MM,'Waiting for Phil' 2.95
5 DCw,MMi,MM,last issue 2.95

RAGMAN
[1st Limited Series] 1976–77
1 I&O:Ragman 5.00
2 I:Opal 3.50
3 V:Mr. Big 3.00
4 JKu(1st interior on character) . . . 3.00
5 JKu,O:Ragman,final issue. 3.00
[2nd Limited Series] 1991–92
1 PB,O:Ragman 3.00
2 PB,O:Ragman Powers 3.00
3 PB,Original Ragman 2.75
4 PB,Gang War 2.75
5 PB,V:Golem 2.75
6 PB,V:Golem,A:Batman 2.75
7 PB,V:Golem,A:Batman 2.75
8 PB,V:Golem,A:Batman 2.75

RAGMAN: CRY OF THE DEAD
1993–94
1 JKu(c),R:Ragman 2.00
2 JKu(c),A:Marinette 2.00
3 JKu(c),V:Marinette 2.00
4 JKu(c),Exorcism 2.00
5 JKu(c),V:Marinette 2.00
6 JKu(c),final issue 2.00

THE RAY
[Limited Series] 1992
1 JQ,ANi,I&O:Ray(Ray Torril). . . . 5.00
2 JQ,ANi,I:G.A. Ray. 4.00
3 JQ,ANi,A:G.A. Ray. 3.00
4 JQ,ANi,V:Dr.Polaris 4.00
5 JQ,ANi,V:Dr.Polaris 3.00
6 JQ,ANi,C:Lobo,final issue 3.00
TPB In A Blaze of Power 9.95
[Regular Series] 1994–96
1 JQ(c),RPr,V:Brinestone,
   A:Superboy, ... 3.00
1a Newsstand Ed. 1.75
2 RPr,V:Brinestone,A:Superboy . . 1.75
3 RPr,I:Death Masque 2.00
4 JQ(c),RPr,I:Death Masque,
   Dr. Polarus 2.00
5 JQ(c),RPr,V:G.A.Ray 2.00
6 JQ(c),RPr,V:Black Canary. 2.00
7 JQ(c),RPr,V:Canary/Ray 2.00
8 V:Lobo,Black Canary 2.00
9 Ray Undoes the past 2.00

The Ray, Ann. #1 © DC Comics, Inc.

10 F:Happy Terril 2.00
11 30 years in future. 2.00
12 V:Mystech 2.00
13 V:Death Masque 2.25
14 The Ray needs help, V:Death
   Masque 2.25
15 F:Vandal Savage 2.25
16 D:Happy Terrill. 2.25
17 I:Josh Terrill,V:Atomic Skull . . . 2.25
18 Underworld Unleashed tie-in . . 2.25
19 Underworld Unleashed tie-in . . 2.25
20 F:Black Condor 2.25
21 Black Condor captured 2.25
22 . . . . 2.25
23 V:Death Masque 2.25
24 . . . . 2.25
25 double size 3.50
26 . . . . 2.25
27 . . . . 2.25
28 CPr,final issue 2.25
Ann.#1 Year One Annual 3.95

REAL FACT COMICS
March-April, 1946
1 S&K,Harry Houdini story 500.00
2 S&K, Rin-Tin-Tin story 350.00
3 H.G. Wells story 300.00
4 Jimmy Stewart story,B:Just
   Imagine 350.00
5 Batman & Robin(c) 1,500.00
6 O:Tommy Tomorrow. 1,000.00
7 'The Flying White House' 150.00
8 VF,A:Tommy Tomorrow. 500.00
9 S&K,Glen Miller story 250.00
10 'The Vigilante' by MMe 250.00
11 EK,'How the G-Men Capture
   Public Enemies!'. 150.00
12 'How G-Men are Trained'. . . . 150.00
13 Dale Evans story 450.00
14 Will Rogers story,'Diary of
   Death' 125.00
15 A:The Master Magician-
   Thurston. 125.00
16 A:Four Reno Brothers,
   T.Tommorow 400.00
17 'I Guard an Armored Car' . . . 125.00
18 'The Mystery Man of
   Tombstone'. 125.00
19 'The Weapon that Won the
   West'. 125.00
20 JKu 150.00
21 JKu,July-Aug., 1949. . . . . . . 125.00

REAL SCREEN COMICS
Spring, 1945
1 B:Fox & the Crow,Flippity
  & Flop 850.00
2 (fa) 400.00
3 (fa) 200.00
4 thru 7 (fa) . . . . @150.00
8 thru 11 (fa) . . . . @125.00
12 thru 20 (fa) . . . . @90.00
21 thru 30 (fa) . . . . @75.00
31 thru 40 (fa) . . . . @50.00
41 thru 128 (fa) . . . . @35.00
Becomes:

TV SCREEN CARTOONS
129 thru 137 . . . . @40.00
138 Jan.–Feb., 1961 . . . . 40.00

R.E.B.E.L.S '94
0 New team. 2.00
1 L.E.G.I.O.N.,Green Lantern 2.00
2 Dissent. 2.00
3 . . . . 2.00
4 Ship goes Insane 2.00

R.E.B.E.L.S '95
5 F:Dox. 2.00
6 Dox Defeated 2.00
7 John Sin. 2.00
8 V:Galactic Bank 2.25
9 F:Dox,Ignea,Garv,Strata 2.25
10 V:World Bank. 2.25
11 . . . . 2.25
12 F:Iceman Assassin 2.25
13 Underworld Unleashed tie-in . . . 2.25
14 F:Lyrl Dox 2.25

R.E.B.E.L.S. '96
15 V:Lyrl Dox 2.25
16 V:Lyrl Dox's satellite. 2.25

RED TORNADO
1985
1 Cl/FMc. 1.25
2 Cl/FMc,A:Superman 1.25
3 Cl/FMc. 1.25
4 Cl/FMc 1.25

RESTAURANT AT THE END OF THE UNIVERSE
1994
1 Adapt. 2nd book in Hitchhikers'
  Guide to the Galaxy,
  I:The Restaurant 7.00
2 V:The Meal. 7.00
3 Final issue 7.00

RESURRECTION MAN
March 1997
1 DAn(s),JG,lenticular death's
  head cover. 7.00
2 DAn(s),JG,V:Amazo 5.00
3 DAn(s),JG,"Scorpion Memories"
  pt.1 (of 3) 2.50
4 DAn(s),JG,"Scorpion Memories"
  pt.2 . . . . 2.50
5 DAn(s),JG,"Scorpion Memories"
  pt.3 concl. 2.50
6 DAn&ALa(s),JoP,Genesis tie-in . . 2.50
7 DAn&ALa(s),TGb,BG,A:Batman . 2.50
8 DAn&ALa(s),BG,Big Howler 2.50
9 DAn&ALa(s),F:Hitman, pt.1 . . . . 2.50
10 DAn&ALa(s),F:Hitman, pt.2 . . . 2.50
11 DAn&ALa(s), Origin of the
  Species, pt.1 . . . . 2.50
12 DAn&ALa(s), Origin of the

Species, pt.2 . . . . 2.50
13 DAn&ALa(s),Candy Man 2.50
14 DAn&ALa(s),really dead?. 2.50
15 DAn&ALa(s),JG,V:Rider. 2.50
16 DAn&ALa(s),BG,Avenging
  Angels x-over pt.1 . . . . 2.50
17 DAn&ALa(s),BG,Avenging
  Angels x-over pt.3 . . . . 2.50
18 DAn&ALa(s),A:Phantom Stranger,
  Deadman 2.50
19 DAn&ALa(s),Cape Fear, pt.1 . . . 2.50
20 DAn&ALa(s),Cape Fear, pt.2 . . . 2.50
21 DAn&ALa(s),Cape Fear, pt.3 . . . 2.50
22 DAn&ALa(s) 2.50
23 DAn&ALa(s),Resurrection
  Woman 2.50
24 DAn&ALa(s) 2.50
25 DAn&ALa(s)Millennium
  Meteor,pt.1 . . . . 2.50
26 DAn&ALa(s)Millennium Meteor,
  pt.2,A:Superman, Titans 2.50
27 DAn&ALa(s)Millennium Meteor,
  pt.3,final issue 2.50
Spec.#1,000,000 DAn&ALa(s) 2.50

RICHARD DRAGON, KUNG FU FIGHTER
April-May, 1975
1 O:Richard Dragon. 1.50
2 JSn/AM 1.50
3 JK 1.25
4 RE/WW 1.25
5 RE/WW 1.25
6 RE/WW 1.25
7 RE/WW 1.25
8 RE/WW 1.25
9 RE 1.25
10 RE. 1.25
11 RE. 1.25
12 RE. 1.25
13 thru 17 RE . . . . @1.25
18 Nov.–Dec., 1977 . . . . 1.25

RIMA, THE JUNGLE GIRL
April-May, 1974
1 NR,I:Rima,O:Pt. 1 . . . . 2.00
2 NR,O:Pt.2. . . . . 1.50
3 NR,O:Pt.3. . . . . 1.25
4 NR,O:Pt.4. . . . . 1.25
5 NR 1.25

Rima, The Jungle Girl #6
© DC Comics Inc.

6 NR 1.25
7 April-May, 1975 . . . . 1.25

RING, THE
1 GK,Opera Adaption 12.00
2 GK,Sigfried's Father's Sword . . . 7.00
3 GK,to save Brunhilde 6.00
4 GK, final issue 6.00
TPB rep.#1 thru #4. . . . . 19.95

RIP HUNTER, TIME MASTER
March-April, 1961
1 . . . . 500.00
2 . . . . 250.00
3 thru 5 . . . . @150.00
6 and 7 Ath . . . . @125.00
8 thru 15 . . . . @75.00
16 thru 20 . . . . @75.00
21 thru 28 . . . . @75.00
29 Nov.–Dec., 1965 . . . . 75.00

ROAD TO PERDITION
DC/Paradox/Pocket (April, 1998)
TPB 6"x8" 304pg., b&w 14.00

ROBIN
[1st Limited Series] 1991
1 TL,BB(c),Trial,pt.1(&Poster) 5.00
1a 2nd printing 2.50
1b 3rd printing 1.50
2 TL,BB(c) Trial,pt.2 . . . . 2.50
2a 2nd printing 1.50
3 TL,BB(c) Trial,pt.3 . . . . 2.00
4 TL,Trial,pt.4 . . . . 2.00
5 TL,Final issue,A:Batman. 2.00
TPB BB(c),rep.#1–#5,Batman
  #455–#457. . . . . 7.95
[2nd Limited Series] 1991
[ROBIN II: THE JOKER'S WILD]
1 Direct,Hologram(c)Joker face . . . 2.00
1a (c)Joker straightjacket. 2.00
1b (c)Joker standing 2.00
1c (c)Batman. 2.00
1d Newsstand(no hologram) 1.00
1e collectors set,extra holo. 5.00
2 Direct,Hologram(c) Robin/Joker
  Knife 1.50
2a (c)Joker/Robin-Dartboard 1.50
2b (c)Robin/Joker-Hammer 1.50
2c Newsstand(no hologram) 1.00
2d collectors set,extra holo. 5.00
3 Direct,Holo(c)Robin standing . . . 1.50
3a (c)Robin swinging 1.50
3b Newsstand(no hologram) 1.50
3c collectors set,extra holo. 3.00
4 Direct,Hologram 1.50
4a Newsstand (no hologram) 1.25
4b collectors set,extra holo. 2.00
Collectors set (#1 thru #4). 30.00
[3rd Limited Series] 1992–93
[ROBIN III: CRY OF THE HUNTRESS]
1 TL,A:Huntress,Collector's Ed.
  movable(c),poster. 3.00
1a MZ(c),Newsstand Ed. 1.50
2 TL,V:KGBeast,A:Huntress. 2.75
2a MZ(c),Newsstand Ed 1.50
3 TL,V:KGBeast,A:Huntress. 2.75
3a MZ(c),newsstand Ed. 1.50
4 TL,V:KGBeast,A:Huntress. 2.75
4a MZ(c),newsstand Ed. 1.50
5 TL,V:KGBeast,A:Huntress. 2.75
5a MZ(c),newsstand Ed. 1.50
6 TL,V:KGBeast,King Snake,

Robin #1 © DC Comics, Inc.

A:Huntress. 2.75
6a MZ(c),Newsstand Ed. 1.50

[Regular Series] 1993–99
1 B:CDi(s),TG,SHa,V:Speedboyz . . 4.00
1a Newstand Ed. 2.00
2 TG,V:Speedboyz 2.00
3 TG,V:Cluemaster,
   Electrocutioner 1.75
4 TG,V:Cluemaster,Czonk,
   Electrocutioner 1.75
5 TG,V:Cluemaster,Czonk,
   Electrocutioner 1.75
6 TG,A:Huntress 1.75
7 TG,R:Robin's Father. 2.00
8 TG,KnightsEnd#5,A:Shiva 3.00
9 TG,Knights End:Aftermath 2.25
10 TG,Zero Hour,V:Weasel. 1.50
11 New Batman 1.50
12 Robin vs. thugs 1.50
13 V:Steeljacket 1.50
14 CDi(s),TG,Return of Bruce
   Wayne,Troika,pt.4. . . . . 1.50
14a Collector's edition 2.50
15 Cluemaster Mystery. 1.50
16 F:Spoiler 1.50
17 I:Silver Monkey,V:King Snake,Lynx
   [New Miraweb format begins] . . 2.00
18 Gotham City sabotaged 2.00
19 V:The General 2.00
20 F:Robin 2.00
21 Ninja Camp,pt.1. . . . . 2.00
22 CDi,TG,Ninja Camp,pt.2 . . . . . . 2.00
23 CDi,Underworld Unleashed tie-in 2.00
24 CDi,V:Charaxes 2.00
25 CDi,F:Green Arrow 2.00
26 . . . . 2.00
27 . . . . 2.00
28 CDi,Contagion: conclusion 2.00
29 CDi,FFo,SnW,A:Maxie Zeus . . . 2.00
30 CDi,FFo,SnW,A:Maxie Zeus . . . 2.00
31 CDi(s),A:Wildcat 2.00
32 CDi(s),Legacy, pt. 3 x-over. 2.00
33 CDi(s),Legacy, pt. 7 x-over. 2.00
34 CDi(s),JhD,action at a
   Shakespear play 2.00
35 CDi(s),Robin & Spoiler, Final
   Night tie-in 2.00
36 CDi(s),V:Toyman, The General . 2.00
37 CDi(s),V:The General, Toyman . 2.00
38 CDi(s), ... 2.00
39 CDi(s), pt.2 . . . . 2.00
40 CDi(s), ... 2.00
41 CDi(s),F:Tim and Ariana 2.00
42 CDi(s),F:Crocky the Crocodile . . 2.00

43 CDi(s),A:Spoiler. 2.00
44 CDi(s) Pt.2 (of 2) 2.00
45 CDi(s) Tim Drake grounded 2.00
46 CDi(s) Genesis tie-in 2.00
47 CDi,V:General, pt.1 . . . . 2.00
48 CDi,V:General, pt.2 . . . . 2.00
49 CDi,to Paris 2.00
50 CDi(s),F:Lady Shiva & King
   Snake, 48pg. 3.00
51 CDi(s) 2.00
52 CDi(s) Cataclysm x-over,pt.7 . . . 2.00
53 CDi(s),SnW,Cataclysm concl. . . . 2.00
54 CDi(s),SnW,Aftershock 2.00
55 CDi(s),SnW, Brotherhood of
   the Fist x-over, pt.3. . . . . 2.00
56 CDi(s),SnW,tearful turning point . 2.00
57 CDi(s),SnW,A:Spoiler. 2.00
58 CDi(s),SnW,A:Spoiler. 2.00
59 CDi(s),SnW,V:Steeljacket. 2.00
60 CDi(s),SnW,Alvin Draper 2.00
61 CDi(s),SnW,V:Phil Delinger 2.00
62 CDi(s),SnW,A:Flash, pt.1 . . . . . 2.00
63 CDi(s),SnW,A:Flash, pt.2 . . . . . 2.00
64 CDi(s),SnW,A:Flash, pt.3 . . . . . 2.00
65 CDi(s),SnW,A:Spoiler. 2.00
66 CDi(s),SnW,V:demons 2.00
67 CDi(s),SnW,No Man's Land 2.00
68 CDi(s),No Man's Land 2.00
69 CDi(s),No Man's Land 2.00
Ann.#1 TL,Eclipso tie-in,V:Anarky . . 3.00
Ann.#2 KD,JL,Bloodlines#10,
   I:Razorsharp 2.75
Ann.#3 Elseworlds Story. 3.25
Ann.#4 Year One Annual 2.95
Ann.#5 CDi,Legends of the Dead
   Earth 2.95
Ann.#5 Legends o/t Dead Earth . . . 2.95
Ann.#6 Pulp Heroes (Western),
   CDi(s) 3.95
Spec.#1,000,000 CDi(s),SnW 2.00
Spec. Robin/Argent Double Shot
   DJu,CDi,V:Spoiler x-over (1997) 2.00
TPB A Hero Reborn,JAp,TL 4.95
TPB Tragedy and Triumph,
   TL,NBy. 9.95

ROBIN PLUS
1 MWa&BAu(s), F:Bart Allen, skiing
   rips, V:Mystral 2.95
2 LKa,CDi,AWi,ALa,F:Fang 3.00

ROBIN 3000
1 CR,Elseworlds,V:Skulpt 5.25
2 CR,Elseworlds,V:Skulpt 5.25

ROBIN HOOD TALES
**Jan.–Feb., 1957–Mar.–Apr.,
1958**
7 . . . . 250.00
8 thru 14 . . . . @200.00

ROBOTECH DEFENDERS
1 MA,mini-series 3.50
2 MA. 3.00

ROGAN GOSH
Vertigo 1994
1 PF PrM(s) (From Revolver). 7.25

RONIN
July, 1983
1 FM,1:Billy 6.00
2 FM,I:Casey. 5.00
3 FM,V:Agat 5.00
4 FM,V:Agat 5.00

5 FM,V:Agat 6.00
6 FM,D:Billy. 8.00
Paperback, FM inc. Gatefold. 12.00

ROOTS OF THE SWAMP THING
July, 1986
1 BWr,rep.SwampThing#1&#2 . . . . 3.00
2 BWr,rep.SwampThing#3&#4 . . . . 3.00
3 BWr,rep.SwampThing#5&#6 . . . . 3.00
4 BWr,rep.SwampThing#7&#8 . . . . 3.00
5 BWr,rep.SwampThing#9&#10,
   H.O.S. #92, final issue 3.00

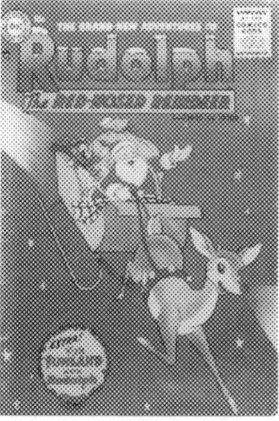

*Rudolph The Red-Nosed Reindeer
© DC Comics, Inc.*

RUDOLPH THE RED -NOSED REINDEER
Dec., 1950
1950 . . . . 60.00
1951 thru 1954. . . . . @50.00
1955 thru 1962 Winter . . . . @30.00

RUSSIAN ROULETTE
Vertigo 1999
1 (of 3) 3.00

SAGA OF RAS AL GHUL
1988
1 NA,DG, reprints. 5.00
2 rep. 4.00
3 rep.Batman #242&#243 . . . . . . 4.00
4 rep.Batman #244&#245,
   Detective #410. . . . . 4.00
TPB reps. 17.95

SAGA OF THE SWAMP THING
1982–85
1 JmP(s),TY,DSp,O:Swamp Thing,
   BU:PhantomStranger 4.00
2 Ph(c),TY,DSp,I:Grasp 2.00
3 TY,DSp,V:Vampires 2.00
4 TY,TD,V:Demon 2.00
5 TY 2.00
6 TY,I:General Sunderland. 2.00
7 TY 2.00
8 TY 2.00
9 TY 2.00
10 TY 2.00

11 TY,I:Golem. 2.00
12 LWn(s),TY 2.00
13 TY,D:Grasp 2.00
14 A:Phantom Stranger 2.00
15 . . . . 2.00
16 SBi,JTo. 2.00
17 I:Matthew Cable. 4.00
18 JmP(s),LWn(s),SBi,JTo,BWr,
   R:Arcane 2.00
19 JmP(s),SBi,JTo,V:Arcane 2.00
20 B:AMo(s),Day,JTo(i),D:Arcane
   (Original incarnation) 15.00
21 SBi,JTo,O:Swamp Thing,I:Floronic
   Man,D:General Sunderland . . 13.00
22 SBi,JTo,O:Floronic Man 10.00
23 SBi,JTo,V:Floronic Man 10.00
24 SBi,JTo,V:Floronic Man,A:JLA,
   In Arkham 10.00
25 SBi,A:Jason Blood,I:Kamara . . . 8.00
26 SBi,A:Demon,
   D:Matthew Cable 8.00
27 SBi,D:Kamara,A:Demon 7.00
28 SwM,Burial of Alec Holland 7.00
29 SBi,JTo,R:Arcane. 7.00
30 SBi,AA,D:Abby,C:Joker,
   V:Arcane 9.00
31 RV,JTo,D:Arcane 6.00
32 SwM,Tribute to WK Pogo strip . . 6.00
33 rep.H.O.S.#92,A:Cain & Abel . . . 6.00
34 SBi,JTo,Swamp Thing & Abby
   Fall in Love 8.00
35 SBi,JTo,Nukeface,pt.1 . . . . 5.00
36 SBi,JTo,Nukeface,pt.2 . . . . 5.00
37 RV,JTo,I:John Constantine,
   American Gothic,pt.1 . . . . . . 17.00
38 SnW,JTo,V:Water-Vampires
   (Pt.1) A:J.Constantine 6.00
39 SBi,JTo,V:Water-Vampires
   (Pt.2) A:J.Constantine 5.00
40 SBi,JTo,C:J.Constantine,
   The Curse 5.00
41 SBi,AA,Voodoo Zombies #1 . . . . 3.00
42 SBi,JTo,RoR,
   Voodoo Zombies #2 . . . . 3.00
43 SnW,RoR,Windfall,
   I:Chester Williams 3.00
44 SBi,JTo,RoR,V:Serial Killer,
   C:Batman,Constantine,Mento . . 5.00
45 SnW,AA,Ghost Dance 3.00
Ann.#1 MT,TD,Movie Adaption . . . 2.00
Ann.#2 AMo(s),E:Arcane,A:Deadman,
   Phantom Stranger,Spectre,
   Demon,Resurrection of Abby . . 7.00
Ann.#3 AMo(s),Ape issue 4.00
TPB rep.#21-#27 . . . . 12.95
TPB rep.#28-#34,Ann.#2 . . . . . . 14.95
Becomes:

SWAMP THING

SANDMAN

[1st Regular Series] 1974–75
1 JK,I&O:Sandman,I:General
   Electric. 12.00
2 V:Dr.Spider. 5.00
3 Brain that Blanked
   out the Bronx 5.00
4 JK,Panic in the Dream Stream . . 5.00
5 JK,Invasion of the Frog Men 5.00
6 JK,WW,V:Dr.Spider. 6.00

[2nd Regular Series] 1989–93
1 B:NGa(s),SK,I:2nd Sandman . . 50.00
2 SK,A:Cain,Abel. 20.00
3 SK,A:John Constantine. 18.00
4 SK,A:Demon. 10.00
5 SK,A:Mr.Miracle,J'onnJ'onzz . . . 10.00
6 V:Doctor Destiny. 9.00
7 V:Doctor Destiny. 8.00
8 Sound of her wings,F:Death . . . 30.00
8a Guest Ed.Pin-Up Cover 75.00

Sandman, 1st Series #1
© DC Comics Inc.

9 Tales in the Sand,Doll's House
   prologue. 7.00
10 B:Doll's House,A:Desire
   & Despair,I:Brut & Glob 7.00
11 MovingIn,A:2ndS-man 7.00
12 Play House,D;2ndS'man 7.00
13 Men of Good Fortune,A:Death,
   Lady Constantine 7.00
14 Collectors,D:Corinthian 8.00
15 Into' Night,DreamVortex. 6.00
16 E:Doll's House,Lost Hearts 6.00
17 Calliope. 6.00
18 Dream of a 1000 Cats 6.00
18a error pg.1. . . . . 20.00
19 Midsummer Nights Dream 5.00
19a error copy 15.00
20 Strange Death Element Girl,
   A:Death 5.00
21 Family Reunion,B:Season
   of Mists 6.00
22 Season of Mists,I:Daniel Hall . . 13.00
23 Season of Mists. 6.00
24 Season of Mists. 6.00
25 Season of Mists. 6.00
26 Season of Mists. 5.00
27 E:Season of Mists 5.00
28 Ownership of Hell 5.00
29 A:Lady J.Constantine. 4.00
30 Ancient Rome;A:Death,Desire . . 4.00
31 Ancient Rome,pt.2 . . . . 4.00
32 B:The Game of You 4.00
33 The Game of You 4.00
34 The Game of You 3.00
35 The Game of You 3.00
36 The Game of You,48pgs 4.00
37 The Game of You,Epilogue 3.00
38 Convergence. 2.50
39 Convergence,A:Marco Polo 2.50
40 Convergence,A:Cain,Abel,Eve,
   Matthew the Raven 2.50
41 JIT,VcL,(i),B:Brief Lives,
   F:Endless. 3.00
42 JIT,VcL,(i),F:Delirium,Dream. . . 2.50
43 JIT,VcL,(i),A:Death,Etain 2.50
44 JIT,VcL,(i),R:Corinthian,
   Destruction. 2.50
45 JIT,VcL,(i),F:Tiffany,
   Ishtar(Belli). 2.50
46 JIT,VcL,(i),F:Morpheus/Bast,A:AIDS
   insert story,F:Death 3.00

Vertigo 1994–96
47 JIT,VcL,(i),A:Endless 3.50
48 JIT,VcL,(i),L:Destruction 3.50
49 JIT,VcL,(i),E:Brief Lives,

F:Orpheus 3.50
50 DMc(c),CR,Tales of Baghdad,
   pin-upsby TM,DMc,MK. 4.00
50a Gold Ed. 25.00
51 BT,MBu(i),B:Inn at the end of
   the World,Gaheris' tale 3.00
52 BT,MBu(i),JWk,Cluracan's
   Story 3.00
53 BT,DG,MBu(i),MZi,Hob's
   Leviathan 3.00
54 BT,MiA,MBu(i),R:Prez 3.00
55 SAp,VcL,BT,MBu(i),F:Klaproth
   Cerements's Story 3.00
56 BT,MBu(i),DG(i),SLi(i),GyA,TyH(i),
   E:Inn at the end of the World,
   C:Endless 3.00
57 MaH,B:Kindly Ones,Inc.American
   Freak Preview 4.00
58 MaH,Kindly Ones,pt.2,
   A:Lucifer. 2.50
59 MaH,Kindly Ones,pt.3,R:Fury. . . 2.00
60 MaH,Kindly Ones,pt.4 . . . . 2.00
61 MaH,Kindly Ones,pt.5 . . . . 2.00
62 Kindly Ones,pt.6,Murder 2.00
63 MaH,Kindly Ones,pt.7,
   A:Rose Walker 2.00
64 Kindly Ones,pt.8 . . . . 2.00
65 MaH,Kindly Ones,pt.9,Dream
   Kingdom. 2.00
66 MaH,Kindly Ones,pt.10 . . . . 2.00
67 MaH,Kindly Ones,pt.11 . . . . 2.00
68 MaH,Kindly Ones,pt.12 . . . . 2.00
69 MaH,Kindly Ones finale 3.00
70 The Wake,pt.1 . . . . 2.00
71 The Wake,pt.2 . . . . 2.00
72 NGa,DMc,The Wake,pt.3 . . . . . . 2.00
73 NGa,Sunday Mourning 2.00
74 NGa,V:Lord of Dreams 2.00
TPB Preludes & Nocturnes,
   rep. #1–#8 . . . . 20.00
TPB Doll's House, rep #8–#16 . . 18.00
HC The Doll's House 30.00
TPB Dream Country,Rep.#17-#20. 15.00
TPB Fables & Reflections,rep. . . . 20.00
HC Fables and Reflections 30.00
TPB Season of Mists,rep.#21-#28. 20.00
HC Season of Mists 40.00
TPB A Game of You,rep.#32–#37. 20.00
HC A Game of You,rep.#32–#37 . 32.00
TPB Brief Lives 20.00
HC Brief Lives 30.00
TPB The Wake, rep. #70–#75. . . 20.00
HC The Wake. 30.00
TPB World's End DMc(c) 20.00
Sandman Covers, 1989–96 . . . . 40.00
Spec.BT,Glow in the Dark(c),The
   Legend of Orpheus,
   (inc. Portrait Gallery) 6.00

SANDMAN MYSTERY THEATRE

Vertigo 1993–99
1 B:MWg(s),GyD,R:G.A.Sandman,
   B:Tarantula,I:Mr.Belmont,
   Dian Belmont 5.00
2 GyD,V:Tarantula 3.00
3 GyD,V:Tarantula 3.00
4 GyD,E:Tarantula 3.00
5 JWk,The Face 3.00
6 JWk,The Face #2 . . . . 3.00
7 JWk,The Face #3 . . . . 3.00
8 JWk,E:The Face 3.00
9 RGT,B:The Brute,I:Rocket
   Ramsey 3.00
10 RGT,The Brute#2. . . . . 3.00
11 RGT,The Brute#3. . . . . 3.00
12 RGT,E:The Brute 3.00
13 GyD,B:The Vamp. 3.00
14 GyD,The Vamp#2 . . . . 3.00
15 GyD,The Vamp#3 . . . . 3.00

16 GyD,E:The Vamp. 3.00
17 GyD,B:The Scorpion 3.00
18 GyD,The Scorpion,pt.2 . . . . . . 3.00
19 GyD,The Scorpion,pt.3 . . . . . . 3.00
20 GyD,The Scorpion,pt.4 . . . . . . 3.00
21 Dr. Death. 3.00
22 Dr. Death,pt.2 . . . . 3.00
23 Dr. Death,pt.3 . . . . 3.00
24 Dr. Death,pt.4 . . . . 3.00
25 The Butcher,pt.1 . . . . 3.00
26 The Butcher,pt.2 . . . . 3.00
27 The Butcher,pt.3 . . . . 3.00
28 The Butcher,pt.4 . . . . 3.00
29 The Hourman,pt.1 . . . . 3.00
30 The Hourman,pt.2 . . . . 3.00
31 The Hourman,pt.3 . . . . 3.00
32 The Hourman,pt.4 . . . . 3.00
33 The Python,pt.1 . . . . 3.00
34 The Python,pt.2 . . . . 3.00
35 The Python,pt.3 . . . . 3.00
36 The Python,pt.4 . . . . 3.00
37 The Mist,pt.1 . . . . 3.00
38 The Mist,pt.2 . . . . 3.00
39 The Mist,pt.3 . . . . 3.00
40 The Mist,pt.4 . . . . 3.00
41 MWg&SSe(s),GyD, Phantom of
   the Fair pt. 1. . . . . 2.50
42 MWg&SSe(s),GyD, Phantom of
   the Fair pt. 2. . . . . 2.50
43 MWg&SSe(s),GyD, Phantom of
   the Fair pt. 3. . . . . 2.50
44 MWg&SSe(s),GyD, Phantom of
   the Fair pt. 4. . . . . 2.50
45 MWg&SSe(s),"The Blackhawk,"
   pt.1 . . . . 2.50
46 MWg&SSe(s),"The Blackhawk,"
   pt.2 . . . . 2.50
47 MWg&SSe(s),"The Blackhawk,"
   pt.3 . . . . 2.50
48 MWg&SSe(s),RCa,"The
   Blackhawk" concl. 2.50
49 MWg&SSe(s),"The Scarlet
   Ghost," pt.1 . . . . 2.50
50 MWg&SSe(s),"The Scarlet
   Ghost," pt.2, 48pg 3.50
51 MWg&SSe(s),"The Scarlet
   Ghost," pt.3 . . . . 2.50
52 MWg&SSe(s),"The Scarlet
   Ghost," pt.4 . . . . 2.50
53 MWg&SSe(s),The Crone,pt.1. . . 2.50
53 MWg&SSe(s),The Crone,pt.2. . . 2.50
54 SSe&MWg(s),The Crone,pt.3. . . 2.50
55 SSe&MWg(s),The Crone,pt.4. . . 2.50
56 SSe&MWg(s),The Crone, concl. 2.50
57 SSe&MWg(s),The Cannon,pt.1 . 2.50
58 SSe&MWg(s),The Cannon,pt.2 . 2.50
59 SSe&MWg(s),The Cannon,pt.3 . 2.50
60 SSe&MWg(s),The Cannon,pt.4 . 2.50
61 SSe(s),GyD,The City, pt.1 . . . . 2.50
62 SSe(s),GyD,The City, pt.2 . . . . 2.50
63 SSe(s),GyD,The City, pt.3 . . . . 2.50
64 SSe(s),GyD,The City, pt.4 . . . . 2.50
65 SSe,GyD,The Goblin, pt.1 . . . . 2.50
66 SSe,GyD,The Goblin, pt.2 . . . . 2.50
67 SSe,GyD,The Goblin, pt.3 . . . . 2.50
68 SSe,GyD,The Goblin, pt.4 . . . . 2.50
69 SSe,GyD. 2.50
70 SSe,GyD,final issue. 2.50
Ann.#1 . . . . 3.95
TPB The Tarantula 14.95

SANDMAN PRESENTS:
LOVE STREET
Vertigo 1999
1 (of 3) MZi,VcL. 3.00
2 MZi,VcL,F:John Constantine. . . . 3.00
3 MZi,VcL,Concl. 3.00

SANDMAN PRESENTS:
LUCIFER
Vertigo 1999
1 (of 3) SHp, Morningstar Option . . 3.00
2 SHp 3.00
3 SHp, conclusion 3.00

SCARAB
Vertigo 1993–94
1 GF(c),B:JnS(s),SEa,MkB(i),
   R&O:Scarab,V:Halaku-umid . . . 2.25
2 GF(c),SEa,MkB(i),A:Phantom
   Stranger. 2.25
3 GF(c),SEa,MkB(i),in North
   Carolina. 2.25
4 GF(c),SEa,MkB(i),V:Rathoroch . . 2.25
5 GF(c),SEa,MkB(i) 2.25
6 GF(c),SEa,MkB(i),V:Gloryboys . . 2.25
7 GF(c),SEa,MkB(i),V:Scientists . . 2.25
8 GF(c),SEa,MkB(i),Final Issue . . . 2.25

SCARE TACTICS
Oct. 1996
1 LKa(s),AWi,ALa,monsters of
   the MTV age 2.25
2 LKa(s),AWi,ALa,I:Scaremobile . . 2.25
3 LKa(s),AWi,ALa, ... 2.25
4 LKa(s),AWi,ALa, "Big For His
   Age," O:Grossout 2.25
5 LKa(s),AWi,ALa, Valentine's Day
   issue 2.25
6 LKa(s),AWi,ALa, F:Fang 2.25
7 LKa(s),AWi,ALa, F:The Children
   of the Beast 2.25
8 LKa(s),AWi,ALa, Convergence,
   x-over, concl. 2.25
9 LKa(s),AWi,ALa,"Snake Oil"
   concl. 2.25
10 LKa(s),AWi,ALa,in Gotham 2.25
11 LKa(s),AWi,ALa,A:Batman 2.25

Scarlet #14 © DC Comics, Inc.

SCARLETT
1993–94
1 I:Scarlett,Blood of the Innocent. . 3.50
2 Blood of the Innocent cont. 1.75
3 Blood of the Innocent cont. 1.75
4 V:The Nomads 1.75
5 GM,O:Nomads 1.75
6 thru 8 GM,Blood of the Damned . 1.75
9 GM,V:Undead. 1.75
10 B:Blood of the City. 1.75

11 I:Afterburn 1.75
12 V:Sligoth 1.75
13 V:Gearsman 1.75
14 final issue 1.75

SCENE OF THE CRIME
Vertigo 1999
1 (of 4) 2.50
2 thru 4 . . . . @2.50

SCRIBBLY
Aug. 1948–Dec.–Jan. 1951–52
1 SM. 700.00
2 . . . . 500.00
3 . . . . 400.00
4 . . . . 400.00
5 . . . . 400.00
6 thru 10 . . . . @275.00
11 thru 15 . . . . @250.00

SCOOBY-DOO
Warner Bros./DC June 1997
1 . . . . 1.75
2 . . . . 1.75
3 A wedding 1.75
4 Mad Hounds of the Hunt. 2.00
5 Freddy's Grampa Ted. 2.00
6 Ghost Riders in Disguise 2.00
7 Mystery of the Missing Cargo . . . 2.00
8 . . . . 2.00
9 Mardi Gras 2.00
10 mystery convention 2.00
11 evil genie 2.00
12 comic book con. 2.00
13 real monster 2.00
14 beneath New York City 2.00
15 Big Puce 2.00
16 . . . . 2.00
17 . . . . 2.00
18 . . . . 2.00
19 Ghost of Holiday Presents 2.00
20 Wraithcar Driver. 2.00
21 . . . . 2.00
22 Curse of Wrangler Field. 2.00
23 two fish stories. 2.00
24 Surf's up 2.00
25 Phantom of the Mosh Pit 2.00
26 One Night in Roswell, pt.1 . . . . 2.00
27 One Night in Roswell, pt.2 . . . . 2.00

SEA DEVILS
Sept.–Oct., 1961
1 RH. 500.00
2 RH 250.00
3 RH 175.00
4 RH 150.00
5 RH 150.00
6 thru 10 RH . . . . @85.00
11 . . . . 65.00
12 . . . . 65.00
13 JKu,GC,RA 65.00
14 thru 20 . . . . @65.00
21 I:Capt X,Man Fish 40.00
22 thru 35, May-June, 1967. . . . @40.00

SEBASTIAN O
Vertigo 1993
1 GMo(s),SY,I:Sebastian O,A:Lord
   Lavender,Roaring Boys 2.50
2 GMo(s),SY,V:Roaring Boys,
   Assassins,A:Abbe 2.50
3 GMo(s),SY,D:Lord Lavender. . . . 2.50

SECRET HEARTS
Sept.–Oct., 1949–July 1971
1 'Make Believe Sweetheart' . . . 400.00

2 ATh,`Love Is Not A Dream'. . . 200.00
3 `Sing Me A Love Song'. 175.00
4 ATh 175.00
5 ATh 175.00
6 . . . . 175.00
7 . . . . 300.00
8 . . . . 125.00
9 . . . . 125.00
10 thru 20 . . . . @125.00
21 thru 26 . . . . @75.00
27 B:Comics Code 50.00
28 thru 30 . . . . @50.00
31 thru 70 . . . . @45.00
71 thru 110 . . . . @25.00
111 thru 120 . . . . @20.00
121 thru 150 . . . . @12.00
151 thru 153 . . . . @10.00

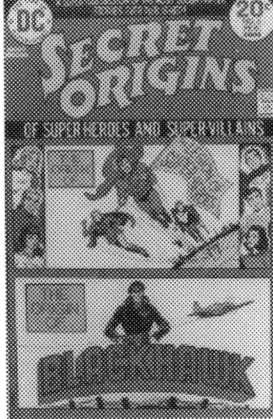

Secret Origins #6 © DC Comics Inc.

SECRET ORIGINS
Feb. 1973–Oct. 1974

1 O:Superman,Batman,Ghost,
    Flash 20.00
2 O:Green Lantern,Atom,
    Supergirl 10.00
3 O:Wonder Woman,Wildcat 10.00
4 O:Vigilante by MMe 10.00
5 O:The Spectre 10.00
6 O:Blackhawk,Legion of Super
    Heroes 10.00
7 O:Robin, Aquaman 10.00

SECRET ORIGINS
April, 1986

1 JOy,WB,F:Superman 4.00
2 GK,F:Blue Beetle 3.50
3 JBi,F:Captain Marvel 3.00
4 GT,F:Firestorm 2.75
5 GC,F:Crimson Aventer 3.00
6 DG,MR,F:Batman. 5.00
7 F:Sandman,Guy Gardner 3.50
8 MA,F:Shadow Lass,Dollman. . . . 2.50
9 GT,F:Skyman,Flash 2.50
10 JL,JO,JA,F:Phantom Stranger . . 2.25
11 LMc,TD,F:Hawkman,Powergirl . . 2.00
12 F:Challengers of the Unknown
    I:G.A. Fury 2.00
13 EL,F:Nightwing 3.00
14 F:Suicide Squad 2.25
15 KMo,DG,F:Deadman,Spectre. . . 2.25
16 AKu,F:Hourman,Warlord 2.00
17 KGi,F:Green Lantern 2.25
18 . . . . 2.00
19 JM(c),MA. 2.00

Secret Origins #17 © DC Comics Inc.

20 RL,DG,F:Batgirl 3.00
21 GM,MA,F:Jonah Hex 2.00
22 F:Manhunter,Millenium tie-in . . 2.00
23 F:Manhunter,Millenium tie-in . . . 2.00
24 F:Dr.Fate,Blue Devil. 2.00
25 F:The Legion 2.00
26 F:Black Lightning 2.00
27 F:Zatanna,Zatara. 2.00
28 RLd,GK,F:Nightshade,Midnight . 2.00
29 F:Atom,Red Tornado 2.00
30 F:Elongated Man 2.00
31 F:Justice Society of America. . . 2.00
32 F:Justice League America. 3.00
33 F:Justice League Inter.. . . . . . . 2.00
34 F:Justice League Inter.. . . . . . . 2.00
35 KSu,F:Justice League Inter. 2.00
36 F:Green Lantern 3.00
37 F:Legion of Subst. Heroes 2.00
38 F:Green Arrow,Speedy 2.00
39 F:Batman,Animal Man 3.50
40 F:Gorilla City 2.00
41 F:Flash Villains 2.50
42 DC,F:Phantom Girl 2.00
43 TVE,TT,F:Hawk & Dove 2.00
44 F:Batman,Clayface tie-in 3.00
45 F:Blackhawk,El Diablo 2.00
46 CS,F:All Headquarters 2.00
47 CS,F:The Legion 2.00
48 KG,F:Ambush Bug. 2.00
49 F: The Cadmus Project 2.50
50 GP,CI,DG,F:Batman,Robin,
    Flash,Black Canary 4.00
Ann.#1 JBy,F:Doom Patrol 3.00
Ann.#2 CI,MA,F:Flash 2.00
Ann.#3 F:The Teen Titans. 3.00
Spec.#1 SK,PB,DG,F:Batman's worst
    Villians,A:Penguin. 4.00
TPB DG,New Origin Batman. 4.50
GN rep of 1961 Annual. 5.00
Replica Edition 80-page 5.00

SECRET SOCIETY OF SUPER-VILLAINS
May-June, 1976

1 A:Capt.Boomerang, Grodd,
    Sinestro 2.50
2 R:Capt.Comet,A:Green Lantern . 2.50
3 A:Mantis, Darkseid 2.00
4 A:Kalibak,Darkseid,Gr.Lantern . 2.00
5 RB,D:Manhunter,A:JLA. 2.00
6 RB/BL,A:Black Canary 1.50
7 RB/BL,A:Hawkgirl,Lex Luthor . . . 1.50
8 RB/BL,A:Kid Flash 1.50

9 RB/BMc,A:Kid Flash, Creeper. . . 1.50
10 DAy/JAb,A:Creeper 1.25
11 JO,N:Wizard 1.25
12 BMc,A:Blockbuster 1.25
13 A:Crime Syndicate of America . . 1.00
14 A:Crime Syndicate of America . . 1.00
15 A:G.A.Atom, Dr. Mid Nite 1.25

SECRETS OF HAUNTED HOUSE
April-May, 1975

1 LD(c),Dead Heat. 25.00
2 ECh(c),A Dead Man 12.00
3 ECh(c),Pathway To Purgatory. . 12.00
4 LD(c),The Face of Death 12.00
5 BWr(c),Gunslinger! 15.00
6 JAp(c),Deadly Allegiance 10.00
7 JAp(c),It'll Grow On You 10.00
8 MK(c),Raising The Devil 10.00
9 LD(c),The Man Who Didn't
    Believe in Ghosts 10.00
10 MK(c),Ask Me No Questions . . 10.00
11 MK(c),Picasso Fever!. 10.00
12 JO&DG(c),Yorick's Skull. 10.00
13 JO&DG(c),The Cry of the
    Warewolf 10.00
14 MK(c),Selina 10.00
15 LD(c),Over Your Own Dead
    Body 7.00
16 MK(c),Water, Water Every Fear . 7.00
17 LD(c),Papa Don. 7.00
18 LD(c),No Sleep For The Dying . . 7.00
19 LD(c),The Manner of Execution . 7.00
20 JO(c),The Talisman of the
    Serpent 7.00
21 LD(c),The Death's Head
    Scorpion. 7.00
22 LD(c),See How They Die 7.00
23 LD(c),The Creeping Red Death . 7.00
24 LD(c),Second Chance To Die. . . 7.00
25 LD(c),The Man Who Cheated
    Destiny. 7.00
26 MR(c),Elevator to Eternity 7.00
27 DH(c),Souls For the Master 7.00
28 DH(c),Demon Rum 7.00
29 MK(c),Duel of Darkness. 7.00
30 JO(c),For the Love of Arlo 7.00
31 I:Mister E. 8.00
32 The Legend of the Tiger's Paw . 4.00
33 In The Attic Dwells Dark Seth . . 4.00
34 Double Your Pleasure 4.00
35 Deathwing, Lord of Darkness. . . 4.00
36 RB&DG(c),Sister Sinister 4.00
37 RB&DG(c),The Third Wish Is
    Death. 4.00
38 RB&DG(c),Slaves of Satan 4.00
39 RB&DG(c),The Witch-Hounds
    of Salem 4.00
40 RB&DG(c),The Were-Witch
    of Boston 4.00
41 JKu(c),House at Devil's Tail 4.00
42 JKu(c),Mystic Murder. 4.00
43 JO(c),Mother of Invention. 4.00
44 BWr(c),Halloween God 4.00
45 EC&JO(c),Star-Trakker 4.00
46 March, 1982 . . . . 4.00

SINISTER HOUSE OF SECRET LOVE
Oct.–Nov., 1971

1 . . . . 35.00
2 JJ(c). 15.00
3 ATh 14.00
4 April-May, 1972 . . . . 12.00

Becomes:

SECRETS OF SINISTER HOUSE
June-July, 1972

5	18.00
6	10.00
7 NR	10.00
8	10.00
9	10.00
10 NA(i)	20.00
11	7.00
12	7.00
13	7.00
14	7.00
15	7.00
16	7.00
17 DBa	7.00
18 June-July, 1974	7.00

SECRETS OF THE LEGION OF SUPER-HEROES
Jan., 1981

1 O:Legion	1.50
2 O:Brainiac 5	1.00
3 March, 1981,O:Karate Kid	1.00

SEEKERS
Vertigo

1 & 2	@2.50

SEEKERS INTO THE MYSTERY

1	2.50
2	2.50
3	2.50
4 JMD,Lucas Hart spirit resurrected	2.50
5 JMD,JMu,	2.50
6	2.50
7	2.50
8	2.50
9 JMD(s),MZi,"Falling Down from Heaven," pt.4 concl.	2.50
10 JMD(s),JMu,F:Charlie Limbo	2.50
11 JMD(s),JIT,"God's Shadow" pt.1	2.50
12 JMD(s),JIT,"God's Shadow" pt.2	2.50
13 JMD(s),JIT,"God's Shadow" pt.3	2.50
14 JMD(s),JIT,"In God's Shadow," concl.	2.50
15 JMD(s),JMu,Hart meets Magician, final issue	2.95

SENSATION COMICS
1942–52

1 I:Wonder Woman,Wildcat	22,000.00
2 I:Etta Candy & the Holiday Girls, Dr. Poison	3,500.00
3 Diana Price joins Military Intelligence	2,000.00
4 I:Baroness PaulaVonGunther	1,500.00
5 V:Axis Spies	1,200.00
6 Wonder Woman receives magic lasso,V:Baroness Gunther	1,200.00
7 V:Baroness Gunther	850.00
8 Meets Gloria Bullfinch	850.00
9 A:The Real Diana Prince	850.00
10 V:Ishti	850.00
11 I:Queen Desira	850.00
12 V:Baroness Gunther	750.00
13 V:Olga,Hitler(c)	1,000.00
14	800.00
15 V:Simon Slikery	800.00
16 V:Karl Schultz	800.00
17 V:Princess Yasmini	800.00

18 V:Quito	800.00
19 Wonder Woman goes berserk	800.00
20 V:Stoffer	800.00
21 V:American Adolf	600.00
22 V:Cheetah	600.00
23 'War Laugh Mania'	600.00
24 I:Wonder Woman's mental radio	600.00
25	600.00
26 A:Queen Hippolyte	600.00
27 V:Ely Close	600.00
28 V:Mayor Prude	600.00
29 V:Mimi Mendez	600.00
30 V:Anton Unreal	600.00
31 'Grow Down Land'	450.00
32 V:Crime Chief	450.00
33 Meets Percy Pringle	450.00
34 I:Sargon	500.00
35 V:Sontag Henya in Atlantis	400.00
36 V:Bedwin Footh	400.00
37 A:Mala((1st app. All-Star #8)	400.00
38 V:The Gyp	400.00
39 V:Nero	400.00
40 I:Countess Draska Nishki	400.00
41 V:Creeper Jackson	350.00
42 V:Countess Nishki	350.00
43 Meets Joel Heyday	350.00
44 V:Lt. Sturm	350.00
45 V:Jose Perez	350.00
46 V:Lawbreakers Protective League	350.00
47 V:Unknown	350.00
48 V:Topso and Teena	350.00
49 V:Zavia	350.00
50 V:`Ears' Fellock	350.00
51 V:Boss Brekel	300.00
52 Meets Prof. Toxino	300.00
53 V:Wanta Wynn	300.00
54 V:Dr. Fiendo	300.00
55 V:Bughumans	300.00
56 V:Dr. Novel	300.00
57 V:Syonide	300.00
58 Meets Olive Norton	300.00
59 V:Snow Man	300.00
60 V:Bifton Jones	300.00
61 V:Bluff Robust	300.00
62 V:Black Robert of Dogwood	300.00
63 V:Prof. Vibrate	300.00
64 V:Cloudmen	300.00
65 V:Lim Slait	300.00
66 V:Slick Skeener	300.00
67 V:Daredevil Dix	300.00
68 'Secret of the Menacing Octopus'	325.00
69 V:Darcy Wells	275.00
70 Unconquerable Woman of Cocha Bamba	275.00
71 V:Queen Flaming	275.00
72 V:Blue Seal Gang	275.00
73 Wonder Woman time travel story	275.00
74 V:Spug Spangle	275.00
75 V:Shark	275.00
76 V:King Diamond	275.00
77 V:Boss Brekel	275.00
78 V:Furiosa	275.00
79 Meets Leila and Solala	275.00
80 V:Don Enrago	275.00
81 V:Dr. Frenzi	300.00
82 V:King Lunar	225.00
83 V:Prowd	225.00
84 V:Duke Daxo	225.00
85 Meets Leslie M. Gresham	225.00
86 'Secret of the Amazing Bracelets'	225.00
87 In Twin Peaks(in Old West)	225.00
88 Wonder Woman in Holywood	225.00
89 V:Abacus Rackeett gang	225.00
90 'The Secret of the Modern Sphinx'	225.00

Sensation #21 © DC Comics, Inc.

91	225.00
92 V:Duke of Deceptions	225.00
93 V:Talbot	225.00
94 Girl Isue	325.00
95	300.00
96	300.00
97	300.00
98 'Strange Mission'	300.00
99 I:Astra	300.00
100	450.00
101 'Battle for the Atom World'	300.00
102 'Queen of the South Seas'	300.00
103 V:Robot Archers	300.00
104 'The End of Paradise Island'	300.00
105 'Secret of the Giant Forest'	300.00
106 E:Wonder Woman	300.00
107 ATh,Mystery issue	550.00
108 ATh,I:Johnny Peril	450.00
109 Ath,A:Johnny Peril	550.00

Becomes:

SENSATION MYSTERY
1952–53

110 B:Johnny Peril	300.00
111 'Spectre in the Flame'	275.00
112 'Death has 5 Guesses'	275.00
113	275.00
114 GC,'The Haunted Diamond'	275.00
115 'The Phantom Castle'	275.00
116 'The Toy Assassins', July-Aug., 1953	275.00

SENSATION COMICS
1999

1 JeR(s),ScB, F:Wonder Woman & Hawkgirl	2.00

SERGEANT BILKO
May-June, 1957

1 Based on TV show	550.00
2	275.00
3	250.00
4	200.00
5	200.00
6 thru 17	@175.00
18 March-April, 1960	175.00

SERGEANT BILKO'S PVT. DOBERMAN
June-July, 1958

1	300.00
2	175.00

3 . . . . 125.00
4 . . . . 125.00
5 . . . . 125.00
6 thru 10 . . . . @100.00
11 Feb.–March, 1960 . . . . 100.00

SGT. ROCK
(See: OUR ARMY AT WAR)

SGT. ROCK SPECIAL
Oct., 1988
#1 rep.Our Army at War#162-#63 . . 2.00
#2 rep.Brave & Bold #52. . . . . 2.00
#3 rep.Showcase #45. . . . . 2.00
#4 rep.Our Army at War#147-#48. . 2.00
#5 rep.Our Army at War#81&#103 . 2.00
#6 rep.Our Army at War #160 . . . . . 2.00
#7 rep.Our Army at War #85 . . . . . . 2.00
#8 rep. 2.00
#9 thru #20 reprints. . . . . @2.00
Spec. #1 TT,MGo,JKu,CR,(new
  stories). 2.95

SGT. ROCK'S PRIZE BATTLE TALES
Winter, 1964
1 . . . . 225.00

SHADE
June-July, 1977
(1st Regular Series)
1 SD,I&O: Shade. 4.00
2 SD,V:Form 3.25
3 SD,V:The Cloak 2.75
4 SD,Return to Meta-Zone. 2.75
5 SD,V:Supreme Decider. 2.75
6 SD,V:Khaos 2.75
7 SD,V:Dr.Z.Z. 2.75
8 SD,last issue 2.75

SHADE, THE
Feb. 1997
1 (of 4) JeR(s),GeH,A:Ludlows . . . 2.25
2 JeR(s),JWi,MGy,poisoned by love
  of his life 2.25
3 JeR(s),BBI,Golden Age Flash Jay
  Garrick retiring 2.25
4 JeR(s),MZi,V:last of the Ludlows. 2.25

SHADE, THE CHANGING MAN
July, 1990
1 B:PrM(s),CBa,MPn,I:Kathy George,
  I&D:Troy Grezer. 5.00
2 CBa,MPn,Who Shot JFK#1. . . . . 4.00
3 CBa,MPn,Who Shot JFK#2. . . . . 3.00
4 CBa,MPn,V:American Scream . . 3.00
5 CBa,MPn,V:Hollywood
  Monsters 3.00
6 CBa,MPn,V:Ed Loot 3.00
7 CBa,MPn,I:Arnold Major. 3.00
8 CBa,Mpn,I:Lenny 3.00
9 CBa,MPn,V:Arnold Major 3.00
10 CBa,MPn,Paranioa 2.75
11 CBa,MPn,R:Troy Grezer 2.50
12 CBa,MPn,V:Troy Grezer 2.50
13 CBa,MPn,I:Fish Priest 2.50
14 CBa,MPn,V:Godfather of Guilt . . 2.50
15 CBa,MPn,I:Spirit 2.50
16 CBa,MPn,V:American Scream . . 2.50
17 RkB(i),V:Rohug 2.50
18 MPn,E:American Scream. 2.50
19 MPn,V:Dave Messiah Seeker. . . 2.50
20 JD,CBa,MPn,RkB,R:Roger 2.50

Shade, The Changing Man #3
© DC Comics Inc.

21 MPn,The Road,A:Stringer 2.25
22 The Road,Childhood 2.25
23 The Road 2.25
24 The Road 2.25
25 The Road 2.25
26 MPn(i),F:Lenny 2.25
27 MPn(i),Shade becomes female . 2.25
28 MPn(i),Changing Woman#2 . . . . 2.25
29 MPn(i),Changing Woman#3 . . . . 2.25
30 Another Life. 2.25
31 Ernest & Jim#1 . . . . 2.25
32 Ernest & Jim#2 . . . . 2.25

Vertigo
33 CBa,B:Birth Pains 2.25
34 CBa,RkB(i),GID(i),A:Brian Juno,
  Garden of Pain. 2.25
35 CBa,RkB(i),E:Birth Pains,
  V:Juno. 2.25
36 CBa,PrG(i),RkB(i),B:Passion child,
  I:Miles Laimling 2.25
37 CBa,RkB(i),Shade/Kathy 2.25
38 CBa,RkB(i),Great American
  Novel 2.25
39 CBa,SEa,RkB(i),Pond Life 2.25
40 PBd,at Hotel Shade 2.25
41 GID,Pandora's Story,Kathy is
  pregnant. 2.25
42 CBa,RkB(i),SY,B:History Lesson,
  A:John Constantine 2.50
43 CBa,RkB(i),PBd,Trial of William
  Matthieson,A:J.Constantine . . . 2.50
44 CBa,RkB(i),E:History Lesson,
  D:William Matthieson,A:John
  Constantine 2.50
45 CBa,B:A Season in Hell. 2.25
46 CBa(c),GID,Season in Hell#2. . . 2.25
47 CBa(c),GID,A:Lenny 2.25
48 CBa(c),GID 2.25
49 CBa(c),GID,Kathy's Past 2.25
50 GID,BBI,MiA,pin-up gallery. 3.25
51 GID,BBI,MiA,Masks,pt.1 . . . . . . 2.00
52 GID,BBI,MiA,Masks,pt.2. . . . . . . 2.00
53 GID,BBI,MiA,Masks,pt.3. . . . . . . 2.00
54 Meeting. 2.00
55 . . . . 2.00
56 . . . . 2.00
57 MBu,PrM,F:George 2.00
58 PrM,Michael Lark. 2.00
59 MBu,PrM,Nasty Infections,pt.1 . . 2.25
60 MBu,PrM,Nasty Infections,pt.2. . 2.25
61 MBu,PrM,Nasty Infections,pt.3. . 2.25
62 Nasty Infections,pt.4 . . . . 2.25
63 Nasty Infections,finale 2.25

Shade, The Changing Man #35
© DC Comics Inc.

64 The Madness. 2.25
65 The Roots of Madness,pt.1 . . . . 2.25
66 The Roots of Madness,pt.2 . . . . 2.25
67 The Roots of Madness,pt.3 . . . . 2.25
68 After Kathy,pt.1 . . . . 2.25
69 After Kathy,pt.2 . . . . 2.25
70 After Kathy,pt.3, final issue. 2.25

SHADO, SONG OF THE DRAGON
1992
1 GM(i),From G.A. Longbow
  Hunters 5.50
2 GM(i),V:Yakuza 5.00
3 GM(i),V:Yakuza 5.00
4 GM(i),V:Yakuza 5.00

SHADOW, THE
[1st Regular Series] 1973–75
1 MK,The Doom Puzzle. 28.00
2 MK,V:Freak Show Killer 18.00
3 MK,BWr 20.00
4 MK,Ninja Story 18.00
5 FR 10.00
6 MK 18.00
7 FR 9.00
8 FR 9.00
9 FR 9.00
10 . . . . 9.00
11 A:Avenger 9.00
12 . . . . 9.00

[Limited Series] 1986
1 HC,R:Shadow. 6.00
2 HC,O:Shadow 4.00
3 HC,V:Preston Mayrock 3.00
4 HC,V:Preston Mayrock 3.00
TPB rep. #1 thru #4 . . . . 12.95

[2nd Regular Series] 1987–89
1 BSz,Shadows & Light,pt.1 . . . . . 3.50
2 BSz,Shadows & Light,pt.2 . . . . . 3.50
3 BSz,Shadows & Light,pt.3 . . . . . 3.50
4 BSz,Shadows & Light,pt.4 . . . . . 3.50
5 BSz,Shadows & Light,pt.5 . . . . . 3.50
6 BSz,Shadows & Light,pt.6 . . . . . 3.50
7 MR,KB,Harold Goes to
  Washington 2.00
8 KB,Seven Deadly Finns,pt.1 . . . . 2.00
9 KB,Seven Deadly Finns,pt.2 . . . . 2.00
10 KB,Seven Deadly Finns,pt.3 . . . . 2.00
11 KB,Seven Deadly Finns,pt.4 . . . . 2.00

DC COMICS

12 KB,Seven Deadly Finns,pt.5 . . . 2.00
13 KB,Seven Deadly Finns,pt.6 . . . 2.00
14 KB,Body And Soul,pt.1 . . . . . . 2.00
15 KB,Body And Soul,pt.2 . . . . . . 2.00
16 KB,Body And Soul,pt.3 . . . . . . 2.00
17 KB,Body And Soul,pt.4 . . . . . . 2.00
18 KB,Body And Soul,pt.5 . . . . . . 2.00
19 KB,Body And Soul,pt.6 . . . . . . 2.00
Ann.#1 JO,AA,Shadows & Light
   prologue 3.00
Ann.#2 KB,Agents 2.50

Shadow Cabinet #11 © DC Comics, Inc.

SHADOW CABINET
Milestone 1994–95
0 WS(c),3RL,Shadow War,Foil(c),A:All
   Milestone characters 3.00
1 JBy(c),3RW,I&D:Corpsicle. 2.00
2 3RW,V:Arcadian League. 1.75
3 3RW,F:Sideshow 2.00
4 3RW,F:Sideshow 2.00
5 . . . . 1.75
6 . . . . 1.75
7 . . . . 1.75
8 New Cabinet. 1.75
9 R:Old Cabinet. 1.75
10 V:Red Dog. 1.75
11 Death Issue 1.75
12 SYSTEM 1.75
13 A:Hardware,Starlight 1.75
14 Long Hot Summer, Iron Butterfly
   Starlight 2.50
15 Long Hot Summer 2.50
16 Changing of the Guard 2.50
17 V:Dharma,final issue 2.50

SHADOWDRAGON ANNUAL
1995
Ann.#1 Year One Annual 3.50

SHADOW OF BATMAN
1 reprints of Detective Comics . . . 10.00
2 thru 4 . . . . @7.50

SHADOW OF THE BATMAN
1985–86
1 WS,AM,MR,rep. 7.00
2 MR,TA,rep.A:Hugo Strange 5.00
3 MR,TA,rep.A:Penguin 5.00

4 MR,TA,rep.A:Joker 6.00
5 MR,DG,rep. 5.00

SHADOW'S FALL
1994–95
1 JVF,Voyage of self-discovery . . . 2.95
2 JVF,More of tale 2.95
3 JVF,Shen confronts shadow 2.95
4 JVF,Gale wounded 2.95
5 JVF,Shadow goes Berserk 2.95
6 JVF,F:Warren Gale,final issue . . . 2.95

SHADOW STRIKES!, THE
1989–92
1 EB,Death's Head 3.00
2 EB,EB,PoliticalKiller,V:Rasputin . 2.50
3 EB,V:Mad Monk,V:Rasputin 2.50
4 EB,D:Mad Monk,V:Rasputin 2.50
5 EB,Shadow & Doc Savage#1 . . . 2.50
6 Shadow & Doc Savage #3 . . . . . 2.50
7 RM,A:Wunderkind,O:Shadow's
   Radio Show 2.50
8 EB,A:Shiwan Khan 2.50
9 Fireworks#2 . . . . 2.50
10 EB,Fireworks#3 . . . . 2.50
11 EB,O:Margo Lane 2.50
12 EB,V:Chicago Mob 2.50
13 EB,V:Chicago Mob 2.50
14 EB,V:Chicago Mob 2.50
15 EB,V:Chicago Mob 2.50
16 Assassins,pt.1 . . . . 2.50
17 Assassins,pt.2 . . . . 2.50
18 Shrevvie 2.50
19 NY,NJ Tunnel. 2.50
20 Shadow+Margo Vs.Nazis. 2.50
21 V:Shiwan Khan 2.50
22 V:Shiwan Khan 2.50
23 V:Shiwan Khan 2.50
24 Search for Margo Lane 2.50
25 In China. 2.50
26 V:Shiwan Khan 2.50
27 V:Shiwan Khan,Margo
   Rescued. 2.50
28 SL,In Hawaii 2.50
29 DSp,`Valhalla',V:Nazis 2.50
30 The Shadow Year One,pt.1 . . . . 2.50
31 The Shadow Year One,pt.2 . . . . 2.50
Ann.#1 DSp `Crimson Dreams'. . . . 4.00

SHADOW WAR OF HAWKMAN
May, 1985
1 AA,V:Thangarians. 1.50
2 AA,V:Thangarians. 1.25
3 AA,V:Thangarians,A:Aquaman,
   Elong.Man 1.25
4 AA,V:Thangarians. 1.25
Spec.#1 V:Thangarians 1.25

SHAZAM!
1973–78
[1st Regular Series]
1 B:DON(s),CCB,O:Capt.Marvel . 10.00
2 CCB,A:Mr.Mind. 5.00
3 CCB,V:Shagg Naste 4.00
4 E:DON(s),CCB,V:Ibac. 4.00
5 B:ESM(s),CCB,A:Leprechaun . . . 4.00
6 B:DON(s),CCB,Dr,Sivana 4.00
7 CCB,A:Capt Marvel Jr. 4.00
8 CCB,O:Marvel Family 25.00
9 E:DON(S)DC,CCB,A:Mr.Mind,
   Captain Marvel Jr. 4.00
10 ESM(s)CCB,BO. 4.00
11 ViCKS,BO,rep. 4.00
12 BO,DG 15.00
13 BO,KS,A:Luthor. 15.00
14 KS,A:Monster Society 15.00

Shazam #1 © DC Comics, Inc.

15 KS,BO,Luther 15.00
16 KS,BO. 15.00
17 KS,BO. 15.00
18 KS,BO. 4.00
19 KS,BO,Mary Marvel 4.00
20 KS,A:Marvel Family 4.00
21 reprint 4.00
22 reprint 4.00
23 reprint 4.00
24 reprint 4.00
25 KS,DG,I&O:Isis 5.00
26 KS. 4.00
27 KS,A:Kid Eternity 5.00
28 KS. 4.00
29 KS. 4.00
30 KS. 4.00
31 KS,A:Minute Man 4.00
32 KS. 4.00
33 KS. 4.00
34 O:Capt.Marvel Jr. 4.00
35 DN,KS,A:Marvel Family 4.00

SHAZAM ARCHIVES
1 Rep.Whiz Comics#2-#15 . . . . 49.95

SHAZAM, THE NEW BEGINNING
April, 1987
1 O:Shazam & Capt.Marvel 1.50
2 V:Black Adam. 1.25
3 V:Black Adam. 1.25
4 V:Black Adam. 1.25

SHERLOCK HOLMES
Sept.–Oct., 1975
1 . . . . 1.00

SHEVA'S WAR
DC/Helix (Aug., 1998)
1 (of 5) CsM,Iron Empires 3.00
2 CsM,Iron Empires. 3.00
3 CsM,Iron Empires. 3.00
4 CsM. 3.00
5 CsM. 3.00

SHOWCASE
1956–70, 1977–78
1 F:Fire Fighters 3,200.00
2 JKu,F:Kings of Wild 850.00
3 F:Frogmen 800.00

DC COMICS

4 CI,JKu,I&O:S.A. Flash	
(Barry Allen) 26,000.00	
5 F:Manhunters 1,000.00	
6 JK,I&O:Challengers of the	
Unknown 3,600.00	
7 JK,F:Challengers 1,800.00	
8 CI,F:Flash,I:Capt.Cold 12,000.00	
9 F:Lois Lane 6,000.00	
10 F:Lois Lane 2,500.00	
11 JK(c),F:Challengers 1,500.00	
12 JK(c),F:Challengers 1,500.00	
13 CI,F:Flash,Mr.Element. 4,200.00	
14 CI,F:Flash,Mr.Element. 5,000.00	
15 I:Space Ranger. 1,800.00	
16 F:Space Ranger 1,000.00	
17 GK(c),I:Adam Strange 2,200.00	
18 GK(c),F:Adam Strange . . . 1,200.00	
19 GK(c),F:Adam Strange . . . 1,300.00	
20 I:Rip Hunter 900.00	
21 F:Rip Hunter 500.00	
22 GK,I&O:S.A. Green Lantern	
(Hal Jordan) 4,800.00	
23 GK,F:Green Lantern 1,600.00	
24 GK,F:Green Lantern 1,600.00	
25 JKu,F:Rip Hunter 300.00	
26 JKu,F:Rip Hunter 300.00	
27 RH,I:Sea Devils 800.00	
28 RH,F:Sea Devils 400.00	
29 RH,F:Sea Devils 400.00	
30 O:Aquaman 750.00	
31 GK(c),F:Aquaman 400.00	
32 F:Aquaman 400.00	
33 F:Aquaman 450.00	
34 GK,MA,I&O:S.A. Atom 1,400.00	
35 GK,MA,F:Atom. 800.00	
36 GK,MA,F:Atom. 600.00	
37 RA,I:Metal Man 550.00	
38 RA,F:Metal Man 500.00	
39 RA,F:Metal Man 350.00	
40 RA,F:Metal Man 325.00	
41 F:Tommy Tomorrow 175.00	
42 F:Tommy Tomorrow 175.00	
43 F:Dr.No(James Bond 007) . . . 450.00	
44 F:Tommy Tomorrow 125.00	
45 JKu,O:Sgt.Rock 250.00	
46 F:Tommy Tomorrow 100.00	
47 F:Tommy Tomorrow 100.00	
48 F:Cave Carson 75.00	
49 F:Cave Carson 75.00	
50 MA,CI,F:I Spy 75.00	
51 MA,CI,F:I Spy 75.00	
52 F:Cave Carson 75.00	
53 JKu(c),RH,F:G.I.Joe. 75.00	
54 JKu(c),RH,F:G.I.Joe. 75.00	
55 MA,F:Dr.Fate,Spectre,1st S.A.	

Showcase #39 © DC Comics Inc.

Green Lantern,Solomon	
Grundy. 260.00	
56 MA,F:Dr.Fate 75.00	
57 JKu,F:Enemy Ace 150.00	
58 JKu,F:Enemy Ace 125.00	
59 F:Teen Titans 100.00	
60 MA,F:Spectre. 250.00	
61 MA,F:Spectre. 150.00	
62 JO,I:Inferior 5. . . . . 75.00	
63 JO,F:Inferior 5. . . . . 50.00	
64 MA,F:Spectre. 150.00	
65 F:Inferior 5. . . . . 50.00	
66 I:B'wana Beast. 30.00	
67 F:B'wana Beast 30.00	
68 I:Maniaks 30.00	
69 F:Maniaks 30.00	
70 I:Binky 30.00	
71 F:Maniaks 30.00	
72 JKu,ATh,F:Top Gun 30.00	
73 SD,I&O:Creeper. 125.00	
74 I:Anthro 75.00	
75 SD,I:Hawk & Dove 100.00	
76 NC,I:Bat Lash 50.00	
77 BO,I:Angel & Ape 50.00	
78 I:Jonny Double. 30.00	
79 I:Dolphin 50.00	
80 NA(c),F:Phantom Stranger. . . 65.00	
81 I:Windy & Willy 25.00	
82 I:Nightmaster. 60.00	
83 BWr,MK,F:Nightmaster 50.00	
84 BWr,MK,F:Nightmaster 50.00	
85 JKu,F:Firehair 18.00	
86 JKu,F:Firehair 18.00	
87 JKu,F:Firehair 18.00	
88 F:Jason's Quest 10.00	
89 F:Jason's Quest 10.00	
90 F:Manhunter 9.00	
91 F:Manhunter 9.00	
92 F:Manhunter 9.00	
93 F:Manhunter 9.00	
94 JA,JSon,I&O:2nd	
Doom Patrol. 12.00	
95 JA,JSon,F:2nd Doom Patrol. . . 9.00	
96 JA,JSon,F:2nd Doom Patrol. . . 9.00	
97 JO,JSon,O:Power Girl 6.00	
98 JSon,DG,Power Girl 6.00	
99 JSon,DG,Power Girl 6.00	
100 JSon,all star issue 7.00	
101 JKu(c),AM,MA,Hawkman . . . 6.00	
102 JKu(c),AM,MA,Hawkman . . . 6.00	
103 JKu(c),AM,MA,Hawkman . . . 6.00	
104 RE,OSS Spies 6.00	
TPB Rep.1956–59 . . . . 20.00	

SHOWCASE '93

1 AAd(c),EH,AV,F:Catwoman,	
Blue Devil,Cyborg. 4.00	
2 KM(c),EH,AV,F:Catwoman,	
Blue Devil,Cyborg. 3.50	
3 KM(c),EH,TC,F:Catwoman,	
Blue Devil,Flash 3.00	
4 F:Catwoman,Blue Devil,	
Geo-Force 2.50	
5 F:KD,DG,BHi,F:Robin,Blue	
Devil,Geo-Force 2.50	
6 MZ(c),KD,DG,F:Robin,Blue	
Devil,Deathstroke. 2.50	
7 BSz(c),KJ,Knightfall#13,F:Two-	
Face,Jade&Obsidian 5.00	
8 KJ,Knightfall#14,F:Two-Face,	
Peacemaker,Fire and Ice 4.00	
9 F:Huntress,Peacemaker,Shining	
Knight 2.50	
10 BWg,SI,F:Huntress,Batman,	
Dr.Light,Peacemaker,Deathstroke,	
Katana,M.Manhunter 2.50	
11 GP(c),F:Robin,Nightwing,	
Peacemaker,Deathstroke,Deadshot,	
Katana,Dr.Light,Won.Woman . . 2.50	
12 AD(c),BMc,F:Robin,Nightwing,	
Green Lantern,Creeper. 2.50	

SHOWCASE '94

1 KN,F:Joker,Gunfire,Orion,Metro . 2.25	
2 KON(c),E:Joker,B:Blue Beetle. . . 2.25	
3 MMi(c),B:Razorsharpe 2.25	
4 AIG(s),DG,F:Arkham Asylum inmates	
E:Razorsharpe,Blue Bettle 2.25	
5 WS(c),CDi(s),PJ,B:Robin & Huntress,	
F:Bloodwynd,Loose Cannon. . . 2.25	
6 PJ,KK(s),F:Robin & Huntress . . 2.25	
7 JaL(c),PDd(s),F:Comm. Gordon . 2.25	
8 AIG(s),O:Scarface,Ventriloquist,	
F:Monarch,1st Wildcat 3.00	
9 AIG(s),DJ,O:Scarface,Ventriloquist,	
F:Monarch,Waverider. 2.75	
10 JQ(c),AIG(s),F:Azrael,Zero Hour,	
B:Black Condor. 3.00	
11 Black Condor, Man-Bat 2.25	
12 Barbara Gordon. 2.00	

SHOWCASE '95

1 Supergirl. 2.50	
2 . . . . 2.50	
3 F:Eradicator,Claw 2.25	
4 A:Catwoman,Hawke 3.00	
5 F:Thorne,Firehawk 3.00	
6 DRo(c&a),F:Lobo,Bibbo 3.00	
7 F:Mongul 3.00	
8 . . . . 3.00	
9 F:Lois Lane 3.00	
10 F:Gangbuster 3.00	
11 F:Agent Liberty 3.00	
12 F:Supergirl,Maitresse 3.00	

SHOWCASE '96

1 F:Steel & Warrior 3.00	
2 F:Steel and Warrior 3.00	
3 . . . . 3.00	
4 F:Firebrand. 3.00	
5 F:Green Arrow & Thorn 3.00	
6 F:Superboy, Animated Series . . . 3.00	
7 F:Mary Marvel 3.00	
8 F:Superman, Superboy &	
Supergirl 4.00	
9 F:Lady Shiva & Shadowdragon,	
Martian Manhunter 3.00	
10 F:Ultra Boy, Captain Comet . . . 3.00	
11 Legion of Super-Heroes 3.00	
12 "10,000 Brainiacs" 3.00	

SILVER AGE
DC CLASSICS

Action #252(rep). 1.50	
Adventure #247(rep). 1.50	
Brave and Bold #28 (rep) 1.50	
Detective #225 (rep) 1.50	
Detective #327 (rep) 1.50	
Green Lantern #76 (rep) 1.50	
House of Secrets #92 (rep). 2.00	
Showcase #4 (rep) 1.75	
Showcase #22 (rep) 1.50	
Sugar & Spike #99(1st printing) . . . 1.50	

SILVER BLADE
Sept., 1987

1 KJ,GC,maxi-series 1.50	
2 thru 12 GC . . . . @1.50	

SKIN GRAFT
Vertigo 1993

1 B:JeP(s),WaP,I:John Oakes,	
A:Tattooed Man(Tarrant) 3.25	
2 WaP,V:Assassins 3.00	
3 WaP,In Kyoto,I:Mizoguchi Kenji . . 3.00	
4 E:JeP(s),WaP,V:Tarrant,Kenji . . . 3.00	

SKREEMER
May, 1989
1 . . . . 1.50
2 thru 6 . . . . @2.00

SKULL AND BONES
1992
1 EH,I&O:Skull & Bones 4.95
2 EH,V:KGB 4.95
3 EH,V:KGB 4.95

SLASH MARAUD
Nov., 1987
1 PG 2.25
2 PG 2.00
3 thru 10 PG . . . . @2.00

SMASH COMICS
1999
1 TPe(s),F:Doctor Mid-Nite
& Hourman. 2.00

SONIC DISRUPTORS
1987–88
1 thru 10 . . . . @1.75

SON OF AMBUSH BUG
July, 1986
1 . . . . 1.00
2 thru 6 KG . . . . @1.00

SOVEREIGN SEVEN
1995–98
1 CCI(s),DT,I:Sovereign Seven,
V:Female Furies,A:Darkseid . . . 3.00
2 I:Nike,Kratos,Zelus,Bia 2.00
3 V:Nike,Kratos,Zelus,Bia 2.00
4 I:Skin Dance 2.00
5 CCI,DT,V:Skin Dance 2.00
6 CCI,DT,V:Force Majeure 2.00
7 CCI,DT,Wild Hunt,pt.2. . . . . 2.00
8 CCI,DT,Clv,Wild Hunt,pt.3. . . . . 2.00
9 CCI,DT,Clv. 2.00
10 CCI,DT,Clv,Road Trip,pt.1 . . . . 2.00
11 CCI,DT,Clv,Road Trip,pt.2 (of 3). 2.00
12 CCI(s) 2.00
13 CCI(s) 2.00

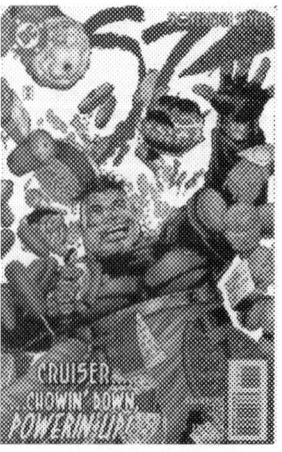

Sovereign Seven #19
© DC Comics, Inc.

14 CCI(s) 2.00
15 CCI,DT,Clv,Sovereign team
betrayed. 2.00
16 CCI,DT,Clv,Network betrays
Sovereigns, Final Night tie-in . . 2.00
17 CCI(s),RLm,Clv,V:Network. 2.00
18 CCI(s),RLm,Clv,V:Network and
Kim 2.00
19 CCI(s) 2.00
20 CCI(s),VGi,Finale trapped in
Forest Fire 2.00
21 CCI(s),RLm,DC,Clv,Danae's
secret 2.00
22 CCI(s),RLm,DC,Clv,Indigo &
Rampart fall 2.00
23 CCI(s),RLm,DC,Clv,Finale
hallucinates 2.00
24 CCI(s),RLm,Clv,A:Superman . . 2.00
25 CCI(s),RLm,Clv,V:Power Girl . . 2.00
26 CCI(s),RLm,Clv,A:Hitman. 2.00
27 CCI(s),RLm,Clv,Genesis tie-in . 2.25
28 CCI(s),RLm,Clv,A:Impulse 2.00
29 CCI(s),RLm,Clv,Sovereign dies . 2.00
30 CCI(s),RLm,Clv,revenge 2.00
31 CCI(s),RLm,Clv,F:Power Girl . . 2.25
32 CCI(s),RLm,Clv,F:Power Girl . . 2.25
33 CCI(s),RLm,Clv,F:Power Girl . . 2.25
34 CCI(s),RLm,Clv,in Kuristan 2.25
35 CCI(s),RLm,Clv,The Rapture . . 2.25
36 CCI(s),RLm,Clv,final issue 2.25
Ann.#1 CCI, Year One Annual . . . 4.00
Ann.#2 CCI(s),RL,KJ,Legends of
the Dead Earth. 3.00
TPB CCI(s),DT, rep.#1–#5 . . . . . 12.95

SOVEREIGN SEVEN PLUS
1 one-shot. 2.95

SPACE JAM
Warner Bros./DC Oct. 1996
one-shot comic adaptation of movie 5.95

SPANNER'S GALAXY
Dec., 1984
1 mini-series 1.50
2 thru 6 . . . . @1.00

SPECTRE, THE
1967–69
1 MA,V:Captain Skull. 100.00
2 NA,V:Dirk Rawley. 75.00
3 NA,A:Wildcat 75.00
4 NA 75.00
5 NA 75.00
6 MA 45.00
7 MA,BU:Hourman 45.00
8 MA,Parchment of Power
Perilous 45.00
9 BWr(2nd BWr Art). 50.00
10 MA 45.00

[2nd Regular Series] 1987–89
1 GC,O:Spectre. 3.00
2 GC,Cult of BRM 2.50
3 GC,Fashion Model Murders 2.00
4 GC 2.00
5 GC,Spectre's Murderer. 2.00
6 GC,Spectre/Corrigan separated . 2.00
7 A:Zatanna,Wotan 2.00
8 A:Zatanna,Wotan 2.00
9 GM,Spectre's Revenge. 2.00
10 GM,A:Batman,Millenium 2.25
11 GM,Millenium. 2.00
12 GM,The Talisman,pt.1 . . . . 2.00
13 GM,The Talisman,pt.2 . . . . 2.00
14 GM,The Talisman,pt.3 . . . . 2.00
15 GM,The Talisman,pt.4 . . . . 2.00
16 Jim Corrigan Accused 2.00

The Spectre, 2nd Series #28
© DC Comics, Inc.

17 New Direction,`Final Destiny' . . . 2.00
18 Search for Host Body. 2.00
19 `Dead Again' 2.00
20 Corrigan Detective Agency 2.00
21 A:Zoran 1.75
22 BS,Sea of Darkness,A:Zoran . . 1.75
23 A:Lords of Order,
Invasion x-over. 1.75
24 BWg,Ghosts i/t Machine#1. . . . 1.75
25 Ghosts in the Machine #2 . . . . 1.75
26 Ghosts in the Machine #3 . . . . 1.75
27 Ghosts in the Machine #4 . . . . 1.75
28 Ghosts in the Machine #5 . . . . 1.75
29 Ghosts in the Machine #6 . . . . 1.75
30 Possession 1.75
31 Spectre possessed, final issue. . 1.75
Ann.#1, A:Deadman 2.75

[3rd Regular Series] 1992–97
1 B:JOs(s),TMd,R:Spectre,
Glow in the dark(c) 7.00
2 TMd,Murder Mystery. 6.00
3 TMd,O:Spectre. 4.00
4 TMd,O:Spectre. 4.00
5 TMd,BB(c),V:Kidnappers 3.50
6 TMd,Spectre prevents evil 3.50
7 TMd 3.50
8 TMd,Glow in the dark(c) 5.00
9 TMd,MWg(c),V:The Reaver . . . 3.00
10 TMd,V:Michael. 3.00
11 TMd,V:Azmodeus. 3.00
12 V:Reaver 3.00
13 TMd,V:Count Vertigo,
Glow in the Dark(c) 3.00
14 JoP,A:Phantom Stranger 2.00
15 TMd,A:Phantom Stranger,Demon,
Doctor Fate,John Constantine . 2.00
16 JAp,V:I.R.A. 2.00
17 TT(c),TMd,V:Eclipso. 2.00
18 TMd,D:Eclipso 2.00
19 TMd,V:Hate 2.00
20 A:Lucien 2.00
21 V:Naiad,C:Superman 3.00
22 A:Superman 2.25
23 Book of Judgment, pt.1 . . . . . . 2.00
24 Book of Judgment, pt.2 . . . . . . 2.00
25 Book of Judgment, pt.3 . . . . . . 2.00
26 . . . . 2.00
27 R:Azmodus 2.00
28 V:Azmodus 2.00
29 V:Azmodus 2.00
30 V:Azmodus 2.00
31 Descent into Pandemonium 2.25
32 V:Killo 2.25
33 . . . . 2.25

All comics prices listed are for *Near Mint* condition.

34 Power of the Undead........ 2.25
35 JOs,TMd,Underworld
  Unleashed tie-in............ 2.25
36 JOs,TMd,Underworld
  Unleashed tie-in............ 2.25
37 JOs,TMd,The Haunting of
  America,pt.1............... 2.25
38 JOs,TMd,The Haunting of
  America,pt.2............... 2.25
39 JOs,TMd,The Haunting of
  America,pt.3............... 2.25
40 JOs,TMd,The Haunting of
  America,pt.4............... 2.25
41 JOs,TMd,The Haunting of
  America,pt.5............... 2.25
42 JOs,TMd,The Haunting of
  America,pt.6............... 2.25
43 Witchcraft................ 2.25
44 Madame Xanadu............ 2.25
45 .... 2.25
46 JOs(s),TMd,discovery of the
  Spear of Destiny........... 2.25
47 JOs(s),TMd,"The Haunting of
  America" Final Night tie-in 2.25
48 JOs(s),TMd,"The Haunting of
  America" 2.25
49 JOs(s),TMd,"The Haunting of
  America" 2.25
50 JOs(s),TMd,............. 2.25
51 JOs(s),TMd,A:Batman,Joker ... 2.25
52 JOs(s),TMd,Nate Kane discovers
  murder evidence 2.25
53 JOs(s),TMd,"Haunting of Jim
  Corrigan" cont............. 2.25
54 JOs(s),TMd,hunt for murderer of
  Mister Terrific 2.25
55 JOs(s),TMd,Corrigan implicated
  in murder 2.25
56 JOs(s),TMd,JTo "Haunting if Jim
  Corrigan" 2.50
57 JOs(s),TMd,Spectre & Jim
  Corrigan in Heaven 2.50
58 JOs,TMd,Genesis tie-in 2.50
59 JOs,TMd,BWr(c), alien pod 2.50
60 JOs,TMd,Quest for God, cont... 2.50
61 JOs,TMd,Quest for God, concl. . 2.50
62 JOs,TMd,final issue 2.50
Ann.#1 JOs,TMd,Year One...... 3.95
TPB Punishment and Crimes 9.95
TPB Crimes & Punishments,
  JOs,TMd 10.00

SPEED FORCE
Sept., 1997
1 MWa,BAu,JBy,BML,JAp,BSn,
  Flash stories, 64pg. 4.00

SPELLJAMMER
Sept., 1990
1 RogueShip#1 .... 3.00
2 RogueShip#2 .... 2.50
3 RogueShip#3 .... 2.00
4 RogueShip#4 .... 2.00
5 New Planet............... 1.75
6 Tember, Planet contd 1.75
7 Planet contd.............. 1.75
8 conclusion 1.75
9 Meredith Possessed......... 1.75
10 Tie-in w/Dragonlance #33&34 .. 1.75
11 Dwarf Citidel 1.75
12 Kirstig Vs. Meredith 1.75
13 Tember to the Rescue 1.75
14 Meredith's Son #1 .... 1.75
15 Meredith's Son #2 .... 1.75

STALKER
1975–1976
1 O&I:Stalker............... 5.00

2 thru 4 .... @2.50

STANLEY & HIS MONSTER
(see FOX AND THE CROW)

STANLEY & HIS MONSTER
1 R:Stanley................ 1.25
2 I:Demon Hunter 1.25
3 A:Ambrose Bierce........... 1.25
4 final issue............... 1.25

S.T.A.R. CORPS
1 A:Superman 2.00
2 I:Fusion,A:Rampage......... 1.75
3 I:Brainstorm 1.75
4 I:Ndoki 1.75
5 I:Trauma................ 1.75
6 I:Mindgame 1.75

STAR CROSSED
DC/Helix April 1997
1 (of 3) MHo,Dyltah's romance
  with Saa............... 2.50
2 MHo,"Love During Wartime" ... 2.50
3 (of 3) 2.50

[NEIL GAIMAN & CHARLES VESS'] STARDUST
DC/Vertigo Oct., 1997
1 (of 4) NGa(s),CV 6.00
2 NGa(s),CV adult faerie tale..... 6.00
3 NGa(s),CV 6.00
4 NGa(s),CV 6.00

Starfire #3 © DC Comics Inc.

STARFIRE
1976–77
1 .... 1.50
2 thru 8 .... @1.00

STAR HUNTERS
Oct.–Nov., 1977
1 DN&BL................. 1.00
2 LH&BL................. 1.00
3 MN&BL,D:Donovan Flint...... 1.00
4 thru 7 .... @1.00

STARMAN
1988–92
1 TL,I&O:New Starman 4.00
2 TL,V:Serial Killer,C:Bolt....... 3.00
3 TL,V:Bolt 3.00
4 TL,V:Power Elite............ 2.50
5 TL,Invasion,A:PowerGirl,
  Firestorm 2.50
6 TL,Invasion,A:G.L.,Atom...... 2.00
7 TL,Soul Searching Issue...... 2.00
8 TL,V:LadyQuark........... 2.00
9 TL,A:Batman,V:Blockbuster 2.00
10 TL,A:Batman,V:Blockbuster ... 2.00
11 TL,V:Power Elite 2.00
12 TL,V:Power Elite,A:Superman . . 2.00
13 TL,V:Rampage 2.00
14 TL,A:A:Superman,V:Parasite ... 2.00
15 TL,V:Deadline............ 2.00
16 TL,O:Starman 2.00
17 TL,V:Dr.Polaris,A:PowerGirl 2.00
18 TL,V:Dr.Polaris,A:PowerGirl 2.00
19 TL,V:Artillery 2.00
20 TL,FireFighting 2.00
21 TL,Starman Quits 2.00
22 TL,V:Khunds 2.00
23 TL,A:Deadline 2.00
24 TL,A:Deadline 2.00
25 TL,V:Deadline 2.00
26 V:The Mist.............. 2.00
27 V:The Mist.............. 2.00
28 A:Superman 7.00
29 V:Plasmax.............. 2.00
30 Seduction of Starman #1 ..... 2.00
31 Seduction of Starman #2 ..... 2.00
32 Seduction of Starman #3 ..... 2.00
33 Seduction of Starman #4 ..... 2.00
34 A:Batman 2.00
35 A:Valor,Mr.Nebula,ScarletSkier. . 2.00
36 A:Les Mille Yeux 2.00
37 A:Les Mille Yeux 2.00
38 War of the Gods X-over....... 2.00
39 V:Plasmax.............. 2.00
40 V:Las Vegas 2.00
41 V:Maaldor.............. 2.00
42 Star Shadows,pt.1,A:Eclipso ... 3.00
43 Star Shadows,pt.2,A:Lobo,
  Eclipso................. 2.50
44 Star Shadows,pt.3,A:Eclipso
  V:Lobo................ 2.50
45 Star Shadows,pt.4, V:Eclipso ... 2.50
2nd Series 1994–99
0 New Starman............. 8.00
1 Threat of the Mist........... 8.00
2 .... 4.00
3 V:Son of the Mist 4.00
4 .... 4.00
5 V:Starman 4.00
6 Times Past Features......... 4.00
7 Sinister Circus 3.00
8 TyH(c),Sinister Circus......... 3.00
9 TyH(c),Mist's daughter breaks
  out of prison............ 3.00
10 Sins of the Chile,prelude 3.00
11 .... 3.00
12 JeR,TyH,Sins of the Child,pt.1 .. 3.00
13 JeR,TyH,Sins of the Child,pt.2 .. 3.00
14 JeR,TyH,Sins of the Child,pt.3 .. 3.00
15 JeR,TyH,Sins of the Child,pt.4 .. 3.00
16 JeR,TyH,Sins of the Child,pt.5 .. 3.00
17 JeR,TyH 3.00
18 JeR,TyH,Orig.Starman
  vs.The Mist 3.00
19 JeR,TyH,Talking with David 2 .. 3.00
20 JeR(s),TyH,GyD,"Sand and
  Stars," pt.1 .... 3.00
21 JeR(s),TyH,GyD,"Sand and
  Stars," pt.2 .... 2.50
22 JeR(s),TyH,GyD,"Sand and
  Stars," pt.3 .... 2.50
23 JeR(s),TyH,GyD,"Sand and

DC COMICS

Starman #25 © DC Comics, Inc.

Stars," pt.4 concl 2.50
24 JeR(s),TyH,"Hell & Back," pt.1 . 2.50
25 JeR(s),TyH,"Hell & Back," pt.2 . 2.50
26 JeR(s),TyH,"Hell & Back," pt.3 . 2.50
27 . . . . 2.50
28 JeR(s)Superfreaks and
  Backstabbers 2.50
29 JeR(s),TyH,GyD,V:The Shade,
  Starman history 2.50
30 JeR(s),TyH,"Infernal Devices"
  pt.1 (of 6) 2.50
31 JeR(s),TyH,"Infernal Devices"
  pt.2 . . . . 2.50
32 JeR(s),TyH,"Infernal Devices"
  pt.3 . . . . 2.50
33 JeR(s),TyH,"Infernal Devices"
  pt.4,A:Batman, Sentinel 2.50
34 JeR(s),TyH,A:Batman, Sentinel,
  Floronic Man 2.25
35 JeR(s),TyH,A:Batman, Floronic
  Man, Sentinel 2.25
36 JeR(s),TyH,F:Will Payton 2.25
37 JeR(s),TyH,F:GoldenAgeHeroes 2.25
38 JeR(s),TyH,new JLE 2.25
39 JeR(s),TyH,Lightning &
  Stars, pt.1 x-over 2.25
40 JeR(s),TyH 2.25
41 JeR(s),GEr,TyH 2.25
42 JeR(s),MS,Nazis,Demon 2.25
43 JeR(s),TyH,help from JLA 2.25
44 JeR(s),times past story 2.50
45 JeR(s),search for Will Payton. . 2.50
46 JeR(s),TyH,Bobo 2.50
47 JeR,SY,TyH, ... 2.50
48 JeR,SY,A:Swamp Thing. 2.50
49 JeR,SY,Talking with David 2.50
50 JeR(s),PSj,48-page 4.00
51 JeR(s),PSj,to Krypton 2.50
52 JeR(s),PSj,A:Adam Strange. . . 2.50
53 JeR(s),PSj,A:Adam Strange. . . 2.50
54 JeR(s),Times Past tale. 2.50
55 JeR(s),PSj,A:Space Cabby . . . 2.50
56 JeR(s),PSj,A:ElongatedMan. . . 2.50
57 JeR(s),PSj,TyH,AxR,A:Tigorr
  & Fastbak, pt.1 . . . . 2.50
58 JeR,TyH,AxR, pt.2 . . . . 2.50
Ann.#1 Legends o/t Dead Earth . . 3.50
Ann.#2 Pulp Heroes (Romance) . . 3.95
Spec.#1,000,000 JeR(s),PSj. 2.50
Secret Files #1,O:Starmen 5.00
Giant #1 80-page 5.00
Spec. Starman: The Mist, F:Mary
  Marvel, Girlfrenzy (1998) . . . 2.00
TPB Sins of the Father,rep.#0–#5 . 12.95
TPB Night and Day, rep. stories

from #7–#16. . . . . 14.95
TPB A Wicked Inclination, rep. . . 18.00
TPB Times Past 18.00

STARS AND S.T.R.I.P.E.
1999
0 LMd,DDv,I:Courtney Whitman. . . 3.00
1 LMd,DDv,O:Star-Spangled Kid . . 2.50
2 LMd,DDv,V:Paintball 2.50
3 LMd,DDv,V:Skeeter 2.50

STAR SPANGLED
COMICS
Oct., 1941
1 O:Tarantula,B:Captain X of the
  R.A.F.,Star Spangled Kid,
  Armstrong of the Army. . . . 4,000.00
2 V:Dr. Weerd. 1,400.00
3 . . . . 800.00
4 V:The Needle 800.00
5 V:Dr. Weerd 800.00
6 E:Armstrong 550.00
7 S&K,O&1st app:The Guardian,
  B:Robotman,The Newsboy
  Legion, TNT 6,500.00
8 O:TNT & Dan the Dyna-Mite 1,800.00
9 . . . . 1,400.00
10 . . . . 1,400.00
11 . . . . 1,100.00
12 Newsboy Legion stories,
  `Prevue of Peril!' 1,100.00
13 `Kill Dat Story!' 1,100.00
14 `Meanest Man on Earth' . . . 1,100.00
15 `Playmates of Peril' 1,100.00
16 `Playboy of Suicide Slum!'. . 1,100.00
17 V:Rafferty Mob 1,100.00
18 O:Star Spangled Kid 1,300.00
19 E:Tarantula 1,000.00
20 B:Liberty Belle. 1,000.00
21 . . . . 800.00
22 `Brains for Sale'. 800.00
23 `Art for Scrapper's Sake' . . . 800.00
24 . . . . 800.00
25 `Victuals for Victory' 800.00
26 `Louie the Lug goes Literary' . 800.00
27 `Turn on the Heat!" 800.00
28 `Poor Man's Rich Man'. 800.00
29 `Cabbages and Comics'. 800.00
30 . . . . 400.00
31 `Questions Please!' 400.00
32 . . . . 400.00
33. . . . . 400.00
34 `From Rags to Run!'. 400.00
35 `The Proud Poppas' 400.00
36 `Cowboy of Suicide Slum' . . . 400.00
37 . . . . 400.00
38 . . . . 400.00
39 `Two Guardians are a Crowd'. 400.00
40 . . . . 400.00
41 Back the 6th War Loan(c) . . . 375.00
42 . . . . 375.00
43 American Red Cross(c) 375.00
44 . . . . 375.00
45 7th War Loan (c) 375.00
46 . . . . 375.00
47 . . . . 375.00
48 . . . . 375.00
49 . . . . 375.00
50 . . . . 375.00
51 A:Robot Robber. 375.00
52 `Rehearsal for Crime'. 375.00
53 `The Poet of Suicide Slum'. . . 375.00
54 `Dead-Shot Daisy's Revenge'. 375.00
55 `Gabby Strikes a Gusher'. . . . 375.00
56 `The Treasuer of Araby'. 375.00
57 `Recruit for the Legion'. 375.00
58 `Matadors of Suicide Slum' . . 375.00
59 . . . . 375.00
60 . . . . 375.00

Star Spangled Comics #15
© DC Comics, Inc.

61 . . . . 375.00
62 `Prevue of Tomorrow'. 375.00
63 . . . . 375.00
64 `Criminal Cruise' 375.00
65 B:Robin,(c) & stories 1,200.00
66 V:No Face 700.00
67 `The Castle of Doom' 550.00
68 . . . . 550.00
69 `The Stolen Atom Bomb' 850.00
70 V:The Clock. 550.00
71 `Perils of the Stone Age' 550.00
72 `Robin Crusoe'. 550.00
73 V:The Black Magician 550.00
74 V:The Clock. 550.00
75 The State vs. Robin 550.00
76 V:The Fence 550.00
77 `The Boy who Wanted Robin
  for Christmas'. 550.00
78 `Rajah Robin' 550.00
79 V:The Clock,`The Tick-Tock
  Crimes'. 550.00
80 `The Boy Disc Jockey' 550.00
81 `The Seeing-Eye Dog Crimes' 450.00
82 `The Boy who Hated Robin' . . 450.00
83 `Who is Mr. Mystery',B:Captain
  Compass backup story. 450.00
84 How can we Fight Juvenile
  Delinquency? 650.00
85 `Peril at the Pole'. 450.00
86 . . . . 475.00
87 V:Sinister Knight 650.00
88 Robin Declares War on
  Batman, B:Batman app. 525.00
89 `Batman's Utility Belt?' 525.00
90 `Rancho Fear!'. 525.00
91 `Cops 'n' Robbers?' 525.00
92 `Movie Hero No. 1?'. 525.00
93 . . . . 525.00
94 `Underworld Playhouse'. 525.00
95 `The Man with the Midas Touch',
  E:Robin(c),Batman story. . . . 525.00
96 B:Tomahawk(c) & stories . . . 350.00
97 `The 4 Bold Warriors'. 300.00
98 . . . . 300.00
99 `The Second Pocahontas' . . . 300.00
100 `The Frontier Phantom' 300.00
101 Peril on the High Seas 250.00
102 . . . . 250.00
103 `Tomahawk's Death Duel!' . . 250.00
104 `Race with Death!' 250.00
105 `The Unhappy Hunting
  Grounds' 250.00
106 `Traitor in the War Paint'. . . 250.00
107 `The Brave who Hunted
  Tomahawk'. 250.00
108 `The Ghost called Moccasin

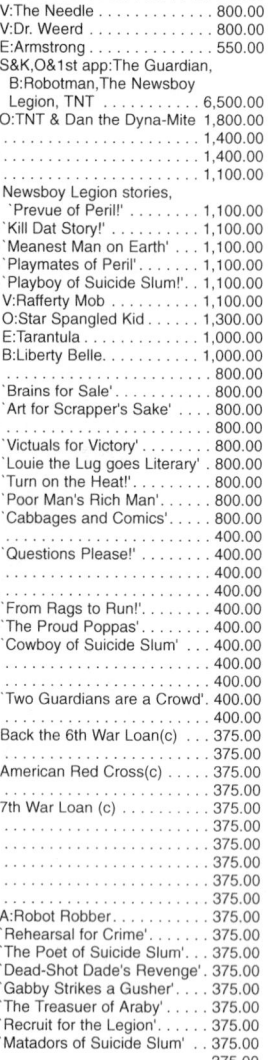

DC COMICS

Foot!' 250.00	41 IN(c),A Gunner's Hands 85.00	Armored Giants 350.00
109 'The Land Pirates of	42 JGr(c),Sniper Alley 85.00	91 JGr(c),The Train of Terror 55.00
Jolly Roger Hill!' 250.00	43 JGr(c),Top Kick Brother 85.00	92 Last Battle of the
110 'Sally Raines Frontier Girl' . 275.00	44 JGr(c),Tank 711	Dinosaur Age 125.00
111 'The Death Map of Thunder	Doesn't Answer 85.00	93 Goliath of the Western Front . . 55.00
Hill' 275.00	45 JGr(c),Flying Heels 85.00	94 JKu(c),The Frogman and
112 . . . . 300.00	46 JGr(c),Gunner's Seat 85.00	the Dinosaur 125.00
113 FF,V:'The Black Cougar' . . . 325.00	47 JGr(c),Sidekick 85.00	95 Guinea Pig Patrol,Dinosaurs . 125.00
114 'Return of the Black Cougar' 350.00	48 JGr(c),Battle Hills 85.00	96 Mission X,Dinosaur 125.00
115 'Journey of a Thousand	49 JGr(c),Payload 85.00	97 The Sub-Crusher, Dinosaur . . 125.00
Deaths' 300.00	50 JGr(c),Combat Dust 85.00	98 Island of Thunder, Dinosaur . . 125.00
116 'The Battle of Junction Fort' . 300.00	51 JGr(c),Battle Pigeon 70.00	99 The Circus of Monsters,
117 'Siege?' 300.00	52 JGr(c),Cannon-Man 70.00	Dinosaur 125.00
118 V:Outlaw Indians 250.00	53 JGr(c),Combat Close-Ups 70.00	100 The Volcano of Monsters,
119 'The Doomed Stockade?' . . . 225.00	54 JGr(c),Flying Exit 70.00	Dinosaur. 150.00
120 'Revenge of Raven Heart!' . . 225.00	55 JKu(c),The Burning Desert . . . 70.00	101 The Robot and the Dinosaur 125.00
121 'Adventure in New York!' . . . 225.00	56 JKu(c),The Walking Sub 70.00	102 Punchboard War,Dinosaur . . 125.00
122 'I:Ghost Breaker,(c)& stories 250.00	57 JGr(c),Call For a Frogman 70.00	103 Doom at Dinosaur Island,
123 'The Dolls of Doom' 200.00	58 JGr(c),MD,Waist Punch 70.00	Dinosaur. 125.00
124 'Suicide Tower' 200.00	59 JGr(c),Kick In The Door 70.00	104 The Tree of Terror,
125 The Hermit's Ghost Dog!' . . . 200.00	60 JGr(c),Hotbox 70.00	Dinosaurs 125.00
126 'The Phantom of Paris!' 200.00	61 JGr(c),MD,Tow Pilot 70.00	105 The War of Dinosaur Island . 125.00
127 'The Supernatural Alibi!' . . . 200.00	62 JGr(c),The Three GIs 70.00	106 The Nightmare War,
128 C:Batman,'The Girl who	63 JGr(c),Flying Range Rider 70.00	Dinosaurs 125.00
lived 5,000 Years!' 200.00	64 JGr(c),MD,Frogman Ambush . . 70.00	107 Battle of the Dinosaur
129 'The Human Orchids' 250.00	65 JGr(c),JSe,Frogman Block 70.00	Aquarium 125.00
130 'The Haunted Town',	66 JGr(c),Flattop Pigeon 70.00	108 Dinosaur D-Day 125.00
July, 1952 . . . . 275.00	67 RH(c),MD,Ashcan Alley 70.00	109 The Last Soldiers 125.00
Becomes:	68 JGr(c),The Long Step 70.00	110 thru 133 . . . . @125.00
STAR SPANGLED	69 JKu(c),Floating Tank, The' 70.00	134 NA 100.00
WAR STORIES	70 JKu(c),No Medal For	135 . . . . 75.00
Aug., 1952	Frogman 65.00	136 . . . . 75.00
131 CS&StK(c),I Was A Jap	71 JKu(c),Shooting Star 65.00	137 Dinosaur 75.00
Prisoner of War 900.00	72 JGr(c),Silent Fish 65.00	138 Enemy Ace 100.00
132 CS&StK(c),The G.I. With	73 JGr(c),MD,The Mouse &	139 O:Enemy Ace 90.00
The Million-Dollar Arm 600.00	the Tiger 65.00	140 . . . . 65.00
133 CS&StK(c),Mission-San	74 JGr(c),MD,Frogman Bait 65.00	141 . . . . 65.00
Marino 500.00	75 JGr(c),MD,Paratroop	142 . . . . 50.00
3 CS&StK(c),Hundred-Mission	Mousketeers 65.00	143 . . . . 50.00
Mitchell 275.00	76 MD,JKu(c),Odd Man 65.00	144 NA,JKu 60.00
4 CS&StK(c),The Hot Rod Tank . 275.00	77 MD,JKu(c),Room to Fight. 65.00	145 . . . . 50.00
5 LSt(c),Jet Pilot 275.00	78 MD,JGr(c),Fighting Wingman . . 65.00	146 . . . . 50.00
6 CS(c),Operation Davy Jones . 275.00	79 MD,JKu(c),Zero Box 65.00	147 . . . . 50.00
7 CS(c),Rookie Ranger,The . . . 200.00	80 MD,JGr(c),Top Gunner 65.00	148 . . . . 50.00
8 CS(c),I Was A	81 MD,RH(c),Khaki Mosquito 65.00	149 . . . . 50.00
Holywood Soldier 200.00	82 MD,JKu(c),Ground Flier 65.00	150 JKu,Viking Prince 50.00
9 CS&StK(c),Sad Sack Squad . . 200.00	83 MD,JGr(c),Jet On	151 I:Unknown Soldier 50.00
10 CS,The G.I. & The Gambler . . 200.00	My Shoulder 65.00	152 . . . . 15.00
11 LSt(c),The Lucky Squad 200.00	84 MD,IN(c),O:Mademoiselle	153 . . . . 15.00
12 CS(c),The Four Horseman of	Marie 150.00	154 O:Unknown Soldier 40.00
Barricade Hill 200.00	85 IN(c),A Medal For Marie 80.00	155 . . . . 10.00
13 No Escape 200.00	86 JGr(c),A Medal For Marie 80.00	156 I:Battle Album 8.00
14 LSt(c),Pitchfork Army 200.00	87 JGr(c),T.N.T. Spotlight 75.00	157 thru 160 . . . . 6.00
15 The Big Fish 200.00	88 JGr(c),The Steel Trap 75.00	161 E:Enemy Ace 6.00
16 The Yellow Ribbon 200.00	89 IN(c),Trail of the Terror 75.00	162 thru 170 . . . . @10.00
17 IN(c),Prize Target 200.00	90 RA(c),Island of	171 thru 200 . . . . @8.00
18 IN(c),The Gladiator 200.00		201 thru 204 . . . . @2.50
19 IN(c),The Big Lift 200.00		**Becomes:**
20 JGr(c),The Battle of		**UNKNOWN SOLDIER**
the Frogmen 200.00		**April-May, 1977**
21 JGr(c),Dead Man's Bridge . . . 150.00		205 thru 247 . . . . @1.25
22 JGr(c),Death Hurdle 150.00		248 and 249 O:Unknown Soldier . @1.25
23 JGr(c),The Silent Frogman . . . 150.00		250 . . . . 1.25
24 JGr(c),Death Slide 150.00		251 B:Enemy Ace 1.25
25 JGr(c),S.S. Liferaft 150.00		252 thru 268 . . . . @1.25
26 JGr(c),Bazooka Man 150.00		
27 JGr(c),Taps for a Tail Gunner . 150.00		**STAR SPANGLED COMICS**
28 JGr(c),Tank Duel 150.00		**1999**
29 JGr(c),A Gun Called Slugger . 150.00		1 CWn, F:Sandman & Star
30 JGr(c),The Thunderbolt Tank . 150.00		Spangled Kid 2.00
31 IN(c),Tank Block. 100.00		
32 JGr(c),Bridge to Battle 100.00		**STAR TREK**
33 JGr(c),Pocket War 100.00		**1984–88**
34 JGr(c),Fighting...Snowbirds . . 100.00		**[1st Regular Series]**
35 JGr(c),Zero Hour 100.00		1 TS,The Wormhole Connection . 15.00
36 JGr(c),A G.I. Passed Here . . . 100.00		2 TS,The Only Good Klingon 8.00
37 JGr(c),A Handful of T.N.T. . . . 100.00		3 TS,Errand of War 7.00
38 RH(c),One-Man Army 100.00		4 TS,Deadly Allies 7.00
39 JGr(c),Flying Cowboy 100.00		
40 JGr(c),Desert Duel 100.00		

Star Spangled War Stories 15
© DC Comics Inc.

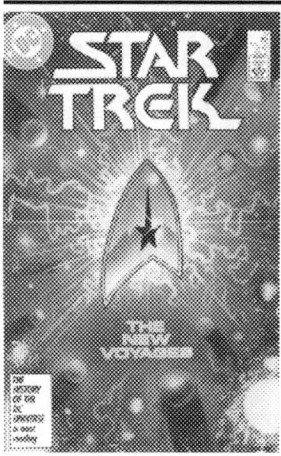

Star Trek #37 © DC Comics, Inc.

5 TS,Mortal Gods 7.00
6 TS,Who is Enigma? 6.00
7 EB,O:Saavik. 6.00
8 TS,Blood Fever 6.00
9 TS,Mirror Universe Saga #1 . . . 6.00
10 TS,Mirror Universe Saga #2. . . . 6.00
11 TS,Mirror Universe Saga #3. . . . 6.00
12 TS,Mirror Universe Saga #4. . . . 6.00
13 TS,Mirror Universe Saga #5. . . . 5.00
14 TS,Mirror Universe Saga #6. . . . 5.00
15 TS,Mirror Universe Saga #7. . . . 5.00
16 TS,Mirror Universe Saga end. . . 5.00
17 TS,The D'Artagnan Three 5.00
18 TS,Rest & Recreation 5.00
19 DSp,W.Koenig story. 5.00
20 TS,Girl. 5.00
21 TS,Dreamworld 5.00
22 TS,The Wolf #1 . . . . 5.00
23 TS,The Wolf #2 . . . . 4.00
24 TS,Double Blind #1 . . . . 4.00
25 TS,Double Blind #2.. . . . . 4.00
26 TSV:Romulans 4.00
27 TS,Day in the Life 4.00
28 GM,The Last Word 4.00
29 Trouble with Bearclaw 4.00
30 CI,F:Uhura. 4.00
31 TS,Maggie's World. 4.00
32 TS,Judgment Day 4.00
33 TS,20th Anniv. 4.50
34 V:Romulans. 2.50
35 GM,Excelsior. 2.50
36 GM,StarTrek IV tie-in 2.50
37 StarTrek IV tie-in 2.50
38 AKu,The Argon Affair. 2.50
39 TS,A:Harry Mudd. 2.50
40 TS,A:Harry Mudd. 2.50
41 TS,V:Orions. 2.50
42 TS,The Corbomite Effect 2.50
43 TS,Paradise Lost #1 . . . . 2.50
44 TS,Paradise Lost #2 . . . . 2.50
45 TS,Paradise Lost #3 . . . . 2.50
46 TS,Getaway. 2.50
47 TS,Idol Threats 2.50
48 TS,The Stars in Secret
   Influence 2.50
49 TS,Aspiring to be Angels 2.50
50 TS,Anniv. 3.50
51 TS,Haunted Honeymoon 2.50
52 TS,'Hell in a Hand Basket' 2.50
53 `You're Dead,Jim'. 2.50
54 Old Loyalties 2.50
55 TS,Finnegan's Wake 2.50
56 GM,Took place during 5 year
   Mission 2.50
Ann.#1 All Those Years Ago 4.00

Ann.#2 DJw,The Final Voyage 3.00
Ann.#3 CS,F:Scotty 3.00
Star Trek III Adapt.TS. 2.50
Star Trek IV Adapt. TS 2.50
StarTrek V Adapt. 2.50

[2nd Regular Series]
1989–96

1 The Return 10.00
2 The Sentence. 5.00
3 Death Before Dishonor 4.00
4 Reproccussions 4.00
5 Fast Friends 4.00
6 Cure All 4.00
7 Not Sweeney! 4.00
8 Going,Going. 3.50
9 ...Gone. 3.50
10 Trial of James Kirk #1 . . . . 3.50
11 Trial of James Kirk #2 . . . . 3.50
12 Trial of James Kirk #3 . . . . 3.50
13 Return of Worthy #1 . . . . 3.50
14 Return of Worthy #2 . . . . 3.50
15 Return of Worthy #3 . . . . 3.50
16 Worldsinger 3.00
17 Partners? #1 . . . . 3.00
18 Partners? #2 . . . . 3.00
19 Once A Hero 3.00
20 . . . . 3.00
21 Kirk Trapped 3.00
22 A:Harry Mudd 3.00
23 The Nasgul,A:Harry Mudd 3.00
24 25th Anniv.,A:Harry Mudd 3.50
25 Starfleet Officers Reunion 2.50
26 Pilkor 3 . . . . 2.50
27 Kirk Betrayed. 2.50
28 V:Romulans. 2.50
29 Mediators 2.50
30 Veritas #1 . . . . 2.50
31 Veritas #2 . . . . 2.50
32 Veritas #3 . . . . 2.50
33 Veritas #4 . . . . 2.50
34 JD,F:Kirk,Spock,McCoy 2.50
35 Tabukan Syndrome#1 . . . . 2.50
36 Tabukan Syndrome#2 . . . . 2.50
37 Tabukan Syndrome#3 . . . . 2.50
38 Tabukan Syndrome#4 . . . . 2.50
39 Tabukan Syndrome#5 . . . . 2.50
40 Tabukan Syndrome#6 . . . . 2.50
41 Runaway 2.50
42 Helping Hand. 2.50
43 V:Binzalans 2.50
44 Acceptable Risk. 2.50
45 V:Trelane. 2.50
46 V:Captain Klaa. 2.50
47 F:Spock & Saavik 2.50
48 The Neutral Zone. 2.50
49 weapon from Genesis 2.50
50 "The Peacemaker". 4.00
51 "The Price" 2.00
52 V:Klingons. 2.00
53 Timecrime #1. . . . . 2.00
54 Timecrime #2. . . . . 2.00
55 Timecrime #3. . . . . 2.00
56 Timecrime #4. . . . . 2.00
57 Timecrime #5. . . . . 2.00
58 F:Chekov. 2.00
59 Uprising. 2.00
60 Hostages. 2.00
61 On Talos IV 2.25
62 Alone,pt.1, V:aliens 2.25
63 Alone,pt.2 . . . . 2.25
64 Kirk 2.25
65 Kirk in Space. 2.25
66 Spock 2.25
67 Ambassador Stonn 2.25
68 . . . . 2.25
69 Wolf in Cheap Clothing,pt.1 . . . . 2.25
70 Wolf in Cheap Clothing,pt.2 . . . . 2.25
71 Wolf in Cheap Clothing,pt.3 . . . . 2.50
72 Wolf in Cheap Clothing,pt.4 . . . . 2.50
73 Star-crossed,pt.1 . . . . 2.50

Star Trek, 2nd Series #56
© DC Comics, Inc.

74 Star-crossed,pt.2 . . . . 2.25
75 Star-crossed,pt.3 . . . . 4.00
76 Tendar. 2.25
77 to the Romulan Neutral Zone . . . 2.50
78 The Chosen,pt.1 (of 3). 2.50
79 The Chosen,pt.2 . . . . 2.50
80 The Chosen,pt.3 . . . . 2.50
Ann.#1 GM,sty by G.Takei(Sulu) . . . 4.00
Ann.#2 Kirks 1st Yr At Star
   Fleet Academy 4.00
Ann #3 KD,F:Ambassador Sarek . . 3.50
Ann.#4 F:Spock on Pike's ship 3.50
Ann.#6 Convergence,pt.1 . . . . 3.95
Spec.#1 PDd(s),BSz. 3.75
Spec.#2 The Defiant. 3.95
Spec.#3 V:Orion pirates 3.95
Debt of Honor,AH,CCl(s),HC. 27.00
Debt of Honor SC 14.95
Spec. 25th Anniv.. . . . . 6.95
Star Trek VI,movie adapt(direct) . . . 5.95
Star Trek VI,movie(newsstand) 2.95
TPB Best of Star Trek reps. 19.95
TPB Star Trek: Revisitations
   rep. #22–#24,F:Gary Seven,
   #49–#50,F:Harry Mudd, 176pg 19.95
TPB Who Killed Captain Kirk?,
   rep.Star Trek#49–#55 . . . . . . 16.95
TPB The Ashes of Eden, Shatner
   novel adapt. 14.95

STAR TREK: THE MODALA IMPERATIVE
1991

1 Planet Modula 6.00
2 Modula's Rebels. 4.50
3 Spock/McCoy rescue Attempt. . . 4.00
4 Rebel Victory 4.00
TPB reprints both minis 19.95

STAR TREK: THE NEXT GENERATION
Feb., 1988
[1st Regular Series]

1 based on TV series,Where No
   Man Has Gone Before 15.00
2 Spirit in the Sky 10.00
3 Factor Q. 8.00
4 Q's Day 8.00
5 Q's Effects 8.00
6 Here Today. 8.00

[2nd Regular Series] 1989–95

1 Return to Raimon	16.00
2 Murder Most Foul	9.00
3 Derelict	7.50
4 The Hero Factor	7.50
5 Serafin's Survivors	6.00
6 Shadows in the Garden	6.00
7 The Pilot	5.00
8 The Battle Within	5.00
9 The Pay Off	5.00
10 The Noise of Justice	5.00
11 The Imposter	4.00
12 Whoever Fights Monsters	4.00
13 The Hand of the Assassin	4.00
14 Holiday on Ice	4.00
15 Prisoners of the Ferengi	3.50
16 I Have Heard the Mermaids Singing	3.50
17 The Weapon	3.50
18 MM,Forbidden Fruit	3.50
19 The Lesson	3.50
20 Lost Shuttle	3.50
21 Lost Shuttle cont.	3.50
22 Lost Shuttle cont.	3.50
23 Lost Shuttle cont.	3.50
24 Lost Shuttle conc.	3.50
25 Okona S.O.S.	3.50
26 Search for Okona	3.50
27 Worf,Data,Troi,Okona trapped on world	3.50
28 Worf/K'Ehleyr story	3.50
29 Rift,pt.1	3.50
30 Rift,pt.2	3.50
31 Rift conclusion	3.50
32	3.50
33 R:Mischievous Q	3.50
34 V:Aliens,F:Mischievous Q	3.50
35 Way of the Warrior	3.50
36 Shore Leave in Shanzibar#1	3.25
37 Shore Leave in Shanzibar#2	3.25
38 Shore Leave in Shanzibar#3	3.25
39 Divergence #1	3.25
40 Divergence #2	3.25
41 V:Strazzan Warships	3.25
42 V:Strazzans	3.25
43 V:Strazzans	3.25
44 Disrupted Lives	3.25
45 F:Enterprise Surgical Team	3.25
46 Deadly Labyrinth	3.25
47 Worst of Both World's#1	3.00
48 Worst of Both World's#2	3.00
49 Worst of Both World's#3	3.00
50 Double Sized,V:Borg	4.00
51 V:Energy Beings	3.00
52 in the 1940's	3.00
53 F:Picard	3.00
54 F:Picard	3.00
55 Data on Trial	3.00
56 Abduction	3.00
57 Body Switch	3.00
58 Body Switch	3.00
59 B:Children in Chaos	3.00
60 Children in Chaos#2	3.00
61 E:Children in Chaos	3.00
62 V:Stalker	3.00
63 A:Romulans	3.00
64 Geordie	3.00
65 Geordie	3.00
66	3.00
67 Friends/Strangers	3.00
68 Friends/Strangers,pt.2	3.00
69 Friends/Strangers,pt.3	3.00
70 Friends/Strangers,pt.4	3.00
71 War of Madness,pt.1	2.50
72 War of Madness,pt.2	2.50
73 War of Madness,pt.3	2.50
74 War of Madness,pt.4	2.50
75 War of Madness,pt.5	4.00
76 F:Geordi	2.50
77 Gateway, pt.1	2.50
78 Gateway, pt.2	2.50
79 Crew transformed into androids	2.50
80 Mysterious illness	2.50
Ann.#1 A:Mischievous Q.	4.50
Ann.#2 BP,V:Parasitic Creatures	4.00
Ann.#3	2.50
Ann.#4 MiB(s),F:Dr.Crusher	4.00
Ann.#6 Convergence,pt.2	3.95
Series Finale	4.25
Spec.#1	3.75
Spec.#2 CCl(s)	4.00
Star Trek N.G.:Sparticus.	5.00
TPB Beginnings, BSz(c) rep.	19.95

STAR TREK: THE NEXT GENERATION DEEP SPACE NINE
1994–95

1 Crossover with Malibu	2.50
2	2.50

Star Trek, The Next Generation, III Wind #4 © DC Comics Inc.

STAR TREK: THE NEXT GENERATION ILL WIND
1995–96

1 Solar-sailing race	2.50
2 Explosion Investigated	2.50
3 A bomb aboard ship	2.50
4 finale	2.50

STAR TREK THE NEXT GENERATION MODALA IMPERATIVE
1991

1 A:Spock,McCoy	6.00
2 Modula Overrun by Ferengi	5.00
3 Picard,Spock,McCoy & Troi trapped	4.00
4 final issue	4.00

STAR TREK THE NEXT GENERATION SHADOWHEART
1994–95

1 thru 3	@2.25
4 Worf Confront Nikolai	2.25

STATIC
Milestone 1993–96

1 JPL,I:Static,Hotstreak,Frieda Goren, w/poster,card,D puzzle piece	4.00
1a Newstand Ed.	2.00
1b Platinum Ed.	8.00
2 JPL,V:Hotstreak,I:Tarmack	2.00
3 JPL,V:Tarmack	1.75
4 JPL,A:Holocaust,I:Don Cornelius	1.75
5 JPL,I:Commando X	1.75
6 JPL,V:Commando X	1.75
7 3RW,V:Commando X	1.75
8 WS(c),3RW,Shadow War,I:Plus.	1.75
9 3RW,I:Virus	1.75
10 3RW,I:Puff,Coil	1.75
11 3RW,V:Puff,Coil	1.75
12 3RW,I:Joyride	1.75
13 I:Shape Changer	1.75
14 Worlds Collide,V:Rift	2.75
15 V:Paris Bloods	1.75
16 Revelations	1.75
17 Palisade	1.75
18 Princess Nightmare	1.75
19	1.75
20	1.75
21 A:Blood Syndicate	1.75
22 V:Rabis	1.75
23 A:Boogieman	1.75
24 A:Dusk	1.75
25 Long Hot Summer, V:Dusk, 48pgs.	3.95
26 Long Hot Summer	2.50
27	2.50
28 Drug Raid	2.50
29 HC(c), Friend Drug Dealer	2.50
30 Deals with Friend's Death	2.50
31 GK	2.50
32 V:Swarm	2.50
33	2.50
34 V:Ruberband Man	2.50
35 new Prometheus	2.50
36 JP,V:Sinister Botanist	2.50
37	2.50
38	2.50
39	2.50
40 JMr	2.50
41 Virgil's relationship with Daisy	2.50
42 V:six enemies	2.50
43 A:Brickhouse, V:Frieda Goren	2.50
44	2.50
45 MBr(s),JMr,Static lays a trap for Laserjet.	2.50
46 MBr(s),JMr	2.50
47 DMD(s),JMr, final issue	2.50

STEEL
1994–98

1 JBg(c),B:LSi(s),CsB,N:Steel	3.00
2 JBg(c),CsB,V:Toastmaster	2.00
3 JBg(c),CsB,V:Amertek	2.00
4 JBg(c),CsB.	2.00
5 JBg(c),CsB,V:Sister's Attacker	2.00
6 JBg(c),CsB,Worlds Collide,pt.5	2.00
7 Worlds Collide,pt.6	1.75
8 Zero Hour,I:Hazard.	1.75
9 F:Steel	1.50
10 F:Steel.	1.50
11	1.50
12	1.50
13 A:Maxima	1.50
14 A:Superman	1.50
15 R:White Rabbit	1.50
16 V:White Rabbit [new Miraweb format begins]	2.00
17 Steel controls armor powers	2.00
18 Abduction	2.00
19	2.00
20 Body Rejects Armor.	2.00
21 LSi,Underworld Unleashed tie-in	2.00
22 Steel separated from Superboy	2.00

Steel #14 © DC Comics, Inc.

23 Steel attacked 2.00
24 V:Hazard's 2.00
25 . . . . 2.00
26 Natasha gains superpowers. . . . 2.00
27 LSi,V:Hazard 2.00
28 . . . . 2.00
29 . . . . 2.00
30 . . . . 2.00
31 LSi(s),V:Armorbeast. 2.00
32 V:Blockbuster 2.00
33 JAp,DG,Natasha's drug abuse . . 2.00
34 CPr(s),DCw,TP,A:Natasha, in
    Jersey City 2.00
35 CPr(s),DCw,TP, ... 2.00
36 CPr(s),DCw,TP,Combing the
    sewers of Jersey City 2.00
37 CPr(s),DCw,TP,John Irons,
    Amanda Quick & Skorpio a
    romantic triangle. 2.00
38 CPr(s),DCw,TP,A:The Question . 2.00
39 CPr(s),DCw,TP,V:Crash 2.00
40 CPr(s),VGi,Steel tries out
    new hammer 2.00
41 CPr(s),DCw,TMo, John Irons
    guilty of murder? 2.00
42 CPr(s),DCw,TP,Irons and
    Amanda assaulted 2.00
43 CPr(s),DCw,TP,to Metropolis . . . 2.00
44 CPr(s),DCw,TP,Genesis tie-in . . 2.50
45 CPr(s),DCw,TP,seek policeman . 2.50
46 CPr(s),DCw,TP,F:Superboy 2.50
47 CPr(s),DCw,TP,F:Amanda 2.50
48 . . . . 2.50
49 CPr(s),DCw,TP,V:Deadline 2.50
50 CPr(s),DCw,TP,Millennium
    Giants 2.50
51 CPr(s),DCw,TP,bounty hunter . . 2.50
52 CPr(s),final issue 2.50
1-shot, movie adaptation. 5.00
Ann.#1 Elseworlds story 2.95
TPB THe Forging of a Hero LSi(s) 19.95

STEEL, THE
INDESTRUCTIBLE MAN
March, 1978

1 DH,I:Steel. 5.00
2 DH 3.00
3 DH 3.00
4 DH 3.00
5 Oct.–Nov., 1978 . . . . 5.00

STRANGE ADVENTURES
1950–74

1 The Menace of the Green
    Nebula. 2,600.00
2 S&K,JM(c),Doom From
    Planet X 1,200.00
3 The Metal World 800.00
4 BP,The Invaders From the
    Nth Dimension 800.00
5 The World Inside the Atom . . : 700.00
6 The Confessions of a Martian . 700.00
7 The World of Giant Ants 700.00
8 MA,ATh,Evolution Plus 700.00
9 MA,B:Captain Comet,The
    Origin of Captain Comet . . 1,600.00
10 MA,CI,The Air Bandits
    From Space 700.00
11 MA,CI,Day the Past
    Came Back 500.00
12 MA,CI,GK(c),The Girl From
    the Diamond Planet 500.00
13 MA,CI,GK(c),When the Earth
    was Kidnapped. 500.00
14 MA,CI,GK(c),Destination
    Doom 500.00
15 MA,CI,GK(c),Captain Comet-
    Enemy of Earth 450.00
16 MA,CI,GK(c),The Ghost of
    Captain Comet 450.00
17 MA,CI,GK(c),Beware the
    Synthetic Men 450.00
18 CI,MA(c),World of Flying Men 450.00
19 CI,MA(c),Secret of the
    Twelve Eternals 450.00
20 CI,Slaves of the Sea Master. . 450.00
21 CI,MA(c),Eyes of the
    Other Worlds 400.00
22 CI,The Guardians of the
    Clockwork Universe 400.00
23 CI,MA(c),The Brain Pirates
    of Planet X 400.00
24 CI,MA(c),Doomsday on Earth. 400.00
25 CI,GK(c),The Day
    That Vanished 400.00
26 CI,Captain Vs. Miss Universe. 400.00
27 CI,MA(c),The Counterfeit
    Captain Comet 400.00
28 CI,Devil's Island in Space. . . . 400.00
29 CI,The Time Capsule From
    1,000,000 B.C. 400.00
30 CI,MA(c),Menace From the
    World of Make-Believe 350.00
31 CI,Lights Camera Action 350.00
32 CI,MA(c),The Challenge of
    Man-Ape the Mighty 350.00
33 CI,MA(c),The Human Beehive 350.00
34 CI,MA(c) 350.00
35 CI,MA(c),Cosmic Chessboard 350.00
36 CI,MA(c),The Grab-Bag
    Planet. 350.00
37 CI,MA(c),The Invaders From
    the Golden Atom 350.00
38 CI,MA(c),Seeing-Eye Humans 350.00
39 CI,MA(c),The Guilty Gorilla . . 400.00
40 CI,MA(c),The Mind Monster . . 300.00
41 CI,MA(c),The Beast From Out
    of Time. 300.00
42 CI,MD,MA(c),The Planet of
    Ancient Children. 300.00
43 CI,MD,MA(c),The Phantom
    Prize Fighter. 300.00
44 CI,MA(c),The Planet That
    Plotted Murder 300.00
45 CI,MD,MA(c),Gorilla World. . . 300.00
46 CI,MA(c),E:Captain Comet
    Interplanetary War Base 300.00
47 CI,MA(c),The Man Who Sold
    the Earth 300.00
48 CI,MA(c),Human Phantom . . . 300.00
49 CI,MA(c),The Invasion
    from Indiana 300.00

Strange Adventures #231
© DC Comics, Inc.

50 CI,MA(c),The World Wrecker . 250.00
51 CI,MA(c),The Man Who
    Stole Air 250.00
52 CI,MA(c),Prisoner of the
    Parakeets. 250.00
53 CI,MA(c),The Human Icicle . . 250.00
54 CI,MA(c),The Electric Man . . . 175.00
55 CI,MA(c),The Gorilla Who
    Challanged the World,pt.I . . . 175.00
56 CI,The Jungle Emperor,pt.II . . 175.00
57 CI,The Spy from Saturn 175.00
58 CI,I Hunted the Radium Man . 175.00
59 CI,The Ark From Planet X . . . 175.00
60 CI,Across the Ages 175.00
61 CI,The Mirages From Space . 175.00
62 CI,The Fireproof Man. 175.00
63 CI,I Was the Man in the Moon 175.00
64 CI,GK(c),Gorillas In Space . . . 175.00
65 CI,GK(c),Prisoner From Pluto. 175.00
66 CI,GK(c),The Human Battery . 175.00
67 CI,GK(c),Martian Masquerader175.00
68 CI,The Man Who Couldn't
    Drown 175.00
69 CI,Gorilla Conquest of Earth . 175.00
70 CI,Triple Life of Dr. Pluto 175.00
71 CI,MSy,Zero Hour For Earth . . 150.00
72 CI,The Skyscraper That Came
    to Life. 150.00
73 CI,Amazing Rain of Gems . . . 150.00
74 CI,The Invisible Invader
    From Dimension X 150.00
75 CI,Secret of the Man-Ape. . . . 150.00
76 CI,B:Darwin Jones,The Robot
    From Atlantis 150.00
77 CI,A:Darwin Jones,The World
    That Slipped Out of Space . . 150.00
78 CI,The Secret of the Tom
    Thumb Spaceman 150.00
79 CI,A:Darwin Jones,Invaders
    from the Ice World 150.00
80 CI,Mind Robbers of Venus . . . 150.00
81 CI,The Secret of the
    Shrinking Twins 150.00
82 CI,Giants of the Cosmic Ray . 125.00
83 CI,Assignment in Eternity. . . . 125.00
84 CI,Prisoners of the Atom
    Universe. 125.00
85 CI,The Amazing Human Race 125.00
86 CI,The Dog That Saved the
    Earth 125.00
87 CI,New Faces For Old 125.00
88 CI,A:Darwin Jones,The Gorilla
    War Against Earth 125.00
89 CI,Earth For Sale. 125.00

DC COMICS

90 CI,The Day I Became a
Martian 125.00
91 CI,Midget Earthmen of Jupiter 125.00
92 CI,GK(c),The Amazing Ray
of Knowledge 125.00
93 CI,GK,c;A:Darwin Jones,
Space-Rescue By Proxy. . . . 125.00
94 MA,CI,GK(c),Fisherman of
Space. 125.00
95 CI,The World at my Doorstep. 125.00
96 CI,MA,(c),The Menace of
Saturn's Rings 125.00
97 CI,MA(c),MSy,Secret of the
Space-Giant 125.00
98 CI,GK(c),MSy,Attack on Fort
Satellite 125.00
99 CI,MSy,GK(c),Big Jump Into
Space. 125.00
100 CI,MSy,The Amazing Trial
of John (Gorilla) Doe 135.00
101 CI,MSy,GK(c),Giant From
Beyond. 100.00
102 MSy,GK(c),The Three Faces
of Barry Morrell. 100.00
103 GK(c),The Man Who
Harpooned Worlds 100.00
104 MSy,GK(c),World of Doomed
Spacemen 100.00
105 MSy,GK(c),Fisherman From
the Sea 100.00
106 MSy,CI,GK(c),Genie in the
Flying Saucer. 100.00
107 MSy,CI,GK(c),War of the
Jovian Bubble-Men. 100.00
108 MSy,CI,GK(c),The Human
Pet of Gorilla Land 100.00
109 MSy,CI,GK(c),The Man Who
Weighted 100 Tons. 100.00
110 MSy,CI,GK(c),Hand From
Beyond. 100.00
111 MSy,CI,GK(c),Secret of
the Last Earth-Man. 100.00
112 MSy,CI,GK(c),Menace of
the Size-Changing Spaceman 100.00
113 MSy,CI,GK(c),Deluge From
Space. 100.00
114 MSy,CI,GK(c),Secret of the
Flying Buzz Saw. 100.00
115 MSy,CI,GK(c),The Great
Space-Tiger Hunt 100.00
116 MSy,CI,RH,GK(c),Invasion
of the Water Warriors 100.00
117 MSy,CI,GK(c),I:Atomic
Knights. 600.00
118 MSy,CI,The Turtle-Men of
Space. 125.00
119 MSy,CI,MA(c),Raiders
From the Giant World 100.00
120 MSy,CI,MA,Attack of the Oil
Demons 250.00
121 MSy,CI,MA(c),Invasion of the
Flying Reptiles 75.00
122 MSy,CI,MA(c),David and the
Space-Goliath 75.00
123 MSy,CI,MA(c),Secret of the
Rocket-Destroyer 150.00
124 MSy,CI,MA(c),The Face-Hunter
From Saturn. 85.00
125 MSy,CI,The Flying Gorilla
Menace 75.00
126 MSy,CI,MA(c),Return of the
Neanderthal Man 150.00
127 MSy,CI,MA(c),Menace
From the Earth-Globe. 75.00
128 MSy,CI,MA(c),The Man
With the Electronic Brain . . . 75.00
129 MSy,CI,MA(c),The Giant
Who Stole Mountains 80.00
130 MSy,CI,MA.War With the
Giant Frogs 75.00
131 MSy,CI,MA(c),Emperor

of the Earth 75.00
132 MSy,CI,MA(c),The Dreams
of Doom. 80.00
133 MSy,CI,MA(c),The Invisible
Dinosaur 75.00
134 MSy,CI,MA(c), The Aliens
Who Raided New York 80.00
135 MSy,CI,MA(c),Fishing Hole
in the Sky. 75.00
136 MSy,CI,MA(c),The Robot
Who Lost Its Head 50.00
137 MSy,CI,MA(c),Parade of the
Space-Toys 50.00
138 MSy,CI,MA(c),Secret of the
Dinosaur Skeleton 80.00
139 MSy,CI,MA(c),Space-Roots
of Evil. 50.00
140 MSy,CI,MA(c),Prisoner of
the Space-Patch. 50.00
141 MSy,CI,MA(c),Battle Between
the Two Earths 75.00
142 MSy,CI,MA(c),The Return of
the Faceless Creature 50.00
143 MSy,CI,MA(c),The Face in
the Atom-Bomb Cloud 50.00
144 MSy,CI,MA(c),A:Atomic
Knights, When the Earth
Blacked Out 100.00
145 MSy,CI,MA,The Man Who
Lived Forever. 50.00
146 MSy,CI,MA(c),Perilous Pet
of Space. 50.00
147 MSy,CI,MA(c),The Dawn-
World Menace 70.00
148 MSy,CI,MA(c),Earth Hero,
Number One 50.00
149 MSy,CI,MA(c),Raid of
the Rogue Star. 50.00
150 MSy,CI,MA(c),When Earth
Turned into a Comet. 70.00
151 MSy,CI,MA(c),Invasion Via
Radio-Telescope. 50.00
152 MSy,MA(c),The Martian
Emperor of Earth 50.00
153 MSy,MA(c),Threat of the
Faceless Creature 50.00
154 CI,MSy,MA,GK(c),Earth's
Friendly Invaders 50.00
155 MSy,MA,GK(c),Prisoner
of the Undersea World 50.00
156 MSy,CI,MA(c),The Man
With the Head of Saturn 50.00
157 MSy,CI,MA(c),Plight of
the Human Cocoons. 50.00

Strange Adventures #243
© DC Comics Inc.

158 MSy,CI,MA(c),The Mind
Masters of Space 50.00
159 MSy,CI,MA(c),The Maze
of Time. 50.00
160 MSy,CI,MA(c),A:Atomic
Knights, Here Comes the
Wild Ones 50.00
161 MSy,CI,MA(c),Earth's Frozen
Heat Wave,E:Space Museum . 40.00
162 CI,MA(c),Mystery of the
12 O'Clock Man 40.00
163 MA(c),The Creature in
the Black Light 40.00
164 DD&SMo(c),I Became
a Robot 40.00
165 DD&SMo(c),I Broke the
Supernatural Barrier. 40.00
166 DD&SMo(c),I Lived in
Two Bodies 40.00
167 JkS(c),The Team That
Conqured Time. 40.00
168 JkS(c),I Hunted Toki
the Terrible 40.00
169 DD&SMo(c),The Prisoner
of the Hour Glass 40.00
170 DD&SMo(c),The Creature
From Strange Adventures. . . . 40.00
171 The Diary of the
9-Planet Man? 40.00
172 DD&SMo(c),I Became
the Juggernaut Man 40.00
173 The Secret of the
Fantasy Films. 40.00
174 JkS(c),The Ten Ton Man . . . 40.00
175 Danger: This Town is
Shrinking 40.00
176 DD&SMo(c),The Case of
the Cosmonik Quartet. 40.00
177 I Lived a Hundred Lives,
O:Immortal Man 40.00
178 JkS(c),The Runaway Comet. . 40.00
179 JkS(c),I Buried Myself Alive . . 40.00
180 CI,I:Animal Man,`I Was the
Man With Animal Powers . . . 225.00
181 The Man of Two Worlds. 25.00
182 JkS(c),The Case of the
Blonde Bombshell 25.00
183 JM(c),The Plot to Destroy
the Earth 25.00
184 GK(c),A:Animal Man,The
Return of the Man With
Animal Powers 150.00
185 JkS(c),Ilda-Gangsters Inc. . . . 25.00
186 Beware the Gorilla Witch 25.00
187 JkS(c),O:The Enchantress . . . 28.00
188 SD,JkS(c),I Was the
Four Seasons. 25.00
189 SD,JkS(c),The Way-Out
Worlds of Bertram Tilley 25.00
190 CI,A:Animal Man,A-Man-the
Hero with Animal Powers . . . 150.00
191 JkS(c),Beauty vs. the Beast . . 25.00
192 Freak Island. 25.00
193 The Villian Maker. 25.00
194 JkS(c),The Menace of the
Super- Gloves 25.00
195 JkS(c),Secret of the Three
Earth Dooms,A:Animal Man . 100.00
196 JkS(c),Mystery of the
Orbit Creatures. 25.00
197 The Hostile Hamlet 22.00
198 JkS(c),Danger! Earth
is Doomed 22.00
199 Robots of the Round Table. . . 22.00
200 . . . . 22.00
201 JkS,Animal Man. 50.00
202. . . . . 22.00
203. . . . . 22.00
204. . . . . 22.00
205 CI,I&O:Deadman 100.00
206 NA,MSy. 75.00

207 NA.	50.00
208 NA.	50.00
209 NA.	50.00
210 NA.	50.00
211 NA.	50.00
212 NA.	50.00
213 NA.	50.00
214 NA.	50.00
215 NA.	50.00
216 NA.	50.00
217 MA,MSy,A:Adam Strange.	12.00
218 MA,CI,MSy	11.00
219 CI,JKu	11.00
220 CI,JKu	11.00
221 CI	11.00
222 MA,New Adam Strange	13.00
223 MA,CI	11.00
224 MA,CI	11.00
225 MA,JKu	11.00
226 MA,JKu,New Adam Strange.	13.00
227 JKu	11.00
228 NA(c).	25.00
229	11.00
230 GM(c)	11.00
231 E:Atomic Knights	11.00
232 JKu	10.00
233 JKu	10.00
234 JKu	10.00
235 NA(c).	20.00
236.	10.00
237.	10.00
238 MK(c)	10.00
239	10.00
240 MK(c)	10.00
241	10.00
242 MA	10.00
243 F:Adam Strange.	10.00
244 Oct.–Nov., 1974.	10.00

STRANGE SPORTS STORIES
Sept.–Oct. 1973

1 CS,DG	25.00
2 thru 6	@15.00

STREETS
1993

1 Tenderloin	4.95
2 Procurement.	4.95
3	4.95

SUGAR & SPIKE
April-May, 1956

1 SM	1,400.00
2 SM	500.00
3 SM	400.00
4 SM	350.00
5 SM	350.00
6 thru 10 SM	@250.00
11 thru 20 SM	@200.00
21 thru 29 SM	@100.00
30 SM,A:Scribbly	125.00
31 thru 50 SM	@100.00
51 thru 70 SM	@70.00
71 thru 79 SM	@50.00
80 SM,I:Bernie the Brain.	50.00
81 thru 97 SM	@30.00
98 SM,Oct.–Nov., 1971.	30.00

STUCK RUBBER BABY SOFTCOVER
DC/Paradox Press

GN by Howard Cruise.	14.00

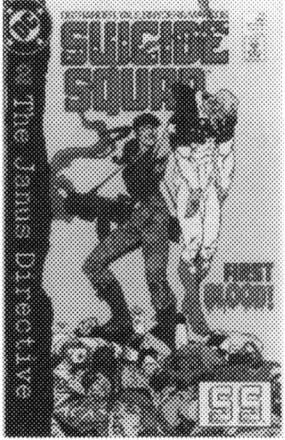

Suicide Squad #27 © DC Comics, Inc.

SUICIDE SQUAD
1987–91

1 LMc,Legends,I:Jihad.	2.50
2 LMc,V:The Jihad.	2.00
3 LMc,V:Female Furies	1.75
4 LMc,V:William Hell	1.75
5 LM,A:Penguin.	2.50
6 LM,A:Penguin.	2.50
7 LMc,V:Peoples Hero.	1.50
8 LMc,O:SquadMembers	1.50
9 LMc,Millenium	1.50
10 LMc,A:Batman.	1.50
11 LMc,A:Vixen,Speedy	1.50
12 LMc,Enchantress, V:Nightshade	1.50
13 LMc,X-over,JLI#13.	2.00
14 Nightshade Odyssey #1.	1.50
15 Nightshade Odyssey #2.	1.50
16 R:Shade	3.00
17 LMc,V:The Jihad	1.25
18 LMc,V:Jihad.	1.25
19 LMc,Personal Files 1988	1.25
20 LMc,V:Mirror Master	1.25
21 LMc,bonus book #10	1.25
22 LMc,D:Senator Cray	1.25
23 LMc,Invasion	1.25
24 LMc,V:Guerillas	1.25
25 L:Nightshade	1.25
26 D:Rick Flag,Jihad	1.25
27 Janus Directive #2.	1.25
28 Janus Directive #4.	1.25
29 Janus Directive #8.	1.25
30 Janus Directive #10.	1.25
31 Personal Files 1989.	1.25
32 V:Female Furies	1.25
33 GI,V:Female Furies	1.25
34 GI,V:Granny Goodness	1.25
35 LMc,GI,V:Female Furies	1.25
36 GI,D:Original Dr.Light.	1.25
37 GI,A:Shade,The Changing Man,V:Loa	1.50
38 LMc,GI,O:Bronze Tiger	1.25
39 GI,D:Loa	1.25
40 Phoenix Gambit #1,A:Batman Int. Poster	1.50
41 Phoenix Gambit #2	1.25
42 Phoenix Gambit,A:Batman.	1.25
43 Phoenix Gambit,A:Batman.	1.25
44 I:New Atom,O:Captain Boomerang	1.25
45 A:Kobra.	1.00
46 A:Kobra.	1.00
47 GI,A:Kobra,D:Ravan	1.00
48 GI,New Thinker.	1.00

49 GI,New Thinker	1.00
50 GI,50 Years of S.Squad	2.00
51 A:Deadshot	1.00
52 R:Docter Light	1.00
53 GI,The Dragon's Horde #1.	1.00
54 GI,The Dragon's Horde #2.	1.00
55 GI,The Dragon's Horde #3.	1.00
56 GI,The Dragon's Horde #4.	1.00
57 GI,The Dragon's Horde conc..	1.00
58 GI,War of the Gods x-over.	1.00
59 GI,A:Superman, Batman, Aquaman,A:Jihad, Hayoth	1.25
60 GI,A:Superman,Batman, Aquaman,Jihad,The Hayoth	1.25
61 GI,A:Superman,Batman, Aquaman,V:Jihad.	1.25
62 GI,R:Ray Palmer,A:Batman Superman,Aquaman.	1.25
63 GI,I:Gvede, Lord of Death	1.25
64 GI,A:Task Force X	1.25
65 GI,Bronze Tiger	1.25
66 GI,Final Iss.E:Suicide Squad	1.25
Ann.#1 GN,V:Argent,A:Manhunter	1.75

SUPERBOY
1949–76

1 `Superman (c).	6,800.00
2 `Superboy Day'	1,500.00
3	1,200.00
4 The Oracle of Smallville	800.00
5 Superboy meets Supergirl, Pre-Adventure #252.	750.00
6 I:Humpty Dumpty,the Hobby Robber.	700.00
7 WB,V:Humpty Dumpty	700.00
8 CS,I:Superbaby,V:Humpty Dumpty	650.00
9 V:Humpty Dumpty.	650.00
10 CS,I:Lana Lang	650.00
11 CS,2nd Lang,V:Humpty Dumpty	550.00
12 CS,The Heroes Club	550.00
13 CS,Scout of Smallville	550.00
14 CS,I:Marsboy	550.00
15 CS,A:Superman.	550.00
16 CS,A:Marsboy	375.00
17 CS,Superboy's Double.	375.00
18 CS,Lana Lang-Hollywood Star.	375.00
19 CS,The Death of Young Clark Kent	375.00
20 CS,The Ghost that Haunted Smallville	375.00
21 CS,Lana Lang-Magician.	275.00

Superboy #143 © DC Comics, Inc.

22 CS,The New Clark Kent. . . . 275.00	
23 CS,The Super Superboy 275.00	
24 CS,The Super Fat Boy of	
Steel 275.00	
25 CS,Cinderella of Smallville . . . 275.00	
26 CS,A:Superbaby 275.00	
27 CS,Clark Kent-Runaway. . . . 275.00	
28 CS,The Man Who Defeated	
Superboy 275.00	
29 CS,The Puppet Superboy . . . 275.00	
30 CS,I:Tommy Tuttle 200.00	
31 CS,The Amazing Elephant	
Boy From Smallville 200.00	
32 CS,His Majesty King	
Superboy 200.00	
33 CS,The Crazy Costumes of	
the Boy of Steel. 200.00	
34 CS,Hep Cats o/Smallville 200.00	
35 CS,The Five Superboys. 200.00	
36 . . . . 200.00	
37 CS,I:Thaddeus Lang 200.00	
38 CS,Public Chimp #1. . . . . 200.00	
39 CS,Boy w/Superboy Powers . 200.00	
40 CS,The Magic Necklace. 175.00	
41 CS,Superboy Meets	
Superbrave. 175.00	
42 CS,Gaucho of Smallville 175.00	
43 CS,Super-Farmer o/Smallville 175.00	
44 The Amazing Adventure of	
Superboy's Costume 175.00	
45 A Trap For Superboy 175.00	
46 The Battle of Fort Smallville . . 175.00	
47 CS,A:Superman. 175.00	
48 CS,Boy Without Super-Suit . . 175.00	
49 I:Metallo (Jor-El's Robot) 200.00	
50 The Super-Giant of Smallville. 175.00	
51 I:Krypto 150.00	
52 CS,The Powerboy from Earth. 150.00	
53 CS,A:Superman. 150.00	
54 CS,The Silent Superboy. 150.00	
55 CS,A:Jimmy Olson. 150.00	
56 CS,A:Krypto. 150.00	
57 CS,One-Man Baseball Team . 150.00	
58 CS,The Great Kryptonite	
Mystery 150.00	
59 CS,A:Superbaby 150.00	
60 The 100,000 Cowboy. 150.00	
61 The School For Superboys. . . 125.00	
62 I:Gloria Kent 125.00	
63 CS,The Two Boys of Steel . . . 125.00	
64 CS,A:Krypto. 125.00	
65 Superboy's Moonlight Spell . . 125.00	
66 The Family with X-Ray Eyes . 125.00	
67 I:Klax-Ar 125.00	
68 O&I:Bizarro 500.00	
69 How Superboy Learned	
To Fly. 100.00	
70 O:Superboy's Glasses 100.00	
71 A:Superbaby 100.00	
72 The Flying Girl of Smallville . . 100.00	
73 CS,A:Superbaby 100.00	
74 A:Jor-El & Lara 100.00	
75 A:Superbaby 100.00	
76 I:Super Monkey 100.00	
77 Superboy's Best Friend 100.00	
78 O:Mr.Mzyzptik 150.00	
79 A:Jar-El & Lara 85.00	
80 Superboy meets Supergirl . . . 125.00	
81 The Weakling From Earth 75.00	
82 A:Bizarro Krypto 75.00	
83 I:Kryptonite Kid 75.00	
84 A:William Tell. 75.00	
85 Secret of Mighty Boy 75.00	
86 I:PeteRoss,A:Legion 150.00	
87 I:Scarlet Jungle of Krypton. . . . 80.00	
88 The Invader from Earth 80.00	
89 I:Mon-El. 250.00	
90 A:Pete Ross 75.00	
91 CS,Superboy in Civil War. 75.00	
92 CS,I:Destructo,A:Lex Luthor. . . 75.00	
93 A:Legion 65.00	

Superboy #206 © DC Comics Inc.

94 I:Superboy Revenge Squad,	
A:Pete Ross. 50.00	
95 Imaginary Story,The Super	
Family From Krypton 50.00	
96 A:Pete Ross,Lex Luther. 50.00	
97 Krypto Story. 40.00	
98 Legion,I&O:Ultraboy. 55.00	
99 O: The Kryptonite Kid 45.00	
100 I:Phantom Zone 175.00	
101 The Handsome Hound	
of Steel 35.00	
102 O:Scarlet Jungle of Krypton. . 35.00	
103 CS,A:King Arthur,Jesse James	
Red Kryptonite 35.00	
104 O:Phantom Zone 35.00	
105 CS,`The Simpleton of Steel'. . 35.00	
106 CS,A:Brainiac 35.00	
107 CS,I:Superboy Club of	
Smallville 40.00	
108 The Kent's First Super Son . . 35.00	
109 The Super Youth of Bronze . . 35.00	
110 A:Jor-El 35.00	
111 Red Kryptonite Story 35.00	
112 CS,A:Superbaby 35.00	
113 `The Boyhood of Dad Kent' . . 35.00	
114 A:Phantom Zone,	
Mr.Mxyzptlk 35.00	
115 A:Phantom Zone,Lex Luthor. . 35.00	
116 `The Wolfboy of Smallville' . . 35.00	
117 A:Legion 35.00	
118 CS,`The War Between	
Superboy and Krypto' 35.00	
119 V:Android Double. 30.00	
120 A:Mr.Mxyzptlk 30.00	
121 CS,A:Jor-El,Lex Luthor 30.00	
122 Red Kryptonite Story 30.00	
123 CS,The Curse of the	
Superboy Mummy 30.00	
124 I:Insect Queen 30.00	
125 O:Kid Psycho. 30.00	
126 O:Krypto 30.00	
127 A:Insect Queen 32.00	
128 A:Phantom Zone,Kryptonite	
Kid,Dev En. 32.00	
129 rep.A:Mon-El,SuperBaby . . . 35.00	
130. . . . . 20.00	
131 A;Lex Luthor,Mr.Mxyzptlk,I:	
Space Canine Patrol Agents. . 20.00	
132, CS,A:Space Canine	
Patrol Agents 20.00	
133 A:Robin, repr. 20.00	
134 `The Scoundrel of Steel'. . . . 20.00	
135 A:Lex Luthor 20.00	
136 A:Space Canine Agents. . . . 20.00	
137 Mysterious Mighty Mites. . . . 20.00	

138 giant, Superboy's Most	
Terrific Battles. 35.00	
139 `The Samson of Smallville'. . . 15.00	
140 V:The Gambler 15.00	
141 No Mercy for a Hero 15.00	
142 A:Super Monkey 15.00	
143 NA(c),`The Big Fall' 15.00	
144 `Superboy's Stolen Identity' . . 15.00	
145 NA(c)Kents become young . . 15.00	
146 NA(c),CS,`The Runaway' 15.00	
147 giant O:Legion 25.00	
148 NA(c),CS,C:PolarBoy. 14.00	
149 NA(c),A:Bonnie & Clyde. 14.00	
150 JAb,V:Mr.Cipher. 14.00	
151 NA(c),A:Kryptonite Kid 14.00	
152 NA(c),WW 14.00	
153 NA(c),WW,A;Prof Mesmer . . . 12.00	
154 WW(i),A:Jor-El & Lara	
`Blackout For Superboy' 12.00	
155 NA(c),WW,`Revolt of the	
Teenage Robots' 12.00	
156 giant 16.00	
157 WW 12.00	
158 WW,A:Jor-El & Lara. 12.00	
159 WW(i),A:Lex Luthor 12.00	
160 WW,`I Chose Eternal Exile' . . 12.00	
161 WW,`The Strange Death of	
Superboy'. 12.00	
162 A:Phantom Zone 12.00	
163 NA(c),`Reform School Rebel'. 12.00	
164 NA(c),`Your Death Will	
Destroy Me' 12.00	
165 giant 16.00	
166 NA(c),A:Lex Luthor 12.00	
167 NA(c),MA,A:Superbaby 12.00	
168 NA(c),MA,Hitler 12.00	
169 MA,A:Lex Luthor 12.00	
170 MA,A:Genghis Khan 12.00	
171 MA,A:Aquaboy. 12.00	
172 MA(i),GT,A:Legion,	
O:Lightning Lad,Yango 13.00	
173 NA(c),GT,DG,O:CosmicBoy . . 12.00	
174 giant 16.00	
175 NA(c),MA,Rejuvenation of	
Ma & Pa Kent. 12.00	
176 NA(c),MA,GT,WW,A:Legion . 12.00	
177 MA,A:Lex Luthor 8.00	
178 NA(c),MA,Legion Reprint 8.00	
179 MA,A:Lex Luthor 8.00	
180 MA,O:Bouncing Boy. 8.00	
181 MA 8.00	
182 MA,A:Bruce Wayne. 8.00	
183 MA,GT,CS(rep),A:Legion 8.00	
184 MA,WW,O:Dial H rep. 8.00	
185 A:Legion 10.00	
186 MA 5.00	
187 MA 5.00	
188 MA,DC,O:Karkan,A:Legn 5.00	
189 MA 5.00	
190 MA,WW. 5.00	
191 MA,DC O:SunBoy retold 5.00	
192 MA 5.00	
193 MA,WW,N:Chameleon Boy,	
Shrinking Violet 5.00	
194 MA 5.00	
195 MA,WW,I:Wildfire,	
N:Phantom Girl. 5.00	
196 last Superboy solo. 8.00	
197 DC,Legion begins, New	
Costumes,I:Tyr 11.00	
198 DC N:Element Lad,	
Princess Projects 6.00	
199 DC,A:Tyr, Otto Orion 6.00	
200 DC,M:Bouncing Boy	
& Duo Damsel 11.00	
201 DC,Wildfire returns 6.00	
202 N:Light Lass 3.00	
203 MGr,D:Invisible Kid 18.00	
204 MGr,A:Supergirl 5.00	
205 MGr,CG,100 pages 6.00	
206 MGr,A:Ferro Lad 5.00	

All comics prices listed are for *Near Mint* condition.

DC COMICS

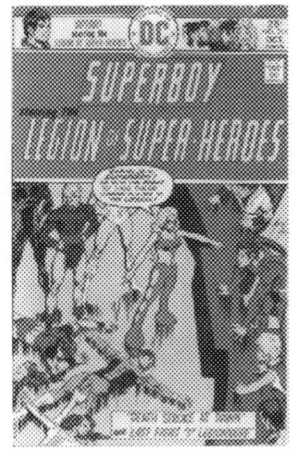

Superboy #212 © DC Comics, Inc.

207 MGr,O:Lightning Lad 5.00
208 MGr,CS,68pp,Legion of
   Super Villains. 7.00
209 MGr,N:Karate Kid. 5.00
210 MGr,O:Karate Kid. 7.00
211 MGr. 4.00
212 MGr,L:Matter Eater Lad 4.00
213 MGr,V:Benn Pares. 4.00
214 MGr,V:Overseer. 4.00
215 MGr,A:Emerald Empress 4.00
216 MGr,I:Tyroc 4.00
217 MGr,I:Laurel Kent. 4.00
218 J:Tyroc,A:Fatal Five 4.00
219 MGr,A:Fatal Five 4.00
220 MGi,BWi 4.00
221 MGr,BWi,I:Grimbor. 3.00
222 MGr,BWi,MN,BL,A:Tyroc 3.00
223 MGr,BWi 3.00
224 MGr,BWi,V:Pulsar Stargrave . . 3.00
225 MGr(c),BWi,JSh,MN 3.00
226 MGr(c),MN,JSh,JA,
   I:Dawnstar 3.00
227 MGr(c),JSon,JA,V:Stargrave . . 3.00
228 MGr(c),JSh,JA,
   D:Chemical King 3.00
229 MGr(c),JSh,JA,V:Deregon . . . 3.00
230 MGr(c),JSh,V:Sden 3.00
Becomes:

SUPERBOY & THE
LEGION OF
SUPER-HEROES
1976–79

231 MGr(c),JSh,MN,JA,doub.size
   begins,V:Fatal Five. 5.00
232 MGr(c),JSh,RE,JA,V:
   Dr.Regulus 5.00
233 MGr(c),JSh,BWi,MN,BL,
   I:Infinite Man 5.00
234 MGr(c),RE,JA,V:Composite
   Creature. 5.00
235 MGr,GT 5.00
236 MGr(c),BMc,JSh,MN,JRu,
   V:Khunds 5.00
237 MGr(c),WS,JA 5.00
238 JSn(c),reprint. 5.00
239 MGR(c),JSn,JRu,Ultra Boy
   accused 5.00
240 MGr(c),HC,BWi,JSh,BMc,
   O:Dawnstar;V:Grimbor 5.00
241 JSh,BMc,A:Ontir 5.00
242 JSh,BMc,E:Double Size 5.00
243 MGr(c),JA,JSon 5.00
244 JSon,V:Dark Circle. 5.00

245 MA,JSon,V:Mordu 5.00
246 MGr(c),JSon,DG,MA,
   V:Fatal Five 3.00
247 JSon,JA,anniv.issue. 3.00
248 JSon 3.00
249 JSon,JA. 3.00
250 JSn,V:Omega 3.00
251 JSn,Brainiac 5 goes insane . . 3.00
252 JSon,V:Starburst bandits 2.00
253 JSon,I:Blok,League of
   Super Assassins 2.00
254 JSon,V:League of Super
   Assassins. 2.00
255 JSon,A:Jor-El. 2.00
256 JSon 2.00
257 SD,JSon,DA,V:Psycho
   Warrior 2.00
258 JSon,V:Psycho Warrior 2.00
Becomes:

Legion of Super Heroes
[2nd Series]

[NEW ADVENTURES OF]
SUPERBOY
Jan., 1980

1 KS 1.50
2 KS 1.25
3 KS 1.25
4 KS 1.25
5 KS 1.25
6 KS 1.25
7 KS,JSa 1.25
8 thru 33 KS . . . . @1.25
34 KS,I:Yellow Peri 1.25
35 thru 44 KS . . . . @1.25
45 KS,I:Sunburst 1.25
46 KS,A:Sunburst. 1.25
47 KS,A:Sunburst. 1.25
48 KS 1.25
49 KS,A:Zatara. 1.25
50 KS,KG,A:Legion 1.50
51 KS,FM(c)In Between Years . . . 1.25
52 KS 1.25
53 KS 1.25
54 KS 1.25

SUPERBOY
1990–91

1 TV Tie-in,JM,photo(c) 1.25
2 JM,T.J.White Abducted 1.25
3 JM,'Fountain of Youth' 1.25
4 JM,'Big Man on Campus' 1.25
5 JM,Legion Homage 1.25
6 JM,Luthor. 1.25
7 JM,Super Boy Arrested. 1.25
8 JM,AAd(i),Bizarro 1.25
9 JM/CS,PhantomZone#1 . . . . . . 1.25
10 JM/CS,PhantomZone#2. . . . . . 1.25
11 CS. 1.25
12 CS,X-Mas in Smallville. 1.25
Becomes:

ADVENTURES OF
SUPERBOY
1991

13 A:Mr.Mxyzptlk 1.75
14 CS,A:Brimstone 1.25
15 CS,Legion Homage 1.25
16 CS,Into the Future 1.25
17 CS,A:Luthor. 1.25
18 JM,'At the Movies'. 1.25
19 JM,Blood Transfusion 1.25
20 JM,O:Nicknack,(G.Gottfried
   script). 1.25
21 V:Frost Monster 1.25
22 . . . . 1.25
Spec.#1 CS,A:Ma Kent. 1.75

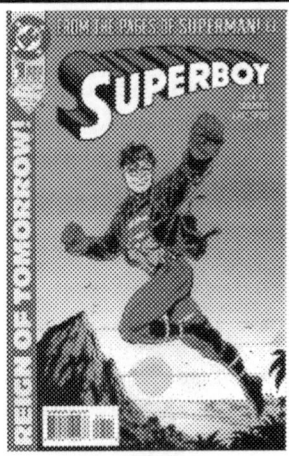

Superboy #1 © DC Comics, Inc.

SUPERBOY
[2nd Series]
1994–99

1 B:KK(s),TG,DHz,V:Sidearm 3.00
2 TG,DHz,I:Knockout. 2.50
3 TG,DHz,I:Scavenger. 2.00
4 TG,DHz,MeP,I:Lock n' Load 2.00
5 TG,DHz,I:Silver Sword 2.00
6 TG,DHz,Worlds Collide,pt.3
   C:Rocket 1.75
7 Worlds Collide, pt.8,V:Rift 1.75
8 Zero Hour,A:Superboy 1.50
9 Silican Dragon 1.50
10 Monster. 1.50
11 Techno. 1.50
12 Copperhead. 1.50
13 Watery Grave,pt.1 . . . . 1.50
14 Watery Grave,pt.2 . . . . 1.50
15 Watery Grave,pt.3 . . . . 1.50
16 TG,DHz,KK,V:Loose Cannon
   [New Miraweb format begins] . . 2.00
17 TG,DHz,KK Looking for
   Roxy Leech 2.00
18 V:Valor. 2.00
19 . . . . 2.00
20 R:Scavenger 2.00
21 KK,TG,DHz,Future Tense,Pt.1 . . 2.00
22 KK,TG,DHz,Underworld
   Unleashed x-over. 2.00
23 KK,TG,DHz,V:Technician 2.00
24 KK,TG,DHz,V:Silversword 2.00
25 New Gods 3.00
26 KK,DHz,Losin'it,pt.2 . . . . 2.00
27 KK,DHz,Losin'it,pt.3 . . . . 2.00
28 KK,DHz,Losin'it,pt.4 (of 6) 2.00
29 . . . . 2.00
30 . . . . 2.00
31 . . . . 2.00
32 RMz(s),RBe,DHz,V:King Shark . 2.00
33 RMz(s),RBe,DHz, survivors flee
   to Hawaii, Final Night tie-in. . . . 2.00
34 RMz(s),RBe,DHz, V:Dubbilex. . . 2.00
35 RMz(s),RBe,DHz, Superboy
   abducted 2.00
36 RMz(s),RBe,DHz,V:King SHark . 2.00
37 RMz(s),SB,V:Sledge 2.00
38 RMz(s),RBe,DHz,"Meltdown,"
   pt.1 (of 3) 2.00
39 RMz(s),RBe,DHz,"Meltdown,"
   pt.2 . . . . 2.00
40 RMz(s),RBe,DHz,"Meltdown,"
   pt.2 x-over 2.00
41 RMz(s),RBe,DHz,"Meltdown,"
   pt.3 concl. 2.00

42 SB, ... 2.00
43 SB,Lanie & Ken. 2.00
44 SB,island of teenagers. 2.00
45 RMz,DHz,TGu,A:Legion. 2.00
46 RMz,DHz,TGu,V:Silver Sword . . 2.00
47 RMz,DHz,TGu,F:Green Lantern . 2.00
48 BKs,DHz,TGu,theme park 2.00
49 DHz. 2.00
50 KK,TGu,Last Boy on Earth pt.1 . 2.00
51 KK,TGu,Last Boy on Earth pt.2 . 2.00
52 KK,TGu,Last Boy on Earth pt.3 . 2.00
53 KK,TGu,Last Boy on Earth pt.4 . 2.00
54 KK,TGu,A:Wild Men. 2.00
55 KK,TGu,V:Grokk, Hex 2.00
56 KK,TGu,Project Cadmus 2.00
57 KK,TGu,Demolition Run,pt.1 . . 2.00
58 KK,TGu,Demolition Run,pt.2 . . . 2.00
59 KK,DAb,A:Superman. 2.00
60 KK,TGu,A:JLA,Hyper-
    Tension,pt.1 . . . . 2.00
61 KK,TGu,Hyper-Tension,pt.2 . . . 2.00
62 KK,TGu,Hyper-Tension,pt.3 . . . 2.00
63 KK,TGu,Hyper-Tension,pt.4 . . . 2.00
64 KK,TGu,Hyper-Tension,pt.5 . . . 2.00
65 KK,TGu,guest-star packed. 2.00
66 KK,TGu,Wild Lands 2.00
67 KK,AaL, in Wild Lands. 2.00
Ann.#1 Elseworlds Story. 3.25
Ann.#2 KK,BKs, Year One 3.95
Ann.#3 Legends o/t Dead Earth . . . 2.95
Ann.#4 Pulp Heroes (High-
    Adventure) 3.95
Spec.#1,000,000 KK,TGu. 2.00

SUPERBOY
& THE RAVERS

1 KK&SMt(s),PaP,DDv, ... 2.00
2 KK&SMt(s),PaP,DDv,InterC.E.P.T.
    pursues Superboy and Kaliber . 2.00
3 KK&SMT(s),PaP,DDv,teleported
    to Rann,V:Half-Life 2.00
4 KK&SMt(s),PaP,DDv,A:Adam
    Strange 2.00
5 KK&SMt(s),PaP,DDv,O:Hero. . . . 2.00
6 KK&SMt(s),PaP,DDv, ... 2.00
7 KK&SMt(s),PaP,DDv, "Road Trip,"
    pt.1,A:Impulse 2.00
8 KK&SMt(s),PaP,DDv, "Road Trip,"
    pt.2,A:Guy Gardner 2.00
9 KK&SMt(s),PaP,DDv, "Road Trip,"
    pt.3,A:Aura 2.00
10 KK&SMt(s),DDv, "Meltdown,"
    pt. 4 . . . . 2.00
11 KK&SMt(s),PaP,DDv, Superboy
    presumed dead 2.00
12 KK(s),AaL,. 2.00
13 KK(s),SMt,F:Hero,Sparx 2.00
14 KK&SMt(s),Genesis tie-in 2.00
15 KK&SMt(s),new Rave 2.00
16 KK&SMt(s),Half-Life. 2.00
17 KK&SMt(s),Kaliber. 2.00
18 KK&SMt(s),V:Qward 2.00
19 . . . . 2.00

SUPERBOY PLUS
Nov. 1996

1 RMz(s),ASm,F:Captain
    Marvel Jr.. . . . . 2.95
2 LKa,AWi,ALa,F:Slither 3.00

SUPERBOY/RISK
DOUBLE-SHOT
Dec., 1997

1 DJu,JoP,x-over. 2.00

Super DC Giant, S-14
© *DC Comics Inc.*

SUPER DC GIANT
1970–71, 1976

S-13 Binky 70.00
S-14 Top Guns of the West. 20.00
S-15 Western Comics. 20.00
S-16 Best of the Brave & the Bold 25.00
S-17 Love 1970 . . . . 35.00
S-18 Three Mouseketeers. 20.00
S-19 Jerry Lewis. 25.00
S-20 House of Mystery 25.00
S-21 Love 1971 . . . . 35.00
S-22 Top Guns of the West. 20.00
S-23 The Unexpected. 25.00
S-24 Supergirl 25.00
S-25 Challengers of the Unknown. 25.00
S-26 Aquaman 25.00
S-27 Strange Flying Saucer
    Advengures (1976). 20.00

SUPER FRIENDS
Nov., 1976

1 ECh(c),JO,RE,'Fury of the
    Superfoes',A:Penguin. 18.00
2 RE,A:Penguin. 10.00
3 RF(c),RF,A:JLA 7.00
4 RF,V:Riddler,I:Skyrocket 7.00
5 RF(c),RF,V:Greenback 7.00
6 RF(c),RF,A:Atom 5.00
7 RF(c),RF,I:Zan & Jana,
    A:Seraph 5.00
8 RF(c),RF,A:JLA 5.00
9 RF(c),RF,A:JLA,I:Iron Maiden . . . 5.00
10 RF(c),RF'TheMonkeyMenace' . . 5.00
11 RF(c),RF 4.00
12 RF(c),RF,A:TNT. 4.00
13 RF(c),RF 4.00
14 RF(c),RF 4.00
15 RF(c),RF, A:The Elementals. . . . 4.00
16 RF(c),RF,V:The Cvags. 4.00
17 RF(c),RF,A:Queen Hippolyte . . . 4.00
18 KS(c),V:Tuantra,Time Trapper . . 4.00
19 RF(c),RF,V:Menagerie Man . . . 4.00
20 KS(c),KS,V:Frownin' Fritz. 4.00
21 RF(c),RF,V:Evil Superfriends
    Doubles 3.50
22 RF(c),RF,V:Matador Mob 3.50
23 FR(c),RF,V:Mirror Master 3.50
24 RF(c),RF,V:Exorians 3.50
25 RF(c),RF,V:Overlord,
    A:Green Lantern, Mera. 3.50
26 RF(c),RF,A:Johnny Jones 3.50
27 RF(c),RF,'The Spaceman Who
    Stole the Stars 3.50

28 RF(c),RF,A:Felix Faust. 3.50
29 RF(c),RF,B.U.KS,'Scholar From
    the Stars 3.50
30 RF(c),RF,V:Grodd & Giganta . . 3.50
31 RF(c),RF,A:Black Orchid 4.00
32 KS(c),KS,A:Scarecrow. 3.00
33 RF(c),RF,V:Menagerie Man . . . 3.00
34 RF(c)RF,'The Creature That
    Slept a Million Years' 3.00
35 RT,'Circus o/t Super Stars 3.00
36 RF(c),RF,A:Plastic Man
    & Woozy 3.00
37 RF(c),RF,A:Supergirl;
    B.U. A:Jack O'Lantern 3.00
38 RF(c),RF,V:Grax;
    B.U. A:Serpah 3.00
39 RF(c),RF,A:Overlord;
    B.U. A:Wonder Twins 3.00
40 RF(c),RF,V:The Monacle;
    B.U. Jack O'Lantern 3.00
41 RF(c),RF,V:Toyman;
    B.U. A:Seraph 3.00
42 RT,A:Flora,V:Flame; B.U.Wonder
    Twins' Christmas Special 3.00
43 KS(c),RT,V:Futuro; B.U.JSon
    A:Plastic Man 3.00
44 KS(c),RT,'Peril o/t Forgotten
    Identities'; B.U.Jack O'Lantern . 3.00
45 KS(c),RT,A:Bushmaster,
    Godiva, Rising Sun, Olympian,
    Little Mermaid, Wild Huntsman;
    B.U. Plastic Man,V: Sinestro. . . 3.00
46 RT,V:The Conqueror;
    B.U. BO,Seraph 3.00
47 KS(c),RT,A:Green Fury
    Aug. 1981 . . . . 4.00

SUPERGIRL
[1st Regular Series]
Nov., 1972—Sept. 1974

1 'Trail of the Madman';
    Superfashions From Fans;
    B:B.U. DG,Zatanna 25.00
2 BO(c)A:Prof.Allan,Bottle
    City of Kandor 10.00
3 BO(c),'The Garden of Death' . . 10.00
4 V:Super Scavanger. 10.00
5 BO(c),A:Superman,V:Dax; B.U.
    MA:Rep.Hawkman #4. . . . . . . 15.00
6 BO(c),'Love & War'. 10.00
7 BO(c),A:Zatanna. 10.00
8 BO(c),A:Superman,Green
    Lantern, Hawkman 15.00
9 BO(c),V:Sharkman 10.00
10 A:Prey,V:Master Killer 10.00

[DARING NEW
ADVENTURES OF]
SUPERGIRL
[2nd Regular Series]
Nov. 1982

1 CI,BO,I:Psi; B:B.U:Lois Lane . . . 1.50
2 CI,BO,C:Decay. 1.50
3 CI,BO,V:Decay,'Decay Day' 1.50
4 CI,BO, V:The Gang 1.50
5 CI,BO,V:The Gang 1.50
6 CI,BO,V:The Gang 1.50
7 CI,BO,V:The Gang 1.50
8 CI,BO,A:Doom Patrol 1.50
9 CI,BO,V:Reactron
    A:Doom Patrol 1.50
10 CI,BO,'Radiation Fever'. 1.50
11 CI,BO,V:Chairman 1.50
12 CI,BO,V:Chairmann 1.50
13 CI,BO,N:Supergirl,A:Superman
    V:Blackstarr 1.50
Becomes:

SUPERGIRL
Dec., 1983–Sept. 1984

14 GK(c),CI,BO,V:Blackstarr
  A:Rabbi Nathan Zuber 1.50
15 CI,BO,V:Blackstarr,
  A:Blackstarr's Mom. 1.50
16 KG/BO(c),CI,BO,
  A:Ambush Bug 1.50
17 CI/DG(c),CI,BO,V:Matrix
  Prime 1.50
18 DG(c),CI,BO, V:Kraken 1.50
19 EB/BO(c),CI,BO,`Who Stole
  Supergirl's Life'. 1.50
20 CI,BO,C:JLA,Teen Titans:
  Teh Parasite. 1.50
21 EB/BO(c),EB,Kryptonite Man . . . 1.50
22 EB(c),CI,BO,`I Have Seen the
  Future & it is Me' 1.50
23 EB(c),CI,BO,`The Future
  Begins Today 1.50
Spec.#1 JL/DG(c),GM,Movie Adapt. 1.50
Spec.#1 AT,Honda give-away 1.50

[Limited Series] 1994

1 KGa(c),B:RSt(s),JBr,O:Supergirl . 5.00
2 KGa(c),JBr. 4.00
3 KGa(c),JBr,D:Clones 3.00
4 KGa(c),RSt(s),JBr,final Issue . . . 3.00

SUPERGIRL
Sept. 1996

1 PDd(s),GFr,CaS,. 11.00
2 PDd(s),GFr,CaS,V:Chakat 5.00
3 PDd(s),GFr,CaS,V:Grodd, Final
  Night tie-in 4.00
4 PDd(s),GFr,CaS,transformed into
  savage. 3.00
5 PDd(s),GFr,CaS,Supergirl visits
  the Kents,V:Chemo 3.00
6 PDd(s),GFr,CaS, ... 3.00
7 PDd(s),GFr,CaS,Supergirl learns
  about Linda Danvers 3.00
8 PDd(s),GFr,CaS,Buzz gets date
  with Supergirl 3.00
9 PDd(s),GFr,CaS,V:Tempus 3.00
10 PDd(s),Linda tries to relax 3.00
11 PDd(s),CaS,V:Silver Banshee . . 3.00
12 PDd(s),Mattie possessed by
  Silver Banshee 3.00
13 CaS, 3 girls dreams invaded by
  incubus 2.50
14 PDa,CaS,Genesis tie-in 2.00
15 PDa,CaS,V:Extremists 2.00
16 PDa,CaS,F:Power Girl 2.00

Supergirl #1 © DC Comics, Inc.

17 PDa,CaS,L-Ron, Despero 2.00
18 PDa,CaS,V:Despero 2.00
19 . . . . 2.00
20 PDa,CaS,Millennium Giants. . . . 2.00
21 PDa,CaS,Comet 2.00
22 PDa, ... 2.00
23 PDa,A:Steel. 2.00
24 PDa,Avenging Angels x-over . . . 2.00
25 PDa,truth about Comet 2.00
26 PDd,truth discovered 2.00
27 PDd(s),V:Female Furies,pt.1 . . . 2.00
28 PDd(s),V:Female Furies,pt.2 . . . 2.00
29 PDd(s),V:Female Furies,pt.3 . . . 2.00
30 PDd(s),V:Matrix 2.00
31 PDd(s),A:Superman. 2.00
32 PDd(s),SeP,V:Mr.Carnivean . . . 2.00
33 PDd(s),V:Mr.Carnivean 2.00
34 PDd(s),V:Parasite 2.00
35 PDd(s),V:Parasite, concl.. . . . . . 2.00
36 PDd(s),Young Justice
  x-over,Hell's Angel's,pt.2. . . . . . 2.00
37 PDd(s),Hell's Angels,pt.4 . . . . . 2.00
Ann.#1 Legends o/t Dead Earth . . . 2.95
Ann. #2 TPe,CDi,ACa, Pulp Heroes 4.00
Spec.#1,000,000 PDd(s),DAb. 2.00
TPB rep. Supergirl #1–#9 . . . . 15.00
Spec. Supergirl/Lex Luthor JBr,
  F:Lex Luthor (1993) 4.00
Spec. Supergirl/Prism Double-Shot
  DJu,TGb,Clv, x-over (1997) . . . 2.00

SUPER HEROES BATTLE SUPER GORILLA
Winter, 1976

1 Superman Flash rep. 1.00

SUPERMAN
1939–86

1 JoS,O:Superman,reprints Action
  Comics #1-#4 . . . . 130,000.00
2 JoS,I:George Taylor 10,000.00
3 JoS,V:Superintendent
  Lyman 6,500.00
4 JoS,V:Lex Luthor 5,000.00
5 JoS,V:Lex Luthor 3,500.00
6 JoS,V:`Brute' Bashby 2,500.00
7 JoS,I:Perry White. 2,400.00
8 JoS,V:Jackal 2,200.00
9 JoS,V:Joe Gatson 2,200.00
10 JoS,V:Lex Luthor 2,100.00
11 JoS,V:Rolf Zimba 1,600.00
12 JoS,V:Lex Luthor 1,600.00
13 JoS,I:Jimmy Olsen,V:Lex
  Luthor,`The Archer' 1,600.00
14 JoS,I:Lightning Master. 2,600.00
15 JoS,V:The Evolution King . . 1,500.00
16 JoS,V:Mr. Sinus 1,400.00
17 JoS,V:Lex Luthor,Lois Lane
  first suspects Clark is
  Superman 1,400.00
18 JoS,V:Lex Luthor 1,300.00
19 JoS,V:Funnyface,
  1st Imaginary story 1,300.00
20 JoS,V:Puzzler,Leopard 1,300.00
21 JoS,V:Sir Gauntlet. 1,000.00
22 JoS,V:Prankster 1,000.00
23 JoS,Propaganda story. 1,000.00
24 V:Cobra King 1,400.00
25 Propaganda story 1,000.00
26 I:J.Wilbur Wolfingham,
  A:Mercury 1,000.00
27 V:Toyman 1,000.00
28 V:J.Wilbur Wolfingham,
  A:Hercules. 1,000.00
29 V:Prankster. 1,000.00
30 I&O:Mr. Mxyztplk. 1,500.00
31 V:Lex Luthor 900.00
32 V:Toyman 900.00
33 V:Mr. Mxyztptlk 900.00

Superman #76 © DC Comics, Inc.

34 V:Lex Luthor 900.00
35 V:J.Wilbur Wolfingham. 900.00
36 V:Mr. Mxyztptlk 900.00
37 V:Prankster,A:Sinbad 900.00
38 V:Lex Luthor 900.00
39 V:J.Wilbur Wolfingham. 900.00
40 V:Mr. Mxyztptlk,A:Susie
  Thompkins 900.00
41 V:Prankster 600.00
42 V:J.Wilbur Wolfingham 600.00
43 V:Lex Luthor 600.00
44 V:Toyman,A:Shakespeare . . 600.00
45 A:Hocus & Pocus,Lois Lane
  as Superwoman 600.00
46 V:Mr. Mxyztptlk,Lex Luthor,
  Superboy flashback 600.00
47 V:Toyman 600.00
48 V:Lex Luthor 600.00
49 V:Toyman 600.00
50 V:Prankster 600.00
51 V:Mr. Mxyztptlk 500.00
52 V:Prankster 500.00
53 WB,O:Superman. 2,200.00
54 V:Wrecker 500.00
55 V:Prankster 500.00
56 V:Prankster 500.00
57 V:Lex Luthor 500.00
58 V:Tiny Trix 500.00
59 V:Mr.Mxyzptlk 500.00
60 V:Toyman 500.00
61 I:Kryptonite,V:Prankster. . . 1,000.00
62 V:Mr.Mxyzptlk,A:Orson
  Welles 500.00
63 V:Toyman 500.00
64 V:Prankster 500.00
65 V:Mala,Kizo and U-Ban 500.00
66 V:Prankster 500.00
67 A:Perry Como,I:Brane
  Taylor. 500.00
68 V:Lex Luthor 500.00
69 V:Prankster,A:Inspector
  Erskine Hawkins 500.00
70 V:Prankster 500.00
71 V:Lex Luthor 450.00
72 V:Prankster 450.00
72a giveaway 750.00
73 Flashback story 450.00
74 V:Lex Luthor 450.00
75 V:Prankster 450.00
76 A:Batman (Superman &
  Batman revel each other's
  identities) 1,300.00
77 A:Pocahontas 425.00
78 V:Kryptonian snagriff,
  A:Lana Lang. 425.00

79 V:Lex Luthor,A:Inspector
  Erskine Hawkins......... 425.00
80 A:Halk Kar............... 425.00
81 V:Lex Luthor 425.00
82 V:Mr. Mxyzptlk 400.00
83 V:`The Brain' 400.00
84 Time-travel story 400.00
85 V:Lex Luthor 400.00
86 V:Mr.Mxyzptlk 400.00
87 WB,V:The Thing from
  40,000 AD'............. 400.00
88 WB,V:Lex Luthor,Toyman,
  Prankster team.......... 425.00
89 V:Lex Luthor 400.00
90 V:Lex Luthor 425.00
91 `The Superman Stamp' 400.00
92 Goes back to 12th Century
  England 400.00
93 V:`The Thinker' 400.00
94 `Clark Kent's Hillbilly Bride'... 400.00
95 A:Susie Thompkins 400.00
96 V:Mr. Mxyzptlk 350.00
97 `Superboy's Last Day In
  Smallville'.............. 350.00
98 `Clark Kent, Outlaw!' 350.00
99 V:Midnite gang........... 350.00
100 F:Superman-Substitute
  Schoolteacher 1,700.00
101 A:Lex Luthor 275.00
102 I:Superman Stock
  Company 275.00
103 A:Mr.Mxyzptlk 275.00
104 F:Clark Kent,Jailbird...... 275.00
105 A:Mr.Mxyzptlk 275.00
106 A:Lex Luthor 300.00
107 F:Superman In 30th century
  (pre-Legion) 275.00
108 I:Perry White Jr.......... 275.00
109 I:Abner Hokum........... 275.00
110 A:Lex Luthor 275.00
111 Becomes Mysto the Great .. 250.00
112 A:Lex Luthor 250.00
113 A:Jor-El 250.00
114 V:The Great Mento........ 250.00
115 V:The Organizer.......... 250.00
116 Return to Smallville 250.00
117 A:Lex Luthor 250.00
118 F:Jimmy Olsen........... 250.00
119 A:Zoll Orr............... 250.00
120 V:Gadget Grim........... 250.00
121 I:XL-49 (Futureman)....... 200.00
122 In the White House........ 200.00
123 CS,pre-Supergirl tryout
  A:Jor-El & Lara.......... 225.00
124 F:Lois Lane 200.00
125 F:Superman College Story.. 200.00
126 F:Lois Lane 200.00
127 WB,I&O:Titano........... 225.00
128 V:Vard & Boka 200.00
129 WB,I&O:Lori Lemaris 225.00
130 A:Krypto,the Superdog.... 200.00
131 A:Mr. Mxyzptlk 150.00
132 A:Batman & Robin 150.00
133 F:Superman Joins Army.... 150.00
134 A:Supergirl & Krypto 150.00
135 A:Lori Lemaris,Mr.Mxyzptlk . 150.00
136 O:Discovery Kryptonite.... 150.00
137 CS,I:Super-Menace....... 150.00
138 A:Titano,Lori Lemaris 150.00
139 CS,O:Red Kryptonite 150.00
140 WB,I:Bizarro Jr,Bizarro
  Supergirl,Blue Kryptonite.... 175.00
141 I:Lyla Lerrol,A:Jor-EL
  & Lara 125.00
142 WB,CS,A:Al Capone 125.00
143 WB,F:Bizarro meets
  Frankenstein 125.00
144 O:Superboy's 1st Public
  Appearance 125.00
145 F:April Fool's Issue 125.00
146 F:Superman's life story..... 175.00

147 CS,I:Adult Legion......... 150.00
148 CS,V:Mxyzptlk 150.00
149 CS:A:Luthor,C:JLA........ 150.00
150 CS,KS,V:Mxyzptlk 75.00
151 CS..................... 75.00
152 A:Legion 75.00
153 CS..................... 75.00
154 CS,V:Mzyzptlk 75.00
155 WB,CS,V:Cosmic Man 75.00
156 CS,A:Legion,Batman 75.00
157 CS,I:Gold kryptonite...... 80.00
158 CS,I:Nightwing&Flamebird ... 75.00
159 CS,Imaginary Tale
  F:Lois Lane 75.00
160 CS,F:Perry White......... 75.00
161 D:Ma & Pa Kent.......... 80.00
162 A:Legion 80.00
163 CS..................... 60.00
164 CS,Luthor,I:Lexor........ 60.00
165 CS,A:Saturn Woman 60.00
166 CS..................... 60.00
167 CS,I:Ardora,Brainiac 100.00
168 CS..................... 60.00
169 Great DC Contest 60.00
170 CS,A:J.F.Kennedy,Luthor ... 60.00
171 CS,Mxyzptlk............. 60.00
172 CS,Luthor,Brainiac........ 60.00
173 CS,A:Batman........... 60.00
174 Mxyzptlk 60.00
175 CS,Luthor 60.00
176 CS,Green Kryptonite 60.00
177 Fortress of Solitude 60.00
178 CS, Red Kryptonite 60.00
179 CS,Clark Kent in Marines... 60.00
180 CS..................... 60.00
181 Superman 2965.......... 60.00
182 CS,Toyman 60.00
183 giant 60.00
184 Secrets of the Fortress...... 50.00
185 JM,Superman's Achilles
  Heel.................. 50.00
186 CS,The Two Ghosts of
  Superman 50.00
187 giant 50.00
188 V:Zunial,The Murder Man.... 55.00
189 WB,The Mystery of Krypton's
  Second Doom 50.00
190 WB,I:Amalak 50.00
191 The Prisoner of Demon 50.00
192 CS,Imaginary Story,
  I:Superman Jr. 50.00
193 giant 50.00
194 CS,Imaginary,A:Supes Jr. ... 50.00
195 CS,V:Amalak 50.00
196 WB,reprint 50.00

Superman #226 © DC Comics Inc.

197 giant 50.00
198 CS,F:The Real Clark Kent ... 50.00
199 CS,F:Superman/Flash race,
  A:JLA................. 225.00
200 WB,A:Brainiac 50.00
201 CS,F:Clark Kent Abandons
  Superman 35.00
202 A:Bizarro,(giant size) 40.00
203 F:When Superman Killed His
  Friends 35.00
204 NA(c),RA,A:Lori Lemaris 35.00
205 NA(c),I:Black Zero 35.00
206 NA(c),F:The Day Superman
  Became An Assistant 35.00
207 CS,F:The Case Of the
  Collared Crimefighter 40.00
208 NA(c),CS.............. 35.00
209 CS,F:The Clark Kent Monster 35.00
210 CS,F:Clark Kent's Last Rites . 35.00
211 CS,RA 35.00
212 giant 45.00
213 CS,JA,V:Luthor,C:Brainiac 5.. 35.00
214 NA(c),CS,JA,F:The Ghosts
  That Haunted Superman 30.00
215 NA(c),CS,JA,V:Luthor,
  Imaginary Story 30.00
216 JKu(c),RA,Superman in Nam . 30.00
217 CS,A:Mr.Mxyzptlk........ 35.00
218 CS,JA,A:Mr.Mxyzptlk 30.00
219 CS,F:Clark Kent-Hero,
  Superman Public Enemy 30.00
220 CS,A:Flash 30.00
221 CS,F:The Two Ton Superman 30.00
222 giant 45.00
223 CS,A:Supergirl........... 30.00
224 CS,Imaginary Story 30.00
225 CS,F:The Secret of the
  Super Imposter.......... 30.00
226 CS,F:When Superman Became
  King Kong 30.00
227 Krypton,(giant)............ 35.00
228 CS,DA................. 30.00
229 WB,CS 30.00
230 CS,DA,Luthor 30.00
231 CS,DA,Luthor 30.00
232 F:Krypton,(giant)......... 35.00
233 CS,MA,I:Quarrum 30.00
234 NA(c),CS,MA........... 30.00
235 CS,MA................ 30.00
236 CS,MA,DG,A:Green Arrow... 30.00
237 NA(c),CS,MA........... 30.00
238 CS,MA,GM 30.00
239 giant 40.00
240 CS,DG,MK,A:I-Ching 12.00
241 CS,MA,A:Wonder Woman ... 15.00
242 CS,MA,A:Wonder Woman ... 15.00
243 CS,MA................ 15.00
244 CS,MA................ 15.00
245 100 pg reprints........... 25.00
246 CS,MA,RB,I:S.T.A.R. Labs .. 15.00
247 CS,MA,Guardians o/Universe. 15.00
248 CS,MA:A:Luthor,I:Galactic
  Golem 15.00
249 CS,MA,DD,NA,I:Terra-Man... 20.00
250 CS,MA,Terraman 15.00
251 CS,MA,RB.............. 15.00
252 NA(c),rep.100pgs......... 25.00
253 CS,MA................ 15.00
254 CS,MA,NA.............. 20.00
255 CS,MA,DG.............. 7.00
256 CS,MA................ 7.00
257 CS,MA,DD,DG,A:Tomar-Re ... 7.00
258 CS,MA,DC.............. 7.00
259 CS,MA,A:Terra-Man 7.00
260 CS,DC,I:Valdemar 7.00
261 CS,MA,V:Star Sapphire 7.00
262 CS,MA................ 7.00
263 CS,MA,DD,FMc.......... 7.00
264 DC,CS,I:SteveLombard 7.00
265 CS,MA................ 7.00
266 CS,MA,DD,V:Snowman 7.00

Superman #235 © DC Comics, Inc.

267 CS,MA,BO. 7.00
268 CS,BO,DD,MA,A:Batgirl. 7.00
269 CS,MA. 7.00
270 CS,MA,V:Valdemar 7.00
271 CS,BO,DG,V:Brainiac 7.00
272 100pg.reprints 25.00
273 CS,DG. 7.00
274 CS. 7.00
275 CS,DG,FMc. 7.00
276 CS,BO,I&O:Captain Thunder . . 7.00
277 CS. 7.00
278 CS,BO,Terraman,100page . . . 25.00
279 CS,Batgirl,Batman 7.00
280 CS,BO. 7.00
281 CS,BO,I:Vartox 7.00
282 CS,KS,N:Luthor. 7.00
283 CS,BO,Mxyzptlk. 7.00
284 CS,BO,100p reprint 25.00
285 CS,BO. 7.00
286 CS,BO. 7.00
287 CS,BO,R:Krypto. 7.00
288 CS,BO. 7.00
289 CS,BO,JL 7.00
290 CS,V:Mxyzptlk 7.00
291 CS,BO. 7.00
292 CS,BO,AM,O:Luthor 7.00
293 CS,BO. 7.00
294 CS,JL,A:Brain Storm 7.00
295 CS,BO. 7.00
296 CS,BO,Identity Crisis #1 . . . . 7.00
297 CS,BO,Identity Crisis #2 . . . . 7.00
298 CS,BO,Identity Crisis #3 . . . . 7.00
299 CS,BO,Identity Crisis #4
    A:Luthor,Brainiac,Bizarro 7.00
300 CS,BO,2001,anniversary 22.00
301 BO,JL,V:Solomon Grundy 4.00
302 JL,BO,V:Luthor,A:Atom 4.00
303 CS,BO,I:Thunder&Lightning . . . 4.00
304 CS,BO,V:Parasite 4.00
305 CS,BO,V:Toyman. 4.00
306 CS,BO,V:Bizarro 4.00
307 NA(c),JL,FS,A:Supergirl. 4.00
308 NA(c),JL,FS,A:Supergirl. 4.00
309 JL,FS,A:Supergirl. 3.50
310 CS,V:Metallo 3.50
311 CS,FS,A:Flash 2.50
312 CS,FS,A:Supergirl 3.50
313 NA(c),CS,DA,A:Supergirl 3.50
314 NA(c),CS,DA,A:Gr.Lantern. . . . 3.50
315 CS,DA,V:Blackrock 3.50
316 CS,DA,V:Metallo 3.50
317 NA(c),CS,DA,V:Metallo 3.50
318 CS. 3.00
319 CS,V:Solomon Grundy. 3.00
320 CS,V:Solomon Grundy. 3.00

321 CS,V:Parasite 3.00
322 CS,V:Solomon Grundy. 3.00
323 CS,DA,I:Atomic Skull 3.00
324 CS,A:Atomic Skull 3.00
325 CS. 3.00
326 CS,V:Blackrock 3.00
327 CS,KS,V:Kobra,C:JLA 3.00
328 CS,KS,V:Kobra 3.00
329 KS,CS 3.00
330 CS,F:glasses explained 3.00
331 CS,I:Master Jailer 3.00
332 CS,V:Master Jailer. 3.00
333 CS,V:Bizarro 3.00
334 CS. 3.00
335 CS,W:Mxyzptlk 3.00
336 CS,V:Rose And Thorn 3.00
337 CS,A:Brainiac,Bizarro 3.00
338 CS,F:Kandor enlarged 3.00
339 CS,I:N.R.G.X 3.00
340 CS,V:N.R.G.X 3.00
341 CS,F:Major Disaster. 3.00
342 CS,V:Chemo 3.00
343 CS. 3.00
344 CS,A:Phantom Stranger. 3.00
345 CS,`When time ran backward' . 3.00
346 CS,`Streak of Bad Luck'. 3.00
347 JL 3.00
348 CS. 3.00
349 CS,V:Mxyzptlk 3.00
350 CS,`Clark Kent's Vanishing
    Classmate'. 3.00
351 CS,JL,A:Mxyzptlk. 3.00
352 CS,RB 3.00
353 CS,origin 3.00
354 CS,JSon,I:Superman 2020. . . . 3.00
355 CS,JSon,F:Superman 2020 . . . 3.00
356 CS,V:Vartox 3.00
357 CS,DCw,F:Superman 2020 . . . 3.00
358 CS,DG,DCw 3.00
359 CS. 3.00
360 CS,AS,F:World of Krypton 3.00
361 CS,AS 3.00
362 CS,KS,DA 3.00
363 CS,RB,C:Luthor. 3.00
364 GP(c),RB,AS 3.00
365 CS,KS 3.00
366 CS,KS 3.00
367 CS,GK,F:World of Krypton 3.00
368 CS,AS 3.00
369 RB,FMc,V:Parasite 3.00
370 CS,KS,FMc,A:Chemo 3.00
371 CS 3.00
372 CS,GK,F:Superman 2021 . . . . 3.00
373 CS,V:Vartox 3.00
374 GK(c),CS,DA,KS,V:Vartox . . . 3.00
375 CS,DA,GK,V:Vartox 3.00
376 CS,DA,CI,BO,SupergirlPrev. . . 2.75
377 GK(c),CS,V:Terra-Man 2.75
378 CS. 2.75
379 CS,V:Bizarro 2.75
380 CS. 2.75
381 GK(c),CS. 2.75
382 GK(c),CS. 2.75
383 CS. 2.75
384 GK(c),CS. 2.75
385 GK(c),CS,V:Luthor. 2.75
386 GK(c),CS,V:Luthor. 2.75
387 GK(c),CS. 2.75
388 GK(c),CS. 2.75
389 GK(c),CS. 2.75
390 GK(c),CS,V:Vartox 2.75
391 GK(c),CS,V:Vartox 2.75
392 GK(c),CS,V:Vartox 2.75
393 IN,DG,V:Master Jailer 2.75
394 CS,V:Valdemar 2.75
395 CS,V:Valdemar 2.75
396 CS. 2.75
397 EB,V:Kryptonite Man 2.75
398 CS,AS,DJ 2.75
399 CS,BO,EB 2.75
400 HC(c),FM,AW,JO,JSo,MR,

Superman #299 © DC Comics, Inc.

    TA,WP,MK,KJ,giant 8.00
401 CS,BO,V:Luthor. 2.75
402 CS,BO,WB 2.75
403 CS,BO,AS 2.75
404 CI,BO,V:Luthor 2.75
405 KS,KK,AS,F:Super-Batman . . . 2.75
406 IN,AS,KK. 2.75
407 IN,V:Mxyzptlk 2.75
408 CS,AW,JRu,F:Nuclear
    Holocaust. 2.75
409 CS,AW,KS. 2.75
410 CS,AW,V:Luthor. 2.75
411 CS,MA,F:End Earth-Prime 2.75
412 CS,AW,V:Luthor. 2.75
413 CS,AW,V:Luthor. 2.75
414 CS,AW,Crisis tie-in. 3.00
415 CS,AW,Crisis,W:Super Girl . . . 3.00
416 CS,AW,Luthor 2.75
417 CS,V:Martians 2.75
418 CS,V:Metallo 2.75
419 CS,V:Iago 2.75
420 CS,F:Nightmares 2.75
421 CS,V:Mxyzptlk 2.75
422 BB(c),CS,TY,LMa,V:Werewolf . 2.75
423 AMo(s),CS,GP,F:Last
    Superman 8.00
Ann.#1 I:Supergirl Rep. 1,000.00
Ann.#2 I&O:Titano 450.00
Ann.#3 I:Legion 300.00
Ann.#4 O:Legion 250.00
Ann.#5 A:Krypton 200.00
Ann.#6 A:Legion. 200.00
Ann.#7 O:Superman,Silver Anniv. 150.00
Ann.#8 F:Secret origins 125.00
Ann.#9 GK(c),ATh,TA,CS,
    A:Batman. 6.00
Ann.#10 CS,MA,F:Sword of
    Superman 5.00
Ann.#11 AMo(s),DGb,A:Batman,
    Robin,Wonder Woman 6.00
Ann.#12 BB(c),AS,A:Lex Luthor,
    Last War Suit 3.00
Game Give-away 10.00
Giveaway CS,AT 2.00
Pizza Hut 1977. . . . . 6.00
Radio Shack 1980 JSw,DG. 5.00
Radio Shack 1981 CS 5.00
Radio Shack 1982 CS 5.00
Spec.#1 GK 3.50
Spec.#2 GK,V:Brainiac 3.50
Spec.#3 IN,V:Amazo 3.50
Superman III Movie,CS. 1.50
Superman IV Movie,DH,DG,FMc . . 1.50
Becomes:

DC COMICS

ADVENTURES OF
SUPERMAN
1987

424 JOy,I:Man O'War 2.50
425 JOy,Man O'War 2.25
426 JOy,Legends,V:Apokolips. . . . 2.25
427 JOy,V:Qurac 2.25
428 JOy,V:Qurac,I:JerryWhite 2.25
429 JOy,V:Concussion 2.25
430 JOy,V:Fearsome Five. 2.25
431 JOy,A:Combattor 2.00
432 JOy,I:Jose Delgado 2.00
433 JOy,V:Lex Luthor 2.00
434 JOy,I:Gang Buster 2.50
435 JOy,A:Charger. 2.00
436 JOy,Millenium X-over 2.00
437 JOy,Millenium X-over 2.00
438 JOy,N:Brainiac. 2.50
439 JOy,R:Superman Robot 2.00
440 JOy,A:Batman,Wond.Woman . . 2.00
441 JOy,V:Mr.Mxyzptlk 2.00
442 JOy,V:Dreadnaught,A:JLI 2.00
443 JOy,DHz,I:Husque 2.00
444 JOy,Supergirl SagaPt.2 . . . . . 2.00
445 JOy,V:Brainiac 2.00
446 JOy,A:Gangbuster,
    A:Luthor's Old Costume 2.00
447 JOy,A:Gangbuster 2.00
448 JOy,I:Dubbilex,A:Gangbuster . . 2.00
449 JOy,Invasion X-over. 2.00
450 JOy,Invasion X-over. 2.00
451 JOy,`Superman in Space'. 2.00
452 DJu,V:Wordbringer. 2.00
453 JOy,DJu,A:Gangbuster 2.00
454 JOy,DJu,I:New Mongul. 2.50
455 DJu,ATb,A:Eradicator. 3.50
456 DJu,ATb,V:Turmoil 2.00
457 DJu,V:Intergang. 2.00
458 DJu,KJ,R:Elastic Lad
    (Jimmy Olsen) 2.00
459 DJu,V:Eradicator 3.00
460 DJu,NKu,V:Eradicator 3.00
461 DJu,GP,V:Eradicator 3.00
462 DJu,ATb,Homeless
    Christmas Story 2.00
463 DJu,ATb,Superman Races
    Flash 3.00
464 DJu,ATb,Day of Krypton
    Man #2,A:Lobo. 3.50
465 DJu,ATb,Day of Krypton
    Man #5,V:Draaga 3.00
466 DJu,DG,V:Team Excalibur
    Astronauts,I:Hank Henshaw
    (becomes Cyborg Superman). . 4.50
467 DJu,ATb,A:Batman 2.50
468 DJu,ATb,Man Of Steel's
    Journal,V:Hank Henshaw 3.00
469 DJu,ATb,V:Dreadnaught. 2.00
470 DJu,ATb,Soul Search #3,
    D:Jerry White 2.00
471 CS,Sinbad Contract #2 . . . . . 2.00
472 DJu,ATb,Krisis of Krimson
    Kryptonite #2 . . . . 3.00
473 DJu,ATb,A:Green Lantern,
    Guy Gardner 2.00
474 DJu,ATb,Drunk Driving issue . . 2.00
475 DJu,ATb,V:Kilgrave,Sleez 2.00
476 DJu,BBr,Time & Time Again,pt.1,
    A:Booster Gold,Legion 2.00
477 DJu,BBr,T & T Again,pt.4,
    A:Legion. 2.00
478 DJu,BBr,T & T Again,pt.7,
    A:Legion,Linear Man 2.00
479 EH,Red Glass Trilogy#2. . . . . 2.00
480 JOy,DJu,BMc,TG,BBr,CS,
    Revenge of the Krypton
    Man,pt.3. . . . . 3.00
481 1st TG Supes,DHz,V:Parasite . 2.00
482 TG,DHz,V:Parasite 2.00
483 TG,DHz,V:Blindspot. 2.00

484 TG,Blackout #1,V:Mr.Z 2.00
485 TG,DHz,Blackout #5,A:Mr.Z . . 2.00
486 TG,V:Purge 2.00
487 TG,DHz,X-mas,A:Agent
    Liberty 2.00
488 TG,Panic in the Sky,pt.3,
    V:Brainiac. 3.00
489 TG,Panic in the Sky,Epiloge. . . 2.50
490 TG,A:Agent Liberty,Husque . . 1.75
491 TG,DHz,V:Cerberus,Metallo. . . 1.75
492 WS(c),V:Sons of Liberty,
    A:Agent Liberty. 1.75
493 TG,Blaze/Satanus War,pt.1 . . . 1.75
494 TG,DHz,I:Kismet 1.75
495 TG,DHz,A:Forever People,
    Darkseid. 1.75
496 V:Mr.Mxyzptlk,C:Doomsday . . 2.00
496a 2nd printing 1.50
497 TG,Doomsday Pt.3,A:Maxima,
    Bloodwynd 5.00
497a 2nd printing 1.75
498 TG,Funeral for a Friend#1 . . . . 4.00
498a 2nd Printing 1.25
499 TG,DHz,Funeral for a
    Friend#5. . . . . 3.50
500 JOy(c),B:KK(s),TG,DJu,JBg,JG,
    BBr,Bagged,Superman in limbo,
    I:Four Supermen,Direct Sales. . 3.50
500a Newsstand Ed. 3.00
500b Platinum Ed. 15.00
501 TG,Reign of Supermen#2,Direct
    Sales,Die-Cut(c),Mini-poster
    F:Superboy 3.00
501a Newstand Ed. 2.00
502 TG,A:Supergirl,V:Stinger 2.00
503 TG,Cyborg Superman Vs.
    Superboy 2.50
504 TG,DHz,A:All Supermen,
    V:Mongul 2.50
505 TG,DHz,Superman returns to
    Metropolis,Holografx(c). 2.50
505a Newstand Ed. 2.00
506 TG,DHz,A:Guardian. 1.75
507 Spilled Blood#1,V:Bloodsport. . 1.75
508 BKi,A:Challengers of the
    Unknown 1.75
509 BKi,A:Auron. 1.75
510 BKi,Bizarro's World#2,
    V:Bizarro 1.75
511 BKi,A:Guardian 1.75
512 BKi,V:Parasite 1.75
513 BKi,Battle for Metropolis #4 . . . 1.75
514 BKi,Fall of Metropolis #4 . . . . 1.75
515 BKi,Massacre in Metropolis . . . 1.75

The Adventures of Superman #499
© DC Comics Inc.

516 BKi,Zero Hour,I:Alpha
    Centurion. 1.50
517 BKi,deathtrap. 1.50
518 BKi 1.50
519 KK,BKi,Secret of Superman's
    Tomb 1.50
520 SI,KK,JMz,100 crimes at
    midnight. 1.50
521 SI,KK,R:Thorn 1.50
522 SI,KKIdentity known. 1.50
523 SI,KK,Death of C.Kent,pt.2. . . . 1.50
524 SI,KK,Death of C.Kent,pt.6
    [New Miraweb format begins] . . 2.00
525 SI,KK. 2.00
526 Bloodsport vs. Bloodsport 2.00
527 . . . . 2.00
528 Trial of Superman,prelude 2.00
529 Trial of Superman 2.00
530 KK,SI,JMz,Trial of Superman . . 2.00
531 KK,SI,JMz,Trial of Superman,
    concl. 2.00
532 KK,SI,JMz, return of Lori
    Lemaris 2.00
533 KK,SI,JMz 2.00
534 KK,SI,JMz,V:Lord Satannus . . . 2.00
535 KK,SI,JMz,Lois & LoriLemaris . . 2.00
536. . . . . 2.00
537. . . . . 2.00
538. . . . . 2.00
539 F:Guardian and the Newsboy
    Legion 2.00
540 KK(s),TyD,KIS,A:Ferro, Final
    Night tie-in 2.00
541 KK(s),SI,JMz,on Honeymoon,
    A:Superboy,Tana Moon,Kekona 2.00
542 KK&JOy(s),PR,JMz,V:Misa . . . 2.00
543 . . . . 2.00
544 KK(s),SI,JMz,"Who Killed Clark
    Kent in braod daylight?. 2.00
545 KK(s),SEa,JMz,Return of the
    Atomic Skull,new blue costume 2.00
546 KK(s),SI,JMz,V:Metallo, uses
    new powers 2.00
547 KK(s),SI,JMz,Superman goes
    to Kandor,A:The Atom 2.00
548 KK(s),SI,JMz,V:Lex Luthor 2.00
549 KK(s),SI,JMz,F:Jimmy Olsen . . 2.00
550 KK(s),SI,TGu,JMz,DRo, 48pg . 3.50
551 DJu,TGu,DRo,Genesis,
    V:Cyborg 2.00
552 KK,TGu,DRo,V:Parasite. 2.00
553 KK,TGu,DRo,disappearances . 2.00
554 KK,TGu,DRo,disappearances . 2.00
555 KK,TRu,DRo,Red/Blue x-over . 2.00
556 KK,TRu,DRo,Red & Blue 2.00
557 KK,VS,DRo,Millennium Giants
    x-over. 2.00
558 KK,JOy,DRo,silver age?,pt.1 . . 2.00
559 KK,JOy,DRo,silver age?,pt.2 . . 2.00
560 KK,JOy,DRo,silver age?,pt.3 . . 2.00
561 KK,JOy,TGu,DRo,Waverider . . 2.00
562 KK(s),JOy,TGu,DRo,Lexcom . . 2.00
563 RMz,TGb,TP,City of the
    Future, pt.4 x-over 2.00
564 KK&JOy(s),TGu,DRo,
    A:Geo-Force 2.00
565 KK&JOy(s),TGu,DRo,A:JLA . . . 2.00
566 KK&JOy(s),TGu,DRo,V:Lex
    Luthor 2.00
567 KK&JOy(s),DRo,PR, ... 2.00
568 LSi(s),TMo,DRo,V:Metallo 2.00
569 LSi(s),TMo,DRo,V:S.C.U. 2.00
570 RMz&TPe(s),TGb,TP,
    A:JLA,pt.2 x-over 2.00
571 LSi(s),DRo,V:Atomic Skull 2.00
Ann.#1 JSn(c),DJu,I:Word Bringer . 3.00
Ann.#2 CS/JBy,KGa/DG,BMc,
    A:L.E.G.I.O.N.'90 (Lobo). 4.00
Ann.#3 BHi,JRu,DG,
    Armageddon 2001. . . . . 3.00
Ann.#4 BMc,A:Lobo,Guy Gardner,

DC COMICS

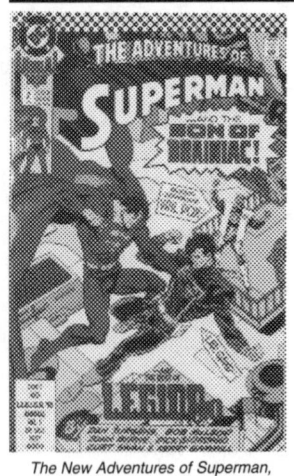

The New Adventures of Superman, Ann. #2 © DC Comics, Inc.

Eclipso tie-in. 3.00
Ann.#5 TG,I:Sparx 2.75
Ann.#6 MMi(c),Elseworlds Story . . . 3.00
Ann.#7 Year One Story 4.00
Ann.#8 Legends o/t Dead Earth . . . 2.95
Ann.#9 Pulp Heroes (Western) 3.95
Spec.#1,000,000 ALa&DAn(s)LMa,
A:Teen Titans, V:Solaris 2.00

SUPERMAN'S BUDDY
1954
1 w/costume 1,000.00
1 w/out costume 400.00

SUPERMAN'S
CHRISTMAS ADVENTURE
1 (1940) 4,000.00
2 (1944). 900.00

SUPERMAN AND THE
GREAT CLEVELAND FIRE
1948
1 for Hospital Fund 500.00

SUPERMAN (miniature)
1942
1 Py-Co-Pay Tooth Powder
Give- Away. 650.00
2 CS,Superman Time Capsule. . 450.00
3 CS,Duel in Space 400.00
4 CS,Super Show in Metropolis . 400.00

SUPERMAN RECORD
COMIC
1966
1 w/record 125.00
1 w/out record 75.00

SUPERMAN
SPECTACULAR
1982
1 A:Luthor & Terra-Man 2.50

SUPERMAN-TIM
STORE PAMPHLETS
1942
Superman-Tim store Monthly
Membership Pamphlet, 16
pages of stories, games,
puzzles (1942), each 700.00
Superman-Tim store Monthly
Membership Pamphlet, 16
pages of stories, games,
puzzles (1943), each 300.00
Superman-Tim store Monthly
Membership Pamphlet, 16
pages of stories, games,
puzzles (1944), each 225.00
Superman-Tim store Monthly
Membership Pamphlet, 16
pages of stories, games,
puzzles (1945), each 175.00
Superman-Tim store Monthly
Membership Pamphlet, 14-16
pages of stories, games,
puzzles, 5"x8" color(c),
(1946), each. 300.00
Superman-Tim stamp
album, 1946 . . . . 250.00
Superman-Tim store Monthly
Membership Pamphlet, 14-16
pages of stories, games,
puzzles, 5"x8" color(c),
(1947), each. 200.00
Superman-Tim stamp album,
Superman story, 1947. . . . . . 275.00
Superman-Tim store Monthly
Membership Pamphlet, 14-16
pages of stories, games,
puzzles, 5"x8" color(c),(1948),
each 150.00
Superman-Tim stamp
album, 1948 . . . . 175.00
Superman-Tim store Monthly
Membership Pamphlet, 14-16
pages of stories, games,
puzzles, 5"x8" color(c),
(1949), each. 150.00
Superman-Tim store Monthly
Membership Pamphlet, 14-16
pages of stories, games,
puzzles, 5"x8" color(c)
(1950), each. 200.00

SUPERMAN WORKBOOK
1945
1 rep. Superman #14 . . . . 1,000.00

SUPERMAN
[2nd Regular Series] 1987–99
1 JBy,TA,I:Metallo 5.00
2 JBy,TA,V:Luthor 3.00
3 JBy,TA,Legends tie-in 2.50
4 JBy,KK,V:Bloodsport. 2.25
5 JBy,KK,V:Host 2.00
6 JBy,KK,V:Host 2.00
7 JBy,KK,V:Rampage 2.00
8 JBy,KK,A:Superboy,Legion 2.00
9 JBy,KK,V:Joker. 4.00
10 JBy,KK,V:Rampage 2.00
11 JBy,KK,V:Mr.Mxyzptlk 2.00
12 JBy,KK,A:Lori Lemerias 2.00
13 JBy,KK,Millenium. 2.00
14 JBy,KK,A:Green Lantern 2.00
15 JBy,KK,I:New Prankster. 2.00
16 JBy,KK,A:Prankster 2.00
17 JBy,KK,O:Silver Banshee. 2.00
18 MMi,KK,A:Hawkman 2.00
19 JBy,V:Skyhook. 2.00
20 JBy,KK,A:Doom Patrol 2.50
21 JBy,A:Supergirl 2.00

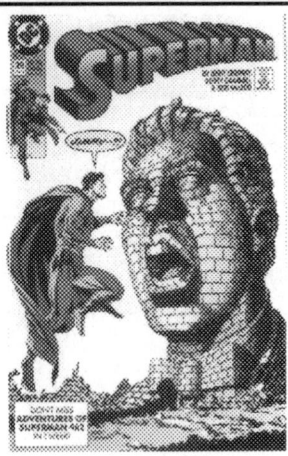

Superman #39 © DC Comics, Inc.

22 JBy,A:Supergirl 2.00
23 MMi,CR,O:Silver Banshee 2.00
24 KGa,V:Rampage 2.00
25 KGa,V:Brainiac 2.00
26 KGa,BBr,V:Baron Sunday 2.00
27 KGa,BBr,V:Guardian 2.00
28 KGa,BBr,Supes Leaves Earth . . 2.00
29 DJu,BBr,V:Word Bringer. 2.00
30 KGa,DJu,A:Lex Luthor. 2.00
31 DJu,PCu,V:Mxyzptlk 2.00
32 KGa,V:Mongul 2.00
33 KGa,A:Cleric 2.00
34 KGa,V:Skyhook. 2.00
35 CS,KGa,A:Brainiac 2.00
36 JOy,V:Prankster. 2.00
37 JOy,A:Guardian 2.00
38 JOy,Jimmy Olsen Vanished 2.00
39 JOy,KGa,V:Husque 2.00
40 JOy,V:Four Armed Terror 2.00
41 JOy,Day of Krypton Man #1,
A:Lobo 3.50
42 JOy,Day of Krypton Man #4,
V:Draaga 3.50
43 JOy,V:Krypton Man 2.00
44 JOy,A:Batman 2.00
45 JOy,F:Jimmy Olsen's Dairy 2.00
46 DJu,JOy,A:Jade,Obsidian,
I:New Terra-Man. 2.00
47 JOy,Soul Search #2,V:Blaze . . . 2.00
48 CS,Sinbad Contract #1 . . . . . . 2.00
49 JOy,Krisis of K.Kryptonite#1. . . . 3.00
50 JBy,KGa,DJu,JOy,BBr,CS,Krisis
of Krimson Kryptonite #4,
Clark Proposes To Lois. 6.00
50a 2nd printing 1.50
51 JOy,I:Mr.Z 1.75
52 KGa,V:Terra-Man. 1.75
53 JOy,Superman reveals i.d. 3.50
53a 2nd Printing. 1.25
54 JOy,KK,Time & Time Again#3 . . 1.75
55 JOy,KK,Time & Time Again#6 . . 1.75
56 EH,KK,Red Glass Trilogy#1 . . . 1.75
57 JOy,DJu,BBr,ATi,JBg,BMc,TG,
Revenge o/t Krypton Man #2 . . 3.50
58 DJu,BBr,I:Bloodhounds 1.75
59 DJu,BBr,A:Linear Men 1.75
60 DJu,EB,I:Agent Liberty,
V:Intergang 2.00
61 DJu,BBr,A:Waverider,
V:Linear Men 1.75
62 DJu,BBr,Blackout #4,A:Mr.Z. . . . 1.75
63 DJu,A:Aquaman 1.75
64 JG,Christmas issue 1.75
65 DJu,Panic in the Sky#2,
I:New Justice League 3.50

66 DJu,Panic in the Sky#6,	Super Heroes. 2.00	Adventure) DJu 3.95
V:Brainiac. 8.00	120 DJu(s),RF,JRu, ... 2.00	Ann.#10 DJu(s),PR,Clv,BWr,
67 DJu,Aftermath 1.75	121 DJu(s),RF,JRu,"They Call it	Ghosts 3.00
68 DJu,V:Deathstroke. 1.75	Suicide Slum". 2.00	Ann.#11 JoP,AAd(c),JLApe:Gorilla
69 WS(c),DJu,A:Agent Liberty 1.75	122 DJu(s),RF,JRu,Lois visits	Warfare 2.95
70 DJu,BBr,A:Robin,V:Vampires . . . 1.75	Fortress of Solitude 2.00	Spec.#1,000,000 DAn&ALa(s),NBy . 2.00
71 DJu,Blaze/Satanus War 1.75	123 DJu(s),RF,Jru,Superman gets	Giant Ann.#1 Replica edition. 5.00
72 DJu,Crisis at Hand#2. . . . . . . 1.75	New Costume 2.00	Giant #1 80-page 5.00
73 DJu,A:Waverider,V:Linear	123a collector's edition, glow-in-	Giant #2 80-page 5.00
Men,C:Doomsday. 4.00	the-dark cover, ... 2.00	Spec.#0 PeerPressure,pt.3 (1994) . 2.00
73a 2nd printing 1.50	124 DJu(s),RF,JRu,A:Scorn, prince	Spec.King of the World, foil. 5.00
74 DJu,V:Doomsday,A:JLA 7.00	of Kandor 2.00	Spec.King of the World, reg. 4.00
74a 2nd printing 1.75	125 DJu(s),RF,JRu,Kandor and	Spec. Superman: Lois Lane,
75 DJu,V:Doomsday,D:Superman,	Metropolis,A:Atom 2.00	Girlfrenzy (1998) 2.00
Collectors Ed. 15.00	126 DJu(s),RF,JRu,A:Batman. 2.00	Spec.#1 WS,V:L.Luthor,`Sandman' . 6.00
75a newstand Ed. 9.00	127 DJu(s),RF,JRu,F:Jimmy Olsen . 2.00	Spec. Superman Plus One (1997) . 3.00
75b 2nd printing 4.00	128 DJu(s),RF,JRu, Genesis tie-in . 2.00	Spec.#1 Superman: The Earth
75c 3rd printing 1.50	129 DJu(s),PR,JRu,A:Scorn 2.00	Stealers, JBy,CS,JOy (1988) . . 3.50
75d 4th Printing 1.50	130 DJu(s),RF,JRu,dragon's tooth. . 2.00	2nd printing 3.00
75e Platinum Ed. 60.00	131 DJu(s),RF,JRu,Luthor &	Spec. Superman Forever, KK,DJu,LSi,
76 DJu,BBr,Funeral for Friend#4. . . 3.00	Contessa's kid 2.00	JBy,SI,DG, Luthor's kidnapped
77 DJu,BBr,Funeral for Friend#8. . . 3.00	132 DJu,RF,JRu,Red/Blue x-over . . 2.00	daughter (1998) 5.00
78 DJu,BBr,Reign of Supermen#3,	133 . . . . 2.00	Deluxe ed.,AxR(c), lenticular . . 6.00
Die-Cut(c),Mini poster,F:Cyborg	134 DJu,RF,JRu,Millennium Giants. 2.00	Spec.#1 Superman: The Legacy of
Supes,A:Doomsday 2.50	135 DJu,RF,JRu,aftermath 2.00	Superman,WS,JG,F:Guardian,
78a Newsstand Ed. 2.00	136 DJu,PR,JRu,The Superman	Waverider,Sinbad (1993) 4.00
79 DJu,BBr,Memorial Service for	of 2999 A.D., pt.1 . . . . 2.00	Spec. Superman/Toyman (1996). . . 2.00
Clark 2.00	137 DJu,PR,JRu,2999 AD,pt.2 . . . . 2.00	Spec. Team Superman, MMr(s),
80 DJu,BBr,Coast City Blows up,	138 DJu,PR,JRu,2999 AD,pt.3 . . . . 2.00	DHz,48-page,F:Superboy,
V:Mongul. 4.00	139 DJu(s),JSn,JRu,V:Dominus . . . 2.00	Supergirl & Steel 3.00
81 DJu,O:Cyborg Superman. 3.50	140 RMz(s),TGb,TP,City of the	Spec. Team Superman Secret Files 5.00
82 DJu,Chromium(c),A:All Supermen,	Future, pt.3 x-over 2.00	Spec. 3-D #1 LSi,V:Mainframe 4.00
V:Cyborg Superman. 5.00	141 DJu(s),SEa,JRu,I:Outburst. . . . 2.00	Spec. Whatever Happened to the
82a Newstand Ed. 2.25	142 DJu(s),JRu,F:Outburst 2.00	Man of Tomorrow 6.00
83 DJu,A:Batman 1.75	143 DJu(s),SEp,JRu, ... 2.00	Newstime-The Life and Death of
84 DJu,V:Toyman 1.75	144 DJu(s),SEp,JRu,V:Lex Luthor. . 2.00	the Man of Steel-Magazine,
85 DJu,V:Toyman 1.75	145 DJu(s),SEp,JRu,hate mail 2.00	DJu,BBr,JOy,JG,JBg. 3.25
86 DJu,A:Sun Devils. 1.75	146 DJu(s),SEp,JRu,V:Toyman. . . . 2.00	Spec.#1 Superman Gallery (1993) . 2.95
87 DJu(c&s),SI,JRu,Bizzaro's	147 RMz(s),TGb,BAn,A:JLA,pt.1. . . 2.00	Secret Files #1 Superman Villains . 5.00
World#1, R:Bizarro. 1.75	148 DJu(s),SEp,JRu, ... 2.00	Secret Files #2. . . . . 5.00
88 DJu(c&s),SI,JRu,Bizzaro's	149 RF,SB,Strange Visitor,pt.1 . . . . 2.00	GN The Death of Superman rep. Man
World#5, D:Bizarro. 1.75	Ann.#1 RF,BBr,A:Titano 2.00	of Steel #17–#19, Superman
89 DJu(c&s),V:Cadmus Project. . . . 1.75	Ann.#2 RF,BBr,R:Newsboy Legion	#73–#75,Adventures of Superman
90 DJu(c&s),Battle for	& Guardian. 3.00	#496–#497, Action Comics
Metropolis#3 . . . . 1.75	Ann.#3 DAb(1st Work),TA,DG,	#683–#684 & Justice League
91 DJu(c&s),Fall of Metropolis#3 . . 1.75	Armageddon 2001. . . . . 9.00	#69 (1993). 6.00
92 Massacre in Metropolis 1.75	Ann.#3a 2nd printing(silver) 2.00	Later printings 5.95
93 Zero Hour,A:Batman 1.75	Ann.#4 Eclipso 2.75	Platinum Edition 15.00
94 Conduit 1.75	Ann.#5 Bloodlines#6,DL,I:Myriad . . 2.75	GN Superman At Earth's End
95 Brainiac. 1.75	Ann.#6 Elseworlds Story. 2.95	(Elseworlds 1995). 4.95
96 Virtual Reality 1.75	Ann.#7 WS(c),Year One Annual	GN Superman: Distant Fires, HC,GK,
97 Shadow Dragon. 1.75	A:Dr. Occult 3.95	nuclear winter (1997) 6.00
98 R:Shadow Strike 1.75	Ann.#8 Legends o/t Dead Earth . . . 2.95	GN Superman: Earth Day 1991, KGa
99 R:Agent Liberty 1.75	Ann.#9 Pulp Heroes (High–	Metropolis `Clean-Up'. 5.50
100 BBr,DJu,Death of C.Kent,pt.1 . . 2.95		GN Superman For Earth (1991) . . . 4.95
100a Collectors Edition. 3.95		GN Superman: Kal, Medieval
101 Death of Clark Kent,pt.5		Superman (Elseworlds 1995) . . 5.95
[New Miraweb format begins] . . 2.00		GN Superman: Last God of Krypton 5.00
102 DJu,A:Captain Marvel 2.00		GN Superman's Metropolis, RLo &
103 O:Arclight 2.00		RTs(s),TMK, in Fritz Lang's
104 . . . . 2.00		Metropolis (Elseworlds 1996) . . 5.95
105 A:Green Lantern 2.00		GN The Superman Monster 7.00
106 DJu,RF,The Trial of Superman . 2.00		GN A Nation Divided 5.00
107 DJu,RF,The Trial of Superman . 2.00		GN Superman: The Odyssey 5.00
108 DJu,RF,The Trial of Superman . 2.00		GN Peace on Earth, oversized 10.00
109 DJu,RF,V:Kill Fee. 2.00		GN Superman Red/Superman Blue,
110 . . . . 2.00		V:Toyman, Cyborg, Superman
111 DJu,RF,Cat Grant in charge . . . 2.00		split into two entities (1997) . . . 4.00
112 DJu,RF,Lois & Clark. 2.00		Deluxe, 3-D cover 5.00
113 DJu(s),RF,JRu, ... 2.00		GN Superman Secret Files, DJu,JOy,
114 DJu(s),RF,JRu,A:Brainiac. . . . 2.00		etc.,inc. O:Superman (1997). . . 5.00
115 DJu(s),RF,JRu,Lois leaves		GN Superman Secret Files: Villains
Metropolis 2.00		(1997) 5.00
116 DJu(s),RF,JRu,battle city siga		GN Superman: Silver Banshee, 48pg,
concl., V:Daxamite,B.U. Teen		prestige format (1998) 5.00
Titans preview 2.00		GN Superman: Speeding Bullets,
117 DJu(s),RF,JRu,V: his own		EB (Elseworlds 1993) 6.00
robots, Final Night tie-in 2.00		GN Superman, Under a Yellow Sun
118 DJu(s),RF,JRu,F:time-lost		by Clark Kent,KGa,EB (1994). . 5.95
Legion of Super Heroes 2.00		GN Superman: The Wedding Album,
119 DJu(s),RF,JRu,A:Legion of		collector's edition, 96 pg.,

Superman #85 © DC Comics Inc.

Superman Spec. #1 © DC Comics, Inc.

cardstock cover 4.95
GN War of the Worlds,Elseworlds . . 6.00
TPB Superman: Bizarro's World . . 10.00
TPB Superman: The Death of Clark
   Kent, rep.Superman:Man of Steel
   #43–#46, Superman #99–#102,
   Action Comics #709–#711, Adv.
   of Superman #523–#525, Super-
   man: Man of Tomorrow #1
   (1997) 20.00
TPB Eradication 13.00
TPB Exile 15.00
TPB Superman/Fantastic Four . . . 10.00
TPB Krisis of the Krimson Kryptonite
   rep. Superman #49–#50, Adven-
   tures of Superman #472–#473,
   Action Comics #659–#660 and
   Starman #28 . . . . 12.95
TPB Panic in the Sky rep. 9.95
TPB Return of Superman rep. Reign
   of Superman 14.95
TPB Superman Vs. Revenge
   Squad 13.00
TPB Time and Time Again (1994) . . 7.50
TPB The Wedding and
   Beyond rep. 15.00
TPB World Without Superman 7.50
Archives, Vol. 1 S&S rep. 50.00
Archives, Vol. 2 S&S rep. 50.00
Archives, Vol. 3 S&S rep. 50.00
Archives, Vol. 4 S&S rep. 50.00
Superman Archives HC rep 39.95
Greatest Superman Stories Ever Told:
   HC 75.00
   TPB 15.95

SUPERMAN
ADVENTURES
Sept. 1996

1 PDi(s),RBr,TA, from animated
   TV show 1.75
2 SMI,RBr,TA,V:Metallo 1.75
3 SMI(s),RBr,TA,V:Brainiac 1.75
4 SMI(s) 1.75
5 SMI,BBl,TA,V:Livewire 1.75
6 SMI(s),RBr,TA,Metropolis
   in ruins 1.75
7 SMI(s),RBr,TA,V:Jax-Ur, Mala . . . 1.75
8 SMI(s),RBr,TA,V:Jax-Ur 1.75
9 SMI(s),MM,TA,"Return of
   the Hero" 1.75
10 SMI(s),RBr,TA,V:Toyman 1.75
11 SMI(s),RBr,TA,struck down

by strange malady 1.75
12 SMI(s),RBr,TA,BB, Kryptonian
   virus, concl. 1.75
13 SMI(s),RBr,TA,BB, alien races . . 2.00
14 TA,Angela Chen 2.00
15 RBr,TA,Superman's pal Bibbo . . 2.00
16 MMr(s),TA, meets Man of Steel . 2.00
17 . . . . 2.00
18 TA,should Clark quit? 2.00
19 TA,V:Multi-Face 2.00
20 RBr,TA,V:MasterTrax 2.00
21 Supergirl Adventures, 64pg. . . . 4.00
22 MMr,TA,RBr,War Games, pt.1 . . 2.00
23 MMr,TA,RBr,War Games, pt.2 . . 2.00
24 MMr,TA,RBr,V:Parasite 2.00
25 MMr,TA,RBr,F:Batgirl,C:Batman,
   Robin, Nightwing 2.00
26 MMr,TA,V:Mr.Mxyzptlk 2.00
27 MMr,TA,F:Lex Luthor 2.00
28 MMr,MM,TA,F:Jimmy Olsen . . . 2.00
29 MMr,TA,A:Lobo, Bizarro 2.00
30 MMr,TA,A:Lara, pt.1 . . . . 2.00
31 MMr,TA,A:Lara, pt.2 . . . . 2.00
32 DvM(s),Lois Hypnotized 2.00
33 DvM(s),TA,Secret Identity 2.00
34 MMr(s),TA,MM,A:Dr.Fate 2.00
35 MMr(s),TA,A:Toyman 2.00
36 MMr(s),TA, many emergencies . 2.00
Ann.#1 JoS,DDv,V:Akamin 4.00
TPB rep.#1–#6 . . . . 8.00
Spec. #1 Superman vs. Lobo –
   Misery in Space, DvM,MM,
   A:Man of Tomorrow 3.00

SUPERMAN & BATMAN:
GENERATIONS —
AN IMAGINARY TALE
1998

1 (of 4) JBy, Elseworlds 5.00
2 JBy,V:Bat-Mite 5.00
3 JBy. 5.00
4 JBy, conclusion. 5.00

SUPERMAN
& BUGS BUNNY
1999

1 JSon,TP 2.50

SUPERMAN:
THE DARK SIDE
Elseworlds, Aug., 1998

1 JFM,KD,First Son of Apokolips . . 5.00
2 . . . . 5.00
3 KD, conclusion 5.00
TPB Superman: The Dark Side. . . 13.00

SUPERMAN/DOOMSDAY:
HUNTER/PREY
1994

1 DJu(a&s),BBr,R:Doomsday,R:Cyborg
   Superman,A:Darkseid. 5.50
2 DJu(a&s),BBr,V:Doomsday,Cyborg
   Superman,A:Darkseid. 5.25
3 DJu(a&s),BBr,V:Doomsday 5.25
TPB Rep. #1-#3 . . . . 14.95

SUPERMAN:
THE DOOMSDAY WARS
1998

1 (of 3) DJu,BBr,R:Doomsday 5.00
2 DJu,V:Doomsday 5.00
3 DJu, conclusion 5.00

*Superman/Doomsday, Hunter/Prey
#3 © DC Comics, Inc.*

SUPERMAN FAMILY
Prev: Superman's Pal,
Jimmy Olsen
1974–82

164 KS,NC(c),Jimmy Olsen:`Death
   Bites with Fangs of Stone' . . . 35.00
165 KS,NC(c),Supergirl:`Princess
   of the Golden Sun' 22.00
166 KS,NC(c),Lois Lane:`The
   Murdering Arm of Metropolis' . 20.00
167 KS,NC(c),Jimmy Olsen:`A
   Deep Death for Mr. Action' . . . 20.00
168 NC(c),Supergirl:`The Girl
   with the See-Through Mind' . . 20.00
169 NC(c),Lois Lane:`Target of
   the Tarantula' 20.00
170 KS(c),Jimmy Olsen:`The Kid
   Who Adopted Jimmy Olsen' . . 15.00
171 ECh(c),Supergirl:`Cleopatra-
   Queen of America' 15.00
172 KS(c),Lois Lane:`The Cheat
   the Whole World Cheered' . . . 15.00
173 KS(c),Jimmy Olsen:`Menace
   of the Micro-Monster' 15.00
174 KS(c),Supergirl:`Eyes of
   the Serpent' 15.00
175 KS(c),Lois Lane:`Fadeout
   For Lois' 15.00
176 KS(c),Jimmy
   Olsen:`Nashville, Super-Star' . 15.00
177 KS(c),Supergirl:`Bride
   of the Stars' 7.00
178 KS(c),Lois Lane:`The Girl
   With the Heart of Steel'. 7.00
179 KS(c),Jimmy Olsen:`I Scared
   Superman to Death' 7.00
180 KS,Supergirl:`The Secret of
   the Spell-Bound Supergirl' 7.00
181 ECh(c),Lois Lane:`The Secret
   Lois Lane Could Never Tell' . . . 7.00
182 CS&NA(c),Jimmy Olsen:
   `Death on Ice'. 8.00
183 NA(c),Supergirl:`Shadows
   of Phantoms' 6.00
184 NA(c),Supergirl:`The
   Visitors From The Void'. 6.00
185 NA(c),Jimmy Olsen: The
   Fantastic Fists and Fury
   Feet of Jimmy Olsen' 6.00
186 JL&DG(c),Jimmy Olsen:
   `The Bug Lady'. 6.00
187 JL(c),Jimmy Olsen:`The
   Dealers of Death' 6.00

188 JL&DG(c),Jimmy Olsen:
`Crisis in Kandor' 6.00
189 JL(c),Jimmy Olsen:`The
Night of the Looter'. 6.00
190 Jimmy Olsen:`Somebody
Stole My Town' 6.00
191 Superboy:`The Incredible
Shrinking Town' 6.00
192 RA&DG(c),Superboy:`This
Town For Plunder' 6.00
193 RA&DG(c),Superboy:`Menace
of the Mechanical Monster'. . . . 6.00
194 MR,Superboy:`When
the Sorcerer Strikes'. 7.00
195 RA&DG(c),Superboy:`The Curse
of the Un-Secret Identity' 5.00
196 JL&DG(c),Superboy:`The
Shadow of Jor-El'. 5.00
197 JL(c),Superboy:`Superboy's
Split Personality'. 5.00
198 JL(c),Superboy:`Challenge
of the Green K-Tastrophe'. 5.00
199 RA&DG(c),Superboy:`The
Case of Cape Caper' 5.00
200 RA&DG(c),Lois Lane:
`Unhappy Anniversary'. 7.00
201 RA&DG(c),Supergirl:`The
Face on Cloud 9' 3.00
202 RA&DG(c),Supergirl:`The
Dynamic Duel' 3.00
203 RA&DG(c),Supergirl:`The
Supergirl From Planet Earth'. . . 3.00
204 RA&DG(c),Supergirl:`The
Earth-quake Enchantment' 3.00
205 RA&DG(c),Supergirl:`Magic
Over Miami' 3.00
206 RA&DG(c),Supergirl:`Strangers
at the Heart's Core' 3.00
207 RA&DG(c),Supergirl:`Look
Homeward, Argonian'. 3.00
208 RA&DG(c),Supergirl:`The
Super-Switch to New York' 3.00
209 Supergirl:`Strike Three-
You're Out' 3.00
210 Supergirl:`The Spoil Sport
of New York'. 3.00
211 RA&DG(c):Supergirl:`The Man
With the Explosive Mind'. 3.00
212 RA&DG(c):Supergirl:`Payment
on Demand' 3.00
213 . . . . 3.00
214 . . . . 3.00
215 . . . . 3.00
216 thru 222 . . . . @3.00

SUPERMAN FOR
ALL SEASONS
June, 1998
1 (of 4) JLb,TSe, from farmboy
to superhero. 5.00
2 JLb,TSe,V:Lex Luthor. 5.00
3 JLb,TSe,V:Lex Luthor. 5.00
4 JLb,TSe, conclusion 5.00

SUPERMAN:
THE MAN OF STEEL
1991–97
1 B:LSi(s),DJu,BMc,JOy,BBr,TG,
Revenge o/t Krypton Man#1 . . . 5.00
2 JBg,V:Cerberus 3.00
3 JBg,War of the Gods X-over . . . 2.50
4 JBg,V:Angstrom 2.50
5 JBg,CS,V:Atomic Skull 2.50
6 JBg,Blackout#3,A:Mr.Z 2.50
7 JBg,V:Cerberus 2.50
8 KD,V:Jolt,Blockhouse 2.50
9 JBg,Panic in the Sky#1,
V:Brainiac. 3.00

10 JBg,Panic in the Sky#5,
D:Draaga 2.50
11 JBg,V:Flashpoint 2.00
12 JBg,V:Warwolves. 2.00
13 JBg,V:Cerberus 2.00
14 JBg,A:Robin,V:Vampires 2.00
15 KG,KGa,Blaze/Satanus War . . . 2.00
16 JBg,Crisis at Hand#1 . . . . 2.00
17 JBg,V:Underworld,
C:Doomsday 6.00
17a 2nd printing 1.50
18 JBg,I:Doomsday,V:Underworld. . 8.00
18a 2nd printing 4.00
18b 3rd printing 2.00
19 JBg,Doomsday,pt.5 . . . . 5.00
19a 2nd printing 2.00
20 JBg,Funeral for a Friend#3 . . . 3.00
21 JBg,Funeral for a Friend#7 . . . 3.00
22 JBg,Reign of Supermen#4,Direct
Sales,Die-Cut(c),mini-poster,
F:Man of Steel 2.50
22a Newsstand Ed. 1.75
23 JBg,V:Superboy. 2.00
24 JBg,V:White Rabbit,A:Mongul . . 2.00
25 JBg,A:Real Superman 3.00
26 JBg,A:All Supermen,V:Mongul,
Cyborg Superman 2.50
27 JBg,A:Superboy,Lex Luthor . . . 2.00
28 JBg(c),A:Steel 1.75
29 LSi(s),JBg,Spilled Blood#3,
V:Hi-Tech,Blood Thirst 1.75
30 LSi(s),JBg,V:Lobo,Vinyl(c) 2.50
30a Newstand Ed. 1.75
31 MBr,A:Guardian. 1.75
32 MBr,Bizarro's World#4,
V:Bizarro 1.75
33 MBr,V:Parasite. 1.75
34 JBg,A:Lex Men,Dubbile Men . . . 1.75
35 JBg,Worlds Collide#1,
I:Fred Bentson 1.75
36 JBf,Worlds Collide,pt.10,V:Rift
A:Icon 1.75
37 JBg,Zero Hour,A:Batman 1.75
38 Mystery 1.50
39 JBg,Luthor. 1.50
40 . . . . 1.50
41 Locke 1.50
42 F:Locke 1.50
43 V:Deathtrap 1.50
44 Prologue to Death 1.50
45 JGb,DJa,Death of Clark Kent,pt.4
[New Miraweb format begins] . . 2.00
46 JBg,DJa,A:Shadowdragon 2.00
47 O:Bloodsport 2.00

Superman: The Man of Steel #12
© DC Comics Inc.

48 . . . . 2.00
49 Skyhook 2.00
50 JBg,DJa,The Trial of
Superman, 48pg. 2.95
51 JBg,DJa,The Trial of Superman . 2.00
52 JBg,The Trial of Superman . . . 2.00
53 JBg,DRo,A:Lex Luthor,Contessa 2.00
54 JBg 2.00
55 JBg,DJa, Clark dates Lori
Lemaris 2.00
56 JBg,DJa, manipulator revealed . 2.00
57 RSt,JBg,DJa, more twisters . . . 2.00
58 LSi(s),JBg,DJa,A:Supergirl. . . . 2.00
59 LSi(s),JBg,DJa,Parasite, Steel . . 2.00
60 LSi(s),JBg,DJa,R:Bottled City
of Kandor. 2.00
61 LSi(s),JBg,DJa,V:Riot 2.00
62 LSi(s),JBg,DJa, Superman
looses powers, Final Night tie-in 2.00
63 LSi(s),JBg,DJa,Clark is
kidnapped & revealed identity. . 2.00
64 LSi(s),JBg,DJa,Superman tries to
restore his powers 2.00
65 LSi(s),SB,DJa,V:Superman
Revenge Squad 2.00
66 LSi(s),JBg,DJa,V:Rajiv. 2.00
67 LSi(s),JBg,DJa,New powers
prequel. 2.00
68 LSi(s),JBg,DJa,V:Metallo 2.00
69 KK&LSi(s),SEa,DJa,A:Atom,
in Kandor 2.00
70 LSi(s),SEa,DJa,V:Saviour 2.00
71 LSi(s),SEa,DJa,V:Mainframe,
Superman Revenge Squad. . . . 2.00
72 LSi(s),SEa,JP,DJa,JBg,Genesis
V:Mainframe. 2.00
73 LSi&MWa(s),SEa,DJa,V:Revenge
Squad 2.00
74 LSi(s),SEa,DJa,dragon's tooth . 2.00
75 LSi(s),DJa,JBg,Mr.Mxyzptlk dies
parody of Superman #75 . . . . . 2.00
76 LSi(s),JBb,DJa,V:Mokkari 2.00
77 . . . . 2.00
78 JBg, Millennium Giants, pt.1
x-over. 2.00
79 JBg, Millennium Giants 2.00
80 LSi,JBg,DJa,golden age?,pt.1 . . 2.00
81 LSi,JBg,DJa,golden age?,pt.2 . . 2.00
82 LSi,JBg,DJa,golden age?,pt.3 . . 2.00
83 LSi,SEa,DJa,Dominus 2.00
84 RMz(s),TGb,TP,City of the
Future, pt.2 x-over 2.00
85 JBg,DJa,V:Simyan & Mokkari. . . 2.00
86 LSi(s),SEa,DJa,dreams
of disasters 2.00
87 MSh(s),DoM,DJa,A:Steel,
Superboy, Supergirl 2.00
88 MSh(s),DoM,DJa. 2.00
89 MSh(s),DoM,V:Dominus. 2.00
90 MSh(s),V:Superman's Robot . . . 2.00
91 MSh(s),DoM,paranoia 2.00
92 TPe(s),TGb,TP,Secret
origins,concl. 2.00
93 MSh,DoM 2.00
Ann.#1 Eclipso tie-in,A:Starman . . 2.75
Ann.#2 Bloodlines#2,I:Edge 2.75
Ann.#3 MBr,Elseworlds Story 2.95
Ann.#4 Year One Annual 2.95
Ann.#5 Legends o/t Dead Earth . . 2.95
Ann.#6 Pulp Heroes (Hard Boiled)
LSi(s),DJa. 3.95
Spec.#1,000,000 KK&JOy(s),
AWi,DJa. 2.00
Gallery 1 . . . . 3.50
TPB 7.50

SUPERMAN:
THE MAN OF TOMORROW
1995–96
1 TGu,BBr,RSt(s),V:Lex Luthor . . . 2.00

All comics prices listed are for *Near Mint* condition.

Superman: The Man of Tomorrow #1
© DC Comics, Inc.

2 v:Parasite 2.00
3 TG,BBr, The Trial of Superman . . 2.00
4 RSt(s),PR,BBr,A:Shazam 2.00
5 RSt(s),PR,BBr,Wedding of Lex
    Luthor 2.00
6 RSt(s),PR,BBr,Superman V:
    Jackal again. 2.00
7 RSt(s),PR,BBr, ... 2.00
8 RSt(s),PR,BBr,V:Carbide 2.00
9 RSt(s),PR,BBr,Ma and Pa Kent
    open their album 2.00
10 . . . .
11 LSi(s),PR,DJa,BBr 2.00
12 LSi(s),PR,DJa, ... 2.00
13 LSi(s),PR,DJa,A:JLA 2.00
14 LSi(s),PR,DJa,V:Riot 2.00
Spec.#1,000,000 MSh(s),DRo 2.00

SUPERMAN'S GIRL FRIEND, LOIS LANE
1958–74

1 CS,KS 3,200.00
2 CS,KS 800.00
3 CS,KS,spanking panel shown . 550.00
4 CS,KS 450.00
5 CS,KS 425.00
6 CS,KS 350.00
7 CS,KS 350.00
8 CS,KS 300.00
9 CS,KS, A:Pat Boone. 300.00
10 CS,KS 300.00
11 CS,KS 200.00
12 CS,KS 200.00
13 CS,KS 175.00
14 KS,`Three Nights in the
    Fortress of Solitude' 165.00
15 KS,I:Van-Zee 165.00
16 KS, Lois' Signal-Watch. 165.00
17 KS,CS,A:Brainiac. 165.00
18 KS,A:Astounding Man 165.00
19 KS,`Superman of the Past'. . . 135.00
20 KS,A:Superman. 135.00
21 KS,A:Van-Zee 135.00
22 KS,A:Robin Hood. 135.00
23 KS,A:Elastic Lass, Supergirl. . 135.00
24 KS,A:Van-Zee, Bizarro 135.00
25 KS,`Lois Lane's
    Darkest Secret'. 125.00
26 KS,A:Jor-El 125.00
27 KS,CS,A:Bizarro 125.00
28 KS,A:Luthor. 125.00
29 CS,A:Aquaman,Batman,Green
    Arrow 125.00

30 KS,A:Krypto,Aquaman 75.00
31 KS,A:Lori Lemaris 70.00
32 KS,CS,A:Bizarro 70.00
33 KS,CS,A:Phantom Zone,Lori
    Lemaris, Mon-El. 75.00
34 KS,A:Luthor,Supergirl. 70.00
35 KS,CS,A:Supergirl 70.00
36 KS,CS,Red Kryptonite Story . . 70.00
37 KS,CS,`The Forbidden Box' . . . 70.00
38 KS,CS,A:Prof.Potter,
    Supergirl 70.00
39 KS,CS,A:Supergirl,Jor-El,
    Krypto, Lori Lemaris 70.00
40 KS,`Lois Lane, Hag!' 70.00
41 KS,CS,`The Devil and
    Lois Lane'. 70.00
42 KS,A:Lori Lemaris 70.00
43 KS,A:Luthor. 70.00
44 KS,A:Lori Lemaris,Braniac,
    Prof. Potter. 70.00
45 KS,CS,`The Superman-Lois
    Hit Record'. 70.00
46 KS,A:Luthor. 70.00
47 KS,`The Incredible Delusion' . . 70.00
48 KS,A:Mr. Mxyzptlk 70.00
49 KS,The Unknown Superman . . 70.00
50 KS,A:Legion 60.00
51 KS,A:Van-Zee & Lori Lemaris . 50.00
52 KS,`Truce Between Lois
    Lane and Lana Lang' 50.00
53 KS,A:Lydia Lawrence. 50.00
54 KS,CS,`The Monster That
    Loved Lois Lane' 50.00
55 KS,A:Supergirl. 50.00
56 KS,`Lois Lane's
    Super-Gamble!' 55.00
57 KS,`The Camera From
    Outer Space' 50.00
58 KS,`The Captive Princess' . . . 50.00
59 KS,CS,A:Jor-El & Batman 50.00
60 KS,`Get Lost,Superman!' 50.00
61 KS,A:Mxyzptlk 50.00
62 KS,A:Mxyzptlk 50.00
63 KS,`The Satanic Schemes
    of S.K.U.L.'. 50.00
64 KS,A:Luthor. 50.00
65 KS,A:Luthor. 50.00
66 KS,`They Call Me the Cat!'. . . . 50.00
67 KS,`The Bombshell of
    the Boulevards'. 50.00
68 giant size. 60.00
69 KS,Lois Lane's Last Chance . . 50.00
70 KS,I:Silver Age Catwoman,
    A:Batman,Robin,Penguin . . . 250.00
71 KS,A:Catwoman,Batman,
    Robin,Penguin 150.00
72 KS,CS,A:Ina Lemaris. 25.00
73 KS,`The Dummy and
    the Damsel!' 25.00
74 KS,A:Justice League & Bizarro
    World,I:Bizarro Flash 35.00
75 KS,`The Lady Dictator'. 25.00
76 KS,A:Hap-El 25.00
77 giant size. 50.00
78 KS,Courtship,Kryptonian Style . 25.00
79 KS,B:NA(c) 20.00
80 KS,`Get Out of My Life,
    Superman' 20.00
81 KS,`No Witnessesin
    Outerspace' 20.00
82 GT,A:Brainiac&Justice League . 20.00
83 GT,`Witch on Wheels' 20.00
84 GT,KS,`Who is Lois Lane?' . . 20.00
85 GT,KS,A:Kandorians 20.00
86 giant size. 40.00
87 GT,KS,A:Cor-Lar 20.00
88 GT,KS,`Through a Murderer's
    Eyes' 20.00
89 CS,A:Batman & Batman Jr. . . . 25.00
90 GT,A:Dahr-nel 20.00
91 GT,A:Superlass 20.00

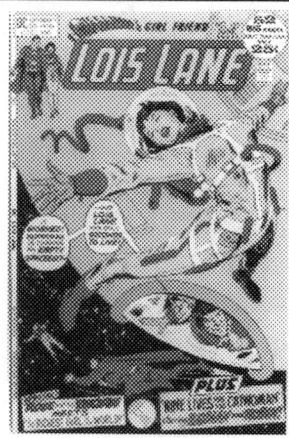

Superman's Girl Friend Lois Lane
#123 © DC Comics, Inc.

92 GT,A:Superhorse 20.00
93 GT,A:Wonder Woman 20.00
94 GT,KS,A:Jor. 20.00
95 giant size. 40.00
96 GT,A:Jor 15.00
97 GT,KS,A:Lori Lemaris,
    Luma Lynai,Lyla Lerrol 15.00
98 GT,A:Phantom Zone 15.00
99 GT,KS,A:Batman 15.00
100 GT,A:Batman. 15.00
101 GT,KS,`The Super-Reckless
    Lois Lane'. 15.00
102 GT,KS,When You're Dead,
    You're Dead 15.00
103 GT,KS,A:Supergirl 15.00
104 giant size 40.00
105 RA,I&O:Rose & Thorn 40.00
106 WR,`I am Curious Black!' 15.00
107 WR,The Snow-Woman Wept . 15.00
108 WR,The Spectre Suitor 15.00
109 WR,`I'll Never Fall
    in Love Again'. 15.00
110 WR,`Indian Death Charge!'. . . 15.00
111 WR,A:Justice League 15.00
112 WR,KS,A:Lori Lemaris 15.00
113 giant size 40.00
114 WR,KS,A:Rose & Thorn 15.00
115 WR,A:The Black Racer 15.00
116 WR,A:Darkseid & Desaad . . . 15.00
117 WR,`S.O.S From Tomorrow!' . 15.00
118 WR,A:Darkseid & Desaad . . . 15.00
119 WR,A:Darkseid & Lucy Lane . 15.00
120 WR,`Who Killed Lucy Lane?' . 15.00
121 WR,A:The Thorn 15.00
122 WR,A:The Thorn 15.00
123 JRo,`Ten Deadly Division
    of the 100' 15.00
124 JRo,`The Hunters' 8.00
125 JRo,`Death Rides Wheels!' . . . 8.00
126 JRo,`The Brain Busters' 8.00
127 JRo,`Curse of the Flame' 8.00
128 JRo,A:Batman & Aquaman . . . 8.00
129 JRo,`Serpent in Paradise' 8.00
130 JRo,`The Mental Murster' 8.00
131 JRo,Superman–Marry Me!'. . . . 8.00
132 JRo,Zatanna B.U. 8.00
133 JRo,`The Lady is a Bomb' 8.00
134 JRo,A:Kandor 8.00
135 JRo,`Amazing After-Life
    of Lois Lane'. 8.00
136 JRo,A:Wonder Woman 8.00
137 JRo,`The Stolen Subway'. . . . 10.00
Ann.#1 . . . . 175.00
Ann.#2 . . . . 125.00

SUPERMAN: SILVER BANSHEE
1998
1 (of 2) DIB(s),ALa. 2.25
2 DIB(s),ALa, conclusion 2.25

SUPERMAN'S NEMESIS, LEX LUTHOR
1999
1 (of 4) VS,DJa,. 2.50
2 VS,DJa. 2.50
3 VS,DJa. 2.50
4 VS,DJa, conclusion 2.50

SUPERMAN'S PAL, JIMMY OLSEN
1954–74
1 CS,`The Boy of 100 Faces!'. 4,200.00
2 CS,The Flying Jimmy Olsen. 1,200.00
3 CS,`The Man Who Collected
    Excitement 700.00
4 CS,`King For A Day!' 500.00
5 CS,`The Story of Superman's
    Souvenirs 450.00
6 CS,Kryptonite story 350.00
7 CS,`The King of Marbles' 350.00
8 CS,`Jimmy Olsen, Crooner'. . . . 325.00
9 CS,`The Missile of Steel'. 325.00
10 CS,`Jungle Jimmy Olsen'. . . . 325.00
11 CS,`TNT.Olsen,The Champ'. . . 250.00
12 CS,`Invisible Jimmy Olsen'. . . 250.00
13 CS,`Jimmy Olsen's
    Super Issue' 225.00
14 CS,`The Boy Superman' 225.00
15 CS,`Jimmy Olsen,Speed
    Demon'. 225.00
16 CS,`The Boy Superman' 225.00
17 CS,J.Olsen as cartoonist 225.00
18 CS,A:Superboy 225.00
19 CS,`Supermam's Kid Brother . 200.00
20 CS,`Merman of Metropolis'. . . 200.00
21 CS,`The Wedding of Jimmy
    Olsen'. 175.00
22 CS,`The Super Brain of
    Jimmy Olsen' 175.00
23 CS,`The Adventure of
    Private Olsen'. 175.00
24 CS,`The Gorilla Reporter'. . . . 175.00
25 CS,`The Day There Was
    No Jimmy Olsen. 175.00
26 CS,`Bird Boy of Metropolis' . . 150.00
27 CS,`The Outlaw Jimmy Olsen' 150.00
28 CS,`The Boy Who Killed
    Superman' 150.00
29 CS,A:Krypto. 150.00
30 CS,`The Son of Superman' . . . 150.00
31 CS,I:Elastic Lad. 125.00
32 CS,A:Prof.Potter. 125.00
33 CS,`Human Flame Thrower'. . . 125.00
34 CS,`Superman's Pal of Steel'. 125.00
35 CS,`Superman's Enemy' 125.00
36 CS,I:Lois Lane,O:Jimmy Olsen
    as Superman's Pal 125.00
37 CS,O:Jimmy Olsen's SignalWatch,
    A:Elastic Lad(Jimmy Olsen) . 125.00
38 CS,`Olsen's Super-Supper' . . 125.00
39 CS,`The Super-Lad of Space' 125.00
40 CS,A:Supergirl,Hank White
    (Perry White's son) 125.00
41 CS,`The Human Octopus' 90.00
42 CS,`Jimmy The Genie'. 90.00
43 WB,CS,`Jimmy Olsen's Private
    Monster'. 90.00
44 CS,`Miss Jimmy Olsen' 90.00
45 CS,A:Kandor 90.00
46 CS,A:Supergirl,Elastic Lad . . 90.00
47 CS,`Monsters From Earth!'. . . . 90.00

48 CS,I:Superman Emergency
    Squad 90.00
49 CS,A:Congorilla & Congo Bill. . 90.00
50 CS,A:Supergirl,Krypto,Bizarro . 90.00
51 CS,A:Supergirl. 75.00
52 CS,A:Mr. Mxyzptlk,
    Miss Gzptlsnz. 75.00
53 CS,A:Kandor,Lori Lemaris,
    Mr.Mxyztlk 75.00
54 CS,A:Elastic Lad 75.00
55 CS,A:Aquaman,Thor 75.00
56 KS,Imaginary story 75.00
57 KS,A:Supergirl,Imaginary story. 40.00
58 CS,C:Batman. 40.00
59 CS,A:Titano. 40.00
60 CS,`The Fantastic Army of
    General Olsen' 40.00
61 CS,Prof. Potter 40.00
62 CS,A:Elastic Lad,Phantom
    Zone 40.00
63 CS,A:Supergirl,Kandor 45.00
64 CS,`Jimmy Olsen's
    Super-Romance 35.00
65 CS,A:Miss Gzptlsnz 35.00
66 CS,KS,A:Mr. Mxyzptlk 35.00
67 CS,`The Dummy That Haunted
    Jimmy Olsen' 35.00
68 CS,`The Helmet of Hate' 35.00
69 CS,A:Nightwing,Flamebird . . . 35.00
70 A:Supergirl,Lori Lemaris,
    Element Lad. 35.00
71 CS,A:Mr. Mxyzptlk 30.00
72 CS,A:Legion of Super-Heroes,
    Jimmy Olsen becomes honorary
    member. 35.00
73 A:Kandor. 35.00
74 CS,A:Mr. Mxyzptlk,Lex Luthor . 30.00
75 CS,A:Supergirl. 30.00
76 CS,A:Legion of Super-Heroes . 30.00
77 CS,Jimmy Olsen becomes
    Colossal Boy, A:Titano 30.00
78 CS,A:Aqualad 30.00
79 CS,`The Red-Headed Beetle
    of 1,000 B.C.'. 30.00
80 CS,A:Bizarro. 30.00
81 CS,KS,A:Lori Lemaris,I&O
    only A:Mighty Eagle 30.00
82 CS,`The Unbeatable Jimmy
    Olsen'. 30.00
83 CS,A:Kandor 30.00
84 CS,A:Titano 30.00
85 CS,C:Legion of Super-Heroes . 35.00
86 CS,A:Congorilla,Braniac. 30.00
87 A:Lex Luthor,Brainiac,Legion

Superman's Pal, Jimmy Olsen #149
© DC Comics Inc.

    of Super-Villians 35.00
88 C:Legion of Super-Heroes 30.00
89 I:Agent Double-Five,C:John F.
    Kennedy. 30.00
90 CS,A:Mr. Mxyzptlk 30.00
91 CS,C:Batman & Robin. 30.00
92 JM,A:Batman,Robin,Supergirl . 30.00
93 `The Batman-Superman of
    Earth-X!' 30.00
94 O:Insect Queen retold 30.00
95 Giant 35.00
96 I:Tempus 25.00
97 A:Fortress of Solitude 25.00
98 `The Bride of Jungle Jimmy'. . . 25.00
99 A:Legion of Super-Heroes . . . 25.00
100 A:Legion of Super-Heroes . . . 35.00
101 A:Jor-El and Lara. 15.00
102 `Superman's Greatest Double
    Cross!' 15.00
103 `The Murder of Clark Kent!' . . 15.00
104 Giant 30.00
105 V:Tempus 12.00
106 CS,A:Legion of Super-Heroes 12.00
107 A:Krypto 12.00
108 CS,`The Midas of Metropolis'. 12.00
109 A:Lex Luthor 12.00
110 CS,`Jimmy Olsen's Blackest
    Deeds!'. 12.00
111 . . . . 12.00
112 . . . . 12.00
113 V:Magnaman 35.00
114 `The Wrong Superman!' 12.00
115 A:Aquaman 12.00
116 A:Brainiac 12.00
117 `Planet of the Capes' 12.00
118 A:Lex Luthor 12.00
119 `Nine Lives Like a Cat!' 12.00
120 V:Climate King. 12.00
121 thru 125 . . . . @12.00
126 CS,Riddle of Kryptonite Plus . 12.00
127 CS,Jimmy in Revolutionary
    War. 12.00
128 I:Mark Olsen(Jimmy's Father) 12.00
129 MA,A:Mark Olsen. 12.00
130 MA,A:Robin,Brainiac 12.00
131 . . . . 30.00
132 MA,When Olsen Sold out
    Superman 12.00
133 JK,B:New Newsboy Legion,
    I:Morgan Edge. 45.00
134 JK,I:Darkseid. 70.00
135 JK,I:New Guardian. 22.00
136 JK,O:New Guardian,
    I:Dubbilex. 15.00
137 JK,I:Four Armed Terror. 15.00
138 JK,V:Four Armed Terror 15.00
139 JK,A:Don Rickles,I:Ugly
    Mannheim 15.00
140 . . . . 14.00
141 JK,A:Don Rickles,Lightray
    B:Newsboy Legion rep 14.00
142 JK,I:Count Dragorian 14.00
143 JK,V:Count Dragorian 14.00
144 JK,A Big Thing in a Deep
    Scottish Lake 14.00
145 JK,Brigadoon. 14.00
146 JK,Homo Disastrous 14.00
147 JK,Superman on New
    Genesis,A:High Father,
    I:Victor Volcanium. 14.00
148 JK,V:Victor Volcanium,
    E:Newsboy Legion rep 14.00
149 BO(i), The Unseen Enemy,
    B:Plastic Man rep 10.00
150 BO(i) A Bad Act to Follow . . . 10.00
151 BO(i),A:Green Lantern 10.00
152 MSy,BO,I:Real Morgan Edge. 10.00
153 MSy,Murder in Metropolis. . . . 10.00
154 KS,The Girl Who Was Made
    of Money 10.00
155 KS,Downfall of Judas Olsen. . 10.00

156 KS,Last Jump for
  a Skyjacker 10.00
157 KS,Jimmy as Marco Polo. . . . 10.00
158 KS,A:Lena Lawrence
  (Lucy Lane) 10.00
159 KS,Jimmy as Spartacus 10.00
160 KS,A:Lena Lawrence
  (Lucy Lane) 10.00
161 KS,V:Lucy Lane 10.00
162 KS,A:Lex Luthor. 10.00
163 KS,Jimmy as Marco Polo. . . . 10.00

SUPERMAN: SAVE THE PLANET
Aug., 1998
1 LSi,SEa,DRo,JP,KN, last
  front page. 3.00
1 collector's edition 4.00

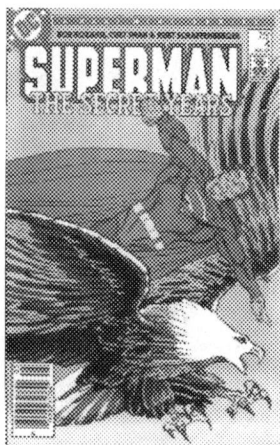

Superman, The Secret Years #4
© DC Comics, Inc.

SUPERMAN, THE SECRET YEARS
Feb., 1985
1 CS,KS,FM(c) 1.50
2 CS,KS,FM(c) 1.25
3 CS,KS,FM(c) 1.25
4 CS,KS,FM(c), May 1985. . . . . . . 1.25

SUPERMAN VS. AMAZING SPIDER-MAN
April, 1976
1 RA/DG,oversized 75.00
1a 2nd printing, signed 125.00

SUPERMAN/ WONDER WOMAN: WHOM GODS DESTROY
Elseworlds Oct. 1996
Mini-series
1 CCI(s),DAb, Lois becomes the
  immortal Wonder Woman 4.95
2 CCI(s),DAb, search for Lana
  Lang 4.95
3 . . . . 4.95
4 CCI(s),DAb, romance of the
  century, concl. 4.95

SUPERMEN OF AMERICA
1999
GN with membership kit 5.00
GN standard edition 4.00

SUPER POWERS
1984
[Kenner Action Figures]
1 A:Batman & Joker 3.50
2 A:Batman & Joker 3.50
3 A:Batman & Joker 3.50
4 A:Batman & Joker 3.50
5 JK(c),JK,A:Batman & Joker. . . . 3.50
[2nd Series] 1985–86
1 JK,`Seeds of Doom' 2.00
2 JK,`When Past & Present Meet' . 2.00
3 JK,`Time Upon Time' 2.00
4 JK,There's No Place Like Rome . 2.00
5 JK,`Once Upon a Tomorrow' 2.00
6 JK,`Darkkseid o/t Moon' 2.00
[3rd Series] 1986
1 CI,`Threshold'. 1.50
2 CI,`Escape'. 1.50
3 CI,`Machinations' 1.50
4 CI,`A World Divided' 1.50

SUPER-TEAM FAMILY
1975–78
1 rep. 15.00
2 Creeper/Wildcat 7.00
3 RE/WW,Flash & Hawkman 7.00
4 . . . . 8.00
5 . . . . 8.00
6 . . . . 8.00
7 . . . . 8.00
8 JSh,Challengers 8.00
9 JSh,Challengers 8.00
10 JSh,Challengers 8.00
11 Supergirl,Flash,Atom 8.00
12 Green Lantern,Hawkman 8.00
13 Aquaman, Capt. Comet 8.00
14 Wonder Woman,Atom 8.00
15 Flash & New Gods. 11.00

SWAMP THING
[1st Regular Series]
Oct.–Nov., 1972
1 B:LWn(s),BWr,O:Swamp Thing . 80.00
2 BWr,I:Arcane 40.00
3 BWr,I:Patchwork Man 30.00
4 BWr 25.00
5 BWr 25.00
6 BWr 25.00
7 BWr,A:Batman 30.00
8 BWr,Lurker in Tunnel 13 . . . . . 20.00
9 BWr 20.00
10 E:BWr,A;Arcane. 20.00
11 thru 22 NR . . . . @8.00
23 NR,reverts to Dr.Holland 8.00
24 NR 8.00
TPB rep.#1-#10,House of Secrets
  #92, Dark Genesis Saga. 19.95

SWAMP THING
1986–96
Previously:
SAGA OF THE SWAMP THING
46 B:AMo(s) cont'd,SBi,JTo,Crisis,
  A:John Constantine,Phantom
  Stranger. 4.00
47 SBi,Parliment of Trees,Full
  origin,A:Constantine 3.00
48 SBi,JTo,V:Brujeria,
  A:Constantine. 3.00
49 SBi,AA,A:Constantine,Demon,Ph.

Swamp Thing #57 © DC Comics, Inc.

  Stranger,Spectre,Deadman. . . . 3.00
50 SBi,RV,JTo,concl.American
  Gothic,D:Zatara&Sargon,
  Double Size 6.00
51 RV,AA,L:Constantine 3.00
52 RV,AA,Arkham Asylum,A:Flor.
  Man,Lex Luthor,C:Joker,
  2-Face,Batman. 4.00
53 JTo,V:Batman,Swamp Thing
  Banished to Space 4.00
54 JTo script,RV,AA,C:Batman . . . 3.00
55 RV,AA,JTo,A:Batman,. 3.00
56 RV,AA,My Blue Heaven 3.00
57 RV,AA,A:Adam Strange 3.00
58 RV,AA,A:Adam Strange,GC,
  Spectre preview 3.00
59 JTo,RV,AA,D:Patchwork Man . . . 3.00
Direct Sales Only
60 JTo,Loving the Alien. 3.00
61 RV,AA,All Flesh is Grass
  G.L.Corps X-over 3.00
62 RV(&script),AA,Wavelength,
  A:Metron,Darkseid 3.00
63 RV,AA,Loose Ends(reprise) 3.00
64 E:AMo(s),SBi,TY,RV,AA,
  Return of the Good Gumbo . . . 3.00
65 RV,JTo,A:Constantine 3.50
66 RV,Elemental Energy. 2.50
67 RV,V:Solomon Grundy,
  Hellblazer preview 4.00
68 RV,O:Swamp Thing 2.50
69 RV,O:Swamp Thing 2.50
70 RV,AA,Quest for SwampThing . . 2.50
71 RV,AA,Fear of Flying 2.50
72 RV,AA,Creation 2.50
73 RV,AA,A:John Constantine. 3.00
74 RV,AA,Abbys Secret 2.50
75 RV,AA,Plant Elementals. 2.50
76 RV,AA,A:John Constantine. 3.00
77 TMd,AA,A:John Constantine . . . 3.00
78 TMd,AA,Phantom Pregnancy . . . 2.50
79 RV,AA,A:Superman,Luthor. 2.50
80 RV,AA,V:Aliends 2.50
81 RV,AA,Invasion x-over 2.50
82 RV,AA,A:Sgt.Rock & Easy Co. . . 2.50
83 RV,AA,A:Enemy Ace 2.50
84 RV,AA,A:Sandman. 10.00
85 RV,TY,Time Travel contd. 2.50
86 RV,TY,A:Tomahawk 2.50
87 RV,TY,Camelot,A:Demon 2.50
88 RV,TY,A:Demon,Golden
  Gladiator 2.50
89 MM,AA,The Dinosaur Age 2.50
90 BP,AA,Birth of Abbys Child

(Tefe) 2.75
91 PB,AA,Abbys Child (New
 Elemental) 2.50
92 PB,AA,Ghosts of the Bayou. . . . 2.50
93 PB,AA,New Power. 2.50
94 PB,AA,Ax-Murderer 2.50
95 PB,AA,Toxic Waste Dumpers. . . 2.50
96 PB,AA,Tefes Powers 2.50
97 PB,AA,Tefe,V:Nergal,
 A:Arcane 2.50
98 PB,AA,Tefe,in Hell 2.50
99 PB,AA,Tefe,A:Mantago,
 John Constantine 3.00
100 PB,AA,V:Angels of Eden,
 (48 pages) 3.50
101 AA,A:Tefe 2.50
102 V:Mantagos Zombies,inc. prev.
 of Worlds Without End 2.50
103 Green vs. Grey 2.50
104 Quest for Elementals,pt.1 . . . . 2.50
105 Quest for Elementals,pt.2 . . . . 2.50
106 Quest for Elementals,pt.3 . . . . 2.50
107 Quest for Elementals,pt.4 . . . . 2.50
108 Quest for Elementals,pt.5 . . . . 2.50
109 Quest for Elementals,pt.6 . . . . 2.50
110 TMd,A:Father Tocsin 2.50
111 V:Ghostly Zydeco Musician . . . 2.50
112 TMd,B:Swamp Thing
 for Governor 2.50
113 E:Swamp Thing for Governor . . 2.50
114 TMd,Hellblazer 2.75
115 TMd,A:Hellblazer,V:Dark
 Conrad 2.75
116 From Body of Swamp Thing . . . 2.25
117 JD,The Lord of Misrule,
 Mardi Gras 2.25
118 A Childs Garden,A:Matthew
 the Raven 2.25
119 A:Les Perdu 2.25
120 F:Lady Jane. 2.25
121 V:Sunderland Corporation . . . 2.25
122 I:The Needleman 2.25
123 V:The Needleman 2.25
124 In Central America 2.25
125 V:Anton Arcane,20th Anniv. . . . 3.75
126 Mescalito 2.25
127 Project Proteus #1 . . . . 2.25
128 Project proteus #2 . . . . 2.25

Vertigo
129 CV(c),B:NyC(s),SEa,KDM(i),
 Sw.Thing's Deterioration 2.25
130 CV(c),SEa,KDM(i),A:John
 Constantine,V:Doctor Polygon . 2.25
131 CV(c),SEa,KDM(i),I:Swamp
 Thing's,Doppleganger,
 F:The Folk 3.00
132 CV(c),SEa,KDM(i),
 V:Doppleganger 3.00
133 CV(c),SEa,KDM(i),R:General
 Sunderland,V:Thunder Petal . . . 3.00
134 CV(c),SEa,KDM(i),Abby Leaves,
 C:John Constantine 3.00
135 CV(c),SEa,KDM(i),A:J.Constantine,
 Swamp Thing Lady Jane meld . 3.00
136 CV(c),RsB,KDM(i),A:Lady Jane,
 Dr.Polygon,John Constantine . . 3.00
137 CV(c),E:NyC(s),RsB,KDM(i),
 IR:Sunderland is Anton Arcane,
 A:J.Constantine 3.00
138 CV(c),DiF(s),RGu,KDM,B:Mind
 Fields 3.00
139 CV(c),DiF(s),RGu,KDM,A:Black
 Orchid,In Swamp Thing's mind,
 cont'd fr.Black Orchid #5 . . . . . 3.00
140 B:Bad Gumbo 3.00
140a Platinum Ed. 10.00
141 A:Abigail Arcane 3.00
142 Bad Gumbo#3 . . . . 3.00
143 E:Bad Gumbo 3.00
144 In New York City 3.00
145 In Amsterdam 3.00

146 V:Nelson Strong. 3.00
147 Hunter 3.00
148 Sargon 3.00
149 Sargon 3.00
150 V:Sargon 3.50
151 . . . . 2.25
152 River Run,pt.1 . . . . 2.25
153 River Run 2.25
154 River Run 2.25
155 River Run 2.25
156 PJ,River Run 2.25
157 . . . . 2.25
158 . . . . 2.25
159 Swamp Dog 2.25
160 PhH,KDM,Atmospheres 2.25
161 Atmospheres 2.25
162 Atmospheres 2.25
163 Atmospheres 2.25
164 . . . . 2.25
165 CS,KDM,F:Chester Williams . . 2.25
166 PhH,KDM,Trial by Fire,pt.1 . . 2.25
167 PhH,KDM,Trial by Fire,pt.2 . . . 2.25
168 MMr(s),PhH,KDM,Trial by Fire,
 pt.3 . . . . 2.25
169 MMr(s),PhH,KDM,Trial by Fire,
 pt.4 . . . . 2.25
170 MMr(s),PhH,KDM,Trial by Fire,
 pt.5 . . . . 2.25
171 MMr(s),PhH,KDM,"Trial by Fire,"
 pt.6 last issue 2.25
Ann.#4 PB/AA,A:Batman 2.75
Ann.#5 A:BrotherPower Geek 3.25
Ann.#6 Houma 3.50
Ann.#7 CV(c),NyC(s),MBu(i),Childrens
 Crusade,F:Tefe,A:Maxine,BU:
 Beautyand the Beast 4.25

Sword of Sorcery #5 © DC Comics Inc.

SWORD OF SORCERY
Feb.–March, 1973
1 MK(c),HC 25.00
2 BWv,NA,Hc. 30.00
3 BWv,HC,MK,WS 25.00
4 HC,WS 10.00
5 Nov.–Dec., 1973 . . . . 10.50

SWORD OF THE ATOM
Sept., 1983
1 GK 1.50
2 thru 4 GK . . . . @1.25
Spec.#1 GK 1.25
Spec.#2 GK 1.25
Spec.#3 PB 1.50

SYSTEM, THE
DC/Vertigo 1996
TPB by Peter Kuper 12.95

TAILGUNNER JO
Sept., 1988
1 . . . . 1.25
2 . . . . 1.25
3 . . . . 1.25
4 . . . . 1.25
5 . . . . 1.25
6 . . . . 1.25

TAKION
1996
1 PuK,AaL,Josh Sanders
 becomes Takion 1.75
2 thru 4 . . . . @1.75
5 PuK,AaL,Adventures of Source
 Elemental" cont. 1.75
6 PuK,AaL,Final Night tie-in. 1.75
7 PuK,AaL,Arzaz trains Takion,
 final issue 1.75

TALES OF THE GREEN LANTERN CORPS
May, 1981
1 JSon,FMc,O:Green Lantern 1.50
2 JSon,FMc. 1.25
3 JSon,FMc. 1.25

TALES OF THE LEGION OF SUPER HEROES
Aug., 1984
(Previously:
Legion of Super Heroes)
314 KG,V:Ontiir 1.50
315 KG(i),V:Dark Circle 1.50
316 KG(i),O:White Witch. 1.50
317 KG(i),V:Dream Demon. 1.50
318 KG(i),V:Persuader 1.50
319 KG(i),V:Persuader,
 A:Superboy 1.50
320 DJu,V:Magpie 1.50
321 DJu,Exile,V:Kol 1.50
322 DJu,Exile,V:Kol 1.50
323 DJu,Exile,V:Kol 1.50
324 DJu,EC,V:Dev-Em 1.50
325 DJu,V:Dark Circle 1.50
326 reprint of Baxter #1 . . . . 1.00
327 reprint of Baxter #2 . . . . 1.00
328 reprint of Baxter #3 . . . . 1.00
329 reprint of Baxter #4 . . . . 1.00
330 reprint of Baxter #5 . . . . 1.00
331 reprint of Baxter #6 . . . . 1.00
332 reprint of Baxter #7 . . . . 1.00
333 reprint of Baxter #8 . . . . 1.00
334 reprint of Baxter #9 . . . . 1.00
335 reprint of Baxter #10 . . . . 1.00
336 reprint of Baxter #11 . . . . 1.00
337 reprint of Baxter #12 . . . . 1.00
338 reprint of Baxter #13 . . . . 1.00
339 reprint of Baxter #14 . . . . 1.00
340 reprint of Baxter #15 . . . . 1.00
341 reprint of Baxter #16 . . . . 1.00
342 reprint of Baxter #17 . . . . 1.00
343 reprint of Baxter #19 . . . . 1.00
344 reprint of Baxter #19 . . . . 1.00
345 reprint of Baxter #20 . . . . 1.00
346 reprint of Baxter #21 . . . . 1.00
347 reprint of Baxter #22 . . . . 1.00
348 reprint of Baxter #23 . . . . 1.00
349 reprint of Baxter #24 . . . . 1.00
350 reprint of Baxter #25 . . . . 1.00
351 reprint of Baxter #26 . . . . 1.00

DC COMICS

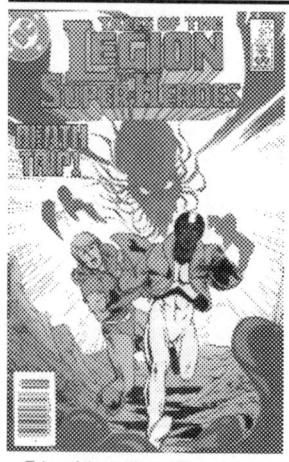

Tales of the Legion of Super Heroes
#317 © DC Comics, Inc.

352 reprint of Baxter #27 . . . . 1.00
353 reprint of Baxter #28 . . . . 1.00
354 reprint of Baxter #29 . . . . 1.00
Ann.#4 rep. Baxter Ann.#1 . . . . . . 1.00
Ann.#5 rep. Baxter Ann.#2 . . . . . . 1.00

TALES OF THE
NEW TEEN TITANS
June, 1982
1 GP, O:Cyborg 2.00
2 GP, O:Raven 2.00
3 GD, O:Changling 2.00
4 GP/EC,O:Starfire 2.00

TALES OF THE
TEEN TITANS
(see NEW TEEN TITANS)

TALES OF THE
UNEXPECTED
1956–68
1 The Out-Of-The-World Club . 1,000.00
2 . . . . 500.00
3 . . . . 375.00
4 Seven Steps to the Unknown . 375.00
5 . . . . 375.00
6 `The Girl in the Bottle' 275.00
7 NC(c),Pen That Never Lied . . . 275.00
8 . . . . 275.00
9 LSt(c),The Amazing Cube 275.00
10 MMe(c),The Strangest Show
   On Earth 275.00
11 LSt(c),Who Am I? 175.00
12 JK,Four Threads of Doom . . . 200.00
13 JK(c),Weapons of Destiny . . . 200.00
14 SMo(c),The Forbidden Game . 175.00
15 JK,MMe,Three Wishes
   to Doom 200.00
16 JK,The Magic Hammer 200.00
17 JK,Who Is Mr. Ashtar? 200.00
18 JK(c),MMe,A Man Without A
   World 200.00
19 NC,Man From Two Worlds . . . 150.00
20 NC(c),The Earth Gladiator . . . 150.00
21 JK,The Living Phantoms 200.00
22 JK(c),The Man From Robot
   Island 200.00
23 JK,The Invitation From Mars! . 200.00
24 LC,The Secret Of Planetoid

Zero! 175.00
25 The Sorcerer's Asteroid! 175.00
26 MMe,The Frozem City 175.00
27 MMe,The Prison In Space . . . 175.00
28 The Melting Planet 175.00
29 The Phantom Raider 175.00
30 The Jinxed Planet 175.00
31 RH,Keep Off Our Planet 125.00
32 Great Space Cruise Mystery . 125.00
33 The Man Of 1,000 Planets . . . 125.00
34 Ambush In Outer Space 125.00
35 MMe,I was a Space Refugee . 125.00
36 The Curse Of The
   Galactic Goodess 125.00
37 The Secret Prisoners
   Of Planet 13 . . . . 125.00
38 The Stunt Man Of Space 125.00
39 The Creatures From The
   Space Globe 125.00
40 B:Space Ranger,The Last
   Days Of Planet Mars! 900.00
41 SMo(c),The Destroyers From
   The Stars! 300.00
42 The Secret Of The
   Martian Helmet 300.00
43 The Riddle Of The Burning
   Treasures,I:Space Ranger . . 700.00
44 DD&SMo(c),The Menace Of
   The Indian Aliens 225.00
45 DD&SMo(c),The Sheriff
   From Jupiter 225.00
46 DD&SMo(c),The
   Duplicate Doom! 225.00
47 DD(c),The Man Who Stole
   The Solar System 150.00
48 Bring 'Em Back Alive-
   From Space 150.00
49 RH,The Fantastic Lunar-Land 150.00
50 MA,King Barney The Ape 150.00
51 Planet Earth For Sale 125.00
52 Prisoner On Pluto 125.00
53 InterplanetaryTroubleShooter . 125.00
54 The Ugly Sleeper Of Klanth,
   Dinosaur 150.00
55 The Interplanetary
   Creature Trainer 125.00
56 B:Spaceman At Work,Invaders
   From Earth 125.00
57 The Jungle Beasts Of Jupiter . 125.00
58 The Boss Of The
   Saturnian Legion 125.00
59 The Man Who Won A World . . 125.00
60 School For Space Sleuths . . . 125.00
61 The Mystery Of The
   Mythical Monsters 100.00
62 The Menace Of The Red
   Snow Crystals 100.00
63 Death To Planet Earth 100.00
64 Boy Usurper Of Planet Zonn . 100.00
65 The Creature That
   Couldn't Exist 100.00
66 MMe,Trap Of The Space
   Convict 100.00
67 The Giant That
   Devoured A Village 100.00
68 Braggart From Planet Brax . . . 75.00
69 Doom On Holiday Asteroid . . . 75.00
70 The Hermit Of Planetoid X . . . 75.00
71 Manhunt In Galaxy G-2! 75.00
72 The Creature Of 1,000 Dooms . 75.00
73 The Convict Defenders
   Of Space! 75.00
74 Prison Camp On Asteroid X-3! . 75.00
75 The Hobo Jungle Of Space . . . 75.00
76 The Warrior Of Two Worlds! . . 75.00
77 Dateline-Outer Space 75.00
78 The Siren Of Space 75.00
79 Big Show On Planet Earth! . . . 75.00
80 The Creature Tamer! 75.00
81 His Alien Master! 75.00
82 Give Us Back Our Earth!,

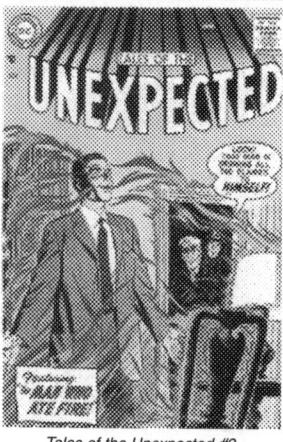

Tales of the Unexpected #9
© DC Comics, Inc.

E:Space Ranger 75.00
83 DD&SMo(c),The Anti-Hex
   Merchant! 45.00
84 DD&SMo(c),The Menace Of
   The 50-Fathom Men 45.00
85 JkS(c),The Man Who Stole My
   Powers,B:Green Glob 45.00
86 DD&SMo(c),They'll Never
   Take Me Alive! 40.00
87 JkS(c),The Manhunt Through
   Two Worlds 40.00
88 DD&SMo(c),GK,The Fear
   Master 40.00
89 DD,SMo(c),Nightmare on Mars 40.00
90 JkS(c),The Hero Of 5,000 BC . 40.00
91 JkS(c),The Prophetic Mirages,
   I:Automan 40.00
92 The Man Who Dared To Die! . . 40.00
93 JkS(c),Prisoners Of Hate
   Island 40.00
94 The Monster Mayor - USA . . . 40.00
95 The Secret Of Chameleo-Man . 40.00
96 Wanted For Murder...1966...
   6966 . . . . 40.00
97 One Month To Die 40.00
98 Half-Man/Half Machine 40.00
99 JkS(c),Nuclear Super-Hero! . . 40.00
100 Judy Blonde, Secret Agent! . . 40.00
101 The Man In The Liquid Mask! . 35.00
102 Bang!Bang! You're Dead 35.00
103 JA,ABC To Disaster 35.00
104 NA(c),Master Of The
    Voodoo Machine 35.00
Becomes:

UNEXPECTED, THE
1968–82
105 The Night I Watched
    Myself Die 40.00
106 B:Johnny Peril,The Doorway
    Into Time 25.00
107 MD,JkS(c),The Whip Of Fear! 28.00
108 JkS(c),Journey To
    A Nightmare 25.00
109 JkS(c),Baptism By Starfire! . . 25.00
110 NA(c),Death Town, U.S.A.! . . . 30.00
111 NC(c),Mission Into Eternity . . 25.00
112 NA(c),The Brain Robbers! . . . 30.00
113 NA(c),The Shriek Of
    Vengeance 30.00
114 NA(c),My Self-My Enemy! . . . 30.00
115 BWr,NA(c),Diary Of
    A Madman 30.00
116 NC(c),Express Train
    To Nowhere! 25.00

117 NC(c),Midnight Summons
  The Executioner! 18.00
118 NA(c),A:Judge Gallows,Play
  A Tune For Treachery. 18.00
119 BWr,NC(c),Mirror,Mirror
  On The Wall 25.00
120 NC(c),Rambeau's Revenge . . 18.00
121 BWr,NA(c),Daddy's
  Gone-A-Hunting 25.00
122 WW,DG(c),The Phantom
  Of The Woodstock Festival. . . 18.00
123 NC(c),Death Watch! 18.00
124 NA(c),These Walls Shall
  Be Your Grave 20.00
125 NC(c),Screech Of Guilt! 18.00
126 ATh,NC(c),You Are Cordially
  Invited To Die! 18.00
127 GT,JK,ATh,NC(c),Follow The
  Piper To Your Grave 18.00
128 DW,BWr,NC(c),Where Only
  The Dead Are Free! 25.00
129 NC(c),Farewell To A
  Fading Star 18.00
130 NC(c),One False Step 18.00
131 NC(c),Run For Your Death! . . 18.00
132 MD,GT,NC(c),The Edge Of
  Madness 18.00
133 WW,JkS(c),A:Judge Gallows,
  Agnes Doesn't Haunt Here
  Anymore! 20.00
134 GT,NC(c),The Restless Dead. 18.00
135 NC(c),Death, Come
  Walk With Me! 15.00
136 SMo,GT,NC(c),An Incident
  of Violence 15.00
137 WW,NC(c),Dark Vengeance! . 18.00
138 WW,NC(c),Strange Secret of
  the Huan Shan Idol. 18.00
139 GT,NC(c),The 2 Brains of
  Beast Bracken! 15.00
140 JkS(c),The Anatomy of Hate . 12.00
141 NC(c),Just What Did Eric
  See? 12.00
142 NC(c),Let The Dead Sleep! . . 12.00
143 NC(c),Fear is a Nameless
  Voice 12.00
144 NC(c),The Dark Pit of
  Dr. Hanley 12.00
145 NC(c),Grave of Glass. 12.00
146 NC(c),The Monstrosity! 12.00
147 NC(c),The Daughter of
  Dr. Jekyll 12.00
148 NC(c),Baby Wants Me Dead! . 12.00
149 NC(c),To Wake the Dead 12.00
150 NC(c),No One Escapes From
  Gallows Island 12.00
151 NC(c),Sorry, I'm Not Ready
  To Die! 12.00
152 GT,NC(c),Death Wears Many
  Faces. 12.00
153 NC(c),Who's That Sleeping
  In My Grave? 12.00
154 NC(c),Murder By Madness. . . 12.00
155 NC(c),Non-Stop Journey
  Into Fear 12.00
156 NC(c),A Lunatic Is Loose
  Among Us! 12.00
157 NC(c),The House of
  the Executioner 12.00
158 NC(c),Reserved for Madmen
  Only 12.00
159 NC(c),A Cry in the Night 12.00
160 NC(c),Death of an Exorcist. . . 12.00
161 BWr,NC(c),Has Anyone
  Seen My Killer 25.00
162 JK,NC(c),I'll Bug You
  To Your Grave 18.00
163 DD,LD(c),Room For Dying . . . 7.00
164 House of the Sinister Sands. . 7.00
165 LD(c),Slayride in July. 7.00
166 LD(c),The Evil Eyes of Night . . 7.00

167 LD(c),Scared Stiff 7.00
168 LD(c),Freak Accident 7.00
169 LD(c),What Can Be Worse
  Than Dying?. 7.00
170 LD(c),Flee To Your Grave 7.00
171 LD(c),I.O.U. One Corpse 7.00
172 LD(c),Strangler in Paradise . . . 7.00
173 LD(c),What Scared Sally? 7.00
174 LD(c),Gauntlet of Fear 7.00
175 LD(c),The Haunted Mountain . . 7.00
176 JkS(c),Having A
  Wonderful Crime 7.00
177 ECh(c),Reward for the Wicked . 7.00
178 LD(c),Fit To Kill! 7.00
179 LD(c),My Son, The Mortician . . 7.00
180 GT,LD(c),The Loathsome
  Lodger of Nightmare Inn. 9.00
181 LD(c),Hum of the Haunted 7.00
182 LD(c),Sorry, This Coffin
  is Occupied 7.00
183 LD(c),The Dead Don't
  Always Die. 7.00
184 LD(c),Wheel of Misfortune! 7.00
185 LD(c),Monsters from a
  Thousand Fathoms 7.00
186 LD(c),To Catch a Corpse 7.00
187 LD(c),Mangled in Madness 7.00
188 LD(c),Verdict From The Grave . 7.00
189 SD,LD(c),Escape From the
  Grave. 7.00
190 LD(c),The Jigsaw Corpse. 6.00
191 MR,JO(c),Night of the Voodoo
  Curse. 7.00
192 LD(c),A Killer Cold & Clammy . 6.00
193 DW,LD(c),Don't Monkey the
  Murder. 6.00
194 LD(c),Have I Got a Ghoul
  For You 6.00
195 JCr,LD(c),Whose Face is at
  My Window 7.00
196 LD(c),The Fear of Number 13 . 4.00
197 LD(c),Last Laugh of a Corpse . 4.00
198 JSn(c),Rage of the
  Phantom Brain 4.00
199 LD(c),Dracula's Daughter. 4.00
200 GT,RA&DG(c),A:Johnny Peril,
  House on the Edge of Eternity . 6.00
201 Do Unto Others 4.00
202 JO,LD(c),Death Trap 4.00
203 MK(c),Hang Down Your
  Head, Joe Mundy. 4.00
204 DN,JKu(c),Twinkle, Twinkle
  Little Star 4.00
205 JkS,A:Johnny Peril,The Second
  Possession of Angela Lake . . . 4.00
206 JkS,A:Johnny Peril,The
  Ultimate Assassin. 4.00
207 JkS,A:Johnny Peril,Secret of
  the Second Star 4.00
208 JkS,A:Johnny Peril,Factory
  of Fear 4.00
209 JkS,Game for the Ghastly 4.00
210 Vampire of the Apes,Time
  Warp 4.00
211 A:Johnny Peril,The Temple
  of the 7 Stars 4.00
212 JkS,MK(c),A:Johnny Peril,The
  Adventure of the Angel's Smile. 4.00
213 A:Johnny Peril,The Woman
  Who Died Forever 4.00
214 JKu(c),Slaughterhouse Arena . 4.00
215 JKu(c),Is Someone
  Stalking Sandra 4.00
216 GP,JKu(c),Samurai Nightmare . 4.00
217 ShM,DSp,EC(c),Dear Senator . 4.00
218 KG,ECh&DG(c),I'll Remember
  You Yesterday 4.00
219 JKu(c),A Wild Tale 4.00
220 ShM,JKu(c),The Strange
  Guide 4.00
221 SD,ShM,JKu(c),Em the

Energy Monster 4.00
222 KG,SD(c). 4.00

TALES OF THE WILDERNESS
1 GK,special 2.00

Talos of the Wilderness Sea #1
© DC Comics Inc.

TALOS OF THE WILDERNESS SEA
Aug. 1987
1-shot GK 2.00

TANGENT COMICS
(All Oct. 1997)
The Atom #1 DJu,PR,V:Fatal Five . 3.00
The Flash #1, TDz,GFr,CaS 3.00
Doom Patrol #1 DJu,SCh,. 3.00
Green Lantern #1 JeR,JWi,MGy . . . 3.00
The Joker #1 KK,MHy, ... 3.00
Metal Men #1 MRz,MkK 3.00
Nightwing #1 JOs,JD 3.00
Sea Devils #1 KBk,VGi,TP 3.00
The Secret Six #1 CDi,TG, ... 3.00

TANGENT '98
(All June 1998)
The Batman #1 DJu,KJ. 2.00
JLA #1 DJu,DBk,V:UltraHumanites . 2.00
Joker's Wild #1 KK 2.00
Nightwing: Night Force #1 JOs 2.00
Powergirl #1 RMz. 2.00
The Superman #1 Harvey Dent . . . 2.00
Tales of the Green Lantern #1 . . . . 2.00
The Trials of the Flash #1,
  V:Plastic Man 2.00
Wonder Woman #1 PDa, ... 2.00

TANK GIRL
1995
1 Movie Adaptation 5.95

TANK GIRL: APOCALYPSE
1995–96
1 AIG,BBo(c). 2.25
2 AIG,BBo(c)Tank Girl Pregnant. . . 2.25
3 AIG,BBo(c). 2.25
4 AIG, finale 2.25

TANK GIRL: THE ODYSSEY
Vertigo 1995
1 New Limited Series. 2.25
2 BBo(c),Land of Milk & Honey . . . 2.25
3 I:The Sirens 2.25

Tarzan #212 © DC Comics, Inc.

TARZAN
April, 1972
(Prev. published by Gold Key)
207 JKu,O:Tarzan,pt.1 . . . . 5.00
208 thru 210 JKu,O:Tarzan,pt.2–4. . 3.00
211 thru 258 Feb., 1977 . . . . . . @2.00

TARZAN FAMILY
Nov.–Dec., 1975
(Prev.: Korak, Son of Tarzan)
60 B:Korak. 1.25
61 thru 66 Nov.–Dec.,1976 . . . . . @1.25

TATTERED BANNERS
1998
1 (of 4) AIG(s),MMc. 3.00
2 AIG&KG(s),MMc. 3.00
3 AIG(s),MMc. 3.00
4 AIG(s),MMc, conclusion 3.00

TEAM TITANS
1992–94
1 KM,Total Chaos#3,A:New Titans,
   Deathstroke,V:Lord Chaos,
   BU:KGa,Killowat. 2.50
1a BU:AV(i),Mirage 2.50
1b BU:MN,GP,Nightrider 2.50
1c BU:AH,Redwing 2.50
1d BU:GP(i),Terra 2.50
2 KM,Total Chaos#6,A:New
   Titans, V:Chaos,C:Battalion . . . 2.00
3 KM,Total Chaos#9,V:Lord
   Chaos, A:New Titans 2.00
4 KM,Titans Sell-Out#4,
   J:Battalion, Troia 2.00
5 KM,A:Battalion. 2.00
6 ANi,A:Battalion. 2.00
7 PJ,I:Nightwing of 2001 . . . . 2.00
8 PJ,A:Raven 2.00
9 PJ,V:Bloodwing 2.00
10 PJ,V:Vampiric Creatures 2.00
11 PJ,F:Battalion 2.00

12 PJ,F:Battalion 2.00
13 PJ,New Direction. 2.00
14 PJ,V:Clock King,Chronos,Calander
   Man,Time Commander. 2.00
15 PJ 2.00
16 PJ,F:Nightrider. 2.00
17 PJ,A:Deathwing. 2.00
18 IR:Leader 2.00
19 V:Leader 2.00
20 PJ,V:Lazarium 2.00
21 PJ,V:US Government. 2.00
22 PJ,A:Chimera 2.25
23 PJ,I:Warhawk(Redwing). 2.25
24 PJ,Zero Hour,R.Kole,last issue. 2.25
Ann.#1 I:Chimera 3.50
Ann.#2 PJ,Elseworlds Story 3.75

TEEN BEAT
Nov.–Dec., 1967
1 Monkees photo. 17.00
Becomes:
TEEN BEAM
2 Monkees 14.00

TEEN TITANS
[1st Series]
Jan., 1966
1 NC,Titans join Peace Corps . . 200.00
2 NC,I:Garn Akaru. 100.00
3 NC,I:Ding Dong Daddy 60.00
4 NC,A:Speedy 60.00
5 NC,I:Ant 60.00
6 NC,A:Beast Boy 45.00
7 NC,I:Mad Mod 45.00
8 IN/JAb,I:Titans Copter. 45.00
9 NC,A:Teen Titan Sweatshirts . . 45.00
10 NC,I:Bat-Bike. 45.00
11 IN/NC A:Speedy 40.00
12 NC,in Spaceville 45.00
13 NC,Christmas story 40.00
14 NC,I:Gargoyle 40.00
15 NC,I:Capt. Rumble. 40.00
16 NC,I:Dimension X 40.00
17 NC,A:Mad Mod 40.00
18 NC,1:Starfire (Russian) 40.00
19 GK,WW,J:Speedy 40.00
20 NA,NC J:Joshua 42.00
21 NA,NC,A:Hawk,Dove 42.00
22 NA,NC,O:Wondergirl 42.00
23 GK,NC,N:Wondergirl 20.00
24 GK,NC. 20.00
25 NC,I:Lilith,A:J.L.A. 20.00
26 NC,I:Mal 20.00
27 NC. 20.00
28 NC,A:Ocean Master. 20.00
29 NC,A:Ocean Master. 20.00
30 NC,A:Aquagirl 20.00
31 NC,GT,A:Hawk,Dove 20.00
32 NC,I:Gnarrk. 12.00
33 GT,NS,A:Gnarrk. 12.00
34 GT,NC. 12.00
35 GT,NC,O:Mal 12.00
36 GT,NC,JAp,V:Hunchback. 12.00
37 GT,NC. 12.00
38 GT,NC. 12.00
39 GT,NC,Rep.Hawk & Dove 12.00
40 NC,A:Aqualad 12.00
41 NC,DC,Lilith Mystery 12.00
42 NC. 12.00
43 NC,Inherit the Howling Night . . 12.00
44 C:Flash 12.00
45 IN,V:Fiddler 12.00
46 IN,A:Fiddler 12.00
47 C:Two-Face 6.00
48 I:Bumblebee,Harlequin,
   A:Two-Face 11.00
49 R:Mal As Guardian 6.00
50 DH,I:Teen Titans West 10.00
51 DH,A:Teen Titans West 6.00

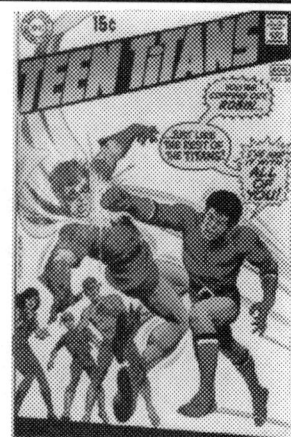

Teen Titans #28 © DC Comics, Inc.

52 DH,A:Teen Titans West 6.00
53 O:Teen Titans, A:JLA. 8.00

TEEN TITANS, THE
Aug. 1996
1 DJu(s),GP,"Titan's Children,"
   pt.1 (of 3) 4.00
2 DJu(s),GP,"Titan's Children,"
   pt.2,V:Prysm. 3.00
3 DJu(s),GP,"Titan's Children,"
   pt.3 . . . . 2.50
4 DJu(s),GP,"Coming Out," pt.1,
   A:Robin 2.00
5 DJu(s),GP,"Coming Out," pt.2 . . 2.00
6 DJu(s),DJu,GP,F:Risk. 2.00
7 DJu(s),DJu,GP,The Atom quits
   team 2.00
8 DJu(s),DJu,GP,J:Atom,V:Dark
   Nemesis. 2.00
9 DJu(s),DJu,GP,"Lost World of
   Skartaris," pt.1 . . . . 2.00
10 DJu(s),DJu,GP,"Lost World of
   Skartaris," pt.2 . . . . 2.00
11 DJu(s),DJu,GP,"Lost World of
   Skartaris" concl.,A:Warlord, . . . 2.00
12 DJu(s),DJu,GP,Original Titans,
   pt.1 (of 4) 48pg. 2.95
13 DJu,GP,Original Titans, pt.2
   Genesis tie-in 2.00
14 DJu,GP,Original Titans, pt.3 . . . 2.00
15 DJu,GP,Original Titans, pt.4. . . . 2.00
16 DJu,GP,aftermath 2.00
17 DJu,PJ,team reunites. 2.00
18 DJu,PR 2.00
19 DJu,PJ,Millennium Giants,
   A:Superman Red 2.00
20 DJu, night with the Titans. 2.00
21 DJu,Titans Hunt,pt.1 . . . . 2.00
22 DJu,Titans Hunt,pt.2 . . . . 2.00
23 DJu,Titans Hunt,pt.3 . . . . 2.00
24 DJu,Titans Hunt,pt.4, final
   issue 2.00
Ann.#1 Pulp Heroes (High-
   Adventure). 3.95
Annual #1 (1967) 80-page, rep. . . . 5.00

TEEN TITANS SPOTLIGHT
Aug., 1986
1 DCw,DG,Starfire "Apartheid". . . . 1.50
2 DCw,DG,Starfire Apartheid#2 . . . 1.00
3 RA,Jericho 1.00
4 RA,Jericho 1.00

5 RA,Jericho 1.00
6 RA,Jericho 1.00
7 JG,Hawk 1.50
8 JG,Hawk 1.00
9 Changeling. 1.00
10 EL,Aqualad And Mento 1.50
11 JO,Brotherhood of Evil. 1.00
12 EC,Wondergirl 1.00
13 Cyborg 1.00
14 1stNightwing/Batman
　　Team-up. 2.50
15 EL,Omega Men 1.50
16 Thunder And Lightning. 1.00
17 DH,Magennta 1.00
18 ATi,Aqualad,A:Aquaman 1.50
19 Starfire,A:Harbinger,Millenium
　　X-over 1.00
20 RT(i),Cyborg 1.00
21 DSp,Flashback sty w/orig.Teen
　　Titans. 1.25

TEMPEST
Mini-series Sept. 1996
1 (of 4) from Aquaman. 1.75
2 new costume 1.75
3 O:Tempest 1.75
4 finale 1.75

TEMPUS FUGITIVE
1990
1 KSy,Time Travel,I:Ray 27 . . . . . . 4.95
2 KSy,Viet Nam 4.95
3 KSy,World War I 4.95
4 KSy,final issue 4.95

TERMINAL CITY
DC/Vertigo 1996–97
1 thru 3 DMt(s),MLr,. . . . . @2.50
4 DMt(s),MLr,I:Kid Gloves 2.50
5 DMt(s),MLr,Missing link on
　　the loose 2.50
6 DMt(s),MLr, ... 2.50
7 DMt(s),MLr,A:Lady in Red. 2.50
8 DMt(s),MLr, ... 2.50
9 (of 9) DMt(s),MLr,finale 2.50
TPB rep. mini-series 20.00

TERMINAL CITY: AERIAL GRAFFITI
DC/Vertigo (Sept., 1997)
1 (of 5) DMt,MLr,MCo(c) 2.50
2 DMt,MLr,MCo(c),F:Cosmo Quinn 2.50
3 DMt,MLr,MCo(c), ... 2.50
4 DMt,MLr,MCo(c) 2.50

3-D BATMAN
1953, 1966
1 rep.Batman #42 & #48 . . . . . . 900.00
1a A:Tommy Tomorrow (1966) . . 250.00

THRILLER
Nov., 1983
1 TVE 1.75
2 TVE,O:Thriller. 1.50
3 TVE 1.50
4 TVE 1.50
5 TVE,DG,Elvis satire 1.50
6 TVE,Elvis satire 1.50
7 TVE 1.50
8 TVE 1.50
9 TVE 1.50
10 TVE. 1.50
11 AN. 1.50
12 AN. 1.50

THRILLING COMICS
1999
1 CDi(s),RH,F:Hawkman &
　　Wildcat. 2.00

THRILLKILLER
Elseworlds
1 HC(s),DIB,F:Robin and Batgirl . . 3.50
2 HC(s),DIB, ... 3.00
3 HC(s),DIB,conl. 3.00

THRILLKILLERS '62
Feb., 1998
GN HC,DIB. 5.00

TIMBER WOLF
1992–93
1 AG(i),V:Thrust 2.00
2 V:Captain Flag 1.50
3 AG(i),V:Creeper 1.50
4 AG(i),V:Captain Flag. 1.50
5 AG(i),V:Dominators,Capt.Flag. . . 1.50

TIME BREAKERS
DC/Helix
1 (of 5) RaP(s),CWn,time
　　paradoxes created 2.50
2 RaP(s),CWn, ... 2.50
3 RaP(s),CWn,expedition to 20th
　　century England 2.50
4 RaP(s),CWn,Angela travels back
　　in time 2.50
5 RaP(s),CWn,final issue. 2.50

TIME MASTERS
Feb., 1990
1 ATi,O:Rip Hunter,A:JLA. 2.50
2 ATi,A:Superman 2.00
3 ATi,A:Jonah Hex, Cave Carson. . 2.00
4 ATi,Animal Man #22 x-over. 2.00
5 ATi,A:Viking Prince 2.00
6 ATi,A:Dr.Fate 2.00
7 ATi,A:GrLantern,Arion. 2.00
8 ATi,V:Vandal Savage 2.00

TIME WARP
Oct.–Nov., 1979
1 JAp,RB,SD,MK(c),DN,TS 15.00

Time Warp #5 © DC Comics Inc.

2 DN,JO,TS,HC,SD,MK(c),GK . . . 10.00
3 DN,SD,MK(c),TS 10.00
4 MN,SD,MK(c),DN 10.00
5 DN,MK(c),July 1980 . . . . 1.00

TITANS
1999
1 MBu, new team, two covers 2.50
2 MBu,A:Superman 2.50
3 MBu 2.50
4 MBu,V:Goth 2.50
5 MBu,A:Siren 2.50
6 MBu,A:Green Lantern 2.50
7 MBu,Velocity 10, pt.1 . . . . 2.50
8 MBu,Velocity 10, pt.2 . . . . 2.50
Secret Files #1 . . . . 5.00
GN Scissors, Paper, Stone, manga
　　style (1997) 5.00

TITANS SELL-OUT SPECIAL
1 SE,AV,I:Teeny Titans,
　　w/Nightwing poster. 3.75

TOMAHAWK
1950–72
1 Prisoner Called Tomahawk. . 1,200.00
2 FF(4pgs),Four Boys
　　Against the Frontier 500.00
3 Warpath 325.00
4 Tomahawk Wanted: Dead
　　or Alive. 325.00
5 The Girl Who Was Chief 325.00
6 Tomahawk-King of the Aztecs. 250.00
7 Punishment of Tomahawk 250.00
8 The King's Messenger 250.00
9 The Five Doomed Men 250.00
10 Frontied Sabotage 250.00
11 Girl Who Hated Tomahawk . . . 200.00
12 Man From Magic Mountain. . . 200.00
13 Dan Hunter's Rival 200.00
14 The Frontier Tinker 200.00
15 The Wild Men of
　　Wigwam Mountain 200.00
16 Treasure of the Angelique . . . 200.00
17 Short-Cut to Danger. 200.00
18 Bring In M'Sieur Pierre. 200.00
19 The Lafayette Volunteers 200.00
20 NC(c),The Retreat of
　　Tomahawk 200.00
21 NC(c),The Terror of the
　　Wrathful Spirit. 125.00
22 CS(c),Admiral Tomahawk. . . . 125.00
23 CS(c),The Indian Chief
　　From Oxford. 125.00
24 NC(c),Adventure In the
　　Everglades 125.00
25 NC(c),The Star-Gazer of
　　Freemont 125.00
26 NC(c),Ten Wagons For
　　Tomahawk 125.00
27 NC(c),Frontier Outcast. 125.00
28 I:Lord Shilling. 150.00
29 The Conspiracy of Wounded
　　Bear. 175.00
30 The King of the Thieves 125.00
31 NC(c),The Buffalo Brave
　　From Misty Mountain 100.00
32 NC(c),The Clocks That
　　Went to War 100.00
33 The Paleface Tribe. 100.00
34 The Capture of General
　　Washington 100.00
35 Frontier Feud. 100.00
36 NC(c),A Cannon for Fort
　　Reckless 100.00
37 NC(c),Feathered Warriors . . . 100.00
38 The Frontier Zoo 100.00
39 The Redcoat Trickster 100.00
40 Fearless Fettle-Daredevil 100.00
41 The Captured Chieftain 100.00

Tomahawk-2 © DC Comics, Inc.

42 The Prisoner Tribe	100.00
43 Tomahawk's Little Brother	100.00
44 The Brave Named Tomahawk	100.00
45 The Last Days of Chief Tory	100.00
46 The Chief With 1,000 Faces	75.00
47 The Frontier Rain-Maker	75.00
48 Indian Twin Trouble	75.00
49 The Unknown Warrior	75.00
50 The Brave Who Was Jinxed	75.00
51 General Tomahawk	75.00
52 Tom Thumb of the Frontier	75.00
53 The Four-Footed Renegade	75.00
54 Mystery of the 13th Arrows	75.00
55 Prisoners of the Choctaw	75.00
56 The Riddle of the Five Little Indians	75.00
57 The Strange Fight at Fort Bravo	100.00
58 Track of the Mask	50.00
59 The Mystery Prisoner of Lost Island	50.00
60 The Amazing Walking Fort	50.00
61 Tomahawk's Secret Weapons	50.00
62 Strongest Man in the World	50.00
63 The Frontier Super Men	50.00
64 The Outcast Brave	50.00
65 Boy Who Wouldn't Be Chief	50.00
66 DD&SMo(c),A Trap For Tomahawk	50.00
67 DD&SMo(c),Frontier Sorcerer	50.00
68 DD&SMo(c),Tomahawk's Strange Ally	50.00
69 DD&SMo(c),Tracker-King of the Wolves	50.00
70 DD&SMo(c),Three Tasks for Tomahawk	50.00
71 DD&SMo(c),The Boy Who Betrayed His Country	50.00
72 DD&SMo(c),The Frontier Pupil	50.00
73 DD&SMo(c),The Secret of the Indian Sorceress	50.00
74 DD&SMo(c),The Great Paleface Masquerade	50.00
75 DD&SMo(c),The Ghost of Lord Shilling	50.00
76 DD&SMo(c),The Totem-Pole Trail	50.00
77 DD&SMo(c),The Raids of the One-Man Tribe	50.00
78 DD&SMo(c),The Menace of the Mask	50.00
79 DD&SMo(c),Eagle Eye's Debt of Honor	50.00
80 DD&SMo(c),The Adventures of Tracker	35.00

81 The Strange Omens of the Indian Seer	35.00
82 The Son of the Tracker	35.00
83 B:Tomahawk Rangers, Against the Tribe	35.00
84 There's a Coward Among the Rangers	35.00
85 The Wispering War	35.00
86 Rangers vs. King Colossus	20.00
87 The Secrets of Sgt. Witch Doctor	20.00
88 The Rangers Who Held Back the Earth	20.00
89 The Terrible Tree-Man	20.00
90 The Prisoner In The Pit	20.00
91 The Tribe Below the Earth	20.00
92 The Petrified Sentry of Peaceful Valley	20.00
93 The Return of King Colosso	20.00
94 Rip Van Ranger	20.00
95 The Tribe Beneath the Sea	20.00
96 The Ranger Killers	20.00
97 The Prisoner Behind the Bull's-Eye	20.00
98 The Pied Piper Rangers	20.00
99 The Rangers vs.ChiefCobweb	20.00
100 The Weird Water-Tomahawk	30.00
101 Tomahawk, Enemy Spy	15.00
102 The Dragon Killers	15.00
103 The Frontier Frankenstein	15.00
104 The Fearful Freak of Dunham's Dungeon	15.00
105 The Attack of the Gator God	15.00
106 The Ghost of Tomahawk	15.00
107 Double-Cross of the Gorilla Ranger	15.00
108 New Boss For the Rangers	15.00
109 The Caveman Ranger	15.00
110 Tomahawk Must Die	15.00
111 Vengeance of the Devil-Dogs	15.00
112 The Rangers vs. Tomahawk	15.00
113 The Mad Miser of Carlisle Castle	15.00
114 The Terrible Power of Chief Iron Hands	15.00
115 The Deadly Flaming Ranger	15.00
116 NA(c),The Last Mile of Massacre Trail	15.00
117 NA(c),Rangers'Last Stand	15.00
118 NA(c),Tomahawk, Guilty of Murder	15.00
119 NA(c),Bait For a Buzzard	15.00
120 NC(c),The Coward Who Lived Forever	15.00
121 NA(c),To Kill a Ranger	15.00
122 IN(c),Must the Brave Die	15.00
123 NA(c),The Stallions of Death	15.00
124 NA(c),The Valley of No Return	15.00
125 NA(c),A Chief's Feather For Little Bear	15.00
126 NA(c),The Baron of Gallows Hill	15.00
127 NA(c),The Devil is Waiting	15.00
128 NA(c),Rangers-Your 9 Lives For Mine	15.00
129 NA(c),Treachery at Thunder Ridge	15.00
130 NA(c),Deathwatch at Desolation Valley	15.00
131 JKu(c),B:Son of Tomahawk, Hang Him High	15.00
132 JKu(c),Small Eagle...Brother Hawk	10.00
133 JKu(c),Scalp Hunter	10.00
134 JKu(c),The Rusty Ranger	10.00
135 JKu(c),Death on Ghost Mountain	10.00
136 JKu(c),A Piece of Sky	15.00
137 JKu(c),Night of the Knife	15.00
138 JKu(c),A Different Kind	

of Christmas	15.00
139 JKu(c),Death Council	20.00
140 Jku(c),The Rescue	15.00

TOR
May-June, 1975

1 JKu,O:Tor	1.25
2 thru 6, Tor reprints	@1.25

TOTAL JUSTICE
Sept. 1996

1 thru 3 CPr(s),RBe,DG, toy line tie-in	@2.25

TOTAL RECALL
1990

1 Movie Adaption	3.00

TOXIC GUMBO
DC/Vertigo (March, 1998)

1-shot GN	6.00

TRANSMETROPOLITAN
DC/Helix July 1997

1 WEI,DaR,JeM, gonzo journalism in 21st century	2.50
2 WEI,DaR,Angels 8 district	2.50
3 WEI,DaR, riot in Angels 8	2.50
4 WEI,DaR, Vs President of US	2.50
5 WEI,DaR, Watches TV	2.50
6 WEI,DaR,evangelicals	2.50
7 WEI,DaR	2.50
8 WEI,DaR,AnotherColdMorning	2.50
9 WEI,DaR,Wild in the Country	2.50
10 WEI,DaR,Freeze Me with Your Kiss, pt.1	2.50
11 WEI,DaR,Freeze Me, pt.2	2.50
12 WEI,DaR,Freeze Me, pt.3	2.50
13 WEI,DaR,JaL(c),Year of the Bastard, pt.1	2.50
14 WEI,DaR,JaL(c),Bastard,pt.2	2.50
15 WEI,DaR,JaL(c),Bastard,pt.3	2.50
16 WEI,DaR,Bastard,pt.4	2.50
17 WEI,DaR,Bastard,pt.5	2.50
18 WEI,DaR,Bastard, concl.	2.50
19 WEI,DaR,New Scum,pt.1	2.50
20 WEI,DaR,New Scum,pt.2	2.50
21 WEI,DaR,New Scum,pt.3	2.50
22 WEI,DaR,New Scum,pt.4	2.50

Transmetropolitan #8
© DC Comics, Inc.

23 WEl,DaR,New Scum,pt.5 . . . . . . 2.50
24 WEl,DaR,New Scum,pt.6 . . . . . . 2.50
25 WEl,DaR,JLe(c),Days in
    the City #1 . . . . 2.50
26 WEl,DaR,RyR,JLe(c),Days in
    the City #2 . . . . 2.50
TPB Back on the Street 8.00
TPB Lust For Life 15.00

TRENCHCOAT BRIGADE
Vertigo 1999
1 (of 4) JNR(s),F:John Constantine,
    Mister E, Dr.Occult, Phantom
    Stranger 2.50
2 JNR 2.50
3 JNR 2.50
4 JNR, conclusion 2.50

TRIUMPH
[Mini-Series] 1995
1 From Zero Hour 1.75
2 Teamates Peril 1.75
3 V:Mind Readers 1.75

TRUE FAITH
DC/Vertigo (Aug., 1997)
TPB GEn,WaP, series rep. 13.00

TSR WORLDS
TSR 1990
1 I:SpellJammer 4.50

TV SCREEN CARTOONS
(see REAL SCREEN COMICS)

2020 VISIONS
DC/Vertigo April 1997
1 (of 12) the Disunited States
    of America 2.25
2 JaD(s), ... 2.25
3 JaD(s), ... 2.25
4 JaD(s),WaP, "La Tormenta"
    pt.1 (of 3) 2.25
5 JaD(s),WaP, "La Tormenta" pt.2 . 2.25
6 JaD(s),WaP,"La Tormenta,pt.3 . . . 2.25
7 JaD(s), "Renegade," pt.1 . . . . . . 2.25
8 JaD(s), "Renegade," pt.2 . . . . . . 2.25
9 JaD(s), "Renegade," pt.3 . . . . . . 2.25
10 JaD(s),Repro-Man,pt.1. . . . . . . 2.25
11 JaD(s),Repro-Man,pt.2. . . . . . . 2.25
12 JaD(s),Repro-Man,pt.3. . . . . . . 2.25

TWILIGHT
1990–91
1 JL,Last Frontier 5.50
2 JL,K.SorensenVs.T.Tomorrow . . . 4.95
3 JL,K.SorensenVs.T.Tomorrow . . . 4.95

UNAUTHORIZED BIO
OF LEX LUTHOR
1 EB 3.95

UNCLE SAM
DC/Vertigo (Nov, 1997)
GN 1 (of 2) AxR 5.00
GN 2 AxR. 5.00

UNDERWORLD
Dec., 1987
1 EC,New Yorks Finest 1.25
2 EC,A:Black Racer. 1.25
3 EC,V:Black Racer. 1.25

---

4 EC,final issue 1.25

UNDERWORLD
UNLEASHED
1995–96
1 PWa,F:Neron 5.00
2 PWa,Neron Vs.Green Lantern . . 4.00
3 PWa,conclusion 4.00
Abyss—Hell's Sentinel 1-shot . . . 3.00
Apokolips-Dark Uprising 1-shot. . . 3.00
Batman—Devil's Asylum 1-shot
    AIG,BSz 3.00
Patterns of Fear 1-shot 3.00

UNEXPECTED, THE
(see TALES OF
THE UNEXPECTED)

UNKNOWN SOLDIER
(see STAR SPANGLED)

UNKNOWN SOLDIER
April, 1977
1 True Origin revealed,Viet
    Nam 1970 . . . . 1.50
2 Origin contd.,Iran 1977 . . . . 1.50
3 Origin contd.Afghanistan1982 . . . 1.50
4 Nicaragua. 1.50
5 Nicaragua contd. 1.50
6 . . . . 1.50
7 Libia 1.50
8 Siberia, U.S.S.R. 1.75
9 North Korea 1952 . . . . 1.75
10 C.I.A. 1.75
11 C.I.A., Army Intelligence. 1.75
12 final issue,Oct.1982 . . . . 1.75

UNKNOWN SOLDIER
DC/Vertigo Feb. 1997
1 (of 4) GEn(s),KPI,F:maverick
    CIA agent. 2.50
2 GEn(s),KPI,search for Unknown
    Soldier continues 2.50
3 GEn(s),KPI,search for Unknown
    Soldier continues 2.50
4 GEn(s),KPI,intrigue, finale. 2.50
TPB series rep.. . . . . 13.00

UNTOLD LEGEND
OF BATMAN
July, 1980
1 JA,JBy,(1st DC work)O:Batman . 6.00
2 JA,O:Joker&Robin 4.50
3 JA,O:Batgirl 4.50

V
(TV Adaptation)
Feb., 1985
1 CI/TD 1.35
2 thru 5 CI/TD . . . . @1.25
6 thru 16 CI/TD . . . . @1.25
17 & 18 DG. . . . . @1.25

VALOR
1992–94
1 N:Valor,A:Lex Luthor Jr. 2.00
2 MBr,AG,V:Supergirl 1.50
3 MBr,AG,V:Lobo. 1.50
4 MBr,AG,V:Lobo. 1.50
5 MBr,A:Blasters 1.50
6 A:Blasters,V:Kanjar Ru 1.50

Valor #12 © DC Comics Inc.

7 A:Blasters. 1.50
8 AH(c),V:The Unimaginable 1.50
9 AH(c),PCu,A:Darkstar. 1.50
10 AH(c),V:Unimaginable 1.50
11 A:Legionnaires. 1.50
12 AH(c),B:D.O.A. 3.00
13 AH(c),D:Valor's Mom 3.00
14 AH(c),A:JLA,Legionnaires 2.50
15 SI(c),D.O.A #4. . . . . 2.00
16 CDo,D.O.A #5. . . . . 2.00
17 CDo,LMc,D:Valor. 1.75
18 A:Legionnaires. 1.75
19 CDo,A:Legionnaires,V:Glorith. . 1.75
20 CDo,A:Wave Rider 1.75
21 . . . . 1.75
22 End of an Era,pt.2 . . . . 1.75
23 Zero Hour 2.50

VAMPS
Vertigo 1994–95
1 BB(c) 3.00
2 BB(c) 2.50
3 thru 5 BB(c) . . . . @2.25
6 BB(c),last issue 2.25
TPB 9.95

VAMPS:
HOLLYWOOD & VEIN
Vertigo 1996
1 F:Mink 2.25
2 . . . . 2.25
3 I:Maggot 2.25
4 F:Mink,Screech 2.25
5 off to rescue Hugh Evans (of 6) . 2.25
6 . . . . 2.25

VAMPS: PUMPKIN TIME
Vertigo 1998
1 (of 3) Halloween mini-series . . . 2.50
2 . . . . 2.50
3 . . . . 2.50

VERMILLION
DC/Helix Aug. 1996
1 ADv,MKu(c) Lucius Shepard
    story. 2.50
2 ADv,MKu(c) Jonathan Cave's
    cover blown 2.50
3 ADv,riot aboard space ship,
    Ildiko's tale 2.50

Vamps Pumpkin Time #2
© DC Comics, Inc.

4 ADv,Starship's engines run wild . 2.50
5 ADv 2.50
6 ADv,Creation of Vermillion 2.50
7 ADv,Jonathan Cave discovers
　hiding place of enemy 2.50
8 ADv,"Joyland" 2.50
9 GEr, the library in Kaia Mortai . . . 2.50
10 GEr, "Lord Iron and Lady
　Manganese, pt.2 . . . . 2.50
11 GEr,"Lord Iron and Lady
　Manganese" concl 2.50
12 final issue 2.50

V FOR VENDETTA
Sept., 1988
1 Reps.Warrior Mag(U.K.),I:V,
　A:M.Storm (Moore scripts) 5.00
2 Murder Spree 3.50
3 Govt. Investigators close in 3.00
4 T.V. Broadcast take-over 3.00
5 Govt.Corruption Expose 3.00
6 Evey in Prison 3.00
7 Evey released 2.50
8 Search for V,A:Finch 2.50
9 V:Finch 2.50
10 D:V 2.50
TPB 1990 . . . . 14.95

VERTIGO GALLERY: DREAMS AND NIGHTMARES
1995
1 Various artists 3.50

VERTIGO JAM
1993
1 GF(c),NGa(s),ANo(s),PrM(s),GEn(s),
　JaD(s),KN,SDi,SEa,NyC(s),EiS,PhH,
　KDM(i),SeP,MiA,RaP(s),MPn(i),
　Vertigo Short Stories 4.50

VERTIGO PREVIEW
1992
Preview of new Vertigo titles,
　new Sandman story 1.75

VERTIGO VERITE: HELL ETERNAL
Feb, 1998
1-shot JaD,SeP 7.00

VERTIGO VERITE: THE SYSTEM
1 thru 3 . . . . @2.95
GN Seven Miles a Second 7.95

VERTIGO VERITE: THE UNSEEN HAND
DC/Vertigo 1996
1 thru 3 TLa . . . . @2.50
4 TLa, final issue 2.50

VERTIGO VISIONS: DR. OCCULT
1 F:Dr. Occult 3.95

VERTIGO VISIONS: DR. THIRTEEN
DC/Vertigo July 1998
GN evil artificial intelligence 6.00

VERTIGO VISIONS: THE GEEK
1993
1 RaP(s),MiA,V:Dr.Abuse4.25

VERTIGO VISIONS: PHANTOM STRANGER
1993
1 AaK(s),GyD,The Infernal House . 3.75

VERTIGO VISIONS: THE EATERS
1995
1 I:The Quills 4.95

VERTIGO VISIONS: TOMAHAWK
DC/Vertigo May, 1998
GN RaP,TY 5.00

VERTIGO: WINTER'S EDGE
DC/Vertigo 1998
TPB BB(c) rep. 8.00
GN Winter's Edge II 7.00

VEXT
1999
1 KG,MMK,MkM 2.50
2 KG,MMK,MkM 2.50
3 KG,MMK,MkM 2.50
4 KG,MMK,MkM 2.50
5 KG,MMK,MkM 2.50
6 KG,MMK,MkM, final issue 2.50

VIGILANTE
Oct., 1983
1 KP,DG,F:Adrian Chase 3.50
2 KP 3.00
3 KP,Cyborg 2.50
4 DN,V:Exterminator 2.50

Vigilante #34 DC Comics, Inc.

5 KP 2.50
6 O:Vigilante 3.00
7 O:Vigilante 3.00
8 RA,V:Electrocutioner 2.50
9 RA,V:Electrocutioner 2.50
10 RA,DG,avenges J.J. 2.50
11 RA,V:Controller 2.00
12 GK,"Journal" 2.00
13 GK,"Locke Room Murder" 2.00
14 RA,V:Hammer 2.00
15 RA,V:Electrocutioner 2.00
16 RA 2.00
17 Moore 3.00
18 Moore 3.00
19 RA 2.00
20 A:Nightwing 2.50
21 A:Nightwing 2.50
22 . . . . 2.00
23 V:Electrocutioner 2.00
24 "Mother's Day" 2.00
25 RM,V:Police Torturers 2.00
26 V:Electrocutioner 2.00
27 V:Electrocutioner 2.00
28 New Vigilante 2.00
29 RM,New Vigilante 2.00
30 RM,D:Glitz Jefferson 2.00
31 RM,New York Violence 2.00
32 RM,New York Violence 2.00
33 RM,V:Rapist 2.00
34 . . . . 2.00
35 JBy(c),O:MadBomber 2.00
36 MGr(c),V:Peacemaker 2.25
37 MGr,RM,V:Peacemaker 2.25
38 MGr,PeaceMaker 2.25
39 White Slavery 2.00
40 HC(c),White Slavery 2.00
41 . . . . 2.00
42 A:Peacemaker,V:Terrorists . . . 2.00
43 V:PeaceMaker 2.00
44 DC,V:Qurac 2.00
45 I:Black Thorn 2.00
46 Viigilante in Jail 2.00
47 A:Batman 2.50
48 I:Homeless Avenger 2.00
49 . . . . 2.00
50 KSy(c)D:Vigilante 2.50
Ann.#1 . . . . 3.00
Ann.#2 V:Cannon 2.50

VIGILANTE: CITY LIGHTS, PRAIRIE JUSTICE
1995–96
1 JeR,MCo,(of 4)	2.50
2 JeR,V:Bugsy Siegel	2.50
3 JeR	2.50
4 finale	2.50

VIPER
1994
1 Based on the TV Show	2.25
2	2.00
3	2.00
4 final issue	2.00

WANDERERS
June, 1988
1 I:New Team	1.25
2 V:The Performer	1.25
3 A:Legion of Superheroes	1.25
4 V:Controller Hunters	1.25
5 O:Wanderers	1.25
6 V:Terrorists	1.25
7 V:Medtorians	1.25
8 O:Psyche	1.25
9 O:Psyche	1.25
10 F:Quantum Queen	1.25
11 F:Quantum Queen	1.25
12 V:Aliens	1.25
13 V:Dinosaurs	1.25

WANTED: THE WORLD'S MOST DANGEROUS VILLIANS
July-Aug., 1972
1 rep. Batman,Green Lantern	4.00
2 Batman/Joker/Penguin	5.00
3	3.00
4	3.00
5	3.00
6	3.00
7	3.00
8	3.00
9	3.00

WARLORD
Jan., 1976
1 MGr,O:Warlord	15.00
2 MGr,I:Machiste	10.00
3 MGr,`War Gods of Skartaris'	7.00
4 MGr,`Duel of the Titans'	7.00
5 MGr,`The Secret of Skartaris'	7.00
6 MGr,I:Mariah,Stryker	5.00
7 MGr,O:Machiste	5.00
8 MGr,A:Skyra	5.00
9 MGr,N:Warlord	5.00
10 MGr,I:Ashiya	5.00
11 MGr,rep.1st Issue special #8	4.00
12 MGr,I:Aton	4.00
13 MGr,D:Stryker	4.00
14 MGr,V:Death	4.00
15 MGr,I:Joshua	4.00
16 MGr,I:Saaba	4.00
17 MGr,`Citadel of Death'	4.00
18 MGr,I:Shadow	4.00
19 MGr,`Wolves of the Steppes'	4.00
20 MGr,I:Joshua clone	5.00
21 MGr,D:Joshua clone,Shadow	3.00
22 MGr`Beast in the Tower'	3.00
23 MGr,`Children of Ba'al'	3.00
24 MGr,I:Iligia	3.00
25 MGr,I:Ahir	3.00
26 MGr,`The Challenge'	3.00
27 MGr,`Atlantis Dying'	3.00

28 MGr,I:Wizard World'	3.00
29 MGr,I:Mongo Ironhand'	3.00
30 MGr,C:Joshua	3.00
31 MGr,`Wing over Shamballah'	3.00
32 MGr,I:Shakira	3.00
33 MGr,Birds of Prey,A:Shakira	3.00
34 MGr,Sword of the Sorceror, I:Hellfire	3.00
35 MGr,C:Mike Grell	3.00
36 MGr,`Interlude'	3.00
37 MGr,JSn,I:Firewing,B:Omac	6.00
38 MGr,I:Jennifer,A:Omac	3.00
39 MGr,JSn,`Feast of Agravar'	4.00
40 MGr,N:Warlord	3.00
41 MGr,A:Askir	2.50
42 MGr,JSn,A:Tara,Omac	3.50
43 MGr,JSn,`Berserk'A:Omac	3.50
44 MGr,`The Gamble'	3.00
45 MGr,`Nightmare in Vista Vision',A:Omac	3.00
46 MGr,D:Shakira	3.00
47 MGr,I:Mikola,E:Omac	3.00
48 MGr,EC,TY,I:Arak,Claw(B)	3.00
49 MGr,TY,A:Shakira,E:Claw	2.50
50 MGr,`By Fire and Ice'	2.50
51 MGr,TY,rep.#1, I(B):Dragonsword	2.00
52 MGr,TY,`Back in the U.S.S.R.	2.50
53 MT,TY,`Sorcerer's Apprentice'	2.00
54 MT,`Sorceress Supreme', E:Dragonsword	2.00
55 MT,`Have a Nice Day'	2.00
56 MT,JD,I:Gregmore,(B):Arion	2.00
57 MT,`The Two Faces of Travis Morgan'	2.00
58 MT,O:Greamore	2.00
59 MGr,A:Joshua	2.00
60 JD,`Death Dual'	2.00
61 JD,A:Greamore	2.00
62 JD,TMd,A:Mikola,E:Arion	2.00
63 JD,RR,I(B):Barren Earth	2.00
64 DJu,RR`Elsewhere'	2.00
65 DJu,RR,A:Wizard World, No Barren Earth	2.00
66 DJu`Wizard World', No Barren Earth	2.00
67 DJu,RR,`The Mark'	2.00
68 DJu,RR	2.00
69 DJu,RR	2.00
70 DJu,`Outback'	2.00
71 DJu/DA,`The Journey Back' No Barren Earth	2.00
72 DJu,DA,I:Scarhart,No Barren Earth	2.00

Warlord #72 © DC Comics Inc.

73 DJ,DA,`Cry Plague'	2.00
74 DJu,No Barren Earth	2.00
75 DJu,`All Dreams Must Pass' No Barren Earth	2.00
76 DJu,DA,RR,A:Sarga	2.00
77 DJu,DA,RR,Let My People Go	2.00
78 DJu,RR,`Doom's Mouth'	2.00
79 PB,RM,`Paradox',No Barren Earth	2.00
80 DJu,DA,RR,`Future Trek'	2.00
81 DJu,DA,RR,`Thief's Magic'	2.00
82 DJu,DA,RR,`Revolution'	2.00
83 DJu,RR,`All the President's Men'	2.00
84 DJu,DA,RR,`Hail to the Chief'	2.00
85 DJu,RR,`The Price of Change'	2.00
86 DJ,DA,No Barren Earth	2.00
87 DJu,RB,RR,I:Hawk	2.00
88 DJu,RB,RR,I:Patch,E:Barren Earth	2.00
89 RB,I:Sabertooth	2.00
90 RB,`Demon's of the Past'	2.00
91 DJu,DA,I:Maddox,O:Warlord O:Jennifer	1.75
92 NKu,`Evil in Ebony'	2.00
93 RR,A:Sabertooth	1.75
94 `Assassin's Prey'	1.75
95 AKu,`Dragon's Doom'	2.00
96 `Nightmare Prelude'	1.75
97 RB,A:Saaba,D:Scarhart	1.75
98 NKu,Crisis tie-in	2.00
99 NKu`Fire and Sword'	2.00
100 AKu,D:Greamore,Sabertooth	2.00
101 MGr,`Temple of Demi-god'	1.75
102 I:Zuppara,Error-Machiste with two hands	1.75
103 JBi,`Moon Beast'	1.75
104 RR,`Dragon Skinner'	1.75
105 RR,`Staliiers of Skinner'	1.75
106 RR,I:Daimon	1.75
107 RR,`Bride of Yano'	1.75
108 RR,I:Mortella	1.75
109 RR,A:Mortella	1.75
110 RR,A:Skyra III	1.75
111 RR,`Tearing o/t Island Sea'	1.75
112 RR,`Obsession'	1.75
113 RR,`Through Fiends Destroy Me'	1.75
114 RR,`Phenalegeno Dies'	1.75
115 RR,`Citadel of Fear'	1.75
116 RR,`Revenge of the Warlord'	1.75
117 RR,A:Power Girl	1.75
118 RR,A:Power Girl	1.75
119 RR,A:Power Girl	1.75
120 ATb,A:Power Girl	1.75
121 ATb,A:Power Girl	1.75
122 ATb,A:Power Girl	1.75
123 JD,TMd,N:Warlord	1.75
124 JD,TMd,I:Scavenger	1.75
125 JD,TMd,D:Tara	1.75
126 JD,TMd,A:Machiste	1.75
127 JD,`The Last Dragon'	1.75
128 JD,I:Agife	1.75
129 JD,Vision of Quest	1.75
130 JD,A:Maddox	1.75
131 JD,RLd,`Vengeful Legacies	3.00
132 `A New Beginning'	1.75
133 JD,final issue (44pg)	2.00
Ann.#1 MGr,A:Shakira	3.00
Ann.#2 I:Krystovar	1.75
Ann.#3 DJu,`Full Circle'	1.75
Ann.#4 A:New Gods, Legends tie-in	1.75
Ann.#5 AKu,Hellfire	1.75
Ann.#6 F:New Gods	1.50
TPB Warlord:Savage Empire, Rep.#1-#10,#12,Special #8	19.95

[Limited Series]
1 Travis Morgan retrospective	1.75
2 Fate of T. Morgan revealed	1.75
3 Return of Deimos	1.75

DC COMICS

4 V:Deimos 1.75
5 MGr(c),Skartaros at War. 1.75
6 finale 1.75

WAR OF THE GODS
1 GP,A:Lobo,Misc.Heroes,Circe
   (direct) 1.75
2 GP,A:Misc.Heroes,V:Circe,
   w/poster. 1.75
2a (Newsstand) 1.75
3 GP,A:Misc.Heroes,V:Circe,
   w/poster 1.75
3a Newsstand 1.75
4 GP,A:Misc.Heroes,V:Circe,
   w/poster. 1.75
4a Newsstand 1.75

Wasteland #11 © DC Comics, Inc.

WASTELAND
Dec., 1987
1 Selection of Horror stories 1.75
2 . . . . 1.75
3 . . . . 1.75
4 . . . . 1.75
5 `The big crossover story'. 1.75
6 . . . . 1.75
7 `Great St.Louis Electrical
   Giraffe Caper'. 1.75
8 `Dead Detective'. 1.75
9 . . . . 1.75
10 TT,African Folk Tale 1.75
11 `Revenge o/t Swamp Creature' . 1.75
12 JO,`After the Dead Detective'. . . 1.75
13 TT(c),JO 2.00
14 JO,RM,`Whistling Past the
   Graveyard' 2.00
15 JO,RM. 2.00
16 JO. 2.00
17 JO. 2.00
18 JO,RM,final issue 2.00

WATCHMEN
Sept., 1986
1 B:AMo,DGb,D:Comedian 7.50
2 DGb,Funeral for Comedian. 5.00
3 DGb,F:Dr.Manhattan. 5.00
4 DGb,O:Dr.Manhattan 5.00
5 DGb,F:Rorschach. 5.00
6 DGb,O:Rorschach 5.00
7 DGb,F:Nite Owl 5.00
8 DGb,F:Silk Spectre 5.00
9 DGb,O:Silk Spectre 5.00
10 DGb,A:Rorschach 5.00

11 DGb,O:Ozymandius. 5.00
12 DGb,D:Rorsharch 5.00
TPB rep.#1-#12 . . . . 14.95
TPB 20.00

WEB, THE
Impact 1991–92
1 I:Gunny, Bill Grady, Templar 1.25
2 O:The Web, I:Brew, Jump,
   Sunshine Kid 1.00
3 Minions of Meridian, I:St.James . 1.00
4 Agent Jump vs. UFO 1.00
5 Agent Buster/Fly team-up
   V:Meridian 1.00
6 I:Posse,A:Templar 1.00
7 V:Meridian's Forces 1.00
8 R: Studs. 1.00
9 Earthquest,pt.1 . . . . 2.50
10 V:Templar 1.25
11 V:Templar 1.25
12 "The Gauntlet",A:Shield 1.25
13 Frenzy#1 . . . . 1.25
14 Frenzy#2 . . . . 1.25
Ann.#1 Earthquest,w/trading card . . 2.50

Weird #2 © DC Comics, Inc.

WEIRD, THE
April, 1988
1 BWr,A:JLI. 4.00
2 BWr,A:JLI. 3.00
3 BWr,V:Jason. 3.00
4 final issue. 2.50

WEIRD
DC/Paradox Press 1997
1 B&W magazine. 3.00
2 . . . . 3.00
3 . . . . 3.00

WEIRD WAR TALES
Sept.–Oct., 1971
1 JKu(c),JKu,RH,Fort which
   Did Not Return 175.00
2 JKu,MD,Military Madness 60.00
3 JKu(c),RA,The Pool 55.00
4 JKu(c),Ghost of Two Wars 50.00
5 JKu(c),RH,Slave. 50.00
6 JKu(c),Pawns, The Sounds
   of War 25.00
7 JKu(c),JKu,RH,Flying Blind. . . . 25.00
8 NA(c),The Avenging Grave. . . . 45.00
9 NC(c),The Promise. 25.00

10 NC(c),Who is Haunting
   the Haunted Chateau 25.00
11 NC(c),ShM,Oct. 30, 1918:
   The German Trenches, WWI . 20.00
12 MK(c),God of Vengeance. 20.00
13 LD(c),The Die-Hards 20.00
14 LD(c),ShM,The Ghost of
   McBride's Woman 20.00
15 LD(c),Ace King Just Flew
   In From Hell 20.00
16 LD(c),More Dead Than Alive . . 20.00
17 GE(c),Dead Man's Hands 20.00
18 GE(c),Captain Dracula. 20.00
19 LD(c),The Platoon That
   Wouldn't Die. 20.00
20 LD(c),Operation Voodoo 20.00
21 LD(c),One Hour To Kill. 15.00
22 LD(c),Wings of Death. 15.00
23 LD(c),The Bird of Death. 15.00
24 LD(c),The Invisible Enemy 15.00
25 LD(c),Black Magic...White
   Death 15.00
26 LD(c),Jump Into Hell 15.00
27 LD(c),Survival of the
   Fittest. 15.00
28 LD(c),Isle of Forgotten
   Warriors 15.00
29 LD(c),Breaking Point 15.00
30 LD(c),The Elements of Death. . 15.00
31 LD(c),Death Waits Twice 15.00
32 LD(c),The Enemy, The Stars . . 15.00
33 LD(c),Pride of the Master
   Race 15.00
34 LD(c),The Common Enemy . . . 15.00
35 LD(c),The Invaders 15.00
36 JKu(c),Escape 20.00
37 LD(c),The Three Wars of
   Don Q 7.00
38 JKu(c),Born To Die 7.00
39 JKu(c),The Spoils of War. 7.00
40 ECh(c),Back From The Dead. . . 7.00
41 JL(c), The Dead Draftees of
   Regiment Six 7.00
42 JKu(c),Old Soldiers Never
   Die 7.00
43 ECh(c),Bulletproof 7.00
44 JKu(c),ShM,The Emperor
   Weehawken 7.00
45 JKu(c),The Battle of Bloody
   Valley. 7.00
46 Kill Or Be Killed 7.00
47 JKu(c),Bloodbath of the Toy
   Soldiers 7.00
48 JL(c),Ultimate Destiny 7.00
49 The Face Of The Enemy 7.00
50 ECh(c),-An Appointment With
   Destiny. 7.00
51 JKu(c),Secret Weapon. 7.00
52 JKu(c),The Devil Is A
   Souvenir Hunter 7.00
53 JAp(c), Deadly Dominoes 7.00
54 GM(c),Soldier of Satan 7.00
55 JKu(c),A Rebel Shall Rise
   From The Grave. 7.00
56 AM(c),The Headless Courier . . . 7.00
57 RT(c),Trial By Combat 7.00
58 JKu(c),Death Has A Hundred
   Eyes 7.00
59 The Old One 7.00
60 JKu(c),Night Flight 7.00
61 HC(c),Mind War. 4.00
62 JKu(c),The Grubbers 4.00
63 JKu(c),Battleground. 4.00
64 JKu(c),Deliver Me For D-Day . . 4.00
65 JKu(c),The Last Cavalry
   Charge 4.00
66 JKu(c),The Iron Star 4.00
67 JKu(c),The Attack of the
   Undead 4.00
68 FM,JKu(c),The Life and Death of
   Charlie Golem 4.00

69 JKu(c),The Day After Doomsday 4.00
70 LD(c),The Blood Boat 4.00
71 LD(c),False Prophet. 4.00
72 JKu(c),Death Camp 4.00
73 GE(c),The Curse of Zopyrus . . . 4.00
74 GE(c),March of the Mammoth . . 4.00
75 JKu(c),The Forgery 4.00
76 JKu(c),The Fire Bug. 4.00
77 JKu(c),Triad. 4.00
78 JKu(c),Indian War In Space 4.00
79 JKu(c),The Gods Themselves . . 4.00
80 JKu(c),An Old Man's Profession. 4.00
81 JKu(c),It Takes Brains To
    Be A Killer 4.00
82 GE(c),Funeral Fire. 4.00
83 GE(c),Prison of the Mind 4.00
84 JKu(c),Devil's Due 4.00
85 thru 124 June 1983 . . . . @4.00

WEIRD WAR TALES
DC/Vertigo April 1997
1 (of 4) anthology 2.50
2 MK(c) 2.50
3 . . . . 2.50
4 . . . . 2.50

All-Star Western #3 © DC Comics Inc.

ALL-STAR WESTERN
Aug.–Sept. 1970
1 NA(c),CI 30.00
2 NA(c),GM,B:Outlaw 15.00
3 NA(c),GK,O:El Diablo 12.00
4 NA(c),GK,JKu,GM 12.00
5 NA(c),JAp,E:Outlaw 12.00
6 GK,B:Billy the Kid. 12.00
7 . . . . 15.00
8 E:Billy the Kid. 15.00
9 FF 15.00
10 GM,I:Jonah Hex. 200.00
11 GM,A:Jonah Hex 100.00
Becomes:

WEIRD WESTERN TALES
June-July, 1972
12 NA,BWr,JKu 75.00
13 . . . . 50.00
14 ATh 25.00
15 NA(c),GK. 25.00
16 thru 28 . . . . @15.00
29 O:Jonah Hex 25.00
30 . . . . 10.00
31 thru 38 . . . . @10.00
39 I&O:Scalphunter 10.00
40 thru 70 . . . . @6.00

WEIRD WORLDS
Aug.–Sept., 1971
1 JO,MA,John Carter. 30.00
2 NA,JO(c),MA,BWr. 25.00
3 MA,NA 15.00
4 MK(c),MK 10.00
5 MK(c),MK. 10.00
6 MK(c),MK. 10.00
7 John Carter ends 10.00
8 HC,I:Iron Wolf. 10.00
9 and 10 HC . . . . @10.00

WESTERN COMICS
Jan.–Feb., 1948
1 MMe,B:Vigilante,Podeo Rick,
    WyomingKid,CowboyMarshal 600.00
2 MMe,Vigilante vs. Dirk Bigger . 300.00
3 MMe,Vigilante vs. Pecos Kid. . 225.00
4 MMe,Vigilante as Pecos Kid . . 225.00
5 I:Nighthawk. 200.00
6 Wyoming Kid vs. `The
    Murder Mustang'. 175.00
7 Wyoming Kid in `The Town
    That Was Never Robbed . . . 175.00
8 O:Wyoming Kid. 200.00
9 Wyoming Kid vs. Jack
    Slaughter 150.00
10 Nighthawk in `Tunnel ofTerror' 150.00
11 Wyoming Kid vs. Mayor Brock 125.00
12 Wyoming Kid vs. Baldy Ryan . 125.00
13 I:Running Eagle 125.00
14 Wyoming Kid in `The Siege
    of Praire City 125.00
15 Nighthawk in `Silver, Salt
    and Pepper 125.00
16 Wyoming Kid vs. Smilin' Jim . 125.00
17 BP,Wyoming Kid vs. Prof.
    Penny. 125.00
18 LSt on Nighthawk,WyomingKid
    in `Challenge of the Chiefs'. . 125.00
19 LSt,Nighthawk in `The
    Invisible Rustlers 125.00
20 LSt,Nighthawk in `The Mystery
    Mail From Defender Dip' 100.00
21 LSt,Nighthawk in `Rattlesnake
    Hollow' 100.00
22 LSt,I:Jim Pegton 100.00
23 LSt,Nighthawk reveals
    ID to Jim. 100.00
24 The $100,000 Impersonation . 100.00
25 V:Souix Invaders 100.00
26 The Storming of the Sante
    Fe Trail. 100.00
27 The Looters of Lost Valley . . . 100.00
28 The Thunder Creek Rebellion 100.00
29 Six Guns of the Wyoming Kid. 100.00
30 V:Green Haired Killer 100.00
31 The Sky Riding Lawman 100.00
32 Death Rides the Stage Coach 100.00
33 . . . . 100.00
34 Prescription For Killers. 100.00
35 The River of Rogues 100.00
36 Nighthawk(c),Duel in the Dark . 75.00
37 The Death Dancer 75.00
38 Warpath in the Sky 75.00
39 Death to Fort Danger. 75.00
40 Blind Man's Bluff 75.00
41 thru 60 . . . . @75.00
61 thru 85 . . . . @50.00

WHERE IN THE WORLD
IS CARMEN SANDIEGO?
DC/Helix 1996
1 thru 3 . . . . @1.75
4 . . . . 1.75

WHO'S WHO
1985–87
1 . . . . 2.00
2 thru 9 . . . . @1.50
10 inc. 1.25
11 inc. Infinity Inc. 1.25
12 inc. Kamandi 1.25
13 inc. Legion of Super Heroes/
    Villains 1.25
14 inc. 1.25
15 inc. Metal Men 1.25
16 inc. New Gods. 1.25
17 inc. Outsiders 1.25
18 inc. Power Girl. 1.25
19 inc. Robin 1.25
20 inc. 1.25
21 inc. The Spectre 1.25
22 inc. Superman 1.25
23 inc. Teen Titans 1.25
24 inc. Unknown Soldier. 1.25
25 inc. 1.25
26 inc. 1.25

WHO'S WHO
(PACKET)
1 inc. Superman 6.00
1a 2nd printing 5.50
2 inc. Flash 5.50
2a 2nd printing 5.00
3 inc. Green Lantern 5.50
4 inc. Wonder Woman 5.50
5 inc. Batman. 5.50
6 inc. Hawkman. 5.50
7 inc. Shade 5.50
8 inc. Lobo 6.00
9 inc. Legion of Super-Heroes 5.50
10 inc. Robin 5.50
11 inc. L.E.G.I.O.N. '91 . . . . 5.50
12 inc. Aquaman 5.50
13 Villains issue, inc. Joker. 6.00
14 inc. New Titans 5.50
15 inc. Doom Patrol 5.50
16 inc. Catwoman,final issue 5.00

WHO'S WHO
IN IMPACT
1 Shield. 4.95
2 Black Hood. 4.95

WHO'S WHO
IN THE LEGION
1987–88
1 History/Bio of Legionnaires 1.25
2 inc. Dream Girl. 1.25
3 inc. Karate Kid 1.25
4 inc. Lightning Lad 1.25
5 inc. Phantom Girl 1.25
6 inc. Timber Wolf 1.25
7 wraparound(c) 1.25

WHO'S WHO
IN STAR TREK
1987
1 HC(c) 6.00
2 HC(c) 6.00

WHO'S WHO
UPDATE '87
1 inc. Blue Beetle 1.50
2 inc. Catwoman 1.25
3 inc. Justice League. 1.25
4 . . . . 1.25
5 inc. Superboy 1.25

WHO'S WHO
UPDATE '88
1 inc. Brainiac 1.25
2 inc. JusticeLeagueInternational. . 1.25
3 inc. Shado 1.25
4 inc. Zatanna 1.25
WHO'S WHO UPDATE '93
1 F:Eclipso,Azrael 5.25

WILD DOG
Sept., 1987
1 mini series DG(i),I:Wild Dog 1.00
2 DG(i),V:Terrorists 1.00
3 DG(i) 1.00
4 DG(i),O:Wild Dog, final issue . . . 1.00
Spec.#1 . . . . 2.50

WILD WILD WEST
1999
1-shot movie adaptation 5.00

WINDY & WILLY
May-June, 1969
1 thru 4 . . . . @20.00

WISE SON:
THE WHITE WOLF
DC/Milestone Sept. 1996
1 by Ho Che Anderson 2.50
2 thru 4 . . . . @2.50

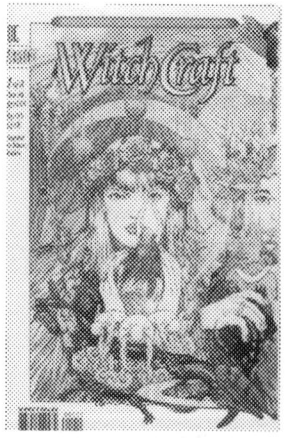

Witchcraft #1 © DC Comics, Inc.

WITCHCRAFT
Vertigo 1994
1 CV(c),Three Witches from
Sandman 4.00
2 F:Mildred 3.50
3 Final issue 3.25
TPB rep. mini-series 14.95

WITCHCRAFT:
LA TERREUR
Feb., 1998
1 (of 3) JeR, sequel 2.50
2 JeR 2.50
3 JeR 2.50

WONDER WOMAN
1942–86
1 O:Wonder Woman,A:Paula
Von Gunther 17,000.00
2 I:Earl of Greed,Duke of
Deception and Lord Conquest,
A:Mars. 2,500.00
3 Paula Von Gunther reforms . 1,500.00
4 A:Paula Von Gunther 1,200.00
5 I:Dr. Psycho,A:Mars 1,200.00
6 I:Cheetah. 1,000.00
7 . . . . 1,000.00
8 I:Queen Clea 1,000.00
9 I:Giganto 1,000.00
10 I:Duke Mephisto Saturno . . . 1,000.00
11 I:Hypnoto 750.00
12 I:Queen Desira 750.00
13 V:King Rigor & the Seal Men . 750.00
14 I:Gentleman Killer 750.00
15 I:Solo. 750.00
16 I:King Pluto 750.00
17 Wonder Woman goes to
Ancient Rome. 750.00
18 V:Dr. Psycho 750.00
19 V:Blitz 750.00
20 V:Nifty and the Air Pirates . . . 750.00
21 I:Queen Atomia 650.00
22 V:Saturno 650.00
23 V:Odin and the Valkyries 650.00
24 I:Mask 650.00
25 V:Purple Priestess 650.00
26 I:Queen Celerita. 650.00
27 V:Pik Socket 650.00
28 V:Cheetah,Clea,Dr. Poison,
Giganta,Hypnata,Snowman,
Zara (Villainy,Inc.). 550.00
29 V:Paddy Gypso 550.00
30 `The Secret of the
Limestone Caves'. 550.00
31 V:Solo 450.00
32 V:Uvo 450.00
33 V:Inventa. 450.00
34 V:Duke of Deception 450.00
35 `Jaxo,Master of Thoughts' . . . 450.00
36 V:Lord Cruello 450.00
37 A:Circe 450.00
38 V:Brutex. 450.00
39 `The Unmasking of Wonder
Woman' 450.00
40 `Hollywood Goes To Paradise
Island' 450.00
41 `Wonder Woman,Romance
Editor'. 350.00
42 V:General Vertigo. 350.00
43 `The Amazing Spy Ring
Mystery' 350.00
44 V:Master Destroyer 350.00
45 `The Amazon and the
Leprachaun'. 700.00
46 V:Prof. Turgo 300.00
47 V:Duke of Deception 300.00
48 V:Robot Woman. 300.00
49 V:Boss. 300.00
50 V:Gen. Voro 300.00
51 V:Garo. 225.00
52 V:Stroggo 225.00
53 V:Crime Master of Time 225.00
54 A:Merlin 225.00
55 `The Chessmen of Doom' . . . 225.00
56 V:Plotter Gang 225.00
57 V:Mole Men 225.00
58 V:Brain 225.00
59 V:Duke Dozan 225.00
60 A:Paula Von Gunther 225.00
61 `Earth's Last Hour' 175.00
62 V:Angles Andrews 175.00
63 V:Duke of Deception 175.00
64 V:Thought Master 175.00
65 V:Duke of Deception 175.00
66 V:Duke of Deception 175.00
67 `Confessions of a Spy' 175.00

Wonder Woman #17 © DC Comics, Inc.

68 `Landing of the Flying
Saucers' 175.00
69 A:Johann Gutenberg,Chris.
Columbus, Paul Revere
and the Wright Brothers 175.00
70 I:Angle Man 175.00
71 `One-Woman Circus' 165.00
72 V:Mole Goldings 150.00
73 V:Prairie Pirates. 150.00
74 `The Carnival of Peril' 150.00
75 V:Angler. 150.00
76 . . . . 150.00
77 V:Smokescreen gang. 150.00
78 V:Angle Man 150.00
79 V:Spider. 150.00
80 V:Machino 150.00
81 V:Duke of Deception,
Angle Man 150.00
82 A:Robin Hood 150.00
83 `The Boy From Nowhere' 150.00
84 V:Duke of Deception,
Angle Man 150.00
85 V:Capt. Virago 150.00
86 V:Snatcher. 150.00
87 `The Day the Clocks Stopped' 150.00
88 V:Duke of Deception 150.00
89 `The Triple Heroine' 150.00
90 Wonder Woman on Jupiter. . . 150.00
91 `The Interplanetary Olympics'. 125.00
92 V:Angle Man 125.00
93 V:Duke of Deception 125.00
94 V:Duke of Deception,
A:Robin Hood. 125.00
95 O:Wonder Woman's tiara 135.00
96 V:Angle Man 125.00
97 `The Runaway Time Express'. 125.00
98 . . . . 125.00
99 V:Silicons. 125.00
100 Anniversary Issue 150.00
101 V:Time Master 100.00
102 F:Steve Trevor 100.00
103 V:Gadget-Maker. 100.00
104 A:Duke of Deception 100.00
105 O,I:Wonder Woman 500.00
106 W.Woman space adventure . 100.00
107 Battles space cowboys. 100.00
108 Honored by U.S. Post Off. . . 100.00
109 V:Slicker 100.00
110 I:Princess 1003 . . . . 100.00
111 I:Prof. Menace 100.00
112 V:Chest of Monsters. 75.00
113 A:Queen Mikra. 75.00
114 V:Flying Saucers 75.00
115 A:Angle Man 75.00
116 A:Professor Andro 75.00
117 A:Etta Candy 75.00
118 A:Merman 75.00

119 A:Mer Boy 75.00	197 MSy,DG 15.00	249 A:Hawkgirl 3.00
120 A:Hot & Cold Alien 75.00	198 MSy,DG 15.00	250 I:Orana 3.00
121 A:Wonder Woman Family . . . 60.00	199 JJ(c),DG 25.00	251 O:Orana 3.00
122 I:Wonder Tot 60.00	200 JJ(c),DG 15.00	252 . . . . 3.00
123 I:Wonder Girl,Wonder Tot . . . 60.00	201 DG,A:Catwoman 10.00	253 . . . . 3.00
124 A:Wonder Girl,Wonder Tot . . . 60.00	202 DG,A:Catwoman,I:Fafhrd	254 . . . . 3.00
125 WW-Battle Prize 60.00	& the Gray Mouser 10.00	255 V:Bushmaster 3.00
126 I:Mr.Genie 60.00	203 DG,Womens lib 10.00	256 V:Royal Flush Gang 3.00
127 Suprise Honeymoon 50.00	204 DH,BO,rewears costume 15.00	257 . . . . 3.00
128 O:InvisiblePlane 45.00	205 DH,BO 10.00	258 . . . . 3.00
129 A:WonderGirl,WonderTot . . . 45.00	206 DH,O:Wonder Woman 10.00	259 . . . . 3.00
130 A:Angle Man 45.00	207 RE 10.00	260 . . . . 3.00
131 . . . . 45.00	208 RE 10.00	261 . . . . 3.00
132 V:Flying Saucer 45.00	209 RE 10.00	262 RE,A:Bushmaster 3.00
133 A:Miss X 45.00	210 RE 10.00	263 . . . . 3.00
134 V:Image-Maker 45.00	211 RE,giant 10.00	264 . . . . 3.00
135 V:Multiple Man 45.00	212 CS,A:Superman,tries to	265 . . . . 3.00
136 V:Machine Men 45.00	rejoin JLA 10.00	266 . . . . 3.00
137 V:Robot Wonder Woman 45.00	213 IN,A:Flash 5.00	267 R:Animal Man 12.00
138 V:Multiple Man 45.00	214 CS,giant,A:Green Lantern 8.00	268 A:Animal Man 10.00
139 Amnesia revels Identity 45.00	215 A:Aquaman 5.00	269 WW(i),Rebirth of Wonder
140 A:Morpheus,Mr.Genie 45.00	216 A:Black Canary 5.00	Woman,pt.1 . . . . 2.50
141 A:Angle Man 45.00	217 DD,A:Green Arrow 5.00	270 Rebirth,pt.2 . . . . 2.50
142 A:Mirage Giants 45.00	218 KS,Red Tornado 5.00	271 JSon,B:Huntress,Rebirth,pt.3 . . 2.50
143 A:Queen Hippolyte 45.00	219 CS,A:Elongated Man 5.00	272 JSon 2.50
144 I:Bird Boy 45.00	220 DG,NA,A:Atom 5.00	273 JSon,A:Angle Man 2.50
145 V:Phantom Sea Beast 45.00	221 CS,A:Hawkman 5.00	274 JSon,I:Cheetah II 2.50
146 $1,000 Dollar Stories 45.00	222 A:Batman 5.00	275 JSon,V:Cheetah II 2.50
147 Wonder Girl becomes Bird Girl	223 R:Steve Trevor 5.00	276 JSon,V:Kobra 2.50
and Fish Girl. 45.00	224 . . . . 5.00	277 JSon,V:Kobra 2.50
148 A:Duke of Deception 45.00	225 . . . . 5.00	278 JSon,V:Kobra 2.50
149 Last Day of the Amazons 45.00	226 . . . . 5.00	279 JSon,A:Demon,Catwoman . . . 3.00
150 V:Phantome Fish Bird 45.00	227 . . . . 5.00	280 JSon,A:Demon,Catwoman . . . 3.00
151 F:1st Full Wonder Girl story . . 30.00	228 B:War stories 5.00	281 JSon,Earth 2 Joker 3.50
152 F:Wonder Girl 30.00	229 . . . . 5.00	282 JSon,Earth 2 Joker 3.50
153 V:Duke of Deception 30.00	230 V:Cheetah 5.00	283 Earth 2 Joker 3.50
154 V:Boiling Man 30.00	231 . . . . 5.00	284. . . . . 2.00
155 I married a monster 30.00	232 MN,A:JSA 5.00	285 JSon,V:Red Dragon 2.00
156 V:Brain Pirate 30.00	233 GM 5.00	286. . . . . 2.00
157 A:Egg Fu,the First 30.00	234 . . . . 5.00	287 DH,RT,JSon,Teen Titans 2.25
158 A:Egg Fu,the First 30.00	235 . . . . 5.00	288 GC,RT,New Wonder Woman . . 2.00
159 Origin 35.00	236. . . . . 5.00	289 GC,RT,JSon,New W.Woman . . 2.00
160 A:Cheetah,Dr. Psycho 30.00	237 RB(c),O:Wonder Woman 6.00	290 GC,RT,JSon,New W.Woman . . 2.00
161 A:Angle Man 30.00	238 RB(c). 4.00	291 GC,FMc,A:Zatanna 2.00
162 O:Diana Prince 30.00	239 RB(c). 4.00	292 GC,FMc,RT,Supergirl. 2.00
163 A:Giganta 30.00	240. . . . . 4.00	293 GC,FMc,Starfire,Raven 2.00
164 A:Angle Man 30.00	241 JSon,DG,A:Spectre 4.00	294 GC,FMc,JSon,V:Blockbuster . . 2.00
165 A:Paper Man,Dr.Psycho 30.00	242 . . . . 3.00	295 GC,FMc,JSon,Huntress 2.00
166 A:Egg Fu,The Fifth 30.00	243 . . . . 3.00	296 GC,Fmc,JSon 2.00
167 A:Crimson Centipede 30.00	244 . . . . 3.00	297 MK(c),GC,FMc,JSon 2.00
168 RA,ME,V:Giganta. 30.00	245 . . . . 3.00	298 GC,FMc,JSon 2.00
169 RA,ME,Crimson Centipede . . 30.00	246 . . . . 3.00	299 GC,FMc,JSon 2.00
170 RA,ME,V:Dr.Pyscho 30.00	247 . . . . 3.00	300 GC,FMc,RA,DG,KP,RB,KG
171 A:Mouse Man 20.00	248 D:Steve Trevor 3.00	C:New Teen Titans 3.25
172 IN,A:Android Wonder Woman 20.00		301 GC,FMc. 2.00
173 A:Tonia 20.00		302 GC,FMc,V:Artemis 2.00
174 A:Angle Man 20.00		303 GC,FMc,Huntress 2.00
175 V:Evil Twin 20.00		304 GC,FMc,Huntress 2.00
176 A:Star Brothers 20.00		305 GC,Huntress,I:Circe 5.00
177 A:Super Girl 20.00		306 DH,Huntress 2.00
178 MSy,DG,I:New Wonder		307 DH,Huntress,Black Canary . . . 2.00
Woman 25.00		308 DH,Huntress,Black Canary . . . 2.00
179 D:Steve Trevor,I:Ching 20.00		309 DH,Huntress 2.00
180 MSy,DG,wears no costume		310 DH,Huntress 2.00
I:Tim Trench 15.00		311 DH,Huntress 2.00
181 MSy,DG,A:Dr.Cyber 15.00		312 DH,DSp,A:Gremlins 2.00
182 MSy,DG 15.00		313 DH,V:Circe 2.00
183 MSy,DG,V:War 15.00		314 DH,Huntress 2.00
184 MSy,DG,A:Queen Hippolyte . . 15.00		315 DH,Huntress 2.00
185 MSy,DG,V:Them 15.00		316 DH,Huntress 2.00
186 MSy,DG,I:Morgana 15.00		317 DH,V:Cereberus 2.00
187 MSy,DG,A:Dr.Cyber 15.00		318 DH,V:Space Aliens 2.00
188 MSy,DG,A:Dr.Cyber 15.00		319 DH,V:Dr.Cyber 2.00
189 MSy,DG 15.00		320 DH. 2.00
190 MSy,DG 15.00		321 DH,Huntress 2.00
191 MSy,DG 15.00		322 IN 2.00
192 MSy,DG 15.00		323 DH,A:Cheetah, Angle Man . . . 2.00
193 MSy,DG 15.00		324 DH. 2.00
194 MSy,DG 15.00		325 DH. 2.00
195 MSy,WW 16.00	*Wonder Woman #288*	326 DH. 2.00
196 MSy,DG,giant,Origin rep 18.00	© *DC Comics Inc.*	327 DH,Crisis 2.00

Wonder Woman #288
© *DC Comics Inc.*

Wonder Woman, 2nd Series #3
© DC Comics, Inc.

328 DH,Crisis 2.00
329 DH,Crisis, giant 2.00

WONDER WOMAN
[2nd Regular Series] 1987–97
1 GP,O:Amazons,Wonder Woman . 4.00
2 GP,I:Steve Trevor 3.00
3 GP,I:Julia Vanessa 2.50
4 GP,V:Decay 2.00
5 GP,V:Deimos, Phobos 2.00
6 GP,V:Ares. 1.50
7 GP,I:Myndi Mayer 1.50
8 GP,O:Legends,A:JLA,Flash. 1.50
9 GP,I:New Cheetah 1.50
10 GP,V:Seven Headed Hydra,
    Challenge of the Gods,pt.1,
    gatefold(c) 1.50
10a regular(c). 1.50
11 GP,V:Echidna,Challenge
    of the Gods,pt.3 . . . . 1.50
12 GP,Millenium,V:Pan, Challenge
    of the Gods,pt.3,
    Millenium x-over. 1.50
13 GP,Millenium,A:Ares,Challenge
    of the Gods,pt.4 . . . . 1.50
14 GP,A:Hercules 1.50
15 GP,I:New Silver Swan 1.50
16 GP,V:Silver Swan. 1.50
17 GP,DG,V:Circe. 1.50
18 GP,DG,V:Circe,+Bonus bk#4 . . 1.50
19 GP,FMc,V:Circe 1.50
20 GP,BMc,D:Myndi Mayer. 1.50
21 GP,BMc,L:Greek Gods,
    Destruction of Olympus 1.50
22 GP,BMc,F:Julia, Vanessa. 1.50
23 GP,R:Hermes,V:Phobos,
    Prelude to New Titans #50 . . . . 1.50
24 GP,V:Ixion, Phobos 1.50
25 CMa,Invasion,A:JLA 1.25
26 CMa,Invasion,V:Capt.Atom 1.25
27 CMa,V:Khunds,A:Cheetah 1.25
28 CMa,V:Cheetah 1.25
29 CMa,V:Cheetah 1.25
30 CMa,V:Cheetah 1.25
31 CMa,V:Cheetah 1.25
32 TG,V:Amazons,A:Hermes 1.25
33 CMa,V:Amazons,Cheetah 1.25
34 CMa,I:Shim'Tar 1.25
35 CMa,V:Shim'Tar. 1.25
36 CMa,A:Hermes 1.25
37 CMa,V:Discord,A:Superman . . . 1.25
38 CMa,V:Eris 1.25
39 CMa,V:Eris,A:Lois Trevor 1.25

40 CMa,V:Eris,A:Lois Lane 1.25
41 CMa,RT,F:Julia,Ties that Bind . . 1.25
42 CMa,RT,V:Silver Swan. 1.25
43 CMa,RT,V:Silver Swan 1.25
44 CMa,RT,V:SilverSwan 1.25
45 CM,RT,Pandora's Box 1.25
46 RT,Suicide Issue,D:Lucy 1.50
47 RT,A:Troia 1.25
48 RTP,A:Troia. 1.25
49 recap of 1st four years. 1.25
50 RT,SA,BB,AH,CM,KN,PCR,MW
    A:JLA,Superman 2.00
51 RT,V:Mercury. 1.25
52 CM,KN,Shards,V:Dr.Psycho. . . . 1.25
53 RT,A:Pariah 1.25
54 RT,V:Dr.Psycho 1.25
55 RT,V:Dr.Psycho 1.25
56 RT,A:Comm.Gordon. 1.25
57 RT,A:Clark Kent,Bruce Wayne . . 1.25
58 RT,War of the Gods,V:Atlas 2.00
59 RT,War of the Gods,
    A:Batman Robin. 2.00
60 RT,War of the Gods,
    A:Batman,Robin. 2.00
61 RT,War of the Gods,V:Circe 2.00
62 War o/t Gods,Epilogue. 1.50
63 BB(c)A:Deathstroke,Cheetah . . . 1.75
64 BB(c),Kidnapped Child. 1.50
65 BB(c),PCu,V:Dr.Psycho 1.50
66 BB(c),PCu,Exodus In Space#1 . 1.50
67 BB(c),PCu,Exodus In Space#2 . 1.50
68 BB(c),PCu,Exodus In Space#3 . 1.50
69 PCu, Exodus In Space#4. . . . . . . 1.50
70 PCu,Exodus In Space#5 . . . . . . 1.50
71 BB(c),DC,RT,Return fr.space . . . 1.50
72 BB(c),O:retold 1.75
73 BB(c),Diana gets a job. 1.50
74 BB(c),V:White Magician 1.50
75 BB(c),A:The White Magician 1.50
76 BB(c),A:Doctor Fate. 1.50
77 BB(c). 1.50
78 BB(c),A:Flash 1.50
79 BB(c),V:Mayfly,A:Flash. 1.50
80 BB(c),V:Ares Buchanan 1.50
81 BB(c),V:Ares Buchanan 1.50
82 BB(c),V:Ares Buchanan 1.50
83 BB(c),V:Ares Buchanan 1.50
84 BB(c),V:Ares Buchanan 1.75
85 BB(c). 15.00
86 BB(c),Turning Point 2.50
87 BB(c),No Quarter,NoSanctuary . 2.50
88 BB(c),A:Superman. 8.00
89 BB(c),A:Circle 7.00
90 New Direction 8.00
91 Choosing Wonder Woman 5.00
92 New Wonder Woman. 5.00
93 New Wonder Woman. 4.00
94 . . . . 6.00
95 V:Cheetah 6.00
96 V:The Joker. 6.00
97 V:The Joker. 6.00
98 BB(c),F:Artemis 3.00
99 BB(c),A:White Magician 3.00
100 BB(c) White Magician defeats
    Artemis 6.00
100a Collector's ed., holo(c) 3.95
101 V:White Magician 3.00
102 V:Metron,Darkseid 2.25
103 JBy,A:Darkseid 2.00
104 JBy,Diana takes crown? 2.00
105 JBy,Grecian artifact comes
    to life 2.00
106 JBy,A:The Demon,Phantom
    Stranger. 2.00
107 . . . . 2.00
108 JBy,F:The Demon,Arion,The
    Phantom Stranger 2.00
109 JBy,V:The Flash,I:Champion . 2.00
110 JBy,V:Sinestro 2.00
111 JBy,I:New Wonder Girl,
    V:Doomsday. 2.00

Wonder Woman, 2nd Series #77
© DC Comics, Inc.

112 JBy,V:Doomsday,A:Superman . 2.50
113 JBy,Wonder Girl vs. Decay. . . . 2.00
114 JBy,V:Doctor Psycho 2.00
115 JBy,beneath the Arctic ice 2.00
116 JBy,beneath the Arctic ice 2.00
117 JBy,V:Earth Moovers 2.00
118 JBy 2.00
119 JBy,fight to regain Cheetah's
    humanity, cont. 2.00
120 JBy,48pg., pin-ups 3.00
121 JBy,Wonder Woman reverting
    to clay 2.00
122 JBy,Gods of Olympus are back 2.00
123 JBy,R:Artemis 2.00
124 JBy,A:Demon. 2.00
125 JBy,A:Donna Troy & JLA 2.00
126 JBy,JL,Genesis tie-in 2.00
127 JBy,JL(c),new era 2.00
128 JBy,JL,V:Egg Fu 2.00
129 JBy,JL,Hippolyta debuts as
    replacement Wonder Woman . . 2.00
130 JBy,JL,pt.1,A:Golden-age
    Flash 2.00
131 JBy,pt.2 . . . . 2.00
132 JBy,pt.3,A:Justice Society 2.00
133 . . . . 2.00
134 JBy,Who is Donna Troy? 2.00
135 JBy,secret revealed 2.00
136 JBy,back to Earth. 2.00
137 CPr,V:Circe, pt.1 . . . . 2.00
138 MBr,F:Hippolyta,V:Circe,pt.2 . . 2.00
139 MBr, ... 2.00
140 BMc,A:Superman & Batman . . 2.00
141 BMc,A:Superman & Batman . . 2.00
142 BMc,The Wonder Dome. 2.00
143 BMc,Devastation,pt.1 . . . . 2.00
144 BMc,Devastation,pt.2 . . . . 2.00
145 BMc,Devastation,pt.3 . . . . 2.00
146 BMc,Devastation,pt.4 . . . . 2.00
147 BMc,GodWar begins 2.00
148 BMc,GodWar, pt.2 . . . . 2.00
149 RBr,BMc,GodWar,pt.3 . . . . 2.00
Ann.#1,GP,AAd,RA,BB,JBo,JL,CS
    Tales of Paradise Island 2.00
Ann.#2 CM,F:Mayer Agency. 2.50
Ann.#3 Eclipso tie-in 2.50
Ann.#4 Year One Annual 3.50
Ann.#5 JBy,DC,NBy,Legends of the
    Dead Earth. 2.95
Ann.#6 Pulp Heroes (Macabre). . . . 3.95
Ann.#7 Ghosts 3.00
Ann.#8 JLApe Gorilla Warfare. 3.00
Spec.#1,000,000 CPr(s),MC,BMc . . 2.00
Spec #1 A:Deathstroke,Cheetah . . 2.25

Spec.#0 History of Amazons...... 7.00
TPB The Contest, rep. #90,#0
#91–#93.................. 9.95
TPB The Challenge of Artemas ... 9.95
TPB Second Genesis JBy, rep.
#101–#105.............. 9.95
GN Amazonia, BML........... 8.00
GN The Once and Future Story ... 5.00
GN Amazonia, Elseworlds....... 8.00
Archives, Vol. 1.............. 50.00
Secret Files #2.............. 5.00
Spec. Wonder Woman: Donna Troy
Girlfrenzy (1998)........... 2.00
Spec. Wonder Woman Plus CPr(s),MC,
TP,Jesse Quick & Wonder
Woman (1996)............ 2.95

WORLD OF KRYPTON
July, 1979
1 HC/MA.O:Jor-El............. 1.50
2 HC/MA,A:Superman.......... 1.00
3 HC...................... 1.00

[2nd Series] 1987–88
1 MMi,John Byrne script....... 1.00
2 MMi,John Byrne script....... 1.00
3 MMi,John Byrne script....... 1.00
4 MMi,A:Superman........... 1.00

WORLD OF METROPOLIS
1988
1 DG(i),O:Perry White.......... 1.00
2 DG(i),O:Lois Lane........... 1.00
3 DG(i),Clark Kent............ 1.00
4 DG(i),O:Jimmy Olsen........ 1.00

WORLD OF SMALLVILLE
1988
1 KS/AA,Secrets of Ma&Pa Kent.. 1.25
2 KS/AA,`Stolen Moments'....... 1.25
3 KS/AA,Lana Lang/Manhunter ... 1.25
4 KS/AA,final issue 1.25

WORLDS COLLIDE
1994
1 MBr(c),3RW,CsB,Ccs,DCw,
TG,A:Blood Syndicate,Icon,
Hardware,Static,Superboy,
Superman,Steel,Vinyl Cling(c) . 4.25
1a Newsstand Ed............. 2.75

WORLD'S BEST COMICS
Spring, 1941
1 Superman vs. the Rainmaker,
Batman vs. Wright..... 15,000.00
Becomes:
WORLD'S FINEST
COMICS
1941–86
2 Superman V:`The Unknown X',
Batman V:Ambrose Taylor . 4,000.00
3 I&O:Scarecrow......... 2,900.00
4 Superman V:Dan Brandon,
Batman V:Ghost Gang.... 2,000.00
5 Superman V:Lemuel P.Potts,
Batman V:Brains Kelly 2,000.00
6 Superman V:Metalo,Batman
meets Scoop Scanlon 1,500.00
7 Superman V:Jenkins,Batman
V:Snow Man Bandits 1,500.00
8 Superman:`Talent Unlimited'
Batman V:Little Nap Boyd,
B:Boy Commandos...... 1,400.00
9 Superman:`One Second to
Live',Batman V:Bramwell B.
Bramwell.............. 1,400.00

10 Superman V:The Insect Master,
Batman reforms Oliver Hunt1,300.00
11 Superman V:Charlie Frost,
Batman V:Rob Calendar . . 1,100.00
12 Superman V:Lynx,Batman:
`Alfred Gets His Man'..... 1,100.00
13 Superman V:Dice Dimant,
Batman,V:Swami Pravhoz . 1,100.00
14 Superman V:Al Bandar,Batman
V:Jib Buckler........... 1,100.00
15 Superman V:Derby Bowser,
Batman V:Mennekin....... 1,100.00
16 Superman:`Music for the Masses,
Batman V:Nocky Johnson . 1,100.00
17 Superman:`The Great Godini',
Batman V:Dr.Dreemo.... 1,000.00
18 Superman:`The Junior Reporters,
Batman V:Prof.Brane...... 900.00
19 A:The Joker.............. 900.00
20 A:Toyman 900.00
21 Superman:`Swindle in
Sweethearts!'........... 650.00
22 Batman V:Nails Finney...... 650.00
23 Superman:`The Colossus
of Metropolis'........... 650.00
24 .... 650.00
25 Superman V:Ed Rook,Batman:
`The Famous First Crimes' . . 650.00
26 `Confessions of Superman' . . 650.00
27 `The Man Who Out-Supered
Superman 650.00
28 A:Lex Luther,Batman V:Glass
Man 650.00
29 Superman:`The Books that
couldn't be Bound' 650.00
30 Superman:`Sheriff Clark Kent`,
Batman V:Joe Coyne 650.00
31 `Superman's Super-Rival`,Batman:
`Man with the X-Ray Eyes' . . 600.00
32 Superman visits
Ancient Egypt........... 600.00
33 `Superman Press, Inc.',
Batman V:James Harmon... 600.00
34 `The Un-Super Superman' ... 600.00
35 Daddy Superman,A:Penguin . 600.00
36 Lois Lane,Sleeping Beauty... 600.00
37 `The Superman Story`,Batman
V:T-Gun Jones.......... 600.00
38 If There were No Superman.. 600.00
39 Superman V:Big Jim Martin,
Batman V:J.J.Jason 600.00
40 Superman V:Check,Batman:`4
Killers Against Fate!'....... 600.00
41 I:Supermanium,

World's Finest Comics #106
© *DC Comics Inc.*

E:Boy Commandos........ 425.00
42 Superman goes to Uranus,
A:Marco Polo & Kubla Khan . 425.00
43 A:J.Wilbur Wolfingham..... 425.00
44 Superman:`The Revolt of the
Thought Machine'........ 425.00
45 Superman:`Lois Lane and Clark
Kent,Private Detectives..... 425.00
46 Superman V:Mr. 7 .... 425.00
47 Superman:`The Girl Who
Hated Reporters.......... 425.00
48 A:Joker 425.00
49 Superman meets the
Metropolis Shutterbug
Society, A:Penguin 425.00
50 `Superman Super Wrecker' . . 425.00
51 Superman:`The Amazing
Talents of Lois Lane'...... 425.00
52 A:J.Wilbur Wolfingham..... 425.00
53 Superman V:Elias Toomey... 425.00
54 `The Superman Who Avoided
Danger!' 425.00
55 A:Penguin 425.00
56 Superman V:Dr.Vallin,Batman
V:Big Dan Hooker......... 425.00
57 `The Artificial Superman' 425.00
58 Superman V:Mr.Fenton 425.00
59 A:Lex Luthor,Joker......... 425.00
60 A:J.Wilbur Wolfingham...... 425.00
61 A:Joker,`Superman's
Blackout' 250.00
62 A:Lex Luthor 250.00
63 Superman:`Clark Kent,
Gangster' 250.00
64 Superman:`The Death of Lois
Lane,Batman:`Bruce Wayne...
Amateur Detective'........ 250.00
65 `The Confessions of Superman',
Batman V:The Blaster...... 600.00
66 `Superman,Ex-Crimebuster;
Batman V:Brass Haley...... 425.00
67 Superman:`Metropolis-Crime
Center!' 425.00
68 Batman V:The Crimesmith ... 425.00
69 A:Jor-El,Batman
V:Tom Becket............ 425.00
70 `The Two Faces of Superman',
Batman:`Crime Consultant' . . 425.00
71 B:Superman/Batman
team-ups 850.00
72 V:Heavy Weapon gang 600.00
73 V:Fang................. 600.00
74 `The Contest of Heroes'..... 500.00
75 V:The Purple Mask Mob..... 425.00
76 `When Gotham City
Challenged Metropolis 325.00
77 V:Prof.Pender 325.00
78 V:Varrel mob 325.00
79 A:Aladdin............... 325.00
80 V:Mole 325.00
81 Meet Ka Thar from future.... 275.00
82 A:Three Musketeers........ 275.00
83 `The Case of the Mother
Goose Mystery' 275.00
84 V:Thad Linnis gang 275.00
85 Meet Princess Varina....... 275.00
86 V:Henry Bartle 275.00
87 V:Elton Craig 275.00
88 1st team-up Luthor & Joker .. 300.00
89 I:Club of Heroes.......... 275.00
90 A:Batwoman 275.00
91 V:Rohtul,descendent of Lex
Luthor................. 200.00
92 Ist & only A:Skyboy 175.00
93 V:Victor Danning 200.00
94 O:Superman/Batman team,
A:Lex Luthor............ 550.00
95 `Battle o/t Super Heroes' 175.00
96 `Super-Foes from Planet X' . . 175.00
97 V:Condor Gang 175.00
98 I:Moonman 175.00

World's Finest Comics #172
© DC Comics, Inc.

99 JK,V:Carl Verril 175.00
100 A:Kandor, Lex Luthor 325.00
101 A:Atom Master 150.00
102 V:Jo-Jo Groff gang,
    B:Tommy Tomorrow 150.00
103 `The Secrets of the
    Sorcerer's Treasure 150.00
104 A:Lex Luthor 150.00
105 V:Khalex 150.00
106 V:Duplicate Man. 150.00
107 `The Secret of the Time
    Creature' 150.00
108 `The Star Creatures'. 150.00
109 V:Fangan. 150.00
110 `The Alien Who Doomed
    Robin!' 150.00
111 V:Floyd Frisby 150.00
112 . . . . 150.00
113 1st Bat-Mite/Mr.Mxyzptlk
    team-up 150.00
114 `Captives o/t Space Globes'. 150.00
115 The Curse That Doomed
    Superman 125.00
116 V:Vance Collins 125.00
117 A:Batwoman,Lex Luthor 125.00
118 V:Vath-Gar. 125.00
119 V:General Grambly. 125.00
120 V:Faceless Creature 125.00
121 I:Miss Arrowette. 125.00
122 V:Klor 60.00
123 A:Bat-Mite & Mr. Mxyzptlk . . . 60.00
124 V:Hroguth,E:Tommy
    Tomorrow. 60.00
125 V:Jundy,B:Aquaman. 60.00
126 A:Lex Luthor 60.00
127 V:Zerno 60.00
128 V:Moose Morans 60.00
129 Joker/Luthor T.U. 75.00
130 . . . . 60.00
131 V:Octopus 60.00
132 V:Denny Kale,Shorty Biggs . . 60.00
133 . . . . 60.00
134 V:Band of Super-Villians 60.00
135 V:The Future Man 60.00
136 The Batman Nobody
    Remembered 60.00
137 A:Lex Luthor 60.00
138 V:General Grote. 60.00
139 V:Sphinx Gang,E:Aquaman . . 60.00
140 CS,V:Clayface 60.00
141 CS,A:Jimmy Olsen. 60.00
142 CS,O:Composite Man 60.00
143 CS,A:Kandor,I:Mailbag. 50.00
144 CS,A:Clayface,Brainiac 50.00

145 CS,Prison for Heroes. 50.00
146 CS,Batman,Son of Krypton . . 50.00
147 CS,A:Jimmy Olsen. 50.00
148 CS,A:Lex Luthor,Clayface . . . 50.00
149 CS,The Game of the
    Secret Identities 50.00
150 CS,V:Rokk and Sorban 35.00
151 CS,A:Krypto,BU:Congorilla. . . 35.00
152 CS,A:The Colossal Kids,Bat-
    mite,V:Mr.Mxyzptlk 35.00
153 CS,V:Lex Luthor 35.00
154 CS,The Sons of Batman &
    Superman(Imaginary) 35.00
155 CS,The 1000th Exploit of
    Batman & Superman 35.00
156 CS,I:BizarroBatman,V:Joker. 100.00
157 CS,The Abominable Brats
    (Imaginary story) 35.00
158 CS,V:Brainiac 35.00
159 CS,A:Many Major villians,I:Jim
    Gordon as Anti-Batman & Perry
    White as Anti-Superman. 35.00
160 V:Dr Zodiac.. . . . . 35.00
161 CS,80 page giant 40.00
162 V:The Jousting Master 25.00
163 CS,The Court of No Hope . . . 25.00
164 CS,I:Genia,V:Brainiac 25.00
165 CS,The Crown of Crime. 25.00
166 CS,V:Muto & Joker 28.00
167 CS,The New Superman &
    Batman(Imaginary) V:Luthor . . 25.00
168 CS,R:Composite Superman . . 25.00
169 The Supergirl/Batgirl Plot;
    V:Batmite,Mr.Mxyzptlk 25.00
170 80 page giant,reprint 25.00
171 CS,V:The Executioners 25.00
172 CS,Superman & Batman
    Brothers (Imaginary) 25.00
173 CS,The Jekyll-Hyde Heroes . . 50.00
174 CS,Secrets of the Double
    Death Wish 25.00
175 NA(1st Batman),C:Flash 20.00
176 NA,A:Supergirl & Batgirl. 20.00
177 V:Joker & Luthor 22.00
178 CS,The Has-Been Superman. 20.00
179 CS,giant 30.00
180 RA,ME,Supermans Perfect
    Crime. 20.00
181 RA,ME. 20.00
182 RA,ME,The Mad Manhunter. . 20.00
183 RA,ME,Supermans Crimes
    of the Ages. 20.00
184 RA,ME,A:JLA,Robin. 20.00
185 CS,The Galactic Gamblers. . . 20.00
186 RA,ME,The Bat Witch 20.00
187 RA,ME,Demon Superman . . . 20.00
188 giant,reprint 30.00
189 RA,ME,V:Lex Luthor 20.00
190 RA,V:Lex Luthor 15.00
191 RA,A:Jor-El,Lara 15.00
192 RA,The Prison of No Escape . 15.00
193 The Breaking of Batman
    and Superman 15.00
194 RA,ME,Inside the Mafia 15.00
195 RA,ME,Dig Now-Die Later . . . 15.00
196 CS,The Kryptonite Express,
    E:Batman. 15.00
197 giant 35.00
198 DD,B:Superman T.U.,
    A:Flash. 90.00
199 DD,Superman & Flash race . . 90.00
200 NA(c),DD,Prisoners of the
    Immortal World; A:Robin. 20.00
201 NA(c),DD,A Prize of Peril,
    A:Green Lantern,Dr. Fate. . . . 15.00
202 NA(c),DD,Vengeance of the
    Tomb Thing,A:Batman 15.00
203 NA(c),DD,Who's Minding the
    Earth,A:Quamar 15.00
204 NA(c),DD,Journey to the End
    of Hope,A:Wonder Woman . . . 15.00

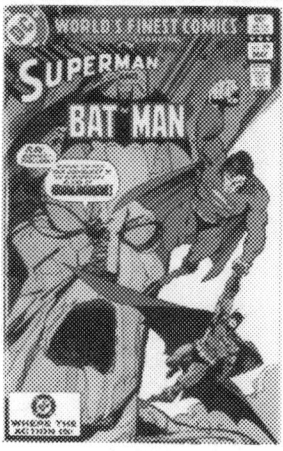

World's Finest Comics #291
© DC Comics, Inc.

205 NA(c),DD,The Computer that
    Captured a Town,Frazetta Ad,
    A:Teen Titans 20.00
206 DD,giant reprint 30.00
207 DD,Superman,A:Batman,
    V:Dr.Light 15.00
208 NA(c),DD,A:Dr Fate 15.00
209 NA(c),DD,A:Green Arrow,
    Hawkman,I&V:The Temper . . 15.00
210 NA(c),DD,A:Batman. 15.00
211 NA(c),DD,A:Batman. 15.00
212 CS(c),And So My World
    Begins,A:Martian Manhunter. . 15.00
213 DD,Peril in a Very Small
    Place,A:The Atom 15.00
214 DD,A:Vigilante 15.00
215 DD,Saga of the Super Sons
    (Imaginary story) 15.00
216 DD,R:Super Sons,Little Town
    with a Big Secret. 15.00
217 DD,MA,Heroes with
    Dirty Hands 15.00
218 DD,DC,A:Batman,
    BU:Metamorpho 15.00
219 DD,Prisoner of Rogues Rock;
    A:Batman 15.00
220 DD,MA,Let No Man Write My
    Epitaph,BU:Metamorpho. 15.00
221 DD,Cry Not For My Forsaken
    Son; R:Super Sons. 15.00
222 DD,Evil In Paradise 15.00
223 DD,giant,A:Deadman,Aquaman
    Robotman 20.00
224 DD,giant,A:Super Sons,
    Metamorpho,Johnny Quick . . . 20.00
225 giant,A:Rip Hunter,Vigilante,
    Black Canary,Robin 15.00
226 A:Sandman,Metamorpho,
    Deadman,Martian Manhunter . 20.00
227 MGr,BWi,A:The Demonic Duo,
    Vigilante,Rip Hunter,Deadman,
    I:Stargrave 20.00
228 ATh,A:Super Sons,Aquaman,
    Robin,Vigilante 20.00
229 I:Powerman,A:Metamorpho . . 15.00
230 A:Super-Sons,Deadman,
    Aquaman 15.00
231 A:Green Arrow,Flash 15.00
232 DD,The Dream Bomb 15.00
233 A:Super-Sons 15.00
234 CS,Family That Fled Earth. . . 15.00
235 DD,V:Sagitaurus 15.00
236 DD,A:The Atom 15.00
237 Intruder from a Dead World . . 15.00

DC COMICS

238 DD,V:Luthor,A:Super-Sons. . . 15.00
239 CS,A:Gold(from Metal Men) . . 15.00
240 DD,A:Kandor 12.00
241 Make Way For a New World . 12.00
242 EC,A:Super-Sons. 12.00
243 CS,AM,A:Robin 12.00
244 NA(c),JL,MA,MN,TA,giant
    B:Green Arrow 12.00
245 NA(C),CS,MA,MN,TA,
    GM,JSh,BWi,giant 12.00
246 NA(c),KS,MA,MN,TA,GM,
    DH,A:JLA. 12.00
247 KS,GM,giant 12.00
248 KS,GM,DG,TVE,A:Sgt.Rock . . 12.00
249 KS,SD,TVE,A:Phantom
    Stranger,B:Creeper. 12.00
250 GT,SD,Superman,Batman,
    Wonder Woman,Green Arrow,
    Black Canary,team-up 10.00
251 GT,SD,JBi,BL,TVE,RE,
    JA,A:Poison Ivy,Speedy,
    I:CountVertigo 10.00
252 GT,TVE,SD,JA,giant. 10.00
253 KS,DN,TVE,SD,B:Shazam 7.00
254 GT,DN,TVE,SD,giant 7.00
255 JL,DA,TVE,SD,DN,KS,
    E:Creeper 7.00
256 MA,DN,KS,DD,Hawkman,Black
    Lightning,giant 7.00
257 DD,FMc,DN,KS,GT,RB,
    RT,giant 7.00
258 NA(c),RB,JL,DG,DN,KS,RT,
    giant. 7.00
259 RB,DG,MR,MN,DN,KS. 7.00
260 RB,DG,MN,DN 7.00
261 RB,DG,AS,RT,EB,DN,
    A:Penguin, Terra Man. 7.00
262 DG,DN,DA,JSon,RT,
    Aquaman 7.00
263 RB,DG,DN,TVE,JSh,Aquaman,
    Adam Strange 7.00
264 RB,DG,TVE,DN,Aquaman 7.00
265 RB,DN,RE,TVE 7.00
266 RB,TVE,DN 7.00
267 RB,DG,TVE,AS,DN,
    A:Challengers of the Unknown . 7.00
268 DN,TVE,BBr,RT,AS 7.00
269 RB,FMc,TVE,BBr,AS,DN,DA . . 7.00
270 NA(c),RB,RT,TVE,AS,
    DN,LMa 7.00
271 GP(c),RB,FMc,O:Superman/
    Batman T.U. 6.00
272 RB,DN,TVE,BBr,AS 5.00
273 TVE,LMa,JSon,AS,DN,DA,
    A:Plastic Man. 5.00
274 TVE,LMa,BBr,GC,AS,DN,
    Green Arrow. 5.00
275 RB,FMc,TVE,LMa,DSp,AS,
    DN,DA,A:Mr.Freeze 5.00
276 GP(c),RB,TVE,LMa,DSp,Cl,
    DN,DA 5.00
277 GP(c),RT,TVE,DSp,AS,DN,
    DH,V:Dr.Double X 5.00
278 GP(c),RB,TVE,LMa,DSp,DN . . 5.00
279 KP,TVE,LMa,AS,DN,
    B:Kid Eternity 5.00
280 RB,TVE,LMa,AS,DN 5.00
281 GK(c),IN,TVE,LMa,AS,DN 5.00
282 IN,FMc,GK,Cl,last giant
    E:Kid Eternity 5.00
283 GT,FMc,GK 5.00
284 GT,DSp,A:Legion,E:G.Arrow . . 5.00
285 FM(c),RB,A:Zatanna 5.00
286 RB,A:Flash 5.00
287 TVE,A:Flash 5.00
288 A:JLA 5.00
289 GK(c),Kryll way of Dying 5.00
290 TD(i),I:Stalagron. 5.00
291 WS(c),TD(i),V:Stalagron. 5.00
292 . . . . 5.00
293 . . . . 5.00

294. . . . . 5.00
295 FMc(i) 5.00
296 RA. 5.00
297 GC,V:Pantheon 5.00
298 V:Pantheon 5.00
299 GC,V:Pantheon 5.00
300 RA,GP,KJ,MT,FMc,A:JLA 5.00
301 Rampage. 2.25
302 DM,NA(rep) 2.25
303 Plague. 2.25
304 SLi,O:Null&Void 2.25
305 TVE,V:Null&Void 2.25
306 SLi,I:Swordfish & Barracuda . . 2.25
307 TVE,V:Null&Void 2.25
308 GT,Night and Day 2.25
309 MT,AA,V:Quantum 2.25
310 I:Sonik 2.25
311 A:Monitor. 2.25
312 AA,I:Network 2.25
313 AA(i),V:Network 2.25
314 AA(i),V:Executrix 2.25
315 V:Cathode 2.25
316 LSn,I:Cheapjack 2.25
317 LSn,V:Cheapjack 2.25
318 AA(i),A:Sonik 2.25
319 AA(i),I:REM 2.25
320 AA(i),V:REM 2.25
321 AA,V:Chronos 2.25
322 KG,The Search 2.25
323 AA(i),final issue 2.25

WORLD'S FINEST
[Limited Series] 1990
1 SR,KK,Worlds Apart 8.00
2 SR,KK,Worlds Collide. 6.00
3 SR,KK,Worlds At War 6.00
TPB rep.#1-#3 . . . . 19.95

WORLD'S FINEST: SUPERBOY/ROBIN
Oct. 1996
1 (of 2) CDi&KK(s),TG,SHa,
    V:Poison Ivy, Metallo 4.95
2 CDi&KK(s),TG,SHa, V:Poison
    Ivy, Metallo. 4.95

WORLD'S GREATEST SUPER-HEROES
1977
1 A:Batman,Robin 2.50

WORLD WITHOUT END
1990
1 The Host, I:Brother Bones 5.00
2 A:Brother Bones. 3.50
3 . . . . 3.50
4 House of Fams. 2.50
5 Female Fury. 2.50
6 conclusion 2.50

WRATH OF THE SPECTRE
May, 1988
1 JAp,rep.Adventure #431-#433 . . 2.50
2 JAp,rep.Adventure #434-#436 . . 2.50
3 JAp,rep.Adventure #437-#440 . . 2.50
4 JAp,reps.,final issue 2.50

XENOBROOD
1994–95
0 New team. 1.50
1 Battles 1.50
2 Bestiary 1.50
3 A:Superman. 1.50

Xenobrood #5 © DC Comics Inc.

4 V:Bestiary. 1.50
5 V:Vimian. 1.50
6 final issue. 1.50

XERO
March 1997
1 Cpr(s),Ccs,Trane Walker/Xero . 1.75
2 CPr(s),Ccs,"The Rookie". 1.75
3 Cpr(s),Ccs,"The Beast". 1.75
4 CPr(s) 1.75
6 CPr, Genesis tie-in 1.75
7 CPr(s),O:Zerp, pt.1 . . . . 1.75
8 CPr,O:Zero. 2.00
9 CPr(s), ... 2.00
10 CPr,a matter of ethics 2.00
11 . . . . 2.00
12 CPr, final issue, Xero dead 2.00

XOMBI
Milestone 1994–96
0 WS(c),DCw,Shadow War,Foil(c),
    I:Xombi,Twilight 2.50
1 JBy(c),B:Silent Cathedrals 2.00
1a Platinum ed. 12.00
2 I:Rabbi Simmowitz,Golms,Liam
    Knight of the Spoken Fire 1.75
3 A:Liam 2.00
4 Silent Cathedrals 2.00
5 Silent Cathedrals 1.75
6 Silent Cathedrals 1.75
7 School of Anguish 1.75
8 School of Anguish,pt.2 . . . . 1.75
9 School of Anguish,pt.3 . . . . 1.75
10 School of Anguish,pt.4 . . . . 1.75
11 School of Anguish,pt.5 . . . . 1.75
12 Truth and Surprises 1.75
13 V:Kinderessen 1.75
14 Long Hot Summer, A:Cheryl
    Saltz 2.50
15 Long Hot Summer 2.50
16 Long Hot Summer 2.50
17 Reader's Choice 2.50
18 Serpent's Tail. 2.50
19 Mister Missy, Bellhop 2.50
20 . . . . 2.50
21 final issue 3.50

YOUNG ALL STARS
June, 1987
1 I:IronMunro&FlyingFox,D:TNT. . . 4.50
2 V:Axis Amerika. 2.50

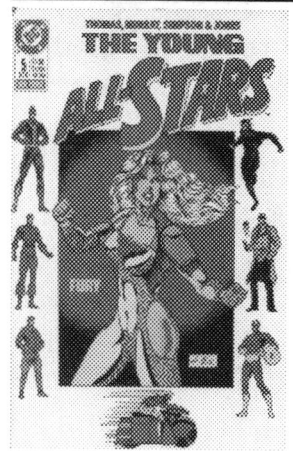

Young All-Stars #5
© DC Comics, Inc.

3 V:Axis Amerika 2.00
4 I:The Tigress 2.00
5 I:Dyna-mite,O:Iron Munro 2.00
6 . . . . 2.00
7 Baseball Game,A:Tigress 2.00
8 Millenium 2.00
9 Millenium 2.00
10 Hugo Danner 2.00
11 `Birth of Iron Munro' 2.00
12 `Secret of Hugo Danner' 2.00
13 `V:Deathbolt,Ultra-Humanite . . 2.00
14 Fury+Ultra Humanite 2.00
15 IronMunro At high school 2.00
16 Ozyan Inheritance 2.00
17 Ozyan Inheritance 2.00
18 Ozyan Inheritance 2.00
19 Ozyan 2.00
20 O:Flying Fox 2.00
21 Atom & Evil#1 . . . . 2.00
22 Atom & Evil#2 . . . . 2.00
23 Atom & Evil#3 . . . . 2.00
24 Atom & Evil#4 . . . . 2.00
25 . . . . 2.00
26 End of the All Stars? 2.00
27 `Sons of Dawn' begins 2.00
28 Search for Hugo Danner 2.00
29 A:Hugo Danner 2.00
30 V:Sons of Dawn 2.00
31 V:Sons of Dawn,last issue 2.00
Ann.#1 MG,V:Mekanique 2.50

YOUNG HEROES IN LOVE
April 1997
1 DeM,F:Hard Drive 1.75
2 DeM,sex, lies and superheroics . 1.75
3 A:Superman 1.75
4 F:Hard Drive 1.75
5 Genesis tie-in 2.00
6 The Rat Pack 2.00
7 Secret Identity Issu 2.00
8 V:Scarecrow 2.00
9 F:Frostbite & Bonfire 2.00
10 V:Grundo'mu 2.00
11 V:Grundo'mu 2.00
12 Hard Drive dead? 2.00
13 New leader picked 2.00
14 Man of Inches vs. Man
    of Candles 2.00
15 Junior vs. Birthday Boy 2.00
16 DeM,Zip-Kid 2.00
17 DeM,Monstergirl's Uncle 2.50
Spec.#1,000,000 DeM final issue . . 2.50

YOUNG JUSTICE
July 1998
1 PDd,TNu,Robin,Superboy,
  Impulse 2.50
2 PDd,TNu,V:Super-Cycle 2.50
3 PDd(s),TNu,V:Mr.Mxyzptlk 2.50
4 PDd(s),TNu,Girls join team 2.50
5 PDd(s),TNu,V:Harm 2.50
6 PDd(s),TNu,F:JLA 2.50
7 PDd(s),TNu,A:Nightwing 2.50
8 CDi(s),TNu,A:Razorsharp 2.50
9 PDd(s),V:Huggathugees 2.50
10 PDd(s),V:The Acolyte 2.50
11 PDd(s),Rescue Red Tornado . . . 2.50
12 PDd(s),TNu,Supergirl x-over
   Hell's Angels,pt.1 . . . . 2.50
13 PDd(s), Hell's Angels,pt.3 . . . . . 2.50
Spec.#1,000,000 PDd(s),TNu 2.50
Giant#1 Secret Origins, 80-page . . . 5.00
Giant#1 80-page 5.00
Secret Files #1 . . . . 5.00
Spec.#1 Young Justice in
  No Man's Land, CDi(s) 4.00
Spec.#1 Young Justice: The Secret
  Impulse, Superboy, Robin
  (1998) 2.00

YOUNG LOVE
Sept.–Oct., 1963
39 . . . . 30.00
40 thru 50 . . . . @20.00
51 thru 70 . . . . @15.00

Zatanna #3 © DC Comics, Inc.

71 thru 80 . . . . @12.00
81 thru 126 . . . . @10.00

ZATANNA
1987
1 R:Zatanna 2.25
2 N:Zatanna 2.25
3 Come Together 2.25
4 V:Xaos 2.25

ZERO HOUR:
CRISIS IN TIME
1994
4 DJu(a&s),JOy,A:All DC Heroes,
  D;2nd Flash 1.50
3 DJu(a&S),JOy,D:G.A.Sandman,
  G:A.Atom,Dr.Fate,1st Wildcat
  IR:Time Trapper is Rokk Krinn,
  Hawkmen merged 1.50
2 DJu(a&s),Joy 1.50
1 DJu(a&s),JOy,b:Power Gir's
  Child 1.50
0 DJu(A&S),JOy,Gatefold(c),Extant
  vs. Spectre 1.50

AMAZON
DC 1996–97
1 JBy,TA 3.00
1 one-shot JBy,Princess Ororo
   is Wonder Woman 2.00

ASSASSINS
DC 1996–97
1 DGC,SMc. 3.00
1 one-shot DGC(s),SMc,F:Dare
   and Catsai 2.00

BAT-THING
DC 1997
1 one-shot LHa(s),RDm,BSz,
   V:motorcycle gang 2.00

BRUCE WAYNE:
AGENT OF S.H.I.E.L.D.
Marvel Comics 1996
1 CDi, ... 3.00

BULLETS & BRACELETS
Marvel Comics 1996
1 JOs,GFr,CaS 3.00

CHALLENGERS OF
THE FANTASTIC
Marvel 1997
1 KK,TGu,AV. 2.00

DARK CLAW
ADVENTURES, THE
DC 1997
1 one-shot TTy,RBr,V:Ladia Talia . . 2.00

DC VERSUS MARVEL
MARVEL VERSUS DC
1 (DC)DJu. 6.00
1a 2nd printing 4.00
2 (Marvel)PDd,DJu 5.00
2a 2nd printing 4.00
3 (Marvel)DJu 4.00
4 (DC)PDd,DJu 4.00
TPB rep. mini series #1–#4. . . . . . 12.95

DOCTOR STRANGEFATE
DC Comics 1996–97
1 RMz,KN 3.00
1 one-shot RMz(s),JL,KN,Supreme
   Lord of Order 2.00

EXCITING X-PATROL
Marvel 1997
1 BKs,BHi 2.00

GENERATION HEX
DC 1997
1 one-shot,PrM(s),AdP,F:Jono Hex,
   Madam Banshee 2.00

IRON LANTERN
Marvel 1997
1 KB,PSm,AW. 2.00

JLX
DC Comics 1996–97
1 MWa,GJ, ... 3.00
1 one-shot,MWa(s),GJ,HPo,JhD . . 2.00

JLX UNLEASHED
DC 1997
1 one-shot, CPr,"The Inextinguish-
   able Flame" 2.00

LEGENDS OF
THE DARK CLAW
DC Comics 1996–97
1 LHa,JBa, ... 3.00
1 one-shot LHa(s),JBa, ... 2.00
1 2nd printing 2.00

LOBO THE DUCK
DC 1997
1 one-shot, AlG,VS, ... 2.00

MAGNETO &
THE MAGNETIC MEN
Marvel Comics 1996
1 MWa,GJ,JMs,ATi 3.00

MAGNETIC MEN
FEATURING MAGNETO
Marvel 1997
1 TPe,BKi,DPs 2.00

SPEED DEMON
Marvel Comics 1996
1 HMe,SvL,AM 3.00

SPIDER-BOY
Marvel Comics 1996
1 KK,MeW. 3.00

SPIDER-BOY TEAM-UP
Marvel Comics 1997
1 KK,RSt. 2.00

SUPER-SOLDIER
DC Comics 1996–97
1 MWa,DGb 3.00
1-shot MWa(s),DGb,V:Ultra-
   Metallo, Green Skull, Hydra . . . 2.00

SUPER SOLDIER:
MAN OF WAR
DC 1997
1 one-shot MWa(s),DGb,JP,
   V:Nazis 2.00

THORION OF
THE NEW ASGODS
Marvel 1997
1 KG,JR2 . . . . 2.00

X-PATROL
Marvel Comics 1996
1 KK,BKs 3.00
The Amalgam Age of Comics: The DC C
   omics Collection TPBs 12.95
The Amalgam Age of Comics: The Marv
   el Comics Collection TPBs 12.95
Return to the Amalgam Age of Comics:
   The DC Comics Collection TPB . . 13.00

Bat-Thing #1 © DC /Marvel

Iron Lantern #1 © DC/Marvel

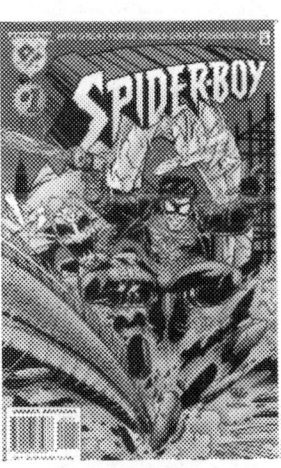

Spider-Boy #1 © DC/Marvel

MARVEL

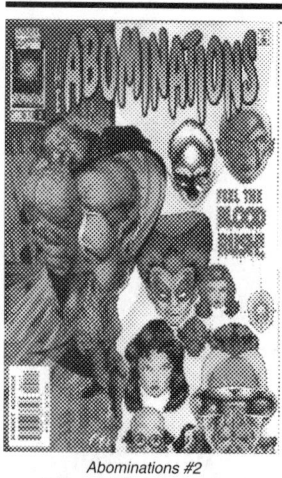

Abominations #2
© Marvel Entertainment Group

ABOMINATIONS
1996
1 (of 3) IV,AMe, Future Imperfect
  spin-off.................. 1.50
2 IV,AMe, ... 1.50
3 IV,AMe, ... 1.50

ABRAHAM STONE
1995
1 JKu, Early 20th century....... 6.95
2 Wandering Man in the 20s 6.95

ACTION FORCE
March, 1987
1 U.K. G.I. Joe Series 1.50
2 thru 39 .... @1.00
40 1988 .... 1.00

ACTUAL CONFESSIONS
See: LOVE ADVENTURES

ACTUAL ROMANCES
Oct., 1949
1 .... 45.00
2 Photo Cover.............. 25.00

ADVENTURE INTO FEAR
See: FEAR

ADVENTURE INTO MYSTERY
Atlas 1956–57
1 BEv(c),Future Tense 250.00
2 Man on the 13th Floor 150.00
3 Next Stop Eternity 125.00
4 AW, The Hex 150.00
5 BEv,The People Who Weren't . 125.00
6 The Wax Man............. 125.00
7 .... 125.00

ADVENTURES INTO TERROR
See: JOKER COMICS

ADVENTURES INTO WEIRD WORLDS
Jan., 1952–June 1954
1 RH,GT,The Walking Death ... 400.00
2 The Thing In the Bottle 250.00
3 The Thing That Waited 175.00
4 BEv,RH,TheVillageGraveyard . 175.00
5 BEv,I Crawl Thru Graves 175.00
6 The Ghost Still Walks 175.00
7 Monsters In Disguise 175.00
8 Nightmares............... 175.00
9 Do Not Feed.............. 175.00
10 BEv,Down In The Cellar..... 175.00
11 Phantom 150.00
12 Lost In the Graveyard 150.00
13 Where Dead Men Walk 150.00
14 A Shriek In the Night 150.00
15 Terror In Our Town......... 150.00
16 The Kiss of Death 150.00
17 RH,He Walks With A Ghost .. 150.00
18 Ivan & Petroff............. 150.00
19 It Happened One Night 150.00
20 The Doubting Thomas 150.00
21 What Happened In the Cave . 150.00
22 RH,The Vampire's Partner ... 150.00
23 The Kiss of Death 125.00
24 Halfway Home 125.00
25 BEv,JSt,The Mad Mamba.... 125.00
26 Good-Bye Earth........... 150.00
27 The Dwarf of Horror Moor ... 250.00
28 DW,Monsters From the Grave 150.00
29 Bone Dry................ 100.00
30 JSt,The Impatient Ghost 100.00

ADVENTURES OF CAPTAIN AMERICA
Sept., 1991
1 KM,JRu,O:Capt. America 5.75
2 KM,KWe,TA,O:Capt.America ... 5.50
3 KM,KWe,JRu,D:Lt.Col.Fletcher.. 5.50
4 KWe,JRu,V:Red Skull......... 5.50

ADVENTURES OF CYCLOPS & PHOENIX
1994
1 SLo(s),GeH,AV,O:Cable 4.00
2 SLo(s),GeH,AV,O:Cable 3.50
3 SLo(s),GeH,AV,O:Cable 3.50
4 SLo(s),GeH,AV,O:Cable 3.50
TPB Rep. #1-#4 .... 14.95

ADVENTURES OF HOMER GHOST
Atlas June–Aug., 1957
1 .... 30.00
2 .... 25.00

ADVENTURES OF PINKY LEE
Atlas July, 1955
1 .... 150.00
2 .... 75.00

3 thru 5 .... @65.00

ADVENTURES OF SNAKE PLISSKIN
1997
1-shot LKa, *Escape From L.A.*
  movie adapt. 3.00

ADVENTURES OF SPIDER-MAN
1996
1 from animated TV show 1.00
2 V:Hammerhead 1.00
3 thru 8 .... 1.00
8 AS,V:Kingpin 1.00
9 MHi,A:Dr. Strange, ... 1.00
10 AS,V:The Beetle 1.00
11 AS,V:Doctor Octopus, Venom .. 1.00
12 AS,V:Doctor Octopus, Venom .. 1.00

ADVENTURES OF THE UNCANNY X-MEN
1995
1 Rep..................... 1.00

Adventures of the X-Men #12
© Marvel Entertainment Group

ADVENTURES OF THE X-MEN
1996–97
1 from animated TV show 1.00
2 X-Factor vs. X-Men.......... 1.00
3 thru 7.................... 1.00
8 RMc,BHr,GyM,Gambit back in
  New Orleans 1.00
9 RMc,GyM,F:Storm 1.00
10 RMc,A:Vanisher........... 1.00
11 RMc,V:Man-Thing 1.00
12 RMc,Age of Apocalypse...... 1.00

All comics prices listed are for *Near Mint* condition.

ADVENTURES ON THE PLANET OF THE APES
Oct., 1975
1 GT,Planet of the Apes Movie
  Adaptation 2.50
2 GT,Humans Captured. 2.50
3 GT,Man Hunt 2.50
4 GT,Trial By Fear. 2.50
5 GT, Fury in the
  Forbidden Zone 2.50
6 GT,The Forbidden Zone,Cont'd. . 2.50
7 AA,Man Hunt Cont'd. 2.50
8 AA,Brent & Nova Enslaved. 2.50
9 AA,Mankind's Demise. 2.50
10 AA,When Falls the Lawgiver . . . 2.50
11 AA,The Final Chapter;
  Dec., 1976 . . . . 2.50

ADVENTURES OF THE THING
April–July 1992
1 rep. Marvel 2 in 1 #50. . . . . 2.50
2 rep. Marvel 2 in 1 #80
  B.U. Ghost Rider 1.50
3 rep. Marvel 2 in 1 #51. . . . . 1.50
4 rep. Marvel 2 in 1 #77. . . . . 1.50

AGE OF INNOCENCE
1995
1-shot Timeslid aftermath 2.50

AIRTIGHT GARAGE
Epic July–Oct. 1993
1 thru 4 rep.Moebius GNv . . . . . @2.50

AKIRA
Epic Sept., 1988
1 The Highway,I:Kaneda,Tetsuo,
  Koy,Ryu,Colonel,Takaski. 15.00
1a 2nd printing 3.00
2 Pursuit,I:Number27,(Masaru) . . . 7.00
2a 2nd printing 3.50
3 Number 41,V:Clown Gang 6.00
4 King of Clowns,V:Colonel 7.00
5 Cycle Wars,V:Clown Gang 6.00
6 D:Yamagota 5.00
7 Prisoners and Players,I:Miyo . . . 5.00
8 Weapon of Vengeance 5.00
9 Stalkers 5.00
10 The Awakening 5.00
11 Akira Rising. 4.50
12 Enter Sakaki 4.50
13 Desperation. 4.50
14 Caught in the Middle 4.50
15 Psychic Duel 4.50
16 Akira Unleashed 4.50
17 Emperor of Chaos 4.50
18 Amid the Ruins 4.00
19 To Save the Children 4.00
20 Revelations 4.00
21 . . . . 4.00
22 . . . . 4.00
23 . . . . 4.00
24 Clown Gang 4.00
25 Search For Kay 4.00
26 Juvenile A Project 4.00
27 Kay and Kaneda 4.00
28 Tetsuo 4.00
29 Tetsuo 4.00
30 Tetsuo,Kay,Kaneda 4.00
31 D:Kaori,Kaneda,Vs.Tetsuo 4.00
32 Tetsuo'sForces vs.U.S.Forces . . 4.00
33 Tetsuo V:Kaneda 4.00
34 64pt. R:Otomo. 7.00
35 Leads toward final battle 7.00
36 Lady Miyako 7.00
37 ghost of Tetsuo 7.00
38 conclusion. 7.00
TPB Akira:Reprints#1-#3 . . . . 13.95
TPB Akira:Reprints#4-#6 . . . . 13.95
TPB Akira:Reprints#7-#9 . . . . 13.95
TPB Akira:Reprints#10-#12. . . . . . 14.95
TPB Akira:Reprints#13-#15. . . . . . 14.95
TPB Akira:Reprints#16-#18. . . . . . 14.95
TPB Akira:Reprints#19-#21. . . . . . 16.95
TPB Akira:Reprints#22-#24. . . . . . 16.95
TPB Akira:Reprints#25-#27. . . . . . 16.95
TPB Akira:Reprints#28-#30. . . . . . 17.95

ALADDIN
1 . . . . 1.50
2 . . . . 1.50
3 . . . . 1.50
4 . . . . 1.50
5 A:Queen Tatiana. 1.50
6 A:Zena 1.50
7 Genie Convention. 1.50
8 Body Switch 1.50
9 Archery Contest 1.50
10 Genie winds back his powers. . . 1.50
11 Magic Carpet Grand Prix 1.50
12 F:Iago 1.50

Alf #5
© *Marvel Entertainment Group*

ALF
Star March, 1988
1 Photo Cover. 1.50
1a 2nd printing 1.00
2 Alf Causes trouble 1.50
3 More adventures 1.50
4 Willie on Melmac 1.50
5 I:Alf's evil twin. 1.50
6 Photo Cover. 1.50
7 Pygm-Alien. 1.50
8 Ochmoneks' Garage. 1.25
9 Alf's Independence Day 1.25
10 Alf goes to College 1.25
11 Halloween special 1.00
12 Alf loses memory. 1.00
13 Racetrack of my Tears. 1.00
14 Night of the Living Bread 1.00
15 Alf on the Road 1.00
16 More Adventures 1.00
17 Future vision 1.00
18 More Adventures 1.00
19 The Alf-strologer 1.00
20 Alf the Baby Sitter,pt.1 . . . . 1.00
21 Alf the Baby Sitter,pt.2 . . . . 1.00
22 X-Men parody 1.00
23 Alf visits Australia 1.00
24 Rhonda visits Earth 1.00
25 More Adventures 1.00
26 Alf gets a job 1.00
27 Alf lost 1.00
28 Alf's Amnesia. 1.00
29 Alf/Brian reporters 1.00
30 Shakespeare Baby 1.00
31 Alf's Summer Camp. 1.00
32 Arnold Schwarzemeimac. 1.00
33 Dungeons & Dragons Spoof . . . 1.00
34 Alf-Red & Alf-Blue(2 Alfs). 1.00
35 Gone with the Wind 1.00
36 More Adventures 1.00
37 Melmacian Gothic 1.00
38 Boundtree Hunters. 1.00
39 Pizarro Alf 1.00
40 A:Zoreo 1.00
41 TV. 1.00
42 V:Alf 1.00
43 House Break-in 1.00
44 A:Fantastic Fur 1.00
45 Melmenopaus 1.00
46 Goes to Center of Earth. 1.00
47 Meteor Bye-Products,pt.1 . . . . . 1.00
48 Meteor Bye-Products,pt.2 . . . . . 1.00
49 1st Rhonda solo story 1.00
50 Final Issue, giant size 1.75
Ann.#1 Evol.War. 3.00
Ann.#2. 1.75
Spring Spec.#1. . . . . 1.75
Holiday Spec.#2 . . . . 2.00

ALIEN LEGION
Epic April, 1984
1 FC,TA,I:Sarigar,Montroc 4.00
2 FC,TA,CP,V:Harkilons. 3.50
3 FC,TA,CW,V:Kroyzo 3.00
4 FC,TA,CW,F:Skob 3.00
5 FC,CW,D:Skob 3.00
6 FC,CW,WPo,V:Harkilons 3.00
7 CW,WPo,I:Lora. 2.50
8 CW,WPo,V:Harkilons 2.50
9 CW,V:Harkilons 2.50
10 CW,LSn,V:Harkilons 2.50
11 CW,LSn,V:Harkilons. 2.50
12 LSn,A:Aob-Sin. 2.50
13 LSn,F:Montroc. 2.50
14 LSn,V:Cordar. 2.50
15 LSn,V:Alphor,Betro,&Gamoid . . . 2.50
16 LSn,J:Tomaro 2.50
17 LSn,Durge on Drugs 2.50
18 LSn,V:Dun. 2.50
19 LSn,A:GalarcyScientist 2.50
20 LSn,L:Skilene 2.50

[2nd Series] Aug. 1987
1 LSn,I:Guy Montroc 3.00
2 LSn,V:Quallians 2.50
3 LSn,Hellscope 2.50
4 LSn,V:Harkillons 2.50
5 LSn,F:JuggerGrimrod 2.50
6 LSn,F:JuggerGrimrod 2.50
7 LSn,A:Guy Montroc 2.50
8 LSn,I:Nakhira 2.50
9 LSn,V:Harkilons 2.50
10 LSn,V:Harkilons. 2.50
11 LSn,V:Harkilons 2.50
12 LSn,Tamara Pregnant 2.50
13 LSn,V:MomojianKndrel 2.50
14 LSn,J:Saravil 2.50
15 LSn,J:Spellik 2.50
16 LSn,D:Jugger's Father. 2.50
17 LSn,O:JuggerGrimrod 2.50
18 LSn,O:JuggerGrimrod 2.50
GN Grimrod 5.95

MARVEL

ALIEN LEGION: BINARY DEEP
Epic 1993
1-shot with trading card 3.50

ALIEN LEGION: JUGGER GRIMROD
Epic Aug. 1992
Book One 5.95

ALIEN LEGION: ONE PLANET AT A TIME
Epic Heavy Hitters May 1993
1 HNg,CDi,One Planet at a Time . . 4.95
2 HNg,CDi. 4.95
3 HNg,CDi. 4.95

ALIEN LEGION: ON THE EDGE
Epic Nov. 1990
1 LSn,V:B'Be No N'ngth. 4.95
2 LSn,V:B'Be No N'ngth. 4.95
3 LSn,V:B'Be No N'ngth. 4.95
4 LSn,V:B'Be No N'ngth. 4.95

All-Select #5
© Marvel Entertainment Group

ALIEN LEGION: TENANTS OF HELL
Epic 1991
1 LSn,Nomad Squad On
  Combine IV 4.50
2 LSn,L:Torie Montroc,I:Stagg 4.50
TPB Alien Legion:Slaughterworld . . 9.95

ALL-SELECT COMICS
Fall, 1943
Timely (Daring Comics)
1 B:Capt.America,Sub-Mariner,
  Human Torch;WWII 7,500.00
2 A:Red Skull,V:Axis Powers. . 2,500.00
3 B:Whizzer,V:Axis 1,500.00
4 V: Axis. 1,300.00
5 E:Sub-Mariner,V:Axis 1,200.00
6 A:The Destroyer,V:Axis 1,000.00
7 E:Whizzer,V:Axis 1,000.00
8 V:Axis Powers 1,000.00
9 V:Axis Powers 1,000.00

10 E:Capt.America,Human Torch;
  A:The Destroyer 1,000.00
11 I:Blonde Phantom,A:Miss
  America. 1,800.00
Becomes:

BLONDE PHANTOM
12 B:Miss America;The Devil's
  Playground 1,200.00
13 B:Sub-Mariner;Horror In
  Hollywood 700.00
14 E:Miss America;Horror At
  Haunetd Castle. 650.00
15 The Man Who Deserved
  To Die 650.00
16 A:Capt.America,Bucky;
  Modeled For Murder. 850.00
17 Torture & Rescue. 600.00
18 Jealously,Hate & Cruelty 600.00
19 Killer In the Hospital. 600.00
20 Blonde Phantom's Big Fall . . . 600.00
21 Murder At the Carnival. 600.00
22 V: Crime Bosses 600.00
Becomes:

LOVERS
23 Love Stories 85.00
24 My Dearly Beloved. 40.00
25 The Man I Love 50.00
26 thru 29 . . . . @30.00
30 MK 50.00
31 thru 36 . . . . @30.00
37 . . . . 50.00
38 BK. 50.00
39 . . . . 30.00
40. . . . . 30.00
41BEv 40.00
42 thru 65 . . . . @30.00
66 . . . . 25.00
67 ATh 40.00
68 thru 86 Aug. 1957 . . . . @25.00

ALL SURPRISE
Timely Fall, 1943
1 (fa),F:Super Rabbit,Gandy,
  Sourpuss 200.00
2 . . . . 100.00
3 . . . . 75.00
4 thru 10 . . . . @75.00
11 HK. 100.00
12 Winter, 1946 . . . . 75.00

ALL-TRUE CRIME
See: OFFICIAL TRUE CRIME CASES

ALL WINNERS COMICS
Summer, 1941
1 S&K,BEv,B:Capt.America & Bucky,
  Human Torch & Toro,Sub-Mariner
  A:The Angel,Black Marvel 15,000.00
2 S&K,B:Destroyer,Whizzer. . . 4,000.00
3 BEv,Bucky & Toro Captured . 2,400.00
4 BEv,Battle For Victory
  For America. 2,500.00
5 V:Nazi Invasion Fleet 1,500.00
6 V:Axis Powers,A:
  Black Avenger 1,600.00
7 V:Axis Powers 1,200.00
8 V:Axis Powers 1,100.00
9 V:Nazi Submarine Fleet 1,100.00
10 V:Nazi Submarine Fleet . . . 1,200.00
11 V: Nazis 1,000.00
12 A:Red Skull,E:Destroyer;
  Jap P.O.W. Camp 1,200.00
13 V:Japanese Fleet 1,000.00
14 V:Japanese Fleet 1,000.00
15 Japanese Supply Train 1,000.00
16 In Alaska V:Gangsters. 1,000.00

17 V:Gansters;Atomic
  Research Department 1,000.00
18 V:Robbers;Internal Revenue
  Department 1,100.00
19 I:All Winners Squad,
  Fall, 1946 . . . . 3,500.00
21 A:All-Winners Squad;Riddle
  of the Demented Dwarf . . . 3,000.00
Becomes:

ALL TEEN COMICS
20 F:Georgie,Willie,
  Mitzi,Patsy Walker 50.00
Becomes:

TEEN COMICS
21 HK,A:George,Willie,Mitzi,
  Patsy Walker, Hey Look 100.00
22 A:George,Willie,Margie,
  Patsy Walker 65.00
23 A:Patsy Walker,Cindy,George . 65.00
24 . . . . 75.00
25. . . . . 65.00
26. . . . . 65.00
27. . . . . 65.00
28. . . . . 75.00
29. . . . . 65.00
30 HK,Hey Look 85.00
31 thru 34 . . . . @65.00
35 May, 1950 . . . . 65.00
Becomes:

JOURNEY INTO UNKNOWN WORLDS
Atlas Sept. 1950
36(1) RH,End of the Earth. . . . 1,800.00
37(2) BEv,GC,When Worlds
  Collide 800.00
38(3) GT,Land of Missing Men . . 650.00
4 MS,RH,Train to Nowhere 400.00
5 MS,Trapped in Space 400.00
6 GC,RH,World Below
  the Atlantic. 400.00
7 BW,RH,House That Wasn't . . . 675.00
8 RH,The Stone Thing 400.00
9 MS,JSt,The People Who
  Couldn't Exist 500.00
10 THe Undertaker. 400.00
11 BEv,Frankie Was Afraid 300.00
12 BK,Last Voice You Hear. . . . 300.00
13 The Witch Woman 225.00
14 BW,BEv,CondemnedBuilding . 500.00
15 They Crawl By Night 500.00
16 Scared to Death. 225.00
17 BEv,GC,RH,The Ice
  Monster Cometh. 225.00

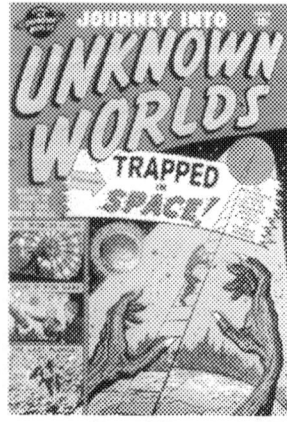

Journey Into Unknown Worlds #5
© Marvel Entertainment Group

18 The Broth Needs Somebody .	250.00
19 MF,GC,The Long Wait	250.00
20 GC,RH,The Race That	
Vanished	225.00
21 MF.	175.00
22 thru 33	@150.00
34 MK,AT	150.00
35 AT	125.00
26 thru 35	@150.00
36 thru 44	@125.00
45 AW,SD.	135.00
46 & 47.	@125.00
48 GW	125.00
49	125.00
50 JDa,RC	125.00
51 WW,SD,JSe.	135.00
52	125.00
53 RC,BP	125.00
54 AT,BP	125.00
55 AW,RC,BEv	125.00
56 BEv	125.00
57 JO	100.00
58 MO	100.00
59 AW,August, 1957	125.00

ALL WINNERS COMICS
[2nd Series] August, 1948
1 F:Blonde Phantom,A:Capt.America
Sub-Mariner,Human Torch 2,000.00
Becomes:

ALL WESTERN WINNERS
2 B,I&O:Black Rider,B:Two-Gun
Kid, Kid-Colt. 600.00
3 Black Rider V: Satan. 300.00
4 Black Rider Unmasked 275.00
Becomes:

WESTERN WINNERS
5 I Challenge the Army 225.00
6 The Mountain Mystery 175.00
7 Ph(c) Randolph Scott 175.00
Becomes:

BLACK RIDER
8 Ph(c),B:Black Rider;Valley
of Giants 350.00
9 Wrath of the Redskin 175.00
10 O:Black Rider 200.00
11 Redmen on the Warpath 125.00
12 GT,The Town That Vanished . 125.00
13 The Terrified Tribe 125.00
14 The Tyrant of Texas 125.00
15 Revolt of the Redskins. 100.00
16 . . . . 100.00
17 . . . . 100.00
18. . . . . 100.00
19 SSh,GT,A:Two-Gun Kid 100.00
20 GT 110.00
21 SSh,GT,A:Two-Gun Kid 100.00
22 SSh,A:Two-Gun Kid 100.00
23 SSh,A:Two-Gun Kid 100.00
24 SSh,JSt 100.00
25 SSh,JSt,A:Arrowhead 100.00
26 SSh,A:Kid-Colt. 100.00
27 SSh,A:Kid-Colt. 110.00
Becomes:

WESTERN TALES OF BLACK RIDER
28 JSe,D:Spider 125.00
29 . . . . 90.00
30 . . . . 90.00
31 . . . . 90.00
Becomes:

GUNSMOKE WESTERN
32 MD,MB,F:Kid Colt,Billy
Buckskin. 125.00
33 MD 100.00
34 MB 75.00

35	100.00
36 AW	100.00
37 JDa	75.00
38	50.00
39	50.00
40 AW	75.00
41	35.00
42.	35.00
43	40.00

Alpha Flight #5
© Marvel Entertainment Group

44 AT	45.00
45 thru 55	@40.00
56 MB	45.00
57 thru 76	@40.00
77 July, 1963	35.00

ALPHA FLIGHT
August, 1983
1 JBy,I:Puck,Marrina,Tundra 3.00
2 JBy,I:Master,Vindicator Becomes
Guardian,B:O:Marrina 2.00
3 JBy,O:Master,A:Namor,Invisible
Girl, ... 2.00
4 JBy,A:Namor,Invisible Girl,
E:O:Marrina,A:Master 2.00
5 JBy,B:O:Shaman,F:Puck. 2.00
6 JBy,E:O:Shaman,I:Kolomag . . . 2.00
7 JBy,B:O:Snowbird,I:Delphine
Courtney & Deadly Ernest 2.00
8 JBy,E:O:Snowbird,O:Deadly
Ernest,I:Nemesis 2.00
9 JBy,O:Aurora,A:Wolverine,
Super Skrull 2.00
10 JBy,O:Northstar,V:SuperSkrull . 2.00
11 JBy,I:Omega Flight,Wild Child
O:Sasquatch 2.00
12 JBy,D:Guardian,V:Omega
Flight 2.00
13 JBy,C:Wolverine,Nightmare 3.00
14 JBy,V:Genocide 2.00
15 JBy,R:Master 2.00
16 JBy,BWi,V:Master,C:Wolverine
I:Madison Jeffries 2.25
17 JBy,BWi,A:Wolverine,X-Men . . . 3.00
18 JBy,BWi,J:Heather,I:Ranaq 2.00
19 JBy,I:Talisman,V:Ranaq 2.00
20 JBy,I:Gilded Lily,N:Aurora. 2.00
21 JBy,BWi,O:Gilded Lily,Diablo . . 2.00
22 JBy,BWi,I:Pink Pearl 2.00
23 JBy,BWi,D:Sasquatch,
I:Tanaraq 2.00
24 JBy,BWi,V:Great Beasts,J:Box . . 2.00
25 JBy,BWi,V:Omega Flight

I:Dark Guardian	2.00
26 JBy,BWi,A:Omega Flight,Dark	
Guardian	2.00
27 JBy,V:Omega Flight.	2.00
28 JBy,Secret Wars II,V:Omega	
Flight,D:Dark Guardian.	2.00
29 MMi,V:Hulk,A:Box	2.00
30 MMi,I&O:Scramble,R:Deadly	
Ernest	2.00
31 MMi,D:Deadly Ernest,	
O:Nemesis	2.00
32 MMi(c),JBg,O:Puck,I:2nd	
Vindicator.	2.00
33 MMi(c),SB,X-Men,I:Deathstrike .	3.00
34 MMi(c),SB,Wolverine,V:	
Deathstrike.	3.00
35 DR,R:Shaman	2.00
36 MMi(c),DR,A:Dr.Strange	2.00
37 DR,O:Pestilence,N:Aurora	2.00
38 DR,A:Namor,V:Pestilence	2.00
39 MMi(c),DR,WPo,A:Avengers . . .	2.25
40 DR,WPo,W:Namor & Marrina. . .	2.25
41 DR,WPo,I:Purple Girl,	
J:Madison Jeffries	2.25
42 DR,WPo,I:Auctioneer,J:Purple Girl,	
A: Beta Flight	2.25
43 DR,WPo,V:Mesmero,Sentinels. .	2.25
44 DR,WPo,D:Snowbird,	
A:Pestilence.	2.25
45 JBr,WPo,R:Sasquatch,	
L:Shaman	2.25
46 JBr,WPo,I:2nd Box.	2.25
47 MMi,WPo,TA,Vindicator solo . . .	2.25
48 SL(i),I:Omega	2.25
49 JBr,WPo,I:Manikin,D:Omega . . .	2.25
50 WS(c),JBr,WPo,L:Northstar,Puck,	
Aurora,A:Loki,Double size	2.50
51 JLe(1st Marv),WPo(i),V:Cody. . .	4.00
52 JBr,WPo(i),I:Bedlam,	
A:Wolverine	3.00
53 JLe,WPo(i),I:Derangers,Goblin	
D&V:Bedlam,A:Wolverine	3.00
54 WPo(i),O&J:Goblyn	2.00
55 JLe,TD,V:Tundra	2.50
56 JLe,TD,V:Bedlamites	2.50
57 JLe,TD,V:Crystals,	
C:Dreamqueen	2.50
58 JLe,AM,V:Dreamqueen	2.50
59 JLe,AM,I:Jade Dragon,R:Puck . .	2.50
60 JLe,AM,V:J.Dragon,D.Queen . . .	2.50
61 JLe,AM,on Trial	
(1st JLe X-Men)	2.50
62 JLe,AM,V:Purple Man	2.50
63 MG,V:U.S.Air Force	2.00
64 JLe,AM,V:Great Beasts	2.50
65 JLe(c),AM(i),Dream Issue	2.00
66 JLe(c),I:China Force	2.00
67 JLe(c),O:Dream Queen	2.00
68 JLe(c),V:Dream Queen	2.00
69 JLe(c),V:Dream Queen	2.00
70 MM(i),V:Dream Queen.	2.00
71 MM(i),I:Sorcerer.	2.00
72 V:Sorcerer.	2.00
73 MM(i),V:Sorcerer.	2.00
74 MM(i),Alternate Earth.	2.00
75 JLe(c),MMi(i),Double Size	3.00
76 MM(i),V:Sorcerer.	2.00
77 MM(i),V:Kingpin	2.00
78 MM(i),A:Dr.Strange,Master. . . .	2.00
79 MM(i),AofV,V:Scorpion,Nekra. . .	2.00
80 MM(i),AofV,V:Scorpion,Nekra. . .	2.00
81 JBy(c),MM(i),B:R:Northstar	2.00
82 JBy(c),MM(i),E:R:Northstar	2.00
83 JSh	2.00
84 MM(i),Northstar	2.00
85 MM(i).	2.00
86 MBa,MM,V:Sorcerer	2.00
87 JLe(c),MM(i),A:Wolverine.	3.00
88 JLe(c),MM(i),A:Wolverine.	3.00
89 JLe(c),MM(i),R:Guardian,A:	
Wolverine.	3.00

All comics prices listed are for *Near Mint* condition.

90 JLe(c),MM(i),A:Wolverine 3.00	15 SSe. 2.00
91 MM(i),A:Dr.Doom 2.00	16 SSe,V:Brass Bishop. 2.00
92 Guardian vs.Vindicator. 2.00	17 SSe,V:X the Unknown 2.00
93 MM(i),A:Fant.Four,I:Headlok . . . 2.00	18 SSe,Alpha:Omega,pt.1 . . . . 2.00
94 MM(i),V:Fant.Four,Headlok 2.00	19 SSe,Alpha:Omega,pt.2 . . . . 2.00
95 MM(i),Lifelines 2.00	20 SSe,Alpha:Omega,pt.3 . . . . 2.00
96 MM(i),A:Master 2.00	Spec. #1 SSe,"In the Beginning,"
97 B:Final Option,A:Her 2.00	Flashback, A:Wolverine 2.00
98 A:Avengers 2.00	Ann.1998 Alpha Flight/Inhumans . . 3.50
99 A:Avengers 2.00	

100 JBr,TMo,DR,LMa,E:Final Option
A:Galactus,Avengers,D:
Guardian,G-Size. 2.50
101 TMo,Final Option Epilogue,
A:Dr.Strange,Avengers 2.00
102 TMo,I:Weapon Omega, ... 2.00
103 TMo,V:Diablo,U.S.Agent 2.00
104 TMo,N:Alpha Flight,Weapon
Omega is Wild Child. 2.00
105 TMo,V:Pink Pearl. 2.00
106 MPa,Aids issue,Northstar
acknowledges homosexuality . . 2.50
106a 2nd printing 2.50
107 A:X-Factor,V:Autopsy. 2.00
108 A:Soviet Super Soldiers 2.00
109 V:Peoples Protectorate 2.00
110 PB,Infinity War,I:2nd Omega
Flight,A:Wolverine 2.00
111 PB,Infinity War,V:Omega
Flight,A:Wolverine 2.00
112 PB,Infinity War,V:Master. 2.00
113 V:Mauler 2.00
114 A:Weapon X 2.00
115 PB,I:Wyre,A:Weapon X 2.00
116 PB,I:Rok,V:Wyre 2.00
117 PB,V:Wyre 2.00
118 PB,V:Thunderball 2.00
119 PB,V:Wrecking Crew 2.00
120 PB,10th Anniv.,V:Hardliners,
w/poster 2.50
121 PCu,V:Brass Bishop,A:Spider-
Man,Wolverine,C:X-Men. 2.00
122 PB,BKi,Inf.Crusade 2.00
123 PB,BKi,Infinity Crusade 2.00
124 PB,BKi,Infinity Crusade 2.00
125 PB,V:Carcass 2.00
126 V:Carcass 2.00
127 SFu(s),Infinity Crusade 2.00
128 B:No Future. 2.00
129 C:Omega Flight 2.00
130 E:No Future,last issue,
Double Sized 2.50
Ann.#1 LSn,V:Diablo,Gilded Lily . . . 3.00
Ann.#2 JBr,BMc 2.00
Spec.#1 PB,A:Wolverine,
O:First Team,V:Egghead. 3.75
Spec.#1–#3 Newsstand versions
of #97–#99 . . . . @1.50
Spec.#4 Newsstand ver.of #100 . . . 2.00

ALPHA FLIGHT
1997
1 SSe,ScC, former team kidnapped,
I:Murmur, Radius,Flex,Guardian . 2.00
2 SSe,ScC 2.00
2 variant cover. 2.00
3 SSe,ScC, ... 2.00
4 SSe,ScC,V:Mesmero 2.00
5 SSe,ScC,A:Mesmero 2.00
6 SSe,What's up with Sasquatch? . 2.00
7 SSe,Evils explode. 2.00
8 SSe,ScC,North & South prelude . 2.00
9 SSe,ScC,North & South pt.1,
X-men x-over 2.00
10 SSe,Flung into Prometheus Pit . 2.00
11 SSe,race to save 2 worlds 2.00
12 SSe,Alphan dies,48pg. double
size 3.00
13 SSe,F:Basil Killbrew 2.00
14 SSe,I:Brass Bishop 2.00

ALPHA FLIGHT SPECIAL
1991
1 thru 4 reprints . . . . @1.50

AMAZING ADVENTURES
June, 1961
1 JK,SD,O&B:Dr.Droom;Torr . 1,200.00
2 JK,SD,This is Manoo 600.00
3 JK,SD,Trapped in the
Twilight World 500.00
4 JK,SD, I Am X 450.00
5 JK,SD, Monsteroso 450.00
6 JK,SD,E:Dr.Droom; Sserpo . . 450.00
Becomes:

AMAZING ADULT FANTASY
Dec., 1961
7 SD,Last Man on Earth 600.00
8 SD,The Coming of the Krills . . 500.00
9 SD,The Terror of Tim Boo Ba . 450.00
10 SD,Those Who Change 450.00
11 SD,In Human Form 450.00
12 SD,Living Statues 450.00
13 SD,At the Stroke of Midnight . 450.00
14 SD,Beware of the Giants 475.00
Becomes:

AMAZING FANTASY
August, 1962
15 JK(c),SD,I&O:Spider-Man,I:Aunt
May, Flash Thompson, Burglar,
I&D:Uncle Ben. 28,000.00
Marvel Milestone rep.#15 (1992). . . 3.00
[Second Series] 1995
15a gold Rep. (1995) 25.00
16 KBk, O:Spider-Man,painted 4.00
17 KBk, More early adventures. . . . 4.00
18 KBk,conclusion 4.00

AMAZING ADVENTURES
August, 1970
[1st Regular Series]
1 JK,JB,B:Inhumans,Bl.Widow . . 40.00
2 JK,JB,A:Fantastic Four. 15.00
3 JK,GC,BEv,V:Mandarin. 15.00
4 JK,GC,BEv,V:Mandarin. 15.00
5 NA,TP,DH,BEv,V:Astrologer . . 25.00
6 NA,DH,SB,V:Maximus 25.00
7 NA,DH,BEv 25.00
8 NA,DH,BEv,E:Black Widow,
A:Thor,(see Avengers #95) . . 25.00
9 MSy,BEv,V:Magneto 12.00
10 GK(c),MSy,V:Magneto,
E:Inhumans 12.00
11 GK(c),TS,B:O:New Beast,
A:X-Men. 75.00
12 GK(c),TS,MP,A:Iron Man 20.00
13 JR(c),TS,V:New Br'hood
Evil Mutants,I:Buzz Baxter
(Mad Dog) 20.00
14 GK(c),TS,JM,V:Quasimodo . . 20.00
15 JSn(c),TS,A:X-Men,V:Griffin. . 20.00
16 JSn(c),FMc(i),V:Juggernaut . . 20.00
17 JSn,A:X-Men,E:Beast 20.00
18 HC,NA,B:Killraven 20.00
19 HC,Sirens on 7th Avenues . . . 6.00
20 Coming of the Warlords 6.00

Amazing Adventures #14
© *Marvel Entertainment Group*

21 Cry Killraven 6.00
22 Killraven 6.00
23 Killraven 6.00
24 New Year Nightmare-2019AD . . 6.00
25 RB,V:Skar 6.00
26 GC,V:Ptson-Rage Vigilante . . . 6.00
27 CR,JSn,V:Death Breeders 6.00
28 JSn,CR,V:Death Breeders 6.00
29 CR,Killraven 6.00
30 CR,Killraven 6.00
31 CR,Killraven 6.00
32 CR,Killraven 6.00
33 CR,Killraven 6.00
34 CR,D:Hawk 6.00
35 KG,Killraven Continued 6.00
36 CR,Killraven Continued 6.00
37 CR,O:Old Skull 6.00
38 CR,Killraven Continued. 6.00
39 CR,E:Killraven. 6.00
[2nd Regular Series]
1 rep.X-Men#1,38,Professor X. . . . 7.00
2 rep.X-Men#1,39,O:Cyclops. 6.00
3 rep.X-Men#2,40,O:Cyclops. 6.00
4 rep.X-Men#2,41,O:Cyclops. 6.00
5 rep.X-Men#3,42,O:Cyclops. 6.00
6 JBy(c),rep.X-Men#3,43,Cyclops . 6.00
7 rep.X-Men#4,44,O:Iceman 6.00
8 rep.X-Men#4,45,O:Iceman 6.00
9 JBy(c),X-Men#5,46,O:Iceman . . . 6.00
10 rep.X-Men#5,47,O:Iceman 6.00
11 rep.X-Men#6,48,Beast. 6.00
12 rep.X-Men#6,Str.Tales#168 . . . 6.00
13 rep.X-Men #7. . . . . 6.00
14 rep.X-Men #8. . . . . 6.00

AMAZING COMICS
Timely Comics Fall, 1944
1 F:Young Allies,Destroyer,
Whizzer, Sergeant Dix . . . 1,500.00
Becomes:

COMPLETE COMICS
2 F:Young Allies,Destroyer,Whizzer
Sergeant Dix; Winter'44-5 . 1,000.00

AMAZING DETECTIVE CASES
Atlas Nov., 1950
3 Detective/Horror Stories 175.00
4 Death of a Big Shot 100.00
5 . . . . 100.00
6 Danger in the City 100.00

7 .... 75.00	C:Avengers,F.F.,Daredevil... 400.00
8 .... 75.00	19 SD,V:Sandman,I:Ned Leeds
9 GC, The Man Who Wasn't ... 75.00	A:Human Torch. 300.00
10 GT. 75.00	20 SD,I&O:Scorpion 400.00
11 The Black Shadow........ 125.00	21 SD,A:Beetle,Human Torch ... 250.00
12 MS,BK, Harrigan's Wake 125.00	22 SD,V:The Clown,Masters of
13 BEv,JSt,.............. 175.00	Menace 225.00
14 Hands Off; Sept., 1952 ..... 125.00	23 SD,V:GreenGoblin(3rd App.) . 350.00
	24 SD,V:Mysterio 200.00

AMAZING HIGH ADVENTURE
August, 1984

1 BSz,JSo,JS 3.00	25 SD,I:Spider Slayer,Spencer Smythe,C:Mary Jane 250.00
2 PS,AW,BSz,TA,MMi,BBl,CP,CW . 2.50	26 SD,I:CrimeMaster,V:Green Goblin 300.00
3 MMi,VM,JS. 2.50	27 SD,V:CrimeMaster, Green Goblin 275.00
4 JBo,JS,SBi.............. 2.50	
5 JBo; Oct., 1986 .... 2.50	28 SD,I:Molten Man,Peter Parker Graduates High School,rare in near-mint condition 400.00

AMAZING SCARLET SPIDER

1 MBa,LMa,VirtualMortality,pt.2 ... 1.95	29 SD,V:Scorpion 175.00
2 TDF,MBa,CyberWar,pt.2 .... 1.95	30 SD,I:Cat Burglar. 175.00
	31 SD,I:Gwen Stacy,Harry Osborn Prof.Warren,V:Dr.Octopus... 175.00

AMAZING SPIDER-MAN
March, 1963

1 JK(c),SED,I:Chameleon,J.Jonah & John Jameson,A:F.Four .. 20,000.00	32 SD,V:Dr.Octopus 175.00
	33 SD,V:Dr.Octopus 175.00
2 SD,I:Vulture,Tinkerer C:Mysterio(disguised) 3,000.00	34 SD,V:Kraven 175.00
	35 SD,V:Molten Man. 175.00
3 SD,I&O:Dr.Octopus 2,400.00	36 SD,I:The Looter 175.00
4 SD,I&O:Sandman,I:Betty Brant,Liz Allen 1,700.00	37 SD,V:Professor Stromm, I:Norman Osborn 175.00
5 SD,V:Dr.Doom,C:Fant.Four . 1,500.00	38 SD,V:Joe Smith(Boxer) 175.00
6 SD,I&O:Lizard,The Connors. 1,300.00	39 JR,IR:Green Goblin is Norman Osborn 225.00
7 SD,V:Vulture. 900.00	
8 SD,JK,I:Big Brain,V:Human Torch,A:Fantastic Four 850.00	40 JR,O:Green Goblin 325.00
9 SD,I&O:Electro 900.00	41 JR,I:Rhino,C:Mary Jane 175.00
10 SD,I:Enforcers,Big Man 850.00	42 JR,V:John Jameson,I:Mary Jane (Face Revealed) 150.00
11 SD,V:Dr.Octopus, D:Bennett Brant 500.00	43 JR,O:Rhino 100.00
12 SD,V:Dr.Octopus 500.00	44 JR,V:Lizard(2nd App.) 100.00
13 SD,I:Mysterio. 650.00	45 JR,V:Lizard 100.00
14 SD,I:Green Goblin, V:Enforcers, Hulk. 1,600.00	46 JR,I&O:Shocker 110.00
	47 JR,V:Kraven 100.00
15 SD,I:Kraven,A:Chameleon ... 600.00	48 JR,I:Fake Vulture,A:Vulture . 100.00
16 SD,A:Daredevil, V:Ringmaster 400.00	49 JR,V:Fake Vulture,Kraven ... 100.00
17 SD,2nd A:Green Goblin, A:Human Torch. 600.00	50 JR,I:Kingpin,Spidey Quits, C:Johnny Carson 400.00
18 SD,V:Sandman,Enforcers,	51 JR,V:Kingpin 175.00

Amazing Spider-Man #26
© Marvel Entertainment Group

52 JR,V:Kingpin,I:Robbie Robertson,D:Fred Foswell ... 85.00	
53 JR,V:Dr.Octopus 75.00	
54 JR,V:Dr.Octopus 75.00	
55 JR,V:Dr.Octopus 75.00	
56 JR,V:Dr.Octopus,I:Capt.Stacy . 75.00	
57 JR,DH,A:Kazar 75.00	
58 JR,DH,V:Spencer Smythe, Spider Slayer 75.00	
59 JR,DH,V:Kingpin 75.00	
60 JR,DH,V:Kingpin 75.00	
61 JR,DH,V:Kingpin 75.00	
62 JR,DH,V:Medusa........... 55.00	
63 JR,DH,V:1st & 2nd Vulture 55.00	
64 JR,DH,V:Vulture. 55.00	
65 JR,JM,V:Prisoners 55.00	
66 JR,DH,V:Mysterio 55.00	
67 JR,JM,V:Mysterio,I:Randy Robertson 55.00	
68 JR,JM,V:Kingpin 60.00	
69 JR,JM,V:Kingpin 60.00	
70 JR,JM,V:Kingpin 60.00	
71 JR,JM,V:Quicksilver,C:Scarlet Witch,Toad,A:Kingpin 50.00	
72 JR,JB,JM,V:Shocker 50.00	
73 JR,JB,JM,I:Man Mountain Marko, Silvermane 50.00	
74 JR,JM,V:Silvermane. 45.00	
75 JR,JM,V:Silvermane,A:Lizard.. 45.00	
76 JR,JM,V:Lizard,A:H.Torch ... 45.00	
77 JR,JM,V:Lizard,A:H.Torch ... 45.00	
78 JR,JM,I&O:Prowler 50.00	
79 JR,JM,V:Prowler 45.00	
80 JR,JB,JM,V:Chameleon 45.00	

Amazing Spider-Man #36
© Marvel Entertainment Group

81 JR,JB,JM,I:Kangaroo 45.00	
82 JR,JM,V:Electro........... 45.00	
83 JR,I:Richard Fisk(as Schemer), Vanessa(Kingpin's wife) V:Kingpin 50.00	
84 JR,JB,JM,V:Schemer,Kingpin.. 45.00	
85 JR,JB,JM,V:Schemer,Kingpin.. 45.00	
86 JR,JM,V:Black Widow, C:Iron Man, Hawkeye 45.00	
87 JR,JM,Reveals ID to his friends,changes mind 45.00	
88 JR,JM,V:Dr.Octopus. 45.00	
89 GK,JR,V:Dr.Octopus 45.00	
90 GK,JR,V:Dr.Octopus D:Capt.Stacy 60.00	
91 GK,JR,I:Bullit. 45.00	
92 GK,JR,V:Bullit,A:Iceman 45.00	
93 JR,V:Prowler 45.00	
94 JR,SB,V:Beetle,O:Spider-Man . 70.00	
95 JR,SB,London,V:Terrorists 45.00	
96 GK,JR,A:Green Goblin,Drug Mention,No Comic Code..... 90.00	
97 GK,V:Green Goblin,Drugs 75.00	
98 GK,V:Green Goblin,Drugs 75.00	
99 GK,Prison Riot,A:Carson 50.00	
100 JR(c),GK,Spidey gets four arms from serum 180.00	
101 JR(c),GK,I:Morbius,the Living Vampire,A:Lizard 135.00	
101a Reprint,Metallic ink. 2.50	
102 JR(c),GK,O:Morbius, V:Lizard 100.00	
103 GK,V:Kraven,A:Kazar. 30.00	
104 GK,V:Kraven,A:Kazar. 30.00	
105 GK,V:Spenser Smythe, Spider Slayer 30.00	
106 JR,V:Spenser Smythe, Spider Slayer 30.00	
107 JR,V:Spenser Smythe, Spider Slayer 30.00	
108 JR,R:Flash Thompson, I:Sha-Shan,V:Vietnamese.... 30.00	
109 JR,A:Dr.Strange, V:Vietnamese............. 30.00	
110 JR,I:The Gibbon. 30.00	
111 JR,V:The Gibbon,Kraven 30.00	
112 JR,Spidey gets an Ulcer..... 30.00	
113 JSn,JR,I:Hammerhead V:Dr.Octopus 30.00	
114 JSn,JR,V:Hammerhead,Dr. Octopus,I:Jonas Harrow 30.00	
115 JR,V:Hammerhead, Dr.Octopus............. 30.00	
116 JR,JM,V:The Smasher 30.00	

All comics prices listed are for *Near Mint* condition.   **CVA Page 155**

117 JR,JM,V:Smasher,Disruptor . . 30.00	183 RA,BMc,V:Rocket Racer 7.00
118 JR,JM,V:Smasher,Disruptor . . 30.00	184 RA,V:White Tiger 7.00
119 JR,A:Hulk. 45.00	185 RA,V:White Tiger 7.00
120 GK,JR,V:Hulk. 45.00	186 KP,A:Chameleon,Spidey
121 GK,JR,V:Green Goblin	cleared by police of charges . . . 7.00
D:Gwen Stacy,Drugs 125.00	187 JSn,BMc,A:Captain
122 GK,JR,D:Green Goblin 135.00	America,V:Electro 8.00
123 GK,JR,A:Powerman. 25.00	188 KP,A:Jigsaw. 7.00
124 GK,JR,I:Man-Wolf 26.00	189 JBy,JM,A:Man-Wolf 8.00
125 RA,JR,O:Man-Wolf 25.00	190 JBy,JM,A:Man-Wolf 8.00
126 JM(c),RA,JM,V:Kangaroo,	191 KP,V:Spiderslayer 6.00
A: Human Torch 25.00	192 KP,JM,V:The Fly 6.00
127 JR(c),RA,V:3rd Vulture,	193 KP,JM,V:The Fly 6.00
A:Human Torch 25.00	194 KP,I:Black Cat 16.00
128 JR(c),RA,V:3rd Vulture 25.00	195 KP,AM,JM,O:Black Cat 7.00
129 K&R(c),RA,I:Punisher,	196 AM,JM,D:Aunt May,A:Kingpin . 6.00
Jackal. 135.00	197 KP,JM,V:Kingpin 6.00
130 JR(c),RA,V:Hammerhead,	198 SB,JM,V:Mysterio 6.00
Dr.Octopus,I:Spider-Mobile . . . 22.00	199 SB,JM,V:Mysterio 6.00
131 GK(c),RA,V:Hammerhead,	200 JR(c),KP,JM,D:Burglar,Aunt May
Dr.Octopus 22.00	alive,O:Spider-Man. 25.00
132 GK(c),JR,V:Molten Man 20.00	201 KP,JM,A:Punisher 10.00
133 JR(c),RA,V:Molten Man 20.00	202 KP,JM,A:Punisher 10.00
134 JR(c),RA,I:Tarantula,C:	203 FM(c),KP,A:Dazzler 7.00
Punisher(2nd App.). 27.00	204 JR2(c),KP,V:Black Cat 6.00
135 JR(c),RA,V:Tarantula,	205 KP,JM,V:Black Cat. 6.00
A:Punisher 55.00	206 JBy,GD,V:Jonas Harrow. 8.00
136 JR(c),RA,I:2nd GreenGoblin. . 40.00	207 JM,V:Mesmero. 6.00
137 GK(c),RA,V:Green Goblin . . . 35.00	208 JR2,AM,BBr,V:Fusion(1stJR2
138 K&R(c),RA,I:Mindworm 25.00	SpM art),I:Lance Bannon 7.00
139 K&R(c),RA,I:Grizzly,V:Jackal . 25.00	209 KJ,BMc,JRu,BWi,AM,
140 GK(c),RA,I:Gloria Grant,	I:Calypso,V:Kraven 8.00
V:Grizzly,Jackal 25.00	210 JR2,JSt,I:Madame Web 8.00
141 JR(c),RA,V:Mysterio. 25.00	211 JR2,JM,A:Sub-mariner 6.00
142 JR(c),RA,V:Mysterio. 25.00	212 JR2,JM,I:Hydro-Man 6.00
143 K&R(c),RA,I:Cyclone 25.00	213 JR2,JM,V:Wizard 6.00
144 K&R(c),RA,V:Cyclone 25.00	214 JR2,JM,V:Frightful Four,
145 K&R(c),RA,V:Scorpion 25.00	A: Namor,Llyra 6.00
146 RA,JR,V:Scorpion 25.00	215 JR2,JM,V:Frightful Four,
147 JR(c),RA,V:Tarantula 25.00	A: Namor,Llyra 6.00
148 GK(c),RA,V:Tarantula,IR:Jackal	216 JR2,JM,A:Madame Web 6.00
is Prof.Warren 30.00	217 JR2,JM,V:Sandman,
149 K&R(c),RA,D:Jackal. 45.00	Hydro-Man 6.00
150 GK(c),RA,V:Spenser Smythe . 20.00	218 FM(c),JR2,JM,AM,V:Sandman
151 RA,JR,V:Shocker. 17.00	Hydro-Man 6.00
152 K&R(c),RA,V:Shocker 17.00	219 FM(c),LMc,JM,V:Grey
153 K&R(c),RA,V:Paine 17.00	Gargoyle,A:Matt Murdock 6.00
154 JR(c),SB,V:Sandman 17.00	220 BMc,A:Moon Knight 6.00
155 JR(c),SB,V:Computer. 16.00	221 JM(i),A:Ramrod 5.00
156 JR(c),RA,I:Mirage,W:Ned	222 WS(c),BH,JM,I:SpeedDemon. . 5.00
Leeds & Betty Brant 16.00	223 JR2,AM,A:Red Ghost. 5.00
157 JR(c),RA,V:Dr.Octopus 16.00	224 JR2,V:Vulture. 5.00
158 JR(c),RA,V:Dr.Octopus 16.00	225 JR2,BWi,V:Foolkiller 5.00
159 JR(c),RA,V:Dr.Octopus 16.00	226 JR2,JM,A:Black Cat 5.00
160 K&R(c),RA,V:Tinkerer 16.00	
161 K&R(c),RA,A:Nightcrawler,	
C:Punisher 16.00	
162 JR(c),RA,Nightcrawler,	
Punisher,I:Jigsaw 16.00	
163 JR(c),RA,Kingpin 10.00	
164 JR(c),RA,Kingpin 10.00	
165 JR(c),RA,Lizard 10.00	
166 JR(c),RA,Lizard 10.00	
167 JR(c),RA,V:Spiderslayer,	
I:Will-o-the Wisp 10.00	
168 JR(c),KP,V:Will-o-the Wisp . . . 12.00	
169 RA,V:Dr.Faustas 10.00	
170 RA,V:Dr.Faustas 10.00	
171 RA,A:Nova. 11.00	
172 RA,V:Molten Man. 10.00	
173 JR(c),RA,JM,V:Molten Man . . 10.00	
174 RA,TD,JM,A:Punisher 15.00	
175 RA,JM,A:Punisher,D:Hitman. . 15.00	
176 RA,TD,V:Green Goblin. 12.00	
177 RA,V:Green Goblin 12.00	
178 RA,JM,V:Green Goblin 12.00	
179 RA,V:Green Goblin 12.00	
180 RA,IR&V:Green Goblin is Bart	
Hamilton). 12.00	
181 GK(c),SB,O:Spider-Man... . . . 8.00	
182 RA,A:Rocket Racer 7.00	

227 JR2,JM,A:Black Cat. 5.00
228 RL,Murder Mystery 5.00
229 JR2,JM,V:Juggernaut. 7.00
230 JR2,JM,V:Juggernaut. 7.00
231 JR2,AM,V:Cobra 5.00
232 JR2,JM,V:Mr.Hyde. 5.00
233 JR2,JM,V:Tarantula 5.00
234 JR2,DGr,V:Tarantula 5.00
235 JR2,V:Tarantula,C:Deathlok
O:Will-o-the Wisp 5.00
236 JR2,D:Tarantula 5.00
237 BH,A:Stilt Man 5.00
238 JR2,JR,I:Hobgoblin (inc.
Tattoo transfer) 75.00
238a w/out Tattoo 12.00
239 JR2,V:Hobgoblin 35.00
240 JR2,BL,Vulture. 5.00
241 JR2,O:Vulture 5.00
242 JR2,Mad Thinker 5.00
243 JR2,Peter Quits School 5.00
244 JR2,KJ,V:Hobgoblin. 9.00
245 JR2,V:Hobgoblin 12.00
246 JR2,DGr,Daydreams issue. . . . 5.00
247 JR2,JR,V:Thunderball 5.00
248 JR2,BBr,RF,TA,V:Thunderball,
Kid who Collects Spider-Man . . 5.00
249 JR2,DGr,V:Hobgoblin,
A:Kingpin 10.00
250 JR2,KJ,V:Hobgoblin 10.00
251 RF,KJ,V:Hobgoblin,Spidey
Leaves for Secret Wars 10.00
252 RF,BBr,returns from Secret
Wars,N:Spider-Man 25.00
253 RL,I:Rose 8.00
254 RL,JRu,V:Jack O'Lantern. 5.00
255 RF,JRu,Red Ghost. 5.00
256 RF,JRu,I:Puma,A:Black Cat . . . 6.00
257 RF,JRu,V:Puma,
A:Hobgoblin 8.00
258 RF,JRu,A:Black Cat,Fant.Four,
Hobgoblin,V:Black Costume . . 11.00
259 RF,JRu,A:Hobgoblin,O:
Mary Jane 12.00
260 RF,JRu,BBr,V:Hobgoblin 8.00
261 CV(c),RF,JRu,V:Hobgoblin. . . . 8.00
262 Ph(c),BL,Spidey Unmasked . . . 7.00
263 RF,BBr,I:Spider-Kid 4.00
264 Paty,V:Red Nine 4.00
265 RF,JRu,V:Black Fox,
I:Silver Sable 10.00
265a 2nd printing 1.50
266 RF,JRu,I:Misfits,Toad. 4.00
267 BMc,PDd(s),A:Human Torch . . 4.00
268 JBy(c),RF,JRu,Secret WarsII . . 4.00
269 RF,JRu,V:Firelord. 4.00
270 RF,BMc,V:Firelord,
A:Avengers,I:Kate Cushing. . . . 4.00
271 RF,JRu,A:Crusher Hogan,
V:Manslaughter 4.00
272 SB,KB,I&O:Slyde. 4.00
273 RF,JRu,Secret Wars II,
A:Puma 4.00
274 TMo,JR,Secret Wars II,
Beyonder V:Mephisto,A:1st
Ghost Rider 6.00
275 RF,JRu,V:Hobgoblin,O:Spidey
(From Amaz.Fantasy#15) 7.00
276 RF,BBr,V:Hobgoblin 6.00
277 RF,BL,CV,A:Daredevil,
Kingpin. 5.00
278 A:Hobgoblin,V:Scourge,
D:Wraith. 4.00
279 RL,A:Jack O'Lantern,
2nd A:Silver Sable 4.00
280 RF,BBr,V:Sinister Syndicate,
A:Silver Sable,Hobgoblin,
Jack O'Lantern 4.00
281 RF,BBr,V:Sinister Syndicate,
A:Silver Sable,Hobgoblin,
Jack O'Lantern. 10.00
282 RL,BL,A:X-Factor. 4.00

Amazing Spider-Man #228
© Marvel Entertainment Group

Amazing Spider-Man #266
© Marvel Entertainment Group

283 RF,BL,V:Titania,Absorbing
    Man,C:Mongoose 4.00
284 RF,BBr,JRu,B:Gang War,
    A: Punisher,Hobgoblin 7.00
285 MZ(c),A:Punisher,Hobgoblin . . . 9.00
286 ANi(i),V:Hobgoblin,A:Rose . . . 8.00
287 EL,ANi,A:Daredevl,Hobgoblin . 6.00
288 E:Gang War,A:Punisher,
    Falcon,Hobgoblin,Daredevil,
    Black Cat, Kingpin 7.00
289 TMo,IR:Hobgoblin is Ned Leeds,
    I:2nd Hobgoblin (Jack O'
    Lantern) 20.00
290 JR2,Peter Proposes. 4.00
291 JR2,V:Spiderslayer 4.00
292 AS,V:Spiderslayer,Mary
    Jane Accepts proposal 4.00
293 MZ,BMc,V:Kraven 10.00
294 MZ,BMc,D:Kraven 10.00
295 BSz(c),KB(i),Mad Dog,pt.#2 . . . 4.00
296 JBy(c),AS,V:Dr.Octopus 4.00
297 AS,V:Dr.Octopus 4.00
298 TM,BMc,V:Chance,C:Venom
    (not in costume) 35.00
299 TM,BMc,V:Chance,I:Venom . . 20.00
300 TM,O:Venom 65.00
301 TM,A:Silver Sable 15.00
302 TM,V:Nero,A:Silver Sable. . . . 15.00
303 TM,A:Silver Sable,Sandman . 15.00
304 TM,JRu,V:Black Fox,Prowler
    I:Jonathan Caesar 12.00
305 TM,JRu,V:BlackFox,Prowler. . 12.00
306 TM,V:Humbug,Chameleon . . . 11.00
307 TM,O:Chameleon 11.00
308 TM,V:Taskmaster,J.Caesar. . . 11.00
309 TM,I:Styx & Stone 11.00
310 TM,V:Killershrike 11.00
311 TM,Inferno,V:Mysterio 11.00
312 TM,Inferno,Hobgoblin V:
    Green Goblin 15.00
313 TM,Inferno,V:Lizard 10.00
314 TM,X-mas issue,V:J.Caesar. . 10.00
315 TM,V:Venom,Hydro-Man 20.00
316 TM,V:Venom 20.00
317 TM,V:Venom,A:Thing 20.00
318 TM,V:Scorpion 8.00
319 TM,V:Scorpion,Rhino 8.00
320 TM,B:Assassin Nation Plot
    A:Paladin,Silver Sable 8.00
321 TM,A:Paladin,Silver Sable 6.00
322 TM,A:Silver Sable,Paladin 6.00
323 TM,A:Silver Sable,Paladin,
    Captain America. 6.00
324 TM(c),EL,AG,V:Sabretooth,A:

Capt.America,Silver Sable 9.00
325 TM,E:Assassin Nation Plot,
    V:Red Skull,Captain America,
    Silver Sable 6.00
326 V:Graviton,A of V. 4.00
327 EL,AG,V:Magneto,A of V. 5.00
328 TM,V:Hulk,A of V. 8.00
329 EL,V:Tri-Sentinel 6.00
330 EL,A:Punisher,Black Cat 6.00
331 EL,A:Punisher,C:Venom. 6.00
332 EL,V:Venom,Styx & Stone . . . 7.00
333 EL,V:Venom,Styx & Stone 7.00
334 EL,B:Sinister Six,A:Iron Man . . 4.00
335 EL,TA,A:Captain America. 4.00
336 EL,D:Nathan Lubensky,
    A:Dr.Strange,Chance 3.50
337 WS(c),EL,TA,A:Nova 3.50
338 EL,A:Jonathan Caesar. 3.50
339 EL,JR,E:Sinister Six,A:Thor
    D:Jonathan Caesar 3.50
340 EL,V:Femme Fatales 3.00
341 EL,V:Tarantula,Powers Lost . . . 3.00
342 EL,A:Blackcat,V:Scorpion. 3.00
343 EL,Powers Restored,
    C:Cardiac,V:Chameleon 3.00
344 EL,V:Rhino,I:Cardiac,Cletus
    Kassady(Carnage),A:Venom. . . 8.00
345 MBa,V:Boomerang,C:Venom,
    A:Cletus Kassady(infected
    with Venom-Spawn) 9.00
346 EL,V:Venom. 6.00
347 EL,V:Venom. 6.00
348 EL,A:Avengers. 3.00
349 EL,A:Black Fox 3.00
350 EL,V:Doctor Doom,Black Fox. . 4.00
351 MBa,A:Nova,V:Tri-Sentinal 4.00
352 MBa,A:Nova,V:Tri-Sentinal 3.00
353 MBa,B:Round Robin:The Side
    Kick's Revenge,A:Punisher,
    Nova,Moon Knight,Darkhawk . . 3.00
354 MBa,A:Nova,Punisher,
    Darkhawk,Moon Knight. 3.00
355 MBa,A:Nova,Punisher,
    Darkhawk,Moon Knight. 3.00
356 MBa,A:Moon Knight,
    Punisher,Nova 3.00
357 MBa,A:Moon Knight,
    Punisher,Darkhawk,Nova 3.00
358 MBa,E:Round Robin:The Side
    Kick's Revenge,A:Darkhawk,
    Moon Knight,Punisher,Nova,
    Gatefold(c) 3.00
359 CMa,A:Cardiac,C:Cletus
    Kasady (Carnage) 4.00
360 CMa,V:Cardiac,C:Carnage. . . . 5.00
361 MBa,I:Carnage 9.00
361a 2nd printing 1.50
362 MBa,V:Carnage,Venom 6.00
362a 2nd printing 1.50
363 MBa,V:Carnage,Venom,. 5.00
364 MBa,V:Shocker 2.50
365 MBa,JR,V:Lizard,30th Anniv.,
    Hologram(c),w/poster,Prev.of
    Spider-Man 2099 by RL 6.00
366 JBi,A:Red Skull,Taskmaster . . . 2.50
367 JBi,A:Red Skull,Taskmaster . . . 2.50
368 MBa,B:Invasion of the Spider
    Slayers #1,BU:Jonah Jameson. 2.00
369 MBa,V:Electro,BU:Green
    Goblin 2.00
370 MBa,V:Scorpion,BU:A.May . . . 2.00
371 MBa,V:Spider-Slayer,
    BU:Black Cat 2.00
372 MBa,V:Spider-Slayer 2.00
373 MBa,V:Sp.-Slayer,BU:Venom . . 3.00
374 MBa,V:Venom 4.00
375 MBa,V:Venom,30th Anniv.,Holo
    graphx(c) 5.00
376 V:Styx&Stone,A:Cardiac 2.00
377 V:Cardiac,O:Styx&Stone 2.00
378 MBa,Total Carnage#3,V:Shriek,

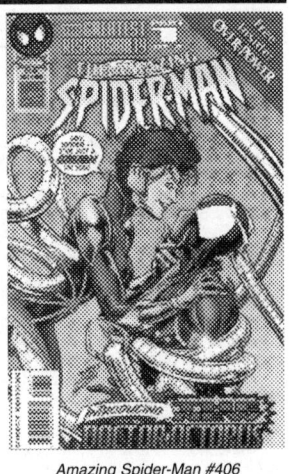

Amazing Spider-Man #406
© Marvel Entertainment Group

    Carnage,A:Venom,Cloak 2.00
379 MBa,Total Carnage#7,
    V:Carnage,A:Venom. 2.00
380 MBa,Maximum Carnage#11 . . . 2.00
381 MBa,V:Dr.Samson,A:Hulk 1.75
382 MBa,V:Hulk,A:Dr.Samson 1.75
383 MBa,V:Jury 1.75
384 MBa,AM,V:Jury 1.75
385 B:DvM(s),MBa,RyE,V:Jury 1.50
386 MBa,RyE,B:Lifetheft,V:Vulture . 3.00
387 MBa,RyE,V:Vulture 3.00
388 Blue Foil(c),MBa,RyE,RLm,TP,
    E:Lifetheft,D:Peter's Synthetic
    Parents,BU:Venom,Cardiac,
    Chance,. 4.00
388a Newsstand Ed. 3.00
389 MBa,RyE,E:Pursuit,
    V:Chameleon, ... 1.75
390 MBa,RyE,B:Shrieking,
    A:Shriek,w/cel 3.25
390a Newsstand Ed. 1.75
391 MBa,RyE,V:Shriek,Carrion. . . . 2.00
392 MBa,RyE,V:Shriek,Carrion. . . . 2.00
393 MBa,RyE,E:Shrieking,
    V:Shriek,Carrion 2.00
394 MBa,RyE,Power & Responsibility,
    pt.2,V:Judas Traveller, ... 4.00
394a w/flip book,2 covers 2.00
395 MBa,RyE,R:Puma 1.75
396 MBa,RyE,A:Daredevil,
    V:Vulture, Owl 1.75
397 MBa,Web of Death,pt.1,
    V:Stunner,Doc Ock. 2.50
398 MBa,Web of Death,pt.3 . . . . . . 1.75
399 MBa,Smoke and Mirrors,pt.2 . . 1.75
400 MBa,Death of a Parker 7.00
400a die-cut cover 3.00
401 MBa,The Mark of Kaine,pt.2. . . 1.75
402 MBa,R:Judas Travellor. 1.75
403 MBa,JMD,LMa The Trial of
    Peter Parker,pt.2 . . . . 1.75
404 Maximum Clonage. 1.75
405 JMD,DaR,LMa,Exiled,pt.2,. . . . 1.75
406 I:New Doc Ock 1.75
407 TDF,MBa,LMa,Return of
    Spider-Man,pt.2 . . . . 1.75
408 TDF,MBa,LMa,Media
    Blizzard,pt.2 . . . . 1.75
409 . . . . 1.75
410 . . . . 1.75
411 TDF,MBa,LMa,Blood
    Brothers,pt.2 . . . . 1.75
412 . . . . 1.75
413 . . . . 1.75

MARVEL

414 A:The Rose 1.75
415 Onslaught saga,V:Sentinels . . . 2.50
416 Onslaught epilogue 3.00
417 TDF,RG,secrets of Scrier &
   Judas Traveler 2.00
418 Revelations,pt.3, R:Norman
   Osborn. 2.50
419 TDF,SSr,V:Black Tarantula 1.75
420 TDF,SSr,X-Man x-over,pt.1 . . . 1.75
421 TDF,SSr,I:Dragonfly; Electro
   Kidnapped 2.50
422 TDF,SSr,V:Electro,Tarantula . . . 2.50
423 TDF,V:Electro 1.75
424 TDF,JoB,V:Black Tarantula, The
   Hand, Dragonfly, Delilah,
   The Rose, Elektra 1.75
425 TDF,SSr,V:Electro,double size. 3.50
426 TDF,SSr,V:Doctor Octopus. . . . 1.50
427 TDF,SSr,JR gatefold cover,
   V:Doctor Octopus 2.50
428 TDF,V:Doctor Octopus. 2.00
429 TDF,A:Daredevil, X-Man,
   Absorbing Man, Titania. 2.00
430 TDF,SSr,V:Carnage,A:Silver
   Surfer. 2.00
431 TDF,SSr,V:Carnage (with Silver
   Surfer's powers). 2.00
432 SSr,JR2,Spider-Hunt,pt.2
   x-over. 2.00
432a variant cover 3.50
433 TDF,TL,Identity Crisis prelude,
   good-bye to Joe Robertson . . . 2.00
434 TDF,JoB,Identity Crisis, as
   Ricochet vs. Black Tarantula. . . 2.00
435 TDF,MD2,Ricochet,A:Delilah . . 2.00
436 TDF,JoB,V:Black Tarantula. . . . 2.00
437 TDF,JoB,V:Plant Man. 2.00
Bi-weekly
438 TDF,V:Daredevil. 2.00
439 TDF,future history chronicle . . . 2.00
440 JBy,The Gathering of the Five,
   Pt.2 (of 5) x-over 2.00
441 JBy,V:Green Goblin, The
   Final Chapter, pt.1 . . . . 2.00
Minus 1 Spec., TDF,JBe, flashback,
   early Kingpin. 2.00
Ann.#1 SD,I:Sinister Six 600.00
Ann.#2 SD,A:Dr.Strange. 250.00
Ann.#3 JR,DH,A:Avengers 100.00
Ann.#4 A:H.Torch,V:Mysterio,
   Wizard 90.00
Ann.#5 JR(c),A:Red Skull,I:Peter
   Parker's Parents. 100.00
Ann.#6 JR(c),Rep.Ann.#1,Fant.
   Four Ann.#1,SpM #8 . . . . 35.00
Ann.#7 JR(c),Rep.#1,#2,#38. . . . 28.00
Ann.#8 Rep.#46,#50. . . . . 28.00
Ann.#9 JR(c),Rep.Spec.SpM #2 . 20.00
Ann.#10 JR(c),GK,V:Human Fly . 12.00
Ann.#11 GK(c),DP,JM,JR2,AM,. . 12.00
Ann.#12 JBy(c),KP,Rep.#119,
   #120. . . . . 12.00
Ann.#13 JBy,TA,V:Dr.Octopus. . . 10.00
Ann.#14 FM,TP,A:Dr.Strange,
   V:Dr.Doom,Dormammu. 12.00
Ann.#15 FM,KJ,BL,Punisher. 15.00
Ann.#16 JR2,JR,I:New Captain
   Marvel,A:Thing 7.00
Ann.#17 EH,JM,V:Kingpin. 5.00
Ann.#18 RF,BL,JG,V:Scorpion . . . 5.00
Ann.#19 JR(c),MW,V:Spiderslayer . 5.00
Ann.#20 BWi(i),V:Iron Man 2020. . 5.00
Ann.#21 JR(c),PR,W:SpM,direct . 16.00
Ann.#21a W:SpM,news stand . . . 12.00
Ann.#22 JR(c),MBa(1stSpM),SD,
   JG,RLm,TD,Evolutionary War,
   I:Speedball,New Men 7.00
Ann.#23 JBy(c),RLd,MBa,RF,
   AtlantisAttacks#4,A:She-Hulk . . 7.00
Ann.#24 GK,SD,MZ,DGr,
   A:Ant Man 4.00

Ann.#25 EL(c),SB,PCu,SD,
   Vibranium Vendetta#1,Venom. . 6.00
Ann.#26 Hero Killers#1,A:New
   Warriors,BU:Venom,Solo 5.00
Ann.#27 TL,I:Annex,w/card. 3.50
Ann.#28 SBt(s),V:Carnage,BU:Cloak &
   Dagger,Rhino 3.25
Ann. '96 two new stories, 48pg, . . 3.00
Ann. '97 RSt,TL,RJn, 48pg, ... 3.00
Ann. '98 TL,TDF,F:Spider-Man & Devil
   Dinosaur, 48pg. 3.00
G-Size Superheroes #1 GK,
   A:Morbius,Man-Wolf. 30.00
G-Size #1 JR(c),RA,DH,
   A:Dracula 12.00
G-Size #2 K&R(c),RA,AM,
   A:Master of Kung Fu 10.00
G-Size #3 GK(c),RA,DocSavage. . 10.00
G-Size #4 GK(c),RA,Punisher. . . . 35.00
G-Size #5 GK(c),RA,V:Magnum . . 8.00
G-Size #6 Rep.Ann.#4 . . . . 7.00
G-Size.Spec.#1 O:Symbiotes 4.50
Marvel Milestone rep. #1 (1993) . . 2.95
Marvel Milestone rep. #3 (1995) . . 2.95
Marvel Milestone rep. #129 (1992) . 2.95
Marvel Milestone rep. #149 (1994) . 2.95
GNv Fear Itself RA,A:S.Sable 12.95
GNv Spirits of the Earth CV,Scotland,
   V:Hellfire Club 25.00
TPB Assassination Plot,
   rep.#320-325 . . . . 14.95
TPB Carnage,rep.#361-363 . . . . . 6.95
TPB Cosmic Adventures rep.
   Amaz.SpM #327-329,Web #59
   61,Spec.SpM #158-160 . . . . . 19.95
TPB Kraven's Last Hunt, Reps. AS
   #293,294,Web.#31,32,P.Parker
   #131,132,SC 15.95
   HC 19.95
TPB Origin of the Hobgoblin rep.#238,
   239,244,245,249-251 . . . . 14.95
TPB Saga of the Alien Costume,reps.
   #252-259 . . . . 9.95
TPB Spider-Man Vs. Venom,reps.
   A.SpM#298-300,315-317 . . . . 10.00
TPB Venom Returns rep.Amaz.SpM.
   #331-333,344-347 . . . . 12.95
TPB The Wedding,Reps.A.S.
   #290-292,Ann#21 . . . . 12.95
Nothing Can Stop the Juggernaut,
   reps.#229,230 . . . . 3.95
Sensational Spider-Man,reps.
   Ann.#14,15; 4.95
Skating on Thin Ice(Canadian) . . . 15.00
Skating on Thin Ice(US) 1.50
Soul of the Hunter MZ,BMc,
   R:Kraven 7.00
Unicef:Trial of Venom,
   A:Daredevil,V:Venom 50.00
See Also:
PETER PARKER;
SPECTACULAR SPIDER-MAN;
WEB OF SPIDER-MAN

AMAZING SPIDER-MAN
Nov. 1998
1 HMe,JBy,DHz,V:Scorpion,48-page
   prismatic etched (c) 3.00
1a signed 19.63
2 HMe,JBy,DHz,I:Shadrac 2.00
2a variant BiT cover 2.00
3 HMe,JBy,DHz,V:Shadrac,
   A:Iceman 2.00
4 HMe,JBy,SHa,A:Fantastic Four. . 2.00
5 HMe,JBy,SHa,I:new
   Spider-Woman 2.00
6 JBy,HMe,SHa,F:Spider-Woman . 2.00
7 JBy,HMe,SHa,Reality Bent 2.00
8 JMy,HMe,SHa,JR2(c),
   Reality Bent x-over. 2.00

9 JMy,HMe,SHa,JR2(c),V:Scorpion 2.00
10 JMy,HMe,SHa,JR2(c),Mary Jane 2.00
Ann.1999 JB,HMe, 48-page 3.50
Coll.Classics rep. #300. . . . . 2.50
Coll.Classics rep. #300 signed . . . 30.00
Coll.Classics rep. Sp-M #1 . . . . . . 2.50
Coll.Classics rep. Sp-M #1 signed. 30.00

AMAZING SPIDER-MAN
INDEX
See: OFFICIAL MARVEL
INDEX TO THE AMAZING
SPIDER-MAN

AMAZING SPIDER-MAN
COLLECTION
1 Mark Bagley card set 2.95
2 and 3 MBa, from card set . . . . @2.95

AMAZING X-MEN, THE
March–June 1995
1 X-Men after Xavier 4.00
2 Exodus,Dazzler,V:Abyss. 3.00
3 F:Bishop. 3.00
4 V:Apocalypse 2.50
TPB Rep. #1-#4 . . . . 8.95

AMERICAN TAIL II
Dec., 1991
1 movie adaption. 1.00
2 movie adaption. 1.00

A-NEXT
Aug. 1998
1 TDF,RF,BBr,Next Generation of
   Avengers 2.00
2 TDF,RF,BBr,V:Kree & Sentry. . . . 2.00
2a variant cover. 2.00
3 TDF,RF,BBr,Orig.Defenders
   vs. New Avengers 2.00
4 TDF,RF,BBr,turning points. 2.00
5 TDF,RF,BBr,SB,Ghosts of
   the Past 2.00
6 TDF,RF,BBr,Majority Rules 2.00
7 TDF,RF,BBr,Last Days of
   the Avengers 2.00
8 TDF,RF,BBr,A:Ant-Man,Uneasy
   Allies 2.00

A-Next #4
© Marvel Entertainment Group

9 TDF,RF,BBr,Critical Choices 2.00
10 TDF,RF,BBr,Incredible Journeys. 2.00
11 TDF,RF,BBr,A:Captain America
   & Doctor Doom 2.00
12 TDF,RF,BBr,I:Revengers 2.00

ANIMAX
Star Comics Dec., 1986–June 1987
1 Based on Toy Line 1.00
2 thru 4 .... @1.00

Annex #1
© Marvel Entertainment Group

ANNEX
Aug.–Nov. 1994
1 WMc,I:Brace, Crucible of Power . 2.00
2 WMc,V:Brace, Crucible, pt.2 .... 1.75
3 Crucible of Power, pt.3 .... 1.75
4 Crucible of Power, pt.4 .... 1.95

ANNIE
(Treasury Edition)
Oct., 1982
1 Movie Adaptation 1.25
2 Nov., 1982 .... 1.25

ANNIE OAKLEY
Atlas Spring, 1948
1 A:Hedy Devine 300.00
2 CCB,I:Lana,A:Hedy Devine .. 175.00
3 .... 150.00
4 .... 150.00
5 .... 100.00
6 thru 8 .... @75.00

9 AW, ... 80.00
10 .... 60.00
11 June, 1956. .... 65.00

A-1
1993
1 The Edge 5.95
2 Cheeky,Wee Budgie Boy 5.95
3 King Leon. 5.95
4 King Leon. 5.95

APOCALYPSE STRIKEFILES
1 After Xavier special. 2.50

ARCHANGEL
1996
1-shot B&W 2.50

ARIZONA KID
Atlas March, 1951
1 RH,Coming of the Arizons Kid. 125.00
2 RH,Code of the Gunman 50.00
3 RH(c) 45.00
4 .... 45.00
5 .... 45.00
6 Jan., 1952 .... 45.00

ARRGH!
Dec., 1974
Satire
1 Vampire Rats 15.00
2 .... 10.00
3 Beauty And the Big Foot 10.00
4 The Night Gawker 10.00
5 Sept., 1975 .... 10.00

ARROWHEAD
April, 1954
1 Indian Warrior Stories 100.00
2 .... 50.00
3 .... 50.00
4 Nov., 1954 .... 50.00

ASTONISHING
See: MARVEL BOY

ASTONISHING TALES
August, 1970
1 BEv(c),JK,WW,KaZar,Dr.Doom . 40.00
2 JK,WW,Ka-Zar,Dr.Doom 20.00
3 BWS,WW,Ka-Zar,Dr.Doom 25.00
4 BWS,WW,Ka-Zar,Dr.Doom 25.00
5 BWS,GT,Ka-Zar,Dr.Doom 25.00
6 BWS,BEv,GT,I:Bobbi Morse . . 25.00
7 HT,GC,Ka-Zar,Dr.Doom 15.00
8 HT,TS,GT,GC,TP,Ka-Zar. 15.00
9 GK(c),JB,Ka-Zar,Dr.Doom. 12.00
10 GK(c),BWS,SB,Ka-Zar. 15.00
11 GK,O:Kazar 12.00
12 JB,DA,NA,V:Man Thing. 12.00
13 JB,RB,DA,V:Man Thing 7.00
14 GK(c),rep. Kazar 7.00
15 GK,TS,Kazar 7.00
16 RB,AM,A:Kazar 7.00
17 DA,V:Gemini 7.00
18 JR(c),DA,A:Kazar 7.00
19 JR(c),DA,JSn,JA,I:Victorious . . . 7.00
20 JR(c),A:Kazar 7.00
21 RTs(s),DAy,B:It 7.00
22 RTs(s),DAy,V:Granitor 7.00
23 RTs(s),DAy,A:Fin Fang Foom. . . 7.00
24 RTs(s),DAy,E:It 7.00
25 RB(a&s),B:I&O:Deathlok,
   GP(1st art) 30.00
26 RB(a&s),I:Warwolf 7.00
27 RB(a&s),V:Warwolf 7.00
28 RB(a&s),V:Warwolf 7.00
29 rep.Marv.Super Heroes #18 .... 8.00
30 RB(a&s),KP, ... 7.00
31 RB(a&s),BW,KP,V:Ryker 7.00
32 RB(a&s),KP,V:Ryker 6.00
33 RB(a&s),KJ,I:Hellinger 6.00
34 RB(a&s),KJ,V:Ryker 6.00
35 RB(a&s),KJ,I:Doomsday-Mech. . 6.00
36 RB(a&s),KP,E:Deathlok,
   I:Godwulf 20.00

ASTONISHING X-MEN
March–June 1995
1 Uncanny X-Men 5.00
2 V:Holocaust 3.50
3 V:Abyss 3.00
4 V:Beast,Infinities............. 2.50
TPB Rep. #1-#4 .... 8.95

ASTONISHING X-MEN
July 1999
1 (of 3) BPe,HMe,new X-Men team 2.50
2 BPe,HMe,The Shattering x-over . 2.50

A-TEAM
March, 1984
1 .... 1.00
2 .... 1.00
3 May, 1984 .... 1.00

ATOMIC AGE
Epic Nov., 1990
1 AW...................... 4.50
2 AW...................... 4.50
3 AW,Feb., 1991 .... 4.50

AVENGERS
Sept., 1963
1 JK,O:Avengers,V:Loki 2,500.00
2 JK,V:Space Phantom 650.00
3 JK,V:Hulk,Sub-Mariner 400.00
4 JK,R&J:Captain America ... 1,500.00
5 JK,L:Hulk,V:Lava Men. 250.00
6 JK,I:Masters of Evil........ 200.00
7 JK,V:Baron Zemo,
   Enchantress 200.00
8 JK,I:Kang 190.00
9 JK(c),DH,I&D:Wonder Man ... 215.00
10 JK(c),DH,I:Immortus........ 175.00
11 JK(c),DH,A:Spider-Man,
   V:Kang 200.00
12 JK(c),DH,V:Moleman,
   Red Ghost 125.00
13 JK(c),DH,I:Count Nefaria 125.00
14 JK,DH,V:Count Nefaria 125.00
15 JK,DH,D:Baron Zemo 100.00
16 JK,J:Hawkeye,Scarlet Witch,
   Quicksilver 135.00
17 JK(c),DH,V:Mole Man,A:Hulk . 100.00
18 JK(c),DH,V:The Commisar... 100.00
19 JK(c),DH,I&O:Swordsman,
   O:Hawkeye 90.00

Avengers #28
© Marvel Entertainment Group

MARVEL

20 JK(c),DH,WW,V:Swordsman,
   Mandarin 60.00
21 JK(c),DH,WW,V:Power Man
   (not L.Cage),Enchantress. . . . 60.00
22 JK(c),DH,WW,V:Power Man. . . 60.00
23 JK(c),DH,JR,V:Kang 45.00
24 JK(c),DH,JR,V:Kang 45.00
25 JK(c),DH,V:Dr.Doom 50.00
26 DH,V:Attuma 45.00
27 DH,V:Attuma,Beetle 45.00
28 JK(c),DH,I:1st Goliath,
   I:Collector. 50.00
29 DH,V:Power Man,Swordsman . 45.00
30 JK(c),DH,V:Swordsman 45.00
31 DH,V:Keeper of the Flame 45.00
32 DH,I:Bill Foster 30.00
33 DH,V:Sons of the Serpent
   A:Bill Foster 30.00
34 DH,V:Living Laser 30.00
35 DH,V:Mandarin 30.00
36 DH,V:The Ultroids 30.00
37 GK(c),DH,V:Ultroids. 30.00
38 GK(c),DH,V:Enchantress,
   Ares,J:Hercules 30.00
39 DH,V:Mad Thinker 30.00
40 DH,V:Sub-Mariner 30.00
41 JB,V:Dragon Man,Diablo 25.00
42 JB,V:Dragon Man,Diablo 25.00
43 JB,V:Red Guardian 25.00
44 JB,V:Red Guardian,
   O:Black.Widow. 25.00
45 JB,V:Super Adoptoid 25.00
46 JB,V:Whirlwind. 25.00
47 JB,GT,V:Magneto. 28.00
48 GT,I&O:New Black Knight 28.00
49 JB,V:Magneto 28.00
50 JB,V:Typhon 25.00
51 JB,GT,R:Iron Man,Thor
   V:Collector. 25.00
52 JB,J:Black Panther,
   I:Grim Reaper. 30.00
53 JB,GT,A:X-Men; x-over
   X-Men #45. . . . . 40.00
54 JB,GT,V:Masters of Evil
   I:Crimson Cowl(Ultron) 25.00
55 JB,I:Ultron,V:Masters of Evil. . . 20.00
56 JB,D:Bucky retold,
   V:Baron Zemo 20.00
57 JB,I:Vision,V:Ultron 70.00
58 JB,O&J:Vision 45.00
59 JB,I:Yellowjacket 20.00
60 JB,W:Yellowjacket & Wasp. . . . 18.00
61 JB,A:Dr.Strange,x-over
   Dr. Strange #178 . . . . 17.00
62 JB,I:Man-Ape,A:Dr.Strange . . . 17.00
63 GC,I&O:2nd Goliath(Hawkeye)
   V:Egghead 16.00
64 GC,V:Egghead,O:Hawkeye . . . 16.00
65 GC,V:Swordsman,Egghead . . . 16.00
66 BWS,I:Ultron 6,Adamantium. . . 17.00
67 BWS,V:Ultron 6 . . . . 17.00
68 SB,V:Ultron 13.00
69 SB,I:Nighthawk,Grandmaster,
   Squadron Supreme, V:Kang . . 15.00
70 SB,O:Squadron Supreme
   V:Kang. 13.00
71 SB,I:Invaders,V:Kang. 25.00
72 SB,A:Captain Marvel,
   I:Zodiac 12.00
73 HT(i),V:Sons of Serpent. 12.00
74 JB,TP,V:Sons of Serpent,
   IR:Black Panther on TV 12.00
75 JB,TP,I:Arkon 13.00
76 JB,TP,V:Arkon 12.00
77 JB,TP,V:Split-Second Squad . . 12.00
78 SB,TP,V:Lethal Legion 12.00
79 JB,TP,V:Lethal Legion 12.00
80 JB,TP,I&O:Red Wolf. 13.00
81 JB,TP,A:Red Wolf 12.00
82 JB,TP,V:Ares,A:Daredevil. 12.00
83 JB,TP,I:Valkyrie,

V:Masters of Evil 20.00
84 JB,TP,V:Enchantress,Arkon . . . 12.00
85 JB,V:Squadron Supreme 12.00
86 JB,JM,A:Squad Supreme. 12.00
87 SB(i),O:Black Panther,
   V: A.I.M. 30.00
88 SB,JM,V:Psyklop,A:Hulk,
   Professor.X 12.00
89 SB,B:Kree/Skrull War. 12.00
90 SB,V:Sentry #459,Ronan,
   Skrulls 12.00
91 SB,V:Sentry #459,Ronan,
   Skrulls 12.00
92 SB,V:Super Skrull,Ronan, ... 12.00
93 NA,TP,V:Super-Skrull,G-Size . . 55.00
94 NA,JB,TP,V:Super-Skrull,
   I:Mandroids 35.00
95 NA,TP,V:Maximus,Skrulls,
   A:Inhumans,O:Black Bolt 35.00
96 NA,TP,V:Skrulls,Ronan 35.00
97 GK&BEv(c),JB,TP,E:Kree-Skrull
   War,V:Annihilus,Ronan,Skrulls,
   A:Golden Age Heroes. 18.00
98 BWS,SB,V:Ares,R:Hercules.
   R&N:Hawkeye 25.00
99 BWS,TS,V:Ares 25.00
100 BWS,JSr,V:Ares & Kratos . . . 75.00
101 RB,DA,A:Watcher 9.00
102 RB,JSt,V:Grim Reaper,
   Sentinels 9.00
103 RB,JSt,V:Sentinels. 9.00
104 RB,JSt,V:Sentinels. 9.00
105 JB,JM,V:Savage Land
   Mutates; A:Black Panther 9.00
106 GT,DC,RB,V:Space Phantom. . 9.00
107 GT,DC,JSn,V:Space
   Phantom, Grim Reaper. 11.00
108 DH,DC,JSt,V:Space
   Phantom,Grim Reaper 9.00
109 DH,FMc,V:Champion,
   L:Hawkeye 9.00
110 DH,V:Magneto,A:X-Men 22.00
111 DH,J:Bl.Widow,A:Daredevil,
   X-Men,V:Magneto. 22.00
112 DH,I:Mantis,V:Lion-God,
   L:Black Widow 15.00
113 FBe(i),V:The Living Bombs. . . . 8.00
114 JR(c),V:Lion-God,J:Mantis,
   Swordsman 8.00
115 JR(c),A:Defenders,V:Loki,
   Dormammu 9.00
116 JR(c),A:Defenders,S.Surfer
   V:Loki,Dormammu 9.00
117 JR(c),FMc(i),A:Defenders,Silv.
   Surfer,V:Loki,Dormammu 9.00

Avengers #83
© *Marvel Entertainment Group*

118 JR(c),A:Defenders,S.Surfer
   V:Loki,Dormammu 9.00
119 JR(c),DH(i),V:Collector 7.00
120 JSn(c),DH(i),V:Zodiac 7.00
121 JR&JSn(c),JB,DH,V:Zodiac . . . 7.00
122 K&R(c),V:Zodiac 7.00
123 JR(c),DH(i),O:Mantis 7.00
124 JR(c),JB,DC,V:Kree,O:Mantis . 7.00
125 JR(c),JB,DC,V:Thanos 16.00
126 DC(i),V:Klaw,Solarr 8.00
127 GK(c),SB,JSon,A:Inhumans,
   V:Ultron,Maximus 8.00
128 K&R(c),SB,JSon,V:Kang 7.00
129 SB,JSon,V:Kang 7.00
130 GK(c),SB,JSon,V:Slasher,
   Titanic Three 7.00
131 GK(c),SB,JSon,V:Kang,
   Legion of the Unliving. 7.00
132 SB,JSon,Kang,Legion
   of the Unliving 6.00
133 GK(c),SB,JSon,O:Vision 7.00
134 K&R(c),SB,JSon,O:Vision 7.00
135 JSn&JR(c),GT,O:Mantis,
   Vision,C:Thanos 8.00
136 K&R(c),rep Amazing Adv#12 . . 7.00
137 JR(c),GT,J:Beast,
   Moondragon. 7.00
138 GK(c),GT,V:Toad 6.00
139 K&R(c),GT,V:Whirlwind 6.00
140 K&R(c),GT,V:Whirlwind 6.00
141 GK(c),GP,V:Squad.Sinister. . . . 5.00
142 K&R(c),GP,V:Squadron
   Sinister,Kang 5.00
143 GK(c),GP,V:Squadron
   Sinister,Kang 5.00
144 GP,GK(c),V:Squad.Sinister,
   O&J:Hellcat,O:Buzz Baxter. . . . 5.00
145 GK(c),DH,V:Assassin 5.00
146 GK(c),DH,KP,V:Assassin 5.00
147 GP,V:Squadron Supreme 5.00
148 JK(c),GP,V:Squad.Supreme. . . 5.00
149 GP,V:Orka 7.00
150 GP,JK,rep.Avengers #16 . . . . . 5.00
151 GP,new line-up,
   R:Wonder Man 4.50
152 JB,JSt,I:New Black Talon 5.00
153 JB,JSt,V:L.Laser,Whizzer. 4.50
154 GP,V:Attuma 4.50
155 SB,V:Dr.Doom,Attuma 4.50
156 SB,I:Tyrak,V:Attuma. 4.50
157 DH,V:Stone Black Knight 4.50
158 JK(c),SB,I&O:Graviton. 4.50
159 JK(c),SB,V:Graviton, ... 4.50
160 GP,V:Grim Reaper 4.50
161 GP,V:Ultron,A:Ant-Man. 4.50
162 GP,V:Ultron,I:Jocasta 4.50
163 GT,A:Champions,V:Typhon . . . 4.50
164 JBy,V:Lethal Legion 6.00
165 JBy,V:Count Nefario. 6.00
166 JBy,V:Count Nefario. 6.00
167 GP,A:Guardians,A:Nighthawk,
   Korvac,V:Porcupine 4.00
168 GP,A:Guardians,V:Korvac,
   I:Gyrich 4.00
169 SB,I:Eternity Man. 4.00
170 GP,R:Jocasta,C:Ultron,
   A:Guardians. 4.00
171 GP,V:Ultron,A:Guardians,
   Ms Marvel 4.00
172 SB,KJ,V:Tyrak 4.00
173 SB,V:Collector 4.00
174 GP(c),V:Collector. 4.00
175 V&O:Korvac,A:Guardians. 4.00
176 V:Korvac,A:Guardians 4.00
177 DC(c),D:Korvac,A:Guardians . . 4.00
178 CI,V:Manipulator 4.00
179 JM,AG,V:Stinger,Bloodhawk. . . 4.00
180 JM,V:Monolith,Stinger,
   D:Bloodhawk 4.00
181 JBy,GD,I:Scott Lang. 5.00
182 JBy,KJ,V:Maximoff 4.00

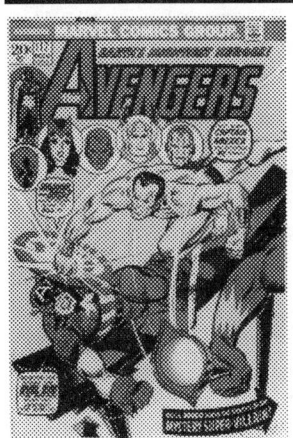

Avengers #117
© *Marvel Entertainment Group*

183 JBy,KJ,J:Ms.Marvel 4.00
184 JBy,KJ,J:Falcon,
    V:Absorbing Man 4.00
185 JBy,DGr,O:Quicksilver & Scarlet
    Witch,I:Bova,V:Modred 4.00
186 JBy,DGr,V:Modred,Chthon 4.00
187 JBy,DGr,V:Chthon,Modred 4.00
188 JBy,DGr,V:The Elements 4.00
189 JBy,DGr,V:Deathbird 4.00
190 JBy,DGr,V:Grey Gargoyle,
    A:Daredevil 4.00
191 JBy,DGr,V:Grey Gargoyle,
    A:Daredevil 4.00
192 I:Inferno. 3.00
193 FM(c),SB,DGr,O:Inferno. 3.00
194 GP,JRu,J:Wonder Man. 3.00
195 GP,JRu,A:Antman,
    I&C:Taskmaster 5.00
196 GP,JA,A:Antman,
    V:Taskmaster,. 3.00
197 CI,JAb,V:Red Ronin 3.00
198 GP,DGr,V:Red Ronan 3.00
199 GP,DGr,V:Red Ronan 3.00
200 GP,DGr,V:Marcus,
    L:Ms.Marvel 5.00
201 GP,DGr,F:Jarvis 3.00
202 GP,V:Ultron 3.00
203 CI,V:Crawlers,F:Wonderman . . 3.00
204 DN,DGr,V:Yellow Claw. 3.00
205 DGr,V:Yellow Claw. 3.00
206 GC,DGr,V:Pyron 3.00
207 GC,DGr,V:Shadowlord. 3.00
208 GC,DGr,V:Berserker 3.00
209 DGr,A:Mr.Fantastic,V:Skrull . . . 3.00
210 GC,DGr,V:Weathermen 3.00
211 GC,DGr,Moon Knight,J:Tigra . . 3.00
212 DGr,V:Elfqueen 3.00
213 BH,DGr,L:Yellowjacket 3.00
214 BH,DGr,V:Gh.Rider,A:Angel . . 5.00
215 DGr,A:Silver Surfer,
    V:Molecule Man 2.50
216 DGr,A:Silver Surfer,
    V:Molecule Man 2.50
217 BH,DGr,V:Egghead,
    R:Yellowjacket,Wasp3 . . . . 2.50
218 DP,V:M.Hardy 2.50
219 BH,A:Moondragon,Drax 2.50
220 BH,DGr,D:Drax,V:MnDragon . . 2.50
221 J:She Hulk. 2.50
222 V:Masters of Evil 2.50
223 A:Antman 2.50
224 AM,A:Antman 2.50
225 A:Black Knight. 2.50
226 A:Black Knight. 2.50
227 J:2nd Captain Marvel,

O:Avengers 2.50
228 V:Masters of Evil 2.50
229 JSt,V:Masters of Evil 2.50
230 A:Cap.Marvel,L:Yellowjacke . . 2.50
231 AM,JSi,J:2nd Captain Marvel,
    Starfox 2.50
232 AM,JSi. 2.50
233 JBy,V:Annihilus 2.50
234 AM,JSi,O:ScarletWitch. 2.50
235 AM,JSi,V:Wizard. 2.50
236 AM,JSi,A:SpM,V:Lava Men . . . 2.50
237 AM,JSi,A:SpM,V:Lava Men . . . 2.50
238 AM,JSi,V:Moonstone,
    O:Blackout 3.00
239 AM,JSi,A:David Letterman 3.50
240 AM,JSi,A:Dr.Strange 2.50
241 AM,JSi,V:Morgan LeFey 2.50
242 AM,JSi,Secret Wars 2.50
243 AM,JSi,Secret Wars. 2.50
244 AM,JSi,V:Dire Wraiths 2.50
245 AM,JSi,V:Dire Wraiths 2.50
246 AM,JSi,V:Eternals 2.50
247 AM,JSi,A:Eternals,V:Deviants . 2.50
248 AM,JSi,A:Eternals,V:Deviants . 2.50
249 AM,JSi,A:Maelstrom 2.50
250 AM,JSi,A:W.C.A.
    V:Maelstrom. 3.50
251 BH,JSi,A:Paladin 2.50
252 BH,JSi,J:Hercules
    V:Blood Brothers 2.50
253 BH,JSi,J:Black Knight 2.50
254 BH,JSi,A:W.C.A. 2.50
255 TP,p(c),JB,Legacy of
    Thanos/Santuary II 2.50
256 JB,TP,A:Kazar 2.50
257 JB,TP,D:Savage Land,
    I:Nebula 3.00
258 JB,TP,A:SpM,Firelord,Nebula . . 2.50
259 JB,TP,V:Nebula 2.50
260 JB,TP,SecretWarsII, IR:Nebula
    is Thanos' Granddaughter 2.50
261 JB,TP,Secret Wars II 2.50
262 JB,TP,J:Submariner 2.50
263 JB,TP,X-Factor tie-in,
    Rebirth,Marvel Girl,pt.1 . . . . . . 6.00
264 JB,TP,I:2nd Yellow Jacket 2.50
265 JB,TP,Secret Wars II 2.50
266 JB,TP,Secret Wars II,A:
    Silver Surfer. 2.50
267 JB,TP,V:Kang. 2.50
268 JB,TP,V:Kang. 2.50
269 JB,TP,V:Kang,A:Immortus 2.50
270 JB,TP,V:Moonstone 2.50
271 JB,TP,V:Masters of Evil 2.50
272 JB,TP,A:Alpha Flight 2.50
273 JB,TP,V:Masters of Evil 2.50
274 JB,TP,V:Masters of Evil 2.50
275 JB,TP,V:Masters of Evil 2.50
276 JB,TP,V:Masters of Evil 2.50
277 JB,TP,V:Masters of Evil 2.50
278 JB,TP,V:Tyrok,J:Dr.Druid 2.50
279 JB,TP,new leader. 2.50
280 BH,KB,O:Jarvis 2.50
281 JB,TP,V:Olympian Gods. 2.50
282 JB,TP,V:Cerberus 2.50
283 JB,TP,V:Olympian Gods. 2.50
284 JB,TP,V:Olympian Gods. 2.50
285 JB,TP,V:Zeus. 2.50
286 JB,TP,V:Fixer. 2.50
287 JB,TP,V:Fixer. 2.50
288 JB,TP,V:Sentry 459 . . . . 2.50
289 JB,TP,J:Marrina 2.50
290 JB,TP,V:Adaptoid. 2.50
291 JB,TP,V:Marrina. 2.50
292 JB,TP,V:Leviathon 2.50
293 JB,TP,V:Leviathon 2.50
294 JB,TP,V:Nebula. 2.50
295 JB,TP,V:Nebula. 2.50
296 JB,TP,V:Nebula. 2.50
297 JB,TP,V:Nebula. 2.50
298 JB,TP,Inferno,Edwin Jarvis. . . . 2.50

Avengers #262
© *Marvel Entertainment Group*

299 JB,TP,Inferno,V:Orphan
    Maker,R:Gilgemesh. 2.50
300 JB,TP,WS,Inferno,V:Kang,
    O:Avengers,J:Gilgemesh,
    Mr.Fantastic,Invis.Woman. 4.00
301 BH,DH,A:SuperNova 2.00
302 RB,TP,V:SuperNova,
    A:Quasar 2.00
303 RB,TP,V:SuperNova,A:FF 2.00
304 RB,TP,V:U-Foes,Puma. 2.00
305 PR,TP,V:Lava Men. 2.00
306 PR,TP,O:Lava Men. 2.00
307 PR,TP,V:Lava Men. 2.00
308 PR,TP,A:Eternals,J:Sersi 2.00
309 PR,TP,V:Blastaar 2.00
310 PR,TP,V:Blastaar 2.00
311 PR,TP,Acts of Veng.,V:Loki . . . 2.00
312 PR,TP,Acts of Vengeance,
    V:Freedom Force 2.00
313 PR,TP,Acts of Vengeance,
    V:Mandarin,Wizard. 2.00
314 PR,TP,J:Sersi,A:Spider-Man,
    V:Nebula 2.00
315 PR,TP,A:SpM,V:Nebula 2.00
316 PR,TP,J:Spider-Man 2.00
317 PR,TP,A:SpM,V:Nebula 2.00
318 PR,TP,A:SpM,V:Nebula 2.00
319 PR,B:Crossing Line 2.00
320 PR,TP,A:Alpha Flight 2.00
321 PR,Crossing Line#3 . . . . 2.00
322 PR,TP,Crossing Line#4 . . . . . . 2.00
323 PR,TP,Crossing Line#5 . . . . . . 2.00
324 PR,TP,E:Crossing Line. 2.00
325 V:MotherSuperior,
    Machinesmith. 2.00
326 TP,I:Rage 5.00
327 TP,V:Monsters 2.00
328 TP,O:Rage. 4.00
329 TP,J:Sandman,Rage 2.00
330 TP,V:Tetrarch of Entropy 2.00
331 TP,J:Rage,Sandman 2.00
332 TP,V:Dr.Doom 2.00
333 HT,V:Dr.Doom 2.00
334 NKu,TP,B:Collector,
    A:Inhumans 2.00
335 RLm(c),SEp,TP,V:Thane
    Ector,A:Collector, ... 1.75
336 RLm(c),SEp,TP 1.75
337 RLm(c),SEp,TP,V:ThaneEctor . 1.75
338 RLm(c),SEp,TP,A:Beast, ... 1.75
339 RLm(c),SEp,TP,E:Collector . . . 1.75
340 RLm(c),F:Capt.Amer.,Wasp . . . 1.75
341 SEp,TP,A:New Warriors,V:Sons
    of Serpents 1.75

342 SEP,TP,A:New Warriors,
  V:Hatemonger 1.75
343 SEp,TP,J:Crystal,C&I:2nd
  Swordsman,Magdalene 2.00
344 SEp,TP,I:Proctor 2.00
345 SEp,TP,Oper. Galactic Storm
  Pt.5,V:Kree,Shiar 1.75
346 SEp,TP,Oper. Galactic Storm
  Pt.12,I:Star Force 1.75
347 SEp,TP,Oper. Galactic Storm
  Pt.19,D:Kree Race,Conclusion . 2.00
348 SEp,TP,F:Vision 1.75
349 SEp,TP,V:Ares 1.75
350 SEp,TP,rep.Avengers#53,A:Prof.
  X,Cyclops,V:StarJammers 3.00
351 KWe,V:Star Jammers. 1.75
352 V:Grim Reaper. 1.75
353 V:Grim Reaper. 1.75
354 V:Grim Reaper. 1.75
355 BHs(s),SEp,I:Gatherers,
  Coal Tiger 2.00
356 B:BHs(s),SEp,TP,A:Bl.Panther
  D:Coal Tiger. 1.75
357 SEp,TP,A:Watcher 1.75
358 SEp,TP,V:Arkon. 1.75
359 SEp,TP,A:Arkon. 1.75
360 SEp,TP,V:Proctor,double-size,
  bronze foil(c) 4.00
361 SEp,I:Alternate Vision 1.50
362 SEp,TP,V:Proctor. 1.50
363 SEp,TP,V:Proctor,D:Alternate
  Vision,C:Deathcry,Silver Foil(c),
  30th Anniv., ... 3.00
364 SEp,TP,I:Deathcry,V:Kree 1.50
365 SEp,TP,V:Kree. 1.50
366 SEp,TP,V:Kree,N:Dr.Pym,Gold
  Foil(c). 4.50
367 F:Vision 2.00
368 SEp,TP,Bloodties#1,
  A:X-Men. 3.00
369 SEp,TP,E:BHs(s),Bloodties#5,
  D:Cortez,V:Exodus,Platinum
  Foil(c). 3.00
370 SEp(c),TP(c),GI,V:Deviants,
  A:Kro,I:Delta Force. 1.50
371 GM,TP,V:Deviants,A:Kro 1.50
372 B:BHs(s),SEp,TP,I:2nd
  Gatherers,A:Proctor 1.50
373 SEp,TP,I:Alternate Jocasta,
  V:Sersi 1.50
374 SEp,TP,O&IR:Proctor is Alternate
  Black Knight. 1.50
375 SEp,TP,Double Sized,D:Proctor,
  L:Sersi,Black Knight 3.25
376 F:Crystal,I:Terrigen. 1.75
377 F:Quicksilver 1.50
378 TP,I:Butcher. 1.50
379 TP,Hercules,V:Hera 1.50
379a Avengers Double Feature #1
  flip-book with Giant-Man #1 . . . 2.50
380 Hera 6.00
380a Avengers Double Feature #2
  flip-book with Giant Man #2 . . . 5.00
381 Quicksilvr, Scarlet Witch. 4.00
381a Avengers Double Feature #3
  flip-book with Giant Man #3 . . . 2.50
382 Wundagore 1.50
382a Avengers Double Feature #4
  flip-book with Giant Man #4 . . . 2.50
383 A:Fantastic Force,V:Arides. . . . 3.00
384 Hercules Vs. Stepmom 4.00
385 V:Red Skull 3.00
386 F:Black Widow. 3.00
387 Taking A.I.M.,pt.2. . . . . 3.00
388 Taking A.I.M.,pt.4. . . . . 3.00
389 B:Mike Deodato 3.00
390 BHs,TP,The Crossing, prelude . 3.00
391 BHs,Cont. From Avg. Crossing 3.00
392 BHs,TP,The Crossing. 3.00
393 BHs,TP,The Crossing. 3.00
394 BHs,TP,The Crossing. 3.00

395 BHs,TP,Timeslide concludes . . 3.00
396 . . . . 3.00
397 TP,Incred.Hulk #440 x-over . . . 3.00
398 TP,V:Unknown foe 3.00
399 . . . . 3.00
400 MeW,MWa,double size 4.50
401 MeW,MWa,Onslaught saga . . . 3.00
402 MWa,MD2,Onslaught, finale. . . 3.00
Ann.#1 DH,V:Mandarin,
  Masters of Evil 60.00
Ann.#2 DH,JB,V:Scar.Centurion . . 35.00
Ann.#3 rep.#4,T.ofSusp.#66-68 . . 25.00
Ann.#4 rep.#5,#6 . . . . 12.00
Ann.#5 JK(c),rep.#8,#11 . . . . 12.00
Ann.#6 GP,HT,V:Laser,Nuklo,
  Whirlwind 10.00
Ann.#7 JSn,JRu,V:Thanos,A:Captain
  Marvel,D:Warlock(2nd) 15.00
Ann.#8 GP,V:Dr.Spectrum. 6.00
Ann.#9 DN,V:Arsenal 5.00
Ann.#10 MGo,A:X-Men,Spid.Woman,
  I:Rogue,V:Br.o/Evil Mutants . . 30.00
Ann.#11 DP,V:Defenders 5.00
Ann.#12 JG,V:Inhumans,Maximus . 4.00
Ann.#13 JBy,V:Armin Zola 4.00
Ann.#14 JBy,KB,V:Skrulls 4.00
Ann.#15 SD,KJ,V:Freedom Force . . 4.00
Ann.#16 RF,BH,TP,JR2,BSz,KP,AW,
  MR,BL,BWi,JG,KN,A:Silver
  Surfer,Rebirth Grandmaster . . . 4.50
Ann.#17 MBr,MG,Evol.Wars,J:2nd
  Yellow Jacket. 4.00
Ann.#18 MBa,MG,Atlan.Attack#8,
  J:Quasar 3.00
Ann.#19 HT,Terminus Factor. 2.50
Ann.#20 Subterran.Odyssey#1 . . . 2.50
Ann.#21 Citizen Kang#4 . . . . 2.50
Ann.#22 I:Bloodwraith,w/card 3.25
Ann.#23 JB 3.25
G-Size#1 JR(c),RB,DA,I:Nuklo . . . 10.00
G-Size#2 JR(c),DC,O:Kang,
  D:Swordsman,O:Rama-Tut. . . . 7.00
G-Size#3 GK(c),DC,V:Kang,Legion
  of the Unliving 5.00
G-Size#4 K&R(c),DH,W:Scarlet Witch
  &Vision,O:Mantis,Moondragon . 7.00
G-Size#5 rep,Annual #1. . . . . 3.00
GNv Death Trap:The Vault RLm,
  A:Venom 20.00
Marvel Milestone rep. #1 (1993) . . 2.95
Marvel Milestone rep. #4 (1995) . . 2.95
Marvel Milestone rep. #16 (1993) . . 2.95
TPB Greatest Battles of the
  Avengers 15.95
TPB Korvac Saga,rep.#167-177 . . 12.95

Avengers King Size Spec. #1
© Marvel Entertainment Group

TPB Yesterday Quest,Rep.#181,182
  185-187 . . . . 6.95

AVENGERS
Nov. 1996

1 RLd,JV,CYp,JSb,Heroes Reborn,
  F:Thor, Captain America,
  V:Loki. 6.00
1A Variant cover 7.50
1 gold signature edition, bagged . 20.00
2 RLd,JV,CYp,JSb,V:Kang. 2.50
3 RLd,JV,CYp,JSb,V:Kang,A:Nick
  Fury. 2.50
4 RLd,JLb,CYp,JSb, ... 2.50
4A variant cover 2.50
5 RLd,CYp,JSb,V:Hulk,concl. 2.00
6 RLd,JLb,CYp,JSb,"Industrial
  Revolution," pt.1 x-over 2.00
7 RLd,JLb,IaC,JSb, ... 2.00
8 RLd,JLb,IaC,JSb,F:Simon
  Williams (Wonder Man),V:Ultron,
  Lethal Legion 2.00
9 JLb,RLd,IaC,F:Vision, Wonder
  Man 1.95
10 WS, ... 1.95
11 . . . . 2.00
12 WS,Galactus Saga, x-over. . . . 2.00
13 JeR, Wildstorm x-over 2.00
Minus 1 Spec., JLb,RLd,IaC,JSb,
  flashback 1.95

AVENGERS
Dec. 1997

1 GP,KBk,AV,F:Everyone,48 pg. . . 3.00
2 KBk,GP,AV,A:Scarlet Witch. 2.00
3 KBk,GP,AV,trapped in midieval
  present. 2.00
4 KBk,GP,AV,who makes the team?2.00
5 KBk,GP,AV,Squadron Supreme. . 2.00
6 KBk,GP,AV,V:SquadronSupreme. 2.00
7 KBk,GP,AV,Live Kree or Die, pt.4,
  concl 2.00
8 KBk,GP,AV,I:Triathlon 2.00
9 KBk,GP,AV,V:Moses Magnum . . 2.00
10 KBk,GP,AV,V:Grim Reaper. . . . 2.00
11 KBk,GP,AV,V:Grim Reaper. . . . 2.00
12 KBk,GP,AV,V:Thunderbolts
  48-page 3.00
13 KBk,GP,AV,R:New Warriors . . . 2.00
14 KBk,GP,AV,R:Beast 2.00
15 KBk,GP,AV,A:Iron Man. 2.00
16 JOy,AG,R:Photon 2.00
16a variant JOy,GP cover. 2.00
17 JOy,AG,A:Warbird &
  Black Knight 2.00
18 JOy,AG,V:Wrecking Crew 2.00
19 KBk,GP,AV,Ultron,pt.1 . . . . 2.00
19a signed 30.00
20 KBk,GP,AV,Ultron,pt.2 . . . . 2.00
21 KBk,GP,AV,Ultron,pt.3 . . . . 2.00
Ann. '98 Avengers/Squadron Supreme
  KBk,CPa,GP, 48pg. 2.50
Ann.1999 KBk,JFM, Why Avengers
  disbanded, 48-page 3.50
Rough Cut Edition KBk,GP, 48pg,
  original pencils of #1, b&w . . . 3.00
TPB Essential Avengers 14.95
TPB Avengers: Under Siege 16.95
TPB Avengers Visionaries:
  George Perez, 176-page 16.95

AVENGERS FOREVER
Oct. 1998

1 (of 12) GP,KBk,CPa,Rick Jones
  radiation poisoning 3.00
2 GP,KBk,CPa,new Avengers 3.00
3 GP,KBk,CPa,Kang/Immortus. . . . 3.00
4 KBk,different eras. 3.00

Avengers Forever #1
© Marvel Entertainment Group

4a, b & c variant covers . . . . @3.00
5 KBk,RSt,A:1950s Avengers 3.00
6 KBk,RSt,V:Immortus. 3.00
7 KBk,RSt,reunited 3.00
8 KBk,Immortus' plan. 3.00
9 KBk,RSt,Kang the Conqueror . . . 3.00
10 KBk,RSt,V:Immortus 3.00
11 KBk,RSt,V:Avengers Battalion . . 3.00

AVENGERS INDEX
See: OFFICIAL MARVEL INDEX TO THE AVENGERS

AVENGERS LOG
1994
1 GP(c),History of the Avengers . . 2.25

AVENGERS SPOTLIGHT
August, 1989
Formerly: Solo Avengers
21 AM,DH,TMo,JRu,Hawkeye,
    Starfox 1.25
22 AM,DH,Hawkeye,O:Swordsman. 1.25
23 AM,DH,KD,Hawkeye,Vision 1.25
24 AM,DH,Hawkeye,O:Espirita 1.25
25 AM,TMo,Hawkeye,Rick Jones . . 1.25
26 A of V,Hawkeye,Iron Man. 1.25
27 A of V,AM,DH,DT,Hawkeye,
    Avengers 1.25
28 A of V,AM,DH,DT,Hawkeye,
    Wonder Man,Wasp. 1.25
29 A of V,DT,Hawkeye,Iron Man . . . 1.25
30 AM,DH,Hawkeye,New Costume. 1.25
31 AM,DH,KW,Hawkeye,US.Agent. 1.25
32 AM,KW,Hawkeye,U.S.Agent . . . 1.25
33 AM,DH,KW,Hawkeye,US.Agent . 1.25
34 AM,DH,KW,SLi(c),Hawkeye
    U.S.Agent 1.25
35 JV,Gilgamesh 1.25
36 AM,DH,Hawkeye 1.25
37 BH,Dr.Druid. 1.25
38 JBr,Tigra 1.25
39 GCo,Black Knight 1.25
40 Vision,Last Issue 1.25

AVENGERS STRIKEFILE
1994
1 BHa(s),Avengers Pin-ups 2.00

AVENGERS: THE CROSSING
1995
1 BHs,Death of an Avenger,
    chromium cover,48pg. 6.00

AVENGERS: THE TERMINATRIX OBJECTIVE
1993
1 B:MGu(s),MG,Holografx(c),
    V:Terminatrix 2.75
2 MG,V:Terminatrix,A:Kangs 2.00
3 MG,V:Terminatrix,A:Kangs 2.00
4 MG,Last issue 2.00

AVENGERS: TIMESLIDE
1996
1 BHs,TKa,End of the Crossing
    Megallic chrome cover 4.95

AVENGERS/ULTRAFORCE
1995
1 V:Malibu's Ultraforce. 3.95

AVENGERS UNLEASHED
1 V:Count Nefarious 1.00
Becomes:
AVENGERS UNPLUGGED
1996
2 Crushed by Graviton. 1.00
3 x-over with FF Unplugged. 1.00
4 . . . . 1.00
5 . . . . 1.00

AVENGERS WEST COAST
Sept., 1989
Prev: West Coast Avengers
47 JBy,V:J.Random 2.00
48 JBy,V:J.Random 2.00
49 JBy,V:J.Random,W.Man. 2.00
50 JBy,R:G.A.Human Torch 2.00
51 JBy,R:Iron Man 2.00
52 JBy,V:MasterPandmonum 2.00
53 JBy,Acts ofVeng.,V:U-Foes 2.00
54 JBy,Acts ofVeng.,V:MoleMan . . . 2.00
55 JBy,Acts ofVeng.finale,V:Loki
    Magneto kidnaps Sc.Witch 2.50
56 JBy,V:Magneto. 2.50
57 JBy,V:Magneto. 2.50
58 V:Vibro, ... 2.00
59 TMo,V:Hydro-Man,A:Immortus . . 2.00
60 PR,V:Immortus, ... 2.00
61 PR,V:Immortus 2.00
62 V:Immortus 2.00
63 PR,I:Living Lightning 2.00
64 F:G.A.Human Torch. 2.00
65 PR,V:Ultron,Grim Reaper. 2.00
66 PR,V:Ultron,Grim Reaper. 2.00
67 PR,V:Ultron,Grim Reaper. 2.00
68 PR,V:Ultron 2.00
69 PR,USAgent vs Hawkeye,
    I:Pacific Overlords 2.50
70 DR,V:Pacific Overlords 1.75
71 DR,V:Pacific Overlords 1.75
72 DR,V:Pacific Overlords 1.75
73 DR,V:Pacific Overlords 1.75
74 DR,J:Living Lightning,Spider
    Woman,V:Pacific Overlords. . . . 1.75
75 HT,A:F.F,V:Arkon,double 2.00

Avengers West Coast #96
© Marvel Entertainment Group

76 DR,Night Shift,I:Man-Demon . . . 1.50
77 DR,A:Satannish & Nightshift . . . 1.50
78 DR,V:Satannish & Nightshift . . . 1.50
79 DR,A:Dr.Strange,V:Satannish. . . 1.50
80 DR,Galactic Storm,pt.2 . . . . 1.50
81 DR,Galactic Storm,pt.9 . . . . 1.50
82 DR,Galactic Storm,pt.16
    A:Lilandra. 1.50
83 V:Hyena 1.50
84 DR,I:Deathweb,A:SpM,
    O:Spider-Woman 1.75
85 DR,A:SpM,V:Death Web 1.50
86 DR,A:SpM,V:Death Web 1.50
87 DR,A:Wolverine,V:Bogatyri 1.75
88 DR,A:Wolverine,V:Bogatyri 1.75
89 DR,V:Ultron 1.50
90 DR,A:Vision,V:Ultron 1.50
91 DR,V:Ultron,I:War Toy 1.50
92 DR,V:Goliath(Power Man) 1.50
93 DR,V:Doctor Demonicus 1.50
94 DR,J:War Machine. 1.75
95 DR,A:Darkhawk,V:Doctor
    Demonicus. 1.50
96 DR,Inf.Crusade x-over 1.50
97 ACe,Inf.Crusade,V:Power
    Platoon 1.50
98 DR,I:4th Lethal Legion 1.50
99 DR,V:4th Lethal Legion 1.50
100 DR,D:Mockingbird,V:4th Lethal
    Legion,Red Foil(c) 3.50
101 DR,Bloodties#3,V:Exodus 4.00
102 DR,L:Iron Man,Spider-Woman,
    US Agent,Scarlet Witch,War
    Machine,last issue 4.00
Ann.#4 JBy,TA,MBa,Atlan.Attacks
    #12,V:Seven Brides of Set 4.00
Ann.#5 Terminus Factor 3.50
Ann.#6 Subterranean Odyssey#5 . . 2.50
Ann.#7 Assault on Armor City#4 . . . 2.25
Ann.#8 DR,I:Raptor w/card 3.25

BALDER THE BRAVE
Nov., 1985
1 WS,SB,V:Frost Giants 1.50
2 WS,SB,V:Frost Giants 1.25
3 WS,SB,V:Frost Giants 1.25
4 WS,SB,V:Frost Giants;Feb,1986. 1.25

BARBIE
Jan., 1991
1 polybagged with Credit Card. . . . 7.00
2 . . . . 3.50

3	3.00
4 Ice Skating	3.00
5 Sea Cruise	3.00
6 Sun Runner Story	3.00
7 Travel issue	3.00
8 TV Commercial	3.00
9 Music Tour Van	3.00
10 Barbie in Italy	3.00
11 Haunted Castles	3.00
12 Monkey Bandit	3.00
13 MW,A:Skipper,Ken	3.00
14 Country Fair	3.00
15 Barbie in Egypt,pt.1	3.00
16 Barbie in Egypt,pt.2	3.00
17 Weightwatchers/Art issue	3.00
18 V:heavy Metal Band	3.00
19 A:Surfer Pal	3.00
20 Skipper at Special Olympics	3.00
21 I:Whitney,female fire fighter	3.00
22 Barbie in Greece	3.00
23 thru 27	@3.00
28 Valentine's Day Issue	3.00
29 Skipper babysits	3.00
30 Cowgirls on the Range	3.00
31 Rest and Relaxation	3.00
32 A:Dandy the Gorilla	3.00
33 thru 41	@3.00
42 thru 49	@3.00
50 Anniv. issue, Disney World(c)	3.00
51 Vet's assistant	2.00
52 Valentines Day Special	2.00
53 Marooned	2.00
54 Female Inventors	2.00
55 in Nashville	2.00
56 Sherlock Barbie	2.00
57 Nashville	2.00
58 Barbie Teaches Skating	2.00
59 Famous Females	2.00
60 Halloween Hero	2.00
61 Alaska Gold Rush	2.00
62 Christmas/Nutcracker	2.00
63	2.00
64	2.00
65 Under Antarctica	2.00
66	2.00

BARBIE FASHION
Jan., 1991

1 polybagged with dorknob hanger	5.00
2 thru 63	@2.50

BATTLE
Atlas March, 1951

1 They called Him a Coward	200.00
2 The War Department Secrets	100.00
3 The Beast of the Bataan	60.00
4 I:Buck Private O'Toole	60.00
5 Death Trap Of Gen. Wu.	60.00
6 RH	60.00
7 Enemy Sniper	60.00
8 A Time to Die	60.00
9 RH	50.00
10	50.00
11 thru 20	@40.00
21	45.00
22	40.00
23	45.00
24	40.00
25	35.00
26 JR	35.00
27	35.00
28 JSe	35.00
29	35.00
30	35.00
31 RH	35.00
32 JSe,GT	35.00
33 GC,JSe,JSt	35.00
34 JSe	35.00
35	35.00

36 BEv	35.00
37 RA,JSt	40.00
38	30.00
39	30.00
40	30.00
41	30.00
42 thru 46	@30.00
47 JO	30.00
48	30.00
49 JDa	40.00
50 BEv	30.00
51	30.00
52 GWb	30.00
53 BP	30.00
54	30.00
55 GC,AS,BP	40.00
56	30.00
57	30.00
58	30.00
59	30.00
60 A:Combat Kelly	30.00
61 A:Combat Kelly	30.00
62 A:Combat Kelly	30.00
63 SD	55.00
64 JK	75.00
65 JK	75.00
66 JSe,JK,JDa	75.00
67 JSe,JK,AS,JDa	75.00
68 JSe,JK,AW,SD	75.00
69 RH,JSe,JK,SW	60.00
70 BEv,SD; June, 1960	60.00

BATTLE ACTION
Atlas Feb., 1952

1	150.00
2	75.00
3	40.00
4	40.00
5	40.00
6	40.00
7	40.00
8	40.00
9	40.00
10	40.00
11 thru 15	@35.00
16 thru 26	@32.00
27	35.00
28	30.00
29	30.00
30 August, 1957	35.00

BATTLEBOOKS
Nov. 1998

Captain America, BiT(c)	4.00
Citizen V, BiT(c)	4.00
Colossus, BiT(c)	4.00
Elektra, BiT(c)	4.00
Gambit, BiT(c)	4.00
Iron Man, BiT(c)	4.00
Rogue, BiT(c)	4.00
Spider-Girl, BiT(c)	4.00
Spider-Man, BiT(c)	4.00
Storm, BiT(c)	4.00
Thor, BiT(c)	4.00
Wolverine, BiT(c)	4.00

BATTLE BRADY
See: MEN IN ACTION

BATTLEFIELD
Atlas April, 1952

1 RH, Slaughter on Suicide Ridge	125.00
2	50.00
3 Ambush Patrol	50.00
4	50.00
5 Into the Jaws of Death	50.00

6 thru 10	@35.00
11 GC,May, 1953	35.00

BATTLEFRONT
Atlas June, 1952

1 RH(c),Operation Killer	175.00
2	75.00
3 Spearhead	60.00
4 Death Trap of General Chun	60.00
5 Terror of the Tank Men	55.00
6 A:Combat Kelly	50.00
7 A:Combat Kelly	50.00
8 A:Combat Kelly	50.00
9 A:Combat Kelly	50.00
10 A:Combat Kelly	50.00
11 thru 20	@40.00
21 thru 39	@30.00
40 AW	50.00
41	30.00
42 AW	50.00
43 thru 48 August,1957	@35.00

BATTLEGROUND
Atlas Sept., 1954

1	125.00
2 JKz.	65.00
3 thru 8	@50.00
9	50.00
10	35.00
11 AW	60.00
12	30.00
13 AW	60.00
14 JD	35.00
15	30.00
16	30.00
17	30.00
18 AS	60.00
19	30.00
20 August, 1957	30.00

BATTLESTAR GALACTICA
March, 1979

1 EC,B:TV Adaptation; Annihalation	3.00
2 EC,Exodus	2.50
3 EC,Deathtrap	2.50
4 WS,Dogfight	2.50
5 WS,E:TV Adaptation;Ambush	2.50
6 Nightmare	2.00

Battlestar Galactica #4
© Marvel Entertainment Group

---

7 Commander Adama Trapped . . . 2.00
8 Last Stand 2.00
9 Space Mimic 2.00
10 This Planet Hungers 2.00
11 WS,Starbuck's Dilemma. 2.00
12 WS,Memory Ends 2.00
13 WS,All Out Attack 2.00
14 Radiation Threat 2.00
15 Ship of Crawling Death 2.00
16 . . . . 2.00
17 Animal on the Loose 2.00
18 Battle For the Forbidden Fruit . . 2.00
19 Starbuck's Back. 2.00
20 Duel to the Death 2.00
21 To Slay a Monster..To Deatroy
    a World 2.00
22 WS,A Love Story?. 2.00
23 Dec., 1981. . . . . 2.00

BATTLETIDE
1990
1 thru 4 F: Death's Head II and
    Killpower. . . . . @1.75

BATTLETIDE II
1993
1 Foil embossed cover 2.95
2 thru 8 F: Death's Head II and
    Killpower. . . . . @1.75

Beast #1
© Marvel Entertainment Group

BEAST
March 1997
1 (of 3) KG,CNn,F:Karma, Cannon-
    ball, V:Viper & Spiral. 2.50
2 KG,CNn,V:Spiral. 2.50
3 KG,CNn, concl.. . . . . 2.50

BEAUTY AND THE BEAST
Jan., 1985
1 DP,Beast & Dazzler,direct. 3.00
1a DP,Beast & Dazzler,UPC 2.00
2 DP,Beast & Dazzler 2.00
3 DP,Beast & Dazzler 2.00
4 DP,Beast & Dazzler 2.00

BEAUTY AND THE BEAST
1992
1 . . . . 1.50

2 Wardrobe's birthday party. 1.50
3 . . . . 1.50
4 . . . . 1.50
5 . . . . 1.50
6 Lumiere takes Cogsworth's job . . 1.50
7 Belle & Chip caught in snow 1.50
8 . . . . 1.50
9 Can Beast prove his love? 1.50
10 Chip & Belle have a snow ball . . 1.50
11 History of Beast's Castle 1.50
12 . . . . 1.50
13 The Dessert Disaster. 1.50

Beavis & Butt-Head #4
© Marvel Entertainment Group

BEAVIS & BUTT-HEAD
March 1994
1 Based on the MTV Show 5.00
1a 2nd Printing 2.50
2 Dead from the Neck up. 3.50
3 Break out at Burger World 3.00
4 Tattoo Parlor. 2.25
5 Field Day 2.25
6 Revulsion 2.25
7 Oldies bot. 2.25
8 Be a clown. 2.25
9 Makin' movies. 2.25
10 Halloween 2.25
11 . . . . 2.00
12 . . . . 2.00
13 . . . . 2.00
14 Join Biker Gang. 2.00
15 Spring Break 2.00
16 Capture The Flag. 2.00
17 with video camera 2.00
18 Woodsuck 2.00
19 break-up? 2.00
20 Solar Eclipse 2.00
21 Male Cheerleaders 2.00
22 Antics at theme park 2.00
23 Witless 2.00
24 Holiday suck-tacular 2.00
25 . . . . 1.95
26 . . . . 1.95
27 Easter spirit 1.95
28 . . . . 1.95
TPB Greatest Hits, rep.#1–#4. . . 12.95
TPB Holidazed and Confused. . . . 12.95

BEST OF MARVEL '96
TPB 224pg. 19.95

BEST WESTERN
June, 1949
58 A:KidColt,BlackRider,Two-
    Gun Kid;Million DollarTrain
    Robbery. 150.00
59 A:BlackRider,KidColt,Two-Gun
    Kid;The Black Rider Strikes . 125.00
Becomes:

WESTERN OUTLAWS
& SHERIFFS
60 PH(c),Hawk Gaither. 100.00
61 Ph(c),Pepper Lawson 75.00
62 Murder at Roaring
    House Bridge 75.00
63 thru 65. . . . . @75.00
66. . . . . 50.00
67. . . . . 70.00
68 thru 72. . . . . @50.00
73 June, 1952 . . . . 40.00

BEWARE
March, 1973
1 Reprints 4.50
2 thru 8 . . . . @2.50
Becomes:

TOMB OF DARKNESS
9 Reprints 2.00
10 thru 22 . . . . @1.00
23 November, 1976 . . . . 2.00

BIKER MICE FROM MARS
1993
1 I:Biker Mice 1.50
2 thru 3. 1.50

BILL & TED'S
BOGUS JOURNEY
Nov., 1991
1 Movie Adaption. 3.25

BILL & TED'S
EXCELLENT COMICS
Dec., 1991
1 From Movie; Wedding Reception 1.25
2 Death Takes a Vacation 1.25
3 `Daze in the Lives' 1.25
4 Station Plague 1.25
5 Bill & Ted on Trial 1.25
6 Time Trial. 1.25
7 Time Trial, Concl 1.25
8 History Final. 1.25
9 I:Morty(new Death). 1.25
10 'Hyperworld'. 1.25
11 Lincoln assassination. 1.25
12 Last issue 1.25

BILLY BUCKSKIN
WESTERN
Atlas Nov., 1955
1 MD,Tales of the Wild Frontier . 100.00
2 MD,Ambush 75.00
3 MD,AW, Thieves in the Night . . 75.00
Becomes:

2-GUN KID
4 SD,A: Apache Kid 75.00
Becomes:

TWO-GUN WESTERN
5 B:Apache Kid,Doc Holiday,
    Kid Colt Outlaw 75.00
6 . . . . 40.00
7 . . . . 40.00
8 RC. 50.00

MARVEL

9 AW	60.00
10	35.00
11 AW	60.00
12 Sept., 1957,RC	45.00

BISHOP
1994
1 Mountjoy, foil cover	4.50
2 foil stamped cover	4.00
3 JOs	3.50
4 V:Mountjoy	3.50

BISHOP:
THE LAST X-MAN
Aug. 1999
1 R:Bishop, 48-page debut	3.00

BISHOP: XAVIER'S
SECURITY ENFORCER
Nov., 1997
1 (of 3) JOs,SEp	2.50
2 JOs,SEp,hunted by X.S.E.	2.50
3 JOs,SEp,Bishop v. Rook, concl.	2.50

BIZARRE ADVENTURES
See: MARVEL PREVIEW

BLACK AXE
1 JR2(c),A:Death's Head II	2.00
2 JR2(2),A:Sunfire,V:The Hand	2.00
3 A:Death's Head II,V:Mesphisto	2.00
4 in ancient Egypt	2.00
5 KJ(c),In Wakanda	2.00
6 KJ(c),A:Black Panther	2.00
7 KJ(c),A:Black Panther	1.75
8 thru 13	@1.75

BLACK CAT
Limited Series]
1 Wld,A:Spider-Man,V:Cardiac, I:Faze	1.75
2 Wld,V:Faze	1.50
3 Wld,Cardiac	1.50
4 Wld,V:Scar	1.50

BLACK DRAGON
Epic May 1985
1 JBo	4.00
2 thru 6 JBo	@3.00

BLACK GOLIATH
Feb., 1976—Nov., 1976
1 GT,O:Black Goliath,Cont's From Powerman #24	5.00
2 GT,V:Warhawk	4.00
3 GT,D:Atom-Smasher	4.00
4 KP,V:Stilt-Man	4.00
5 D:Mortag	4.00

BLACK KNIGHT, THE
Atlas May, 1955—April, 1956
1 O: Crusader;The Black Knight Rides	650.00
2 Siege on Camelot	500.00
3 Blacknight Unmasked	400.00
4 Betrayed	400.00
5 SSh,The Invincible Tartar	400.00

BLACK KNIGHT
June, 1990—Sept., 1990
1 TD,R:Original Black Knight	2.00

2 TD,A:Dreadknight	1.75
3 RB,A:Dr.Strange	1.75
4 RB,TD,A:Dr Strange, Valkyrie	1.75

BLACK KNIGHT: EXODUS
1996
1-shot R:Black Knight,A:Sersi, O:Exodus	2.50

Black Panther #7
© Marvel Entertainment Group

BLACK PANTHER
[1st Series]
Jan., 1977—May, 1979
1 JK,V:Collectors	9.00
2 JK,V:Six Million Year Man	5.00
3 JK,V:Ogar	3.50
4 JK,V:Collectors	3.50
5 JK,V:Yeti	3.50
6 JK,V:Ronin	3.50
7 JK,V:Mister Little	3.50
8 JK,D:Black Panther	3.50
9 JK,V:Jakarra	3.50
10 JK,V:Jakarra	3.50
11 JK,V:Kilber the Cruel	3.50
12 JK,V:Kilber the Cruel	3.50
13 JK,V:Kilber the Cruel	3.50
14 JK,A:Avengers,V:Klaw	3.50
15 JK,A:Avengers,V:Klaw	3.50

BLACK PANTHER
July 1988—Oct. 1988
[1st Mini-Series]
1 I:Panther Spirit	2.50
2 V:Supremacists	2.50
3 A:Malaika	2.50
4 V:Panther Spirit	2.50

[2nd Mini-Series]
PANTHER'S PREY
May, 1991
1 DT,A:W'Kabi,V:Solomon Prey	4.95
2 thru 4 DT,V:Solomon Prey	@4.95

BLACK PANTHER
Sept. 1998
1 CPr,MT,A:T'Challa	2.50
2 CPr,MT,A:Mephisto	2.50
2a variant cover	2.50
3 CPr,MT,JQ,I:Achebe	2.50

4 CPr,MT,JQ,V:Mephisto	2.50
5 CPr,V:Mephisto	2.50
6 CPr,JJu,V:Kraven the Hunter	2.50
7 CPr,JJu,V:Kraven, round 2	2.50
8 CPr,JJu,A:Avengers	2.50
9 CPr,MM,A:Avengers	2.50
10 CPr,MM,political counter-attack	2.50
11 CPR,MBr,Enemy of the State,pt.3	2.50

BLACK RIDER
See: ALL WINNERS
COMICS

BLACK RIDER
RIDES AGAIN
Atlas Sept., 1957
1 JK,Treachery at Hangman's Ridge	175.00

BLACKSTONE, THE
MAGICIAN
May, 1948—Sept., 1948
2 B:Blonde Phantom	450.00
3	300.00
4 Bondage(c)	325.00

BLACK WIDOW
Apr. 1999
1 (of 3) Black Widow replaced?	3.50
1a variant cover (1:4)	3.50
2 A:Daredevil	3.00
3 conclusion	3.00
TPB Web of Intrigue, rep. Marvel Fanfare #10–#13	4.00

BLACKWULF
1994–95
1 AMe,Embossied(c),I:Mammoth, Touchstone,Toxin,D:Pelops, V:Tantalus,	2.75
2 AMe,I:Sparrow,Wildwind	1.75
3 AMe,I:Scratch	1.50
4 AMe,I:Giant-man	1.50
5 AMe	1.50
6 AMe,Tantalus	1.50
7 AMe,V:Tantalus	1.50
8 AMe	1.50
9 Seven Worlds of Tantalus,pt.1 A:Daredevil	1.50
10 Seven Worlds of Tantalus,pt.2, last issue	1.50

BLADE,
THE VAMPIRE HUNTER
1994–95
1 Foil(c),Clv(i),R:Dracula	3.00
2 Clv(i),V:Dracula	1.95
3 Clv(i)	1.95
4 Clv(i)	1.95
5 Clv(i)	1.95
6 Clv(i)	1.95
7 Clv(i)	1.95
8 Bible John, Morbius	1.95
9	1.95
10 R:Dracula	1.95
11 Dracula Untombed,pt.2	1.95

BLADE
(Sept., 1998)
1 (of 6) DMG,40-page, photo(c)	3.50

1a variant cover (1:4). 3.50
2 DMG,A:Morbius,Dominique. 3.00
2a variant cover. 3.00
3 DMG, ... 3.00
4 DMG,F:Morbius 3.00
1-shot Blade: Crescent City Blues,
   MPe,V:Deacon Frost (1-98) . . . 3.50
1-shot DMG, movie tie-in (2-98) . . . 3.00
1-shot movie adaptation,48 pg 6.00

Blade Runner #1
© Marvel Entertainment Group

BLADE RUNNER
Oct., 1982
1 AW, Movie Adaption 2.00
2 AW, ... 2.00

BLAZE
[Limited Series] 1993–94
1 HMe(s),RoW,A:Clara Menninger . 2.00
2 HMe(s),RoW,I:Initiate 2.00
3 HMe(s),RoW, ... 2.00
4 HMe(s),RoW,D:Initiate,Last
   issue 2.00
[Regular Series] Aug. 1994
1 HMz,LHa,foil (c) 3.25
2 HMz,LHa,I:Man-Thing. 2.25
3 HMz,LHa,V:Ice Box Bob 1.95
4 HMz,LHa,Apache Autumn,pt.1 . . 1.95
5 HMz,LHa,Apache Autumn,pt.2 . . 1.95
6 Apache Autumn,pt.3 . . . . 1.95
7 Carnivale Quintano. 1.95
8 A:Arcae 1.95
9 Clara's Eyeballs 1.95
10 Undead M.C. 1.95
11 A:Punisher. 1.95
12 reunited with children, final iss. . 1.95

BLAZE CARSON
Sept., 1948
1 SSh(c),Fight,Lawman
   or Crawl 175.00
2 Guns Roar on Boot Hill 150.00
3 A:Tex Morgan 150.00
4 A:Two-Gun Kid 150.00
5 A:Tex Taylor 150.00
Becomes:

REX HART
6 CCB,Ph(c),B:Rex Hart,
   A:Black Rider 150.00
7 Ph(c),Mystery at Bar-2 Ranch 125.00
8 Ph(c),The Hombre Who
   Killed His Friends 125.00

Becomes:
WHIP WILSON
9 Ph(c),B:Whip Wilson,O:Bullet;
   Duel to the Death 450.00
10 Ph(c),Wanted for Murder 250.00
11 Ph(c) 250.00
Becomes:
GUNHAWK, THE
12 The Redskin's Revenge 100.00
13 GT,The Man Who Murdered
   Gunhawk 75.00
14 . . . . 75.00
15 . . . . 75.00
16 . . . . 75.00
17 . . . . 75.00
18 Dec., 1951. . . . . 75.00

BLAZE, THE WONDER COLLIE
Oct., 1949
2 Ph(c),Blaze-Son of Fury 150.00
3 Ph(c), Lonely Boy;Feb.,1950. . 125.00

BLONDE PHANTOM
See: ALL-SELECT COMICS

BLOOD
Feb., 1988—April, 1988
1 . . . . 6.00
2 thru 4 . . . . @5.00

BLOOD & GLORY
1993
1 KJ Cap & the Punisher 5.95
2 KJ Cap & the Punisher 5.95
3 KJ Cap & the Punisher 5.95

BLOODLINES
Epic 1992
1 F:Kathy Grant-Peace Corps 5.95

BLOODSEED
1993
1 LSh,I:Bloodseed 2.25
2 LSh,V:Female Bloodseed 2.25

BOOK OF THE DEAD
1993–94
1 thru 4 Horror rep . . . . @2.00
5 and 6 . . . . @1.75

BOZZ CHRONICLES, THE
Epic Dec., 1985
1 thru 5 . . . . @1.75
6 May, 1986 . . . . 1.75

BRATS BIZARRE
Epic *Heavy Hitters* 1994
1 with trading card 3.25
2 thru 4 with trading card . . . . . @2.50

BREAK THE CHAIN
1 KB,KRS-One,w/audio tape 7.00

BRUTE FORCE
August, 1990
1 JD/JSt 1.00
2 . . . . 1.00

---

3 . . . . 1.00
4 November, 1990. . . . . 1.00

BUCK DUCK
Atlas June, 1953
1 (fa)stories. 60.00
2 and 3 . . . . @25.00
4 Dec., 1953 . . . . 25.00

BUCKAROO BANZAI
Dec., 1984
1 Movie Adaption. 3.00
2 Conclusion, Feb., 1985. . . . . . . 2.00

Bug #1
© Marvel Entertainment Group

BUG
1997
1-shot 48pg. 3.00

BULLWINKLE & ROCKY
Star Nov., 1987
1 EC&AM,Based on 1960's TV
   Series 3.00
2 EC&AM, ... 2.00
3 EC&AM,Rumpled Mudluck
   Thyme Mag 2.00
4 EC&AM,Boris and Natasha. . . . 2.00
5 EC&AM, ... 2.00
6 EC&AM,Wassamatta Me 2.00
7 EC&AM,Politics,Moose V:Boris . . 2.00
8 EC&AM,Superhero, March,1989 . 2.00
9 EC 2.00
TPB, Bullwinkle & Rocky Collection
   AM,early stories 4.95

CABLE
[Limited Series] 1992
1 JR2,DGr,V:Mutant Liberation
   Front,A:Weapon X 4.00
2 JR2,DGr,V:Stryfe,O:Weapon X . . 3.00
[Regular Series] May 1993
1 B:FaN(s),ATi,O:Cable,V:New
   Canaanites,A:Stryfe,foil(c) 5.00
2 ATi,V:Stryfe 2.50
3 ATi,A:Six Pack 2.25
4 ATi,A:Six Pack 2.25
5 DaR,V:Sinsear 2.25
6 DT,A:Tyler,Zero,Askani,
   Mr.Sinister,C:X-Men 2.50
7 V:Tyler,A:Askani,X-Men,Domino . 2.50
8 O:Cable,V:Tyler,A:X-Men,Cable is

Nathan Summers 2.50
9 MCW,B:Killing Field,A:Excalibur,
 V:Omega Red 2.25
10 MCW,A:Acolytes,Omega Red . . 2.25
11 MCW,E:Killing Field,D:Katu 2.25
12 SLo(s),B:Fear & Loathing,
 V:Senyaka 2.25
13 V:D'Spayre 2.00
14 V:S'yM 2.25
15 A:Thorn 2.25
16 Foil(c),Dbl-size,A:Jean,Scott
 Logan,V:Phalanx 7.00
16a Newsstand ed 2.50
17 Deluxe ed 2.25
17a Newsstand ed 1.50
18 Deluxe ed 2.25
18a Newsstand ed 1.50
19 Deluxe ed 2.25
19a Newsstand ed 1.50
20 V:Legion, Deluxe ed. w/card . . . 4.00
20a Newsstand ed 1.50
21 Cable makes tough decisions,
 A:Domino 2.25
22 V:Fortress 2.25
23 IaC,A:Domino 2.25
24 F:Blaquesmith 2.00
25 IaC,SHa,F:Cable's Wife,foil(c) . . 5.00
26 Tries to return to X-Mansion . . . 2.00
27 IaC, A:Domino 2.00
28 IaC,SHa,concl. war in Genosha . 2.00
29 . . . . 2.00
30 . . . . 2.00
31 IaC, cont.X-Men/Cable war 2.00
32 Onslaught saga 3.00
33 Onslaught saga 3.00
34 Onslaught saga 3.00
35 Onslaught saga 2.00
36 . . . . 2.00
37 JLb,IaC,SHa,V:Askani'son,Kane 2.00
38 JLb,IaC,SHa,V:PSycho-Man,
 A:Kane 2.00
39 JLb,IaC,SHa,V:Psycho-Man 2.00
40 TDz,IaC,SHa,V:Renee Majcomb 2.00
41 TDz,SHa,F:Bishop 2.00
42 TDz,RGr,SHa,"The Prophecy
 of the Twelve" 2.00
43 TDz,RGr,Images of Nathan's
 past 2.00
44 TDz,RGr,SHa,A:Madelyne Pryor
 (Cable's mom) 2.00
45 JeR,RGr,Zero Tolerance,
 "No Escape,"pt.2 . . . . 2.00
46 JeR,RGr,SHa,Zero Tolerance,
 "No Escape", pt.2 (of 3) 2.00
47 JeR,RGr,SHa, Operation Zero
 Tolerance, V:Batsion 2.00
48 JeR,SHa,V:Hellfire Club 2.00
49 JeR,SHa,V:Hellfire Club 2.00
50 JeR,SHa,A:Cyclops, Phoenix,
 Union Jack, 48pg 3.00
51 JeR,Hellfire Hunt 2.00
52 JeR,Hellfire Hunt, pt.5 . . . . 2.00
53 JoC,Hellfire Hunt, concl. 2.00
54 JoC,A:Black Panther,V:Klaw . . . 2.00
55 JoC,A:Irene Merryweather,
 Domino 2.00
56 JoC,V:Stilt-Man & Hydro-Man . . 2.00
57 JoC,Cable powers altered by
 EMP wave 2.00
58 JoC,Persecution, pt.1 . . . . 2.00
59 JoC,I:Agent 18,V:Zzaxx 2.00
60 JoC,Nemesis Contract,pt.2 . . . . 2.00
61 JoC,Nemesis Contract,pt.3 . . . . 2.00
62 JoC,Nemesis Contract,pt.4 . . . . 2.00
63 JoC,Blood Brothers,pt.2,x-over . 2.00
64 JoC,O:Cable 2.00
65 JoC,Millennium countdown 2.00
66 JoC,Sign of the End Times,pt.1 . 2.00
67 JoC,Sign of the End Times,pt.2 . 2.00
68 JoC,Sign of the End Times,pt.3 . 2.00
69 JoC,A:Blaquesmith,Archangel . . 2.00

70 JoC,A:Archangel 2.00
71 RLd,abandons his destiny,
 with RLd poster 2.00
72 RLd,reunited with X-force 2.00
Ann. '98 AOI(c) F:Cable vs. Machine
 Man, O:Bastion 3.00
Ann.1999 48-page 3.50
Minus 1 Spec., TDz,JeR, flashback. 1.95
GN Cable/Wolverine Guts 'N' Glory. 6.00
Cable: Second Genesis 4.00
TPB Cable,rep.New Mutants
 #87-94 . . . . 15.95

CABLE & X-FORCE
Cable & X-Force '95 Spec 3.95
Cable & X-Force '96 Spec.48pg 3.00
Cable & X-Force '97 Spec.#1
 JFM,CJ,V:Malekith,48pg 3.00

CADILLACS & DINOSAURS
Epic Nov., 1990
1 Rep.Xenozoic Tales 3.00
2 Rep.Xenozoic Tales 2.50
3 Rep.Xenozoic Tales 2.50
4 Rep.Xenozoic Tales 2.50
5 Rep.Xenozoic Tales 2.50
6 Rep.Xenozoic Tales, April,1991 . 2.50

CAGE
1992–93
1 DT,R:Luke Cage,I:Hardcore, ... 2.50
2 DT,V:Hammer 1.50
3 DT,A:Punisher,V:Untouchables . . 1.50
4 DT,A:Punisher,V:Untouchables . . 1.50
5 DT,I:New Power Man 1.50
6 DT,V:New Power Man 1.50
7 DT,A:Avengers West Coast 1.50
8 DT,V:Steele,Wonder Man 1.50
9 V:Rhino,A:Hulk 1.50
10 DT,V:Hulk,Rhino 1.50
11 DT,V:Rapidfire 1.50
12 A:Iron Fist,double size 2.00
13 V:The Thinker 1.50
14 PCu,I:Coldfire 1.50
15 DT,For Love Nor Money#2,
 A:Silver Sable,Terror. 1.50
16 DT,For Love Nor Money#5,
 A:Silver Sable,Terror. 1.50
17 DT,Infinty Crusade 1.50
18 A:Dred,V:Creed 1.50

Cage #5
© *Marvel Entertainment Group*

19 A:Dakota North 1.50
20 Last issue 1.50

CAMP CANDY
May, 1990
1 thru 6, Oct. 1990 . . . . @1.00

CAPTAIN AMERICA COMICS
Timely/Atlas May, 1941
1 S&K,Hitler(c),I&O:Capt.America &
 Bucky,A:Red Skull,B:Hurricane,
 Tuk the Caveboy 55,000.00
2 S&K,RC,AAv,Hitler(c),
 I:Circular Shield;Trapped
 in the Nazi Stronghold . . 10,000.00
3 S&K,RC,AAv,Stan Lee's 1st Text,
 A:Red Skull,Bondage(c) . . 8,500.00
4 S&K,AAv,Horror Hospital . . . 5,000.00
5 S&K,AAv,Ringmaster's
 Wheel of Death 4,500.00
6 S&K,AAv,O:Father Time,
 E:Tuk 4,000.00
7 S&K,A: Red Skull 4,500.00
8 S&K, The Tomb 4,000.00
9 S&K,RC,V:Black Talon 3,500.00
10 S&K,RC,Chamber
 of Horrors 3,500.00
11 AAv,E:Hurricane;Feuding
 Mountaineers 3,000.00
12 AAv,B:Imp,E:Father Time;
 Pygmie's Terror 2,800.00
13 AAv,O:Secret Stamp;All Out
 For America 3,000.00
14 AAv,V:Japs;Pearl Harbor
 Symbol cover 2,800.00
15 AAv,Den of Doom 2,800.00
16 AAv,A:R.Skull;CapA
 Unmasked 3,500.00
17 AAv,I:Fighting Fool;
 Graveyard 2,500.00
18 AAv,V:Japanese 2,200.00
19 AAv,V:Ghouls,
 B:Human Torch 1,800.00
20 AAv,A:Sub-Mariner,V:Nazis . 1,800.00
21 SSh(c),Bucky Captured 1,700.00
22 SSh(c),V:Japanese 1,700.00
23 SSh(c),V:Nazis 1,700.00
24 SSh(c),V:Black
 Dragon Society 1,700.00
25 SSh(c),V:Japs;Drug Story . . 1,700.00
26 ASh(c),V:Nazi Fleet 1,600.00
27 ASh(c)CapA&Russians
 V:Nazis, E:Secret Stamp . . 1,600.00
28 ASh(c),NaziTortureChamber 1,600.00
29 ASh(c),V:Nazis;French
 Underground 1,600.00
30 SSh(c),Bucky Captured 1,600.00
31 ASh(c),Bondage(c) 1,500.00
32 SSh(c),V: Japanese Airforce 1,500.00
33 ASh(c),V:Nazis;BrennerPass 1,500.00
34 SSh(c),Bondage(c) 1,500.00
35 SSh(c),CapA in Japan 1,500.00
36 SSh(c),V:Nazis;Hitler(c) 2,000.00
37 ASh(c),CapA in Berlin,
 A:Red Skull 1,600.00
38 ASh(c),V:Japs;Bondage(c) . 1,400.00
39 ASh(c),V:Japs;Boulder Dam 1,400.00
40 SSh(c),V:Japs;Ammo Depot 1,400.00
41 ASh(c),FinalJapaneseWar(c) 1,300.00
42 ASh(c),V:Bank Robbers . . . 1,300.00
43 ASh(c),V:Gangsters 1,300.00
44 ASh(c),V:Gangsters 1,300.00
45 ASh(c),V:Bank Robbers . . . 1,300.00
46 ASh(c),Holocaust(c) 1,300.00
47 ASh(c),Final Nazi War(c) . . . 1,300.00
48 ASh(c),V:Robbers 1,200.00
49 ASh(c),V:Sabatuers 1,200.00
50 ASh(c),V:Gorilla Gang 1,300.00

51 ASh(c),V:Gangsters 1,200.00
52 ASh(c),V:AtomBombThieves 1,200.00
53 ASh(c),V:Burglars 1,200.00
54 ASh(c),TV Studio,
    V:Gangsters 1,200.00
55 V:Counterfeiters 1,200.00
56 SSh(c),V:Art Theives...... 1,200.00
57 Symbolic CapA(c) 1,200.00
58 ASh(c),V:Bank Robbers .. 1,200.00
59 SSh(c)O:CapA Retold;Private
    Life of Captain America ... 2,500.00
60 V:The Human Fly 1,200.00
61 SSh(c),V:Red Skull;
    Bondage(c) 1,900.00
62 SSh(c),Kingdom of Terror . 1,200.00
63 SSh(c),I&O:Asbestos Lady;
    The Parrot Strikes 1,300.00
64 Diamonds Spell Doom 1,200.00
65 When Friends Turn Foes... 1,200.00
66 O:Golden Girl;Bucky Shot . 1,400.00
67 E:Toro(in Human Torch);
    Golden Girl Team-Up..... 1,200.00
68 A:Golden Girl;Riddle of
    the Living Dolls 1,200.00
69 Weird Tales of the Wee
    Males, A:Sun Girl........ 1,200.00
70 A:Golden Girl,Sub-Mariner,
    Namora;Worlds at War.... 1,200.00
71 A:Golden Girl; Trapped ... 1,200.00
72 Murder in the Mind 1,200.00
73 The Outcast of Time 1,200.00
74 A:Red Skull;Capt.America's
    Weird Tales 3,800.00
75 Thing in the Chest........ 1,200.00
76 JR(c),Capt.America,Commie
    Smasher 1,200.00
77 Capt.A,Commie Smasher.... 800.00
78 JR(c),V:Communists;
    Sept.,1954 .... 800.00
Marvel Milestone rep. #1 (1995) ... 3.95

CAPTAIN AMERICA
Prev: Tales of Suspense
April, 1968

100 JK,A:Avengers 300.00
101 JK,I:4th Sleeper........... 75.00
102 JK,V:Red Skull,4th Sleeper .. 40.00
103 JK,V:Red Skull.............. 40.00
104 JK,DA,JSo,V:Red Skull 40.00
105 JK,DA,A:Batroc 40.00
106 JK,Cap.Goes Wild 40.00
107 JK,Red Skull 40.00
108 JK,Trapster 40.00
109 JK,O:Captain America 50.00
110 JSo,JSt,A:Hulk, Rick Jones
    in Bucky Costume 55.00
111 JSo,JSt,I:Man Killer 55.00
112 JK,GT,Album 35.00
113 JSo,TP,Avengers,
    D:Madame Hydra......... 55.00
114 JR,SB,C:Avengers 20.00
115 JB,SB,A:Red Skull 20.00
116 GC,JSt,A:Avengers 20.00
117 JR(c),GC,JSt,I:Falcon 50.00
118 JR(c),GC,JSt,A:Falcon 20.00
119 GC,JSt,O:Falcon 20.00
120 GC,JSt,A:Falcon 20.00
121 GC,JSt,V:Man Brute........ 15.00
122 GC,JSt,Scorpion 12.00
123 GC,JSt,A:NickFury,
    V:Suprema............. 12.00
124 GC,JSt,I:Cyborg........... 12.00
125 GC,Mandarin 12.00
126 JK&BEv(c),GC,A:Falcon ... 12.00
127 GC,WW,A:Nick Fury 12.00
128 GC,V:Satan's Angels 12.00
129 GC,Red Skull............. 12.00
130 GC,I:Batroc 15.00
131 GC,V:Hood 11.00
132 GC,A:Bucky Barnes 11.00

Captain America #132
© *Marvel Entertainment Group*

133 GC,O:Modok,B:Capt.America/
    Falcon Partnership 11.00
134 GC,V:Stone Face........... 11.00
135 JR(c),GC,TP,A:Nick Fury 11.00
136 GC,BEv,V:Tyrannus 11.00
137 GC,BEv,A:Spider-Man 13.00
138 JR,A:Spider-Man 12.00
139 JR,Falcon solo............ 9.00
140 JR,O:Grey Gargoyle 9.00
141 JR,JSt,V:Grey Gargoyle..... 7.00
142 JR,JSt,Nick Fury 7.00
143 JR,Red Skull 10.00
144 GM,JR,N:Falcon,V:Hydra.... 7.00
145 GK,JR,V:Hydra 7.00
146 JR(c),SB,V:Hydra.......... 6.00
147 GK(c),SB,V:Hydra 6.00
148 SB,JR,Red Skull 6.00
149 GK(c),SB,JM,V:Batroc 6.00
150 K&R(c),SB,V:The Stranger.... 6.00
151 SB,V:Mr.Hyde............. 6.00
152 SB,V:Scorpion,Mr.Hyde 6.00
153 SB,JM,V:50's Cap 6.00
154 SB,V:50's Cap 6.00
155 SB,FMc,O:50's Cap 6.00
156 SB,FMc,V:50's Cap 6.00
157 SB,I:The Viper 6.00
158 SB,V:The Viper 6.00
159 SB,V:PlantMan,Porcupine 6.00
160 SB,FMc,V:Solarr.......... 6.00
161 SB,V:Dr.Faustus 6.00
162 JSn(c),SB,V:Dr.Faustus 6.00
163 SB,I:Serpent Squad........ 7.00
164 JR(c),I:Nightshade 7.00
165 SB,FMc,V:Yellow Claw...... 6.00
166 SB,FMc,V:Yellow Claw...... 6.00
167 SB,V:Yellow Claw 6.00
168 SB,I&O:Phoenix
    (2nd Baron Zemo) 7.00
169 SB,FMc,C:Black Panther 6.00
170 K&R(c),SB,C:Black Panther... 6.00
171 JR(c),SB,A:Black Panther ... 6.00
172 GK(c),SB,C:X-Men........ 15.00
173 GK(c),SB,A:X-Men......... 16.00
174 GK(c),SB,A:X-Men......... 16.00
175 SB,A:X-Men............. 16.00
176 JR(c),SB,O:Capt.America 8.00
177 JR(c),SB,A:Lucifer,Beast 6.00
178 SB,A:Lucifer 6.00
179 SB,A:Hawkeye............ 6.00
180 GK(c),SB,I:1st Nomad(Cap).. 8.00
181 GK(c),SB,I&O:New Cap 7.00
182 FR,Madam Hydra 7.00
183 GK(c),FR,R:Cap,D:New Cap . 8.00
184 K&R(c),HT,A:Red Skull 5.00

Captain America #237
© *Marvel Entertainment Group*

185 GK(c),SB,FR,V:Red Skull..... 5.00
186 GK(c),FR,O:Falcon 6.00
187 K&R(c),FR,V:Druid.......... 5.00
188 GK(c),SB,V:Druid.......... 5.00
189 GK(c),FR,V:Nightshade 5.00
190 GK(c),FR,A:Nightshade 5.00
191 FR,A:Stilt Man,N.Fury 5.00
192 JR(c),FR,A:Dr.Faustus...... 5.00
193 JR(c),JK,`Mad Bomb'........ 5.00
194 JK,I:Gen.Heshin............ 5.00
195 JK,1984................. 5.00
196 JK,Madbomb............. 5.00
197 JK,Madbomb............. 5.00
198 JK,Madbomb............. 5.00
199 JK,Madbomb............. 5.00
200 JK,Madbomb............. 7.00
201 JK,Epilogue.............. 4.00
202 JK,Night People........... 4.00
203 JK,Night People........... 4.00
204 JK,I:Argon 4.00
205 JK,V:Argon 4.00
206 JK,I:Swine 4.00
207 JK,V:Swine 4.00
208 JK,I:Arnim Zola,D:Swine 4.00
209 JK,O:Arnim Zola,I:Primus 4.00
210 JK,A:Red Skull........... 4.00
211 JK,A:Red Skull........... 4.00
212 JK,A:Red Skull........... 4.00
213 JK,I:Night Flyer 4.00
214 JK,D:Night Flyer 4.00
215 GT,Redwing 4.00
216 Reprint,JK 4.00
217 JB, I:Quasar(Marvel Boy)
    I:Vamp................ 5.00
218 SB,A:Iron Man............ 4.00
219 SB,JSt,V:TheCorporation.... 4.00
220 SB,D:L.Dekker............ 4.00
221 SB,Ameridroid 4.00
222 SB,I:Animus(Vamp)........ 4.00
223 SB,Animus.............. 4.00
224 MZ,V:Animus............ 4.00
225 SB,A:Nick Fury 4.00
226 SB,A:Nick Fury 4.00
227 SB,A:Nick Fury 4.00
228 SB,Constrictor 4.00
229 SB,R:SuperAgents of Shield .. 4.00
230 SB,A:Hulk.............. 4.00
231 SB,DP,A:Grand Director...... 4.00
232 SB,DP,V:Grand Director...... 4.00
233 SB,DP,D:Sharon Carter 4.00
234 SB,DP,A:Daredevil......... 4.00
235 SB,FM,A:Daredevil 4.00
236 SB,V:Dr.Faustus 4.00
237 SB,`From the Ashes' 4.00

238 SB,V:Hawk Riders 4.00	312 PNe,I:Flag Smasher. 2.00	357 KD,AM,V:Sisters of Sin
239 JBy(c),SB,V:Hawk Riders. 4.00	313 PNe,D:Modok 2.00	Baron Zemo,Batroc 2.00
240 SB,V:A Guy Named Joe. 4.00	314 PNe,A:Nighthawk. 2.00	358 KD,B:Blood Stone Hunt 2.00
241 A:Punisher. 9.00	315 PNe,V:Serpent Society 2.00	359 KD,V:Zemo,C:Crossbones 2.00
242 JSt,A:Avengers 3.00	316 PNe,A:Hawkeye. 2.00	360 KD,I:Crossbones 2.00
243 GP(c),RB,V:Adonis 3.00	317 PNe,I:Death-Throws 2.00	361 KD,V:Zemo,Batroc 2.00
244 TS,`A Monster Berserk' 3.00	318 PNe,V&D:Blue Streak 2.00	362 KD,V:Zemo,Crossbones. 2.00
245 CI,JRn,Nazi Hunter 3.00	319 PNe,V:Scourge,D:Vamp 2.00	363 KD,E:Blood Stone Hunt,
246 GP(c),JBi,V:Joe 3.00	320 PNe,V:Scourge 2.00	V:Crossbones,C:Wolverine 2.00
247 JBy,V:BaronStrucker 4.00	321 PNe,V:Flagsmasher,	364 KD,V:Crossbones 2.00
248 JBy,JRu,Dragon Man 4.00	I:Ultimatum. 2.00	365 KD,Acts of Vengeance,
249 JBy,O:Machinesmith,	322 PNe,V:Flagsmasher. 2.00	V:SubMariner,Red Skull 2.00
A:Air-Walker. 4.00	323 PNe,I:Super Patriot	366 1st RLm Capt.Amer.,Acts of
250 JBy,Cap for Pres 4.00	(US Agent) 5.00	Vengeance,V:Controller 2.00
251 JBy,V:Mr.Hyde 4.00	324 PNe,V:Whirlwind,Trapster 2.00	367 KD,Acts of Vengeance,
252 JBy,V:Batrok 4.00	325 I:Slug,A:Nomad 2.00	Magneto Vs. Red Skull. 2.50
253 JBy,V:Baron Blood. 4.00	326 V:Dr.Faustus. 2.00	368 RLm,V:Machinesmith 2.00
254 JBy,D:B.Blood,UnionJack,I:3rd	327 MZ(c)V:SuperPatriot 3.00	369 RLm,I:Skeleton Crew 2.00
Union Jack. 4.00	328 MZ(c),I:Demolition Man 2.00	370 RLm,V:Skeleton Crew 2.00
255 JBy,40th Anniv.,O:Cap 4.00	329 MZ(c),A:Demolition Man 2.00	371 RLm,V:Trump,Poundcakes. . . . 2.00
256 GC,V:Demon Druid 2.50	330 A:Night Shift,Shroud 2.00	372 RLm,B:Streets of Poison,
257 A:Hulk 2.50	331 A:Night Shift,Shroud 2.00	Cap on Drugs,C:Bullseye 2.50
258 MZ,V:Blockbuster. 2.50	332 BMc,Rogers resigns. 7.00	373 RLm,V:Bullseye,A:Bl.Widow. . . 2.00
259 MZ,V:Dr. Octopus 2.50	333 B:John Walker Becomes	374 RLm,V:Bullseye,A:Daredevil. . . 2.00
260 AM,In Jail 2.50	6th Captain America. 5.00	375 RLm,V:Daredevil. 2.00
261 MZ,A:Nomad 3.00	334 I:4th Bucky 4.00	376 RLm,A:Daredevil. 2.00
262 MZ,V:Ameridroid 2.50	335 V:Watchdogs 3.00	377 RLm,V:Crossbones,Bullseye . . 2.00
263 MZ,V:Red Skull 2.50	336 A:Falcon 2.50	378 RLm,E:Streets of Poison,Red
264 MZ,X-Men 4.00	337 TMo,I:The Captain. 2.50	Skull vs Kingpin,V:Crossbones . 2.00
265 MZ,A:Spider-Man,N.Fury 3.00	338 KD,AM,V:Professor Power . . . 2.50	379 RLm(c),V:Serpent Society 2.00
266 MZ,A:Spider-Man. 3.00	339 KD,TD,Fall of Mutants,	380 RLm,V:Serpent Society 2.00
267 MZ,V:Everyman 2.50	V:Famine 2.50	381 RLm,V:Serpent Society 2.00
268 MZ,A:Defenders(x-over from	340 KD,AM,A:Iron Man, ... 2.00	382 RLm,V:Serpent Society 2.00
Def.#106) 2.50	341 KD,AM,I:Battlestar,A:Viper 2.00	383 RLm(c),RLm,50th Anniv.
269 MZ,A:Team America 2.50	342 KD,AM,A:D-Man,Falcon,	64Pages. 4.00
270 MZ,V:Tess-One 2.50	Nomad,Viper 2.00	384 RLm,A:Jack Frost 2.00
271 MZ,V:Mr.X 2.50	343 KD,AM,A:D-Man,Falcon,	385 RLm,A:USAgent 2.00
272 MZ,I:Vermin 3.00	Nomad 2.00	386 RLm,Cap./USAgent T.U. 2.00
273 MZ,A:Nick Fury 2.50	344 KD,AM,A:D-Man,Nomad 2.50	387 B:Superia Strategem 2.00
274 MZ,D:SamSawyer 2.50	345 KD,AM,V:Watchdogs 2.00	388 A:Paladin 2.00
275 MZ,V:Neo-Nazis 2.50	346 KD,AM,V:Resistants. 2.00	389 Superia Strategem #3 . . . . 2.00
276 MZ,V:Baron Zemo 2.50	347 KD,AM,V:RWinger&LWinger . . 2.00	390 Superia Strategem #4 . . . . 2.00
277 MZ,V:Baron Zemo 2.50	348 KD,AM,V:Flag Smasher 2.00	391 Superia Strategem #5 . . . . 2.00
278 MZ,V:Baron Zemo 2.50	349 KD,AM,V:Flag Smasher 2.00	392 E:Superia Strategem 2.00
279 MZ,V:Primus 2.50	350 KD,AM,doub-size,Rogers Ret.	393 V:Captain Germany 2.00
280 MZ,V:Scarecrow 2.50	as Captain Am,V:Red Skull,	394 A:Red Skull,Diamondback 2.00
281 MZ,A:Spider Woman,	E:6th Cap 4.00	395 A:Red Skull,Crossbones 2.00
R:'50's Bucky 2.50	351 KD,AM,V:Nick Fury 2.00	396 I:2nd Jack O'Lantern 2.00
282 MZ,I:2nd Nomad 4.00	352 KD,AM,I:Supreme Soviets 2.00	397 V:Red Skull,X-Bones,Viper. . . . 2.00
282a (second primting) 2.00	353 KD,AM,V:Supreme Soviets . . . 2.00	398 Operation:Galactic Storm
283 MZ,A:Viper 4.00	354 KD,AM,I:USAgent,	Pt.1,V:Warstar 2.00
284 SB,Nomad. 3.00	V:Machinesmith 3.00	399 Operation Galactic Storm
285 MZ,V:Porcupine 3.00	355 RB,AM,A:Falcon,Battlestar. . . . 2.00	Pt.8,V:Kree Empire. 2.00
286 MZ,V:Deathlok 5.00	356 AM,V:Sisters of Sin 2.00	400 Operation Galactic Storm
287 MZ,V:Deathlok 5.00		Pt.15,BU:rep.Avengers #4 . . . . 4.00
288 MZ,V:Deathlok,D:Hellinger. . . . 5.00		401 R:D-Man,A:Avengers 2.00
289 MZ,A:Red Skull 2.50		402 RLe,B:Man & Wolf,
290 JBy(c),RF,A:Falcon 2.50		A:Wolverine 2.00
291 JBy(c),HT,V:Tumbler 2.50		403 RLe,A:Wolverine 2.00
292 I&O:Black Crow 2.50		404 RLe,A:Wolverine 2.00
293 V:Mother Superior 2.50		405 RLe,A:Wolverine 2.00
294 R:Nomad 2.50		406 RLe,A:Wolverine 2.00
295 V:Sisters of Sin 2.50		407 RLe,A:Wolverine,Cable 2.00
296 V:Baron Zemo 2.50		408 RLe,E:Man & Wolf. 1.50
297 O:Red Skull 2.50		409 RLe,V:Skeleton Crew. 1.50
298 V:Red Skull 2.50		410 RLe,V:Crossbones,Skel.Crew . 1.50
299 V:Red Skull 2.50		411 RLe,V:Snapdragon. 1.50
300 D:Red Skull 4.00		412 RLe,V:Batroc,A:Shang-Chi. . . . 1.50
301 PNe,A:Avengers 2.00		413 A:Shang-Chi,V:Superia 1.50
302 PNe,I:Machete,V:Batroc. 2.00		414 RLe,A:Kazar,Black Panther . . . 1.50
303 PNe,V:Batroc. 2.00		415 RIe,A:Black Panther,Kazar . . . 1.50
304 PNe,V:Stane Armor 2.00		416 RLe,Savage Land Mutates,
305 PNe,A:Capt.Britain,V:Modred . . 2.00		A:Black.Panther,Kazar 1.50
306 PNe,A:Capt.Britain,V:Modred . . 2.00		417 RLe,A:Black Panther,Kazar,
307 PNe,I:Madcap 2.00		V:AIM. 1.50
308 PNe,I:Armadillo,		418 RLe,V:Night People 1.50
Secret WarsII 2.00		419 RLe,V:Viper. 1.50
309 PNe,V:Madcap. 2.00		420 RLe,I:2nd Blazing Skull,
310 PNe,V:Serpent Society,I:Cotton		A:Nightshift. 3.00
Mouth,Diamondback. 2.50	*Captain #275*	421 RLe,V:Nomad 1.50
311 PNe,V:Awesome Android 2.00	© Marvel Entertainment Group	422 RLe,I:Blistik 1.50

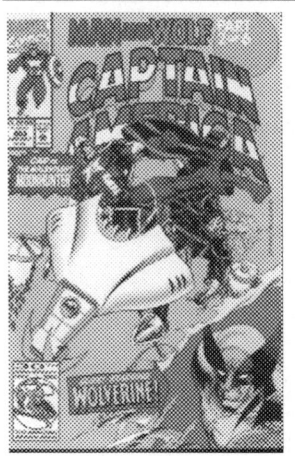

Captain America #403
© Marvel Entertainment Group

423 RTs(s),MCW,V:Namor 1.50
424 MGv(s),A:Sidewinder 1.50
425 B:MGu(s),DHv,Embossed(c),I:2nd
    Super Patriot,Dead Ringer 3.50
426 DHv,A:Super Patriot,Dead Ringer,
    V:Resistants 1.50
427 DHv,V:Super Patriot,Dead
    Ringer 1.75
428 DHv,I:Americop 1.75
429 DHv,V:Kono 1.50
430 Daemon Dran, Americop 1.75
431 DHv,I:Free Spirit 1.50
432 DHv,Fighting Chance 1.50
433 DHv,Baron Zemo 1.50
434 DHv,A:Fighting Spirit,
    V:King Cobra 1.50
435 DHv,Fighting Chance 1.50
436 V:King Cobra, Mister Hyde,
    Fighting Chance conclusion . . . 1.50
437 Cap in a Coma 1.50
438 I:New Body Armor 1.50
439 Dawn's Early Light,pt.2 . . . . . . 1.50
440 Taking A.I.M.,pt.1 . . . . 1.50
441 Taking A.I.M.,pt.3 . . . . 1.50
442 Batroc, Cap,V:Zeitgeist 1.50
443 MGu,24 hours to live 1.50
444 MWa,RG,President Kidnapped. 6.00
445 MWa,RG,R:Captain America . . 4.00
446 MWa,RG,Operation
    Rebirth,pt.2 . . . . 3.50
447 MWa,RG,Op.Rebirth,pt.3 . . . . . 3.50
448 MWa,RG,Operation
    Rebirth,pt.4,double size 6.00
449 MWa,RG,A:Thor 2.50
450 MWa,RG,Man Without a
    Country, pt,1 . . . . 2.50
450a alternate cover 4.00
451 MWa,RG,DRo,Man Without
    A Country,pt.2,new costume . . . 2.00
452 MWa,RG,Man Without a
    Country, pt.3 . . . . 2.00
453 MWa,RG Man Without a
    Country, concl.,old costume . . . 2.00
454 MWa,RG,A:Avengers 2.00
Ann.#1 rep.. . . . . 22.00
Ann.#2 rep.. . . . . 11.00
Ann.#3 JK, ... 5.00
Ann.#4 JK,V:Magneto,I:Mutant
    Force 10.00
Ann.#5 `Deathwatcher' 4.00
Ann.#6 A:Contemplator. 4.00
Ann.#7 O:Shaper of Worlds 4.00
Ann.#8 MZ,A:Wolverine 30.00
Ann.#9 MBa,SD,Terminus Factor

#1,N:Nomad. 4.50
Ann.#10 MM,Baron Strucker,pt.3
    (see Punisher Ann.#4) 2.50
Ann.#11 Citizen Kang#1 . . . . 2.50
Ann.#12 I:Bantam,w/card 3.25
Ann.#13 RTs(s),MCW, ... 3.25
Drug Wars PDd(s),SaV,A:New
    Warriors 2.00
G-Size#1 GK(c),rep.O:Cap.Amer. . . 7.00
HC vol.Slipcase Rep.#1
    thru #10 (From 1940's) 75.00
Medusa Effect RTs(s),MCW,RB,
    V:Master Man. 2.95
Movie Adapt 2.00
Spec.#1 Rep.Cap.A #110,#111 . . . 2.00
Spec.#2 Rep.Cap.A.#113
    & Strange Tales #169 . . . . 2.00
TPB Bloodstone Hunt,rep.
    #357-364 . . . . 15.95
TPB Captain America: Man Without
    a Country, MWa,RG,SK, rep.
    (1998) 15.00
TPB War and Remembrance,
    rep. #247-#255 . . . . 12.95
Collector's Preview 1.95
Ashcan 75

[2nd Series] Nov. 1996

1 RLd,CDi,JSb, Heroes Reborn,
    I:Nick Fury,48pg. 5.00
1A Stars and stripes background
    variant cover 7.50
1b gold signature edition,
    cardstock cover 18.00
1c San Diego Con edition 25.00
2 RLd,JLb,JSb,Falcon & Red Skull 3.00
3 RLd,JLb,JSb,A:Hulk,V:Red Skull
    & Master Man. 2.50
4 RLd,JLb,JSb,F:Prince Namor,. . . 2.50
5 RLd,JLb,JSb,V:Crossbones 2.50
6 RLd,JLb,JSb,"Industrial
    Revolution," epilogue,A:Cable. . 2.50
7 RLd,JLb,DaF, ... 2.00
8 RLd,JLb,SPa,A:Nick Fury,
    WWII story 2.00
9 JLb,RLd,SPa,WWII story. 2.00
10 JLb,RLd,SPa,WWII story, concl.. 2.00
11 JeR,JoB,Odyssey across
    America, pt.4, concl. 2.00
12 JeR,JoB,Heroes Reborn, Galactus
    concl. 3.00
13 JeR,RLm,Wildstorm x-over 2.50
Ashcan, ComicCon. 5.00

[3rd Series] Nov. 1997

1 MWa,RG,BWi,A:Lady Deathstrike,
    Red Skull, Sharon Carter, 48pg 3.00
1a variant cover. 15.00
2 MWa,RG,BWi,A devastating loss 5.00
2a variant cover. 4.00
3 MWa,RG,BWi,V:Hydra 4.00
4 MWa,RG,BWi,F:Batroc 3.00
5 MWa,RG,BWi,V:Hordes of Hydra 3.00
6 MWa,RG,V:Skrulls 3.00
7 MWa,NKu,Power & Glory concl. . 2.00
8 MWa,Nku,Live Kree or Die, pt.2
    x-over. 3.50
9 MWa,NKu,American Nightmare,
    pt.1 . . . . 3.00
10 MWa,NKu,American Nightmare,
    pt.2 . . . . 3.00
11 MWa,NKu,American
    Nightmare, pt.3. . . . . 3.00
12 MWa,NKu,American Night-
    mare, pt.4, 48-page 3.00
13 MWa,MFm,R:Red Skull 2.00
14 MWa,MFm,R:Red Skull 2.00
15 MWa,NKu,V:Red Skull 2.00
16 MWa,NKu,V:Red Skull 2.00
17 MWa,NKu,V:Red Skull 2.00
18 MWa,LW,RbC,V:Cosmic Cube
    double sized. 3.00

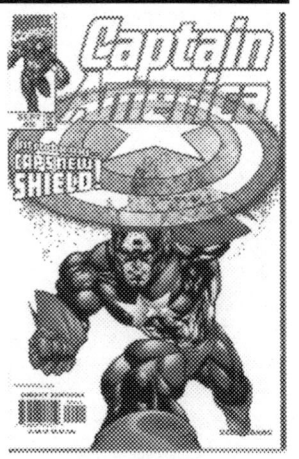

Captain America 3rd Series, #9
© Marvel Entertainment Group

19 MWa,NKu,V:2 foes 2.00
20 MWa,NKu,Shield secrets 2.00
21 MWa,NKu,A:Black Panther 2.00
22 MWa,NKu,A:Black Panther 2.00
Ann.1998 Captain America/
    Citizen V,KBk,KK, 48-page 3.50
Ann. 1999 JoC,V:Flag Smasher,
    48-page 3.50

CAPTAIN AMERICA: SENTINEL OF LIBERTY
July 1998

1 MWa,RG,new foe, in future. 2.00
1 signed by MWa & RG 5.00
2A MWa,RG(c&a) F:Invaders,
    V:Nazis 2.00
2B variant JSm(c) 2.00
3 MWa,RG,DGr,A:Sub-Mariner . . . 2.00
4 MWa,RG,DGr,A:Human Torch. . . 2.00
5 MWa,RG,MFm,Tales of
    Suspense pt.1 . . . . 2.00
6 MWa,RG,MFm,Tales of
    Suspense pt.2 . . . . 3.00
7 RSt,RF,civil war tale concl. 2.00
8 MWa,R:Falcon 2.00
9 MWa,A:Falcon 2.00
10 psychedelic look back 2.00
11 MWa,A:Human Torch 2.00
12 MWa,DGr,F:Bucky,48-page 3.00
Spec.RoughCut #1,MWa,RG,48-pg. 3.00

CAPTAIN BRITAIN CLASSICS

1 AD rep.. . . . . 2.50

CAPTAIN CONFEDERACY
Epic Nov., 1991

1 I:Capt.Confederacy,Kid Dixie . . . 2.25
2 Meeting of Superhero Reps 2.25
3 Framed for Murder 2.25
4 Superhero conference,final iss.. . 2.25

CAPTAIN JUSTICE
March, 1988

1 Based on TV Series 1.00
2 April, 1988 . . . . 1.00

CAPTAIN MARVEL
May, 1968
1 GC,O:retold,V:Sentry#459 .... 75.00
2 GC,V:Super Skrull 25.00
3 GC,V:Super Skrull 25.00
4 GC,Sub-Mariner 20.00
5 DH,I:Metazoid. 20.00
6 DH,I:Solam. 12.00
7 JR(c),DH,V:Quasimodo. 12.00
8 DH,I:Cuberex 12.00
9 DH,D:Cuberex 12.00
10 DH,V:Number 1 .... 12.00
11 BWS(c),I:Z0 .... 12.00
12 K&R(c),I:Man-Slayer 9.00
13 FS,V:Man-Slayer 9.00
14 FS,Iron Man 9.00
15 TS,DA,Z0 .... 8.00
16 DH,Ronan 8.00
17 GK,DA,O:R.Jones ret,N:Capt.
  Marvel 9.00
18 GK,JB,DA,I:Mandroid. 8.00
19 GK,DA,Master.of.MM 8.00
20 GK,DA,I:Rat Pack 8.00
21 GK,DA,Hulk. 8.00
22 GK(c),WB,V:Megaton. 8.00
23 GK(c),WB,FMc,V:Megaton..... 8.00

Captain Marvel #24
© Marvel Entertainment Group

24 GK(c),WB,ECh,I:L.Mynde 8.00
25 1st JSn,Cap.Marvel,Cosmic
  Cube Saga Begins 15.00
26 JSn,DC,Thanos(2ndApp.)
  A:Thing 20.00
27 JSn,V:Thanos,A:Mentor,
  Starfox, I:Death 12.00
28 JSn,DGr,Thanos Vs.Drax,
  A:Avengers 12.00
29 JSn,AM,O:Zeus,C:Thanos
  I:Eon,C:Mentor. 9.00
30 JSn,AM,Controller,C:Thanos ... 9.00
31 JSn,AM,Avengers,
  Thanos,Drax,Mentor. 9.00
32 JSn,AM,DGr,O:Drax,
  Moondragon,A:Thanos 9.00
33 JSn,KJ,E:Cosmic Cube Saga
  1st D:Thanos. 12.00
34 JSn,JA,V:Nitro(leads to
  his Death) 7.00
35 GK(c),AA,Ant Man. 5.00
36 AM,Watcher,Rep.CM#1 ...... 5.00
37 AM,KJ,Nimrod 5.00
38 AM,KJ,Watcher 5.00
39 AM,KJ,Watcher 5.00
40 AM,AMc,Watcher. 5.00
41 AM,BWr,CR,BMc,TA,Kree 4.00
42 AM,V:Stranger,C:Drax 4.00

43 AM,V:Drax. 4.00
44 GK(c),AM,V:Drax 4.00
45 AM,I:Rambu 4.00
46 AM,TA,D:Fawn 4.00
47 AM,TA,A:Human Torch 4.00
48 AM,TA,I:Chetah. 4.00
49 AM,V:Ronan,A:Cheetah. 4.00
50 AM,TA,Avengers,
  V:Super Adaptiod. 3.00
51 AM,TA,V:Mercurio,4-D Man ... 3.00
52 AM,TA,V:Phae-dor. 3.00
53 AM,TA,A:Inhumans 3.00
54 PB,V:Nitro 3.00
55 PB,V:Death-grip. 3.00
56 PB,V:Death-grip. 3.00
57 PB,V:Thor,A;Thanos 5.00
58 PB,Drax/Titan 3.00
59 PB,Drax/Titan,I:Stellarax 3.00
60 PB,Drax/Titan 3.00
61 PB,V:Chaos. 3.00
62 PB,V:Stellarax 3.00
G-Size #1 reprints 8.00

CAPTAIN MARVEL
1989
1 MBr,I:Powerkeg,V:Moonstone... 3.00
1 DyM(s),MBr,V:Skinhead(1993) .. 2.00
PF Death of Captain Marvel 7.95
TPB Life of Captain Marvel,JSn .. 14.95

CAPTAIN MARVEL
1995
1 FaN,R:Captain Marvel(son of)... 3.00
2 FaN,V:X-Treme,Erik the Red ... 3.00
3 FaN,V:X-treme 3.00
4 thru 6 FaN .... @3.00

CAPTAIN PLANET
Oct., 1991
1 I&O:Captain Planet. 2.00
2 V:Dr.Blights' Smog Monster 2.00
3 V:Looten Plunder 2.00
4 `Pollutionland'. 2.00
5 V:Duke Nukem. 2.00
6 A:Capt.Pollution,Eco-Villains.... 2.00
7 thru 9 .... @2.00
10 V:Litterbug. 2.00
11 BHi,V:Greedly 2.00
12 V:Looten Plunder,last issue ... 2.00

CAPT. SAVAGE & HIS
LEATHERNECK RAIDERS
Jan., 1968
1 SSh(c),C:Sgt Fury;The Last
  Bansai 35.00
2 SSh(c),O:Hydra;Return of Baron
  Strucker 20.00
3 SSh,Two Against Hydra 20.00
4 SSh,V:Hydra;The Fateful Finale 20.00
5 SSh,The Invincible Enemy 20.00
6 Mission;Save a Howler 20.00
7 SSh,Objective:Ben Grimm 22.00
8 Mission:Foul Ball 20.00
Becomes:

CAPT. SAVAGE & HIS
BATTLEFIELD RAIDERS
9 .... 6.00
10 To the Last Man. 5.00
11 A:Sergeant Fury. 5.00
12 V:The Japanese 3.75
13 The Junk Heap Juggernauts ... 5.00
14 Savage's First Mission. 5.00
15 Within the Temple Waits Death . 5.00
16 V:The Axis Powers 5.00
17 V:The Axis Powers 5.00
18 V:The Axis Powers 5.00

19 March, 1970 .... 5.00

CARE BEARS
Star Nov., 1985
1 .... 2.00
2 thru 14 .... @2.00

Marvel
15 thru 20 .... @2.00

CARNAGE
1-shot Carnage: Its a Wonderful
  Life (1996) 2.00
1-shot Carnage: Mindbomb
  foil cover (1996). 2.95

CARTOON KIDS
Atlas 1957
1 A:Dexter the Demon,Little
  Zelda,Willie,Wise Guy. 50.00

CAR WARRIORS
Epic 1990
1 Based on Roll Playing Game ... 2.25
2 Big Race Preparations 2.25
3 Ft.Deloran-Lansing Race begin. 2.25
4 Race End, Final issue. 2.25

CASEY–CRIME
PHOTOGRAPHER
August, 1949
1 Ph(c),Girl on the Docks. 150.00
2 Ph(c),Staats Cotsworth. 100.00
3 Ph(c),He Walked With Danger 100.00
4 Ph(c),Lend Me Your Life 100.00
Becomes:

TWO GUN WESTERN
[1st Series]
5 JB,B,I&O:Apache Kid 150.00
6 The Outcast 100.00
7 Human Sacrifice 100.00
8 JR,DW,A:Kid Colt,Texas Kid,
  Doc Holiday 100.00
9 A:Kid Colt,Marshall"Frosty"
  Bennet Texas Kid 100.00
10. .... 100.00
11 thru 14 June, 1952 .... @75.00

CASPER
1996
1 From Animated TV show 1.50
2 visit to Harvey Castle 1.50
3 and 4 .... 1.00

CAT, THE
Nov., 1972—June 1973
1 JM,I&O:The Cat 22.00
2 JM,V:The Owl 15.00
3 BEv,V:Kraken 15.00
4 JSn,V:Man-Bull 15.00

CENTURY:
DISTANT SONS
1996
1-shot DAn,48pg. 2.95

CHAMBER OF CHILLS
Nov., 1972
1 SSh,A Dragon Stalks By
  Night,(H.Ellison Adapt.) 25.00
2 FB,BEv,SD,Monster From the
  Mound,(RE Howard Adapt.) .. 15.00

3 FB,BEv,SD, Thing on the Roof . 15.00
4 FB,BEv,SD, Opener of the
    Crypt,(J.Jakes,E.A.Poe Adapt) 15.00
5 FB,BEv,SD, Devils Dowry 15.00
6 FB,BEv,SD, Mud Monster 15.00
7 thru 24 FB,BEv,SD . . . . @15.00
25 FB,BEv,SD November, 1976 . . 15.00

Chamber of Darkness #2
© Marvel Entertainment Group

CHAMBER OF DARKNESS
Oct., 1969
1 JB, Tales of Maddening Magic . 50.00
2 NA(script),Enter the Red Death. 25.00
3 JK,BWS,JB, Something Lurks
    on Shadow Mountain 30.00
4 JK Monster Man Came Walking,
    BU:BWS. 60.00
5 JCr,JK,SD, And Fear Shall
    Follow, plus Lovecraft adapt. . 20.00
6 SD 20.00
7 SD,JK,BWr, Night of the
    Gargoyle 35.00
8 DA,BEv, Beast that Walks Like
    a Man Special, 5 Tales of
    Maddening Magic,Jan. 1972. . 20.00
Becomes:

MONSTERS ON
THE PROWL
9 SAD,BWS,Monster Stories
    Inc,Gorgilla. 25.00
10 JK,Roc 15.00
11 JK,A Titan Walks the Land 15.00
12 HT,JK,Gomdulla The Living
    Pharoah 15.00
13 HT,JK,Tragg. 15.00
14 JK,SD,Return of the Titan 15.00
15 FrG,JK,The Thing Called It . . . 15.00
16 JSe,SD,JK, Serpent God of
    Lost Swamp,A:King Kull 15.00
17 JK,SD,Coming of Colossus . . . 15.00
18 JK,SD,Bruttu 15.00
19 JK,SD,Creature From the
    Black Bog. 15.00
20 JK,SD,Oog Lives Again 15.00
21 JK,SD,A Martian Stalks
    the City 15.00
22 JK,SD,Monster Runs Amok . . . 12.00
23 JK,The Return of Grogg. 12.00
24 JK,SD, Magnetor 12.00
25 JK,Colossus Lives Again 12.00
26 JK,SD,The Two Headed Thing . 12.00
27 JK,Sserpo 12.00
28 JK,The Coming of Monsteroso. 12.00
29 JK,SD Monster at my Window . 12.00

30 JK,Diablo Demon from the 5th
    Dimension, Oct., 1974 . . . . . . 12.00

CHAMPIONS
June, 1986
1 GK(c),DH,I&O:Champions 20.00
2 DH,O:Champions 14.00
3 GT,Assault on Olympus 13.00
4 GT,`Murder at Malibu' 12.00
5 DH,I:Rampage 12.00
6 JK(c),GT,V:Rampage 12.00
7 GT,O:Black Widow,I:Darkstar . . 12.00
8 BH,O:Black Widow 12.00
9 BH,BL,V:Crimson Dynamo 12.00
10 BH,BL,V:Crimson Dynamo 12.00
11 JBy,A:Black Goliath,Hawkeye. . 13.00
12 JBy,BL,V:Stranger 13.00
13 JBy,BL,V:Kamo Tharn 13.00
14 JBy,I:Swarm 13.00
15 JBy,V:Swarm 13.00
16 BH,A:Magneto,Dr.Doom,
    Beast 12.00
17 GT,JBy,V:Sentinels,last issue . . 13.00

CHILDREN OF THE
VOYAGE
Frontier 1993
1 F:Sam Wantling 3.25
2 Counterfeit Man 2.25
3 V:Voyager. 2.25
4 Last Issue. 2.25

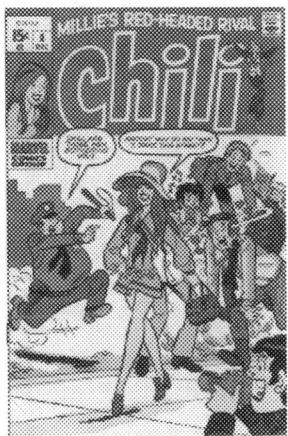

Chili #8
© Marvel Entertainment Group

CHILI
May, 1969
1 Millie's Rival 50.00
2 . . . . 25.00
3 . . . . 15.00
4 . . . . 15.00
5 . . . . 15.00
6 thru 15 . . . . @12.00
16 thru 20 . . . . @10.00
21 thru 25 . . . . @8.00
26 Dec., 1973 . . . . 8.00
Spec.#1, 1971 . . . . 15.00

CHUCK NORRIS
Star Jan.–Sept., 1987
1 SD 2.00
2 thru 5 . . . . @2.00

CINDY COMICS
See: KRAZY COMICS

CLANDESTINE
Oct. 1994–Sept. 1995
Preview issue, Intro (1994) 1.50
1 MFm,AD,foil(c) 3.25
2 Wraparound (c),A:Silver Surfer . . 2.50
3 I:Argent,Kimera,A:SilverSurfer . . 2.50
4 R:Adam 2.50
5 MFm,AD,O:Adam Destine. 2.50
6 A:Spider-Man 2.50
7 A:Spider-Man 2.50
8 A:Dr.Strange. 2.50
9 Training Time 2.50
10 A:Britanic. 2.50
11 V:Modan 2.50
12 Aftermath. 2.50
13 Who Will Lead 2.50
14 Vincent Vs. Adam 2.50
TPB AD,MFm (1997) 12.00

CLASSIC CONAN
See: CONAN SAGA

CLASSIC X-MEN
See: X-MEN

CLIVE BARKER'S
BOOK OF THE DAMNED
Epic Nov., 1991
1 JBo,Hellraiser companion 5.00
2 MPa,Hellraiser Companion 5.00

CLIVE BARKER'S
HELLRAISER
Epic 1989–93
1 BWr,DSp 7.00
2 . . . . 6.00
3 . . . . 6.50
4 . . . . 4.50
5 . . . . 4.50
6 . . . . 7.00
7 The Devil's Brigade #1 . . . . 7.00
8 The Devil's Brigade #2&3 . . . . . 7.00
9 The Devil's Brigade #4&5 . . . . . 7.00
10 The Devil's Brigade #6&7
    foil Cover 5.00
11 The Devil's Brigade #8&9. . . . . 4.50
12 The Devil's Brigade #10-12 . . . . 4.50
13 MMi,RH,Devil's Brigade #13 . . . 4.50
14 The Devil's Brigade #14. . . . . . . 5.00
15 The Devil's Brigade #15. . . . . . . 5.00
16 E:Devil's Brigade 5.00
17 BHa,DR,The Harrowing 10.00
18 O:Harrowers 5.00
19 A:Harrowers 5.00
20 NGa(s),DMc,Last Laugh 9.00
Dark Holiday Spec.#1 (1992) 5.00
Spring Slaughter Spec.#1 (1994) . . 7.00
Summer Spec.#1 (1992 . . . . 6.00

CLOAK & DAGGER
(Limited Series) Oct., 1983
1 RL,TA,I:Det.O'Reilly,
    Father Delgado 2.50
2 RL,TA,V:Duane Hellman 2.00
3 RL,TA,V:Street Gang 2.00
4 RL,TA,O:Cloak & Dagger, ... 2.00

MARVEL

CLOAK & DAGGER
[1st Regular Series] July 1985
1 RL,Pornography 2.00
2 RL,Dagger's mother 1.50
3 RL,A:Spider-Man 2.00
4 RL,Secret Wars II 1.50
5 RL,I:Mayhem 1.50
6 RL,A:Mayhem 1.50
7 RL,A:Mayhem. 1.50
8 TA, Drugs 1.50
9 AAd,TA,A:Mayhem 2.50
10 BBI,TA,V:Dr. Doom 1.50
11 BBI,TA,Last Issue 1.50

[Mutant Misadventures of]
CLOAK & DAGGER
[2nd Regular Series]
Oct., 1988
1 CR(i),A:X-Factor 3.00
2 CR(i),C:X-Factor,V:Gromitz. . . . 2.50
3 SW(i),JLe(c),A:Gromitz 2.00
4 TA(i),Inferno,R:Mayhem 2.00
5 TA(i),R:Mayhem. 2.00
6 TA(i),A:Mayhem 1.75
7 A:Crimson Daffodil,V:Ecstacy 1.75
8 Acts of Vengeance prelude 1.75
9 Acts of Vengeance 2.00
10 Acts of Vengeance,"X-Force"
   name used,Dr.Doom. 2.00
11 . . . . 1.50
12 A:Dr.Doom. 1.50
13 A:Dr.Doom. 1.50
14 & 15 RL . . . . @1.50
16 RL,A:Spider-Man 2.00
17 A:Spider-Man, ... 2.00
18 Inf.Gauntlet X-over,
   A:Spider-Man, Ghost Rider. . . . 2.50
19 O:Cloak & Dagger,final issue . . . 2.50
GNv Predator and Prey 14.95

A CLUELESS VALENTINE
1 characters from movie, 48pg. . . . 2.50

CODENAME: GENETIX
1993
1 PGa,A:Wolverine 2.00
2 PGa,V:Prime EvilA:Wolverine . . . 2.00
3 . . . . 2.00
4 A:Wolverine,Kazar 2.00

CODE OF HONOR
1996
1 (of 4) CDi,TnS,I:Jeff Piper,
   fully painted 5.95
2 thru 4 CDi, ... @5.95

CODE NAME: SPITFIRE
See: SPITFIRE AND
THE TROUBLESHOOTERS

COLOSSUS
Aug., 1997
1-shot BRa,Colossus & Meggan
   V:Arcade, 48pg 3.00

COLOSSUS:
GOD'S COUNTRY
PF V:Cold Warriors 7.00

COMBAT
Atlas June, 1952
1 War Stories, Bare Bayonets . . 150.00

2 RH, Break Thru,(Dedicated to
   US Infantry) 75.00
3 . . . . 50.00
4 BK 60.00
5 thru 10 . . . . @45.00
11 April, 1953 . . . . 50.00

COMBAT CASEY
See: WAR COMBAT

COMBAT KELLY AND
THE DEADLY DOZEN
Atlas Nov., 1951
1 RH,Korean war stories 175.00
2 Big Push. 75.00
3 The Volunteer. 60.00
4 V:Communists 60.00
5 OW,V:Communists 60.00
6 V:Communists 60.00
7 V: Communists 60.00
8 Death to the Reds 60.00
9 . . . . 60.00
10 . . . . 60.00
11 . . . . 45.00
12 thru 16 . . . . @50.00
17 A:Combat Casey 75.00
18 A:Battle Brady 35.00
19 V:Communists 35.00
20 V:Communists 35.00
21 Transvestite Cover. 40.00
22 thru 40 . . . . @30.00
41 thru 44 August, 1957 . . . . . @30.00

COMBAT KELLY
June, 1972
1 JM, Stop the Luftwaffe 20.00
2 The Big Breakout 10.00
3 O:Combat Kelly 10.00
4 Mutiny,A:Sgt.Fury and the
   Howling Commandoes 10.00
5 Escape or Die 10.00
6 The Fortress of Doom. 10.00
7 Nun Hostage,V:Nazis 10.00
8 V:Nazis. 10.00
9 Oct., 1973 . . . . 10.00

COMET MAN
Feb., 1987
1 BSz(c),I:Comet Man 1.50
2 BSz(c),A:Mr.Fantastic 1.00
3 BSz(c),A:Hulk. 1.00
4 BSz(c),A:Fantistic Four 1.00
5 BSz(c),A:Fantastic Four 1.00
6 BSz(c),Last issue, July,1987 . . . 1.00

COMIX BOOK
(black & white magazine) 1974
1 . . . . 25.00
2 . . . . 20.00
3 . . . . 25.00
4 . . . . 12.00
5 1976 . . . . 12.00

COMIX ZONE
1 video game tie-in 2.50
2 video game tie-in 2.50

COMMANDO
ADVENTURES
Atlas June, 1957
1 Seek, Find and Destroy 55.00
2 MD, Hit 'em and Hit 'em
   Hard, August,1957 . . . . 50.00

Commando Adventures #2
© Marvel Entertainment Group

COMPLETE COMICS
See: AMAZING COMICS

COMPLETE MYSTERY
August, 1948
1 Seven Dead Men 350.00
2 Jigsaw of Doom 300.00
3 Fear in the Night. 300.00
4 A Squealer Dies Fast 300.00
Becomes:

TRUE COMPLETE
MYSTERY
5 Rice Mancini,
   The Deadly Dude 175.00
6 Ph(c),Frame-up that Failed . . 125.00
7 Ph(c),Caught 125.00
8 Ph(c),The Downfall of Mr.
   Anderson, Oct., 1949 . . . . . 125.00

CONAN
1995–96
1 Pit Fighter. 3.00
2 LHa,Hyborean tortue factory 3.00
3 V:Cannibals 3.00
4 LHa,JP,Rune Conan Prelude . . . 3.00
5 LHa,V:yeti. 3.00
6 LHa, the plague 3.00
7 LHa,BBI,V:The Iron Man. 3.00
8 . . . . 3.00
9 . . . . 3.00
10 Conan kidnapped by Amazons . 3.00
11 . . . . 3.00

CONAN: DEATH
COVERED IN GOLD
July 1999
1 (of 3) RTs 3.00
2 RTs 3.00

CONAN
THE ADVENTURER
1994–95
1 RT(s),RK, Red Foil(c) 3.00
2 RT(s),RK 1.75
3 RT(s),RK 1.50
4 . . . . 1.50
5 . . . . 1.50
6 . . . . 1.50
7 . . . . 1.50

MARVEL

8 . . . . 1.50
9 . . . . 1.50
10 . . . . 1.50
11 Torture Chamber 1.50
12 Abominations of Yondo 1.50
13 Seven Warriors 1.50
14 RTs,Young Conan,last issue. . . . 1.50

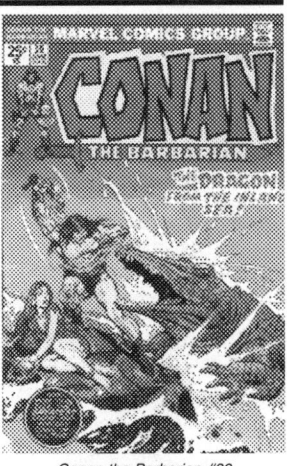

Conan the Barbarian #1
© Marvel Entertainment Group

CONAN THE BARBARIAN
Oct., 1979

1 BWS/DA,O:Conan,A:Kull 225.00
2 BWS/SB,Lair o/t Beast-Men . . . 80.00
3 BWS,SB,Grey God Passes. . . 135.00
4 BWS,SB,Tower o/t Elephant . . . 60.00
5 BWS,Zukala's Daughter 60.00
6 BWS,SB,Devil Wings Over
   Shadizar. 35.00
7 BWS,SB,DA,C:Thoth-Amon,
   I:Set. 35.00
8 BWS,TS,TP,Keepers o/t Crypt . 35.00
9 BWS,SB,Garden of Fear. 35.00
10 BWS,SB,JSe,Beware Wrath of
   Anu;BU:Kull 50.00
11 BWS,SB,Talons of Thak. 50.00
12 BWS,GK,Dweller in the Dark,
   Blood of the Dragon B.U. 25.00
13 BWS,SB,Web o/t Spider-God. . 25.00
14 BWS,SB,Green Empress of
   Melnibone 40.00
15 BWS,SB 40.00
16 BWS,Frost Giant's Daughter . . 25.00
17 GK,Gods of Bal-Sagoth,
   A:Fafnir 11.00
18 GK,DA,Thing in the Temple,
   A:Fafnir 11.00
19 BWS,DA,Hawks from
   the Sea 22.00
20 BWS,DA,Black Hound of
   Vengeance,A:Fafnir 22.00
21 BWS,CR,VM,DA,SB, Monster
   of the Monoliths 20.00
22 BWS,DA,rep.Conan #1 . . . . . . 22.00
23 BWS,DA,Shadow of the
   Vulture,I:Red Sonja 30.00
24 BWS,Song of Red Sonja 38.00
25 JB,SB,JSe,Mirrors of Kharam
   Akkad,A:Kull. 8.00
26 JB,Hour of the Griffin 6.00
27 JB,Blood of Bel-Hissar. 5.00
28 JB,Moon of Zembabwei 5.00
29 JB,Two Against Turan 5.00
30 JB,The Hand of Nergal 5.00
31 JB,Shadow in the Tomb. 4.00
32 JB,Flame Winds of Lost Khitai . 4.00

33 JB,Death & 7 Wizards 4.00
34 JB,Temptress in the Tower
   of Flame. 4.00
35 JB,Hell-Spawn of Kara-Shehr . . 4.00
36 JB,Beware of Hyrkanians
   bearing Gifts. 4.00
37 NA,Curse of the Golden Skull . 10.00
38 JB,Warrior & Were-Woman 3.50
39 JB,Dragon from the
   Inland Sea. 3.50
40 RB,Fiend from Forgotten City. . . 3.50
41 JB,Garden of Death & Life 5.00
42 JB,Night of the Gargoyle 5.00
43 JB,Tower o/Blood,A:RedSonja . . 5.00
44 JB,Flame&Fiend,A:RedSonja. . . 6.00
45 JB,Last Ballad of Laza-Lanti . . . 6.00
46 JB,JSt,Curse of the Conjurer . . . 4.00
47 JB,DA,Goblins in the
   Moonlight 4.00
48 JB,DG,DA,Rats Dance at Raven
   gard,BU:Red Sonja 4.00
49 JB,DG,Wolf-Woman. 4.00
50 JB,DG,Dweller in the Pool 4.00
51 JB,DG,Man Born of Demon 4.00
52 JB,TP,Altar and the Scorpion . . . 4.00
53 JB,FS,Brothers of the Blade. . . . 4.00
54 JB,TP,Oracle of Ophir 4.00
55 JB,TP,Shadow on the Land 4.00
56 JB,High Tower in the Mist 4.00
57 MP,Incident in Argos 4.00
58 JB,Queen o/tBlackCoast,
   2nd A:Belit 6.00
59 JB,Ballad of Belit,O:Belit 3.50
60 JB,Riders o/t River Dragons. . . . 3.50
61 JB,She-Pirate,I:Amra 3.50
62 JB,Lord of the Lions,O:Amra . . . 3.50
63 JB,Death Among Ruins,
   V&D:Amra 3.50
64 JSon,AM,rep.Savage Tales#5 . . 3.50
65 JB,Fiend o/tFeatheredSerpent . . 3.50
66 JB,Daggers & Death Gods,
   C:Red Sonja. 3.50
67 JB,Talons of the Man-Tiger,
   A:Red Sonja. 3.50
68 JB,Of Once & Future Kings,
   V:KingKull,A:Belit,Red Sonja . . 3.50
69 VM,Demon Out of the Deep. . . . 3.50
70 JB,City in the Storm. 3.50
71 JB,Secret of Ashtoreth. 3.50
72 JB,Vengeance in Asgalun 3.50
73 JB,..In the Well of Skelos. 3.50
74 JB,Battle at the Black Walls
   C:Thoth-Amon. 3.50
75 JB,Hawk-Riders of Harakht 3.50
76 JB,Swordless in Stygia 3.50
77 JB,When Giants Walk
   the Earth 3.50
78 JB,rep.Savage Sword #1,
   A:Red Sonja. 3.50
79 HC,Lost Valley of Iskander. 3.50
80 HC,Trial By Combat. 3.50
81 HC,The Eye of the Serpent 3.00
82 HC,The Sorceress o/t Swamp . . 3.00
83 HC,The Dance of the Skull 3.00
84 JB,Two Against the Hawk-City,
   I:Zula 3.00
85 JB,Of Swordsmen & Sorcerers,
   O:Zulu 3.00
86 JB,Devourer of the Dead 3.00
87 TD, rep. Savage Sword #3. . . . . 3.00
88 JB,Queen and the Corsairs 3.00
89 JB,Sword & the Serpent,
   A:Thoth-Amon 3.00
90 JB,Diadem of the Giant-Kings . . 3.00
91 JB,Savage Doings in Shem 3.00
92 JB,The Thing in the Crypt 3.00
93 JB,Of Rage & Revenge 3.00
94 JB,BeastKing ofAbombi,L:Zulu . 3.00
95 JB,The Return of Amra 3.00
96 JB,Long Night of Fang
   & Talon,pt.1 . . . . 3.00

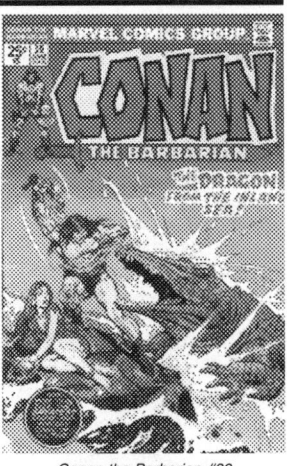

Conan the Barbarian #39
© Marvel Entertainment Group

97 JB,Long Night of Fang
   & Talon,pt.2 . . . . 3.00
98 JB,Sea-Woman 3.00
99 JB,Devil Crabs o/t Dark Cliffs. . . 3.00
100 JB,Death on the Black Coast,
   D:Belit (double size) 3.50
101 JB,The Devil has many Legs . . 1.75
102 JB,The Men Who
   Drink Blood 1.75
103 JB,Bride of the Vampire 1.75
104 JB,The Vale of Lost Women. . . 1.75
105 JB,Whispering Shadows 1.75
106 JB,Chaos in Kush 1.75
107 JB,Demon of the Night. 1.75
108 JB,Moon-Eaters of Darfar 1.75
109 JB,Sons o/t Bear God 1.75
110 JB,Beward t/Bear o/Heaven . . . 1.75
111 JB,Cimmerian Against a City . . 1.75
112 JB,Buryat Besieged 1.75
113 JB,A Devil in the Family 1.75
114 JB,The Shadow of the Beast . . 1.75
115 JB,A War of Wizards, A:Red
   Sonja Double size 10th Anniv.
   (L:Roy Thomas script) 2.50
116 JB,NA,Crawler in the Mist . . . : 1.75
117 JB,Corridor of Mullah-Kajar . . . 1.75
118 JB,Valley of Forever Night 1.75
119 JB,Voice of One Long Gone. . . 1.75
120 JB,The Hand of Erlik 1.75
121 JB,BMc,Price of Perfection. . . . 1.75
122 JB,BMc,The City Where Time
   Stood Still. 1.75
123 JB,BMc,Horror Beneath the
   Hills 1.75
124 JB,BMc,the Eternity War 1.75
125 JB,BMc,the Witches ofNexxx . . 1.75
126 JB,BMc,Blood Red Eye
   of Truth 1.75
127 GK,Snow Haired Woman
   of the Wastes 1.75
128 GK,And Life Sprang Forth
   From These 1.75
129 GK,The Creation Quest 1.75
130 GK,The Quest Ends. 1.75
131 GK,The Ring of Rhax. 1.75
132 GK,Games of Gharn 1.75
133 GK,The Witch of Widnsor. 1.75
134 GK,A Hitch in Time 1.75
135 MS,JRu,The Forest o/t Night . . 1.75
136 JB,The River of Death 1.75
137 AA,Titans Gambit. . : 1.75
138 VM,Isle of the Dead 1.75
139 VM,In the Lair of
   the Damned 1.75

MARVEL

MARVEL

140 JB,Spider Isle	1.75
141 JB,The Web Tightens.	1.75
142 JB,The Maze,the Man,	
the Monster	1.75
143 JB,Life Among the Dead	1.75
144 JB,The Blade & the Beast	1.75
145 Son of Cimmeria	1.75
146 JB,Night o/t Three Sisters	1.75
147 JB,Tower of Mitra.	1.75
148 JB,The Plague of Forlek	1.75
149 JB,Deathmark	1.75
150 JB,Tower of Flame.	1.75
151 JB,Vale of Death	1.50
152 JB,Dark Blade of	
Jergal Zadh	1.50
153 JB,Bird Men of Akah Ma'at.	1.50
154 JB,the Man-Bats of	
Ur-Xanarrh	1.50
155 JB,SL,The Anger of Conan	1.50
156 JB,The Curse	1.50
157 JB,The Wizard	1.50
158 JB,Night of the Wolf.	1.50
159 JB,Cauldron of the Doomed.	1.50
160 Veil of Darkness.	1.50
161 JB,House of Skulls,A:Fafnir	1.50
162 JB,Destroyer in the Flame,	
A:Fafnir	1.50
163 JB,Cavern of the Vines of	
Doom,A:Fafnir	1.50
164 The Jeweled Sword of Tem	1.50
165 JB,V:Nadine.	1.50
166 JB,GI,Blood o/t Titan,A:Fafnir	1.50
167 JB,Creature From Time's	
Dawn,A:Fafnir	1.50
168 JB,Bird Woman & the Beast.	1.50
169 JB,Tomb of the Scarlet Mage	1.50
170 JB,Dominion of the Dead,	
A&D:Fafnir	1.50
171 JB,Barbarian Death Song	1.50
172 JB,Reavers in Borderland	1.50
173 JB,Honor Among Thieves	1.50
174 JB,V:Tetra	1.50
175 JB,V:Spectre ofDeath.	1.50
176 JB,Argos Rain	1.50
177 JB,V:Nostume	1.50
178 JB,A:Tetra,Well of Souls.	1.50
179 JB,End of all there is,A:Kiev.	1.50
180 JBV:AnitRenrut	1.50
181 JB,V:KingMaddoc II	1.50
182 JB,V:King of Shem.	1.50
183 JB,V:Imhotep.	1.50
184 JB,V:Madoc.	1.50
185 JB,R:Tetra	1.50
186 JB,The Crimson Brotherhood.	1.50
187 JB,V:Council of Seven.	1.50
188 JB,V:Devourer-Souls	1.50
189 JB,V:Devourer-Souls	1.50
190 JB,Devourer-Souls.	1.50
191 Deliverance	1.50
192 JB,V:TheKeeper	1.50
193 Devourer-Souls	1.50
194 V:Devourer-Souls.	1.50
195 Blood of Ages	1.50
196 V:Beast.	1.50
197 A:Red Sonja	1.50
198 A:Red Sonja	1.50
199 O:Kaleb.	1.50
200 JB,D.sizeV:Dev-Souls	2.00
201 NKu,GI,Thulsa Doom.	1.50
202	1.50
203 V:Thulsa Doom	1.50
204 VS,GI,A:Red Sonja,I:Strakkus	1.50
205 A:Red Sonja	1.50
206 VS,GI,Heku trilogy,pt.1.	1.50
207 VS,GI,Heku,pt.2,O:Kote.	1.50
208 VS,GI,Heku,pt.3.	1.50
209 VS,GI,Heku epilogue	1.50
210 VS,GI,V:Sevante	1.50
211 VS,GI,V:Sevante	1.50
212 EC,GI	1.50
213 V:Ghamud Assassins.	1.50

214 AA.	1.50
215 VS,AA,Conan Enslaved	1.50
216 V:Blade of Zed.	1.50
217 JLe(c),V:Blade of Zed	1.50
218 JLe(c),V:Picts	1.50
219 JLe(c),V:Forgotten Beasts	1.50
220 Conan the Pirate	1.50
221 Conan the Pirate	1.50
222 AA,DP,Revenge.	1.50
223 AA,Religious Cult.	1.50
224 AA,Cannibalism.	1.50
225 AA,Conan Blinded	1.50
226 AA,Quest for Mystic Jewel	1.50
227 AA,Mystic Jewel,pt.2	1.50
228 AA,Cannibalism,pt.1	1.50
229 AA,Cannibalism,pt.2	1.50
230 FS,SDr,Citadel,pt.1	1.50
231 FS,DP,Citadel,pt.2	1.50
232 RLm,Birth of Conan	3.00
233 RLm,DA,B:Conan as youth	2.00
234 RLm,DA	2.00
235 RLm,DA	2.00
236 RLm,DA	2.00
237 DA,V:Jormma	1.50
238 DA,D:Conan	1.50
239 Conan Possessed	1.50
240 Conan Possessed	1.50
241 TM(c),R:RoyThomasScript.	3.50
242 JLe(c),A:Red Sonja	2.50
243 WPo(c),V:Zukala,.	2.00
244 A:Red Sonja,Zula.	1.50
245 A:Red Sonja,V:King	
of Vampires	1.50
246 A:Red Sonja,V:MistMonster	1.50
247 A:Red Sonja,Zula.	1.50
248 V:Zulu	1.50
249 A:Red Sonja,Zula.	1.50
250 A:RedSonja,Zula,V:Zug	
double size.	2.00
251 Cimmeria,V:Shumu Gorath	1.50
252 ECh.	1.50
253 ECh,V:Kulan-Goth(X-Men	
Villain)	1.50
254 ECh,V:Shuma-Gorath (Dr.	
Strange Villain).	1.50
255 ECh,V:Shuma-Gorath	1.50
256 ECh,D:Nemedia's King	1.50
257 ECh,V:Queen Vammator	1.50
258 AA(i),A:Kulan Gath	1.50
259 V:Shuma-Gorath	1.50
260 AA(i),V:Queen Vammatar	1.50
261 V:Cult of the Death Goddess	1.50
262 V:The Panther	1.50
263 V:Malaq.	1.50

Conan the Barbarian, Giant-Size #1
© Marvel Entertainment Group

264 V:Kralic	1.50
265 V:Karlik	1.50
266 Conan the Renegade(adapt)	1.50
267 adaption of Tor.	1.50
268 adaption of Tor.	1.50
269 V:Agohoth,Prince Borin	1.50
270 Devourer of the Dead	1.50
271 V:Devourer of Souls.	1.50
272 V:Devourer	1.50
273 V:Purple Lotus	1.50
274 V:She-Bat	1.50
275 RTs(s),Last Issue cont. in	
Savage Sword of Conan.	5.00
G-Size#1 GK,TS,Hour of the	
Dragon, inc.rep.Conan#3,	
I:Belit	8.00
G-Size#2 GK,TS,Conan Bound,	
inc. rep Conan #5.	5.00
G-Size#3 GK,TS,To Tarantia	
& the Tower,inc.rep.Conan#6	5.00
G-Size#4,GK,FS,Swords of the	
South,inc.rep.Conan #7	5.00
G-Size#5 rep.Conan #14,#15	
& Back-up story #12.	5.00
KingSz.#1 rep.Conan #2,#4	13.00
Ann.#2 BWS,Phoenix on the Sword	
A:Thoth-Amon	4.00
Ann.#3 JB,HC,Mountain of	
the Moon God, B.U.Kull story	2.00
Ann.#4 JB,Return of	
Conqueror,A:Zenobia	2.00
Ann.#5 JB,W:Conan/Zenobia	2.00
Ann.#6 GK,King of the	
Forgotten People	2.00
Ann.#7 JB,Red Shadows	
& Black Kraken	1.50
Ann.#8 VM,Dark Night of the	
White Queen	1.50
Ann.#9	1.50
Ann.#10 Scorched Earth	
(Conan #176 x-over)	1.50
Ann.#11	1.50
Conan-Barbarian Movie Spec.#1	1.25
Conan-Barbarian Movie Spec.#2	1.25
Conan-Destroyer Movie Spec.#1	1.25
Red Nails Special Ed.BWS.	4.00
TPB Conan & Ravagers Out	
of Time.	9.95
TPB Conan the Reaver.	9.95
TPB Conan the Rogue,JB,V:Romm	9.95
TPB Horn of Azroth	9.95
TPB Skull of Set.	9.95

CLASSIC CONAN
June, 1987

1 BWS,rep.	2.00
2 BWS,rep.	2.00
3 BWS,rep.	2.00

Becomes:

CONAN SAGA

4 rep.	3.00
5 rep.	3.00
6 rep.	3.00
7 rep.	3.00
8 rep.	3.00
9 rep.	3.00
10 rep.	3.00
11 rep.	2.50
12 rep.	2.50
13 rep.	2.50
14 rep.Savage Sword #5	2.50
15 rep.Savage Sword #7	2.50
16 rep.Savage Sword #12	2.50
17 rep.Savage Sword	2.50
18 rep.Savage Sword	2.50
19 rep.Savage Sword #28	2.50
20 rep.Savage Sword #25	2.50
21 rep.Savage Sword	2.50
22 rep.Giant Size Conan #1&2	2.50
23 rep.Hour of the Dragon	2.50

24 rep.Hour of the Dragon 2.50	
25 rep.Savage Sword 2.50	
26 rep.Savage Sword #11. . . . . . . 2.50	
27 rep.Savage Sword #15 . . . . . . 2.50	
28 rep.Savage Sword #16 . . . . . . 2.25	
29 rep.Savage Sword #17 . . . . . . 2.25	
30 rep.Savage Sword #18 . . . . . . 2.25	
31 rep.Savage Sword #19 . . . . . . 2.25	
32 rep.Savage Sword #5 . . . . 2.25	
33 rep.Savage Sword #5 . . . . 2.25	
34 rep.Savage Sword # 2.25	
35 rep.Savage Sword #32 . . . . . . 2.25	
36 rep.Savage Sword #12 . . . . . . 2.25	
37 rep.Savage Sword #34 . . . . . . 2.25	
38 rep.Conan #94&#95. . . . . 2.25	
39 rep.Conan #96&#97. . . . . 2.25	
40 rep.Savage Sword #26 . . . . . . 2.25	
41 rep.Savage Sword #27 . . . . . . 2.25	
42 rep.Savage Sword #40 . . . . . . 2.25	
43 rep.Savage Sword #41 . . . . . . 2.25	
44 rep.Savage Sword #42 . . . . . . 2.25	
45 rep.Savage Sword #43 . . . . . . 2.25	
46 rep.Savage Sword #15 . . . . . . 2.25	
47 rep.Savage Sword #22 . . . . . . 2.25	
48 rep.Savage Sword #23 . . . . . . 2.25	
49 rep.Sav.Sword Super Spec#2 . . 2.25	
50 rep.Conan #58. . . . . 2.25	
51 rep.Conan #59&#60. . . . . 2.25	
52 rep.Conan #61. . . . . 2.25	
53 thru 63 rep.Savage Sword . . . @2.25	
64 thru 94 rep. . . . . @2.25	
95 D:Belit 2.25	
96 . . . . 2.25	
97 Red Sonja rep. 2.25	
98 rep. #106–#108 . . . . 2.25	

CONAN CLASSICS
1994–95
1 rep. Conan #1 . . . . 2.00
2 rep. Conan #2 . . . . 2.00
3 rep. Conan #3 . . . . 1.75
4 thru 8 rep. Conan #4–#8. . . . . . . 1.50
9 Garden of Fear. 1.50
10 V:Anu 1.50
11 New Sword Manuever 1.50

CONAN/RUNE
1995
1 BWS,Conan Vs. Rune 3.50

CONAN
1 CCt, ... 2.00
2 CCt,V:Sorcerer. 2.00
3 (of 3) CCt, ... 2.00

CONAN:
RIVER OF BLOOD
April 1998
1 (of 3) Valeria, vs. giant crocs. . . . 2.50
2 Caught in the middle of a war . . . 2.50
3 Lord of the Crocodiles, concl. . . . 2.50

CONAN THE BARBARIAN
VS. THE LORD OF
THE SPIDERS
Jan., 1998
1 (of 3) RTs,V:Harpagus 2.50
2 RTs, ... 2.50
3 RTs,V:Harpagus 2.50

CONAN:
THE RETURN OF STYRM
July 1998
1 (of 3) V:Mecora. 2.50

2 (of 3) V:Mecora. 3.00
3 conclusion 3.00

Conan: The Scarlet Sword #1
© Marvel Entertainment Group

CONAN:
THE SCARLET SWORD
Oct. 1998
1 (of 3) RTs,V:Thun'da 3.00
2 RTs,A:Helliana 3.00
3 RTs,conclusion 3.00

CONAN: THE USURPER
Oct., 1997
1 (of 3) CDi,KJ,Conan attacks
  Cimmeria? 2.50
2 CDi,KJ, ... 2.50
3 CDi,KJ, concl. 2.50

KING CONAN
March, 1980
1 JB/ECh,I:Conn,V:Thoth-Amon. . . 3.00
2 JB,Black Sphinx of Nebthu 2.50
3 JB,Dragon Wings Over
  Zembabwei 2.50
4 JB,V:Thoth-Amon 2.50
5 JB,The Sorcerer in the Realm
  of Madness 2.50
6 JB,The Lady's Name Is..Trouble . 2.50
7 PS,JB. 2.75
8 A:Queen Reclaimed 2.75
9 JB,V:Medusa Monster. 2.25
10 V:Sea Monster. 2.25
11 V:Giant Totem Monster. 1.75
12 V:Monster 1.75
13 V:Monster 1.75
14 V:Demon 1.75
15 V:Sea Monster. 1.75
16 Conan Into Battle. 1.75
17 A:Conn 1.75
18 King of the Freaks? 1.75
19 MK(c),Skull & X-Bones cover. . . 1.75
Becomes:

CONAN THE KING
20 MS,The Prince is Dead 2.00
21 MS,Shadows. 2.00
22 GI/MS,The Black Dragons,Prince
  Conan II back-up story begins . 2.00
23 MS/GI,Ordeal 2.00
24 GI/MS,Fragments:AWitch'sTale . 2.00
25 MS/GI,Daggers 2.00
26 MS/GI,PrinceConanII B.U.ends . 2.00
27 MS/GI,A Death in Stygia 2.00

Conan the King #21
© Marvel Entertainment Group

28 MS/GI,Call of the Wild,
  A:Red Sonja. 2.00
29 MS,The Sleeping Lion 2.00
30 GI,Revenge on the Black River . 2.00
31 GI,Force of Arms 2.00
32 GI,Juggernaut 2.00
33 . . . . 2.00
34 . . . . 2.00
35 . . . . 2.00
36 . . . . 2.00
37 AW,Sack of Belverus 2.00
38 MM,A:Taurus,Leora 2.00
39 The Tower 2.00
40 . . . . 2.00
41 V:Leora 2.00
42 Thee Armada,A:Conn 2.00
43 . . . . 2.00
44 . . . . 2.00
45 V:Caliastros 2.00
46 V:Caliastros 2.00
47 TD,V:Caliastros 2.00
48 . . . . 2.00
49 . . . . 2.00
50 GI,50th Anniversary issue 2.00
51 GI,Death of Prince Conn 2.00
52 GI,Prince Conn story contd 2.00
53 GI,A:Thoth-Amon. 2.00
54 GI,V:Thoth-Amon. 2.00
55 GI,Sorcerers Ring,final issue . . . 2.00

CONAN THE SAVAGE
1995–96
(Black & White Magazine)
1 New Series. 3.00
2 CDi,Conan a gladiator 3.00
3 V:Monster. 3.00
4 CDi,Conan vs. Rune. 3.00
5 MBn,VMk,Ice age tale. 3.00
6 Bros.Hildebrandt(c),V:FallenIdol . 3.00
7 CDi,F:Iron Maidens. 3.00
8 & 9 . . . . @3.00
10 JB story, 48pg. 3.00

CONEHEADS
1994
1 Based Saturday Night Live 2.00
2 There Goes the Neighborhood . . 2.00
3 In Paris. 1.75

All comics prices listed are for *Near Mint* condition.   **CVA Page 177**

Coneheads #2
© Marvel Entertainment Group

CONSPIRACY
Dec., 1997
1 (of 2) DAn,Were the origins of
Marvel's superheroes really a
conspiracy, not an accident?. . . 3.00
2 DAn,concl. 3.00

CONTEST OF CHAMPIONS
June, 1982
1 JR2,Grandmaster vs. Mistress
Death, A:Alpha Flight 7.00
2 JR2,Grandmaster vs. Mistress
Death, A:X-Men 5.00
3 JR2,D:Grandmaster, Rebirth
Collector, A:X-Men 5.00

CONTEST OF
CHAMPIONS II
July 1999
1 (of 5) CCI,Marvel vs. Marvel 2.50
2 CCI,Atlas vs. Storm 2.50
3 CCI,super hero slugfest 2.50
4 CCI. 2.50
TPB Contest of Champions,
160-page, '70s rep.. . . . . 17.95

COPS: THE JOB
1992
1 MGo(c),V:Serial killer 1.50
2 MGo(c). 1.25
3 MGo(c),V:Eviscerator 1.25
4 MGo(c),D:Eviscerator,Nick 1.25

COSMIC POWERS
1994
1 RMz(s),RLm,JP,F:Thanos 2.75
2 RMz(s),JMr,F:Terrax 2.75
3 RMz(s),F:Jack of Hearts 2.75
4 RMz(s),RLm,F:Legacy 2.75
5 RMz(s),F&O:Morg 2.75
6 RMz(s),F&O:Tyrant. 2.75

COSMIC POWERS
UNLIMITED
1995–96
1 Surfer vs. Thanos 3.95
2 Jack of Hearts vs. Jakar 3.95
3 GWt,JB,F:Lunatik,64pg. 3.95

4 GWt,SEa,cont.StarMasters#3 . . . 3.95
5 GWt,SEa,R:Captain Universe . . . 3.95

COUNT DUCKULA
Star Nov., 1988
1 O:CountDuckula,B:DangerMouse 1.25
2 A:Danger Mouse 1.00
3 thru 15 . . . . @1.00

COWBOY ACTION
See: WESTERN
THRILLERS

COWBOY ROMANCES
Oct., 1949
1 Ph(c),Outlaw and the Lady . . . 150.00
2 Ph(c),William Holden/Mona
Freeman,Streets of Laredo . . 100.00
3 Phc,Romance in
Roaring Valley 75.00
Becomes:

YOUNG MEN
4 A Kid Names Shorty 125.00
5 Jaws of Death 75.00
6 Man-Size 75.00
7 The Last Laugh 75.00
8 Adventure stories continued . . . 75.00
9 Draft Dodging story. 75.00
10 US Draft Story 75.00
11 Adventure stories continued . . . 50.00
12 B:On the Battlefield,
inc.Spearhead 50.00
13 RH,Break-through 50.00
14 RH,Fox Hole 50.00
15 Battlefield stories cont,. 50.00
16 Sniper Patrol 50.00
17 Battlefield stories cont,. 50.00
18 BEv,Warlord. 50.00
19 BEv. 50.00
20 BEv,E:On the Battlefield 50.00
21 B:Flash Foster and his High
Gear Hot Shots 50.00
22 Screaming Tires. 50.00
23 E:Flash Foster and his High
Gear Hot Shots 50.00
24 BEv,B:Capt. America,Human
Torch,Sub-Mariner,O:Capt.
America,Red Skull 1,500.00
25 BEv,JR, Human Torch,Capt.
America,Sub-Mariner 800.00
26 BEv,Human Torch, Capt.
America,Sub Mariner 800.00
27 Bev, Human Torch/Toro
V:Hypnotist 800.00
28 E:Human Torch, Capt.America,
Sub Mariner,June, 1954 . . . . 800.00

COWGIRL ROMANCES
See: DARING MYSTERY

COYOTE
Epic June, 1983
1 SL,. 1.50
2 SL 1.50
3 BG 1.50
4 SL 1.50
5 SL 1.50
6 SL 1.50
7 SL,SD 1.50
8 SL 1.50
9 SL,SD 1.50
10 SL 1.50
11 FS,1st TM art,O:Slash 4.00
12 TM 2.00
13 TM 2.00

14 FS,TM,A:Badger 2.00
15 SL 1.50
16 SL,A:Reagan,Gorbachev 1.50

CRASH RYAN
Epic Oct., 1984
1 War Story 1.75
2 Doomsday 1.50
3 Fortress Japan 1.50
4 Jan., 1985 . . . . 1.50

CRAZY
Atlas Dec., 1953
1 BEv,satire, Frank N.Steins
Castle. 175.00
2 BEv,Beast from 1000 Fathoms 150.00
3 Bev,Madame Knockwurst's
Whacks Museum 125.00
4 BEv,I Love Lucy satire 125.00
5 BEv,Censorship satire. 125.00
6 BEv,satire. 125.00
7 BEv,satire,July, 1954 . . . . 125.00

CRAZY
Feb., 1973–June 1973
1 Not Brand Echh reps,
Forbushman. 20.00
2 Big,Batty Love & Hisses issue . 15.00
3 Stupor-Man,A:FantasticalFour. . 15.00

CREATURES ON
THE LOOSE
See: TOWER OF
SHADOWS

CRIME CAN'T WIN
See: KRAZY COMICS

CRIME FIGHTERS
April, 1948—Nov., 1949
1 Police Stories 175.00
2 Jewelry robbery 75.00
3 The Nine who were Doomed. . . 75.00
4 Human Beast at Bay. 50.00
5 V:Gangsters 50.00
6 Pickpockets 50.00
7 True Cases, Crime Can't Win . . 50.00
8 True Cases, Crime Can't Win . . 50.00
9 Ph(c),It Happened at Night 50.00
10 Ph(c),Killer at Large 50.00
Atlas Sept., 1954—Jan., 1955
11 V:Gangsters. 75.00
12 V:Gangsters. 75.00
13 Clay Pidgeon. 75.00

CRITICAL MASS
Epic Jan.–July, 1990
1 KS,GM,BSzF:ShadowlineSaga . . 4.95
2 . . . . 4.95
3 GM,SDr,JRy 4.95
4 . . . . 4.95
5 JZ 4.95
6 . . . . 4.95
7 July, 1990. . . . . 4.95

CROSSOVER CLASSICS
TPB Marvel and D.C. GP(c),reprints
both Spider-Man/Superman,the
Batman/Hulk and the X-Men/New
Teen Titans Battles 18.00

MARVEL

CRYPT OF SHADOWS
Jan., 1973
1 BW,RH,Midnight on Black
Mountain 20.00
2 Monster at the Door 15.00
3 Dead Man's Hand. 15.00
4 Cl,Secret in the Vault 15.00
5 JM,The Graveyard Ghoul 15.00
6 BEv,Don't Bury Me Deep 15.00
7 JSt,The Haunting of Bluebeard . 15.00
8 How Deep my Grave 15.00
9 Beyond Death. . . . .
15.00 10 A Scream in the Dark. . . 15.00
11 The Ghouls in my Grave 10.00
12 Behind the Locked Door 10.00
13 SD,Back From the Dead 10.00
14 The Thing that Creeps 10.00
15 My Coffin is Crowded. 10.00
16 . . . . 10.00
17 In the Hands of Shandu 10.00
18 SD,Face of Fear 10.00
19 SD,Colossus that Challenged
the World 10.00
20 A Monster walks Among Us . . . 10.00
21 SD,Death Will Be Mine,
Nov. 1975. . . . . 10.00

CUPID
Dec., 1949
1 Ph(c),Cora Dod's Amazing
Decision. 100.00
2 Ph(c),Betty Page, Mar. 1950 . . 200.00

CURSE OF THE WEIRD
1993–94
1 thru 4 SD,rep. 50's Sci-Fi 1.50

CUTTING EDGE
1995
1 WML,F:Hulk,Ghosts of the
Future tie-in 2.95

CYBERSPACE 3000
1 A:Dark Angel,Galactus,V:Badoon,
Glow in the dark(c) 3.00
2 SeT,A:Galactus,Dark Angel. . . . 2.00
3 SeT,A:Galactus,Keeper. 2.00
4 SeT,A:Keeper. 2.00
5 SeT,A:Keeper. 2.00
6 SeT,A:Warlock 2.00

Dakota North #3
© Marvel Entertainment Group

7 SeT,I:Gamble 2.00
8 SeT,A:Warlock 2.00
9 SeT 1.75
10 SeT 1.75
11 SeT 1.75

DAILY BUGLE
B&W 1996
1 (of 3) KIK,GA 2.50
2 KIK,GA. 2.50
3 KIK,GA. 2.50

DAKOTA NORTH
1986
1 (Now in Cage) 1.50
2 . . . . 1.25
3 . . . . 1.25
4 . . . . 1.25
5 Feb., 1987 . . . . 1.25

DAMAGE CONTROL
May, 1989
1 EC/BWi;A:Spider-Man 2.50
2 EC/BWi;A:Fant.Four 2.00
3 EC/BWi;A:Iron Man 2.00
4 EC/BWi;A:X-Men 2.00
[2nd Series] 1989–90
1 EC,A:Capt.America&Thor 3.00
2 EC,A:Punisher 2.50
3 EC 2.00
4 EC,Punisher. 2.00
[3rd Series]1991
1 Clean-up Crew Returns 1.50
2 A:Hulk,New Warriors 1.50
3 A:Avengers W.C.,Wonder Man,
Silver Surfer. 1.50
4 A:SilverSurfer & others 1.50

DANCES WITH DEMONS
Frontier 1993
1 CAd 2.95
2 CAd,V:Manitou 1.95
3 CAd,V:Manitou 1.95
4 CAd,last issue 1.95
5 Okay, there's more!. 1.95
6 . . . . 1.95

DAREDEVIL
April, 1964
1 B:StL(s),JK(c),BEv,I&O:Daredevil,
I:Karen Page,Foggy Nelson 2,000.00
2 JK(c),JO,V:Electro 550.00
3 JK(c),JO,I&O:The Owl 375.00
4 JK(c),JO,I&O:Killgrave 325.00
5 JK(c),WW,V:Masked Matador . 225.00
6 WW,I&O Original Mr. Fear. . . . 150.00
7 WW,I:Red Costume,V:Namor . 275.00
8 WW,I&O:Stiltman 150.00
9 WW(i),Killers Castle 150.00
10 WW(i),V:Catman 150.00
11 WW(i),R:Cat. 125.00
12 JK,JR,2nd A:Kazar. 125.00
13 JK,JR,O:Ka-Zar 75.00
14 JR,If This Be Justice 75.00
15 JR,A:Ox. 75.00
16 JR,A:Spider-Man,
I:Masked Marauder. 125.00
17 JR,A:Spider-Man 100.00
18 DON(s),JR,I:Gladiator 60.00
19 JR,V:Gladiator 60.00
20 JR(c),GC,V:Owl 50.00
21 GC,BEv,V:Owl 40.00
22 GC,V:Tri-man. 40.00
23 GC,V:Tri-man. 40.00
24 GC,A:Ka-Zar 40.00
25 GC,V:Leapfrog. 40.00

26 GC,V:Stiltman 40.00
27 GC,Spider-Man 40.00
28 GC,V:Aliens. 40.00
29 GC,V:The Boss 40.00
30 BEv(c),GC,A:Thor 40.00
31 GC,V:Cobra. 30.00
32 GC,V:Cobra. 30.00
33 GC,V:Beetle. 30.00
34 BEv(c),GC,O:Beetle. 30.00
35 BEv(c),GC,A:Susan Richards. . 30.00
36 GC,A:FF 30.00
37 GC,V:Dr.Doom. 30.00
38 GC,A:FF 30.00
39 GC,GT,V:Unholy Three 30.00
40 GC,V:Unholy Three 30.00
41 GC,D:Mike Murdock. 25.00
42 GC,DA,I:Jester 25.00
43 JK(c),GC,A:Capt.America 24.00
44 JSo(c),GC,V:Jester 20.00
45 GC,V:Jester. 20.00
46 GC,V:Jester. 20.00
47 GC,`Brother Take My Hand' . . . 20.00
48 GC,V:Stiltman 20.00
49 GC,V:Robot,I:Starr Saxon 20.00
50 JR(c),BWS,JCr,V:Robot 25.00
51 B:RTs(s),BWS,V:Robot 25.00
52 BWS,JCr,A:Black Panther 25.00
53 GC,O:Daredevil. 27.00
54 GC,V:Mr.Fear,A:Spidey 17.00
55 GC,V:Mr.Fear 15.00
56 GC,V:Death Head 15.00
57 GC,V:Death Head 15.00
58 GC,V:Stunt Master. 13.00
59 GC,V:Torpedo. 13.00
60 GC,V:Crime Wave 13.00
61 GC,V:Cobra. 13.00
62 GC,O:Night Hawk 13.00
63 GC,V:Gladiator 13.00
64 GC,A:Stuntmaster. 13.00
65 GC,V:BrotherBrimstone 13.00
66 GC,V:BrotherBrimstone 13.00
67 BEv(c),GC,Stiltman 13.00
68 AC,V:Kragg Blackmailer,
a:Bl.Panther,DD'sID Rev. . . . 13.00
69 E:RTs(s),GC,V:Thunderbolts,
A:Bl.Panther(DD's ID Rev) . . . 13.00
70 GC,V:Terrorists 13.00
71 RTs(s),GC,V:Terrorists. 16.00
72 GyC(s),GC,Tagak,V:Quother . . 12.00
73 GC,V:Zodiac 12.00
74 B:GyC(s),GC,I:Smasher. 12.00
75 GC,V:El Condor. 12.00
76 GC,TP,V:El Condor 12.00
77 GC,TP,V:Manbull 12.00

78 GC,TP,V:Manbull 12.00	157 GC,V:Death Stalker 3.00
79 GC,TP,V:Manbull 12.00	158 FM,V:Death Stalker 40.00
80 GK(c),GC,TP,V:Owl 12.00	159 FM,V:Bullseye 22.00
81 GK(c),GC,JA,A:Black Widow . . 22.00	160 FM,Bullseye. 10.00
82 GK(c),GC,JA,V:Scorpion 12.00	161 FM,V:Bullseye 10.00
83 JR(c),BWS,BEv,V:Mr.Hyde. . . . 14.00	162 SD,JRu,`Requiem' 3.50
84 GK(c),GC,Assassin 12.00	163 FM,V:Hulk,I:Ben Urich 10.00
85 GK(c),GC,A:Black Widow. . . . 12.00	164 FM,KJ,A:Avengers 10.00
86 GC,TP,V:Ox 12.00	165 FM,KJ,V:Dr.Octopus 10.00
87 GC,TP,V:Electro. 12.00	166 FM,KJ,V:Gladiator 10.00
88 GK(c),GC,TP,O:Black Widow . . 12.00	167 FM,KJ,V:Mauler. 10.00
89 GC,TP,A:Black Widow 12.00	168 FM,KJ,I&O:Elektra 45.00
90 E:StL(s),GK(c),GC,TP,V:Ox . . 12.00	169 FM,KJ,V:Bullseye 12.00
91 GK(c),GC,TP,I:Mr. Fear III 12.00	170 FM,KJ,V:Bullseye. 12.00
92 GK(c),GC,TP,A:BlackPanther. . 13.00	171 FM,KJ,V:Kingpin 7.00
93 GK(c),GC,TP,A:Black Widow . . 12.00	172 FM,KJ,V:Bullseye. 7.00
94 GK(c),GC,TP,V:Damon Dran . . 12.00	173 FM,KJ,V:Gliadator 7.00
95 GK(c),GC,TP,V:Manbull 12.00	174 FM,KJ,A:Gladiator 7.00
96 GK(c),GC,ECh,V:Manbull. 12.00	175 FM,KJ,A:Elektra,V:Hand 8.00
97 GK(c),V:Dark Messiah 12.00	176 FM,KJ,A:Elektra. 7.00
98 E:GyC(s),GC,ECh,V:Dark	177 FM,KJ,A:Stick 8.00
Messiah 12.00	178 FM,KJ,A:PowerMan&I.Fist . . . 7.00
99 B:SvG(s),JR(c),V:Hawkeye . . 12.00	179 FM,KJ,V:Elektra. 7.00
100 GC,V:Angar the Screamer . . 25.00	180 FM,KJ,V:Kingpin 7.00
101 RB,A:Angar the Screamer . . . 8.00	181 FM,KJ,V:Bullseye,D:Elektra,
102 A:Black Widow. 7.00	A:Punisher 12.00
103 JR(c),DH,A:Spider-Man 7.00	182 FM,KJ,A:Punisher 7.00
104 GK(c),DH,V:Kraven 7.00	183 FM,KJ,V:PunisherDrug. 7.00
105 DH,JSn,DP,C:Thanos. 15.00	184 FM,KJ,V:PunisherDrug. 7.00
106 JR(c),DH,A:Black Widow 7.00	185 FM,KJ,V:King Pin 5.00
107 JSn(c),JB(i),A:Capt.Marvel. . . 7.00	186 FM,KJ,V:Stiltman. 5.00
108 K&R(c),PG(i),V:Beetle 7.00	187 FM,KJ,A:Stick 5.00
109 GK(c),DH(i),V:Beetle 7.00	188 FM,KJ,A:Black Widow 5.00
110 JR(c),GC,A:Thing,O:Nekra . . . 7.00	189 FM,KJ,A:Stick,A:BlackWidow . . 5.00
111 JM(i),I:Silver Samurai. 8.50	190 FM,KJ,R:Elektra. 6.00
112 GK(c),GC,V:Mandrill. 7.00	191 FM,TA,A:Bullseye 5.00
113 JR(c),V:Gladiator 7.00	192 KJ,V:Kingpin 3.00
114 GK(c),I:Death Stalker. 7.00	193 KJ,Betsy 3.00
115 V:Death Stalker 6.00	194 KJ,V:Kingpin 3.00
116 GK(c),GC,V:Owl. 6.00	195 KJ,Tarkington Brown 3.00
117 E:SvG(s),K&R(c),V:Owl 6.00	196 KJ,A:Wolverine 9.00
118 JR(c),DH,I:Blackwing 6.00	197 V:Bullseye 2.50
119 GK(c),DH(i),V:Crusher 6.00	198 V:Dark Wind 2.50
120 GK(c),V:Hydra,I:El Jaguar . . . 6.00	199 V:Dark Wind 2.50
121 GK(c),A:Shield. 5.00	200 JBy(c),V:Bullseye. 3.00
122 GK(c),V:Blackwing. 5.00	201 JBy(c),A:Black Widow 2.50
123 V:Silvermane,I:Jackhammer. . 5.00	202 I:Micah Synn 2.50
124 B:MWn(s),GK(c),GC,KJ,	203 JBy(c),I:Trump. 2.50
I:Copperhead 5.00	204 BSz(c),V:Micah Synn 2.50
125 GK(c),KJ(i),V:Copperhead . . . 5.00	205 I:Gael 2.50
126 GK(c),KJ(i),D: 2nd Torpedo . . 5.00	206 V:Micah Synn 2.50
127 GK(c),KJ(i),V:3rd Torpedo . . . 5.00	207 BSz(c),A:Black Widow 2.50
128 GK(c),KJ(i),V:Death Stalker . . 5.00	208 Harlan Ellison 3.00
129 KJ(i),V:Man Bull 5.00	209 Harlan Ellison 3.00
130 KJ(i),V:Brother Zed 5.00	210 DM,V:Micah Synn 2.50
131 KJ(i),I&O:2nd Bullseye 20.00	
132 KJ(i),V:Bullseye 5.00	211 DM,V:Micah Synn 2.50
133 JM(i),GK(c),V:Jester. 4.00	212 DM,V:Micah Synn 2.50
134 JM(i),V:Chameleon 4.00	213 DM,V:Micah Synn 2.50
135 JM(i),V:Jester 4.00	214 DM,V:Micah Synn 2.50
136 JB,JM,V:Jester. 4.00	215 DM,A:Two-Gun Kid 2.50
137 JB,V:Jester 4.00	216 DM,V:Gael. 2.50
138 JBy,A:Ghost Rider 7.00	217 BS(c),V:Gael 2.50
139 SB,V:A Bomber 4.00	218 KP,V:Jester 2.50
140 SB,V:Gladiator. 4.00	219 FM,JB 3.00
141 GC,Bullseye 4.00	220 DM,D:Heather Glenn 2.50
142 GC,V:Cobra. 4.00	221 DM,Venice. 2.50
143 E:MWn(s),GC,V:Cobra. 4.00	222 DM,A:Black Widow 2.50
144 GT,V:Manbull 4.00	223 DM,Secret Wars II 2.50
145 GT,V:Owl 4.00	224 DM,V:Sunturion 2.50
146 GC,V:Bullseye 5.00	225 DM,V:Vulture 2.50
147 GC,V:Killgrave 3.00	226 FM(plot),V:Gladiator. 3.00
148 GC,V:Deathstalker. 3.00	227 FM,Kingpin,Kar.Page 6.00
149 KI,V:Smasher 3.00	228 FM,DM,V:Kingpin. 4.00
150 GC,KJ,I:Paladin 4.00	229 FM,Kingpin,Turk 4.00
151 GC,Daredevil Unmasked 3.00	230 R:Matt's Mother 4.00
152 KJ,V:Paladin 3.00	231 FM,DM,V:Kingpin. 4.00
153 GC,V:Cobra. 3.00	232 FM,V:Kingpin,Nuke 4.00
154 GC,V:Mr. Hyde 3.00	233 FM,Kingpin,Nuke,Capt.Am. . . . 4.00
155 V:Avengers 3.00	234 SD,KJ,V:Madcap 2.00
156 GC,V:Death Stalker 3.00	235 SD,KJ,V:Mr. Hyde 2.00
	236 BWS,A:Black Widow 4.00
	237 AW(i),V:Klaw 2.00
	238 SB,SL,AAd(c)V:Sabretooth . . . 6.00
	239 AAd(c),AW,GI(i),V:Rotgut 2.00
	240 AW,V:Rotgut 2.00
	241 MZ(c),TM,V:Trixter 3.00
	242 KP,V:Caviar Killer. 2.00
	243 AW,V:Nameless One 2.00
	244 TD(i),V:Nameless One 2.00
	245 TD(i),A:Black Panther 2.00
	246 TD(i),V:Chance 2.00
	247 KG,A:Black Widow. 2.00
	248 RL,AW,A:Wolverine,
	V:Bushwhacker 6.00
	249 RL,AW,V:Wolverine,
	Bushwhacker 6.00
	250 JR2,AW,I:Bullet 3.50
	251 JR2,AW,V:Bullet. 3.00
	252 JR2,AW,Fall o/Mutants. 4.50
	253 JR2,AW,V:Kingpin 3.00
	254 JR2,AW,I:Typhoid Mary 7.00
	255 JR2,AW,A:Kingpin,TMary 5.00
	256 JR2,AW,A:Kingpin,TMary. . . . 5.00
	257 JR2,AW,A:Punisher 5.00
	258 RLm,V:Bengal 3.50
	259 JR2,AW,V:TyphoidMary 4.00
	260 JR2,AW,V:T.Mary,K.pin 4.00
	261 JR2,AW,HumanTorch. 2.50
	262 JR2,AW,Inferno 2.50
	263 JR2,AW,Inferno 2.50
	264 SD,AW,MM,V:The Owl 2.50
	265 JR2,AW,Inferno 2.50
	266 JR2,AW,V:Mephisto 2.50
	267 JR2,AW,V:Bullet. 2.50
	268 JR2,AW,V:TheMob. 2.50
	269 JR2,AW,V:Pyro&Blob 2.50
	270 JR2,AW,A:Spider-Man,
	I:Blackheart 3.00
	271 JR2,AW,I:Number9 . . . . 2.50
	272 JR2,AW,I:Shotgun 3.00
	273 JR2,AW,V:Shotgun 2.50
	274 JR2,AW,V:Inhumans 2.50
	275 JR2,AW,ActsOfVen.,V:Ultron . 2.50
	276 JR2,AW,ActsOfVen.,V:Ultron . . 2.50
	277 RL,AW,Vivian's Story 2.00
	278 JR2,AW,V:Blackheart,
	A:Inhumans 2.50
	279 JR2,AW,V:Mephisto,
	A:Inhumans 2.50
	280 JR2,AW,V:Mephisto,
	A:Inhumans 2.50
	281 JR2,AW,V:Mephisto,
	A:Inhumans 2.50
	282 JR2,AW,V:Mephisto,
	A:Silver Surfer, Inhumans 2.50
	283 MBa,AW,A:Captain America . . 2.00

Daredevil #113
© Marvel Entertainment Group

Daredevil #182
© *Marvel Entertainment Group*

284 LW,AW,R:Bullseye 2.00
285 LW,AW,B:Bullseye
become DD#1 . . . . 2.00
286 LW,AW,GCa,Fake
Daredevil #2. . . . . 2.00
287 LW,AW,Fake Daredevil #3 . . . . 2.00
288 LW,AW,A:Kingpin. 2.00
289 LW,AW,A:Kingpin. 2.00
290 LW,AW,E:Fake Daredevil 2.00
291 LW,AW,V:Bullet 2.00
292 LW,A:Punisher,V:Tombstone . . 2.00
293 LW,A:Punisher,V:Tombstone . . 2.00
294 LW,V:The Hand. 1.75
295 LW,V:The Hand,
A:GhostRider. 1.75
296 LW,AW,V:The Hand 1.75
297 B:DGC(s),LW,AW,B:Last Rites,
V:Typhoid Mary,A:Kingpin. 3.50
298 LW,AW,A:Nick Fury,Kingpin . . . 2.50
299 LW,AW,A:Nick Fury,Kingpin . . . 2.50
300 LW,AW,E:Last Rites, ... 4.00
301 V:The Owl 1.75
302 V:The Owl 1.75
303 V:The Owl. 1.75
304 AW,Non-action issue 1.75
305 AW,A:Spider-Man 1.75
306 AW,A:Spider-Man 1.75
307 1st SMc DD,Dead Man's Hand #1,
A:Nomad 3.00
308 SMc,Dead Man's Hand #5,
A:Punisher,V:Silvermane 2.00
309 SMc,Dead Man's Hand#7,
A:Nomad,Punisher 2.00
310 SMc,Inf.War,V:Calipso 2.00
311 SMc,V:Calypso 2.00
312 Firefighting issue 1.75
313 SMc,V:Pyromaniac 2.00
314 SMc,V:Mr.Fear,I:Shock. 2.00
315 SMc,V:Mr.Fear. 2.00
316 Goes Underground 1.75
317 SMc,Comedy Issue 2.00
318 SMc,V:Taskmaster. 2.00
319 SMc,Fall from Grace Prologue,
A:Silver Sable,Garrett,Hand . . . 5.00
319a 2nd Printing 2.00
320 SMc,B:Fall from Grace,
V:Crippler,S.Sable,A:Stone 5.00
321 SMc,N:Daredevil,A:Venom,
Garret, V:Hellspawn,Glow
in the Dark(c) 3.00
321a Newsstand Ed. 3.00
322 SMc,A:Venom,Garret,Siege . . . 3.00
323 SMc,V:Venom,A:Siege,Garret,
I:Erynys 2.50

324 SMc,A:Garret,R:Elektra,
A:Stone , Morbius 2.50
325 SMc,E:Fall from Grace, A:Garret,
Siege,Elektra,Morbius,V:Hand,
D:Hellspawn,Double size 3.00
326 SMc,B:Tree of Knowledge,
I:Killobyte,A:Capt.America 2.00
327 E:DGC(s),SMc,A:Capt.Amer. . . 2.00
328 GtW(s),V:Wirehead,A:Captain
America,S.Sable, Wild Pack . . . 2.00
329 B:DGC(s),SMc,A:Captain
America, S.Sable,Iron Fist 2.00
330 SMc,A:Gambit 2.00
331 SMc,A:Captain America,
VLHydra. 2.00
332 A:Captain America,Gambit. . . . 2.00
333 TGb,GWt. 2.00
334 TGb,GWt. 2.00
335 . . . . 2.00
336 . . . . 2.00
337 V:Kingpin,A:Blackwulf 2.00
338 Wages of Sin,pt.1 . . . . 2.00
339 Wages of Sin,pt.2 . . . . 2.00
340 R:Kingpin 2.00
341 Kingpin 2.00
342 DGc,KP,V:Kingpin 2.00
343 Without Costume 2.00
344 Identity Crisis,pt.1 . . . . 2.00
345 Identity Crisis,pt.2 . . . . 2.00
346 V:Sir 2.00
347 V:mystery man. 2.00
348 In NY City 2.00
349 Retreats to the Chaste 2.00
350 Double size 3.50
351 . . . . 2.50
352 Return of Matt Murdock 2.50
353 KK,CNr,A:Mr. Hyde 2.00
354 KK,CNr,A:Spider-Man 2.00
355 KK,CNr,A:Pyro. 2.00
356 KK,CNr, ... 2.00
357 KK,CNr, ... 2.00
358 KK,CNr,MRy,A:Mysterio 2.00
359 KK,CNr,A:Absorbing Man. 2.00
360 KK,CNr,MRy,V:Onslaught. 2.00
361 KK,CNr,MRy,A:Black Widow . . 2.00
362 KK,CNr,Romance 2.00
363 KK,GC,CaS,V:Insomnia 2.00
364 KK,CNr,MRy,V:Insomnia 2.00
365 CNr,MRy,V:Mr. Fear,
A:Molten Man. 2.00
366 GC,V:Gladiator 2.00
367 GC,V:Gladiator, concl. 2.00
368 GC,A:Black Widow and Omega
Red 2.00
369 AOI,V:Soviet Super Soldiers. . . . 2.00
370 GC,Black Widow, concl. 2.00
371 AOI,Matt Murdock & Karen
Page's relationship 2.00
372 AOI,Killers after Karen Page . . 2.00
373 AOI,V:The 3 . . . . 2.00
374 AOI,V:Mr. Fear. 2.00
375 AOI,RL,V:Mr. Fear,double size . 3.00
376 SLo,CHm,Daredevil deep
undercover. 2.00
377 SLo,TMo,SHa,Flying Blind,pt.2 2.00
378 SLo,TMo,SHa,Flying Blind,pt.3. 2.00
379 SLo,CHm,Flying Blind,concl. . . 2.00
380 DGC,LW,RbC, V:Bullseye,Bush-
wacker,Kingpin, double size . . . 3.00
Minus 1 Spec., GC, flashback. 1.95
Ann.#1 GC 30.00
Ann.#2 reprints. 8.00
Ann.#3 reprints. 8.00
Ann.#4 (1976)GT,A:Black
Panther,Namor. 6.00
Ann.#5 (1989)MBa,JLe,JR2,KJ,
WPo,AM,Atlantis Attacks,
A:Spider-Man. 5.00
Ann.#6 TS,Lifeform#2,A:Typhoid
Mary 2.75
Ann.#7 JG,JBr,Von Strucker

Daredevil #225
© *Marvel Entertainment Group*

Gambit,pt.1,A:Nick Fury 2.50
Ann.#8 Sys.Bytes#2,A:Deathlok . . . 2.75
Ann.#9 MPa,I:Devourer,w/card,tie-in
to "Fall From Grace". 5.00
Ann.#10 I:Ghostmaker,A:Shang
Chi, Elektra 3.25
G-Size #1 GK(c),reprints. 12.00
TPB Born Again,rep.#227-#233 . . 10.95
TPB Fall of the Kingpin,
rep.#297-300 . . . . 15.95
TPB Gangwar,Reprints
#169-#172,#180. . . . . 12.95
TPB Marked for Death,reps#159-
161,163,164 . . . . 9.95
Daredevil/Punisher:Child's Play
reprints#182-#184 . . . . 7.00
TPB Daredevil: Man Without Fear. 15.95

DAREDEVIL
Sept. 1998

1 JP,JQ,F:Matt Murdock 2.50
2 JP,JQ,blind faith dilemma 2.50
2a variant JSC cover. 2.50
3 JP,JQ,Guardian Devil,pt.3. . . . . . 2.50
4 JP,JQ,Guardian Devil,pt.4. . . . . . 2.50
5 JP,JQ,Guardian Devil,pt.5. . . . . . 2.50
6 JP,JQ,Guardian Devil,pt.6 . . . . . 2.50
7 JP,JQ,Guardian Devil,pt.7. . . . . . 2.50
8 JP,JQ,Guardian Devil,concl. 2.50
8a signed 30.00
9 JP,JQ,DMk,V:Kingpin 2.50
9a signed 30.00
10 JP,JQ,DMk,I:Echo 2.50
11 JP,JQ,DMk,A:Kingpin 2.50
TPB rep. #1–#3 . . . . 9.95

DAREDEVIL/BATMAN
1997

Spec. DGC,SMc, 48pg 6.00

DAREDEVIL/
DEADPOOL '97

Spec, BCh, JHo, Two annuals in
one, 48pg. 5.00

DAREDEVIL/SHI
SHI/DAREDEVIL
Marvel/Crusade 1996

1 (Daredevil/Shi) TSg,AW,
x-over,pt.1 . . . . 2.95

MARVEL

1 (Shi/Daredevil)x-over, pt.2 . . . . . 2.95

DAREDEVIL: THE MAN WITHOUT FEAR
1993–94
1 B:FM(s),JR2,AW,O:Daredevil,
A:Stick,D:Daredevil's Father . . . 7.00
2 JR2,AW,A:Stick,Stone,Elektra . . 6.00
3 JR2,AW,A:Elektra,Kingpin 5.00
4 JR2,AW,A:Kingpin,I:Mickey 5.00
5 JR2,AW,A:Mickey,Last Issue . . . 5.00
TPB rep.#1#5 . . . . 15.95

DARING MYSTERY COMICS
Timely Jan., 1940
1 ASh(c),JSm,O:Fiery Mask,
A:Monako John Steele,Doc Doyle,
Flash FosterBarney Mullen,
Sea Rover, Bondage (c) . . 17,500.00
2 ASh(c),JSm,O:Phantom Bullet
A:Zephyr Jones & K4,Laughing
Mask Mr.E,B:Trojak 6,500.00
3 ASh(c),JSm,A:Phantom
Reporter,Marvex,Breeze
Barton, B:Purple Mask . . . 4,000.00
4 ASh(c),A:G-Man Ace,K4,
Monako,Marvex,E:Purple
Mask,B:Whirlwind Carter . . 2,400.00
5 JSm,B:Falcon,A:Fiery Mask,K4,
Little Hercules,Bondage(c) 2,400.00
6 S&K,O:Marvel Boy,A:Fiery
Mask, Flying Fame,Dynaman,
Stuporman,E:Trojak 3,000.00
7 S&K,O:Blue Diamond,A:The Fin,
Challenger,Captain Daring,
Silver Scorpion,Thunderer . 2,500.00
8 S&K,O:Citizen V,A:Thunderer,
Fin Silver Scorpion,Captain
Daring Blue Diamond 2,000.00
Becomes:

DARING COMICS
9 ASh(c),B:Human Torch,Toro,
Sub Mariner 900.00
10 ASh(c),A:The Angel 750.00
11 ASh(c),A:The Destroyer 750.00
12 E:Human Torch,Toro,Sub-
Mariner, Fall, 1945 . . . . 750.00
Becomes:

JEANIE COMICS
13 B:Jeanie,Queen of the
Teens Mitzi,Willie 100.00
14 Baseball(c) 75.00
15 Schoolbus(c) 75.00
16 Swimsuit(c) 100.00
17 HK,Fancy dress party(c),
Hey Look 75.00
18 HK,Jeanie'sDate(c),Hey Look . . 75.00
19 Ice-Boat(c),Hey Look 75.00
20 Jukebox(c). 50.00
21 . . . . 50.00
22 HK,Hey Look 75.00
23 . . . . 50.00
24. . . . . 50.00
25. . . . . 50.00
26. . . . . 50.00
27 E:Jeanie,Queen of Teens 50.00
Becomes:

COWGIRL ROMANCES
28 Ph(c),Mona Freeman/MacDonald
Carey,Copper Canyon 150.00

DARK ANGEL
See: HELL'S ANGEL

DARK CRYSTAL
April, 1983
1 movie adaption 1.00
2 movie adaption,May 1983 . . . . . 1.00

DARK GUARD
1993–94
1 A:All UK Heroes 2.95
2 A:All UK Heroes 1.75
3 V:Leader,MyS-Tech 1.75
4 V:MyS-Tech 1.75
5 . . . . 1.75
6 and 7 . . . . @1.75

DARKHAWK
March, 1991
1 MM,I&O:Darkhawk,
A:Hobgoblin 3.00
2 MM,A:Spider-Man,V:Hobgoblin . . 2.50
3 MM,A:Spider-Man,V:Hobgoblin . . 2.50
4 MM,I:Savage Steel 2.50
5 MM,I:Portal. 2.50
6 MM,A:Cap.Am,D.D.,Portal,
V:U-Foes 2.50
7 MM,I:Lodestone 2.00
8 MM,V:Lodestone 2.00
9 MM,A:Punisher,V:Savage Steel . 2.00
10 MM,A&N:Tombstone 2.00
11 MM,V:Tombstone 2.00
12 MM,V:Tombstone,R:Dark
Hawks'Father 2.00
13 MM,V:Venom 3.00
14 MM,V:Venom,D:Dark
Hawks Father. 3.00
15 MM,Heart of the Hawk,concl . . . 2.00
16 MM,V:Terrorists 2.00
17 MM,I:Peristrike Force. 2.00
18 MM,V:Mindwolf 2.00
19 MM,R:Portal,A:Spider-Man,V:The
Brotherhood of Evil Mutants . . . 2.00
20 MM,A:Spider-Man,Sleepwalker,
V:Brotherhood of Evil Mutants . 2.00
21 MM,B:Return to Forever 1.75
22 MM,A:Ghost Rider. 1.75
23 MM,I:Evilhawk 1.75
24 V:Evilhawk. 1.50
25 MM,O:Darkhawk,V:Evilhawk,
Holo-graphx(c) 3.50
26 A:New Warriors 1.50
27 A:New Warriors,V:Zarrko 1.50
28 A:New Warriors,Zarrko. 1.50
29 A:New Warriors 1.50
30 I:Purity. 1.50
31 Infinity Crusade 1.50
32 R:Savage Steel 1.50
33 I:Cuda 1.50
34 V:Cuda 1.50
35 DFr(s),V:Venom 1.50
36 DFr(s),V:Scokers,A:Venom 1.50
37 DFr(s),V:Venom 1.50
38 DFr(s),N:Darkhawk 1.50
39 DFr(s) 1.50
40 DFr(s) 1.75
41 DFr(s) 1.75
42 DFr(s), V:Portal,I:Shaper 1.75
43 DFr(s) 1.75
44 DFr(s) 1.75
45 DFr(s),A:Portal. 1.75
46 DFr(s) 1.75
47 . . . . 1.50
48 R:Darkhawk,V:Mahari 1.50
49 V:Overhawk. 1.50
50 V:Overhawk. 2.50
Ann.#1 MM,Assault on ArmorCity . . 3.00

Ann.#2 GC,AW,I:Dreamkiller,
w/Trading card 3.00
Ann.#3 I:Damek 3.00

Darkhold #7
© Marvel Entertainment Group

DARKHOLD
1992–94
1 RCa,I:Redeemers,Polybagged
w/poster,A:Gh.Rider,Blaze 3.00
2 RCa,R:Modred 2.50
3 A:Modred,Scarlet Witch 2.00
4 V:Sabretooth,N'Garai 2.00
5 A:Punisher, Ghost Rider. 2.00
6 RCa,V:Dr.Strange. 2.00
7 A:Dr.Strange,V:Japanese Army. . 2.00
8 Betrayal #1. . . . . 2.00
9 Diabolique 2.00
10 V:Darkholders 2.00
11 Midnight Massacre#3,D:Modred,
Vicki. 2.50
12 V:Chthon 2.00
13 V:Missing Link 2.00
14 Vicki's Secret revealed. 2.00
15 Siege of Darkness,pt.#4. . . . . . 2.00
16 Siege of Darkness,pt.#12. . . . . 2.00

DARK MAN
MOVIE ADAPTION
Sept., 1990
1 BH/MT/TD 2.00
2 BH/TD 1.50
3 BH/TD,final issue 1.50

DARKMAN
Sept., 1990
1 JS,R:Darkman 3.50
2 JS,V:Witchfinder 3.00
3 JS,Witchfinder 3.00
4 JS,V:Dr.West 3.00
5 JS,Durant 3.00
6 JS,V:Durant 3.00

DATE WITH MILLIE
Atlas Oct., 1956
[1st Series]
1 . . . . 125.00
2 . . . . 75.00
3 thru 7 . . . . @50.00
[2nd Series] Oct., 1959
1 . . . . 60.00
2 thru 7 . . . . @40.00

All comics prices listed are for *Near Mint* condition.

Becomes:

LIFE WITH MILLIE

8	40.00
9 & 10	@30.00
11 thru 20	@25.00

Becomes:

MODELING WITH MILLIE

21	35.00
22 thru 54 June, 1967	@25.00

DATE WITH PATSY
Sept., 1957

1 A:Patsy Walker	50.00

DAYDREAMERS
Aug., 1997

1 (of 3) JMD,MEg,HSm	2.50
2 JMD,MEg,HSm,	2.50
3 JMD,TDz,MEg,HSm,concl.	2.50

DAZZLER
March, 1981

1 AA,JR2,A:X-Men,Spm, O:Dazzler.	2.50
2 WS,JR2,AA,X-Men,A:SpM	2.00
3 JR2,Dr.Doom	1.50
4 FS,Dr.Doom	1.50
5 FS,I:Blue Shield	1.50
6 FS,Hulk	1.50
7 FS,Hulk	1.50
8 FS,Quasar	1.50
9 FS,D:Klaw	1.50
10 FS,Galactus	1.50
11 FS,Galactus.	1.50
12 FS,The Light That Failed	1.50
13 FS,V:Grapplers	1.50
14 FS,She Hulk	1.50
15 FS,BSz,Spider Women	1.50
16 FS,BSz,Enchantress	1.50
17 FS,Angel,V:Doc Octopus	1.50
18 FS,BSz,A:Fantastic Four,Angel, V:Absorbing Man	1.50
19 FS,Blue Bolt,V:Absorbing Man	1.50
20 FS,V:Jazz and Horn.	1.50
21 FS,A:Avengers,F.F.,C:X-Men, (double size)	1.50
22 FS,V:Rogue,Mystique	3.50
23 FS,V:Rogue,A:Powerman, Iron Fist	2.00
24 FS,V:Rogue,A:Powerman,	

Dazzler #20
© Marvel Entertainment Group

Iron Fist	3.00
25 FS,`The Jagged Edge'	1.50
26 FS,Lois London	1.50
27 FS,Fugitive	2.50
28 FS,V:Rogue.	3.00
29 FS,Roman Nekoboh	1.50
30 FS,Moves to California.	1.50
31 FS,The Last Wave	1.50
32 FS,A:Inhumans	1.50
33 Chiller	2.50
34 FS,Disappearance	1.50
35 FS,V:Racine Ramjets.	1.50
36 JBy(c),FS,V:Tatterdemalion	1.50
37 JBy(c),FS	1.50
38 PC,JG,X-Men	5.00
39 PC,JG,Caught in the grip of death	1.50
40 PC,JG,Secret Wars II.	2.50
41 PC,JG,A:Beast	2.50
42 PC,JG,A:Beast,last issue	2.50

DEADLIEST HEROES OF KUNG FU
Summer, 1975

1 Magazine size	3.50

DEADLY FOES OF SPIDER-MAN
May, 1991

1 AM,KGa,V:Sinister Syndicate	4.00
2 AM,Boomerang on Trial	3.00
3 AM,Deadly Foes Split.	3.00
4 AM,Conclusion	3.00
TPB rep. #1–#4	12.95

DEADLY HANDS OF KUNG FU
April, 1974

1 NA(c),JSa,JSon,O:Sons of the Tiger, B:Shang-Chi, Bruce Lee Pin-up	30.00
2 NA(c),JSa	25.00
3 NA(c),JSon,A:Sons of the Tiger	20.00
4 NA(Bruce Lee)(c),JSon,Bruce Lee biography	20.00
5 BWS,PG.	15.00
6 GP,JSon,A:Sons of the Tiger	15.00
7 GP,JSon,A:Sons of the Tiger	20.00
8 GP,JSon,A:Sons of the Tiger	12.00
9 GP,JSon,A:Sons of the Tiger	12.00
10 GP,JSon,A:Sons of the Tiger	20.00
11 NA(c),GP,JSon,A:Sons of the Tiger.	12.00
12 NA(c),GP,JSon,A:Sons of the Tiger.	10.00
13 GP,JSon,A:Sons of the Tiger	10.00
14 NA(c),GP,HC,JSon,A:Sons of the Tiger.	35.00
15 JS.PG,JSn,,Annual #1	15.00
16 JSn,A:Sons of the Tiger.	10.00
17 NA(c),JSn,KG,A:Sons of the Tiger.	10.00
18 JSn,A:Sons of the Tiger	10.00
19 JSn,I:White Tiger	15.00
20 GP,O:White Tiger	10.00
21	8.00
22 KG,C:Jack of Hearts	10.00
23 GK,Jack of Hearts	15.00
24 KG,Ironfist	15.00
25 I:Shimaru.	15.00
26	15.00
27	9.00
28 Bruce Lee Special	40.00
29 Ironfist vs. Shang Chi.	15.00
30 Swordquest	10.00
31 JSon, Jack of Hearts	10.00
32 MR,JSon,Daughters of the	

Dragon.	10.00
33 MR,Feb., 1977	
12.00 Spec. Album Ed.,NA, Sum.1974 .	
15.00	

DEAD OF NIGHT
Dec., 1973

1 JSt,Horror reprints,A Haunted House is not a Home	15.00
2 BEv(c),House that Fear Built	10.00
3 They Lurk Below.	10.00
4 Warewolf Beware	10.00
5 Deep Down	10.00
6 Jack the Ripper	10.00
7 SD,The Thirteenth Floor	10.00
8 Midnight Brings Dark Madness	10.00
9 Deathride	10.00
10 SD,I Dream of Doom	10.00
11 GK/BWr(c),I:Scarecrow, Fires of Rebirth,Fires of Death August, 1975	18.00

DEADPOOL
1993

1 B:FaN(s),JMd,MFm(i), V:Slayback,Nyko	4.00
2 JMd,MFm(i),V:Black Tom Cassidy,Juggernaut	3.00
3 JMd,MFm(i),I:Comcast, Makeshift,Rive,A:Slayback	2.50
4 E:FaN(s),JMd,MFm(i), A:Slayback,Kane	2.50

[2nd Limited Series] 1994

1 A:Banshee,Syrin,Juggernaut Black Tom	2.00
2 A:Banshee,Syrin,V:Juggernaut	2.00
3 A:Syrin,Juggernaut	2.00
4 Final issue	2.00

DEADPOOL
1996

1 NMa,V:Sasquatch,48pg,	3.50
2 NMa,A:Copycat	3.00
3 NMa,A:Siryn.	2.50
4 NMa,Will Hulk cure him?	2.00
5 NMa,A:Siryn,T-Ray.	2.00
6 NMa,I:	2.00
7 AaL,A:Typhoid Mary.	2.00
8 NMa, cont. from Daredevil/ Deadpool '97,A:Gerry	2.00
9 NMa, new villain.	2.00
10 NMa,A:Great Lake Avengers	2.00
11 NMa,Fall through time, A:Alfred	5.00
12 NMa,Typhoid Mary, Zoe Cullodon & Siryn return	2.00
13 NMa,V:T-Ray.	2.00
14 WMc,Deal of a Lifetime	2.00
15 WMc,A:Landau, Luckman & Lake	2.00
16 WMc, in middle east	2.00
17 WMc, Landau, Luckman & Lake's plan	2.00
18 WMc,V:Ajax.	2.00
19 WMc,more secrets of blind AI	2.00
20 Cosmic Messiah	2.00
21	2.00
22 WMc,A:Cable	2.00
23 WMc,Dead Reckoning,pt.1 48-page	3.00
24 WMc,Dead Reckoning,pt.2.	2.00
25 WMc,Dead Reckoning,pt.3.	2.00
26 Dead Reckoning,aftermath.	2.00
27 V:A.I.M. concl.	2.00
28 R:Weasel.	2.00
29 V:Bullseye.	2.00
30 A:Mercedes,T-Ray.	2.00
31 V:T-Ray.	2.00
32 V:T-Ray,A:Mercedes	2.00

33 V:T-Ray 2.00
Ann. '98 BCh(c) F:Deadpool & Death,
48pg 3.00
Minus 1 Spec., ALo, flashback,
O:Deadpool 1.95
Spec. Deadpool Team-Up,2 Deadpools
F:Widdle Wade. 3.00
Spec. Baby's First Deadpool Book . 3.00
Spec. Encyclopedia Deadpoolica . . 3.00
TPB Circle Chase,FaN,JMd,MFm, 12.95
TPB Mission Improbable. 14.95
TPB MWa,IaC,Sins of the Past,
rep. limited series 6.00

DEATH3
1993
1 I:Death Metal,Death Wreck. 2.95
2 V:Ghost Rider. 1.75
3 A:Hulk,Cable,Storm,Thing. 1.75
4 Last issue. 1.75

DEATHLOK
[Limited Series] July, 1990
1 JC,SW,I:Michael Colins
(2nd Deathlok) 4.00
2 JC,SW,V:Wajler 3.00
3 DCw,SW,V:Cyberants 3.00
4 DCw,SW,V:Sunfire,final issue . . . 3.00

[Regular Series] 1991–94
1 DCw,MM,V:Warwolf 2.50
2 DCw,MM,A:Dr.Doom,Machine Man,
Forge 2.50
3 DCw,MM,V:Dr.Doom,
A:Mr.Fantastic 2.50
4 DCw,MM,A:X-Men,F.F.,Vision,
O:Mechadoom 2.50
5 DCw,MM,V:Mechadoom,
A:X-Men,Fantastic Four 2.50
6 DCw,MM,A:Punisher,
V:Silvermane 2.50
7 DCw,MM,A:Punisher,
V:Silvermane 2.50
8 A:Main Frame,Ben Jacobs 2.00
9 DCw,MM,A:Ghost Rider,
V:Nightmare 2.50
10 DCw,MM,A:GhR,V:Nightmare . . 2.50
11 DCw,MM,V:Moses Magnum . . . 2.00
12 DCw,MM,Biohazard Agenda . . . 2.00
13 DCw,MM,Biohazard Agenda . . . 2.00
14 DCw,MM,Biohazard Agenda . . . 2.00
15 DCw,MM,Biohazard Agenda . . . 2.00
16 DCw,MM,Inf.War,V:Evilok. 2.00

Deathlok #5
© Marvel Entertainment Group

17 WMc,MM,B:Cyberwar 2.00
18 WMc,A:Silver Sable 2.00
18a Newstand Ed. 1.75
19 SMc,Cyberwar#3 . . . . 2.00
20 SMc,Cyberwar#4 . . . . 2.00
21 E:Cyberwar,A:Cold Blood
Nick Fury 2.00
22 V:MosesMagnum,A:Bl.Panther. . 2.00
23 A:Bl.Panther,V:Phreak,Stroke. . . 2.00
24 V:MosesMagnum,A:Bl.Panther. . 2.00
25 WMc,V:MosesMagnum,A:Black
Panther,holo-grafx(c) 2.50
26 V:Hobogoblin. 2.00
27 R:Siege 2.00
28 Infinty Crusade 2.00
29 Inner Fears 2.00
30 KHd,V:Hydra 2.00
31 GWt(s),KoK,B:Cyberstrike,
R:1st Deathlok 2.00
32 GWt(s),KoK,A:Siege 2.00
33 GWt(s),KoK,V:Justice Peace . . . 2.00
34 GWt(s),KoK,E:Cyberstrike,V:Justice
Peace,final issue 2.00
Ann.#1 JG,I:Timestream 2.75
Ann.#2 I:Tracer,w/card 2.95

DEATHLOK
July 1999
1 JoC,JQ&JaL(c),Marvel Tech 2.00
2 JoC,A:Nick Fury 2.00
2a variant cover. 2.00
3 JoC,I:Billy Bailey. 2.00

DEATHLOK SPECIAL
1991
1 Rep.Mini Series 2.50
2 Rep.Mini Series 2.50
3 Rep.Mini Series 2.50
4 Rep.Mini Series, final issue. 2.50

DEATH METAL
Marvel UK 1994
1 JRe,I:Argon,C:Alpha Flight 1.95
2 JRe,V:Alpha Flight 1.95
3 JRe,I:Soulslug 1.95
4 Re,Last Issue. 1.95

DEATH METAL
VS. GENETIX
Marvel UK 1993–94
1 PaD,w/card. 2.95
2 PaD,w/card. 2.95

DEATH'S HEAD
Marvel UK Dec., 1988
1 V:Backbreaker 5.00
2 A:Dragons Claws 4.00
3 . . . . 4.00
4 V:Plague Dog 3.00
5 V:Big Shot 3.00
6 V:Big Shot 3.00
7 & 8 . . . . @3.00
9 A:Fantastic Four. 3.50
10 A:Iron Man. 3.50
TPB Reprints#1-#10 . . . . 12.95

DEATH'S HEAD
[Limited Series]
1 A:`Old' Death's Head 1.95

DEATH'S HEAD II
Marvel UK March, 1992
[Limited Series]
1 LSh,I:2nd Death's Head,

Death's Head II #9
© Marvel Entertainment Group

D:1st Death's Head 4.00
1a 2nd printing,Silver. 2.50
2 LSh,A:Fantastic Four 3.00
2a 2nd printing,Silver. 3.00
3 LSh,I:Tuck 3.50
4 LSh,A:Wolverine,Spider-Man,
Punisher. 3.50

[Regular Series] 1992
1 LSh,A:X-Men,I:Wraithchilde . . . 3.00
2 LSh,A:X-Men 2.25
3 LSh,A:X-Men,V:Raptors 2.25
4 LSh,A:X-Men,V:Wraithchilde . . . 2.25
5 V:UnDeath's Head II,
A:Warheads 2.25
6 R:Tuck,V:Major Oak 2.25
7 V:Major Oak 2.25
8 V:Wizard Methinx 2.25
9 BHi,V:Cybernetic Centaurs 2.25
10 DBw,A:Necker 2.25
11 SCy,R:Charnel. 2.25
12 DAn(s),SvL,V:Charnel 2.25
13 SvL,A:Liger 2.25
14 SvL,Brain Dead Cold,Blue
Foil(c). 3.25
15 SvL,V:Duplicates 2.25
16 SvL,DAn 2.25
17 SvL,DAn 1.95
18 SvL,DAn 1.95
Spec. Gold Ed. LSh(a&s) 3.95

DEATH'S HEAD II/DIE CUT
Marvel UK 1993
1 I:Die Cut. 3.25
2 O:Die Cut 1.75

DEATH'S HEAD II/
KILLPOWER: BATTLETIDE
[1st Limited Series]
1 GSr,A:Wolverine. 2.50
2 thru 4 GSr,A:Wolverine . . . . . . @2.00
[2nd Limited Series]
1 A:Hulk 3.25
2 V:Hulk 1.75
3 A:Hulk 1.75
4 last issue 1.75

DEATH-WRECK
Marvel UK 1994
1 A:Death's Head II 1.95
2 V:Gangsters 1.95

3 A:Dr.Necker 1.95
4 last issue 1.95

DEEP, THE
Nov., 1977
1 CI,Movie Adaption 2.00

DEFENDERS
August, 1972
1 SB,I&D:Necrodames. 65.00
2 SB,V:Calizuma 30.00
3 GK(c),SB,JM,V:UndyingOne . . . 25.00
4 SB,FMc,Bl.Knight,V:Valkyrie . . . 25.00
5 SB,FMc,D:Omegatron. 25.00
6 SB,FMc,V:Cyrus Black 20.00
7 SB,FBe,A:Hawkeye 20.00
8 SB,FBe,Avengers,SilverSurfer . 20.00
9 SB,FMc,Avengers. 20.00
10 SB,FBe,Thor vs. Hulk 22.00
11 SB,FBe,A:Avengers 10.00
12 SB,JA,Xemnu 8.00
13 GK(c),SB,KJ,J:Night Hawk. . . . 8.00
14 SB,DGr,O:Hyperion 8.00
15 SB,KJ,A:Professor X,V:Magneto,
Savage Land Mutates. 12.00
16 GK(c),SB,Professor X,V:Magneto,
Savage Land Mutates. 12.00
17 SB,DGr,Power Man 7.00
18 GK(c),SB,DGr,A:Power Man . . . 7.00
19 GK(c),SB,KJ,A:Power Man 7.00
20 K&R(c),SB,A:Thing 7.00
21 GK(c),SB,O:Valkyrie 5.00
22 GK(c),SB,V:Sons o/t Serpent . . 5.00
23 GK(c),SB,A:Yellow Jacket 5.00
24 GK(c),SB,BMc,A:Daredevil 5.00
25 GK(c),SB,JA,A:Daredevil 5.00
26 K&R(c),SB,A:Guardians. 8.00
27 K&R(c),SB,A:Guardians
C:Starhawk 8.00
28 K&R(c),SB,A:Guardians
I:Starhawk 7.00
29 K&R(c),SB,A:Guardians. 7.00
30 JA(i),A:Wong 4.00
31 SB,JM,Nighthawk 4.00
32 GK(c),SB,JM,O:Nighthawk. 4.00
33 GK(c),SB,JM,V:Headmen 4.00
34 SB,JM,V:Nebulon 4.00
35 GK(c),SB,KJ,I:Red Guardian . . . 4.00
36 GK(c),SB,KJ,A:Red Guardian . 12.00
37 GK(c),SB,KJ,J:Luke Cage 4.00
38 SB,KJ,V:Nebulon 12.00
39 SB,KJ,V:Felicia 4.00

Defenders #35
© Marvel Entertainment Group

40 SB,KJ,V:Assassin 4.00
41 KG,KJ,Nighthawk. 4.00
42 KG,KJ,V:Rhino 4.00
43 KG,KJ,Cobalt Man,Egghead . . . 4.00
44 KG,KJ,J:Hellcat,V:Red Rajah . . . 4.00
45 KG,KJ,Valkyrie V:Hulk 4.00
46 KG,KJ,L:DrStrange,LukeCage . . 4.00
47 KG,KJ,Moon Knight 4.00
48 KG,A:Wonder Man. 4.00
49 KG,O:Scorpio 4.00
50 KG,Zodiac,D:Scorpio 4.00
51 KG,Moon Knight 4.00
52 KG,Hulk,V:Sub Mariner 4.00
53 KG,DC,MG,TA,C&I:Lunatik 3.00
54 MG,Nigh Fury 3.00
55 CI,O:Red Guardian 3.00
56 CI,KJ,Hellcat,V:Lunatik 3.00
57 DC,Ms.Marvel 3.00
58 Return of Dr.Strange 3.00
59 I:Belathauzer. 3.00
60 V:Vera Gemini 3.00
61 Spider-Man,A:Lunatik 2.50
62 Hercules,C:Polaris 2.50
63 Mutli Heroes 2.50
64 Mutli Heroes 2.50
65 Red Guardian 2.50
66 JB,Valkyrie I 2.50
67 Valkryie II 2.50
68 HT,When Falls the Mountain . . . 2.50
69 HT,A:The Anything Man. 2.50
70 HT,A:Lunatik 2.50
71 HT,O:Lunatik 2.50
72 HT,V:Lunatik 2.50
73 HT,Foolkiller,V:WizardKing 5.00
74 HT,Foolkiller,L:Nighthawk. 5.00
75 HT,Foolkiller. 4.00
76 HT,O:Omega 2.00
77 HT,Moon Dragon 2.00
78 HT,Yellow Jacket 2.00
79 HT,Tunnel World 2.00
80 HT,DGr,Nighthawk. 2.00
81 HT,Tunnel World 2.00
82 DP,JSt,Tunnel World 2.00
83 DP,JSt,Tunnel World 2.00
84 DP,JSt,Black Panther. 2.00
85 DP,JSt,Black Panther. 2.00
86 DP,JSt,Black Panther. 2.00
87 DP,JSt,V:Mutant Force. 2.00
88 DP,JSt,Matt Mardock 2.00
89 DP,JSt,D:Hellcat's
Mother, O:Mad-Dog 2.00
90 DP,JSt,Daredevil 2.00
91 DP,JSt,Daredevil 2.00
92 DP,JSt,A:Eternity,
Son of Satan 3.00
93 DP,JSt,Son of Satan 3.00
94 DP,JSt,I:Gargoyle. 2.00
95 DP,JSt,V:Dracula,O:Gargoyle. . . 2.00
96 DP,JSt,Ghost Rider 3.00
97 DP,JSt,False Messiah 2.00
98 DP,JSt,A:Man Thing. 2.00
99 DP,JSt,Conflict. 2.00
100 DP,JSt,DoubleSize,V:Satan . . . 3.00
101 DP,JSt,Silver Surfer 2.00
102 DP,JSt,Nighthawk 2.00
103 DP,JSt,I:Null 2.00
104 DP,JSt,Devilslayer,J:Beast 2.00
105 DP,JSt,V:Satan 2.00
106 DP,Daredevil,D:Nighthawk 2.00
107 DP,JSt,Enchantress,A:D.D. . . . 2.00
108 DP,A:Enchantress 2.00
109 DP,A:Spider-Man 2.50
110 DP,A:Devilslayer 2.00
111 DP,A:Hellcat. 2.00
112 DP,A:SquadronSupreme 2.00
113 DP,A:SquadronSupreme 2.00
114 DP,A:SquadronSupreme 2.00
115 DP,A:Submariner 2.00
116 DP,Gargoyle. 2.00
117 DP,Valkyrie. 2.00
118 DP,V:Miracleman 2.00

Defenders #108
© Marvel Entertainment Group

119 DP,V:Miracleman 2.00
120 DP,V:Miracleman 2.00
121 DP,V:Miracleman 2.00
122 DP,A:Iceman 2.00
123 DP,I:Cloud,V:Secret Empire . . . 2.00
124 DP,V:Elf. 2.00
125 DP,New Line-up:Gargoyle,Moon
dragon,Valkyrie,Iceman,Beast,
Angel,W:Son of Satan & Hellcat
I:Mad Dog 3.00
126 DP,A:Nick Fury 2.00
127 DP,V:Professor Power 2.00
128 DP,V:Professor Power 2.00
129 DP,V:Professor Power,New
Mutants X-over. 2.00
130 DP,V:Professor Power 2.00
131 DP,V:Walrus,A:Frogman 2.00
132 DP,V:Spore Monster. 2.00
133 DP,V:Spore Monster. 2.00
134 DP,I:Manslaughter 2.00
135 DP,V:Blowtorch Brand 2.00
136 DP,V:Gargoyle. 2.00
137 DP,V:Gargoyle. 2.00
138 DP,O:Moondragon 2.00
139 DP,A:Red Wolf,V:Trolls. 2.00
140 DP,V:Asgardian Trolls 2.00
141 DP,All Flesh is Grass 2.00
142 DP,V:M.O.N.S.T.E.R. 2.00
143 DP,I:Andromeda,Runner 2.00
144 DP,V:Moondragon 2.00
145 DP,V:Moondragon 2.00
146 DP,Cloud 2.00
147 DP,A:Andromeda,I:Interloper . . 2.00
148 DP,A:Nick Fury 2.00
149 DP,V:Manslaughter,O:Cloud. . . 2.00
150 DP,O:Cloud,double-size 3.00
151 DP,A:Interloper 2.00
152 DP,Secret Wars II,D:Moon-
dragon,Valkyrie,Gargoyle 3.00
G-Size#1 GK(c),JSn,AM,O:Hulk . . 12.00
G-Size#2 GK,KJ,Son of Satan . . . 8.00
G-Size#3 JSn,DA,JM,DN,A:D.D.. . . 6.00
G-Size#4 GK(c),DH,A:YellowJack. . 6.00
G-Size#5 K&R(c),DH,A:Guardians . 6.00
Ann.#1 SB,KJ. 6.00

DEFENDERS OF
DYNATRON CITY
1992
1 FC,I:Defenders of Dynatron City
(from video game & TV ser.) . . . 1.25
2 FC,O:Defender of D.City. 1.25
3 FC,A:Dr Mayhem 1.25

4 FC 1.25
5 FC,V:Intelligent Fleas 1.25
6 FC,V:Dr.Mayhem 1.25

DEFENDERS OF THE EARTH
Jan., 1987—Sept., 1984
1 AS,Flash Gordon & Mandrake . . 2.00
2 AS,Flash Gordon & Mandrake . . 2.00
3 AS,O:Phantom 2.00
4 AS,O:Mandrake 2.00

DELLA VISION
Atlas April, 1955
1 The Television Queen 80.00
2 . . . . 55.00
3 . . . . 55.00
Becomes:

PATTY POWERS
4 . . . . 35.00
5 . . . . 22.00
6 . . . . 22.00
7 Oct., 1956 . . . . 22.00

DENNIS THE MENACE
Nov., 1981–Nov., 1982
1 . . . . 1.25
2 thru 13 . . . . @1.00

Destroyer #7
© Marvel Entertainment Group

DESTROYER, THE
Nov., 1989
1 Black & White Mag. 3.50
2 thru 9 . . . . @2.25
10 June 1990 . . . . 2.25
TPB rep. B/w mag(color) 9.95

THE DESTROYER: TERROR
Dec., 1991
1 V:Nuihc 1.95
2 V:Nuihc 1.95
3 GM,V:Nuihc 1.95
4 DC,'The Last Dinosaur' 1.95

DEVIL DINOSAUR
April, 1978—Dec., 1978
1 JK,I:Devil Dinosaur,Moon Boy . 10.00
2 JK,War With the Spider God 5.00
3 JK,Giant 5.00
4 JK,Objects From the Sky 5.00
5 JK,The Kingdom of the Ants . . . 5.00

6 JK.The Fall 5.00
7 JK,Prisoner of the Demon Tree . 5.00
8 JK,V:Dino Riders 5.00
9 JK,Lizards That Stand 5.00

DEVIL DINOSAUR SPRING FLING
1997
Spec. F:Devil Dinosaur,
Moon-Boy, 48pg 3.00

DEVIL-DOG DUGAN
Atlas July, 1956
1 War Stories 75.00
2 . . . . 50.00
3 . . . . 35.00
Becomes:

TALE OF THE MARINES
4 BP,War Stories 40.00
Becomes:

MARINES AT WAR
5 War Stories 30.00
6 . . . . 30.00
7 The Big Push,August, 1957 . . . 30.00

DEXTER THE DEMON
See: MELVIN THE MONSTER

DIE-CUT
Marvel UK 1993–94
1 A:Beast 2.50
2 V:X-Beast 1.75
3 A:Beast,Prof.X 1.75
4 V:Red Skull 1.75

DIE-CUT VS. G-FORCE
Marvel UK 1993
1 SFr(s),LSh(c),I:G-Force 2.75
2 SFr(s),LSh(c),Last issue 2.75

DIGITEK
Marvel UK 1992–93
1 DPw,I:Digitek,C:Deathlok 2.25
2 DPw,A:Deathlok,V:Bacillicons . . 2.25
3 DPw,A:Deathlok,V:Bacillicons . . 2.25
4 DPw,V:Bacillicons 2.25

DINO RIDERS
Feb., 1989
1 Based on Toys 1.00
2 . . . . 1.00
3 May, 1989 . . . . 1.00

DINOSAURS: A CELEBRATION
Epic 1992
Horns and Heavy Armor 4.95
Bone-Heads and Duck-Bills 4.95
Terrible Claws and Tyrants 4.95
Egg Stealers and Earth Shakers . . . 4.95
TPB 192pg 12.95

DISNEY AFTERNOON
1994–95
1 DarkwingDuck vs.FearsomeFive . 2.00
2 . . . . 2.00
3 . . . . 2.00
4 DarkwingDuck:Gum w/t Wind . . 2.00
5 F:Baloo, Mrs. Cunningham 2.00

6 . . . . 2.00
7 F:Darkwing Duck 2.00
8 . . . . 2.00
9 DarkwingDuck:Borsht to Death . . 2.00
10 F:Scrooge & Mrs. Beakley 2.00

DISNEY COMIC HITS
1995
1 . . . . 3.00
2 F:Lion King 3.00
3 F:Pocahontas 3.00
4 F:Toy Story 3.00
5 Holiday 3.00
6 Aladdin 3.00
7 . . . . 3.00
8 Lion King story 3.00
9 . . . . 3.00
10 Hunchback of Notre Dame 4.00
11 thru 13 . . . . @3.00
14 F:Toy Story characters 3.00
15 101 Dalmations 3.00
16 101 Dalmatians 3.00
17 final issue 3.00

DISNEY PRESENTS
1 F:Aladdin 2.00
2 F:Timon & Pummba 2.00
3 . . . . 2.00

DOC SAMSON
1996
1 From The Incredible Hulk 1.95
2 A:She-Hulk 1.95
3 . . . . 1.95
4 . . . . 1.95

DOC SAVAGE
Oct., 1972
1 JM,Pulp Adapts,Death Eighty
Stories High 15.00
2 JSo(c),The Feathered Serpent
Strikes 10.00
3 JSo(c),Silver Death's Head 10.00
4 JSo(c),The Hell Diver 9.00
5 GK(c),Night of the Monsters . . . 9.00
6 JSo(c),Where Giants Walk 9.00
7 JSo(c),Brand of the Werewolfs . . 9.00
8 In the Lair of the Werewolf
Jan., 1974 . . . . 9.00
G-Size#1 thru #2 Reprints 8.00

DOC SAVAGE
August, 1975
(black & white magazine)
1 JB,Ph(c),Ron Ely 8.00
2 JB 6.00
3 JB 6.00
4 . . . . 6.00
5 thru 7 . . . . @6.00
8 Spring 1977 . . . . 6.00

DR. STRANGE
[1st Series] June, 1968
Prev: Strange Tales
169 DA,O:Dr.Strange 125.00
170 DA,A:Ancient One 40.00
171 TP,DA,V:Dormammu 35.00
172 GC,TP,V:Dormammu 35.00
173 GC,TP,V:Dormammu 35.00
174 GC,TP,I:Satannish 35.00
175 GC,TP,I:Asmodeus 35.00
176 GC,TP,V:Asmodeus 35.00
177 GC,TP,D:Asmodeus,
N:Dr.Strange 35.00
178 GC,TP,A:Black Knight 35.00

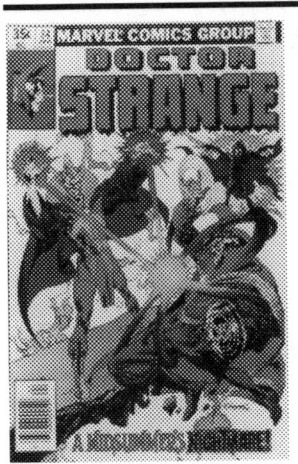

Doctor Strange, 2nd Series #34
© Marvel Entertainment Group

179 BWS(c),rep.Amazing Spider-
   Man Ann.#2 . . . . 35.00
180 GC,TP,V:Nightmare 35.00
181 FB(c),GC,TP,I:Demons of
   Despair 35.00
182 GC,TP,V:Juggernaut 40.00
183 BEv(c),GC,TP,
   I:Undying Ones 40.00

[2nd Regular Series] 1974–87
1 FB,DG,I:Silver Dagger 35.00
2 FB,DG,I:Soul Eater. 15.00
3 FB,A:Dormammu 7.00
4 FB,DG,V:Death. 6.00
5 FB,DG,A:Silver Dagger. 6.00
6 FB(c),GC,KJ,A:Umar,I:Gaea 5.00
7 GC,JR,A:Dormammu 5.00
8 GK(c),GC,TP,O:Clea. 5.00
9 GK(c),GC,A:Dormammu,O:Clea . 5.00
10 B:MWn(s),GK(c),GC,A:Eternity . 5.00
11 JR(c),GC,TP,A:Eternity. 4.50
12 GC,TP,A:Eternity 4.50
13 GC,TP,A:Eternity 4.50
14 GC,TP,A:Dracula 4.50
15 GC,TP,A:Devil 4.50
16 GC,TP,A:Devil 4.50
17 GC,TP,A:Styggro 4.50
18 GC,A:Styggro 4.50
19 GC,AA,I:Xander. 4.50
20 A:Xander. 4.50
21 DA,O:Dr.Strange 4.00
22 I:Apalla 4.00
23 E:MWn(s),JSn,A:Wormworld . . 4.00
24 JSn,A:Apalla,I:Visamajoris 4.00
25 AM,V:Dr.Strange Yet 4.00
26 JSn,A:The Ancient One 4.00
27 TS,A:Stygyro,Sphinx 4.00
28 TS,A:Ghost Rider,
   V:In-Betweener. 5.00
29 TS,A:Nighthawk. 4.00
30 I:Dweller 3.50
31 TS,A:Sub Mariner 3.50
32 A:Sub Mariner 3.50
33 TS,A:The Dreamweaver. 3.50
34 TS,A:Nightmare,D:CyrusBlack . 3.50
35 TS,V:Dweller,I:Ludi 3.50
36 Thunder of the Soul 3.50
37 Fear,the Final Victor. 3.50
38 GC,DG,A:Baron Mordo 3.50
39 GC,DG,A:Baron Mordo 3.50
40 GC,A:Asrael 3.50
41 GC,A:Man Thing 3.00
42 GC,A:Black Mirror 3.00
43 V:Shadow Queen. 3.00

44 GC,A:Princess Shialmar 3.00
45 GC,A:Demon in the Dark 3.00
46 FM,A:Sibylis 3.00
47 MR,TA,I:Ikonn 3.00
48 MR,TA,Brother Voodoo 3.00
49 MR,TA,A:Baron Mordo. 3.00
50 MR,TA,A:Baron Mordo. 3.00
51 MR,TA,A:Sgt. Fury,
   V:Baron Mordo 3.00
52 MR,TA,A:Nightmare 2.50
53 MR,TA,A:Nightmare,Fantastic
   Four,V:Rama-Tut 2.50
54 PS,V:Tiboro 2.50
55 MGo,TA,V:Madness. 2.50
56 PS,TA,O:Dr.Strange. 4.00
57 KN,TA,A:Dr.Doom 2.50
58 DGr,TA,V:Dracula 2.50
59 DGr,TA,V:Dracula 2.50
60 DGr,TA,Scarlet Witch 2.50
61 DGr,TA,V:Dracula 2.50
62 SL,V:Dracula 2.50
63 CP,V:Topaz 2.50
64 TSa,`Art Rage'. 2.50
65 PS,Charlatan 2.50
66 PS,`The Cosen One' 2.50
67 SL,A:Jessica Drew,Shroud. . . . 2.50
68 PS,A:Black Knight 2.25
69 PS,A:Black Knight 2.25
70 BBI,V:Umar 2.25
71 DGr,O:Dormammu 2.25
72 PS,V:Umar 2.25
73 PS,V:Umar 2.25
74 MBg,Secret Wars II 2.25
75 A:Fantastic Four 2.25
76 A:Fantastic Four 2.25
77 A:Topaz 2.25
78 A:Cloak,I:Ecstasy. 3.00
79 A:Morganna. 2.00
80 A:Morganna,C:Rintah 2.00
81 V:Urthona,I:Rintah 2.00
Ann.#1 CR,`Doomworld'. 4.50
G-Size#1 K&R(c),reps Strange
   Tales#164-#168 . . . . 6.00
GN Dr.Strange: What is it that
   Distrubs you, Stephen?, CR,
   revised from Dr.Strange Ann.#1,
   48pg bookshelf (Aug. 1997) . . . 6.00

[3rd Regular Series] 1988–96
1 V:Dorammu 4.00
2 V:Dorammu 3.00
3 I:Dragon Force 3.00
4 EL(c),A:Dragon Force. 3.00
5 JG,V:Baron Mordo 3.50
6 JG,I:Mephista 3.00
7 JG,V:Agamotto,Mephisto 3.00
8 JG,V:Mephisto & Satanish 3.00
9 JG,O:Dr.Strange. 3.50
10 JG,V:Morbius. 3.50
11 JG,A of V,V:Hobgoblin,
   C:Morbius 4.00
12 JG,A of V,V:Enchantress 2.75
13 JG,A of V,V:Arkon 2.75
14 JG,B:Vampiric Verses,
   A:Morbius. 3.50
15 JG,A:Morbius,Amy Grant(C) . . . 5.00
16 JG,A:Morbius,Brother Voodoo . 3.50
17 JV,TD,A:Morbius,Br.Voodoo. . . 3.50
18 JG,E:Vampiric Verses,A:Morbius,
   Brother Voodoo,R:Varnae. . . . 3.50
19 GC,A:Azrael 2.50
20 JG,TD,A:Morbius,V:Zom 3.50
21 JG,TD,B:Dark Wars,
   R:Dormammu. 2.50
22 JG,TD,LW,V:Dormammu 2.50
23 JG,LW,V:Dormammu 2.50
24 JG,E:Dark Wars,V:Dormammu. . 2.50
25 RLm,A:Red Wolf, Black Crow . . 2.50
26 GI,V:Werewolf By Night 2.50
27 GI,V:Werewolf By Night 2.50
28 X-over Ghost Rider #12,
   V:Zodiac. 3.00

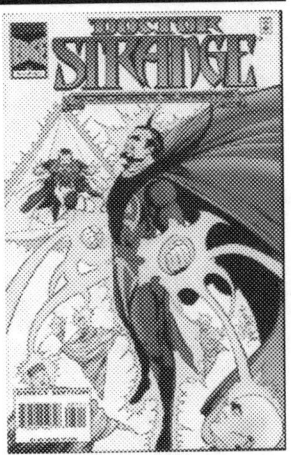

Doctor Strange, 3rd Series #87
© Marvel Entertainment Group

29 A:Baron Blood 2.50
30 Topaz' Fate 2.50
31 TD,Inf.Gauntlet,A:Silver Surfer. . 3.00
32 Inf.Gauntlet,A:Warlock,Silver
   Surfer,V:Silver Dagger 2.50
33 Inf.Gauntlet,V:Thanos,
   Zota,A:Pip 2.50
34 Inf.Gauntlet,V:Dr.Doom,
   A:Pip,Scarlet Witch 2.50
35 Inf.Gauntlet,A:Thor,Pip,
   Scarlet Witch 2.50
36 Inf.Gauntlet,A:Warlock(leads
   into Warlock&Inf.Watch#1) 3.00
37 GI,V:Frankensurfer 2.00
38 GI,Great Fear #1 . . . . 2.00
39 GI,Great Fear #2 . . . . 2.00
40 GI,Great Fear #3,A:Daredevil. . . 2.00
41 GI,A:Wolverine 3.00
42 GI,Infinity War,V:Galactus,A:
   Silver Surfer. 2.25
43 GI,Infinity War,Galactus Vs.
   Agamotto,A:Silver Surfer 2.00
44 GI,Infinity War,V:Juggernaut. . . . 2.00
45 GI,Inf.War,O:Doctor Strange . . . 2.00
46 GI,Inf.War,R:old costume. 2.00
47 GI,Inf.War,V:doppleganger. 2.00
48 GI,V:The Vishanti. 2.00
49 GI,R:Dormammu 2.00
50 GI,A:Hulk,Ghost Rider,Silver
   Surfer,V:Dormammu(leads into
   Secret Defenders)holo-grafx(c). 3.50
51 GI,V:Religious Cult 2.00
52 GI,A:Morbius. 2.00
53 GI,Closes Mansion,L:Wong . . . 2.00
54 GI,Infinity Crusade. 2.00
55 GI,Inf.Crusade. 2.00
56 GI,Inf.Crusade. 2.00
57 A:Kyllian,Urthona. 2.00
58 V:Urthona. 2.00
59 GI,V:Iskelior. 2.00
60 B:DQ(s),Siege of
   Darkness,pt.#7 . . . . 4.00
61 Siege of Darkness,pt.#15. . . . . . 3.25
62 V:Dr.Doom. 2.25
63 JJ(c),V:Morbius 2.00
64 MvR,V:Namor 2.00
65 MvR,V:Namor,Vengeance 2.25
66 A:Wong 2.25
67 R:Clea. 2.25
68 MvR 2.00
69 MvR 2.00
70 A:Hulk 2.00
71 V:Hulk 2.00
72 Metallic(c),Last Rites,pt.1 . . . . . 2.00

All comics prices listed are for *Near Mint* condition.   **CVA Page 187**

MARVEL

73 Last Rites,pt.2 . . . . 2.00
74 SY,DQ,Last Rites,pt.3 . . . . 2.00
75 Prismatic cover 3.50
76 I:New Costume 2.00
77 Mob Clean-up 2.00
78 R:Chton. 2.00
79 Doc's new Asylum 2.00
80 Missing for four months? 2.00
81 A:Nick Fury 2.00
82 A:Hellstorm 2.00
83 V:Tempo Mob,Dormammu 2.00
84 The Homecoming,pt.1 . . . . 2.00
85 The Homecoming,pt.2 . . . . 2.00
86 The Homecoming,pt.3 . . . . 2.00
87 The Homecoming,pt.4 . . . . 2.00
88 The Fall of the Tempo,pt.1 . . . . 2.00
89 The Fall of the Tempo,pt.2 . . . . 2.00
90 final issue 2.00
Ann #2 Return of Defenders,Pt4 . . 5.00
Ann #3 GI,I:Killiam,w/card. 3.25
Ann.#4 V:Salome 3.00
Spec. Dr. Strange/Ghost Rider#1
   Newsstand vers. of Dr.
   Strange #28 (1991) 6.00
Spec.#1 Dr. Strange vs. Dracula
   rep. MWn(s),GC (1994) 2.00
GNv Triumph and Torment MBg,
   F:Dr. Strange & Dr.Doom 9.95
   HC 14.95
Ashcan. 75

DOCTOR STRANGE
Dec. 1998
1 (of 4) TyH,killer pursued 3.00
2 TyH,secrets in Topaz 3.00
3 TyH,magic in Manhattan 3.00
4 TyH,PC,conclusion 3.00

DR. STRANGE CLASSICS
March, 1984
1 SD,Reprints 2.00
2 . . . . 2.00
3 . . . . 2.00
4 June, 1984 . . . . 2.00

DOCTOR WHO
1984–86
1 BBC TV Series,UK reprints,
   Return of the Daleks. 4.50
2 Star Beast 3.00
3 Transformation 3.00

Doctor Who #5
© Marvel Entertainment Group

4 A:K-9,Daleks 3.00
5 V:Time Witch,Colin Baker
   interview 3.00
6 B:Ancient Claw saga 3.00
7 . . . . 3.00
8 The Collector 3.00
9 The Life Bringer 3.00
10 This is your Life 3.00
11 The Deal 3.00
12 End of the Line 3.00
13 V:The Cybermen 3.00
14 Clash of the Neutron Knight. . . 3.00
15 B:Peter Davison-Dr. Who. 3.00
16 Into the Realm of Satan, ... 3.00
17 Peter Davison Interview. 3.00
18 A:Four Dr.Who's 3.00
19 A:The Sontarans 3.00
20 The Stockbridge Horror 3.00
21 The Stockbridge Horror 3.00
22 The Stockbridge Horror 3.00
23 The Unearthly Child. 3.00

DR. ZERO
Epic April, 1988
1 BSz,DCw,I:Dr.Zero 2.00
2 BSz,DCw 1.50
3 BSz,DCw 1.50
4 thru 6 . . . . @1.50
7 DSp 1.50
8 End series, August, 1989 . . . . . 1.50

DOLLY DILL
1945
1 Newsstand 80.00

DOMINO
1996
1 thru 3 . . . . @1.95

DOOM 2099
1993–96
1 PB,I:Doom 2099,V:Tiger Wylde,
   foil(c) 3.00
2 I:Rook Seven 2.00
3 PB,V:Tiger Wylde 2.00
4 PB,V:Tiger Wylde 2.00
5 PB,I:Fever 2.00
6 I:Duke Stratosphear 2.00
7 PB,I:Paloma,V:Duke,Fever Haze 2.00
8 PB,C:Ravage 2.00
9 EC,V:Jack the Ripper 2.00
10 PB,w/Poster. 2.00
11 PB,I:Thandaza 1.75
12 PB,V:Thandaza 1.75
13 PB(c),JFm(s),V:Necrotek 1.75
14 RLm(c),PB,Fall o/t Hammer#4 . 1.75
15 PB,I:Radian 1.75
16 EC(a&s), ... 1.75
17 PB,V:Radian,w/card. 1.75
18 PB, ... 1.75
19 PB,C:Bloodhawk 1.75
20 PB,A:Bloodhawk 1.75
21 PB,Shadow King 1.75
22 PB,R:Duke Stratosphere 1.50
23 PB,R:Tyger Wylde 1.50
24 PB. 1.50
25 PB. 2.50
25a foil cover 3.25
26 . . . . 1.50
27 Revolution 1.50
28 Prologue to D-Day 1.50
Becomes:

DOOM 2099 A.D.
29 Doom Invades America 1.95
29a Chromium Cover 3.50
30 D:Corporate Head 1.95
31 PB,One Nation Under Doom . . 1.95

32 Ravage Aftermath 1.95
33 . . . . 1.95
34 I:Anthony Herod. 1.95
35 E:One Nation Under Doom . . . 1.95
36 . . . . 1.95
37 . . . . 1.95
38 . . . . 1.95
39 . . . . 1.95
40 Rage Against Time,pt.1 . . . . . . 1.95
41 Rage Against Time,pt.2 . . . . . . 1.95

DOPEY DUCK COMICS
Timely Fall, 1945
1 A:Casper Cat,Krazy Krow . . . 100.00
2 A:Casper Cat,Krazy Krow 90.00
Becomes:

WACKY DUCK
3 Paperchase(c) 75.00
4 Wacky Duck(c) 100.00
5 Duck & Devil(c) 65.00
6 Cliffhanger(c) 65.00
1 Baketball(c) 50.00
2 Traffic Light(c). 50.00
Becomes:

JUSTICE COMICS

DOUBLE DRAGON
July, 1991
1 I:Billy&Jimmy Lee 1.00
2 Dragon Statue Stolen,V:Stelth . . 1.00
3 Billy Vs. Jimmy 1.00
4 Dragon Force out of control 1.00
5 V:Stealth 1.00
6 V:Nightfall, final issue 1.00

DOUBLE EDGE
1995
Alpha Punisher vs. Nick Fury 4.95
Omega D:Major Character 4.95

D.P. 7
Nov., 1986
1 O:DP7 . . . . 1.00
2 V:Headhunter. 1.00
3 RT,Headhunters 1.00
4 RT,V:Wompus. 1.00
5 RT,Exorcist 1.00
6 RT,I:The Sweat Shop 1.00
7 RT,V:Clinic 1.00
8 RT,V:Clinic 1.00
9 RT,AW,I:New Paranormals 1.00
10 RT,I:Mysterious People 1.00
11 AW(i)V:Regulator 1.00
12 O:Randy 1.00
13 O:Charly 1.00
14 AW 1.00
15 . . . . 1.00
16 V:BlackPower 1.00
17 . . . . 1.00
18 Pitt tie-in 1.00
19 . . . . 1.25
20 Spitfire 1.25
21 . . . . 1.25
22 . . . . 1.25
23 A:PsiForce 1.25
24 A:Mastodon. 1.25
25 V:Famileech 1.50
26 V:Famileech 1.50
27 The Pitt 1.50
28 V:The Candidate 1.25
29 Deadweight 1.50
30 V:Para-troop 1.25
31 A:Chrome 1.50
32 I:The Cure,last issue,
   June 1989 . . . . 1.50
Ann.#1,I:Witness 1.00

DRACULA LIVES
B&W Magazine, 1973—75
1 GC	35.00
2 NA,GC,JSn,O:Dracula	30.00
3 NA,JB,	25.00
4 MP	20.00
5 GC	20.00
6 JB,GC	20.00
7 GE	20.00
8 GC	20.00
9 AA,RG	20.00
10	25.00
11 thru 13	@20.00

DRACULA: LORD OF THE UNDEAD
Oct. 1998
1 (of 3) PO,TP,R:Dracula	3.00
2 PO,TP,V:Seward	3.00
3 PO,TP,conclusion	3.00

DRAFT, THE
1988
1 Sequel to The Pit	3.75

DRAGON LINES
Epic *Heavy Hitters* 1993
[1st Limited Series]
1 RLm,V:Terrorist on Moon, Embossed(c)	3.00
2 RLm,V:Kuei Emperor	2.25
3 RLm,V:Spirit Boxer	2.25
4 RLm,K:Kuei Emperor	2.25
[Regular Series]
1 B:PQ(s),RLm,I:Tao	2.50
2 RLm,	2.50

DRAGONSLAYER
Oct.–Nov., 1981
1 Movie adapt.	1.25
2 Movie adapt.	1.25

DRAGON STRIKE
1 Based on TSR Game	1.50

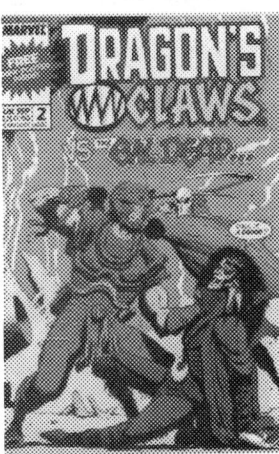

Dragon's Claws #2
© Marvel Entertainment Group

DRAGON'S TEETH/ DRAGON'S CLAWS
July, 1988
1 GSr,I:Mercy Dragon, Scavenger,Digit Steel	1.75
2 GSr,V:Evil Dead	1.50
3 GSr,Go Home	1.50
4 GSr	1.50
5 GSr,I:Death's Head	18.00
6 thru 10 GSr	@1.75

DREADLANDS
Epic
1 Post-Apocalyptic Mini-series	4.00
2 Trapped in Prehistoric Past	4.00
3 V:Alien Time Travelers	4.00
4 Final Issue	4.00

DREADSTAR
Epic Nov., 1982
1 JSn,I:Lord Papal	4.00
2 JSn,O:Willow	2.50
3 JSn,V:Lord Papal	2.25
4 JSn,I:Z	2.25
5 JSn,V:Teutun	2.25
6 JSn,BWr,Interstellar Toybox	2.25
7 JSn,BWr,V:Dr.Mezlo	2.25
8 JSn,V:Z	2.25
9 JSn,V:Z	2.25
10 JSn,V:Z	2.25
11 JSn,O:Lord Papal	2.00
12 JSn,I:Dr.Delphi	2.00
13 JSn,V:Infra Red & Ultra Violet	2.00
14 JSn,V:Lord Papal	2.00
15 JSn,new powers	2.00
16 JSn,V:Lord Papal	2.00
17 JSn,V:Willows father	2.00
18 JSn,V:Dr.Mezlo	2.00
19 JSn,V:Dr Mezlo	2.00
20 JSn,D:Oedi	2.00
21 JSn,D:Dr.Delphi	2.00
22 JSn,V:Lord Papal	2.00
23 JSn,V:Lord Papal	2.00
24 JSn,JS,V:Lord Papal	2.00
25 JSn,V:Lord Papal	2.00
26 JSn,R:Oedi	2.00
Ann.#1 JSn,The Price	2.50

See COLOR COMICS section

DREADSTAR & COMPANY
July, 1985
1 JSo,reprint	1.25
2 JSo,rep.	1.00
3 JSo,rep.	1.00
4 JSo,rep.	1.00
5 JSo,rep,Dec., 1985.	1.00

DROIDS
Star April, 1986
1 JR	3.00
2 AW	3.00
3 JR/AW	3.00
4 AW	3.00
5 AW	3.00
6 EC/AW,A:Luke Skywalker	3.00
7 EC/AW,A:Luke Skywalker	3.00
8 EC/AW,A:Luke Skywalker	3.00

DRUID
1995
1 R:Dr. Druid Surprise!!!	2.50
2 F:Nekra	1.95
3 deranged canibal wisemen	1.95
4 Why Must He Die?	1.95

Dune #1
© Marvel Entertainment Group

DUNE
April–June, 1985
1 Movie Adapt,Rep. Marvel Super Spec,BSz	1.50
2 Movie Adapt,BSz	1.50
3 Movie Adapt,BSz,	1.50

DYNOMUTT
Nov., 1977
1 Based on TV series	10.00
2 thru 5	@8.00
6 Sept., 1978	8.00

EARTHWORM JIM
1995–96
1 I:Earthworm Jim	2.25
2 Cow tipping	2.25
3 V:Lawyers,conclusion	2.25

EARTH X
Jan. 1999
0 (of 14) AxR,JPL,Machine Man & Watcher	4.00
0a signed	30.00
1 AxR,JPL,V:Inhumans,32-page	3.00
1a signed	30.00
2 AxR,JPL,fate of Fant.Four	3.00
3 AxR,JPL,World Super Powers	3.00
4 JPL,AxR(c),A:new Hulk.	3.00
5 JPL,AxR(c),V:Doombots	3.00
6 JPL,AxR(c),different X-Men	3.00
7 JPL,AxR(c),A:Hulk	3.00
Sketchbook	4.00

ECTOKID
Razorline 1993–94
1 I:Dex Mungo,BU:Hokum & Hex.	2.75
2 O:Dex.	2.00
3 I:Ectosphere	2.00
4 I:Brothers Augustine	2.00
5 A:Saint Sinner	2.00
6 Highway 61 Revisited	2.00
7	2.00
8 V:Ice Augustine	1.75
9 Love is like a Bullet.	2.00
10	2.00
Ectokid Unleashed	2.95

ELECTRIC UNDERTOW
Dec., 1989
1 MBa,Strike Force 4.00
2 MBa, Will Deguchis 4.00
3 MBa, Alien Invaders 4.00
4 MBa,Attack on Beijing 4.00
5 MBa, Morituri defeated,March,
1990 . . . . 4.00

ELEKTRA
Nov. 1996
1 PrM,MD2, ... 2.95
1A variant (c). 4.00
2 PrM,MD2,V:Bullseye, round two . 2.00
3 PrM,MD2, ... 2.00
4 PrM,MD2 . . . . 2.00
5 PrM,MD2, ... 2.00
6 PrM,MD2 . . . . 2.00
7 PrM,MD2,A:Konrad,The Architect 2.00
8 PrM,MD2,V:The Architect 2.00
9 PrM,MD2,V:The Four Winds 2.00
10 PrM,MD2,V:Daredevil,"American
Samurai," pt.1 . . . . 2.00
11 PrM,MD2,F:Daredevil. 2.00
12 PrM,MD2,F:Daredevil,V:American
Samuri 2.00
13 PrM,MD2,F:Daredevil, concl. . . . 2.00
14 LHa,MD2,A:Wolverine 2.00
15 LHa,MD2,A:Silver Samurai . . . 2.00
16 LHa,MD2,A Hole in the Soul . . . 2.00
17 LHa,MD2,V:The Hand 2.00
18 LHa,MD2,A:Shang-Chi&Kingpin. 2.00
19 LHa,MD2,last issue 2.00
Minus 1 Spec.,PMg,MD2,flashback. 1.95

ELEKTRA: ASSASSIN
August, 1986
1 FM,BSz,V:Shield 6.00
2 FM,BSz,I:Garrett. 5.00
3 FM,BSz,V:Shield,A:Garrett 5.00
4 FM,BSz,V:Shield,A:Garrett 5.00
5 FM,BSz,I:Chastity,A:Garrett 5.00
6 FM,BSz,A:Nick Fury,Garrett 5.00
7 FM,BSz,V:Ken Wind,A:Garrett . . 5.00
8 FM,BSz,V:Ken Wind,A:Garrett . . 6.00
TPB Rep #1-8 . . . . 12.95

ELEKTRA LIVES AGAIN
Graphic Novel FM,R:Elektra,A:Matt
Murdock,V:The Hand 30.00
TPB FM, rep. of HC, 80pg. 6.95

Elektra #12
© Marvel Entertainment Group

ELEKTRA: ROOT OF EVIL
1 V:Snakeroot 3.00
2 V:Snakeroot 3.00
3 Elektra's Brother. 3.00
4 V:The Hand 3.00

ELEKTRA: SAGA
Feb., 1984
1 FM,rep.Daredevil 7.00
2 FM,rep.Daredevil 7.00
3 FM,rep.Daredevil 7.00
4 FM,rep.Daredevil 7.00
TPB Reprints#1-#4. . . . . 16.95
GN Book One FM,KJ, rep. from
Daredevil, 96pg 3.95
GN Book Two FM,KJ, rep. from
Daredevil, 96pg 3.95

ELEKTRA/WITCHBLADE
1-shot "Devil's Reign,"
pt.6, x-over. 3.00

ELFQUEST
August, 1985
1 WP,reprints. 4.00
2 WP. 2.50
3 WP. 2.50
4 WP. 2.50
5 WP. 2.50
6 WP,Young Cutter V:Mad Coil . . . 2.50
7 WP,Young Cutter V:Mad Coil . . . 2.25
8 WP. 2.25
9 WP. 2.25
10 WP,A:Cutter, Skywise 2.25
11 WP,I:Two Edge 2.25
12 WP,The Mysterious Forest. 2.25
13 WP,The Forest, A:Leetah 2.25
14 WP,A:The Bone Woman 2.25
15 WP,The Forest, continued 2.25
16 WP,Forbidden Grove 2.00
17 WP,Blue Mountain 2.00
18 WP,Secrets 2.00
19 WP,Twisted Gifts 2.00
20 WP,Twisted Gifts 2.00
21 WP 2.00
22 WP,A:Winnowill 2.00
23 WP,Blue Mountain,A:Winnowill. . 2.00
24 WP,The Quest Usurped 2.00
25 WP,Northern Wastelands 2.00
26 WP,Rayeks Story. 2.00
27 WP,Battle Preparations 2.00
28 WP,Elves vs. Trolls 2.00
29 WP,Battle Beneath Blue
Mountain 2.00
30 and 31 WP. . . . . @2.00
32 WP,Conclusion, March 1988 . . . 2.00

ELSEWHERE PRINCE
Epic May–Oct., 1990
1 thru 6 . . . . @2.00

ELVIRA
Oct., 1988
Spec.B&W, Movie Adapt. 2.00

EPIC
1992
1 Wildcards,Hellraiser 4.95
2 Nightbreed,Wildcards 4.95
3 DBw,MFm,Alien Legion, ... 4.95
4 Stalkers,Metropol,Wildcards 4.95

EPIC GRAPHIC NOVEL
Moebius 1: Upon a Star 10.00
Moebius 2: Arzach 10.00

Moebius 3: Airtight Garage 10.00
Moebius 4: Long Tomorrow. 10.00
Moebius 5: 10.00
Moebius 6: Pharadonesia 10.00
Last of Dragons 7.00
The Incal 1 Moebius 11.00
The Incal 2 Moebius 11.00
The Incal 3 Moebius 11.00
JBo,Someplace Strange 7.00
MZ,Punisher. 16.95

EPIC ILLUSTRATED
Spring, 1980
1 Black and White/Color Mag. . . . 6.00
2 thru 10 . . . . @4.50
11 thru 15 . . . . @3.50
16 . . . . 4.00
17 thru 20 . . . . @3.00
21 thru 25 . . . . @3.00
26 thru 34, March, 1986 . . . . @5.50

EPIC LITE
Epic Nov., 1991
One-shot short stories 3.95

ESSENTIAL SPIDER-MAN
1997
Vol. 1 StL,SD, rep. Amaz. Fant. #15,
Amaz Sp.-M #1–#20, Ann. #1. 13.00
Vol. 2 StL,SD, rep. Amaz. Sp.-M
#21–#43, Ann.#2&#3 . . . . 13.00
Vol. 3 StL,JR,Lizard,Vulture,
Kraven 13.00

ESSENTIAL WOLVERINE
May 1998
Vol 3 TPB 13.00

ESSENTIAL X-MEN
Vol. 2 rep. Uncanny X-Men #120-
#145. . . . . 14.95
Vol. 3 rep. Uncanny X-Men #145-
#161, Annuals #3-#5 . . . . 14.95

ETERNALS
[1st Series] July, 1976
1 JK,I:Ikaris,25 cent edition 6.00
2 JK,I:Ajak,25 cent edition 5.00
3 JK,I:Sersi 5.00
4 JK,Night of the Demons 4.00
5 JK,I:Makarri,Zuras Thena,Domo. 4.00
6 JK,Gods & Men at City College. . 4.00
7 JK,V:Celestials 4.00
8 JK,I:Karkas, Reject. 4.00
9 JK,I:Sprite,Reject vs. Karkas. . . 4.00
10 JK,V:Celestials 4.00
11 JK,I:Kingo Sunen 4.00
12 JK,I:Uni-Mind. 4.00
13 JK,I:FOrgottenOne(Gilgamesh) . 4.00
14 JK,V:Hulk 4.00
15 JK,V:Hulk 4.00
16 JK,I:Dromedan. 4.00
17 JK,I:Sigmar 4.00
18 JK,I:Nerve Beast 4.00
19 JK,Secret o/t Pyramid 4.00
Ann.#1 JK,V:Timekillers 3.00
[2nd Series] Oct., 1985
1 SB,I:Cybele 1.50
2 SB,V:Deviants 1.50
3 SB,V:Deviants 1.50
4 SB,V:Deviants 1.50
5 SB,V:Deviants 1.50
6 SB,V:Deviants 1.50
7 SB,V:Deviants 1.50
8 WS,SB,V:Deviants 1.50
9 WS,SB,V:Deviants 1.50

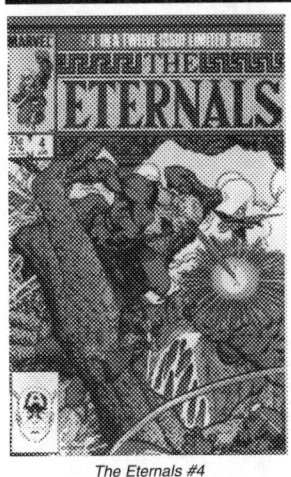

The Eternals #4
© Marvel Entertainment Group

10 WS,SB,V:Deviants 1.50
11 WS,KP,V:Deviants 1.50
12 WS,KP,V:Deviants 1.50

ETERNALS: HEROD FACTOR
Nov., 1991
1 MT/BMc,A:Sersi (giant size) 2.50

EVERYMAN
Epic 1991
1-shot Supernatural Story
(Animated Cel Artwork) 4.50

EWOKS
Star June, 1985—Sept., 1987
1 Based on TV Series 3.00
2 . . . . 2.50
3 . . . . 2.50
4 A:Foonars 2.50
5 Wicket vs. Ice Demon. 2.50
6 Mount Sorrow, A:Teebo 2.50
7 A:Logray,V:Morag. 2.50
8 . . . . 2.50
9 Lost in Time 2.50
10 Lost in Time. 1.50
11 Kneesaa Shrunk,A:Fleebogs . . 1.50
12 . . . . 1.50
13 . . . . 1.50
14 Teebo- King for a Day 1.50
15 . . . . 1.50

EXCALIBUR
April, 1988
1 AD,Special,O:Excalibur,
V:Technet. 5.00
1a 2nd Printing. 2.50
1b 3rd Printing. 2.00
2 AAd,Mojo Mayhem,A:X-Babies . . 2.50
3 Air Apparent Spec.RLm,KJ,JG,TP,
RL,EL,JRu,A:Coldblood 3.00

[Regular Series]
1 B:CCl(s),AD,V:Warwolves,
I:Widget 5.00
2 AD,V:Warwolves,I:Kylun 4.00
3 AD,V:Juggernaut 3.50
4 AD,V:Arcade,Crazy Gang 3.00
5 AD,V:Arcade. 3.00
6 AD,Inferno,I:Alistaire Stuart. . . . 3.00

7 AD,Inferno 3.00
8 RLm,JRu,A:New Mutants 3.00
9 AD,I:Nazi-Excalibur. 3.00
10 MR,V:Nazi-Excalibur. 3.00
11 MR,V:Nazi-Excalibur 3.00
12 AD,Fairy Tale Dimension 3.00
13 AD,The Prince,N:Capt.Britian. . . 3.00
14 AD,Too Many Heroes. 2.50
15 AD,I:US James Braddock 2.50
16 AD,V:Anjulie 2.50
17 AD,C:Prof.X,Starjammers 2.50
18 DJ,DA,V:Jamie Braddock. 2.50
19 RL,TA,AM,V:Jamie Braddock . . . 2.50
20 RLm,JRu,V:Demon Druid. 2.50
21 I:Crusader X 2.50
22 V:Crusader X. 2.50
23 AD,V:Magik 2.50
24 AD,Return Home,C:Galactus . . 2.50
25 E:CCl(s),AM,A:Galactus,Death,
Watcher 2.50
26 RLm,JRu,V:Mastermind 2.50
27 BWS,BSz,A:Nth Man 3.00
28 BBI,Night at Bar. 2.50
29 JRu,V:Nightmare,A:PowerPack . 2.50
30 DR,AM,A:Doctor Strange. 2.50
31 DR,AM,V:Son of Krakoa 2.50
32 V:Mesmero 2.50
33 V:Mesmero 2.50
34 V:Mesmero 2.50
35 AM,Missing Child. 2.50
36 AM,V:Silv.Sable,Sandman 2.50
37 A:Avengers W.C.,Dr.Doom. . . . 2.50
38 A:Avengers W.C.,Dr.Doom. . . . 2.50
39 A:Avengers W.C.,Dr.Doom. . . . 2.50
40 O:Excalibur,Trial-Lockheed . . . 2.50
41 V:Warwolves,C:Cable 3.00
42 AD,Team Broken Up 3.50
43 AD,Nightcrawler,V:Capt.Brit. . . 3.00
44 AD,Capt.Britain On Trial. 3.00
45 AD,I:N-Men,. 3.00
46 AD,Return of Kylun,C:Cerise . . . 3.00
47 AD,I:Cerise 3.00
48 AD,A:Anti-Phoenix 3.00
49 AD,MFm,V:Necrom,R:Merlyn . . 3.00
50 AD,Phoenix,V:Necrom,Merlyn . . 4.00
51 V:Giant Dinosaurs 2.00
52 O:Phoenix,A:Prof X,MarvGirl . . 2.00
53 A:Spider-Man,V:The Litter 2.00
54 AD,MFm,V:Crazy Gang 2.50
55 AD,MFm,A:Psylocke 2.50
56 AD,MFm,A:Psylocke,
V:Saturyne,Jamie Braddock . . . 2.50
57 A:X-Men,Alchemy,V:Trolls 2.75
58 A:X-Men,Alchemy,V:Trolls 2.75
59 A:Avengers 2.25
60 A:Avengers 2.25
61 AD,MFm,Phoenix Vs.Galactus . 2.25
62 AD,MFm,A:Galactus 2.25
63 AD,MFm,V:Warpies 2.25
64 AD,MFm,V:RCX,R:Rachel 2.25
65 AD,MFm,R:Dark Phoenix. 2.25
66 AD,MFm,V:Ahab,Sentinels,
O:Widget 2.25
67 AD,MFm,V:Ahab,Sentinels. . . . 2.25
68 V:Starjammers. 2.00
69 A:Starjammers. 2.00
70 A:Starjammers. 2.00
71 DaR,Hologram(c),N:Excalibur . 4.00
72 KeL,V:Siena Blaze 2.00
73 TSr,V:Siena Blaze 2.00
74 InC,A:Mr.Sinster,Siena Blaze . . 2.00
75 SLo(s),KeL,I:Daytripper(Amanda
Sefton),Britannic(Capt.Britain),
BU:Nightcrawler 3.50
75a Newstand Ed. 2.25
76 KeL,V:D'spayre 2.00
77 KeL,R:Doug Ramsey. 2.00
78 A:Zero,Doug Ramsey 2.25
79 A:Zero,Doug Ramsey 2.25
80 A:Zero,Doug Ramsey 2.25
81 Doug Ramsey 2.25

Excalibur #17
© Marvel Entertainment Group

82 . . . . 2.50
82a foil(c) 3.50
83 regular ed. 1.50
83a Deluxe ed. Kitty,Nightcrawler . . 2.25
84 regular ed. 1.50
84a Deluxe ed. 2.25
85 regular ed. 1.50
85a Deluxe ed. 2.25
86 regular ed. 1.50
86a Deluxe ed. 2.25
87 KeL,Secrets of the Genoshan
Mutate Technology 2.00
88 Dream Nails,pt.1 . . . . 2.00
89 Dream Nails,pt.2 . . . . 2.00
90 Between Uncreated,Phalanx . . . 3.00
91 F:Colossus 2.00
92 F:Colossus 2.00
93 F:Wolfsbane 2.00
94 A:Karma & Psylocke 2.00
95 . . . . 2.00
96 . . . . 2.00
97 BWi,B.Braddock's secrets told . . 2.00
98 . . . . 2.00
99 European Hellfire Club,
Onslaught 2.00
100 Onslaught saga, double size . . 3.00
101 . . . . 2.00
102 . . . . 2.00
103 WEl,F:Colossus,Kitty &
Nichtcrawler 2.00
104 JAr,BHi,PNe,Douglock's
dark side 2.00
105 JAr,BHi,PNe,V:Moonstar, ... 2.00
106 . . . . 2.00
107 SvL,New direction 2.00
108 Dragons of the Crimson Dawn . 2.00
109 V:Spiral,A:Captain Britain. 2.00
110 V:The Dragons of the
Crimson Dawn 2.00
111 F:Shadowcat,R:Rory Cambell
(Ahab?) 2.00
112 Quicksilver tie-in 2.00
113 BRa,Colossus & Meggan 2.00
114 BRa,Vanisher. 2.00
115 BRa,Quarantine,F:GenerationX 2.00
116 BRa,Legacy Virus, cont. 2.00
117 BRa,F:Kitty Pryde, Colossus &
Nightcrawler. 2.00
118 BRa,V:Creatures from the
Shadows 2.00
119 BRa,V:Nightmare 2.00
120 BRa,F:Kitty Pryde & Pete
Wisdom 2.00
121 BRa,to Egypt. 2.00

MARVEL

MARVEL

122 BRa,V:Original X-Men?	2.00
123 BRa,V:Mimic	2.00
124 BBr,Captain Britain's bachelor party	2.00
125 TvS,SHa, W:Captain Britain & Meggan, final issue	3.00
Minus 1 Spec., flashback, F:Nightcrawler	2.00
Ann.#1 I:Khaos,w/card	3.25
Spec #1 The Possession	4.00
Spec #2 RLm,DT,JG,RL, A:Original X-Men	2.75
PF Cold Blood	4.95
GN Weird War III	9.95
TPB Wild, Wild Life	5.95

FACTOR X
1995
1 After Xavier	4.00
2 Scott vs. Alex Summers	3.00
3 Cyclops vs. Havok	2.50
4 Jean & Scott	2.50
TPB Rep. #1-#4	8.95

FAFHRD AND THE GRAY MOUSER
Epic Oct., 1990
1 MMi,Fritz Leiber adapt.	5.00
2 & 3 MMi	@5.00
4 MMi, Feb. 1991	5.00

FAITHFUL
Nov., 1949
1 Ph(c),I Take This Man	75.00
2 Ph(c),Love Thief,Feb.,1950.	60.00

FALCON
Nov., 1983
1 PS,V:Nemesis	2.00
2 V:Sentinels	1.50
3 V:Electro	1.50
4 A:Capt.America, Feb., 1984	1.50

FALLEN ANGELS
April, 1987
1 KGa,TP,A:Sunspot,Warlock	3.00
2 KGa,TP,I:Gomi,Fallen Angels	2.50
3 KGa,TP,A:X-Factor	2.50
4 KGa,TP,A:Moon Boy, Devil Dinosaur	2.50
5 JSon,D:Angel,Don	2.50
6 JSon,Coconut Grove	2.50
7 KGa,Captured in CoconutGrove	2.50
8 KGa,L:Sunspot,Warlock	2.50

FANTASTIC FIVE
Aug. 1999
1 TDF,PR,AM,New Team:Human Torch Thing,Ms.Fantastic,Psilord & Big Brain	2.00

FANTASTIC FORCE
1994–96
1 Foil stamped cover	2.50
2 Moses	2.25
3	2.25
4 A:Captain America	2.25
5 I:Dreadface	2.25
6 F:Vibraxis	1.75
7 V:Doom	1.75
8 V:Crimson Cadre	1.75
9 Atlantis Rising	1.75
10 A:Human Torch	1.75
11 A:Black Panther	1.75

12 V:Vanguard	1.75
13 J:She-Hulk	1.75
14 V:Wakanda	1.75
15 End of the Fantastic Force?	1.75
16 End of the Fantastic Force?	1.75
17	1.75
18	1.75

FANTASTIC FOUR
Nov., 1961
1 JK,I&O:Mr.Fantastic,Thing Invisible Girl,Human Torch Mole Man	20,000.00
2 JK,I:Skrulls	3,800.00
3 JK,I:Miracleman	2,500.00
4 JK,R:Submariner	3,000.00
5 JK,JSt,I&O:Doctor Doom	3,300.00
6 JK,V:Doctor Doom	1,700.00
7 JK,I:Kurrgo	875.00
8 JK,I:Alicia Masters,I&O: Puppet Master	875.00
9 JK,V:Submariner	850.00
10 JK,V:Doctor Doom,I:Ovoids	850.00
11 JK,I:Impossible Man	700.00
12 JK,V:Hulk	1,200.00
13 JK,SD,I&O:Red Ghost, I:Watcher	500.00
14 JK,SD,V:Submariner	300.00
15 JK,I:Mad Thinker	300.00
16 JK,V:Doctor Doom	300.00
17 JK,V:Doctor Doom	300.00
18 JK,I:Super Skrull	300.00
19 JK,I&O:Rama Tut	300.00
20 JK,I:Molecule Man	325.00
21 JK,I:Hate Monger	250.00
22 JK,V:Mole Man	250.00
23 JK,V:Doctor Doom	250.00
24 JK,I:Infant Terrible	250.00
25 JK,Thing vs.Hulk	450.00
26 JK,V:Hulk,A:Avengers	375.00
27 JK,A:Doctor Strange	175.00
28 JK,1st X-Men x-over	250.00
29 JK,V:Red Ghost	150.00
30 JK,I&O:Diablo	150.00
31 JK,V:Mole Man	125.00
32 JK,V:Superskrull	125.00
33 JK,I:Attuma	125.00
34 JK,I:Gideon	125.00
35 JK,I:Dragon Man,A:Diablo	125.00
36 JK,I:Medusa,Frightful Four	125.00
37 JK,V:Skrulls	100.00
38 JK,V:Frightful Four,I:Trapster	100.00
39 JK,WW,A:Daredevil	100.00

Fantastic Four #27
© Marvel Entertainment Group

40 JK,A:Daredevil,Dr.Doom	100.00
41 JK,V:Fright.Four,A:Medusa	75.00
42 JK,V:Frightful Four	75.00
43 JK,V:Frightful Four	75.00
44 JK,JSt,I:Gorgon, V:Dragon Man	100.00
45 JK,JSt,I:Inhumans(Black Bolt, Triton,Lockjaw,Crystal, Karnak)	100.00
46 JK,JSt,V:Seeker	100.00
47 JK,JSt,I:Maximus,Attilan, Alpha Primitives	100.00
48 JK,JSt,I:Silver Surfer, C:Galactus	900.00
49 JK,JSt,A:Silver Surfer, V:Galactus	250.00
50 JK,JSt,V:Galactus,Silver Surfer,I:Wyatt Wingfoot	275.00
51 JK,JSt,I:Negative Zone	65.00
52 JK,JSt,I:Black Panther	125.00
53 JK,JSt,I:Klaw,Vibranium	100.00
54 JK,JSt,I:Prester John	60.00
55 JK,JSt,A:Silver Surfer	90.00
56 JK,JSt,O:Klaw,A:Inhumans, C:Silver Surfer	65.00
57 JK,JSt,V:Doc Doom, A:Silver Surfer	65.00
58 JK,JSt,V:Doc Doom, A:Silver Surfer	65.00
59 JK,JSt,V:Doc Doom, A:Silver Surfer	65.00
60 JK,JSt,V:Doc Doom, A:Silver Surfer	65.00
61 JK,JSt,V:Sandman, A:Silver Surfer	65.00
62 JK,JSt,I:Blastaar	45.00
63 JK,JSt,V:Blastaar	50.00
64 JK,JSt,I:The Kree,Sentry	50.00
65 JK,JSt,I:Ronan,Supreme Intelligence	50.00
66 JK,JSt,O:Him,A:Crystal	100.00
67 JK,JSt,I:Him	125.00
68 JK,JSt,V:Mad Thinker	60.00
69 JK,JSt,V:Mad Thinker	50.00
70 JK,JSt,V:Mad Thinker	50.00
71 JK,JSt,V:Mad Thinker	50.00
72 JK,JSt,A:Watcher,S.Surfer	50.00
73 JK,JSt,A:SpM,DD,Thor	35.00
74 JK,JSt,A:Silver Surfer	45.00
75 JK,JSt,A:Silver Surfer	45.00
76 JK,JSt,V:Psycho Man,S.Surf	45.00
77 JK,JSt,V:Galactus,S.Surfer	45.00
78 JK,JSt,V:Wizard	40.00
79 JK,JSt,A:Crystall,V:Mad Thinker	40.00
80 JK,JSt,A:Crystal	40.00
81 JK,JSt,J:Crystal,V:Wizard	40.00
82 JK,JSt,V:Maximus	40.00
83 JK,JSt,V:Maximus	40.00
84 JK,JSt,V:Doctor Doom	30.00
85 JK,JSt,V:Doctor Doom	30.00
86 JK,JSt,V:Doctor Doom	30.00
87 JK,JSt,V:Doctor Doom	30.00
88 JK,JSt,V:Mole Man	30.00
89 JK,JSt,V:Mole Man	30.00
90 JK,JSt,V:Skrulls	25.00
91 JK,JSt,V:Skrulls,I:Torgo	25.00
92 JK,JSt,V:Torgo,Skrulls	25.00
93 JK,JSt,V:Torgo,Skrulls	25.00
94 JK,JSt,I:Agatha Harkness	25.00
95 JK,JSt,I:Monocle	25.00
96 JK,JSt,V:Mad Thinker	25.00
97 JK,JSt,V:Monster from Lost Lagoon	25.00
98 JK,JSt,V:Kree Sentry	25.00
99 JK,JSt,A:Inhumans	25.00
100 JK,JSt,V:Puppetmaster	100.00
101 JK,JSt,V:Maggia	25.00
102 JK,JSt,V:Magneto	25.00
103 JR,V:Magneto	25.00
104 JR,V:Magneto	22.00

Fantastic Four #88
© *Marvel Entertainment Group*

105 JR,L:Crystal 20.00
106 JR,JSt,`Monster's Secret' 20.00
107 JB,JSt,V:Annihilus 20.00
108 JK,JB,JR,JSt, V:Annihilus . . . 20.00
109 JB,JSt,V:Annihilus 20.00
110 JB,JSt,V:Annihilus 20.00
111 JB,JSt,A:Hulk 20.00
112 JB,JSt,Thing vs. Hulk 60.00
113 JB,JSt,I:Overmind 15.00
114 JR(c),JB,V:Overmind 15.00
115 JR(c),JB,JSt,I:Eternals 15.00
116 JB,JSt,O:Stranger 15.00
117 JB,JSt,V:Diablo 11.00
118 JR(c),JB,JM,V:Diablo 11.00
119 JB,JSt,V:Klaw 11.00
120 JB,JSt,I:Gabriel(Airwalker)
     (Robot) 11.00
121 JB,JSt,V:Silver Surfer,D:
     Gabriel Destroyer 15.00
122 JR(c),JB,JSt,V:Galactus,
     A:Silver Surfer 15.00
123 JB,JSt,V:Galactus,
     A:Silver Surfer 14.00
124 JB,JSt,V:Monster 9.00
125 E:StL(s),JB,JSt,V:Monster 9.00
126 B:RTs(s),JB,JSt,
     O:FF,MoleMan 9.00
127 JB,JSt,V:Mole Man 9.00
128 JB,JSt,V:Mole Man 10.00
129 JB,JSt,I:Thundra,
     V:Frightful Four 9.00
130 JSo(c),JB,JSt,V:Frightful Four . 8.00
131 JSo(c),JB,JSt,V:QuickSilver . . 8.00
132 JB,JSt,J:Medusa 8.00
133 JSt(i),V:Thundra 8.00
134 JB,JSt,V:Dragon Man 8.00
135 JB,JSt,V:Gideon 8.00
136 JB,JSt,A:Shaper 8.00
137 JB,JSt,A:Shaper 8.00
138 JB,JSt,O:Miracle Man 8.00
139 JB,V:Miracle Man 8.00
140 JB,JSt,O:Annihilus 8.00
141 JR(c),JB,JSt,V:Annihilus 8.00
142 RB,JSt,A:Doc Doom 8.00
143 GK(c),RB,V:Doc Doom 8.00
144 RB,JSt,V:Doc Doom 8.00
145 JSt&GK(c),RA,I:Ternak 8.00
146 RA,JSt,V:Ternak 8.00
147 RB,JSt,V:Subby 8.00
148 RB,JSt,V:Frightful Four 8.00
149 RB,JSt,V:Sub-Mariner 8.00
150 GK(c),RB,JSt,W:Crystal &
     Quicksilver,V:Ultron 9.00
151 RB,JSt,O:Thundra 7.00

152 JR(c),RB,JM,A:Thundra 7.00
153 GK(c),RB,JSt,A:Thundra 7.00
154 GK(c),rep.Str.Tales #127 . . . . 7.00
155 RB,JSt,A:Surfer 8.00
156 RB,JSt,A:Surfer,V:Doom 8.00
157 RB,JSt,A:Surfer 8.00
158 RB,JSt,V:Xemu 7.00
159 RB,JSt,V:Xemu 7.00
160 K&R(c),JB,V:Arkon 7.00
161 RB,JSt,V:Arkon 5.00
162 RB,DA,JSt,V:Arkon 5.00
163 RB,JSt,V:Arkon 5.00
164 JK(c),GP,JSt,V:Crusader,R:
     Marvel Boy,I:Frankie Raye 5.00
165 GP,JSt,O:Crusader,
     O&D:Marvel Boy 5.00
166 GP,V:Hulk 6.00
167 JK(c),GP,JSt,V:Hulk 6.00
168 RB,JSt,J:Luke Cage 5.00
169 RB,JSt,V:Puppetmaster 5.00
170 GP,JSt,L:Luke Cage 5.00
171 JK(c),RB,GP,JSt,I:Gor 4.00
172 JK(c),GP,JSt,V:Destroyer 5.00
173 JB,JSt,V:Galactus,O:Heralds . . 5.00
174 JB,V:Galactus 5.00
175 JB,A:High Evolutionary 4.00
176 GP,JSt,V:Impossible Man 4.00
177 JP,JS,A:Frightful Four
     I:Texas Twister,Capt.Ultra 4.00
178 GP,V:Frightful Four,Brute 4.00
179 JSt,V:Annihilus 4.00
180 reprint #101 . . . . 4.00
181 E:RTs(s),JSt,V:Brute,
     Annihilus 4.00
182 SB,JSt,V:Brute,Annihilus 4.00
183 SB,JSt,V:Brute,Annihilus 4.00
184 GP,JSt,V:Eliminator 4.00
185 GP,JSt,V:Nich.Scratch 4.00
186 GP,JSi,I:Salem's Seven 4.00
187 GP,JSt,V:Klaw,Molecule Man . 4.00
188 GP,JSt,V:Molecule Man 4.00
189 reprint FF Annual #4 . . . . 4.00
190 SB,O:Fantastic Four 5.00
191 GP,JSt,V:Plunderer,
     Team Breaks Up 4.00
192 GP,JSt,V:Texas Twister 4.00
193 KP,JSt,V:Darkoth,Diablo 4.00
194 KP,V:Darkoth,Diablo 4.00
195 KP,A:Sub-Mariner 4.00
196 KP,V:Invincible Man (Reed),
     A:Dr.Doom,Team Reunited 4.00
197 KP,JSt,Red Ghost 4.00
198 KP,JSt,V:Doc Doom 4.00
199 KP,JSt,V:Doc Doom 4.00
200 KP,JSt,V:Doc Doom 5.00
201 KP,JSt,FF's Machinery 3.00
202 KP,JSt,V:Quasimodo 3.00
203 KP,JSt,V:Mutant 3.00
204 KP,JSt,V:Skrulls 3.00
205 KP,JSt,V:Skrulls 3.00
206 KP,JSt,V:Skrulls,A:Nova 3.00
207 SB,JSt,V:Monocle,A:SpM 3.00
208 SB,V:Sphinx,A:Nova 2.50
209 JBy,JSt,I:Herbie,A:Nova 4.00
210 JBy,JS,A:Galactus 3.00
211 JBy,JS,I:Terrax,A:Galactus . . . 4.00
212 JBy,JSt,V:Galactus,Sphinx . . . 3.00
213 JBy,JSt,V:Terrax,Galactus
     Sphinx 3.00
214 JBy,JSt,V:Skrull 3.00
215 JBy,JSt,V:Blastaar 3.00
216 JBy,V:Blastaar 3.00
217 JBy,JSt,A:Dazzler 3.00
218 JBy,JSt,V:FrightfulFour,
     A:Spider-Man 4.00
219 BSz,JSt,A:Sub-Mariner 3.00
220 JBy,JSt,A:Vindicator 3.50
221 JBy,JSt,V:Vindicator 3.50
222 BSz,JSt,V:Nicholas Scratch . . . 3.00
223 BSz,JSt,V:Salem's Seven 3.00
224 BSz,A:Thor 3.00

Fantastic Four #285
© *Marvel Entertainment Group*

225 BSz,A:Thor 3.00
226 BSz,A:Shogun 3.00
227 BSz,JSt,V:Ego-Spawn 3.00
228 BSz,JSt,V:Ego-Spawn 3.00
229 BSz,JSt,I:Firefrost,Ebon
     Seeker 3.00
230 BSz,JSt,A:Avengers,
     O:Firefrost & Ebon Seeker 3.00
231 BSz,JSt,V:Stygorr 3.00
232 JBy,New Direction,V:Diablo . . . 5.00
233 JBy,V:Hammerhead 3.50
234 JBy,V:Ego 3.50
235 JBy,O:Ego 3.50
236 JBy,V:Dr.Doom,A:Puppet
     Master, 20th Anniv. 4.50
237 JBy,V:Solons 3.50
238 JBy,O:Frankie Raye,
     new Torch 3.50
239 JBy,I:Aunt Petunia,
     Uncle Jake 4.50
240 JBy,A:Inhumans,b:Luna 3.50
241 JBy,A:Black Panther 3.50
242 JBy,A:Daredevil,Thor,Iron Man
     Spider-Man,V:Terrax 3.50
243 JBy,A:Daredevil,Dr.Strange,
     Spider-Man,Avengers,V:Galactus,
     Terrax 4.00
244 JBy,A:Avengers,Dr.Strange,
     Galactus, Frankie Raye
     Becomes Nova 4.00
245 JBy,V:Franklin Richards 3.00
246 JBy,V:Dr.Doom,
     A:Puppet Master 3.00
247 JBy,A:Dr.Doom,I:Kristoff,
     D:Zorba 3.00
248 JBy,A:Inhumans 3.00
249 JBy,V:Gladiator 3.00
250 JBy,A:Capt.America,SpM
     V:Gladiator 3.00
251 JBy,A:Annihilus 2.50
252 JBy,1st sideways issue,V:
     Ootah,A:Annihilus,w/tattoo 3.00
252a w/o tattoo 2.00
253 JBy,V:Kestorans,A:Annihilus . . 3.00
254 JBy,V:Mantracora,
     A:She-Hulk,Wasp 3.00
255 JBy,A:Daredevil,Annihilus,
     V:Mantracora 3.00
256 JBy,A:Avengers,Galactus,
     V:Annihilus,New Costumes 3.00
257 JBy,A:Galactus,Death,Nova,
     Scarlet Witch 3.50
258 JBy,A:Dr.Doom,D:Hauptmann . 3.00
259 JBy,V:Terrax,Dr.Doom,

MARVEL

C:Silver Silver 3.00
260 JBy,V:Terrax, Dr.Doom,
    A:Silver Surfer,Sub-Mariner . . . 4.00
261 JBy,A:Sub-Mariner,Marrina,
    Silver Surfer,Sc.Witch,Lilandra . 4.00
262 JBy,O:Galactus,A:Odin,
    (J.Byrne in story) 3.00
263 JBy,V:Messiah,A:Mole Man . . . 3.00
264 JBy,V:Messiah,A:Mole Man . . . 3.00
265 JBy,A:Trapster,Avengers,
    J:She-Hulk,Secret Wars 3.00
266 KGa,JBy,A:Hulk,Sasquatch,
    V:Karisma 3.00
267 JBy,A:Hulk,Sasquatch,Morbius,
    V:Dr.Octopus,Sue miscarries . . 3.00
268 JBy,V:Doom's Mask 3.00
269 JBy,R:Wyatt Wingfoot,
    I:Terminus 3.00
270 JBy,V:Terminus 3.00
271 JBy,V:Gormuu 3.00
272 JBy,I:Warlord (Nathaniel
    Richards) 3.00
273 JBy,V:Warlord 3.00
274 JBy,AG,cont.from Thing#19,
    A:Spider-Man's Black Costume. 3.00
275 JBy,AG,V:T.J.Vance 3.00
276 JBy,JOy,V:Mephisto,
    A:Dr.Strange 3.00
277 JBy,JOy,V:Mephisto,
    A:Dr.Strange,R:Thing 3.00
278 JBy,JOy,O:Dr.Doom,A:Kristoff
    (as Doom) 3.00
279 JBy,JOy,V:Dr.Doom(Kristoff),
    I:New Hate-Monger 3.00
280 JBy,JOy,I:Malice,
    V:Hate-Monger 3.00
281 JBy,JOy,A:Daredevil,V:Hate
    Monger,Malice 3.00
282 JBy,JOy,A:Power Pack,Psycho
    Man,Secret Wars II 3.00
283 JBy,JOy,V:Psycho-Man 3.00
284 JBy,JOy,V:Psycho-Man 3.00
285 JBy,JOy,Secret Wars II
    A:Beyonder 3.00
286 JBy,TA,R:Jean Grey,
    A:Hercules Capt.America 3.50
287 JBy,JSt,A:Wasp,V:Dr.Doom . . . 3.00
288 JBy,JSt,V:Dr.Doom,Secret
    Wars II 3.50
289 JBy,AG,D:Basilisk,V:Blastaar,
    R:Annihilus 3.00
290 JBy,AG,V:Annihilus 3.00
291 JBy,CR,A:Nick Fury 3.00
292 JBy,AG,A:Nick Fury,V:Hitler . . . 3.00

293 JBy,AG,A:Avengers.W.C. 3.00
294 JOy,AG,V:FutureCentralCity . . . 2.50
295 JOy,AG,V:Fut.Central City 2.50
296 BWS,KGa,RF,BWi,AM,KJ,JB,
    SL,MS,JRu,JOy,JSt,25th
    Anniv.,V:MoleMan. 3.00
297 JB,SB,V:Umbra-Sprite 2.50
298 JB,SB,V:Umbra-Sprite 2.50
299 JB,SB,She-Hulk,V:Thing,
    A:Spider-Man,L:She-Hulk 2.50
300 JB,SB,W:Torch & Fake Alicia
    (Lyja),A:Puppet-Master,Wizard,
    Mad Thinker,Dr.Doom. 3.00
301 JB,SB,V:Wizard,MadThinker . . 2.25
302 JB,SB,V:Project Survival 2.25
303 JB,RT,A:Thundra,V:Machus . . 2.25
304 JB,JSt,V:Quicksilver,
    A:Kristoff 2.25
305 JB,JSt,V:Quicksilver,
    J:Crystal,A:Dr.Doom 2.25
306 JB,JSt,A:Capt.America,
    J:Ms.Marvel,V:Diablo 2.25
307 JB,JSt,L:Reed&Sue,V:Diablo . . 2.25
308 JB,JSt,I:Fasaud 2.25
309 JB,JSt,V:Fasaud 2.25
310 KP,JSt,V:Fasaud,N:Thing
    & Ms.Marvel 2.25
311 KP,JSt,A:Black Panther,
    Dr.Doom,V:THRob 2.25
312 KP,JSt,A:Black Panther,
    Dr.Doom,X-Factor 2.25
313 SB,JSt,V:Lava Men,
    A:Moleman. 2.00
314 KP,JSt,V:Belasco 2.00
315 KP,JSt,V:Mast.Pandem. 2.00
316 KP,JSt,A:CometMan 2.00
317 KP,JSt,L:Crystal 2.00
318 KP,JSt,V:Dr.Doom 2.00
319 KP,JSt,G-Size,O:Beyonder. . . . 2.25
320 KP,JSt,Hulk vs Thing 2.50
321 RLm,RT,A:She-Hulk. 2.00
322 KP,JSt,Inferno,V:Graviton. 2.00
323 KP,JSt,RT,Inferno A:Mantis . . . 2.00
324 KP,JSt,RT,A:Mantis 2.00
325 RB,RT,A:Silver Surfer,
    D:Mantis. 2.50
326 KP,RT,I:New Frightful Four 2.00
327 KP,RT,V:Frightful Four 2.00
328 KP,RT,V:Frightful Four 2.00
329 RB,RT,V:Mole Man 2.00
330 RB,RT,V:Dr.Doom 2.00
331 RB,RT,V:Ultron 2.00
332 RB,RT,V:Aron 2.00
333 RB,RT,V:Aron,Frightful Four . . . 2.00
334 RB,Acts of Vengeance 2.00
335 RB,RT,Acts of Vengeance 2.00
336 RLm,Acts of Vengeance. 2.00
337 WS,A:Thor,Iron Man,
    B:Timestream saga 4.00
338 WS,V:Deathshead,A:Thor,
    Iron Man 2.50
339 WS,V:Gladiator 2.50
340 WS,V:Black Celestial 2.50
341 WS,A:Thor,Iron Man 2.50
342 A:Rusty,C:Spider-Man 2.50
343 WS,V:Stalin 2.50
344 WS,V:Stalin 2.50
345 WS,V:Dinosaurs 2.50
346 WS,V:Dinosaurs 2.50
347 AAd,ATi(i)A:Spider-Man,
    GhostRider,Wolverine,Hulk . . 4.00
347a 2nd printing 2.00
348 AAd,ATi(i)A:Spider-Man,
    GhostRider,Wolverine,Hulk . . 4.00
348a 2nd printing 2.00
349 AAd,ATi(i),AM(i)A:Spider-Man,
    Wolverine,GhostRider,Hulk,
    C:Punisher. 3.50
350 WS,Am(i),R:Ben Grimm as
    Thing,(48p). 3.00
351 MBa,Kubic. 2.50

352 WS,Reed Vs.Dr.Doom 2.50
353 WS,E:Timestream Saga,
    A:Avengers, ... 2.50
354 WS,Secrets of the Time
    Variance Authority 2.50
355 AM,V:Wrecking Crew 2.00
356 B:TDF(s),PR,A:New Warriors,
    V:Puppet Master. 2.00
357 PR,V:Mad Thinker,
    Puppetmaster. 2.00
358 PR,AAd,30th Anniv.,1st Marv. Die
    Cut(c),D:Lyja,V:Paibok,BU:
    Dr.Doom. 3.00
359 PR,I:Devos the Devastator. . . . 2.00
360 PR,V:Dreadface 2.00
361 PR,V:Dr.Doom,X-masIssue . . . 2.00
362 PR,A:Spider-Man,
    I:WildBlood. 2.00
363 PR,I:Occulus,A:Devos 2.00
364 PR,V:Occulus 2.00
365 PR,V:Occulus 2.00
366 PR,Infinity War,R:Lyja 2.00
367 PR,Inf.War,A:Wolverine 2.00
368 PR,V:Infinity War X-Men 2.00
369 PR,Inf.War,R:Malice,
    A:Thanos 2.00
370 PR,Inf.War,V:Mr.Fantastic
    Doppleganger. 2.00
371 PR,V:Lyja,foil(c) 4.00
371a 2nd Printing 3.00
372 PR,A:Spider-Man,Silver
    Sable 2.00
373 PR,V:Aron,Silver sable. 2.00
374 PR,V:Secret Defenders 2.00
375 V:Dr.Doom,A:Inhumans,Lyja,
    Holo-Grafix(c). 3.00
376 PR,A:Nathan Richards,V:Paibok,
    Devos,w/Dirt Magazine. 2.75
376a w/out Dirt Magazine 2.00
377 PR,V:Paibok,Devos,Klaw,
    I:Huntara 2.00
378 PR,A:Sandman,SpM,DD 2.00
379 PR,V:Ms.Marvel 2.00
380 PR,A:Dr.Doom,V:Hunger 2.00
381 PR,D:Dr.Doom,Mr.Fantastic,
    V:Hunger 5.00
382 PR,V:Paibok,Devos,Huntara . . 3.00
383 PR,V:Paibok,Devos,Huntara . . 2.00
384 PR,A:Ant-Man,V:Franklin
    Richards. 2.00
385 PR,A:Triton,Tiger Shark,
    Starblast#7 . . . . 2.00
386 PR,Starblast#11,A:Namor,Triton,
    b:Johnny & Lyja child 1.75

Fantastic Four #367
© Marvel Entertainment Group

Fantastic Four #404
© Marvel Entertainment Group

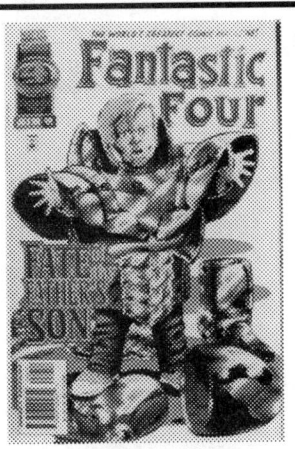

Fantastic Four #414
© Marvel Entertainment Group

387 Die-Cut & Foil (c),PR,N:Invisible
    Woman,J:Ant-Man,A:Namor . . . 3.25
387a Newsstand Ed. 1.75
388 PR,I:Dark Raider,V:FF,
    Avengers,w/cards 2.00
389 PR,I:Raphael Suarez,A:Watcher,
    V:Collector 2.00
390 PR,A:Galactus. 2.00
391 PR,I:Vibraxas. 1.75
392 Dark Raider 1.75
393 . . . . 1.75
394 Neon(c) w/insert print. 2.95
394a Newsstand ed.,no bag/inserts 1.75
395 Thing V:Wolverine 1.75
396 . . . . 1.75
397 Resurrection,pt.1 . . . . 1.75
398 regular edition 1.50
398a Enhanced cover. 2.75
399 Watcher's Lie. 1.75
399a Foil stamped cover 2.50
400 Watcher's Lie,pt.3 . . . . 3.95
401 V:Tantalus 1.50
402 Atlantis Rising,Namor
    vs. Black Bolt 1.50
403 TDF,PR,DBi,F:Thing,Medusa . 1.50
404 R:Namor,I:New Villian 1.50
405 J:Namor. 1.50
406 TDF,PR,DBi,R:Dr. Doom,
    I:Hyperstorm 1.50
407 TDF,PR,DBi,Return of
    Reed Richards 1.50
408 TDF,PR,DBi,Original FF unite. . 1.50
409 TDF,PR,DBi,All new line-up . . . 1.50
410 . . . . 1.50
411 . . . . 1.50
412 TDF,PR,DBi,Mr.Fantastic
    vs. Sub-Mariner 1.50
413 . . . . 1.50
414 Galactus vs. Hyperstorm 1.50
415 Onslaught saga, A:X-Men . . . 2.50
416 Onslaught saga, A:Dr. Doom,
    double size, finale 2.50
Ann.#1 JK,SD,I:Atlantis,Dorma,
    Krang,V:Namor,O:FF 550.00
Ann.#2 JK,JSt,O:Dr.Doom. 350.00
Ann.#3 JK,W:Reed and Sue . . . 145.00
Ann.#4 JK,JSt,I:Quasimodo 75.00
Ann.#5 JK,JSt,A:Inhumans,Silver
    Surfer,Black Panther,
    I:Psycho Man 120.00
Ann.#6 JK,JSt,I:Annihilus,
    Franklin Richards 50.00
Ann.#7 JK(c),reprints 25.00
Ann.#8 JR(c),reprints 15.00
Ann.#9 JK(c),reprints. 15.00

Ann.#10 reprints Ann.#3 . . . . 15.00
Ann.#11 JK(c),JB,A:The Invaders . . 7.00
Ann.#12 A:The Invaders 7.00
Ann.#13 V:The Mole Man 7.00
Ann.#14 GP,V:Salem's Seven 7.00
Ann.#15 GP,V:Dr.Doom,Skrulls 5.00
Ann.#16 V:Dragonlord 5.00
Ann.#17 JBy,V:Skrulls. 5.00
Ann.#18 KGa,V:Skrulls,W:Black
    Bolt and Medusa,A:Inhumans . . 5.00
Ann.#19 JBy,V:Skrulls. 5.00
Ann.#20 TD(i),V:Dr.Doom 4.00
Ann.#21 JG,JSt,Evol.Wars 4.00
Ann.#22 RB,Atlantis Attacks,
    A:Avengers 4.00
Ann.#23 JG,GCa,Days of Future
    Present #1 . . . . 5.00
Ann.#24 JG,AM,Korvac Quest #1,
    A:Guardians of the Galaxy 3.00
Ann.#25 Citizen Kang #3 . . . . 2.50
Ann.#26 HT,I:Wildstreak,
    V:Dreadface,w/card 3.25
Ann.#27 MGu,V:Justice Peace 3.25
G-Size#1 RB,Thing/Hulk. 15.00
G-Size#2 K&R(c),JB,Time to Kill. . . 9.00
G-Size#3 RB,JSt,Four Horseman . . 9.00
G-Size#4 JB,JSt,I:Madrox. 10.00
G-Size#5 JK(c),V:Psycho Man,
    Molecule Man. 7.00
G-Size#6 V:Annihilus 7.00
Spec.#1 Rep.Ann.#1 JBy(c) 2.00
TPB Rep.#347-349. . . . . 5.95
TPB Nobody Gets Out Alive, rep.
    Fant.Four #387–#392 + new. . 15.95
TPB Trial of Galactus,reprints
    #242-244,#257-262 . . . . 9.95
Marvel Milestone rep. #1 (1991) . . 2.95
Marvel Milestone rep. #5 (1992) . . 2.95
Ashcan. 75
Spec. The Origin of Galactus 2.50

[2nd Series] Nov. 1996

1 JLe,BCi,SW, 48pg 5.00
1A Mole Man cover 12.00
1B Gold signature, bagged,
    limited 25.00
2 JLe,BCi,V:Namor 4.00
3 JLe,BCi,SW,A:Avengers 3.00
4 JLe,BCi,SW,I:Black Panther 3.00
4A x-mas cover 3.50
5 JLe,BCi,SW,V:Dr. Doom 3.50
6 JLe,BCi,SW,Industrial Revolution
    prologue 2.50
7 JLe,BCi,BBh,V:Blastaar 2.00
8 JLe,BCi,BBh,V:Inhumans 2.00
9 JLe,BCi,BBh,V:Inhumans 2.50
10 JLe,BCi,BBh,A:Silver Surfer,
    Tyrax 2.50
11 JLe,BCi,BBh,A:Silver Surfer,
    Firelord, Terrax. 2.50
12 JLe,BCi,BBh,GalactusSaga,pt.1,
    reunited 2.50
13 JeR,Wildstorm x-over. 2.50
Ashcan, signed, numbered 10.00

[3rd Series] Nov. 1997

1 SLo,AD,MFm, The Ruined, 48pg
    debut 5.00
2 SLo,AD,MFm,A:Iconoclast 2.00
3 SLo,AD,MFm,V:Red Ghost 2.00
4 SLo,SvL,ATi,A:Silver Surfer,
    double size. 3.00
4 signed by SLo, (500 copies) . . . 20.00
5 SLo,SvL,ATi,V:The Crucible 2.00
6 CCi,SvL, new villains 2.00
7 CCi,SvL,ATi,V:Technet 2.00
8 CCi,SvL,V:Captain Britain corp. . 2.00
9 CCi,SvL,A:Spider-Man 2.00
10 CCi,SvL,ATi 2.00
11 CCi,SvL,ATi,Crucible—unleashed
    in Genosha 2.00
12 CCi,SvL,ATi, V:Fantastic Four

double-size. 3.00
13 CCi,SvL,A:Ronan the Accuser . . 2.00
14 CCi,SvL,V:Ronan. 2.00
15 CCi,SvL,ATi,Iron Man x-over . . . 2.00
16 CCi,SvL,ATi,V:Kree Avengers . . 2.00
17 CCi,SvL,ATi,I:Lockdown. 2.00
18 CCi,SvL,ATi,Jail Break. 2.00
19 CCi,SvL,ATi,V:Annihilus 2.00
20 CCi,SvL,ATi,V:Ruined 2.00
21 CCi,SvL,ATi,V:Hades 2.00
22 CCi,SvL,ATi,V:Valeria
    Von Doom 2.00
Ann.1998 Fant.Four & Fant.Four . . 3.50
TPB Heroes Return, 96-page 10.95
TPB Essential Fantastic Four 14.95

FANTASTIC FOUR: ATLANTIS RISING
1995

1 B:Atlantis Rising 3.95
2 TDF,MCW,finale, acetate(c) 3.95

FANTASTIC FOUR INDEX
See: OFFICIAL MARVEL INDEX TO THE FANTASTIC FOUR

FANTASTIC FOUR ROAST
1 FH/MG/FM/JB/MA/TA,May,1982 . 5.00

FANTASTIC FOUR 2099
1996

1 Cont. from 2099 Genesis 3.95
2 V:Stark/Fujikawa elite guard 2.00
3 . . . . 2.00
4 . . . . 2.00
5 A:Spider-Man 2099. . . . . 2.00

FANTASTIC FOUR UNLIMITED
1993–96

1 HT,A:Bl.Panther,V:Klaw. 4.50
2 HT,JQ(c),A:Inhumans 4.25
3 HT,V:Blastaar,Annihilus. 4.25
4 RTs(s),HT,V:Mole Man,A:Hulk . . 4.25
5 RTs(s),HT,V:Frightful Four. 4.25
6 RTs(s),HT,V:Namor. 4.00
7 HT,V:Monsters 4.00
8 . . . . 4.00
9 A:Antman 4.00
10 RTs,HT,V:Maelstrom,A:Eternals . 4.00
11 RTs,HT,Atlantis Rising fallout . . . 4.00
12 RTs,TDF,V:Hyperstorm. 4.00
13 . . . . 4.00

FANTASTIC FOUR UNPLUGGED
1995–96

1 comic for a buck. 1.00
2 Reed Richard's Will 1.00
3 F:Mr. Fantastic 1.00
4 . . . . 1.00
5 Back in NY,V:Blastaar. 1.00

FANTASTIC FOUR VS. X-MEN
Feb., 1987

1 JBg,TA,V:Dr.Doom 4.00
2 JBg,TA,V:Dr.Doom 3.00
3 JBg,TA,V:Dr.Doom 3.00
4 JBg,TA,V:Dr.Doom, June 1987 . . 3.00
TPB Reprints Mini-series 12.95

MARVEL

FANTASTIC WORLD OF HANNA-BARBERA
Dec., 1977
1	1.00
2	1.00
3 June, 1978	1.00

FANTASY MASTERPIECES
Feb., 1966
1 JK/DH/SD,reprints	75.00
2 JK,SD,DH,Fin Fang Foom	35.00
3 GC,DH,JK,SD,Capt.A rep.	25.00
4 JK,Capt.America rep.	25.00
5 JK,Capt.America rep.	25.00
6 JK,Capt.America rep.	25.00
7 SD,Sub Mariner rep.	25.00
8 H.Torch & Sub M.rep.	30.00
9 SD,MF,O:Human Torch Rep	30.00
10 rep.All Winners #19	25.00
11 JK,(rep),O:Toro	25.00
Becomes:

MARVEL SUPER-HEROES

FANTASY MASTERPIECES
[Volume 2] Dec., 1979
1 JB,JSt,Silver Surfer rep.	5.00
2 JB,JSt,Silver Surfer rep.	5.00
3 JB,JSt,Silver Surfer rep.	5.00
4 JB,JSt,Silver Surfer rep.	5.00
5 JB,JSt,Silver Surfer rep.	5.00
6 JB,JSt,Silver Surfer rep.	5.00
7 JB,JSt,Silver Surfer rep.	5.00
8 JB/JSn,Warlock rep.Strange Tales #178	4.00
9 JB,JSn,rep.StrangeTales#179	4.00
10 JB,JSn,rep.StrangeTales#180	4.00
11 JB,JSn,rep.StrangeTales#181	4.00
12 JB,JSn,rep.Warlock #9	4.00
13 JB,JSn,rep.Warlock #10	4.00
14 JB,JSn,rep.Warlock #11	4.00

FAREWELL TO WEAPONS
1 DirtBag,W/Nirvana Tape	3.50

FEAR
Nov., 1970
1 1950's Monster rep. B:I Found Monstrum,The Dweller in the Black Swamp	30.00
2 X The Thing That Lived	20.00
3 Zzutak, The Thing That Shouldn't Exist	20.00
4 I Turned Into a Martian	20.00
5 I Am the Gorilla Man.	20.00
6 The Midnight Monster.	20.00
7 I Dream of Doom	12.00
8 It Crawls By Night!	12.00
9 Dead Man's Escape	12.00
Becomes:

ADVENTURE INTO FEAR
1972
10 GM,B:Man-Thing	25.00
11 RB,I:Jennifer Kale,Thog	10.00
12 JSn,RB	10.00
13 VM,Where World's Collide	8.00
14 VM,Plague o/t Demon Cult.	8.00
15 VM,Lord o/t Dark Domain	8.00
16 VM,ManThing in Everglades	8.00
17 VM,I:Wundarr(Aquarian)	8.00
18 VM	8.00
19 VM,FMc,I:Howard the Duck, E:Man-Thing	25.00
20 PG,B:Morbius	28.00
21 GK,V:Uncanny Caretaker.	8.00
22 RB,V:Cat-Demond.	8.00

23 1st CR art,A World He Never Made	8.00
24 CR,V:Blade, The Vampire Slayer	20.00
25 You Always Kill the One You Love	7.00
26 V:Uncanny Caretaker.	7.00
27 V:Simon Stroud	7.00
28 Doorway Down into Hell.	7.00
29 Death has a Thousand Eyes	7.00
30 Bloody Sacrifice.	7.00
31 last issue,Dec. 1975	7.00

FEUD
Epic 1993
1 I:Skids,Stokes,Kite	2.50
2 V:Grunts,Skide,Stockers	2.25
3	2.25
4	2.25

FIGHT MAN
1993
1 I:Fight Man	2.00

FIRESTAR
March, 1986
1 MW,SL,O:Firestar,A:X-Men, New Mutants	4.00
2 MW,BWI,A:New Mutants.	4.00
3 AAd&BSz(c),MW,SL, A:White Queen.	3.00
4 MW,SL,V:White Queen	3.00

FISH POLICE
1992–93
1 V:S.Q.U.I.D,Hook	1.25
2 V:Hook	1.25
3 V:Hook.	1.25
4 V:Hook.	1.25
5 V:Goldie Prawn	1.25
6 Shark Bait #1	1.25

Flash Gordon #1
© Marvel Entertainment Group

FLASH GORDON
1995
1 R:Flash Gordon	2.00
2 AW,V:Ming, final issue	2.95

FLINTSTONE KIDS
Star Comics August, 1987
1 thru 10	@1.00

11 April, 1989	1.00

FLINTSTONES
Oct., 1977–Feb. 1979
1 From TV Series	1.50
2	1.25
3	1.25
4 A:Jetsons	1.25
5 thru 7	@1.25

FLYING HERO BARBIE
1 Super Hero Barbie	1.50

FOOLKILLER
Oct., 1990
1 I:Kurt Gerhardt (Foolkiller III)	3.50
2 O:Foolkiller I & II	3.00
3 Old Costume	3.00
4 N:Foolkiller.	2.50
5 Body Count	2.50
6 Fools Paradise	2.00
7 Who the Fools Are	2.00
8 Sane Must Inherit Earth,A:SpM.	2.00
9 D:Darren Waite.	2.00
10 New Identity, July 1991	2.00

FOORFUR
Star Comics August, 1987
1 thru 6	@1.00

FORCE WORKS
1994–96
1 TmT,Pop-up(c),I:Century,V:Kree, N:US Agent	4.00
2 TmT,V:Scatter.	1.75
3 TmT,V:Scatter.	1.50
4 Civil War.	1.50
5 regular cover	1.50
5a Neon(c),bagged w/print.	2.95
6 Hands of the Mandarin,pt.1.	1.50
7 Hands of the Mandarin,pt.2.	1.50
8 DAn,ALa,Christmas Party	1.50
9 I:Dream Guard	1.50
10 V:Dream Guard	1.50
11 F:War Machine	1.50
12 V:Recorder	2.50
13 DAn,ALa,A:Avengers	1.50
14	1.50
15 DAn,ALa,O:Century.	1.50
16	1.50
17 DAn,ALa,The Crossing	1.50
18 DAn,ALa,The Crossing	1.50
19 DAn,ALa,The Crossing	1.50
20 DAn,cont.Avengers:Timeslide	1.50

FOR YOUR EYES ONLY
1 HC,James Bond rep.	2.00
2 HC,James Bond rep.	2.00

FRAGGLE ROCK
1985
1 thru 8	@1.00
[Volume 2] April, 1988
1 thru 5 rep.	@1.00
6 Sept., 1988	1.00

FRANCIS, BROTHER OF THE UNIVERSE
1980
1-shot SB.	2.50

FRANKENSTEIN
See: MONSTER OF
FRANKENSTEIN

FRED HEMBECK
1-shot Destroys the Marvel
  Universe, parody (1989) 2.00
1-shot Sells the Marvel Universe
  parody (1990). 1.50

FRIGHT
June, 1975
1 Son of Dracula 10.00

FRONTIER WESTERN
Feb., 1956
1 RH,. 125.00
2 AW,GT 75.00
3 MD. 75.00
4 MD. 50.00
5 RC 60.00
6 AW, ... 75.00
7 JR 50.00
8 RC 50.00
9 . . . . 50.00
10 August, 1957 . . . . 50.00

FUNNY FROLICS
Summer, 1945
1 (fa) 125.00
2 . . . . 75.00
3 . . . . 50.00
4 . . . . 50.00
5 HK 60.00

FURTHER ADVENTURES
OF CYCLOPS
AND PHOENIX
1996
1 thru 4 . . . . 1.95
TPB PrM,JPL, O:Mr. Sinister, ... 12.00

FURY
1994
1 MCW,O:Fury,A:S.A. Heroes 3.25

FURY/AGENT 13
March 1998
1 (of 2) TKa,is Nick Fury alive? . . . 3.00
2 TKa,MZ(c),Sharon Carter's searches
  for Nick 3.00

FURY OF S.H.I.E.L.D.
1995
1 Foil etched cover 2.50
2 A:Iron Man 1.95
3 J:Hydra 1.95
4 w/decoder card. 2.50

GALACTIC GUARDIANS
1994
1 KWe,C:Woden 1.75
2 KWe,I:Hazmat,Savant,Ganglia . . 1.50
3 KWe. 1.50
4 KWe,final issue. 1.50

GALACTUS
THE DEVOURER
April 1999
1 (of 6) JMu,LSi,A:Silver Surfer,
  Fant.Four & Avengers,48-page . 3.50
2 LSi,JB,BSz 2.50

GAMBIT
1997
1 HMe(c),LW,KJ,V:Assassin'sGuild,
  D:Henri LeBeau,Embossed(c) . 5.00
1a Gold Ed. 15.00
2 LW,KJ,C:Gideon,A:Rogue. 3.00
3 LW,KJ,A:Candra,Rogue,
  D:Gambit's Father 3.00
4 LW,KJ,A:Candra,Rogue,D:Tithe
  Collector. 3.00
TPB Rep.#1-#4. . . . . 8.95

GAMBIT
1997
1 (of 4) HMe,KJ,In Miami. 2.50
2 HMe,KJ, ... 2.50
3 HMe,KJ,in the Vatican 2.50
4 HMe V:Stoker, concl. 2.50

GAMBIT
Dec. 1998
1 FaN,SSr,O:Gambit,48-page 3.00
1a signed 24.95
2 FaN,SSr,V:Storm 3.00
2a variant cover. 3.00
3 FaN,SSr,V:Mengo Brothers. . . . 2.00
4 FaN,SSr,A:Blade 2.00
5 FaN,SSr,R:Rogue. 2.00
6 FaN,SSr,I:The Pig. 2.00
7 FaN,SSr, ... 2.00
8 FaN,A:Sinister,Sabretooth. 2.00
9 FaN,The Shattering,x-over 2.00
Ann.1999 48-page 3.50
Giant Sized Gambit, 96-page, rep. . 4.00

GAMBIT AND
THE X-TERNALS
1995
1 X-Force after Xavier 3.50
2 V:Deathbird,Starjammers 2.50
3 V:Imperial Guard 2.25
4 Charles Kidnapped 2.25

GARGOYLE
June, 1985
1 BWr(c),from `Defenders'. 2.00
2 thru 4 . . . . @1.50

GARGOYLES
1995–96
1 TV Series 2.50
2 TV Series 1.50
3 F:Broadway 1.50
4 V:Statues 1.50
5 Humanoid Gargoyles 1.50
6 Medusa Project concl. 1.50
7 Demona & Triad 1.50
8 I:The Pack 1.50
9 V:Demonia,Triad. 1.50
10 Demonia gains magical powers . 1.50
11 Elisa turns to Xanatos 1.50
12 Sorceress traps Gargoyles. . . . 1.50
13 Behind Enemy Lines 1.50
14 . . . . 1.50
15 . . . . 1.50
16 Hammer of Fear 1.50

Gargoyle #4
© Marvel Entertainment Group

GENE DOGS
Marvel UK 1993–94
1 I:Gene DOGS,w/cards 2.75
2 V:Genetix 2.00
3 V:Hurricane 2.00
4 last issue 1.75

GENERATION NEXT
1995
1 Generation X AX 3.50
2 Genetic Slave Pens 2.50
3 V:Sugar Man 2.25
4 V:Sugar Man 2.25

GENERATION X
Oct. 1994
1 CBa,Banshee & White Queen. . . 5.00
2 CBa,SLo. 2.00
2a Deluxe edition. 3.50
3 CBa 2.00
3a Deluxe edition. 3.50
4 CBa,V:Nanny,Orphanmaker 2.00
4a Deluxe edition. 3.00
5 SLo,CBa,MBu,two new young

Generation X #45
© Marvel Entertainment Group

MARVEL

mutants at the Academy...... 2.25
6 A:Wolverine 2.25
7 SLo,F:Banshee,A:White Queen . 2.25
8 F:Banshee 2.00
9 SLo,TG,Chamber in a kilt 2.00
10 SLo,TG,MBu,Banshee vs.
  OmegaRed............... 2.00
11 SLo,TG,V:Omega Red........ 2.00
12 SLo,TG,V:Emplate........... 2.00
13 .... 2.00
14 .... 2.00
15 SLo,MBu,Synch goes psycho . 2.00
16 .... 2.00
17 SLo,CBa,Onslaught saga,
  X-Cutioner vs. Skin........ 2.00
18 SLo,CBa,Onslaught saga..... 2.00
19 SLo,CBa,.................. 2.00
20 SLo,CBa,.................. 2.00
21 SLo,CBa,MBu,F:Skin & Chamber,
  A:Beverly Switzer, Howard
  the Duck 2.00
22 SLo,CBa,.................. 2.00
23 SLo,CBa,V:Black Tom Cassidy . 2.00
24 SLo,MBy,F:Monet,Emplate..... 2.00
25 SLo,CBa,double size 3.00
26 SLo,CBa,Shot down over the
  Atlantic................. 2.00
27 SLo,CBa,on nuclear sub...... 2.00
28 SLo,CBa,No Exit prelude..... 2.00
29 JeR,CBa, V:Sentinels 2.00
30 JeR,CBa, V:Zero Tolerance ... 2.00
31 JeR,CBa, ... 2.00
32 TDF,MBu,F:Banshee, Moira
  McTaggert 2.00
33 LHa,MBu,new direction 2.00
34 LHa,Truth behind M........ 2.00
35 LHa,Jubilee,V:Emplate....... 2.00
36 LHa,Final Fate of M......... 2.00
37 LHa,Final Fate of M......... 2.00
38 LHa,TyD,kids save universe.... 2.00
39 LHa,TyD, multi-dimensional trip . 2.00
40 LHa,TyD,Penance mystery
  revealed................ 2.00
41 LHa,TyD,Jubilee,V:Bastion,
  Omega Red, Sabretooth.... 2.00
42 LHa,TyD,results of EMP wave .. 2.00
43 LHa,TyD,V:Bianca LaNiege ... 2.00
44 LHa,TyD,V:White Queen 2.00
45 LHa,TyD,F:Banshee......... 2.00
46 LHa,TyD,F:Forge........... 2.00
47 LHa,TyD,Danger Room 2.00
48 TyD,Jubilee vs. M 2.00
49 TyD,V:Maggott............. 2.00
50 TyD,War of the Mutants,pt.1 ... 3.00
50a signed 20.00
51 V:Hunter Brawn 2.00
52 TyD,blackmail 2.00
53 TyD,V:Rising Sons,A:Paladin ... 2.00
54 TyD,A:Paladin 2.00
55 TyD,in bodies of Hellions 2.00
56 TyD,A:X-Men of past 2.00
Minus 1 Spec., JeR,CBa, flashback,
  F:Banshee 1.95
Ann. '95 SLo,J:Mondo,
  V:Hellfire Club 3.95
Ann. '96 GN MGo,JJ,DPs,V:Fenris . 2.95
Ann. '97, Haunted by Ghosts
  of Hellions 2.00
Ann.1998 Generation X/Dracula ... 3.50
Holliday Spec. 48-page 1-shot ... 3.50

GENERATION X/GEN 13
Dec., 1997
1-shot JeR,SvL,V:Mr. Pretorious ... 4.00
1a variant cover CBa (1:4) 4.00

GENERATION X:
UNDERGROUND
March 1998
1-shot by Jim Mahfood, b&w..... 2.50

GENERIC COMIC
1 .... 1.50

GENETIX
Marvel UK 1993–94
1 B:ALa(s),w/cards 2.75
2 I:Tektos 2.00
3 V:Tektos 1.75
4 PGa,V:MyS-Tech 1.75
5 PGa,V:MyS-Tech 1.75
6 V:Tektos 1.95

GEORGIE COMICS
Spring, 1945
1 Georgie stories begin 120.00
2 Pet Shop (c) 55.00
3 Georgie/Judy(c) 40.00
4 Wedding Dress(c) 40.00
5 Monty/Policeman(c) 40.00
6 Classroom(c) 40.00
7 Fishing(c) 45.00
8 Soda Jerk(c) 35.00
9 Georgie/Judy(c),HK,Hey Look . 45.00
10 Georgie/Girls(c),HK,Hey Look . 45.00
11 Table Tennis(c),A:Margie,Millie . 30.00
12 Camping(c) 30.00
13 Life Guard(c),HK,Hey Look ... 40.00
14 Classroom(c),HK,Hey Look ... 45.00
15 Winter Sports(c)........... 25.00
16 .... 25.00
17 HK,Hey Look 25.00
18 .... 25.00
19 Baseball(c) 25.00
20 Title change to Georgie
  & Judy Comics 25.00
21 Title change to Georgie
  & Judy Comics........... 20.00
22 Georgie comics........... 20.00
23 .... 20.00
24 .... 20.00
25 .... 40.00
26 .... 20.00
27 .... 20.00
28 .... 20.00
29 .... 35.00
30 thru 38................. @20.00
39 Oct., 1952 .... 20.00

GETALONG GANG
May, 1985—March, 1986
1 thru 6 .... @1.00

GHOST RIDER
[1st Regular Series] Sept., 1973
1 GK,JSt,C:Son of Satan....... 60.00
2 GK,I:Son of Satan,A:Witch
  Woman 25.00
3 JR,D:Big Daddy Dawson,
  new Cycle 15.00
4 GK,A:Dude Jensen.......... 15.00
5 GK,JR,I:Roulette........... 15.00
6 JR,O:Ghost Rider 11.00
7 JR,A:Stunt Master.......... 11.00
8 GK,A:Satan,I:Inferno....... 10.00
9 GK,TP,O:Johnny Blaze 11.00
10 JSt,A:Hulk 11.00
11 GK,KJ,SB,A:Hulk 10.00
12 GK,KJ,FR,A:Phantom Eagle ... 8.00
13 GK,JS,GT,A:Trapster........ 8.00
14 GT,A:The Orb 8.00
15 SB,O:The Orb 8.00

16 DC,GT,Blood in the Water 8.00
17 RB,FR,I:Challenger 8.00
18 RB,FR,A:Challenger,
  Spider-Man 9.00
19 GK,FR,A:Challenger 8.00
20 GK,KJ,JBy,A:Daredevil 10.00
21 A:Gladiator,D:Eel 5.00
22 AM,DH,KP,JR,A:Enforcer...... 5.00
23 JK,DH,DN,I:Water Wiz. 5.00
24 GK,DC,DH,A:Enforcer 5.00
25 GK,DH,A:Stunt Master....... 5.00
26 GK,DP,A:Dr. Druid 5.00
27 SB,DP,A:Hawkeye 5.00
28 DP,A:The Orb 5.00
29 RB,DP,A:Dormammu 5.00
30 DP,A:Dr.Strange 5.00
31 FR,DP,BL,A:Bounty Hunt. 5.00
32 KP,BL,DP,A:Bounty Hunt...... 5.00
33 DP,I:Dark Riders 5.00
34 DP,C:Cyclops 5.00
35 JSn,AM,A:Death 6.00
36 DP,Drug Mention 5.00
37 DP,I:Dick Varden 5.00
38 DP,A:Death Cult. 5.00
39 DP,A:Death Cult. 5.00
40 DP,I:Nuclear Man. 5.00
41 DP,A:Jackal Gang 5.00
42 DP,A:Jackal Gang 5.00
43 CI:Crimson Mage. 5.00
44 JAb,CI,A:Crimson Mage. 5.00
45 DP,I:Flagg Fargo 5.00
46 DP,A:Flagg Fargo 5.00
47 AM,DP. 5.00
48 BMc,DP. 5.00
49 DP,I:The Manitou 5.00
50 DP,A:Night Rider 6.00
51 AM,PD,A:Cycle Gang 4.00
52 AM,DP. 4.00
53 DP,I:Lord Asmodeus 4.00
54 DP,A:The Orb 4.00
55 DP,A:Werewolf By Night. 4.00
56 DP,A:Moondark,I:Night Rider .. 4.00
57 AM,DP,I:The Apparition 4.00
58 DP,FM,A:Water Wizard 4.00
59 V:Water Wizard,Moon Dark 4.00
60 DP,HT,A:Black Juju 4.00
61 A:Arabian Knight 4.00
62 KJ,A:Arabian Knight. 4.00
63 LMc,A:The Orb 4.00
64 BA,V:Azmodeus........... 4.00
65 A:Fowler 4.00
66 BL,A:Clothilde 4.00
67 DP,A:Sally Stantop. 4.00
68 O:Ghost Rider 4.00

Ghost Rider #4
© Marvel Entertainment Group

   All comics prices listed are for *Near Mint* condition.

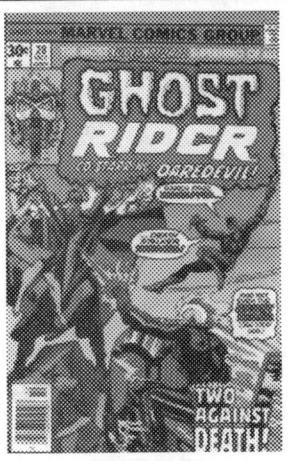

Ghost Rider #20
© Marvel Entertainment Group

69 . . . . 4.00
70 I:Jeremy 4.00
71 DP,I:Adam Henderson 4.00
72 A:Circus of Crime 4.00
73 A:Circus of Crime 4.00
74 A:Centurions 4.00
75 I:Steel Wind 4.00
76 DP,A:Mephisto,I:Saturnine 4.00
77 O:Ghost Rider's Dream 4.00
78 A:Nightmare 4.00
79 A:Man Cycles 4.00
80 A:Centurions 4.00
81 D:Ghost Rider 9.00

[2nd Regular Series] 1990–98
1 JS,MT,I:2nd Ghost Rider,
   Deathwatch 4.00
1a 2nd printing 2.00
2 JS,MT,I:Blackout 3.00
3 JS,MT,A:Kingpin,V:Blackout,
   Deathwatch 3.00
4 JS,MT,V:Mr.Hyde 3.00
5 JLe(c),JS,MT,A:Punisher 3.00
5a rep.Gold 2.50
6 JS,MT,A:Punisher 3.00
7 MT,V:Scarecrow 3.00
8 JS,MT,V:H.E.A.R.T 3.00
9 JS,MT,A:Morlocks,X-Factor 2.50
10 JS,MT,V:Zodiac 2.50
11 LSn,MT,V:Nightmare,
   A:Dr.Strange 2.50
12 JS,MT,A:Dr.Strange 2.50
13 MT,V:Snow Blind,R:J.Blaze 2.50
14 MT,Blaze Vs.Ghost Rider 2.50
15 MT,A:Blaze,V:Blackout
   Glow in Dark(c) 3.00
15a 2nd printing (gold) 2.50
16 MT,A:Blaze,Spider-Man,
   V:Hobgoblin 2.50
17 MT,A:Spider-Man,Blaze,
   V:Hobgoblin 2.50
18 MT,V:Reverend Styge 2.25
19 MT,A:Mephisto 2.25
20 MT(i),O:Zodiac 2.25
21 MT(i),V:Snowblind,
   A:Deathwatch 2.25
22 MT,A:Deathwatch,Ninjas 2.25
23 MT,I:Hag & Troll,A:Deathwatch . 2.25
24 MT,V:Deathwatch,D:Snowblind,
   C:Johnny Blaze 2.25
25 V:Blackout (w/Center spread
   pop-up) 2.50
26 A:X-Men,V:The Brood 2.50
27 A:X-Men,V:The Brood 2.50

28 NKu,JKu,Rise of the Midnight
   Sons#1,V:Lilith,w/poster 2.50
29 NKu,JKu,A:Wolverine,Beast 2.50
30 NKu,JKu,V:Nightmare 2.25
31 NKu,JKu,Rise o/t Midnight
   Sons#6, A:Dr.Strange,Morbius,
   Nightstalkers,Redeemers,
   V:Lilith,w/poster 2.25
32 BBi,A:Dr.Strange 2.00
33 BBi,AW,V:Madcap (inc.Superman
   tribute on letters page) 2.00
34 BBi,V:Deathwatchs' ninja 2.00
35 BBi,AW,A:Heart Attack 2.00
36 BBi,V:Mr.Hyde,A:Daredevil 2.00
37 BBi,A:Archangel,V:HeartAttack . 2.00
38 MM,V:Scarecrow 2.00
39 V:Vengeance 2.00
40 Midnight Massacre#2,
   D:Demogblin 2.50
41 Road to Vengeance#1 . . . . 2.00
42 Road to Vengeance#2 . . . . 2.00
43 Road to Vengeance#3 . . . . 2.00
44 Siege of Darkness,pt.#2 . . . . . . 2.00
45 Siege of Darkness,pt.#10 . . . . . 2.00
46 HMe(s),New Beginning 2.00
47 HMe(s),RG, ... 2.00
48 HMe(s),RG,A:Spider-Man 2.00
49 HMe(s),RG,A:Hulk,w/card 2.25
50 Red Foil(c),AKu,SMc,A:Blaze,
   R:2nd Ghost Rider 3.25
50a Newsstand Ed. 2.75
51 SvL 2.25
52 SvL 2.00
53 SvL,V:Blackout 2.00
54 SvL,V:Blackout 2.00
55 V:Mr.Hyde 2.00
56 The Next Wave 2.00
57 A:Wolverine 2.00
58 HMe,SvL,Betrayal,pt.1 . . . . 2.00
59 Betrayal,pt.2 . . . . 2.00
60 Betrayal,pt.3 . . . . 2.00
61 Betrayal,pt.4 . . . . 2.00
62 EventInChains,pt.1,A:Fury 2.00
63 EventInChains,pt.2 . . . . 2.00
64 EventInChains,pt.3 . . . . 2.00
65 EventInChains,pt.4,R:Blackout . . 2.00
66 V:Blackout 2.00
67 A:Gambit,V:Brood 2.00
68 A:Gambit,Wolverine,V:Brood . . . 2.00
69 Domestic Violence 2.00
70 New Home in Bronx 2.00
71 . . . . 2.00
72 . . . . 2.00
73 John Blaze is back 2.00
74 A:Blaze, Vengeance 2.00
75 . . . . 1.50
76 V:Vengeance 1.50
77 A:Dr. Strange 1.50
78 new costume, A:Dr. Strange . . . 1.50
79 IV,New costume, A:Valkyrie, . . . 1.50
80 IV,V:Furies,Valkyrie,
   A:Black Rose 1.50
81 IV,A:Howard the Duck,
   Devil Dinosaur 1.50
82 IV,A:Devil Dinosaur, ... 1.50
83 IV,A:Scarecrow,Lilith 1.50
84 IV,A:Scarecrow, Lilith 2.00
85 IV,V:Lilith, Scarecrow 2.00
86 IV,rampage through the Bronx . . 2.00
87 IV,KIK,AM, ... 2.00
88 IV, V:Pao Fu,Blackheart 2.00
89 IV,JS,. 2.00
90 IV,JS,Last Temptation, pt.1 . . . . 2.00
91 IV,JS,A:Blackheart 2.00
92 IV,JS,Journey into the past 2.00
93 IV,JS,MT,Last Temptation concl.,
   double sized 3.00
94 IV,JS,MT,Becomes Lord of the
   Underworld, last issue 2.00
Ann.#1 I:Night Terror,w/card 3.25
Ann.#2 F:Scarecrow 2.95

GN Ghost Rider/Captain America:
   Fear, AW, V:Scarecrow (1992) . 6.25
TPB Midnight Sons,rep.GhR#28,31,
   Morbius#1,Darkhold#1,Spirirts of
   Vengeance#1,Nightstalkers#1. 19.95
TPB Resurrected rep.#1-#7 . . . . . 12.95
TPB Ghost Rider/Wolverine/Punisher:
   Dark Design (1994) 5.95
TPB Ghost Rider/Wolverine/Punisher:
   Hearts of Darkness, JR2/KJ,V:
   Blackheart, double gatefold cover
   (1991) 5.50
Poster Book 4.95
Spec. Crossroads 3.95
Minus 1 Spec., IV,JS, flashback . . 1.95

GHOST RIDER/BALLISTIC
Marvel/Top Cow 1996
1-shot WEI,BTn,"Devil's
   Reign," pt.3, x-over 2.95

GHOST RIDER/BLAZE
SPIRITS OF VENGEANCE
1992–94
1 AKu,polybagged w/poster,V:Lilith,
   Rise of the Midnight Sons#2 . . . 3.50
2 AKu,V:Steel Wind 2.50
3 AKu,CW,V:The Lilin 2.00
4 AKu,V:Hag & Troll,C:Venom 3.00
5 AKu,BR,Spirits of Venom#2,
   A:Venom,Spidey,Hobgoblin 5.00
6 AKu,Spirits of Venom#4,A:Venom,
   Spider-Man,Hobgoblin 3.50
7 AKu,V:Steel Vengeance 2.00
8 V:Mephisto 2.00
9 I:Brimstone 2.00
10 AKu,V:Vengeance 2.00
11 V:Human Spider Creature 2.00
12 AKu,BR,Vengeance,glow in the
   dark(c) 3.25
13 AKu,Midnight Massacre#5 . . . . 2.50
14 Missing Link#2 . . . . 2.00
15 Missing Link#3 . . . . 2.00
16 V:Zarathos,Lilith 2.00
17 HMe(s),Siege/Darkness,pt.8 . . . 2.00
18 HMe(s),Siege/Darkness,pt.13 . . 2.00
19 HMe(s),HMz,V:Vampire 2.00
20 HMe(s),A:Steel Wind 2.00
21 HMe(s),HMz,V:Werewolves 2.00
22 HMe(s),HMz,V:Cardiac 2.25
23 HMe(s),HMz,A:Steel Wind 2.25

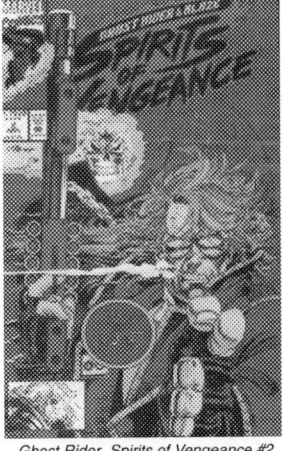

Ghost Rider ,Spirits of Vengeance #2
© Marvel Entertainment Group

MARVEL

GHOST RIDER/CYBLADE
Marvel/Top Cow 1996
1-shot IV,ACh,"Devil's Reign,"
pt.2, x-over.............. 2.95

GHOST RIDER 2099
1994–96
1 Holografx(c),LKa,CBa,MBu,I:Ghost
   Rider 2099,w/card 2.75
1a Newsstand Ed............... 1.75
2 LKa,CBa,MBu, ... 1.75
3 LKa,CBa,MBu,I:Warewolf 1.75
4 LKa,CBa,MBu,V:Warewolf 1.75
5 LKa,CBa,MBu. 1.75
6 LKa,CBa,MBu. 1.75
7 LKa,CBa,MBu. 1.75
8 LKa,CBa,MBu. 1.75
9 .... 1.50
10 .... 1.50
11 V:Bloodsport Society 1.50
12 I:Coda.................... 1.50
Becomes:

GHOST RIDER 2099 A.D.
13 F:Doom................... 2.00
14 Deputized by Doom......... 2.00
15 One Nation Under Doom 2.00
16 V:Max Synergy 2.00
17 .... 2.00
18 V:L-Cipher................ 2.00
19 V:L-Cipher................ 2.00
20 .... 2.00
21 V:Vengeance 2099 .... 2.00
22 V:Vengeance 2099 .... 2.00
23 .... 2.00
24 .... 2.00
25 Double size final issue....... 3.00

GIANT-SIZE CHILLERS
1975
1 AA,....................... 15.00
2 .... 10.00
3 BWr,Night of the Gargoyle 15.00

GIANT-SIZE CHILLERS
1974
1 I&O:Lilith,F:Curse of Dracula... 25.00
Becomes:

GIANT-SIZE DRACULA
2 Vengeance of the Elder Gods.. 15.00
3 rep. Uncanny Tales #6 .... 12.00

Giant Size Chillers #1
© Marvel Entertainment Group

---

4 SD,Demon of Devil's Lake 12.00
5 JBy, 1st Marvel art 20.00

G.I. JOE:
A REAL AMERICAN HERO
June, 1982
1 HT,BMc,Baxter paper 3.00
2 DP,JAb,North Pole 2.50
3 HT,JAb,Trojan Robot 2.00
4 HT,JAb,Wingfield 2.00
5 DP,Central Park 2.00
6 HT,V:Cobra................. 2.00
7 HT,Walls of Death........... 2.00
8 HT,Sea Strike 2.00
9 The Diplomat 2.00
10 Springfield................. 2.00
11 Alaska Pipeline 2.00
12 V:Snake Eyes 2.50
13 Rio Lindo................. 2.00
14 V:Destro.................. 2.00
15 A:Red Eye................. 2.00
16 V:Cobra.................. 2.00
17 Loose Ends 2.00
18 V:Destro.................. 2.00
19 D:General Kwinn 2.00
20 JBy(c),GI,Clutch 2.00
21 SL(i),Silent Interlude 2.00
22 V:Destro.................. 2.00
23 I:Duke................... 1.75
24 RH,I:Storm Shadow......... 2.00
25 FS,I:Zartan............... 2.00
26 SL(i),O:Snake Eyes 2.50
27 FS,O:Snake Eyes 2.00
28 Swampfire 2.00
29 FS,V:Destro................ 2.00
30 JBy(c),FS,V:Dreddnoks 2.00
31 V:Destro.................. 1.75
32 FS,V:Dreddnoks 2.00
33 FS,Celebration.............. 1.75
34 Shakedown 1.75
35 JBy(c),MBr,V:Dreddnoks 1.75
36 MBr,Shipwar 1.75
2a to 36a 2nd printings ... @1.00
37 FS,Twin Brothers,I:Flint 2.00
38 V:Destro.................. 2.00
39 Jungle 2.00
40 Hydrofoil 2.00
41 .... 2.00
42 A:Stormshadow............ 2.00
43 Death Issue,New Joe........ 2.00
44 V:Cobra.................. 2.00
45 V:Cobra.................. 2.00
46 V:Cobra.................. 2.00
47 V:Cobra,D:Stormshadow 2.00
48 V:Cobra.................. 2.00
49 V:Cobra,I:Serpentor 2.00
50 I:G.I.Joe Missions,R:S'shadow.. 2.25
51 V:Cobra Emperor........... 1.50
52 V:Stormshadow 1.50
53 Hawk V:Cobra 1.50
54 V:Destro.................. 1.50
55 The Pit 1.50
56 V:Serpentor 1.50
57 V:Destro.................. 1.50
58 V:Cobra.................. 1.50
59 Armor 1.50
60 TM,I:Zanzibar 2.50
61 MR,D:Cobra Commander 1.25
62 Trial..................... 1.25
63 A:GI Joe Snow Job 1.25
64 V:Baroness 1.25
65 V:Cobra.................. 1.25
66 Stalker Rescued 1.25
67 .... 1.25
68 I:Battleforce 2000 .... 1.25
69 TSa...................... 1.25
70 V:Destro.................. 1.25
71 .... 1.25
72 .... 1.25
73 .... 1.25

---

74 .... 1.25
75 MR 1.25
76 D:Serpentor................ 1.25
77 MR,V:Cobra................ 1.25
78 V:Cobra.................. 1.25
79 MR,V:Dreadnoks 1.25
80 V:Cobra.................. 1.25
81 MR,V:Dreadnoks 1.00
82 MR,V:Cobra................ 1.00
83 I:RoadPig 1.00
84 MR,O:Zartan............... 1.00
85 Storm Shadow,Vs.Zartan...... 1.00
86 MR,25th Anniv. 1.00
87 TSa,V:Cobra 1.00
88 TSa,V:Python Patrol 1.00
89 MBr,V:Road Pig 1.00
90 MBr,R:Red Ninjas 1.00
91 TSa,V:Red Ninjas,D:Blind
   Masters 1.00
92 MBr,V:Cobra Condor 1.00
93 MBr,V:Baroness............ 1.00
94 MBr,A:Snake Eyes.......... 1.00
95 MBr,A:Snake Eyes.......... 1.00
96 MBr,A:Snake Eyes.......... 1.00
97 .... 1.00
98 MBr,R:Cobra Commander 1.00
99 HT....................... 1.00
100 MBr...................... 1.50
101 MBr...................... 1.00
102 MBr...................... 1.00
103 MBr,A:Snake Eyes......... 1.00
104 MBr,A:Snake Eyes......... 1.00
105 MBr,A:Snake Eyes......... 1.00
106 MBr,StormShadowStalker 1.00
107 .... 1.00
108 I:G.I.Joe Dossiers 1.00
109 Death Issue............... 1.00
110 Mid-East Crisis............. 1.00
111 A:Team Ninjas 1.00
112 A:Team Ninjas 1.00
113 V:Cobra.................. 1.00
114 V:Cobra.................. 1.00
115 Story Concl.Dusty Dossier 1.00
116 Destro:Search&Destroy #1.... 1.00
117 Destro:Search&Destroy #2.... 1.00
118 Destro:Search&Destroy #3.... 1.00
119 HT,Android Dopplegangers ... 1.00
120 V:Red Ninjas,Slice & Dice 1.00
121 V:Slice & Dice 1.25
122 V:Slice & Dice 1.25
123 I:Eco-Warriors,A:Big Man..... 1.25
124 V:Headman 1.25
125 V:Headhunters............. 1.25
126 R:Firefly.................. 1.25

G.I. Joe #16
© Marvel Entertainment Group

G.I. Joe #59
© *Marvel Entertainment Group*

127 R:Original G.I.Joe	1.25
128 V:Firefly	1.25
129 V:Cobra Commander	1.25
130 V:Cobra Commander	1.25
131 V:Cobra Commander	1.25
132 V:Cobra	1.25
133 V:Cobra	1.25
134 V:Red Ninjas, Firefly, Hostilities	1.25
135 V:Cobra Ninja w/card	1.75
136 w/Trading Card	1.75
137 V:Night Creepers,w/card	1.75
138 V:Night Creepers,w/card	1.75
139 R:Transformers,V:Cobra	1.25
140 A:Transformers	1.25
141 A:Transformers	1.25
142 A:Transformers	1.25
143 F:Scarlet	1.25
144 O:Snake Eyes	1.25
145 V:Cobra	1.25
146 F:Star Brigade	1.25
147 F:Star Brigade	1.25
148 F:Star Brigade	1.25
149.	1.25
150 Cobra Commander vs. Snake Eyes	2.00
151 V:Cobra	1.50
152 First G.I. Joe	1.50
153 V:Cobra	1.50
154	1.50
155 final issue	1.50
SC GI Joe and the Transformers	4.95
Spec. TM rep.#61	1.50
Ann.#1	3.00
Ann.#2	2.00
Ann.#3	2.00
Ann.#4	2.00
Ann.#5	2.00
Yearbook #1 (1985)	2.50
Yearbook #2 (1986)	2.50
Yearbook #3 (1987)	2.50
Yearbook #4 (1988)	2.50

G.I. JOE
EUROPEAN MISSIONS
June, 1988

1 British rep.	1.25
2	1.50
3	1.50
4	1.50
5 thru 15	@1.75

G.I. JOE
SPECIAL MISSIONS
Oct., 1986

1 HT,New G.I. Joe	1.75
2 HT	1.50
3 HT	1.50
4 HT	1.50
5 HT	1.50
6 HT,Iron Curtain	1.50
7 HT	1.50
8 HT	1.50
9 HT	1.50
10 thru 21 HT	@1.00
22	1.00
23 HT	1.00
24	1.00
25 HT	1.00
26 HT	1.00
27	1.00
28 HT,final	1.00

G.I. JOE AND
THE TRANSFORMERS
1987

1 HT,mini-series	1.75
2 HT,Cobra	1.50
3 HT,Cobra,Deceptions	1.00
4 HT,Cobra,Deceptions	1.00

G.I. JOE UNIVERSE

1 Biographies rep.#1	2.50
2	2.00
3 MZ(c)	2.00
4	1.25

G.I. TALES
See: SERGEANT BARNEY
BARKER

GIRL COMICS
Atlas Nov., 1949

1 Ph(c),True love stories,I Could Escape From Love	125.00
2 Ph(c),JKu,Blind Date	75.00
3 BEv,Ph(c),Liz Taylor	100.00
4 PH(c),Borrowed Love	45.00
5 Love stories	45.00
6 same	45.00
7 same	45.00
8 same	45.00
9 same	45.00
10 The Deadly Double-Cross	45.00
11 Love stories	45.00
12 BK,The Dark Hallway	50.00
Becomes:	

GIRL CONFESSIONS

13	50.00
14	30.00
15	30.00
16 BEv	35.00
17 BEv	35.00
18 BEv	35.00
19	25.00
20	25.00
21 thru 34	@17.00
35 August, 1954	17.00

GIRLS' LIFE
Atlas Jan., 1954

1	50.00
2	25.00
3	20.00
4	20.00
5	20.00

6 November, 1954	20.00

GLADIATOR/SUPREME
1997

1 KG,ASm,x-over	5.00

GODZILLA
August, 1977

1 HT,JM,Based on Movie Series	8.00
2 HT,FrG,GT,Seattle Under Seige	6.00
3 HT,TD,A;Champions	4.00
4 TS,TD,V;Batragon	4.00
5 TS,KJ,Isle of the Living Demons	6.00
6 HT,A Monster Enslaved	6.00
7 V:Red Ronin	6.00
8 V:Red Ronin	6.00
9 Las Gamble in Las Vegas	6.00
10 V:Yetrigar	6.00
11 V;Red Ronin,Yetrigar	4.00
12 Star Sinister	4.00
13 V:Mega-Monster	4.00
14 V:Super-Beasts	4.00
15 Stampede	4.00
16 Jaws of Fear	4.00
17 Godzilla Shrunk	4.00
18 Battle Beneath Eighth Avenue	4.00
19 Panic on the Pier	4.00
20 A;Fantastic Four	4.50
21 V;Devil Dinosaur	4.00
22 V:Devil Dinosaur	4.00
23 A;Avengers	4.50
24 July, 1979	4.00

GOLDEN AGE
OF MARVEL

TPB RyL	10.00
Vol.1, 176-page	20.00
Vol.2, 176-page	20.00

GREATEST SPIDER-MAN
& DAREDEVIL TEAM-UPS

TPB 175pg	10.00

GREEN GOBLIN
1995–96

1 I:New Green Goblin	2.95
2 TDF,SMc,V:Rhino	1.95
3 TDF,SMc,CyberWar tie-in	1.95
4 TDF,SMc,V:Hobgoblin	1.95
5 TDF,V:Hobgoblin	1.95
6	1.95
7	1.95
8 TDF,SMc,I:Angelface	1.95
9	1.95
10	1.95
11	1.95
12 Onslaught saga	1.95
13 Onslaught saga	1.95

GROO CHRONICLES
Epic 1989

1 SA	5.00
2 SA	4.00
3 SA	4.00
4 SA	4.00
5 SA	4.00
6 SA	3.50

[SERGIO ARAGONE'S]
GROO, THE WANDERER
(see Pacific, Eclipse)
Epic 1985–95

1 SA,I:Minstrel	9.00

MARVEL

2 SA,A:Minstrel	6.00
3 SA,Medallions	5.00
4 SA,Airship	4.00
5 SA,Slavers	4.00
6 SA,The Eye of the Kabala	4.00
7 SA,A:Sage	4.00
8 SA,A:Taranto	4.00
9 SA,A:Sage	4.00
10 SA,I:Arcadio	4.00
11 SA,A:Arcadio	4.00
12 SA,Groo Meets the Thespians	4.00
13 SA,A:Sage	4.00
14 SA	4.00
15 SA,Monks	4.00
16 SA,A:Taranto	4.00
17 SA,Pirannas	4.00
18 SA,I:Groo Ella	4.00
19 SA,A:Groo Ella	3.00
20 SA,A:Groo Ella	3.00
21 SA,I:Arba,Dakarba	3.00
22 SA,Ambassador	3.00
23 SA,I:Pal,Drumm	3.00
24 SA,Arcadio's	3.00
25 SA,Taranto	3.00
26 SA,A:Arba,Taranto	3.00
27 SA,A:Minstrel,Sage	3.00
28 SA	3.00
29 SA,I:Ruferto	4.00
30 SA,A:Ruferto	3.00
31 SA,A:Pal,Drumm	2.00
32 SA,C:Sage	2.00
33 SA,Pirates	2.00
34 SA,Wizard's amulet	2.00
35 SA,A:Everybody	2.00
36 SA,A:Everybody	2.00
37 SA,A:Ruferto	2.00
38 SA,Dognappers	2.00
39 SA,A:Pal,Drumm	2.00
40 SA	2.00
41 SA,I:Granny Groo	2.00
42 SA,A:Granny Groo	2.00
43 SA,A:Granny Groo	2.00
44 SA,A:Ruferto	2.00
45 SA	2.00
46 SA,New Clothes	2.00
47 SA,A:Everybody	2.00
48 SA,A:Ruferto	2.00
49 SA,C:Chakaal	2.00
50 SA,double size	3.00
51 SA,A:Chakaal	2.00
52 SA,A:Chakaal	2.00
53 SA,A:Chakaal	2.00
54 SA,A:Ahak	2.00
55 SA,A:Ruferto	2.00
56 SA,A:Minstrael	2.00
57 SA,A:Ruferto	2.00
58 SA,A:Idol	2.00
59 SA	2.00
60 SA,A:Ruferto	2.00
61 SA,A:Horse	2.00
62 SA,A:Horse	1.75
63 SA,A:Drumm	1.75
64 SA,A:Artist	1.75
65 SA	1.75
66 SA	1.75
67 SA	1.75
68 SA	1.75
69 SA	1.75
70 SA	1.50
71 SA	1.50
72 SA	1.50
73 SA,Amnesia,pt1	1.50
74 SA,Amnesia,pt2	1.50
75 SA,Memory Returns	1.50
76 SA	1.50
77 SA	1.50
78 SA,R:Weaver,Scribe	1.50
79 SA,Groo the Assassin	1.50
80 SA,I:Thaiis,pt.1	1.50
81 SA,Thaiis,pt.2	1.50
82 SA,Thaiis,pt.3	1.50

Groo The Wanderer #1
© Marvel Entertainment Group

83 SA,Thaiis,pt.4	1.50
84 SA,Thaiis Conclusion	1.50
85 SA,Groo turns invisible	1.50
86 SA,Invisible Groo	1.50
87 SA,Groo's Army	1.50
88 SA,V:Cattlemen,B.U. Sage	2.50
89 SA,New Deluxe Format	2.25
90 SA,Worlds 1st Lawyers	2.25
91 SA,Bonus Pages	2.25
92 SA,Groo Becomes Kid Groo	2.25
93 SA,Groo destroys glacier	2.25
94 SA	2.25
95 SA,Endangered Species	2.25
96 SA,Wager of the Gods#1	2.25
97 SA,Wager of the Gods#2	2.25
98 SA,Wager of the Gods#3	2.25
99 SA,E:Wager of the Gods	2.25
100 SA,Groo gets extra IQ points	2.75
101 SA,Groo loses intelligence	2.25
102 SA,F:Newly literate Groo	2.25
103 SA,General Monk	2.25
104 SA,F:Oso,Ruferto	2.25
105 SA,V:Minotaurs	2.25
106 SA,B:Man of the People	2.25
107 SA,Man of the People#2	2.25
108 SA,Man of the People#3	2.25
109 SA,E:Man of the People	2.25
110 SA,Mummies	2.25
111 SA,The Man who Killed Groo	2.25
112 SA,Rufferto Avenged	2.25
113 SA	2.25
114 SA,V:Vultures	2.25
115 SA	2.25
116 SA,Early unto Morning	2.25
117 SA	2.25
118 SA	2.25
119 SA	2.25
120 Groo hangs up swords	2.25
GNv Death of Groo	8.00
GNv 2nd print	8.00
TPB Groo Adventures	8.95
TPB Groo Carnival	8.95
TPB Groo Expose	8.95
TPB GRoo Festival	8.95
TPB Groo Garden	10.95

GROOVY
March, 1968—July, 1968

1 Monkeys,Ringo Starr,Photos	50.00
2 Cartoons,Gags,Jokes	40.00
3	40.00

GUARDIANS OF THE GALAXY
June, 1990

1 B:JV(a&s),I:Taserface,R:Aleta	3.00
2 MZ(c),JV,V:Stark,C:Firelord	2.50
3 JV,V:Stark,I:Force,C:Firelord	2.50
4 JV,V:Stark,A:Force,Firelord	2.50
5 JV,TM(c),V:Force,I:Mainframe (Vision)	2.50
6 JV,V:Force,Vance Possesses Capt.America Shield	2.50
7 GP(c),JV,I:Malevolence, O:Starhawk	3.00
8 SLi(c),JV,V:Yondu,C:Rancor	3.00
9 RLd(c),JV,I:Replica,Rancor	3.00
10 JLe(c),JV,V:Rancor,The Nine I&C:Overkill(Taserface)	3.00
11 BWi(c),JV,V:Rancor,I:Phoenix	3.00
12 ATb(c),JV,V:Overkill A:Firelord	2.50
13 JV,A:Ghost Rider,Force, Malevolence	3.00
14 JS(c),JV,A:Ghost Rider,Force, Malevolence	3.00
15 JSn(c),JV,I:Protege,V:Force	2.50
16 JV,V:Force,A:Protege, Malevolence,L:Vance Astro	2.50
17 JV,V:Punishers(Street Army), L:Martinex,N:Charlie-27,	2.50
18 JV,V:Punishers,I&C:Talon,A: Crazy Nate	3.00
19 JV,V:Punishers,A:Talon	2.50
20 JV,I:Major Victory (Vance Astro) J:Talon & Krugarr	2.50
21 JV,V:Rancor	2.50
22 JV,V:Rancor	2.50
23 MT,V:Rancor,C:Silver Surfer	2.50
24 JV,A:Silver Surfer	3.00
25 JV, Prismatic Foil(c) V:Galactus,A:SilverSurfer	3.50
25a 2nd printing,Silver	2.50
26 JV,O:Guardians(retold)	2.00
27 JV,Infinity War,O:Guardian A:Inhumans	2.00
28 JV,Inf.War,V:Various Villians	2.00
29 HT,Inf.War,V:Various Villians	2.00
30 KWe,A:Captain America	2.00
31 KWe,V:Badoon,A:Capt.A	1.75
32 KWe,V:Badoon Gladiator	1.75
33 KWe,A:Dr.Strange,R:Aleta	1.50
34 KWe,J:Yellowjacket II	1.50
35 KWe,A:Galatic Guardians, V:Bubonicus	1.50
36 KWe,A:Galatic Guardians, V:Dormammu	1.50
37 KWe,V:Dormammu,A:Galatic Guardians	1.50
38 KWe,N:Y.jacket,A:Beyonder	1.50
39 KWe,Rancor Vs. Dr.Doom,Holo- grafx(c)	3.25
40 KWe,V:Loki,Composite	1.50
41 KWe,V:Loki,A:Thor	1.50
42 KWe,I:Woden	1.50
43 KWe,A:Woden,V:Loki	1.50
44 KWe,R:Yondu	1.50
45 KWe,O:Starhawk	1.50
46 KWe,N:Major Victory	1.50
47 KWe,A:Beyonder,Protoge, Overkill	1.50
48 KWe,V:Overkill	1.75
49 KWe,A:Celestial	1.75
50 Foil(c),R:Yondu,Starhawk sep- arated,BU:O:Guardians	3.25
51 KWe,A:Irish Wolfhound	1.50
52 KWe,A:Drax	1.50
53 KWe,V:Drax	1.50
54 KWe,V:Sentinels	1.50
55 KWe,Ripjack	1.50
56 Ripjack	1.50
57 R:Keeper	1.50

MARVEL

Guardians of the Galaxy #33
© Marvel Entertainment Group

58	1.50
59 A:Keeper	1.50
60 F:Starhawk	1.50
61 F:Starhawk	1.50
62 Guardians Stop War of the Worlds last issue	1.50
Ann.#1 Korvac Quest #4,I:Krugarr	3.00
Ann.#2 HT,I:Galactic Guardians, System Bytes #4	3.00
Ann.#3 CDo,I:Irish Wolfhound, w/Trading card	3.25
Ann.#4 V:Nine	3.25
TPB rep #1 thru #6	12.95

GUNHAWK, THE
See: BLAZE CARSON

GUNHAWKS
Oct., 1972

1 SSh,B:Reno Jones & Kid Cassidy Two Rode Together	10.00
2 Ride out for Revenge	8.00
3 Indian Massacre	8.00
4 Trial by Ordeal	8.00
5 The Reverend Mr. Graves	8.00
6 E:Reno Jones & Kid Cassidy D:Kid Cassidy	8.00
7 A Gunhawks Last Stand A;Reno Jones, Oct., 1973	8.00

GUNRUNNER
Marvel UK 1993–94

1 I:Gunrunner,w/trading cards	2.95
2 A:Ghost Rider	2.00
3 V:Cynodd	2.00
4	2.00
5 A:Enhanced	2.00
6 final issue	1.75

GUNSLINGER
See: TEX DAWSON,
GUNSLINGER

GUNSMOKE WESTERN
See: ALL WINNERS
COMICS

HARROWERS
1993–94

1 MSt(s),GC,F:Pinhead	3.25
2 GC,AW(i),	2.75
3 GC,AW(i),	2.75
4 GC,AW(i),	2.75
5 GC,AW(i),Devil's Pawn#1	2.75
6 GC,AW(i),Devil's Pawn#2	2.75

Harvey #1
© Marvel Entertainment Group

HARVEY
Oct., 1970–Dec., 1972

1	40.00
2 thru 6	@25.00

HARVEY PRESENTS:
CASPER

1	1.50

HAVOK & WOLVERINE
Epic March, 1988

1 JMu,KW,V:KGB,Dr.Neutron	5.00
2 JMu,KW,V:KGB,Dr.Neutron	4.00
3 JMu,KW,V:Meltdown	4.00
4 JMu,KW,V:Meltdown,Oct.1989	4.00
TPB rep.#1-4	16.95

HAWKEYE
[1st Limited Series] Sept., 1983

1 A:Mockingbird	3.00
2 I:Silencer	2.50
3 I:Bombshell,Oddball	2.00
4 V:Crossfire,W:Hawkeye & Mockingbird, (Dec. 1983)	2.00

[2nd Limited Series] 1994

1 B:CDi(s),ScK,V:Trickshot, I:Javelynn,Rover	2.00
2 ScK,V:Viper	2.00
3 ScK,A:War Machine,N:Hawkeye, V:Secret Empire	2.00
4 E:CDi(s),ScK,V:Trickshot,Viper, Javelynn	2.00

HAWKEYE: EARTH'S
MIGHTIEST MARKSMAN
Aug. 1998

1-shot TDF,MBa,JJ,DR,AM 48pg	3.00

HEADMASTERS
STAR July, 1987

1 FS,Transformers	1.25
2 and 3	@1.00
4 Jan., 1988	.75

HEATHCLIFF
Star April, 1985

1 thru 16	@1.00
17 Masked Moocher	1.00
18 thru 49	@1.00
50 Double-size	1.00
51 thru 55	@1.00

HEATHCLIFF'S
FUNHOUSE
Star May, 1987

1 thru 9	@1.00
10 1988	1.00

HEAVY HITTERS
Ann.#1 (1993)	4.00

HEDY DEVINE COMICS
Aug., 1947—Sept., 1952

22 I:Hedy Devine	80.00
23 BW,Beauty and the Beach, HK,Hey Look	90.00
24 High Jinx in Hollywood, HK, Hey Look	90.00
25 Hedy/Bull(c),HK,Hey Look	80.00
26 Skating(c),HK,Giggles&Grins	60.00
27 Hedy at Show(c),HK,Hey Look	70.00
28 Hedy/Charlie(c),HK,Hey Look	70.00
29 Tennis(c),HK,Hey Look	70.00
30	70.00
31 thru 50	@40.00

HEDY WOLFE
Atlas August, 1957

1 Patsy Walker's Rival	50.00

HELLHOUND
1993–94

1 Hellhound on my Trial	2.50
2 Love in Vain	2.50
3 Last Fair Deal Gone Down	2.25

HELLRAISER
See: CLIVE BARKER'S
HELLRAISER

HELLRAISER III
HELL ON EARTH

1 Movie Adaptation,(prestige)	4.95
1a Movie Adapt.(magazine)	2.95

HELLSTORM,
PRINCE OF LIES
1993

1 R:Daimon Hellstrom, Parchment(c)	3.50
2 A:Dr.Strange,Gargoyle	3.00
3 O:Hellstorm	2.75
4 V:Ghost Rider	2.75
5 MB	2.50
6 MB,V:Dead Daughter	2.50
7 A:Armaziel	2.50
8 Hell is where the heart is	2.25
9 LKa(s),Highway to Heaven	2.25
10 LKa(s),Heaven's Gate	2.25

11 LKa(s),PrG,Life in Hell 2.25
12 Red Miracles 2.25
13 Red Miracles Sidewalking 2.25
14 Red Miracles Murder is Easy . . . 2.25
15 Cigarette Dawn 2.75
16 Down Here 2.25
17 The Saint of the Pit 2.00
18 . . . . 2.00
19 . . . . 2.00
20 . . . . 2.00
21 final issue 2.00

HELL'S ANGEL
1992
1 GSr,A:X-Men,O:Hell's Angel 3.00
2 GSr,A:X-Men,V:Psycho Warriors . 2.50
3 GSr,A:X-Men,V:MyS-Tech 2.00
4 GSr,A:X-Men,V:MyS-Tech 2.00
5 GSr,A:X-Men,V:MyS-Tech 2.00
6 Gfr,A:X-Men,V:MyS-Tech 2.00
Becomes:

DARK ANGEL
7 DMn,A:Psylocke,V:MyS-Tech . . . 2.00
8 DMn,A:Psylocke 2.00
9 A:Punisher 2.00
10 MyS-Tech Wars tie-in. 2.00
11 A:X-Men,MyS-Tech wars tie-in . . 2.00
12 A:X-Men 2.00
13 A:X-Men,Death's Head II 2.00
14 Aftermath#2. . . . . 1.75
15 Aftermath#3. . . . . 1.75
16 SvL,E:Aftermath,last issue 1.75

HERCULES AND THE HEART OF CHAOS
Limited Series Aug., 1997
1 (of 3) TDF,RF,PO,. 2.50
2 TDF,RF,PO, ... 2.50
3 TDF,RF,PO,V:Ares, concl.. . . . . . 2.50

HERCULES PRINCE OF POWER
Sept., 1982
1 BL,I:Recorder. 3.00
2 BL,I:Layana Sweetwater. 2.00
3 BL,V:The Brothers,C:Galactus . . 2.00
4 BL,A:Galactus 2.00
[2nd Series] March, 1984
1 BL,I:Skyypi. 2.50
2 BL,A:Red Wolf 1.50
3 BL,A:Starfox 1.50
4 BL,D:Zeus, June, 1984. . . . . 1.50
TPB BL rep. Vol.1 #1–#4 and
Vol.2 #1–#4 . . . . 6.00

HERO
May, 1990
1 . . . . 2.50
2 . . . . 2.00
3 . . . . 1.50
4 RH 1.50
5 RH 1.50
6 Oct., 1990 . . . . 1.50

HERO FOR HIRE
June, 1972
1 GT,JR,I&O:Power Man 35.00
2 GT,A:Diamond Back 12.00
3 GT,I:Mace. 10.00
4 V:Phantom of 42nd St. 10.00
5 GT,A:Black Mariah 10.00
6 V:Assassin 7.00
7 GT,Nuclear Bomb issue 7.00
8 GT,A:Dr.Doom 7.00
9 GT,A:Dr.Doom,Fant.Four 7.00

Hero For Hire #15
© Marvel Entertainment Group

10 GT,A:Dr.Death,Fant.Four 7.00
11 GT,A:Dr.Death 5.00
12 GT,C:Spider-Man. 5.00
13 A:Lion Fang. 5.00
14 V:Big Ben 5.00
15 Cage Goes Wild 5.00
16 O:Stilletto,D:Rackham 5.00
Becomes:

POWER MAN

HEROES FOR HIRE
July, 1997
1 JOs,PFe,F:Iron Fist 3.00
2 JOs,PFe,V:Nitro 2.00
2A Variant PFe cover. 2.00
3 JOs,PFe,V:Nitro 2.00
4 JOs,Power Man vs. Iron Fist. . . . 2.00
5 JOs,V:Sersi, Diabolical Deviants . 2.00
6 JOs,PFe, Deviants 2.00
7 JOs V:Thunderbolts 2.00
8 JOs,Iron Fist's agenda revealed . 2.00
9 JOs,Search for Punisher. 2.00
10 JOs,Deadpool hired. 2.00
11 JOs,PFe,A:Deadpool, V:Silver
Sable and Wild Pack 2.00
12 JOs,PFe,Traitor revealed, 48pg . 3.00
13 JOs,PFe,V:Master 2.00
14 JOs,F:Black Knight 2.00
15 JOs,PFe,Siege of Wundagore,
pt.1 (of 5) 2.00
16 JOs,PFe,Siege of Wundagore,
pt.3 . . . . 2.00
17 JOs,DBw,F:Luke Cage
& She-Hulk. 2.00
18 JOs,PFe,A:Wolverine. 2.00
19 JOs,PFe,F:Wolverine. 2.00
Ann.'98 JOs,BWi,PFe,Heroes For
Hire/Quicksilver, The Siege of
Wundagore, pt.5 (of 5) 48pg . . . 3.00

HEROES FOR HOPE
1 TA/JBy/HC/RCo/BWr,A:XMen . . . 7.00

HEROES REBORN: THE RETURN
Oct., 1997
½ Heroes Reborn prequel, (Marvel/
Wizard 1996) 7.50
1 (of 4) PDd,ATi,SvL,F:Franklin
Richards. 2.50

2 PDd,ATi,SvL, F:Spider-Man,
Thunderbolts & Doctor Strange. 2.50
3 PDd,SvL,ATi,A UniverseMayDie . 2.50
4 PDd,SvL,ATi, crossover to Marvel
Universe?. 2.50
TPB Return of the Heroes. 14.95

HOKUM & HEX
Razorline 1993–94
1 BU:Saint Sinner 2.75
2 I:Analyzer. 2.00
3 I:Wrath 2.00
4 I:Z-Man 2.00
5 V:Hyperkind 2.00
6 B:Bloodshed. 2.00
7 V:Bloodshed. 2.00
8 V:Bloodshed. 2.00
9 E:Bloodshed,final issue. 2.25

HOLIDAY COMICS
Jan., 1951
1 LbC(c),Christmas(c) 175.00
2 LbC(c),Easter Parade(c) 200.00
3 LbC(c),4th of July(c) 125.00
4 LbC(c),Summer Vacation 75.00
5 LbC(c),Christmas(c) 80.00
6 LbC(c),Birthday(c). 90.00
7 LbC(c),Rodeo (c) 75.00
8 LbC(c),Christmas(c)
Oct., 1952 . . . . 75.00

HOLLYWOOD SUPERSTARS
Epic Nov., 1990
1 DSp 2.00
2 thru 5 DSp, March, 1991. . . . . @2.25

HOMER, THE HAPPY GHOST
March, 1955
1 . . . . 75.00
2 . . . . 35.00
3 . . . . 20.00
4 thru 15 . . . . @20.00
16 thru 22 . . . . @18.00
[2nd Series] Nov., 1969
1 . . . . 15.00
2 thru 5 . . . . @10.00

HOOK
1992
1 JRy,GM,movie adaption 1.00
2 JRy,Return to Never Land. 1.00
3 Peter Pans Magic. 1.00
4 conclusion 1.00
Hook Super Spec.#1 . . . . 2.95

HORRORS, THE
Jan., 1953—April, 1954
11 LbC(c),The Spirit of War. 200.00
12 LbC(c),Under Fire 175.00
13 LbC(c),Terror Castle. 175.00
14 LbC(c),Underworld Terror. . . . 175.00
15 LbC(c),The Mad Bandit 175.00

HOT SHOTS
AVENGERS
1 Painted Pin-ups (1995). 2.95
SPIDER-MAN
1 Painted pin-ups 2.95
X-MEN
1 Painted pin-ups 2.95

Howard The Duck #27
© Marvel Entertainment Group

HOUSE II
1 1987, Movie Adapt.......... 2.00

HOWARD THE DUCK
Jan., 1976
1 FB,SL,A:Spider-Man,I:Beverly... 7.00
2 FB,V:TurnipMan&Kidney Lady .. 2.00
3 JB,Learns Quack Fu.......... 1.50
4 GC,V:Winky Man 1.50
5 GC,Becomes Wrestler 1.50
6 GC,V:Gingerbread Man 1.50
7 GC,V:Gingerbread Man 1.50
8 GC,A:Dr.Strange,ran for Pres.... 1.50
9 GC,V:Le Beaver 1.25
10 GC,A:Spider-Man 2.00
11 GC,V:Kidney Lady 1.25
12 GC,I:Kiss................. 4.00
13 GC,A:Kiss 4.00
14 GC,Howard as Son of Satan ... 2.00
15 GC,A:Dr.Strange,A:Dr.Bong .. 1.25
16 GC,DC,JB,DG,TA,
   V:Incredible Creator 1.25
17 GC,D:Dr.Bong............. 1.25
18 GC,Howard the Human #1..... 1.25
19 GC,Howard the Human #2..... 1.25
20 GC,V:Sudd 1.25
21 GC,V:Soofi 1.25
22 A:ManThing,StarWars Parody . 1.25
23 A:ManThing,StarWars Parody .. 1.25
24 GC,NightAfter..SavedUniverse.. 1.25
25 GC,V:Circus of Crime 1.25
26 GC,V:Circus of Crime 1.25
27 GC,V:Circus of Crime 1.25
28 GC,Cooking With Gas 1.25
29 Duck-Itis Poster Child 1978 .... 1.25
30 Iron Duck,V:Dr. Bong......... 1.25
31 Iron Duck,V:Dr. Bong......... 1.25
32 V:Gopher................. 1.25
33 BB(c),The Material Duck 1.25
Ann.#1, V:Caliph of Bagmom ... 1.25
Holiday Spec. LHa,ATi,PFe (1996) . 3.00

HOWARD THE DUCK MAGAZINE
(B&W) Oct., 1979–March 1981
1 .... 2.50
2 & 3 .... @1.50
4 Beatles,Elvis,Kiss........... 5.00
5 thru 9 .... @1.50

HUGGA BUNCH
Star Oct., 1986—Aug., 1987
1 .... 1.25
2 thru 6 .... @1.00

HULK, THE
Feb. 1999
1 JBy,RG,DGr,48-page 3.00
1a signed 20.00
1b gold foil cover........... 10.00
2 JBy,RG,DGr,Hulk unleashed.... 2.00
2a variant AdP cover.......... 2.00
3 JBy,RG,DGr,Hulk berserk 2.00
4 JBy,RG,DGr,old foe 2.00
5 JBy,RG,DGr,V:Man-Thing 2.00
6 JBy,RG,DGr,V:Man-Thing 2.00
7 JBy,RG,DGr,A:Avengers...... 2.00
Ann. 1999 JBy,DGr,48-page 3.50

HULK 2099
1994–95
1 GJ,Foil(c),V:Draco 2.50
2 GJ,V:Draco............... 1.50
3 I:Golden Boy 1.50
4 .... 1.50
5 Ultra Hulk................ 1.50
Becomes:

HULK 2099 A.D.
6 Gamma Ray Scientist........ 1.50
7 A:Doom,Dr.Apollo........... 1.95
8 One Nation Under Doom 1.95
9 California Quake............. 1.95

HUMAN FLY
July, 1987
1 I&O:Human Fly,A:Spider-Man .. 5.00
2 A:Ghost Rider............... 7.50
3 DC,JSt(c),DP,`Fortress of Fear' . 1.75
4 JB/TA(c),`David Drier' 1.75
5 V:Makik 1.75
6 Fear in Funland 1.75
7 ME,Fury in the Wind 1.75
8 V:White Tiger 1.75
9 JB/TA(c),ME,V:Copperhead,A:
   White Tiger,Daredevil 1.75
10 ME,Dark as a Dungeon 1.75
11 ME,A:Daredevil 1.75
12 ME,Suicide Sky-Dive 1.75
13 BLb/BMc(c),FS,V:Carl Braden .. 1.75
14 BLb/BMc(c),SL,Fear Over
   Fifth Avenue 1.75
15 BLb/BMc(c),War in the
   Washington Monument....... 1.75
16 BLb/BMc(c),V:Blaze Kendall ... 1.75
17 BLb,DP,Murder on the Midway.. 1.75
18 V:Harmony Whyte 1.75
19 BL(c),V:Jacopo Belbo
   March, 1979............... 1.75

RED RAVEN COMICS
Timely Comics August, 1940
1 JK,O:Red Raven,I:Magar,A:Comet
   Pierce & Mercury,Human Top,
   Eternal Brain 11,000.00
Becomes:

HUMAN TORCH
Fall, 1940–Aug. 1954
2 (#1)ASh(c),BEv,B:Sub-Mariner
   A:Fiery Mask,Falcon,Mantor,
   Microman 22,000.00
3 (#2)Ash(c),BEv,V:Sub-
   Mariner,Bondage(c) 4,500.00
4 (#3)ASh(c),BEv,O:Patriot ... 3,500.00
5 (#4)V:Nazis,A:Patriot,Angel
   crossover 2,500.00
5a(#5)ASh(c),V:Sub-Mariner .. 4,000.00

6 ASh(c),Doom Dungeon 1,500.00
7 ASh(c),V:Japanese 1,600.00
8 ASh(c),BW,V:Sub-Mariner .. 2,800.00
9 ASh(c),V:General Rommel .. 1,500.00
10 ASh(c),BW,V:Sub-Mariner .. 2,100.00
11 ASh(c),Nazi Oil Refinery ... 1,300.00
12 ASh(c),V:Japanese,
   Bondage(c) 2,000.00
13 ASh(c),V:Japanese,
   Bondage(c) 1,300.00
14 ASh(c),V:Nazis 1,300.00
15 ASh(c),Toro Trapped...... 1,300.00
16 ASh(c),V:Japanese 900.00
17 ASh(c),V:Japanese 900.00
18 ASh(c),V:Japanese,
   MacArthurs HQ........... 900.00
19 ASh(c),Bondage(c) 900.00
20 ASh(c),Last War Issue 900.00
21 ASh(c),V:Organized Crime... 900.00
22 ASh(c),V:Smugglers....... 900.00
23 ASh(c),V:Giant Robot 1,000.00
24 V:Mobsters 900.00
25 The Masked Monster....... 900.00
26 Her Diary of Terror........ 900.00
27 SSh(c),BEv,V:The Asbestos
   Lady 900.00
28 BEv,The Twins Who Weren't . 900.00
29 You'll Die Laughing 900.00
30 BEv,The Stranger,A:Namora . 800.00
31 A:Namora................ 700.00
32 A:Sungirl,Namora.......... 700.00
33 Capt.America crossover..... 750.00
34 The Flat of the Land....... 700.00
35 A;Captain America,Sungirl ... 750.00
36 A:Submariner............. 700.00
37 BEv,A:Submariner 700.00
38 BEv,A:Submariner 700.00

HUMAN TORCH
Sept., 1974
1 JK,rep.StrangeTales #101..... 12.00
2 rep.Strange Tales #102....... 8.00
3 rep.Strange Tales #103....... 8.00
4 rep.Strange Tales #104....... 8.00
5 rep.Strange Tales #105....... 8.00
6 rep.Strange Tales #106....... 8.00
7 rep.Strange Tales #107....... 8.00
8 rep.Strange Tales #108....... 8.00

HUMAN TORCH COMICS
Feb. 1999
1-shot V:Sub-Mariner, 48-page 4.00

Human Torch #3
© Marvel Entertainment Group

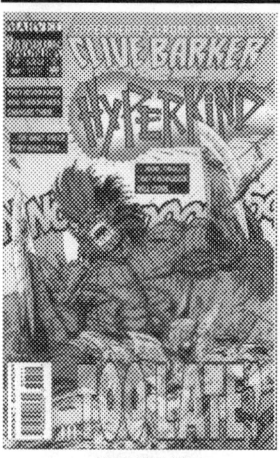

Hyperkind #7
© *Marvel Entertainment Group*

HYPERKIND
Razorline
1 I:Hyperkind,BU:EctoKid	2.75
2 I:Bliss	2.00
3 V:Living Void	2.00
4 FBk(s),I:Paragon John	2.00
5 V:Paragon John	2.00
6 Vetus Unleashed	2.00
7 Ambertrance	2.00
8 I:Tempest	2.00
9 I:Lazurex,w/card	2.25

HYPERKIND UNLEASHED
1994
1 BU,V:Thermakk	2.95

ICEMAN
Dec., 1984
1 DP,mini-series	2.00
2 DP,V:Kali	1.50
3 DP,A;Original X-Men,Defenders Champions	1.50
4 DP,Oblivion,June, 1985	1.50

IDEAL
Timely July, 1948
1 Antony and Cleopatra	250.00
2 The Corpses of Dr.Sacotti	225.00
3 Joan of Arc	200.00
4 Richard the Lionhearted A:The Witness	325.00
5 Phc,Love and Romance	125.00
Becomes:	

LOVE ROMANCES
6 Ph(c),I Loved a Scoundrel	75.00
7 Ph(c)	50.00
8 Ph(c)	55.00
9 thru 12 Ph(c)	@35.00
13 thru 20	@35.00
21 BK	50.00
22	30.00
23	30.00
24 BK	45.00
25	45.00
26 thru 35	@30.00
36 BK	45.00
37	30.00
38 BK	45.00
39 thru 44	@30.00
45 MB	40.00

46	30.00
47	30.00
48	25.00
49 ATh	45.00
50	25.00
51	25.00
52	25.00
53 ATh	45.00
54	25.00
55	25.00
56	25.00
57 MB	40.00
58 thru 74	@25.00
75 MB	35.00
76	25.00
77 MB	35.00
78	25.00
79	25.00
80 RH(c)	30.00
81	25.00
82 MB,JK(c)	30.00
83 JSe,JK(c)	40.00
84 JK	30.00
85 JK	30.00
86 thru 95	@20.00
96 JK	45.00
97	25.00
98 JK	45.00
99 JK	45.00
100 thru 104	@25.00
105 JK	40.00
106 JK,July, 1963	40.00

IDEAL COMICS
Timely Fall, 1944
1 B:Super Rabbit,Giant Super Rabbit V:Axis(c)	125.00
2 Super Rabbit at Fair(c)	75.00
3 Beach Party(c)	65.00
4 How to Catch Robbers	65.00
Becomes:	

WILLIE COMICS
5 B:Willie,George,Margie,Nellie Football(c)	80.00
6 Record Player(c)	50.00
7 Soda Fountain(c),HK,Hey Look	55.00
8 Fancy Dress(c)	50.00
9	50.00
10 HK,Hey Look	50.00
11 HK,Hey Look	50.00
12	40.00
13	50.00
14 thru 18	@35.00
19	50.00
20 Li'L Willie Comics	35.00
21 Li'L Willie Comics	35.00
22	35.00
23 May, 1950	35.00

IDOL
Epic 1992
1 I:Idol	2.95
2 Phantom o/t Set	2.95
3 Conclusion	2.95

ILLUMINATOR
1993
1	5.00
2	5.00
3	3.00
4	3.00

IMMORTALIS
1 A:Dr.Strange	1.95
2 A:Dr.Strange	1.95
3 A:Dr.Strange,V:Vampires	1.95
4 Mephisto, final issue	1.75

IMPERIAL GUARD
[Limited Series] 1997
1 (of 3) BAu,Woj	2.00
2 and 3 BAu,Woj	@2.00

IMPOSSIBLE MAN
SUMMER VACATION
1990–91
1 GCa,DP	2.50
2	2.00
Summer Fun Spec. TPe, Vacation on Earth	2.50

INCAL, THE
Epic Nov., 1988
1 Moebius,Adult	2.50
2 Moebius,Adult	2.00
3 Moebius,Adult, Jan., 1989	2.00

INCOMPLETE
DEATH'S HEAD
1993
1 thru 10 rep.Death's Head #1 thru #10	@2.00
11 rep.Death's Head #11	1.75

INCREDIBLE HULK
May, 1962
1 JK,I:Hulk(Grey Skin),Rick Jones, Thunderbolt Ross,Betty Ross, Gremlin,Gamma Base	12,000.00
2 JK,SD,O:Hulk,(Green skin)	2,500.00
3 JK,O:rtd.,I:Ring Master, Circus of Crime	1,600.00
4 JK,V:Mongu	1,400.00
5 JK,I:General Fang	1,400.00
6 SD,I:Metal Master	2,000.00
See: Tales to Astonish #59-#101	

April, 1968
102 MSe,GT,O:Retold	175.00
103 MSe,I:Space Parasite	75.00
104 MSe,O&N:Rhino	65.00
105 MSe,GT,I:Missing Link	60.00
106 MSe,HT,GT	55.00
107 HT,V:Mandarin	55.00
108 HT,JMe,A:Nick Fury	55.00
109 HT,JMe,A:Ka-Zar	55.00
110 HT,JMe,A:Ka-Zar	55.00
111 HT,DA,I:Galaxy Master	30.00
112 HT,DA,O:Galaxy Master	30.00
113 HT,DA,V:Sandman	30.00
114 HT,DA	30.00
115 HT,DA,A:Leader	30.00
116 HT,DA,V:Super Humanoid	30.00
117 HT,DA,A:Leader	30.00
118 HT,V:Sub-Mariner	30.00
119 HT,V:Maximus	22.00
120 HT,V:Maximus	22.00
121 HT,I:The Glob	22.00
122 HT,V:Thing	40.00
123 HT,V:Leader	20.00
124 HT,SB,V:Rhino,Leader	20.00
125 HT,V:Absorbing Man	20.00
126 HT,A:Dr.Strange	20.00
127 HT,Moleman vs.Tyrannus I:Mogol	15.00
128 HT,A:Avengers	15.00
129 HT,V:Glob	15.00
130 HT,Banner Vs Hulk	15.00
131 HT,A:Iron Man	12.00
132 HT,JSe,V:Hydra	12.00
133 HT,JSe,I:Draxon	12.00
134 HT,SB,I:Golem	12.00
135 HT,SB,V:Kang	12.00
136 HT,SB,I:Xeron	12.00
137 HT,V:Abomination	12.00

Incredible Hulk #4
© Marvel Entertainment Group

138 HT,V:Sandman 12.00
139 HT,V:Leader 12.00
140 HT,V:Psyklop 12.00
141 HT,JSe,I&O:Doc Samson . . . 14.00
142 HT,JSe,V:Valkyrie,A:Doc
    Samson 7.00
143 DA,JSe,V:Dr.Doom 7.00
144 DA,JSe,V:Dr.Doom 7.00
145 HT,JSe,O:Retold 9.00
146 HT,JSe,Leader 7.00
147 HT,JSe,Doc Samson loses
    Powers 7.00
148 HT,JSe,I:Fialan 7.00
149 HT,JSe,I:Inheritor 7.00
150 HT,JSe,I:Viking,A:Havoc 10.00
151 HT,JSe,C:Ant Man 7.00
152 HT,DA,Many Cameos 7.00
153 HT,JSe,C:Capt.America 7.00
154 HT,JSe,A:Ant Man,
    V:Chameleon 7.00
155 HT,JSe,I:Shaper of Worlds . . . 7.00
156 HT,V:Hulk 7.00
157 HT,I:Omnivac,Rhino 7.00
158 HT,C:Warlock,V:Rhino 7.00
159 HT,V:Abomination,Rhino 7.00
160 HT,V:Tiger Shark 6.00
161 HT,V:Beast 8.00
162 HT,I:Wendigo I 9.50
163 HT,I:Gremlin 6.00
164 HT,I:Capt.Omen 6.00
165 HT,I:Aquon 6.00
166 HT,I:Zzzax 6.00
167 HT,JAb,V:Modok 6.00
168 HT,JAb,I:Harpy 6.00
169 HT,JAb,I:Bi-Beast 6.00
170 HT,JAb,V:Volcano 6.00
171 HT,JAb,A:Abomination,Rhino . . 6.00
172 HT,JAb,X:X-Men 12.00
173 HT,V:Cobolt Man 6.00
174 HT,V:Cobolt Man 6.00
175 JAb,V:Inhumans 6.00
176 HT,JAb,A:Man-Beast,C:Warlock
    Crisis on Counter-Earth 14.00
177 HT,JAb,D:Warlock 15.00
178 HT,JAb,Warlock Lives 15.00
179 HT,JAb, ... 6.00
180 HT,JAb,I:Wolverine
    V:Wendigo I 100.00
181 HT,JAb,A:Wolverine (1st
    Full Story),V:Wendigo II 525.00
182 HT,JAb,I&D:Crackajack
    Jackson,C:Wolverine 65.00
183 HT,V:Zzzaz 5.00
184 HT,V:Living Shadow 5.00

185 HT,V:General Ross 5.00
186 HT,I:Devastator 5.00
187 HT,JSt,V:Gremlin 5.00
188 HT,JSt,I:Droog 5.00
189 HT,JSt,I:Datrine 5.00
190 HT,MSe,Toadman 5.00
191 HT,JSt,Toadman,I:Glorian 5.00
192 HT,V:The Lurker 5.00
193 HT,JSt,Doc.Samson regains
    Powers 5.00
194 SB,JSt,V:Locust 5.00
195 SB,JSt,V:Abomination 5.00
196 SB,JSt,V:Army 5.00
197 BWr(c),SB,JSt,A:Man-Thing . . . 5.00
198 SB,JSt,A:Man-Thing 5.00
199 SB,JSt,V:Shield,Doc Samson . . 5.00
200 SB,JSt,Multi,Hulk in Glenn
    Talbots Brain 30.00
201 SB,JSt,V:Fake Conan 4.00
202 SB,JSt,A:Jarella 4.00
203 SB,JSt,A:Jarella 4.00
204 SB,JStl:Kronus 4.00
205 SB,JSt,D:Jarella 4.00
206 SB,JSt,C:Dr.Strange 4.00
207 SB,JSt,A:Dr.Strange 4.00
208 SB,JSt,V:Absorbing Man 4.00
209 SB,JSt,V:Absorbing Man 4.00
210 SB,A:Dr.Druid,O:Merlin II 4.00
211 SB,A:Dr.Druid 4.00
212 SB,I:Constrictor 4.50
213 SB,TP,I:Quintronic Man 4.00
214 SB,Jack of Hearts 4.00
215 SB,V:Bi-Beast 3.50
216 SB,Gen.Ross 3.50
217 SB,I:Stilts,A:Ringmaster 3.50
218 SB,KP,Doc Samson versus
    Rhino 3.50
219 SB,V:Capt.Barravuda 3.50
220 SB,Robinson Crusoe 3.50
221 SB,AA,A:Sting Ray 3.50
222 JSn,AA,Cavern of Bones 3.50
223 SB,V:Leader 3.50
224 SB,V:The Leader 3.50
225 SB,V:Leader,A:Doc Samson . . 3.50
226 SB,JSt,A:Doc Samson 3.50
227 SB,JK,A:Doc Samson 3.50
228 SB,BMc,I:Moonstone,V:Doc
    Samson 6.00
229 SB,O:Moonstone,V:Doc
    Samson 3.50
230 JM,BL,A:Bug Thing 3.50
231 SB,I:Fred Sloan 3.50
232 SB,A:Capt.America 3.50
233 SB,A:Marvel Man 3.50
234 SB,Marvel Man Changes name
    to Quasar 3.50
235 SB,A:Machine Man 3.50
236 SB,A:Machine Man 3.50
237 SB,A:Machine Man 3.50
238 SB,JAb,Jimmy Carter 3.50
239 SB,I:Gold Bug 3.50
240 SB,Eldorado 3.50
241 SB,A:Tyrannus 3.00
242 SB,Eldorado 3.00
243 SB,A:Gammernon 3.00
244 SB,A:It 3.00
245 SB,A:Super Mandroid 3.00
246 SB,V:Capt.Marvel 3.00
247 SB,A:Bat Dragon 3.00
248 SB,V:Gardener 3.00
249 SD,R:Jack Frost 3.00
250 SB,A:Silver Surfer 10.00
251 MG,A:3-D Man 3.00
252 SB,A:Woodgod 3.00
253 SB,A:Woodgod 3.00
254 SB,I:U-Foes 3.00
255 SB,V:Thor 3.00
256 SB,I&O:Sabra 3.00
257 SB,I&O:Arabian Knight 3.00
258 I:Soviet Super Soldiers 3.00
259 SB,A:Soviet Super-Soldiers

Incredible Hulk #278
© Marvel Entertainment Group

  O:Darkstar 3.00
260 SB,Sugata 3.00
261 SB,V:Absorbing Man 3.00
262 SB,I:Glazer 3.00
263 SB,Avalanche 3.00
264 SB,A:Corruptor 3.00
265 SB,I:Rangers 3.50
266 SB,V:High Evolutionary 2.50
267 SB,V:Rainbow,O:Glorian 2.50
268 SB,I:Pariah 2.50
269 SB,I:Bereet 2.50
270 SB,A:Abomination 2.50
271 SB,I:Rocket Raccoon,
    20th Anniv. 2.50
272 SB,C:X-Men,I:Wendigo III . . . 5.00
273 SB,A:Alpha Flight 4.00
274 SB,Beroct 2.50
275 SB,JSt,I:Megalith 2.50
276 SB,JSt,V:U-Foes 2.50
277 SB,JSt,U-Foes 2.50
278 SB,JSt,C:X-Men,
    Avengers,Fantastic Four 2.50
279 SB,JSt,C:X-Men,
    Avengers,Fantastic Four 2.50
280 SB,JSt,Jack Daw 2.50
281 SB,JSt,Trapped in Space 2.50
282 SB,JSt,A:She Hulk 2.50
283 SB,JSt,A:Avengers 2.50
284 SB,JSt,A:Avengers 2.50
285 SB,JSt,Northwind,V:Zzzax 2.50
286 SB,JSt,V:Soldier 2.50
287 SB,JSt,V:Soldier 2.50
288 SB,JSt,V:Abomination 2.50
289 SB,JSt,V:Modok 2.50
290 SB,JSt,V:Modok 2.50
291 SB,JSt,V:Thunderbolt Ross . . . 2.50
292 SB,JSt,V:Dragon Man 2.50
293 SB,V:Nightmare 2.50
294 SB,V:Boomerang 2.50
295 SB,V:Boomerang 2.50
296 SB,A:Rom 2.50
297 SB,V:Nightmare 2.50
298 KN(c),SB,V:Nightmare 2.50
299 SB,A:Shield 2.50
300 SB,A:Spider-Man,Avengers
    Doctor Strange 6.00
301 SB,Crossroads 2.50
302 SB,Crossroads 2.50
303 SB,V:The Knights 2.50
304 SB,V:U-Foes 2.50
305 SB,V:U-Foes 2.50
306 SB,V:Klaatu 2.50
307 SB,V:Klaatu 2.50
308 SB,V:Puffball Collective 2.50

MARVEL

309 SB,V:Goblin & Glow. 2.50
310 Crossroads 2.50
311 Crossroads 2.50
312 Secret Wars II,O:Bruce 3.50
313 A:Alpha Flight 2.50
314 JBy,V:Doc Samson 5.00
315 JBy,A:Doc Samson,Banner
     & Hulk Separated. 3.00
316 JBy,A:Avengers,N:Doc
     Samson 3.00
317 JBy,I:Hulkbusters,A:Doc
     Samson 3.00
318 JBy,A:Doc Samson 3.00
319 JBy,W:Bruce & Betty 5.00
320 AM,A:Doc Samson 2.50
321 AM,A:Avengers 2.50
322 AM,A:Avengers 2.50
323 AM,A:Avengers 2.50
324 AM,R:Grey Hulk(1st since #1),
     A:Doc Samson 10.00
325 AM,Rick Jones as Hulk . . . 3.50
326 A:Rick Jones,New Hulk 6.00
327 AM,F:General Ross 2.50
328 AM,1st PDd(s),Outcasts. 7.00
329 AM,V:Enigma. 5.00
330 1st TM Hulk,D:T-bolt Ross . . 15.00
331 TM,V:Leader 11.00
332 TM,V:Leader 7.00
333 TM,V:Leader 7.00
334 TM,I:Half-life 7.00
335 HorrorIssue 4.00
336 TM,A:X-Factor 5.00
337 TM,A:X-Factor,
     A:Doc Samson 5.00
338 TM,I:Mercy,V:Shield. 5.00
339 TM,A:RickJones. 5.00
340 TM,Hulk vs Wolverine 25.00
341 TM,V:Man Bull 4.00
342 TM,V:Leader 4.00
343 TM,V:Leader 4.00
344 TM,V:Leader 4.00
345 TM,V:Leader,Double-Size 7.00
346 TM,EL,L:Rick Jones 6.00
347 In Las Vegas,I:Marlo Chandler,
     V:Absorbing Man 4.00
348 V:Absorbing Man 3.00
349 A:Spider-Man. 3.50
350 Hulk vs Thing,A:Beast
     V:Dr.Doom 4.00
351 R:Jarella's World 3.00
352 V:Inquisitor 3.00
353 R:Bruce Banner. 3.00
354 V:Maggia 3.00
355 V:Glorian 3.00
356 V:Glorian,Cloot 3.00
357 V:Glorian,Cloot 3.00
358 V:Glorian,Cloot 3.00
359 JBy(c),C:Wolverine(illusion) . . . 4.00
360 V:Nightmare & Dyspare 3.00
361 A:Iron Man,V:Maggia 3.00
362 V:Werewolf By Night 3.00
363 Acts of Vengeance. 3.00
364 A:Abomination,B:Countdown . . 3.00
365 A:Fantastic Four 3.00
366 A:Leader,I:Riot Squad 3.00
367 1st DK Hulk,I:Madman(Leader's
     brother),E:Countdown. 8.00
368 SK,V:Mr.Hyde 4.00
369 DK,V:Freedom Force 3.00
370 DK,R:Original Defenders 3.00
371 DK,BMc,A:Orig.Defenders . . . 3.00
372 DK,R:Green Hulk. 9.00
373 DK,Green Hulk & Grey Hulk. . . 4.00
374 DK,BMc,Skrulls,
     R:Rick Jones 4.00
375 DK,BMc,V:Super Skrull 4.00
376 DK,BMc,Green Hulk,Grey
     Hulk & Banner fight 5.00
377 DK,BMc,New Green Hulk,
     combination of green,grey, and
     Bruce Banner,A:Ringmaster . . . 9.00

Incredible Hulk #369
© Marvel Entertainment Group

377a 2nd printing (gold) 5.00
378 V:Rhino,Christmas Issue 3.00
379 DK,MFm,I:Pantheon 4.00
380 A:Nick Fury,D:Crazy-8 . . . . . . 3.00
381 DK,MFm,Hulk J:Pantheon 4.00
382 DK,MFm,A:Pantheon 4.00
383 DK,MFm,Infinity Gauntlet. 4.00
384 DK,MFm,Infinity Gauntlet. 4.00
385 DK,MFm,Infinity Gauntlet. 4.00
386 DK,MFm,V:Sabra,A:Achilles. . . 4.00
387 DK,MFm,V:Sabra,A:Achilles. . . 4.00
388 DK,MFm,I:Speed Freak,Jim
     Wilson,revealed to have AIDS . 5.00
389 1st Comic art By Gary Barker
     (Garfield),A:Man-Thing,Glob . . . 4.00
390 DK,MFm,B:War & Pieces,
     C:X-Factor 4.00
391 DK,MFm,V:X-Factor. 4.00
392 DK,MFm,E:War & Pieces,
     A:X-Factor 4.00
393 DK,MFm,R:Igor,A:Soviet Super Sol-
     diers,30th Anniv.,Green foil(c). . 5.00
393a 2nd printing,Silver 2.50
394 MFm(i),F:Atalanta,I:Trauma . . . 3.00
395 DK,MFm,A:Punisher,
     I:Mr.Frost 3.00
396 DK,MFm,A:Punisher,
     V:Mr.Frost 3.00
397 DK,MFm,B:Ghost of the
     Past,V:U-Foes,A:Leader 3.00
398 DK,MFm,D:Marlo,V:Leader . . . 3.00
399 JD,A:FF,Dr.Strange 3.00
400 JD,MFm,E:Ghost of the Past,
     V:Leader,1st Holo-grafx(c),1st
     GFr Hulk(pin-up) 3.50
400a 2nd Printing 2.50
401 JDu,O:Agememnon 2.00
402 JDu,V:Juggernaut 2.00
403 GFr,V:Red Skull,A:Avengers . . 3.00
404 GFr,V:Red Skull,Juggernaut,
     A:Avengers 3.50
405 GFr,Ajax Vs. Achilles 2.75
406 GFr,V:Captain America 2.00
407 GFr,I:Piecemeal,A:Madman,
     B:O:Ulysses 2.00
408 GFr,V:Madman,Piecemeal,
     D:Perseus,A:Motormouth,
     Killpower 1.75
409 GFr,A:Motormouth,Killpower,
     V:Madman 1.75
410 GFr,A:Nick Fury,S.H.I.E.L.D.,
     Margo agrees to marry Rick . . . 1.75
411 GFr,V:Nick Fury,S.H.I.E.L.D.. . . 1.75
412 PaP,V:Bi-Beast,A:She-Hulk . . . 1.75

413 GFr,CaS,B:Troyjan War,
     I:Cassiopea,Armageddon,
     V:Trauma 1.75
414 GFr,CaS,V:Trauma,C:S.Surfer . 1.75
415 GFr,CaS,V:Trauma,A:Silver
     Surfer,Starjammers. 1.75
416 GFr,CaS,E:Troyjan War,D:Trauma,
     A:S.Surfer,Starjammers 1.75
417 GFr,CaS,Rick's/Marlo's Bachelor/
     Bachelorette Party 1.75
418 GFr,CaS,W:Rick & Marlo,
     A:Various Marvel persons,
     Die Cut(c). 2.75
418a Newsstand Ed. 1.75
419 CaS,V:Talos. 1.75
420 GFr,CaS,AIDS Story,
     D: Jim Wilson. 1.75
421 CaS,B:Myth Conceptions 1.75
422 GFr,Myth Conceptions,pt.2 . . . 1.75
423 GFr,CaS,MythConcept.,pt.3 . . . 1.50
424 B:Fall of the Hammer. 1.50
425 Regular Edition 1.50
425a Enhanced cover. 3.50
426 PDa,LSh,R:Mercy 1.50
426a Deluxe edition 1.95
427 A:Man-Thing 1.50
427a Deluxe edition 1.95
428 Suffer The Children 1.95
429 Abortion Issue 1.95
430 A:Speed Freak. 1.95
431 PDa,LSh R:Abomination 1.95
432 V:Abomination 1.95
433 PDd,V:Abomination 1.95
434 Funeral of the Year 1.95
435 Hulk Vs. Rhino baseball. 2.50
436 PDd,Ame,Ghosts of the
     Future,pt.1 . . . . 1.95
437 PDd,AMe,Ghosts of the
     Future,pt.2 . . . . 1.95
438 PDd,AMe,Ghosts of the
     Future,pt.3 . . . . 1.95
439 PDd,AMe,Ghosts of the
     Future,pt.4 . . . . 1.95
440 PDd,AMe, ... 1.95
441 PDd,AMe,A:She-Hulk. 1.95
442 A:Molecule Man, She-Hulk. . . . 1.95
443 Janis 1.50
444 Onslaught saga, V:Cable 1.50
445 Onslaught saga 1.50
446 blamed for loss of Fantastic Four
     and Avengers. 1.50
447 PDd,MD2,F:The Unleashed
     Hulk. 1.50
447a Variant Tank Smashing cover. 5.00
448 PDd,MD2,V:The Pantheon 1.50
449 PDd,MD2,I:Thunderbolts 1.50
450 PDd,MD2,F:Doctor Strange,
     56pg. 2.95
451 PDd,MD2, ... 1.50
452 PDd,MD2, ... 1.50
453 PDd,MD2,V:Future Hulk. 1.50
454 PDd,AKu,MFm,A God,
     in Savage Land 1.50
455 PDd,AKu,MFm,in X-Mansion . . 2.00
456 PDd,AKu,MFm,A:Apocalypse. . 2.00
457 PDd,Hulk vs. Juggernaut 2.00
458 PDd,AKu,MFm,V:Mercy 2.00
459 PDd,AKu,MFm,V:Abomination . 2.00
460 PDa,AKu,MFm, Return of Bruce
     Banner. 2.00
461 PDa,V:Thunderbolt Ross 2.00
462 PDa,AKu,MFm,V:Thunderbolt
     Ross 2.00
463 PDa,AKu,MFm,V:Thunderbolt
     Ross 2.00
464 PDa,AKu,MFm,V:Troygens & Silver
     Surfer. 2.00
465 PDa,MFm,Poker game. 2.00
466 PDa,AKu,MFm,tragic loss 2.00
467 PDa,AKu,MFm,Hulk attempts
     suicide 2.00

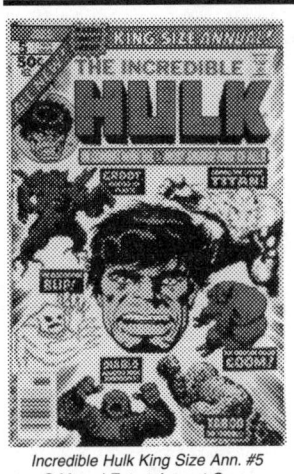

Incredible Hulk King Size Ann. #5
© Marvel Entertainment Group

468 JoC,new direction,. 2.00
469 JoC,LMa,F:Super-Adaptoid . . . 2.00
470 JoC,NMa,V:Ringmaster
    & Circus of Crime. 2.00
471 JoC,NMa,Circus of
    Crime,concl. 2.00
472 JoC,Great Astonishment,pt.1 . . 2.00
473 JoC,Great Astonishment,pt.2 . . 2.00
474 JoC,Great Astonishment,pt.3 . . 2.00
Spec.#1,A:Inhumans (1968) 75.00
Spec.#2 rep.O:Hulk,A:Leader
    (1969) 50.00
Spec.#3 rep.A:Leader (1971) 18.00
Spec.#4 IR:Hulk/Banner (1972). . . 15.00
Ann.#5 V:Xemnu,Diablo (1976). . . 10.00
Ann.#6 HT,A:Dr.Strange,I:Paragon
    (Her) (1977). 6.00
Ann.#7 JBy,BL,A:Angel,Iceman
    A:Doc Samson (1978) 7.00
Ann.#8 Alpha Flight (1979). 6.00
Ann.#9 Checkmate (1980) 3.00
Ann.#10,A:CaptainUniverse(1981) . 3.00
Ann.#11 RB,JSt,A:Spider-Man,
    Avengers,V:Unis (1982) 4.00
Ann.#12 (1983). 3.00
Ann.#13 (1984). 3.00
Ann.#14 JBy,SB (1985) 3.00
Ann.#15 V:Abomination (1986) 3.00
Ann.#16 HT,Life Form #3,
    A:Mercy (1990). 3.00
Ann.#17 Subterran.Odyssey #2
    (1991) 3.00
Ann #18 KM,TA,TC(1st Work),Return
    of the Defenders,Pt.1 (1992). . . 7.00
Ann.#19 I:Lazarus,w/card (1993) . . 3.25
Ann.#20 SvL,SI (1994) 1.75
Ann.'98 F:Hulk&Sub-Mariner, 48pg . 3.00
Ann. Hulk 1999. . . . . 3.50
Marvel Milestone rep. #1 (1991) . . . 2.95
G-Size#1 rep.Greatest Foes 10.00
Minus 1 Spec., PDd,AKu,MFm,
    flashback 1.95
Spec. '97 Onslaught aftermath . . . 3.00
Spec. Incredible Hulk
    vs. Superman, 48-page 6.00
Spec. Hulk vs. Superman, signed . 20.00
TPB Ground Zero rep.#340-345 . . 12.95
TPB Future Imperfect, PDd,GP,
    96pg. 12.00
TPB Ghosts of the Past,
    Rep. #396–#400. . . . . 12.00
TPB Transformations, 176pg. 12.00
TPB Beauty and the Beast, ... 17.00
TPB Essential Incredible Hulk. . . . 14.95

INCREDIBLE HULK: FUTURE IMPERFECT
1 GP,V:Maestro 10.00
2 GP,V:Maestro 8.00
TPB Rep. 12.95

INCREDIBLE HULK MEGAZINE
TPB six stories, 96pg 3.95

INCREDIBLE HULK/PITT
1997
Spec. PDd,DK,x-over 6.00

INCREDIBLE HULK VS. WOLVERINE
Oct., 1986
1 HT,rep #181 B:,V:Wolverine. . . . 12.00

INDEPENDENCE DAY
1996
0 . . . . 1.50
1 . . . . 1.50
2 . . . . 1.50
TPB rep. #0–#2, 96pg 6.95

[Further Adventures of] INDIANA JONES
Jan., 1983
1 JBy/TA 2.00
2 JBy/TA 1.50
3 . . . . 1.50
4 KGa 1.50
5 KGa 1.50
6 HC/TA 1.50
7 thru 24 KGa . . . . @1.50
25 SD,What Lurks Within the Tomb 1.50
26 SD. 1.50
27 SD. 1.50
28 SD. 1.50
29 SD. 1.50
30 SD. 1.50
31 SD,The Summit Meeting 1.50
32 SD,Fly the Friendly Skies. 1.50
33 SD. 1.50
34 SD, March, 1986 . . . . 1.50

INDIANA JONES AND THE LAST CRUSADE
1 B&W,Mag.,movie adapt, 1989. . . 2.95
[Mini-Series] 1989
1 Rep,Movie adapt, 1989. . . . . . . 1.25
2 Rep,Movie adapt. 1.25
3 Rep,Movie adapt 1.25
4 Rep,Movie adapt. 1.25

INDIANA JONES AND THE TEMPLE OF DOOM
1984
1 Movie adapt 1.25
2 Movie adapt.. . . . . 1.25
3 Movie adapt.. . . . . 1.25

INFINITY CRUSADE
1993
1 RLm,AM,I:Goddess,A:Marvel
    Heroes,foil(c) 4.00
2 RLm,AM,V:Goddess 3.00
3 RLm,AM,V:Goddess,Mephisto . . 3.00
4 RLm,AM,V:Goddess,A:Magnus . . 3.00
5 RLm,AM,V:Goddess 3.00

6 RLm,AM,V:Goddess. 3.00

INFINITY GAUNTLET
July, 1991
1 GP,O:Infinity Gauntlet 5.00
2 GP,JRu,2ndRebirth:Warlock 4.00
3 GP,JRu,I:Terraxia 4.00
4 GP,JRu,RLm, V:Thanos. 4.00
5 JRu,RLm,V:Thanos,D:Terraxia . . 4.00
6 RLm,JRu,V:Nebula. 4.00
TPB rep. #1 thru 6 . . . . 24.95

INFINITY WAR
1992
1 RLm,AM,R:Magus,Thanos 5.00
2 RLm,AM,V:Magus,A:Everyone . . 3.00
3 RLm,AM,V:Magus,A:Everyone . . 2.50
4 RLm,AM,Magus gets Gauntlet . . 2.50
5 RLm,AM,V:Magus. 2.50
6 RLm,AM,V:Magus. 2.50

Inhumanoids #3
© Marvel Entertainment Group

INHUMANOIDS
Star Jan.–July, 1987
1 Hasbro Toy. 1.25
2 O:Inhumanoids 1.25
3 V:D'Compose 1.25
4 A:Sandra Shore 1.25

INHUMANS
Oct., 1975
1 GP,V:Blastaar. 10.00
2 GP,V:Blastaar. 5.00
3 GP,I:Kree S 4.00
4 GK,Maximus 4.00
5 GK,V:Maximus 4.00
6 GK,Maximus. 4.00
7 GK,DP,I:Skorn 4.00
8 GP,DP,Skorn. 4.00
9 reprint,V:Mor-Tog 4.00
10 KP,D:Warkon 4.00
11 KP,JM,I:Pursuer 4.00
12 KP,Hulk 4.00
Spec.#1(The Untold Saga),
    O:Inhumans 4.00
Spec. Atlantis Rising story 2.95

INHUMANS
Sept. 1998
1 (of 12) PJe,JaL,F:Black Bolt,
    Medusa, Karnak, Triton, Gorgon,

MARVEL

Crystal, Lockjaw	3.00
2 PJe,JaL,F:Tonaje	3.00
2a variant cover	3.00
3 PJe,JaL,Attilan's dark side	3.00
4 PJe,JaL,War against Attilan	3.00
5 PJe,JaL,Earth vs. Attilan	3.00
6 PJe,JaL,V:Maximus	3.00
7 PJe,JaL,F:Black Bolt	3.00
8 PJe,JaL,F:Lockjaw	3.00
9 PJe,JaL,F:Triton	3.00
10 PJe,JaL,F:Woz & Medusa	3.00

INTERFACE
Epic Dec., 1989

1 ESP	2.50
2 thru 7	@2.00
8	2.25

Invaders #6
© Marvel Entertainment Group

INVADERS
August, 1975

1 FR,JR(c),A:Invaders, A:Mastermind	20.00
2 FR,JR(c)I:Brain Drain	7.00
3 FR,JR(c),I:U-Man	6.00
4 FR,O&V:U-Man	5.00
5 RB,JM,V:Red Skull	5.00
6 FR,V:Liberty Legion	5.00
7 FR,I:Baron Blood, 1st Union Jack	5.00
8 FR,FS,J:Union Jack	5.00
9 FR,FS,O:Baron Blood	5.00
10 FR,FS,rep.Captain America Comics#22	5.00
11 FR,FS,I:Blue Bullet	4.00
12 FR,FS,I:Spitfire	4.00
13 FR,FS,GK(c),I:Golem, Half Face	4.00
14 FR,FS,JK(c),I:Crusaders	4.00
15 FR,FS,JK(c),V:Crusaders	4.00
16 FR,JK(c),V:Master Man	4.00
17 FR,FS,GK(c),I:Warrior Woman	4.00
18 FR,FS,GK(c),R:1st Destroyer	4.00
19 FR,FS,V:Adolph Hitler	4.00
20 FR,FS,GK(c),I&J:2nd Union Jack BU:rep.Marvel Comics #1	7.50
21 FR,FS,GK(c),BU:rep.Marvel Mystery #10	5.50
22 FR,FS,GK(c),O:Toro	3.00
23 FR,FS,GK(c),I:Scarlet Scarab	3.00
24 FR,FS,GK(c),rep.Marvel Mystery #17	4.00
25 FR,FS,GK(c),V:Scarlet Scarab	3.00
26 FR,FS,GK(c),V:Axis Agent	3.00

27 FR,FS,GK(c),V:Axis Agent	3.00
28 FR,FS,I:2nd Human Top, Golden Girl,Kid Commandos	3.00
29 FR,FS,I:Teutonic Knight	3.00
30 FR,FS,V:Teutonic Knight	3.00
31 FR,FS,V:Frankenstein	3.00
32 FR,FS,JK(c),A:Thor	4.50
33 FR,FS,JK(c),A:Thor	4.50
34 FR,FS,V:Master Man	3.00
35 FR,FS,I:Iron Cross	3.00
36 FR,FS,O:Iron Cross	3.00
37 FR,FS,V:Iron Cross	3.00
38 FR,FS,V:Lady Lotus	3.00
39 FR,FS,O:Lady Lotus	3.00
40 FR,FS,V:Baron Blood	3.00
41 E:RTs(s)FR,FS,V:Super Axis, double-size	5.00
Ann.#1 A:Avengers,R:Shark	5.00
G-Size#1 FR,rep.Submariner#1	5.00

[Limited Series] 1993

1 R:Invaders	2.00
2 V:Battle Axis	2.00
3 R:Original Vison (1950's)	2.00
4 V:The Axis	2.00

IRON FIST
Nov., 1975

1 JBy,A:Iron Man	35.00
2 JBy,V:H'rythl	17.00
3 JBy,KP,KJ,V:Ravager	12.00
4 JBy,V:Radion	14.00
5 JBy,V:Scimitar	12.00
6 JBy,O:Misty Knight	10.00
7 JBy,V:Khimbala Bey	10.00
8 JBy,V:Chaka	10.00
9 JBy,V:Chaka	10.00
10 JBy,DGr,A:Chaka	10.00
11 JBy,V:Wrecking Crew	10.00
12 JBy,DGr,V:Captain America	10.00
13 JBy,A:Boomerang	10.00
14 JBy,I:Sabretooth	125.00
15 JBy,A&N:Wolverine,A:X-Men Sept. 1977	35.00
Marvel Milestone rep. #14 (1992)	4.00

IRON FIST
May 1998

1 (of 3) DJu,JG, from Heroes For Hire	2.50
2 DJu,JG,search for Scorpio Key, V:S.H.I.E.L.D.	2.50
3 DJu,JG,concl.	2.50

IRON MAN
May, 1968

1 B:StL,AGw(s),JCr,GC, I:Mordius	350.00
2 JCr,I:Demolisher	125.00
3 JCr,V:The Freak	75.00
4 JCr,A:Unicorn	65.00
5 JCr,GT,I:Cerebos	55.00
6 JCr,GT,V:Crusher	60.00
7 JCr,GT,V:Gladiator	45.00
8 JCr,GT,O:Whitney Frost	45.00
9 JCr,GT,A:Mandarin	45.00
10 JCr,GT,V:Mandarin	45.00
11 JCr,GT,V:Mandarin	28.00
12 JCr,GT,I:Controller	28.00
13 JCr,GT,A:Nick Fury	28.00
14 JCr,V:Night Phantom	28.00
15 JCr,GT,A:Red Ghost	28.00
16 JCr,GT,V:Unicorn	20.00
17 JCr,GT,I:Madam Masque, Midas	22.00
18 JCr,GT,V:Madame Masque	20.00
19 JCr,GT,V:Madame Masque	20.00
20 JCr,I:Charlie Gray	20.00
21 JCr,I:Eddie	15.00

22 JCr,D:Janice Cord	15.00
23 JCr,I:Mercenary	17.00
24 JCr,GT,V:Madame Masque	15.00
25 JCr,A:Sub-Mariner	17.00
26 JCr,DH,J:Val-Larr	15.00
27 JCr,DH,I:Firebrand	15.00
28 E:AGw(s),JCr,DH, V:Controller	15.00
29 B:StL,AyB(s),DH,V:Myrmidon	15.00
30 DH,I:Monster Master	15.00
31 DH,I:Mastermind	15.00
32 GT,I:Mechanoid	15.00
33 DH,I:Spy Master	15.00
34 DH,A:Spy Master	15.00
35 DH,A:Daredevil,Spymaster	15.00
36 E:AyB(s),DH,I:RamRod	15.00
37 DH,A:Ramrod	15.00
38 GT,Jonah	15.00
39 HT,I:White Dragon	14.00
40 GT,A:White Dragon	14.00
41 GT,JM,I:Slasher	14.00
42 GT,I:Mikas	14.00
43 GT,JM,A:Mikas,I:Guardsmen	15.00
44 GT,A:Capt.America	14.00
45 GT,A:Guardsman	14.00
46 GT,D:Guardsman	14.00
47 BS,JM,O:Iron Man	15.00
48 GT,V:Firebrand	12.00
49 GT,V:Adaptoid	12.00
50 B:RTs(s),GT,V:Prin.Python	12.00
51 GT,C:Capt.America	12.00
52 GT,I:Raga	12.00
53 GT,JSn,I:BlackLama	12.00
54 GT,BEv,Sub-Mariner,I:Madame MacEvil (Moondragon)	17.00
55 JSn,I:Destroyer,Thanos,Mentor Starfox(Eros),Blood Bros.	85.00
56 JSn,I:Fangor	18.00
57 GT,R:Mandarin	10.00
58 GT,V:Mandarin	10.00
59 GT,A:Firebrand	10.00
60 GT,C:Daredevil	10.00
61 GT,Marauder	10.00
62 whiplash	10.00
63 GT,A:Dr.Spectrum	10.00
64 GT,I:Rokk	10.00
65 GT,O:Dr.Spectrum	10.00
66 GT,V:Thor	10.00
67 GT,V:Freak	10.00
68 GT,O:Iron Man	12.00
69 GT,V:Mandarin	9.00
70 GT,A:Sunfire	9.00
71 GT,V:Yellow Claw	7.50
72 E:RTs(s),GT,V:Black Lama	7.50
73 B:LWn(s),KP,JM,V:Titanic Three	7.50
74 KP,V:Modok	7.50
75 V:Black Lama	7.50
76 Rep,A:Hulk	7.50
77 V:Thinker	7.50
78 GT,V:Viet Cong	7.50
79 GT,I:Quasar(not Current one).	7.50
80 JK(c),O:Black Lama	7.50
81 A:Black Lama	6.00
82 MSe,A:Red Ghost	6.00
83 E:LWn(s),HT,MSe,Red Ghost	6.00
84 HT,A:Dr.Ritter	6.00
85 HT,MSe,A:Freak	6.00
86 B:MWn(s),GT,I:Blizzard	7.00
87 GT,V:Blizzard	6.00
88 E:MWn(s),GT, V:Blood Brothers	6.00
89 GT,A:D.D.,Blood Bros.	6.00
90 JK(c),GT,Controller,A:Thanos.	7.50
91 GT,BL,A:Controller	6.00
92 JK(c),GT,V:Melter	6.00
93 JK(c),HT,V:Kraken	6.00
94 JK(c),HT,V:Kraken	6.00
95 JK(c),GT,PP,V:Ultimo	6.00
96 GT,DP,V:Ultimo	6.00
97 GT,DP,I:Guardsman II	6.00

Iron Man #11
© *Marvel Entertainment Group*

98 GT,DP,A:Sunfire. 6.00
99 GT,V:Mandarin. 6.00
100 JSn(c),GT,V:Mandarin. 16.00
101 GT,I:Dread Knight 5.00
102 GT,O:Dread Knight 5.00
103 GT,V:Jack of Hearts. 5.00
104 GT,V:Midas 5.00
105 GT,V:Midas 5.00
106 GT,V:Midas 5.00
107 KP,V:Midas 5.00
108 CI,A:Growing Man 5.00
109 JBy(c),CI,V:Van Guard. 5.00
110 KP,I:C.Arcturus. 5.00
111 KP,O:Rigellians 5.00
112 AA,KP,V:Punisher from
    Beyond 5.00
113 KP,HT,V:Unicorn,Spymaster . . 5.50
114 KG,I:Arsenal 5.00
115 JR2,O:Unicorn,V:Ani-men . . . 5.00
116 JR2,BL,V:MadameMasque. . . 5.00
117 BL,JR2,1st Romita Jr 6.00
118 JBy,BL,A:Nick Fury 8.00
119 BL,JR2,Alcholic Plot. 6.00
120 JR2,BL,A:Sub-Mariner,
    I:Rhodey(becomes War Machine),
    Justin Hammer. 6.00
121 BL,JR2,A:Submariner 5.00
122 DC,CI,BL,O:Iron Man. 5.00
123 BL,JR2,V:Blizzard 5.00
124 BL,JR2,A:Capt.America 4.00
125 BL,JR2,A:Ant-Man 4.00
126 BL,JR2,V:Hammer. 4.00
127 BL,JR2,Battlefield 4.00
128 BL,JR2,Alcohol 6.00
129 SB,A:Dread Night 3.50
130 BL,V:Digital Devil 3.50
131 BL,V:Hulk 3.50
132 BL,V:Hulk 3.50
133 BL,A:Hulk,Ant-Man 3.50
134 BL,V:Titanium Man 3.50
135 BL,V:Titanium Man 3.50
136 V:Endotherm 3.50
137 BL,Fights oil rig fire 3.50
138 BL,Dreadnought,Spymaster . . 3.50
139 BL,Dreadnought,Spymaster . . 3.50
140 BL,V:Force 3.50
141 BL,JR2,V:Force 3.50
142 BL,JR2,Space Armor 3.50
143 BL,JR2,V:Sunturion 3.50
144 BL,JR2,Sunturion,O:Rhodey . . 3.50
145 BL,JR2,A:Raiders 3.50
146 BL,JR2,I:Black Lash. 3.50
147 BL,JR2,V:Black Lash 3.00
148 BL,JR2,V:Terrorists 3.00

149 BL,JR2,V:Dr.Doom. 3.00
150 BL,JR2,V:Dr.Doom,Dble. 5.00
151 TA,BL,A:Antman 3.00
152 BL,JR2,New Armor 3.00
153 BL,JR2,V:Living Laser 3.00
154 BL,JR2,V:Unicorn 3.00
155 JR2,V:Back-Getters 3.00
156 JR2,I:Mauler 3.25
157 V:Spores 3.00
158 CI,AM,Iron Man Drowning 3.00
159 PS,V:Diablo 3.00
160 SD,V:Serpent'sSquad 3.00
161 A:Moon Knight 3.00
162 V:Space Ships 3.00
163 V:Chessmen 3.00
164 LMc,A:Bishop 3.00
165 LMc,Meltdown 3.00
166 LMc,V:Melter 2.50
167 LMc,Alcholic Issue. 2.50
168 LMc,A:Machine Man 2.50
169 LMc,B:Rhodey as 2nd
    Ironman 13.00
170 LMc,2nd Ironman. 12.00
171 LMc,2nd Ironman. 3.00
172 LMc,V:Firebrand 3.00
173 LMc,Stane International 3.00
174 LMc,Alcoholism 3.50
175 LMc,Alcoholism 3.50
176 LMc,Alcoholism 3.50
177 LMc,Alcoholism 3.50
178 LMc,V:Wizard 3.00
179 LMc,V:Mandarin. 3.00
180 LMc,V:Mandarin. 3.00
181 LMc,V:Mandarin. 3.00
182 LMc,Secret Wars 3.00
183 LMc,Turning Point 3.00
184 LMc,Moves to California. 3.00
185 LMc,V:Zodiac Field 3.00
186 LMc,I:Vibro 3.00
187 LMc,V:Vibro 3.00
188 LMc,I:New Brother's Grimm . . . 3.00
189 LMc,I:Termite. 3.00
190 LMc,O:Termite,A:Scar.Witch. . . 3.00
191 LMc,New Grey Armor 5.00
192 LMc,V:Iron Man(Tony Stark). . . 5.00
193 LMc,V:Dr.Demonicus 3.00
194 LMc,I:Scourge,A:West Coast
    Avengers 3.00
195 LMc,A:Shaman 3.00
196 LMc,V:Dr.Demonicus 3.00
197 LMc,Secret Wars II 3.00
198 SB,V:Circuit Breaker 3.00
199 LMc,E:Rhodey as 2nd Ironman,
    V:Obadiah Stone 3.00
200 LMc,D:Obadiah Stone 6.00
201 MBr,V:Madam Masque. 2.00
202 A:Kazar 2.00
203 MBr,A:Hank Pym 2.00
204 MBr,V:Madame Masque. 2.00
205 MBr,V:A.I.M. 2.00
206 MBr,V:Goliath 2.00
207 MBr,When t/Sky Rains Fire . . 2.00
208 MBr,V:A.I.M. 2.00
209 V:Living Laser 2.00
210 MBr,V:Morgan Le Fey 2.00
211 AS,V:Living Laser. 2.00
212 DT,V:Iron Monger. 2.00
213 A:Dominic Fortune 2.00
214 A:Spider-Woman 2.00
215 BL,AIM 2.00
216 BL,MBr,D:Clymenstra. 2.00
217 BL,MRr,V:Hammer. 2.00
218 BL,MBr,Titanic 2.00
219 BL,V:The Ghost 2.00
220 BL,MBr,V:The Ghost,
    D:Spymaster 2.00
221 BL,MBr,V:The Ghost 2.00
222 BL,MBr,R:Abrogast 2.00
223 BL,MBr,V:Blizzard,Beetle 2.00
224 BL,V:Justin Hammer,Force. . . . 2.00
225 BL,MBr,B:Armor Wars 5.00

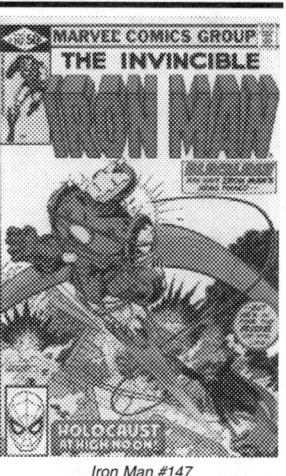

Iron Man #147
© *Marvel Entertainment Group*

226 BL,MBr,V:Stingray 4.50
227 BL,MBr,V:Mandroids, ... 4.00
228 BL,MBr,V:Guardsmen 4.00
229 BL,D:Titanium Man 4.00
230 V:Firepower, ... 4.00
231 V:Firepower,N:Iron Man 4.00
232 BWS,Nightmares,E:Armor
    Wars 4.50
233 JG,BL,A:AntMan 2.00
234 JG,BL,A:Spider-Man 3.00
235 JG,BL,V:Grey Gargoyle 2.00
236 JG,BL,V:Grey Gargoyle 2.00
237 JG,BL,V:SDI Monster. 2.00
238 JG,BL,V:Rhino,D:M.Masque. . . 2.00
239 JG,BL,R:Ghost 2.00
240 JG,BL,V:Ghost. 2.00
241 BL,V:Mandarin. 2.00
242 BL,BWS,V:Mandarin 3.00
243 BL,BWS,Stark Paralyzed 3.00
244 BL,V:Fixer,A:Force(D.Size) . . . 5.00
245 BL(c),V:Dreadnaughts 2.00
246 BL,HT,V:A.I.M.,Maggia 2.00
247 BL,A:Hulk 2.25
248 BL,Tony Stark Cured 2.25
249 BL,V:Dr.Doom 2.00
250 BL,V:Dr.Doom,A of V 2.00
251 HT,AM,V:Wrecker,A of V 2.00
252 HT,AM,V:Chemistro,A of V 2.00
253 BL,V:Slagmire 2.00
254 BL,V:Spymaster. 2.00
255 HT,V:Devestator
    I:2nd Spymaster. 2.00
256 JR2,V:Space Station 2.00
257 V:Samurai Steel. 2.00
258 JR2,BWi,B:Armor Wars II,V:
    Titanium Man 2.25
259 JR2,BWi,V:Titanium Man 2.00
260 JR2,BWi,V:Living Laser 2.00
261 JR2,BWi,A:Mandarin 2.00
262 JR2,BWi,A:Mandarin 2.00
263 JR2,BWi,A:Wonderman,
    V:Living Laser 2.00
264 JR2,BWi,A:Mandarin 2.00
265 JR2,BWi,V:Dewitt. 2.00
266 JR2,BWi,E:Armor Wars II. 2.00
267 PR,BWi,B:New O:Iron Man,
    Mandarin,V:Vibro 2.00
268 PR,BWi,E:New O:Iron Man. . . . 2.00
269 PR,BWi,A:Black Widow 2.00
270 PR,BWi,V:Fin Fang Foom 2.00
271 PR,BWi,V:Fin Fang Foom 2.00
272 PR,BWi,O:Mandarin. 2.00
273 PR,BWi,V:Mandarin. 2.00
274 MBr,BWi,V:Mandarin 2.00

MARVEL

275 PR,BWi,A:Mandarin,Fin Fang
   Foom (Double size) 4.00
276 PR,BWi,A:Black Widow 2.00
277 PR,BWi,A:Black Widow 2.00
278 BWi,Galactic Storm,pt.6
   A:Capt.America,V:Shatterax . . . 2.00
279 BWi,Galactic Storm,pt.13,
   V:Ronan,A:Avengers 2.00
280 KHd,V:The Stark 2.00
281 KHd,I&V:Masters of Silence,
   C:War Machine Armor 3.50
282 KHd,I:War Machine Armor,
   V:Masters of Silence. 3.50
283 KHd,V:Masters of Silence 2.50
284 KHd,Stark put under Cryogenic
   Freeze,B:Rhodey as Iron Man . 3.50
285 KHd,BWi(i),Tony's Funeral 2.00
286 KHd,V:Avengers West Coast . . 2.00
287 KHd,I:New Atom Smasher 2.00
288 KHd,30th Anniv.,V:Atom
   Smasher,foil(c) 4.50
289 KHd,V:Living Laser,
   R:Tony Stark 2.00
290 KHd,30th Anniv.,N:Iron Man,
   Gold foil(c) 4.50
291 KHd,E:Rhodey as Iron Man,
   Becomes War Machine. 2.00
292 KHd,Tony reveals he is alive . . 2.00
293 KHd,V:Controller 2.00
294 KHd,Infinity Crusade 2.00
295 KHd,Infinity Crusade 2.00
296 KHd,V:Modam,A:Omega Red. . 2.00
297 KHd,V:Modam,Omega Red . . . 2.00
298 KHd(c),I:Earth Mover 2.00
299 KHd(c),R:Ultimo 2.00
300 KHd,TMo,N:Iron Man,I:Iron
   Legion,A:War Machine,V:Ultimo
   Foil(c). 5.00
300a Newstand Ed. 2.75
301 KHd,B:Crash and Burn,
   A:Deathlok,C:Venom 2.00
302 KHd,V:Venom 2.00
303 KHd,V:New Warriors,
   C:Thundrstrike 2.00
304 KHd,C:Hulk,V:New Warriors,
   Thundrstrike,N:Iron Man 2.00
305 KHd,V:Hulk,. 2.00
306 KHd,Stark Enterprise 2.00
307 TMo,I:Vor/Tex,R:Mandarin 2.00
308 TMo,Vor/Tex 2.00
309 TMo,Vor/Tex 2.00
310 regular. 2.00
310a Neon(c),with insert print 3.50
311 V:Mandarin 2.00
312 double size 3.00
313 LKa,TMo,AA Meeting. 2.00
314 LKa,TMo,new villain. 2.00
315 A:Black Widow. 2.00
316 I:Slag,A:Crimson Dynamo 2.00
317 In Dynamos Armor. 3.00
318 LKa,TMo,V:Slag. 2.00
319 LKa,TMo,New Space Armor. . . 2.00
320 F:Hawkeye 2.00
321 Cont. From Avg. Crossing 2.00
322 TKa,TheCrossing,V:JackFrost . 2.00
323 TKa,V:Avengers. 2.00
324 TKa,The Crossing 2.00
325 TKa,Avengers:Timeslide after . 3.50
326 . . . . 2.00
327 . . . . 2.00
328 TKa,Tony Stark at ColumbiaU . 2.00
329 thru 332 final issue 2.00
Ann.#1 rep.Iron Man #25 . . . . . . 25.00
Ann.#2 rep.Iron Man #6 . . . . . . 10.00
Ann.#3 SB,Manthing. 6.00
Ann.#4 DP,GT,V:Modok,
   A:Champions 4.00
Ann.#5 JBr,A:Black Panther 2.50
Ann.#6 A:Eternals,V:Brother
   Tode. 2.50
Ann.#7 LMc,A:West Coast

Avengers, I:New Goliath. 2.50
Ann.#8 A:X-Factor 3.00
Ann.#9 V:Stratosfire,A:Sunturion. . 2.50
Ann.#10 PS,BL,Atlantis Attacks #2
   A:Sub-Mariner 3.00
Ann.#11 SD,Terminus Factor #2 . . 2.00
Ann.#12 Subterran.Odyssey #4 . . 2.00
Ann.#13 GC,AW,Assault on Armor
   City,A:Darkhawk. 2.50
Ann.#14 TMo,A:Face Theif,w/card,
   BU:War Machine 3.25
Ann.#15 GC,V:Controller 3.25
Spec.#1 rep.Sub-Mariner x-over . . 20.00
Spec.#2 rep.(1971). 8.00
Marvel Milestone rep. #55 (1992) . . 2.95
G-Size#1 Reprints 8.00
1-shot Iron Man/Force Works Collec-
   tors' Preview, Neon wrap-around
   cover, double size, X-over 2.00
1-shot Iron Manual, BSz(c),Guide
   to Iron Man's technology. 2.00
GN Iron Man 2020 . . . . 5.95
TPB Armor Wars rep.#225-#232 . . 12.95
TPB Many Armors of Iron Man . . . 15.95
TPB Power of Iron Man 9.95
TPB JR2,BL,Iron Man vs. Dr. Doom
   rep. #149-#150,#249-#250 . . 12.95
Iron Manual BSz(c),guide to Iron
Man's technology 2.00

[2nd Series] Nov. 1996
1 JLe,SLo,WPo,SW,A:Bruce
   Banner, New O:Hulk,48pg., . . . 4.00
1A variant Hulk showing cover. . . . 5.00
1 gold signature edition, bagged . 25.00
2 JLe,SLo,WPo,SW. 3.00
3 JLe,SLo,WPo,SW,Heroes brawl . 2.50
4 JLe,SLo,WPo,SW,V:Laser 2.25
4A X-mas cover. 4.00
5 JLe,SLo,WPo,SW, Whirlwind . . . 2.00
6 JLe,SLo,WPo,SW,"Industrial
   Revolution," pt.2 x-over 2.00
7 JLe,SLo,WPo,SW,A:Pepper
   Potts,Villain revealed 2.00
8 JLe,SLo,RBn,fate of Rebel 2.00
9 JLe,SLo,RBn,V:Mandarin 2.00
10 JLe,SLo,RBn,F:The Hulk 2.00
11 JLb,RBn,V:Dr. Doom,A:Hydra. . 2.00
12 WPo,JLe,JLb,F:Dr. Doom,
   Galactus. 2.00
13 JeR,LSn,Wildstorm x-over 2.00

[3rd Series] 1997
1 SCh,KBk,V:Mastermind,48 pg. . . 3.00
2 KBk,SCh,in Switzerland 2.00

Iron Man, 2nd Series #5
© Marvel Entertainment Group

3 KBk,SCh,V:Hydra Dreadnought
   Robot. 2.00
4 KBk,SCh,R:Firebrand 2.00
5 KBk,SCh,V:Firebrand 2.00
6 KBk,F:Black Widow 2.00
7 KBk,SCh,Live Kree or Die, pt.1
   x-over. 2.00
8 KBk,SCh,secret identity out 2.00
9 KBk,SCh,A:Black Widow 2.00
10 KBk,SCh,A:Avengers. 2.00
11 KBk,SCh,A:Warbird &
   War Machine 2.00
12 KBk,V:War Machine. 2.00
13 KBk,SCh,V:Controller,48-page . . 3.00
13a signed 20.00
14 KBk,SCh,Fant.Four x-over. 2.00
15 KBk,SCh,V:Nitro 2.00
16 KBk,RSt,V:Dragon Lord 2.00
17 KBk,RSt,SCh,V:Fin Fang Foom . 2.00
18 KBk,RSt,SCh,V:War Machine. . . 2.00
19 KBk,RSt,SCh,V:War Machine. . . 2.00
20 KBk,SCh,V:War Machine. 2.00
21 KBk,RSt,TGu,MBa,
   Eighth Day prologue. 2.00
Ann. 1998 Iron Man/Captain
   America, KBk,MWa, 48-page . . 3.50
Ann. 1999 KBk,JoC,48-page. 3.50

IRON MAN:
AGE OF INNOCENCE
1-shot Avengers:Timeslide. 2.50

IRON MAN &
SUBMARINER
April 1968
1 GC, 2 stories 225.00

IRON MAN:
THE IRON AGE
June 1998
1 (of 2) KBk,48pg bookshelf. 6.00
2 KBk,48pg bookshelf, concl. 6.00

ISLAND OF DR. MOREAU
Oct., 1977
1 GK(c),movie adapt. 2.00

IT'S A DUCK'S LIFE
Feb., 1950
1 F;Buck Duck,Super Rabbit 75.00
2 . . . . 35.00
3 thru 10 . . . . @25.00
11 Feb., 1952 . . . . 25.00

JACK OF HEARTS
Jan., 1984
1 Mini series 1.50
2 O:Jack of Hearts. 1.00
3 . . . . 1.00
4 Final issue,April 1984 . . . . 1.00

JAMES BOND JR.
1992
1 I&O:JamesBondJr.(TVseries) . . . 3.00
2 Adventures Contd. 1.50
3 V:Goldfinger,Odd Job 1.50
4 thru 6 . . . . @1.50
V:Scumlord 1.50
8 V:Goldfinger,Walter D.Plank 1.50
9 V:Dr.No in Switzerland 1.50
10 V:Robot,Dr.DeRange 1.50
11 V:S.C.U.M. 1.50
12 V:Goldfinger,Jaws 1.50

JANN OF THE JUNGLE
See: JUNGLE TALES

JEANIE COMICS
See: DARING MYSTERY

JIHAD
Epic
1 Cenobites vs. Nightbreed 4.50
2 E:Cenobites vs. Nightbreed 4.50

JOHN CARTER, WARLORD OF MARS
June, 1977
1 GK,DC,O:John Carter,Created
　by Edgar Rice Burroughs 5.00
2 GK/DC(c),GK,RN, White Apes
　of Mars. 3.00
3 GK,RN,Requiem for a Warlord . . 3.00
4 GK,RN, Raiding Party. 3.00
5 GK,RN,Giant Battle Issue 3.00
6 GK/DC(c),GK,Alone Against a
　World 3.00
7 GK,TS,Showdown 3.00
8 GK,RN,Beast With Touch of
　Stone 3.00
9 GK,RN,Giant Battle Issue 3.00
10 GK,The Death of Barsoom?. . . . 3.00
11 RN,O:Dejah Thoris. 2.00
12 RN,City of the Dead. 2.00
13 RN,March of the Dead 2.00
14 RN,The Day Helium Died. 2.00
15 RN,GK,Prince of Helium
　Returns 2.00
16 RN,John Carters Dilemna 2.00
17 BL,What Price Victory 5.00
18 FM,Tars Tarkas Battles Alone. . . 1.50
19 RN(c),War With the Wing Men . . 1.50
20 RN(c),Battle at the Bottom
　of the World 1.50
21 RN(c),The Claws of the Banth . 1.50
22 RN(c),The Canyon of Death. . . . 1.50
23 Murder on Mars. 1.50
24 GP/TA(c),Betrayal 1.50
25 Inferno. 1.50
26 Death Cries the Guild of
　Assassins 1.50
27 Death Marathon. 1.50
28 Guardians of the Lost

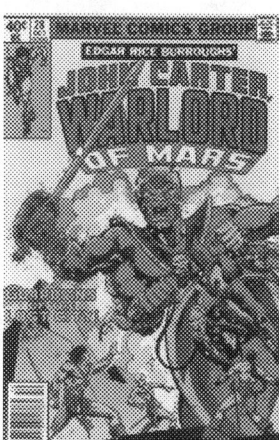

John Carter, Warlord of Mars #28
© Marvel Entertainment Group

City Oct., 1979 . . . . 2.50
Ann.#1 RN(c),GK,Battle story 2.00
Ann.#2 RN(c),GK,Outnumbered . . . 2.00
Ann.#3 RN(c),GK,Battle story 2.00

JOKER COMICS
Timely April, 1942
1 BW,I&B:Powerhouse Pepper,
　A:Stuporman 1,600.00
2 BW,I:Tessie the Typist 650.00
3 BW,A:Tessie the Typist,
　Squat Car Squad 450.00
4 BW,Squat Car (c) 450.00
5 BW,same 450.00
6 BW, ... 250.00
7 BW 250.00
8 BW 250.00
9 BW 250.00
10 BW,Shooting Gallery (c). 250.00
11 BW 200.00
12 BW 200.00
13 BW 200.00
14 BW 200.00
15 BW 200.00
16 BW 200.00
17 BW 200.00
18 BW 200.00
19 BW 200.00
20 BW 200.00
21 BW 175.00
22 BW 175.00
23 BW,HK,`Hey Look' 175.00
24 BW,HK,`Laff Favorites'. 175.00
25 BW,HK,same 175.00
26 BW,HK,same 175.00
27 BW 175.00
28 . . . . 50.00
29 BW 175.00
30 BW 175.00
31 BW 125.00
32 B:Millie,Hedy 50.00
33 HK. 50.00
34 . . . . 35.00
35 HK. 50.00
36 HK. 50.00
37 . . . . 35.00
38 . . . . 35.00
39 . . . . 35.00
40 . . . . 35.00
41 A:Nellie the Nurse 35.00
42 I:Patty Pin-up. 50.00
Becomes:

ADVENTURES INTO TERROR
43(1)AH,B:Horror Stories 500.00
44(2)AH,`Won't You Step Into
　My Palor'. 325.00
3 GC,`I Stalk By Night' 175.00
4 DR,`The Torture Room' 175.00
5 GC,DR,`The Hitchhiker' 225.00
6 RH,`The Dark Room' 175.00
7 GT(c),BW,`Where Monsters
　Dwell' 450.00
8 JSt,`Enter... the Lizard' 150.00
9 RH(c),JSt,`The Dark
　Dungeon' 165.00
10 `When the Vampire Calls'. . . . 165.00
11 JSt,`Dead Man's Escape' 125.00
12 BK,`The Man Who Cried
　Ghost' 150.00
13 BEv(c),`The Hands of Death' . 150.00
14 GC,`The Hands'. 125.00
15 `Trapped by the Tarantula' . . 125.00
16 RH(c),`Her Name Is Death' . . 125.00
17 `I Die Too Often',Bondage(c) . 125.00
18 `He's Trying To Kill Me' 125.00
19 `The Girl Who Couldn't Die' . . 150.00
20 . . . . 150.00
21 GC 125.00

22 . . . . 125.00
23. . . . . 125.00
24 MF,GC. 125.00
25 MF. 150.00
26 GC 125.00
27 . . . . 125.00
28 GC 125.00
29 GC 125.00
30 . . . . 125.00
31 May, 1954 . . . . 125.00

JOURNEY INTO MYSTERY
June, 1952
1 RH(c),B:Mystery/Horror
　stories 2,800.00
2 `Don't Look' 850.00
3 `I Didn't See Anything' 650.00
4 RH,BEv(c),`I'm Drowning,'
　severed hand (c) 650.00
5 RH,BEv(c),`Fright' 425.00
6 BEv(c),`Till Death Do
　Us Part' 425.00
7 BEv(c),`Ghost Guard' 425.00
8 `He Who Hesitates' 425.00
9 BEv(c),`I Made A Monster' . . . 425.00
10 `The Assassin of Paris' 425.00
11 RH,GT,`Meet the Dead' 375.00
12 `A Night At Dragmoor Castle' . 325.00
13 `The Living and the Dead' . . . 325.00
14 DAy,RH,`The Man Who
　Owned A World' 325.00
15 RH(c),`Till Death Do
　Us Part' 325.00
16 DW,`Vampire Tale' 325.00
17 SC,`Midnight On Black
　Mountain' 325.00
18 `He Wouldn't Stay Dead' 325.00
19 JF,`The Little Things' 325.00
20 BEv,BP,`After Man, What'. . . . 325.00
21 JKu,`The Man With No Past'. . 325.00
22 `Haunted House' 325.00
23 GC,`Gone, But Not Forgotten' 200.00
24 `The Locked Drawer' 200.00
25 `The Man Who Lost Himself' . 200.00
26 `The Man From Out There'. . . 200.00
27 `BP,JSe,`Masterpiece' 200.00
28 `The Survivor' 200.00
29 `Three Frightened People' . . . 200.00
30 JO,`The Lady Who Vanished'. 200.00
31 `The Man Who Had No Fear' . 200.00
32 `Elevator In The Sky' 200.00
33 SD,AW,`There'll Be Some
　Changes Made' 225.00

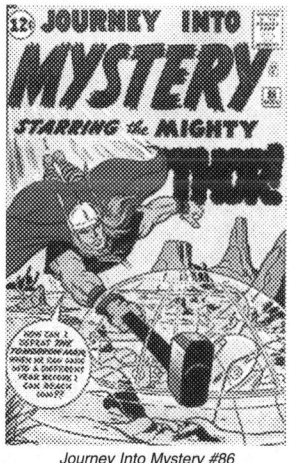

Journey Into Mystery #86
© Marvel Entertainment Group

34 BP,BK,`The Of The
  Mystic Ring' 200.00
35 LC,JF,`Turn Back The Clock' . 200.00
36 `I, The Pharaoh'. 200.00
37 BEv(c),`The Volcano' 200.00
38 SD,`Those Who Vanish' 200.00
39 BEv(c),DAy,WW,`The
  Forbidden Room' 200.00
40 BEv(c),JF,`The Strange
  Secret Of Henry Hill' 200.00
41 BEv(c),GM,RC,`I Switched
  Bodies' 175.00
42 BEv(c),GM,`What Was
  Farley's Other Face 175.00
43 AW,`Ghost Ship'. 200.00
44 SD,JK,BEv. 200.00
45 BEv,JO 175.00
46 . . . . 175.00
47 BEv 175.00
48 . . . . 175.00
49 . . . . 175.00
50 SD 175.00
51 SD,JK 200.00
52 JK 175.00
53 DH. 175.00
54 AW 200.00
55 . . . . 175.00
56 thru 61 SD,JK. . . . . @175.00
62 SD,JK,I:Xemnu 225.00
63 thru 68 SD,JK. . . . . @175.00
69 thru 82 . . . . @225.00
83 JK,SD,I&O:Thor 4,500.00
84 JK,SD,DH,I:Executioner . . . 1,000.00
85 JK,SD,I:Loki,Heimdall,Balder,
  Tyr,Odin,Asgard 600.00
86 JK,SD,DH,V:Tomorrow Man . . 400.00
87 JK,SD,V:Communists. 300.00
88 JK,SD,V:Loki. 300.00
89 JK,SD,O:Thor(rep). 300.00
90 SD,I:Carbon Copy 150.00
91 JSt,SD,I:Sandu 175.00
92 JSt,SD,V:Loki,I:Frigga 175.00
93 DAy,JK,SD,I:Radioactive
  Man 175.00
94 JSt,SD,V:Loki. 135.00
95 JSt,SD,I:Duplicator. 135.00
96 JSt,SD,I:Merlin II 125.00
97 JK,I:Lava Man,O:Odin 150.00
98 DH,JK,I&O:Cobra. 125.00
99 DH,JK,I:Mr.Hyde,Surtur 125.00
100 DH,JK,V:Mr.Hyde. 125.00
101 JK,V:Tomorrow Man. 100.00
102 JK,I:Sif,Hela. 100.00
103 JK,I:Enchantress,
  Executioner 100.00
104 JK,Giants. 100.00
105 JK,V:Hyde,Cobra 100.00
106 JK,O:Balder 100.00
107 JK,I:Grey Gargoyle,Karnilla . 100.00
108 JK,A:Dr.Strange. 100.00
109 JK,V:Magneto 135.00
110 JK,V:Hyde,Cobra,Loki 75.00
111 JK,V:Hyde,Cobra,Loki 75.00
112 JK,V:Hulk,O:Loki 200.00
113 JK,V:Grey Gargoyle 75.00
114 JK,I&O:Absorbing Man 75.00
115 JK,O:Loki,V:Absorbing Man . 100.00
116 JK,V:Loki,C:Daredevil. 75.00
117 JK,V:Loki 75.00
118 JK,I:Destroyer 75.00
119 JK,V:Destroyer,I:Hogun,
  Fandrall,Volstagg 75.00
120 JK,A:Avengers,Absorbing
  Man 75.00
121 thru 123 JK,V:AbsorbingMan. @75.00
124 JK,A:Hercules 75.00
125 JK,A:Hercules. 75.00
Annual #1, JK,I:Hercules. 160.00
Becomes:

THOR

JOURNEY INTO MYSTERY
[2nd series] Oct., 1972
1 GK,TP,MP,`Dig Me No Grave' . 15.00
2 GK,`Jack the Ripper' 8.00
3 JSn,TP,`Shambler From
  the Stars'. 8.00
4 GC,DA,`Haunter of the Dark',
  H.P. Lovecraft adaptation. 8.00
5 RB,FrG,`Shadow From the
  Steeple',R. Bloch adaptation . . 8.00
6 Mystery Stories 7.00
7 thru 19 . . . . @7.00

JOURNEY INTO UNKNOWN WORLDS
See: ALL WINNERS COMICS

J-2
Aug. 1998
1 TDF,RLm,AM,F:J2 with the powers
  of Juggernaut 2.00
2 TDF,RLm,AM,V:Buffer Zone,
  Enthralla & Uncanny X-People . 2.00
2a variant cover. 2.00
3 TDF,RLm,AM,V:Hulk. 2.00
4 TDF,RLm,AM,turning points . . . 2.00
5 TDF,RLm,AM,Ghosts of the Past 2.00
6 TDF,RLm,AM,Majority Rules. . . 2.00
7 TDF,RLm,AM,Last Days of
  the Original Juggernaut 2.00
8 TDF,RLm,AM,Uneasy Allies . . . 2.00
9 TDF,RLm,AM,Critical Choices. . . 2.00
10 TDF,RLm,AM,Incredible
  Journeys 2.00
11 TDF,RLm,AM,Master of Jug-Fu . 2.00
12 TDF,RLm,AM,A:Juggernaut,
  last issue 2.00

JUGGERNAUT
1997
1-shot 48pg. 3.00

JUNGLE ACTION
Atlas Oct., 1954
1 JMn,JMn(c),B:Leopard Girl . . 250.00
2 JMn,JMn(c) 275.00
3 JMn,JMn(c) 150.00
4 JMn,JMn(c) 150.00
5 JMn,JMn(c) 150.00
6 JMn,JMn(c),August, 1955 . . . 150.00

JUNGLE ACTION
Oct., 1972—Nov., 1976
1 JB(c),Lorna,Tharn,Jann
  reprints 15.00
2 GK(c),same 10.00
3 JSn(c),same 10.00
4 GK(c),same 10.00
5 JR(c),JB,B:Black Panther,
  V:Man-Ape 15.00
6 RB/FrG(c),RB,V:Kill-Monger . . . 10.00
7 RB/KJ(c),RB,V:Venomn 10.00
8 RB/KJ(c),RB,GK,
  O:Black Panther 10.00
9 GK/KJ(c),RB,V:Baron Macabre 10.00
10 GK/FrG(c),V:King Cadaver. . . 10.00
11 GK(c),V:Baron Macabre,Lord
  Karnaj 10.00
12 RB/KJ(c),V:Kill Monger 8.00
13 GK/JK(c),V:White Gorilla,
  Sombre. 8.00
14 GK(c),V:Prehistoric

Jungle Action #1
© *Marvel Entertainment Group*

  Monsters 8.00
15 GK(c),V:Prehistoric
  Monsters 8.00
16 GK(c),V:Venomm. 8.00
17 GK(c),V:Kill Monger. 8.00
18 JKu(c),V:Madame Slay 8.00
19 GK(c),V:KKK,`Sacrifice
  of Blood'. 8.00
20 V:KKK,`Slaughter In The
  Streets' 8.00
21 V:KKK,`Cross Of Fire, Cross
  Of Death' 7.00
22 JB(c),V:KKK,Soul Stranger . . . 7.00
23 JBy(c),V:KKK. 7.00
24 GK(c),I:Wind Eagle 7.00

JUNGLE TALES
Atlas Sept., 1954
1 B:Jann of the Jungle,Cliff
  Mason,Waku 250.00
2 GT,Jann Stories cont. 200.00
3 Cliff Mason,White Hunter,
  Waku Unknown Jungle . . . 175.00
4 Cliff Mason,Waku,Unknown
  Jungle 175.00
5 RH(c),SSh,Cliff Mason,Waku,
  Unknown Jungle 175.00
6 DH,SSh,Cliff Mason,Waku,
  Unknown Jungle 175.00
7 DH,SSh,Cliff Mason,Waku,
  Unknown Jungle. 175.00
Becomes:

JANN OF THE JUNGLE
8 SH,SSh,`The Jungle Outlaw' . 200.00
9 `With Fang and Talons' 125.00
10 AW,`The Jackal's Lair' 110.00
11 `Bottomless Pit'. 100.00
12 `The Lost Safari' 100.00
13 `When the Trap Closed' 100.00
14 V:Hunters 100.00
15 BEv(c),DH,V:Hunters. 100.00
16 BEv(c),AW,`Jungle
  Vengeance' 125.00
17 BEv(c),DH,AW,June, 1957 . . . 125.00

JUSTICE
Nov., 1986
1 I:Justice 1.25
2 . . . . 1.00
3 Yakuza Assassin 1.00
4 thru 8 . . . . @1.00

9 KG 1.00
10 thru 18 . . . . @1.00
19 thru 31 . . . . @1.25
32 Last issue,A:Joker 1.50

JUSTICE COMICS
Atlas Fall, 1947
7(1) B:FBI in Action,`Mystery of
  White Death'. 200.00
8(2),HK,`Crime is For Suckers' . . 150.00
9(3),FBI Raid 125.00
4 Bank Robbery 125.00
5 Subway(c) 100.00
6 E:FBI In Action 100.00
7 Symbolic(c) 100.00
8 Funeral(c) 100.00
9 B:`True Cases Proving Crime
  Can't Win'. 100.00
10 Ph(c),Bank Hold Up 100.00
11 Ph(c),Behind Bars 100.00
12 Ph(c),The Crime of
  Martin Blaine 75.00
13 Ph(c),The Cautiouc Crook 75.00
14 Ph(c) 75.00
15 Ph(c) 75.00
16 F:"Ears"Karpik-Mobster 60.00
17 `The Ragged Stranger'. 60.00
18 `Criss-Cross' 60.00
19 `Death Of A Spy' 60.00
20 `Miami Mob'. 60.00
21 `Trap'. 60.00
22 `The Big Break' 60.00
23 thru 40 . . . . @50.00
41 Electrocution cover 100.00
42 thru 51 . . . . @50.00
52 `Flare Up' 50.00
Becomes:

TALES OF JUSTICE
May, 1955—Aug., 1957
53 BEv,`Keeper Of The Keys' . . . 125.00
54 thru 57 . . . . @85.00
58 BK 100.00
59 BK 100.00
60 thru 63 . . . . @50.00
64 RC,DW,JSe 75.00
65 RC. 75.00
66 JO,AT 75.00
67 DW 75.00

JUSTICE: FOUR BALANCE
1 A:Thing, Yancy Street Gang 1.75
2 V:Hate Monger. 1.75

Ka-Zar Reprint Series #1
© Marvel Entertainment Group

3 the story continues... . . . . 1.75
4 ...to its conclusion. 1.75

KATHY
Atlas Oct., 1959—Feb., 1964
1 `Teenage Tornado' 45.00
2 . . . . 25.00
3 thru 15 . . . . @20.00
16 thru 27 . . . . @15.00

KA-ZAR
[Reprint Series] Aug., 1970
1 X-Men ID 17.00
2 Daredevil 12, 13. . . . . 12.00
3 DDH,Spider-Man,March, 1971 . 12.00
[1st Series] Jan., 1974
1 O:Savage Land 3.00
2 DH,JA,A:Shanna The She-Devil . 2.50
3 DH,V:Man-God,A:El Tigre. 2.50
4 DH,V:Man-God. 2.50
5 DH,D:El-Tigre. 2.50
6 JB/AA,V:Bahemoth. 2.00
7 JB/BMc`Revenge of the
  River-Gods' 2.00
8 JB/AA,`Volcano of
  Molten Death'. 2.00
9 JB,`Man Who Hunted Dinosaur' . 2.00
10 JB,`Dark City of Death' 2.00
11 DH/FS,`Devil-God of Sylitha' . . . 2.00
12 RH,`Wizard of Forgotten
  Death' 2.00
13 V:Lizard Men 2.00
14 JAb,V:Klaw 2.00
15 VM,V:Klaw,`Hellbird'. 2.00
16 VM,V:Klaw. 2.00
17 VM,V:Klaw. 2.00
18 VM,V:Klaw,Makrum 2.00
19 VM,V:Klaw,Raknor the Slayer . . 2.00
20 VM,V:Klaw,`Fortress of Fear' . . . 2.00
[2nd Series] Apr. 1981
1 BA,O:Ka-Zar. 2.00
2 thru 7 BA . . . . @2.00
8 BA,Kazar Father. 2.00
9 BA 2.00
10 BA,Direct D 2.00
11 BA/GK,Zabu 2.00
12 BA,Panel Missing 2.00
12a Scarce Reprint. 2.00
13 BA. 2.00
14 BA/GK,Zabu 2.00
15 BA. 2.00
16 . . . . 2.00
17 Detective 2.00
18 . . . . 2.00
19 . . . . 2.00
20 A:Spider-Man 2.00
21 . . . . 2.00
22 A:Spider-Man 2.00
23 A:Spider-Man 2.00
24 A:Spider-Man 2.00
25 A:Spider-Man 2.00
26 A:Spider-Man 2.00
27 A:Buth. 2.00
28 Pangea 2.00
29 W:Kazar & Shanna, Doub.Size . 2.00
30 V:Pterons 2.00
31 PangeaWarII 2.00
32 V:Plunderer 2.00
33 V:Plunderer 2.00
34 Last Issue Doub.Size. 2.00
[3rd Series] 1997
1 MWa,NKu,Ka-Zar, Shanna, Zabu,
  V:Gregor, 40pg. 5.00
1a 2nd printing 2.50
2 MWa,NKU,V:Gregor 4.00
2A NKu variant cover. 3.00
3 MWa,NKu,Ka-Zar's son dead? . . 3.00
4 MWa,NKu,in New York City 3.00

Ka-Zar 2nd Series #32
© Marvel Entertainment Group

5 MWa,NKu,. 2.50
6 MWa,V:Rampaging Rhino. 2.00
7 MWa,NKu,F:Shanna the
  She-Devil 2.00
8 MWa,NKu, Urban Jungle, pt.1. . . 2.00
9 MWa,NKu, Urban Jungle, pt.2. . . 2.00
10 MWa,NKu, Urban Jungle, pt.3 . . 2.00
11 MWa,NKu, Urban Jungle, pt.4,
  concl. 2.00
12 MWa,A:High Evolutionary 2.00
13 MWa,A:High Evolutionary 2.00
14 MWa,NKu,end old & begin new
  storyline, double size 3.00
15 A:Punisher 3.00
16 A:Punisher. 2.00
17 Ka-Zar clears his name,
  A:Jameka. 2.00
18 People of the Savage Land
  revolt 2.00
19 V:Gregor 2.00
20 A:Gregor,Zira, final issue 2.00
Ann. '97 V:Garrok, the Petrified
  Man 2.50
Ann. '98 Kazar/Daredevil heroes
  unite. 3.00

KA-ZAR OF THE SAVAGE LAND
1996
1-shot CDi,V:Sauron, 48pg.
  prelude to series. 3.00

KA-ZAR: SIBLING RIVALRY
1997
1 MWa,TDz, Flashback 1.95

KELLYS, THE
See: KID KOMICS

KENT BLAKE OF THE SECRET SERVICE
May, 1951—July, 1953
1 U.S. Govt. Secret Agent
  stories,Bondage cover 125.00
2 JSt,Drug issue,`Man with
  out A Face 75.00
3 `Trapped By The Chinese

Reds' 50.00
4 Secret Service Stories 50.00
5 RH(c),`Condemned To Death' . 50.00
6 Cases from Kent Blake files ... 50.00
7 RH(c),Behind Enemy Lines ... 50.00
8 V:Communists 50.00
9 thru 14 .... @50.00

KICKERS INC.
Nov., 1986
1 SB,O:Kickers 1.25
2 SB 1.00
3 RF,Witches............... 1.00
4 RF,FIST 1.00
5 RF,A:D.P.7 .... 1.00
6 thru 8 RF .... @1.00
9 .... 1.00
10 TD.................... 1.00
11 .... 1.00
12 Oct., 1987 .... 1.00

KID & PLAY
1 Based on Rap Group 1.25
2 Drug Issue 1.25
3 At your Friends Expense 1.25
4 .... 1.25
5 .... 1.25
6 Record Contract............ 1.25
7 Fraternity Pledging......... 1.25
8 Kid and Cindy become an item.. 1.25
9 C:Marvel Heroes 1.25

KID COLT OUTLAW
Atlas Aug., 1948
1 B:Kid Colt,A:Two-Gun Kid ... 700.00
2 `Gun-Fighter and the Girl' ... 350.00
3 `Colt-Quick Killers
  For Hire'............... 250.00
4 `Wanted',A:Tex Taylor 250.00
5 `Mystery of the Misssing
  Mine',A:Blaze Carson...... 250.00
6 A:Tex Taylor,`Valley of
  the Warewolf'........... 175.00
7 B:Nimo the Lion 175.00
8 .... 175.00
9 .... 175.00
10 `The Whip Strikes',E:Nimo
  the Lion' 175.00
11 O:Kid Colt 200.00
12 .... 125.00
13 DRi 125.00

Kid Colt #103
© Marvel Entertainment Group

14 .... 125.00
15 `Gun Whipped in Shotgun
  City' 125.00
16 .... 125.00
17 .... 125.00
18 DRi 125.00
19 .... 100.00
20 `The Outlaw' 100.00
21 thru 30 .... @100.00
31 .... 100.00
32 .... 100.00
33 thru 45 A:Black Rider ... @75.00
46 RH(c). 50.00
47 DW 50.00
48 RH(c),JKu 50.00
49 .... 50.00
50 .... 50.00
51 thru 56 .... @45.00
57 AW 50.00
58 AW 50.00
59 AW 50.00
60 AW 50.00
61 .... 25.00
62 .... 25.00
63 .... 25.00
64 .... 30.00
65 .... 30.00
66 thru 78 .... @25.00
79 Origin Retold 30.00
80 thru 86 .... @25.00
87 JDa(reprint) 30.00
88 AW 35.00
89 AW,Matt Slade.......... 35.00
90 thru 99 .... @15.00
100 .... 25.00
101 .... 20.00
102 .... 15.00
103 `The Great Train Robbery' ... 15.00
104 JKu(c),DH,`Trail of
  Kid Colt' 15.00
105 DH,V:Dakota Dixon 15.00
106 JKu(c),`The Circus
  of Crime' 15.00
107 .... 15.00
108 BEv 15.00
109 DAy,V:The Barracuda....... 15.00
110 GC,V:Iron Mask 15.00
111 JKu(c),V:Sam Hawk, The
  Man Hunter 15.00
112 JKu(c),V:Mr. Brown 15.00
113 JKu(c),GC,V:Bull Barton.... 15.00
114 JKu(c),Return of Iron Mask.. 15.00
115 JKu(c),V:The Scorpion 15.00
116 JKu(c),GC,V:Dr. Danger &
  Invisible Gunman......... 15.00
117 JKu(c),GC,V:The Fatman &
  His Boomerang 15.00
118 V:Scorpion,Bull Barton,
  Dr. Danger 15.00
119 DAy(c),JK,V:Bassett The
  Badman 15.00
120 `Cragsons Ride Again' 15.00
121 A:Rawhide Kid,Iron Mask.... 10.00
122 V:Rattler Ruxton 10.00
123 V:Ringo Barker 10.00
124 A:Phantom Raider 10.00
125 A:Two-Gun Kid 10.00
126 V:Wes Hardin 9.00
127 thru 129 .... @9.00
130 O:Kid Colt 9.00
131 thru 150............ @9.00
151 thru 200 reprints ...... @7.00
201 thru 228 reprints ...... @6.00
229 April, 1979............. 6.00

KID FROM DODGE CITY
Atlas July, 1957—Sept., 1957
1 .... 50.00
2 .... 25.00

KID FROM TEXAS
Atlas June, 1957—Aug., 1957
1 .... 50.00
2 .... 25.00

KID KOMICS
Timely Feb., 1943
1 SSh(c),BW,O:Captain Wonder
  & Tim Mulrooney I:Whitewash,
  Knuckles,Trixie Trouble,
  Pinto Pete Subbie 3,300.00
2 AsH(c),F:Captain Wonder
  Subbie, B:Young Allies,
  B:Red Hawk,Tommy Tyme 1,400.00
3 ASh(c),A:The Vision &
  Daredevils 1,000.00
4 ASh(c),B:Destroyer,A:Sub-Mariner,
  E:Red Hawk,Tommy Tyme .. 900.00
5 ASh(c),V:Nazis 650.00
6 ASh(c),V:Japanese 650.00
7 ASh(c),B;Whizzer 600.00
8 ASh(c),V:Train Robbers 600.00
9 ASh(c),V:Elves 600.00
10 ASh(c),E:Young Allies,
  The Destoyer,The Whizzer . 600.00
Becomes:

KID MOVIE KOMICS
11 F:Silly Seal,Ziggy Pig
  HK,Hey Look........... 175.00
Becomes:

RUSTY COMICS
12 F:Rusty,A:Mitzi........... 100.00
13 Do not Disturb(c) 50.00
14 Beach(c),BW,HK,Hey Look .. 75.00
15 Picnic(c),HK,Hey Look...... 60.00
16 Juniors Grades,HK,HeyLook . 60.00
17 John in Trouble,HK,HeyLook . 60.00
18 John Fired............. 40.00
19 Fridge raid(c),HK........ 40.00
20 And Her Family,HK 65.00
21 And Her Family,HK 100.00
22 .... 100.00
Becomes:

KELLYS, THE
23 F:The Kelly Family(Pop,
  Mom,Mike,Pat & Goliath) 75.00
24 Mike's Date,A;Margie........ 50.00
25 Wrestling(c) 50.00
Becomes:

SPY CASES
26(#1) Spy stories 150.00
27(#2) BEv,Bondage(c)........ 100.00
28(#3) Sabotage,A:Douglas
  Grant Secret Agent 100.00
4 The Secret Invasion 90.00
5 The Vengeance of Comrade
  de Casto 90.00
6 A:Secret Agent Doug Grant ... 90.00
7 GT,A:Doug Grant 90.00
8 Atom Bomb(c),Frozen
  Horror 75.00
9 Undeclared War 70.00
10 Battlefield Adventures 65.00
11 Battlefield Adventures 60.00
12 Battlefield Adventures 60.00
13 Battlefield Adventures 60.00
14 Battlefield Adventures 60.00
15 Doug Grant 60.00
16 Doug Grant 60.00
17 Doug Grant 60.00
18 Contact in Ankara 60.00
19 Final Issue,Oct., 1953 ...... 60.00

KID SLADE GUNFIGHTER
See: MATT SLADE

KILLFRENZY
1 .... 1.95
2 Castle Madspike............ 1.95

KILLPOWER:
THE EARLY YEARS
1993
1 B:MiB,Goes on Rampage..... 3.25
2 thru 3 O:Killpower........... 2.00
4 E:MiB,last issue 2.00

KING ARTHUR & THE
KNIGHTS OF JUSTICE
1993–94
1 Based on Cartoon 1.25
2 Based on Cartoon 1.25
3 Based on Cartoon 1.25

KING CONAN:
See: CONAN THE KING

KINGPIN
Nov., 1997
1-shot StL,JR, bookshelf 48pg 6.00

KISSNATION
1997
1 Rock & Roll, A:X-Men........ 10.00

KITTY PRYDE:
AGENT OF S.H.I.E.L.D.
Oct., 1997
1 (of 3) LHa,V:Ogun 2.50
2 LHa,V:Ogun 2.50
3 LHa,Ogun's Slave?.......... 2.50

KITTY PRYDE
& WOLVERINE
Nov., 1984
1 AM,V:Ogun................. 6.00

Kitty Pryde & Wolverine #3
© Marvel Entertainment Group

2 AM,V:Ogun................ 4.00
3 thru 5 AM,V:Ogun .... @4.00
6 AM,D:Ogun, April, 1985 ...... 3.00

KNIGHTS OF
PENDRAGON
[1st Regular Series] July, 1990
1 GEr 2.75
2 thru 7 .... @2.25
8 inc.SBi Poster.............. 2.25
9 V:Bane Fisherman 2.25
10 Cap.Britain/Union Jack 2.25
11 A:Iron Man................ 2.25
12 A:Iron Man,Union Jack....... 2.25
13 O:Pendragon............... 2.25
14 A:Mr.Fantastic,Invisible Woman
    Black Panther............. 2.25
15 BlackPanther/Union Jack T.U. .. 2.25
16 A:Black Panther............. 2.25
17 D:Albion, Union Jack,
    A:Black Panther............ 2.25
18 A:Iron Man,Black Panther 2.25

[2nd Regular Series]
1 GEr,A:Iron Man,R:Knights of
    Pendragon,V:MyS-TECH 2.25
2 A:Iron Man,Black Knight....... 2.00
3 PGa,A:Iron Man,Black Knight ... 2.00
4 Gawain Vs. Bane 2.00
5 JRe,V:Magpie............... 2.00
6 A:Spider-Man............... 2.00
7 A:Spider-Man,V:Warheads..... 2.00
8 JRe,A:Spider-Man............ 2.00
9 A:Spider-Man,Warheads....... 2.00
10 V:Baron Blood.............. 2.00
11........................... 2.00
12 MyS-TECH Wars,V:Skire 2.00
13 A:Death's Head II 2.00
14 A:Death's Head II 2.00
15 D:Adam,A:Death's Head II..... 2.00

KRAZY KOMICS
Timely July, 1942
1 B:Ziggy Pig,Silly Seal 400.00
2 Toughy Tomcat(c) 200.00
3 Toughy Tomcat/Bunny(c) 125.00
4 Toughy Tomcat/Ziggy(c) 125.00
5 Ziggy/Buzz Saw(c) 125.00
6 Toughy/Cannon(c) 125.00
7 Cigar Store Indian(c) 125.00
8 Toughy/Hammock(c) 125.00
9 Hitler(c).................. 125.00
10 Newspaper(c) 150.00
11 Canoe(c) 150.00
12 Circus(c) 150.00
13 Pirate Treasure(c) 100.00
14 Fishing(c)................. 100.00
15 Ski-Jump(c)............... 100.00
16 Airplane(c)................. 75.00
17 Street corner(c) 75.00
18 Mallet/Bell(c) 75.00
19 Bicycle(c)................. 75.00
20 Ziggy(c) 75.00
21 Toughy's date(c) 75.00
22 Crystal Ball(c) 75.00
23 Sharks in bathtub(c)........ 75.00
24 Baseball(c) 75.00
25 HK,Krazy Krow(c) 100.00
26 Super Rabbit(c)............ 75.00
Becomes:

CINDY COMICS
27 HK,B:Margie,Oscar 135.00
28 HK,Snow sled(c) 75.00
29 .... 75.00
30 .... 75.00
31 HK....................... 75.00
32 .... 50.00
33 A;Georgie................ 50.00
34 thru 40................. @50.00

Becomes:
CRIME CAN'T WIN
41 Crime stories 175.00
42 .... 100.00
43 GT,Horror story 120.00
4 thru 11 .... @75.00
12 Sept., 1953 .... 75.00

KRAZY KOMICS
Timely
[2nd Series] Aug., 1948
1 BW,HK,B:Eustice Hayseed .. 300.00
2 BW,O:Powerhouse Pepper
    November, 1948 .... 225.00

KRAZY KROW
Summer, 1945
1 B:Krazy Krow 100.00
2 .... 65.00
3 Winter, 1945-46 .... 65.00

KREE-SKRULL WAR
Sept.–Oct., 1983
1 & 2 JB,NA,reprints .... @5.00

KRULL
Nov.–Dec., 1983
1 Ph(c),BBI,movie adapt 1.00
2 BBI,rep.,Marvel Super Spec.... 1.00

KULL THE CONQUEROR
[1st Series] June, 1971
1 MSe,RA,WW,A King Comes
    Riding,O:Kull 20.00
2 MSe,JSe,Shadow Kingdom 9.00
3 MSe,JSe,Death Dance of
    Thulsa Doom 9.00
4 MSe,JSe,Night o/t Red Slayers.. 6.00
5 MSe,JSe,Kingdom By the Sea .. 4.00
6 MSe,JSe,Lurker Beneath
    the Sea 3.00
7 MSe,JSe,Delcardes'Cat,
    A:Thulsa Doom 3.00
8 MSe,JSe,Wolfshead 3.00
9 MSe,JSe,The Scorpion God ... 3.00
10 MSe,Swords o/t White Queen .. 3.00
11 MP,King Kull Must Die, O:Kull
    cont.,A:Thulsa Doom 3.00
12 MP,SB,Moon of Blood,V:Thulsa

Kull The Conqueror #1
© Marvel Entertainment Group

Kull The Conqueror #11
© Marvel Entertainment Group

Doom,B:SD,B.U.stories 3.00
13 MP,AM,Torches From Hell,
   V:Thulsa Doom 3.00
14 MP,JA,The Black Belfry,
   A:Thulsa Doom 3.00
15 MP,Wings o/t Night-Beast,
   E:SD,B.U.stories 3.00
16 EH,Tiger in the Moon,
   A:Thulsa Doom 3.00
17 AA,EH,Thing from Emerald
   Darkness 3.00
18 EH,AA,Keeper of Flame
   & Frost 3.00
19 EH,AA,The Crystal Menace . . . 3.00
20 EH,AA,Hell Beneath Atlantis . . . 3.00
21 City of the Crawling Dead 3.00
22 Talons of the Devil-Birds 2.00
23 Demon Shade 2.00
24 Screams in the Dark 2.00
25 A Lizard's Throne 2.00
26 Into Death's Dimension 2.00
27 The World Within 2.00
28 Creature and the Crown,
   A:Thulsa Doom 2.00
29 To Sit the Topaz Throne,
   V:Thulsa Doom, final issue . . . 2.00

[2nd Series] 1982

1 JB,Brule 2.50
2 Misareenia 2.00

[3rd Series] 1983–85

1 JB,BWi,DG,Iraina 1.50
2 JB,Battle to the Death. 1.25
3 JB 1.00
4 JB 1.00
5 JB 1.00
6 JB 1.00
7 JB,Masquerade Death 1.00
8 JB 1.00
9 JB 1.00
10 JB 1.00

KULL AND THE
BARBARIANS
May, 1975

1 NA,GK,reprint Kull #1 . . . . 5.00
2 BBI,reprint,Dec., 1983 . . . . 2.00
3 NA,HC,O:Red Sonja 3.00

LABRYNTH
1986–87

1 Movie adapt 2.00

---

2 and 3 . . . . @1.50

LAFF-A-LYMPICS
1978–79

1 F;Hanna Barbera 12.00
2 thru 5 . . . . @10.00
6 thru 13 . . . . @10.00

LANA
August, 1948

1 F:Lana Lane The Show Girl,
   A:Rusty,B:Millie 100.00
2 HK,Hey Look,A:Rusty 60.00
3 Show(c),B:Nellie 40.00
4 Ship(c) 40.00
5 Audition(c) 40.00
6 Stop sign(c) 40.00
7 Beach(c) 40.00
Becomes:

LITTLE LANA

8 Little Lana(c) 26.00
9 Final Issue,March, 1950 . . . . . . 26.00

LANCE BARNES:
POST NUKE DICK
Epic 1993

1 I:Lance Barnes 2.50
2 Cigarettes. 2.50
3 Warring Mall Tribe 2.50
4 V:Ex-bankers,last issue 2.50

LAST AMERICAN
Epic 1990–91

1 . . . . 3.50
2 . . . . 3.00
3 . . . . 2.50
4 Final issue. 2.25

THE LAST
AVENGERS STORY

1 PDd, Alterverse,Future world . . . 5.95
2 PDd, Final fate,fully painted 5.95
TPB PDd,AOl, rep. Alterniverse
   story, 96pg. 12.95

LAST STARFIGHTER, THE
Oct.–Dec., 1984

1 JG(c),BBI,Movie adapt. 1.00
2 Movie adapt 1.00
3 BBI 1.00

LAWBREAKERS
ALWAYS LOSE!
Spring, 1948–Oct. 1949

1 Partial Ph(c),Adam and Eve,
   HK,Giggles and Grins 225.00
2 FBI V:Fur Theives 125.00
3 . . . . 85.00
4 Asylum(c) 100.00
5 . . . . 75.00
6 Pawnbroker(c) 75.00
7 Crime at Midnight 75.00
8 Prison Break 75.00
9 Ph(c),He Prowled at Night 75.00
10 Phc(c),I Met My Murderer . . . 75.00

LAWDOG

1 B:CDi(s),FH,I:Lawdog 2.50
2 FH,V:Vocal-yokel Cultist 2.25
3 FH,Manical Nazis 2.25
4 FH,V:Zombies 2.25
5 FH 2.25
6 FH 2.25

---

7 FH,V:Zombies 2.25
8 FH,w/card. 2.25
9 FH,w/card. 2.25
10 last issue, w/card. 2.25

LAWDOG & GRIMROD:
TERROR AT THE
CROSSROADS
1993

1 . . . . 3.50

LEGION OF MONSTERS
Sept., 1975
(black & white magazine)

1 NA(c),GM,I&O:Legion of
   Monsters,O:Manphibian 30.00

LEGION OF NIGHT
Oct., 1991

1 WPo/SW,A:Fin Fang Foom 5.50
2 WPo,V:Fin Fang Foom 5.50

LETHAL FOES OF
SPIDER-MAN
1993

1 B:DFr(s),SMc,R:Stegron 2.00
2 SMc,A:Stegron 2.00
3 SMc,V:Spider-Man 2.00
4 E:DFr(s),SMc,Last Issue. 2.00

LIFE OF
CAPTAIN MARVEL
August, 1985

1 rep.Iron Man #55,
   Capt.Marvel #25,26 . . . . 9.00
2 rep.Capt.Marvel#26-28 . . . . 6.50
3 rep.Capt.Marvel#28-30
   Marvel Feature #12 . . . . 6.00
4 rep.Marvel Feature #12,Capt.
   Marvel #31,32,Daredevil#105 . . 6.00
5 rep.Capt.Marvel #32-#34 . . . . . . 6.00

LIFE OF CHRIST
1993

1 Birth of Christ 3.00
2 MW,The Easter Story 3.00

LIFE OF POPE
JOHN-PAUL II
1983

1 JSt, Jan., 1983 . . . . 5.00
1a Special reprint 3.00

LIFE WITH MILLIE
See: DATE WITH MILLIE

LIGHT AND
DARKNESS WAR
Epic Oct., 1988

1 . . . . 4.00
2 . . . . 3.00
3 thru 6 Dec., 1989 . . . . @2.50

LINDA CARTER,
STUDENT NURSE
Atlas Sept., 1961

1 . . . . 40.00
2 thru 9, Jan., 1963 . . . . @30.00

MARVEL

LION KING
1 based on Movie 2.75

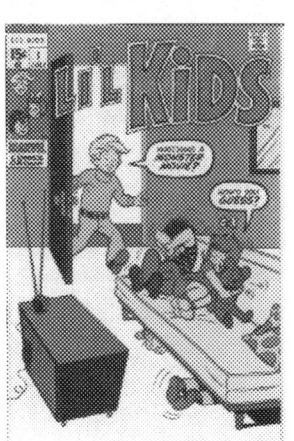

Li'l Kids #1
© Marvel Entertainment Group

LI'L KIDS
Aug., 1970–June 1973
1 . . . . 30.00
2 thru 12 . . . . @15.00

LI'L PALS
Sept., 1972
1 . . . . 20.00
2 thru 5, May, 1973 . . . . @18.00

LITTLE ASPRIN
July, 1949
1 HK,A;Oscar 100.00
2 HK 50.00
3 Dec., 1949 . . . . 35.00

LITTLE LANA
See: LANA

LITTLE LENNY
June, 1949
1 . . . . 50.00
2 . . . . 35.00
3 November, 1949 . . . . 35.00

LITTLE LIZZIE
June, 1949
1 Roller Skating(c) 60.00
2 Soda(c) 40.00
3 Movies(c) 40.00
4 Lizzie(c) 40.00
5 Lizzie/Swing(c) April,1950 . . . 40.00
[2nd Series] Sept., 1953
1 . . . . 40.00
2 . . . . 30.00
3 Jan., 1954 . . . . 30.00

LITTLE MERMAID, THE
1993
1 . . . . 1.50
2 Reception for Pacifica royalty . . . 1.50
3 TrR,Ariel joins fish club 1.50

4 . . . . 1.50
5 . . . . 1.50
6 TrR,Ariel decorates coral"tree" . . 1.50
7 TrR,Flogglefish banished 1.50
8 . . . . 1.50
9 Annual Sea Horse Tournament . . 1.50
10 TrR,AnnualBlowfishTournament . 1.50
11 TrR,Sharkeena,King Triton 1.50
12 . . . . 1.50
13 Lobster Monster. 1.50

LOGAN
1-shot HMe,48pg 5.95
1-shot Logan: Path of the
  Warrior (1996) 5.00
1-shot Logan: Shadow Society,
  HMe,TCk Early life of
  Wolverine (1996) 5.00

LOGAN'S RUN
Jan., 1977
1 GP,From Movie. 6.00
2 GP,Cathedral Kill 5.00
3 GP,Lair of Laser Death 5.00
4 GP,Dread Sanctuary. 5.00
5 GP,End Run 5.00
6 MZ,B.U.Thanos/Drax 10.00
7 TS,Cathedral Prime 5.00

LONGSHOT
Sept., 1985
1 AAd,WPo(i),BA,I:Longshot 8.00
2 AAd,WPo(i),I:RicoshetRita 6.00
3 AAd,WPo(i),I:Mojo,Spiral 6.00
4 AAd,WPo(i),A:Spider-Man 6.00
5 AAd,WPo(i),A:Dr. Strange. 6.00
6 AAd,WPo(i),A:Dr. Strange. 6.00
TPB Reprints #1-#6 . . . . 16.95
1-shot, JMD,MZi,AW, 48pg
  (Dec. 1997) 4.00

LOOSE CANNONS
1 and 2 DAn . . . . @2.50
3 DAn 2.75

LORNA, THE JUNGLE GIRL
Atlas 1953–57
1 Terrors of the Jungle,O:Lorna . 250.00
2 Headhunter's Strike
  I:Greg Knight 125.00
3 . . . . 100.00
4 . . . . 100.00
5 . . . . 100.00
6 RH(c),GT 90.00
7 RH(c) 90.00
8 Jungle Queen Strikes Again . . . 90.00
9 . . . . 90.00
10 White Fang 90.00
11 Death From the Skies 90.00
12 Day of Doom 75.00
13 thru 17 . . . . @75.00
18 AW(c) 85.00
19 thru 26 . . . . @60.00

LOVE ADVENTURES
Atlas Oct., 1949
1 Ph(c) 100.00
2 Ph(c),Tyrone Power/Gene
  Tierney 100.00
3 thru 12 . . . . @50.00
Becomes:
ACTUAL CONFESSIONS
13 . . . . 16.00
14 Dec., 1952. . . . . 16.00

LOVE DRAMAS
Oct., 1949
1 Ph(c),JKa 100.00
2 Jan., 1950 . . . . 75.00

LOVE ROMANCES
See: IDEAL

LOVERS
See: ALL-SELECT COMICS

LOVE SECRETS
Oct., 1949
1 . . . . 70.00
2 Jan., 1950 . . . . 40.00

LUNATIK
1995
1 KG 1.95
2 V:The Avengers 1.95
3 conclusion 1.95

MACHINE MAN
April, 1978
1 JK,From 2001. . . . . 3.00
2 JK 2.50
3 JK,V:Ten-For,The Mean
  Machine. 2.50
4 JK,V:Ten-For,Battle on A
  Busy Street 2.50
5 JK,V:Ten-For,Day of the
  Non-Hero. 2.50
6 JK,V:Ten-For 2.50
7 JK,With A Nation Against Him. . . 2.50
8 JK,Escape:Impossible. 2.50
9 JK,In Final Battle 2.50
10 SD,Birth of A Super-Hero. 2.50
11 SD,V;Binary Bug 2.50
12 SD,"Where walk the Gods" . . . 2.50
13 SD,Xanadu 2.50
14 SD,V:Machine Man 2.50
15 SD,A:Thing,Human Torch 2.50
16 SD,I:Baron Brimstone And the
  Satan Squad 2.50
17 SD,Madam Menace. 2.50
18 A:Alpha Flight 3.50
19 I:Jack o'Lantern 15.00

Machine Man #10
© Marvel Entertainment Group

MARVEL

MACHINE MAN
[Limited-Series]
Oct., 1984

1 HT,BWS,V:Baintronics	2.50
2 HT,BWS,C:Iron Man of 2020	2.50
3 HT,BWS,I:Iron Man of 2020	3.00
4 HT,BWS,V:Iron Man of 2020	2.50
TPB rep.#1-4	5.95

MACHINE MAN 2020
1994

1 rep. limited series #1–#2.	2.00
2 rep. limited series #3–#4.	2.00

MAD ABOUT MILLIE
April, 1969

1	35.00
2 thru 16	@15.00
17 Dec., 1970.	15.00
Ann.#1	12.00

MADBALLS
Star Sept., 1986

1 Based on Toys	1.25
2 thru 9	@1.00
10 June, 1988	1.00

MAD DOG
1 from Bob TV Show	1.50
2 V:Trans World Trust Corp.	1.25
3 V:Cigarette Criminals	1.25
4 V:Dogs of War	1.25
5 thru 6	@1.95

MADE MEN
May 1998

1-shot HMe gangster epic.	6.00

MAGIK
Dec., 1983

1 JB,TP,F:Storm and Illyana	3.50
2 JB,TP,A:Belasco,Sym.	3.00
3 TP,A:New Mutants,Belasco.	3.00
4 TP,V:Belasco,A:Sym.	3.00

MAGNETO
1993

0 JD,JBo,rep. origin stories.	6.00
0a Gold ed.	8.00
0b Platinum ed.	10.00

MAGNETO
1996

1 (of 4) PrM,KJo,JhB, Joseph	2.00
2 PrM,KJo,JhB, Joseph's search for his past life	2.00
3 PrM,KJo,JhB	2.00
4 PrM,KJo,JhB, concl.	2.00

MAGNETO REX
March 1999

1 (of 3) BPe,takes over Genosha.	2.50
1a signed	19.95
2 BPe,V:Rogue	2.50
3 BPe,A:Rogue,Quicksilver	2.50
GN Magneto Ascendant, 96-page rep.	4.00

MAN COMICS
Atlas 1949–53

1 GT, Revenge	150.00

2 GT, Fury in his Fists	85.00
3 Mantrap	75.00
4 The Fallen Hero	75.00
5 Laugh,Fool,Laugh	75.00
6 Black Hate	60.00
7 The Killer	60.00
8 BEv,An Eye For an Eye	75.00
9 B:War Issues,Here Comes Sergeant Smith	40.00
10 Korean Communism	40.00
11 RH,Cannon Fodder	40.00
12 The Black Hate	40.00
13 GC,RH,Beach Head.	40.00
14 GT,No Prisoners	50.00
15	40.00
16	35.00
17 RH.	35.00
18 thru 20	@35.00
21 GC	35.00
22 BEv,BK,JSt	60.00
23 thru 26	@35.00
27 E:War Issues	35.00
28 Where Mummies Prowl	35.00

MANDRAKE
1995

1 fully painted series	2.95
2 V:Octon	2.95
3 final issue	2.95

MAN FROM ATLANTIS
Feb., 1978–Aug., 1978

1 TS,From TV Series,O:Mark Harris	5.00
2 FR,FS,The Bermuda Triangle Trap	3.00
3 FR,FS,Undersea Shadow	3.00
4 FR,FS,Beware the Killer Spores	3.00
5 FR,FS,The Ray of the Red Death	3.00
6 FR,FS,Bait for the Behemoth	3.00
7 FR,FS,Behold the Land Forgotten	3.00

MAN-THING
[1st Series] Jan., 1974

1 FB,JM,A:Howard the Duck	14.00
2 VM,ST,Hell Hath No Fury	7.00
3 VM,JA,I:Original Foolkiller.	6.00
4 VM,JA,O&D:Foolkiller	4.00

Man-Thing #3
© *Marvel Entertainment Group*

5 MP,Night o/t Laughing Dead	4.00
6 MP,V:Soul-Slayers,Drug Issue	4.00
7 MP,A Monster Stalks Swamp	4.00
8 MP,Man Into Monster	4.00
9 MP,Deathwatch	4.00
10 MP,Nobody Dies Forever	4.00
11 MP,Dance to the Murder	4.00
12 KJ,Death-Cry of a Dead Man	4.00
13 TS,V:Captain Fate	4.00
14 AA,V:Captain Fate	4.00
15 A Candle for Saint Cloud	4.00
16 JB,TP,Death of a Legend	4.00
17 JM,Book Burns in Citrusville	4.00
18 JM,Chaos on the Campus	4.00
19 JM,FS,I:Scavenger	4.00
20 JM,A:Spider-Man,Daredevil, Shang-Chi,Thing	4.50
21 JM,O:Scavenger,Man Thing.	4.00
22 JM,C:Howard the Duck	4.00
G-Size #1 MP,SD,JK,rep.TheGlob	5.00
G-Size #2 JB,KJ,The Monster Runs Wild.	4.00
G-Size #3 AA,A World He Never Made	4.00
G-Size #4 FS,EH,inc.Howard the Duck vs.Gorko	4.00
G-Size #5 DA,EH,inc.Howard the Duck vs.Vampire	6.00

[2nd Series] 1979—1981

1 JM,BWi	2.00
2 BWi,JM,Himalayan Nightmare	1.50
3 BWi.JM,V:Snowman	1.50
4 BWi,DP,V:Mordo,A:Dr Strange	1.50
5 DP,BWi,This Girl is Terrified	1.50
6 DP,BWi,Fraternity Rites	1.25
7 BWi,DP Return of Captain Fate	1.25
8 BWi,DP,V:Captain Fate.	1.25
9 BWi(c),Save the Life of My Own Child	1.25
10 BWi,DP,Swampfire.	1.25
11 Final issue	1.25

[3rd Series] Oct., 1997

1 JMD,LSh, non-code	3.00
2 JMD,LSh, reunion with ex-wife, A:Dr. Strange	3.00
3 JMD,LSh, visit to Devil Slayer.	3.00
4 JMD,LSh, V:Devil-Slayer.	3.00
5 JMD,LSh, new abilities revealed.	3.00
6 JMD,LSh, V:Cult of Entropy	3.00
7 JMD,LSh, Muck Monster, Namor	3.00
8 JMD,LSh, Muck Monster turned back into Ted Sallis.	3.00
Storyline continues in Strange Tales	

MARINES AT WAR
See: DEVIL-DOG DUGAN

MARINES IN ACTION
Atlas June, 1955

1 B:Rock Murdock,Boot Camp Brady	75.00
2 thru 13	@40.00
14 Sept., 1957	40.00

MARINES IN BATTLE
Atlas Aug., 1954

1 RH,B:Iron Mike McGraw	125.00
2	75.00
3 thru 6	@45.00
7	50.00
8	45.00
9	45.00
10	45.00
11 thru 16	@40.00
17	60.00
18 thru 22	@40.00
23	60.00

MARVEL (vertical sidebar)

24	40.00
25 Sept., 1958	50.00

MARK HAZZARD: MERC
Nov., 1986–Oct. 1987

1 GM,O:Mark Hazard	1.50
2 GM	1.00
3 M,Arab Terrorists	1.00
4 GM	1.00
5 GM	1.00
6 GM	1.00
7 GM	1.00
8 GM	1.00
9 NKu/AKu	1.00
10 thru 12	@1.00
Ann.#1 D:Merc	1.25

MARSHALL LAW
Epic 1987–89

1	4.50
2	3.00
3 thru 6	@2.50

MARVEL ACTION HOUR: FANTASTIC FOUR
1994–95

1 regular	1.50
1a bagged with insert print from animated series	3.00
2 V:Puppet Master	1.50
3	1.50
4 V:Sub-Mariner	1.50
5	1.50
6 R:Skrulls	1.50
7 V:Doctor Doom	1.50
8 Wanted by the Law	1.50

MARVEL ACTION HOUR: IRON MAN
1994–95

1 regular	1.50
1a bagged with insert print from animated series	3.25
2 V:War Machine	1.50
3 V:Ultimo	1.50
4 A:Force Works, Hawkeye, War Machine	1.50
5 O:Iron Man	1.50
6 V:Fing Fang Foom	1.50
7 V:Mandarin	1.50

Marvel Action Hour #5
© Marvel Entertainment Group

8 V:Robots	1.50

MARVEL ACTION UNIVERSE
TV Tie-in, Jan., 1989

1 Rep.Spider-Man & Friends	2.50

MARVEL ADVENTURES STARRING DAREDEVIL
Dec., 1975–Oct. 1976

1 Rep,Daredevil #22	5.00
2 thru 5, Rep,Daredevil #23-26	@3.00
6 DD #27	3.00

MARVEL ADVENTURES
Feb. 1997

1 RMc,F:The Hulk	1.50
2 RMc,F:Spider-Man	1.50
3 RMc,F:Quicksilver & Scarlet Witch	1.50
4 RMc,BHr,F:Hulk,V:Brotherhood of Evil Mutants	1.50
5 RMc,BHr,F:Spider-Man, The X-Men	1.50
6 RMc,BHr,A:Spider-Man,Invisible Woman, Human Torch	1.50
7 RMc,F:Hulk,V:Tyrannus	1.50
8 RMc,V:Molto	1.50
9 RMc,F:Fantastic Four, Subterranean War, concl.	1.50
10 RMc,Sky-Rider vs. Gladiator	1.50
11 RMc,F:Spider-Man,Sandman	1.50
12 RMc,F:Fantastic Four,V:Frightful Four	1.50
13 AM,F:Spider-Man, Silver Surfer	1.50
14 RMc,F:The Hulk,A:Dr. Strange, Juggernaut	1.50
15 RMc,F:X-Men,V:Beast's army	1.50
16 RMc,F:Silver Surfer	1.50
17 RMc,F:Spider-Man, Iron Man	1.50
18 RMc,F:Sentinel of Liberty	1.50
19 RMc,F:The Avengers	1.50
20 RMc,F:Iron Man	1.50

MARVEL & DC PRESENTS
Nov., 1982

1 WS,TA,X-Men & Titans,A:Darkseid, Deathstroke(3rd App.),	18.00

MARVEL BOY
Dec., 1950

1 RH,O:Marvel Boy,Lost World	750.00
2 BEv,The Zero Hour	600.00

Becomes:

ASTONISHING

3 BEv,Marvel Boy,V:Mr Death	750.00
4 BEv,Stan Lee,The Screaming Tomb	500.00
5 BEv,Horro in the Caves of Doom	500.00
6 BEv,My Coffin is Waiting E:Marvel Boy	500.00
7 JR,Nightmare	200.00
8 RH,Behind the Wall	200.00
9 RH(c),The Little Black Box	200.00
10 BEv,Walking Dead	200.00
11 BF,JSt.Mr Mordeau	175.00
12 GC,BEv,Horror Show	175.00
13 BK,MSy,Ghouls Gold	200.00
14 BK,The Long Jump Down	200.00
15 BEv(c),Grounds for Death	175.00
16 BEv(c),DAy,SSh,Don't Make a Ghoul of Yourself	200.00
17 Who Was the Wilmach	

Astonishing #5
© Marvel Entertainment Group

Werewolf?	175.00
18 BEv(c),JR,Vampire at my Window	200.00
19 BK,Back From the Grave	200.00
20 GC,Mystery at Midnight	175.00
21 Manhunter	150.00
22 RH(c),Man Against Werewolf	150.00
23 The Woman in Black	175.00
24 JR,The Stone Face	150.00
25 RC,I Married a Zombie	175.00
26 RH(c),I Died Too Often	150.00
27	150.00
28 No Evidence	150.00
29 BEv(c),GC,Decapitation(c)	150.00
30 Tentacled eyeball story	200.00
31	125.00
32 A Vampire Takes a Wife	125.00
33 SMo	125.00
34 Transformation	125.00
35	125.00
36 Pithecanthrope Giant	125.00
37 BEv,Poor Pierre	125.00
38 The Man Who Didn't Belong	100.00
39	100.00
40	100.00
41	100.00
42	100.00
43	100.00
44 RC	110.00
45 BK	110.00
46	100.00
47 BK	110.00
48	100.00
49	100.00
50	100.00
51	100.00
52	100.00
53	110.00
54	110.00
55	125.00
56	100.00
57	150.00
58	100.00
59	100.00
60	100.00
61	100.00
62	100.00
63 August, 1957	100.00

MARVEL CHILLERS
Oct., 1975

1 GK(c),I:Mordred the Mystic	6.00
2 E:Mordred	4.00
3 HC/BWr(c),B:Tigra,The Were	

Marvel Chillers #1
© Marvel Entertainment Group

Marvel Classic Comics #8
© Marvel Entertainment Group

Marvel Collectors' Item Classic #20
© Marvel Entertainment Group

Woman 4.00
4 V:Kraven The Hunter 4.00
5 V:Rat Pack,A:Red Wolf 4.00
6 RB(c),JBy,V:Red Wolf 4.00
7 JK(c),GT,V:Super Skrull
  E:Tigra,Oct., 1976 . . . . 4.00
GN MGu(s),LSh,F:The Hulk 5.00
GN LHa(s) F:Wolverine 5.00

MARVEL CHRISTMAS SPECIAL

1 DC/AAd/KJ/SB/RLm,A:Ghost Rider
  X-Men,Spider-Man 2.25

MARVEL CLASSICS COMICS

1976–78

1 GK/DA(c),B:Reprints from
  Pendulum Illustrated Comics
  Dr.Jekyll & Mr. Hyde 15.00
2 GK(c),AN,Time Machine 10.00
3 GK/KJ(c) The Hunchback of
  Notre Dame 10.00
4 GK/DA(c),20,000 Leagues–
  Beneath the Sea by Verne. . . 10.00
5 GK(c),RN,Black Beauty 10.00
6 GK(c),Gullivers Travels 10.00
7 GK(c),Tom Sawyer 10.00
8 GK(c),AN,Moby Dick 10.00
9 GK(c),NR,Dracula. 10.00
10 GK(c),Red Badge of Courage . 10.00
11 GK(c),Mysterious Island 10.00
12 GK/DA(c),AN,3 Musketeers . . 10.00
13 GK(c),Last of the Mohicans . . 10.00
14 GK(c),War of the Worlds 10.00
15 GK(c),Treasure Island 10.00
16 GK(c),Ivanhoe. 9.00
17 JB/ECh(c),The Count of
   Monte Cristo 9.00
18 ECh(c),The Odyssey 9.00
19 JB(c),Robinson Crusoe 9.00
20 Frankenstein 9.00
21 GK(c),Master of the World 9.00
22 GK(c),Food of the Gods. 9.00
23 Moonstone by Wilkie Collins . . 9.00
24 GK/RN(c),She 9.00
25 The Invisible Man by H.G.Wells . 9.00
26 JB(c),The Illiad by Homer 9.00
27 Kidnapped. 9.00
28 MGo(1st art) The Pit and
   the Pendulum. 12.00

29 The Prisoner of Zenda. 9.00
30 The Arabian Nights 9.00
31 The First Men in the Moon. . . . 9.00
32 GK(c),White Fang 9.00
33 The Prince and the Pauper 9.00
34 AA,Robin Hood 9.00
35 FBe,Alice in Wonderland 9.00
36 A Christmas Carol 9.00

MARVEL COLLECTORS ITEM CLASSICS

Feb., 1965

1 SD,JK,reprint FF #2 . . . . 75.00
2 SD,JK,reprint FF #3 . . . . 35.00
3 SD,JK,reprint FF #4 . . . . 35.00
4 SD,JK,reprint FF #7 . . . . 35.00
5 SD,JK,reprint FF #8 . . . . 25.00
6 SD,JK,reprint FF #9 . . . . 25.00
7 SD,JK,reprint FF #13 . . . . 25.00
8 SD,JK,reprint FF #10 . . . . 25.00
9 SD,JK,reprint FF #14 . . . . 25.00
10 SD,JK,reprint FF #15 . . . . 25.00
11 SD,JK,reprint FF #16 . . . . 20.00
12 SD,JK,reprint FF #17 . . . . 20.00
13 SD,JK,reprint FF #18 . . . . 20.00
14 SD,JK,reprint FF #20 . . . . 20.00
15 SD,JK,reprint FF #21 . . . . 20.00
16 SD,JK,reprint FF #22 . . . . 20.00
17 SD,JK,reprint FF #23 . . . . 20.00
18 SD,JK,reprint FF #24 . . . . 20.00
19 SD,JK,reprint FF #27 . . . . 20.00
20 SD,JK,reprint FF #28 . . . . 20.00
21 SD,JK,reprint FF #29 . . . . 20.00
22 SD,JK,reprint FF #30 . . . . 20.00
Becomes:

MARVEL'S GREATEST COMICS

23 SD,JK,reprint FF#31 . . . . 4.00
24 SD,JK,reprint FF#32 . . . . 4.00
25 SD,JK,reprint FF#33 . . . . 4.00
26 SD,JK,reprint FF#34 . . . . 4.00
27 SD,JK,reprint FF#35 . . . . 4.00
28 SD,JK,reprint FF#36 . . . . 4.00
29 JK,reprint FF#37 . . . . 4.00
30 JK,reprint FF#38 . . . . 4.00
31 JK,reprint FF#40 . . . . 4.00
32 JK,reprint FF#42 . . . . 4.00
33 JK,reprint FF#44 . . . . 4.00
34 JK,reprint FF#47 . . . . 4.00
35 JK,reprint FF#48 . . . . 8.50
36 JK,reprint FF#49 . . . . 7.00
37 JK,reprint FF#50 . . . . 7.00

38 JK,reprint FF#51 . . . . 3.00
39 JK,reprint FF#52 . . . . 3.00
40 JK,reprint FF#53 . . . . 3.00
41 JK,reprint FF#54 . . . . 3.00
42 JK,reprint FF#55 . . . . 3.00
43 JK,reprint FF#56 . . . . 3.00
44 JK,reprint FF#61 . . . . 3.00
45 JK,reprint FF#62 . . . . 3.00
46 JK,reprint FF#63 . . . . 3.00
47 JK,reprint FF#64 . . . . 3.00
48 JK,reprint FF#65 . . . . 3.00
49 JK,reprint FF#66 . . . . 6.00
50 JK,reprint FF#67 . . . . 6.00
51 thru 75 JK,reprint FF . . . . . . @1.75
76 thru 82 JK,reprint FF . . . . . . @1.25
83 thru 95 Reprint FF . . . . @1.25
96 Reprint FF#, Jan., 1981 . . . . . 1.25

MARVEL COMICS

Oct.-Nov., 1939

1 FP(c),BEv,CBu,O:Sub-Mariner
  I&B:The Angel,A:Human Torch,
  Kazar,Jungle Terror,
  B:The Masked Raider . . 110,000.00
Becomes:

MARVEL MYSTERY COMICS

2 CSM(c),BEv,CBu,PGn,
  B:American, Ace,Human
  Torch,Sub-Mariner,Kazar . 21,000.00
3 ASh(c),BEv,CBu,PGn,
  E:American Ace 9,000.00
4 ASh(c),BEv,CBu,PGn,
  I&B:Electro,The Ferret,
  Mystery Detective 7,200.00
5 ASh(c),BEv,CBu,PGn,
  Human Torch(c) 16,000.00
6 ASh(c),BEv,CBu,PGn,
  Angle(c) 5,000.00
7 ASh(c),BEv,CBu,PGn,
  Bondage(c) 5,000.00
8 ASh(c),BEv,CBu,PGn,Human
  TorchV:Sub-Mariner 7,200.00
9 ASh(c),BEv,CBu,PGn,Human
  Torch V:Sub-Mariner(c) . . 20,000.00
10 ASh(c),BEv,CBu,PGn,B:Terry
   Vance Boy Detective 5,000.00
11 ASh(c),BEv,CBu,PGn,
   Human Torch V:Nazis(c) . . 2,800.00
12 ASh(c),BEv,CBu,
   PGn,Angel(c). 3,000.00
13 ASh(c),BEv,CBu,PGn,S&K,

I&B:The Vision 3,800.00
14 ASh(c),BEv,CBu,PGn,S&K,
  Sub-Mariner V:Nazis 1,800.00
15 ASh(c),BEv,CBu,PGn,S&K,
  Sub-Mariner(c) 1,900.00
16 ASh(c),BEv,CBu,PGn,S&K,
  HumanTorch/NaziAirbase . . 1,800.00
17 ASh(c),BEv,CBu,PGn,S&K
  Human Torch/Sub-Mariner 2,000.00
18 ASh(c),BEv,CBu,PGn,S&K,
  Human Torch & Toro(c) . . . 1,600.00
19 ASh(c),BEv,CBu,PGn,S&K,
  O:Toro,E:Electro 1,800.00
20 ASh(c),BEv,CBu,PGn,S&K,
  O:The Angel 1,800.00
21 ASh(c),BEv,CBu,PGn,S&K,
  I&B:The Patriot 1,600.00
22 ASh(c),BEv,CBu,PGn,S&K,
  Toro/Bomb(c) 1,400.00
23 ASh(c),BEv,CBu,PGn,S&K,
  O:Vision,E:The Angel 1,400.00
24 ASh(c),BEv,CBu,S&K,
  Human Torch(c) 1,400.00
25 BEv,CBu,S&K,ASh Nazi(c) . 1,400.00
26 ASh(c),BEv,CBu,S&K,
  Sub-Mariner(c) 1,300.00
27 ASh(c),BEv,CBu,
  S&K,E:Kazar 1,300.00
28 ASh(c),BEv,CBu,S&K,Bondage
  (c),B:Jimmy Jupiter 1,300.00
29 ASh(c),BEv,CBu,Bondage(c) 1,300.00
30 BEv,CBu,Pearl Harbor(c) . 1,300.00
31 BEv,CBu,HUman Torch(c) . . 1,100.00
32 CBu,I:The Boboes 1,100.00
33 ASHc(c),CBu,Japanese(c) . . 1,100.00
34 ASh(c),CBu,V:Hitler 1,300.00
35 ASh(c),Beach Assault(c) . . . 1,100.00
36 ASh(c),Nazi Invasion of
  New York(c) 1,100.00
37 SSh(c),Nazi(c) 1,100.00
38 SSh(c),Battlefield(c) 1,100.00
39 ASh(c),Nazis/U.S(c) 1,100.00
40 ASh(c),Zeppelin(c) 1,100.00
41 ASh(c),Jap. Command(c) . . 1,000.00
42 ASh(c),Japanese Sub(c) . . . 1,000.00
43 ASh(c),Destroyed Bridge(c). 1,000.00
44 ASh(c),Nazi Super Plane(c) 1,000.00
45 ASh(c),Nazi(c) 1,000.00
46 ASh(c),Hitler Bondage(c). . . 1,000.00
47 ASh(c),Ruhr Valley Dam(c) . 1,000.00
48 ASh(c),E:Jimmy Jupiter,
  Vision,Allied Invasion(c) . . . 1,000.00
49 SSh(c),O:Miss America,
  Bondage(c) 1,300.00
50 ASh(c),Bondage(c),Miss
  Patriot 1,100.00
51 ASh(c),Nazi Torture(c) 900.00
52 ASh(c),Bondage(c) 900.00
53 ASh(c),Bondage(c) 900.00
54 ASh(c),Bondage(c) 900.00
55 ASh(c),Bondage(c) 900.00
56 ASh(c),Bondage(c) 900.00
57 ASh(c),Torture/Bondage(c) . . 900.00
58 ASH(c),Torture(c) 900.00
59 ASh(c),Testing Room(c) 900.00
60 ASh(c),Japanese Gun(c) 900.00
61 Torturer Chamber(c) 900.00
62 ASh(c),Violent(c) 900.00
63 ASh(c),NaziHighCommand(c) 900.00
64 ASh(c),Last Nazi(c) 900.00
65 ASh(c),Bondage(c) 900.00
66 ASh(c),Last Japanese(c) 900.00
67 ASh(c),Treasury raid(c) 800.00
68 ASh(c),Torture Chamber(c) . . 800.00
69 ASh(c),Torture Chamber(c) . . 800.00
70 Cops & Robbers(c) 800.00
71 ASh(c),Egyptian(c) 800.00
72 Police(c) 800.00
73 Werewolf Headlines(c) 800.00
74 ASh(c),Robbery(c),E:The
  Patriot 800.00

75 Tavern(c),B:Young Allies 800.00
76 ASh(c),Shoot-out(c),B:Miss
  America 800.00
77 Human Torch/Sub-Mariner(c) . 800.00
78 Safe Robbery(c) 800.00
79 Super Villians(c),E:The
  Angel 800.00
80 I:Capt.America(in Marvel) . . 1,000.00
81 Mystery o/t Crimson Terror . . . 850.00
82 I:Sub-Mariner/Namora Team-up
  O:Namora,A:Capt.America. 2,000.00
83 The Photo Phantom,E;Young
  Allies 750.00
84 BEv,B:The Blonde Phantom 1,000.00
85 BEv,A:Blonde Phantom,
  E;Miss America 750.00
86 BEv,Blonde Phantom ID
  Revealed,E:Bucky 850.00
87 BEv,I:Capt.America/Golden
  Girl Team-up. 900.00
88 BEv,E:Toro. 800.00
89 BEv,I:Human Torch/Sun Girl
  Team-up 850.00
90 BEv,Giant of the Mountains . . 850.00
91 BEv,I:Venus,E:Blonde
  Phantom,Sub-Mariner. 850.00
92 BEv,How the Human Torch was
  Born,D:Professor Horton,I:The
  Witness,A:Capt.America . . 2,000.00
92a Marvel #33(c)rare,reprints 10,000.00
Becomes:

MARVEL TALES
August, 1949
93 The Ghoul Strikes 1,100.00
94 BEv,The Haunted Love 750.00
95 The Living Death 500.00
96 MSy,The Monster Returns . . . 500.00
97 DRi,MSy,The Wooden Horror. 600.00
98 BEv,BK,MSy,The Curse of
  the Black Cat 500.00
99 DRi,The Secret of the Wax
  Museum 500.00
100 The Eyes of Doom 500.00
101 The Man Who Died Twice . . 500.00
102 BW,A Witch Among Us 650.00
103 RA,A Touch of Death 550.00
104 RH(c),BW,BEv,The Thing
  in the Mirror 700.00
105 RH(c),GC,JSt,The Spider . . . 500.00
106 RH(c),BK,BEv,In The Dead of
  the Night 400.00
107 GC,OW,BK,The Thing in the
  Sewer. 400.00
108 RH(c),BEv,JR,Horror in the
  Moonlight 300.00
109 BEv(c),Sight for Sore Eyes. . 300.00
110 RH,SSh,A Coffin for Carlos . 300.00
111 BEv,Horror Under the Earth . 300.00
112 The House That Death Built . 300.00
113 RH,Terror Tale 300.00
114 BEv(c),GT,JM,2 for Zombie . 300.00
115 The Man With No Face 300.00
116 JSt. 300.00
117 BEv(c),GK,Terror in the
  North. 300.00
118 RH,DBr,GC,A World
  Goes Mad 300.00
119 RH,They Gave Him A Grave 300.00
120 GC,Graveyard(c) 300.00
121 GC,Graveyard(c) 250.00
122 JKu,Missing One Body. 250.00
123 No Way Out. 250.00
124 He Waits at the Tombstone . 250.00
125 JF,Horror House. 250.00
126 DW,It Came From Nowhere . 200.00
127 BEv(c),GC,MD,Gone is the
  Gargoyle 200.00
128 Emily,Flying Saucer(c) 200.00
129 You Can't Touch Bottom . . . 200.00
130 RH(c),JF,The Giant Killer . . . 200.00

131 GC,BEv,Five Fingers 200.00
132 . . . . 150.00
133 . . . . 150.00
134 BK,JKu,Flying Saucer(c) . . . 150.00
135 thru 141 . . . . @125.00
142 . . . . 125.00
143 . . . . 125.00
144 . . . . 135.00
145 . . . . 125.00
146 . . . . 100.00
147 . . . . 125.00
148 . . . . 100.00
149 . . . . 100.00
150 . . . . 100.00
151 . . . . 100.00
152 . . . . 125.00
153 . . . . 135.00
154 . . . . 100.00
155 . . . . 100.00
156 . . . . 100.00
157 . . . . 125.00
158 . . . . 100.00
159 August, 1957 . . . . 125.00

MARVEL COMICS PRESENTS
Sept., 1988
1 WS(c),B:Wolverine(JB,KJ),Master
  of Kung Fu(TS),Man-Thing(TGr,DC)
  F:Silver Surfer(AM). 10.00
2 F:The Captain(AM) 5.00
3 JR2(c),F:The Thing(AM) 4.00
4 F:Thor(AM). 4.00
5 F:Daredevil(DT,MG) 4.00
6 F:Hulk 4.00
7 F:Submariner(SD) 4.00
8 CV(c),E:Master of Kung Fu,F:
  Iron Man(JS) 4.00
9 F:Cloak,El Aquila 4.00
10 E:Wolverine,B:Colossus(RL,CR),
  F:Machine Man(SD,DC) 4.00
11 F:Ant-Man(BL),Slag(RWi). 3.00
12 E:Man-Thing,F:Hercules(DH),
  Namorita(FS) 3.00
13 B:Black Panther(GC,TP),F:
  Shanna,Mr.Fantastic &
  Invisible Woman. 3.00
14 F:Nomad(CP),Speedball(SD) . . . 3.00
15 F:Marvel Girl(DT,MG),Red
  Wolf(JS). 3.00
16 F:Kazar(JM),Longshot(AA) 3.00
17 E:Colossus,B:Cyclops(RLm),
  F:Watcher(TS) 4.00

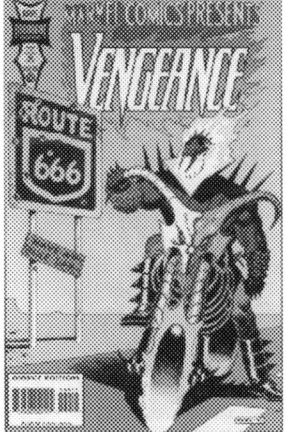

Marvel Comics Presents #149
© Marvel Entertainment Group

18 F:She-Hulk(JBy,BWi),Willie
Lumpkin(JSt) 3.00
19 RLd(c)B:Dr.Strange(MBg),
I:Damage Control(EC,AW) 3.00
20 E:Dr.Strange,F:Clea(RLm) 3.00
21 F:Thing,Paladin(RWi,DA) 3.00
22 F:Starfox(DC),Wolfsbane &
Mirage 3.00
23 F:Falcon(DC),Wheels(RWi) 3.00
24 E:Cyclops,B:Havok(RB,JRu),
F:Shamrock(DJ,DA) 3.00
25 F:Ursa Major,I:Nth Man 4.00
26 B&I:Coldblood(PG),F:Hulk 2.50
27 F:American Eagle(RWi) 2.50
28 F:Triton(JS) 2.50
29 F:Quasar(PR) 2.50
30 F:Leir(TMo) 2.50
31 EL,E:Havok,B:Excalibur
(EL,TA). 4.00
32 TM(c),F:Sunfire(DH,DC) 3.00
33 F:Namor(JLe) 3.00
34 F:Captain America(JsP) 3.00
35 E:Coldblood,F:Her(EL,AG) 4.00
36 BSz(c),F:Hellcat(JBr) 4.00
37 E:Bl.Panther,F:Devil-Slayer 3.00
38 E:Excalibur,B:Wonderman(JS),
Wolverine(JB),F:Hulk(MR,DA) . 4.00
39 F:Hercules(BL),Spider-Man 3.50
40 F:Hercules(BL),Overmind(DH) . . 3.50
41 F:Daughters of the Dragon(DA),
Union Jack(KD) 3.50
42 F:Iron Man(MBa),Siryn(LSn) . . . 3.50
43 F:Iron Man(MBa),Siryn(LSn) . . . 3.50
44 F:Puma(BWi),Dr.Strange 3.50
45 E:Wonderman,F:Hulk(HT),
Shooting Star 3.50
46 RLd(c),B:Devil-Slayer,F:Namor,
Aquarian 3.50
47 JBy(c),E:Wolverine,F:Captain
America,Arabian Knight(DP) . . 3.50
48 B:Wolverine&Spider-Man(EL),
F:Wasp,Storm&Dr.Doom 5.00
49 E:Devil-Slayer,F:Daredevil(RWi),
Gladiator(DH) 4.50
50 E:Wolverine&Spider-Man,B:Comet
Man(KJo),F:Captain Ultra(DJ),
Silver Surfer(JkS) 4.50
51 B:Wolverine(RLd),F:Iron Man
(MBr,DH),Le Peregrine 4.00
52 F:Rick Jones,Hulk(RWi,TMo) . . . 4.00
53 E:Wolverine,Comet Man,F:
Silver Sable&Black Widow
(RLd,BWi),B:Stingray 4.00
54 B:Wolverine&Hulk(DR),
Werewolf,F:Shroud(SD,BWi). . . 6.00
55 F:Collective Man(GLa) 6.00
56 E:Stingray,F:Speedball(SD) 6.00
57 DK(c),B:Submariner(MC,MFm),
Black Cat(JRu) 6.00
58 F:Iron Man(SD) 6.00
59 E:Submariner,Werewolf,
F:Punisher 6.00
60 B:Poison,Scarlet Witch,
F:Captain America(TL) 6.00
61 E:Wolverine&Hulk,
F:Dr.Strange. 6.00
62 F:Wolverine(PR),Deathlok(JG). . 6.00
63 F:Wolverine(PR),E:Scarlet
Witch,Thor(DH) 4.00
64 B:Wolverine&Ghost Rider(MT),
Fantastic Four(TMo),F:Blade . . 4.00
65 F:Starfox(ECh). 3.50
66 F:Volstagg. 3.50
67 E:Poison,F:Spider-Man(MG) . . . 3.50
68 B:Shanna(PG),E:Fantastic Four
F:Lockjaw(JA,AM) 3.50
69 B:Daredevil(DT),F:Silver Surfer . 3.50
70 F:BlackWidow&Darkstar(AM) . . 3.50
71 E:Wolverine&Ghost Rider,F:
Warlock(New Mutants)(SMc) . . 3.50
72 B:Weapon X(BWS),E:Daredevil,

F:Red Wolf(JS). 7.00
73 F:Black Knight(DC),
Namor(JM). 5.00
74 F:Constrictor(SMc),Iceman &
Human Torch(JSon,DA) 5.00
75 F:Meggan & Shadowcat,
Dr.Doom(DC) 5.00
76 F:Death's Head(BHi,MFm),
A:Woodgod(DC). 5.00
77 E:Shanna,B:Sgt.Fury&Dracula
(TL,JRu),F:Namor 4.50
78 F:Iron Man(KSy),Hulk&Selene . . 4.50
79 E:Sgt.Fury&Dracula,F:Dr.Strange,
Sunspot(JBy) 4.50
80 F:Daughters of the Dragon,Mister
Fantastic(DJ),Captain America
(SD,TA) 4.50
81 F:Captain America(SD,TA),
Daredevil(MR,AW),Ant-Man . . . 4.00
82 B:Firestar(DT),F:Iron Man(SL),
Power Man. 4.00
83 F:Hawkeye,Hum.Torch(SD,EL) . 4.00
84 E:Weapon X 4.00
85 B:Wolverine(SK),Beast(RLd,JaL-
1st Work),F:Speedball(RWi),
I:Cyber. 7.00
86 F:PaladinE:RLd on Beast. 5.00
87 E:Firestar,F:Shroud(RWi) 5.00
88 F:Solo,Volcana(BWi) 5.00
89 F:Spitfire(JSn),Mojo(JMa) 5.00
90 B:Ghost Rider & Cable,F:
Nightmare 4.50
91 F:Impossible Man 3.50
92 E:Wolverine,Beast,
F:Northstar(JMa) 3.50
93 SK(c),B:Wolverine,Nova,
F:Daredevil. 3.00
94 F:Gabriel 3.00
95 SK(c),E:Wolverine,F:Hulk. 3.00
96 B:Wolverine(TT),E:Nova,
F:Speedball 3.00
97 F:Chameleon,Two-Gun Kid,
E:Ghost Rider/Cable. 2.50
98 E:Wolverine,F:Ghost Rider,
Werewolf by Night 2.50
99 F:Wolverine,Ghost Rider,
Mary Jane,Captain America. . . . 2.50
100 SK,F:Ghost Rider,Wolverine,
Dr.Doom,Nightmare 3.00
101 SK(c),B:Ghost Rider&Doctor
Strange,Young Gods,Wolverine
&Nightcrawler,F:Bar With
No Name 2.00
102 RL,GC,AW,F:Speedball 2.00

Marvel Comics Presents #163
© Marvel Entertainment Group

103 RL,GC,AW,F:Puck 2.00
104 RL,GC,AW,F:Lockheed 2.00
105 RL,GC,AW,F:Nightmare 2.00
106 RL,GC,AW,F:Gabriel,E:Ghost
Rider&Dr.Strange 2.00
107 GC,AW,TS,B:Ghost Rider&
Werewolf 2.00
108 GC,AW,TS,SMc,E:Wolverine&
Nightcrawler,B:Thanos 2.00
109 SLi,TS,SMc,B:Wolverine&
Typhoid Mary,E:Young Gods. . . 2.00
110 SLi,SMc,F:Nightcrawler 2.00
111 SK(c),SLi,RWi,F:Dr.Strange,
E:Thanos 2.00
112 SK(c),SLi,F:Pip,Wonder Man,
E:Ghost Rider&Werewolf 2.00
113 SK(c),SLi,B:Giant Man,
Ghost Rider&Iron Fist. 1.75
114 SK(c),SLi,F:Arabian Knight. . . . 1.75
115 SK(c),SLi,F:Cloak&Dagger. . . . 1.75
116 SK(c),SLi,E:Wolverine &
Typhoid Mary 1.75
117 SK,PR,B:Wolverine&Venom,
I:Ravage 2099 . . . . 4.00
118 SK,PB,RWi,E:Giant Man,
I:Doom 2099 . . . . 3.00
119 SK,GC,B:Constrictor,E:Ghost
Rider&Iron Fist,F:Wonder Man . 3.00
120 SK,GC,E:Constrictor,B:Ghost
Rider/Cloak & Dagger,
F:Spider-Man 2.50
121 SK,GC,F:Mirage,Andromeda . . 2.50
122 SK(c),GK,E:Wolverine&Venom,
Ghost Rider&Cloak&Dagger,F:
Speedball&Rage,Two-Gun Kid . 2.50
123 SK(c),DJ,SLi,B:Wolverine&Lynx,
Ghost Rider&Typhoid Mary,
She-Hulk,F:Master Man. 1.75
124 SK(c),DJ,MBa,SLi,F:Solo 1.75
125 SLi,SMc,DJ,B:Iron Fist. 1.75
126 SLi,DJ,E:She-Hulk 1.75
127 SLi,DJ,DP,F:Speedball. 1.75
128 SLi,DJ,RWi,F:American Eagle . 1.75
129 SLi,DJ,F:Ant Man. 1.75
130 DJ,SLi,RWi,E:Wolverine&Lynx,
Ghost Rider&Typhoid Mary,Iron
Fist,F:American Eagle 1.75
131 MFm,B:Wolverine,Ghost Rider&
Cage,Iron Fist&Sabretooth,
F:Shadowcat 1.75
132 KM(c),F:Iron Man. 1.75
133 F:Cloak & Dagger 1.75
134 SLi,F:Vance Astro 1.75
135 SLi,F:Daredevil 1.75
136 B:Gh.Rider&Masters of Silence,
F:Iron Fist,Daredevil. 1.75
137 F:Ant Man 1.75
138 B:Wolverine,Spellbound 1.75
139 F:Foreigner 1.75
140 F:Captain Universe 1.75
141 BCe(s),F:Iron Fist 1.75
142 E:Gh.Rider&Masters of Silence,
F:Mr.Fantastic 1.75
143 Siege of Darkness,pt.#3,
B:Werewolf,Scarlet Witch,
E:Spellbound 2.00
144 Siege of Darkness,pt.#6,
B:Morbius. 2.00
145 Siege of Darkness,pt.#11 . . . . . 2.00
146 Siege of Darkness,pt.#14. . . . . 1.75
147 B:Vengeance,F:Falcon,Masters of
Silence,American Eagle 1.75
148 E:Vengeance,F:Capt.Universe,
Black Panther. 1.75
149 F:Daughter o/t Dragon,Namor,
Vengeance,Starjammers. 1.75
150 ANo(s),SLi,F:Typhoid Mary,DD,
Vengeance,Wolverine. 1.75
151 ANo(s),F:Typhoid Mary,DD,
Vengeance. 1.75
152 CDi(s),PR,B:Vengeance,Wolverine,

War Machine,Moon Knight 1.75
153 CDi(s),A:Vengeance,Wolverine,
   War Machine,Moon Knight . . . 1.75
154 CDi(s),E:Vengeance,Wolverine,
   War Machine,Moon Knight 1.75
155 CDi(s),B:Vengeance,Wolverine,
   War Machine,Kymaera 1.75
156 B:Shang Chi,F:Destroyer 1.50
157 F:Nick Fury 1.50
158 AD,I:Clan Destine,E:Kymaera,
   Shang Chi,Vengeance 1.75
159 B:Hawkeye, New Warriors,
   F:Fun,E:Vengeance 1.75
160 B:Vengeance,Mace 2.00
161 E:Hawkeye 1.75
162 B:Tigra,E:Mace 1.75
163 E:New Warriors 1.75
164 Tigra, Vengeance. 1.75
165 Tigra, Vengeance. 1.75
166 Turbo, Vengeance 1.75
167 Turbo, Vengeance 1.75
168 Thing, Vengeance 1.75
169 Mandarin, Vengeance 1.75
170 Force, Vengeance 1.75
171 Nick Fury. 1.75
172 Lunatik 1.75
173 . . . . 1.75
174 . . . . 1.75
175 . . . . 1.75
TPB Ghost Rider & Cable,rep
   #90-97 . . . . 3.95
TPB Save the Tyger,rep.Wolverine
   story from #1-10 . . . . 3.95

MARVEL COMICS SUPER SPECIAL
[Magazine, 1977]
1 JB,WS,Kiss,Features &Photos . 65.00
2 JB,Conan(1978) 6.00
3 WS,Close Encounters 5.00
4 GP,KJ,Beatles story 25.00
Becomes:
MARVEL SUPER SPECIAL
5 Kiss 1978 . . . . 35.00
6 GC,Jaws II 3.00
7 Does Not Exist
8 Battlestar Galactica(Tabloid) . . . 3.00
9 Conan 4.00
10 GC,Starlord 3.00
11 JB,RN,Weirdworld,. 3.00
12 JB,Weirdworld, ... 3.00
13 JB,Weirdworld, ... 3.00
14 GC,Meteor,adapt 3.00
15 Star Trek 6.00
15a Star Trek 9.00
16 AW,B:Movie Adapts,Empire
   Strikes Back. 7.00
17 Xanadu 2.00
18 HC(c),JB,Raiders of the Lost
   Ark. 2.00
19 HC,For Your Eyes Only 5.00
20 Dragonslayer 2.50
21 JB,Conan 1.00
22 JSo(c),AW,Bladerunner 2.00
23 Annie 2.00
24 Dark Crystal 2.00
25 Rock and Rule. 2.00
26 Octopussy 2.50
27 AW,Return of the Jedi 6.00
28 PH(c),Krull. 2.00
29 DSp,Tarzan of the Apes. 2.00
30 Indiana Jones and the Temple
   of Doom 2.50
31 The Last Star Fighter. 2.00
32 Muppets Take Manhattan. 2.00
33 Buckaroo Banzai 2.00
34 GM,Sheena 2.00
35 JB,Conan The Destroyer 2.00
36 Dune 2.00

37 2010 . . . . 2.00
38 Red Sonja 2.00
39 Santa Claus. 2.00
40 JB,Labrynth 2.00
41 Howard the Duck,Nov.,1986. . . . 2.00

MARVEL DOUBLE FEATURE
Dec., 1973
1 JK,GC,B:Tales of Suspense
   Reprints,Capt.America,
   Iron-Man 4.00
2 JK,GC ,A:Nick Fury 2.50
3 JK,GC 2.50
4 JK,GC,Cosmic Cube 2.50
5 JK,GC,V:Red Skull 2.50
6 JK,GC,V:Adaptoid 2.50
7 JK,GC,V:Tumbler 2.50
8 JK,GC,V:Super Adaptoid 2.50
9 GC,V:Batroc 2.50
10 GC 2.50
11 GC,Capt.America Wanted 2.50
12 GC,V:Powerman,Swordsman. . . 2.50
13 GC,A:Bucky. 2.50
14 GC,V:Red Skull 2.50
15 GK,GC,V:Red Skull 2.50
16 GC,V:Assassin 2.50
17 JK,GC,V:Aim,Iron Man &
   Sub-Mariner #1 . . . . 4.00
18 JK,GC,V:Modok,Iron Man #1 . . . 5.00
19 JK,GC,E:Capt.America 5.00
20 JK(c) 2.50
21 Capt.America,Black Panther
   March, 1977. . . . . 2.50

MARVEL FANFARE
March, 1972
1 MG,TA,PS,F:Spider-Man,
   Daredevil,Angel 7.00
2 MG,SM,FF,TVe,F:SpM,Ka-Zar . . 5.00
3 DC,F:X-Men 5.00
4 PS,TA,MG,F:X-Men,Deathlok . . . 5.00
5 MR,F:Dr.Strange. 4.00
6 F:Spider-Man,Scarlet Witch . . . 4.50
7 F:Hulk/Daredevil 3.00
8 CI,TA,GK,F:Dr.Strange 3.00
9 GM,F:Man Thing 3.00
10 GP,B:Black Widow 3.50
11 GP,D:M.Corcoran. 3.50
12 GP,V:Snapdragon 3.50
13 GP,E:B.Widow,V:Snapdragon. . 3.50
14 F:Fantastic Four,Vision 2.75
15 BWS,F:Thing,Human Torch . . . 3.00
16 DC,JSt,F:Skywolf 2.50
17 DC,JSt,F:Skywolf 2.50
18 FM,JRu,F:Captain America . . . 3.00
19 RL,F:Cloak and Dagger 2.50
20 JSn,F:Thing&Dr.Strange 3.00
21 JSn,F:Thing And Hulk 3.00
22 KSy,F:Iron Man 2.50
23 KSy,F:Iron Man 2.50
24 F:Weird World 3.00
25 F:Weird World 2.50
26 F:Weird World 2.50
27 F:Daredevil 2.50
28 KSy,F:Alpha Flight 2.50
29 JBy,F:Hulk. 3.00
30 BA,AW,F:Moon Knight 2.50
31 KGa,F:Capt.America,
   Yellow Claw 2.50
32 KGa,PS,F:Capt.America,
   Yellow Claw 2.50
33 JBr,F:X-Men 5.00
34 CV,F:Warriors Three 2.50
35 CV,F:Warriors Three 2.50
36 CV,F:Warriors Three 2.50
37 CV,F:Warriors Three 2.50
38 F:Captain America 2.50
39 JSon,F:Hawkeye,Moon Knight . . 2.50

Marvel Fanfare #33
© Marvel Entertainment Group

40 DM,F:Angel,Storm,Mystique. . . . 3.00
41 DGb,F:Dr.Strange 2.50
42 F:Spider-Man. 3.00
43 F:Sub-Mariner,Human Torch . . . 2.50
44 KSy,F:Iron Man vs.Dr.Doom. . . . 2.50
45 All Pin-up Issue,WS,AAd,MZ,
   JOy,BSz,KJ,HC,PS,JBy 3.00
46 F:Fantastic Four 2.50
47 MG,F:Spider-Man,Hulk 3.00
48 KGa,F:She-Hulk 2.50
49 F:Dr.Strange 2.50
50 JSon,JRu,F:Angel 3.00
51 JB,JA,GC,AW,F:Silver Surfer . . . 4.00
52 F:Fantastic Four 2.50
53 GC,AW,F:Bl.Knight,Dr.Strange . . 2.50
54 F:Black Knight,Wolverine 3.50
55 F:Powerpack,Wolverine 3.50
56 CI,DH,F:Shanna t/She-Devil . . . 2.50
57 BBl,AM,F:Shanna,Cap.Marvel . . 2.50
58 BBl,F:Shanna,Vision/Sc.Witch . . 2.50
59 BBl,F:Shanna,Hellcat. 2.50
60 PS,F:Daredevil,Capt.Marvel. . . . 2.50

MARVEL FANFARE
Second Series 1996
1 Captain America, Falcon. 1.00
2 New Fantastic Four 1.00
3 BbB,F:Spider-Man, Ghost Rider,. 1.00
4 F:Longshot. 1.00
5 F:Longshot. 1.00
6 F:Power Man & Iron Fist V.
   Sabretooth 1.00

MARVEL FEATURE
[1st Regular Series]
Dec., 1971
1 RA,BE,NA,I&O:Defenders &
   Omegatron. 100.00
2 BEv,F:The Defenders 50.00
3 BEv,F:The Defenders 45.00
4 F:Ant-Man 15.00
5 F:Ant-Man. 11.00
6 F:Ant-Man 10.00
7 CR,F:Ant-Man 10.00
8 JSc,CR,F:Ant-Man,O:Wasp. . . . 10.00
9 CR,F:Ant-Man 10.00
10 CR,F:Ant-Man 10.00
11 JSn,JSt,F:Thing & Hulk 15.00
12 JSn,JSt,F:Thing,Iron Man,
   Thanos,Blood Brothers. 12.00

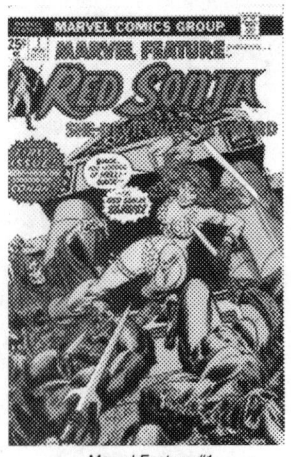

Marvel Feature #1
© Marvel Entertainment Group

[2nd Regular Series]
(All issues feature Red Sonja)
1 DG,The Temple of Abomination . 5.00
2 FT,Blood of the Hunter 2.00
3 FT,Balek Lives 2.00
4 FT,Eyes of the Gorgon 2.00
5 FT,The Bear God Walks 2.00
6 FT,C:Conan,Belit 2.00
7 FT,V:Conan,A:Belit,Conan#68 . . 2.00

MARVEL FRONTIER
COMICS SPECIAL
1 All Frontier Characters 3.25
1994 . . . . 2.95

MARVEL FUMETTI BOOK
April, 1984
1 NA(c),Stan Lee, All photos 1.25

MARVEL GRAPHIC NOVEL
1982
1 JSn,D:Captain Marvel,A:Most
  Marvel Characters 30.00
1a 2nd printing 10.00
1b 3rd-5th printing 7.00
2 F:Elric,Dreaming City 12.00
2a 2nd printing 7.00
3 JSn,F:Dreadstar 12.00
3a 2nd-3rd printing 7.00
4 BMc,I:New Mutants,Cannonball
  Sunspot,Psyche,Wolfsbane . . 22.00
4a 2nd printing 10.00
4b 3rd-4th printing 8.00
5 BA,F:X-Men 17.00
5a 2nd printing 9.00
5b 3rd-5th printing 7.00
6 WS,F:Starslammers 10.00
6a 2nd printing 7.00
7 CR,F:Killraven 7.00
8 RWi,AG,F:Super Boxers 8.00
8a 2nd printing 7.00
9 DC,F:Futurians 12.00
9a 2nd printing 7.00
10 RV,F:Heartburst 8.00
10a 2nd printing 6.00
11 VM,F:Void Indigo 12.00
12 F:Dazzler the Movie 10.00
12a 2nd printing 6.00
13 MK,F:Starstruck 7.00
14 JG,F:SwordsofSwashbucklers . . 6.00
15 CV,F:Raven Banner 6.00

16 GLa,F:Alladin Effect 6.00
17 MS,F:Living Monolith 7.00
18 JBy,F:She-Hulk 9.00
18 later printings 8.00
19 F:Conan 6.00
20 F:Greenberg the Vampire 6.00
21 JBo,F:Marada the She-wolf . . . 6.00
22 BWr,Hooky,F:Spider-Man 12.00
23 DGr,F:Dr.Strange 6.00
24 FM,BSz,F:Daredevil 10.00
25 F:Dracula 8.00
26 FC,TA,F:Alien Legion 6.00
27 BH,F:Avengers 6.00
28 JSe,F:Conan the Reaver 6.50
29 BWr,F:Thing & Hulk 8.00
30 F:A Sailor's Story 6.00
31 F:Wolf Pack 6.00
32 SA,F:Death of Groo 15.00
33 F:Thor 6.00
34 AW,F:Cloak & Dagger 6.00
35 MK/RH,F:The Shadow 12.00
36 F:Willow movie adaption 7.00
37 BL,F:Hercules 7.00
38 JB,F:Silver Surfer 15.00
39 F:Iron Man,Crash 14.50
40 JZ,F:The Punisher 12.00
41 F:Roger Rabbit 7.00
42 F:Conan of the Isles 9.00
43 EC,F:Ax 6.00
44 BJ,F:Arena 6.00
45 JRy,F:Dr.Who 9.00
46 TD,F:Kull 7.00
47 GM,F:Dreamwalker 7.00
48 F:Sailor's Storm II 7.00
49 MBd,F:Dr.Strange&Dr.Doom . . 16.00
50 F:Spider-Man,Parallel Lives . . . 9.00
51 F:Punisher,Intruder 10.00
52 DSp,F:Roger Rabbit 9.00
53 PG,F:Conan 6.95
54 HC,F:Wolverine & Nick Fury . . 17.00

MARVEL HALLOWEEN:
THE SUPERNATURALS
TOUR BOOK
Sept. 1999
1-shot, 16-page, cardstock cov 3.00

MARVEL HEROES
1 StL,FaN,Mega-Jam,48pg 2.95

MARVEL: HEROES
AND LEGENDS 1997
Aug., 1997
1-shot, Stan Lee, JR(c) 6.00

MARVEL HOLIDAY
SPECIAL
1 StG(s),PDd(s),SLo(s),RLm,PB, . . 3.25
1-shot MWa,KK 2.95

MARVEL KIDS
1999
Fantastic Four: Franklin's
  Adventures 3.50
Incredible Hulk: Project Hide 3.50
Spider-Man Mysteries 3.50
X-Men: Mutant Search R.U.1 . . . . 3.50

MARVEL KNIGHTS
TOUR BOOK
Aug. 1998
1-shot, cardstock cover 3.00

MARVEL MASTERPIECES
COLLECTION
1993
1 Joe Jusko Masterpiece Cards . . . 3.25
2 F:Wolverine,Thanos,Apocalypse . 3.00
3 F:Gambit,Venom,Hulk 3.00
4 F:Wolverine Vs. Sabretooth . . . 3.00

MARVEL MASTERPIECES
II COLLECTION
1994
1 thru 3 w/cards . . . . @3.00

MARVEL MILESTONE
EDITIONS 1991–95
See: ORIGINAL TITLES

MARVEL MINI-BOOKS
1966
(black & white)
1 F:Capt.America,Spider-Man,Hulk
  Thor,Sgt.Fury 12.00
2 F:Capt.America,Spider-Man,Hulk
  Thor,Sgt.Fury 12.00
3 F:Capt.America,Spider-Man,Hulk
  Thor,Sgt.Fury 12.00
4 thru 6 F:Capt.America,Spider-Man,
  Hulk,Thor,Sgt.Fury . . . . @12.00

MARVEL MOVIE
PREMIERE
B&W Magazine, 1975
1 Land That Time Forgot,
  Burroughs adapt 5.00

MARVEL MOVIE
SHOWCASE FEATURING
STAR WARS
Nov., 1982
1 Rep,Stars Wars #1-6 . . . . 4.00
2 Dec., 1982 . . . . 4.00

MARVEL MOVIE
SPOTLIGHT FEATURING
RAIDERS OF
THE LOST ARK
Nov., 1982
1 Rep,Raiders of Lost Ark#1-3 . . . 3.00

MARVEL
MYSTERY COMICS
See: MARVEL COMICS

MARVEL NO-PRIZE BOOK
Jan., 1983
1 MGo(c),Stan Lee as
  Dr Doom(c) 3.00

MARVEL: PORTRAITS
OF A UNIVERSE
1 Fully painted moments 3.00
2 Fully painted moments 3.00
3 F:Death of Elektra 3.00
4 final issue 3.00

Marvel Premiere #35
© Marvel Entertainment Group

MARVEL PREMIERE
April, 1972

1 GK,O:Warlock,Receives Soul Gem,
  Creation of Counter Earth. . . . 40.00
2 GK,JK,F:Warlock 25.00
3 BWS,F:Dr.Strange 28.00
4 FB,BWS,F:Dr.Strange. 14.00
5 MP,CR,F:Dr.Strange,I:Sligguth . 10.00
6 MP,FB,F:Dr.Strange 10.00
7 MP,CR,F:Dr.Strange,I:Dagoth . . 10.00
8 JSn,F:Dr.Strange 10.00
9 NA,FB,F:Dr.Strange 10.00
10 FB,F:Dr.Strange,
  D:Ancient One 10.00
11 NA,FB,F:Dr.Strange,I:Shuma . . 10.00
12 NA,FB,F:Dr.Strange 10.00
13 NA,FB,F:Dr.Strange 10.00
14 NA,FB,F:Dr.Strange 10.00
15 GK,DG,I&O:Iron Fist,pt.1 . . . . . 50.00
16 DG,O:Iron Fist,pt.2,V:Scythe . . 25.00
17 DG,`Citadel on the
  Edge of Vengeance' 15.00
18 DG,V:Triple Irons 15.00
19 DG,A:Ninja 13.00
20 I:Misty Knight. 13.00
21 V:Living Goddess. 13.00
22 V:Ninja. 13.00
23 PB,V:Warhawk. 13.00
24 PB,V:Monstroid 13.00
25 1st JBy,AMc,E:Iron Fist 18.00
26 JK,GT,F:Hercules. 7.00
27 F:Satana 7.00
28 F:Legion Of Monsters,A:Ghost
  Rider,Morbius,Werewolf. 15.00
29 JK,I:Liberty Legion,
  O:Red Raven 5.00
30 JK,F:Liberty Legion 5.00
31 JK,I:Woodgod 5.00
32 HC,F:Monark 5.00
33 HC,F:Solomon Kane 5.00
34 HC,F:Solomon Kane 5.00
35 I&O:Silver Age 3-D Man. 5.00
36 F:3-D Man. 5.00
37 F:3-D Man 5.00
38 AN,MP,I:Weird World 5.00
39 AM,I:Torpedo(1st solo). 5.00
40 AM,F:Torpedo 5.00
41 TS,F:Seeker 3000 . . . . 5.00
42 F:Tigra. 5.00
43 F:Paladin. 5.00
44 KG,F:Jack of Hearts(1stSolo). . 5.00
45 GP,F:Manwolf 5.00
46 GP,F:Manwolf 5.00

47 JBy,I:2nd Antman(Scott Lang) . . 5.00
48 JBy,F:2nd Antman 4.00
49 F:The Falcon. 4.00
50 TS,TA,F:Alice Cooper 7.00
51 JBi,F:Black Panther,V:Klan . . 3.00
52 JBi,F.B.Panther,V:Klan. 3.00
53 JBi,F:B.Panther,V:Klan. 3.00
54 GD,TD,I:Hammer. 3.00
55 JSt,F:Wonderman(1st solo) 4.00
56 HC,TA,F:Dominic Fortune 2.50
57 WS(c),I:Dr.Who 3.50
58 TA(c),FM,F:Dr.Who 3.00
59 F:Dr.Who. 3.00
60 WS(c),DGb,F:Dr.Who 3.00
61 TS,F:Starlord. 3.00

MARVEL PRESENTS
Oct., 1975

1 BMc,F:Bloodstone 10.00
2 BMc,O:Bloodstone 9.00
3 AM,B:Guardians/Galaxy 16.00
4 AM,I:Nikki 12.00
5 AM,`Planet o/t Absurd' 12.00
6 AM,V:Karanada 12.00
7 AM,`Embrace the Void' 12.00
8 AM,JB,JSt,reprint.S.Surfer#2 . . 15.00
9 AM,O:Starhawk 12.00
10 AM,O:Starhawk 12.00
11 AM,D:Starhawk's Children 12.00
12 AM,E:Guardians o/t Galaxy . . . 12.00

Marvel Preview #13
© Marvel Entertainment Group

MARVEL PREVIEW
Feb., 1975
(black & white magazine)

1 NA,AN,Man Gods From
  Beyond the Stars 5.00
2 GM(c),O:Punisher 80.00
3 GM(c),Blade the Vampire Slayer. 8.00
4 GM(c),I&O:Starlord 9.00
5 Sherlock Holmes 9.00
6 Sherlock Holmes 9.00
7 KG,Satana,A:Sword in the Star . 9.00
8 GM,MP,Legion of Monsters . . 11.00
9 Man-God,O:Starhawk. 6.00
10 JSn,Thor the Mighty. 6.00
11 JBy,I:Starlord 6.00
12 MK,Haunt of Horror 3.50
13 JSn(c),Starhawk 5.00
14 JSn(c),Starhawk 5.00
15 MK(c),Starhawk 3.50
16 GC,Detectives 3.00
17 GK,Black Mask 3.00
18 GC,Starlord 3.00
19 Kull 3.00
20 HC,NA,GP,Bizarre Adventures . . 4.00

21 SD,Moonlight. 4.00
22 JB,King Arthur 3.00
23 JB,GC,FM,Bizarre Adventures . . 5.00
24 Debut Paradox 3.00
Becomes:

BIZARRE ADVENTURES
25 MG,TA,MR,Lethal Ladies 3.00
26 JB(c),King Kull. 3.00
27 JB,AA,GP,Phoenix,A:Ice-Man . . 6.00
28 MG,TA,FM,NA,The Unlikely
  Heroes,Elektra 4.00
29 JB,WS,Horror 3.50
30 JB,Tomorrow 3.00
31 JBy,After the Violence Stops . . . 3.50
32 Gods 3.00
33 Ph(c),Horror. 3.00
34 PS,Christmas Spec,Son of Santa
  Howard the Duck,Feb.,1983 . . . 3.50

MARVEL PREVIEW
1993
Preview of 1993 . . . . 3.95

MARVEL REMIX
Nov. 1998
1 (of 3) Fantastic Four 3.00
1a signed 20.00
2 Fantastic Four:Fireworks 3.00
3 Fantastic Four:Fireworks 3.00

MARVELS
1 B:KBk(s),AxR,I:Phil Sheldon,
  A:G.A.Heroes,Human Torch Vs
  Namor 8.00
2 AxR,A:S.A.Avengers,FF,X-Men. . 6.00
3 AxR,FF vs Galactus 5.00
4 AxR,Final issue 5.00
HC rep.#1-#4 . . . . 34.95

MARVEL SAGA
Dec., 1985
1 JBy,Fantastic Four,Wolv. 2.50
2 Hulk 1.50
3 Spider-Man. 2.50
4 X-Men 2.50
5 Thor 1.50
6 Fantastic Four 1.50
7 Avengers 1.50
8 X-Men 2.00
9 Angel 1.50
10 X-Men 2.00
11 X-Men 2.00
12 O:Capt. America 1.50
13 O:Daredevil,Elektra 2.00
14 O:Green Goblin 2.00
15 Avengers 1.50
16 Daredevil,X-Men 2.00
17 Kazar,X-Men 2.00
18 Hawkeye-Quicksilver 1.50
19 SpM,Thor,Daredevil 2.00
20 Daredevil,Giant Man 1.50
21 FF,V:Frightful Four 1.50
22 Wedding 1.50
23 . . . . 1.50
24 . . . . 1.50
25 O:Silver Surfer,Dec.,1987 . . . . 2.25

MARVEL:
SHADOWS & LIGHT
B&W 1996
1-shot MGo,JPL,KJ,48pg. 3.00

MARVEL SPECTACULAR
August, 1973
1 JK,rep Thor #128 . . . . 8.00

MARVEL

2 JK,rep Thor #129 . . . . 5.00
3 JK,rep Thor #130 . . . . 5.00
4 JK,rep Thor #133 . . . . 5.00
5 JK,rep Thor #134 . . . . 5.00
6 JK,rep Thor #135 . . . . 5.00
7 JK,rep Thor #136 . . . . 5.00
8 JK,rep Thor #137 . . . . 5.00
9 JK,rep Thor #138 . . . . 5.00
10 JK,rep Thor #139 . . . . 5.00
11 JK,rep Thor #140 . . . . 4.00
12 JK,rep Thor #141 . . . . 4.00
13 JK,rep Thor #142 . . . . 4.00
14 JK,rep Thor #143 . . . . 4.00
15 JK,rep Thor #144 . . . . 4.00
16 JK,rep Thor #145 . . . . 4.00
17 JK,rep Thor #146 . . . . 4.00
18 JK,rep Thor #147 . . . . 4.00
19 JK,rep Thor#148,Nov.,1975 . . . 4.00

MARVEL SPOTLIGHT
[1st Regular Series] Nov., 1971
1 NA(c)WW,F:Red Wolf 25.00
2 MP,BEv,NA,I&O:Werewolf 75.00
3 MP,F:Werewolf 30.00
4 SD,MP,F:Werewolf 30.00
5 SD,MP,I&O:Ghost Rider 75.00
6 MP,TS,F:Ghost Rider 35.00
7 MP,TS,F:Ghost Rider 35.00
8 JM,MB,F:Ghost Rider 35.00
9 TA,F:Ghost Rider 25.00
10 SD,JM,F:Ghost Rider 25.00
11 SD,F:Ghost Rider 25.00
12 SD,2nd A:Son of Satan 25.00
13 F:Son of Satan 10.00
14 JM,F:Son of Satan,I:Ikthalon . . 10.00
15 JM, F:Son of Satan,
    I:Baphomet 7.00
16 JM,F:Son of Satan 7.00
17 JM,F:Son of Satan 7.00
18 F:Son of Satan, I:Allatou 7.00
19 F:Son of Satan 7.00
20 F:Son of Satan 7.00
21 F:Son of Satan 7.00
22 F:Son of Satan, Ghost Rider . . . 8.00
23 F:Son of Satan 7.00
24 JM,F:Son of Satan 7.00
25 GT,F:Sinbad 4.00
26 F:The Scarecrow 4.00
27 F:The Sub-Mariner 4.00
28 F:Moon Knight (1st full solo) . . 11.00
29 F:Moon Knight 10.00
30 JSt,JB,F:Warriors Three 6.00
31 HC,JSn,F:Nick Fury 6.00

Marvel Spotlight #25
© Marvel Entertainment Group

32 I:Spiderwoman, Jessica Drew . . 9.00
33 F:Deathlok, I:Devilslayer 6.00
[2nd Regualar Series] 1979
1 PB,F:Captain Marvel 2.50
1a No`1' on Cover 4.00
2 FM(c),F:Captain Marvel,A:Eon . . 2.00
3 PB,F:Captain Marvel 2.00
4 PB,F:Captain Marvel 2.00
5 FM(c),SD,F:Dragon Lord 2.00
6 F:Star Lord 2.00
7 FM(c),F:StarLord 2.00
8 FM,F:Captain Marvel 2.50
9 FM(c),SD,F:Captain Universe . . . 2.00
10 SD,F:Captain Universe 2.00
11 SD,F:Captain Universe 2.00

MARVEL SPOTLIGHT ON CAPTAIN AMERICA
1 thru 4, Captain America rep. . . @2.95

MARVEL SPOTLIGHT ON DR. STRANGE
1 thru 4, Dr. Strange, rep . . . . . . @2.95

MARVEL SPOTLIGHT ON SILVER SURFER
1 thru 4, Silver Surfer, rep . . . . . @2.95

MARVEL SUPER ACTION
Jan., 1976
1-shot TD,GE,FS,MP,HC,F:Punisher,
    Weirdworld,Dominic Fortune,
    I:Huntress(Mockingbird) 50.00

MARVEL SUPER ACTION
May, 1977–Nov. 1981
1 JK,reprint,Capt.America #100 . . . 8.00
2 JK,reprint,Capt.America #101 . . . 6.00
3 JK,reprint,Capt.America #102 . . . 6.00
4 BEv,RH,reprint,Marvel Boy #1 . . . 6.00
5 JK,reprint,Capt.America #103 . . . 6.00
6 JK,reprint,Capt.America #104 . . . 5.00
7 JK,reprint,Capt.America #105 . . . 5.00
8 JK,reprint,Capt.America #106 . . . 5.00
9 JK,reprint,Capt.America #107 . . . 5.00
10 JK,reprint,Capt.America #108 . . 5.00
11 JK,reprint,Capt.America #109 . . 5.00
12 JSo,reprint,Capt.America #110 . . 5.00
13 JSo,reprint,Capt.America #111 . . 5.00
14 JB,reprint,Avengers #55 . . . . . . 5.00
15 JB,reprint,Avengers #56 . . . . . . 5.00
16 Reprint,Avengers,annual #2 . . . 4.00
17 Reprint,Avengers # 4.00
18 JB(c),reprint,Avengers #57 . . . . 4.00
19 JB(c),reprint,Avengers #58 . . . . 4.00
20 JB(c),reprint,Avengers #59 . . . . 4.00
21 Reprint,Avengers #60 . . . . 3.00
22 JB(c),reprint,Avengers #61 . . . . 3.00
23 Reprint,Avengers #63 . . . . 3.00
24 Reprint,Avengers #64 . . . . 3.00
25 Reprint,Avengers #65 . . . . 3.00
26 Reprint,Avengers #66 . . . . 3.00
27 BWS,Reprint,Avengers #67 . . . 3.00
28 BWS,Reprint,Avengers #68 . . . 3.00
29 Reprint,Avengers #69 . . . . 3.00
30 Reprint,Avengers #70 . . . . 3.00
31 Reprint,Avengers #71 . . . . 3.00
32 Reprint,Avengers #72 . . . . 3.00
33 Reprint,Avengers #73 . . . . 3.00
34 Reprint,Avengers #74 . . . . 3.00
35 JB(c),Reprint,Avengers #75 . . . 3.00
36 JB(c),Reprint,Avengers #75 . . . 3.00
37 JB(c),Reprint,Avengers #76 . . . 3.00

MARVEL SUPERHEROES
Oct., 1966
1-shot Rep. D.D. #1, Avengers #2,
    Marvel Mystery #8 . . . . 75.00

MARVEL SUPER-HEROES
[1st Regular Series] 1967–71
(Prev.: Fantasy Masterpieces)
12 GC,I&O:Captain Marvel 100.00
13 GC,2nd A:Captain Marvel 65.00
14 F:Spider-Man 90.00
15 GC,F:Medusa 30.00
16 I:Phantom Eagle 30.00
17 O:Black Knight 30.00
18 GC,I:Guardians o/t Galaxy 50.00
19 F:Kazar 15.00
20 F:Dr.Doom,Diablo 15.00
21 thru 31 reprints . . . . @12.00
32 thru 55 rep. Hulk/Submariner
    from Tales to Astonish . . . . . . @5.00
56 reprints Hulk #102 . . . . 3.50
57 thru 105 reps.Hulk issues . . . . @3.00

MARVEL SUPERHEROES
[2nd Regular Series] May, 1990
1 RLm,F:Hercules,Moon Knight,
    Magik,Bl.Panther,Speedball . . . 4.00
2 . . . . 3.50
3 F:Captain America,Hulk,Wasp . . 4.00
4 AD,F:SpM,N.Fury,D.D.,Speedball
    Wond.Man,Spitfire,Bl.Knight . . . 3.50
5 F:Thor,Thing,Speedball,
    Dr.Strange 3.50
6 RB,SD,F:X-Men,Power Pack,
    Speedball,Sabra 3.00
7 RB,F:X-Men,Cloak & Dagger . . . 2.75
8 F:X-Men,Iron Man,Namor 2.50
9 F:Avengers W.C.,Thor,Iron Man . . 3.00
10 DH,F:Namor,Fantastic Four,
    Ms.Marvel#24 . . . . 3.50
11 F:Namor,Ms.Marvel#25 . . . . . . 3.00
12 F:Dr.Strange,Falcon,Iron Man . . 3.00
13 F:Iron Man 2.75
14 BMc,RWi,F:Iron Man,
    Speedball, Dr.Strange 2.75
15 KP,DH,F:Thor,Iron Man,Hulk . . 2.75
Holiday Spec.#1 AAd,DC,JRu,F:FF,
    X-Men,Spider-Man,Punisher . . . 3.25
Holiday Spec.#2 AAd(c),SK,MGo,
    RLm,SLi,F:Hulk,Wolverine,
    Thanos,Spider-Man 3.25
Fall Spec.RB,A:X-Men,Shroud,
    Marvel Boy,Cloak & Dagger . . . 2.25

MARVEL SUPERHEROES MEGAZINE
1 thru 6 rep . . . . @2.95

MARVEL SUPER SPECIAL
See: MARVEL COMICS

MARVEL SWIMSUIT
1992
1 Schwing Break 4.95

MARVEL TAILS
Nov., 1983
1 ST,Peter Porker 2.00

MARVEL TALES
1964
1 All reprints,O:Spider-Man 275.00
2 rep.Avengers #1,X-Men #1,

Marvel Tales #134
© Marvel Entertainment Group

Hulk #3. . . . . 100.00
3 rep.Amaz.SpM.#6. . . . . 45.00
4 rep.Amaz.SpM.#7. . . . . 30.00
5 rep.Amaz.SpM.#8. . . . . 30.00
6 rep.Amaz.SpM.#9. . . . . 30.00
7 rep.Amaz.SpM.#10. . . . . 30.00
8 rep.Amaz.SpM.#13. . . . . 20.00
9 rep.Amaz.SpM.#14. . . . . 24.00
10 rep.Amaz.SpM.#15 . . . . 24.00
11 rep.Amaz.SpM.#16 . . . . 24.00
12 rep.Amaz.SpM.#17 . . . . 24.00
13 rep.Amaz.SpM.#18
   rep.1950's Marvel Boy 20.00
14 rep.Amaz.SpM.#19,
   reps.Marvel Boy 18.00
15 rep.Amaz.SpM.#20,
   reps.Marvel Boy 18.00
16 rep.Amaz.SpM.#21,
   reps.Marvel Boy 18.00
17 thru 22 rep.Amaz.SpM.
   #22-#27 . . . . @15.00
23 thru 27 rep.Amaz.SpM.
   #30-#34 . . . . @15.00
28 rep.Amaz.SpM.#35&36 . . . . . 15.00
29 rep.Amaz.SpM.#39&40 . . . . . 15.00
30 rep.Amaz.SpM.#58&41 . . . . . 15.00
31 rep.Amaz.SpM.#42 . . . . 15.00
32 rep.Amaz.SpM.#43&44 . . . . . 15.00
33 rep.Amaz.SpM.#45&47 . . . . . 15.00
34 rep.Amaz.SpM.#48 . . . . 6.00
35 rep.Amaz.SpM.#49 . . . . 6.00
36 thru 41 rep.
   Amaz.SpM.#51-#56 . . . . @6.00
42 thru 53 rep.
   Amaz.SpM.#59-#70 . . . . @6.00
54 thru 80 rep.
   Amaz.SpM.#73-#99 . . . . @6.00
81 rep.Amaz.SpM.#103 . . . . 6.00
82 rep.Amaz.SpM.#103-4 . . . . . . 6.00
83 thru 97 rep.
   Amaz.SpM.#104-#118 . . . . . @6.00
98 rep.Amaz.SpM.#121 . . . . 6.00
99 rep.Amaz.SpM.#122 . . . . 6.00
100 rep.Amaz.SpM.#123,BU:Two
   Gun Kid,Giant-Size. 3.50
101 thru 105 rep.Amaz.
   SpM.#124-#128 . . . . @3.00
106 rep.Amaz.SpM.#129,
   (I:Punisher) 4.00
107 thur 110 rep.Amaz.
   SpM.#130-133 . . . . @2.00
111 Amaz.SpM.#134,A:Punisher . . . 4.00
112 Amaz.SpM.#135,A:Punisher . . . 3.00
113 thru 125 rep.Amaz.Spider

Man #136-#148 . . . . @2.00
126 rep.Amaz.Spider-Man#149. . . . 4.00
127 rep.Amaz.Spider-Man#150. . . . 3.00
128 rep.Amaz.Spider-Man#151. . . . 4.00
129 thru 136 rep.Amaz.Spider
   Man #152-#159 . . . . @2.50
137 rep.Amaz.Fantasy#15 . . . . 7.00
138 rep.Amaz.SpM.#1 . . . . 7.00
139 thru 149 rep.
   AmazSpM#2-#12 . . . . @2.50
150 rep.AmazSpM Ann#1. . . . . . . 2.50
151 rep.AmazSpM#13 . . . . 2.50
152 rep.AmazSpM#14 . . . . 4.00
153 thru 190
   rep.AmazSpM#15-52 . . . . . @2.00
191 rep. #96-98 . . . . 2.25
192 rep. #121-122 . . . . 2.25
193 thru 198 rep.Marv.Team
   Up#59-64 . . . . @2.00
199 . . . . 2.00
200 rep. SpM Annual 14. . . . . 2.00
201 thru 206 rep.Marv.
   Team Up#65-70 . . . . @2.00
207 . . . . 2.00
208 . . . . 2.00
209 MZ(c),rep.SpM#129,Punisher. . 3.00
210 MZ(c),rep.SpM#134. . . . . 4.00
211 MZ(c),rep.SpM#135. . . . . 4.00
212 MZ(c),rep.Giant-Size#4 . . . . . 4.00
213 MZ(c),rep.Giant-Size#4 . . . . . 4.00
214 MZ(c),rep.SpM#161 . . . . 4.00
215 MZ(c),rep.SpM#162 . . . . 3.00
216 MZ(c),rep.SpM#174. . . . . 3.00
217 MZ(c),rep.SpM#175. . . . . 3.00
218 MZ(c),rep.SpM#201. . . . . 3.00
219 MZ(c),rep.SpM#202. . . . . 3.00
220 MZ(c),rep.Spec.SpM #81 . . . . 3.00
221 MZ(c),rep.Spec.SpM #82 . . . . 3.00
222 MZ(c),rep.Spec.SpM #83 . . . . 2.00
223 thru 227 TM(c),rep.
   SpM #88-92 . . . . @2.25
228 TM(c),rep.Spec.SpM.#17 . . . . 2.00
229 TM(c),rep.Spec.SpM.#18 . . . . 2.00
230 TM(c),rep.SpM #203 . . . . 2.00
231 TM(c),rep.Team-Up#108 . . . . 2.00
232 TM(c),rep. 2.00
233 TM(c),rep. X-Men. 2.00
234 TM(c),rep. X-Men. 2.00
235 TM(c),rep. X-Men. 2.00
236 TM(c),rep. X-Men. 2.00
237 TM(c),rep. 2.00
238 TM(c),rep. 2.00
239 TM(c),rep.SpM,Beast. 2.00
240 rep.SpM,Beast,MTU#90 . . . . . 1.50
241 rep.MTU#124. . . . . 1.50
242 rep.MTU#89,Nightcrawler 1.50
243 rep.MTU#117,SpM,Wolverine. . 1.50
244 MR(c),rep. 1.50
245 MR(c),rep. 1.50
246 MR(c),rep. 1.50
247 MR(c),rep.MTU Annual #6 . . . . 1.50
248 MR(c),rep. 1.50
249 MR(c),rep.MTU #14 . . . . 1.50
250 MR(c),rep.MTU #100 . . . . 1.50
251 rep.Amaz.SpM.#100 . . . . 1.50
252 rep.Amaz.SpM.#101 . . . . 3.50
253 rep.Amaz.SpM.#102 . . . . 3.00
254 rep.MTU #15,inc.2 Ghost
   Rider pin-ups by JaL 3.00
255 SK(c),rep.MTU #58,
   BU:Ghost Rider 1.75
256 rep. MTU. 1.50
257 rep.Amaz.SpM.#238 . . . . 1.50
258 rep.Amaz.SpM.#239 . . . . 1.50
259 thru 261 rep.Amaz.SpM.#249
   thru 251 . . . . 1.50
262 rep Marvel Team-Up #53 . . . . 1.25
263 rep Marvel Team-Up #54 . . . . 1.25
264 rep.B:Amaz.SpM.Ann.#5 . . . . 1.25
265 rep.E:Amaz.SpM.Ann.#5 . . . . 1.25
266 thru 274 rep.Amaz.SpM#252

Marvel Team-Up #36
© Marvel Entertainment Group

   thru #260. . . . . @1.25
275 rep.Amaz.SpM#261 . . . . 1.25
276 rep.Amaz.SpM#263 . . . . 1.25
277 rep.Amaz.SpM#265 . . . . 1.25
278 thru 282 rep.Amaz.SpM#268
   thru 272 . . . . 1.25
283 rep.Amaz.SpM#273 . . . . 1.25
284 rep.Amaz.SpM#275 . . . . 1.25
285 rep.Amaz.SpM#276 . . . . 1.25
286 rep.Amaz.SpM#277 . . . . 1.25
287 rep.Amaz.SpM#278 . . . . 1.25
288 rep.Amaz.SpM#280 . . . . 1.50
289 rep.Amaz.SpM#281 . . . . 1.25
290 & 291 rep.Amaz.SpM. 1.50

MARVEL TALES
See: MARVEL COMICS

MARVEL TEAM-UP
March, 1972
(Spider-Man in all,unless *)
1 RA,F:Hum.Torch,V:Sandman . 120.00
2 RA,F:Hum.Torch,V:Sandman . . 35.00
3 F:Human Torch,V:Morbius. . . . 50.00
4 GK,F:X-Men,A:Morbius. 50.00
5 GK,F:Vision 20.00
6 GK,F:Thing,O:Puppet Master,
   V:Mad Thinker 20.00
7 RA,F:Thor. 20.00
8 JM,F:The Cat 20.00
9 RA,F:Iron Man 20.00
10 JM,F:Human Torch 20.00
11 JM,F:The Inhumans 18.00
12 RA,F:Werewolf 20.00
13 GK,F:Captain America 25.00
14 GK,F:Sub-Mariner 15.00
15 RA,F:Ghostrider. 15.00
16 GK,JM,F:Captain Marvel 14.00
17 GK,F:Mr.Fantastic,
   A:Capt.Marvel 14.00
18 *F:Hulk,Human Torch. 14.00
19 SB,F:Ka-Zar 14.00
20 SB,F:Black Panther 17.00
21 SB,F:Dr.Strange 7.00
22 SB,F:Hawkeye. 7.00
23 *F:Human Torch,Iceman,
   C:Spider-Man,X-Men 8.00
24 JM,F:Brother Voodoo. 7.00
25 JM,F:Daredevil 7.00
26 *F:H.Torch,Thor,V:Lavamen . . 7.00
27 JM,F:The Hulk. 7.00

28 JM,F:Hercules 7.00	105 *F:Powerman,Iron Fist,Hulk . . . 3.00	Strange 2.00
29 *F:Human Torch,Iron Man 7.00	106 HT,F:Captain America 3.00	9 TPe,F:Sub-Mariner & Captain
30 JM,F:The Falcon 7.00	107 HT,F:She-Hulk 3.00	America 2.00
31 JM,F:Iron Fist 7.00	108 HT,F:Paladin 3.00	10 TPe,AW,F:Sub Mariner & Thing . 2.00
32 *F:Hum.Torch,Son of Satan 7.00	109 HT,F:Dazzler 3.00	11 TPe,AW,PO,F:Sub-Mariner & Iron
33 SB,F:Nighthawk 7.00	110 HT,F:Iron Man 3.00	Man, final issue 2.00
34 SB,F:Valkyrie 7.00	111 HT,F:Devil Slayer 3.00	
35 SB,*F:H.Torch,Dr.Strange 7.00	112 HT,F:King Kull 3.00	
36 SB,F:Frankenstein 6.00	113 HT,F:Quasar,V:Lightmaster. . . . 3.00	
37 SB,F:Man-Wolf 6.00	114 HT,F:Falcon 3.00	
38 SB,F:Beast 5.00	115 HT,F:Thor 3.00	
39 SB,F:H.Torch,I:Jean Dewolff . . . 5.00	116 HT,F:Valkyrie 3.00	
40 SB,F:Sons of the Tiger. 5.00	117 HT,F:Wolv,V:Prof Power 12.00	
41 SB,F:Scarlet Witch. 5.00	118 HT,F:Professor X 4.00	
42 SB,F:Scarlet Witch,Vision 5.00	119 KGa,F:Gargoyle 3.00	
43 SB,F:Dr.Doom 5.00	120 KGa,F:Dominic Fortune 3.00	
44 SB,F:Moon Dragon 5.00	121 KGa,F:Human Torch,I:Leap	
45 SB,F:Killraven 5.00	Frog(Frog Man) 3.00	
46 SB,F:Deathlok 6.00	122 KGa,F:Man-Thing 3.00	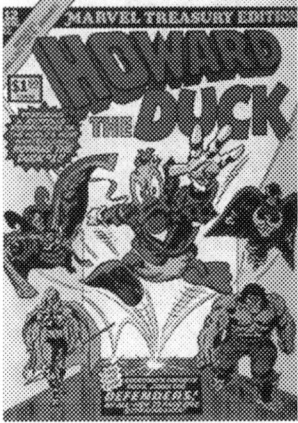
47 F:The Thing. 5.00	123 KGa,F:Daredevil 3.00	
48 SB,F:Iron Man,I:Wraith 5.00	124 KGa,F:Beast 3.50	
49 SB,F:Iron Man 5.00	125 KGa,F:Tigra 3.00	
50 SB,F:Dr.Strange 5.00	126 BH,F:Hulk 3.00	
51 SB,F:Iron Man 4.00	127 KGa,F:Watcher,X-mas issue . . 3.00	
52 SB,F:Captain America 4.00	128 Ph(c)KGa,F:Capt.America. . . . 3.00	
53 1st JBy New X-Men,F:Hulk . . . 25.00	129 KGa,F:The Vision 3.00	
54 JBy,F:Hulk,V:Woodgod 6.00	130 KGa,F:The Scarlet Witch 3.00	
55 JBy,F:Warlock,I:Gardener 8.00	131 KGa,F:Leap Frog. 3.00	
56 SB,F:Daredevil 5.00	132 KGa,F:Mr.Fantastic 3.00	
57 SB,F:Black Widow. 5.00	133 KGa,F:Fantastic Four. 3.00	
58 SB,F:Ghost Rider,V:Trapster . . . 5.00	134 F:Jack of Hearts 3.00	
59 JBy,F:Yellowjacket,V:Equinox. . . 5.00	135 F:Kitty Pryde 3.00	*Marvel Treasury Edition #12*
60 JBy,F:Wasp,V:Equinox. 5.00	136 F:Wonder Man. 3.00	*© Marvel Entertainment Group*
61 JBy,F:Human Torch 5.00	137 *F:Aunt May & F.Richards 3.00	
62 JBy,F:Ms.Marvel 5.00	138 F:Sandman,I:New Enforcers . . 3.00	
63 JBy,F:Iron Fist 5.50	139 F:Sandman,Nick Fury 3.00	**MARVEL**
64 JBy,F:Daughters o/t Dragon. . . . 5.00	140 F:Black Widow. 3.00	**TREASURY EDITION**
65 JBy,I:Captain Britain(U.S.)	141 SpM(2nd App Black Costume)	**Sept., 1974**
I:Arcade 7.50	F:Daredevil. 4.00	1 SD,Spider-Man,I:Contemplator . 25.00
66 JBy,F:Captain Britain 6.00	142 F:Captain Marvel(2nd one). . . . 3.00	2 JK,F:Fant.Four,Silver Surfer . . . 12.00
67 JBy,F:Tigra,V:Kraven 5.00	143 F:Starfox 3.00	3 F:Thor 10.00
68 JBy,F:Man-Thing,I:D'Spayre. . . . 5.00	144 F:M.Knight,V:WhiteDragon. . . . 3.00	4 BWS,F:Conan 9.00
69 JBy,F:Havok 6.00	145 F:Iron Man. 3.00	5 O:Hulk 8.00
70 JBy,F:Thor. 5.00	146 F:Nomad 3.50	6 GC,FB,SD,F:Dr.Strange 8.00
71 F:The Falcon,V:Plantman. 4.00	147 F:Human Torch 3.00	7 JB,JK,F:The Avengers 9.00
72 F:Iron Man. 4.00	148 F:Thor 3.00	8 F:X-Mas stories 10.00
73 F:Daredevil 4.00	149 F:Cannonball. 3.50	9 F:Super-Hero Team-Up. 8.00
74 BH,F:Not ready for prime time	150 F:X-Men,V:Juggernaut 5.50	10 F:Thor. 8.00
players(Saturday Night Live). . . 5.00	Ann.#1 SB,F:New X-Men 16.00	11 F:Fantastic Four. 8.00
75 JBy,F:Power Man 4.00	Ann.#2 F:The Hulk 5.00	12 F:Howard the Duck 8.00
76 HC,F:Dr.Strange 4.00	Ann.#3 F:Hulk,PowerMan. 4.00	13 F:X-Mas stories 8.00
77 HC,F:Ms.Marvel. 4.00	Ann.#4 F:Daredevil,Moon Knight. . 3.00	14 F:Spider-Man. 8.00
78 DP,F:Wonderman 4.00	Ann.#5 F:Thing,Scarlet Witch,	15 BWS,F:Conan,Red Sonja. 10.00
79 JBy,TA,F:Red Sonja. 5.00	Quasar,Dr.Strange 3.00	16 F:Defenders. 8.00
80 SpM,F:Dr.Strange,Clea 4.00	Ann.#6 F:New Mutants,Cloak &	17 F:The Hulk. 8.00
81 F:Satana 4.00	Dagger(cont.New Mutants#22) . 4.00	18 F:Spider Man,X-Men 10.00
82 SB,F:Black Widow 5.00	Ann.#7 F:Alpha Flight. 3.00	19 F:Conan 10.00
83 SB,F:Nick Fury 5.00		20 F:Hulk 10.00
84 SB,F:Master of Kung Fu 5.00		21 F:Fantastic Four 10.00
85 SB,F:Bl.Widow,Nick Fury 5.00	**MARVEL TEAM-UP INDEX**	22 F:Spider-Man. 10.00
86 BMc,F:Guardians o/t Galaxy . . . 4.00	**See: OFFICIAL MARVEL**	23 F:Conan 10.00
87 GC,F:Black Panther. 4.00	**INDEX TO**	24 F:The Hulk. 10.00
88 SB,F:Invisible Girl 4.00	**MARVEL TEAM-UP**	25 F:Spider-Man,Hulk. 10.00
89 RB,F:Nightcrawler 4.50		26 GP,F:Hulk,Wolverine,Hercules . 12.00
90 BMc,F:The Beast. 4.00		27 HT,F:Hulk,Spider-Man 10.00
91 F:Ghost Rider 4.00	**MARVEL TEAM-UP**	28 JB,JSt,F:SpM/Superman 18.00
92 CI,F:Hawkeye,I:Mr.Fear IV 3.50	**1997**	
93 CI,F:Werewolf	1 TPe,PO,AW, F:Spider-Man,	**MARVEL TREASURY**
I:Tatterdemalion (named) 4.00	Generation X 2.00	**OF OZ**
94 MZ,F:Shroud 3.50	2 TPe,PO,AW, F:Spider-Man &	**(oversized) 1975**
95 I:Mockingbird(Huntress). 4.00	Hercules. 2.00	1 JB,movie adapt. 4.00
96 F:Howard the Duck 3.50	3 TPe,DaR,AW, F:Spider-Man &	
97 *F:Hulk,Spiderwoman 3.50	Sandman 2.00	**MARVEL TREASURY**
98 F:Black Widow. 3.50	4 TPe,DaR,F:Spider-Man &	**SPECIAL**
99 F:Machine Man 3.50	Man-Thing 2.00	Vol. I Spider-Man, 1974 . . . . 4.00
100 FM,JBy,F:F.F.,I:Karma,	5 TPe,DaR,F:Spider-Man &	Vol. II Capt. America, 1976 . . . . . . 3.50
BU:Storm & Bl.Panther. 8.00	Mystery guest. 2.00	
101 F:Nighthawk 3.00	6 TPe,F:Spider-Man & Sub-Mariner 2.00	
102 F:Doc Samson,Rhino. 3.00	7 MWn,TPe,F:Spider-Man & Blade 2.00	
103 F:Antman. 3.00	8 TPe,F:Sub-Mariner & Doctor	
104 *F:Hulk,Ka-zar 3.00		

Marvel Triple Action #46
© Marvel Entertainment Group

MARVEL TRIPLE ACTION
Feb., 1972

1 Rep.	4.00
2 thru 47 rep.	@1.50
G-Size#1 F:Avengers	3.00
G-Size#2 F:Avengers	3.00

MARVEL TWO-IN-ONE
Jan., 1974
(Thing in all, unless *)

1 GK,F:Man-Thing	40.00
2 GK,JSt,F:Namor,Namorita	14.00
3 F:Daredevil	14.00
4 F:Capt.America,Namorita	14.00
5 F:Guardians of the Galaxy	15.00
6 F:Dr.Strange	15.00
7 F:Valkyrie	6.00
8 F:Ghost Rider	7.00
9 F:Thor	5.00
10 KJ,F:Black Widow	5.00
11 F:Golem	4.00
12 F:Iron Man	4.00
13 F:Power Man	4.00
14 F:Son of Satan	5.00
15 F:Morbius	5.00
16 F:Ka-zar	4.00
17 F:Spider-Man	4.50
18 F:Spider-Man	4.50
19 F:Tigra	4.00
20 F:The Liberty Legion	4.00
21 F:Doc Savage	3.50
22 F:Thor,Human Torch	3.50
23 F:Thor,Human Torch	3.50
24 SB,F:Black Goliath	3.50
25 F:Iron Fist	4.00
26 F:Nick Fury	3.00
27 F:Deathlok	4.00
28 F:Sub-Mariner	3.00
29 F:Master of Kung Fu	3.00
30 JB,F:Spiderwoman	4.00
31 F:Spiderwoman	3.00
32 F:Invisible girl	3.00
33 F:Modred the Mystic	3.00
34 F:Nighthawk,C:Deathlok	3.50
35 F:Skull the Slayer	3.00
36 F:Mr.Fantastic	3.00
37 F:Matt Murdock	3.00
38 F:Daredevil	3.00
39 F:The Vision	3.00
40 F:Black Panther	3.00
41 F:Brother Voodoo	3.00
42 F:Captain America	3.00

43 JBy,F:Man-Thing	5.00
44 GD,F:Hercules	3.00
45 GD,F:Captain Marvel	4.50
46 F:The Hulk	5.00
47 GD,F:Yancy Street Gang,	
I:Machinesmith	3.00
48 F:Jack of Hearts	3.00
49 GD,F:Dr.Strange	3.00
50 JBy,JS,F:Thing & Thing	3.50
51 FM,BMc,F:Wonderman,Nick	
Fury, Ms.Marvel	4.00
52 F:Moon Knight,I:Crossfire	3.00
53 JBy,JS,F:Quasar,C:Deathlok	3.50
54 JBy,JS,D:Deathlok,	
I:Grapplers	6.00
55 JBy,JS,I:New Giant Man	3.00
56 GP,GD,F:Thundra	2.50
57 GP,GD,F:Wundarr	2.50
58 GP,GD,I:Aquarian,A:Quasar	2.50
59 F:Human Torch	2.50
60 GP,GD,F:Impossible Man,	
I:Impossible Woman	2.50
61 GD,F:Starhawk,I&O:Her.	3.00
62 GD,F:Moondragon	3.00
63 GD,F:Warlock	3.00
64 DP,GD,F:Stingray,	
I:Serpent Squad	2.50
65 GP,GD,F:Triton	2.50
66 GD,F:Scarlet Witch,	
V:Arcade	2.50
67 F:Hyperion,Thundra	2.50
68 F:Angel,V:Arcade	2.50
69 GD,F:Guardians o/t Galaxy	2.50
70 F:The Inhumans	2.50
71 F:Mr.Fantastic,I:Deathurge,	
Maelstrom	2.50
72 F:Stingray	2.50
73 F:Quasar	2.50
74 F:Puppet Master,Modred	2.50
75 F:The Avengers,O:Blastaar	2.50
76 F:Iceman,O:Ringmaster	2.50
77 F:Man-Thing	2.50
78 F:Wonder Man	2.50
79 F:Blue Diamond,I:Star Dancer	2.50
80 F:Ghost Rider	2.00
81 F:Sub-Mariner	2.00
82 F:Captain America	2.00
83 F:Sasquatch	3.00
84 F:Alpha Flight	3.00
85 F:Giant-Man	2.00
86 O:Sandman	2.25
87 F:Ant-Man	2.00
88 F:She-Hulk	2.00
89 F:Human Torch	2.00

Marvel Two-In-One #84
© Marvel Entertainment Group

90 F:Spider-Man	2.25
91 V:Sphinx	2.00
92 F:Jocasta,V:Ultron	2.00
93 F:Machine Man,D:Jocasta	2.25
94 F:Power Man,Iron Fist	2.00
95 F:Living Mummy	2.00
96 F:Sandman,C:Marvel Heroes	2.00
97 F:Iron Man	2.00
98 F:Franklin Richards	2.00
99 JBy(c),F:Rom	2.00
100 F:Ben Grimm	2.50
Ann.#1 SB,F:Liberty Legion	5.00
Ann.#2 JSn,2nd D:Thanos,A:Spider	
Man,Avengers,Capt.Marvel,	
I:Lord Chaos,Master Order	12.00
Ann.#3 F:Nova	4.00
Ann.#4 F:Black Bolt	3.50
Ann.#5 F:Hulk,V:Pluto	3.00
Ann.#6 I:American Eagle	3.00
Ann.#7 I:Champion,A:Hulk,Thor,	
DocSamson,Colossus,Sasquatch,	
WonderMan	3.50

OFFICIAL HANDBOOK OF THE MARVEL UNIVERSE
Jan., 1983

1 Abomination-Avengers'	
Quintet	7.50
2 BaronMordo-Collect.Man	6.00
3 Collector-Dracula	5.00
4 Dragon Man-Gypsy Moth	5.00
5 Hangman-Juggernaut	5.00
6 K-L	4.00
7 Mandarin-Mystique	4.00
8 Na,oria-Pyro	4.00
9 Quasar to She-Hulk	4.00
10 Shiar-Sub-Mariner	4.00
11 Subterraneans-Ursa Major	4.00
12 Valkyrie-Zzzax	4.00
13 Book of the Dead	4.00
14 Book of the Dead	4.00
15 Weaponry	4.00

[2nd Series]

1 Abomination-Batroc	5.00
2 Beast-Clea	4.00
3 Cloak & D.-Dr.Strange	4.00
4 Dr.Strange-Galactus	4.00
5 Gardener-Hulk	4.00
6 Human Torch-Ka-Zar	3.25
7 Kraven-Magneto	3.25
8 Magneto-Moleman	3.25
9 Moleman-Owl	3.25
10	3.25
11	2.50
12 S-T	2.50
13	2.50
14 V-Z	2.50
15	2.50
16 Book of the Dead	2.50
17 Handbook of the Dead,inc.	
JLe illus.	2.50
18	2.50
19	2.50
20 Inc.RLd illus.	2.50

Marvel Universe Update

1 thru 8	@1.75

Marvel Universe Packet

1 inc. Spider-Man	5.50
2 inc. Captain America	4.50
3 inc. Ghost Rider	5.00
4 inc. Wolverine	4.50
5 inc. Punisher	4.25
6 inc. She-Hulk	4.00
7 inc. Daredevil	4.00
8 inc. Hulk	4.00
9 inc. Moon Knight	4.00
10 inc. Captain Britain	4.00
11 inc. Storm	4.00
12 inc. Silver Surfer	4.00

MARVEL

13 inc. Ice Man. 4.50
14 inc. Thor 4.50
15 thru 22. . . . . @4.50
23 inc. Cage. 4.50
24 inc. Iron Fist. 4.50
25 inc.Deadpool,Night Thrasher . . 4.50
26 inc. Wonderman 5.00
27 inc.Beta Ray Bill,Pip 5.00
28 inc.X-Men 5.00
29 inc.Carnage. 5.00
30 thru 36. . . . . @5.00

MARVEL UNIVERSE
1996
1 Post Onslaught. 2.95

MARVEL UNIVERSE
April 1998
1 CPa(c),RSt,SEp,AW,F:Human
   Torch,Capt.Am.,Namor,48pg. . 3.00
2A JBy(c),RSt,SEp,AW,V:Hydra,
   Baron Strucker. 2.00
2B DGb(c). 2.00
3 RSt,SEp,AW,V:Hydra 2.00
4 RSt,MM, all-star jam cover,
   F:Monster Hunters 2.00
5 MM,RSt,F:The Monster Hunters . 2.00
6 MM,RSt,F:Monster Hunters,pt.3 . 2.00
7 MM,RSt,F:Monster Hunters,pt.4 . 2.00

MARVEL VALENTINE'S SPECIAL
1997
1-shot MWa,TDF, 48pg 3.00

MARVEL X-MEN COLLECTION
1994
1 thru 3 JL from the 1st series
   X-Men Cards 3.25

MARVIN MOUSE
Atlas Sept., 1957
1 BEv,F:Marvin Mouse 30.00

MASTER OF KUNG FU, SPECIAL MARVEL ED.
April, 1974
Prev: Special Marvel Edition
17 JSn,I:Black Jack Tarr. 20.00
18 PG,1st Gulacy Art 14.00
19 PG,A:Man-Thing 10.00
20 GK(c),PG,AM,V:Samurai 10.00
21 AM,Season of Vengeance..
   Moment of Death 8.00
22 PG,DA,Death. 8.00
23 AM,KJ,River of Death 8.00
24 JSn,WS,AM,ST,Night of the
   Assassin 8.00
25 JSt(c),PG,ST,Fists Fury...
   Rites of Death 8.00
26 KP,ST,A:Daughter of
   Fu Manchu. 7.00
27 SB,FS,A:Fu Manchu 7.00
28 EH,ST,Death of a Spirit 7.00
29 PG,V:Razor-Fist. 7.00
30 PG,DA,Pit of Lions. 7.00
31 GK&DA(c),PG,DA,Snowbuster... 7.00
32 GK&ME(c),SB,ME,Assault on an
   Angry Sea 7.00
33 PG,Messenger of Madness,
   I:Leiko Wu 7.00
34 PG,Captive in A Madman's
   Crown 7.00

35 PG,V:Death Hand 7.00
36 The Night of the Ninja's 7.00
37 V:Darkstrider & Warlords of
   the Web 5.00
38 GK(c),PG,A:The Cat 5.00
39 GK(c),PG,A:The Cat 5.00
40 PG,The Murder Agency 5.00
41 . . . . 5.00
42 GK(c),PG,TS,V:Shockwave . . . 5.00
43 PG,V:Shockwave. 5.00
44 SB(c),PG,V:Fu Manchu 5.00
45 GK(c),PG,Death Seed 5.00
46 PG,V:Sumo 5.00
47 PG,The Cold White
   Mantle of Death 5.00
48 PG,Bridge of a 1,000 Dooms . . 5.00
49 PG,V:Shaka Kharn,The
   Demon Warrior. 5.00
50 PG,V:Fu Manchu 5.00
51 PG(c),To End...To Begin 5.00
52 Mayhem in Morocco 4.00
53 . . . . 4.00
54 JSn(c),Death Wears Three
   Faces. 4.00
55 PG(c),The Ages of Death. 4.00
56 V:The Black Ninja 4.00
57 V:Red Baron 4.00
58 Behold the Final Mask 4.00
59 GK(c),B:Phoenix Gambit,
   Behold the Angel of Doom 4.00
60 A:Dr.Doom,Doom Came 4.00
61 V:Skull Crusher 3.50
62 Coast of Death 3.50
63 GK&TA(c),Doom Wears
   Three Faces. 3.50
64 PG(c),To Challenge a Dragon . . 3.50
65 V:Pavane. 3.50
66 V:Kogar. 3.50
67 PG(c),Dark Encounters 3.50
68 Final Combats,V:The Cat. 3.50
69 . . . . 3.50
70 A:Black Jack Tarr,Murder
   Mansion 3.50
71 PG(c),Ying & Yang (c) 3.50
72 V:Shockwave. 3.50
73 RN(c),V:Behemoths 3.50
74 TA(c),A:Shockwave 3.50
75 Where Monsters Dwell. 3.50
76 GD,Battle on the Waterfront. . . 3.75
77 GD,I:Zaran 3.75
78 GD,Moving Targets 3.75
79 GD,This Side of Death. 3.75
80 GD,V:Leopard Men 3.75
81 GD,V:Leopard Men 3.75

82 GD,Flight into Fear 3.75
83 GD,. 3.75
84 GD,V:Fu Manchu. 3.75
85 GD,V:Fu Manchu. 3.75
86 GD,V:Fu Manchu. 3.75
87 GD,V:Zaran. 3.75
88 GD,V:Fu Manchu. 3.75
89 GD,D:Fu Manchu. 3.75
90 MZ,Death in Chinatown 3.75
91 GD,Gang War,drugs 4.00
92 GD,Shadows of the Past 3.75
93 GD,Cult of Death 3.75
94 GD,V:Agent Synergon 3.75
95 GD,Raid 3.75
96 GD,I:Rufus Carter 3.75
97 GD,V:Kung Fu's Dark Side. . . . 3.75
98 GD,Fight to the Finish 3.75
99 GD,Death Boat 3.75
100 GD,Doublesize 5.00
101 GD,Not Smoke,Nor Beads,
   Nor Blood. 3.75
102 GD,Assassins,1st GD(p) 4.00
103 GD,V:Assassins. 3.75
104 GD,Fight without Reason,
   C:Cerberus. 3.75
105 GD,I:Razor Fist 3.75
106 GD,C:Velcro 3.75
107 GD,A:Sata 3.75
108 GD 3.75
109 GD,Death is a Dark Agent 3.75
110 GD,Perilous Reign 3.75
111 GD 3.75
112 GD(c),Commit and Destroy . . . 3.75
113 GD(c),V:Panthers. 3.75
114 Fantasy o/t Autumn Moon . . . 3.75
115 GD. 3.75
116 GD. 3.75
117 GD,Devil Deeds Done
   in Darkness 3.75
118 GD,D:Fu Manchu,double 3.75
119 GD. 3.75
120 GD,Dweller o/t Dark Stream. . . 3.75
121 Death in the City of Lights'. . . . 2.00
122 . . . . 2.00
123 V:Ninjas. 2.00
124 . . . . 2.00
125 . . . . 2.00
G-Size#1,CR,PG 3.00
G-Size#2 PG,V:Yellow Claw 2.00
G-Size#3 . . . . 2.00
G-Size#4 JK,V:Yellow Claw 2.00
Spec.#1 Bleeding Black 3.25

MASTER OF KUNG FU: BLEEDING BLACK
1 V:ShadowHand, 1991. . . . . 2.95

MASTERS OF TERROR
July–Sept., 1975
1 GM(c),FB,BWS,JSn,NA 3.00
2 JSn(c),GK,VM, ... 2.00

MASTERS OF THE UNIVERSE
Star May, 1986—March, 1988
1 I:Hordak. 1.50
2 thru 12 . . . . @1.00
Movie #1 GT 2.00

MATT SLADE, GUNFIGHTER
Atlas May, 1956
1 AW,AT,F:Matt Slade,Crimson
   Avenger 100.00
2 AW,A:Crimson Avenger 75.00
3 A:Crimson Avenger 60.00

Master of Kung Fu #84
© Marvel Entertainment Group

4 A:Crimson Avenger 60.00
Becomes:

KID SLADE GUNFIGHTER
5 F:Kid Slade 60.00
6 . . . . 40.00
7 AW,Duel in the Night 60.00
8 July, 1957 . . . . 40.00

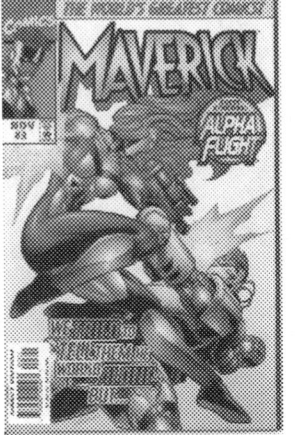

Maverick #3
© Marvel Entertainment Group

MAVERICK
1997
1 JGz,F:Christopher Nord/David
North/Maverick, 48pg 3.00
2 JGz,A:Victor Creed and Logan . . 2.00
2a variant cover. 2.00
3 JGz,V:Puck & Vindicator. 2.00
4 JGz,A:Wolverine. 2.00
5 JGz,A:The Blob 2.00
6 JGz,V:Sabretooth 2.00
7 JGz,V:Sabretooth 2.00
8 JGz,V:The Confessor 2.00
9 JGz,Maverick's secrets 2.00
10 JGz,V:Ivan the Terrible, Chris
Bradley becomes Bolt. 2.00
11 JGz,A:Darkstar,Vanguard,
Ursa Major 2.00
12 JGz, double sized last issue. . . . 3.00
1-shot LHa, V:Sabretooth,48pg. . . . 2.95

MELVIN THE MONSTER
Atlas July, 1956
1 . . . . 60.00
2 thru 6 . . . . @40.00
Becomes:

DEXTER THE DEMON
Sept., 1957
7 . . . . 25.00

MEMORIES
Epic
1 Space Adventures 2.50

MENACE
Atlas May, 1953
1 RH,BEv,GT,One Head Too
Many 500.00
2 RH,BEv,GT,JSt,Burton'sBlood . 350.00
3 BEv,RH,JR,The Werewolf . . . 250.00
4 BEv,RH,The Four Armed Man. 250.00

5 BEv,RH,GC,GT,I&O:Zombie . . 400.00
6 BEv,RH,JR,The Graymoor
Ghost 250.00
7 JSt,RH,Fresh out of Flesh. . . . 200.00
8 RH,The Lizard Man 200.00
9 BEv,The Walking Dead 225.00
10 RH(c),Half Man,Half... . . . . . 200.00
11 JKz,JR,Locked In,May, 1954 . 200.00

MEN IN ACTION
Atlas April, 1952
1 Sweating it Out 60.00
2 US Infantry stories 35.00
3 RH 25.00
4 War stories 25.00
5 Squad Charge 25.00
6 War stories 25.00
7 RH(c),BK,No Risk Too Great . . 45.00
8 JRo(c),They Strike By Night . . . 25.00
9 SSh(c),Rangers Strike Back . . 25.00
Becomes:

BATTLE BRADY
10 SSh(c),F:Battle Brady 100.00
11 SSh(c) 75.00
12 SSh(c),Death to the Reds 50.00
13 . . . . 50.00
14 Final Issue,June, 1953. . . . . . 50.00

MEN IN BLACK
1 ANi, prequel to movie (1997) . . . 4.00
Spec. Movie Adaptation (1997). . . . 4.00

MEN IN BLACK: RETRIBUTION
Aug., 1997
1 continuation from movie 2.50

MEN'S ADVENTURES
See: TRUE WESTERN

MEPHISTO vs. FOUR HEROES
April–July, 1987
1 JB,BWi,A:Fantastic Four. 2.50
2 JB,BWi,A:X-Factor 2.25
3 JB,AM,A:X-Men 2.25
4 JB,BWi,A:Avengers 2.00

METEOR MAN
1993–94
1 R:Meteor Man 1.25
2 V:GhostStrike,Malefactor,Simon . 1.25
3 A:Spider-Man 1.25
4 A:Night Thrasher 1.25
5 Exocet 1.25
6 final issue 1.25

[TED McKEEVER'S} METROPOL
Epic 1991–92
1 Ted McKeever 2.95
2 . . . . 2.95
3 . . . . 2.95
4 . . . . 2.95
5 . . . . 2.95
6 . . . . 2.95
7 . . . . 2.95
8 Return of Eddy Current. 2.95
9 `Wings of Silence'. 2.95
10 `Rotting Metal,Rusted Flesh' . . 2.95
11 `Diagram of the Heart' 2.95
12 . . . . 2.95

METROPOL A.D.
Epic 1992
1 R:The Angels 3.50
2 V:Demons 3.50
3 V:Nuclear Arsenal. 3.50

Micronauts #1
© Marvel Entertainment Group

MICRONAUTS
[1st Series] Jan., 1979
1 MGo,JRu,O:Micronauts 3.00
2 MGo,JRu,Earth. 2.50
3 MGo,JRu 2.00
4 MGo. 2.00
5 MGo,V:Prometheus 2.00
6 MGo. 2.00
7 MGo,A:Man Thing 2.00
8 MGo,BMc,I:Capt. Univ. 2.50
9 MGo,I:Cilicia. 2.00
10 MGo 2.00
11 MGo 2.00
12 MGo 2.00
13 HC,F:Bug 1.50
14 HC,V:Wartstaff. 1.50
15 HC,AM,A:Fantastic Four 1.50
16 HC,AM,A:Fantastic Four 1.50
17 HC,AM,A:Fantastic Four 1.50
18 HC,Haunted House Issue 1.50
19 PB,V:Odd John 1.50
20 PB,A:Antman. 1.50
21 PB,I:Microverse 1.50
22 PB. 1.50
23 PB,V:Molecule Man 1.50
24 MGo,V:Computrex 1.50
25 PB,A:Mentallo 1.50
26 PB,A:Baronkarza 1.25
27 PB,V:Hydra,A:Shield 1.25
28 PB,V:Hydra,A:Shield 1.25
29 PB,Doc Samson 1.25
30 PB,A:Shield. 1.25
31 PB,A:Dr.Strange 1.25
32 PB,A:Dr.Strange 1.25
33 PB,A:Devil of Tropica. 1.25
34 PB,A:Dr.Strange 1.25
35 O:Microverse 1.50
36 KG,Dr.Strange 1.50
37 KG,Nightcrawler 3.50
38 GK,1st direct 2.50
39 SD. 1.75
40 GK,A:FF 1.75
41 GK,Dr.Doom 1.25
42 GK 1.25
43 . . . . 1.25

44 . . . . 1.25	
45 Arcade. 1.25	
46 . . . . 1.25	
47 . . . . 1.25	
48 JG 2.00	
49 JG,V:BaronKarza. 1.50	
50 JG,V:BaronKarza. 1.50	
51 JG. 1.50	
52 JG. 1.50	
53 JG,V:Untouchables 1.50	
54 JG,V:Tribunal. 1.50	
55 JG,V:KarzaWorld. 1.50	
56 JG,Kaliklak 1.50	
57 JG,V:BaronKarza. 1.50	
58 JG,V:BaronKarza. 1.50	
59 JG,V:TheMakers. 1.50	
Ann.#1,SD 2.00	
#2 SD. 1.50	

[2nd Series]

1 V:The Makers. 1.50
2 AAd(c),V:The Makers 1.50
3 Huntarr'sEgg 1.00
4 V:The Makers. 1.00
5 The Spiral Path 1.00
6 L:Bug 1.00
7 Acroyear. 1.00
8 V:Scion 1.00
9 R:Devil 1.00
10 V:Enigma Force. 1.00
11 V:Scion 1.00
12 V:Scion 1.00
13 V:Dark Armada 1.00
14 V:Keys of the Zodiac 1.00
15 O:Marionette 1.50
16 Secret Wars II 1.50
17 V:Scion 1.00
18 Acroyear 1.00
19 R:Baron Karza 1.00
20 Last Issue 1.25

MICRONAUTS
(Special Edition) Dec., 1983
1 MGo/JRu,rep. 2.00
2 MGo/JRu,rep. 2.00
3 Rep.MG/JRu 2.00
4 Rep.MG/JRu 2.00
5 Rep.MG/JRu,April, 1984. . . . . 2.00

MIDNIGHT MEN
Epic *Heavy Hitters* 1993
1 HC,I:Midnight Men 2.75
2 HC,J:Barnett. 2.25
3 HC,Pasternak is Midnight Man . . 2.25
4 HC,Last issue. 2.25

MIDNIGHT SONS UNLIMITED
1993–95
1 JQ,JBi,MT(c),A:Midnight Sons . . 4.25
2 BSz(c),F:Midnight Sons 4.25
3 JR2(c),JS,A:Spider-Man 4.25
4 Siege of Darkness #17,
  D:2nd Ghost Rider 4.25
5 DQ(s),F:Mordred,Vengeance,
  Morbius,Werewolf,Blaze,
  I:Wildpride 4.25
6 DQ(s),F:Dr.Strange. 3.95
7 DQ(s),F:Man-Thing. 3.95
8 . . . . 3.95
9 J:Mighty Destroyer 3.95

MIGHTY MARVEL WESTERN
Oct., 1968
1 JK,All reprints,B:Rawhide Kid
  Kid Colt,Two-Gun Kids 25.00

---

2 JK,DAy,Beware of the Barker
  Brothers 20.00
3 HT(c),JK,DAy,Walking Death . . 20.00
4 HT(c),DAy 20.00
5 HT(c),DAy,Ambush 20.00
6 HT(c),DAy Doom in the Desert . 20.00
7 DAy,V:Murderous Masquerader 20.00
8 HT(c),DAy,Rustler's on the
  Range 20.00
9 JSe(c),JK,DAy,V:Dr Danger . . . 20.00
10 OW,DH,Cougar 20.00
11 V:The Enforcers 15.00
12 JK,V:Blackjack Bordon. 15.00
13 V:Grizzly 15.00
14 JK.V:The Enforcers 15.00
15 Massacre at Medicine Bend. . . 15.00
16 JK,Mine of Death. 15.00
17 Ambush at Blacksnake Mesa. . 15.00
18 Six-Gun Thunderer 15.00
19 Reprints cont 15.00
20 same 15.00
21 same 10.00
22 . . . . 10.00
23 same 10.00
24 JDa,E:Kid Colt. 10.00
25 B:Matt Slade 10.00
26 thru 31 Reprints . . . . @10.00
32 JK,AW,Ringo Kid #23. . . . . . . 7.00
33 thru 36 Reprints . . . . @7.00
37 JK,AW Two-Gun #51 . . . . 7.00
38 thru 45 Reprints . . . . @7.00
46 same,Sept., 1976 . . . . 7.00

MIGHTY HEROES
Nov., 1997
1-shot SLo, Diaper Man, Rope Man,
  Cuckoo Man, Tornado Man, Strong
  Man, etc. 3.00

SABAN'S MIGHTY MORPHIN POWER RANGERS
1 SLo,FaN,New ongoing series . . . 2.25
2 FaN,RLm,JP,more 1.75
3 FaN,RLm,JP,more adventures . . 1.75
4 LSn,JP,V:Glob monster. 1.75
5 . . . . 1.75
6 . . . . 1.75
7 Close Encounter with Alien 1.75
Photo Adaptation 2.95

SABAN'S MIGHTY MORPHIN POWER RANGERS: NINJA RANGERS/ VR TROOPERS
1 FaN,RLm,JP,flip book 1.75
2 JP,flip book. 1.75
3 New outfits 1.75
4 . . . . 1.75
5 . . . . 1.75
6 . . . . 1.75

MIGHTY MOUSE
[1st Series] Fall, 1946
1 Terytoons Presents 900.00
2 . . . . 450.00
3 . . . . 300.00
4 Summer, 1947 . . . . 300.00

MIGHTY MOUSE
Oct., 1990
1 EC,Dark Mite Returns. 3.00
2 EC,V:The Glove 2.00

Mighty Mouse #3
© *Marvel Entertainment Group*

3 EC/JBr(c)Prince Say More 1.50
4 EC/GP(c)Alt.Universe #1 . . . . . . 1.50
5 EC,Alt.Universe #2 . . . . 1.50
6 `Ferment',A:'MacFurline'. 1.50
7 EC,V:Viral Worm 1.25
8 EC,BAT-BAT:Year One,
  O:Bug Wonder 1.25
9 EC,BAT-BAT:Year One,
  V:Smoker. 1.25
10 `Night o/t Rating Lunatics' 1.25

MILLIE THE MODEL
Winter, 1945
1 O:Millie the Model,
  Bowling(c) 450.00
2 Totem Pole(c) 275.00
3 Anti-Noise(c) 175.00
4 Bathing Suit(c) 175.00
5 Blame it on Fame 175.00
6 Beauty and the Beast 175.00
7 Bathing Suit(c) 175.00
8 Fancy Dress(c),HK,Hey Look . 175.00
9 Paris(c),BW 200.00
10 Jewelry(c),HK,Hey Look. . . . 175.00
11 HK,Giggles and Grins 125.00
12 A;Rusty,Hedy Devine 100.00
13 A;Hedy Devine,HK,Hey Look. 125.00
14 HK,Hey Look 125.00
15 HK,Hey Look 75.00
16 . . . . 100.00
17 thru 20 . . . . @80.00
21 thru 30 . . . . @60.00
31 thru 75 . . . . @50.00
76 thru 99 . . . . @30.00
100 . . . . 35.00
101 thru 126 . . . . @25.00
127 Millie/Clicker 30.00
128 A:Scarlet Mayfair 25.00
129 The Truth about Agnes 25.00
130 thru 153 . . . . @25.00
154 B:New Millie. 25.00
155 thru 206 . . . . @25.00
207 Dec., 1973. . . . . 25.00
Ann.#1 How Millie Became
  a Model 150.00
Ann.#2 Millies Guide to
  the world of Modeling 125.00
Ann.#3 Many Lives of Millie 75.00
Ann.#4 Many Lives of Millie 30.00

MARVEL

MISS AMERICA COMICS
1944
1 Miss America(c),pin-ups ... 1,200.00

MISS AMERICA MAGAZINE
Nov., 1944—Nov. 1958
2 Ph(c),Miss America costume
  I;Patsy Walker,Buzz Baxter,
  Hedy Wolfe 1,000.00
3 Ph(c),A:Patsy Walker,Miss
  America............... 400.00
4 Ph(c),Betty Page,A:Patsy
  Walker,Miss America...... 400.00
5 Ph(c),A:Patsy Walker,Miss
  America 400.00
6 Ph(c),A:Patsy Walker 75.00
7 Patsy Walker stories........ 50.00
8 same 50.00
9 same 50.00
10 same 50.00
11 same 50.00
12 same 50.00
13 thru 18 .... @50.00
21 .... 55.00
22 thru 45 .... @35.00
46 thru 93 .... @30.00

MISS FURY COMICS
Timely Winter, 1942-43
1 Newspaper strip reprints,
  ASh(c) O:Miss Fury 2,700.00
2 V:Nazis(c) 1,200.00
3 Hitler/Nazi Flag(c) 1,000.00
4 ASh(c),Japanese(c) 750.00
5 ASh(c),Gangster(c) 700.00
6 Gangster(c) 650.00
7 Gangster(c) 600.00
8 Atom-Bomb Secrets(c)
  Winter, 1946 .... 600.00

MISTY
Star Dec., 1985
1 F:Millie the Models Niece 1.50
2 thru 5 .... @1.00
6 May, 1986 .... 1.00

MITZI COMICS
Timely Spring, 1948
1 HK:Hey Look,Giggles
  and Grins 125.00
Becomes:
MITZI'S BOYFRIEND
2 F:Chip,Mitzi/Chip(c) 50.00
3 Chips adventures 35.00
4 thru 7 same .... @35.00
Becomes:
MITZI'S ROMANCES
8 Mitzi/Chip(c) 40.00
9 .... 35.00
10 Dec., 1949................ 35.00

MODELING WITH MILLIE
See: DATE WITH MILLIE

MOEBIUS
Epic Oct., 1987
1 .... 12.00
2 .... 12.00
3 .... 15.00
4 .... 12.00
5 .... 12.00
6 1988 .... 12.00

MOEBIUS: FUSION
1 128pg Sketchbook 19.95

MOLLY MANTON'S ROMANCES
Sept., 1949
1 Ph(c),Dare Not Marry 85.00
2 Ph(c),Romances of 60.00
Becomes:
ROMANTIC AFFAIRS
3 Ph(c) 35.00

MONSTER MENACE
1 thru 4 SD,rep.............. @1.25

Frankenstein #13
© Marvel Entertainment Group

MONSTER OF FRANKENSTEIN
Jan., 1973
1 MP,Frankenstein's Monster.... 40.00
2 MP,Bride of the Monster 25.00
3 MP,Revenge................ 25.00
4 MP,Monster's Death 25.00
5 MP,The Monster Walks
  Among Us............... 25.00
Becomes:
FRANKENSTEIN
1973–75
6 MP,Last of the Frankensteins .. 15.00
7 JB,The Fiend and the Fury ... 15.00
8 JB,A:Dracula 25.00
9 JB,A:Dracula 25.00
10 JB,Death Strikes Frankenstein. 15.00
11 Carnage at CastleFrankenstein 10.00
12 Frankenstein's Monster today . 10.00
13 Undying Fiend 10.00
14 Fury of the Night Creature 10.00
15 Trapped in a Nightmare 10.00
16 The Brute and the Berserker .. 10.00
17 Phoenix Aflame 10.00
18 Children of the Damned
  Sept., 1975.............. 10.00

MONSTERS ON THE PROWL
See: CHAMBER OF DARKNESS

MONSTERS UNLEASHED
July, 1973
1 GM(c),GC,DW,B&W Mag 30.00
2 JB,FB,BEv,B:Frankenstein 25.00
3 NA(c),GK,GM,GT,B:Man-Thing 25.00
4 JB,GC,BK,I:Satana 25.00
5 JB 15.00
6 MP 15.00
7 AW 15.00
8 GP,NA 20.00
9 A:Wendigo 20.00
10 O:Tigra 20.00
11 FB(C),April, 1975.......... 20.00
Ann.#1 GK 20.00

MOON KNIGHT
[1st Regular Series] Nov., 1980
1 BSz,O:Moon Knight 5.00
2 BSz,V:Slasher 3.50
3 BSz,V:Midnight Man 3.50
4 BSz,V:Committee of 5 .... 3.50
5 BSz,V:Red Hunter 3.50
6 BSz,V:White Angels 3.50
7 BSz,V:Moon Kings 3.50
8 BSz,V:Moon Kings, Drug 3.00
9 BSz,V:Midnight Man 3.00
10 BSz,V:Midnight Man 3.00
11 BSz,V:Creed (Angel Dust) 3.00
12 BSz,V:Morpheus 3.00
13 BSz,A:Daredevil & Jester..... 3.00
14 BSz,V:Stained Glass Scarlet . . 3.00
15 FM(c),BSz,1st Direct 3.50
16 V:Blacksmith 3.00
17 BSz,V:Master Sniper 3.00
18 BSz,V:Slayers Elite 3.00
19 BSz,V:Arsenal 3.00
20 BSz,V:Arsenal 3.00
21 A:Bother Voodoo 2.25
22 BSz,V:Morpheus 2.50
23 BSz,V:Morpheus 2.50
24 BSz,V:Stained Glass Scarlet . . 2.50
25 BSz,Black Specter........... 2.50
26 KP,V:Cabbie Killer 2.00
27 A:Kingpin................. 2.00
28 BSz,"Spirits in the Sands" ... 2.00
29 BSz,V:Werewolf............. 2.50
30 BSz,V:Werewolf............. 2.50
31 TA,V:Savage Studs 2.00
32 KN,Druid Walsh 2.00
33 KN,V:Druid Walsh 2.00
34 KN,Marc Spector 2.00
35 KN,X-Men,FF,V:The Fly

Moon Knight #1
© Marvel Entertainment Group

MARVEL

DoubleSized.	3.00
36 A:Dr.Strange	2.00
37 V:Zohar	2.00
38 V:Zohar	2.00

[2nd Regular Series] 1985

1 O:Moon Knight,DoubleSize	2.00
2 Yucatan	2.00
3 V:Morpheus	2.00
4 A:Countess	2.00
5 V:Lt.Flint	2.00
6 GI,LastIssue	2.00

[3rd Regular Series] 1989–94

1 V:Bushmaster	4.00
2 A:Spider-Man	3.00
3 V:Bushmaster	2.50
4 RH,A:Midnight,Black Cat	2.50
5 V:Midnight,BlackCat	2.50
6 A:BrotherVoodoo	2.50
7 A:BrotherVoodoo	2.50
8 TP,A:Punisher,A of V	3.00
9 TP,A:Punisher,A of V	3.00
10 V:Killer Shrike,A of V	2.00
11 TP,V:Arsenal	2.00
12 TP,V:Bushman,A:Arsenal	2.00
13 TP,V:Bushman	2.00
14 TP,V:Bushman	2.00
15 TP,Trial o/Marc Spector #1,A:	
Silv.Sable,Sandman,Paladin . .	3.00
16 TP,Trial o/Marc Spector #2,A:	
Silv.Sable,Sandman,Paladin . .	3.00
17 TP,Trial o/Marc Spector #3	3.00
18 TP,Trial o/Marc Spector #4	3.00
19 RLd(c),TP,SpM,Punisher	3.00
20 TP,A:Spider-Man,Punisher	3.00
21 TP,Spider-Man,Punisher	3.00
22 I:Harbinger	2.00
23 Confrontation	2.00
24 A:Midnight	2.00
25 MBa,TP,A:Ghost Rider	3.00
26 BSz(c),TP,B:Scarlet Redemption	
V:Stained Glass Scarlet	2.00
27 TP,V:Stained Glass Scarlet	2.00
28 TP,V:Stained Glass Scarlet	2.00
29 TP,V:Stained Glass Scarlet	2.00
30 TP,V:Stained Glass Scarlet	2.00
31 TP,E:Scarlet Redemption,	
A:Hobgoblin	2.50
32 TP,V:Hobgoblin,SpM(in Black) . .	3.00
33 TP,V:Hobgoblin,A:Spider-Man . .	3.00
34 V:Killer Shrike	2.00
35 TP,Return of Randall Spector	
Pt.1,A:Punisher	2.00
36 TP,A:Punisher,Randall	2.00
37 TP,A:Punisher,Randall	2.00
38 TP,A:Punisher,Randall	2.00
39 TP,N:Moon Knight,A:Dr.Doom . .	2.00
40 TP,V:Dr.Doom	2.00
41 TP,Infinity War,I:Moonshade . . .	2.00
42 TP,Infinity War,V:Moonshade . . .	2.00
43 TP(i),Infinity War	2.00
44 Inf.War,A:Dr.Strange.FF	2.00
45 V:Demogoblin	2.00
46 V:Demogoblin	2.00
47 Legacy Quest Scenario	2.00
48 I:Deadzone	2.00
49 V:Deadzone	2.00
50 A:Avengers,I:Hellbent,	
Die-cut(c)	3.50
51 A:Gambit,V:Hellbent	2.00
52 A:Gambit,Werewolf	2.00
53 "Pang"	2.00
54	2.00
55 SPa,V:Sunstreak	6.00
56 SPa,V:Seth	6.00
57 SPa,Inf.Crusade	4.00
58 SPa(c),A:Hellbent	3.00
59 SPa(c)	3.00
60 E:TKa(s),SPa,D:Moonknight . . .	4.00
Spec.#1 ANi,A:Shang-Chi.	2.50
1-shot Moon Knight: Divided We Fall	

DCw,V:Bushman (1992)	4.95

MOON KNIGHT
(Special Edition) Nov., 1983

1 BSz,reprints	2.00
2 BSz,reprints	2.00
3 BSz,reprints,Jan., 1984.	2.00

MOON KNIGHT
Nov. 1997–Feb. 1998

1 (of 4) DgM, Moon Knight returns .	2.50
1 signed by Tommy Lee Edwards	
(250 copies)	20.00
2 DgM,A:Scarlet	2.50
3 DgM,Resurrection War,V:Black	
Spectre	2.50
4 DgM,Resurrecton War, concl. . . .	2.50

MOON KNIGHT
Dec. 1998

1 (of 4) DgM,MT,A:Marlene	3.00
2 DgM,MT	3.00
3 DgM,MT	3.00
4 DgM,MT,concl.	3.00

MOONSHADOW
Epic May, 1985

1 JMu,O:Moonshadow	4.00
2 JMu,Into Space	3.50
3 JMu,The Looney Bin	3.50
4 JMu,Fights Ira	3.50
5 JMu,Prisoner	3.50
6 JMu,Hero of War	3.50
7 JMu,UnkshussFamily	3.50
8 JMu,Social Outcast.	3.50
9 JMu,Search For Ira.	3.50
10 JMu,Internat.House of T	3.50
11 JMu,UnkshussFamily	3.50
12 JMu,UnkshussFamily,Feb.1987 .	3.50

MORBIUS
1992–95

1 V:Lilith,Lilin,A:Blaze,Gh.Rider,	
Rise o/t Midnight Sons #3,	
polybagged w/poster	3.00
2 V:Simon Stroud	2.50
3 A:Spider-Man	2.00
4 I:Dr.Paine,C:Spider-Man	2.00
5 V:Basilisk,(inc Superman tribute	

Morbius #11
© *Marvel Entertainment Group*

---

on letters page)	2.00
6 V:Basilisk	2.00
7 V:Vic Slaughter.	2.00
8 V:Nightmare	2.00
9 V:Nightmare	2.00
10 Two Tales	2.00
11 A:Nightstalkers	2.00
12 Midnight Massacre#4	2.50
13 R:Martine,A:Lilith	2.00
14 RoW,V:Nightmare,A:Werewolf . .	2.00
15 A:Ghost Rider,Werewolf.	2.00
16 GWt(s),Siege of Darkness#5 . . .	2.00
17 GWt(s),Siege of Darkness#17 . .	2.00
18 GWt(s),A:Deathlok	2.00
19 GWt(s),A:Deathlok	2.00
20 GWt(s),I:Bloodthirst	2.00
21 B:Dance of the Hunter,A:SpM . .	2.25
22 A:Spider-Man	2.25
23 E:Dance of the Hunter,A:SpM . .	2.25
24 Return of the Dragon	2.25
25 RoW	2.50
26	2.00
27	2.00
28 A:Werewolf	2.00
29	2.00
30 New Morbius	2.00
31 A:Mortine.	2.00
32 Another Kill	2.00

MORBIUS REVISITED
1993

1 WMc,rep.Fear #20	2.00
2 WMc,rep.Fear #28	2.00
3 WMc,rep.Fear #29	2.00
4 WMc,rep.Fear #30	2.00
5 WMc,rep.Fear #31	2.00

MORT THE DEAD TEENAGER
1993–94

1 LHa(s),I:Mort	1.75
2 thru 4 LHa(s), ...	1.75

MOTHER TERESA
1984

1 Mother Teresa Story	2.00

MOTOR MOUTH & KILLPOWER
Marvel UK 1992–93

1 GFr,A:Nick Fury,I:Motor	
Mouth,Killpower	2.50
2 GFr,A:Nick Fury, ...	2.00
3 GFr,V:Killpower,A:Punisher	2.00
4 GFr,A:Nick Fury,Warheads,	
Hell's Angel,O:Killpower	2.00
5 GFr,A:Excalibur,Archangel	2.00
6 GFr,A:Cable,Punisher.	2.00
7 EP,A:Cable,Nick Fury	2.00
8 JFr,A:Cable,Nick Fury.	2.00
9 JFr,A:Cable,N.Fury,V:Harpies . . .	2.00
10 V:Red Sonja	2.00
11 V:Zachary Sorrow	2.00
12 A:Death's Head II	2.00
13 A:Death's Head II	2.00

MS. MARVEL
Jan., 1977

1 JB,O:Ms Marvel	7.00
2 JB,JSt,V:Scorpion	5.00
3 JB,JSt,V:Doomsday Man	3.00
4 JM,JSt,V:Destructor	3.00
5 JM,JSt,A:V:Vision	3.00
6 JM,JSt,V:Grotesk	3.00
7 JM,JSt,V:Modok	3.00
8 JM,JSt,V:Grotesk	3.00

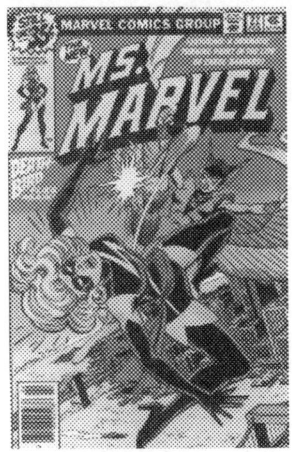

Ms. Marvel #22
© Marvel Entertainment Group

Mutant X #4
© Marvel Entertainment Group

9 KP,JSt,I:Deathbird 5.00
10 JB,TP,V:Deathbird,Modok 3.00
11 V:Elementals 3.00
12 V:Hecate 3.00
13 Bedlam in Boston 2.00
14 V:Steeplejack. 2.00
15 V:Tigershark. 2.00
16 V:Tigershark,A:Beast 14.00
17 . . . . 6.00
18 I:Mystique,A;Avengers 17.00
19 A:Captain Marvel. 3.00
20 V:Lethal Lizards,N:Ms.Marvel . . 2.00
21 V:Lethal Lizards. 2.00
22 V:Deathbirds 2.00
23 The Woman who Fell to Earth
   April, 1979 . . . . 2.00

MUPPET BABIES
Star August, 1984
1 thru 10 . . . . @1.00
11 thru 20 . . . . @1.00
21 thru 25 July, 1989 . . . . @1.00

MUPPETS TAKE MANHATTAN
1 movie adapt,November, 1984 . . . 1.00
2 movie adapt 1.00
3 movie adapt,Jan., 1985 . . . . 1.00

MUTANTS: THE AMAZING X-MEN
1 X-Men After Xavier 3.50
2 Exodus, Dazzler,V:Abyss 2.25
3 F:Bishop. 2.00
4 V:Apocalypse 2.00

MUTANTS: THE ASTONISHING X-MEN
1 Uncanny X-Men 3.50
2 V:Holocaust 2.25
3 V:Abyss 2.00
4 V:Beast,Infinities. 2.00

MUTANTS: GENERATION NEXT
1 Generation X Ax. 3.50
2 Genetic Slave Pens 2.25
3 V:Sugar Man 2.00
4 V:Sugar Man 2.00

MUTANT X
Aug. 1998
1 HMe,TR,F:Havok, 48pg 3.00
2 HMe,TR,F:Havok 2.00
2a variant cover. 2.00
3 HMe,TR,V:Pack 2.00
4 HMe,TR,V:Goblin Queen 2.00
5 HMe,F:Brute, Fallen 2.00
6 HMe,A:Mutant-X Spider-Man . . . 2.00
7 HMe,Trial of the Brute. 2.00
8 HMe,V:Goblin Queen 2.00
9 HMe,V:Sentinels. 2.00
10 HMe,V:The Six 2.00
11 HMe,Bloodstorm vs. Havok 2.00
12 HMe,O:Goblin Queen,Havok,
   48-page 3.00
13 O:Bloodstorm 2.00
GN Mutant X, rep.#1 & #2 . . . . . . 6.00
Ann. 1999, 48-page 3.50

MUTATIS
Epic
1 I:Mutatis 2.25
2 O:Mutatis 2.25
3 A:Mutatis 2.25

MY DIARY
Dec., 1949–March 1950
1 Ph(c),The Man I Love 75.00
2 Ph(c),I Was Anybody's Girl 60.00

MY LOVE
July, 1949
1 Ph(c),One Heart to Give 75.00
2 Ph(c),Hate in My Heart 50.00
3 Ph(c), ... 50.00
4 Ph(c),Betty Page, April,1950. . 200.00

MY LOVE
Sept., 1969
1 Love story reprints 25.00
2 thru 9 . . . . @4.00
10 . . . . 5.00
11 thru 38 . . . . @3.00
39 March, 1976 . . . . 3.00

MY ROMANCE
Sept., 1948
1 Romance Stories 75.00

2 . . . . 50.00
3 . . . . 50.00
Becomes:

MY OWN ROMANCE
4 Romance Stories Continue 75.00
5 thru 10 . . . . @40.00
11 thru 20 . . . . @35.00
21 thru 50 . . . . @30.00
51 thru 54 . . . . @25.00
55 ATh 35.00
56 thru 60 . . . . @25.00
61 thru 70 . . . . @20.00
71 AW 55.00
72 thru 76 . . . . @20.00
Becomes:

TEENAGE ROMANCE
77 Romance Stories Continue . . . 20.00
78 thru 85 . . . . @20.00
86 March, 1962 . . . . 20.00

MYS-TECH WARS
Marvel UK 1993
1 BHi,A:FF,X-Men,Avengers 2.00
2 A:FF,X-Men,X-Force. 2.00
3 BHi,A:X-Men,X-Force 2.00
4 A:Death's Head II 2.00

MYSTERY TALES
Atlas March, 1952
1 GC,Horror Strikes at Midnight . 650.00
2 BK,BEv,OW,The Corpse
   is Mine 325.00
3 RH,GC,JM, The Vampire
   Strikes 250.00
4 Funeral of Horror 250.00
5 Blackout at Midnight 250.00
6 . . . . 250.00
7 JRo,The Ghost Hunter 250.00
8 BEv 250.00
9 BEv(c),the Man in the Morgue 250.00
10 BEV(c),GT,What Happened
   to Harry 250.00
11 BEv(c) 200.00
12 GT,MF 225.00
13 . . . . 200.00
14 BEv(c),GT 200.00
15 RH(c),EK. 200.00
16 . . . . 200.00
17 RH(c). 200.00
18 AW,DAy,GC. 210.00
19 . . . . 185.00
20 Electric Chair 185.00
21 JF,MF,BP,Decapitation 200.00
22 JF,MF 200.00
23 thru 27 . . . . @150.00
28 . . . . 125.00
29 thru 32 . . . . @135.00
33 BEv 125.00
34 . . . . 125.00
35 BEv,GC 125.00
36 . . . . 135.00
37 DW,BP,JR 125.00
38 BP 125.00
39 BK 135.00
40 . . . . 135.00
41 MD,BEv. 125.00
42 . . . . 125.00
41 GC 125.00
44 AW 150.00
45 SD. 135.00
46 RC,SD,JP 150.00
47 DAy,BP 150.00
48 . . . . 125.00
49 GM,AT,DAy 125.00
50 JO,AW,GM. 150.00
51 DAy,JO 150.00
52 . . . . 125.00
53 . . . . 125.00

54 RC,August, 1957 . . . . 150.00

MYSTICAL TALES
Atlas June, 1956
1 BEv,BP,JO,Say the Magical
   Words 350.00
2 BEv(c),JO,Black Blob 200.00
3 BEv(c),RC,Four Doors To . . . 175.00
4 BEv(c).The Condemned 175.00
5 AW,Meeting at Midnight 175.00
6 BK,AT,He Hides in the Tower . 150.00
7 BEv,JF,JO,AT,FBe,The
   Haunted Tower 150.00
8 BK,SC, Stone Walls Can't
   Stop Him,August, 1957 . . . . 150.00

MYSTIC COMICS
Timely March, 1940
[1st Series]
1 ASh(c),O;The Blue Blaze,Dynamic
   Man,Flexo,B:Dakor the Magician
   A:Zephyr Jones,3X's,Deep Sea
   Demon,Bondage(c) 13,000.00
2 ASh(c),B:The Invisible Man
   Mastermind, ... 3,500.00
3 ASh(c),O:Hercules 2,500.00
4 ASh(c),O:Thin Man,Black Widow
   E:Hercules,Blue Blazes,Dynamic
   Man,Flexo,Invisible Man . . 2,800.00
5 ASh(c)O:The Black Marvel,
   Blazing Skull,Super Slave
   Terror,Sub-Earth Man 2,500.00
6 ASh(c),O:The Challenger,
   B:The Destroyer 2,800.00
7 S&K(c),B:The Witness,O:Davey
   and the Demon,E;The Black
   Widow,Hitler(c) 3,000.00
8 Bondage(c) 1,500.00
9 MSy,DRi,Hitler/Bondage(c) . 1,500.00
10 E:Challenger,Terror 1,500.00

[2nd Series] Oct., 1944
1 B:The Angel,Human Torch,
   Destroyer,Terry Vance,
   Tommy Tyme,Bondage(c) . 1,800.00
2 E:Human Torch,Terry
   Vance,Bondage(c) 1,000.00
3 E:The Angel,Tommy Tyme
   Bondage(c) 900.00
4 ASh(c),A:Young Allies
   Winter, 1944-45 . . . . 800.00

MYSTIC
[3rd Series] March, 1951
1 MSy,Strange Tree 650.00
2 MSy,Dark Dungeon 350.00
3 GC,Jaws of Creeping Death . 300.00
4 BW,MSy,The Den of the
   Devil Bird 600.00
5 MSy,Face 200.00
6 BW,She Wouldn't Stay Dead . 550.00
7 GC,Untold Horror waits
   in the Tomb 200.00
8 DAy(c),BEv,GK,A Monster
   Among Us 200.00
9 BEv 200.00
10 GC 200.00
11 JR,The Black Gloves 175.00
12 GC 175.00
13 In the Dark. 175.00
14 The Corpse and I 175.00
15 GT,JR,House of Horror. 175.00
16 A Scream in the Dark. 175.00
17 BEv,Behold the Vampire. 175.00
18 BEv(c),The Russian Devil . . . 175.00
19 Swamp Girl 175.00
20 RH(c). 175.00
21 BEv(c),GC. 150.00
22 RH(c). 150.00

23 RH(c),RA,Chilling Tales 150.00
24 GK,How Many Times Can
   You Die 150.00
25 RH(c),RA,E.C.Swipe 150.00
26 Severed Head(c) 150.00
27 Who Walks with a Zombie . . . 135.00
28 DW,Not Enough Dead 135.00
29 SMo,The Unseen. 135.00
30 RH(c),DW 135.00
31 SC,JKz 135.00
32 The Survivor 135.00
33 thru 36 . . . . @135.00
37 thru 51 . . . . @125.00
52. . . . . 125.00
53 thru 57 . . . . @125.00
58 thru 60 . . . . @110.00
61. . . . . 100.00

'NAM, THE
Dec., 1986
1 MGo,Vietnam War 3.00
1a 2nd printing 1.50
2 MGo,Dust Off 2.50
3 MGo,Three Day Pass 2.00
4 MGo,TV newscrew 2.00
5 MGo,Top Sgt. 2.00
6 MGo,Monsoon 2.00
7 MGo,Cedar Falls 2.00
8 MGo,5th to the 1st 2.00
9 MGo,ActionIssue 2.00
10 MGo,Saigon 2.00
11 MGo,Christmas 1.75
12 MGo,AgentOrange. 1.75
13 MGo 1.75
14 . . . . 1.75
15 ReturningVets 1.75
16 . . . . 1.75
17 Vietcong 1.75
18 . . . . 1.75
19 . . . . 1.75
20 . . . . 1.75
21 . . . . 1.75
22 Thanksgiving 1.75
23 XmasTruce of'67 . . . . 1.75
24 TetOffensive 1.75
25 TetOffensive-KheSanh 1.75
26 HomefrontIssue 1.75
27 Candle in the Wind 1.75
28 Borderline 1.75
29 PeaceTalks 1.75
30 TheBunker. 1.75
31 Fire and Ice 1.75

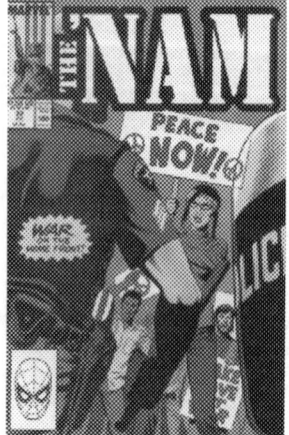

The 'Nam #32
© *Marvel Entertainment Group*

32 Nam in America. 1.75
33 SpecialistDaniels 1.75
34 OperationPhoenix 1.75
35 Xmas-BobHope 1.75
36 RacialTension 1.75
37 Colorblind 1.75
38 Minefields 1.75
39 . . . . 1.75
40 . . . . 1.75
41 ,A:Thor,Iron Man, Cap.Am 1.75
42 . . . . 1.75
43 . . . . 1.75
44 SDr 1.75
45 . . . . 1.75
46 . . . . 1.75
47 TD. 1.75
48 TD. 1.75
49 Donut Dolly #1. . . . . 1.75
50 HT,Donut Dolly #2 DoubSz 2.00
51 HT,Donut Dolly #3 . . . . 1.75
52 Frank Castle(Punisher)#1 . . . . 3.00
52a 2nd printing 2.00
53 Punisher #2. . . . . 2.00
54 Death of Joe Hallen #1 . . . . . . 1.75
55 TD,Death of Joe Hallen #2. . . . 1.50
56 TD,Death of Joe Hallen #3. . . . 1.50
57 TD,Death of Joe Hallen #4. . . . 1.50
58 TD,Death of Joe Hallen #5. . . . 1.50
59 P.O.W. Story #1 . . . . 1.50
60 P.O.W. Story #2 . . . . 1.50
61 P.O.W. Story #3 . . . . 1.50
62 Speed & Ice,pt.1 . . . . 1.50
63 Speed & Ice,pt.2 . . . . 1.50
64 Speed & Ice,pt.3 . . . . 1.50
65 Speed & Ice,pt.4 . . . . 1.75
66 RH,Speed & Ice,pt.5 . . . . 1.75
67 A:Punisher. 2.00
68 A:Punisher. 2.00
69 A:Punisher. 2.00
70 Don Lomax writes 1.75
71 Vietnamese Point of View 1.75
72 The trials of war. 1.75
73 War on the Homefront 1.75
74 Seige at An Loc. 1.75
75 My Lai Massacre 2.25
76 R:Rob Little 1.75
77 Stateside 1.75
78 . . . . 1.75
79 Beginning of the End#1 . . . . . . 1.75
80 MGo(c),'68 Tet Offensive 1.75
81 MGo(c),TET Offensive ends. . . . 1.75
82 TET Offensive 1.75
83 thru 84 Last issue 1.75
TPB rep. #1–#4 (1999) 14.95

'NAM MAGAZINE, THE
(B&W) Aug., 1988–May 1989
1 Reprints 3.00
2 thru 10 . . . . @2.50

NAMORA
Fall–Dec., 1948
1 BEv,DR 1,800.00
2 BEv,A:Sub-Mariner,Blonde
   Phantom 1,100.00
3 BEv,A:Sub-Mariner 1,000.00

NAMOR THE
SUB-MARINER
April, 1990
1 JBy,BWi,I:Desmond
   & Phoebe Marrs 3.50
2 JBy,BWi,V:Griffin 2.50
3 JBy,BWi,V:Griffin 2.50
4 JBy,A:Reed & Sue Richards,
   Tony Stark 2.50
5 JBy,A:FF,IronMan,C:Speedball . . 2.50
6 JBy,V:Sluj. 2.50

MARVEL

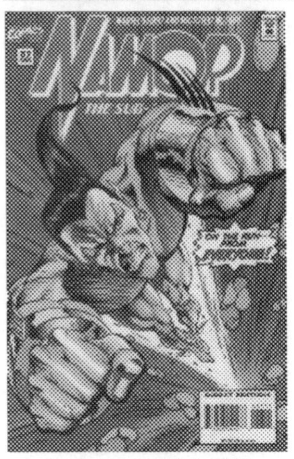

Namor, The Sub-Mariner #57
© Marvel Entertainment Group

52 Gl,I:Sea Leopard 1.75
53 Gl,V:Sea Leopard 1.75
54 Gl,I:Llyron 1.50
55 Gl,V:Llyron 1.50
56 Gl,V:Llyron 1.50
57 A:Capt. America, V:Llyron 1.50
58 . . . . 1.50
59 Gl,V:Abomination. 1.50
60 A:Morgan Le Fay. 1.50
61 Atlantis Rising 1.50
62 V:Triton 1.50
Ann.#1 Subterran.Odyssey #3 . . . 2.00
Ann.#2 Return o/Defenders,pt.3 . . 4.00
Ann.#3 I:Assassin,A:Iron Fist,
  w/Trading card 3.25
Ann.#4 V:Hydra 3.25

NAVY ACTION
August, 1954
1 US Navy War Stories 100.00
2 Navy(c) 50.00
3 thru 17 . . . . @35.00
18 August, 1957 . . . . 35.00

NAVY COMBAT
Atlas June, 1955
1 DH,B;Torpedo Taylor. 100.00
2 DH 50.00
3 DH 35.00
4 DH 35.00
5 DH 35.00
6 A:Battleship Burke 35.00
7 thru 10 . . . . @35.00
11 MD 30.00
12 RC. 55.00
13 . . . . 25.00
14 . . . . 30.00
15 . . . . 25.00
16 . . . . 25.00
17 AW 65.00
18 . . . . 25.00
19 . . . . 25.00
20 Oct., 1958 . . . . 25.00

NAVY TALES
Atlas Jan., 1957
1 BEv(c),BP,Torpedoes 125.00
2 AW,RC,One Hour to Live 80.00
3 JSe(c) 65.00
4 JSe(c),GC,JSt,RC,July, 1957 . . 65.00

NELLIE THE NURSE
Atlas 1945
1 Beach(c) 225.00
2 Nellie's Date(c) 100.00
3 Swimming Pool(c) 85.00
4 Roller Coaster(c) 85.00
5 Hospital(c),HK,Hey Look. 85.00
6 Bedside Manner(c) 75.00
7 Comic book(c)A:Georgie 75.00
8 Hospital(c),A:Georgie 75.00
9 BW,Nellie/Swing(c)A:Millie . . . 100.00
10 Bathing Suit(c),A:Millie. 80.00
11 HK,Hey Look 100.00
12 HK,Giggles `n' Grins 90.00
13 HK. 60.00
14 HK. 75.00
15 HK. 75.00
16 HK. 75.00
17 HK.A:Annie Oakley 75.00
18 HK. 75.00
19 . . . . 60.00
20 . . . . 60.00
21 . . . . 50.00
22 . . . . 50.00
23 . . . . 50.00
24 . . . . 50.00

7 JBy,V:Sluj 2.50
8 JBy,V:Headhunter,R:D.Rand. . . . 2.50
9 JBy,V:Headhunter. 2.50
10 JBy,V:Master Man,Warrior
  Woman 2.00
11 JBy,V:Mast.Man,War.Woman . . 2.00
12 JBy,R:Invaders,Spitfire 2.00
13 JBy,Namor on Trial,A:Fantastic
  Four,Captain America,Thor. . . . 2.00
14 JBy,R:Lady Dorma,A:Kazar
  Griffin 2.00
15 JBy,A:Iron Fist 2.00
16 JBy,A:Punisher,V:Iron Fist 2.00
17 JBy,V:Super Skrull(Iron Fist) . . 2.00
18 JBy,V:SuperSkrull,A:Punisher . . 2.00
19 JBy,V:Super Skrull,D:D.Marrs. . 2.00
20 JBy,Search for Iron Fist,
  O:Namorita. 2.00
21 JBy,Visit to K'un Lun 2.00
22 JBy,Fate of Iron Fist,
  C:Wolverine 2.00
23 JBy,BWi,Iron Fist Contd.,
  C:Wolverine 2.00
24 JBy,BWi,V:Wolverine 2.50
25 JBy,BWi,V:Master Khan 2.00
26 JaL,BWi,Search for Namor 5.00
27 JaL,BWi,V:Namorita. 4.00
28 JaL,BWi,A:Iron Fist 3.00
29 JaL,BWi,After explosion. 2.50
30 JaL,A:Doctor Doom 2.50
31 JaL,V:Doctor Doom. 2.50
32 JaL,V:Doctor Doom,
  Namor regains memory 2.50
33 JaL,V:Master Khan 2.00
34 JaL,R:Atlantis 2.00
35 JaL,V:Tiger Shark 2.00
36 JaL,I:Suma-Ket,A:Tiger Shark . . 2.00
37 JaL,Blue Holo-Grafix,Altantean
  Civil War,N:Namor 2.50
38 JaL,O:Suma-Ket 2.00
39 A:Tigershark,V:Suma-Ket. 1.50
40 V:Suma-Ket. 1.50
41 V:War Machine 1.50
42 MCW,A:Stingray,V:Dorcas 1.50
43 MCW,V:Orka,Dorcas 1.50
44 I:Albatross 1.50
45 Gl,A:Sunfire,V:Attuma 1.50
46 Gl,. 1.50
47 Gl,Starblast #2 . . . . 1.50
48 Gl,Starblast #9,A:FF 1.50
49 Gl,A:Ms. Marrs 1.50
50 Gl,Holo-grafx(c),A:FF. 3.00
50a Newsstand Ed. 2.00
51 AaL, ... 1.75

25 . . . . 50.00
26 . . . . 50.00
27 . . . . 50.00
28 HK,Rusty Reprint. 55.00
29 thru 35 . . . . @40.00
36 Oct., 1952 . . . . 40.00

NEW ADVENTURES OF CHOLLY & FLYTRAP
Epic
1 . . . . 4.95
2 . . . . 3.95
3 . . . . 3.95

NEW MUTANTS, THE
March, 1983
1 BMc,MG,O:New Mutants 5.00
2 BMc,MG,V:Sentinels. 4.00
3 BMc,MG,V:Brood Alien. 3.00
4 SB,BMc,A:Peter Bristow 3.00
5 SB,BMc,A:Dark Rider 3.00
6 SB,AG,V:Viper 3.00
7 SB,BMc,V:Axe 3.00
8 SB,BMc,I:Amara Aquilla 3.00
9 SB,TMd,I:Selene 3.00
10 SB,BMc,C:Magma 3.00
11 SB,TMd,I:Magma 3.00
12 SB,TMd,J:Magma 3.00
13 SB,TMd,I:Cypher(Doug Ramsey)
  A:Kitty Pryde,Lilandra. 4.00
14 SB,TMd,J:Magik,A:X-Men 3.00
15 SB,TMd,Mass.Academy. 3.00
16 SB,TMd,V:Hellions,I:Warpath
  I:Jetstream 4.00
17 SB,TMd,V:Hellions,A:Warpath . . 4.00
18 BSz,V:Demon Bear,I:New
  Warlock,Magus. 5.00
19 BSz,V:Demon Bear 3.00
20 BSz,V:Demon Bear 3.00
21 BSz,O&J:Warlock,doub.sz 5.00
22 BSz,A:X-Men. 3.50
23 BSz,Sunspot,Cloak & Dagger . . 3.00
24 BSz,A:Cloak & Dagger. 3.00
25 BSz,A:Cloak & Dagger. 6.00
26 BSz,I:Legion(Prof.X's son) 7.00
27 BSz,V:Legion. 4.00
28 BSz,O:Legion 4.00
29 BSz,V:Gladiators,I:Guido
  (Strong Guy) 3.00
30 BSz,A:Dazzler. 3.00
31 BSz,A:Shadowcat 3.00
32 SL,V:Karma. 3.00

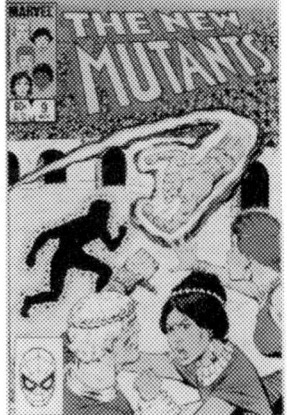

New Mutants #9
© Marvel Entertainment Group

33 SL,V:Karma 3.00
34 SL,V:Amahl Farouk 3.00
35 BSz,J:Magneto 3.00
36 BSz,A:Beyonder 3.00
37 BSz,D:New Mutants 3.00
38 BSz,A:Hellions 3.00
39 BSz,A:White Queen 3.00
40 JG,KB,V:Avengers 3.00
41 JG,TA,Mirage 3.00
42 JG,KB,A:Dazzler 3.00
43 SP,V:Empath,A:Warpath 3.00
44 JG,V:Legion 5.00
45 JG,A:Larry Bodine 3.00
46 JG,KB,Mutant Massacre 3.50
47 JG,KB,V:Magnus 3.00
48 JG,CR,Future 3.00
49 VM,Future 3.00
50 JG,V:Magus,R:Prof.X 4.00
51 KN,A:Star Jammers 3.00
52 RL,DGr,Limbo 3.00
53 RL,TA,V:Hellions 3.00
54 SB,TA,N:New Mutants 3.00
55 BBI,TA,V:Aliens 3.00
56 JBr,TA,V:Hellions,A:Warpath . . . 3.00
57 BBI,TA,I&J:Bird-Boy 3.00
58 BBI,TA,Bird-Boy 3.00
59 BBI,TA,Fall of Mutants,
   V:Dr.Animus 3.00
60 BBI,TA,F.of M.,D:Cypher 2.50
61 BBI,TA,Fall of Mutants 2.50
62 JMu,A:Magma,Hellions 2.50
63 BHa,JRu,Magik 2.50
64 BBI,TA,R:Cypher 2.50
65 BBI,TA,V:FreedomForce 2.50
66 BBI,TA,V:Forge 2.50
67 BBI,I:Gosamyr 2.50
68 BBI,V:Gosamyr 2.50
69 BBI,AW,I:Spyder 2.50
70 TSh,AM,V:Spyder 2.50
71 BBI,AW,V:N'Astirh 2.50
72 BBI,A,Inferno 2.50
73 BBI,W,A:Colossus 3.00
74 BBI,W,A:X-Terminators 2.50
75 JBy,Mc,Black King,V:Magneto . . 3.50
76 RB,TP,J:X-Terminators 2.50
77 RB,V:Mirage 2.50
78 RL,AW,V:FreedomForce 2.50
79 BBI,AW,V:Hela 2.50
80 BBI,AW,Asgard 2.50
81 LW,TSh,JRu,A:Hercules 2.50
82 BBI,AW,Asgard 2.50
83 BBI,Asgard 2.50
84 TSh,AM,A:QueenUla 2.50
85 RLd&TMc(c),BBI,V:Mirage 5.00
86 RLd,BWi,V:Vulture,C:Cable 6.00
87 RLd,BWi,I:Mutant Liberation
   Front,Cable 15.00
87a 2nd Printing 2.00
88 RLd,2nd Cable,V:Freedom
   Force 7.00
89 RLd,V:Freedom Force 6.00
90 RLd,A:Caliban,V:Sabretooth . . . 6.00
91 RLd,A:Caliban,Masque,
   V:Sabretooth 6.00
92 RLd(c),BH,V:Skrulls 4.00
93 RLd,A:Wolverine,Sunfire,
   V:Mutant Liberation Front 6.00
94 RLd,A:Wolverine,Sunfire,
   V:Mutant Liberation Front 5.00
95 RLd,Extinction Agenda,V:Hodge
   A:X-Men,X-Factor,D:Warlock . . 5.00
95a 2nd printing(gold) 5.00
96 RLd,ATb,JRu,Extinction Agenda
   V:Hodge,A:X-Men,X-Factor . . . 5.00
97 E:LSi(s),RLd(c),JRu,Extinction
   Agenda,V:Hodge 5.00
98 FaN(s),RLd,I:Deadpool,Domino,
   Gideon,L:Rictor 9.00
99 FaN(s),RLd,I:Feral,Shatterstar,
   L:Sunpst,J:Warpath 5.00
100 FaN(s),RLd,J:Feral,Shatterstar,

I:X-Force,V:Masque,Imperial
   Protectorate,A:MLF 6.00
100a 2nd Printing(Gold) 4.00
100b 3rd Printing(Silver) 3.50
Ann.#1 BMc,TP,L.Cheney 7.00
Ann.#2 AD,V:Mojo,I:Psylocke,Meggan
   (American App.) 9.00
Ann.#3 AD,PN,V:Impossible Man . . 4.00
Ann.#4 JBr,BMc,Evol.Wars 6.00
Ann.#5 RLd,JBg,MBa,KWi,Atlantis
   Attacks,A:Namorita,I:Surf 8.00
Ann.#6 RLd(c),Days o/Future Present
   V:FranklinRichards,(Pin-ups) . . 6.00
Ann.#7 JRu,RLd,Kings of Pain,
   I:Piecemeal & Harness,
   Pin-ups X-Force 5.00
Spec #1,AAd,TA,Asgard War 6.00
Summer Spec.#1 BBI,Megapolis . . 3.50
TPB New Mutants: Demon Bear,
   CCI/BSz,Rep #18–#21 . . . . . . 8.95

NEW MUTANTS
Sept. 1997
1 (of 3) BRa,BCh,F:Cannonball,
   Moonstar, Wolfsbane,Karma &
   Sunspot 2.50
2 BRa,BCh,meeting with mutants
   of the past 2.50
3 BRa,BCh, will Magik return
   for good? 2.50

NEW WARRIORS
July, 1990
1 B:FaN(s),MBa,AW,V:Terrax,
   O:New Warriors 4.00
1a Gold rep. 2.50
2 FaN(s),MBa,AW,I:Midnight's Fire,
   Silhouette 3.50
3 MBa,LMa(i),V:Mad Thinker 3.50
4 MBa,LMa(i),I:Psionex 3.50
5 MBa,LMa(i),V:Star Thief,
   C:White Queen 3.50
6 MBa,LMa(i),V:StarThief,
   A:Inhumans 3.50
7 MBa,LMa(i),V:Bengal,
   C:Punisher 3.50
8 MBa,LMa(i),V:Punisher,
   I:Force of Nature 3.50
9 MBa,LMa(i),V:Punisher,Bengal,
   Force of Nature 3.50
10 MBa,LMa(i),V:Hellions,White
   Queen,I:New Sphinx 3.50

New Warriors #10
© *Marvel Entertainment Group*

11 MBa,LMa(i),V:Sphinx,
   B:Forever Yesterday 2.50
12 MBa,LMa(i),V:Sphinx 2.50
13 MBa,LMa(i),V:Sphinx,
   E:Forever Yesterday 2.50
14 MBa,LMa(i),A:Namor,
   Darkhawk 2.50
15 MBa,LMa(i),V:Psionex,
   R:Terrax,N:Nova 2.50
16 MBa,LMa(i),A:Psionex,
   V:Terrax 2.50
17 MBa,LMa(i),A:Silver Surfer,Fant.
   Four,V:Terrax,I:Left Hand 2.50
18 MBa,LMa(i),O:Night Thrasher . . 2.00
19 MBa,LMa(i),V:Gideon 2.00
20 MBa,LMa(i),V:Clan Yashida,
   Marvel Boy kills his father 2.00
21 MBa,LMa(i),I:Folding Circle 2.00
22 MBa,LMa(i),A:Darkhawk,Rage . . 2.00
23 MBa,LMa(i),V:Folding Circle 2.00
24 LMa(i),V:Folding Circle 2.00
25 MBa,LMa(i),Die-Cut(c),Marvel Boy
   found guilty of murder,D:Tai,
   O:Folding Circle 2.50
26 DaR,LMa(i),V:Guardsmen 2.00
27 DaR,LMa(i),Inf.War,Speedball Vs.
   his doppelganger,N:Rage 2.00
28 DaR,LMa(i),I:Turbo,Cardinal . . . 2.00
29 DaR,LMa(i),V:Trans-Sabal 2.00
30 DaR,LMa(i),V:Trans Sabal 2.00
31 DaR,LMa(i)A:Cannonball,Warpath,
   Magma,O&N:Firestar 2.00
32 DaR,LMa(i),B:Forces of Darkness,
   Forces of Light,A:Spider-Man,
   Archangel,Dr.Strange 1.75
33 DaR,LMa(i),A:Cloak & Dagger,
   Turbo,Darkhawk 1.75
34 DaR,LMa(i),A:Avengers,SpM,
   Thing,Torch,Darkhawk,
   C:Darkling 1.75
35 DaR,LMa(i),A:Turbo 1.75
36 DaR,LMa(i),A:Turbo 1.75
37 F:Marvel Boy,V:Wizard 1.75
38 DaR,LMa(i),D:Rage's granny,
   V:Poison Memories 1.75
39 DaR,LMa(i),L:Namorita 1.75
40 DaR,LMa(i),B:Starlost,
   V:Supernova 2.50
40a Newsstand Ed. 1.50
41 DaR,LMa(i),V:Supernova 1.75
42 DaR,LMa(i),E:Starlost,N:Nova,
   V:Supernova 1.75
43 DaR,LMa(i),N&I:Justice
   (Marvel Boy) 1.75
44 Ph(c),DaR,LMa(i),N&I:Kymaera
   (Namorita) 1.75
45 DaR,LMa(i),Child's Play#2,
   N:Silhouette,Speedball,
   V:Upstarts 1.75
46 DaR,LMa(i),Child's Play#4,
   V:Upstarts 1.75
47 DaR,LMa(i),Time&TimeAgain,pt.1,
   A:Sphinx,I:Powerpax 1.75
48 DaR,LMa(i),Time&TimeAgain,pt.4,
   J:Cloak&Dagger,Darkhawk,Turbo,
   Powerpax,Bandit 1.75
49 DaR,LMa(i),Time&TimeAgain,pt.8
   V:Sphinx 1.75
50 reg. (c) 2.00
50a Glow-in-the-dark(c),V:Sphinx . . 3.25
51 revamp 1.50
52 R:Psionex 1.50
53 V:Psionex 1.50
54 V:Speedball 1.50
55 V:Soldiers of Misfortune 1.50
56 V:Soldiers 1.50
57 A:Namor 1.50
58 F:Psionex 1.50
59 F:Speedball 1.50
60 Nova Omega,pt.2 . . . . 2.50
61 J:Scarlet Spider,Maximum

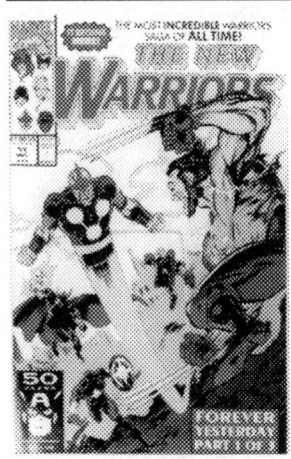

New Warriors #11
© Marvel Entertainment Group

Clonage prologue 1.50
62 F:Scarlet Spider,Maximum
　Clonage tie-in 1.50
63 F:Firestar. 1.50
64 I:Psionix 1.50
65 F:Scarlet Spider,V:Kymaera 1.50
66 F:Speedball 1.50
67 Nightmare in Scarlet,pt.2 . . . . . 1.50
68 Future Shock,pt.1 . . . . 1.50
69 . . . . 1.50
70 . . . . 1.50
71 Future Shock,pt.4 . . . . 1.50
Ann.#1 MBa,A:X-Force,V:Harness,
　Piecemeal,Kings of Pain #2 . . . 4.00
Ann.#2 Hero Killers #4,V:Sphinx . . . 2.75
Ann.#3 LMa(i),E:Forces of Light,
　Forces of Darkness,I:Darkling
　w/card 3.25
Ann.#4 DaR(s),V:Psionex 3.25
TPB New Beginnings rep.Thor #411,
　412,New Warriors #1-#4 . . . 12.95

NEW WARRIORS
Aug. 1999
1 F:Speedball,48-page 3.00

NFL SUPERPRO
1 . . . . 7.00
Spec.#1 reprints 2.00
[Regular Series] Oct., 1991
1 A:Spider-Man,I:Sanzionaire 2.50
2 V:Quickkick 1.25
3 I:Instant Replay 1.00
4 V:Sanction 1.00
5 A:Real NFL Player 1.25
6 Racism Iss.,recalled by Marvel . . 6.00
7 thru 11 . . . . @1.25
12 V:Nefarious forces of evil 1.25

NICK FURY, AGENT
OF S.H.I.E.L.D.
[1st Regular Series] June, 1968
1 JSo/JSt,I:Scorpio 75.00
2 JSo,A:Centaurius 40.00
3 JSo,DA,V:Hell Hounds 35.00
4 FS,O:Nick Fury 30.00
5 JSo,V:Scorpio 30.00
6 FS,"Doom must Fall" 15.00
7 FS,V:S.H.I.E.L.D. 15.00
8 FS,Hate Monger 8.00
9 FS,Hate Monger 8.00

10 FS,JCr,Hate Monger 8.00
11 BS(c),FS,Hate Monger 8.00
12 BS 10.00
13 . . . . 6.00
14 . . . . 6.00
15 I:Bullseye 28.00
16 JK,rep 4.00
17 JK,rep 4.00
18 JK,rep 4.00
[Limited Series] 1983–94
1 JSo,rep 3.00
2 JSo,rep 2.00
[2nd Regular Series] 1989–93
1 BH,I:New Shield,V:Death's
　Head(not British hero) 3.00
2 KP,V:Death's Head 2.00
3 KP,V:Death's Head 1.50
4 KP,V:Death's Head 1.50
5 KP,V:Death's Head 1.50
6 KP,V:Death's Head 1.50
7 KP,Chaos Serpent #1 . . . . 1.50
8 KP,Chaos Serpent #2 . . . . 1.50
9 KP,Chaos Serpent #3 . . . . 1.50
10 KP,Chaos Serpent ends,
　A:Capt.America 1.50
11 D:Murdo MacKay 1.50
12 Hydra Affair #1 . . . . 1.50
13 Hydra Affair #2 . . . . 1.50
14 Hydra Affair #3 . . . . 1.50
15 Apogee of Disaster #1 . . . . 1.50
16 Apogee of Disaster #2 . . . . 1.50
17 Apogee of Disaster #3 . . . . 1.50
18 Apogee of Disaster #4 . . . . 1.50
19 Apogee of Disaster #5 . . . . 1.50
20 JG,A:Red Skull 2.50
21 JG,R:Baron Strucker 2.00
22 JG,A:Baron Strucker,R:Hydra . . 2.00
23 JG,V:Hydra 2.00
24 A:Capt.Am,Thing,V:Mandarin . . 1.75
25 JG,Shield Vs. Hydra 2.00
26 JG,A:Baron Strucker,
　C:Wolverine 2.50
27 JG,V:Hydra,A:Wolverine 2.50
28 V:Hydra,A:Wolverine 2.50
29 V:Hydra,A:Wolverine 2.50
30 R:Leviathan,A:Deathlok 2.00
31 A:Deathlok,V:Leviathan 2.00
32 V:Leviathan 2.00
33 Super-Powered Agents 2.00
34 A:Bridge(X-Force),V:Balance
　of Terror 2.00
35 A:Cage,V:Constrictor 2.00
36 . . . . 2.00

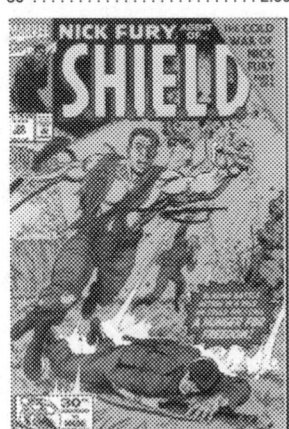

Niick Fury, Agent of S.H.I.E.L.D. #39
© Marvel Entertainment Group

37 . . . . 2.00
38 Cold War of Nick Fury #1 . . . . . 2.00
39 Cold War of Nick Fury #2 . . . . . 2.00
40 Cold War of Nick Fury #3 . . . . . 2.00
41 Cold War of Nick Fury #4 . . . . . 2.00
42 I:Strike Force Shield 2.00
43 R:Clay Quatermain 2.00
44 A:Captain America 2.00
45 A:Bridge 2.00
46 V:Gideon,Hydra 2.00
47 V:Baron Strucker,last issue . . . 2.00
TPB Death Duty V:Night Raven . . . 5.95
TPB Captain America 5.95
TPB Scorpion Connection 7.95
Ashcan 75

NICK FURY, VERSUS
S.H.I.E.L.D.
June, 1988
1 JSo(c),D:Quartermail 6.00
2 BSz(c),Into The Depths 5.00
3 Uneasy Allies 4.00
4 V:Hydra 3.00
5 V:Hydra 3.00
6 V:Hydra, Dec., 1988 . . . . 3.00
TPB Reprints #1-#6 . . . . 15.95

NIGHTBREED
Epic April, 1990
1 . . . . 4.00
2 . . . . 3.00
3 . . . . 2.50
4 . . . . 2.50
5 JG 2.50
6 BBl,Blasphemers,pt.1 . . . . 2.50
7 JG,Blasphemers,pt.2 . . . . 2.50
8 BBl,MM,Blasphemers,pt.3 . . . . . 2.50
9 BBl,Blasphemers,pt.4 . . . . 2.50
10 BBl,Blasphemers,pt.5 . . . . 2.50
11 South America,pt.1 . . . . 2.25
12 South America,pt.2 . . . . 2.25
13 Emissaries o/Algernon Kinder . . 2.25
14 Rawhead Rex Story 2.25
15 Rawhead Rex 2.25
16 Rawhead Rex 2.25
17 KN(i),V:Werewolves 2.25
18 V:Werewolves 2.25
19 V:Werewolves 2.25
20 Trapped in the Forest 2.25
21 V:Ozymandias 2.50
22 V:Ozymandias 2.50
23 F:Peloquin 2.50
24 Search for New Midian 2.50
25 Search for New Midian 2.50
Nightbreed:Genesis, Rep.#1-#4 . . . 9.95

NIGHTCAT
1 DCw,I&O:Night Cat 4.50

NIGHTCRAWLER
Nov., 1985
1 DC,A:Bamfs 4.00
2 DC 3.00
3 DC,A:Other Dimensional X-Men . 3.00
4 DC,A:Lockheed,V:Dark Bamf
　Feb., 1986 . . . . 3.00

NIGHTHAWK
July 1998
1 (of 3) RCa,BWi,Nighthawk shake
　off coma 2.50
2 (of 3) RCa,BWi,V:Mephisto 2.50
3 RCa,BWi,conclusion 2.50

MARVEL

NIGHTMARE
1994
1 ANo	2.00
2 ANo	2.00
3 ANo	2.00

NIGHTMARE CIRCUS
1 video-game tie-in	2.50
2 video-game tie-in	2.50

NIGHTMARE ON ELM STREET
Oct., 1989
1 RB/TD/AA.,Movie adapt	3.00
2 AA,Movie adapt,Dec., 1989	2.25

NIGHTMASK
Nov., 1986
1 O:Night Mask	1.25
2 V:Gnome	1.00
3 V:Mistress Twilight	1.00
4 EC,D:Mistress Twilight	1.00
5 EC,Nightmare.	1.00
6 EC	1.00
7 EC	1.00
8 EC	1.00
9	1.00
10 Lucian	1.00
11	1.00
12 Oct. 1987	1.00

NIGHT NURSE
Nov., 1972
1 The Making of a Nurse	100.00
2 Moment of Truth	60.00
3	60.00
4 Final Issue,May, 1973	60.00

NIGHT RIDER
Oct., 1974
1 Reprint Ghost Rider #1	10.00
2 Reprint Ghost Rider #2	7.00
3 Reprint Ghost Rider #3	7.00
4 Reprint Ghost Rider #4	7.00
5 Reprint Ghost Rider #5	7.00
6 Reprint Ghost Rider #6 August, 1975	7.00

NIGHTSTALKERS
1992–94
1 TP(i),Rise o/t Midnight Sons#5 A:GR,J.Blaze,I:Meatmarket, polybagged w/poster	3.00
2 TP(i),V:Hydra	2.50
3 TP(i),V:Dead on Arrival	2.00
4 TP(i),V:Hydra	2.00
5 TP(i),A:Punisher	2.00
6 TP(i),A:Punisher	2.00
7 TP(i),A:Ghost Rider	2.00
8 Hannibal King vs Morbius	2.00
9 MPa,A:Morbius	2.00
10 Midnight Massacre#1,D:Johnny Blaze,Hannibal King	2.50
11 O:Blade	2.00
12 V:Vampires	2.00
13 V:Vampires	2.00
14 Wld,Siege of Darkness#1.	2.00
15 Wld,Siege of Darkness#9.	2.00
16 V:Dreadnought	2.00
17 F:Blade	2.00
18 D:Hannibal King,Frank Drake, last issue	2.00

Night Thrasher #5
© Marvel Entertainment Group

NIGHT THRASHER
[Limited Series] 1992–93
1 B:FaN(s),DHv,N:Night Thrasher, V:Bengal	2.50
2 DHv,I:Tantrium	2.25
3 DHv,V:Gideon.	2.25
4 E:FaN(s),DHv,A:Silhoutte	2.25

[Regular Series] 1993–95
1 B:FaN(s),MBa,JS,V:Poison Memories	3.25
2 JS,V:Concrete Dragons	2.00
3 JS(c),I:Aardwolf,A:Folding Circle.	2.00
4 JS(c),V:Aardwolf,I:Air Force	2.00
5 JS,V:Air Force	2.00
6 Face Value,A:Rage.	2.00
7 DdB,V:Bandit	2.00
8 DdB,V:Bandit	2.00
9 DdB,A:Tantrum.	2.00
10 DdB,A:Iron Man,w/card	2.25
11 DdB,Time & Time Again,pt.2	2.25
12 DdB,Time & Time Again,pt.5	2.25
13 Lost in the Shadows,pt.1	1.95
14 Lost in the Shadows,pt.2	1.95
15 Money Don't Buy,pt.1	1.95
16 A:Prowler.	1.95
17	1.95
18	1.95
19 V:Tantrum	1.95
20	1.95
21 Rage vs. Grind	1.95

NIGHTWATCH
1994–95
1 RLm,I:Salvo,Warforce Holo(c).	3.00
1a Newsstand ed.	1.75
2 RLm,AM,I:Flashpoint	1.50
3 RLm,AM,V:Flashpoint	1.50
4 RLm,A:Warrent,V:Gauntlet	1.75
5 I:Sunstreak,A:Venom	1.50
6 V:Venom	1.50
7 I:Cardiaxe.	1.50
8 V:Cardiaxe	1.50
9 origins	1.50
10	1.50
11	1.50
12	1.50

NOCTURNE
1995
1 DAn, in London	1.50
2 DAn,O:Nocturne	1.50

3 Interview with Amy	1.50
4 V:Dragon	1.50

NO ESCAPE
1994
1 & 2 Movie adaptation	@1.50

NOMAD
[Limited Series] Nov., 1990
1 B:FaN(s),A:Capt.America	3.00
2 A:Capt.America	2.50
3 A:Capt.America	2.50
4 A:Capt.America, final issue, Feb. 1989.	2.50

[Regular Series] 1992–94
1 B:FaN(s),R:Nomad,[Gatefold(c), map]	3.00
2 V:Road Kill Club	2.50
3 V:U.S.Agent	2.50
4 DeadMan's Hand#2,V:Deadpool	2.00
5 DeadMan's Hand#4,V:Punisher	2.00
6 DeadMan's Hand#8,A:Punisher, Daredevil	2.00
7 Infinity War,V:Gambit, Doppleganger.	2.00
8 L.A.Riots	2.00
9 I:Ebbtide.	2.00
10 A:Red Wolf	2.00
11 in Albuquerque	2.00
12 In Texas.	2.00
13 AIDS issue	2.00
14 Hidden in View	2.00
15 Hidden in View	2.00
16 A:Gambit.	2.00
17 Bucky Kidnapped.	2.00
18 A:Captain America,Slug.	2.00
19 FaN(s),Faustus Affair.	2.00
20 A:Six Pack.	2.00
21 A:Man-Thing.	2.00
22 American Dreamers#1,V:Zaran	2.00
23 American Dreamers#2.	2.00
24 American Dreamers#3.	2.00
25 American Dreamers#4, finale.	2.00

NORTHSTAR
1994
1 SFr,DoC,V:Weapon:P.R.I.M.E.	2.00
2 SFr,DoC,V:Arcade	2.00
3 SFr,DoC,V:Arcade	2.00
4 SFr,DoC,final issue.	2.00
N Presents James O'Barr	2.50

NOT BRAND ECHH
August, 1967
1 JK(c),BEv,Forbush Man(c)	35.00
2 MSe,FrG,Spidey-Man,Gnat-Man & Rotten	25.00
3 MSe(C),TS,JK,FrG,O:Charlie America	25.00
4 GC,JTg,TS,Scaredevil, ECHHs-Men	25.00
5 JK,TS,GC,I&O:Forbush Man	25.00
6 MSe(c),GC,TS,W:Human Torch	25.00
7 MSe(c),JK,GC,TS,O:Fantastical Four,Stupor Man	25.00
8 MSe(c),GC,TS,C:Beatles	28.00
9 MSe,GC,TS,Bulk V:Sunk-Mariner	25.00
10 JK,TS,MSe,The Worst of...	30.00
11 King Konk	30.00
12 MSe,Frankenstein,A:Revengers	30.00
13 GC,MSe,Stamp Out Trading Cards(c).	30.00

MARVEL

NOTHING CAN STOP THE JUGGERNAUT
1989
1 JR2,rep.SpM#229&#230. . . . . . 4.00

NOVA
[1st Regular Series] Sept., 1976
1 B:MWn(s),JB,JSt,I&O:Nova 5.00
2 JB,JSt,I:Condor,Powerhouse . . . 3.00
3 JB,JSt,I:Diamondhead 2.50
4 SB,TP,A:Thor,I:Corruptor 2.50
5 SB,V:Earthshaker. 2.50
6 SB,V:Condor,Powerhouse,
   Diamondhead,I:Sphinx 2.50
7 SB,War in Space,O:Sphinx 2.50
8 V:Megaman 2.50
9 V:Megaman 2.50
10 V:Condor,Powerhouse,
   Diamond-head Sphinx 2.50
11 V:Sphinx 2.00
12 A:Spider-Man 2.50
13 I:Crimebuster,A:Sandman 2.50
14 A:Sandman 2.00
15 CI,C:Spider-Man, Hulk. 2.00
16 CI,A:Yellow Claw 2.00
17 A:Yellow Claw 2.00
18 A:Yellow Claw, Nick Fury 2.00
19 CI,TP,I:Blackout 2.00
20 What is Project X?. 2.00
21 JB,BMc,JRu. 2.00
22 CI,I:Comet 2.00
23 CI,V:Dr.Sun 2.00
24 CI,I:New Champions,V:Sphinx . . 2.00
25 E:MWn(s),CI,A:Champions,
   V:Sphinx 2.00

[2nd Regular Series] 1994–95
1 B:FaN(s),ChM,V:Gladiator,Foil
   Embossed(c) 3.00
2 ChM,V:Tail Hook Rape 2.00
3 ChM,A:Spider-Man,Corruptor . . . 2.00
4 ChM,I:NovaO:O 2.00
5 ChM,R:Condor,w/card. 2.25
6 ChM,Time & Time Again,pt.3 . . . 2.25
7 ChM,Time & Time Again,pt.6 . . . 2.25
8 ChM,I:Shatterforce 2.25
9 ChM,V:Shatterforce 2.00
10 ChM,V:Diamondhead. 2.00
11 ChM,V:Diamondhead. 2.00
12 ChM,A:Inhumans. 2.00
13 ChM,A:Inhumans. 2.00
14 A:Condor. 2.00
15 V:Brethern of Zorr 2.00

Nova #9
© Marvel Entertainment Group

16 Countdown Conclusion 2.00
17 Nova Loses Powers. 2.00
18 Nova Omega,pt.1 . . . . 2.00

NOVA
March 1999
1 EL,JoB,F:Rich Rider,48-page . . . 3.00
2 EL,JoB,A:Capt.America 2.00
2a variant JoB cover 2.00
3 EL,JoB,A:Capt.America & Hulk . . 2.00
4 EL,JoB,A:Mr.Fantastic 2.00
5 EL,JoB,A:Spider-Man 2.00
6 EL,JoB,V:Sphinx. 2.00

Nth MAN
August, 1989
1 . . . . 2.00
2 . . . . 1.00
3 . . . . 1.00
4 . . . . 1.00
5 thru 7 . . . . @1.00
8 DK 2.00
9 thru 16, finale, Sept., 1990 . . . @1.00

Obnoxio the Clown #1
© Marvel Entertainment Group

OBNOXIO THE CLOWN
April, 1983
1 X-Men 2.00

OFFCASTES
Epic *Heavy Hitters* 1993
1 MV,I:Offcastes 2.50
2 MV,V:Kaoro 1.95
3 MV,Last Issue. 1.95

OFFICIAL MARVEL INDEX: 1985–88
TO THE AMAZING SPIDER-MAN
Index 1 . . . . 3.00
Index 2 thru 9 . . . . @2.50

TO THE AVENGERS
Index 1 thru 7 . . . . @2.50

TO THE FANTASTIC FOUR
Index 1 thru 12 . . . . @2.25

TO MARVEL TEAM-UP
Index 1 thru 6 . . . . @1.75

TO THE X-MEN
Index 1 thru 7 . . . . @2.95
[Vol. 2] 1994
Index 1 thru 5 . . . . @1.95

OFFICIAL MARVEL TIMELINE
1-shot, 48pg 5.95

OFFICIAL TRUE CRIME CASES
Fall, 1947
24 (1)SSh(c),The Grinning Killer . 175.00
25 (2)She Made Me a Killer,HK. . 125.00
Becomes:
ALL-TRUE CRIME
26 SSh(c),The True Story of Wilbur
   Underhill. 200.00
27 Electric Chair(c),Robert Mais . 150.00
28 Cops V:Gangsters(c) 75.00
29 Cops V:Gangsters(c) 75.00
30 He Picked a Murderous Mind . 75.00
31 Hitchiking Thugs(c) 75.00
32 Jewel Thieves(c) 75.00
33 The True Story of Dinton
   Phillips 75.00
34 Case of the Killers Revenge. . . 75.00
35 Ph(c),Date with Danger 75.00
36 Ph(c) 75.00
37 Ph(c),Story of Robert Marone . 75.00
38 Murder Weapon,Nick Maxim . . 75.00
39 Story of Vince Vanderee 75.00
40 . . . . 75.00
41 Lou "Lucky" Raven 75.00
42 BK,Baby Face Nelson 85.00
43 Doc Channing Paulson 70.00
44 Murder in the Big House 70.00
45 While the City Sleeps. 70.00
46 . . . . 70.00
47 Gangster Terry Craig 70.00
48 GT,They Vanish By Night 70.00
49 BK,Squeeze Play. 75.00
50 Shoot to Kill. 70.00
51 Panic in the Big House 70.00
52 Prison Break, Sept., 1952 . . . . 70.00

OLYMPIANS
Epic July, 1991
1 Spoof Series. 3.95
2 Conclusion. 3.95

OMEGA THE UNKNOWN
March, 1976
1 JM,I:Omega 4.00
2 JM,A:Hulk. 2.50
3 JM,A:Electro. 2.00
4 JM,V:Yellow Claw 2.00
5 JM,V:The Wrench. 2.00
6 JM,V:Blockbuster 2.00
7 JM,V:Blockbuster 2.00
8 JM,C:New Foolkiller,V:Nitro. 5.00
9 JM,A:New Foolkiller,
   D:Blockbuster. 7.00
10 JM,D:Omega the Unknown 2.00

ONE, THE
Epic July, 1985
1 thru 5 . . . . @1.75
6 Feb., 1986 . . . . 1.75

101 WAYS TO END THE CLONE SAGA
1-shot (1997). 2.50

ONSLAUGHT
1996–97
Marvel Universe: AKu,SLo,MWd,
  Marvel Heroes vs. Onslaught . . 7.00
Marvel Universe: Gold edition. . . . 15.00
X-Men: AKu,SLo,MWd (1996). 6.00
X-Men: Gold editon. 15.00
Onslaught: Epilogue (1997) 3.00
TPB Book 1, rep. X-Men #53 & #54,
  Uncanny X-Men 322 & 334
  and Onslaught X-Men. 12.95
TPB Book 2, rep. X-Man #18 & #19
  and X-Force #57 & 58 . . . . 9.95
TPB Book 3, rep. Uncanny X-Men
  #335, Avengers #401, FF #415,
  X-Men #55. . . . . 9.95
TPB Book 4, rep. Inc.Hulk #444
  & #445, Cable #34 & #35 . . . . . 9.95
TPB Book 5, rep. X-Factor #125,
  Punisher #11, Green Goblin #12,
  Amaz. Sp.-M. #415, Sp.-M. #72 9.95
TPB Book 6, rep. Uncanny X-Men
  #336, X-Men #56, Avengers #402,
  FF #416 & Onslaught: Marvel
  Universe. 12.95

ONYX OVERLORD
Epic 1992–93
1 JBi,Sequel to Airtight Garage . . . 3.00
2 JBi,The Joule 2.75
3 JBi,V:Overlord 2.75
4 V:Starbilliard. 2.75

OPEN SPACE
Dec., 1989–Aug. 1990
1 . . . . 6.00
2 thru 4 . . . . @5.25

ORIGINAL GHOST RIDER
1992–94
1 MT(c),rep Marvel Spotlight#5 . . . 2.25
2 rep.Marvel Spotlight#6 . . . . 2.00
3 rep.Marvel Spotlight#7 . . . . 2.00
4 JQ(c),rep.Marvel Spotlight#8. . . 2.00
5 KM(c),rep.Marvel spotlight#9 . . 2.00
6 rep.Marvel Spotlight#10 . . . . . . 2.00
7 rep.Marvel Spotlight#11 . . . . . . 2.00
8 rep.Ghost Rider#1 . . . . 2.00
9 rep.Ghost Rider#2 . . . . 2.00
10 rep.Marvel Spotlight#12. . . . . . 2.00
11 rep.Ghost Rider#3 . . . . 2.00
12 rep.Ghost Rider#4 . . . . 2.00
13 rep.Ghost Rider#38 . . . . 2.00
14 rep.Ghost Rider#6 . . . . 1.75
15 rep.Ghost Rider#7 . . . . 1.75
15 rep.Ghost Rider#8 . . . . 1.75
18 rep.Ghost Rider#9 . . . . 1.75
18 rep.Ghost Rider#10 . . . . 1.75
19 rep.Ghost Rider#11 . . . . 1.75
20 rep.Ghost Rider#12 . . . . 1.75
21 rep.Ghost Rider#13 . . . . 1.75
22 rep.Ghost Rider#14 . . . . 1.75
23 rep.Ghost Rider#15 . . . . 1.95

ORIGINAL GHOST RIDER RIDES AGAIN
July, 1991
1 rep.GR#68+#69(O:JohnnyBlaze) 3.00
2 rep.G.R. #70,#71 . . . . 2.00
3 rep.G.R. #72,#73 . . . . 2.00
4 rep.G.R. #74,#75 . . . . 2.00

5 rep.G.R. #76,#77 . . . . 2.00
6 rep.G.R. #78,#79 . . . . 2.00
7 rep.G.R. #80,#81 . . . . 2.00

ORIGINS OF MARVEL COMICS
TPB StL,JK,SD reprinting, 260pg . 25.00

OSBORN JOURNALS, THE
1997
1-shot KHt,F:Norman Osborn 3.00

OUR LOVE
Sept., 1949
1 Ph(c),Guilt of Nancy Crane . . 100.00
2 Ph(c),My Kisses Were Cheap . 50.00
Becomes:

TRUE SECRETS
3 Love Stories,continued 75.00
4 . . . . 50.00
5 . . . . 50.00
6 BEv 60.00
7 . . . . 50.00
8 . . . . 50.00
9 . . . . 50.00
10 . . . . 50.00
11 thru 21 . . . . @35.00
22 BEv. 50.00
23 thru 39 . . . . @30.00
40 Sept., 1956 . . . . 30.00

OUR LOVE STORY
Oct., 1969
1 . . . . 30.00
2 . . . . 15.00
3 . . . . 15.00
4 . . . . 15.00
5 JSo 50.00
6 thru 13 . . . . @15.00
14 Gary Friedrich &Tarpe Mills . . . 20.00
15 thru 37 . . . . @10.00
38 Feb., 1976. . . . . 10.00

OUTLAW FIGHTERS
Atlas August, 1954
1 GT,Western Tales 85.00
2 GT 50.00
3 . . . . 50.00
4 A;Patch Hawk 50.00
5 RH, Final Issue,April, 1955 . . . 50.00

OUTLAW KID
Atlas Sept., 1954
1 SSh,DW,B&O:Outlaw Kid,A;Black
  Rider 175.00
2 DW,A:Black Rider 60.00
3 DW,AW,GWb 75.00
4 DW(c),Death Rattle 65.00
5 . . . . 65.00
6 . . . . 65.00
7 . . . . 65.00
8 AW,DW 80.00
9 . . . . 75.00
10 . . . . 75.00
11 thru 17 . . . . @50.00
18 AW 60.00
19 Sept., 1957 . . . . 50.00

[2nd series] August, 1970
1 JSe(c),DW,Jo,Showdown,rep . . 20.00
2 DW,One Kid Too Many 15.00
3 HT(c),DW,Six Gun Double
  Cross 15.00
4 DW 12.00
5 DW 12.00
6 DW 12.00

Outlaw Kid #2
© Marvel Entertainment Group

7 HT(c),DW,Treachery on
  the Trail 12.00
8 HT(c),DW,RC,Six Gun Pay Off . 12.00
9 JSe(c),DW,GWb,The Kids
  Last Stand 10.00
10 GK(c),DAy,NewO:Outlaw Kid . . 10.00
11 GK(c),Thunder Along the
  Big Iron 10.00
12 The Man Called Bounty Hawk . 10.00
13 The Last Rebel 10.00
14 The Kid Gunslingers of
  Calibre City 10.00
15 GK(c),V:Madman of Monster
  Mountain 10.00
16 The End of the Trail 10.00
17 thru 29. . . . . @10.00
30 Oct., 1975 . . . . 10.00

OVER THE EDGE AND UNDER A BUCK
1995–96
1 F:Daredevil vs. Mr. Fear 1.00
2 F:Doctor Strange 1.00
3 F:Hulk 1.00
4 in Cypress Hills 1.00
5 . . . . 1.00
6 F:Daredevil. 1.00
7 Doc & Nightmare 1.00

PARAGON
1 I:Paragon,Nightfire 5.00

PATSY & HEDY
Atlas Feb., 1952
1 B:Patsy Walker&Hedy Wolfe . 125.00
2 Skating(c) 75.00
3 Boyfriend Trouble 50.00
4 Swimsuit(c) 50.00
5 Patsy's Date(c). 50.00
6 Swimsuit/Picnic(c) 50.00
7 Double-Date(c) 50.00
8 The Dance 50.00
9 . . . . 50.00
10 . . . . 50.00
11 thru 25 . . . . @35.00
26 thru 50 . . . . @25.00
51 thru 60. . . . . @20.00
61 thru 109 . . . . @15.00
110 Feb., 1967 . . . . 15.00

PATSY & HER PALS
May, 1953
1 MWs(c),F:Patsay Walker 90.00
2 MWs(c),Swimsuit(c) 60.00
3 MWs(c),Classroom(c) 50.00
4 MWs(c),Golfcourse(c) 50.00
5 MWs(c).Patsy/Buzz(c) 50.00
6 thru 10 . . . . @50.00
11 thru 28 . . . . @35.00
29 August, 1957 . . . . 35.00

PATSY WALKER
1945–Dec. 1965
1 F:Patsy Walker Adventures . . 350.00
2 Patsy/Car(c) 175.00
3 Skating(c) 125.00
4 Perfume(c) 125.00
5 Archery Lesson(c) 125.00
6 Bus(c) 125.00
7 Charity Drive(c) 125.00
8 Organ Driver Monkey(c) 125.00
9 Date(c) 125.00
10 Skating(c),Wedding Bells . . 125.00
11 Date with a Dream 100.00
12 Love in Bloom,Artist(c) 100.00
13 Swimsuit(c),There Goes My
  Heart;HK,Hey Look 100.00
14 An Affair of the Heart,
  HK,Hey Look 100.00
15 Dance(c) 75.00
16 Skating(c) 75.00
17 Patsy's Diary(c),HK,Hey Look 100.00
18 Autograph(c) 75.00
19 HK,Hey Look 100.00
20 HK,Hey Look 100.00
21 HK,Hey Look 100.00
22 HK,Hey Look 100.00
23 . . . . 65.00
24 . . . . 65.00
25 HK,Rusty 100.00
26 . . . . 50.00
27 . . . . 50.00
28 . . . . 50.00
29 . . . . 50.00
30 HK,Egghead Double 75.00
31 . . . . 50.00
32 thru 57 . . . . @30.00
58 thru 99 . . . . @25.00
100 . . . . 25.00
101 thru 124 . . . . @15.00
Fashion Parade #1 . . . . 75.00

PETER PARKER,
THE SPECTACULAR
SPIDER-MAN
Dec., 1976
1 SB,V:Tarantula 30.00
2 SB,V:Kraven,Tarantula 15.00
3 SB,I:Lightmaster 10.00
4 SB,V:Vulture,Hitman 10.00
5 SB,V:Hitman,Vulture 10.00
6 SB,V:Morbius,rep.M.T.U.#3 . . 12.00
7 SB,V:Morbius,A:Human Torch . . 15.00
8 SB,V:Morbius 12.00
9 SB,I:White Tiger 6.00
10 SB,A:White Tiger 6.00
11 JM,V:Medusa 5.00
12 SB,V:Brother Power 5.00
13 SB,V:Brother Power 5.00
14 SB,V:Brother Power 5.00
15 SB,V:Brother Power 5.00
16 SB,V:The Beetle 5.00
17 SB,A:Angel & Iceman
  Champions disbanded 6.00
18 SB,A:Angel & Iceman 6.00
19 SB,V:The Enforcers 5.00
20 SB,V:Lightmaster 5.00
21 JM,V:Scorpion 5.00

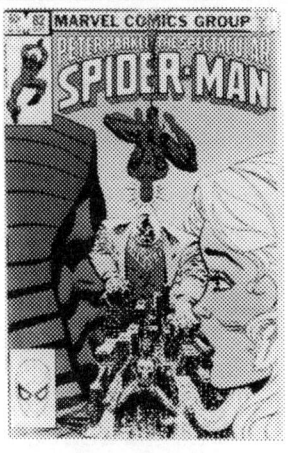
Peter Parker #82
© *Marvel Entertainment Group*

22 MZ,A:Moon Knight,V:Cyclone . . 5.00
23 A:Moon Knight,V:Cyclone 5.00
24 FS,A:Hypno-Hustler 4.00
25 JM,FS,I:Carrion 5.00
26 JM,A:Daredevil,V:Carrion 4.00
27 DC,FM,I:Miller Daredevil,
  V:Carrion 20.00
28 FM,A:Daredevil,V:Carrion 15.00
29 JM,FS,V:Carrion 5.00
30 JM,FS,V:Carrion 5.00
31 JM,FS,D:Carrion 5.00
32 BL,JM,FS,V:Iguana 5.00
33 JM,FS,O:Iguana 5.00
34 JM,FS,V:Iguana,Lizard 5.00
35 V:Mutant Mindworm 5.00
36 JM,V:Swarm 5.00
37 DC,MN,V:Swarm 5.00
38 SB,V:Morbius 5.00
39 JM,JR2,V:Schizoid Man 5.50
40 FS,V:Schizoid Man 5.50
41 JM,V:Meteor Man,A:GiantMan . . 5.00
42 JM,A:Fant.Four,V:Frightful 4. . . . 5.00
43 JBy(c),MZ,V:The Ringer,
  V:Belladonna 5.00
44 JM,V:The Vulture 5.00
45 MSe,V:The Vulture 5.00
46 FM(c),MZ,V:Cobra 5.00
47 MSe,A:Prowler II 5.00
48 MSe,A:Prowler II 5.00
49 MSe,I:Smuggler 5.00
50 JR2,JM,V:Mysterio 5.00
51 MSe&FM(c),V:Mysterio 5.00
52 FM(c),D:White Tiger 5.00
53 JM,FS,V:Terrible Tinkerer 5.00
54 FM,WS,MSe,V:Silver Samurai . . 5.00
55 LMc,JM,V:Nitro 5.00
56 FM,JM,V:Jack-o-lantern 12.00
57 JM,V:Will-o-the Wisp 5.00
58 JBy,V:Ringer,A:Beetle 6.00
59 JM,V:Beetle 5.00
60 JM&FM(c),O:Spider-Man,
  V:Beetle 5.50
61 JM,V:Moonstone 4.50
62 JM,V:Goldbug 4.50
63 JM,V:Molten Man 4.50
64 JM,I:Cloak&Dagger 8.00
65 BH,JM,V:Kraven,Calypso 4.50
66 JM,V:Electro 4.00
67 AMb,V:Boomerang 4.00
68 LMc,JM,V:Robot of Mendell
  Stromm 4.00
69 AM,A:Cloak & Dagger 5.00
70 A:Cloak & Dagger 5.00
71 JM,Gun Control issue 4.00

72 AM,V:Dr.Octopus 4.00
73 AM,JM,V:Dr.Octopus,A:Owl 4.00
74 AM,JM,V:Dr.Octopus,R:Bl.Cat . . 4.00
75 AM,JM,V:Owl,Dr.Octopus 5.00
76 AM,Black Cat on deathbed 4.00
77 AM,V:Gladiator,Dr.Octopus 4.00
78 AM,V:Dr.Octopus,C:Punisher . . . 4.00
79 AM,V:Dr.Octopus,A:Punisher . . . 4.00
80 AM,F:J.Jonah Jameson 3.50
81 A:Punisher 6.00
82 A:Punisher 6.00
83 A:Punisher 6.00
84 AM,F:Black Cat 3.50
85 AM,O:Hobgoblin powers
  (Ned Leeds) 12.00
86 FH,V:Fly 3.50
87 AM,Reveals I.D.to Black Cat . . . 3.50
88 AM,V:Cobra,Mr.Hyde 3.50
89 AM,Secret Wars,A:Kingpin 4.00
90 AM,Secret Wars 5.00
91 AM,V:Blob 3.50
92 AM,I:Answer 3.50
93 AM,V:Answer 3.50
94 AM,A:Cloak & Dagger,V:
  Silver Mane 3.50
95 AM,A:Cloak & Dagger,V:
  Silvermane 3.50
96 AM,A:Cloak & Dagger,V:
  Silvermane 3.50
97 HT,JM,A:Black Cat 3.50
98 HT,JM,I:Spot 3.50
99 HT,JM,V:Spot 3.50
100 AM,V:Kingpin,C:Bl.Costume . . . 6.00
101 JBy(c),AM,V:Killer Shrike 3.00
102 JBy(c),AM,V:Backlash 3.00
103 AM,V:Blaze;Not John Blaze . . . 3.00
104 JBy(c),AM,V:Rocket Racer 3.00
105 AM,A:Wasp 3.00
106 AM,A:Wasp 3.00
107 RB,D:Jean DeWolf,I:SinEater . . 4.00
108 RB,A:Daredevil,V:Sin-Eater . . . 3.00
109 RB,A:Daredevil,V:Sin-Eater . . . 3.00
110 RB,A:Daredevil,V:Sin-Eater . . . 3.00
111 RB,Secret Wars II 3.00
112 RB,A:Santa Claus,Black Cat . . 3.00
113 RB,Burglars,A:Black Cat 3.00
114 BMc,V:Lock Picker 3.00
115 BMc,A:Black Cat,Dr.Strange,
  I:Foreigner 3.50
116 A:Dr.Strange, Foreigner,
  Black Cat, Sabretooth 5.00
117 DT,C:Sabretooth,A:Foreigner,
  Black Cat,Dr.Strange 4.00
118 MZ,D:Alexander,V:SHIELD 3.00

Peter Parker #123
© *Marvel Entertainment Group*

119 RB,BMc,V:Sabretooth,
  A:Foreigner,Black Cat. 5.00
120 KG. 3.00
121 RB,BMc,V:Mauler 3.00
122 V:Mauler 3.00
123 V:Foreigner,Black Cat 3.00
124 V:Dr.Octopus 3.00
125 V:Wr.Crew,A:Spiderwoman . . . 3.00
126 JM,A:Sp.woman,V:Wrecker . . . 3.00
127 AM,V:Lizard. 3.00
128 C:DDevil,A:Bl.Cat,Foreigner. . . 3.50
129 A:Black Cat,V:Foreigner. 3.00
130 A:Hobgoblin. 6.00
131 MZ,BMc,V:Kraven 7.00
132 MZ,BMc,V:Kraven 7.00
133 BSz(c),Mad Dog,pt.3 . . . . 5.00
Ann.#1 RB,JM,V:Dr.Octopus 5.00
Ann.#2 JM,I&O:Rapier 4.50
Ann.#3 JM,V:Manwolf. 4.50
Ann.#4 AM,O:Aunt May,A:Bl.Cat. . . 5.00
Ann.#5 I:Ace,Joy Mercado 4.50
Ann.#6 V:Ace 4.50
Ann.#7 Honeymoon iss,A:Puma . . . 4.50
Becomes:

SPECTACULAR
SPIDER-MAN

PETER PARKER:
SPIDER-MAN
Nov. 1998
1 JR2,HMe,SHa,A:new Spider-Man,
  V:Ranger,48-page 3.00
1a signed 35.00
2 JR2,HMe,SHa,A:Thor. 2.00
2a variant cover. 2.00
3 HMe,JR2,SHa,A:Iceman,
  V:Shadrac 2.00
4 HMe,JR2,SHa,V:Marrow. 2.00
5 HMe,SHa,BS,JBy(c),F:Spider-
  Woman,Aunt May, Black Cat . . 2.00
6 HMe,SHa,RJ2,JBy(c),V:Kingpin . 2.00
7 JR2,HMe,SHa,Reality Bent. 2.00
8 JR2,HMe,SHa,V:Bullseye. 2.00
9 JR2,HMe,SHa,R:Venom 2.00
10 JR2,HMe,SHa,R:Carnage 2.00
Ann. 1999,CCs, 48-page 3.50

PETER PORKER
Star May, 1985
1 Parody 2.50
2 . . . . 1.50
3 . . . . 1.50
4 . . . . 1.50
5 V:Senior Simians 1.50
6 A Blitz in Time 1.50
7 . . . . 1.50
8 Kimono My House 1.25
9 Uncouth my Tooth 1.25
10 Lost Temple of the Golden
  Retriever 1.25
11 Dog Dame Afternoon 1.25
12 The Gouda,Bad & Ugly 1.25
13 Halloween issue 1.25
14 Heavy Metal Issue. 1.25
15 . . . . 1.25
16 Porker Fried Rice,Final Issue . . 1.25
17 Sept., 1987 . . . . 1.25

PETER, THE LITTLE PEST
Nov., 1969
1 F:Peter 35.00
2 Rep,Dexter & Melvin 25.00
3 Rep,Dexter & Melvin 25.00
4 Rep,Dexter & Melvin,
  May, 1970 . . . . 25.00

Phantom 2040, #3
© Marvel Entertainment Group

PHANTOM
1 Lee Falk's Phantom 4.00
2 V:General Babalar 4.00
3 final issue. 4.00

PHANTOM 2040
1 Based on cartoon 2.50
2 V:Alloy 2.50
3 MPa,V:Crime Syndicate 2.50
4 Vision Quest. 2.50

PHOENIX
(UNTOLD STORY)
April, 1984
1 JBy,O:Phoenix (R.Summers) . . 12.00

PILGRIM'S PROGRESS
1 adapts John Bunyans novel . . . 10.00

PINHEAD
1993–94
1 Red Foil(c),from Hellraiser 3.00
2 DGC(s),V:Cenobites 2.50
3 DGC(s),V:Cenobites 2.50
4 DGC(s),V:Cenobites 2.50
5 DGC(s),Devil in Disguise 2.50
6 DGC(s), ... 2.50

PINHEAD VS.
MARSHALL LAW
1993
1 KON,In Hell 3.00
2 KON. 3.00

PINOCHIO & THE
EMPEROR OF THE NIGHT
March, 1988
1 Movie adapt.. . . . . 1.25

PINT-SIZED X-BABIES:
MURDERAMA
June 1998
1-shot, Mojo, Arcade, 48pg, ... 3.00

PIRATES OF
DARK WATERS
Nov., 1991
1 based on T.V. series 1.00
2 Search for 13 Treasures. 1.00
3 V:Albino Warriors,Konk. 1.00
4 A:Monkey Birds 1.25
5 Tula Steals 1st Treasuer. 1.25
6 thru 9 . . . . @1.25

PITT, THE
March, 1988
1 SB,SDr,A:Spitfire 4.00

PLANET OF THE APES
Aug., 1974–Feb. 1977
(black & white magazine)
1 MP 30.00
2 MP 20.00
3 . . . . 10.00
4 . . . . 10.00
5 . . . . 10.00
6 thru 10 . . . . @10.00
11 thru 20 . . . . @10.00
21 thru 29. . . . . @15.00

Planet Terry #12
© Marvel Entertainment Group

PLANET TERRY
Star April, 1985
1 thru 11 . . . . @1.00
12 March, 1986 . . . . 1.00

PLASMER
Marvel UK 1993–94
1 A:Captain America 3.50
2 A:Captain Britain,Black Knight . . 2.25
3 A:Captain Britain 2.25
4 A:Captain Britain 2.25
5 thru 7 . . . . 1.95

PLASTIC FORKS
Epic 1990
1 . . . . 5.50
2 thru 5 . . . . @5.25

POLICE ACADEMY
Nov., 1989
1 Based on TV Cartoon 1.25
2 . . . . 1.00

3 . . . . 1.00	
4 and 5 . . . . @1.00	
6 Feb., 1990 . . . . 1.00	

POLICE ACTION
Jan., 1954

1 JF,GC,Riot Squad 125.00	
2 JF,Over the Wall 75.00	
3 . . . . 50.00	
4 DAy 50.00	
5 DAy 50.00	
6 . . . . 50.00	
7 BPNov., 1954 . . . . 50.00	

POLICE BADGE
See: SPY THRILLERS

POPPLES
Star Dec., 1986

1 Based on Toys 1.00	
2 . . . . 1.00	
3 . . . . 1.00	
4 . . . . 1.00	
5 August, 1987 . . . . 1.00	

POWDERED TOAST-MAN
Spec. F:Powder Toast-Man 3.25

POWERHOUSE PEPPER COMICS
1943—Nov., 1948

1 BW,Movie Auditions(c) 1,200.00	
2 BW,Dinner(c) 650.00	
3 BW,Boxing Ring(c) 600.00	
4 BW,Subway(c) 600.00	
5 BW,Bankrobbers(c) 750.00	

POWER LINE
Epic May, 1988

1 BMc(i) 2.25	
2 Aw(i) 2.00	
3 A:Dr Zero 2.00	
4 . . . . 2.00	
5 thru 7 GM . . . . @2.00	
8 GM Sept., 1989 . . . . 2.00	

POWER MAN
Prev: Hero for Hire
Feb., 1974

17 GT,A:Iron Man 9.00	
18 GT,V:Steeplejack 6.00	
19 GT,V:Cottonmouth 6.00	
20 GT,Heroin Story 6.00	
21 V:Original Power Man 5.00	
22 V:Stiletto & Discus 5.00	
23 V:Security City 5.00	
24 GT,I:BlackGoliath(BillFoster) . . . 5.00	
25 A:Circus of Crime 5.00	
26 GT,V:Night Shocker 5.00	
27 GP,AMc,V:Man Called X 5.00	
28 V:Cockroach 5.00	
29 V:Mr.Fish 5.00	
30 RB,KJ,KP,I:Piranha 5.00	
31 SB,NA(i),V:Piranha 5.00	
32 JSt,FR,A:Wildfire 3.50	
33 FR,A:Spear 3.50	
34 FR,A:Spear,Mangler 3.50	
35 DA,A:Spear,Mangler 3.50	
36 V:Chemistro 3.50	
37 V:Chemistro. 3.50	
38 V:Chemistro. 3.50	
39 KJ,V:Chemistro,Baron 3.50	
40 V:Baron 3.50	
41 TP,V:Thunderbolt,Goldbug 3.50	

42 V:Thunderbolt,Goldbug 3.50	
43 AN,V:Mace 3.50	
44 TP,A:Mace 3.50	
45 JSn,A:Mace. 4.00	
46 GT,I:Zzzax(recreated) 3.50	
47 BS,A:Zzzax 4.00	
48 JBy,A:Iron Fist. 4.00	
49 JBy,A:Iron Fist 4.00	

Becomes:

POWER MAN & IRON FIST

50 JBy,I:Team-up with Iron Fist. . . . 2.50	
51 MZ,Night on the Town 2.50	
52 MZ,V:Death Machines 2.50	
53 SB,O:Nightshade. 2.50	
54 TR,O:Iron Fist 2.50	
55 Chaos at the Coliseum 2.50	
56 Mayhem in the Museum. 2.50	
57 X-Men,V:Living Monolith 6.00	
58 1st El Aguila(Drug) 2.00	
59 BL(c),TVE,V:Big Apple	
Bomber. 1.75	
60 BL(c),V:Terrorists 1.75	
61 BL(c),V:The Maggia 1.75	
62 BL(c),KGa,V:Man Mountain	
D:Thunerbolt 1.75	
63 BL(c),Cage Fights Fire. 1.75	
64 DGr&BL(c),V:Suetre,Muerte . . . 1.75	
65 BL(c),A:El Aquila, ... 1.75	
66 FM(c),Sabretooth(2nd App.) . . . 30.00	
67 V:Bushmaster 1.75	
68 FM(c),V:Athur Nagan 2.00	
69 V:Soldier 2.00	
70 FM(c)V:El Supremo 1.75	
71 FM(c),I:Montenegro 1.75	
72 FM(c),V:Chako 1.75	
73 FM(c),V:Rom 1.75	
74 FM(c),V:Ninja. 1.75	
75 KGa,O:IronFist. 2.50	
76 KGa,V:Warhawk 2.50	
77 KGa,A:Daredevil 2.50	
78 KGa,A:El Aguila,Sabretooth	
(Slasher)(3rd App.) 20.00	
79 V:Dredlox 1.75	
80 KJ(c),V:Montenegro 1.75	
81 V:Black Tiger 1.75	
82 V:Black Tiger 1.75	
83 V:Warhawk 1.75	
84 V:Constrictor,A:Sabertooth	
(4th App.) 18.00	
85 KP,V:Mole Man 1.75	
86 A:Moon Knight 1.75	
87 A:Moon Kinght. 1.75	
88 V:Scimtar. 1.75	
89 V:Terrorists 1.75	
90 V:Unus BS(c). 1.75	
91 "Paths and Angles" 1.75	
92 V:Hammeread,I:New Eel 1.75	
93 A:Chemistro. 1.75	
94 V:Chemistro. 1.75	
95 Danny Rand 1.75	
96 V,Chemistro. 1.75	
97 K'unlun,A:Fera. 1.75	
98 V:Shades & Commanche. 1.75	
99 R:Daught.of Dragon. 1.75	
100 O:K'unlun,DoubleSize 1.75	
101 A:Karnak 1.75	
102 V:Doombringer. 1.75	
103 O:Doombringer. 1.75	
104 V:Dr.Octopus,Lizard. 1.75	
105 F:Crime Buster 1.75	
106 Luke Gets Shot 1.75	
107 JBy(c),Terror issue. 1.75	
108 V:Inhuman Monster 1.75	
109 V:The Reaper 1.75	
110 V:Nightshade,Eel 1.75	
111 I:Captain Hero 1.75	
112 JBy(c),V:Control7. . . . . 1.75	
113 JBy(c),A:Capt.Hero 1.75	
114 JBy(c),V:Control7. . . . . 1.75	
115 JBy(c),V:Stanley. 1.75	
116 JBy(c),V:Stanley. 1.75	

Power Pack #7
© Marvel Entertainment Group

117 R:K'unlun 1.75	
118 A:Colleen Wing 1.75	
119 A:Daught.of Dragon 1.75	
120 V:Chiantang. 1.75	
121 Secret Wars II 1.75	
122 V:Dragonkin. 1.75	
123 V:Race Killer 1.75	
124 V:Yellowclaw 1.75	
125 MBr,LastIssue;D:Iron Fist. 3.00	
G-Size#1 reprints 4.00	
Ann.#1 Earth Shock 5.00	

POWER PACHYDERMS
Sept., 1989

1 Elephant Superheroes 1.50	

POWER PACK
August, 1984

1 JBr,BWi,I&O:Power Pack,	
I:Snarks 2.50	
2 JBr,BWi,V:Snarks 2.00	
3 JBr,BWi,V:Snarks 2.00	
4 JBr,BWi,V:Snarks 2.00	
5 JBr,BWi,V:Bogeyman 2.00	
6 JBr,BWi,A:Spider-Man 2.00	
7 JBr,BWi,A:Cloak & Dagger 2.00	
8 JBr,BWi,A:Cloak & Dagger 2.00	
9 BA,BWi,A:Marrina. 1.50	
10 BA,BWi,A:Marrina 1.50	
11 JBr,BWi,V:Morlocks 2.00	
12 JBr,BWi,A:X-Men,V:Morlocks . . . 3.00	
13 BA,BWi,Baseball issue 1.50	
14 JBr,BWi,V:Bogeyman. 1.50	
15 JBr,BWi,A:Beta Ray Bill 1.50	
16 JBr,BWi,I&O:Kofi,J:Tattletale	
(Franklin Richards). 2.00	
17 JBr,BWi,V:Snarks 1.50	
18 BA,SW,Secret Wars II,	
V:Kurse 2.00	
19 BA,SW,Doub.size,Wolverine . . . 4.00	
20 BMc,A:NewMutants 1.50	
21 BA,TA,C:Spider-Man 1.50	
22 JBg,BWi,V:Snarks 1.50	
23 JBg,BWi,V:Snarks,C:FF. 1.50	
24 JBg,BWi,V:Snarks,C:Cloak 2.00	
25 JBg,BWi,A:FF,V:Snarks 1.25	
26 JBg,BWi,A:Cloak & Dagger 1.25	
27 JBg,AG,A:Wolverine,X-Factor,	
V:Sabretooth 3.00	
28 A:Fantastic Four,Hercules 1.25	
29 JBg,DGr,A:SpM,V:Hobgoblin . . . 2.00	
30 VM,Crack 1.25	

31 JBg,I:Trash	1.25
32 JBg,V:Trash	1.25
33 JBg,A:Sunspot,Warlock,	
C:Spider-Man	1.75
34 TD,V:Madcap	1.25
35 JBg,A:X-Factor,D:Plague	1.75
36 JBg,V:Master Mold	1.25
37 SDr(i),I:Light-Tracker	1.25
38 SDr(i),I:Molecula	1.25
39 V:Bogeyman	1.25
40 A:New Mutants,V:Bogeyman	1.75
41 SDr(i),V:The Gunrunners	1.25
42 JBg,SDr,Inferno,V:Bogeyman	2.00
43 JBg,SDr,AW,Inferno,	
V:Bogeyman	2.00
44 JBr,Inferno,A:New Mutants	2.25
45 JBr,End battle w/Bogeyman	1.50
46 WPo,A:Punisher,Dakota North	2.00
47 JBg,I:Bossko	1.50
48 JBg,Toxic Waste #1	1.50
49 JBg,JSh,Toxic Waste #2	1.50
50 AW(i),V:Snarks	1.50
51 GM,I:Numinus	1.50
52 AW(i),V:Snarks,A:Numinus	1.50
53 EC,A of V,A:Typhoid Mary	1.50
54 JBg,V:Mad Thinker	1.50
55 DSp,V:Mysterio	1.50
56 TMo,A:Fant.Four,Nova	1.50
57 TMo,A:Nova,V:Star Stalker	1.50
58 TMo,A:Galactus,Mr.Fantastic	1.50
59 TMo,V:Ringmaster	1.50
60 TMo,V:Puppetmaster	1.50
61 TMo,V:Red Ghost & Apes	1.50
62 V:Red Ghost & Apes	
(last issue)	1.50
Holiday Spec.JBr,Small Changes	2.25

PRINCE NAMOR, THE SUB-MARINER
Sept., 1984

1 I:Dragonrider,Dara	2.50
2 I:Proteus	1.50
3	1.25
4 Dec., 1984	1.25

PRINCE VALIANT
1994–95

1 JRy,CV,Thule, Camelot	
and the Misty Isles	4.00
2 JRy,CV	4.00
3 JRy,CV	4.00
4 JRy,CV, final issue	4.00

PRIVATE EYE
Atlas Jan., 1951

1	150.00
2	100.00
3 GT	100.00
4	75.00
5	75.00
6 JSt	75.00
7	75.00
8 March, 1952	75.00

PROFESSOR XAVIER AND THE X-MEN
1995

1 1st Year Together	1.00
2 V:The Vanisher	1.00
3 FaN,F:The Blob	1.00
4 V:Magneto & Brotherhood	1.00
5	1.00
6	1.00
7 FdS,Sub-Mariner	1.00
8 thru 12	1.00
13 AHo,F:Juggernaut	1.00

14 JGz,V:Juggernaut,	1.00
15 JGz,F:Quicksilver & Scarlet	
Witch	1.00
16	1.00
17 JGz,V:Sentinels,F:Beast	1.00
18 JGz,X-Men vs. Sentinels,	
final issue	1.00

PROWLER, THE
1994

1 Creatures of the Night, pt.1	1.75
2 V:Nightcreeper, Creatures, pt.2	1.75
3 Creatures of the Night, pt.3	1.75
4 V:Vulture, Creatures, pt.4	1.75

Psi Force #9
© Marvel Entertainment Group

PSI FORCE
Nov., 1986

1 MT,O:PSI Force	1.25
2 MT	1.00
3 MT,CIA	1.00
4 MT,J:Network	1.00
5 MT	1.00
6 MT(c)	1.00
7 MT(c)	1.00
8 MT	1.00
9 MT(c)	1.00
10 PSI Hawk	1.00
11	1.00
12 MT(c)	1.00
13	1.00
14 AW	1.00
15	1.00
16 RLm	1.25
17 RLm	1.25
18 RLm	1.25
19 RLm	1.25
20 RLm,V:Medusa Web;Rodstvow	1.50
21 RLm	1.50
22 RLm,A:Nightmask	1.50
23 A:D.P.7	1.50
24	1.50
25	1.25
26	1.25
27 thru 31	@1.50
32 June, 1989	1.50
Ann.#1	1.25

PSYCHONAUTS
Epic 1993–94

1 thru 4 War in the Future	4.95

PSYLOCKE & ANGEL: CRIMSON DAWN
1997

1 SvL,ATi,V:Obsideon	3.00
2 SvL,ATi,	3.00
3 BRa,SvL,ATi	3.00
4 (of 4) BRa,SvL,ATi	3.00

PUNISHER
[Limited Series] Jan., 1986

1 MZ,Circle of Blood,double size	6.00
2 MZ,Back to the War	5.00
3 MZ,V:The Right	4.00
4 MZ,V:The Right	3.00
5 V:Jigsaw,end Mini-Series	3.00

[Regular Series] 1987–95

1 KJ,V:Wilfred Sobel,Drugs	5.00
2 KJ,V:General Trahn,Bolivia	3.00
3 KJ,V:Colonel Fryer	2.50
4 KJ,I:The Rev,Microchip Jr.	2.50
5 KJ,V:The Rev	2.50
6 DR,KN,V:The Rosettis	2.50
7 DR,V:Ahmad,D:Rose	2.50
8 WPo,SW(1st Punisher),	
V:Sigo & Roky	3.00
9 WPo,SW,D:MicrochipJr,V:Sigo	2.50
10 WPo,SW,A:Daredevil (x-over	
w/Daredevil #257)	3.00
11 WPo,SW,O:Punisher	2.00
12 WPo,SW,V:Gary Saunders	2.00
13 WPo,SW,V:Lydia Spoto	2.00
14 WPo,SW,I:McDowell,Brooks	2.00
15 WPo,SW,V:Kingpin	2.00
16 WPo,SW,V:Kingpin	2.00
17 WPo,SW,V:Kingpin	2.00
18 WPo,SW,V:Kingpin,C:X-Men	2.00
19 LSn,In Australia	2.00
20 WPo(c),In Las Vegas	2.00
21 EL,SW,Boxing Issue	2.00
22 EL,SW,I:Saracen	2.00
23 EL,SW,V:Scully	2.00
24 EL,SW,A:Shadowmasters	2.00
25 EL,AW,A:Shadowmasters	2.00
26 RH,Oper.Whistle Blower#1	2.00
27 RH,Oper.Whistle Blower#2	2.00
28 BR,A:Dr.Doom,A of Veng.	2.00
29 BR,A:Dr.Doom,A of Veng.	2.00
30 BR,V:Geltrate	2.00
31 BR,V:Bikers #1	2.00
32 BR,V:Bikers #2	2.00
33 BR,V:The Reavers	2.00
34 BR,V:The Reavers	2.00
35 BR,MF,Jigsaw Puzzle #1	2.00
36 MT,MF,Jigsaw Puzzle #2	2.00
37 MT,Jigsaw Puzzle #3	2.00
38 BR,MF,Jigsaw Puzzle #4	2.00
39 JSh,Jigsaw Puzzle #5	2.00
40 BR,JSh,Jigsaw Puzzle #6	2.00
41 BR,TD,V:Terrorists	2.00
42 MT,V:Corrupt Mili. School.	2.00
43 BR,Border Run	2.00
44 Flag Burner	2.00
45 One Way Fare	2.00
46 HH,Cold Cache	2.00
47 HH,Middle East #1	2.00
48 HH,Mid.East #2,V:Saracen	2.00
49 HH,Punisher Hunted	2.00
50 HH,MGo(c),I:Yo Yo Ng	2.00
51 Chinese Mafia	2.00
52 Baby Snatchers	2.00
53 HH,in Prison	2.00
54 HH,in Prison	2.00
55 HH,in Prison	2.00
56 HH,in Prison	2.00
57 HH,in Prison	2.00
58 V:Kingpin's Gang,A:Micro	2.50
59 MT(c),V:Kingpin	2.00
60 VM,AW,Black Punisher,	
A:Luke Cage	2.00

Punisher #25
© Marvel Entertainment Group

61 VM,A:Luke Cage 2.00
62 VM,AW,A:Luke Cage 1.50
63 MT(c),VM,V:Thieves 1.50
64 Eurohit #1 . . . . 1.50
65 thru 70 Eurohit . . . . @1.50
71 AW(i) 1.50
72 AW(i) 1.50
73 AW(i),Police Action #1 . . . . . . 1.50
74 AW(i),Police Action #2 . . . . . . 1.50
75 AW(i),Police Action #3,foil(c),
  double size. 2.50
76 LSn,in Hawaii 1.50
77 VM,Survive#1 . . . . 1.50
78 VM,Survive#2 . . . . 1.50
79 VM,Survive#3 . . . . 1.50
80 Goes to Church 1.50
81 V:Crooked Cops 1.50
82 B:Firefight 1.50
83 Firefight#2 . . . . 1.50
84 E:Firefight 1.50
85 Suicide Run 2.00
86 Suicide Run#3,Foil(c), ... 2.00
87 Suicide Run#6 . . . . 1.50
88 LSh(c),Suicide Run#9 . . . . 1.50
89 . . . . 1.75
90 Hammered 1.75
91 Silk Noose 1.75
92 Razor's Edge 1.75
93 Killing Streets 1.75
94 B:No Rules 1.50
95 No Rules 1.50
96 . . . . 1.50
97 CDi 1.50
98 . . . . 1.50
99 . . . . 1.50
100 New Punisher 3.00
100a Enhanced ed. 4.00
101 CC,Raid's Franks Tomb 1.50
102 A:Bullseye 1.50
103 Countdown 4 . . . . 1.50
104 CDi,Countdown 1, V:Kingpin,
  final issue. 1.50
Ann.#1 MT,A:Eliminators,
  Evolutionary War. 4.00
Ann.#2 JLe,Atlantis Attacks #5,
  A:Moon Knight 3.50
Ann.#3 LS,MT,Lifeform #1 . . . . . . 3.00
Ann.#4 Baron Strucker,pt.2
  (see D.D.Annual #7) 3.00
Ann.#5 System Bytes #1 . . . . 2.50
Ann.#6 I:Eradikator,w/card 3.25
GNv 5.00
Summer Spec.#1 VM,MT 3.50
Summer Spec.#2 SBs(c) 2.50

Summer Spec.#3 V:Carjackers 2.50
Summer Spec.#4 . . . . 3.25
Spec. Punisher/Batman,CDi,JR2,
  48pg (1994) 5.00
Spec.#1 Punisher/Daredevil, rep.
  Daredevil 6.00
Punisher:No Escape A:USAgent,
  Paladin (1990) 5.50
Punisher Movie Spec.BA (1989) . . . 5.95
GNv Punisher: The Prize (1990) . . 5.50
Punisher:Bloodlines DC 6.25
Punisher:Blood on the Moors . . 16.95
Punisher:G-Force 5.25
Punisher:Origin of Mirco Chip #1,
  O:Mirco Chip 2.00
Punisher:Origin of Mirco Chip #2
  V:The Professor 2.00
Classic Punisher rep early
  B&W magazines. 7.00
Punisher:Back To School Spec.
  #1 JRy,short stories 3.25
  #2 BSz 2.95
Punisher:Die Hard in the Big
  Easy Mardi Gras 5.25
Holiday Spec.#1 V:Young
  Mob Capo 3.25
Holiday Spec #2 . . . . 2.95
Punisher:Ghosts of the Innocent#1
  TGr, V:Kingpin's Dead Men . . . 5.95
Punisher:Ghosts of the Innocent#2
  TGr, V:Kingpin,Snake 5.95
TPB Punisher: Eye For An Eye. . . 9.95

[2nd Regular Series] 1995
1 JOs,TL,Clv,Punisher sent to
  the Electric Chair, foil(c) 2.95
2 JOs,TL,Clv,Crime family boss . . 1.95
3 JOs,TL,Clv,V:Hatchetman. 1.95
4 JOs,TL,Clv,A:Daredevil,Jigsaw . 1.95
5 . . . . 1.95
6 . . . . 1.95
7 JOs,TL,Clv,V:Son of Nick Fury . 1.95
8 . . . . 1.50
9 . . . . 1.50
10 . . . . 1.50
11 Onslaught saga 1.50
12 A:X-Cutioner 3.00
13 JOs,TL, Working for S.H.I.E.L.D.?,
  A:X-Cutioner 1.50
14 . . . . 1.50
15 JOs,TL, X-Cutioner 1.50
16 JOS,TL, concl.? 1.50
17 JOS,TL,A:Daredevil,Doc Samson,
  Spider-Man 1.50
18 JOS,TL,Frank Castle amnesia? . 1.95
19 JOS,TL,V:Taskmaster 1.95
20 JOS,TL, fugitive Punisher 1.95

PUNISHER
Sept. 1998
1 (of 4) BWr,JP,TSg,F:Frank
  Castle 3.00
2 BWr,JJu,JP,A:Hellstrom 3.00
3 BWr,JJu,TSg,JP,A:Gadriel. 3.00
4 BWr,JJu,TSg,JP,Hell on Earth. . . 3.00

PUNISHER ARMORY
July, 1990
1 JLe(c) 3.00
2 JLe(c) 2.00
3 . . . . 2.00
4 thru 6 . . . . @2.00
7 thru 10 . . . . @2.00

PUNISHER/
CAPTAIN AMERICA:
BLOOD AND GLORY
1 thru 3 KJ,V:Drug Dealers. . . . . @6.25

CLASSIC PUNISHER
1 TDz 4.95

PUNISHER KILLS
THE MARVEL UNIVERSE
1995
1-shot Alterniverse. 5.95

PUNISHER MAGAZINE
Oct., 1989
1 MZ,rep.,Punisher #1 . . . . 2.50
2 MZ,rep 2.25
3 thru 13 KJ,rep. . . . . @2.25
14 rep. PWJ #1&#2 . . . . 2.25
15 rep. PWJ 2.25
16 rep.,1990. . . . . 2.25

PUNISHER
MEETS ARCHIE
1994
1 JB 4.25
1a newsstand ed. 3.25

PUNISHER MOVIE COMIC
Nov., 1989
1 Movie adapt.. . . . . 1.50
2 Movie adapt.. . . . . 1.50
3 Movie adapt,Dec., 1989 . . . . . . 1.50

PUNISHER P.O.V.
July, 1991
1 BWr,Punisher/Nick Fury 5.50
2 BWr,A:Nick Fury,Kingpin 5.50
3 BWr,V:Mutant Monster,
  A:Vampire Slayer 5.50
4 BWr,A:Nick Fury 5.25

PUNISHER 2099
1993–95
1 TMo,Jake Gallows family
  Killed, foil(c) 2.50
2 TMo,I:Fearmaster,Kron,Multi
  Factor 2.25
3 TMo,V:Frightening Cult. 2.25
4 TMo,V:Cyber Nostra 1.75
5 TMo,V:Cyber Nostra,Fearmaster. 1.75
6 TMo,V:Multi-Factor 1.75

Punisher 2099 #12
© Marvel Entertainment Group

7 TMo,Love and Bullets#1 . . . . . . 1.75
8 TMo,Love and Bullets#2 . . . . 1.75
9 TMo,Love and Bullets#3 . . . . 1.75
10 TMo,I:Jigsaw 1.50
11 TMo,V:Jigsaw 1.50
12 TMo,A:Spider-Man 2099 . . . . . 1.50
13 TMo,Fall of the Hammer#5 . . . . 1.50
14 WSm, ... 1.50
15 TMo,V:Fearmaster,
   I:Public Enemy 1.50
16 TMo,V:Fearmaster,
   Public Enemy 1.75
17 TMo,V:Public Enemy 1.75
18 TMo,I:Goldheart. 1.75
19 TMo,I:Vendetta 1.50
20 . . . . 1.50
21 . . . . 1.50
22 V:Hotwire. 1.50
23 I:Synchron,V:Hotwire 1.50
24 V:Synchron 1.50
25 Enhanced cover. 2.95
25a newsstand ed. 2.25
26 V:Techno-Shaman 1.50
27 R:Blue Max 1.50
Becomes:

PUNISHER 2099 A.D.

28 Minister of Punishment 1.95
29 Minister of Punishment 1.95
30 One Nation Under Doom 1.95
31 . . . . 1.95
32 Out of Ammo 1.95
33 Counddown to final issue. 1.95
34 final issue 1.95

Punisher War Journal #2
© *Marvel Entertainment Group*

PUNISHER WAR JOURNAL
Nov., 1988

1 CP,JLe,O:Punisher 3.00
2 CP,JLe,A:Daredevil. 2.50
3 CP,JLe,A:Daredevil. 2.50
4 CP,JLeV:The Sniper 2.50
5 CP,JLe,V:The Sniper. 2.50
6 CP,JLe,A:Wolverine 2.50
7 CP,JLe,A:Wolverine 2.50
8 JLe,I:Shadowmasters 2.50
9 JLe,A:Black Widow. 2.50
10 JLe,V:Sniper 2.50
11 JLe,Shock Treatment 2.00
12 JLe,AM,V:Bushwacker. 2.00
13 JLe(c),V:Bushwacker 2.00
14 JLe(c),DR,RH,A:Spider-Man . . 2.00
15 JLe(c),DR,RH,A:Spider-Man . . 2.00
16 MT(i),Texas Massacre 2.00

17 JLe,AM,Hawaii. 2.00
18 JLe,AM,Kahuna,Hawaii 2.00
19 JLe,AM,Traume in Paradise. . . 2.00
20 AM 2.00
21 TSm,AM 2.00
22 TSm,AM,Ruins #1 . . . . 2.00
23 TSm,AM,Ruins #2 . . . . 2.00
24 . . . . 2.00
25 MT 2.00
26 MT,A:Saracen 2.00
27 MT,A:Saracen 2.00
28 MT 2.00
29 MT,A:Ghostrider. 2.00
30 MT,A:Ghostrider. 2.00
31 NKu,Kamchatkan
   Konspiracy#1 . . . . 2.00
32 Kamchatkan Konspiracy #2 . . . 2.00
33 Kamchatkan Konspiracy #3 . . . 2.00
34 V:Psycho 2.00
35 Movie Stuntman. 2.00
36 Radio Talk Show #1 . . . . 2.00
37 Radio Talk Show #2. . . . . 2.00
38 . . . . 2.00
39 DGr,V:Serial Killer 2.00
40 MWg 1.75
41 Armageddon Express 1.75
42 Mob run-out. 1.75
43 JR2(c) 1.75
44 Organ Donor Crimes 1.75
45 Dead Man's Hand #3,V:Viper. . . 2.00
46 Dead Man's Hand #6,V:Chainsaw
   and the Praetorians 1.75
47 Dead Man's Hand #7,A:Nomad,
   D.D,V:Hydra,Secret Empire . . 1.75
48 B:Payback. 1.75
49 JR2(c),V:Corrupt Cop 1.75
50 MT,V:Highjackers,I:Punisher
   2099 . . . . 2.00
51 E:Payback. 1.75
52 A:Ice(from The'Nam) 1.75
53 A:Ice(from the Nam) 1.75
54 Hyper#1 . . . . 1.75
55 Hyper#2 . . . . 1.75
56 Hyper#3 . . . . 1.75
57 A:Ghost Rider,Daredevil. 1.75
58 A:Ghost Rider,Daredevil. 1.75
59 F:Max the Dog. 1.75
60 CDi(s),F:Max the Dog 1.75
61 CDi(s),Suicide Run#1,Foil(c) . . . 3.00
62 CDi(s),Suicide Run#4 . . . . 2.00
63 CDi(s),Suicide Run#7 . . . . 2.00
64 CDi(s),Suicide Run#10 . . . . . . 3.00
64a Newsstand Ed. 2.50
65 B:Pariah 2.00
66 A:Captain America. 2.25
67 Pariah#3 . . . . 2.25
68 A:Spider-Man 2.25
69 E:Pariah 1.95
70 . . . . 1.95
71 . . . . 1.95
72 V:Fake Punisher 1.95
73 E:Frank Castle. 1.95
74 . . . . 1.95
75 MT(c) 2.50
76 First Entry 1.95
77 R:Stone COld 1.95
78 V:Payback,Heathen. 1.95
79 Countdown 3 . . . . 1.95
80 Countdown 0, A:Nick Fury,
   V:Bullseye, final issue. 1.95
TPB reprints #6,7 . . . . 4.95

PUNISHER WAR ZONE
1992

1 JR2,KJ,Punisher As Johnny Tower
   Die-Cut Bullet Hole(c). 3.00
2 JR2,KJ,Mafia Career 2.00
3 JR2,KJ,Punisher/Mafia,contd . . . 2.00
4 JR2,KJ,Cover gets Blown 2.00
5 JR2,KJ,A:Shotgun 2.00

6 JR2,KJ,A:Shotgun 2.00
7 JR2,V:Rapist in Central Park . . . 2.00
8 JR2,V:Rapist in Central Park . . . 2.00
9 JR2,V:Magnificent Seven. 2.00
10 JR2,V:Magnificent Seven. 2.00
11 JR2,MM,V:Magnificent Seven. . 2.00
12 Punisher Married 2.00
13 Self-Realization 2.00
14 Psychoville#3 . . . . 2.00
15 Psychoville#4 . . . . 2.00
16 Psychoville#5 . . . . 2.00
17 Industrial Esponiage 2.00
18 Jerico Syndrome#2 . . . . 2.00
19 Jerico Syndrome#3 . . . . 2.00
20 B:2 Mean 2 Die 2.00
21 2 Mean 2 Die#2 . . . . 2.00
22 A:Tyger Tyger 2.00
23 Suicide Run#2,Foil(c). 3.25
24 Suicide Run#5, ... 2.00
25 Suicide Run#8, ... 2.50
26 CDi(s),JB,Pirates 2.00
27 CDi(s),JB, ... 2.25
28 CDi(s),JB,Sweet Revenge 2.25
29 CDi(s),JB,The Swine 2.25
30 CDi(s),JB, ... 1.95
31 CDi(s),JB,River of Blood,pt.1 . . 1.95
32 CDi(s),JB,River of Blood,pt.2 . . 1.95
33 CDi(s),JB,River of Blood,pt.3 . . 1.95
34 CDi(s),JB,River of Blood,pt.4 . . 1.95
35 River of Blood,pt.5. . . . . 1.95
36 River of Blood,pt.6. . . . . 1.95
37 O:Max 1.95
38 Dark Judgment,pt.1 . . . . 1.95
39 Dark Judgment,pt.2 . . . . 1.95
40 In Court 1.95
41 CDi,Countdown 2, final issue . . 1.95
Ann.#1 Jb,MGo,(c),I:Phalanx,
   w/Trading card 3.25
Ann.#2 CDi(s),DR. 2.95

PUNISHER: YEAR ONE
1994

1 O:Punisher 2.50
2 O:Punisher 2.50
3 O:Punisher 2.50
4 finale 2.50

PUSSYCAT
(B&W Magazine) Oct., 1968
1 BEv,BWa,WW 175.00

QUASAR
Oct., 1989

1 O:Quasar 2.50
2 V:Deathurge,A:Eon. 2.00
3 A:Human Torch,V:The Angler . . . 2.00
4 Acts of Vengeance,A:Aquarian . . 2.00
5 A of Veng,V:Absorbing Man 2.00
6 V:Klaw,Living Laser,Venom,
   Red Ghost 3.00
7 MM,A:Cosmic SpM,V:Terminus. . 2.50
8 MM,A:New Mutants,BlueShield. . 2.00
9 MM,A:Modam. 2.00
10 MM,A:Dr.Minerva. 2.00
11 MM,A:Excalibur,A:Modred 2.00
12 MM,A:Makhari,Blood Bros.. . . . 1.75
13 JLe(c)MM,J.into Mystery #1 . . . . 1.75
14 TM(c)MM,J.into Mystery #2 . . . . 2.00
15 MM,Journey into Mystery #3 . . . 1.75
16 MM,Double sized. 2.00
17 MM,Race,A:Makkari,Whizzer,
   Quicksilver,Capt.Marv,Super
   Sabre,Barry Allen Spoof 2.25
18 GCa,N:Quasar. 1.75
19 GCa,B:Cosmos in Collision,
   C:Thanos 2.00
20 GCa,A:Fantastic Four 2.00
21 GCa,V:Jack of Hearts 2.00

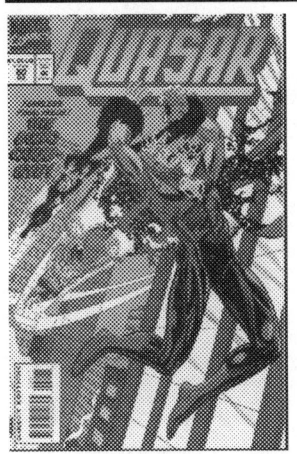

Quasar #60
© Marvel Entertainment Group

22 GCa,D:Quasar,A:Ghost Rider . . 2.00
23 GCa,A:Ghost Rider 2.00
24 GCa,A:Thanos,Galactus,
   D:Maelstrom. 2.00
25 GCa,Eternity & Infinity,N:Quasar,
   E:Cosmos Collision 2.00
26 GCa,Inf.Gauntlet,A:Thanos 2.50
27 GCa,Infinity Gauntlet,I:Epoch. . . 2.00
28 GCa,A:Moondragon,Her,
   X-Men 2.00
29 GCa,A:Moondragon,Her 1.50
30 GCa,What If? tie-in 1.50
31 GCa,R:New Universe. 1.50
32 GCa,Op.GalacticStorm,pt.3 . . . 1.50
33 GCa,Op.GalacticStorm,pt.10 . . . 1.50
34 GCa,Op.GalacticStorm,pt.17 . . . 1.50
35 GCa,Binary V:Her 1.50
36 GCa,V:Soul Eater 1.50
37 GCa,V:Soul Eater 1.50
38 GCa,Inf.War,V:Warlock 1.50
39 SLi,Inf.War,V:Deathurge. 1.50
40 SLi,Inf.War,V:Deathurge. 1.50
41 R:Marvel Boy 1.50
42 V:Blue Marvel 1.50
43 V:Blue Marvel 1.50
44 V:Quagmire. 1.50
45 V:Quagmire,Antibody. 1.50
46 Neutron,Presence 1.50
47 1st Full Thunderstrike Story 1.50
48 A:Thunderstrike 1.50
49 Kalya Vs. Kismet 1.50
50 A:Man-Thing,Prism(c) 3.25
51 V:Angler,A:S.Supreme 1.50
52 V:Geometer. 1.50
53 . . . . 1.50
54 MGu(s),Starblast #2. . . . . 1.50
55 MGu(s),A:Stranger. 1.50
56 MGu(s),Starblast #10. . . . . 1.50
57 MGu(s),A:Kismet 1.50
58 . . . . 1.50
59 A:Thanos,Starfox. 1.50
60 final issue 1.50

QUESTPROBE
August, 1984
1 JR,A:Hulk,I:Chief Examiner. 2.00
2 AM,JM,A:Spider-Man 1.75
3 JSt,A:Thing & Torch 1.50

QUICKSILVER
Sept. 1997
1 CJ,TPe, V:Exodus, cont. from

Excalibur #113 . . . . 3.00
2 TPe,CJ,A:Knights of Wundagore. 2.00
3 TPe,CJ,V:Arkon 2.00
4 TPe, Crystal returns 2.00
5 TPe,V:Inhumans. 2.00
6 TPe,Inhumands trilogy concl. . . . 2.00
7 JOs,F:The Black Knight 2.00
8 JOs,F:Pietro,V:Pyro 2.00
9 JOs,Savage Land concl.,A:High
   Evolutionary 2.00
10 JOS,Live Kree or Die, pt.3,
   x-over. 2.00
11 JOs,The Seige of Wundagore,
   pt.2 (of 5) 2.00
12 JOs,The Seige of Wundagore,
   pt.4 (of 5) 48pg. 3.00
13 JOs,Seige of Wundagore,pt.5,
   final issue. 2.00

QUICK-TRIGGER WESTERN
See: WESTERN THRILLERS

RAIDERS OF THE LOST ARK
Sept., 1981
1 JB/KJ,movie adaption 2.00
2 JB/KJ, ... 1.75
3 JB/KJ,Nov.,1981 . . . . 1.75

RAMPAGING HULK, THE
May 1998
1 RL,double size, savage Hulk era. 3.00
2A RL,DGr,I:Ravage 2.00
2B JQ,JP,variant cover 2.00
3 RL,DGr,V:Ravage, concl. 2.00
4 DR,Trapped by an Avalanche . . . 2.00
5 RL,F:Fantastic Four 2.00
6 RL,DGr,V:Puma 2.00

RAVAGE 2099
1992–95
1 PR,I:Ravage. 2.50
2 PR,V:Deathstryk 2.00
3 PR,V:Mutroids 2.00
4 PR,V:Mutroids 1.50
5 PR,Hellrock 1.50
6 PR,N:Ravage 1.50
7 PR,new Powers 1.50
8 V:Deathstryke 1.50
9 PR,N:Ravage 1.50
10 V:Alchemax 1.50
11 A:Avatarr 1.50
12 Ravage Transforms 1.50
13 V:Fearmaster. 1.50
14 V:Punisher 2099 . . . . 1.50
15 Fall of the Hammer #2 . . . . 1.50
16 I:Throwback. 1.50
17 GtM,V:Throwback,O:X-11. . . . . 1.50
18 GtM,w/card 1.75
19 GtM, ... 1.75
20 GtM,V:Hunter. 1.50
21 Savage on the Loose. 1.50
22 Exodus 1.50
23 Blind Justice 1.50
24 Unleashed. 1.50
25 Flame Bearer. 2.25
25a Deluxe ed. 2.95
26 V:Megastruck. 1.50
27 V:Deathstryke 1.50
28 R:Hela. 1.50
29 V:Deathstryke 1.50
30 King Ravage 1.50
Becomes:

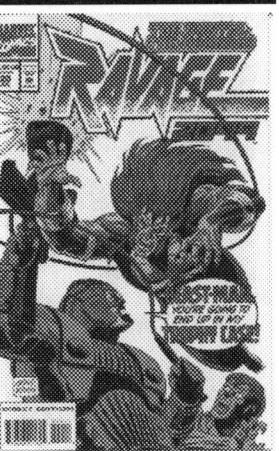

Ravage 2099 #20
© Marvel Entertainment Group

RAVAGE 2099 A.D.
31 V:Doom. 1.95
32 One Nation Under Doom 1.95
33 Final issue. 1.95

RAWHIDE KID
Atlas March, 1955—May, 1979
1 B:Rawhide Kid & Randy,
   A:Wyatt Earp 650.00
2 Shoot-out(c) 250.00
3 V:Hustler 175.00
4 Rh(c) 175.00
5 GC 175.00
6 Six-Gun Lesson 150.00
7 AW 150.00
8 . . . . 150.00
9 . . . . 150.00
10 thru 16 . . . . @100.00
17 JK,O:Rawhide Kid 100.00
18 thru 20 . . . . @100.00
21 . . . . 90.00
22 . . . . 90.00
23 JK,O:Rawhide Kid Retold. . . . 150.00
24 thru 30 . . . . @75.00
31 JK,DAy,No Law in Mesa. 85.00
32 JK,DAy,Beware of the
   Parker Brothers 85.00
33 JK(c),JDa,V:Jesse James 75.00
34 JDa,JK,V:Mister Lightning . . . 75.00
35 JK(c),GC,JDa,I&D:The Raven . 75.00
36 DAy,A Prisoner in
   Outlaw Town 65.00
37 JK(c),DAy,GC,V:The Rattler . . . 65.00
38 DAy.V:The Red Raven 65.00
39 DAy 65.00
40 JK(c),DAy,A:Two Gun Kid 65.00
41 JK(c),The Tyrant of
   Tombstone Valley 65.00
42 JK 65.00
43 JK 65.00
44 JK(c),V:The Masked Maverick . 65.00
45 JK(c),O:Rawhide Kid Retold. . . 75.00
46 JK(c),ATh 50.00
47 JK(c),The Riverboat Raiders . . 40.00
48 GC,V:Marko the Manhunter . . . 35.00
49 The Masquerader 35.00
50 A:Kid Colt,V:Masquerader 35.00
51 DAy,Trapped in the
   Valley of Doom. 35.00
52 DAy,Revenge at
   Rustler's Roost. 35.00
53 Guns of the Wild North 35.00
54 DH,BEv,The Last Showdown . . 35.00

MARVEL

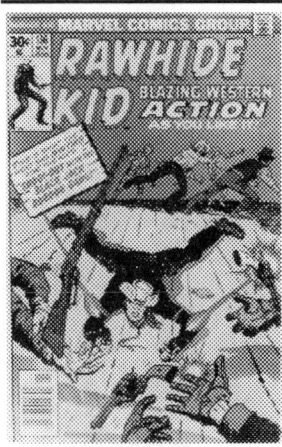

Rawhide Kid #136
© Marvel Entertainment Group

55 . . . . 35.00
56 DH,JTgV:The Peacemaker. . . . 35.00
57 V:The Scorpion 35.00
58 DAy. 35.00
59 V:Drako. 35.00
60 DAy,HT,Massacre at Medicine
  Bend 35.00
61 DAy,TS,A:Wild Bill Hickok 30.00
62 Gun Town,V:Drako. 30.00
63 Shootout at Mesa City 30.00
64 HT,Duel of the Desparadoes . . 30.00
65 JTg,HT,BE 30.00
66 JTg,BEv,Death of a Gunfighter. 30.00
67 Hostage of Hungry Hills 30.00
68 JB,V:The Cougar 30.00
69 JTg,The Executioner 30.00
70 JTg,The Night of the Betrayers 25.00
71 JTg,The Last Warrior 25.00
72 JTg,The Menace of Mystery
  Valley. 25.00
73 JTg,The Manhunt. 25.00
74 JTg,The Apaches Attack 25.00
75 JTg,The Man Who Killed
  The Kid 25.00
76 JTg,V:The Lynx 25.00
77 JTg,The Reckoning 25.00
78 JTg 25.00
79 JTg,AW,The Legion of the Lost 25.00
80 Fall of a Hero 25.00
81 thru 85 . . . . @25.00
86 JK,O:Rawhide Kid retold 25.00
87 thru 99 . . . . @12.00
100 O:Rawhide Kid retold. 15.00
101 thru 135 . . . . @12.00
126 thru 151 . . . . @10.00

RAWHIDE KID
August, 1985
1 JSe,mini-series. 1.50
2 thru 4 . . . . @1.25

RAZORLINE FIRST CUT
1993
1 Intro Razorline 1.00

REAL EXPERIENCES
See: TESSIE THE TYPIST

RED RAVEN
See: HUMAN TORCH

Red Sonja #1
© Marvel Entertainment Group

RED SONJA
[1st Series] Jan., 1977
1 FT,O:Red Sonja,`Blood of the
  Unicorn' 3.50
2 FT,`Demon of the Maze' 2.50
3 FT,`The Games of Gita' 2.00
4 FT,`The Lake of the Unknown' . . 2.00
5 FT,`Master of the Bells'. 2.00
6 FT,`The Singing Tower' 1.25
7 FT,`Throne of Blood' 1.25
8 FT,Vengeance o/t Golden Circle . 1.25
9 FT,`Chariot o/t Fire-Stallions'. . . . 1.25
10 FT,Red Lace,pt.1 . . . . 1.25
11 FT,Red Lace,pt.2 . . . . 1.25
12 JB/JRu,`Ashes & Emblems' 1.25
13 JB/AM,`Shall Skranos Fall'. 1.25
14 SB/AM,`Evening on the Border' . 1.25
15 JB/TD,`Tomb of 3 Dead Kings'
  May, 1979 . . . . 1.25
[2nd Series] Feb., 1983
1 TD,GC, The Blood That Binds . . 1.25
2 GC, March,1983 . . . . 1.00
[3rd Series] August, 1983
1 . . . . 1.25
2 thru 13 . . . . @1.25
1 movie adaption, 1985 . . . . 1.25
2 movie adaption, 1985 . . . . 1.25

RED SONJA
1-shot Bros.Hildebrandt(c),48pg . . . 2.95

RED WARRIOR
Atlas Jan.–Dec., 1951
1 GT,Indian Tales 100.00
2 GT(c),The Trail of the Outcast . 65.00
3 The Great Spirit Speaks 50.00
4 O:White Wing 50.00
5 . . . . 50.00
6 Final Issue 50.00

RED WOLF
May, 1972–Sept. 1973
1 SSh(c),GK,JSe,F:Red Wolf
  & Lobo 18.00
2 GK(c),SSh,Day of the Dynamite
  Doom 10.00
3 SSh,War of the Wolf Brothers . 10.00
4 SSh,V:Man-Bear 10.00
5 GK(c),SSh 10.00
6 SSh,JA,V;Devil Rider 10.00

7 SSh,JA,Echoes from a Golden
  Grave 10.00
8 SSh,Hell on Wheels 10.00
9 DAy,To Die Again,O:Lobo 10.00

REN AND STIMPY SHOW
1992–96
1 Polybagged w/Air Fowlers,
  Ren(c) 5.00
1a Stimpy(c) 4.00
1b 2nd Printing 3.00
1c 3rd Printing. 2.00
2 Frankenstimpy 3.00
2a 2nd Printing 2.00
3 Christmas issue 3.00
3a 2nd Printing 2.00
4 Where's Stimpy? 3.00
5 Teacher Bingo 3.00
6 A:SpM,V:Powdered Toast Man . . 3.00
7 F:Offical Yak Shaving Day 3.00
8 F:Bun Boy Burger Bunny 3.00
9 Untamed World 3.00
10 Bug Out. 3.00
11 Ren's Peaceful Place. 3.00
12 Teacher Bingo 3.00
13 Halloween issue 2.50
14 Mars needs Vecro 2.50
15 Christmas Spec. 2.25
16 . . . . 2.25
17 This Year's Model 2.25
18 U.S. Ohhhhh No!. 2.25
19 Minimalist issue 2.25
20 F:Muddy Mudskipper 2.25
21 I'm The Cat 2.25
22 Badtime Stories 2.00
23 Athletics 2.00
24 Halloween 2.00
25 regular (c) 2.00
25a die-cut(c),A new addition 3.00
26 . . . . 2.00
27 . . . . 2.00
28 Filthy the Monkey 2.00
29 Loch Ness Mess 2.00
30 Pinata game 2.00
31 Sausage Castle 2.00
32 Join Circus, UFO Abduction. . . . 2.00
33 Bowling 2.00
34 lottery ticket. 2.00
35 Pasta Monster 2.00
36 Ren Cabby Driver 2.00
37 Medical experiment 2.00
38 Cat who Knew too Much 2.00
39 Mad Computer. 2.00
40 . . . . 2.00
41 . . . . 2.00
42 at Cap'n Salty Wet World. 2.00
Spec.#1 . . . . 3.25
Spec.#2 . . . . 3.25
Spec.#3 Powder Toast Man 3.00
Spec.#4 . . . . 3.00
Spec.#5 Virtual Stupidity. 3.00
Spec.#6 History of Music 3.00
Holiday Special. 3.00
Spec. Radio Dazed & Confused . . . 2.00
Spec. Around the World in a Daze . 3.00
TPB Running Joke,rep.#1-4,w/new
  material 13.25
TPB Pick of the Litter 13.25
TPB Tastes Like Chicken 13.25
TPB Your Pals 12.95
TPB Seech Little Monkeys 12.95

RETURN OF THE JEDI
1 AW,movie adapt 3.00
2 AW,movie adapt 3.00
3 AW,movie adapt 3.00
4 AW,movie adapt 3.00

REX HART
See: BLAZE CARSON

RICHIE RICH
1 Movie Adaptation 2.95

RINGO KID
[2nd Series] Jan., 1970
1 AW,Reprints 15.00
2 JSe,Man Trap 8.00
3 JR,the Man From the Panhandle 8.00
4 HT(c),The Golden Spur 8.00
5 JMn,Ambush 8.00
6 Capture or Death 8.00
7 HT(c),JSe,JA,Terrible Treasure
   of Vista Del Oro 8.00
8 The End of the Trail 8.00
9 JSe,Mystery of the Black
   Sunset 8.00
10 Bad day at Black Creek 8.00
11 Bullet for a Bandit 8.00
12 A Badge to Die For 15.00
13 DW,Hostage at Fort Cheyenne . 6.00
14 Showdown in the Silver
   Cartwheel 6.00
15 Fang,Claw, and Six-Gun 6.00
16 Battle of Cattleman's Bank 6.00
17 Gundown at the Hacienda 6.00
18 . . . . 6.00
19 Thunder From the West 6.00
20 AW 6.00
21 thru 29 . . . . @6.00
30 Nov., 1973 . . . . 6.00

RINGO KID WESTERN
Atlas August, 1954
1 JSt,O:Ringo Kid,B:Ringo Kid . 200.00
2 I&O:Arab,A:Black Rider 100.00
3 . . . . 75.00
4 . . . . 75.00
5 . . . . 75.00
6 . . . . 75.00
7 . . . . 75.00
8 JSe 75.00
9 . . . . 50.00
10 JSe(c),AW 60.00
11 JSe(c) 50.00
12 JO 50.00
13 AW 60.00
14 thru 20 . . . . @50.00
21 Sept., 1957 . . . . 50.00

ROBOCOP
March, 1990
1 LS,I:Nixcops 6.00
2 LS,V:Nixcops 4.00
3 LS 3.00
4 LS 3.00
5 LS,WarzonePt1 . . . . 3.00
6 LS,WarzonePt2 . . . . 3.00
7 LS 2.50
8 LS,V:Gang-5. . . . . 2.50
9 LS,V:Vigilantes 2.50
10 LS 2.50
11 HT 2.50
12 LS,Robocop Army #1. . . . . 2.00
13 LS,Robocop Army #2. . . . . 2.00
14 LS,Robocop Army #3. . . . . 2.00
15 LS,Robocop Army #4. . . . . 2.00
16 TV take over 2.00
17 LS,V:The Wraith 2.00
18 LS,Mindbomb #1 . . . . 2.00
19 LS,Mindbomb #2 . . . . 2.00
20 In Detroit 2.00
21 LS,Beyond the Law,pt.1 . . . . . . 2.00
22 LS,Beyond the Law,pt.2 . . . . . . 2.00
23 LS,Beyond the Law,pt.3,final . . . 2.00

Robocop Movie Adapt 4.95
Robocop II Movie Adapt 4.95

ROBOCOP II
August, 1990
1 MBa,rep.Movie Adapt. 2.00
2 and 3 MBa,rep.Movie adapt . . @1.50

ROBOTIX
Feb., 1986
1 Based on toys 1.00

ROCKET RACCOON
May, 1985—Aug., 1985
1 thru 4 MM . . . . @1.50

Rocko's Modern Life #1
© Marvel Entertainment Group

ROCKO'S MODERN LIFE
1994
1 and 2 . . . . @2.25
3 and 4 . . . . @1.95

ROGUE
1995
1 Enhanced cover 4.50
2 A:Gambit 4.00
3 Gamtit or Rogue? 2.95
4 final issue 2.95

ROM
Dec., 1979
1 SB,I&O:Rom. 3.00
2 FM(c),SB,V:Dire Wraiths 2.50
3 FM(c),SB,I:Firefall. 2.50
4 SB,A:Firefall 2.00
5 SB,A:Dr.Strange 2.00
6 SB,V:Black Nebula 1.50
7 SB,V:Dark Nebula 1.50
8 SB,V:Dire Wraiths. 1.50
9 SB,V:Serpentyne 1.50
10 SB,V:U.S.Air Force 1.50
11 SB,V:Dire Wraiths 1.50
12 SB,A:Jack O' Hearts 1.75
13 SB,V:Plunderer 1.25
14 SB,V:Mad Thinker 1.25
15 SB,W:Brandy and Dire Wraith . . 1.25
16 SB,V:Watchwraith 1.25
17 SB,A:X-Men. 3.00
18 SB,A:X-Men. 3.00
19 SB,JSt,C:X-Men 1.50

20 SB,JSt,A:Starshine 1.25
21 SB,JSt,A:Torpedo 1.25
22 SB,JSt,A:Torpedo 1.25
23 SB,JSt,A:Powerman,Iron Fist. . . 1.25
24 SB,JSt,A:Nova. 1.25
25 SB,JSt,Double-Sized 1.50
26 SB,JSt,V:Galactus 1.00
27 SB,JSt,V:Galactus 1.00
28 SB,JSt,D:Starshine 1.00
29 SB,Down in the Mines 1.00
30 SB,JSt,A:Torpedo 1.00
31 SB,JSt,V:Evil Mutants,Rogue . . . 2.00
32 SB,JSt,V:Evil Mutants 2.00
33 SB,V:Sybil 1.00
34 SB,A:Sub-Mariner 1.00
35 SB,A:Sub-Mariner 1.00
36 SB,V:Scarecrow. 1.00
37 SB,A:Starshine 1.00
38 SB,A:Master of Kung Fu 1.00
39 SB,A:Master of Kung Fu 1.00
40 SB,A:Torpedo 1.00
41 SB,A:Dr.Strange 1.00
42 SB,A:Dr.Strange 1.00
43 SB,Rom Becomes Human 1.00
44 SB,A:Starshine,O:Gremlin 1.00
45 SB,V:Soviet Super Soldiers 1.00
46 SB,V:Direwraiths 1.00
47 SB,New Look for Wraiths 1.00
48 SB,V:Dire Wraiths 1.00
49 SB,V:Dire Wraiths 1.00
50 SB,D:Torpedo,V:Skrulls 1.25
51 SB,F:Starshine 1.00
52 BSz(c),SB,V:Dire Wraiths. 1.00
53 SB,BSz,V:Dire Wraiths. 1.00
54 V:Dire Wraiths 1.00
55 V:Dire Wraihs 1.00
56 A:Alpha Flight 2.00
57 A:Alpha Flight 2.00
58 JG(c),A:Antman 1.00
59 SD,BL,V:Microbe Menace 1.00
60 SD,TP,V:Dire Wraiths. 1.00
61 SD,V:Wraith-Realm 1.00
62 SD,A:Forge 1.25
63 SD,V:Dire Wraiths 1.00
64 SD,V:Dire Wraiths 1.00
65 SD,A:X-Men,Avengers. 1.25
66 SD,Rom leaves Earth 1.25
67 SD,V:Scorpion 1.00
68 BSz(c)SD,Man & Machine 1.00
69 SD,V:Ego 1.00
70 SD. 1.00
71 SD,V:Raak. 1.00
72 SD,Secret Wars II 1.25
73 SD,JSt. 1.00

Rom #1
© Marvel Entertainment Group

MARVEL (side tab)

74 SD,JBy,Code of Honor. 1.00
75 SD,CR,Doublesize,last issue . . . 1.50
Ann.#1 PB,A:Stardust. 1.50
Ann.#2 I:Knights of Galador 1.25
Ann.#3 A:New Mutants. 2.00
Ann.#4 V:Gladiator 1.25

ROMANCE DIARY
Dec., 1949
1 . . . . 75.00
2 March, 1950 . . . . 60.00

ROMANCES OF
THE WEST
Nov., 1949
1 Ph(c),Calamity Jane,
  Sam Bass. 150.00
2 March, 1950 . . . . 100.00

ROMANCE TALES
Oct., 1949
(no #1 thru 6)
7 . . . . 75.00
8 . . . . 50.00
9 March, 1950 . . . . 50.00

ROMANTIC AFFAIRS
See: MOLLY MANTON'S
ROMANCES

ROYAL ROY
Star May, 1985
1 thru 5 . . . . @1.00
6 March, 1986 . . . . 1.00

RUGGED ACTION
Atlas Dec., 1954
1 Man-Eater 100.00
2 JSe,DAy.Manta-Ray 60.00
3 DAy 60.00
4 . . . . 60.00
Becomes:

STRANGE STORIES
OF SUSPENSE
5 RH,The Little Black Box 300.00
6 BEv,The Illusion 150.00
7 JSe(c),BEv,Old John's House . 165.00
8 AW,BP,TYhumbs Down 165.00
9 BEv(c),Nightmare 150.00
10 RC,MME,AT. 165.00
11 BEv(c) 125.00
12 AT 125.00
13 BEv,GM 100.00
14 AW 150.00
15 BK 135.00
16 MF,BP, August, 1957 . . . . . . 135.00

RUINS
1995
1 Marvel's Alterverse 4.95
2 Fully painted, 32pg. 4.95

RUSTY COMICS
See: KID KOMICS

SABRETOOTH
[Limited Series] 1993
1 B:LHa(s),MT,A:Wolverine 5.00
2 MT,A:Mystique,C:Wolverine . . . 4.00
3 MT,A:Mystique,Wolverine 3.50

4 E:LHa(s),MT,D:Birdy 3.00
TPB rep. #1–#4. . . . . 12.95

SABRETOOTH CLASSICS
1994–95
1 rep. Power Man/Iron Fist #66 . . . 1.75
2 rep. Power Man/Iron Fist #78 . . . 1.75
3 rep. Power Man/Iron Fist #84 . . . 1.75
4 rep. Spider-Man #116 . . . . 1.75
5 rep. Spider-Man #119 . . . . 1.50
6 reprints. 1.50
7 reprints. 1.50
8 reprints. 1.50
9 reprints. 1.50
10 Morlock Massacre 1.50
11 rep. Daredevil #238 . . . . 1.50
12 rep. V:Wolverine 1.50
13 rep. 1.50
14 A:Mauraders 1.50
15 Mutant Massacre, rep.
   Uncanny X-Men #221. . . . . . . 1.50

SABRETOOTH
Spec.#1 FaN, cont.from X-Men#48 . 4.95

SABRETOOTH
Oct., 1997
1-shot,F:Wildchild 2.50

SABRETOOTH
& MYSTIQUE
1 JGz,AOI,. 1.95
2 thru 4 JGz,AOI . . . . @1.95

SACHS & VIOLENS
Epic 1993–94
1 GP,PDd(s) 3.00
2 GP,PDd(s),V:Killer 2.50
3 GP,PDd(s),V:White Slavers. 2.50
4 GP,PDd(s),D:Moloch. 2.25

SAGA OF CRYSTAR
May, 1983
1 O:Crystar 2.25
2 A:Ika 1.50
3 A:Dr.Strange. 1.50
4 . . . . 1.50
5 . . . . 1.50
6 A:Nightcrawler 2.00
7 I:Malachon 1.50
8 . . . . 1.50
9 . . . . 1.50
10 Chaos 1.50
11 Alpha Flight,Feb., 1985 . . . . . . 2.00

SAGA OF ORIGINAL
HUMAN TORCH
1 RB,O:Original Human Torch 3.00
2 RB,A:Toro. 2.50
3 RB,V:Adolph Hitler 2.50
4 RB,Torch vs. Toro. 2.50

ST. GEORGE
Epic June, 1988
1 KJ,Shadow Line 1.25
2 KJ,I:Shrek 1.25
3 KJ 1.50
4 KJ 1.50
5 . . . . 1.50
6 . . . . 1.50
7 DSp 1.50
8 Oct., 1989 . . . . 1.50

SAINT SINNER
Razorline 1993–94
1 I:Phillip Fetter. 2.75
2 F:Phillip Fetter 2.00
3 in Vertesque. 2.00
4 . . . . 2.00
5 Arcadia. 2.00
6 . . . . 2.00
7 The Child Stealer 2.00
8 . . . . 1.95

SAM & MAX
GO TO THE MOON
1 Dirtbag Special,w/Nirvana Tape . 4.00
[Regular Series]
1 MMi,AAd,F:Skull Boy 3.25
2 AAd,MMi 2.95
3 . . . . 2.95

SAMURAI CAT
Epic 1991
1 I:MiaowaraTomokato. 2.25
2 I:Con-Ed,V:Thpaghetti-Thoth. . . . 2.25
3 EmpireStateStrikesBack 2.25

SATANA
Nov., 1997
1 JaL,WEI,AOI,V:Doctor Strange,
  non-code series 3.00
2 WEI,AOI,to the gates of Hell 3.00

Savage Sword of Conan #4
© Marvel Entertainment Group

SAVAGE SWORD
OF CONAN
August, 1974
(black & white magazine)
1 BWS,JB,NA,GK,O:Blackmark,
  3rdA:Red Sonja,Boris(c) . . . 75.00
2 NA(c),HC,GK, `Black Colossus,'
  B.U.King Kull;B.U.Blackmark . 35.00
3 JB,BWS,GK, `At The Mountain
  of the Moon God;B.U.s:
  Kull;Blackmark 30.00
4 JB,RCo,GKIron Shadows in the
  Moon B.U.Blackmark,Boris(c) . 15.00
5 JB,A WitchShall beBorn,Boris(c) 15.00
6 AN,`Sleeper `Neath the Sands' . 12.50
7 JB,Citadel at the Center
  of Time Boris(c) 12.50
8 inc.GK,`Corsairs against Stygia. 12.50
9 Curse of the Cat-Goddess,

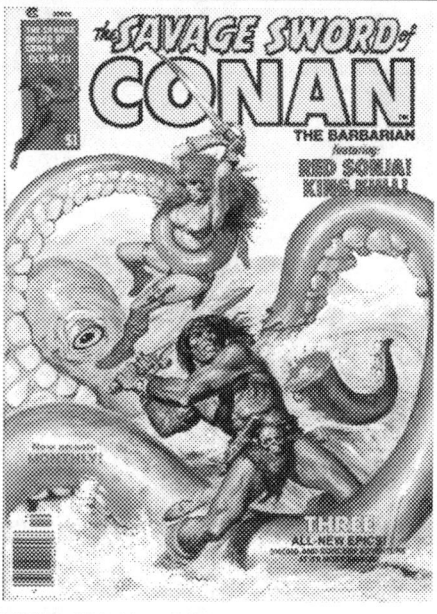

Savage Sword of Conan #18 & #23 © Marvel Entertainment Group

Boris(c),B.U.King Kull 12.50
10 JB,`Sacred Serpent of Set'
   Boris(c) 10.00
11 JB,`The Abode of the Damned' 10.00
12 JB,Haunters of Castle Crimson
   Boris(c) 10.00
13 GK,The Thing in the Temple,
   B.U. Solomon Kane 10.00
14 NA,Shadow of Zamboula,
   B.U.Solomon Kane 10.00
15 JB,Boris(c),`Devil in Iron' 10.00
16 JB,BWS,People of the Black
   Circle,B.U.Bran Mak Morn . . . 10.00
17 JB,`On to Yimsha!,
   B.U.Bran Mak Morn 10.00
18 JB,`The Battle of the Towers'
   B.U. Solomon Kane 10.00
19 JB,`Vengeance in Vendhya'
   B.U.Solomon Kane 10.00
20 JB,`The Slithering Shadow'
   B.U. Solomon Kane 10.00
21 JB,`Horror in the Red Tower' . . 10.00
22 JB,`Pool o/t Black One'
   B.U. Solomon Kane 10.00
23 JB,FT,`Torrent of Doom'
   B.U. Solomon Kane 10.00
24 JB,BWS,`Tower of the
   Elephant'B.U.Cimmeria 10.00
25 DG,SG,Jewels of Gwahlur,
   B.U.Solomon Kane. 10.00
26 JB/TD,Beyond the Black River,
   B.U.Solomon Kane. 8.00
27 JB/TD,Children of Jhebbal Sag . 8.00
28 JB/AA,Blood of the Gods 8.00
29 ECh,FT,Child of Sorcery,
   B.U. Red Sonja 8.00
30 FB,The Scarlet Citadel. 8.00
31 JB/TD,The Flaming Knife,pt.1 . . 8.00
32 JB/TD,Ghouls of Yanaldar,pt.2 . . 8.00
33 GC,Curse of the Monolith,
   B.U.Solomon Kane. 8.00
34 CI/AA,MP,Lair o/t Ice Worm;B.U.
   Solomon Kane,B.U.King Kull . . 8.00
35 ECh,Black Tears 8.00
36 JB,AA,Hawks over Shem. 8.00
37 SB,Sons of the White Wolf

B.U. Solomon Kane 8.00
38 JB/TD,The Road of the Eagles. . 8.00
39 SB/TD,The Legions of the Dead,
   B.U.Solomon Kane concl.. . . . . 8.00
40 JB/TD,A Dream of Blood 8.00
41 JB/TD,Quest for the Cobra Crown
   A:Thoth-Amon,B.U.Sol.Kane . . 8.00
42 JB/TD,Devil-Tree of Gamburu,
   A:Thoth-Amon,B.U.Sol.Kane . . 8.00
43 JB/TD,King Thoth-Amon,
   B.U.King Kull 8.00
44 SB/TD,The Star of Khorala 8.00
45 JB/TD,The Gem in the Tower,
   B.U. Red Sonja 8.00
46 EC/TD,Moon of Blood,
   B.U. Hyborian Tale 8.00
47 GK/JB/JRu,Treasure of Tranicos
   C:Thoth-Amon 8.00
48 JB/KJ,A Wind Blows from Stygia
   C:Thoth-Amon 8.00
49 JB/TD,When Madness Wears the
   Crown, B.U.Hyborian Tale 6.00
50 JB/TD,Swords Across the
   Alimane 6.00
51 JB/TD,Satyrs' Blood 6.00
52 JB/TD,Conan the Liberator 6.00
53 JB,The Sorcerer and the Soul,
   B.U. Solomon Kane 6.00
54 JB,The Stalker Amid the Sands,
   B.U. Solomon Kane 6.00
55 JB,Black Lotus & Yellow Death
   B.U. King Kull. 6.00
56 JB/TD,The Sword of Skelos. . . . 6.00
57 JB/TD,Zamboula 6.00
58 JB/TD,KGa,For the Throne of
   Zamboula,B.U.OlgerdVladislav . 6.00
59 AA,ECh,City ofSkulls,B.U.Gault . 6.00
60 JB,The Ivory Goddess 6.00
61 JB,Wizard Fiend of Zingara 6.00
62 JB/ECh,Temple of the Tiger,
   B.U. Solomon Kane 6.00
63 JB/ECh,TP/BMc,GK,Moat of Blood
   I:Chane of the Elder Earth . . . 6.00
64 JB/ECh,GK,Children of Rhan,
   B.U. Chane 6.00
65 GK,JB,Fangs of the Serpent,

B.U. Bront 6.00
66 thru 75. . . . . @6.00
76 thru 80 . . . . @5.00
81 JB/ECh,Palace of Pleasure,
   B.U. Bront 5.00
82 AA,BWS,Devil in the Dark.Pt.1
   B.U.repConan#24,Swamp Gas. 5.00
83 AA,MW,NA,ECh,Devil in the Dark
   Pt.2,B.U. Red Sonja,Sol.Kane . 5.00
84 VM,Darksome Demon of
   Rabba Than 5.00
85 GK,Daughter of the God King . . 5.00
86 GK,Revenge of the Sorcerer . . . 5.00
87 . . . . 5.00
88 JB,Isle of the Hunter 5.00
89 AA,MW,Gamesman of Asgalun,
   B.U. Rite of Blood. 5.00
90 JB,Devourer of Souls. 5.00
91 JB,VM,Forest of Friends,
   B.U. The Beast,The Chain 5.00
92 JB,The Jeweled Bird 5.00
93 JB/ECh,WorldBeyond the Mists . 5.00
94 thru 101 . . . . @5.00
102 GD,B.U.Bran Mac Morn. 4.00
103 GD,White Tiger of Vendhya,
   B.U. Bran Mac Morn. 4.00
104 . . . . 4.00
105 . . . . 4.00
106 Feud of Blood 4.00
107 thru 118 . . . . @4.00
119 ECh,A:Conan's Sister. 4.00
120 Star of Thama-Zhu. 4.00
121 . . . . 4.00
122 . . . . 4.00
123 ECh,Secret of the GreatStone . 4.00
124 ECh,Secret of the Stone 4.00
125 Altar of the Goat God. 4.00
126 The Mercenary 4.00
127 Reunion in Scarlet,Return
   of Valeria 4.00
128 . . . . 4.00
129 . . . . 4.00
130 Reavers of the Steppes 4.00
131 GI,Autumn of the Witch 4.00
132 ECh,Masters o/t Broadsword . . 4.00
133 . . . . 4.00

All comics prices listed are for *Near Mint* condition.   CVA Page 255

134 Conan the Pirate 4.00	198 RTs,JB,EC,Red Hand 2.25	10 RH,NA,AW,A:Shanna. 5.00
135 Conan the Pirate 4.00	199 RTs,JB,EC,V:Black Zarona. . . . 2.25	11 RH. 5.00
136 NKu,Stranded on DesertIsland. 4.00	200 RTs,JB,ECh,JJu(c),The Barbarian	12 Summer, 1975. . . . . 5.00
137 ECh,The Lost Legion 4.00	from Cross Plains. 2.25	Ann.#1 GM,GK,BWS,O:Kazar. 6.00
138 ECh,Clan o/t Lizard God 4.00	201 RTs,MCW,return to Tarantia . . . 2.25	
139 ECh,A:Valeria 4.00	202 RTs,JB,ECh,Conan in the City	**SAVAGE TALES**
140 ECh,The Ghost's Revenge. . . . 4.00	City of Magicians,pt.1 . . . . 2.25	**Nov., 1985**
141 ECh. 4.00	203 RTs,JB,ECh,Conan in the City	
142 ECh,V:Warlord. 4.00	City of Magicians,pt.2 . . . . 2.25	**(black & white magazine)**
143 ECh. 4.00	204 RTs,JB,ECh,Conan in the City	1 MGo,I:The `Nam 3.00
144 ECh. 4.00	City of Magicians,pt.3 . . . . 2.25	2 MGo 2.00
145 ECh. 4.00	205 RTs,JB,ECh,Conan in the City	3 MGo 2.00
146 ECh. 4.00	City of Magicians,pt.4 . . . . 2.25	4 MGo 2.00
147 ECh. 4.00	206 RTs,JB,ECh,BLr(c),Conan in the	5 MGo 2.00
148 BMc. 4.00	City of Magicians,concl. 2.25	6 MGo 2.00
149 TGr,BMc,Conan Enslaved 4.00	207 RTs,JB,ECh,MK(c), Conan and	7 MGo 2.00
150 ECh. 4.00	the Spider God, pt.1 . . . . 2.25	8 MGo 2.00
151 ECh. 4.00	208 RTs,JB,ECh, Conan and the	9 MGo,March, 1987 . . . . 2.00
152 ECh,Valley Beyond the Stars . . 4.00	Spider God, pt.2. . . . . 2.25	
153 Blood on the Sand,Pt.1 . . . . . . 4.00	209 RTs,JB,Conan and the	**SCARLET SPIDER**
154 Blood on the Sand,Pt.2 . . . . . . 4.00	Spider God,pt.3 . . . . 2.25	**1995–96**
155 ECh,V:Vampires. 4.00	210 RTs,Conan and the	1 HMe,GK,TP,VirtualMortality,pt.3 . 2.00
156 V:Corinthian Army 4.00	Spider God,pt.4 . . . . 2.25	2 HMe,JR2,AW,CyberWar,pt.3. . . . 2.00
157 V:Hyborians. 4.00	211 RTs,Conan and the Gods of	3 and 4 HMe . . . . @2.00
158 ECh,The Talisman-Gem. 4.00	the Mountain,pt.1 . . . . 2.25	
159 Conan Enslaved 4.00	212 RTs,Conand and the Gos of	**SCARLET SPIDER**
160 . . . . 4.00	the Mountain,pt.2 . . . . 2.25	**UNLIMITED**
161 V:Magician/Monsters 4.00	213 RTs,Conan and the Gods of	**1995**
162 AW,Horned God,B.U.Sol.Kane . 3.00	the Mountain,pt.3 . . . . 2.25	1 True Origin,64pg. 3.95
163 V:Picts. 3.00	214 RTs,Conan and the Gods of	
164 Conan's Revenge 3.00	the Mountain,pt.4 . . . . 2.25	**SCARLET WITCH**
165 B.U. King Kull 3.00	215 RTs,JuB(c),Conan and the Gods	**1994**
166 ECh,Conan in New World,Pt.1 . 3.00	of the Mountain,concl.. . . . . 2.25	1 ALa(s),DAn(s),JH,I:Gargan,
167 ECh,Conan in New World,Pt.2 . 3.00	216 RTs,AA,Vengeance of Nitocris . 2.25	C:Master Pandemonium. 2.00
168 ECh,Conan in New	217 RTs,Conan theMercenary,pt.1 . 2.25	2 C:Avengers West Coast 2.00
World,concl 3.00	218 RTs,Conan theMercenary,pt.2 . 2.25	3 A:Avengers West Coast 2.00
169 . . . . 3.00	219 RTs,A:Solomon Kane. 2.25	4 V:Lore,last issue. 2.00
170 AW,A:Red Sonja,Valeria	220 RTs,V:Skull Out of Time 2.25	
B.U. Solomon Kane 3.00	221 RTs,C.L.Moore story adapt. . . . 2.25	**SCOOBY-DOO**
171 TD,Conan Youth Story 2.50	222 RTs,The Haunter of the Towers	**Oct., 1977**
172 JS,JRu,Haunted Swamp,	B.U.JB,Conan Barbarian #1 . . . 2.25	1 B:DynoMutt 9.00
B.U.King Kull,Valeria,	223 RTs,A:Tuzune Thune 2.25	2 thru 8 . . . . @8.00
Red Sonja 2.50	224 RTs,JWk,The Dwellers Under the	9 Feb., 1979 . . . . 8.00
173 ECh,Under Siege. 2.50	Tombs,adapt. B.U.V:Dinosaurs . 2.25	
174 AA,Red Stones of	225 . . . . 2.25	**SECRET DEFENDERS**
Rantha Karn. 2.50	226 RTs,EN(c),The Four Ages	**1993–95**
175 The Demonslayer Sword 2.50	of Conan, A:Red Sonja. 2.25	1 F:Dr.Strange(in all),Spider
176 FH,TT,V:Wizard,B.U. Witch	227 RTs,JBu, besieged in a lost	Woman,Nomad,Darkhawk,
Queen,Dagon,Ghouls. 2.50	city, B.U. Kull,Red Sonja. 2.25	
177 LMc,TD,ECh,Conan the Prey,	228 RTs,AN,Conan in chains! 2.25	
B.U.King Conan,Red Sonja . . . 2.50	229 RTs 2.25	
178 AA,The Dinosaur God 2.50	230 RTs, Acheron falls, Ring of	
179 ECh,A:Red Sonja,Valeria,	Tkrubu,pt.2, R:Kull 2.25	
B.U.Conan 2.50	231 RTs, V:Tuzoun Thune, B.U.	
180 ECh,Sky-God Bardisattva,	EM,Red Sonja 2.25	
B.U. King Kull. 2.50	232 RTs 2.25	
181 TD,Conan the Pagan God?,	233 A:Juma the Black, Kull. 2.25	
B.U. Voodoo Tribe 2.50	234 RTs,JBu, A:Nefartari;	
182 RB/RT,V:Killer Ants 2.50	A:Red Sonja, Zula 2.25	
183 ECh,V:Kah-Tah-Dhen,	235 RTs,JBu,The Daughter of	
B.U.King Kull 2.50	Raktauanishi, final issue. 2.25	
184 AA,Return of Sennan 2.50	Ann.#1 SB,BWS,inc.`Beware the	
185 The Ring of Molub 2.50	Wrath of Anu',B.U. King	
186 AW,A:Thulsa Doom 2.50	Kull Vs.Thulsa Doom 2.25	
187 ECh,A:Conan's Brother? 2.50		
188 V:Kharban the Sorcerer 2.50	**SAVAGE TALES**	
189 A:Search Zukala for Gem. 2.50	**May, 1971**	
190 JB/TD,Skull on the Seas,pt.1 . . 2.25		
191 JB/ECh,Skull on the Seas,pt.2	**(black & white magazine)**	
Thulsa Doom Vs.Thoth-Amon. . 2.25	1 GM,BWS,JR,I&O:Man-Thing,	
192 JB/ECh,Skull on the Seas,pt.3	B:Conan,Femizons,A:Kazar . 150.00	
B.U. King Kull. 2.25	2 GM,FB,BWS,AW,BWr,A:King	
193 JB/ECh,Skull on the Seas concl.	Kull rep,Creatures on	
V:Thulsa Doom & Thoth-Amon . 2.25	the Loose #10 . . . . 50.00	
194 JB/ECh,Wanted for Murder,	3 FB,BWS,AW,JSo 35.00	
B.U. Li-Zya. 2.25	4 NA(c),E:Conan 20.00	
195 JB/ECh,V:Yamatains,	5 JSn,JB,B:Brak the Barbarian . . 20.00	
Giant Tortoise. 2.25	6 NA(c),JB,AW,B:Kazar 8.00	
196 JB/ECh,Treasure of the Stygian	7 GM,NA 6.00	
Prince-Toth-Mekri,A:Valeria. . . 2.25	8 JB,A:Shanna,E:Brak 5.00	*Secret Defenders #22*
197 RTs,JB,EC,Red Hand 2.25	9 MK,A:Shanna 5.00	*© Marvel Entertainment Group*

Wolverine,V:Macabre 3.25	
2 F:Spider Woman,Nomad,Darkhawk,	
Wolverine,V:Macabre 2.50	
3 F:Spider Woman,Nomad,Darkhawk,	
Wolverine,V:Macabre 2.00	
4 F:Namorita,Punisher,	
Sleepwalker,V:Roadkill 2.00	
5 F:Naromita,Punisher,	
Sleepwalker, V:Roadkill 2.00	
6 F:Spider-Man,Scarlet Witch,Captain	
America,V:Suicide Pack 2.00	
7 F:Captain America,Scarlet Witch,	
Spider-Man 2.00	
8 F:Captain America,Scarlet Witch,	
Spider-Man 2.00	
9 F:War Machine,Thunderstrike,	
Silver Surfer 2.00	
10 F:War Machine,Thunderstrike,	
Silver Surfer 2.00	
11 TGb,F:Hulk,Nova,Northstar 2.00	
12 RMz(s),TGb,F:Thanos 2.75	
13 RMz(s),TGb,F:Thanos,Super Skrull,	
Rhino,Nitro,Titanium Man 2.00	
14 RMz(s),TGb,F:Thanos,Super Skrull,	
Rhino,Nitro,Titanium Man,	
A:Silver Surfer 2.00	
15 F:Dr.Druid,Cage,Deadpool 2.25	
16 F:Dr.Druid,Cage,Deadpool 2.25	
17 F:Dr.Druid,Cage,Deadpool 2.25	
18 F:Iron Fist,Giant Man 2.25	
19 F:Dr.Druid,Cadaver,	
Shadowoman 1.95	
20 V:Venom 1.95	
21 V:Slaymaker 1.95	
22 Final Defense,pt.1 . . . . 1.95	
23 Final Defense,pt.2 . . . . 1.95	
24 Final Defense,pt.3 . . . . 1.95	
25 V:Dr.Druid 1.95	

SECRET WARS
May, 1984

1 MZ,A:X-Men,Fant.Four,Avengers,
   Hulk,SpM in All,I:Beyonder. . . . 4.00
2 MZ,V:Magneto 3.00
3 MZ,I:Titania & Volcana 3.00
4 BL,V:Molecule Man. 3.00
5 BL,F:X-Men 3.00
6 MZ,V:Doctor Doom 3.00
7 MZ,I:New Spiderwoman 3.50
8 MZ,I:Alien Black Costume
   (for Spider-Man) 12.00
9 MZ,V:Galactus 2.00
10 MZ,V:Dr.Doom. 2.00

Secret Wars II #6
© Marvel Entertainment Group

---

11 MZ,V:Dr.Doom 2.00
12 MZ,Beyonder Vs. Dr.Doom . . . 2.50
TPB rep #1-#12 . . . . 19.95

SECRET WARS II
July, 1985

1 AM,SL,A:X-Men,New Mutants. . . 2.00
2 AM,SL,A:Fantastic Four 1.50
3 AM,SL,A:Daredevil 1.50
4 AM,I:Kurse 1.50
5 AM,SL,I:Boom Boom 2.50
6 AM,SL,A:Mephisto 1.50
7 AM,SL,A:Thing 1.50
8 AM,SL,A:Hulk. 1.50
9 AM,SL,A:Everyone,double-size. . 2.00

SECTAURS
June, 1985

1 Based on toys 1.50
2 . . . . 1.00
3 . . . . 1.00
4 . . . . 1.00
5 thru 10 1986 . . . . @1.00

SEEKER 3000
April 1998

1 (of 4) DAn,IEd,sci-fi adventure,
   48pg 3.00
2 DAn,IEd,encounter with aliens . . 3.00
3 DAn,IEd,V:Hkkkt, ... 2.50
4 DAn,IEd,V:Hkkkt, concl. 2.50

SEMPER FI
Dec., 1988

1 JSe 2.00
2 JSe 1.50
3 JSe 1.50
4 JSe 1.50
5 JSe 1.50
6 . . . . 1.50
7 and 8 . . . . @1.00
9 August, 1989,final issue 1.00

SENSATIONAL
SPIDER-MAN

1 KM/TP/KJ,rep. (1989) 5.95

SENSATIONAL
SPIDER-MAN
Jan. 1996

0 DJu,KJ,Return of Spider-Man,pt.1
   Lenticular cover 5.00
1 DJu,KJ,Media Blizzard,pt.1,
   V:New Mysterio 2.00
2 DJu,KJ,Return of Kaine,pt.2 . . . . 2.00
3 DJu,KJ,Web of Carnage,pt.1 . . . 2.00
4 DJu,KJ,Blood Brothers,pt.1. . . . . 2.00
5 DJu 2.00
6 DJu 2.00
7 TDz,A:Onslaught 2.00
8 TDz,The Looter 2.00
9 TDz,Onslaught tie-in 2.00
10 TDz,RCa,V:Swarm. 2.00
11 TDz,Revelations, pt.2 . . . . 2.00
11A bagged with card, etc. 5.00
12 TDz,SwM, V:Trapster 2.00
13 TDz,RCa,A:Ka-zar, Shanna 2.00
14 TDz,RCa,Savage Land saga . . . 2.00
15 TDz,RCa,Savage Land saga . . . 2.00
16 TDz,RCa,R:Black Cat,
   V:Prowler,Vulture 2.00
17 TDz,RCa,V:Black Cat,
   Prowler,Vulture 2.00
18 TDz,RCa,V:Vulture 2.00
19 TDz,RCa,R:Living Monolith 2.00

Sensational Spider-Man #33
© Marvel Entertainment Group

20 TDz,RCa,Living Pharoah, concl. 2.00
21 TDz,RCa,Techomancers 2.00
22 TDz,RCa,A:Doctor Strange 2.00
23 TDz,RCa,A:Doctor Strange 2.00
24 TDz,RCa,A:S.H.I.E.L.D., Looter . 2.00
25 TDz,RCa,Spider-Hunt,pt1 x-over 3.00
26 TDz,RCa,JoB,Identity Crisis
   prelude 2.00
27 TDz,RCa,MeW,Identity Crisis,
   as Hornet V:Phaeton 2.00
28 TDz,RCa,as Hornet, V:Vulture . . 2.00
29 TDz,RCa,V:Arcade, Black Cat . . 2.00
30 TDz,A:Black Cat,V:Arcade 2.00
31 TDz,MeW,RCa,V:Rhino 2.00
32 TDz,JoB,The Gathering of the
   Five, pt.1 (of 5) 2.00
33 TDz,JoB,Gathering of
   the Five,pt.5 . . . . 2.00
Minus 1 Spec.,TDz,RCa, flashback. 1.95
TPB In the Savage Land
   rep.#13-#15 . . . . 6.00
Wizard mini-comic 1.00
TPB Sensational Spider-Man '96
   JMD,SwM, seq. to Kraven's
   Last Hunt, 64pg 2.95

SERGEANT
BARNEY BARKER
August, 1956

1 JSe,Comedy 100.00
2 JSe,Army Inspection(c) 75.00
3 JSe,Tank(c) 75.00
Becomes:

G.I. TALES

4 JSe,At Grips with the Enemy . . 45.00
5 . . . . 30.00
6 JO,BP,GWb, July, 1957 . . . . . . 35.00

SGT. FURY & HIS
HOWLING COMMANDOS
May, 1963–Dec. 1981

1 Seven Against the Nazis . . . 1,100.00
2 JK,Seven Doomed Men 300.00
3 JK,Midnight on Massacre
   Mountain 175.00
4 JK,V:Lord Ha-Ha,D:Junior
   Juniper 175.00
5 JK,V:Baron Strucker 175.00
6 JK,The Fangs of the Fox 125.00
7 JK,Fury Court Martial 125.00
8 JK,V:Dr Zemo,I:Percival

Pinkerton 125.00
9 DAy,V:Hitler 125.00
10 DAy,On to Okinwawa,I:Capt.
   Savage. 125.00
11 DAy,V:Capt.Flint. 75.00
12 DAy,Howler deserts 75.00
13 DAy,JK,A;Capt.America 300.00
14 DAy,V:Baron Strucker 75.00
15 DAy,SD,Too Small to Fight
   Too Young to Die 75.00
16 DAy,In The Desert a Fortress
   Stands 75.00
17 DAy,While the Jungle Sleeps . . 75.00
18 DAy,Killed in Action 75.00
19 DAy,An Eye for an Eye 75.00
20 DAy,V:the Blitz Squad 75.00
21 DAy,To Free a Hostage 50.00
22 DAy,V:Bull McGiveney 50.00
23 DAy,The Man who Failed 50.00
24 DAy,When the Howlers Hit
   the Home Front 50.00
25 DAy,Every Man my Enemy. . . . 50.00
26 DAy,Dum Dum Does it the
   Hard Way. 50.00
27 DAy,O:Fury's Eyepatch 50.00
28 DAy,Not a Man Shall Remain
   Alive. 50.00
29 DAy,V:Baron Strucker 50.00
30 DAy,Incident in Italy 50.00
31 Day,Into the Jaws of Death . . . 25.00
32 DAy,A Traitor in Our Midst . . . 25.00
33 DAy,The Grandeur That was
   Greece. 25.00
34 DAy,O:Howling Commandoes . 25.00
35 DAy,Berlin Breakout,J:Eric
   Koenig. 25.00
36 DAy,My Brother My Enemy . . . 25.00
37 DAy,In the Desert to Die 25.00
38 This Ones For Dino 25.00
39 Into the Fortress of Fear 25.00
40 That France Might be Free . . . 25.00
41 V:The Blitzers 25.00
42 Three Were AWOL 25.00
43 Scourge of the Sahara,A:Bob
   Hope,Glen Miller. 25.00
44 JSe,The Howlers First Mission. 25.00
45 JSe,I:The War Lover 25.00
46 JSe,They Also Serve 25.00
47 Tea and Sabotage 25.00
48 A:Blitz Squad. 25.00
49 On to Tarawa. 25.00
50 The Invasion Begins 25.00
51 The Assassin. 25.00
52 Triumph at Treblinka 25.00
53 To the Bastions of Bavaria . . . 25.00
54 Izzy Shoots the Works 25.00
55 Cry of Battle, Kiss of Death . . 20.00
56 Gabriel Blow Your Horn 20.00
57 TS,The Informer 20.00
58 Second Front. 20.00
59 D-Day for Dum Dum 20.00
60 Authorised Personnel Only . . . 20.00
61 The Big Breakout. 20.00
62 The Basic Training of Fury. . . . 20.00
63 V:Nazi Tanks 20.00
64 The Peacemonger,A:Capt
   Savage. 20.00
65 Eric Koenig,Traitor 20.00
66 Liberty Rides the Underground. 20.00
67 With a Little Help From My
   Friends. 20.00
68 Welcome Home Soldier 20.00
69 While the City Sleeps. 20.00
70 The Missouri Marauders 20.00
71 Burn,Bridge,Burn 20.00
72 Battle in the Sahara 20.00
73 Rampage on the
   Russian Front. 20.00
74 Each Man Alone 20.00
75 The Deserter 15.00
76 He Fought the Red Baron 15.00

Sgt. Fury #26
© Marvel Entertainment Group

77 A Traitor's Trap,A:Eric Koenig . 15.00
78 Escape or Die 15.00
79 Death in the High Castle 15.00
80 To Free a Hostage 15.00
81 The All American 15.00
82 Howlers Hit The
   Home Front,rep 15.00
83 Dum DumV:Man-Mountain
   McCoy 15.00
84 The Devil's Disciple 15.00
85 Fury V:The Howlers 15.00
86 Germ Warfare 15.00
87 Dum Dum does it...rep 15.00
88 Save General Patton 15.00
89 O:Fury's eyepatch,rep 15.00
90 The Chain That Binds 15.00
91 Not A Man...rep 12.00
92 Some Die Slowly 12.00
93 A Traitor...rep 12.00
94 GK(c),Who'll Stop the Bombs. . 12.00
95 7 Doomed Men, rep 12.00
96 GK(c),Dum-Dum Sees it
   Through. 12.00
97 Till the Last Man Shall Fail. . . . 12.00
98 A:Deadly Dozen. 12.00
99 Guerillas in Greece 12.00
100 When a Howler Falls 12.00
101 Pearl Harbor 9.00
102 Death For A Dollar. 9.00
103 Berlin Breakout 9.00
104 The Tanks Are Coming 9.00
105 My Brother,My Enemy 9.00
106 Death on the Rhine 9.00
107 Death-Duel in the Desert 9.00
108 Slaughter From the Skies. 9.00
109 This Ones For Dino,rep 9.00
110 JSe(c),The Reserve 9.00
111 V:Colonel Klaw 9.00
112 V:Baron Strucker 9.00
113 That France Might
   Be Free,rep 9.00
114 Jungle Bust Out 9.00
115 V:Baron Strucker 9.00
116 End of the Road. 9.00
117 Blitz Over Britain 9.00
118 War Machine 9.00
118 War Machine 9.00
119 They Strike by Machine 9.00
120 Trapped in the Compound of
   Death 9.00
121 An Eye for an Eye 8.00
122 A;The Blitz Squad 8.00
123 To Free a Hostage. 8.00
124 A:Bull McGiveney 8.00

125 The Man Who Failed 8.00
126 When the Howlers Hit Home.. . 8.00
127 Everyman My Enemy,rep 8.00
128 Dum Dum does it...rep. 8.00
129 O:Fury's Eyepatch 8.00
130 A:Baron Strucker 8.00
131 Armageddon 8.00
132 Incident in Italy 8.00
133 thru 140 . . . . @8.00
141 thru 150 . . . . @8.00
151 thru 160 . . . . @7.00
161 thru 167 . . . . @7.00
Ann.#1 Korea #4,#5 . . . . 150.00
Ann.#2 This was D-Day 50.00
Ann.#3 Vietnam 30.00
Ann.#4 Battle of the Bulge 20.00
Ann.#5 Desert Fox 15.00
Ann.#6 Blaze of Battle 15.00
Ann.#7 Armageddon. 15.00

SERGIO ARAGONES MASSACRES MARVEL
1996
1-shot Parody. 4.95

SEVEN BLOCK
Epic 1990
1 . . . . 2.50

SHADOWMASTERS
Oct., 1989–Jan. 1990
1 RH 11.00
2 . . . . 7.00
3 . . . . 6.00
4 . . . . 5.00

SHADOWRIDERS
1993
1 I:Shadowriders,A:Cable,
   Ghost Rider 2.00
2 A:Ghost Rider. 2.00
3 A:Cable 2.00
4 A:Cable 2.00

SHADOWS & LIGHT
Dec. 1997
1 BSf,RMz,LWn,BWr,GeH,SD,B&W
   anthology series. 3.00
2 JSn,LW,LSh,GK 3.00
3 BL,JSn. 3.00
4 three new tales. 3.00

SHANNA, THE SHE-DEVIL
Dec., 1972–Aug. 1973
1 GT,F:Shanna 7.50
2 RA,The Dungeon of Doom 5.00
3 RA,The Hour of the Bull 3.00
4 RA,Mandrill. 3.00
5 JR(c),RA,V:Nekra 3.00

SHEENA
Dec., 1984–Feb. 1985
1 and 2 Movie adapt . . . . @1.00

SHE-HULK
[1st Regular Series]Feb., 1980
1 JB,BWi,I&O:She-Hulk. 6.00
2 BWi,D:She-Hulk's best friend . . 3.00
3 BWi,Wanted for Murder 3.00
4 BWi,V:Her Father 3.00
5 BWi,V:Silver Serpent 3.00
6 A:Iron Man 2.50
7 BWi,A:Manthing 2.50

She-Hulk #16
© Marvel Entertainment Group

8 BWi,A:Manthing 2.50
9 BWi,Identity Crisis 2.50
10 V:The Word 2.50
11 BWi,V:Dr.Morbius. 2.50
12 V:Gemini 2.50
13 V:Man-Wolf 2.00
14 V:Hellcat 2.00
15 V:Lady Kills 2.00
16 She Hulk Goes Berserk 2.00
17 V:Man-Elephant. 2.00
18 V:Grappler. 2.00
19 V:Her Father 2.00
20 A:Zapper 2.00
21 V:Seeker 2.00
22 V:Radius 2.00
23 V:Radius 2.00
24 V:Zapper 2.00
25 Double-sized,last issue 2.50
[2nd Regular Series] 1989–94
1 JBy,V:Ringmaster 3.00
2 JBy. 2.25
3 JBy,A:Spider-Man. 2.25
4 JBy,I:Blond Phantom 2.25
5 JBy. 2.25
6 JBy,A:U.S.1,Razorback. 2.25
7 JBy,A:U.S.1,Razorback. 2.25
8 JBy,A:Saint Nicholas. 2.25
9 AM(i) 2.00
10 AM(i) 2.00
11 . . . . 2.00
12 . . . . 2.00
13 SK(c). 2.00
14 MT(c),A:Howard the Duck 2.00
15 SK(c). 2.00
16 SK(c). 2.00
17 SK(c),V:Dr.Angst 2.00
18 SK(c). 2.00
19 SK(c),V:Nosferata 2.00
20 SK(c),Darkham Asylum 2.00
21 SK(c),V:Blonde Phantom 2.00
22 SK(c),V:Blonde Phantom,A:All
   Winners Squad. 2.00
23 V:Blonde Phantom 2.00
24 V:Deaths'Head. 4.00
25 A:Hercules,Thor. 2.00
26 A:Excalibur 2.00
27 Cartoons in N.Y. 2.00
28 Game Hunter Stalks She-Hulk . . 2.00
29 A:Wolv.,Hulk,SpM,Venom 2.50
30 MZ(c),A:Silver Surfer,Thor
   Human Torch 2.25
31 JBy,V:Spragg the Living Hill 2.50
32 JBy,A:Moleman,V:Spragg. 2.00

33 JBy,A:Moleman,V:Spragg. 2.00
34 JBy,Returns to New York 2.00
35 JBy,V:X-Humed Men 2.00
36 JBy,X-mas issue (#8 tie-in) 2.00
37 JBy,V:Living Eraser 2.00
38 JBy,V:Mahkizmo 2.00
39 JBy,V:Mahkizmo 2.00
40 JBy,V:Spraggs,Xemnu 2.00
41 JBy,V:Xemnu 2.00
42 JBy,V:USArcher. 2.00
43 JBy,V:Xemnu 2.00
44 JBy,R:Rocket Raccoon 2.00
45 JBy,A:Razorback. 2.00
46 JBy,A:Rocket Raccoon 2.00
47 V:D'Bari 2.00
48 JBy,A:Rocket Raccoon 2.00
49 V:Skrulls,D'Bari 2.00
50 JBy,WS,TA,DGb,AH,HC,
   D:She-Hulk. 4.00
51 TMo,V:Savage She-Hulk 2.00
52 D:She-Hulk,A:Thing,Mr.Fantastic,
   I:Rumbler,V:Titania 2.00
53 AH(c),A:Zapper 2.00
54 MGo(c),A:Wonder Man 2.00
55 V:Rumbler 2.00
56 A:War Zone 2.00
57 A:Hulk 2.00
58 V:Electro 2.00
59 V:Various Villains. 2.00
60 last issue 2.00
TPB rep. #1-#8. . . . . 12.95

SHE HULK: CEREMONY
1989
1 JBr/SDr 4.00
2 JBr/FS 4.00

SHIELD
Feb., 1973
1 . . . . 9.00
2 . . . . 5.00
3 . . . . 5.00
4 . . . . 5.00
5 Oct., 1973 . . . . 5.00

SHOGUN WARRIORS
Feb., 1979
1 HT,DGr,F:Raydeen, Combatra,
   Dangard Ace 4.00
2 HT,DGr,V:Elementals of Evil 2.50
3 AM(c),HT,DGr,V:Elementals

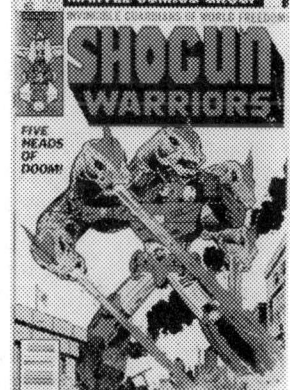

Shogun Warriors #10
© Marvel Entertainment Group

   of Evil 2.50
4 HT,DGr,`Menace of the
   Mech Monsters' 2.50
5 HT,DGr,`Into The Lair
   of Demons' 2.50
6 HT,ME 2.00
7 HT,ME 2.00
8 HT,ME 2.00
9 `War Beneath The Waves' 2.00
10 `Five Heads of Doom' 2.00
11 TA(c) 2.00
12 WS(c) 2.00
13 `Demons on the Moon'. 2.00
14 V:Dr. Demonicus 2.00
15 . . . . 2.00
16 . . . . 2.00
17 . . . . 2.00
18 . . . . 2.00
19 A:Fantastic Four 2.50
20 Sept., 1980 . . . . 2.00

SHROUD
Limited Series 1994
1 B:MiB(s),MCW,A:Spider-Man,
   V:Scorpion 2.00
2 MCW,A:Spider-Man,V:Scorpion . 2.00
3 MCW,I:Kali 2.00
4 MCW,Final Issue 2.00

SILVERHAWKS
August, 1987
1 thru 5 . . . . @1.00
6 June, 1988 . . . . 1.00

SILVER SABLE
1992–95
1 Foil stamped(c),A:Sandman,
   Spider-Man 3.00
2 I:Gattling. 2.00
3 V:Gattling,Foreigner 1.75
4 Infinity War,V:Doctor Doom 1.75
5 Infinity War,V:Doctor Doom 1.50
6 A:Deathlok 1.50
7 A:Deathlok 1.50
8 V:Hydra 1.50
9 O:Silver Sable 1.50
10 A:Punisher,Leviathan. 1.50
11 Cyber Warriors,Hydra. 1.50
12 V:Cyberwarriorss,R:Sandman . . 1.50
13 For Love Nor Money#3,
   A:Cage,Terror. 1.50
14 For Love Nor Money#6,
   A:Cage,Terror. 1.50
15 V:Viper,A:Captain America. 1.50
16 SBt,Infnty Crusade 1.50
17 Infinity Crusade 1.50
18 A:Venom 1.50
19 Siege of Darkness x-over. 1.50
20 GWt(s),StB,BU:Sandman,Fin . . . 1.50
21 Gang War 1.50
22 . . . . 1.50
23 GWt(s),A:Deadpool,Daredevil,
   BU:Sandman 1.50
24 GWt(s),BU:Crippler,w/card. 1.75
25 V:Hydra. 2.25
26 F:Sandman 1.75
27 A:Code Blue 1.50
28 F:Chen 1.50
29 A:Wild Pack. 1.50
30 problems with law 1.50
31 V:terrorists. 1.50
32 A:The Foreigner. 1.50
33 V:Hammerhead 1.50
34 . . . . 1.50
35 Li'l Silvie Tale. 1.50

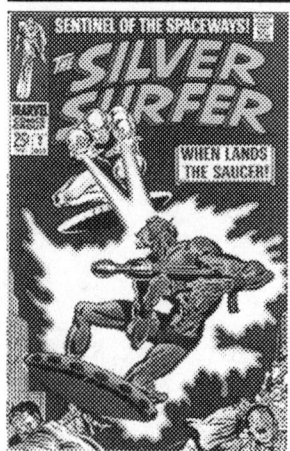

Silver Surfer #2
© *Marvel Entertainment Group*

SILVER SURFER

[1st Series] August, 1968

1 B:StL(s),JB,JSr,GC,O:Silver Surfer,
O:Watcher,I:Shala Bal..... 450.00
2 JB,JSr,GC,A:Watcher 200.00
3 JB,JSr,GC,I:Mephisto 150.00
4 JB,A:Thor,low distribution
scarce 425.00
5 JB,A:Fant.Four,V:Stranger ... 100.00
6 JB,FB,A:Watcher 125.00
7 JB,A:Watcher,I:Frankenstein's
Monster 100.00
8 JB,DA,A:Mephisto,I:Ghost..... 75.00
9 JB,DA,A:Mephisto,A:Ghost..... 75.00
10 JB,DA,South America 75.00
11 JB,DA 60.00
12 JB,DA,V:The Abomination 60.00
13 JB,DA,V:Doomsday Man 60.00
14 JB,DA,A:Spider-Man 75.00
15 JB,DA,A:Human Torch....... 60.00
16 JB,V:Mephisto 60.00
17 JB,V:Mephisto 60.00
18 E:StL(s),JK,V:Inhumans...... 60.00

[2nd Regular Series] 1982

1 JBy,TP,Direct Only,V:Mephisto . 10.00

[3rd Regular Series] July 1987

1 MR,JRu,A:Fantastic Four,
Galactus,V:Champion........ 9.00
2 MR,A:Shalla Bal,V:Skrulls...... 6.00
3 MR,V:Collector & Runner 5.00
4 MR,JRu,A:Elders,I:Obliterator... 5.00
5 MR,JRu,V:Obliterator 5.00
6 MR,JRu,O:Obliterator,A:Kree,
Skrulls 5.00
7 MR,JRu,V:Supremor,Elders/
Soul Gems 5.00
8 MR,JRu,V:Supremor......... 5.00
9 MR,Elders Vs.Galactus........ 5.00
10 MR,A:Galactus,Eternity 5.00
11 JSon,JRu,V:Reptyl.......... 4.50
12 MR,JRu,V:Reptyl,A:Nova...... 4.50
13 JSon,DC,V:Ronan 4.50
14 JSon,DC,V:Skrull Surfer 4.50
15 RLm,JRu,A:Fantastic Four..... 6.00
16 RLm,Inbetweener possesses
Soul Gem,A:Fantastic Four.... 4.00
17 RLm,A:Inbetweener,Galactus,
Fantastic Four,D:Trader,
Possessor,Astronomer 4.00
18 RLm,Galactus V:Inbetweener... 4.00
19 RLm,MR,V:Firelord 4.00
20 RLm,A:Superskrull,Galactus ... 4.00
21 MR,DC,V:Obliterator 4.00

22 RLm,V:Ego 4.00
23 RLm,V:Dragon............ 4.00
24 RLm,V:G.I.G.O............. 4.00
25 RLm,V:Ronan,Kree Skrull War.. 4.00
26 RLm,V:Nenora............ 4.00
27 RLm,V:Stranger........... 4.00
28 RLm,D:Super Skrull,V:Reptyl .. 4.00
29 RLm,V:Midnight Sun 4.00
30 RLm,V:Midnight Sun 4.00
31 RLm,O:Living Tribunal &
Stranger (double size) 4.50
32 RF,JSt,A:Mephisto.......... 4.00
33 Rlm,V:Impossible Man....... 4.00
34 RLm,(1stJSn),2nd R:Thanos ... 5.00
35 RLm,A:Thanos,R:Drax....... 4.00
36 RLm,V:Impossible Man,A:Warlock
Capt.Marvel,C:Thanos 4.00
37 RLm,V:Drax,A:Mentor 4.00
38 RLm,V:Thanos(continued in
Thanos Quest) 4.00
39 JSh,V:Algol 3.00
40 RLm,V:Dynamo City 3.00
41 RLm,V:Dynamo City,A:Thanos.. 3.00
42 RLm,V:Dynamo City,A:Drax.... 3.00
43 RLm,V:DynamoCity 3.00
44 RLm,R:Thanos,Drax,
O:Inf.Gems............... 3.00
45 RLm,Thanos vs. Mephisto 3.00
46 RLm,R:Warlock,A:Thanos 3.00
47 RLm,Warlock V:Drax,
A:Thanos 3.00
48 RLm,A:Galactus,Thanos 3.00
49 RLm,V:Thanos Monster....... 3.00
50 RLm,Silver Stamp(D.size),
V:Thanos Monster 8.00
50a 2nd printing 2.50
50b 3rd printing 2.00
51 RLm,Infinity Gauntlet x-over... 2.50
52 RLm,Infinity Gauntlet x-over... 2.50
53 RLm,Infinity Gauntlet x-over.... 2.50
54 RLm,I.Gauntlet x-over,V:Rhino.. 2.50
55 RLm,I.Gauntlet x-over,Universe
According to Thanos,pt.1 ..... 2.50
56 RLm,I.Gauntlet x-over,Universe
According to Thanos,pt.2 ..... 2.50
57 RLm,Infinity Gauntlet x-over.... 2.50
58 RLm(c),Infinity Gauntlet x-over,
A:Hulk,Namor,Dr.Strange 2.50
59 RLm(c),TR,Infinity Gauntlet,
Thanos V:Silver Surfer 2.50
60 RLm,V:Midnight Sun,
A:Inhumans 2.00
61 RLm,I:Collection.Agency 2.00
62 RLm,O:Collection Agency 2.00
63 RLm,A:Captain Marvel........ 2.00
64 RLm,V:Dark Silver Surfer..... 2.00
65 RLm,R:Reptyl,I:Princess
Alaisa................... 2.00
66 RLm,I:Avatar,Love & Hate 2.00
67 RLm(c),KWe,Inf.War,V:Galactus
A:DrStrange 2.00
68 RLm(c),KWe,Inf.War,O:Nova ... 2.00
69 RLm(c),KWe,Infinity War,
A:Galactus 2.00
70 RLm(c),Herald War#1,I:Morg ... 2.00
71 RLm(c),Herald War#2,V:Morg .. 2.00
72 RLm(c),Herald War#3,R:Nova .. 2.00
73 RLm,R:Airwalker 2.00
74 RLm,V:Terrax.............. 2.00
75 RLm,E:Herald Ordeal,V:Morg,
D:Nova.................. 3.00
76 RLm,A:Jack of Hearts 1.50
77 RLm,A:Jack of Hearts 1.50
78 RLm,R:Morg,V:Nebula 1.50
79 RLm,V:Captain Atlas 1.50
80 RLm,I:Ganymede,Terrax
Vs.Morg 1.50
81 RLm,O:Ganymede,I:Tyrant..... 1.50
82 RLm,V:Tyrant,double sized ... 2.00
83 Infinity Crusade 1.50
84 RLm(c),Infinity Crusade 1.50

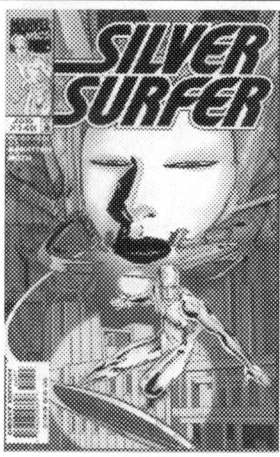

Silver Surfer #140
© *Marvel Entertainment Group*

85 RLm(c),Infinity Crusade 2.00
86 RLm(c), Blood & Thunder,pt.2
V:Thor,A:Beta Ray Bill 1.50
87 RLm(c),Blood & Thunder,pt.7... 1.50
88 RLm(c),Blood & Thunder,pt.10.. 1.50
89 RLm(c),CDo,C:Legacy........ 1.50
90 RLm(c),A:Legacy,C:Avatar..... 1.50
91 RLm 1.75
92 RLm,V:Avatar 1.75
93 V:Human Torch 1.75
94 A:Fantastic Four, Warlock 1.75
95 SEa,A:Fantastic Four.......... 1.50
96 A:Fantastic Four,Hulk......... 1.50
97 A:Fantastic Four,R:Nova 1.50
98 R:Champion 1.50
99 A:Nova 1.50
100 V:Mephisto 2.25
100a enhanced ed.............. 4.50
101 RMz,JoP,A:Shalla Bal 1.50
102 V:Galactus................ 1.50
103 I:Death quad 1.50
104 Surfer Rampage 1.50
105 V:Super Skrull 1.50
106 A:Legacy,Morg............. 1.50
107 TGb,BAn,A:Galactus,Morg,
Tyrant................... 1.50
108 Galactus Vs. Tyrant 1.50
109 Morg has Ultimate Nulifier 1.50
110 JB,F:Nebula................ 1.50
111 GP,TGb,BAn,to Other Side
of Galaxy 2.00
112 GP,BAn,.................. 2.00
113 GP,TGb,BAn,V:Blackbody ... 2.00
114 .... 2.00
115 GP,TGb,BAn,Surfer in pieces.. 2.00
116 GP,TGb,BAn,Pieces cause
trouble.................. 2.00
117 .... 2.00
118 .... 1.50
119 .... 1.50
120 .... 1.50
121 A:Quasar, Beta Ray Bill 1.50
122 GP,SEa, returns to Marvel
Universe................. 1.50
123 GP,RG................... 1.50
124 GP,RG................... 1.50
125 RG,V:Hulk, double size 3.00
126 JMD,RG,BWi,A:Dr. Strange ... 2.00
127 JMD,RG,BWi,A:Alicia Masters. 2.00
128 JMD,RG,BWi,V:Puppet Master. 2.00
129 JMD,RG,BWi,back in time,
late 1940s 2.00
130 JMD,CNr,BWi, trapped in past. 2.00
131 JMD,RG,BWi, ... 2.00

132 JMD,PaP,Puppet Master
  missing 2.00
133 JMD,MRy,PaP,V:PuppetMaster 2.00
134 JMD,TGm,MRy,Regains his
  memories, pt.1 (of 4) 2.00
135 JMD,TGm,MRy,Alicia summons
  Scrier. 2.00
136 JMD,TGm,MRy, ... 2.00
137 JMD,TGm,MRy,Mephisto v.
  Scrier. 2.00
138 JMD,RCz,MRy,A:The Thing,
  tie-in. 2.00
139 JMD,RCz,MRy,V:Gargoyle 2.00
140 JMD,JMu,on Zenn-La untouched
  by Galactus 2.00
141 JMD,JMu,A:Sama-D,Alicia
  Masters 2.00
142 JMD,JMu,Tenebrae,The Union,
  Cipher 2.00
143 JMD,DCw,Tenebrae,V:Psycho
  Man 2.00
Bi-Weekly Issues
144 JMD,JMu,V:Psycho-Man,
  A:Tenebrae. 2.00
145 JMD,JMu,A:Psycho-Man,
  Tenebrae,Cypphyrr. 2.00
146 TDF,DCw,V:Firelord 2.00
Minus 1 Spec., JMD,RG,BWi,
  flashback, first human contact . 2.00
Spec. Silver Surfer: Dangerous Arti-
  facts,RMz, Galactus,T hanos
  (1996) 4.00
Spec. Silver Surfer: Inner Demons,
  rep. JMD,RGa,BWi (1998) 3.00
Ann.#1 RLm,JSon,Evolution War . . 7.00
Ann.#2 RLm,Atlantis Attacks. 5.00
Ann.#3 RLm,Lifeform #4. . . . . 4.00
Ann.#4 RLm,Korvac Quest #3,A:
  Guardians of Galaxy. 3.00
Ann.#5 RLm,Ret.o/Defenders #3 . . 2.50
Ann.#6 RLm(c),I:Legacy,w/card . . . 3.75
Ann.'97 1 JMD,VS,KJ,V:Scrier,
  48pg 2.00
Ann.'98 MPe,RBe,TDF,F:Thor,
  48pg 3.00
TPB Silver Surger, The Enslavers,
  KP 16.95
TPB Homecoming,A:Moondragon . 12.95
TPB Silver Surfer: Parable, StL,Moe,
  rep. of hc, 64pg (1998) 6.00
TPB Rebirth of Thanos,reprints
  #34-38 . . . . 12.95
TPB StL,JK, new origin. 13.00
Ashcan. .75

SILVER SURFER
Epic Dec., 1988
1 Moebius,V:Galactus 3.00
2 Moebius,V:Galactus 3.00
Graphic Novel. 14.95

SILVER SURFER:
LOFTIER THAN MORTALS
Aug. 1999
1 MFr,V:Dr. Doom 2.50
2 MFr,V:Dr. Doom, concl. 2.50

SILVER SURFER/
SUPERMAN
Marvel/DC 1996
Spec. GP,RLm,TA, x-over 5.95

SILVER SURFER VS.
DRACULA
1994
1 rep,MWn(s),GC,TP 1.75

SILVER SURFER/
WARLOCK:
RESURRECTION
1993
1 JSn,V:Mephisto,Death 3.50
2 JSn,TA,V:Death 3.00
3 JSn,TA,V:Mephisto 3.00
4 JSn,TA,V:Mephisto 3.00

SILVER SURFER/
WEAPON ZERO
Marvel/Top Cow 1997
1-shot Devil's Reign, pt.8 . . . . 4.00

SISTERHOOD OF STEEL
Epic Dec., 1984
1 I:Sisterhood 2.00
2 . . . . 2.00
3 . . . . 2.00
4 thru 8 . . . . @1.50

SIX FROM SIRIUS
Epic July, 1984
1 PG,limited series 3.00
2 PG. 2.00
3 PG 2.00
4 PG 2.00

SIX FROM SIRIUS II
Epic Feb., 1986
1 PG. 1.75

SIX-GUN WESTERN
Atlas Jan., 1957
1 JSe(c),RC,JR,'Kid Yukon
  Gunslinger' 125.00
2 SSh,AW,DAy,JO,`His Guns
  Hang Low' 100.00
3 AW,BP,DAy 100.00
4 JSe(c),JR,GWb 60.00

SKELETON WARRIORS
1995
1 based on cartoon 1.50
2 Legion of Light 1.50
3 V:Grimstar 1.50
4 Grimskull abandons Legion
  of Light. 1.50

SKRULL KILL CREW
1995
1 I:Kill Crew. 2.95
2 V:Hydra 2.95
3 V:Captain America 2.95
4 V:Fantastic Four. 2.95
5 Conclusion 2.95

SKULL, THE SLAYER
August, 1975
1 GK(c),O:Skull the Slayer 2.50
2 GK(c),`Man Against Gods' 1.50
3 `Trapped in the Tower
  of Time' 1.50
4 `Peril of the Pyramids',
  A:Black Knight 1.50
5 A:Black Knight 1.50
6 `The Savage Sea' 1.50
7 `Dungeon of Blood'. 1.50
8 JK(c),Nov., 1976 . . . . 1.50

Skull the Slayer #6
© Marvel Entertainment Group

SLAPSTICK
1992–93
1 TA(i),I:Slapstick. 1.50
2 TA(i),A:Spider-Man,V:Overkill . . . 1.25
3 V:Dr.Denton 1.25
4 A:GR,DD,FF,Cap.America 1.25

SLEDGE HAMMER
Feb., 1988
1 . . . . 1.25
2 March, 1988. . . . . 1.00

SLEEPWALKER
June, 1991
1 BBl,I:Rick Sheridan,C:8-Ball 3.00
2 BBl,V:8-Ball 2.00
3 BBl,A:Avengers,X-Men,X-Factor,
  FF,I:Cobweb,O:Sleepwalker . . . 1.75
4 RL,I:Bookworm. 1.75
5 BBl,A:SpM,K.Pin,V:Ringleader . . 1.75
6 BBl,A:SpM,Inf.Gauntlet x-over . . 1.75
7 BBl,Infinity Gauntlet x-over,
  V:Chain Gang. 1.75
8 BBl,A:Deathlok 1.50
9 BBl,I:Lullabye 1.50
10 BBl,MM,I:Dream-Team. 1.50
11 BBl,V:Ghost Rider 1.50
12 JQ,A:Nightmare. 2.50
13 BBl,MM,I:Spectra. 1.50
14 BBl,MM,V:Spectra 1.50
15 BBl,MM,I:Thought Police 1.50
16 BBl,MM,A:Mr.Fantastic,Thing. . . 1.50
17 BBl,A:Spider-Man,Darkhawk,
  V:Brotherhood o/Evil Mutants . . 1.50
18 JQ(c),Inf.War,A:Prof.X 1.50
19 V:Cobweb,w/pop out Mask. . . . 2.00
20 V:Chain Gang,Cobweb 1.50
21 V:Hobgoblin 1.50
22 V:Hobgoblin,8-Ball. 1.50
23 V:Cobweb,Chain Gang 1.50
24 Mindfield#6 . . . . 1.50
25 O:Sleepwalker,Holo-grafx(c). . . . 3.50
26 V:Mindspawn. 1.50
27 A:Avengers 1.50
28 I:Psyko 1.50
29 DG,V:Psyko. 1.50
30 V:Psyko. 1.50
31 DG(ci),A:Spectra 1.50
32 V:Psyko. 1.50
33 V:Mindspawn,Last issue 1.50
Holiday Spec.#1 JQ(c) 2.25

SLEEZE BROTHERS
August, 1989
1 Private Eyes	....	1.75
2	....	1.75
3	....	1.75
4	....	1.75
5	....	1.75
6	....	1.75

SLINGERS
Oct. 1998
1 Ccs,F:Ricochet, Hornet,
Prodigy & Dusk, 48-page:
1a Ricochet edition	3.00
1b Hornet edition.............	3.00
1c Prodigy edition	3.00
1d Dusk edition	3.00
2 CCs,V:Maggia	2.00
2a variant cover.............	2.00
3 CCs,F:Prodigy	2.00
4 CCs,F:Prodigy	2.00
5 CCs,F:Black Marvel	2.00
6 CCs,Truth or Dare	2.00
7 CCs,V:The Griz	2.00
8 CCs,V:The Griz	2.00
9 CCs,A:Ricochet	2.00
10 CCs,Raising Hell'sChildren,pt.1	2.00
11 CCs,Raising Hell'sChildren,pt.2	2.00

SMURFS
Dec., 1982
1	....	3.00
2	....	3.00
3	....	3.00
Treasury Edition	....	15.00

SOLARMAN
Jan., 1989
1 JM	1.25
2 MZ/NR,A:Dr.Doom, May, 1990 . .	1.25

SOLO
[Limited Series] 1994
1 RoR,I:Cygnus..............	1.75
2 RoR,V.A.R.E.S.	1.75
3 RoR,V:Spidey.............	1.75
4 final issue................	1.75

SOLO AVENGERS
Dec., 1987
1 MBr,JRu,JLe,AW,Hawkeye; Mockingbird	4.00
2 MBr,JRu,KD,BMc,Hawkeye; Capt.Marvel	1.50
3 MBr,JRu,BH,SDr,Hawkeye; Moon Knight...............	1.50
4 RLm,JRu,PR,BL,Hawkeye; Black Knight...............	2.00
5 MBr,JRu,JRy,Hawkeye; Scarlet Witch	1.50
6 MBr,JRu,TGr,Hawkeye;Falcon . .	1.25
7 MBr,JG,BL,Hawkeye;Bl.Widow . .	1.25
8 MBr,Hawkeye;Dr.Pym.........	1.25
9 MBr,JBr,SDr,Hawkeye;Hellcat . .	1.25
10 MBr,LW,Hawkeye;Dr.Druid.....	1.25
11 MBr,JG,BL,Hawkeye;Hercules . .	1.25
12 RLm,SDr,Hawkeye; New Yellow Jacket	2.00
13 RLm,JG,Hawkeye;WonderMan .	2.00
14 AM,AD,JRu,Hawkeye;She-Hulk .	1.25
15 AM,Hawkeye;Wasp	1.25
16 AM,DP,JA,Hawkeye; Moondragon..............	1.25
17 AM,DH,DC,Hawkeye; Sub-Mariner...............	1.25
18 RW,DH,Hawkeye;Moondragon. .	1.25

Solo Avengers #3
© *Marvel Entertainment Group*

19 RW,DH,Hawkeye,BlackPanther .	1.25
20 RW,DH,Hawkeye;Moondragon. .	1.25
Becomes:	

AVENGERS SPOTLIGHT

SOLOMON KANE
Sept., 1985
1 F:Solomon Kane	1.50
2	1.00
3 BBl,`Blades of the Brotherhood' .	1.00
4 MMi.......................	1.00
5 `Hills of the Dead'	1.00
6	1.00

SON OF SATAN
Dec., 1975–Feb. 1977
1 GK(c),JM,F:Daimon Hellstrom. .	15.00
2 Demon War,O:Possessor	11.00
3	11.00
4 The Faces of Fear	10.00
5 V:Mind Star	10.00
6 A World Gone Mad..........	10.00
7 Mirror of Judgement	10.00
8 RH,To End in Nightmare......	10.00

SOVIET SUPER SOLDIERS
1 AMe,JS,I:Redmont 4.........	2.00

SPACEMAN
Atlas Sept., 1953
1 BEv(c),F:Speed Carter and the Space Sentinals	500.00
2 JMn,`Trapped in Space'	325.00
3 BEv(c),JMn,V:Ice Monster....	300.00
4 JMn	300.00
5 GT	300.00
6 JMn,`The Thing From Outer Space',Oct., 1954	300.00

SPACE SQUADRON
Atlas June, 1951
1 F:Capt. Jet Dixon,Blast,Dawn, Revere,Rusty Blake	500.00
2 GT(c),...................	450.00
3 `Planet of Madness',GT	350.00
4	350.00
5	350.00
Becomes:	

SPACE WORLDS
April, 1952
6 `Midnight Horror'..........	300.00

SPECIAL COLLECTOR'S EDITION
Dec., 1975
1 Kung-Fu,Iron Fist	6.00

SPECIAL MARVEL EDITION
Jan., 1971
1 JK,B:Thor,B:Reprints	15.00
2 JK,V:Absorbing Man	12.00
3 JK,`While a Universe Trembles'...............	12.00
4 JK,`Hammer and the Holocaust', E:Thor	12.00
5 JSe(c),JK,DAy,B:Sgt. Fury ...	12.00
6 HT(c),DAy,`Death Ray of Dr. Zemo'	7.00
7 DAy,V:Baron Strucker	7.00
8 JSe(c),DAy`On To Okinawa'	7.00
9 DAy,`Crackdown of Captain Flint	7.00
10 DAy........................	7.00
11 JK,DAy,A:Captaim America & Bucky	7.00
12 DAy,V:Baron Strucker	7.00
13 JK/DAy(c),DAy,SD,`Too Small to Fight, Too Young To Die'....	7.00
14 DAy,E:Reprints,Sgt. Fury	7.00
15 JSn,AM,I:Shang-Chi & Master of Kung Fu,I&O:Nayland Smith, Dr. Petrie	45.00
16 JSn,AM,I&O:Midnight........	20.00
KingSz.Ann.#1 A:Iron Fist.......	18.00
Becomes:	

MASTER OF KUNG FU

SPECTACULAR SCARLET SPIDER
1995
1 SB,BSz,Virtual Morality,pt.4	1.95
2 SB,BSz,CyberWar,pt.4	1.95

SPECTACULAR SPIDER-MAN
(Magazine) July–Nov, 1968
1 Lo, This Monster,b&w........	65.00
2 V:Green Goblin, color	110.00

SPECTACULAR SPIDER-MAN
Dec., 1976
Prev: Peter Parker
134 SB,A:Sin-Eater,V:Electro	4.00
135 SB,A:Sin-Eater,V:Electro	3.00
136 SB,D:Sin-Eater,V:Electro	3.00
137 SB,I:Tarantula II............	3.00
138 SB,A:Capt.A.,V:TarantulaII....	3.00
139 SB,O:Tombstone	4.00
140 SB,A:Punisher,V:Tombstone. .	3.00
141 SB,A:Punisher,V:Tombstone. .	3.00
142 SB,A:Punisher,V:Tombstone. .	3.00
143 SB,A:Punisher,D:Persuader, I:Lobo Brothers............	3.00
144 SB,V:Boomerang...........	3.00
145 SB,A:Boomerang...........	3.00
146 SB,R:Green Goblin	5.00
147 SB,V:Hobgoblin (Demonic Power)	15.00

Spectacular Spider-Man #138
© Marvel Entertainment Group

148 SB,Inferno 3.00
149 SB,V:Carrion II. 5.00
150 SB,A:Tombstone,Trial
   J.Robertson. 3.00
151 SB,V:Tombstone 3.00
152 SB,O:Lobo Bros.,A:Punisher,
   Tombstone 4.00
153 SB,V:Hammerhead,A:
   Tombstone 3.00
154 SB,V:Lobo Bros.,Puma 3.00
155 SB,V,Tombstone 3.00
156 SB,V:Banjo,A:Tombstone 3.00
157 SB,V:Shocker,Electro,
   A:Tombstone 3.00
158 SB,Super Spider Spec.,
   I:Cosmic Spider-Man 7.00
159 Cosmic Powers,V:Brothers
   Grimm 5.00
160 SB,A:Hydro Man,Shocker,
   Rhino,Dr.Doom. 4.00
161 SB,V:Hobgoblin,Hammerhead,
   Tombstone 3.00
162 SB,V:Hobgoblin,Carrion II 3.00
163 SB,V:Hobgoblin,D:Carrion II. . . 3.00
164 SB,V:Beetle. 2.50
165 SB,SDr,D:Arranger,I:Knight
   & Fogg. 2.50
166 SB,O:Knight & Fogg 2.50
167 SB,D:Knight & Fogg. 2.50
168 SB,A:Kingpin,Puma,
   Avengers 2.50
169 SB,I:Outlaws,A:R.Racer,
   Prowler,Puma,Sandman 2.50
170 SB,A:Avengers,Outlaws. 2.50
171 SB,V:Puma 2.50
172 SB,V:Puma 2.50
173 SB,V:Puma 2.50
174 SB,A:Dr.Octopus 2.50
175 SB,A:Dr.Octopus 2.50
176 SB,I:Karona 2.50
177 SB,V:Karona,A:Mr.Fantastic. . . 2.50
178 SB,B:Child Within,V:Green
   Goblin, A:Vermin 2.50
179 SB,V:Green Goblin,Vermin. . . . 2.50
180 SB,V:Green Goblin,Vermin. . . . 2.50
181 SB,V:Green Goblin 2.50
182 SB,V:Green Goblin 2.50
183 SB,V:Green Goblin 2.50
184 SB,E:Child Within,V:Green
   Goblin 2.50
185 SB,A:Frogman,White Rabbit . . 2.00
186 SB,B:FuneralArrangements
   V:Vulture 2.00
187 SB,V:Vulture 2.00

188 SB,E:Funeral Arrangements
   V:Vulture 2.00
189 SB,30th Ann.,Hologram(c),
   V:Green Goblin 6.00
189a Gold 2nd printing 3.00
190 SB,V:Rhino,Harry Osborn 2.00
191 SB,Eye of the Puma 1.75
192 SB,Eye of the Puma 1.75
193 SB,Eye of the Puma 1.75
194 SB,Death of Vermin#1 . . . . . . 1.75
195 SB,Death of Vermin#2 . . . . . . 1.75
195a Dirtbag Spec,w/Dirt#2 tape . . 2.50
196 SB,Death of Vermin#3 . . . . . . 1.75
197 SB,A:X-Men,V:Prof.Power . . . 1.75
198 SB,A:X-Men,V:Prof.Power . . . 1.75
199 SB,A:X-Men,Green Goblin . . . 2.00
200 SB,V:Green Goblin,D:Harry
   Osborn,Holografx(c) 4.00
201 SB,Total Carnage,V:Carnage,
   Shriek,A:Black Cat,Venom 1.75
202 SB,Total Carnage#9,A:Venom,
   V:Carnage 1.75
203 SB,Maximum Carnage#13 . . . . 1.75
204 SB,A:Tombstone 1.75
205 StG(s),SB,V:Tombstone,
   A:Black Cat 1.75
206 SB,V:Tombstone 1.75
207 SB,A:The Shroud. 1.50
208 SB,A:The Shroud. 1.50
209 StB,SB,I:Dead Aim,
   BU:Black Cat 1.50
210 StB,SB,V:Dead Aim,
   BU:Black Cat 1.50
211 Pursuit#2,V:Tracer 1.50
212 . . . . 1.75
213 ANo(s),V:Typhiod Mary,w/cel . . 3.50
213a Newsstand Ed. 1.75
214 V:Bloody Mary 1.75
215 V:Scorpion 1.75
216 V:Scorpion. 1.75
217 V:Judas Traveller,clone 2.00
217a Foil(c),bonus stuff 5.00
218 V:Puma 1.75
219 Back from the Edge,pt.2 . . . . . 2.00
220 Web of Death,pt.3 . . . . 2.50
221 Web of Death,finale 3.00
222 The Price of Truth 1.50
223 Aftershocks,pt.4 . . . . 3.00
223a enhanced cover. 2.00
224 The Mark of Kaine,pt.4. . . . . . 2.50
225 SB,TDF,BSz,I:New Green
   Goblin, 48pg.s 3.00
225a 3-D HoloDisk Cover. 5.00
226 SB,BSz,The Trial of Peter
   Parker,pt.4, identity revealed . . 3.00
227 TDF,SB,BSz,Maximum
   Clonage,pt.5. . . . . 1.50
228 Timebomb,pt.1 . . . . 1.50
229 Greatest Responsibility,pt.3 . . . 2.50
229a Special cover. 4.00
230 SB,Return of Spider-Man,pt.4 . 2.00
231 SB,Return of Kaine,pt.1 . . . . . . 2.00
232 . . . . 2.00
233 SB,JP,Web of Carnage,pt.4 . . . 2.00
234 SB,Blood Brothers,pt.4. . . . . . . 2.00
235 . . . . 2.00
236 . . . . 2.00
237 V:Lizard. 2.00
238 V:Lizard. 2.00
239 V:Lizard. 2.00
240 TDz,LRs,"Book of Revelations,"
   pt.1 (of 4) 2.00
241 Revelations epilogue 2.00
242 JMD,LRs,R:Chameleon,
   A:Kangaroo 2.00
243 JMD,LRs,R:Chameleon 2.00
244 JMD,LRs,V:Chameleon 2.00
245 JMD,LRs,V:Chameleon,
   A:Kangaroo 2.00
246 JMD,LRs,V:Kangaroo,Grizzly . . 2.00
247 JMD,LRs,F:JackO'Lantern,pt.1 . 2.00

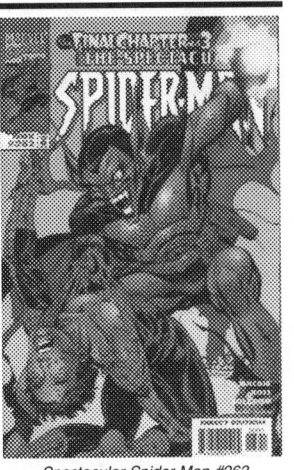

Spectacular Spider-Man #263
© Marvel Entertainment Group

248 JMD,LRs,DGr,F:Jack O'
   Lantern, pt.2. . . . . 2.00
249 JMD,LRs,DGr, Last Temptation
   of Flash Thompson. 2.00
250 JR, V:Original Green Goblin,
   double gatefold cover 3.50
251 JMD,LRs,DGr,V:Kraven the
   Hunter 2.00
252 JMD,LRs,DGr,V:Norman
   Osborn. 2.00
253 JMD,LRs,DGr,V:Norman Osborn,
   Gibbon, Grizzly. 2.00
254 JMD,LRs,DGr,V:Prof.Angst . . . 2.00
255 JMD,LRs,DGr,Spider-Hunt,pt.4
   x-over, double size 3.00
256 JMD,LRs,DGr,Identity Crisis
   prelude, A:Prodigy 2.00
257 JMD,LRs,DGr,Identity Crisis,
   as Prodigy, V:Conundrum 2.00
258 JMD,LRs,DGa,as Prodigy 2.00
259 RSt,LRs,DGa,V:Hobgoblin 2.00
260 JR, RSt,LRs,DGa,Green Goblin
   vs. Hobgoblin 2.00
261 RSt,LRs,AM,Goblins at the
   Gate,pt.3 . . . . 2.00
262 JBy, AM, LRs, The Gathering of
   the Five, pt.4 (of 5) x-over 2.00
263 JBy,AM,LRs,The Final
   Chapter,pt.3 x-over. 2.00
Ann.#8 MBa,RLm,TD,Evolutionary
   Wars,O:Gwen Stacy Clone. . . . 5.00
Ann.#9 DR,MG,DJu,MBa,Atlantis
   Attacks. 4.00
Ann.#10 SLi(c),RB,MM,TM,RA . . . 6.00
Ann.#11 EL(c),RWi,Vib.Vendetta. . 2.50
Ann.#12 Hero Killers#2,A:New
   Warriors,BU:Venom 4.50
Ann.#13 I:Noctune,w/Card 3.25
Ann.#14 V:Green Goblin. 2.95
Super-Size Spec.#1 Planet of the
   Symbiotes,pt.4,64pg flip-book. . 3.95
Minus 1 Spec., JMD,LRs,DGr,
   flashback, F:Flash Thompson. . 1.95

SPEEDBALL
Sept., 1988

1 SD,JG,O:Speedball 2.00
2 SD,JG,V:Sticker,Graffiti Gorillas . 1.50
3 SD,V:Leaper Logan 1.25
4 SD,DA,Ghost Springdale High . . 1.25
5 SD,V:Basher. 1.25
6 SD,V:Bug-Eyed Voice. 1.25
7 SD,V:Harlequin Hit Man 1.25

8 SD,V:Bonehead Gang 1.25
9 SD,V:Nathan Boder 1.25
10 SD,V:Mutated Pigs,Killer
    Chickens, last issue 1.25

SPELLBOUND
Atlas March, 1952
1 `Step into my Coffin' 500.00
2 BEv,RH,`Horror Story',
    A:Edgar A. Poe 250.00
3 RH(c),OW 225.00
4 RH,Decapitation story 225.00
5 BEv,JM,`Its in the Bag' 225.00
6 BK,`The Man Who Couldn't
    be Killed' 225.00
7 BEv,JMn,`Don't Close
    the Door' 175.00
8 BEv(c),RH,JSt,DAy,
    `The Operation' 175.00
9 BEv(c),RH,`The Death of
    Agatha Slurl' 175.00
10 JMn(c),BEv,RH,`The Living
    Mummy' 175.00
11 `The Empty Coffin' 150.00
12 RH,`My Friend the Ghost'. . . . 150.00
13 JM,`The Dead Men' 150.00
14 BEv(c),RH,JMn,`Close Shave' 150.00
15 `Get Out of my Graveyard' . . . 150.00
16 RH,BEv,JF,JSt,`Behind
    the Door' 150.00
17 BEv(c),GC,BK,`Goodbye
    Forever' 150.00
18 BEv(c),JM 150.00
19 BEv(c),BP,`Witch Doctor' . . . 150.00
20 RH(c),BP 150.00
21 RH(c). 135.00
22 . . . . 135.00
23 . . . . 135.00
24 JMn(c),JR 125.00
25 JO,`Look into my Eyes' 125.00
26 JR,`The Things in the Box'. . . 125.00
27 JMn,JR,`Trap in the Mirage' . 125.00
28 BEv 125.00
29 JSe(c),SD 150.00
30 BEv(c) 125.00
31 . . . . 125.00
32 BP,`Almost Human' 125.00
33 AT 125.00
34 June, 1957. . . . . 125.00

SPELLBOUND
Jan., 1988
1 thru 3 . . . . @1.50
4 A:New Mutants. 2.00
5 . . . . 1.50
6 double-size. 2.25

SPIDER-GIRL
August 1998
0 TDF,RF,BSz, cont. from What-If?
    #105, Peter & Mary Jane's
    daughter. 3.00
1 TDF,PO,AW, F:Mayday Parker,
    V:Mr. Nobody 2.00
2 TDF,PO,AW,V:Crazy Eight
    & Darkdevil 2.00
2a variant cover. 2.00
3 TDF,PO,AW,A:Fantastic Five . . . 2.00
4 TDF,PO,AW,turning points 2.00
5 TDF,PO,AW,Ghosts of the Past . . 2.00
6 TDF,PO,AW,Majority Rules. 2.00
7 TDF,PO,AW,Last Days of
    Spider-Man 2.00
8 TDF,PO,AW,A:Spider-Man,
    Uneasy Allies. 2.00
8a autographed 20.00
9 TDF,PO,AW,Critical Choices. . . . 2.00
10 TDF,PO,AW,Incredible Journeys 2.00

11 TDF,PO.AW,V:Spider-Man 2.00
12 TDF,PO,AW,A:Darkdevil. 2.00
13 TDF,Po,AW,Joins A-Next 2.00
Ann.#1 TDF,PO,AW,A:Green Goblin 4.00
TPB rep. #1 & #2 . . . . 9.95

Spider-Man #1
© *Marvel Entertainment Group*

SPIDER-MAN
August, 1990
1 TM Purple Web(c),V:Lizard,
    A:Calypso,B:Torment 5.00
1a Silver Web(c) 6.00
1b Bag,Purple Web 8.00
1c Bag,Silver Web 12.00
1d 2nd print,Gold(c). 5.00
1e 2nd print Gold UPC(rare) 15.00
1f Platinum Ed. 135.00
2 TM,V:Lizard,A:Calypso 4.00
3 TM,V:Lizard,A:Calypso 4.00
4 TM,V:Lizard,A:Calypso 4.00
5 TM,V:Lizard,A:Calypso,
    E:Torment 4.00
6 TM,A:Ghost Rider,V:Hobgoblin . . 4.00
7 TM,A:Ghost Rider,V:Hobgoblin . . 4.00
8 TM,B:Perceptions,A:Wolverine
    I:Wendigo IV 4.00
9 TM,A:Wolverine,Wendigo 4.00
10 TM,RLd,SW,JLe(i),A:Wolv. 4.00
11 TM,A:Wolverine,Wendigo. 4.00
12 TM,E:Perceptions,A:Wolv.. . . . . 4.00
13 TM,V:Morbius,R:Black Cost. . . . 4.00
14 TM,V:Morbius,A:Black Cost.. . . . 4.00
15 EL,A:Beast 4.00
16 TM,RLd,A:X-Force,V:Juggernaut,
    Black Tom,cont.in X-Force#4 . . 4.50
17 RL,AW,A:Thanos,Death 4.00
18 EL,B:Return of the Sinister Six,
    A:Hulk 4.00
19 EL,A:Hulk,Deathlok 4.00
20 EL,A:Nova 4.00
21 EL,A:Hulk,Deathlok,Solo 4.00
22 EL,A:Ghost Rider,Hulk. 2.50
23 EL,E:Return of the Sinister Six,
    A:Hulk,G.Rider,Deathlok,FF . . . 4.00
24 Infinity War,V:Hobgoblin,
    Demogoblin 4.00
25 CMa,A:Excalibur,V:Arcade 4.00
26 RF,MBa,Hologram(c),30th Anniv.
    I:New Burglar. 5.00
27 MR,Handgun issue 2.25
28 MR,Handgun issue 2.25
29 CMa,Ret.to Mad Dog Ward#1 . . 2.25
30 CMa,Ret.to Mad Dog Ward#2 . . 2.25
31 CMa,Ret.to Mad Dog Ward#3 . . 2.25
32 BMc,A:Punisher,V:Master of

Vengeance. 2.25
33 BMc,A:Punisher,V:Master of
    Vengeance. 2.25
34 BMc,A:Punisher,V:Master of
    Vengeance. 2.25
35 TL,Total Carnage#4,V:Carnage,
    Shriek,A:Venom,Black Cat 2.25
36 TL,Total Carnage#8,V:Carnage,
    A:Venom,Morbius 2.25
37 TL,Total Carnage#12,
    V:Carnage 2.25
38 thru 40 KJ,V:Electro. 2.25
41 TKa(s),JaL,I:Platoon,
    A:Iron Fist 2.25
42 TKa(s),JaL,V:Platoon,
    A:Iron Fist 2.25
43 TKa(s),JaL,V:Platoon,
    A:Iron Fist 2.25
44 HMe(s),TL,V:Hobgoblin 2.25
45 HMe(s),TL,SHa,Pursuit#1,
    V:Chameleon 2.25
46 HMe(s),TL,V:Hobgoblin,w/cel . . . 3.25
46a Newsstand Ed. 1.75
47 TL,SHa,V:Demogoblin 2.25
48 TL,SHa,V:Hobgoblin,
    D:Demogoblin 2.25
49 TL,SHa,I:Coldheart 2.25
50 TL,SHa,I:Grim Hunter,foil(c) . . . 5.00
50a newsstand ed. 2.50
51 TL,SHa,Power,pt.3,foil(c) 4.00
51a newsstand ed. 2.25
52 TL,SHa,Spide-clone,V:Venom . . 2.25
53 TL,SHa,Clone,V:Venom 2.25
54 Web of Life,pt.3 . . . . 2.25
55 Web of Life,finale. 2.25
56 Smoke and Mirrors 2.00
57 Aftershocks,pt.1 . . . . 2.50
57a enhanced cover. 3.00
58 The Mark of Kaine,pt.3 . . . . 2.00
59 F:Travellor,Host 2.00
60 TL,SHa,HMa,The Trial of
    Peter Parker,pt.3 . . . . 2.00
61 TL,Maximum Clonage,pt.4 . . . . 2.00
62 HMe,TL,Exiled,pt.3 . . . . 2.00
63 HMe,TL,Greatest
    Responsibility,pt.2. . . . . 2.00
64 HMe,JR2,Return of
    Spider-Man,pt.3 . . . . 2.00
65 HMe,JR2,AW,Media
    Blizzard,pt.3 . . . . 2.00
66 HMe,JR2,Return of Kaine,pt.4 . . 2.00
67 HMe,JR2,Web of Carnage,pt.3 . 2.00
68 HMe,JR2,AW,Blood
    Brothers,pt.3 . . . . 2.00
69 HMe,JR2,Blood Brothers
    aftermath 2.00
70 HMe,JR2,A:Onslaught 3.00
71 HMe,JR2, ... 2.00
72 HMe,JR2,Onslaught saga 2.00
73 HMe,JR2 . . . . 2.00
74 HMe,JR2,AW,A:Daredevil,
    V:Fortunato 2.00
75 HMe,JR2,Revelations, pt.4. . . . . 3.00
76 HMe,JR2,SHa,Post-Onslaught
    world,I:Shoc 2.00
77 HMe,JR2,SHa,V:Morbius 2.00
Becomes:

PETER PARKER,
SPIDER-MAN
78 HMe,JR2,SHa,F:Mary Jane
    Parker 2.00
79 HMe,JR2,SHa,V:Hydra,A:Captain
    Arthur Stacy 2.00
80 HMe,JR2,SHa,V:S.H.O.C. 2.00
81 HMe,JR2,SHa,V:Shang-Chi,pt.1. 2.00
82 HMe,JR2,SHa,Anti-Mutant
    Movement 2.00
83 HMe,JR2,SHa,V:Morbius 2.00
85 HMe,JR2,SHa,V:Friends of
    Humanity 2.00

86 HMe,JR2,SHa,F:Jimmy Six,
　Hammerhead 2.00
87 HMe,JR2,SHa,A:Trapster &
　Shocker. 2.00
88 HMe,JR2,SHa,Spider-Man is
　Public Enemy #1 . . . . 2.00
89 HMe,JR2,SHa,Spider-Hunt,pt.3
　x-over. 2.00
90 HMe,JR2,SHa,Identity Crisis
　prelude. 2.00
91 HMe,JR2,SHa,Identity Crisis,
　as Dusk 2.00
92 HMe,JR2,as Dusk, V:Trapster . . 2.00
93 HMe,JS,R:Ghost Rider 2.00
94 HMe,JR2,SHa,Who wasJoeyZ? . 2.00
95 HMe,JR2,SHa,Trapped in
　elevator shaft 2.00
96 HMe,JR2,SHa,The Gathering of
　the Five (pt. 3 of 5)x-over 2.00
97 HMe,JR2,SHa,JBy(c),The Final
　Chapter,pt.2 x-over. 2.00
98 HMe,JR2,SHa,JBy(c),The Final
　Chapter,pt.4 x-over. 2.00
98a alternate JBy(c) (1:2) 2.00
Minus 1 Spec., HMe,JR2,SHa,
　flashback, A:Stacys 2.00
Ann.'97 Simon Garth—Zombie 2.95
Ann. '98 HMe, Spider-Man/Elektra,
　V:The Silencer, 48pg. 3.00
GN Fear Itself. 12.95
GN Nothing Stops Juggernaut 3.95
GN Parallel Lives 8.95
GN JMD,MZ,Soul of the Hunter . . 5.95
HC Kraven's Last Hunt 19.95
HC CV,Spirits of the Earth 18.95
Spec. Chaos in Calgary 1.50
Spec. Double Trouble 1.50
Spec. Hit and Run, Canadian 1.50
Spec. Skating on Thin Ice. 1.50
Spec. Trial of Venom,UNICEF. . . . 15.00
Sup.Sz.Spec#1 Planet of the
　Symbiotes, pt.2;
　flipbook F:Scarlet Spider. 3.95
Giant-Sized CCl,JBy. 4.00
TPB Assasination Plot 14.95
TPB Carnage 6.95
TPB Cosmic Adventures. 19.95
TPB Death of Gwen Stacy 14.95
TPB Hooky. 6.95
TPB Identity Crisis 19.95
TPB Maximum Carnage 24.95
TPB Origin of the Hobgoblin 14.95
TPB Return of the Sinister Six . . . 15.95
TPB Spider-Man: Revelations,JR2,
　rep. +14 new pages (1997). . . 12.00
TPB Round Robin. 15.95
TPB Saga of the Alien Costume . . 14.00
　2nd printing 12.95
TPB Spider-Man vs. Venom 9.95
TPB Torment Rep.#1-#5. . . . . . . 12.95
TPB Venom Returns. 12.95
TPB Very Best of Spider-Man 15.95
TPB The Wedding 12.95
TPB Invasion Spider Slayers 15.95
TPB Clone Genesis 16.95
TPB V:Green Goblin 15.95
TPB Spider-Man'sGreatestVillains. 15.95
Holiday Spec.'95. . . . . 2.95

SPIDER-MAN
ADVENTURES
1994–96
1 From animated series. 1.50
1a foil (c). 2.95
2 Animated Adventures 1.50
3 V:Spider-Slayer 1.50
4 Animated Adventures 1.50
5 V:Mysterio 1.50
6 V:Kraven 1.50
7 V:Doctor Octopus 1.50

8 O:Venom,pt.1 . . . . 1.50
9 O:Venom,pt.2 . . . . 1.50
10 V:Venom 1.50
11 V:Hobgoblin. 1.50
12 V:Hobgoblin. 1.50
13 V:Chameleon. 1.50
14 V:Doc Octopus 1.50
15 Doc Conners 1.50
TPB Rep.#1-#5, 112pg 8.95

SPIDER-MAN
& AMAZING FRIENDS
Dec., 1981
1 DSp,A:Iceman,I:Firestar 5.50

SPIDER-MAN/BADROCK
Marvel/Maximum Press 1997
1 x-over, pt.1 . . . . 3.00
2 x-over, pt. 2 . . . . 3.00

SPIDER-MAN/BATMAN
1995
1 JMD,MBa,MFm,V:Carnage,Joker 5.95

SPIDER-MAN, CHAPTER 1
Oct. 1998
1 (of 13) JBy,formative years 2.50
1a signed 19.63
2 JBy,A:Fantastic Four. 2.50
2a variant JBy cover 5.00
2b signed, both covers. 30.00
3 JBy,V:J.Jonah Jameson 2.50
4 JBy,V:Dr.Octopus & Dr.Doom . . 2.50
5 JBy,V:Lizard 2.50
6 JBy,V:Electro 2.50
7 JBy,V:Mysterio 2.50
8 JBy,V:Green Goblin 2.50
9 JBy,V:Circus of Crime. 2.50
10 JBy,V:Green Goblin 2.50
11 JBy,V:Giant-Man 2.50
12 JBy,V:Sandman, double size
　final issue. 3.50
Spec.#0 JBy,O:Sandman,Vulture
　& Lizard 2.50

SPIDER-MAN CLASSICS
1993–94
1 rep.Amazing Fantasy#15 . . . . . 1.75
2 thru 11 rep.Amaz.SpM#1-#10 . @1.75
12 rep.Amaz.SpM#11 . . . . 1.50
13 rep.Amaz.SpM#12. . . . . 1.50
14 rep.Amaz.SpM#13. . . . . 1.50
15 rep.Amaz.SpM#14,w/cel 3.25
15a Newsstand Ed. 1.50

SPIDER-MAN
COMICS MAGAZINE
Jan., 1987
1 . . . . 2.50
2 thru 13 . . . . @1.50

SPIDER-MAN:
DEAD MAN'S HAND
1997
1-shot, RSt,DaR,JeM,V:Carrion . . . 3.00

SPIDER-MAN:
THE FINAL ADVENTURE
1995–96
1 FaN,DaR,Clv,I:Tendril 3.00
2 FaN,DaR,JAl,V:Tendril 3.00
3 FaN,DaR,JAl,V:Tendril 3.00

4 FaN,DaR,JAl,V:Tendril,concl. . . . 3.00

SPIDER-MAN:
FRIENDS AND ENEMIES
1995
1 V:Metahumes 2.00
2 A:Nova,Darkhawk,Speedball. . . . 2.00
3 V:Metahumes 2.00
4 F:Metahumes 2.00

SPIDER-MEN: FUNERAL
FOR AN OCTOPUS
1995
1 Doc Oc Dead 2.50
2 A:Sinister Six 2.00
3 Final Issue 2.00

SPIDER-MAN/GEN13
Marvel/Wildstorm 1996
1-shot PDd,SI,CaS x-over 4.95

Spider-Man Hobgoblin Lives #3
© Marvel Entertainment Group

SPIDER-MAN:
HOBGOBLIN LIVES
1997
1 (of 3) RSt,RF,GP 2.50
2 RSt,RF,GP,Who was the original
　Hobgoblin?. 2.50
3 RSt,RF,GP,Original identity
　revealed. 2.50
TPB RF(c), series rep. 15.00

SPIDER-MAN: MADE MEN
June 1998
GN HMe,gangster epic 6.00

SPIDER-MAN:
THE MANGA
Black & White, Oct., 1997
Bi-weekly
1 imported, translated 4.00
2 . . . . 3.00
3 V:Elektro 3.00
4 V:Lizard 3.00
5 V:Lizard 3.00
6 V:Lizard, concl. 3.00
7 V:Kangaroo 3.00
8 V:Kangaroo 3.00

9 V:Kangaroo 3.00
10 Imposter Spider-Man 3.00
11 Real Spider-Man returns 3.00
12 name dragged through the mud. 3.00
13 V:Mysterio 3.00
14 V:Mysterio 3.00
15 V:Mysterio, double size 4.00
16 Human side of Japanese
   Spider-Man 3.00
17 Human side cont.. . . . . 3.00
18 Human side concl.. . . . . 3.00
19 Spidey's vacation. 3.00
20 and 21 . . . . @3.00
22 woman who creates blizzards . . 3.00
23 secrets of the Ice Woman 3.00
24 blood donated 3.00
25 V:Mitsuo Kitano 3.00
26 Mitsuo Kitano insane 3.00
27 Yu refuses costume 3.00
28 JMd(c), Yu puts on costume. . . . 3.00
29 JMd(c), Yu vs. Kitano. 3.00
30 Yu vs. Kitano 3.00
31 . . . . 3.00
32 Yu escapes 3.00
33 V:Motorcyclists 3.00
34 thru 37 . . . . @3.00

SPIDER-MAN:
MAXIMUM CLONAGE
1995
Alpha Maximum Clonage,pt.1 . . . . 5.50
Omega TL,Maximum Clonage,pt.6 . 4.95

SPIDER-MAN MEGAZINE
1994–95
1 thru 4 rep. . . . . @2.95
5 Vision rep. 2.95
6 V:Thing & Torch, rep. 2.95

Spider-Man: Mutant Agenda #1
© Marvel Entertainment Group

SPIDER-MAN:
MUTANT AGENDA
0 thru 2 Paste in Book . . . . @1.50
3 Paste in Book. 1.50

SPIDER-MAN:
POWER OF TERROR
1995
1 R:Silvermane,A:Deathlok 2.00
2 V:Silvermane 2.00
3 New Scorpion. 2.00

4 V:Silvermane 2.00

SPIDER-MAN/PUNISHER
Part 1 TL,A:Tombstone 3.00
Part 2 TL,A:Tombstone 3.00

SPIDER-MAN/PUNISHER/
SABERTOOTH:
DESIGNER GENES
1 SMc,Foil(c). 9.50

SPIDER-MAN:
REDEMPTION
1996
1 thru 4 JMD,MZ,BMc, Mary Jane
   arrested for Murder . . . . @1.50

SPIDER-MAN SAGA
Nov., 1991
1 SLi(c),History from Amazing
   Fantasy #15-Amaz.SpM#100 . . 3.25
2 SLi(c),Amaz.SpM#101-#175 . . . . 3.25
3 Amaz.SpM#176-#238 . . . . 3.25
4 Amaz.SpM #239-#300 . . . . 3.25

SPIDER-MAN
SUPER SIZE SPECIAL
1 Planet of the Symbiotes,pt.2 . . . . 3.95

SPIDER-MAN TEAM-UP
1995–96
1 MWa,KeL,V:Hellfire Club 3.00
2 thru 4 . . . . 3.00
5 SvG,DaR,JFr,F:Gambit,
   Howard the Duck 3.00
6 JMD,LHa,F:Hulk & Doctor
   Strange 3.00
7 KBk,SB,F:Thunderbolts 3.00

SPIDER-MAN:
THE ARACHNIS PROJECT
1984–95
1 Wld, beginnings 1.75
2 Wld,V:Diggers 1.75
3 Wld,V:Jury 1.75
4 Wld,V:Life Foundation 1.75
5 Wld,V:Jury 1.75

SPIDER-MAN:
THE CLONE JOURNALS
1-shot (1995) 1.95

SPIDER-MAN:
THE JACKAL FILES
1 Files of the Jackal (1995) 1.95

SPIDER-MAN:
THE LOST YEARS
1995
0 JMD,JR2,LSh,64pg,rep. 4.00
1 History of Kaine,Ben. 3.00
2 JMD,JR2,KJ,Kaine & Ben 3.00
3 Ben vs. Kaine. 3.00

SPIDER-MAN:
THE PARKER YEARS
1995
1 JR2,JPi,F:The real Clone 2.50

SPIDER-MAN 2099
1992–96
1 RL,AW,I:Spider-Man 2099 . . . . . 4.00
2 RL,AW,O:Spider-Man 2099.. . . . 3.00
3 RL,AW,V:Venture 2.50
4 RL,AW,I:Specialist,
   A:Doom 2099. . . . . 2.00
5 RL,AW,V:Specialist. 2.00
6 RL,AW,I:New Vulture 2.00
7 RL,AW,Vulture of 2099 . . . . 2.00
8 RL,AW,V:New Vulture 2.00
9 KJo,V:Alchemax 2.00
10 RL,AW,O:Wellvale Home 2.00
11 RL,AW,V:S.I.E.G.E. 2.00
12 RL,AW,w/poster. 2.00
13 RL,AW,V:Thanatos 1.75
14 PDd(s),RL(c),TGb,Downtown. . . 1.75
15 PDd(s),RL,I:Thor 2099,
   Heimdall 2099 . . . . 1.75
16 PDd(s),RL,Fall of the
   Hammer#1 . . . . 1.75
17 PDd(s),RL,V:Bloodsword 1.75
18 PDd(s),RLm,V:Lyla 1.75
19 PDd(s),RL,w/card 1.75
20 PDd(s),RL,Crash & Burn 1.75
21 V:Gangs 1.75
22 V:Gangs 1.75
23 RL,I:Risque 3.00
24 Kasey 1.75
25 A:Hulk 2099, dbl-size,foil(c) . . . 3.25
25a Newsstand ed.. . . . . 2.25
26 V:Headhunter, Travesty 1.50
27 V:Travesty 1.50
28 V:Travesty 1.50
29 V:Foragers. 1.50
30 V:Flipside 1.50
31 I:Dash 1.50
Becomes:

SPIDER-MAN 2099 A.D.
32 I:Morgue 2.00
33 One Nation Under Doom 2.00
34 V:Alchemex 2.00
35 . . . . 2.00
36a Spider-Man 2099(c) 2.00
36b Venom 2099(c) 2.00
37a Venom 2099 . . . . 2.00
37b variant cover 2.00
38 . . . . 2.00
39 A:Venom 2099. . . . . 2.00
40 V:Goblin 2099 . . . . 2.00
41 and 42 . . . . @2.00
43 V:Sub-Mariner 2099. . . . . 2.00
Ann.#1 PDd(s),RL 3.00

Spider-Man 2099 #42
© Marvel Entertainment Group

Spec.#1 I:3 new villains 4.00

SPIDER-MAN UNLIMITED
1993
1 RLm,Maximun Carnage#1,I:Shriek,
  R:Carnage 5.00
2 RLm,Maximum Carnage#14 . . . . 4.50
3 RLm,O:Doctor Octopus. 4.50
4 RLm,V:Mystrerio,Rhino. 4.25
5 RLm,A:Human Torch,
  I:Steel Spider 4.25
6 RLm,A:Thunderstrike 4.00
7 RLm,A:Clone 4.00
8 Tom Lyle. 4.00
9 The Mark of Kaine,pt.5 . . . . 4.00
10 SwM,Exiled,pt.4 . . . . 4.00
11 FaN,V:Black Cat 4.00
12 Blood Brother tie-in 4.00
13 . . . . 3.00
14 JoB, an ally dies 3.00
15 TDF,JoB,F:Puma 3.00
16 cont. from X-Force #64 . . . . 3.00
17 JoB, Revelations, sequel 3.00
18 TDF,JoB,F:Doctor Octopus 3.00
19 JoB,F:Lizard 3.00
20 JoB,A:Hannibal King, V:Lilith . . . 3.00
21 MD2,Frankenstein Monster lives . 3.00
22 MD2,V:The Scorpion 3.00

SPIDER-MAN UNMASKED
1996
1-shot 64pg information source . . . 6.00

SPIDER-MAN VS. DRACULA
1994
1 rep. 1.75

SPIDER-MAN vs. VENOM
1990
1 TM(c) 8.95

SPIDER-MAN: THE VENOM AGENDA
Nov., 1997
1-shot LHa,TL, J. Jonah Jameson,
  V:Venom 3.00

SPIDER-MAN vs. WOLVERINE
1990
1 MBr,AW,D:Ned Leeds(the original
  Hobgoblin),V:Charlie. 22.00
1a reprint. 5.00

SPIDER-MAN: WEB OF DOOM
1994
1 3-part series. 1.75
2 Spidey falsely accused 1.75
3 conclusion 1.75

SPIDER-MAN & X-FACTOR: SHADOW GAMES
1 PB,I:Shadowforce 2.25
2 PB,V:Shadowforce 2.25
3 PB,V:Shadowforce, final issue . . 2.25

Spider-Woman #25
© *Marvel Entertainment Group*

SPIDER-WOMAN
April, 1978
1 Cl,TD,O:Spiderwoman 6.00
2 Cl,TD,I:Morgan Le Fey 2.00
3 Cl,TD,I:Brother's Grimm 2.00
4 Cl,TD,V:Hangman 2.00
5 Cl,TD,Nightmares. 2.00
6 Cl,A:Werewolf By Night 2.00
7 Cl,SL,AG,V:Magnus 2.00
8 Cl,AG,"Man who would not die" . 2.00
9 Cl,AG,A:Needle,Magnus. 2.00
10 Cl,AG,I:Gypsy Moth. 2.00
11 Cl,AG,V:Brothers Grimm 1.50
12 Cl,AG,V:Brothers Grimm 1.50
13 Cl,AG,A:Shroud. 1.50
14 BSz(c),Cl,AG,A:Shroud 1.50
15 BSz(c),Cl,AG,A:Shroud 1.50
16 BSz(c),Cl,AG,V:Nekra 1.50
17 Cl,Deathplunge 1.50
18 Cl,A:Flesh 1.50
19 Cl,A:Werewolf By Night,
  V:Enforcer 1.75
20 FS,A:Spider-Man 1.50
21 FS,A:Bounty Hunter. 1.50
22 FS,A:Killer Clown. 1.50
23 TVE,V:The Gamesmen 1.50
24 TVE,V:The Gamesmen 1.50
25 SL,Two Spiderwomen 1.50
26 JBy(c),SL,V:White Gardenia. . . . 1.50
27 BSz(c),JBi,A:Enforcer 1.50
28 BSz(c),SL,A:Enforcer,Spidey . . . 1.50
29 JR2(c),ECh,FS,A:Enforcer,
  Spider-Man 1.50
30 FM(c),SL,JM,I:Dr.Karl Malus . . . 1.50
31 FM(c),SL,JM,A:Hornet 1.50
32 FM(c),SL,JM,A:Werewolf 1.75
33 SL,V:Yesterday's Villian 1.50
34 SL,AM,V:Hammer and Anvil. . . . 1.50
35 SL,AG,V:Angar the Screamer . . 1.50
36 SL,Spiderwoman Shot 1.50
37 SL,TA,BWi,AM,FS,A:X-Men,I:
  Siryn,V:Black Tom 4.00
38 SL,BWi,A:X-Men,Siryn 5.00
39 SL,BWi,Shadows 1.50
40 SL,BWi,V:The Flying Tiger 1.50
41 SL,BWi,V:Morgan LeFay 1.50
42 SL,BWi,V:Silver Samurai 1.50
43 SL,V:Silver Samurai. 1.50
44 SL,V:Morgan LeFay 1.50
45 SL,Spider-Man Thief Cover 1.50
46 SL,V:Mandroids,A:Kingpin 1.50
47 V:Daddy Longlegs 1.50
48 O:Gypsy Moth 1.50

49 A:Tigra 1.50
50 PH(c),D:Spiderwoman 3.50
[Limited Series] 1993–94
1 V:Therak 2.00
2 O:Spider-Woman 2.00
3 V:Deathweb 2.00
4 V:Deathweb,Last issue 2.00

SPIDER-WOMAN
May 1999
1 JBy,BS,48-page 3.00
1a signed 20.00
2 BS,JBy,A:Dr. Octopus. 2.00
2a variant JR2 cover 2.00
3 BS,JBy,V:Flesh & Bones. 2.00
4 BS,JBy,V:Flesh & Bones. 2.00

SPIDEY SUPER STORIES
Oct., 1974
1 Younger reader's series in
  association with the Electric
  Company,O:Spider-Man 12.00
2 A:Kraven 8.00
3 A:Ringleader 8.00
4 A:Medusa 8.00
5 A:Shocker 8.00
6 A:Iceman 8.00
7 A:Lizard, Vanisher 8.00
8 A:Dr. Octopus 8.00
9 A:Dr. Doom 8.00
10 A:Green Goblin 7.00
11 A:Dr. Octopus 7.00
12 A:The Cat,V:The Owl 7.00
13 A:Falcon 7.00
14 A:Shanna 7.00
15 A:Storm 8.00
16 . . . . 6.00
17 A:Captain America 6.00
18 A:Kingpin. 6.00
19 A:Silver Surfer,Dr. Doom 6.00
20 A;Human Torch,Invisible Girl . . . 6.00
21 A:Dr. Octopus 5.00
22 A:Ms. Marvel,The Beetle 5.00
23 A:Green Goblin 5.00
24 A:Thundra 5.00
25 A:Dr. Doom 5.00
26 A:Sandman 5.00
27 A:Thor,Loki 5.00
28 A:Medusa 5.00
29 A:Kingpin. 5.00

Spidey Super Stories #4
© *Marvel Entertainment Group*

MARVEL

MARVEL (sidebar)

30 A:Kang	5.00
31 A:Moondragon,Dr. Doom	4.00
32 A:Spider-Woman,Dr. Octopus	4.00
33	4.00
34 A:Sub-Mariner	4.00
35	4.00
36 A:Lizard	4.00
37 A:White Tiger	4.00
38 A:Fantastic Four	4.00
39 A:Hellcat,Thanos	6.00
40 A:Hawkeye	4.00
41 A:Nova,Dr. Octopus	4.00
42 A:Kingpin	4.00
43 A:Daredevil,Ringmaster	4.00
44 A:Vision	4.00
45 A:Silver Surfer,Dr. Doom	6.00
46 A:Mysterio	4.00
47 A:Spider-Woman,Stilt-Man	4.00
48 A:Green Goblin	4.00
49 Spidey for President	4.00
50 A:She-Hulk	4.00
51 and 52	@4.00
53 A:Dr. Doom	4.00
54 `Attack of the Bird-Man'	4.00
55 A:Kingpin	4.00
56 A:Captain Britain, Jack O'Lantern	4.00
57 March, 1982	4.00

SPITFIRE AND THE TROUBLESHOOTERS
Oct., 1986

1 HT/JSt	1.00
2 HT	1.00
3 HT,Macs Armor	1.00
4 TM/BMc(Early TM work)	3.00
5 HT/TD,A:StarBrand	1.00
6 HT,Trial	1.00
7 HT	1.00
8 HT,New Armor	1.00
9	1.00

Becomes:
CODE NAME: SPITFIRE

10 MR/TD	1.00
11 thru 13	@1.00

SPOOF
Oct., 1970

1 MSe	12.00
2 MSe,`Brawl in the Family'	10.00
3 MSe,Richard Nixon cover	10.00
4 MSe,`Blechhula'	10.00
5 MSe,May, 1973	11.00

SPORT STARS
Nov., 1949

1 The Life of Knute Rockne	250.00

Becomes:
SPORTS ACTION

2 BP(c),Life of George Gipp	250.00
3 BEv,Hack Wilson	165.00
4 Art Houtteman	150.00
5 Nile Kinnick	150.00
6 Warren Gun	150.00
7 Jim Konstanty	150.00
8 Ralph Kiner	175.00
9 Ed "Strangler" Lewis	150.00
10 JMn,`The Yella-Belly'	150.00
11 `The Killers'	150.00
12 BEv,`Man Behind the Mask'	150.00
13 BEv,Lew Andrews	150.00
14 MWs,Ken Roper,Sept.,1952	125.00

SPOTLIGHT
Sept., 1978

1 F:Huckleberry Hound,YogiBear	12.00

2 Quick Draw McDraw	8.00
3 The Jetsons	8.00
4 Magilla Gorilla, March, 1979	8.00

SPUMCO COMIC BOOK

1 I:Jimmy the Hapless Boy	6.95
2	6.95
3 64pgs of sick humor	6.95
4 More sick humor	6.95
TPB	24.95

SPY CASES
See: KID KOMICS

SPY FIGHTERS
March, 1951

1 GT	150.00
2 GT	100.00
3	75.00
4 thru 13	@75.00
14 thru 15 July, 1953	@85.00

SPYKE
Epic *Heavy Hitters* 1993

1 MBn,BR,I:Spyke	2.75
2 MBn,BR,V:Conita	2.75
3 thru 4 MBn,BR	@2.00

SPY THRILLERS
Atlas Nov., 1954

1 `The Tickling Death'	150.00
2 V:Communists	100.00
3	75.00
4	75.00

Becomes:
POLICE BADGE

5 Sept., 1955	75.00

SQUADRON SUPREME
Sept., 1985

1 BH,L:Nighthawk	3.00
2 BH,F:Nuke,A:Scarlet Centurion	2.50
3 BH,D:Nuke	2.50
4 BH,L:Archer	2.00
5 BH,L:Amphibian	2.00
6 PR,J:Institute of Evil	2.00
7 JB,JG,V:Hyperion	2.00
8 BH,V:Hyperion	2.00

Squadron Supreme #4
© Marvel Entertainment Group

9 BSz(c),PR,D:Tom Thumb	2.00
10 PR,V:Quagmire	2.00
11 PR,V:Redeemers	2.00
12 PR,D:Nighthawk,Foxfire, Black Archer	2.50
GN Death of a Universe	9.95
TPB 352 pages.	15.00

STALKERS
Epic 1990–91

1 MT	1.50
2 MT	1.50
3 MT	1.50
4 MT	1.50
5 MT	1.50
6 VM,MT	1.50
7 VM,MT	1.50
8 VM,MT	1.50
9 thru 12 VM	@1.50

STARBLAST
1994

1 MGu(s),HT,After the Starbrand	2.25
2 MGu(s),HT,After the Starbrand	2.00
3 MGu(s),HT,After the Starbrand	2.00
4 MGu(s),HT,Final Issue	2.00

STARBRAND
Oct., 1986

1 JR2,O:Starbrand	1.50
2 JR2/AW	1.00
3 JR2/AW	1.00
4 JR2/AW	1.00
5 JR2/AW	1.00
6 JR2/AW	1.00
7 JR2/AW	1.00
8 JR2/AW	1.00
9 KG/BWi,A:Nightmask	1.00
10	1.00
11 JR2,TP	1.00
12 JR2,TP,X-Men X-over	1.25
13 JR2,TP	1.25
14 JR2,TP	1.25
15	1.25
16	1.25
17 JBy,TP,New Starbrand	1.50
18 JBy/TP	1.50
19 JBy/TP	1.50
Ann.#1	1.25

STAR COMICS MAGAZINE
Dec., 1986 (digest size)

1 F:Heathcliff,Muppet Babies, Ewoks	1.50
2 thru 13 1988	@1.50

STARJAMMERS
1995–96

1 I:The Uncreated	2.95
2 War For the Shi'ar	2.95
3 stuck in deep space	2.95
4 conclusion	2.95

STAR-LORD, SPECIAL EDITION
Feb., 1982

1 JBy reprints	6.00

STARLORD
Mini-Series 1996

1 (of 3) DLw,	2.50
2 DLw	2.50
3 DLw,V:Damyish	2.50

STARLORD MEGAZINE
TPB CCl,JBy,TA, rep., 64pg 2.95

STAR MASTER
1 MGu,Cosmic Avengers assemble 2.00
2 MGu,Worldengine saga 2.00
3 MGu,Cauldron of Conversion . . . 2.00

STARRIORS
August, 1984
1 . . . . 1.50
2 . . . . 1.25
3 . . . . 1.25
4 Feb., 1982 . . . . 1.25

STARSTRUCK
March, 1985
1 MK 2.00
2 MK 1.75
3 thru 8 MK, Feb. 1986 . . . . @1.50

STAR TREK
April, 1980
1 DC,KJ,rep.1st movie Adapt. 8.00
2 DC,KJ,rep.1st movie Adapt. 6.00
3 DC,KJ,rep.1st movie Adapt. 5.00
4 DC,KJ,The Weirdest Voyage . . . 5.00
5 DC,KJ,Dr.McCoy..Killer 5.00
6 DC,KJ,A:Ambassador Phlu 5.00
7 MN,KJ,Kirk/Spock(c). 5.00
8 DC(p),F:Spock 5.00
9 DC,FS,Trapped in a Web of
   Ghostly Vengeance 5.00
10 KJ(i),Spock the Barbarian 5.00
11 TP(i),Like A Woman Scorned . . . 5.00
12 TP(i),Trapped in a Starship
   Gone Mad 5.00
13 TP(i),A:Barbara McCoy 5.00
14 LM,GD,We Are Dying,
   Egypt,Dying 5.00
15 GK,The Quality of Mercy 5.00
16 LM,There's no Space
   like Gnomes 5.00
17 EH,TP,The Long Nights Dawn . . 7.00
18 A Thousand Deaths,last issue . 15.00

STAR TREK:
DEEP SPACE NINE
1996
1 HWe(s),TGb,AM,DS9 in the
   Gamma Quadrant,pt.1 (of 2) . . . 2.00
2 DS9 in Gamma Quadrant,pt.2. . . 2.00
3 TGb,AM,pt.1 (of 2) 2.00
4 TGb,AM,pt.2 . . . . 2.00
5 AM,terrorist attack 2.00
6 HWe(s),TGb,AM,Shirn sentence
   Sisko to Death, "Risk," pt.1 . . . . 2.00
7 HWe(s),TGb,"Risk," pt.2 . . . . . . 2.00
8 TGb,AM,V:Maquis & Romulans. . 2.00
9 TGb,AM,V:Maquis & Romulans,
   pt.2 . . . . 2.00
10 HWe,TGb, trapped in the
   holosuite 2.00
11 HWe,TGb, ... 2.00
12 Telepathy War x-over 2.00
13 Jem'Hadar battle 2.00
14 Why do Klingons hate tribbles? . 2.00
15 The Tailor's deeds 2.00

STAR TREK:
EARLY VOYAGES
Dec. 1996
1 DAn,IEd,Captain Pike's crew,
   double size premier 3.00
2 DAn,IEd,distress signal 2.00

Star Trek: Early Voyages #6
© Marvel Entertainment Group

3 DAn,IEd,on Rigel 7, prologue to
   "The Cage" 2.00
4 DAn,IEd, prologue to "The Cage" 2.00
5 DAn,IEd, V:Vulcans 2.00
6 DAn,IEd, Cloak & Dagger concl. . 2.00
7 DAn,IEd, The wrath of Kaaj 2.00
8 DAn,IEd,F:Dr. Boyce 2.00
9 DAn,IEd,F:Nano 2.00
10 DAn,V:Chakuun, Tholians 2.00
11 DAn,IEd,The Fallen, pt. 2 . . . . . 2.00
12 DAn,IEd, ... 2.00
13 DAn,IEd,F:Yeoman Colt 2.00
14 DAn,IEd,Pike vs. Kirk 2.00
15 DAn,IEd,F:Yeoman Colt 2.00
16 . . . . 2.00
17 DAn,IEd, Pike & Kaaj 2.00

STAR TREK:
FIRST CONTACT
GN Movie Adapt. 6.00

STAR TREK:
MIRROR, MIRROR
1996
1-shot continuation of famous
   classic episode 4.00

STAR TREK: THE NEXT
GENERATION—
RIKER SPECIAL
May 1998
1-shot, DAn,IEd,Riker photo cover . 3.50

STAR TREK: THE NEXT
GENERATION/X-MEN:
SECOND CONTACT
March 1998
1-shot, DAn,IEd,64pg 5.00
1-shot, variant CNr cover (1:5) 5.00

STAR TREK: OPERATION
ASSIMILATION
1-shot Borg story 3.00

Star Trek: Starfleet Academy #8
© Marvel Entertainment Group

STAR TREK:
STARFLEET ACADEMY
1996
1 Cadets vs. Gorns 2.00
2 ALa, R&R in Australia 2.00
3 F:Decker 2.00
4 V:Klingon Bird-of-prey 2.00
5 V:Klingons 2.00
6 Funeral of Kamilah
   Goldstein,I:Edam Astrun 2.00
7 ALa,F:Edam Astrun,Nog 2.00
8 ALa, Return of Charlie X 2.00
9 ALa, on Talos, V:Jem'Hadar . . . 2.00
10 ALa,F:Captain Pike, Jem'Hadar . 2.00
11 F:Christopher Pike 2.00
12 ALa, Telepathy War x-over 2.00
13 Parent's Day 2.00
14 T'Priell revealed, pt.1 (of 3) 2.00
15 T'Priell dead?, pt.2 . . . . 2.00
16 T'Priell Revealed, pt3 . . . . 2.00
17 Battle for T'Priell's mind 2.00
18 Entirely in Klingon language. . . . 2.00
19 Pava vs. Kovold 2.00

STAR TREK:
TELEPATHY WAR
Sept., 1997
1-shot Telepathy War, pt.4
   x-over, 48pg 3.00

STAR TREK: UNLIMITED
1996
1 DAn,IEd,MBu,JeM,AW, Classic
   series & TNG 3.00
2 DAn,IEd,MBu, ... 3.00
3 DAn,IEd,MBu, ... 3.00
4 DAn,IEd,MBu,AW, 2 tales 3.00
5 DAn,IEd,TMo,RoR,AW,ANi,48pg. 3.00
6 DAn, Telepathy War x-over 2.00
7 DAn,IEd,F:Q & Trelane 2.00
8 DAn,IEd,Day of Honor tie-in 2.00
9 DAn,IEd,V:Klingons 2.00
10 A Piece of the Action,
   conclusion of series 2.00

STAR TREK:
THE UNTOLD VOYAGES
Jan., 1998
1 (of 5) Star Trek 2nd Five Year

MARVEL

Mission 2.50	
2 Spock, Savik, Dr. McCoy 2.50	
3 F:McCoy, McCoy's Daughter. . . . 2.50	
4 F:Sulu 2.50	
5 48pg finale 3.50	

STAR TREK: VOYAGER
1996
1 F:Neelix & Talaxians, pt.1 . . . . . . 2.00
2 F:Neelix & Talaxians, pt.2 . . . . . . 2.00
3 F:Neelix & Talaxians, pt.3 . . . . . . 2.00
4 HWe(s),"Homeostasis," pt.1 . . . . 2.00
5 HWe(s),"Homeostasis," pt.2 . . . . 2.00
6 HWe(s),"Homeostasis," pt.3 . . . . 2.00
7 Ancient Relic 2.00
8 Mysterious Relic encountered . . . 2.00
9 DAn,IEd,AM, rescue mission . . . 2.00
10 The Borg are back 2.00
11 Zoological Experiment 2.00
12 Zoological Experiment 2.00
13 Crew loses a member 2.00
14 Distress Call 2.00
15 Tuvok Trapped 2.00

STAR TREK: VOYAGER: SPLASHDOWN
Jan., 1998
1 (of 4) AM,Crash landing on
    water planet 2.00
2 AM,The ship may sink 2.00
3 AM,adventure undersea 2.00
4 AM,escape from sea creatures . . 2.00

STAR TREK/X-MEN
1-shot SLo,MS, 64pg. 5.00
1a rep. of STAR TREK/X-MEN . . . 4.95

STAR WARS
July, 1977
1 HC,30 Cent,movie adaption. . . . 65.00
1a HC,35 Cent(square Box). . . . 400.00
1b "Reprint". 7.50
2 HC,movie adaptation 25.00
2b "Reprint". 4.00
3 HC,movie adaptation 25.00
3b "Reprint". 4.00
4 HC,SL,movie adapt.(low dist.). . 22.00
4b "Reprint". 4.00
5 HC,SL,movie adaptation 22.00
5b "Reprint". 3.00

Star Wars #17
© *Marvel Entertainment Group*

---

6 HC,DSt,E:movie adaption 22.00
6b "Reprint". 3.00
7 HC,FS,F:Luke&Chewbacca . . . 20.00
7b "Reprint". 2.50
8 HC,TD,Eight against a World . . 20.00
8b "Reprint". 2.50
9 HC,TP,V:Cloud Riders. 20.00
9b "Reprint". 2.50
10 HC,TP,Behemoth fr.Below 20.00
11 CI,TP,Fate o/Luke Skywalker . . 18.00
12 TA,CI,Doomworld. 18.00
13 TA,JBy,CI,Deadly Reunion 18.00
14 TA,CI 18.00
15 CI,V:Crimson Jack 18.00
16 WS,V:The Hunter. 18.00
17 Crucible, Low Dist. 18.00
18 CI,Empire Strikes(Low Dist). . . 18.00
19 CI,Ultimate Gamble(Low Dist) . 18.00
20 CI,Death Game(Scarce). 18.00
21 TA,CI,Shadow of a Dark
    Lord(Scarce) 18.00
22 CI,Han Solo vs.Chewbacca . . . 15.00
23 CI,Flight Into Fury 15.00
24 CI,Ben Kenobi Story 15.00
25 CI,Siege at Yavin 15.00
26 CI,Doom Mission 15.00
27 CI,V:The Hunter. 15.00
28 CI,Cavern o/t Crawling Death. . 15.00
29 CI,Dark Encounter 15.00
30 CI,A Princess Alone 15.00
31 CI,Return to Tatooine 15.00
32 CI,The Jawa Express. 15.00
33 CI,GD,V:Baron Tagge 15.00
34 CI,Thunder in the Stars 15.00
35 CI,V:Darth Vader 15.00
36 CI,V:Darth Vader 15.00
37 CI,V:Darth Vader 15.00
38 TA,MG,Riders in the Void. 15.00
39 AW,B:Empire Strikes Back 25.00
40 AW,Battleground Hoth 25.00
41 AW,Imperial Pursuit 25.00
42 AW,Bounty Hunters 25.00
43 AW,Betrayal at Bespin 25.00
44 AW,E:Empire Strikes Back 25.00
45 CI,GD,Death Probe 20.00
46 DI,TP,V:Dreamnaut Devourer . . 20.00
47 CI,GD,Droid World 20.00
48 CI,Leia vs.Darth Vader. 20.00
49 SW,TP,The Last Jedi 20.00
50 WS,AW,TP,G-Size issue 20.00
51 WS,TP,Resurrection of Evil . . . 15.00
52 WS,TP. 15.00
53 CI,WS 15.00
54 CI,WS 15.00
55 thru 66 WS,TP . . . . @15.00
67 TP 15.00
68 GD,TP 20.00
69 GD,TP 20.00
70 A:Han Solo 20.00
71 A:Han Solo 20.00
72 . . . . 20.00
73 Secret of Planet Lansbane 20.00
74 thru 91 . . . . @20.00
92 BSz(c) 20.00
93 thru 97 . . . . @20.00
98 AW 20.00
99 . . . . 20.00
100 Painted(c),double-size 20.00
101 BSz 15.00
102 KRo's Back 15.00
103 thru 106 . . . . @15.00
107 WPo(i),last issue 20.00
Ann.#1 WS(c),V:Winged Warlords. 10.00
Ann.#2 RN 8.00
Ann.#3 RN,Darth Vader(c) 8.00

STEELGRIP STARKEY
Epic July, 1986
1 . . . . 1.75
2 . . . . 1.75

---

3 . . . . 1.75
4 . . . . 1.75
5 . . . . 1.75
6 June, 1987 . . . . 1.75

STEELTOWN ROCKERS
April, 1990—Sept., 1990
1 SL 1.50
2 thru 6 SL. . . . . @1.50

STORM
1 TyD,KIS,V:Candra. 2.95
2 . . . . 2.95
3 . . . . 2.95
4 TyD,KIS, conclusion,foil cover. . . 2.95

STRANGE COMBAT TALES
1 thru 2 . . . . 2.75
3 Tiger by the Tail 2.50
4 Midnight Crusade 2.50

STRANGE STORIES OF SUSPENSE
See: RUGGED ACTION

STRANGE TALES
[1st Regular Series]
June, 1951
1 'The Room' 2,500.00
2 'Trapped In A Tomb' 850.00
3 JMn,'Man Who Never Was' . . 600.00
4 BEv,'Terror in the Morgue' . . . 700.00
5 'A Room Without A Door' 650.00
6 RH(c),'The Ugly Man' 500.00
7 'Who Stands Alone' 500.00
8 BEv(c),'Something in the Fog'. 500.00
9 'Drink Deep Vampire' 500.00
10 BK,'Hidden Head' 550.00
11 BEv(c),GC,'O'Malley's Friend'. 300.00
12 'Graveyard At Midnight' 300.00
13 BEv(c),'Death Makes A Deal'. 300.00
14 GT,'Horrible Herman' 300.00
15 BK,'Don't Look Down' 325.00
16 Decapitation cover. 300.00
17 DBr,JRo,'Death Feud' 300.00
18 'Witch Hunt' 300.00
19 RH(c),'The Rag Doll' 300.00
20 RH(c),GC,SMo,'Lost World' . . 300.00
21 BEv 250.00
22 BK,JF 250.00
23 'The Strangest Tale in
    the World' 250.00
24 'The Thing in the Coffin' 250.00
25 . . . . 250.00
26 . . . . 250.00
27 JF,'The Garden of Death' 250.00
28 'Come into my Coffin' 250.00
29 'Witch-Craft' 225.00
30 'The Thing in the Box' 225.00
31 'The Man Who Played
    with Blocks' 225.00
32 . . . . 225.00
33 JMn(c),'Step Lively Please' . . 225.00
34 'Flesh and Blood' 200.00
35 'The Man in the Bottle'. 200.00
36 . . . . 200.00
37 'Out of the Storm' 200.00
38 . . . . 200.00
39 'Karnoff's Plan'. 200.00
40 BEv,'The Man Who Caught a
    Mermaid' 200.00
41 BEv,'Riddle of the Skull' 225.00
42 DW,BEv,JMn,'Faceless One' . 225.00
43 JF,'The Mysterious Machine'. 200.00

Strange Tales #72
© *Marvel Entertainment Group*

44 . . . . 200.00
45 JKa,`Land of the
  Vanishing Men'. 225.00
46 thru 57 . . . . @175.00
58 AW 175.00
59 BK 175.00
60 . . . . 150.00
61 BK 175.00
62 . . . . 150.00
63 . . . . 175.00
64 AW 175.00
65 . . . . 165.00
66 . . . . 165.00
67 thru 78 . . . . @250.00
79 SD,JK,Dr.Strange Prototype . . 250.00
80 thru 83 SD,JK . . . . @175.00
84 SD,JK,Magneto Prototype . . . 175.00
85 SD,JK 150.00
86 SD,JK,`I Who
  Created Mechano' 150.00
87 SD,JK,`Return of Grogg' 150.00
88 SD,JK,`Zzutak' 150.00
89 SD,JK,`Fin Fang Foom' 450.00
90 SD,JK,`Orrgo the
  Unconquerable' 150.00
91 SD,JK,`The Sacrifice' 150.00
92 SD,JK,`The Thing That Waits
  For Me'. 150.00
93 SD,JK,`The Wax People' 150.00
94 SD,JK,`Pildorr the Plunderer' . 150.00
95 SD,JK,`Two-Headed Thing' . . 150.00
96 SD,JK,`I Dream of Doom'. . . . 150.00
97 SD,JK,`When A Planet Dies' . 350.00
98 SD,JK,`No Human Can
  Beat Me'. 150.00
99 SD,JK,`Mister Morgan's
  Monster' 150.00
100 SD,JK,`I Was Trapped
  in the Crazy Maze' 150.00
101 B:StL(s),SD,JK,
  B:Human Torch. 900.00
102 SD,JK,I:Wizard 300.00
103 SD,JK,I:Zemu 250.00
104 SD,JK,I:The Trapster 250.00
105 SD,JK,V:Wizard 250.00
106 SD,A:Fantastic Four. 175.00
107 SD,V:Sub-Mariner 200.00
108 SD,JK,A:FF,I:The Painter . . . 175.00
109 SD,JK,I:Sorcerer 175.00
110 SD,I&B:Dr.Strange,
  Nightmare 1,200.00
111 SD,I:Asbestos,
  Baron Mordo 350.00
112 SD,I:The Eel 125.00
113 SD,I:Plant Man. 125.00

114 SD,JK,A:Captain America. . . 400.00
115 SD,O:Dr.Strange 500.00
116 SD,V:Thing. 125.00
117 SD,V:The Eel 100.00
118 SD,V:The Wizard 125.00
119 SD,C:Spider-Man 125.00
120 SD,1st Iceman/Torch T.U.. . . 135.00
121 SD,V:Plantman 75.00
122 SD,V:Dr.Doom 65.00
123 SD,A:Thor,I:Beetle 65.00
124 SD,I:Zota 65.00
125 SD,V:Sub-Mariner 65.00
126 SD,I:Dormammu,Clea 65.00
127 SD,V:Dormammu. 60.00
128 SD,I:Demon. 60.00
129 SD,I:Tiboro 60.00
130 SD,C:Beatles. 65.00
131 SD,I:Dr.Vega 55.00
132 SD,I:Orini. 55.00
133 SD,I:Shazana 55.00
134 SD,E:Torch,I:Merlin 55.00
135 SD,JK:I:Shield & Hydra
  B:Nick Fury 125.00
136 SD,JK,V:Dormammu 50.00
137 SD,JK,A:Ancient One. 60.00
138 SD,JK,I:Eternity 45.00
139 SD,JK,V:Dormammu 45.00
140 SD,JK,V:Dormammu 45.00
141 SD,JK,I:Fixer,Mentallo 45.00
142 SD,JK,I:THEM,V:Hydra 45.00
143 SD,JK,V:Hydra. 45.00
144 SD,JK,V:Druid,I:Jasper
  Sitwell 45.00
145 SD,JK,I:Mr.Rasputin. 45.00
146 SD,JK,V:Dormammu,I:AIM. . 45.00
147 BEv,JK,F:Wong 45.00
148 BEv,JK,O:Ancient One. 75.00
149 BEv,JK,V:Kaluu 45.00
150 BEv,JK,JB(1st Marvel Art)
  I:Baron Strucker,Umar 45.00
151 JK,JSo(1st Marvel Art),
  I:Umar 60.00
152 BEv,JK,JSo,V:Umar 40.00
153 JK,JSo,MSe,V:Hydra 40.00
154 JSo,MSe,I:Dreadnought. . . . 40.00
155 JSo,MSe,A:L.B.Johnson . . . 40.00
156 JSo,MSe,I:Zom 40.00
157 JSo,MSe,A:Zom,C:Living
  Tribunal 40.00
158 JSo,MSe,A:Zom,I:Living
  Tribunal(full story). 45.00
159 JSo,MSe,O:Nick Fury,A:Capt.
  America,I:Val Fontaine 50.00
160 JSo,MSe,A:Captain America
  I:Jimmy Woo. 40.00
161 JSo,I:Yellow Claw 40.00
162 JSo,DA,A:Captain America. . 40.00
163 JSo,DA,V:Yellow Claw 40.00
164 JSo,DA,V:Yellow Claw 40.00
165 JSo,DA,V:Yellow Claw 40.00
166 DA,GT,JSo,A:AncientOne. . . 40.00
167 JSo,DA,V:Doctor Doom 50.00
168 JSo,DA,E:Doctor Strange,Nick
  Fury,V:Yandroth 40.00
169 JSo,I&O:Brother Voodoo . . . 15.00
170 JSo,O:Brother Voodoo 12.00
171 GC,V:Baron Samed 12.00
172 GC,DG,V:Dark Lord 12.00
173 GC,DG,I:Black Talon 12.00
174 JB,JM,O:Golem 10.00
175 SD,R:Torr. 10.00
176 F:Golem 10.00
177 FB,F:Golem 10.00
178 JSn,B&O:Warlock,I:Magus . . 27.00
179 JSn,I:Pip,I&D:Capt.Autolycus. 15.00
180 JSn,I:Gamora,Kray-tor 15.00
181 JSn,E:Warlock 15.00
182 SD,GK,rep Str.Tales
  #123,124 . . . . 10.00
183 SD,rep Str.Tales #130,131 . . 10.00
184 SD,rep Str.Tales #132,133 . . 10.00

Strange Tales #170
© *Marvel Entertainment Group*

185 SD,rep Str.Tales #134,135 . . . 10.00
186 SD,rep Str.Tales #136,137 . . . 10.00
187 SD,rep Str.Tales #138,139 . . . 10.00
188 SD,rep Str.Tales #140,141 . . . 10.00
Ann.#1 V:Grottu,Diablo 475.00
Ann.#2 A:Spider-Man 500.00
Marvel Milestone rep. stories from
  #110–#111, #114–#115 (1995) . 2.95

[2nd Regular Series] 1987–88
1 BBI,CW,B:Cloak&Dagger,Dr.
  Strange,V:Lord of Light. 1.50
2 BBI,CW,V:Lord of Light,Demon. . 1.25
3 BBI,AW,CW,A:Nightmare,Khat . . 1.25
4 BBI,CW,V:Nightmare. 1.25
5 BBI,V:Rodent,A:Defenders 1.25
6 BBI,BWi,V:Erlik Khan,
  A:Defenders 1.25
7 V:Nightmare,A:Defenders 1.25
8 BBI,BWi,V:Kaluu 1.25
9 BBI,BWi,A:Dazzler,I:Mr.Jip,
  V:Kaluu 1.25
10 BBI,BWi,RCa,A:Black Cat,
  V:Mr.Jip,Kaluu 1.25
11 RCa,BWi,V:Mr.Jip,Kaluu. 1.25
12 WPo,BWi,A:Punisher,V:Mr.Jip . . 2.00
13 JBr,BWi,RCa,Punisher,
  Power Pack 2.00
14 JBr,BWi,RCa,Punisher,P.Pack . . 2.00
15 RCa,BMc,A:Mayhem 1.25
16 RCa,BWi,V:Mr.Jip 1.25
17 RCa,BWi,V:Night 1.25
18 RCa,KN,A:X-Factor`,V:Night . . 1.50
19 MMi(c),EL,TA,RCa,A:Thing . . . 1.25
TPB Fully painted. 6.95

STRANGE TALES
June 1998
1 JMD,PJe,LSh,Man-Thing, 64pg. . 5.00
2A JMD,PJe,LSh,Man-Thing,
  Werewolf, 64pg 5.00
2B variant cover 5.00
3 JMD,PJe,NA(c),Man-Thing,
  Werewolf, 64pg 5.00
4 JMD,PJe,LSh,F:Man-Thing
  final issue. 5.00

STRANGE TALES:
DARK CORNERS
March 1998
1-shot JEs, three stories, 48pg. . . 4.00

STRANGE TALES
OF THE UNUSUAL
Dec., 1955—Aug., 1957
1 JMn(c),BP,DH,JR,`Man Lost' . 325.00
2 BEv,`Man Afraid' 175.00
3 AW,`The Invaders' 200.00
4 `The Long Wait' 125.00
5 RC,SD,`The Threat' 175.00
6 BEv 150.00
7 JK,JO 150.00
8 . . . . 125.00
9 BEv(c),BK 150.00
10 GM,AT 125.00
11 BEv(c),August, 1957 . . . . . 125.00

STRANGE WORLDS
Dec., 1958
1 JK,SD 650.00
2 SD 350.00
3 JK 300.00
4 AW 250.00
5 SD 225.00

STRAWBERRY
SHORTCAKE
Star June, 1985—April, 1986
1 . . . . 1.25
2 thru 7 . . . . @1.00

STRAY TOASTERS
Epic Jan., 1988
1 BSz 5.00
2 BSz 4.50
3 and 4 BSz. . . . . @4.00

STRIKEFORCE
MORITURI
Dec., 1986
1 BA,SW,WPo(1st pencils-
    3 pages),I:Blackwatch 2.50
2 BA,SW,V:The Horde 1.50
3 BA,SW,V:The Horde 1.50
4 BA,SW,WPo,V:The Horde. . . . 2.00
5 BA,SW,V:The Horde 1.50
6 BA,SW,V:The Horde 1.25
7 BA,SW,V:The Horde 1.25
8 BA,SW,V:The Horde 1.25
9 BA,SW,V:THe Horde 1.25
10 WPo,(1st pencils-full story),
    SW,R:Black Watch,O:Horde . . 3.00
11 BA,SW,V:The Horde 1.25
12 BA,SW,D:Jelene 1.25
13 BA,SW,Old V:NewTeam. 1.25
14 BA,AW,V:The Horde 1.25
15 BA,AW,V:The Horde 1.25
16 WPo,SW,V:The Horde 2.50
17 WPo(c),SW,V:The Horde 1.25
18 BA,SW,V:Hammersmith 1.25
19 BA,SW,V:THe Horde,D:Pilar . . 1.25
20 BA,SW,V:The Horde 1.25
21 MMi(c),TD(i),V:The Horde . . . 1.25
22 TD(i),V:The Horde 1.25
23 MBa,VM,V:The Horde 1.50
24 VM(i),I:Vax,V:The Horde 1.75
25 TD(i),V:The Horde 1.75
26 MBa,VM,V:The Horde 1.75
27 MBa,VM,O:MorituriMaster . . . 1.75
28 MBa,V:The Tiger 1.75
29 MBa,V:Zakir Shastri 1.75
30 MBa,V:Andre Lamont,The Wind. 1.75
31 MBa(c),V:The Wind,last issue . . 1.75

STRONG GUY REBORN
Spec. TDz,ASm,ATi, (1997) 3.00

STRYFE'S STRIKE FILE
1 LSn,NKu,GCa,BP,C:Siena
    Blaze,Holocaust (1993) 4.00
1a 2nd Printing 1.75

SUB-MARINER
May, 1968
1 JB,O:Sub-Mariner. 125.00
2 JB,A:Triton 40.00
3 JB,A:Triton 30.00
4 JB,V:Attuma 30.00
5 JB,I&O:Tiger Shark 30.00
6 JB,DA,V:Tiger Shark. 30.00
7 JB,I:Ikthon 30.00
8 JB,V:Thing 30.00
9 MSe,DA,A:Lady Dorma. 30.00
10 GC,DA,O:Lemuria 30.00
11 GC,V:Capt.Barracuda. 20.00
12 MSe,I:Lyna 20.00
13 MSe,JS,A:Lady Dorma. 20.00
14 MSe,V:Fake Human Torch 25.00
15 MSe,V:Dragon Man 20.00
16 MSe,I:Nekaret,Thakos 12.00
17 MSe,I:Stalker,Kormok 12.00
18 MSe,A:Triton 12.00
19 MSe,I:Stingray. 15.00
20 JB,V:Dr.Doom 12.00
21 MSe,D:Lord Seth. 12.00
22 MSe,A:Dr.Strange 12.00
23 MSe,I:Orka 8.00
24 JB,JM,V:Tiger Shark 8.00
25 SB,JM,O:Atlantis 8.00
26 SB,A:Red Raven 8.00
27 SB,I:Commander Kraken 9.00
28 SB,V:Brutivae 8.00
29 SB,V:Hercules 7.00
30 SB,A:Captain Marvel 8.00
31 SB,A:Triton 7.00
32 SB,JM,I&O:Llyra 7.00
33 SB,JM,I:Namora 7.00
34 SB,JM,AK,1st Defenders 12.00
35 SB,JM,A:Silver Surfer 12.00
36 BWr,SB,W:Lady Dorma 10.00
37 RA,D:Lady Dorma 8.00
38 RA,JSe,O:Rec,I:Thakorr,Fen . . . 8.00
39 RA,JM,V:Llyra 8.00
40 GC,I:Turalla,A:Spidey 10.00
41 GT,V:Rock 6.00
42 GT,JM,V:House Named Death . . 6.00
43 GC,V:Tunal 6.00
44 MSe,JM,V:Human Torch 7.00
45 MSe,JM,V:Tiger Shark 6.00
46 GC,D:Namor's Father 6.00
47 GC,A:Stingray,V:Dr.Doom 6.00

Sub-Mariner #67
© Marvel Entertainment Group

48 GC,V:Dr.Doom. 6.00
49 GC,V:Dr.Doom. 6.00
50 BEv,I:Namorita. 9.00
51 BEv,O:Namorita,C:Namora 7.00
52 GK,V:Sunfire 6.00
53 BEv,V:Sunfire 6.00
54 BEv,AW,V:Sunfire,I:Lorvex 6.00
55 BEv,V:Torg. 6.00
56 DA,I:Coral 6.00
57 BEv,I:Venus 6.00
58 BEv,I:Tamara 6.00
59 BEv,V:Tamara 6.00
60 BEv,V:Tamara 6.00
61 BEv,JM,V:Dr.Hydro 6.00
62 HC,JSt,I:Tales of Atlantis.. . . . . 6.00
63 HC,JSt,V:Dr.Hydro,I:Arkus 6.00
64 HC,JSe,I:Maddox. 6.00
65 DH,DP,V:She-Devil,inc.BEv
    Eulogy Pin-up. 6.00
66 DH,V:Orka,I:Raman 6.00
67 DH,A:FF,V:Triton,N:Namor
    I&O:Force 6.00
68 DH,O:Force. 6.00
69 GT,V:Spider-Man. 7.00
70 GT,I:Piranha 6.00
71 GT,V:Piranha 6.00
72 DA,V:Slime/Thing. 6.00
Spec.#1 Rep. Tales to Astonish
    #70-#73 . . . . 8.25
Spec.#2 Rep. Tales to Astonish
    #74-#76 . . . . 8.25

[Limited Series]
1 RB,BMc,Namor's Birth 2.50
2 RB,BMc,Namor Kills Humans . . . 2.00
3 RB,BMc,V:Surface Dwellers 2.00
4 RB,BMc,V:Human Torch 2.00
5 RB,BMc,A:Invaders 2.00
6 RB,BMc,V:Destiny 2.00
7 RB,BMc,A:Fantastic Four 2.00
8 RB,BMc,A:Hulk,Avengers 2.00
9 RB,BMc,A:X-Men,Magneto 2.00
10 RB,BMc,V:Thing 2.00
11 RB,BMc,A:Namorita,Defenders . 2.00
12 RB,BMc,A:Dr.Doom,
    AlphaFlight. 2.00

(SAGA OF THE)
SUB-MARINER
[Mini-Series] Nov., 1988
1 RB,BMc,Namor's Birth 2.50
2 RB,BMc,Namor Kills Humans . . . 1.50
3 RB,BMc,V:Surface Dwellers 1.50
4 RB,BMc,V:Human Torch 1.50
5 RB,BMc,A:Invaders 1.50
6 RB,BMc,V:Destiny 1.50
7 RB,BMc,A:Fantastic Four 1.50
8 RB,BMc,A:Hulk,Avengers 1.50
9 RB,BMc,A:X-Men,Magneto 1.50
10 RB,BMc,V:Thing 1.50
11 RB,BMc,A:Namorita,Defenders . 1.50
12 RB,BMc,A:Dr.Doom,Alp.Flight . . 1.50

SUB-MARINER COMICS
Timely Spring, 1941
1 ASh(c),BEv,PGn,B:Sub-
    Mariner, The Angel 20,000.00
2 ASh(c),BEv,Nazi
    Submarine (c) 4,500.00
3 ASh(c),BEv 3,000.00
4 ASh(c),BEv,BW 2,500.00
5 . . . . 1,800.00
6 ASh(c) 1,500.00
7 . . . . 1,500.00
8 ASh(c) 1,500.00
9 ASh(c),BW 1,500.00
10 ASh(c) 1,500.00
11 ASh(c) 1,100.00
12 ASh(c) 1,100.00

13 ASh(c) 1,100.00
14 ASh(c) 1,100.00
15 ASh(c) 1,100.00
16 ASh(c) 1,100.00
17 ASh(c) 1,100.00
18 ASh(c) 1,100.00
19 . . . . 1,100.00
20 ASh(c) 1,100.00
21 SSh(c),BEv 800.00
22 SSh(c),BEv 800.00
23 SSh(c),BEv 800.00
24 MSy(c),BEv,A:Namora,
   bondage cover 800.00
25 MSy(c),HK,B:The Blonde
   Phantom, A:Namora,
   bondage(c) 1,000.00
26 BEv,A:Namora 800.00
27 DRi(c),BEv,A:Namora 800.00
28 DRi(c),BEv,A:Namora 800.00
29 BEv,A:Namora,Human Torch . 800.00
30 DRi(c),BEv,`Slaves Under
   the Sea' 800.00
31 BEv,`The Man Who Grew',
   A:Capt. America,E:Blonde
   Phantom. 800.00
32 BEv,O:Sub-Mariner 1,300.00
33 BEv,O:Sub-Mariner,A:Human
   Torch,B:Namora 700.00
34 BEv,A:Human Torch,bondage
   cover 575.00
35 BEv,A:Human Torch. 575.00
36 BEv 575.00
37 JMn(c),BEv 575.00
38 SSh(c),BEv,JMn. 650.00
39 JMn(c),BEv 550.00
40 JMn(c),BEv 550.00
41 JMn(c),BEv 550.00
42 BEv,Oct., 1955. . . . . 700.00

SUBURBAN JERSEY
NINJA SHE-DEVILS
1 I:Ninja She-Devils. 1.50

SUNFIRE & BIG HERO 6
July 1998
1 (of 3) SLo,from Alpha Flight 2.50
2 SLo,V:Everwraith 2.50
3 SLO,conclusion 2.50

SUPERNATURALS
Oct. 1998
1 (of 4) BnP,JBa(c),F:Brother
   Voodoo, V:Jack O'Lantern, with
   mask 4.00
1a signed 30.00
2 BnP,JBa(c), with mask 4.00
3 BnP,JBa(c), with mask 4.00
4 BnP,JBa(c), with mask, concl. . . . 4.00

SUPERNATURAL
THRILLERS
Dec., 1972
1 JSo(c),JSe,FrG,IT! 20.00
2 VM,DA,The Invisible Man 15.00
3 GK,The Valley of the Worm 15.00
4 Dr. Jekyll and Mr. Hyde 15.00
5 RB,The Living Mummy 35.00
6 GT,JA,The Headless Horseman . 8.00
7 VM,B:The Living Mummy,`
   Back From The Tomb' 8.00
8 VM,`He Stalks Two Worlds' 8.00
9 GK/AM(c),VM,DA,`Pyramid of
   the Watery Doom' 8.00
10 VM,`A Choice of Dooms' 8.00
11 VM,`When Strikes the ASP' 8.00
12 VM,KJ,`The War That Shook
   the World'. 8.00

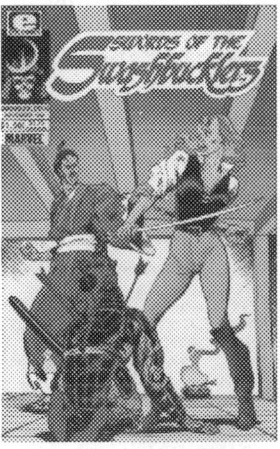

Supernatural Thrillers #6
© Marvel Entertainment Group

13 VM,DGr,`The Tomb of the
   Stalking Dead' 8.00
14 VM,AMc,`All These Deadly
   Pawns'. 8.00
15 TS, E:The Living Mummy,`Night
   of Armageddon',Oct., 1975 . . . . 8.00

SUPER SOLDIERS
Marvel UK 1993
1 I:Super Soldier,A:USAgent 2.75
2 A:USAgent 2.00
3 A:USAgent 2.00
4 A:USAgent,Avengers 2.00
5 A:Captain America,AWC. 2.00
6 O:Super Soldiers 2.00
7 in Savage Land 2.00

SUPER-VILLAIN
CLASSICS
May, 1983
1 O:Galactus 3.50

SUPER-VILLAIN
TEAM-UP
August, 1975
1 GT/BEv(c),B:Dr.Doom/Sub-
   Mariner,A:Attuma,Tiger Shark 10.00
2 SB,A:Tiger Shark, Attuma 7.00
3 EH(c),JA,V:Attuma 4.00
4 HT,JM,Dr.Doom vs. Namor 4.00
5 RB/JSt(c),HT,DP,A:Fantastic
   Four,I:Shroud 4.00
6 HT,JA,A:Shroud,Fantastic Four. . 3.00
7 RB/KJ(c),HT,O:Shroud 3.00
8 KG,V:Ringmaster 3.00
9 ST,A:Avengers,Iron Man 3.00
10 BH,DP,A:Capt.America,
   V:Attuma,Red Skull 3.00
11 DC/JSt(c),BH,DP,B:Dr. Doom,
   Red Skull,A:Capt. America 3.00
12 DC/AM(c),BH,DP,Dr.Doom vs.
   Red Skull 3.00
13 KG,DP,Namor vs. Krang 3.00
14 JBy/TA(c),BH,DP,V:Magneto,
   X-over with Champions #15 . . . 5.00
15 GT,ME,A:Red Skull 3.00
16 CI,A:Dr. Doom 3.00
17 KP(c),Red Skull Vs.Hatemonger
   June 1976 . . . . 3.00
G-Size#1 F:Namor, Dr.Doom 3.00
G-Size#2 F:Namor, Dr.Doom 3.00

SUSPENSE
Atlas Dec., 1949
1 BP,Ph(c),Sidney Greenstreet/
   Peter Lorne (Maltese Falcon) 450.00
2 Ph(c),Dennis O'Keefe/Gale
   Storm (Abandoned) 225.00
3 B:Horror stories,`The Black
   Pit' 225.00
4 `Thing In Black' 200.00
5 BEv,GT,RH,BK,DBr,
   `Hangman's House' 200.00
6 BEv,GT,PAM,RH,`Madness
   of Scott Mannion' 200.00
7 DBr,GT,DR,`Murder' 200.00
8 GC,DRi,RH,`Don't Open
   the Door' 200.00
9 GC,DRi,Back From The Dead. 200.00
10 JMn(c),WIP,RH,`Trapped
   In Time' 200.00
11 MSy,`The Suitcase' 150.00
12 GT,`Dark Road' 150.00
13 JMn(c),`Strange Man',
   bondage cover 150.00
14 RH,Death And Doctor Parker. 150.00
15 JMn(c),OW,`The Machine' . . . 150.00
16 OW,`Horror Backstage' 150.00
17 `Night Of Terror' 150.00
18 BK,`The Cozy Coffin' 175.00
19 BEv,RH 150.00
20 . . . . 150.00
21 BEv(c) 150.00
22 BEv(c),BK,OW. 150.00
23 BEv 150.00
24 RH,GT. 175.00
25 `I Died At Midnight' 175.00
26 BEv(c) 125.00
27 DBr 150.00
28 BEv 150.00
29 JMn,BF,JRo,April, 1953 . . . . . 150.00

SWORDS OF THE
SWASHBUCKLERS
Epic 1985–87
1 JG,Adult theme. 2.25
2 JG 1.75
3 JG 1.75
4 JG 1.50
5 JG 1.50
6 JG 1.50
7 JG 1.50
8 thru 12, June 1987 . . . . @1.50

Swords of the Swashbucklers #10
© Marvel Entertainment Group

TALE OF THE MARINES
See: DEVIL-DOG DUGAN

TALES OF ASGARD
Oct., 1968
1	35.00
Vol.2 #1 Feb,1984	2.00

TALES OF G.I. JOE
Jan., 1988
1 reprints,#1	2.00
2 #2	1.50
3 #3	1.50
4 #4	1.50
5 #5	1.50
6 #6	1.50
7 rep. #7 - #16.	1.50

TALES OF JUSTICE
See: JUSTICE COMICS

TALES OF THE AGE OF APOCALYPSE
1996
1-shot SLo,JoB,Age of Apocalypse stories	5.00
GN, rep.	6.00

TALES OF THE AGE OF APOCALYPSE: SINISTER BLOODLINE
Dec., 1997
GN JFM,SEp, 48pg bookshelf.	6.00

TALES OF THE MARVELS: BLOCKBUSTER
Fully Painted (1995)	5.95

TALES OF THE MARVELS: INNER DEMONS
Fully painted, 48pg. (1996)	5.95

TALES OF THE MARVELS: WONDER YEARS
1 & 2 DAb (1995	@4.95

TALES OF SUSPENSE
Jan., 1959
1 DH(c),AW,`The Unknown Emptiness'	1,500.00
2 SK,JH,`Robot in Hiding'	600.00
3 SD,JK,`The Aliens Who Captured Earth'	500.00
4 JK,AW,`One Of Us Is A Martian'	550.00
5 JF,`Trapped in the Tunnel To Nowhere'	350.00
6 JK(c),`Howl in the Swamp'	350.00
7 SD,JK,Molten Man-Thing	400.00
8 BEv,`Monstro'	325.00
9 JK(c),JF,`Diablo'	425.00
10 RH,`I Bought Cyclops Back To Life'	325.00
11 JK(c),`I Created Sporr'	275.00
12 RC,`Gorkill The Living Demon'	275.00
13 `Elektro'	275.00
14 JK(c),`I Created Colossus'	275.00
15 JK/DAy(c),`Behold...Goom'.	275.00
16 JK/DAy(c),`The Thing Called Metallo'.	325.00
17 JK/DAy(c),`Goo Gam, Son of Goom'	275.00
18 JK/DAy(c),`Kraa the Inhuman'	275.00
19 JK,DAy,SD,`The Green Thing'	275.00
20 JK,DAy,SD,`Colossus Lives Again'.	275.00
21 JK/DAy(c),SD,`This Is Klagg'	225.00
22 JK/DAy(c),SD,`Beware Of Bruttu'	225.00
23 JK,DAy,SD,`The Creature in the Black Bog'.	225.00
24 JK,DAy,SD,`Insect Man'	225.00
25 JK,DAy,SD,`The Death of Monstrollo'	225.00
26 JK,DAy,SD,`The Thing That Crawled By Night'	200.00
27 JK,DAy,SD,`When Oog Lives Again'	200.00
28 JK,DAy,SD,`Back From the Dead'	200.00
29 JK,DAy,SD,DH,`The Martian Who Stole A City'	175.00
30 JK,DAy,SD,DH,`The Haunted Roller Coaster'	200.00
31 JK,DAy,SD,DH,`The Monster in the Iron Mask'.	200.00
32 JK,DAy,SD,DH,`The Man in the Bee-Hive'	350.00
33 JK,DAy,SD,DH,`Chamber of Fear'.	175.00
34 JK,DAy,SD,DH,`Inside The Blue Glass Bottle'	175.00
35 JK,DAy,SD,DH,`The Challenge of Zarkorr'.	200.00
36 SD,`Meet Mr. Meek'.	175.00
37 DH,SD,`Hagg'	175.00
38 JDa,`The Teenager who ruled the World	175.00
39 JK,O&I:Iron Man	4,200.00
40 JK,C:Iron Man.	1,400.00
41 JK,A:Iron Man,V:Dr. Strange	700.00
42 DH,SD,I:Red Pharoah	325.00
43 JK,DH,I:Kala,A:Iron Man	325.00
44 DH,SD,V:Mad Pharoah	325.00
45 DH,V:Jack Frost.	325.00
46 DH,CR,I:Crimson Dynamo	250.00
47 SD,V:Melter.	200.00
48 SD,N:Iron Man.	250.00
49 SD,A:Angel	200.00
50 DH,I:Manderin	150.00
51 DH,I:Scarecrow	125.00
52 DH,I:Black Widow	150.00
53 DH,O:Watcher	135.00
54 DH,V:Mandarin	85.00
55 DH,V:Mandarin	85.00
56 DH,I:Unicorn	85.00
57 DH,I&O:Hawkeye.	175.00
58 DH,GT,B:Captain America	300.00
59 DH,1st S.A. Solo Captain America,I:Jarvis	300.00
60 DH,JK,V:Assassins	125.00
61 DH,JK,V:Mandarin	75.00
62 DH,JK,O:Mandarin.	75.00
63 JK,O:Captain America	225.00
64 DH,JK,A:Black Widow, Hawkeye	85.00
65 DH,JK,I:Red Skull	150.00
66 DH,JK,O:Red Skull	150.00
67 DH,JK,V:Adolph Hitler	50.00
68 DH,JK,V:Red Skull.	50.00
69 DH,JK,I:Titanium Man	50.00
70 DH,JK,GT,V:Titanium Man	45.00
71 DH,JK,WW,GT,V:Titanium Man	55.00
72 DH,JK,GT,V:The Sleeper	45.00
73 JA,JK,GT,A:Black Knight	45.00
74 JA,JK,GT,V:The Sleeper	45.00
75 JA,JK,I:Batroc,Sharon Carter	45.00
76 JA,JR,V:Mandarin	50.00
77 JA,JK,JR,V:Ultimo,I:Peggy Carter.	45.00
78 JA,GC,JK,V:Ultimo.	45.00
79 JA,GC,JK,V:Red Skull, I:Cosmic Cube	75.00
80 JA,GC,JK,V:Red Skull	80.00
81 JA,GC,JK,V:Red Skull	50.00
82 GC,JK,V:The Adaptoid.	50.00
83 GC,JK,V:The Adaptoid.	50.00
84 GC,JK,V:Mandarin	50.00
85 GC,JK,V:Batroc	50.00
86 GC,JK,V:Mandarin	50.00
87 GC,V:Mole Man	50.00
88 GK,JK,GC,V:Power Man	50.00
89 GK,JK,GC,V:Red Skull.	50.00
90 GK,JK,GC,V:Red Skull.	50.00
91 GK,GC,JK,V:Crusher.	50.00
92 GC,JK,A:Nick Fury.	50.00
93 GC,JK,V:Titanium Man.	50.00
94 GC,JK,I:Modok	50.00
95 GC,JK,V:Grey Gargoyle, IR:Captain America	50.00
96 GC,JK,V:Grey Gargoyle	50.00
97 GC,JK,I:Whiplash, A:Black Panther	50.00
98 GC,JK,I:Whitney Frost A:Black Panther	75.00
99 GC,JK,A:Black Panther	85.00
Marvel Milestone rep. #39 (1993)	2.95

Becomes:

CAPTAIN AMERICA

TALES OF THE ZOMBIE
August, 1973
(black & white magazine)
1 Reprint Menace #5,O:Zombie	20.00
2 GC,GT	15.00
3	15.00
4 `Live and Let Die'	15.00
5 BH	15.00
6	15.00
7 thru 9 AA	@15.00
10 March, 1975	15.00

TALES TO ASTONISH
[1st Series] Jan., 1959
1 JDa,`Ninth Wonder of the World'	1,600.00
2 SD,`Capture A Martian'	650.00
3 SD,JK,`The Giant From Outer Space'	450.00
4 SD,JK,`The Day The Martians Struck'	450.00

Tales of Suspense #58
© Marvel Entertainment Group

5 SD,AW,`The Things on
   Easter Island' 475.00
6 SD,JK,`Invasion of the
   Stone Men' 400.00
7 SD,JK,`The Thing on Bald
   Mountain' 400.00
8 DAy,SD,JK,`Mummex, King of
   the Mummies'. 400.00
9 DAy,JK(c),SD,`Droom, the
   Living Lizard' 400.00
10 DAy,JK,SD,`Titano'. 400.00
11 DAy,JK,SD,`Monstrom, the Dweller
   in the Black Swamp' 250.00
12 JK/DAy(c),SD,`Gorgilla' 250.00
13 JK,SD,`Groot, the Monster
   From Planet X' 250.00
14 JK,SD,`Krang' 250.00
15 JK/DAy,`The Blip'. 400.00
16 DAy,JK,SD,`Thorr' 300.00
17 JK,SD,`Vandoom'. 250.00
18 DAy,JK,SD,`Gorgilla Strikes
   Again'. 250.00
19 DAy,JK,SD,`Rommbu' 250.00
20 JK,SD,`X, The Thing
   That Lived' 250.00
21 JK,SD,`Trull the Inhuman' . . . 250.00
22 JK,SD,`The Crawling
   Creature' 200.00
23 JK,SD,`Moomba is Here' 200.00
24 JK,SD,`The Abominable
   Snowman' 200.00
25 JK,SD,`The Creature From
   Krogarr' 200.00
26 JK,SD,`Four-Armed Things' . . 200.00
27 StL(s),SD,JK,I:Antman . . . 3,400.00
28 JK,SD,I Am the Gorilla Man . . 200.00
29 JK,SD,When the Space
   Beasts Attack' 200.00
30 JK,SD,Thing From the
   Hidden Swamp' 200.00
31 JK,SD,The Mummy's Secret . 200.00
32 JK,SD,Quicksand. 200.00
33 JK,SD,Dead Storage 200.00
34 JK,SD,Monster at Window . . . 200.00
35 StL(s),JK,SD, B:Ant Man
   (2nd App.) 1,500.00
36 JK,SD,V:Comrade X 600.00
37 JK,SD,V:The Protector. 375.00
38 JK,SD,Betrayed By the Ants . 375.00
39 JK,DH,V:Scarlet Beetle 375.00
40 JK,SD,DH,The Day Ant-Man
   Failed. 375.00
41 DH,St,SD,V:Kulla 250.00
42 DH,JSe,SD,Voice of Doom. . . 250.00
43 DH,SD,Master of Time. 250.00
44 JK,SD,I&O:Wasp 275.00
45 DH,SD,V:Egghead 175.00
46 DH,SD,I:Cyclops(robot) 175.00
47 DH,SD,V:Trago 175.00
48 DH,SD,I:Porcupine. 175.00
49 JK,DH,AM,Ant-Man Becomes
   Giant-Man 200.00
50 JK,SD,I&O:Human Top 125.00
51 JK,V:Human Top 125.00
52 I&O:Black Knight 125.00
53 DH,V:Porcupine 125.00
54 DH,I:El Toro 125.00
55 V:Human Top. 125.00
56 V:The Magician 125.00
57 A:Spider-Man. 150.00
58 V:Colossus(not X-Men one) . . 125.00
59 V:Hulk,Black Knight 175.00
60 SD,B:Hulk,Giant Man. 200.00
61 SD,I:Glenn Talbot,
   V:Egghead. 75.00
62 I:Leader,N:Wasp 75.00
63 SD,O:Leader(1st full story). . . . 75.00
64 SD,V:Leader 75.00
65 BP,DH,SD,N:Giant-Man,. 75.00
66 BP,JK,SD,V:Leader,Chameleon 75.00
67 BP,JK,SD,I:Kanga Khan. 75.00

68 BP,JK,N:Human Top,V:Leader . 75.00
69 BP,JK,V:Human Top,Leader,
   E:Giant-Man. 75.00
70 GC,JK,B:Sub-Mariner/Hulk,I:
   Neptune 100.00
71 GC,JK,V:Leader,I:Vashti. 60.00
72 GC,JK,V:Leader. 60.00
73 GC,JK,V:Leader,A:Watcher . . . 60.00
74 GC,JK,V:Leader,A:Watcher . . . 60.00
75 GC,JK,A:Watcher. 60.00
76 GC,GK,JK,Atlantis 60.00
77 JK,V:Executioner 60.00
78 BEv,GC,JK,Prince and
   the Puppet 60.00
79 BEv,GC,JK,Hulk vs.Hercules . . 60.00
80 BEv,GC,JK,Moleman vs
   Tyrannus 60.00
81 BEv,GC,JK,I:Boomerang,Secret
   Empire,Moleman vs Tyrannus. 60.00
82 BEv,GC,JK,V:Iron Man. 75.00
83 BEv,JK,V:Boomerang. 50.00
84 BEv,GC,JK,Like a Beast at Bay 50.00
85 BEv,GC,JK,B:Missile &
   the Monster 50.00
86 BEv,JB,V:Warlord Krang 50.00
87 BEv,JB,IR:Hulk 50.00
88 BEv,GK,V:Boomerang 50.00
89 BEv,GK,V:Stranger 50.00
90 JK,GK,BEv,I:Abomination. 50.00
91 GK,BEv,DA,V:Abomination. . . . 50.00
92 MSe,C:Silver Surfer x-over . . . 62.00
93 MSe,Silver Surfer x-over 60.00
94 BEv,MSe,V:Dragorr,High
   Evolutionary. 50.00
95 BEv,MSe,V:High Evolutionary . 50.00
96 MSe,Skull Island,High Evol. . . . 50.00
97 MSe,C:Kazar,X-Men 55.00
98 DA,MSe,I:Legion of the Living
   Lightning,I:Seth 50.00
99 DA,MSe,V:Legion of the Living
   Lighting 50.00
100 MSe,DA,Hulk v.SubMariner . . 60.00
101 MSe,GC,V:Loki 85.00
Becomes:

INCREDIBLE HULK

TALES TO ASTONISH
[2nd Series] Dec., 1979
1 JB,rep.Sub-Mariner#1. . . . . 5.00
2 JB,rep.Sub-Mariner#2. . . . . 3.00
3 JB,rep.Sub-Mariner#3. . . . . 3.00
4 JB,rep.Sub-Mariner#4. . . . . 3.00
5 JB,rep.Sub-Mariner#5. . . . . 3.00

6 JB,rep.Sub-Mariner#6. . . . . 3.00
7 JB,rep.Sub-Mariner#7. . . . . 3.00
8 JB,rep.Sub-Mariner#8. . . . . 3.00
9 JB,rep.Sub-Mariner#9. . . . . 3.00
10 JB,rep.Sub-Mariner#10 . . . . . . 3.00
11 JB,rep.Sub-Mariner#11 . . . . . . 3.00
12 JB,rep.Sub-Mariner#12 . . . . . . 3.00
13 JB,rep.Sub-Mariner#13 . . . . . . 3.00
14 JB,rep.Sub-Mariner#14 . . . . . . 3.00

TARZAN
June, 1977
1 JB,Edgar Rice Burroughs Adapt. 5.00
2 JB,O:Tarzan 4.00
3 JB,`The Alter of the Flaming
   God',I:LA 2.00
4 JB,TD,V:Leopards 2.00
5 JB,TD,`Vengeance',A:LA 2.00
6 JB,TD,`Rage of Tantor,A:LA . . . 2.00
7 JB,TD,`Tarzan Rescues The
   Moon' 2.00
8 JB,`Battle For The Jewel Of
   Opar' 2.00
9 JB,`Histah, the Serpent' 2.00
10 JB,`The Deadly Peril of
   Jane Clayton' 2.00
11 JB 2.00
12 JB,`Fangs of Death'. 2.00
13 JB,`Lion-God'. 2.00
14 JB,`The Fury of Fang and Claw'. 2.00
15 JB,`Sword of the Slaver' 2.00
16 JB,`Death Rides the Jungle
   Winds' 2.00
17 JB,`The Entrance to the
   Earths Core'. 2.00
18 JB,`Corsairs of the Earths Core'. 2.00
19 `Pursuit'. 2.00
20 `Blood Bond' 2.00
21 `Dark and Bloody Sky' 2.00
22 JM,RN,`War In Pellucidar' 2.00
23 `To the Death' 2.00
24 `The Jungle Lord Returns' 2.00
25 RB(c),V:Poachers 2.00
26 RB(c),`Caged' 2.00
27 RB(c),`Chaos in the Caberet' . . 2.00
28 `A Savage Against A City' 2.00
29 Oct., 1979 . . . . 2.00
Ann.#1 JB 2.50
Ann.#2 `Drums of the
   Death-Dancers' 2.00
Ann.#3 `Ant-Men and the
   She-Devils 2.00

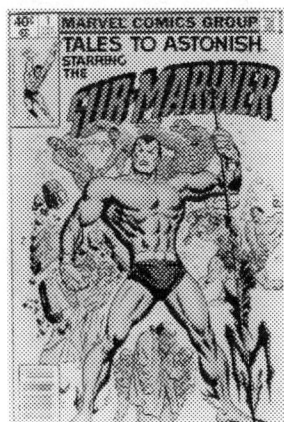

Tales to Astonish #1
© Marvel Entertainment Group

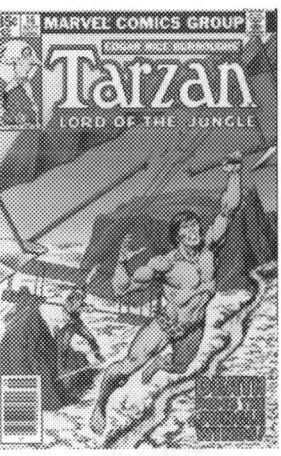

Tarzan #16
© Marvel Entertainment Group

TARZAN OF THE APES
July, 1984
1 (movie adapt.) 1.25
2 . . . . 1.25

Team America #7
© Marvel Entertainment Group

TEAM AMERICA
June, 1982
1 O:Team America. 2.00
2 V:Marauder 1.25
3 LMc,V:Mr.Mayhem. 1.25
4 Lmc,V:Arcade Assassins 1.25
5 A:Marauder 1.25
6 A:R.U. Ready 1.25
7 LMc,V:Emperor of Texas. 1.25
8 DP,V:Hydra. 1.25
9 A:Iron Man 1.25
10 V:Minister Ashe 1.00
11 A:Marauder,V:GhostRider. 3.00
12 DP,Marauder unmasked,
   May, 1983 . . . . 2.50

TEAM HELIX
1993
1 A:Wolverine 2.00
2 A:Wolverine 2.00

TEAM X/TEAM 7
1996
1-shot LHa,SEp,MRy 4.95

TEAM X 2000
Dec. 1998
1-shot, 48-page. 3.50

TEEN COMICS
See: ALL WINNERS
COMICS

TEENAGE ROMANCE
See: MY ROMANCE

TEK WORLD
See: WILLIAM SHATNER'S
TEK WORLD

TERMINATOR 2
Sept., 1991
1 KJ,movie adaption 1.25
2 KJ,movie adaption 1.25
3 KJ,movie adaption 1.25
Terminator II (bookshelf format) . . . 4.95
Terminator II (B&W mag. size) 2.25

TERRARISTS
Epic 1993–94
1 thru 4 w/card. . . . . @2.50
5 thru 7 . . . . @2.50

TERROR INC.
1992–93
1 JZ,I:Hellfire. 3.00
2 JZ,I:Bezeel,Hellfire 2.50
3 JZ,A:Hellfire 2.00
4 JZ,A:Hellfire,V:Barbatos 2.00
5 JZ,V:Hellfire,A:Dr Strange 2.00
6 JZ,MT,A:Punisher. 2.00
7 JZ,V:Punisher. 2.00
8 Christmas issue 2.00
9 JZ,V:Wolverine 2.25
10 V:Wolverine. 2.25
11 A:Silver Sable,Cage. 2.00
12 For Love Nor Money#4,A:Cage,
   Silver Sable 2.00
13 Inf.Crusade,A:Gh.Rider 2.00

TESSIE THE TYPIST
Timely Summer, 1944
1 BW,'Doc Rockblock' 400.00
2 BW,'Powerhouse Pepper' . . . 225.00
3 Football cover 75.00
4 BW 125.00
5 BW 125.00
6 BW,HK,'Hey Look' 125.00
7 BW 125.00
8 BW 125.00
9 BW,HK,'Powerhouse Pepper' . 150.00
10 BW,A:Rusty 150.00
11 BW,A:Rusty 150.00
12 BW,HK. 150.00
13 BW,A:Millie The Model,Rusty . 110.00
14 BW 100.00
15 HK,A:Millie,Rusty 100.00
16 HK. 75.00
17 HK,A:Millie, Rusty 75.00
18 HK. 75.00
19 Annie Oakley story. 50.00
20 . . . . 45.00
21 A:Lana, Millie 45.00
22 . . . . 45.00
23 . . . . 45.00
Becomes:

TINY TESSIE
24 . . . . 45.00
Becomes:

REAL EXPERIENCES
25 Ph(c),Jan., 1950 . . . . 40.00

TEXAS KID
Atlas Jan., 1951
1 GT,JMn,O:Texas Kid 125.00
2 JMn 60.00
3 JMn,'Man Who Didn't Exist' . . . 50.00
4 JMn 50.00
5 JMn 50.00
6 JMn 50.00
7 JMn 50.00
8 JMn 50.00
9 JMn 50.00
10 JMn,July, 1952. . . . . 50.00

TEX DAWSON,
GUNSLINGER
Jan., 1973
1 JSo(c) 15.00
Becomes:

GUNSLINGER
2 . . . . 10.00
3 June, 1973 . . . . 10.00

TEX MORGAN
August, 1948
1 . . . . 175.00
2 'Boot Hill Welcome For A
   Bad Man' 125.00
3 . . . . 100.00
4 'Trapped in the Outlaws Den',
   A:Arizona Annie 75.00
5 'Valley of Missing Cowboys' . . . 75.00
6 'Never Say Murder',
   A:Tex Taylor 75.00
7 CCB,Ph(c), 'Captain Tootsie',
   A:Tex Taylor 125.00
8 Ph(c),'Terror Of Rimrock
   Valley', A:Diablo 125.00
9 Ph(c),'Death to Tex Taylor'
   Feb., 1950 . . . . 125.00

TEX TAYLOR
Sept., 1948
1 'Boot Hill Showdown' 175.00
2 'When Two-Gun Terror Rides
   the Range' 125.00
3 'Thundering Hooves and
   Blazing Guns' 100.00
4 Ph(c),'Draw or Die Cowpoke' . 125.00
5 Ph(c),'The Juggler of Yellow
   Valley',A:Blaze Carson 125.00
6 Ph(c),'Mystery of Howling Gap'
   . . . . 100.00
7 Ph(c),'Trapped in Times' Lost
   Land',A:Diablo 120.00
8 Ph(c),'The Mystery of Devil-
   Tree Plateau',A:Diablo 120.00
9 Ph(c),'Guns Along the Border',
   A:Nimo,March, 1950 . . . . . . 120.00

THANOS QUEST
1990
1 JSn,RLm,V:Elders,
   for Soul Gems 6.00
1a 2nd printing 3.00
2 JSn,RLm,O:SoulGems,I:
   Infinity Gauntlet (story
   cont.in SilverSurfer #44) 5.00
2a 2nd printing 3.00

THING, THE
July, 1983
1 JBy,O:Thing 2.50
2 JBy,Woman from past. 1.75
3 JBy,A:Inhumans 1.50
4 JBy,A:Lockjaw 1.50
5 JBY,A:Spider-Man,She-Hulk 1.50
6 JBy,V:Puppet Master 1.25
7 JBy,V:Goody Two Shoes. 1.25
8 JBy,V:Egyptian Curse 1.25
9 JBy,F:Alicia Masters 1.25
10 JBy,Secret Wars 1.25
11 JBy,B:Rocky Grimm 1.25
12 JBy,F:Rocky Grimm 1.25
13 JBy,F:Rocky Grimm 1.25
14 F:Rocky Grimm 1.25
15 F:Rocky Grimm 1.25
16 F:Rocky Grimm 1.25
17 F:Rocky Grimm 1.25
18 F:Rocky Grimm 1.25

    All comics prices listed are for *Near Mint* condition.

19 F:Rocky Grimm 1.25	
20 F:Rocky Grimm 1.25	
21 V:Ultron 1.25	
22 V:Ultron 1.25	
23 R:Thing to Earth,A:Fant.Four . . . 1.25	
24 V:Rhino,A:Miracle Man 1.25	
25 V:Shamrock 1.25	
26 A:Vance Astro 1.50	
27 I:Sharon Ventura 1.25	
28 A:Vance Astro 1.25	
29 A:Vance Astro 1.25	
30 Secret Wars II,A:Vance Astro. . . 1.25	
31 A:Vance Astro 1.25	
32 A:Vance Astro 1.25	
33 A:Vance Astro,I:NewGrapplers . . 1.25	
34 V:Titania,Sphinx. 1.25	
35 I:New Ms.Marvel,PowerBroker. . 1.25	
36 Last Issue,A:She-Hulk 1.25	

[Mini-Series]

1 rep.Marvel Two-in-One #50. . . . . 1.75
2 rep Marvel Two-in-One,V:GR . . . 1.75
3 rep Marvel Two-in-One #51 . . . . 1.25
4 rep Marvel Two-in-One #43 . . . . 1.25

THING/SHE-HULK

March, 1998

1-shot TDz,V:Dragon Man, 48pg. . . 3.00

THOR, THE MIGHTY

Prev: Journey Into Mystery

March, 1966

126 JK,V:Hercules 135.00	
127 JK,I:Pluto,Volla 55.00	
128 JK,V:Pluto,A:Hercules 55.00	
129 JK,V:Pluto,I:Ares 55.00	
130 JK,V:Pluto,A:Hercules 55.00	
131 JK,I:Colonizers. 55.00	
132 JK,A:Colonizers,I:Ego 55.00	
133 JK,A:Colonizers,A:Ego. 55.00	
134 JK,I:High Evolutionary,	
Man-Beast 60.00	
135 JK,O:High Evolutionary 50.00	
136 JK,F:Odin 45.00	
137 JK,I:Ulik. 45.00	
138 JK,V:Ulik,A:Sif 45.00	
139 JK,V:Ulik 45.00	
140 JK,V:Growing Man. 45.00	
141 JK,V:Replicus 35.00	
142 JK,V:Super Skrull. 35.00	
143 JK,BEv,V:Talisman 35.00	
144 JK,V:Talisman 35.00	
145 JK,V:Ringmaster 35.00	
146 JK,O:Inhumans Part 1 . . . . . . 45.00	

Thor #195
© Marvel Entertainment Group

147 JK,O:Inhumans Part 2 . . . . . . 40.00	
148 JK,I:Wrecker,O:Black Bolt . . . 40.00	
149 JK,O:Black Bolt,Medusa. 40.00	
150 JK,A:Triton. 35.00	
151 JK,V:Destroyer. 35.00	
152 JK,V:Destroyer. 35.00	
153 JK,F:Dr.Blake. 35.00	
154 JK,I:Mangog 35.00	
155 JK,V:Mangog 35.00	
156 JK,V:Mangog 35.00	
157 JK,D:Mangog. 35.00	
158 JK,O:Don Blake Part 1 . . . . . . 75.00	
159 JK,O:Don Blake Part 2 . . . . . . 35.00	
160 JK,I:Travrians. 32.00	
161 JK,Shall a God Prevail 32.00	
162 JK,O:Galactus 45.00	
163 JK,I:Mutates,A:Pluto. 25.00	
164 JK,A:Pluto,V:Greek Gods. . . . 25.00	
165 JK,V:Him/Warlock 60.00	
166 JK,V:Him/Warlock 50.00	
167 JK,F:Sif 23.00	
168 JK,O:Galactus 42.00	
169 JK,O:Galactus 42.00	
170 JK,BEv,V:Thermal Man 25.00	
171 JK,BEv,V:Wrecker 25.00	
172 JK,BEv,V:Ulik. 25.00	
173 JK,BEv,V:Ulik,Ringmaster . . . 25.00	
174 JK,BEv,V:Crypto-Man. 25.00	
175 JK,Fall of Asgard,V:Surtur . . . 25.00	
176 JK,V:Surtur 25.00	
177 JK,I:Igon,V:Surtur. 25.00	
178 JK,C:Silver Surfer 26.00	
179 JK,MSe,C:Galactus 25.00	
180 NA,JSi,V:Loki. 20.00	
181 NA,JSi,V:Loki. 20.00	
182 JB,V:Dr.Doom 10.00	
183 JB,V:Dr.Doom 10.00	
184 JB,I:The Guardian 10.00	
185 JB,JSt,V:Silent One 10.00	
186 JB,JSt,V:Hela. 10.00	
187 JB,JSt,V:Odin 10.00	
188 JB,JM,F:Odin 10.00	
189 JB,JSt,V:Hela. 10.00	
190 JB,I:Durok 10.00	
191 JB,JSt,V:Loki. 10.00	
192 JB 10.00	
193 JB,SB,V:Silver Surfer 45.00	
194 JB,SB,V:Loki 10.00	
195 JB,JR,V:Mangog 10.00	
196 JB,NR,V:Kartag 10.00	
197 JB,V:Mangog. 10.00	
198 JB,V:Pluto 10.00	
199 JB,V:Pluto,Hela 10.00	
200 JB,Ragnarok 12.00	
201 JB,JM,Odin resurrected. 7.00	
202 JB,V:Ego-Prime 7.00	
203 JB,V:Ego-Prime 7.00	
204 JB,JM,Demon from t/Depths . . 7.00	
205 JB,V:Mephisto 7.00	
206 JB,V:Absorbing Man 6.00	
207 JB,V:Absorbing Man 6.00	
208 JB,V:Mercurio 6.00	
209 JB,I:Druid 6.00	
210 JB,DP,I:Ulla,V:Ulik 6.00	
211 JB,DP,V:Ulik. 6.00	
212 JB,JSt,V:Sssthgar 6.00	
213 JB,DP,I:Gregor. 6.00	
214 SB,JM,V:Dark Nebula 6.00	
215 JB,JM,J:Xorr 6.00	
216 JB,JM,V:4D-Man 6.00	
217 JB,SB,I:Krista,V:Odin 6.00	
218 JB,JM,A:Colonizers 6.00	
219 JB,I:Protector. 6.00	
220 JB,V:Avalon. 6.00	
221 JB,V:Olympus 6.00	
222 JB,JSe,A:Hercules,V:Pluto. . . 6.00	
223 JB,A:Hercules,V:Pluto 6.00	
224 JB,V:Destroyer. 6.00	
225 JB,JSi,I:Fire Lord 8.00	
226 JB,A:Watcher,Galactus 5.00	
227 JB,JSi,V:Ego 5.00	

Thor #292
© Marvel Entertainment Group

228 JB,JSi,A:Galactus,D:Ego 5.00	
229 JB,JSi,A:Hercules,I:Dweller . . . 5.00	
230 JB,A:Hercules 5.00	
231 JB,DG,V:Armak 5.00	
232 JB,JSi,A:Firelord 5.00	
233 JB,Asgard Invades Earth 5.00	
234 JB,V:Loki 5.00	
235 JB,JSi,I:Possessor	
(Kamo Tharnn) 5.00	
236 JB,JSi,V:Absorbing Man. 5.00	
237 JB,JSi,V:Ulik 5.00	
238 JB,JSi,V:Ulik 5.00	
239 JB,JSi,V:Ulik 5.00	
240 SB,KJ,V:Seth. 5.00	
241 JB,JGi,I:Geb 5.00	
242 JB,JSt,V:Servitor 5.00	
243 JB,JSt,V:Servitor 5.00	
244 JB,JSt,V:Servitor 5.00	
245 JB,JSt,V:Servitor 5.00	
246 JB,JSt,A:Firelord 5.00	
247 JB,JSt,A:Firelord 5.00	
248 JB,V:Storm Giant 5.00	
249 JB,V:Odin 5.00	
250 JB,D:Igron,V:Mangog. 5.00	
251 JB,A:Sif 3.50	
252 JB,V:Ulik 3.50	
253 JB,I:Trogg 3.50	
254 JK,O:Dr.Blake rep 3.50	
255 Stone Men of Saturn Rep. 3.50	
256 JB,I:Sporr 3.50	
257 JK,JB,I:Fee-Lon. 3.50	
258 JK,JB,V:Grey Gargoyle 3.50	
259 JB,A:Spider-Man 4.00	
260 WS,I:Doomsday Star 4.00	
261 WS,I:Soul Survivors 3.50	
262 WS,Odin Found,I:Odin Force . . 3.50	
263 WS,V:Loki 3.50	
264 WS,V:Loki 3.50	
265 WS,V:Destroyer 3.50	
266 WS,Odin Quest 3.50	
267 WS,F:Odin. 3.50	
268 WS,V:Damocles. 3.50	
269 WS,V:Stilt-Man 3.50	
270 WS,V:Blastaar 3.50	
271 Avengers,Iron Man x-over 3.50	
272 JB,Day the Thunder Failed 3.50	
273 JB,V:Midgard Serpent 3.50	
274 JB,D:Balder,I:Hermod,Hoder . . 3.50	
275 JB,V:Loki,I:Sigyn 3.50	
276 JB,Trial of Loki. 3.50	
277 JB,V:Fake Thor 3.50	
278 JB,V:Fake Thor 3.50	
279 A:Pluto,V:Ulik. 3.50	
280 V:Hyperion. 3.50	
281 O:Space Phantom 3.50	

282 V:Immortus,I:Tempus 3.50	356 BL,BG,V:Hercules 2.25
283 JB,V:Celestials. 3.50	357 WS,A:Beta Ray Bill 2.50
284 JB,V:Gammenon 3.50	358 WS,A:Beta Ray Bill 2.50
285 JB,R:Karkas 3.50	359 WS,V:Loki 2.25
286 KP,KRo,D:Kro,I:Dragona 3.50	360 WS,V:Hela. 2.25
287 KP,2nd App & O:Forgotten	361 WS,V:Hela. 2.25
One(Hero) 3.50	362 WS,V:Hela. 2.25
288 KP,V:Forgotten One 3.50	363 WS,Secret Wars II,V:Kurse . . . 2.50
289 KP,V:Destroyer 3.50	364 WS,I:Thunder Frog 2.25
290 I:Red Bull(Toro Rojo) 3.50	365 WS,A:Thunder Frog. 2.25
291 KP,A:Eternals,Zeus 3.50	366 WS,A:Thunder Frog. 2.25
292 KP,V:Odin 3.50	367 WS,D:Malekith,A:Kurse 2.25
293 KP,Door to Minds Eye 3.50	368 WS,F:Balder t/Brave,Kurse . . . 2.25
294 KP,O:Odin & Asgard,I:Frey. . . 3.50	369 WS,F:Balder the Brave 2.25
295 KP,I:Fafnir,V:Storm Giants . . . 3.50	370 JB,V:Loki 2.25
296 KP,D:Siegmund 3.50	371 SB,I:Justice Peace,V:Zaniac . . 2.25
297 KP,V:Sword of Siegfried 3.50	372 SB,V:Justice Peace 2.25
298 KP,V:Dragon(Fafnir). 3.50	373 SB,A:X-Factor,(Mut.Mass) . . . 5.00
299 KP,A:Valkyrie,I:Hagen 3.50	374 WS,SB,A:X-Factor,(Mut.Mass)
300 KP,giant,O:Odin & Destroyer,	A:Sabretooth 7.00
Rindgold Ring Quest ends,D:Uni-	375 WS,SB,N:Thor(Exoskeleton) . . 2.25
Mind,I:Mother Earth 6.00	376 WS,SB,V:Absorbing Man 2.25
301 KP,O:Mother Earth,V:Apollo . . 3.00	377 WS,SB,N:Thor,A:Ice Man. . . . 2.25
302 KP,V:Locus 3.00	378 WS,SB,V:Frost Giants 2.25
303 Whatever Gods There Be 3.00	379 WS,V:Midgard Serpent 2.25
304 KP,V:Wrecker. 3.00	380 WS,V:Midgard Serpent 2.25
305 KP,R:Gabriel(Air Walker) 3.00	381 WE,SB,A:Avengers 2.50
306 KP,O&V:Firelord,O:AirWalker . 3.00	382 WS,SB,V:Frost Giants,Loki . . . 2.50
307 KP,I:Dream Demon 3.00	383 BBr,Secret Wars story 2.50
308 KP,V:Snow Giants 3.00	384 RF,BBr,I:Future Thor(Dargo) . . 5.00
309 V:Bomnardiers. 3.00	385 EL,V:Hulk 2.00
310 KP,V:Mephisto 3.00	386 RF,BBr,I:Leir 2.00
311 KP,GD,A:Valkyrie 3.00	387 RF,BBr,V:Celestials 2.00
312 KP,V:Tyr. 3.00	388 RF,BBr,V:Celestials 2.00
313 KP,Thor Trial 3.00	389 RF,BBr,V:Celestials 2.00
314 KP,A:Drax,Moondragon 3.00	390 RF,BBr,A:Avengers,V:Seth . . . 2.00
315 KP,O:Bi-Beast 3.00	391 RF,BBr,I:Mongoose,Eric
316 KP,A:Iron Man,Man Thing,	Masterson,A:Spider-Man 5.00
V:Man-Beast 3.00	392 RF,I:Quicksand 2.00
317 KP,V:Man-Beast. 3.00	393 RF,BBr,V:Quicksand,A:DD . . . 2.00
318 GK,V:Fafnir 3.00	394 RF,BBr,V:Earth Force. 2.00
319 KP,I&D:Zaniac 3.00	395 RF,V:Earth Force 2.00
320 KP,V:Rimthursar. 2.75	396 RF,A:Black Knight 2.00
321 I:Menagerie 2.50	397 RF,A:Loki. 2.00
322 V:Heimdall. 2.50	398 RF,DH,R:Odin,V:Seth. 2.00
323 V:Death 2.50	399 RF,RT,R:Surtur,V:Seth 2.00
324 V:Graviton 2.50	400 RF,JSt,CV,V:Surtur,Seth. 5.00
325 JM,O:Darkoth,V:Mephisto . . . 2.75	401 V:Loki 2.00
326 I:New Scarlet Scarab 2.75	402 RF,JSt,V:Quicksand 2.00
327 V:Loki & Tyr. 2.50	403 RF,JSt,V:Executioner 2.00
328 I:Megatak 2.75	404 RF,JSt,TD,V:Annihilus 2.00
329 HT,V:Hrungnir 2.50	405 RF,JSt,TD,V:Annihilus 2.00
330 BH,I:Crusader 2.50	406 RF,JSt,TD,V:Wundagore 2.00
331 Threshold of Death 2.50	407 RF,JSt,R:Hercules,High Evol.. . 2.00
332 V:Dracula. 2.75	
333 BH,V:Dracula. 2.75	
334 Quest For Rune Staff. 2.50	
335 V:Possessor 2.50	
336 A:Captain Ultra 2.75	
337 WS,I:Beta Ray Bill,A:Surtur . . 7.50	
338 WS,O:Beta Ray Bill,I:Lorelei . 5.00	
339 WS,V:Beta Ray Bill 3.50	
340 WS,A:Beta Ray Bill 3.00	
341 WS,V:Fafnir. 2.25	
342 WS,V:Fafnir,I:Eilif. 2.25	
343 WS,V:Fafnir. 2.25	
344 WS,Balder Vs.Loki,I:Malekith. . 2.25	
345 WS,V:Malekith 2.25	
346 WS,V:Malekith 2.25	
347 WS,V:Malekith,I:Algrim	
(Kurse). 2.25	
348 WS,V:Malekith 2.25	
349 WS,R:Beta Ray Bill,O:Odin,	
I&O:Vili & Ve(Odin's brothers). . 2.50	
350 WS,V:Surtur. 2.25	
351 WS,V:Surtur. 2.25	
352 WS,V:Surtur. 2.25	
353 WS,V:Surtur,D:Odin 2.25	
354 WS,V:Hela. 2.25	
355 WS,SB,A:Thor's Great	
Grandfather 2.25	

408 RF,JSt,I:Eric Masterson/Thor
V:Mongoose. 3.50
409 RF,JSt,V:Dr.Doom 2.00
410 RF,JSt,V:Dr.Doom,She-Hulk. . 2.00
411 RF,JSt,C:New Warriors
V:Juggernaut,A of V 3.00
412 RF,JSt,I:New Warriors
V:Juggernaut,A of V 4.00
413 RF,JSt,A:Dr.Strange. 1.75
414 RF,JSt,V:Ulik 1.75
415 HT,O:Thor 1.75
416 RF,JSt,A:Hercules 1.75
417 RF,JSt,A:High Evolutionary . . 1.75
418 RF,JSt,V:Wrecking Crew 1.75
419 RF,JSt,B:Black Galaxy
Saga,I:Stellaris. 1.75
420 RF,JSt,A:Avengers,V:Stellaris. . 1.75
421 RF,JSt,V:Stellaris. 1.75
422 RF,JSt,V:High Evol.,Nobilus . . 1.75
423 RF,JSt,A:High Evol.,Celestials
Count Tagar. 1.75
424 RF,JSt,V:Celestials,E:Black
Galaxy Saga 1.75
425 RF,AM,V:Surtur,Ymir 1.75
426 RF,JSt,HT,O:Earth Force 1.50
427 RF,JSt,A:Excalibur. 1.50
428 RF,JSt,A:Excalibur. 1.50
429 RF,JSt,A:Ghost Rider. 2.00
430 RF,AM,A:Mephisto,Gh.Rider . . 2.00
431 HT,AM,V:Ulik,Loki. 1.75
432 RF,D:Loki,Thor Banished,Eric
Masterson becomes 2nd Thor . 4.00
433 RF,V:Ulik 5.00
434 RF,AM,V:Warriors Three 2.50
435 RF,AM,V:Annihilus 2.50
436 RF,AM,V:Titania,Absorbing
Man,A:Hercules 1.50
437 RF,AM,V:Quasar 1.50
438 RF,JSt,A:Future Thor(Dargo) . . 1.50
439 RF,JSt,A:Drago 1.50
440 RF,AM,I:Thor Corps. 2.50
441 RF,AM,Celestials vs.Ego 2.50
442 RF,AM,Don Blake,Beta Ray
Bill,Mephisto. 1.50
443 RF,AM,A:Dr.Strange,Silver
Surfer,V:Mephisto. 1.50
444 RF,AM,Special X-mas tale . . . 1.50
445 AM,Galactic Storm,pt.7
V:Gladiator. 1.50
446 AM,Galactic Storm,pt.14
A:Avengers 1.50
447 RF,AM,V:Absorbing Man
A:Spider-Man. 1.50
448 RF,AM,V:Titania,A:SpM 1.50
449 RF,AM,V:Ulik 1.50
450 RF,AM,V:Heimdall,A:Code Blue
Double-Sized,Gatefold(c),rep.
Journey Into Mystery#87 . . . . 3.00
451 RF,AM,I:Bloodaxe 1.50
452 RF,AM,V:Bloodaxe. 1.50
453 RF,AM,V:Mephisto 1.50
454 RF,AM,V:Mephisto,Loki,
Karnilla. 1.50
455 AM(i),V:Loki,Karnilla,R:Odin,
A:Dr.Strange 1.50
456 RF,AM,V:Bloodaxe. 1.50
457 RF,AM,R:1st Thor 1.50
458 RF,AM,Thor vs Eric 1.50
459 RF,AM,C&I:Thunderstrike(Eric
Masterson). 2.00
460 I:New Valkyrie 1.50
461 V:Beta Ray Bill. 1.50
462 A:New Valkyrie 1.50
463 Infinity Crusade 1.50
464 Inf.Crusade,V:Loki 1.50
465 Infinity Crusade 1.50
466 Infinity Crusade 1.50
467 Infinity Crusade 1.50
468 RMz(s),Blood & Thunder#1 . . 3.00
469 RMz(s),Blood & Thunder#5 . . 1.50
470 MCW,Blood & Thunder#9 . . . 1.50

Thor #501
© Marvel Entertainment Group

471 MCW,E:Blood & Thunder 1.50
472 B:RTs(s),MCW,I:Godling,C:High
   Evolutionary 1.50
473 MCW,V:Godling,High Evolutionary
   I&C:Karnivore(Man-Beast) 1.75
474 MCW,C:High Evolutionary 1.50
475 MCW,Foil(c),A:Donald Blake,
   N:Thor 3.00
475a Newsstand Ed. 2.00
476 V:Destroyer 1.75
477 V:Destroyer,A:Thunderstrike. . . 1.75
478 V:Norvell Thor 1.75
479 V:Norvell Thor 1.75
480 V:High Evolutionary 1.50
481 V:Grotesk 1.50
482 Don Blake construct. 1.50
483 RTs,MCW,V:Loki 1.50
484 Badoy and Soul 1.50
485 V:The Thing. 1.50
486 High Evolutionary,Godpack . . . 1.50
487 V:Kurse 1.50
488 RTs,MCW,Kurse Saga concl. . . 1.50
489 RTs,V:Kurse,A:Hulk 1.50
490 TDF,after Thunderstrike 1.50
491 N:Thor. 7.50
492 Worldengine's Secrets 5.00
493 Worldengine trigers Ragnarok . 3.00
494 Worldengine saga conclusion. . 3.00
495 BML,Avengers:Timeslice 2.50
496 MD2,BML 2.50
497 MD2,BML 2.50
498 BML,V:Absorbing Man 2.00
499 MD2,BML, ... 2.00
500 MD2,BML,double size,A:Dr.
   Strange 3.00
501 MD2,BML,I:Red Norvell 2.00
502 MD2,BML,Onslaught tie-in, A:Red
   Norvell, Jane Foster, Hela . . . 2.00
Becomes:

JOURNEY INTO MYSTERY
Third Series Nov. 1996
503 TDF,MD2, The Lost Gods, New
   Norse gods?. 1.50
504 TDF,Golden Realm in ruins,
   V:Ulik the Troll 1.50
505 TDF,MD2, V:Wrecker,
   A:Spider-Man 1.50
506 TDF,MD2, R:Heimdall 1.50
507 TDF,Odin kidnapped 1.50
508 TDF, ... 1.95
509 TDF,Battle for the Future
   of Asgard 1.95
510 TDF,Return of Loki,A:Seth 1.95
511 TDF,EBe,Lost Gods reunited
   with Odin 1.95
512 EBe, Odin vs. Seth 1.95
513 TDF,SB,AM, Odin vs. Seth, concl.. .
514 BRa,VRu,F:Shang Chi, Master
   of Kung Fu 2.00
515 BRa,VRu,F:Shang Chi, Master
   of Kung Fu, pt.2 . . . . 2.00
516 BRa,VRu,F:Shang Chi, Master
   of Kung Fu, pt.3 . . . . 2.00
517 SLo,RGr,F:Black Widow. 2.00
518 SLo,RGr,F:Black Widow. 2.00
519 SLo,RGr,F:Black Widow, concl. 2.00
520 MWn,F:Hannibal King pt.1 . . . 2.00
521 MWn,F:Hannibal King, pt.2 . . . 2.00
Ann.#2 JK,V:Destroyer 50.00
Ann.#3 JK,rep,Grey Gargoyle. . . . 13.00
Ann.#4 JK,rep,TheLivingPlanet. . . 11.00
Ann.#5 JK,JB,Hercules,O:Odin . . . 10.00
Ann.#6 JK,JB,A:Guardians of the
   Galaxy,V:Korvac. 10.00
Ann.#7 WS,Eternals 9.00
Ann.#8 JB,V:Zeus. 8.00
Ann.#9 LMc,Dormammu 7.00
Ann.#10 O:Chthon,Gaea,A:Pluto . 6.00
Ann.#11 O:Odin 6.00
Ann.#12 BH,I:Vidar(Odin's son) . . . 6.00

Ann.#13 JB,V:Mephisto 6.00
Ann.#14 AM,DH,Atlantis Attacks. . . 5.00
Ann.#15 HT,Terminus Factor #3 . . . 4.00
Ann.#16 Korvac Quest,pt.2,
   Guardians of Galaxy. 2.50
Ann.#17 Citizen Kang#2 . . . . 2.50
Ann.#18 TGr,I:The Flame,w/card . . 3.25
Ann.#19 V:Flame 3.25
G-Size.#1 Battles,A:Hercules 14.00
TPB Alone Against the Celestials,
   rep.Thor#387-389. . . . . 5.95
TPB Ballad of Beta Ray Bill,rep.
   Thor#337-340. . . . . 8.95
Minus 1 Spec., TDF,EBe,flashback . 1.95
1-shot, Rough Cut, DJu,JR,original
   pencils, b&w 48pg 3.00

THOR
May 1998
1 JR2,KJ,DJu,The hero returns,
   48pg 3.00
2A JR2,KJ,DJu,V:Destroyer,A:Hela,
   Marnot 2.00
2B JR2,KJ variant cover 2.00
3 DJu,JR2,KJ,A:Marnot,V:Sedna . . 2.00
4 DJu,JR2,KJ,A:Namor,Sedna. . . . 2.00
5 DJu,JR2,KJ,V:Charles Diamond . 2.00
6 DJu,JR2,KJ,V:Hercules. 2.00
7 DJu,JR2,KJ,V:Zeus 2.00
8 DJu,JR2,KJ,PeterParker x-over . 2.00
9 DJu,JB,JOy,War on
   Asgard,prelude. 2.00
10 DJu,JR2,KJ,War on Asgard,pt.1. 2.00
11 DJu,JR2,KJ,War on Asgard,pt.2. 2.00
12 DJu,JR2,KJ,War on
   Asgard,concl. 48-page 3.00
12a signed 30.00
13 DJu,JR2,KJ,A:Marnot 2.00
14 DJu,Hammer secret. 2.00
15 DJu,KJ,JR2(c),A:Warriors 3 . . . . 2.00
16 DJu,KJ,JR2,A:Warriors 3 . . . . . . 2.00
Ann.1999 DJu,KJ, 48-page. 3.50
Ann.1999 signed. 20.00
Spec. rep.#1 & #2. . . . . 6.00

THOR CORPS
[Limited Series]
1 TDF(s),PO,V:Demonstaff 2.00
2 TDF(s),PO,A:Invaders 2.00
3 TDF(s),PO,A:Spider-Man 2099 . 2.00
4 TDF(s),PO,Last Issue 2.00

THREE MUSKETEERS
1 thru 2 movie adapt. 1.25

THUNDERBOLTS
Feb. 1997
1 KBk,MBa,VRu,Post-onslaught new
   team:Citizen V, Meteroite, Techno,
   Songbird, Atlas & Mach-1, ... 3.00
1 rep. 2.50
2 KBk,MBa,VRu,V:Mad Thinker. . . 2.00
2a variant cover by MBa&VRu. . . . 2.00
2 rep. 2.00
3 KBk,MBa,VRu,Headquarters at
   Freedom's Plaza 2.00
4 KBk,MBa,VRu,I:Jolt 2.00
5 KBk,MBa,VRu,V:Elements of
   Doom. 2.00
6 KBk,MBa,VRu,V:Elements of
   Doom 2.00
7 KBk,MBa,VRu,F:Citizen V. 2.00
8 KBk,MBa,VRu,Songbird fights
   alone 2.00
9 KBk,MBa,VRu,Black Widow 2.00
10 KBk,MBa,VRu,Secret Identities
   discovered 2.00
11 KBk,MBa,VRu,V:Citizen V 2.00

12 KBk,MBa,VRu,A:Fantastic Four,
   Avengers 2.00
13 KBk,MBa,SHa,on trial 3.00
14 KBk,MBa,VRu,V:Citizen V,
   Meteorite 2.00
15 KBk,MBa,VRu,V:S.H.I.E.L.D. . . . 2.00
16 KBk,MBa,SHa,V:Lightningrods. . 2.00
17 KBk,MBa,SHa,V:Graviton 2.00
18 KBk,MBa,SHa,villains once
   again? 2.00
19 KBk,MBa,SHa,. 2.00
20 KBk,MBa,SHa,V:Masters of Evil. 2.00
21 KBk,MBa,SHa,F:Songbird 2.00
22 KBk,MBa,SHa,A:Hercules 2.00
23 KBk,MBa,SHa,V:U.S.Agent 2.00
24 KBk,MBa,SHa,R:Citizen V 2.00
25 KBk,MBa,SHa,48-page 3.00
25a signed 20.00
26 KBk,MBa,SHa,JoC,A:Mach-1. . . 2.00
27 KBk,MBa,SHa,A:Archangel 2.00
28 KBk,MBa,SHa,V:Graviton 2.00
29 KBk,MBa,SHa,V:Graviton 2.00
30 KBk,MBa,SHa,V:Graviton 2.00
31 KBk,MBa,SHa,R:Citizen V 2.00
Ann. '97 KBk,MBa,TGu,GP,
   O:Thunderbolts, 48pg. 2.95
Spec.#0 Wizard Nov. 1998 . . . .
Spec.First Strikes, rep.#1 & #2 . . . . 5.00
TPB 176pg, secret history. 12.00

THUNDERBOLTS:
DISTANT RUMBLINGS
1997
1 KBk,SEp,Flashback,F:Citizen V . 2.50

THUNDERCATS
Star Dec., 1985
1 JM,TV tie-in 2.00
1a 2nd printing 1.00
2 JM,A:Berbils,V:Mumm-Ra 1.50
3 . . . . 1.50
4 JM,I:Lynxana 1.50
5 JM 1.50
6 JM 1.50
7 Return to Thundera 1.50
8 V:Monkiang 1.50
9 V:Pekmen. 1.00
10 . . . . 1.00
11 I:The Molemen. 1.00
12 `The Protectors'. 1.00
13 EC/AW,V:Safari Joe. 1.00
14 V:Snaf 1.00

Thundercats #1
© Marvel Entertainment Group

Thunderstrike #1
© Marvel Entertainment Group

15 JM,A:Spidera	1.00
16 `Time Capsula'	1.00
17	1.00
18 EC/AW,`Doom Gaze'	1.00
19	1.00
20 EC/AW	1.00
21 JM,A:Hercules Baby	1.00
22 I:Devious Duploids	1.00
23 V:Devious Duploids	1.00
24 June, 1988	1.00

THUNDERSTRIKE
1993–95
1 B:TDF(s),RF,Holografx(c),
  V:Bloodaxe,I:Car Jack 3.25
2 RF,V:Juggernaut. 1.50
3 RF,I:Sangre 1.50
4 RF,A:Spider-Man,I:Pandora 1.50
5 RF,A:Spider-Man,V:Pandora 1.50
6 RF,I:Blackwulf,Bristle,Schizo,Lord
  Lucian,A:SpM,Code:Blue,Stellaris,
  V:SHIELD,Pandora,C:Tantalus . 1.50
7 KP,V:Tantalus,D:Jackson 1.75
8 RF,I&V:Officer ZERO 1.75
9 RF,V:Bloodaxe 1.75
10 RF,A:Thor 1.75
11 RF,A:Wildstreak 1.50
12 RF,A:Whyte Out 1.50
13a Double Feature flip book
  with Code Blue #1 . . . . 2.50
14 RF, Inferno 42 . . . . 1.50
14a Double Feature flip book
  with Code Blue #2 . . . . 2.50
15 RF,V:Methisto 1.50
15a Double Feature flip book
  with Code Blue #3 . . . . 2.50
16 . . . . 1.50
17 V:Bloodaxe 1.50
18 V:New Villain 1.50
19 Shopping Network 1.50
20 A: Black Panther 1.50
21 A:War Machine,V:Loki 1.50
22 TDF,AM,RF,Mystery of Bloodaxe
  blows open. 1.50
23 TDF,A:Avengers 1.50
24 TDF,V:Bloodaxe, final issue 1.50

TIMELY PRESENTS: HUMAN TORCH COMICS
Aug. 1998
1-shot GN. 6.00

TIMESLIP COLLECTION
Sept. 1998
1-shot, 48-page 3.00

TIMESLIP: THE COMING OF THE AVENGERS
Aug. 1998
1-shot GN. 6.00

TIMESPIRITS
Epic Jan., 1985
1 TY 2.00
2 . . . . 1.75
3 . . . . 1.75
4 AW 1.50
5 thru 7 . . . . @1.50
8 March, 1986 . . . . 1.50

TIMESTRYKE
1 . . . . 1.95
2 . . . . 1.95

TINY TESSIE
See: TESSIE THE TYPIST

TOMB OF DARKNESS
See: BEWARE

TOMB OF DRACULA
April, 1972
1 GC,Night of the Vampire 100.00
2 GC,Who Stole My Coffin? 50.00
3 GC,TP,I:Rachel Van Helsing . . . 35.00
4 GC,TP,Bride of Dracula! 35.00
5 GC,TP,To Slay A Vampire 35.00
6 GC,TP,Monster of the Moors. . . 30.00
7 GC,TP,Child is Slayer of
  the Man 30.00
8 GC(p),The Hell-Crawlers. 30.00
9 The Fire Cross 30.00
10 GC,I:Blade Vampire Slayer . . . 32.00
11 GC,TP,Master of the Undead
  Strikes Again! 18.00
12 GC,TP,House that Screams . . . 18.00
13 GC,TP,O:Blade 20.00
14 GC,TP,Vampire has Risen
  from the Grave 18.00
15 GC,TP,Stay Dead 18.00
16 GC,TP,Back from the Grave. . . 18.00
17 GC,TP,A Vampire Rides This
  Train! 18.00
18 GC,TP,A:Werewolf By Night. . . 20.00
19 GC,TP,Snowbound in Hell 18.00
20 GC,TP,ManhuntForAVampire . . 18.00
21 GC,TP,A:Blade 15.00
22 GC,TP,V:Gorna 15.00
23 GC,TP,Shadow over Haunted
  Castle 15.00
24 GC,TP,I am your Death 15.00
25 GC,TP,Blood Stalkers of Count
  Dracula 15.00
26 GC,TP,A Vampire Stalks the
  Night 15.00
27 GC,TP,..And the Moon Spews
  Death! 15.00
28 GC,TP,Five came to Kill a
  Vampire' 15.00

Tomb of Dracula #9
© Marvel Entertainment Group

29 GC,TP,Vampire goes Mad? . . . 15.00
30 GC,TP,A:Blade 15.00
31 GC,TP,Child of Blood. 15.00
32 GC,TP,The Vampire Walks
  Among Us 15.00
33 GC,TP,Blood on My Hands . . . 15.00
34 GC,TP,Bloody Showdown 15.00
35 GC,TP,A:Brother Voodoo 15.00
36 GC,TP,Dracula in America 15.00
37 GC,TP,The Vampire Walks
  Among Us 10.00
38 GC,TP,Bloodlust for a Dying
  Vampire. 15.00
39 GC,TP,Final Death of Dracula . 15.00
40 GC,TP,Triumph of Dr.Sun. 15.00
41 GC,TP,A:Blade 8.00
42 GC,TP,V:Dr.Sun. 7.00
43 GC,TP,A:NewYear'sNightmare . . 7.00
44 GC,TP,A:Dr.Strange. 7.00
45 GC,TP,A:Hannibal King 8.00
46 GC,TP,W:Dracula & Domini . . . 7.00
47 GC,TP,Death-Bites 7.00
48 GC,TP,A:Hannibal King 8.00
49 GC,TP,A:Robin Hood,
  Frankenstein's Monster 7.00
50 GC,TP,A:Silver Surfer 15.00
51 GC,TP,A:Blade 7.50
52 GC,TP,V:Demon 6.50
53 GC,TP,A:Hannibal King,Blade . . 7.50
54 GC,TP,Twas the Night Before
  Christmas. 6.50
55 GC,TP,Requiem for a Vampire . . 6.50
56 GC,TP,A:Harold H. Harold 6.50
57 GC,TP,The Forever Man 6.50
58 GC,TP,A:Blade 7.00
59 GC,TP,The Last Traitor 6.50
60 GC,TP,The Wrath of Dracula . . . 6.50
61 GC,TP,Resurrection. 6.50
62 GC,TP,What Lurks Beneath 6.50
63 GC,TP,A:Janus 6.50
64 GC,TP,A:Satan 6.50
65 GC,TP,Where No Vampire
  Has Gone Before 6.50
66 GC,TP,Marked for Death 6.50
67 GC,TP,A:Lilith 6.50
68 GC,TP,Dracula turns Human . . . 6.50
69 GC,TP,Cross of Fire. 6.50
70 GC,TP,double size,last issue . . . 8.50
Savage Return of Dracula. rep.
  Tomb of Dracula #1,#2 . . . . 2.00
Wedding of Dracula. rep.Tomb
  of Dracula #30,#45,#46 . . . . . . 2.00
Requiem for Dracula. rep.Tomb
  of Dracula #69,70. . . . . 2.00

TOMB OF DRACULA
[Mini-Series] Nov., 1991
1 GC,AW,Day of Blood 6.00
2 GC,AW,Dracula in DC 5.50
3 GC,AW,A:Blade 5.50
4 GC,AW,D:Dracula. 5.50

TOMB OF DRACULA
(B&W Mag.) Nov., 1979
1 . . . . 3.50
2 SD 5.00
3 FM 5.00
4 . . . . 3.00
5 . . . . 3.00
6 Sept., 1980 . . . . 3.00

TOMB OF DRACULA
MEGAZINE
TPB Halloween, MWn,GC,TP . . . 3.95

TOMORROW KNIGHTS
Epic June, 1990
1 . . . . 1.95
2 . . . . 1.50
3 . . . . 1.50
4 Origin. 1.50
5 . . . . 2.25
6 . . . . 2.25

TOP DOG
Star Comics April, 1985
1 . . . . 1.25
2 thru 14, June 1987 . . . . @1.00

TOR
Epic *Heavy Hitters* 1993
1 JKu,R:Tor,Magazine Format 6.25
2 JKu 6.25
3 JKu,V:The Iduard Ring 6.25

TOUGH KID
SQUAD COMICS
Timely March, 1942
1 O:The Human Top,Tough Kid
  Squad,A:The Flying Flame,
  V:Doctor Klutch 8,500.00

TOWER OF SHADOWS
Sept., 1969
1 JR(c),JSo,JCr,`At The Stroke
  of Midnight' 40.00
2 JR(c),DH,DA,NA,`The Hungry
  One' 25.00
3 GC,BWs,GT,`Midnight in the
  Wax Museum' 25.00
4 DH,Within The Witching Circle . 15.00
5 DA,BWS,WW,`Demon That
  Stalks Hollywood' 35.00
6 WW,SD,`Pray For the Man in
  the Rat-Hole 35.00
7 BWS,WW,`Titano' 35.00
8 WW,SD,`Demons of
  Dragon-Henge' 35.00
9 BWr(c),TP,Lovecraft story 35.00
Becomes:

CREATURES ON
THE LOOSE
March, 1971
10 BWr,A:King Kull 50.00
11 DAy,rep Moomba is Here 15.00
12 JK,`I Was Captured By Korilla'. 15.00
13 RC,`The Creature

Creatures on the Loose #27
© *Marvel Entertainment Group*

From Krogarr' 15.00
14 MSe,`Dead Storage' 15.00
15 SD,Spragg the Living Mountain 15.00
16 GK,BEv,GK,B&O:Gullivar Jones,
  Warrior of Mars 10.00
17 GK,`Slaves o/t Spider Swarm' . 10.00
18 RA,`The Fury of Phra' 10.00
19 WB,JM,GK,`Red Barbarian
  of Mars' 10.00
20 GK(c),GM,SD,`The Monster...
  And the Maiden' 10.00
21 JSo(c),GM,`Two Worlds To
  Win',E:Guilliver 8.00
22 JSo(c),SD,VM,B:Thongor,
  Warrior of Lost Lemuria 8.00
23 VM,`The Man-Monster Strikes'. . 8.00
24 VM,`Attack of the Lizard-Hawks' 8.00
25 VM,GK(c),`Wizard of Lemuria' . . 8.00
26 VM,`Doom of the Serpent Gods' 8.00
27 VM,SD,`Demons Dwell in the
  Crypts of Yamath'. 8.00
28 SD,`The Hordes of Hell' 8.00
29 GK(c),`Day of the Dragon Wings',
  E:Thongor,Warrior of Lost
  Lemuria 8.00
30 B:Man-Wolf,`Full Moon, Dark
  Fear' 10.00
31 GT,`The Beast Within' 8.00
32 GT,V:Kraven the Hunter. 8.00
33 GK(c),GP,`The Name of the
  Game is Death' 8.00
34 GP,`Nightflight to Fear'. 8.00
35 GK(c),GP. 8.00
36 GK(c),GP,`Murder by Moonlight'. 8.00
37 GP,Sept., 1975 . . . . 8.00

TOXIC AVENGER
March, 1991
1 VM(i)I&O:Toxic Avenger. 1.50
2 VM(i) 1.50
3 VM(i)`Night of LivingH.bodies . . 1.50
4 Legend of Sludgeface. 1.50
5 I:Biohazard 1.50
6 V:Biohazard 1.50
7 `Sewer of Souviaki'. 1.50
8 `Sewer of Souviaki' conc. 1.50
9 Abducted by Aliens. 1.50
10 `Die,Yuppie Scum',pt.1. . . . . . 1.50

TOXIC CRUSADERS
1992
1 F:Toxic Avengers & Crusaders . . 1.50

2 SK(c),V:Custard-Thing 1.25
3 SK(c),V:Custard-Thing 1.25
4 V:Giant Mutant Rats 1.25
5 V:Dr.Killemoff 1.25
6 V:Dr.Killemoff 1.25
7 F:Yvonne 1.25
8 V:Psycho 1.25
[2nd Series]
1 . . . . 1.25
2 . . . . 1.25

TRANSFORMERS
[1st Regular Series] Sept., 1984
1 FS,Toy Comic. 2.50
2 FS,OptimusPrime V:Megatron. . . 1.75
3 FS.A:Spider-Man 1.75
4 MT(c),FS 1.50
5 Transformers Dead?. 1.50
6 Autobots vs.Decepticons 1.50
7 KB,V:Megatron. 1.50
8 KB,A:Dinobots 1.50
9 MM,A:Circuit Breaker 1.50
10 Dawn of the Devastator 1.50
11 HT. 1.50
12 HT,V:Shockwave 1.50
13 DP,Return of Megatron 1.50
14 DP,V:Decepticons 1.50
15 DP. 1.50
16 KN,A:Bumblebee 1.50
17 DP,I:New Transformers,pt.1 . . . . 1.50
18 DP,I:New Transformers,pt.2 . . . . 1.50
19 DP,I:Omega Supreme 1.50
20 HT,Skid vs.Ravage 1.50
21 DP,I:Aerialbots 1.25
22 DP,I:Stuntacons(Menasor) 1.25
23 DP,Return of Circuit Breaker . . . 1.25
24 DP,D:Optimus Prime 1.25
25 DP,Decpticons (full story). 1.25
26 DP. 1.25
27 DP,V:Head Hunter 1.25
28 DP 1.25
29 DP,I:Scraplets, Triplechangers . 1.25
30 DP,V:Scraplets. 1.25
31 DP,Humans vs. Decepticons . . . 1.25
32 DP,`Autobots for Sale' 1.25
33 DP,Autobots vs.Decepticons . . . 1.25
34 V:Sky Lynx 1.25
35 JRy,I:UK.version Transformers . . 1.25
36 . . . . 1.00
37 . . . . 1.00
38 . . . . 1.00
39 . . . . 1.00
40 Autobots' New Leader 1.00

Transformers #9
© *Marvel Entertainment Group*

MARVEL

41 . . . . 1.00
42 Return of Optimus Prime 1.00
43 Optimus Prime,Goldbug. 1.00
44 FF,Return of Circuit Breaker. . . . 1.00
45 V:The Jammers 1.00
46 I:New Transformers 1.00
47 B:Underbase saga,I:Seacons. . . 1.00
48 Optimus Prime/Megatron
 (past story). 1.00
49 Underbase saga Contd. 1.00
50 E:Underbase saga,I:New
 Characters 1.00
51 I:Pretender Decepticon Beasts. . 1.00
52 I:Mecannibles,pt.1 . . . . 1.00
53 Mecannibles,pt.2 . . . . 1.00
54 I:Micromasters 1.00
55 MG 1.00
56 Return of Megatron 1.00
57 Optimus Prime vs.Scraponok . . 1.00
58 V:Megatron 1.00
59 A:Megatron,D:Ratchet 1.00
60 Battle on Cybertron 1.00
61 O:Transformers 1.00
62 B:Matrix Quest,pt.1 . . . . 1.00
63 . . . . 1.00
64 I:The Klud 1.00
65 GSr 1.00
66 E:Matrix Quest,pt.5 . . . . 1.00
67 V:Unicorn,Also Alternative
 World 1.00
68 I:Neoknights 1.00
69 Fate of Ratchet & Megatron
 revealed. 1.00
70 Megatron/Ratchet fused
 together 1.00
71 Autobots Surrender to
 Decepticons 1.00
72 Decepticon Civil War,
 I:Gravitron 1.00
73 I:Unicron,A:Neoknights 1.00
74 A:Unicron&Brothers of Chaos . . 1.00
75 V:Thunderwing & Dark Matrix . . 1.00
76 Aftermath of War 1.00
77 Unholy Alliance 1.00
78 Galvatron vs.Megatron. 1.00
79 Decepticons Invade Earth 1.00
80 Return of Optimus Prime,final . . 1.00

[2nd Regular Series]
1 Split Foil(c),A:Dinobots 3.00
2 A:G.I.Joe,Cobra 2.00
3 . . . . 2.00
4 MaG,V:Jhiaxus 2.00
5 . . . . 2.00
6 V:Megatron. 2.00
7 V:Darkwing. 2.00
8 V:Darkwing. 2.00
9 . . . . 2.00
10 Total War. 2.00
11 . . . . 1.75

TRANSFORMERS COMICS MAGAZINE
1986–88
1 Digest Size 1.50
2 thru 11 . . . . @1.50

TRANSFORMERS, THE MOVIE
Dec., 1986–Feb. 1987
1 thru 3 Animated Movie adapt. . @1.25

TRANSFORMERS UNIVERSE
Dec., 1986
1 . . . . 1.25
2 & 3. . . . . @1.25
4 March, 1987 . . . . 1.25

TRANSMUTATION OF IKE GARAUDA
Epic 1991
1 JSh,I:IkeGaruda 3.95
2 JSh,conclusion 3.95

Trouble With Girls #1
© Marvel Entertainment Group

TROUBLE WITH GIRLS: NIGHT OF THE LIZARD
Epic *Heavy Hitters* 1993
1 BBI,AW,R:Lester Girls. 2.75
2 BBI,AW,V:Lizard Lady. 2.25
3 BBI,AW,V:Lizard Lady. 2.25
4 BBI,AW,last issue 2.25

TRUE COMPLETE MYSTERY
See: COMPLETE MYSTERY

TRUE SECRETS
See: OUR LOVE

TRUE WESTERN
Dec., 1949
1 Ph(c),Billy the Kid 125.00
2 Ph(c),Alan Ladd,Badmen vs.
 Lawmen 125.00
Becomes:
TRUE ADVENTURES
3 BP,MSy,Boss of Black Devil . . 100.00
Becomes:
MEN'S ADVENTURES
4 He Called me a Coward 225.00
5 Brother Act 150.00
6 Heat of Battle 125.00
7 The Walking Death 125.00
8 RH,Journey Into Death 125.00
9 Bullets,Blades and Death 100.00
10 BEv,The Education of Thomas
 Dillon. 100.00
11 Death of A Soldier 100.00
12 Firing Squad 100.00
13 RH(c),The Three Stripes 100.00
14 GC,BEv,Steel Coffin. 100.00
15 JMn(c). 100.00
16 . . . . 100.00

17 . . . . 100.00
18 . . . . 100.00
19 JRo 100.00
20 RH(c) 100.00
21 BEv(c),JSt,The Eye of Man . . 125.00
22 BEv,JR,Mark of the Witch 125.00
23 BEv(c),RC,The Wrong Body. . 125.00
24 RH,JMn,GT,Torture Master. . . 125.00
25 SSh(c),Who Shrinks My Head 125.00
26 Midnight in the Morgue 125.00
27 CBu(c),A:Capt.America,Human
 Torch,Sub-Mariner 800.00
28 BEv,A:Capt.America,Human Torch,
 Sub-Mariner,July, 1954 . . . . . 750.00

TRY-OUT WINNER BOOK
March, 1988
1 Spider-Man vs. Doc Octopus . . 15.00

TV STARS
August, 1978
1 A:Great Grape Ape 12.00
2 . . . . 10.00
3 . . . . 10.00
4 A:Top Cat,Feb., 1979 . . . . 10.00

2099: MANIFEST DESTINY
March 1998
GN LKa,MMK,F:MiguelO'Hara,48pg 6.00

2-GUN KID
See: BILLY BUCKSKIN

TWO-GUN KID
Atlas March, 1948—April, 1977
1 B:Two-Gun Kid,The Sheriff . . 750.00
2 Killers of Outlaw City 300.00
3 RH,A:Annie Oakley 225.00
4 RH,A:Black Rider 225.00
5 . . . . 275.00
6 . . . . 175.00
7 RH,Brand of a Killer 175.00
8 The Secret of the Castle of
 Slaves 175.00
9 JSe,Trapped in Hidden Valley
 A:Black Rider 175.00
10 JK(c),The Horrible Hermit
 of Hidden Mesa 175.00
11 JMn(c),GT,A:Black Rider 150.00
12 JMn(c),GT,A:Black Rider 150.00
13 thru 24 . . . . @125.00
25 AW 125.00
26 . . . . 100.00
27 . . . . 100.00
28 . . . . 100.00
29 . . . . 100.00
30 AW 100.00
31 thru 44. . . . . 60.00
45 . . . . 55.00
46 . . . . 55.00
47 . . . . 45.00
48 . . . . 50.00
49 . . . . 45.00
50 . . . . 40.00
51 AW 40.00
52 thru 59. . . . . @40.00
60 DAy,New O:Two Gun Kid 25.00
61 JK,DAy,The Killer and The Kid 25.00
62 JK,DAy,At the Mercy of Moose
 Morgan. 25.00
63 DAy,The Guns of Wild Bill
 Taggert. 20.00
64 DAy,Trapped by Grizzly
 Gordon. 20.00
65 DAy,Nothing Can Save Fort
 Henry. 20.00

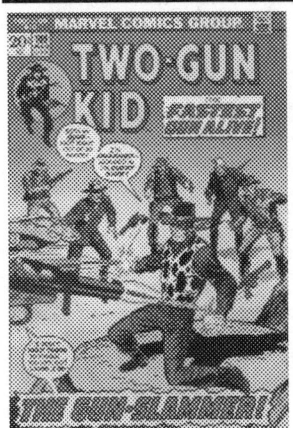

Two-Gun Kid #109
© *Marvel Entertainment Group*

2001: A Space Odyssey #1
© *Marvel Entertainment Group*

66 DAy,Ringo's Raiders 20.00
67 DAy,The Fangs of the Fox 20.00
68 DAy,The Purple Phantom. 20.00
69 DAy,Badman Called Goliath . . . 20.00
70 DAy,Hurricane 20.00
71 DAy,V:Jesse James 20.00
72 DAy,V:Geronimo 20.00
73 Guns of the Galloway Gang . . . 20.00
74 Dakota Thompson 20.00
75 JK,Remember the Alamo 20.00
76 JK,Trapped on the Doom 20.00
77 JK,V:The Panther 20.00
78 V:Jesse James 20.00
79 The River Rats 20.00
80 V:The Billy Kid 20.00
81 The Hidden Gun 15.00
82 BEv,Here Comes the Conchos. 15.00
83 Durango,Two-Gun
    Kid Unmasked 15.00
84 Gunslammer 15.00
85 Fury at Falcon Flats,
    A:Rawhide Kids 15.00
86 V:Cole Younger 15.00
87 OW,The Sidewinder and the
    Stallion. 15.00
88 thru 100 . . . . @15.00
101 . . . . 15.00
102 thru 136 . . . . @10.00

TWO-GUN KID:
SUNSET RIDERS
1995
1 FaN,R:Two-Gun Kid,64pgs 6.95
2 FaN,concl. 64pgs.. . . . . 6.95

TWO GUN WESTERN
See: CASEY–CRIME
PHOTOGRAPHER

TWO-GUN WESTERN
See: BILLY BUCKSKIN

2001: A SPACE ODYSSEY
Oct., 1976
1 JK,FRg,Based on Movie 3.00

2001: A SPACE ODYSSEY
Dec., 1976—Sept., 1977
1 JK,Based on Movie 5.00
2 JK,Vira the She-Demon 3.00
3 JK,Marak the Merciless 3.00
4 JK,Wheels of Death 3.00
5 JK,Norton of New York 3.00
6 JK,Immortality ...Death 3.00
7 JK,The New Seed 3.00
8 JK,Capture of X-51,I&O:Mr.
    Machine(Machine-Man) 4.00
9 JK,A:Mr Machine 3.00
10 Hotline to Hades,A:Mr Machine . 3.00

2010
April, 1985
1 TP,movie adapt. 1.00
2 TP,movie adapt,May, 1985 . . . . . 1.00

2099 A.D.
1995
1 Chromium cover. 4.00

2099 APOCALYPSE
1995
1 . . . . 5.00

2099 GENESIS
1996
1 Chromium Cover 4.00

2099 SPECIAL:
THE WORLD OF DOOM
1995
1 The World of Doom 2.25

2099 UNLIMITED
1993–96
1 DT,I:Hulk 2099,A:Spider-Man 2099,
    I:Mutagen. 4.50
2 DT,F:Hulk 2099,Spider-Man 2099,
    I:R-Gang 4.25
3 GJ(s),JJB,F:Hulk & SpM 2099 . . 4.25
4 PR(c),GJ(s),JJB,I:Metalscream
    2099,Lachryma 2099 . . . . 4.25
5 GJ(s),I:Vulx,F:Hazardd 2099 . . . 3.95
6 . . . . 3.95

Becomes:
2099 A.D. UNLIMITED
7 . . . . 3.95
8 F:Public Enemy 3.95
9 One Nation Under Doom 3.95
10 V:Chameleon 2099 . . . . 3.95
Spec. #1 The World of Doom 2.25

2099:
WORLD OF TOMORROW
1996–97
1 . . . . 2.50
2 . . . . 2.50
3 MMk,MsM,ATi,F:Spider-Man,
    X-Men 2.50
4 ATi,X-Men 2099 discover secret . 2.50
5 ATi 2.50
6 PFe&ATi(c),Phalanx's final
    assault 2.50
7 Spider-Man 2099 searches for his
    brother: Green Goblin. 2.50
8 Phalanx invasion aftermath. . . . 2.50
9 Humanity vs. Lunatika 2.50

TYPHOID
1995–96
1 ANo,JVF,Painted series 3.95
2 ANo,JVF,Hunt for serial killer . . . 3.95
3 ANo,JVF,sex,blood & videotapes . 3.95
4 ANo,JVF,conclusion 3.95

ULTIMATE AGE
OF APOCALYPSE
Rep. #1-#4 Age of Apocalypse stories:
Ultimate Amazing X-Men 8.95
Ultimate Astonishing X-Men 8.95
Ultimate Factor X 8.95
Ultimate Gambit and the X-Ternals . 8.95
Ultimate Generation Next 8.95
Ultimate Weapon X. 8.95
Ultimate X-Calibre 8.95
Ultimate X-Man. 8.95

ULTRAFORCE/AVENGERS
1 V:Loki,A:Malibu's Ultraforce 3.95

ULTRA GIRL
Mini-Series 1996
1 BKs,I&O:Ultra Girl. 1.50
2 BKs, ... 1.50
3 BKs,R:New Warriors. 1.50

ULTRA X-MEN
COLLECTION
1 Metallic(c), art from cards 2.95
2 thru 5 art from cards . . . . @2.95

ULTRA X-MEN III
Preview 2.95

ULTRON
June 1999
1-shot Ultron Unleashed, rep. 3.50

UNCANNY ORIGINS
Sept. 1996
1 F:Cyclops. 1.00
2 F:Quicksilver 1.00
3 DHv,BAn,F:Archangel. 1.00
4 F:Firelord 1.00
5 MHi,F:Hulk 1.00
6 F:Beast 1.00

Uncanny Origins #2
© Marvel Entertainment Group

7 F:Venom	1.00
8 F:Nightcrawler	1.00
9 F:Storm	1.00
10 F:Black Cat	1.00
11 F:Luke Cage	1.00
12 F:Black Knight	1.00
13 LWn,MCa,F:Doctor Strange	1.00
14 LWn,MCW,F:Iron Fist	1.00

UNCANNY TALES
Atlas June, 1952

1 RH,While the City Sleeps	650.00
2 JMn,BEv	350.00
3 Escape to What	300.00
4 JMn,Nobody's Fool	300.00
5 Fear	300.00
6 He Lurks in the Shadows	300.00
7 BEv,Kill,Clown,Kill	250.00
8 JMn,Bring Back My Face	250.00
9 BEv,RC,The Executioner	250.00
10 RH(c),JR,The Man Who Came Back To Life	250.00
11 GC,The Man Who Changed	200.00
12 BP,BEv,Bertha Gets Buried	200.00
13 RH,Scared Out of His Skin	200.00
14 RH,The Victims of Vonntor	200.00
15 RA,JSt,The Man Who Saw Death	200.00
16 JMn,GC,Zombie at Large	200.00
17 GC,I Live With Corpses	200.00
18 JF,BP,Clock Face(c)	200.00
19 DBr,RKr,The Man Who Died Again	200.00
20 DBr,Ted's Head	200.00
21	175.00
22 DAy	175.00
23	175.00
24	175.00
25 MSy	175.00
26	175.00
27 RA	175.00
28	175.00
29	100.00
30	100.00
31	100.00
32 BEv	100.00
33	100.00
34 BP	100.00
35	100.00
36 BP,BEv	100.00
37 MD	100.00
38 BP	100.00
39 BEv	100.00

40	100.00
41	100.00
42 MD	125.00
43	100.00
44	100.00
45 MD	100.00
46 GM	100.00
47 TSe	100.00
48 BEv	100.00
49 JO	100.00
50 JO	100.00
51 GM	125.00
52 GC	100.00
53 JO,AT	100.00
54	120.00
55	100.00
56 Sept., 1957	125.00

UNCANNY TALES FROM THE GRAVE
Dec., 1973—Oct., 1975

1 RC,Room of no Return	15.00
2 DAy,Out of the Swamp	10.00
3 No Way Out	10.00
4 JR,SD,Vampire	10.00
5 GK,GT,Don't Go in the Cellar	10.00
6 JR,SD,The Last Kkrul	10.00
7 RH,SD,Never Dance With a Vampire	10.00
8 SD,Escape Into Hell	10.00
9 JA,The Nightmare Men	10.00
10 SD,DH,Beware the Power of Khan	10.00
11 SD,JF,RH,Dead Don't Sleep	10.00
12 SD,Final Issue	10.00

UNCANNY X-MEN
See: X-MEN

UNKNOWN WORLDS OF SCIENCE FICTION
Jan., 1975
(black & white magazine)

1 AW,RKr,AT,FF,GC	4.00
2 FB,GP	3.25
3 GM,AN,GP,GC	3.25
4	3.25
5 GM,NC,GC	3.25
6 FB,AN,GC,Nov., 1975	3.25
Spec.#1 AN,NR,JB	3.50

UNION JACK
Oct. 1998

1 (of 3) BRa,F:Joey Chapman	3.00
2 BRa,V:Baroness	3.00
3 BRa,conclusion	3.00

U.S.A. COMICS
Timely Aug., 1941

1 S&K(c),BW,Bondage(c),The Defender(c)	9,800.00
2 S&K(c),BW,Capt.Terror(c)	3,000.00
3 S&K(c),Capt.Terror(c)	2,200.00
4	1,600.00
5 Hitler(c),O:AmericanAvenger	1,800.00
6 ASh(c),Capt.America(c)	2,200.00
7 BW,O:Marvel Boy	1,900.00
8 Capt.America (c)	1,500.00
9 Bondage(c), Capt.America	1,500.00
10 SSh(c),Bondage(c), Capt.America	1,500.00
11 SSh(c),Bondage(c), Capt.America	1,200.00
12 ASh(c),Capt.America	1,200.00
13 ASh(c),Capt.America	1,200.00

14 Capt.America	900.00
15 Capt.America	900.00
16 ASh(c),Bondage(c), Capt.America	900.00
17 Bondage(c),Capt.America	900.00

U.S. 1 #2
© Marvel Entertainment Group

U.S. 1
May, 1983–Oct. 1984

1 AM(c),HT,Trucking Down the Highway	1.25
2 HT,Midnight	1.00
3 FS,ME,Rhyme of the Ancient Highwayman	1.00
4 FS,ME	1.00
5 FS,ME,Facing The Maze	1.00
6 FS,ME	1.00
7 FS,ME	1.00
8 FS,ME	1.00
9 FS,ME,Iron Mike-King of the Bike	1.00
10 thru 12 FS,ME	@1.00

U.S. AGENT
June–Dec. 1993

1 V:Scourge,O:U.S.Agent	2.00
2 V:Scourge	2.00
3 V:Scourge	2.00
4 last issue	2.00

UNTAMED
Epic *Heavy Hitters* 1993

1 I:Griffen Palmer	2.75
2 V:Kosansui	2.25
3 V:Kosansui	2.25

UNTOLD LEGEND OF CAPTAIN MARVEL, THE
1997

1 (of 3) Early days of Captain Marvel	2.50
2 Early days of Captain Marvel	2.50
3 V:Kree	2.50

UNTOLD TALES OF SPIDER-MAN
Sept. 1995–Sept. 1997

1 F:Young Spider-Man	3.00
2 V:Batwing	1.50
3 V:Sandman	1.00

4 V:J.Jonah Jameson 1.00
5 V:Vulture 1.00
6 A:Human Torch. 1.00
7 . . . . 1.00
8 . . . . 1.00
9 A:Batwing,Lizard. 1.00
10 KBk,PO,I:Commanda. 1.00
11 KBk,PO, ... 1.00
12 KBk,PO, ... 1.00
13 KBk,PO, ... 1.00
14 KBk,PO, ... 1.00
15 KBk,PO,AV,Gordon's plan to
   control the Bugle 1.00
16 Re-I:Mary Jane Watson 1.00
17 KBk,PO,AV,V:Hawkeye 1.00
18 KBk,PO,AV,A:Green Goblin,
   Headsman 1.00
19 KBk,PO,AW,F:Doctor Octopus . 1.00
20 KBk,PO,AW,V:Vulture 1.00
21 KBk,PO,AW,V:Menace,A:Original
   X-Men 1.00
22 KBk,PO,AW,V:Scarecrow, ... 1.00
23 KBk,PO,AW,V:Crime Master,
   A:Green Goblin 1.00
24 KBk,PO,BMc, Fate of Batwing . . 1.00
25 LBI,PO,BMc, V:Green Goblin,
   final issue. 2.00
Minus 1 Spec., RSt,JR, flashback,
   Peter's parents. 1.95
Ann. '96 1 KBk,MiA,JSt,A date with
   Invisible Girl? 1.95
Ann. '97 KBk,TL,A:everyone, 48pg . 2.95
TPB rep. #1–#8 . . . . 17.00
one-shot GN KBk,SL,Encounter,
   A:Dr. Strange 48pg. 6.00

VALKYRIE
1996
1-shot JMD, ... 2.50

VAMPIRE TALES
August, 1973
(black & white magazine)
1 BEv,B:Morbius the Living
   Vampire. 50.00
2 JSo,I:Satana 40.00
3 A:Satana 20.00
4 GK 30.00
5 GK,O:Morbius The Living
   Vampire 35.00
6 AA,I:Lilith 30.00
7 HC,PG 30.00
8 AA,A:Blade The Vampire
   Slayer 30.00
9 RH,AA 30.00
10 . . . . 30.00
11 June, 1975. . . . . 30.00
Ann.#1 . . . . 15.00

VAULT OF EVIL
Feb., 1973—Nov., 1975
1 B:1950's reps,Come Midnight,
   Come Monster 15.00
2 The Hour of the Witch 10.00
3 The Woman Who Wasn't 10.00
4 Face that Follows 10.00
5 Ghost 10.00
6 The Thing at the Window 10.00
7 Monsters 10.00
8 The Vampire is my Brother . . . 10.00
9 Giant Killer 10.00
10 The Lurkers in the Caves. 10.00
11 Two Feasts For a Vampire 10.00
12 Midnight in the
   Haunted Mansion 10.00
13 Hot as the Devil 10.00
14 Midnight in the Haunted Manor 10.00
15 Don't Shake Hands with the

Vault of Evil #6
© *Marvel Entertainment Group*

Devil. 10.00
16 A Grave Honeymoon 10.00
17 Grave Undertaking. 10.00
18 The Deadly Edge. 10.00
19 Vengeance of Ahman Ra 10.00
20 . . . . 10.00
21 Victim of Valotorr 10.00
22 . . . . 10.00
23 Black Magician Lives Again . . . 10.00

VENOM:
ALONG CAME A SPIDER
1996
1 LHA,GLz,V:New Spider-Man. . . . 3.00
2 LHa,JPi,V:New Spider-Man. . . . 3.00
3 . . . . 3.00
4 conclusion, 48pg 3.00

VENOM:
CARNAGE UNLEASHED
1995
1 Venom vs. Carnage 3.00
2 Venom vs. Carnage 3.00
3 No Spider-Help. 3.00
4 JRu,Wld,LHa,cardstock(c) 3.00

VENOM:
THE ENEMY WITHIN
1994
1 BMc,Glow-in-the-dark(C),
   A:Demogoblin,Morbius 3.25
2 BMc,A:Demogoblin,Morbius . . . 3.25
3 BMc,V:Demogoblin,A:Morbius. . . 3.25

VENOM: FINALE
1997–98
1 thru 3 LHa, ... @3.00

VENOM: FUNERAL PYRE
1993
1 TL,JRu,A:Punisher 3.50
2 TL,JRu,AM,V:Gangs. 3.50
3 TL,JRu,Last issue. 3.50

VENOM: THE HUNGER
1996
1 thru 4 LKa,TeH,V:Dr. Paine . . . @2.00

VENOM: THE HUNTED
1996
1 LHa,3 part mini-series. 3.00

VENOM:
LETHAL PROTECTOR
1993
1 MBa,A:Spider-Man.holo-grafx(c) . 5.00
1a Gold Ed. 8.00
2 MBa,A:Spider-Man 3.50
3 MBa,Families of Venom's
   victims 3.50
4 RLm,A:Spider-Man,V:Life
   Foundation 3.50
5 RLm,V:Five Symbiotes,A:SpM . . 3.50
6 RLm,V:Spider-Man 3.50
Super Size Spec.#1 Planet of
   the Symbiotes,pt.3 . . . . 3.95
Venom:Deathtrap:The Vault,RLm,
   A:Avengers,Freedom Force . . . 6.95
TPB Lethal Protector RLm,DvM . . 15.95

VENOM: LICENSE TO KILL
1997
1 (of 3) LHa,KHt, sequel to Venom
   on trial 2.00
2 LHa,V:Dr. Yes. 2.00
3 LHa,V:Dr. Yes. 2.00

VENOM: THE MACE
1994
1 Embossed(c),CP(s),LSh,I:Mace . 3.25
2 CP(s),LSh,V:Mace 3.25
3 CP(s),LSh,V:Mace,final issue . . . 3.25

VENOM: THE MADNESS
1993–94
1 B:ANi(s),KJo,V:Juggernaut 3.50
2 KJo,V:Juggernaut 3.25
3 E:ANi(s),KJo,V:Juggernaut 3.25

VENOM:
NIGHTS OF VENGEANCE
1994
1 RLm,I:Stalkers,A:Vengeance . . . 3.25
2 RLm,A:Vengeance,V:Stalkers . . . 3.25
3 RLm,V:Stalkers. 3.25
4 RLm,final issue. 3.25

VENOM: ON TRIAL
Jan.–May 1997
1 LHa,Tries to break out 2.00
2 LHa,Defended by Matt Murdock
   (Daredevil),A:Spider-Man 2.00
3 LHa,A:Spider-Man, Carnage,
   Daredevil 2.00

VENOM:
SEED OF DARKNESS
1997
1 LKa,JFy,Flashback, early Eddie
   Brock 2.00

VENOM:
SEPARATION ANXIETY
1994–95
1 Embossed(c) 3.00
2 V:Symbiotes 3.00
3 . . . . 3.00
4 . . . . 3.00
TPB Rep.#1-#4 HMe,RoR,SDR . . . 9.95

MARVEL

VENOM:
SIGN OF THE BOSS
1997
1 (of 2) IV,TDr,V:Ghost Rider 2.00
2 (of 2) IV,TDr,conclusion. 2.00

VENOM:
SINNER TAKES ALL
1995
1 LHa,GLz,I:New Sin-Eater 3.00
2 V:Sineater 3.00
3 Wrong Man 3.00
4 LHa,GLz,V:Sin-Eater 3.00
5 LHa, finale 3.00

VENOM:
TOOTH AND CLAW
1996–97
1 (of 3) LHa,JPi,AM, Dirtnap usurps
   Venom's body. 2.00
2 LHa,JPi,AM,V:Wolverine. 2.00
3 LHa,JPi,AM,V:Wolverine,
   Chimera. 2.00

VENUS
Atlas August, 1948
1 B:Venus,Hedy Devine,HK,Hey
   Look 900.00
2 Venus(c) 550.00
3 Carnival(c) 450.00
4 Cupid(c).HK,Hey Look 475.00
5 Serenade(c) 450.00
6 Wrath of a Goddess,A:Loki . . 400.00
7 The Romance That Could
   Not Be 400.00
8 The Love Trap 400.00
9 Whom the Gods Destroy 400.00
10 B:Scince Fiction/Horror,
   Trapped On the Moon. 450.00
11 The End of the World 550.00
12 GC,The Lost World 400.00
13 BEv,King of the Living Dead. . 600.00
14 BEv,The Fountain of Death . 600.00
15 BEv,The Empty Grave 600.00
16 BEv,Where Gargoyles Dwell . 600.00
17 BEv,Tower of Death,
   Bondage(c). 600.00
18 BEv,Terror in the Tunnel. . . . 600.00
19 BEv,THe Kiss Of Death 600.00

VERY BEST OF
MARVEL COMICS
1-shot reps Marvel Artists
   Favorite Stories 12.95

VIDEO JACK
Nov., 1987
1 KGi,O:Video Jack 2.50
2 KGi. 2.00
3 KGi. 1.75
4 KGi. 1.75
5 KGi. 1.75
6 KGi,NA,BWr,AW. 1.25

VISION, THE
1994–95
1 BHs,mini-series 1.75
2 BHs 1.75
3 BHs 1.75
4 BHs 1.75

Vison & Scarlet Witch #2
© Marvel Entertainment Group

VISION &
SCARLET WITCH
[1st Series] Nov., 1982
1 RL,V:Halloween 2.00
2 RL,V:Isbisa,D:Whizzer 1.50
3 RL,A:Wonderman,V:GrimReaper 1.50
4 RL,A:Magneto,Inhumans 1.50
[2nd Series] 1985–86
1 V:Grim Reaper 2.00
2 V:Lethal Legion,D:Grim Reaper . 1.75
3 V:Salem's Seven 1.75
4 I:Glamor & Illusion 1.75
5 A:Glamor & Illusion. 1.75
6 A:Magneto 1.75
7 V:Toad 1.75
8 A:Powerman. 1.75
9 V:Enchantress 1.75
10 A:Inhumans. 1.75
11 A:Spider-Man. 1.75
12 Birth of V&S's Child 1.25

VISIONARIES
Star Nov., 1987
1 thru 5 . . . . @1.00
6 Sept. 1988 . . . . 1.00

VOID INDIGO
Epic Nov., 1984
1 VM,Epic Comics 2.00
2 VM,Epic Comics,March, 1985. . . 2.00

WACKY DUCK
See: DOPEY DUCK

WALLY THE WIZARD
Star April, 1985
1 . . . .
. . . . 1.25
2 thru 11 . . . . @1.00
12 March, 1986. . . . . 1.00

WAR, THE
1989
1 Sequel to The Draft & The Pit . . 3.50
2 . . . . 3.50
3 . . . . 3.50
4 1990. 3.50

WAR ACTION
Atlas April, 1952
1 JMn,RH,War Stories, Six Dead
   Men 125.00
2 . . . . 75.00
3 Invasion in Korea 50.00
4 thru 10 . . . . @50.00
11 . . . . 65.00
12 . . . . 65.00
13 BK. 65.00
14 Rangers Strike,June, 1953. . . . 55.00

WAR ADVENTURES
Atlas Jan., 1952
1 GT,Battle Fatigue 100.00
2 The Story of a Slaughter 50.00
3 JRo 40.00
4 RH(c) 40.00
5 RH,Violent(c) 40.00
6 Stand or Die 40.00
7 JMn(c) 40.00
8 BK 70.00
9 RH(c) 30.00
10 JRo(c),Attack at Dawn 30.00
11 Red Trap 30.00
12 . . . . 30.00
13 RH(c),The Commies Strike
   Feb., 1953 . . . . 30.00

WAR COMBAT
Atlas March, 1952
1 JMn,Death of Platoon Leader . 100.00
2 . . . . 50.00
3 JMn(c) 35.00
4 JMn(c) 35.00
5 The Red Hordes 35.00
Becomes:

COMBAT CASEY
6 BEv,Combat Casey cont 100.00
7 . . . . 75.00
8 JMn(c) 50.00
9 . . . . 45.00
10 RH(c). 75.00
11 & 12 . . . . @40.00
13 thru 19 . . . . @75.00
20 . . . . 40.00
21 thru 33 . . . . @35.00
34 July, 1957 . . . . 35.00

WAR COMICS
Atlas Dec., 1950
1 You Only Die Twice 175.00
2 Infantry's War 100.00
3 . . . . 75.00
4 GC,The General Said Nuts . . . 75.00
5 . . . . 75.00
6 The Deadly Decision of
   General Kwang 75.00
7 RH 75.00
8 RH,No Survivors 75.00
9 RH 75.00
10 . . . . 75.00
11 thru 21 . . . . @50.00
22. . . . . 65.00
23 thru 37 . . . . @40.00
38 JKu 50.00
39 . . . . 40.00
40 . . . . 40.00
41 . . . . 40.00
42 . . . . 40.00
43 AT 50.00
44 . . . . 40.00
45 . . . . 40.00
46 RC. 55.00
47 . . . . 40.00
48 . . . . 40.00
49 Sept., 1957 . . . . 55.00

WARHEADS
Marvel UK 1992–93
1 GEr,I:Warheads,A:Wolverine, . . . 2.25
2 GEr,V:Nick Fury 2.00
3 DTy,A:Iron Man. 2.00
4 SCy,A:X-Force 2.00
5 A:X-Force,C:Deaths'Head II 2.00
6 SCy,A:Death's Head II 2.00
7 SCy,A:Death's Head II,S.Surfer. . 2.00
8 SCy,V:Mephisto 2.00
9 SCy,V:Mephisto 2.00
10 JCz,V:Mephisto 2.00
11 A:Death's Head II. 2.00
12 V:Mechanix 2.00
13 Xenophiles Reptiles. 2.00
14 last issue. 2.00

WARHEADS: BLACK DAWN
1 A:Gh.Rider,Morbius 3.25
2 V:Dracula 2.00

WAR IS HELL
Jan., 1973—Oct., 1975
1 B:Reprints,Decision at Dawn . . 15.00
2 Anytime,Anyplace,War is Hell . . 9.00
3 Retreat or Die 9.00
4 Live Grenade 9.00
5 Trapped Platoon 9.00
6 We Die at Dawn 9.00
7 While the Jungle Sleeps,A:Sgt
    Fury 9.00
8 Killed in Action,A;Sgt Fury 9.00
9 B:Supernatural,War Stories . . . 20.00
10 Death is a 30 Ton Tank 10.00
11 thru 15 . . . . @10.00

WARLOCK
[1st Regular Series] Aug., 1972
1 GK,I:Counter Earth,A:High
    Evolutionary 15.00
2 JB,TS,V:Man Beast 7.00
3 GK,TS,V:Apollo 6.00
4 JK,TS,V:Triax 5.00
5 GK,TS,V:Dr.Doom 5.00
6 TS(i),O:Brute 5.00
7 TS(i),V:Brute,D:Dr.Doom. 5.00
8 TS(i),R:Man-Beast(cont
    in Hulk #176) 5.00
9 JSn,1st`Rebirth'Thanos,O:Magnus,
    N:Warlock,I:In-Betweener 8.00

Warlock #5
© Marvel Entertainment Group

10 JSn,SL,O:Thanos,V:Magus,
    A:In-Betweener. 15.00
11 JSn,SL,D:Magus,A:Thanos,
    In-Betweener. 10.00
12 JSn,SL,O:Pip,V:Pro-Boscis
    A:Starfox 9.00
13 JSn,SL,I&O:Star-Thief 9.00
14 JSn,SL,V:Star-Thief 9.00
15 JSn,A:Thanos,V:Soul-Gem . . . 15.00

[2nd Regular Series] 1992
1 JSn,rep.Strange Tales #178-180
    Baxter Paper 4.00
2 JSn,rep.Strange Tales #180
    & Warlock #9 . . . . 2.50
3 JSn,rep.Warlock #10-#12 . . . . . 2.50
4 JSn,rep.Warlock #13-#15 . . . . . 2.50
5 JSn,rep.Warlock #15 . . . . 2.50
6 JSn,rep. 2.50

WARLOCK
[Limited Series]
1 Rep.Warlock Series 3.50
2 Rep.Warlock Series 3.00
3 Rep.Warlock Series 3.00
4 Rep.Warlock Series 3.00
5 Rep.Warlock Series 3.00
6 Rep.Warlock Series 3.00

WARLOCK
Sept. 1998
1 (of 4) TL,RJn,R:Adam Warlock . . 3.00
2 TL,murderer revealed 3.00
3 TL,V:Drax 3.00
4 TL,Concl. 3.00

WARLOCK
Aug. 1999
1 LSi,PFe,Marvel Tech. 2.00
2 LSi,PFe,A:Iron Man 2.00
2a variant PFe cover 2.00

WARLOCK AND THE INFINITY WATCH
1992–95
1 AMe, Trial of the Gods(from
    Infinity Gauntlet) 3.00
2 AMe,I:Infinity Watch(Gamora,Pip,
    Moondragon,Drax & 1 other) . . 2.75
3 RL,TA,A:High Evolutionary,
    Nobilus,I:Omega. 2.75
4 RL,TA,V:Omega 2.50
5 AMe,TA,V:Omega. 2.50
6 AMe,V:Omega(Man-Beast) 2.50
7 TR,TA,V:Mole Man,A:Thanos . . . 2.50
8 TR,TA,Infinity War,A:Thanos . . . 2.25
9 AMe,TA,Inf.War,O:Gamora 2.00
10 AMe,Inf.War,Thanos vs
    Doppleganger. 2.50
11 O:Pip,Gamora,Drax,M'dragon . . 2.00
12 TR,Drax Vs.Hulk 2.00
13 TR,Drax vs Hulk 2.00
14 AMe,V:United Nations 2.00
15 AMe,Magnus,Him 2.00
16 TGr,I:Count Abyss 2.00
17 TGr,I:Maxam 2.00
18 AMe,Inf.Crusade,N:Pip 2.00
19 TGr,A:Hulk,Wolverine,Infinity
    Crusade 2.00
20 AMe,Inf.Crusade 2.00
21 V:Thor 2.00
22 AMe,Infinity Crusade 2.00
23 JSn(s),TGb,Blood &
    Thunder#4 . . . . 2.00
24 JSn(s),TGb,V:Geirrodur 2.00
25 JSn(s),AMe,Die-Cut(c),Blood &
    Thunder #12. . . . . 3.25
26 A:Avengers 2.00

Warlock and the Infinity Watch #3
© Marvel Entertainment Group

27 TGb,V:Avengers 2.00
28 TGb,V:Man-Beast 2.00
29 A:Maya 2.25
30 PO 2.25
31 . . . . 1.95
32 Heart & Soul 1.95
33 V:Count Abyss. 1.95
34 V:Count Abyss. 1.95
35 V:Tyrannus 1.95
36 . . . . 1.95
37 A:Zaharius. 1.95
38 . . . . 1.95
39 V:Domitron 1.95
40 A:Thanos. 1.95
41 Monster Island. 1.95
42 Warlock vs. Maxam, Atlantis
    Rising, final issue 1.95

WARLOCK CHRONICLES
1993–94
1 TR,F:Adam Warlock,holo-grafx(c),
    I:Darklore,Meer'lyn 3.25
2 TR,Infinity Crusade,Thanos revealed
    to have the Reality Gem 2.25
3 TR,A:Mephisto 2.25
4 TR,A:Magnus 2.25
5 TR(c),Inf.Crusade 2.25
6 TR,Blood & Thunder,pt.#3 . . . . 2.25
7 TR,Blood & Thunder,pt.#7 . . . . 2.25
8 TR,Blood & Thunder,pt.#11. . . . 2.25
9 TR 2.00
10 TR. 2.00
11 TR. 2.00

WAR MACHINE
1994–96
1 GG,Foil Embossed(c),B:LKa&StB,
    O:War Machine,V:Cable,
    C:Deathlok 3.25
1a Newstand Ed. 2.25
2 GG,V:Cable,Deathlok,w/card . . 1.75
3 GG,V:Cable,Deathlok 1.75
4 GG,C:Force Works 1.75
5 GG,I:Deachtoll 1.50
6 GG,V:Deathtoll 1.50
7 GG,A:Hawkeye. 1.50
8 reg ed. 1.50
8a neon(c),w/insert print 3.00
9 Hands of Mandarin,pt.2 . . . . . . 1.50
10 Hands of Mandarin,pt.5 . . . . . . 1.50
11 X-Mas Party. 1.50
12 V:Terror Device 1.50
13 V:The Rush Team 1.50

MARVEL

14 A:Force Works. 1.50
15 In The Past of WWII 2.50
16 DAn,A:Rick Fury,Cap.America . . 1.50
17 The Man Who Won WWII 1.50
18 DAn,N:War Machine 1.50
19 DAn,A:Hawkeye 1.50
20 DAn,The Crossing 1.50
21 DAn,The Crossing 1.50
22 DAn,V:Iron Man. 1.50
23 DAn,Avengers:Timeslide 1.50

WAR MAN
Epic 1993
1 thru 2 CDi(s). 2.50

WEAPON X
1995
1 Wolverine After Xavier 3.00
2 Full Scale War 2.25
3 Jean Leaves. 2.00
4 F:Gateway 2.00
TPB Rep.#1-#4. . . . . 8.95

WEAVEWORLD
Epic 1991–92
1 MM, Clive Barker adaptation. . . . 4.95
2 MM,`Into the Weave'. 4.95
3 MM. 4.95

WEB OF
SCARLET SPIDER
1995–96
1 TDF,Virtual Mortality,pt.1 . . . . . . 1.95
2 TDF,CyberWar,pt.2 . . . . 1.95
3 Nightmare in Scarlet,pt.1 . . . . . . 1.95
4 Nightmare in Scarlet,pt.3 . . . . . . 1.95

WEB OF SPIDER-MAN
April, 1985
1 JM,V:New Costume 15.00
2 JM,V:Vulture. 8.00
3 JM,V:Vulture. 6.00
4 JM,JBy,V:Dr.Octopus 5.00
5 JM,JBy,V:Dr.Octopus 5.00
6 MZ,BL,JM,Secret Wars II 5.00
7 SB,A:Hulk,V:Nightmare,
   C:Wolverine 5.00
8 V:Smithville Thunder. 5.00
9 V:Smithville Thunder. 5.00
10 JM,A:Dominic Fortune,
   V:Shocker 5.00
11 BMc,V:Thugs. 5.00
12 BMc,SB,V:Thugs 5.00
13 BMc,V:J.JonahJameson. 5.00
14 KB,V:Black Fox 5.00
15 V:Black Fox,I:Chance 4.00
16 MS,KB,V:Magma 4.00
17 MS,V:Magma. 4.00
18 MS,KB,Where is Spider-Man? . . 4.00
19 MS,BMc,I:Solo,Humbug. 4.00
20 MS,V:Terrorists 4.00
21 V:Fake Spider-Man 4.00
22 MS,V:Terrorists 4.00
23 V:Slyde 4.00
24 SB,V:Vulture,Hobgoblin 4.00
25 V:Aliens. 4.00
26 V:Thugs. 4.00
27 V:Headhunter 4.00
28 BL,V:Thugs 4.00
29 A:Wolverine,2nd App:New
   Hobgoblin. 9.00
30 KB,O:Rose,C:Daredevil,Capt.
   America,Wolverine,Punisher. . . 7.00
31 MZ,BMc,V:Kraven 6.00
32 MZ,BMc,V:Kraven 6.00
33 BSz(c),SL,V:Kingpin,Mad

Dog Ward,pt.#1 . . . . 4.00
34 SB,A:Watcher 4.00
35 AS,V:Living Brain. 4.00
36 AS,V:Phreak Out,I:Tombstone . 5.00
37 V:Slasher. 5.00
38 AS,A:Tombstone,V:Hobgoblin . . 5.00
39 AS,V:Looter(Meteor Man) 4.00
40 AS,V:Cult of Love 4.00
41 AS,V:Cult of Love 4.00
42 AS,V:Cult of Love 4.00
43 AS,V:Cult of Love 4.00
44 AS,V:Warzone,A:Hulk 3.00
45 AS,V:Vulture 3.00
46 A:Dr.Pym,V:Nekra 3.00
47 AS,V:Hobgoblin 4.00
48 AS,O:New Hobgoblin's Demonic
   Power 11.00
49 VM,V:Drugs. 3.00
50 AS,V:Chameleon(double size) . . 5.00
51 MBa,V:Chameleon,Lobo Bros. . . 3.00
52 FS,JR,O:J.Jonah Jameson
   V:Chameleon 3.00
53 MBa,V:Lobo Bros.,C:Punisher
   A:Chameleon 3.00
54 AS,V:Chameleon,V:Lobo Bros. . 3.00
55 AS,V:Chameleon,Hammerhead,
   V:Lobo Bros. 3.00
56 AS,I&O:Skin Head,
   A:Rocket Racer 3.00
57 AS,D:SkinHead,
   A:Rocket Racer 3.00
58 AS,V:Grizzly 3.00
59 AS,Acts of Vengeance,V:Titania
   A:Puma,Cosmic Spider-Man. . . 5.00
60 AS,A of V,V:Goliath 3.00
61 AS,A of V,V:Dragon Man 3.00
62 AS,V:Molten Man. 2.00
63 AS,V:Mister Fear 2.00
64 AS,V:Graviton,Titania,Trapster. . 2.00
65 AS,V:Goliath,Trapster,Graviton. . 2.00
66 AS,V:Tombstone,A:G.Goblin . . . 2.50
67 AS,A:GreenGoblin,
   V:Tombstone 2.50
68 AS,A:GreenGoblin,
   V:Tombstone 2.50
69 AS,V:Hulk 2.50
70 AS,I:The Spider/Hulk. 2.50
71 A:Silver Sable 2.00
72 AM,A:Silver Sable 2.00
73 AS,A:Human Torch,
   Colossus,Namor. 2.00
74 AS,I:Spark,V:Bora 2.00
75 AS,C:New Warriors 2.00
76 AS,Spidey in Ice 2.00

Web of Spider-Man #2
© Marvel Entertainment Group

77 AS,V:Firebrand,Inheritor. 2.00
78 AS,A:Firebrand,Cloak&Dagger. . 2.00
79 AS,V:Silvermane 2.00
80 AS,V:Silvermane 2.00
81 I:Bloodshed 2.00
82 V:Man Mountain Marko 2.00
83 V:A.I.M. Supersuit 2.00
84 AS,B:Name of the Rose. 2.50
85 AS,Name of the Rose 2.00
86 AS,I:Demogoblin. 2.50
87 AS,I:Praetorian Guard 2.00
88 AS,Name of the Rose 2.00
89 AS,E:Name of the Rose,
   I:Bloodrose. 2.00
90 AS,30th Ann.,w/hologram,
   polybagged,V:Mysterio 3.00
90a Gold 2nd printing. 2.50
91 AS,V:Whisper And Pulse 2.00
92 AS,V:Foreigner 2.00
93 AS,BMc,V:Hobgoblin,A:Moon
   Knight,Foreigner. 2.00
94 AS,V:Hobgoblin,A:MoonKnight. . 2.00
95 AS,Spirits of Venom#1,A:Venom,
   J.Blaze,GR,V:Hag & Troll 2.50
96 AS,Spirits of Venom#3, A:G.R,
   J.Blaze,Venom,Hobgoblin. 2.00
97 AS,I:Dr.Trench,V:Bloodrose . . . 2.00
98 AS,V:Bloodrose,Foreigner 2.00
99 I:Night Watch,V:New Enforcer . . 2.00
100 AS,JRu,V:Enforcers,Bloodrose,
   Kingpin(Alfredo),I:Spider Armor,
   O:Night Watch,Holografx(c) . . . 4.00
101 AS,Total Carnage:V:Carnage,
   Shriek,A:Cloak and Dagger,
   Venom 2.00
102 Total Carnage#6,V:Carnage,
   A:Venom,Morbius. 2.00
103 AS,Maximum Carnage#10,
   V:Carnage 2.00
104 AS,Infinity Crusade 2.00
105 AS,Infinity Crusade 2.00
106 AS,Infinity Crusade 2.00
107 AS,A:Sandman,Quicksand. . . . 2.00
108 B:TKa(s),AS,I:Sandstorm,
   BU:Cardiac. 2.00
109 AS,V:Shocker,A:Night Thrasher,
   BU:D:Calypso. 2.00
110 AS,I:Warrant,A:Lizard. 2.00
111 AS,V:Warrant,Lizard. 2.00
112 AS,Pursuit#3,V:Chameleon,
   w/card 2.00
113 AS,A:Gambit,Black Cat,w/cel . . 3.50
113a Newsstand Ed. 2.00
114 AS 2.00
115 AS,V:Facade 2.00
116 AS,V:Facade 2.00
117 Foil(c), flip book with
   Power & Responsibility #1 . . . . 5.00
117a Newsstand ed. 2.00
118 Spider-clone, V:Venom. 3.00
119 Clone,V:Venom 2.50
119a bagged with Milestone rep.
   Amazing Sp-Man #150,checklist 6.50
120 Web of Life,pt.1 . . . . 2.50
121 Web of Life,pt.3 . . . . 2.50
122 Smoke and Mirrors,pt.1 . . . . . 2.50
123 The Price of Truth,pt.2. . . . . . 1.50
124 The Mark of Kaine,pt.1. . . . . . 1.50
125 R:Gwen Stacy 3.00
125a 3-D Holodisk cover 4.25
126 The Trial of Peter Parker,pt.1 . . 2.00
127 Maximum Clonage,pt.2 . . . . . . 2.00
128 TDF,Exiled,pt.1 . . . . 2.00
129 Timebomb,pt.2. . . . . 2.00
Ann.#1 V:Future Max 6.00
Ann.#2 AAd,MMi,A:Warlock 8.00
Ann.#3 AS,DP,JRu,JM,BL. 4.50
Ann.#4 AS,TM,RLm,Evolutionary
   Wars,A:Man Thing,V:Slug. 5.00
Ann.#5 AS,SD,JS,Atlantis
   Attacks,A:Fantastic Four. 3.50

Ann.#6 SD,JBr,SB,A:Punisher 4.50
Ann.#7 Vibranium Vendetta #3 . . . . 2.50
Ann.#8 Hero Killers#3,A:New
　Warriors,BU:Venom,Black Cat . 3.00
Ann.#9 CMa,I:Cadre,w/card 3.25
Ann.#10 V:Shriek 3.75
Super Size Spec.#1 Planet of
　the Symbiotes,pt.5 . . . . 3.95

WEBSPINNERS: TALES OF SPIDER-MAN
Nov. 1998

1 JMD,JR,MZi,A:Mysterio,seq.to
　Amaz.Sp-M#38, 48-page 3.00
1a signed 19.63
2 JMD,JR,V:J.Jonah Jameson 2.50
2a variant SR cover 2.50
3 JMD,V:Mysterio, concl 2.50
4 KG,ErS,seq.to Silver Surfer#18 . . 2.50
5 KG,ErS,A:Silver Surfer 2.50
6 KG,ErS,F:Silver Surfer,
　Psycho-Man & Annihilus 2.50
7 BS,MPn,V:Sandman 2.50
8 BS,MPn,V:Sandman 2.50
9 V:Sandman 2.50
10 V:Chameleon, pt.1 . . . . 2.50

WEIRD WONDERTALES
Dec., 1973

1 B:Reprints 15.00
2 I Was Kidnapped by a Flying
　Saucer 10.00
3 The Thing in the Bog 10.00
4 It Lurks Behind the Wall 10.00
5 . . . . 10.00
6 The Man Who Owned a Ghost . 10.00
7 The Apes That Walked
　like Men 10.00
8 Reap A Deadly Harvest 10.00
9 The Murder Mirror 10.00
10 Mister Morgans Monster 10.00
11 Slaughter in Shrangri-La 8.00
12 The Stars Scream Murder 8.00
13 The Totem Strikes 8.00
14 Witching Circle 8.00
15 . . . . 8.00
16 The Shark 8.00
17 Creature From Krogarr 8.00
18 Krang 8.00
19 A:Dr Druid 8.00
20 The Madness 8.00
21 A:Dr Druid 8.00

Weird Wonder Tales #20
© Marvel Entertainment Group

22 The World Below,May, 1975 . . . . 8.00

WEREWOLF BY NIGHT
Sept., 1972

1 MP(cont from Marvel Spotlight)
　FullMoonRise..WerewolfKill . . . 50.00
2 MP,Like a Wild Beast at Bay . . . 20.00
3 MP,Mystery of the Mad Monk . . 13.00
4 MP,The Danger Game 13.00
5 MP,A Life for a Death 13.00
6 MP,Carnival of Fear 10.00
7 MP,JM,Ritual of Blood 8.00
8 MP,Krogg,Lurker from Beyond . . 8.00
9 TS,V:Tatterdemalion 8.00
10 TS,bondage cover 8.00
11 GK,TS,Full Moon..Fear Moon . . 6.00
12 GK,Cry Monster 6.00
13 MP,ManMonsterCalledTaboo . . . 5.00
14 MP,Lo,the Monster Strikes 5.00
15 MP,(new)O:Werewolf,
　V:Dracula 12.00
16 MP,TS,A:Hunchback of Notre
　Dame 5.00
17 Behold the Behemoth 5.00
18 War of the Werewolves 5.00
19 V:Dracula 7.00
20 The Monster Breaks Free 5.00
21 GK(c),To Cure a Werewolf 4.00
22 GK(c),Face of a Friend 4.00
23 Silver Bullet for a Werewolf 4.00
24 GK(c),V:The Brute 4.00
25 GK(c),Eclipse of Evil 4.00
26 GK(c),A Crusade of Murder 4.00
27 GK(c),Scourge o/t Soul-Beast . . 4.00
28 GK(c),V:Dr.Glitternight 4.00
29 GK(c),V:Dr.Glitternight 4.00
30 GK(c),Red Slash across
　Midnight 4.00
31 Death in White 4.00
32 I&O:Moon Knight 65.00
33 Were-Beast..Moon Knight
　A:Moon Knight(2nd App) 30.00
34 GK(c),TS,House of Evil..House
　of Death 4.00
35 TS,JS,BWi,Jack Russell vs.
　Werewolf 4.00
36 Images of Death 4.00
37 BWr(c),BW,A:Moon Knight,
　Hangman,Dr.Glitternight 7.00
38 . . . . 3.50
39 V:Brother Voodoo 3.50
40 A:Brother Voodoo,V:Dr.
　Glitternight 3.50
41 V:Fire Eyes 3.50
42 A:IronMan,Birth of a Monster . . 3.50
43 Tri-Animal Lives,A:Iron Man 3.50
G-Size#2,SD,A:Frankenstein
　Monster (reprint) 3.00
G-Size#3 GK(c),Transylvania 3.50
G-Size#4 GK(c),A:Morbius 10.00
G-Size#5 GK(c),Peril of
　Paingloss 3.00

WEREWOLF BY NIGHT
Dec., 1997

1 PJe,F:Jack Russell returns 3.00
2 PJe,Search for wolf Amulet 3.00
3 PJe,Stuck between man & wolf. . . 3.00
4 PJe,to the depths of hell 3.00
5 PJe, confronts demon 3.00
6 PJe, visit Underworld nightclub . . 3.00
Storyline continues in Strange Tales

WEST COAST AVENGERS
[Limited Series] Sept., 1984

1 BH,A:Shroud,J:Hawkeye,IronMan,
　WonderMan,Mockingbird,Tigra . 4.00
2 BH,V:Blank 3.00

West Coast Avengers #1
© Marvel Entertainment Group

3 BH,V:Graviton 2.00
4 BH,V:Graviton 2.00

[Regular Series] 1985–89

1 AM,JSt,V:Lethal Legion 4.00
2 AM,JSt,V:Lethal Legion 3.00
3 AM,JSt,V:Kraven 3.00
4 AM,JSt,A:Firebird,Thing,I:Master
　Pandemonium 3.00
5 AM,JSt,A:Werewolf,Thing 3.00
6 AM,KB,A:Thing 3.00
7 AM,JSt,V:Ultron 3.00
8 AM,JSt,V:Rangers,A:Thing 3.00
9 AM,JSt,V:Master Pandemonium . 3.00
10 AM,JSt,V:Headlok,Griffen 3.00
11 AM,JSt,A:Nick Fury 2.50
12 AM,JSt,V:Graviton 2.50
13 AM,JSt,V:Graviton 2.50
14 AM,JSt,V:Pandemonium 2.50
15 AM,JSt,A:Hellcat 2.50
16 AM,JSt,V:Tiger Shark,
　Whirlwind 2.50
17 AM,JSt,V:Dominus' Minions 2.50
18 AM,JSt,V:The Wild West 2.50
19 AM,JSt,A:Two Gun Kid 2.50
20 AM,JSt,A:Rawhide Kid 2.50
21 AM,JSt,A:Dr.Pym,Moon Knight . 2.50
22 AM,JSt,A:Fant.Four,Dr.Strange,
　Night Rider 2.00
23 AM,RT,A:Phantom Rider 2.00
24 AM,V:Dominus 2.00
25 AM,V:Abomination 2.00
26 AM,V:Zodiac 2.00
27 AM,V:Zodiac 1.75
28 AM,V:Zodiac 1.75
29 AM,V:Taurus,A:Shroud 1.75
30 AM,C:Composite Avenger 1.75
31 AM,V:Arkon 1.75
32 AM,TD,V:Yetrigar,J:Wasp 1.75
33 AM,O:Ant-Man,Wasp;
　V:Madam X,El Toro 1.75
34 AM,V:Quicksilver,J:Vision &
　Scarlet Witch 1.75
35 AM,V:Dr.Doom,Quicksilver 1.75
36 AM,V:The Voice 1.75
37 V:The Voice,A:Mantis 1.75
38 AM,TMo,V:Defiler 1.50
39 AM,V:Swordsman 1.50
40 AM,MGu,V:NightShift,
　A:Shroud 1.50
41 TMo,I:New Phantom Rider,
　L:Moon Knight 1.50
42 JBy,Visionquest#1,V:Ultron 2.50
43 JBy,Visionquest#2, ... 2.25
44 JBy,Visionquest#3,J:USAgent . . 2.00

45 JBy,Visionquest#4,	
I:New Vision 2.25	
46 JBy,I:Great Lakes Avengers. . . . 2.00	
Ann. #1 MBr,GI,V:Zodiak 2.25	
Ann. #2 AM,A:SilverSurfer,V:Death,	
Collector,R:Grandmaster 2.00	
Ann. #3 AM,RLm,TD,Evolutionary	
Wars,R:Giant Man 3.50	

Becomes:

AVENGERS WEST COAST

WESTERN GUNFIGHTERS
[2nd series] August, 1970
1 JK,JB,DAy,B:Ghost Rider
A:Fort Rango,The Renegades
Gunhawk 12.00
2 HT(c),DAy,JMn,O:Nightwind,
V:Tarantula 7.00
3 DAy,V:Hurricane(reprint) 7.00
4 HT(c),DAy,TS,B:Gunhawk,
Apache Kid,A;Renegades 7.00
5 DAy,FrG,A:Renegades 7.00
6 HT(c),DAy,SSh,Death of
Ghost Rider 8.00
7 HT(c),DAy,SSh,O:Ghost Rider
retold,E:Ghost Rider,Gunhawk 10.00
8 DAy,SSh,B:Black Rider,Outlaw
Kid(rep) 6.00
9 DW,Revenge rides the Range. . . 6.00
10 JK,JMn,O:Black Rider,B:Matt
Slade,E:Outlaw Kid 6.00
11 JK,Duel at Dawn 6.00
12 JMn,O:Matt Slade 6.00
13 Save the Gold Coast Expires. . . 6.00
14 JSo(c),Outlaw Town 6.00
15 E:Matt Slade,Showdown in
Outlaw Canyon. 6.00
16 B:Kid Colt,Shoot-out in Silver
City 6.00
17 thru 20 . . . . @6.00
21 thru 24 . . . . @5.00
25 . . . . 5.00
26 F:Kid Colt,Gun-Slinger,Apache
Kid 5.00
27 thru 32 . . . . @5.00
33 Nov., 1975 . . . . 5.00

WESTERN KID
[1st Series] Dec., 1954
1 JR,B:Western Kid,O:Western Kid
(Tex Dawson) 150.00
2 JMn,JR,Western Adventure . . . 75.00
3 JMn(c),JR,Gunfight(c) 60.00
4 JMn(c),JR,The Badlands 60.00
5 JR 60.00
6 JR 60.00
7 JR 60.00
8 JR 60.00
9 JR,AW 75.00
10 JR,AW,Man in the Middle. 75.00
11 thru 16 . . . . @50.00
17 August, 1957 . . . . 50.00

[2nd Series] Dec., 1971–Aug. 1972
1 Reprints 10.00
2 . . . . 7.00
3 . . . . 7.00
4 . . . . 7.00
5 . . . . 7.00

WESTERN OUTLAWS
Atlas Feb., 1954—Aug., 1957
1 JMn(c),RH,BP,The Greenville
Gallows,Hanging(c) 125.00
2 . . . . 65.00
3 thru 10 . . . . @50.00
11 AW 50.00

12 . . . . 45.00	
13 MB 50.00	
14 AW 55.00	
15 AT,GT 50.00	
16 BP 40.00	
17 . . . . 45.00	
18 . . . . 40.00	
19 . . . . 50.00	
20 and 21 . . . . @45.00	

WESTERN OUTLAWS & SHERIFFS
See: BEST WESTERN

WESTERN TALES OF BLACK RIDER
See: ALL WINNERS COMICS

WESTERN TEAM-UP
Nov., 1973
1 Rawhide Kid/Dakota Kid 2.00

WESTERN THRILLERS
Nov., 1954
1 JMn,Western tales 100.00
2 . . . . 50.00
3 . . . . 50.00
4 . . . . 50.00
Becomes:

COWBOY ACTION
5 JMn(c),The Prairie Kid 60.00
6 . . . . 40.00
7 . . . . 40.00
9 . . . . 40.00
10 . . . . 40.00
11 MN,AW,Ther Manhunter March,
1956. 60.00
Becomes:

QUICK-TRIGGER WESTERN
12 Bill Larson Strikes 75.00
13 The Man From Cheyenne 85.00
14 BEv,RH(c) 60.00
15 AT 50.00
16 JK 45.00
17 GT. 45.00
18 GM 45.00
19 JSe 40.00

WESTERN WINNERS
See: ALL WINNERS COMICS

WHAT IF?
[1st Regular Series] Feb., 1977
1 Spider-Man joined Fant.Four. . . 18.00
2 GK(c),Hulk had Banner brain . . 9.00
3 GK,KJ,F:Avengers 6.00
4 GK(c),F:Invaders 6.00
5 F:Captain America 6.00
6 F:Fantastic Four 6.00
7 GK(c),F:Spider-Man 6.00
8 GK(c),F:Daredevil. 5.50
9 JK(c),F:Avengers of the '50s. . . 6.00
10 JB,F:Thor 5.00
11 JK,F:FantasticFour. 5.00
12 F:Hulk 5.00
13 JB,Conan Alive Today 6.00
14 F:Sgt. Fury 5.00
15 CI,F:Nova 5.00

What If #13
© Marvel Entertainment Group

16 F:Master of Kung Fu 5.00
17 CI,F:Ghost Rider 5.00
18 TS,F:Dr.Strange. 4.00
19 PB,F:Spider-Man 5.00
20 F:Avengers 4.00
21 GC,F:Sub-Mariner 4.00
22 F:Dr.Doom. 4.00
23 JB,F:Hulk. 4.00
24 GK,RB,Gwen Stacy had lived . . 5.00
25 F:Thor,Avengers,O:Mentor. . . . 4.00
26 JBy(c),F:Captain America 4.00
27 FM(c),Phoenix hadn't died 7.00
28 FM,F:Daredevil,Ghost Rider. . . . 6.00
29 MG(c),F:Avengers 4.00
30 RB,F:Spider-Man 10.00
31 Wolverine killed the Hulk 15.00
32 Avengers lost to Korvac. 3.50
33 BL,Dazzler herald of Galactus . . 3.50
34 FH,FM,JBy,BSz:Humor issue. . . 3.50
35 FM,Elektra had lived 6.00
36 JBy,Fant.Four had no powers . . 3.00
37 F:Thing,Beast,Silver Surfer 3.50
38 F:Daredevil,Captain America . . . 3.00
39 Thor had fought Conan 3.00
40 F:Dr.Strange 3.00
41 F:Sub-Mariner 3.50
42 F:Fantastic Four 3.00
43 F:Conan 3.00
44 F:Captain America 3.00
45 F:Hulk,Berserk. 3.50
46 Uncle Ben had lived. 5.00
47 F:Thor,Loki 3.00
Spec.#1 F:Iron Man,Avengers. . . . 4.00
Best of What IF? rep.#1,#24,
#27,#28 . . . . 12.95

[2nd Regular Series]
1 RWi,MG,The Avengers had lost
the Evolutionary War 5.00
2 GCa,Daredevil Killed Kingpin,
A:Hobgoblin, The Rose 4.00
3 Capt.America Hadn't Given Up
Costume,A:Avengers 3.50
4 MBa,Spider-Man kept Black
Costume,A:Avengers,Hulk 4.50
5 Vision Destroyed Avengers,
A:Wonder Man. 3.50
6 RLm,X-Men Lost Inferno,
A:Dr.Strange 6.00
7 RLd,Wolverine Joined Shield,
A:Nick Fury,Black Widow 7.00
8 Iron Man Lost The Armor Wars,
A:Ant Man 3.50
9 RB,New X-Men Died 6.00
10 MZ(c),BMc,Punisher's Family

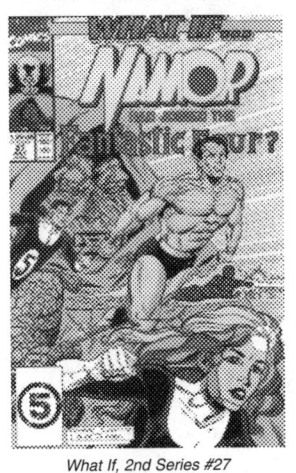

What If, 2nd Series #27
© Marvel Entertainment Group

Didn't Die,A:Kingpin 3.00
11 TM(c),JV,SM,Fant.Four had the
    Same Powers,A:Nick Fury 3.50
12 JV,X-Men Stayed in Asgard,
    A:Thor,Hela 3.00
13 JLe(c),Prof.X Became
    Juggernaut,A:X-Men. 3.50
14 RLm(c),Capt.Marvel didn't die
    A:Silver Surfer 3.00
15 GCa,Fant.Four Lost Trial of
    Galactus,A:Gladiator 3.00
16 Wolverine Battled Conan,
    A:X-Men,Red Sonja 5.00
17 Kraven Killed Spider-Man,
    A:Daredevil,Captain America . . 3.00
18 LMc,Fant.Four fought Dr.Doom
    before they gained powers 2.50
19 RW,Vision took over Earth,
    A:Avengers,Dr.Doom 2.50
20 Spider-Man didn't marry Mary
    Jane,A:Venom,Kraven 3.00
21 Spider-Man married Black Cat,
    A:Vulture,Silver Sable. 2.50
22 RLm,Silver Surfer didn't escape
    Earth,A:F.F,Mephisto,Thanos . . 4.00
23 New X-Men never existed,
    A:Eric the Red,Lilandra. 2.50
24 Wolverine Became Lord of
    Vampires,A:Punisher 3.00
25 Marvel Heroes lost Atlantis
    Attacks,double size 3.25
26 LMc,Punisher Killed Daredevil,
    A:Spider-Man. 2.50
27 Submariner Joined Fantastic
    Four,A:Dr. Doom 2.00
28 RW,Capt.America led Army of
    Super-Soldiers,A:Submariner . . 2.00
29 RW,Capt.America formed the
    Avengers 2.00
30 Inv.Woman's 2nd Child had
    lived,A:Fantastic Four. 2.00
31 Spider-Man/Captain Universe
    Powers. 2.00
32 Phoenix Rose Again,pt.1 . . . . . 2.00
33 Phoenix Rose Again,pt.2 . . . . . 2.00
34 Humor Issue 1.75
35 B:Time Quake,F.F. vs.Dr. Doom
    & Annihilus. 1.75
36 Cosmic Avengers,V:Guardians
    of the Galaxy 1.75
37 X-Vampires,V:Dormammu 1.75
38 Thor was prisoner of Set 1.75
39 E:Time Quake,Watcher saved the
    Universe. 1.75

40 Storm remained A thief? 1.75
41 JV,Avengers fought Galactus . . . 2.00
42 KWe,Spidey kept extra arms 1.75
43 Wolverine married Mariko 1.75
44 Punisher possessedby Venom . . 1.75
45 Barbara Ketch became G.R. . . . 1.75
46 Cable Killed Prof.X,Cyclops &
    Jean Grey 1.75
47 Magneto took over USA. 1.75
48 Daredevil Saved Nuke 1.50
49 Silver Surfer had Inf.Gauntlet? . . 1.50
50 Hulk killed Wolverine 4.00
51 PCu,Punisher is Capt.America . . 1.50
52 BHi,Wolverine led Alpha Flight . . 2.00
53 F:Iron Man,Hulk. 1.50
54 F:Death's Head 1.50
55 LKa(s),Avengers lose G.Storm . . 1.50
56 Avengers lose G.Storm#2 . . . . . 1.50
57 Punisher a member of SHIELD . 1.50
58 Punisher kills SpM 1.50
59 Wolverine lead Alpha Flight 2.00
60 RoR,Scott & Jean's Wedding . . . 1.50
61 Spider-Man's Parents 1.95
62 Woverine vs Weapon X 2.25
63 F:War Machine,Iron Man 1.95
64 Iron Man sold out. 2.25
65 Archangel fell from Grace 1.50
66 Rogue and Thor 1.50
67 Cap.America returns 1.50
68 Captain America story 1.50
69 Stryfe Killed X-Men 1.50
70 Silver Surfer 1.50
71 The Hulk 1.50
72 Parker Killed Burglar 1.50
73 Daredevil,Kingpin. 1.50
74 Sinister Formed X-Men 1.50
75 Gen-X's Blink had lived 1.50
76 Flash Thompson Spider-Man . . . 1.50
77 Legion had killed Magneto 1.50
78 FF had stayed together 1.50
79 Storm had Phoenix's Power. . . . 1.50
80 KGa,Hulk was Cured 1.50
81 Age of Apocalypse didn't end. . . 1.50
82 WML,J.JonahJameson
    adopted Spider-Man. 1.50
83 . . . . 1.50
84 . . . . 1.50
85 Magneto Ruled all mutants 1.50
86 . . . . 1.50
87 . . . . 1.50
88 . . . . 1.50
89 . . . . 1.50
90 . . . . 1.50
91 F:Hulk, nice guy, Banner violent. 1.50
92 F:Cannonball,Husk 1.50
93 F:Wolverine. 1.50
94 JGz,F:Juggernaut 1.50
95 IV,F:Ghost Rider. 1.50
96 CWo,F:Quicksilver, ... 2.00
97 F:Black Knight 2.00
98 F:Nightcrawler & Rogue. 2.00
99 F:Black Cat 2.00
100 IV,KJ,F:Gambit & Rogue, 48pg 3.00
101 ATi,F:Archangel 2.00
102 F:Daredevil's Dad 2.00
103 DaF,F:Captain America 2.00
104 F:Silver Surver,ImpossibleMan. 2.00
105 TDF,RF,F:Spider-Man and
    Mary Jane's Daughter. 25.00
106 TDF,F:X-Men,Gambit
    sentenced to death. 2.00
107 TDF,RF,BSz,F:Thor 2.00
108 TDF,F:The Avengers 2.00
109 TA,F:Fantastic Four 2.00
110 TDF,F:Wolverine 2.00
111 TDF,F:Wolverine. 2.00
112 F:Ka-Zar 2.00
113 F:Iron Man, Dr. Strange 2.00
114 F:Secret Wars, 32-page,
    final issue. 2.50
Minus 1 Spec., AOI, flashback,

F:Bishop. 1.95
TPB Best of What If? 12.95

WHAT THE -?!
[Parodies]
August, 1988
1 . . . . 5.00
2 JBy,JOy,AW, ... 4.00
3 TM, ... 5.00
4 . . . . 3.00
5 EL,JLe,WPo,Wolverine 5.00
6 Wolverine,Punisher. 3.00
7 . . . . 2.50
8 DK 2.50
9 . . . . 1.75
10 JBy,X-Men,Dr.Doom, Cap.
    America 1.75
11 DK,RLd(part) 2.00
12 Conan, F.F.,Wolverine. 1.50
13 Silver Burper,F.F.,Wolverine. . . . 1.50
14 Spittle-Man 1.50
15 Capt.Ultra,Wolverina 1.50
16 Ant Man,Watcher 1.25
17 Wulverean/Pulverizer,Hoagg/
    Spider-Ham,SleepGawker,F.F. . 1.25
18 . . . . 1.25
19 . . . . 1.25
20 Infinity Wart Crossover 1.25
21 Weapon XX,Toast Rider. 1.25
22 F:Echs Farce. 1.25
23 . . . . 1.25
24 Halloween issue 1.25
25 . . . . 1.25
26 Spider-Ham 2099 . . . . 1.25
Summer Spec. 2.50
Fall Spec. 2.50

WHERE CREATURES ROAM
July, 1970—Sept., 1971
1 JK,SD,DAy,B:Reprints
    The Brute That Walks. 25.00
2 JK,SD,Midnight/Monster 15.00
3 JK,SD,DAy,Thorg 15.00
4 JK,SD,Vandoom 15.00
5 JK,SD,Gorgilla 15.00
6 JK,SD,Zog 15.00
7 SD 15.00
8 The Mummy's Secret,E:Reprints 15.00

WHERE MONSTERS DWELL
Jan., 1970
1 B:Reprints,Cyclops 25.00
2 Sporr 15.00
3 Grottu 15.00
4 . . . . 15.00
5 Taboo 15.00
6 Groot 15.00
7 Rommbu 15.00
8 The Four-Armed Men 15.00
9 Bumbu 15.00
10 Monster That Walks
    Like A Man. 15.00
11 Gruto 12.00
12 Orogo 12.00
13 The Thing That Crawl 12.00
14 The Green Thing 12.00
15 Kraa- The Inhuman 12.00
16 Beware the Son Of Goom 12.00
17 The Hidden Vampires 12.00
18 The Mask of Morghum. 12.00
19 The Insect Man 12.00
20 Klagg 12.00
21 Fin Fang Foom 12.00
22 Elektro. 12.00
23 The Monster Waits For Me. . . . 12.00

MARVEL

Where Monsters Dwell #31
© Marvel Entertainment Group

24 The Things on Easter Island	12.00
25 The Ruler of the Earth	12.00
26	12.00
27	12.00
28 Droom,The Living Lizard	12.00
29 thru 37 Reprints	@12.00
38 Reprints,Oct., 1975	12.00

WHIP WILSON
See: BLAZE CARSON

WILD
Atlas Feb., 1954

1 BEv,JMn,Charlie Chan Parody	175.00
2 BEv,RH,JMn,Witches(c)	125.00
3 CBu(c),BEv,RH,JMn,	100.00
4 GC,Didja Ever See a Cannon Brawl.	100.00
5 RH,JMn,August, 1954	100.00

WILD CARDS
Epic Sept., 1990

1 JG	5.50
2 JG,V:Jokers	4.50
3 A:Turtle	4.50

WILDC.A.T.S/X-MEN:
THE DARK AGE
Dec., 1997

1-shot MtB,WEI,V:Daemonites & Sentinels, 48pg.	4.50
1a variant cover MGo	4.50

WILD THING
Marvel UK 1993

1 A:Virtual Reality Venom and Carnage.	3.00
2 A:VR Venom and Carnage	2.00
3 A:Shield	2.00
4	2.00
5 Virtual Reality Gangs	2.00
6 Virtual Reality Villians	2.00
7 V:Trask.	2.00
8	1.75
9	1.75
10	1.75
11	1.75

12	1.75
13	1.75

WILD THING
Aug. 1999

1 RLm,AM,LHa,F:Wolverine's daughter Rina	2.00

WILD WEST
Spring, 1948

1 SSh(c),B:Two Gun Kids,Tex Taylor,Arizona Annie	250.00
2 SSh(c),CCb, Captain Tootsie	200.00

Becomes:

WILD WESTERN

3 SSh(c),B:Tex Morgan,Two Gun Kid,Tex Taylor,Arizona Annie	200.00
4 Rh,SSh,CCB,Capt. Tootsie. A:Kid Colt,E:Arizona Annie	150.00
5 RH,CCB,Captain Tootsie A;Black Rider,Blaze Carson	150.00
6 A:Blaze Carson,Kid Colt	100.00
7	100.00
8 RH	100.00
9 Ph(c),B:Black Rider	150.00
10 Ph(c)	175.00
11	100.00
12	80.00
13	80.00
14	80.00
15	90.00
16 thru 20	@75.00
21 thru 29	@70.00
30 JKa	75.00
31 thru 40	@50.00
41 thru 47	@40.00
48 AW	45.00
49 thru 53	@40.00
54 AW	60.00
55 AW	60.00
56 and 57 Sept. 1957	@40.00

WILLIAM SHATNER'S
TEK WORLD
1992–94

1 LS,Novel adapt.	2.25
2 LS,Novel adapt.cont.	2.00
3 LS,Novel adapt.cont.	2.00
4 LS,Novel adapt.cont.	2.00
5 LS,Novel adapt.concludes	2.00

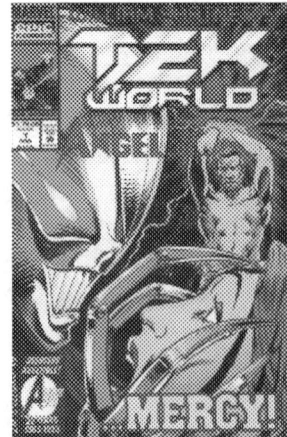

William Shatner's Tek World #7
© Marvel Entertainment Group

6 LS,V:TekLords	2.00
7 E:The Angel	2.00
8	2.00
9	2.00
10	2.00
11 thru 17.	2.00
19 Sims of the Father#1	1.75
20 Sims of the Father#2	1.75
21 Who aren't in Heaven	1.75
22 Father and Guns	1.75
23 We'll be Right Back	2.00
24	1.75

WILLIE COMICS
See: IDEAL COMICS

WILLOW
August, 1988

1 Movie adapt.	1.00
2 Movie adapt.	1.00
3 Movie adapt,Oct., 1988.	1.00

WITNESS, THE
Sept., 1948

1	1,000.00

WOLFPACK
August, 1988

1 I:Wolfpack	1.00
2 thru 11	@1.00
12 July, 1988	1.00

WOLVERINE
[Limited Series] Sept., 1982

1 B:CCl(s),FM,JRu,A:Mariko, I:Shingen	42.00
2 FM,JRu,A:Mariko,I:Yukio.	30.00
3 FM,JRu,A:Mariko,Yukio.	30.00
4 B:CCl(s),FM,JRu,A:Mariko, D:Shingen	32.00

[Regular Series] 1988

1 JB,AW,V:Banipur	25.00
2 JB,KJ,V:Silver Samurai.	12.00
3 JB,AW,V:Silver Samurai	10.00
4 JB,AW,I:Roughouse, Bloodsport	10.00
5 JB,AW,V:Roughouse, Bloodsport	10.00
6 JB,AW,V:Roughouse, Bloodsport	9.00
7 JB,A:Hulk.	8.00
8 JB,A:Hulk	8.00
9 GC,Old Wolverine Story	8.00
10 JB,BSz,V:Sabretooth (1st battle)	22.00
11 JB,BSz,B:Gehenna Stone	7.00
12 JB,BSz,Gehenna Stone	7.00
13 JB,BSz,Gehenna Stone	7.00
14 JB,BSz,Gehenna Stone	7.00
15 JB,BSz,Gehenna Stone	7.00
16 JB,BSz,E:Gehenna Stone	7.00
17 JBy,KJ,V:Roughouse	6.00
18 JBy,KJ,V:Roughouse	6.00
19 JBy,KJ,A of V,I:La Bandera	6.00
20 JBy,KJ,A of V,V:Tigershark.	5.00
21 JBy,KJ,V:Geist.	5.00
22 JBy,KJ,V:Geist,Spore	5.00
23 JBy,KJ,V:Geist,Spore	5.00
24 GC,`Snow Blind'	4.00
25 JB,O:Wolverine(part)	4.00
26 KJ,Return to Japan	4.00
27 thru 30 Lazarus Project	4.00
31 MS,DGr,A:Prince o'Mandripoor	4.00
32 MS,DGr,V:Ninjas	4.00
33 MS,Wolverine in Japan	4.00

Wolverine, Limited Series #1
© *Marvel Entertainment Group*

34 MS,DGr,Wolverine in Canada . . 4.00
35 MS,DGr,A:Puck 4.00
36 MS,DGr,A:Puck,Lady D'strike. . . 4.00
37 MS,DGr,V:Lady Deathstrike 4.00
38 MS,DGr,A:Storm,I:Elsie Dee 4.00
39 MS,DGr,Wolverine Vs. Clone . . . 4.00
40 MS,DGr,Wolverine Vs. Clone . . . 4.00
41 MS,DGr,R:Sabretooth,
    A:Cable 7.00
41a 2nd printing 2.25
42 MS,DGr,A:Sabretooth,Cable 5.00
42a 2nd printing 2.00
43 MS,DGr,A:Sabretooth,C:Cable. . 4.00
44 LSn,DGr 3.00
45 MS,DGr,A:Sabretooth 4.00
46 MS,DGr,A:Sabretooth 4.00
47 V:Tracy 3.00
48 LHa(s),MS,DGr,B:Shiva
    Scenario. 3.00
49 LHa(s),MS,DGr,. 3.00
50 LHa(s),MS,DGr,A:X-Men,Nick Fury,
    I:Shiva,Slash-Die Cut(c) 5.00
51 MS,DGr,A:Mystique,X-Men 2.50
52 MS,DGr,A:Mystique,V:Spiral . . . 2.50
53 MS,A:Mystique,V:Spiral,Mojo . . 2.50
54 A:Shatterstar 2.50
55 MS,V:Cylla,A:Gambit,Sunfire . . . 2.50
56 MS,A:Gambit,Sunfire,V:Hand,
    Hydra. 2.50
57 MS,D:Lady Mariko,A:Gambit . . . 3.00
58 A:Terror 2.00
59 A:Terror 2.00
60 Sabretooth vs.Shiva,
    I:John Wraith 2.50
61 MT,History of Wolverine and
    Sabretooth,A:John Wraith. 2.50
62 MT,A:Sabretooth,Silver Fox 2.00
63 MT,V:Ferro,D:Silver Fox. 2.00
64 MPa,V:Ferro,Sabretooth 2.00
65 MT,A:Professor X. 2.00
66 MT,A:X-Men. 2.00
67 MT,A:X-Men. 2.00
68 MT,V:Epsilon Red 2.00
69 DT,A:Rogue,V:Sauron,tie-in to
    X-Men#300 . . . . 2.00
70 DT,Sauron,A:Rogue,Jubilee 2.00
71 DT,V:Sauron,Brain Child,
    A:Rogue, Jubilee 2.00
72 DT,Sentinels 2.00
73 DT,V:Sentinels 2.00
74 ANi,V:Sentinels 2.00
75 AKu,Hologram(c),Wolv.has
    Bone Claws,leaves X-Men 6.00
76 DT(c),B:LHa(s),A:Deathstrike,
    Vindicator,C:Puck. 2.00

77 AKu,A:Vindicator,Puck,V:Lady
    Deathstrike. 2.00
78 AKu,V:Cylla,Bloodscream 2.00
79 AKu,V:Cyber,I:Zoe Culloden. . . . 2.00
80 IaC,V:Cyber, ... 2.00
81 IaC,V:Cyber,A:Excalibur. 2.00
82 AKu,BMc,A:Yukio,Silver
    Samurai. 2.00
83 AKu,A:Alpha Flight. 2.00
84 A:Alpha Flight 2.00
85 Phalanx Covenant, Final Sanction,
    V:Phalanx,holografx(c) 4.00
85a newsstand ed. 5.00
86 AKu,V:Bloodscream. 2.50
87 AKu,deluxe,V:Juggernaut. 3.00
87a newsstand ed. 2.00
88 AKu,deluxe ed. 3.00
88a newsstand ed. 2.00
89 deluxe ed. 3.00
89a newsstand ed. 1.50
90 V:Sabretooth, deluxe ed. 4.00
90a newsstand ed. 1.50
91 LHa,Logan's future unravels . . . 3.00
92 LHa,AKu,DGr,A:Sabretooth 3.00
93 R:Cyber. 3.00
94 Feral Wolverine 3.00
95 LHa,AKu,DGr,V:Dark Riders . . . 3.00
96 LHa,Aku,DGr,Death of Cyber. . . 3.00
97 LHa,AKu,DGr,A:Genesis 2.50
98 LHa,AKu,F:Genesis 2.50
99 . . . . 2.50
100 LHa,AKu,DG,A:Elektra;double-
    size, Foil Hologram cover 10.00
100a regular edition 4.00
101 LHa,AKu,A:Elektra. 3.00
102 LHa 3.00
103 LHa,Elektra,A:Onslaught 3.00
104 LHa,Gateway, Onslaught 2.00
105 LHa,Gateway, Elektra 2.00
106 LHa 2.00
107 LHa,VS,prologue to Elektra#1 . 2.00
108 LHa,back to Tokyo,A:Yukio. . . . 2.00
109 LHa,DG, ... 2.00
110 LHa,DG,Who's spying on
    Logan. 2.00
111 LHa,DG,Logan moves to NYC . 2.00
112 LHa,DG,Logan in NYC 2.00
113 LHa,R:Ogun,A:Lady Deathstrike
    & Spiral 2.00
114 LHa,back in costume,V:Cyborg
    Donald Pierce 2.00
115 LHa,Zero Tolerance,V:Bastion . 2.00
116 LHa,Zero Tolerance, ... 2.00
117 LHa,Zero Tolerance, V:Prime
    Sentinels 2.00
118 LHa,Zero Tolerance aftermath . 2.00
119 WEI,Pt.1 of 4) 2.00
120 WEI,The White Ghost 2.00
121 WEI,Not Yet Dead, pt.3 . . . . . . 2.00
122 WEI,Not Yet Dead, pt.4 . . . . . . 2.00
123 TDF,DCw,R:Roughouse,
    Bloodscream. 2.00
124 TDF,DCw,A:Captain America,
    V:Rascal 2.00
125 CCl,V:Viper,48pg 8.00
126 CCl,V:Sabretooth. 2.00
127 CCl,Sabretooth takes over. . . . 2.00
128 CCl,V:Hydra, The Hand 2.00
129 TDz,A:Wendigo 2.00
130 TDz,V:Viper. 2.00
131 TDz,V:Viper. 2.00
132 TDz,Halloween in Salem Center
    . . . . 2.00
133 EL,JMs,F:Warbird 2.00
133a variant EL cover (1:4). 2.00
134 EL,JMs,V:Big Apple heroes . . . 2.00
135 EL,JMs,Joins Starjammers. . . . 2.00
136 EL,JMs,on prison planet. 2.00
137 EL,JMs,V:The Collector 2.00
138 EL,JMs,Great Escape concl. . . 2.00
139 EL,A:Cable 2.00

140 EL,Xavier paranoid 2.00
141 EL,Wolverine paranoid. 2.00
142 EL,R:Alpha Flight. 2.00
143 EL,A:Alpha Flight. 2.00
Ann. '97 JOs,V:Volk 3.00
Spec. '95 LHa,F:Nightcrawler 3.95
Minus 1 Spec., LHa,CNn, flashback,
    F:Weapon X 1.95
TPB Wolverine rep Marvel Comics
    Presents #1-#10. . . . . 2.95
Jungle Adventure MMi,(Deluxe) . . . 5.50
SC Acts of Vengeance, rep. 6.95
Bloodlust (one shot),AD
    V:Siberian Were-Creatures. . . . 6.00
Global Jeapordy,PDd(s) 2.95
Killing, KSW,JNR 5.95
Rahne of Terror, C:Cable 8.00
Save the Tiger,rep. 2.95
GNv Bloody ChoicesJB,A:N.Fury . 12.95
Typhoid's Kiss,rep. 6.95
Inner Fury,BSz,V:Nanotech
    Machines 6.25
GN Scorpio Rising, T.U.Fury. 5.95
HC Weapon X 19.95
TPB Triumphs & Tragedies. 16.95
GN Black Rio, 48-page. 6.00
Winter Spec. MWa B&W. 3.00
TPB Not Dead Yet 14.95

WOLVERINE & PUNISHER: DAMAGING EVIDENCE
1993
1 B:CP(s),GEr,A:Kingpin 2.25
2 GEr,A:Kingpin,Sniper 2.25
3 GEr,Last issue 2.25

WOLVERINE: DAYS OF FUTURE PAST
Oct., 1997
1 (of 3) JFM,JoB,JHo, Logan &
    Magneto in far future 2.50
2 JFM,JoB,JHo,with Jubilee. 2.50
3 JFM,JoB,JHo,V:Council of the
    Chosen, concl. 2.50

WOLVERINE: DOOMBRINGER
Nov., 1997
1-shot DgM,JP,F:Silver Samurai . . . 3.00

WOLVERINE ENCYCLOPEDIA
Vol. 1 AKu(c) 48pg. 5.95
Vol. 2 48pg. 5.95
Vol. 3 48pg. 5.95

WOLVERINE/GAMBIT: VICTIMS
1995
1 Takes Place in London 3.00
2 Is Wolverine the Killer? 3.00
3 V:Mastermind 3.00
4 conclusion 3.00

WOLVERINE/PUNISHER: REVELATION
Apr. 1999
1 (of 4) TSg,PtL,Revelation 3.00
1a signed 30.00
2 TSg,PtL,V:Revelation 3.00
3 TSg,PtL,V:Revelation 3.00
4 TsG,PtL,V:Revelation,concl. . . . 3.00

MARVEL

WOLVERINE SAGA
Sept., 1989
1 RLd(c), ... 6.50
2 . . . . 5.00
3 . . . . 5.00
4 Dec., 1989 . . . . 5.00

WONDER DUCK
Sept., 1949
1 Whale(c) 50.00
2 . . . . 33.00
3 March, 1950 . . . . 33.00

WONDERMAN
March, 1986
1 KGa,one-shot special 3.00

Wonder Man #3
© Marvel Entertainment Group

WONDER MAN
Sept., 1991
1 B:GJ(s),JJ,V:Goliath 2.50
2 JJ,A:West Coast Avengers 1.50
3 JJ,V:Abominatrix,I:Spider 1.50
4 JJ,I:Splice,A:Spider. 1.50
5 JJ,A:Beast,V:Rampage. 1.50
6 JJ,A:Beast,V:Rampage. 1.50
7 JJ,Galactic Storm,pt.4,
　A:Hulk & Rich Jones. 1.50
8 JJ,GalacticStorm,pt.11,A:Vision. . 1.50
9 JJ,GalacticStorm,pt.18,A:Vision . 1.50
10 JJ,V:Khmer Rouge. 1.50
11 V:Angkor 1.50
12 V:Angkor 1.50
13 Infinity War 1.50
14 Infinity War,V:Warlock 1.50
15 Inf.War,V:Doppleganger. 1.50
16 JJ,I:Armed Response,
　A:Avengers West Coast 1.50
17 JJ,A:Avengers West Coast. 1.50
18 V:Avengers West Coast. 1.50
19 . . . . 1.50
20 V:Splice,Rampage. 1.50
21 V:Splice,Rampage. 1.50
22 JJ,V:Realm of Death 1.50
23 JJ,A:Grim Reaper,Mephisto 1.50
24 JJ,V:Grim Reaper,Goliath. 1.50
25 JJ,N:Wonder Man,D:Grim Reaper,
　V:Mephisto. 3.25
26 A:Hulk,C:Furor,Plan Master 1.50
27 A:Hulk 1.50
28 RoR,A:Spider-Man. 1.50
29 RoR,A:Spider-Man. 1.50

30 V:Hate Monger 1.25
31 . . . . 1.25
32 . . . . 1.25
33 . . . . 1.25
Spec.#1 (1985),KGa. 3.00
Ann.#1 System Bytes #3 . . . . 2.25
Ann.#2 I:Hit-Maker,w/card. 2.95

WORLD CHAMPIONSHIP WRESTLING
1 F:Lex Luger,Sting 1.50
2 . . . . 1.25
3 . . . . 1.25
4 Luger Vs El Gigante 1.25
5 Rick Rude Vs. Sting 1.25
6 F:Dangerous Alliance,R.Rude. . . 1.25
7 F:Steiner Brothers 1.25
8 F:Sting,Dangerous Alliance. 1.25
9 Bunkhouse Brawl 1.25
10 Halloween Havoc. 1.25
11 Sting vs Grapplers 1.25
12 F:Ron Simmons. 1.25

WORLD OF FANTASY
Atlas May, 1956
1 The Secret of the Mountain. . . 350.00
2 AW,Inside the Tunnel 200.00
3 DAy,SC, The Man in the Cave 175.00
4 BEv(c),BP,JF,Back to the
　Lost City. 150.00
5 BEv(c),BP,In the Swamp. 150.00
6 BEv(c),BP,The Strange Wife
　of Henry Johnson. 150.00
7 BEv(c),GM,Man in Grey 150.00
8 GM,JO,MF,The Secret of the
　Black Cloud 165.00
9 BEv,BK. 150.00
10 . . . . 100.00
11 AT 125.00
12 BEv(c) 100.00
13 BEv,JO 100.00
14 JMn(c),GM,JO,CI,JM 100.00
15 JK(c) 100.00
16 AW,SD,JK 150.00
17 JK(c),SD 135.00
18 JK(c) 135.00
19 JK(c),SD,August, 1959. . . . . . 135.00

WORLD OF MYSTERY
Atlas June, 1956
1 BEv(c),AT,JO,The Long Wait . 350.00
2 BEv(c),The Man From
　Nowhere 125.00
3 SD,AT,JDa, The Bugs 150.00
4 SD(c),BP,What Happened in
　the Basement 150.00
5 JO,She Stands in Shadows . . 125.00
6 AW,SD,GC,Sinking Man 150.00
7 Pick A Door July, 1957 . . . . . . 125.00

WORLD OF SUSPENSE
Atlas April, 1956
1 JO,BEv,MO,A Stranger
　Among Us 250.00
2 SD,LC,When Walks
　the Scarecrow 150.00
3 AW,The Man Who Couldn't
　Be Touched 150.00
4 Something is in This House . . 125.00
5 BEv,DH,JO 125.00
6 BEv(c),BP. 125.00
7 AW,The Face 150.00
8 Prisoner of the Ghost Ship . . . 125.00

World's Unknown #8
© Marvel Entertainment Group

WORLDS UNKNOWN
May, 1973
1 GK,AT,The Coming of the
　Martians,Reprints 15.00
2 GK,TS,A Gun For A Dinosaur. . 10.00
3 The Day the Earth Stood
　Still. 10.00
4 JB,Arena 10.00
5 DA,JM,Black Destroyer. 10.00
6 GK(c),The Thing Called It 10.00
7 GT,The Golden Voyage of
　Sinbad,Part 1 . . . . 10.00
8 The Golden Voyage of
　Sinbad,Part 2, August, 1974 . 10.00

WYATT EARP
Atlas Nov., 1955
1 JMn,F:Wyatt Earp 150.00
2 AW,Saloon(c) 90.00
3 JMn(c),The Showdown,
　A:Black Bart 75.00
4 Ph(c),Hugh O'Brian,JSe,
　India Sundown 75.00
5 Ph(c),Hugh O'Brian,DW,
　Gun Wild Fever 75.00
6 . . . . 75.00
7 AW 75.00
8 . . . . 75.00
9 and 10 . . . . @75.00
11 . . . . 75.00
12 AW 75.00
13 thru 20 . . . . @60.00
21 JDa(c) 50.00
22 thru 29 . . . . @35.00
30 Reprints 15.00
31 thru 33 Reprints . . . . @10.00
34 June, 1973 . . . . 10.00

XAVIER INSTITUTE ALUMNI YEARBOOK
GN 48pg (1996) 5.95

X-CALIBRE
1995
1 Excaliber After Xavier. 4.00
2 V:Callisto & Morlock Crew 3.00
3 D:Juggernaut. 3.00
4 Secret Weapon. 3.00
TPB Rep.#1-#4. . . . . 8.95

X-Factor #18
© *Marvel Entertainment Group*

X-FACTOR
Feb., 1986

1 WS(c),JG,BL,JRu,I:X-Factor,
   Rusty 8.00
2 JG,BL,I:Tower. 5.00
3 JG,BL,V:Tower 4.00
4 KP,JRu,V:Frenzy. 4.00
5 JG,JRu,I:Alliance of Evil,
   C:Apocalypse. 5.00
6 JG,BMc,I:Apocalypse 12.00
7 JG,JRu,V:Morlocks,I:Skids . . 4.00
8 MS,JRu,V:Freedom Force 4.00
9 JRu(i),V:Freedom Force
   (Mutant Massacre) 5.00
10 WS,BWi,V:Marauders(Mut.Mass),
   A:Sabretooth 6.00
11 WS,BWi,A:Thor(Mutant Mass) . 5.00
12 MS,BWi,V:Vanisher 4.00
13 WS,DGr,V:Mastermold. 4.00
14 WS,BWi,V:Mastermold. 4.00
15 WS,BWi,D:Angel 5.00
16 DM,JRu,V:Masque. 4.00
17 WS,BWi,I:Rictor. 5.00
18 WS,BWi,V:Apocalypse. 4.00
19 WS,BWi,V:Horsemen of
   Apocalypse 3.00
20 JBr,A:X-Terminators. 2.50
21 WS,BWi,V:The Right 2.50
22 SB,BWi,V:The Right. 2.50
23 WS,BWi,C:Archangel. 9.00
24 WS,BWi,Fall of Mutants,
   I:Archangel. 12.00
25 WS,BWi,Fall of Mutants 3.00
26 WS,BWi,Fall of Mutants,
   N:X-Factor 3.00
27 WS,BWi,Christmas Issue 2.50
28 WS,BWi,V:Ship 2.00
29 WS,BWi,V:Infectia 2.00
30 WS,BWi,V:Infectia,Free.Force . 2.00
31 WS,BWi,V:Infectia,Free.Force . 2.00
32 SLi,A:Avengers 2.00
33 WS,BWi,V:Tower & Frenzy,
   R:Furry Beast. 2.00
34 WS,BWi,I:Nanny,
   Orphan Maker 2.00
35 JRu(i),WS(c),V:Nanny,
   Orphan Maker 2.00
36 WS,BWi,Inferno,V:Nastirh 2.50
37 WS,BWi,Inferno,V:Gob.Queen . 2.50
38 WS,AM,Inferno,A:X-Men,D:
   MadelynePryor(GoblinQueen). . 2.50
39 WS,AM,Inferno,A:X-Men,
   V:Mr.Sinister. 2.50
40 RLd,AM,O:Nanny,Orphan Maker

   1st Liefeld Marvel work. 6.00
41 AAd,AM,I:Alchemy. 2.50
42 AAd,AM,A:Alchemy 2.50
43 PS,AM,V:Celestials 2.00
44 PS,AM,V:Rejects 2.00
45 PS,AM,V:Rask. 2.00
46 PS,AM,V:Rejects 2.00
47 KD,AM,V:Father. 2.00
48 thru 49 PS,AM,V:Rejects 2.00
50 RLd&TM(c),RB,AM,A:Prof.X
   (double sized),BU:Apocalypse . 3.00
51 AM,V:Sabretooth,Caliban. 4.00
52 RLd(c),AM,V:Sabretooth,
   Caliban 3.00
53 AM,V:Sabretooth,Caliban 3.00
54 MS,AM,A:Colossus,I:Crimson . 2.00
55 MMi(c),CDo,AM,V:Mesmero. . . 2.00
56 AM,V:Crimson 2.00
57 NKu,V:Crimson 2.00
58 JBg,AM,V:Crimson. 2.00
59 AM,V:Press Gang 2.00
60 JBg,AM,X-Tinction Agenda#3 . 3.00
60a 2nd printing(gold). 2.00
61 JBg,AM,X-Tinction Agenda#6 . 3.00
62 JBg,AM,JLe(c),E:X-Agenda . . 3.00
63 WPo,I:Cyberpunks. 3.00
64 WPo,ATb,V:Cyberpunks. 3.00
65 WPo,ATb,V:Apocalypse 3.00
66 WPo,ATb,I:Askani,
   V:Apocalypse. 3.00
67 WPo,ATb,V:Apocalypse,I:Shinobi
   Shaw,D:Sebastian Shaw 2.00
68 WPo,ATb,JLe(c),V:Apocalypse,
   L:Nathan,(taken into future) . . . 3.00
69 WPo,V:Shadow King 2.00
70 MMi(c),JRu,Last old team 2.00
71 LSn,AM,New Team 4.00
71a 2nd printing 1.50
72 LSn,AM,Who shot Madrox
   revealed. 2.00
73 LSn,AM,Mob Chaos in D.C.. . . 2.00
74 LSn,AM,I:Slab 2.00
75 LSn,AM,I:Nasty Boys(doub.sz). . 3.00
76 LSn,AM,A:Hulk,Pantheon. 2.00
77 LSn,AM,V:Mutant Lib. Front. . . 2.00
78 LSn,AM,V:Mutant Lib. Front . . 2.00
79 LSn,AM,V:Helle's Belles. 2.00
80 LSn,AM,V:Helle's Belles,
   C:Cyber 2.00
81 LSn,AM,V:Helle's Belles,Cyber . 2.00
82 JQ(c),LSn,V:Brotherhood of Evil
   Mutants,I:X-iles 2.00
83 MPa,A:X-Force,X-iles 2.00
84 JaL,X-Cutioners Song #2,
   V:X-Force,A:X-Men 2.50
85 JaL,X-Cutioners Song #6,
   Wolv.& Bishop,V:Cable. 2.50
86 JaL,AM,X-Cutioner's Song#10,
   A:X-Men,X-Force,V:Stryfe. . . . 2.50
87 JQ,X-Cutioners Song
   Aftermath 2.50
88 JQ,AM,V:2nd Genegineer,
   I:Random 4.00
89 JQ,V:Mutates,Genosha 2.00
90 JQ,AM,Genosha vs. Aznia. . . . 2.00
91 AM,V:Armageddon. 1.75
92 JQ,AM,V:Fabian Cortez,
   Acolytes,hologram(c) 5.00
93 Magneto Protocols. 3.00
94 PR,J:Forge 3.00
95 B:JMD(s),AM,Polaris
   Vs. Random. 1.75
96 A:Random 1.75
97 JD,I:Haven,A:Random 1.75
98 GLz,A:Haven,A:Random 1.50
99 JD,A:Haven,Wolfsbane returns
   to human 1.50
100 JD,Red Foil(c),V:Haven,
   D:Madrox 3.25
100a Newstand Ed. 2.00
101 JD,AM,Aftermath 1.50

X-Factor #103
© *Marvel Entertainment Group*

102 JD,AM,V:Crimson Commando,
   Avalanche 1.50
103 JD,AM,A:Malice. 1.75
104 JD,AM,V:Malice,
   C:Mr. Sinister. 1.75
105 JD,AM,V:Malice 1.75
106 Phalanx Covenant,Life Signs
   Holografx(c) 3.25
106a newsstand ed 2.00
107 A:Strong Guy. 1.75
108 A:Mystique, deluxe ed. 2.50
108a newsstand ed. 1.50
109 A:Mystique,V:Legion, deluxe . . 2.00
109a newsstand ed. 1.50
110 Invasion. 2.00
110a deluxe ed. 2.00
111 Invasion. 1.50
111a deluxe ed. 2.00
112 AM,JFM,SEp,F:Guido,Havok . 2.00
113 A:Mystique. 2.00
114 AM,Wild Child & Mystique 2.00
115 F:Wild Child,Havok 2.00
116 F:Wild Child 2.00
117 HMe,AM,F:Cyclops 2.00
118 HMe,AM,A:Random,Shard. . . . 2.00
119 HMe,AM,F:Sabretooth 2.00
120 . . . . 2.00
121 . . . . 2.00
122 HMe,SEp,AM,J:Sabretooth . . . 2.00
123 . . . . 2.00
124 A:Onslaught. 3.00
125 Onslaught saga, double size . . 3.00
126 Beast vs. Dark Beast. 2.00
127 Mystique 2.00
128 HMe,JMs,AM,Hound Program . 2.00
129 HMe,JMs,AM,Graydon Creed's
   campaign 2.00
130 HMe,JMs,AM,Assassination of
   Graydon Creed. 2.50
131 HMe,JMs,ATi,Havok strikes
   back. 2.00
132 HMe,JMs,ATi,Break away from
   government 2.00
133 HMe,JMs,ATi,A:Multiple Man &
   Strong Guy. 2.00
134 HMe,JMs,Ati,"Operation X-Factor
   Underground," cont. 2.00
135 HMe,JMs,Strong Guy awakes . 2.00
136 HMe,JMs,ATi, A:Sabretooth . . . 2.00
137 HMe,JMs,ATi, Final fate of
   Shard and Polaris. 2.00
138 HMe,JMs,ATi,Sabertooth,
   V:Maberick 2.00
139 HMe,ATi,Who killed Graydon

MARVEL

Creed.................. 2.00	21 GCa,V:War Machine,SHIELD... 2.00	62 JLb,F:Sunspot............. 2.00
140 HMe,ATi,Who killed Graydon	22 GCa,V:Externals........... 2.00	63 JFM,AdP,F:Risque,Cannonball.. 2.00
Creed, A:Mystique........ 2.00	23 GCa,V:Saul,Gigeon,A:Six Pack . 2.00	64 JFM,AdP,In Latveria, searching
141 HMe,ATi,Shard's Plan..... 2.00	24 GCa,A:Six Pack,A:Deadpool... 1.50	for Doctor Doom's weapons... 2.00
142 ATi,F:Wild Child......... 2.00	25 GCa,A:Mageneto,Exodus,	65 JFM,AdP,Warpath follows Risque
143 HMe,ATi,Havok vs.DarkBeast . 2.00	R:Cable............... 5.00	to Florida............... 2.00
144 HMe,ATi,V:Brotherhood,	26 GCa(c),MtB,I:Reignfire....... 2.00	66 JFM,AdP,A:Risque,James
Dark Beast............ 2.00	27 GCa(c),MtB,V:Reignfire,MLF,	Proudstar.............. 2.00
145 HMe,ATi,Havok vs. X.U.E..... 2.00	I:Moonstar,Locus........... 1.50	67 JFM,AdP,F:Warpath, Risque ... 2.00
146 HMe,ATi,Havok, Multiple	28 MtB,V:Reignfire,MLF....... 1.50	68 JFM,AdP,Zero Tolerance..... 2.00
Man,V:Polaris.............. 2.00	29 MtB,V:Arcade,C:X-Treme...... 1.50	69 JFM,AdP,Zero Tolerance
147 HMe,Havok v. Mandroids..... 2.00	30 TnD,V:Arcade,A:X-Treme...... 1.50	aftermath............. 2.00
148 F:Shard................ 2.00	31 F:Siryn................ 1.50	70 JFM,AdP,new direction starts.. 2.00
149 HMe,Polaris & Madrox rejoin . 2.00	32 Child's Play#1,A:New Warriors.. 1.50	71 JFM,AdP,new direction....... 2.00
Spec #1 JG,Prisoner of Love.... 5.00	33 Child's Play#3,A:New Warriors,	72 JFM,AdP,on the road........ 2.00
Ann.#1 BL,BBr,V:CrimsonDynamo . 5.00	V:Upstarts............. 1.50	73 JFM,AdP,in New Orleans..... 2.00
Ann.#2 TGr,JRu,A:Inhumans..... 4.00	34 F:Rictor,Domino,Cable...... 2.00	74 JFM,ASm,Skids is back..... 2.00
Ann.#3 WS(c),AM,JRu,PC,TD,	35 TnD,R:Nimrod............ 1.50	75 JFM,AdP,A:Reignfire,
Evolutionary War........ 3.50	36 TnD,V:Nimrod............ 1.75	double size............ 3.00
Ann.#4 JBy,WS,JRu,MBa,Atlantis	37 PaP,I&D:Absalom.......... 1.50	76 JFM,AdP,F:Shatterstar..... 2.00
Attacks,BU:Doom & Magneto . . 3.50	38 TaD,Life Signs,pt.2,	77 JFM,AdP,F:Sunfire & Meltdown . 2.00
Ann.#5 JBg,AM,DR,GI,Days of Future	I:Generation X, foil(c)...... 5.00	78 JFM,AdP,Reignfire makes his
Present,A:Fant.Four,V:Ahab . . 4.00	38a newsstand ed........... 2.00	move................ 2.00
Ann.#6 Flesh Tears Saga,pt.4,	39 TaD................ 1.50	79 JFM,AdP,O:Reignfire....... 2.00
A:X-Force, New Warriors..... 4.00	40 TaD, deluxe............. 2.00	80 JFM,AdP,V:Reignfire....... 2.00
Ann #7 JQ,JRu,Shattershot,pt.3 ... 4.00	40a newsstand ed........... 1.50	81 JFM,AdP,trip to Hawaii,
Ann.#8 I:Charon,w/card....... 3.25	41 TaD,O:feral,deluxe........ 2.00	V:Lava Men, AdP Poster..... 2.00
Ann.#9 JMD(s),MtB,V:Prof.Power,	41a newsstand ed........... 1.50	82 JFM,V:Griffin, Damocles
A:Prof.X,O:Haven........ 3.25	42 Emma Frost, deluxe........ 2.00	Foundation............ 2.00
Minus 1 Spec., HMe,JMs,ATi,	42a newsstand ed........... 1.50	83 JFM,F:Cannonball......... 2.00
flashback,F:Havok.......... 1.95	43 Home is Where Heart....... 1.50	84 JFM,V:Deviants.......... 2.00
GN X-Men: Wrath of Apocalypse,	43a deluxe ed.............. 2.00	85 JFM,Return of Skids....... 2.00
rep.X-Factor#65–#68....... 4.95	44 AdP,Prof.X,X-Mansion...... 2.00	86 JFM,A:Hulk............ 2.00
	45 AdP,Caliban vs. Sabretooth.... 2.00	87 JFM,V:new Hellions....... 2.00
### X-51	46 R:The Mimic........... 2.00	88 JFM,V:new Hellions....... 2.00
July 1999	47 A:Deadpool............. 2.00	89 JFM,prisoners of the Hellions... 2.00
1 JQ&JP(c) Marvel Tech........ 2.00	48 AdP,Siryn Takes Charge...... 2.00	90 JFM,Hellion War,concl...... 2.00
2 JoB,V:Brotherhood of Mutants .. 2.00	49 ADp,MBu,Holocaust is here.... 2.00	91 JFM,home to San Francisco.. 2.00
2a variant cover.............. 2.00	50 AdP,MPn,F:Sebastian Shaw... 2.00	92 JFM,F:Domino.......... 2.00
3 JoB,A:X.E.R.O............. 2.00	50a prismatic foil cover....... 4.00	93 JFM,Domino returns....... 2.00
	50b variant RLd(c)......... 6.00	94 JFM,destination Genosha.... 2.00
### X-FORCE	51 AdP,MPn,V:Risque........ 2.00	95 JFM,F:Magneto.......... 2.00
August, 1991	52 A:Onslaught............ 3.50	Ann.#1 Shattershot,pt1....... 2.75
1 RLd,V:Stryfe,Mutant Liberation	53 .... 2.00	Ann.#2 JaL,LSn,I:X-Treme,w/card.. 3.25
Front,bagged, white on black	54 AdP, Can X-Force	Ann.#3............... 2.95
graphics with X-Force Card ... 3.00	protect X-Ternals?........ 2.00	Annual 1998 X-Force/Champions . 6.00
1a with Shatterstar Card........ 2.00	55 .... 2.00	Minus 1 Spec., JFM,AdP, flashback,
1b with Deadpool Card......... 2.00	56 Deadpool, A:Onslaught....... 3.50	F:John Proudstar........... 1.95
1c with Sunspot & Gideon Card... 2.00	57 Onslaught saga.......... 2.00	TPB X-Force & Spider-Man: Sabotage,
1d with Cable Card............ 3.00	58 Onslaught saga.......... 2.00	rep.X-Force #3 & #4 and
1e Unbagged Copy............ 1.50	59 .... 2.00	Spider-Man #16........ 6.95
1f 2nd Printing.............. 1.50	60 JLb,,F:Shatterstar,A:Long Shot . 2.00	
2 RLd,I:New Weapon X,V:	61 JLb,R:Longshot,O:Shatterstar .. 2.00	### X-FORCE MEGAZINE
Deadpool................ 3.00		TPB LSi,RLd, rep. New Mutants
3 RLd,C:Spider-Man,		#99–#100................ 3.95
V:Juggernaut,Black Tom...... 3.00		
4 RLd,SpM/X-Force team-up,		### X-MAN
V:Juggernaut(cont.from SpM#16)		**March 1995**
Sideways format........ 3.00		1 Cable after Xavier........... 5.00
5 RLd,A:Brotherhood Evil Mutants. 2.50		2 Sinister's Plan.............. 4.00
6 RLd,V:Bro'hood Evil Mutants... 2.50		3 V:Domino............... 2.50
7 RLd,V:Bro'hood Evil Mutants... 2.50		4 V:Sinister................ 2.50
8 MMi,O:Cable(Part)........ 2.50		5 Into this World............ 2.50
9 RLd,D:Sauron,Masque........ 2.50		6 V:X-Men................ 2.50
10 MPa,V:Mutant Liberation Front. 2.00		7 Evil from Age of Apocalypse.... 2.25
11 MPa,Deadpool Vs Domino..... 2.00		8 Crossover Adventure......... 2.00
12 MPa,A:Weapon Prime,Gideon .. 2.00		9 F:Nate's Past............. 2.00
13 MPa,V:Weapon Prime....... 2.00		10 Nate's Past............. 2.00
14 TSr,V:Weapon Prime,Krule 2.00		11 Young Nate seeks out X-Men... 2.00
15 GCa,V:Krule,Deadpool....... 2.00		12 F:Excalibur............. 2.00
16 GCa,X-Cutioners Song #4,		13 .... 2.00
X-Factor V:X-Force........ 2.00		14 .... 2.00
17 GCa,X-Cutioners Song#8,		15 JOs,X-Men/Cable war aftermath 3.00
Apocalypse V:Stryfe........ 2.00		16 Holocaust,A:Onslaught..... 2.50
18 GCa,X-Cutioners Song#12,		17 Holocaust,Quicksilver,Scarlet
Cable vs Stryfe.............. 2.00		Witch, A:Onslaught........ 2.50
19 GCa,X-Cutioners Song		18 Onslaught saga.......... 2.50
Aftermath,N:X-Force......... 2.00	*X-Force #62*	19 Onslaught saga.......... 2.50
20 GCa,O:Graymalkin......... 2.00	© Marvel Entertainment Group	20 .... 2.50
		21 TKa,RCz,F:Nate.......... 2.50

X-Men #23
© *Marvel Entertainment Group*

22 TKa,RCz,F:Threnody,A:Madelyne
  Pryor 2.50
23 TKa,RCz,F:Bishop 2.50
24 TKa,RCz,Spider-Man vs. Nate . . 2.50
25 TKa,RCz,Madelyne Pryor,
  double size 4.00
26 TKa,RCz,Nate limps to Muir
  Isle,A:Moira Mactaggert 2.50
27 TKa,RCz,Hellfire Club, concl. . . . 2.50
28 TKa,RCz,Dark Beast's offer 2.50
29 TKa,RCz,Back in New York, ... 2.50
30 TKa,RCz,F:Nate Grey 2.50
31 RL,DGr,F:Nate Grey 2.00
32 TKa,V:Jacknife 2.00
33 TKa,V:Jacknife 2.00
34 TKa,Secret of Nate's popularity . 2.00
35 TKa,Terrorists Strike 2.00
36 TKa,V:Purple Man 2.00
37 TKa,Nate leaves N.Y.,
  A:Spider-Man 2.00
38 TKa,A:Spider-Man, Gwen Stacy. 2.00
39 TKa,AOl,Nate & Madeline Pryor. 2.00
40 TKa,RPc,V:Great Beasts 2.00
41 TKa,RCz,Madelyne Pryor 2.00
42 TKa,RCz,hunted by leprechauns 2.00
43 TKa,RCz,Nate Grey–murderer?! 2.00
44 TKa,RCz,F:Nate Grey,Gauntlet . 2.00
45 TKa,prelude to X-Man/Cable
  x-over. 2.00
46 TKa,Cable x-over. 2.00
47 TKa,Blood Brothers,pt.3 . . . . . . 2.00
48 LRs,V:Crusader. 2.00
49 LRs,TKa,F:Nate. 2.00
50 TKa,LRs,War of the
  Mutants,pt.2, 48-page. 2.00
51 TKa,LRs,V:Psi-Ops 2.00
52 TKa,LRs,V:Psi-Ops 2.00
53 TKa,Strange Relations,pt.1 . . . . 2.00
54 TKa,Strange Relations,pt.2 . . . . 2.00
55 TKa,M'Kraan Crystal 2.00
56 TKa,Nate in Greyville. 2.00
Minus 1 Spec., TKa,RCz,
  flashback,O:Nate Grey 1.95
Spec.#1 X-Man '96. . . . . 2.95
Ann. '97 RBe, Nate, Sugar Man,
  Dark Beast, Holocaust 3.00
Ann. '98 X-Man, The Hulk, Thanos,
  48pg 3.00
GNv X-Man,BRa,TyD, 48pg 6.00

X-MEN

Sept., 1963

1 JK,O:X-Men,I:Professor X,Beast
  Cyclops,Marvel Girl,Iceman

Angel,Magneto 6,200.00
2 JK,I:Vanisher 1,800.00
3 JK,I:Blob. 700.00
4 JK,I:Quicksilver,Scarlet Witch
  Mastermind,Toad 650.00
5 JK,V:Broth. of Evil Mutants . . . 450.00
6 JK,V:Sub-Mariner 350.00
7 JK,V:Broth. of Evil Mutants,
  Blob 325.00
8 JK,I:Unus,1st Ice covered
  Iceman. 325.00
9 JK,A:Avengers,I:Lucifer. 325.00
10 JK,I:Modern Kazar. 325.00
11 JK,I:Stranger 275.00
12 JK,O:Prof.X,I:Juggernaut 350.00
13 JK,JSt,V:Juggernaut 250.00
14 JK,I:Sentinels. 250.00
15 JK,O:Beast,V:Sentinels 250.00
16 JK,V:Mastermold,Sentinels. . . 250.00
17 JK,V:Magneto 150.00
18 V:Magneto 150.00
19 I:Mimic. 150.00
20 V:Lucifer 150.00
21 V:Lucifer,Dominus 135.00
22 V:Maggia 135.00
23 V:Maggia 135.00
24 I:Locust(Prof.Hopper). 135.00
25 JK,I:El Tigre 135.00
26 V:El Tigre. 125.00
27 C:Fant.Four,V:Puppet Master. 125.00
28 I:Banshee 150.00
29 V:Super-Apaptoid. 125.00
30 JK,I:The Warlock 125.00
31 JK,I:Cobalt Man 85.00
32 V:Juggernaut 85.00
33 GK,A:Dr.Strange,Juggernaut . . 85.00
34 V:Tyrannus,Mole Man 85.00
35 JK,A:Spider-Man,Banshee . . . 125.00
36 V:Mekano 85.00
37 DH,V:Blob,Unus. 85.00
38 DH,A:Banshee,O:Cyclops . . . 125.00
39 DH,GT,A:Banshee,V:Mutant
  Master,O:Cyclops 85.00
40 DH,GT,V:Frankenstein,
  O:Cyclops 85.00
41 DH,GT,I:Grotesk,O:Cyclops . . . 75.00
42 DH,GT,JB,V:Grotesk,
  O:Cyclops,D:Prof.X 75.00
43 GT,JB,V:Magneto,Quicksilver,
  Scarlet Witch,C:Avengers 85.00
44 V:Magneto,Quicksilver,Sc.Witch,
  R:Red Raven,O:Iceman 85.00
45 PH,JB,V:Magneto,Quicksilver,
  Scarlet Witch,O:Iceman 85.00
46 DH,V:Juggernaut,O:Iceman . . . 75.00
47 DH,I:Maha Yogi 75.00
48 DH,JR,V:Quasimodo 75.00
49 JSo,DH,C:Magneto,I:Polaris,
  Mesmero,O:Beast. 75.00
50 JSo,V:Magneto,O:Beast. 85.00
51 JSo,V:Magneto,Polaris,
  Erik the Red,O:Beast 75.00
52 DH,MSe,JSt,O:Lorna Dane
  V:Magneto,O:Beast 55.00
53 1st BWS,O:Beast. 85.00
54 BWS,DH,I:Havok,O:Angel 80.00
55 BWS,DH,O:Havok,Angel 75.00
56 NA,V:LivingMonolith,O:Angel . . 75.00
57 NA,V:Sentinels,A:Havok. 75.00
58 NA,A:Havoc,V:Sentinels. 90.00
59 NA,V:Sentinels,A:Havoc. 75.00
60 NA,I:Sauron. 75.00
61 NA,V:Sauron 75.00
62 NA,A:Kazar,Sauron,Magneto . . 75.00
63 A:Ka-Zar,V:Magneto. 60.00
64 DH,A:Havok,I:Sunfire 55.00
65 NA,MSe,A:Havok,Shield,
  Return of Prof.X 60.00
66 SB,MSe,V:Hulk,A:Havok 60.00
67 rep.X-Men #12,#13 . . . . 35.00
68 rep.X-Men #14,#15 . . . . 35.00

X-Men #93
© *Marvel Entertainment Group*

69 rep.X-Men #16,#19 . . . . 35.00
70 rep.X-Men #17,#18 . . . . 35.00
71 rep.X-Men #20. . . . . 35.00
72 rep.X-Men #21,#24 . . . . 35.00
73 thru 93 rep.X-Men #25-45 . . @30.00
94 GK(c),B:CCI(s),DC,BMc,B:2nd
  X-Men,V:Count Nefaria. 475.00
95 GK(c),DC,V:Count Nefaria,
  Ani-Men,D:Thunderbird. 100.00
96 DC,I:Moira McTaggert,
  Kierrok 85.00
97 DC,V:Havok,Polaris,Eric
  the Red,I:Lilandra 75.00
98 DC,V:Sentinels,Stephen Lang . 85.00
99 DC,V:Sentinels,S.Lang. 90.00
100 DC,V:Stephen Lang. 85.00
101 DC,I:Phoenix,Black Tom,
  A:Juggernaut 75.00
102 DC,O:Storm,V:Juggernaut,
  Black Tom 40.00
103 DC,V:Juggernaut,Bl.Tom 40.00
104 DC,V:Magneto,I:Star
  Jammers,A:Lilandra 35.00
105 DC,BL,V:Firelord 35.00
106 DC,TS,V:Firelord 35.00
107 DC,DGr,I:Imperial Guard,Star
  Jammers,Gladiator,Corsair . . . 40.00
108 JBy,TA,A:Star Jammers,
  C:Fantastic Four,Avengers. . . . 80.00
109 JBy,TA,I:Vindicator. 55.00
110 TD,DC,V:Warhawk 35.00
111 JBy,TA,V:Mesmero,A:Beast,
  Magneto 35.00
112 GP(c),JBy,TA,V:Magneto,
  A:Beast 32.00
113 JBy,TA,V:Magneto,A:Beast. . . 32.00
114 JBy,TA,A:Beast,R:Sauron. . . . 32.00
115 JBy,TA,V:Sauron,Garokk,
  A:Kazar,I:Zaladane 30.00
116 JBy,TA,V:Sauron,Garokk,
  A:Kazar 30.00
117 JBy,TA,O:Prof.X,I:Amahl
  Farouk (Shadow King) 35.00
118 JBy,I:Moses Magnum,A:Sunfire
  C:Iron Fist,I:Mariko 32.00
119 JBy,TA,V:Moses Magnum,
  A:Sunfire 32.00
120 JBy,TA,I:AlphaFlight (Shaman,
  Sasquatch,Northstar,Snowbird,
  Aurora). 55.00
121 JBy,TA,V:Alpha Flight 65.00
122 JBy,TA,A:Juggernaut,Black
  Tom,Arcade,Power Man 30.00
123 JBy,TA,V:Arcade,A:SpM. 28.00

MARVEL

124 JBy,TA,V:Arcade 28.00
125 JBy,TA,A:Beast,Madrox the
    Multiple Man,Havok,Polaris. . . 28.00
126 JBy,TA,I:Proteus,
    A:Havok,Madrox. 28.00
127 JBy,TA,V:Proteus,A:Havok,
    Madrox. 28.00
128 GP(c),JBy,TA,V:Proteus,
    A:Havok,Madrox. 28.00
129 JBy,TA,I:Shadow Cat,White
    Queen,C:Hellfire Club. 35.00
130 JR2(c),JBy,TA,I:Dazzler
    V:White Queen. 30.00
131 JBy,TA,V:White Queen,
    A:Dazzler 22.00
132 JBy,TA,I:Hellfire Club,
    V:Mastermind 22.00
133 JBy,TA,V:Hellfire Club,
    Mastermind,F:Wolverine 22.00
134 JBy,TA,V:Hellfire Club,Master
    mind,I:Dark Phoenix,A:Beast . 22.00
135 JBy,TA,V:Dark Phoenix,C:SpM,
    Fant.Four,Silver Surfer 22.00
136 JBy,TA,V:Dark Phoenix,
    A:Beast 22.00
137 JBy,TA,D:Phoenix,V:Imperial
    Guard,A:Beast 28.00
138 JBy,TA,History of X-Men,
    L:Cyclops,C:Shadow Cat 22.00
139 JBy,TA,A:Alpha Flight,R:Wendigo,
    N:Wolverine,J:Shadowcat. . . . 35.00
140 JBy,TA,V:Wendigo,A:Alpha
    Flight 35.00
141 JBy,TA,I:2nd Brotherhood of Evil
    Mutants,I:Rachel (Phoenix II) . 35.00

Becomes:

UNCANNY X-MEN

142 JBy,TA,V:Evil Mutants,
    A:Rachel (Phoenix II) 25.00
143 JBy,TA,V:N'Garai,I:Lee
    Forrester 10.00
144 BA,JRu,A:Man-Thing,
    O:Havok, V:D'Spayre 9.00
145 DC,JRu,V:Arcade,A:DrDoom . . 9.00
146 DC,JRu,V:Dr.Doom,Arcade . . . 9.00
147 DC,JRu,V:Dr.Doom,Arcade . . . 9.00
148 DC,JRu,I:Caliban,A:Dazzler
    Spiderwoman. 9.00
149 DC,JRu,A:Magneto 9.00
150 DC,JRu,BWi,V:Magneto 10.00
151 JSh,BMc,JRu,V:Sentinels. 7.00
152 BMc,JRu,V:White Queen 7.00
153 DC,JRu,I:Bamf. 7.00
154 DC,JRu,BWi,I:Sidrian Hunters
    A:Corsair,O:Cyclops(part) 7.00
155 DC,BWi,V:Deathbird,I:Brood . . 7.00
156 DC,BWi,V:Death Bird,
    A:Tigra, Star Jammers 7.00
157 DC,BWi,V:Deathbird 7.00
158 DC,BWi,2nd A:Rogue,
    Mystique 9.00
159 BSz,BWi,V:Dracula 7.00
160 BA,BWi,V:Belasco,I:Magik 7.00
161 DC,BWi,I:Gabrielle Haller,
    O:Magneto,Professor X 8.00
162 DC,BWi,V:Brood 10.00
163 DC,BWi,V:Brood 7.00
164 DC,BWi,V:Brood,I:Binary 7.00
165 PS,BWi,V:Brood 8.00
166 PS,BWi,V:Brood,A:Binary,
    I:Lockheed 8.00
167 PS,BWi,V:Brood,A:N.Mutants. . 8.00
168 PS,BWi,I:Madelyne Pryor. 7.00
169 PS,BWi,I:Morlocks 7.00
170 PS,BWi,A:Angel,V:Morlocks. . . 7.00
171 WS,BWi,J:Rogue,V:Binary . . . 10.00
172 PS,BWi,V:Viper,Silver
    Samurai, ... 8.00
173 PS,BWi,V:Viper,Silver
    Samurai, ... 5.00
174 PS,BWi,A:Mastermind 5.00

175 PS,JR2,BWi,W:Cyclops and
    Madelyne,V:Mastermind 8.00
176 JR2,BWi,I:Val Cooper 5.00
177 JR2,JR,V:Brotherhood of
    Evil Mutants 5.00
178 JR2,BWi,BBr,V:Brotherhood
    of Evil Mutants 5.00
179 JR2,DGr,V:Morlocks. 5.00
180 JR2,DGr,BWi,Secret Wars 5.00
181 JR2,DGr,A:Sunfire 5.00
182 JR2,DGr,V:S.H.I.E.L.D. 5.00
183 JR2,DGr,V:Juggernaut 5.00
184 JR2,DGr,V:Selene,I:Forge 7.00
185 JR2,DGr,V:Shield,U.S.
    Govt.,Storm loses powers. 5.00
186 BWS,TA,Lifedeath,
    V:Dire Wraiths 6.00
187 JR2,DGr,V:Dire Wraiths 5.00
188 JR2,DGr,V:Dire Wraiths 5.00
189 JR2,SL,V:Selene,A:Magma 5.00
190 JR2,DGr,V:Kulan Gath,A:SpM,
    Avengers,New Mutants. 5.00
191 JR2,DGr,A:Avengers,Spider-Man,
    New Mutants,I:Nimrod 5.00
192 JR2,DGr,V:Magus 5.00
193 JR2,DGr,V:Hellions,I:Firestar
    Warpath,20th Anniv. 8.00
194 JR2,DGr,SL,V:Nimrod 5.00
195 BSz(c),JR2,DGr,A:Power
    Pack,V:Morlocks. 5.00
196 JR2,DGr,J:Magneto 6.00
197 JR2,DGr,V:Arcade 5.00
198 BWS,F:Storm,'Lifedeath II' 5.00
199 JR2,DGr,I:Freedom Force,
    Rachel becomes 2nd Phoenix . 5.00
200 JR2,DGr,A:Magneto,I:Fenris . . 8.00
201 RL,WPo(i),I:Nathan
    Christopher (Cyclops son) 9.00
202 JR2,AW,Secret Wars II 5.00
203 JR2,AW,Secret Wars II 5.00
204 JBr,WPo,V:Arcade 5.00
205 BWS,A:Lady Deathstrike 12.00
206 JR2,DGr,V:Freedom Force. . . . 4.00
207 JR2,DGr,V:Selene 4.00
208 JR2,DGr,V:Nimrod,
    A:Hellfire Club 4.00
209 JR2,CR,V:Nimrod,A:Spiral 4.00
210 JR2,DGr,I:Marauders,
    (Mutant Massacre) 10.00
211 JR2,BBI,AW,V:Marauders,
    (Mutant Massacre) 10.00
212 RL,DGr,V:Sabretooth
    (Mutant Massacre) 12.00
213 AD,V:Sabretooth (Mut.Mass) . 12.00

Uncanny X-Men #195
© Marvel Entertainment Group

214 BWS,BWi,V:Malice,A:Dazzler. . 4.00
215 AD,DGr,I:Stonewall,Super
    Sabre,Crimson Commando . . . 4.00
216 BWS(c),JG,DGr,V:Stonewall . . 4.00
217 WS(c),JG,SL,V:Juggernaut . . . 4.00
218 AAD(c),MS,DGr,V:Juggernaut . 4.00
219 BBI,DGr,V:Marauders,Polaris
    becomes Malice,A:Sabertooth . 5.00
220 MS,DGr,A:Naze 4.00
221 MS,DGr,I:Mr.Sinister,
    V:Marauders. 8.00
222 MS,DGr,V:Marauders,Eye
    Killers,A:Sabertooth 9.00
223 KGa,DGr,A:Freedom Force . . . 4.00
224 MS,DGr,V:Adversary 4.00
225 MS,DGr,Fall of Mutants
    I:1st US App Roma 6.00
226 MS,DGr,Fall of Mutants 6.00
227 MS,DGr,Fall of Mutants,F. 6.00
228 RL,TA,A:OZ Chase 4.00
229 MS,DGr,I:Reavers,Gateway . . . 4.00
230 RL,DGr,Xmas Issue 4.00
231 RL,DGr,V:Limbo. 4.00
232 MS,DGr,V:Brood 4.00
233 MS,DGr,V:Brood 4.00
234 MS,JRu,V:Brood 4.00
235 RL,CR,V:Magistrates 4.00
236 MS,DGr,V:Magistrates 4.00
237 RL,TA,V:Magistrates 4.00
238 MS,DGr,V:Magistrates 4.00
239 MS,DGr,Inferno,A:Mr.Sinister . . 4.00
240 MS,DGr,Inferno,V:Marauders . . 4.00
241 MS,DGr,Inferno,O:Madeline
    Pryor,V:Marauders 4.00
242 MS,DGr,Inferno,D:N'Astirh,
    A:X-Factor,Double-sized 4.00
243 MS,Inferno,A:X-Factor. 4.00
244 MS,DGr,I:Jubilee 15.00
245 RLd,DGr,Invasion Parody. 4.00
246 MS,DGr,V:Mastermold,
    A:Nimrod 4.00
247 MS,DGr,V:Mastermold 3.00
248 JLe(1st X-Men Art),DGr,
    V:Nanny & Orphan Maker. . . . 14.00
248a 2nd printing 2.00
249 MS,DGr,C:Zaladane,
    V:Savage Land Mutates. 3.00
250 MS,SL,I:Zaladane. 3.00
251 MS,DGr,V:Reavers 3.00
252 JLe,BSz(c),RL,SW,V:Reavers . 3.00
253 MS,SL,V:Amahl Farouk 3.00
254 JLe(c),MS,DGr,V:Reavers 3.00
255 MS,DGr,V:Reavers,D:Destiny . . 3.00
256 JLe,SW,Acts of Vengeance,
    V:Manderin,A:Psylocke. 8.00
257 JLe,JRu,AofV,V:Manderin 6.00
258 JLe,SW,AofV,V:Manderin 7.00
259 MS,DGr,V:Magistrates,. 5.00
260 JLe(c),MS,DGr,A:Dazzler 4.00
261 JLe(c),MS,DGr,V:Hardcase &
    Harriers 4.00
262 KD,JRu,V:Masque,Morlocks. . . 4.00
263 JRu(i),O:Forge,V:Morlocks 4.00
264 JLe(c),MC,JRu,V:Magistrate. . . 4.00
265 JRu(i),V:Shadowking 4.00
266 NKu(c),MC,JRu,I:Gambit 30.00
267 JLe,WPo,SW,V:Shadowking . . 15.00
268 JLe,SW,A:Captain America,
    Black Widow,V:The Hand,
    Baron Strucker. 17.00
269 JLe,ATi,Rogue V:Ms.Marvel . . . 4.00
270 JLe,ATi,SW,X-Tinction Agenda
    #1, A:Cable,New Mutants 10.00
270a 2nd printing(Gold) 4.00
271 JLe,SW,X-Tinction Agenda
    #4,A:Cable,New Mutants 5.00
272 JLe,SW,X-Tinction Agenda
    #7,A:Cable,New Mutants 5.00
273 JLe,WPo,JBy,KJ,RL,MS,MGo,
    LSn,SW,A:Cable,N.Mutants . . . 5.00
274 JLe,SW,V:Zaladane,A:Magneto,

Uncanny X-Men #217
© Marvel Entertainment Group

Nick Fury,Kazar 4.00
275 JLe,SW,R:Professor X,A:Star
    Jammers,Imperial Guard 6.00
275a 2nd Printing (Gold). 3.00
276 JLe,SW,V:Skrulls,Shi'ar 3.00
277 JLe,SW,V:Skrulls,Shi'ar 3.00
278 PS,Professor X Returns to
    Earth,V:Shadowking 3.00
279 NKu,SW,V:Shadowking 3.00
280 E:CCl(s),NKu,A:X-Factor,
    D:Shadowking,Prof.X Crippled . 3.00
281 WPo,ATi,new team (From X-Men
    #1),D:Pierce,Hellions,V:Sentinels,
    I:Trevor Fitzroy,Upstarts 5.00
281a 2nd printing,red(c) 1.25
282 WPo,ATi,V:Fitzroy,C:Bishop . . . 9.00
282a 2nd printing,gold(c) of #281
    inside 1.25
283 WPo,ATi,I:Bishop,Malcolm,
    Randall. 10.00
284 WPo,ATi,SOS from USSR. . . . 3.00
285 WPo,I:Mikhail(Colossus'
    brother from Russia) 3.00
286 JLe,WPo,ATi,A:Mikhail. 3.00
287 JR2,O:Bishop,
    D:Malcolm,Randall 3.00
288 NKu,BSz,A:Bishop. 3.00
289 WPo,ATi,Forge proposes
    to Storm 3.00
290 WPo,SW,V:Cyberpunks,
    L:Forge 3.00
291 TR,V:Morlocks. 2.50
292 TR,V:Morlocks 2.50
293 TR,D:Morlocks,Mikhail. 2.50
294 BP,TA,X-Cutioner's Song#1,
    Stryfe shoots Prof X,A:X-Force,
    X-Factor,polybag.w/ProfX card . 3.00
295 BP,TA,X-Cutioners Song #5,
    V:Apocalypse 3.00
296 BP,TA,X-Cutioners Song #9,
    A:X-Force,X-Factor,V:Stryfe . . . 3.00
297 BP,X-Cutioners Song
    Aftermath. 2.00
298 BP,TA,V:Acolytes 2.00
299 BP,A:Forge,Acolytes,I:Graydon
    Creed (Sabretooth's son) 2.00
300 JR2,DGr,BP,V:Acolytes,A:Forge,
    Nightcrawler,Holografx(c) 5.00
301 JR2,DGr,I:Sienna Blaze,
    V:Fitzroy. 2.00
302 JR2,V:Fitzroy. 2.00
303 JR2,V:Upstarts,D:Illyana 2.00
304 JR2,JaL,PS,L:Colossus,
    V:Magneto,Holo-grafx(c) 5.00

305 JD,F:Rogue,Bishop 2.00
306 JR2,V:Hodge 2.00
307 JR2,Bloodties#4,A:Avengers,
    V:Exodus,Cortez 2.00
308 JR2,Scott & Jean announce
    impending marriage 2.00
309 JR2,O:Professor X & Amelia . . 2.00
310 JR2,DG,A:Cable,V:X-Cutioner,
    w/card 4.00
311 JR2,DG,AV,V:Sabretooth,
    C:Phalanx 2.00
312 JMd,DG,A:Yukio,I:Phalanx,
    w/card 2.00
313 JMd,DG,V:Phalanx 2.00
314 LW,BSz,R:White Quen. 2.00
315 F:Acolytes 2.00
316 V:Phalanx,I:M,Phalanx Covenant
    Generation Next,pt.1, holo(c) . . 5.00
316a newsstand ed. 2.00
317 JMd,V:Phalanx,prism(c) 5.00
317a newsstand ed. 2.00
318 JMd,L:Jubilee, deluxe 2.25
318a newsstand ed. 2.00
319 R:Legion, deluxe 2.25
319a newsstand ed. 2.00
320 deluxe ed. 4.00
320 newsstand ed. 2.00
321 R:Lilandra, deluxe ed. 2.25
321 newsstand ed. 2.00
322 SLo,TGu,Rogue,Iceman run from
    Gambit's Secret 6.00
323 I:Onslaught 2.25
324 SLo,F:Cannonball 2.25
325 R:Colossus 4.50
326 SLo,JMd,F:Gambit,Sabretooth . 2.00
327 SLo,JMd,Magneto's Fate 2.00
328 SLo,JMd,Sabretooth freed . . . 2.00
329 SLo,JMd,A:Doctor Strange. . . 2.00
330. . . . . 2.00
331 . . . . 2.00
332 SLo,JMd, cont from
    Wolverine #100 . . . . 2.00
333 SLo,JMd, Operation: Zero
    Tolerance, Onslaught saga 3.00
334 SLo,JMd, Onslaught saga 3.00
335 SLo,JMd, Onslaught saga 3.00
336 Apocalypse vs. Onslaught 2.50
337 Operation: Zero Tolerance 2.50
338 SLo,JMd,R:Angel. 2.50
339 SLo,JMd,F:Cyclops, J.J.
    Jameson, Havok 2.50
340 SLo,JMd,F:Iceman. 2.50
341 SLo,JMd,Rogue gets gift 2.50
342 SLo,JMd, Shi'ar Empire, pt.1 . . 4.00
342a Rogue cover. 17.00
343 SLo,JMd, Shi'ar Empire, pt.2 . . 2.50
344 SLo,JMd, Shi'ar Empire, pt.3 . . 2.50
345 SLo,JMd, trip home, A:Akron . . 5.00
346 SLo,JMd,Zero Tolerance,
    A:Spider-Man 4.00
347 SLo,JMd,Zero Tolerance 2.00
348 SLo,JMd,at Magneto's base . . . 2.00
349 SLo,JMd,Maggot vs. Psylocke
    & Archangel 2.00
350 SSe,JMd,Trial of Gambit,
    double-sized. 4.00
350a Gambit (c) 15.00
351 SSe,JMd,Dr. Cecilia Reyes . . . 3.00
352 SSe,EBe,Cyclops & Phoenix
    leave, Facade arrives 3.00
353 SSe,CBa,Rogues Anguish 2.00
354 SSe,CBa,F:Rogue 2.00
354a Jean Gray (c). 6.00
355 SSe,CBa, North & South
    pt.2 x-over 5.00
356 SSe,CBa, originals V:Phoenix . 2.00
357 SSe,Cyclops & Phoenix. 2.00
358 SSe,CBa,Phoenix collapses. . . 2.00
359 SSe,CBa,Rogue 2.00
360A SSe,CBa, I:New X-Men, foil
    etched cover 5.00

Uncanny X-Men #296
© Marvel Entertainment Group

360B regular cover. 4.00
361 SSe,SSr,R:Gambit. 2.00
362 SSe,CBa,Hunt for Xavier,pt.1 . . 2.00
363 SSe,CBa,Hunt for Xavier,pt.3. . 2.00
364 SSe,Hunt for Xavier,pt.5. . . . . . 2.00
365 SSe,CBa,A:Professor X 2.00
366 AD,BPe,Magneto War,pt.1 . . . . 2.00
367 AD,Magneto War,pt.3. . . . . 2.00
368 AD,AKu,Requiem for an X-Man 2.00
368a signed 19.95
369 AD,AKu,V:Juggernaut 2.00
370 AD,AKu,in the past 2.00
371 AD,AKu(c),Rage Against
    the Machine, pt.1 x-over. 2.00
371a signed 20.00
372 AKu,AD,The Shattering,pt.1 . . . 2.00
373 AKu,AD,The Shattering,pt.2. . . 2.00
Ann.#1 rep.#9,#11 . . . . 75.00
Ann.#2 rep.#22,#23 . . . . 65.00
Ann.#3 GK(c),GP,TA,A:Arkon 20.00
Ann.#4 JR2,BMc,A:Dr.Strange . . . 15.00
Ann.#5 BA,BMc,A:F.F.. . . . . 12.00
Ann.#6 BSz,BWi,Dracula 13.00
Ann.#7 MGo,TMd,BWi,TA,BBr,
    BA,JRu,BBl,SL,AM,
    V:Impossible Man. 10.00
Ann.#8 SL,Kitty's story 10.00
Ann.#9 AAd,AG,MMi,Asgard,V:Loki,
    Enchantress,A:New Mutants. . 15.00
Ann.#10 AAd,TA,V:Mojo,
    J:Longshot,A:New Mutants . . . 13.00
Ann.#11 AD,V:Horde,A:CaptBrit . . . 6.00
Ann.#12 AAd,BWi,RLm,TD,Evol.
    War,V:Terminus,Savage Land. . 6.00
Ann.#13 MBa,JRu,Atlantis Attacks . 5.00
Ann.#14 AAd,DGr,BWi,AM,ATi,
    V:Ahab,A:X-Factor,. 8.00
Ann.#15,TR,JRu,MMi(c),Flesh Tears,
    Pt.3,A:X-Force,New Warriors . . 5.00
Ann.#16 JaL,JRu,Shattershot
    Part.2. . . . . 4.00
Ann.#17 JPe,MFm,I:X-Cutioner,
    D:Mastermind,w/card 4.00
Ann.#18 JR2,V:Caliban,
    BU:Bishop 3.25
Marvel Milestone rep. #1 (1991) . . . 2.95
Marvel Milestone rep. #9 (1993) . . . 2.95
Marvel Milestone rep. #28 (1994) . . 2.95
G-Size #1,GK,DC,I:New X-Men
    (Colossus,Storm,Nightcrawler,
    Thunderbird,3rd A:Wolv.) . . . 500.00
G-Size #2,rep.#57-59 . . . . 55.00
Marvel Milestone rep. Giant
    Size #1 (1991) 3.95

Spec.#1 X-Men: Earth Fall,
  rep. #232–#234 (1996) 2.95
Spec.#1 X-Men vs. Dracula, rep.
  X-Men Ann.#6 (1993) 2.00
GNv X-Men: Days of Future Past
  rep. X-Men #141-142 .... 5.00
GNv Pryde of the X-Men 10.95
GNv God Loves,Man Kills,
  (1994) prestige 6.95
GN X-Men Firsts, I:Wolverine,Rogue,
  Gambit & Mr. Sinister, rep. Avengers
  Ann.#10, Uncanny X-Men
  #221,#266
  & Incredible Hulk #181 (1996) . 5.00
GNv X-Men Rarities,F:Classic
  Stories (1995) 5.95
TPB Asgardian Wars 15.95
TPB Bloodties V:Exodus 15.95
TPB The Coming of Bishop, rep.
  #282–#285,#287–#288 (1995) 12.95
TPB Dark Phoenix Saga 12.95
TPB X-Men: Days of Future Present,
  MMi(c),Rep.F.F.Ann.#23,X-Men
  Ann.#14,X-Factor Ann.#5,
  New Mutant Ann.#10 ...... 14.95
TPB Essential X-Men
  collection, rep. 12.95
TPB Fatal Attractions (1994) ... 17.95
TPB From the Ashes 16.95
TPB Greatest Battles 15.95
TPB X-Men: Inferno, 352pg 19.95
TPB X-Men Megazine, CCl,JLe, rep.
  Uncanny X-Men #273–#275 ... 3.95
TPB X-Men: Mutant Massacre,
  rep. 256pg 24.95
TPB Savage Land 9.95
TPB X-Cutioner's Song 24.95
TPB X-Tinction Agenda, rep.X-Men
  #270-272,X-Factor #60-62,
  New Mutants #95-97 ...... 19.95
X-Men Survival Guide to the
  Mansion, NKu(c) (1993) 6.95

X-MEN

[2nd Regular Series] Oct., 1991
1A(c);Storm,Beast,B:CCl(s),JLe,SW
  I:Fabian Cortez,Acolytes,
  V:Magneto 3.00
1B(c);Colossus,Psylocke 3.00
1C(c);Cyclops,Wolverine 3.00
1D(c);Magneto................ 3.00
1E(c);Gatefold w/pin-ups 6.50
2 JLe,SW,V:Magneto Contd. 4.00
3 E:CCl(s),JLe,SW,V:Magneto ... 4.00
4 JBy(s),JLe,SW,I:Omega Red,
  V:Hand................... 4.00
5 B:SLo(s),JLe,SW,V:Hand,
  Omega Red,I:Maverick....... 4.00
6 JLe,SW,V:Omega Red, Hand,
  Sabretooth 4.00
7 JLe,SW,V:Omega Red,Hand,
  Sabretooth 3.00
8 JLe,SW,Bishop vs. Gambit 3.00
9 JLe,SW,A:Ghost Rider,V:Brood.. 3.00
10 JLe,SW,MT,Longshot Vs. Mojo,
  BU:Maverick............... 3.00
11 E:SLo(s)JLe,MT,V:Mojo,
  BU:Maverick............... 2.50
12 B:FaN(s),ATb,BWi,I:Hazard 2.50
13 ATb,BWi,V:Hazard........... 2.50
14 NKu,X-Cutioners Song#3,A:X-Fact.
  X-Force,V:Four Horsemen 2.50
15 NKu,X-Cutioners Song #7,
  V:Mutant Liberation Front 2.50
16 NKu,MPn,X-Cutioners Song #11,
  A:X-Force,X-Factor,V:Dark Riders,
  Apocalypse Vs.Archangel,IR:Stryfe
  is Nathan Summers 2.50
17 NKu,MPn,R:Illyana,A:Darkstar.. 2.50
18 NKu,MPn,R:Omega Red,V:Soul

Skinner 2.50
19 NKu,MPn,V:Soul Skinner,
  Omega Red.............. 2.50
20 NKu,MPn,J.Grey vs Psylocke .. 2.50
21 NKu,V:Silver Samurai,Shinobi .. 2.50
22 BPe,V:Silver Samurai,Shinobi .. 2.50
23 NKu,MPn,V:Dark Riders,
  Mr.Sinister 2.50
24 NKu,BSz,A Day in the Life..... 2.50
25 NKu,Hologram(c),V:Magneto,
  Wolverine's Adamantium skeleton
  pulled out............... 14.00
25a Gold Edition............. 38.00
25b B&W cover 30.00
26 NKu,Bloodties#2,A:Avengers,
  I:Unforgiven 2.50
27 RiB,I:Threnody............. 2.50
28 NKu,MRy,F:Sabretooth 2.50
29 NKu,MRy,V:Shinobi 2.50
30 NKu,MRy,W:Cyclops&Jean Grey,
  w/card 5.00
31 NKu,MRy,A:Spiral,Matsuo,
  D:Kwannon 2.50
32 NKu,MRy,A:Spiral,Matsuo 2.25
33 NKu,MRy,F:Gambit &
  Sabretooth 2.25
34 NKu,MRy,A:Riptide......... 2.25
35 LSh,A:Nick Fury.............. 2.25
36 NKu,MRy,I:Synch,PhalanxCovenant
  Generation Next,pt.2, deluxe .. 5.00
36a Newsstand ed.............. 1.75
37 NKu,MRy,Generation Next,pt.3
  foil(c) 5.00
37a newsstand ed............. 1.75
38 NKu,MRy,F:Psylocke 2.50
38a newsstand ed.............. 1.50
39 X-Treme, deluxe 2.50
39a newsstand ed.............. 1.50
40 deluxe.................. 3.00
40a newsstand ed............. 1.50
41 V:Legion, deluxe 2.50
41a newsstand ed............. 1.50
42 PS,PaN,Mysterious Visitor.... 2.50
43 Rogue and Iceman 2.50
44 FaN,Mystery of Magneto 2.50
45 20th Anniv.pt.2............. 4.00
46 FaN,Aku,V:Comcast......... 2.00
47 SLo,AKu,CaS,F:Dazzler....... 2.00
48 SLo,AKu,CaS,F:Sabretooth 2.00
49 SLo,AKu,Bishop wanted 3.00
50 Onslaught(c)............. 6.00
50a regular edition 4.00
51 MWa,Onslaught............. 2.50
52 MWa,AKu,CaS,V:Sinister 2.50

X-Men, 2nd Series #1
© *Marvel Entertainment Group*

53 Onslaught saga 6.00
54 Onslaught saga 5.00
55 Onslaught saga 3.00
56 Onslaught saga 3.00
57 Operation: Zero Tolerence 2.50
58 SLo,NKu 2.50
59 .... 2.50
60 SLo,NKu,F:Ororo, V:Candra.... 2.50
61 SLo,CNn,F:Storm, V:Candra ... 2.50
62 SLo,CPa,F:Sebastian Shaw,
  Shang Chi 2.50
62A variant Storm/Wolverine(c).. . 13.00
63 SLo,CPa,ATi,A:Sebastian Shaw,
  Inner Circle 2.50
64 SLo,CPa,ATi,V:Hellfire Club ... 2.50
65 SLo,CPa,ATi, No Exit prelude .. 2.50
66 SLo,CPa,ATi, Zero Tolerance,
  A:Bastion 2.00
67 SLo,CPa,ATi, Zero Tolerance,
  F:Iceman, Cecilia Reyes. 2.00
68 SLo,CPa,ATi, Operation: Zero
  Tolerance 2.00
69 SLo,CPa, Operation: Zero Tolerance,
  concl. 2.00
70 ATi,Who will join X-Men?,
  double-sized. 5.00
71 ATi,Cyclops banished. 4.00
72 ATi,Professor Logan's School of
  Hard Knocks 2.50
73 ATi,Marrow visits Callisto 2.00
74 ATi,Terror in Morlock Tunnels.... 2.00
75 ATi,V:N'Garai, double size 3.00
76 CCl,V:Sabretooth, 35th anniv
  kickoff 2.00
77 ATi,A:Black Panther,Maggott ... 2.00
78 Return of Professor X 2.00
79 ATi,Cannonball must leave team 2.00
80A BPe, ATi, cont. from Uncanny X-
  Men #360, etched foil (c) 4.00
80B regular cover............. 3.00
81 AKu,MFm,Search for Prof.X.... 2.00
82 AKu,MFm,Hunt for Xavier 2.00
83 AKu,MFm,Hunt for Xavier,pt.4 .. 2.00
84 AJu,Hunt for Xavier,concl. 2.00
85 AD,MFm,R:Magneto 2.00
85a signed 30.00
86 AD,MFm,Magneto War,pt.2,
  O:Joseph 2.00
87 AD,MFm,Magneto War,pt.4 .... 2.00
88 AD,MFm,R:Juggernaut 2.00
89 AD,MFm,In the past......... 2.00
90 AD,MFm,In the past,concl...... 2.00
91 AD,AKu,Rage Against
  the Machine, pt.2 x-over...... 2.00
91a signed 30.00
92 AD,MFm,The Shattering x-over . 2.00
93 AD,MFm,The Shattering x-over . 2.00
Ann.#1 JLe,Shattershot,pt.1,
  I:Mojo II 3.50
Ann.#2 I:Empyrean,w/card 3.25
Ann.#3 F:Storm 3.50
Ann. Uncanny X-Men '97, V:Brother-
  hood, 48pg. 3.00
Ann. '98 RMz, F:X-Men & Doctor
  Doom 3.00
Ann. '98 X-Men/Fantastic Four, JoC,
  PaP, 48pg 3.00
Ann.1999 Rage Against the
  Machine, pt.3 x-over, 48-page . 3.50
Uncanny X-Men'95 Spec. F:Husk .. 3.95
Spec.X-Men '95, F:Mr.Sinister.... 3.95
Spec.X-Men'96 LHa, 64pg., F:Gambit,
  Rogue, Magneto, Jubilee
  & Wolverine 2.95
Spec. X-Men'97,JFM,SEp,F:Gambit,
  Joesph & Phoenix 3.00
Minus 1 Spec., SLo,JMd,, flashback,
  discovery of mutants 1.95
Spec.#1 X-Men: Road to Onslaught
  (1996) 2.50
Spec. X-Men Universe: Past,

Present and Future. 3.00
Chrom.Classics, Vol.2,#1,signed . . 30.00
GN TKa,AD,MFm, Age of
    Apocalypse 2.95
TPB Dark Phoenix Saga 15.95
TPB Dawn of the Age of
    Apocalypse, gold foil cover. . . . 8.95
TPB Legion Quest 8.95
TPB Magneto Returns 15.95
TPB Rise of Apocalypse 9.00
TPB Twilight of the Age of
    Apocalypse, gold foil cover. . . . 8.95
TPB Crossroads 15.95
TPB Phoenix Rising 14.95
TPB Road Trippin 20.00

X-MEN ADVENTURES
[1st Season] 1992–94
1 V:Sentinals, Based on TV
    Cartoon 6.00
2 V:Sentinals,D:Morph. 5.00
3 V:Magneto,A:Sabretooth. 4.00
4 V:Magneto 4.00
5 V:Morlocks 4.00
6 V:Sabretooth 3.50
7 V:Cable,Genosha,Sentinels . . . 3.00
8 A:Colossus,A:Juggernaut 3.00
9 I:Colussus(on cartoon),
    V:Juggernaut 3.00
10 A:Angel,V:Mystique 3.00
11 I:Archangel(on cartoon) 2.00
12 V:Horsemen of Apocalypse 2.00
13 RMc(s),I:Bishop(on cartoon) . . . 2.00
14 V:Brotherhood of Evil Mutants . . 2.00
15 . . . . 2.00
TPB Vol.1 . . . . 4.95
TPB Vol.2 . . . . 4.95
TPB Vol.3 . . . . 5.95
TPB Vol.4 rep. Days of Future Past
    and Final Conflict 6.95
[2nd Season] 1994–95
1 R:Morph,I:Mr. Sinister
    (on cartoon) 3.00
2 I:Nasty Boys (on cartoon) 2.00
3 I:Shadow King (on cartoon) 2.00
4 I:Omega Red (on cartoon) 2.00
5 I:Alpha Flight (on cartoon). 2.00
6 F:Gambit 2.00
7 A:Cable,Bishop,Apocalypse . . . 1.75
8 A:Cable,Biship,Apocalypse 1.75
9 O:Rogue. 1.75
10 . . . . 1.75
11 F:Mojo,Longshot 1.75

X-Men Adventures #5
© Marvel Entertainment Group

12 Reunions,pt.1 . . . . 1.75
13 Reunions,pt.1 . . . . 1.75
[3rd Season] 1995–96
1 Out of the Past,pt.1 . . . . 3.00
2 V:Spirit Drinker 1.75
3 Phoenix Saga,pt.1 . . . . 1.75
4 Phoenix Saga,pt.2 . . . . 1.75
5 Phoenix Saga,pt.3 . . . . 1.75
6 Phoenix Saga,pt.4 . . . . 1.75
7 Phoenix Saga,pt.5 . . . . 1.50
8 War in The Savage Land 1.50
9 F:Ka-Zar. 1.50
10 Dark Phoenix,Saga,pt.1 . . . . . . 1.50
11 Dark Phoenix Saga,pt.2 . . . . . . 1.50
12 Dark Phoenix Saga,pt.3 . . . . . . 1.50
13 Dark Phoenix Saga,pt.4 . . . . . . 1.50

X-MEN: ALPHA
1994
1 Age of Apocalypse, double size . 7.00
1a gold edition, 48pp 45.00

X-Men Alpha Flight #1
© Marvel Entertainment Group

X-MEN/ALPHA FLIGHT
Jan., 1986
1 PS,BWi,V:Loki 5.00
2 PS,BWi,V:Loki 4.00

X-MEN/ALPHA FLIGHT: THE GIFT
Jan. 1998
1-shot CCI,PS, rep. of limited series 6.00

X-MEN/ ANIMATION SPECIAL
TV Screenplay Adapt 10.95

X-MEN ARCHIVES: CAPTAIN BRITAIN
1995
1 AMo,AD,Secret History. 3.00
2 AMo,AD,F:Captain Britain. 3.00
3 AMo,AD,Trial of Captain Britain . 3.00
4 AMo,AD,Trial cont. 3.00
5 AD,AMo,F:Captain Britain. 3.00
6 AMo,AD,Final Apocalypse? 3.00
7 AMo,AD,conclusion 3.00

X-MEN: ASKANI'SON
1 SLo,GeH,sequel to Adventures of
    Cyclops & Phoenix 3.00
2 SLo,GeH,A:Stryfe 3.00
3 SLo,GeH 3.00
4 SLo,GeH,conclusion 3.00
Books of Askani, portraits (1995) . . 3.00

X-MEN AT STATE FAIR
1 KGa,Dallas Times Herald 40.00

X-MEN CHRONICLES
1995
1 X-Men Unlimited AX 4.00
2 V:Abbatoir 4.00

X-MEN/CLANDESTINE
1996
1 & 2 AD,MFm,48pg . . . . @3.00

X-MEN CLASSICS
Dec., 1983
1 NA,rep. 3.50
2 NA,rep. 3.50
3 NA,rep. 3.50

CLASSIC X-MEN
Sept., 1986
1 AAd(c),JBo,New stories, rep.
    giant size X-Men 1 . . . . 9.00
2 rep.#94,JBo/AAd(c),BU:
    Storm & Marvel Girl 6.00
3 rep.#95,JBo/AAd(c),BU:
    I:Thunderbird II 4.00
4 rep.#96,JBo/AAd(c),BU:
    Wolverine & N.Crawler 3.50
5 rep.#97,JBo/AAd(c),BU:
    Colossus 3.00
6 rep.#98,JBo/AAd(c),BU:
    JeanGrey,I:Seb.Shaw. 3.00
7 rep.#99,JBo/AAd(c),BU:
    HellfireClub,W.Queen 3.00
8 rep.#100,JBo/AAd(c),BU:
    O:Jean Grey/Phoenix 3.00
9 rep.#101,JBo/AAd(c),BU:
    Nightcrawler 3.00
10 rep.#102,JBo/AAd(c),BU:
    Wolverine,A:Sabretooth 8.00
11 rep.#103,JBo/BL(c),BU:Storm . . 2.50
12 rep.#104,JBo/AAd(c),BU:
    O:Magneto. 7.00
13 rep.#105,JBo/AAd(c),BU:
    JeanGrey & Misty Knight 3.00
14 rep.#107,JBo/AAd(c),BU:
    Lilandra 3.00
15 rep.#108,JBo/AAd(c),BU:
    O:Starjammers 3.00
16 rep.#109,JBo/AAd(c),BU:
    Banshee. 3.00
17 rep.#111,JBo/TA(c),BU:
    Mesmero 5.00
18 rep.#112,JBo/AAd(c),BU:
    Phoenix 4.00
19 rep.#113,JBo/AAd(c),BU:
    Magnetoo 4.00
20 rep.#114,JBo/AAd(c),
    BU:Storm 3.00
21 rep.#115,JBo/AAd(c),
    BU:Colossus. 3.00
22 rep.#116,JBo/AAd(c),
    BU:Storm 3.00
23 rep.#117,JBo/KGa(c),BU:
    Nightcrawler. 3.00
24 rep.#118,JBo/KGa(c),BU:
    Phoenix 3.00
25 rep.#119,JBo/KGa(c),BU:Wolv.. . 3.00
26 rep.#120,JBo/KGa(c),BU:Wolv. . 4.00

Classic X-Men #9
© Marvel Entertainment Group

27 rep.#121,JBo/KD(c),BU:
  Wolverine & Phoenix 3.00
28 rep.#122,JBo/KD(c),BU:X-Men. . 3.00
29 rep.#123,JBo/KD(c),BU:
  Colossus 3.00
30 rep.#124,JBo/SLi(c),BU:
  O:Arcade 3.00
31 rep.#125,JBo/SLi(c),BU:
  Professor.X 3.00
32 rep.#126,JBo/SLi(c),BU:
  Wolverine. 3.00
33 rep.#127,JBo/SLi(c),BU:
  Havok 3.00
34 rep.#128,JBo/SLi(c),BU:
  W.Queen,M.Mind 3.00
35 rep.#129,JBo/SLi(c),BU:
  K.Pryde 3.00
36 rep.#130,MBr/SLi(c),BU:
  Banshee & Moira 3.00
37 rep.#131,RL/SLi(c),BU:
  Dazzler 3.00
38 rep.#132,KB/SLi(c),BU:
  Dazzler 3.00
39 rep.#133,2nd JLe X-Men/SLi(c),
  BU:Storm 11.00
40 rep.#134,SLi(c),BU:N.Crawler . . 2.00
41 rep.#135,SLi(c),BU:
  Mr. Sinister,Cyclops 2.00
42 rep.#136,SLi(c),BU:
  Mr. Sinister,Cyclops 2.00
43 rep.#137,JBy(c),BU:
  Phoenix,Death 2.50
Becomes:

X-MEN CLASSICS
1990
44 rep.#138,KD/SLi(c) 2.00
45 thru 49 rep.#139-#145,SLi(c) . @2.00
50 thru 69 rep.#146-#165 . . . . . @1.50
70 rep.#166 . . . . 1.75
71 thru 99 rep.#167-#195 . . . . . @1.50
100 thru 105 rep. #196-#201 . . . @1.50
106 Phoenix vs. Beyonder 1.50
107 F:Rogue 1.50
108 F:Nightcrawler 1.50
109 Rep. Uncanny X-Men #205 . . . 1.50
110 Rep. Uncanny X-Men #206 . . . 1.50

X-MEN: EARLY YEARS
1 rep. X-Men (first series) #1 . . 1.75
2 rep. X-Men (first series) #2 . . . . 1.75
3 rep. X-Men (first series) #3 . . . . 1.75
4 thru 16 rep. X-Men (first series)
  #4 to #16 . . . . @1.50

---

17 Rep. X-Men #17 & #18 . . . . . . 2.50

X-MEN INDEX
See: OFFICIAL MARVEL
INDEX TO THE X-MEN

X-MEN: LIBERATORS
Sept. 1999
1 (of 4) PJ,F:Wolverine,Nightcrawler
  & Colossus. 3.00
2 PJ,V:Russian army 3.00
3 PJ,V:Nikolas. 3.00
4 PJ,V:Omega Red 3.00

X-MEN: LOST TALES
1997
1 CCi,JBo,rep. from Classic X-Men 3.00
2 CCi,JBo,rep. from Classic X-Men 3.00

X-MEN/MICRONAUTS
Jan., 1984
1 JG,BWi,Limited Series 3.50
2 JG,BWi,KJo,V:Baron Karza. . . . 2.50
3 JG,BWi,V:Baron Karza 2.50
4 JG,BWi,V:Baron Karza,Apr.1984. 2.50

X-MEN: THE MANGA
Jan. 1998
1 b&w,translated,F:Jubilee 3.00
2 Jubilee joins, V:Sentinels 3.00
3 Agent Gyrich strikes 3.00
4 Beast captured, morph dead. . . . 3.00
5 Magneto attempts to rescue
  Beast. 3.00
6 Beast on trial, A:Sabretooth 3.00
7 V:Magneto 3.00
8 V:Magneto 3.00
9 V:Morlocks 3.00
10 V:Morlocks, 40pg finale 3.00
11 Wolverine vs. Sabretooth 3.00
12 Wolverine vs. Sabretooth 3.00
13 F:Storm, Jubilee & Gambit. . . . 3.00
14 . . . . 3.00
15 . . . . 3.00
16 A:Colossus,V:Juggernaut,
  double-size. 4.00
17 F:Cable & Angel 3.00
18 Angel becomes Archangel 3.00
19 Angel becomes Death 3.00
20 Rogue vs. Apocalypse 3.00
21 V:Four Horsemen 3.00
22 V:Sentinels 3.00
23 RGr(c),F:Bishop. 3.00
24 RGr(c),V:Nimrod 3.00
25 Bishop vs. Gambit 3.00
26 V:Brotherhood of Evil Mutants . . 3.00
27 Magneto Returns. 3.00
28 V:Master Mold,A:Magneto 3.00
29 thru 32 . . . . @3.00

X-MEN OMEGA
1995
1 FaN,Slo,After Xavier, concl. . . . 10.00
1a Gold ed. Chromium(c) 48pg. . . 45.00

X-MEN PRIME
1995
1 SLo,FaN,BHi,major plotlines for
  all X books begin, chromium(c)10.00

X-MEN: PRYDE & WISDOM
1 WEI,TyD,KIS. 2.00
2 & 3 WEI,TyD,KIS. . . . . @2.00

X-MEN:
THE MAGNETO WAR
Jan. 1999
1-shot AD, Joseph vs. Magneto . . . 3.00
1a signed 20.00

X-MEN: THE
RISE OF APOCALYPSE
1 TKa,AdP, ancient history of
  X-Men 1.95
2 thru 4 TKa,AdP,. . . . . @1.95
TPB 10.00

X-MEN SPOTLIGHT
ON STARJAMMERS
1990
1 DC,F:Starjammers,A:Prof.X 5.00
2 DC,F:Starjammers,A:Prof.X 5.00

X-MEN: TRUE FRIENDS
July 1999
1 (of 3) CCi,RL,JP,F:Shadowcat. . . 2.00
2 CCi,RL,JP,A:Kitty Pryde 2.00

X-MEN 2099
1993-96
1 B:JFM(s),RLm,JP,I:X-Men 2099 . 3.00
1a Gold Ed. 5.00
2 RLm,JP,V:Rat Pack 2.50
3 RLm,JP,D:Serpentina 2.50
4 RLm,JP,I:Theatre of Pain 2.00
5 RLm,JP,Fall of the Hammer#3 . . 2.00
6 RLm,JP,I:Freakshow. 2.00
7 RLm,JP,V:Freakshow 2.00
8 RLm(c),JS3,JP,N;Metalhead,
  I:2nd X-Men 2099. . . . . 2.00
9 RLm,JP,V:2nd X-Men 2099. . . . 2.00
10 RLm,JP,A:La Lunatica 2.00
11 RLm,JP,V:2nd X-Men 2099 . . . 2.00
12 RLm,JP,A:Junkpile. 2.00
13 RLm,JP 2.00
14 RLm,JP,R:Loki. 2.00
15 RLm,JP,F:Loki,I:Haloween Jack . 1.50
16 . . . . 1.50
17 X'ian 1.50
18 Haloween Jack 1.50
19 Conclusion Halloween Jack . . . 1.50
Becomes:

X-MEN 2099 A.D.
20 F:Bloodhawk 1.95
21 Doom Factor 1.95
22 One Nation Under Doom 1.95
23 V:Junkpile 1.95
24 . . . . 1.95
25 X-Men Reunited. 2.50
25a variant cover 4.25
26 V:Graverobber 1.95
27 . . . . 1.95
28 X-Nation x-over 1.95
29 X-Nation x-over 1.95
30 . . . . 1.95
31 . . . . 1.95
32 V:Foolkiller. 1.95
Spec.#1 Bros.Hildebrandt(c). 3.95
GN X-Men 2099: Oasis, rep.,Greg
  Hildebrandt(c) 64pg, (1998) . . . 6.00

X-MEN UNLIMITED
1993
1 CBa,BP,O:Siena Blaze 7.00
2 JD,O:Magneto 6.00
3 FaN(s),BSz(c),MMK,Sabretooth
  joins X-Men,A:Maverick 7.00
4 SLo(s),RiB,O:Nightcrawler,Rogue,

Mystique,IR:Mystique is
Nightcrawler's mother 5.00
5 JFM(s),LSh,After Shi'ar/
Kree War 4.00
6 JFM(s),PS,Sauron 4.00
7 JR2,HMe,O:Storm 4.00
8 Legacy Virus Victim 4.00
9 LHa,Wolverine & Psylocke 4.00
10 MWa,Dark Beast,Beast,
double-size. 8.00
11 Rogue & Magneto, double-size . 8.00
12 Onslaught x-over,A:Juggernaut . 3.00
13 GP,Binary gone berserk 3.00
14 TKa, Onslaught fallout 3.00
15 HMe,F:Wolverine, Iceman &
Maverick 3.00
16 MvR,F:Banshee, White Queen,
I:Primal 3.00
17 TKa,Wolverine vs. Sabretooth,
minds are switched. 3.00
18 TDF,V:Hydro Man 3.00
19 BRa,Nightcrawler v. Belasco . . . 3.00
20 F:Generation X 3.00
21 TDz,Strong Guy returns 3.00
22 into Marrow's World 3.00
23 F:Professor X 3.00
24 F:Wolverine & Cecilia Reyes . . . 3.00

X-MEN VS. AVENGERS
April, 1987
1 MS,JRu,V:Soviet SuperSoldiers . 4.50
2 MS,JRu,V:Sov.Super Soldiers . . 3.50
3 MS,JRu,V:Sov.Super Soldiers . . 3.50
4 KP,JRu,BMc,AW,AM,V:Magneto
July 1987 . . . . 3.00
TPB 12.95

X-MEN VS. THE BROOD
1996
1 and 2 Day of Wrath . . . . @3.00
TPB rep. #1,#2 and Unc.X-Men
#232–#234 . . . . 17.00

X-NATION 2099
1996
1 . . . . 1.95
2 . . . . 1.95
3 At Herod's Themepark 1.95

X.S.E.
Mini-Series 1996
1 (of 4) JOs,Bishop & Shard's
secrets 2.00

2 JOs, How did Shard die 2.00
3 JOs, How Shard died 2.00
4 JOs, conclusion 2.00

X-TERMINATORS
Oct., 1988—Jan., 1989
1 JBg,AW,AM,I:N'astirh 4.00
2 JBg,AM,V:N'astirh. 3.50
3 JBg,AM,V:N'astirh. 3.00
4 JBg,AM,A:New Mutants 3.00

X-UNIVERSE
1995
1 The Other Heroes. 3.50
2 F:Ben Grimm,Tony Stark. 3.50

YOGI BEAR
Nov., 1977
1 A:Flintstones 15.00
2 . . . . 10.00
3 . . . . 10.00
4 . . . . 10.00
5 . . . . 10.00
6 . . . . 10.00
7 . . . . 10.00
8 . . . . 10.00
9 March, 1979 . . . . 10.00

YOUNG ALLIES COMICS
Timely Summer, 1941—Oct., 1946
1 S&K,Hitler(c),I&O:Young Allies
1st meeting Capt. America &
Human Torch,A:Red Skull 10,000.00
2 S&K,A;Capt.America,Human
Torch. 2,700.00
3 Remember Pearl Harbor(c) . 2,000.00
4 A;Capt. America,Torch,Red Skull
ASh(c),Horror In Hollywood
A:Capt.America,Torch 3,000.00
5 ASh(c) 1,200.00
6 ASh(c) 800.00
7 ASh(c) 800.00
8 ASh(c) 800.00
9 ASh(c),Axis leaders(c),
B:Tommy Type 900.00
10 ASh(c) 800.00
11 ASh(c) 700.00
12 ASh(c) 700.00
13 ASh(c) 700.00
14 . . . . 700.00
15 ASh(c) 700.00
16 ASh(c) 700.00

Young Allies #14
© Marvel Entertainment Group

17 ASh(c) 700.00
18 ASh(c) 700.00
19 ASh(c),E:Tommy Type 700.00
20 . . . . 700.00

YOUNG HEARTS
Nov., 1949—Feb., 1950
1 . . . . 50.00
2 Feb., 1950 . . . . 40.00

YOUNG MEN
See: COWBOY ROMANCES

YUPPIES FROM HELL
1989
1 Satire 2.95
2 . . . . 2.95
3 . . . . 2.95

ZORRO
Marvel UK 1990
1 Don Diego 1.00
2 thru 12 . . . . @1.00

MARVEL

GOLDEN AGE

A-1 COMICS
Magazine Enterprises, 1944
N# F:Kerry Drake,BU:Johnny
  Devildog & Streamer Kelly . . 175.00
1 A:Dotty Driple,Mr. EX,Bush
  Berry and Lew Loyal 90.00
2 A:Texas Slim & Dirty Dalton,
  The Corsair,Teddy Rich, Dotty
  Dripple,Inca Dinca,Tommy Tinker
  Little Mexico and Tugboat. . . . 50.00
3 same 30.00
4 same 30.00
5 same 30.00
6 same 28.00
7 same 25.00
8 same 25.00
9 Texas Slim Issue 28.00
10 Same characters as
  issues #2–#8 . . . . 25.00
11 Teena 40.00
12 Teena 30.00
13 JCr,Guns of Fact and Fiction,
  narcotics & junkies featured . 225.00
14 Tim Holt WesternAdventures . 450.00
15 Teena 35.00
16 Vacation Comics 28.00
17 Tim Holt #2, E:A-1 on cover . . 250.00
18 Jimmy Durante, Ph(c) 350.00
19 Tim Holt #3 . . . . 200.00
20 Jimmy Durante Ph(c) 300.00
21 OW,Joan of Arc movie adapt.. 200.00
22 Dick Powell (1949). 175.00
23 Cowboys N' Indians #6 . . . . . . 35.00
24 FF(c),LbC,Trail Colt #2. . . . . . 275.00
25 Fibber McGee & Molly (1949) . 50.00
26 LbC, Trail Colt #2. . . . . 200.00
27 Ghost Rider#1,O:GhostRider . 550.00
28 Christmas (Koko & Kola) 20.00
29 FF(c), Ghost Rider #2 . . . . . . 475.00
30 BP, Jet Powers #1 . . . . 250.00
31 FF,Ghost Rider#3,O:Ghost
  Rider 450.00
32 AW,GE,Jet Powers #2 . . . . . . 200.00
33 Muggsy Mouse #2 . . . . 28.00
34 FF(c),Ghost Rider #4 . . . . 450.00
35 AW,Jet Powers 275.00
36 Muggsy Mouse 35.00
37 FF(c),Ghost Rider 450.00
38 AW,WW,Jet Powers 275.00
39 Muggsy Mouse 20.00
40 Dogface Dooley 28.00
41 Cowboys N' Indians 22.00
42 BP,Best of the West 325.00
43 Dogface Dooley 20.00
44 Ghost Rider 200.00
45 American Air Forces 35.00
46 Best of the West 175.00
47 FF,Thunda 900.00
48 Cowboys N' Indians 22.00
49 Dogface Dooley 15.00
50 BP,Danger Is Their Busines . . 100.00
51 Ghost Rider 200.00
52 Best of the West 150.00
53 Dogface Dooley 15.00
54 BP,American Air Forces 35.00
55 BP,U.S. Marines 25.00
56 BP,Thunda. 150.00
57 Ghost Rider 175.00
58 American Air Forces 35.00
59 Best of the West 100.00
60 The U.S. Marines. 35.00
61 Space Ace. 375.00
62 Starr Flagg. 300.00
63 FF,Manhunt 275.00

64 Dogface Dooley 15.00
65 BP,American Air Forces 35.00
66 Best of the West 100.00
67 American Air Forces 35.00
68 U.S. Marines 35.00
69 Ghost Rider 175.00
70 Best of the West 100.00
71 Ghost Rider 175.00
72 U.S. Marines 35.00
73 BP,Thunda. 125.00
74 BP,American Air Forces 30.00
75 Ghost Rider 150.00
76 Best of the West 100.00
77 LbC,Grl,Manhunt 225.00
78 BP,Thunda. 100.00
79 American Air Forces 35.00
80 Ghost Rider 150.00
81 Best of the West 100.00
82 BP,Cave Girl 325.00
83 BP,Thunda. 100.00
84 Ghost Rider 150.00
85 Best of the West 100.00
86 BP,Thunda. 100.00
87 Best of the West 100.00
88 Bobby Benson's B-Bar-B 50.00
89 BP,Home Run,Stan Musial . . . 175.00
90 Red Hawk 70.00
91 BP,American Air Forces 30.00
92 Dream Book of Romance 35.00
93 BP,Great Western 150.00
94 FF,White Indian 175.00
95 BP,Muggsy Mouse 15.00
96 BP,Cave Girl 250.00
97 Best of the West 100.00
98 Undercover Girl 275.00
99 Muggsy Mouse 12.00
100 Badmen of the West 175.00
101 FF,White Indian 150.00
101(a) FG, Dream Book of
  Romance, Marlon Brando. . . 125.00
103 BP,Best of the West 100.00
104 FF,White Indian 150.00
105 Great Western 100.00
106 BP,Dream Book of Love 75.00
107 Hot Dog 25.00
108 BP,BC,Red Fox 125.00
109 BP,Dream Book of Romance . 40.00
110 Dream Book of Romance 40.00

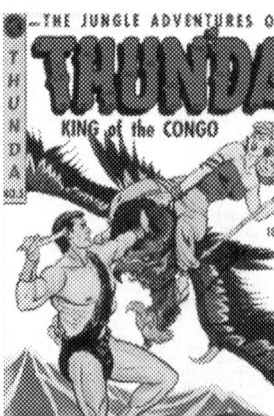

A-1 Comics #83
© Magazine Enterprises

111 BP,I'm a Cop 125.00
112 Ghost Rider 110.00
113 BP,Great Western. 100.00
114 Dream Book of Love 55.00
115 Hot Dog 18.00
116 BP,Cave Girl 200.00
117 White Indian. 75.00
118 BP(c),Undercover Girl 250.00
119 Straight Arrow's Fury 100.00
120 Badmen of the West 125.00
121 Mysteries of the
  Scotland Yard. 125.00
122 Black Phantom. 275.00
123 Dream Book of Love 40.00
124 Hot Dog. 18.00
125 BP,Cave Girl 200.00
126 BP,I'm a Cop. 55.00
127 BP,Great Western 100.00
128 BP,I'm a Cop 55.00
129 The Avenger 275.00
130 BP,Strongman 150.00
131 BP,The Avenger. 200.00
132 Strongman 125.00
133 BP,The Avenger. 200.00
134 Strongman 125.00
135 White Indian 75.00
136 Hot Dog 15.00
137 BP,Africa 135.00
138 BP,Avenger 200.00
139 BP,Strongman, 1955 . . . . . . 100.00

ABBIE AN' SLATS
United Features Syndicate
March–Aug., 1948
1 RvB(c) 225.00
2 RvB(c) 175.00
3 RvB(c) 100.00
4 Aug., 1948 . . . . 100.00
N# 1940,Earlier Issue 275.00
N#. 225.00

ABBOTT AND COSTELLO
St. John Publishing Co.
Feb., 1948
1 PP(c), Waltz Time. 400.00
2 Jungle Girl and Snake(c) 200.00
3 Outer Space cover 150.00
4 MD, Circus cover 125.00
5 MD,Bull Fighting cover 125.00
6 MD,Harem cover 125.00
7 MD,Opera cover 125.00
8 MD,Pirates cover 125.00
9 MD,Polar Bear cover 125.00
10 MD,PP(c),Son of Sinbad tale . 170.00
11 MD 100.00
12 PP(c), Movie issue. 100.00
13 Fire fighters cover 100.00
14 Bomb cover. 100.00
15 Bubble Bath cover 100.00
16 thru 29 MD. . . . . @75.00
30 thru 39 MD. . . . . @50.00
40 MD,Sept., 1956. . . . . 50.00
3-D #1, Nov. 1953. . . . . 250.00

ACE COMICS
David McKay Publications
April, 1937
1 JM, F:Katzenjammer Kids . . 2,800.00
2 JM, A:Blondie 750.00
3 JM, A:Believe It Or Not. 525.00
4 JM, F:Katzenjammer Kids. . . . 500.00

All comics prices listed are for *Near Mint* condition.

5 JM, A:Believe It Or Not 500.00
6 JM, A:Blondie 365.00
7 JM, A:Believe It Or Not 365.00
8 JM, A:Jungle Jim 365.00
9 JM, A:Blondie 365.00
10 JM, F:Katzenjammer Kids . . . 350.00
11 I:The Phantom series 600.00
12 A:Blondie, Jungle Jim 325.00
13 A:Ripley's Believe It Or Not . . 300.00
14 A:Blondie, Jungle Jim 300.00
15 A:Blondie 275.00
16 F:Katzenjammer Kids 275.00
17 A:Blondie 275.00
18 A:Ripley's Believe It Or Not . . 275.00
19 F:Katzenjammer Kids 275.00
20 A:Jungle Jim 275.00
21 A:Blondie 250.00
22 A:Jungle Jim 250.00
23 F:Katzenjammer Kids 250.00
24 A:Blondie 250.00
25 . . . . 250.00
26 O:Prince Valiant 750.00
27 thru 36 . . . . @250.00
37 Krazy Kat Ends 175.00
38 thru 49 . . . . @150.00
50 thru 59 . . . . @125.00
60 thru 69 . . . . @120.00
70 thru 79 . . . . @110.00
80 thru 89 . . . . @100.00
90 thru 99 . . . . @75.00
100 . . . . 100.00
101 thru 109 . . . . @75.00
110 thru 119 . . . . @65.00
120 thru 143 . . . . @60.00
144 Phantom covers begin 100.00
145 thru 150 . . . . @75.00
151 Oct.–Nov., 1949 . . . . 100.00

ACES HIGH
E.C. Comics, March–April, 1955
1 GE(c),JDa,WW,GE,BK 200.00
2 GE(c),JDa,WW,GE,BK 125.00
3 GE(c),JDa,WW,GE,BK 100.00
4 GE(c),JDa,WW,GE,BK 100.00
5 GE(c),JDa,WW,BK,
    Nov.–Dec., 1955 . . . . 100.00

ADVENTURES INTO
DARKNESS
Standard Publications
Aug., 1952
5 JK(c), ATh 225.00

Adventures Into Darkness #10
© *Standard Publications*

6 GT, JK 125.00
7 JK(c) 150.00
8 ATh 160.00
9 JK,ATh 175.00
10 JK,ATh,MSy. 125.00
11 JK,ATh,MSy. 125.00
12 JK,ATh,MYs. 125.00
13 Cannibalism feature 135.00
14 . . . . 100.00

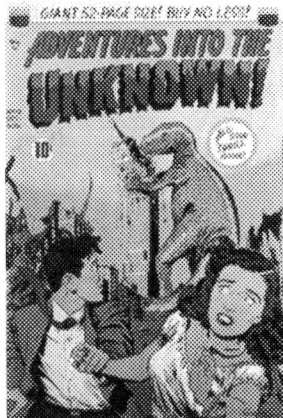

Adventures Into the Unknown #13
© *American Comics Group*

ADVENTURES INTO
THE UNKNOWN!
American Comics Group
Fall 1948
1 FG, Haunted House cover . . 1,500.00
2 Haunted Island cover 600.00
3 AF, Sarcophagus cover 625.00
4 Monsters cover 275.00
5 Monsters cover 275.00
6 Giant Hands cover 225.00
7 Skeleton Pirate cover 225.00
8 Horror 225.00
9 Snow Monster 225.00
10 Red Bats 225.00
11 Death Shadow 225.00
12 OW(c) 225.00
13 OW(c),Dinosaur 175.00
14 OW(c),Cave 175.00
15 Red Demons 175.00
16 . . . . 175.00
17 OW(c),The Thing Type 225.00
18 OW(c),Wolves 175.00
19 OW(c),Graveyard 150.00
20 OW(c),Graveyard 150.00
21 Bats and Dracula 150.00
22 Death 150.00
23 Bats 150.00
24 . . . . 150.00
25 . . . . 150.00
26 . . . . 150.00
27 AW 200.00
28 thru 39 . . . . @125.00
40 thru 49 . . . . @110.00
50 . . . . 125.00
51 Lazarus 235.00
52 Lazarus 235.00
53 . . . . 225.00
54 . . . . 225.00
55 . . . . 225.00
56 Lazarus 225.00
57 . . . . 225.00
58 Lazarus 225.00
59 . . . . 200.00
60 . . . . 75.00

61 . . . . 75.00
62 thru 69 . . . . @60.00
70 thru 79 . . . . @40.00
80 thru 89 . . . . @35.00
90 thru 99 . . . . @50.00
100 . . . . 40.00
101 thru 115 . . . . @35.00
116 AW,AT 40.00
117 thru 127 . . . . @35.00
128 AW,Forbidden Worlds 40.00
129 thru 152 . . . . @30.00
153 A:Magic Agent 30.00
154 O:Nemesis 40.00
155 . . . . 30.00
156 A:Magic Agent 30.00
157 thru 174, Aug. 1967 . . . . . @30.00

ADVENTURES IN
WONDERLAND
Lev Gleason Publications
April, 1955
1 . . . . 50.00
2 . . . . 35.00
3 . . . . 30.00
4 . . . . 30.00
5 . . . . 35.00

ADVENTURES OF
MIGHTY MOUSE
St. John Publishing Co.
Nov., 1951
1 Mighty Mouse Adventures 175.00
2 Menace of the Deep 135.00
3 Storm Clouds of Mystery 100.00
4 Thought Control Machine 85.00
5 Jungle Peril 75.00
6 `The Vine of Destruction' 65.00
7 Space Ship(c) 65.00
8 Charging Alien(c) 65.00
9 Meteor(c) 60.00
10 Revolt at the Zoo" 60.00
11 Jungle(c) 60.00
12 A:Freezing Terror 60.00
13 A:Visitor from Outer Space . . . 60.00
14 V:Cat 55.00
15 . . . . 55.00
16 . . . . 55.00
17 . . . . 55.00
18 May, 1955 . . . . 55.00

AGGIE MACK
Four Star Comics/
Superior Comics, Jan., 1948
1 AF,HR(c) 200.00
2 JK(c) 100.00
3 AF,JK(c) 90.00
4 AF 125.00
5 AF,JK(c) 100.00
6 AF,JK(c) 90.00
7 AF,Burt Lancaster on cover . . . 100.00
8 AF,JK(c), Aug. 1949 . . . . 80.00

BILL BARNES,
AMERICA'S AIR ACE
Street and Smith Publications
July, 1940
1 (Bill Barnes Comics) 650.00
2 Second Battle Valley Forge . . . 350.00
3 A:Aviation Cadets 300.00
4 Shotdown(c) 275.00
5 A:Air Warden, Danny Hawk. . . 225.00
6 A:Danny Hawk,RocketRodney 200.00
7 How to defeat the Japanese . . 200.00
8 Ghost Ship 200.00
9 Flying Tigers, John Wayne . . . 210.00

GOLDEN AGE

10 I:Roane Waring 200.00
11 Flying Tigers 200.00
12 War Workers 200.00
Becomes:

AIR ACE

2-1 Invades Germany 200.00
2-2 Jungle Warfare 100.00
2-3 A:The Four Musketeers 90.00
2-4 A:Russell Swann 90.00
2-5 A:The Four Musketeers 90.00
2-6 Raft(c). 75.00
2-7 BP, What's New In Science . . 75.00
2-8 XP-59 . . . . 75.00
2-9 The Northrop P-61. . . . . 75.00
2-10 NCG-14. . . . . 75.00
2-11 Whip Lanch 75.00
2-12 PP(c). 75.00
3-1 . . . . 60.00
3-2 Atom and It's Future 60.00
3-3 Flying in the Future 60.00
3-4 How Fast Can We Fly 60.00
3-5 REv(c). 60.00
3-6 V:Wolves. 60.00
3-7 BP(c), Vortex of Atom Bomb 150.00
3-8 Feb.–March, 1947 . . . . 75.00

AIRBOY
(see AIR FIGHTERS COMICS)

AIR FIGHTERS COMICS
Hillman Periodicals, Nov., 1941
1 I:Black Commander
  (only App) 1,600.00
2 O:Airboy A:Sky Wolf 2,700.00
3 O:Sky Wolf and Heap 1,400.00
4 A:Black Angel, Iron Ace 900.00
5 A:Sky Wolf and Iron Ace. . . . 675.00
6 Airboy's Bird Plane 650.00
7 Airboy battles Kultur 575.00
8 A:Skinny McGinty 530.00
9 A:Black Prince, Hatchet Man. . 525.00
10 I:The Stinger 525.00
11 Kida(c). 525.00
12 A:Misery 525.00
2-1 A:Flying Dutchman 500.00
2-2 I:Valkyrie. 750.00
2-3 Story Panels cover 500.00
2-4 V:Japanese 500.00
2-5 Air Boy in Tokyo 500.00
2-6 `Dance of Death'. 500.00
2-7 A:Valkyrie. 500.00
2-8 Airboy Battles Japanese . . . 500.00
2-9 Airboy Battles Japanese . . . 500.00
2-10 O:Skywolf 600.00
Becomes:

AIRBOY

2-11. 550.00
2-12 A:Valkyrie 350.00
3-1 . . . . 300.00
3-2 . . . . 275.00
3-3 Never published
3-4 I:The Heap 250.00
3-5 Airboy 225.00
3-6 A:Valkyrie 225.00
3-7 AMc,Witch Hunt. 225.00
3-8 A:Condor. 235.00
3-9 O:The Heap. 250.00
3-10 . . . . 200.00
3-11 . . . . 200.00
3-12 Airboy missing. 250.00
4-1 Elephant in chains cover . . . 235.00
4-2 I:Rackman. 150.00
4-3 Airboy profits on name. 150.00
4-4 S&K. 180.00
4-5 S&K,The American Miracle . 180.00
4-6 S&K,A:Heap and

Flying Fool 180.00
4-7 S&K. 180.00
4-8 S&K,Girlfriend captured . . . 180.00
4-9 S&K,Airboy in quick sand. . . 180.00
4-10 S&K,A:Valkyrie 180.00
4-11 S&K,A:Frenchy 180.00
4-12 FBe. 200.00
5-1 LSt 125.00
5-2 I:Wild Horse of Calabra . . . 125.00
5-3 . . . . 125.00
5-4 CI 125.00
5-5 Skull on cover 125.00
5-6 . . . . 125.00
5-7 . . . . 125.00
5-8 Bondage Cover 150.00
5-9 Zoi,Row. 125.00
5-10 A:Valkyrie,O:The Heap. . . . 135.00
5-11 Airboy vs. The Rats 125.00
5-12 BK,Rat Army captures
  Airboy. 125.00
6-1 . . . . 125.00
6-2 . . . . 125.00
6-3 . . . . 125.00
6-4 Airboy boxes 135.00
6-5 A:The Ice People. 125.00
6-6 . . . . 125.00
6-7 Airboy vs. Chemical Giant . . 125.00
6-8 O:The Heap. 150.00
6-9 . . . . 125.00
6-10 . . . . 125.00
6-11 . . . . 125.00
6-12 . . . . 125.00
7-1 . . . . 120.00
7-2 BP. 120.00
7-3 BP. 120.00
7-4 I:Monsters of the Ice 120.00
7-5 V:Monsters of the Ice. 120.00
7-6 . . . . 120.00
7-7 Mystery of the Sargasso
  Sea 120.00
7-8 A:Centaur 120.00
7-9 I:Men of the StarlightRobot . 120.00
7-10 O:The Heap. 120.00
7-11 . . . . 120.00
7-12 Airboy visits India. 120.00
8-1 BP,A:Outcast and Polo
  Bandits. 100.00
8-2 BP,Suicide Dive cover 100.00
8-3 I:The Living Fuse 100.00
8-4 A:Death Merchants o/t Air . . 120.00
8-5 A:Great Plane from Nowhere 100.00
8-6 . . . . 100.00
8-7 . . . . 100.00
8-8 . . . . 100.00
8-9 . . . . 100.00

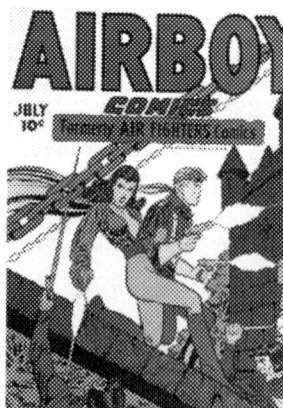

Airboy #3-6
© Hillman Periodicals

8-10 A:Mystery Walkers. 100.00
8-11 . . . . 100.00
8-12 . . . . 120.00
9-1 . . . . 100.00
9-2 A:Valkyrie 90.00
9-3 A:Heap (cover) 90.00
9-4 A:Water Beast, Frog Headed
  Riders 100.00
9-5 A:Heap vs.Man of Moonlight . 90.00
9-6 Heap cover 90.00
9-7 Heap cover 90.00
9-8 Heap cover 90.00
9-9 . . . . 100.00
9-10 Space cover 100.00
9-11 . . . . 90.00
9-12 Heap cover 90.00
10-1 Heap cover 90.00
10-2 Ships on Space 90.00
10-3 . . . . 90.00
10-4 May, 1953 . . . . 90.00

AL CAPP'S
DOG PATCH COMICS
Toby Press, June, 1949
1 . . . . 175.00
2 A:Daisy. 125.00
3 . . . . 110.00
4 Dec., 1949 . . . . 110.00

AL CAPP'S SHMOO
Toby Press, July, 1949
1 100 Trillion Schmoos 250.00
2 Super Shmoo(c) 175.00
3 . . . . 175.00
4 . . . . 150.00
5 April, 1950 . . . . 150.00

AL CAPP'S WOLF GAL
Toby Press, 1951
1 Pin-Up 225.00
2 1952. . . . . 200.00

ALL-FAMOUS CRIME
Star Publications, May, 1951
8 LbC(c) 125.00
9 LbC(c) 200.00
10 LbC(c) 100.00
4 LbC(c) 125.00
5 LbC(c) 125.00
Becomes:

ALL-FAMOUS
POLICE CASES
6 LbC(c) 125.00
7 LbC(c) 100.00
8 LbC(c) 100.00
9 LbC(c) 75.00
10 thru 15 LbC(c) . . . . @75.00
16 Sept., 1954 . . . . 75.00

ALL GOOD COMICS
**R. W. Voight/Fox Publ./
St. John Publ.**
1 1944. . . . . 175.00
1 1946. . . . . 150.00
N# 1949 . . . . 500.00

ALL GREAT COMICS
(see DAGGER, DESERT HAWK)

ALL HERO COMICS
Fawcett Publications
March, 1943
1 A:Capt. Marvel Jr.,Capt.
Midnight,Ibis, Golden Arrow
and Spy Smasher 1,400.00

All-Humor Comics #3
© Quality Comics

ALL HUMOR COMICS
Comic Favorites, Inc.
(Quality Comics), Spring 1946
1 . . . . 125.00
2 PG. 65.00
3 I:Kelly Poole. 40.00
4 thru 7 . . . . @35.00
8 PG 40.00
9 . . . . 40.00
10 . . . . 40.00
11 thru 17 . . . . @30.00

ALL LOVE ROMANCES
(see SCREAM COMICS)

ALL NEGRO COMICS
June,1947
1 . . . . 2,800.00

ALL-NEW COMICS
Family Comics
(Harvey Publ.), Jan., 1943
1 A:Steve Case, Johnny Rebel
I:Detective Shane 2,300.00
2 JKu,O:Scarlet Phantom. 800.00
3 . . . . 550.00
4 AdH 600.00
5 Flash Gordon 500.00
6 I:Boy Heroes and Red Blazer . 500.00
7 JKu,AS(c),A:Black Cat &
Zebra 500.00
8 JKu,A:Shock Gibson. 500.00
9 JKu,A:Black Cat 500.00
10 JKu,A:Zebra. 450.00
11 BP,A:Man in Black, Girl
Commandos. 450.00
12 JKu 450.00
13 Stuntman by S&K,
A:Green Hornet&cover 475.00
14 BP,A:Green Hornet 450.00
15 Smaller size, Distributed
by Mail, March–April, 1947 . . 400.00

ALL TOP COMICS
William H. Wise Co., 1944
N# 132pgs.,A:Capt.
V,Red Robbins 225.00

ALL TOP COMICS
Fox Features Syndicate
Spring 1946
1 A:Cosmo Cat, Flash Rabbit. . . 125.00
2 . . . . 50.00
3 . . . . 40.00
4 . . . . 40.00
5 . . . . 40.00
6 . . . . 40.00
7 . . . . 40.00
7a 85.00
8 JKa(c),I:Blue Beetle 1,750.00
9 JKa(c),A:Rulah 900.00
10 JKa(c),A:Rulah 1,000.00
11 A:Rulah,Blue Beetle 800.00
12 A:Rulah,Jo Jo,Blue Beetle . . 800.00
13 A:Rulah 800.00
14 A:Rulah,Blue Beetle 1,000.00
15 A:Rulah 800.00
16 A:Rulah,Blue Beetle. 800.00
17 A:Rulah,Blue Beetle. 800.00
18 A:Dagar,Jo Jo 500.00
Green Publ.
6 1957 . . . . 20.00
6 1958 . . . . 20.00
6 1959 . . . . 20.00
6 1959 . . . . 20.00
6 Supermouse cover. 20.00

ALLEY OOP
Argo Publications Nov., 1955
1 . . . . 125.00
2 . . . . 100.00
3 March, 1956 . . . . 100.00

AMAZING ADVENTURES
Ziff-Davis Publ. Co., 1950
1 WW, Asteroid Witch 500.00
2 Masters of Living Flame 225.00
3 The Evil Men Do. 225.00
4 Invasion of the Love Robots . . 225.00
5 Secret of the Crater-Men 225.00
6 Man Who Killed a World 250.00

AMAZING GHOST STORIES
(See: WEIRD HORRORS)

AMAZING-MAN COMICS
Centaur Publications
Sept., 1939–Feb. 1942
5 BEv,O:Amazing Man 15,000.00
6 BEv,B:The Shark 2,700.00
7 BEv,I:Magician From Mars . . 1,600.00
8 BEv 1,200.00
9 BEv 1,200.00
10 BEv 1,100.00
11 BEv,I:Zardi 1,000.00
12 SG(c). 900.00
13 SG(c). 900.00
14 B:Reef Kinkaid, Dr. Hypo . . . 750.00
15 A:Zardi. 600.00
16 Mighty Man's powers
revealed. 650.00
17 A:Dr. Hypo. 600.00
18 BLb(a),SG(c) 600.00
19 BLb(a),SG(c) 600.00
20 BLb(a),SG(c) 600.00
21 O:Dash Dartwell. 625.00

22 A:Silver Streak, The Voice . . . 600.00
23 I&O:Tommy the Amazing Kid . 600.00
24 B:King of Darkness,Blue Lady 550.00
25 A:Meteor Marvin 950.00
26 A:Meteor Marvin,ElectricRay . 900.00

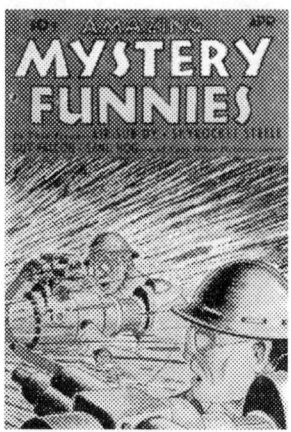

Amazing Mystery Funnies #8
© Centaur Publications

AMAZING MYSTERY FUNNIES
Centaur Publications, 1938
1 Skyrocket Steele in the
Year X. 2,700.00
2 WE,Skyrocket Steele 1,400.00
3 . . . . 500.00
(#4) WE,bondage (c) 700.00
2-1(#5) 650.00
2-2(#6) Drug use 550.00
2-3(#7) Air Sub DX 550.00
2-4(#8) 550.00
2-5(#9) 700.00
2-6(#10) 550.00
2-7(#11) scarce 2,700.00
2-8(#12) Speed Centaur 1,000.00
2-9(#13) 600.00
2-10(#14) 600.00
2-11(#15) 600.00
2-12(#16) BW,I:Space Patrol . . 1,500.00
3-1(#17) I:Bullet 600.00
18 . . . . 600.00
19 BW,Space Patrol 750.00
20 . . . . 600.00
21 BW,Space Patrol 750.00
22 BW,Space Patrol 750.00
23 BW,Space Patrol 750.00
24 BW,Space Patrol 750.00

AMAZING WILLIE MAYS
Famous Funnies, 1954
1 Willie Mays(c). 600.00

AMERICAN LIBRARY
David McKay Publ., 1943
(#1) Thirty Seconds Over
Tokyo, movie adapt. 250.00
(#2) Guadalcanal Diary. 175.00
3 Look to the Mountain 100.00
4 The Case of the Crooked
Candle (Perry Mason). 100.00
5 Duel in the Sun. 100.00
6 Wingate's Raiders. 110.00

AMERICA'S BEST COMICS
Nedor/Better/Standard Publications, Feb. 1942
1 B:Black Terror, Captain Future,
The Liberator,Doc Strange . 1,800.00
2 O:American Eagle. 700.00
3 B:Pyroman 550.00
4 A:Doc Strange, Jimmy Cole . . 450.00
5 Lone Eagle, Capt. Future. . . 425.00
6 A:American Crusader 400.00
7 A:Hitler,Hirohito. 550.00
8 The Liberator ends 400.00
9 ASh(c) 450.00
10 ASh(c) 350.00
11 ASh(c) 350.00
12 Red Cross cover 350.00
13 . . . . 350.00
14 Last American Eagle app . . . 350.00
15 ASh(c) 325.00
16 ASh(c) 335.00
17 Doc Strange carries football. . 325.00
18 Bondage cover 325.00
19 ASh(c) 325.00
20 vs. the Black Market 325.00
21 Infinity cover 300.00
22 A:Captain Future 300.00
23 B:Miss Masque 375.00
24 Bondage cover 350.00
25 A:Sea Eagle 300.00
26 A:The Phantom Detective . . . 300.00
27 ASh(c) 300.00
28 A:Commando Cubs,
Black Terror 300.00
29 A:Doc Strange 300.00
30 ASh(c) 300.00
31 July, 1949 . . . . 300.00

AMERICA'S BIGGEST COMICS BOOK
William H. Wise, 1944
1 196 pgs. A:Grim Reaper, Zudo,
Silver Knight, Thunderhoof,
Jocko and Socko,Barnaby
Beep,Commando Cubs. . . . 300.00

AMERICA'S GREATEST COMICS
Fawcett Publications, Fall 1941
1 MRa(c),A:Capt. Marvel,
Bulletman,Spy Smasher and
Minute Man 2,300.00
2 F:Capt. Marvel 1,200.00
3 F:Capt. Marvel 800.00
4 B:Commando Yank 600.00
5 Capt.Marvel in "Lost Lighting" . 600.00
6 Capt.Marvel fires Machine
Gun 550.00
7 A:Balbo the Boy Magician. . . . 550.00
8 A:Capt.Marvel Jr.,Golden
Arrow, Summer 1943 . . . . . 550.00

AMERICA IN ACTION
Dell Publishing Co., 1942
1 . . . . 125.00

ANDY COMICS
(see SCREAM COMICS)

ANGEL
Dell Publishing Co., Aug., 1954
(1) see Dell Four Color #576
2 . . . . 20.00
3 thru 16 . . . . @15.00

ANIMAL ANTICS
Dell Publishing Co., 1946
1 B:Racoon Kids 350.00
2 . . . . 200.00
3 thru 10 . . . . @125.00
11 thru 23 . . . . @75.00

ANIMAL COMICS
Dell Publishing Co., 1942
1 WK,Pogo 1,000.00
2 Uncle Wiggily(c),A:Pogo 450.00
3 Muggin's Mouse(c),A:Pogo . . . 325.00
4 Uncle Wiggily(c) 250.00
5 Uncle Wiggily(c) 325.00
6 Uncle Wiggily 200.00
7 Uncle Wiggily 200.00
8 Pogo 250.00
9 War Bonds(c),A:Pogo 250.00
10 Pogo 250.00
11 Pogo 175.00
12 Pogo 175.00
13 Pogo 175.00
14 Pogo 175.00
15 Pogo 175.00
16 Uncle Wiggily. 100.00
17 Pogo(c) 125.00
18 Pogo(c) 125.00
19 Pogo(c) 125.00
20 Pogo 100.00
21 Pogo(c) 125.00
22 Pogo 75.00
23 Pogo 75.00
24 Pogo(c) 85.00
25 Pogo(c) 85.00
26 Pogo(c) 85.00
27 Pogo(c) 75.00
28 Pogo(c) 75.00
29 Pogo(c) 75.00
30 Pogo(c) 75.00

ANIMAL FABLES
E.C. Comics, July–Aug. 1946
1 B:Korky Kangaroo,Freddy Firefly
Petey Pig and Danny Demon 275.00
2 B:Aesop Fables 200.00
3 . . . . 150.00
4 . . . . 150.00
5 Firefly vs. Red Ants 150.00
6 . . . . 150.00
7 O:Moon Girls,Nov.–Dec.1947 . 450.00

ANIMAL FAIR
Fawcett Publications, March 1946
1 B:Captain Marvel Bunny,
Sir Spot 150.00
2 A:Droopy, Colonel Walrus 75.00
3 . . . . 35.00
4 A:Kid Gloves, Cub Reporter . . . 35.00
5 thru 7 . . . . 35.00
8 . . . . 25.00
9 . . . . 25.00
10 . . . . 25.00
11 Feb. 1947 . . . . 25.00

ANNIE OAKLEY & TAGG
Dell Publishing Co., 1953
(1) see Dell Four Color #438
(2) see Dell Four Color #481
(3) see Dell Four Color #575
4 . . . . 125.00
5 . . . . 90.00
6 thru 10 . . . . @75.00
11 thru 18 . . . . @50.00

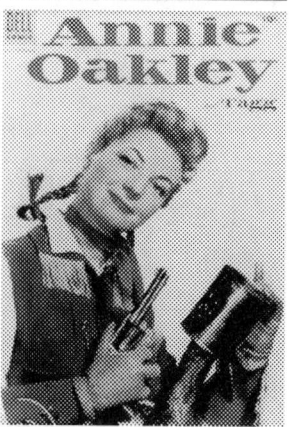

Annie Oakley & Tagg
© Dell Publishing Co.

ARCHIE COMICS
MLJ Magazines Winter, 1942-43
1 I:Jughead & Veronica 11,000.00
2 . . . . 2,500.00
3 . . . . 1,800.00
4 . . . . 1,000.00
5 . . . . 900.00
6 . . . . 700.00
7 thru 11 . . . . @650.00
12 thru 15 . . . . @500.00
16 thru 19 . . . . @450.00
Archie Publications
20 . . . . 450.00
21 . . . . 300.00
22 thru 31 . . . . @275.00
32 thru 42 . . . . @150.00
43 thru 50 . . . . @100.00
51 thru 60 . . . . @75.00
61 thru 70 . . . . @50.00
71 thru 80 . . . . @40.00
81 thru 99 . . . . @30.00
100 . . . . 50.00
101 . . . . 25.00
102 thru 115 . . . . @15.00
116 thru 130 . . . . @12.00
131 thru 145 . . . . @10.00
146 thru 160 . . . . @7.50
161 thru 180 . . . . @5.00
181 thru 200 . . . . @4.00
201 thru 250 . . . . @3.00
251 thru 280 . . . . @3.00
281 thru 389 . . . . @3.00

ARCHIE'S GIANT SERIES MAGAZINE
Archie Publications, 1954
1 . . . . 900.00
2 . . . . 550.00
3 . . . . 400.00
4 . . . . 350.00
5 . . . . 350.00
6 thru 10 . . . . @250.00
11 thru 20 . . . . @200.00
21 thru 29 . . . . @125.00
30 thru 35 . . . . @45.00
136 thru 141 . . . . @45.00
142 . . . . 32.00
143 thru 160 . . . . @12.00
161 thru 199 . . . . @8.00
200 . . . . 5.00
201 thru 250 . . . . @2.50

251 thru 299	@2.00
300 thru 500	@2.00

ARCHIE'S GIRLS BETTY AND VERONICA
Archie Publications, 1950

1	1,100.00
2	500.00
3	350.00
4	250.00
5	240.00
6 thru 10	@200.00
11 thru 15	@150.00
16 thru 20	@100.00
21	90.00
22 thru 29	@85.00
30 thru 40	@60.00
41 thru 50	@50.00
51 thru 60	@40.00
61 thru 70	@35.00
71 thru 80	@30.00
81 thru 90	@25.00
91 thru 99	@20.00
100	25.00
101 thru 120	@12.00
121 thru 140	@10.00
141 thru 160	@7.00
161 thru 180	@3.00
181 thru 199	@2.00
200	3.00
201 thru 220	@2.00
221 thru 240	@2.00
241 thru 347	@2.00

ARCHIE'S JOKE BOOK MAGAZINE
Archie Publications, 1953

1	650.00
2	350.00
3	250.00
15 thru 19	@165.00
20 thru 25	@120.00
26 thru 35	@90.00
36 thru 40	@60.00
41 1st NA art	125.00
42 & 43	60.00
44 thru 48 NA	@70.00
49 thru 60	@20.00
61 thru 70	@15.00
71 thru 80	@10.00
81 thru 100	@5.00
101 thru 200	@2.50
201 thru 288	@2.00

ARCHIE'S MECHANICS
Archie Publications, Sept., 1954

1	550.00
2	400.00
3	300.00

ARCHIE'S PAL, JUGHEAD
Archie Publications, 1949

1	900.00
2	450.00
3	275.00
4	250.00
5	250.00
6	200.00
7 thru 10	@175.00
11 thru 15	@125.00
16 thru 20	@85.00
21 thru 30	@65.00
31 thru 39	@50.00
40 thru 50	@35.00

51 thru 60	@30.00
61 thru 70	@25.00
71 thru 80	@20.00
81 thru 99	@15.00
100	17.00
101 thru 126	@10.00

Archie's Pals 'N' Gals #4
© Archie Publications

ARCHIE'S PALS `N' GALS
Archie Publications 1952–53

1	600.00
2	300.00
3	200.00
4	135.00
5	135.00
6	80.00
7	80.00
8 thru 10	@75.00
11 thru 15	@50.00
16 thru 20	@35.00
21 thru 30	@20.00
31 thru 40	@20.00
41 thru 50	@12.00
51 thru 60	@10.00
61 thru 70	@7.00
71 thru 80	@5.00
81 thru 99	@2.50
100	3.00
101 thru 120	@2.00
121 thru 160	@2.00
161 thru 224	@2.00

ARCHIE'S RIVAL REGGIE
Archie Publications, 1950

1	600.00
2	275.00
3	200.00
4	175.00
5	175.00
6	150.00
7 thru 10	@125.00
11 thru 13	@75.00
14 thru 15	@65.00
16 Aug., 1954	70.00

ARMY & NAVY COMICS
(see SUPERSNIPE COMICS)

ARROW, THE
Centaur Publications
Oct. 1940–Oct. 1941

1 B:Arrow	2,300.00
2 BLB(c)	1,000.00
3 O:Dash Dartwell,Human Meteor, Rainbow, Bondage(c)	900.00

ATOMAN
Spark Publications, Feb. 1946

1 JRo,MMe,O:Atoman,A:Kid Crusaders	450.00
2 JRo,MMe	350.00

ATOMIC COMICS
Green Publishing Co.
Jan., 1946

1 S&S,A:Radio Squad, Barry O'Neal	1,100.00
2 MB,A:Inspector Dayton, Kid Kane	500.00
3 MB,A:Zero Ghost Detective	350.00
4 JKa(c), July–Aug., 1946	325.00

ATOMIC COMICS
Daniels Publications
1946 (Reprints)

1 A:Rocketman,Yankee Boy, Bondage cover,rep.	225.00

ATOMIC MOUSE
Capital Stories/
Charlton Comics, March, 1953

1 AFa,O:Atomic Mouse	150.00
2 AFa,Ice Cream cover	65.00
3 AFa,Genie and Magic Carpet cover	50.00
4 AFa	50.00
5 AFa,A:Timmy the Timid Ghost	50.00
6 thru 10 Funny Animal	@40.00
11 thru 14 Funny Animal	@25.00
15 A:Happy the Marvel Bunny	30.00
16 Funny Animal,Giant	32.00
17 thru 30 Funny Animal	@25.00
31 thru 36 Funny Animal	@20.00
37 A:Atom the Cat	20.00
38 thru 40 Funny Animal	@15.00
41 thru 53 Funny Animal	@10.00
54 June, 1963	10.00

ATOMIC THUNDER BOLT, THE
Regor Company, Feb., 1946

1 I:Atomic Thunderbolt, Mr. Murdo	450.00

AUTHENTIC POLICE CASES
St. John Publ. Co., 1948

1 Hale the Magician	275.00
2 Lady Satan, Johnny Rebel	150.00
3 A:Avenger	300.00
4 Masked Black Jack	175.00
5 JCo	175.00
6 JCo,MB(c)	300.00
7 thru 10	@125.00
11 thru 15	@100.00

16 thru 23	@75.00
24 thru 28	@125.00
29 thru 38	@45.00

AVIATION AND
MODEL BUILDING
(see TRUE AVIATION
PICTURE STORIES)

AVON ONE-SHOTS
Avon Periodicals
1949-1953
{Listed in Alphabetical Order}

1 Atomic Spy Cases	200.00
N# WW,Attack on Planet Mars	600.00
1 Batchelor's Diary	150.00
1 Badmen of the West	200.00
N# Badmen of Tombstone	75.00
1 Behind Prison Bars	150.00
2 Betty and Her Steady	35.00
N# Blackhawk Indian Tomahawk War	75.00
1 Blazing Sixguns	75.00
1 Butch Cassidy	80.00
N# Chief Crazy Horse	100.00
N# FF,Chief Victorio's Apache Massacre	300.00
N# City of the Living Dead	350.00
1 Complete Romance	150.00
N# Custer's Last Fight	75.00
1 Dalton Boys	70.00
N# Davy Crockett	70.00
N# The Dead Who Walk	400.00
1 Diary of Horror,Bondage(c)	275.00
N# WW,An Earth Man on Venus	950.00
1 Eerie, bondage(c)	675.00
1 Escape from Devil's Island	250.00
N# Fighting Daniel Boone	80.00
N# For a Night of Love	125.00
1 WW,Flying Saucers	650.00
N# Flying Saucers	450.00
1 Going Steady with Betty	60.00
N# Hooded Menace	400.00
N# King of the Badmen of Deadwood	100.00
1 King Solomon's Mines	225.00
N# Kit Carson & the Blackfeet Warriors	50.00
N# Last of the Comanches	75.00
N# Masked Bandit	100.00
1 WW,Mask of Dr. Fu Manchu	700.00

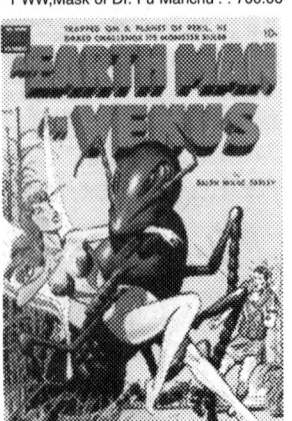

Avon One-Shot: An Earthman on Venus
© *Avon Periodicals*

N# Night of Mystery	300.00
1 Outlaws of the Wild West	175.00
1 Out of this World	475.00
N# Pancho Villa	125.00
1 Phantom Witch Doctor	350.00
1 Pixie Puzzle Rocket to Adventureland	75.00
1 Prison Riot,drugs	175.00
N# Red Mountain Featuring Quantrell's Raiders	150.00
N# Reform School Girl	1,000.00
1 Robotmen of the Lost Planet	800.00
N# WW(c),Rocket to the Moon	850.00
N# JKu,Secret Diary of Eerie Adventures	1,150.00
1 Sheriff Bob Dixon's Chuck Wagon	65.00
1 Sideshow	135.00
1 JKu,Sparkling Love	80.00
N# Speedy Rabbit	30.00
1 Teddy Roosevelt & His Rough Riders	110.00
N# The Underworld Story	200.00
N# The Unknown Man	175.00
1 War Dogs of the U.S. Army	100.00
N# White Chief of the Pawnee Indians	75.00
N# Women to Love	150.00

BABE
Prize/Headline Feature
June–July 1948

1 BRo,A;Boddy Rogers	120.00
2 BRo,same	75.00
3 Bro,same	50.00
4 thru 9 BRo,same	@35.00

BABE RUTH
SPORTS COMICS
Harvey Publications,
April, 1949

1 BP	350.00
2 BP	250.00
3 BP,Joe Dimaggio(c)	300.00
4 BP,Bob Feller(c)	200.00
5 BP,Football(c)	200.00
6 BP,Basketball(c)	200.00
7 BP	200.00
8 BP	200.00
9 BP, Stan Musial(c)	175.00
11 Feb., 1951	175.00

BANNER COMICS
Ace Magazines, Sept., 1941

3 B:Captain Courageous, Lone Warrior	800.00
4 JM(c),Flag(c)	650.00
5	500.00

Becomes:
CAPTAIN COURAGEOUS
COMICS

6 I:The Sword	650.00

BARNYARD COMICS
Animated Cartoons
June, 1944

1 (fa)	80.00
2 (fa)	40.00
3 (fa)	25.00
4 (fa)	25.00
5 (fa)	25.00
6 thru 12 (fa)	@22.00
13 FF(ti)	30.00
14 FF(ti)	30.00
15 FF(ti)	30.00

16	35.00
17 FF(ti)	30.00
18 FF,FF(ti)	75.00
19 FF,FF(ti)	75.00
20 FF,FF(ti)	75.00
21 FF(ti)	30.00
22 FF,FF(ti)	75.00
23 FF(ti)	30.00
24 FF,FF(ti)	75.00
25 FF,FF(ti)	75.00
26 FF(ti)	30.00
27 FF(ti)	30.00
28	20.00
29 FF(ti)	30.00
30 and 31	@20.00

Becomes:
DIZZY DUCK

32 thru 39	@15.00

BASEBALL COMICS
Will Eisner Productions
Spring, 1949

1 A:Rube Rocky	600.00

BASEBALL HEROS
Fawcett Publications, 1952

N# Babe Ruth cover	650.00

BASEBALL THRILLS
Ziff-Davis Publ. Co.
Summer 1951

10 Bob Feller Predicts Pennant Winners	300.00
2 BP, Yogi Berra story	225.00
3 EK, Joe DiMaggio story, Summer 1952	300.00

BATTLEFIELD ACTION
(see DYNAMITE)

BEANY & CECIL
Dell Publishing Co., Jan., 1952

1	150.00
2	100.00
3	100.00
4	100.00
5	100.00

BEN BOWIE & HIS
MOUNTAIN MEN
Dell Publishing Co., 1952

(1) see Dell Four Color #443	
(2 thru 6) see Dell Four Color	
7	15.00
8 thru 10	@15.00
11 I:Yellow Hair	17.00
12	12.00
13	12.00
14	12.00
15	12.00
16	12.00
17	12.00

BEST COMICS
Better Publications, Nov., 1939

1 B:Red Mask	600.00
2 A:Red Mask, Silly Willie	375.00
3 A:Red Mask	375.00
4 Cannibalism story, Feb., 1940	400.00

BEWARE
(see CAPTAIN SCIENCE)

BIG CHIEF WAHOO
Eastern Color Printing
July, 1942

1	300.00
2 BWa(c),Three Ring Circus	150.00
3 BWa(c)	100.00
4 BWa(c)	100.00
5 BWa(c),Wild West Rodeo	100.00
6 A:Minnie-Ha-Cha	75.00
7	50.00
8	50.00
9	50.00
10	60.00
11 thru 22	@40.00
23 1943	40.00

BIG SHOT COMICS
Columbia Comics Group
May, 1940

1 MBI,OW,Skyman,B:The Face, Joe Palooka, Rocky Ryan	1,600.00
2 MBi,OW,Marvelo cover	600.00
3 MBi,Skyman cover	500.00
4 MBi,OW,Joe Palooka cover	450.00
5 MBi,Joe Palooka cover	400.00
6 MBi,Joe Palooka cover	350.00
7 MBi,Elect Joe Palooka and Skyman	325.00
8 MBi,Joe Palooka and Skyman dress as Santa	325.00
9 MBi,Skyman	325.00
10 MBi,Skyman	325.00
11 MBi	275.00
12 MBi,OW	275.00
13 MBi,OW	275.00
14 MBi,OW,O:Sparky Watts	275.00
15 MBi,OW,O:The Cloak	300.00
16 MBi,OW	225.00
17 MBi(c),OW	225.00
18 MBi,OW	225.00
19 MBi,OW,The Face cover	235.00
20 MBi,OW,OW(c),Skyman cov.	235.00
21 MBi,OW,A:Raja the Arabian Knight	200.00
22 MBi,OW,Joe Palooka cover	200.00
23 MBi,OW,Sparky Watts cover	175.00
24 MBi,OW,Uncle Sam cover	200.00
25 MBi,OW,Sparky Watts cover	175.00
26 MBi,OW,Devildog cover	200.00
27 MBi,OW,Skyman cover	200.00

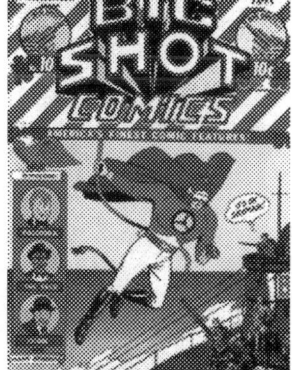

Big Shot Comics #10
© Columbia Comics

28 MBi,OW,Hitler cover	250.00
29 MBi,OW,I:Captain Yank	200.00
30 MBi,OW,Santa cover	165.00
31 MBi,OW,Sparky Watts cover	135.00
32 MBi,OW,B:Vic Jordan newspaper reps	175.00
33 MBi,OW,Sparky Watts cover	135.00
34 MBi,OW	150.00
35 MBi,OW	150.00
36 MBi,OW,Sparky Watts cover	135.00
37 MBi,OW	130.00
38 MBi,Uncle Slap Happy cover	135.00
39 MBi,Uncle Slap Happy cover	135.00
40 MBi,Joe Palooka Happy (c)	135.00
41 MBi,Joe Palooka	125.00
42 MBi,Joe Palooka parachutes	125.00
43 MBi,V:Hitler	135.00
44 MBi,Slap Happy cover	125.00
45 MBi,Slap Happy cover	125.00
46 MBi,Uncle Sam cover,V:Hitler.	135.00
47 MBi,Uncle Slap Happy cover	125.00
48 MBi	125.00
49 MBi	85.00
50 MBi,O:The Face	85.00
51 MBi	85.00
52 MBi,E:Vic Jordan (Hitler cov) newspaper reps	125.00
53 MBi,Uncle Slap Happy cover	85.00
54 MBi,Uncle Slap Happy cover	85.00
55 MBi,Happy Easter cover	85.00
56 MBi	85.00
57 MBi	85.00
58 MBi	85.00
59 MBi,Slap Happy	85.00
60 MBi,Joe Palooka	75.00
61 MBi	60.00
62 MBi	60.00
63 MBi	60.00
64 MBi,Slap Happy	60.00
65 MBi,Slap Happy	60.00
66 MBi,Slap Happy	60.00
67 MBi	60.00
68 MBi,Joe Palooka	60.00
69 MBi	60.00
70 MBi,OW,Joe Palooka cover	60.00
71 MBi,OW	65.00
72 MBi,OW	65.00
73 MBi,OW,The Face cover	65.00
74 MBi,OW	65.00
75 MBi,OW,Polar Bear swim club cover	65.00
76 thru 80 MBi,OW	@50.00
81 thru 84 MBi,OW	@45.00
85 MBi,OW,Dixie Dugan cover	50.00
86 thru 95 MBi,OW	@45.00
96 MBi,OW,X-Mas cover	45.00
97 thru 99 MBi,OW	@45.00
100 MBi,OW,Special issue	50.00
101 thru 103 MBi,OW	@45.00
104 MBi, Aug., 1949	50.00

BIG-3
Fox Features Syndicate
Fall 1940

1 B:BlueBeetle,Flame,Samson	1,700.00
2 A:BlueBeetle,Flame,Samson.	725.00
3 same	550.00
4 same	500.00
5 same	500.00
6 E:Samson, bondage cover	450.00
7 A:V-Man, Jan., 1942	400.00

BILL BARNES,
AMERICA'S AIR ACE
(see AIR ACE)

BILL BOYD WESTERN
Fawcett Publications
Feb., 1950

1 B:Bill Boyd, Midnite,Ph(c)	375.00
2 P(c)	200.00
3 B:Ph(c)	150.00
4	100.00
5	100.00
6	100.00
7	90.00
8	90.00
9	90.00
10	90.00
11	75.00
12	75.00
13	75.00
14	75.00
15 thru 21	@70.00
22 E:Ph(c)	70.00
23 June, 1952	85.00

BILL STERN'S
SPORTS BOOK
Approved Comics
Spring-Summer, 1951

1 Ewell Blackwell	175.00
2	125.00
2-2 EK Giant	150.00

BILLY THE KID
ADVENTURE MAGAZINE
Toby Press, Oct., 1950

1 AW,FF,AW(c),FF(c)	250.00
2 Photo cover	50.00
3 AW,FF	250.00
4	40.00
5	40.00
6 FF,Photo cover	60.00
7 Photo cover	40.00
8	40.00
9 HK Pot-Shot Pete	60.00
10	40.00
11	40.00
12	40.00
13 HK	50.00
14 AW,FF	60.00
15 thru 21	@35.00
22 AW,FF	40.00
23 thru 29	@30.00
30 1955	35.00

BINGO COMICS
Howard Publications, 1945

1	165.00

BLACK CAT COMICS
Harvey Publications
(Home Comics),
June–July, 1946

1 JKu	500.00
2 JKu,JSm(c)	250.00
3 JSm(c)	225.00
4 B:Red Demon	200.00
5 S&K	250.00
6 S&K,A:Scarlet Arrow, O:Red Demon	250.00
7 S&K	250.00
8 S&K,B:Kerry Drake	225.00
9 S&K,O:Stuntman	275.00
10 JK,JSm	175.00
11	175.00
12 "Ghost Town Terror"	175.00
13 thru 16 LEI	@150.00
17 A:Mary Worth, Invisible Scarlet	150.00

GOLDEN AGE

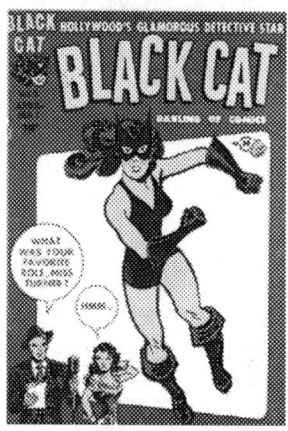

Black Cat #5
© Harvey Publications

GOLDEN AGE

18 LEI. 150.00
19 LEI. 150.00
20 A:Invisible Scarlet 150.00
21 LEI. 150.00
22 LEI thru 26 . . . . @150.00
27 X-Mas issue. 150.00
28 I:Kit,A:Crimson Raider 150.00
29 Black Cat bondage cover. . . . 150.00
Becomes:

BLACK CAT MYSTERY
30 RP,Black Cat(c) 165.00
31 RP. 125.00
32 BP,RP,Bondage cover 135.00
33 BP,RP,Electrocution cover . . . 150.00
34 BP,RP 125.00
35 BP,RP,OK, Atomic Storm 150.00
36 RP. 175.00
37 RP. 125.00
38 RP. 125.00
39 RP. 150.00
40 RP. 125.00
41 . . . . 125.00
42 . . . . 125.00
43 BP 125.00
44 BP,HN,JkS,Oil Burning cover . 150.00
45 BP,HN,Classic cover 175.00
46 BP,HN 125.00
47 BP,HN 125.00
48 BP,HN 125.00
49 BP,HN 125.00
50 BP,Rotting Face. 300.00
51 BP,HN,MMe. 125.00
52 BP 75.00
53 BP. 75.00
Becomes:

BLACK CAT WESTERN
54 A:Black Cat & Story 100.00
55 A:Black Cat 75.00
56 same. 75.00
Becomes:

BLACK CAT MYSTIC
58 JK,Starts Comic Code 125.00
59 KB. 100.00
60 JK. 100.00
61 HN. 90.00
62 . . . . 75.00
63 JK 75.00
64 JK. 90.00
65 April, 1963. . . . . 90.00

BLACK DIAMOND WESTERN
(see DESPERADO)

UNCLE SAM QUARTERLY
Quality Comics Group
Fall, 1941
1 BE,LF(c),JCo. 3,000.00
2 LG(c),BE 1,000.00
3 GT,GT(c) 750.00
4 GT,GF(c) 650.00
5 RC,GT 650.00
6 GT 550.00
7 Hitler, Tojo, Mussolini 700.00
8 . . . . 525.00
Becomes:

BLACKHAWK
Comic Magazines, Winter, 1944
9 Bait for a Death Trap 2,700.00
10 RC. 850.00
11 RC. 600.00
12 Flies to thrilling adventure . . . 550.00
13 Blackhawk Stalks Danger. . . . 550.00
14 BWa 525.00
15 Patrols the Universe. 525.00
16 RC,BWa,Huddles for Action . . 450.00
17 BWa,Prepares for Action 450.00
18 RC,RC(c),BWa,One for All
    and All for One. 425.00
19 RC,RC(c),BWa,Calls
    for Action 425.00
20 RC,RC(c),BWa,Smashes
    Rugoth the ruthless God. . . . 425.00
21 BWa,Battles Destiny
    Written n Blood. 350.00
22 RC,RC(c),BWa,Fear battles
    Death and Destruction 350.00
23 RC,RC(c),BWa,Batters
    Down Oppression. 350.00
24 RC,RC(c),BWa 350.00
25 RC,RC(c),BWa,V:The Evil
    of Mung 350.00
26 RC,RC(c),V:Menace of a
    Sunken World. 325.00
27 BWa,Destroys a War-Mad
    Munitions Magnate 325.00
28 BWa,Defies Destruction in the
    Battle of the Test Tube 325.00
29 BWa,Tale of the Basilisk
    Supreme Chief 325.00
30 BWa,RC,RC(c),The Menace
    of the Meteors 325.00
31 BWa,RC,RC(c),JCo,Treachery
    among the Blackhawks. 250.00
32 BWa,RC,RC(c),A:Delya,
    Flying Fish 250.00
33 RC,RC(c),BWa,
    A:The Mockers. 250.00
34 BWa,A:Tana,Mavis. 250.00
35 BWa,I:Atlo,Strongest Man
    on Earth. 250.00
36 RC,RC(c),BWa,V:Tarya 225.00
37 RC,RC(c),BWa,V:Sari,The
    Rajah of Ramastan. 225.00
38 BWa 225.00
39 RC,RC(c),BWa,V:Lilith. 225.00
40 RC,RC(c),BWa,Valley of
    Yesterday. 225.00
41 RC,RC(c),BWa 200.00
42 RC,RC(c),BWa,
    V:Iron Emperor. 200.00
43 RC,RC(c),BWa,Terror
    from the Catacombs. 200.00
44 RC,RC(c),BWa,The King
    of Winds. 200.00
45 BWa,The Island of Death. . . . 200.00
46 RC,RC(c),BWa,V:DeathPatrol 200.00

47 RC,RC(c),BWa,War! 200.00
48 RC,RC(c),BWa,A:Hawks of
    Horror,Port of Missing Ships . 200.00
49 RC,RC(c),BWa,A:Valkyrie,
    Waters of Terrible Peace. . . . 200.00
50 RC,RC(c),BWa,I:Killer Shark,
    Flying Octopus 225.00
51 BWa,V:The Whip, Whip of
    Nontelon. 175.00
52 RC,RC(c),BWa,Traitor in
    the Ranks. 175.00
53 RC,RC(c),BWa,V:Golden
    Mummy 175.00
54 RC,RC(c),BWa,V:Dr. Deroski,
    Circles of Suicide 175.00
55 RC,RC(c),BWa,V:Rocketmen . 175.00
56 RC,RC(c),BWa,V:The Instructor,
    School for Sabotage 175.00
57 RC,RC(c),BWa,Paralyzed City
    of Armored Men 175.00
58 RC,RC(c),BWa,V:King Cobra,
    The Spider of Delanza 175.00
59 BWa,V:Sea Devil 175.00
60 RC,RC(c),BWa,V:Dr. Mole and
    His Devils Squadron. 175.00
61 V:John Smith, Stalin's
    Ambassador of Murder. 165.00
62 V:General X, Return of
    Genghis Kahn 165.00
63 RC,RC(c),The Flying
    Buzz-Saws. 165.00
64 RC,RC(c),V:Zoltan Korvas,
    Legion of the Damned 165.00
65 Olaf as a Prisoner in Dungeon
    of Fear 165.00
66 RC,RC(c),V:The Red
    Executioner, Crawler. 165.00
67 RC,RC(c),V:Future Fuehrer . . 165.00
68 V:Killers of the Kremlin. 150.00
69 V:King of the Iron Men,
    Conference of the Dictators . 150.00
70 V:Killer Shark. 150.00
71 V:Von Tepp, The Man Who
    could Defeat Blackhawk
    O:Blackhawk 200.00
72 V:Death Legion 150.00
73 V:Hangman,The Tyrannical
    Freaks 150.00
74 Plan of Death. 150.00
75 V:The Mad Doctor Baroc,
    The Z Bomb Menace 150.00
76 The King of Blackhawk Island 150.00
77 V:The Fiendish
    Electronic Brain 150.00
78 V:The Killer Vulture,

Blackhawk #14
© Comic Magazines

Phantom Raider 150.00
79 V:Herman Goering, The
   Human Bomb 150.00
80 V:Fang, the Merciless,
   Dr. Death 150.00
81 A:Killer Shark, The Sea
   Monsters of Killer Shark 150.00
82 V:Sabo Teur, the Ruthless
   Commie Agent 150.00
83 I:Hammmer & Sickle, V:Madam
   Double Cross 150.00
84 V:Death Eye,Dr. Genius,
   The Dreaded Brain Beam . . . 150.00
85 V:The Fiendish Impersonator . 150.00
86 V:The Human Torpedoes 150.00
87 A:Red Agent Sovietta,V:Sea
   Wolf, Le Sabre,Comics Code 125.00
88 V:Thunder the Indestructible,
   The Phantom Sniper. 125.00
89 V:The Super Communists . . . 125.00
90 V:The Storm King, Villainess
   who smashed the Blackhawk
   team. 125.00
91 Treason in the Underground. . 125.00
92 V:The World Traitor 125.00
93 V:Garg the Destroyer,
   O:Blackhawk 135.00
94 V:Black Widow, Darkk the
   Destroyer 125.00
95 V:Madam Fury, Queen of the
   Pirates 125.00
96 Doom in the Deep 125.00
97 Revolt of the Slave Workers. . 125.00
98 Temple of Doom 125.00
99 The War That Never Ended . . 125.00
100 The Delphian Machine 150.00
101 Satan's Paymaster 100.00
102 The Doom Cloud 100.00
103 The Super Race 100.00
104 The Jet Menace 100.00
105 The Red Kamikaze Terror . . 100.00
106 The Flying Tank Platoon . . . 100.00
107 The Winged Menace 100.00
(Please see DC Listings)

BLACK HOOD
(see LAUGH COMICS)

BLACK TERROR
Better Publications/
Standard, Winter, 1942-43
1 Bombing cover 2,100.00
2 V:Arabs,Bondage(c) 750.00
3 V:Nazis,Bondage(c) 550.00
4 V:Sub Nazis 475.00
5 V:Japanese 475.00
6 Air Battle 400.00
7 Air Battle,V:Japanese,
   A:Ghost 400.00
8 V:Nazis 400.00
9 V:Japanese,Bondage(c) 425.00
10 V:Nazis 400.00
11 thru 16 . . . . @300.00
17 Bondage(c) 325.00
18 ASh 300.00
19 ASh 300.00
20 ASh 300.00
21 ASh 325.00
22 FF,ASh 300.00
23 ASh 300.00
24 Bondgae(c) 325.00
25 ASh 300.00
26 GT,ASh 300.00
27 MME,GT,ASh 300.00

BLAZING COMICS
Enwil Associates/Rural Home
June, 1944
1 B:Green Turtle, Red Hawk,
   Black Buccaneer 400.00
2 Green Turtle cover 250.00
3 Green Turtle cover 225.00
4 Green Turtle cover 225.00
5 March, 1945 . . . . 225.00
5a Black Buccaneer(c),1955 . . . 75.00
6 Indian-Japanese(c), 1955 . . . . 75.00

Blondie #167
© King Comics

BLONDIE COMICS
David McKay, Spring, 1947
1 . . . . 150.00
2 . . . . 75.00
3 . . . . 50.00
4 . . . . 50.00
5 . . . . 50.00
6 thru 10 . . . . @30.00
11 thru 15 . . . . @25.00
Harvey Publications
16 . . . . 30.00
17 thru 20 . . . . @20.00
21 thru 30 . . . . @15.00
31 thru 50 . . . . @12.00
51 thru 80 . . . . @10.00
81 thru 99 . . . . @7.50
100 . . . . 10.00
101 thru 124 . . . . @7.50
125 Giant 10.00
126 thru 135 . . . . @7.00
136 thru 140 . . . . @6.00
141 thru 163 . . . . @10.00
King Publications
164 thru 167 . . . . @10.00
168 thru 174 . . . . @4.00
Charlton Comics
175 thru 200 . . . . @3.00
201 thru 220 . . . . @3.00

BLUE BEETLE, THE
Fox Features Syndicate/
Holyoke Publ., Winter 1939
1 O:Blue Beetle,A:Master
   Magician 3,700.00
2 . . . . 1,200.00
3 JSm(c) 800.00
4 Mentions marijuana 550.00
5 A:Zanzibar the Magician 500.00
6 B:Dynamite Thor,
   O:Blue Beetle 500.00

7 A:Dynamo 450.00
8 E:Thor,A:Dynamo 450.00
9 A:Black Bird,Gorilla 450.00
10 A:Black Bird, bondage cover . 450.00
11 A:Gladiator. 400.00
12 A:Black Fury 400.00
13 B:V-Man 500.00
14 JKu,I:Sparky 450.00
15 JKu 450.00
16 . . . . 325.00
17 A:Mimic 300.00
18 E:V-Man,A:Red Knight 300.00
19 JKu,A:Dascomb Dinsmore . . . 325.00
20 I&O:The Flying Tiger
   Squadron 350.00
21 . . . . 225.00
22 A:Ali-Baba 225.00
23 A:Jimmy DooLittle 225.00
24 I:The Halo 225.00
25 . . . . 225.00
26 General Patton story 235.00
27 A:Tamoa 225.00
28 . . . . 200.00
29 . . . . 200.00
30 L:Holyoke 200.00
31 F:Fox. 175.00
32 Hitler cover 225.00
33 Fight for Freedom 175.00
34 A:Black Terror,Menace of K-4. 175.00
35 . . . . 175.00
36 The Runaway House 175.00
37 Inside the House 175.00
38 Revolt of the Zombies 175.00
39 . . . . 175.00
40 . . . . 175.00
41 A:O'Brine Twins 150.00
42 . . . . 150.00
43 . . . . 150.00
44 . . . . 150.00
45 . . . . 150.00
46 A:Puppeteer. 175.00
47 JKa,V:Junior Crime Club . . . 900.00
48 JKa,A:Black Lace. 700.00
49 JKa 700.00
50 JKa,The Ambitious Bride . . . 650.00
51 JKa, Shady Lady 575.00
52 JKa(c),Bondage cover 900.00
53 JKa,A:Jack "Legs"
   Diamond,Bondage(c) 600.00
54 JKa,The Vanishing Nude . . . 1,000.00
55 JKa 550.00
56 JKa,Tri-State Terror 550.00
57 JKa,The Feagle Bros. 550.00
58 . . . . 100.00
59 . . . . 100.00
60 Aug., 1960 . . . . 100.00

Blue Beetle #54
© Fox Features Syndicate

BLUE BEETLE
(see THING!, THE)

BLUE BOLT
Funnies, Inc./Novelty Press/
Premium Service Co,
June, 1940

1 JSm,PG,O:Blue Bolt	2,500.00
2 JSm	1,200.00
3 S&K,A:Space Hawk	1,000.00
4 PG	900.00
5 BEv,B:Sub Zero	850.00
6 JK,JSm	800.00
7 S&K,BEv	850.00
8 S&K(c)	800.00
9	725.00
10 S&K(c)	775.00
11 BEv(c)	800.00
12	800.00
2-1 BEv(c),PG,O:Dick Cole & V:Simba	250.00
2-2 BEv(c),PG	200.00
2-3 PG,Cole vs Simba	175.00
2-4 BD	175.00
2-5 I:Freezum	175.00
2-6 O:Sgt.Spook, Dick Cole	150.00
2-7 BD	125.00
2-8 BD	125.00
2-9 JW	125.00
2-10 JW	125.00
2-11 JW	125.00
2-12 E:Twister	125.00
3-1 A:115th Infantry	100.00
3-2 A:Phantom Sub	100.00
3-3	100.00
3-4 JW(c)	75.00
3-5 Jor	75.00
3-6 Jor	75.00
3-7 X-Mas cover	75.00
3-8	75.00
3-9 A:Phantom Sub	75.00
3-10 DBa	75.00
3-11 April Fools cover	75.00
3-12	75.00
4-1 Hitler,Tojo,Mussolini cover.	135.00
4-2 Liberty Bell cover	50.00
4-3 What are You Doing for Your Country	50.00
4-4 I Fly for Vengence	50.00
4-5 TFH(c)	50.00
4-6 HcK	50.00
4-7 JWi(c).	50.00
4-8 E:Sub Zero	50.00

Blue Bolt 5-6
© Novelty Press

4-9	50.00
4-10	50.00
4-11	50.00
4-12	50.00
5-1 thru 5-12	@50.00
6-1	50.00
6-2 War Bonds (c)	60.00
6-3	50.00
6-4 Racist(c).	85.00
6-5 Soccer cover	50.00
6-6 thru 6-12	@50.00
7-1 thru 7-12	@50.00
8-1 Baseball cover	50.00
8-2 JHa	50.00
8-3 JHe	50.00
8-4 JHa	50.00
8-5 JHe	50.00
8-6 JDo	50.00
8-7 LbC(c).	60.00
8-8	50.00
8-9 AMc(c)	50.00
8-10	50.00
8-11 Basketball cover	55.00
8-12	50.00
9-1 AMc,Baseball cover	50.00
9-2 AMc	45.00
9-3	45.00
9-4 JHe	45.00
9-5 JHe	45.00
9-6 LbC(c),Football cover	60.00
9-7 JHe	45.00
9-8 Hockey cover	50.00
9-9 LbC(c),3-D effect	70.00
9-10	40.00
9-11	40.00
9-12	40.00
10-1 Baseball cover,3-D effect	50.00
10-2 3-D effect	45.00

Star Publications

102 LbC(c),Chameleon	225.00
103 LbC(c),same	200.00
104 LbC(c),same	200.00
105 LbC(c),O:Blue Bolt Space, Drug Story	375.00
106 S&K,LbC(c),A;Space Hawk	350.00
107 S&K,LbC(c),A;Space Hawk	350.00
108 S&K,LbC(c),A:Blue Bolt	350.00
109 BW,LbC(c)	350.00
110 B:Horror covers,A:Target	350.00
111 Weird Tales of Horror, A:Red Rocket	350.00
112 JyD,WiP	300.00
113 BW,JyD,A:Space Hawk	300.00
114 LbC(c),JyD.	300.00
115 LbC(c),JyD,A:Sgt.Spook.	350.00
116 LbC(c),JyD,A:Jungle Joe	350.00
117 LbC(c),A:Blue Bolt,Jo-Jo	350.00
118 WW,LbC(c),A:White Spirit.	350.00
119 LbC(c)	350.00

Becomes:

GHOSTLY WEIRD STORIES
Star Publications, Sept., 1953

120 LbC,A:Jo-Jo	250.00
121 LbC,A:Jo-Jo.	225.00
122 LbC,A:The Mask	225.00
123 LbC,A:Jo-Jo.	225.00
124 LbC, Sept., 1954	225.00

BLUE CIRCLE COMICS
Enwil Associates/
Rural Home, June, 1944

1 B:Blue Circle,O:Steel Fist	200.00
2	150.00
3 Hitler parody cover	175.00
4	75.00
5 E:Steel Fist,A:Driftwood Davey	75.00
6	75.00

BLUE RIBBON COMICS
MLJ Magazines, Nov., 1939

1 JCo,B:Dan Hastings, Richy-Amazing Boy	2,700.00
2 JCo,B:Bob Phantom, Silver Fox	1,000.00
3 JCo,A:Phantom,Silver Fox	700.00
4 O:Fox,Ty Gor,B:Doc Strong, Hercules	750.00
5 Gattling Gun cover	550.00
6 Amazing Boy Richy cover	500.00
7 A:Fox cover,Corporal Collins V:Nazis.	500.00
8 E:Hercules	500.00
9 O&I:Mr. Justice	2,200.00
10 Mr. Justice cover	800.00
11 SCp(c)	800.00
12 E:Doc Strong	800.00
13 B:Inferno	800.00
14 A:Inferno	700.00
15 A:Inferno,E:Green Falcon.	700.00
16 O:Captain Flag	1,400.00
17 Captain Flag V:Black Hand	725.00
18 Captain Flag-Black Hand	700.00
19 Captain Flag cover.	700.00
20 Captain Flag V:Nazis cover	750.00
21 Captain Flag V:Death.	700.00
22 Circus Cover, March, 1942.	700.00

BLUE RIBBON COMICS
St. John Publications
Feb., 1949

1 Heckle & Jeckle	40.00
2 MB(c),Diary Secrets	80.00
3 MB,MB(c),Heckle & Jeckle	35.00
4 Teen-age Diary Secrets	80.00
5 MB,Teen-age Diary Secrets	75.00
6 Dinky Duck	15.00

BO
Charlton Comics, June, 1955

1	40.00
2	30.00
3 Oct., 1955	30.00

BOB COLT
Fawcett Publications
Nov., 1950

1 B:Bob Colt,Buck Skin	350.00
2 Death Round Train	200.00
3 Mysterious Black Knight of the Prairie	175.00
4 Death Goes Downstream	175.00
5 The Mesa of Mystery	175.00
6 The Mysterious Visitors.	175.00
7 Dragon of Disaster	150.00
8 Redman's Revenge	150.00
9 Hidden Hacienda	150.00
10 Fiend from Vulture Mountain	150.00

BOLD STORIES
Kirby Publishing Co.
March, 1950

1 WW,Near nudity cover	1,000.00
2 GI,Cobra's Kiss	850.00
3 WW,Orge of Paris,July, 1950	750.00
4 Case of the Winking Buddha.	300.00
5 It Rhymes with Lust	300.00
6 Candid Tales, April 1950.	300.00

BOMBER COMICS
Elliot Publishing Co.
March, 1944

1 B:Wonder Boy,Kismet,

Eagle Evans	500.00
2 Wonder Boy cover	275.00
3 Wonder Boy-Kismet cover	250.00
4 Hitler,Tojo, Mussolini cover	300.00

BOOK OF ALL COMICS
William H. Wise, 1945
1 A:Green Mask,Puppeteer	300.00

BOOK OF COMICS, THE
William H. Wise, 1945
N# A:Captain V	300.00

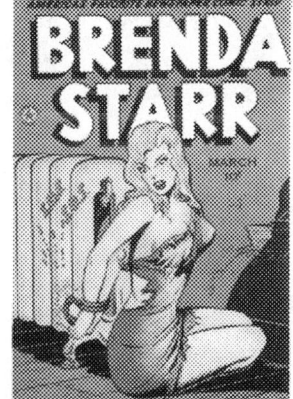

Boy Comics #12
© Lev Gleason Publications

BOY COMICS
Comic House, Inc.
(Lev Gleason Publ.), April, 1942
3 O:Crimebuster,Bombshell,Young Robin, B:Yankee Longago, Swoop Storm	2,400.00
4 Hitler,Tojo,Mussolini cover	1,000.00
5 Crimebuster saves day cover	700.00
6 O:Iron Jaw & Death of Son, B:Little Dynamite	2,000.00
7 Hitler,Tojo,Mussolini cover	650.00
8 D:Iron Jaw	700.00
9 I:He-She	600.00
10 Iron Jaw returns	1,000.00
11 Iron Jaw falls in love	600.00
12 Crimebuster V:Japanese	500.00
13 V:New,more terrible Iron Jaw	500.00
14 V:Iron Jaw	500.00
15 I:Rodent,D:Iron Jaw	550.00
16 Crimebuster V:Knight	250.00
17 Flag cover,Crimebuster V:Moth	275.00
18 Smashed car cover	250.00
19 Express train cover	250.00
20 Coffin cover	250.00
21 Boxing cover	175.00
22 Under Sea cover	175.00
23 Golf cover	175.00
24 County insane asylum cover	175.00
25 52 pgs	175.00
26 68 pgs	175.00
27 Express train cover	200.00
28 E:Yankee Longago	200.00
29 Prison break cover	200.00
30 O:Crimebuster,Murder cover	250.00
31 68 pgs	175.00
32 E:Young Robin Hood	175.00
33	175.00
34 Suicide cover & story	135.00

35	125.00
36	125.00
37	125.00
38	125.00
39 E:Little Dynamite	125.00
40	125.00
41 thru 50	@110.00
51 thru 56	@100.00
57 B:Dilly Duncan	125.00
58	100.00
59	100.00
60 Iron Jaw returns	125.00
61 O:Iron Jaw,Crimebuster	135.00
62 A:Iron Jaw	125.00
63 thru 70	@75.00
71 E:Dilly Duncan	75.00
72	75.00
73	75.00
74 thru 79	@75.00
80 I:Rocky X	60.00
81 thru 88	@60.00
89 A:The Claw	65.00
90 same	65.00
91 same	65.00
92 same	65.00
93 The Claw(c),A:Rocky X	65.00
94	55.00
95	55.00
96	55.00
97	55.00
98 A:Rocky X	65.00
99	55.00
100	65.00
101	65.00
102	65.00
103 thru 118	@65.00
119 March, 1956	65.00

BOY EXPLORERS
(see TERRY AND THE PIRATES)

BRENDA STARR
Four Star Comics Corp./
Superior Comics Ltd.,
Sept., 1947
13(1)	650.00
14(2) JKa,Bondage cover	700.00
2-3	500.00
2-4 JKa,Operating table cover	650.00
2-5 Swimsuit cover	500.00

Brenda Starr #14
© Superior Comics

2-6	500.00
2-7	500.00
2-8 Cosmetic cover	500.00
2-9 Giant Starr cover	500.00
2-10 Wedding cover	500.00
2-11	500.00
2-12	500.00

BRICK BRADFORD
Best Books
(Standard Comics), July, 1949
5	150.00
6 Robot cover	175.00
7 AS	100.00
8	100.00

BROADWAY ROMANCES
Quality Comics Group
Jan., 1950
1 PG,BWa&(c)	225.00
2 BWa,Glittering Desire	175.00
3 BL,Stole My Love	75.00
4 Enslaved by My Past	85.00
5 Flame of Passion,Sept.,1950	85.00

BRONCHO BILL
Visual Editions
(Standard Comics), Jan., 1948
5	75.00
6 AS(c)	45.00
7 AS(c)	35.00
8 ASh	35.00
9 AS(c)	35.00
10 AS(c)	35.00
11 AS(c)	25.00
12 AS(c)	25.00
13 AS(c)	25.00
14 ASh	25.00
15 ASh	25.00
16 AS(c)	25.00

BRUCE GENTRY
Four Star Publ./
Visual Editions/
Superior, Jan., 1948
1 B:Ray Bailey reprints	350.00
2 Plane crash cover	250.00
3 E:Ray Bailey reprints	225.00
4 Tiger attack cover	175.00
5	175.00
6 Help message cover	175.00
7	175.00
8 End of Marriage cover, July, 1949	175.00

BUCCANEERS
(see KID ETERNITY)

BUCK JONES
Dell Publishing Co.,
Oct., 1950
1	150.00
2	75.00
3	60.00
4	60.00
5	60.00
6	60.00
7	60.00
8	60.00

GOLDEN AGE

BUCK ROGERS
Eastern Color Printing
Winter 1940
1 Partial Painted(c) 2,900.00
2 . . . . 1,100.00
3 Living Corpse from Crimson
  Coffin 900.00
4 One man army of greased
  lightning 850.00
5 Sky Roads 800.00
6 Sept., 1943 . . . . 800.00

Toby Press
100 Flying Saucers 200.00
101 . . . . 175.00
9 . . . . 175.00

BUG MOVIES
Dell Publishing Co., 1931
1 . . . . 100.00

BUGS BUNNY
DELL GIANT EDITIONS
Dell Publishing Co.
Christmas
1 Christmas Funnies (1950). . . . 300.00
2 Christmas Funnies (1951). . . . 250.00
3 Christmas Funnies (1952). . . . 200.00
4 Christmas Funnies (1953). . . . 200.00
5 Christmas Funnies (1954). . . . 200.00
6 Christmas Party (1955) 175.00
7 Christmas Party (1956) 185.00
8 Christmas Funnies (1957). . . . 185.00
9 Christmas Funnies (1958). . . . 185.00
1 County Fair (1957) 200.00
Halloween
1 Halloween Parade (1953) 200.00
2 Halloween Parade (1954) 175.00
3 Trick 'N' Treat
  Halloween Fun (1955) 185.00
4 Trick 'N' Treat
  Halloween Fun (1956) 185.00
Vacation
1 Vacation Funnies (1951) 300.00
2 Vacation Funnies (1952) 275.00
3 Vacation Funnies (1953) 250.00
4 Vacation Funnies (1954) 200.00
5 Vacation Funnies (1955) 200.00
6 Vacation Funnies (1956) 175.00
7 Vacation Funnies (1957) 175.00
8 Vacation Funnies (1958) 175.00
9 Vacation Funnies (1959) 175.00

BUGS BUNNY
Dell Publishing Co., 1942
@WP Heading 1:see Four Color for
early years
28 thru 30 . . . . @40.00
31 thru 50 . . . . @30.00
51 thru 70 . . . . @25.00
71 thru 85 . . . . @20.00
86 Giant-Show Time 75.00
87 thru 100 . . . . @10.00
101 thru 120 . . . . @7.00
121 thru 140 . . . . @5.00
141 thru 190 . . . . @4.00
191 thru 245 . . . . @3.00

BULLETMAN
Fawcett Publications
Summer, 1941
1 I:Bulletman & Bulletgirl 2,800.00
2 MRa(c) 1,200.00
3 MRa(c) 900.00
4 V:Headless Horror,

  Guillotine cover. 850.00
5 Riddle of Dr. Riddle. 800.00
6 V:Japanese 650.00
7 V:Revenge Syndicate 625.00
8 V:Mr. Ego 600.00
9 V:Canine Criminals 600.00
10 I:Bullet Dog 625.00
11 V:Fiendish Fiddler 550.00
12 . . . . 500.00
13 . . . . 500.00
14 V:Death the Comedian. 500.00
15 V:Professor D 500.00
16 VanishingElephant,Fall 1946 . 500.00

Buster Crabbe #6
© *Famous Funnies*

BUSTER CRABBE
Famous Funnies, Nov., 1951
1 The Arrow of Death 225.00
2 AW&GE(c) 250.00
3 AW&GE(c) 275.00
4 FF(c) 350.00
5 AW,FF,FF,(c) 900.00
6 Sharks cover 100.00
7 FF 150.00
8 Gorilla cover 100.00
9 FF 150.00
10 . . . . 100.00
11 Snakes cover 75.00
12 Sept., 1953 . . . . 75.00

BUSTER CRABBE
Lev Gleason Pub., 1953
1 Ph(c) 150.00
2 ATh 150.00
3 ATh 150.00
4 F. Gordon(c) 125.00

BUZ SAWYER
Standard Comics, June, 1948
1 . . . . 150.00
2 I:Sweeney 100.00
3 . . . . 75.00
4 . . . . 75.00
5 June, 1949 . . . . 75.00

CALLING ALL BOYS
Parents Magazine Institute
Jan., 1946
1 Skiing 75.00
2 . . . . 30.00
3 Peril Out Post 25.00
4 Model Airplane 25.00
5 Fishing 25.00

---

6 Swimming 25.00
7 Baseball 25.00
8 School 25.00
9 The Miracle Quarterback 25.00
10 Gary Cooper cover 35.00
11 Rin-Tin-Tin cover 25.00
12 Bob Hope cover. 50.00
13 Bing Cosby cover 40.00
14 J. Edgar Hoover cover 25.00
15 Tex Granger cover 20.00
16 . . . . 20.00
17 Tex Granger cover, May, 1948 . 20.00
Becomes:

TEX GRANGER
18 Bandits of the Badlands 55.00
19 The Seven Secret Cities 45.00
20 Davey Crockett's Last Fight . . 35.00
21 Canyon Ambush 35.00
22 V:Hooded Terror 35.00
23 V:Billy the Kid 35.00
24 A:Hector, Sept., 1949. . . . . . . 40.00

CALLING ALL GIRLS
Parent Magazine Press, Inc.
Sept., 1941
1 . . . . 85.00
2 Virginia Weidler cover 40.00
3 Shirley Temple cover 55.00
4 Darla Hood cover 30.00
5 Gloria Hood cover 30.00
6 . . . . 25.00
7 . . . . 25.00
8 . . . . 25.00
9 Flag cover 28.00
10 . . . . 25.00
11 thru 20 . . . . @25.00
21 thru 39 . . . . @15.00
40 Liz Taylor 70.00
41. . . . . 15.00
42. . . . . 15.00
43 Oct., 1945 . . . . 15.00

CALLING ALL KIDS
Quality Comics, Inc.
Dec./Jan., 1946
1 Funny Animal stories 50.00
2 . . . . 25.00
3 . . . . 20.00
4 . . . . 15.00
5 . . . . 15.00
6 . . . . 15.00
7 . . . . 15.00
8 . . . . 15.00
9 . . . . 15.00
10 . . . . 15.00
11 thru 25 . . . . @10.00
26 Aug., 1949. . . . . 10.00

CAMERA COMICS
U.S. Camera Publishing Corp.
July–Sept., 1944
1 Airfighter,Grey Comet 150.00
2 How to Set Up a Darkroom . . 125.00
3 Linda Lens V:Nazi cover 80.00
4 Linda Lens cover 60.00
5 Diving cover 60.00
6 Jim Lane cover 60.00
7 Linda Lens cover 60.00
8 Linda Lens cover 60.00
9 Summer, 1946 . . . . 60.00

CAMP COMICS
Dell Publishing Co., 1942
1 Ph(c),WK,A:Bugs Bunny 400.00
2 Ph(c),WK,A:Bugs Bunny 300.00
3 Ph(c),Wk 400.00

    All comics prices listed are for *Near Mint* condition.

Captain Aero #6
© Holyoke Publishing Co.

CAPTAIN AERO COMICS
Holyoke Publishing Co.
Dec., 1941
1 B:Flag-Man&Solar,Master
of Magic Captain Aero,
Captain Stone 1,200.00
2 A:Pals of Freedom 600.00
3 JKu,B:Alias X,A:Pals of
Freedom 600.00
4 JKu,O:Gargoyle,
Parachute jump 600.00
5 JKu 500.00
6 JKu,Flagman,A:Miss Victory . . 400.00
7 Alias X 250.00
8 O:Red Cross,A:Miss Victory . . 250.00
9 A:Miss Victory,Alias X 200.00
10 A:Miss Victory,Red Cross 175.00
11 A:Miss Victory 150.00
12 same 150.00
13 same 150.00
14 same 150.00
15 AS(c),A:Miss Liberty 150.00
16 AS(c),Leather Face 125.00
17 LbC(c) 225.00
21 LbC(c) 225.00
22 LbC(c),I:Mighty Mite. 225.00
23 LbC(c) 225.00
24 LbC(c) American Planes Dive
Bomb Japan. 250.00
25 LbC(c),Science Fiction(c) 250.00
26 LbC(c) 225.00

CAPTAIN BATTLE
New Friday Publ./
Magazine Press, Summer, 1941
1 B:Captain Battle,O:Blackout 1,000.00
2 Pirate Ship cover 650.00
3 Dungeon cover 550.00
4 . . . . 400.00
5 V:Japanese, Summer, 1943 . . 400.00

CAPTAIN BATTLE, Jr.
Comic House, Fall, 1943
1 Claw V:Ghost, A:Sniffer 850.00
2 Man who didn't believe
in Ghosts 600.00

CAPTAIN COURAGEOUS
(see BANNER COMICS)

CAPTAIN EASY
Standard Comics, 1939
N# Swash Buckler 750.00
10 . . . . 80.00
11 . . . . 60.00
12 . . . . 60.00
13 ASh(c). 60.00
14 . . . . 60.00
15 . . . . 60.00
16 ASh(c). 60.00
17 Sept., 1949 . . . . 60.00

CAPTAIN FEARLESS COMICS
Helnit Publishing Co.
Aug., 1941
1 O:Mr. Miracle,Alias X,Captain
Fearless Citizen Smith,
A:Miss Victory 650.00
2 A:Border Patrol, Sept.,1941 . . 400.00

CAPTAIN FLASH
Sterling Comics, Nov., 1954
1 O:Captain Flash 275.00
2 V:Black Knight 150.00
3 Beasts from 1,000,000 BC . . . 150.00
4 Flying Saucer Invasion 150.00

CAPTAIN FLEET
Approved Comics, Fall, 1952
1 Storm and Mutiny ...Typhoon . 100.00

CAPTAIN FLIGHT COMICS
Four Star Publications
March, 1944
N# B:Captain Flight,Ace Reynolds
Dashthe Avenger,Professor X 300.00
2 . . . . 150.00
3 . . . . 125.00
4 B:Rock Raymond Salutes
America's Wartime Heroines . 150.00
5 Bondage cover,B:Red Rocket
A:The Grenade 500.00
6 Girl tied at the stake 150.00
7 Dog Fight cover 350.00
8 B:Yankee Girl,A:Torpedoman . 350.00
9 Dog Fight cover 350.00
10 Bondage cover 350.00
11 LBc(c),Future(c),
Feb-March, 1947 . . . . 500.00

CAPTAIN GALLANT
Charlton Comics, 1955
1 Ph(c),Buster Crabbe. 55.00
2 . . . . 45.00
3 . . . . 45.00
4 Sept., 1956 . . . . 45.00

CAPTAIN JET
Four Star Publ., May, 1952
1 Factory bombing cover 150.00
2 Parachute jump cover 90.00
3 Tank bombing cover 75.00
4 Parachute cover 75.00
5 . . . . 50.00

CAPTAIN KIDD
(see ALL GREAT COMICS)

CAPTAIN MARVEL ADVENTURES
Fawcett Publications
Spring, 1941
N# JK, B:Captain Marvel &
Sivana 29,000.00
2 GT,JK(c),Billy Batson (c) . . . 3,500.00
3 JK(c),Thunderbolt (c) 2,200.00
4 Shazam(c). 1,500.00
5 V:Nazis 1,100.00
6 Solomon, Hercules, Atlas, Zeus,
Achilles & Mercury cover . . . 900.00
7 Ghost of the White Room 900.00
8 Forward America 900.00
9 A:Ibac the Monster, Nippo
the Nipponese, Relm of
the Subconscious 900.00
10 V:Japanese 900.00
11 V:Japanese and Nazis 700.00
12 Joins the Army 700.00
13 V:Diamond-Eyed Idol of
Doom. 700.00
14 Nippo meets his Nemesis . . . 700.00
15 Big "Paste the Axis" contest. . 700.00
16 Uncle Sam cover, Paste
the Axis 700.00
17 P(c), Paste the Axis 650.00
18 P(c), O:Mary Marvel 1,500.00
19 Mary Marvel & Santa cover . . 550.00
20 Mark of the Black
Swastika 3,400.00
21 Hitler cover 3,300.00
22 B:Mr. Mind serial,
Shipyard Sabotage. 700.00
23 A:Steamboat 500.00
24 Minneapolis Mystery 500.00
25 Sinister Faces cover 500.00
26 Flag cover 500.00
27 Joins Navy. 400.00
28 Uncle Sam cover 400.00
29 Battle at the China Wall 400.00
30 Modern Robinson Crusoe . . . 400.00
31 Fights his own Conscience. . . 400.00
32 V:Mole Men, Dallas 400.00
33 Mt. Rushmore parody
cover, Omaha. 375.00
34 Oklahoma City. 375.00
35 O:Radar the International
Policeman, Indianapolis 350.00

Captain Marvel #21
© Fawcett Publications

GOLDEN AGE

36 Missing face contest, St. Louis. 350.00
37 V:Block Busting Bubbles, Cincinnati. 350.00
38 V:Chattanooga Ghost, Rock Garden City. 350.00
39 V:Mr. Mind's Death Ray, Pittsburgh. 350.00
40 V:Ghost of the Tower,Boston . 350.00
41 Runs for President, Dayton . . 250.00
42 Christmas special, St. Paul . . 250.00
43 V:Mr. Mind,I:Uncle Marvel, Chicago 250.00
44 OtherWorlds,Washington,D.C. 250.00
45 V:Blood Bank Robbers. 250.00
46 E: Mr. Mind Serial, Tall Stories of Jonah Joggins . . . 250.00
47 . . . . 235.00
48 Signs Autographs cover. . . . 225.00
49 V: An Unknown Killer. 225.00
50 Twisted Powers. 225.00
51 Last of the Batsons 175.00
52 O&I:Sivana Jr.,V:Giant Earth Dreamer. 200.00
53 Gets promoted. 175.00
54 Marooned in the Future, Kansas City. 200.00
55 Endless String, Columbus . . . 175.00
56 Goes Crazy, Mobile 175.00
57 A:Haunted Girl, Rochester . . . 175.00
58 V:Sivana 175.00
59 . . . . 175.00
60 Man who made Earthquakes . 175.00
61 I&V: Oggar, the Worlds Mightiest Immortal 225.00
62 The Great Harness Race 175.00
63 Stuntman. 175.00
64 . . . . 175.00
65 V:Invaders from Outer Space. 175.00
66 Atomic War cover 200.00
67 Hartford. 175.00
68 Scenes from the Past, Baltimore 175.00
69 Gets Knighted 175.00
70 Horror in the Box 175.00
71 Wheel of Death 175.00
72 . . . . 175.00
73 Becomes a Petrophile 175.00
74 Who is the 13th Guest 175.00
75 V:Astonishing Yeast Menace . 175.00
76 A:Atom Ambassador 175.00
77 The Secret Life 175.00
78 O:Mr. Tawny 200.00
79 O:Atom,A:World's Worst Actor 250.00
80 Twice told story 400.00
81 A:Mr. Atom. 150.00
82 A:Mr. Tawny. 150.00
83 Indian Chief. 150.00
84 V:Surrealist Imp 150.00
85 Freedom Train. 200.00
86 A:Mr. Tawny. 150.00
87 V:Electron Thief. 150.00
88 Billy Batson's Boyhood. 150.00
89 V:Sivana 150.00
90 A:Mr. Tawny. 150.00
91 A:Chameleon Stone. 150.00
92 The Land of Limbo. 150.00
93 Book of all Knowledge 150.00
94 Battle of Electricity. 150.00
95 The Great Ice Cap. 150.00
96 V:Automatic Weapon 150.00
97 Wiped Out. 150.00
98 United Worlds 150.00
99 Rain of Terror. 150.00
100 V:Sivana,Plot against the Universe. 300.00
101 Invisibility Trap 150.00
102 Magic Mix-up 150.00
103 Ice Covered World of 1,000,000 AD 150.00

104 Mr. Tawny's Masquerade . . . 150.00
105 The Dog Catcher 150.00
106 V:Menace of the Moon 150.00
107 V:Space Hunter 150.00
108 V:Terrible Termites 150.00
109 The Invention Inventor 150.00
110 V:Sivana 150.00
111 The Eighth Sea 150.00
112 . . . . 150.00
113 Captain Marvel's Feud 150.00
114 V:The Ogre 150.00
115 . . . . 150.00
116 Flying Saucer. 175.00
117 . . . . 135.00
118 V:Weird Water Man 150.00
119 . . . . 150.00
120 . . . . 150.00
121 . . . . 150.00
122 . . . . 150.00
123 . . . . 150.00
124 V:Discarded Instincts 150.00
125 V:Ancient Villain. 150.00
126 thru 130 . . . . @150.00
131 . . . . 150.00
132 V:Flood 150.00
133 . . . . 150.00
134 . . . . 150.00
135 Perplexing Past Puzzle 150.00
136 . . . . 150.00
137 . . . . 150.00
138 V:Haunted Horror. 150.00
139 . . . . 150.00
140 Hand of Horror 150.00
141 Horror 150.00
142 . . . . 150.00
143 Great Stone Face on the Moon. 150.00
144 thru 147 . . . . @150.00
148 V:The World. 150.00
149 . . . . 150.00
150 Captains Marvel's Wedding, Nov., 1953 . . . . 300.00

CAPTAIN MARVEL JR.
Fawcett Publications
Nov., 1952
1 O:Captain Marvel, Jr., A:Capt. Nazi 4,500.00
2 O:Capt.Nippon,V:Capt. Nazi 1,500.00
3 Parade to Excitement 800.00
4 V:Invisible Nazi 800.00
5 V:Capt. Nazi 700.00
6 Adventure of Sabbac. 600.00
7 City under the Sea 600.00

Captain Marvel Jr. #2
© Fawcett Publications

8 Dangerous Double 550.00
9 Independence cover 550.00
10 Hitler cover 575.00
11 . . . . 450.00
12 Scuttles the Axis Isle in the Sky. 500.00
13 V:The Axis,Hitler,cover. 475.00
14 X-Mas cover, Santa wears Capt. Marvel uniform 400.00
15 . . . . 450.00
16 A:Capt. Marvel, Sivana, Pogo 400.00
17 Meets his Future self 400.00
18 V:Birds of Doom. 400.00
19 A:Capt. Nazi & Capt. Nippon . 400.00
20 Goes on the Warpath 375.00
21 Buy War Stamps 300.00
22 Rides World's oldest steamboat 300.00
23 . . . . 300.00
24 V:Weather Man 300.00
25 Flag cover. 300.00
26 Happy New Year 300.00
27 Jungle Thrills. 300.00
28 V:Sivana's Crumbling Crimes. 300.00
29 Blazes a Wilderness Trail. . . . 300.00
30 . . . . 300.00
31 . . . . 200.00
32 Keeper of the Lonely Rock. . . 200.00
33 . . . . 200.00
34/35 I&O:Sivana Jr. 200.00
36 Underworld Tournament. 200.00
37 FreddyFreeman'sNews-stand. 200.00
38 A:Arabian Knight 200.00
39 V:Sivana Jr., Headline Stealer. 200.00
40 Faces Grave Situation 200.00
41 I:The Acrobat. 150.00
42 V:Sivana Jr. 150.00
43 V:Beasts on Broadway. 150.00
44 Key to the Mystery. 150.00
45 A:Icy Fingers 150.00
46 . . . . 150.00
47 V:Giant of the Beanstalk 150.00
48 Whale of a Fish Story 150.00
49 V:Dream Recorder. 150.00
50 Wanted: Freddy Freeman . . . 150.00
51 The Island Riddle. 125.00
52 A:Flying Postman. 125.00
53 Atomic Bomb on the Loose . . 175.00
54 V:Man with 100 Heads. 150.00
55 Pyramid of Eternity 150.00
56 Blue Boy's Black Eye. 150.00
57 Magic Ladder. 150.00
58 Amazing Mirror Maze. 150.00
59 . . . . 150.00
60 V:Space Menace 150.00
61 V:Himself. 125.00
62 . . . . 125.00
63 V:Witch of Winter. 125.00
64 thru 70 . . . . @125.00
71 thru 74 . . . . @125.00
75 V:Outlaw of Crooked Creek . . 125.00
76 thru 85 . . . . @125.00
86 Defenders of time 125.00
87 thru 89 . . . . @125.00
90 The Magic Trunk 100.00
91 thru 99 . . . . @100.00
100 V:Sivana Jr 125.00
101 thru 106 . . . . @100.00
107 The Horror Dimension . . . . . @100.00
108 thru 118 . . . . @100.00
119 Condemned to Die, June, 1953. . . . . 100.00

CAPTAIN MIDNIGHT
Fawcett Publications
Sept., 1942
1 O:Captain Midnight, Capt. Marvel cover 2,300.00
2 Smashes Jap Juggernaut. . . 1,100.00

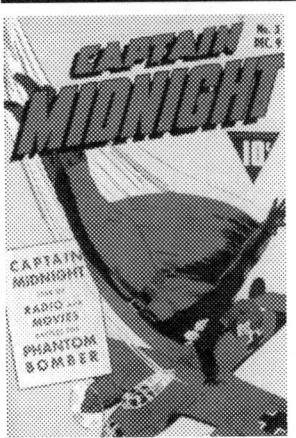

Captain Midnight #3
© *Fawcett Publications*

3 Battles the Phantom Bomber . 750.00
4 Grapples the Gremlins 700.00
5 Double Trouble in Tokyo 700.00
6 Blasts the Black Mikado 600.00
7 Newspaper headline cover . . . 600.00
8 Flying Torpedoes
   Berlin-Bound 550.00
9 MRa(c), Subs in Mississippi . . 550.00
10 MRa(c), Flag cover 550.00
11 MRa(c), Murder in Mexico . . . 400.00
12 V:Sinister Angels 400.00
13 Non-stop Flight around
   the World 400.00
14 V:King of the Villains 400.00
15 V:Kimberley Killer. 400.00
16 Hitler's Fortress Breached . . . 400.00
17 MRa(c), Hello Adolf 375.00
18 Death from the Skies 375.00
19 Hour of Doom for the Axis . . . 375.00
20 Brain and Brawn against Axis 375.00
21 Trades with Japanese 300.00
22 Plea for War Stamps 300.00
23 Japanese Prison cover. 300.00
24 Rising Sun Flag cover 300.00
25 Amusement Park Murder 300.00
26 Hotel of Horror. 300.00
27 Death Knell for Tyranny 300.00
28 Gliderchuting to Glory 300.00
29 Bomb over Nippon. 300.00
30 . . . . 300.00
31 . . . . 200.00
32 . . . . 200.00
33 V:Shark 200.00
34 . . . . 200.00
35 thru 40 . . . . @200.00
41 thru 50 . . . . @150.00
51 thru 63 . . . . @150.00
64 V:XOG, Ruler of Saturn 150.00
65 . . . . 150.00
66 V:XOG. 150.00
67 Fall, 1948 . . . . 150.00
Becomes:

SWEET HEART
68 Robert Mitchum 75.00
69 thru 118 . . . . @25.00
111 Ronald Reagan story 30.00
119 Marilyn Monroe 150.00
120 Atomic Bomb story . . . . @35.00
121 . . . . 20.00
122 1954 . . . . 15.00

CAPTAIN SCIENCE
Youthful Magazines
Nov., 1950
1 WW,O:Captain Science,
   V:Monster God of Rogor. . . . 650.00
2 WW,V:Cat Men of Phoebus,
   Space Pirates. 350.00
3 Ghosts from the Underworld . 350.00
4 WW,Vampires 600.00
5 WW,V:Shark Pirates of Pisces 600.00
6 WW,V:Invisible Tyrants,
   bondage cover 500.00
7 WW,Bondage(c) Dec., 1951 . . 500.00
Becomes:

FANTASTIC
8 Isle of Madness 300.00
9 Octopus cover 225.00
Becomes:

BEWARE
10 SHn,Doll of Death 275.00
11 SHn,Horror Head 225.00
12 SHn,Body Snatchers 200.00
Becomes:

CHILLING TALES
13 MF,Screaming Skull 400.00
14 SHn,Smell of Death 225.00
15 SHn,Curse of the Tomb 225.00
16 HcK,Mark of the Beast
   Bondage(c) 225.00
17 MFc(c),Wandering Willie,
   Oct.,1953 . . . . 250.00

CAPTAIN STEVE SAVAGE
Avon Periodicals
[1st Series] 1950
N# WW 300.00
2 EK(c),The Death Gamble 125.00
3 EK(c),Crash Landing in
   Manchuria 75.00
4 EK(c),V:Red Raiders from
   Siang-Po 50.00
5 EK(c),Rockets of Death 50.00
6 Operation Destruction 50.00
7 EK(c),Flight to Kill 50.00
8 EK(c),V:Red Mystery Jet 50.00
9 EK(c) 50.00
10 . . . . 50.00
11 EK(c). 55.00
12 WW 75.00
13 . . . . 65.00

[2nd Series] Sept./Oct., 1954
5 . . . . 35.00
6 WW 50.00
7 thru 13 . . . . @20.00

CAPTAIN VIDEO
Fawcett Publications
Feb., 1951
1 GE,Ph(c) 850.00
2 Time when Men could not
   Walk. 600.00
3 GE,Indestructible Antagonist . 500.00
4 GE,School of Spies 500.00
5 GE,Missiles of Doom,
   photo cover 500.00
6 GE,Island of Conquerors,
   Photo cover; Dec. 1951 . . . . 500.00

CASPER, THE FRIENDLY GHOST
St. John Publishing
Sept., 1949
1 O:Baby Huey 1,300.00
2 . . . . 500.00

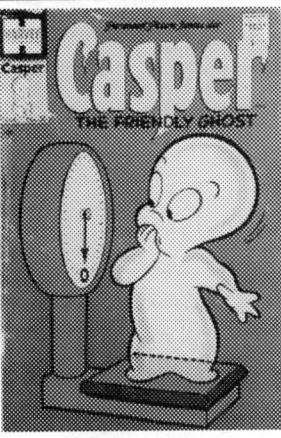

Casper #30
© *Harvey Publications*

3 . . . . 450.00
4 . . . . 350.00
5 . . . . 350.00

Harvey Publications
7 . . . . 275.00
8 thru 9 . . . . @150.00
10 I:Spooky 175.00
11 A:Spooky 100.00
12 thru 18 . . . . @75.00
19 I:Nightmare 85.00
20 I:Wendy the Witch 85.00
21 thru 30 . . . . @50.00
31 thru 40 . . . . @40.00
41 thru 50 . . . . @30.00
51 thru 60 . . . . @25.00
61 thru 69 . . . . @20.00
70 July, 1958 . . . . 22.00

CAT MAN COMICS
Helnit Publ. Co./
Holyoke Publ. Co./
Continental Magazine
May, 1941
1 O:Deacon&Sidekick Mickey,
   Dr. Diamond & Ragman,A:Black
   Widow, B:Blaze Baylor. . . . 2,600.00
2 Ragman 900.00
3 B:Pied Piper 600.00
4 CQ 550.00
5 I&O: The Kitten 500.00
6 CQ 450.00
7 CQ 450.00
8 JKa, I:Volton 600.00
9 JKa 400.00
10 JKa,O:Blackout,
   B:Phantom Falcon 400.00
11 JKa,DRi,BF 410.00
12 . . . . 350.00
13 . . . . 350.00
14 CQ 350.00
15 Rajah of Destruction 350.00
16 Bye-Bye Axis. 425.00
17 Buy Bonds and Stamps 400.00
18 Buy Bonds and Stamps 400.00
19 CQ,Hitler,Tojo and
   Mussolini cover. 450.00
20 CQ,Hitler,Tojo and
   Mussolini cover. 450.00
21 CQ 300.00
22 CQ 300.00
23 CQ 300.00
N# V:Japanese,Bondage(c) 350.00
N# V:Demon. 300.00

N# A:Leather Face 300.00
27 LbC(c),Flag cover,O:Kitten . . . 500.00
28 LbC(c),Horror cover 550.00
29 LbC(c),BF 500.00
30 LbC(c),Bondage(c). 575.00
31 LbC(c) 500.00
32 Aug., 1946 . . . . 400.00

CHALLENGER, THE
Interfaith Publications, 1945
N# O:The Challenger Club 250.00
2 JKa 200.00
3 JKa 200.00
4 JKa,BF 200.00

Chamber of Chills #23
© *Harvey Publications*

CHAMBER OF CHILLS
Harvey Publications/
Witches Tales, June, 1951
21 . . . . 350.00
22 . . . . 200.00
23 Eyes Ripped Out 200.00
24 Bondage cover 225.00
5 Shrunken Skull,
   Operation Monster 225.00
6 Seven Skulls of Magondi 200.00
7 Pit of the Damned 175.00
8 Formula for Death 200.00
9 Bondage cover 150.00
10 Cave of Death 150.00
11 Curse of Morgan Kilgane 125.00
12 Swamp Monster 125.00
13 The Lost Race 150.00
14 Down to Death 125.00
15 Nightmare of Doom 150.00
16 Cycle of Horror 150.00
17 Amnesia 150.00
18 Hair cut-Atom Bomb 175.00
19 Happy Anniversary 150.00
20 Shock is Struck 150.00
21 BP,Nose for News 160.00
22 Is Death the End? 125.00
23 BP,Heartline 125.00
24 BP,Bondage(c) 175.00
25 . . . . 75.00
26 HN,Captains Return 75.00
Becomes:

CHAMBER OF CLUES
27 BP,A:Kerry Drake 100.00
28 A:Kerry Drake 50.00

CHAMPION COMICS
Worth Publishing Co.
Dec., 1939
2 B:Champ, Blazing Scarab, Neptina,
   Liberty Lads, Jingleman . . . 1,200.00
3 . . . . 600.00
4 Bailout(c) 625.00
5 Jungleman(c) 625.00
6 MNe 625.00
7 MNe,Human Meteor 650.00
8 . . . . 900.00
9 . . . . 900.00
10 Bondage cover 1,000.00
Becomes:

CHAMP COMICS
11 Human Meteor 650.00
12 Human Heteor 500.00
13 Dragon's Teeth 450.00
14 Liberty Lads 450.00
15 Liberty Lads 450.00
16 Liberty Lads 450.00
17 Liberty Lads 450.00
18 Liberty Lads 600.00
19 A:The Wasp 625.00
20 A:The Green Ghost 450.00
21 . . . . 350.00
22 A:White Mask 425.00
23 Flag cover 425.00
24 . . . . 350.00
25 . . . . 350.00
26 thru 29 . . . . 350.00

CHARLIE McCARTHY
Dell Publishing Co.
Nov., 1947
1 . . . . 150.00
2 . . . . 75.00
3 . . . . 75.00
1 . . . . 75.00
2 . . . . 75.00
3 . . . . 75.00
4 . . . . 75.00
5 . . . . 75.00
6 . . . . 75.00
7 . . . . 75.00
8 . . . . 75.00
9 . . . . 75.00

CHIEF, THE
Dell Publishing Co.
Aug., 1950
(1) see Dell Four Color #290
2 . . . . 30.00

CHILLING TALES
(see CAPTAIN SCIENCE)

CHUCKLE THE GIGGLY
BOOK OF COMIC
ANIMALS
R. B. Leffing Well Co., 1944
1 . . . . 125.00

CINEMA COMICS
HERALD
Paramount/Universal/RKO/
20th Century Fox
Giveaways 1941-43
N# Mr. Bug Goes to Town 75.00
N# Bedtime Story 75.00
N# Lady for a Night,J.Wayne . . . 100.00
N# Reap the Wild Wind 75.00

N# Thunderbirds 75.00
N# They All Kissed Me 75.00
N# Bombardier 75.00
N# Crash Dive 75.00
N# Arabian Nights 75.00

CIRCUS THE
COMIC RIOT
Globe Syndicate, June, 1938
1 BKa,WE,BW 5,000.00
2 BKa,WE,BW 2,700.00
3 BKa,WE,BW, Aug., 1938 . . . 2,700.00

CISCO KID, THE
Dell Publishing Co.
(1) *See Dell Four Color #292*
2 Jan., 1951 . . . . 275.00
3 thru 5 . . . . @125.00
6 thru 10 . . . . @ 90.00
11 thru 20 . . . . @ 75.00
21 thru 36 . . . . @ 60.00
37 thru 41 Ph(c)'s . . . . @100.00

CLAIRE VOYANT
Leader Publ./Visual Ed./
Pentagon Publ., 1946-47
N# 450.00
2 JKa(c) 400.00
3 Case of the Kidnapped Bride . 350.00
4 Bondage cover 400.00

CLOAK AND DAGGER
Approved Comics
(Ziff-Davis), Fall, 1952
1 NS(c),Al Kennedy of the Secret
   Service 175.00

CLUE COMICS
Hillman Periodicals
Jan., 1943
1 O:Boy King,Nightmare,Micro-Face,
   Twilight,Zippo 850.00
2 . . . . 400.00
3 Boy King V:The Crane 400.00
4 V:The Crane 300.00
5 V:The Crane 300.00
6 Hells Kitchen 175.00
7 V:Dr. Plasma,Torture(c) 200.00
8 RP,A:The Gold Mummy King . 250.00
9 I:Paris 175.00
10 O:Gun Master 175.00
11 A:Gun Master 125.00
12 O:Rackman 175.00
2-1 S&K,O:Nightro,A:Iron Lady . 325.00
2-2 S&K,Bondage(c) 350.00
2-3 S&K 300.00
Becomes:

REAL CLUE
CRIME STORIES
2-4 DBw,S&K,True Story of
   Ma Barker 375.00
2-5 S&K, Newface surgery cover 275.00
2-6 S&K, Breakout cover 250.00
2-7 S&K, Stick up cover 250.00
2-8 Kidnapping cover 75.00
2-9 DBa,Boxing fix cover 75.00
2-10 DBa,Murder cover 75.00
2-11 Attempted bank
   robbery cover 75.00
2-12 Murder cover 75.00
3-1 thru 3-12 . . . . @ 50.00
4-1 thru 4-12 . . . . @ 75.00
5-1 thru 5-12 . . . . @ 40.00
6-1 thru 6-12 . . . . @ 40.00

6-10 Bondage(c). 70.00
7-1 thru 7-12. . . . . @30.00
8-1 thru 8-4. . . . . @30.00
8-5 May, 1953 . . . . 30.00

C-M-O COMICS
Comic Corp. of America
(Centaur), May, 1942
1 Invisible Terror 750.00
2 Super Ann 500.00

COCOMALT BIG BOOK
OF COMICS
Harry A. Chesler, 1938
1 BoW,PGn,FG,JCo,(Give away)
  Little Nemo 1,800.00

COLOSSUS COMICS
Sun Publications
March, 1940
1 A:Colossus 2,800.00

COLUMBIA COMICS
William H. Wise Co., 1944
1 Joe Palooka,Charlie Chan . . . 200.00

COMICS, THE
Dell Publishing Co.
March, 1937
1 I:Tom Mix & Arizona Kid. . . . 1,500.00
2 A:Tom Mix & Tom Beaty 650.00
3 A:Alley Oop 500.00
4 same 500.00
5 same 500.00
6 thru 11 same. . . . . @500.00

COMICS ON PARADE
United Features Syndicate
April 1938–Feb. 1955
1 B:Tarzan,Captain and the Kids,
  Little Mary, Mixup,Abbie & Slats,
  Broncho Bill,Li'l Abner 3,000.00
2 Circus Parade of all 1,100.00
3 . . . . 800.00
4 On Rocket 750.00
5 All at the Store 750.00
6 All at Picnic. 450.00
7 Li'l Abner(c) 450.00
8 same 450.00
9 same 450.00
10 same 450.00
11 same 350.00
12 same 350.00
13 same 350.00
14 Abbie n' Slats (c) 350.00
15 Li'l Abner(c) 350.00
16 Abbie n' Slats(c). 350.00
17 Tarzan,Abbie n' Slats(c) 375.00
18 Li'l Abner(c) 350.00
19 same 350.00
20 same 300.00
21 Li'l Abner(c) 300.00
22 Tail Spin Tommy(c) 300.00
23 Abbie n' Slats(c). 300.00
24 Tail Spin Tommy(c) 300.00
25 Li'l Abner(c) 300.00
26 Abbie n' Slats(c) 300.00
27 Li'l Abner(c) 300.00
28 Tail Spin Tommy(c) 300.00
29 Abbie n' Slats(c). 300.00
30 Li'l Abner(c) 200.00
31 The Captain & the Kids(c) . . . 175.00
32 Nancy and Fritzi Ritz(c) 125.00
33 Li'l Abner(c) 150.00

Comics on Parade #9
© United Features Syndicate

34 The Captain & the Kids(c) . . . 125.00
35 Nancy and Fritzi Ritz(c) 125.00
36 Li'l Abner(c) 145.00
37 The Captain & the Kids(c) . . . 125.00
38 Nancy and Fritzi Ritz(c) 110.00
39 Li'l Abner(c) 135.00
40 The Captain & the Kids(c) . . . 125.00
41 Nancy and Fritzi Ritz(c) 75.00
42 Li'l Abner(c) 125.00
43 The Captain & the Kids(c) . . . 125.00
44 Nancy and Fritzi Ritz(c) 75.00
45 Li'l Abner(c) 125.00
46 The Captain & the Kids(c) 90.00
47 Nancy and Fritzi Ritz(c) 75.00
48 Li'l Abner(c) 125.00
49 The Captain & the Kids(c) 90.00
50 Nancy and Fritzi Ritz(c) 75.00
51 Li'l Abner(c) 125.00
52 The Captain & the Kids(c) 75.00
53 Nancy and Fritzi Ritz(c) 125.00
54 Li'l Abner(c) 125.00
55 Nancy and Fritzi Ritz(c) 75.00
56 The Captain & the Kids(c) 75.00
57 Nancy and Fritzi Ritz(c) 70.00
58 Li'l Abner(c) 125.00
59 The Captain & the Kids(c) 70.00
60 Nancy and Fritzi Ritz(c) 55.00
61 thru 76 same . . . . @55.00
77 Nancy & Sluggo(c). 50.00
78 thru 104 same . . . . @50.00

COMPLETE BOOK OF
COMICS AND FUNNIES
William H. Wise & Co., 1945
1 Wonderman-Magnet 300.00

CONFESSIONS OF LOVE
Artful Publications
April, 1950
1 . . . . 200.00
2 July, 1950. . . . . 125.00

CONFESSIONS OF LOVE
Star Publications, July, 1952
11 AW,LbC(c)Intimate Secrets of
  Daring Romance 75.00
12 AW,LbC(c),I Couldn't Say No . 75.00
13 AW,LbC(c),Heart Break 75.00
14 AW,LbC(c),My Fateful Love . . 50.00
4 JyD,AW,LbC(c),The Longing
  Heart 50.00

5 AW,LbC(c),I Wanted Love. 50.00
6 AW,LbC(c),My Jealous Heart . . 50.00
Becomes:

CONFESSIONS OF
ROMANCE
7 LbC(c)Too Good 100.00
8 AW,LbC(c),I Lied About Love . . 60.00
9 WW,AW,LbC(c),I Paid
  Love's Price 100.00
10 JyD,AW,LbC(c),My Heart Cries
  for Love 60.00
11 JyD,AW,LbC(c),Intimate
  Confessions, Nov., 1954. . . . . 60.00

CONFESSIONS OF
LOVELORN
(see LOVELORN)

CONQUEROR COMICS
Albrecht Publications
Winter, 1945
1 . . . . 125.00

CONTACT COMICS
Aviation Press, July, 1944
N# LbC(c),B:Black Venus,
  Golden Eagle 400.00
2 LbC(c),Peace Jet 300.00
3 LbC(c),LbC,E:Flamingo 275.00
4 LbC(c),LbC 275.00
5 LbC(c),A:Phantom Flyer 300.00
6 LbC(c),HK 350.00
7 LbC(c),Flying Tigers 250.00
8 LbC(c),Peace Jet 250.00
9 LbC(c),LbC,A:Marine Flyers . . 250.00
10 LbC(c),A:Bombers of the AAF 250.00
11 LbC(c),HK,AF,Salutes Naval
  Aviation 350.00
12 LbC(c),A:Sky Rangers, Air Kids,
  May, 1946 . . . . 350.00

COO COO COMICS
Nedor/Animated Cartoons
(Standard), Oct., 1942
1 O&I:Super Mouse 200.00
2 . . . . 100.00
3 . . . . 50.00
4 . . . . 50.00
5 . . . . 50.00
6 . . . . 40.00
7 thru 10 . . . . @35.00
11 thru 33 . . . . @35.00
34 thru 40 FF illustration . . . . . . @50.00
41 FF 125.00
42 FF 125.00
43 FF illustration. 75.00
44 FF illustration. 75.00
45 FF illustration. 75.00
46 FF illustration 45.00
47 FF 75.00
48 FF illustration 50.00
49 FF illustration 60.00
50 FF illustration 60.00
51 thru 61 . . . . @25.00
62 April, 1952. . . . . 25.00

"COOKIE"
Michel Publ./Regis Publ.
(American Comics Group)
April, 1946
1 . . . . 125.00
2 . . . . 50.00
3 . . . . 40.00

GOLDEN AGE

4	40.00
5	40.00
6 thru 20	@35.00
21 thru 30	@30.00
31 thru 54	@25.00
55 Aug., 1955	25.00

COSMO CAT
Fox Features Syndicate
July/Aug., 1946

1	175.00
2	85.00
3 O:Cosmo Cat	65.00
4 thru 10	@35.00

COURAGE COMICS
J. Edward Slavin, 1945

1	75.00
2 Boxing cover	80.00
77 Naval rescue, PT99 cover	80.00

COWBOY COMICS
(see STAR RANGER)

COWBOYS `N' INJUNS
Compix
(M.E. Enterprises), 1946-47

1 Funny Animal Western	40.00
2 thru 8	@25.00

COWBOY WESTERN
COMICS/HEROES
(see YELLOWJACKET
COMICS)

COWGIRL ROMANCES
Fiction House Magazine, 1952

1 The Range of Singing Guns	225.00
2 The Lady of Lawless Range	125.00
3 Daughter of the Devil's Band	100.00
4 Bride Wore Buckskin	90.00
5 Taming of Lone-Star Lou	90.00
6 Rose of Mustang Mesa	85.00
7 Nobody Loves a Gun Man	85.00
8 Wild Beauty	85.00
9 Gun-Feud Sweethearts	85.00
10 JKa,AW,No Girl of Stampede Valley	90.00
11 Love is Where You Find It	85.00
12 Dec., 1952	85.00

COW PUNCHER
Avon Periodicals/
Realistic Publ., Jan., 1947

1 JKu	275.00
2 JKu,JKa(c),Bondage cover	225.00
3 AU(c)	150.00
4	150.00
5	150.00
6 WJo(c),Drug story	200.00
7	150.00
1 JKu	150.00

CRACK COMICS
Comic Magazines
(Quality Comics Group)
May, 1940

1 LF,O:Black Condor,Madame Fatal, Red Torpedo, Rock Bradden, Space Legion, B:The Clock,Wizard Wells	4,200.00
2 Black Condor cover	1,700.00
3 The Clock cover	1,200.00
4 Black Condor cover	1,000.00
5 LF,The Clock cover	850.00
6 PG,Black Condor cover	800.00
7 Clock cover	800.00
8 Black Condor cover	800.00
9 Clock cover	800.00
10 Black Condor cover	800.00
11 LF,PG,Clock cover	700.00
12 LF,PG,Black Condor cover	700.00
13 LF,PG,Clock cover	700.00
14 AMc,LF,PG,Clack Condor(c)	700.00
15 AMc,LF,PG,Clock cover	700.00
16 AMc,LF,PG,Black Condor(c)	700.00
17 FG,AMc,LF,PG,Clock cover	700.00
18 AMc,LF,PG,Black Condor(c)	700.00
19 AMc,LF,PG,Clock cover	700.00
20 AMc,LF,PG,Black Condor(c)	700.00
21 AMc,LF,PG,same	600.00
22 LF,PG,same	600.00
23 AMc,LF,PG,same	600.00
24 AMc,LF,PG,same	600.00
25 AMc,same	500.00
26 AMc,same	500.00
27 AMc,I&O:Captain Triumph	800.00
28 Captain Triumph cover	500.00
29 A:Spade the Ruthless	500.00
30 I:Biff	400.00
31 Helps Spade Dig His Own Grave	200.00
32 Newspaper cover	200.00
33 V:Men of Darkness	200.00
34	200.00
35 V:The Man Who Conquered Flame	200.00
36 Good Neighbor Tour	200.00
37 V:The Tyrant of Toar Valley	200.00
38 Castle of Shadows	200.00
39 V:Crime over the City	200.00
40 Thrilling Murder Mystery	125.00
41	125.00
42 All that Glitters is Not Gold	125.00
43 Smashes the Evil Spell of Silent	125.00
44 V:Silver Tip	125.00
45 V:King-The Jack of all Trades	125.00
46 V:Mr. Weary	125.00
47 V:Hypnotic Eyes Khor	135.00
48 Murder in the Sky	135.00
49	135.00
50 A Key to Trouble	135.00
51 V:Werewolf	135.00

Crack Comics #32
© Quality Comics Group

52 V:Porcupine	135.00
53 V:Man Who Robbed the Dead	135.00
54 Shoulders the Troubles of the World	135.00
55 Brain against Brawn	135.00
56 Gossip leads to Murder	135.00
57 V:Sitok–Green God of Evil	135.00
58 V:Targets	125.00
59 A Cargo of Mystery	125.00
60 Trouble is no Picnic	125.00
61 V:Mr. Pointer-Finger of Fear	125.00
62 V:The Vanishing Vandals	125.00

Becomes:

CRACK WESTERN

63 PG, I&O:Two-Gun Lil, B:Frontier Marshal,Arizona Ames,	150.00
64 RC,Arizona AmesV:Two-Legged Coyote	100.00
65 RC,Ames Tramples on Trouble	100.00
66 Arizona Ames Arizona Raines, Tim Holt,Ph(c)	90.00
67 RC, Ph(c)	100.00
68	75.00
69 RC	75.00
70 O&I:Whip and Diablo	90.00
71 RC(c)	100.00
72 RC,Tim Holt,Ph(c)	72.00
73 Tim Holt,Ph(c)	55.00
74 RC(c)	60.00
75 RC(c)	60.00
76 RC(c),Stage Coach to Oblivion	60.00
77 RC(c),Comanche Terror	60.00
78 RC(c),Killers of Laurel Ridge	60.00
79 RC(c),Fires of Revenge	60.00
80 RC(c),Mexican Massacre	60.00
81 RC(c),Secrets of Terror Canyon	60.00
82 The Killer with a Thousand Faces	40.00
83 Battlesnake Pete's Revenge	40.00
84 PG(c),Revolt at Broke Creek May,1951	40.00

CRACKAJACK FUNNIES
Dell Publishing Co.
June, 1938

1 AMc,A:Dan Dunn,The Nebbs, Don Winslow	2,000.00
2 AMc,same	800.00
3 AMc,same	600.00
4 AMc,same	450.00
5 AMc,Naked Women(c)	500.00
6 AMc,same	350.00
7 AMc,same	350.00
8 AMc,same	350.00
9 AMc,A:Red Ryder	1,000.00
10 AMc,A:Red Ryder	350.00
11 AMc,A:Red Ryder	300.00
12 AMc,A:Red Ryder	300.00
13 AMc,A:Red Ryder	300.00
14 AMc,A:Red Ryder	300.00
15 AMc,A:Tarzan	350.00
16 AMc	250.00
17 AMc	250.00
18 AMc	250.00
19 AMc	250.00
20 AMc	250.00
21 AMc	250.00
22 AMc	250.00
23 AMc	250.00
24 AMc	250.00
25 AMc,I:The Owl	600.00
26 AMc	400.00
27 AMc	400.00
28 AMc,A:The Owl	400.00
29 AMc,A:Ellery Queen	400.00
30 AMc,A:Tarzan	400.00
31 AMc,A:Tarzan	400.00

GOLDEN AGE

Crackajack #38
© *Dell Publishing Co.*

32 AMc,O:Owl Girl 450.00
33 AMc,A:Tarzan 300.00
34 AMc,same 300.00
35 AMc,same 300.00
36 AMc,same 300.00
37 AMc 300.00
38 AMc 300.00
39 AMc,I:Andy Panada 400.00
40 AMc,A:Owl(c). 300.00
41 AMc 300.00
42 AMc 300.00
43 AMc,A:Owl(c). 275.00

CRASH COMICS
Tem Publishing Co.
May, 1940
1 S&K,O:Strongman, B:Blue Streak,
 Perfect Human, Shangra . . 2,500.00
2 S&K 1,200.00
3 S&K 1,000.00
4 S&K,O&I:Catman 2,400.00
5 S&K, Nov., 1940 . . . . 1,000.00

CRIME AND PUNISHMENT
Lev Gleason Publications
April, 1948
1 CBi(c),Mr.Crime(c) 250.00
2 CBi(c). 100.00
3 CBi(c),BF 125.00
4 CBi(c),BF 75.00
5 CBi(c). 75.00
6 thru 10 CBi(c) . . . . @65.00
11 thru 15 CBi(c). . . . . @50.00
16 thru 27 CBi(c). . . . . @40.00
28 thru 38 . . . . @35.00
39 Drug issue 60.00
40 thru 44 . . . . @35.00
45 Drug issue 60.00
46 thru 73 . . . . @35.00
66 ATh 250.00
67 Drug Storm 200.00
68 ATh(c) 175.00
69 Drug issue 55.00
74 Aug., 1955 . . . . 30.00

CRIME DETECTIVE COMICS
Hillman Publications
March–April, 1948
1 BFc(c),A:Invisible 6 . . . . 200.00
2 Jewel Robbery cover 75.00
3 Stolen cash cover. 60.00
4 Crime Boss Murder cover 60.00
5 BK,Maestro cover. 60.00
6 AMc,Gorilla cover 50.00
7 GMc,Wedding cover 50.00
8 . . . . 40.00
9 Safe Robbery cover
 (a classic). 225.00
10 . . . . 60.00
11 BP 60.00
12 BK 60.00
2-1 Bluebird captured 75.00
2-2 . . . . 40.00
2-3 . . . . 40.00
2-4 BK. 45.00
2-5 . . . . 40.00
2-6 . . . . 40.00
2-7 BK, GMc. 45.00
2-8 . . . . 40.00
2-9 . . . . 40.00
2-10 . . . . 40.00
2-11 . . . . 40.00
2-12 . . . . 40.00
3-1 Drug Story. 40.00
3-2 thru 3-7 . . . . @40.00
3-8 May/June, 1953 . . . . 30.00

CRIME DOES NOT PAY
(see SILVER STREAK COMICS)

CRIME ILLUSTRATED
E.C. Comics, Nov.–Dec., 1955
1 Grl,RC,GE,JO. 125.00
2 Grl,RC,JCr,JDa,JO 100.00

CRIME MUST STOP
Hillman Periodicals, Oct., 1952
1 BK 450.00

CRIME MYSTERIES
Ribage Publishing Corp.
May, 1952
1 Transvestism,Bondage(c) 375.00
2 A:Manhunter, Lance Storm,
 Drug. 250.00
3 FF-one page, A:Dr. Foo 200.00
4 A:Queenie Star, Bondage Star 300.00
5 Claws of the Green Girl 175.00
6 . . . . 175.00
7 Sons of Satan 175.00
8 Death Stalks the Crown,
 Bondage(c) 200.00
9 You are the Murderer 175.00
10 The Hoax of the Death. 175.00
11 The Strangler. 175.00
12 Bondage(c) 190.00
13 AT,6 lives for one 200.00
14 Painted in Blood 175.00
15 Feast of the Dead,Acid Face . 250.00
Becomes:

SECRET MYSTERIES
16 Hiding Place,Horror 150.00
17 The Deadly Diamond,Horror. . 100.00
18 Horror 125.00
19 Horror,July, 1955 . . . . 125.00

CRIMES ON THE WATERFRONT
(see FAMOUS GANGSTERS)

INTERNATIONAL COMICS
E.C. Publ. Co., Spring, 1947
1 KS,I:Manhattan's Files 650.00
2 KS,A: Van Manhattan &
 Madelon 500.00
3 KS,same 300.00
4 KS,same 300.00
5 I:International Crime-Busting
 Patrol 300.00
Becomes:

INTERNATIONAL CRIME PATROL
6 A:Moon Girl & The Prince . . . 550.00
Becomes:

CRIME PATROL
7 SMo,A:Capt. Crime Jr.,Field
 Marshall of Murder 450.00
8 JCr,State Prison cover 400.00
9 AF,JCr,Bank Robbery 400.00
10 AF,JCr,Wanted:James Dore . . 400.00
11 AF,JCr 400.00
12 AF,Grl,JCr,Interrogation(c) . . . 400.00
13 AF,JCr 400.00
14 AF,JCr,Smugglers cover. 400.00
15 AF,JCr,Crypt of Terror 2,000.00
16 AF,JCr,Crypt of Terror 1,400.00
Becomes:

CRYPT OF TERROR
E.C. Comics, April, 1950
17 JCr&(c),AF,`Werewolf
 Strikes Again' 2,400.00
18 JCr&(c),AF,WW,HK
 `The Living Corpse' 1,400.00
19 JCr&(c),AF,Grl,
 `Voodoo Drums'. 1,400.00
Becomes:

TALES FROM THE CRYPT
Oct., 1950
20 JCr&(c),AF,Gl,JKa
 `Day of Death' 1,100.00
21 AF&(c),WW,HK,Gl,`Cooper
 Dies in the Electric Chair . . . 800.00

Tales From the Crypt #43
© *E.C. Comics*

Crime—Crown

22 AF, JCr(c) 750.00
23 AF&(c),JCr,JDa,Grl
   `Locked in a Mauseleum' . . . 500.00
24 AF(c),WW,JDa,JCr,Grl
   `Danger...Quicksand' 500.00
25 AF(c),WW,JDa,JKa,Grl
   `Mataud Waxworks' 500.00
26 WW(c),JDa,Grl,
   `Scared Graveyard'. 350.00
27 JKa, WW(c), Guillotine cover . 350.00
28 AF(c),JDa,JKa,Grl,JO
   `Buried Alive' 350.00
29 JDa&(c),JKa,Grl,JO
   `Coffin Burier' 350.00
30 JDa&(c),JO,JKa,Grl
   `Underwater Death' 350.00
31 JDa&(c),JKa,Grl,AW
   `Hand Chopper' 400.00
32 JDa&(c),GE,Grl,`Woman
   Crushed by Elephant' 300.00
33 JDa&(c),GE,JKa,Grl,`Lower
   Berth',O:Crypt Keeper. 500.00
34 JDa&(c),GE,Grl,`Jack the
   Ripper,'Ray Bradbury adapt.. 300.00
35 JDa&(c),JKa,JO,Grl,
   `Werewolf' 300.00
36 JDa&(c),JKa,GE,Grl, Ray
   Bradbury adaptation 300.00
37 JDa(c),JO,BE. 300.00
38 JDa(c),BE,RC,Grl,`Axe Man'. 300.00
39 JDa&(c),JKa,JO,Grl,`Children
   in the Graveyard' 300.00
40 JDa&(c),GE,BK,Grl,
   `Underwater Monster' 300.00
41 JDa&(c),JKa,GE,Grl,
   `Knife Thrower'. 275.00
42 JDa(c),JO,Vampire cover 275.00
43 JDa(c),JO,GE 275.00
44 JO,RC,Guillotine cover. 275.00
45 JDa&(c),JKa,BK,Gl,`Rat
   Takes Over His Life' 275.00
46 JDa&(c),GE,JO,Gl,`Werewolf
   man being hunted,Feb.1955 . 350.00

CRIME REPORTER
St. John Publishing Co.
Aug., 1948
1 Death Makes a Deadline 300.00
2 GT,MB(c),Matinee Murders . . 550.00
3 GT,MB(c),Dec., 1948 . . . . 250.00

CRIMES BY WOMEN
Fox Features Syndicate
June, 1948
1 Bonnie Parker 900.00
2 Vicious Female 500.00
3 Prison break cover 425.00
4 Murder cover 400.00
5 . . . . 400.00
6 Girl Fight cover. 500.00
7 . . . . 400.00
8 . . . . 400.00
9 . . . . 400.00
10 . . . . 400.00
11 . . . . 400.00
12 . . . . 400.00
13 ACME jewelry robbery cover . 400.00
14 Prison break cover. 400.00
15 Aug., 1951. . . . . 400.00

CRIME SMASHER
Fawcett Publications
Summer, 1948
1 The Unlucky Rabbit's Foot . . . 300.00

CRIME SMASHERS
Ribage Publishing Corp.
Oct., 1950
1 Girl Rape 650.00
2 JKu,A:Sally the Sleuth, Dan
   Turner, Girl Friday, Rat Hale . 300.00
3 MFa 200.00
4 Zak(c) 200.00
5 WW 250.00
6 . . . . 150.00
7 Bondage cover,Drugs 175.00
8 . . . . 150.00
9 Bondage cover 175.00
10 . . . . 150.00
11 . . . . 150.00
12 FF 175.00
13 . . . . 165.00
14 . . . . 150.00
15 . . . . 150.00

CRIME SUSPENSTORIES
L.L. Publishing Co.
(E.C. Comics), Oct.–Nov., 1950
1a JCr,Grl 1,000.00
1 JCr,WW,Grl 800.00
2 JCr,JKa,Grl 450.00
3 JCr,WW,Grl 350.00
4 JCr,Gln,Grl,JDa 325.00
5 JCr,JKa,Grl,JDa 300.00
6 JCr,JDa,Grl 250.00
7 JCr,Grl 250.00
8 JCr,Grl 250.00
9 JCr,Grl 250.00
10 JCr,Grl. 250.00
11 JCr,Grl. 200.00
12 JCr,Grl. 200.00
13 JCr,AW 225.00
14 JCr 200.00
15 JCr 200.00
16 JCr,AW 225.00
17 JCr,FF,AW, Ray Bradbury . . . 275.00
18 JCr,RC,BE 200.00
19 JCr,RC,GE,AF(c) 200.00
20 RC,JCr, Hanging cover 250.00
21 JCr 150.00
22 RC,JO,JCr(c),
   Severed head cover 175.00
23 JKa,RC,GE 175.00
24 BK,RC,JO 150.00
25 JKa,(c),RC. 150.00
26 JKa,(c),RC,JO 150.00
27 JKa,(c),GE,Grl,March, 1955. . 150.00

Crime SuspenStories #24
© E.C. Comics

CRIMINALS ON THE RUN
Premium Group of Comics
Aug., 1948
4-1 LbC(c) 175.00
4-2 LbC(c), A:Young King Cole . 150.00
4-3 LbC(c), Rip Roaring Action
   in Alps 150.00
4-4 LbC(c), Shark cover 150.00
4-5 AMc 150.00
4-6 LbC 125.00
4-7 LbC 325.00
5-1 LbC 125.00
5-2 LbC 125.00
10 LbC 150.00
Becomes:

CRIME-FIGHTING DETECTIVE
11 LbC, Brodie Gang Captured. . 100.00
12 LbC(c), Jail Break Genius . . . 100.00
13 . . . . 50.00
14 LbC(c), A Night of Horror. . . . 75.00
15 LbC(c). 75.00
16 LbC(c), Wanton Murder 75.00
17 LbC(c), The Framer
   was Framed 75.00
18 LbC(c), A Web of Evil 75.00
19 LbC(c), Lesson of the Law . . . 75.00
Becomes:

SHOCK DETECTIVE CASE
20 LbC(c), The Strangler 100.00
21 LbC(c), Death Ride 100.00
Becomes:

SPOOK DETECTIVE CASES
22 Headless Horror. 225.00
Becomes:

SPOOK SUSPENSE AND MYSTERY
23 LbC,Weird Picture of Murder . 150.00
24 LbC(c),Mummy's Case. 175.00
25 LbC(c),Horror Beyond Door . . 150.00
26 LbC(c),JyD,Face of Death . . . 150.00
27 LbC(c),Ship of the Dead. 150.00
28 LbC(c),JyD,Creeping Death . . 150.00
29 LbC(c),Solo for Death 150.00
30 LbC(c),JyD,Nightmare,
   Oct.,1954 . . . . 150.00

CROWN COMICS
Golfing/McCombs Publ.
Winter 1944
1 Edgar Allen Poe adapt. 275.00
2 MB,I:Mickey Magic 200.00
3 MB,Jungle adventure cover . . 200.00
4 MB(c) 200.00
5 MB(c),Jungle adventure cover 200.00
6 MB(c),Jungle adventure cover 200.00
7 JKa,AF,MB(c),Race Car driving
   cover 200.00
8 MB 135.00
9 . . . . 85.00
10 Plane crash cover 85.00
11 LSt 75.00
12 LSt 75.00
13 LSt 75.00
14 . . . . 95.00
15 FBe 75.00
16 FBe,Jungle adventure(c) 75.00
17 FBe 75.00
18 FBe 75.00
19 BP,July, 1949. . . . . 75.00

GOLDEN AGE

CRUSADER FROM MARS
Approved Publ.
(Ziff-Davis), Jan.–March, 1952
1 Mission Thru Space, Death in
the Sai 600.00
2 Beachhead on Saturn's Ring,
Bondage(c),Fall, 1952 . . . . . 450.00

CRYIN' LION, THE
William H. Wise Co.
Fall, 1944
1 . . . . 75.00
2 . . . . 60.00
3 Spring, 1945 . . . . 60.00

CRYPT OF TERROR
(see CRIME PATROL)

CYCLONE COMICS
Bibara Publ. Co., June, 1940
1 O:Tornado Tom 1,200.00
2 . . . . 550.00
3 . . . . 500.00
4 Voltron 450.00
5 A:Mr. Q,Oct., 1940 . . . . 450.00

ALL GREAT COMICS
Fox Features Syndicate
Oct., 1947
12 A:Brenda Starr. 400.00
13 JKa,O:Dagger, Desert Hawk . 350.00
Becomes:

DAGAR, DESERT HAWK
14 JKa,Monster of Mura 550.00
15 JKa,Curse of the Lost
Pharaoh 350.00
16 JKa,Wretched Antmen 300.00
19 Pyramid of Doom. 275.00
20 . . . . 275.00
21 JKa(c),The Ghost of Fate. . . . 300.00
22 . . . . 275.00
23 Bondage cover 300.00
Becomes:

CAPTAIN KIDD
24 Blackbeard the Pirate. 100.00
25 Sorceress of the Deep. 100.00
Becomes:

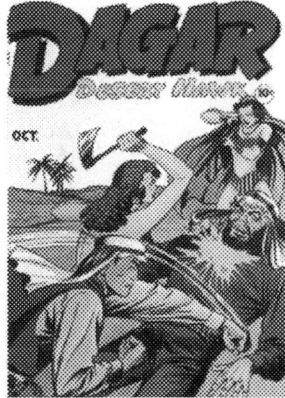

Dagar Desert Hawk #20
© Fox Features Syndicate

MY SECRET STORY
26 He Wanted More Than Love . . 85.00
27 My Husband Hated Me 50.00
28 I Become a Marked Women. . . 50.00
29 My Forbidden Rapture,
April, 1950 . . . . 50.00

DAFFY
Dell Publishing Co.,
March, 1953
(1) *see Dell Four Color #457*
(2) *see Dell Four Color #536*
(3) *see Dell Four Color #615*
4 thru 7 . . . . @25.00
8 thru 11 . . . . @20.00
12 thru 17 . . . . @15.00
Becomes:
DAFFY DUCK
18 . . . . 15.00
19 . . . . 15.00
20 . . . . 15.00
21 thru 30 . . . . @10.00
Gold Key
31 thru 40. . . . . @8.00
41 thru 59. . . . . @6.00
60 B&A:Road Runner. 3.00
61 thru 90 same . . . . @3.00
91 thru 127 . . . . @2.00
Whitman
128 thru 145 . . . . @2.00

DAGWOOD
Harvey Publications
Sept., 1950
1 . . . . 100.00
2 . . . . 50.00
3 thru 10 . . . . @35.00
11 thru 20 . . . . @30.00
21 thru 30 . . . . @20.00
31 thru 50 . . . . @15.00
51 thru 70 . . . . @10.00
71 thru 109 . . . . @8.00
110 thru 140 . . . . @7.00

DANGER AND
ADVENTURE
(see THIS MAGAZINE
IS HAUNTED)

DANGER IS OUR
BUSINESS
Toby Press/
I.W. Enterprises, 1953
1 AW,FF,Men who Defy Death
for a Living 325.00
2 Death Crowds the Cockpit 75.00
3 Killer Mountain 60.00
4 . . . . 60.00
5 thru 9 . . . . @50.00
10 June, 1955 . . . . 60.00

DAREDEVIL COMICS
Lev Gleason Publications
July, 1941
1 Daredevil Battles Hitler, A:Silver
Streak, Lance Hale, Dickey Dean,
Cloud Curtis,V:The Claw,
O:Hitler 10,000.00
2 I:The Pioneer, Champion of
American,B:London,Pat
Patriot,Pirate Prince. 2,600.00
3 CBi(c),O:Thirteen 1,500.00

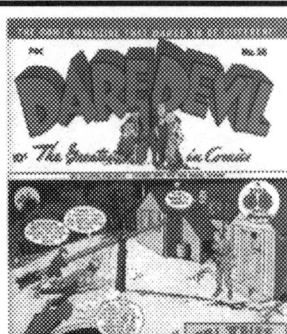

Daredevil #38
© Lev Gleason

4 CBi(c),Death is the Refere . . 1,300.00
5 CBi(c),I:Sniffer&Jinx, Claw
V:Ghost,Lottery of Doom . . 1,100.00
6 CBi(c) 850.00
7 CBi(c), What Ghastly Sight Lies
within the Mysterious Trunk . 750.00
8 V:Nazis cover, E:Nightro 700.00
9 V:Double 700.00
10 America will Remember
Pearl Harbor. 700.00
11 Bondage cover, E:Pat
Patriot, London. 750.00
12 BW,CBi(c), O:The Law 1,100.00
13 BW,I:Little Wise Guys 1,000.00
14 BW,CBi(c) 500.00
15 BW,CBi(c), D:Meatball 700.00
16 BW,CBi(c) 475.00
17 BW,CBi(c), Into the Valley
of Death 450.00
18 BW,CBi(c), O:Daredevil,
double length story 1,000.00
19 BW,CBi(c), Buried Alive 375.00
20 BW,CBi(c), Boxing cover 375.00
21 CBi(c), Can Little Wise Guys
Survive Blast of Dynamite?. . 650.00
22 CBi(c) 300.00
23 CBi(c), I:Pshyco. 300.00
24 CBi(c), Punch and Judy
Murders 300.00
25 CBi(c), baseball cover 325.00
26 CBi(c) 275.00
27 CBi(c), Bondage cover. 300.00
28 CBi(c) 275.00
29 CBi(c) 275.00
30 CBi(c), Ann Hubbard White
1922-1943 . . . . 275.00
31 CBi(c), D:The Claw 600.00
32 V:Blackmarketeers. 200.00
33 CBi(c) 200.00
34 CBi(c) 200.00
35 B:Two Daredevil stories
every issue. 175.00
36 CBi(c) 175.00
37 CBi(c) 175.00
38 CBi(c), O:Daredevil 350.00
39 CBi(c) 175.00
40 CBi(c) 175.00
41 . . . . 150.00
42 thru 50 CBi(c). . . . . @150.00
51 CBi(c) 125.00
52 CBi(c),Football cover 150.00
53 thru 57 . . . . @125.00
58 Football cover 150.00
59 . . . . 125.00
60 . . . . 125.00

GOLDEN AGE

61 thru 68 . . . . @125.00	2-3 . . . . 45.00	The Mummy & Other Stories 300.00
69 E:Daredevil 125.00	2-4 . . . . 45.00	Western Roundup #1 . . . . 350.00
70 . . . . 100.00	2-5 thru 2-12 . . . . @25.00	Western Roundup #2 . . . . 200.00
71 thru 78 . . . . @75.00	3-1 . . . . 25.00	Western Roundup #3 . . . . 175.00
79 B:Daredevil 85.00		Western Roundup #4 thru #5. . @150.00
80 . . . . 80.00	**DEADWOOD GULCH**	Western Roundup #6 thru #10. @140.00
81 . . . . 55.00	**Dell Publishing Co., 1931**	Western Roundup #11 thru #17 @135.00
82 . . . . 55.00	1 . . . . 125.00	Western Roundup #18 . . . . 125.00
83 thru 99 . . . . @55.00		Western Roundup #19 thru #25 . 125.00
100 . . . . 75.00	**DEAR BEATRICE**	Woody Woodpecker Back
101 thru 133 . . . . @50.00	**FAIRFAX**	to School #1 . . . . 165.00
134 Sept., 1956 . . . . 50.00	**Best Books**	Woody Woodpecker Back
	(Standard Comics), Nov., 1950	to School #2 . . . . 120.00
DARING CONFESSIONS	5 . . . . 40.00	Woody Woodpecker Back
(see YOUTHFUL HEART)	6 thru 9 . . . . @25.00	to School #3 . . . . 90.00
		Woody Woodpecker Back
		to School #4 . . . . 90.00
DARING LOVE	**DEAR LONELY HEART**	Woody Woodpecker County
(see YOUTHFUL	**Artful Publications**	Fair #5 . . . . 90.00
ROMANCES)	**March, 1951**	Woody Woodpecker Back
	5 . . . . 100.00	to School #6 . . . . 80.00
	6 . . . . 35.00	Woody Woodpecker County
DARK MYSTERIES	7 MB,Jungle Girl 75.00	Fair #2 . . . . 75.00
Merit Publications	8 . . . . 30.00	Also See:
June–July, 1951	9 . . . . 30.00	**Bugs Bunny**
1 WW, WW(c), Curse of the		**Marge's Little Lulu**
Sea Witch. 750.00	**DEAR LONELY HEARTS**	**Tom and Jerry, and**
2 WW, WW(c), Vampire Fangs	**Comic Media, Aug., 1953**	**Walt Disney Dell Giant Editions**
of Doom 500.00	1 Six Months to Live 38.00	
3 Terror of the Unwilling	2 Date Hungry, Price of Passion . 22.00	**DELL GIANT COMICS**
Witch 250.00	3 thru 8 . . . . @22.00	**Dell Publishing Co.**
4 Corpse that Came Alive 250.00		**Sept. 1959**
5 Horror of the Ghostly Crew . . 225.00	**DEARLY BELOVED**	21 M.G.M. Tom & Jerry
6 If the Noose Fits Wear It! 225.00	**Approved Comics**	Picnic Time. 200.00
7 Terror of the Cards of Death . . 225.00	**(Ziff-Davis), Fall, 1952**	22 W.Disney's Huey, Dewey & Louie
8 Terror of the Ghostly Trail . . . 225.00	1 Ph(c) 100.00	Back to School (Oct 1959) . . 135.00
9 Witch's Feast at Dawn 225.00		23 Marge's Little Lulu &
10 Terror of the Burning Witch . . 275.00	**DEBBIE DEAN,**	Tubby Halloween Fun. 200.00
11 The River of Blood. 200.00	**CAREER GIRL**	24 Woody Woodpeckers
12 Horror of the Talking Dead . . . 200.00	**Civil Service Publishing**	Family Fun 125.00
13 Terror of the Hungry Cats. . . . 200.00	**April, 1945**	25 Tarzan's Jungle World 175.00
14 Horror of the Fingers of Doom 225.00	1 . . . . 75.00	26 W.Disney's Christmas
15 Terror of the Vampires Teeth . 200.00	2 . . . . 70.00	Parade,CB 375.00
16 Horror of the Walking Dead . . 200.00		27 W.Disney's Man in
17 Terror of the Mask of Death . . 200.00	**DELL GIANT EDITIONS**	Space (1960) 200.00
18 Terror of the Burning Corpse . 200.00	**Dell Publishing Co.**	28 Bugs Bunny's Winter Fun. . . 175.00
19 The Rack of Terror. 250.00	**1953-58**	29 Marge's Little Lulu &
20 Burning Executioner 225.00	Abe Lincoln Life Story. 125.00	Tubby in Hawaii 200.00
21 The Sinister Secret 150.00	Cadet Gray of West Point 100.00	30 W.Disney's DisneylandU.S.A.. 175.00
22 The Hand of Destiny 150.00	Golden West Rodeo Treasury . . . 150.00	31 Huckleberry Hound
23 The Mardenburg Curse 125.00	Life Stories of	Summer Fun 225.00
24 Give A Man enough Rope,	American Presidents 90.00	32 Bugs Bunny Beach Party . . . 100.00
July, 1955. . . . . 125.00	Lone Ranger Golden West 300.00	33 W.Disney's Daisy Duck &
	Lone Ranger Movie Story 500.00	Uncle Scrooge Picnic Time. . 175.00
DAVY CROCKETT	Lone Ranger Western	
Avon Periodicals, 1951	Treasury('53) 275.00	
1 . . . . 125.00	Lone Ranger Western	
	Treasury('54) 175.00	
DEAD END	Moses & Ten Commandments . . 75.00	
CRIME STORIES	Nancy & Sluggo Travel Time. . . 100.00	
Kirby Publishing Co.	Pogo Parade 450.00	
April, 1949	Raggedy Ann & Andy 275.00	
N# BP 400.00	Santa Claus Funnies 150.00	
	Tarzan's Jungle Annual #1 . . . . 200.00	
DEAD-EYE	Tarzan's Jungle Annual #2 . . . . 150.00	
WESTERN COMICS	Tarzan's Jungle Annual #3 . . . . 125.00	
Hillman Periodicals	Tarzan's Jungle Annual #4 . . . . 125.00	
Nov.–Dec., 1948	Tarzan's Jungle Annual #5 . . . . 125.00	
1 BK 125.00	Tarzan's Jungle Annual #6 . . . . 125.00	
2 . . . . 60.00	Tarzan's Jungle Annual #7 . . . . 125.00	
3 . . . . 50.00	Treasury of Dogs 100.00	
4 thru 12 . . . . @35.00	Treasury of Horses 100.00	
2-1 . . . . 30.00	Universal Presents-Dracula-	
2-2 . . . . 30.00		

Dell Giant #51
© Dell Publishing Co.

34 Nancy&SluggoSummerCamp. 120.00
35 W.Disney's Huey, Dewey &
  Louie Back to School 150.00
36 Marge's Little Lulu & Witch
  Hazel Halloween Fun 200.00
37 Tarzan, King of the Jungle . . . 150.00
38 W.Disney's Uncle Donald and
  his Nephews Family Fun . . . 125.00
39 W.Disney's Merry Christmas . 125.00
40 Woody Woodpecker
  Christmas Parade. 100.00
41 Yogi Bear's Winter Sports . . . 225.00
42 Marge's Little Lulu &
  Tubby in Australia. 100.00
43 Mighty Mouse in OuterSpace. 400.00
44 Around the World with
  Huckleberry & His Friends . . 225.00
45 Nancy&SluggoSummerCamp. 100.00
46 Bugs Bunny Beach Party 100.00
47 W.Disney's Mickey and
  Donald in Vacationland. 175.00
48 The Flintstones #1
  (Bedrock Bedlam). 275.00
49 W.Disney's Huey, Dewey &
  Louie Back to School 150.00
50 Marge's Little Lulu &
  Witch Hazel Trick 'N' Treat . . 225.00
51 Tarzan, King of the Jungle . . . 150.00
52 W.Disney's Uncle Donald &
  his Nephews Dude Ranch . 150.00
53 W.Disney's Donald Duck
  Merry Christmas. 135.00
54 Woody Woodpecker
  Christmas Party 120.00
55 W.Disney's Daisy Duck & Uncle
  Scrooge Show Boat (1961). . 075.00

DELL JUNIOR TREASURY
Dell Publishing Co.
June, 1955
1 Alice in Wonderland 100.00
2 Aladdin. 65.00
3 Gulliver's Travels 50.00
4 Adventures of Mr. Frog 55.00
5 Wizard of Oz 60.00
6 Heidi. 65.00
7 Santa & the Angel 65.00
8 Raggedy Ann 65.00
9 Clementina the Flying Pig. 60.00
10 Adventures of Tom Sawyer . . . 60.00

DENNIS THE MENACE
Visual Editions/Literary Ent.
(Standard, Pines)
Aug., 1953
1 . . . . 425.00
2 . . . . 200.00
3 . . . . 125.00
4 . . . . 125.00
5 thru 10 . . . . @100.00
11 thru 20 . . . . @75.00
21 thru 31 . . . . @50.00

Hallden (Fawcett)
32 thru 40 . . . . @30.00
41 thru 50 . . . . @25.00
51 thru 60 . . . . @20.00
61 thru 70 . . . . @15.00
71 thru 90 . . . . @10.00
91 thru 140 . . . . @5.00
141 thru 166 . . . . @4.00

DESPERADO
Lev Gleason Publications
June, 1948
1 CBi(c) 75.00
2 CBi(c) 40.00
3 CBi(c) 30.00

4 CBi(c) 25.00
5 CBi(c) 25.00
6 CBi(c) 25.00
7 CBi(c) 25.00
8 CBi(c) 25.00

Black Diamond Western #37
© Lev Gleason

Becomes:

BLACK DIAMOND
WESTERN
9 CBi(c) 125.00
10 CBi(c) 60.00
11 CBi(c) 50.00
12 CBi(c) 50.00
13 CBi(c) 50.00
14 CBi(c) 50.00
15 CBi(c) 50.00
16 thru 28 BW,Big Bang Buster. @65.00
29 thru 40 . . . . @30.00
41 thru 52 . . . . @25.00
53 3-D 60.00
54 3-D 50.00
55 thru 60 . . . . @25.00

DETECTIVE EYE
Centaur Publications
Nov., 1940
1 B:Air Man, The Eye Sees,
  A:Masked Marvel 1,700.00
2 O:Don Rance, Mysticape,
  Dec., 1940 . . . . 1,200.00

DETECTIVE
PICTURE STORIES
Comics Magazine Co.
Dec., 1936
1 The Phantom Killer 3,600.00
2 . . . . 1,700.00
3 . . . . 1,100.00
4 WE, Muss Em Up 1,000.00
5 Trouble, April, 1937 . . . . 1,200.00

DEXTER COMICS
Dearfield Publications
Summer, 1948–July 1949
1 . . . . 40.00
2 . . . . 30.00
3 thru 5 . . . . @20.00

DIARY CONFESSIONS
(see TENDER ROMANCE)

DIARY LOVES
Comic Magazines
(Quality Comics Group)
Sept., 1949
1 BWa. 100.00
2 BWa. 80.00
3 . . . . 30.00
4 RC 45.00
5 . . . . 25.00
6 . . . . 25.00
7 . . . . 25.00
8 BWa. 75.00
9 BWa 60.00
10 BWa 75.00
11 . . . . 25.00
12 . . . . 25.00
13 . . . . 25.00
14 . . . . 25.00
15 BWa 50.00
16 BWa 50.00
17 . . . . 25.00
18 . . . . 25.00
19 . . . . 25.00
20 . . . . 25.00
21 BWa 40.00
22 thru 31 . . . . @15.00
Becomes:

G.I. SWEETHEARTS
32 Love Under Fire. 25.00
33 . . . . 25.00
34 . . . . 25.00
35 . . . . 25.00
36 Lend Lease Love Affair 25.00
37 thru 45 . . . . @25.00
Becomes:

GIRLS IN LOVE
46 Somewhere I'll Find You 30.00
47 thru 56 . . . . @20.00
57 MB,MB(c), Can Love Really
  Change Him, Dec., 1956 . . . . 40.00

DIARY SECRETS
(see TEEN-AGE DIARY
SECRETS)

DICK COLE
Curtis Publ./
Star Publications
Dec.–Jan., 1949
1 LbC,LbC(c),CS,All sports(c) . . 175.00
2 LbC 90.00
3 LbC, LbC(c) 100.00
4 LbC, LbC(c),Rowing cover . . . 100.00
5 LbC,LbC(c) 100.00
6 LbC,LbC(c), Rodeo cover . . . 100.00
7 LbC,LbC(c) 100.00
8 LbC,LbC(c), Football cover . . 100.00
9 LbC,LbC(c), Basketball cover . 100.00
10 Joe Louis 100.00
Becomes:

SPORTS THRILLS
11 Ted Williams & Ty Cobb 275.00
12 LbC, Joe Dimaggio & Phil
  Rizzuto, Boxing cover. 200.00
13 LbC(c),Basketball cover. 150.00
14 LbC(c),Baseball cover 150.00
15 LbC(c),Baseball cover,
  Nov., 1951 . . . . 150.00

GOLDEN AGE

DICKIE DARE
Eastern Color Printing Co.
1941
1 BEv(c)	250.00
2	175.00
3	175.00
4 1942.	200.00

DICK TRACY
MONTHLY
Dell Publishing Co.
Jan., 1948
1 ChG,'Dick Tracy & the Mad Doctor'	450.00
2 ChG,A:MarySteele,BorisArson	250.00
3 ChG,A:Spaldoni,Big Boy	250.00
4 ChG,A:Alderman Zeld	200.00
5 ChG,A:Spaldoni,Mrs.Spaldoni	200.00
6 ChG,A:Steve the Tramp	200.00
7 ChG,A:Boris Arson,Mary Steele	200.00
8 ChG,A:Boris & Zora Arson . . .	200.00
9 ChG,A:Chief Yellowpony	200.00
10 ChG,A:Cutie Diamond	200.00
11 ChG,A:Toby Townly, Bookie Joe	150.00
12 ChG,A:Toby Townly, Bookie Joe	150.00
13 ChG,A:Toby Townly, Blake . . .	160.00
14 ChG,A:Mayor Waite Wright . .	150.00
15 ChG,A:Bowman Basil.	150.00
16 ChG,A:Maw,'Muscle' & 'Cut' Famon	150.00
17 ChG,A:Jim Trailer, Mary Steele	150.00
18 ChG,A:Lips Manlis, Anthel Jones	150.00
19 'Golden Heart Mystery'	200.00
20 'Black Cat Mystery'	200.00
21 'Tracy Meets Number One' . .	200.00
22 'Tracy and the Alibi Maker'. . .	150.00
23 'Dick Tracy Meets Jukebox' . .	150.00
24 'Dick Tracy and Bubbles'	150.00
Becomes:	

DICK TRACY
COMICS MONTHLY
Harvey
25 ChG,A:Flattop	175.00
26 ChG,A:Vitamin Flintheart	150.00
27 ChG,'Flattop Escapes Prision'	150.00
28 ChG,'Case o/t Torture Chamber'	160.00
29 ChG,A:Brow,Gravel Gertie . . .	150.00
30 ChG,'Blackmail Racket'	150.00
31 ChG,A:Snowflake Falls	125.00
32 ChG,A:Shaky,Snowflake Falls	125.00
33 ChG,'Strange Case of Measles'.	150.00
34 ChG,A:Measles,Paprika.	125.00
35 ChG,'Case of Stolen $50,000'	125.00
36 ChG,'Case of the Runaway Blonde'	150.00
37 ChG,'Case of Stolen Money' .	125.00
38 ChG,A:Breathless Mahoney. .	125.00
39 ChG,A:Itchy,B.O.Pleanty	125.00
40 ChG,'Case of Atomic Killer' . .	125.00
41 ChG,Pt.1'Murder by Mail'. . . .	100.00
42 ChG,Pt.2'Murder by Mail'. . . .	100.00
43 ChG,'Case of the Underworld Brat'.	100.00
44 ChG,'Case of the Mouthwash Murder'.	100.00
45 ChG,'Case of the Evil Eyes'. .	100.00
46 ChG,'Case of the Camera Killers'.	100.00
47 ChG,'Case of the Bloodthirsty Blonde'	100.00

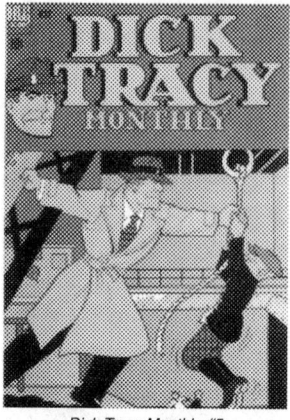

Dick Tracy Monthly #5
© Dell Publishing Co.

48 ChG, 'Case of the Murderous Minstrel'	100.00
49 ChG,Pt.1'Killer Who Returned From the Dead	100.00
50 ChG,Pt.2'Killer Who Returned From the Dead' . . .	100.00
51 ChG,'Case of the High Tension Hijackers'	75.00
52 ChG, 'Case of the Pipe-Stem Killer'	75.00
53 ChG,Pt.1'Dick Tracy Meets the Murderous Midget'	75.00
54 ChG,Pt.2'Dick Tracy Meets the Murderous Midget'	75.00
55 ChG,Pt.3'Dick Tracy Meets the Murderous Midget'	75.00
56 ChG,'Case of the Teleguard Terror'	75.00
57 ChG,Pt.1'Case of the Ice Cold Killer'	100.00
58 ChG,Pt.2'Case of the Ice Cold Killer'	75.00
59 ChG,Pt.1'Case of the Million Dollar Murder'	75.00
60 ChG,Pt.2'Case of the Million Dollar Murder'	65.00
61 ChG,'Case of the Murderers Mask'.	65.00
62 ChG,Pt.1'Case of the White Rat Robbers'	65.00
63 ChG,Pt.2'Case of the White Rat Robbers'	65.00
64 ChG,Pt.1'Case of the Interrupted Honeymoon'	65.00
65 ChG,Pt.2'Case of the Interrupted Honeymoon'	65.00
66 ChG,Pt.1'Case of the Killer's Revenge'.	65.00
67 ChG,Pt.2'Case of the Killer's Revenge'.	65.00
68 ChG,Pt.1'Case of the TV Terror'.	65.00
69 ChG,Pt.2'Case of the TV Terror'	65.00
70 ChG,Pt.3'Case of the TV Terror'.	65.00
71 ChG,A:Mrs. Forchune,Opal . .	65.00
72 ChG,A:Empty Wiliams,Bonny .	65.00
73 ChG,A:Bonny Braids	65.00
74 ChG,A:Mr. & Mrs. Fortson Knox	65.00
75 ChG,A:Crewy Lou, Sphinx	65.00
76 ChG,A:Diet Smith,Brainerd . .	65.00
77 ChG,A:Crewy Lou, Bonny Braids	65.00
78 ChG,A:Spinner Records.	65.00

79 ChG,A:Model Jones, Larry Jones	65.00
80 ChG,A:Tonsils,Dot View.	65.00
81 ChG,A:Edward Moppet,Tonsils.	65.00
82 ChG,A:Dot View,Mr. Crime. . . .	65.00
83 ChG,A:Rifle Ruby,Newsuit Nan	65.00
84 ChG,A:Mr. Crime,Newsuit Nan.	65.00
85 ChG,A:Newsuit Nan, Mrs.Lava.	65.00
86 ChG,A:Mr. Crime, Odds Zonn .	65.00
87 ChG,A:Odds Zonn,Wingy.	65.00
88 ChG,A:Odds Zonn,Wingy.	65.00
89 ChG,Pt.1'Canhead'	65.00
90 ChG,Pt.2'Canhead'	65.00
91 ChG,Pt.3'Canhead'	65.00
92 ChG,Pt.4'Canhead'	65.00
93 ChG,Pt.5'Canhead'	65.00
94 ChG,Pt.6'Canhead'	65.00
95 ChG,A:Mrs. Green,Dewdrop . .	65.00
96 ChG,A:Dewdrop,Sticks	65.00
97 ChG,A:Dewdrop,Sticks	65.00
98 ChG,A:Open-Mind Monty, Sticks.	65.00
99 ChG,A:Open-Mind Monty, Sticks.	70.00
100 ChG,A:Half-Pint,Dewdrop. . . .	75.00
101 ChG,A:Open-Mind Monty	65.00
102 ChG,A:Rainbow Reiley,Wingy	65.00
103 ChG,A:Happy,Rughead	65.00
104 ChG,A:Rainbow Reiley,Happy	65.00
105 ChG,A:Happy,Rughead	65.00
106 ChG,A:Fence,Corny,Happy . .	65.00
107 ChG,A:Rainbow Reiley	65.00
108 ChG,A:Rughead,Corny,Fence	65.00
109 ChG,A:Rughead,Mimi,Herky .	65.00
110 ChG,A:Vitamin Flintheart	65.00
111 ChG,A:Shoulders,Roach.	65.00
112 ChG,A:Brilliant,Diet Smith . . .	65.00
113 ChG,A:Snowflake Falls	65.00
114 ChG,A:'Sketch'Paree.	65.00
115 ChG,A:Rod & Nylon Hoze . . .	65.00
116 ChG,A:Empty Williams.	65.00
117 ChG,A:Spinner Records.	65.00
118 ChG,A:Sleet.	65.00
119 ChG,A:Coffyhead.	65.00
120 ChG,'Case Against Mumbles Quartet'.	60.00
121 ChG,'Case of the Wild Boys' .	60.00
122 ChG,'Case of the Poisoned Peliet'	60.00
123 ChG,'Case of the Deadly Treasure Hunt'	60.00
124 ChG,'Case of Oodles Hears Only Evil	60.00
125 ChG,'Case of the Desparate Widow'	60.00
126 ChG,'Case of Oodles' Hideout'	60.00
127 ChG,'Case Against Joe Period'.	60.00
128 ChG,'Case Against Juvenile Delinquent'.	60.00
129 ChG,'Case of Son of Flattop' .	60.00
130 ChG,'Case of Great Gang Roundup'	60.00
131 ChG,'Strange Case of Flattop's Conscience'	65.00
132 ChG,'Case of Flattop's Big Show'.	65.00
133 ChG,'Dick Tracy Follows Trail of Jewel Thief Gang'.	60.00
134 ChG,'Last Stand of Jewel Thieves'	60.00
135 ChG,'Case of the Rooftop Sniper'.	60.00
136 ChG,'Mystery of the Iron Room'.	60.00
137 ChG,'Law Versus Dick Tracy'.	60.00
138 ChG,'Mystery of Mary X'	60.00
139 ChG,'Yogee the Merciless'. . .	60.00
140 ChG,'The Tunnel Trap'	60.00
141 ChG,'Case of Wormy &	

His Deadly Wagon 60.00
142 ChG,`Case of the
Killer's Revenge'. 60.00
143 ChG,`Strange Case of
Measles'. 60.00
144 ChG,`Strange Case of
Shoulders' 60.00
145 ChG,`Case of the Feindish
Photo-graphers';April, 1961 . . 60.00

DIME COMICS
Newsbook Publ. Corp., 1945
1 LbC,A:Silver Streak 400.00

DING DONG
Compix
(Magazine Enterprises), 1947
1 (fa). 90.00
2 (fa) 50.00
3 thru 5 (fa) . . . . @40.00

DINKY DUCK
St. John Publ. Co./Pines
Nov., 1951
1 . . . . 50.00
2 . . . . 30.00
3 thru 10 . . . . @20.00
11 thru 15 . . . . @15.00
16 thru 18. . . . . @10.00
19 Summer, 1958. . . . . 10.00

DIXIE DUGAN
Columbia Publ./
Publication Enterprises
July, 1942
1 Boxing cover,Joe Palooka. . . . 225.00
2 . . . . 125.00
3 . . . . 85.00
4 . . . . 60.00
5 . . . . 60.00
6 thru 12 . . . . @45.00
13 1949 . . . . 45.00

DIZZY DAMES
B&M Distribution Co.
(American Comics)
Sept.–Oct., 1952
1 . . . . 60.00
2 . . . . 40.00
3 thru 6 July–Aug., 1953 . . . . . @25.00

DIZZY DON COMICS
Howard Publications/
Dizzy Dean Ent., 1943
1 B&W interior. 45.00
2 B&W Interior. 20.00
3 B&W Interior. 15.00
4 B&W Interior. 15.00
5 thru 21 . . . . @15.00
22 Oct., 1946. . . . . 40.00
1a thru 3a. . . . . @30.00

DIZZY DUCK
(see BARNYARD COMICS)

DOC CARTER
V.D. COMICS
Health Publ. Inst., 1949
N# 150.00
N# 100.00

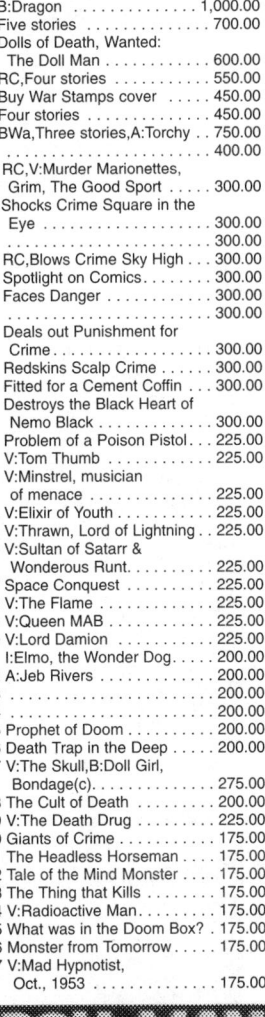

Doc Savage #5
© Street & Smith

DOC SAVAGE COMICS
Street & Smith, May, 1940
1 B:Doc Savage, Capt. Fury, Danny
Garrett, Mark Mallory, Whisperer,
Capt. Death, Treasure
Island, A: The Magician . . . 4,200.00
2 O:Ajax,The Sun Man,E:The
Whisperer 1,200.00
3 Artic Ice Wastes 1,000.00
4 E:Treasure Island, Saves
U.S. Navy. 800.00
5 O:Astron, the Crocodile
Queen, Sacred Ruby 600.00
6 E: Capt. Fury, O:Red Falcon,
Murderous Peace Clan . . . 500.00
7 V:Zoombas 500.00
8 Finds the Long Lost Treasure . 500.00
9 Smashes Japan's Secret Oil
Supply 500.00
10 O:Thunder Bolt, The Living
Dead A:Lord Manhattan 500.00
11 V:Giants of Destruction. 400.00
12 Saves Merchant Fleet from
Complete Destruction. 400.00
2-1 The Living Evil 400.00
2-2 V:Beggar King 400.00
2-3 . . . . 400.00
2-4 Fight to Death. 400.00
2-5 Saves Panama Canal from
Blood Raider 400.00
2-6 . . . . 400.00
2-7 V:Black Knight 400.00
2-8 Oct., 1943 . . . . 400.00

DR. ANTHONY KING
HOLLYWOOD LOVE
DOCTOR
Harvey, Publ., 1952
1 . . . . 75.00
2 . . . . 40.00
3 . . . . 40.00
4 BP,May, 1954 . . . . 40.00

DOLL MAN
Comic Favorites
(Quality Comics Group)
Fall, 1941
1 RC,B:Doll Man & Justine
Wright 2,700.00

2 B:Dragon 1,000.00
3 Five stories 700.00
4 Dolls of Death, Wanted:
The Doll Man 600.00
5 RC,Four stories 550.00
6 Buy War Stamps cover 450.00
7 Four stories 450.00
8 BWa,Three stories,A:Torchy . . 750.00
9 . . . . 400.00
10 RC,V:Murder Marionettes,
Grim, The Good Sport 300.00
11 Shocks Crime Square in the
Eye 300.00
12 . . . . 300.00
13 RC,Blows Crime Sky High . . 300.00
14 Spotlight on Comics. 300.00
15 Faces Danger 300.00
16 . . . . 300.00
17 Deals out Punishment for
Crime. 300.00
18 Redskins Scalp Crime 300.00
19 Fitted for a Cement Coffin . . . 300.00
20 Destroys the Black Heart of
Nemo Black 300.00
21 Problem of a Poison Pistol. . . 225.00
22 V:Tom Thumb 225.00
23 V:Minstrel, musician
of menace 225.00
24 V:Elixir of Youth 225.00
25 V:Thrawn, Lord of Lightning . . 225.00
26 V:Sultan of Satarr &
Wonderous Runt. 225.00
27 Space Conquest 225.00
28 V:The Flame 225.00
29 V:Queen MAB 225.00
30 V:Lord Damion 225.00
31 I:Elmo, the Wonder Dog. . . . 200.00
32 A:Jeb Rivers 200.00
33 . . . . 200.00
34 . . . . 200.00
35 Prophet of Doom 200.00
36 Death Trap in the Deep 200.00
37 V:The Skull,B:Doll Girl,
Bondage(c). 275.00
38 The Cult of Death 200.00
39 V:The Death Drug 225.00
40 Giants of Crime 175.00
41 The Headless Horseman 175.00
42 Tale of the Mind Monster . . . 175.00
43 The Thing that Kills 175.00
44 V:Radioactive Man. 175.00
45 What was in the Doom Box? . 175.00
46 Monster from Tomorrow 175.00
47 V:Mad Hypnotist,
Oct., 1953 . . . . 175.00

Doll Man #32
© Quality Comics Group

FAMOUS GANG, BOOK OF COMICS
Firestone Tire & Rubber Co.
1942
N# 800.00
Becomes:

DONALD AND MICKEY MERRY CHRISTMAS
N# (2),CB, 1943 . . . . 750.00
N# (3),CB, 1944 . . . . 700.00
N# (4),CB, 1945 . . . . 1,000.00
N# (5),CB, 1946 . . . . 750.00
N# (6),CB, 1947 . . . . 650.00
N# (7),CB, 1948 . . . . 650.00
N# (8),CB, 1949 . . . . 675.00

DONALD DUCK
Whitman
W.Disney's Donald Duck ('35) . 2,200.00
W.Disney's Donald Duck ('36) . 2,000.00
W.Disney's Donald Duck ('38) . 2,200.00

DONALD DUCK GIVEAWAYS
Donald Duck Surprise Party (Icy
  Frost Ice Cream 1948)WK . . 900.00
Donald Duck (Xmas Giveaway
  1944) 350.00
Donald Duck Tells About Kites
  (P.G.&E., Florida 1954) . . . 2,000.00
Donald Duck Tells About Kites
  (S.C.Edison 1954) 1,800.00
Donald Duck and the Boys
  (Whitman 1948) 125.00
Donald Ducks Atom Bomb
  (Cherrios 1947) 275.00

(WALT DISNEY'S) DONALD DUCK
Dell Publishing Co.
Nov. 1952
(#1-#25) See Dell Four Color
26 CB;"Trick or Treat" (1952) . . . 350.00
27 CB(c);"Flying Horse"('53) . . . 150.00
28 CB(c); Robert the Robot. 125.00
29 CB(c). 125.00
30 CB(c). 125.00
31 thru 39 . . . . @65.00
40 thru 44 . . . . @60.00
45 CB 160.00
46 CB; "Secret of Hondorica" . . . 250.00
47 thru 51 . . . . @60.00
52 CB; "Lost Peg-Leg Mine" 150.00
53 . . . . 40.00
54 CB; "Forbidden Valley". 150.00
55 thru 59 . . . . @40.00
60 CB; "Donald Duck & the
  Titanic Ants" 150.00
61 thru 67 . . . . @40.00
68 CB. 125.00
69 thru 78 . . . . @35.00
79 CB (1 page). 45.00
80 . . . . 30.00
81 CB (1 page). 35.00
82 . . . . 30.00
83 . . . . 30.00
84 . . . . 30.00
See: Independent Color Listings

DON FORTUNE MAGAZINE
Don Fortune Publ. Co.
Aug., 1946
1 CCB 150.00

---

2 CCB 100.00
3 CCB,Bondage(c) 75.00
4 CCB 75.00
5 CCB 75.00
6 CCB, Jan., 1947 . . . . 75.00

DON NEWCOMBE
Fawcett Publications, 1950
1 Baseball Star 300.00

DON WINSLOW OF THE NAVY
Fawcett Publ./
Charlton Comics, Feb., 1943
1 Captain Marvel cover 900.00
2 Nips the Nipponese in
  the Solomons 400.00
3 Single-Handed invasion of
  the Philippines 300.00
4 Undermines the Nazis! 250.00
5 Stolen Battleship Mystery . . . 250.00
6 War Stamps for Victory cover . 250.00
7 Coast Guard 150.00
8 U.S. Marines 150.00
9 Fighting Marines 150.00
10 Fighting Seabees. 150.00
11 . . . . 125.00
12 Tuned for Death. 125.00
13 Hirohito's Hospitality. 135.00
14 Catapults against the Axis . . . 135.00
15 Fighting Merchant Marine. . . . 120.00
16 V:The Most Diabolical Villain
  of all Time 120.00
17 Buy War Stamps cover 120.00
18 The First Underwater Convoy. 100.00
19 Bonape Excersion 100.00
20 The Nazi Prison Ship 100.00
21 Prisoner of the Nazis 90.00
22 Suicide Football 90.00
23 Peril on the High Seas 90.00
24 Adventures on the High Seas. . 90.00
25 Shanghaied Red Cross Ship . . 90.00
26 V:The Scorpion 90.00
27 Buy War Stamps 90.00
28 . . . . 90.00
29 Invitation to Trouble 90.00
30 . . . . 90.00
31 Man or Myth? 75.00
32 Return of the Renegade. 75.00
33 Service Ribbons 75.00
34 Log Book. 75.00
35 . . . . 75.00

Don Winslow of the Navy #6
© Fawcett Publications

---

36 . . . . 75.00
37 V: Sea Serpent 75.00
38 Climbs Mt. Everest. 75.00
39 Scorpion's Death Ledger 75.00
40 Kick Off! 75.00
41 Rides the Skis! 70.00
42 Amazon Island. 70.00
43 Ghastly Doll Murder Case 70.00
44 The Scorpions Web 70.00
45 V:Highwaymen of the Seas . . . 70.00
46 Renegades Jailbreak 70.00
47 The Artic Expedition. 70.00
48 Maelstrom of the Deep. 70.00
49 The Vanishing Ship! 70.00
50 V:The Snake 70.00
51 A:Singapore Sal. 60.00
52 Ghost of the Fishing Ships. . . . 60.00
53 . . . . 60.00
54 . . . . 60.00
55 . . . . 60.00
56 Far East 60.00
57 A:Singapore Sal. 60.00
58 . . . . 60.00
59 . . . . 60.00
60 thru 63 . . . . @60.00
64 MB 70.00
65 Ph(c) 75.00
66 Ph(c) 75.00
67 Ph(c) 75.00
68 Ph(c) 75.00
69 Ph(c), Jaws of Destruction . . . 75.00
70 . . . . 50.00
71 . . . . 50.00
72 . . . . 50.00
73 Sept., 1955 . . . . 50.00

DOPEY DUCK
Non-Pareil Publ. Corp.
Fall, 1945
1 A:Krazy Krow,Casper Cat 125.00
2 same 100.00
Becomes:

WACKY DUCK
3 . . . . 65.00
4 . . . . 50.00
5 . . . . 50.00
6 Summer, 1947 . . . . 50.00

DOROTHY LAMOUR (see JUNGLE LIL)

DOTTY DRIPPLE
Magazine Enterprises/
Harvey Publications, 1946
1 . . . . 60.00
2 . . . . 30.00
3 thru 10 . . . . @15.00
11 thru 20 . . . . @10.00
21 thru 23 . . . . @8.00
24 June, 1952 . . . . 8.00
Becomes:

HORACE & DOTTY DRIPPLE
25 thru 42. . . . . @6.00
43 Oct., 1955 . . . . 6.00

DOUBLE COMICS
Elliot Publications
1 ('40),Masked Marvel. 1,700.00
2 ('41),Tornado Tim. 1,200.00
3 ('42) 1,000.00
4 ('43) 750.00
5 ('44) 750.00

DOUBLE UP
Elliot Publications, 1941
1 . . . . 600.00

DOWN WITH CRIME
Fawcett Publications
Nov., 1951
1 A:Desarro 200.00
2 BP, A:Scanlon Gang 125.00
3 H-is for Heroin 100.00
4 BP, A:Desarro 75.00
5 No Jail Can Hold Me 100.00
6 The Puncture-Proof Assassin . . 75.00
7 The Payoff, Nov., 1952 . . . . . . 75.00

DUDLEY
Prize Publications
Nov.–Dec., 1952
1 . . . . 100.00
2 . . . . 75.00
3 March–April, 1950 . . . . 65.00

DUMBO WEEKLY
The Walt Disney Co., 1942
1 Gas giveaways 400.00
2 . . . . 125.00
3 . . . . 125.00
4 . . . . 125.00
5 thru 16 . . . . @125.00

DURANGO KID
Magazine Enterprises
Oct.–Nov., 1949
1 FF, Charles Starrett photo cover
  B:Durango Kid & Raider . . . 550.00
2 FF, Charles Starrett Ph(c) 300.00
3 FF, Charles Starrett Ph(c) . . . 275.00
4 FF, Charles Starrett Ph(c),
  Two-Timing Guns 250.00
5 FF, Charles Starrett Ph(c),
  Tracks Across the Trail 250.00
6 FF 150.00
7 FF,Atomic(c) 165.00
8 FF thru 10 . . . . @150.00
11 FF 125.00
12 FF 125.00
13 FF 125.00
14 thru 16 FF . . . . @125.00
17 O:Durango Kid 150.00
18 FMe,DAy(c) 75.00
19 FMe,FG 60.00
20 FMe,FG 60.00
21 FMe,FG 60.00
22 FMe,FG 65.00
23 FMe,FG,I:Red Scorpion 65.00
24 thru 30 FMe,FG . . . . @65.00
31 FMe,FG 65.00
32 thru 40 FG . . . . @60.00
41 FG,Oct., 1941 . . . . 70.00

DYNAMIC COMICS
Dynamic Publications
(Harry 'A' Chesler)
Oct., 1941
1 EK,O:Major Victory, Dynamic Man,
  Hale the Magician, A:Black
  Cobra 1,300.00
2 O:Dynamic Boy & Lady
  Satan,I:Green Knight,
  Lance Cooper 600.00
3 GT 500.00
8 Horror cover 500.00
9 MRa,GT,B:Mr.E 500.00
10 . . . . 400.00

Dynamic Comics #13
© Harry A Chesler

11 GT 325.00
12 GT 300.00
13 GT 325.00
14 . . . . 300.00
15 . . . . 300.00
16 GT,Bondage(c),Marijuana. . . . 325.00
17 . . . . 425.00
18 Ric. 250.00
19 A:Dynamic Man 235.00
20 same,Nude Woman 350.00
21 same 225.00
22 same 225.00
23 A:Yankee Girl,1.0948 . . . . . . 225.00

DYNAMITE
Comic Media/Allen Hardy Publ.
May, 1953
1 DH(c),A:Danger#6 . . . . 120.00
2 . . . . 75.00
3 PAM, PAM(c),B:Johnny
  Dynamite,Drug 75.00
4 PAM, PAM(c),Prostitution 100.00
5 PAM, PAM(c) 75.00
6 PAM, PAM(c) 75.00
7 PAM, PAM(c) 75.00
8 PAM, PAM(c) 75.00
9 PAM, PAM(c) 75.00
Becomes:

JOHNNY DYNAMITE
Charlton Comics
10 PAM(c) 50.00
11 . . . . 35.00
12 . . . . 40.00
Becomes:

FOREIGN INTRIGUES
13 A:Johnny Dynamite 35.00
14 same 30.00
15 same 30.00
Becomes:

BATTLEFIELD ACTION
16 . . . . 25.00
17 . . . . 15.00
18 . . . . 15.00
19 . . . . 15.00
20 . . . . 15.00
21 thru 30 . . . . @10.00
31 thru 70 . . . . @5.00
71 thru 84 Oct. 1984 . . . . @2.00

EAGLE, THE
Fox Features Syndicate
July, 1941
1 B:The Eagle,A:Rex Dexter
  of Mars 1,500.00
2 B:Spider Queen 700.00
3 B:Joe Spook 550.00
4 Jan., 1942 . . . . 500.00

EAGLE
Rural Home Publ.
Feb.–March, 1945
1 LbC 250.00
2 LbC,April–May, 1945 . . . . 150.00

EAT RIGHT
TO WORK AND WIN
Swift Co., 1942
N# Flash Gordon,Popeye 250.00

EDDIE STANKY
Fawcett Publications, 1951
N# New York Giants 250.00

EERIE
Avon Periodicals
May–June, 1951–
Aug.–Sept. 1954
1 JKa,Horror from the Pit,
  Bondage(c) 2,500.00
2 WW,WW(c), Chamber
  of Death 450.00
3 WW,WW(c),JKa,JO
  Monster of the Storm 500.00
4 WW(c),Phantom of Reality . . . 400.00
5 WW(c), Operation Horror 350.00
6 Devil Keeps a Date 200.00
7 WW(c),JKa,JO,Blood for
  the Vampire 300.00
8 EK, Song of the Undead 200.00
9 JKa, Hands of Death 200.00
10 Castle of Terror 200.00
11 Anatomical Monster 175.00
12 Dracula 225.00
13 . . . . 200.00
14 Master of the Dead 200.00
15 . . . . 125.00
16 WW, Chamber of Death 150.00
17 WW(c),JO,JKa, ... 200.00

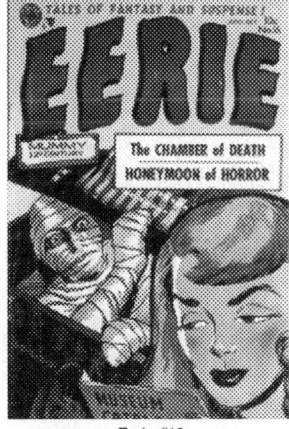

Eerie #16
© Avon Periodicals

EERIE ADVENTURES
Approved Comics
(Ziff-Davis), Winter, 1951
1 BP,JKa,Bondage 275.00

EGBERT
Arnold Publications/
Comic Magazine
Spring, 1946
1 I:Egbert & The Count 150.00
2 . . . . 75.00
3 . . . . 40.00
4 . . . . 40.00
5 . . . . 40.00
6 . . . . 50.00
7 . . . . 40.00
8 . . . . 40.00
9 . . . . 40.00
10 . . . . 40.00
11 thru 17 . . . . @25.00
18 1950 . . . . 25.00

EH!
Charlton Comics
Dec., 1953
1 DAy(c),DG 200.00
2 DAy(c) 150.00
3 DAy(c) 125.00
4 DAy(c) 125.00
5 DAy(c) 125.00
6 DAy(c) 125.00
7 DAy(c),Nov., 1954 . . . . 125.00

EL BOMBO COMICS
Frances M. McQueeny, 1945
1 . . . . 50.00

ELLERY QUEEN
Superior Comics
May–Nov., 1949
1 LbC(c),JKa,Horror. 400.00
2 . . . . 300.00
3 Drug issue 275.00
4 The Crooked Mile 250.00

ELLERY QUEEN
Approved Comics
(Ziff-Davis)
Jan.–March, 1952
1 NS(c),The Corpse the Killed . . 350.00
2 NS,Killer's Revenge,
   Summer, 1952 . . . . 275.00

ELSIE THE COW
D.S. Publishing Co.
Oct.–Nov., 1949
1 P(c) 175.00
2 Bondage(c). 200.00
3 July–Aug., 1950 . . . . 175.00

ENCHANTING LOVE
Kirby Publishing Co.
Oct., 1949
1 Branded Guilty, Ph(c) 100.00
2 Ph(c),BP. 50.00
3 Ph(c),Utter Defeat was our
   Victory; Jan.–Feb., 1950 . . . . 40.00

ETTA KETT
Best Books, Inc.
(Standard Comics)
Dec., 1948
11 . . . . 75.00
12 . . . . 40.00
13 . . . . 40.00
14 Sept., 1949 . . . . 40.00

ERNIE COMICS
(see SCREAM COMICS)

EXCITING COMICS
Better Publ./Visual Editions
(Standard Comics)
April, 1940
1 O:Mask, Jim Hatfield,
   Dan Williams 3,400.00
2 B:Sphinx 1,400.00
3 V;Robot 900.00
4 V:Sea Monster 600.00
5 V:Gargoyle 600.00
6 . . . . 650.00
7 AS(c) 450.00
8 . . . . 450.00
9 O:Black Terror & Tim,
   Bondage(c) 7,000.00
10 A:Black Terror. 2,000.00
11 same. 1,000.00
12 Bondage(c) 650.00
13 Bondage(c) 650.00
14 O:Sphinx 450.00
15 O:Liberator 475.00
16 Black Terror 400.00
17 same 400.00
18 same 400.00
19 same 400.00
20 E:Mask,Bondage(c) 375.00
21 A:Liberator 350.00
22 O:The Eaglet,B:American
   Eagle 400.00
23 Black Terror 300.00
24 Black Terror 300.00
25 Bondage(c) 325.00
26 ASh(c). 300.00
27 ASh(c) 300.00
28 ASh(c) 400.00
29 ASh(c) 400.00
30 ASh(c),Bondage(c) 425.00
31 ASh(c). 350.00

Exciting Comics #4
© Standard Comics

32 ASh(c) 350.00
33 ASh(c) 350.00
34 ASh(c) 350.00
35 ASh(c),E:Liberator 350.00
36 ASh(c) 350.00
37 ASh(c) 350.00
38 ASh(c) 350.00
39 ASh(c)O:Kara, Jungle
   Princess. 450.00
40 ASh(c) 400.00
41 ASh(c) 400.00
42 ASh(c),B:Scarab 450.00
43 ASh(c) 400.00
44 ASh(c) 400.00
45 ASh(c),V:Robot 400.00
46 ASh(c) 400.00
47 ASh(c) 400.00
48 ASh(c) 400.00
49 ASh(c),E:Kara &
   American Eagle 400.00
50 ASh(c),E:American Eagle . . . 400.00
51 ASh(c),B:Miss Masque. 450.00
52 ASh(c),Miss Masque 375.00
53 ASh(c),Miss Masque 375.00
54 ASh(c),E:Miss Masque. 375.00
55 ASh(c),O&B:Judy o/t Jungle. . 400.00
56 ASh(c) 375.00
57 ASh(c) 375.00
58 ASh(c) 375.00
59 ASh(c),FF,Bondage(c) 400.00
60 ASh(c),The Mystery Rider . . . 350.00
61 ASh(c) 325.00
62 ASh(c) 325.00
63 thru 65 ASh(c) . . . . @350.00
66 . . . . 325.00
67 GT. 325.00
68 . . . . 325.00
69 Sept., 1949 . . . . 325.00

EXCITING ROMANCES
Fawcett Publications, 1949
1 Ph(c) 75.00
2 thru 3 . . . . @40.00
4 Ph(c) 45.00
5 thru 14 . . . . @30.00

EXOTIC ROMANCE
(see TRUE WAR
ROMANCES)

EXPLORER JOE
Approved Comics
(Ziff-Davis)
Winter, 1951
1 NS,The Fire Opal
   of Madagscar 75.00
2 BK, Oct.–Nov., 1952. . . . . 85.00

EXPOSED
D.S. Publishing Co.
March–April, 1948
1 Corpses Cash and Carry 150.00
2 Giggling Killer 175.00
3 One Bloody Night 75.00
4 JO,Deadly Dummy 75.00
5 Body on the Beach 75.00
6 Grl,The Secret in the Snow . . 250.00
7 The Gypsy Baron,
   July–Aug., 1949 . . . . 275.00

EXTRA
Magazine Enterprises, 1947
1 . . . . 400.00

EXTRA!
E.C. Comics,
March–April, 1955
1 JCr,RC,JSe 150.00
2 JCr,RC,JSe 100.00
3 JCr,RC,JSe 100.00
4 JCr,RC,JSe 100.00
5 Nov.–Dec., 1955 . . . . 100.00

FACE, THE
Publication Enterprises
(Columbia Comics), 1942
1 MBi(c),The Face 700.00
2 MBi(c) 450.00
Becomes:

TONY TRENT
3 MBi,A:The Face 75.00
4 1949 . . . . 55.00

FAIRY TALE PARADE
Dell Publishing Co., 1942
1 WK,Giant 1,400.00
2 WK,Flying Horse. 600.00
3 WK. 425.00
4 WK. 400.00
5 WK. 400.00
6 WK. 300.00
7 WK. 300.00
8 WK. 300.00
9 WK. 300.00

FAMOUS COMICS
Zain-Eppy Publ.
N# Joe Palooka 350.00

FAMOUS CRIMES
Fox Features Syndicate
June, 1948
1 Cold Blooded Killer 400.00
2 Near Nudity cover 300.00
3 Crime Never Pays 350.00
4 . . . . 150.00
5 . . . . 150.00
6 . . . . 150.00
7 Drug issue 300.00
8 thru 19 . . . . @100.00
20 Aug., 1951 . . . . 100.00
51 1952 . . . . 50.00

FAMOUS FAIRY TALES
K.K. Publication Co., 1942
N# WK, Giveaway 325.00
N# WK, Giveaway 250.00
N# WK, Giveaway 250.00

FAMOUS FEATURE
STORIES
Dell Publishing Co., 1938
1A:Tarzan, Terry and the Pirates
Dick Tracy,Smilin' Jack 550.00

FAMOUS FUNNIES
Eastern Color Printing Co.
1933
N# A Carnival of Comics 8,500.00
N# Feb., 1934,
1st 10› comic. 22,000.00
1 July, 1934 . . . . 16,000.00
2 . . . . 3,000.00
3 B:Buck Rogers 4,000.00
4 Football cover 1,300.00
5 . . . . 1,000.00

6 . . . . 750.00
7 . . . . 750.00
8 . . . . 750.00
9 . . . . 750.00
10 . . . . 750.00
11 Four pages of Buck Rogers . . 650.00
12 Four pages of Buck Rogers . . 650.00
13 . . . . 550.00
14 . . . . 500.00
15 Football cover 500.00
16 . . . . 500.00
17 Christmas cover. 500.00
18 Four pages of Buck Rogers . . 650.00
19 . . . . 500.00
20 . . . . 500.00
21 Baseball 400.00
22 Buck Rogers 400.00
23 . . . . 375.00
24 B: War on Crime 375.00
25 . . . . 375.00
26 . . . . 375.00
27 G-Men cover 375.00
28 . . . . 375.00
29 . . . . 375.00
30 . . . . 375.00
31 . . . . 300.00
32 . . . . 300.00
33 A:Baby Face Nelson &
John Dillinger 300.00
34 . . . . 300.00
35 Buck Rogers 325.00
36 . . . . 275.00
37 . . . . 275.00
38 Portrait,Buck Rogers 300.00
39 . . . . 275.00
40 . . . . 275.00
41 thru 50 . . . . @250.00
51 thru 57 . . . . @200.00
58 Baseball cover. 200.00
59 . . . . 200.00
60 . . . . 200.00
61 . . . . 175.00
62 . . . . 175.00
63 . . . . 175.00
64 . . . . 175.00
65 JK 175.00
66 . . . . 175.00
67 . . . . 175.00
68 JK 175.00
69 . . . . 175.00
70 . . . . 175.00
71 BEv 125.00
72 BEv,B:Speed Spaulding 125.00
73 BEv 125.00
74 BEv 125.00
75 BEv 125.00
76 BEv 125.00
77 BEv,Merry Christmas cover . . 125.00
78 BEv 125.00
79 BEv 125.00
80 BEv,Buck Rogers 125.00
81 O:Invisible Scarlet O'Neil 100.00
82 Buck Rogers cover 125.00
83 Dickie Dare 100.00
84 Scotty Smith 100.00
85 Eagle Scout,Roy Rogers 100.00
86 Moon Monsters 100.00
87 Scarlet O'Neil. 100.00
88 . . . . 100.00
89 O:Fearless Flint 100.00
90 Bondage cover 110.00
91 . . . . 75.00
92 . . . . 75.00
93 . . . . 75.00
94 War Bonds. 85.00
95 Invisible Scarlet O'Neil 75.00
96 . . . . 75.00
97 War Bonds Promo 75.00
98 . . . . 75.00
99 . . . . 75.00
100 Anniversary issue 75.00

Famous Funnies #210
© Eastern Color Printing

101 thru 110 . . . . @75.00
111 thru 130 . . . . @60.00
131 thru 150 . . . . @50.00
151 thru 162 . . . . @50.00
163 Valentine's Day cover. 45.00
164 . . . . 40.00
165 . . . . 40.00
166 . . . . 40.00
167 . . . . 40.00
168 . . . . 40.00
169 AW 75.00
170 AW 75.00
171 thru 190 . . . . @40.00
191 thru 203 . . . . @35.00
204 War cover 32.00
205 thru 208 . . . . @30.00
209 FF(c),Buck Rogers. 650.00
210 FF(c),Buck Rogers. 650.00
211 FF(c),Buck Rogers. 650.00
212 FF(c),Buck Rogers. 650.00
213 FF(c),Buck Rogers. 650.00
214 FF(c),Buck Rogers. 650.00
215 FF(c),Buck Rogers. 650.00
216 FF(c),Buck Rogers. 650.00
217 . . . . 40.00
218 July, 1955 . . . . 40.00

FAMOUS GANG, BOOK
OF COMICS
(see DONALD AND
MICKEY
MERRY CHRISTMAS)

FAMOUS GANGSTERS
Avon Periodicals
April, 1951
1 Al Capone, Dillinger,
Luciano & Shultz 250.00
2 WW(c),Dillinger Machine-
Gun Killer 250.00
3 Lucky Luciano & Murder Inc. . . 250.00
Becomes:

CRIME ON
THE WATERFRONT
4 Underworld Gangsters who
Control the Shipment of Drugs!,
May, 1952 . . . . 225.00

All comics prices listed are for *Near Mint* condition. **CVA Page 333**

GOLDEN AGE

FAMOUS STARS
Ziff-Davis Publ. Co.
Aug., 1950
1 OW,Shelley Winter,Susan Peters
  & Shirley Temple 225.00
2 BEv,Betty Hutton, Bing Crosby 150.00
3 OW,Judy Garland, Alan Ladd . 165.00
4 RC,Jolson, Bob Mitchum 125.00
5 BK,Elizabeth Taylor,
  Esther Williams. 175.00
6 Gene Kelly, Spring, 1952 . . . . 125.00

FAMOUS STORIES
Dell Publishing Co., 1942
1 Treasure Island 200.00
2 Tom Sawyer 200.00

FAMOUS WESTERN
BADMEN
(see REDSKIN)

FANTASTIC
(see CAPTAIN SCIENCE)

Fantastic Comics #4
© *Fox Features Syndicate*

FANTASTIC COMICS
Fox Features Syndicate
Dec., 1939
1 LF(c),I&O:Samson,B:Star
  Dust, Super Wizard, Space
  Smith & Capt. Kid 3,800.00
2 BP,LF(c),Samson destroyed the
  Battery and Routed the Foe 1,600.00
3 BP,LF(c),Slays the Iron
  Monster. 5,000.00
4 GT,LF(c),Demolishes the
  Closing Torture Walls. 1,500.00
5 GT,LF(c),Crumbles the
  Mighty War Machine 1,400.00
6 JSm(c),Bondage(c) 1,000.00
7 JSm(c) 1,000.00
8 GT,Destroys the Mask of
  Fire,Bondage(c) 750.00
9 Mighty Muscles saved the
  Drowning Girl 750.00
10 I&O:David 750.00
11 Wrecks the Torture Machine
  to save his fellow American . 600.00
12 Heaved the Huge Ship high
  into the Air 600.00

13 . . . . 600.00
14 . . . . 600.00
15 . . . . 600.00
16 E:Stardust 600.00
17 . . . . 600.00
18 I:Black Fury & Chuck 650.00
19 . . . . 600.00
20 . . . . 600.00
21 B&I: The Banshee,Hitler(c). . . 625.00
22 . . . . 600.00
23 O:The Gladiator, Nov., 1941. . 625.00

FARGO KID
(see JUSTICE TRAPS OF
THE GUILTY)

FAST FICTION
Seaboard Publ./
Famous Author Illustrated
Oct., 1949
1 Scarlet Pimpernel 275.00
2 HcK,Captain Blood 250.00
3 She 350.00
4 The 39 Steps 200.00
5 HcK,Beau Geste 200.00
Becomes:

STORIES BY FAMOUS
AUTHORS ILLUSTRATED
1a Scarlet Pimpernel 250.00
2a Captain Blood. 250.00
3a She 300.00
4a The 39 Steps 200.00
5a Beau Geste 175.00
6 HcK,MacBeth 200.00
7 HcK,Window. 165.00
8 HcK,Hamlet 175.00
9 Nicholas Nickleby 150.00
10 HcK,Romeo & Juliet. 150.00
11 GS,Ben Hur 165.00
12 GS,La Svengali 165.00
13 HcK,Scaramouche 165.00

FAWCETT
FUNNY ANIMALS
Fawcett Publications
Dec., 1942
1 I:Hoppy the Marvel,
  Captain Marvel cover 450.00
2 X-Mas Issue 225.00
3 Spirit of '43 . . . . 150.00
4 and 5 . . . . @150.00
6 Buy War Bonds and Stamps . 100.00
7 . . . . 100.00
8 Flag cover 100.00
9 and 10 . . . . @100.00
11 thru 20 . . . . @75.00
21 thru 30 . . . . @50.00
31 thru 40 . . . . @35.00
41 thru 83 . . . . @25.00

Charlton Comics
84 . . . . 25.00
85 thru 91 Feb. 1956. . . . . @20.00

FAWCETT MOVIE
COMICS
Fawcett Publications, 1949
N# Dakota Lil 250.00
N#a Copper Canyon 200.00
N# Destination the Moon 650.00
N# Montana 175.00
N# Pioneer Marshal 175.00
N# Powder River Rustlers 200.00
N# Singing Guns 160.00

7 Gunmen of Abilene 175.00
8 King of the Bull Whip 275.00
9 BP,The Old Frontier 160.00
10 The Missourians 160.00
11 The Thundering Trail 225.00
12 Rustlers on Horseback. 165.00
13 Warpath. 125.00
14 Last Outpost,RonaldReagan . 300.00
15 The Man from Planet-X 1,800.00
16 10 Tall Men 100.00
17 Rose Cimarron 55.00
18 The Brigand. 65.00
19 Carbine Williams 75.00
20 Ivanhoe, Dec., 1952 . . . . . . 150.00

FEATURE BOOKS
David McKay Publications
May, 1937
N# Dick Tracy 7,000.00
N# Popeye 7,000.00
1 Zane Grey's King of the
  Royal Mounted 650.00
2 Popeye 650.00
3 Popeye and the "Jeep" 600.00
4 Dick Tracy 1,000.00
5 Popeye and his Poppa 600.00
6 Dick Tracy 800.00
7 Little Orphan Annie 900.00
8 Secret Agent X-9 . . . . 550.00
9 Tracy & the Famon Boys . . . 800.00
10 Popeye & Susan 600.00
11 Annie Rooney 250.00

Feature Books #2
© *David McKay Publications*

12 Blondie 600.00
13 Inspector Wade 200.00
14 Popeye in Wild Oats 700.00
15 Barney Baxter in the Air. . . . 250.00
16 Red Eagle 275.00
17 Gang Busters. 500.00
18 Mandrake the Magician 400.00
19 Mandrake 400.00
20 The Phantom 750.00
21 Lone Ranger 600.00
22 The Phantom. 600.00
23 Mandrake in Teibe Castle. . . 400.00
24 Lone Ranger 600.00
25 Flash Gordon on the
  Planet Mongo. 750.00
26 Prince Valiant. 750.00
27 Blondie 125.00
28 Blondie and Dagwood 100.00
29 Blondie at the Home
  Sweet Home. 100.00
30 Katzenjammer Kids 125.00

31 Blondie Keeps the Home
   Fires Burning 100.00
32 Katzenjammer Kids 100.00
33 Romance of Flying. 85.00
34 Blondie Home is Our Castle. . . 90.00
35 Katzenjammer Kids 100.00
36 Blondie on the Home Front . . 100.00
37 Katzenjammer Kids 100.00
38 Blondie the ModelHomemaker. 80.00
39 The Phantom. 400.00
40 Blondie 80.00
41 Katzenjammer Kids 90.00
42 Blondie in Home-Spun Yarns . . 80.00
43 Blondie Home-Cooked Scraps . 80.00
44 Katzenjammer Kids in
   Monkey Business 80.00
45 Blondie in Home of the Free
   and the Brave. 75.00
46 Mandrake in Fire World 275.00
47 Blondie in Eaten out of
   House and Home 80.00
48 The Maltese Falcon 450.00
49 Perry Mason - The Case of
   the Lucky Legs. 175.00
50 The Shoplifters Shoe,
   P. Mason 175.00
51 Rip Kirby - Mystery of
   the Mangler 250.00
52 Mandrake in the Land of X . . . 275.00
53 Phantom in Safari Suspense . 350.00
54 Rip Kirby - Case of the
   Master Menace. 250.00
55 Mandrake in 5-numbers
   Treasue Hunt 275.00
56 Phantom Destroys the
   Sky Band 300.00
57 Phantom in the Blue Gang,
   1948. . . . . 300.00

FEATURE FUNNIES
Harry A. Chesler Publ./
Comic Favorites
Oct., 1937–May 1950
1 RuG,RuG(c),A:Joe Palooka,
   Mickey Finn, Bungles, Dixie
   Dugan, Big Top, Strange as
   It Seems, Off the Record . . 2,200.00
2 A: The Hawk 1,000.00
3 WE,Joe Palooka,The Clock. . . 750.00
4 RuG,WE,RuG(c),Joe Palooka. 550.00
5 WE, Joe Palooka drawing . . . 550.00
6 WE, Joe Palooka cover 550.00
7 WE,LLe, Gallant Knight story

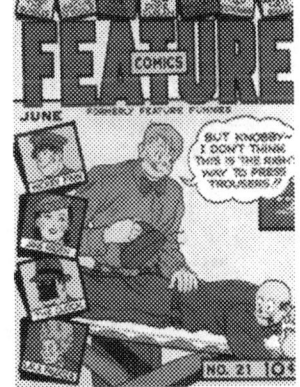

Feature Comics #21
© Quality Comics Group

by Vernon Henkel 450.00
8 WE 375.00
9 WE, Joe Palooka story 400.00
10 WE,Micky Finn(c). 375.00
11 WE,LLe,The Bungles(c) 375.00
12 WE, Joe Palooka(c). 400.00
13 WE,LLe, World Series(c) 450.00
14 WE,Ned Brant(c) 325.00
15 WE,Joe Palooka(c) 350.00
16 Mickey Finn(c) 325.00
17 WE 325.00
18 Joe Palooka cover 350.00
19 WE,LLe,Mickey Finn(c) 325.00
20 WE,LLe 325.00
Becomes:

FEATURE COMICS
Quality Comics Group
21 Joe Palooka(c). 450.00
22 LLe(c),Mickey Finn(c). 350.00
23 B:Charlie Chan 375.00
24 AAr,Joe Palooka(c) 325.00
25 AAr,The Clock(c) 325.00
26 AAr,The Bundles(c) 325.00
27 WE,AAr,I:Doll Man 3,200.00
28 LF,AAr,The Clock(c) 1,400.00
29 LF,AAr,The Clock(c) 750.00
30 LF,AAr,Doll Man(c) 750.00
31 LF,AAr,Mickey Finn(c) 600.00
32 PGv,LF,GFx,Doll Man(c). . . . 425.00
33 PGv,LF,GFx,Bundles(c) 400.00
34 PGv,LF,GFx,Doll Man(c). . . . 425.00
35 PGv,LF,GFx,Bundles(c) 400.00
36 PGv,LF,GFx,Doll Man(c). . . . 425.00
37 PGv,LF,GFx,Bundles(c) 400.00
38 PGv,GFx,Doll Man(c) 325.00
39 PGv,GFx,Bundles(c) 350.00
40 PGv,GFx,WE(c),Doll Man(c) . 325.00
41 PGv,GFx,WE(c),Bundles(c) . . 350.00
42 GFx,Doll Man(c). 250.00
43 RC,GFx,Bundles(c) 225.00
44 RC,GFx,Doll Man(c). 325.00
45 RC,GFx,Bundles(c) 225.00
46 RC,PGv,GFx,Doll Man(c) . . . 250.00
47 RC,GFx,Bundles(c) 225.00
48 RC,GFx,Doll Man(c) 250.00
49 RC,GFx,Bundles(c) 250.00
50 RC,GFx,Doll Man(c) 250.00
51 RC,GFx,Bundles(c) 225.00
52 RC,GFx,Doll Man(c) 225.00
53 RC,GFx,Bundles(c) 200.00
54 RC,GFx,Doll Man(c) 225.00
55 RC,GFx,Bundles(c) 200.00
56 RC,GFx,Doll Man(c). 250.00
57 RC,GFx,Bundles(c) 200.00
58 RC,GFx,Doll Man cover 225.00
59 RC,GFx,Mickey Finn(c) 200.00
60 RC,GFx,Doll Man(c) 225.00
61 RC,GFx,Bundles(c) 185.00
62 RC,GFx,Doll Man(c). 190.00
63 RC,GFx,Bundles(c) 175.00
64 BP,GFx,Doll Man(c) 185.00
65 BP,GFx(c),Bundles(c) 175.00
66 BP,GFx,Doll Man(c) 175.00
67 BP 150.00
68 BP,Doll Man vs.BeardedLady. 175.00
69 BP,GFx(c),Devil cover 165.00
70 BP,Doll Man(c) 175.00
71 BP,GFx(c) 125.00
72 BP,Doll Man(c). 125.00
73 BP,GFx(c),Bundles(c) 110.00
74 Doll Man(c) 125.00
75 GFx(c) 100.00
76 GFx(c) 100.00
77 Doll Man cover until #140. . . . 110.00
78 Knows no Fear but the
   Knife Does 100.00
79 Little Luck God. 100.00
80 . . . . 100.00
81 Wanted for Murder. 100.00
82 V:Shawunkas the Shaman . . . 100.00

83 V:Mechanical Man 100.00
84 V:Masked Rider, Death
   Goes to the Rodeo 100.00
85 V:King of Beasts 100.00
86 Is He A Killer? 100.00
87 The Maze of Murder 100.00
88 V:The Phantom Killer. 100.00
89 Crook's Goose 100.00
90 V:Whispering Corpse 100.00
91 V:The Undertaker. 100.00
92 V:The Image 100.00
93 . . . . 100.00
94 V:The Undertaker. 100.00
95 Flatten's the Peacock's Pride . 100.00
96 Doll Man Proves
   Justice is Blind 100.00
97 V:Peacock 100.00
98 V:Master Diablo 100.00
99 On the Warpath Again!. 100.00
100 Crushes the City of Crime . . 125.00
101 Land of the Midget Men! 75.00
102 The Angle 75.00
103 V:The Queen of Ants 75.00
104 V:The Botanist 75.00
105 Dream of Death 75.00
106 V:The Sword Fish 75.00
107 Hand of Horror! 75.00
108 V:Cateye 75.00
109 V:The Brain 75.00
110 V:Fat Cat 75.00
111 V:The Undertaker. 75.00
112 I:Mr. Curio & His Miniatures . . 75.00
113 V:Highwayman. 75.00
114 V:Tom Thumb. 75.00
115 V:The Sphinx 75.00
116 V:Elbows 75.00
117 Polka Dot on the Spot 75.00
118 thru 144 . . . . @75.00

FEDERAL MEN COMICS
Gerard Publ. Co., 1942
2 S&S,Spanking 250.00

FELIX THE CAT
Dell Publishing Co.
Feb.–March 1948
1 . . . . 250.00
2 . . . . 150.00
3 . . . . 100.00
4 . . . . 100.00
5 . . . . 100.00
6 . . . . 75.00
7 . . . . 75.00

Felix the Cat #36
© Dell Publishing Co./Toby Press

8 . . . . 75.00
9 . . . . 75.00
10 . . . . 75.00
11 thru 19 . . . . @65.00

Toby Press

20 thru 30 . . . . @125.00
31 . . . . 25.00
32 . . . . 60.00
33 . . . . 60.00
34 . . . . 25.00
35 . . . . 25.00
36 thru 59 . . . . @60.00
60 . . . . 55.00
61 . . . . 55.00

Harvey

62 thru 80 . . . . @18.00
81 thru 99 . . . . @15.00
100 . . . . 20.00
101 thru 118 . . . . @12.00
Spec., 100 pgs, 1952 . . . . 175.00
Summer Ann., 100 pgs. 1953 . . . 150.00
Winter Ann.,#2 100 pgs, 1954. . . 125.00

FERDINAND THE BULL
Dell Publishing Co., 1938
1 . . . . 140.00

FIGHT AGAINST CRIME
Story Comics May, 1951
1 Scorpion of Crime Inspector
  "Brains" Carroway 225.00
2 Ganglands Double Cross 125.00
3 Killer Dolan's Double Cross . . 100.00
4 Hopped Up Killers - The
  Con's Slaughter,Drug issue . 100.00
5 Horror of the Avenging Corpse 100.00
6 Terror of the Crazy Killer 100.00
7 . . . . 100.00
8 Killer with the Two-bladed
  Knife 75.00
9 Rats Die by Gas,Horror. 200.00
10 Horror of the Con's Revenge . 200.00
11 Case of the Crazy Killer 200.00
12 Horror,Drug issue. 225.00
13 The Bloodless Killer. 200.00
14 Electric Chair cover 225.00
15 . . . . 175.00
16 RA,Bondage(c) 225.00
17 Knife in Neck(c). 225.00
18 Attempted hanging cover 250.00
19 Bondage(c) 250.00
20 Severed Head cover 400.00
21 . . . . 175.00
Becomes:

FIGHT AGAINST THE GUILTY
22 RA,Electric Chair 200.00
23 March, 1955 . . . . 125.00

FIGHT COMICS
Fight Comics Inc.
(Fiction House Magazines)
Jan., 1940
1 LF,GT,WE(c),O:Spy Fighter . 2,200.00
2 GT,WE(c),Joe Lewis 900.00
3 WE(c),GT,B:Rip Regan,
  The Powerman 650.00
4 GT,LF(c). 550.00
5 WE(c) 550.00
6 GT,BP(c) 400.00
7 GT,BP(c),Powerman-Blood
  Money 400.00
8 GT,Chip Collins-Lair of
  the Vulture 400.00
9 GT,Chip Collins-Prey of the
  War Eagle 400.00

10 GT,Wolves of the Yukon. . . . 400.00
11 . . . . 350.00
12 RA,Powerman-Monster of
  Madness 350.00
13 Shark Broodie-Legion
  of Satan 350.00
14 Shark Broodie-Lagoon
  of Death 350.00
15 Super-American-Hordes of
  the Secret Dicator. 500.00
16 B:Capt.Fight,SwastikaPlague . 500.00
17 Super-American-Blaster of
  the Pig-Boat Pirates 400.00
18 Shark Broodie-Plague of
  the Yellow Devils 400.00
19 E:Capt. Fight 400.00
20 . . . . 300.00
21 Rip Carson-Hell's Sky-Riders . 250.00
22 Rip Carson-Sky Devil's
  Mission. 250.00
23 Rip Carson-Angels of
  Vengeance 250.00
24 Baynonets for the Banzai
  Breed! Bondage(c) 225.00
25 Rip Carson-Samurai
  Showdown 200.00
26 Rip Carson-Fury of
  the Sky-Brigade 200.00
27 War-Loot for the Mikado,
  Bondage(c). 200.00
28 Rip Carson 200.00
29 Rip Carson-Charge of the
  Lost Region 200.00
30 Rip Carson-Jeep-Raiders of
  the Torture Jungle 200.00
31 Gangway for the Gyrenes,
  Decapitation cover 225.00
32 Vengeance of the Hun-
  Hunters,Bondage(c) 225.00
33 B:Tiger Girl 150.00
34 Bondage(c) 165.00
35 MB 150.00
36 MB 150.00
37 MB 150.00
38 MB,Bondage(c) 175.00
39 MB,Senorita Rio-Slave Brand
  of the Spider Cult 150.00
40 MB,Bondage cover 175.00
41 MB,Bondage cover 175.00
42 MB 150.00
43 MB,Senorita Rio-The Fire-Brides
  of the Lost Atlantis,
  Bondage(c). 175.00
44 MB,R:Capt. Fight 150.00
45 MB,Tonight Don Diablo Rides. 150.00

Fight Comics #4
© Fiction House Magazines

46 MB 150.00
47 MB,SenoritaRio-Horror's
  Hacienda 150.00
48 MB 150.00
49 MB,JKa,B:Tiger Girl(c) 150.00
50 MB 150.00
51 MB,O:Tiger Girl 300.00
52 MB,Winged Demons of Doom 125.00
53 MB,Shadowland Shrine 125.00
54 MB,Flee the Cobra Fury. . . . 125.00
55 MB,Jungle Juggernaut 125.00
56 MB 125.00
57 MB,Jewels of Jeopardy 125.00
58 MB 125.00
59 MB,Vampires ofCrystalCavern 125.00
60 MB,Kraal of DeadlyDiamonds 125.00
61 MB,Seekers of the Sphinx,
  O:Tiger Girl. 175.00
62 MB,Graveyard if the
  Tree Tribe. 110.00
63 MB. 110.00
64 MB,DawnBeast from
  Karama-Zan!. 110.00
65 Beware the Congo Girl. 110.00
66 Man or Ape!. 100.00
67 Head-Hunters of Taboo Trek . 100.00
68 Fangs of Dr. Voodoo 100.00
69 Cage of the Congo Fury. . . . 100.00
70 Kraal of Traitor Tusks 100.00
71 Captives for the Golden
  Crocodile 100.00
72 Land of the Lost Safaris. . . . 100.00
73 War-Gods of the Jungle 100.00
74 Advengers of the Jungle 100.00
75 Perils of Momba-Kzar 100.00
76 Kraal of Zombi-Zaro. 100.00
77 Slave-Queen of the Ape Man. 100.00
78 Great Congo Diamond
  Robbery 125.00
79 A:Space Rangers. 125.00
80 . . . . 100.00
81 E:Tiger Girl(c) 100.00
82 RipCarson-CommandoStrike . 100.00
83 NobodyLoves a Minesweeper 100.00
84 Rip Carson-Suicide Patrol . . 100.00
85 . . . . 100.00
86 GE,Tigerman,Summer,1954 . . 110.00

FIGHTING AMERICAN
Headline Publications
(Prize), April–May, 1954
1 S&K,O:Fighting American &
  Speedboy 1,400.00
2 S&K,S&K(c) 650.00
3 S&K,S&K(c) 500.00
4 S&K,S&K(c) 500.00
5 S&K,S&K(c) 500.00
6 S&K,S&K(c),O:Fighting
  American 475.00
7 S&K,S&K(c), April–May, 1955 425.00

FIGHTING DAVY CROCKETT
(see KIT CARSON)

FIGHTING INDIANS OF THE WILD WEST
Avon Periodicals
March, 1952
1 EK,EL,Geronimo, Crazy Horse,
  Chief Victorio 100.00
2 EK,Same, Nov., 1952 . . . . . . 75.00

GOLDEN AGE

FIGHTING LEATHERNECKS
Toby Press, Feb., 1952
1 JkS,Duke's Diary 100.00
2 . . . . 65.00
3 . . . . 50.00
4 . . . . 50.00
5 . . . . 45.00
6 Dec., 1952 . . . . 40.00

FIGHTIN' TEXAN
(see TEXAN, THE)

FIGHTING YANK
Nedor Publ./Better Publ.
(Standard Comics) Sept., 1942
1 B:Fighting Yank, A:Wonder Man,
Mystico, Bondage cover. . . 1,700.00
2 JaB 750.00
3 . . . . 550.00
4 AS(c) 450.00
5 AS(c) 450.00
6 AS(c) 450.00
7 AS(c),A:Fighting Yank 400.00
8 AS(c) 400.00
9 AS(c) 400.00
10 AS(c). 400.00
11 AS(c), A:Grim Reaper, Nazis
bomb Washington cover. . . . 350.00
12 AS(c), Hirohito bondage cover 350.00
13 AS(c). 300.00
14 AS(c). 300.00
15 AS(c). 300.00
16 AS(c). 300.00
17 AS(c). 300.00
18 AS(c), A:American Eagle 300.00
19 AS(c). 300.00
20 AS(c) 300.00
21 AS(c) A:Kara,Jungle
Princess. 325.00
22 AS(c) A:Miss Masque-
cover story 350.00
23 AS(c) Klu Klux Klan
parody cover 350.00
24 A:Miss Masque 325.00
25 JRo,MMe,A:Cavalier 400.00
26 JRo,MMe,A:Cavalier 325.00
27 JRo,MMe,A:Cavalier 325.00
28 JRo,MMe,AW,A:Cavalier 350.00
29 JRo,MMe,Aug., 1949 . . . . . . 350.00

FILM STAR ROMANCES
Star Publications, 1950
1 LbC(c), Rudy Valentino story . 300.00
2 Liz Taylor & Robert Taylor,
photo cover 275.00
3 May–June, 1950, photo(c) . . . 175.00

FIREHAIR COMICS
Flying Stories, Inc.
(Fiction House Magazine)
Winter, 1948
1 I:Firehair, Riders on the
Pony Express 450.00
2 Bride of the Outlaw Guns 200.00
3 Kiss of the Six-Gun Siren! . . . 150.00
4 & 5 . . . . @150.00
6 . . . . 125.00
7 War Drums at Buffalo Bend . . 125.00
8 Raid on the Red Arrows 125.00
9 French Flags and Tomahawks 125.00
10 Slave Maiden of the Crees. . . 125.00
11 Wolves of the Overland
Trail,Spring, 1952 . . . . 125.00

Flame #1
© *Fox Feature Syndicate*

FLAME, THE
Fox Feature Syndicate
Summer, 1940
1 LF,O:The Flame 2,700.00
2 GT,LF 1,000.00
3 BP 750.00
4 . . . . 700.00
5 GT 700.00
6 GT 700.00
7 A:The Yank 700.00
8 The Finger of the Frozen
Death!, Jan., 1942 . . . . 700.00

FLAMING LOVE
Comic Magazines
(Quality Comics Group)
Dec., 1949
1 BWa,BWa(c),The Temptress
I Feared in His Arms 250.00
2 Torrid Tales of Turbulent
Passion 100.00
3 BWa,RC,My Heart's at Sea . . 175.00
4 One Women who made a
Mockery of Love, Ph(c). 75.00
5 Bridge of Longing, Ph(c) 75.00
6 Men both Loved & Feared Me,
Oct., 1950 . . . . 75.00

FLASH GORDON
Harvey Publications
Oct., 1950
1 AR,Bondage(c) 200.00
2 AR 150.00
3 AR Bondage(c). 165.00
4 AR, April, 1951 . . . . 150.00

FLIP
Harvey Publications
April, 1954
1 HN 150.00
2 HN,BP,June, 1954 . . . . 150.00

FLY BOY
Approved Comics
(Ziff-Davis) Spring, 1952
1 NS(c),Angels without Wings . . 125.00
2 NS(c),Flyboy's Flame-Out,
Oct.–Nov., 1952 . . . . 75.00

THE FLYING A'S RANGE RIDER
Dell Publishing Co.
June–Aug., 1953
(1) = *Dell Four Color #404*
2 Ph(c) all 75.00
3 . . . . 50.00
4 . . . . 50.00
5 . . . . 50.00
6 . . . . 50.00
7 . . . . 50.00
8 . . . . 50.00
9 . . . . 50.00
10 . . . . 50.00
11 . . . . 40.00
12 . . . . 40.00
13 . . . . 40.00
14 . . . . 40.00
15 . . . . 40.00
16 . . . . 40.00
17 ATh 55.00
19 . . . . 40.00
20 . . . . 40.00
21 . . . . 40.00
22 . . . . 40.00
23 . . . . 40.00
24. . . . . 40.00

FOODINI
Continental Publications
March, 1950
1 . . . . 90.00
2 . . . . 50.00
3 . . . . 40.00
4 Aug., 1950 . . . . 40.00

FOOTBALL THRILLS
Approved Comics
(Ziff-Davis)
Fall-Winter, 1952
1 BP,NS(c),Red Grange story . . 200.00
2 NS(c),Bronko Nagurski,
Spring,1952 . . . . 150.00

FORBIDDEN LOVE
Comic Magazine
(Quality Comics Group)
March, 1950
1 RC,Ph(c),Heartbreak Road . . 550.00
2 Ph(c),I loved a Gigolo 225.00
3 Kissless Bride 225.00
4 BWa,Brimstone Kisses,
Sept., 1950 . . . . 250.00

FORBIDDEN WORLDS
American Comics Group
July–Aug., 1951
1 AW,FF 1,000.00
2 . . . . 500.00
3 AW,WW,JD. 500.00
4 Werewolf cover 250.00
5 AW 400.00
6 AW,King Kong cover 350.00
7 . . . . 200.00
8 . . . . 200.00
9 Atomic Bomb 225.00
10 JyD 175.00
11 The Mummy's Treasure 150.00
12 Chest of Death. 150.00
13 Invasion from Hades 150.00
14 Million-Year Monster 150.00
15 The Vampire Cat 150.00
16 The Doll. 150.00
17 . . . . 150.00

Forbidden Worlds #14
© American Comics Group

18 The Mummy	150.00
19 Pirate and the Voodoo Queen	150.00
20 Terror Island	150.00
21 The Ant Master	100.00
22 The Cursed Casket	100.00
23 Nightmare for Two	100.00
24	100.00
25 Hallahan's Head	100.00
26 The Champ	100.00
27 SMo,The Thing with the Golden Hair	100.00
28 Portrait of Carlotta	100.00
29 The Frogman	100.00
30 The Things on the Beach	100.00
31 SMo,The Circle of the Doomed	80.00
32 The Invasion of the Dead Things	80.00
33	80.00
34 Atomic Bomb	110.00
35 Comics Code	75.00
36 thru 62	@50.00
63 AW	75.00
64	45.00
65	45.00
66	45.00
67	45.00
68 OW(c)	45.00
69 AW	75.00
70	45.00
71	45.00
72 OW,I:Herbie	150.00
73	45.00
74	45.00
75 JB	40.00
76 AW	60.00
77	40.00
78 AW,OW(c)	60.00
79 thru 85 JB	@40.00
86 Flying Saucer	50.00
87	40.00
88	40.00
89	40.00
90	40.00
91	40.00
92	40.00
93	40.00
94 OW(c),A:Herbie	75.00
95	30.00
96 AW	50.00
97 thru 115	@30.00
116 OW(c)A:Herbie	35.00
117	30.00
118	30.00
119	30.00
120 thru 124	@30.00

125 I:O:Magic Man	35.00
126 A:Magic Man	25.00
127 same	25.00
128 same	25.00
129 same	25.00
130 same	25.00
131 same	25.00
132 same	25.00
133 I:O:Dragona	25.00
134 A:Magic Man	25.00
135 A:Magic Man	25.00
136 A:Nemesis	25.00
137 A:Magic Man	25.00
138 A:Magic Man	25.00
139 A:Magic Man	25.00
140 SD,A:Mark Midnight	25.00
141 thru 145	@15.00

FOREIGN INTRIGUES
(see DYNAMITE)

FOUR COLOR
Dell Publishing Co., 1939

N# Dick Tracy	7,000.00
N# Don Winslow of the Navy	1,400.00
N# Myra North	800.00
4 Disney'sDonaldDuck(1940)	11,000.00
5 Smilin' Jack	600.00
6 Dick Tracy	1,500.00
7 Gang Busters	400.00
8 Dick Tracy	800.00
9 Terry and the Pirates	650.00
10 Smilin' Jack	600.00
11 Smitty	400.00
12 Little Orphan Annie	500.00
13 Walt Disney's Reluctant Dragon (1941)	1,700.00
14 Moon Mullins	400.00
15 Tillie the Toiler	400.00
16 W.Disney's Mickey Mouse Outwits the Phantom Blob (1941)	9,500.00
17 W.Disney's Dumbo the Flying Elephant (1941)	2,000.00
18 Jiggs and Maggie	450.00
19 Barney Google and Snuffy Smith	450.00
20 Tiny Tim	350.00
21 Dick Tracy	675.00
22 Don Winslow	350.00
23 Gang Busters	300.00
24 Captain Easy	450.00
25 Popeye	750.00

[Second Series]

1 Little Joe	500.00
2 Harold Teen	300.00
3 Alley Oop	500.00
4 Smilin' Jack	475.00
5 Raggedy Ann and Andy	550.00
6 Smitty	250.00
7 Smokey Stover	350.00
8 Tillie the Toiler	250.00
9 Donald Duck finds Pirate Gold!	8,500.00
10 Flash Gordon	850.00
11 Wash Tubs	350.00
12 Bambi	600.00
13 Mr. District Attorney	350.00
14 Smilin' Jack	400.00
15 Felix the Cat	750.00
16 Porky Pig	850.00
17 Popeye	600.00
18 Little Orphan Annie's Junior Commandos	450.00
19 W.Disney's Thumper meets the Seven Dwarfs	600.00
20 Barney Baxter	275.00
21 Oswald the Rabbit	550.00
22 Tillie the Toiler	225.00

23 Raggedy Ann and Andy	400.00
24 Gang Busters	300.00
25 Andy Panda	500.00
26 Popeye	600.00
27 Mickey Mouse and the Seven Colored Terror	1,000.00
28 Wash Tubbs	250.00
29 CB,Donald Duck and the Mummy's Ring	7,000.00
30 Bambi's Children	600.00
31 Moon Mullins	200.00
32 Smitty	175.00
33 Bugs Bunny	1,200.00
34 Dick Tracy	475.00
35 Smokey Stover	175.00
36 Smilin' Jack	250.00
37 Bringing Up Father	200.00
38 Roy Rogers	2,200.00
39 Oswald the Rabbit	400.00
40 Barney Google and Snuffy Smith	250.00
41 WK,Mother Goose	250.00
42 Tiny Tim	175.00
43 Popeye	350.00
44 Terry and the Pirates	450.00
45 Raggedy Ann	350.00
46 Felix the Cat and the Haunted House	450.00
47 Gene Autry	450.00
48 CB,Porky Pig o/t Mounties	1,100.00
49 W.Disney's Snow White and the Seven Dwarfs	700.00
50 WK,Fairy Tale Parade	325.00
51 Bugs Bunny Finds the Lost Treasure	400.00
52 Little Orphan Annie	350.00
53 Wash Tubbs	150.00
54 Andy Panda	300.00
55 Tillie the Toiler	125.00
56 Dick Tracy	350.00
57 Gene Autry	375.00
58 Smilin' Jack	250.00
59 WK,Mother Goose	200.00
60 Tiny Folks Funnies	150.00
61 Santa Claus Funnies	250.00
62 CB,Donald Duck in Frozen Gold	2,300.00
63 Roy Rogers-photo cover	600.00
64 Smokey Stover	150.00
65 Smitty	125.00
66 Gene Autry	400.00
67 Oswald the Rabbit	200.00
68 WK,Mother Goose	225.00
69 WK,Fairy Tale Parade	275.00
70 Popeye and Wimpy	300.00

Four Color #10
© Dell Publishing Co.

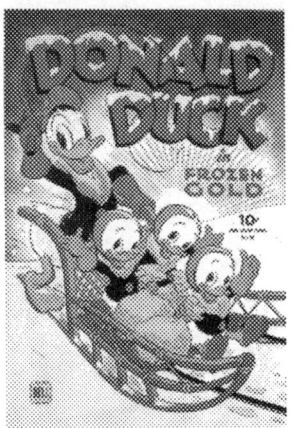

Four Color #62
© Dell Publishing Co.

71 WK,Walt Disney's
   Three Caballeros 850.00
72 Raggedy Ann. 250.00
73 The Grumps 125.00
74 Marge's Little Lulu. 1,000.00
75 Gene Autry and the Wildcat . . 300.00
76 Little Orphan Annie 275.00
77 Felix the Cat 450.00
78 Porky Pig & the Bandit Twins. 275.00
79 Mickey Mouse in the Riddle
   of the Red Hat. 1,200.00
80 Smilin' Jack 175.00
81 Moon Mullins 125.00
82 Lone Ranger 450.00
83 Gene Autry in Outlaw Trail . . . 325.00
84 Flash Gordon. 450.00
85 Andy Panda and the
   Mad Dog Mystery 175.00
86 Roy Rogers-photo cover 400.00
87 WK,Fairy Tale Parade 275.00
88 Bugs Bunny. 250.00
89 Tillie the Toiler 150.00
90 WK,Christmas with
   Mother Goose 200.00
91 WK,Santa Claus Funnies. . . . 200.00
92 WK,W.Disney's Pinocchio . . . 700.00
93 Gene Autry 250.00
94 Winnie Winkle 125.00
95 Roy Rogers,Ph(c) 400.00
96 Dick Tracy 275.00
97 Marge's Little Lulu 500.00
98 Lone Ranger 325.00
99 Smitty 100.00
100 Gene Autry Comics-photo
    cover 275.00
101 Terry and the Pirates 300.00
102 WK,Oswald the Rabbit. 175.00
103 WK,Easter with
    Mother Goose 200.00
104 WK,Fairy Tale Parade 225.00
105 WK,Albert the Aligator 700.00
106 Tillie the Toiler 100.00
107 Little Orphan Annie 250.00
108 Donald Duck in the
    Terror of the River 1,600.00
109 Roy Rogers Comics. 300.00
110 Marge's Little Lulu 350.00
111 Captain Easy 150.00
112 Porky Pig's Adventure in
    Gopher Gulch. 150.00
113 Popeye 150.00
114 WK,Fairy Tale Parade 200.00
115 Marge's Little Lulu 350.00
116 Mickey Mouse and the
    House of Many Mysteries . . . 275.00

117 Roy Rogers Comics,
    Ph(c) 250.00
118 Lone Ranger 325.00
119 Felix the Cat 300.00
120 Marge's Little Lulu 300.00
121 Fairy Tale Parade. 100.00
122 Henry. 125.00
123 Bugs Bunny's Dangerous
    Venture 165.00
124 Roy Rogers Comics,Ph(c) . . 250.00
125 Lone Ranger 225.00
126 WK,Christmas with
    Mother Goose 175.00
127 Popeye 150.00
128 WK,Santa Claus Funnies. . . 150.00
129 W.Disney's Uncle Remus
    & his tales of Brer Rabbit . . . 300.00
130 Andy Panda 100.00
131 Marge's Little Lulu 300.00
132 Tillie the Toiler 100.00
133 Dick Tracy 250.00
134 Tarzan and the Devil Ogre . . 650.00
135 Felix the Cat 250.00
136 Lone Ranger 225.00
137 Roy Rogers Comics. 250.00
138 Smitty 75.00
139 Marge's Little Lulu 275.00
140 WK,Easter with
    Mother Goose 175.00
141 Mickey Mouse and the
    Submarine Pirates 250.00
142 Bugs Bunny and the
    Haunted Mountain 175.00
143 Oswald the Rabbit & the
    Prehistoric Egg. 100.00
144 Poy Rogers Comics,Ph(c) . . 250.00
145 Popeye 150.00
146 Marge's Little Lulu 275.00
147 W.Disney's Donald Duck
    in Volcano Valley 1,100.00
148 WK,Albert the Aligator
    and Pogo Possum 650.00
149 Smilin' Jack 125.00
150 Tillie the Toiler 100.00
151 Lone Ranger 200.00
152 Little Orphan Annie 150.00
153 Roy Rogers Comics. 200.00
154 Andy Panda. 100.00
155 Henry 75.00
156 Porky Pig and the Phantom . 100.00
157 W.Disney's Mickey Mouse
    and the Beanstalk. 250.00
158 Marge's Little Lulu 275.00
159 CB,W.Disney's Donald Duck
    in the Ghost of the Grotto . . . 900.00
160 Roy Rogers Comics,Ph(c) . . 175.00
161 Tarzan & the Fires of Tohr . . 600.00
162 Felix the Cat 175.00
163 Dick Tracy 175.00
164 Bugs Bunny Finds the
    Frozen Kingdom. 175.00
165 Marge's Little Lulu 275.00
166 Roy Rogers Comics,Ph(c) . . 200.00
167 Lone Ranger 175.00
168 Popeye 150.00
169 Woody Woodpecker,Drug. . . 165.00
170 W.Disney's Mickey Mouse
    on Spook's Island. 200.00
171 Charlie McCarthy 250.00
172 WK,Christmas with
    Mother Goose 150.00
173 Flash Gordon. 150.00
174 Winnie Winkle 75.00
175 WK,Santa Claus Funnies. . . 150.00
176 Tillie the Toiler 75.00
177 Roy Rogers Comics,Ph(c) . . 175.00
178 CB,W.Disney's Donald
    Duck Christmas on Bear
    Mountain. 1,400.00
179 WK,Uncle Wiggily 150.00
180 Ozark the Ike 85.00

Four Color #167
© Dell Publishing Co.

181 W.Disney's Mickey Mouse
    in Jungle Magic 200.00
182 Porky Pig in Never-
    Never Land 125.00
183 Oswald the Rabbit 75.00
184 Tillie the Toiler 75.00
185 WK,Easter with
    Mother Goose 150.00
186 W.Disney's Bambi 175.00
187 Bugs Bunny and the
    Dreadful Bunny 125.00
188 Woody Woodpecker. 125.00
189 W.Disney's Donald Duck in
    The Old Castle's Secret 800.00
190 Flash Gordon 150.00
191 Porky Pig to the Rescue. . . . 125.00
192 WK,The Brownies 135.00
193 Tom and Jerry 150.00
194 W.Disney's Mickey Mouse
    in the World Under the Sea. . 200.00
195 Tillie the Toiler 50.00
196 Charlie McCarthy in The
    Haunted Hide-Out. 175.00
197 Spirit of the Border. 125.00
198 Andy Panda. 100.00
199 W.Disney's Donald Duck in
    Sheriff of Bullet Valley. 900.00
200 Bugs Bunny, Super Sleuth . 125.00
201 WK,Christmas with
    Mother Goose 125.00
202 Woody Woodpecker. 75.00
203 CB,W.Disney's Donald Duck in
    The Golden Christmas Tree . 650.00
204 Flash Gordon. 100.00
205 WK,Santa Claus Funnies. . . 150.00
206 Little Orphan Funnies. 75.00
207 King of the Royal Mounted. . 175.00
208 W.Disney's Brer Rabbit
    Does It Again 125.00
209 Harold Teen 50.00
210 Tippe and Cap Stubbs 45.00
211 Little Beaver. 60.00
212 Dr. Bobbs 40.00
213 Tillie the Toiler 50.00
214 W.Disney's Mickey Mouse
    and his Sky Adventure 175.00
215 Sparkle Plenty 100.00
216 Andy Panda and the
    Police Pup 75.00
217 Bugs Bunny in Court Jester . 125.00
218 W.Disney's 3 Little Pigs 150.00
219 Swee'pea. 120.00
220 WK,Easter with
    Mother Goose 150.00
221 WK,Uncle Wiggly 125.00

GOLDEN AGE

222 West of the Pecos 75.00
223 CB,W.Disney's Donald Duck in
    Lost in the Andes 850.00
224 Little Iodine 75.00
225 Oswald the Rabbit 50.00
226 Porky Pig and Spoofy 75.00
227 W.Disney's Seven Dwarfs . . 125.00
228 The Mark of Zorro 250.00
229 Smokey Stover 50.00
230 Sunset Press 60.00
231 W.Disney's Mickey Mouse
    and the Rajah's Treasure . . . 150.00
232 Woody Woodpecker 75.00
233 Bugs Bunny 125.00
234 W.Disney's Dumbo in Sky
    Voyage 125.00
235 Tiny Tim 45.00
236 Heritage of the Desert 75.00
237 Tillie the Toiler 50.00
238 CB,W.Disney's Donald Duck
    in Voodoo Hoodoo 600.00
239 Adventure Bound 50.00
240 Andy Panda 60.00
241 Porky Pig 75.00
242 Tippie and Cap Stubbs 35.00
243 W.Disney's Thumper
    Follows His Nose 125.00
244 WK,The Brownies 125.00
245 Dick's Adventures in
    Dreamland 40.00
246 Thunder Mountain 45.00
247 Flash Gordon 125.00
248 W.Disney's Mickey Mouse
    and the Black Sorcerer 150.00
249 Woody Woodpecker 65.00
250 Bugs Bunny in
    Diamond Daze 135.00
251 Hubert at Camp Moonbeam . . 50.00
252 W.Disney's Pinocchio 125.00
253 WK,Christmas with
    Mother Goose 140.00
254 WK,Santa Claus Funnies,
    A:Pogo 140.00
255 The Ranger 45.00
256 CB,W.Disney's Donald Duck in
    Luck of the North 450.00
257 Little Iodine 50.00
258 Andy Panda and the
    Ballon Race 75.00
259 Santa and the Angel 50.00
260 Porky Pig, Hero of the
    Wild West 75.00
261 W.Disney's Mickey Mouse
    and the Missing Key 150.00
262 Raggedy Ann and Andy 60.00
263 CB,W.Disney's Donald Duck in
    Land of the Totem Poles 450.00
264 Woody Woodpecker in
    the Magic Lantern 60.00
265 King of the Royal Mountain . . 85.00
266 Bugs Bunny on the Isle of
    Hercules 125.00
267 Little Beaver 40.00
268 W.Disney's Mickey Mouse's
    Surprise Visitor 150.00
269 Johnny Mack Brown,Ph(c) . . 200.00
270 Drift Fence 40.00
271 Porky Pig 75.00
272 W.Disney's Cinderella 125.00
273 Oswald the Rabbit 45.00
274 Bugs Bunny 125.00
275 CB,W.Disney's Donald Duck
    in Ancient Persia 425.00
276 Uncle Wiggly 75.00
277 PorkyPig in DesertAdventure . 75.00
278 Bill Elliot Comics,Ph(c) 150.00
279 W.Disney's Mickey Mouse &
    Pluto Battle the Giant Ants . . 125.00
280 Andy Panda in the Isle
    of the Mechanical Men 60.00
281 Bugs Bunny in The Great

Circus Mystery 125.00
282 CB,W.Disney's Donald Duck in
    The Pixilated Parrot 450.00
283 King of the Royal Mounted . . 100.00
284 Porky Pig in the Kingdom
    of Nowhere 75.00
285 Bozo the Clown 200.00
286 W.Disney's Mickey Mouse
    and the Uninvited Guest 125.00
287 Gene Autry's Champion in the
    Ghost of BlackMountain,Ph(c)100.00
288 Woody Woodpecker 75.00
289 BugsBunny in IndianTrouble . 120.00
290 The Chief 50.00
291 CB,W.Disney's Donald Duck in
    The Magic Hourglass 450.00
292 The Cisco Kid Comics 150.00
293 WK,The Brownies 125.00
294 Little Beaver 45.00
295 Porky Pig in President Pig . . . 75.00
296 W.Disney's Mickey Mouse
    Private Eye for Hire 125.00
297 Andy Panda in The
    Haunted Inn 50.00
298 Bugs Bunny in Sheik
    for a Day 125.00
299 Buck Jones & the Iron Trail . 175.00
300 CB,W.Disney's Donald Duck in
    Big-Top Bedlam 450.00
301 The Mysterious Rider 40.00
302 Santa Claus Funnies 35.00
303 Porky Pig in The Land of
    the Monstrous Flies 65.00
304 W.Disney's Mickey Mouse
    in Tom-Tom Island 100.00
305 Woody Woodpecker 30.00
306 Raggedy Ann 35.00
307 Bugs Bunny in Lumber
    Jack Rabbit 85.00
308 CB,W.Disney's Donald Duck in
    Dangerous Disguise 375.00
309 Dollface and Her Gang 40.00
310 King of the Rotal Mounted . . 55.00
311 Porky Pig in Midget Horses
    of Hidden Valley 55.00
312 Tonto 150.00
313 W.Disney's Mickey Mouse in
    the Mystery of the Double-
    Cross Ranch 125.00
314 Ambush 40.00
315 Oswald Rabbit 30.00
316 Rex Allen,Ph(c) 150.00
317 Bugs Bunny in Hare Today
    Gone Tomorrow 75.00
318 CB,W.Disney's Donald Duck in
    No Such Varmint 375.00

Four Color #355
© Dell Publishing Co.

319 Gene Autry's Champion 40.00
320 Uncle Wiggly 60.00
321 Little Scouts 30.00
322 Porky Pig in Roaring Rockies . 50.00
323 Susie Q. Smith 30.00
324 I Met a Handsome Cowboy . . 75.00
325 W.Disney's Mickey Mouse
    in the Haunted Castle 125.00
326 Andy Panda 35.00
327 Bugs Bunny and the
    Rajah's Treasure 100.00
328 CB,W.Disney's Donald Duck
    in Old California 400.00
329 Roy Roger's Trigger,Ph(c) . . 150.00
330 Porky Pig meets the
    Bristled Bruiser 50.00
331 Disney's Alice in
    Wonderland 150.00
332 Little Beaver 35.00
333 Wilderness Trek 40.00
334 W.Disney's Mickey Mouse
    and Yukon Gold 120.00
335 Francis the Famous
    Talking Mule 75.00
336 Woody Woodpecker 35.00
337 The Brownies 35.00
338 Bugs Bunny and the
    Rocking Horse Thieves 90.00
339 W.Disney's Donald Duck
    and the Magic Fountain 100.00
340 King of the Royal Mountain . . 65.00
341 W.Disney's Unbirthday Party
    with Alice in Wonderland 150.00
342 Porky Pig the Lucky
    Peppermint Mine 45.00
343 W.Disney's Mickey Mouse in
    Ruby Eye of Homar-Guy-Am 100.00
344 Sergeant Preston from
    Challenge of the Yukon 125.00
345 Andy Panda in Scotland Yard . 35.00
346 Hideout 40.00
347 Bugs Bunny the Frigid Hare . . 75.00
348 CB,W.Disney's Donald Duck
    The Crocodile Collector 250.00
349 Uncle Wiggly 60.00
350 Woody Woodpecker 35.00
351 Porky Pig and the Grand
    Canyon Giant 50.00
352 W.Disney's Mickey Mouse
    Mystery of Painted Valley 85.00
353 CB(c),W.Disney'sDuckAlbum 100.00
354 Raggedy Ann & Andy 45.00
355 Bugs Bunny Hot-Rod Hair . . . 75.00
356 CB(c),W.Disney's Donald
    Duck in Rags to Riches 250.00
357 Comeback 35.00
358 Andy Panada 35.00
359 Frosty the Snowman 60.00
360 Porky Pig in Tree Fortune . . . 45.00
361 Santa Claus Funnies 35.00
362 W.Disney's Mickey Mouse &
    the Smuggled Diamonds 100.00
363 King of the Royal Mounted . . . 60.00
364 Woody Woodpecker 35.00
365 The Brownies 30.00
366 Bugs Bunny Uncle
    Buckskin Comes to Town 75.00
367 CB,W.Disney's Donald Duck in
    A Christmas for Shacktown . . 375.00
368 Bob Clampett's
    Beany and Cecil 300.00
369 Lone Ranger's Famous
    Horse Hi-Yo Silver 75.00
370 Porky Pig in Trouble
    in the Big Trees 45.00
371 W.Disney's Mickey Mouse
    the Inca Idol Case 85.00
372 Riders of the Purple Sage . . . 30.00
373 Sergeant Preston 75.00
374 Woody Woodpecker 30.00
375 John Carter of Mars 275.00

376 Bugs Bunny 75.00
377 Susie Q. Smith 30.00
378 Tom Corbett, Space Cadet . . 200.00
379 W.Disney's Donald Duck in
     Southern Hospitality 100.00
380 Raggedy Ann & Andy 40.00
381 Marge's Tubby 150.00
382 W.Disney's Show White and
     the Seven Dwarfs 150.00
383 Andy Panda 25.00
384 King of the Royal Mounted . . . 50.00
385 Porky Pig 45.00
386 CB,W.Disney's Uncle Scrooge
     in Only A Poor Old Man . . . 1,000.00
387 W.Disney's Mickey Mouse
     in High Tibet 85.00
388 Oswald the Rabbit 45.00
389 Andy Hardy Comics 30.00
390 Woody Woodpecker 35.00
391 Uncle Wiggly 60.00
392 Hi-Yo Silver 50.00
393 Bugs Bunny 75.00
394 CB(c),W.Disney's Donald Duck
     in Malayalaya 250.00
395 Forlorn River 35.00
396 Tales of the Texas Rangers,
     Ph(c) 100.00
397 Sergeant Preston o/t Yukon . . 75.00
398 The Brownies 30.00
399 Porky Pig in the Lost
     Gold Mine 45.00
400 AMc,Tom Corbett 125.00
401 W.Disney's Mickey Mouse &
     Goofy's Mechanical Wizard . . . 75.00
402 Mary Jane and Sniffles 75.00
403 W.Disney's Li'l Bad Wolf 100.00
404 The Ranger Rider,Ph(c) 100.00
405 Woody Woodpecker 30.00
406 Tweety and Sylvester 75.00
407 Bugs Bunny, Foreign-
     Legion Hare 65.00
408 CB,W.Disney's Donald Duck
     and the Golden Helmet 400.00
409 Andy Panda 25.00
410 Porky Pig in the
     Water Wizard 40.00
411 W.Disney's Mickey Mouse
     and the Old Sea Dog 75.00
412 Nevada 35.00
413 Disney's Robin Hood(movie),
     Ph(c) 125.00
414 Bob Clampett's Beany
     and Cecil 175.00
415 Rootie Kazootie 125.00
416 Woody Woodpecker 30.00
417 Double Trouble with Goober . . 25.00
418 Rusty Riley 40.00
419 Sergeant Preston 75.00
420 Bugs Bunny 65.00
421 AMc,Tom Corbett 125.00
422 CB,W.Disney's Donald Duck
     and the Gilded Man 375.00
423 Rhubarb 30.00
424 Flash Gordon 150.00
425 Zorro 140.00
426 Porky Pig 35.00
427 W.Disney's Mickey Mouse &
     the Wonderful Whizzix 65.00
428 Uncle Wiggily 35.00
429 W.Disney's Pluto in
     Why Dogs Leave Home 100.00
430 Marge's Tubby 100.00
431 Woody Woodpecker 30.00
432 Bugs Bunny and the
     Rabbit Olympics 60.00
433 Wildfire 35.00
434 Rin Tin Tin,Ph(c) 165.00
435 Frosty the Snowman 35.00
436 The Brownies 30.00
437 John Carter of Mars 175.00
438 W.Disney's Annie

Oakley (TV) 150.00
439 Little Hiawatha 50.00
440 Black Beauty 30.00
441 Fearless Fagan 25.00
442 W.Disney's Peter Pan 100.00
443 Ben Bowie and His
     Mountain Men 50.00
444 Marge's Tubby 75.00
445 Charlie McCarthy 40.00
446 Captain Hook and Peter Pan 100.00
447 Andy Hardy Comics 25.00
448 Beany and Cecil 175.00
449 Tappan's Burro 35.00
450 CB(c),W.Disney's DuckAlbum 75.00
451 Rusty Riley 30.00
452 Raggedy Ann and Andy 40.00
453 Susie Q. Smith 30.00
454 Krazy Kat Comics 35.00
455 Johnny Mack Brown Comics,
     Ph(c) 50.00
456 W.Disney's Uncle Scrooge
     Back to the Klondike 650.00
457 Daffy 75.00
458 Oswald the Rabbit 35.00
459 Rootie Kazootie 75.00
460 Buck Jones 75.00
461 Marge's Tubby 75.00
462 Little Scouts 15.00
463 Petunia 30.00
464 Bozo 100.00
465 Francis the Talking Mule 50.00
466 Rhubarb, the Millionaire Cat . . 30.00
467 Desert Gold 30.00
468 W.Disney's Goofy 125.00
469 Beetle Bailey 110.00
470 Elmer Fudd 35.00
471 Double Trouble with Goober . . 20.00
472 Wild Bill Elliot,Ph(c) 55.00
473 W.Disney's Li'l Bad Wolf 65.00
474 Mary Jane and Sniffles 70.00
475 M.G.M.'s the Two
     Mouseketeers 75.00
476 Rin Tin Tin,Ph(c) 60.00
477 Bob Clampett's Beany and
     Cecil 150.00
478 Charlie McCarthy 40.00
479 Queen o/t West Dale Evans . 150.00
480 Andy Hardy Comics 25.00
481 Annie Oakley and Tagg 65.00
482 Brownies 30.00
483 Little Beaver 30.00
484 River Feud 30.00
485 The Little People 40.00
486 Rusty Riley 35.00
487 Mowgli, the Jungle Book 35.00
488 John Carter of Mars 175.00
489 Tweety and Sylvester 30.00
490 Jungle Jim 50.00
491 EK,Silvertip 75.00
492 W.Disney's Duck Album 65.00
493 Johnny Mack Brown,Ph(c) . . . 45.00
494 The Little King 125.00
495 CB, W.Disney's Uncle
     Scrooge 500.00
496 The Green Hornet 275.00
497 Zorro, (Sword of) 150.00
498 Bugs Bunny's Album 45.00
499 M.G.M.'s Spike and Tyke 25.00
500 Buck Jones 65.00
501 Francis the Famous
     Talking Mule 35.00
502 Rootie Kazootie 60.00
503 Uncle Wiggily 40.00
504 Krazy Kat 35.00
505 W.Disney's the Sword and
     the Rose (TV),Ph(c) 100.00
506 The Little Scouts 20.00
507 Oswald the Rabbit 25.00
508 Bozo 100.00
509 W.Disney's Pluto 65.00
510 Son of Black Beauty 35.00

Four Color #462
© Dell Publishing Co.

511 EK,Outlaw Trail 40.00
512 Flash Gordon 60.00
513 Ben Bowie and His
     Mountain Men 30.00
514 Frosty the Snowman 30.00
515 Andy Hardy 25.00
516 Double Trouble With Goober . 20.00
517 Walt Disney's Chip 'N' Dale . 100.00
518 Rivets 25.00
519 Steve Canyon 100.00
520 Wild Bill Elliot,Ph(c) 50.00
521 Beetle Bailey 40.00
522 The Brownies 25.00
523 Rin Tin Tin,Ph(c) 75.00
524 Tweety and Sylvester 25.00
525 Santa Claus Funnies 30.00
526 Napoleon 20.00
527 Charlie McCarthy 35.00
528 Queen o/t West Dale Evans,
     Ph(c) 75.00
529 Little Beaver 25.00
530 Bob Clampett's Beany
     and Cecil 150.00
531 W.Disney's Duck Album 55.00
532 The Rustlers 35.00
533 Raggedy Ann and Andy 40.00
534 EK,Western Marshal 40.00
535 I Love Lucy,Ph(c) 550.00
536 Daffy 35.00
537 Stormy, the Thoroughbred . . . 25.00
538 EK,The Mask of Zorro 165.00
539 Ben and Me 25.00
540 Knights of the Round Table,
     Ph(c) 75.00
541 Johnny Mack Brown,Ph(c) . . . 50.00
542 Super Circus Featuring
     Mary Hartline 50.00
543 Uncle Wiggly 35.00
544 W.Disney's Rob Roy(Movie),
     Ph(c) 100.00
545 The Wonderful Adventures
     of Pinocchio 100.00
546 Buck Jones 75.00
547 Francis the Famous
     Talking Mule 40.00
548 Krazy Kat 30.00
549 Oswald the Rabbit 25.00
550 The Little Scouts 15.00
551 Bozo 100.00
552 Beetle Bailey 45.00
553 Susie Q. Smith 30.00
554 Rusty Riley 30.00
555 Range War 30.00
556 Double Trouble with Goober . . 20.00
557 Ben Bowie and His

All comics prices listed are for *Near Mint* condition.

Mountain Men 30.00	
558 Elmer Fudd 30.00	
559 I Love Lucy,Ph(c) 400.00	
560 W.Disney's Duck Album 60.00	
561 Mr. Magoo 125.00	
562 W.Disney's Goofy 85.00	
563 Rhubarb, the Millionaire Cat. . 30.00	
564 W.Disney's Li'l Bad Wolf. . . . 60.00	
565 Jungle Jim 30.00	
566 Son of Black Beauty 30.00	
567 BF,Prince Valiant,Ph(c). . . . 125.00	

629 Lady & The Tramp with Jock . 75.00
630 Priscilla's Pop 30.00

the River Pirates(TV),Ph(c). . 125.00
672 Quentin Durward,Ph(c) 60.00

Four Color #711
© Dell Publishing Co.

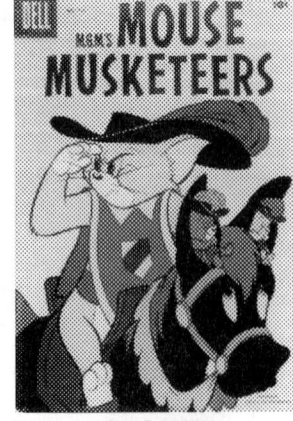

738 Westward Ho, the Wagons,
    Ph(c) 90.00
739 MD,Bounty Guns 30.00
740 Chilly Willy 30.00
741 The Fastest Gun Alive,Ph(c) . 60.00
742 Buffalo Bill Jr.,Ph(c) 55.00
743 Daisy Duck's Diary. 45.00
744 Little Beaver 25.00
745 Francis the Famous
    Talking Mule 30.00
746 Dotty Dripple and Taffy. 25.00
747 Goofy 90.00
748 Frosty the Snowman 30.00
749 Secrets of Life,Ph(c) 50.00
750 The Great Cat 50.00
751 Our Miss Brooks,Ph(c). 75.00
752 Mandrake, the Magician. . . . 125.00
753 Walt Scott's Little People 30.00
754 Smokey the Bear. 60.00
755 The Littlest Snowman 30.00
756 Santa Claus Funnies 30.00
757 The True Story of
    Jesse James,Ph(c). 90.00
758 Bear Country 45.00
759 Circus Boy,Ph(c) 100.00
760 W.Disney's Hardy Boys(TV) . 125.00
761 Howdy Doody 125.00
762 SB,The Sharkfighters,Ph(c) . 100.00
763 GrandmaDuck'sFarmFriends . 75.00
764 M.G.M.'s Mouse Musketeers . 20.00
765 Will-Yum! 20.00
766 Buffalo Bill,Ph(c) 35.00
767 Spin and Marty 75.00
768 EK,Steve Donovan, Western
    Marshal,Ph(c). 45.00
769 Gunsmoke. 75.00
770 Brave Eagle,Ph(c) 30.00
771 MD,Brand of Empire 30.00
772 Cheyenne,C.Walker Ph(c) . . 65.00
773 The Brave One,Ph(c). 35.00
774 Hi and Lois 25.00
775 SB,Sir Lancelot and
    Brian,Ph(c). 85.00
776 Johnny Mack Brown,Ph(c) . . 40.00
777 Scamp. 75.00
778 The Little Rascals 50.00
779 Lee Hunter, Indian Fighter . . 40.00
780 Captain Kangaroo,Ph(c). . . . 150.00
781 Fury,Ph(c) 50.00
782 Duck Album. 50.00
783 Elmer Fudd 20.00
784 Around the World in 80
    Days,Ph(c) 75.00
785 Circus Boys,Ph(c) 100.00
786 Cinderella 50.00
787 Little Hiawatha. 40.00
788 BF,Prince Valiant 75.00
789 EK,Silvertip-Valley Thieves. . 45.00
790 ATh,The Wings of Eagles,
    J.Wayne Ph(c) 175.00
791 The 77th Bengal Lancers,
    Ph(c) 65.00
792 Oswald the Rabbit 20.00
793 Morty Meekle. 25.00
794 SB,The Count of Monte
    Cristo 85.00
795 Jiminy Cricket 65.00
796 Ludwig Bemelman's
    Madeleine and Genevieve . . 35.00
797 Gunsmoke,Ph(c) 75.00
798 Buffalo Bill,Ph(c) 40.00
799 Priscilla's Pop 30.00
800 The Buccaneers,Ph(c) 50.00
801 Dotty Dripple and Taffy 25.00
802 Goofy 75.00
803 Cheyenne,C.Walker Ph(c) . . . 60.00
804 Steve Canyon 50.00
805 Crusader Rabbit 250.00
806 Scamp. 65.00
807 MB,Savage Range 30.00
808 Spin and Marty,Ph(c) 75.00

Four Color #938
© Dell Publishing Co.

809 The Little People 30.00
810 Francis the Famous
    Talking Mule 25.00
811 Howdy Doody 100.00
812 The Big Land,A.Ladd Ph(c) . 100.00
813 Circus Boy,Ph(c) 100.00
814 Covered Wagon,A:Mickey
    Mouse 80.00
815 Dragoon Wells Massacre 75.00
816 Brave Eagle,Ph(c) 30.00
817 Little Beaver 25.00
818 Smokey the Bear. 60.00
819 Mickey Mouse in Magicland . . 45.00
820 The Oklahoman,Ph(c) 120.00
821 Wringle Wrangle,Ph(c). 75.00
822 ATh,W.Disney's Paul Revere's
    Ride (TV) 125.00
823 Timmy 25.00
824 The Pride and the Passion,
    Ph(c) 100.00
825 The Little Rascals 50.00
826 Spin and Marty and Annette,
    Ph(c) 150.00
827 Smokey Stover 30.00
828 Buffalo Bill, Jr,Ph(c). 35.00
829 Tales of the Pony Express,
    Ph(c) 40.00
830 The Hardy Boys,Ph(c) 100.00
831 No Sleep 'Til Dawn,Ph(c). . . . 60.00
832 Lolly and Pepper 30.00
833 Scamp. 75.00
834 Johnny Mack Brown,Ph(c) . . 50.00
835 Silvertip- The Fake Rider 40.00
836 Man in Fight. 75.00
837 All-American Athlete
    Cotton Woods 40.00
838 Bugs Bunny's Life
    Story Album 60.00
839 The Vigilantes 50.00
840 Duck Album. 55.00
841 Elmer Fudd 20.00
842 The Nature of Things 70.00
843 The First Americans. 85.00
844 Gunsmoke,Ph(c) 100.00
845 ATh,The Land Unknown. . . . 150.00
846 ATh,Gun Glory 125.00
847 Perri 65.00
848 Marauder's Moon 40.00
849 BF,Prince Valiant 75.00
850 Buck Jones 30.00
851 The Story of Mankind,
    V.Price Ph(c) 60.00
852 Chilly Willy 30.00
853 Pluto 50.00
854 Hunchback of Notre Dame,

    Ph(c) 125.00
855 Broken Arrow,Ph(c) 45.00
856 Buffalo Bill, Jr.,Ph(c). 40.00
857 The Goofy Adventure Story . . 75.00
858 Daisy Duck's Diary. 50.00
859 Topper and Neil 30.00
860 Wyatt Earp,Ph(c) 100.00
861 Frosty the Snowman 30.00
862 Truth About Mother Goose. . . 65.00
863 Francis the Famous
    Talking Mule. 30.00
864 The Littlest Snowman 30.00
865 Andy Burnett,Ph(c). 75.00
866 Mars and Beyond. 100.00
867 Santa Claus Funnies 30.00
868 The Little People 30.00
869 Old Yeller,Ph(c) 75.00
870 Little Beaver 25.00
871 Curly Kayoe. 25.00
872 Captain Kangaroo,Ph(c). . . . 150.00
873 Grandma Duck's
    Farm Friends 50.00
874 Old Ironsides 60.00
875 Trumpets West 30.00
876 Tales of Wells Fargo,Ph(c) . . . 75.00
877 ATh,Frontier Doctor,Ph(c). . . 100.00
878 Peanuts. 150.00
879 Brave Eagle,Ph(c) 30.00
880 MD,Steve Donovan,Ph(c). . . . 40.00
881 The Captain and the Kids. . . . 25.00
882 ATh,W.DisneyPresentsZorro 200.00
883 The Little Rascals 50.00
884 Hawkeye and the Last
    of the Mohicans,Ph(c). 75.00
885 Fury,Ph(c) 60.00
886 Bongo and Lumpjaw 30.00
887 The Hardy Boys,Ph(c) 75.00
888 Elmer Fudd 20.00
889 ATh,W.Disney's Clint
    & Mac(TV),Ph(c). 100.00
890 Wyatt Earp,Ph(c) 60.00
891 Light in the Forest,
    C.Parker Ph(c) 75.00
892 Maverick,J.Garner Ph(c) . . . 300.00
893 Jim Bowie,Ph(c). 50.00
894 Oswald the Rabbit 20.00
895 Wagon Train,Ph(c). 150.00
896 Adventures of Tinker Bell 60.00
897 Jiminy Cricket 50.00
898 EK,Silvertip 45.00
899 Goofy 60.00
900 BF,Prince Valiant 75.00
901 Little Hiawatha 60.00
902 Will-Yum! 25.00
903 Dotty Dripple and Taffy. 25.00
904 Lee Hunter, Indian Fighter . . . 30.00
905 W.Disney's Annette (TV),
    Ph(c) 300.00
906 Francis the Famous
    Talking Mule. 30.00
907 Ath,Sugarfoot,Ph(c) 150.00
908 The Little People
    and the Giant 30.00
909 Smitty 25.00
910 ATh,The Vikings,
    K.Douglas Ph(c) 100.00
911 The Gray Ghost,Ph(c) 100.00
912 Leave it to Beaver,Ph(c). . . . 200.00
913 The Left-Handed Gun,
    Paul Newman Ph(c) 100.00
914 ATh,No Time for Sergeants,
    Ph(c) 125.00
915 Casey Jones,Ph(c). 50.00
916 Red Ryder Ranch Comics . . . 25.00
917 The Life of Riley,Ph(c) 125.00
918 Beep Beep, the Roadrunner. 100.00
919 Boots and Saddles,Ph(c) 75.00
920 Ath,Zorro,Ph(c) 150.00
921 Wyatt Earp.Ph(c) 60.00
922 Johnny Mack Brown,Ph(c) . . 50.00
923 Timmy 20.00

924 Colt .45,Ph(c). 75.00
925 Last of the Fast Guns,Ph(c) . . 60.00
926 Peter Pan 35.00
927 SB,Top Gun. 30.00
928 Sea Hunt,L.Bridges Ph(c). . . 125.00
929 Brave Eagle,Ph(c) 30.00
930 Maverick,J. Garner Ph(c) . . 125.00
931 Have Gun, Will Travel,Ph(c) . 150.00
932 Smokey the Bear. 60.00
933 ATh,W.Disney's Zorro. 150.00
934 Restless Gun 100.00
935 King of the Royal Mounted. . . 30.00
936 The Little Rascals 50.00
937 Ruff and Ready 125.00
938 Elmer Fudd 20.00
939 Steve Canyon 60.00
940 Lolly and Pepper 25.00
941 Pluto 40.00
942 Pony Express 40.00
943 White Wilderness. 60.00
944 SB,7th Voyage of Sinbad . . . 150.00
945 Maverick,J.Garner Ph(c) . . . 125.00
946 The Big Country,Ph(c) 60.00
947 Broken Arrow,Ph(c) 40.00
948 Daisy Duck's Diary 50.00
949 High Adventure,Ph(c). 45.00
950 Frosty the Snowman 30.00
951 ATh,Lennon Sisters
    Life Story,Ph(c). 150.00
952 Goofy 60.00
953 Francis the Famous
    Talking Mule. 30.00
954 Man in Space 75.00
955 Hi and Lois 25.00
956 Ricky Nelson,Ph(c) 225.00
957 Buffalo Bee 75.00
958 Santa Claus Funnies 30.00
959 Christmas Stories 30.00
960 ATh,W.Disney's Zorro. 150.00
961 Jace Pearson's Tales of
    Texas Rangers,Ph(c). 40.00
962 Maverick,J.Garner Ph(c) . . . 125.00
963 Johnny Mack Brown,Ph(c) . . . 40.00
964 The Hardy Boys,Ph(c). 85.00
965 GrandmaDuck'sFarmFriends . 55.00
966 Tonka,Ph(c). 75.00
967 Chilly Willy. 25.00
968 Tales of Wells Fargo,Ph(c) . . . 75.00
969 Peanuts 125.00
970 Lawman,Ph(c). 125.00
971 Wagon Train,Ph(c). 75.00
972 Tom Thumb 85.00
973 SleepingBeauty & the Prince 150.00
974 The Little Rascals 50.00
975 Fury,Ph(c) 50.00
976 ATh,W.Disney's Zorro,Ph(c) . 150.00
977 Elmer Fudd 20.00
978 Lolly and Pepper 20.00
979 Oswald the Rabbit 20.00
980 Maverick,J.Garner Ph(c) . . . 125.00
981 Ruff and Ready 100.00
982 The New Adventures of
    Tinker Bell 65.00
983 Have Gun, Will Travel,Ph(c). 100.00
984 Sleeping Beauty's Fairy
    Godmothers 75.00
985 Shaggy Dog,Ph(c) 75.00
986 Restless Gun,Ph(c) 75.00
987 Goofy 60.00
988 Little Hiawatha. 30.00
989 Jimmy Cricket 50.00
990 Huckleberry Hound 125.00
991 Francis the Famous
    Talking Mule 30.00
992 ATh,Sugarfoot,Ph(c) 100.00
993 Jim Bowie,Ph(c). 50.00
994 Sea HuntL.Bridges Ph(c) . . . 100.00
995 Donald Duck Album 55.00
996 Nevada 30.00
997 Walt Disney Presents,Ph(c) . . 65.00
998 Ricky Nelson,Ph(c) 225.00

999 Leave It To Beaver,Ph(c) . . . 175.00
1000 The Gray Ghost,Ph(c) 100.00
1001 Lowell Thomas' High
    Adventure,Ph(c) 45.00
1002 Buffalo Bee 50.00
1003 ATh,W.Disney's Zorro,Ph(c) 150.00
1004 Colt .45,Ph(c). 60.00
1005 Maverick,J.Garner Ph(c). . . 125.00
1006 SB,Hercules 100.00
1007 John Paul Jones,Ph(c) 45.00
1008 Beep, Beep, the
    Road Runner 50.00
1009 CB,The Rifleman,Ph(c) . . . 250.00
1010 Grandma Duck's Farm
    Friends. 125.00
1011 Buckskin,Ph(c). 75.00
1012 Last Train from Gun
    Hill,Ph(c) 75.00
1013 Bat Masterson,Ph(c) 135.00
1014 ATh,The Lennon Sisters,
    Ph(c) 150.00
1015 Peanuts 100.00
1016 Smokey the Bear 50.00
1017 Chilly Willy 25.00
1018 Rio Bravo,J.Wayne Ph(c) . . 225.00
1019 Wagon Train,Ph(c). 75.00
1020 Jungle 25.00
1021 Jace Pearson's Tales of
    the Texas Rangers,Ph(c) . . . 45.00
1022 Timmy 25.00
1023 Tales of Wells Fargo,Ph(c) . . 75.00
1024 ATh,Darby O'Gill and
    the Little People,Ph(c) 100.00
1025 CB,W.Disney's Vacation in
    Disneyland 225.00
1026 Spin and Marty,Ph(c) 60.00
1027 The Texan,Ph(c) 60.00
1028 Rawhide,
    Clint Eastwood Ph(c) 250.00
1029 Boots and Saddles,Ph(c) . . . 50.00
1030 Spanky and Alfalfa, the
    Little Rascals 50.00
1031 Fury,Ph(c) 60.00
1032 Elmer Fudd 20.00
1033 Steve Canyon,Ph(c). 60.00
1034 Nancy and Sluggo
    Summer Camp. 25.00
1035 Lawman,Ph(c) 75.00
1036 The Big Circus,Ph(c) 60.00
1037 Zorro,Ph(c) 175.00
1038 Ruff and Ready 75.00
1039 Pluto 40.00
1040 Quick Draw McGraw 150.00
1041 ATh,Sea Hunt,
    L.Bridges Ph(c). 100.00
1042 The Three Chipmunks 40.00

Four Color #1013
© Dell Publishing Co.

1043 The Three Stooges,Ph(c) . . 225.00
1044 Have Gun,Will Travel,Ph(c) 100.00
1045 Restless Gun,Ph(c) 75.00
1046 Beep Beep, the
    Road Runner 50.00
1047 CB,W.Disney's
    GyroGearloose 200.00
1048 The Horse Soldiers
    J.Wayne Ph(c) 165.00
1049 Don't Give Up the Ship
    J.Lewis Ph(c) 60.00
1050 Huckleberry Hound 75.00
1051 Donald in Mathmagic Land. 100.00
1052 RsM,Ben-Hur. 125.00
1053 Goofy. 60.00
1054 Huckleberry Hound
    Winter Fun 75.00
1055 CB,Daisy Duck's Diary 125.00
1056 Yellowstone Kelly,
    C.Walker Ph(c) 50.00
1057 Mickey Mouse Album. 40.00
1058 Colt .45,Ph(c). 60.00
1059 Sugarfoot. 75.00
1060 Journey to the Center of the
    Earth, P.Boone Ph(c) 125.00
1061 Buffalo Bill 50.00
1062 Christmas Stories. 35.00
1063 Santa Claus Funnies 35.00
1064 Bugs Bunny's Merry
    Christmas. 55.00
1065 Frosty the Snowman 30.00
1066 ATh,77 Sunset Strip,Ph(c) . 150.00
1067 Yogi Bear. 120.00
1068 Francis the Famous
    Talking Mule 30.00
1069 ATh,The FBI Story,Ph(c). . . 125.00
1070 Soloman and Sheba,Ph(c) . . 75.00
1071 ATh,TheRealMcCoys,Ph(c) 125.00
1072 Blythe 40.00
1073 CB,Grandma Duck's Farm
    Friends. 150.00
1074 Chilly Willy. 25.00
1075 Tales of Wells Fargo,Ph(c) . . 75.00
1076 MSy,The Rebel,Ph(c) 125.00
1077 SB,The Deputy,
    H.Fonda Ph(c) 150.00
1078 The Three Stooges,Ph(c). . . 125.00
1079 The Little Rascals 50.00
1080 Fury,Ph(c) 60.00
1081 Elmer Fudd 20.00
1082 Spin and Marty 60.00
1083 Men into Space,Ph(c). 75.00
1084 Speedy Gonzales. 35.00
1085 ATh,The Time Machine . . . 175.00
1086 Lolly and Pepper 25.00
1087 Peter Gunn,Ph(c). 110.00
1088 A Dog of Flanders,Ph(c). . . . 35.00
1089 Restless Gun,Ph(c) 70.00
1090 Francis the Famous
    Talking Mule 30.00
1091 Jacky's Diary 40.00
1092 Toby Tyler,Ph(c). 50.00
1093 MacKenzie's Raiders,Ph(c) . 60.00
1094 Goofy. 55.00
1095 CB,W.Disney's
    GyroGearloose 125.00
1096 The Texan,Ph(c) 60.00
1097 Rawhide,C.Eastwood Ph(c) 175.00
1098 Sugarfoot,Ph(c) 75.00
1099 CB(c),Donald Duck Album . . 75.00
1100 W.Disney's Annette's
    Life Story (TV),Ph(c). 225.00
1101 Robert Louis Stevenson's
    Kidnapped,Ph(c). 60.00
1102 Wanted: Dead or Alive,
    Ph(c) 150.00
1103 Leave It To Beaver,Ph(c) . . . 175.00
1104 Yogi Bear Goes to College . . 75.00
1105 ATh,Gale Storm,Ph(c) 125.00
1106 ATh,77 Sunset Strip,Ph(c) . 125.00
1107 Buckskin,Ph(c). 60.00

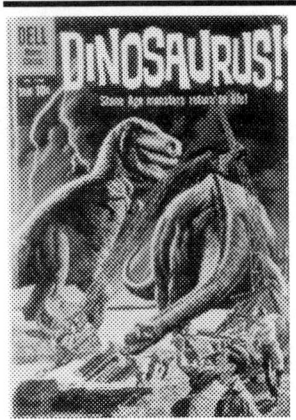

Four Color #1120
© Dell Publishing Co.

1108 The Troubleshooters,Ph(c) . . 50.00
1109 This Is Your Life, Donald
    Duck,O:Donald Duck 175.00
1110 Bonanza,Ph(c) 400.00
1111 Shotgun Slade 50.00
1112 Pixie and Dixie
    and Mr. Jinks 60.00
1113 Tales of Wells Fargo,Ph(c) . . 75.00
1114 Huckleberry Finn,Ph(c) 40.00
1115 Ricky Nelson,Ph(c) 165.00
1116 Boots and Saddles,Ph(c) . . . 50.00
1117 Boy and the Pirate,Ph(c) 50.00
1118 Sword and the Dragon,Ph(c) 60.00
1119 Smokey and the Bear
    Nature Stories 50.00
1120 Dinosaurus,Ph(c) 75.00
1121 RC,GE,HerculesUnchained 120.00
1122 Chilly Willy 25.00
1123 Tombstone Territory,Ph(c). . . 75.00
1124 Whirlybirds,Ph(c) 60.00
1125 GK,RH,Laramie,Ph(c). 125.00
1126 Sundance,Ph(c) 75.00
1127 The Three Stooges,Ph(c) . . 125.00
1128 Rocky and His Friends 425.00
1129 Pollyanna,H.Mills Ph(c) 85.00
1130 SB,The Deputy,
    H.Fonda Ph(c) 125.00
1131 Elmer Fudd 20.00
1132 Space Mouse. 30.00
1133 Fury,Ph(c) 50.00
1134 ATh,Real McCoys,Ph(c) . . . 110.00
1135 M.G.M.'s Mouse Musketeers 60.00
1136 Jungle Cat,Ph(c) 45.00
1137 The Little Rascals 50.00
1138 The Rebel,Ph(c) 100.00
1139 SB,Spartacus,Ph(c) 150.00
1140 Donald Duck Album 65.00
1141 Huckleberry Hound for
    President 75.00
1142 Johnny Ringo,Ph(c) 65.00
1143 Pluto 40.00
1144 The Story of Ruth,Ph(c) . . . 110.00
1145 GK,The Lost World,Ph(c) . . 125.00
1146 Restless Gun,Ph(c) 65.00
1147 Sugarfoot,Ph(c) 75.00
1148 I aim at the Stars,Ph(c) 75.00
1149 Goofy 55.00
1150 CB,Daisy Duck's Diary . . . 125.00
1151 Mickey Mouse Album 40.00
1152 Rocky and His Friends 275.00
1153 Frosty the Snowman 30.00
1154 Santa Claus Funnies 30.00
1155 North to Alaska 175.00
1156 Walt Disney Swiss
    Family Robinson. 65.00
1157 Master of the World 50.00

1158 Three Worlds of Gulliver. . . . 50.00
1159 ATh,77 Sunset Strip 125.00
1160 Rawhide 175.00
1161 CB,Grandma Duck's
    Farm Friends 150.00
1162 Yogi Bera joins the Marines . 75.00
1163 Daniel Boone 50.00
1164 Wanted: Dead or Alive 100.00
1165 Ellery Queen 125.00
1166 Rocky and His Friends 275.00
1167 Tales of Wells Fargo,Ph(c) . . 65.00
1168 The Detectives,
    R.Taylor Ph(c) 125.00
1169 New Adventures of
    Sherlock Holmes 150.00
1170 The Three Stooges,Ph(c) . 125.00
1171 Elmer Fudd 20.00
1172 Fury,Ph(c) 50.00
1173 The Twilight Zone. 235.00
1174 The Little Rascals 40.00
1175 M.G.M.'s Mouse Musketeers 25.00
1176 Dondi,Ph(c) 45.00
1177 Chilly Willy 25.00
1178 Ten Who Dared 60.00
1179 The Swamp Fox,
    L.Nielson Ph(c) 75.00
1180 The Danny Thomas Show . 165.00
1181 Texas John Slaughter,Ph(c) . 60.00
1182 Donald Duck Album 45.00
1183 101 Dalmatians 125.00
1184 CB,W.Disney's
    Gyro Gearloose 125.00
1185 Sweetie Pie 30.00
1186 JDa,Yak Yak. 100.00
1187 The Three Stooges,Ph(c) . . 125.00
1188 Atlantis the Lost
    Continent,Ph(c) 110.00
1189 Greyfriars Bobby,Ph(c) 50.00
1190 CB(c),Donald and
    the Wheel 75.00
1191 Leave It to Beaver,Ph(c). . . 175.00
1192 Rocky Nelson,Ph(c) 175.00
1193 The Real McCoys,Ph(c) . . . 100.00
1194 Pepe,Ph(c). 45.00
1195 National Velvet,Ph(c) 65.00
1196 Pixie and Dixie
    and Mr. Jinks 40.00
1197 The Aquanauts,Ph(c) 60.00
1198 Donald in Mathmagic Land. . 75.00
1199 Absent-Minded Professor,
    Ph(c) 75.00
1200 Hennessey,Ph(c) 60.00
1201 Goofy 55.00
1202 Rawhide,C.Eastwood Ph(c) 175.00
1203 Pinocchio. 60.00
1204 Scamp. 40.00
1205 David & Goliath,Ph(c). 50.00
1206 Lolly and Pepper 25.00
1207 MSy,The Rebel,Ph(c) 100.00
1208 Rocky and His Friends. . . . 275.00
1209 Sugarfoot,Ph(c) 75.00
1210 The Parent Trap,
    H.Mills Ph(c) 85.00
1211 RsM,77 Sunset Strip,Ph(c) . 100.00
1212 Chilly Willy. 25.00
1213 Mysterious Island,Ph(c) . . . 100.00
1214 Smokey the Bear 50.00
1215 Tales of Wells Fargo,Ph(c) . . 65.00
1216 Whirlybirds,Ph(c) 75.00
1218 Fury,Ph(c) 50.00
1219 The Detectives,
    Robert Taylor Ph(c) 85.00
1220 Gunslinger,Ph(c) 75.00
1221 Bonanza,Ph(c) 200.00
1222 Elmer Fudd 20.00
1223 GK,Laramie,Ph(c) 75.00
1224 The Little Rascals 40.00
1225 The Deputy,H.Fonda Ph(c). . 85.00
1226 Nikki, Wild Dog of the North . 50.00
1227 Morgan the Pirate,Ph(c) 75.00
1229 Thief of Bagdad,Ph(c) 70.00

1230 Voyage to the Bottom
    of the Sea,Ph(c) 125.00
1231 Danger Man,Ph(c) 125.00
1232 On the Double 40.00
1233 Tammy Tell Me True. 60.00
1234 The Phantom Planet 75.00
1235 Mister Magoo. 125.00
1236 King of Kings,Ph(c) 100.00
1237 ATh,The Untouchables,
    Ph(c) 250.00
1238 Deputy Dawg. 125.00
1239 CB(c),Donald Duck Album . . 65.00
1240 The Detectives,
    R.Taylor Ph(c) 85.00
1241 Sweetie Pies 30.00
1242 King Leonardo and
    His Short Subjects 150.00
1243 Ellery Queen 75.00
1244 Space Mouse. 30.00
1245 New Adventures of
    Sherlock Holmes 150.00
1246 Mickey Mouse Album. 40.00
1247 Daisy Duck's Diary 45.00
1248 Pluto 40.00
1249 The Danny Thomas Show,
    Ph(c) 175.00
1250 Four Horseman of the
    Apocalypse,Ph(c) 75.00
1251 Everything's Ducky. 60.00
1252 The Andy Griffith Show,
    Ph(c) 325.00
1253 Spaceman 100.00
1254 "Diver Dan" 50.00
1255 The Wonders of Aladdin. . . . 50.00
1256 Kona, Monarch of
    Monster Isle 50.00
1257 Car 54, Where Are You?,
    Ph(c) 100.00
1258 GE,The Frogmen. 60.00
1259 El Cid,Ph(c) 60.00
1260 The Horsemasters,Ph(c) . . 125.00
1261 Rawhide,C.Eastwood Ph(c) 175.00
1262 The Rebel,Ph(c). 100.00
1263 RsM,77 Sinset Strip,Ph(c) . 100.00
1264 Pixie & Dixie & Mr.Jinks 40.00
1265 The Real McCoys,Ph(c) . . . 100.00
1266 M.G.M.'s Spike and Tyke . . . 15.00
1267 CB,GyroGearloose. 75.00
1268 Oswald the Rabbit 20.00
1269 Rawhide,C.Eastwood Ph(c) 175.00
1270 Bullwinkle and Rocky 225.00
1271 Yogi Bear Birthday Party . . . 50.00
1272 Frosty the Snowman 25.00
1273 Hans Brinker,Ph(c). 60.00
1274 Santa Claus Funnies 30.00
1275 Rocky and His Friends. . . . 225.00
1276 Dondi. 30.00
1278 King Leonardo and
    His Short Subjects 150.00
1279 Grandma Duck's Farm
    Friends. 55.00
1280 Hennessey,Ph(c) 50.00
1281 Chilly Willy. 25.00
1282 Babes in Toyland,Ph(c) . . . 100.00
1283 Bonanza,Ph(c) 200.00
1284 RH,Laramie,Ph(c) 75.00
1285 Leave It to Beaver,Ph(c). . . 175.00
1286 The Untouchables,Ph(c). . . 175.00
1287 Man from Wells Fargo,Ph(c). 40.00
1288 RC,GE,The Twilight Zone. . 150.00
1289 Ellery Queen 75.00
1290 M.G.M.'s Mouse
    Musketeers 25.00
1291 RsM,77 Sunset Strip,Ph(c). 100.00
1293 Elmer Fudd 20.00
1294 Ripcord 60.00
1295 Mr. Ed, the Talking Horse,
    Ph(c) 100.00
1296 Fury,Ph(c) 50.00
1297 Spanky, Alfalfa and the
    Little Rascals 40.00

GOLDEN AGE

1298 The Hathaways,Ph(c)...... 35.00	16 Bondage(c)............. 200.00	3-9 AFa.................... 15.00
1299 Deputy Dawg.......... 125.00	17 Magno Lighting.......... 150.00	3-10 AFa................... 15.00
1300 The Comancheros...... 175.00	18 Magno Lighting........ 150.00	3-11 AFa,1948(c)........... 15.00
1301 Adventures in Paradise.... 40.00	19 RP,RP(c)............... 150.00	3-12 AFa................... 15.00
1302 JohnnyJason,TeenReporter . 25.00	20 RP,RP(c)............... 150.00	4-1 thru 4-7 AFa...........@15.00
1303 Lad: A Dog,Ph(c)......... 30.00	21 RP,RP(c)............... 125.00	5-1 AFa................... 15.00
1304 Nellie the Nurse......... 75.00	22 RP(c).................. 125.00	5-2 AFa................... 15.00
1305 Mister Magoo.......... 125.00	23 RP(c).................. 125.00	5-3....................... 15.00
1306 Target: The Corruptors,	24 RP(c).................. 125.00	5-4 Star Publications........ 15.00
Ph(c).................... 55.00	25 RP(c).................. 125.00	39 LbC(c)................. 50.00
1307 Margie................. 45.00	26 RP(c).................. 125.00	40 LbC(c)................. 50.00
1308 Tales of the Wizard of Oz... 75.00	27 RP(c).................. 110.00	41 LbC(c)................. 50.00
1309 BK,87th Precinct,Ph(c)..... 85.00	28........................ 100.00	42 LbC(c)................. 50.00
1310 Huck and Yogi Winter	29........................ 100.00	43 LbC(c)................. 20.00
Sports.................. 75.00	30........................ 100.00	**Becomes:**
1311 Rocky and His Friends.... 275.00	31........................ 100.00	**FRISKY ANIMALS**
1312 National Velvet,Ph(c)...... 35.00	32........................ 100.00	**Star Publications**
1313 Moon Pilot.Ph(c)........ 75.00		44 LbC.................... 70.00
1328 GE,The Underwater	**FRANKENSTEIN COMICS**	45 LbC................... 100.00
City,Ph(c)................ 60.00	**Crestwood Publications**	46 LbC,Baseball........... 60.00
1330 GK,Brain Boy.......... 100.00	**(Prize Publ.)**	47 LbC................... 60.00
1332 Bachelor Father........... 75.00	**Summer, 1945**	48 LbC................... 60.00
1333 Short Ribs............. 40.00	1 B:Frankenstein,DBr,DBr(c)... 800.00	49 LbC................... 60.00
1335 Aggie Mack............ 30.00	2 DBr,DBr(c)............. 400.00	50 LbC................... 60.00
1336 On Stage.............. 40.00	3 DBr,DBr(c)............. 275.00	51 LbC(c)................. 60.00
1337 Dr. Kildare,Ph(c)....... 100.00	4 DBr,DBr(c)............. 275.00	52 LbC(c)................. 75.00
1341 The Andy Griffith Show,	5 DBr,DBr(c)............. 275.00	53 LbC(c)................. 55.00
Ph(c)................... 300.00	6 DBr,DBr(c),S&K......... 250.00	54 LbC(c),Supercat(c)...... 55.00
1348 JDa,Yak Yak.......... 100.00	7 DBr,DBr(c),S&K......... 250.00	55 LbC(c),same........... 55.00
1349 Yogi Berra Visits the U.N... 100.00	8 DBr,DBr(c),S&K......... 250.00	56 LbC(c),same........... 55.00
1350 Commanche,Ph(c)...... 50.00	9 DBr,DBr(c),S&K......... 250.00	57 LbC(c),same........... 55.00
1354 Calvin and the Colonel.... 60.00	10 DBr,DBr(c),S&K........ 250.00	58 LbC(c),same,July, 1954...... 55.00
	11 DBr, DBr(c)A:Boris Karloff.... 200.00	
	12 DBr,DBr(c)............ 200.00	**FRITZI RITZ**
	13 DBr,DBr(c)............ 200.00	**United Features Syndicate/**
	14 DBr,DBr(c)............ 200.00	**St. John Publications**
	15 DBr,DBr(c)............ 200.00	**Fall, 1948**
	16 DBr,DBr(c)............ 200.00	N# Special issue........... 100.00
	17 DBr,DBr(c)............ 200.00	2....................... 50.00
	18 B:Horror.............. 300.00	3....................... 40.00
	19...................... 175.00	4 thru 7................@30.00
	3-4..................... 150.00	6 A:Abbie & Slats.......... 35.00
	3-5..................... 150.00	8 thru 10...............@25.00
	3-6..................... 150.00	11 1958................. 25.00
	4-1 thru 4-6..............@150.00	
	5-1 thru 5-4..............@150.00	**FROGMAN COMICS**
	5-5 Oct.–Nov., 1954......... 150.00	**Hillman Periodicals**
		Jan.–Feb., 1952–May 1953
	FRISKY FABLES	1....................... 75.00
	Novelty Press/Premium Group	2....................... 40.00
	Spring, 1945	3....................... 40.00
	1 AFa.................... 75.00	4 MMe.................. 30.00
	2 AFa.................... 40.00	5 BK,AT................. 40.00
	3 AFa.................... 35.00	6....................... 25.00
	4 AFa.................... 28.00	7....................... 25.00
	5 AFa.................... 28.00	8 thru 11...............@25.00
	6 AFa.................... 28.00	
	7 AFa,Flag (c)............. 30.00	**FRONTIER ROMANCES**
	2-1 AFa,Rainbow(c).......... 25.00	**Avon Periodicals**
	2-2 AFa.................. 20.00	**Nov.–Dec., 1949**
	2-3 AFa.................. 20.00	1 She Learned to Ride and Shoot,
	2-4 AFa.................. 20.00	and Kissing Came Natural.. 400.00
	2-5 AFa.................. 20.00	2 Bronc-Busters Sweetheart,
	2-6 AFa.................. 20.00	Jan.–Feb., 1950......... 250.00
	2-7 AFa.................. 20.00	
	2-8 AFa,Halloween (c)....... 20.00	**FRONTLINE COMBAT**
	2-9 AFa,Thanksgiving(c)....... 18.00	**Tiny Tot Publications**
	2-10 AFa,Christmas cover.... 20.00	**(E.C. Comics),**
	2-11 AFa................. 20.00	**July–Aug., 1951**
	2-12 AFa,Valentines Day cover... 18.00	1 HK(c),WW, JSe,JDa,Hanhung
	3-1 AFa.................. 15.00	Changjn cover.......... 500.00
	3-2 AFa.................. 15.00	2 HK(c),WW,Tank Battle cover . 300.00
	3-3 AFa.................. 18.00	3 HK(c),WW,Naval Battleship
	3-4 AFa.................. 15.00	fire cover.............. 275.00
	3-5 AFa.................. 15.00	4 HK(c),WW, Bazooka cover... 225.00
	3-6 AFa.................. 15.00	
	3-7 AFa.................. 15.00	
	3-8 AFa,Turkey (c)........ 15.00	

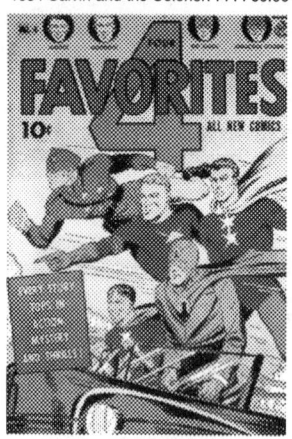

Four Favorites #4
© Ace Magazines

FOUR FAVORITES
Ace Magazines
Sept., 1941

1 B:Vulcan, Lash Lighting, Magno	
the Magnetic Man, Raven,	
Flag cover,Hitler......... 1,100.00	
2 A: Black Ace............. 450.00	
3 E:Vulcan............... 350.00	
4 E:Raven,B:Unknown Soldiers 350.00	
5 B:Captain Courageous..... 325.00	
6 A: The Flag, B: Mr. Risk..... 325.00	
7 JM.................... 300.00	
8....................... 300.00	
9 RP,HK................. 300.00	
10 HK................... 350.00	
11 HK,LbC,UnKnown Soldier... 325.00	
12 LbC.................. 225.00	
13 LbC.................. 175.00	
14 Fer................... 175.00	
15 Fer................... 175.00	

GOLDEN AGE

5 HK(c),JSe 200.00
6 HK(c),WW,JSe 175.00
7 HK(c),WW,JSe,Document of the
   Action at Iwo Jima 175.00
8 HK(c),WW,ATh 175.00
9 HK(c),WW,JSe,Civil War iss. . 175.00
10 GE,HK(c),WW,
   Crying Child cover 225.00
11 GE 150.00
12 GE,Air Force issue 150.00
13 JSe,GE,WW(c),
   Bi-Planes cover 150.00
14 JKu,GE,WW(c) 150.00
15 JSe,GE,WW(c), Jan., 1954 . . 150.00

FRONT PAGE
COMIC BOOK
Front Page Comics, 1945
1 JKu,BP,BF(c),I:Man in Black . 275.00

FUGITIVES FROM
JUSTICE
St. John Publishing Co.
Feb., 1952
1 . . . . 125.00
2 MB, Killer Boomerang 150.00
3 GT 125.00
4 . . . . 50.00
5 Bondage cover, Oct., 1952 . . . 70.00

FUNNIES, THE
(1ST SERIES)
Dell Publishing Co.
1929-30
1 B:Foxy Grandpa, Sniffy 600.00
2 thru 21 . . . . @250.00
N#(22) 225.00
N#(23) thru (36) . . . . @200.00

FUNNIES, THE
(2ND SERIES)
Dell Publishing Co.
Oct., 1936
1 Tailspin Tommy,Mutt & Jeff,
   Capt. Easy,D.Dixon 2,400.00
2 Scribbly 1,000.00
3 . . . . 750.00
4 Christmas issue 600.00
5 . . . . 600.00
6 thru 22 . . . . @450.00
23 thru 29 . . . . @325.00
30 B:John Carter of Mars 1,000.00
31 inc. Dick Tracy 600.00
32 . . . . 600.00
33 . . . . 600.00
34 . . . . 600.00
35 John Carter (c) 600.00
36 John Carter (c) 600.00
37 John Carter (c) 600.00
38 Rex King of the Deep (c) . . . 600.00
39 Rex King (c) 600.00
40 John Carter (c) 600.00
41 Sky Ranger (c) 600.00
42 Rex King (c) 600.00
43 Rex King (c) 600.00
44 Rex King (c) 600.00
45 I&O:Phantasmo:Master of
   the World 500.00
46 Phantasmo (c) 500.00
47 Phantasmo (c) 400.00
48 Phantasmo (c) 350.00
49 Phantasmo (c) 350.00
50 Phantasmo (c) 350.00
51 Phantasmo (c) 350.00

52 Phantasmo (c) 375.00
53 Phantasmo (c) 375.00
54 Phantasmo (c) 375.00
55 Phantasmo (c) 375.00
56 Phantasmo (c) E:John Carter 375.00
57 I&O:Captain Midnight 1,500.00
58 Captain Midnight (c) 600.00
59 Captain Midnight (c) 600.00
60 Captain Midnight (c) 600.00
61 Captain Midnight (c) 500.00
62 Captain Midnight (c) 500.00
63 Captain Midnight (c) 500.00
64 B: Woody Woodpecker 800.00
Becomes:

New Funnies #94
© Dell Publishing Co.

NEW FUNNIES
Dell Publishing Co. July, 1942
65 Andy Panda, Ragady Ann &
   Andy, Peter Rabbit 700.00
66 same 350.00
67 Felix the Cat 350.00
68 . . . . 350.00
69 WK, The Brownies 350.00
70 . . . . 350.00
71 . . . . 200.00
72 WK 200.00
73 . . . . 200.00
74 . . . . 200.00
75 WK,Brownies 200.00
76 CB,Andy Panda, Woody
   Woodpecker 1,100.00
77 same 200.00
78 Andy Panda 200.00
79 . . . . 150.00
80 . . . . 150.00
81 . . . . 150.00
82 WK,Brownies 175.00
83 WK,Brownies 175.00
84 WK,Brownies 150.00
85 WK,Brownies 175.00
86 . . . . 125.00
87 Woody Woodpecker 100.00
88 same 100.00
89 same 100.00
90 same 100.00
91 thru 99 . . . . @75.00
100 . . . . 85.00
101 thru 110 . . . . @50.00
111 thru 118 . . . . @40.00
119 Christmas 35.00
120 thru 142 . . . . @30.00
143 Christmas cover 35.00
144 thru 149 . . . . @30.00
150 thru 154 . . . . @20.00
155 Christmas cover 22.00

156 thru 167 . . . . @20.00
168 Christmas cover 22.00
169 thru 181 . . . . @20.00
182 I&O:Knothead & Splinter . . . 20.00
183 thru 200 . . . . @20.00
201 thru 240 . . . . @15.00
241 thru 288 . . . . @10.00

FUNNY BOOK
Funny Book Publ. Corp.
(Parents Magazine) Dec., 1952
1 Alec, the Funny Bunny,
   Alice in Wonderland 100.00
2 Gulliver in Giant-Land 45.00
3 . . . . 35.00
4 Adventures of Robin Hood 30.00
5 . . . . 30.00
6 . . . . 30.00
7 . . . . 30.00
8 . . . . 30.00
9 . . . . 30.00

FUNNY FILMS
Best Syndicated Features
(American Comics Group)
Sept.–Oct., 1949
1 B:Puss An' Boots,
   Blunderbunny 125.00
2 . . . . 75.00
3 . . . . 40.00
4 . . . . 35.00
5 . . . . 35.00
6 . . . . 35.00
7 . . . . 35.00
8 . . . . 35.00
9 . . . . 35.00
10 . . . . 35.00
11 thru 20 . . . . @25.00
21 thru 28 . . . . @22.00
29 May–June, 1954 . . . . 22.00

FUNNY FUNNIES
Nedor Publ. Co.
April, 1943
1 Funny Animals 135.00

FUNNYMAN
Magazine Enterprises of
Canada
Dec., 1947
1 S&K,S&K(c) 300.00
2 S&K,S&K(c) 175.00
3 S&K,S&K(c) 150.00
4 S&K,S&K(c) 150.00
5 S&K,S&K(c) 150.00
6 S&K,S&K(c), Aug., 1948 . . . . 150.00

FUTURE COMICS
David McKay Publications
June, 1940
1 Lone Ranger,Phantom 2,000.00
2 Lone Ranger 950.00
3 Lone Ranger 800.00
4 Lone Ranger,Sept., 1940 . . . . 750.00

FUTURE WORLD
COMICS
George W. Dougherty
Summer, 1946
1 . . . . 165.00
2 Fall, 1946 . . . . 150.00

GABBY HAYES WESTERN
Fawcett Publ./Charlton Comics
Nov., 1948
1 Ph(c) 350.00
2 Ph(c) 150.00
3 The Rage of the Purple Sage,
Ph(c) 100.00
4 Ph(c) 100.00
5 Ph(c) 85.00
6 Ph(c) 85.00
7 Ph(c) 75.00
8 Ph(c) 75.00
9 Ph(c),V:The Kangaroo Crook . . 75.00
10 Ph(c) 75.00
11 Ph(c), Chariot Race 75.00
12 V:Beaver Ben, The Biting Bandit,
Ph(c) 65.00
13 thru 15 . . . . @65.00
16 . . . . 50.00
17 . . . . 50.00
18 thru 20 . . . . @50.00
21 thru 51 . . . . @35.00
51 thru 59 Dec., 1954 . . . . @20.00

GANGSTERS AND GUN MOLLS
Realistic Comics
(Avon)
Sept., 1951
1 WW,A:Big Jim Colosimo,
Evelyn Ellis 325.00
2 JKa, A:Bonnie Parker, The
Kissing Bandit 250.00
3 EK, A:Juanita Perez, Crimes
Homicide Squad 225.00
4 A:Mara Hite, Elkins Boys,
June, 1952 . . . . 175.00

GANGSTERS CAN'T WIN
D.S. Publishing Co.
Feb.–March, 1948
1 Shot Cop cover 225.00
2 A:Eddie Bentz 100.00
3 Twin Trouble Trigger Man 75.00
4 Suicide on SoundStageSeven . 75.00
5 Trail of Terror 75.00
6 Mystery at the Circus 75.00
7 Talisman Trail 60.00
8 . . . . 60.00
9 Suprise at Buoy 13,
June–July, 1949 . . . . 60.00

GANG WORLD
Literary Enterprises
(Standard Comics)
Oct., 1952
5 Bondage cover 150.00
6 Mob Payoff, Jan., 1953 . . . . . 100.00

GASOLINE ALLEY
Star Publications
Oct., 1950
1 . . . . 150.00
2 LBc 90.00
3 LBc(c), April, 1950 . . . . 125.00

GEM COMICS
Spotlight Publ.
April, 1945
1 A:Steve Strong,Bondage(c) . . 175.00

GENE AUTRY COMICS
Fawcett Publications
Jan., 1942
1 The Mark of Cloven Hoof . . 7,500.00
2 . . . . 1,200.00
3 Secret of the Aztec Treasure 1,000.00
4 . . . . 650.00
5 Mystery of PaintRockCanyon . 700.00
6 Outlaw Round-up 650.00
7 Border Bullets 650.00
8 Blazing Guns 600.00
9 Range Robbers 600.00
10 Fightin' Buckaroo, Danger's
Trail, Sept., 1943 . . . . 600.00
11 . . . . 625.00
12 . . . . 600.00

GENE AUTRY COMICS
Dell Publishing Co.
May/June 1946
1 . . . . 450.00
2 Ph(c) 250.00
3 Ph(c) 175.00
4 Ph(c),I:Flap Jack. 175.00
5 Ph(c), all. 150.00
6 thru 10 . . . . @135.00
11 thru 19 . . . . @125.00
20 . . . . 135.00
21 thru 29 . . . . @100.00
30 thru 40, B:Giants . . . . @75.00
41 thru 56 E:Giants. . . . . @60.00
57 . . . . 35.00
58 Christmas cover. 40.00
59 thru 66 . . . . @35.00
67 thru 80, B:Giant . . . . @40.00
81 thru 90, E:Giant . . . . @30.00
91 thru 93 . . . . @25.00
94 Christmas cover. 28.00
95 thru 99 . . . . @25.00
100 . . . . 30.00
101 thru 111 . . . . @25.00
112 thru 121 . . . . @20.00

GENE AUTRY'S CHAMPION
Dell Publishing Co.
Aug., 1950
(1) see Dell Four Color #287
(2) see Dell Four Color #319
3 . . . . 35.00
4 . . . . 35.00
5 thru 19 . . . . @35.00

Gene Autry and Champion
© Dell Publishing Co.

GEORGE PAL'S PUPPETOON'S
Fawcett Publications
Dec., 1945
1 Captain Marvel (c) 350.00
2 . . . . 150.00
3 . . . . 100.00
4 thru 17 . . . . @90.00
18 Dec., 1947. . . . . 90.00

GERALD McBOING-BOING AND THE NEARSIGHTED MR. MAGOO
Dell Publishing Co.
Aug.–Oct., 1952
1 . . . . 100.00
2 . . . . 75.00
3 . . . . 75.00
4 . . . . 75.00
5 . . . . 75.00

GERONIMO
Avon Periodicals, 1950
1 Massacre at San Pedro Pass . 125.00
2 EK(c), Murderous Battle
at Kiskayah 75.00
3 EK(c) 75.00
4 EK(c),Apache Death Trap,
Feb., 1952 . . . . 75.00

GET LOST
Mikeross Publications
Feb.–March, 1954
1 . . . . 200.00
2 . . . . 150.00
3 June–July, 1954 . . . . 100.00

GHOST
Fiction House Magazine
Winter, 1951
1 The Banshee Bells 500.00
2 I Woke In Terror 250.00
3 The Haunted Hand of X 200.00
4 Flee the Mad Furies 200.00
5 The Hex of Ruby Eye 200.00
6 The Sleepers in the Crypt . . . 225.00
7 When Dead Rogues Ride . . . 225.00
8 Curse of the Mist-Thing 225.00
9 It Crawls by Night,Bondage(c). 250.00
10 Halfway to Hades. 225.00
11 GE, The Witch's Doll,
Summer, 1954 . . . . 225.00

GHOST BREAKERS
Street & Smith, Sept., 1948
1 BP,BP(c), A:Dr. Neff 275.00
2 BP,BP(c), Breaks the Voodoo
Hoodoo,Dec., 1948. . . . . . . 225.00

GHOSTLY WEIRD STORIES
(see BLUE BOLT)

GIANT BOY BOOK OF COMICS
Newsbook Publ.
(Lev Gleason), 1945
1 A:Crime Buster & Young
Robin Hood 750.00

All comics prices listed are for *Near Mint* condition.

GIANT COMICS EDITION
St. John Publ., 1948

1 Mighty Mouse 450.00
2 Abbie and Slats 200.00
3 Terry Toons 350.00
4 Crime Comics 500.00
5 MB, Police Case Book 500.00
6 MB,MB(c), Western
   Picture Story............. 475.00
7 May not exist
8 The Adventures of Mighty
   Mouse 300.00
9 JKu,MB,Romance & Confession
   Stories,Ph(c) 450.00
10 Terry Toons 300.00
11 MB,MB(c),JKu,Western
   Picture Stories 450.00
12 MB,MB(c),Diary Secrets,
   Prostitute 750.00
13 MB,JKu, Romances........ 425.00
14 Mighty Mouse Album 350.00
15 MB(c),Romance........... 425.00
16 Little Audrey 300.00
N#, Mighty Mouse Album 300.00

GIANT COMICS EDITION
United Features Syndicate
1945

1 A:Abbie & Slats, Jim Hardy,
   Ella Cinders,Iron Vic 275.00
2 Elmo, Jim Hardy, Abbie &
   Slats, 1945............. 200.00

G.I. COMBAT
Quality Comics Group
Oct., 1952

1 RC(c), Beyond the Call
   of Duty 450.00
2 RC(c), Operation Massacre .. 200.00
3 An Indestructible Marine 175.00
4 Bridge to Blood Hill 175.00
5 Hell Breaks loose on
   Suicide Hill.............. 175.00
6 Beachhead Inferno 150.00
7 Fire Power Assault 125.00
8 RC(c),Death-trap Hill 125.00
9 Devil Riders 125.00
10 RC(c), Two-Ton Booby Trap.. 150.00
11 Hell's Heroes 100.00
12 Hand Grenade Hero....... 100.00
13 Commando Assault 100.00
14 Spear Head Assault....... 100.00

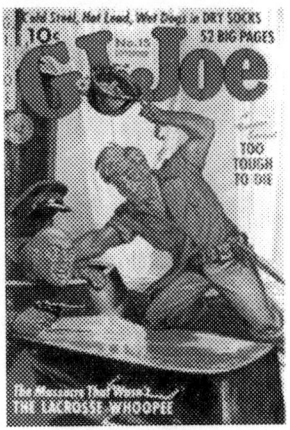

G.I. Combat #2
© Quality Comics Group

15 Vengeance Assault 100.00
16 Trapped Under Fire 90.00
17 Attack on Death Mountain 90.00
18 Red Battle Ground.......... 90.00
19 Death on Helicopter Hill...... 90.00
20 Doomed Legion-Death Trap .. 90.00
21 Red Sneak Attack 75.00
22 Vengeance Raid 75.00
23 No Grandstand in Hell 75.00
24 Operation Steel
   Trap,Comics Code 75.00
25 Charge of the CommieBrigade. 70.00
26 Red Guerrilla Trap 70.00
27 Trapped Behind Commie Lines 70.00
28 Atomic Battleground......... 70.00
29 Patrol Ambush............. 70.00
30 Operation Booby Trap 70.00
31 Human Fly on Heartbreak Hill . 70.00
32 Atomic Rocket Assault...... 90.00
33 Bridge to Oblivion 70.00
34 RC,Desperate Mission...... 85.00
35 Doom Patrol 70.00
36 Fire Power Assault......... 70.00
37 Attack at Dawn 70.00
38 Get That Tank 70.00
39 Mystery of No Man's Land 70.00
40 Maneuver Battleground 70.00
41 Trumpet of Doom........... 70.00
42 March of Doom 70.00
43 Operation Showdown........ 70.00
See DC Comics for 44-120

GIFT COMICS
Fawcett Publications
March, 1942

1 A:Captain Marvel, Bulletman,
   Golden Arrow,Ibis, the
   Invincible, Spy Smasher .. 2,400.00
2 .... 1,650.00
3 .... 1,100.00
4 A:Marvel Family, 1949 ..... 650.00

GIGGLE COMICS
Creston Publ./
American Comics Group
Oct., 1943

1 (fa)same................ 175.00
2 KHu 90.00
3 KHu 55.00
4 KHu 50.00
5 KHu 50.00
6 KHu 45.00
7 KHu 45.00
8 KHu 45.00
9 I:Super Katt 50.00
10 KHu................... 45.00
11 thru 20 KHu .... @30.00
21 thru 30 KHu .... @25.00
31 thru 40 KHu .... @20.00
41 thru 94 KHu .... @18.00
95 A:Spencer Spook.......... 20.00
96 KHu................... 18.00
97 KHu................... 18.00
98 KHu................... 18.00
99 KHu................... 18.00
100 and 101 March–April,1955 . @18.00

G.I. JANE
Stanhall Publ.
May, 1953

1 .... 60.00
2 thru 6 .... @25.00
7 thru 9 .... @20.00
10 Dec., 1954............... 18.00

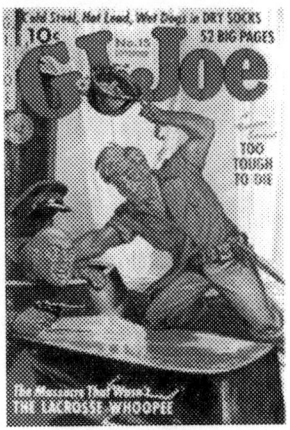

G.I. Joe #15
© Ziff-Davis Publication Co.

G.I. JOE
Ziff-Davis Publication Co.
1950

10 NS(c),Red Devils of Korea,
   V:Seoul City Lou.......... 75.00
11 NS(c),The Guerrilla's Lair..... 50.00
12 NS(c)................... 50.00
13 NS(c),Attack at Dawn....... 50.00
14 NS(c),Temple of Terror,
   A:Peanuts the Great........ 45.00
2-6 It's a Foot Soldiers Job,
   I:Frankie of the Pump..... 45.00
2-7 BP,NS(c),The Rout at
   Sugar Creek 45.00
8 BP,NS(c),Waldo'sSqueezeBox . 45.00
9 NS(c),Dear John........... 45.00
10 NS(c),Joe Flies the Payroll ... 45.00
11 NS(c),For the Love of Benny . 45.00
12 NS(c),Patch work Quilt....... 45.00
13 NS(c)................... 45.00
14 NS(c),The Wedding Ring...... 45.00
15 The Lacrosse Whoopee 45.00
16 Mamie's Mortar 45.00
17 A Time for Waiting 45.00
18 Giant 125.00
19 Old Army Game..Buck Passer . 40.00
20 General Confusion 40.00
21 Save 'Im for Brooklyn........ 40.00
22 Portrait of a Lady 40.00
23 Take Care of My Little Wagon . 40.00
24 Operation 'Operation'........ 40.00
25 The Two-Leaf Clover 40.00
26 NS(c),Nobody Flies Alone
   Mud & Wings 40.00
27 "Dear Son...Come Home" ... 40.00
28 They Alway's Come Back
   Bondage cover........... 40.00
29 What a Picnic 35.00
30 NS(c),The One-Sleeved
   Kimono 35.00
31 NS(c),Get a Horse.......... 30.00
32 thru 47 .... @30.00
48 Atom Bomb 35.00
49 thru 51 June, 1957........ @30.00

GINGER
Close-Up Publ.
(Archie Publications)
Jan., 1951

1 GFs 75.00
2 .... 40.00
3 .... 30.00

GOLDEN AGE

4	30.00
5	25.00
6	25.00
7 thru 9	@35.00
10 A:Katy Keene,Summer,1954	40.00

GIRLS IN LOVE
Fawcett Publications
May, 1950

1	55.00
2 Ph(c),July, 1950	50.00

GIRLS IN LOVE
(see DIARY LOVES)

G.I. SWEETHEARTS
(see DIARY LOVES)

G.I. WAR BRIDES
Superior Publ. Ltd.
April, 1954

1	30.00
2	25.00
3 thru 7	@15.00
8 June, 1955	15.00

GOING STEADY
(see TEEN-AGE
TEMPTATIONS)

GOLDEN ARROW
Fawcett Publications
Spring, 1942

1 B:Golden Arrow	650.00
2	300.00
3	250.00
4	225.00
5 Spring, 1947	225.00
6 BK	250.00
6a 1944 Well Known Comics (Giveaway)	275.00

GOLDEN LAD
Spark Publications
July, 1945

1 MMe,MMe(c),A:Kid Wizards, Swift Arrow,B:Golden Ladd	550.00
2 MMe,MMe(c)	250.00
3 MMe,MMe(c)	250.00
4 MMe,MMe(c), The Menace of the Minstrel	250.00
5 MMe,MMe(c),O:Golden Girl, June, 1946	250.00

GOLDEN WEST LOVE
Kirby Publishing Co.
Sept.–Oct., 1949

1 BP,I Rode Heartbreak Hill, Ph(c)	125.00
2 BP	85.00
3 BP,Ph(c)	85.00
4 BP,April, 1950	85.00

GOLD MEDAL COMICS
Cambridge House, 1945

N# Captain Truth	200.00

GOOFY COMICS
Nedor Publ. Co./
Animated Cartoons
(Standard Comics)
June, 1943

1 (fa)	135.00
2	70.00
3 VP	45.00
4 VP	35.00
5 VP	35.00
6 thru 10 VP	@35.00
11 thru 15	@30.00
15 thru 19	@25.00
20 thru 35 FF	@40.00
36 thru 48	@25.00

GREAT AMERICAN
COMICS PRESENTS–
THE SECRET VOICE
4 Star Publ., 1944

1 Hitler,Secret Weapon	225.00

GREAT COMICS
Novak Publ. Co., 1945

1 LbC(c)	275.00

GREAT COMICS
Great Comics Publications
Nov., 1941

1 I:The Great Zorro	1,000.00
2 Buck Johnson	500.00
3 The Lost City, Jan., 1942	1,200.00

GREAT LOVER
ROMANCES
Toby Press, March, 1951

1 Jon Juan,A:Dr. King	100.00
2 Hollywood Girl	50.00
3 Love in a Taxi	30.00
4 The Experimental Kiss	30.00
5 After the Honeymoon	30.00
6 HK,The Kid Sister Falls in Love	50.00
7 Man Crazy	25.00
8 Stand-in Boyfriend	25.00
9 The Cheat	25.00
10 Heart Breaker	25.00
11	25.00
12	25.00
13 Powerhouse of Deciet	25.00
14	25.00
15 Ph(c),Still Undecided, Liz Taylor	60.00
16 thru 21	@25.00
22 May, 1955	25.00

GREEN GIANT COMICS
Pelican Publications, 1941

1 Black Arrow, Dr. Nerod O:Colossus	9,000.00

GREEN HORNET
COMICS
Helnit Publ. Co./
Family Comics
(Harvey Publ.), Dec., 1940

1 B:Green Hornet,P(c)	4,400.00
2	1,400.00
3 BWh(c)	1,200.00
4 BWh(c)	800.00
5 BWh(c)	800.00

Green Hornet #11
© Harvey Publications

6	800.00
7 BP, O:Zebra, B:Robin Hood & Spirit of 76	700.00
8 BP,Bondage cover	600.00
9 BP, Behind the Cover	600.00
10 BP	600.00
11 Who is Mr. Q?	600.00
12 BP,A:Mr.Q	600.00
13 Hitler cover	650.00
14 BP,Spirit of 76-Twinkle Twins, Bondage(c)	475.00
15 ASh(c),Nazi Ghost Ship	450.00
16 BP,Prisoner of War	450.00
17 BP,ASh(c),Nazis' Last Stand	450.00
18 BP,ASh(c),Jap's Treacherous Plot,Bondage cover	475.00
19 BP,ASh(c),Clash with the Rampaging Japs	450.00
20 BP,ASh(c),Tojo's Propaganda Hoax	475.00
21 BP,ASh(c),Unwelcome Cargo.	375.00
22 ASh(c),Rendezvous with Jap Saboteurs	375.00
23 BF,ASh(c),Jap's Diabolical Plot #B2978	375.00
24 BF,Science Fiction cover	400.00
25 thru 29	@375.00
30 BP,JKu	375.00
31 BP,JKu	400.00
32 BP,JKu	325.00
33 BP,JKu	325.00
34 BP,JKu	325.00
35 BP,JKu	325.00
36 BP,JKu,Bondage cover	350.00
37 BP,JKu	325.00
38 BP,JKu	325.00
39 S&K	325.00
40 thru 45	@225.00
46 Drug	250.00
47 Sept., 1949	225.00

GREEN LAMA
Spark Publications/Prize Publ.
Dec., 1944

1 I:Green Lama, Lt. Hercules & Boy Champions	1,000.00
2 MRa,Forward to Victory in 1945	600.00
3 MRa,The Riddles of Toys	500.00
4 MRa,Dive Bombs Japan	475.00
5 MRa,MRa(c),Fights for the Four Freedoms	475.00
6 MRa,Smashes a Plot against America	475.00

   All comics prices listed are for *Near Mint* condition.

7 MRa,Merry X-Mas 400.00
8 MRa,Smashes Toy Master
   of Crime, March, 1946 . . . . . 400.00

Green Mask #12
© Fox Features Syndicate

GREEN MASK, THE
Fox Features Syndicate
Summer, 1940
1 O:Green Mask & Domino . . 3,000.00
2 A:Zanzibar 1,100.00
3 BP 650.00
4 B:Navy Jones 500.00
5 . . . . 450.00
6 B:Nightbird,E:Navy Jones,
   Bondage cover 350.00
7 B:Timothy Smith &
   The Tumbler 275.00
8 JSs 250.00
9 E:Nightbird, Death Wields
   a Scalpel! 275.00
10 . . . . 225.00
11 The Banshee of Dead
   Man's Hill 225.00
2-1 Election of Skulls 175.00
2-2 Pigeons of Death 175.00
2-3 Wandering Gold Brick 150.00
2-4 Time on His Hands 150.00
2-5 JFe,SFd 175.00
2-6 Adventure of the Disappearing
   Trains, Oct.–Nov., 1946 . . . . 175.00

GUMPS, THE
Dell Publishing Co., 1945
1 . . . . 100.00
2 . . . . 75.00
3 . . . . 50.00
4 . . . . 50.00
5 . . . . 50.00

GUNS AGAINST GANGSTERS
Curtis Publ./Novelty Press
Sept.–Oct., 1948
1 LbC,LbC(c),B:Toni Gayle 250.00
2 LbC,LbC(c) 175.00
3 LbC,LbC(c) 150.00
4 LbC,LbC(c) 150.00
5 LbC,LbC(c) 150.00
6 LbC,LbC(c),Shark 150.00
2-1 LbC,LbC(c),
   Sept.–Oct., 1949 . . . . 150.00

GUNSMOKE
Western Comics, Inc.
April–May, 1949
1 GRi,GRi(c),Gunsmoke & Masked
   Marvel,Bondage cover 350.00
2 GRi,GRi(c) 200.00
3 GRi,GRi(c) 150.00
4 GRi(c),Bondage(c) 125.00
5 GRi(c) 125.00
6 . . . . 65.00
7 . . . . 65.00
8 . . . . 65.00
9 . . . . 65.00
10. . . . . 65.00
11 thru 15 . . . . @50.00
16 Jan., 1952 . . . . 50.00

HA HA COMICS
Creston Publ.
(American Comics Group)
Oct., 1943
1 Funny Animal, all 175.00
2 . . . . 75.00
3 . . . . 55.00
4 . . . . 55.00
5 . . . . 55.00
6 thru 10 . . . . @40.00
11 . . . . 30.00
12 thru 15 KHu . . . . @30.00
16 thru 20 KHu . . . . @28.00
21 thru 30 KHu . . . . @25.00
31 thru 101 . . . . @20.00
102 Feb.–March, 1955 . . . . 20.00

MISTER RISK
Humor Publ.
(Ace Magazines)
Oct., 1950
1 (7) B:Mr. Risk 30.00
2 . . . . 25.00
Becomes:

MEN AGAINST CRIME
3 A:Mr. Risk, Case of the Carnival
   Killer 60.00
4 Murder-And the Crowd Roars . 35.00
5 . . . . 35.00
6 . . . . 35.00
7 Get Them! 35.00
Becomes:

HAND OF FATE
Ace Magazines
8 . . . . 250.00
9 LC 175.00
10 LC 150.00
11 Genie(c). 125.00
12 . . . . 125.00
13 Hanging(c). 150.00
14 . . . . 125.00
15 . . . . 125.00
16 . . . . 100.00
17 . . . . 100.00
18 . . . . 100.00
19 Drug issue,Quicksand(c) 125.00
20 . . . . 100.00
21 Drug issue 125.00
22 . . . . 100.00
23 Graveyard(c) 100.00
24 LC,Electric Chair 175.00
25 Nov., 1954 . . . . 75.00
25a Dec., 1954 . . . . 100.00

HANGMAN COMICS
(see LAUGH COMICS)

HAP HAZARD COMICS
A.A. Wyn/Red Seal Publ./
Readers Research
Summer, 1944
1 Funny Teen 60.00
2 Dog Show 30.00
3 Sgr, ... 28.00
4 Sgr, ... 28.00
5 thru 10 Sgr, ... @20.00
11 thru 13 Sgr, ... @15.00
14 AF(c) 35.00
15 . . . . 15.00
16 thru 24 . . . . @15.00
Becomes:

REAL LOVE
25 Dangerous Dates. 50.00
26 . . . . 25.00
27 LbC(c), Revenge Conquest . . . 35.00
28 thru 40 . . . . @18.00
41 thru 66 . . . . @15.00
67 Comics code 12.00
68 thru 76, Nov. 1956 . . . . @12.00

HAPPY COMICS
Nedor Publications/
Animated Cartoons
(Standard Comics)
Aug., 1943
1 Funny Animal in all 125.00
2 . . . . 75.00
3 . . . . 45.00
4 . . . . 40.00
5 thru 10 . . . . @40.00
11 thru 20 . . . . @35.00
21 thru 30 . . . . @30.00
31 and 32 . . . . @50.00
33 FF 125.00
34 thru 37 FF . . . . @50.00
38 thru 40 . . . . @20.00
Becomes:

HAPPY RABBIT
41 Funny Animal in all 25.00
42 thru 50 . . . . @15.00
Becomes:

HARVEY COMIC HITS
51 Phantom 200.00
52 Steve Canyon's Air Power 85.00
53 Mandrake 150.00
54 Tim Tyler's Tales of Jungle
   Terror 75.00
55 Love Stories of Mary Worth . . . 30.00
56 Phantom, Bondage cover. . . . 175.00
57 AR,Kidnap Racket 110.00
58 Girls in White. 30.00
59 Tales of the Invisible 75.00
60 Paramount Animated Comics 275.00
61 Casper the Friendly Ghost . . . 300.00
62 Paramount Animated Comics,
   April, 1953 . . . . 100.00

HAPPY HOULIHANS
(see SADDLE JUSTICE)

HAUNTED THRILLS
Four Star Publ.
(Ajax/Farrell)
June, 1952
1 Ellery Queen 300.00
2 LbC,Ellery Queen 200.00

GOLDEN AGE

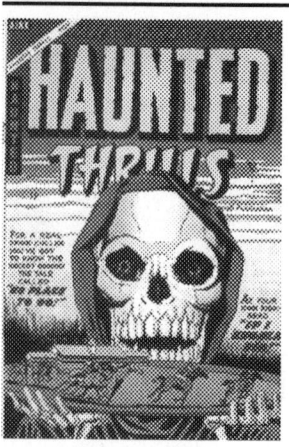

Haunted Thrills #18
© Four Star Publications

3 Drug Story 175.00
4 Ghouls Castle 150.00
5 Fatal Scapel 150.00
6 Pit of Horror 125.00
7 Trail to a Tomb 125.00
8 Vanishing Skull 125.00
9 Madness of Terror 125.00
10 . . . . 125.00
11 Nazi Concentration Camp . . . 150.00
12 RWb 100.00
13 . . . . 100.00
14 RWb 125.00
15 The Devil Collects 100.00
16 . . . . 100.00
17 Mirror of Madness 100.00
18 No Place to Go,
    Nov.–Dec., 1954 . . . . 110.00

HAUNT OF FEAR
Fables Publ.
(E.C. Comics)
May–June, 1950
15 JCr,JCr(c),AF,WW 2,400.00
16 JCr,JCr(c),AF,WW 1,000.00
17 JCr,JCr(c),AF,WW,O:Crypt
    of Terror,Vault of Horror
    & Haunt of Fear 900.00
4 AF(c),WW,JDa 600.00
5 JCr,JCr(c),WW,JDa,Eye Injury 500.00
6 JCr,JCr(c),WW,JDa. 350.00
7 JCr,JCr(c),WW,JDa. 350.00
8 AF(c),JKa,JDa,
    Shrunken Head 350.00
9 AF(c),JCr,JDa. 350.00
10 AF(c),Grl,JDa 325.00
11 JKa,Grl,JDa 275.00
12 JCr,Grl,JDa 275.00
13 Grl,JDa 275.00
14 Grl,Grl(c),JDa,O:Old Witch. . 325.00
15 JDa 275.00
16 GRi(c),JDa,Ray Bradbury
    adaptation 275.00
17 JDa,Grl(c),Classic
    Ghastly (c) 275.00
18 JDa,Grl(c),JKa,Ray Bradbury
    adaptation 300.00
19 JDa,Guillotine (c),
    Bondage cover 300.00
20 RC,JDa,Grl,Grl(c) 250.00
21 JDa,Grl,Grl(c) 200.00
22 same. 200.00
23 same 200.00
22 same 200.00

23 same 200.00
24 same 200.00
25 same 200.00
26 RC,same 250.00
27 same, Cannibalism 225.00
28 Dec., 1954 . . . . 225.00

HAWK, THE
Approved Comics
(Ziff-Davis)
Winter, 1951
1 MA,The Law of the Colt,P(c) . 150.00
2 JKu,Iron Caravan of the
    Mojave, P(c) 100.00
3 Leverett's Last Stand,P(c) . . . 75.00
4 Killer's Town,P(c) 60.00
5 . . . . 50.00
6 . . . . 50.00
7 . . . . 50.00
8 MB(c),Dry River Rampage 60.00
9 MB,MB(c),JKu 75.00
10 MB(c) 60.00
11 MB(c). 60.00
12 MB,MB(c), May, 1955 . . . . . . 60.00

HEADLINE COMICS
American Boys Comics/
Headline Publ. (Prize Publ.)
Feb., 1943
1 B:Jr. Rangers 350.00
2 JaB,JaB(c) 150.00
3 JaB,JaB(c) 110.00
4 . . . . 100.00
5 HcK 100.00
6 HcK 100.00
7 HcK,Jr. Rangers 100.00
8 HcK,Hitler cover 250.00
9 HcK 100.00
10 HcK,Hitler story,Wizard(c) . . . 150.00
11 . . . . 65.00
12 HcK,Heroes of Yesterday. 65.00
13 HcK,A:Blue Streak. 75.00
14 HcK,A:Blue Streak. 75.00
15 HcK,A:Blue Streak. 75.00
16 HcK,O:Atomic Man 175.00
17 Atomic Man(c) 100.00
18 Atomic Man(c) 100.00
19 S&K,Atomic Man(c) 200.00
20 Atomic Man(c) 100.00
21 E:Atomic Man 100.00
22 HcK 50.00
23 S&K,S&K(c),Valentines Day
    Massacre 175.00
24 S&K,S&K(c),You can't Forget
    a Killer 175.00
25 S&K,S&K(c),CrimeNeverPays 175.00
26 S&K,S&K(c),CrimeNeverPays 175.00
27 S&K,S&K(c),CrimeNeverPays 175.00
28 S&K,S&K(c),CrimeNeverPays 175.00
29 S&K,S&K(c),CrimeNeverPays 175.00
30 S&K,S&K(c),CrimeNeverPays 175.00
31 S&K,S&K(c),CrimeNeverPays 175.00
32 S&K,S&K(c),CrimeNeverPays 175.00
33 S&K,S&K(c),Police and FBI
    heroes 175.00
34 S&K,S&K(c),same 175.00
35 S&K,S&K(c),same 175.00
36 S&K,S&K(c),same,Ph(c) 100.00
37 S&K,S&K(c),MvS,same,Ph(c). 125.00
38 S&K,S&K(c),same,Ph(c) 40.00
39 S&K,S&K(c),same,Ph(c) 40.00
40 S&K,S&K(c),Ph(c)Violent
    Crime 40.00
41 Ph(c),J.Edgar Hoover(c) 40.00
42 Ph(c) 30.00
43 Ph(c) 30.00
44 MMe,MvS,WE,S&K 50.00
45 JK 25.00

46 . . . . 20.00
47 . . . . 20.00
48 . . . . 20.00
49 MMe 20.00
50 . . . . 20.00
51 JK 22.00
52 . . . . 20.00
53 . . . . 20.00
54 . . . . 20.00
55 . . . . 20.00
56 S&K. 40.00
57 . . . . 20.00
58 . . . . 20.00
59 . . . . 20.00
60 MvS(c). 20.00
61 MMe,MvS(c) 20.00
62 MMe,MMe(c). 20.00
63 MMe,MMe(c). 20.00
64 MMe,MMe(c). 20.00
65 MMe,MMe(c). 20.00
66 MMe,MMe(c). 20.00
67 MMe,MMe(c). 20.00
68 MMe,MMe(c). 20.00
69 MMe,MMe(c). 20.00
70 MMe,MMe(c). 20.00
71 MMe,MMe(c). 20.00
72 MMe,MMe(c). 20.00
73 MMe,MMe(c). 20.00
74 MMe,MMe(c). 20.00
75 MMe,MMe(c). 20.00
76 MMe,MMe(c). 20.00
77 MMe,MMe(c),Oct., 1956 . . . . 20.00

HEART THROBS
Comics Magazines
(Quality)
Aug., 1949
1 BWa(c),PG,Spoiled Brat 300.00
2 BWa(c),PG,Siren of
    the Tropics 175.00
3 PG 50.00
4 BWa(c),Greed Turned Me into
    a Scheming Vixen,Ph(c) 100.00
5 Ph(c) 30.00
6 BWa 85.00
7 . . . . 30.00
8 BWa 85.00
9 I Hated Men,Ph(c) 45.00
10 BWa,My Secret Fears 50.00
11 . . . . 18.00
12 . . . . 15.00
13 . . . . 18.00
14 BWa 18.00
15 My Right to Happiness,Ph(c) . . 45.00
16 . . . . 16.00
17 . . . . 16.00
18 . . . . 16.00
19 . . . . 16.00
20 . . . . 16.00
21 BWa 35.00
22 BWa 30.00
23 BWa 30.00
24 thru 30 . . . . @15.00
31 thru 33 . . . . @15.00
34 thru 39 . . . . @15.00
40 BWa 25.00
41 . . . . 15.00
42 . . . . 15.00
43 thru 45 . . . . @15.00
(Please see DC listings)

HECKLE AND JECKLE
St. John Publ./Pines
Nov., 1951
1 Blue Ribbon Comics 200.00
2 Blue Ribbon Comics 125.00
3 . . . . 85.00
4 . . . . 75.00

5	75.00
6	75.00
7	55.00
8	50.00
9	50.00
10	50.00
11 thru 15	@40.00
16 thru 20	@35.00
21 thru 33	@30.00
34 June, 1959	32.00

HELLO PAL COMICS
Harvey Publications
Jan., 1943

1 B:Rocketman & Rocket Girl, Mickey Rooney cover, Ph(c) all	500.00
2 Charlie McCarthy cover	400.00
3 Bob Hope cover, May, 1943	375.00

HENRY
Dell Publishing Co.
Oct., 1946

1	100.00
2	50.00
3 thru 10	@35.00
11 thru 20	@25.00
21 thru 30	@20.00
31 thru 40	@15.00
41 thru 50	@12.00
51 thru 65	@10.00

Henry Aldrich Comics #3
© Dell Publishing Co.

HENRY ALDRICH COMICS
Dell Publishing Co.
Aug.–Sept., 1950

1	90.00
2	45.00
3	30.00
4	30.00
5	30.00
6 thru 10	@25.00
11 thru 22	@20.00

HEROIC COMICS
Eastern Color Printing Co./
Famous Funnies
Aug., 1940

1 BEv,BEv(c),O:Hydroman,Purple Zombie, B:Man of India	1,200.00
2 BEv,BEv(c),B:Hydroman covers	600.00

3 BEv,BEv(c)	375.00
4 BEv,BEv(c)	350.00
5 BEv,BEv(c)	325.00
6 BEv,BEv(c)	300.00
7 BEv,BEv(c),O:Man O'Metal	350.00
8 BEv,BEv(c)	200.00
9 BEv	200.00
10 BEv	200.00
11 BEv,E:Hydroman covers	200.00
12 BEv,B&O:Music Master	225.00
13 BEv,RC,LF	200.00
14 BEv	225.00
15 BEv,I:Downbeat	225.00
16 BEv,CCB(c),A:Lieut Nininger, Major Heidger,Lieut Welch,B:P(c)	150.00
17 BEv,A:JohnJames Powers,Hewitt T.Wheless, Irving Strobing	150.00
18 HcK,BEv,Pass the Ammunition	150.00
19 HcK,BEv,A:Barney Ross	150.00
20 HcK,BEv	135.00
21 HcK,BEv	100.00
22 HcK,BEv,Howard Gilmore	100.00
23 HcK,BEv	100.00
24 HcK,BEv	100.00
25 HcK,BEv	100.00
26 HcK,BEv	100.00
27 HcK,BEv	100.00
28 HcK,BEv,E:Man O'Metal	100.00
29 HcK,BEv,E:Hydroman	100.00
30 BEv	100.00
31 BEv,CCB,Capt. Tootsie	25.00
32 ATh,CCB,WWII(c), Capt. Tootsie	45.00
33 ATh,	45.00
34 WWII(c)	25.00
35 Ath,B:Rescue(c)	45.00
36 HcK,ATh	45.00
37 same	45.00
38 ATh	45.00
39 HcK,ATh	45.00
40 ATh,Boxing	45.00
41 Grl(c),ATh	45.00
42 ATh	45.00
43 ATh	35.00
44 HcK,ATh	35.00
45 HcK	35.00
46 HcK	35.00
47 HcK	35.00
48 HcK	35.00
49 HcK	35.00
50 HcK	35.00
51 HcK,ATh,AW	40.00
52 HcK,AW	40.00
53 HcK	35.00
54	25.00
55 ATh	25.00
56 ATh(c)	30.00
57 ATh(c)	25.00
58 ATh(c)	25.00
59 ATh(c)	25.00
60 ATh(c)	25.00
61 BEv(c)	20.00
62 BEv(c)	20.00
63 BEv(c)	20.00
64 GE,BEv(c)	22.00
65 HcK(c),FF,ATh,AW,GE	50.00
66 HcK(c),FF	35.00
67 HcK(c),FF,Korean War(c)	35.00
68 HcK(c),Korean War(c)	35.00
69 HcK(c),FF	50.00
70 HcK(c),FF,B:Korean War(c)	35.00
71 HcK(c),FF	35.00
72 HcK(c),FF	50.00
73 HcK(c),FF	35.00
74 HcK(c)	35.00
75 HcK(c),FF	35.00
76 HcK,HcK(c)	20.00
77 same	20.00
78 same	20.00

Heroic Comics #4
© Eastern Color Printing

79 same	20.00
80 same	20.00
81 FF,HcK(c)	22.00
82 FF,HcK(c)	22.00
83 FF,HcK(c)	22.00
84 HcK(c)	22.00
85 HcK(c)	22.00
86 FF,HcK(c)	25.00
87 FF,HcK(c)	25.00
88 HcK(c),E:Korean War covers	20.00
89 HcK(c)	20.00
90 HcK(c)	20.00
91 HcK(c)	20.00
92 HcK(c)	20.00
93 HcK(c)	20.00
94 HcK(c)	20.00
95 HcK(c)	20.00
96 HcK(c)	20.00
97 HcK(c),E:P(c),June, 1955	20.00

HICKORY
Comic Magazine
(Quality Comics Group)
Oct., 1949

1 ASa,	75.00
2 ASa,	35.00
3 ASa,	25.00
4 ASa,	25.00
5 ASa,	25.00
6 ASa,Aug., 1950	25.00

HI-HO COMICS
Four Star Publications, 1946

1 LbC(c)	200.00
2 LbC(c)	100.00
3 1946	100.00

HI-JINX
B & I Publ. Co.
(American Comics Group)
July–Aug., 1947

1 (fa) all	100.00
2	60.00
3	50.00
4 thru 7	@40.00
N#	75.00

HI-LITE COMICS
E.R. Ross Publ.
Fall, 1945
1 .... 100.00

Hit Comics #2
© Quality Comics Group

HIT COMICS
Comics Magazine
(Quality Comics Group)
July, 1940
1 LF(c),O:Neon,Hercules,I:The
  Red Bee, B:Bob & Swab,
  Blaze Barton Strange
  Twins,X-5 Super Agent
  Casey Jones,Jack & Jill . . 5,500.00
2 GT,LF(c),B:Old Witch 2,000.00
3 GT,LF(c),E:Casey Jones . . . 1,800.00
4 GT,LF(c),B:Super Agent &
  Betty Bates,E:X-5 . . . . 1,500.00
5 GT,LF(c),B:Red Bee cover . . 4,400.00
6 GT,LF(c) 1,500.00
7 GT,LF(c),E:Red Bee cover . . 1,550.00
8 GT,LF(c),B:Neon cover 1,500.00
9 JCo,LF(c),E:Neon cover. . . . 1,500.00
10 JCo,RC,LF(c),B:Hercules(c) 1,500.00
11 JCo,RC,LF(c),A:Hercules 950.00
12 JCo,RC,LF(c),A:Hercules. . . . 950.00
13 JCo,RC,LF(c),A:Hercules. . . . 950.00
14 JCo,RC,LF(c),A:Hercules. . . . 950.00
15 JCo,RC,A:Hercules 900.00
16 JCo,RC,LF(c),A:Hercules. . . . 900.00
17 JCo,RC,LF(c),E:Hercules(c). . 900.00
18 JCo,RC,RC(c),O:Stormy
  Foster,B:Ghost of Flanders 1,000.00
19 JCo,RC(c),B:StormyFoster . . 850.00
20 JCo,RC(c),A:Stormy Foster . . 850.00
21 JCo,RC(c) 800.00
22 JCo 800.00
23 JCo,RC,RC(c) 750.00
24 JCo,E:Stormy Foster cover . . 750.00
25 JCo,RP,O:Kid Eternity 1,400.00
26 JCo,RP,A:Black Hawk 800.00
27 JCo,RP,B:Kid Eternity covers . 400.00
28 JCo,RP,A:Her Highness 400.00
29 JCo,RP 400.00
30 JCo,RP,HK,V:Julius Caesar
  and his Legion of Warriors . . 350.00
31 JCo,RP 350.00
32 JCo,RP,V:Merlin the Wizard . . 200.00
33 JCo,RP 175.00
34 JCo,RP,E:Stormy Foster 175.00
35 JCo,Kid Eternity accused
  of Murder 175.00
36 JCo,The Witch's Curse 175.00

37 JCo,V:Mr. Silence 175.00
38 JCo 175.00
39 JCo,Runaway River Boat. . . . 175.00
40 PG,V:Monster from the Past . 175.00
41 PG,Did Kid Eternity Lose
  His Power?. 125.00
42 PG,Kid Eternity Loses Killer
  Cronson 125.00
43 JCo,PG,V:Modern Bluebeard . 125.00
44 JCo,PG,Trips up the Shoe . . . 125.00
45 JCo,PG,Pancho Villa against
  Don Pablo 125.00
46 JCo,V:Mr. Hardeel 125.00
47 A Polished Diamond can be
  Rough on Rats 125.00
48 EhH,A Treasure Chest
  of Trouble. 125.00
49 EhH,V:Monsters from
  the Mirror 125.00
50 EhH,Heads for Trouble 125.00
51 EhH,Enters the Forgotten
  World 100.00
52 EhH,Heroes out of the Past . . 100.00
53 EhH,V:Mr. Puny 100.00
54 V:Ghost Town Killer 100.00
55 V:The Brute 100.00
56 V:Big Odds 100.00
57 Solves the Picture in
  a Frame 100.00
58 Destroys Oppression!. 100.00
59 Battles Tomorrow's Crimes
  Today! 100.00
60 E:Kid Eternity covers,
  V:The Mummy 100.00
61 RC,RC(c),I:Jeb Rivers 125.00
62 RC(c). 100.00
63 RC(c),A:Jeb Rivers 125.00
64 RC,A:Jeb Rivers 125.00
65 Bondage cover,RC,July, 1950 135.00

HOLIDAY COMICS
Fawcett Publ.
Nov., 1942
1 Captain Marvel (c) 1,500.00

HOLIDAY COMICS
Star Publ.
Jan., 1951
1 LbC(c),(fa),Christmas cover . . 250.00
2 LbC(c),Parade(c) 275.00
3 LbC(c),July 4th(c) 175.00
4 LbC(c),Vacation(c) 175.00
5 LbC(c),Christmas(c) 175.00
6 LbC(c),Birthday(c). 175.00
7 LbC(c) 150.00
8 LbC(c),Christmas(c) 175.00

HOLLYWOOD COMICS
New Age Publishers
Winter, 1944
1 (fa). 125.00

HOLLYWOOD CONFESSIONS
St. John Publ. Co.
Oct., 1949
1 JKu,JKu(c) 175.00
2 JKu,JKu(c), Dec., 1949 . . . . 225.00

HOLLYWOOD DIARY
Comics Magazine
(Quality Comics), Dec., 1949
1 . . . . 125.00
2 Photo cover 75.00

3 Photo cover 60.00
4 . . . . 60.00
5 Photo cover, Aug., 1950 . . . . 60.00

HOLLYWOOD FILM STORIES
Feature Publications
(Prize)
April, 1950
1 June Allison,Ph(c) 125.00
2 Lizabeth Scott,Ph(c) 75.00
3 Barbara Stanwick,Ph(c) 75.00
4 Beth Hutton, Aug., 1950 . . . . 75.00

HOLLYWOOD SECRETS
Comics Magazine
(Quality Comics Group)
Nov., 1949
1 BWa,BWa(c) 225.00
2 BWa,BWa(c),RC 125.00
3 Ph(c) 75.00
4 Ph(c),May, 1950 . . . . 75.00
5 Ph(c) 75.00
6 Ph(c) 75.00

HOLYOKE ONE-SHOT
Tem Publ.
(Holyoke Publ. Co.), 1944
1 Grit Grady 75.00
2 Rusty Dugan 65.00
3 JK,Miss Victory,O:Cat Woman. 150.00
4 Mr. Miracle 55.00
5 U.S. Border Patrol 50.00
6 Capt. Fearless 50.00
7 Strong Man 55.00
8 Blue Streak 50.00
9 S&K, Citizen Smith 80.00
10 S&K, Capt. Stone 75.00

HONEYMOON ROMANCE
Artful Publications
(Digest Size)
April, 1950
1 . . . . 250.00
2 July, 1950 . . . . 225.00

HOODED HORSEMAN
(see OUT OF THE NIGHT)

HOPALONG CASSIDY
Fawcett Publications
Feb., 1943
1 B:Hopalong Cassidy & Topper,
  Captain Marvel cover 4,500.00
2 . . . . 650.00
3 Blazing Trails 300.00
4 5-full length story 275.00
5 Death in the Saddle, Ph(c) . . 250.00
6 . . . . 200.00
7 . . . . 200.00
8 Phantom Stage Coach 200.00
9 The Last Stockade 200.00
10 4-spine tingling adventures . . 200.00
11 Desperate Jetters! Ph(c) 150.00
12 The Mysterious Message. . . . 150.00
13 The Human Target, Ph(c). . . . 150.00
14 Land of the Lawless, Ph(c). . . 150.00
15 Death holds the Reins, Ph(c) . 150.00
16 Webfoot's Revenge, Ph(c) . . . 150.00
17 The Hangman's Noose, Ph(c) 150.00

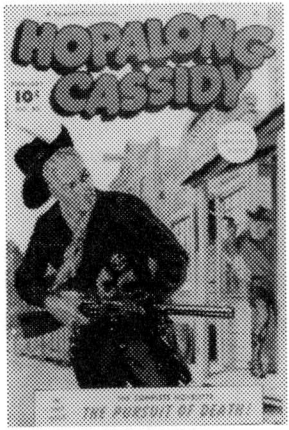

Hopalong Cassidy #40
© Fawcett Publications

18 The Ghost of Dude Ranch, Ph(c)	150.00
19 A:William Boyd,Ph(c)	150.00
20 The Notorious Nellie Blaine!, B:P(c)	125.00
21 V:Arizona Kid	125.00
22 V:Arizona Kid	125.00
23 Hayride Horror	125.00
24 Twin River Giant	125.00
25 On the Trails of the Wild and Wooly West	125.00
26 thru 30	@100.00
31 52 pages	75.00
32 36 pages	75.00
33 thru 35, 52 pages	@75.00
36 36 pages	60.00
37 thru 40, 52 pages	@75.00
40 36 pages	60.00
41 E:P(c)	40.00
42 B:Ph(c)	75.00
43	75.00
44	50.00
45	60.00
46 thru 51	@50.00
52	45.00
53	50.00
54	50.00
55	45.00
56	50.00
57	50.00
58 thru 70	@50.00
71 thru 84	@40.00
85 E:Ph(c),Jan., 1954	50.00

(Please see DC listings)

HOPPY THE MARVEL BUNNY
Fawcett Publications
Dec., 1945

1 A:Marvel Bunny	150.00
2	75.00
3	50.00
4	50.00
5	50.00
6 thru 14	@40.00
15 Sept., 1947	40.00

HORRIFIC
Artful/Comic Media/ Harwell Publ./Mystery
Sept., 1952

1 Conductor in Flames(c)	275.00
2 Human Puppets(c)	150.00
3 DH(c),Bullet hole in head(c)	250.00
4 DH(c),head on a stick (c)	100.00
5 DH(c)	125.00
6 DH(c),Jack the Ripper	100.00
7 DH(c),Shrunken Skulls	100.00
8 DH(c),I:The Teller	125.00
9 DH(c),Claws of Horror, Wolves of Midnight	100.00
10 DH(c),The Teller-four eerie tales of Horror	100.00
11 DH(c),A:Gary Ghoul,Freddie, Demon,Victor Vampire, Walter Werewolf	75.00
12 DH(c),A:Gary Ghoul,Freddie Demon,Victor Vampire, Walter Werewolf	75.00
13 DH(c),A:Gary Ghoul,Freddie Demom,Victor Werewolf, Walter Werewolf	75.00

Becomes:

TERRIFIC COMICS

14	175.00
15	125.00
16 B:Wonderboy	125.00

Becomes:

WONDERBOY

17 The Enemy's Enemy	350.00
18 Success is No Accident, July, 1955	300.00

HORROR FROM THE TOMB
(see MYSTERIOUS STORIES)

HORRORS, THE
Star Publications
Jan., 1953

11 LbC(c),JyD,of War	200.00
12 LbC(c),of War	175.00
13 LbC(c),of Mystery	150.00
14 LbC(c),of the Underworld	175.00
15 LbC(c),of the Underworld, April, 1954	175.00

HORSE FEATHER COMICS
Lev Gleason Publications
Nov., 1947

1 BW	135.00
2	55.00
3	50.00
4 Summer, 1948	50.00

HOT ROD AND SPEEDWAY COMICS
Hillman Periodicals
Feb.–March, 1952

1	225.00
2 BK	100.00
3	50.00
4	50.00
5 April–May, 1953	50.00

HOT ROD COMICS
Fawcett Publications
Feb., 1952–53

N# BP,BP(c),F:Clint Curtis	200.00
2 BP,BP(c),Safety comes First	125.00
3 BP,BP(c),The Racing Game	100.00
4 BP,BP(c),Bonneville National Championships	100.00
5 BP,BP(c),	100.00
6 BP,BP(c),Race to Death	100.00

HOT ROD KING
Approved Comics
(Ziff-Davis), Fall, 1952

1 P(c)	175.00

HOWDY DOODY
Dell Publishing Co.
Jan., 1950

1 Ph(c)	950.00
2 Ph(c)	400.00
3 Ph(c)	225.00
4 Ph(c)	225.00
5 Ph(c)	225.00
6 P(c)	150.00
7	135.00
8	135.00
9	135.00
10	135.00
11	125.00
12	125.00
13 Christmas (c)	125.00
14 thru 20	@125.00
21 thru 38	@100.00

HOW STALIN HOPES WE WILL DESTROY AMERICA
Pictorial News, 1951

N# (Giveaway)	400.00

HUMBUG
Harvey Kurtzman, 1957

1 JDa,WW,WE,End of the World	225.00
2 JDa,WE,Radiator	100.00
3 JDa,WE	75.00
4 JDa,WE,Queen Victoria(c)	75.00
5 JDa,WE	75.00
6 JDa,WE	75.00
7 JDa,WE,Sputnik(c)	80.00
8 JDa,WE,Elvis/George Washington(c)	75.00
9 JDa,WE	75.00
10 JDa,Magazine	100.00
11 JDw,WE,HK,Magazine	100.00

HUMDINGER
Novelty Press/ Premium Service
May–June, 1946

1 B:Jerkwater Line,Dink, Mickey Starlight	225.00
2	100.00
3	75.00
4	75.00
5	75.00
6	75.00
2-1	60.00
2-2 July–Aug., 1947	60.00

HUMPHREY COMICS
Harvey Publications
Oct., 1948
1 BP,Joe Palooka 80.00
2 BP 35.00
3 BP 30.00
4 BP,A:Boy Heroes 40.00
5 BP 25.00
6 BP 25.00
7 BP,A:Little Dot 25.00
8 BP,O:Humphrey 30.00
9 BP 20.00
10 BP..................... 20.00
11 thru 21 .... @20.00
22 April, 1952................ 20.00

HYPER MYSTERY COMICS
Hyper Publications
May, 1940
1 B:Hyper 1,600.00
2 June, 1940 .... 900.00

Ibis The Invincible #5
© Fawcett Publications

IBIS, THE INVINCIBLE
Fawcett Publications
Jan., 1942
1 MRa(c),O:Ibis 1,400.00
2 Bondage cover 700.00
3 BW 600.00
4 BW,A:Mystic Snake People .. 400.00
5 BW,Bondage cover,The
   Devil's Ibistick 425.00
6 BW, The Book of Evil,
   Spring, 1948 .... 425.00

IDEAL ROMANCE
(see TENDER ROMANCE)

IF THE DEVIL WOULD TALK
Catechetical Guild, 1950
N# Rare................... 600.00
N#, 1958 Very Rare......... 450.00

ILLUSTRATED STORIES OF THE OPERA
B. Bailey Publ. Co., 1943
N# Faust................. 500.00

N# Aida 450.00
N# Carman 450.00
N# Rigoletto 450.00

I LOVED
(see ZOOT COMICS)

I LOVE LUCY COMICS
Dell Publishing Co.
Feb., 1954
(1) see Dell Four Color #535
(2) see Dell Four Color #559
3 Lucile Ball Ph(c) all........ 225.00
4 .... 200.00
5 .... 200.00
6 thru 10 .... @175.00
11 thru 20................ 125.00
21 thru 35................ 100.00

IMPACT
E.C. Comics
March–April, 1955
1 RC,GE,BK,Grl 125.00
2 RC,JDu,Grl,BK,JO 100.00
3 JO,RC,JDU,Grl,JKa,BK 80.00
4 RC,JO,JDa,GE,Grl,BK 80.00
5 Nov.–Dec., 1955 .... 80.00

INCREDIBLE SCIENCE FANTASY
(see WEIRD SCIENCE)

INCREDIBLE SCIENCE FICTION
E.C. Comics
July–Aug., 1955
30 .... 300.00
31 .... 300.00
32 Jan.–Feb., 1956.......... 300.00
33....................... 250.00

INDIAN CHIEF
Dell Publishing Co.
July–Sept., 1951
3 P(c) all 30.00
4 .... 15.00
5 .... 15.00
6 A:White Eagle............ 15.00
7 .... 15.00
8 .... 15.00
9 .... 15.00
10 .... 15.00
11 .... 15.00
12 I:White Eagle........... 25.00
13 thru 29 .... @10.00
30 SB.................... 15.00
31 SB.................... 15.00
32 SB.................... 15.00
33 SB.................... 15.00

INDIAN FIGHTER
Youthful Magazines
May, 1950
1 Revenge of Chief Crazy Horse 60.00
2 Bondage cover 35.00
3 .... 20.00
4 Cheyenne Warpath 20.00
5 .... 20.00
6 Davy Crockett in Death Stalks
   the Alamo 20.00
7 Tom Horn-Bloodshed at

Massacre Valley 20.00
8 Tales of Wild Bill Hickory,
   Jan., 1952 .... 20.00

INDIANS
Wings Publ. Co.
(Fiction House)
Spring, 1950
1 B:Long Bow, Manzar, White
   Indian & Orphan 150.00
2 B:Starlight 75.00
3 Longbow(c) 60.00
4 Longbow(c) 50.00
5 Manzar(c)................ 60.00
6 Captive of the Semecas 50.00
7 Longbow(c) 50.00
8 A:Long Bow 50.00
9 A:Long Bow 50.00
10 Manzar(c) 50.00
11 thru 16 .... @40.00
17 Spring, 1953,Longbow(c).... 40.00

INDIANS ON THE WARPATH
St. John Publ. Co., 1950
N# MB(c)................. 225.00

INFORMER, THE
Feature Television Productions
April, 1954
1 MSy,The Greatest Social
   Menace of our Time! 65.00
2 MSy..................... 35.00
3 MSy 30.00
4 MSy 30.00
5 Dec., 1954 .... 30.00

IN LOVE
Mainline/Charlton Comics
Aug., 1954
1 S&K,Bride of the Star 225.00
2 S&K,Marilyn's Men 125.00
3 S&K 100.00
4 S&K,Comics Code 60.00
5 S&K(c) 60.00
6 .... 30.00
Becomes:

I LOVE YOU
7 JK(c),BP 75.00
8 .... 25.00
9 .... 25.00
10 .... 25.00
11 thru 16 .... @20.00
17 .... 15.00
18 .... 10.00
19 .... 10.00
20...................... 10.00
21 thru 50 .... @7.00
51 thru 59 .... @5.00
60 Elvis 85.00
61 thru 100 .... @4.00
101 thru 130 .... @3.00

INTERNATIONAL COMICS
(see CRIME PATROL)

INTERNATIONAL CRIME PATROL
(see CRIME PATROL)

INTIMATE CONFESSIONS
Fawcett Publ./
Realistic Comics, 1951

1a P(c) all, Unmarried Bride . . .	550.00
1 EK,EK(c),Days of Temptation... Nights of Desire	150.00
2 Doomed to Silence	135.00
3 EK(c), The Only Man For Me .	125.00
3a Robert Briffault	125.00
4 EK(c),Tormented Love	125.00
5 Her Secret Sin	125.00
6 Reckless Pick-up	125.00
7 A Love Like Ours,Spanking. . .	150.00
8 Fatal Woman, March, 1953 . .	125.00

INTIMATE LOVE
Standard Magazines
Jan., 1950

5 Wings on My Heart,Ph(c)	40.00
6 WE,JSe,Ph(c).	45.00
7 WE,JSe,Ph(c),I Toyed with Love	45.00
8 WE,JSe,Ph(c).	45.00
9 Ph(c)	25.00
10 Ph(c),My Hopeless Heart. . . .	35.00
11	15.00
12	15.00
13 thru 18 . . . . @	15.00
19 ATh	35.00
20	15.00
21 ATh	35.00
22 ATh	35.00
23 ATh	15.00
24 ATh	35.00
25 ATh	15.00
26 ATh	35.00
27 ATh	15.00
28 ATh,Aug., 1954	15.00

INTIMATE SECRETS OF ROMANCE
Star Publications
Sept., 1953

1 LbC(c)	100.00
2 LbC(c)	85.00

INVISIBLE SCARLET O'NEIL
Harvey Publications
Dec., 1950

1	100.00
2	75.00
3 April, 1951	75.00

IT REALLY HAPPENED
William H. Wise/
Visual Editions, 1945

1 Benjamin Franklin, Kit Carson	125.00
2 The Terrible Tiddlers	75.00
3 Maid of the Margiris	50.00
4 Chaplain Albert J. Hoffman . .	50.00
5 AS(c),Monarchs of the Sea,Lou Gehrig, Amelia Earhart	100.00
6 AS(c),Ernie Pyle	50.00
7 FG,Teddy Roosevelt,Jefferson Davis, Story of the Helicopter	50.00
8 FG,Man O' War,Roy Rogers . .	125.00
9 AS(c),The Story of Old Ironsides	50.00
10 AS(c),Honus Wagner, The Story of Mark Twain	75.00
11 AS(c),MB,Queen of the Spanish Main, Oct., 1947	65.00

JACK ARMSTRONG
Parents' Institute
Nov., 1947

1 Artic Mystery	350.00
2 Den of the Golden Dragon . . .	150.00
3 Lost Valley of Ice	125.00
4 Land of the Leopard Men	125.00
5 Fight against Racketeers of the Ring	125.00
6	75.00
7 Baffling Mystery on the Diamond	80.00
8	80.00
9 Mystery of the Midgets	80.00
10 Secret Cargo	80.00
11	75.00
12 Madman's Island, rare	125.00
13 Sept., 1949	75.00

JACE PEARSON OF THE TEXAS RANGERS
Dell Publishing Co.
May, 1952

(1) see Dell Four Color #396	
2 Ph(c),Joel McRae	50.00
3 Ph(c),Joel McRae	50.00
4 Ph(c),Joel McRae	50.00
5 Ph(c),Joel McRae	50.00
6 Ph(c),Joel McRae	50.00
7 Ph(c),Joel McRae	50.00
8 Ph(c),Joel McRae	50.00
9 Ph(c),Joel McRae	50.00
(10) see Dell Four Color #648	

Becomes:

TALES OF JACE PEARSON OF THE TEXAS RANGERS

11	30.00
12	30.00
13	30.00
14	30.00
15 ATh	40.00
16 ATh	40.00
17 thru 20 . . . . @	30.00

JACKIE GLEASON
St. John Publishing Co.
Sept., 1955

1 Ph(c)	700.00
2	500.00

Jackie Gleason #4
© St. John Publishing Co.

3	400.00
4 Dec., 1955	375.00

JACKIE ROBINSON
Fawcett Publications
May, 1950

N# Ph(c) all issues.	700.00
2	500.00
3 thru 5 . . . . @	400.00
6 May, 1952	350.00

JACK IN THE BOX
(see YELLOW JACKET COMICS)

JACKPOT COMICS
MLJ Magazines
Spring, 1941

1 CBi(c),B:Black Hood,Mr.Justice, Steel Sterling,Sgt.Boyle . .	2,400.00
2 SCp(c), ...	1,000.00
3 Bondage cover	750.00
4 First Archie	2,600.00
5 Hitler(c)	1,200.00
6 Son of the Skull v:Black Hood, Bondage(c)	850.00
7 Bondage (c)	850.00
8 Sal(c), ...	800.00
9 Sal(c), ...	800.00

Becomes:

JOLLY JINGLES

10 Super Duck,(fa)	250.00
11 Super Duck	135.00
12 Hitler parody cover,A:Woody Woodpecker	75.00
13 Super Duck	50.00
14 Super Duck	50.00
15 Super Duck	50.00
16 Dec., 1944.	50.00

JACK THE GIANT KILLER
Bimfort & Co.
Aug.–Sept., 1953

1 HcK,HcK(c).	135.00

JAMBOREE
Round Publishing Co.
Feb., 1946

1	125.00
2 March, 1946	75.00

JANE ARDEN
St. John Publ. Co.
March, 1948

1	120.00
2 June, 1948	70.00

JEEP COMICS
R.B. Leffingwell & Co.
Winter, 1944

1 B;Captain Power.	300.00
2	200.00
3 LbC(c),March–April, 1948 . . .	300.00

JEFF JORDAN, U.S. AGENT
D.S. Publ. Co., Dec., 1947

1	55.00

GOLDEN AGE

JESSE JAMES
Avon Periodicals/
Realistic Publ.
Aug., 1950
1 JKu,The San Antonio Stage
   Robbery 125.00
2 JKu,The Daring Liberty Bank
   Robbery 100.00
3 JKu,The California Stagecoach
   Robberies 75.00
4 EK(c),Deadliest Deed! 35.00
5 JKu,WW,Great Prison Break . 100.00
6 JKu,Wanted Dead or Alive . . . 100.00
7 JKu,Six-Gun Slaughter at
   San Romano! 75.00
8 EK,Daring Train Robbery! 50.00
9 EK 25.00
10 thru 14 {Do not exist}
15 . . . . 40.00
16 . . . . 30.00
17 . . . . 25.00
18 JKu 25.00
19 JKu 25.00
20 AW,FF,A:Chief Vic,Kit West . . 100.00
21 . . . . 25.00
22 . . . . 25.00
23 . . . . 25.00
24 EK,B:New McCarty 25.00
25 EK. 25.00
26 EK. 25.00
27 EK,E:New McCarty 25.00
28 . . . . 25.00
29 Aug., 1956. . . . . 25.00

JEST
Harry 'A' Chesler, 1944
10 J. Rebel,Yankee Boy 100.00
11 1944,Little Nemo 125.00

JET ACES
Real Adventure Publ. Co.
(Fiction House), 1952
1 Set 'em up in MIG Alley 100.00
2 Kiss-Off for Moscow Molly 60.00
3 Red Task Force Sighted 60.00
4 Death-Date at 40,000, 1953 . . . 60.00

JET FIGHTERS
Standard Magazines
Nov., 1953
5 ATh,Korean War Stories 85.00
6 Circus Pilot 35.00
7 ATh, Iron Curtains for Ivan,
   March, 1953 . . . . 50.00

JETTA OF THE
21st CENTURY
Standard Comics
Dec., 1952
5 Teen Stories 150.00
6 . . . . 100.00
7 April, 1953 . . . . 100.00

JIGGS AND MAGGIE
Best Books (Standard)/
Harvey Publ.
June, 1949
11 . . . . 60.00
12 thru 21 . . . . @30.00
22 thru 26 . . . . @22.00
27 Feb.–March, 1954 . . . . 22.00

JIM HARDY
Spotlight Publ., 1944
N# Dynamite Jim,Mirror Man . . . 300.00

JIM RAY'S AVIATION
SKETCH BOOK
Vital Publishers
Feb., 1946
1 Radar, the Invisible eye 175.00
2 Gen.Hap Arnold, May, 1946 . . . 150.00

JINGLE JANGLE
COMICS
Eastern Color Printing Co.
Feb., 1942
1 B:Benny Bear,Pie Face Prince,
   Jingle Jangle Tales,Hortense 350.00
2 GCn 175.00
3 GCn 150.00
4 GCn,Pie Face cover 150.00
5 GCn,B:Pie Face 150.00
6 GCn, ... 125.00
7 . . . . 125.00
8 . . . . 125.00
9 . . . . 125.00
10 . . . . 125.00
11 thru 15 E:Pie Face . . . . @100.00
16 thru 20 . . . . @75.00
21 thru 25 . . . . @60.00
26 thru 30 . . . . @50.00
31 thru 41 . . . . @40.00
42 Dec., 1949. . . . . 40.00

JING PALS
Victory Publ. Corp.
Feb., 1946
1 Johnny Rabbit 60.00
2 . . . . 30.00
3 . . . . 30.00
4 Aug., 1948 . . . . 30.00

JOE COLLEGE
Hillman Periodicals
Fall, 1949
1 BP,DPr 50.00
2 BP, Winter, 1949 . . . . 45.00

JOE LOUIS
Fawcett Periodicals
Sept., 1950
1 Ph(c),Life Story. 450.00
2 Ph(c),Nov., 1950 . . . . 300.00

JOE PALOOKA
Publication Enterprises
(Columbia Comics Group)
1943
1 Lost in the Desert 600.00
2 Hitler cover 400.00
3 KO's the Nazis! 250.00
4 Eiffel tower cover, 1944 . . . . . 225.00

JOE PALOOKA
Harvey Publications
Nov., 1954–March 1961
1 Joe Tells How he became
   World Champ 350.00
2 Skiing cover 175.00
3 . . . . 100.00
4 Welcome Home Pals! 100.00

Joe Palooka #1
© Harvey Publications

5 S&K,The Great Carnival
   Murder Mystery 150.00
6 Classic Joe Palooka (c) 100.00
7 BP,V:Grumpopski 100.00
8 BP,Mystery of the Ghost Ship . 75.00
9 Drooten Island Mystery 75.00
10 BP. 75.00
11 . . . . 65.00
12 BP,Boxing Course 65.00
13 . . . . 60.00
14 BP,Palooka's Toughest Fight . . 60.00
15 BP,O:Humphrey 100.00
16 BP,A:Humphrey 60.00
17 BP,A:Humphrey 60.00
18 . . . . 60.00
19 BP,Freedom Train(c) 75.00
20 Punch Out(c) 60.00
21 . . . . 50.00
22 V:Assassin. 50.00
23 Big Bathing Beauty Issue 50.00
24 . . . . 50.00
25 . . . . 50.00
26 BP,Big Prize Fight Robberies . . 50.00
27 BP,Mystery of Bal
   Eagle Cabin 50.00
28 BP,Fights out West 50.00
29 BP,Joe Busts Crime
   Wide Open. 50.00
30 BP,V:Hoodlums 40.00
31 BP. 40.00
32 BP,Fight Palooka was sure
   to Lose. 40.00
33 BP,Joe finds Ann 40.00
34 BP,How to Box like a Champ . . 40.00
35 BP,More Adventures of Little
   Max 40.00
36 BP. 40.00
37 BP,Joe as a Boy 40.00
38 BP. 40.00
39 BP,Original Hillbillies with
   Big Leviticus. 40.00
40 BP,Joe's Toughest Fight 40.00
41 BP,Humphrey's Grudge Fight . . 40.00
42 BP. 40.00
43 BP. 40.00
44 BP,M:Ann Howe. 50.00
45 BP. 35.00
46 Champ of Champs. 35.00
47 BreathtakingUnderwaterBattle . 35.00
48 BP,Exciting Indian Adventure . . 35.00
49 BP. 35.00
50 BP,Bondage(c) 35.00
51 BP. 35.00
52 BP,V:Balonki 35.00
53 BP. 35.00

54 V:Bad Man Trigger McGehee . . 35.00
55 . . . . 35.00
56 Foul Play on the High Seas . . . 35.00
57 Curtains for the Champ 35.00
58 V:The Man-Eating Swamp
    Terror 35.00
59 The Enemy Attacks 35.00
60 Joe Fights Escaped Convict . . 35.00
61 . . . . 30.00
62 S&K 45.00
63 . . . . 30.00
64 . . . . 30.00
65 . . . . 30.00
66 . . . . 30.00
67 . . . . 30.00
68 . . . . 30.00
69 A Package from Home 30.00
70 BP 30.00
71 . . . . 30.00
72 . . . . 30.00
73 BP 30.00
74 thru 118 . . . . @30.00
Giant 1 Body Building 65.00
Giant 2 Fights His Way Back . . . 125.00
Giant 3 Visits Lost City 60.00
Giant 4 All in Family 65.00

JOE YANK
Visual Editions
(Standard Comics)
March, 1952
5 ATh,WE,Korean Jackpot! 60.00
6 Bacon and Bullets,
    G.I.Renegade 40.00
7 Two-Man War,A:Sgt. Glamour . 30.00
8 ATh(c),Miss Foxhole of 1952, . 30.00
9 G.I.'s and Dolls,Colonel Blood . 25.00
10 A Good Way to Die,
    A:General Joe 25.00
11 . . . . 25.00
12 RA 25.00
13 . . . . 25.00
14 . . . . 25.00
15 . . . . 25.00
16 July, 1954 . . . . 25.00

JOHN HIX SCRAPBOOK
Eastern Color Printing Co.
1937
1 Strange as It Seems 250.00
2 Strange as It Seems 200.00

JOHNNY DANGER
Toby Press, Aug., 1954
1 Ph(c),Private Detective 125.00

JOHNNY DYNAMITE
(see DYNAMITE)

JOHNNY HAZARD
Best Books
(Standard Comics)
Aug., 1948
5 FR 100.00
6 FR,FR(c) 75.00
7 FR(c) 60.00
8 FR,FR(c), May, 1949 . . . . 60.00

JOHNNY LAW,
SKY RANGER
Good Comics (Lev Gleason)
April, 1955
1 . . . . 50.00

---

2 . . . . 30.00
3 . . . . 30.00
4 Nov., 1955 . . . . 30.00

JOHN WAYNE
ADVENTURE COMICS
Toby Press, Winter, 1949
1 Ph(c),The Mysterious Valley
    of Violence 1,200.00
2 AW,FF,Ph(c) 500.00
3 AW,FF,Flying Sheriff 500.00
4 AW,FF,Double-Danger,Ph(c) . 500.00
5 Volcano of Death,Ph(c) 450.00
6 AW,FF,Caravan of Doom,
    Ph(c) 450.00
7 AW,FF,Ph(c) 400.00
8 AW,FF,Duel of Death,Ph(c) . . 425.00
9 Ghost Guns,Ph(c) 300.00
10 Dangerous Journey,Ph(c) . . . 250.00
11 Manhunt!,Ph(c) 250.00
12 HK,Joins the Marines,Ph(c) . . 275.00
13 V:Frank Stacy 225.00
14 Operation Peeping John 225.00
15 Bridge Head 250.00
16 AW,FF,Golden Double-Cross . 250.00
17 Murderer's Music 250.00
18 AW,FF,Larson's Folly 275.00
19 . . . . 200.00
20 Whale Cover 200.00
21 . . . . 200.00
22 Flash Flood! 200.00
23 Death on Two Wheels 200.00
24 Desert 200.00
25 AW,FF,Hondo!,Ph(c) 275.00
26 Ph(c) 225.00
27 Ph(c) 225.00
28 Dead Man's Boots! 225.00
29 AW,FF,Ph(c),Crash in
    California Desert 275.00
30 The Wild One, Ph(c) 225.00
31 AW,FF,May, 1955 . . . . 250.00

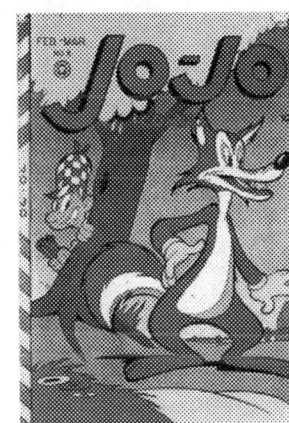

Jo-Jo #5
© Fox Features Syndicate

JO-JO COMICS
Fox Features Syndicate
Spring, 1946
N# (fa) 50.00
2 (fa) 25.00
3 (fa) 25.00
4 (fa) 25.00
5 (fa) 25.00
6 (fa) 25.00
7 B:Jo-Jo Congo King 650.00

---

8 (7)B:Tanee,V:The
    Giant Queen 500.00
9 (8)The Mountain of Skulls 400.00
10 (9)Death of the Fanged Lady . 375.00
11 (10) 375.00
12 (11)Bondage(c),
    Water Warriors 350.00
13 (12) Jade Juggernaut 325.00
14 The Leopards of Learda 325.00
15 The Flaming Fiend 325.00
16 Golden Gorilla,bondage(c) . . . 325.00
17 Stark-Mad Thespian,
    bondage(c) 350.00
18 The Death Traveler 325.00
19 Gladiator of Gore 325.00
20 . . . . 325.00
21 . . . . 325.00
22 . . . . 325.00
23 . . . . 325.00
24 . . . . 325.00
25 Bondage(c) 350.00
26 . . . . 325.00
27 . . . . 325.00
28 . . . . 325.00
29 July, 1949 . . . . 350.00

JOURNEY INTO FEAR
Superior Publications
May, 1951
1 MB,Preview of Chaos 450.00
2 Debt to the Devil 300.00
3 Midnight Prowler 250.00
4 Invisible Terror 250.00
5 Devil Cat 175.00
6 Partners in Blood 175.00
7 The Werewolf Lurks 175.00
8 Bells of the Damned 175.00
9 Masked Death 175.00
10 Gallery of the Dead 175.00
11 Beast of Bedlam 150.00
12 No Rest for the Dead 150.00
13 Cult of the Dead 150.00
14 Jury of the Undead 150.00
15 Corpse in Make-up 165.00
16 Death by Invitation 150.00
17 Deadline for Death 150.00
18 Here's to Horror 150.00
19 This Body is Mine! 150.00
20 Masters of the Dead 150.00
21 Horror in the Clock,
    Sept., 1954 . . . . 150.00

JUDO JOE
Jay-Jay Corp.
Aug., 1952
1 Drug 50.00
2 . . . . 35.00
3 Drug, Dec., 1953 . . . . 35.00

JUDY CANOVA
Fox Features Syndicate
May, 1950
23 (1)WW,WW(c) 125.00
24 (2)WW,WW(c) 120.00
3 JO,WW,WW(c)
    Sept., 1950 . . . . 150.00

JUKE BOX
Famous Funnies
March, 1948
1 ATh(c),Spike Jones 300.00
2 Dinah Shore,Transvestism . . 200.00
3 Vic Damone 150.00
4 Jimmy Durante 150.00
5 . . . . 125.00
6 Jan., 1949,Desi Arnaz 175.00

JUMBO COMICS
Real Adventure Publ. Co.
(Fiction House)
Sept., 1938

1 LF,BKa,JK,WE,WE(c),B:Sheena
  Queen of the Jungle,The Hawk
  The Hunchback 17,000.00
2 LF,JK,WE,BKa,BP,
  O:Sheena 5,500.00
3 JK,WE,WE(c),BP,LF,BKa . . 4,000.00
4 WE,WE(c),MMe,LF,BKa,
  O:The Hawk 3,800.00
5 WE,WE(c),BP,BKa 3,200.00
6 WE,WE(c),BP,BKa 2,800.00
7 WE,BKa,BP 2,700.00
8 LF(c),BP,BKa,World of
  Tommorow. 2,700.00
9 LF(c),BP 2,400.00
10 WE,LF(c),BKa,Regular size
  issues begin 1,400.00
11 LF(c),WE&BP,War of the
  Emerald Gas 1,000.00
12 WE(c),WE&BP,Hawk in Buccaneer
  Vengeance,Bondage(c) . . . 1,100.00
13 WE(c),BP,Sheena in The
  Thundering Herds 1,000.00
14 WE(c),LF,BP,Hawk in Siege
  of Thunder Isle,B:Lightning 1,200.00
15 BP(c),BP,Sheena(c) 650.00
16 BP(c),BP,The Lightning
  Strikes Twice 750.00
17 BP(c), all Sheena covers
  and lead stories 650.00
18 BP 600.00
19 BP(c),BKa,Warriors of
  the Bush. 600.00
20 BP,BKa,Spoilers of
  the Wild 600.00
21 BP,BKa,Prey of the
  Giant Killers 500.00
22 BP,BKa,Victims of the
  Super-Ape,O:Hawk. 550.00
23 BP,BKa,Swamp of the
  Green Terror. 550.00
24 BP,BKa,Curse of the Black
  Venom 550.00
25 BP,BKa,Bait for the Beast . . . 500.00
26 BP,BKa,Tiger-Man Terror . . . 500.00
27 BP,BKa,Sabre-Tooth Terror . . 500.00
28 BKa,RWd,The Devil of
  the Congo 500.00
29 BKa,RWd,Elephant-Scourge . 500.00
30 BKa,RWd,Slashing Fangs . . . 500.00

Jumbo #10
© Fiction House

31 BKa,RWd,Voodoo Treasure
  of Black Slave Lake 450.00
32 BKa,RWd,AB,Captives of
  the Gorilla-Men. 450.00
33 BKa,RWd,AB,Stampede
  Tusks 450.00
34 BKa,RWd,AB,Claws of the
  Devil-Cat 450.00
35 BKa,RWd,AB,Hostage of the
  Devil Apes 450.00
36 BKa,RWd,AB,Voodoo Flames 450.00
37 BKa,RWd,AB,Congo Terror . . 450.00
38 BKa,RWd,ABDeath-Trap of
  the River Demons. 450.00
39 BKa,RWd,AB,Cannibal Bait . . 450.00
40 BKa,RWd,AB,
  Assagai Poison 450.00
41 BKa,RWd,AB,Killer's Kraal,
  Bondage(c). 350.00
42 BKa,RWd,AB,Plague of
  Spotted Killers 350.00
43 BKa,RWd,AB,Beasts of the
  Devil Queen 350.00
44 BKa,RWd,AB,Blood-Cult of
  K'Douma 350.00
45 BKa,RWd,AB,Fanged
  Keeper of the Fire-Gem 350.00
46 BKa,RWd,AB,Lair of the
  Armored Monsters 350.00
47 BKa,RWd,AB,The Bantu
  Blood-Monster 350.00
48 BKa,RWd,AB,Red Meat for
  the Cat-Pack 350.00
49 BKa,RWd,AB,Empire of the
  Hairy Ones. 350.00
50 BKa,RWd,AB,Eyrie of the
  Leopard Birds 350.00
51 BKa,RWd,AB,Monsters with
  Wings. 275.00
52 BKa,RWd,AB,Man-Eaters
  Paradise. 275.00
53 RWd,AB,Slaves of the
  Blood Moon 275.00
54 RWd,AB,Congo Kill 275.00
55 RWd,AB,Bait for the Silver
  King Cat 275.00
56 RWd,AB,Sabre Monsters of
  the Aba-Zanzi,Bondage(c) . . 275.00
57 RWd,AB,Arena of Beasts. . . . 275.00
58 RWd,AB,Sky-Atlas of the
  Thunder-Birds. 275.00
59 RWd,AB,Kraal of Shrunken
  Heads 275.00
60 RWd,AB,Land of the
  Stalking Death 200.00
61 RWd,AB,King-Beast of
  the Masai. 200.00
62 RWd,AB,Valley of Golden
  Death. 200.00
63 RWd,AB,The Dwarf Makers . . 200.00
64 RWd,The Slave-Brand of Ibn
  Ben Satan,Male Bondage. . . 200.00
65 RWd,The Man-Eaters of
  Linpopo 200.00
66 RWd,Valley of Monsters. 200.00
67 RWd,Land of Feathered Evil . 200.00
68 RWd,Spear of Blood Ju-Ju. . . 200.00
69 RWd,AB,MB,Slaves for the
  White Sheik 200.00
70 RWd,AB,MB,The Rogue
  Beast's Prey. 200.00
71 RWd,AB,MB,The Serpent-
  God Speaks 175.00
72 RWd,AB,MB,Curse of the
  Half-Dead. 175.00
73 RWd,AB,MB,War Apes of
  the T'Kanis 175.00
74 RWd,AB,MB,Drums of the
  Voodoo God 175.00
75 RWd,AB,MB,Terror Trail of
  the Devil's Horn 175.00

76 RWd,AB,MB,Fire Gems of
  Skull Valley. 175.00
77 RWd,AB,MB,Blood Dragons
  from Fire Valley 175.00
78 RWd,AB,MB,Veldt of the
  Vampire Apes. 175.00
79 RWd,AB,MB,Dancing
  Skeletons 175.00
80 RWd,AB,MB,Banshee Cats . . 175.00
81 RWd,MB,AB,JKa,Heads for
  King' Hondo's Harem 160.00
82 RWd,MB,AB,JKa,Ghost Riders
  of the Golden Tuskers 160.00
83 RWd,MB,AB,JKa,Charge of
  the Condo Juggernauts . . . 160.00
84 RWd,MB,AB,JKa,Valley of
  the Whispering Fangs. 160.00
85 RWd,MB,AB,JKa,Red Tusks
  of Zulu-Za'an 160.00
86 RWd,MB,AB,JKa,Witch-Maiden
  of the Burning Blade. 160.00
87 RWd,AB,MB,JKa,Sargasso of
  Lost Safaris 160.00
88 RWd,AB,MB,JKa,Kill-Quest
  of the Ju-Ju Tusks 160.00
89 RWd,AB,MB,JKa,Ghost Slaves
  of Bwana Rojo 160.00
90 RWd,AB,MB,JKa,Death Kraal
  of the Mastadons 160.00
91 RWd,AB,MB,JKa,Spoor of
  the Sabre-Horn Tiger 150.00
92 RWd,MB,JKa,Pied Piper
  of the Congo 150.00
93 RWd,MB,JKa,The Beasts
  that Dawn Begot. 150.00
94 RWd,MB,JKa,Wheel of a
  Thousand Deaths 150.00
95 RWd,MB,JKa,Flame Dance
  of the Ju-Ju Witch. 150.00
96 RWd,MB,JKa,Ghost Safari. . . 150.00
97 RWd,MB,JKa,Banshee Wail
  of the Undead,Bondage(c) . . 150.00
98 RWd,MB,JKa,Seekers of
  the Terror Fangs. 150.00
99 RWd,MB,JKa,Shrine of
  the Seven Souls. 150.00
100 RWd,MB,Slave Brand
  of Hassan Bey 175.00
101 RWd,MB,Quest of the
  Two-Face Ju Ju 135.00
102 RWd,MB,Viper Gods of
  Vengeance Veldt 135.00
103 RWd,MB,Blood for the
  Idol of Blades 135.00
104 RWd,MB,Valley of Eternal
  Sleep 135.00
105 RWd,MB,Man Cubs from
  Momba-Zu 200.00
106 RWd,MB,The River of
  No-Return 200.00
107 RWd,MB,Vandals of
  the Veldt. 135.00
108 RWd,MB,The Orphan of
  Vengeance Vale 135.00
109 RWd,MB,The Pygmy's Hiss
  is Poison 135.00
110 RWd,MB,Death Guards the
  Congo Keep 135.00
111 RWd,MB,Beware of the
  Witch-Man's Brew. 135.00
112 RWd,MB,The Blood-Mask
  from G'Shinis Grave 125.00
113 RWd,MB,The Mask's of
  Zombi-Zan 125.00
114 RWd,MB 125.00
115 RWd,MB,Svengali of
  the Apes. 125.00
116 RWd,MB,The Vessel of
  Marbel Monsters. 125.00
117 RWd,MB,Lair of the Half-
  Man King 125.00

GOLDEN AGE

Jumbo Comics #27
© Fiction House

118 RWd,MB,Quest of the
   Congo Dwarflings 125.00
119 RWd,MB,King Crocodile's
   Domain 125.00
120 RWd,MB,The Beast-Pack
   Howls the Moon 125.00
121 RWd,MB,The Kraal of
   Evil Ivory 125.00
122 RWd,MB,Castaways of
   the Congo 125.00
123 RWd,MB, ... 125.00
124 RWd,MB,The Voodoo Beasts
   of Changra-Lo 125.00
125 RWd,MB,JKa(c),The Beast-
   Pack Strikes at Dawn 125.00
126 RWd,MB,JKa(c),Lair of the
   Swamp Beast 125.00
127 RWd,MB,JKa(c),The Phantom
   of Lost Lagoon 125.00
128 RWd,MB,JKa(c),Mad Mistress
   of the Congo-Tuskers 125.00
129 RWd,MB,JKa(c),Slaves of
   King Simbas Kraal 125.00
130 RWd,MB,JKa(c),Quest of
   the Pharaoh's Idol 125.00
131 RWd,JKa(c),Congo Giants
   at Bay 125.00
132 RWd,JKa(c),The Doom of
   the Devil's Gorge 125.00
133 RWd,JKa(c),Blaze the
   Pitfall Trail 125.00
134 RWd,JKa(c),Catacombs of
   the Jackal-Men 125.00
135 RWd,JKa(c),The 40 Thieves
   of Ankar-Lo 125.00
136 RWd,JKa(c),The Perils of
   Paradise Lost 125.00
137 RWd,JKa(c),The Kraal of
   Missing Men 125.00
138 RWd,JKa(c),The Panthers
   of Kajo-Kazar 125.00
139 RWd,JKa(c),Stampede of
   the Congo Lancers 125.00
140 RWd,JKa(c),The Moon
   Beasts from Vulture Valley . . 125.00
141 RWd,JKa(c),B:Long Bow . . . 135.00
142 RWd,JKa(c),Man-Eaters
   of N'Gamba 135.00
143 RWd,JKa(c),The Curse of
   the Cannibal Drum 135.00
144 RWd,JKa(c),The Secrets of
   Killers Cave 135.00
145 RWd,JKa(c),Killers of
   the Crypt 135.00
146 RWd,JKa(c),Sinbad of the

Lost Lagoon 135.00
147 RWd,JKa(c),The Wizard of
   Gorilla Glade 135.00
148 RWd,JKa(c),Derelict of
   the Slave King 135.00
149 RWd,JKa(c),Lash Lord of
   the Elephants 135.00
150 RWd,JKa(c),Queen of
   the Pharaoh's Idol 125.00
151 RWd,The Voodoo Claws
   of Doomsday Trek 125.00
152 RWd,Red Blades of Africa . . 125.00
153 RWd,Lost Legions of the Nile 125.00
154 RWd,The Track of the
   Black Devil 125.00
155 RWd,The Ghosts of
   Blow- Gun Trail 125.00
156 RWd,The Slave-Runners
   of Bambaru 125.00
157 RWd,Cave of the
   Golden Skull 125.00
158 RWd,Gun Trek to
   Panther Valley 125.00
159 RWd,A:Space Scout 110.00
160 RWd,Savage Cargo,
   E:Sheena covers 110.00
161 RWd,Dawns of the Pit 110.00
162 RWd,Hangman's Haunt 110.00
163 RWd,Cagliostro Cursed
   Thee 110.00
164 RWd,Death Bars the Door . . 110.00
165 RWd,Day off from a Corpse . 110.00
166 RWd,The Gallows Bird 110.00
167 RWd,Cult of the Clawmen,
   March, 1953 . . . . 110.00

JUNGLE COMICS
Glen Kel Publ./Fiction House
Jan., 1940

1 HcK,DBr,LF(c),O:The White
   Panther,Kaanga,Tabu, B:The
   Jungle Boy,Camilla, all
   Kaanga covers & stories . . 3,800.00
2 HcK,DBr,WE(c),B:Fantomah 1,200.00
3 HcK,DBr,GT,The Crocodiles
   of Death River 1,100.00
4 HcK,DBr,Wambi in
   Thundering Herds 1,000.00
5 WE(c),GT,HcK,DBr,Empire
   of the Ape Men 1,000.00
6 WE(c),GT,DBr,HcK,Tigress
   of the Deep Jungle Swamp. . 600.00
7 BP(c),DBr,GT,HcK,Live
   Sacrifice,Bondage(c) 550.00
8 BP(c),GT,HcK,Safari into
   Shadowland 550.00
9 GT,HcK,Captive of the
   Voodoo Master 550.00
10 GT,HcK,BP,Lair of the
   Renegade Killer 550.00
11 GT,HcK,V:Beasts of Africa's Ancient
   Primieval Swamp Land 400.00
12 GT,HcK,The Devil's
   Death-Trap 400.00
13 GT(c),GT,HcK,Stalker of
   the Beasts 425.00
14 HcK,Vengeance of the
   Gorilla Hordes 400.00
15 HcK,Terror of the Voodoo
   Cauldron 400.00
16 HcK,Caveman Killers 400.00
17 HcK,Valley of the Killer-Birds . 400.00
18 HcK,Trap of the Tawny
   Killer, Bondage(c) 425.00
19 HcK,Revolt of the Man-Apes . 400.00
20 HcK,One-offering to
   Ju-Ju Demon 400.00
21 HcK,Monster of the Dismal
   Swamp, Bondage(c) 375.00
22 HcK,Lair o/t Winged Fiend . . 350.00

Jungle Comics #1
© Fiction House

23 HcK,Man-Eater Jaws 350.00
24 HcK,Battle of the Beasts 350.00
25 HcK,Kaghis the Blood God,
   Bondage(c) 375.00
26 HcK,Gorillas of the
   Witch-Queen 350.00
27 HcK,Spore o/t Gold-Raiders . . 350.00
28 HcK,Vengeance of the Flame
   God, Bondage(c) 375.00
29 HcK,Juggernaut of Doom 350.00
30 HcK,Claws o/t Black Terror . . 350.00
31 HcK,Land of Shrunken Skulls. 350.00
32 HcK,Curse of the King-Beast . 350.00
33 HcK,Scaly Guardians of
   Massacre Pool,Bondage(c). . 350.00
34 HcK,Bait of the Spotted
   Fury,Bondage(c) 350.00
35 HcK,Stampede of the
   Slave-Masters 350.00
36 HcK,GT,The Flame-Death of
   Ju Ju Mountain 350.00
37 HcK,GT,Scaly Sentinel of
   Taboo Swamp 350.00
38 HcK,GT,Duel of the Congo
   Destroyers 350.00
39 HcK,Land of Laughing Bones. 350.00
40 HcK,Killer Plague 350.00
41 Hck,The King Ape
   Feeds at Dawn 250.00
42 HcK,RC,Master of the
   Moon-Beasts 250.00
43 HcK,The White Shiek 250.00
44 HcK,Monster of the
   Boiling Pool 255.00
45 HcK,The Bone-Grinders of
   B'Zambi, Bondage(c) 250.00
46 HcK,Blood Raiders of
   Tree Trail 250.00
47 HcK,GT,Monsters of the Man
   Pool, Bondage(c) 250.00
48 HcK,GT,Strangest Congo
   Adventure 200.00
49 HcK,GT,Lair of the King
   -Serpent 200.00
50 HcK,GT,Juggernaut of
   the Bush. 200.00
51 HcK,GT,The Golden Lion of
   Genghis Kahn 200.00
52 HcK,Feast for the River
   Devils, Bondage(c) 225.00
53 HcK,GT,Slaves for Horrors
   Harem 225.00
54 HcK,GT,Blood Bride of
   the Crocodile 200.00
55 HcK,GT,The Tree Devil 200.00

---

56 HcK,Bride for the Rainmaker Raj 200.00	104 AgF 135.00	138 BWg(c),HcK,Track of the Black Terror Bondage(c) 125.00
57 HcK,Fire Gems of T'ulaki 200.00	105 AgF,The Red Witch of Ubangi-Shan 135.00	139 BWg(c),HcK,Captain Kidd of the Congo 125.00
58 HcK,Land of the Cannibal God 200.00	106 AgF,Bondage(c) 150.00	140 BWg(c),HcK,The Monsters of Kilmanjaro 125.00
59 HcK,Dwellers of the Mist Bondage(c). 225.00	107 Banshee Valley 150.00	141 BWg(c)HcK,The Death Hunt
60 HcK,Bush Devil's Spoor 200.00	108 HcK,Merchants of Murder . . 150.00	of the Man Cubs 125.00
61 HcK,Curse of the Blood Madness 200.00	109 HcK,Caravan of the Golden Bones 135.00	142 BWg(c),Hck,Sheba of the Terror Claws,Bondage(c) . . . 150.00
62 Bondage(c) 210.00	110 HcK,Raid of the Fire-Fangs . 135.00	143 BWg(c)Hck,The Moon of Devil Drums 150.00
63 HcK,Fire-Birds for the Cliff Dwellers 175.00	111 HcK,The Trek of the Terror-Paws 135.00	144 BWg(c)Hck,Quest of the Dragon's Claw 150.00
64 Valley of the Ju-Ju Idols 175.00	112 HcK,Morass of the Mammoths 135.00	145 BWg(c)Hck,Spawn of the Devil's Moon. 150.00
65 Shrine of the Seven Ju Jus, Bondage(c). 185.00	113 HcK,Two-Tusked Terror 135.00	146 BWg(c),HcK,Orphans of the Congo 150.00
66 Spoor of the Purple Skulls . . . 175.00	114 HcK,Mad Jackals Hunt by Night 135.00	147 BWG(c),HcK,The Treasure of Tembo Wanculu 150.00
67 Devil Beasts of the Golden Temple 175.00	115 HcK,Treasure Trove in Vulture Sky. 135.00	148 BWg(c),HcK,Caged Beasts of Plunder-Men,Bondage(c) . 150.00
68 Satan's Safari 175.00	116 HcK,The Banshees of Voodoo Veldt 135.00	149 BWg(c),HcK. 125.00
69 Brides for the Serpent King . . 175.00	117 HcK,The Fangs of the Hooded Scorpion 135.00	150 BWg(c),HcK,Rhino Rampage, Bondage(c) 150.00
70 Brides for the King Beast, Bondage(c) 185.00	118 HcK,The Muffled Drums of Doom 135.00	151 BWg(c),HcK. 125.00
71 Congo Prey,Bondage(c). 185.00	119 HcK,Fury of the Golden Doom. 135.00	152 BWg(c),HcK,The Rogue of Kopje Kull. 125.00
72 Blood-Brand o/t Veldt Cats . . . 150.00	120 HcK,Killer King Domain 135.00	153 BWg(c),HcK,The Wild Men of N'Gara 125.00
73 The Killer of M'omba Raj, Bondage(c). 175.00	121 HcK,Wolves of the Desert Night 135.00	154 BWg(c),HcK,The Fire Wizard 125.00
74 AgF,GoldenJaws,Bondage(c) . 175.00	122 HcK,The Veldt of Phantom Fangs 135.00	155 BWg(c),HcK,Swamp of the Shrieking Dead. 125.00
75 AgF,Congo Kill. 150.00	123 HcK,The Ark of the Mist-Maids 135.00	156 BWg(c),HcK. 125.00
76 AgF,Blood Thrist of the Golden Tusk. 150.00	124 HcK,The Trail of the Pharaoh's Eye 135.00	157 BWg(c),HcK. 125.00
77 AgF,The Golden Gourds Shriek Blood,Bondage(c) . . . 175.00	125 HcK,Skulls for Sale on Dismal River. 135.00	158 BWg(c),HcK,A:Sheena. 125.00
78 AgF,Bondage(c). 175.00	126 HcK,Safari Sinister. 150.00	159 BWg(c),HcK,The Blow-Gun Kill 125.00
79 AgF,Death has a Thousand Fangs 150.00	127 Hck,Bondage(c). 125.00	160 BWg,HcK,King Fang 125.00
80 AgF,Salome of the Devil-Cats Bondage(c) 175.00	128 HcK,Dawn-Men of the Congo 125.00	161 BWg(c),HcK,The Barbarizi Man-Eaters 125.00
81 AgF,Colossus of the Congo . . 150.00	129 Hck,The Captives of Crocodile Swamp 125.00	162 BWg(c) 125.00
82 AgF,Blood Jewels of the Fire-Bird 150.00	130 HcK,Phantoms of the Congo 125.00	163 BWg(c),Jackals at the Kill, Summer,1954 . . . . 125.00
83 AgF,Vampire Veldt, Bondage(c). 175.00	131 HcK,Treasure-Tomb of the Ape-King 125.00	
84 AgF,Blood Spoor of the Faceless Monster 150.00	132 HcK,Bondage(c). 150.00	**JUNGLE JIM**
85 AgF,Brides for the Man-Apes Bondage(c). 175.00	133 HcK,Scourge of the Sudan Bondage(c). 150.00	**Best Books** **(Standard Comics)**
86 AgF,Firegems of L'hama Lost, Bondage(c) 175.00	134 HcK,The Black Avengers of Kaffir Pass 125.00	**Jan., 1949**
87 AgF,Horror Kraal of the Legless One,Bondage(c) . . . 150.00	135 Hck 125.00	11 . . . . 40.00
88 AgF,Beyond the Ju-Ju Mists. . 165.00	136 HcK,The Death Kraals of Kongola 125.00	12 Mystery Island 25.00
89 AgF,Blood-Moon over the Whispering Veldt 150.00	137 BWg(c),HcK,The Safari of Golden Ghosts 125.00	13 Flowers of Peril 25.00
90 AgF,The Skulls for the Altar of Doom,Bondage(c) . . 165.00		14 . . . . 25.00
91 AgF,Monsters from the Mist Lands, Bondage(c) 165.00		15 . . . . 25.00
92 AgF,Vendetta of the Tree Tribes. 150.00		16 . . . . 25.00
93 AgF,Witch Queen of the Hairy Ones 150.00		17 . . . . 25.00
94 AgF,Terror Raid of the Congo Caesar 150.00		18 . . . . 25.00
95 Agf,Flame-Tongues of the Sky Gods 150.00		19 . . . . 25.00
96 Agf,Phantom Guardians of the Enchanted Lake,Bondage(c). 135.00		20 1951 . . . . 25.00
97 AgF,Wizard of the Whirling Doom,Bondage(c) 165.00		**JUNGLE JIM**
98 AgF,Ten Tusks of Zulu Ivory . . 200.00	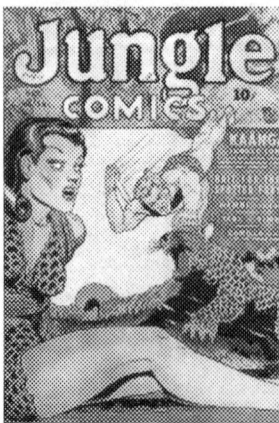	**Dell Publishing Co.**
99 AgF,Cannibal Caravan, Bondage(c). 150.00		**Aug., 1953**
100 AgF,Hate has a Thousand Claws. 150.00		(1) see Dell Four Color #490
101 AgF,The Blade of Buddha, Bondage(c). 150.00		(1) see Dell Four Color #565
102 AgF,Queen of the Amazon Lancers 135.00		3 P(c) all 30.00
103 AgF,The Phantoms of Lost Lagoon 135.00		4 . . . . 25.00

Jungle Comics #34
© Fiction House

5 . . . . 25.00
6 . . . . 20.00
7 . . . . 20.00
8 . . . . 20.00
9 . . . . 20.00
10 . . . . 20.00
11 . . . . 20.00
12 . . . . 20.00
13 `Mystery Island' 20.00
14 `Flowers of Peril' 20.00
15 thru 20 . . . . @20.00

JUNGLE JO
Hero Books
(Fox Features Syndicate)
March, 1950
N#	300.00
1 Mystery of Doc Jungle	350.00
2	250.00
3 The Secret of Youth, Sept., 1950	225.00

JUNGLE LIL
Hero Books
(Fox Features Syndicate)
April, 1950
1 Betrayer of the Kombe Dead.	250.00

Becomes:
DOROTHY LAMOUR
2 WW,Ph(c)The Lost Safari	175.00
3 WW,Ph(c), Aug., 1950	125.00

JUNGLE THRILLS
(see TERRORS OF
THE JUNGLE)

JUNIE PROM
Dearfield Publishing Co.
Winter, 1947
1 Teenage Stories	50.00
2	25.00
3 thru 5	@20.00
6 June, 1949	20.00

Junior #15
© Fox Features Syndicated

JUNIOR COMICS
Fox Features Syndicate
Sept., 1947
9 AF,AF(c) ,Teenage Stories	550.00
10 AF,AF(c)	500.00
11 AF,AF(c)	500.00
12 AF,AF(c)	500.00
13 AF,AF(c)	500.00
14 AF,AF(c)	500.00
15 AF,AF(c)	500.00
16 AF,AF(c),July,1948	500.00

JUNIOR HOOP COMICS
Stanmor Publications
Jan., 1952
1	40.00
2	20.00
3 July, 1952	20.00

JUSTICE TRAPS
THE GUILTY
Headline Publications
(Prize)
Oct.–Nov., 1947
2-1 S&K,S&K(c),Electric chair cover	450.00
2 S&K,S&K(c)	225.00
3 S&K,S&K(c)	200.00
4 S&K,S&K(c),True Confession of a Girl Gangleader	200.00
5 S&K,S&K(c)	200.00
6 S&K,S&K(c)	200.00
7 S&K,S&K(c)	200.00
8 S&K,S&K(c)	200.00
9 S&K,S&K(c)	200.00
10 S&K,S&K(c).	200.00
11 S&K,S&K(c)	100.00
12	40.00
13	50.00
14	40.00
15	40.00
16	40.00
17	50.00
18 S&K,S&K(c)	50.00
19 S&K,S&K(c).	50.00
20	40.00
21 S&K.	75.00
22 S&K(c).	75.00
23 S&K(c).	75.00
24	30.00
25	30.00
26	30.00
27 S&K(c).	50.00
28	30.00
29	30.00
30 S&K.	50.00
31 thru 50	@30.00
51	25.00
52	25.00
53	25.00
54	25.00
55	25.00
56	25.00
57	25.00
58 Drug	175.00
59 thru 92	@25.00

Becomes:
FARGO KID
Headline Publications
(Prize)
93 AW,JSe,O:Kid Fargo	120.00
94 JSe	75.00
95 June–July, 1958,JSe	75.00

KA'A'NGA COMICS
Glen-Kel Publ.
(Fiction House)
Spring, 1949
1 Phantoms of the Congo	400.00
2 V:The Jungle Octopus	200.00
3	150.00
4 The Wizard Apes of Inkosi-Khan	135.00
5	100.00
6 Captive of the Devil Apes	75.00
7 GT,Beast-Men of Mombassa	85.00
8 The Congo Kill-Cry	75.00

Ka'a'nga #9
© Fiction House

9	75.00
10 Stampede for Congo Gold	75.00
11 Claws of the Roaring Congo	60.00
12 Bondage(c)	75.00
13 Death Web of the Amazons	60.00
14 Slave Galley of the Lost Nile Bondage(c)	75.00
15 Crocodile Moon,Bondage(c).	75.00
16 Valley of Devil-Dwarfs	70.00
17 Tembu of the Elephants	60.00
18 The Red Claw of Vengeance	60.00
19 The Devil-Devil Trail.	60.00
20 The Cult of the Killer Claws, Summer, 1954	60.00

KASCO COMICS
Kasco Grainfeed
(Giveaway), 1945
1 BWo	85.00
2 1949,BWo	75.00

KATHY
Standard Comics
Sept., 1949
1 Teen-Age Stories	40.00
2 ASh	22.00
3 thru 6	@15.00
7 thru 17	@12.00

KATY KEENE
Archie Publications/Close-Up
Radio Comics, 1949
1 BWo	750.00
2 BWo	400.00
3 BWo	300.00
4 BWo	300.00
5 BWo	275.00
6 BWo	250.00
7 BWo	250.00
8 thru 12 BWo	@225.00
13 thru 20 BWo	@200.00
21 thru 29 BWo	@150.00
30 thru 38 BWo.	@125.00
39 thru 62 BWo	@100.00
Ann.#1	375.00
Ann.#2 thru #6	225.00

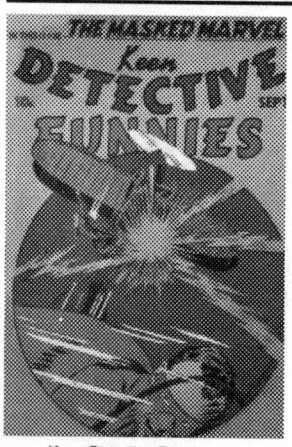

Keen Detective Funnies #13
© Centaur Publications

KEEN DETECTIVE FUNNIES
Centaur Publications
July, 1938

1-8 B:The Clock,	1,500.00
1-9 WE	600.00
1-10	550.00
1-11 Dean Denton	550.00
2-1 The Eye Sees	500.00
2-2 JCo	500.00
2-3 TNT	500.00
2-4 Gabby Flynn	500.00
5	525.00
6	500.00
7 Masked Marvel	1,500.00
8 PGn,Gabby Flynn,Nudity Expanded 16 pages	600.00
9 Dean Denton	525.00
10	525.00
11 BEv,Sidekick	500.00
12 Masked Marvel(c)	650.00
3-1 Masked Marvel(c)	500.00
3-2 Masked Marvel(c)	500.00
3-3 BEv	500.00
16 BEv	500.00
17 JSm	500.00
18 The Eye Sees,Bondage(c)	550.00
19 LFe	500.00
20 BEv,The Eye Sees	500.00
21 Masked Marvel(c)	500.00
22 Masked Marvel(c)	500.00
23 B:Airman	600.00
24 Airman	600.00

KEEN KOMICS
Centaur Publications
May, 1939

1 Teenage Stories	750.00
2 PGn,JaB,CBu	500.00
3 JCo	500.00

KEEN TEENS
Life's Romances Publ./Leader/
Magazine Enterprises, 1945

N# P(c)	175.00
N# Ph(c),Van Johnson	150.00
3 Ph(c)	50.00
4 Ph(c),Glenn Ford	50.00
5 Ph(c),Perry Como	50.00
6	50.00

KEN MAYNARD WESTERN
Fawcett Publications
Sept., 1950

1 B:Ken Maynard & Tarzan (horse) The Outlaw Treasure Trail	400.00
2 Invasion of the Badmen	250.00
3 Pied Piper of the West	200.00
4 Outlaw Hoax	200.00
5 Mystery of Badman City	200.00
6 Redwood Robbery	200.00
7 Seven Wonders of the West	200.00
8 Mighty Mountain Menace, Feb.,1952	200.00

KEN SHANNON
Quality Comics Group
Oct., 1951

1 RC, Evil Eye of Count Ducrie	250.00
2 RC, Cut Rate Corpses	200.00
3 RC, Corpse that Wouldn't Sleep	150.00
4 RC, Stone Hatchet Murder	125.00
5 RC, Case of the Carney Killer	125.00
6 Weird Vampire Mob	150.00
7 RC,Ugliest Man in the World	125.00
8 Chinatown Murders,Drug	150.00
9 RC, Necklace of Blood	100.00
10 RC, Shadow of the Chair, Apr. 1953	100.00

KERRY DRAKE DETECTIVE CASES
Life's Romances/M.E./, 1944

(1) *see N# A-1 Comics*	200.00
2 A:The Faceless Horror	125.00
3	100.00
4 A:Squirrel, Dr. Zero, Caresse	100.00
5 Bondage cover	110.00

Harvey Publ.

6 A:Stitches	50.00
7 A:Shuteye	60.00
8 Bondage cover	65.00
9 Drug	100.00
10 BP,A:Meatball,Drug	100.00
11 BP,I:Kid Gloves	40.00
12 BP	40.00
13 BP,A:Torso	35.00
14 BP,Bullseye Murder Syndicate	35.00
15 BP,Fake Mystic Racket	35.00
16 BP,A:Vixen	30.00
17 BP,Case of the $50,000 Robbery	30.00
18 BP,A:Vixen	30.00
19 BP,Case of the Dope Smugglers	35.00
20 BP,Secret Treasury Agent	30.00
21 BP,Murder on Record	25.00
22 BP,Death Rides the Air Waves	25.00
23 BP,Blackmailer's Secret Weapon	25.00
24 Blackmailer's Trap	25.00
25 Pretty Boy Killer	25.00
26	25.00
27	25.00
28 BP	25.00
29 BP	25.00
30 Mystery Mine,Bondage(c)	35.00
31	25.00
32	25.00
33 Aug., 1952	25.00

KEWPIES
Will Eisner Publications
Spring, 1949

1	350.00

KEY COMICS
Consolidated Magazines
Jan., 1944

1 B:The Key, Will-O-The-Wisp	275.00
2	150.00
3	100.00
4 O:John Quincy,B:The Atom	110.00
5 HoK,Aug., 1946	100.00

KID COWBOY
Approved Comics/
St. John Publ. Co., 1950

1 B:Lucy Belle & Red Feather	65.00
2 Six-Gun Justice	35.00
3 Shadow on Hangman's Bridge	30.00
4 Red Feather V:Eagle of Doom	25.00
5 Killers on the Rampage	25.00
6 The Stovepipe Hat	25.00
7 Ghost Town of Twin Buttes	25.00
8 Thundering Hoofs	25.00
9 Terror on the Salt Flats	25.00
10 Valley of Death	25.00
11 Vanished Herds,Bondage(c)	35.00
12	25.00
13	25.00
14 1954	25.00

KIDDIE KARNIVAL
Approved Comics, 1952

N#	250.00

KID ETERNITY
Comics Magazine
(Quality Comics Group)
Spring, 1946

1	650.00
2	300.00
3 Follow Him Out of This World	200.00
4 Great Heroes of the Past	200.00
5 Don't Kid with Crime	175.00
6 Busy Battling Crime	175.00
7 Protects the World	175.00
8 Fly to the Rescue	175.00
9 Swoop Down on Crime	175.00
10 Golden Touch from Mr. Midas	175.00
11 Aid the Living by Calling the Dead	150.00
12 Finds Death	150.00
13 Invades General Poschka	150.00
14 Battles Double	150.00
15 A: Master Man	150.00
16 Balance Scales of Justice	125.00
17 A:Baron Roxx	125.00
18 A:Man with Two Faces	125.00
Becomes:	

BUCCANEERS

19 RC,Sword Fight(c)	400.00
20 RC,Treasure Chest	275.00
21 RC,Death Trap	325.00
22 A:Lady Dolores,Snuff, Bondage(c)	225.00
23 RC,V:Treasure Hungry Plunderers of the Sea	250.00
24 A:Adam Peril,Black Roger, Eric Falcon	175.00
25 V:Clews	175.00
26 V:Admiral Blood	175.00
27 RC,RC(c)May, 1951	275.00

KID ZOO COMICS
Street & Smith, July, 1948
1 (fa) 125.00

KILLERS, THE
Magazine Enterprises, 1947
1 LbC(c),Thou Shall Not Kill. . . . 750.00
2 Grl,OW,Assassins Mad Slayers
 of the East,Hanging(c),Drug . 650.00

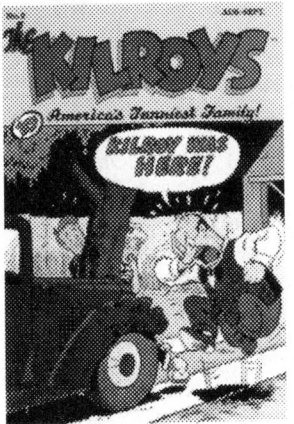

Kilroys #2
© American Comics

KILROYS, THE
B&L Publishing Co./
American Comics
June–July, 1947
1 Three Girls in Love(c) 125.00
2 Flat Tire(c) 60.00
3 Right to Swear(c) 45.00
4 Kissing Booth(c) 45.00
5 Skiing(c) 45.00
6 Prom(c) 30.00
7 To School 30.00
8 . . . . 30.00
9 . . . . 30.00
10 B:Solid Jackson solo 30.00
11 . . . . 25.00
12 Life Guard(c) 25.00
13 thru 21 . . . . @25.00
22 thru 30 . . . . @20.00
31 thru 40 . . . . @18.00
41 thru 47 . . . . @15.00
48 3-D effect 100.00
49 3-D effect. 100.00
50 thru 54, July 1954 . . . . @15.00

KING COMICS
David McKay Publications
April, 1936
(all have Popeye covers)
1 AR,EC,B:Popeye,Flash Gordon,B:
 Henry,Mandrake 8,000.00
2 AR,EC,Flash Gordon 2,400.00
3 AR,EC,Flash Gordon 1,500.00
4 AR,EC,Flash Gordon 1,200.00
5 AR,EC,Flash Gordon 900.00
6 AR,EC,Flash Gordon 650.00
7 AR,EC,King Royal Mounties . 625.00
8 AR,EC,Thanksgiving(c) 600.00
9 AR,EC,Christmas(c) 600.00
10 AR,EC,Flash Gordon 600.00
11 AR,EC,Flash Gordon 500.00
12 AR,EC,Flash Gordon 500.00

13 AR,EC,Flash Gordon 500.00
14 AR,EC,Flash Gordon 500.00
15 AR,EC,Flash Gordon 500.00
16 AR,EC,Flash Gordon 500.00
17 AR,EC,Flash Gordon 475.00
18 AR,EC,Flash Gordon 475.00
Covers say: "Starring Popeye"
19 AR,EC,Flash Gordon 475.00
20 AR,EC,Football(c) 475.00
21 AR,EC,Flash Gordon 350.00
22 AR,EC,Flash Gordon 350.00
23 AR,EC,Flash Gordon 350.00
24 AR,EC,Flash Gordon 350.00
25 AR,EC,Flash Gordon 350.00
26 AR,EC,Flash Gordon 325.00
27 AR,EC,Flash Gordon 325.00
28 AR,EC,Flash Gordon 325.00
29 AR,EC,Flash Gordon 325.00
30 AR,EC,Flash Gordon 325.00
31 AR,EC,Flash Gordon 325.00
32 AR,EC,Flash Gordon 325.00
33 AR,EC,Skiing(c) 325.00
34 AR,Ping Pong(c) 275.00
35 AR,Flash Gordon 275.00
36 AR,Flash Gordon 275.00
37 AR,Flash Gordon 275.00
38 AR,Flash Gordon 275.00
39 AR,Baseball(c). 275.00
40 AR,Flash Gordon 275.00
41 AR,Flash Gordon 250.00
42 AR,Flash Gordon 250.00
43 AR,Flash Gordon 250.00
44 AR,Popeye golf(c) 250.00
45 AR,Flash Gordon 250.00
46 AR,B:Little Lulu 250.00
47 AR,Flash Gordon 250.00
48 AR,Flash Gordon 250.00
49 AR,Weather Vane 250.00
50 AR,B:Love Ranger 250.00
51 AR,Flash Gordon 250.00
52 AR,Flash Gordon 175.00
53 AR,Flash Gordon 175.00
54 AR,Flash Gordon 175.00
55 AR,Magic Carpet 175.00
56 AR,Flash Gordon 175.00
57 AR,Cows Over Moon(c) 175.00
58 AR,Flash Gordon 175.00
59 AR,Flash Gordon 175.00
60 AR,Flash Gordon 175.00
61 AR,B:Phantom,Baseball(c). . . 175.00
62 AR,Flash Gordon 175.00
63 AR,Flash Gordon 150.00
64 AR,Flash Gordon 150.00
65 AR,Flash Gordon 150.00
66 AR,Flash Gordon 150.00
67 AR,Sweet Pea 150.00
68 AR,Flash Gordon 150.00
69 AR,Flash Gordon 150.00
70 AR,Flash Gordon 150.00
71 AR,Flash Gordon 150.00
72 AR,Flash Gordon 125.00
73 AR,Flash Gordon 125.00
74 AR,Flash Gordon 125.00
75 AR,Flash Godron 125.00
76 AR,Flag(c) 135.00
77 AR,Flash Gordon 125.00
78 AR,Popeye,Olive Oil(c) 125.00
79 AR,Sweet Pea 125.00
80 AR,Wimpy(c). 125.00
81 AR,B:Blondie(c) 125.00
82 thru 91 AR . . . . @100.00
92 thru 98 AR . . . . @85.00
99 AR,Olive Oil(c). 100.00
100 . . . . 125.00
101 thru 116 AR . . . . @85.00
117 O:Phantom 75.00
118 Flash Gordon. 85.00
119 Flash Gordon. 75.00
120 Wimpy(c). 60.00
121 thru 140 . . . . @75.00
141 Flash Gordon. 60.00

142 Flash Gordon. 60.00
143 Flash Gordon. 60.00
144 Flash Gordon. 60.00
145 Prince Valiant. 55.00
146 Prince Valiant. 55.00
147 Prince Valiant. 55.00
148 thru 154 . . . . @45.00
155 E:Flash Gordon 45.00
156 Baseball(c) 45.00
157 thru 159 . . . . @35.00

KING OF THE
ROYAL MOUNTED
Dell Publishing Co.
Dec., 1948–1958
(1) *see Dell Four Color #207*
(2) *see Dell Four Color #265*
(3) *see Dell Four Color #283*
(4) *see Dell Four Color #310*
(5) *see Dell Four Color #340*
(6) *see Dell Four Color #363*
(7) *see Dell Four Color #384*
8 Zane Grey adapt. 40.00
9 . . . . 40.00
10 . . . . 40.00
11 thru 28 . . . . @30.00

KIT CARSON
Avon Periodicals, 1950
N# EK(c) Indian Scout 75.00
2 EK(c),Kit Carson's Revenge,
 Doom Trail 50.00
3 EK(c),V:Comanche Raiders . . . 35.00
4 . . . . 30.00
5 EK(c),Trail of Doom 30.00
6 EK(c) 30.00
7 EK(c) 35.00
8 EK(c) 30.00
Becomes:

FIGHTING DAVY
CROCKETT
9 EK(c),Oct./Nov., 1955 . . . . 35.00

KOKO AND KOLA
Compix/Magazine Enterprises
Fall, 1946
1 (fa) 40.00
2 X-Mas Issue 20.00
3 . . . . 15.00
4 . . . . 15.00
5 . . . . 15.00
6 May, 1947 . . . . 15.00

KO KOMICS
Gerona Publications
Oct., 1945
1 . . . . 400.00

KOMIK PAGES
Harry 'A' Chestler
April, 1945
1 JK,Duke of Darkness 300.00

KRAZY KAT COMICS
Dell Publishing Co.
May–June, 1951
1 . . . . 60.00
2 . . . . 40.00
3 . . . . 40.00
4 . . . . 40.00
5 . . . . 40.00

GOLDEN AGE

KRAZY LIFE
(See PHANTOM LADY)

LABOR IS A PARTNER
Catechetical Guild
Educational Society, 1949
1 . . . . 175.00

LAFFY-DAFFY COMICS
Rural Home Publ. Co.
Feb., 1945
1 (fa) 30.00
2 . . . . 30.00

LANCE O'CASEY
Fawcett, 1946–47
1 High Seas Adventure
　from Whiz comics 250.00
2 thru 4 . . . . @150.00

LAND OF THE LOST
EC Comics
July–Aug. 1946–Spring 1948
1 Radio show adapt. 225.00
2 . . . . 150.00
3 thru 9 . . . . @125.00

LARGE FEATURE
COMICS
Dell Publishing Co., 1939
1 Dick Tracy vs. the Blank. . . . 1,500.00
2 Terry and the Pirates. 700.00
3 Heigh-Yo Silver!
　the Lone Ranger. 900.00
4 Dick Tracy gets his man 700.00
5 Tarzan of the Apes. 1,300.00
6 Terry and the Pirates. 650.00
7 Lone Ranger to the rescue . . . 800.00
8 Dick Tracy, Racket Buster. . . . 675.00
9 King of the Royal Mounted . . . 450.00
10 Gang Busters. 600.00
11 Dick Tracy, Mad Doc Hump . . 800.00
12 Smilin' Jack 550.00
13 Dick Tracy and Scottie
　of Scotland Yard. 800.00
14 Smilin' Jack helps G-Men. . . . 575.00
15 Dick Tracy and
　the kidnapped princes. 800.00
16 Donald Duck, 1st Daisy. . . . 5,500.00
17 Gang Busters. 425.00
18 Phantasmo The Master
　of the World 325.00
19 Walt Disney's Dumbo 2,400.00
20 Donald Duck. 5,500.00
21 Private Buck 100.00
22 Nuts and Jolts 100.00
23 The Nebbs. 125.00
24 Popeye in `Thimble Theatre' . 450.00
25 Smilin'Jack. 500.00
26 Smitty 225.00
27 Terry and the Pirates 550.00
28 Grin and Bear It. 75.00
29 Moon Mullins. 200.00
30 Tillie the Toiler 175.00

[Series 2]
1 Peter Rabbit. 350.00
2 Winnie Winkle. 150.00
3 Dick Tracy 600.00
4 Tiny Tim 250.00
5 Toots and Casper 100.00
6 Terry and the Pirates. 550.00
7 Pluto saves the Ship 1,200.00
8 Bugs Bunny 750.00
9 Bringing Up Father 150.00

Large Feature Comics #14
© Dell Publishing Co.

10 Popeye 400.00
11 Barney Google&SnuffySmith . 200.00
12 Private Buck 100.00
13 1001 Hours of Fun. 150.00

LARRY DOBY,
BASEBALL HERO
Fawcett Publications, 1950
1 Ph(c),BW 575.00

LARS OF MARS
Ziff-Davis Publishing Co.
April–May, 1951
10 MA,`Terror from the Sky' 600.00
11 GC, The Terror Weapon. 500.00

LASH LARUE WESTERN
Fawcett Publications
Summer, 1949
1 Ph(c),The Fatal Roundups . . . 750.00
2 Ph(c),Perfect Hide Out 325.00
3 Ph(c),The Suspect 275.00
4 Ph(c),Death on Stage 275.00
5 Ph(c),Rustler's Haven 275.00
6 Ph(c) 250.00
7 Ph(c),Shadow of the Noose . . 200.00
8 Ph(c),Double Deadline 200.00
9 Ph(c),Generals Last Stand . . . 200.00
10 Ph(c) 200.00
11 Ph(c) 175.00
12 thru 20 Ph(c) . . . . @125.00
21 thru 29 Ph(c) . . . . @100.00
30 thru 46 Ph(c) . . . . @75.00
46 Ph(c),Lost Chance 75.00

LASSIE
(& SEVERAL SPECIAL
ISSUES)
Dell Publishing Co.
Oct.–Dec., 1950
1 Ph(c) all 125.00
2 . . . . 50.00
3 . . . . 35.00
4 . . . . 35.00
5 . . . . 35.00
6 . . . . 35.00
7 . . . . 35.00
8 . . . . 35.00
9 . . . . 35.00

10 . . . . 35.00
11 . . . . 25.00
12 Rocky Langford 27.00
13 . . . . 25.00
14 . . . . 25.00
15 I:Timbu 27.00
16 . . . . 25.00
17 . . . . 25.00
18 . . . . 25.00
19 . . . . 25.00
20 MB 30.00
21 MB 30.00
22 MB 30.00
23 thru 38 . . . . @20.00
39 I:Timmy 22.00
40 thru 62 . . . . @18.00
63 E:Timmy 12.00
64 thru 70 . . . . @10.00

LATEST COMICS
Spotlight Publ./
Palace Promotions
March, 1945
1 Funny Animal-Super Duper. . . . 60.00
2 . . . . 40.00

SPECIAL COMICS
MLJ Magazines
(Archie Publ.)
Winter, 1941
1 O:Boy Buddies & Hangman,
　D:The Comet 2,000.00
Becomes:

HANGMAN COMICS
2 B:Hangman & Boy Buddies . 1,300.00
3 V:Nazis cover,Bondage(c) . . . 800.00
4 V:Nazis cover 750.00
5 Bondage cover 700.00
6 . . . . 675.00
7 BF,Graveyard cover 675.00
8 BF 675.00
Becomes:

BLACK HOOD
9 BF 800.00
10 BF,A:Dusty, the
　Boy Detective. 450.00
11 Here lies the Black Hood 325.00
12 . . . . 300.00
13 EK(c). 300.00
14 EK(c). 300.00
15 EK. 300.00
16 EK(c). 300.00
17 Bondage cover 325.00
18 . . . . 300.00
19 I.D. Revealed. 400.00
Becomes:

LAUGH COMICS
20 BWo,B:Archie,Katy Keene . . . 500.00
21 BWo 225.00
22 BWo 225.00
23 Bwo. 225.00
24 BWo,JK,Pipsy 250.00
25 BWo 225.00
26 BWo 125.00
27 BWo 125.00
28 BWo 125.00
29 BWo 125.00
30 BWo 125.00
31 thru 40 BWo. . . . . @75.00
41 thru 50 BWo. . . . . @55.00
51 thru 60 BWo. . . . . @50.00
61 thru 80 BWo. . . . . @25.00
81 thru 99 BWo. . . . . @20.00
100 BWo 30.00
101 thru 126 BWo . . . . @20.00
127 A:Jaguar 22.00
128 A:The Fly. 22.00

　　　All comics prices listed are for *Near Mint* condition.

GOLDEN AGE

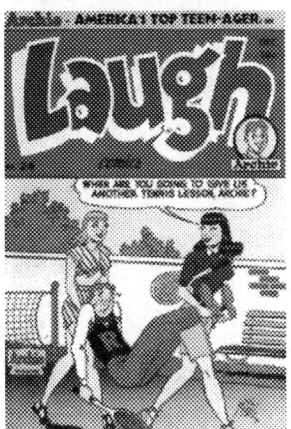

Laugh #24
© Archie Publications

Lawbreakers Suspense Stories #11
© Charlton

129 A:The Fly 22.00
130 A:Jaguar 22.00
131 A:Jaguar 22.00
132 A:The Fly 22.00
133 A:Jaguar 22.00
134 A:The Fly 22.00
135 A:Jaguar 22.00
136 A:Fly Girl 22.00
137 A:Fly Girl 22.00
138 A:The Fly 22.00
139 A:The Fly 22.00
140 A:Jaguar 22.00
141 A:Jaguar 22.00
142 thru 144 . . . . @22.00
145 A:Josie 15.00
146 thru 165 . . . . @10.00
166 Beatles cover. 15.00
167 thru 220 . . . . @5.00
221 thru 250 . . . . @2.50
251 thru 300 . . . . @2.00
301 thru 400 . . . . @1.00

LAUGH COMIX
(see TOP-NOTCH COMICS)

LAUREL AND HARDY
St. John Publishing Co.
March, 1949
1 . . . . 500.00
2 . . . . 300.00
3 . . . . 200.00
26 Rep #1 . . . . 125.00
27 Rep #2 . . . . 125.00
28 Rep #3 . . . . 125.00

LAWBREAKERS
Law & Order Magazines
(Charlton)
March, 1951
1 . . . . 225.00
2 . . . . 125.00
3 . . . . 100.00
4 Drug. 125.00
5 . . . . 100.00
6 LM(c) 125.00
7 Drug 125.00
8 . . . . 100.00
9 StC(c). 100.00
Becomes:

LAWBREAKERS
SUSPENSE STORIES
Jan., 1953
10 StC(c) 200.00
11 LM(c),Negligee(c). 600.00
12 LM(c). 100.00
13 DG(c) 100.00
14 DG(c),Sharks. 100.00
15 DG(c),Acid in Face(c) 300.00
Becomes:

STRANGE SUSPENSE
STORIES
16 DG(c); Jan., 1954 . . . . 200.00
17 DG(c) 175.00
18 SD,SD(c). 125.00
19 SD,SD(c),Electric Chair 325.00
20 SD,SD(c) 250.00
21 SD,SD(c) 175.00
22 SD,SD(c) 225.00
Becomes:

THIS IS SUSPENSE
23 WW; Feb., 1955Comics Code 150.00
24 GE,DG(c) 70.00
25 DG(c) 50.00
26 DG(c) 50.00
Becomes:

STRANGE SUSPENSE
STORIES
27 Oct., 1955 . . . . 100.00
28 . . . . 50.00
29 . . . . 50.00
30 . . . . 50.00
31 SD 125.00
32 SD 125.00
33 SD 125.00
34 SD 125.00
35 SD 125.00
36 SD 125.00
37 SD 125.00
38 . . . . 50.00
39 SD 150.00
40 SD 150.00
41 SD 150.00
42 . . . . 40.00
43 . . . . 40.00
44 . . . . 40.00
45 . . . . 40.00
46 . . . . 40.00
47 SD 100.00
48 SD 100.00
49 . . . . 40.00
50 SD 100.00

51 SD. 100.00
52 SD. 100.00
53 SD. 100.00
54 thru 60 . . . . @35.00
61 thru 74 . . . . @20.00
75 SD,SD(c) 150.00
77 Oct 1965 . . . . 50.00

LAWBREAKERS
ALWAYS LOSE
Crime Bureau Stories
Spring, 1948
1 HK; FBI Reward Poster Photo. 225.00
2 . . . . 125.00
3 . . . . 100.00
4 Vampire 100.00
5 . . . . 75.00
6 Anti Wertham Edition 75.00
7 Drug. 200.00
8 . . . . 75.00
9 Ph(c) 75.00
10 Ph(c), Oct. 1949 . . . . 75.00

LAW-CRIME
Essenkay Publications
April, 1948
1 LbC,LbC-(c);Raymond Hamilton
    Dies In The Chair 500.00
2 LbC,LbC-(c);Strangled
    Beauty Puzzles Police 400.00
3 LbC,LbC-(c);Lipstick Slayer
    Sought; Aug. 1943 . . . . 500.00

LEROY
Visual Editions
(Standard Comics)
Nov., 1949
1 FunniestTeenager of them All . 25.00
2 . . . . 20.00
3 thru 6 . . . . @15.00

LET'S PRETEND
D.S. Publishing Company
May–June, 1950
1 From Radio Nursery Tales . . . 100.00
2 . . . . 75.00
3 Nov., 1950 . . . . 75.00

MISS LIBERTY
Burten/Green Publishing
Circa 1944
1 Reprints-Shield,Wizard 300.00
Becomes:

LIBERTY COMICS
10 Reprints,Hangman. 125.00
11 . . . . 90.00
12 Black Hood 90.00
14 . . . . 90.00
15 . . . . 75.00

LIBERTY GUARDS
Chicago Mail Order
(Comic Corp of America)
Circa 1942
1 PG(c),Liberty Scouts. 275.00
Becomes:

LIBERTY SCOUTS
June, 1941
PG,PG(c)O:Fireman,Liberty
    Scouts 1,000.00
3 PG,PG(c) Aug.,1941

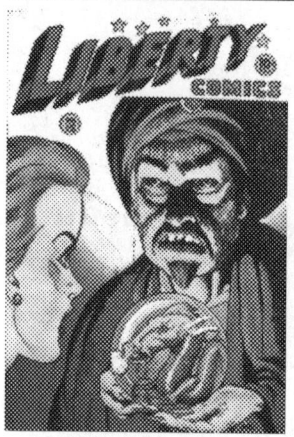

Liberty Comics #15
© Green Publishing
O:Sentinel 750.00

LIFE STORY
Fawcett Publications
April, 1949

1 Ph(c)	75.00
2 Ph(c)	35.00
3 Ph(c)	30.00
4 Ph(c)	30.00
5 Ph(c)	30.00
6 Ph(c)	30.00
7 Ph(c)	25.00
8 Ph(c)	25.00
9 Ph(c)	25.00
10 Ph(c)	25.00
11	20.00
12	20.00
13 WW,Drug	100.00
14 thru 21	@20.00
22 Drug	35.00
23 thru 35	@20.00
36 Drug	25.00
37 thru 42	@18.00
43 GE	25.00
44	18.00
45 1952	18.00

LIFE WITH SNARKY PARKER
Fox Feature Syndicate
Aug., 1950

1	150.00

LI'L ABNER
Harvey Publications
Dec., 1947

61 BP,BW,Sadie Hawkins Day	250.00
62	150.00
63	150.00
64	150.00
65 BP	150.00
66	100.00
67	100.00
68 FearlessFosdick V:Any Face	125.00
69	100.00
70	100.00

Toby Press

71	100.00
72	100.00
73	100.00

74	100.00
75 HK	125.00
76	100.00
77 HK	125.00
78 HK	125.00
79 HK	125.00
80	100.00
81	75.00
82	75.00
83 Baseball	85.00
84	75.00
85	75.00
86 HK	125.00
87	75.00
88	75.00
89	75.00
90	75.00
91 Rep. #77	80.00
92	75.00
93 Rep. #71	80.00
94	75.00
95 Fearless Fosdick	100.00
96	75.00
97 Jan., 1955	75.00

LI'L GENIUS
Charlton Comics, 1955

1	50.00
2	20.00
3 thru 15	@15.00
16 Giants	25.00
17 Giants	25.00
18 Giants,100 pages	30.00
19 thru 40	@10.00
41 thru 54	@7.00
55 1965	7.00

LI'L PAN
Fox Features Syndicate
Dec.–Jan., 1946-47

6	35.00
7	25.00
8 April–May, 1947	25.00

LINDA
(see PHANTOM LADY)

LITTLE AUDREY
St. John Publ. Co./ Harvey Comics
April, 1948

1	300.00
2	150.00
3 thru 6	@100.00
7 thru 10	@60.00
11 thru 20	@35.00
21 thru 24	@25.00
25 B:Harvey Comics	85.00
26 A: Casper	50.00
27 A: Casper	50.00
28 A: Casper	50.00
29 thru 31	@30.00
32 A: Casper	35.00
33 A: Casper	35.00
34 A: Casper	35.00
35 A: Casper	35.00
36 thru 53	@20.00

LITTLE BIT
Jubilee Publishing Company
March, 1949

1	30.00
2 June, 1949	30.00

LITTLE DOT
Harvey Publications
Sept., 1953

1 I: Richie Rich & Little Lotta	800.00
2	350.00
3	200.00
4	150.00
5 O:Dots on Little Dot's Dress	200.00
6 1st Richie Rich(c)	175.00
7	135.00
8	75.00
9	75.00
10	75.00
11 thru 20	@60.00
21 thru 30	@35.00
31 thru 38	@30.00
39	50.00
40 thru 50	@20.00
51 thru 60	@15.00
61 thru 70	@12.00
71 thru 80	@10.00
81 thru 100	@8.00
101 thru 130	@7.00
131 thru 140	@7.00
141 thru 145, 52 pages	@7.00
146 thru 163	@3.00

LITTLE EVA
St. John Publishing Co.
May, 1952

1	60.00
2	30.00
3	18.00
4	18.00
5 thru 10	@12.00
11 thru 30	@10.00
31 Nov., 1956	10.00

LITTLE GIANT COMICS
Centaur Publications
July, 1938

1 PG, B&W with Color(c)	500.00
2 B&W with Color(c)	400.00
3 B&W with Color(c)	425.00
4 B&W with Color(c)	425.00

LITTLE GIANT DETECTIVE FUNNIES
Centaur Publications
Oct., 1938

1 B&W	550.00
2 B&W	400.00
3 B&W	400.00
4 Jan. 1939	400.00

LITTLE GIANT MOVIE FUNNIES
Centaur Publications
Aug., 1938

1 Ed Wheelan-a	550.00
2 Ed Wheelan-a, Oct., 1938	400.00

LITTLE IKE
St. John Publishing Co.
April, 1953

1	50.00
2	25.00
3	20.00
4 Oct., 1953	20.00

All comics prices listed are for *Near Mint* condition.

LITTLE IODINE
Dell Publishing Co.
April, 1949

1	75.00
2	30.00
3	30.00
4	30.00
5	30.00
6 thru 10	@20.00
11 thru 30	@15.00
31 thru 50	@10.00
51 thru 56	@8.00

LITTLE JACK FROST
Avon Periodicals, 1951

1	35.00

LITTLE LULU
(see MARGE'S LITTLE LULU)

LITTLE MAX COMICS
Harvey Publications
Oct., 1949

1 I: Little Dot,Joe Palooka	125.00
2 A: Little Dot	60.00
3 A: Little Dot,Joe Palooka(c)	40.00
4	25.00
5 C: Little Dot	25.00
6 thru 10	@20.00
11 thru 22	@18.00
23 A: Little Dot	12.00
24 thru 37	@10.00
38 Rep. #20	10.00
39 thru 72	@10.00
73 A: Richie Rich; Nov.'61	10.00

LITTLE MISS MUFFET
Best Books
(Standard Comics)
Dec., 1948

11 Strip Reprints	45.00
12 Strip Reprints	30.00
13 Strip Reprints; Mar.'49	30.00

LITTLE MISS SUNBEAM COMICS
Magazine Enterprises
June–July, 1950

1	75.00
2	40.00
3	40.00
4 Dec.–Jan., 1951	40.00

LITTLE ORPHAN ANNIE
Dell Publishing Co., 1941

1	150.00
2 Orphan Annie and the Rescue	100.00
3	100.00

LITTLE ROQUEFORT
St. John Publishing Co.
June,1952

1	40.00
2	20.00
3 thru 9	@15.00

Pines

10 Summer 1958	18.00

LITTLE SCOUTS
Dell Publishing Co.
March, 1951

(1) see Dell Four Color #321	
2	20.00
3	20.00
4	20.00
5	20.00
6	20.00

LITTLEST SNOWMAN
Dell Publishing Co.
Dec., 1956

1	20.00

LIVING BIBLE, THE
Living Bible Corp.
Autumn, 1945

1 LbC-(c) Life of Paul	300.00
2 LbC-(c) Joseph &His Brethern	150.00
3 LbC-(c) Chaplains At War	250.00

LONE EAGLE
Ajax/Farrell
April–May, 1954

1	50.00
2	30.00
3 Bondage(c)	35.00
4 Oct.–Nov., 1954	30.00

LONE RANGER
Dell Publishing Co.
Jan.–Feb. 1948

1 B:Lone Ranger & Tonto B:Strip Reprint	650.00
2	300.00
3	250.00
4	250.00
5	250.00
6	200.00
7	200.00
8 O:Retold	250.00
9	200.00
10	200.00
11 B:Young Hawk	125.00
12 thru 20	@125.00
21	100.00
22	100.00
23 O:Retold	125.00
24 thru 30	@100.00
31 (1st Mask Logo)	110.00
32 thru 36	@75.00
37 (E:Strip reprints)	75.00
38 thru 50	@60.00
51 thru 75	@50.00
76 thru 99	@45.00
100	75.00
101 thru 111	@40.00
112 B:Clayton Moore Ph(c)	135.00
113 thru 117	@75.00
118 O:Lone Ranger & Tonto retold, Anniv. issue	150.00
119 thru 144	@75.00
145 final issue,May/July 1962	75.00

THE LONE RANGER'S COMPANION TONTO
Dell Publishing Co.
Jan., 1951

(1) see Dell Four Color #312	
2 P(c) all	60.00
3	60.00
4	50.00

5	50.00
6 thru 10	@50.00
11 thru 20	@40.00
21 thru 25	@30.00
26 thru 33	@25.00

THE LONE RANGER'S FAMOUS HORSE HI-YO SILVER
Dell Publishing Co.
Jan., 1952

(1) see Dell Four Color #369	
(1) see Dell Four Color #392	
3 P(c) all	35.00
4	35.00
5	35.00
6 thru 10	@35.00
11 thru 36	@30.00

The Lone Rider #3
© Superior Comics

LONE RIDER
Farrell (Superior Comics) April, 1951

1	125.00
2 I&O: Golden Arrow; 52 pgs.	60.00
3	50.00
4	50.00
5	50.00
6 E: Golden Arrow	60.00
7 G. Arrow Becomes Swift Arrow	65.00
8 O: Swift Arrow	70.00
9 thru 14	@30.00
15 O: Golden Arrow Rep. #2.	35.00
16 thru 19	@25.00
20	20.00
21 3-D (c)	75.00
22	20.00
23 A: Apache Kid	25.00
24	20.00
25	20.00
26 July, 1955	20.00

LONG BOW
Real Adventures Publ.
(Fiction House)
Winter, 1950

1	100.00
2	50.00
3 "Red Arrows Means War"	45.00
4 "Trial of Tomahawk"	45.00
5	45.00
6 "Rattlesnake Raiders"	35.00

All comics prices listed are for *Near Mint* condition.

7	35.00
8	35.00
9 Spring, 1953	35.00

LOONEY TUNES AND MERRIE MELODIES
Dell Publishing Co., 1941

1 B:&1st Comic App. Bugs Bunny Daffy Duck,Elmer Fudd	10,000.00
2 Bugs/Porky(c)	1,500.00
3 Bugs/Porky(c) B:WK, Kandi the Cave	1,200.00
4 Bugs/Porky(c),WK	1,000.00
5 Bugs/Porky(c),WK, A:Super Rabbit	1,000.00
6 Bugs/Porky/Elmer(c),E:WK, Kandi the Cave.	700.00
7 Bugs/Porky(c)	500.00
8 Bugs/Porky swimming(c),F:WK, Kandi the Cave	700.00
9 Porky/Elmer car painted(c)	500.00
10 Porky/Bugs/Elmer Parade(c)	500.00
11 Bugs/Porky(c),F:WK, Kandi the Cave.	500.00
12 Bugs/Porky rollerskating(c).	400.00
13 Bugs/Porky(c)	400.00
14 Bugs/Porky(c)	400.00
15 Bugs/Porky X-Mas(c),F:WK Kandi the Cave.	350.00
16 Bugs/Porky ice-skating(c).	350.00
17 Bugs/Petunia Valentines(c)	350.00
18 Sgt.Bugs Marine(c)	350.00
19 Bugs/Painting(c)	350.00
20 Bugs/Porky/ElmerWarBonds(c), B:WK,Pat,Patsy&Pete.	350.00
21 Bugs/Porky 4th July(c)	300.00
22 Porky(c).	300.00
23 Bugs/Porky Fishing(c)	300.00
24 Bugs/Porky Football(c).	300.00
25 Bugs/Porky/Petunia Halloween (c),E:WK,Pat, Patsy & Pete	300.00
26 Bugs Thanksgiving(c).	250.00
27 Bugs/Porky New Years(c)	250.00
28 Bugs/Porky Ice-Skating(c)	250.00
29 Bugs Valentine(c).	250.00
30 Bugs(c)	250.00
31 Bugs(c)	200.00
32 Bugs/Porky Hot Dogs(c).	200.00
33 Bugs/Porky War Bonds(c)	210.00
34 Bugs/Porky Fishing(c)	200.00
35 Bugs/Porky Swimming(c)	200.00
36 Bugs/Porky(c)	200.00
37 Bugs Halloween(c).	200.00

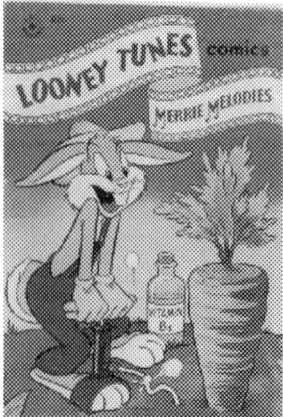

Looney Tunes and Merrie Melodies
© Dell PublishingCo.

Looney Tunes and Merrie Melodies
© Dell Publishing Co.

38 Bugs Thanksgiving(c).	200.00
39 Bugs X-Mas(c).	200.00
40 Bugs(c)	200.00
41 Bugs Washington's Birthday(c)	150.00
42 Bugs Magician(c).	150.00
43 Bugs Dream(c)	150.00
44 Bugs/Porky(c)	150.00
45 Bugs War Bonds(c)	150.00
46 Bugs/Porky(c)	125.00
47 Bugs Beach(c).	125.00
48 Bugs/Porky Picnic(c)	125.00
49 Bugs(c)	125.00
50 Bugs(c)	125.00
51 thru 60	@100.00
61 thru 80	@75.00
81 thru 86	@50.00
87 Bugs X-Mas(c).	55.00
88 thru 99	@50.00
100.	55.00
101 thru 110	@35.00
111 thru 125	@30.00
126 thru 150	@25.00
151 thru 165	@20.00

Becomes:

LOONEY TUNES
Aug., 1955

166 thru 200	@15.00
201 thru 245	@12.00
246 final issue,Sept.1962	12.00

LOST WORLD
Literacy Enterprises (Standard Comics) Oct., 1952

5 ATh, Alice in Terrorland	300.00
6 ATh	250.00

LOVE AND MARRIAGE
Superior Comics Ltd. March, 1952

1	50.00
2	25.00
3	20.00
4	20.00
5	20.00
6	20.00
7	20.00
8 thru 15	@20.00
16 Sept., 1954	20.00

LOVE AT FIRST SIGHT
Periodical House (Ace Magazines) Oct., 1949

1 P(c)	60.00
2 P(c)	25.00
3	15.00
4 P(c)	15.00
5 thru 10	@15.00
11 thru 33	@10.00
34 1st Edition Under Code	7.00
35 thru 41	@7.00
42 1956	7.00

LOVE CONFESSIONS
Comics Magazine (Quality Comics Group) Oct., 1949

1 PG,BWa(c)& Some-a	200.00
2 PG	100.00
3	40.00
4 RC	60.00
5 BWa	85.00
6 Ph(c)	20.00
7 Ph(c) Van Johnson	20.00
8 BWa	75.00
9 Ph(c)Jane Russell/Robert Mitchum	20.00
10 BWa	75.00
11 thru 18 Ph(c)	@35.00
19	25.00
20 BWa	75.00
21	20.00
22 BWa	60.00
23 thru 28	@15.00
29 BWa	75.00
30 thru 38	@15.00
39 MB	20.00
40	15.00
41	15.00
42	15.00
43 1st Edition Under Code	15.00
44 thru 46	@15.00
47 BWa(c)	60.00
48 thru 54 Dec., 1956	@15.00

LOVE DIARY
Our Publishing Co./Toytown July, 1949

1 BK,Ph(c)	100.00
2 BK,Ph(c)	75.00
3 BK,Ph(c)	75.00
4 thru 9 Ph(c)	@30.00
10 BEv,Ph(c)	25.00
11 thru 24 Ph(c)	@22.00
25	20.00
26	20.00
27 Ph(c)	22.00
28	20.00
29 Ph(c)	22.00
30	20.00
31 JB(c)	20.00
32 thru 41	@20.00
42 MB(c)	20.00
43 thru 47	@20.00
48 1st Edition Under Code, Oct.'55	20.00

LOVE DIARY
Quality Comics Group Sept., 1949

1 BWa(c)	200.00

LOVE LESSONS
Harvey Publications
Oct., 1949

1	65.00
2	30.00
3 Ph(c)	20.00
4	20.00
5 June, 1950	20.00

LOVE LETTERS
Comic Magazines
(Quality Comics Group)
Nov., 1949

1 PG,BWa(c)	175.00
2 PG,BWa(c)	150.00
3 PG	75.00
4 BWa	125.00
5	25.00
6	25.00
7	25.00
8	25.00
9 Ph(c) of Robert Mitchum	35.00

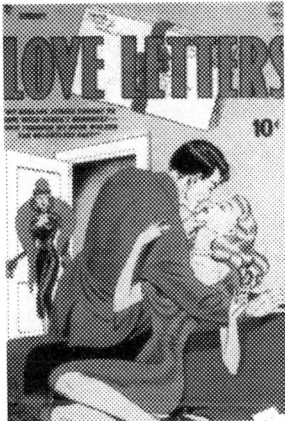

Love Letters #2
© Quality Comics Group

10	25.00
11 BWa	60.00
12	20.00
13	20.00
14	20.00
15	20.00
16 Ph(c) of Anthony Quinn	22.00
17 BWa, Ph(c) of Jane Russell	22.00
18 thru 30	@15.00
31 BWa	25.00
Becomes:

LOVE SECRETS

32	32.00
33	15.00
34 BWa	50.00
35 thru 39	@15.00
40 MB(c)1st Edition Under Code	25.00
41 thru 50	@12.00
50 MB	12.00
51 MB(c)	12.00
52 thru 56	@10.00

LOVELORN
Best Syndicated/Michel Publ.
(American Comics Group)
Aug.–Sept., 1949

1	100.00
2	50.00

3 thru 10	@35.00
11 thru 17	@25.00
18 2pgs. MD-a	20.00
19	25.00
20	25.00
21 Prostitution Story	45.00
22 thru 50	@12.00
51 July, 1954 3-D	100.00
Becomes:

CONFESSIONS OF LOVELORN

52 3-D	125.00
53	35.00
54 3-D	125.00
55	25.00
56 Communist Story	40.00
57 Comics Code	15.00
58 thru 90	@15.00
91 AW	35.00
92 thru 105	@10.00
106 P(c)	10.00
107 P(c)	10.00
108 thru 114	@10.00

LOVE MEMORIES
Fawcett Publications
Autumn, 1949

1 Ph(c)	50.00
2 Ph(c)	25.00
3 Ph(c)	25.00
4 Ph(c)	25.00

LOVE MYSTERY
Fawcett Publications
June, 1950

1 GE, Ph(c)	150.00
2 GE, Ph(c)	125.00
3 GE & BP, Ph(c); Oct., 1950	125.00

LOVE PROBLEMS AND ADVICE ILLUSTRATED
McCombs/Harvey Publications
Home Comics, June, 1949

1 BP	85.00
2 BP	35.00
3	25.00
4	25.00
5 L. Elias(c)	22.00
6	20.00
7 BP	20.00
8 BP	20.00
9 BP	20.00
10 BP	20.00
11 BP	18.00
12 BP	18.00
13 BP	18.00
14 BP	18.00
15	15.00
16	15.00
17 thru 23 BP	@15.00
24 BP, Rape Scene	20.00
25 BP	12.00
26	12.00
27	12.00
28 BP	12.00
29 BP	12.00
30	12.00
31	12.00
32 Comics Code	8.00
33 BP	8.00
34	8.00
35	8.00
36	8.00
37	8.00
38 S&K (c)	8.00
39	8.00

40 BP	8.00
41 BP	8.00
42	8.00
43	8.00
44 March, 1957	8.00

LOVERS LANE
Lev Gleason Publications
Oct., 1949

1 CBi (c),FG-a	50.00
2 P(c)	35.00
3 P(c)	18.00
4 P(c)	18.00
5 P(c)	18.00
6 GT,P(c),	18.00
7 P(c),	18.00
8 P(c),	18.00
9 P(c),	18.00
10 P(c)	18.00
11 thru 19 P(c)	@15.00
20 Ph(c); FF 1 page Ad,	20.00
21 Ph(c)	10.00
22 Ph(c)	10.00
23	10.00
24	10.00
25	10.00
26 Ph(c)	10.00
27 Ph(c)	10.00
28 Ph(c)	10.00
29 thru 38	@10.00
39 Story Narrated by Frank Sinatra	30.00
40	9.00
41 June, 1954	9.00

LOVE SCANDALS
Comic Magazines
(Quality Comics Group)
Feb., 1950

1 BW(c)&a	175.00
2 PG-a, Ph(c)	65.00
3 PG-a, Ph(c)	65.00
4 BWa(c)&a 18Pgs.; GFx-a	135.00
5 Ph(c), Oct., 1950	50.00

LOVE STORIES OF MARY WORTH
Harvey Publications
Sept., 1949

1 Newspaper Reprints	40.00
2 Newspaper Reprints	25.00
3 Newspaper Reprints	20.00
4 Newspaper Reprints,	20.00
5 May, 1950	20.00

LUCKY COMICS
Consolidated Magazines
Jan., 1944

1 Lucky Star	125.00
2 Henry C. Kiefer(c)	75.00
3	75.00
4	75.00
5 Summer, 1946,Devil(c)	75.00

LUCKY DUCK
Standard Comics
(Literary Enterprises)
Jan., 1953

5 IS (c)&a	40.00
6 IS (c)&a	30.00
7 IS (c)&a	30.00
8 IS (c)&a, Sept., 1953	30.00

GOLDEN AGE

LUCKY FIGHTS IT THROUGH
Educational Comics, 1949
N# HK-a, V.D. Prevention . . . 1,300.00

LUCKY "7" COMICS
Howard Publications, 1944
1 Bondage(c) Pioneer 250.00

LUCKY STAR
Nationwide Publications
1950
1 JDa,B:52 pages western 75.00
2 JDa 40.00
3 JDa 40.00
4 JDa 35.00
5 JDa 35.00
6 JDa 35.00
7 JDa 35.00
8 thru 13 . . . . @25.00
14 1955,E:52 pages western 25.00

LUCY, THE REAL GONE GAL
St. John Publishing Co.
June, 1953
1 Negligee Panels,Teenage 65.00
2 . . . . 35.00
3 MD-a 25.00
4 Feb., 1954 . . . . 22.00
Becomes:

MEET MISS PEPPER
St. John Publishing Co.
April, 1954
5 JKu-a 100.00
6 JKu (c)&a, June,1954 . . . . 90.00

MAD
E.C. Comics
Oct.–Nov., 1952
1 JSe,HK(c),JDa,WW 5,600.00
2 JSe,JDa(c),JDa,WW 1,400.00
3 JSe,HK(c),JDa,WW 750.00
4 JSe,HK(c),JDa-Flob Was
   A Slob,JDa,WW 750.00
5 JSe,BE(c).JDa,WW 1,400.00
6 JSe,HK(c),Jda,WW 575.00
7 HK(c),JDa,WW 575.00
8 HK(c),JDa,WW 575.00
9 JSe,HK(c),JDa,WW 575.00
10 JSe,HK(c),JDa,WW 575.00
11 BW,BW(c),JDa,WW,Life(c) . . . 575.00
12 BK,JDa,WW 475.00
13 HK(c),JDa,WW,Red(c) 475.00
14 RH,HK(c),JDa,WW,
   Mona Lisa(c) 475.00
15 JDa,WW,Alice in
   Wonderland(c) 475.00
16 HK(c),JDa,WW,Newspaper(c) 475.00
17 BK,BW,JDa,WW 475.00
18 HK(c),JDa,WW 475.00
19 JDa,WW,Racing Form(c) 350.00
20 JDa,WW,Composition(c) 350.00
21 JDa,WW,1st A.E.Neuman(c) . 350.00
22 BE,JDa,WW,Picasso(c) 350.00
23 Last Comic Format Edition,
   JDa,WW Think(c) 350.00
24 BK,WW, HK Logo & Border;
   1st Magazine Format 850.00
25 WW, Al Jaffee Sterts As Reg.. 350.00
26 BK,WW,WW(c) 300.00
27 WWa,RH,JDa(c) 275.00
28 WW,BE(c),RH Back(c) 275.00
29 JKa,BW,WW,WW(c);

1st Don Martin Artwork 275.00
30 BE,WW,RC; 1st A.E.
   Neuman(c) By Mingo 400.00
31 JDa,WW,BW,Mingo(c) 225.00
32 MD,JO 1st as reg.;Mingo(c);
   WW-Back(c) 200.00
33 WWa,Mingo(c);JO-Back(c) . . 200.00
34 WWa,Mingo(c);1st Berg
   as Reg. 175.00
35 WW,RC,Mingo Wraparound(c) 175.00
36 WW,BW,Mingo(c),JO,MD . . . 125.00
37 WW,Mingo(c)JO,MD 125.00
38 WW,JO,MD 125.00
39 WW,JO,MD 125.00
40 WW,BW,JO,MD 125.00
41 WW,JO,MD 100.00
42 WW,JO,MD 100.00
43 WW,JO,MD 100.00
44 WW,JO,MD 100.00
45 WW,JO,MD 100.00
46 JO,MD 100.00
47 JO,MD 100.00
48 JO,MD 100.00
49 JO,MD 100.00
50 JO,MD 100.00
51 JO,MD 75.00
52 JO,MD 75.00
53 JO,MD 75.00
54 JO,MD 75.00
55 JO,MD 75.00
56 JO,MD 70.00
57 JO,MD 60.00
58 JO,MD 70.00
59 WW,JO,MD 75.00
60 JO,MD 70.00
61 JO,MD 60.00
62 JO,MD 60.00
63 JO,MD 60.00
64 JO,MD 60.00
65 JO,MD 60.00
66 JO,MD 55.00
67 JO,MD 55.00
68 Don Martin(c),JO,MD 55.00
69 JO,MD 55.00
70 JO,MD 55.00
71 JO,MD 55.00
72 JO,MD 55.00
73 JO,MD 55.00
74 JO,MD 55.00
75 Mingo(c),JO,MD 50.00
76 Mingo(c),SA,JO,MD 50.00
77 Mingo(c),SA,JO,MD 50.00
78 Mingo(c),SA,JO,MD 50.00
79 Mingo(c),SA,JO,MD 50.00
80 Mingo(c),SA,JO,MD 50.00

Mad #9
© E.C. Comics

81 Mingo(c),SA,JO,MD 50.00
82 BW,Mingo(c),SA,JO,MD 50.00
83 Mingo(c),SA,JO,MD 50.00
84 Mingo(c),SA,JO,MD 50.00
85 Mingo(c)SA,JO,MD 50.00
86 Mingo(c);1st Fold-in Back(c),
   SA,JO,MD 50.00
87 Mingo(c),JO,MD. 45.00
88 Mingo(c),JO,MD. 45.00
89 WK,Mingo(c),JO,MD 50.00
90 Mingo(c); FF-Back(c),JO,MD . . 45.00
91 Mingo(c),JO,MD. 40.00
92 Mingo(c),JO,MD. 40.00
93 Mingo(c),JO,MD. 40.00
94 Mingo(c),JO,MD. 40.00
95 Mingo(c),JO,MD. 40.00
96 Mingo(c),JO,MD. 40.00
97 Mingo(c),JO,MD. 40.00
98 Mingo(c),JO,MD. 40.00
99 JDa,Mingo(c),JO,MD 50.00
100 Mingo(c),JO,MD. 40.00
101 Infinity(c) by Mingo,JO,MD . . . 30.00
102 Mingo(c)JO,MD 30.00
103 Mingo(c)JO,MD 30.00
104 Mingo(c)JO,MD 30.00
105 Mingo(c);Batman TV Spoof
   ,JO,MD. 35.00
106 Mingo(c);FF-Back(c),JO,MD. . 35.00
107 Mingo(c),JO,MD. 30.00
108 Mingo(c),JO,MD. 30.00
109 Mingo(c),JO,MD. 30.00
110 Mingo(c),JO,MD. 30.00
111 Mingo(c),JO,MD. 30.00
112 JO,MD 30.00
113 JO,MD 30.00
114 JO,MD 30.00
115 JO,MD 30.00
116 JO,MD 30.00
117 JO,MD 30.00
118 JO,MD 30.00
119 JO,MD 30.00
120 JO,MD 30.00
121 Beatles,JO,MD. 30.00
122 MD & Mingo(c),JO,MD,
   Reagan 25.00
123 JO,MD. 20.00
124 JO,MD. 20.00
125 JO,MD. 20.00
126 JO,MD. 20.00
127 JO,MD. 20.00
128 Last JO;MD. 20.00
129 MD 20.00
130 MD 20.00
131 MD 20.00
132 MD 20.00
133 MD 20.00
134 MD 20.00
135 JDa(c),MD. 17.00
136 MD 15.00
137 BW,MD 15.00
138 MD 15.00
139 JDa(c),MD. 16.00
140 thru 153 MD . . . . @16.00
154 Mineo(c),MD 16.00
155 . . . . 16.00
156 . . . . 16.00
157 . . . . 16.00
158 . . . . 16.00
159 . . . . 16.00
160 Mingo(c),JDa,AT 16.00
161 . . . . 14.00
162 Mingo(c),MD,AT 14.00
163 . . . . 14.00
164 Mingo,PaperMoon(c),AT,
   MD,SA 14.00
165 Don Martin(c),At,MD 14.00
166 . . . . 14.00
167 . . . . 14.00
168 Mingo(c),AT,MD 14.00
169 MD(c) 14.00
170 . . . . 14.00

171 Mingo(c) 12.00	
172 Mingo(c) 12.00	
173 JDa(c) 12.00	
174 . . . . 12.00	
175 . . . . 12.00	
176 MD(c) 12.00	
177 . . . . 12.00	
178 JDa(c) 12.00	
179 . . . . 12.00	
180 Jaws(c),SA,MD,JDA,AT 12.00	
181 G.Washington(c),JDa. 12.00	
182 . . . . 12.00	
183 Mingo(c),AT,SA,MD 12.00	
184 Mingo(c),Md,AT 12.00	
185 . . . . 12.00	
186 Star Trek Spoof 14.00	
187 . . . . 12.00	
188 . . . . 12.00	
189 . . . . 12.00	
190 . . . . 12.00	
191 Clark(c),JDa,MD,AT 12.00	
192 . . . . 12.00	

193 Charlies Angels(c),
    Rickart,JDa,SA,MD. 12.00
194 Rocky(c),Rickart,AT,MD 12.00
195 . . . . 12.00
196 Star Wars Spoof,
    Rickart,AT,JDa 18.00
197 . . . . 12.00
198 UPC(c),AT,MD 12.00
199 Jaffee(c),AT,JDa,SA,MD. 12.00
200 Rickart(c),Close Encounters . 15.00
201 Rickart(c),Sat.Night Fever 7.50
202 . . . . 7.50
203 Star Wars Spoof,Rickart(c). . . . 8.50
204 Hulk TV Spoof,JawsII(c). 7.50
205 Rickart(c),Grease. 7.50
206 Mingo,(c),AT,JDa,Md 7.50
207 Jones(c),Animal House(c) 7.50
208 Superman Movie Spoof,
    Rickart(c) 7.50
209 Mingo(c),AT,MD 7.50
210 Mingo,Lawn Mower,AT,
    JDa,MD 7.50
211 Mingo(c) 7.50
212 Jda(c),AT,MD 8.00
213 JDa(c),SA,AT,JDa 8.00
214 . . . . 7.00
215 Jones(c),MD,AT,JDa 7.00
216 . . . . 7.00
217 Jaffee(c),For Pres,AT,MD 7.00
218 Martin(c),AT,MD 7.00
219 thru 250 . . . . @7.00
251 thru 260 . . . . @5.00
261 thru 299 . . . . @4.00
300 thru 303 . . . . 6.00
304 thru 330 . . . . 3.00

MAGIC COMICS
David McKay Publications
Aug., 1939

1 Mandrake the Magician,
    Henry,Popeye,Blondie,
    Barney Baxter,Secret Agent
    X-9, Bunky,Henry on(c) . . . 2,200.00
2 Henry on(c) 750.00
3 Henry on(c) 550.00
4 Henry on(c),Mandrake-Logo . 500.00
5 Henry on(c),Mandrake-Logo . 350.00
6 Henry on(c),Mandrake-Logo . 325.00
7 Henry on(c),Mandrake-Logo . 325.00
8 B:Inspector Wade,Tippie 300.00
9 Henry-Mandrake Interact(c) . . 300.00
10 Henry-Mandrake Interact(c) . 300.00
11 Henry-Mandrake Interact(c) . 275.00
12 Mandrake on(c) 275.00
13 Mandrake on(c) 275.00
14 Mandrake on(c) 275.00
15 Mandrake on(c) 275.00
16 Mandrake on(c) 275.00

Magic Comics #8
© David McKay Publications

17 B:Lone Ranger 275.00
18 Mandrake/Robot on(c) 250.00
19 Mandrake on(c) 250.00
20 Mandrake on(c) 250.00
21 Mandrake on(c) 175.00
22 Mandrake on(c) 175.00
23 Mandrake on(c) 175.00
24 Mandrake on(c) 175.00
25 B:Blondie; Mandrake in
    Logo for Duration 175.00
26 Blondie (c) 150.00
27 Blondie (c); High
    School Heroes 150.00
28 Blondie (c); High
    School Heroes 150.00
29 Blondie (c); High
    School Heroes 150.00
30 Blondie (c) 150.00
31 Blondie(c);High School
    Sports Page 125.00
32 Blondie (c);Secret Agent X-9 . 125.00
33 C.Knight's-Romance of Flying 125.00
34 ClaytonKnight's-War in the Air 125.00
35 Blondie (c) 125.00
36 July'42; Patriotic-(c) 125.00
37 Blondie (c) 125.00
38 ClaytonKnight's-Flying Tigers 125.00
39 Blondie (c) 125.00
40 Jimmie Doolittle bombs Tokyo 125.00
41 How German Became
    British Censor. 100.00
42 Joe Musial's-Dollar-a-Dither . . 100.00
43 Clay Knight's-War in the Air . . 100.00
44 Flying Fortress in Action. . . . 100.00
45 Clayton Knight's-Gremlins . . . 100.00
46 Adventures of Aladdin Jr. 100.00
47 Secret Agent X-9 . . . . 100.00
48 General Arnold U.S.A.F. 100.00
49 Joe Musial's-Dollar-a-Dither . . 100.00
50 The Lone Ranger 100.00
51 Joe Musial's-Dollar-a-Dither . . 75.00
52 C. Knights-Heroes on Wings . . 75.00
53 C. Knights-Heroes on Wings . . 75.00
54 High School Heroes 75.00
55 Blondie (c) 80.00
56 High School Heroes 75.00
57 Joe Musial's-Dollar-a-Dither . . 75.00
58 Private Breger Abroad 75.00
59 . . . . 75.00
60 . . . . 75.00
61 Joe Musial's-Dollar-a-Dither . . 60.00
62 . . . . 60.00
63 B:Buz Sawyer, Naval Pilot . . . 60.00
64 thru 70 . . . . @60.00
71 thru 80 . . . . @45.00

80 thru 90 . . . . @40.00
91 thru 99 . . . . @40.00
100 . . . . 50.00
101 thru 108 . . . . @35.00
108 Flash Gordon. 40.00
109 Flash Gordon. 40.00
110 thru 113 . . . . @30.00
114 The Lone Ranger. 30.00
115 thru 119 . . . . @30.00
120 Secret Agent X-9 . . . . 35.00
121 Secret Agent X-9 . . . . 35.00
122 Secret Agent X-9 . . . . 35.00
123 Sec. Agent X-9;Nov-Dec.'49. . 35.00

MAJOR HOOPLE COMICS
Nedor Publications, 1942

1 Mary Worth,Phantom Soldier;
    Buy War Bonds On(c) 300.00

MAJOR VICTORY COMICS
H. Clay Glover Svcs./
Harry A. Chestler, 1944

1 O:Major Victory,I:Spider
    Woman 450.00
2 A: Dynamic Boy 300.00
3 A: Rocket Boy 250.00

MAN HUNT!
Magazine Enterprises
Oct., 1953

1 LbC,FG,OW(c);B:Red Fox,
    Undercover Girl, Space Ace   375.00
2 LbC,FG,OW(c);
    Electrocution(c) 300.00
3 LbC,FG,OW,OW(c) 250.00
4 LbC,FG,OW,OW(c) 250.00
5 LbC,FG,OW,OW(c) 250.00
6 LbC,OW,OW(c) 225.00
7 LbC,OW; E:Space Ace 225.00
8 LbC,OW,FG(c);B:Trail Colt . . 225.00
9 LbC,OW 225.00
10 LbC,OW,OW(c),Gwl. 225.00
11 LbC,FF,OW;B:The Duke,
    Scotland Yard. 300.00
12 LbC,OW 150.00
13 LbC,FF,OW;Rep.Trail Colt #1 . 250.00
14 LbC,OW;Bondage,
    Hypo-(c);1953. . . . . 225.00

MAN OF WAR
Comic Corp. of America
(Centaur Publ.), Nov., 1941

1 PG,PG(c);Flag(c);B:The Fire-
    Man,Man of War,The Sentinel,
    Liberty Guards,Vapoman . . 1,300.00
2 PG,PG(c);I: The Ferret 1,000.00

MAN O'MARS
Fiction House/
I.W. Enterprises, 1953

1 MA, Space Rangers 300.00
1 MA, Rep. Space Rangers 50.00

MARCH OF COMICS
K.K. Publications/
Western Publ., 1946
(All were Giveaways)

N# WK back(c),Goldilocks 300.00
N# WK,How Santa got His
    Red Suit 300.00
N# WK,Our Gang 400.00

GOLDEN AGE

N# CB,Donald Duck;
  "Maharajah Donald" 7,500.00
5 Andy Panda 150.00
6 WK,Fairy Tales 200.00
7 Oswald the Lucky Rabbit 150.00
8 Mickey Mouse 550.00
9 Gloomey Bunny 75.00
10 Santa Claus.............. 65.00
11 Santa Claus............. 50.00
12 Santa's Toys 50.00
13 Santa's Suprise 50.00
14 Santa's Kitchen 50.00
15 Hip-It-Ty Hop 75.00
16 Woody Woodpecker....... 150.00
17 Roy Rogers 225.00
18 Fairy Tales.............. 90.00
19 Uncle Wiggily........... 75.00
20 CB,Donald Duck 4,500.00
21 Tom and Jerry 100.00
22 Andy Panda............. 65.00
23 Raggedy Ann and Andy..... 125.00
24 Felix the Cat; By
   Otto Messmer............ 200.00
25 Gene Autrey 200.00
26 Our Gang 200.00
27 Mickey Mouse 400.00
28 Gene Autry 200.00
29 Easter 30.00
30 Santa 25.00
31 Santa................. 25.00
32 Does Not Exist
33 A Christmas Carol 25.00
34 Woody Woodpecker........ 75.00
35 Roy Rogers 225.00
36 Felix the Cat 175.00
37 Popeye 150.00
38 Oswald the Lucky Rabbit..... 50.00
39 Gene Autry 185.00
40 Andy and Woody 50.00
41 CB,DonaldDuck,SouthSeas. 3,600.00
42 Porky Pig............... 60.00
43 Henry 40.00
44 Bugs Bunny 75.00
45 Mickey Mouse 300.00
46 Tom and Jerry 70.00
47 Roy Rogers 175.00
48 Santa................. 20.00
49 Santa................. 20.00
50 Santa 20.00
51 Felix the Cat 150.00
52 Popeye 125.00
53 Oswald the Lucky Rabbit..... 50.00
54 Gene Autrey 150.00
55 Andy and Woody 45.00
56 CB back(c),Donald Duck 275.00
57 Porky Pig............... 55.00
58 Henry 30.00
59 Bugs Bunny 70.00
60 Mickey Mouse 275.00
61 Tom and Jerry 50.00
62 Roy Rogers 175.00
63 Santa.................. 20.00
64 Santa................. 20.00
65 Jingle Bells 20.00
66 Popeye 100.00
67 Oswald the Lucky Rabbit..... 30.00
68 Roy Rogers 175.00
69 Donald Duck 250.00
70 Tom and Jerry 40.00
71 Porky Pig............... 55.00
72 Krazy Kat............... 50.00
73 Roy Rogers 150.00
74 Mickey Mouse 250.00
75 Bugs Bunny............. 65.00
76 Andy and Woody 35.00
77 Roy Rogers 100.00
78 Gene Autrey; last regular
   sized issue 100.00
79 Andy Panda,5"x7" format..... 25.00
80 Popeye 65.00
81 Oswald the Lucky Rabbit 25.00

82 Tarzan 150.00
83 Bugs Bunny............. 50.00
84 Henry 25.00
85 Woody Woodpecker...... 25.00
86 Roy Rogers 125.00
87 Krazy Kat............... 25.00
88 Tom and Jerry 30.00
89 Porky Pig............... 25.00
90 Gene Autrey 90.00
91 Roy Rogers and Santa..... 125.00
92 Christmas w/Santa........ 15.00
93 Woody Woodpecker....... 25.00
94 Indian Chief............. 65.00
95 Oswald the Lucky Rabbit 20.00
96 Popeye 60.00
97 Bugs Bunny 40.00
98 Tarzan,Lex Barker Ph(c) 150.00
99 Porky Pig............... 25.00
100 Roy Rogers 100.00
101 Henry 20.00
102 Tom Corbet,P(c)........ 135.00
103 Tom and Jerry 25.00
104 Gene Autrey 75.00
105 Roy Rogers 100.00
106 Santa's Helpers 15.00
107 *Not Published*
108 Fun with Santa. 15.00
109 Woody Woodpecker........ 20.00
110 Indian Chief 30.00
111 Oswald the Lucky Rabbit .. 20.00
112 Henry................. 20.00
113 Porky Pig.............. 25.00
114 Tarzan,RsM 150.00
115 Bugs Bunny 40.00
116 Roy Rogers 100.00
117 Popeye 60.00
118 Flash Gordon, P(c)....... 120.00
119 Tom and Jerry 20.00
120 Gene Autrey 65.00
121 Roy Rogers 100.00
122 Santa's Suprise 15.00
123 Santa's Christmas Book.... 15.00
124 Woody Woodpecker........ 20.00
125 Tarzan, Lex Barker Ph(c) .. 150.00
126 Oswald the Lucky Rabbit 20.00
127 Indian Chief............. 20.00
128 Tom and Jerry 20.00
129 Henry 20.00
130 Porky Pig 25.00
131 Roy Rogers 100.00
132 Bugs Bunny............. 30.00
133 Flash Gordon,Ph(c) 100.00
134 Popeye 45.00
135 Gene Autrey 60.00
136 Roy Rogers 75.00

March of Comics #41
© Walt Disney

137 Gifts from Santa. 10.00
138 Fun at Christmas 10.00
139 Woody Woodpecker....... 20.00
140 Indian Chief 25.00
141 Oswald the Lucky Rabbit 15.00
142 Flash Gordon............ 80.00
143 Porky Pig.............. 20.00
144 RsM,Ph(c),Tarzan 135.00
145 Tom and Jerry 20.00
146 Roy Rogers,Ph(c) 100.00
147 Henry 15.00
148 Popeye 35.00
149 Bugs Bunny............. 25.00
150 Gene Autrey 60.00
151 Roy Rogers 75.00
152 The Night Before Christmas.. 12.00
153 Merry Christmas 12.00
154 Tom and Jerry 20.00
155 Tarzan,Ph(c) 125.00
156 Oswald the Lucky Rabbit 15.00
157 Popeye 30.00
158 Woody Woodpecker....... 20.00
159 Indian Chief............. 20.00
160 Bugs Bunny 20.00
161 Roy Rogers 75.00
162 Henry 15.00
163 Rin Tin Tin 32.00
164 Porky Pig.............. 20.00
165 The Lone Ranger........ 65.00
166 Santa & His Reindeer 12.00
167 Roy Rogers and Santa..... 75.00
168 Santa Claus' Workshop 12.00
169 Popeye 30.00
170 Indian Chief 25.00
171 Oswald the Lucky Rabbit .. 20.00
172 Tarzan 100.00
173 Tom and Jerry 15.00
174 The Lone Ranger. 60.00
175 Porky Pig.............. 20.00
176 Roy Rogers 60.00
177 Woody Woodpecker....... 15.00
178 Henry 15.00
179 Bugs Bunny 20.00
180 Rin Tin Tin 25.00
181 Happy Holiday 10.00
182 Happi Tim 10.00
183 Welcome Santa 10.00
184 Woody Woodpecker....... 15.00
185 Tarzan, Ph(c)........... 100.00
186 Oswald the Lucky Rabbit 12.00
187 Indian Chief............. 25.00
188 Bugs Bunny 25.00
189 Henry 15.00
190 Tom and Jerry 18.00
191 Roy Rogers 60.00
192 Porky Pig.............. 20.00
193 The Lone Ranger. 60.00
194 Popeye 25.00
195 Rin Tin Tin............. 30.00
196 *Not Published*
197 Santa is Coming 10.00
198 Santa's Helper........... 10.00
199 Huckleberry Hound 50.00
200 Fury 30.00
201 Bugs Bunny 25.00
202 Space Explorer 50.00
203 Woody Woodpecker....... 15.00
204 Tarzan 55.00
205 Mighty Mouse 35.00
206 Roy Rogers,Ph(c) 60.00
207 Tom and Jerry 15.00
208 The Lone Ranger,Ph(c) 90.00
209 Porky Pig.............. 15.00
210 Lassie 30.00
211 *Not Published*
212 Christmas Eve 10.00
213 Here Comes Santa 10.00
214 Huckleberry Hound 50.00
215 Hi Yo Silver 35.00
216 Rocky & His Friends 75.00
217 Lassie 20.00

GOLDEN AGE

March of Comics #70
© M. G. M.

218 Porky Pig. 20.00
219 Journey to the Sun. 30.00
220 Bugs Bunny 20.00
221 Roy and Dale,Ph(c) 60.00
222 Woody Woodpecker. 15.00
223 Tarzan 75.00
224 Tom and Jerry 15.00
225 The Lone Ranger. 40.00
226 Christmas Treasury 10.00
227 Not Published
228 Letters to Santa 10.00
229 The Flintstones 100.00
230 Lassie 20.00
231 Bugs Bunny. 20.00
232 The Three Stooges 75.00
233 Bullwinkle 75.00
234 Smokey the Bear. 20.00
235 Huckleberry Hound 35.00
236 Roy and Dale. 50.00
237 Mighty Mouse 20.00
238 The Lone Ranger. 40.00
239 Woody Woodpecker. 15.00
240 Tarzan 60.00
241 Santa Around the World. 10.00
242 Santa Toyland 10.00
243 The Flintstones 100.00
244 Mr.Ed,Ph(c) 25.00
245 Bugs Bunny. 20.00
246 Popeye 20.00
247 Mighty Mouse 20.00
248 The Three Stooges 75.00
249 Woody Woodpecker. 10.00
250 Roy and Dale 50.00
251 Little Lulu & Witch Hazel . . . 100.00
252 P(c),Tarzan 45.00
253 Yogi Bear. 25.00
254 Lassie 20.00
255 Santa's Christmas List 10.00
256 Christmas Party 10.00
257 Mighty Mouse 20.00
258 The Sword in the Stone
     (Disney Version) 50.00
259 Bugs Bunny. 20.00
260 Mr. Ed 20.00
261 Woody Woodpecker. 15.00
262 Tarzan 55.00
263 Donald Duck 75.00
264 Popeye 25.00
265 Yogi Bear. 30.00
266 Lassie 20.00
267 Little Lulu. 90.00
268 The Three Stooges 75.00
269 A Jolly Christmas. 10.00
270 Santa's Little Helpers 10.00
271 The Flintstones 75.00

272 Tarzan 45.00
273 Bugs Bunny. 20.00
274 Popeye 20.00
275 Little Lulu. 75.00
276 The Jetsons. 100.00
277 Daffy Duck. 15.00
278 Lassie 20.00
279 Yogi Bear. 30.00
280 Ph(c),The Three Stooges. . . . 75.00
281 Tom & Jerry 15.00
282 Mr. Ed 20.00
283 Santa's Visit 10.00
284 Christmas Parade 10.00
285 Astro Boy. 325.00
286 Tarzan. 40.00
287 Bugs Bunny. 20.00
288 Daffy Duck. 15.00
289 The Flintstones 65.00
290 Ph(c), Mr. Ed. 18.00
291 Yogi Bear. 25.00
292 Ph(c), The Three Stooges . . . 70.00
293 Little Lulu. 55.00
294 Popeye 20.00
295 Tom & Jerry 15.00
296 Lassie 20.00
297 Christmas Bells 10.00
298 Santa's Sleigh 10.00
299 The Flintstones 60.00
300 Tarzan 40.00
301 Bugs Bunny. 15.00
302 Ph(c), Laurel & Hardy 30.00
303 Daffy Duck. 10.00
304 Ph(c), The Three Stooges . . . 70.00
305 Tom & Jerry. 10.00
306 Ph(c), Daniel Boone. 40.00
307 Little Lulu. 45.00
308 Ph(c), Lassie 15.00
309 Yogi Bear. 25.00
310 Ph(c) of Clayton Moore;
     The Lone Ranger. 75.00
311 Santa's Show 8.00
312 Christmas Album 8.00
313 Daffy Duck. 12.00
314 Laurel & Hardy 25.00
315 Bugs Bunny. 15.00
316 The Three Stooges 60.00
317 The Flintstones 30.00
318 Tarzan 35.00
319 Yogi Bear. 20.00
320 Space Family Robinson 100.00
321 Tom & Jerry 12.00
322 The Lone Ranger. 40.00
323 Little Lulu. 30.00
324 Ph(c), Lassie 12.00
325 Fun With Santa 9.00
326 Christmas Story 9.00
327 The Flintstones 55.00
328 Space Family Robinson 55.00
329 Bugs Bunny. 15.00
330 The Jetsons. 75.00
331 Daffy Duck. 12.00
332 Tarzan 35.00
333 Tom & Jerry 12.00
334 Lassie 15.00
335 Little Lulu. 25.00
336 The Three Stooges 55.00
337 Yogi Bear. 20.00
338 The Lone Ranger. 35.00
339 Not Published
340 Here Comes Santa 9.00
341 The Flintstones 55.00
342 Tarzan 30.00
343 Bugs Bunny. 20.00
344 Yogi Bear. 23.00
345 Tom & Jerry 12.00
346 Lassie 15.00
347 Daffy Duck. 12.00
348 The Jetsons. 65.00
349 Little Lulu. 25.00
350 The Lone Ranger. 30.00
351 Beep-Beep, The

Road Runner 20.00
352 Space Family Robinson 75.00
353 Beep-Beep, The Road
     Runner. 20.00
354 Tarzan 25.00
355 Little Lulu. 25.00
356 Scooby Doo, Where Are You . 22.00
357 Daffy Duck & Porky Pig 12.00
358 Lassie 15.00
359 Baby Snoots 12.00
360 Ph(c), H.R. Pufnstuf. 15.00
361 Tom & Jerry 12.00
362 Smokey the Bear. 15.00
363 Bugs Bunny & Yosemite Sam. 15.00
364 Ph(c), The Banana Splits 11.00
365 Tom & Jerry 12.00
366 Tarzan 25.00
367 Bugs Bunny & Porky Pig 15.00
368 Scooby Doo. 20.00
369 Little Lulu. 20.00
370 Ph(c), Lassie 12.00
371 Baby Snoots 9.00
372 Smokey The Bear 11.00
373 The Three Stooges 50.00
374 Wacky Witch 8.00
375 Beep-Beep & Daffy Duck 12.00
376 The Pink Panther. 15.00
377 Baby Snoots 9.00
378 Turok, Son of Stone. 95.00
379 Heckle & Jeckle. 10.00
380 Bugs Bunny & Yosemite Sam. 15.00
381 Lassie 12.00
382 Scooby Doo. 18.00
383 Smokey the Bear. 9.00
384 The Pink Panther. 12.00
385 Little Lulu. 15.00
386 Wacky Witch 7.00
387 Beep-Beep & Daffy Duck 10.00
388 Tom & Jerry 10.00
389 Little Lulu. 15.00
390 The Pink Panther. 12.00
391 Scooby Doo. 18.00
392 Bugs Bunny & Yosemite Sam. 15.00
393 Heckle & Jeckle. 8.00
394 Lassie 10.00
395 Woodsy the Owl . . . . , . 6.00
396 Baby Snoots 6.00
397 Beep-Beep & Daffy Duck 7.00
398 Wacky Witch 6.00
399 Turok, Son of Stone. 65.00
400 Tom & Jerry 8.00
401 Baby Snoots 6.00
402 Daffy Duck. 8.00
403 Bugs Bunny. 10.00
404 Space Family Robinson 40.00
405 Cracky. 6.00
406 Little Lulu. 15.00
407 Smokey the Bear. 6.00
408 Turok, Son of Stone. 45.00
409 The Pink Panther. 10.00
410 Wacky Witch 6.00
411 Lassie 10.00
412 New Terrytoons 4.00
413 Daffy Duck. 4.00
414 Space Family Robinson 35.00
415 Bugs Bunny. 10.00
416 The Road Runner 6.00
417 Little Lulu. 15.00
418 The Pink Panther. 10.00
419 Baby Snoots 4.00
420 Woody Woodpecker. 4.00
421 Tweety & Sylvester 4.00
422 Wacky Witch 4.00
423 Little Monsters. 4.00
424 Cracky. 4.00
425 Daffy Duck. 4.00
426 Underdog. 18.00
427 Little Lulu. 10.00
428 Bugs Bunny. 6.00
429 The Pink Panther. 6.00
430 The Road Runner 7.00

431 Baby Snoots 4.00
432 Lassie 5.00
433 Tweety & Sylvester 4.00
434 Wacky Witch 4.00
435 New Terrytoons 4.00
436 Cracky. 4.00
437 Daffy Duck. 4.00
438 Underdog. 10.00
439 Little Lulu. 10.00
440 Bugs Bunny. 7.00
441 The Pink Panther. 5.00
442 The Road Runner 5.00
443 Baby Snoots 3.00
444 Tom & Jerry. 3.00
445 Tweety & Sylvester 3.00
446 Wacky Witch 2.00
447 Mighty Mouse 5.00
448 Cracky. 2.00
449 The Pink Panther. 5.00
450 Baby Snoots 3.00
451 Tom & Jerry. 4.00
452 Bugs Bunny. 4.00
453 Popeye 3.00
454 Woody Woodpecker. 4.00
455 The Road Runner 4.00
456 Little Lulu. 3.00
457 Tweety & Sylvester 3.00
458 Wacky Witch 2.00
459 Mighty Mouse 5.00
460 Daffy Duck. 3.00
461 The Pink Panther. 4.00
462 Baby Snoots 2.00
463 Tom & Jerry. 4.00
464 Bugs Bunny. 5.00
465 Popeye 4.00
466 Woody Woodpecker. 4.00
467 Underdog. 8.00
468 Little Lulu. 4.00
469 Tweety & Sylvester 3.00
470 Wacky Witch 3.00
471 Mighty Mouse 5.00
472 Heckle & Jeckle. 4.00
473 The Pink Panther. 5.00
474 Baby Snoots 2.00
475 Little Lulu. 3.00
476 Bugs Bunny. 5.00
477 Popeye 3.00
478 Woody Woodpecker. 5.00
479 Underdog. 10.00
480 Tom & Jerry. 8.00
481 Tweety & Sylvster 3.00
482 Wacky Witch 3.00
483 Mighty Mouse 5.00
484 Heckle & Jeckle. 3.00
485 Baby Snoots 3.00
486 The Pink Panther. 5.00
487 Bugs Bunny. 5.00
488 April, 1982; Little Lulu 3.00

MARGE'S LITTLE LULU
Dell Publishing Co.
1 B:Lulu's Diary 600.00
2 I:Gloria,Miss Feeny. 300.00
3 . . . . 275.00
4 . . . . 275.00
5 . . . . 275.00
6 . . . . 200.00
7 I:Annie,X-Mas Cover. 200.00
8 . . . . 200.00
9 . . . . 200.00
10 . . . . 200.00
11 thru 18 . . . . @175.00
19 I:Wilbur. 175.00
20 I:Mr.McNabbem. 175.00
21 thru 25 . . . . @150.00
26 rep.Four Color#110 . . . . 150.00
27 thru 29. . . . . @150.00
30 Christmas cover. 150.00
31 thru 34 . . . . @125.00
35 B:Mumday Story 125.00

36 thru 38 . . . . @125.00
39 I:Witch Hazel 150.00
40 Halloween Cover 125.00
41 . . . . 125.00
42 Christmas Cover 125.00
43 Skiing Cover 125.00
44 Valentines Day Cover 125.00
45 2nd A:Witch Hazel. 125.00
46 thru 60 . . . . @125.00
61 . . . . 75.00
62 . . . . 75.00
63 I:Chubby 75.00
64 thru 67 . . . . @75.00
68 I:Professor Cleff. 75.00
69 thru 77 . . . . @75.00
78 Christmas Cover 75.00
79 . . . . 75.00
80 . . . . 75.00
81 thru 89 . . . . @60.00
90 Christmas Cover 60.00
91 thru 99 . . . . @60.00
100 . . . . 75.00
101 thru 122 . . . . @60.00
123 I:Fifi 50.00
124 thru 164 . . . . @40.00
165 giant sized 150.00
166 giant sized 150.00
167 thru 169 . . . . @35.00
170 . . . . 15.00
171 . . . . 15.00
172 . . . . 18.00
173 . . . . 15.00
174 . . . . 15.00
175 . . . . 18.00
176 . . . . 18.00
177 . . . . 15.00
178 thru 196 . . . . @18.00
197 . . . . 15.00
198 thru 200 . . . . @18.00
201 . . . . 8.00
202 . . . . 12.00
203 . . . . 8.00
204 . . . . 12.00
205 . . . . 12.00
206 . . . . 8.00

MARMADUKE MOUSE
Quality Comics Group
(Arnold Publications)
Spring, 1946
1 Funny Animal 85.00
2 Funny Animal 32.00
3 thru 8 Funny Animal . . . . . . @25.00
9 Funny Animal 22.00
10 Funny Animal 22.00
11 thru 20 Funny Animal . . . . . @20.00
21 thru 30 Funny Animal . . . . . @18.00
31 thru 40 Funny Animal . . . . . @15.00
41 thru 50 Funny Animal . . . . . @12.00
51 thru 65 Funny Animal . . . . . @10.00

MARTIN KANE
Hero Books
(Fox Features syndicate)
June, 1950
1 WW,WW-(c) 200.00
2 WW,JO, Auguat, 1950 . . . . . 150.00

MARVEL FAMILY, THE
Fawcett Publications
Dec., 1945
1 O:Captain Marvel,Captain Marvel Jr.,
  Mary Marvel,Uncle Marvel;
  V:Black Adam 1,200.00
2 . . . . 550.00
3 . . . . 400.00
4 The Witch's Tale 350.00

5 Civilization of a
  Prehistoric Race 325.00
6 . . . . 275.00
7 The Rock of Eternity 250.00
8 The Marvel Family
  Round Table 250.00
9 V: The Last Vikings 250.00
10 V: The Sivana Family. 250.00
11 V: The Well of Evil 225.00
12 V: The Iron Horseman 225.00
13 . . . . 225.00
14 Captain Marvel Invalid 225.00
15 V: Mr. Triangle 200.00
16 World's Mightiest Quarrell . . . 200.00
17 . . . . 200.00
18 . . . . 200.00
19 V: The Monster Menace. 200.00
20 The Marvel Family Feud 200.00
21 V: The Trio of Terror. 160.00
22 V: The Triple Threat. 160.00
23 March of Independence (c) . . 175.00
24 V: The Fighting Xergos 160.00
25 Trial of the Marvel Family. . . . 160.00
26 V: Mr. Power 150.00
27 V: The Amoeba Men 150.00
28 . . . . 150.00
29 V: The Monarch of Money . . . 150.00
30 A:World's Greatest Magician . 150.00
31 V:Sivana & The Great Hunger 125.00
32 The Marvel Family Goes
  Into Buisness 125.00
33 I: The Hermit Family 125.00
34 V: Sivana's Miniature Menace 125.00
35 V: The Berzerk Machines. . . . 125.00
36 V: The Invaders From Infinity . 125.00
37 V: The Earth Changer 125.00
38 V: Sivana's Instinct
  Exterminator Gun 125.00
39 The Legend of Atlantis. 125.00
40 Seven Wonders of the
  Modern World 125.00
41 The Great Oxygen Theft 125.00
42 V: The Endless Menace. 100.00
43 . . . . 100.00
44 V: The Rust That Menaced
  the World 100.00
45 The Hoax City 100.00
46 The Day Civilization Vanished 100.00
47 V: The Interplanetary Thieves 150.00
48 V: The Four Horsemen. 100.00
49 ...Proves Human Hardness . . 100.00
50 The Speech Scrambler
  Machine 100.00
51 The Living Statues. 120.00
52 The School of Witches. 100.00

Marvel Family #9
© Fawcett Publications

53 V: The Man Who Changed
the World 100.00
54 . . . . 100.00
55 . . . . 100.00
56 The World's Mightiest Project. 100.00
57 . . . . 100.00
58 The Triple Time Plot. 100.00
59 . . . . 100.00
60 . . . . 100.00
61 . . . . 90.00
62 . . . . 90.00
63 V: The Pirate Planet. 90.00
64 . . . . 90.00
65 . . . . 90.00
66 The Miracle Stone 90.00
67 . . . . 90.00
68 . . . . 90.00
69 V: The Menace of Old Age. . . 90.00
70 V: The Crusade of Evil 90.00
71 . . . . 90.00
72 . . . . 90.00
73 . . . . 90.00
74 . . . . 90.00
75 The Great Space Struggle 90.00
76 . . . . 125.00
77 Anti-Communist. 150.00
78 V: The Red Vulture 125.00
79 . . . . 90.00
80 . . . . 90.00
81 . . . . 90.00
82 . . . . 90.00
83 V: The Flying Skull. 90.00
84 thru 87 . . . . @90.00
88 Jokes of Jeopardy 90.00
89 And Then There Were None;
Jan., 1954 . . . . 90.00

MARVELS OF SCIENCE
Charlton Comics
March, 1946
1 1st Charlton Book; Atomic
Bomb Story 150.00
2 . . . . 100.00
3 . . . . 100.00
4 President Truman(c); Jun.`6 . . 100.00

MARY MARVEL COMICS
Fawcett Publications/
Charlton Comics
Dec., 1945
1 Intro: Mary Marvel 1,500.00
2 . . . . 600.00
3 . . . . 400.00
4 On a Leave of Absence 375.00
5 Butterfly (c). 275.00
6 A:Freckles,Teenager of
Mischief 275.00
7 The Kingdom Undersea 275.00
8 Holiday Special Issue 275.00
9 Air Race (c) 225.00
10 A: Freckles 225.00
11 A: The Sad Dryads. 175.00
12 Red Cross Appeal on(c). 175.00
13 Keep the Homefires Burning . 175.00
14 Meets Ghosts (c) 175.00
15 A: Freckles 175.00
16 The Jukebox Menace. 150.00
17 Aunt Agatha's Adventures . . . 150.00
18 . . . . 150.00
19 Witch (c) 150.00
20 . . . . 150.00
21 V: Dice Head. 125.00
22 The Silver Slippers. 125.00
23 The Pendulum Strikes 125.00
24 V: The Nightowl 125.00
25 A: Freckles 125.00
26 A:Freckles dressed as Clown. 125.00
27 The Floating Oceanliner. 125.00

Mary Marvel #4
© Fawcet Publications

28 Sept., 1948 . . . . 125.00
Becomes:

MONTE HALE WESTERN
29 Ph(c),B:Monte Hale & His
Horse Pardner 350.00
30 Ph(c),B:Big Bow-Little
Arrow; CCB,Captain Tootsie 225.00
31 Ph(c),Giant 175.00
32 Ph(c),Giant 175.00
33 Ph(c),Giant 175.00
34 Ph(c),E:Big Bow-Little
Arrow;B:Gabby Hayes,Giant. 175.00
35 Ph(c),Gabby Hayes, Giant . . . 175.00
36 Ph(c),Gabby Hayes, Giant . . . 175.00
37 Ph(c),Gabby Hayes 125.00
38 Ph(c),Gabby Hayes, Giant . . . 150.00
39 Ph(c);CCB, Captain Tootsie;
Gabby Hayes, Giant. 150.00
40 Ph(c),Gabby Hayes, Giant . . . 150.00
41 Ph(c),Gabby Hayes 75.00
42 Ph(c),Gabby Hayes, Giant . . . 90.00
43 Ph(c),Gabby Hayes, Giant . . . 90.00
44 Ph(c),Gabby Hayes, Giant . . . 90.00
45 Ph(c),Gabby Hayes 75.00
46 Ph(c),Gabby Hayes, Giant . . . 75.00
47 Ph(c),A:Big Bow-Little Arrow;
Gabby Hayes, Giant. 75.00
48 Ph(c),Gabby Hayes, Giant . . . 75.00
49 Ph(c),Gabby Hayes 75.00
50 Ph(c),Gabby Hayes, Giant . . . 75.00
51 Ph(c),Gabby Hayes, Giant . . . 70.00
52 Ph(c),Gabby Hayes, Giant . . . 70.00
53 Ph(c),A:Slim Pickens;
Gabby Hayes 50.00
54 Ph(c),Gabby Hayes, Giant . . . 70.00
55 Ph(c),Gabby Hayes, Giant . . . 70.00
56 Ph(c),Gabby Hayes, Giant . . . 70.00
57 Ph(c),Gabby Hayes 50.00
58 Ph(c),Gabby Hayes, Giant . . . 60.00
59 Ph(c),Gabby Hayes, Giant . . . 60.00
60 thru 79 Ph(c),Gabby Hayes . @45.00
80 Ph(c),E: Gabby Hayes 45.00
81 Ph(c). 45.00
82 Final Ph(c), Last Fawcett
Edition 45.00
83 1st Charlton Edition, R:G.
Hayes Back B&W Ph(c) 45.00
84 . . . . 45.00
85 . . . . 42.00
86 E: Gabby Hayes 42.00
87 . . . . 42.00
88 Jan., 1956 . . . . 42.00

MASK COMICS
Rural Home Publications
Feb.–March, 1945
1 LbC,LbC-(c), Evil (c) 2,000.00
2 LbC-(c),A:Black Rider,The
Collector The Boy Magician;
Apr-May'45, Devil (c) 1,400.00

MASKED MARVEL
Centaur Publications
Sept., 1940
1 I: The Masked Marvel 1,300.00
2 PG, ... 900.00
3 Dec., 1940 . . . . 850.00

MASKED RANGER
Premier Magazines
April, 1954
1 FF,O&B:The Masked Ranger,
Streak the Horse,The
Crimson Avenger 250.00
2 . . . . 75.00
3 . . . . 75.00
4 B: Jessie James,Billy the Kid,
Wild Bill Hickock,
Jim Bowie's Life Story 90.00
5 . . . . 90.00
6 . . . . 90.00
7 . . . . 90.00
8 . . . . 90.00
9 AT,E:All Features; A:Wyatt
Earp Aug., 1955 . . . . 100.00

MASTER COMICS
Fawcett Publications
March, 1940
1-6 Oversized,7-Normal Format
1 O:Master Man; B:The Devil's
Dagger, El Carin-Master of
Magic, Rick O'Say, Morton
Murch, White Rajah, Shipwreck
Roberts, Frontier Marshall,
Mr. Clue, Streak Sloan. . . . 7,000.00
2 Master Man (c) 1,800.00
3 Master Man (c) Bondage . . 1,500.00
4 Master Man (c) 1,400.00
5 Master Man (c) 1,400.00
6 E: All Above Features 1,500.00
7 B:Bulletman,Zorro,The Mystery
Man, Lee Granger, Jungle
King,Buck Jones 2,200.00
8 B:The Red Gaucho,Captain
Venture, Planet Princess . . 1,200.00
9 Bulletman & Steam Roller. . . . 900.00
10 E: Lee Granger 900.00
11 O: Minute Man 2,000.00
12 Minute Man (c) 1,100.00
13 O:Bulletgirl; E:Red Gaucho . 1,600.00
14 B: The Companions Three . . . 800.00
15 MRa, Bulletman & Girl (c) . . . 800.00
16 MRa, Minute Man (c) 800.00
17 B:MRa on Bulletman 750.00
18 MRa, ... 750.00
19 MRa, Bulletman & Girl (c) . . . 750.00
20 MRa,C:Cap.Marvel-Bulletman 750.00
21 MRa-(c),Capt. Marvel in
Bulletman,I&O:CaptainNazi 4,500.00
22 MRa-(c),E:Mystery Man,Captain
Venture; Bondage(c);Capt.
Marvel Jr. X-Over In
Bulletman; A:Capt. Nazi. . . 4,200.00
23 MRa,MRa(c),B:Capt.
Marvel Jr. V:Capt. Nazi . . . 2,200.00
24 MRa,MRa(c),Death By Radio. 775.00
25 MRa,MRa(c),The Jap
Invasion 775.00

GOLDEN AGE

GOLDEN AGE

Master Comics #7
© *Fawcett Publications*

26 MRa,MRa(c),Capt. Marvel Jr.
Avenges Pearl Harbor 700.00
27 MRa.MRa(c),V For Victory(c) . 700.00
28 MRa,MRa(c)Liberty Bell(c) . . . 700.00
29 MRa,MRa(c),Hitler &
Hirohito(c) 700.00
30 MRa,MRa(c),Flag (c);Capt.
Marvel Jr, V: Capt. Nazi 700.00
31 MRa,MRa(c),E:Companions
Three,Capt.Marvel Jr,
V:Mad Dr. Macabre. 500.00
32 MRa,MRa(c),E: Buck Jones;
CMJr Strikes Terror Castle . . 500.00
33 MRa,MRa(c),B:Balbo the Boy
Magician, Hopalong Cassidy. 500.00
34 MRa,MRa(c),Capt.Marvel Jr
V: Capt.Nazi. 500.00
35 MRa,MRa(c),CMJr Defies
the Flame. 500.00
36 MRa,MRa(c),Statue Of
Liberty(c) 500.00
37 MRa,MRa(c),CMJr Blasts
the Nazi Raiders. 450.00
38 MRa,MRa(c),CMJr V:
the Japs. 450.00
39 MRa,MRa(c),CMJr Blasts
Nazi Slave Ship 450.00
40 MRa,MRa(c),Flag (c) 450.00
41 MRa,MRa(c),Bulletman,Bulletgirl,
CMJr X-Over In Minuteman . 500.00
42 MRa,MRa(c),CMJr V: Hitler's
Dream Soldier 300.00
43 MRa(c),CMJr Battles For
Stalingrad. 300.00
44 MRa(c),CMJr In Crystal City
of the Peculiar Penguins. . . . 300.00
45 MRa(c), ... 300.00
46 MRa(c) 300.00
47 MRa(c),A:Hitler; E: Balbo 325.00
48 MRa(c),I:Bulletboy;Capt.
Marvel A: in Minuteman 350.00
49 MRa(c),E: Hopalong Cassidy,
Minuteman 300.00
50 I&O: Radar,A:Capt. Marvel,
B:Nyoka the Jungle Girl 300.00
51 MRa(c),CMJr V: Japanese . . . 175.00
52 MRa(c),CMJr & Radar Pitch
War Stamps on (c) 175.00
53 CMJR V: Dr. Sivana. 175.00
54 MRa(c),Capt.Marvel Jr
Your Pin-Up Buddy. 175.00
55 . . . . 175.00
56 MRa(c) 150.00
57 CMJr V: Dr. Sivana 150.00
58 MRA,MRa(c), ... 150.00

59 MRa(c),A:The Upside
Downies. 165.00
60 MRa(c) 165.00
61 CMJr Meets Uncle Marvel . . . 165.00
62 Uncle Sam on (c). 165.00
63 W/ Radar (c) 125.00
64 W/ Radar (c) 125.00
65 . . . . 125.00
66 CMJr & Secret Of the Sphinx . 125.00
67 Knight (c). 125.00
68 CMJr in the Range of
the Beasts 125.00
69 . . . . 125.00
70 . . . . 125.00
71 CMJr,V:Man in Metal Mask. . . 110.00
72 CMJr V: Sivana & The Whistle
That Wouldn't Stop 110.00
73 CMJr V: The Ghost of Evil . . . 110.00
74 CMJr & The Fountain of Age . 110.00
75 CMJr V: The Zombie Master. . 110.00
76 . . . . 110.00
77 Pirate Treasure (c). 110.00
78 CMJr in Death on the Scenic
Railway. 110.00
79 CMJr V: The Black Shroud . . . 110.00
80 CMJr-The Land of Backwards 110.00
81 CMJr & The Voyage 'Round
the Horn. 100.00
82 CMJr,IN,Death at the
Launching 100.00
83 . . . . 100.00
84 CMJr V: The Human Magnet . 100.00
85 CMJr-Crime on the Campus . 100.00
86 CMJr & The City of Machines. 100.00
87 CMJr & The Root of Evil 100.00
88 CMJr V: The Wreckers;
B: Hopalong Cassidy 100.00
89 . . . . 100.00
90 CMJr V: The Caveman 100.00
91 CMJr V: The Blockmen 100.00
92 CMJr V: The Space Slavers . . 100.00
93 BK,CMJr,V:TheGrowingGiant. 125.00
94 E: Hopalong Cassidy 100.00
95 B: Tom Mix; CMJr Meets
the Skyhawk. 100.00
96 CMJr Meets the Worlds
Mightiest Horse 100.00
97 CMJr Faces the Doubting
Thomas 100.00
98 KKK Type 100.00
99 Witch (c) 100.00
100 CMJr V: The Ghost Ship . . . 120.00
101 thru 105 . . . . @100.00
106 E: Bulletman 100.00
107 CMJr Faces the Disappearance
of the Statue of Liberty 100.00
108 . . . . 80.00
109 . . . . 80.00
110 CMJr & The Hidden Death . . 80.00
111 thru 122 . . . . @80.00
123 CMJr V: The Flying
Desperado. 80.00
124 . . . . 80.00
125 CMJr & The Bed of Mystery . 80.00
126 thru 131 . . . . @80.00
132 V: Migs 90.00
133 E: Tom Mix; April, 1953 . . . . 100.00

MD
E.C. Comics
April 1955–Jan. 1956
1 RC,GE,Grl,JO,JCr(c) 125.00
2 thru 5 RC,GE,Grl,JO,JCr(c). @100.00

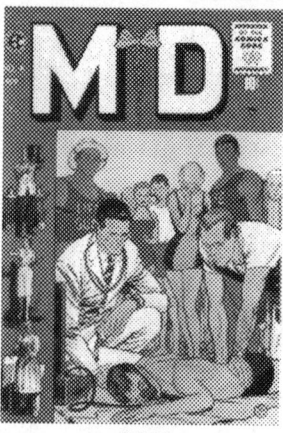

MD #4
© *E.C. Publications*

MEDAL OF
HONOR COMICS
Stafford Publication
Spring, 1947
1 True Stories of Medal of Honor
Recipants 55.00

MEET CORLISS
ARCHER
Fox Features Syndicate
March, 1948
1 AF,AF(c), Teenage 450.00
2 AF(c) 400.00
3 . . . . 300.00
Becomes:

MY LIFE
4 JKa,AF, ... 225.00
5 JKa, ... 150.00
6 JKa,AF, ... 150.00
7 Watercolor&Ink Drawing on(c) . 75.00
8 . . . . 50.00
9 . . . . 50.00
10 WW, July, 1950 . . . . 85.00

MEET MERTON
Toby Press, Dec., 1953
1 Dave Berg-a,Teen Stories. 30.00
2 Dave Berg-a 15.00
3 Dave Berg-a 12.00
4 Dave Berg-a; June, 1954 . . . . . 12.00

MEET THE NEW
POST GAZETTE
SUNDAY FUNNIES
Pitsberg Post Gazette
N# One Shot Insert F: Several
Syndicated Characters in Stories
Exclusive to This Edition. . . . 750.00

MEL ALLEN
SPORTS COMICS
Visual Editions, 1949
1 GT 175.00
2 Lou Gehrig. 125.00

MEN AGAINST CRIME
(see HAND OF FATE)

MERRY-GO-ROUND
COMICS
LaSalle/Croyden/
Rotary Litho., 1944
1 LaSalle Publications Edition . . 100.00
1a 1946, Croyden Edition 35.00
1b Sept-Oct.'47,Rotary Litho Ed. . 50.00
2 . . . . 50.00

MERRY MOUSE
Avon Periodicals
June, 1953
1 (fa),F. Carin (c)&a 35.00
2 (fa),F. Carin (c)&a 20.00
3 (fa),F. Carin (c)&a 20.00
4 (fa),F. Carin (c)&a;Jan.'54 . . . . 20.00

METEOR COMICS
Croyden Publications
Nov., 1945
1 Captain Wizard & Baldy Bean. 250.00

MICKEY FINN
Eastern Color/
Columbia Comics Group, 1942
1 . . . . 225.00
2 . . . . 125.00
3 A: Charlie Chan 75.00
4 . . . . 60.00
5 thru 9 . . . . @40.00
10 thru 15 . . . . @30.00

(WALT DISNEY'S)
MICKEY MOUSE
Dell Publishing Co.
Dec. 1952
#1-#27 Dell Four Color
28 . . . . 40.00
29 . . . . 35.00
30 . . . . 35.00
31 . . . . 35.00
32 thru 34 . . . . @35.00
35 thru 50 . . . . @25.00
51 thru 73 . . . . @15.00
74 . . . . 20.00
75 thru 99 . . . . @15.00
100 thru 105 rep. . . . . @20.00
106 thru 120 . . . . @15.00
121 thru 130 . . . . @10.00
131 thru 146 . . . . @10.00
147 rep,Phantom Fires 15.00
148 rep. 15.00
149 thru 158 . . . . @8.00
159 rep. 12.00
160 thru 170 . . . . @7.00
171 thru 199 . . . . @3.00
200 rep. 5.00
201 thru 218 . . . . @3.00
See: Independent Color Comics

MICKEY MOUSE
MAGAZINE
Kay Kamen
1 (1933) scarce. 3,200.00
2 . . . . 1,000.00
3 thru 8 . . . . @950.00
9 . . . . 900.00

Mickey Mouse Magazine #c
© Walt Disney

MICKEY MOUSE MAGAZINE
Kay Kamen
1 digest size (1933) 1,200.00
2 dairy give-away promo(1933) . 400.00
3 dairy give-away promo(1934) . 350.00
4 dairy give-away promo(1934) . 350.00
5 dairy give-away promo(1934) . 350.00
6 dairy give-away promo(1934) . 350.00
7 dairy give-away promo(1934) . 350.00
8 dairy give-away promo(1934) . 350.00
9 dairy give-away promo(1934) . 350.00
10 dairy give-awaypromo(1934) . 350.00
11 dairy give-awaypromo(1934) . 350.00
12 dairy give-away promo(1934) . 350.00
Volume II
1 dairy give-away promo(1934) . 250.00
2 dairy give-away promo(1934) . 250.00
3 dairy give-away promo(1935) . 250.00
4 dairy give-away promo(1935) . 250.00
5 dairy give-away promo(1935) . 250.00
6 dairy give-away promo(1935) . 250.00
7 dairy give-away promo(1935) . 250.00
8 dairy give-away promo(1935) . 250.00
9 dairy give-away promo(1935) . 250.00
10 dairy give-awaypromo(1935) . 250.00
11 dairy give-awaypromo(1935) . 250.00
12 dairy give-awaypromo(1935) . 250.00

MICKEY MOUSE MAGAZINE
K.K. Pub./Westen Pub
1 (1935) 13¼"x10¼" 12,000.00
2 . . . . 1100.00
3 . . . . 600.00
4 . . . . 600.00
5 (1936) Donald Duck solo 700.00
6 Donald Duck editor. 600.00
7 . . . . 600.00
8 Donald Duck solo 600.00
9 . . . . 600.00
10 . . . . 600.00
11 Mickey Mouse, editor. 550.00
12 . . . . 550.00
Volume II
1 . . . . 550.00
2 . . . . 550.00
3 Christmas issue, 100pg . . . 2,500.00
4 (1937) Roy Ranger adv.strip . . 500.00
5 Ted True strip 400.00
6 Mickey Mouse cut-outs. 375.00
7 Mickey Mouse cut-outs. 375.00
8 Mickey Mouse cut-outs. 375.00
9 Mickey Mouse cut-outs. 375.00
10 Full color 550.00
11. . . . . 400.00

12 Hiawatha. 400.00
13 . . . . 400.00
Volume III
2 Big Bad Wolf (c) 450.00
3 First Snow White 750.00
4 (1938) Snow White. 600.00
5 Snow White (c). 700.00
6 Snow White ends 500.00
7 7 Dwarfs Easter (c). 375.00
8 . . . . 350.00
9 Dopey(c). 350.00
10 Goofy(c) 350.00
11 Mickey Mouse Sheriff. 350.00
12 A:Snow White 350.00
Volume IV
1 Practile Pig. 350.00
2 I:Huey,Louis & Dewey(c). 400.00
3 Ferdinand the Bull 350.00
4 (1939),B:Spotty. 325.00
5 Pluto solo 350.00
7 Ugly Duckling 325.00
7a Goofy & Wilber 350.00
8 Big Bad Wolf(c) 350.00
9 The Pointer. 350.00
10 July 4th 450.00
11 . . . . 300.00
12 Donald's Penguin. 400.00
Volume V
1 Black Pete 400.00
2 Goofy(c). 600.00
3 Pinochio 600.00
4 (1940). 350.00
5 Jimmy Crickett(c) 375.00
6 Tugboat Mickey 375.00
7 Huey, Louis & Dewey(c) 400.00
8 Figaro & Cleo 375.00
9 Donald(c),J.Crickett 450.00
10 July 4th 425.00
11 Mickey's Tailor 450.00
12 Change of format 3,500.00
becomes:

WALT DISNEY COMICS
& STORIES

MICKEY MOUSE
Whitman
904 W.Disney's Mickey Mouse
and his friends (1934) 1,100.00
948 Disney'sMickeyMouse('34) 1,100.00

MIDGET COMICS
St. John Publishing Co.
Feb., 1950
1 MB(c),Fighting Indian Stories . 100.00
2 April, 1950;Tex West-Cowboy
Marshall 50.00

MIGHTY ATOM, THE
(see PIXIES)

MIGHTY MIDGET
COMICS
Samuel E. Lowe & Co., 1942-43
4"x5" Format
1 Bulletman. 125.00
2 Captain Marvel 125.00
3 Captain Marvel Jr. 100.00
4 Golden Arrow 100.00
5 Ibis the Invincible 100.00
6 Spy Smasher 100.00
7 Balbo, The Boy magician 40.00
8 Bulletman 75.00
9 Commando Yank 50.00

GOLDEN AGE

10 Dr. Voltz, The Human
   Generator. 40.00
11 Lance O'Casey 40.00
12 Leatherneck the Marine 40.00
13 Minute Man 75.00
14 Mister Q 40.00
15 Mr. Scarlet & Pinky 60.00
16 Pat Wilson & His
   Flying Fortress 40.00
17 Phantom Eagle 50.00
18 State Trooper Stops Crime. . . . 40.00
19 Tornado Tom 40.00

MIGHTY MOUSE
Fall, 1946
[1st Series]
1 Terytoons Presents 900.00
2 . . . . 400.00
3 . . . . 275.00
4 Summer, 1947 . . . . 275.00

MIGHTY MOUSE
St. John Publishing
Aug., 1947
5 . . . . 275.00
6 thru 10 . . . . @150.00
11 thru 20 . . . . @100.00
21 thru 25 . . . . @75.00
26 thru 30 . . . . @60.00
31 thru 34 . . . . @50.00
35 Flying Saucer 65.00
36 . . . . 50.00
37 . . . . 50.00
38 thru 45 Giant 100 pgs. . . . . @150.00
46 thru 66 . . . . @50.00
67 P(c), ... 50.00
Pines
68 thru 81 Funny Animal . . . . . @40.00
82 Infinity (c). 40.00
83 June, 1959 . . . . 40.00

MIGHTY MOUSE
ADVENTURE STORIES
St. John Publishing Co., 1953
N# 384 Pages,Rebound. 350.00

MIKE BARNETT,
MAN AGAINST CRIME
Fawcett Publications
Dec., 1951
1 The Mint of Dionysosi 125.00
2 Mystery of the Blue Madonna . 75.00
3 Revenge Holds the Torch 50.00
4 Special Delivery 50.00
5 Market For Morphine 75.00
6 Oct., 1952 . . . . 50.00

MILITARY COMICS
Comics Magazines
(Quality Comics Group)
Aug., 1941
1 JCo,CCu,FG,BP,WE(c),O:Blackhawk,
   Miss America, Death Patrol,
   Blue Tracer; B:X of the Underground, Yankee Eagle,Q-Boat,
   Shot & Shell, Archie Atkins,
   Loops & Banks 8,000.00
2 JCo,FG,BP,CCu,CCu(c),B:
   Secret War News 2,000.00
3 JCo,FG,BP,AMc,CCu,CCu(c),
   I&O:Chop Chop 1,800.00
4 FG,BP,AMc,CCu,CCu(c), . . 1,400.00
5 FG,BP,AMc,CCu,CCu(c),

B: The Sniper 1,200.00
6 FG,BP,AMc,CCu,CCu(c) 900.00
7 FG,BP,AMc,CCu,CCu(c)
   E:Death Patrol 900.00
8 FG,BP,AMc,CCu,CCu(c) 900.00
9 FG,BP,AMc,CCu,CCu(c),
   B: The Phantom Clipper . . . 900.00
10 FG,BP,CCu,AMc,WE(c) . . . 1,000.00
11 FG,BP,CCu,AMc,
   WE(c),Flag(c) 750.00
12 FG,BP,AMc,RC,RC(c) 900.00
13 FG,BP,AMc,RC,RC(c),E:X of
   the Underground 700.00
14 FG,AMc,RC,RC(c),B:Private
   Dogtag 700.00
15 FG,AMc,RC,RC(c), ... 700.00
16 FG,AMc,RC,RC(c),E:The
   Phantom Clipper,Blue Tracer 600.00
17 FG,AMc,RC,RC(c),
   B:P.T. Boat 600.00
18 FG,AMc,RC,RC(c), V:
   The Thunderer 600.00
19 FG,RC,RC(c), V:King Cobra . 600.00
20 GFx,RC,RC(c), Death Patrol . 600.00
21 FG,GFx 550.00
22 FG,GFx 550.00
23 FG,GFx 550.00
24 FG,GFx,V: Man-Heavy
   Glasses 550.00
25 FG,GFx,V: Wang The Tiger . . 550.00
26 FG,GFx,V: Skull. 500.00
27 FG,JCo,R:The Death Patrol . . 500.00
28 FG,JCo, Dungeon of Doom . . 500.00
29 FG,JCo,V: Xanukhara 500.00
30 FG,JCo,BWa,BWa(c),B.Hwk
   V: Dr. Koro 500.00
31 FG,JCo,BWa,E:Death
   Patrol; I: Captain Hitsu 500.00
32 JCo,A: Captain Hitsu 450.00
33 W/ Civil War Veteran 450.00
34 A: Eve Rice 450.00
35 Shipwreck Island 450.00
36 Cult of the Wailing Tiger. 450.00
37 Pass of Bloody Peace 450.00
38 B.Hwk Faces Bloody Death . . 450.00
39 A: Kwan Yin. 450.00
40 V: Ratru 425.00
41 W/ Chop Chop (c) 425.00
42 V: Jap Mata Hari 425.00
43 . . . . 425.00
Becomes:

MODERN COMICS
44 Duel of Honor 450.00
45 V: Sakyo the Madman 350.00

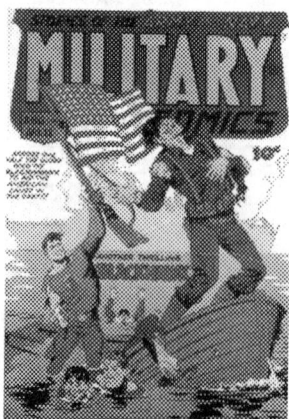

Military Comics #11
© Quality Comics Group

46 RC, Soldiers of Fortune 350.00
47 RC,PG,V:Count Hokoy. 350.00
48 RC,PG,V:Pirates of Perool . . . 350.00
49 RC,PG,I:Fear,Lady
   Adventuress 350.00
50 RC,PG 350.00
51 RC,PG, Ancient City of Evil . . 300.00
52 PG,BWa,V: The Vulture 300.00
53 PG,BWa,B: Torchy. 350.00
54 PG,RC,RC/CCu,BWa. 275.00
55 PG,RC,RC/CCu,BWa. 275.00
56 PG,RC/CCu,BWa. 275.00
57 PG,RC/CCu,BWa. 275.00
58 PG,RC,RC/CCu,BWa,
   V:The Grabber 275.00
59 PG,RC/CCu,BWa. 275.00
60 PG,RC/CCu,BWa,RC(c),
   V:Green Plague 275.00
61 PG,RC/CCu,BWa,RC(c). 275.00
62 PG,RC/CCu,BWa,RC(c). 275.00
63 PG,RC/CCu,BWa,RC(c). 250.00
64 PG,RC/CCu,BWa,RC(c). 250.00
65 PG,RC/CCu,BWa,RC(c). 250.00
66 PG,RC/CCu,BWa. 250.00
67 PG,RC/CCu,BWa,RC(c). 250.00
68 PG,RC/CCu,BWa,RC(c);
   I:Madame Butterfly 250.00
69 PG,RC/CCu,BWa,RC(c). 250.00
70 PG,RC/CCu,BWa,RC(c) 250.00
71 PG,RC/CCu,BWa,RC(c). 250.00
72 PG,RC/CCu,BWa,RC(c). 225.00
73 PG,RC/CCu,BWa,RC(c). 225.00
74 PG,RC/CCu,BWa,RC(c). 225.00
75 PG,RC/CCu,BWa,RC(c). 225.00
76 PG,RC/CCu,BWa,RC(c). 225.00
77 PG,RC/CCu,BWa,RC(c). 225.00
78 PG,RC/CCu,BWa,JCo,RC(c) . 250.00
79 PG,RC/CCu,BWa,JCo,RC(c) . 225.00
80 PG,RC/CCu,BWa,JCo,RC(c) . 225.00
81 PG,RC/CCu,BWa,JCo,RC(c) . 225.00
82 PG,RC/CCu,BWa,JCo,RC(c) . 225.00
83 PG,RC/CCu.BWa,JCo,RC(c);
   E: Private Dogtag 225.00
84 PG,RC/CCu,BWa,RC(c). 225.00
85 PG,RC/CCu,BWa,RC(c). 225.00
86 PG,RC/CCu,BWa,RC(c). 225.00
87 PG,RC/CCu,BWa,RC(c). 225.00
88 PG,RC/CCu,BWa,RC(c). 225.00
89 PG,RC/CCu,BWa,RC(c). 225.00
90 PG,RC/CCu,GFx,RC(c) 225.00
91 RC/CCu,GFx,RC(c) 225.00
92 RC/CCu,GFx,RC(c) 225.00
93 RC/CCu,GFx,RC(c) 225.00
94 RC/CCu,GFx,RC(c) 225.00
95 RC/CCu,GFx,RC(c) 225.00
96 RC/CCu,GFx,RC/CCu(c) 225.00
97 RC/CCu,GFx,RC/CCu(c) 225.00
98 RC/CCu,GFx,RC/CCu(c) 225.00
99 RC/CCu,GFx,JCo,RC/CCu(c). 225.00
100 GFx,JCo,RC/CCu(c) 225.00
101 GFx,JCo,RC/CCu(c) 225.00
102 GFx,JCo,WE,BWa,
   RC/CCu(c) 250.00

MILT GROSS FUNNIES
Milt Gross, Inc.
Aug., 1947
1 Gag Oriented Caricature 50.00
2 Gag Oriented Caricature 45.00

MINUTE MAN
Fawcett Publications
Summer, 1941
1 V: The Nazis 1,300.00
2 V: The Mongol Horde 900.00
3 V: The Black Poet;Spr'42 . . . . 850.00

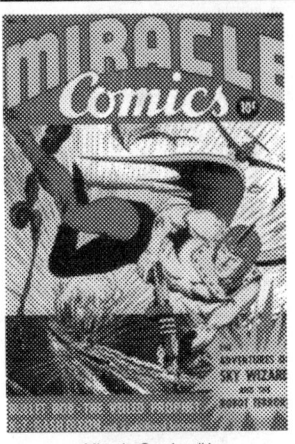

Miracle Comics #4
© Hillman Periodicals

MIRACLE COMICS
Hillman Periodicals
Feb.,1940
1 B:Sky Wizard,Master of Space,
Dash Dixon,Man of Might,Dusty
Doyle,Pinkie Parker, The Kid
Cop,K-7 Secret Agent,Scorpion
& Blandu,Jungle Queen . . 1,400.00
2 . . . . 700.00
3 B:Bill Colt,The Ghost Rider . . 750.00
4 A:The Veiled Prophet,
Bullet Bob; Mar'41 . . . . 700.00

MISS CAIRO JONES
Croyden Publishers, 1944
1 BO,Rep. Newspaper Strip . . . 150.00

MR. ANTHONY'S
LOVE CLINIC
Hillman Periodicals, 1945
1 Ph(c) 75.00
2 . . . . 50.00
3 . . . . 40.00
4 . . . . 40.00
5 Ph(c),Apr/May'50 . . . . 40.00

MR. MUSCLES
(see THING, THE)

MISTER MYSTERY
Media Publ./SPM Publ./
Aragon Publ.
Sept., 1951
1 HK,RA,Horror 600.00
2 RA,RA(c) 400.00
3 RA(c) 400.00
4 Bondage(c) 425.00
5 Lingerie(c) 400.00
6 Bondage(c) 425.00
7 BW,Bondage(c);The Brain
Bats of Venus 800.00
8 Lingerie(c) 375.00
9 HN 350.00
10 . . . . 350.00
11 BW,Robot Woman 600.00
12 Flaming Object to Eye (c). . . . 800.00
13 . . . . 250.00
14 . . . . 250.00

15 The Coffin & Medusa's Head . 275.00
16 Bondage(c) 275.00
17 . . . . 250.00
18 BW,Bondage(c) 450.00

MISTER RISK
(see HAND OF FATE)

MISTER UNIVERSE
Mr. Publ./Media Publ./
Stanmore
July, 1951
1 . . . . 150.00
2 RA(c);Jungle That time Forgot 125.00
3 Marijuana Story 100.00
4 Mr. Universe Goes to War. 50.00
5 Mr. Universe Goes to War;
April, 1952 . . . . 60.00

MODERN COMICS
(see MILITARY COMICS)

MODERN LOVE
Tiny Tot Comics
(E.C. Comics)
June–July, 1949
1 Stolen Romance 450.00
2 JcR,AF(c),I Craved
Excitement 350.00
3 AF(c);Our Families Clashed . . 300.00
4 AF(c);I Was a B Girl 400.00
5 AF(c);Saved From Shame . . . 400.00
6 AF(c);The Love That
Might Have Been 400.00
7 AF(c);They Won't Let Me
Love Him 300.00
8 AF(c);Aug-Sept'50 . . . . 300.00

MOE & SHMOE COMICS
O.S. Publishing Co.
Spring, 1948
1 Gag Oriented Caricature 35.00
2 Gag Oriented Caricature 25.00

MOLLY O'DAY
Avon Periodicals
Feb., 1945
1 GT;The Enchanted Dagger . . 350.00

MONKEYSHINES COMICS
Publ. Specialists/Ace/
Summer, 1944
1 (fa),Several Short Features . . . 50.00
2 (fa),Same Format Throughout
Entire Run 25.00
3 thru 16 Funny Animal . . . . . . @20.00
Ace
17 Funny Animal 20.00
18 thru 21 . . . . @15.00
Unity Publ.
22 (fa) 15.00
23 (fa) 15.00
24 (fa),AFa,AFa(c) 15.00
25 (fa) 15.00
26 (fa) 15.00
27 (fa),July, 1949 . . . . 15.00

MONSTER
Fiction House Magazines, 1953
1 Dr. Drew. 400.00

2 . . . . 275.00

MONSTER CRIME
COMICS
Hillman Periodicals
Oct., 1952
1 52 Pgs,15 Cent Cover Price . . 750.00

MONTE HALL
WESTERN
(see MARY MARVEL
COMICS)

MONTY HALL OF
THE U.S. MARINES
Toby Press, Aug., 1951
1 B:Monty Hall,Pin-Up Pete;
(All Issues) 50.00
2 . . . . 30.00
3 thru 5 . . . . @25.00
6 . . . . 20.00
7 The Fireball Express 20.00
8 . . . . 20.00
9 . . . . 20.00
10 The Vial of Death. 20.00
11 Monju Island Prison Break 20.00

MOON GIRL AND
THE PRINCE
E.C. Comics, Autumn, 1947
1 JCr(c),O:Moon Girl 750.00
2 JCr(c),Battle of the Congo . . . 400.00
3 . . . . 350.00
4 V: A Vampire 350.00
5 1st E.C. Horror-Zombie Terror. 850.00
6 . . . . 450.00
7 O:Star;The Fient Who
Fights With Fire 450.00
8 True Crime Feature 450.00
Becomes:

A MOON, A GIRL
...ROMANCE
9 AF,Grl,AF(c),C:Moon Girl;
Spanking Panels 550.00
10 AF,Grl,WW,AF(c),Suspicious
of His Intentions 500.00
11 AF,Grl,WW,AF(c),Hearts
Along the Ski Trail 500.00
12 AF,Grl,AF(c),
March–April, 1950 . . . . 600.00

MOPSY
St. John Publishing Co.
Feb., 1948
1 Paper Dolls Enclosed 100.00
2 . . . . 55.00
3 . . . . 50.00
4 Paper Dolls Enclosed 50.00
5 Paper Dolls Enclosed 50.00
6 Paper Dolls Enclosed 50.00
7 . . . . 40.00
8 Paper Dolls Enclosed;
Lingerie Panels 45.00
9 . . . . 40.00
10 . . . . 40.00
11 . . . . 30.00
12 . . . . 30.00
13 Paper Dolls Enclosed. 35.00
14 thru 18 . . . . @30.00
19 Lingerie(c);Paper
Dolls Enclosed 35.00

MORTIE
Magazine Publishers
Dec., 1952
1 ...Mazie's Friend 30.00
2 . . . . 18.00
3 . . . . 15.00

MOTION PICTURE
COMICS
Fawcett Publications
Nov., 1950
101 Ph(c),Monte Hale's-
Vanishing Westerner. 225.00
102 Ph(c),Rocky Lane's-Code
of the Silver Sage. 200.00
103 Ph(c),Rocky Lane's-Covered
Wagon Raid 200.00
104 BP,Ph(c),Rocky Lane's-
Vigilante Hideout 200.00
105 BP,Ph(c),Audie Murphy's-
Red Badge of Courage. 250.00
106 Ph(c),George Montgomery's-
The Texas Rangers 200.00
107 Ph(c),Rocky Lane's-Frisco
Tornado 200.00
108 Ph(c),John Derek's-Mask
of the Avenger 150.00
109 Ph(c),Rocky Lane's-Rough
Rider of Durango 200.00
110 GE,Ph(c), When Worlds
Collide 700.00
111 Ph(c),Lash LaRue's-The
Vanishing Outpost 225.00
112 Ph(c),Jay Silverheels'-
Brave Warrior 125.00
113 KS,Ph(c),George Murphy's-
Walk East on Beacon 100.00
114 Ph(c),George Montgomery's-
Cripple Creek;Jan, 1953. . . . 100.00

MOTION PICTURES
FUNNIES WEEKLY
1st Funnies Incorporated, 1939
1 BEv,1st Sub-Mariner 18,000.00
2 Cover Only 250.00
3 Cover Only 250.00
4 Cover Only 250.00

MOVIE CLASSICS
(NO #S)
Dell Publishing Co.
Jan., 1953
1 Around the World Under
the Sea 30.00
2 Bambi 35.00
3 Battle of the Buldge 25.00
4 Ph(c),Beach Blanket Bingo . . 50.00
5 Ph(c),Bon Voyage 25.00
6 Castilian 30.00
7 Cat 20.00
8 Cheyenne Autumn 45.00
9 Ph(c),Circus World,
John Wayne (c) 100.00
10 Ph(c),Countdown,J.Caan(c). . 30.00
11 Creature 50.00
12 Ph(c),David Ladd's Life Story. . 75.00
13 Ph(c),Die Monster Die 50.00
14 Dirty Dozen 40.00
15 Ph(c),Dr. Who & the Daleks . . 125.00
16 Dracula 40.00
17 El Dorado,J.WaynePh(c) 125.00
18 Ensign Pulver 25.00
19 Frankenstein 40.00
20 Ph(c),Great Race. 40.00
21 B.LancasterPh(c). 40.00

22 Hatari 65.00
23 Horizontal Lieutenant. 25.00
24 Ph(c) Mr. Limpet 25.00
25 Jack the Giant Killer. 60.00
26 Ph(c),Jason & the Argonauts . . 100.00
27 Lancelot & Guinevere 55.00
28 Lawrence. 55.00
29 Lion of Sparta 25.00
30 Mad Monster Party 55.00
31 Magic Sword 45.00
32 Ph(c),Masque of Red Death. . . 40.00
33 Maya. 35.00
34 McHale's Navy. 40.00
35 Ph(c) Merrills' Marauders 25.00
36 Ph(c),Mouse on the Moon 20.00
37 Mummy. 40.00
38 Music Man. 30.00
39 Ph(c),Naked Prey 50.00
40 Ph(c),Night of the Grizzly 35.00
41 None but the Brave 55.00
42 Ph(c),Operation Bikini 30.00
43 Operation Cross Bold. 30.00
44 Prince & the Pauper. 30.00
45 Raven,V.Price(c) 45.00
46 Ring of Bright Water 35.00
47 Runaway 20.00
48 Ph(c),Santa Claus Conquers
the Martians 65.00
49 Ph(c),Six Black Horses 30.00
50 Sky Party. 35.00
51 Smoky. 25.00
52 Ph(c),Sons of Katie Elder. . . . 125.00
53 GE,Tales of Terror 30.00
54 Ph(c),3 Stooges meet
Hercules. 75.00
55 Tomb of Legeia 25.00
56 Treasure Island 25.00
57 Twice Told Tales(V.Price) 35.00
58 Two on a Guillotine 25.00
59 Valley of Gwangi 45.00
60 War Gods of the Deep 20.00
61 War Wagon (John Wayne) 85.00
62 Who's Minding the Mint 25.00
63 Wolfman 35.00
64 Ph(c),Zulu 30.00
65 . . . . 25.00

MOVIE COMICS
Fiction House Magazines
Dec., 1946
1 Big Town on(c) 450.00
2 MB,White Tie & Tails 325.00
3 MB,Andy Hardy Laugh Hit . . . 325.00
4 MB,Slave Girl 400.00

MOVIE LOVE
Famous Funnies Publications
Feb., 1950
1 Ph(c),Dick Powell(c) 100.00
2 Ph(c),Myrna Loy(c) 50.00
3 Ph(c),Cornell Wilde(c) 35.00
4 Ph(c),Paulette Goddard(c) 35.00
5 Ph(c),Joan Fontaine(c) 35.00
6 Ph(c),Ricardo Montalban(c) . . . 35.00
7 Ph(c),Fred Astaire(c) 35.00
8 AW,FF,Ph(c),Corinne
Calvert(c) 250.00
9 Ph(c),John Lund(c) 35.00
10 Ph(c),Mona Freeman(c) 275.00
11 Ph(c),James Mason(c) 35.00
12 Ph(c),Jerry Lewis &
Dean Martin(c) 50.00
13 Ph(c),Ronald Reagan(c). 150.00
14 Ph(c),Janet Leigh,Gene Kelly. . 40.00
15 Ph(c), ... 35.00
16 Ph(c),Angela Lansbury. 60.00
17 FF,Ph(c),Leslie Caron 30.00
18 Ph(c),Cornel Wilde. 30.00
19 Ph(c),John Derek. 30.00

20 Ph(c),Debbie Reynolds 35.00
21 Ph(c),Patricia Medina. 30.00
22 Ph(c),John Payne 30.00

MOVIE THRILLERS
Magazine Enterprises 1949
1 Ph(c),Burt Lancaster's-
Rope of Sand 225.00

MR. MUSCLES
(see THING!, THE)

MUGGY-DOO, BOY CAT
Stanhall Publications
July, 1953
1 . . . . 30.00
2 and 3 . . . . @20.00
4 Jan., 1954 . . . . 20.00

Murder Incorporated #4
© Fox Features Incorporated

MURDER,
INCORPORATED
Fox Features Incorporated
Jan., 1948
1 For Adults Only-on(c) 400.00
2 For Adults Only-on(c);Male
Bondage(c),Electrocution sty 275.00
3 Dutch Schultz-Beast of Evil . . 150.00
4 The Ray Hamilton Case,
Lingerie(c) 150.00
5 thru 8 . . . . @150.00
9 Bathrobe (c) 165.00
9a Lingerie (c) 175.00
10 . . . . 125.00
11 . . . . 110.00
12 . . . . 110.00
13 . . . . 125.00
14 Bill Hale-King o/t Murderers . . 110.00
15 . . . . 110.00
16(5),Second Series 90.00
17(2) 90.00
18(3), Bondage(c) w/Lingerie,
Aug., 1951 . . . . 125.00

MURDEROUS
GANGSTERS
Avon Periodicals/Realistic
July, 1951
1 WW,Pretty Boy Floyd,
Leggs Diamond 350.00

All comics prices listed are for *Near Mint* condition.

2 WW,Baby Face Nelson,Mad
  Dog Esposito 225.00
3 P(c),Tony & Bud Fenner,
  Jed Hawkins 200.00
4 EK(c),Murder By Needle-
  Drug Story, June, 1952. . . . . 200.00

MUTINY
Aragon Magazines
Oct., 1954
1 AH(c),Stormy Tales of the
  Seven Seas 100.00
2 AH(c) 75.00
3 Bondage(c),Feb., '55 . . . . 75.00

MY CONFESSIONS
(see WESTERN TRUE
CRIME)

MY DATE COMICS
Hillman Periodicals
July, 1944
1 S&K,S&K (c), Teenage 225.00
2 S&K,DB,S&K(c) 150.00
3 S&K,DB,S&K(c) 150.00
4 S&K,DB,S&K(c) 150.00

MY DESIRE
Fox Features Syndicate
Oct., 1949
1 Intimate Confessions 100.00
2 WW,They Called Me Wayward . 60.00
3 I Hid My Lover 40.00
4 WW, April, 1950 . . . . 125.00

MY GREAT LOVE
Fox Features Syndicate
Oct., 1949
1 Reunion In a Shack 75.00
2 My Crazy Dreams 40.00
3 He Was Ashamed of Me 35.00
4 My Two Wedding Rings;Apr'50 40.00

MY INTIMATE AFFAIR
Fox Features Syndicate
March, 1950
1 I Sold My Love 75.00
2 I Married a Jailbird;May'50 . . . . 45.00

MY LIFE
(see MEET CORLISS
ARCHER)

MY LOVE AFFAIR
Fox Features Syndicate
July, 1949
1 Truck Driver's Sweetheart 75.00
2 My Dreadful Secret 50.00
3 WW,I'll Make Him Marry Me . . 100.00
4 WW,They Called Me Wild . . . 100.00
5 WW,Beauty Was My Bait 100.00
6 WW,The Man Downstairs 100.00

MY LOVE MEMORIES
(see WOMEN OUTLAWS)

MY LOVE LIFE
(see TEGRA, JUNGLE
EMPRESS)

MY LOVE STORY
Fox Features Syndicate
Sept., 1949
1 Men Gave Me Jewels 75.00
2 He Dared Me 50.00
3 WW,I Made Love a Plaything . 100.00
4 WW,I Tried to Be Good 100.00

MY PAST
CONFESSIONS
(see WESTERN
THRILLERS)

MY PRIVATE LIFE
Fox Features Syndicate
Feb., 1950
16 My Friendship Club Affair. 75.00
17 My Guilty Kisses;April'50 . . . . . 50.00

MY SECRET
Superior Comics
Aug., 1949
1 True Love Stories 75.00
2 I Was Guilty of Being a
  Cheating Wife 50.00
3 Was I His Second Love?; 50.00
Becomes:

OUR SECRET
4 JKa,She Loves Me,She Loves
  Me Not; Nov., 1949. . . . . 60.00
5 . . . . 40.00
6 . . . . 40.00
7 How Do You Fall In Love? 45.00
8 His Kiss Tore At My
  Heart; June, 1950. . . . . 40.00

MY SECRET AFFAIR
Hero Books
(Fox Features Syndicate)
Dec., 1949
1 WW,SHn,My Stormy
  Love Affair 150.00
2 WW,I Loved a Weakling 100.00
3 WW, April, 1950 . . . . 125.00

MY SECRET LIFE
Fox Features Syndicate
July, 1949
22 I Loved More Than Once. 75.00
23 WW. 125.00
24 Love Was a Habit 30.00
25 . . . . 30.00
Becomes:

ROMEO TUBBS
26 WW,That Lovable Teen-ager . 125.00

MY SECRET LOVE
(see PHANTOM LADY)

MY SECRET MARRIAGE
Superior Comics
May, 1953
1 I Was a Cheat 75.00
2 . . . . 30.00
3 We Couldn't Wait 20.00
4 . . . . 20.00
5 . . . . 20.00
6 . . . . 20.00
7 thru 23 . . . . @20.00
24 1956 . . . . 20.00

MY SECRET ROMANCE
Hero Books
(Fox Features Syndicate)
Jan., 1950
1 WW,They Called Me 'That'
  Woman 100.00
2 WW,They Called Me Cheap . . 100.00

MYSTERIES WEIRD
AND STRANGE
Superior Comics/
Dynamic Publ.
May, 1953
1 The Stolen Brain 200.00
2 The Screaming Room,
  Atomic Bomb 125.00
3 The Avenging Corpse 100.00
4 Ghost on the Gallows 100.00
5 Horror a la Mode 100.00
6 Howling Horror 100.00
7 Demon in Disguise 100.00
8 The Devil's Birthmark 100.00
9 . . . . 100.00
10 . . . . 110.00
11 . . . . 100.00

MYSTERIOUS
ADVENTURES
Story Comics
March, 1951
1 Wild Terror of the
  Vampire Flag 375.00

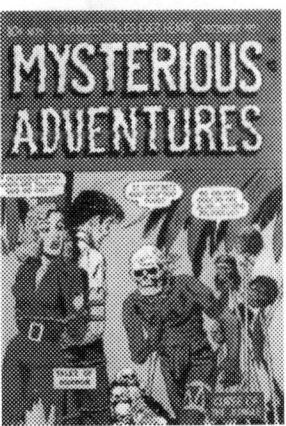

Mysterious Adventures #5
© Story Comics

2 Terror of the Ghoul's Corpse . 200.00
3 Terror of the Witche's Curse . . 175.00
4 The Little Coffin That Grew . . 175.00
5 LC,Curse of the Jungle,
    Bondage(c). 220.00
6 LC,Ghostly Terror in the
    Cave 150.00
7 LC,Terror of the Ghostly
    Castle 275.00
8 Terror of the Flowers of Deat. . 275.00
9 The Ghostly Ghouls-
    Extreme Violence 225.00
10 Extreme Violence. 175.00
11 The Trap of Terror 225.00
12 SHn,Vultures of Death-
    Extreme Violence 225.00
13 Extreme Violence. 225.00
14 Horror of the Flame Thrower
    Extreme Violence 225.00
15 DW,Ghoul Crazy 275.00
16 Chilling Tales of Horror. 275.00
17 DW,Bride of the Dead 275.00
18 Extreme Violence. 275.00
19 The Coffin 275.00
20 Horror o/t Avenging Corpse . . 275.00
21 Mother Ghoul's Nursery
    Tales, Bondage (c) 275.00
22 RA,Insane 175.00
23 RA,Extreme Violence. 200.00
24 KS, ... 150.00
25 KS,Aug., 1955 . . . . 150.00

HORROR FROM
THE TOMB
Premier Magazines
Sept., 1954
1 AT,GWb,The Corpse Returns . 250.00
Becomes:

MYSTERIOUS STORIES
2 GWb(c),Eternal Life 250.00
3 GWb,The Witch Doctor 175.00
4 That's the Spirit 160.00
5 King Barbarossa 160.00
6 GWb,Strangers in the Night . . 175.00
7 KS,The Pipes of Pan;Dec'55. . 160.00

MYSTERIOUS TRAVELER
COMICS
Trans-World Publications
Nov., 1948
1 BP,BP(c),Five Miles Down . . . 450.00

MYSTERY COMICS
William H. Wise & Co., 1944
1 AS(c),B:Brad Spencer-Wonderman,
    King of Futeria,The Magnet, Zudo-
    Jungle Boy,The Silver Knight 800.00
2 AS(c),Bondage (c) 550.00
3 AS(c),Robot(c),LanceLewis,B . 500.00
4 AS(c),E:All Features,
    KKK Type(c). 500.00

MYSTERY MEN COMICS
Fox Features Syndicate
Aug., 1939
1 GT,DBr,LF(c),Bondage(c);I:Blue
    Beetle,Green Mask,Rex Dexter
    of Mars,Zanzibar,Lt.Drake,D-13
    Secret Agent,Chen Chang,
    Wing Turner,Capt. Denny 10,000.00
2 GT,BP,DBr,LF(c),
    Rex Dexter (c) 2,800.00
3 LF(c) 3,500.00
4 LF(c),B:Captain Savage. . . . 2,000.00
5 GT,BP,LF(c),Green Mask (c) 2,000.00

Mystery Men Comics #3
© Fox Features Syndicate

6 GT,BP 1,800.00
7 GT,BP,Bondage(c),
    Blue Beetle(c) 2,000.00
8 GT,BP,LF(c),Bondage(c),
    Blue Beetle 1,800.00
9 GT,BP,DBr(c),B:The Moth 900.00
10 GT,BP,JSm(c),A:Wing
    Turner; Bondage(c). 800.00
11 GT,BP,JSm(c),I:The Domino. . 800.00
12 GT,BP,JSm(c),BlueBeetle(c). . 800.00
13 GT,I:The Lynx & Blackie. 525.00
14 GT,Male Bondage (c) 475.00
15 GT,Blue Beetle (c) 450.00
16 GT,Hypo(c),MaleBondage(c) . 475.00
17 GT,BP,Blue Beetle (c) 450.00
18 GT,Blue Beetle (c) 450.00
19 GT,I&B:Miss X 500.00
20 GT,DBr,Blue Beetle (c). 425.00
21 GT,E:Miss X. 425.00
22 GT,CCu(c),Blue Beetle (c) . . 425.00
23 GT,Blue Beetle (c) 425.00
24 GT,BP,DBr, Blue Beetle (c). . . 425.00
25 GT,Bondage(c);
    A:Private O'Hara. 450.00
26 GT,Bondage(c);B:The Wraith . 450.00
27 GT,Bondage(c),BlueBeetle(c) . 450.00
28 GT,Bondage(c);Satan's
    Private Needlewoman. 450.00
29 GT,Bondage(c),Blue
    Beetle (c) 450.00
30 Holiday of Death 425.00
31 Bondage(c);Feb'42. . . . . 450.00

MY STORY
(see ZAGO, JUNGLE
PRINCE)

NATIONAL COMICS
Comics Magazines
(Quality Comics Group)
July, 1940
1 GT,HcK,LF(c),B:Uncle Sam,Wonder
    Boy,Merlin the Magician,Cyclone,
    Kid Patrol,Sally O'Neil-Police-
    woman, Pen Miller,Prop
    Powers, Paul Bunyan . . 4,500.00
2 WE,GT,HcK,LF&RC(c) 1,800.00
3 GT,HcK,WE&RC(c) 1,300.00
4 GT,HcK,LF&RC(c),E:Cyclone;
    Torpedo Islands of Death . . 1,000.00
5 GT,LF&RC(c),B:Quicksilver;
    O:Uncle Sam 1,100.00

6 GT,LF&RC(c) 1,000.00
7 GT,LF&RC(c) 1,100.00
8 GT,LF&RC(c) 1,000.00
9 JCo,LF&RC(c) 1,000.00
10 RC,JCo,LF&RC(c). 1,000.00
11 RC,JCo,LF&RC(c). 1,000.00
12 RC,JCo,LF&RC(c). 750.00
13 RC,JCo,LF,LF&RC(c). 700.00
14 RC,JCo,LF,PG,LF&RC(c). . . . 700.00
15 RC,JCo,LF,PG,LF&RC(c). . . . 700.00
16 RC,JCo,LF,PG,LF&RC(c). . . . 700.00
17 RC,JCo,LF,PG,LF&RC(c). . . . 500.00
18 JCo,LF,PG,LF&RC(c),
    Pearl Harbor. 900.00
19 JCo,LF,PG,RC(c),The Black
    Fog Mystery 500.00
20 JCo,LF,PG,LF&RC(c) 500.00
21 LF,JCo,PG,LF(c) 500.00
22 JCo,LF,PG,FG,GFx,LF(c),
    E:Jack & Jill,Pen Miller,
    Paul Bunyan 500.00
23 JCo,PG,FG,GFx,AMc,LF
    & GFx(c),B:The Unknown,
    Destroyer 171. . . . . 550.00
24 JCo,PG,RC,AMc,FG,
    GFx,RC(c) 500.00
25 AMc,RC,JCo,PG,FG,
    GFx,RC(c) 350.00
26 AMc,Jco,RC,PG,RC(c),
    E:Prop Powers,WonderBoy. . 350.00
27 JCo,AMc 350.00
28 JCo,AMc 350.00
29 JCo,O:The Unknown;U.Sam
    V:Dr. Dirge 375.00
30 JCo,RC(c) 365.00
31 JCo,RC(c) 350.00
32 JCo,RC(c) 350.00
33 JCo,GFx,RC(c),B:Chic Carter;
    U.Sam V:Boss Spring. 350.00
34 JCo,GFx,U.Sam V:Big John
    Fales 350.00
35 JCo,GFx,E:Kid Patrol. 250.00
36 JCo 250.00
37 JCo,FG,A:The Vagabond . . . 250.00
38 JCo,FG,Boat of the Dead. . . . 250.00
39 JCo,FG,Hitler(c);U.Sam
    V:The Black Market 250.00
40 JCo,FG,U.Sam V:The
    Syndicate of Crime 175.00
41 JCo,FG 175.00
42 JCo,FG,JCo(c),B:The Barker . 150.00
43 JCo,FG,JCo(c). 150.00
44 JCo,FG 150.00
45 JCo,FG,E:Merlin the Magician 150.00
46 JCo,JCo(c),Murder is no Joke 150.00
47 JCo,JCo(c),E:Chic Carter. . . . 150.00

National Comics #6
© Quality Comics Group

48 JCo,O:The Whistler 150.00
49 JCo,JCo(c),A Corpse
   for a Cannonball. 150.00
50 JCo,JCo(c),V:Rocks Myzer . . 150.00
51 JCo,BWa,JCo(c),
   A:Sally O'Neil 200.00
52 JCo,A Carnival of Laughs . . . 125.00
53 PG,V:Scramolo 125.00
54 PG,V:Raz-Ma-Taz 125.00
55 JCo,AMc,V:The Hawk 125.00
56 GFx,JCo,AMc,V:The Grifter . . 125.00
57 GFX,JCo,AMc,V:Witch Doctor 125.00
58 GFz,JCo,AMc,Talking Animals 125.00
59 GFx,JCo,AMc,V:The Birdman 125.00
60 GFx,JCo,AMc,V:Big Ed Grew 125.00
61 GFx,AMc,Trouble Comes in
   Small Packages 90.00
62 GFx,AMc,V:Crocodile Man. . . . 90.00
63 GFx,AMc,V:Bearded Lady 90.00
64 GFx,V:The Human Fly 90.00
65 GFx,GFx(c)V:The King. 90.00
66 GFx,GFx(c)V:THe Man Who
   Hates the Circus. 90.00
67 GFx,Gfx(c),A:Quicksilver;
   V:Ali Ben Riff Raff. 90.00
68 GFx,GFx(c),V:Leo the LionMan 90.00
69 GFx,Gfx(c),A:Percy the
   Powerful. 90.00
70 GFx,GFx(c),Barker Tires
   of the Big Top 90.00
71 PG,GFx(c),V:SpellbinderSmith . 90.00
72 PG,GFx(c),The Oldest Man
   in the World 90.00
73 PG,GFx(c),V:A CountrySlicker . 90.00
74 PG,GFx(c),V:Snake Oil Sam . . 90.00
75 PG,GFx(c),Barker Breakes the
   Bank at Monte Marlo;Nov'49. . 90.00

NEBBS, THE
Dell Publishing Co., 1941
1 rep. 60.00

NEGRO ROMANCE
Fawcett Publications
June, 1950
1 GE,Ph(c), Love's Decoy 900.00
2 GE,Ph(c), A Tragic Vow 700.00
3 GE,Ph(c), My Love
   Betrayed Me 700.00
Charlton Comics
4 Rep.FawcettEd.#2;May,1955 . 500.00

NEW ROMANCES
Standard Comics
May, 1951
5 Ph(c), The Blame I Bore 75.00
6 Ph(c), No Wife Was I 40.00
7 Ph(c), My Runaway Heart,
   Ray Miland. 35.00
8 Ph(c) 35.00
9 Ph(c) 35.00
10 ATh,Ph(c) 50.00
11 ATh,Ph(c) of Elizabeth Taylor . . 80.00
12 Ph(c) 25.00
13 Ph(c) 25.00
14 ATh,Ph(c) 40.00
15 Ph(c) 25.00
16 ATh,Ph(c) 40.00
17 Ath, ... 40.00
18 and 19 . . . . @25.00
20 GT, ... 30.00
21 April, 1954. . . . . 25.00

NICKEL COMICS
Dell Publishing Co., 1938
1 Bobby & Chip. 550.00

NICKEL COMICS
Fawcett Publications
May, 1940
1 JaB(c),O&I: Bulletman 3,500.00
2 JaB(c), ... 1,000.00
3 JaB(c), ... 750.00
4 JaB(c), B: Red Gaucho 650.00
5 CCB(c),Bondage(c) 650.00
6 and 7 CCB(c) . . . . @600.00
8 CCB(c),Aug. 23, 1940,
   World's Fair 650.00

NIGHTMARE
(see WEIRD HORRORS)

NIGHTMARE
Ziff-Davis Publishing Co.
1 EK,GT,P(c),The Corpse That
   Wouldn't Stay Dead 400.00
2 EK,P(c),Vampire Mermaid . . . 300.00
St. John Publishing Co.
3 EK,P(c),The Quivering Brain . 250.00
4 P(c),1953 . . . . 200.00

NORTHWEST MOUNTIES
Jubilee Publications/
St. John Publ. Co.
Oct., 1948
1 MB,BLb(c),Rose of the Yukon 350.00
2 MB,BLb(c),A:Ventrilo. 275.00
3 MB, Bondage(c) 250.00
4 MB(c),A:Blue Monk,July'49 . 250.00

NURSERY RHYMES
Ziff-Davis Publishing Co., 1950
1 How John Came Clean 75.00
2 The Old Woman Who
   Lived in a Shoe 50.00

NUTS!
Premere Comics Group
March, 1954
1 . . . . 200.00
2 . . . . 150.00
3 Mention of "Reefers". 165.00
4 . . . . 150.00
5 Captain Marvel Spoof;Nov.'54 150.00

NUTTY COMICS
Fawcett Publications
Winter, 1946
1 (fa),F:Capt. Kid,Richard Richard,
   Joe Miller...Among others . . 100.00

NUTTY LIFE
(see PHANTOM LADY)

NYOKA THE
JUNGLE GIRL
Fawcett Publications
Winter, 1945
1 Bondage(c);Partial Ph(c) of
   Kay Aldridge as Nyoka 450.00
2 . . . . 225.00
3 . . . . 225.00
4 Bondage(c) 225.00
5 Barbacosi Madness;
   Bondage(c) 225.00
6 . . . . 175.00

7 North Pole Jungle;Bondage(c) 165.00
8 Bondage(c) 165.00
9 . . . . 150.00
10 . . . . 150.00

Nyoka The Jungle Girl #5
© Fawcett Publications

11 Danger! Death! in an
   Unexplored Jungle 125.00
12 . . . . 90.00
13 The Human Leopards 125.00
14 The Mad Witch Doctor;
   Bondage(c). 125.00
15 Sacred Goat of Kristan. 125.00
16 BK,The Vultures of Kalahari . . 150.00
17 BK 150.00
18 BK,The Art of Murder. 150.00
19 The Elephant Battle 150.00
20 Explosive Volcano Action . . . 150.00
21 . . . . 75.00
22 The Weird Monsters 75.00
23 Danger in Duplicate 75.00
24 The Human Jaguar;
   Bondage(c) 80.00
25 Hand Colored Ph(c). 60.00
26 A Jungle Stampede 60.00
27 Adventure Laden 60.00
28 The Human Statues of
   the Jungle 60.00
29 Ph(c) 60.00
30 Ph(c) 60.00
31 thru 40 Ph(c) . . . . @50.00
41 thru 50 Ph(c) . . . . @40.00
51 thru 59 Ph(c) . . . . @35.00
60 Ph(c) 30.00
61 Ph(c),The Sacred Sword of
   the Jungle 30.00
62 & 63 Ph(c) . . . . @30.00
64 Ph(c), The Jungle Idol 30.00
65 Ph(c) 30.00
66 Ph(c) 30.00
67 Ph(c), The Sky Man. 30.00
68 thru 74 Ph(c) . . . . @30.00
75 Ph(c), The Jungle Myth
   of Terror 30.00
76 Ph(c) 30.00
77 Ph(c),The Phantoms of the
   Elephant Graveyard;Jun'53. . . 30.00

OAKY DOAKS
Eastern Color Printing Co.
July, 1942
1 Humor Oriented 225.00

OH, BROTHER!
Stanhall Publications
Jan., 1953
1 Bill Williams-a 25.00
2 thru 5 . . . . @15.00

OK COMICS
United Features Syndicate
July, 1940
1 B:Pal Peyton,Little Giant, Phantom
Knight,Sunset Smith,Teller Twins,
Don Ramon, Jerrry Sly,Kip Jaxon,
Leatherneck,Ulysses 600.00
2 Oct., 1940 . . . . 575.00

100 PAGES OF COMICS
Dell Publishing Co., 1937
101 Alley Oop,OG,Wash Tubbs,
Tom Mix,Dan Dunn 1,200.00

ON THE AIR
NBC Network Comics, 1947
1 Giveaway, no cover 175.00

ON THE SPOT
Fawcett Publications
Autumn, 1948
N# Bondage(c),PrettyBoyFloyd . . 250.00

OPERATION PERIL
American Comics Group
(Michel Publ.)
Oct.–Nov., 1950
1 LSt,OW,OW(c),B:TyphoonTyler,
DannyDanger,TimeTravellers 275.00
2 OW,OW(c) 150.00
3 OW,OW(c),Horror 125.00
4 OW,OW(c), Flying Saucers . . . 125.00
5 OW,OW(c), Science Fiction. . . 125.00
6 OW, Tyr. Rex 125.00
7 OW,OW(c) 100.00
8 OW,OW(c) 100.00
9 OW,OW(c) 100.00
10 OW,OW(c) 100.00
11 OW,OW(c), War 100.00
12 OW,OW(c),E:Time Travellers . 100.00
13 OW,OW(c),War Stories 50.00
14 OW,OW(c),War Stories 50.00

Operation Peril #2
© American Comics Group

15 OW,OW(c),War Stories 50.00
16 OW,OW(c),April–May,1953,
War Stories 50.00

OUR FLAG COMICS
Ace Magazines
Aug., 1941
1 MA,JM,B:Capt.Victory,Unknown
Soldier,The Three Cheers . 1,700.00
2 JM,JM(c),O:The Flag 900.00
3 Tank Battle (c) 700.00
4 MA 700.00
5 I:Mr. Risk;April, 1942,
Male Bondage 725.00

Our Gang #4
© Dell Publishing Co.

OUR GANG COMICS
Dell Publishing Co.
Sept.–Oct., 1942
1 WK,Barney Bear, Tom &
Jerry 1,000.00
2 WK. 500.00
3 WK,Benny Burro 350.00
4 WK 350.00
5 WK. 350.00
6 WK. 500.00
7 WK 250.00
8 WK,CB,Benny Burro 600.00
9 WK,CB,Benny Burro 550.00
10 WK,CB,Benny Burro 400.00
11 WK,I:Benny Bear 550.00
12 thru 20 WK. . . . . @250.00
21 thru 29 WK. . . . . @175.00
30 WK,Christmas(c) 150.00
31 thru 34 WK. . . . . @125.00
35 WK,CB 125.00
36 WK,CB 125.00
37 thru 40 WK. . . . . @60.00
41 thru 50 WK. . . . . @50.00
51 thru 56 WK. . . . . @35.00
57 . . . . 30.00
58 Our Gang 30.00
59 Our Gang 30.00
Becomes:

TOM AND JERRY
July, 1949
60 . . . . 60.00
61 . . . . 50.00
62 . . . . 45.00
63 . . . . 45.00
64 . . . . 45.00
65 . . . . 45.00

66 Christmas (c) 50.00
67 thru 70 . . . . @45.00
71 thru 76 . . . . @35.00
77 Christmas (c) 40.00
78 thru 80 . . . . @35.00
81 thru 89 . . . . @30.00
90 Christmas (c) 35.00
91 thru 99 . . . . @30.00
100 . . . . 35.00
101 thru 120 . . . . @25.00
121 thru 150 . . . . @20.00
151 thru 212 . . . . @12.00

OUR SECRET
(see MY SECRET)

OUTLAWS
D.S. Publishing Co.
Feb.–March, 1948
1 HcK,Western Crime Stories . . 225.00
2 Grl,Doc Dawson's Dilema . . . 200.00
3 Cougar City Cleanup 100.00
4 JO,Death Stakes A Claim . . . 125.00
5 RJ,RJ(c),Man Who Wanted
Mexico 100.00
6 AMc,RJ,RJ(c),The Ghosts of
Crackerbox Hill 100.00
7 Grl,Dynamite For Boss Cavitt . 150.00
8 Grl,The Gun & the Pen 150.00
9 FF,Shoot to Kill;June–
July, 1949 . . . . 325.00

WHITE RIDER AND SUPER HORSE
Star Publications
Sept., 1950
1 LbC(c) 75.00
2 LbC(c) 30.00
3 LbC(c) 30.00
4 LbC(c) 35.00
5 LbC(c),Stampede of Hard
Riding Thrills 35.00
6 LbC(c),Drums of the Sioux 35.00
Becomes:

INDIAN WARRIORS
7 LbC(c),Winter on the Great
Plains 50.00
8 LbC(c) 30.00
Becomes:

WESTERN CRIME CASES
9 LbC(c),The Card Sharp Killer . . 60.00
Becomes:

OUTLAWS, THE
10 LbC(c),Federated Express . . . 75.00
11 LbC(c),Frontier Terror!!! 50.00
12 LbC(c),Ruthless Killer!!! 50.00
13 LbC(c),The Grim Avengers . . . 50.00
14 AF,JKa,LbC(c),Trouble in
Dark Canyon,April'54 . . . . . . 50.00

OUT OF THE NIGHT
American Comics Group/
Best Synd. Feature
Feb.–March, 1952
1 AW 500.00
2 AW 400.00
3 . . . . 200.00
4 AW 325.00
5 . . . . 200.00
6 The Ghoul's Revenge 200.00
7 . . . . 200.00
8 The Frozen Ghost 200.00

9 Death Has Wings,
   Science Fiction 200.00
10 Ship of Death 200.00
11 . . . . 175.00
12 Music for the Dead 175.00
13 HN,From the Bottom of
   the Well 175.00
14 Out of the Screen 175.00
15 The Little Furry Thing 150.00
16 Nightmare From the Past 150.00
17 The Terror of the Labyrinth . . . 150.00
Becomes:

HOODED HORSEMAN
18 B: The Hooded Horseman . . . 75.00
19 The Horseman's Strangest
   Adventure 100.00
20 OW,O:Johnny Injun 65.00
21 OW,OW(c) 50.00
22 OW 50.00
23 . . . . 50.00
24 . . . . 50.00
25 . . . . 50.00
26 O&I:Cowboy Sahib 70.00
27 Jan.–Feb., 1953. . . . . 60.00

OUT OF THE SHADOWS
Visual Editions
(Standard Comics)
July, 1952
5 ATh,GT,The Shoremouth
   Horror 375.00
6 ATh,JKz,Salesman of Death . 250.00
7 JK,Plant of Death 175.00
8 Mask of Death 150.00
9 RC,Till Death Do Us Part 175.00
10 MS,We Vowed,Till Death
   Do Us Part 125.00
11 ATh,Fountain of Fear 175.00
12 ATh,Hand of Death 250.00
13 MS,The Cannibal 200.00
14 ATh,The Werewolf,
   Aug., 1954 . . . . 225.00

OXYDOL-DREFT
Giveaways, 1950
The Set is More Valuable if the
Original Envelope is Present
1 L'il Abner 75.00
2 Daisy Mae 75.00
3 Shmoo 80.00
4 AW&FF(c),John Wayne 135.00
5 Archie 65.00
6 Terry Toons Comics 75.00

OZZIE AND BABS
Fawcett Publications
Winter, 1946
1 Humor Oriented, Teenage 45.00
2 Humor Oriented 20.00
3 Humor Oriented 15.00
4 Humor Oriented 15.00
5 Humor Oriented 15.00
6 Humor Oriented 15.00
7 Humor Oriented 15.00
8 Humor Oriented 15.00
9 Humor Oriented 15.00
10 Humor Oriented 15.00
11 Humor Oriented 15.00
12 Humor Oriented 15.00
13 Humor Oriented;1949 . . . . . . 15.00

PAGEANT OF COMICS
St. John Publishing Co.
Sept., 1947
1 Rep. Mopsy 75.00

2 Rep. Jane Arden,Crime
   Reporter 75.00

PANHANDLE PETE AND JENNIFER
J. Charles Lave
Publishing Co.
July, 1951
1 (fa) 40.00
2 (fa) 30.00
3 (fa),Nov.'51 . . . . 30.00

PANIC
Tiny Tot Publications
(E.C. Comics), March, 1954
"Humor in a Jugular Vein"
1 BE,JKa,JO,JDa,AF(c) 250.00
2 BE,JO,WW,JDa,A:Bomb 125.00
3 BE,JO,BW,WW,JDa,AF(c) . . . 110.00
4 BE,JO,WW,JDa,BW(c),
   Infinity(c) 110.00
5 BE,JO,WW,JDa,AF(c) 90.00
6 BE,JO,WW,JDa,Blank (c) 90.00
7 BE,JO,WW,JDa 90.00
8 BE,JO,WW,JDa,Eye Chart (c) . . 90.00
9 BE,JO,WW,JDa,Ph(c),
   Confidential(c) 90.00
10 BE,JDa, Postal Package(c) . . . 90.00
11 BE,WW,JDa,Wheaties parody
   as Weedies (c) 90.00
12 BE,WW,JDa,JDa(c);
   Dec.–Jan. 1955–56 . . . . 125.00

PARAMOUNT ANIMATED COMICS
Family Publications
(Harvey Publ.) June, 1953
1 (fa),B:Baby Herman & Katnip,
   Baby Huey,Buzzy the Crow . 110.00
2 (fa) 60.00
3 (fa) 45.00
4 (fa) 45.00
5 (fa) 45.00
6 (fa) 45.00
7 (fa), Baby Huey (c) 120.00
8 (fa), Baby Huey (c) 50.00
9 (fa), Infinity(c),Baby Huey (c) . . 50.00
10 thru 21 (fa),Baby Huey(c) . . . @30.00
22 (fa), July, 1956, Baby Huey (c) . 30.00

PAROLE BREAKERS
Avon Periodicals/Realistic
Dec., 1951
1 P(c),Hellen Willis,Gun
   Crazed Gun Moll 325.00
2 JKu,P(c),Vinnie Sherwood,
   The Racket King 250.00
3 EK(c),John "Slicer" Berry,
   Hatchetman of Crime;
   July,1952 . . . . 200.00

PATCHES
Rural Home Publ./
Patches Publ.
March–April, 1945
1 LbC(c),Imagination In Bed(c) . 250.00
2 Dance (c) 100.00
3 Rocking Horse (c) 75.00
4 Music Band (c) 75.00
5 LbC(c),A:Danny Kaye,Football 125.00
6 A: Jackie Kelk 75.00
7 A: Hopalong Cassidy 125.00
8 A: Smiley Burnettte 75.00

9 BK,A: Senator Claghorn 75.00
10 A: Jack Carson 75.00
11 A: Red Skeleton; Dec'47 . . . . 100.00

PAWNEE BILL
Story Comics
Feb.–July, 1951
1 A:Bat Masterson,Wyatt Earp,
   Indian Massacre
   at Devil's Gulch 55.00
2 Blood in Coffin Canyon 35.00
3 LC,O:Golden Warrior,Fiery
   Arrows at Apache Pass; 35.00

PAY-OFF
D.S. Publishing Co.
July–Aug., 1948–
March–April, 1949
1 . . . . 150.00
2 The Pennsylvania Blue-Beard 100.00
3 The Forgetful Forger 75.00
4 RJ(c),Lady and the Jewels 75.00
5 The Beautiful Embezzeler 75.00

PEDRO
Fox Features Syndicate
Jan., 1950
1 WW,WW(c),Humor Oriented . 165.00
2 Aug., 1950 . . . . 110.00

PENNY
Avon Publications, 1947
1 The Slickest Chick of 'em All . . 60.00
2 . . . . 30.00
3 America's Teen-age
   Sweetheart 30.00
4 . . . . 30.00
5 . . . . 30.00
6 Perry Como Ph(c),Sept.–
   Oct., 1949 . . . . 35.00

PEP COMICS
MJL Magazines/
Archie Publications
Jan., 1940
1 IN,JCo,MMe,IN(c),I:Shield,
   O:Comet,Queen of Diamonds,
   B:The Rocket,Press Guardian,
   Sergeant Boyle Chang,Bently

Pep #26
© *Archie Publications*

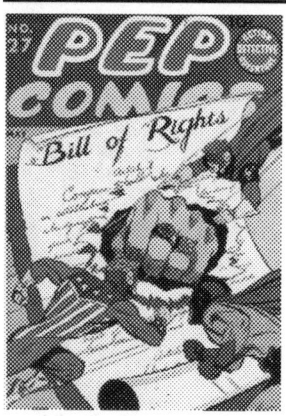

Pep Comics #27
© Archie Publications

of Scotland Yard	7,000.00
2 CBi,JCo,IN,IN(c),O:Rocket	1,700.00
3 JCo,IN,IN(c),Shield (c)	1,200.00
4 Cbi,JCo,MMe,IN,IN(c),	
C:Wizard(not Gareb)	1,000.00
5 Cbi,JCo,MMe,IN,IN(c),	
C:Wizard	1,000.00
6 IN,IN(c), Shield (c)	750.00
7 IN,IN(c),Bondage(c),Shield(c)	750.00
8 JCo,IN, Shield (c)	725.00
9 IN, Shield (c)	725.00
10 IN,IN(c), Shield (c)	725.00
11 MMe,IN,IN(c),I:Dusty,	
Boy Detective	800.00
12 IN,IN(c),O:Fireball	
Bondage(c), E:Rocket,	
Queen of Diamonds	1,000.00
13 IN,IN(c),Bondage(c)	625.00
14 IN,IN(c)	600.00
15 IN,Bondage(c)	625.00
16 IN,O:Madam Satan	1,000.00
17 IN,IN(c),O:Hangman,	
D:Comet	2,700.00
18 IN,IN(c),Bondage(c)	600.00
19 IN	575.00
20 IN,IN(c),E:Fireball	575.00
21 IN,IN(c),Bondage(c),	
E: Madam Satan	600.00
22 IN,IN(c)I:Archie,	
Jughead, Betty	11,000.00
23 IN,IN(c)	1,100.00
24 IN,IN(c)	900.00
25 IN,IN(c)	900.00
26 IN,IN(c),I:Veronica	1,250.00
27 IN,IN(c),Bill of Rights (c)	700.00
28 IN,IN(c), V:Capt. Swastika	700.00
29 ASH (c)	700.00
30 B:Capt.Commando	700.00
31 Bondage(c)	700.00
32 Bondage(c)	550.00
33	500.00
34 Bondage(c)	550.00
35	500.00
36 1st Archie(c)	1,200.00
37 Bondage(c)	425.00
38 ASH(c)	400.00
39 ASH(c), Human Shield	400.00
40	400.00
41 2nd Archie; I:Jughead	275.00
42 F:Archie & Jughead	250.00
43 F:Archie & Jughead	250.00
44	250.00
45	250.00
46	250.00
47 E:Hangman,Infinity(c)	250.00
48 B:Black Hood	250.00

49	250.00
50	250.00
51	200.00
52 B:Suzie	200.00
53	200.00
54 E:Captain Commando	200.00
55	200.00
56 thru 58	@175.00
59 E:Suzie	175.00
60 B:Katy Keene	175.00
61	150.00
62 I L'il Jinx	150.00
63	150.00
64	150.00
65 E:Shield	150.00
66 thru 71	@100.00
72 thru 80	@85.00
81 thru 90	@65.00
91 thru 99	@50.00
100	85.00
101 thru 110	@40.00
111 thru 120	@35.00
121 thru 130	@30.00
131 thru 140	@25.00
141 thru 150	@20.00
151 thru 160,A:Super Heroes	@18.00
161 thru 200	@10.00
201 thru 250	@5.00
251 thru 300	@5.00
301 thru 350	@4.00
351 thru 411	@3.00

PERFECT CRIME, THE
Cross Publications
Oct., 1949

1 BP,DW	200.00
2 BP	125.00
3	100.00
4 BP	100.00
5 DW	100.00
6	100.00
7 B:Steve Duncan	100.00
8 Drug Story	125.00
9	100.00
10	100.00
11 Bondage (c)	125.00
12	75.00
13	75.00
14 Poisoning (c)	75.00
15 "The Most Terrible Menace",	
Drug	100.00
16	75.00
17	75.00
18 Drug (c)	125.00
19	75.00
20 thru 25	@50.00
26 Drug w/ Hypodermic (c)	150.00
27	75.00
28	75.00
29	75.00
30 E:Steve Duncan, Rope	
Strangulation (c)	125.00
31	60.00
32	60.00
33	60.00

PERFECT LOVE
Approved Comics(Ziff-Davis)/
St. John Publ. Co.
Aug.–Sept., 1951

1 (10),P(c),Our Kiss was a	
Prelude to Love Adrift	125.00
2	75.00
3 P(c)	50.00
4	50.00
5	50.00
6	50.00
7	50.00

8 EK	55.00
9 EK,P(c)	40.00
10 Ph(c), Dec '53	40.00

PERSONAL LOVE
Famous Funnies, Jan., 1950

1 Ph(c) Are You in Love	100.00
2 Ph(c) Serenade for Suzette	
Mario Lanzo	50.00
3 Ph(c)	40.00
4 Ph(c)	40.00
5 Ph(c)	40.00
6 Ph(c) Be Mine Forever	45.00
7 Ph(c) You'll Always Be	
Mine, Robert Walker	45.00
8 EK,Ph(c),Esther Williams &	
Howard Keel	50.00
9 EK,Ph(c),Debra Paget & Louis	
Jordan	50.00
10 Ph(c),Loretta Young	
Joseph Cotton	45.00
11 ATh, Ph(c),Gene Tierney &	
Glenn Ford	75.00
12 Ph(c) Jane Greer &	
William Lundigan	40.00
13 Ph(c) Debra Paget &	
Louis Jordan	35.00
14 Ph(c) Kirk Douglas &	
Patrice Wymore	50.00
15 Ph(c) Dale Robertson &	
Joanne Dru	35.00
16 Ph(c) Take Back Your Love	35.00
17 Ph(c) My Cruel Deception	35.00
18 Ph(c) Gregory Peck &	
Susan Hayward	45.00
19 Ph(c) Anthony Quinn	45.00
20 Ph(c) The Couple in the	
Next Apartment, Bob Wagner	40.00
21 Ph(c) I'll Make You Care	35.00
22 Ph(c) Doorway To Heartbreak	35.00
23 Ph(c) SaveMe from that Man	35.00
24 FF, Ph(c) Tyrone Power	300.00
25 FF, Ph(c) The Dark Light	300.00
26 Ph(c) Love Needs A Break	35.00
27 FF, Ph(c) Champ or Chump?	300.00
28 FF, Ph(c) A Past to Forget	300.00
29 Ph(c) Charlton Heston	45.00
30 Ph(c) The Lady is Lost	35.00
31 Ph(c) Marlon Brando	60.00
32 FF, Ph(c) The Torment,	
Kirk Douglas	350.00
33 Ph(c) June ,1955	35.00

PETER COTTONTAIL
Key Publications
Jan., 1954

1 No 3-D (fa)	40.00
1 Feb '54 3-D (fa)	100.00
2 Rep of 3-D #1,not in 3-D	30.00

PETER PAUL'S 4 IN 1
JUMBO COMIC BOOK
Capitol Stories, 1953

1 F: Racket Squad in Action,	
Space Adventures,Crime &	
Justice,Space Western	300.00

PETER PENNY AND HIS
MAGIC DOLLAR
American Bakers Assn., 1947

1 History from Colonial	
America to the 1950's	125.00
2	75.00

PETER RABBIT
Avon Periodicals, 1947
1 H. Cady art 225.00
2 H. Cady art 175.00
3 H. Cady art 150.00
4 H. Cady art 150.00
5 H. Cady art 150.00
6 H. Cady art 150.00
7 thru 10 . . . . @30.00
11 . . . . 15.00

KRAZY LIFE
Fox Features Syndicate, 1945
1 (fa) 55.00
Becomes:
NUTTY LIFE
2 (fa) 45.00
Becomes:
WOTALIFE
Fox Features Synd./
Green Publ., Aug.–Sept., 1946
3 (fa)B:L'il Pan,Cosmo Cat 35.00
4 . . . . 25.00
5 thru 11 . . . . @20.00
12 July, 1947 . . . . 20.00
Becomes:

PHANTOM LADY
Fox Features Syndicate
Aug., 1947
13(#1) MB,MB(c) Knights of
  the Crooked Cross 3,200.00
14(#2) MB,MB(c) Scoundrels
  and Scandals 2,000.00
15 MB,MB(c) The Meanest
  Crook In the World 1,800.00
16 MB,MB(c) Claa Peete The
  Beautiful Beast, Negligee . . 1,800.00
17 MB.MB(c) The Soda Mint
  Killer, Bondage (c) 4,500.00
18 MB,MB(c) The Case of
  Irene Shroeder 1,400.00
19 MB,MB(c) The Case of
  the Murderous Model 1,400.00
20 MB,MB(c) Ace of Spades . . 1,000.00
21 MB,MB(c) 1,000.00
22 MB,JKa 1,000.00
23 MB,JKa Bondage (c) 1,100.00
Becomes:

MY LOVE SECRET
24 JKa, My Love Was For Sale . . . 90.00
25 Second Hand Love 50.00
26 WW I Wanted Both Men 100.00
27 I Was a Love Cheat 40.00
28 WW, I Gave Him Love 100.00
29 . . . . 40.00
30 Ph(c) 40.00

LINDA
Ajax/Farrell, April–May, 1954
1 . . . . 75.00
2 Lingerie section 55.00
3 . . . . 40.00
4 Oct.–Nov.,1954 . . . . 40.00
Becomes:

PHANTOM LADY
5(1) MB,Dec-Jan'54-55 . . . . 900.00
2 Last Pre-Code Edition 650.00
3 Comics Code 500.00
4 Red Rocket,June, 1955 . . . . . 500.00

PHIL RIZZUTO
Fawcett Publications, 1951
Ph(c) The Sensational Story of
  The American Leagues MVP 500.00

Phantom Lady #16
© Fox Feature Syndicate

PICTORIAL CONFESSIONS
St. John Publishing Co.
Sept., 1949
1 MB,MB(c),I Threw Away My Repu-
  tation on a Worthless Love . 200.00
2 MB,Ph(c) I Tried to be a
  Hollywood Glamour Girl 125.00
3 JKY,MB,MB(c),They Caught
  Me Cheating 125.00
Becomes:

PICTORIAL ROMANCES
4 Ph(c) MB, Trapped By Kisses
  I Couldn't Resist 200.00
5 MB,MB(c) 150.00
6 MB,MB(c) I Was Too Free
  With Boys 100.00
7 MB,MB(c) 100.00
8 MB,MB(c) I Made a
  Sinful Bargain 100.00
9 MB,MB(c) Dishonest Love . . . 100.00
10 MB,MB(c) I Was The
  Other Woman 75.00
11 MB,MB(c) The Worst
  Mistake A Wife Can Make . . . 85.00
12 MB,MB(c) Love Urchin 60.00
13 MB,MB(c) Temptations of a
  Hatcheck Girl 60.00
14 MB,MB(c) I Was A
  Gamblers Wife 60.00
15 MB,MB(c) Wife Without
  Pride or Principles 60.00
16 MB,MB(c) The Truth of My
  Affair With a Farm Boy 60.00
17 MB,MB(c) True Confessions
  of a Girl in Love 175.00
18 MB,MB(c) 175.00
20 MB,MB(c) 175.00
21 MB,MB(c) 50.00
22 MB,MB(c) 50.00
23 MB,MB(c) 50.00
24 MB,MB(c) March,1954 . . . . . . 50.00

PICTORIAL LOVE STORIES
St. John Publishing Co.
Oct., 1952
1 MB,MB(c) I Lost My Head, My
  Heart and My Resistance . . . 175.00

PICTURE NEWS
299 Lafayette Street Corp.
Jan., 1946
1 Will The Atom Blow The
  World Apart 275.00
2 Meet America's 1st Girl Boxing
  Expert,Atomic Bomb 150.00
3 Hollywood's June Allison Shows
  You How to be Beautiful,
  Atomic Bomb 100.00
4 Amazing Marine Who Became
  King of 10,000 Voodoos,
  Atomic Bomb 125.00
5 G.I.Babies,Hank Greenberg . . . 90.00
6 Joe Louis(c) 125.00
7 Lovely Lady, Englands
  Future Queen 80.00
8 Champion of them All 75.00
9 Bikini Atom Bomb,
  Joe DiMaggio 100.00
10 Dick Quick, Ace Reporter,
  Atomic Bomb
  Jan./Feb. 1947 . . . . 100.00

PICTURE STORIES FROM SCIENCE
Educational Comics
Spring, 1947
1 Understanding Air and Water . 200.00
2 Fall '47 Amazing Discoveries
  About Food & Health 175.00

PICTURE STORIES FROM WORLD HISTORY
E.C. Comics, Spring, 1947
1 Ancient World to the
  Fall of Rome 250.00
2 Europes Struggle for
  Civilization 200.00

PINHEAD AND FOODINI
Fawcett Publications
July, 1951–Jan. 1952
1 Ph(c) 175.00
2 Ph(c) 100.00
3 Ph(c) Too Many Pinheads 60.00
4 Foodini's Talking Camel 60.00

PIN-UP PETE
Minoan Magazine Publishers
1952
1 Loves of a GI Casanova 100.00

PIONEER PICTURE STORIES
Street & Smith, Dec., 1941
1 Red Warriors in Blackface 200.00
2 Life Story Of Errol Flynn 100.00
3 Success Stories of Brain
  Muscle in Action 75.00
4 Legless Ace & Boy Commando
  Raid Occupied France 75.00
5 How to Tell Uniform and
  Rank of Any Navy Man 75.00
6 General Jimmy Doolittle 85.00
7 Life Story of Admiral Halsey . . . 85.00
8 Life Story of Timoshenko 75.00
9 Dec. '43,Man Who Conquered
  The Wild Frozen North 75.00

GOLDEN AGE

All comics prices listed are for *Near Mint* condition. | **CVA Page 389**

PIRACY
E.C. Comics, Oct.–Nov., 1954
1 WW,JDa,AW,WW(c),RC,AT . . 225.00
2 RC,JDa(c),WW,AW,AT 175.00
3 RC,GE, RC(c),Grl 150.00
4 RC,GE,RC(c),Grl 125.00
5 RC,GE,BK(c),Grl 125.00
6 JDa,RC,GE,BK(c),Grl 125.00
7 Oct Nov GE(c),RC,GE,Grl . . . 125.00

PIRATE COMICS
Hillman Periodicals, Feb., 1950
1 . . . . 175.00
2 . . . . 120.00
3 . . . . 100.00
4 Aug–Sept., 1950. . . . . 90.00

PIXIES, THE
Magazine Enterprises
Winter, 1946
1 Mighty Atom 45.00
2 . . . . 25.00
3 . . . . 20.00
4 . . . . 20.00
5 . . . . 25.00
Becomes:

MIGHTY ATOM, THE
6 . . . . 25.00

PLANET COMICS
Love Romance Publ.
(Fiction House Magazines)
Jan., 1940
1 AB,DBR,HCk, Planet Comics,
WE&LF,O:Aura,B:Flint Baker,
Red Comet,Spurt Hammond,
Capt. Nelson Cole 10,000.00
2 HcK,LF(c) 3,500.00
3 WE(c),HcK. 2,500.00
4 HcK,B:Gale Allan and
the Girl Squad 2,000.00
5 BP,HcK 1,900.00
6 BP,HcK,BP(c),The Ray
Pirates of Venus 2,000.00
7 BP,AB,HcK,BP(c) B:Buzz
Crandall Planet Payson . . 1,600.00
8 BP,AB HcK 1,500.00
9 BP,AB,GT,HcK,B:Don
Granville Cosmo Corrigan . 1,500.00
10 BP,AB,GT HcK 1,500.00
11 HcK, B:Crash Parker. 1,500.00
12 Dri,B:Star Fighter 1,500.00
13 Dri,B:Reef Ryan 1,300.00
14 Dri B:Norge Benson 1,200.00
15 B: Mars,God of War 2,300.00
16 Invasion From The Void . . . 1,100.00
17 Warrior Maid of Mercury . . . 1,100.00
18 Bondage(c) 1,200.00
19 Monsters of the Inner World 1,100.00
20 RP, Winged Man Eaters
of the Exile Star. 1,100.00
21 RP,B:Lost World
Hunt Bowman 1,200.00
22 Inferno on the Fifth Moon . . 1,100.00
23 GT,Lizard Tyrant of
the Twilight World 1,000.00
24 GT,Grl Raiders From
The Red Moon. 1,000.00
25 Grl,B:Norge Benson 1,000.00
26 Grl,B:The Space Rangers
Bondage(c) 1,100.00
27 Grl, The Fire Eaters of
Asteroid Z. 800.00
28 Grl, Bondage (c) 850.00
29 Grl,Dragon Raiders of Aztla . . 800.00
30 GT,Grl City of Lost Souls 800.00

Planet Comics #2
© Fiction House Magazines

31 Grl,Fire Priests of Orbit6X . . . 675.00
32 Slaver's Planetoid 800.00
33 MA 675.00
34 MA,Bondage 850.00
35 MA B:Mysta of The Moon. . . . 700.00
36 MA Collosus of the
Blood Moon 700.00
37 MA, Behemoths of the
Purple Void. 700.00
38 MA 600.00
39 MA. Death Webs Of Zenith 3 . 600.00
40 Chameleon Men from
Galaxy 9. . . . . 600.00
41 MA,Aaf,New O: Auro
Bondage (c) 650.00
42 MA,AaF,E:Gale Allan 600.00
43 MA,AaF Death Rays
From the Sun. 600.00
44 MA,Bbl,B:Futura 600.00
45 Ma,Bbl,Her Evilness
from Xanado. 600.00
46 MA,Bbl,GE The Mecho-Men
From Mars 600.00
47 MA,Bbl,GE,The Great
Green Spawn 550.00
48 MA,GE. 550.00
49 MA,GE, Werewolves From
Hydra Hell 550.00
50 MA,GE,The Things of Xeves . 550.00
51 MA,GE, Mad Mute X-Adapts . 500.00
52 GE,Mystery of the Time
Chamber 500.00
53 MB,GE,Bondage(c)
Dwarflings From Oceania . . 500.00
54 MB,GE,Robots From Inferno . 500.00
55 MB,GE,Giants of the
Golden Atom 500.00
56 MB,GE,Grl. 475.00
57 MB,GE,Grl. 475.00
58 MB,GE,Grl. 475.00
59 MB,GE,Grl,LSe 475.00
60 GE,Grl,Vassals of Volta 475.00
61 GE,Grl, The Brute in the
Bubble 350.00
62 GE,Musta,Moon Goddess . . . 350.00
63 GE,Paradise or Inferno 350.00
64 GE,Monkeys From the Blue . . 350.00
65 The Lost World 350.00
66 The Plague of the
Locust Men 350.00
67 The Nymphs of Neptune 350.00
68 Synthoids of the 9th Moon . . . 350.00
69 The Mentalists of Mars. 350.00
70 Cargo For Amazonia 350.00
71 Sandhogs of Mars 250.00

72 Last Ship to Paradise. 250.00
73 The Martian Plague,
Winter 1953 . . . . 250.00

PLASTIC MAN
Comics Magazines
(Quality Comics Group)
Summer, 1943
1 JCo,JCo(c)Game of Death. . 3,000.00
2 JCo,JCo(c)The Gay Nineties
Nightmare 1,300.00
3 JCo,JCo(c) 800.00
4 JCo,JCo(c) 650.00
5 JCo,JCo(c) 550.00
6 JCo,JCo(c) 450.00
7 JCo,JCo(c) 450.00
8 JCo,JCo(c) 450.00
9 JCo,JCo(c) 450.00
10 JCo,JCo(c) 450.00
11 JCo,JCo(c). 400.00
12 JCo,JCo(c),V:Spadehead. . . . 400.00
13 JCo,JCo(c),V:Mr.Hazard. . . . 400.00
14 JCo,JCo(c),Words,Symbol
of Crime 400.00
15 JCo,JCo(c),V:BeauBrummel. . 400.00
16 JCo,JCo(c),Money
Means Trouble 400.00
17 JCo,JCo(c),A:The Last
Man on Earth 400.00
18 JCo,JCo(c),Goes Back
to the Farm. 400.00
19 JCo,JCo(c),V;Prehistoric
Plunder 400.00
20 JCo,JCo(c),A:Sadly,Sadly . . . 400.00
21 JCo,JCo(c),V:Crime Minded
Mind Reader. 300.00
22 JCo,JCo(c), Which Twin
is the Phony 300.00
23 JCo,JCo(c),The Fountain
of Age 300.00
24 JCo,JCo(c),The Black Box
of Terror 300.00
25 JCo,JCo(c),A:Angus
MacWhangus 300.00
26 JCo,JCo(c),On the Wrong
Side of the Law? 300.00
27 JCo,JCo(c),V:The Leader. . . . 300.00
28 JCo,JCo(c),V:Shasta 300.00
29 JCo,JCo(c),V:Tricky Toledo . . 300.00
30 JCo,JCo(c),V:Weightless
Wiggins 300.00
31 JCo,JCo(c),V:Raka the
Witch Doctor. 225.00
32 JCo,JCo(c),V:Mr.Fission. 225.00
33 JCo,JCo(c),V:The Mad
Professor 225.00
34 JCo,JCo(c),Smuggler'sHaven. 225.00
35 JCo,JCo(c),V:The Hypnotist . . 225.00
36 JCo,JCo(c),The Uranium
Underground 225.00
37 JCo,JCo(c),V:Gigantic Ants . . 225.00
38 JCo,JCo(c),The Curse of
Monk Mauley 225.00
39 JCo,JCo(c),The Stairway
to Madness 225.00
40 JCo,JCo(c),The Ghoul of
Ghost Swamp. 225.00
41 JCo,JCo(c),The Beast with
the Bloody Claws 200.00
42 JCo,JCo(c),The King of
Thunderbolts 200.00
43 JCo,JCo(c),The Evil Terror. . . 200.00
44 JCo,JCo(c),The Magic Cup . . 200.00
45 The Invisible Raiders 200.00
46 V:The Spider 200.00
47 The Fiend of a
Thousand Faces. 200.00
48 Killer Crossbones. 200.00
49 JCo,The Weapon for Evil 200.00
50 V:Iron Fist 200.00

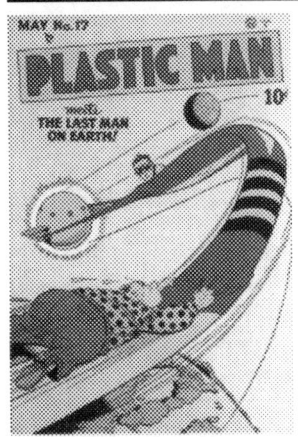

Plastic Man #17
© Quality Comics Group

51 Incredible Sleep Weapon 175.00
52 V:Indestructible Wizard 185.00
53 V:Dazzia,Daughter of
    Darkness 185.00
54 V:Dr.Quomquat 185.00
55 The Man Below Zero 185.00
56 JCo, The Man Who Broke
    the Law of Gravity 185.00
57 The Chemist's Cauldron 185.00
58 JCo,The Amazing
    Duplicating Machine 185.00
59 JCo,V:The Super Spy 185.00
60 The Man in the Fiery
    Disguise 175.00
61 V:King of the Thunderbolts. . . 175.00
62 V:The Smokeweapon. 175.00
63 V:Reflecto 175.00
64 Nov'56 The Invisible
    Raiders 175.00

POCAHONTAS
Pocahontas Fuel Co.
Oct., 1941
N# 65.00
2 . . . . 50.00

POCKET COMICS
Harvey Publications,
Aug., 1941
1 100 pages,O:Black Cat,Spirit
    of '76,Red Blazer Phantom
    Sphinx & Zebra,B:Phantom
    Ranger,British Agent #99,
    Spin Hawkins,Satan 750.00
2 . . . . 500.00
3 . . . . 400.00
4 Jan.'42,All Features End 350.00

POGO POSSUM
Dell Publishing Co.
1 WK,A:Swamp Land Band 550.00
2 WK. 400.00
3 WK. 375.00
4 WK. 375.00
5 WK. 375.00
6 thru 10 WK . . . . @250.00
11 WK, Christmas cover . . . . . @300.00
12 thru 16 WK. . . . . @200.00

POLICE COMICS
Comic Magazines
(Quality Comics Group)
Aug., 1941
1 GFx,JCo,WE.PGn,RC,FG,AB,
    GFx(c),B&O:Plastic Man
    The Human Bomb,#711,I&B,
    Chic Canter,The Firebrand
    Mouthpiece,Phantom Lady
    The Sword. 6,500.00
2 JCo,GFx,PGn,WE,RC,FG,
    GFx(c) 2,400.00
3 JCo,GFx,PGn,WE,RC,FG,
    GFx(c) 1,600.00
4 JCo,GFx,PGn,WE,RC,FG,
    GFx&WEC(c). 1,500.00
5 JCo,GFx,PGn,WE,RC,FG,
    GFx(c) 1,300.00
6 JCo,GFx,PGn,WE,RC,FG,
    GFx(c) 1,200.00
7 JCo,GFx,PGn,WE,RC,FG,
    GFx(c) 1,100.00
8 JCo,GFx,PGn,WE,RC,FG,
    GFx(c),B&O:Manhunter . . 1,500.00
9 JCo,GFx,PGn,WE,RC,FG,
    GFx(c) 1,100.00
10 JCo,GFx,PGn,WE,RC,FG,
    GFx(c) 1,000.00
11 JCo,GFx,PGn,WE,RC,FG,
    GFx(c),B:Rep:Rep.Spirit
    Strips. 1,700.00
12 JCo,GFX,PGn,WE,FG,AB,
    RC(c) I:Ebony 1,000.00
13 JCo,GFx,PGn,WE,FG,AB,RC(c)
    E:Firebrand,I:Woozy Winks 1,000.00
14 JCo,GFx,PGn,WE,Jku,GFX(c) 750.00
15 JCo,GFx,PGn,WE,Jku,GFX(c)
    E:#711,B:Destiny. 750.00
16 JCo,PGn,WE,JKu 750.00
17 JCo,PGn,WE,JKu,JCo(c) 750.00
18 JCo,PGn,WE,JCo(c) 750.00
19 JCo,PGn,WE,JCo(c) 750.00
20 JCo,PGn,WE,JCo(c),A:Jack
    Cole in Phantom Lady 750.00
21 JCo,PGn,WE,JCo(c) 600.00
22 JCo,PGn,WE,RP,JCo(c)
    The Eyes Have it 600.00
23 JCo,WE,RP,JCo(c),E:Phantom
    Lady. 550.00
24 JCo,WE,HK,JCo(c),B:Flatfoot
    Burns. 550.00
25 JCo,WE,HK,RP,JCo(c),The
    Bookstore Mysrery 550.00
26 JCo,WE,Hk,JCo,(c)E:Flatfoot
    Burns. 550.00
27 JCo,WE,JCo(c) 550.00
28 JCo,WE,JCo(c) 550.00
29 JCo,WE,JCo(c) 550.00
30 JCo,WE,JCo(c),A Slippery
    Racket 550.00
31 JCo,WE,JCo(c),Is Plastic
    Man Washed Up?. 400.00
32 JCo,WE,JCo(c),Fiesta Turns
    Into a Fracas 400.00
33 JCo,WE. 400.00
34 JCo,WE,JCO(c) 400.00
35 JCo,WE,JCO(c) 400.00
36 JCo,WE,JCO(c),Rest
    In Peace. 400.00
37 JCo,WE,PGn,JCo(c),Love
    Comes to Woozy 400.00
38 JCo,WE,PGn,JCo(c) 400.00
39 JCo,WE,PGn,JCo(c) 400.00
40 JCo,WE,PGn,JCo(c) 400.00
41 JCo,WE,PGn,JCo(c),E:Reps.
    of Spirit Strip 300.00
42 JCo,LF&WE,PGn,JCo(c),
    Woozy Cooks with Gas. . . . 300.00
43 JCo,LF&WE,PGn,JCo(c) 300.00
44 JCo,PGn,LF,JCo(c) 275.00

Police Comics #13
© Quality Comics Group

45 JCo,PGn,LF,JCo(c) 275.00
46 JCo,PGn,LF,JCo(c) 275.00
47 JCo,PGn,LF,JCo(c),
    V:Dr.Slicer 275.00
48 JCo,PGn,LF,JCo(c),V:Big
    Beaver 275.00
49 JCo,PGn,LF,JCo(c),V:Thelma
    Twittle. 275.00
50 JCo,PGn,LF,JCo(c) 275.00
51 JCo,PGn,LF,JCo(c),V:The
    Granite Lady. 225.00
52 JCo,PGn,LF,JCo(c) 225.00
53 JCo,PGn,LF,JCo(c),
    V:Dr.Erudite 225.00
54 JCo,PGn,LF,JCo(c) 225.00
55 JCo,PGn,LF,JCo(c),V:The
    Sleepy Eyes. 225.00
56 JCo,PGn,LF,JCo(c),V:The
    Yes Man. 225.00
57 JCo,PGn,LF,JCo(c),
    V:Mr.Misfit 225.00
58 JCo,PGn,LF,JCo(c),E:The
    Human Bomb. 225.00
59 JCo,PGn,LF,JCo(c),A:Mr.
    Happiness 225.00
60 JCo,PGn,LF,JCo(c) 175.00
61 JCo,PGn,LF,JCo(c) 175.00
62 JCo,PGn,LF,JCo(c) 175.00
63 JCo,PGn,LF,JCo(c),
    V:The Crab. 175.00
64 JCo,PGn,LF,HK,JCo(c) 175.00
65 JCo,PGn,LF,JCo(c) 175.00
66 JCo,PGn,LF,JCo(c) Love
    Can Mean Trouble 175.00
67 JCo,LF,JCo(c),
    V:The Gag Man 175.00
68 JCo,LF,JCo(c) 175.00
69 JCo,LF,JCo(c),V:Strecho 175.00
70 JCo,LF,JCo(c) 175.00
71 JCo,LF,JCo(c) 175.00
72 JCo,LF,JCo(c),V:Mr.Cat 175.00
73 JCo,LF,JCo(c) 175.00
74 JCo,LF,JCo(c),V:Prof.Dimwit . 175.00
75 JCo,LF,JCo(c) 175.00
76 JCo,LF,JCo(c),V:Mr.Morbid. . . 175.00
77 JCo,LF,JCo(c),V:Skull Face
    & Eloc 175.00
78 JCo,LF,JCo(c),A Hot Time In
    Dreamland 175.00
79 JCo,LF,JCo(c),V:Eaglebeak . . 175.00
80 JCo,LF,JCo(c),V:Penetro 175.00
81 JCo,LF,JCo(c),V:A Gorilla. . . . 175.00
82 JCo,LF,JCo(c) 175.00
83 JCo,LF,JCo(c) 175.00
84 JCo,LF,JCo(c) 175.00

85 JCo,LF,JCo(c),V:Lucky 7 . . . . 175.00	
86 JCo,LF,JCo(c),V:The Baker . . 175.00	
87 JCo,LF,JCo(c) 175.00	
88 JCo,LF,JCo(c),V:The Seen. . . 175.00	
89 JCo,JCo(c),V:The Vanishers . 150.00	
90 JCo,LF,JCo(c),V:Capt.Rivers . 150.00	
91 JCo,JCo(c),The	
Forest Primeval 160.00	
92 JCo,LF,JCo(c),V:Closets	
Kennedy. 160.00	
93 JCo,JCo(c),V:The Twinning	
Terror 160.00	
94 JCo,JCo(c),WE 250.00	
95 JCo,JCo(c),WE,V:Scowls. . . . 250.00	
96 JCo,JCo(c),WE,V:Black	
Widow 250.00	
97 JCo,JCo(c),WE,V:The Mime. . 250.00	
98 JCo,JCo(c),WE 250.00	
99 JCo,JCo(c),WE 250.00	
100 JCo,JCo(c). 300.00	
101 JCo,JCo(c). 300.00	
102 JCo,JCo(c),E:Plastic Man. . . 300.00	
103 JCo,LF,B&I:Ken Shannon;	
Bondage(c). 175.00	
104 The Handsome of Homocide 150.00	
105 Invisible Hands of Murder. . . 150.00	
106 Museum of Murder. 150.00	
107 Man with the ShrunkenHead 150.00	
108 The Headless Horse Player . 150.00	
109 LF,Bondage(c),Blood on the	
Chinese Fan. 150.00	
110 Murder with a Bang 150.00	
111 Diana, Homocidal Huntress . 150.00	
112 RC,The Corpse on the	
Sidewalk. 165.00	
113 RC,RC(c), The Dead Man	
with the Size 13 Shoe. 165.00	
114 The Terrifying Secret of	
the Black Bear 150.00	
115 Don't Let Them Kill Me. 150.00	
116 Stage Was Set For Murder. . 150.00	
117 Bullet Riddled Bookkeeper . . 150.00	
118 Case of the Absent Corpse . 150.00	
119 A Fast & Bloody Buck 150.00	
120 Death & The Derelict 150.00	
121 Curse of the Clawed Killer . . 150.00	
122 The Lonely Hearts Killer. . . . 150.00	
123 Death Came Screaming. . . . 150.00	
124 Masin Murder. 150.00	
125 Bondage(c),The Killer of	
King Arthur's Court. 165.00	
126 Hit & Run Murders. 150.00	
127 Oct'53,Death Drivers 150.00	

POLICE LINE-UP
Avon Periodicals/
Realistic Comics, Aug., 1951

1 WW,P(c). 250.00	
2 P(c),Drugs 175.00	
3 JKu,EK,P(c). 125.00	
4 July '52,EK. 125.00	

POLICE TRAP
Mainline Sept., 1954

1 S&K(c). 200.00	
2 S&K(c) 100.00	
3 S&K(c) 100.00	
4 S&K(c) 100.00	

Charlton Comics

5 S&K,S&K(c) 150.00	
6 S&K,S&K(c) 150.00	

Becomes:

PUBLIC DEFENDER
IN ACTION

7 . . . . 50.00	
8 thru 12, Oct. 1957. . . . . @40.00	

GOLDEN AGE

POLLY PIGTAILS
Parents' Magazine Institute
Jan., 1946

1 Ph(c) 55.00	
2 Ph(c) 25.00	
3 Ph(c) 20.00	
4 Ph(c) 20.00	
5 Ph(c) 20.00	
6 Ph(c) 20.00	
7 Ph(c) 15.00	
8 . . . . 15.00	
9 . . . . 15.00	
10 . . . . 15.00	
11 thru 22 . . . . @10.00	
22 Ph(c). 10.00	
23 Ph(c) 10.00	
34 thru 43 . . . . @10.00	

Popeye #3
© Dell Publishing Co.

POPEYE
Dell Publishing Co., 1948

1 . . . . 325.00	
2 . . . . 150.00	
3 `Welcome to Ghost Island' . . . 125.00	
4 . . . . 125.00	
5 . . . . 125.00	
6 . . . . 125.00	
7 . . . . 125.00	
8 . . . . 125.00	
9 . . . . 125.00	
10 . . . . 125.00	
11 . . . . 100.00	
12 . . . . 100.00	
13 . . . . 100.00	
14 thru 20 . . . . @100.00	
21 thru 30 . . . . @75.00	
31 thru 40 . . . . @65.00	
41 thru 45 . . . . @50.00	
46 O:Sweat Pea 65.00	
47 thru 50 . . . . @45.00	
51 thru 60 . . . . @35.00	
61 thru 65 . . . . @25.00	

POPULAR COMICS
Dell Publishing Co.
Feb., 1936

1 Dick Tracy, Little Orphan	
Annie. 3,800.00	
2 Terry Pirates 1,300.00	
3 Terry,Annie,Dick Tracy 1,000.00	
4 . . . . 800.00	
5 B:Tom Mix 800.00	
6 . . . . 650.00	
7 . . . . 650.00	

8 . . . . 650.00	
9 . . . . 650.00	
10 Terry,Annie,Tracy 650.00	
11 Terry,Annie,Tracy 500.00	
12 Christmas(c) 500.00	
13 Terry,Annie,Tracy 500.00	
14 Terry,Annie,Tracy 500.00	
15 same 500.00	
16 same 500.00	
17 same 500.00	
18 same 500.00	
19 same 500.00	
20 same 500.00	
21 same 400.00	
22 same 400.00	
23 same 400.00	
24 same 400.00	
25 same 400.00	
26 same 400.00	
27 E:Terry,Annie,Tracy 400.00	
28 A:Gene Autry. 300.00	
29 . . . . 300.00	
30 . . . . 300.00	
31 A:Jim McCoy 300.00	
32 A:Jim McCoy 300.00	
33 . . . . 300.00	
34 . . . . 300.00	
35 Christmas(c),Tex Ritter. 300.00	
36 . . . . 300.00	
37 . . . . 300.00	
38 B:Gang Busters 325.00	
39 . . . . 300.00	
40 . . . . 300.00	
41 . . . . 300.00	
42 . . . . 300.00	
43 F:Gang Busters 325.00	
44 . . . . 225.00	
45 Tarzan(c) 225.00	
46 O:Martan the Marvel Man . . . 350.00	
47 F:Martan the Marvel Man . . . 225.00	
48 F:Martan the Marvel Man . . . 225.00	
49 F:Martan the Marvel Man 225.00	
50 . . . . 225.00	
51 B&O:Voice. 225.00	
52 A:Voice 175.00	
53 F:The Voice 175.00	
54 F:Gang Busters,A:Voice. 175.00	
55 F:Gang Busters 185.00	
56 F:Gang Busters 175.00	
57 F:The Marvel Man 175.00	
58 F:The Marvel Man 175.00	
59 F:The Marvel Man 175.00	
60 O:Prof. Supermind 185.00	
61 Prof. Supermind & Son 150.00	
62 Supermind & Son 150.00	
63 B:Smilin' Jack 150.00	
64 Smilin'Jack,Supermind. 150.00	
65 Professor Supermind 150.00	
66 . . . . 150.00	
67 Gasoline Alley 150.00	
68 F:Smilin' Jack 150.00	
69 F:Smilin' Jack 150.00	
70 F:Smilin' Jack 150.00	
71 F:Smilin' Jack 150.00	
72 B:Owl,Terry & the Pirates. . . . 300.00	
73 F:Terry and the Pirates. 175.00	
74 F:Smilin' Jack 175.00	
75 F:Smilin'Jack,A:Owl 175.00	
76 Captain Midnight 250.00	
77 Captain Midnight 250.00	
78 Captain Midnight 250.00	
79 A:Owl 175.00	
80 F:Smilin' Jack,A:Owl 175.00	
81 F: Terry&thePirates,A:Owl . . . 175.00	
82 F:Smilin' Jack,A:Owl 175.00	
83 F:Smilin'Jack,A:Owl 175.00	
84 F:Smilin' Jack,A:Owl 175.00	
85 F:ThreeLittleGremlins,A:Owl. . 175.00	
86 F:Three Little Gremlins. 125.00	
87 F:Smilin' Jack 125.00	
88 F:Smilin' Jack 125.00	

All comics prices listed are for *Near Mint* condition.

89 F:Smokey Stover 125.00
90 F:Terry and the Pirates 125.00
91 F:Smokey Stover 125.00
92 F:Terry and the Pirates 125.00
93 F:Smilin' Jack 125.00
94 F:Terry and the Pirates 125.00
95 F:Smilin' Jack 125.00
96 F:Gang Busters 125.00
97 F:Smilin' Jack 125.00
98 B:Felix Cat 135.00
99 F:Bang Busters 125.00
100 . . . . 150.00
101 thru 141 . . . . 75.00
142 E:Terry & the Pirates 70.00
143 . . . . 70.00
144 . . . . 70.00
145 F:Harold Teen 70.00

POPULAR ROMANCES
Better Publications
(Standard Comics), Dec., 1949
5 B:Ph(c) 40.00
6 Ph(c) 25.00
7 RP 25.00
8 Ph(c) 25.00
9 Ph(c) 25.00
10 WW 40.00
11 thru 16 . . . . @20.00
17 WE 25.00
18 thru 21 . . . . @25.00
22 thru 27 ATh,Ph(c) . . . . @50.00

SCHOOL DAY ROMANCES
Star Publications
Nov.–Dec., 1949
1 LbC(c),Teen-Age 125.00
2 LbC(c) 85.00
3 LbC(c),Ph(c) 85.00
4 LbC(c),JyD,RonaldReagan . . 135.00
Becomes:

POPULAR TEEN-AGERS
5 LbC(c),Toni Gay,
   Eve Adams 175.00
6 LbC(c),Ginger Bunny,
   Midge Martin 150.00
7 LbC(c) 150.00
8 LbC(c) 150.00
9 LbC(c) 75.00
10 LbC(c) 75.00
11 LbC(c) 50.00
12 LbC(c) 50.00
13 LbC(c),JyD 50.00
14 LbC,WW,Spanking 125.00
15 LbC(c),JyD 40.00
16 . . . . 35.00
17 LbC(c),JyD 35.00
18 LbC(c) 35.00
19 LbC(c) 35.00
20 LbC(c),JyD 45.00
21 LbC(c),JyD 45.00
22 LbC(c) 30.00
23 LbC(c) 30.00

POWER COMICS
Holyoke/Narrative Publ., 1944
1 LbC(c) 1,100.00
2 B:Dr.Mephisto,Hitler(c) 1,200.00
3 LbC(c) 1,200.00
4 LbC(c) 1,100.00

PRIDE OF THE YANKEES
Magazine Enterprises, 1949
1 N#,OW,Ph(c),The Life
   of Lou Gehrig 650.00

PRISON BREAK
Avon Periodicals/Realistic
Sept., 1951
1 WW(c),WW 300.00
2 WW(c),WW,JKu 200.00
3 JD,JO 175.00
4 EK 150.00
5 EK,CI 150.00

Prize Comics #45
© Prize Publications

PRIZE COMICS
Feature Publications
(Prize Publ.), March, 1940
1 O&B:Power Nelson,Jupiter.
   B:Ted O'Neil,Jaxon of
   the Jungle,Bucky Brady,
   Storm Curtis, Rocket(c) . . . 1,700.00
2 B:The Owl 800.00
3 Power Nelson(c) 700.00
4 Power Nelson(c) 700.00
5 A:Dr.Dekkar 650.00
6 A:Dr.Dekkar 650.00
7 S&K,DBr,JK(c),O&B DR Frost,
   Frankenstein,B:GreenLama,
   Capt Gallant,Voodini
   Twist Turner 1,400.00
8 S&K,DBr 750.00
9 S&K,DBr,Black Owl(c) 700.00
10 DBr,Black Owl(c) 600.00
11 DBr,O:Bulldog Denny 550.00
12 DBr 550.00
13 DBR,O&B:Yank and
   Doodle,Bondage(c) 600.00
14 DBr,Black Owl(c) 550.00
15 DBr,Black Owl(c) 550.00
16 DBr,JaB,B:Spike Mason 550.00
17 DBr,Black Owl(c) 550.00
18 DBr,Black Owl(c) 550.00
19 DBr,Yank&Doodle(c) 550.00
20 DBr,Yank&Doodle(c) 550.00
21 DBr,JaB(c),Yank&Doodle(c) . 350.00
22 DBr,Yank&Doodle(c) 350.00
23 DBr,Uncle Sam(c) 350.00
24 DBr,Abe Lincoln(c) 350.00
25 DBr,JaB,Yank&Doodle(c) . . . 350.00
26 DBr,JaB,JaB(c),Liberty
   Bell(c) 350.00
27 DBr,Yank&Doodle(c) 225.00
28 DBr,Yank&Doodle(c) 200.00
29 DBr,JaB(c)Yank&Doodle(c) . . 200.00
30 DBr,Yank&Doodle(c) 225.00
31 DBr,Yank&Doodle(c) 200.00
32 DBr,Yank&Doodle(c) 200.00

33 DBr,Bondage(c),Yank
   & Doodle 225.00
34 DBr,O:Airmale;New
   Black Owl 225.00
35 DBr,B:Flying Fist & Bingo 125.00
36 DBr,Yank&Doodle(c) 125.00
37 DBr,I:Stampy,Hitler(c) 200.00
38 DBr,B.Owl,Yank&Doodle(c) . . 125.00
39 DBr,B.Owl,Yank&Doodle(c) . . 125.00
40 DBr,B.Owl,Yank&Doodle(c) . . 125.00
41 DBr,B.Owl,Yank&Doodle(c) . . 125.00
42 DBr,B.Owl,Yank&Doodle(c) . . 100.00
43 DBr,B.Owl,Yank&Doodle(c) . . 100.00
44 DBr, B&I:Boom Boom
   Brannigan 100.00
45 DBr 100.00
46 DBr 100.00
47 DBr 100.00
48 DBr,B:Prince Ra;Bondage(c) . 125.00
49 DBr,Boom Boom(c) 90.00
50 DBr,Farnkenstein(c) 100.00
51 DBr 90.00
52 DBr, B:Sir Prize 90.00
53 DBr, The Man Who Could
   Read Features 100.00
54 DBr 90.00
55 DBr,Yank&Doodle(c) 90.00
56 DBr,Boom Boom (c) 90.00
57 DBr,Santa Claus(c) 90.00
58 DBr,The Poisoned Punch 90.00
59 DBr,Boom Boom(c) 90.00
60 DBr,Sir Prise(c) 90.00
61 DBr,The Man wih the
   Fighting Feet 90.00
62 DBr,Hck(c),Yank&Doodle(c) . . . 90.00
63 DBr,S&K,S&K(c),Boom
   Boom(c) 100.00
64 DBr,Blackowl Retires 90.00
65 DBr,DBr(c),Frankenstein 90.00
66 DBr,DBr(c),Frankenstein 90.00
67 DBr,B:Brothers in Crime 90.00
68 DBr,RP(c) 90.00
Becomes:

PRIZE COMICS WESTERN
69 ACa(c),B:Dusty Ballew 100.00
70 ACa(c) 75.00
71 ACa(c) 75.00
72 ACa(c),JSe 75.00
73 ACa(c) 75.00
74 ACa(c) 75.00
75 JSe,S&K(c),6-Gun Showdown
   at Rattlesnake Gulch 80.00
76 Ph(c),Randolph Scott 100.00
77 Ph(c),JSe,Streets of
   Laredo,movie 75.00
78 Ph(c),JSe,HK,Bullet
   Code, movie 120.00
79 Ph(c),JSe,Stage to
   China, movie 120.00
80 Ph(c),Gunsmoke Justice 75.00
81 Ph(c),The Man Who Shot
   Billy The Kid 75.00
82 Ph(c),MBi,JSe&BE,Death
   Draws a Circle 75.00
83 JSe,S&K(c) 70.00
84 JSe 50.00
85 JSe,B:American Eagle 150.00
86 JSe 60.00
87 JSe&BE 65.00
88 JSe&BE 65.00
89 JSe&BE 65.00
90 JSe&BE 65.00
91 JSe&BE,JSe&BE(c) 65.00
92 JSe,JSe&BE(c) 65.00
93 JSe,JSe&BE(c) 65.00
94 JSe&BE,JSe&BE(c) 65.00
95 JSe,JSe&BE(c) 65.00
96 JSe,JSe&BE,JSe&BE(c) 65.00
97 JSe,JSe&BE,JSeBE(c) 65.00

GOLDEN AGE

98 JSe&BE,JSe&BE(c) 65.00
99 JSe&BE,JSe&BE(c) 65.00
100 JSe,JSe(c). 85.00
101 JSe 65.00
102 JSe 65.00
103 JSe 65.00
104 JSe 65.00
105 JSe 65.00
106 JSe 50.00
107 JSe 50.00
108 JSe 70.00
109 JSe&AW 80.00
110 JSe&BE 75.00
111 JSe&BE 75.00
112 . . . . 50.00
113 AW&JSe 75.00
114 MMe,B:The Drifter 35.00
115 MMe 35.00
116 MMe 35.00
117 MMe 35.00
118 MMe,E:The Drifter 35.00
119 Nov/Dec'56 . . . . 35.00

PSYCHOANALYSIS
E.C. Comics
March–April, 1955
1 JKa,JKa(c) 150.00
2 JKa,JKa(c) 125.00
3 JKa,JKa(c) 125.00
4 JKa,JKa(c) Sept.–Oct. 1955 . . 125.00

PUBLIC ENEMIES
D.S. Publishing Co., 1948
1 AMc. 150.00
2 AMc 150.00
3 AMc 75.00
4 AMc 75.00
5 AMc 75.00
6 AMc 75.00
7 AMc,Eye Injury 90.00
8 . . . . 75.00
9 . . . . 75.00

PUNCH AND JUDY COMICS
Hillman Periodicals, 1944
1 (fa) 100.00
2 . . . . 50.00
3 . . . . 40.00
4 thru 12 . . . . @35.00
2-1 . . . . 30.00
2-2 JK 100.00
2-3 . . . . 30.00
2-4 . . . . 30.00
2-5 . . . . 30.00
2-6 . . . . 30.00
2-7 . . . . 30.00
2-8 . . . . 30.00
2-9 . . . . 30.00
2-10 JK 100.00
2-11 JK. 100.00
2-12 JK. 100.00
3-1 JK 100.00
3-2 . . . . 90.00
3-3 . . . . 25.00
3-4 . . . . 25.00
3-5 . . . . 25.00
3-6 . . . . 25.00
3-7 . . . . 25.00
3-8 . . . . 25.00
3-9 . . . . 25.00

PUNCH COMICS
Harry 'A' Chesler, Dec., 1941
1 B:Mr.E,The Sky Chief,Hale
  the Magician,Kitty Kelly . . . 1,000.00
2 A:Capt.Glory. 650.00

Punch Comics #17
© Harry A Chesler

3-8 Do Not Exist
9 B:Rocket Man & Rocket
  girl,Master Ken. 550.00
10 JCo,A:Sky Chief. 500.00
11 JCo,O:Master Key,A:Little
  Nemo 500.00
12 A:Rocket Boy,Capt.Glory 650.00
13 Ric(c). 500.00
14 GT. 400.00
15 FSm(c) 400.00
16 . . . . 400.00
17 . . . . 400.00
18 FSm(c),Bondage(c),Drug 500.00
19 FSm(c) 400.00
20 Women semi-nude(c). 650.00
21 Drug 400.00
22 I:Baxter,Little Nemo 200.00
23 A:Little Nemo. 200.00

PUPPET COMICS
Dougherty, Co., Spring, 1946
1 Funny Animal 35.00
2 . . . . 30.00

PURPLE CLAW, THE
Minoan Publishing Co./
Toby Press, Jan., 1953
1 O:Purple Claw 200.00
2 and 3 . . . . @150.00

PUZZLE FUN COMICS
George W. Dougherty Co.
Spring, 1946
1 PGn 150.00
2 . . . . 125.00

QUEEN OF THE WEST, DALE EVANS
Dell Publishing Co.
July, 1953
(1) *see Dell Four Color #479*
(1) *see Dell Four Color #528*
3 ATh, Ph(c) all 75.00
4 ATh,RsM 65.00
5 RsM. 45.00
6 RsM. 45.00
7 RsM. 45.00
8 RsM. 45.00
9 RsM. 45.00
10 RsM. 45.00

11 . . . . 32.00
12 RsM 40.00
13 RsM 40.00
14 RsM 40.00
15 RsM 40.00
16 RsM 40.00
17 RsM 40.00
18 RsM 40.00
19 . . . . 30.00
20 RsM 40.00
21 . . . . 30.00
22 RsM 40.00

RACKET SQUAD IN ACTION
Capitol Stories/
Charlton Comics
May–June, 1952
1 Carnival(c) 200.00
2 . . . . 100.00
3 Roulette 100.00
4 FFr(c) 100.00
5 Just off the Boat 125.00
6 The Kidnap Racket. 85.00
7 . . . . 75.00
8 . . . . 75.00
9 2 Fisted fix 75.00
10 . . . . 75.00
11 SD,SD(c),Racing(c) 175.00
12 JoS,SD(c),Explosion(c) 325.00
13 JoS(c),The Notorious Modelling
  Agency Racket,Acid 75.00
14 DG(c),Drug 100.00
15 Photo Extortion Racket 60.00
16 thru 28 . . . . @60.00
29,March, 1958 . . . . 75.00

RAGGEDY ANN AND ANDY
Dell Publishing Co., 1942
1 Billy & Bonnie Bee 250.00
2 . . . . 125.00
3 DNo,B:Egbert Elephant 125.00
4 DNo,WK 150.00
5 DNo 100.00
6 DNo 100.00
7 Little Black Sambo 100.00
8 . . . . 100.00
9 . . . . 100.00
10 . . . . 100.00
11 . . . . 75.00
12 . . . . 75.00
13 . . . . 75.00
14 . . . . 75.00
15 . . . . 75.00
16 thru 20. . . . . @75.00
21 Alice in Wonderland. 65.00
22 thru 27. . . . . @45.00
28 WK 50.00
29 thru 39. . . . . @45.00

RALPH KINER HOME RUN KING
Fawcett Publications, 1950
1 N#, Life Story of the
  Famous Pittsburgh Slugger. . 450.00

RAMAR OF THE JUNGLE
Toby Press/
Charlton Comics, 1954
1 Ph(c),TV Show 125.00
2 Ph(c) 75.00
3 . . . . 75.00

4	75.00
5 Sept '56	75.00

RANGE ROMANCES
Comics Magazines
(Quality Comics), Dec., 1949

1 PGn(c),PGn	150.00
2 RC(c),RC	175.00
3 RC,Ph(c)	125.00
4 RC,Ph(c)	125.00
5 RC,PGn,Ph(c)	125.00

RANGERS OF FREEDOM
Flying Stories, Inc.
(Fiction House), Oct., 1941

1 I:Ranger Girl & Rangers of Freedom;V:Super-Brain	1,700.00
2 V:Super -Brain	700.00
3 Bondage(c) The Headsman of Hate	600.00
4 Hawaiian Inferno	500.00
5 RP,V:Super-Brain	500.00
6 RP,Bondage(c);Bugles of the Damned	500.00
7 RP,Death to Tojo's Butchers	400.00

Becomes:

Rangers #7
© Fiction House

RANGERS COMICS

8 RP,B:US Rangers	400.00
9 GT,BLb,Commando Steel for Slant Eyes	400.00
10 BLb,Bondage (c)	425.00
11 Raiders of the Purple Death	350.00
12 A:Commando Rangers	350.00
13 Grl,B:Commando Ranger	350.00
14 Grl,Bondage(c)	350.00
15 GT,Grl,Bondage(c)	350.00
16 Grl,GT;Burma Raid	375.00
17 GT,GT,Bondage(c),Raiders of the Red Dawn	375.00
18 GT	375.00
19 GE,Blb,GT,Bondage(c)	300.00
20 GT	275.00
21 GT,Bondage(c)	300.00
22 GT,B&O:Firehair	225.00
23 GT,BLb,B:Kazanda	200.00
24 Bondage(c)	225.00
25 Bondage(c)	225.00
26 Angels From Hell	200.00
27 Bondage(c)	225.00
28 BLb,E:Kazanda;B&O Tiger	

Man	225.00
29 Bondage(c)	225.00
30 BLb,B:Crusoe Island	235.00
31 BLb,Bondage(c)	200.00
32 BLb	175.00
33 BLb,Drug	175.00
34 BLb	175.00
35 BLB,Bondage(c)	200.00
36 BLb,MB	175.00
37 BLb,Mb	175.00
38 BLb,MB,GE,Bondage(c)	200.00
39 BLb,GE	175.00
40 BLb,GE,BLb(c)	175.00
41 BLb,GE	150.00
42 BLb,GE	150.00
43 BLb,GE	150.00
44 BLb,GE	150.00
45 BLb,GEl	150.00
46 BLb,GE	135.00
47 BLb,JGr	135.00
48 BLb,JGr	135.00
49 BLb,JGr	135.00
50 BLb,JGr,Bondage(c)	150.00
51 BLb,JGr	135.00
52 BLb,JGr,Bondage(c)	150.00
53 BLb,JGr,Prisoners of Devil Pass	135.00
54 JGr,When The Wild Commanches Ride	135.00
55 JGr,Massacre Guns at Pawnee Pass	135.00
56 JGr, Gun Smuggler of Apache Mesa	135.00
57 JGr,Redskins to the Rescue	135.00
58 JGr,Brides of the Buffalo Men	135.00
59 JGr,Plunder Portage	135.00
60 JGr, Buzzards of Bushwack Trail	135.00
61 BWh(c)Devil Smoke at Apache Basin	100.00
62 BWh(c)B:Cowboy Bob	100.00
63 BWh(c)	100.00
64 BWh(c)B:Suicide Smith	100.00
65 BWh(c):Wolves of the Overland Trail,Bondage(c)	110.00
66 BWh(c)	100.00
67 BWh(c)B:Space Rangers	100.00
68 BWh(c);Cargo for Coje	100.00
69 BWh(c);Great Red Death Ray	100.00

REAL CLUE CRIME STORIES
(see CLUE COMICS)

REAL FUNNIES
Nedor Publishing Co.
Jan., 1943

1 (fa)	135.00
2 and 3 (fa)	@65.00

REAL HEROES COMICS
Parents' Magazine Institiute
Sept., 1941

1 HcK,Franklin Roosevelt	250.00
2 J, Edgar Hoover	125.00
3 General Wavell	100.00
4 Chiang Kai Shek	100.00
5 Stonewall Jackson	100.00
6 Lou Gehrig	150.00
7 Chennault and his Flying Tigers	75.00
8 Admiral Nimitz	75.00
9 The Panda Man	60.00
10 Carl Akeley-Jungle	

Adventurer	60.00
11 Wild Jack Howard	55.00
12 General Robert L Eichelberger	50.00
13 HcK,Victory at Climback	50.00
14 Pete Gray	50.00
15 Alexander Mackenzie	50.00
16 Balto of Nome Oct '46	50.00

REAL LIFE STORY OF FESS PARKER
Dell Publishing Co., 1955

1	75.00

REALISTIC ROMANCES
Avon Periodicals/
Realistic Comics
July–Aug., 1951

1 Ph(c)	150.00
2 Ph(c)	75.00
3 P(c)	60.00
4 P(c)	60.00
5 thru 14	@60.00
15	50.00
16 Drug	75.00
17	50.00

REAL LIFE COMICS
Visual Editions/Better/
Standard/Nedor, Sept., 1941

1 ASh(c),Lawrence of Arabia,Uncle Sam(c)	400.00
2 ASh(c),Liberty(c)	175.00
3 Adolph Hitler(c)	450.00
4 ASh(c)Robert Fulton, Charles DeGaulle	125.00
5 ASh(c)Alexander the Great	125.00
6 ASh(c)John Paul Jones,CDR	100.00
7 ASh(c)Thomas Jefferson	100.00
8 Leonardo Da Vinci	100.00
9 US Coast Guard Issue	100.00
10 Sir Hubert Wilkens	100.00
11 Odyssey on a Raft	75.00
12 ImpossibleLeatherneck	75.00
13 ASh(c)The Eternal Yank	75.00
14 Sir Isaac Newton	75.00
15 William Tell	75.00
16 Marco Polo	75.00
17 Albert Einstein	85.00
18 Ponce De Leon	75.00
19 The Fighting Seabees	75.00
20 Joseph Pulitzer	75.00
21 Admiral Farragut	50.00
22 Thomas Paine	50.00
23 Pedro Menendez	50.00
24 Babe Ruth	125.00
25 Marcus Whitman	50.00
26 Benvenuto Cellini	50.00
27 A Bomb Story	125.00
28 Robert Blake	50.00
29 Daniel DeFoe	50.00
30 Baron Robert Clive	50.00
31 Anthony Wayne	50.00
32 Frank Sinatra	75.00
33 Frederick Douglas	50.00
34 Paul Revere,Jimmy Stewart	60.00
35 Rudyard Kipling	50.00
36 Story of the Automobile	50.00
37 Francis Manion	50.00
38 Richard Henry Dana	45.00
39 Samuel FB Morse	40.00
40 FG,ASh(c),Hans Christian Anderson	45.00
41 Abraham Lincoln,Jimmy Foxx	60.00
42 Joseph Conrad,Fred Allen	50.00
43 Louis Braille,O.W.Holmes	45.00
44 Citizens of Tomorrow	45.00

GOLDEN AGE

Real Life Comics #25
© *Standard Comics*

45 ASh(c),Francois Villon 65.00
46 The Pony Express 65.00
47 ASh(c),Montezuma 45.00
48 . . . . 45.00
49 ASh(c),Gene Bearden,
    Baseball 50.00
50 FF,ASh(c),Lewis & Clark 175.00
51 GE,ASh(c),Sam Houston 125.00
52 GE,FF,ASh(c),JSe&BE
    Leif Erickson. 160.00
53 JSe&BE,Henry Wells &
    William Fargo 65.00
54 GT,Alexander Graham Bell. . . . 65.00
55 ASh(c),JSe&BE, The James
    Brothers 65.00
56 JSe&BE. 65.00
57 JSe&BE. 65.00
58 JSe&BE,Jim Reaves 75.00
59 FF,JSe&BE,Battle Orphan
    Sept '52 . . . . 65.00

REAL LOVE
(see HAP HAZARD
COMICS)

REAL WEST ROMANCES
**Crestwoood Publishing Co./
Prize Publ., April–May, 1949**
1 S&K,Ph(c) 125.00
2 Ph(c),Spanking. 90.00
3 JSe,BE,Ph(c) 40.00
4 S&K,JSe,BE,Ph(c) 75.00
5 S&K,MMe,JSe,Audie
    Murphy Ph(c) 65.00
6 S&K,JSe,BE,Ph(c) 50.00

RECORD BOOK OF
FAMOUS POLICE CASES
St. John Publishing Co., 1949
1 N#,JKu,MB(c) 275.00

RED ARROW
**P.L. Publishing Co.
May, 1951**
1 Bondage(c). 75.00
2 . . . . 50.00
3 P(c) 40.00

RED BAND COMICS
**Enwil Associates
Nov., 1944**
1 The Bogeyman 250.00
2 O:Bogeyman,same(c)as#1 . . . 200.00
3 A:Captain Wizard 175.00
4 May '45,Repof#3,Same(c). . . . 175.00

RED CIRCLE COMICS
**Enwil Associates
(Rural Home Public)
Jan., 1945**
1 B:Red Riot,The Prankster 225.00
2 LSt,A:The Judge. 175.00
3 LSt,LSt(c) 150.00
4 LSt,LSt(c) covers of #4
    stapled over other comics. . . 150.00

TRAIL BLAZERS
Street & Smith, Jan., 1942
1 Wright Brothers. 150.00
2 Benjamin Franklin,Dodgers . . . 175.00
3 Red Barber,Yankees 255.00
4 Famous War song 125.00
Becomes:

RED DRAGON COMICS
5 JaB(c),B&O:Red Rover:
    B:Capt.Jack Comkmando
    Rex King&Jet,Minute Man . . 800.00
6 O:Red Dragon 1,500.00
7 The Curse of the
    Boneless Men 1,000.00
8 China V:Japan 550.00
9 The Reducing Ray,Jan '44 . . . 550.00
(2nd Series) Nov., 1947
1 B:Red Dragon. 700.00
2 BP 500.00
3 BP,BP(c),I:Dr Neff 450.00
4 BP,BP(c). 550.00
5 BP,BP(c). 400.00
6 BP,BP(c). 400.00
7 BP,BP(c),May 49 . . . . 400.00

RED MASK
(see TIM HOLT)

RED RABBIT
**Dearfield/
J. Charles Lave Publ. Co.
Jan., 1941**
1 (fa) 55.00
2 . . . . 30.00
3 thru 10 . . . . @20.00
11 thru 22 . . . . @18.00

RED SEAL COMICS
**Harry 'A' Chesler, Jr./Superior
Oct., 1945**
14 GT,Bondage(c),Black Dwarf . . 500.00
15 GT,Torture 325.00
16 GT. 450.00
17 GT,Lady Satan,Sky Chief 325.00
18 Lady Satan,Sky Chief 325.00
19 Lady Satan,Sky Chief 300.00
20 Lady Satan,Sky Chief 300.00
21 Lady Satan,Sky Chief 300.00
22 Rocketman 200.00

REDSKIN
**Youthful Magazines
Sept., 1950**
1 Redskin,Bondage(c) 75.00
2 Apache Dance of Death 50.00
3 Daniel Boone 35.00
4 Sitting Bull- Red Devil
    of the Black Hills. 35.00
5 . . . . 35.00
6 Geronimo- Terror of the
    Desert,Bondage 45.00
7 Firebrand of the Sioux 35.00
8 . . . . 35.00
9 . . . . 35.00
10 Dead Man's Magic. 35.00
11 . . . . 35.00
12 Quanah Parker,Bondage(c) . . . 45.00
Becomes:

FAMOUS WESTERN
BADMEN
13 Redskin- Last of the
    Comanches 40.00
14 . . . . 25.00
15 The Dalton Boys Apr '52 . . . . . 25.00

REMEMBER
PEARL HARBOR
Street & Smith, 1942
1 N# JaB,Battle of the
    Pacific,Uncle Sam(c) 350.00

RETURN OF THE
OUTLAW
**Minoan Publishing Co.
Feb., 1953**
1 Billy The Kid 50.00
2 . . . . 30.00
3 thru 11 . . . . @20.00

REVEALING ROMANCES
**A.A. Wyn
(Ace Magazines), Sept., 1949**
1 . . . . 40.00
2 . . . . 20.00
3 thru 6 . . . . @15.00

REX ALLEN COMICS
**Dell Publishing Co.
Feb., 1951**
(1) *see Dell Four Color #316*
2 Ph(c) all 75.00
3 thru 10 . . . . @60.00
11 thru 23 . . . . @40.00
24 ATh 50.00
25 thru 31 . . . . @40.00

REX DEXTER OF MARS
**Fox Features Syndicate
Autumn, 1940**
1 DBr,DBr(c) Battle ofKooba . . 1,500.00

RIBTICKLER
Fox Features Syndicate, 1945
1 . . . . 70.00
2 . . . . 35.00
3 Cosmo Cat. 25.00
4 thru 6 . . . . @20.00
7 Cosmo Cat. 22.00
8 thru 9 . . . . @20.00

RIN TIN TIN
Dell Publishing Co.
Nov., 1952
(1) *see Dell Four Color #434*
(1) *see Dell Four Color #476*
(1) *see Dell Four Color #523*
4 thru 10 Ph(c) all . . . . @50.00
11 thru 20 . . . . @70.00

Rocket Comics #2
© *Hillman Periodicals*

ROCKET COMICS
Hillman Periodicals
March, 1940
1 O:Red Roberts;B:Rocket
Riley,Phantom Ranger,Steel
Shank,Buzzard Baynes,Lefty
Larson,The Defender,Man
with 1,000 Faces 2,000.00
2 . . . . 600.00
3 May '40 E:All Features 1,000.00

ROCKET KELLY
Fox Features Syndicate
Autumn, 1945–Oct. Nov. 1946
N#. 200.00
1 . . . . 200.00
2 A:The Puppeteer 150.00
3 thru 6 . . . . @125.00

ROCKETMAN
Ajax/Farrell Publications
June, 1952
1 Space Stories of the Future . . 300.00

ROCKET SHIP X
Fox Features Syndicate
Sept., 1951
1 . . . . 500.00
2 N# Variant of Original 325.00

ROCKY LANE WESTERN
Fawcett/Charlton Comics
May, 1949
1 Ph(c)B:Rocky Lane,Slim
Pickins 800.00
2 Ph(c) 300.00
3 Ph(c) 200.00
4 Ph(c)CCB,Rail Riders
Rampage,F Capt Tootsie . . . 200.00
5 Ph(c)The Missing

Stagecoaches. 200.00
6 Ph(c)Ghost Town Showdown . 150.00
7 Ph(c)The Border Revolt 175.00
8 Ph(c)The Sunset Feud 175.00
9 Ph(c)Hermit of the Hills. 175.00
10 Ph(c)Badman's Reward 150.00
11 Ph(c)Fool's Gold Fiasco 125.00
12 Ph(c),CCB,Coyote Breed
F:Capt Tootsie,Giant. 125.00
13 Ph(c),Giant 125.00
14 Ph(c) 100.00
15 Ph(c)B:Black Jacks
Hitching Post,Giant. 110.00
16 Ph(c),Giant 100.00
17 Ph(c),Giant 100.00
18 Ph(c) 110.00
19 Ph(c),Giant 115.00
20 Ph(c)The Rodeo Rustler
E:Slim Pickens 115.00
21 Ph(c)B: Dee Dickens 100.00
22 Ph(c). 90.00
23 thru 30 . . . . @100.00
31 thru 40 . . . . @90.00
41 thru 55 . . . . @90.00
56 thru 60 . . . . @65.00
61 thru 70 . . . . @60.00
71 thru 87 . . . . @50.00

ROD CAMERON WESTERN
Fawcett Publications
Feb., 1950
1 Ph(c) 400.00
2 Ph(c) 175.00
3 Ph(c),Seven Cities of Cipiola . 150.00
4 Ph(c),Rip-Roaring Wild West . 125.00
5 Ph(c),Six Gun Sabotage 125.00
6 Ph(c),Medicine Bead Murders 125.00
7 Ph(c),Wagon Train Of Death . 125.00
8 Ph(c),Bayou Badman 125.00
9 Ph(c),Rustlers Ruse 125.00
10 Ph(c),White Buffalo Trail . . . 125.00
11 Ph(c),Lead Poison 100.00
12 thru 19 Ph(c) . . . . @100.00
20 Phc(c),Great Army Hoax . . . 100.00

ROLY-POLY COMICS
Green Publishing Co., 1945
1 B:Red Rube&Steel Sterling . . 200.00
6 A:Blue Cycle 100.00
10 A:Red Rube. 100.00
11 . . . . 100.00
12 . . . . 100.00
13 . . . . 100.00
14 A:Black Hood. 100.00
15 A:Steel Fist;1946 . . . . 225.00

ROMANCE AND CONFESSION STORIES
St. John Publishing Co., 1949
1 MB(c),MB. 250.00

ROMANTIC LOVE
Avon Periodicals/Realistic
Sept.–Oct., 1949
1 P(c) 135.00
2 P(c) 85.00
3 P(c) 75.00
4 Ph(c) 75.00
5 P(c) 75.00
6 Ph(c),Drug,Thrill Crazy 100.00
7 P(c) 75.00
8 P(c) 75.00
9 EK,P(c). 85.00

10 thru 11 P(c) . . . . @80.00
12 EK. 85.00
20 . . . . 75.00
21 . . . . 75.00
22 EK. 75.00
23 EK. 75.00

ROMANTIC MARRIAGE
Ziff-Davis/
St. John Publishing Co.
Nov.–Dec., 1950
1 Ph(c),Selfish wife 125.00
2 P(c),Mother's Boy. 60.00
3 P(c),Hen Peck House 50.00
4 P(c) 50.00
5 Ph(c) 50.00
6 Ph(c) 40.00
7 Ph(c) 40.00
8 P(c) 40.00
9 P(c) 40.00
10 P/PH(c) 100.00
11 . . . . 40.00
12 . . . . 40.00
13 Ph(c) 40.00
14 thru 20 . . . . @40.00
20 Ph(c) 40.00
21 . . . . 40.00
22 . . . . 40.00
23 MB 45.00
24 . . . . 40.00

ROMANTIC PICTURE NOVELETTES
Magazine Enterprises, 1946
1 Mary Wothr adventure 125.00

ROMANTIC SECRETS
Fawcett Publ./Charlton Comics
Sept., 1949
1 Ph(c) 100.00
2 MSy(c). 50.00
3 MSy(c) 50.00
4 GE 60.00
5 BP 55.00
6 . . . . 25.00
7 BP 25.00
8 . . . . 25.00
9 GE 35.00
10 BP 30.00
11 . . . . 25.00
12 BP 30.00
13 . . . . 25.00
14 . . . . 25.00
15 . . . . 25.00
16 BP,MSy 30.00
17 BP 30.00
18 . . . . 25.00
19 . . . . 25.00
20 BP.MBi 30.00
21 . . . . 20.00
22 . . . . 20.00
23 . . . . 18.00
24 GE. 40.00
25 MSy. 18.00
26 BP,MSy 20.00
27 MSy. 18.00
28 . . . . 18.00
29 BP 20.00
30 thru 32 . . . . @18.00
33 MSy. 20.00
34 BP 20.00
35 . . . . 18.00
36 BP 20.00
37 BP 20.00
38 thru 52 . . . . @18.00

All comics prices listed are for *Near Mint* condition.

ROMANTIC STORY
Fawcett Publ./Charlton Comics
Nov., 1949
1 Ph(c)	75.00
2 Ph(c)	40.00
3 Ph(c)	30.00
4 Ph(c)	30.00
5 Ph(c)	30.00
6 Ph(c)	30.00
7 BP,Ph(c)	25.00
8 BP,Ph(c)	25.00
9 Ph(c)	22.00
10 Ph(c)	22.00
11 Ph(c)	22.00
12 Ph(c)	22.00
13 Ph(c)	22.00
14 Ph(c)	22.00
15 GE,Ph(c)	35.00
16 BP,Ph(c)	25.00
17 Ph(c)	20.00
18 Ph(c)	20.00
19 Ph(c)	20.00
20 BP,Ph(c)	22.00
22 ATh,Ph(c)	18.00

Charlton Comics
23.	15.00
24 Ph(c)	15.00
25 thru 29	@15.00
30 BP	20.00
31 thru 39	@15.00

ROMANTIC WESTERN
Fawcett Publications
Winter, 1949
1 Ph(c)	125.00
2 Ph(c),AW,AMc	135.00
3 Ph(c)	100.00

ROMEO TUBBS
(see MY SECRET LIFE)

ROUNDUP
D.S. Publishing Co.
July–Aug., 1948
1 HcK	125.00
2 Drug	100.00
3	75.00
4	75.00
5 Male Bondage	85.00

ROY CAMPANELLA, BASEBALL HERO
Fawcett Publications, 1950
N# Ph(c),Life Story of the
   Battling Dodgers Catcher . . . 500.00

ROY ROGERS
Dell Publishing Co.
1 photo (c)	850.00
2	300.00
3	200.00
4	200.00
5	200.00
6 thru 10	@150.00
11 thru 20	@125.00
21 thru 30	@100.00
31 thru 46	@75.00
47 thru 50	@65.00
51 thru 56	@50.00
57 Drug	65.00
58 thru 70	@50.00
71 thru 80	@40.00
81 thru 91	@35.00
Becomes:

Roy Rogers and Trigger
© Dell Publishing Co.

ROY ROGERS AND TRIGGER
92 thru 99	@35.00
100	50.00
101 thru 118	@35.00
119 thru 125 ATn	@50.00
126 thru 131	@40.00
132 thru 144 RsM	@45.00
145	50.00

ROY ROGER'S TRIGGER
Dell Publishing Co.
May, 1951
(1) *see Dell Four Color #329*	
2 Ph(c)	125.00
3 P(c)	40.00
4 P(c)	40.00
5 P(c)	40.00
6 thru 17 P(c)	@30.00

RULAH, JUNGLE GODDESS
(see ZOOT COMICS)

SAARI, THE JUNGLE GODDESS
P.L. Publishing Co.
Nov., 1951
1 The Bantu Blood Curse 300.00

SABU, ELEPHANT BOY
Fox Features Syndicate
June, 1950
1(30) WW,Ph(c)	175.00
2 JKa,Ph(c),Aug.'50	125.00

HAPPY HOULIHANS
Fables Publications
(E.C. Comics), Autumn, 1947
1 O:Moon Girl	400.00
2	250.00
Becomes:

SADDLE JUSTICE
3 HcK,JCr,AF	300.00
4 AF,JCr	275.00
5 AF,Grl,WI	250.00

6 AF,Grl	250.00
7 AF,Grl	250.00
8 AF,Grl,WI	250.00
Becomes:

SADDLE ROMANCES
9 Grl(c),Grl	300.00
10 AF(c),WW	325.00
11 AF(c),Grl	275.00

SAD SACK
Harvey Publications
Sept. 1949
1 I:Little Dot	400.00
2	200.00
3	100.00
4 thru 10	@75.00
11 thru 21	50.00
22 Back in the Army Again, The Specialist	35.00
23 thru 50	@20.00
51 thru 100	@15.00
100 thru 150	@7.50
151 thru 200	@5.00
200 thru 287	@4.00
See also Other Pub. (Color)

The Saint #1
© Avon Periodicals

SAINT, THE
Avon Periodicals
Aug., 1947
1 JKa,JKa(c),Bondage(c)	550.00
2	300.00
3 Rolled Stocking Leg(c)	225.00
4 MB(c)	200.00
5 Spanking Panel	275.00
6 B:Miss Fury	325.00
7 P(c),Detective Cases(c)	175.00
8 P(c),Detective Cases"(c)	150.00
9 EK(c),The Notorious Murder Mob	150.00
10 WW,P(c),V:The Communist Menace	175.00
11 P(c),Wanted For Robbery	100.00
12 P(c),The Blowpipe Murders March, 1952	125.00

SAM HILL PRIVATE EYE
Close-Up Publications, 1950
1 The Double Trouble Caper	100.00
2	55.00
3	50.00
4 Negligee panels	65.00
5 thru 7	@40.00

SAMSON
Fox Features Syndicate
Autumn, 1940
1 BP,GT,A:Wing Turner 1,700.00
2 BP,A:Dr. Fung 700.00
3 JSh(c),A:Navy Jones 500.00
4 WE,B:Yarko 450.00
5 WE 450.00
6 WE,O:The Topper;Sept'41 . . . 450.00

SAMSON
Ajax Farrell Publ
(Four Star)
April, 1955
12 The Electric Curtain 200.00
13 Assignment Danger 175.00
14 The Red Raider;Aug'55 . . . . . 175.00

SANDS OF THE
SOUTH PACIFIC
Toby Press, Jan., 1953
1 2-Fisted Romantic Adventure . 150.00

SCHOOL DAY
ROMANCES
(see POPULAR TEEN-
AGERS)

Science Comics #7
© Fox Features Syndicate

SCIENCE COMICS
Fox Features Syndicate
Feb., 1940
1 GT,LF(c),O&B:Electro,Perisphere
Payne,The Eagle,Navy Jones;
B:Marga,Cosmic Carson,
Dr. Doom; Bondage(c) . . . 3,500.00
2 GT,LF(c) 1,600.00
3 GT,LF(c),Dynamo. 1,400.00
4 JK,Cosmic Carson 1,200.00
5 Giant Comiscope Offer
Eagle(c) 700.00
6 Dynamop(c) 700.00
7 Bondage(c),Dynamo 700.00
8 Sept., 1940 Eagle(c) 650.00

SCIENCE COMICS
Humor Publications
Jan., 1946
1 RP(c),Story of the A-Bomb . . . 100.00
2 RP(c),How Museum Pieces
Are Assembled 45.00
3 AF,RP(c),How Underwater
Tunnels Are Made 75.00
4 RP(c),Behind the Scenes at
A TV Broadcast 30.00
5 The Story of the World's
Bridges; Sept., 1946 . . . . 35.00

SCIENCE COMICS
Ziff-Davis Publ. Co.
May, 1946
N# Used For A Mail Order
Test Market 300.00

SCIENCE COMICS
Export Publication Enterprises
March, 1951
1 How to resurrect a dead rat . . . 50.00

SCOOP COMICS
Harry 'A' Chesler Jr.
Nov., 1941
1 I&B:Rocketman&Rocketgirl;B:Dan
Hastings;O&B:Master Key . 1,000.00
2 A:Rocketboy,Eye Injury 1,100.00
3 Partial rep. of #2 . . . . 500.00
4 thru 7 do not exist
8 1945 . . . . 350.00

SCREAM COMICS
Humor Publ./Current Books
(Ace Magazines)
Autumn, 1944
1 . . . . 100.00
2 . . . . 50.00
3 . . . . 40.00
4 thru 15 . . . . @40.00
16 I:Lily Belle 45.00
17 . . . . 30.00
18 Drug 40.00
19 . . . . 30.00
Becomes:

ANDY COMICS
20 Teenage 25.00
21 . . . . 25.00
Becomes:

ERNIE COMICS
22 Teenage 30.00
23 thru 25 . . . . @20.00
Becomes:

ALL LOVE ROMANCES
26 Ernie 25.00
27 LbC 32.00
28 thru 32 . . . . @15.00

(Capt. Silvers Log of...)
SEA HOUND, THE
Avon Periodicals, 1945
N# The Esmerelda's Treasure . . . 90.00
2 Adventures in Brazil 70.00
3 Louie the Llama 70.00
4 In Greed & Vengence;
Jan-Feb, 1946 . . . . 70.00

SECRET LOVES
Comics Magazines
(Quality Comics)
Nov., 1949
1 BWa(c) 150.00
2 BWa(c),Lingerie(c) 125.00
3 RC 75.00
4 . . . . 50.00
5 Boom Town Babe 75.00
6 . . . . 50.00

SECRET MYSTERIES
(see CRIME MYSTERIES)

SELECT DETECTIVE
D.S. Publishing Co.
Aug.–Sept., 1948
1 MB,Exciting New Mystery
Cases. 150.00
2 MB,AMc,Dead Men.... . . . . . . 100.00
3 Face in theFrame;Dec-Jan'48 . . 75.00

SERGEANT PRESTON
OF THE YUKON
Dell Publishing Co., Aug., 1951
(1 thru 4) *see Dell Four Color #344;*
#373, 397, 419
5 thru 10 P(c). . . . . @65.00
11 P(c) 50.00
12 P(c). 50.00
13 P(c),O:Sergeant Preston 55.00
14 thru 17 P(c) . . . . @50.00
18 P(c). 50.00
19 thru 29 Ph(c) . . . . @55.00

Seven Seas #5
© Universal Phoenix

SEVEN SEAS COMICS
Universal Phoenix Features/
Leader Publ., April, 1946
1 MB,RWb(c),B:South Sea
Girl, Captain Cutlass 700.00
2 MB,RWb(c) 600.00
3 MB,AF,MB(c) 500.00
4 MB,MB(c) 500.00
5 MB,MB(c),Hangman's Noose . 500.00
6 MB,MB(c);1947 . . . . 500.00

SHADOW COMICS
Street & Smith, March, 1940
1-1 P(c),B:Shadow,Doc Savage,
 Bill Barnes,Nick Carter,
 Frank Merriwell,Iron Munro 4,000.00
1-2 P(c),B: The Avenger 1,500.00
1-3 P(c),A: Norgill the
 Magician 1,000.00
1-4 P(c),B:The Three
 Musketeers 850.00
1-5 P(c),E: Doc Savage 850.00
1-6 A: Captain Fury 700.00
1-7 O&B: The Wasp 750.00
1-8 A:Doc Savage 700.00
1-9 A:Norgill the Magician 700.00
1-10 O:Iron Ghost;B:The Dead
 End Kids 650.00
1-11 O:Hooded Wasp 700.00
1-12 Crime Does Not pay 550.00
2-1 . . . . 550.00
2-2 Shadow Becomes Invisible . 500.00
2-3 O&B:supersnipe;
 F:Little Nemo 725.00
2-4 F:Little Nemo 500.00
2-5 V:The Ghost Faker 500.00
2-6 A:Blackstone the Magician . . 400.00
2-7 V:The White Dragon 400.00
2-8 A:Little Nemo 400.00
2-9 The Hand of Death 400.00
2-10 A:Beebo the WonderHorse . 400.00
2-11 V:Devil Kyoti 400.00
2-12 V:Devil Kyoti 375.00
3-1 JaB(c),V:Devil Kyoti 375.00
3-2 Red Skeleton Life Story 375.00
3-3 V:Monstrodamus 375.00
3-4 V:Monstrodamus 375.00
3-5 V:Monstrodamus 375.00
3-6 V:Devil's of the Deep 375.00
3-7 V: Monstrodamus 375.00
3-8 E: The Wasp 375.00
3-9 The Stolen Lighthouse 375.00
3-10 A:Doc Savage 375.00
3-11 P(c),V: Thade 375.00
3-12 V: Thade 375.00
4-1 Red Cross Appeal on (c) . . . 350.00
4-2 V:The Brain of Nippon 350.00
4-3 Little Men in Space 350.00
4-4 ...Mystifies Berlin 350.00
4-5 ...Brings Terror to Tokio . . . 350.00
4-6 V:The Tarantula 350.00
4-7 Crypt of the Seven Skulls . . . 350.00
4-8 V:the Indigo Mob 350.00
4-9 Ghost Guarded Treasure
 of the Haunted Glen 350.00
4-10 V:The Hydra 350.00
4-11 V:The Seven Sinners 350.00
4-12 Club Curio 300.00
5-1 A:Flatty Foote 300.00
5-2 Bells of Doom 300.00
5-3 The Circle of Death. 300.00
5-4 The Empty Safe Riddle. 300.00
5-5 The Mighty Master Nomad . . 300.00
5-6 ...Fights Piracy Among
 the Golden Isles 300.00
5-7 V:The Talon 300.00
5-8 V:The Talon 300.00
5-9 V:The Talon 300.00
5-10 V:The Crime Master 300.00
5-11 The Clutch of the Talon 300.00
5-12 Most Dangerous Criminal . . 300.00
6-1 Double Z 300.00
6-2 Riddle of Prof.Mentalo 300.00
6-3 V:Judge Lawless 300.00
6-4 V:Dr. Zenith 300.00
6-5 . . . . 300.00
6-6 ...Invades the
 Crucible of Death 300.00
6-7 Four Panel Cover 300.00
6-8 Crime Among the Aztecs . . . 300.00
6-9 I:Shadow Jr. 350.00
6-10 Devil's Passage 300.00

6-11 The Black Pagoda. 300.00
6-12 BP,BP(c),Atomic Bomb
 Secrets Stolen 325.00
7-1 The Yellow Band 325.00
7-2 A:Shadow Jr. 325.00
7-3 BP,BP(c),Crime Under
 the Border 350.00
7-4 BP,BP(c),One Tree Island,
 Atomic Bomb 375.00
7-5 A:Shadow Jr. 325.00
7-6 BP,BP(c),The Sacred Sword
 of Sanjorojo 350.00
7-7 Crime K.O. 350.00
7-8 ...Raids Crime Harbor 350.00
7-9 BP,BP(c),Kilroy Was Here . . 350.00
7-10 BP,BP(c),The Riddle of
 the Flying Saucer 400.00
7-11 BP,BP(c),Crime
 Doesn't Pay 350.00
7-12 BP,BP(c)Back From
 the Grave 350.00
8-1 BP,BP(c),Curse of the Cat . . 350.00
8-2 BP,BP(c),Decay,Vermin &
 Murder in the Bayou 350.00
8-3 BP,BP(c),The Spider Boy . . . 350.00
8-4 BP,BP(c),Death Rises
 Out of the Sea 350.00
8-5 BP,BP(c),Jekyll-
 Hyde Murders. 350.00
8-6 Secret of Valhalla Hall 350.00
8-7 BP,BP(c),Shadow in Danger 350.00
8-8 BP,BP(c),...Solves a
 Twenty Year Old Crime 350.00
8-9 BP,BP(c),3-D Effect(c). 350.00
8-10 BP,BP(c),Up&Down(c) 350.00
8-11 BP,BP(c) 350.00
8-12 BP,BP(c),Arabs,Boat(c). . . . 350.00
9-1 Airport(c) 350.00
9-2 BP,BP(c),Flying Cannon(c) . . 350.00
9-3 BP,BP(c),Shadow's Shadow . 350.00
9-4 BP,BP(c) 350.00
9-5 Death in the Stars;Aug'49 . . 350.00

SHARP COMICS
H.C. Blackerby
Winter, 1945
1 O:Planetarian(c) 300.00
2 O:The Pioneer 250.00

SHEENA, QUEEN OF THE JUNGLE
Real Adventures
(Fiction House)
Spring, 1942
1 Blood Hunger 1,900.00
2 Black Orchid of Death 900.00
3 Harem Shackles 700.00
4 The Zebra Raiders 400.00
5 War of the Golden Apes 350.00
6 . . . . 325.00
7 They Claw By Night 300.00
8 The Congo Colossus 300.00
9 and 10 . . . . @275.00
11 Red Fangs of the Tree Tribe. . 275.00
12 . . . . 225.00
13 Veldt o/t Voo Doo Lions 225.00
14 The Hoo Doo Beasts of
 Mozambique. 225.00
15 . . . . 225.00
16 Black Ivory. 225.00
17 Great Congo Treasure Trek . . 225.00
18 Doom of the Elephant Drum
 Winter, 1952. . . . . 225.00

SHIELD-WIZARD COMICS
MLJ Magazines
Summer, 1940
1 IN,EA,O:Shield. 3,400.00
2 O:Shield;I:Roy 1,500.00
3 Roy,Child Bondage(c) 900.00
4 Shield,Roy,Wizard 900.00
5 B:Dusty-Boy Dectective,Child
 Bondage. 800.00
6 B:Roy the Super Boy,Child
 Bondage 750.00
7 Shield(c),Roy Bondage(c) . . . 770.00
8 Bondage(c) 750.00
9 Shield/Roy(c) 650.00
10 Shield/Roy(c) 650.00
11 Shield/Roy(c) 650.00
12 Shield/Roy(c) 650.00
13 Bondage (c);Spring'44 . . . . . 675.00

SHIP AHOY
Spotlight Publishers
Nov., 1944
1 LbC(c) 75.00

SHOCK DETECTIVE CASE(S)
(see CRIMINALS ON THE RUN)

SHOCK SUSPENSTORIES
Tiny Tot Comics
(E.C. Comics)
Feb.–March, 1952
1 JDa,JKa,AF(c),ElectricChair . . 650.00
2 WW,JDa,Grl,JKa,WW(c). 400.00
3 WW,JDa,JKa,WW(c). 300.00
4 WW,JDa,JKa,WW(c). 300.00
5 WW,JDa,JKa,WW(c),Hanging . 250.00
6 WW,AF,JKa,WW(c),
 Bondage(c). 300.00
7 JKa,WW,GE,AF(c),Face
 Melting 300.00
8 JKa,AF,AW,GE,WW,AF(c). . . . 300.00
9 JKa,AF,RC,WW,AF(c) 300.00
10 JKa,WW,RC,JKa(c),Drug 300.00
11 JCr,JKa,WW,RC,JCr(c) 275.00
12 AF,JKa,WW,RC,AF(c)Drug(c). 300.00

Shock SuspenStories #12
© E.C. Comics

13 JKa,WW,FF,JKa(c). 350.00	
14 JKa,WW,BK,WW(c) 275.00	
15 JKa,WW,RC,JDa(c)	
Strangulation 225.00	
16 GE,RC,JKa,GE(c),Rape. 225.00	
17 GE,RC,JKa,GE(c) 200.00	
18 GE,RC,JKa,GE(c);Jan'55. . . . 200.00	

SHOCKING MYSTERY CASES
(see THRILLING CRIME CASES)

SILVER STREAK COMICS
**Your Guide/New Friday/
Comic House/Newsbrook
Publications/Lev Gleason
Dec., 1939**

1 JCo,JCo(c),I&B:The Claw,Red
  Reeves Capt.Fearless;B:Mr.
  Midnight,Wasp;A:Spiritman11,000.00
2 JSm,JCo,JSm(c) 3,500.00
3 JaB(c),I&O:Silver Streak;
  B:Dickie Dean,Lance Hale,
  Ace Powers,Bill Wayne,
  Planet Patrol 3,000.00
4 JCo,JaB(c)B:Sky Wolf;
  N:Silver Streak,I:Lance
  Hale's Sidekick-Jackie 1,300.00
5 JCo,JCo(c),Dickie Dean
  V:The Raging Flood. 1,600.00
6 JCo,JaB,JCo(c),O&I:Daredevil
  [Blue & Yellow Costume];
  R:The Claw 12,000.00
7 JCo,N: Daredevil 7,500.00
8 JCo,JCo(c) 2,500.00
9 JCo,BoW(c) 1,500.00
10 BoW,BoW(c) 1,300.00
11 DRi(c) I:Mercury. 900.00
12 DRi(c) 700.00
13 JaB,JaB(c),O:Thun-Dohr 700.00
14 JaB,JaB(c),A:Nazi
  Skull Men 700.00
15 JaB,DBr,JaB(c),
  B:Bingham Boys. 600.00
16 DBr,BoW(c),Hitler(c). 650.00
17 DBr,JaB(c),E:Daredevil 600.00
18 DBr,JaB(c),B:The Saint 500.00
19 DBr,EA 400.00

*Silver Streak Comics #13
© Lev Gleason*

20 BW,BEv,EA 400.00	
21 BW,BEv. 400.00	

Becomes:

CRIME DOES NOT PAY

22(23) CBi(c),The Mad Musician
  & Tunes of Doom 1,700.00
23 CBi(c),John Dillinger-One
  Man Underworld 1,000.00
24 CBi(c),The Mystery of the
  Indian Dick. 800.00
25 CBi(c),Dutch Shultz-King
  of the Underworld. 450.00
26 CBi(c),Lucky Luciano-The
  Deadliest of Crime Rats 450.00
27 CBi(c),Pretty Boy Floyd 450.00
28 CBi(c),. 450.00
29 CBi(c),Two-Gun Crowley-The
  Bad Kid with the Itchy
  Trigger Finger. 350.00
30 CBi(c),"Monk"Eastman
  V:Thompson's Mob. 350.00
31 CBi(c) The Million Dollar
  Bank Robbery 250.00
32 CBi(c),Seniorita of Sin 250.00
33 CBi(c),Meat Cleaver Murder. . 250.00
34 CBi(c),Elevator Shaft 250.00
35 CBi(c),Case o/t MissingToe . . 250.00
36 CBi(c) 225.00
37 CBi(c) 225.00
38 CBi(c) 225.00
39 FG,CBi(c) 225.00
40 FG,CBi(c) 225.00
41 FG,RP,CBi(c),The Cocksure
  Counterfeiter 175.00
42 FG,RP,CBi(c). 200.00
43 FG,RP,CBi(c). 150.00
44 FG,CBi(c),The Most Shot
  At Gangster 150.00
45 FG,CBi(c) 150.00
46 FG,CBi(c),ChildKidnapping(c) 160.00
47 FG,CBi(c),ElectricChair 200.00
48 FG,CBi(c) 150.00
49 FG,CBi(c) 150.00
50 FG,CBi(c) 150.00
51 FG,GT,CBi(c),1st Monthly Iss. 125.00
52 FG,GT,CBi(c). 125.00
53 FG,CBi(c) 125.00
54 FG,CBi(c) 125.00
55 FG,CBi(c) 125.00
56 FG,GT,CBi(c). 125.00
57 FG,CBi(c) 125.00
58 FG,CBi(c) 125.00
59 FG,Cbi(c) 125.00
60 FG,CBi(c) 125.00
61 FG,GT,CBi(c) 100.00
62 FG,CBi(c),Bondage(c) 125.00
63 FG,CBi(c) 100.00
64 FG,GT,CBi(c). 100.00
65 FG,CBi(c) 100.00
66 FG,GT,CBi(c). 100.00
67 FG,GT,CBi(c). 100.00
68 FG,CBi(c) 100.00
69 FG,CBi(c) 100.00
70 FG,Cbi(c) 100.00
71 FG,CBi(c) 75.00
72 FG,CBi(c) 75.00
73 FG,CBi(c) 75.00
74 FG,CBi(c) 75.00
75 FG,CBi(c) 75.00
76 FG,CBi(c) 75.00
77 FG,CBi(c),Electrified Safe . . . 100.00
78 FG,CBi(c) 75.00
79 FG. 75.00
80 FG. 75.00
81 FG. 75.00
82 FG. 75.00
83 FG. 75.00
84 FG. 75.00
85 FG. 75.00
86 FG. 70.00
87 FG,P(c),The Rock-A-Bye

Baby Murder 70.00	
88 FG,P(c),Death Carries a Torch. 70.00	
89 FG,BF,BF P(c),The Escort	
Murder Case 70.00	
90 FG,BF P(c),The Alhambra	
Club Murders 70.00	
91 FG,AMc,BF P(c),Death	
Watches The Clock 70.00	
92 BF,FG,BF P(c). 70.00	
93 BF,FG,AMc,BF P(c). 70.00	
94 BF,FG,BF P(c). 70.00	
95 FG,AMc,BF P(c) 70.00	
96 BF,FG,BF P(c),The Case of	
the Movie Star's Double 70.00	
97 FG,BF P(c) 70.00	
98 BF,FG,BF P(c),Bondage(c) . . . 70.00	
99 BF,FG,BF P(c) 70.00	
100 FG,BF,AMc,P(c),The Case	
of the Jittery Patient 100.00	
101 FG,BF,AMc,P(c). 60.00	
102 FG,BF,AMc,P(c). 60.00	
103 FG,BF,AMc,BF P(c) 60.00	
104 thru 110 FG . . . . @60.00	
111 thru 120 . . . . @60.00	
121 thru 140 . . . . @45.00	
141 JKu 40.00	
142 JKu,CBi(c). 40.00	
143 JKu,Comic Code 40.00	
144 I Helped Capture"Fat Face"	
George Klinerz. 35.00	
145 RP,Double Barrelled Menace . 35.00	
146 BP,The Con & The Canary. . . 35.00	
147 JKu,BP,A Long Shoe On the	
Highway;July, 1955. . . . . 50.00	

SINGLE SERIES
United Features Syndicate
1938

1 Captain & The Kids 550.00
2 Bronco Bill 300.00
3 Ella Cinders 250.00
4 Li'l Abner 500.00
5 Fritzi Ritz 175.00
6 Jim Hardy 225.00
7 Frankie Doodle 175.00
8 Peter Pat 175.00
9 Strange As it Seems 200.00
10 Little Mary Mixup 165.00
11 Mr. & Mrs. Beans 165.00
12 Joe Jinx. 165.00
13 Looy Dot Dope. 165.00
14 Billy Make Believe 165.00
15 How It Began. 175.00
16 Illustrated Gags 125.00
17 Danny Dingle. 125.00
18 Li'l Abner 400.00
19 Broncho Bill 225.00
20 Tarzan 1,200.00
21 Ella Cinders 200.00
22 Iron Vic 175.00
23 Tailspin Tommy 200.00
24 Alice In Wonderland. 250.00
25 Abbie an' Slats. 200.00
26 Little Mary Mixup 150.00
27 Jim Hardy 175.00
28 Ella Cinders & Abbie AN'
  Slats 1942 . . . . 175.00

SKELETON HAND
American Comics Group
Sept.–Oct., 1952

1 . . . . 300.00
2 The Were-Serpent of Karnak . 200.00
3 Waters of Doom 175.00
4 Black Dust 175.00
5 The Rise & Fall of the
  Bogey Man. 175.00
6 July–Aug., 1953 . . . . 175.00

GOLDEN AGE

SKY BLAZERS
Hawley Publications
Sept., 1940
1 Flying Aces,Sky Pirates 500.00
2 Nov., 1940 . . . . 300.00

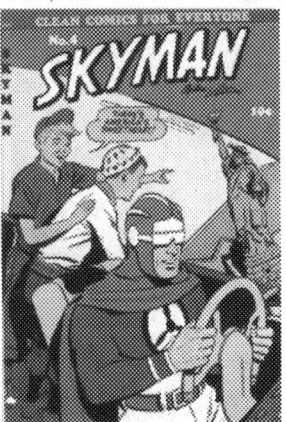

Skyman #4
© Columbia Comics Group

SKYMAN
Columbia Comics Group, 1941
1 OW,OW(c),O:Skyman,Face . . 900.00
2 OW,OW(c),Yankee Doodle . . . 450.00
3 OW,OW(c) 300.00
4 OW,OW(c),Statue of
   Liberty(c) 1948 . . . . 300.00

SKY PILOT
Ziff-Davis Publishing Co.
1950
10 NS P(c),Lumber Pirates 100.00
11 Ns P(c),The 2,00 Foot Drop;
   April–May, 1951 . . . . 75.00

SKY ROCKET
Home Guide Publ.
(Harry 'A' Chesler), 1944
1 Alias the Dragon,Skyrocket. . . 200.00

SKY SHERIFF
D.S. Publishing
Summer, 1948
1 I:Breeze Lawson & the Prowl
   Plane Patrol 75.00

SLAM BANG COMICS
Fawcett Publications
Jan., 1940
1 B:Diamond Jack,Mark Swift,
   Lee Granger,Jungle King . . 1,600.00
2 F:Jim Dolan Two-Fisted
   Crime Buster 700.00
3 A: Eric the Talking Lion 1,000.00
4 F: Hurricane Hansen-Sea
   Adventurer 550.00
5 . . . . 550.00
6 I: Zoro the Mystery Man;
   Bondage(c) 550.00
7 Bondage(c);Sept., 1940 . . . . 550.00

SLAPSTICK COMICS
Comic Magazine Distrib., Inc.
1945
N# Humorous Parody 150.00

SLAVE GIRL COMICS
Avon Periodicals
Feb., 1949
1 . . . . 700.00
2 April, 1949 . . . . 500.00

SLICK CHICK COMICS
Leader Enterprises, Inc., 1947
1 Teen-Aged Humor 65.00
2 Teen-Aged Humor 45.00
3 1947. . . . . 45.00

SMASH COMICS
Comics Magazine, Inc.
(Quality Comics Group)
Aug., 1939
1 WE,O&B:Hugh Hazard, Bozo
   the Robot,Black X, Invisible
   Justice: B:Wings Wendall,
   Chic Carter 2,000.00
2 WE,A:Lone Star Rider 800.00
3 WE,B:Captain Cook,JohnLaw 500.00
4 WE,PGn,B:Flash Fulton 450.00
5 WE,PGn,Bozo Robot 450.00
6 WE,PGn,GFx,Black X(c). 450.00
7 WE,PGn,GFx,Wings
   Wendell(c) 400.00
8 WE,PGn,GFx,Bozo Robot. . . . 400.00
9 WE,PGn,GFx,Black X(c). 400.00
10 WE,PGn,GFx,Bozo robot(c) . . 400.00
11 WE,PGn,GFx,BP,Black X(c) . . 400.00
12 WE,PGn,GFx,BP,Bozo(c). . . . 400.00
13 WE,PGn,GFx,AB,BP,B:Mango,
   Purple Trio,BlackX(c) 400.00
14 BP,LF,AB,PGn,I:The Ray. . . 2,200.00
15 BP,LF,AB,PGn,The Ram(c) . 1,000.00
16 BP,LF,AB,PGn,Bozo(c) 1,000.00
17 BP,LF,AB,PGn,JCo,
   The Ram(c) 1,000.00
18 BP,LF,AB,JCo,PGn,
   B&O:Midnight 1,200.00
19 BP,LF,AB,JCo,PGn,Bozo(c) . . 650.00
20 BP,LF,AB,JCo,PGn,
   The Ram(c) 650.00
21 BP,LF,AB,JCo,PGn 650.00
22 BP,LF,AB,JCo,PGn,
   B:The Jester. 650.00
23 BP,AB,JCo,RC,PGn,
   The Ram(c) 500.00
24 BP,AB,JCo,RC,PGn,A:Sword,
   E:ChicCarter,
   N:WingsWendall. 500.00
25 AB,JCo,RC,PGn,O:Wildfire . . 600.00
26 AB,JCo,RC,PGn,Bozo(c) 500.00
27 AB,JCo,RC,PGn,The Ram(c). 500.00
28 AB,JCo,RC,PGn,
   1st Midnight (c) 500.00
29 AB,JCo,Rc,PGn,B:Midnight(c) 450.00
30 AB,JCo,PGn 450.00
31 AB,JCo,PGn 400.00
32 AB,JCo,PGn 400.00
33 AB,JCo,PGn,O:Marksman . . . 500.00
34 AB,JCo,PGn 400.00
35 AB,JCo,RC,PGn 400.00
36 AB,JCo,RC,PGn,E:Midnight(c) 400.00
37 AB,JCo,RC,PGn,Doc
   Wacky becomes Fastest
   Human on Earth. 400.00
38 JCo,RC,PGn,B:Yankee Eagle 450.00
39 PGn,B:Midnight(c) 350.00
40 PGn,E:Ray 350.00

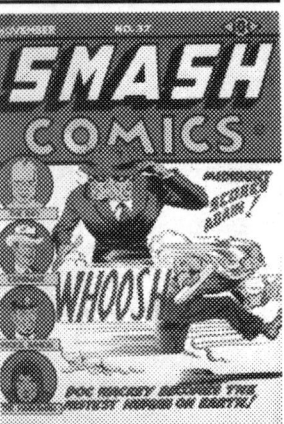

Smash #37
© Quality Comics Group

41 PGn. 225.00
42 PGn,B:Lady Luck. 250.00
43 PGn. 250.00
44 PGn. 225.00
45 PGn,E:Midnight(c) 225.00
46 RC,Twelve Hours to Live 225.00
47 Wanted Midnight,
   Dead or Alive 225.00
48 Midnight Meets the
   Menace from Mars 225.00
49 PGn,FG,Mass of Muscle 225.00
50 I:Hyram the Hermit. 225.00
51 A:Wild Bill Hiccup. 175.00
52 PGn,FG,Did Ancient Rome Fall,
   or was it Pushed?. 175.00
53 Is ThereHonorAmongThieves. 175.00
54 A:Smear-Faced Schmaltz . . . 175.00
55 Never Trouble Trouble until
   Trouble Troubles You 175.00
56 The Laughing Killer 175.00
57 A Dummy that Turns Into
   A Curse 175.00
58 . . . . 175.00
59 A Corpse that Comes Alive . . 175.00
60 The Swooner & the Trush . . . 175.00
61 . . . . 150.00
62 V:The Lorelet. 150.00
63 PGn 150.00
64 PGn,In Search of King Zoris. . 150.00
65 PGn,V:Cyanide Cindy 150.00
66 Under Circle's Spell 150.00
67 A Living Clue 150.00
68 JCo,Atomic Dice 150.00
69 JCo,V:Sir Nuts 150.00
70 . . . . 150.00
71 . . . . 125.00
72 JCo,Angela,the Beautiful
   Bovine 125.00
73 . . . . 125.00
74 . . . . 125.00
75 The Revolution 125.00
76 Bowl Over Crime 125.00
77 Who is Lilli Dilli?. 125.00
78 JCo,Win Over Crime 125.00
79 V:The Men From Mars. 125.00
80 JCo,V:Big Hearted Bosco. . . . 125.00
81 V:Willie the Kid 125.00
82 V:Woodland Boy 125.00
83 JCo,Quizmaster. 125.00
84 A Date With Father Time 125.00
85 JCo,A Singing Swindle. 125.00

GOLDEN AGE

SMASH HITS
SPORTS COMICS
Essankay Publications
Jan., 1949
1 LbC,LbC(c) 225.00

SMILEY BURNETTE
WESTERN
Fawcett Publications
March, 1950
1 Ph(c),B:Red Eagle 350.00
2 Ph(c) 250.00
3 Ph(c) 250.00
4 Ph(c) 250.00

SMILIN' JACK
Dell Publishing Co., 1940
1 .... 125.00
2 .... 65.00
3 thru 8 .... @40.00

SMITTY
Dell Publishing Co., 1940
1 .... 100.00
2 .... 50.00
3 .... 40.00
4 thru 7 .... @30.00

SNAP
Harry 'A' Chesler Jr.
Publications, 1944
N# Humorous 100.00

SNAPPY COMICS
Cima Publications
(Prize), 1945
1 A:Animale 175.00

SNIFFY THE PUP
Animated Cartoons
(Standard Comics)
Nov., 1949
5 FF,Funny Animal 45.00
6 thru 9 Funny Animal ...... @20.00
10 thru 17 Funny Animal ..... @15.00
18 Sept., 1953 .... 15.00

SOLDIER COMICS
Fawcett Publications
Jan., 1952
1 Fighting Yanks on Flaming
  Battlefronts 70.00
2 Blazing Battles Exploding
  with Combat 35.00
3 .... 30.00
4 A Blow for Freedom 25.00
5 Only The Dead Are Free 25.00
6 Blood & Guts 18.00
7 The Phantom Sub 18.00
8 More Plasma! 18.00
9 Red Artillery 18.00
10 .... 18.00
11 Sept., 1953 .... 18.00

SOLDIERS OF FORTUNE
Creston Publications
(American Comics Group)
Feb.–March, 1952
1 OW(c),B:Ace Carter,

Crossbones, Lance Larson . 150.00
2 OW(c) 75.00
3 OW(c) 60.00
4 .... 60.00
5 OW(c) 60.00
6 OW(c),OW,Bondage(c) 65.00
7 .... 60.00
8 OW thru 10 .... @60.00
11 OW,Format Change to War ... 30.00
12 .... 30.00
13 OW,Feb.–March, 1953....... 30.00

SON OF SINBAD
St. John Publishing Co.
Feb., 1950
1 JKu,JKu(c),The Curse of the
  Caliph's Dancer 300.00

SPACE ACTION
Junior Books
(Ace Magazines)
June, 1952
1 Invaders from a Lost Galaxy . 550.00
2 The Silicon Monster from
  Galaxy X 450.00
3 Attack on Ishtar,
  Oct.., 1952 .... 450.00

Space Adventures #3
© Charlton Comics

SPACE ADVENTURES
Capitol Stories/
Charlton Comics
July, 1952
1 AFa&LM(c) 350.00
2 .... 175.00
3 DG(c) 150.00
4 DG(c) 150.00
5 StC(c) 150.00
6 StC(c),Two Worlds 125.00
7 DG(c),Transformation 150.00
8 DG(c),All For Love 125.00
9 DG(c) 125.00
10 SD,SD(c)............... 350.00
11 SD,JoS 400.00
12 SD(c)................. 400.00
13 A:Blue Beetle........... 150.00
14 A:Blue Beetle........... 150.00
15 Ph(c) of Rocky Jones 150.00
16 BKa,A:Rocky Jones....... 150.00
17 A:Rocky Jones.......... 125.00
18 A:Rocky Jones.......... 125.00
19 .... 100.00

20 First Trip to the Moon...... 200.00
21 .... 100.00
22 Does Not Exist
23 SD,Space Trip to the Moon .. 150.00
24 .... 125.00
25 Brontosaurus............ 125.00
26 SD,Flying Saucers......... 150.00
27 SD,Flying Saucers......... 150.00
28 Moon Trap.............. 45.00
29 Captive From Space 45.00
30 Peril in the Sky 45.00
31 SD,SD(c),Enchanted Planet.. 125.00
32 SD,SD(c),Last Ship
  from Earth 125.00
33 Galactic Scourge,
  I&O:Captain Atom........ 400.00
34 SD,SD(c),A:Captain Atom ... 150.00
35 thru 40 SD,SD(c),
  A:Captain Atom........ @150.00
41 .... 25.00
42 SD,A:Captain Atom 25.00
43 .... 25.00
44 A:Mercury Man 25.00
45 A:Mercury Man 25.00
46 thru 58............... @25.00
59 Nov., 1964.............. 25.00

SPACE BUSTERS
Ziff-Davis Publishing Co.
Spring, 1952
1 BK,NS(c),Ph(c),Charge of
  the Battle Women 650.00
2 EK,BK,MA,NS(c),
  Bondage(c),Ph(c) 500.00
3 Autumn, 1952 .... 450.00

SPACE COMICS
Avon Periodicals
March–April, 1954
4 (fa),F:Space Mouse 30.00
5 (fa),F:Space Mouse,
  May–June, 1954 .... 25.00

SPACE DETECTIVE
Avon Periodicals
July, 1951
1 WW,WW(c),Opium Smugglers
  of Venus 800.00
2 WW,WW(c),Batwomen of
  Mercury 550.00
3 EK(c),SeaNymphs ofNeptune 300.00
4 EK,Flame Women of Vulcan,
  Bondage(c) 325.00

SPACE MOUSE
Avon Periodicals
April, 1953
1 Funny Animal 45.00
2 Funny Animal............ 35.00
3 thru 5 Funny Animal ...... @20.00

SPACE PATROL
Approved Comics
(Ziff-Davis)
Summer, 1952
1 BK,NS,Ph(c), The Lady of
  Diamonds 700.00
2 BK,NS,Ph(c),Slave King of
  Pluto,Oct.–Nov., 1952 ..... 500.00

SPACE THRILLERS
Avon Periodicals, 1954
N# Contents May Vary....... 850.00

SPACE WESTERN COMICS
(see YELLOWJACKET COMICS)

SPARKLER COMICS
United Features Syndicate
July, 1940
1 Jim Handy 300.00
2 Frankie Doodle,Aug., 1940 . . 225.00

SPARKLER COMICS
United Features Syndicate
July, 1941
1 BHg,O:Sparkman;B:Tarzan,Captain
   & the Kids,Ella Cinders,Danny
   Dingle,Dynamite Dunn, Nancy,
   Abbie an' Slats, Frankie
   Doodle,Broncho Bill 1,800.00
2 BHg, The Case of Poisoned
   Fruit 650.00
3 BHg 500.00
4 BHg,Case of Sparkman &
   the Firefly 500.00
5 BHg,Sparkman,Natch 450.00
6 BHg,Case o/t Bronze Bees . . 425.00
7 BHg,Case o/t Green Raiders . 425.00
8 BHg,V:River Fiddler 425.00
9 BHg,N:Sparkman 425.00
10 BHg,B:Hap Hopper,
   Sparkman's ID revealed . . . 425.00
11 BHg,V:Japanese 375.00
12 BHg,Another N:Sparkman . . . 375.00
13 BHg,Hap Hopper Rides
   For Freedom 375.00
14 BHg,BHg(c),Tarzan
   V:Yellow Killer 400.00
15 BHg 350.00
16 BHg,Sparkman V:Japanese . . 350.00
17 BHg,Nancy(c) 350.00
18 BHg,Sparkman in Crete 350.00
19 BHg,I&B:Race Riley,
   Commandos 350.00
20 BHg,Nancy(c) 350.00
21 BHg,Tarzan(c) 350.00
22 BHg,Nancy(c) 275.00
23 BHg,Capt&Kids(c) 275.00
24 BHg,Nancy(c) 275.00
25 BHg,BHg(c),Tarzan(c) 300.00
26 BHg,Capt&Kids(c) 275.00
27 BHg,Nancy(c) 275.00
28 BHg,BHg(c),Tarzan(c) 300.00
29 BHg,Capt&Kids(c) 275.00
30 BHg,Nancy(c) 275.00
31 BHg,BHg(c),Tarzan(c) 300.00
32 BHg,Capt&Kids(c) 125.00
33 BHg,Nancy(c) 125.00
34 BHg,BHg(c),Tarzan(c) 250.00
35 BHg,Capt&Kids(c) 125.00
36 BHg,Nancy(c) 125.00
37 BHg,BHg(c),Tarzan(c) 250.00
38 BHg,Capt&Kids(c) 125.00
39 BHg,BHg(c),Tarzan(c) 250.00
40 BHg,Nancy(c) 125.00
41 BHg,Capt&Kids(c) 100.00
42 BHg,BHg,Tarzan(c) 200.00
43 BHg,Nancy(c) 100.00
44 BHg,Tarzan(c) 100.00
45 BHg,Capt&Kids(c) 100.00
46 BHg,Nancy(c) 100.00
47 BHg,Tarzan(c) 200.00
48 BHg,Nancy(c) 100.00
49 BHg,Capt&Kids(c) 100.00
50 BHg,BHg(c),Tarzan(c) 165.00
51 BHg,Capt&Kids(c) 100.00
52 BHg,Nancy(c) 100.00

53 BHg,BHg(c),Tarzan(c) 150.00
54 BHg,Capt&Kids(c) 75.00
55 BHg,Nancy(c) 75.00
56 BHg,Capt&Kids(c) 75.00
57 BHg,F:Li'l Abner. 75.00
58 BHg,A:Fearless Fosdick. 90.00
59 BHg,B:Li'l Abner 90.00
60 BHg,Nancy(c) 75.00
61 BHg,Capt&Kids(c) 75.00
62 BHg,Li'L Abner(c) 75.00
63 BHg,Capt&Kids(c) 75.00
64 BHg,Valentines (c). 75.00
65 BHg,Nancy(c) 75.00
66 BHg,Capt&Kids(c) 75.00
67 BHg,Nancy(c) 75.00
68 BHg, ... 75.00
69 BHg,B:Nancy (c) 75.00
70 BHg. 75.00
71 thru 80 BHg . . . . @60.00
81 BHg,E:Nancy(c). 60.00
82 BHg. 60.00
83 BHg,Tarzan(c) 50.00
84 BHg. 50.00
85 BHg,E:Li'l Abner 50.00
86 BHg. 50.00
87 BHg,Nancy(c) 50.00
88 thru 96 BHg . . . . @50.00
97 BHg,O:Lady Ruggles 100.00
98 BHg. 50.00
99 BHg,Nancy(c) 50.00
100 BHg,Nancy(c) 60.00
101 thru 108 BHg . . . . @35.00
109 BHg,ATh 40.00
110 BHg. 35.00
111 BHg 35.00
112 BHg. 35.00
113 BHg,ATh 60.00
114 thru 120 BHg . . . . @35.00

SPARKLING STARS
Holyoke Publishing Co.
June, 1944
1 B:Hell's Angels,Ali Baba,FBI,
   Boxie Weaver,Petey & Pop . 125.00
2 . . . . 75.00
3 . . . . 50.00
4 thru 12 . . . . @45.00
13 O&I:Jungo, The Man-Beast . . . 50.00
14 thru 19 . . . . @45.00
20 I:Fangs the Wolfboy. 45.00
21 thru 28 . . . . @45.00
29 Bondage(c) 35.00
30 thru 32 . . . . @30.00
33 March, 1948 . . . . 30.00

SPARKMAN
Frances M. McQueeny, 1944
1 O:Sparkman. 225.00

SPARKY WATTS
Columbia Comics Group, 1942
1 A:Skyman,Hitler(c) 350.00
2 . . . . 200.00
3 . . . . 125.00
4 O:Skyman 125.00
5 A:Skyman 100.00
6 . . . . 75.00
7 . . . . 75.00
8 . . . . 75.00
9 . . . . 75.00
10 1949 . . . . 75.00

[STEVE SAUNDERS] SPECIAL AGENT
Parents Magazine/ Commended Comics, Dec., 1947
1 J. Edgar Hoover, Ph(c) 60.00
2 . . . . 30.00
3 thru 7 . . . . @25.00
8 Sept., 1949. . . . . 25.00

SPECIAL COMICS
(see LAUGH COMICS)

SPECIAL EDITION COMICS
Fawcett Publications
Aug., 1940
1 CCB,CCB(c),F:Captain
   Marvel 8,500.00

Speed Comics #10
© Harvey Publications

SPEED COMICS
Brookwood/Speed Publ.
Harvey Publications
Oct., 1939
1 BP,B&O:Shock Gibson,B:Spike
   Marlin,Biff Bannon 2,500.00
2 BP ,B:Shock Gibson(c) 800.00
3 BP,GT 500.00
4 BP 400.00
5 BP,DBr 400.00
6 BP,GT 350.00
7 GT,JKu,B:Mars Mason 350.00
8 JKu 325.00
9 JKu 325.00
10 JKu,E:Shock Gibson(c) 325.00
11 JKu,E:Mars Mason. 325.00
12 B:The Wasp. 400.00
13 I:Captain Freedom;B:Girls
   Commandos,Pat Parker 450.00
14 Pocket sized format-100pgs. . 450.00
15 Pocket size 450.00
16 JKu,Pocket size 450.00
17 O:Black Cat 550.00
18 B:Capt.Freedom,Bondage(c) . 425.00
19 . . . . 400.00
20 . . . . 400.00
21 JKu(c) 400.00
22 JKu(c) 400.00
23 JKu(c),O:Girl Commandos . . . 425.00

24	300.00
25	275.00
26 Flag (c)	275.00
27	275.00
28 E:Capt Freedom	275.00
29 Case o/t Black Marketeers	275.00
30 POW Death Chambers	275.00
31 ASh(c),Nazi Thrashing(c)	350.00
32 ASh(c)	325.00
33 ASh(c)	325.00
34 ASh(c)	325.00
35 ASh(c),BlackCat'sDeathTrap	350.00
36 ASh(c)	325.00
37 RP(c)	325.00
38 RP(c),War Bond Plea with Iwo Jima flag allusion(c)	325.00
39 RP(c),B:Capt Freedom(c)	275.00
40 RP(c)	275.00
41 RP(c)	275.00
42 JKu,RP(c)	275.00
43 JKu,E:Capt Freedom(c)	275.00
44 BP,JKu,Four Kids on a raft, Jan.–Feb., 1947	300.00

SPEED SMITH THE HOT ROD KING
Ziff-Davis Publishing Co.
Spring, 1952

1 INS,Ph(c),A:Roscoe the Rascal	125.00

SPIRIT, THE
Will Eisner
(Weekly Coverless Comic Book), June, 1940

WE,O:SPirit	600.00
6/9/40 WE	250.00
6/16/40 WE,Black Queen	175.00
6/23/40 WE,Mr Mystic.	150.00
6/30/40 WE	150.00
7/7/40 WE,Black Queen	150.00
7/14/40 WE	100.00
7/21/40 WE	100.00
7/28/40 WE	100.00
8/4/40 WE	100.00
7/7/40-11/24/40,WE	70.00
12/1/40 WE,Ellen Spanking(c)	125.00
12/8/40-12/29/40	60.00
1941 WE Each	50.00
3/16 WE I:Silk Satin	95.00
6/15 WE I Twilight	60.00
6/22 WE Hitler	60.00
1942 WE Each	40.00
2-1	60.00
2-15	45.00
2-23	65.00
1943 WE Each,LF,WE scripts	30.00
1944 JCo,LF.	15.00
1945 LF Each,	15.00
1946 WE Each	30.00
1/13 WE,O:The Spirit	50.00
1/20 WE,Satin	50.00
3/17 WE,I:Nylon	50.00
4/21 WE,I:Mr.Carrion	55.00
7/7 WE,I:Dulcet Tone&Skinny	50.00
10/6 WE,I:F:Gell.	60.00
1947 WE Each	30.00
7/13.,WE,Hansel &Gretel	45.00
7/20,WE,A:Bomb	50.00
9/28,WE,Flying Saucers	65.00
10/5,WE, Cinderella	32.00
12/7,WE,I:Power Puff	32.00
1948 WE Each	30.00
1/11,WE,Sparrow Fallon	35.00
1/25,WE,I:Last A Net	40.00
3/14,WE,A:Kretuama	35.00
4/4,WE,A:Wildrice.	35.00

Spirit #19
© Will Eisner

7/25,The Thing	60.00
8/22,Poe Tale,Horror	65.00
9/18, A:Lorelei	35.00
11/7,WE,A:Plaster of Paris	40.00
1949 WE Each	30.00
1/23 WE,I:Thorne	40.00
8/21 WE,I:Monica Veto	40.00
9/25 WE,A:Ice	40.00
12/4 WE,I:Flaxen	35.00
1950 WE Each	30.00
1/8 WE,I:Sand Saref.	70.00
2/10, Horror Issue.	35.00
1951 WE(Last WE 8/12/51)	@30.00
Non-Eisners	@12.00
1952 Non-Eisners	@12.00
7/27 WW,Denny Colt	350.00
8/3 WW,Moon.	350.00
8/10 WW.Moon.	350.00
8/17 WW,WE,Heart	300.00
8/24 WW,Rescue	300.00
8/31 WW,Last Man	300.00
9/7 WW,Man Moon	380.00
9/14 WE.	80.00
9/21 WE Space	250.00
9/28 WE Moon	300.00
10/5 WE Last Story	125.00

SPIRIT, THE
Quality Comics Group/
Vital Publ., 1944

N# Wanted Dead or Alive!	550.00
N# ...in Crime Doesn't Pay.	350.00
N# ...In Murder Runs Wild	250.00
4 ...Flirts with Death.	200.00
5 ...Wanted Dead or Alive	175.00
6 ...Gives You Triple Value.	150.00
7 ...Rocks the Underworld	150.00
8	150.00
9 ...Throws Fear Into the Heart of Crime	150.00
10 ...Stalks Crime	150.00
11 ...America's Greatest Crime Buster	150.00
12 WE(c),...The Famous Outlaw Who Smashes Crime	250.00
13 WE(c),...and Ebony Cleans Out the Underworld;Bondage(c)	250.00
14 WE(c)	250.00
15 WE(c),Bank Robber at Large	250.00
16 WE(c),The Caase of the Uncanny Cat	250.00
17 WE(c),The Organ Grinding Bank Robber	250.00

18 WE,WE(c),`The Bucket of Blood	300.00
19 WE,WE(c),`The Man Who Murdered the Spirit'	300.00
20 WE,WE(c),`The Vortex'	300.00
21 WE,WE(c),`P'Gell of Paris'	300.00
22 WE(c),TheOctopus,Aug.1950.	450.00

SPIRIT, THE
Fiction House Magazines
1952

1 Curse of Claymore Castle	275.00
2 WE,WE(c),Who Says Crime Doesn't Pay	300.00
3 WE/JGr(c),League of Lions	200.00
4 WE,WE&JGr(c),Last Prowl of Mr. Mephisto;Bondage (c)	250.00
5 WE, WE(c),Ph(c)1954	250.00

SPIRITMAN
Will Eisner, 1944

1 3 Spirit Sections from 1944 Bound Together	150.00
2 LF, 2 Spirit Sections from 1944 Bound Together	125.00

SPITFIRE COMICS
Harvey Publ., Aug., 1941

1 MKd(c), 100pgs., Pocket size	550.00
2 100 pgs.,Pocket size, Oct., 1941`	500.00

SPOOK COMICS
Baily Publications, 1946

1 A:Mr. Lucifer	200.00

SPOOK DETECTIVE CASES
(see CRIMINALS ON THE RUN)

SPOOKY
Harvey Publications
Nov., 1955

1 Funny Apparition	225.00
2 same	100.00
3 thru 10 same	@45.00
11 thru 20 same	@25.00
21 thru 30 same	@20.00
31 thru 40 same	@15.00
41 thru 70 same	@9.00
71 thru 90 same	@5.00
91 thru 120 same	@3.00
121 thru 160 same	@2.50
161 same,Sept., 1980.	2.50

SPOOKY MYSTERIES
Your Guide Publishing Co.
1946

1 Rib-Tickling Horror	75.00

SPORT COMICS
(see TRUE SPORT PICTURE STORIES)

SPORTS THRILLS
(see DICK COLE)

GOLDEN AGE

SPOTLIGHT COMICS
Harry 'A' Chesler Jr.
Publications
Nov., 1944
1 GT,GT(c),B:Veiled Avenger,
  Black Dwarf,Barry Kuda 500.00
2 .... 400.00
3 1945,Eye Injury............ 425.00

SPUNKY
Standard Comics
April, 1949
1 FF,Adventures of a Junior
  Cowboy 40.00
2 FF 25.00
3 .... 20.00
4 .... 20.00
5 .... 20.00
6 .... 20.00
7 Nov., 1951 .... 20.00

SPY AND
COUNTER SPY
Best Syndicated Features
(American Comics Group)
Aug.–Sept., 1949
1 I&O:Jonathan Kent 175.00
2 .... 100.00
Becomes:

SPY HUNTERS
3 Jonathan Kent 135.00
4 J.Kent.................... 75.00
5 J.Kent.................... 75.00
6 J.Kent.................... 75.00
7 OW(c),J.Kent 75.00
8 OW(c),J.Kent 75.00
9 OW(c),J.Kent 75.00
10 OW(c),J.Kent 75.00
11 .... 50.00
12 OW(c),MD 50.00
13 and 14 .... @45.00
15 OW(c) 50.00
16 AW 100.00
17 .... 35.00
18 War (c) 45.00
19 and 20 .... @45.00
21 B:War Content............ 45.00
22 .... 45.00
23 Torture................. 125.00
24 `BlackmailBrigade',July,1953 .. 45.00

SPY SMASHER
Fawcett Publications
Autumn, 1941
1 B;Spy Smasher 3,000.00
2 Mra(c) 1,300.00
3 Bondage (c) 900.00
4 .... 800.00
5 Mra,Mt. Rushmore(c) 900.00
6 Mra,Mra(c),V:The Sharks
  of Steel 750.00
7 Mra 750.00
8 AB 600.00
9 AB,Hitler,Tojo, Mussolini(c) ... 700.00
10 AB,Did Spy Smasher
  Kill Hitler?............. 700.00
11 AB,Feb., 1943 .... 600.00

SQUEEKS
Lev Gleason Publications
Oct., 1953
1 CBi(c),(fa) 30.00
2 CBi(c),(fa) 15.00
3 CBi(c),(fa) 12.00

4 (fa) 12.00
5 (fa),Jan., 1954 .... 12.00

STAMP COMICS
Youthful Magazines/Stamp
Comics, Inc.
Oct., 1951
1 HcK,Birth of Liberty 250.00
2 HcK,RP,Battle of White Plains 125.00
3 HcK,DW,RP,Iwo Jima 100.00
4 HcK,DW,RP 100.00
5 HcK,Von Hindenberg disaster . 110.00
6 HcK,The Immortal Chaplains . 100.00
7 HcK,RKr,RP,B&O:Railroad ... 150.00
Becomes:

THRILLING ADVENTURES
IN STAMPS
8 HcK, 100 Pgs.,Jan.,1953 .... 500.00

STAR COMICS
Comic Magazines/Ultem
Publ./Chesler
Centaur Publications
Feb., 1937
1 B:Dan Hastings 1,200.00
2 .... 550.00
3 .... 500.00
4 WMc(c) 525.00
5 WMc(c),A:Little Nemo 525.00
6 CBi(c),FG 500.00
7 FG 450.00
8 BoW,BoW(c),FG,A:Little
  Nemo,Horror 475.00
9 FG,CBi(c) 450.00
10 FG,CBi(c),BoW,A:Impyk.... 650.00
11 FG,BoW,JCo 450.00
12 FG,BoW,B:Riders of the
  Golden West 425.00
13 FG,BoW 400.00
14 FG,GFx(c)............... 400.00
15 CBu,B:The Last Pirate 400.00
16 CBu,B:Phantom Rider 400.00
2-1 CBu,B:Phantom Rider(c) .. 400.00
2-2 CBu,A:Diana Deane 375.00
2-3 GFx(c),CBu 350.00
2-4 CBu 350.00
2-5 CBu 350.00
2-6 CBu,E:Phanton Rider 350.00
2-7 CBu,Aug., 1939 .... 350.00

Star Comics #14
© Centaur Publications

STARLET O'HARA IN
HOLLYWOOD
Standard Comics
Dec., 1948
1 The Terrific Tee-Age Comic... 100.00
2 Her Romantic Adventures in
  Movie land 75.00
3 and 4, Sept., 1949 .... @50.00

STAR RANGER
Comics Magazines/Ultem/
Centaur Publ.
Feb., 1937
1 FG,I:Western Comic 1,300.00
2 .... 525.00
3 FG 500.00
4 .... 500.00
5 .... 500.00
6 FG 400.00
7 FG 375.00
8 GFx,FG,PGn,BoW 375.00
9 GFx,FG,PGn,BoW 375.00
10 JCo,GFx,FG,PGn,BoW 700.00
11 .... 500.00
12 JCo,JCo(c),FG,PGn....... 500.00
Becomes:

COWBOY COMICS
13 FG,PGn................. 750.00
14 FG,PGn................. 600.00
Becomes:

STAR RANGER
FUNNIES
15 WE,PGn 750.00
2-1(16) JCo,JCo(c).......... 600.00
2-2(17) PGn,JCo,A:Night Hawk. 500.00
2-3(18) JCo,FG 450.00
2-4(19) A:Kit Carson 450.00
2-5(20) Oct., 1939 .... 450.00

STARS AND STRIPES
COMICS
Comic Corp of America
(Centaur Publications)
May, 1941
2 PGn,PGn(c),`Called to Colors',
  The Shark,The Voice 1,700.00
3 PGn,PGn(c),O:Dr.Synthe .. 1,000.00
4 PGn,PGn(c),I:The Stars
  & Stripes 875.00
5 .... 600.00
6(5), Dec., 1941 .... 600.00

STAR STUDDED
Cambridge House, 1945
N# 25 cents (c) price;128 pgs.;
  32 F:stories 200.00
N# The Cadet,Hoot Gibson,
  Blue Beetle............. 150.00

STARTLING COMICS
Better Publ./Nedor Publ.
June, 1940
1 WE,LF,B&O:Captain Future,
  Mystico, Wonder Man;
  B:Masked Rider 1,800.00
2 Captain Future(c) 700.00
3 same 600.00
4 same 450.00
5 same 375.00
6 same 350.00
7 same 350.00
8 ASh(c) 350.00
9 Bondage(c)............. 375.00

10 O:Fighting Yank 2,700.00
11 Fighting Yank(c). 800.00
12 Hitler,Mussolini,Tojo cover . . . 600.00
13 JBi. 450.00
14 JBi. 450.00
15 Fighting Yank (c) 450.00
16 Bondage(c),O:FourComrades 500.00
17 Fighting Yank (c),
    E:Masked Rider 350.00
18 JBi,B&O:Pyroman 750.00
19 Pyroman(c) 350.00
20 Pyroman(c),B:Oracle 350.00
21 HcK,ASh(c)Bondage(c)O:Ape 375.00
22 HcK,ASh(c),Fighting Yank(c) . 350.00
23 HcK,BEv,ASh(c),Pyroman(c) . 325.00
24 HcK,BEv,ASh(c),Fighting
    Yank(c). 325.00
25 HcK,BEv,ASh(c),Pyroman(c) . 325.00
26 BEv,ASh(c),Fighting Yank(c) . 325.00
27 BEv,ASh(c),Pyroman(c) 325.00
28 BEv,ASh(c),Fighting Yank(c) . 325.00
29 BEv,ASh(c),Pyroman(c) 325.00
30 ASh(c),Fighting Yank(c) 325.00
31 ASh(c),Pyroman(c) 325.00
32 ASh(c),Fighting Yank(c) 325.00
33 ASh(c),Pyroman(c) 325.00
34 ASh(c),Fighting Yank(c),
    O:Scarab 325.00
35 ASh(c),Pyroman(c) 335.00
36 ASh(c),Fighting Yank(c) 300.00
37 ASh(c),Bondage (c) 300.00
38 ASh(c),Bondage(c) 300.00
39 ASh(c),Pyroman(c) 300.00
40 ASh(c),E:Captain Future 300.00
41 ASh(c),Pyroman(c) 300.00
42 ASh(c),Fighting Yank(c) 300.00
43 ASh(c),Pyroman(c),
    E:Pyroman 300.00
44 Grl(c),Lance Lewis(c). 450.00
45 Grl(c),I:Tygra 450.00
46 Grl,Grl(c),Bondage(c) 450.00
47 ASh(c),Bondage(c) 450.00
48 ASh(c),Lance Lewis(c). 400.00
49 ASh(c),Bondage(c),
    E:Fighting Yank 2,500.00
50 ASh(c),Lance Lewis(c),
    Sea Eagle 400.00
51 ASh(c),Sea Eagle 400.00
52 ASh(c). 400.00
53 ASh(c),Sept., 1948. . . . . 400.00

STARTLING TERROR TALES
Star Publications
May, 1952
10 WW,LbC(c),The Story Starts . 550.00
11 LbC(c),The Ghost Spider
    of Death 500.00
12 LbC(c),White Hand Horror . . . 175.00
13 JyD,LbC(c),Love From
    a Gorgor. 175.00
14 LbC(c),Trapped by the
    Color of Blood 175.00
4 LbC(c),Crime at the Carnival . 150.00
5 LbC(c),The Gruesome
    Demon of Terror 150.00
6 LbC(c),Footprints of Death . . . 150.00
7 LbC(c),The Case of the
    Strange Murder 175.00
8 RP,LbC(c),Phantom Brigade . . 175.00
9 LbC(c),The Forbidden Tomb . 150.00
10 LbC(c),The Horrible Entity . . . 175.00
11 RP,LbC(c),The Law Will
    Win, July, 1954. . . . . 175.00

Steve Canyon #6
© Harvey Publications

STEVE CANYON COMICS
Harvey Publications
Feb., 1948
1 MC,BP,O:Steve Canyon 150.00
2 MC,BP 125.00
3 MC,BP,Canyon's Crew 100.00
4 MC,BP,Chase of Death 100.00
5 MC,BP,A:Happy Easter 100.00
6 MC,BP,A:Madame Lynx,
    Dec., 1948 . . . . 110.00

STEVE ROPER
Famous Funnies
April, 1948
1 Reprints newspaper strips 65.00
2 . . . . 35.00
3 . . . . 25.00
4 . . . . 25.00
5 Dec., 1948 . . . . 25.00

STORIES BY FAMOUS AUTHORS ILLUSTRATED
(see FAST FICTION)

STORY OF HARRY S. TRUMAN, THE
Democratic National Committee, 1948
N# Giveaway-The Life of Our
    33rd President 85.00

STRAIGHT ARROW
Magazine Enterprises
Feb.–March, 1950
1 OW,B:Straight Arrow & his
    Horse Fury 350.00
2 BP,B&O:Red Hawk 150.00
3 BP,FF(c) 250.00
4 BP,Cave(c) 150.00
5 BP,StraightArrow'sGreatLeap . 150.00
6 BP 125.00
7 BP,The Railroad Invades
    Comanche Country 125.00
8 BP 125.00
9 BP 125.00
10 BP. 125.00

Straight Arrow #24
© Magazine Enterprises

11 BP,The Valley of Time 150.00
12 thru 19 BP . . . . @100.00
20 BP,Straight Arrow's
    Great War Shield 125.00
21 BP,O:Fury 150.00
22 BP,FF(c) 150.00
23 BP. 75.00
24 BP,The Dragons of Doom 75.00
25 BP. 75.00
26 BP. 75.00
27 BP. 75.00
28 BP,Red Hawk 50.00
29 thru 35 BP . . . . @50.00
36 BP Drug 55.00
37 BP. 55.00
38 BP. 55.00
39 BP,The Canyon Beasts 60.00
40 BP,Secret of the
    Spanish Specters 60.00
41 BP. 40.00
42 BP. 40.00
43 BP,I:Blaze 55.00
44 BP. 40.00
45 BP. 40.00
46 thru 53 BP . . . . @40.00
54 BP,March, 1956. . . . . 40.00

STRANGE CONFESSIONS
Approved Publications
(Ziff-Davis)
Spring, 1952
1 EK,Ph(c). 350.00
2 . . . . 225.00
3 EK,Ph(c),Girls reformatory . . . 225.00
4 Girls reformatory. 225.00

STRANGE FANTASY
Farrell Publications/
Ajax Comics
Aug., 1952
(2)1. . . . . 300.00
2 . . . . 250.00
3 The Dancing Ghost 250.00
4 Demon in the Dungeon,
    A:Rocketman 225.00
5 Visiting Corpse 150.00
6 . . . . 150.00
7 A:Madam Satan 225.00
8 A:Black Cat 150.00
9 S&K,SD 175.00
10 . . . . 150.00
11 Fearful Things Can Happen

All comics prices listed are for *Near Mint* condition.   **CVA Page 407**

in a Lonely Place 150.00	
12 The Undying Fiend 150.00	
13 Terror in the Attic,	
Bondage(c). 200.00	
14 Monster in the Building,	
Oct.–Nov., 1954 . . . . 150.00	

UNKNOWN WORLD
Fawcett Publications
June, 1952

1 NS(c),Ph(c),Will You Venture
  to Meet the Unknown 350.00
Becomes:

STRANGE STORIES FROM ANOTHER WORLD

2 NS(c),Ph(c),Will You?
  Dare You 350.00
3 NS(c),Ph(c),The Dark Mirror . 275.00
4 NS(c),Ph(c),Monsters of
  the Mind 275.00
5 NS(c),Ph(c),Dance of the
  Doomed Feb., 1953 . . . . . . 275.00

STRANGE SUSPENSE STORIES
Fawcett Publications
June, 1952

1 BP,MSy,MBi 550.00
2 MBi,GE 350.00
3 MBi,GE(c) 300.00
4 BP 300.00
5 MBi(c),Voodoo(c) 300.00
6 BEv 125.00
7 BEv 150.00
8 AW 150.00
9 . . . . 125.00
10 . . . . 150.00
11 . . . . 100.00
12 . . . . 100.00
13 . . . . 100.00
14 . . . . 125.00
15 AW,BEv(c) 125.00

Charlton Comics

16 . . . . 200.00
17 . . . . 150.00
18 SD,SD(c) 250.00
19 SD,SD(c) 350.00
20 SD,SD(c) 250.00
21 . . . . 125.00
22 SD(c) 225.00
Becomes:

THIS IS SUSPENSE!

23 WW 200.00
24 . . . . 75.00
25 . . . . 50.00
26 . . . . 50.00
Becomes:

STRANGE SUSPENSE STORIES

27 . . . . 75.00
28 . . . . 50.00
29 . . . . 50.00
30 . . . . 50.00
31 SD(c) 125.00
32 SD 125.00
33 SD 125.00
34 SD,SD(c) 250.00
35 SD 125.00
36 SD,SD(c) 125.00
37 SD 150.00
38 . . . . 125.00
39 SD 175.00
40 SD 125.00
41 SD 125.00

42 . . . . 35.00
43 . . . . 35.00
44 . . . . 35.00
45 SD 75.00
46 . . . . 35.00
47 SD 75.00
48 SD 75.00
49 . . . . 35.00
50 SD 90.00
51 thru 53 SD . . . . @50.00
54 thru 60 . . . . @30.00
61 thru 74 . . . . @15.00
75 . . . . 100.00
76 . . . . 30.00
77 . . . . 30.00

STRANGE SUSPENSE STORIES
(see LAWBREAKERS)

STRANGE TERRORS
St. John Publishing Co.
June, 1952

1 The Ghost of Castle
  Karloff, Bondage(c). 350.00
2 UnshackledFlight intoNowhere 200.00
3 JKu,Ph(c),The Ghost Who
  Ruled Crazy Heights 250.00
4 JKu,Ph(c),Terror from
  the Tombs 350.00
5 JKu,Ph(c),No Escaping
  the Pool of Death 250.00
6 LC,PAM,Bondage(c),Giant . . . 350.00
7 JKu,JKu(c),Cat's Death,Giant . 375.00

STRANGE WORLD OF YOUR DREAMS
Prize Group
Aug., 1952

1 S&K(c),What Do They Mean–
  Messages Rec'd in Sleep . . 500.00
2 MMe,S&K(c),Why did I Dream
  That I Was Being Married
  to a Man without a Face? . . . 400.00
3 S&K(c) 350.00
4 MMe,S&K(c),The Story of
  a Man Who Dreamed a Murder
  that Happened 300.00

Strange Worlds #4
© Avon Periodicals

STRANGE WORLDS
Avon Periodicals
Nov., 1950

1 JKu,Spider God of Akka 700.00
2 WW,Dara of the Vikings 650.00
3 AW&FF,EK(c),WW,JO 1,300.00
4 JO,WW,WW(c),The
  Enchanted Dagger 650.00
5 WW,WW(c),JO,Bondage(c);
  Sirens of Space 450.00
6 EK,WW(c),JO,SC,
  Maid o/t Mist 300.00
7 EK, Sabotage on
  Space Station 1 . . . . 250.00
8 JKu,EK,The Metal Murderer . . 250.00
9 The Radium Monsters 250.00
18 JKu 250.00
19 Astounding Super
  Science Fantasies 250.00
20 WW(c),Fighting War Stories. . . 50.00
21 EK(c) 40.00
22 EK(c),Sept.–Oct., 1955 . . . . . . 40.00

STRICTLY PRIVATE
Eastern Color Printing
July, 1942

1 You're in theArmyNow-Humor . 150.00
2 F:Peter Plink, 1942 . . . . 150.00

STUNTMAN COMICS
Harvey Publications
April–May, 1946

1 S&K,O:Stuntman 800.00
2 S&K,New Champ of Split-
  Second Action 550.00
3 S&K,Digest sized,Mail Order
  Only, B&W interior,
  Oct.–Nov., 1946 . . . . 550.00

SUGAR BOWL COMICS
Famous Funnies
May, 1948

1 ATh,ATh(c),The Newest in
  Teen Age! 80.00
2 . . . . 30.00
3 ATh 60.00
4 . . . . 30.00
5 Jan., 1949 . . . . 30.00

SUN FUN KOMIKS
Sun Publications, 1939

1 F:Spineless Sam the
  Sweetheart 200.00

SUNNY, AMERICA'S SWEETHEART
Fox Features Syndicate
Dec., 1947

11 AF,AF(c) 550.00
12 AF,AF(c) 450.00
13 AF,AF(c) 450.00
14 AF,AF(c) 450.00

SUNSET CARSON
Charlton Comics
Feb., 1951

1 Painted, Ph(c);Wyoming
  Mail 700.00
2 Kit Carson-Pioneer 500.00
3 . . . . 375.00
4 Panhandle Trouble,
  Aug., 1951 . . . . 375.00

SUPER BOOK OF COMICS

Western Publishing Co. 1943

N# Dick Tracy 300.00
1 Dick Tracy 250.00
2 Smitty,Magic Morro 80.00
3 Capt. Midnight 150.00
4 Red Ryder,Magic Morro 70.00
5 Don Winslow,Magic Morro 70.00
5 Dom Winslow,Stratosphere Jim. 70.00
5 Terry & the Pirates 80.00
6 Don Winslow 75.00
7 Little Orphan Annie. 70.00
8 Dick Tracy 100.00
9 Terry & the Pirates 100.00
10 Red Ryder, Magic Morro 70.00

SUPER-BOOK OF COMICS

Western Publishing Co., 1944

1 Dick Tracy (Omar) 175.00
1 Dick Tracy (Hancock) 125.00
2 Bugs Bunny (Omar) 40.00
2 Bugs Bunny (Hancock) 30.00
3 Terry & the Pirates (Omar) 75.00
3 Terry & the Pirates (Hancock) . . 65.00
4 Andy Panda (Omar) 35.00
4 Andy Panda (Hancock) 30.00
5 Smokey Stover (Omar) 30.00
5 Smokey Stover (Hancock) 20.00
6 Porky Pig (Omar) 35.00
6 Porky Pig (Hancock) 30.00
7 Smilin' Jack (Omar) 40.00
7 Smilin' Jack (Hancock) 35.00
8 Oswald the Rabbit (Omar) 30.00
8 Oswald the Rabbit (Hancock) . . 20.00
9 Alley Oop (Omar) 80.00
9 Alley Oop (Hancock) 70.00
10 Elmer Fudd (Omar) 30.00
10 Elmer Fudd (Hancock) 20.00
11 Little Orphan Annie (Omar) . . . 45.00
11 Little Orphan Amnie (Hancock). 35.00
12 Woody Woodpecker (Omar). . . 35.00
12 WoodyWoodpecker(Hancock) . 25.00
13 Dick Tracy (Omar) 80.00
13 Dick Tracy (Hancock). 75.00
14 Bugs Bunny (Omar) 30.00
14 Bugs Bunny (Hanock) 25.00
15 Andy Panda (Omar). 20.00
15 Andy Panda (Hancock) 15.00
16 Terry & the Pirates (Omar) . . . 70.00
16 Terry & the Pirates (Hancock) . 50.00
17 Smokey Stover (Omar) 30.00
17 Smokey Stover (Hancock) 30.00
18 Porky Pig (Omar). 25.00
18 Smokey Stover (Hancock) 20.00
19 Smilin' Jack (Omar) 35.00
N# Smilin' Jack (Hancock) 20.00
20 Oswald the Rabbit (Omar) 25.00
N# Oswald the Rabbit (Hancock) . 15.00
21 Gasoline Alley (Omar) 45.00
N# Gasoline Alley (Hancock) 35.00
22 Elmer Fudd (Omar) 25.00
N# Elmer Fudd (Hancock) 30.00
23 Little Orphan Annie (Omar) . . . 30.00
N# Little Orphan Annie (Hancock). 25.00
24 Woody Woodpecker (Omar). . . 22.00
N# WoodyWoodpecker(Hancock) . 18.00
25 Dick Tracy (Omar) 70.00
N# Dick Tracy (Hancock) 50.00
26 Bugs Bunny (Omar). 25.00
N# Bugs Bunny (Hancock) 20.00
27 Andy Panda (Omar). 20.00
27 Andy Panda (Hancock) 15.00
28 Terry & the Pirates (Omar) . . . 70.00
28 Terry & the Pirates (Hancock) . 50.00
29 Smokey Stover (Omar) 25.00
29 Smokey Stover (Hancock) 20.00
30 Porky Pig (Omar). 25.00

30 Porky Pig (Hancock) 20.00
N# Bugs Bunny (Hancock) 20.00

SUPER CIRCUS

Cross Publishing Co.

Jan., 1951

1 Partial Ph(c) 55.00
2 . . . . 40.00
3 . . . . 30.00
4 . . . . 30.00
5 1951 . . . . 30.00

Super Comics #33
© Cross Publishing Co.

SUPER COMICS

Dell Publishing Co.

May 1938

1 Dick Tracy,Terry and the
  Pirates,Smilin'Jack,Smokey
  Stover,Orphan Annie,etc. . . 2,000.00
2 . . . . 700.00
3 . . . . 650.00
4 . . . . 550.00
5 Gumps(c) 500.00
6 . . . . 400.00
7 Smokey Stover(c) 400.00
8 Dick Tracy(c) 375.00
9 . . . . 375.00
10 Dick Tracy(c) 375.00
11 . . . . 325.00
12 . . . . 325.00
13 . . . . 325.00
14 . . . . 325.00
15 . . . . 325.00
16 Terry & the Pirates 300.00
17 Dick Tracy(c) 300.00
18 . . . . 300.00
19 . . . . 300.00
20 Smilin'Jack(c). 325.00
21 B:Magic Morro 275.00
22 Magic Morro(c) 300.00
23 all star(c) 275.00
24 Dick Tracy(c) 300.00
25 Magic Morro(c) 275.00
26 . . . . 275.00
27 Magic Morro(c) 275.00
28 Jim Ellis(c) 300.00
29 Smilin'Jack(c). 275.00
30 inc.The Sea Hawk 300.00
31 Dick Tracy(c) 225.00
32 Smilin' Jack(c) 235.00
33 Jim Ellis(c). 225.00
34 Magic Morro(c) 225.00
35 thru 40 Dick Tracy(c) . . . . . @225.00
41 B:Lightning Jim 200.00

42 thru 50 Dick Tracy(c) . . . . @200.00
51 thru 54 Dick Tracy(c) . . . . . @150.00
55 . . . . 150.00
56 . . . . 150.00
57 Dick Tracy(c) 150.00
58 Smitty(c) 150.00
59 . . . . 150.00
60 Dick Tracy(c) 175.00
61 . . . . 135.00
62 Flag(c). 135.00
63 Dick Tracy(c) 135.00
64 Smitty(c) 125.00
65 Dick Tracy(c) 135.00
66 Dick Tracy(c) 135.00
67 Christmas(c) 135.00
68 Dick Tracy(c) 135.00
69 Dick Tracy(c) 135.00
70 Dick Tracy(c) 135.00
71 Dick Tracy(c) 100.00
72 Dick Tracy(c) 100.00
73 Smitty(c) 100.00
74 War Bond(c) 100.00
75 Dick Tracy(c) 100.00
76 Dick Tracy(c) 100.00
77 Dick Tracy(c) 100.00
78 Smitty(c) 90.00
79 Dick Tracy(c) 90.00
80 Dick Tracy(c) 90.00
81 Dick Tracy(c) 90.00
82 Dick Tracy(c) 90.00
83 Smitty(c) 85.00
84 Dick Tracy(c) 90.00
85 Smitty(c) 85.00
86 All on cover 90.00
87 All on cover 90.00
88 Dick Tracy(c) 90.00
89 Smitty(c) 75.00
90 Dick Tracy(c) 85.00
91 Smitty(c) 75.00
92 Dick Tracy(c) 85.00
93 Dick Tracy(c) 85.00
94 Dick Tracy(c) 85.00
95 thru 99 . . . . @75.00
100 . . . . 90.00
101 thru 115 . . . . @50.00
116 Smokey Stover(c) 40.00
117 Gasoline Alley(c) 40.00
118 Smokey Stover(c) 40.00
119 Terry and the Pirates(c) 45.00
120 . . . . 45.00
121 . . . . 45.00

SUPER-DOOPER COMICS

Able Manufacturing Co., 1946

1 A:Gangbuster 125.00
2 . . . . 75.00
3 & 4 . . . . @50.00
5 A:Captain Freedom,Shock
  Gibson 50.00
6 & 7 same . . . . @50.00
8 A:Shock Gibson, 1946 . . . . . . 50.00

SUPER DUCK COMICS

**MLJ Magazines/Close-Up
(Archie Publ.)**

Autumn, 1944

1 O:Super Duck. 350.00
2 . . . . 200.00
3 I:Mr. Monster 150.00
4 & 5 . . . . @125.00
6 thru 10 . . . . @100.00
11 thru 20 . . . . @75.00
21 thru 40 . . . . @60.00
41 thru 60 . . . . @40.00
61 thru 94 . . . . @30.00

GOLDEN AGE

SUPER FUNNIES
Superior Comics Publishers
March, 1954
1 Dopey Duck 275.00
2 Out of the Booby-Hatch 50.00
Becomes:

SUPER WESTERN FUNNIES
3 F:Phantom Ranger 30.00
4 F:Phantom Ranger,Sept. 1954 . 30.00

SUPER MAGICIAN COMICS
Street & Smith, May, 1941
1 B:The Mysterious Blackstone . 450.00
2 V:Wild Tribes of Africa 275.00
3 V:Oriental Wizard 250.00
4 V:Quetzal Wizard,O:Transo. . . 225.00
5 A:The Moylan Sisters 225.00
6 JaB,JaB(c),The Eddie
   Cantor story 225.00
7 In the House of Skulls 250.00
8 A:Abbott & Costello 250.00
9 V:Duneen the Man-Ape 250.00
10 V:Pirates o/t Sargasso Sea . 250.00
11 JaB(c),V:Fire Wizards. 250.00
12 V:Baal 250.00
2-1 A:The Shadow 250.00
2-2 In the Temple of the
   10,00 Idols 125.00
2-3 Optical Illusion on (c)-
   turn Jap into Monkey 125.00
2-4 V:Cannibal Killers 125.00
2-5 V:The Pygmies of Lemuria¡ . 125.00
2-6 V;Pirates & Indians 125.00
2-7 Can Blackstone Catch the
   Cannonball? 125.00
2-8 V:Marabout,B:Red Dragon . . 125.00
2-9 . . . . 125.00
2-10 Pearl Dives Swallowed By
   Sea Demons 125.00
2-11 Blackstone Invades
   Pelican Islands. 125.00
2-12 V:Bubbles of Death. 125.00
3-1 . . . . 135.00
3-2 Bondage(c),Midsummers
   Eve 125.00
3-3 The Enchanted Garden 125.00
3-4 Fabulous Aztec Treasure . . . 125.00
3-5 A:Buffalo Bill 125.00
3-6 Magic Tricks to Mystify 125.00
3-7 V:Guy Fawkes 125.00
3-8 V:Hindu Spook Maker 125.00
3-9 . . . . 125.00
3-10 V:The Water Wizards 125.00
3-11 V:The Green Goliath 125.00
3-12 Lady in White 125.00
4-1 Cannibal of Crime 100.00
4-2 The Devil's Castle 100.00
4-3 V:Demons of Golden River . . 100.00
4-4 V:Dr. Zero 100.00
4-5 Bondage(c) 100.00
4-6 V:A Terror Gang 100.00
4-7 . . . . 100.00
4-8 Mystery of the
   Disappearing Horse 100.00
4-9 A Floating Light? 100.00
4-10 Levitation 100.00
4-11 Lost, Strange Land
   of Shangri. 100.00
4-12 I:Nigel Elliman. 100.00
5-1 V:Voodoo Wizards of the
   Everglades,Bondage (c) . . . 100.00
5-2 Treasure of the Florida
   Keys; Bondage (c) 100.00
5-3 Elliman Battles Triple Crime . 100.00
5-4 Can A Human Being Really
   Become Invisible 100.00

5-5 Mystery of the Twin Pools . . 100.00
5-6 A:Houdini 100.00
5-7 F:Red Dragon. 225.00
5-8 F:Red Dragon,
   Feb.–March, 1947 . . . . 225.00

SUPERMOUSE
Standard Comics/Pines
Dec., 1948
1 FF,(fa) 150.00
2 FF,(fa) 85.00
3 FF,(fa) 65.00
4 FF,(fa) 70.00
5 FF,(fa) 65.00
6 FF,(fa) 65.00
7 thru 10 (fa) . . . . @25.00
11 thru 20 (fa) . . . . @20.00
21 thru 44 (fa) . . . . @15.00
45 (fa),Autumn, 1958 . . . . 15.00

SUPER-MYSTERY COMICS
Periodical House
(Ace Magazines)
July, 1940
1 B:Magno,Vulcan,Q-13,Flint
   of the Mountes 1,400.00
2 Bondage (c) 650.00
3 JaB,B:Black Spider 550.00
4 O:Davy;A:Captain Gallant . . . 450.00
5 JaB,JM(c),I&B:The Clown . . . 450.00
6 JM,JM(c),V:The Clown 350.00
2-1 JM,JM(c),O:Buckskin,
   Bondage(c) 350.00
2-2 JM,JM(c),V:The Clown 325.00
2-3 JM,JM(c),V:The Clown 325.00
2-4 JM,JM(c),V:The Nazis 325.00
2-5 JM,JM(c),Bondage(c) 350.00
2-6 JM,JM(c),Bondage(c),
   `Foreign Correspondent' . . . 350.00
3-1 B:Black Ace 375.00
3-2 A:Mr, Risk, Bondage(c) 375.00
3-3 HK,HK(c),I:Lancer;B:Dr.
   Nemesis, The Sword 350.00
3-4 HK 350.00
3-5 HK,LbC,A:Mr. Risk 375.00
3-6 HK,LbC,A:Paul Revere Jr. . . 375.00
4-1 HK,LbC,A:Twin Must Die . . . 325.00
4-2 A:Mr. Risk 225.00
4-3 Mango out to Kill Davey! . . . 225.00
4-4 Danger Laughs at Mr. Risk . 225.00

Super Magician Comics #56
© Street & Smith

4-5 A:Mr. Risk 225.00
4-6 RP,A:Mr. Risk 225.00
5-1 RP 200.00
5-2 RP,RP(c),The Riddle of the
   Swamp-Land Spirit. 200.00
5-3 RP,RP(c),The Case of the
   Whispering Death 200.00
5-4 RP,RP(c) 200.00
5-5 RP,Harry the Hack 200.00
5-6 . . . . 200.00
6-1 . . . . 175.00
6-2 RP,A:Mr. Risk 175.00
6-3 Bondage (c) 175.00
6-4 E:Mango;A:Mr. Risk 175.00
6-5 Bondage(c) 175.00
6-6 A:Mr. Risk 175.00
7-1 . . . . 175.00
7-2 KBa(c) 175.00
7-3 Bondage(c). 175.00
7-4 . . . . 175.00
7-5 . . . . 175.00
7-6 . . . . 175.00
8-1 The Riddle of the Rowboat . . 150.00
8-2 Death Meets a Train. 150.00
8-3 The Man Who Couldn't Die . 150.00
8-4 RP(c) 150.00
8-5 GT,MMe,Staged for Murder . 150.00
8-6 Unlucky Seven,July, 1949 . . 150.00

ARMY AND NAVY COMICS
Street & Smith, May, 1941
1 Hawaii is Calling You,Capt.
   Fury,Nick Carter 400.00
2 Private Rock V;Hitler 250.00
3 The Fighting Fourth 250.00
4 The Fighting Irish 250.00
5 I:Super Snipe 350.00
Becomes:

SUPERSNIPE COMICS
6 A "Comic" With A Sense
   of Humor 650.00
7 A:Wacky, Rex King 400.00
8 Axis Powers & Satan(c),
   Hitler(c) 450.00
9 Hitler Voodoo Doll (c) 500.00
10 Lighting (c). 400.00
11 A:Little Nemo 400.00
12 Football(c) 400.00
2-1 B:Huck Finn 275.00
2-2 Battles Shark 275.00
2-3 Battles Dinosaur 275.00
2-4 Baseball(c) 275.00
2-5 Battles Dinosaur 275.00
2-6 A:Pochontas 275.00
2-7 A:Wing Woo Woo 275.00
2-8 A:Huck Finn 275.00
2-9 Dotty Loves Trouble 275.00
2-10 Assists Farm Labor
   Shortage 275.00
2-11 Dotty & the Jelly Beans. . . . 275.00
2-12 Statue of Liberty 275.00
3-1 Ice Skating(c) 225.00
3-2 V:Pirates(c). 225.00
3-3 Baseball(c). 225.00
3-4 Jungle(c) 225.00
3-5 Learn Piglatin 225.00
3-6 Football Hero 225.00
3-7 Saves Girl From Grisley 225.00
3-8 Rides a Wild Horse. 225.00
3-9 Powers Santa's Sleigh 225.00
3-10 Plays Basketball 225.00
3-11 Is A Baseball Pitcher. 225.00
3-12 Flies with the Birds 225.00
4-1 Catches A Whale 175.00
4-2 Track & Field Athlete 175.00
4-3 Think Machine(c) 175.00
4-4 Alpine Skiier 175.00
4-5 Becomes a Boxer. 175.00

4-6 Race Car Driver 175.00	
4-7 Bomber(c) 175.00	
4-8 Baseball Star 175.00	
4-9 Football Hero 175.00	
4-10 Christmas(c) 175.00	
4-11 Artic Adventure 175.00	
4-12 The Ghost Remover 175.00	
5-1 Aug.–Sept., 1949 . . . . 175.00	

SUPER SPY
Centaur Publications
Oct.–Nov., 1940

1 O:Sparkler 900.00
2 A:Night Hawk, Drew Ghost, Tim
 Blain, S.S. Swanson the Inner
 Circle, Duke Collins, Gentlemen
 of Misfortune 550.00

SUPER WESTERN COMICS
Youthful Magazines Aug., 1950

1 BP,BP,(c),B;Buffalo Bill,Wyatt
 Earp,CalamityJane,SamSlade 55.00
2 thru 4 March, 1951 . . . . @35.00

SUPER WESTERN FUNNIES
(see SUPER FUNNIES)

SUPERWORLD COMICS
Komos Publications
(Hugo Gernsback)
April, 1940

1 FP,FP(c),B:MilitaryPowers,BuzzAllen
 Smarty Artie, Alibi Alige . . . 4,800.00
2 FP,FP(c),A:Mario 2,900.00
3 FP,FP(c),V:Vest Wearing
 Giant Grasshoppers 2,000.00

SUSPENSE COMICS
Et Es Go Mag. Inc.
(Continental Magazines)
Dec., 1945

1 LbC, Bondage(c),B:Grey
 Mask 3,200.00
2 DRi,I:The Mask 2,400.00
3 LbC,ASh(c),Bondage(c) . . . 8,000.00

Suspense Comics #9
© Continental Magazines

---

4 LbC,LbC(c),Bondage(c) . . . 1,800.00	
5 LbC,LbC(c) 1,700.00	
6 LbC,LbC(c),The End of	
the Road 1,700.00	
7 LbC,LbC(c) 1,300.00	
8 LbC,LbC(c) 3,500.00	
9 LbC,LbC(c) 1,300.00	
10 RP,LbC,LbC(c) 1,300.00	
11 RP,LbC,LbC(c),Satan(c) . . . 3,500.00	
12 LbC,LbC(c),Dec., 1946 . . . . 1,300.00	

SUSPENSE DETECTIVE
Fawcett Publications
June, 1952

1 GE,MBi,MBi(c),Death Poised
 to Strike 300.00
2 GE,MSy 175.00
3 A Furtive Footstep 150.00
4 MBi,MSy,Bondage(c),A Blood
 Chilling Scream 135.00
5 MSy,MSy(c),MBi,A Hair-Trigger
 from Death, March, 1953 . . . 150.00

SUZIE COMICS
(see TOP-NOTCH COMICS)

SWEENEY
Standard Comics
June, 1949

4 Buzz Sawyer's Pal 45.00
5 Sept., 1949 . . . . 40.00

SWEETHEART DIARY
Fawcett
Winter, 1949

1 . . . . 75.00
2 . . . . 40.00
3 and 4 WW. . . . . @75.00
5 thru 10 . . . . @30.00
11 thru 14 . . . . @20.00

SWEETHEART DIARY
Charlton Comics
Jan. 1953

32 . . . . 22.00
33 thru 40 . . . . @10.00
41 thru 65 . . . . @6.00

SWEET HEART
(see CAPTAIN MIDNIGHT)

SWEET LOVE
Harvey Publications
(Home Comics)
Sept., 1949

1 Ph(c) 35.00
2 Ph(c) 20.00
3 BP 20.00
4 Ph(c) 15.00
5 BP,JKa,Ph(c) 30.00

SWEET SIXTEEN
Parents' Magazine Group
Aug.–Sept., 1946

1 Van Johnson story 125.00
2 Alan Ladd story 100.00
3 Rip Taylor. 60.00
4 E:Taylor 60.00
5 Gregory Peck story (c) 55.00
6 Dick Hammes(c). 50.00

---

7 Ronald Reagan(c). 125.00	
8 Shirley Jones(c) 50.00	
9 William Holden(c) 50.00	
10 James Stewart(c). 55.00	
11 . . . . 50.00	
12 Bob Cummings(c) 50.00	
13 Robert Mitchum(c) 60.00	

SWIFT ARROW
Farrell Publications(Ajax)
Feb.–March, 1954

1 Lone Rider's Redskin Brother . 60.00
2 . . . . 35.00
3 . . . . 30.00
4 . . . . 30.00
5 Oct.–Nov., 1954 . . . . 30.00

(2nd Series) April, 1957

1 . . . . 30.00
2 B:Lone Rider 20.00
3 Sept., 1957 . . . . 20.00

TAFFY
Orbit Publications/Rural Home/
Taffy Publications
March–April, 1945

1 LbC(c),(fa),Bondage(c) 300.00
2 LbC(c),(fa) 125.00
3 (fa) 60.00
4 (fa) 50.00
5 LbC(c),A:Van Johnson 125.00
6 A:Perry Como 60.00
7 A:Dave Clark 75.00
8 A:Glen Ford 60.00
9 A:Lon McCallister 60.00
10 A:John Hodiak 60.00
11 A:Mickey Rooney 60.00
12 Feb., 1948. . . . . 60.00

TAILSPIN
Spotlight Publications
Nov., 1944

N# LbC(c),A:Firebird 200.00

TALES FROM THE CRYPT
(see CRIME PATROL)

TALES FROM THE TOMB
(see Dell Giants)

TALES OF HORROR
Toby Press/Minoan Publ. Corp
June, 1952

1 Demons of the Underworld . . . 250.00
2 What was the Thing in
 the Pool?,Torture 200.00
3 The Big Snake 125.00
4 The Curse of King Kala! 125.00
5 Hand of Fate 125.00
6 The Fiend of Flame 125.00
7 Beast From The Deep 125.00
8 The Snake that Held A
 City Captive 125.00
9 It Came From the Bottom
 of the World 150.00
10 The Serpent Strikes. 150.00
11 Death Flower? 150.00
12 Guaranteed to Make Your
 Hair Stand on End 165.00
13 Ghost with a Torch;
 Oct., 1954 . . . . 135.00

GOLDEN AGE

TALES OF TERROR
Toby Press, 1952
1 Just A Bunch of Hokey
Hogwash 175.00

Tales of TerrorAnnual #3
© E.C. Comics

TALES OF TERROR
ANNUAL
E.C. 1951
N# AF 3,500.00
2 AF 1,500.00
3 . . . . 1,100.00

TALLY-HO COMICS
Baily Publishing Co.
Dec., 1944
N# FF,A:Snowman 250.00

TARGET COMICS
Funnnies Inc./Novelty Publ./
Premium Group/Curtis
Circulation Co./Star
Publications, Feb., 1940
1 BEv,JCo,CBu,JSm;B,O&I:Manowar,
White Streak,Bull's-Eye;B:City
Editor,High Grass Twins,T-Men,
Rip Rory,Fantastic Feature
Films, Calling 2-R 3,700.00
2 BEv,JSm,JCo,CBu,White
Streak(c) 2,000.00
3 BEv,JSm,JCo,CBu 1,100.00
4 JSm,JCo 1,100.00
5 CBu,BW,O:White Streak . . . 3,500.00
6 CBu,BW,White Streak(c) . . . 1,300.00
7 CBu,BW,BW(c),V:Planetoid
Stories,Space Hawk(c) . . . 4,000.00
8 CBu,BW,White Shark(c) 1,000.00
9 CBu,BW,White Shark(c) 1,000.00
10 CBu,BW,JK(c),The
Target(c) 1,300.00
11 BW,The Target(c) 1,100.00
12 BW,same 1,000.00
2-1 BW,CBu 700.00
2-2 BW,BoW(c) 550.00
2-3 BW,BoW(c),The Target(c) . . . 450.00
2-4 BW,B:Cadet 450.00
2-5 BW,BoW(c),The Target(c) . . . 425.00
2-6 BW,The Target(c) 425.00
2-7 BW,The Cadet(c) 425.00
2-8 BW,same 425.00

2-9 BW,The Target(c) 425.00
2-10 BW,same 700.00
2-11 BW,The Cadet(c) 425.00
2-12 BW,same 425.00
3-1 BW,same 400.00
3-2 BW 400.00
3-3 BW,The Target(c) 400.00
3-4 BW,The Cadet(c) 400.00
3-5 BW 400.00
3-6 BW,War Bonds(c) 400.00
3-7 BW 400.00
3-8 BW,War Bonds(c) 400.00
3-9 BW 400.00
3-10 BW 400.00
3-11 . . . . 90.00
3-12 . . . . 90.00
4-1 JJo(c) 65.00
4-2 ERy(c) 65.00
4-3 AVi 65.00
4-4 . . . . 65.00
4-5 API(c),Statue of Liberty(c) . . . 75.00
4-6 BW 65.00
4-7 AVi 65.00
4-8,Christmas(c) 65.00
4-9 . . . . 65.00
4-10 . . . . 65.00
4-11 . . . . 65.00
4-12 . . . . 65.00
5-1 . . . . 50.00

Target #18
© Star Publications

5-2 The Target 55.00
5-3 Savings Checkers(c) 50.00
5-4 War Bonds Ph(c) 50.00
5-5 thru 5-12 . . . . @50.00
6-1 The Target(c) 55.00
6-2 . . . . 50.00
6-3 Red Cross(c) 50.00
6-4 . . . . 50.00
6-5 Savings Bonds(c) 50.00
6-6 The Target(c) 50.00
6-7 The Cadet(c) 50.00
6-8 AFa 50.00
6-9 The Target(c) 50.00
6-10 . . . . 50.00
6-11 . . . . 50.00
6-12 . . . . 50.00
7-1 . . . . 50.00
7-2 Bondage(c) 50.00
7-3 The Target(c) 50.00
7-4 DRi,The Cadet(c) 50.00
7-5 . . . . 50.00
7-6 DRi(c) 50.00
7-7 The Cadet(c) 50.00
7-8 DRi(c) 50.00
7-9 The Cadet(c) 50.00

7-10 DRi,DRi(c) 50.00
7-11 . . . . 50.00
7-12 JH(c) 50.00
8-1 . . . . 50.00
8-2 DRi,DRi(c),BK 50.00
8-3 DRi,The Cadet(c) 50.00
8-4 DRi,DRi(c) 50.00
8-5 DRi,The Cadet(c) 50.00
8-6 DRi,DRi(c) 50.00
8-7 BK,DRi,DRi(c) 50.00
8-8 DRi,The Cadet(c) 50.00
8-9 DRi,The Cadet(c) 50.00
8-10 DRi,KBa,LbC(c) 200.00
8-11 DRi,The Cadet 50.00
8-12 DRi,The Cadet 50.00
9-1 DRi,LbC(c) 200.00
9-2 DRi. 50.00
9-3 DRi,Bondage(c),The Cadet(c) . 50.00
9-4 DRi,LbC(c) 200.00
9-5 DRi,Baseball(c) 50.00
9-6 DRi,LbC(c) 200.00
9-7 DRi 50.00
9-8 DRi,LbC(c) 200.00
9-9 DRi,Football(c) 50.00
9-10 DRi,LbC(c) 200.00
9-11,The Cadet. 50.00
9-12 LbC(c),Gems(c) 200.00
10-1,The Cadet 50.00
10-2 LbC(c) 200.00
10-3 LbC(c) 200.00
Becomes:

TARGET WESTERN
ROMANCES
Star Publications
Oct.–Nov., 1949
106 LbC(c),The Beauty Scar. . . . 250.00
107 LbC(c),The Brand Upon His
Heart 200.00

TARZAN
Dell Publishing Co.
Jan.–Feb. 1948
1 V:White Savages of Vari. . . . 1,000.00
2 Captives of Thunder Valley . . . 550.00
3 Dwarfs of Didona 400.00
4 The Lone Hunter. 400.00
5 The Men of Greed 400.00
6 Outlwas of Pal-ul-Don 300.00
7 Valley of the Monsters 300.00
8 The White Pygmies 300.00
9 The Men of A-Lur 300.00
10 Treasure of the Bolgani 300.00

Tarzan #8
© Dell Publishing Co.

11 The Sable Lion	250.00
12 The Price of Peace	250.00
13 B:Lex Barker photo(c)	225.00
14	225.00
15	225.00
16	200.00
17	200.00
18	200.00
19	200.00
20	200.00
21 thru 30	@150.00
31 thru 54 E:L.Barker Ph(c)	@100.00
55 thru 70	@75.00
71 thru 79	@50.00
80 thru 90 B:ScottGordonPh(c)	@30.00
91 thru 99	@28.00
100	40.00
101 thru 110 E:S.GordonPh(c)	@25.00
111 thru 120	@20.00
121 thru 131	@20.00

TEEN-AGE DIARY SECRETS
St. John Publishing Co.
Oct., 1949

6 MB,PH(c)	75.00
7 MB,PH(c)	85.00
8 MB,PH(c)	75.00
9 MB,PH(c)	85.00

Becomes:

DIARY SECRETS

10 MB	65.00
11 MB	55.00
12 thru 19 MB	@50.00
20 MB,JKu	55.00
21 thru 28 MB	@30.00
29 MB,Comics Code	25.00
30 MB	25.00

TEEN-AGE ROMANCES
St. John Publishing Co.
Jan., 1949

1 MB(c),MB	275.00
2 MB(c),MB	150.00
3 MB(c),MB	175.00
4 Ph(c)	150.00
5 MB,Ph(c)	150.00
6 MB,Ph(c)	150.00
7 MB,Ph(c)	150.00
8 MB,Ph(c)	150.00
9 MB,MB(c),JKu	160.00
10 thru 27 MB,MB(c),JKu	@125.00
28 thru 30	@50.00
31 thru 34 MB(c)	@50.00
35 thru 42 MB(c),MB	@60.00
43 MB(c),MB,Comics Code	40.00
44 MB(c),MB	40.00
45 MB(c),MB	40.00

TEEN-AGE TEMPTATIONS
St. John Publishing Co.
Oct., 1952

1 MB(c),MB	325.00
2 MB(c),MB	125.00
3 MB(c),MB	150.00
4 MB(c),MB	150.00
5 MB(c),MB	150.00
6 MB(c),MB	150.00
7 MB(c),MB	150.00
8 MB(c),MB,Drug	175.00
9 MB(c),MB	150.00

Becomes:

GOING STEADY

10 MB(c),MB	85.00
11 MB(c),MB.	60.00
12 MB(c),MB	60.00

13 MB(c),MB	60.00
14 MB(c),MB	60.00

TEENIE WEENIES, THE
Ziff-Davis Publishing Co.
1951

10	85.00
11	80.00

TEEN LIFE
(see YOUNG LIFE)

TEGRA, JUNGLE EMPRESS
(see ZEGRA, JUNGLE EMPRESS)

TELEVISION COMICS
Animated Cartoons
(Standard Comics), Feb., 1950

5 Humorous Format,I:Willie Nilly	50.00
6	35.00
7	35.00
8 May, 1950	35.00

TELEVISION PUPPET SHOW
Avon Periodicals, 1950

1 F:Sparky Smith,Spotty, Cheeta, Speedy	80.00
2 Nov., 1950	75.00

TELL IT TO THE MARINES
Toby Press, March, 1952

1 I:Spike & Pat	125.00
2 A:Madame Cobra	60.00
3 Spike & Bat on a Commando Raid!	40.00
4 Veil Dancing(c)	42.00
5	42.00
6 To Paris	35.00
7 Ph(c),The Chinese Bugle	30.00
8 Ph(c),V:Communists in South Korea	30.00
9 Ph(c)	30.00
10	30.00
11	30.00
12	30.00
13 John Wayne Ph(c)	75.00
14 Ph(c)	30.00
15 Ph(c),July, 1955	30.00

TENDER ROMANCE
Key Publications
Dec., 1953

1	65.00
2	35.00

Becomes:

IDEAL ROMANCE

3	35.00
4 thru 8	@20.00

Becomes:

DIARY CONFESSIONS

9	25.00
10	15.00

TERRIFIC COMICS
(see HORRIFIC)

Terrific Comics
© *Continental Magazines*

TERRIFIC COMICS
Et Es Go Mag. Inc./
Continental Magazines
Jan., 1944

1 LbC,DRi(c),F:Kid Terrific Drug	2,700.00
2 LcC,ASh(c),B:Boomerang, `Comics' McCormic	2,000.00
3 LbC,LbC(c)	2,000.00
4 LbC,RP(c)	3,500.00
5 LbC,BF,ASh(c),Bondage(c)	4,000.00
6 LbC,LbC(c),BF,Nov.,1944	1,700.00

TERROR ILLUSTRATED
E.C. Comics
Nov.–Dec., 1955

1 JCr,GE,Grl,JO,RC(c)	125.00
2 Spring, 1956	100.00

TERRIFYING TALES
Star Publications
Jan., 1953

11 LbC,LbC(c),`TyrantsofTerror'.	375.00
12 LbC,LbC(c),`Bondage(c), `Jungle Mystery'	300.00
13 LbC(c),Bondage(c),`The Death-Fire,Devil Head(c)	375.00
14 LbC(c),Bondage(c),`The Weird Idol'	325.00
15 LbC(c),`The Grim Secret', April, 1954	325.00

Becomes:

JUNGLE THRILLS
Star Publications Feb., 1952

16 LbC(c),`Kingdom of Unseen Terror'	300.00

Becomes:

TERRORS OF THE JUNGLE

17 LbC(c),Bondage(c)	300.00
18 LbC(c),Strange Monsters	225.00
19 JyD,LbC(c),Bondage(c),The Golden Ghost Gorilla	225.00
20 JyD,LbC(c),The Creeping Scourge	225.00

All comics prices listed are for *Near Mint* condition.   **CVA Page 413**

GOLDEN AGE

21 LbC(c),Evil Eyes of Death!. . . 250.00
4 JyD,LbC(c),Morass of Death . 175.00
5 JyD,LbC(c),Bondage's,
  Savage Train 200.00
6 JyD,LbC(c),Revolt of the
  Jungle Monsters 200.00
7 JyD,LbC(c) 175.00
8 JyD,LbC(c),Death's Grim
  Reflection 175.00
9 JyD,LbC(c),Doom to
  Evil-Doers 175.00
10 JyD,LbC(c),Black Magic,
  Sept., 1954. . . . . 175.00

BOY EXPLORERS
1 S&K(c),S&K,The Cadet. 650.00
2 S&K(c),S&K 750.00
Becomes:

TERRY AND THE PIRATES
3 S&K,MC(c),MC,Terry and
  Dragon Lady. 300.00
4 S&K,MC(c),MC. 175.00
5 S&K,MC(c),MC,BP,
  Chop-Chop(c). 100.00
6 S&K,.MC(c),MC 100.00
7 S&K,MC(c),MC,BP 100.00
8 S&K,MC(c),MC,BP 100.00
9 S&K,MC(c),MC,BP 100.00
10 S&K,MC(c),MC,BP. 100.00
11 S&K,MC(c),MC,BP,
  A:Man in Black. 75.00
12 S&K,MC(c),MC,BP. 75.00
13 S&K,MC(c),MC,Belly Dancers . 75.00
14 thru 20 S&K,MC(c),MC. . . . @60.00
22 thru 26 S&K,MC(c),MC. . . . @55.00
27 Charlton Comics 50.00
28. . . . . 50.00

TERRY-BEARS COMICS
St. John Publishing Co.
June, 1952
1 . . . . 20.00
2 & 3 . . . . @15.00

TERRY-TOONS COMICS
Select, Timely, Marvel,
St. Johns, 1942
1 Paul Terry (fa) 1,300.00
2 . . . . 500.00
3 thru 6 . . . . @350.00
7 Hitler,Hirohito,Mussolini(c) 300.00
8 thru 20 . . . . @225.00
21 thru 37 . . . . @150.00
38 I&(c):Mighty Mouse 850.00
39 Mighty Mouse 250.00
40 thru 49 All Mighty Mouse . . @125.00
50 I:Heckle & Jeckle. 250.00
51 thru 60. . . . . @75.00
61 thru 70. . . . . @65.00
71 thru 86 . . . . @60.00

TEXAN, THE
St. John Publishing Co.
Aug., 1948
1 GT,F:Buckskin Belle,The Gay
  Buckaroo,Mustang Jack 80.00
2 GT 40.00
3 BLb(c) 35.00
4 MB,MB(c) 60.00
5 MB,MB(c),Mystery Rustlers
  of the Rio Grande 60.00
6 MB,MB(c),Death Valley
  Double-Cross 50.00
7 MB,MB(c),Comanche Justice
  Strikes at Midnight 60.00
8 MB,MB(c),Scalp Hunters

Hide their Tracks 60.00
9 MB(c),Ghost Terror of
  the Blackfeet 60.00
10 MB,MB(c),Treason Rides
  the Warpath 50.00
11 MB,MB(c),Hawk Knife 60.00
12 MB 60.00
13 MB,Doublecross at Devil'sDen . 60.00
14 MB,Ambush at Buffalo Trail . . . 60.00
15 MB,Twirling Blades Tame
  Treachery 60.00
Becomes:

FIGHTIN' TEXAN
16 GT,Wanted Dead or Alive 45.00
17 LC,LC(c);Killers Trail,
  Dec., 1952 . . . . 40.00

TEX FARRELL
D.S. Publishing Co.
March–April, 1948
1 Pride of the Wild West 75.00

TEX GRANGER
(see CALLING ALL BOYS)

TEX RITTER WESTERN
Fawcett Publications/
Charlton Comics
Oct., 1950–May 1959
1 Ph(c),B:Tex Ritter, his Horse
  White Flash, his dog Fury, and
  his mom Nancy 525.00
2 Ph(c),Vanishing Varmints 250.00
3 Ph(c),Blazing Six-Guns 175.00
4 Ph(c),The Jaws of Terror 150.00
5 Ph(c),Bullet Trail 150.00
6 Ph(c),Killer Bait 150.00
7 Ph(c),Gunsmoke Revenge . . . 125.00
8 Ph(c),Lawless Furnace Valley 125.00
9 Ph(c),The Spider's Web 125.00
10 Ph(c),The Ghost Town 125.00
11 Ph(c),Saddle Conquest 125.00
12 Ph(c),Prairie Inferno. 75.00
13 Ph(c). 75.00
14 Ph(c). 75.00
15 Ph(c). 75.00
16 thru 19 Ph(c) . . . . @75.00
20 Ph(c),Stagecoach To Danger . . 75.00
21 . . . . 75.00
22 Panic at Diamond B. 60.00
23 A:Young Falcon 50.00
24 A:Young Falcon 50.00
25 A:Young Falcon 50.00
26 thru 38 . . . . @45.00
39 AW,AW(c) 45.00
40 thru 46 . . . . @40.00

THING!, THE
Song Hits/Capitol Stories/
Charlton Comics, Feb., 1952
1 Horror. 600.00
2 Crazy King(c) 400.00
3 . . . . 400.00
4 AFa(c),I Was A Zombie 350.00
5 LM(c),Severed Head(c). 375.00
6 . . . . 350.00
7 Fingenail to Eye(c) 500.00
8 . . . . 350.00
9 Severe 550.00
10 Devil(c) 350.00
11 SC,Cleaver 450.00
12 SD,SD(c),Neck Blood
  Sucking 600.00
13 SD,SD(c). 600.00
14 SD,SD(c). 600.00

The Thing #3
© Charlton Comics

15 SD,SD(c). 600.00
16 Eye Torture 400.00
17 BP,SD(c). 550.00
Becomes:

BLUE BEETLE
18 America's Fastest Moving
  Crusader Against Crime 125.00
19 JKa,Lightning Fast. 150.00
20 JKa 150.00
21 The Invincible 100.00
Becomes:

MR. MUSCLES
22 World's Most Perfect Man 30.00
23 Aug., 1956. . . . . 20.00

THIS IS SUSPENSE
(see LAWBREAKERS)

THIS IS WAR
Standard Comics
July, 1952
5 ATh,Show Them How To Die . . 80.00
6 ATh,Make Him A Soldier 75.00
7 One Man For Himself 25.00
8 Miracle on Massacre Hill 25.00
9 ATh,May, 1953 . . . . 60.00

THIS IS SUSPENSE!
(see STRANGE SUSPENSE STORIES)

THIS MAGAZINE IS HAUNTED
Fawcett Publications/
Charlton Comics
Oct., 1951
1 MBi,F:Doctor Death 450.00
2 GE 300.00
3 MBi,Quest of the Vampire . . . 200.00
4 BP,The Blind, The Doomed
  and the Dead 200.00
5 BP,GE,The Slithering Horror
  of Skontong Swamp! 300.00
6 Secret of the Walking Dead . . 150.00
7 The Man Who Saw Too Much . 150.00
8 The House in the Web 150.00
9 The Witch of Tarlo. 150.00

GOLDEN AGE

This Magazine is Haunted #5
© Fawcett Publications

10 I Am Dr Death,
  Severed Head(c) 225.00
11 BP,Touch of Death 125.00
12 BP. 125.00
13 BP,Severed Head(c) 200.00
14 BP,Horrors of the Damned . . . 125.00
15 DG(c) 100.00
16 SD(c). 250.00
17 SD,SD(c) 265.00
18 SD,SD(c) 265.00
19 SD(c). 225.00
20 SMz(c). 125.00
21 SD(c). 200.00
Becomes:

DANGER AND ADVENTURE

22 The Viking King,F:Ibis the
  Invincible 50.00
23 F:Nyoka the Jungle Girl
  Comics Code 45.00
24 DG&AA(c) 35.00
25 thru 27 . . . . @30.00
Becomes:

ROBIN HOOD AND HIS MERRY MEN

28 . . . . 40.00
29 thru 37 . . . . @30.00
38 SD,Aug., 1958. . . . . 75.00

3-D-ELL

Dell Publishing Co., 1953
1 Rootie Kazootie 300.00
2 Rootie Kazootie 275.00
3 Flunkey Louise 275.00

THREE RING COMICS

Spotlight Publishers
March, 1945
1 Funny Animal 50.00

THREE STOOGES

Jubilee Publ.
Feb., 1949
1 JKu,Infinity(c) 850.00
2 JKu,On the Set of the
  `The Gorilla Girl' 600.00

St. John Publishing Co.
1 JKu,`Bell Bent for
  Treasure, Sept., 1953. . . . . . 500.00

2 JKu. 350.00
3 JKu,3D 350.00
4 JKu,Medical Mayhem 250.00
5 JKu,Shempador-Matador
  Supreme 250.00
6 JKu, ... 250.00
7 JKu,Ocotber, 1954 . . . . 250.00

THRILLING COMICS

Better Publ./Nedor/
Standard Comics
Feb., 1940
1 B&O:Doc Strange,B:Nickie
  Norton 2,400.00
2 B:Rio Kid,Woman in Red
  Pinocchio 1,000.00
3 B:Lone Eagle,The Ghost 650.00
4 Dr Strange(c) 500.00
5 Bondage(c) 450.00
6 Dr Strange(c) 450.00
7 Dr Strange(c) 450.00
8 V:Pirates 450.00
9 Bondage(c) 450.00
10 V:Nazis 450.00
11 ASh(c),V:Nazis. 425.00
12 ASh(c) 400.00
13 ASh(c),Bondage(c) 450.00
14 ASh(c). 425.00
15 ASh(c),V:Nazis 425.00
16 Bondage(c) 450.00
17 Dr Strange(c). 450.00
18 Dr Strange(c). 450.00
19 I&O:American Crusader 450.00
20 Bondage(c) 450.00
21 American Crusader(c) 325.00
22 Bondage(c) 350.00
23 American Crusader 325.00
24 I:Mike in Doc Strange. 325.00
25 DR Strange(c) 325.00
26 Dr Strange(c). 325.00
27 Bondage(c) 350.00
28 Bondage(c) 350.00
29 E:Rio Kid;Bondage(c). 350.00
30 Bondage(c) 350.00
31 Dr Strange(c). 300.00
32 Dr Strange(c). 275.00
33 Dr Strange(c). 275.00
34 Dr Strange(c). 275.00
35 Dr Strange 275.00
36 ASh(c),B:Commando 300.00
37 BO,ASh(c) 275.00
38 ASh(c) 275.00
39 ASh(c),E:American Crusader . 275.00
40 ASh(c) 275.00
41 ASh(c),F:American Crusader . 275.00
42 ASh(c) 200.00
43 ASh(c) 200.00
44 ASh(c),Hitler(c) 300.00
45 EK,ASh(c) 210.00
46 ASh(c) 210.00
47 ASh(c) 200.00
48 EK,ASh(c) 200.00
49 ASh(c) 200.00
50 ASh(c) 200.00
51 ASh(c) 200.00
52 ASh(c),E:Th Ghost;
  Peto-Bondage(c) 225.00
53 ASh(c),B:Phantom Detective . 200.00
54 ASh(c),Bondage(c) 225.00
55 ASh(c),E:Lone Eagle 200.00
56 ASh(c),B:Princess Pantha . . 325.00
57 ASh(c) 250.00
58 ASh(c) 250.00
59 ASh(c) 250.00
60 ASh(c) 250.00
61 ASh(c),GRi,A:Lone Eagle. . . 250.00
62 ASh(c) 250.00
63 ASh(c),GT 250.00
64 ASh(c) 250.00
65 ASh(c),E:Commando Cubs,

Thrilling Comics #29
© Standard Comics

Phantom Detective 250.00
66 ASh(c). 250.00
67 FF,ASh(c) 350.00
68 FF,ASh(c) 350.00
69 FF,ASh(c) 350.00
70 FF,ASh(c) 350.00
71 FF,ASh(c) 350.00
72 FF,ASh(c) 350.00
73 FF,ASh(c) 350.00
74 E:Princess Pantha;
  B:Buck Ranger. 200.00
75 B:Western Front. 100.00
76 . . . . 100.00
77 ASh(c) 100.00
78 Bondage(c) 110.00
79 BK. 100.00
80 JSe,BE,April, 1951. . . . . 110.00

THRILLING CRIME CASES

Star Publications
June–July, 1950
41 LbC(c),The Unknowns 175.00
42 LbC(c),The Gunmaster 150.00
43 LbC,LbC(c),The Chameleon. . 175.00
44 LbC(c),Sugar Bowl Murder. . . 175.00
45 LbC(c),Maze of Murder 175.00
46 LbC,LbC(c),Modern
  Communications. 125.00
47 LbC(c),The Careless Killer . . . 125.00
48 LbC(c),Road Black. 125.00
49 LbC(c),The Poisoner 225.00
Becomes:

SHOCKING MYSTERY CASES

50 JyD,LbC(c),Dead Man's
  Revenge. 275.00
51 JyD,LbC(c),A Murderer's
  Reward 150.00
52 LbC(c),The Carnival Killer . . . 150.00
53 LbC(c),The Long Shot of Evil . 150.00
54 LbC(c),Double-Cross of Death 150.00
55 LbC(c),Return from Death . . . 150.00
56 LbC(c),The Chase 175.00
57 LbC(c),Thrilling Cases 125.00
58 LbC(c),Killer at Large. 125.00
59 LbC(c),Relentless Huntdown. . 125.00
60 LbC(c),Lesson of the Law,
  Oct., 1954 . . . . 125.00

THRILLING ROMANCES
Standard Comics
Dec., 1949
5 Ph(c) 55.00
6 Ph(c) 25.00
7 Ph(c),JSe,BE 35.00
8 Ph(c) 25.00
9 Ph(c),GT 30.00
10 Ph(c),JSe,BE. 30.00
11 Ph(c),JSe,BE 30.00
12 Ph(c),WW 45.00
13 Ph(c),JSe 25.00
14 Ph(c),Danny Kaye 18.00
15 Ph(c),Tony Martin,Ph(c) 18.00
16 Ph(c) 15.00
17 Ph(c) 15.00
18 Ph(c) 15.00
19 Ph(c) 15.00
20 Ph(c) 15.00
21 Ph(c) 15.00
22 Ph(c),ATn 35.00
23 Ph(c),ATn 35.00
24 Ph(c),ATn3 . . . . 35.00
25 Ph(c),ATn 35.00

THRILLING TRUE STORY OF THE BASEBALL GIANTS
Fawcett Publications, 1952
N# Partial Ph(c),Famous Giants
   of the Past 550.00
2 Yankees Ph(c),Joe DiMaggio,
   Yogi Berra,Mickey Mantle,
   Casey Stengel 550.00

TICK TOCK TALES
Magazine Enterprises
Jan., 1946
1 (fa) Koko & Kola 65.00
2 (fa) Calender 35.00
3 thru 10 (fa) . . . . @25.00
11 thru 18 (fa) . . . . @20.00
19 (fa),Flag(c). 20.00
20 (fa) 20.00
21 (fa) 15.00
22 (fa) 15.00
23 (fa),Mugsy Mouse 15.00
24 thru 33 (fa) . . . . @15.00
34 (fa), 1951. . . . . 15.00

TIM HOLT
Magazine Enterprises
Jan.–Feb., 1949
4 FBe,Ph(c). 350.00
5 FBe,Ph(c). 200.00
6 FBe,Ph(c),I:Calico Kid 225.00
7 FBe,Ph(c),Man-Killer Mustang 175.00
8 FBe,Ph(c) 175.00
9 FBe,DAy(c),TerribleTenderfoot 175.00
10 FBe,DAy(c),The Devil Horse . 175.00
11 FBe,DAy(c),O&I:Ghost Rider . 275.00
12 FBe,DAy(c),Battle at
   Bullock Gap 80.00
13 FBe,DAy(c),Ph(c). 80.00
14 FBe,DAy(c),Ph(c),The
   Honest Bandits. 80.00
15 FBe,DAy,Ph(c) 80.00
16 FBe,DAy,Ph(c) 80.00
17 FBe,DAy,Ph(c). 250.00
18 FBe,DAy,Ph(c) 75.00
19 FBe,DAy,They Dig By Night . . 60.00
20 FBe,DAy,O:Red Mask 90.00
21 FBe,DAy,FF(c). 225.00
22 FBe,DAy 55.00
23 FF,FBe,DAy 175.00
24 FBe,DAy,FBe(c). 55.00

25 FBe,DAy,FBe(c). 100.00
26 FBe,DAy,FBe(c). 50.00
27 FBe,DAy,FBe(c),V:Straw Man . 50.00
28 FBe,DAy,FBe(c),Ph(c) 50.00
29 FBe,DAy,FBe,Ph(c),. 50.00
30 FBe,DAy,FBe(c),Lady Doom
   & The Death Wheel 45.00
31 FBe,DAy,FBe(c). 45.00
32 FBe,DAy,FBe(c). 45.00
33 FBe,DAy,FBe(c). 45.00
34 FBe,DAy,FBe(c). 60.00
35 FBe,DAy,FBe(c). 60.00
36 FBe,DAy,FBe(c),Drugs. 65.00
37 FBe,DAy,FBe(c). 65.00
38 FBe,DAy,FBe(c). 65.00
39 FBe,DAy,FBe(c),3D Effect . . . 70.00
40 FBe,DAy,FBe(c). 70.00
41 FBe,DAy,FBe(c). 70.00
Becomes:

RED MASK
42 FBe,DAy,FBe(c),3D 125.00
43 FBe,DAy,FBe(c),3D 100.00
44 FBe,DAy,FBe(c),Death at
   Split Mesa,3D. 90.00
45 FBe,DAy,FBe(c),V:False Red
   Mask 90.00
46 FBe,DAy,FBe(c). 90.00
47 FBe,DAy,FBe(c). 90.00
48 FBe,DAy,FBe(c),Comics Code . 85.00
49 FBe,DAy,FBe(c). 85.00
50 FBe,DAy 85.00
51 FBe,DAy,The Magic of `The
   Presto Kid' 85.00
52 FBe,DAy,O:Presto Kid 90.00
53 FBe,DAy 70.00
54 FBe,DAy,Sept., 1957 . . . . 90.00

TIM TYLER COWBOY
Standard Comics
Nov., 1948
11 . . . . 40.00
12 . . . . 30.00
13 The Doll Told the Secret. 30.00
14 Danger at Devil's Acres 30.00
15 Secret Treasure. 30.00
16 . . . . 30.00
17 . . . . 30.00
18 1950 . . . . 30.00

TINY TOTS COMICS
Dell Publishing Co., 1943
1 . . . . 300.00

TINY TOTS COMICS
E.C. Comics, March, 1946
N# Your First Comic Book
   B:Burton Geller(c) and art. . . 225.00
2 . . . . 125.00
3 Celebrate the 4th 100.00
4 Go Back to School 120.00
5 Celebrate the Winter 100.00
6 Do Their Spring Gardening . . . 90.00
7 On a Thrilling Ride 100.00
8 On a Summer Vacation 100.00
9 On a Plane Ride 100.00
10 Merry X-Mas Tiny Tots
   E:Burton Geller(c)and art . . . 100.00

TIP TOP COMICS
United Features,St. John,Dell
1930
1 HF,Li'l Abner 6,500.00
2 HF 1,600.00
3 HF,Tarzan(c) 1,500.00
4 HF,Li'l Abner(c). 900.00
5 HF,Capt&Kids(c). 675.00

6 HF 650.00
7 HF 650.00
8 HF,Li'l Abner(c). 650.00
9 HF,Tarzan(c). 800.00
10 HF,Li'l Abner(c). 650.00
11 HF,Tarzan(c) 600.00
12 HF,Li'l Abner 500.00
13 HF,Tarzan(c) 525.00
14 HF,Li'l Abner(c). 500.00
15 HF,Capt&kids(c). 500.00
16 HF,Tarzan(c) 525.00
17 HF,Li'l Abner(c). 500.00
18 HF,Tarzan(c) 525.00
19 HF,Football(c) 450.00
20 HF,Capt&Kids(c) 450.00
21 HF,Tarzan(c) 450.00
22 HF,Li'l Abner(c) 350.00
23 HF,Capt&Kids(c) 350.00
24 HF,Tarzan(c) 450.00
25 HF,Capt&Kids(c) 350.00
26 HF,Li'L Abner(c) 350.00
27 HF,Tarzan(c) 450.00
28 HF,Li'l Abner(c) 350.00
29 HF,Capt&Kids(c) 350.00
30 HF,Tarzan(c) 450.00
31 HFCapt&Kids(c). 350.00
32 HF Tarzan(c) 350.00
33 HF,Tarzan(c). 400.00
34 HF,Capt&Kids(c) 400.00
35 HF 300.00
36 HF,HK,Tarzan(c) 400.00
37 HF,Tarzan 400.00
38 HF 300.00
39 HF,Tarzan 400.00
40 HF 300.00
41 Tarzan(c) 450.00
42 . . . . 300.00
43 Tarzan(c) 325.00
44 HF 300.00
45 HF,Tarzan(c) 325.00
46 HF 300.00
47 HF,Tarzan(c). 325.00
48 HF 300.00
49 HF 300.00
50 HF,Tarzan(c) 325.00
51 . . . . 250.00
52 Tarzan(c) 300.00
53 . . . . 250.00
54 . . . . 325.00
55 . . . . 250.00
56 . . . . 250.00
57 BHg. 250.00
58 . . . . 225.00
59 BHg. 250.00
60 . . . . 200.00

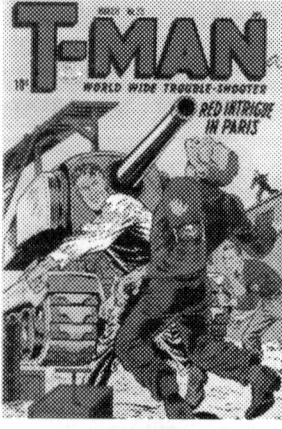

T-Man #21
© Quality Comics Group

GOLDEN AGE

61 and 62 BHg	@250.00
63 thru 90	@125.00
91 thru 99	@100.00
100	125.00
101 thru 150	@65.00
151 thru 188	@40.00
189 thru 225	@40.00

T-MAN
Comics Magazines
(Quality Comics Group)
Sept., 1951

1 JCo,Pete Trask-the Treasury Man	275.00
2 RC(c),The Girl with Death in Her Hands	175.00
3 RC,RC(c),Death Trap in Iran	150.00
4 RC,RC(c),Panama Peril	150.00
5 RC,RC(c),Violence in Venice	150.00
6 RC(c),The Man Who Could Be Hitler	150.00
7 RC(c),Mr. Murder & The Black Hand	125.00
8 RC(c),Red Ticket to Hell	125.00
9 RC(c),Trial By Terror	125.00
10	125.00
11 The Voice of Russia	100.00
12 Terror in Tokyo	100.00
13 Mind Assassins	100.00
14 Trouble in Bavaria	100.00
15 The Traitor,Bondage(c)	100.00
16 Hunt For a Hatchetman	100.00
17 Red Triggerman	100.00
18 Death Rides the Rails	100.00
19 Death Ambush	100.00
20 The Fantastic H-Bomb Plot	125.00
21 The Return of Mussolini	75.00
22 Propaganda for Doom	90.00
23 Red Intrigue in Parid,H-Bomb	75.00
24 Red Sabotage	50.00
25 RC,The Ingenious Red Trap	75.00
26	50.00
27	50.00
28	50.00
29	50.00
30 thru 37	@50.00
38 Dec., 1956	50.00

TNT COMICS
Charles Publishing Co.
Feb., 1946

1 FBI story,YellowJacket	200.00

TODAY'S BRIDES
Ajax/Farrell Publishing Co.
Nov., 1955

1	35.00
2	20.00
3	20.00
4 Nov., 1956	20.00

TODAY'S ROMANCE
Standard Comics
March, 1952

5	35.00
6 ATh	40.00
7	20.00
8	20.00

TOM AND JERRY
DELL GIANT EDITIONS
Dell Publishing Co.
1952–58

Back to School	200.00

Tom and Jerry Winter Carnival #1
© Dell Publishing Co.

Picnic Time	150.00
Summer Fun 1	250.00
Summer Fun 2	100.00
Winter Carnival 1	350.00
Winter Carnival 2	175.00
Winter Fun 3	100.00
Winter Fun 4	90.00
Winter Fun 5	80.00
Winter Fun 6	75.00
Winter Fun 7	75.00

TOMB OF TERROR
Harvey Publications
June, 1952

1 BP,The Thing From the Center of the Earth	300.00
2 RP,The Quagmire Beast	150.00
3 BP,RP,Caravan of the Doomed, Bondage(c)	175.00
4 RP,I'm Going to Kill You, Torture	150.00
5 RP	150.00
6 RP,Return From the Grave	150.00
7 RP,Shadow of Death	150.00
8 HN,The Hive	150.00
9 BP,HN,The Tunnel	150.00
10 BP,HN,The Trial	150.00
11 BP,HN,The Closet	150.00
12 BP,HN,Tale of Cain	165.00
13 BP,What Was Out There	175.00
14 BP,SC,End Result	175.00
15 BP,HN,Break-up	225.00
16 BP,Going,Going,Gone	175.00
Becomes:	

THRILLS OF TOMORROW

17 RP,BP,The World of Mr. Chatt	40.00
18 RP,BP,The Dead Awaken	30.00
19 S&K,S&K(c),A:Stuntman	275.00
20 S&K,S&K(c),A:Stuntman	225.00

TOM CORBETT SPACE CADET
Dell Publishing Co.
Jan., 1952
See also Dell Four Color

4 based on TV show	100.00
5	75.00
6	70.00
7	60.00
8	50.00

9	50.00
10	50.00
11	50.00

Tom Corbett Space Cadet #2
© Prize Publications

TOM CORBETT SPACE CADET
Prize Publications
May–June, 1955

1	225.00
2	200.00
3 Sept.–Oct., 1955	200.00

TOM MIX
Ralston-Purina Co.
Sept., 1940

1 O:Tom Mix	2,800.00
2	850.00
3	550.00
4 thru 9	@500.00
Becomes:	

TOM MIX COMMANDOS COMICS

10	450.00
11 Invisible Invaders	450.00
12 Terrible Talons Of Tokyo	450.00

TOM MIX WESTERN
Fawcett Publications
Jan., 1948

1 Ph(c),Two-Fisted Adventures	800.00
2 Ph(c),Hair-Triggered Action	350.00
3 Ph(c),Double Barreled Action	250.00
4 Ph(c),Cowpunching	250.00
5 Ph(c),Two Gun Action	250.00
6 CCB,Most Famous Cowboy	200.00
7 CCB,A Tattoo of Thrills	200.00
8 EK,Ph(c),Gallant Guns	185.00
9 CCB,Song o/t Deadly Spurs	175.00
10 CCB,Crack Shot Western	175.00
11 CCB,EK(C),Triple Revenge	175.00
12 King of the Cowboys	150.00
13 Ph(c),Leather Burns	150.00
14 Ph(c),Brand of Death	150.00
15 Ph(c),Masked Treachery	150.00
16 Ph(c),Death Sputing Guns	150.00
17 Ph(c),Trail of Doom	150.00
18 Ph(c),Reign of Terror	100.00
19 Hand Colored Ph(c)	125.00
20 Ph(c),CCB,F:Capt Tootsie	100.00
21 Ph(c)	100.00

GOLDEN AGE

22 Ph(c),The Human Beast. 100.00
23 Ph(c),Return of the Past. 100.00
24 Hand Colored Ph(c),
The Lawless City 100.00
25 Hand Colored Ph(c),
The Signed Death Warrant . . 100.00
26 Hand Colored Ph(c),
Dangerous Escape. 100.00
27 Hand Colored Ph(c),
Hero Without Glory. 100.00
28 Ph(c),The Storm Kings. 100.00
29 Hand Colored Ph(c),The
Case of the Rustling Rose . . 100.00
30 Ph(c),Disappearance
in the Hills 100.00
31 Ph(c). 80.00
32 Hand Colored Ph(c),
Mystery of Tremble Mountain . 75.00
33 . . . . 75.00
34 . . . . 65.00
35 Partial Ph(c),The Hanging
at Hollow Creek 75.00
36 Ph(c). 75.00
37 Ph(c). 75.00
38 Ph(c),36 pages 65.00
39 Ph(c). 75.00
40 Ph(c). 75.00
41 Ph(c). 70.00
42 Ph(c). 75.00
43 Ph(c). 50.00
44 Ph(c). 50.00
45 Partial Ph(c),The Secret
Letter. 50.00
46 Ph(c). 50.00
47 Ph(c). 50.00
48 Ph(c). 50.00
49 Partial Ph(c),Blind Date
With Death 50.00
50 Ph(c). 50.00
51 Ph(c). 50.00
52 Ph(c). 50.00
53 Ph(c). 50.00
54 Ph(c). 50.00
55 Ph(c). 50.00
56 Partial Ph(c),Deadly Spurs. . . . 50.00
57 Ph(c)5 . . . . 50.00
58 Ph(c). 50.00
59 Ph(c). 50.00
60 Ph(c). 50.00
61 Partial Ph(c),Lost in the
Night,May 1953 . . . . 75.00

TOMMY OF THE
BIG TOP
**King Features/
Standard Comics, 1948**
10 Thrilling Circus Adventures . . . 30.00
11 . . . . 20.00
12 March, 1949 . . . . 20.00

TOM-TOM THE
JUNGLE BOY
Magazine Enterprises, 1946
1 (fa) 40.00
2 (fa) 30.00
3 Winter 1947,(fa),X-mas issue . . 15.00
1 . . . . 15.00

TONTO
(See LONE RANGER'S
COMPANION TONTO)

TONY TRENT
(see FACE, THE)

TOP FLIGHT COMICS
**Four Star/St. John Publ. Co.
July, 1949**
1 . . . . 60.00
1 Hector the Inspector 40.00

TOP LOVE STORIES
**Star Publications
May, 1951**
3 LbC(c) 125.00
4 LbC(c) 100.00
5 LbC(c) 100.00
6 LbC(c),WW 150.00
7 LbC(c) 100.00
8 LbC(c) 100.00
9 LbC(c) 100.00
10 thru 16 LbC(c) . . . . @100.00
17 LbC(c),WW 125.00
18 LbC(c) 100.00
19 LbC(c),JyD 100.00

TOP-NOTCH COMICS
**MLJ Magazines
Dec., 1939**
1 JaB,JCo,B&O:The Wizard,
B:Kandak,Swift of the Secret
Service,The Westpointer,
Mystic, Air Patrol,Scott
Rand, Manhunter 5,000.00
2 JaB,JCo,B:Dick Storm,
E:Mystic, B:Stacy Knight . . 1,800.00
3 JaB,JCo,EA(c),E:Swift of the
Secret Service,Scott Rand 1,200.00
4 JCo,EA(c),MMe,O&I:Streak,
Chandler 1,000.00
5 Ea(c),MMe,O&I:Galahad,
B:Shanghai Sheridan 1,000.00
6 Ea(c),MMe,A:The Sheild . . . 900.00
7 Ea(c),MMe,N:The Wizard . 1,000.00
8 E:Dick Sorm,B&O:Roy The
Super Boy,The Firefly 1,000.00
9 O&I:Black Hood,
B:Fran Frazier 4,700.00
10 . . . . 1,300.00
11 . . . . 750.00
12 . . . . 750.00
13 . . . . 750.00

*Top-Notch Comics #4
© MLJ Magazines*

14 Bondage(c) 800.00
15 MMe 750.00
16 . . . . 700.00
17 Bondage(c) 725.00
18 . . . . 675.00
19 Bondage(c) 725.00
20 . . . . 675.00
21 . . . . 550.00
22 . . . . 550.00
23 Bondage(c) 575.00
24 Black Hood Smashes
Murder Ring 550.00
25 E:Bob Phantom 550.00
26 . . . . 550.00
27 E:The Firefly 550.00
28 B:Suzie,Pokey Okay,
Gag Oriented 550.00
29 E:Kandak. 550.00
30 . . . . 550.00
31 . . . . 300.00
32 . . . . 300.00
33 BWo,B:Dotty&Ditto. 300.00
34 BWo 300.00
35 BWo 300.00
36 BWo 300.00
37 thru 40 BWo. . . . . @300.00
41 . . . . 300.00
42 BWo 300.00
43 . . . . 300.00
44 EW:Black Hood,I:Suzie 275.00
45 Suzie(c). 275.00
Becomes:

LAUGH COMIX
46 Suzie & Wilbur. 100.00
47 Suzie & Wilbur. 85.00
48 Suzie & Wilbur. 85.00
Becomes:

SUZIE COMICS
49 B:Ginger 150.00
50 AFy(c) 90.00
51 AFy(c) 90.00
52 AFy(c) 90.00
53 AFy(c) 90.00
54 AFy(c) 100.00
55 AFy(c) 110.00
56 BWo,B;Katie Keene. 65.00
57 thru 70 BWo . . . . @65.00
71 thru 79 BWo . . . . @55.00
80 thru 99 BWo . . . . @45.00
100 Aug., 1954, BWo 45.00

TOPS
**Tops Mag. Inc.
(Lev Gleason), July, 1949**
1 RC&BLb,GT,DBa,CBi(c),I'll Buy
That Girl,Our Explosive
Children 900.00
2 FG,BF,CBi(c),RC&BLb 800.00

TOPS COMICS
**Consolidated Book Publishers
1944**
2000 Don on the Farm 200.00
2001 The Jack of Spades
V:The Hawkman 100.00
2002 Rip Raiders 75.00
2003 Red Birch 20.00

TOP SECRET
**Hillman Publications
Jan., 1952**
1 The Tricks of the Secret
Agent Revealed 150.00

GOLDEN AGE

TOP SECRETS
Street & Smith, Nov., 1947
1 BP,BP(c),Of the Men Who
  Guard the U.S. Mail 250.00
2 BP,BP(c),True Story of Jim
  the Penman 175.00
3 BP,BP(c),Crime Solved by
  Mental Telepathy 150.00
4 Highway Pirates 150.00
5 BP,BP(c),Can Music Kill 150.00
6 BP,BP(c),The Clue of the
  Forgotten Film 150.00
7 BP,BP(c),Train For Sale 225.00
8 BP,BP(c) 150.00
9 BP,BP(c) 150.00
10 BP,BP(c),July–Aug., 1949 . . . 225.00

TOPS IN ADVENTURE
Approved Comics
(Ziff-Davis)
Autumn, 1952
1 BP,Crusaders From Mars 350.00

TOP SPOT COMICS
Top Spot Publishing Co.
1945
1 The Duke Of Darkness 200.00

TOPSY-TURVY
R.B. Leffingwell Publ.
April, 1945
1 I:Cookie 50.00

TOR
St. John Publishing Co.
Sept., 1953
1 JKu,JKu(c),O;Tor,One Million
  Years Ago 85.00
2 JKu,JKu(c),3-D Issue 75.00
3 JKu,JKu(c),ATh,historic Life . . . 80.00
4 JKu,JKu(c),ATh 80.00
5 JKu,JKu(c),ATh,Oct., 1954 . . . . 80.00

TORCHY
Quality Comics Group
Nov., 1949
1 GFx,BWa(c),The Blonde
  Bombshell 1,000.00

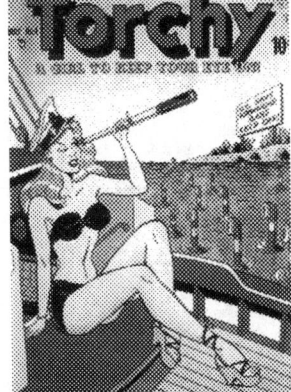

Torchy #4
© Quality Comics Group

---

2 GFx,GFx(c),Beauty at
  its' Best 500.00
3 GFx,GFx(c),You Can't
  Beat Nature 500.00
4 GFx,GFx(c),The Girl to
  Keep Your Eye On 600.00
5 BWa,GFx,BWa(c),At the
  Masquerade Party 800.00
6 Sept., 1950,BWa,GFx,
  BWa(c),The Libido Driven
  Boy Scout. 800.00

TORMENTED, THE
Sterling Comics
July, 1954
1 Buried Alive 150.00
2 Sept., 1954,The Devils
  Circus 125.00

TOYLAND COMICS
Fiction House Magazines
Jan., 1947
1 Wizard of the Moon 175.00
2 Buddy Bruin & Stu Rabbit . . . 125.00
3 GT,The Candy Maker 150.00
4 July, 1947 . . . . 125.00

TOY TOWN COMICS
Toytown Publ./Orbit Publ.
Feb., 1945
1 LbC,LbC(c)(fa) 225.00
2 LbC,(fa) 150.00
3 LbC,LbC(c),(fa) 125.00
4 LbC,(fa) 125.00
5 LbC,(fa) 125.00
6 LbC,(fa) 125.00
7 LbC,(fa),May, 1947 . . . . 125.00

TRAIL BLAZERS
(see RED DRAGON
COMICS)

TREASURE COMICS
Prize Comics Group, 1943
1 S&K,Reprints of Prize Comics
  #7 through #11 . . . . 1,600.00

TREASURE COMICS
American Boys Comics
(Prize Publications)
June–July, 1945
1 HcK,B:PaulBunyan,MarcoPolo 225.00
2 HcK,HcK(c),B:Arabian Knight,
  Gorilla King,Dr.Styx 125.00
3 HcK 100.00
4 HcK 100.00
5 HcK,JK 150.00
6 HcK,BK,HcK(c) 125.00
7 HcK,FF,HcK(c) 250.00
8 HcK,FF 250.00
9 HcK,DBa 100.00
10 JK,DBa,JK(c) 225.00
11 BK,HcK,DBa,The Weird
  Adventures of Mr. Bottle 150.00
12 DBa,DBa(c),Autumn, 1947 . . . 100.00

TREASURY OF COMICS
St. John Publishing Co., 1947
1 RvB,RvB(c),Abbie an' Slats . 125.00
2 Jim Hardy 75.00
3 Bill Bimlin 75.00
4 RvB,RvB(c),Abbie an' Slats . . . 75.00

---

5 Jim Hardy,Jan., 1948 . . . . 70.00

TRIPLE THREAT
Gerona Publications
Winter, 1945
1 F:King O'Leary,The Duke of
  Darkness,Beau Brummell . . 175.00

TRUE AVIATION
PICTURE STORIES
Parents' Institute/P.M.I.
Aug., 1942
1 How Jimmy Doolittle
  Bombed Tokyo 100.00
2 Knight of the Air Mail 50.00
3 The Amazing One-Man
  Air Force 40.00
4 Joe Foss America's No. 1
  Air Force 40.00
5 Bombs over Germany 40.00
6 Flight Lt. Richard
  Hillary R.A.F. 40.00
7 "Fatty" Chow China's
  Sky Champ 40.00
8 Blitz over Burma 40.00
9 Off the Beam 40.00
10 "Pappy" Boyington 40.00
11 Ph(c) 40.00
12 . . . . 40.00
13 Ph(c),Flying Facts 40.00
14 . . . . 40.00
15 . . . . 40.00
Becomes:

AVIATION AND MODEL
BUILDING
16 . . . . 45.00
17 Feb., 1947 . . . . 50.00

TRUE COMICS
True Comics/
Parents' Magazine Press
April, 1941
1 My Greatest Adventure-by
  Lowell Thomas 225.00
2 BEv,The Story of the
  Red Cross 125.00
3 Baseball Hall of Fame. 135.00
4 Danger in the Artic 100.00
5 Father Duffy-the Fighting
  Chaplin 120.00
6 The Capture of Aquinaldo . . . 120.00
7 JKa,Wilderness Adventures of
  George Washington 120.00
8 U.S. Army Wings 75.00
9 A Pig that Made History 75.00
10 Adrift on an Ice Pan. 75.00
11 Gen. Douglas MacArthur 65.00
12 Mackenzie-King of Canada . . 60.00
13 The Real Robinson Crusoe . . . 65.00
14 Australia war base of
  the South Pacific 65.00
15 The Story of West Point 75.00
16 How Jimmy Doolittle
  Bombed Tokyo 70.00
17 The Ghost of Captain Blig,
  B.Feller 75.00
18 Battling Bill of the
  Merchant Marine 80.00
19 Secret Message Codes 50.00
20 The Story of India 45.00
21 Timoshenko the Blitz Buster. . . 50.00
22 Gen. Bernard L. Montgomery. . 45.00
23 The Story of Steel 45.00
24 Gen. Henri Giraud-Master
  of Escape. 45.00
25 Medicine's Miracle Men 45.00

---

26 Hero of the Bismarck Sea 45.00
27 Leathernecks have Landed . . . 50.00
28 The Story of Radar 40.00
29 The Fighting Seabees 40.00
30 Dr. Norman Bethune-Blood
    Bank Founder. 40.00
31 Our Good Neighbor Bolivia,
    Red Range 50.00
32 Men against the Desert 35.00
33 Gen. Clark and his Fighting
    5th 40.00
34 Angel of the Battlefield. 35.00
35 Carlson's Marine Raiders. 35.00
36 Canada's Sub-Busters 35.00
37 Commander of the Crocodile
    Fleet. 35.00
38 Oregon Trailblazer. 35.00
39 Saved by Sub 35.00
40 Sea Furies. 35.00
41 Cavalcade of England 30.00
42 Gen. Jaques Le Clerc-Hero
    of Paris 30.00
43 Unsinkable Ship. 35.00
44 El Senor Goofy. 30.00
45 Tokyo Express. 25.00
46 The Magnificent Runt. 30.00
47 Atoms Unleashed,
    Atomic Bomb 75.00
48 Pirate Patriot 30.00
49 Smiking Fists. 30.00
50 Lumber Pirates 30.00
51 Exercise Musk-Ox 30.00
52 King of the Buckeneers 30.00
53 Baseline Booby 30.00
54 Santa Fe Sailor 30.00
55 Sea Going Santa 30.00
56 End of a Terror. 30.00
57 Newfangled Machines 30.00
58 Leonardo da Vinci-500 years
    too Soon 30.00
59 Pursuit of the Pirates 35.00
60 Emmett Kelly-The World's
    Funniest Clown 30.00
61 Peter Le Grand-
    Bold Buckaneer 30.00
62 Sutter's Gold 30.00
63 Outboard Outcome 30.00
64 Man-Eater at Large 30.00
65 The Story of Scotland Yard . . . 30.00
66 Easy Guide to Football
    Formations. 35.00
67 The Changing Zebra 30.00
68 Admiral Byrd 25.00
69 FBI Special Agent Steve
    Saunders 35.00
70 The Case of the Seven
    Hunted Men 30.00
71 Story of Joe DiMaggio 150.00
72 FBI,Jackie Robinson 60.00
73 The 26 Mile Dash-Story of
    the Marathon 35.00
74 A Famous Coach's Special
    Football Tips. 35.00
75 King of Reporters. 35.00
76 The Story of a Buried
    Treasure. 35.00
77 France's Greatest Detective. . . 35.00
78 Cagliostro-Master Rogue 50.00
79 Ralph Bunche-Hero of Peace. . 35.00
80 Rocket Trip to the Moon. 150.00
81 Red Grange. 150.00
82 Marie Celeste Ship of
    Mystery 125.00
83 Bullfighter from Brooklyn 125.00
84 King of the Buckaneers,
    Aug., 1950 . . . . 125.00

TRUE CONFIDENCES
Fawcett Publications
Autumn, 1949
1 . . . . 75.00
2 and 3 . . . . @45.00
4 DP 45.00

True Crime #3
© Magazine Village

TRUE CRIME COMICS
Magazine Village, Inc.
May, 1947
2 JCo(c),JCo(c),James Kent-
    Crook,Murderer,Escaped
    Convict; Drug. 1,000.00
3 JCo,JCo(c),Benny Dickson-
    Killer;Drug 750.00
4 JCo,JCo(c),Little Jake-
    Big Shot 700.00
5 JCo(c),The Rat & the Blond
    Gun Moll;Drug 450.00
6 Joseph Metley-Swindler,
    Jailbird, Killer 350.00
2-1(7) ATh,WW,Ph(c),Phil
    Coppolla,Sept., 1949 . . . . . 600.00

TRUE LIFE SECRETS
Romantic Love Stories/
Charlton Comics
March–April, 1951
1 . . . . 70.00
2 . . . . 40.00
3 . . . . 30.00
4 . . . . 30.00
5 thru 20 . . . . @30.00
21 thru 25 . . . . @20.00
26 Comics Code 15.00
27 thru 29 . . . . @15.00

TRUE LIFE ROMANCES
Ajax/Farrell Publications
Dec., 1955
1 . . . . 50.00
2 . . . . 30.00
3 Aug., 1956 . . . . 35.00

TRUE LOVE PICTORIAL
St. John Publishing Co., 1952
1 Ph(c) 100.00
2 MB. 65.00

3 MB(c),MB,JKu 200.00
4 MB(c),MB,JKu 200.00
5 MB(c),MB,JKu 200.00
6 MB(c) 100.00
7 MB(c) 100.00
8 MB(c) 75.00
9 MB(c) 75.00
10 MB(c),MB 75.00
11 MB(c),MB. 75.00

TRUE MOVIE AND TELEVISION
Toby Press, Aug., 1950
1 Liz Taylor, Ph(c) 300.00
2 FF,Ph(c),John Wayne,
    L.Taylor 225.00
3 June Allyson,Ph(c) 200.00
4 Jane Powell,Ph(c),Jan.,1951. . 100.00

SPORT COMICS
Street & Smith, Oct., 1940
1 F:Lou Gehrig 400.00
2 F:Gene Tunney 250.00
3 F:Phil Rizzuto 250.00
4 F:Frank Leahy 200.00
Becomes:

TRUE SPORT PICTURE STORIES
5 Joe DiMaggio 275.00
6 Billy Confidence 125.00
7 Mel Ott. 150.00
8 Lou Ambers 125.00
9 Pete Reiser 125.00
10 Frankie Sinkwich 125.00
11 Marty Serfo 125.00
12 JaB(c),Jack Dempsey 135.00
2-1 JaB(c),Willie Pep 125.00
2-2 JaB(c). 125.00
2-3 JaB(c),Carl Hubbell. 135.00
2-4 Advs. in Football & Battle . . . 150.00
2-5 Don Hutson 125.00
2-6 Dixie Walker. 150.00
2-7 Stan Musial 175.00
2-8 Famous Ring Champions
    of All Time 150.00
2-9 List of War Year Rookies . . . 175.00
2-10 Connie Mack 150.00
2-11 Winning Basketball Plays . . 125.00
2-12 Eddie Gottlieb. 125.00
3-1 Bill Conn 125.00
3-2 Philadelphia Athletics 100.00
3-3 Leo Durocher 125.00
3-4 Rudy Dusek 100.00
3-5 Ernie Pyle 100.00
3-6 Bowling with Ned Day 100.00
3-7 Return of the Mighty (Home
    from War);Joe DiMaggio(c) . . 250.00
3-8 Conn V:Louis 200.00
3-9 Reuben Shark 100.00
3-10 BP,BP(c),Don "Dopey"
    Dillock 100.00
3-11 BP,BP(c),Death
    Scores a Touchdown 100.00
3-12 Red Sox V:Senators 100.00
4-1 Spring Training in
    Full Spring 100.00
4-2 BP,BP(c),How to Pitch 'Em
    Where They Can't Hit 'Em . . 100.00
4-3 BP,BP(c),1947 Super Stars . 125.00
4-4 BP,BP(c),Get Ready for
    the Olympics 125.00
4-5 BP,BP(c),Hugh Casey 100.00
4-6 BP,BP(c),Phantom Phil
    Hergesheimer 100.00
4-7 BP,BP(c),How to Bowl Better 100.00
4-8 Tips on the Big Fight 125.00
4-9 BP,BP(c),Bill McCahan 100.00
4-10 BP,BP(c),Great Football

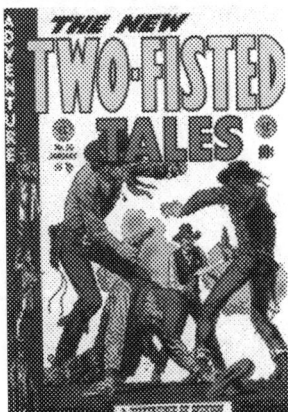

Two-Fisted Tales #36
© E.C. Comics

Plays 100.00
4-11 BP,BP(c),Football 100.00
4-12 BP,BP(c),Basketball 100.00
5-1 Satchel Paige 150.00
5-2 History of Boxing,
    July–Aug., 1949 . . . . 100.00

TRUE SWEETHEART SECRETS
Fawcett Publications
May, 1950
1 Ph(c) 75.00
2 WW 125.00
3 BD 50.00
4 BD 50.00
5 BD 50.00
6 thru 11 . . . . @40.00

TRUE-TO-LIFE ROMANCES
Star Publications
Nov.–Dec., 1949
3 LbC(c),GlennFord/JanetLeigh . 150.00
4 LbC(c) 100.00
5 LbC(c) 100.00
6 LbC(c) 100.00
7 LbC(c) 100.00
8 LbC(c) 100.00
9 LbC(c) 100.00
10 LbC(c) 100.00
11 LbC(c) 100.00
12 LbC(c) 100.00
13 LbC(c),JyD 100.00
14 LbC(c),JyD 100.00
15 LbC(c),WW,JyD 125.00
16 LbC(c),WW,JyD 125.00
17 LbC(c),JyD 100.00
18 LbC(c),JyD 100.00
19 LbC(c),JyD 100.00
20 LbC(c),JyD 100.00
21 LbC(c),JyD 100.00
22 LbC(c) 90.00
23 LbC(c) 90.00

TRUE WAR ROMANCES
Comic Magazines, Inc.
(Quality Comics)
Sept., 1952
1 Ph(c) 75.00
2 . . . . 40.00

3 thru 10 . . . . @20.00
11 thru 20 . . . . @15.00
21 Comics Code 15.00
Becomes:
EXOTIC ROMANCES
22 . . . . 35.00
23 thru 26 . . . . @20.00
27 MB 35.00
28 MB 35.00
29 . . . . 20.00
30 MB 35.00
31 MB 35.00

TUROK, SON OF STONE
Dell Publishing Co.
Dec., 1954
(1) *see Dell Four Color #596*
(2) *see Dell Four Color #656*
3 . . . . 250.00
4 and 5 . . . . @225.00
6 thru 10 . . . . @150.00
11 thru 20 . . . . @90.00
21 thru 29 . . . . @60.00
See Other Color section

TWEETY AND SYLVESTER
Dell Publishing Co.
June, 1952
(1) *see Dell Four Color #406*
(2) *see Dell Four Color #489*
(3) *see Dell Four Color #524*
4 thru 20 . . . . @20.00
21 thru 37 . . . . @10.00

TWINKLE COMICS
Spotlight Publications
May, 1945
1 Humor Format 70.00

TWO-FISTED TALES
Fables Publications
(E.C. Comics)
Nov.–Dec., 1950
18 HK,JCr,WW,JSe,HK(c) 800.00
19 HK,JCr,WW,JSe,HK(c) 550.00
20 JDa,HK,WW,JSe,HK(c) 350.00
21 JDa,HK,WW,JSe,HK(c) 300.00
22 JDa,HK,WW,JSe,HK(c) 300.00
23 JDa,HK,WW,JSe,HK(c) 225.00
24 JDa,HK,WW,JSe,HK(c) 200.00
25 JDa,HK,WW,JSe,HK(c) 200.00
26 JDa,JSe,HK(c),Action at
    the Changing Reservoir 150.00
27 JDa,JSe,HK(c) 150.00
28 JDa,JSe,HK(c) 150.00
29 JDa,JSe,HK(c) 200.00
30 JDa,JSe,JDa(c) 200.00
31 JDa,JSe,HK(c),Civil
    War Story 160.00
32 JDa,JKu,WW(c) 160.00
33 JDa,JKu,WW(c) 175.00
34 JDa,JSe,JDa(c) 160.00
35 JDa,JSe,JDa(c),Civil
    War Story 175.00
36 JDa,JSe,JSe(c),A
    Difference of Opinion 100.00
37 JSe,JSe(c),Bugles &
    Battle Cries 100.00
38 JSe,JSe(c) 100.00
39 JSe,JSe(c) 100.00
40 JDa,JSe,GE,GE(c) 150.00
41 JSe,GE,JDa(c),March, 1955. . 100.00

UNCLE CHARLIE'S FABLES
Lev Gleason Publications
Jan., 1952
1 CBi(c),Ph(c) 55.00
2 BF,CBi(c),Ph(c) 30.00
3 CBi(c),Ph(c) 35.00
4 CBi(c),Ph(c) 35.00
5 CBi,Ph(c),Sept., 1952 . . . . . . 30.00

UNCLE SAM
(see BLACKHAWK)

UNCLE SCROOGE
Dell Publishing Co.
March, 1952
(1) *see Dell Four Color #386*
(2) *see Dell Four Color #456*
(3) *see Dell Four Color #495*
4 . . . . 400.00
5 . . . . 300.00
6 . . . . 250.00
7 CB 225.00
8 . . . . 200.00
9 . . . . 200.00
10 . . . . 200.00
11 thru 20 . . . . @175.00
21 thru 30 . . . . @150.00
31 thru 39 . . . . @100.00
See Other Pub. section

UNDERWORLD
D.S. Publishing Co.
Feb.–March, 1948
1 SMo(c),Violence 350.00
2 SMo(c),Electrocution. 350.00
3 AMc,AMc(c),The Ancient Club 275.00
4 Grl,The Beer Baron Murder . . 200.00
5 Grl,The Postal Clue 175.00
6 The Polka Dot Gang 125.00
7 Mono-The Master 125.00
8 The Double Tenth 125.00
9 Thrilling Stories of the Fight
    against Crime,June, 1953 . . 125.00

Underworld #9
© DS Publishing

UNDERWORLD CRIME
Fawcett Publications
June, 1952
1 The Crime Army 225.00
2 Jailbreak 150.00
3 Microscope Murder 125.00
4 Death on the Docks 125.00
5 River of Blood 125.00
6 The Sky Pirates 125.00
7 Bondage & Torture(c) 175.00
8 .... 125.00
9 June, 1953............... 125.00

UNITED COMICS
United Features Syndicate
1950
8 thru 26 Bushmiller(c),
   Fritzi Ritz .... @25.00

UNITED STATES FIGHTING AIR FORCE
Superior Comics, Ltd.
Sept., 1952
1 Coward's Courage 50.00
2 Clouds that Killed 25.00
3 Operation Decoy 15.00
4 thru 28 .... @15.00
29 Oct., 1959............... 15.00

UNITED STATES MARINES
Wm. H. Wise/Magazine Ent/
Toby Press, 1943
N# MBi,MBi(c),Hellcat out
   of Heaven 50.00
2 MBi,Drama of Wake Island ... 35.00
3 A Leatherneck Flame Thrower . 30.00
4 MBi 30.00
5 BP 25.00
6 BP 25.00
7 BP 20.00
8 thru 10 .... @20.00
11 1952 .... 20.00

UNKEPT PROMISE
Legion of Truth, 1949
1 Anti:Alcoholic Drinking 50.00

UNKNOWN WORLDS
(see STRANGE STORIES FROM ANOTHER WORLD)

UNSEEN, THE
Visual Editions
(Standard Comics), 1952
5 ATh,The Hungry Lodger 250.00
6 JKa,MSy,Bayou Vengeance .. 200.00
7 JKz,MSy,Time is the Killer ... 175.00
8 JKz,MSy,The Vengance Vat .. 175.00
9 JKz,MSy,Your Grave is Ready 175.00
10 JKz,MSy 175.00
11 JKz,MSy 175.00
12 ATh,GT,Till Death Do Us Part. 175.00
13 .... 125.00
14 .... 125.00
15 ATh,The Curse of the
   Undead!, July, 1954 .... 175.00

UNTAMED LOVE
Comic Magazines
(Quality Comics Group)
Jan., 1950
1 BWa(c),PGn............. 175.00
2 Ph(c) 100.00
3 PGn................... 100.00
4 .... 100.00
5 PGn 100.00

USA IS READY
Dell Publishing Co., 1941
1 Propaganda WWII 300.00

U.S. JONES
Fox Features Syndicate
Nov., 1941
1 Death Over the Airways ... 1,000.00
2 Jan., 1942 .... 700.00

U.S. MARINES IN ACTION!
Avon Periodicals
Aug.–Dec., 1952
1 On Land,Sea & in the Air 50.00
2 The Killer Patrol 20.00
3 EK(c),Death Ridge 22.00

U.S. TANK COMMANDOS
Avon Periodicals
June, 1952
1 EK(c),Fighting Daredevils
   of the USA 50.00
2 EK(c) 25.00
3 EK,EK(c),Robot Armanda 25.00
4 EK,EK(c),March, 1953 .... 25.00

VALOR
E.C. Comics, March, 1955
1 AW,AT,WW,WW(c),Grl,BK.... 250.00
2 AW(c),AW,WWGrl,BK....... 200.00
3 AW,RC,BK,JOc(c)......... 150.00
4 WW(c),RC,Grl,BK,JO 150.00
5 WW(c),WW,AW,GE,Grl,BK ... 125.00

VARIETY COMICS
Rural Home Publ./
Croyden Publ. Co., 1944
1 MvS,MvS(c),O:Capt, Valiant .. 175.00
2 MvS,MvS(c) 125.00
3 MvS,MvS(c) 100.00
4 .... 75.00
5 1946 .... 60.00

VAULT OF HORROR
(see WAR AGAINST CRIME)

V...COMICS
Fox Features Syndicate
Jan., 1942
1 V:V-Man 1,000.00
2 The Horror of the
   Dungeons, March, 1942 ... 750.00

VERI BEST SURE SHOT COMICS
Holyoke Publishing Co. 1945
1 reprint Holyoke One-Shots ... 275.00

VIC FLINT
St. John Publishing Co.
Aug., 1948
1 ...Crime Buster 60.00
2 .... 40.00
3 .... 35.00
4 .... 35.00
5 April, 1949 .... 35.00

VIC JORDAN
Civil Service Publications
April, 1945
1 Escape From a Nazi Prison ... 75.00

VIC TORRY AND HIS FLYING SAUCER
Fawcett Publications, 1950
1 Ph(c),Revealed at Last 450.00

VICTORY COMICS
Hillman Periodicals
Aug., 1941
1 BEv,BEv(c),F:TheConqueror 2,500.00
2 BEv,BEv(c) 1,000.00
3 The Conqueror(c) 700.00
4 Dec., 1941 .... 650.00

VIC VERITY MAGAZINE
Vic Verity Publications
1945
1 CCB,CCB(c),B:Vic Verity,Hot-
   Shot Galvan, Tom Travis ... 125.00
2 CCB,CCB(c),Annual Classic
   Dance Recital 75.00
3 CCB 60.00
4 CCB,I:Boomer Young;The
   Bee-U-TiFul Weekend 60.00
5 CCB,Championship Baseball
   Game 60.00
6 CCB,High School Hero 60.00
7 CCB,CCB(c),F:Rocket Rex ... 60.00

Vic Verity Magazine #6
© Vic Verity Publications

VOODOO
Four Star Publ./Farrell/
Ajax Comics May, 1952

1 MB,South Sea Girl	400.00
2 MB	300.00
3 Face Stabbing	200.00
4 MB,Rendezvous	200.00
5 Ghoul For A Day,Nazi	175.00
6 The Weird Dead, Severed Head	185.00
7 Goodbye World	175.00
8 MB, Revenge	200.00
9 Will this thing Never Stew?	175.00
10 Land of Shadows & Screams	175.00
11 Human Harvest	150.00
12 The Wazen Taper	150.00
13 Bondage(c),Caskets to Fit Everybody	165.00
14 Death Judges the Beauty Contest	150.00
15 Loose their Heads	165.00
16 Fog Was Her Shroud	150.00
17 Apes Laughter,Electric Chair	165.00
18 Astounding Fantasy	150.00
19 MB,Bondage(c); Destination Congo	200.00
Ann.#1	550.00

Becomes:

VOODA

20 MB,MB(c),Echoes of an A-Bomb	225.00
21 MB,MB(c),Trek of Danger	200.00
22 MB,MB(c),The Sun Blew Away, Aug., 1955	200.00

WACKY DUCK
(see DOPEY DUCK)

WALT DISNEY'S
COMICS & STORIES
Dell Publishing Co.

N# 1943 dpt.store giveway	400.00
N# 1945 X-mas giveaway	150.00

WALT DISNEY'S
COMICS & STORIES
Dell Publishing Co.
Oct., 1940

1 (1940)FG,Donald Duck & Mickey Mouse	17,000.00
2	6,500.00
3	2,000.00
4 Christmas(c)	1,400.00
4a Promo issue	1,500.00
5	1,100.00
6	900.00
7	900.00
8	900.00
9	900.00
10	900.00
11 1st Huey,Louie,Dewey	750.00
12	800.00
13	750.00
14	750.00
15 3 Little Kittens	700.00
16 3 Little Pigs	650.00
17 The Ugly Ducklings	700.00
18	550.00
19	525.00
20	525.00
21	550.00
22	500.00
23	475.00
24	475.00
25	475.00

Walt Disney's Comics & Stories #116
© Walt Disney

26	475.00
27	500.00
28	475.00
29	475.00
30	475.00
31 CB; Donald Duck	3,000.00
32 CB	1,400.00
33 CB	1,000.00
34 CB;WK; Gremlins	800.00
35 CB;WK; Gremlins	750.00
36 CB;WK; Gremlins	750.00
37 CB;WK; Gremlins	375.00
38 CB;WK; Gremlins	475.00
39 CB;WK; Gremlins	475.00
40 CB;WK; Gremlins	475.00
41 CB;WK; Gremlins	425.00
42 CB	425.00
43 CB	400.00
44 CB	400.00
45 CB	400.00
46 CB	400.00
47 CB	375.00
48 CB	375.00
49 CB	375.00
50 CB	375.00
51 CB	300.00
52 CB; Li'l Bad Wolf begins	300.00
53 CB	300.00
54 CB	300.00
55 CB	300.00
56 CB	300.00
57 CB	300.00
58 CB	300.00
59 CB	300.00
60 CB	300.00
61 CB; Dumbo	225.00
62 CB	225.00
63 CB; Pinocchio	225.00
64 CB; Pinocchio	225.00
65 CB; Pluto	225.00
66 CB	225.00
67 CB	225.00
68 CB	225.00
69 CB	225.00
70 CB	225.00
71 CB	175.00
72 CB	175.00
73 CB	175.00
74 CB	175.00
75 CB; Brer Rabbit	175.00
76 CB; Brer Rabbit	175.00
77 CB; Brer Rabbit	175.00
78 CB	175.00
79 CB	175.00
80 CB	175.00

81 CB	150.00
82 CB;Bongo	175.00
83 CB;Bongo	175.00
84 CB;Bongo	175.00
85 CB	175.00
86 CB;Goofy & Agnes	175.00
87 CB;Goofy & Agnes	150.00
88 CB;Goofy & Agnes, I:Gladstone Gander	175.00
89 CB;Goofy&Agnes,Chip'n'Dale	150.00
90 CB;Goofy & Agnes	150.00
91 CB	125.00
92 CB	125.00
93 CB	125.00
94 CB	125.00
95	125.00
96 Little Toot	125.00
97 CB; Little Toot	125.00
98 CB; Uncle Scrooge	275.00
99 CB	125.00
100 CB	175.00
101 CB	125.00
102 CB	125.00
103 CB	110.00
104	110.00
105 CB	125.00
106 CB	125.00
107 CB	125.00
108	110.00
109	110.00
110 CB	125.00
111 CB	125.00
112 CB; drugs	125.00
113 CB	125.00
114 CB	125.00
115	40.00
116	40.00
117	40.00
118	40.00
119	40.00
120	40.00
121 Grandma Duck begins	40.00
122	40.00
123	40.00
124 CB	110.00
125 CB;I:Junior Woodchucks	125.00
126 CB	75.00
127 CB	75.00
128 CB	75.00
129 CB	75.00
130 CB	75.00
131 CB	75.00
132 CB A:Grandma Duck	75.00
133 CB	75.00
134 I:The Beagle Boys	175.00
135 CB	75.00
136 CB	75.00
137 CB	75.00
138 CB	75.00
139 CB	75.00
140 CB; I:Gyro Gearloose	175.00
141 CB	60.00
142 CB	60.00
143 CB; Little Hiawatha	60.00
144 CB; Little Hiawatha	60.00
145 CB; Little Hiawatha	60.00
146 CB; Little Hiawatha	60.00
147 CB; Little Hiawatha	60.00
148 CB; Little Hiawatha	60.00
149 CB; Little Hiawatha	60.00
150 CB; Little Hiawatha	60.00
151 CB; Little Hiawatha	60.00
152 thru 200 CB	@50.00
201 CB	40.00
202 CB	40.00
203 CB	40.00
204 CB, Chip 'n' Dale & Scamp	40.00
205 thru 240 CB	@40.00
241 CB; Dumbo x-over	30.00
242 CB	30.00
243 CB	30.00

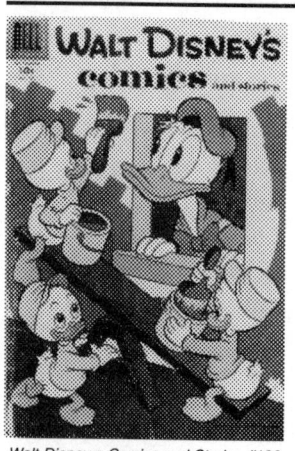

Walt Disney;s Comics and Stories #192
© Walt Disney

244 CB. 30.00
245 CB. 30.00
246 CB. 30.00
247 thru 255 CB;GyroGearloose @30.00
256 thru 263 CB;Ludwig Von
Drake & Gearloose . . . . @30.00
See: **Independent Color Comics**

WALT DISNEY ANNUALS
Walt Disney's Autumn Adventure . . 4.00
Walt Disney's Holiday Parade. 3.50
Walt Disney's Spring Fever. 3.25
Walt Disney's Summer Fun. 3.25

WALT DISNEY
DELL GIANT EDITIONS
Dell Publishing Co.
1 CB,W.Disney's Xmas
Parade('49) 900.00
2 CB,W.Disney'sXmas
Parade('50) 700.00
3 W.Disney'sXmas Parade('51) . 225.00
4 W.Disney'sXmas Parade('52) . 200.00
5 W.Disney'sXmas Parade('53) . 200.00
6 W.Disney'sXmas Parade('54) . 200.00
7 W.Disney'sXmas Parade('55) . 200.00
8 CB,W.Disney'sXmas
Parade('56) 350.00
9 CB,W.Disney'sXmas
Parade('57) 300.00
1 CB,W.Disney's Christmas in
Disneyland (1957) 400.00
1 CB,W.Disney's Disneyland
Birthday Party (1958) 400.00
1 W.Disney's Donald and Mickey
in Disneyland (1958). 175.00
1 W.Disney's Donald Duck
Beach Party (1954). 225.00
2 W.Disney's Donald Duck
Beach Party (1955). 175.00
3 W.Disney's Donald Duck
Beach Party (1956). 175.00
4 W.Disney's Donald Duck
Beach Party (1957). 175.00
5 W.Disney's Donald Duck
Beach Party (1958). 175.00
6 W.Disney's Donald Duck
Beach Party (1959). 175.00
1 W.Disney's Donald Duck
Fun Book (1954). 600.00
2 W.Disney's Donald Duck
Fun Book (1954). 550.00
1 W.Disney's Donald Duck

in Disneyland (1955). 200.00
1 W.Disney's Huey, Dewey
and Louie (1958) 150.00
1 W.Disney's DavyCrockett('55) . 135.00
1 W.Disney's Lady and the
Tramp (1955) 275.00
1 CB,W.Disney's Mickey Mouse
Almanac (1957) 400.00
1 W.Disney's Mickey Mouse
Birthday Party (1953) 500.00
1 W.Disney's Mickey Mouse
Club Parade (1955) 400.00
1 W.Disney's Mickey Mouse
in Fantasyland (1957). 200.00
1 W.Disney's Mickey Mouse
in Frontierland (1956). 200.00
1 W.Disney's Summer Fun('58) . 200.00
2 CB,W.Disney'sSummer
Fun('59) 200.00
1 W.Disney's Peter Pan
Treasure Chest (1953). . . . 1,500.00
1 Disney Silly Symphonies('52) . 450.00
2 Disney Silly Symphonies('53) . 400.00
3 Disney Silly Symphonies('54) . 350.00
4 Disney Silly Symphonies('54) . 350.00
5 Disney Silly Symphonies('55) . 300.00
6 Disney Silly Symphonies('56) . 300.00
7 Disney Silly Symphonies('57) . 300.00
8 Disney Silly Symphonies('58) . 300.00
9 Disney Silly Symphonies('59) . 300.00
1 Disney SleepingBeauty('59) . . 450.00
1 CB,W.Disney's Uncle Scrooge
Goes to Disneyland (1957) . . 400.00
1 W.Disney's Vacation in
Disneyland (1958) 175.00
1 CB,Disney's Vacation
Parade('50) 1,300.00
2 Disney'sVacation Parade('51) . 450.00
3 Disney'sVacation Parade('52) . 225.00
4 Disney'sVacation Parade('53) . 225.00
5 Disney'sVacation Parade('54) . 225.00
6 Disney's Picnic Party (1955) . 175.00
7 Disney's Picnic Party (1956) . 175.00
8 CB,Disney's Picnic
Party (1957) 350.00

DELL JUNIOR TREASURY
1 W.Disney's Alice in Wonderland
(1955) 85.00

WALT DISNEY
PRESENTS
Dell Publishing Co.
June–Aug., 1952
1 Ph(c), Four Color 60.00
2 Ph(c) 50.00
3 Ph(c) 50.00
4 Ph(c) 50.00
5 and 6 Ph(c). . . . . @50.00

WAMBI
JUNGLE BOY
Fiction House Magazines
Spring, 1942
1 HcK,HcK(c),Vengence of
the Beasts 700.00
2 HcK,HcK(c),Lair of the
Killer Rajah 400.00
3 HcK,HcK(c) 250.00
4 HcK,HcK(c),The Valley of
the Whispering Drums 150.00
5 HcK,HcK(c),Swampland Safari 150.00
6 Taming of the Tigress 100.00
7 Duel of the Congo Kings 100.00
8 AB(c),Friend of the Animals . . 100.00
9 Quest of the Devils Juju 100.00
10 Friend of the Animals. 75.00

11 . . . . 75.00
12 Curse of the Jungle Jewels . . . 75.00
13 New Adventures of Wambi. . . . 75.00
14 . . . . 75.00
15 The Leopard Legions. 75.00
16 . . . . 75.00
17 Beware Bwana! 75.00
18 Ogg the Great Bull Ape,
Winter, 1952. . . . . 75.00

WANTED COMICS
Toytown Comics/
Orbit Publications
Sept.–Oct., 1947
9 Victor Everhart 125.00
10 Carlo Banone 75.00
11 Dwight Band 75.00
12 Ralph Roe. 80.00
13 James Spencer;Drug 80.00
14 John "Jiggs" Sullivan;Drug. . . . 80.00
15 Harry Dunlap;Drug. 50.00
16 Jack Parisi;Drug 50.00
17 Herber Ayers;Drug. 50.00
18 Satan's Cigarettes;Drug 135.00
19 Jackson Stringer 45.00
20 George Morgan 45.00
21 BK,Paul Wilson 50.00
22. . . . . 50.00
23 George Elmo Wells 40.00
24 BK,Bruce Cornett;Drug 65.00
25 Henry Anger 30.00
26 John Wormly 30.00
27 Death Always Knocks Twice . . 30.00
28 Paul H. Payton 30.00
29 Hangmans Holiday 30.00
30 George Lee 30.00
31 M Consolo. 30.00
32 William Davis. 30.00
33 The Web of Davis 30.00
34 Dead End 30.00
35 Glen Roy Wright 50.00
36 SSh,SSh(c),Bernard Lee
Thomas 30.00
37 SSh,SSh(c),Joseph M. Moore . 30.00
38 SSh,SSh(c) 30.00
39 The Horror Weed;Drug 75.00
40. . . . . 30.00
41. . . . . 30.00
42. . . . . 30.00
43. . . . . 30.00
44. . . . . 30.00
45 Killers on the Loose;Drug. 50.00
46 Chalres Edward Crews 30.00
47 . . . . 30.00
48 SSh,SSh(c) 30.00
49 . . . . 30.00
50 JB(c),Make Way for Murder . . . 75.00
51 JB(c),Dope Addict on a
Holiday of Murder;Drug. 65.00
52 The Cult of Killers;
Classic Drug. 65.00
53 April, 1953. . . . . 30.00

WAR AGAINST CRIME
L.L. Publishing Co.
(E.C. Comics), Spring, 1948
1 Grl 550.00
2 Grl,Guilty of Murder 300.00
3 JCr(c) 300.00
4 AF,JCr(c) 250.00
5 JCr(c) 250.00
6 AF,JCr(c) 250.00
7 AF,JCr(c) 250.00
8 AF,JCr(c) 250.00
9 AF,JCr(c),The Kid 250.00
10 JCr(c),I:Vault Keeper 1,600.00
11 JCr(c) 1,000.00

The Vault of Horror #25
© E.C. Comics

Becomes:

VAULT OF HORROR
12 AF,JCr,JCr(c),Wax Museum 4,000.00
13 AF,WW,JCr(c),Grl,Drug 900.00
14 AF,WW,JCr(c),Grl 750.00
15 AF,JCr,JCr(c),Grl,JKa. 650.00
16 Grl,JKa,JCr,JCr(c) 550.00
17 JDa,Grl,JKa,JCr,JCr(c). 400.00
18 JDa,Grl,JKa,JCr,JCr(c). 400.00
19 JDa,Grl,JKa,JCr,JCr(c). 400.00
20 JDa,Grl,JKa,JCr,JCr(c). 300.00
21 JDa,Grl,JKa,JCr,JCr(c). 300.00
22 JDa,JKa,JCr,JCr(c) 300.00
23 JDa,Grl,JCr,JCr(c) 300.00
24 JDa,Grl,JO,JCr,JCr(c) 300.00
25 JDa,Grl,JKa,JCr,JCr(c). 300.00
26 JDa,Grl,JCr,JCr(c) 300.00
27 JDa,Grl,JCr,GE,JCr(c) 250.00
28 JDa,Grl,JCr,JCr(c) 250.00
29 JDa,Grl,JCr,JKa,JCr(c),
  JDa,Grl,JCr,JCr(c)
  Bradbury Adapt 250.00
30 JDa,Grl,JCr,JCr(c) 250.00
31 JDa,Grl,JCr,JCr(c),
  Bradbury Adapt 200.00
32 JDa,Grl,JCr,JCr(c) 200.00
33 JDa,Grl,RC,JCr(c) 200.00
34 JDa,Grl,JCr,RC,JCr(c) 200.00
35 JDa,Grl,JCr,JCr(c) 200.00
36 JDa,Grl,JCr,BK,JCr(c),Drug . . 200.00
37 JDa,Grl,JCr,AW,JCr(c)
  Hanging 200.00
38 JDa,Grl,JCr,BK,JCr(c) 200.00
39 GRi,JCr,BK,RC,JCr(c)
  Bondage(c). 200.00
40 Jan., 1955, Grl,JCr,BK,JO
  JCr(c). 225.00

WAR BATTLES
Harvey Publications
Feb., 1952
1 BP,Devils of the Deep 75.00
2 BP,A Present From Benny 40.00
3 BP 30.00
4 . . . . 30.00
5 . . . . 30.00
6 HN 30.00
7 BP 35.00
8 . . . . 30.00
9 Dec., 1953 . . . . 30.00

WAR BIRDS
Fiction House Magazines, 1952
1 Willie the Washout 100.00
2 Mystery MIGs of Kwanjamu . . . 50.00
3 thru 6 . . . . @40.00
7 Winter, 1953,Across the
  Wild Yalu 40.00

WAR COMICS
Dell Publishing Co.
May, 1940
1 AMc,Sky Hawk 450.00
2 O:Greg Gildam 250.00
3 . . . . 150.00
4 O:Night Devils 200.00

WAR HEROES
Dell Publishing Co.
July–Sept., 1942
1 Gen. Douglas MacArthur (c) . . 175.00
2 . . . . 100.00
3 . . . . 75.00
4 A:Gremlins 125.00
5 . . . . 45.00
6 thru 11 . . . . @40.00

WAR HEROES
Ace Magazines
May, 1952
1 Always Comin' 50.00
2 LC,The Last Red Tank 30.00
3 You Got it 20.00
4 A Red Patrol 20.00
5 Hustle it Up 20.00
6 LC,Hang on Pal 25.00
7 . . . . 25.00
8 LC,April, 1953 . . . . 25.00

WARPATH
Key Publications/
Stanmore
Nov., 1954
1 Red Men Raid 50.00
2 AH(c),Braves Battle 30.00
3 April, 1955 . . . . 30.00

WARRIOR COMICS
H.C. Blackerby, 1944
1 Ironman wing Brady 150.00

WAR SHIPS
Dell Publishing Co., 1942
1 AMc 75.00

WAR STORIES
Dell Publishing Co., 1942
5 O:The Whistler 175.00
6 A:Night Devils. 125.00
7 A:Night Devils 125.00
8 A:Night Devils 125.00

WARTIME ROMANCES
St. John Publishing Co.
July, 1951
1 MB(c),MB 225.00
2 MB(c),MB 150.00
3 MB(c),MB 125.00
4 MB(c),MB 125.00
5 MB(c),MB 100.00
6 MB(c),MB 125.00
7 MB(c),MB 100.00
8 MB(c),MB 100.00
9 MB(c),MB 75.00
10 MB(c),MB 75.00
11 MB(c),MB. 75.00
12 Mb(c),MB. 75.00
13 MB(c) 50.00
14 MB(c) 50.00
15 MB(c) 50.00
16 MB(c),MB 50.00
17 MB(c) 50.00
18 MB(c),MB 50.00

WAR VICTORY COMICS
U.S. Treasury/War Victory/
Harvey Publ.
Summer, 1942
1 Savings Bond Promo with
  Top Syndicated Cartoonists,
  benefit USO 275.00
Becomes:

WAR VICTORY
ADVENTURES
2 BP,2nd Front Comics 150.00
3 BP,F:Capt Cross of the
  Red Cross 125.00

WEB OF EVIL
Comic Magazines, Inc.
(Quality Comics Group)
Nov., 1952
1 Custodian of the Dead 450.00
2 JCo,Hangmans Horror 300.00
3 JCo 300.00
4 JCo,JCo(c),Monsters of
  the Mist 300.00
5 JCo,JCo(c),The Man who Died
  Twice,Electric Chair(c) 325.00
6 JCo,JCo(c),Orgy of Death . . . 300.00
7 JCo,JCo(c),The Strangling
  Hands 300.00
8 JCo,Flaming Vengeance 250.00
9 JCo,The Monster in Flesh . . . 250.00
10 JCo,Brain that Wouldn't Die . . 250.00
11 JCo,Buried Alive 250.00
12 Phantom Killer 150.00
13 Demon Inferno 150.00
14 RC(c),The Monster Genie . . . 150.00
15 Crypts of Horror 150.00
16 Hamlet of Horror 150.00
17 Terror in Chinatown 135.00
18 Scared to Death,Acid Face . . 150.00

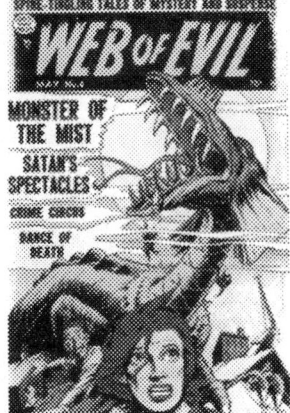

Web of Evil #4
© Quality Comics Group

19 Demon of the Pit 135.00
20 Man Made Terror 135.00
21 Dec., 1954, Death's Ambush . 135.00

WEB OF MYSTERY
A.A. Wyn Publ.
(Ace Magazines), Feb., 1951
1 MSy,Venom of the Vampires . 375.00
2 MSy,Legacy of the Accursed . 200.00
3 MSy,The Violin Curse 175.00
4 GC 175.00
5 . . . . 175.00
6 LC 175.00
7 MSy 175.00
8 LC,LC(c),MSy,The Haunt of
   Death Lake 175.00
9 LC,LC(c) 175.00
10 . . . . 175.00
11 MSy 175.00
12 LC 150.00
13 LC,LC(c) 150.00
14 MSy 150.00
15 . . . . 150.00
16 . . . . 150.00
17 LC,LC(c) 150.00
18 LC 150.00
19 LC 150.00
20 LC 150.00
21 MSy 150.00
22 . . . . 150.00
23 . . . . 150.00
24 LC 150.00
25 LC 150.00
26 . . . . 150.00
27 LC 150.00
28 RP,1st Issue under Comics
   Code Authority 125.00
29 MSy,Sept., 1955 . . . . 125.00

WEDDING BELLS
Quality Comics Group
Feb., 1954
1 OW. 100.00
2 . . . . 45.00
3 . . . . 25.00
4 . . . . 25.00
5 . . . . 25.00
6 . . . . 25.00
7 . . . . 25.00
8 . . . . 25.00
9 Comics Code 25.00
10 BWa 75.00
11 . . . . 25.00
12 . . . . 20.00
13 . . . . 20.00
14 . . . . 20.00
15 MB(c) 25.00
16 MB(c),MB 35.00
17 . . . . 20.00
18 MB 25.00
19 MB 25.00

WEEKENDER, THE
Rucker Publishing Co.
Sept., 1945
3 . . . . 125.00
4 . . . . 100.00
2-1(5)JCo,WMc,Jan., 1946 . . . . 145.00

WEIRD ADVENTURES
P.L. Publishing
May, 1951
1 MB,Missing Diamonds 400.00
2 Puppet Peril 300.00
3 Blood Vengeance,
   Oct. 1951 . . . . 250.00

WEIRD ADVENTURES
Approved Comics
(Ziff-Davis)
July–Aug., 1951
10 P(c),Seeker from Beyond. . . . 300.00

WEIRD CHILLS
Key Publications
July, 1954
1 MBi(c),BW 550.00
2 Eye Torture(c) 500.00
3 Bondage(c),Nov., 1954 . . . . . 325.00

Weird Comics #1
© Fox Features Syndicate

WEIRD COMICS
Fox Features Syndicate
April, 1940
1 LF(c),Bondage(c),B:Birdman,
   Thor,Sorceress of Doom,
   BlastBennett,Typhon,Voodoo
   Man, Dr.Mortal 3,700.00
2 LF(c),Mummy(c) 1,600.00
3 JSm(c) 900.00
4 JSm(c) 900.00
5 Bondage(c),I:Dart,Ace;E:Thor 900.00
6 Dart & Ace(c) 750.00
7 Battle of Kooba 750.00
8 B:Panther Woman,Dynamo,
   The Eagle 750.00
9 V:Pirates 650.00
10 A:Navy Jones 650.00
11 Dart & Ace(c) 450.00
12 Dart & Ace(c) 450.00
13 Dart & Ace(c) 450.00
14 The Rage(c) 450.00
15 Dart & Ace (c) 450.00
16 Flag,The Encore(c) 450.00
17 O:Black Rider 475.00
18 . . . . 450.00
19 . . . . 450.00
20 Jan., 1941,I'm The Master
   of Life and Death 450.00

WEIRD FANTASY
I.C. Publishing Co.
(E.C. Comics)
May–June, 1950
13(1)AF,HK,JKa,WW,AF(c),
   Roger Harvey's Brain 1,700.00
14(2)AF,HK,JKa,WW,AF(c),
   Cosmic Ray Brain Explosion. 650.00
15(3)AF,HK,JKa,WW,AF(c),Your
   Destination is the Moon 500.00
16(4)AF,HK,JKa,WW,AF(c) 500.00
17(5)AF,HK,JKa,WW,AF(c),Not
   Made by Human Hands 450.00
6 AF,HK,JKa,WW,AF(c) 325.00
7 AF,JKa,WW,AF(c) 325.00
8 AF,JKa,WW,AF(c) 325.00
9 AF,Jka,WW,JO,AF(c) 325.00
10 AF,Jka,WW,JO,AF(c) 350.00
11 AF,Jka,WW,JO,AF(c) 250.00
12 AF,Jka,WW,JO,AF(c) 250.00
13 AF,Jka,WW,JO,AF(c) 250.00
14 AF,Jka,WW,JO,AW&FF,AF(c) 350.00
15 AF,JKa,JO,AW&RKr,AF(c),
   Bondage(c). 250.00
16 AF,JKa,JO,AW&RKr,AF(c) . . . 225.00
17 AF,JOP,JKa,AF(c),Bradbury . 225.00
18 AF,JO,JKa,AF(c),Bradbury . . 225.00
19 JO,JKa,JO(c),Bradbury 225.00
20 JO,JKa,AF,AF(c) 225.00
21 JO,JKa,AW&FF(c) 350.00
22 JO,JKa,JO(c),Nov.,1953 . . . . 200.00

WEIRD HORRORS
St. John Publishing Co.
June, 1952
1 GT,Dungeon of the Doomed . 400.00
2 Strangest Music Ever 300.00
3 PAM,Strange Fakir From
   the Orient 300.00
4 Murderers Knoll 175.00
5 Phantom Bowman 175.00
6 Monsters from Outer Space . . 350.00
7 LC,Deadly Double 375.00
8 JKu,JKu(c),Bloody Yesterday . 300.00
9 JKu,JKu(c),Map Of Doom . . . 300.00
Becomes:

NIGHTMARE
10 JKu(c),The Murderer's Mask . 375.00
11 BK,Ph(c),Fangs of Death . . . 300.00
12 JKu(c),The Forgotten Mask . . 250.00
13 BP,Princess of the Sea 225.00
Becomes:

AMAZING GHOST STORIES
14 EK,MB(c), ... 150.00
15 BP. 125.00
16 Feb., 1955, EK,JKu 150.00

WEIRD MYSTERIES
Gilmore Publications
Oct., 1952
1 BW(c) 550.00
2 BWi 750.00
3 Severed Heads(c). 400.00
4 BW,Human headed ants(c) . . . 650.00
5 BW,Brains From Head(c) 650.00
6 Severed Head(c) 400.00
7 Used in "Seduction" 600.00
8 The One That Got Away 400.00
9 Epitaph,Cyclops 400.00
10 The Ruby. 300.00
11 Voodoo Dolls 300.00
12 Sept., 1954 . . . . 300.00

WEIRD SCIENCE
E.C. Comics, 1950
1 AF(c),AF,JKu,HK,WW 1,700.00
2 AF(c),AF,JKu,HK,WW,Flying
   Saucers(c) 750.00
3 AF(c),AF,JKu,HK. 700.00
4 AF(c),AF,JKu,HK 675.00
5 AF(c),AF,JKu,HK,WW,
   Atomic Bomb(c) 425.00
6 AF(c),AF,JKu,HK 400.00

7 AF(c),AF,JKu,HK,Classic(c)... 425.00
8 AF(c),AF,JKu 400.00
9 WW(c),JKu,Classic(c) 425.00
10 WW(c),JKu,JO,Classic(c)... 425.00
11 AF,JKu,Space war 275.00
12 WW(c),JKu,JO,Classic(c)... 275.00
13 WW(c),JKu,JO. 300.00
14 WW(c),WW,JO. 300.00
15 WW(c),WW,JO,GRi,AW,
    RKr,JKa 300.00
16 WW(c),WW,JO,AW,RKr,JKa.. 300.00
17 WW(c),WW,JO,AW,RKr,JKa.. 300.00
18 WW(c),WW,JO,AW,RKr,
    JKa,Atomic Bomb........ 250.00
19 WW(c),WW,JO,AW,
    FF,Horror(c) 400.00
20 WW(c),WW,JO,AW,FF,JKa... 400.00
21 WW(c),WW,JO,AW,FF,JKa... 400.00
22 WW(c),WW,JO,AW,FF 400.00
Becomes:

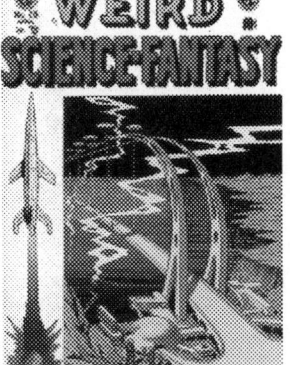

Weird Science Fantasy #28
© E.C. Comics

WEIRD SCIENCE
FANTASY
23 WW(c),WW,AW,BK 275.00
24 WW,AW,BK,Classic(c) 250.00
25 WW,AW,BK,Classic(c) 300.00
26 AF(c),WW,RC,
    Flying Saucer(c)......... 250.00
27 WW(c),WW,RC 250.00
28 AF(c),WW 250.00
29 AF(c),WW,Classic(c) 500.00
Becomes:

INCREDIBLE SCIENCE
FANTASY
30 WW,JDa(c),BK,AW,RKr,JO .. 250.00
31 WW,JDa(c),BK,AW,RKr 300.00
32 JDa(c),BK,WW,JO 300.00
33 WW(c),BK,WW,JO 300.00

WEIRD TALES OF
THE FUTURE
S.P.M. Publ./
Aragon Publications
March, 1952
1 RA 600.00
2 BW,BW(c) 900.00
3 BW,BW(c) 850.00
4 BW,BW(c) 600.00
5 BW,BW(c),Jumpin' Jupiter
    Lingerie(c)............. 850.00
6 Bondage(c) 350.00
7 BW,Devil(c). 550.00

8 July–Aug. 1953 .... 450.00

WEIRD TERROR
Allen Hardy Associates
(Comic Media), Sept., 1952
1 RP,DH,DH(c),Dungeon of the
    Doomed;Hitler 350.00
2 HcK(c),PAM 250.00
3 PAM,DH,DH(c) 250.00
4 PAM,DH,DH(c) 275.00
5 PAM,DH,RP,DH(c),Hanging(c) 225.00
6 DH,RP,DH(c),Step into
    My Parlour. 250.00
7 DH,PAM,DH(c),Blood o/t Bats. 200.00
8 DH,RP,DH(c),Step into
    My Parlour 250.00
9 DH,PAM,DH(c),The Fleabite . 200.00
10 DH,BP,RP,DH(c) 200.00
11 DH,DH(c),Satan's Love Call .. 250.00
12 DH,DH(c),King Whitey 200.00
13 DH,DH(c),Sept., 1954,
    Wings of Death.......... 200.00

WEIRD THRILLERS
Approved Comics
(Ziff-Davis)
Sept.–Oct., 1951
1 Ph(c),Monsters & The Model.. 550.00
2 AW,P(c),The Last Man 400.00
3 AW,P(c),Princess o/t Sea ... 500.00
4 AW,P(c),The Widows Lover .. 375.00
5 BP,Oct., 1952,AW,P(c),
    Wings of Death 375.00

WESTERN ACTION
THRILLERS
Dell Publishing Co.
April, 1937
1 .... 650.00

WESTERN ADVENTURES
COMICS
A.A. Wyn, Inc.
(Ace Magazines), Oct., 1948
N#(1)Injun Gun Bait 150.00
N#(2)Cross-Draw Kid 75.00
N#(3)Outlaw Mesa 75.00
4 Sheriff 50.00
5 .... 50.00
6 Rip Roaring Adventure 50.00
Becomes:

WESTERN LOVE TRAILS
7 .... 75.00
8 Maverick Love 50.00
9 March, 1950 .... 40.00

WESTERN BANDIT
TRAILS
St. John Publishing Co.
Jan., 1949
1 GT,MB(c) 150.00
2 GT,MB(c) 100.00
3 GT,MB,MB(c),Gingham Fury . 125.00

WESTERN CRIME-
BUSTERS
Trojan Magazines
Sept., 1950
1 Gunslingin' Galoots 200.00
2 K-Bar Kate 100.00
3 Wilma West 100.00

4 Bob Dale 100.00
5 Six-Gun Smith 100.00
6 WW 200.00
7 WW,Wells Fargo Robbery ... 200.00
8 .... 100.00
9 WW,Lariat Lucy 200.00
10 WW,April 1952;Tex Gordon . 200.00

WESTERN CRIME CASES
(see WHITE RIDER)

WESTERNER, THE
Wanted Comics Group/
Toytown Publ.
June, 1948
14 F:Jack McCall 75.00
15 F:Bill Jamett. 35.00
16 F:Tom McLowery 35.00
17 F:Black Bill Desmond. 35.00
18 BK,F:Silver Dollar Dalton 50.00
19 MMe,F:Jess Meeton 30.00
20 .... 25.00
21 BK,MMe 50.00
22 BK,MMe 50.00
23 BK,MMe 50.00
24 BK,MMe 50.00
25 O,I,B:Calamity Jane 50.00
26 BK,F:The Widowmaker 65.00
27 .... 75.00
28 thru 31 .... @25.00
32 E:Calamity Jane 25.00
33 A:Quest 25.00
34 .... 25.00
35 SSh(c)................ 25.00
36 .... 25.00
37 Lobo-Wolf Boy........... 25.00
38 .... 25.00
39 .... 25.00
40 SSh(c)................ 25.00
41 Dec., 1951............. 25.00

WESTERN FIGHTERS
Hillman Periodicals
April–May, 1948
1 S&K(c)................ 250.00
2 BF(c) 60.00
3 BF(c) 50.00
4 BK,BF 55.00
5 .... 35.00
6 .... 34.00
7 BK 60.00
8 .... 35.00
9 .... 35.00
10 BK. 60.00
11 AMC&FF 200.00
2-1 BK 60.00
2-2 BP 40.00
2-3 thru 2-12 .... @20.00
3-1 thru 3-11............ @20.00
3-12 BK 40.00
4-1 .... 20.00
4-2 BK 50.00
4-3 BK 50.00
4-4 BK 50.00
4-5 BK 50.00
4-6 BK 50.00
4-7 March–April 1953 .... 20.00

WESTERN FRONTIER
P.L. Publishers
(Approved Comics)
May, 1951
1 Flaming Vengeance 75.00
2 .... 35.00
3 Death Rides the Iron Horse ... 25.00

4 thru 6 . . . . @25.00
7 1952. . . . . 25.00

WESTERN HEARTS
Standard Magazine, Inc.
Dec., 1949
1 Ph(c),JSe 125.00
2 Ph(c),AW,FF. 150.00
3 Ph(c) 65.00
4 Ph(c),JSe,BE 65.00
5 Ph(c),JSe,BE 65.00
6 Ph(c),JSe,BE 65.00
7 Ph(c),JSe,BE 65.00
8 Ph(c) 75.00
9 Ph(c),JSe,BE 75.00
10 Ph(c),JSe,BE 50.00

WESTERN LOVE
Feature Publications
(Prize Comics Group)
July–Aug., 1949
1 S&K 200.00
2 S&K 150.00
3 JSE,BE. 100.00
4 JSE,BE. 100.00
5 JSE,BE. 100.00

WESTERN PICTURE STORIES
Comics Magazine Co.
Feb., 1937
1 WE,Treachery Trail,
  1st Western 1,400.00
2 WE,Weapons of the West . . . 850.00
3 WE,Dragon Pass 650.00
4 June, 1937,CavemanCowboy 650.00

Western Thrillers #3
© Fox Features Syndicate

WESTERN THRILLERS
Fox Features Syndicate
Aug., 1948
1 . . . . 350.00
2 . . . . 125.00
3 GT,RH(c) 100.00
4 . . . . 125.00
5 . . . . 125.00
6 June, 1949 . . . . 100.00
Becomes:

MY PAST CONFESSIONS
7 . . . . 60.00
8 . . . . 40.00
9 . . . . 40.00
10 . . . . 40.00
11. . . . . 75.00
12. . . . . 20.00

WESTERN TRUE CRIME
Fox Features Syndicate
Aug., 1948
1 . . . . 175.00
2 . . . . 150.00
3 . . . . 125.00
4 JCr 150.00
5 . . . . 100.00
6 . . . . 100.00
Becomes:

MY CONFESSION
7 WW 150.00
8 WW,My Tarnished Reputation 125.00
9 I:Tormented Men 40.00
10 Feb., 1950,I Am Damaged
  Goods 40.00

WHACK
St. John Publishing Co.
Dec., 1953
1 Steve Crevice,Flush Jordan
  V:Bing(Crosby)The Merciful . 225.00
2 . . . . 125.00
3 F:Little Awful Fannie 125.00

WHAM COMICS
Centaur Publications
Nov., 1940
1 PG,The Sparkler & His
  Disappearing Suit 1,300.00
2 Dec., 1940,PG,PG(C),
  Men Turn into Icicles 1,000.00

WHIRLWIND COMICS
Nita Publications
June, 1940
1 F:The Cyclone 1,200.00
2 A:Scoops Hanlon,Cyclone(c). . 800.00
3 Sept., 1940,A:Magic
  Mandarin,Cyclone(c). 750.00

WHITE PRINCESS OF THE JUNGLE
Avon Periodicals
July, 1951
1 EK(c),Terror Fangs 400.00
2 EK,EK(c),Jungle Vengeance . 300.00
3 EK,EK(c),The Blue Gorilla . . . 250.00
4 Fangs of the Swamp Beast . . 225.00
5 EK,Coils of the Tree Snake
  Nov., 1952 . . . . 225.00

WHIZ COMICS
Fawcett Publications
Feb., 1940
1 O:Captain Marvel,B:Spy
  Smasher,Golden Arrow,Dan
  Dare, Scoop Smith,Ibis
  the Invincible, Sivana . . . 65,000.00
2 . . . . 4,500.00
3 Make way for
  Captain Marvel 4,000.00
4 Captain Marvel
  Crashes Through 2,500.00

5 Captain Marvel
  Scores Again! 2,000.00
6 Circus of Death 1,800.00
7 B:Dr Voodoo,Squadron
  of Death 1,500.00
8 Saved by Captain Marvel! . . 1,300.00
9 MRa,Captain Marvel
  on the Job 1,300.00
10 Battles the Winged Death . . 1,300.00
11 Hurray for Captain Marvel . . 1,000.00
12 Captain Marvel rides
  the Engine of Doom. 1,000.00
13 Worlds Most Powerful Man! . . 900.00
14 Boomerangs the Torpedo. . . . 900.00
15 O:Sivana. 1,000.00
16 . . . . 1,000.00
17 Knocks out a Tank 1,000.00
18 V:Spy Smasher. 1,000.00
19 Crushes the Tiger Shark 650.00
20 V:Sivana 650.00
21 O:Lt. Marvels. 700.00
22 Mayan Temple 550.00
23 GT,A:Dr. Voodoo 550.00
24 . . . . 550.00
25 O&I:Captain Marvel Jr.,
  Stops the Turbine of Death 5,000.00
26 . . . . 475.00
27 V:Death God of the Katonkas. 500.00
28 V:Mad Dervish of Ank-Har . . . 500.00
29 Three Lt. Marvels (c), Pan
  American Olympics 500.00
30 . . . . 450.00
31 Douglass MacArthur&Spy
  Smasher(c). 400.00
32 Spy Smasher(c). 400.00
33 Spy Smasher(c). 450.00
34 Three Lt. Marvels (c) 350.00
35 Capt. Marvel and the
  Three Fates 375.00
36 Haunted Hallowe'en Hotel . . . 325.00
37 Return of the Trolls 325.00
38 Grand Steeplechase 325.00
39 A Nazi Utopia 325.00
40 A:Three Lt. Marvels, The
  Earth's 4 Corners 325.00
41 Captain Marvel 1,000 years
  from Now 250.00
42 Returns in Time Chair 250.00
43 V:Sinister Spies,
  Spy Smasher(c) 250.00
44 Life Story of Captain Marvel. . 275.00
45 Cures His Critics 250.00
46. . . . . 250.00
47 Captain Marvel needs
  a Birthday. 250.00
48 . . . . 250.00
49 Writes a Victory song 250.00
50 Captain Marvel's most
  embarrassing moment 250.00
51 Judges the Ugly-
  Beauty Contest. 200.00
52 V:Sivana, Chooses
  His Birthday 200.00
53 Captain Marvel fights
  Billy Batson 200.00
54 Jack of all Trades. 200.00
55 Family Tree. 200.00
56 Tells what the Future Will Be . 200.00
57 A:Spy Smasher,Golden Arrow,
  Ibis. 200.00
58 . . . . 200.00
59 V:Sivana's Twin 200.00
60 Missing Person's Machine . . . 200.00
61 Gets a first name 175.00
62 Plays in a Band 175.00
63 Great Indian Rope Trick. 175.00
64 Suspected of Murder 175.00
65 Lamp of Diogenes 175.00
66 The Trial of Mr. Morris!. 175.00
67 . . . . 175.00
68 Laugh Lotion, V:Sivana 175.00

GOLDEN AGE

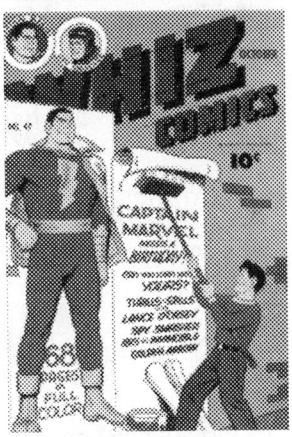

Whiz Comics #47
© Fawcett Publications

69 Mission to Mercury. 175.00
70 Climbs the World's Mightiest
Mountain 175.00
71 Strange Magician 150.00
72 V:The Man of the Future 150.00
73 In Ogre Land 150.00
74 Old Man River 150.00
75 The City Olympics 150.00
76 Spy Smasher become
Crime Smasher 150.00
77 . . . . 150.00
78 . . . . 150.00
79 . . . . 150.00
80 . . . . 150.00
81 . . . . 150.00
82 The Atomic Ship 150.00
83 Magic Locket 150.00
84 . . . . 150.00
85 The Clock of San Lojardo. . . . 150.00
86 V:Sinister Sivanas 150.00
87 The War on Olympia 150.00
88 The Wonderful Magic Carpet . 150.00
89 Webs of Crime. 150.00
90 . . . . 150.00
91 Infinity (c). 150.00
92 . . . . 150.00
93 Captain America become
a Hobo? 150.00
94 V:Sivana 150.00
95 Captain Marvel is grounded . . 150.00
96 The Battle Between Buildings. 150.00
97 Visits Mirage City 150.00
98 . . . . 150.00
99 V:Menace in the Mountains . . 150.00
100 . . . . 200.00
101 . . . . 150.00
102 A:Commando Yank 150.00
103 . . . . 150.00
104 . . . . 150.00
105 . . . . 150.00
106 A:Bulletman 150.00
107 The Great Experiment 175.00
108 thru 114 . . . . @150.00
115 The Marine Invasion. 150.00
116 . . . . 150.00
117 V:Sivana 150.00
118 . . . . 150.00
119 . . . . 150.00
120 . . . . 150.00
121 . . . . 150.00
122 V:Sivana 150.00
123. . . . . 150.00
124 . . . . 150.00
125 Olympic Games of the Gods 150.00
126 . . . . 150.00

127 . . . . 150.00
128 . . . . 150.00
129 . . . . 150.00
130 . . . . 150.00
131 The Television Trap 150.00
132 thru 142 . . . . @150.00
143 Mystery of the Flying Studio. 150.00
144 V:The Disaster Master 150.00
145 . . . . 150.00
146 . . . . 150.00
147 . . . . 150.00
148 . . . . 150.00
149 . . . . 150.00
150 V:Bug Bombs 150.00
151 . . . . 150.00
152 . . . . 150.00
153 V:The Death Horror 200.00
154 Horror Tale, I:Dr.Death 200.00
155 V:Legend Horror,Dr.Death . . 225.00

WHODUNIT?
D.S. Publishing Co.
Aug.–Sept., 1948
1 MB,Weeping Widow 150.00
2 Diploma For Death 100.00
3 Dec.–Jan., 1949 . . . . 100.00

WHO IS NEXT?
Standard Comics
Jan., 1953
5 ATh,RA,Don't Let Me Kill 125.00

WILD BILL ELLIOT
Dell Publishing Co.
May, 1950
(1) see Dell Four Color #278
2 . . . . 45.00
3 thru 5 . . . . @35.00
6 thru 10 . . . . @35.00
(11-12) see Four Color #472, 520
13 thru 17 . . . . @30.00

WILD BILL HICKOK
AND JINGLES
(see YELLOWJACKET
COMICS)

WILBUR COMICS
MLJ Magazines
(Archie Publications)
Summer, 1944
1 F:Wilbur Wilkin-America's Song
of Fun 400.00
2 . . . . 200.00
3 . . . . 150.00
4 . . . . 135.00
5 I:Katy Keene 500.00
6 . . . . 125.00
7 . . . . 125.00
8 . . . . 125.00
9 . . . . 125.00
10 . . . . 125.00
11 thru 20 . . . . 75.00
21 thru 30 . . . . @45.00
31 thru 40 . . . . @35.00
41 thru 50 . . . . @25.00
51 thru 89 . . . . @20.00
90 Oct., 1965 . . . . 20.00

WILD BILL HICKOK
Avon Periodicals
Sept.–Oct., 1949
1 GRI(c),Frontier Fighter 150.00
2 Ph(c),Gambler's Guns 60.00
3 Ph(c),Great Stage Robbery . . . 30.00
4 Ph(c),Guerilla Gunmen 30.00
5 Ph(c),Return of the Renegade . 30.00
6 EK,EK(c),Along the Apache
Trail 30.00
7 EK,EK(c)Outlaws of
Hell's Bend 30.00
8 Ph(c),The Border Outlaws 30.00
9 PH(c),Killers From Texas 30.00
10 Ph(c) 30.00
11 EK,EK(c),The Hell Riders. . . . 30.00
12 EK,EK(c),The Lost Gold MIne . 35.00
13 EK,EK(c),Bloody Canyon
Massacre 35.00
14 . . . . 35.00
15 . . . . 20.00
16 JKa 30.00
17 thru 23 . . . . @25.00
24 EK,EK(c) 30.00
25 EK,EK(c) 30.00
26 EK,EK(c) 30.00
27 EK,EK(c) 30.00
28 EK,EK(c),May–June, 1956. . . . 30.00

WILD BOY OF
THE CONGO
Approved(Ziff-Davis)/
St. John Publ. Co.
Feb.–March, 1951
10(1)NS,PH(c),Bondage(c),The
Gorilla God. 150.00
11(2)NS,Ph(c),Star of the Jungle. . 75.00
12(3)NS,Ph(c),Ice-Age Men 75.00
4 NS.Ph(c),Tyrant of the Jungle . 85.00
5 NS,Ph(c),The White Robe
of Courage 50.00
6 NS,Ph(c) 50.00
7 MB,EK.Ph(c) 60.00
8 Ph(c),Man-Eater 50.00
9 Ph(c),Killer Leopard 50.00
10 . . . . 50.00
11 MB(c). 60.00
12 MB(c) 60.00
13 MB(c) 60.00
14 MB(c) 60.00
15 June, 1955 . . . . 40.00

WINGS COMICS
Wings Publ.
(Fiction House Magazines)
Sept., 1940
1 HcK,AB,GT,Ph(c),B:Skull Squad,
Clipper Kirk,Suicide Smith,
War Nurse,Phantom Falcons,
GreasemonkeyGriffin,Parachute
Patrol,Powder Burns 1,800.00
2 HCk,AB,GT,Bomber Patrol . . . 750.00
3 HcK,AB,GT. 500.00
4 HcK,AB,GT,B:Spitfire Ace 500.00
5 HcK,AB,GT,Torpedo Patrol . . . 500.00
6 HcK,AB,GT,Bombs for Berlin . . 425.00
7 HcK,AB 425.00
8 HcK,AB,The Wings of Doom . 425.00
9 Sky-Wolf 400.00
10 The Upside Down 400.00
11 . . . . 350.00
12 Fury of the fire Boards 350.00
13 Coffin Slugs For The
Luftwaffe 350.00
14 Stuka Buster 350.00
15 Boomerang Blitz 350.00

16 O:Capt.Wings 400.00
17 Skyway to Death 300.00
18 Horsemen of the Sky 300.00
19 Nazi Spy Trap 300.00
20 The One Eyed Devil. 300.00
21 Chute Troop Tornado. 275.00
22 TNT for Tokyo 275.00
23 RP,Battling Eagles of Bataan . 275.00
24 RP,The Death of a Hero. 275.00
25 RP,Suicide Squeeze 275.00
26 Tojo's Eagle Trap 275.00
27 Blb,Mile High Gauntlet 275.00
28 Blb,Tail Gun Tornado 275.00
29 Blb,Buzzards from Berlin 275.00
30 Blb,Monsters of the
    Stratosphere. 225.00
31 BLb,Sea Hawks away 225.00
32 BLb,Sky Mammoth. 225.00
33 BLb,Roll Call of the Yankee
    Eagles 225.00
34 BLb,So Sorry,Mr Tojo. 225.00
35 BLb,RWb,Hell's Lightning. . . . 225.00
36 RWb,The Crash-Master 225.00
37 RWb,Sneak Blitz 225.00
38 RWb,Rescue Raid of the
    Yank Eagle 225.00
39 RWb,Sky Hell/Pigboat Patrol . 225.00
40 RWb,Luftwaffe Gamble 225.00
41 RWb,.50 Caliber Justice. 175.00
42 RWb,PanzerMeat forMosquito 175.00
43 RWb,Suicide Sentinels. 175.00
44 RWb,Berlin Bombs Away 175.00
45 RWb,Hells Cargo. 175.00
46 RWb,Sea-Hawk Patrol 175.00
47 RWb,Tojo's Tin Gibraltar. 175.00
48 RWb 175.00
49 RWb,Rockets Away 175.00
50 RWb,Mission For a Madman . 175.00
51 RWb,Toll for a Typhoon 150.00
52 MB,Madam Marauder 150.00
53 MB,Robot Death Over
    Manhattan 150.00
54 MB,Juggernauts of Death. . . . 150.00
55 MB 150.00
56 MB,Sea Raiders Grave 150.00
57 MB,Yankee Warbirds over
    Tokyo 150.00
58 MB 150.00
59 MB,Prey of the Night Hawks . 150.00
60 MB,E:Skull Squad,
    Hell's Eyes 150.00
61 MB,Raiders o/t Purple Dawn . 135.00
62 Twilight of the Gods 135.00
63 Hara Kiri Rides the Skyways . 135.00
64 Taps For Tokyo 135.00
65 AB,Warhawk for the Kill 135.00
66 AB,B:Ghost Patrol 135.00
67 AB 125.00
68 AB,ClipperKirkBecomesPhantom
    Falcon;O:Phantom Falcon . . 125.00
69 AB,O:cont,Phantom Falcon . . 125.00
70 AB,N:Phantom Falcon;
    O:Final Phantom Falcon 125.00
71 Ghost Patrol becomes
    Ghost Squadron 125.00
72 V:Capt. Kamikaze 125.00
73 Hell & Stormoviks 125.00
74 BLb(c),Loot is What She
    Lived For 125.00
75 BLb(c),The Sky Hag. 125.00
76 BLb(c),Temple of the Dead. . . 125.00
77 BLb(c),Sky Express to Hell. . . 125.00
78 BLb(c),Loot Queen of
    Satan's Skyway 125.00
79 BLb(c),Buzzards of
    Plunder Sky 125.00
80 BLb(c),Port of Missing Pilots . 125.00
81 BLb(c),Sky Trail of the
    Terror Tong. 125.00
82 BLb(c),Bondage(c),Spider &
    The Fly Guy 135.00

83 BLb(c),GE,Deep Six For
    Capt. Wings 125.00
84 BLb(c),GE,Sky Sharks to
    the Kill 125.00
85 BLb(c),GE 125.00
86 BLb(c),GE,Moon Raiders 125.00
87 BLb(c),GE 125.00
88 BLb(c),GE,Madmans Mission. 125.00
89 BLb(c),GE,Bondage(c),
    Rockets Away. 135.00
90 BLb(c),GE,Bondage(c),The
    Radar Rocketeers. 135.00
91 BLb(c),GE,Bondage(c),V-9 for
    Vengeance 135.00
92 BLb(c),GE,Death's red Rocket 125.00
93 BLb(c),GE,Kidnap Cargo 125.00
94 BLb(c),GE,Bondage(c),Ace
    of the A-Bomb Patrol 135.00
95 BLb(c),GE,The Ace of
    the Assassins. 125.00
96 BLb(c),GE 125.00
97 BLb(c),GE,The Sky Octopus . 125.00
98 BLb(c),GE,The Witch Queen
    of Satan's Skyways 125.00
99 BLb(c),GE,The Spy Circus. . . 125.00
100 BLb(c),GE,King o/t Congo . . 150.00
101 BLb(c),GE,Trator of
    the Cockpit. 125.00
102 BLb(c),GE,Doves of Doom. . 125.00
103 BLb(c),GE 125.00
104 BLb(c),GE,Fireflies of Fury. . 125.00
105 BLb(c),GE 125.00
106 BLb(c),GE,Six Aces & A
    Firing Squad. 125.00
107 BLb(c),GE,Operation Satan . 125.00
108 BLb(c),GE,The Phantom
    of Berlin 125.00
109 GE,Vultures of
    Vengeance Sky 125.00
110 GE,The Red Ray Vortex. . . . 125.00
111 GE,E:Jane Martin 100.00
112 The Flight of the
    Silver Saucers 100.00
113 Suicide Skyways 100.00
114 D-Day for Death Rays 100.00
115 Ace of Space 100.00
116 Jet Aces of Korea. 100.00
117 Reap the Red Wind 100.00
118 Vengeance Flies Blind 100.00
119 The Whistling Death. 100.00
120 Doomsday Mission. 100.00
121 Ace of the Spyways 100.00
122 Last Kill Korea 100.00
123 The Cat & the Canaries 100.00
124 Summer, 1954, Death

FIGHTING ACES OF WAR SKIES

Wings #33
© Fiction House

Below Zero. 100.00

WINNIE WINKLE
Dell Publishing Co., 1941
1 . . . . 45.00
2 . . . . 30.00
3 . . . . 20.00
4 thru 7 . . . . @20.00

WITCHCRAFT
Avon Periodicals
March–April, 1952
1 SC,JKu,Heritage of Horror . . . 500.00
2 SC,JKu,The Death Tattoo . . . 375.00
3 EK,Better off Dead 250.00
4 Claws of the Cat,
    Boiling Humans 300.00
5 Ph(c),Where Zombies Walk . . 350.00
6 March, 1953 Mysteries of the
    Moaning Statue 250.00

WITCHES TALES
Harvey Publications
Jan., 1951
1 RP,Bondage(c),Weird Yarns
    of Unseen Terror. 350.00
2 RP,We Dare You 175.00
3 RP,Bondage(c)Forest of
    Skeletons. 125.00
4 BP 125.00
5 BP,Bondage(c),Share
    My Coffin 135.00
6 BP,Bondage(c),Servants of
    the Tomb 135.00
7 BP,Screaming City 135.00
8 Bondage(c). 150.00
9 Fatal Steps. 125.00
10 BP,....,IT! 125.00
11 BP,Monster Maker 100.00
12 Bondage(c);The Web
    of the Spider. 125.00
13 The Torture Jar 100.00
14 Transformation. 125.00
15 Drooling Zombie 100.00
16 Revenge of a Witch 100.00
17 Dimension IV. 135.00
18 HN,Bird of Prey 125.00
19 HN,The Pact 125.00
20 HN,Kiss & Tell 125.00
21 HN,The Invasion 125.00
22 HN,A Day of Panic. 125.00
23 HN,The Wig Maker 125.00
24 HN,The Undertaker 125.00
25 What Happens at 8:30 PM?
    Severed Heads(c). 125.00
26 Up There 100.00
27 The Thing That Grew. 100.00
28 Demon Flies 100.00
Becomes:

WITCHES WESTERN TALES
29 S&K,S&K(c),F:Davy Crockett . 125.00
30 S&K.S&K(c). 150.00
Becomes:

WESTERN TALES
31 S&K,S&K(c),F:Davy Crockett . 100.00
32 S&K,S&K(c). 100.00
33 S&K,S&K(c),July–Sept.,1956 . 100.00

WITH THE MARINES ON THE BATTLEFRONTS OF THE WORLD
Toby Press, June, 1953
1 Ph(c),Flaming Soul 250.00
2 Ph(c),March, 1954 . . . . 50.00

WITTY COMICS
Irwin H. Rubin/Chicago Nite Life News, 1945
1 . . . . 100.00
2 1945. . . . . 50.00
3 thru 7 . . . . @40.00

WOMEN IN LOVE
Fox Features Synd./ Hero Books/ Ziff-Davis, Aug., 1949
1 . . . . 400.00

WOMEN OUTLAWS
Fox Features Syndicate July, 1948
1 . . . . 550.00
2 . . . . 450.00
3 . . . . 450.00
4 . . . . 450.00
5 thru 8 . . . . @350.00
Becomes:

MY LOVE MEMORIES
9 . . . . 75.00
10 . . . . 35.00
11 . . . . 70.00
12 WW. 75.00

WONDERBOY
(see HORRIFIC)

WONDER COMICS
Great Publ./Nedor/ Better Publications May, 1944
1 SSh(c),B:Grim Reaper,
  Spectro Hitler(c) 1,000.00
2 ASh(c),O:Grim Reaper,B:Super
  Sleuths,Grim Reaper(c) 500.00
3 ASh(c),Grim Reaper(c) 475.00
4 ASh(c),Grim Reaper(c) 450.00
5 ASh(c),Grim Reaper(c) 450.00
6 ASh(c),Grim Reaper(c) 350.00
7 ASh(c),Grim Reaper(c) 350.00
8 ASh(c),E:Super Sleuths,
  Spectro 350.00
9 ASh(c),B:Wonderman 350.00
10 ASh(c),Wonderman(c) 425.00

Wonder Comics #2
© Better Publications

11 Grl(c),B:Dick Devins. 425.00
12 Grl(c),Bondage(c) 425.00
13 ASh(c),Bondage(c) 425.00
14 ASh(c),Bondage(c)
  E:Dick Devins. 425.00
15 ASh(c),Bondage(c),B:Tara . . . 500.00
16 ASh(c),A:Spectro,
  E:Grim Reaper. 450.00
17 FF,ASh(c),A:Super Sleuth . . . 475.00
18 ASh(c),B:Silver Knight 450.00
19 ASh(c),FF 425.00
20 FF,Oct., 1948. . . . . 500.00

WONDERLAND COMICS
Feature Publications (Prize Comics Group) Summer, 1945
1 (fa),B:Alex in Wonderland 60.00
2 . . . . 35.00
3 thru 8 . . . . @25.00
9 1947. . . . . 25.00

WONDER COMICS
Fox Features Syndicate May, 1930–Jan. 1942
1 BKa,WE,WE(c),B:Wonderman,
  DR.Kung,K-51 . . . . 15,000.00
2 WE,BKa,LF(c),B:Yarko the
  Great,A:Spark Stevens . . 4,500.00
Becomes:

WONDERWORLD COMICS
3 WE,LF,BP,LF&WE,I:Flame . . 6,500.00
4 WE,LF,BP,LF(c) 2,700.00
5 WE,LF,BP,GT,LF(c),Flame . . 1,600.00
6 WE,LF,BP,GT,LF(c),Flame . . 1,400.00
7 WE,LF,BP,GT,LF(c),Flame . . 1,500.00
8 WE,LF,BP,GT,LF(c),Flame . . 1,600.00
9 WE,LF,BP,GT,LF(c),Flame . . 1,400.00
10 WE,LF,BP,LF(c),Flame 1,400.00
11 WE,LF,BP,LF(c),O:Flame. . . 1,100.00
12 BP,LF(c),Bondage(c),Flame . . 900.00
13 E:Dr Fung,Flame 850.00
14 JoS,Bondage(c),Flame. 900.00
15 JoS&LF(c),Flame. 800.00
16 Flame(c) 650.00
17 Flame(c) 650.00
18 Flame(c) 650.00
19 Male Bondage(c),Flame. 675.00
20 Flame(c) 650.00
21 O:Black Club &Lion,Flame . . . 600.00
22 Flame(c) 550.00
23 Flame(c) 500.00
24 Flame(c) 500.00
25 A:Dr Fung,Flame 500.00
26 Flame(c) 500.00
27 Flame(c) 450.00
28 Bondage(c)I&O:US Jones,
  B:Lu-nar,Flame. 650.00
29 Bondage(c),Flame. 400.00
30 O:Flame(c),Flame 700.00
31 Bondage(c),Flame 400.00
32 Hitler(c),Flame. 450.00
33 Male Bondage(c) 400.00

WORLD FAMOUS HEROES MAGAZINE
Comic Corp. of America (Centaur) Oct., 1941
1 BLb,Paul Revere 1,000.00
2 BLb,Andrew Jackson,V:
  Dickinson 450.00
3 BLb,Juarez-Mexican patriot . . 400.00
4 BLb,Canadian Mounties 400.00

WORLD'S GREATEST STORIES
Jubilee Publications Jan., 1949
1 F:Alice in Wonderland. 200.00
2 F:Pinocchio 175.00

WORLD WAR III
Ace Periodicals March–May, 1953
1 Atomic Bomb cover. 500.00
2 The War That Will Never
  Happen 450.00

WOTALIFE COMICS
(see PHANTOM LADY)

WOW COMICS
David McKay/Henle Publ. July, 1936
1 WE,DBr(c),Fu Manchu,
  Buck Jones 2,200.00
2 WE,Little King 1,400.00
3 WE,WE(c) 1,400.00
4 WE,BKa,AR,DBr(c),Popeye,
  Flash Gordon,Nov.,1936 . . 1,700.00

Wow #7
© Fawcett Publications

WOW COMICS
Fawcett Publications Winter, 1940
N#(1)S&K,CCB(c),B&O:Mr Scarlett;
  B:Atom Blake,Jim Dolan,Rick
  O'Shay,Bondage(c) 14,000.00
2 B:Hunchback 1,800.00
3 V:Mummy Ray Gun 900.00
4 O:Pinky 900.00
5 F:Pinky the Whiz Kid 600.00
6 O:Phantom Eagle;
  B:Commando Yank 600.00
7 Spearhead of Invasion 500.00
8 All Three Heroes. 500.00
9 A:Capt Marvel,Capt MarvelJr.
  Shazam,B:Mary Marvel . . . 1,000.00
10 The Sinister Secret of
  Hotel Hideaway 450.00
11 . . . . 350.00
12 Rocketing adventures 350.00
13 Thrill Show. 350.00

14 V:Mr Night 350.00	85 Ph(c) 100.00
15 The Shazam Girl of America . 325.00	86 Ph(c),The Case of the
16 Ride to the Moon 325.00	Extra Buddy, giant 100.00
17 V:Mary Batson,Alter Ego	87 Ph(c),The Strange Lands . . . 100.00
Goes Berserk 325.00	88 Ph(c),A:Senor Diablo 100.00
18 I:Uncle Marvel,Infinity(c)	89 Ph(c),The Hypnotist 100.00
V is For Victory 325.00	90 Ph(c),The Menace of
19 A Whirlwind Fantasy 325.00	the Cougar, giant 90.00
20 Mary Marvel's Magic Carpet . 325.00	91 Ph(c),Song of Death 90.00
21 Word That Shook the World . . 200.00	92 Ph(c),The Fatal Hide-out,
22 Come on Boys-	giant 90.00
Everybody Sing 200.00	93 Ph(c),Treachery at
23 Trapped by the Terror of	Triple T, giant 90.00
the Future. 200.00	94 Ph(c),Bank Busters,giant 90.00
24 Mary Marvel. 200.00	95 Ph(c),Rampaging River 80.00
25 Mary Marvel Crushes Crime. . 200.00	96 Ph(c),Range Robbers,giant . . . 90.00
26 Smashing Star-	97 Ph(c),Death on the
Studded Stories 175.00	Hook,giant 90.00
27 War Stamp Plea(c). 175.00	98 Ph(c),Web of Death,giant 90.00
28 . . . . 175.00	99 Ph(c),The Hidden Evidence . . 80.00
29 . . . . 175.00	100 Ph(c),A:Red Eagle,Giant 90.00
30 In Mirror Land 175.00	101 Ph(c) 90.00
31 Stars of Action. 125.00	102 thru 111 Ph(c). . . . . @80.00
32 The Millinery Marauders. . . . 125.00	112 Ph(c),March, 1952 . . . . 100.00
33 Mary Marvel(c). 125.00	
34 A:Uncle Marvel 125.00	**YANKEE COMICS**
35 I:Freckles Marvel 125.00	**Chesler Publications**
36 Secret of the Buried City . . . 125.00	**(Harry A. Chesler)**
37 7th War loan plea. 125.00	**Sept., 1941**
38 Pictures That Came to Life. . . 125.00	1 F:Yankee Doodle Jones . . . 1,200.00
39 The Perilous Packages 125.00	2 The Spirit of `41 . . . . 600.00
40 The Quarrel of the Gnomes . . 125.00	3 Yankee Doodle Jones. 450.00
41 Hazardous Adventures. 100.00	4 JCo,Yankee Doodle Jones
42 . . . . 100.00	March, 1942 . . . . 450.00
43 Curtain Time 100.00	
44 Volcanic Adventure 100.00	**YELLOWJACKET**
45 . . . . 100.00	**COMICS**
46 . . . . 100.00	**Levy Publ./Frank Comunale/**
47 . . . . 100.00	**Charlton**
48 . . . . 100.00	**Sept., 1944**
49 . . . . 100.00	1 O&B:Yellowjackets,B:Diana
50 Mary Marvel/Commando Yank 100.00	the Huntress 450.00
51 . . . . 75.00	2 Rosita &The Filipino Kid 250.00
52 . . . . 75.00	3 . . . . 225.00
53 Murder in the Tall Timbers . . . 75.00	4 Fall of the House of Usher . . . 250.00
54 Flaming Adventure. 75.00	5 King of Beasts 250.00
55 Earthquake!. 75.00	6 . . . . 225.00
56 Sacred Pearls of Comatesh . . . 75.00	7 I:Diane Carter;The
57 . . . . 75.00	Lonely Guy 225.00
58 E:Mary Marvel;The Curse	8 The Buzzing Bee Code 225.00
of the Keys 75.00	9 . . . . 225.00
59 B:Ozzie the Hilarious	10 Capt Grim V:The Salvage
Teenager 75.00	Pirates 225.00
60 thru 64 . . . . @75.00	**Becomes:**
65 A:Tom Mix 75.00	**JACK IN THE BOX**
66 A:Tom Mix 75.00	11 Funny Animal,Yellow Jacket . . 55.00
67 A:Tom Mix 75.00	12 Funny Animal 25.00
68 A:Tom Mix 75.00	13 BW,Funny Animal 80.00
69 A:Tom Mix,Baseball 75.00	14 thru 16 Funny Animal . . . . . @30.00
Becomes:	**Becomes:**
REAL WESTERN HERO	**COWBOY WESTERN**
70 It's Round-up Time. 250.00	**COMICS**
71 CCB,P(c),A Rip	17 Annie Oakley,Jesse James . . . 75.00
Roaring Rodeo 150.00	18 JO,JO(c) 50.00
72 w/Gabby Hayes 150.00	19 JO,JO(c),Legends of Paul
73 thru 75 . . . . @150.00	Bunyan. 50.00
Becomes:	20 JO(c),Jesse James 35.00
WESTERN HERO	21 Annie Oakley VisitsDryGulch . 35.00
76 Partial Ph(c)&P(c) 200.00	22 Story of the Texas Rangers . . . 35.00
77 Partial Ph(c)&P(c) 125.00	23 . . . . 35.00
78 Partial Ph(c)&P(c) 125.00	24 Ph(c),F:James Craig 35.00
79 Partial Ph(c)&P(c),	25 Ph(c),F:Sunset Carson. 35.00
Shadow of Death 100.00	26 Ph(c) 65.00
80 Partial Ph(c)&P(c) 125.00	27 Ph(c),Sunset Carson movie . . 150.00
81 CCB,Partial Ph(c)&P(c),	28 Ph(c),Sunset Carson movie . . 100.00
F:Tootsie 125.00	29 Ph(c),Sunset Carson movie . . 100.00
82 Partial Ph(c)&P(c),	
A:Hopalong Cassidy 125.00	
83 Partial Ph(c)&P(c) 125.00	
84 Ph(c) 100.00	

30 Ph(c),Sunset Carson movie . . 150.00	
31 Ph(c). 30.00	
32 thru 34 Ph(c) . . . . @25.00	
35 thru 37 Sunset Carson . . . . @75.00	
38 and 39 . . . . @25.00	
Becomes:	

Space Western Comics #40
© Charlton Comics

SPACE WESTERN COMICS

40 Spurs Jackson,V:The	
Saucer Men 450.00	
41 StC(c),Space Vigilantes 300.00	
42 StC(c) 350.00	
43 StC(c),Battle of	
Spacemans Gulch 300.00	
44 StC(c),The Madman of Mars . 300.00	
45 StC(c),The Moon Bat 300.00	
Becomes:	

COWBOY WESTERN COMICS

46 . . . . 70.00	
Becomes:	

COWBOY WESTERN HEROES

47 . . . . 25.00	
48 . . . . 25.00	
Becomes:	

COWBOY WESTERN

49 . . . . 25.00	
50 F:Jesse James 20.00	
51 thru 56 . . . . @20.00	
58, giant 25.00	
59 thru 66 . . . . @20.00	
67 AW&AT 50.00	
Becomes:	

WILD BILL HICKOK AND JINGLES

68 AW 50.00	
69 AW 35.00	
70 AW 30.00	
71 thru 73 . . . . @20.00	
74 1960 . . . . 20.00	

YOGI BERRA
Fawcett 1957

1 Ph(c) 550.00	

GOLDEN AGE

YOUNG BRIDES
Feature Publications
(Prize Comics) Sept.–Oct., 1952

1 S&K,Ph(c)	200.00
2 S&K,Ph(c)	100.00
3 S&K,Ph(c)	75.00
4 S&K	75.00
5 S&K	75.00
6 S&K	75.00
2-1 S&K	50.00
2-2 S&K	35.00
2-3 S&K	40.00
2-4 S&K	40.00
2-5 S&K	40.00
2-6 S&K	40.00
2-7 S&K	40.00
2-8 S&K	25.00
2-9 S&K	25.00
2-10 S&K	40.00
2-11 S&K	40.00
2-12 S&K	40.00
3-1	15.00
3-2	18.00
3-3	18.00
3-4	18.00
3-5	18.00
3-6	18.00
4-1	18.00
4-2 S&K	50.00
4-3	18.00
4-4 S&K	40.00
4-5	18.00

YOUNG EAGLE
Fawcett Publications/
Charlton Comics
Dec., 1950

1 Ph(c)	125.00
2 Ph(c),Mystery of Thunder Canyon	60.00
3 Ph(c),Death at Dawn	50.00
4 Ph(c)	50.00
5 Ph(c),The Golden Flood	50.00
6 Ph(c),The Nightmare Empire	50.00
7 Ph(c),Vigilante Veangeance	50.00
8 Ph(c),The Rogues Rodeo	50.00
9 Ph(c),The Great Railroad Swindle	50.00
10 June, 1952, Ph(c),Thunder Rides the Trail,O:Thunder	30.00

YOUNG KING COLE
Novelty Press/Premium
Svcs. Co., Autumn, 1945

1-1 Detective Toni Gayle	200.00
1-2	100.00
1-3	75.00
1-4	50.00
2-1	50.00
2-2	50.00
2-3	50.00
2-4	50.00
2-5	50.00
2-6	50.00
2-7	50.00
3-1	45.00
3-2 LbC	45.00
3-3 The Killer With The Hat	40.00
3-4 The Fierce Tiger	40.00
3-5 AMc	40.00
3-6	50.00
3-7 LbC(c),Case of the Devil's Twin	75.00
3-8	60.00
3-9 The Crime Fighting King	60.00
3-10 LbC(c)	75.00
3-11 LbC(c)	75.00

Young King Cole #3-1
© Novelty Press

3-12 July, 1948,AMc(c)	40.00

YOUNG LIFE
New Age Publications
Summer, 1945

1 Partial Ph(c),Louis Palma	75.00
2 Partial Ph(c),Frank Sinatra	80.00

Becomes:

TEEN LIFE

3 Partial Ph(c),Croon without Tricks,June Allyson(c)	50.00
4 Partial Ph(c),Atom Smasher Blueprints,Duke Ellington(c)	45.00
5 Partial Ph(c), Build Your Own Pocket Radio, Jackie Robinson(c)	60.00

YOUNG LOVE
Feature Publ.
(Prize Comics Group)
Feb.–March, 1949

1 S&K,S&K(c)	300.00
2 S&K,Ph(c)	150.00
3 S&K,JSe,BE,Ph(c)	125.00
4 S&K,Ph(c)	75.00
5 S&K,Ph(c)	75.00
2-1 S&K,Ph(c)	125.00
2-2 Ph(c)	50.00
2-3 Ph(c)	50.00
2-4 Ph(c)	50.00
2-5 Ph(c)	50.00
2-6 S&K(c)	75.00
2-7 S&K(c),S&K	75.00
2-8 S&K	75.00
2-9 S&K(c),S&K	75.00
2-10 S&K(c),S&K	75.00
2-11 S&K(c),S&K	75.00
2-12 S&K(c),S&K	75.00
3-1 S&K(c),S&K	75.00
3-2 S&K(c),S&K	75.00
3-3 S&K(c),S&K	75.00
3-4 S&K(c),S&K	75.00
3-5 Ph(c)	50.00
3-6 BP,Ph(c)	50.00
3-7 Ph(c)	50.00
3-8 Ph(c)	50.00
3-9 MMe,Ph(c)	50.00
3-10 Ph(c)	50.00
3-11 Ph(c)	50.00
3-12 Ph(c)	50.00
4-1 S&K	50.00
4-2 Ph(c)	40.00

4-3 Ph(c)	40.00
4-4 Ph(c)	40.00
4-5 Ph(c)	40.00
4-6 S&K,Ph(c)	40.00
4-7 thru 4-12 Ph(c)	@35.00
5-1 thru 5-12 Ph(c)	@25.00
6-1 thru 6-9	@20.00
6-10 thru 6-12	@20.00
7-1 thru 7-7	@15.00
7-8 thru 7-11	@15.00
7-12 thru 8-5	@15.00
8-6 thru 8-12	@20.00

YOUNG ROMANCE COMICS
Feature Publ./Headline/
Prize Publ., Sept.–Oct., 1947

1 S&K(c),S&K	300.00
2 S&K(c),S&K	200.00
3 S&K(c),S&K	175.00
4 S&K(c),S&K	175.00
5 S&K(c),S&K	175.00
6 S&K(c),S&K	150.00
2-1 S&K(c),S&K	150.00
2-2 S&K(c),S&K	150.00
2-3 S&K(c),S&K	150.00
2-4 S&K(c),S&K	150.00
2-5 S&K(c),S&K	150.00
2-6 S&K(c),S&K	100.00
3-1 thru 3-12 S&K(c),S&K	@100.00
4-1 thru 4-12 S&K(c),S&K	@100.00
5-1 ATh,S&K	100.00
2	100.00
3	100.00
5-4 thru 5-12 S&K	@100.00
6-1 thru 6-3	@35.00

YOUR UNITED STATES
Lloyd Jacquet Studios, 1946

1N# Teeming nation of Nations	175.00

YOUTHFUL HEART
Youthful Magazines
May, 1952

1 Frankie Lane(c)	175.00
2 Vic Damone	125.00
3 Johnnie Ray	125.00

Becomes:

DARING CONFESSIONS

4 DW,Tony Curtis	50.00
5	35.00
6 DW	40.00
7	35.00
8 DW	40.00

YOUTHFUL ROMANCES
Pix Parade/Ribage/
Trojan, Aug.–Sept., 1949

1	150.00
2	75.00
3 Tex Beneke	50.00
4	50.00
5	35.00
6	35.00
7 Tony Martin(c)	40.00
8 WW(c)	125.00
9 thru 14	@35.00

Becomes:

DARLING LOVE

15 WD	40.00
16	30.00
17 DW,Ph(c)	30.00

ZAGO, JUNGLE PRINCE
Fox Features Syndicate
Sept., 1948
1 A:Blue Beetle 450.00
2 JKa. 350.00
3 JKa. 300.00
4 MB(c) 300.00
Becomes:

MY STORY
5 JKa,Too Young To Fall in Love . 75.00
6 I Was A She-Wolf 35.00
7 I Lost My Reputation 35.00
8 My Words Condemned Me . . . 35.00
9 WW,Wayward Bride 85.00
10 WW,March, 1950,Second
    Rate Girl. 85.00
11 . . . . 35.00
12 . . . . 35.00

TEGRA, JUNGLE EMPRESS
Fox Features Syndicate
Aug., 1948
1 Blue Bettle,Rocket Kelly 375.00
Becomes:

ZEGRA, JUNGLE EMPRESS
2 JKa 450.00
3 . . . . 350.00
4 . . . . 350.00
5 . . . . 350.00
Becomes:

MY LOVE LIFE
6 I Put A Price Tag On Love 65.00
7 An Old Man's Fancy 35.00
8 My Forbidden Affair 35.00
9 I Loved too Often 35.00
10 My Secret Torture 35.00
11 I Broke My Own Heart 35.00
12 I Was An Untamed Filly 35.00
13 I Can Never Marry You,
    Aug. 1950 . . . . 30.00

ZIP COMICS
MLJ Magazines
Feb., 1940
1 MMe,O&B:Kalathar,The Scarlet
    Avenger,Steel Sterling,B:Mr
    Satan,Nevada Jones,War Eagle
    Captain Valor. 3,700.00
2 MMe,CBi(c)B:Steel
    Sterling(c) 1,600.00
3 CBi,MMe,CBi(c) 1,100.00
4 CBi,MMe,CBi(c) 900.00
5 CBi,MMe,CBi(c) 900.00
6 CBi,MMe,CBi(c) 750.00
7 CBi,MMe,CBi(c) 750.00
8 CBi,MMe,CBi(c),Bondage(c) . 750.00
9 CBi,MMe,CBi(c)E:Kalathar,
    Mr Satan;Bondage(c) 950.00
10 CBi,MMe,CBi(c),B:Inferno . . 850.00
11 CBi,MMe,CBi(c) 700.00
12 CBi,MMe,CBi(c),Bondage(c) . 700.00
13 CBi,MMe,CBi(c)E:Inferno,
    Bondage(c),Woman in
    Electric Chair 725.00
14 CBi,MMe,CBi(c),Bondage(c) . 675.00
15 CBi,MMe,CBi(c),Bondage(c) . 675.00
16 CBi,MMe,CBi(c),Bondage(c) . 675.00
17 CBi,CBI(c),E:Scarlet

Zip Comics #22
© MLJ Magazines

    Avenger Bondage(c). 675.00
18 IN(c),B:Wilbur 700.00
19 IN(c),Steel Sterling(c). 675.00
20 IN(c),O&I:Black Jack
    Hitler(c) 1,000.00
21 IN(c),V:Nazis 600.00
22 IN(c) 650.00
23 IN(c),Flying Fortress 600.00
24 IN(c),China Town Exploit 600.00
25 IN(c),E:Nevada Jones 600.00
26 IN(c),B:Black Witch,
    E:Capt Valor. 600.00
27 IN(c),I:Web,V:Japanese. . . . 1,000.00
28 IN(C),O:Web,Bondage(c) . . 1,000.00
29 Steel Sterling & Web 450.00
30 V:Nazis 450.00
31 IN(c) 350.00
32 . . . . 350.00
33 Bondage(c) 375.00
34 I:Applejack;Bondage(c) 375.00
35 E:Zambini 350.00
36 I:Senor Banana 350.00
37 . . . . 350.00
38 E:Web 350.00
39 O&B:Red Rule. 350.00
40 . . . . 250.00
41 . . . . 250.00
42 . . . . 250.00
43 . . . . 250.00
44 . . . . 250.00
45 E:Wilbur. 250.00
46 . . . . 250.00
47 Crooks Can't Win,
    Summer, 1944 . . . . 250.00

ZIP-JET
St. John Publishing Co.
Feb., 1953
1 Rocketman 500.00
2 April–May, 1953, Assassin
    of the Airlanes 400.00

ZOOM COMICS
Carlton Publishing Co.
Dec., 1945
N# O:Captain Milksop 300.00

Zoot #9
© Fox Features Syndicate

ZOOT COMICS
Fox Features Syndicate
Spring, 1946
N#(1)(fa) 100.00
2 A:Jaguar(fa) 85.00
3 (fa) 50.00
4 (fa) 50.00
5 (fa) 35.00
6 (fa) 35.00
7 B:Rulah 700.00
8 JKa(c),Fangs of Stone 500.00
9 JKa(c),Fangs of Black Fury . . . 500.00
10 JKa(c),Inferno Land 500.00
11 JKa,The Purple Plague,
    Bondage(c). 525.00
12 JKa(c),The Thirsty Stone,
    Bondage(c). 350.00
13 Bloody Moon 325.00
14 Pearls of Pathos,Woman
    Carried off by Bird 450.00
15 Death Dancers. 350.00
16 . . . . 350.00
Becomes:

RULAH, JUNGLE GODDESS
17 JKa(c),Wolf Doctor. 700.00
18 JKa(c),Vampire Garden 500.00
19 JKa(c) 450.00
20 . . . . 450.00
21 JKa(c) 450.00
22 JKa(c) 450.00
23 . . . . 375.00
24 . . . . 350.00
25 . . . . 350.00
26 . . . . 350.00
27 . . . . 375.00
Becomes:

I LOVED
28 . . . . 35.00
29 thru 31 . . . . @25.00
32 My Poison Love, March, 1950 . 25.00

ACCLAIM

ACCLAIM

ACCLAIM ADVENTURE ZONE
Acclaim Young Readers 1997
Digest Size
Ninjak
Spec. "The Boss" 4.50
Turok
Spec. "Extinction" 4.50
Spec. "Dinosaur Rodeo" 4.50
Spec. "Scrounge Rules" 4.50

Archer & Armstrong #6
© Valiant

ARCHER & ARMSTRONG
Valiant 1992
0 JiS(s),BWS,BL,I&O:Archer,
   I:Armstrong,The Sec. 3.00
0 Gold Ed. 5 . . . . 4.00
1 FM(c),B:JiS(s),BWS,BL,Unity #3,
   A:Eternal Warrior 2.25
2 WS(c),E:JiS(s),BWS,BL,Unity
   #11,2nd A:Turok,A:X-O. 2.25
3 B:BWS(a&s), BWi, V:Sect in
   Rome 2.25
4 BWS,BWi,V:Sect in Rome 2.25
5 BWS,BWi,I:Andromeda. 2.25
6 BWS,BWi, A:Andromeda,
   V:Medoc. 2.25
7 BWS,ANi,BWi,V:Sect in England 2.25
8 BWS,as Eternal Warrior #8,
   Three Musketeers,I:Ivan. 2.25
9 BCh,BWi,in Britain 2.00
10 BWS,A:Ivar 2.00
11 BWS,A:Solar,Ivar. 2.00
12 BWS,V:The Avenger 2.00
13 B:MBn(s),RgM,In Los Angeles . 2.00
14 In Los Angeles. 2.00
15 E:MBn(s),In LasVegas, I:Duerst . 2.00
16 V:Sect 2.00
17 B:MBn(s),In Florida 2.00
18 MV,in Heaven 2.00
19 MV,V:MircoboticCult,D:Duerst . . 2.00
20 MV,Chrismas Issue 2.00
21 MV,A:Shadowman,Master
   Darque. 2.00
22 MV,A:Shadowman,Master
   Darque,w/Valiant Era card 2.00
23 MV, ... 2.00
24 MV, ... 2.00
25 MV,A:Eternal Warrior 2.00
26 Chaos Effect-Gamma #4, A:Ivar,
   Et. Warrior 2.00

ARMED & DANGEROUS
Valiant (B&W) 1995
1 thru 4 . . . . @2.95
Spec.#1 . . . . 2.95

ARMED & DANGEROUS
Acclaim (B&W) 1996
1 BH,"Hell's Slaughterhouse" Pt.1 . 2.95
2 BH,"Hell's Slaughterhouse" Pt.2 . 2.95
3 BH,"Hell's Slaughterhouse" Pt.3 . 2.95
4 BH,"Hell's Slaughterhouse" Pt.4 . 2.95

ARMED & DANGEROUS
No. 2
Acclaim (B&W) Dec. 1996
1 BH,"When Irish Eyes are
   Dying," pt.1 . . . . 2.95
2 BH,"When Irish Eyes," pt.2 . . . . 2.95
3 BH,"When Irish Eyes," pt.3 . . . . 2.95
4 BH,"When Irish Eyes," pt.4 . . . . 2.95

ARMORINES
Valiant 1994
0 (from X-O #25),Card Stock (c),
   Diamond Distributors "Fall Fling"
   Retailer Meeting. 2.50
0a Gold Ed. 3.00
1 JGz(s),JCf,B:White Death. 2.25
2 JGz(s),JCf,E:White Death. 2.25
3 JGz(s),JCf,V:Spider Aliens 2.25
4 JCf, V: Spider Aliens. 2.00
5 JCf, Chaos Effect-Delta #2,
   A:H.A.R.D. Corp. 2.00
6 Spider Alien Mothership 2.00
7 Rescue. 2.00
8 Rescue in Iraq 2.00
9 . . . . 2.00
10 Protect Fidel Castro. 2.00
11 V: Spider Super Suit 2.00
12 F: Sirot 2.00
Yearbook I:Linoff. 3.00

BAD EGGS
Acclaim 1996
1 thru 4 BL,DP,"That Dirty Yellow
   Mustard". . . . . @2.95

BAR SINISTER
Windjammer 1995
1 From Shaman's Tears. 2.50
2 V:SWAT Team 2.50
3 F: Animus Prime. 2.50
4 MGe,RHo,V:Jabbersnatch 2.50

BART SEARS' X-O MANOWAR
Valiant 1995
HC Bart Sears' Artwork. 17.95

BLOODSHOT
Valiant 1992
0 KVH(a&s),DG(i),Chromium (c),
   O:Bloodshot,A:Eternal Warrior . 3.00
0a Gold Ed.,w/Diamond "Fall Fling"
   logo 4.00
1 BWS(c),B:KVH(s),DP,BWi, V:Mafia,
   I:Carboni,1st Chromium(c) 2.50
2 DP,I:Durkins,V:Ax 2.50
3 DP,V:The Mob 2.50
4 DP,A:Eternal Warrior. 2.00
5 DP,A:Eternal Warrior,Rai. 2.00
6 DP,I:Ninjak (Not in Costume) . . . 2.00
7 DP,JDx,A:Ninjak (1st appearance
   in costume) 2.00
8 DP,JDx,A:Geoff. 2.00
9 DP,JDx,V:Slavery Ring 2.00
10 DP,JDx,V:Tunnel Rat 2.00
11 DP,JDx,V:Iwatsu 2.00
12 DP,JDx,Day Off 2.00
13 DP,JDx,V:Webnet 2.00
14 DP,JDx,V:Carboni 2.00
15 DP,JDx,V:Cinder 2.00
16 DP,JDx,w/Valiant Era Card. . . . 2.00
17 DP,JDx,A:H.A.R.D.Corps 2.00
18 DP,KVH,After the Missile 2.00
19 DP,KVH,I:Uzzi the Clown 2.00
20 DP,KVH, Chaos Effect-Gamma
   #1, V:Immortal Enemy 2.00
21 DP,V: Immortal Enemy, Ax 2.00
22 Immortal Enemy 2.00
23 Cinder 2.00
24 Geomancer, Immortal Enemy. . . 2.00
25 V:Uzzi the Clown 2.00
26 V:Uzzi the Clown 2.00
27 Rampage Pt. 1 . . . . 2.00
28 Rampage Pt. 3 . . . . 2.00
29 Rampage Conc. A:Ninjak. 2.00
30 V:Shape Shifter 2.00
31 Nanite Killer. 2.00
32 KVH,SCh,V: Vampires 2.00
33 KVH,SCh,V: Vampires 2.00
34 NBy,KVH,new villains spawned . 2.00
35 NBY,KVH,attempts to control . . . 2.00
36 V:Voodoo Drug Dealer. 2.00
37 V:Voodoo Drug Dealer. 2.00
38 V:Rampage 2.00
39 V:Rampage 2.00
40 USA wants Bloodshot 2.00
41 F:Jillian Alcott 2.00
42 Virtual Nightmare. 2.00
43 V:U.S. Troops 2.00
44 I:Deathangel, V:Speedshots. . . . 2.00
45 thru 51 . . . . @2.00
Yearbook #1 KVH,briefcase bomb . 4.25
Yearbook 1995 Villagers 2.95
Spec.GN Last Stand. 5.95

BLOODSHOT Series Two
Acclaim March 1997
1 LKa(s),SaV "Behold, a Pale
   Horseman". 2.50
1a variant cover. 3.00
2 LKa(s),SaV "Dead Man Walking" 2.50
3 LKa(s),SaV "ChainsawMassacre" 2.50
4 LKa(s),SaV Search for Identity . 2.50
5 LKa(s),SaV V:Simon Oreck. . . . 2.50
6 LKa(s),SaV "Bloodwhispers" 2.50
7 LKa(s),SaV "To the Bitter End..",
   pt.1 . . . . 2.50
8 LKa(s),SaV "To the Bitter End..",
   pt.2 . . . . 2.50
9 LKa(s),SaV "Suicide" 2.50

ACCLAIM

10 LKa(s),SaV "Dreamland" 2.50
11 LKa(s),SaV 2.50
12 LKa(s),SaV "Cat Scratch Fever". 2.50
13 LKa(s),SaV in Russia. 2.50
14 LKa(s),SaV to the Vatican 2.50
15 LKa(s),SaV DOA Headquarters . 2.50
16 LKa(s),SaV final issue 2.50

Captain Johner & The Aliens #1
© Valiant

CAPTAIN JOHNER
& THE ALIENS
Valiant May 1995
1 Rep. Magnus Robot Fighter #1–7
(Gold Key 1963–64) 2.95

CHAOS EFFECT
Valiant 1994
Alpha DJ(c), BCh, JOy, A:All
   Valiant Characters 2.25
Alpha Red (c) 3.50
Omega DJ(c), BCh, JOy, A:All
   Valiant Characters 2.25
Omega Gold(c) 3.50
Epilogue pt.1 . . . . 2.95
Epilogue pt.2 . . . . 2.95

CITY KNIGHTS, THE
Windjammer 1995
1 I:Michael Walker 2.50
2 I:Herald 2.50
3 & 4 V:Herald . . . . @2.50

CONCRETE JUNGLE:
THE LEGEND OF
THE BLACK LION
Acclaim 1998
1 (of 6) CPr,JFy,F:Terry Smalls . . . 2.50
2 CPr,JFy,Black Lion Order 2.50
3 CPr,JFy,The Man 2.50
4 CPr,JFy 2.50
5 CPr,JFy 2.50

DARQUE PASSAGES
Acclaim 1997
1 (of 4) sequal to Master Darque . . 2.50
1 signed edition 4.00
2 . . . . 2.50
3 A:Pere Jean, Voodoo King 2.50
4 conclusion 2.50

DEADSIDE
Acclaim 1998
1 (of 4) PJe, ... 2.50
2 thru 4 . . . . @2.50

DEATHMATE
Valiant/Image 1993
Preview (Advanced Comics) 2.00
Preview (Previews) 2.00
Preview (Comic Defense Fund) . . . 4.00
Prologue BL,JLe,RLd,Solar meets
   Void 3.25
Prologue Gold 4.00
Blue SCh, HSn, F:Solar, Magnus,
   Battlestone, Livewire, Stronghold,
   Impact, Striker, Harbinger, Brigade,
   Supreme 3.00
Blue Gold Ed. 4.00
Yellow BCh,MLe,DP,F:Armstrong,
   H.A.R.D.C.A.T.S.,Ninjak,Zealot,
   Shadowman,Grifter,Ivar 3.00
Yellow Gold Ed. 4.00
Black JLe,MS,F:Warblade,Ripclaw,
   Turok,X-O Manowar 4.00
Black Gold Ed. 6.00
Red RLd,JMs, ... 4.00
Red Gold Ed. 3.00
Epilogue 2.50
Epilogue Gold. 3.00

DESTROYER
Valiant 1994
0 MM 41st Century 2.95

DR. TOMORROW
Acclaim May 1997
1 (of 12) BL,Bart Simms finds
   Angel Computer 2.50
2 BL,V:Teutonic Knight 2.50
3 BL,V:Teutonic Knight concl. . . . 2.50
4 BL,V:Joe McCarthy. 2.50
5 BL,V:J. Edgar Hoover 2.50
6 BL,DG,V:Mushroom Cloud 2.50
7 BL,DG,A:Mushroom Cloud 2.50
8 BL,GK,Vietnam. 2.50
9 BL, ... 2.50
10 BL,SMc,on *Oprah* 2.50
11 BL,the time capsule 2.50
12 BL,MBu(c),final issue 2.50

DISNEY'S ACTION CLUB
Acclaim Young Readers 1997
Digest Size
Aladdin
Spec."An Imp-Perfect Day" 4.50
Spec."Monkey Business" 4.50
Buzz Lightyear
Spec."Antique Attack" 4.50
Hercules
Spec."My Fill of Phil". 4.50
The Lion King
Spec."Lurkers in the Water" 4.50
Mighty Ducks
Spec."Puck Power". 4.50
Spec."Rough Stuff". 4.50

DISNEY'S
BEAUTY AND THE BEAST
Acclaim Young Readers 1997
Spec. Holiday Special, digest size . 4.50

DISNEY'S
ENCHANTING STORIES
Acclaim Young Readers 1997
Digest Size
Beauty and the Beast
Spec."The Book Crook" 4.50
Hercules
Spec."A Torch for Meg" 4.50
Hunchback of Notre Dame
Spec."Veiled Beauty" 4.50
The Little Mermaid
Spec."Seal of Approval" 4.50
101 Dalmatians
Spec."Star Search" 4.50
Pocahontas
Spec."River of Youth" 4.50
Snow White and the Seven Dwarfs
Spec."Mirror,Mirror,on the Floor" . . 4.50
Spec."Dopey the Genius" 4.50

DISNEY'S HERCULES
Acclaim Young Readers 1997
1-shot Movie adaptation, 64pg 4.50
Spec. Making of a Hero 6.00

DISNEY'S HERCULES:
THE GREATEST BATTLES
Acclaim Young Readers 1997
HC 96pg. 24.00
TPB 13.00

DISNEY'S
THE LITTLE MERMAID
Acclaim 1997
Spec. Underwater Engagements flip
   book, digest size 4.50

DISNEY'S
101 DALMATIANS
Acclaim 1997
HC Bad to the Bone 24.00
TPB Bad to the Bone 13.00

ETERNAL WARRIOR
Valiant 1992
1 FM(c),JDx,Unity #2,O:Eternal
   Warrior,Armstrong 3.00
1a Gold Ed. 4.00
1b Gold Foil Logo 5.00
2 WS(c),JDx,Unity #10,A:Solar,
   Harbinger,Eternal Warrior
   of 4001. . . . . 2.50
3 JDx,V:Armstrong,I:Astrea 2.50
4 JDx(i),I:Caldone, C:Bloodshot . . 2.50
5 JDx,I:Bloodshot,V:Iwatsu's Men . 2.50
6 BWS,JDx,V:Master Darque. 2.50
7 BWS,V:Master Darque, D:Uncle
   Buck 2.50
8 BWS,as Archer & Armstrong #8
   Three Musketeers,I:Ivar 2.50
9 MMo,JDx,B:Book of the
   Geomancer 2.50
10 JDx,E:Bk. o/t Geomancer. 2.50
11 B:KVH(s),JDx(i), V:Neo-Nazis . . 2.50
12 JDx(i),V:Caldone 2.50
13 MMo,JDx(i),V:Caldone,
   A:Bloodshot 2.50
14 E:KVH(s),MMo,V:Caldone,
   A:Geoff. 2.50
15 YG,A:Bloodshot,V:Tanaka 2.50
16 YG,A:Bloodshot. 2.50
17 A:Master Darque 2.50
18 C:Doctor Mirage 2.50
19 KVH(s),TeH,A:Doctor Mirage . . . 2.50

20 KVH(s),Access Denied 2.50
21 KVH(s),TeH,V:Dr. Steiner 2.50
22 V:Master Darque,w/Valiant Era
   Card. 2.50
23 KVH(s),TeH,Blind Fate. 2.50
24 KVH(s),TeH,V:Immortal Enemy . 2.50
25 MBn(s),A:Archer,Armstrong 2.50
26 Double(c), Chaos Effect-Gamma
   #4, A:Archer, Armstrong, Ivar . . 3.00
27 JOs(s) 2.25
28 War on Drugs 2.25
29 Immortal Enemy 2.25
30 Lt. Morgan. 2.25
31 JD,JOs 2.25
32 . . . . 2.25
33 Mortal Kin Pt.1. . . . . 2.25
34 Mortal Kin Pt.2. . . . . 2.25
35 Mortal Kin Finale 2.50
36 Fenris League 2.50
37 Youthful Tale 2.50
38 V:Niala, The Dead Queen 2.50
39 JOs,JG,PG(c),V:body thieves. . . 2.50
40 JOs,JG,PG(c),finds organ farm . 2.50
41 War in Herznia. 2.50
42 I: Brisbane. 2.50
43 V:Neo Nazi 2.50
44 V:Neo Nazi 2.50
45 R:Fenris Society 2.50
46 V:Fenris Society 2.50
47 Jihad. 2.50
48 Immortal Life in Danger 2.50
49 JOs,JG,Hallucinations 2.50
50 . . . . 2.50
Yearbook #1. . . . . 4.25
Yearbook #2. . . . . 4.00
Wings of Justice WWI. 2.50
Quarterly
Time and Treachery 3.95
Digital Alchemy. 3.95
Spec. Blackworks AHo, ... 4.00

ETERNAL WARRIORS
Acclaim 1997
Quarterly
Archer & Armstrong AHo 3.95
Mog AHo 3.95
The Immortal Enemy AHo. 3.95

FOX FUNHOUSE
Acclaim Young Readers 1997
Digest Size, Featuring The Tick
Spec. "Spoo-o-o-o-nn" 4.50
Spec. "A World of Pain(t)" 4.50
Spec. "Raw, Uncooked Justice" . . . 4.50
Spec. "Way Out of Tuna" 4.50
Spec. "Tick vs. the Entire Ocean. . . 4.50
Spec. Neato-Keen Holiday Special . 4.50

FOX PRESENTS
Acclaim Young Readers 1997
The Tick "No Time For Sanity" . . . 10.00

GEOMANCER
Valiant 1994
1 RgM, I:Geomancer. 3.00
2 RgM, Eternal Warrior 2.00
3 RgM, Darque Elementals 2.00
4 RgM. 2.00
5 Riot Gear pt. 1 . . . . 2.00
6 Riot Gear pt. 2 . . . . 2.00
7 F:Zorn 2.00
8 v:Zorn. 2.00

GOAT, THE: H.A.E.D.U.S.
Acclaim 1998
Spec. CPr,KG,F:Vincent Van Goat . 3.95

GRACKLE, THE
Acclaim (B&W) Sept. 1996
1 MBn,PG,"Double Cross" Pt.1 . . . 2.95
2 MBn,PG,"Double Cross" Pt.2 . . . 2.95
3 MBn,PG,"Double Cross" Pt.3 . . . 2.95
4 MBn,PG,"Double Cross" Pt.4 . . . 2.95

GRAVEDIGGERS
Acclaim (B&W) 1996
1 (of 4) 2.95
2 thru 4 . . . . @2.95

Harbinger #19 © Valiant

HARBINGER
Valiant 1992
0 DL,O:Sting,V:Harada, from TPB
   (Blue Bird Ed.) 2.00
0 from coupons 4.00
1 DL,JDx,I:Sting,Torque,
   Zeppelin,Flamingo,Kris. 3.00
1a w/o coupon. 1.00
2 DL,JDx,V:Harbinger Foundation,
   I:Dr.Heyward 2.00
2a w/o coupon. 1.00
3 DL,JDx,I:Ax,Rexo, V:Spider
   Aliens. 2.00
3a w/o coupon. 1.00
4 DL,JDx,V:Ax,I:Fort,
   Spikeman,Dog,Bazooka 2.00
4a w/o coupon. 1.00
5 DL,JDx,I:Puff,Thumper,
   A:Solar,V:Harada 2.00
5a w/o coupon. 1.00
6 DL,D:Torque,A:Solar,
   V:Harada,Eggbreakers 2.00
6a w/o coupon. 1.00
7 DL,Torque's Funeral 2.00
8 FM(c),DL,JDx,Unity#8,
   A:Magnus,Eternal Warrior. 2.00
9 WS(c),DL,Unity #16,
   A:Magnus,Armstrong,Rai,
   Archer,Eternal Warrior 2.00
10 DL,I:H.A.R.D.Corps, Daryl,
   Shetiqua. 2.00
11 DL,V:H.A.R.D.Corps. 2.00
12 DL,F:Zeppelin,A:Elfquest 2.00
13 Flamingo Vs. Rock 2.00
14 A:Magnus(Dream Sequence),
   C:Stronghold 2.00
15 I:Livewire,Stronghold 2.00
16 A:Livewire,Stronghold 2.00
17 HSn,I:Simon 2.00
18 HSn,I:Screen 2.00
19 HSn,I:Caliph 2.00

20 HSn,V:Caliph. 2.00
21 I:Pete's Father. 2.00
22 HSn,A:Archer & Armstrong 2.00
23 HSn,B:Twilight of the
   Eighth Day. 2.00
24 HSn,V:Eggbreakers 2.00
25 HSn,V:Harada,E:Twlight of the
   Eighth Day 2.50
26 SCh,AdW,I:Jolt,Amazon,
   Mircowave,Anvil,Sonix 2.00
27 SCh,AdW,Chrismas issue 2.00
28 SCh,AdW,O:Sonix,J:Tyger 2.00
29 SCh,AdW,A:Livewire,Stronghold,
   w/Valiant Era card 2.00
30 SCh,AdW,A:Livewire,Stronghold 2.00
31 SCh,AdW,V:H.A.R.D.Corps 2.00
32 SCh,AdW,A:Eternal Warrior 2.00
33 SCh, V:Dr. Eclipse. 2.00
34 SCh,Chaos Effect-Delta#1, A:X-
   O, Dr. Eclipse. 2.00
35 Zephyr. 2.00
36 Zephyr, Magnus. 2.00
37 Magnus, Harada 2.00
38 A:Spikeman. 2.00
39 Zepplin vs. Harada 2.00
40 V:Harbinger. 2.00
41 V:Harbinger. 2.00
TPB w/#0,rep#1-4. . . . . 25.00
TPB 2nd Printing w/o #0. . . . . 9.95
TPB #2, Rep. 6-7,10-11 . . . . 9.95

HARBINGER FILES:
HARADA
Valiant 1994
1 BL,DC,O:Harada 2.75
2 Harada's ultimate weapon. 2.50

H.A.R.D. CORPS
Valiant 1992
1 JLe(c),DL,BL,V:Harbinger
   Foundation,I:Flatline,D:Maniac . 2.50
1a Gold Ed.. . . . . 2.50
2 DL,BL,V:Harb.Foundation 2.50
3 DL,BL,J:Flatline 2.50
4 BL 2.50
5 BCh,BL(i),A:Bloodshot 2.50
5a Comic Defense System Ed. . . . 2.50
6 MLe,A:Spider Aliens. 2.50
7 MLe,V:Spider Aliens, I:Hotshot . 2.50
8 MLe,V:Harada,J:Hotshot. 2.50
9 MLe,V:Harada,A:Turok 2.00
10 MLe,A:Turok,V:Dinosaurs 2.00
11 YG,I:Otherman. 2.00
12 MLe,V:Otherman. 2.00
13 YG,D:Superstar. 2.50
14 DvM(s),YG,V:Edie Simkus 2.00
15 DvM(s),YG,V:Edie Simkus 2.00
16 DvM(s),YG. 2.00
17 DvM(s),RLe,V:Armorines. 2.00
18 DvM(s),RLe,V:Armorines,
   w/Valiant Era card 2.00
19 RLe,A:Harada 2.00
20 RLe,V:Harbingers 2.00
21 RLe,New Direction. 2.00
22 RLe,V:Midnight Earl. 2.00
23 RLe,Chaos Effect-Delta #4,
   A:Armorines, X-O. 2.00
24 Ironhead 2.00
25 Midnight Earl. 2.00
26 Heydrich, Omen. 2.00
27 Heydrich shows evil. 2.00
28 New Hardcorps 2.00
29 V:New Guard. 2.00
30 Final Issue. 2.00

KILLER INSTINCT
1 thru 3 . . . . @2.50
Spec. Brothers by Art Holcomb. . . 2.50

KNIGHTHAWK
Windjammer 1995
1 NA(c&a),I:Knighthawk the
Protector,V:Nemo 2.75
2 NA(c&a),Birth of Nemo 2.50
3 NA,V:Nemo 2.50
4 NA,V:Nemo 2.50
5 I:Cannon, Brick 2.50
6 V:Cannon, Brick 2.50

MAGIC THE GATHERING: ANTIQUITIES WAR
Armada 1995
1 Based on the Antiquities Set 2.75
2 F:Urza, Mishra 2.50
3 I:Tawnos, Ashod 2.50
4 The War Begins 2.50

MAGIC THE GATHERING: ARABIAN KNIGHTS
Armada 1995
1 Based on Rare Card set 2.75
2 V:Queen Nailah 2.50

MAGIC THE GATHERING: CONVOCATIONS
Armada 1995
1 Gallery of Art from Game 2.50

MAGIC THE GATHERING: FALLEN EMPIRES
[Mini-series]
Armada
1 with pack of cards 2.75
2 F:Tymolin 2.50
TPB Rep. #1-#2 . . . . 4.95

MAGIC THE GATHERING: HOMELANDS
Armada 1995
1 I:Feroz, Serra 5.95

MAGIC THE GATHERING: ICE AGE
Armada 1995
1 Dominaia, from card game 3.00
2 Ice Age Adventures 2.50
3 CV(c) Planeswalker battles 2.50
4 final issue 2.50
TPB Rep. #1-#2 . . . . 4.95
TPB Rep. #3-#4 . . . . 4.95

MAGIC THE GATHERING: SHADOW MAGE
Armada 1995
1 I:Jared 3.00
2 F:Hurloon the Minotaur 2.75
3 VMk(c&a),V:Juggernaut 2.50
4 Final issue 2.50
TPB Rep. #1-#2 . . . . 4.95
TPB Rep. #3-#4 . . . . 4.95

MAGIC THE GATHERING: THE URZA-MISHRA WAR
Armada
1 & 2 with Ice Age II card 5.95

MAGIC THE GATHERING: WAYFARER
Armada 1995
1 R:Jared 2.75
2 I:New Land 2.50
3 R:Liana, Ravidel 2.50
4 I:Golthonor 2.50
5 . . . . 2.50

MAGIC THE GATHERING: THE LEGENDS OF: THE ELDER DRAGONS
1 & 2 . . . . @2.50
JEDIT OJANEN
1 & 2 . . . . @2.50
SHANDALAR
1 & 2 . . . . @2.50

[ON THE WORLD OF] MAGIC THE GATHERING
GN Serra Angel + card 5.95
GN Legend of the Fallen Angel +
card 5.95
GN Dakkon Blackblade + card 5.95

Magnus Robot Fighter #27
© *Valiant*

MAGNUS: ROBOT FIGHTER
Valiant 1991
0 PCu,BL,"Emancipator",w/ BWS
card 6.00
0a PCu,BL,w/o card 3.00
1 ANi,BL,B:Steel Nation 4.00
1a w/o coupon 1.00
2 ANi,BL,Steel Nation #2 . . . . 3.00
2a w/o coupon 1.00
3 ANi,BL,Steel Nation #3 . . . . 3.00
3a w/o coupon 1.00
4 ANi,BL,E:Steel Nation 3.00
4a w/o coupon 1.00
5 DL,BL(i),I:Rai(#1),V:Slagger
Flipbook format 3.00
5a w/o coupon 1.00
6 DL,A:Solar,V:Grandmother
A:Rai(#2) 2.50
6a w/o coupon 1.00
7 DL,EC,V:Rai(#3) 2.50
7a w/o coupon 1.00
8 DL,A:Rai(#4),Solar,X-O

Armor.E:Flipbooks 2.50
8a w/o coupon 1.00
9 EC,V:Xyrkol,E-7 . . . . 2.50
10 V:Xyrkol 2.50
11 V:Xyrkol 2.50
12 I:Turok,V:Dr. Noel,
I:Asylum,40pgs 6.00
13 EC,Asylum Pt 1 . . . . 2.50
14 EC,Asylum Pt2 . . . . 2.50
15 FM(c),EC,Unity#4,I:Eternal
Warrior of 4001, O:Unity 2.50
16 WS(c),EC,Unity#12,A:Solar,
Archer,Armstrong,Harbinger, X-
O,Rai,Eternal Warrior 2.50
17 JaB,V:Talpa 2.50
18 SD,R:Mekman,V:E-7 . . . . 2.50
19 SD,V:Mekmen 2.50
20 EC,Tale of Magnus' past 2.50
21 JaB,R:Malevalents, Grand-
mother 3.00
21a Gold Ed. 4.00
22 JaB,D:Felina,V:Malevalents,
Grandmother 2.50
23 V:Malevolents 2.50
24 V:Malevolents 2.50
25 N:Magnus,R:1-A,silver-foil(c) . . . 3.00
26 I:Young Wolves 2.50
27 V:Dr.Lazlo Noel 2.50
28 V:The Malevs 2.25
29 JCf,A:Eternal Warrior 2.25
30 JCf,V:The Malevs 2.25
31 JCf,V:The Malevs 2.25
32 JCf,Battle for South Am 2.25
33 B:JOs(s),JCf,A:Ivar 2.25
34 JCf,Captured 2.25
35 JCf,V:Mekman 2.25
36 JCf,w/Valiant Era Card 2.25
37 JCf,A:Starwatchers 2.25
38 JCf, ... 2.25
39 JCf,F:Torque 2.25
40 JCf,F:Torque, A:Rai 2.25
41 JCf,Chaos Effect-Epsilon#4
A:Solar, Psi-Lords,Rai 2.50
42 JCf, F:Torque,A:Takashi 2.25
43 JCf,F:Torque,Immortal E 2.25
44 JCf,F:Torque,Stagger 2.25
45 V:Immortal Enemy 2.25
46 V:Immortal Enemy 2.25
47 Cold Blooded,pt.1 . . . . 2.25
48 Cold Blooded,pt.2 . . . . 2.25
49 F:Slagger 2.25
50 V:Invisible Legion 2.25
51 KoK,RyR,Return of the
Robots,pt.1 . . . . 2.25
52 KoK,RyR,Robots,pt.2 . . . . 2.25
53 KoK,RyR,Robots,pt.3 . . . . 2.25
54 KoK,RyR,Robots,pt.4 . . . . 2.25
55 KG,A:Rai 2.50
56 Magnus in Japan 2.50
57 . . . . 2.50
58 . . . . 2.50
59 V:Rai 2.50
60 R:The Malevs 2.50
61 Secrets of the Malevs 2.50
62 V:Leeja 2.50
63 R:Destroyer 2.50
64 Ultimatum, F:Destroyer 2.50
Yearbook #1 . . . . 3.95
TPB 1-4 . . . . 9.95

MAGNUS (ROBOT FIGHTER)
Acclaim Jan. 1997
1 Magnus back from the future . . . 2.50
2 "Tomorrow Never Knows" 2.50
3 "Tomorrow Never Knows" 2.50
4 "Tomorrow Never Knows" 2.50
5 "Tomorrow Never Knows" 2.50
6 A:Janice Whitcraft 2.50
7 "When Titans Clash" 2.50

Magnus Robot Fighter #16
© Acclaim

8 TPe,DdB,"When Titans Clash" . . 2.50
9 TPe,"See Tirana and Die" 2.50
10 TPe,"The Memory" 2.50
11 TPe,"Where Angels Fear" 2.50
12 TPe,"Showdown" 2.50
13 TPe, ... 2.50
14 TPe,"Wild in the Streets" 2.50
15 TPe,Magnus stands alone 2.50
16 TPe,"Hart's Home" 2.50
17 TPe,"Invasive Procedures" 2.50
18 TPe,"Welcome to Salvation" 2.50

MAN OF THE ATOM
Valiant Heroes Special Project
Acclaim Jan 1997
Spec. 3.95
TPB The Rebirth of Solar 8.00

MASTER DARQUE
Acclaim 1997
Spec. F:Brixton Sound, 48pg 4.00

MUTANT CHRONICLES—
GOLGOTHA
Valiant
1 thru 4 + game trading card . . . @2.95
TPB, Vol. 1 rep. Pt.#1–#4 . . . . . . 10.95

NINJAK
Valiant 1994
0: O:Ninjak, Pt. 1 . . . . 2.50
00: O:Ninjak, Pt.2 . . . . 2.50
1 B:MMo(s),JQ,JP,Chromium(c),
   I:Dr.Silk,Webnet 3.00
1a Gold Ed 4.00
2 JQ,JP,V:Dr.Silk,Webnet 2.50
3 JQ,JP,I:Seventh Dragon 2.25
4 MMo(a&s),V:Seventh Dragon,
   w/Valiant Era card 2.25
5 MMo(a&s),A:X-O Manowar 2.25
6 MMo(a&s),A:X-O Manowar,
   V:Dr.Silk,Webnet 2.25
7 MMo(a&s),I:Rhaman. 2.25
8 MMo(a&s),Chaos Effect-Gamma
   #3, A:Madame Noir 2.25
9 Dogs of War 2.00
10 Cantebury Tale #1 . . . . 2.00
11 Cantebury Tale #2 . . . . 2.00
12 . . . . 2.00

13 Mad Dogs and English. 2.00
14 Cry Wolf pt. 1 . . . . 2.00
15 Cry Wolf pt. 2 . . . . 2.25
16 Plague Pt. 1. . . . . 2.25
17 Plague Pt. 2. . . . . 2.25
18 Computer Virus 2.25
19 DAn,ALa,MM,Breaking the
   Web,pt.1 . . . . 2.25
20 DAn,ALa,MM,Breaking the
   Web,pt.2 . . . . 2.25
21 DAn,ALa,MM,Breaking the
   Web,pt.3 . . . . 2.25
22 Bitter Wind. 2.25
23 w/o arsenal 2.25
24 Unusual sidekick 2.25
25 . . . . 2.25
26 . . . . 2.25
27 Diamond Smugglers 2.25
28 F:Sister Gabriela 2.25
Yearbook #1, Dr. Silk 3.95

Ninjak #3 © Valiant

NINJAK
Acclaim 1996
1 KBk(s), Denny Meechum
   becomes Ninjak 2.50
2 KBk(s) video game spin-off 2.50
3 KBk(s) video game spin-off 2.50
4 KBk(s) video game spin-off 2.50
5 KBk(s) video game spin-off 2.50
6 KBk(s) "The World's Finest" 2.50
7 KBk(s) video game spin-off 2.50
8 KBk(s) video game spin-off 2.50
9 KBk(s) video game spin-off 2.50
10 KBk(s) F:Maria Barbella 2.50
11 KBk(s) Trial Continues 2.50
12 KBk(s) final issue. 2.50

N.I.O.
Acclaim 1998
1 (of 4) by Shon Bury & JPi 2.50
2 . . . . 2.50
3 . . . . 2.50
4 conclusion 2.50

OPERATION:
STORMBRINGER
**Acclaim Special Event, April
1997**
Spec. F:Teutonic Knight 3.95

ORIGINAL CAPTAIN
JOHNAR AND
THE ALIENS
Valiant 1995
1 Reprint from Magnus 2.95
2 Russ Manning rep. 2.95

ORIGINAL DR. SOLAR
MAN OF THE ATOM
Valiant 1995
1 Reprint 2.95
2 Reprints 2.95
3 Reprints 2.95

ORIGINAL MAGNUS
ROBOT FIGHTER
Valiant 1995
1 Reprint 2.95
2 Russ Manning Art. 2.95
3 Russ Manning 2.95

ORIGINAL TUROK,
SON OF STONE
Valiant 1995
1 Reprint 2.95
2 Alberto Gioletti art. 2.95
3 Alberto Gioletti 2.95
4 Reprints 2.95

OUTCAST SPECIAL
Valiant 1995
1 R:The Outcast 2.50

PLANESWALKER WAR
Acclaim Aug. 1996
GN #1 Magic: The Gathering tie-in . 5.95

PSI-LORDS: REIGN OF
THE STARWATCHERS
Valiant 1994
1 MLe,DG,Chromium(c),Valiant
   Vision,V:Spider Aliens 3.00
2 MLe,DG,V:Spider Aliens 2.25
3 MLe,DG,Chaos Effect-Epsilon#2,
   A:Solar. 2.25
becomes:

PSI-LORDS
4 V:Ravenrok 2.25
5 V:Ravenrok 2.25
6 . . . . 2.25
7 Micro-Invasion 2.25
8 A:Solar the Destroyer 2.25
9 Frozen Harbingers 2.25
10 F:Ravenrok 2.25

PUNX
Windjammer 1995
1 KG,I:Punx 2.50
2 KG,A:Harbinger. 2.50
3 KG,F:P.M.S 2.50
4 KG,final issue 2.50
Spec.#1 . . . . 2.50

PUNX REDUX
1 thru 4 . . . . @2.50

ACCLAIM

ACCLAIM

PUNX
Acclaim Jan. 1997
One Shot Spec. F:Big Max 2.50

QUANTUM LEAP
Acclaim Jan. 1997
1 BML(s),"Into the Void", pt.1 . . . . . 2.50
2 BML(s),"Into the Void", pt.2 . . . . . 2.50
3 BML(s),"Into the Void", pt.3 . . . . . 2.50
Spec. "The Leaper Before. 3.95

QUANTUM & WOODY
Acclaim Feb. 1997
1 CPr(s),MBr Woodrow Van
  Chelton & Eric Henderson
  become unlikely superheros . . . 4.00
1a Variant (c). 5.00
2 CPr(s),MBr,World's worst
  superhero team 3.00
3 CPr(s),MBr,Woody buys a goat. . 3.00
4 CPr(s),MBr. 3.00
5 CPr(s),MBr. 2.75
6 CPr(s),MBr. 2.75
7 CPr(s),MBr. 2.75
8 CPr(s),MBr,R:Warrant. 2.75
9 CPr(s),DCw,Woody is dying 2.75
10 CPr(s),MBr,trapped in each
  other's bodies, Goat month. . . . 2.75
11 CPr(s),MBr,switched body
  delimma 2.50
12 CPr(s),MBr,switched bodies 2.50
13 CPr(s),MBr,back in own bodies . 2.50
14 CPr(s),MBr,Magnum Force,pt.1 . 2.50
15 CPr(s),MBr,Magnum Force,pt.2 . 2.50
16 CPr(s),MBr,Magnum Force,pt.3 . 2.50
17 CPr(s),MBr,Magnum Force,pt.4 . 2.50
TPB Director's Cut, rep.#1–#4 . . . . 8.00
TPB Kiss Your Ass Goodbye 8.00
TPB Holy S-word We're Cancelled . 8.00
TPB Magnum Force 8.00

RAI
Valiant 1991
0 DL,O:Bloodshot,I:2nd Rai,D:X-O,
  Archer,Shadowman,F:all Valiant
  heroes,bridges Valiant Universe
  1992-4001 . . . . 3.00
1 V:Grandmother. 5.00
2 V:Icespike. 2.50
3 V:Humanists,Makiko 3.00
4 V:Makiko,rarest Valiant 4.00
5 Rai leaves earth, C:Eternal
  Warrior. 2.50
6 FM(c),Unity#7,V:Pierce. 2.50
7 WS(c),Unity#15,V:Pierce,
  D:Rai,A:Magnus 2.50
8 Epilogue of Unity in 4001 . . . . . . 2.50
Becomes:

RAI AND THE
FUTURE FORCE
Valiant 1993
9 F:Rai,E.Warrior of 4001,Tekla,
  X-O Commander,Spylocke 2.50
9a Gold Ed. 3.00
10 Rai vs. Malev Emperor 2.25
11 SCh,V:Malevolents. 2.25
12 V:Cyber Raiders 2.25
13 Spylocke Revealed 2.25
14 SCh,D:M'Ree. 2.25
15 SCh,V:X-O. 2.25
16 SCh,V:Malevs 2.25
17 . . . . 2.25
18 JOs(s),Spk,V:Malevs 2.25
19 JCf,V:Malves. 2.25
20 JOs(s),DR,V:Malves,Spylocke
  realed to be Spider Alien 2.25

Rai #27 © Valiant

21 DR,I:Starwatchers,b:Torque,
  w/Valiant Era card 2.25
22 DR,D:2nd Rai, A:Starwatchers. . 2.25
23 DR,A:Starwatchers, ... 2.25
24 DR,in Tibet 2.00
25 DR,F:Spylocke. 2.00
26 DR,Chaos Effect-Epsilon#3,
  A:Solar Magnus,Psi-Lords 2.00
Becomes:

RAI
Valiant 1994
27 "Rising Son" 2.00
28 V:Takashi. 2.00
29 A:Rentaro Nakadai 2.00
30 Splocke 2.00
31 Bad Penny pt. 1 . . . . 2.00
32 Bad Penny pt. 2, F:Axscan 2.00
33 F:Spylocke, Rentaro 2.00
TPB #0-#4 . . . . 11.95
TPB Star System ed. 11.95

REVELATIONS
one-shot by Jim Krueger. 3.95

SABAN POWERHOUSE
Acclaim Young Readers 1997
**Digest Size, F: Power Rangers
Turbo**
Spec. "Simple Simon Says" 4.50
Spec. "Into the Fire" 4.50
Spec. "Mystery of the Phantom
  Ranger" 4.50

SABAN PRESENTS
Acclaim 1997
Spec. Power Rangers Turbo vs. Big
  Bad Beetleborgs. 4.50

SAMUREE
Windjammer 1995
1 I:Samuree 2.50
2 V: The Dragon 2.50
3 V: The Dragon 2.50

THE SECOND LIFE
OF DR. MIRAGE
Valiant 1993
1 B:BL(s),BCh,V:Mast.Darque 2.50
1a Gold Ed. 3.00

2 BCh,V:Master Darque. 2.50
3 BCh 2.50
4 BCh,V:Bhrama 2.50
5 BCh,A:Shadowman,V:Master
  Darque. 2.50
6 BCh,V:Dr.Eclipse 2.50
7 BCh,V:Dr.Eclipse,w/card 2.50
8 BCh,. 2.50
9 BCh,A:Otherman 2.50
10 BCh,V:Otherman 2.50
11 BCh,Chaos Effect-Beta#2, ... 2.50
12 BCh. 2.25
13 BCh. 2.25
14 . . . . 2.25
15 Chaos Effect 2.25
16 . . . . 2.25
17 . . . . 2.25
18 F:Deathsmith 2.25
19 R:Walt Wiley 2.25

SECRETS OF THE
VALIANT UNIVERSE
Valiant 1994
1 from Wizard 2.50
2 BH,Chaos Effect-Beta#4,A:Master
  Darque,Dr.Mirage,Max St.James,
  Dr. Eclipse 2.25

SECRET WEAPONS
Valiant 1993
1 JSP(a&s),BWi(i),I:Dr.Eclipse,
  A:Master Darque,A:Geoff,
  Livewire,Stronghold,Solar,X-O,
  Bloodshot,Shadowman. 2.75
1a Gold Ed. 4.00
2 JSP(a&s),V:Master Darque,
  Dr.Eclipse. 2.25
3 JSP(a&s),V:Speedshots 2.25
4 JSP(a&s),V:Scatterbrain 2.25
5 JSP(a&s),A:Ninjak 2.25
6 JPS(s),JPh(pl),TeH, V:Spider
  Aliens. 2.25
7 JPS(s),V:Spider Aliens 2.25
8 JSP(a&pl),V:Harbingers 2.25
9 JSP(a&s),V:Webnet, w/Valiant
  Era card. 2.25
10 JSP(a&s),V:Webnet. 2.25
11 PGr,New Line-up 2.25
12 PGr,A:Bloodshot 2.25
13 PGr,Chaos Effect-Gamma#2 . . . 2.25
14 PGr,F:Bloodshot 2.00
15 . . . . 2.00
16 . . . . 2.00
17 V:Dr. Silk 2.00
18 Gigo 2.00
19 A:Ninjak 2.00
20 Bloodshot Rampage Pt.2 . . . . . . 2.00
21 Bloodshot Rampage Pt.4 . . . . . . 2.00
22 I:Gestalt, Pyroclast. 2.00
23 A:Bloodshot. 2.00

SECRET WEAPONS:
PLAYING WITH FIRE
Valiant
1 & 2 . . . . @2.50

SHADOW MAN
Valiant 1992
0 BH,TmR,Chromium (c),O:Maxim
  St.James,Shadowman 3.00
0a Newstand ed. 2.50
0b Gold Ed. 4.00
1 DL,JRu,I&O:Shadowman 5.00
2 DL,V:Serial Killer 3.00
3 V:Emil Sosa 3.00
4 DL,FM(c),Unity#6,A:Solar 2.50

All comics prices listed are for *Near Mint* condition.

Shadowman #18 © Valiant

5 DL,WS(c),Unity#14, A:Archer &
   Armstrong 2.50
6 SD,L:Lilora 2.50
7 DL,V:Creature 2.50
8 JDx(i),I:Master Darque 3.00
9 JDx(i),V:Darque's Minions 3.00
10 BH,I:Sandria 2.50
11 BH,N:Shadowman 2.50
12 BH,V:Master Darque 2.50
13 BH,V:Rev.Shadow Man 2.50
14 BH,JDx,V:Bikers 2.50
15 BH,JDx,V:JB,Fake Shadow
   Man,C:Turok 2.50
16 BH,JDx,I:Dr.Mirage, Carmen . . . 3.00
17 BH,JDx,A:Archer & Armstrong . . 2.25
18 BH,JDx,A:Archer & Armstrong . . 2.25
19 BH,A:Aerosmith 2.25
20 BH,A:Master Darque,
   V:Shadowman's Father. 2.50
21 BH,I:Maxim St.James (1895
   Shadowman) 2.25
22 V:Master Darque 2.25
23 BH(a&s),A:Doctor Mirage,
   V:Master Darque 2.25
24 BH(a&s),V:H.A.T.E. 2.25
25 RgM,w/Valiant Era card 2.25
26 w/Valiant Era card 2.50
27 BH,V:Drug Lord 2.25
28 BH,A:Master Darque 2.25
29 Chaos Effect-Beta#1,V:Master
   Darque 2.25
30 R:Rotwak. 2.25
31 thru 33 . . . . @2.25
34 Voodoo in Carribean 2.25
35 A:Ishmael 2.25
36 F:Ishmael 2.25
37 A:X-O, V:Blister 2.25
38 V:Ishmael, Blister. 2.25
39 BH,TmR,Explores Powers 2.25
40 BH,TmR,I,Vampire! 2.25
41 A:Steve Massarsky 2.25
42 . . . . 2.25
43 V:Smilin Jack. 2.25
TPB rep.#1-#3,#6 . . . . 9.95

SHADOWMAN
Acclaim Nov. 1996
1 GEn(s),"Deadside," pt.1 . . . . 2.50
2 GEn(s),"Deadside," pt.2 . . . . 2.50
3 GEn(s),"Deadside," pt.3 . . . . 2.50
4 GEn(s),"Deadside," pt.4 . . . . 2.50
5 JaD,CAd,"Nothing is True," pt.1 . 2.50
6 JaD,CAd,"Nothing is True," pt.2 . 2.50

7 JaD,CAd,"Nothing is True," pt.3 . 2.50
8 JaD,CAd,"Nothing is True," pt.4 . 2.50
9 JaD,CAd,"The Buzz," pt.1 . . . . . 2.50
10 JaD,CAd,"The Buzz," pt.2 . . . . 2.50
11 JaD,CAd,"ClearBlueSkies,"pt.1 . 2.50
12 JaD,CAd,"ClearBlueSkies,"pt.2 . 2.50
13 JaD,CAd,"Hoodoo Bash,"pt.1 . . 2.50
14 JaD,CAd,"Hoodoo Bash,"pt.2 . . 2.50
15 JaD,CAd,"Hoodoo Bash,"pt.3 . . 2.50
16 Mask of Shadows ripped out . . . 2.50
17 Mask of Shadows, pt.2 . . . . 2.50
18 Claudine kidnapped? 2.50
19 pursuit of Mah 2.50
20 Deadside vortes. 2.50

SHADOWMAN
Acclaim 1999
1 DAn,ALa,48-page 3.95
2 . . . . 2.50

SLIDERS
Valiant 1996
1 & 2 . . . . @2.50

SLIDERS: DARKEST HOUR
1 DGC,DG. 2.50
2 DGC,DG. 2.50
3 DGC,DG, Concl. 2.50
Spec. RgM, Montezuma IV rules the
   world 3.95
Spec. #2 "Secrets" 3.95
TPB from TV show 9.00

SLIDERS: ULTIMATUM
Valiant 1996
1 & 2 . . . . @2.50

SOLAR: HELL ON EARTH
Acclaim 1997
1 (of 4) CPr,DCw,Seleski twins
   have power of God. 2.50
2 CPr,Goat Month prelude 2.50
3 CPr,RT,V:Jimmy Six 2.50
4 CPr, ... 2.50

SOLAR: MAN OF THE ATOM
Valiant 1991
1 BWS,DP,BL,B:2nd Death B:Alpha
   & Omega 4.00
2 BWS,DP,BL,V:Dr Solar 3.00
3 BWS,DP,BL,V:Harada I:Harbinger
   Foundation 3.00
4 BWS,DP,BL,E:2nd Death V:Dr
   Solar 2.50
5 BWS,EC,V:Alien Armada 2.50
6 BWS,DP,SDr, V:Alien Armada X-
   O Armor. 2.50
7 BWS,DP,SDr, V:Alien Armada X-
   O Armor. 2.50
8 BWS,V:Dragon of Bangkok. 2.50
9 BWS,DP,SDr, V:Erica's Baby . . . 2.50
10 BWS,DP,SDr,JDx,I:Eternal
   Warrior,E:Alpha&Omega. 3.00
10a 2nd printing 2.00
11 SDr,A:Eternal Warrior, Prequel
   to Unity #0 . . . . 3.00
12 SDr,FM(c),Unity#9,O:Pierce,
   Albert. 2.50
13 DP,SDr,WS(c),Unity #17,
   V:Pierce. 2.50
14 DP,SDr,I:Bender (becomes
   Dr.Eclipse) 3.00
15 SD,V:Bender 3.00

16 Solar moves to California 2.50
17 SDr(i),V:X-O Manowar 2.50
18 SDr(i),A:X-Manowar 2.50
19 SDr(i),V:Videogame 2.50
20 SDr(i),Dawn of the Malevolence. 2.50
21 SDr(i),Master Darque. 2.50
22 SDr(i), V:Master Darque,A:
   Bender(Dr.Eclipse) 2.50
23 SDr(i),JQ(c),V:Master
   Darque,I:Solar War God 2.50
24 SDr(i),A:Solar War God 2.50
25 V:Dr.Eclpise. 2.25
26 Phil and Gayle on vaction 2.25
27 in Austrialia 2.25
28 A:Solar War God 2.25
29 KVH(s),JP(i),Valiant Vision,
   A:Solar War God 2.50
30 KVH(s),JP,V:Energy Parasite . . . 2.25
31 KVH(s),JP,Chrismas Issue 2.25
32 KVH(s),JP,Parent's Night 2.25
33 KVH(s),PGr,JP,B:Solar the
   Destroyer,w/Valiant Era card. . . 2.25
34 KVH(s),PGr,V:Spider Alien. 2.25
35 KVH(s),PGr,JP,E:Solar the
   Destroyer,Valiant Vision 2.25
36 KVH(s),PGr,JP,B:Revenge times
   two,V:Doctor Eclipse, Ravenus. 2.25
37 PGr,JP,E:Revenge times two,
   V:Doctor Eclipse,Ravenus 2.00
38 PGr,JP,Chaos Effect-Epsilon#1 . 2.00
39 thru 41 . . . . @2.00
42 Elements of Evil pt.1 . . . . 2.00
43 Elements of Evil pt.2 . . . . 2.00
44 I:New Character. 2.00
45 Explores Powers 2.00
46 I:The Sentry. 2.25
47 DJu,DG,Brave New World,pt.2 . . 2.25
48 DJu,DG,Brave New World,pt.3 . . 2.25
49 DJu,DG,Brave New World,pt.4 . . 2.25
50 DJu,DG,Brave New World,pt.5 . . 2.25
51 I:Aliens on the Moon 2.25
52 Solar Saves Earth 2.25
53 I:Marauder. 2.25
54 V:Marauder. 2.25
55 I:Black Star 2.25
56 V:Black Star. 2.25
57 A:Armorines. 2.25
58 I:Atman, The Inquisitor. 2.25
59 and 60 KG . . . . @2.25
TPB #0 JiS,BWS,BL,Alpha and
   Omega rep. from Solar #1–#10 9.95
TPB #1 JiS,BWS,GL,V:Doctor Solar
   rep. from Solar #1–#4. . . . . . . 9.95

Solar, Man of the Atom #50
© Valiant

ACCLAIM

STARSLAYER DIRECTORS CUT
Windjammer 1995
1 R:Starslayer, Mike Grell 2.50
2 I:New Star Slayer 2.50
3 Jolly Rodger 2.50
4 V:Battle Droids 2.50
5 I:Baraka Kuhi 2.50
6 V:Valkyrie 2.50
7 MGr(c&a),Can Torin destroy? . . . 2.50
8 MGr(c&a),JAI, Can Torin live with
 his deeds?,final issue 2.50

STARWATCHERS
Valiant
1 MLe,DG,Chromium(c),Valiant
 Vision, ... 3.50

SUPER MARIO BROS.
Valiant 1991
1 thru 6 . . . . @1.95
Spec. #1 . . . . 1.95

TICK, THE
Spec. digest size 4.50

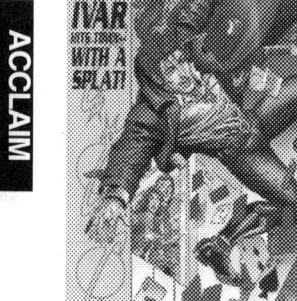

Timewalker #3 © Valiant

TIMEWALKER
Valiant 1994
0 BH,DP,O:3 Immortals 2.95
1 DP, BH 2.50
2 DP,BH 2.50
3 DP BH 2.50
4 Ten Commandments. 2.50
5 DP,BH 2.50
6 Harbinger Wars Pt.1 . . . . 2.50
7 Harbinger Wars Pt.2 . . . . 2.50
8 Harbinger Wars Pt.3 . . . . 2.50
9 V:Jahk rt. 2.50
10 Last God of Dura-Europus,pt.1
 time: 260 A.D. 2.50
11 Last God of Dura-Europus,pt.2. . 2.50
12 3RW,DP,Ashes to Ashes,pt.1 . . 2.50
13 3RW,DP,Ashes to Ashes,pt.2 . . 2.50
14 Meets Mozart. 2.50
15 26th Century 2.50
Yearbook F:Harada. 2.95
TPB F:Archer & Armstrong 9.95

TRINITY ANGELS
Acclaim March 1997
1 KM,DPs, Maria, Gianna &
 Theresa Barbella become Trinity
 Angels 2.50
2 KM,DPs, V:The 99 . . . . 2.50
3 KM,DPs, looking for a little head. 2.50
4 KM,DPs, V:Flaming Queen 2.50
5 KM, New costumes. 2.50
6 KM, in Las Vegas 2.50
7 KM, in Las Vegas 2.50
8 KM, "A Woman Scorned" 2.50
9 KM, A:Rumblin' Guys 2.50
10 KM, Mad Cow 2.50
11 KM, ... 2.50
12 KM, Final issue 2.50

TROUBLEMAKERS
Acclaim Dec. 1996
1 FaN(s) 2.50
2 FaN(s) go back in time 2.50
3 FaN(s) Jane has a big problem. . 2.50
4 FaN(s) Can Blur prevent parents
 divorce? 2.50
5 FaN(s) A:Ninjak 2.50
6 FaN(s) in outer space 2.50
7 FaN(s) I:The Rabble Rousers . . . 2.50
8 FaN(s) Rabble Rousers,pt.2 . . . . 2.50
9 FaN(s) F:Christine 2.50
10 FaN(s) F:Zach 2.50
11 FaN(s) F:Calamity Jane 2.50
12 FaN(s) a Troublemaker dead . . . 2.50
13 FaN(s) F:XL. 2.50
14 FaN(s) 2.50
15 FaN(s) Is Parker alive? 2.50
16 FaN(s) Andrew Chase 2.50
17 FaN(s) V:Turnabout 2.50
18 FaN(s) Jacinda Monroe 2.50
19 FaN(s) V:Rabblerousers 2.50

TUROK: CHILD OF BLOOD
Acclaim 1997
1-shot FaN, 48pg 4.00

TUROK: DINOSAUR HUNTER
Valiant 1993
1 BS,Chromium(c),O:Turok
 retold,V:Monark 3.00
1a Gold Ed. 4.00
2 BS,V:Monark 2.75
3 BCh,V:Monark 2.75
4 TT(s),RgM,O:Turok. 2.75
5 TT(s),RgM,V:Dinosaurs 2.75
6 TT(s),RgM,V:Longhunter 2.75
7 TT(a&s),B:People o/t Spider . . . 2.75
8 TT(a&s),V:T-Rex 2.75
9 TT(a&s),E:People o/t Spider . . . 2.75
10 MBn,RgM,A:Bile 2.75
11 MBn,RgM,V:Chun Yee,w/card . . 2.75
12 MBn,RgM,V:Dinosaur 2.75
13 B:TT(c&s),RgM, ... 2.75
14 V:Dino-Pirate 2.50
15 RgM,V:Dino-Pirate. 2.25
16 Chaos Effect-Beta#3, V:Evil
 Shaman 2.75
17 V:C.I.A. 2.50
18 V:Bionosaurs 2.50
19 A:Manowar 2.50
20 Chichak 2.50
21 Ripsaw 2.50
22 . . . . 2.50
23 A:Longhunter. 2.50
24 R:To The Lost Land 2.50
25 I:Warrior of Mother God 2.50
26 V:Overlord 2.50
27 TT,RgM,Lost Land,pt.4. . . . . . . 2.50

(Turok: Dinosaur Hunter cont.)
28 MBn,DEA hunts rogue T-Rex. . . 2.50
29 SFu,Manhunt,pt.1 . . . . 2.50
30 SFu,Manhunt,pt.2 . . . . 2.50
31 F:Darwin Challenger 2.50
32 V:Special Effects 2.50
33 V:Aliens. 2.50
34 V:Alien Ooze 2.50
35 Early Years 2.50
36 Confronts Past. 2.50
37 V:Nazi Women. 2.50
38 V:Bigfoot 2.50
39 TT,Shainer Silver. 2.50
40 A:Longhunter. 2.50
41 Church of the Poison Mind. 2.50
42 Church of the Poison Mind. 2.50
43 thru 47 . . . . @2.50
Yearbook #1 MBn(s),DC, N&V:Mon
 Ark. 4.25
Yearbook 1995 MGr,The Hunted. . . 2.95
Spec. Tales of the Lost Land. 4.00
TPB FaN 112pgs.rep. game 10.00

TUROK
Acclaim 1998
1 FaN 3-D cover 2.50
2 FaN,A:Armorines 2.50
3 FaN,Lazarus Concordance 2.50
4 FaN, real President?. 2.50
TPB Dinosaur Hunter, FaN 9.95

TUROK: COMIC BOOK MAGAZINE
Acclaim 1998
Seeds of Evil 5.00
Adon's Curse 5.00
Turok/Shadowman 5.00

TUROK: THE HUNTED
Valiant
1 & 2. . . . . 2.50

TUROK QUARTERLY— REDPATH
March 1997, FaN(s),"Spring Break
 in the Lost Land" 3.95
June 1997, FaN(s), Killer loose in
 Oklahoma City 3.95

TUROK/SHADOWMAN
Acclaim 1999
1-shot 3.95

TUROK/SHAMAN'S TEARS
Valiant 1995
1 MGr,Ghost Dance Pt. 1. . . . . 2.50
2 MGr,JAI,White Buffalo
 kidnapped,V:Bar Sinister 2.50
3 V:Supremeists/Circle Sea 2.50

TUROK/TIMEWALKER
Acclaim 1997
1 of 2 FaN(s),"Seventh Sabbath" . . 2.50
2 of 2 FaN(s),"Seventh Sabbath" . . 2.50

UNITY
Valiant 1992
0 BWS,BL,Chapter#1,A:All Valiant
 Heroes,V:Erica Pierce 3.00
0a Red ed.,w/red logo 4.00
1 BWS,BL,Chapter#18,A:All Valiant
 Heroes,D:Erica Pierce 3.00
1a Gold logo 4.00
1b Platinum. 4.00

TPB Previews Exclusive,Vol.I
Chap.#1-9 . . . . 8.00
TPB Previews Exclusive,Vol.II
Chap.#10-18 . . . . 3.00
TPB #1 rep Chapters #1-4 . . . . . . 10.95
TPB #2 rep Chapters #5-9 . . . . . . 9.95
TPB #3 rep Chapters #10-14 . . . . 9.95

VALERIA, THE SHE-BAT
Windjammer 1995
1 (of 2) NA,Valeria & 'Rilla 2.50
2 (of 2) NA,BSz, final issue 2.50

VALIANT ERA
Valiant
TPB rep.Magnus #12,Shadowman
#8, Solar #10-11,Eternal
Warrior#4-5 . . . . 13.95

VALIANT READER: GUIDE TO THE VALIANT UNIVERSE
1 O:Valiant Universe 1.00

VALIANT VISION STARTER KIT
Valiant
1 w/3-D Glasses 2.95
2 F:Starwatchers 2.95

VINTAGE MAGNUS ROBOT FIGHTER
Valiant
1 rep. Gold Key Magnus #22
(which is #1) 5.00
2 rep. Gold Key Magnus #3 . . . . . 4.50
3 rep. Gold Key Magnus #13 . . . . 3.50
4 rep. Gold Key Magnus #15 . . . . 3.50

Visitor #12 © Valiant

VISITOR
Valiant 1994
1 New Series. 2.50
2 F:The Harbinger 2.50

3 The Bomb 2.50
4 V:F/X Specialists 2.50
5 R:Harbinger 2.50
6 KVH,BS(c),V:Men in Black 2.50
7 KVH,BS(c),V:Men in Black,pt.2 . . 2.50
8 KVH,V:Harbinger identity 2.50
9 KVH,A:Harbinger,Flamingo 2.50
10 Weather Problems 2.50
11 V:Cannibals 2.50
12 V:Harada, Men in Black 2.50
13 Visitor is the Future Harbinger . . 2.50

VISITOR VS. VALIANT
Valiant 1994
1 V:Solar 2.95
2 . . . . 2.95

WATERWORLD
Acclaim 1997
1 of 4 V:Leviathan 2.50
2 of 4 "Children of Leviathan". 2.50
3 of 4 KoK 2.50
4 of 4 KoK "Children of Leviathan". 2.50

WWF BATTLEMANIA
Valiant
1 WWF Action 2.50
2 thru 5 . . . . @2.50

X-O MANOWAR
Valiant 1992
0 JQ,O:Aric,1st Full Chromium(c) . 3.00
0a Gold Ed. 3.50
1 BL,BWS,I:Aric,Ken 4.00
2 BL(i),V:Lydia,Wolf-Class Armor . . 3.00
3 I:X-Caliber,A:Solar 3.00
4 MM,A:Harbinger,C:Shadowman
(Jack Boniface) 3.00
5 BWS(c),V:AX 3.00
5a w/Pink logo. 3.00
6 SD,V:Ax(X-O Armor). 3.00
7 FM(c),Unity#5,V:Pierce 2.75
8 WS(c),Unity#13,V:Pierce 2.75
9 Aric in Italy,408 A.D. 2.75
10 N:X-O Armor 2.75
11 V:Spider Aliens 2.50
12 A:Solar 2.50
13 V:Solar 2.50
14 BS,A:Turok,I:Randy Cartier 3.00
15 BS,A:Turok 2.50
15a Red Ed. 3.00
16 V:The Mob. 2.50
17 BL 2.50
18 JCf,V:CIA,A:Randy,I:Paul 2.50
19 JCf,V:US Government 2.50
20 A:Toyo Harada. 2.50
21 V:Ax 2.50
22 Aria in S.America. 2.50
23 Aria in S.America. 2.50
24 Aria comes back 2.50
25 JCf,JGz,PaK,I:Armories,
BU:Armories#0. . . . . 3.00
26 JGz(s),RLv,F:Ken 2.50
27 JGz,RLe,A:Turok,Geomancer,
Stronghold,Livewire 2.50
28 JGz,RLe,D:X-O,V:Spider
Aliens,w/Valiant Era card 2.75
29 JGz,RLe,A:Turok,V:SpiderAliens 2.50
30 JGz,RLe,A:Solar 2.50
31 JGz,RLe, ... 2.50
32 JGz,RLe,at Orb,Inc. 2.25
33 JGz,RLe,Chaos Effect-Delta#3,
A:Armorines,H.A.R.D. Corps. . . 2.25
34 thru 36 . . . . @2.25

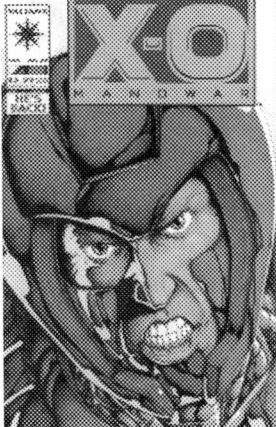

X-O Manowar #24 © Valiant

37 Wolfbridge Affair pt.1 . . . . 2.25
38 Wolfbridge Affair pt.2 . . . . 2.25
39 Wolfbridge Affair pt.3 . . . . 2.25
40 Wolfbridge Affair pt.4 . . . . 2.25
41 Aftermath. 2.25
42 A:Shadowman Surprise 2.25
43 Chasitty's Boys 2.25
44 Bart Sears New Direction. 2.50
45 RMz,V:Crescendo 2.50
46 RMz,V:Crescendo 2.50
47 RMz,V:Crescendo 2.50
48 RMz,BS,A:Turok 2.50
49 RMz,loses control of armor 2.50
50-X R:Paul, I:Alloy 2.50
50-O V:Alloy 2.50
51 V:Lummox 2.50
52 V:A Blast From the Past. 2.50
53 Returns To Space 2.50
54 I:New Aliens 2.50
55 V:Aliens 2.50
56 V:Aliens 2.50
57 I:Gamin 2.50
58 I:Volt 2.50
59 thru 67 . . . . @2.50
TPB rep.#1-4,w/X-O Manual 11.00

X-O MANOWAR
Series Two, Acclaim, Oct. 1997
1 Rand Banion v. R.A.G.E. 2.50
2 v. R.A.G.E. 2.50
3 . . . . 2.50
4 R.A.G.E. is back. 2.50
5 Donovan Wylie vs. Internaut 2.50
6 Internaut controls X-O suit 2.50
7 SEa, Donovan wears his armor . 2.50
8 SEa, V:Basilisk. 2.50
9 SEa, A: new Hard Corps. 2.50
10 SEa, R:Bravado. 2.50
11 BAu,MWa,SEa,alien creators . . . 2.50
12 BAu,MWa,SEa,O:armor 2.50
13 BAu,SEa,V:Alien creators 2.50
14 BAu,SEa,V:Aliens of Unity 2.50
15 BAu,SEa,out of armor 2.50
16 BAu,SEa,. 2.50
17 DMD,SEa,civil war. 2.50
18 DMD,SEa,Rand Banion 2.50
19 DMD,SEa,V:Master Blaster 2.50
20 DMD,trapped in a sleep-state. . . 2.50
TPB MWa,BAu rep.#1–#4 . . . . . . 10.00

DARK HORSE

ABE SAPIEN:
DRUMS OF THE DEAD
March 1998
1-shot Hellboy spin-off 3.00

ABYSS, THE
1 MK,Movie Adaptation pt.1 . . . . . 2.50
2 MK,Movie Adaptation pt.2 . . . . . 2.50

ACCIDENT MAN
(B&W)
1 I:Accident Man 2.50
2 and 3 . . . . @2.50

ADVENTURES OF
LUTHER ARKWRIGHT
Valkyrie Press/Dark Horse
(B&W) 1987–89
1 thru 9 . . . . @2.00
(B&W) 1990
1 thru 9 Rep. . . . . @1.95
TPB 14.95

ADVENTURES OF
THE MASK
1996
1 thru 12 by Michael Eury & Marc
 Campos, TV cartoon adapt. . @2.50

AGENTS OF LAW
Comics' Greatest World 1995
1 KG, I:Law 2.50
2 A:Barb Wire 2.50
3 KG,DLw,The Judgment Gate . . . 2.50
4 Open Golden City 2.50
5 Who is the Mystery figure 2.50
6 V:Predator 2.50

AGE OF REPTILES
1993–94
1 DRd,Story on Dinosaurs 3.00
2 DRd,Story on Dinosaurs 3.00
3 DRd,Story on Dinosaurs 3.00
4 DRd,Story on Dinosaurs 3.00
TPB Tribal Warfare 14.95

AGE OF REPTILES:
THE HUNT
1996
1 thru 5 by Ricardo Delgado . . . . @3.00
TPB The Hunt 17.95

ALIENS
(B&W) 1988
1 Movie Sequel,R:Hicks,Newt . . 15.00
1a 2nd printing 3.00
1b 3rd printing 2.00
1c 4th printing 1.50
2 Hicks raids Mental Hospital 8.00
2a 2nd printing 2.50
2a 3rd printing 1.50
3 Realize Queen is on Earth 4.00
3a 2nd printing 1.50
4 Queen is freed, Newton on

Aliens World 3.00
5 All out war on Aliens World 3.00
6 Hicks & Newt return to Earth . . . 3.00
TPB rep.#1–#6 & DHP #24 . . . . . 11.00
TPB 2nd printing, DvD(c) 11.00
HC rep..#1–#6 & DHP #24 . . . . . 25.00

ALIENS (II)
[Mini-Series] 1989
1 DB,Hicks,Newt hijack ship 4.00
1a 2nd Printing 3.00
2 DB,Crazed general trains aliens . 3.00
2a 2nd Printing 3.00
3 DB,HicksV:General Spears 3.00
3a 2nd Printing 2.50
4 DB,Heroes reclaim earth
 from aliens 3.00
HC, 2,500 made 80.00
HC, 1,000 made 100.00

Aliens: Purge
© Dark Horse Comics

ALIENS
1-shot Earth Angel, JBy 3.00
HC rep. Earth Angel 15.00
1-shot Glass Corridor, DvL 3.00
1-shot Mondo Heat, I:Herk Mondo . 2.50
1-shot Mondo Pest 3.00
1-shot Purge, IEd,PhH 3.00
1-shot Pig, CDi,FH 3.00
1-shot Sacrifice, rep.Aliens UK . . . 4.95
1-shot Salvation DGb,MMi,KN,
 F:Selkirk 4.95
1-shot Special 2.50
1-shot Stalker 2.50
1-shot Wraith 3.00
GN Female War, remastered 16.95
GN Genocide, remastered 16.95
GN Labyrinth, remastered 17.95
GN Nightmare Asylum, remaster. . 16.95
GN Outbreak, remastered 17.95
GN Rogue, Remastered 16.95

ALIENS: ALCHEMY
Sept. 1997
1 (of 3) JAr,RCo 3.00
2 thru 3 . . . . @3.00

ALIENS: APOCALYPSE
— DESTROYING ANGELS
Jan. 1999
1 (of 4) MSh 3.00
2 thru 4 MSh . . . . @3.00

ALIENS: BERSERKER
1 I:Crew of the Nemesis 2.50
2 Terminall 949 . . . . 2.50
3 Traitor 2.50
4 Finale 2.50

ALIENS:
COLONIAL MARINES
1 I: Lt. Joseph Henry 3.00
2 I: Pvt. Carmen Vasquez 2.75
3 V:Aliens 2.75
4 F:Lt.Henry 2.75
5 V:Aliens 2.75
6 F:Herk Mondo 2.75
7 A:Beliveau 2.75
8 F:Lt.Joseph Henry 2.75
9 F:Lt.Joseph Henry 2.75
10 final issue 2.50

ALIENS: EARTH WAR
1 SK,JBo(c),Alien's War renewed . 4.00
1a 2nd Printing 2.50
2 SK,JBo(c),To trap the Queen . . . 4.00
3 SK,JBo(c) Stranded on
 Alien's planet 3.00
4 SK,JBo(c),Resolution,final 3.00
HC Earth War, rep. #1–#4, signed and n
 umbered edition 60.00

ALIENS: GENOCIDE
1 Aliens vs. Aliens 3.50
2 Alien Homeworld 3.00
3 Search for Alien Queen 3.00
4 Conclusion, inc. poster 3.00
TPB Genocide rep. #1–#4 . . . . . . 13.95

ALIENS: HIVE
1 KJo,I:Stanislaw Mayakovsky . . . 4.00
2 KJo,A:Norbert 3.50
3 KJo,A:Julie,Gill 3.25
4 KJo,A:Stan,Final 3.00
TPB Hive rep. #1–#4 . . . . 14.00

ALIENS: HAVOC
1 (of 2) "over 40 creators" 3.00
2 . . . . 3.00

ALIENS: KIDNAPPED
Dec. 1997–Feb. 1998
1 (of 3) 2.50
2 thru 3 . . . . @2.50
TPB Aliens:Kidnapped 9.95

ALIENS: LABYRINTH
1 F:Captured Alien 3.00
2 . . . . 2.50
3 O:Dr.Church 2.50
4 D:Everyone 2.50
TPB rep. #1–#4 . . . . 17.95
TPB remastered 17.95

All comics prices listed are for *Near Mint* condition.

ALIENS: MUSIC OF THE SPEARS
1 I:Damon Eddington 3.00
2 TBd(c),A:Damon Eddington 2.75
3 TBd(c),A:Damon Eddington 2.75
4 TBd(c),last issue. 2.75

ALIENS: NEWT'S TALE
1 How Newt Survived 5.50
2 JBo(c),Newt's point of view
  on how `Aliens' ended 4.95

Alien Resurrection #2
© Dark Horse Comics

ALIEN RESURRECTION
Oct. 1997
1 (of 2) movie adaptation. 2.50
2 DMc(c) 2.50

ALIENS: ROGUE
1 F:Mr.Kay. 3.00
2 V:Aliens 3.00
3 V:Aliens 3.00
4 V:Aliens King 3.00
TPB Nel(c),rep.#1–#4 . . . . 14.95

ALIENS: STRONGHOLD
1 DoM,JP 2.50
2 DoM,JP 2.50
3 DoM,JP 2.50
4 DoM,JP 2.50
TPB 16.95

ALIENS: SURVIVAL
Feb.–Apr. 1998
1 (of 3) TyH(c). 3.00
2 thru 3 . . . . @3.00

ALIENS: TRIBES
HC DvD(c) 24.95
TPB 11.95
HC SBi,DvD 24.95

ALIENS/PREDATOR: DEADLIEST OF THE SPECIES
1 B:CCi(s),JG,F:Caryn Delacroix . . 3.75
2 JG,V:Predator. 3.00
3 JG,F:Caryn Delacroix 3.00
4 JG,V:Predator. 3.00

5 JG,Roadtrip 3.00
6 JG,in Space Station 3.00
7 JG,EB 2.50
8 JG,EB 2.50
9 JG,EB 2.50
10 CCi(s), Human Predators. 2.50
11 CCi,EB,JBo(c),Delacroix vs.
   DeMatier 2.50
12 Caryn's Fate 2.50
TPB. 29.95
Lim. Ed. hc 99.95

ALIENS VS. PREDATOR
0 PN,KS,Rep.DHP#34-36,(B&W) . . 5.00
1 Duel to the Death 4.00
1a 2nd Printing 3.00
2 Dr. Revna missing 3.00
3 Predators attack Aliens. 3.00
4 CW,F:Machiko & Predator 3.00
TPB Rep.#1–#4 . . . . 19.95
TPB PN,KS,rep.DHP#34-36 . . . . . 19.95
HC PN,KS,rep.DHP#34-36 . . . . . 79.95
Ann.#1 (1999) 4.95

ALIENS VS. PREDATOR: BOOTY
1-shot Rep. Diamond Previews . . . 2.50

ALIENS VS. PREDATOR: DUEL
1 Trap, JS 2.50
2 War 2.50

ALIENS VS. PREDATOR: ETERNAL
June 1998
1 (of 4) IEd,GF(c) 2.50
2 thru 4 IEd,GF(c) . . . . @2.50
TPB 9.95

ALIENS VS. PREDATOR: WAR
0 Prelude to New Series 2.50
1 RSd,MM,RCo(c) F:Machiko 2.50
2 I:Machiko Naguchi 2.50
3 F:Machiko Naguchi. 2.50
4 final issue. 2.50
TPB 19.95

ALIENS: XENOGENESIS
Aug. 1999
1 (of 4) 3.00

ALIEN 3
1 thru 3 Movie Adaptation . . . . . @2.50

AMERICAN, THE
(B&W)
1 CW,`Chinese Boxes,'D:Gleason . 5.00
2 CW,`Nightmares. 4.00
3 CW,Secrets of the American. . . . 4.00
4 CW,American vs.Kid America . . . 4.00
5 A:Kiki the Gorilla. 4.00
6 Rashomon-like plot. 3.50
7 Pornography business issue. . . . 3.50
8 Deals with violence issue 3.50
9 American Falls into a cult 3.50

THE AMERICAN: LOST IN AMERICA
1 CMa, American joins a cult 2.50
2 CMa, V:"Feel-Good" cult 2.50

3 CMa, "ApeMask" cult 2.50
4 CMa, Final issue. 2.50
ColorSpec.#1 . . . . 2.95

AMERICAN SPLENDOR
1-shot Letterman by Harvey Pekar . 2.95
1-shot A Step Out of the Nest. 2.95
1-shot On the Job. 2.95
1-shot Comics Con, JZe 2.95
1-shot Music Comics 2.95
1-shot Odds & Ends 2.95
1-shot Transatlantic Comics 2.95

AMERICAN SPLENDOR WINDFALL
(B&W) 1995
1 Windfall Gained,pt.1 . . . . 3.95
2 Windfall Lost. 3.95

ANOTHER CHANCE TO GET IT RIGHT
1 B&W. 14.95
TPB AVs, GfD(c) 9.95

APPLESEED
(B&W) Manga
TPB Book One: The Promethean
  Challenge. 14.95
TPB Book Two: Promethus
  Unbound 14.95
TPB Book Three: The Scales of
  Prometheus 14.95
TPB Book Four: The Promethean
  Balance 14.95

APPLESEED DATABOOK
(B&W) Manga
1 Flip Book, by Masamune Shirow. 5.00
1a 2nd printing 3.50
2 Flip Book 3.50
TPB Rep. #1–#2. . . . . 12.95

ARZACH
TPB by Moebius. 6.95

A SMALL KILLING
GN by Alan Moore & Oscar Zarate 11.95

Atlas #2
© Dark Horse Comics

ATLAS
1 BZ,I:Atlas 2.75
2 BZ,V:Sh'en Chui 2.75
3 BZ,V:Sh'en Chui 2.50
4 BZ, final issue. 2.50

BABE
Legend 1994
1 JBy(a&s) 3.00
2 thru 4 JBy(a&s) . . . . @2.50

BABE 2
Legend 1995
1 V:Shrewmanoid 2.50
2 A:Abe Sapien 2.50

BACCHUS
COLOR SPECIAL
1 A:Thor 2.95
2 A:Abe Sapien 2.50

BADGER:
SHATTERED MIRROR
1 R:Badger 2.50
2 R:Badger 2.50
3 Badger 2.50
4 Phantom, final issue 2.50

BADGER: ZEN POP
FUNNY ANIMAL VERSION
1 MBn,R:Badger 2.50
2 Ham 2.50

BADLANDS
(B&W)
1 I:Connie Bremen 3.50
2 Anne Peck, C.I.A. 3.00
3 Assassination Rumor 2.50
4 Connie heads South 2.50
5 November 22, 1963, Dallas . . . 2.25
6 . . . . 2.25

BARB WIRE
Comics' Greatest World
1 Foil(c),I:Deathcard 2.25
2 DLw,I:Hurricane Max 2.25
3 V:Mace Blitzkrieg 2.00
4 Ghost pt.1 . . . . 2.00
5 Ghost pt.2 . . . . 2.00
6 Hardhide, Ignition 2.50
7 A:Motorhead 2.50
8 V:Ignition 2.50
9 A:Mecha, V:Ignition 2.50
Movie Spec. 3.95
TPB 8.95

BARB WIRE:
ACE OF SPADES
1 thru 4 by CW, TBd & DoM. . . . @2.95

BARRY WINDSOR-SMITH:
STORYTELLER
Oct. 1996
TPBs 1 thru 9 9"x12½". . . . . . . @4.95

BASEBALL GREATS
1 Jimmy Piersall story 3.25

Basil Wolverton's Fantastic Fables #1
© Dark Horse Comics

BASIL WOLVERTON'S
FANTASTIC FABLES
(B&W)
1 BW. 2.50
2 BW. 2.50

BASIL WOLVERTON
IN SPACE
Feb. 1999
TPB 240-page 16.95

BATMAN/ALIENS
Dark Horse/DC March 1997
1 (of 2) RMz,BWr. 4.95
2 conclusion 4.95
TPB 14.95

BETTIE PAGE
1-shot, some nudity 3.95

BETTIE PAGE COMICS:
SPICY ADVENTURE
1-shot by Jim Silke 2.95

BETTIE PAGE:
QUEEN OF HEARTS
1 Movie adaptation 2.00
TPB 19.95

BIG
1 Movie Adaptation 2.00

BIG BLOWN BABY
(B&W) Aug. 1996
1 thru 4 by Bill Wray. . . . . @2.95

BIG GUY AND
RUSTY THE ROBOT BOY
1 V:Monster. 4.95
2 V:Monster. 4.95
TPB FM & GfD 14.95
TPB King Size 29.95

BILLI 99
(B&W)
1 `Pray for us Sinners'. 4.50
2 `Trespasses'. 4.00
3 `Daily Bread'. 4.00

BLACK CROSS:
DIRTY WORK
April 1997
1-shot by Chris Warner. 2.95

BLACK DRAGON, THE
(B&W)
TPB Chris Claremont & John Bolton . . .
17.95

BLACK MAGIC
B&W 1998
TPB 16.95

BLACK PEARL, THE
Sept. 1996
1 by Mark Hamill 2.95
2 thru 5 . . . . @2.95
TPB by Mark Hamill 16.95

BLADE OF THE
IMMORTAL
(B&W) Manga
Conquest, 1996
2 Conquest, pt. 1 . . . . 3.50
3 Conquest, pt. 2 . . . . 3.50
4 Conquest, pt. 3 . . . . 3.50
Genius, 1996
5 Genius, pt. 1 . . . . 3.50
6 Genius, pt.2 . . . . 3.50
Fanatic, 1997
7 Fanatic, pt.1 . . . . 3.50
8 Fanatic, pt.2 . . . . 3.50
Call of the Worm, April 1997
9 pt. 1 by Hiroaki Samura 3.95
10 pt. 2 . . . . 3.95
11 pt. 3 . . . . 3.95
TPB Cry of the Worm 12.95
Dreamsong, July 1997
12 pt. 1 (of 7) by Hiroaki Samura . . 2.95
13 pt. 2 F:Makie, Manji 2.95
14 pt. 3 . . . . 2.95
15 pt. 4 . . . . 2.95
16 pt. 5 . . . . 2.95
17 pt. 6 . . . . 2.95
18 pt. 7 . . . . 2.95
TPB Dreamsong. 12.95
Rin's Bane, March 1998
19 pt.1, by Hiroaki Samura 2.95
20 pt.2 . . . . 2.95
On Silent Wings, May 1998
21 pt. 1 (of 8) 2.95
22 pt. 2. 2.95
23 pt. 3. 2.95
24 pt. 4. 2.95
25 pt. 5. 2.95
26 pt. 6. 2.95
27 pt. 7. 2.95
28 pt. 8. 2.95
TPB On Silent Wings 14.95
TPB Blood of a Thousand. 12.95
Dark Shadows, Jan. 1999
29 pt. 1 (of 5) 2.95
30 pt. 2. 2.95
31 pt. 3. 2.95
32 pt. 4. 2.95
33 pt. 5. 2.95
Food, June 1999
34 . . . . 2.95

DARK HORSE

Heart of Darkness
35 pt.1 (of 8). 2.95
36 pt.2 . . . . 2.95

BLANCHE GOES TO NEW YORK
1 Turn of the Century N.Y. 2.95

BLAST CORPS
Sept. 1998
1-shot F:demolition experts 2.50

BLUE LILY
1 thru 3 . . . . @4.00

BODY BAGS
Aug. 1996
1 (of 4) by Jason Pearson and
   Ken Bruzinak 3.00
2 and 3 . . . . @3.00
TPB 12.95

BOOK OF NIGHT
(B&W)
1 CV 2.50
2 CV 2.00
TPB Children of the Stars 12.95

BOOK OF NIGHT
1 thru 3 . . . . 3.95

BORIS THE BEAR
(B&W)
1 V:Funny Animals 3.00
1a 2nd printing 2.00
2 V:Robots 2.00
3 V:Super Heroes 2.00
4 Bear of Steel 2.00
5 Dump Thing 2.00
6 Bat Bear. 2.00
7 Elves 2.00
8 LargeSize. 2.50
9 Awol. 2.00
10 thru 12. . . . . @2.00
See: B & W Pub. section

BORIS THE BEAR
Color Classics
1 thru 7 . . . . @1.95

BRAVE
March 1997
1 by Cully Hamner & Jason Martin. 2.95

BUBBLE GUM CRISIS: GRAND MAL
Manga
1 . . . . 2.75
2 and 3 . . . . @2.75
4 final issue. 2.50
TPB Rep.#1–#4 . . . . 14.95

BUFFY THE VAMPIRE SLAYER
Sept. 1998
1 JoB,AAd(c) foil, Wu-Tang Fang . . 3.00
1a 2nd printing 2.50
2 JoB, Halloween 3.00
2a newsstand, photo(c) 3.00
3 JoB, Cold Turkey 3.00
3a newsstand, photo(c) 3.00
4 White Christmas 3.00
4a newsstand, photo(c) 3.00
5 Happy New Year 3.00
5a newsstand, photo(c) 3.00
6 New Kid on the Block, pt.1 . . . . 3.00
6a newsstand, photo(c) 3.00
7 JoB, New Kid on the Block, pt.2 . 3.00
7a newsstand, photo(c) 3.00
8 The Final Cut 3.00
8a newsstand, photo(c) 3.00
9 Hey, Good Lookin,pt.1 . . . . 3.00
9a newsstand, photo(c) 3.00
10 Hey, Good Lookin,pt.2 . . . . 3.00
10a newsstand, photo(c) 3.00
11 A Boy Named Sue 3.00
11a newsstand, photo(c) 3.00
12 A Nice Girl Like You 3.00
12a newsstand, photo(c) 3.00
TPB The Dust Waltz 10.00
TPB The Remaining Sunlight 10.00
Spec. 1-shot Spike and Dru 3.00
Ann. 1999, 64-page 4.95

BUFFY THE VAMPIRE SLAYER: ANGEL
May 1999
1 (of 3) 3.00
2 & 3 . . . . @3.00
1a thru 3a newsstand, photo(c) . @3.00

BUFFY THE VAMPIRE SLAYER: THE ORIGIN
Feb. 1999
1 (of 3) DIB,JoB. 3.00
2 & 3 . . . . @3.00
2a & 3a newsstand, photo(c) . . . @3.00
TPB rep. 9.95

BY BIZARRE HANDS
(B&W)
1 JLd(s). 2.50
2 JLd(s). 2.50
3 JLd(s). 2.50

CARAVAN KIDD
(B&W) Manga
1 thru 10 by Johji Manabe . . . . . @2.50
[2nd Series]
1 thru 10 F:Miam . . . . @2.50
TPB Rep. #1–#10. . . . . 19.95
Holiday Spec. 2.50
Valentine's Day Spec. 2.50
[3rd Series]
1 thru 8 . . . . @2.50
Christmas Special. 2.50
TPB Vol. 2 . . . . 19.95
TPB Vol. 3 . . . . 19.95

CATALYST: AGENTS OF CHANGE
Comics' Greatest World
1 JPn(c),V:US Army 2.25
2 JPn(c),I:Grenade 2.25
3 JPn(c),Rebel vs. Titan 2.25
4 JPn(c),Titan vs. Grace 2.00
5 JPn(c),V:Ape 2.00
6 and 7 . . . . @2.00

CHEVAL NOIR
(B&W)
1 DSt(c). 4.00
2 thru 6 . . . . @3.50
7 DSt(c). 3.50
8 . . . . 3.50
9 . . . . 3.50
10 80 page 4.50
11 80 page 4.50
12 MM(c) 3.95
13 . . . . 3.95
14 . . . . 3.95
15 . . . . 3.95
16 thru 19 with 2-card strip . . . . @3.95
20 Great Power o/t Chninkel. 4.50
21 Great Power o/t Chninkel. 3.95
22 Great Power o/t Chninkel,concl.. 4.50
23 inc.`Rork',`Forever War' concl... 3.95
24 In Dreams, Pt.1 . . . . 3.95
25 In Dreams, Pt.2 . . . . 3.95
26 In Dreams, Pt.3 . . . . 3.95
27 I:The Man From Ciguri (Airtight
   Garage sequel) Dreams Pt.4 . . 2.95
28 Ciguri cont. 2.95
29 Ciguri cont. 2.95
30 Ciguri,cont. 2.95

Boris the Bear #7
© Dark Horse Comics

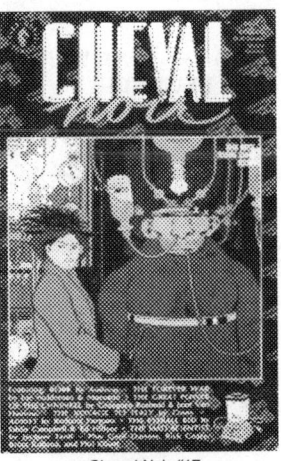

Cheval Noir #17
© Dark Horse Comics

DARK HORSE

DARK HORSE

31 Angriest Dog in the World	2.95
32	2.95
33	2.95
34	2.95
35	2.95
36	2.95
37	2.95
38	2.95
39 In Search of Peter Pan	2.95
40	2.95
41 F:Demon	2.95
42 F:Demon	2.95
43 F:Demon	2.95
44 F:Demon	2.95
45	2.95
46	2.95
47	2.95
48 SwM(c)	2.95
49 F:Rork	2.95
50 F:Rork	2.95

CHRONOWAR
(B&W) Manga Aug. 1996

1 (of 9) by Kazumasa Takayama	2.95
2 thru 9	@2.95

CLASSIC STAR WARS

1 AW,newspaper strip reps.	6.00
2 AW,newspaper strip reps.	4.00
3 AW,newspaper strip reps.	4.00
4 AW,newspaper strip reps.	4.00
5 AW,newspaper strip reps.	4.00
6 AW,newspaper strip reps.	4.00
7 AW,newspaper reps.	4.00
8 AW,newspaper reps. w/card	4.00
9 AW,newspaper reps.	3.50
10 AW,newspaper reps.	3.50
11 thru 19 AW,newspaper reps.	@3.00
20 AW,newspaper strip reps., with trading card, final issue.	4.00
TPB Vol. 1, "In Deadly Pursuit," rep.#1–#7.	15.99
TPB Vol. 1, rep. 2nd edition	16.95
TPB Vol. 2, "Rebel Storm," rep. #8–#14	16.95
TPB Vol. 3, "Escape to Hoth," rep. #15–#20	16.95

CLASSIC STAR WARS: A NEW HOPE

1 AAd(c), rep.	4.25
2 AH(c), rep.	3.95
TPB Rep. #1–#2.	9.95

CLASSIC STAR WARS: DEVILWORLDS
Aug. 1996

1 (of 2) by Alan Moore	2.50
2	2.50

CLASSIC STAR WARS: EARLY ADVENTURES
Aug. 1994–April 1995

1 MiA(c), Gambler's World.	3.00
2 RHo&MGr(c),Blackhole.	2.50
3 EiS(c),Rebels of Vorzyd-5.	2.50
3 bagged with trading card DH2.	5.00
4 RHo(c),Tatooine	2.50
5 RHo(c),A:Lady Tarkin	2.50
6 Weather Dominator	2.50
7 RHo(c),V:Darth Vader.	2.50
8 KPl(c),X-Wing Secrets	2.50
9 KPl(c),A:Boba Fett	2.50
TPB RsM & AGw, AW(c).	19.95

Classic Star Wars: Devilworlds #1
© Dark Horse Comics

CLASSIC STAR WARS: EMPIRE STRIKES BACK

1 Movie Adaptation	4.00
2 Movie Adaptation	4.00
TPB Rep.#1–#2 AW&CG(c)	9.95
TPB reprint, Hildebrandt(c)	9.95

CLASSIC STAR WARS: HAN SOLO AT STAR'S END
March 1997

1 (of 3) by Alfredo Alcala	3.00
2 thru 3	@3.00
TPB rep. AW(c)	6.95

CLASSIC STAR WARS: A LONG TIME AGO
(B&W) March 1999

1 (of 6) rep. Marvel comics	6.00
2 thru 6	@6.00

CLASSIC STAR WARS: RETURN OF THE JEDI

1 Movie Adaptation	4.00
2 Movie Adaptation	3.50
TPB Rep.#1–#2	9.95
TPB rep. Hildebrandt(c)	9.95

CLASSIC STAR WARS: VANDELHELM MISSION
1995

1-shot F:Han Solo, Lando	3.95

CLONEZONE
(B&W)

Spec #1	2.00

CLOWNS, THE (PAGLIACCI)
April 1998

1-shot B&W, CR	2.95

COLORS IN BLACK
Comics From Spike

1 B:Passion Play	2.95
2 Images	2.95
3 Back on the Bus	2.95
4 final issue	2.95

COMIC BOOK

1 thru 4 9"x12" John Kricfalusi	@5.95

COMICS AND STORIES

4 (of 4) by Martin & Millionaire	2.95

COMICS' GREATEST WORLD
(Arcadia)

1 B:MRi(s),FM(c),B:LW,B:O:Vortex, F:X,I:Seekers	3.00
1a B&W proof ed. (1,500 made)	9.00
1b Hologram(c), with cards	7.00
2 JoP,I:Pit Bulls	1.50
3 AH,I:Ghost	5.00
4 I:Monster	1.50
TPB Arcadia	25.00

(Golden City)

1 B:BKs(s),JOy(c),I:Rebel, Amaz.Grace,V:WarMaker	1.25
1a Gold Ed.	5.00
2 I:Mecha	1.25
3 WS(c),I:Titan	1.25
4 E:BKs(s),GP(c),JD,I:Catalyst	1.25
TPB Golden City	11.00

(Steel Harbor)

1 B:CW(s),PG,I:Barb Wire, V:Ignition	1.25
2 MMi(c),TNa,I:Machine.	1.25
3 CW(a&s),I:Wolf Gang	1.25
4 E:CW(s),VGi,I:Motorhead	1.25
TPB Steel Harbor	11.00

(Vortex)

1 B:RSd(s),LW,DoM,I:Division 13.	1.25
2 I:Hero Zero	1.25
3 PC,I:King Tiger	1.25
4 B:RSd(s),E:MRi(s)BMc,E:LW, E:O:Vortex,C:Vortex	1.25
TPB Vortex	11.00
Sourcebook	10.00

CONCRETE
(B&W)

1 PC,R:Concrete, A Stone among Stones	7.00
1a 2nd printing	3.00
2 PC,`Transatlantic Swim'	5.00
3 PC	4.00
4 PC	3.50
5 PC,`An Armchair Stuffed with Dynamite'.	3.50
6 PC,Concrete works on farm	3.50
7 PC,Concrete grows horns.	3.50
8 PC,Climbs Mount Everest.	3.50
9 PC,Mount Everest Pt.2	3.50
10 PC,last Issue	3.50
TPB The Complete Concrete	25.00

CONCRETE

1 PC,ColorSpec.	4.00
EarthDay Spec. PC,Moebius	4.00

CONCRETE: A NEW LIFE

1	3.50
Spec.Land & Sea,rep.	3.25

CONCRETE CELEBRATES EARTH DAY 1990
1-shot. 2.50

CONCRETE: ECLECTICA
1 PC,The Ugly Boy 3.25
2 PC 3.25

CONCRETE: FRAGILE CREATURE
1 PC,`Rulers o/t Omniverse'Pt.1 . . 4.00
2 PC,`Rulers o/t Omniverse'Pt.2 . . 3.00
3 PC,`Rulers o/t Omniverse'Pt.3 . . 3.00
4 PC,`Rulers o/t Omniverse'Pt.3 . . 3.00
TPB 15.95

Concrete Killer Smile #1
© Dark Horse Comics

CONCRETE: KILLER SMILE
Dark Horse-Legend 1994
1 PC 3.50
2 PC 3.00
3 PC 3.00
4 PC, final issue 3.00
TPB Rep.#1–#4 . . . . 16.95

CONCRETE: ODD JOBS
(B&W)
1-shot. 3.50

[PAUL CHADWICK'S] CONCRETE: STRANGE ARMOR
Dec. 1997–Apr. 1998
1 (of 5) 3.00
2 thru 5 . . . . @3.00
TPB Strange Armor 17.00

CONCRETE: THINK LIKE A MOUNTAIN
1 thru 6 PC,GfD(c). . . . . @3.00
TPB PC,GfD(c). 17.95

CORMAC MAC ART
1 Robert E. Howard adapt. 2.25
2 . . . . 2.25
3 . . . . 2.25

CORNY'S FETISH
April 1998
GN by Renee French, 64pg. 4.95

COUTOO
1 Lt. Joe Kraft 3.50

CREEPY
(B&W)
1 KD,TS,GC,SL,Horror 3.95
2 TS,CI,DC,Demonic Baby 3.95
3 JM,TS,JG,V:Killer Clown. 3.95
4 TS,Final issue 3.95

CREATURE FROM THE BLACK LAGOON
1 Movie Adaptation 4.95

CRITICAL ERROR
1 rep.Classic JBy story 2.75

[ANDREW VACHSS'] CROSS
0 GfD(c),I:Cross,Rhino,Princess . . 2.50
1 thru 7 . . . . @2.95

CUD COMICS
(B&W) 1995
1 thru 8 by Terry LaBan . . . . @2.95

THE CURSE OF DRACULA
July 1998
1 (of 3) MWn,GC. 3.00
2 thru 3 . . . . @3.00

CYBERANATICS
HC by Jerry Prosser & Rick Geary 14.95

DANGER UNLIMITED
Dark Horse-Legend
1 JBy(a&s),KD,I:Danger Unlimited, B:BU:Torch of Liberty 2.50
2 JBy(a&s),KD,O:DangerUnlimited. 2.25
3 JBy(a&s),KD,O:Torch of Liberty . 2.25
4 JBy(a&s),KD,Final Issue. 2.25
TPB rep. #1–#4 . . . . 14.95

DARK HORSE CLASSICS
(B&W)
1 Last of the Mohicans 3.95
2 20,000 Leagues Under the Sea . 3.95

DARK HORSE CLASSICS: ALIENS VS. PREDATOR
Feb. 1997
1 thru 6 Rep. . . . . @3.00

DARK HORSE CLASSICS: GODZILLA, KING OF THE MONSTERS
July 1998
1 RSd,SBi,now color 3.00
2 rep. from 1995 . . . . 3.00
3 rep. from 1995 . . . . 3.00
4 rep. Godzilla #2, from 1995. . . . . 3.00
5 . . . . 3.00
6 V:Bagorah 3.00

DARK HORSE CLASSICS: PREDATOR: JUNGLE TALES
1-shot Rep. 3.00

DARK HORSE CLASSICS: STAR WARS— DARK EMPIRE
1997
1 rep. by Tom Veitch,CK,DvD(c) . . 3.00
2 thru 6 rep., DvD(c) . . . . @3.00

DARK HORSE CLASSICS: TERROR OF GODZILLA
Aug. 1998
1 by Kazuhisa Iwata, AAd(c) 3.00
2 . . . . 3.00
3 . . . . 3.00
4 rep. of 1988 B&W. 3.00
5 AAd(c) 3.00
6 AAd(c) 3.00

DARK HORSE COMICS
1 RL,CW,F:Predator,Robocop, I:Renegade,Time Cop,(double gatefold cover) 4.00
2 RL,CW,F:Predator,Robocop, Renegade,Time Cop 3.00
3 CW,F:Robocop,Time Cop,Aliens, Indiana Jones. 3.00
4 F:Predator,Aliens,Ind.Jones . . . 2.75
5 F:Predator,E:Aliens. 2.75
6 F:Robocop,Predator, E:Indiana Jones 2.75
7 F:Robocop,Predator,B:StarWars . 6.00
8 B&I:X,Robocop. 8.00
9 F:Robocop,E:Star Wars 4.00
10 E:X,B:Godzilla,Predator, James Bond. 3.50
11 F:Godzilla,Predator,James Bond,B:Aliens. 2.75
12 F:Predator. 2.75
13 F:Predator,B:Thing. 2.75
14 MiB(s),B:The Mark. 2.75
15 MiB(s),E:The Mark,B:Aliens . . . 2.75
16 B:Predator,E:Thing,Aliens 2.75
17 B:Aliens,Star Wars:Droids 2.75
18 E:Predator. 2.75
19 RL(c),B:X,E:Star Wars:Droids,

Dark Horse Comics #6
© Dark Horse Comics

Aliens.	2.75
20 B:Predator.	2.75
21 F:Mecha	2.75
22 B:Aliens, E:Mecha	2.75
23 B:The Machine	2.50
24 The Machine	2.50
25 Final issue.	2.50

DARK HORSE DOWNUNDER
(B&W)

1 F:Australian Writers	2.50
2 Australian Writers	2.50
3 Australian Writers, finale	2.50

DARK HORSE MONSTERS
Feb. 1997

1-shot.	3.00

DARK HORSE PRESENTS
(B&W)

1 PC,I:Concrete.	10.00
1a 2nd printing	2.50
2 PC,Concrete.	7.00
3 Boris the Bear,Concrete.	4.00
4 PC,Concrete.	4.00
5 PC,Concrete.	4.00
6 PC,Concrete.	4.00
7 I:MONQ	3.50
8 PC,Concrete.	3.50
9	3.50
10 PC,Concrete, I:Masque	7.00
11 Masque	6.00
12 PC,Concrete, Masque	5.00
13 Masque	5.00
14 PC,Concrete, Masque	5.00
15 Masque	5.00
16 PC,Concrete, Masque	5.00
17	3.00
18 PC,Concrete, Mask	5.00
19 Masque	5.00
20 double,Flaming Carrot	6.00
21 Masque	5.00
22	3.00
23	3.00
24 PC,I:Aliens.	10.00
25 thru 31	@3.00
32	4.00
33	3.00
34 Aliens	4.00
35 Predator	4.00
36 Aliens vs.Predator	4.00
36a painted cover.	5.00
37	2.50
38	2.50
39	2.50
40 I:The Aerialist	2.50
41	2.50
42 Aliens	5.00
43 Aliens	4.00
44	2.50
45	2.50
46 Predator	4.00
47	2.50
48 with 2-card strip	2.50
49 with 2-card strip	2.50
50 inc.`Heartbreakers', with 2-card strip.	2.50
51 FM(c),inc.`Sin City'	4.00
52 FM,inc. `Sin City'	3.00
53 FM,inc. `Sin City'	3.00
54 FM,Sin City;JBy Preview of Next Men Pt.1	5.00
55 FM,Sin City;JBy Preview of Next Men (JBy) Pt.2	4.00
56 FM,Sin City,JBy,Next MenPt.3	

Dark Horse Presents #50
© *Dark Horse Comics*

Aliens Genocide(prologue)	3.00
57 FM,SinCity;JBy Next Men Pt.4	3.00
58 FM,Sin City,Alien Fire	2.50
59 FM,Sin City,Alien Fire	2.50
60 FM,Sin City	2.50
61 FM,Sin City	2.50
62 FM,E:Sin City	2.50
63 Moe,Marie Dakar.	2.50
64 MWg,R:The Aerialist	2.50
65 B:Accidental Death	2.50
66 PC,inc.Dr.Giggles	2.50
67 B:Predator story (lead in to "Race War"),double size.	3.95
68 F:Predator,Swimming Lessons (Nestrobber tie-in)	2.50
69 F:Predator	2.50
70 F:Alec	2.50
71 F:Madwoman.	2.50
72 F:Eudaemon	2.50
73 F:Eudaemon	2.50
74	2.50
75 F:Chairman	2.50
76 F:Hermes Vs.the Eye,Ball Kid	2.50
77 F:Hermes Vs.the Eye,Ball Kid	2.50
78 F:Hermes Vs.the Eye,Ball Kid	2.50
79 B:Shadow Empires Slaves.	2.50
80 AAd,I:Monkey Man & O'Brien.	5.00
81 B:Buoy	2.50
82 B:Just Folks.	2.50
83 Last Impression	2.50
84 MBn,F:Nexus,E:Hermes Vs.the Eye Ball Kid	2.50
85 Winner Circle.	2.50
86	2.50
87 F:Concrete	2.50
88 Hellboy	3.00
89 Hellboy	3.00
90 Hellboy	3.00
91 Blackheart, Baden	3.00
92 Too Much Coffee Man	6.00
93 Cud, Blackheart,Coffee Man	8.00
94 A:Eyeball Kid,Coffee Man	6.00
95 Too Much Coffee Man	7.00
96 Kabuli Kid	2.50
97 F:Kabuki Kid	2.50
98 Pot Full of Noodles	2.50
99 Anthology title	2.50
100–#1 Lance Blastoff	2.50
100–#2 Hellboy	2.50
100–#3 Concrete	2.50
100–#4 Black Cross	2.50
100–#5 Pan Fried Girl	2.50
101 BW,F:Aliens.	2.50
102 F:Mr. Painter	2.50

103 F:The Pink Tornado	3.00
104 F:The Pink Tornado	3.00
105 F:The Pink Tornado	3.00
106 F:Godzilla	3.00
107 F:Rusty Razorclam	3.00
108.	3.00
109.	3.00
110.	3.00
111.	3.00
112 three stories, concl.	3.00
113 F:Trypto the Acid Dog	3.00
114 F:Star Slammers	3.00
115 flip-book.	3.00
116.	3.00
117 F:Aliens	3.00
118.	3.00
119.	3.00
120 "One Last Job".	3.00
121 F:Imago.	3.00
122 "Lords of Misrule".	3.00
123 F: Jack Zero	3.00
124 F:Predator	3.00
125 F:Nocturnals	3.00
126 flip book, 48pg.	3.95
127 F:The Nocturnals.	3.00
128 F:Dan & Larry	3.00
129 F:Hammer	3.00
130 F:Zombie Worl	3.00
131 F:Girl Crazy	3.00
132 flip book.	3.00
133 F:Tarzan	3.00
134 F:The Dirty Pair	3.00
135 F:The Fall, concl.	3.00
136 The Ark	3.00
137 Predator	3.00
138 F:Terminators.	3.00
139 F:Roachmill	3.00
140 F:Aliens	3.00
141 F:Buffy the Vampire Slayer.	3.00
142 F:Lovecraftian tales	3.00
143 F:Tarzan tales	3.00
144 F:Ghost, Burgler Girls, Galactic Jack	3.00
145 F:Ghost	3.00
Fifth Anniv. Special DGi,PC, SBi,CW,MW,FM,Sin City, Aliens,Give Me Liberty	8.00
Milestone Ed.#1,rep.DHP#1	2.25
TPB rep.Sin City.	6.00
TPB Best of DHP #1–#20.	9.95
TPB Best of DHP #1–#20 2nd edition	9.95
TPB Best of DHP #21–#30	8.95
TPB Best of DHP #31–#50	8.95
Ann. 1997.	4.95
Ann. 1998.	4.95
Ann. 1999.	4.95

DARK HORSE PRESENTS: ALIENS

1 Rep.	4.95
1a Platinum Edition	8.00

DEADFACE: DOING ISLANDS WITH BACCHUS
(B&W)

1 rep. Bacchus apps.	2.95
2 rep. inc.`Book-Keeper of Atlantis.	2.95

DEADFACE: EARTH, WATER, AIR & FIRE
(B&W)

1 Bacchus & Simpson in Sicily.	2.50
2 A:Don Skylla.	2.50
3 Mafia/Kabeirol-War prep.	2.50
4 Last issue.	2.50

DARK HORSE

DEAD IN THE WEST
(B&W)
1 TT,Joe Landsdale adapt........ 5.00
2 TT,adapt. 5.00

DEAD IN THE WEST
1 TT(c) 3.95

DEAD OR ALIVE—
A CYBERPUNK WESTERN
April 1998
1 (of 4) by Tatjana and Alberto
   Ponticelli 2.50
2 thru 4 .... @2.50

DEADLINE USA
(B&W)
1 rep. Deadline UK,Inc. Tank Girl
   Johnny Nemo............. 9.95
2 inc. Tank Girl,Johnny Nemo 9.95

DECADE OF
DARK HORSE, A
1 (of 4) inc. Star Wars, Nexus,
   Ghost................... 2.95
2 thru 4 .... @2.95

[RANDY BOWEN'S]
DECAPITATOR
June 1998
1 (of 4) GEr,DoM............ 3.00
2 GEr................... 3.00
3 MMi,KJo,AAl.............. 3.00
4 MMi, conclusion........... 3.00

DEVIL CHIEF
1 I:Devil Chief 2.50

DIRTY PAIR
(B&W) Manga
TPB Book 3 A Plague of Angels by
   Adam Warren & Toren Smith . 12.95
TPB Dangerous Acquaintances .. 12.95
TPB Biohazards 12.95

DIRTY PAIR: FATAL
BUT NOT SERIOUS
Manga
1 R:Kei,Yuri................ 2.95
2 V:Kevin Sleet,Yuri........... 2.95
3 Anti Yuri 2.95
4 V:Terrorists............... 2.95
5 conclusion 2.95

DIRTY PAIR: SIM HELL
(B&W) Manga
1 thru 4 by Adam Warren...... @3.25
TPB rep. #1–#4 .... 13.95

DISNEY'S TARZAN
June 1999
1 (of 2) Animated movie adapt. ... 2.95
2 conclusion 2.95

DIVISION 13
1 .... 2.50
2 .... 2.50
3 A:Payback 2.50
4 Carnal Genesis............. 2.50

DOC SAVAGE: CURSE
OF THE FIRE GOD
1 R:Man of Bronze 2.95
2 Exploding Plane 2.95
3 & 4 .... @2.95

DR. GIGGLES
1 Horror movie adapt. 2.50
2 Movie adapt.contd. 2.50

DOMINION
(B&W) Manga
TPB 1 by Masamune Shirow..... 15.00
TPB 2nd printing............. 14.95

DOMINION: CONFLICT 1
— NO MORE NOISE
(B&W) Manga 1996
1 thru 6 by Masamune Shirow .. @2.95
TPB series rep............... 14.95

DOMINION SPECIAL:
PHANTOM OF
THE AUDIENCE
(B&W) Manga
1-shot by Masamune Shirow...... 2.50

DOMU:
A CHILD'S DREAMS
(B&W) Manga
1 Psychic Warfare 5.95
2 Murders Continue........... 5.95
3 Psychic war conclusion. 5.95
TPB by Katsuhiro Otomo 17.95

DRACULA
1 Movie Adaptation 4.95

DRAKUUN:
(B&W) Manga Feb. 1997
Rise of the Dragon Princess
1 by Johji Manabe............ 2.95
2 Part 2.................. 2.95
3 Part 3.................. 2.95
4 Part 4.................. 2.95

5 Part 5.................. 2.95
6 Part 6.................. 2.95
TPB rep................... 12.95
The Revenge of Gustav, Aug. 1997
7 Revenge of Gustav,pt.1 .... 2.95
8 Revenge of Gustav,pt.2 .... 2.95
9 Revenge of Gustav,pt.3 .... 2.95
10 Revenge of Gustav,pt.4 ...... 2.95
11 Revenge of Gustav,pt.5 ...... 2.95
12 Revenge of Gustav,pt.6 ...... 2.95
TPB, rep.................. 14.95
Shadow of the Warlock, Feb. 1998
13 Shadow of the Warlock, pt.1 ... 2.95
14 Shadow of the Warlock, pt.2 ... 2.95
15 Shadow of the Warlock, pt.3 ... 2.95
16 Shadow of the Warlock, pt.4 ... 2.95
17 Shadow of the Warlock, pt.5 ... 2.95
18 Shadow of the Warlock, pt.6 ... 2.95
TPB rep................... 14.95
The Hidden War, Oct. 1998
19 The Hidden War,pt.1 .... 2.95
20 The Hidden War,pt.2 .... 2.95
21 The Hidden War,pt.3 .... 2.95
22 The Hidden War,pt.4 .... 2.95
23 The Hidden War,pt.5 .... 2.95
24 The Hidden War,pt.6 .... 2.95

DYLAN DOG
(B&W) DH/Bonelli Mar. 1999
1 (of 6) by Tiziano Di Sclavi & Angelo
   Stano, MMi(c), 96-page 4.95
2 thru 6 .... @4.95

EDGAR RICE
BURROUGHS'
RETURN OF TARZAN
April 1997
1 adapted by Thomas Yeates
   & John Totleben 3.00
2 .... 3.00
3 .... 3.00

EDGAR RICE
BURROUGHS' TARZAN:
CARSON OF VENUS
May 1998
1 (of 4) by Darko Macan and
   Igor Kordey, F:Carson Napier .. 3.00
2 thru 4 novels adapt. .... @3.00

DARK HORSE

TPB Carson of Venus 12.95

EDGAR RICE BURROUGHS' TARZAN: THE LOST ADVENTURE
1 Lost Manuscript 3.00
2 V:Gorgo the Buffalo 3.00
3 V:Bandits 3.00
4 V:Bandits 3.00
HC 19.95
HC lim. ed. 100.00

EDGAR RICE BURROUGHS' TARZAN
Mugambi
1 by Bruce Jones, Christopher
　Schenck & TY, Betrayed by 3
　man-beasts 3.00
2 "Tarzan's Jungle Fury" 3.00
3 "Tarzan's Jungle Fury" 3.00
4 vs. the Tara virus 3.00
5 Cure to the Tara virus 3.00
6 . . . . 3.00
Tarzan and the Legion of Hate
7 by Allan Gross, Christopher
　Schenck, George Freeman 3.00
8 pt.2. . . . . 3.00
9 pt.3. . . . . 3.00
10 pt.4, concl.. . . . . 3.00
Le Monstre, June 1997
11 pt.1 . . . . 3.00
12 pt.2 Bernie Wrightson(c) 3.00
Modern Prometheus, Aug. 1997
13 pt.1 MK(c) in New York 3.00
14 pt.2 MK(c) 3.00
Tooth and Nail, Oct. 1997
15 pt.1 MSh(c) 3.00
16 pt.2 . . . . 3.00
TPB adapts #11–#16 . . . . 16.95
Tarzan vs. the Moon Men
17 pt.1 TT,AW,TY 3.00
18 pt.2 TT,AW,TY 3.00
19 pt.3 TT,AW,TY 3.00
20 pt.4 TT,AW,TY 3.00
Primeval
21 pt.1 MGr 3.00
22 pt.2 MGr 3.00
23 pt.3 MGr 3.00
24 pt.4 MGr 3.00
TPB RsM,The Land That Time
　Forgot 12.95
TPB Tarzan of the Apes 12.95
TPB The Jewls of Opar. 10.95

EDGAR RICE BURROUGHS' TARZAN— THE SAVAGE HEART
Apr. 1999
1 (of 4) MGr Jane is dead 3.00
2 thru 4 . . . . @3.00

EGON
Jan.–Feb. 1998
1 and 2 . . . . @2.95

EIGHTH WONDER, THE
Nov. 1997
1-shot by Peter Janes & Killian
　Plunkett 2.95

ELRIC: STORMBRINGER
Dark Horse/Topps 1996
1 by Michael Moorcock & CR. 3.00
2 thru 7 (of 7). . . . . @3.00

Elric Stormbringer #2
© Dark Horse Comics

TPB rep. series. 17.95

ENEMY
1 MZ(c),StG(s),I:Enemy. 2.75
2 MZ(c),StG(s),F:Heller 2.75
3 MZ(c),StG(s),A:Heller 2.50
4 . . . . 2.50
5 final issue. 2.95
TPB 14.95

ENO AND PLUM
Sept. 1997
TPB 12.95

EUDAEMON, THE
1 Nel,I:New Eudaemon 3.00
2 Nel,V:Mordare 2.75
3 Nel,V:Mordare 2.75

EVIL DEAD III: ARMY OF DARKNESS
1 JBo,Movie adaptation 4.00
2 JBo,Movie adaptation 3.50
3 JBo,Movie adaptation 3.00

EXOTICS, THE
TPB by Moebius. 7.95

EYEBALL KID
(B&W)
1 I:Eyeball Kid. 2.25
2 V:Stygian Leech 2.25
3 V:Telchines Brothers,last iss. . . . 2.25

FAT DOG MENDOZA
(B&W)
1 I&O:Fat Dog Mendoza 2.50

FAX FROM SARAJEVO
Oct. 1996
GN JKu, 224 pg. 24.95

FLAMING CARROT
(B&W)
18 . . . . 3.50
18a Ash-Can-Limited 4.00

19 . . . . 2.00
20 . . . . 2.00
21 . . . . 2.00
22 . . . . 2.00
23 . . . . 2.00
24 . . . . 3.00
25 F:TMNT,Mysterymen, with
　2-card strip. 3.00
26 A:TMNT. 2.50
27 TM(c),A:TMNT conclusion 2.50
28 . . . . 2.50
29 Man in the Moon,Iron City 2.50
30 V:Man in the Moon 2.50
31 A:Fat Fury 2.50
Ann. 1 by Bob Burden 5.00
TPB Man of Mystery, B&W 12.95
TPB The Wild Shall Wild Remain
　rep. #4–#11 . . . . 17.95
TPB Flaming Carrot's Greatest Hits,
　rep. #12–#18 . . . . 17.95
TPB Fortune Favors the Bold,
　rep.#19–#24 . . . . 16.95

FLAXEN
1 Based on Model,w/poster 2.95

FLOATERS
(B&W)
1 thru 6 From Spike Lee 2.50

FOOT SOLDIERS, THE
1 thru 4 by Jim Krueger. 2.95
TPB 14.95
See also Image Comics

FRANKENSTEIN
1 Movie Adaptation 3.95

FREAKSHOW
1 JBo,DMc,KB, "Wanda the Worm
　Woman," "Lillie" 9.95

GAMERA
Aug. 1996
1 (of 4) by Dave Chipps &
　Mozart Couto 2.95
2 thru 4 . . . . @2.95

GARY GIANNI'S MONSTERMEN
Aug. 1999
1-shot. 2.95

GHOST
Comics' Greatest World
Spec. AH(c) 3.95

GHOST
1 by Eric Luke, R:Ghost. 2.50
2 AH,MfM,Arcadia Nocturne,pt.2 . . 2.50
3 Arcadia Nocturn,pt.3. . . . . 2.50
4 . . . . 2.50
5 V:Predator 2.50
6 . . . . 2.50
7 Hell Night 2.50
8 thru 20 . . . . @2.50
21 Two heroes, one room 2.50
22 "The key is forever beyond
　your reach". 2.50
23 I: The Goblins 2.50
24 X is dead. 2.50
25 double issue 3.95
26 Fairytale version 2.95
27 . . . . 2.95

Ghost #15
© Dark Horse Comics

28 CW(c),Painful Music, pt.1 . . . . . 2.95
29 CW(c),Painful Music, pt.2 . . . . . 2.95
30 CW(c),Painful Music, pt.3 . . . . . 2.95
31 CW(c),Painful Music, pt.4 . . . . . 2.95
32 A Pathless Land 2.95
33 Jade Cathedral, pt.1 . . . . 2.95
34 Jade Cathedral, pt.2 . . . . 2.95
35 Jade Cathedral, pt.3 . . . . 2.95
36 Jade Cathedral, pt.4 . . . . 2.95
Spec.#2 Immortal Coil 3.95
Spec.#3 Scary Monsters 3.95
TPB Ghost Stories 8.95
TPB Ghost: Nocturnes 9.95
TPB Exhuming Elisa 17.95

GHOST
Sept. 1998
1 CW,O:Ghost 2.95
2 CW,V:Dr.Trouvaille 2.95
3 CW,V:Silhouette 2.95
4 CW,The Devil Inside,O:pt.1 . . . . 2.95
5 CW,Stare at the Sun,O:pt.2 . . . . 2.95
6 CW,Stare at the Sun,O:pt.3 . . . . 2.95
7 CW,Shifter,pt.1,F:King Tiger 2.95
8 CW,Shifter,pt.2 . . . . 2.95
9 CW,Shifter,pt.3 . . . . 2.95
10 CW,Shifter,pt.4 . . . . 2.95
11 CW,back in Arcadia 2.95
TPB Black October 14.95
TPB Painful Music 9.95
Spec. Handbook #1 . . . . 2.95

GHOST/HELLBOY
COLLECTION
TPB MMi 4.95

GHOST AND
THE SHADOW
Spec. 1-shot 2.95

GHOST IN THE SHELL
Manga
1 Manga Style 3.95
2 Wetware Virus 3.95
3 Killer Robots 3.95
4 Rookie Cop Killed 3.95
5 F:Major Kusangi 3.95
6 . . . . 3.95
7 Kusanagi in Jail 3.95
8 final issue 3.95

TPB by Masamune Shirow 24.95

G.I. JOE
1 by Mike Barr & Tatsuya Ishida . . 1.95
2 thru 4 . . . . @2.50

GIRL CRAZY
TPB by GHe, rep.#1–#3 . . . . 9.95

GIVE ME LIBERTY
1 FM/DGb, Homes & Gardens 6.00
2 FM/DGb 5.00
3 and 4 FM/DGb . . . . @5.00
TPB 16.00

GODZILLA
(B&W) 1988
1 Japanese Manga 3.50
2 thru 6 . . . . @2.50
Spec #1 . . . . 1.50
TPB 2nd printing 17.95

GODZILLA
COLOR SPECIAL
1 AAd,R:Godzilla,V:Gekido-Jin 3.50
1a rep (1998) 2.95

GODZILLA
1995
0 RSd,The King of Monsters
 is back! 3.00
1 R:Godzill 2.50
2 V:Cybersaur 2.50
3 I:Bagorah the Bat Creature 2.50
4 V:Bagorah,Cybersaur 2.50
5 V:U.S. Army 2.50
6 thru 14 . . . . @2.50
15 "Thunder Downunder" 2.95
16 "Thunder in the Past" 2.95
TPB Past, Present, Future 17.95
TPB Godzilla: Age of Monsters . . . 17.95

GODZILLA VS. BARKLEY
1 MBn(s),JBt,DvD 3.50

GODZILLA VS.
HERO ZERO
1 Tatsuya Ishida 2.50

GRENDEL: BLACK,
WHITE, AND RED
B&W&R, Nov. 1998
1 (of 4) MWa, 48-page 4.00
2 thru 4 MWa,48-page . . . . @4.00

GRENDEL CLASSICS
1 Rep.#18–#19 Comico series 3.95

GRENDEL CYCLE
1 Grendel History 5.95

GRENDEL: DEVIL BY
THE DEED
1993
1 MWg,RRa 3.95
1 representation (1997) 3.95
TPB Devil Tales 9.95

GRENDEL: DEVIL CHILD
June 1999
1 (of 2) MWg, ... 2.95
2 conclusion 2.95

GRENDEL:
DEVIL'S LEGACY
Aug. 1996
1 (of 12) by Matt Wagner 2.75
2 thru 3 . . . . @2.75
TPB Devils and Deaths 16.95

GRENDEL: HOMECOMING
1 Babylon Crash 2.95
2 Babylon Crash pt. 2 . . . . 2.95
3 Too Dead To Die 2.95

GRENDEL: WAR CHILD
1 MWg 4.00
2 thru 9 MWg 3.00
10 MWg, final issue, dbl.size 4.00
TPB 18.95
HC signed and numbered 70.00

GRENDEL TALES:
DEVIL'S APPRENTICE
Sept. 1997
1 (of 3) 2.95
2 thru 3 . . . . @2.95

GRENDEL TALES:
DEVILS AND DEATHS
1 . . . . 2.95
2 . . . . 2.95
TPB rep. Devils and Deaths plus
 Devil's Choices 16.95

GRENDEL TALES:
DEVIL'S CHOICES
1 F:Goran 2.95
2 Marica 2.95
3 Marica vs. Goran 2.95
4 conclusion 2.95

Grendel Tales: The Devil in our
Midst #2 © Dark Horse Comics

DARK HORSE

GRENDEL TALES:
FOUR DEVILS, ONE HELL
1 MWg(c),F:Four Grendels 3.50
2 MWg(c),F:Four Grendels 3.50
3 MWg(c),F:Four Grendels 3.50
4 MWg(c),F:Four Grendels 3.50
5 MWg(c),F:Four Grendels 3.50
6 MWg(c),last issue. 3.25
TPB Rep. #1–#6. . . . . 17.95

GRENDEL TALES:
THE DEVIL IN
OUR MIDST
1 MWg(c) 3.50
2 MWg(c) 3.25
3 MWg(c) 2.95
4 & 5 . . . . @2.95
TPB series rep.. . . . . 15.95

GRENDEL TALES:
THE DEVIL MAY CARE
1 thru 6 mini-series 2.95

GRENDEL TALES:
THE DEVIL'S HAMMER
1 MWg(a&s),I:Petrus Christus 3.50
2 MWg(a&s),A:P.Christus 3.25
3 MWg(a&s),last issue. 3.25

GRIFTER AND THE MASK
Sept. 1996
1 by Seagle, Lima & Pimentel 2.50
2 . . . . 2.50

GUFF
April 1998
1-shot by Sergio Aragones, flip
    book, with Meanie Babies
    card, B&W 1.95

GUNSMITH CATS
(B&W) Manga
1 I:Rally & Mini May. 2.95
2 Revolver Freak. 2.50
3 . . . . 2.95
4 V:Bonnie and Clyde 2.95
5 V:Bonnie and Clyde 2.95
6 Hostage Situation 2.95
7 thru 10 (10 part series) 2.95
TPB Misfire rep. #7–#10 &
    Return of Gray #1–#3 . . . . . . 12.95

GUNSMITH CATS:
BAD TRIP
(B&W) June 1998
1 (of 6) by Kenichi Sonoda 2.95
2 thru 4 . . . . @2.95

GUNSMITH CATS:
BEAN BANDIT
(B&W) June 1998
1 (of 9) by Kenichi Sonoda 2.95
2 thru 8 . . . . @2.95

GUNSMITH CATS:
BONNIE & CLYDE
TPB by Kenichi Sonoda 12.95

GUNSMITH CATS:
GOLDIE VS. MISTY
(B&W) Nov. 1997
1 (of 7) by Kenichi Sonoda 2.95
2 thru 7 . . . . @2.95
TPB Goldie vs. Misty 12.95

GUNSMITH CATS:
SHADES OF GRAY
(B&W) May 1997
1 (of 5) by Kenichi Sonoda 2.95
2 thru 5 (of 5). . . . . @2.95

GUNSMITH CATS:
THE RETURN OF GRAY
(B&W) Aug. 1996
1 thru 7 by Kenichi Sonoda . . . . @2.95
TPB rep. series. 17.95

HAMMER OF
GOD: PENTATHLON
1 MiB(s),NV. 2.50

HAMMER OF GOD:
BUTCH
1 MBn 2.50
2 and 3 MBn . . . . @2.50

THE HAMMER:
UNCLE ALEX
Aug. 1998
1-shot KJo. 2.95

HAPPY BIRTHDAY
MARTHA WASHINGTON
1 Frank Miller 2.95

HARD BOILED
1 GfD 6.00
2 and 3 . . . . @5.00
TPB 14.95
HC 99.95
TPB Big Damn Hard Boiled 29.95

Hard Looks #6
© *Dark Horse Comics*

HARD LOOKS
(B&W)
1 thru 10 AVs Adaptations . . . . . @2.50
Book One. 14.95
TPB AVs. 17.95

HARLAN ELLISON'S
DREAM CORRIDOR
1 Various stories 2.95
2 Various stories 2.95
3 JBy, I Have No Mouth and I
    Must Scream & other stories . . 2.95
4 Catman 2.95
5 . . . . 2.95
6 Opposites Attract 2.95
Spec.#1 Various stories 4.95
TPB 18.95
HC, vol. 1 limited 70.00

HARLAN ELLISON'S
DREAM CORRIDOR
QUARTERLY
Aug. 1996
1 . . . . 5.95
2 . . . . 5.95

HEARTBREAKERS
1 . . . . 2.95

HEART OF EMPIRE:
THE LEGACY OF
LUTHER ARKWRIGHT
April 1999
1 (of 9) BT. 2.95
2 thru 5 . . . . @2.95

HELLBOY
Christmas Special (1997) MMi,
    48pg. 3.95
Hellboy Junior Halloween Special . . 3.95
Hellboy Junior Lurid Easter Special. 3.95
TPB The Lost Army 14.95
TPB The Chained Coffin & Others 17.95

HELLBOY:
ALMOST COLOSSUS
1 (of 2) MMi, sequel to *Wake the
    Devil* 2.95
2 (of 2) 2.95

HELLBOY:
BOX FULL OF EVIL
Aug. 1999
1 (of 2) MMi. 2.95

HELLBOY: SEEDS
OF DESTRUCTION
Legend/Dark Horse
1 JBy,MMi,AAd,V:Vampire Frog,
    BU:Monkeyman & O'Brien 3.50
2 MMi(c),JBy,AAd,BU:Monkeyman
    & O'Brien 3.00
3 MMi(c),JBy,AAd,BU:Monkeyman
    & O'Brien 3.00
4 MMi(c),JBy,AAd,BU:Monkeyman
    & O'Brien 3.00
TPB Seed of Destruction 17.95

All comics prices listed are for *Near Mint* condition.

HELLBOY:
WAKE THE DEVIL
Legend
1 (of 5) MMi 2.95
2 thru 5 . . . . @2.95
TPB Wake The Devil 17.95

HELLHOUNDS
(B&W)
1 I:Hellhounds 2.50
2 thru 6 A:Hellhounds . . . . @2.50

HELLHOUNDS:
PANZER CORPS
(B&W) 1994
1 thru 6 . . . . @2.95
TPB 14.95

HERBIE
1 JBy,reps.& new material 2.50
2 Reps.& new material 2.50

HERETIC, THE
Nov. 1996
1 (of 4) by Rich DiLeonardo, Joe
   Phillips & Dexter Vines 2.95
2 thru 4 . . . . @2.95

HERMES VS. THE
EYEBALL KID
1 thru 3 Symphony of Blood 2.95

HERO ZERO
1 First and last issue 2.50

H.P.'S ROCK CITY
TPB by Moebius 7.95

HYPERSONIC
Nov. 1997
1 (of 4) DAn,GEr 2.95
2 thru 4 . . . . @2.95

Hypersonic #1
© Dark Horse Comics

INDIANA JONES AND
THE ARMS OF GOLD
1 In South America 2.75
2 In South America 2.75
3 V:Incan Gods 2.75
4 . . . . 2.50

INDIANA JONES AND
THE FATE OF ATLANTIS
1 DBa,Search for S.Hapgood with
   2-card strip 4.00
1a 2nd printing 3.00
2 DBa,Lost Dialogue of Plato with
   2-card strip 3.00
3 Map Room of Atlantis 3.00
4 Atlantis, Last issue 3.00
TPB 13.95

INDIANA JONES AND
THE GOLDEN FLEECE
1 SnW 2.75
2 SnW 2.50

INDIANA JONES AND
THE IRON PHOENIX
1 . . . . 2.50
2 V:Nazis 2.50
3 A:Nadia Kirov 2.50
4 V:Undead 2.50

INDIANA JONES AND
THE SARGASSO PIRATES
1 thru 4 . . . . @2.50

INDIANA JONES AND
THE SHRINE OF
THE SEA DEVIL
1 . . . . 2.50

INDIANA JONES AND
THE SPEAR OF DESTINY
1 I:Spear T/Pierced Christ 2.50
2 DSp, with Henry Jones 2.50
3 Search for the Shaft 2.50

Indiana Jones and the Fate of Atlantis
#1 © Dark Horse Comics

INDIANA JONES:
THUNDER IN THE
ORIENT
1 DBa(a&s),in Tripoli 2.75
2 DBa(a&s),Muzzad Ram 2.75
3 DBa(a&s),V:Sgt.Itaki 2.75
4 DBa(a&s),In Hindu Kush 2.75
5 DBa(a&s),V:Japanese Army 2.75
6 DBa(a&s),last issue 2.75

INSTANT PIANO
1 Offbeat humor 3.95
2 . . . . 3.95
3 Various stories 3.95
4 Devil Puppet 3.95

INTRON DEPOT
Nov. 1998
TPB Intron Depot 40.00
TPB Intron Depot 2: Blades . . . 37.95

IRON HAND OF ALMURIC
(B&W)
1 Robert E. Howard adaption 2.00
2 A:Cairn,V:Yagas 2.25
3 V:Yasmeena,The Hive Queen . . . 2.00
4 Conclusion 2.25
GN 10.95

JAMES BOND 007:
QUASIMODO GAMBIT
1 I:Maximillion Quasimodo 3.95
2 V:Fanatical Soldiers 3.95
3 V:Steel 3.95

JAMES BOND 007:
SERPENT'S TOOTH
1 PG,DgM,V:Indigo 5.50
2 PG,DgM,V:Indigo 5.00
3 PG,DgM 5.25
TPB 15.95

JAMES BOND 007:
SHATTERED HELIX
1 V:Cerberus 2.50
2 V:Cerberus 2.50

JAMES BOND 007: A
SILENT ARMAGEDDON
1 V:Troy 3.25
2 V:Omega 3.25
3 V:Omega 3.25

JOHN BOLTON'S
STRANGE WINK
March 1998
1 (of 3) 2.95
2 thru 3 . . . . @2.95

JOHNNY DYNAMITE
1 . . . . 2.95
2 . . . . 2.95
3 V:Faust 2.95
4 Last issue 2.95

JONNY DEMON
1 SL(c),KBk,NV 2.75
2 SL(c),KBk,NV 2.75
2 SL(c),KBk,NV, final issue 2.50

JUNIOR CARROT PATROL
(B&W)
1	2.00
2	2.00

KELLEY JONES'
THE HAMMER
Sept. 1997
1 (of 4) KJo, horror series	2.95
2 thru 4 KJo,	@2.95
TPB	12.95

KELLEY JONES'
THE HAMMER:
THE OUTSIDER
Feb. 1999
1 (of 3) KJo	2.95
2 & 3	@2.95

KINGS OF THE NIGHT
1	2.25
2 end Mini-Series	2.25

KING TIGER/MOTORHEAD
1 (of 2) by D.G. Chichester, Karl Waller & Eric Shanower	2.95
2	2.95

KLING KLANG KLATCH
GN	11.95

LAND OF NOD
(B&W) July 1997
1 (of 4) by Jay Stephens	2.95
2 thru 4	@2.95
TPB Rockabye Book	13.95

THE LEGEND OF
MOTHER SARAH
(B&W) Manga, 1995
1 I:Mother Sarah	2.50
2 Sarah and Tsutsu	2.50
3 Firing Squad	2.50
4 F:Toki	2.50
5 Yunnel Town	2.50
6 Kill or Be Killed	2.95
7 Firing Squad	2.95
8 Conclusion	2.95
TPB The Tunnel Town	18.95

THE LEGEND OF
MOTHER SARAH:
CITY OF THE ANGELS
(B&W) Manga, Oct. 1996
1 (of 9) by Katsuhiro Otomo and Takumi Nagayasu, 48-page	3.95
1 rep. (1997)	3.95
2 thru 4, 48-page	3.95
2 thru 4 rep. (1997)	3.95
5 Tsue a victim, 48-page	3.95
6 Mother Teres questioned, 48pg.	3.95
7 put in front trenches, 48-page	3.95
8 Teres suicide run, 48-page	3.95
9 Conclusion, 32-page	2.95

THE LEGEND OF
MOTHER SARAH:
CITY OF THE CHILDREN
(B&W) Manga 1996
1 thru 7 (7 part mini-series)	@3.95

LORDS OF MISRULE
(B&W) Jan. 1997
1 by DAn, PSj	2.95
2 thru 6	@2.95
TPB The Lords of Misrule	17.95

Lost in Space #2
© Dark Horse Comics

LOST IN SPACE
April 1998
1 (of 3) sequel to film	2.95
2 thru 3 GEr(c)	@2.95
TPB rep. series, GEr(c)	7.95

THE LUCK IN THE HEAD
TPB	11.95

THE MACHINE
Comics Greatest World 1994
1 (a) The Barb Wire spin	2.50
2 V:Salvage	2.50
3 Freak Show	2.50
4 I:Skion	2.50

MADMAN
Legend 1994
1 MiA(s)	8.00
2 MiA(s)	6.00
3 MiA(s)	5.00
4 MiA(s),Muscleman	5.00
5 MiA(s),I:The Blast	4.00
6 MiA(s),A:Big Guy, Big Brain-o-rama,pt.1	12.00
7 MiA(s),FM,A:Big Guy, Big Brain-o-rama,pt.2	6.00
8 MiA(s)	4.00
9 Micro Madman	4.00
10 and 11	@4.00
12 thru 14	@5.00
15	7.00
Yearbook '95 TPB	17.95
Yearbook '96 TPB	17.95
TPB Vol. 1	17.95
TPB Vol. 2	17.95
HC Vol. 1 & Vol. 2, set	100.00

MADMAN/THE JAM
July 1998
1 (of 2) MiA	2.95
2 MiA	2.95

MADMAN COMICS
Apr. 1999
12 MiA	2.95
13 MiA	2.95
14 MiA	2.95
15 MiA	2.95
TPB Boogaloo	8.95

MADWOMAN OF THE
SACRED HEART, THE
(B&W)
TPB by Alex Jodorowsky & Moe	12.95

MAGIC: THE GATHERING
March 1998
1 (of 4) MGr,Initiation	2.95
2 MGr, Legacy	2.95
3 MGr, Crucible	2.95
4 MGr, Destiny	2.95
TPB Gerrard's Quest	11.95

MAGNUS/NEXUS
Dark Horse/Valiant
1 MBn(s), SR	3.25
2 MBn(s), SR	3.25

MAN FROM THE CIGUIRI
TPB by Moebius	7.95

MARK, THE
1 LSn, in America	1.75
2 LSn	1.95
3 LSn	1.95
4	1.95

MARK, THE
(B&W)
1	1.95
2 thru 7	@1.75

MARK, THE
1 MiB(s),V:Archon	2.75
2 MiB(s),V:Archon	2.75
3 MiB(s),V:Archon,A:Pierce	2.75
4 MiB(s),last issue	2.75

MARK, THE
1 I:The Mark	2.50
2 V:Child Killer	2.50

MARSHALL LAW: BLOOD,
SWEAT, AND FEARS
Feb. 1998
TPB	15.95

MARSHALL LAW:
CAPE FEAR
1 KON	2.95

MARSHALL LAW:
SECRET TRIBUNAL
1 KON	2.95
2 KON	2.95

MARSHALL LAW: SUPER BABYLON
1 KON.................... 4.95

MARTHA WASHINGTON GOES TO WAR
Dark Horse-Legends
1 FM(s),DGb, V:Fat Boys Corp.... 3.25
2 FM(s),DGb, V:Fat Boys Corp.... 3.25
3 FM(s),DGb, V:Fat Boys Corp.... 3.25
4 FM(s),DGb, V:Fat Boys Corp.... 3.25
5 FM(s),DBb, final issue 3.25
TPB Rep.#1–#5 .... 17.95

Martha Washington Saves the World #1 © Dark Horse Comics

MARTHA WASHINGTON SAVES THE WORLD
Dec. 1997
1 (of 3) FM,DGb 2.95
2 thru 3 ....@2.95
TPB rep.................... 12.95

MARTHA WASHINGTON STRANDED IN SPACE
1 .... 2.95

MARTIAN MYSTRY
(B&W) DH/Bonelli Mar. 1999
1 by Alfredo Castelli & Giancarlo Alessandrini, DGb(c) 92-page.. 4.95
2 thru 6 .... @4.95

MASAKAZU KATSURA'S SHADOW LADY I
Manga (B&W) Oct. 1998
Dangerous Love
1 (of 7) Masakazu Katsura....... 2.50
2 .... 2.50
3 thru 7 .... @2.50
The Eyes of a Stranger, May 1999
8 thru 11, pt.1–pt.4 .... 2.50

MASK, THE
0 .... 3.00
1 I:Lt.Kellaway Mask........... 5.00
2 V:Rapaz & Walter........... 4.00
3 O:Mask 4.00
4 final issue............... 4.00

TPB 14.95

MASK, THE
1 Movie Adaptation 3.00
2 Movie Adaptation 2.50

MASK, THE (B&W)
0 `Who's Laughing Now' 5.00

MASK/MARSHALL LAW
Feb. 1998
1 (of 2) by Pat Mills and Kevin O'Neill 2.95
2 concl.................... 2.95

The Mask Returns #1 © Dark Horse Comics

MASK RETURNS, THE
1 inc.cut-out Mask............ 5.00
2 Mask's crime spree.......... 4.00
3 .... 4.00
4 .... 4.00
TPB by John Arcudi & Doug Mahnke 14.95

MASK STRIKES BACK, THE
[Mini-series]
1 Mask Strikes Back pt.1 .... 2.50
2 Mask Strikes Back pt.2....... 2.50
3 Mask Strikes Back pt.3....... 2.50
4 DoM,Mask Strikes Back pt.4.... 2.50
5 Mask Strikes Back,pt.5....... 2.50
TPB by John Arcudi, Doug Mahnke & Keith Williams 14.95

MASK, THE: THE HUNT FOR GREEN OCTOBER
1 .... 2.50
2 Kellaway vs. Ray Tuttle 2.50
3 F:Emily Tuttle............. 2.50
4 final issue............... 2.50

MASK, THE: SOUTHERN DISCOMFORT
1 Mardi Gras time 2.50

MASK, THE: VIRTUAL SURREALITY
1-shot F: MMi,SA 2.95

MASK, THE: WORLD TOUR
1 thru 4 .... @2.50

MASK: TOYS IN THE ATTIC
Aug. 1998
1 (of 4) 2.95
2 thru 4 .... @2.95

MAXIMUM OVERLOAD
1 Masque (Mask)............ 12.00
2 thru 4 Mask............. @8.00

MAXIMUM OVERLOAD
1 thru 5 .... @3.95

MECHA
Comics Greatest World 1995
1 color...................... 1.75
2 color...................... 1.75
3 thru 6 B&W.............. @1.75
Spec.(#1) CW(c),color 2.95

MEDAL OF HONOR
1 Ace of Aces 2.50
2 .... 2.50
3 Andrew's Raid 2.50
4 Frank Miller(c) 2.50
5 final issue............... 2.50

MEDAL OF HONOR SPECIAL
1 JKu 2.50

MEZZ GALACTIC TOUR
1 MBn,MV.................. 2.50

THE MINOTAUR'S TALE
TPB by Al Davison 11.95

MR. MONSTER (B&W)
1 .... 3.50
2 .... 2.50
3 Alan Moore story 2.50
4 .... 2.50
5 I:Monster Boy............. 2.00
6 .... 2.00
7 .... 2.00
8 V:Vampires (giant size)....... 4.95

MONKEYMAN & O'BRIEN
Legend
1 by Arthur Adams............ 2.95
2 and 3 .... @2.95
Spec.................... 2.95
TPB 16.95

MOTORHEAD
Comics Greatest World 1995
1 V:Predator 2.50
2 Laughing Wolf Carnival....... 2.50
3 V:Jackboot 2.50

DARK HORSE

MOTORHEAD SPECIAL
1 JLe(c),V:Mace Blitzkrieg 3.95

[BOB BURDEN'S ORIGINAL] MYSTERYMEN
July 1999
1 . . . . 2.95
2 The Amazing Disc Man. 2.95

MYSTERY MEN
July 1999
1 (of 2) Movie adapt. 2.95

MYST: THE BOOK OF THE BLACK SHIPS
Aug. 1997
1 (of 4) from CD-Rom game 2.95
2 thru 4 . . . . @2.95

NATHAN NEVER
(B&W) DH/Bonelli Mar. 1999
1 (of 6) by Michele Medda & Nicola
 Mari, AAd(c) 102-page 4.95
2 thru 6 . . . . @4.95

NEW FRONTIER
(B&W)
1 From series in Heavy Metal 2.75
2 Who Killed Ruby Fields?. 2.75
3 Conclusion 2.75

NEW TWO FISTED TALES: VOL II
1 War stories 4.95

Next Men #11
© Dark Horse Comics

[JOHN BYRNE'S] NEXT MEN
0 Rep Next Men from Dark Horse
 Presents. 3.00
1 JBy,`Breakout'inc.trading card
 certificate 5.00
1a 2nd Printing Blue 3.00
2 JBy,World View. 4.00
3 JBy,A:Sathanis 4.00
4 JBy,A:Sathanis 4.00
5 JBy,A:Sathanis 4.00
6 JBy,O:Senator Hilltop,
 Sathanis,Project Next Men 3.50
7 JBy,I:M-4,Next Men Powers
 explained 3.50
8 JBy,I:Omega Project,A:M-4 . . . . 3.00
9 JBy,A:Omega Project,A:M-4 . . . 3.00
10 JBy,V:OmegaProject,A:M-4 . . . 3.00
11 JBy,V:OmegaProject,A:M-4 . . . 3.00
12 JBy,V:Dr.Jorgenson 3.00
13 JBy,Nathan vs Jack 3.00
14 JBy,I:Speedboy 2.75
15 JBy,in New York. 2.75
16 JBy,Jasmine's Pregnant. 2.75
17 FM(c),JBy,Arrested 2.75
18 JBy,On Trial. 2.75
TPB rep.#1-6 . . . . 16.95
TPB Parallel Collection 16.95

NEXT MEN: FAITH
Dark Horse-Legend 1993
1 JBy(a&s),V:Dr.Trogg, Blue Dahila 3.25
2 JBy,(a&s),F:Jack. 2.75
3 MMi(c),JBy(a&s),I:Hellboy. 3.50
4 JBy(a&s),Last issue 2.75
TPB Book Four. 14.95

NEXT MEN: LIES
Dark Horse-Legend 1994
1 JBy. 2.50
2 JBy. 2.50
3 JBy. 2.50
4 JBy. 2.50
Book 6 TPB Lies. 16.95

NEXT MEN: POWER
Dark Horse-Legend 1994
1 JBy(a&s) 2.75
2 JBy(a&s) 2.75
3 JBy(a&s) 2.75
4 JBY(a&s), final issue 2.50

NEXUS: ALIEN JUSTICE
1 . . . . 4.25
2 . . . . 4.25
3 . . . . 3.95
TPB 16.95

NEXUS: EXECUTIONER'S SONG
1 (of 4) by Mike Baron, Steve
 Rude & Gary Martin 2.95
2 thru 4 . . . . @2.95

NEXUS: GOD CON
April 1997
1 (of 2) by Mike Baron, Steve
 Rude & Gary Martin 2.95
2 . . . . 2.95

NEXUS: THE LIBERATOR
1 "Waking Dreams" 2.75
2 Civil War,D:Gigo. 2.75
3 Civil War contd. 2.75
4 Last issue. 2.75

NEXUS MEETS MADMAN
1-shot. 2.95

NEXUS: NIGHTMARE IN BLUE
(B&W) July 1997
1 (of 4) MBn,SR,GyM 2.95

2 thru 4 . . . . @2.95

NEXUS: THE ORIGIN
1 SR,O:Nexus 4.95

NEXUS: OUT OF THE VORTEX
1 R:Nexus. 2.50
2 Zolot & Nexus Together 2.50
3 O:Vortex. 2.50

NEXUS: THE WAGES OF SIN
1 The Client. 2.95
2 V:Munson. 2.95
3 SR(c&a) Murders in New Eden. . 2.95

NIGHT BEFORE CHRISTMASK
1 Rick Geary 9.95

NINA'S NEW AND IMPROVED ALL-TIME GREATEST
1 Anthology: Nina Paley 2.50

NINTH GLAND, THE
(B&W) March 1997
1-shot by Renee French 3.95

NOCTURNALS: WITCHING HOUR
May 1998
1-shot by Dan Brereton. 4.95

NOSFERATU
(B&W)
1 The Last Vampire 3.95
2 . . . . 2.95

OH MY GODDESS!
(B&W) Manga, 1994–95
1 by Kosuke Fujishima 5.00
2 . . . . 4.00
3 . . . . 4.00

Oh My Goddess! Vol. 4 #2
© Dark Horse Comics

DARK HORSE

4 6	3.00
5	3.00
6	3.00
TPB 1-555-Goddess	12.95

Part II, 1995

1 F:Keiichi	4.00
2	3.00
3	3.00
4	3.00
5	3.00
6	3.00
7	3.00
8	3.00
9	3.00
TPB Love Potion Number 9	12.95
TPB Sympathy for the Devil	12.95

Part III, 1996

1 Wishes are Granted	3.00
2 Love Potion Number 9	3.00
3	3.00
4	3.00
5	3.00
6 Terrible Master Urd, pt.1	3.00
7 Terrible Master Urd, pt.2	3.00
8 Terrible Master Urd, pt.3	3.00
9 Terrible Master Urd, pt.4	3.00
10 Terrible Master Urd, pt.5	3.00
11 Terrible Master Urd, pt.6	3.00

Part IV, 1996–97

1 Robot Wars	3.00
2 The Trials of Morisato, pt.1	3.00
3 The Trials of Morisato, pt.2	3.00
4 The Trials of Morisato, pt.3	3.00
5 The Queen of Vengeance	3.00
6 Mara Strikes Back, pt.1,48-page	4.00
7 Mara Strikes Back, pt.2	3.00
8 Mara Strikes Back, pt.3	@3.00

Part V, 1997–98

1 The Forgotten Promise	3.00
2 The Lunch Box of Love	3.00
3 Meet Me by the Seashore, 48pg.	4.00
4 You're So Bad, 48-page	4.00
5 Ninja Master, pt.1	3.00
6 Ninja Master, pt.2, 48-page	4.00
7 Miss Keiichi, pt.1, 48-page	4.00
7 & 8 Miss Keiichi, pt.2	3.00
9 It's Lonely at the Top	3.50
10 Fallen Angel, 48-page	4.00
11 Play the Game, 48-page	4.00
12 Sorrow, Fear Not	4.00

Part VI, 1998–99

1 Devil in Miss Urd, pt.1, 40pg	@3.50
2 Devil in Miss Urd, pt.2	3.00
3 Devil in Miss Urd, pt.3	3.00
4 Devil in Miss Urd, pt.4	3.00
5 Devil in Miss Urd, pt.5	3.00
6 SuperUrd	3.00

Part VII, 1999

1 (of 8)The Fourth Goddess, pt.1	3.00
2 The Fourth Goddess, pt.2	3.00
3 The Fourth Goddess, pt.3	3.00
4 The Fourth Goddess, pt.4,40pg	3.50
5 The Fourth Goddess, pt.5,40pg	3.50

OKTANE

1 R:Oktane	2.50
2 V:God Zero	2.50
3 V:God Zero	2.50
4 conclusion	2.50

ONE BAD RAT

1 BT	2.95
2 thru 4	@2.95

ORION
(B&W) Manga

1 SF by Masamune Shirow	2.50

2 F:Yamata Empire	2.95
3 thru 6	@2.95
TPB	15.95

OTIS GOES HOLLYWOOD
(B&W) April 1997

1 (of 2) by Bob Fingerman	2.95
2	2.95

OUTLANDERS
(B&W) Manga

1	3.00
2	2.50
3 thru 7	@2.00
8 thru 20	@2.25
21 Operation Phoenix	2.25
22 thru 24	@2.50
25 thru 29 with 2-card strip	@2.50
30	2.50
31 Tetsua dying	2.50
32 D:The Emperor	2.50
33 Story finale	2.50
#0 The Key of Graciale	2.75
TPB Vol. 1 by Johji Manabe	13.95
TPB Vol. 1 2nd edition	13.95
TPB Vol. 2	13.95
TPB Vol. 2 2nd edition	13.95
TPB Vol. 3	13.95
TPB Vol. 4	12.95
TPB Vol. 5	14.95
TPB Vol. 6	14.95
TPB Vol. 7	14.95

OUTLANDERS: EPILOGUE
(B&W)

1	2.75

OUT OF THE VORTEX
Comics' Greatest World 1993

1 B:JOs(s),V:Seekers	2.25
2 MMi(c),DaW,A:Seekers	2.25
3 WS(c),E:JOs(s),DaW,A:Seeker, C:Hero Zero	2.25
4 DaW,A:Catalyst	2.25
5 V:Destroyers,A:Grace	2.25
6 V:Destroyers,A:Hero Zero	2.25
7 AAd(c),DaW,V:Destroyers, A:Mecha	2.25
8 DaW,A:Motorhead	2.25
9 DaW,V:Motorhead	2.25

Out of the Vortex #1
© Dark Horse Comics

10 MZ(c), A:Division 13	2.25
11 V:Reaver Swarm	2.50
12 Final issue	2.50

OZ
by Eric Shanower

TPB The Blue Witch of Oz	9.95
TPB The Forgotten Forest of Oz	8.95
TPB The Ice King of Oz	8.95
TPB The Secret Island of Oz	8.95

PETE & MOE VISIT PROFESSOR SWIZZLE'S ROBOTS

HC	14.95

PI: THE BOOK OF ANTS
Artisan Entertainment Sept. 1998

1-shot, movie adapt.	2.95

PREDATOR

1 CW,Mini Series	6.00
1a 2ndPrinting	3.00
1b 3rdPrinting	2.50
2 CW	5.00
2a 2ndPrinting	3.00
3 CW	4.00
3a 2ndPrinting	2.50
4 CW	3.00
4a 2ndPrinting	2.50

PREDATOR: BAD BLOOD

1 CW,I:John Pulnick	2.75
2 CW,V:Predator	2.75
3 CW,V:Predator,C.I.A.	2.75
4 Last issue	2.50

PREDATOR: BIG GAME

1 Corp.Nakai Meets Predator	3.50
2 Army Base Destroyed, with 2-card strip	3.50
3 Corp.Nakai Arrested, with 2-card strip	3.50
4 Nakai vs. Predator	3.50
TPB rep. #1–#4	13.95
TPB rep. #1–#4, 2nd edition	14.95

Predator: Big Game #2
© Dark Horse Comics

DARK HORSE

PREDATOR: BLOODY SANDS OF TIME
1 DBa,CW,Predator in WWI 3.50
2 DBa,CW, WWII cont'd. 3.25

PREDATOR: CAPTIVE
April 1998
1-shot 2.95

PREDATOR: COLD WAR
1 Predator in Siberia 3.50
2 U.S. Elite Squad in Siberia . . . 3.25
3 U.S. vs. USSR commandos . . . 3.25
4 U.S. vs. USSR in Siberia 3.00
TPB 13.95
TPB 2nd printing. 13.95

PREDATOR: CONCRETE JUNGLE
TPB 14.95

PREDATOR: DARK RIVER
1 thru 4 by Verheiden,RoR,RM. . @2.95

PREDATOR: HELL & HOT WATER
1 thru 3 MSh, GC & GWt . . . . . . @2.95
TPB rep.. 9.95

PREDATOR: HELL COME A WALKIN'
Feb. 1998
1 (of 2) by Nancy Collins,
  Dean Ormston 2.95
2 concl. 2.95

PREDATOR: HOMEWORLD
Mar. 1999
1 (of 4) 2.95
2 thru 4 . . . . @2.95

PREDATOR: INVADERS FROM THE FOURTH DIMENSION
1 . . . . 3.95

PREDATOR JUNGLE TALES
1 Rite of Passage 2.95

PREDATOR: KINDRED
1 . . . . 2.50
2 thru 4 . . . . @2.95
TPB Predator: Kindred 14.95

PREDATOR: NEMESIS
Dec. 1997
1 (of 2) TTg(c). 2.95
2 . . . . 2.95

PREDATOR: PRIMAL
1997
1 (of 2) Kevin J. Anderson(s),
  ScK,Low. 2.95
2 (of 2) 2.95

PREDATOR: RACE WAR
0 F:Serial Killer 2.75
1 V:Serial Killer 2.75
2 D:Serial Killer 2.75
3 in Prison. 2.75
4 Last Issue. 2.75
TPB Race War, serie rep. 17.95

PREDATOR: STRANGE ROUX
1-shot. 2.95

PREDATOR 2
1 DBy, Movie Adapt Pt1 . . . . 3.50
2 MBr, Movie Adapt. Pt2 with
  2-card strip. 3.00

PREDATOR VS. JUDGE DREDD
Sept. 1997
1 (of 3) by John Wagner and
  Enrique Alcatena 2.50
2 thru 3 . . . . @2.50
TPB Predator vs. Judge Dredd . . . 8.95

PREDATOR VS. MAGNUS ROBOT FIGHTER
Valiant/Dark Horse 1992
1 LW,A:Tekla 3.00
1a Platinum Ed. 5.00
1b Gold Ed. 3.00
2 LW,Magnus Vs. Predator, with
  2-card strip. 3.00
TPB Rep. #1–#2. . . . . 7.95

PREDATOR: XENOGENESIS
Aug. 1999
1 (of 4) 2.95

PRIMAL
1 Contd.from Primal:from the
  Cradle to the Grave 2.95
2 A:TJ Cyrus 2.50

PRIMAL FROM THE CRADLE TO THE GRAVE
GN 9.95

PROPELLER MAN
1 I:Propeller Man. 2.95
2 O:Propeller Man,w/2 card strip . 2.95
3 V:Manipulator 2.95
4 V:State Police,w/2 card strip . . . 2.95
5 V:Manipulator 2.95
6 V:Thing, w/2 card strip 2.95
7 . . . . 2.95
8 Last issue,w/2 card strip 2.95

PUMPKINHEAD
1 Based on the movie 2.50

RACE OF SCORPIONS
(B&W)
1 A:Argos,Dito,Alma,Ka 2.25

RACE OF SCORPIONS
Book 1 short stories 5.00
Book 2 . . . . 4.95
Book 3 . . . . 2.50
Book 4 Final issue 2.50

Rack & Pain #2
© Dark Horse Comics

RACK & PAIN
1 GCa(c),I:Rack,Pain. 2.50
2 GCa(c),V:Web 2.50
3 GCa(c),V:Web 2.50
4 GCa(c),Final Issue 2.50

RASCALS IN PARADISE
1 I:Spicy Sanders 3.95
2 . . . . 3.95
3 last issue 3.95
TPB Rep.#1–#3 . . . . 16.95

REAL ADVENTURES OF JONNY QUEST, THE
Sept. 1996
1 . . . . 2.95
3 thru 12 . . . . @2.95

REBEL SWORD
(B&W) Manga
1 by Yoshikazu Yashiko 2.50
2 . . . . 2.50
3 . . . . 2.50
4 V:Ruken 2.50
5 Choice of Jiro 2.50
6 R:Ruken. 2.50

REDBLADE
1 V:Demons 2.50
2 V:Tull 2.50
3 Last Issue. 2.50

RED ROCKET 7
Aug. 1997
1 (of 7) MiA 3.95
2 thru 7 . . . . @3.95
TPB rep. series, 208 pg 29.95

RING OF ROSES
(B&W)
1 Alternate world,1991 . . . . 2.50
2 Plague in London 2.50
3 Plague cont.A:Secret Brother-
  hood of the Rosy Cross 2.50
4 Conclusion 2.50

RIO AT BAY
1 F:Doug Wildey art. 2.95

All comics prices listed are for *Near Mint* condition.

2 F:Doug Wildey art. 2.95
TPB 6.95

ROACHMILL
(B&W)
1 thru 8 . . . . @3.50
9 and 10 . . . . @2.00

ROBOCOP: MORTAL
COILS
1 V:Gangs. 2.75
2 V:Gangs. 2.75
3 V:Coffin,V:Gangs 2.75

ROBOCOP VERSUS
TERMINATOR
1 FM(s),WS,w/Robocop cut-out. . . 3.50
2 FM(s),WS,w/Terminator cut-out. . 3.00
3 FM(s),WS,w/cut-out 3.00
4 FM(s),WS,Conclusion. 3.00

ROBOCOP: PRIME
SUSPECT
1 Robocop framed. 2.75
2 thru 4 V:ZED-309s . . . . @2.50
Collected 13.95

ROBOCOP: ROULETTE
1 V:ED-309s 2.75
2 I:Philo Drut. 2.75
3 V:Stealthbot 2.75
4 last issue 2.75

ROBOCOP 3
1 B:StG(s),Movie Adapt. 2.75
2 V:Aliens,OCP 2.75
3 HNg,ANi(i) 2.75

ROCCO VARGAS
HC by Daniel Torres 30.00

ROCKETEER ADVENTURE
MAGAZINE
1988–95
1 and 2 . . . . @4.00
3 . . . . 2.95
TPB Cliff's New York Adventure

Rocketeer Adventure Magazine #3
© Dark Horse Comics

by Dave Stevens 9.95

THE SAFEST PLACE
SC, SD. 2.50

SCATTERBRAIN
June 1998
1 (of 4) MMi, ... 2.95
2 thru 4 . . . . @2.95

SECRET OF
THE SALAMANDER
(B&W)
1 Jacquestardi, rep 2.95

SERGIO ARAGONES'
BOOGEYMAN
(B&W) June 1998
1 (of 4) 2.95
2 thru 4 . . . . @2.95
TPB, rep. 9.95

SERGIO ARAGONES'
DAY OF THE DEAD
Oct. 1998
1-shot. 2.95

SERGIO ARAGONES'
GROO
Jan.–April 1998
1 (of 4) 2.95
2 thru 4 . . . . @2.95
TPB The Most Intelligent Man
   in the World 9.95
TPB Houndbook. 9.95

SERGIO ARAGONES'
GROO & RUFFERTO
Dec. 1998
1 (of 4) 2.95
2 thru 4 . . . . @2.95

SERGIO ARAGONES'
LOUDER THAN WORDS
(B&W) July–Dec. 1997
1 (of 6) SA. 2.95
2 thru 6 . . . . @2.95
TPB rep. series. 12.95

SEX WARRIORS
1 I:Dakini. 2.50
2 V:Steroids. 2.50

THE SHADOW
1 MK. 2.75
2 MK. 2.50

THE SHADOW AND
DOC SAVAGE
1 . . . . 2.95
2 The Shrieking Skeletons 2.95

THE SHADOW:
HELL'S HEAT WAVE
1 Racial War 2.95
2 MK,V:Ghost 2.95
3 Final issue 2.95

The Shadow #2
© Dark Horse Comics

THE SHADOW: IN THE
COILS OF LEVIATHAN
1 MK,V:Monster. 3.25
2 MK. 3.25
3 MK,w/ GfD poster. 3.25
4 MK,Final issue 3.25
TPB, reprints #1–#4 . . . . 13.95

THE SHADOW AND
THE MYSTERIOUS 3
1 Three stories 2.95

SHADOW EMPIRE:
FAITH CONQURES
1 CsM. 2.95
2 CsM,V:Vaylen. 2.95
3 CsM. 2.95
4 CsM, final issue 2.95

SIGNAL TO NOISE
April 1999
TPB NGa,DMc 14.95

SIN CITY: A DAME
TO KILL FOR
Dark Horse-Legend (B&W)
1 FM(a&s),I:Dwight,Ava. 5.00
1a 2nd printing 3.00
2 FM(a&s),A:Ava. 4.00
2a 2nd printing 2.50
3 FM(a&s),D:Ava's Husband 4.00
3a 2nd printing 2.95
4 FM(a&s) 4.00
5 FM(a&s) 4.00
6 FM(a&s),Final issue 4.00
TPB rep. #1–#6, new pages 15.00
HC rep. #1–#6, new pages 25.00
HC signed, limited 90.00

SIN CITY:
A SMALL KILLING
Dark Horse-Legend
1 GN. 14.00

All comics prices listed are for *Near Mint* condition.   **CVA Page 461**

SIN CITY: FAMILY VALUES
(B&W) 1997
GN 128pg by Frank Miller. 10.00

SIN CITY: HELL AND BACK
July 1999
1 (of 9) FM 2.95
2 . . . . 2.95

SIN CITY: LOST, LONELY, AND LETHAL
Dark Horse–Legend
1-shot, two color. 2.95

SIN CITY: JUST ANOTHER SATURDAY NIGHT
Dark Horse/Wizard
1/2 (Wizard, 24-page) 2.50
1/2 rep., Dark Horse, new (c). 2.50

SIN CITY: SEX AND VIOLENCE
(B&W)
1-shot by Frank Miller. 3.00

SIN CITY: SILENT NIGHT
Dark Horse-Legend
(B&W) 1995
1-Shot. 2.95

SIN CITY: THAT YELLOW BASTARD
(B&W)
1 F.Miller. 4.00
2 . . . . 3.00
3 thru 6 . . . . @3.00
TPB by Frank Miller 15.00
HC. 25.00
HC limited 90.00

SIN CITY: THE BABE WORE RED
Dark Horse-Legend 1994
1 PM. 3.50

SIN CITY: THE BABE WORE RED AND OTHER STORIES
(B&W) 1996
1-shot, some nudity. 3.00

SIN CITY: THE BIG FAT KILL
Dark Horse-Legend 1994
1 FM. 4.00
2 FM. 3.50
3 FM, Dump the Stiffs 3.50
4 FM, Town Without Pity 3.50
5 FM, final issue 3.50
TPB 15.00
HC 25.00

SOCK MONKEY
(B&W) Sept. 1998
1 by Tony Millionaire 2.95
2 F:Uncle Gabby 2.95
VOLUME 2
1 (of 2) 2.95
2 . . . . 2.95

SOLO
1 and 2 . . . . @.50

SPACEHAWK
(B&W)
1 BW reps. 2.25
2 thru 4 BW . . . . @2.00
5 BW. 2.50

SPACE USAGI
1 thru 3 Stan Sakai . . . . @2.95
TPB 16.95

SPECIES
1 Alien Human Hybrid 2.50
2 thru 4 SIL . . . . @2.50

Species: Human Race #4
© Dark Horse Comics

SPECIES: HUMAN RACE
1 PhH 2.95
2 . . . . 2.95
3 SBi 2.95
4 (of 4) 2.95
TPB 11.95

SPIRIT OF WONDER
(B&W) Manga
1 thru 5 by Kenji Tsuruia . . . . . . @2.95
TPB 12.95

STAN SHAW'S BEAUTY & THE BEAST
1 Based on the book 4.95

STARSTRUCK: THE EXPANDING UNIVERSE
(B&W)
1 Pt1 . . . . 2.95
2 Pt2, with 2-card strip. 2.95

STAR WARS
Dec. 1998
1 F:Ki-Adi-Mundi 2.50
2 F:Ki-Adi-Mundi 2.50
3 F:Ki-Adi-Mundi 2.50
4 F:Sylvn. 2.50
5 V:Ephant Mon. 2.50
6 V:Jabba the Hutt. 2.50
7 Outlander 2.50
8 A:Jabba the Hutt. 2.50
9 A:Tusken Raiders. 2.50

STAR WARS: A NEW HOPE— SPECIAL EDITION
Jan.–April 1997
1 EB, AW 6.00
2 thru 4 . . . . @5.00
TPB Rep. #1–#4 Hildebrandt(c) . . . 9.95
Spec. Edition boxed set 30.00

STAR WARS: A NEW HOPE
(B&W) Manga July 1998
1 (of 4) by Tamaki Hisao, 96pg. . . . 9.95
2 thru 4 . . . . @9.95

STAR WARS: THE EMPIRE STRIKES BACK
(B&W) Manga Dec. 1998
1 (of 4) by Toshiki Dudo, 96pg. . . . 9.95
2 thru 4 . . . . @9.95

STAR WARS: THE RETURN OF THE JEDI
(B&W) Manga June 1999
1 (of 4) by Shin-ichi Hiromoto,
96pg. 9.95
2 thru 4 . . . . @9.95

STAR WARS: BATTLE OF THE BOUNTY HUNTERS
July 1996
Pop-up Comic. 17.95

STAR WARS: BOBA FETT—
1-shot Bounty on Bar-Kooda,48pg . 9.00
1-shot When the Fat Lady Swings . 7.00
1-shot Murder Most Foul. 7.00
1-shot Twin Engins of Destruction . 6.00
TPB Death, Lies & Treachery 12.95

STAR WARS: BOBA FETT— ENEMY OF THE EMPIRE
Jan. 1999
1 (of 4) V:Dark Lord of the Sith . . . 3.00
2 thru 4 IG. . . . . @3.00

STAR WARS: BOUNTY HUNTERS —AURRA SING
Aug. 1999
1-shot TT 3.00

Star Wars: Crimson Empire II #4
© Dark Horse Comics

STAR WARS: CRIMSON EMPIRE
Dec. 1997–May 1998

1 PG,CR,DvD(c)	7.00
2 thru 5 PG,CR,DvD(c)	@4.00
TPB Crimson Empire	17.95

VOLUME II: COUNCIL OF BLOOD

1 MRi,RSd,PG,DvD(c)	3.00
2 thru 6 RSd,PG,DvD(c)	@3.00

STAR WARS: DARK EMPIRE

1 CK,Destiny of a Jedi	18.00
1a 2nd Printing	5.00
1b Gold Ed.	15.00
2 CK,Destroyer of worlds, very low print run	22.00
2a 2nd Printing	5.00
2b Gold Ed.	15.00
3 CK,V:The Emperor	10.00
3a 2nd printing	4.00
3b Gold Ed.	10.00
4 CK,V:The Emperor	7.00
4a Gold Ed.	7.00
5 CK,V:The Emperor	7.00
5a Gold Ed.	10.00
6 CK,V:Emperor,last issue	5.00
6a Gold Ed.	9.00
Gold editions, foil logo set	75.00
Platinum editions, embossed set.	135.00
TPB Preview 32pg.	1.00
TPB rep.#1–#6	19.95
TPB CK & Tom Veitch 2nd ed.	17.95
HC leather bound	125.00

STAR WARS DARK EMPIRE II

1 2nd chapter	6.00
2 F:Boba Fett	5.00
3 V:Darksiders	5.00
4 Luke Vs. Darksiders	5.00
5 Creatures	5.00
6 CK,DvD(c), save the twins	5.00
Platinum editions, set	50.00
TPB CK & Tom Veitch rep.#1–#6	17.95
HC Leather bound	100.00

STAR WARS: DARK FORCE RISING
May–Oct. 1997

1 thru 6 (of 6) MBn,TyD,KN	@6.00
TPB series rep	17.95

STAR WARS: DARK FORCES— JEDI KNIGHT
Sept. 1998

HC by William C. Dietz & Dave Dorman	24.95
TPB	14.95

STAR WARS: DARK FORCES— REBEL AGENT
March 1998

HC by William C. Dietz & Dean Williams	24.95
TPB	14.95

STAR WARS: DARK FORCES— SOLDIER FOR THE EMPIRE

HC by William C. Dietz and Dean Williams	24.95
TPB	14.95

STAR WARS: DROIDS
April–Sept. 1994

1 F:C-3PO,R2-D2	4.00
2 V:Thieves	3.00
3 on the Hosk moon	3.00
4	3.00
5 A meeting	2.50
6 final issue	2.50
Spec.#1 I:Olag Greck	2.50
TPB The Kalarba Adventures, rep.	17.95

2nd Series

1 Deputized Droids	3.00
2 Marooned on Nar Shaddaa	2.50
3 C-3PO to the Rescue	2.50
4	2.50
5 Caretaker virus	2.50

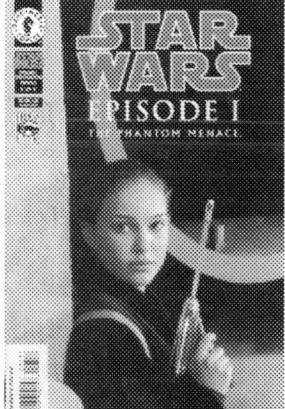

Star Wars Episode 1, #4
© Dark Horse Comics

6 Revolution	2.50
7 & 8	@2.50
TPB Droids—Rebellion, rep.	17.95

STAR WARS: EMPIRE'S END
Oct.–Nov. 1995

1 R:Emperor Palpatine	3.50
2 conclusion	3.50
TPB rep.	6.00

STAR WARS: EPISODE I THE PHANTOM MENACE
Apr. 1999

1 RdM,AW	3.00
1a newsstand edition, photo (c)	3.00
2 RdM,AW	3.00
2a newsstand edition, photo (c)	3.00
3 RdM,AW	3.00
3a newsstand edition, photo (c)	3.00
4 RdM,AW	3.00
4a newsstand edition, photo (c)	3.00
1 RdM,AW	3.00
1a newsstand edition, photo (c)	3.00
GN The Phantom Menace RdM,AW	12.95
Spec. Anakin Skywalker	3.00
Spec. Anakin Skywalker, newsstand	3.00
Spec. Obi-Wan Kenobi	3.00
Spec. Obi-Wan Kenobi, newsstand	3.00
Spec. Queen Amidala	3.00
Spec. Qui-Gon Jinn	3.00

STAR WARS HANDBOOK
July 1998

1 X-Wing Rogue Squadron	3.50
2 Crimson Empire	3.00

STAR WARS: HEIR TO THE EMPIRE
Oct. 1995–April 1996

1 I:Grand Admiral Thrawn	4.00
2 thru 6	3.50
TPB from novel by Timothy Zahn	19.95
HC signed, slipcase	100.00

STAR WARS: JABBA THE HUTT—
1995–1996

1-shot The Garr Suppoon Hit	3.00
1-shot Hunger of Princess Nampi	3.00
1-shot The Dynasty Trap	3.00
1-shot Betrayal	3.00
1-shot The Jabba Tape	3.00

STAR WARS: JEDI ACADEMY LEVIATHAN
Oct. 1998

1 (of 4) by Kevin J. Anderson	3.00
2 thru 4	@3.00

STAR WARS: THE LAST COMMAND
Nov. 1997–July 1998

1 thru 6 MBn	@3.50
TPB, rep.	17.95

All comics prices listed are for *Near Mint* condition.

Star Wars: Mara Jade #3
© Dark Horse Comics

STAR WARS: MARA JADE— BY THE EMPEROR'S HAND
Aug. 1998
1 (of 6) by Timothy Zahn 3.50
2 thru 6 . . . . @3.00
TPB rep. 15.95

STAR WARS: THE PROTOCOL OFFENSIVE
Sept. 1997
1-shot written by Anthony Daniels. . 4.95

STAR WARS: RETURN OF THE JEDI—SPECIAL EDITION
TPB Hildebrandt(c). 9.95

STAR WARS: RIVER OF CHAOS
May–Nov. 1995
1 LSi,JBr,Emperor sends spies . . . 3.00
2 Imperial in Allies Clothing 3.00
3 . . . . 3.00
4 F:Ranulf 3.00

STAR WARS: SHADOWS OF THE EMPIRE
1 (of 6) by John Wagner, Kilian
  Plunkett & P. Craig Russell. . . . 3.50
2 thru 6 . . . . @3.50
TPB 17.95
HC 80.00

STAR WARS: SHADOWS OF THE EMPIRE — EVOLUTION
Feb.–June 1998
1 thru 5 . . . . @3.50

STAR WARS: SHADOW STALKER
Nov. 1997
1-shot from Galaxy Mag. 3.50

STAR WARS: SPLINTER OF THE MIND'S EYE
Dec. 1995–June 1996
1 thru 4 A.D.Foster novel adapt.. @3.50
TPB 14.95

STAR WARS: TALES FROM MOS EISLEY
1-shot, from Star Wars Galaxy
  Mag. #2–#4 . . . . 3.50

STAR WARS: TALES OFTHE JEDI
1 RV,I:Ulic Qel-Droma 6.00
2 RV,A:Ulic Qel-Droma 5.00
3 RV,D:Andur 4.00
4 RV,A:Jabba the Hut 3.50
5 RV,last issue. 3.50
TPB 14.95
TPB 2nd printing. 14.95

STAR WARS: TALES OF THE JEDI: DARK LORDS OF THE SITH
Oct. 1994–March 1995
1 Bagged with card 3.00
2 . . . . 2.50
3 Krath Attack 2.50
4 F:Exar Kun 2.50
5 V:TehKrath 2.50
6 Final battle 2.50
TPB 17.95

STAR WARS: TALES OF THE JEDI: THE FREEDON NADD UPRISING
Aug.–Sept. 1997
1 and 2 . . . . @2.75
2 . . . . 2.50
TPB series rep. 5.95

STAR WARS: TALES OF THE JEDI: THE SITH WAR
Aug. 1995–Jan. 1996
1 F:Exar Kun 3.00
2 F:Ulic Oel-Droma 2.50
3 F:Exar Kun 2.50
4 thru 6 (6 part mini-series) . . . . @2.50
TPB 17.95

STAR WARS: TALES OF THE JEDI—THE FALL OF THE SITH EMPIRE
June–Oct. 1997
1 (of 5) 3.50
2 thru 5 . . . . @3.00

STAR WARS: TALES OF THE JEDI—THE GOLDEN AGE OF THE SITH
Oct. 1996–Feb. 1997
1 thru 5 . . . . @3.50
TPB 16.95

STAR WARS: TALES OF THE JEDI— THE REDEMPTION OF ULIC QEL-DROMA
July 1998
1 (of 5) by Kevin J. Anderson 3.50
2 thru 5 . . . . @3.50

STAR WARS: THE EMPIRE STRIKES BACK
TPB Hildebrandt(c). 10.00

STAR WARS: VADER'S QUEST
Feb. 1999
1 (of 4) DGb,AMK 3.00
2 thru 4 . . . . @3.00

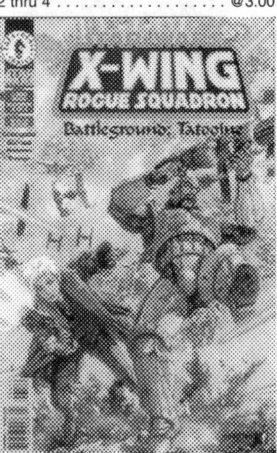

Star Wars: X-Wing Rogue Squadron
#12 © Dark Horse Comics

STAR WARS: X-WING ROGUE SQUADRON
July 1995
The Rebel Opposition
1 F:Wedge Antilles 6.00
2 . . . . 3.50
3 F:Tycho Clehu 3.50
4 F:Tycho Clehu 3.50
½ Wizard limited exclusive 6.00
The Phantom Affair
5 thru 8 . . . . @3.50
TPB rep. 12.95
Battleground Tatooine
9 thru 12 . . . . @3.50
TPB rep. 12.95
The Warrior Princess
13 thru 16 . . . . @3.50
TPB rep. 13.95
Requiem for a Rogue
17 thru 20 . . . . @3.50
TPB rep. 12.95
In the Empire's Service
21 thru 24 . . . . @3.50
TPB rep. 12.95
Making of Baron Fell
25 . . . . 5.00
Family Ties
26 thru 27 . . . . @3.50
Masquerade
28 thru 31 . . . . @3.50
Mandatory Retirement

DARK HORSE

32 thru 35 . . . . @3.50
TPB Blood and Honor. 12.95

STARSHIP TROOPERS
Sept. 1997
1 (of 2) movie adaptation. 3.00
2 movie adaptation, concl. 3.00
TPB rep., inc. Brute Creations,
    Insect Touch, & movie 152 pg. 14.95

Starship Troopers: Brute Creations
© Dark Horse Comics

STARSHIP TROOPERS:
BRUTE CREATIONS
1997
1-shot RbC. 3.00

STARSHIP TROOPERS:
DOMINANT SPECIES
Aug. 1998
1 (of 4) 3.00
2 JoB,RyE. 3.00
3 & 4 . . . . @3.00

STARSHIP TROOPERS:
INSECT TOUCH
1 by Warren Ellis & Paolo Parente . 3.00
2 and 3 (of 3) . . . . @3.00

SUBHUMAN
Nov. 1998
1 (of 4) MSh 3.00
2 thru 4 MSh . . . . @3.00

SUPERMAN/MADMAN
HULLABALOO
June–Aug. 1997
1 (of 3) MiA 3.00
2 and 3 (of 3) . . . . @3.00

SUPERMAN VS. ALIENS
DC/Dark Horse
1 DJu,KN 6.00
2 V:Queen Alien 5.00
TPB 14.95

TALE OF ONE BAD RAT
1 BT 3.00

2 thru 4 . . . . 3.00
TPB Rep.#1–#4 . . . . 14.95

TALES OF
ORDINARY MADNESS
(B&W)
1 JBo(c),Paranoid 3.00
2 JBo(c),Mood. 2.50
3 JBo(c),A Little Bit of Neurosis . . . 2.50

TALES TO OFFEND
July 1997
1-shot by Frank Miller. 2.95

TANK GIRL
(B&W) 1991
1 Rep. from U.K.Deadline Mag.
    with 2-card strip 4.50
2 V:Indiana Potato Jones. 4.00
3 On the Run. 4.00
4 . . . . 4.00
TPB colorized. 14.95
[2nd Series]
1 . . . . 3.50
2 . . . . 3.00
3 and 4 . . . . @3.00

TANK GIRL
1 and 2 . . . . @3.00

TARZAN/JOHN CARTER:
WARLORDS OF MARS
1 thru 4 E.R.Burroughs adapt. . . @2.50

TARZAN VS. PREDATOR
AT THE EARTH'S CORE
1 Tarzan vs. Predator 2.50
2 V:Predator 2.50
3 Tarzan on the Hunt. 2.50
4 . . . . 2.50
TPB series rep.. . . . . 12.95

TERMINAL POINT
1 . . . . 2.50
2 . . . . 2.50

TERMINATOR
1 CW,Tempest. 4.00
2 CW,Tempest. 3.00
3 CW. 3.00
4 CW, conclusion. 3.00

TERMINATOR
1-shot MW,3-D const(c2,
    pop-up inside 5.00
Spec. AlG,GyD,GeD(1998) 2.95

TERMINATOR, THE
Sept. 1998
1 AlG,StP, ... 2.95
2 F:Sarah Connor 2.95
3 F:Killerman. 2.95
4 F:D-800L & D-810X 2.95
TPB Death Valley 14.95

TERMINATOR:
END GAME
1 JG,Final *Terminator* series 3.00
2 JG,Cont.last Term.story 2.75
3 JG, Concl. 2.75
TPB Endgame 9.95

The Terminator #1
© Dark Horse Comics

TERMINATOR:
ENEMY WITHIN
1 cont. from Sec.Objectives 4.00
2 C890.L.threat contd. 3.00
3 Secrets of Cyberdyne 3.00
4 Conclusion 3.00
SC rep #1–#4 . . . . 13.95

TERMINATOR: HUNTERS
& KILLERS
1 V:Russians. 3.00
2 V:Russians. 2.75
3 V:Russians. 2.75

TERMINATOR:
SECONDARY
OBJECTIVES
1 cont. 1st DH mini-series 4.00
2 PG,A:New Female Terminator. . . 3.00
3 PG,Terminators in L.A.&Mexico . 3.00
4 PG,Terminator vs Terminator
    concl. 3.00

TERRITORY, THE
Jan. 1999
1 (of 4) JaD,DvL,F:Ishmael 2.95
2 thru 4 . . . . @2.95

TEX AVERY'S DROOPY
1 Dr. Droopenstein 2.50
2 & 3 . . . . @2.50

TEX AVERY'S
SCREWBALL SQUIRREL
1 I:Screwball Squirrel. 2.50
2 Cleaning House 2.50
3 School of Hard Rocks. 2.50

THING, THE
1 JHi, Movie adaptation 4.00
2 JHi, Movie adaptation 3.50

THE THING: COLD FEAR
1 R:Thing. 3.00
2 . . . . 2.75

DARK HORSE

THING FROM ANOTHER WORLD: CLIMATE OF FEAR
1 Argentinian Military Base
(Bahiathetis)............... 2.75
2 Thing on Base 2.75
3 Thing/takeover 2.75
4 Conclusion.................. 2.75
TPB 15.95

THING FROM ANOTHER WORLD: ETERNAL VOWS
1 PG,I:Sgt. Rowan............. 2.75
2 PG........................ 2.75
3 PG,in New Zealand 2.75
4 PG,Last issue.............. 2.75

THIRTEEN O'CLOCK
(B&W)
1 Mr.Murmer,from Deadline USA .. 2.95

3 X 3 EYES
(B&W) Manga
1 I:Pai,Yakumo, (Manga)....... 2.95
2 & 3 (5-part mini-series) ...... @2.95
TPB Curse of the Gesu, by Yuzo
Takada.................. 12.95
TPB House of Demons........ 12.95

300
May 1998
1 (of 5) FM & Lynn Varley 2.95
2 thru 5 F:Spartans .... @2.95

TIME COP
1 Movie Adaptation 2.75
2 Movie Adaptation 2.50

TITAN
Spec.#1 BS(c),I:Inhibitors 4.25

TONGUE*LASH
Aug. 1996
1 by Randy and Jean-Marc
Lofficier & Dave Taylor 2.95
2 .... 2.95
VOLUME II
1 (of 2) 2.95
2 .... 2.95

TOO MUCH COFFEE MAN
(B&W) July 1997
1-shot by Shannon Wheeler...... 2.95
TPB Guide for the Perplexed 10.95
HC lim. Guide for the Perplexed .. 50.00

TREKKER
(B&W)
1 thru 4 .... @1.50
5 thru 7 .... @1.75
8 O:Trekker................. 1.50
9 .... 1.50

TREKKER
1 .... 2.95

TRIPLE X
(B&W)
TPB by Arnold & Jacob Pander .. 24.95

The Two Faces of Tomorrow #2
© Dark Horse Comics

TWO FACES OF TOMORROW, THE
(B&W) Manga 1997–98
1 (of 13) from James P. Hogan
novel, by Yukinobu Hoshino ... 2.95
2 thru 4 .... @2.95
5 thru 13 .... @3.95

TWO FISTED TALES
Spec. WW,WiS............... 4.95

2112
GN JBy,A:Next Men 2.00
2nd Printing 5.00
TPB GNv, JBy,A:Next Men 10.00
2nd & 3rd printing............. 9.95

[ANDREW VACHSS'] UNDERGROUND
(B&W)
1 AVs(s) 4.25
2 thru 4 AVs(s).............. @3.95

UNIVERSAL MONSTERS
1 AAd,Creature From The
Black Lagoon............. 5.50
2 The Mummy............... 5.50

USAGI YOJIMBO
(B&W)
1 by Stan Sakai 2.95
2 thru 9.................... 2.95
10 with Sergio Aragones........ 2.95
11 "The Lord of Owls".......... 2.95
12 "Vampire Cat of the Geishu".... 2.95
13 thru 22 "Grasscutter," pt.1
thru pt. #10............. 2.95
23 My Father's Sword.......... 2.95
24 The Demon Flute........... 2.95
25 Momo-Usagi-Taro.......... 2.95
26 The Hairpin Murders,pt.1...... 2.95
27 The Hairpin Murders,pt.2...... 2.95
28 Courtesan conspiracy,pt.1 ..... 2.95

29 Courtesan conspiracy,pt.2 ..... 2.95
30 Inspector Ishida mystery 2.95
TPB Shades of Death, rep. of
Mirage series 14.95
HC Shades of Death, lim........ 50.00
TPB Daisho, rep. Mirage........ 14.95
HC Daisho, 200 pg. signed..... 50.00
TPB The Brink of Life & Death .. 14.95
TPB Seasons............... 14.95
HC Seasons, signed........... 55.00
TPB Grasscutter.............. 16.95
HC Grasscutter............... 60.00

USAGI YOJIMBO
1996
1 SS,color spec............... 4.00
2 SS,color spec............... 3.00
3 SS,color spec............... 3.00
4 thru 6 .... @3.00

USAGI YOJIMBO COLOR SPECIAL: GREEN PERSIMMON
1-shot by Stan Sakai 2.95

VAMPIRELLA
(B&W)
1 `The Lion and the Lizard'Pt.1 ... 4.50
2 `The Lion and the Lizard'Pt.2 ... 3.95
3 `The Lion and the Lizard'Pt.3 ... 3.95
4 `The Lion and the Lizard'Pt.3 ... 3.95

VENUS WARS
(B&W) Manga
1 Aphrodia V:Ishtar, with
2-card strip.............. 3.00
2 I: Ken Seno 2.50
3 Aphrodia V:Ishtar 2.50
4 Seno Joins Hound Corps...... 2.50
5 SenoV:Octopus Supertanks 2.50
6 Chaos in Aphrodia 2.50
7 All Out Ground War 2.50
8 Ishtar V:Aphrodia contd....... 2.50
9 Ishtar V:Aphrodia contd....... 2.50
10 Supertanks of Ishtar Advance .. 2.50
11 Aphrodia Captured.......... 2.50
12 A:Miranda,48pgs 2.75
13 Hound Brigade-Suicide Assault. 2.25
14 V:Army 2.50
15 .... 2.50
TPB Vol. 1 .... 13.95

VENUS WARS II
1 V:Security Police 2.75
2 Political Unrest............. 2.25
3 Conspiracy................ 2.25
4 A:Lupica.................. 2.25
5 Love Hotel 2.25
6 Terran Consulate 2.25
7 Doublecross............... 2.25
8 D:Lupisa.................. 2.95
9 A:Matthew 2.95
10 A:Mad Scientist 2.95
11 thru 15 V:Troopers .... @2.95

VIRUS
1 MP(c),F:The Wan Xuan & the
crew of the Electra 3.00
2 MP(c),V:Captian Powell 3.00
3 MP(c),V:Virus.............. 3.00
4 MP(c),Last issue............ 3.00
TPB rep.#1–#4 .... 16.95

All comics prices listed are for *Near Mint* condition.

VERSION
(B&W) Manga
1.1 by Hisashi Sakaguchi 2.50
1.2 thru 1.8 . . . . @2.50

VERSION II
(B&W) Manga
1.1 by Hisashi Sakaguchi 2.50
1.2 thru 1.6 . . . . @2.50

VORTEX, THE
1 . . . . 2.00

WALTER:
CAMPAIGN OF TERROR
1 thru 3 . . . . @2.50

WARRIOR OF
WAVERLY STREET, THE
Nov. 1996
1 (of 2) by Manny Coto and
   John Stokes 2.95

WARRIOR OF WAVERLY
STREET, THE:
BROODSTORM
March 1997
1-shot Manny Coto & John Stokes . 2.95

WARWORLD!
(B&W)
1 . . . . 1.75

WHAT'S MICHAEL?
(B&W) Manga
TPB by Makoto Kobayashi 5.95
TPB Living Together 5.95
TPB Off the Deep End 5.95

WHITE LIKE SHE
(B&W)
1 thru 4 by Bob Fingerman 2.95

WILL TO POWER
Comics' Greatest World 1994
1 BS, A:X 1.25
2 BS, A:X,Monster 1.25
3 BS, A:X 1.25
4 BS, In Steel Harbor 1.25
5 V:Wolfgang 1.00
6 V:Motorhead 1.00
7 JOy(c),V:Amazing Grace 1.00
8 V:Catalyst 1.00
9 Titan, Grace 1.00
10 Vortex alien, Grace 1.00
11 Vortex alien, King Titan 1.00
12 Vortex alien 1.00

WIZARD OF
FOURTH STREET
(B&W)
1 thru 4 . . . . @1.75

WOLF & RED
1 Looney Tunes 2.50
2 Watchdog Wolf 2.50
3 Red Hot Riding Hood 2.50

WOLVERTON IN SPACE
(B&W) April 1997
TPB by Basil Wolverton 16.95

WORLD BELOW, THE
Mar. 1999
1 PC 2.50
2 PC 2.50
3 PC 2.50
4 PC 2.50

X #8 © Dark Horse Comics

X
Comics' Greatest World 1994
1 B:StG(s),DoM,JP,I:X-Killer 3.00
2 DoM,JP,V:X-Killer 2.25
3 DoM,JP,A:Pit Bulls 2.25
4 DoM,JP 2.25
5 DoM,JP,V:Chaos Riders 2.00
6 Cyberassassins 2.00
7 Alamout 2.00
8 A:Ghost 2.50
9 War for Arcadia 2.50
10 War for Arcadia 2.50
11 I:Coffin, War 2.50
12 V:Coffin, A:Monster 2.50
13 D:X 2.50
14 conclusion to War 2.50
15 JS,SiG,war survivors 2.50
16 V:Headhunter 2.50
17 . . . . 2.50
18 V:Predator 2.50
19 V:Challenge 2.50
20 thru 24 . . . . @2.50

X: ONE SHOT
TO THE HEAD
1 . . . . 2.50

XXX
1 . . . . 3.95
2 V:Dr. Zemph 3.95
3 . . . . 3.95
4 V:Rhine Lords 3.95
5 I:Klaar 3.95
6 Klaar captured 4.95
7 Revolution Consequences 4.95

YOUNG CYNICS CLUB
(B&W)
1 . . . . 2.50

THE YOUNG INDIANA
JONES CHRONICLES
1 DBa,FS,TV Movie Adapt 3.25
2 DBa,TV Movie Adapt 2.75
3 thru 5 DBa,GM . . . . @2.75
6 BBa,GM,WW1,French Army 2.75
7 The Congo 2.75
8 Africa,A:A.Schweitzer 2.50
9 Vienna,Sophie-daughter of Arch-
   Duke Ferdinand 2.50
10 In Vienna continued 2.50
11 Far East 2.50
12 Fever Issue 2.50

YOU'RE UNDER ARREST!
(B&W) Manga 1995–96
1 by Kosuke Fujishima 2.95
2 thru 8 (mini-series) . . . . @2.95
TPB rep 12.95

ZOMBIEWORLD:
1-shot Eat Your Heart Out, KJo . . . 2.95
1-shot Home for the Holidays 2.95

ZOMBIEWORLD:
DEAD END
Jan. 1998
1 (of 2) by Stephen Blue 2.95
2 . . . . 2.95

ZOMBIEWORLD:
CHAMPION
OF THE WORMS
Sept. 1997
1 (of 3) MMi 2.95
2 thru 3 . . . . @2.95
Spec. Home for the Holidays 2.95
TPB 8.95

ZOMBIEWORLD:
THE TREE OF DEATH
May 1999
1 (of 4) by Pat Mills & J.
   Deadstock 2.95
2 thru 4 . . . . @2.95

ZOMBIEWORLD:
WINTER'S DREGS
May 1998
1 (of 4) by Bob Fingerman and
   Tommy Lee Edwards 2.95
2 thru 4 . . . . @2.95

DARK HORSE

IMAGE

AARON STRIPS
Image (B&W) April 1997
1 thru 4 rep. from Sunday comic
  strips, by Aaron Warner .... @2.95

ACTION PLANET
Image (B&W) Sept. 1997
Prev. ?
3 .... 3.95

A DISTANT SOIL
Image/Highbrow
(B&W) Prev: Warp Graphics
15 CDo, ... 3.00
16 CDo,A:Bast, Avatar 3.00
17 CDo,D'mer & Bast conflict 3.00
18 CDo,"Ascension" finale 3.00
19 CDo,"Spires of Heaven" pt.1 ... 3.00
20 CDo,Lord Merai's suicide
  weakens Hierachy 3.00
21 CDo,"Exile for D'mer?"........ 3.00
22 CDo,Avatar's secrets,32pg..... 3.00
23 CDo,three stories.............. 3.00
24 CDo,malfunctioning spacesuit .. 3.00
25 CDo,NGa,Troll Bridge,48pg.... 3.95
26 CDo,B.U.:Red-Cloak by
  E.Kushner 2.95
27 CDo,B.U.Liaden tale 2.95
28 CDo,B.U.Liaden tale, concl.... 2.95
29 CDo,B.U.Delia Sherman story .. 2.95
Images of A Distant Soil 3.00
Images of A Distant Soil, signed,
  limited 34.95
GN The Gathering, rep.#1–#11 ... 18.95
GN The Gathering, 2nd printing .. 19.95
TPB The Ascendant, rep.#13–#24 18.95

ADRENALYNN
Image Aug. 1999
1 F:Sabina Nikoli.............. 2.50

ADVENTURES OF AARON
Image March 1997
(B&W) by Aaron Warner
1 "Baby-sitter Gone Bad"........ 2.95
2 "Thunder Thighs of the
  Terrordome" 2.95
3 Babysitter Gone Bad, concl..... 2.95
100 Super Special 2.95
Christmas Spectacular #1........ 2.95

ADVENTURES OF BARRY WEEN, BOY GENIUS, THE
Image (B&W) March 1999
1 (of 3) by Judd Winick 2.95
2 Growing Pains 2.95
3 School 2.95

ADVENTURE STRIP DIGEST
Image (B&W) April 1998
1 by Randy Reynaldo 2.95
2 F:Rob Hanes, detective 2.95

AGE OF BRONZE
Image (B&W) Nov. 1998
1 EiS,The Trojan War 2.95
2 EiS,Death of Paris 2.95
3 EiS,F:Herakles, Hektor 2.95
4 EiS,I:Helen................. 2.95
Spec.#1 EiS, House of Horror..... 2.95
Spec.#2 .... 2.95

AGE OF HEROES, THE
Image/Halloween 1996
(B&W)
1 JHI & JRy................. 2.95
2 JHI & JRy................. 2.95
3 JHI & JRy,Luko,Trickster &
  Aerwyn try to steal treasure
  of the gods............... 2.95
4 JHI & JRy,Drake, the blind
  swordsman returns......... 2.95
5 JHI & JRy,O:Conor One-Arm ... 2.95
Spec. #1 rep. #1 & #2........... 4.95
Spec. #2 rep. #3 & #4........... 6.95

AGE OF HEROES: WEX
Image (B&W) Aug. 1998
1 by JHI,Vurtex 2.95

ALLEGRA
Image/Wildstorm 1996
1 ScC,SSe 2.50
2 thru 4 .... @2.50

ALLEY CAT
Image July 1999
1 BNa,MHw,F:Alley Baggett...... 2.50
1a variant painted cover (1:4) 2.50
2 BNa,MHw,women murdered 2.50

ALLIANCE, THE
Image/Shadowline 1995
1 I:The Alliance 2.50
1a variant cover.............. 2.50

The Alliance #3
© Shadowline

2 Team Comes Together 2.50
2a variant cover.............. 2.50
3 I:Slash C 2.50
3a variant cover.............. 2.50
4 .... 2.50
4a variant cover.............. 2.50

ALLIES, THE
Image/Extreme 1995
1 thru 4 mini-series .... @2.50

ALTERED IMAGE
Image April 1998
1 JV,The Day Reality Went Wild .. 2.50
2 JV,F:Everybody smooshed 2.50
3 JV,Middle Age Crisis, concl. 2.50
TPB F:everybody 9.95

AMANDA AND GUNN
Image (B&W) April 1997
1 JeR, Montana 2036 .... 2.95
2 (of 4) JeR................. 2.95
3 (of 4) JeR................. 2.95
4 (of 4) JeR, conclusion......... 2.95

ANGELA
Image/TMP 1994–95
1 NGa(s),GCa,A:Spawn. 15.00
2 NGa(s),GCa,Angela's trial 14.00
3 NGa(s),GCa,In Hell. 12.00
Spec. Pirate Spawn(c) 32.00
Spec. Pirate Angela(c) 30.00
TPB Rep.#1–#3 .... 9.95

ANGELA/GLORY: RAGE OF ANGELS
Image/TMP/Extreme 1996
1 x-over begins 5.00

ARCANUM
Image/Top Cow March 1997
Mini-series
1 BPe, from Medieval
  Spawn/Witchblade 2.50
1a variant MS(s) (1:4) 2.50
2 BPe, Chi in Asylum.......... 2.50
3 BPe, Ming Chang captive in
  Atlantis.................. 2.50
4 BPe,"The End?" 2.50
5 BPe,Royale's secret journal 2.50
6 BPe,Safe Haven?............ 2.50
7 BPe,Egypt 2.50

ARIA
Image/Avalon Nov. 1998
1 by Brian Holguin & Jay Anacleto. 2.50
1a variant cover.............. 2.50
2 A:Mad Gwynnion 2.50
3 English Countryside 2.50
4 V:Dark One 2.50
4a glow-in-the-dark(c) 6.95
5 London, 1966.............. 2.50
6 Subterranean Homesick Blues . 2.50
Preview Ed. F:Kildare........... 2.95
Spec.#1 Blanc & Noir, sketchbook . 2.95
Spec.#1 alternate cover 6.95

All comics prices listed are for *Near Mint* condition.

ARKAGA
Image Sept. 1997
1 by Arnie Tang Jorgensen 2.95
2 Desire for revenge 2.95

ART OF ERIK LARSEN
1 Sketchbook 4.95

ART OF
HOMAGE STUDIOS
1 Various Pin-ups 4.95

ASCENSION
Image/Top Cow Sept. 1997
1 by David Finch, F:Angels 2.50
2 Andromeda fights alone 2.50
3 reunited with Lucien 2.50
4 . . . . 2.50
5 Gregorieff and Dayak Army 2.50
6 Voivodul returns, concl.. . . . . . . 2.50
7 Andy's problems worsen 2.50
8 revenge on Dayaks & Mineans . . 2.50
9 Andy exiled 2.50
10 A:D. Gavin Taylor. 2.50
11 A:D. Gavin Taylor. 2.50
12 A:turning point 2.50
13 A:Grigorieff, Petra 2.50
14 V:Marcus,A:Andromeda 2.50
15 Rowena's secrets 2.50
16 Petra joins Lucien 2.50
17 a schism 2.50
18 V:new entity. 2.50
Coll.Ed.#1, rep.#1–#2. . . . . 4.95
Coll.Ed.#2 . . . . 4.95

ASTRO CITY
See: KURT BUSIEK'S
ASTRO CITY

ATOMIC TOYBOX
Image April 1999
Odyssey Line
1 AaL, F:Ken Logan 2.50
2 AaL, The Aliens are comming. . . 2.50
2a variant cover (1:2). 2.50

AUTOMATION
Image/Flypaper 1998
1 Robots sent to Mars, and back . . 2.95
2 One goes mad 2.95
3 Sherzad vs. Konak 2.95
TPB rep. #1–#3 . . . . 12.95

THE AWAKENING
Image (B&W) Oct. 1997
1 (of 4) by Stephen Blue 2.95
2 thru 4 . . . . @2.95
TPB Rep. #1–#4. . . . . 9.95

BACKLASH
Image/Wildstorm 1994
1 Taboo, 2 diff. covers 4.00
1a variant edition, 2 covers 3.00
2 Savage Dragon 2.50
3 V:Savage Dragon 2.50
4 SRf,A:Wetworks 2.50
5 SRf,A:Dane 2.50
6 BBh,SRf,A:Wetworks 2.50
7 BBh,SRf,V:Bounty Hunters 2.50
8 RMz,BBh,BWS(c),WildStorm
    Rising,pt.8,w/2 cards 2.50
8a Newsstand ed. 1.95

9 F:Dingo,V:Chasers 2.50
10 I:Crimson. 2.50
11 R:Bloodmoon. 2.50
12 R:Taboo,Crimson's Costume . . . 3.00
13 Taboo to the Rescue 2.50
14 A:Deathblow 2.50
15 F:Cyberjack. 2.50
16 thru 18 . . . . @2.50
19 Fire From Heaven,pt.2 . . . . 2.50
20 SRf,BBh 2.50
21 SRf,BBh 2.50
22 SRf,BBh 2.50
23 SRf,BBh 2.50
24 SRf,BBh,return of Dingo 2.50
25 SRf,BBh,56pg. special 4.00
26 SRf,BBh,Gramalkin identity
    revealed. 2.50
27 SRf,BBh, ... 2.50
28 SRf,BBh,Backlash leads PSI
    team to Europe 2.50
29 SRf,BBh,Haroth raises the
    remnants of Atlantis 2.50
30 SRf,BBh,Backlash confronts
    Kherubim lords. 2.50
31 SRf,BBh,team returns to PSI . . . 2.50
32 SRf,BBh,earth-shattering final
    issue 2.50
TPB Backlash/Spider-Man, Webs &
    Whips, crossover 4.95
TPB The Drahn War, rep.#27–#32 15.00

BACKLASH/SPIDER-MAN
Image/Wildstorm/Marvel 1996
1 . . . . 2.50
1a variant cover. 3.00
2 . . . . 2.50

BADGER
Image (B&W) May 1997
1 MBn,"Betelgeuse". 2.95
2 MBn,"Beefalo don't like fences". . 2.95
3 MBn,"Loose Eel". 2.95
4 MBn,"Hot House" 2.95
5 MBn,Octopi in the hot tub 2.95
6 MBn,Prime Minister of
    Klactoveedesteen. 2.95
7 MBn,Crime Comics. 2.95
8 MBn,Root. 2.95
9 MBn, ... 2.95
10 MBn,Tuesday Ruby 2.95
11 MBn,Watch the Skies. 2.95
12 MBn,The Lady Cobras. 2.95
13 MBn,Horse Police 2.95
14 MBn,Badger Sells Out 2.95

BADROCK
Image/Extreme 1995
1a RLd(p),TM(c), A:Dragon 1.75
1b SPa(ic),A:Savage Dragon 1.75
1c DF(ic) 1.75
2 RLd,ErS(s),V:Girth,A:Savage
    Dragon. 2.50
3 RLd,ErS,V:The Overlord 2.50
Ann.#1 I:Gunner. 2.95
Super-Spec. #1 A:Grifter & The
    Dragon. 2.50

BADROCK
AND COMPANY
Image/Extreme 1994–95
1 KG(s), ... 2.50
1a San Diego Comic Con Ed. 3.00
2 RLd(c),Fuji 2.50
3 Overtkill 2.50
4 TBm,MBm,TNu,A:Velocity. 2.50
5 A:Grifter 2.50
6 Finale, A:ShadowHawk. 2.50

BALLISTIC
Image/Top Cow 1995
1 A:Wetworks 2.50
2 Jesters Transformation 2.50
3 final issue. 2.50

BALLISTIC ACTION
Image/Top Cow 1996
1 MSi(c) pin-ups 2.95

BALLISTIC IMAGERY
Image/Top Cow 1995
1 anthology 2.50

BALLISTIC/WOLVERINE
Image/Top Cow 1996
1 Devil's Reign, pt.4. . . . . 4.00

BATTLESTONE
Image/Extreme 1994
1 New Series. 2.50
1a variant cover. 3.00
2 RLd,ErS,MMy,AV,I&D:Roarke,
    finale 2.50

BATTLE CHASERS
Image/Cliffhanger April 1998
1 JMd, fantasy, team-up 2.50
1a Chromium edition (5,000 made) 3.00
2 JMd,F:Gully 2.50
3 JMd,new ally 2.50
4 JMd,Red Monika 2.50
4a,b,c JMd variant covers . . . . . @2.50
5 JMd,V:Lord August,with 8-page
    Planetary #0. . . . . 2.50
6 JMd,. 2.50
6a variant cover AWa 2.50
7 JMd, Create a Monster. 2.50
TPB Coll.Ed.#1, rep.#1 & #2. . . . . 5.95
TPB Collected Edition #2 . . . . 6.00
Prelude #1, JMd, 16pg 10.00

BEETLEBORGS
Image/Extreme Nov. 1996
1 from TV show. 2.50

IMAGE

BERZERKERS
Image/Extreme 1995
1 From Youngblood #2 . . . . 2.50
2 Escape from Darkthorne. 2.50
3 In the Darklands 2.50
4 final issue. 2.50

Big Bang #22
© *Big Bang Studios*

BIG BANG COMICS
**Image/Big Bang Studios 1996
(B&W) Prev. Caliber**
1 F:Mighty Man 2.00
2 Silver Age Shadowhawk 2.00
3 . . . . 2.00
4 . . . . 2.50
5 Top Secret Origins 2.95
6 Round Table of America and
  Knights of Justice meet, orig.
  mini-series #3 (color) 2.95
7 . . . . 2.95
8 F:Mister U.S. 2.95
9 I:Peter Chefren. 2.95
10 F:Galahad 2.95
11 Faulty Towers is destroying
   Midway City 2.95
12 F:The Savage Dragon 2.95
13 by Jeff Weigel, 40pg spec. 2.95
14 RB,A:The Savage Dragon 2.95
15 SBi(c),F:Dr. Weird 2.95
16 F:Thunder Girl 2.95
17 . . . . 2.95
18 Savage Dragon on Trial 2.95
19 O:Beacon,Hummingbird. 2.95
20 F:Knight Watchman,Blitz 2.95
21 F:Shadow Lady 2.95
22 The Bird-Man of Midway City . . 2.95
23 Riddle of the Sphinx, sequel . . . 2.95
24 History of Big Bang,Vol.1 . . . . . 3.95
25 Anniv. iss. 3.95
26 Murder by Microphone, concl. . . 2.95
TPB rep. 1994 mini-series. 11.00

BLACK AND WHITE
Image/Hack Studios 1996
1 New heroes 1.95
2 ATi(p),apparent death 1.95
3 V:Chang. 1.95
Ashcan. 5.00

BLACK ANVIL
Image/Top Cow 1996
1 & 2. . . . . 2.50

BLACK FLAG
Image/Extreme 1994
1 B&W Preview 3.00

BLACK OPS
Image/Wildstorm 1996
1 thru 5 . . . . @2.50
TPB 14.95

BLINDSIDE
Image/Extreme Aug. 1996
1 MMy & AV, F:Nucgaek Jeno 2.50
2 MMy & AV, Origin continues 2.50

BLISS ALLEY
Image (B&W) July 1997
1 BML 2.95
2 BML,F:Wizard Walker 2.95
3 BML,Inky-Dinks 2.95

BLOODHUNTER
Image/Extreme Nov. 1996
1 RV, Cabbot Stone rises from the
  slab 2.95

BLOODPOOL
Image/Exteme 1995
1 I:Seoul,Rubbe,Wylder 2.50
1a variant cover. 2.50
2 New Neighborhood. 2.50
3 The Mummy's Curse. 2.50
4 final issue. 2.50
TPB Rep. #1-#4 . . . . 12.95
[Regular Series] 1996
1 thru 3 JDy . . . . @2.50

BLOODSTRIKE
Image/Extreme 1993
1 A:Brigade,Rub the Blood(c) 3.00
2 V:Brigade,B:BU:Knight 2.50
3 B:ErS(s),ATi(c),V:Coldsnap 2.25
4 ErS(s), ... 2.25
5 KG,A:Supreme, ... 2.25
6 KG(s),CAx,C&J:Chapel. 2.25
7 KG,RHe,A:Badrock 2.25
8 RHe,A:Spawn. 2.25
9 RHe,Extreme Prejudice #3,
  I:Extreme Warrior,ATh,BU: Black
  & White 2.25
10 V:Brigade, B:BU:Knight 1.95
25 I:Cabbot Bloodstrike 2.50
11 ErS(s),ATi(c),V:Coldsnap 1.95
12 ErS(s) 1.95
13 KG,A:Supreme 1.95
14 KG(s),CAx,C&J:Chapel 1.95
15 KG,RHe,A:Badrock 1.95
16 KG,RHe. 1.95
17 KIA,V:The Horde 2.50
18 ExtremeSacrifice x-over,pt.2 . . . 2.50
19 V:The Horde 2.50
20 R:Deadlock New Order 2.50
21 KA,V:Epiphany New Order. 2.50
22 V:The Horde, last issue 2.50
25 see above, after #10
Ashcan. 5.00

BLOODSTRIKE: ASSASSIN
Image/Extreme 1995
0 R:Battlestone 2.50
1 Debut new series 2.50
1a alternate cover 2.50
2 V:M.D.K. Assassins 2.50

3 V:Persuasion 2.50

BLOODWULF
[Miniseries]
1 RLd,R:Bloodwulf. 2.50
1b Run OJ Run 2.50
1c Alternate cover 2.50
1d Alternate cover 2.50
2 A:Hot Blood 2.50
3 Slippery When Wet. 2.50
4 final issue. 2.50
Spec.#1 V:Supreme Freeferall 2.50

BLUE
Image Aug. 1999
1 Android teenager 2.50

BULLETPROOF MONK
Image/Flypaper Nov. 1998
1 in San Francisco. 2.95
2 N.Y. Chinatown. 2.95
3 conclusion 2.95

BODY COUNT
1 & 2 . . . . @2.50

BOHOS
Image/Flypaper (B&W) 1998
1 by Maggie Whorf & B.Penaranda 2.95
2 F:teenage bohemians 2.95
3 concl 2.95
TPB Bohos. 12.95

BONE
**(B & W)
[Previously by Cartoon Books]**
21 thru 25 . . . . @2.95
26 The Turning. 2.95
27 end of dragonslayer storyline . . . 2.95
Bone Sourcebook. 25
HC#1 Out of Boneville, rep. 19.95
HC#2 The Great Cow Race, rep. . . 19.95
HC#3 Gran'ma's Story, rep. 19.95
Image reprints with new covers
#1 thru #9 . . . . @2.95
10 rep. "Great Cow Race". 2.95
Image/Cartoon Books
11 Aftermath of the Great Cow

Bone #22
© *Jeff Smith*

IMAGE

Race	2.95
12	2.95
13 Thar she blows	2.95
14	2.95
15 Double or nothing	2.95
16 hiding from the Rat Creatures . .	2.95
17 with 5 new pages.	2.95
18 Betrayed	2.95
19 three cheers for dragon-slayer	
Phoney Bone	2.95
20 Phoney Bone vs. Lucius	2.95

BOOF

1	1.95
2 Meathook.	1.95
3 Joyride	1.95
4 Beach.	1.95
5 Down on the Farm	1.95
6 V:Gangster Chimps	1.95

BOOF AND THE BRUISE CREW

1 thru 4 . . . . @1.95
5 Supermarket. 1.95
6 I:Mortar, O:Bruise Crew 1.95

BRASS
Image/Wildstorm

1 Rib,AWa,Folio Edition	3.50
2 Rib,AWa, ...	2.50
3 Rib,AWa,concl.	2.50

Brigade #4
© Rob Liefeld

BRIGADE
Image/Extreme 1993
[1st Series]

1 RLd(s),MMy,I:Brigade	3.50
1a Gold Ed.	4.00
2 RLd(s),V:Genocide,w/coupon#4 .	4.00
2a w/o coupon.	1.00
2b Gold Ed.	4.00
3 V:Genocide	2.00
4 CyP,Youngblood#5 flip	2.00

[2nd Series]

0 RLd(s),ATi(c),JMs,NRd,I:Warcry,	
A:Emp,V:Youngblood	2.25
1 V:Bloodstrike	2.75
1a Gold Ed.	3.00
2 C:Coldsnap	3.00
3 ErS(s),GP(c),MMy,NRd(i),	
V:Bloodstrike	2.25

4 Rip(s),MMy,RHe,I:Roman,	
BU:Lethal.	2.25
5 Rip(s),MMy, ...	2.25
6 Rip(s),MMy,I:Coral,BU:Hackers	
Tale	2.25
7 Rip(s),MMy,V:Worlok	2.25
8 ErS(s),MMy,Extreme Prejudice	
#2,BU:Black & White	2.25
9 ErS(s),MMy,Extreme Prejudice	
#6,ATh,BU:Black & White	2.25
25 ErS(s),MMy,D:Kayo,Coldsnap,	
Thermal, ...	2.25
26 Images of Tomorrow	2.25
10 Extreme Prejudice	1.95
11 WildC.A.T.S	2.50
12 Battlestone	2.50
13 Thermal.	1.95
14 Teamate deaths	1.95
15 MWm,R:Roman Birds of Prey . .	1.95
16 ExtremeSacrifice x-over,pt.3 . . .	2.50
17 MWn,I:New Team	2.50
18 I:The Shape New Order.	2.50
19 MWn,F:Troll.	2.50
20 MWn,alien cult saga,concl.	2.50
21 F:ShadowHawk	2.50
22 F:Brigade Team	2.50
23 & 24. . . . . @2.50
25 & 26 see above	
27 Extreme Babewatch.	2.50
Sourcebook	2.95

BUGBOY
Image (B&W) June 1998

1-shot, by Mark Lewis, 48pg	3.95

CARVERS
Image/Flypaper Oct. 1998

1 F:five snowboarders	2.95
2 J:Crazy Jack.	2.95
3 V:Evil Yeti.	2.95
TPB rep. #1–#3	9.95

CASUAL HEROES

1 thru 5 . . . . @2.50

CATHEDRAL CHILD
Image 1998

GN by Lea Hernandez	9.95
GN 2nd printing	9.95

CELESTINE
Image/Extreme 1996

1	2.50
2	2.50

CHANNEL ZERO
Image (B&W) 1998

1 by Brian Wood	2.95
2	2.95
3 gone global	2.95
4 Filter.	2.95
5 Brink of Millennium crash	2.95
6 Sound system	2.95
TPB Collection	11.95

CHAPEL
Image/Extreme 1995

1 BWn,F:Chapel	3.50
2 V:Colonel Black	3.00
2a variant cover.	2.50

[Regular Series]

1 BWn,F:Chapel	2.50
1a variant cover.	2.50
2 V:Giger.	2.50

Celestine #2
© Extreme Studios

3 V:Giger.	2.50
4 Extreme Babewatch	2.50
5 Hell on Earth,pt.1	2.50
6 Hell on Earth,pt.2	2.50
7 Shadowhunt x-over,pt.2	2.50

CHILDHOOD'S END
Image (B&W) Oct. 1997

1 (of 5) JCf, comunity playground .	2.95

CHILLER
Image Dec. 1998

TPB JHl,F:Brian Marx	17.95

THE C.H.I.X. THAT TIME FORGOT
Image/Studiosaurus Aug. 1998

1 F:Good Girl	2.95

CLOCKWORK ANGELS
Image (B&W) March 1999

GN seq. to Cathedral Child.	9.95

CODE BLUE
Image (B&W) April 1998

1 by Jimmie Robinson	2.95
2 F.I.T.E. creates havoc	2.95

CODENAME: STYKE FORCE
Image/Top Cow 1994

1A MS(s),BPe,JRu(i), ...	3.50
1B Gold Embossed Cover	6.00
1C Blue Embossed Cover	9.00
2 MS(s),BPe,JRu(i), ...	2.50
3 MS(s),BPe,JRu(i), ...	2.50
4 MS(s),BPe,JRu(i), ...	2.50
5 MS(s),BPe,JRu(i), ...	2.50
6 MS(s),BPe,JRu(i), ...	2.25
7 MS(s),BPe,JRu(i), ...	2.25
8A Cyblade poster (Tucci)	4.00
8B Shi poster (Silvestri)	4.00
8C Tempest poster (Tan)	2.25
9 New Teamate	2.25
10 SvG, B:New Adventure	2.25
11 F:Bloodbow	1.95
12 F:Stryker	1.95

IMAGE

13 SvG(s),F:Strkyer 2.25
14 New Jobs 2.25
Spec.#0 O:Stryke Force 2.50
TPB Rep. Death's Angel Saga 9.95

COMBAT

1 . . . . 2.50

COMPLETE ALEX TOTH ZORRO

Image (B&W) April 1999
TPB Complete Alex Toth Zorro . . . 18.95

COSMIC RAY

Image June 1999
1 by Stephen Blue 2.95
1a alternate cover (1:2) 2.95
2 F:Raymond Mann 2.95

CREECH, THE

Image/TMP Oct. 1997
1 GCa,DaM,F:Chirs Rafferty 1.95
2 GCa,DaM,F:Dennis Dross 1.95
TPB Race Against Death 9.95

CRIMSON

Image/Cliffhanger May 1998
1 BAu,HuR,F:Alex Elder, vampire . 2.50
1a variant AWa(c) 2.50
1b Chromium Edition 3.00
2 BAu,HuR,V:Jelly-Bats 2.50
2a variant AAd(c) 2.50
3 BAu,HuR,V:Rose 2.50
4 BAu,HuR,F:Red Hood 2.50
5 BAu,HuR,A:Red Hood 2.50
6 BAu,HuR,A:Red Hood 2.50
7 BAu,HuR,Christmas day 2.50
½ Dynamic Forces exclusive . . . . . . ?

Wildstorm/DC 1999
8 BAu,HuR 2.50
9 BAu,HuR 2.50
10 BAu,HuR 2.50
11 BAu,HuR 2.50
12 BAu,HuR 2.50
13 BAu,HuR 2.50
Spec.#1 Scarlet X: Blood on the
    Moon BAu,HuR,one-shot 4.00
TPB Crimson, rep.#1–#6 . . . . 13.00

CROW, THE

Image/TMP Feb. 1999
1 JMu,F:Eric Draven 2.50
1a variant TP cover (1:4) 2.50
2 JMu,hunt for killers 2.50
3 JMu,justice for killers 2.50
4 JMu,Line Between Devil's Teeth . 2.50
5 JMu,Skin of an Angel,pt.1 . . . . . . 2.50
6 JMu,Skin of an Angel,pt.2 . . . . . . 2.50
7 JMu,Touch of Evil, pt.1 . . . . 2.50

CRUSH, THE

Image/Motown Jan. 1996
1 thru 5 mini-series . . . . @2.50

CRYPT

Image/Extreme 1995
1 A:Prophet 2.50
1a Variant cover 2.50
2 A:Prophet 2.50

The Crush #1
© Motown

CURSE OF THE SPAWN

Image/TMP Sept. 1996
1 DT,DaM,F:Daniel Lianso 9.00
1a B&W Variant 25.00
2 DT,DaM,Dark Future, Pt. 2:
    Blood Lust 7.00
3 DT,DaM,Dark Future, Pt. 3:
    Corpse Candles 7.00
4 DT,DaM, ... 5.00
5 DT,DaM,Sam & Twitch search
    for Gretchen Culver 4.00
6 DT,DaM,Sam & Twitch pursue
    Suture 4.00
7 DT,DaM,Suture is captured 3.50
8 DT,DaM,Suture escapes police
    custody 3.50
9 DT,DaM,Angela's secret origin . 5.00
10 DT,DaM,Angela, Spawn Slayer . 4.00
11 DT,DaM,Angela's story, concl. . . 3.50
12 DT,DaM,Jessica Priest, movie
    photo(c) 3.50
13 DT,DaM "Heart of Darkness" . . . 3.50
14 DT,DaM,Jessica, concl. 3.50
15 DT,DaM,Tempt an Angel,pt.1 . . 3.50
16 DT,DaM,Tempt an Angel,pt.2 . . 3.50
17 DT,DaM 3.50
18 DT,DaM,F:Tony Twist 3.50
19 DT,Curse & Tony Twist 3.50
20 DT,DaM,Monsters & Mythology . 3.50
21 DT,DaM,Zeus Must Die 3.50
22 DT,F:Ryan Hatchett 3.50
23 DT,TM,R:Overtkill 3.50
24 DT,TM,Pandemic 3.50
25 DT,TM,"Heart of Hell" 2.00
26 DT,TM,V:The Crocodile 2.00
27 DT,TM,F:Marc Simmons 2.00
28 DT,TM,V:Suture 2.00
29 DT,TM,A:Jonathan Edward
    Custer 2.00
TPB Vol. 1 Sacrifice the Soul 9.95

CYBERFORCE

Image/Top Cow
[Limited Series] 1992–93
0 WS,O:Cyber Force 2.50
1 MS,I:Cyberforce,w/coupon#3 . . . 5.00
1a w/o coupon 3.00
2 MS,V:C.O.P.S. 3.50
3 MS 2.50
4 MS,V:C.O.P.S,BU:Codename
    Styke Force 2.50
TPB Rep. mini-series 12.95

[Regular Series] 1993
1 EcS(s),MS,SW, ... 2.50
1B Gold Foil Logo 6.00
2 EcS(s),MS,SW,Killer Instinct
    #2,A:Warblade 2.25
2B Silver Embossed Cover 6.00
3 EcS(s),MS,SW,Killer Instinct #4,
    A:WildC.A.T.S. 2.25
3B Gold Embossed Cover 6.00
4 EcS(s),MS,Ballistic 2.00
5 EcS(s),MS 2.00
6 EcS(s),MS,Ballistic's Past 2.00
7 S.H.O.C.s 2.00
8 . . . . 2.50
9 A:Huntsman 2.00
10 A:Huntsman 2.00
10a Alternate Cover 4.00
10b Silver Seal Oz-Con 500c 9.00
11 . . . . 2.00
12 T.I.M.M.I.E. goes wild 2.00
13 EcS,MS,O:Cyberdata 2.25
14 EcS,MSI,V:T.I.M.M.I.E. 2.25
15 New Cyberdata Threat 2.25
16 O:Ripclaw 2.25
17 Regrouping 2.25
18 thru 25 . . . . @2.50
26 KWo 2.50
27 F:Ash 2.50
27a variant cover by JQ&JP (1:4) . . 4.00

Top Cow 1996
28 A:Gabriel 2.50
29 . . . . 2.50
30 ScL,"Devil's Reign" tie-in 2.50
31 The team in conflict 2.50
32 Cyblade leads rejuvenated team 2.50
33 KWo, Cheleene in midst of
    civil war 2.50
34 KWo,Royal Blood, pt.3 . . . . 2.50
35 BTn,Royal Blood, concl. 2.50
Ashcan 1 (San Diego) 4.00
Ashcan 1 (signed) 6.00
Sourcebook 1 . . . . 2.50
Sourcebook 2 I:W.Zero 2.50
Ann.#1 O:Velocity 2.50
Ann.#2 . . . . 2.95
TPB new art 12.95
TPB EcS,MS,SW,Assault with a
    Deadly Woman 9.95

Cyberforce #4
© Top Cow

IMAGE

CYBERFORCE/ CODENAME STRYKEFORCE: OPPOSING FORCES

1 V:Dangerous Threat	2.50
2 Team Vs. Team	2.50

CYBERFORCE ORIGINS

Image/Top Cow 1995

1 O:Cyblade	2.50
1B Gold Seal 1000c	6.00
2 O:Stryker	2.50
3 O:Impact	2.50
4 Misery	3.00

CYBERFORCE UNIVERSE SOURCEBOOK

Image/Top Cow 1994–95

1 and 2	@2.50

CYBERNARY

Image/Wildstorm 1995–96

1 thru 5 mini-series	@2.50

CYBERPUNX

Image/Extreme 1996

1 & 2	@2.50
3 RLe & Ching Lau,F:Drake	2.50

CY-GOR

Image/TMP July 1999

1 RV,I:Fatima,Frankie & Zevon	2.50
2 RV,Fire in the Mind,pt.2	2.50

DAMNED

Image/Homage June 1997

1 (of 4) StG, MZ & DRo	2.50
2 StG, MZ & DRo,F:Mick Thorne	2.50
3 StG, MZ & DRo	2.50
4 StG, MZ & DRo	2.50

DANGER GIRL

Wildstorm/Cliffhanger 1998

1 JSC,AGo, spy, 40 pg	2.95
1a chromium edition, 40pg.	5.00

Daring Escapes #2
© Tod McFarlane

2 I:Johnny Barracuda	2.50
3 in Switzerland	2.50
3a variant AH(c)	2.50
3b variant TC(c)	2.50
4 I:Major Maxim	2.50
5 JSC,AGo	2.50
6 JSC,AGo	2.50
TPB Dangerous Coll.,Vol.1	5.95
TPB Dangerous Coll.,Vol.2,rep 2&3	5.95

DARING ESCAPES

Image/TMP 1998

1 ANi,F:Harry Houdini	2.50
2 ANi,search for Mystical Heart	2.50
3 A:Kimiel	2.50
4 conclusion	2.50

DARKCHYLD/GLORY

Image/Extreme

1-shot, four variant covers, by RLd, RQu, JDy & PtL	2.95

DARKCHYLDE

Image/TMP

1	4.00
1a remastered, RLd(c).	6.00
1b American Entertainment	4.00
2	3.00
2a Variant cover	3.00
2b Remastered, with poster	2.50
3	3.00
3a Remastered, with poster	2.50
4 RQu,Ariel & Kauldron's past	2.50
5 RQu,No one here gets out alive	2.50
TPB Rep. #1–#5.	12.95

Series Two, March 1998

0 RQu,Ariel's back, Ariel's past	2.50

DARKCHYLDE: THE DIARY

Image May 1997

1-shot, RQu et al,diary excerpts	2.50

DARKCHYLDE: THE LEGACY

Image/Majesty Aug. 1998

1 RQu,F:Ariel	2.50
2 RQu	2.50

Darkchylde: The Legacy #2
© Wildstorm

Wildstorm/DC 1999

3 RQu,A:Silencer.	2.50
4 RQu,Carnival of Fools	2.50
4a RQu,AAd(c) variant cover	2.50
Summer Swimsuit Spectacular #1.	4.00
Spec.Dreams of the Darkchylde #0.	2.50
TPB Darkchylde	20.00

DARKER IMAGE

1 BML,BCi(s),RLd,SK,JLe,I:Blood Wulf,Deathblow,Maxx	4.00
1a Gold logo(c)	8.00
1b White(c)	6.00
Ashcan 1	4.00

DARKMINDS

Image 1998

1 PtL,cyberpunk,detective	2.50
2 Neon Dragon	2.50
2a variant cover.	2.50
3 PtL,A:Neon Dragons.	2.50
4 PtL,Paradox killer	2.50
5 PtL,Unlikely friends, enemies	2.95
6 PtL,Aurora Industries	2.95
7 PtL,V:Mamuro Hayabusa	2.95
8 Conclusion, 1st story arc	2.50
½ PtL,Cyborg dreams	2.50
TPB Collection #1 rep. #1–#3.	7.95
TPB Collection #2 rep. #4–#6.	7.95
TPB Collection #3 rep. #7 & #8.	5.95

DARKNESS, THE

Image/Top Cow 1996

0 Preview Edition, B&W.	20.00
½	15.00
½ variant cover	30.00
1 GEn, MS	15.00
1a Dark cover	20.00
1b Platinum cover	15.00
2 GEn, MS	14.00
3 GEn,MS,Jackie pursued by many foes	10.00
4 GEn,MS,Jackie explores Darkness power	8.00
5 GEn,MS,New York gangs on verge of all-out war	8.00
6 GEn,MS,F:JackieEstacado,concl.	5.00
7 MS	5.00
7a variant (c)	18.00
8 JBz,retribution	15.00
8a MS(c)(1:4)	18.00
9 Family Ties,pt.2,x-over	10.00
10 Family Ties,pt.3,x-over	12.00
11 GEn,MS,Hearts of Darkness	3.00
11a Chromium (c)	35.00
11b variant (c)	7.00
12 GEn,Hearts of Darkness	3.00
13 GEn,Hearts of Darkness	3.00
14 GEn,JBz,Hearts of Darkness, concl.	3.00
15 JBz,Spear of Destiny,pt.1	3.00
16 JBz,Spear of Destiny,pt.2	3.00
17 JBz,Spear of Destiny,pt.3	3.00
18 JBz,aftermath	3.00
19 JBz,No Mercy,pt.1	2.50
20 JBz,No Mercy,pt.2	2.50
21 JBz,Wynnwood	2.50
22 JBz,Where is Jenny.	2.50
23 JBz,SLo,new characters	2.50
24 JBz,SLo,road trip to Vegas.	2.50
25 JBz,SLo,48-page	3.50
26 JBz,SLo,A:Joey Scarpaggio.	2.50
GN rep. #1–#2	4.95
GN rep. #3–#4, 56 pg.	4.95
GN rep. #5–#6, 56 pg.	4.95
GN rep. #5–#6, with slipcase	10.00
GN rep. #7–#8	4.95
Slipcase and all 3 GNs	25.00

IMAGE

Signed Slipcase and all 3 GNs . . . 50.00	18 F:Cybernary. 2.50
Spec. Infinity, SLo. 3.50	19 F:Cybernary. 2.50
TPB Coll.Ed.,Vol.V,rep.#11–#12 . . . 5.95	20 A:Gen 13. . . . . 3.50
TPB Coll.Ed. deluxe, rep.#1–#6 . . 14.95	21 Brothers in Arms,pt.2,A:Gen13. . 3.50

DARKNESS, THE/BATMAN
Image/Top Cow April 1999
Spec. SLo,MS x-over 5.95

Dart #2
© Image

DART
Image 1996
1 thru 3 Jozef Szekeres . . . . . . @2.50

DEADLANDS
Image July 1999
GN 1-shot role-play tie-in 6.95

DEADLY DUO, THE
Image/Highbrow 1994–95
1 A:Kill-Cat 2.50
2 A:Pitt, O:Kid Avenger 2.50
3 A:Roman, O:Kill-Cat 2.50

[Second Series] 1995
1 A:Spawn. 2.50
2 A:Savage Dragon. 2.50
3 A:Grunge, Gen13 . . . . 2.50
4 Movie Mayhem. 2.50

DEATHBLOW
Image/Wildstorm 1993
1 JLe,MN,I:Cybernary 3.00
2 JLe,BU:Cybernary 2.50
3 JLe(a&s),BU:Cybernary 3.00
4 JLe(s),TSe,BU:Cybernary 2.50
5 JLe(s),TSe,BU:Cybernary 2.50
5a different cover. 5.00
6 Black Angel 2.00
7 . . . . 2.00
8 Black Angel 2.00
9 The Four Horseman 2.00
10 Michael Cray, Sister Mary 2.00
11 A:Four Horseman 2.00
12 Final Battle 2.50
13 New Story Arc 2.50
14 A:Johnny Savoy. 2.50
15 F:Michael Cray 2.50
16 TvS,BWS(c),WildStorm	
Rising,pt.6,w/2 cards 2.50
16a Newsstand ed.. . . . . 2.00
17 V:Gammorran Hunter Killers . . . 2.50

22 Brothers in Arms,pt.3 . . . . 2.50
23 Brothers in Arms,pt.4 . . . . 2.50
24 Brothers in Arms,pt.5 . . . . 3.00
25 Brothers in Arms,pt.6 . . . . 2.50
26 Fire From Heaven prelude. 2.50
27 Fire From Heaven,pt.8 . . . . 3.00
28 . . . . 2.50
29 . . . . 2.50
Ashcan 1 . . . . 4.00
TPB Dark Angel Saga,rep.,216pg. 29.95

DEATHBLOW/WOLVERINE
Image/Wildstorm
1 RiB, AWs,crossover, set in San	
Francisco's Chinatown 2.50
2 RiB, AWs,concl. 2.50
TPB rep. series 8.95

DECEPTION, THE
Image/Flypaper (B&W)
Jan. 1999
1 (of 3) F:Jordan Risk, magician . . 2.95
2 Framed for murder 2.95
3 V:South American Drug Cartel . . 2.50

DEFCON 4
Image/Wildstorm 1996
1 thru 4 mini-series . . . . @2.50

DEITY
Image
Collected Ed. Vol. 1 . . . . 9.95
Collected Ed. Vol. 2 . . . . 9.95

DEITY: REVELATIONS
Image June 1999
1 F:Jamie 2.95
2 F:Joe Tripoli 2.95

DERRING RISK
Image June 1999
1 Fantasy Adventure 2.50
1a variant cover AWa 2.50

DESPERADOS
Image/Homage Sept. 1997
1 by JMi & John Cassaday 7.00
2 V:Leander Peik. 3.00
2a 2nd printing 2.50
3 V:Leander Peik. 3.00
4 V:Leander Peik, concl. 3.00
5 V:Gideon Brood, pt.1. . . . . 3.00
TPB A Moment's Sunlight,rep.	
#1–#5. 16.95

DESPERATE TIMES
Image (B&W) June 1998
1 by Chris Eliopoulos. 2.95
2 Strip joint 2.95
3 EL(c) 2.95
4 Christmas special 2.95
5 EL(c), sideways 2.95
6 . . . . 2.95

DETECTIVES INC.
Image March 1999
TPB Vol. 1 . . . . 14.95
TPB Vol. 2 A Terror of Dying. 19.95

Desperate Times #3
© Image

DEVASTATOR
Image (B&W) April 1998
1 JHl and Greg Horn 2.95
2 book 1, pt.2 . . . . 2.95
3 concl to book 1. . . . . 2.95

DIVINE RIGHT:
THE ADVENTURES OF
MAX FARADAY
Image/Wildstorm Sept. 1997
1 JLe,SW 7.00
1a variant cover. 7.50
1b variant, signed 29.95
1c Voyager pollybaged pack 6.00
1d Spanish edition. 5.00
2 JLe,SW,search for lost love 4.00
2a variant (c). 5.00
3 JLe,SW,F:Christie Blaze 4.00
4 JLe,SW,F:Lynch 2.50
4a variant (c). 4.00
5 JLe,SW,V:Dominique Faust 2.50
6 JLe,SW,Susanna Chaste located 2.50
7 JLe,SW,Into the Hollow Realm . . 2.50
8 JLe,SW,Tobru,V:Acheron 2.50
8a variant SW(c) 2.50
TPB Collected Edition #1 . . . . 5.95
TPB Collected Edition #2 . . . . 5.95

Wildstorm/DC 1999
9 JLe,SWi,Final Stand in	
Hollow Realm. 2.50
10 JLe,SWi, ... 2.50
11 JLe,SWi,Divine Intervention . . . 2.50
Collected Ed.#3, rep.#5 & #6 . . . . 6.00

DOOM'S IV
Image/Extreme 1994
1 I:Doom's IV. 2.50
1a Variant(c) 2.50
2 MECH-MAX 2.50
2a variant cover. 2.50
3 Dr. Lychee, Brick 2.50
4 Dr. Lyche, Syber-idol 2.50
Sourcebook 2.50

DRACULA VS. ZORRO
(B&W) Image Sept. 1998
1 DMG,RM 2.95
2 DMG,RM, conclusion 2.95

DRAGON, THE
1 Rep. of Savage Dragon 0.99
2 Rep. of Savage Dragon 0.99

THE DRAGON:
BLOOD AND GUTS
Image/Highbrow 1995
1 I:Grip 2.50
2 and 3 JPn,KIS. . . . . @2.50

DUSTY STAR
Image (B&W) April 1997
0 sci-fi,western,adventure 2.95
1 thru 3 . . . . @2.95

DV8
Image/Wildstorm 1996
1 WEl(s),HuR 4.00
1a JLe(c). 5.00
1b Kevin Nowlan(c) 4.00
2 WEl(s),HuR,Gen-active serial
   killers are reported 3.00
3 WEl(s), Evo & Frostbite go
   for a walk 2.50
4 Ivana tries to tighten her control
   on Threshold 2.50
5 Ivana sends DV8 to Japan 2.50
6 idle hands are the devil's tools . . 2.50
7 Sideways Bob's bedtime story . . 2.50
8 Sublime, Evo & Frostbite
   abandoned. 2.50
9 "Ivana Dead?!" 2.50
10 "A Team Divided," pt.2 . . . . 2.50
11 F:Copycat 2.50
12 F:Freestyle,V:Sen.Killory 2.50
13 MHs,prelude to New Horizons . . 2.50
14 MHs,TR,New Horizon,TR(c). . . 2.50
14a TC(c). 2.50
14b Voyager bagged pack 3.50
15 MHs,F:Ivana Baiul 2.50
16 MHs,V:Dominique Faust 2.50
17 MHs, ... 2.50
18 MHs,Team 7 . . . . 2.50
19 MHs,First Mision,pt.1 . . . . 2.50
20 MHs,First Mision,pt.2 . . . . 2.50
21 MHs,First Mision,pt.3,Arthrax . . . 2.50
22 MHs,V:Copycat 2.50
22a variant(c) JMd(1:4). 2.50
23 MHs,F:Threshold 2.50
24 MHs,F:Sublime 2.50
25 MHs,Slipstream,pt.1 . . . . 2.50
Wildstorm/DC 1999
26 MHs,TVs, ... 2.50
27 MHs,TVs,V:Gen-Actives. 2.50
28 MHs,TVs,F:Evo 2.50
29 MHs,TVs, ... 2.50
30 MHs,TVs,Things Fall Apart,pt.1 . 2.50
31 MHs,TvS,Things Fall Apart,pt.2 . 2.50
Annual'99 Slipstream 3.50
#0 40-pages 3.00

DV8 VS. BLACK OPS
Image/Wildstorm (Oct. 1997)
1 Techromis Design, pt.1 . . . . 2.50
2 Techromis Design, pt.2 . . . . 2.50
3 Techromis Design, pt.3 . . . . 2.50

ELEKTRA/CYBLADE
Image/Top Cow Jan 1997
1-shot "Devil's Reign" pt.7 (of 8) . . . 2.95

ESPers #4
© Image

ESPERS
Image April 1997
(B&W) Vol. 3
1 JHI,A:Brian Marx,V:Architects . . . 2.95
1a 2nd printing 2.95
2 JHI, ... 2.95
3 JHI,Black Magic 2.95
4 JHI,Black Magic, concl. 2.95
5 JHI,two stories 2.95
6 JHI,F:Simon Ashley,Alan Black . . 2.95
7 JHI,Feel the Rapture. 2.95
8 JHI, trip to Hong Kong 2.95
9 JHI, V:Architects 2.95
TPB Undertow, rep.Halloween
   Comics series. 14.95
TPB Black Magic, rep.Vol.3,#1–4 . 14.95
TPB The Storm, rep.. . . . . 15.95
TPB Interface, rep.2nd series 15.95

[ADVENTURES OF]
EVIL AND MALICE
Image June 1999
1 by Jimmie Robinson 3.50
2 F:Max 2000 . . . . 3.50
TPB F:Evelyn & Malinda. 12.95

EXPOSURE
Image July 1999
1 F:Shawna & Lisa 2.50

EXTREME ANTHOLOGY
1 . . . . 2.50

EXTREME
CHRISTMAS SPECIAL
Various artists, new work 2.95

EXTREME HERO
1 . . . . 2.95

EXTREME PREJUDICE
0 Prelude to X-over 2.50

EXTREME SACRIFICE
Prelude A:Everyone + card 2.50
Epiloque, conclusion + card 2.50
TPB Rep. whole x-over series. . . . 16.95

EXTREME 3000
Prelude 2.50

EXTREME TOUR BOOK
Tour Book 1992 . . . . 3.00
Tour Book 1994 . . . . 25.00

EXTREMELY
YOUNGBLOOD
Image/Extreme Sept 1997
1 TBm&MBm(s). 3.50

EXTREME ZERO
0 RLd,CYp,ATi(i),I:Cybrid, Law &
   Order, Risk, Code 9, Lancers,
   Black Flag 2.75
0a Variant cover 2.75

FALLING MAN
Image (B&W) Dec. 1997
1 (of 3) BMC,PhH 2.95
2 thru 3 Floyd vs. Duncan . . . . . @2.95

Fathom #3
© Top Cow

FATHOM
Image/Top Cow 1998
1 by Michael Turner,F:Aspen 2.50
2 war beneath the waves. 2.50
3 Life changed forever. 2.50
4 Connection to water 2.50
5 Aspen's connection to water 2.50
6 Admiral's plans revealed. 2.50
7 finale, pt.1 . . . . 2.50
8 finale, pt.2 . . . . 2.50
9 finale, conclusion, end 2.50
TPB Coll. Ed. Vol.I, rep.#1 . . . . . . 5.95
TPB Coll. Ed. Vol.II, rep.#2&#3 . . . 5.95
Spec. Swimsuit Ed.. . . . . 2.95

FIRE
Image (B&W) Dec. 1998
TPB International intelligence 9.95

FIRE FROM HEAVEN
1 x-over. 3.50

FIRSTMAN
Image April 1997
1 ASm,LukeHenry becomesApollo. 2.50

FOOT SOLDIERS, THE
Image (B&W) Sept. 1997
Prev. Dark Horse
1 by Jim Krueger, Graveyard of
　　Forgotten Heroes 2.95
2 Tragedy o/t Travesty Tapestry. . . 2.95
3 Arch enemies, pt.3 . . . . 2.95
4 It's a Wicker World Afterall 2.95
5 Loose Ends 2.95

FOREVER AMBER
Image (B&W) July 1999
1 by Don Hudson 2.95
1a variant cover (1:2). 2.95
2 Lady fights back 2.95

FREAK FORCE
Image/Highbrow 1993–95
1 EL(s),KG 2.25
2 EL(s),KG 2.25
3 EL(s),KG 2.25
4 EL(s),KG,A:Vanguard 2.25
5 EL(s),KG 2.25
6 EL(s),KG 2.25
7 EL(s),KG 2.25
8 EL(s),space ants 2.25
9 EL(s),Cyberforce 2.25
10 EL(s),Savage Dragon 2.25
11 EL(s),Invasion pt.1 . . . . 2.50
12 EL(s),Invasion pt.2 . . . . 2.50
13 EL(s),Invasion pt.3. . . . . 2.50
14 EL(s),Team Defeated 2.50
15 EL(s),F:Barbaric 2.50
16 KG,EL(s),V:Chelsea Nirvana . . 2.50
17 EL,KG,major plots converge . . 2.50
18 Final Issue 2.50
TPB 448pg 29.95

Series Two
Image March 1997
1 EL,Star joins team,V:The
　　Frightening Force 2.95
2 EL,Dart quits team 2.95
3 EL,"Lo there shall come..an
　　ending". 2.95

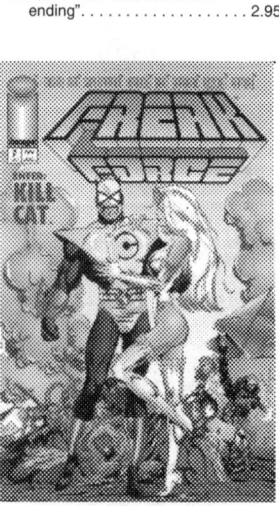
Freak Force #7
© Highbrow

FRIENDS OF MAXX
Image/I Before E
1 WML&SK 2.95
2 MHs&SK 2.95

GAZILLION
Image Nov. 1998
1 HSm, Mars vs. Xof 2.50
1a variant cover (1:4). 2.50

GEN[13]
Image/Wildstorm
0 Individual Hero Stories 4.00
1 JLe(s),BCi(s),I:Fairchild,Grunge,
　　Freefall,Burnout 20.00
1a 2nd printing 4.00
2 JLe(s),BCi(s), ... 16.00
3 JLe(s),BCi(s),A:Pitt 10.00
4 JLe(s),BCi(s) 8.00
5 Final issue 5.00
5a WP variant cover 10.00
TPB 12.95
HC 1,000 copies. 40.00

Regular Series 1995
1a BCi(s),V:Mercenaries 5.00
1b Common Cover 2 . . . . 5.00
1c Heavy Metal Gen 10.00
1d Pulp Fiction Parody. 12.00
1e Gen 13 Bunch 10.00
1f Lin-Gen-re 12.00
1g Lil Gen 13. . . . . 10.00
1h Friendly Neighbor Grunge. . . . 10.00
1i Gen 13 Madison Ave 12.00
1j Gen-Et Jackson 10.00
1k Gen Dress Up cover 10.00
1l Verti-Gen. 10.00
1m Do It Yourself Cover. 10.00
2 BCi,BWS(c),WildStorm Rising,
　　pt.4, w/2 cards 3.00
2a Newstand Edition 2.25
3 Coda Island 3.00
4 Coda Island 2.50
5 I:New Member 2.50
6 I:The Deviants 3.00
7 European Vacation,pt.2. . . . . . . 3.00
8 . . . . 2.50
9 . . . . 2.50
10 Fire From Heaven, pt.3 . . . . . . 2.50
11 . . . . 2.50
12 . . . . 2.50
13 A, B & C, each . . . . @1.30
14 back to school 2.50
15 Fraternity and Sorority rush . . . 2.50
16 . . . . 2.50
17 BCi,JSC,AGo,battle royale
　　in Tower of Luv. 2.50
18 BCi, JSC,AGo,V:Keepers 2.50
19 BCi,JSC,AGo,Lynch & kids flee
　　to Antarctica. 2.50
20 BCi,JSC,AGo,"Spaced Out" . . . 2.50
21 BCi,JSC,AGo,V:D'Rahn 2.50
22 BCi,global civil war 2.50
23 BCi,21st century 2.50
24 BCi,V:D'Rahn 2.50
25 BCi,Homecoming,JsC(c) 3.50
25a TC(c) 3.50
25b Voyager bagged pack 3.50
26 JAr,GFr,CaS,back in NYC 2.50
27 JAr,GFr,CaS,bailed out of jail . . . 2.50
28 JAr,GFr,CaS, new villain 2.50
29 JAr,GFr,CaS,I:Tindalos 2.50
30 JAr,GFr,CaS,to Florida Keys . . . 2.50
31 JAr,GFr,CaS,Roxy's Big Score . . . 2.50
32 JAr,GFr,CaS,Hard Wind 2.50
33 JAr,GFr,CaS,aftermaths, with
　　8-page Planetary #0 . . . . 2.50
34 JAr,GFr,CaS,AAd,A:Roxy
　　& Sarah 2.50

Gen 13 #29
© Jim Lee

35 JAr,GFr,CaS,John Lynch resigns 2.50
36 JAr,GFr,CaS,F:John Lynch. 2.50
College Yearbook 1997. . . . . 2.50
Ann. #1 WEI,SDi"London'sBrilliant" . 2.95
3-D Spec. #1, with glasses 4.95
3-D Spec. #1, variant cover 4.95
TPB rep.1–#5 of original mini-
　　series, 3rd printing 12.95
TPB Lost in Paradise, rep. #3–#5 . . 6.95
TPB EuropeanVacation,rep.#6–#7 . 6.95
TPB rep. #13 A, B & C 6.95
TPB Ordinary Heroes 12.95
TPB Wildstorm Archives, rep. mini-
　　series, #0–#13, covers, etc. . . . 13.00

Wildstorm/DC 1999
37 JAr,GFr,CaS,Reaper 2.50
38 JAr,GFr,CaS,BU:Grunge 2.50
38a variant cover 2.50
39 JAr,GFr,CaS,Genocide. 2.50
40 JAr,GFr,CaS,V:Reaper. 2.50
41 JAr,GFr,CaS, ... 2.50
42 JoC(s),KM,pro wrestlers. 2.50
43 AWa(s&c),F:Fairchild 2.50
44 AWa(s&c),A:Mr.Magestic 2.50
Annual'99 JAr(s). 3.50
TPB Gen13 . . . . 13.00
Spec. Wired 2.50
GN Grunge Saves the World 6.00
GN Bootleg: Grunge— The Movie. 10.00
Spec. 1-shot Going West 2.50
TPB Interactive Plus 12.00
TPB Starting Over 15.00

GEN[13] BOOTLEG
Image/Wildstorm Nov. 1996
1 MFm&AD,lost in the "Linquist
　　Fault" 2.50
1a signed 15.00
2 . . . . 3.50
3 On the banks of the River Plin . . 3.50
4 WS&LSi,F:Valaria 3.50
5 Fairchild looses 30 minutes of
　　her life 3.50
6 Fairchild goes back in time,pt.2. . 3.50
7 Day before a big exam 3.50
8 AWa, pt.1 (of 3) 2.50
9 AWa, pt.2 (of 3) 2.50
10 AWa, pt.3 (of 3) 2.50
11 AaL,WS,Chupacabra,pt.1. . . . . 2.50
12 AaL,WS,Chupacabra,pt.2. . . . . 2.50
13 F:Grunge. 2.50
14 JMi,JoP,GL, bad neighbors 2.50

IMAGE

15 KNo,V:Trance, pt.1	2.50
16 KNo,V:Trance, pt.2	2.50
17 Video arcade challenge	2.50
18 MFm,Grunge-mania.	2.50
19 BKs,JhB,Satyr	2.50
20 CAd,F:John Lynch	2.50
21 StG,DdW,Grunge, Gorilla Guy	2.50
Ann.#1 WEI,SDi, to NYC	2.95
TPB Grunge: The Movie,AWa.	9.95
TPB Vol.1, rep.#1–#4	11.95

GEN13: INTERACTIVE
Image/Wildstorm Oct. 1997

1 vote via internet	2.50
2 MHs,vote via internet	2.50
3 MHs,conclusion	2.50
TPB Gen13 Interactive Plus, rep.	11.95

GEN13/ GENERATION X
Image/Wildstorm July 1997

1 BCi&AAd	2.95
1 variant cover by JSC	2.95
3-D Edition, with glasses	4.95
3-Da variant cover, with glasses	4.95

GEN13: MAGICAL DRAMA QUEEN ROXY
Image/Wildstorm Oct. 1998

1 (of 3) AWa,Mall of Doom.	3.50
2 AWa,V:Caitlin	3.50
3 AWa,dream sequence concl.	3.50

GEN13/MAXX

1	4.00

GEN13/MONKEY MAN & O'BRIEN
Image/Wildstorm June 1998

1 (of 2) AAd.	2.50
1a chromium edition	4.50
2 AAd,alternate universe, concl.	2.50
2a variant AAd(c).	2.50

GEN13: ORDINARY HEROES

1	2.50
2	2.50

GEN12
Image/Wildstorm Feb. 1998

1 BCi,Team 7 tie-in	2.50
2 BCi,F:Morgan of I.O.	2.50
3 BCi,Dominique Faust	2.50
4 BCi,F:Miles Craven.	2.50
5 BCi,Team 7 re-unites	2.50

GLORY
Image/Extreme 1995

0 JDy	2.50
1 JDy,F:Glory	4.00
1a variant cover.	4.00
2 JDy,V:Demon Father.	3.00
3 JDy,A:Rumble & Vandal	2.50
4 Vandal vs. Demon Horde	2.50
4a JDy variant cover	3.00
5 F:Vandal.	2.50
6 Drug Problem.	2.50
7 F:Superpatriot.	2.50
8 Extreme Babewatch	2.50
9 thru 11	@2.50

12 JDy, EBe & JSb.	3.50
13 JDy, EBe & JSb.	2.50
14 JDy, EBe & JSb.	2.50
15 JDy, EBe & JSb, Out for vengeance	2.50
continued: see Color Comics section	
TPB Rep.#1-#4.	9.95

GLORY/ANGELA HELL'S ANGELS

1	4.00

GLORY/AVENGELYNE

1 V:B'lial,I:Faith	4.00
1a no chrome (c)	3.00

GLORY/AVENGELYNE: THE GODYSSEY
Image/Extreme

1 RLd & JDy	3.00
1a photo (c).	4.00

GLORY/CELESTINE: DARK ANGEL
Image/Extreme Sept. 1996

1 (of 3) JDy,PtL,sequel to Rage of Angels, A:Maximage.	2.50
2 JDy,PtL,"Doomsday+1".	2.50

GLORY & FRIENDS BIKINI FEST

1 Nuff said.	2.50

GOLDFISH
Image (B&W) 1998

TPB by Brian Michael Bendis	16.95

GREASE MONKEY
Image March 1998

1 TEI.	2.95
2 TEI.	2.95
3 TEI, The Calling; Rewards	2.95

GRIFTER
Image/Wildstorm 1995

1 BWS(c), WildStorm

Glory #15
© *Extreme Studios*

Rising,pt.5,w/2 cards	2.50
1a Newsstand Ed.	1.95
2 City of Angels,pt.1	2.50
3 City of Angels,pt.2	2.50
4 R:Forgotten Hero	2.50
5 Rampage of a Fallen Hero	2.50
6 V:Poerhouse.	2.50
7 & 8	@2.50

GRIFTER/BADROCK

1 To Save Badrock's Mom	3.00
1a Variant cover	2.50
2	3.00
3 double size.	3.50

GRIFTER-ONE SHOT

1 SS,DN	4.00

GRIFTER
Image/Wildstorm

1 StG	4.00
2 StG	3.00
3 StG,captured by MadJackPower.	3.00
4 StG,vs. Condition Red	2.50
5 StG,Grifter gambles his soul.	2.50
6 StG,	2.50
7 StG,MtB,I:Charlatan	2.50
8 StG,MtB,Zealot disappears,V:Soldier.	2.50
9 StG,Zealot captured?, secret history of Quiet Men	2.50
10 StG,Grifter & Soldier go to rescue Zealot	2.50
11 StG, renegade former agent.	2.50
12 StG,"Who is Tanager?"	2.50
13 StG,"Family Feud".	2.50
14 StG,V:Joe the Dead.	2.50

GRIFTER/SHI

1 & 2.	3.00
HC	29.95
HC signed & numbered(Lee)	50.00
HC signed & numbered(Tucci)	50.00
HC signed & numbered(Charest)	35.00
HC signed & numbered(Hubbs)	25.00

GROO

1 SA	2.25
2 A:Arba, Dakarba.	2.00
3 The Generals Hat	2.00
4 A Drink of Water.	2.00
5 SA,A Simple Invasion	2.00
6 SA,A Little Invention	2.00
7 The Plight of the Drazils	2.00
8	2.25
9 I:Arfetto	2.25
10 The Sinkes	2.25
11 The Gamblers	2.25
12	2.25

HAZARD
Image/Wildstorm 1996

1 JMi,RMr	2.50
2 JMi,RMr	1.75
3 JMi,RMr	1.75
4 JMi,RMr	1.75
5 JMi,RMr,Hazard finds Dr. D'Oro	1.75
6 JMi,RMr	2.25
7 JMi,RMr,Hazard meets Prism	2.25

HEADHUNTERS
Image April 1997 (B&W)

1 ChM,V:Army of Wrath	2.95
2 ChM,V:undead militia	2.95
3 ChM,"Slaughterground"	2.95

IMAGE

All comics prices listed are for *Near Mint* condition.   **CVA Page 477**

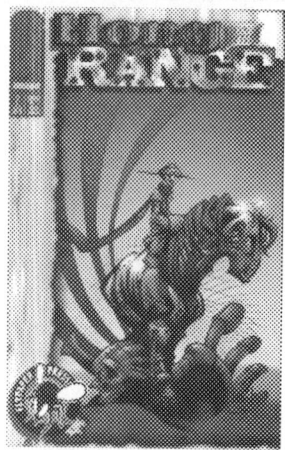

Hong on the Range #2
© Flypaper

HEARTBREAKERS
Image July 1998
Superdigest, 6"x9"
1 B&W and color 104pg. 9.95

HEARTBREAKERS VERSUS BIOVOC
Image
TPB "Bust Out". 9.95
TPB PGn 14.95

HELLCOP
Image/Avalon Oct. 1998
1 JoC,F:Virgil Hilts. 2.50
2 JoC,It's a small underworld
    after all. 2.50
3 JoC,new circles of Hell 2.50
4 JoC,secrets of Hell revealed. . . 2.50
5 JoC,Hell & High Water 2.50
5a variant cover. 2.95

HELLHOLE
Image/Top Cow May 1999
1 SLo,AdP,F:Michael Cabrini 2.50
2 SLo,AdP,The Devil's Candy 2.50
3 SLo,AdP,power brokers 2.50

HELLSHOCK
Image 1994
1 I:Hellshock. 3.50
2 Powers & Origin. 3.50
3 New foe 3.50
4 . . . . 3.50

HELLSHOCK
Image Jan. 1997
1 JaL,Something wrong with
    Daniel, 48pg. 3.00
2 JaL,Daniel learns to control
    powers. 2.50
3 JaL,Daniel free of madness 2.50
4 JaL,Daniel searches for his
    mother, Jonakand plans escape
    from Hell 2.50
5 JaL,Jonakand and fallen angels
    tear hell apart. 2.50
6 JaL,"The Milk of Paradise" 2.50
7 JaL,"A Mother's Story",

double size. 3.95
8 JaL,House of Torture 2.50

HOMAGE STUDIOS
Swimsuit Spec.#1 JLe,WPo, MS. . . 2.25

HONG ON THE RANGE
Image/Matinee Entertainment/Flypaper
1 (of 3) by William Wu & Jeff
    Lafferty 2.50
2 in Washout. 2.50
3 Duke Goslin. 2.50
TPB Hong on the Range. 12.95

IMAGE ZERO
Image 1993
0 I:Troll,Deathtrap,Pin-ups,rep.
    Savage Dragon #4,O:Stryker,
    F:ShadowHawk 15.00

IMAGES OF SHADOWHAWK
Image 1993–94
1 KG,V:Trencher 2.25
2 thru 3 V:Trencher 2.25

IMMORTAL TWO
Image May 1997 (B&W) Half-Tone
1 MsM,F:Gaijin & Gabrielle 2.50
2 MsM. 2.50
3 MsM. 2.50
4 MsM,V:Okami Red 2.50
5 MsM,new drug epidemic. 2.50
6 MsM,First Order, cont. 2.50
7 MsM,vs. impossible odds 2.50
7 MsM,flip photo cover 2.50

INTRIGUE
Image Aug. 1999
1 F:Kirk Best 2.50
1a variant cover (1:4). 2.50

INVISIBLE 9
Image/Flypaper
TPB 12.95

JACKIE CHAN'S SPARTAN X
Image (B&W) March 1998
1 MGo,RM,Hell-Bent Hero for Hire. 2.95
2 MGo,to Russia 2.95
3 MGo,V:Kenshi 2.95
4 MGo,RM, in Istanbul. 2.95
5 MGo,RM, Mind of God 2.95
5a MGo,RM, photo cover 2.95
6 MGo,RM, The Armor of Heaven . 2.95
6a MGo,RM, photo cover. 2.95

JADE WARRIORS
Image Aug. 1999
1 MD2,Destruction of Japan 2.50
1a variant photo cover (1:2). 2.50

JIM LEE'S C-23
Image/Wildstorm April 1998
1 BCi,JMi,F:Corben Helix. 2.50
2 JMi,TC(c),V:Angelans 2.50
3 JMi,TC(c),with trading card 2.50
4 JMi,Corbin, banished 2.50

Immortal Two #1
© Image

5 JMi,RCo(c),Queen Mother 2.50
5a variant JLe(c) (1:4) 2.50
6 JMi,RCo(c),V:HyperShock
    Troopers 2.50
7 JMi,RCo(c),Hail to the Queen . . . 2.50
8 JMi,RCo(c). 2.50

JINX
Image (B&W) June 1997
1 by Brian Michael Bendis 2.95
1a 2nd printing 2.95
2 F:Jinx, female bounty hunter. . . . 2.95
3 thru 5 . . . . @3.95
TPB rep. prev. #1–#4 . . . . 9.95
TPB The Essential Collection 17.95
Spec.#1 Buried Treasure 3.95
Spec.#1 True Crime Confessions . . 3.95

JINX: TORSO
Image (B&W) Aug. 1998
1 by Brian Michael Bendis, 48pg . . 3.95
2 search continues 3.95
3 Torso Killer. 3.95
4 breaking the law. 3.95
5 48-page 4.95
6 conclusion, 48-page 4.95
Spec. #@%!! short stories 3.95

JOURNEYMAN
Image Aug. 1999
1 by Brandon McKinney. 2.95

KABUKI
Image Sept. 1997
1 DMk,O:Kabuki 4.00
1a variant JSo(c). 6.00
2 DMk,O:Kabuki, pg.2 . . . . 3.00
3 DMk,surprise visitor 3.00
4 DMk,Akemi, romance 3.00
5 DMk,action 3.00
6 DMk. 2.95
7 DMk. 2.95
7a DMk variant cover (1:2) 2.95
8 DMk. 2.95
9 DMk, finale. 2.95
TPB Circle of Blood,rep. orig. series
    plus "Fear the Reaper," B&W . 17.95
HC Circle of Blood 29.95
HC Circle of Blood, S&N. 49.95
TPB Dreams. 10.00

IMAGE

TPB Masks of the Noh 10.95
TPB Masks of the Noh, 2nd pr. . . . 12.95
HC Masks of the Noh 39.95
TPB Skin Deep. 9.95
HC Skin Deep 23.95
HC Skin Deep, sign & num. 39.95
TPB Images, part rep. #1, 48pg. . . . 4.95
Reflections #1, 48pg. 4.95
Reflections #2 art & stories 4.95
Spec. #2 Images, rep. #2 & #3 . . . 5.95

KABUKI AGENTS
Image (B&W) Aug. 1999
1 F:Scarab 2.95

KABUKI CLASSICS
Image/
1 Fear the Reaper, rep. 3.95
2 Dance of Death 2.95
3 Circle of Blood, act 1, 48-page . . 3.95
4 Circle of Blood, act 2 . . . . 2.95
5 Circle of Blood, act 3 . . . . 2.95
6 Circle of Blood, act 4 . . . . 2.95
7 Circle of Blood, act 5 . . . . 2.95
8 Circle of Blood, conclusion 2.95

KID SUPREME
Image/Supreme 1996–97
1 & 2 . . . . 2.50
3 DaF,ErS 2.50
4 DaF,ErS,Party time 2.50
5 DaF,ErS,"Birds of a Feather" . . . 2.50
6 DaF,ErS,I: The Sensational
    Spinner 2.50
7 DaF,ErS,Everything falls apart . . 2.50

KID TERRIFIC
(B&W) Image Nov. 1998
1 A:Snedak & Manny Stellar 2.95

KILLER INSTINCT
TOUR BOOK
1 All Homage Artist,I:Crusade 5.00
1a signed 45.00

KILLRAZOR SPECIAL
1 O:Killrazor 2.50

KINDRED
Image/Wildstorm 1994
1 JLe,BCi(s),BBh,I:Knidred 5.00
2 JLe,BCi(s),BBh,V:Kindred 3.50
3 JLe,BCi(s),BBh,V:Kindred 3.00
3a WPo(c),Alternate(c) 6.00
4 JLe,BCi(s),BBh,V:Kindred 3.00
TPB rep. #1–#4 . . . . 9.95

'KINI
Image/Flypaper Feb. 1999
1 KK,BKs,F:Kim Walters 2.50

KISS:
THE PSYCHO CIRCUS
Image/TMP July 1997
1 SvG,AMe 8.00
2 AMe, unearthly origins 6.00
3 AMe, Judgment o/t Elementals . . 5.00
4 AMe,Smoke and Mirrors, pt.1 . . 4.00
5 AMe,Smoke and Mirrors, pt.2 . . 3.00
6 AMe,Smoke and Mirrors, concl. . 3.00
7 AMe,Creatures of the Night 3.00
8 AMe,Forever 3.00

Kiss: The Psycho Circus #5
© Todd McFarlane

9 AMe,Four Sides to Every Story . . 2.50
10 AMe,Destroyer, pt.1 . . . . 2.50
11 AMe,Destroyer, pt.2 . . . . 2.50
12 AMe,Destroyer, pt.3 (of 4) 2.50
13 AMe, Destroyer, pt.4 . . . . 2.50
14 AMe, in Feudal Japan 2.50
15 AMe, in Feudal Japan, choices . 2.25
16 AMe, Ticket for Terror 2.25
17 AMe, World Without Heroes,pt.2 2.25
18 AMe, Sunburst Finish 2.25
19 Fate of the Psycho Circus 2.25
20 Mr. Makebelieve 2.25
21 Don't Talk to Strangers. 2.25
22 Twin sisters 2.25
23 Tribunal of souls 2.25
TPB Vol. I, rep. #1–#6 . . . . 12.95
TPB Vol. II rep. #10–#13 . . . . 9.95

KNIGHTMARE
Image/Extreme 1995
0 O:Knightmare 2.50
1 I:Knightmare MMy 2.50
2 I:Caine 2.50
3 RLd,AV,The New Order,
    F:Detective Murtaugh 2.50
4 RLd,AV,MMy,I:Thrillkill. 2.50
5 V:Thrillkill 2.50
6 Extreme Babewatch 2.50
7 . . . . 2.50
8 I:Acid 2.50

KNIGHT WATCHMAN
Image (B&W) May 1998
1 by Gary Carlson & Chris Ecker . . 2.95
2 Graveyard Shift, pt.2. . . . . 2.95
3 Graveyard Shift, pt.3. . . . . 2.95
4 Graveyard Shift, concl. 2.95

KOSMIC KAT
Image July 1999
Activity Book. 2.95

KURT BUSIEK'S
ASTRO CITY
1 I:Samaritan 11.00
1a 2nd printing 2.00
2 V:Shirak the Devourer 6.00
3 F:Jack in the Box 5.00
4 thru 6 . . . . @7.00
TPB 19.95

HC 39.95

KURT BUSIEK'S
ASTRO CITY VOL.2
Homage Comics 1996–97
½ 5.00
1 KBk(s),BA 6.00
1a Trunk(c) 8.00
1b 2nd printing 2.50
2 KBk(s),BA,F:Astra 6.00
2b 2nd printing 2.50
3 KBk(s),BA, ... 2.50

Image/Homage Comics
4 KBk,BA,Teenager seeks to
    become teen sidekick,pt.1 (of 6) 5.00
5 . . . . 5.00
6 V: creatures of Shadow Hill. 5.00
7 Aliens invade Astro City 3.00
8 The aliens are out there 2.50
9 Honor Guard vs. Aliens finale . . . 2.50
10 meet the junkman 2.50
11 . . . . 2.50
12 F:Jack-In-The-Box 2.50
13 F:Looney Leo 2.50
14 F:Steeljack 2.50
15 F:supervillains 2.50
16 F:El Hombre 2.50
17 F:Steeljack, staying straight . . . 2.50
TPB Confession, rep.#4–#9 . . . . . 19.95
HC Confession 50.00
3-D #1 . . . . 4.95
TPB Life in the Big City. 19.95
HC Life in the Big City. 34.95
TPB Family Album 19.95
HC Family Album 49.95

Homage/DC 1999
VOLUME 2
16 KBk(s), El Hombre 2.50
17 KBk(s), Mock Turtle 2.50
18 KBk(s), F:Steeljack 2.50
Spec.1/2 KBk(s) 2.50

LABMAN
1 . . . . 3.50
1a variant cover. 3.50
2 and 3 . . . . @2.95

LADY PENDRAGON
Image Nov. 1998
1 MHw,Destiny's Embrace 2.50
1a remastered, new cover 2.50
1b Dynamic Forces variant cover. . 6.95
1c JeL (c) glow-in-the-dark 19.95
1d Tour Edition . . . . ??.00
2 MHw,Destiny's Embrace,pt.2 . . . 2.50
3 MHw,Destiny's Embrace,pt.3 . . . 2.50
3a variant cover (1:4). 2.50
0 MHw, Secrets & Origins 2.50
0a Eurosketch cover 10.00
Preview (Wizard, Chicago Comicon) 4.95

LADY PENDRAGON:
DRAGON BLADE
Image April 1999
1 MHw,Merlin trains Jennifer 2.50
1a variant cover (1:4). 2.50
1b Chrome Edition. . . . . ??.00
2 MHw,F:Morgana. 2.50
2a variant cover (1:4). 2.50
3 MHw,B.U.I:Alley Cat. 2.50
4 MHw,Morgana returns 2.50
5 MHw,Spear of Destiny 2.50

IMAGE

IMAGE

LADY PENDRAGON: MORE THAN MORTAL
Image May 1999
1 MHw,Pendragon vs. Protector.	2.50
1a variant cover (1:4).	6.95
1b Gold foil (c).	6.95

LADY SUPREME
Image/Extreme
1 TMr	2.50
2 TMr	2.50
3 TMr,V:Manassa	2.50
4 TMr,"Lady Supreme goes undercover"	2.50

LEAVE IT TO CHANCE
Homage Comics Sept. 1996
1 JeR,PS,I:Chance Falconer	2.50
2	2.50

Image/Homage Comics
3 Chance and St. George race against time	2.50
4	2.50
5 Halloween Night in Devil's Echo	2.50
6 Chance sent to private school.	2.50
7 Falconer's battle with Captain Hitch, pt.2.	2.50
8 "The Phantom of the Mall"	2.50
9 Menace from the Matinee	2.50
10 Terror off the silver screen	2.50
11 Sudden Death	2.50
12 visits her friend Dash	2.50
TPB rep. #1–#4	9.95
TPB Vol. II, rep. #5–#8	12.95
HC Shaman's Rain.	24.95
HC Shaman's Rain, signed	34.95

Homage/DC 1999
12 JeR(s),F:Dash	3.00

LEGEND OF SUPREME
1 KG(s),JJ,DPs,Revelations pt.1	2.50
2 Revelations pt.2	2.50
3 Conclusion	2.50

LETHAL
Image 1996
1 and 2	@2.50

LITTLE-GREYMAN
Image (B&W)
TPB by C. Scott Morse	6.95

LITTLE RED HOT: CHANE OF FOOLS
Image (B&W) Feb. 1999
1 (of 3) by Dawn Brown, F:Chane	2.95
2 stranded in desert.	2.95
3 Heaven vs. Hell	2.95
TPB The Foolish Collection, rep.	12.95

LYNCH
Image/Wildstorm June 1997
1 TVs,"Terror in the Jungle"	2.50

MAN AGAINST TIME
1	2.50
2	2.50

MAGE: THE HERO DEFINED
Image 1997
1 MWg,F:Kevin Matchstick	4.00
2 MWg,Kirby Hero, V:harpies.	3.00
3 MWg,Isis, Gretch	3.00
4 MWg,Isis, drug	3.00
5 MWg,into Canada.	3.00
6 MWg,V:Dragonslayer	2.50
7 MWg,	2.50
8 MWg,V:Red Caps.	2.50
9 MWg,Sibling Trio	2.50
10 MWg,enchanted by a succubus.	2.50
11 MWg,Joe Phat, missing	2.50
12 MWg,Pale Incanter's Lair	2.50
13 MWg,What color is magic	2.50
14 MWg,Man Mountain of????	2.50
Spec. 3-D #1	4.95
TPB Vol. 1 rep.	9.95
TPB Vol. II, rep. #5–#8	9.95
Coll.Ed.Vol.1,rep.#1–#2	5.95
Coll.Ed.Vol.2,rep.#3–#4	5.95
Coll.Ed.Vol.3,rep.#5–#6	5.95
Coll.Ed.Vol.4,rep.#7–#8	4.95
Coll.Ed.Vol.5,rep.#9–#10	4.95
Coll.Ed.Vol.6,rep.#11–#12.	4.95
Coll.Ed.Vol.7,rep.#13–#14	5.50
Coll.Ed.Vol.8,rep.#15–#16	4.95

Mars Attacks Image #1
© Image

MARS ATTACKS IMAGE
Image 1996
1 KG,BSz(of 4)	2.50
2	2.50
3	2.50
4 End of their world as they knew it	2.50

MASK OF ZORRO, THE
Image July 1998
1 (of 4) DMG,RoW,RM,MGo(c), movie adapt.	2.95
2 DMG,RoW, RM,MGo(c)	2.95
3 DMG,RoW,MGo(c)	2.95
4 DMG,RoW,MGo concl.	2.95
4a photo cover	2.95

MAXIMAGE
1 thru 8	@2.50
9 BML, Sex Slaves of Bomba Island.	2.50
10 BML, The King of Emotion is	

The Maxx #24
© Sam Kieth
back.	2.50

MAXX, THE
1/2 SK,from Wizard	7.00
1 SK,I:The Maxx	4.00
1a glow in the dark(c)	12.00
2 SK,V:Mr.Gone	4.00
3 SK,V:Mr.Gone	4.00
4 SK,	4.00
5 SK,	3.00
6 SK,	3.00
7 SK,A:Pitt.	3.50
8 SK,V:Pitt.	3.50
9 SK	3.00
10 SK.	3.00
11 SK.	2.50
12 SK.	2.50
13 Maxx Wanders in Dreams	2.50
14 R:Julie.	2.50
15 Julia's Pregnant.	2.50
16 SK,Is Maxx in Danger?	2.50
17 Gardener Maxx	2.25
18	1.95
19 V:Hooley	1.95
20 Questions are answered	2.25
21 AM story	1.95
22 SK.	1.95
23 SK.	1.95
24 SK.	1.95
25 SK.	1.95
26 SK.	1.95
27 V:Iago the Killer Slug	1.95
28 Sara and Norberg look for Julie	1.95
29 Sara and Gone defeat Iago the Slug	1.95
30 Lil' Sara faces her fears	1.95
31 F:The Library girl	1.95
32 F:The Library girl,pt.2.	1.95
33 Sara's back	1.95
34 Mark and Julia.	1.95
35 who knows?	1.95
36 bumfuzzled	1.95
37 Megan's story concl.	1.95
38 Mark,Julie,Larry, pt.1 (of 4)	1.95
Spec. Friends of Maxx	2.95
TPB Rep. #1–#5	12.95
TPB Vol. 2	12.95

MECHANIC, THE
Image/Homage Aug. 1998
GN JCh,JPe,time travel	5.95

MEDIEVAL SPAWN/ WITCHBLADE

1	11.00
2	9.00
3	7.00
TPB collected	9.95

MEGADRAGON & TIGER
Image March 1999

1 by Tony Wong, from Hong Kong	2.95
2 F:Red Tiger	2.95
3 V:Single-Minded Arhat	2.95
4 V:Fiery Lord	2.95
5 F:Gigi	2.95

Megahurtz #2
© Image

MEGAHURTZ
Image (B&W) Aug. 1997

1 JPi,I:Megahurtz	2.95
2 JPi,visit to Wonderland	2.95
3 JPi,V:N-Filtraitors	2.95
4 JPi,Liberaiders	2.95

MEGATON MAN: BOMBSHELL
Image July 1999

1 DSs,V:Unleash	2.95

MEGATON MAN: HARDCOPY
Image/Fiasco (B&W) Feb. 1999

1 by Don Simpson	2.95
2 with 6 new pages	2.95

MIKE GRELL'S MAGGIE THE CAT

1 thru 4	@2.50

MISERY SPECIAL

1 Cyberforce Origins	2.95

MONSTER FIGHTERS, INC.
Image April 1999

1 Who you gonna call	2.95
2 Wake the dead	2.95

MONSTERMAN
Image (B&W) Sept. 1997

1 MM,from Action Planet	2.95
2 MM,Inhuman monsters	2.95
3 MM,King of Monsters	2.95
4 MM, conclusion	2.95

MORE THAN MORTAL/ LADY PENDRAGON
Image June 1999

1 MHw,x-over	2.50
Prev. Edition 16-page, B&W	4.95

MORE THAN MORTAL: OTHERWORLDS
Image/Liar Comics July 1999

1 F:Derdre & Morand	2.95
1a variant cover (1:2)	2.95
2 in Otherworld	2.95
2a variant cover (1:2)	2.95

MR. MONSTER VS. GORZILLA
Image (2 color) July 1998

1-shot, MGi	2.95

MS. FORTUNE
Image (B&W) 1998

1 by Chris Marrinan	2.95
2 Carnage in the Caribbean	2.95
3 Doom at the Dawn of Time	2.95

MYSTERY, INC.

Ashcan 1	4.00

NAMELESS, THE
Image (B&W) May 1997

1 PhH,I:The Nameless, protector of Mexico City's lost children	2.95
2	2.95
3	2.95
4	2.95
5 V:Huitzilopochtili	2.95

NASH
Image July 1999

1 MMy, by & starring Kevin Nash	2.50
1a variant cover (1:2)	2.95
Preview edition MMy,F:Kevin Nash	2.50
Preview ed.A variant cover (1:2)	2.50

NEON CYBER
Image July 1999

1 F:Neon Dragons	2.50
1a variant cover (1:2)	2.50
2 gang alliance	2.50
2a variant cover (1:2)	2.50

NEW ADVENTURES OF ABRAHAM LINCOLN
Image/Homage Feb. 1998

TPB SMI, 144pg.	19.95

NEW FORCE

1 thru 4 mini-series	@2.50

THE NEW ORDER HANDBOOK

Various artists	1.50

NEW MAN

1 thru 3	@2.50
4 Shadowhunt x-over,pt.5	2.50

NEWMEN
Image/Extreme 1994

1 JMs,	3.00
2 JMs,I:Girth	2.25
3 JMs,V:Girth,I:Ikonna	2.25
4 JMs,A:Ripclaw	1.95
5 JMs,Ripclaw,V:Ikonn.	2.50
6 JMs	2.50
7 JMs	2.50
8 JMs,Team Youngblood	2.50
9 ErS(s),JMs,Kodiak Kidnapped	2.50
10 ExtremeSacrifice x-over,pt.4	2.50
11 F:Reign	2.50
12 R:Elemental	2.50
13 ErS,I:Bootleg	2.50
14 ErS,Dominion's Secret	2.50
15 I:Time Guild	2.50
16	2.50
16a variant cover	3.00
17 R:Girth	2.50
18 F:Byrd	2.50
19 I:Bordda Khan,Shepherd	2.50
20 Extreme Babewatch	2.50
21 ErS,CSp,(1 of 5)	2.50
22 ErS,CSp, Who Needs the Newmen?	2.50
23 ErS,CSp,Who are the Newmen?	2.50

NEW SHADOWHAWK, THE

1 I:New ShadowHawk	2.50
2 V:Mutants	2.50
3 I:Trophy	2.50
4 V:Blowfish	2.50
5 thru 7	@2.50

1963

1 AnM(s),RV,DGb,I:Mystery, Inc.	2.50
1a Gold Ed.	4.00
1b Bronze Ed.	3.00
2 RV,SBi,DGb,JV,I:The Fury	2.25
3 RV,SBi,I:U.S.A.	2.25
4 JV,SBi,I:N-Man, Johnny Beyond	2.25
5 JV,SBi,I:Horus	2.25
6 JV,SBi,I:Tommorow Synicate, C:Shaft.	2.25
Ashcan #1	3.00
Ashcan #2	2.50
Ashcan #4	2.00

NINE VOLT
Image/Top Cow 1997

1 ACh	3.00
1a Variant (c)	4.00
2 ACh	3.00
3 ACh,V:crazed junkie terrorists	2.50
4 ACh,V:Rev. Cyril Gibson	2.50

NORMAL MAN/ MEGATON MAN SPECIAL

1	2.50

OPERATION KNIGHTSTRIKE

1 RHe,A:Chapel,Bravo,Battlestone	2.50
2 In Afganistan	2.50
3 final issue	2.50

THE OTHERS

0 JV(s),From ShadowHawk	2.50
1 JV(s)V:Mongrel.	2.50
2 JV,Mongrel takes weapons	2.50

IMAGE

3 War	2.50
4 O:Clone	2.50

PACT
Image 1994

1 JV(s),WMc,I:Pact, C:Youngblood	2.25
2 JV(s),V:Youngblood	1.95
3 JV(s),V:Atrocity.	1.95

PHANTOM FORCE

1 RLd,JK,w/card	2.75
2 JK,V:Darkfire	1.95

See also Color Comics section

PHANTOM GUARD
Image/Wildstorm Oct. 1997

1 by Sean Ruffner, Ryan Benjamin	2.50
1a variant cover	2.50
1b Voyager bagged pack	3.50
2 Martian wasteland	2.50
3 Lowell Zerium Mines.	2.50
4	2.50
5 V:Vanox,	2.50
6 Countdown to Armageddon	2.50

PITT
Image/Top Cow 1993–95

1 DK,I:Pitt,Timmy.	4.00
2 DK,V:Quagg.	3.00
3 DK,V:Zoyvod	4.00
4 DK,V:Zoyvod	3.00
5 DK	2.50
6 DK	2.50
7 DK	2.50
8 Ransom	2.50
9 DK,Artic Adventures	2.00
Ashcan 1	3.00

POWER OF THE MARK

1 I:Ted Miller	2.50
2 V:The Fuse.	2.50
3 TMB(s), The Mark	2.50
4 TMB,Mark's secrets revealed	2.50

POWER RANGERS ZEO
Image/Extreme Sept. 1997

1 thru 3 TBm&MBm(s),TNu,NRd	@2.50

POWER RANGERS ZEO YOUNGBLOOD
Image/Extreme Oct. 1997

1 thru 2 RLd,TBm,MBm	@2.95

PROPHET
Image/Extreme 1993–95

0 San Diego Comic-Con Ed.	4.00
1 RLd(s)DPs,O:Prophet.	3.00
1a Gold Ed.	4.00
2 RLd(s),DPs,C:Bloodstrike	2.50
3 RLd(s),DPs, V:Bloodstrike, I:Judas.	2.50
4 RLd(s),DPs,A:Judas	2.50
4a SPa(c),Limited Ed.	3.00
5 SPa	3.00
6 SPa	2.50
7 SPa War Games pt.1	2.25
8 SPa War Games pt.2	2.50
9 SPa,Extreme Sacrifice Prelude.	2.50
10 ExtremeSacrifice x-over,pt.6	2.50
Sourcebook	2.95
Ashcan #1	3.00
Ashcan #2	3.00

[Regular Series]

1 SPI, New Series	2.75

Prophet #2
© Extreme Studios

2 SPI, New Direction	2.50
2a variant cover.	2.50
3 True Nature	2.50
4 The Dying Factor	2.50
5 and 6	@2.50
7 CDi,SPa	2.50
8 and 9	@2.50
TPB	12.95
Ann.#1 Supreme Apocalypse	2.50
Spec.#1 Babewatch special	2.50

PROPHET/AVENGELYNE

1	3.00

RAGMOP
Image (B&W)

Vol.2 #1 by Rob Walton	2.95
Vol.2 #2	2.95

REGULATORS
June 1995

1 F:Blackjack,"Touch of Scandal".	2.50
2 F:Vortex	2.50
3 F:Arson	2.50
4 F:Scandal.	2.50

REPLACEMENT GOD AND OTHER STORIES, THE
Image (B&W) May 1997

1 Knute vs. King Ursus	2.95
2 by Zander Cannon	2.95
3 thru 4	@2.95

RESIDENT EVIL
Image/Wildstorm March 1998

1 comic/game magazine 56pg	4.95
2 thru 4 comic/game mag. 56pg.	@4.95

RIPCLAW
Image/Top Cow 1995

1/2 Prelude to Series (Wizard)	3.00
1/2a Con versions	7.00
1 A:Killjoy, I:Shadowblade	3.00
2 Cyblade, Heatwave	2.50
3 EcS,BPe,AV,Alliance with S.H.O.C.s.	2.50
4 conclusion	2.50
Spec.#1 I:Ripclaw's Brother	3.00

[1st Regular Series]

1 thru 5	@2.50

RIPTIDE
Image 1995

1 O:Riptide	2.50
2 O:Riptide	2.50

RISING STARS
Image/Top Cow March 1999

1 A celestial event	2.50
1a, b, & c variant covers	2.50
Preview by J. Michael Straczynski, 16-page, B&W	5.00

SABRE
(B&W) Image 1998

TPB 20th Anniversary.	12.95

SAM & TWITCH
Image/TMP Aug. 1999

1 AMe,Spawn tie-in	2.50

SAVAGE DRAGON
Image/Highbrow

1 EL,I:Savage Dragon	3.00
2 EL,I:Superpatriot.	3.50
3 EL,V:Bedrock,w'coupon#6	2.50
3a EL,w/o coupon	2.50
Spec. Savage Dragon Versus Savage Megaton Man #1 EL,DSm	2.50
Gold Ed.	12.00
TPB	9.95

[2nd Series] 1993

1 EL,I:Freaks.	2.50
2 EL,V:Teen.Mutant Ninja Turtles, Flip book Vanguard #0	2.50
3 EL,A:Freaks	2.25
4 EL,A:Freaks	2.25
5 EL,Might Man flip book	2.25
6 EL,A:Freaks	2.25
7 EL,Overlord	2.25
8 EL,V:Cutthroat,Hellrazor	2.25
9 thru 10 EL,	2.25
11 EL,A:Overlord	1.95
12 EL	1.95
13 EL,Mighty Man,Star,I:Widow (appeared after issue #20)	2.50
13a Larsen version of 13	2.50

Savage Dragon #28
© Erik Larsen

14 Possessed pt.1	2.50
15 Possessed pt.2	2.50
16 Possessed pt.3,V:Mace	2.50
17 V:Dragonslayer	2.50
18 R:The Fiend	2.50
19 V:The Fiend	2.50
20 Rematch with Ovrlord	2.50
21 V:Overlord	2.50
22 A:Teenage Mutant Turtles	2.50
23 Rapture vs. SheDragon	2.50
24 Gang War pt.1	2.50
25 Gang War,pt.2 double size	4.00
26	2.50
27	2.50
28	2.50
29	2.50
30	2.50
31 "The Dragon is trapped in Hell"	2.50
32 Kill-Cat vs. Justice	2.50
33 fatherhood	2.50
34 F:Hellboy, pt.1	3.00
35 F:Hellboy, pt.2	2.50
36 Dragon & Star try to rescue Peter Klaptin	2.50
37 mutants struggle in ruins of Chicago	2.50
38 Dragon vs. Cyberface	2.50
39 Dragon vs. Dung	2.50
40 "G-Man"	2.50
41 Wedding issue	2.50
42 V:Darklord	2.50
43 Stranded on another world	2.50
44 in flying saucer,	2.50
45	2.50
46 She-Dragon vs. Vicious Circle	2.50
47 A knight and a mummy	2.50
48 Unfinished Business, pt.1	2.50
49 Unfinished Business, pt.2	2.50
50 Unfinished Business, pt.3, some reps., 96pg	5.95
51 F:She-Dragon	2.50
52 F:She-Dragon,V:Hercules	2.50
53 EL,F:She Dragon	2.50
54 EL,V:imposter Dragon	2.50
55 EL,Dragon & She-Dragon	2.50
56 EL,Rita Medermade kidnapped	2.50
57 EL,V:Overlord	2.50
58 EL,Dragon's Resurrection	2.50
59 EL,return of Savage Dragon	2.50
60 EL,R:Devastator	2.50
61 EL,R:Rapture	2.50
62 EL,Savage Dragon married	2.50
63 EL,Dragon's honeymoon	2.50
64 EL,Overlord's secrets	2.50
65 EL,Possessed	2.50
66 EL,Dragon shrunk	2.50
TPB A Talk With God	17.95
HC A Talk With God, signed	74.95
TPB The Fallen, rep.#7–#11	12.95
HC The Fallen	29.95
TPB Possessed, rep.#12–#16	12.95
HC Possessed, rep.	89.95
TPB Archives #2, B&W,1982 rep.	2.95
TPB Archives #3, B&W,1984 rep.	2.95
TPB Archives #4, B&W,1986 rep.	2.95
TPB Revenge	13.95
TPB Greatest Team-ups	19.95

SAVAGE DRAGON DESTROYER DUCK
Image Comics
1 SvG,ChM,EL	3.95

SAVAGE DRAGON, THE: RED HORIZON
Image Comics Feb. 1997
1 MsM	2.50
2 MsM,Dragon in the ER,A:Freak	

Force	2.50
3 (of 3) MsM,Freak Force beaten	2.50

SAVAGE DRAGON: MARSHAL LAW
Image July 1997
(B&W)
1 (of 2) PMs,KON,F:Marshal Law	2.50
2 PMs,KON, concl.	2.95

SAVAGE DRAGON: SEX & VIOLENCE
Image July 1997
1 (of 2) TBm,MBm	2.50
2 TBm,MBm,AH, concl.	2.50

SAVANT GARDE
Image/Wildstorm March 1997
1 "A team without a rule book"	2.50
2 Between killer & killer cat	2.50
3 V: strange Tapestry	2.50
4 "Any super-villain can take over the world"	2.50
5 "The Final Showdown"	2.50
6 BKs,Guilty until proven innocent	2.50
7 BKs,death of John Colt	2.50

SHADOWHAWK
Image/Shadowline
1 JV,I:ShadowHawk,Black Foil(c), Pin-up, with coupon#1	3.00
1a w/o coupon	2.00
2 JV,V:Arsenal,A:Spawn, I:Infiniti	3.00
3 JV,V:Arsenal,w/glow-in-the-dark(c)	2.50
4 V:Savage Dragon	2.50
TPB rep.#1-4	19.95
Ashcan #1	2.00
Ashcan #2	2.00
Ashcan #3	2.00
Ashcan #4	2.00

[2nd Series] 1993
1 JV,Die Cut(c)	2.50
1a Gold Ed.	3.00
2 JV,ShadowHawk I.D.	2.50
2a Gold Ed.	2.50
3 Poster(c),JV,w/Ash Can	2.50
TPB	19.95

Shadowhawk #3
© Shadowline

[3rd Series] 1993
0 Zero issue	2.25
1 JV,CWf,V:Vortex,Hardedge, Red Foil(c)	2.50
1a Gold Ed.	3.00
1b signed	6.00
2 JV,CWf,MA,I:Deadline, BU&I:US Male	2.50
3 JV(a&s),ShadowHawk has AIDS, V:Hardedge,Blackjak	2.25
4 JV(a&s),V:Hardedge,	2.25

Note: #5 to #11 not used; #12 below is the next issue, the 12th overall.

12 Monster Within, pt.1	1.95
13 Monster Within, pt.2	1.95
14 Monster Within, pt.3	2.50
15 Monster Within, pt.4	2.50
16 Monster Within, pt.5	2.50
17 Monster Within, pt.6	2.50
18 JV,D:ShadowHawk	2.50
Spec.#1	3.50
Gallery#1	1.95

SHADOWHAWK/ VAMPIRELLA
Book 2 V:Kaul	4.95

Book #1: see Vampi/ShadowHawk

SHADOWHUNT SPECIAL
1 Shadowhunt x-over, pt.1	2.50

SHAMAN'S TEARS
0	2.50
1 MGr,I:Shaman,B:Origin.	3.00
1a Siver Prism Ed.	5.00
2 MGr,Poster(c)	2.50
3 MGr,V:Bar Sinister	2.50
4 MGr,V:Bar Sinister,E:Origin.	1.95
5 MGr,R:Jon Sable	1.95
6 MGr,V:Jon Sable	1.95
7 MGr,V:Rabids	1.95
8 MGr,A:Sable	1.95
9 MGr,Becoming of Broadarrow	1.95
10 Becoming of Broadarrow,pt.2	2.50
11 Becoming of Broadarrow,pt.3	2.50
12 Becoming of Broadarrow,pt.4	2.50
13 The Offspring,pt.1	2.50

SHARKY
Image 1998
1 by Dave Elliott & Alex Horley	2.50
1a variant cover (5,000 made)	2.95
2 coma over	2.50
2a variant cover.	2.95
3 R:Blazin' Glory	2.50
3a variant SBi(c)	2.95
4 tons of guest stars, concl	2.50
4a variant DAy(c)	2.50

SHATTERED IMAGE
Image/Wildstorm
1 KBk,TnD,crossover	2.50
2 KBk,TnD,	2.50
3 KBk,TnD,	2.50
4 KBk,TnD,concl.	2.50

SHIP OF FOOLS
Image (B&W) Sept. 1997
0 Bryan J.L. Glass, Michael Avon Oeming	2.95
1 Death & Taxes, pt.1	2.95
2 Death & Taxes, pt.2	2.95
3 Death & Taxes, pt.3	2.95
4 Death & Taxes, pt.4	2.95
TPB rep. Caliber series	14.95

IMAGE

SHUT UP & DIE
Image (B&W) 1998
1 JHI and Kevin Stokes 2.95
2 JHI,Angry White Man 2.95
3 JHI,Wife abducted 2.95
4 JHI 2.95
5 JHI,A:Earl Jackson 2.95

SIEGE
Image/Wildstorm Jan. 1997
1 JPe,AV,Nothing you believe
    is real 2.50
2 JPe,AV,Omega goes to Hawaii
    for funeral 2.50
3 JPe,AV,Zontarian Crab Ships vs.
    Drop Ship 2.50
4 JPe,AV,Raid to rescue Omega
    Squad 2.50

SIGMA
1 Fire From Heaven prelude 2.50
2 Fire From Heaven, pt.6 . . . . 2.50

SINKING
Image March 1999
GN JHI 14.95

SIREN
Image (B&W) May 1998
1 by J. Torres & Tim Levins 2.95
2 F:Zara Rush, private eye 2.95
3 cpmc;isopm 2.95
TPB rep. Shapes 9.95

SOLAR LORD
Image March 1999
1 by Khoo Fuk Lung 2.50
2 Nickson is Solar Lord 2.50
3 V:5 enemies 2.50
4 V:5 enemies 2.50
5 V:The Emperor of Darkness 2.50
6 O:Nickson 2.50

SOULWIND
Image (B&W) March 1997
1 quest for Soulwind begins 2.95
2 Nick becomes "Captain Crash" . . 2.95
3 Captain Crash & Poke pursue
    Soulwind info 2.95
4 concl. of story arc 2.95
5 The Day I Tried to Live,pt.1 . . . . 2.95
6 The Day I Tried to Live,pt.2 . . . . 2.95
7 The Day I Tried to Live,pt.3 . . . . 2.95
8 The Day I Tried to Live,pt.4 . . . . 2.95
TPB rep #1–#4 . . . . 9.95

SPARTAN:
WARRIOR SPIRIT
1 thru 4 . . . . @2.95

SPARTAN X
(B&W) Image Sept. 1998
1 MGo,RM,"Plague Train" 2.95
2 MGo,RM,"Plague Train," pt.2 . . . 2.95
3 MGo,RM,"Plague Train," pt.3 . . . 2.95

SPAWN
Image/TMP May 1992
1 TM,I:Spawn,w/GP,DK pinups . . 16.00
2 TM,V:The Violator 12.00
3 TM,V:The Violator 11.00
4 TM,V:The Violator,+coupon #2 . 16.00

Spawn #10
© Todd McFarlane

4a w/o coupon 3.00
5 TM,O:Billy Kincaid 12.00
6 TM,I:Overt-Kill 7.00
7 TM,V:Overt-Kill 7.00
8 TM,AMo(s),F:Billy Kincaid 7.00
9 NGa(s),TM,I:Angela 9.00
10 DS(s),TM,A:Cerebus 5.00
11 FM(s),TM 5.00
12 TM,Chapel killed Spawn 5.00
13 TM,A:Youngblood 5.00
14 TM,A:The Violator 6.00
15 TM 4.00
16 GCa,I:Anti-Spawn 6.00
17 GCa,V:Anti-Spawn 8.00
18 GCa,ATi,D:Anti-Spawn 15.00
19 & 20 see after #25
21 TM,The Hunt,pt.1 . . . . 15.00
22 TM,The Hunt,pt.2 . . . . 4.00
23 TM,The Hunt,pt.3 . . . . 4.00
24 TM,The Hunt,pt.4 . . . . 4.00
25 Image X Book,MS,BTn 7.00
19 I:Houdini 7.00
20 J:Houdini 7.00
26 TM 5.00
27 I:The Curse 5.00
28 Faces Wanda 5.00
29 Returns From Angela 5.00
30 A:KKK 5.00
31 R:Redeemer 4.00
32 TM,GCa,New Costume 5.00
33 R:Violator 4.00
34 V:Violator 4.00
35 F:Sam & Twitch 4.00
36 Talks to Wanda 4.00
37 I:The Freak 4.00
38 & 39 . . . . @4.00
40 & 41 V:Curse . . . . @4.00
42 thru 49 . . . . @4.00
50 48pgs 7.00
51 and 52 . . . . @4.00
53 A:Malebolgia 4.00
54 return to New York, alliance
    with Terry Fitzgerald 4.00
55 plans to defeat Jason Wynn . . . 4.00
56 efforts to defeat Jason Wynn . . . 4.00
57 . . . . 3.50
58 sequel to Spawn #29 . . . . 3.50
59 . . . . 3.50
60 battle between Spawn and
    Clown concl. 3.50
61 battle with Clown concl. 3.50
62 Spawn is Al Simmons for 1 day . 3.50
63 Operation: Wynn fall, pt.1 . . . . . 2.50
64 Wynn falls, bagged with toy

Spawn #78
© Todd McFarlane

catalog 2.50
65 recap issue 2.50
66 TM,GCa,lives of alley bums 2.50
67 TM,GCa,Sam and Twitch 2.50
68 TM,GCa,R:Freak 2.50
69 TM,GCa,F:Freak 2.50
70 TM,GCa 2.50
71 TM,GCa,Cold Blooded Truth . . . 2.50
72 TM,GCa,Haunting of the Heap . . 2.25
73 TM,GCa,R:The Heap 2.25
74 TM,GCa,pathway to misery 2.25
75 TM,GCa,Deadly Revelations . . . 2.25
76 TM,GCa,Granny Blake 2.25
77 TM,GCa,confronts 2.25
78 TM,GCa,DaM,"Sins of Excess" . 1.95
79 TM,GCa,DaM,Killer in N.Y. 1.95
80 TM,GCa,DaM,F:Sam & Twitch . . 1.95
81 TM,GCa,DaM,Sins are reborn . . 1.95
82 TM,GCa,DaM,sea of self-doubt . 1.95
83 TM,GCa,DaM,V:Jason Wynn . . . 1.95
84 TM,GCa,DaM,Helle's Belles . . . 1.95
85 TM,GCa,DaM,Legend of Hellspawn .
    1.95
86 TM,GCa,DaM,V:Al Simmons . . . 1.95
87 TM,GCa,DaM,Al Simmons fate . 1.95
88 TM,GCa,DaM,Seasons of
    change 1.95
89 TM,GCa,DaM,secrets revealed . 1.95
TPB Capital Collection rep.#1-3
    limited to 1,200 copies 300.00
TPB TM,rep.#1–#5 . . . . 9.95
TPB Spawn III rep. #12–#15 . . . . . 9.95
TPB Spawn IV rep. #16–#20 . . . . 9.95
TPB Spawn V rep.#21–#25 . . . . . 9.95
TPB Spawn VI, rep.#26–#30 . . . . 9.95
GN Spawn Movie adapt 5.00
Ann.#1 Blood & Shadows, 64-page. 4.95
TPB Angela's Hunt 9.95
TPB Vol. VII Deadman's Touch 9.95
TPB Vol. VIII Betrayal of Blood 9.95

SPAWN/BATMAN
Image/DC
1 FM(s),TM, ... 5.00

SPAWN BLOOD FEUD
1 V:Vampires 4.00
2 . . . . 4.00
3 Hunted as a Vampire 4.00
4 V:Heartless John 4.00

SPAWN BIBLE
Image/TMP
1 TM,GCa 2.00

SPAWN: THE DARK AGES
Image/TMP March 1999
1 GF,LSh, from 12th century 2.50
1a variant TM (c) (1:4) 2.50
2 LSh,A:Black Knight 2.50
3 LSh,A:Black Knight 2.50
4 LSh,Lord Covenant 2.50
5 LSh,Lord Covenant 2.50
6 LSh,Sister Immaculata 2.50

SPAWN THE IMPALER
Image/TMP
Mini-series
1 (of 3) MGr, fully painted 5.00
2 and 3 MGr . . . . @4.00

SPAWN: BLOODFEUD
1 thru 4 reoffered 4.00

SPAWN: THE UNDEAD
Image/TMP May 1999
1 PJe,DT,CWf,F:Spawn 1.95
2 PJe,DT,CWf,F:Travis Ward 1.95
3 PJe,DT,CWf,Heaven vs. Hell . . 1.95

SPAWN/WILDC.A.T.S
1 thru 4 mini-series 3.50

SPIRIT OF THE TAO
Image/Top Cow May 1998
1 BTn,F:Lance & Jasmine 2.50
2 BTn,mission to destroy base . . . 2.50
3 BTn,V:Jaikap Clan 2.50
4 BTn,F:Jasmine & Lance 2.50
5 BTn, Antidote to virus 2.50
6 BTn, Tao grows stronger 2.50
7 BTn, V:Menicus 2.50
8 BTn, A:Messiah 2.50
9 BTn, The Dragon is Loose 2.50
10 BTn, Jasmine out of control . . . 2.50
11 BTn, Dragon ash race 2.50
12 BTn, F:Disciple 2.50

SPLITTING IMAGE
1 DsM,A:Marginal Seven 2.25
2 DsM,A:Marginal Seven 2.25

STAR
1 F:Star from Savage Dragon 2.50
2 Buried Alive 2.50
3 A:Savage Dragon,Rapture 2.50
4 A:Savage Dragon,Rapture 2.50

STARCHILD: MYTHOPOLIS
Image (B&W) 1997
0 JOn, "Prologue" 2.95
1 JOn, "Pinehead" 2.95
2 JOn, "Pinehead," pt.2 . . . . 2.95
3 JOn, "Pinehead," pt.3 . . . . 2.95
4 JOn, "Fisher King," pt.1 . . . . 2.95
5 JOn, "Fisher King," pt.2 . . . . 2.95

STONE
Image/Avalon Sept. 1998
2 WPo,V:Rook 2.50
3 WPo,A:Bann 2.50
4 WPo, conclusion 2.50

VOL. II
1 WPo 2.50
1a Chromium Edition 6.95
2 WPo, search for murderer 2.50
2 Stonechrome edition 14.95
3 WPo,Blood from a Stone 2.50
4 WPo,A Rose by Any Other Name 2.50

STORMWATCH
Image/Wildstorm 1993
0 JSc(c),O:StormWatch,
  V:Terrorists,w/card 2.50
1 JLe(c&s),ScC,TvS(i),
  I:StormWatch 2.25
1a Gold Ed. 4.00
2 JLe(c&s),ScC,TvS(i),I:Cannon,
  Winter,Fahrenheit,Regent 2.25
3 JLe(c&s),ScC,TvS(i),V:Regent,
  I:Backlash 4.00
4 V:Daemonites 2.50
5 SRf(s),BBh,V:Daemonites 2.25
6 BCi,ScC,TC,A:Mercs 2.25
7 BCi,ScC,TC,A:Mercs 2.25
8 BCi,ScC,TC,A:Mercs 2.25
9 BCi,I:Defile 2.25
25 BCi,A:Spartan 2.50
10 V:Talos 2.00
10a variant (c) 3.00
11 the end? 2.00
12 V:Hellstrike 2.00
13 V:M.A.D.-1 . . . . 2.00
14 Despot 2.00
15 Batallion, Flashpoint 2.00
16 V:Defile 2.00
17 D:Batallion 2.00
18 R:Argos 2.50
19 R:M.A.D.-1,L:Winter 2.50
20 F:Cannon,Winter,Bendix 2.50
21 V:Wildcats 2.50
22 RMz,BWS(c),WildStorm
  Rising,pt.9,w/2 cards 2.50
22a Newsstand ed. 1.95
23 R:Despot,Warguard 2.50
24 V:Despot 2.50
25 BCi,A:Spartan 2.75
26 V:Despot 2.50
27 Rebuilding 2.50
28 New Adventures 2.50
29 Reorganization 2.50
30 . . . . 2.50
31 V:Middle Eastern Terrorists . . . 2.50
32 thru 34 . . . . @2.50
35 Fire From Heaven,pt.5 . . . . 2.50

Stormwatch #44
© Jim Lee

36 Fire From Heaven 2.50
37 Double size 3.50
38 . . . . 2.50
39 . . . . 2.50
40 virus 2.50
41 . . . . 2.50
42 Weatherman discovers a
  conspiracy 2.50
43 . . . . 2.50
44 history of Jenny Sparks 2.50
45 Battalion visits his family 2.50
46 secrets and more secrets,
  prologue 2.50
47 WEI(s), JLe, SW, dangerous
  experiment gone awry 2.50
48 "Change or Die" pt.1 . . . . 2.50
49 "Change or Die" pt.2 . . . . 2.50
50 "Change or Die" concl.large size 4.50
Sourcebok JLe(s),DT 2.75
Spec.#1 RMz(s),DT, ... 4.25
Spec.#2 F:Fleshpoint 2.50
Ashcan 1 . . . . 3.00
TPB Change the World 9.95

STORMWATCH
Image/Wildstorm Oct. 1997
1 WEI,bacterial horror 2.50
1a Variant cover 2.50
1b Voyager bagged pack 3.50
2 WEI,Stormwatch Black team . . . 2.50
3 WEI,Black team,concl. 2.50
4 WEI,A Finer World, pt.1 . . . . 2.50
5 WEI,A Finer World, pt.2 . . . . 2.50
6 WEI,A Finer World, pt.3 . . . . 2.50
7 WEI,Bleed, pt.1. . . . . 2.50
8 WEI,Bleed, pt.2. . . . . 2.50
9 WEI,Bleed, pt.3. . . . . 2.50
10 WEI,call it quits? 2.50
11 WEI,BHi,PNe,F:Jackson King . . 2.50
TPB Change or Die 15.00

STRANGERS IN PARADISE VOL. 3
Homage Comics (B&W) 1996
1 TMr 6.00
2 TMr 4.00

Image/Homage Comics
3 TMr,David & Katchoo fight 2.75
4 TMr,Katchoo makes startling
  discovery 2.75
5 TMr,Francine's college days 2.75
6 TMr,Katchoo searches for David . 2.75
7 TMr, ... 2.75
8 TMr,demons of the past 2.75

STREETS
Image April 1999
TPB Streets 16.95

STRIKEBACK!
1 thru 4 . . . . @2.50

SUPER-PATRIOT
1 N:Super-Patriot. 2.25
2 KN(i),O:Super-Patriot 2.25
3 A:Youngblood 2.25
4 . . . . 1.95

SUPER-PATRIOT: LIBERTY AND JUSTICE
1 R:Covenant 2.50
2 Tokyo 2.50
3 Tokyo gets Trashed 2.50
4 Final issue 2.50

IMAGE

Supreme #29
© Rob Liefeld

SUPREME
Image/Supreme 1992
0 O:Supreme	2.50
1 B:RLd(s&i),BrM, V:Youngblood	3.00
1a Gold Ed.	5.00
2 BrM,I:Heavy Mettle	2.50
3 thru 4 BrM	2.50
5 BrM(a&s),Clv(i),I:Thor,V:Chrome.	2.50
6 BrM,Clv(i),I:Starguard, A:Thor,V:Chrome	2.50
7 Rip,ErS(s),SwM,A:Starguard, A:Thor,	2.50
8 Rip(s),SwM,V:Thor,	2.50
9 Rip&KtH(s),BrM,Clv(i), V:Thor.	2.50
10 KrH(s),BrM,JRu(i), BU:I:Black & White	2.50
11 I:Newmen	2.50
12 SPa(c),RLd(s),SwM,	4.00
25 SPa(c),RLd(s),SwM,V:Simple Simon,Images of Tomorrow	6.00
13 B:Supreme Madness	2.50
14 Supreme Madness, pt.2	2.50
15 RLd(s)A:Spawn	2.50
16 V:StormWatch	2.50
17 Supreme Madness, pt.5	2.50
18 E:Supreme Madness	2.50
19 V:The Underworld	2.50
20 V:The Underworld	2.50
21 God Wars	2.50
22 RLd,CNn,God Wars, V:Thor.	2.50
23 ExtremeSacrifice x-over,pt.1	2.50
24 Identity Questions	2.50
#25, see above, after #12	
26 F:Kid Supreme	2.50
27 Rising Son,I:Cortex	2.50
28 Supreme Apocalypse:Prelude	2.50
29 Supreme Apocalypse,pt.1	2.50
30	2.50
31 V:Equinox	2.50
32 V:Cortex	2.50
33 Extreme Babewatch	2.50
34 She-Supreme	2.50
35 thru 38	@2.50
39 AMo	2.50
40 AMo	2.50
41 AMo	5.00
42 AMo,"Secret Origins"	5.00
43 AMo,"Secrets of the Citadel Supreme"	2.50
44 See Color Comics section	
Ann.#1 TMB,CAd,KG,I:Vergessen.	2.95
Ashcan #1	3.00
Ashcan #2	2.00

SUPREME: GLORY DAYS
1 Supreme in WWI	2.95
2 (of 2) BNa&KIA(s),DdW,GyM, A:Superpatriot	2.95

SWORD OF DAMOCLES
1 prelude to Fire From Heaven x-over.	2.50

TALES OF THE DARKNESS
Image/Top Cow
1 WPo,F:Jackie Estacado	2.95
2 WPo,concl. first story	2.95
3 Dungeon, Fire, and Sword,pt.1	2.95
4 Dungeon, Fire & Sword	2.95
5 in Dark Ages	2.95

TALES OF THE WITCHBLADE
Image/Top Cow 1996
1 TnD,F:Anne Bonney	9.00
1a TnD, variant cover (1:4)	12.00
2 TnD,F:Annabella	6.00
3 WEl,BTn,future	5.00
4 WEl,BTn,future, pt.2	4.00
5 RiB,past	3.00
6 RGr, time of Celts	3.00
7 in Ancient Egypt	2.95
7a variant cover (1:4).	2.95
Coll.Ed.#1, rep. #1–#2	4.95

TEAM 1: STORMWATCH
1 I:First StormWatch Team	2.50
2 V:Helspont,D:Think Tank.	2.50

TEAM 1: WILDCATS
1 I:First Wildcats Team	2.50
2 B:Cabal	2.50

TEAM 7
Image/Wildstorm 1994–95
1 New team	4.00
2 New powers	2.50
3 Members go insane	2.50
4 final issue,V:A Nuke	2.50
Ashcan	2.00
TPB	9.95

TEAM 7 OBJECTIVE: HELL
1 CDi,CW,BWS(c),WildStorm Rising,Prologue,w/2 cards	2.50
1a Newsstand ed.	1.95
2 Cambodia	2.50

TEAM 7 III: DEAD REACONING
1 thru 4	@2.50

TEAM YOUNGBLOOD
Image/Extreme 1993
1 B:ErS(s),ATi(c),CYp,NRD(i), I:Masada,Dutch,V:Giger	2.50
2 ATi(c),CYp,NRd(i),V:Giger.	2.25
3 RLd(s),CYp,NRd(i),C:Spawn, V:Giger.	2.25
4 ErS(s),	2.25
5 ErS(s),CNn,V:Lynx	2.25
6 ErS(s),N:Psi-Fire, BU:Black&White	2.25
7 ErS(s),CYp,ATh,Extreme	

Team Youngblood #17
© Extreme Studios

Prejudice#1,I:Quantum, BU:Black & White	2.25
8 ErS(s),CYp,ATh,Extreme Pre-judice #5, V:Quantum, BU:B&W	2.25
9 RLd	2.50
10 ErS(s),CYp,ATh,	2.50
11 RLd,ErS,Cyp	2.00
12 RLd,ErS,Cyp	2.50
13 ErS,Cyp.	2.50
14 RLd,ErS,Cya	2.50
15 New Blood.	2.50
16 RLd,ErS,TNu,I:New Sentinel, A:Bloodpool	2.50
17 ExtremeSacrifice x-over,pt.5	2.50
18 MS, membership drive	2.50
19 R:Brahma	2.50
20 Contact,pt.1 1000 yr Badrock.	2.50
21 Contact,pt.2	2.50
22 Shadowhunt x-over,pt.4	2.50

TEENAGE MUTANT NINJA TURTLES
Image/Highbrow (B&W)
1 thru 3	@2.00
4 Donatello resurrected	2.00
5 FFo,Warlord Komodo uses Splinter as guinea pig.	2.50
6 FFo	2.50
7 FFo,Raphael joins Foot Clan?	2.50
8 FFo,Michelangelo tries to rescue Casey Jones' daughter.	2.95
9 Enter: the Knight Watchman	2.95
10 "Enter: The Dragon".	2.95
11 V:DeathWatch,A:Vanguard.	2.95
12 F:Raph, Foot Gang warfare	2.95
13 Shredder is back!.	2.95
14 Shredder vs. Splinter	2.95
15 F:Donatello	2.95
16 reunited with Splinter	2.95
17 F:Leonardo	2.95
18 UFO Sightings	2.95
19 F:Leatherhead	2.95
20 F:Triceraton	2.95
21 A:Pimiko	2.95
22 F:Lady Shredder	2.95
23 F:Lady Shredder	2.95
TPB A New Beginning	9.95

TELLOS
Image May 1999
1 TDz, The Joining, part 1	2.50

2 TDz, The Joining, part 2 . . . . . . 2.50
3 TDz, The Joining, part 3 . . . . . . 2.50

TENTH, THE
Image Comics
1 BSt,TnD,Last stand against
  Hell on Earth 6.00
2 BSt,TnD,invasion of Darklon
  Corp. begins. 4.00
3 BSt,TnD,Tenth & Espy team-up . 3.00
4 BSt,TnD.confrontation with
  possible Armageddon. 2.50
TPB rep.#1–#4 . . . . 10.95
Regular Series
1 TnD,BSt,V:Blackspell 5.00
2 TnD,BSt,V:Blackspell 4.00
3 TnD,BSt,Gozza,Eve 4.00
4 TnD,BSt,teleported to Japan. . . . 4.00
5 TnD,BSt 3.50
6 TnD,BSt,CollateralDamage,pt.1 . 3.50
7 TnD,BSt,CollateralDamage,pt.2 . 4.00
8 TnD,BSt,Darkk Wind At
  Your Back 2.50
9 TnD,BSt,F:Adrenalynn 2.50
10 TnD,pt.1 (of 3). 2.50
10a variant TnD(c) 2.50
11 TnD,Victor retains Tenth. 2.50
11a variant cover 2.50
12 TnD,Black reign begins 2.50
13 TnD,V:Rhazes Darkk 2.50
14 TnD,V:Rhazes Darkk 2.50
Coll.Ed.Vol.1 rep. #1–#2 . . . . 4.95
Spec.Configuration#1, sourcebook . 2.50
TPB rep.#1–#4 . . . . 11.95

TENTH, THE:
BLACK EMBRACE
Image Feb. 1999
1 TnD,SLo, V:Gozza 2.95
1a variant cover (1:2). 2.95
2 TnD,SLo, F:Esperanza 2.50
3 TnD,SLo, F:Adrenalynn 2.50
4 TnD,SLo, conclusion. 2.50

TOMB RAIDER/
WITCHBLADE REVISITED
Image/Top Cow Dec. 1998
1 Video game tie-in 00

TOOTH & CLAW
Image Aug. 1999
1 Reborn to rage 2.95

TOP COW/BALLISTIC
Swimsuit Spec.#1 MS(c) (1995). . . 4.00

TOP COW SECRETS
Winter Lingerie Spec. (1996) 3.00

A TOUCH OF SILVER
Image (B&W) Jan. 1997
1 JV,"Birthday". 2.95
2 JV,"Dance" 2.95
3 JV,"Bullies" 2.95
4 JV,"Separation". 2.95
5 JV,inc. Tomorrow Syndicate vs.
  Round Table of America, 12pg.
  color section. 2.95
6 JV "Choices" Aug. 1963 . . . . 2.95
TPB A Sociopath in Training 12.95

TREKKER
Image May 1999
1 RoR, in New Gelaph. 00

TRENCHER
1 KG,I:Trencher. 2.25
2 KG, ... 2.25
3 KG,V:Supreme 2.25
4 KG,V:Elvis 2.25

TRIBE
1 TJn(s),LSn,I:The Tribe 2.50
1a Ivory(White) Editon 3.00
2 . . . . 2.25
Ashcan 1 . . . . 3.00

TROLL
Image/Extreme Dec. 1993
1 RLd(s),JMs,I:Evangeliste, V:Katellan
  Command, ... 2.50
2 . . . . 2.50
Halloween Spec.#1. . . . . 2.50
X-Mas Stocking Stuffer #1 . . . . . . 2.95

TROLL: ONCE A HERO
1 Troll in WWII. 2.50

Troubleman #1
© Motown

TROUBLEMAN
Image/Motown June 1996
1 and 2 Charles Drost . . . . @2.50

TSUNAMI GIRL
Image/Flypaper Jan. 1999
1 F:Michelle Vincent 2.95
2 Sorayama (c), A:Alan Poe 2.95
3 Sorayama(c), Surreal conspiracy 2.95

TUG & BUSTER
Image (B&W) June 1998
1 MaH, humor, F:Stinkfinger 2.95

"21"
Image/Top Cow
1 thru 3 LWn,MDa, ... @2.50
4 LWn,MDa,"Time Bomb" pt.1 . . . . 2.50
5 LWn,MDa,"Time Bomb" pt.2 . . . . 2.50
6 LWn,MDa,"Time Bomb" pt.3

"Detonation" 2.50

UNBOUND
Image (B&W) Jan. 1998
1 by Joe Pruett & Michael Peters. . 2.95
2 . . . . 2.95
3 F:Marta & Erik 2.95

UNION
Image/Wildstorm
0 O:Union 2.50
0a WPo(c), ... 3.00
1 MT,I:Union,A:StormWatch 2.75
2 MT 2.75
3 MT 2.75
4 MT,Good Intentions 2.75
Regular Series 1995
1 R:Union, Crusade 2.50
2 V:Crusade & Mnemo 2.50
3 A:Savage Dragon 2.50
4 JRo,BWS(c), WildStorm
  Rising,pt.3,w/2 cards 2.50
4a Newsstand ed. 1.95
5 V:Necros 2.50
6 V:Necros 2.50
7 Jill's Surprise 2.50
8 Regal Vengeance,pt.1 . . . . 2.50
9 Regal Vengeance,pt.2 . . . . 2.50
10 Regal Vengeance,pt.3 . . . . 2.50
1-shot Final Vengeance, MHs,
  V:Regent (1997). 2.50

UNION
Image/Wildstorm 1996
1 MHs,RBn 2.50
2 MHs,RBn 2.50
3 MHs,RBn 1.75

VANGUARD
Image/Highbrow 1993–94
1 EL(s),BU:I:Vanguard. 2.25
2 EL(s),Roxann, ... 2.25
3 AMe, ... 2.25
4 AMe, ... 2.25
5 AMe,V:Aliens 2.25
6 V:Bank Robber. 1.95

VANGUARD:
STRANGE VISITORS
1 (of 4) SEa,BAn,A:Amok 2.95
2 SEa,BAn, ... 2.95
3 SEa,BAn, ... 2.95
4 SEa,BAn,finale 2.95

VELOCITY
1 V:Morphing Opponent. 2.50
2 V:Charnel 2.50
3 & 4 conclusion . . . . @2.50

VIOLATOR
1 AMo(s),BS,I:Admonisher. 2.25
2 AMo(s),BS 1.95
3 AMo(s),BS,last issue 1.95

VIOLATOR/BADROCK
1 AMo(s),A:Celestine. 2.50
2 V:Celestine 2.50
3 F:Dr. McAllister. 2.50
4 Final issue 2.50
TPB Rep. 9.95

IMAGE

All comics prices listed are for *Near Mint* condition.

VISITATIONS
Image (B&W) 1997
GN by C. Stott Morse 6.95

VOGUE
1 F:Vogue,I:Redbloods 2.50
2 & 3 conclusion 2.50

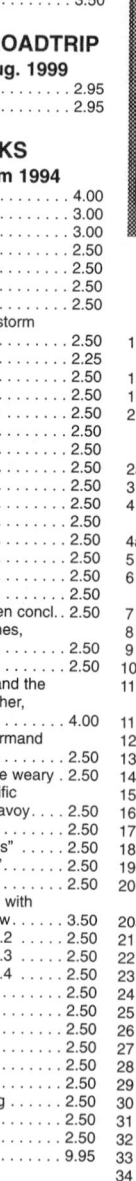

Voodoo #2
© Wildstorm

VOODOO
Image/Wildstorm Nov. 1997
1 AMo(s),WildStorm universe 2.50
2 AMo(s),in old New Orleans 2.50
3 AMo(s), ... 2.50
4 AMo(s), Christian Charles 2.50
TPB Voodoo Dancing in the Dark . 10.00

WARBLADE:
ENDANGERED SPECIES
1 I:Pillar 2.95
2 V:Ripclaw 2.50
3 I:Skinner 2.50
4 final issue 2.50

WARLANDS
Image Aug. 1999
1 by Pat Lee 2.50
1a, b & c variant covers 2.50
1d Armore Chrome edition 12.95

WAY OF THE CODA:
THE COLLECTED
WILDC.A.T.S
TPB VOL.II 12.95

WEAPON ZERO
Image/Top Cow
T-Minus-4 WS 8.00
T-Minus-3 Alien Invasion 5.00
T-Minus-2 Formation of a Team . . 5.00
T-Minus-1 Alien Invasion 5.00
0 Whole Team Together 4.00
1 . . . . 5.00
2 . . . . 3.50
3 . . . . 3.50
4 WS,JBz 3.00
5 WS,JBz 3.00

6 WS,JBz 3.00
7 WS,JBz 3.00
8 WS,JBz 3.00
9 WS,JBz 3.00
10 WS,ScL,"Devil's Reign" tie-in . . . 3.00
11 WS,JBz,Weapon Zero & Lilith
   return to T'srii moonbase . . . 3.00
12 WS,JBz, What's wrong with
   Jamie 3.00
13 WS,JBz,problems with Jamie . . . 3.00
14 JBz,T'Srrii have returned 3.00
15 JBz,T'Srrii,concl.,48pg 3.50

WEASEL GUY: ROADTRIP
Image (B&W) Aug. 1999
1 by Steve Buccellato 2.95
1a variant cover (1:4) 2.95

WETWORKS
Image/Wildstorm 1994
1 WPo 4.00
2 WPo,BCi 3.00
3 WPo,BCi,V:Vampire 3.00
4 WPo,BCi,Dozer 2.50
5 WPo,BCi,Pilgrim's Turn 2.50
6 WPo,BCi,Civil War 2.50
7 WPo,BCi,F:Pilgrim 2.50
8 WPo,SW,BWS(c), Wildstorm
   Rising,pt.7,w/2 cards 2.50
8a Newsstand ed. 2.25
9 F:Jester,Pilgrim Dozer 2.50
10 R:Dozer to Action 2.50
11 Blood Queen Vs. Dane 2.50
12 V:Vampire Nation 2.50
13 Fire From Heaven,pt.1 . . . . 2.50
14 Fire From Heaven,pt.2 . . . . 2.50
15 Fire From Heaven,pt.3 . . . . 2.50
16 Fire From Heaven,pt.4 . . . . 2.50
17 FTa, ... 2.50
18 FTa, ... 2.50
19 FTa, ... 2.50
20 FTa, ... 2.50
21 FTa, ... 2.50
22 FTa,Dave vs.Bloodqueen concl. . 2.50
23 FTa,Flattop & Crossbones,
   V:Lady Feign 2.50
24 FTa, ... 2.50
25 FTa,Can Pilgrim withstand the
   beast that lurks within her,
   double size 4.00
26 team parts ways with Armand
   Waering 2.50
27 V:Craven, no rest for the weary . 2.50
28 Vampire tracked in Pacific
   Northwest,A:Johnny Savoy . . . 2.50
29 V:Soulbender 2.50
30 "Secret of the Symbiotes" 2.50
31 "Time of the Blood War" 2.50
32 StG,PtL,V:Drakkar 2.50
32a Voyager pack, bagged with
   Phantom Guard preview 3.50
33 StG,PtL,Sacraments, pt.2 . . . . 2.50
34 StG,PtL,Sacraments, pt.3 . . . . 2.50
35 StG,PtL,Sacraments, pt.4 . . . . 2.50
36 StG 2.50
37 StG,V:St.Crispin 2.50
38 StG,on West Coast 2.50
39 StG,in South America 2.50
40 StG,in the crosshairs 2.50
41 StG,V:Stormwatch 2.50
42 StG,Mother One missing 2.50
43 StG,Mother One concl. 2.50
Sourcebook 2.50
TPB Rebirth 9.95

WETWORKS/VAMPIRELLA
Image/Wildstorm
1 JMi & GK, x-over 2.95

WildC.A.T.S. #20
© Jim Lee

WILDC.A.T.S.
Image/Wildstorm 1992
1 B:BCi(s),JLe, SW(i), I:Wild-
   C.A.T.S. 5.00
1a Gold Ed. 5.00
1b Gold and Signed 10.00
2 JLe,SW(i),V:Master Gnome,
   I:Wetworks, Prism foil(c),
   with coupon #5 . . . . 5.00
2a w/o coupon 2.00
3 RLd(c),JLe,SW(i), V:Youngblood . 4.00
4 E:BCi(s),JLe,LSn,SW(i),w/card,
   A:Youngblood,BU:Tribe 4.00
4a w/red card 4.00
5 BCi(s),JLe,SW,I:Misery 3.00
6 BCi(s),JLe,SW,Killer Instinct,
   A:Misery,C:Ripclaw 3.00
7 BCi(s),JLe,SW, A:Cyberforce . . . 3.00
8 BCi(s),JLe,SW, ... 3.00
9 BCi(s),JLe,SW, ... 3.00
10 CCi(s),JLe,SW,I:Huntsman . . . 2.50
11 CCi(s),JLe,SW,V:Triad,
   A:Huntsman 2.50
11a WPo(c) 4.00
12 JLe,CCi,A:Huntsman 3.00
13 JLe,CCi,A:Huntsman 4.00
14 X book 4.00
15 F:Black Razors 4.00
16 Black Razors 4.00
17 A:StormWatch 4.00
18 R:Hightower 4.00
19 V:Hightower 4.00
20 TC,JeR,BWS(c),WildStorm
   Rising,pt.2,w/2 cards 2.50
20a Newsstand ed. 2.00
21 Into Space Back Home 2.50
22 Space Adventures 2.50
23 F:Mr. Majestic's Team 2.50
24 O:Maul 2.50
25 double sized 5.00
26 . . . . 2.50
27 . . . . 2.50
28 . . . . 2.50
29 Fire From Heaven,pt.7 . . . . 2.50
30 BKs, ... 2.50
31 BKs 2.50
32 BKs 2.50
33 BKs,gang war rages on 2.50
34 AMo,MtB,New York seconds
   away from nuclear disaster 2.50
35 AMo,MtB,BKs,V:Crusade 2.50
36 AMo,MtB,BKs,V:Crusade,
   A:Union, pt.2 . . . . 2.50

37 BCi,JPe,MtB,WildC.A.T.s
   team divided. 2.50
38 BCi,JPe,MtB,Puritans debut . . . 2.50
39 BCi,JPe,MtB,"C.A.T. Fight". 2.50
40 BCi,JPe,MtB,MtB(c). 2.50
40a variant cover by TC 2.50
41 BCi,JPe,MtB,backwards in time . 2.50
42 BCi,JPe,MTb,in WWI 2.50
43 BCi,JPe,MTb,in ancient China . . 2.50
44 BCi,JPe,MTb,Renaissance 2.50
45 BCi,JPe,MTb 2.50
46 BCi,JPe,MTb,escape from
   Rome. 2.50
47 BCi,JPe,MTb,time trip concl. . . . 2.50
47a variant JMd(c) 2.50
48 BCi,JPe,trapped in mothership. . 2.50
49 BCi,JPe,return to present. 2.50
50 BCi,JPe,AMo,new
   costumes,40pg. 3.50
TPB A Gathering of Eagles. 9.95
Spec.#1 SrG(s),TC,SW,I:Destine,
   Pin-ups 3.50
Spec.#2 . . . . 2.50
3-D #1 rep. #1, with glasses 4.95
3-Da variant cover, glasses. 4.95
TPB rep. #1-4,w/0. . . . . 11.00
TPB Homecoming rep.#21–#27 . . 19.95
Ann.#1 JRo,LSn (1998) 2.95
TPB WildC.A.T.S/Cyberforce
   Killer Instinct. 16.95
TPB Gathering of Eagles 9.95
TPB Gang War,rep.#28–34 . . . . . . 16.95
Volume 2: See COLOR

WILDC.A.T.S ADVENTURES
Image/Wildstorm 1994
1 From animated TV series 2.50
2 Helspont,Troika 2.00
3 Caught in war. 2.00
4 V:The President 2.50
5 I:Lonely 2.50
6 I:Majestics 2.50
7 . . . . 2.50
8 Betrayed. 2.50
9 V:Black Razors. 2.50
10 F:Voodoo. 2.50
Sourcebook (JS(c)) 2.95

WILDC.A.T.S/ALIENS
Image/Wildstorm 1998
1-shot WEI,CSp,KN 4.95
1-shotA, variant GK&KN(c)(1:4) . . 4.95

WILDC.A.T.S. TRILOGY
1 BCi(s),JaL,V:Artemis. 2.50
2 BCi(s),JaL,V:Artemis. 2.25
3 BCi(s),JaL,V:Artemis. 2.25

WILDC.A.T.S/X-MEN
Image/Wildstorm Feb. 1997
1 (of 4) SLo,TC, giant Marvel/Image
   crossover. 4.50
1a alternate cover by JLe 4.50
2 & 4 see Marvel
TPB WildC.A.T.S/X-Men, rep. 18.50

WILDC.A.T.S/X-MEN
Image/Wildstorm June 1997
Golden Age #1. . . . . 4.95
Golden Age #1a variant JLe(c) 4.95
3-D Golden Age #1, with glasses . . 4.95
3-D Golden Age #1, variant cover. . 4.95
Silver Age #1 SLo, JLe & SW, cross ove
   r. 4.50
Silver Age #1a signed. 19.95

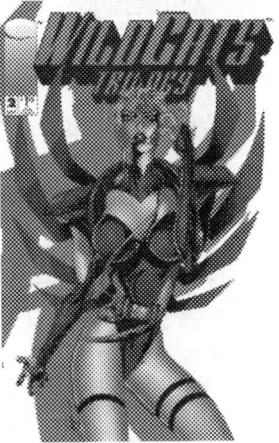

WildC.A.T.s Trilogy #2
© Jim Lee

Silver Age #1b signed, deluxe. . . . 29.95
3-D Silver Age #1, with glasses . . . 6.50
3-D Silver Age #1, NA(c) variant . . 6.50
Modern Age #1, JRo,AHu,MFm . . . 4.50
Modern Age #1a variant cover 4.50
3-D Modern Age #1, with glasses . . 4.95
3-D Modern Age #1, variant cover . 4.95

WILDCORE
Image/Wildstorm Nov. 1997
1 BBh,SRf,BBh(c), V:Drahn 2.50
1a variant TC(c) 2.50
1b Voyager bagged pack 3.00
2 BBh, SRf,Brawl joins 2.50
3 BBh,SRf,V:D'rahn. 2.50
4 BBh,SRf,A:Majestic 2.50
5 BBh,SRf,Tapestry 2.50
6 BBh,SRf,Zealot missing 2.50
7 BBh,SRf,caught in fantasy world. 2.50
8 RBn,SRf,V:Tapestry 2.50
9 RBn,SRf,Zealot's soul restored . . 2.50
10 RBn, SRf,Trans-dimensional
   trauma 2.50
GN Backlash & Taboo's African
   Vacation. 6.00

WILDSTAR
1 JOy,AG,I:WildStar. 2.25
1a Gold Ed. 3.00
2 JOy,AG 2.25
3 JOy,AG,V:Savage Dragon,
   D:WildStar 2.25
4 JOy,AG,Last Issue,Pin-ups 2.25
TPB 12.95
[Regular Series]
1 R:WildStar 2.00
2 V:Mighty Man 2.50
3 . . . . 2.50
Ashcan. 1.00
TPB WildStar Sky Zero. 12.95

WILDSTORM!
Image/Wildstorm
1 F:Spartan,Black Razors 2.50
2 F:Deathblow. 2.50
3 F:Taboo,Spartan. 2.50
4 . . . . 2.50
Winter Wonderfest Spec.#1 . . . . . . 3.50
Spec. #1 Chamber of Horrors 3.50
Spec. Swimsuit Special '97 . . . . . . 2.50
Spec. Ultimate Sports Official

Program. 2.50
Sketchbook 2.95
Spec. Halloween '97 . . . . 2.50

WILDSTORM ARCHIVES GENESIS
Image/Wildstorm June 1998
1 The #1 Collection, 238 pg. 7.00

Wildstorm Rising #1
© Jim Lee

WILDSTORM RISING
Image/Wildstorm
1 JeR,BWS(c&a) WildStorm Rising,
   pt.1:Tricked by Defile,w/2 cards 2.50
1a Newsstand ed. 1.95
2 RMz,BBo,BWS(c) WildStorm
   Rising,pt.10,w/2 cards 2.50
2a Newsstand ed. 1.95
Wildstorm Sourcebook #1. . . . . . . 2.50
TPB Rep. Mini-series 16.95

WILDSTORM SPOTLIGHT
Image/Wildstorm Feb. 1997
1 AMo,F:Majestic, at the end of
   time 2.50
2 StG,RMr,Loner returns 2.50
3 StG,RMr,Secret past of original
   Loner. 2.50
4 F:Hellstrike 2.50

WILDSTORM UNIVERSE '97
Image/Wildstorm Nov. 1997
Sourcebook #1 thru #3 . . . . @2.50

WITCHBLADE
Image/Top Cow 1995–96
1 I:Witchblade 32.00
1A Special retailer edition 40.00
1B Wizard Ace edition,acetate(c). . 45.00
2 . . . . 30.00
2 encore edition. 7.00
3 . . . . 25.00
4 . . . . 15.00
5 . . . . 14.00
6 . . . . 8.00
7 and 8 . . . . @7.00
Top Cow 1996
9 . . . . 7.00

IMAGE

Witchblade #20 © Top Cow

9A variant cover. 11.00
10 I:Darkness (Jackie Estacado). . . 5.00
10a variant Darkness cover (1:4) . 15.00
11 . . . . 5.00
12 Connection between Lisa,
   Microwave Murderer and
   Kenneth Irons. 4.00

Image/Top Cow 1997
13 Dannette Boucher's secret past . 4.00
14 Sara searches for Microwave
   Murderer 4.00
15 "There is a war brewing...". . . . 4.00
16 "Will Witchblade come between
   Sarah and Jake?". 3.50
17 New York City in shambles . . . 3.50
18 Family Ties, pt.1,x-over 3.50
18a variant (c) 7.00
19 Family Ties, pt.4,x-over 3.50
20 Chief Siry, Ian Nottingham 3.00
21 another big surprise. 3.00
22 F:Sara 3.00
23 F:Ian Nottingham. 3.00
24 JPn,Sara learns truth. 3.00
25 Save Jake's Life, 32 pg 3.50
26 "Grey" 2.50
27 A:Kenneth Irons. 2.50
27a variant cover, all villains 2.50
28 A:Jackie Estacado. 2.50
29 A:Kenneth Irons. 2.50
30 Siry & Irons 2.50
31 How Sara's father died. 2.50
32 answers and questions 2.50
33 F:Eric 2.50
34 F:Tommy Gallo 2.50
Coll.Ed.Vol.#1. . . . . 4.95
Coll.Ed.Vol.#2. . . . . 4.95
Coll.Ed.Vol.#3. . . . . 4.95
Coll.Ed.Vol.#4, rep. #7 & #8 . . . . 4.95
Coll.Ed.Vol.#5, rep. #9 & #10 . . . 4.95
Coll.Ed.Vol.#6, rep. #11 & #12 . . 4.95
Coll.Ed.Vol.#7, rep. #13 & #14 . . 4.95
Coll.Ed.Vol.#8, rep. #15–#17 . . . 6.95
Delux Coll.Ed. rep.1–#8 . . . . . . 24.95
Spec. Infinity SLo,AdP 3.50
TPB Collects Witchblade/Darkness
   Family Ties x-over 9.95
Spec. Tomb Raider. 3.95

WIZARDS TALE, THE
Image/Homage Comics 1997
TPB KBk,DWe 19.95
TPB 2nd printing. 19.95
HC 29.95
HC, signed, limited 39.95

WOLVERINE/
WITCHBLADE
Image/Top Cow Jan. 1997
1-shot "Devil's Reign" pt.5 (of 8) . . . 4.00

WYNONNA EARP
Image/Wildstorm
1 BSt, ... 2.50
2 BSt,The Law comes to San
   Diablo 2.50
3 BSt,desperate to stop Hemo
   from going nationwide 2.50
4 BSt,goes to New York,
   V:ancient evil 2.50
5 BSt,battle with Raduk—Eater
   of the Dead concl. 2.50

YOUNGBLOOD
Image/Extreme
0 RLd,O:Youngblood,w/coupon#7 . 3.00
0a without coupon 1.50
0b gold coupon 9.00
1 RLd,I:Youngblood(flipbook) 5.00
1a 2nd print.,gold border 2.50
1b RLD,Silent Edition. 12.95
2 RLd,I:ShadowHawk 5.00
3 RLd,I:Supreme 3.00
4 RLd,DK,A:Prophet,BU:Pitt 3.00
5 RLd,Flip book,w/Brigade #4 . . . 2.50
6 RLd(a&s),J:Troll,Knight Sabre,
   2nd Die Hard, Proposal to Girl
   friend 3.50
7 Badrock, V:Overkill 2.50
8 Chapel, V:Spawn 2.50
9 . . . . 2.50
9a variant cover. 5.00
10 Bravo, Badrock, Troll 2.50
Yr.Bk.#1 CYp,I:Tyrax. 2.75
Ashcan #1 . . . . 8.00
Ashcan #2 . . . . 4.00
TPB rep. #1–#5. . . . . 16.95

[Volume 2] 1995
1 New Roster 2.50
2 The Program Continues 2.50
3 Extreme Babewatch 2.50
4 thru 6 . . . . @2.50
7 Shadowhunt x-over,pt.3 . . . . . . 2.50
8 thru 10, ErS,RCz. . . . . @2.50
TPB Baptism of Fire, F:Spawn . . . .
See Color Pub. section

YOUNGBLOOD
BATTLEZONE
1 BrM 2.25
2 . . . . 2.95

YOUNGBLOOD
STRIKEFILE
Image/Extreme 1993
1 JaL,RLd,I:Allies,A:Al Simmons
   (Spawn) 3.00
1a Gold Ed. 4.00
2 JaL,RLd,V:Super Patriot, Giger. . 2.50
2a Gold Ed. 3.50
3 RLd,JaL,DaM(i), A:Super Partiot. 2.50
4 I:Overtkill 2.25
5 . . . . 3.00
6 flip book 3.00
7 flip book 3.00
8 Shaft 3.00
9 Knight Sabre 3.00
10 RLd,TNu,I:Bloodpool,Task,
   Psilence,Wylder,Rubble 3.50
11 O:Link Crypt 2.50
TPB rep.#1–#3,sketchbook 12.95

*Youngblood Strikefile #6
© Rob Liefeld*

Ashcan. 3.00

YOUNGBLOOD/X-FORCE
Image/Extreme/Marvel 1996
1-shot Mojo visits Image x-over . . . 5.00
1-shot RLd variant cover 5.00

YOUNGBLOOD
YEARBOOK
1 CYp,I:Tyrax. 2.75

YOUNGBLOOD:
YEAR ONE
1 KBk(s),RLd, the early years 2.50
2 KBk(s),RLd,V:Giger,Cybernet . . . 2.50

ZEALOT
Image/Wildstorm 1995
1 O:Zealot. 2.50
2 In Japan. 2.50
3 V:Prometheus. 2.50

ZORRO
Image (B&W) 1998
TPB #1 rep. classic Alex Toth 15.95
TPB #2 rep. classic Alex Toth 15.95
TPB The Lady Wears Red 12.95

ZORRO'S LADY RAWHIDE:
OTHER PEOPLE'S BLOOD
Image (B&W) Feb. 1999
1 DMG,EM,JuB(c),cont. from Topps 2.95
2 DMG,EM,V:Scarlet Fever 2.95
3 DMG,EM,V:Ansel Plague 2.95
4 DMG,EM,V:Scarlet Fever 2.95
5 DMG,EM,Whiplash. 2.95

ZORRO'S RENEGADES
Image
TPB Zorro's Renegades, B&W . . . 14.95
TPB Vol. 2, Lady Rawhide 14.95

All comics prices listed are for *Near Mint* condition.

IMAGE

MALIBU

Airman #1
© Malibu Comics

AIRMAN
1 I:Thresher. 1.95

ALL NEW EXILES
Ultraverse 1995–96
Infinity F:Juggernaut, Blaze 2.50
1 TKa,KeL,Beginning the Quest. . . 1.50
1a Computer painted cover (1:6) . . 2.50
1b signed edition 4.00
2 I:Hellblade, Phoenix flip issue . . . 1.50
3 TKa,KeL,Phoenix Resurrection . . 1.50
4 . . . . 1.50
5 . . . . 1.50
6 I:Moloch 1.50
7 . . . . 1.50
8 I:Maxis 1.50
9 . . . . 1.50
10 "Aladdin Attacks" 1.50
11 V:Maxis,A:Ripfire 1.50

ANGEL OF DESTRUCTION
Oct. 1996
1 . . . . 2.50

ARROW
1 V:Dr.Sheldon,A:Man O'War 1.95

BATTLETECH
Feb. 1995
0 . . . . 2.95

BATTLETECH: FALLOUT
Dec. 1994–Mar. 1995
1 3 tales, Based on FASA game . . 2.95
1a gold foil limited edition 3.50
1b limited holographic editon 5.00
2 V:Clan Jade Falcon 2.95
3 R:Lea 2.95
4 Conclusion 2.95

BLACK SEPTEMBER
Ultraverse 1995
Infinity End of Black September . . . 2.95

BRAVURA
1995
0 Preview book, mail-in 5.00

BREAK-THRU
Ultraverse 1993–94
1 GJ(s),GP,AV(i),A:All Ultraverse
  Heroes. 2.75
1a Foil Edition 7.50
2 GJ(s),GP,AV(i),A:All Ultraverse
  Heroes. 2.75

'BREED
Bravura
[Limited Series] 1994
1 JSn(a&s),Black (c),I:Stoner. 3.00
2 JSn(a&s),I:Rachel. 2.75
3 JSn(a&s),V:Rachel 2.75
4 JSn(a&s),I:Stoner's Mom 2.75
5 JSn(a&s),V:Rachel 2.75
6 JSn(a&s),final issue 2.50
TPB Book of Genesis, rep.#1-#6. . 12.95

'BREED II
Bravura
[Limited Series] 1994–95
1 JSn,The Book of Revelation 2.95
1a gold foil edition 4.00
2 JSn,A:Rachel 2.95
3 JSn,V:Actual Demon. 2.95
4 JSn,Language of Demons 2.95
5 JSn,R:Rachael 2.95
6 JSn,final issue 2.95

BRUCE LEE
1994
1 MBn(s), Stories of B.Lee. 2.95
2 MBn(s) 2.95
3 MBn(s) 2.95
4 thru 6 . . . . @2.95

CODENAME: FIREARM
Ultraverse 1995
0 I:New Firearm. 2.95
1 F:Alec Swan. 2.95
2 Dual Identity 2.95
3 F:Hitch and Lopez 2.95
4 F:Hitch and Lopez 2.95
5 Working Together 2.95

CURSE OF RUNE
Ultraverse 1995
1A CU,Rune/Silver Surfer tie-in . . . 2.50
1B CU, alternate cover 2.50
2 COntrol of the Soul Gem 2.50
3 F:Marvel's Adam Warlock 2.50
4 N:Adam Warlock. 2.50

DEAD CLOWN
1 I:Force America 2.50
2 I:Sadistic Six. 2.50
3 TMs(s),last issue 2.50

Dinosaurs for Hire #3
© Malibu Comics

DINOSAURS FOR HIRE
1 3-D rep. B&W . . . .
3.00@WP Heading 1:[2nd Series] 1993–94
1 B:TMs(s),A:Reese,Archie,
  Lorenzo 3.00
2 BU:Dinosaurs 2099 . . . . 2.50
3 A:Ex-Mutants 2.50
4 V:Poacher,Revenue 2.50
5 . . . . 2.50
6 V:Samantha 2.50
7 V:Turret 2.50
8 Genesis #2, with Skycap 2.50
9 Genesis #5. . . . . 2.50
10 Flip(c) 2.50
11 V:Tiny Lorenzo. 2.50
12 I:Manhatten Bob 2.50
13 I:Lil' Billy Frankenstein 2.50
14 final issue 2.50

DREADSTAR
Bravura 1994–95
1 JSn(c),PDd(s),EC,I:New Dreadstar
  (Kalla),w/stamp 2.75
2 JSn(c),PDd(s),EC,w/stamp 2.50
3 JSn(c),PDd(s),EC,w/stamp 2.75
4 PDd,EC,Kalla's origin,w/stamp . . 2.50
5 PDd,F:Vanth,w/stamp 2.50
6 PDd,w/stamp 2.50

EDGE
Bravura 1994–95
1 GK,I:Edge 2.50
2 GK,STg,Gold Stamp. 2.50
3 GK,The Ultimates 2.50
4 GK,V:Mr. Ultimate. 2.50

ELIMINATOR
Ultraverse 1995
0 Man,DJa,MZ,Zothros tries to re-
  open passage to the Godwheel 2.95
1 MZ,Man,DRo, The Search for the
  Missing Infinity Gems,I:Siren . . 2.95
1a Black Cover ed. 3.95

2 MZ 2.50
3 MZ, Infinity Gem tie-in,finale 2.50

ELVEN
Ultraverse 1994
0 Rep.,A:Prime, double size 2.95
Mini-Series 1994–95
1 A:Prime, Primevil 2.50
2 AaL,R:Maxi-Man 2.50
3 AaL,V:Duey, Primevil 2.50
4 AaL,F:Primevil 2.50

ETERNITY TRIPLE ACTION
B&W
1 F:Gazonga 1.95
2 F:Gigantor 2.50

EXILES
Ultraverse 1993
1 TMs(s),PaP,I:Exiles 4.00
1a w/out card 2.25
1b Gold hologram ed. 10.00
1c Ultra-limited 12.00
2 V:Kort 3.00
3 BWS,Mastodon,BU:Rune 4.00
4 V:Kort 3.00

EX-MUTANTS
Nov. 1992–Apr. 1994
1 I&O:Ex-Mutants 2.25
2 V:El Motho,Beafcake,Brickhouse 2.25
3 A:Sliggo,Zygote 2.25
4 . . . . 2.25
5 Piper Kidnapped 1.95
6 A:Dr.Kildare 1.95
7 V:Dr.Kildare 1.95
8 O:Gelson 1.95
9 F:Dillion 1.95
10 F:Sluggtown 1.95
11 Man(s),Genesis#1,w/card 2.25
12 R0M(s),Genesis#4 . . . . 2.25
13 J:Gravestone,Arc 2.25
14 C:Eye 2.25
15 A:Arrow 2.50
16 A:Arrow,I:KillCorp 2.50
17 A:Arrow,V:KillCorp 2.50
18 A:Arrow,V:KillCorp 2.50

Ex-Mutants #12
© Malibu Comics

FERRET
1 (From Protectors),DZ,V:Purple
   Dragon Tong,A:Iron Skull 2.25
[Regular Series] 1992–93
1 thru 3 . . . . 2.50
4 V:Toxin 2.50
4a Newstand Ed 2.25
5 SEr,Genesis 2.25
6 SEr,Genesis crossover 2.25
7 V:Airman 2.25
8 I:Posse 2.25
9 DZ,R:Iron Skull,I:Deathsong 2.25
10 DZ 2.25
11 . . . . 2.25

FIREARM
Ultraverse 1993–95
0 w/video,I:Duet 3.00
1 I:Firearm,Alec Swan 2.50
1 silver foil, limited edition 4.00
2 BWS,A:Hardcase,BU:Rune 2.75
3 V:Sportsmen 2.25
4 HC,Break-Thru x-over 2.25
5 O:Prime,I:Ellen 2.25
6 A:Prime 2.25
7 V:Killer 2.25
8 DIB(c) 2.25
9 at the Rose Bowl 1.95
10 The Lodge 2.25
11 Ultraverse Premier #5,BU:Prime 3.50
12 Rafferty Saga,pt.1 . . . . 1.95
13 Rafferty Saga,pt.2 . . . . 1.95
14 Swan 1.95
15 Rafferty Saga,pt.3 . . . . 1.95
16 Rafferty Saga,pt.4 . . . . 1.95
17 Rafferty Saga,pt.5 . . . . 1.95
18 JeR,HC(c),Rafferty Saga,finale . 2.50

FLOOD RELIEF
Ultraverse 1994
TPB Ultraverse Heroes 5.00

FOXFIRE
Ultraverse 1996
1 From Phoenix Resurrection 1.50
2 Fate of Mastodon revealed 1.50
3 & 4 . . . . @1.50

FRANKENSTEIN
1 thru 3 movie promo . . . . @2.50

FREEX
Ultraverse 1993–95
1 I:Freex w/Ultraverse card 3.00
1a Ultra-Limited 4.00
1b Full Hologram (c) 5.00
2 L:Valerie,I:Rush 3.00
3 A:Rush 3.00
4 GJ(s),DdW,BWS,BU:Rune 2.75
5 GJ(s),V:Master of the Hunt 2.50
6 GJ(s),BH,Break Thru x-over,
   A:Night Man 2.25
7 BHr,MZ,O:Hardcase 2.25
8 BHr,V:Lost Angel 2.25
9 BHr,A:Old Man 2.25
10 BHr,V:Ms. Contrary 2.25
11 BHr,E:Origins 2.25
12 GJ,Ultraforce 1.95
13 New look 1.95
14 R:Boomboy 1.95
15 Death of Teamate 3.50
16 Prelude to Godwheel 1.95
17 A:Rune 2.50
18 GJ,A:Contray, Cayman, Juice . . 2.50
Giant Size#1 A:Prime 2.50

GENESIS
0 GP,w/Pog,F:Widowmaker, A:Arrow . .
3.50
0a Gold Ed 5.00

GODWHEEL
Ultraverse 1995
0 R:Argus to Godwheel 2.50
1 I:Primevil 2.50
2 Hardcase new costume 2.50
3 F:Lord Pumpkin 2.50
TPB Wheel of Thunder,rep.#0–#3 . . 9.95

GRAVESTONE
July 1993–Feb. 1994
1 D:Gravestone,V:Wisecrack 2.25
1a Newstand Ed 1.95
2 A:Eternal Man, V:Night Plague . . 2.25
2a Newstand Ed 1.95
3 Genesis Tie in,w/skycap 2.25
4 Genesis 2.25
5 V:Scythe 2.25
6 V:Jug 1.95
7 R:Bogg 2.25
8 & 9 . . . . @2.25

HARDCASE
Ultraverse 1993–95
1 I:Hardcase,D:The Squad 3.00
1a Ultra-Limited, silver foil 4.00
1b Full Hologram (c) 5.00
1c Platinum edition 3.50
2 w/Ultraverse card 3.00
3 Hard decisions 2.75
4 A:Strangers 2.75
5 BWS,V:Hardwire,BU:Rune 2.75
6 V:Hardwire 2.50
7 ScB,Break-Thru x-over,
   I:Nanotech,A:Solution 2.25
8 GP,O:Solitare 2.25
9 B:O:Choice,I:Turf 2.25
10 O:Choice 2.25
11 ScB,V:Aladdin 2.25
12 AV,A:Choice 1.95
13 A:Choice 2.25
14 A:Choice 2.25
15 Hardwires, NIM-E 1.95
16 NIM-E 3.50
17 Prime,NIM-E 1.95
18 V:Nim-E, Battle Royale 1.95
19 Prelude to Godwheel 1.95

Hardcase #13
© Malibu Comics

MALIBU

20 R:Rex Mindi	2.50
21 Mundiquest prelude	2.50
22 Mundiquest	2.50
23 A:Loki	2.50
24 Mundiquest,pt.3	2.50
25 Mundiquest,concl.	2.95
26 Time Gem Disaster	2.95

HOSTILE TAKEOVER
1 ashcan Ultraverse x-over 75

LITA FORD
Rock-It Comix
1 JBa 3.95

LORD PUMPKIN
Oct. 1994
0 Sludge 2.50

MAN CALLED A-X
Bravura 1994–95
[Limited Series]
0 1st Puzzle piece	2.95
1 MWn,SwM	2.95
1a Gold foil Edition	4.00
2 MWn,SwM,VLElectobot	2.95
3 MWn,SwM,Mercy Island	2.95
4 MWn,SwM,One Who Came Before	2.95
5 MWn,SwM,Climax	2.95

Man of War #6
© Malibu Comics

MAN OF WAR
1993–94
1 thru 3 V:Lift	2.50
1a thru 5a Newsstand Ed.	1.95
4 w/poster	2.50
5 V:Killinger	2.50
6 KM,Genesis Crossover	2.50
7 DJu,Genesis Crossover	2.50
8 TMs(s),A:Rocket Ranger	2.25
9 thru 12	@2.25

MANTRA
Ultraverse 1993–95
1 AV,I:Mantra,w/Ultraverse card	3.00
1a Full Hologram (c)	12.00
1b Silver foil (c)	5.00
2 AV,V:Warstrike	2.50
3 AV,V:Kismet Deadly	2.50

4 BWS,Mantra's marriage, BU:Rune story	2.50
5 MiB(s),AV(i),V:Wiley Wolf	2.00
6 MiB(s),AV(i),Break Thru x-over	2.00
7 DJu,TA,A:Prime, O:Prototype	2.00
8 B:MiB(s),A:Warstrike	2.00
9 V:Iron Knight,Puppeteer	2.00
10 NBy(c),DaR,B:Archmage Quest, Flip/UltraversePremiere #2	3.00
11 MiB(s),V:Boneyard	2.00
12 MiB(s),A:Strangers	2.00
13 Topaz, Boneyard	2.00
14 Tradesmen, Boneyard	2.00
15 A:Prime,Doc Gross	2.00
16 A:Prime	2.00
17 A:Necromantra	2.00
18 Pregnancy	2.25
19 MiB,Pregnancy	2.25
20 Aftermath of Godwheel	2.25
21 TyD,MiB,Mantra goes bad	2.25
22 A:Marvel's Loki	2.25
23 I:Tremblor, A:Prime	2.25
24 V:Topaz	2.25
Giant Sized#1 GP(c),I:Topaz.	2.25
Ashcan #1	2.00

MANTRA
Ultraverse 1995–96
Infinity N:Mantra	2.50
1 Mantra in all Female Body	1.50
1a Computer Painted Cover	1.50
2 Phoenix flip issue	1.50
3 Phoenix Resurrection	1.50
4	1.50
5	1.50
6 TMs,I:Tattoo,A:Rush	1.50
7	1.50

MANTRA: SPEAR OF DESTINY
Ultraverse 1995
1 Search for Artifact	2.50
2 MiB,Eden vs. Aladdin	2.50

MARVEL/ULTRAVERSE BATTLEZONES
Ultraverse 1996
1 DPs(c),The Battle of the Heroes . 3.95

MEGADETH
Rock-it Comix
1 . . . . 4.25

METALLICA
Rock-it Comix
1 . . . . 4.25

METAPHYSIQUE
Bravura 1995
1 NBy,I:Metaphysique	2.95
1a Gold foil edition	4.00
2 NBy,Mandelbrot malfunctions	2.95
3 I:Harridas	2.95
4 D:Maj.Character,B:Superious	2.95
5 V:Astral Kid	2.95
6 Apocalyptic Armageddon, finale	2.95
Ashcan NBy,B&W	1.00

MIGHTY MAGNOR, THE
1 thru 6 SA . . . . @1.95

Mighty Magnor #2
© Malibu Comics

MONSTER POSSE
B&W
1 I:Monster Posse	2.50
2 I:P.O.N.E,Wack Mack Dwac's sister,D-Vicious	2.50

MORTAL KOMBAT
1994
0 Four stories	2.95
1 Based on the Video Game	2.95
1a Foil Ed	4.00
1b with new material	2.95
2	2.95
3	2.95
4	2.95
5 I:Mortal Kombat II	2.95
6 Climax	2.95
Spec. #1 Tournament edition	3.95
Spec. #2 Tournament edition II	3.95
TPB rep. #1–#6	14.95

MORTAL KOMBAT: BARAKA
1 V:Scorpion 2.95

MORTAL KOMBAT: BATTLEWAVE
1 New series	2.95
2 Action, Action, Action	2.95
3 The Gathering	2.95
4 F:Goro	2.95
5 F:Scorpion	2.95
6 final issue	2.95

MORTAL KOMBAT: GORO, PRINCE OF PAIN
1 Goro	2.95
1a Platinum Edition	6.25
2 Goro, V:Kombatant	2.95
3 Goro, V:God of Pain	2.95

MORTAL KOMBAT: KITANA & MILEENA
1 Secrets of Outworld 2.95

MALIBU

MORTAL KOMBAT: KUNG LAO

1 one-shot Battlewave tie-in. 2.95

MORTAL KOMBAT: RAYDEN AND KANO

1 J:Rayden Kano. 2.95
1a Deluxe Edition 4.95
2 A:Reptile 2.95
3 Kano, conclusion 2.95

MORTAL KOMBAT: U.S. SPECIAL FORCES

1 V:Black Dragon 3.50
2 V:Black Dragon 2.95

NECROMANTRA/ LORD PUMPKIN
Ultraverse 1995

1 A:Loki (from Marvel) 2.95
2 MiB,V:Godwheel, flipbook. 2.95
3 O:Lord Pumpkin 2.95
4 Infinity Gem tie-in 2.95
4a variant cover. 3.50

NECROSCOPE

1 Novel adapt., holo(c) 3.25
1a 2nd printing 2.95
2 thru 4 Adapt. cont. . . . . @2.95

Book II

1 thru 5 . . . . 2.95

NIGHT MAN, THE
Ultraverse 1993–95

1 I:Night Man,Deathmask 2.75
1a Silver foil (c) 4.00
2 GeH,V:Mangle 2.25
3 SEt,GeH,A:Freex,Mangle 2.25
4 HC,I:Scrapyard,O:Firearm 2.25
5 SEt(s). 2.25
6 V:TNTNT 2.25
7 V:Nick 2.25
8 V:Werewolf. 1.95
9 V:Werewolf. 2.25
10 . . . . 1.95
11. . . . . 1.95
12 . . . . 1.95
13 . . . . 1.95
14 V:Rafferty 1.95
15 I:Rigoletto 1.95
16 I:Bloodfly 3.50
17 D:Playland. 2.50
18 DZ,SEt,V:Bloodfly 2.50
19 DZ,SEt,V:Deathmask. 2.50
20 DZ,V:Bloody fly 2.50
21 Identity Revealed. 2.50
22 Infinity Gem tie-in,A:Loki 2.50
23 R:Rhianon 2.50
Ann.#1 V:Pilgrim, 64pg. 3.95

NIGHT MAN, THE
Ultraverse 1995

Infinity Night Man vs. Night Man . . . 2.50
1 Discovers New powers 1.50
1a Computer Painted Cover 1.50
2 phoenix flip issue 1.50
3 Phoenix Resurrection 1.50
4 final issue. 1.50

NIGHT MAN/GAMBIT
1996

1 thru 3 . . . . @2.50

NOCTURNALS
Bravura 1995

1 DIB,I:Nocturnals 2.95
1a Glow-in-the-Dark 4.00
2 DIB,I:Komodo, Mister Fane. . . . 2.95
3 DIB,F:Raccoon. 2.95
4 DIB,I:The Old Wolf 2.95
5 Discovered by Police 2.95
6 DIB, ... 2.95

ORIGINS
Ultraverse

1 O:Ultraverse Heroes. 1.25

OZZY OSBORNE
Rock-It Comix

1 w/guitar pick. 3.95

PANTERA
Rock-it Comix

1 . . . . 3.95
1a Gold Ed. 19.95

PHOENIX RESURRECTION
Ultraverse 1995–96

0 Intro to Phoenix Resurrection . . 1.95
Genesis, A:X-Men 3.95
Revelations, A:X-Men. 3.95
Aftermath, A:X-Men 3.95

PLAN 9 FROM OUTER SPACE

GNv Movie Adapt. 4.95

POWER & GLORY
Bravura 1994

1A HC(a&s),I:American
    Powerhouse. 3.00
1B alternate cover. 3.00
1c Blue Foil (c) 5.00
1d w/seirgraph. 5.00
1e Newsstand 3.00
2 HC(a&s), O:American
    Powerhouse. 2.75
3 HC(a&s) 2.50
4 HC(a&s) 2.50
Winter Special 2.95
TPB Series reprint, w/stamp 12.95

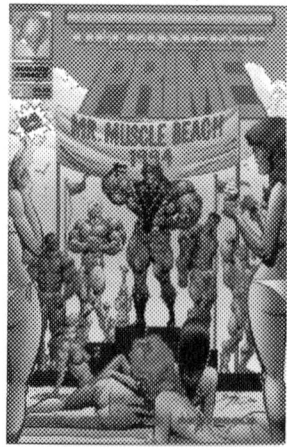

Prime #12
© Malibu Comics

POWER OF PRIME
Ultraverse 1995

1 O:Prime Powers,Godwheel tie-in 2.50
2 V:Doc Gross, Godwheel tie-in . . . 2.50
3 F:Prime Phade 2.50
4 F:Elven,Turbocharge 2.50

PRIME
Ultraverse 1993–95

1 B:GJ(s),I:Prime. 4.00
1a Ultra-Limited. 5.00
1b Full Hologram (c) 5.00
2 V:Organism 8, with Ultraverse
    card 3.00
3 NBy,I:Prototype 3.00
4 NBy,V:Prototype 3.00
5 NBy,BWS,I:Maxi-Man, BU:Rune . 3.00
6 NBy,A:Pres. Clinton 2.75
7 NBy,Break-Thru x-over 2.25
8 NBy,A:Mantra 2.25
9 NBy,Atomic Lies 2.25
10 NBy,A:Firearm,N:Prime 2.25
11 NBy 2.25
12 NBy,(Ultraverse Premiere#3)
    I:Planet Class. 3.50
13 NBy,V:Kutt,Planet Class. 2.95
14 DaR,I:Voodoo Master. 2.25
15 abused kids. 2.00
16 I:Turbo. 2.00
17 Atalon 2.00
18 Prime's new partner. 2.00
19 Prime accused. 2.00
20 GJ,LeS,A:Rafferty 2.50
21 GJ,LeS,World without Prime . . 2.50
22 GJ,LeS,F:Primevil 2.50
23 F:Prime's Mother 2.50
24 F:Prime's Mother 2.50
25 A:Chelsea Clinton 2.50
26 True Powers. 2.50
Ashcan (first) 7.00
Ashcan #1 BV(c),B&W 75
Ann.#1 R:Doc Gross. 3.95
TPB Rep. #1-#4 . . . . 9.95

PRIME
Ultraverse 1995–96

Infinty I:Spider-Prime 3.00
1 Spider-Prime vs. Lizard 1.50
1a Computer painted cover 2.00
2 Phoenix flip issue 1.50
3 Phoenix Resurrection 1.50

Prime, Vol 2, #8
© Malibu Comics

MALIBU

4 & 5 . . . . @1.50
6 Prime on Drugs,pt.1,F:Solitaire . . 1.50
7 F:Solitaire, pt.2 . . . . 1.50
8 F:Solitaire, pt.3 . . . . 1.50
9 and 10 . . . . @1.50
11 "Absolute Power Corrupts?
   Absolutely!" 1.50
12 HuR,KG, pt.3 (of 3) 1.50
13 KG,Prime exposed, V:Colonel
   Rinaldo 1.50
14 KG, Return of Lord Pumpkin . . . 1.50
15 Return of Lord Pumpkin. 1.50

PRIME/CAPTAIN AMERICA
Ultraverse 1996
1 GJ,NBy 3.95

PRIME VS. HULK
0 . . . . 10.00
0a signed premium edition. 20.00

PROJECT A-KO
1 thru 4 Based on anime movie . @2.95

PROTECTORS
1992–94
1 I:Protectors, inc. JBi poster
   (direct) 3.00
1a thru 12a Newsstand . . . . @1.95
2 V:Mr.Monday,w/poster. 2.50
3 V:Steel Army,w/poster. 2.50
4 V:Steel Army 2.50
5 Die Cut(c),V:Mr.Monday 2.50
6 V:Mr.Monday 2.50
7 A:Thresher 2.50
8 V:Wisecrack 1.95
9 V:Wisecrack 2.50
10 I:Mantoka 2.50
11 A:Ms.Fury,V:Black Fury 2.50
12 A:Arrow 2.50
13 RAJ(s),Genesis#3 . . . . 2.25
14 RB(c),RAJ(s),Genesis#6 . . . . . 2.25
15 RAJ(s),J:Chalice 2.25
16 So Help Me God 2.25
17 L:Ferret 2.25
18 V:Regulators,BU:Mantako, R:Mr.
   Monday 2.25
19 A:Gravestone,Arc 2.50
20 V:Nowhere Man. 2.50
Protectors Handbook 2.50

PROTOTYPE
Ultraverse 1993–95
1 V:Ultra-Tech,w/card 2.50
1a Ultra-lim. silver foil(c) 5.00
1b Hologram 6.00
2 I:Backstabber 2.50
3 LeS(s),DvA,JmP,BWS, V:Ultra-
   Tech,BU:Rune 2.50
4 TMs(s),V:Wrath 2.25
5 TMs(s),A:Strangers,Break-
   Thru x-over 2.25
6 TMs(s),Origins Month C:Arena . 2.25
7 TMs(s),V:Arena 2.25
8 TMs(s),V:Arena 2.25
9 Prototype Unplugged 2.25
10 TMs(s),V:Prototype 1.95
11 TMs(s),R:Glare 2.25
12 V:Ultratech. 1.95
13 Ultraverse Premiere #6 . . . . . . 3.50
14 Jimmy Ruiz, new boss. 1.95
15 Techuza, Donovan. 1.95
16 New CEO for Terrordy 1.95
17 Ranger Vs. Engine 1.95
18 Turf War 2.50
G-Size, Hostile Takeover 2.50
Spec.#0 LeS,JQ/JP(c) 2.50

PROTOTYPE: TURF WAR
Ultraverse
1 LeS,V:Techuza 2.50
2 LeS,F:Ranger,Arena 2.50
3 . . . . 2.50

RAFFERTY
1 Ashcan. 1.00

RAVER
1 Prism cover 3.00
1a Newsstand 2.25
2 . . . . 1.95
3 Walter Koenig(s). 1.95
4 and 5 . . . . @1.95

RIPFIRE
0 Prequel to Ripfire Series. 2.50

Rune #2
© Malibu Comics

RUNE
Ultraverse 1994–95
0 BWS(a&s) 4.00
1 BWS(a&s),from Ultraverse 2.50
1a Foil cover 4.00
2 CU(s),BWS,V:Aladdin 2.25
3 DaR,BWS,(Ultraverse Premiere
   #1), Flip book 3.75
4 BWS,V:Twins 2.25
5 BWS 1.95
6 BWS 1.95
7 CU,JS 1.95
8 Rise of Gods,pt.2 . . . . 1.95
9 Prelude to Godwheel 1.95
G-Size #1. . . . . 2.50
TPB BWS(c&a),CU,The Awakening,
   rep.#1–#5. . . . . 12.95

RUNE
Ultraverse 1995–96
Infinity V:Annihilus 2.50
1 A:Adam Warlock. 1.50
1a Computer painted cover 1.50
2 Phoenix flip issue,A:Adam
   Warlock 1.50
3 Phoenix Resurrection 1.50
4 . . . . 1.50
5 . . . . 1.50
6 LKa,A:Warlock 1.50
Spec. #1 Rune vs. Venom x-over . . 1.95

RUNE: HEARTS OF DARKNESS
Ultraverse 1996
1 DgM(s),KHt,TBd, flip book 1.50
2 DgM,KHt,TBd, flip book 1.50
3 DgM,KHt,TBd, flip book 1.50

RUNE/SILVER SURFER
Ultravrse 1995
1 BWS(c),A:Adam Warlock 5.95
1a Lim. edition (5,000 made) 8.00
1b Standard ed.newsprint 2.95

RUST
1 O:Rust 2.95
2 V:Marion Labs 2.95
3 I:Ashe Sapphire,5th Anniv. 2.95
4 I:Rustmobile. 2.95

SANTANA
Rock-it Comix
1 TT(c&s),TY 3.95

Siren #3
© Malibu Comics

SIREN
Ultraverse 1995
Infinity V:War Machine 2.50
1 V:War Machine 1.50
1a Computer painted cover 1.50
2 Phoenix flip issue 1.50
3 Phoenix Resurrection 1.50
Spec. #1 O:Siren 1.95

SLUDGE
Ultraverse 1993–94
1 BWS,I:Sludge,BU:I:Rune 2.75
1a Ultra-Limited. 5.00
2 AaL,I:Bloodstorm 2.25
3 AaL,V:River Men 2.50
4 AaL,Origins Month,V:Alligator . . 2.25
5 AaL,V:Garret Whale 2.25
6 AaL,A:Dragon Fang,Lord
   Pumpkin. 2.25
7 V:Frank Hoag. 2.25
8 AaL,V:Monsters 2.25
9 AaL,O:Sludge. 2.25
10 AaL,O:Sludge. 1.95
11 AaL,V:Bash Brothers 1.95
12 AaL,V:Prime, w/flip book
   w/Ultraverse Premiere #8 . . . . 3.50

13 . . . . 1.95
Red X-Mas. 2.50

SOLITAIRE
Ultraverse 1993–94
1 black baged edition with playing
    card: Ace of Clubs, Diamonds,
    Hearts or Spades 2.75
1d Newsstand edition,no card 2.25
2 GJ(s),JJ,Break-Thru x-over,
    V:Moon Man. 2.25
3 Origins Month, I:Monkey-Woman 2.25
4 O:Solitaire 2.25
5 JJ,V:Djinn. 2.25
6 JJ,V:Lone 1.95
7 JJ,I:Double Edge 2.25
8 GJ,I:Degenerate 1.95
9 GJ,Degenerate Rafferty 1.95
10 Hostile Takeover #2 . . . . 1.95
11 V:Djinn. 1.95
12 V:Anton Lowe 1.95

SOLUTION
Ultraverse 1993–95
0 DaR,O:Solution 4.00
1 DaR,I:Solution 2.50
1a foil cover. 4.00
2 DaR,BWS,V:Rex Mundi,Quatro,
    BU:Rune 2.50
3 DaR,A:Hardcase,Choice. 2.50
4 DaR,Break-Thru x-over,
    A:Hardcase,Choice. 2.50
5 F:Dropkick 2.25
6 B:O:Solution. 2.25
7 KM,O:Solution 2.25
8 KM(c),E:O:Solution. 2.25
9 F:Shadowmage 2.25
10 V:Vyr 2.25
11 V:Vorlexx 2.25
12 JHi 1.95
13 Hostile Takeover pt.3 . . . . 1.95
14 old foes 1.95
15 V:Casino 1.95
16 Flip/UltraverePremiere#10 . . . . 3.50
17 F:Casino, Dragons Claws 2.50

SQUAD, THE
0-A Hardcase's old team 2.50
0-B 2.50
0-C L.A.Riots. 2.50

Solution #6 © Malibu Comics

STAR SLAMMERS
Bravura 1994
1 WS(a&s). 2.75
2 WS(a&s),F:Meredith 2.75
3 WS(a&s). 2.50
4 WS(a&s). 2.50
5 WS,Rojas Choice 2.50

STAR TREK: DEEP SPACE NINE
1 Direct ed. 3.25
1a Photo(c). 3.00
1b Gold foil 5.00
2 w/skycap 3.50
3 Murder on DS9. . . . . 2.75
4 MiB(s),F:Bashir,Dax 2.75
5 MiB(s),V:Slaves 2.75
6 MiB(s),Three Stories. 2.75
7 F:Kira 2.75
8 B:Requiem 2.75
9 E:Requiem 2.75
10 Descendants 2.50
11 A Short Fuse 2.75
12 Baby on Board. 2.50
13 Problems with Odo 2.75
14 on Bejor. 2.75
15 mythologic dilemma 2.75
16 Shangheid 2.50
17 Voyager preview 2.50
18 V:Gwyn 2.50
19 Wormhole Mystery. 2.50
20 Sisko Injured 2.50
21 Smugglers attack DS9 . . . . . . 2.50
22 Commander Quark 2.50
23 Secret of the Lost Orb,pt.1 . . . 2.50
24 Secret of the Lost Orb,pt.2. . . . 2.50
25 Secret of the Lost Orb,pt.3. . . . 2.50
26 Mudd's Pets, pt.1. . . . . 2.50
27 Mudd's Pets, pt.2. . . . . 2.50
28 F:Ensign Ro 2.50
29 F:Thomas Riker,Tuvok. 2.50
30 F:Thomas Riker. 2.50
31 thru 32 . . . . @2.50
Ann.#1 Looking Glass. 3.95
Spec. #1Collision Course 3.50
Spec. #0 Terok Nor. 3.00

STAR TREK: DEEP SPACE NINE CELEBRITY SERIES: BLOOD AND HONOR
1 Mark Lenard(s). 2.95
2 Rules of Diplomacy. 2.95

STAR TREK: DEEP SPACE NINE: LIGHTSTORM
1 Direct ed. 3.50
1a Silver foil 8.00

STAR TREK: DEEP SPACE NINE: HEARTS AND MINDS
[Limited Series]
1 . . . . 3.00
2 . . . . 2.50
3 Into the Abyss,X-over preview . 2.50
4 final issue. 2.50

STAR TREK: DEEP SPACE NINE: THE MAQUIS
[Limited Series]
1 Federation Renegades 2.50
1a Newsstand, photo(c). 2.50

Star Trek: Deep Space Nine #16
© Malibu Comics

2 Garack 2.50
3 F:Quark, Bashir 2.50

STAR TREK: DEEP SPACE NINE/ THE NEXT GENERATION
1 Prophet & Losses, pt.2 . . . . 2.50
2 Prophet & Losses, pt.4 . . . . 2.50

STAR TREK: VOYAGER
A V:Maquis. 2.75
Aa Newsstand, photo(c) 2.75
B conclusion. 2.75
Ba Newsstand, photo(c) 2.50

STRANGERS, THE
Ultraverse 1993–95
1 I:Strangers 3.00
1a Ultra-Limited. 4.00
1b Full Hologram (c) 5.00
2 A:J.D.Hunt,w/Ultraverse card . . 3.00
3 I:TNTNT 2.50
4 A:Hardcase 2.50
5 BWS,BU:Rune 2.50
6 J:Yrial,I:Deathwish 2.25
7 Break-Thru x-over. 2.25
8 RHo,ANi,O:Solution 2.25
9 AV(i),I:Ulta Pirates 2.25
10 AV(i),V:Bastinado. 2.25
11 in Alderson Disk. 2.25
12 O:Yrial. 2.25
13 (Ultraverse Premiere#4). 3.50
14 . . . . 2.25
15 Zip-Zap, Yrail. 1.95
16 Ultras, Teknight 1.95
17 Rafferty 1.95
18 Ultra Pirates 1.95
19 V:Pilgrim 1.95
20 Stranger Destroyed 1.95
21 A:Rex Mundi 2.50
22 SEt,V:Guy Hunt 2.50
23 SEt,RHo,V:Tabboo. 2.50
24 RHo,SEt,V:Taboo. 2.50
25 V:Godwheel Aliens 2.50
26 RHo,SEt,V:Aladdin. 2.50
Ann.#1 Death 3.95
TPB rep. #1-#4. . . . . 9.95
Ashcan 1 (signed) 8.00
Ashcan 1 (unsigned). 8.00

MALIBU

STREET FIGHTER
1 thru 3 Based on Video Game . @3.00

STRIKEBACK
Bravura 1994–95
1 . . . . 2.95
2 . . . . 2.95
3 V:Doberman 2.95
4 V:Dragonryder Island 2.95
Spec.#1 KM,JRu,V:Dragon 3.50

TARZAN: THE BECKONING
1 TY,I:The Spider Man 2.75
2 TY,Going back to Africa 2.50
3 thru 6 . . . . 2.50

TARZAN THE WARRIOR
1 SBs(c),O:Tarzan 3.50
2 . . . . 2.75
3 . . . . 2.75
4 Wom'cha's Ship 2.75
5 . . . . 2.75

TARZAN: LOVE, LIES,
AND THE LOST CITY
1 MWg&WS(s),Short Stories 3.95
2 The lost city of Opar 2.50
3 Final issue 2.50

TERMINATOR 2: CYBERNETIC DAWN
1995–96
1 thru 4 . . . . @2.50
0 flip-book/T2 Nuclear Twilight 2.50

TERMINATOR 2: NUCLEAR TWILIGHT
1995–96
1 thru 4 . . . . @2.50
0 flip-book, see above

ULTRAFORCE
Ultraverse 1994–95
1 Prime, Prototype 2.50
2 . . . . 1.95
3 . . . . 1.95

UltraForce #3
© Malibu Comics

4 . . . . 1.95
5 V:Atalon 1.95
6 V:Atalon 2.50
7 CU,GP(c),F:Ghoul 2.50
8 MWn,CV,GP,F:Black Knight 2.50
9 A:Marvel's Black Knight 2.50
10 . . . . 2.50
Spec.#0 . . . . 2.50

ULTRAFORCE
Ultraverse 1995–96
Infinity Fant. Ultraforce Four 2.50
1 George Perez cover 1.50
1a Computer painted cover 1.50
2 Phoenix flip issue,I:Lament 1.50
3 . . . . 1.50
4 . . . . 1.50
5 . . . . 1.50
6 Smoke and Bone,pt.2 . . . . 1.50
7 . . . . 1.50
8 . . . . 1.50
9 . . . . 1.50
10 A:Sersi,Eliminator 1.50
11 . . . . 1.50
12 MD2,LWn, cont. from All-New
   Exiles #12 . . . . 1.50
13 LWn,MD2,new UltraForce lineup 1.50
14 LWn,MD2,Hardcase returns 1.50
15 LWn,MD2,Hardcase returns 1.50

ULTRAFORCE/AVENGERS
Ultraverse Aug. 1995
1 GP 3.95

ULTRAFORCE/ SPIDER-MAN
Ultraverse 1996
1 . . . . 3.95

ULTRAVERSE DOUBLE FEATURE
Ultraverse
1 F:Prime, Solitaire 3.95

ULTRAVERSE FUTURE SHOCK
Ultraverse 1996
1 one-shot,MPc,alternate futures . . 2.50

ULTRAVERSE ORIGINS
Ultraverse
1 O:Ultraverse Heroes 1.25
1a Silver foil cover 12.50

ULTRAVERSE UNLIMITED
Ultraverse 1996
1 F:Warlock 1.50
2 LWn,KWe, A:All-New Exiles,
   V:Maxis 1.50

ULTRAVERSE: YEAR ZERO: THE DEATH OF THE SQUAD
Ultraverse 1995
0-A hardcase's old team 2.50
0-B 2.50
0-C L.A. Riots 2.50
1 JHI,A:Squad, Mantra 2.95
2 JHI,DaR(c) prequel to Prime#1 . . 2.95
3 Cont. Year Zero Story 2.95
4 I:NM-E 2.95

ULTRAVERSE: YEAR ONE
Ultraverse 1995
1 Handbook, double size 4.95
2 Prime 1.95

ULTRAVERSE: YEAR TWO
Ultraverse 1996
1 Marvel/Ultraverse/Info 4.95

VIRTUA FIGHTER
1 New Video Game Comic 2.95

WARSTRIKE
Ultraverse 1994–95
1 HNg,TA,in South America 1.95
2 HNg,TA,Gatefold(c) 1.95
3 in Brazil 1.95
4 HNg,TA,V:Blind Faith 1.95
5 . . . . 1.95
6 Rafferty 1.95
7 Origin 1.95

WARSTRIKE: PRELUDE TO GODWHEEL
Ultraverse 1994
1 Blind Faith/Lord Pumpkin 1.95

WORLD DOMINATION
1 . . . . 3.95
1a 3.95

WRATH
Ultraverse 1994–95
1 B:MiB(s),DvA,JmP,C:Mantra 2.25
1a Silver foil 3.00
2 DvA,JmP,V:Hellion 2.25
3 DvA,JmP,V:Radicals, I:Slayer . . . 2.25
4 DvA,JmP,V:Freex 2.25
5 DvA,JmP,V:Freex 1.95
6 DvA,JmP 2.25
7 DvA,JmP,I:Pierce,Ogre, Doc
   Virtual 1.95
8 . . . . 1.95
9 A:Prime 2.25
G-Size #1 . . . . 2.50

Wrath #1
© Malibu Comics

MALIBU

COLOR COMICS

ABBOTT AND COSTELLO
Charlton Comics 1968–71
1 . . . . 70.00
2 thru 9 . . . . @40.00
10 thru 21 . . . . @25.00
22 . . . . 20.00

ACCIDENT MAN: THE DEATH TOUCH
Apocalypse
One Shot rep.Toxic #10-#16 . . . . . 3.95

ACES HIGH
Gemstone 1999
1 (of 5) EC Comics reprint 2.50
2 . . . . 2.50
3 . . . . 2.50
4 . . . . 2.50
5 . . . . 2.50
Annual rep. #1–#5 . . . . 13.50
HC 20.00

ACME NOVELTY LIBRARY
Fantagraphics 1994–98
1 thru 5 . . . . @4.50
6 thru 11 Jimmy Corrigan Meets
His Dad, pt. 1 – pt. 6 (of 8) . . @4.50
12 Jimmy & Dad have lunch 4.95
13 Jimmy's Grandfather, 80-page . 10.95
1 thru 7, 2nd printings . . . . @3.95

A.D.A.M.
Toyman 1998
1 . . . . 2.50
2 . . . . 2.50

ADAM-12
Gold Key 1973–76
1 Photo(c), From TV show 70.00
2 thru 9 . . . . @30.00
10 . . . . 25.00

ADAPTERS, THE
1 and 2 . . . . @2.00

ADDAMS FAMILY
Gold Key 1974–75
1 TV cartoon adapt. 100.00
2 . . . . 50.00
3 . . . . 35.00

ADLAI STEVENSON
Dell Publishing Co. Dec., 1966
1 Political Life Story 25.00

ADVENTURES OF BARON MUNCHAUSEN
Now Comics 1989
1 thru 4 movie adapt. series . . . . @1.75

ADVENTURES OF CHRISSIE CLAUS, THE
Hero Graphics
1 Trouble in Toyland 2.95

ADVENTURES OF FELIX THE CAT
Harvey 1992
1 Short Stories 1.25

ADVENTURES OF KUNG FU PIG NINJA FLOUNDER AND 4-D MONKEY
1 thru 6 . . . . @1.80
7 thru 10 . . . . @2.00

ADVENTURES OF ROBIN HOOD
Gold Key 1974–75
1 From Disney cartoon 6.00
2 thru 7 . . . . @3.50

ADVENTURES OF ROGER WILCO
Adventure
1 Based on Space-Quest
Computer games 2.95

Adventures of the Fly #14
© Archie Publications

ADVENTURES OF THE FLY
Archie Publications/ Radio Comics 1959–65
1 JSm/JK,O:Fly,I:SpiderSpry
A:Lancelot Strong/Shield . . . 550.00
2 JSm/JK,DAy,AW 300.00
3 Jack Davis Art, O:Fly 250.00
4 V:Dazzler NA panel 125.00
5 A:Spider Spry 75.00
6 V:Moon Men 75.00
7 A:Black Hood 75.00
8 A:Lancelot Strong/Shield 75.00
9 A:Lancelot Strong/Shield
I:Cat Girl 75.00
10 A:Spider Spry 75.00
11 V:Rock Men 50.00
12 V:Brute Invaders 50.00
13 I:Kim Brand 55.00
14 I:Fly-Girl(Kim Brand) 75.00
15 A:Spider 50.00
16 A:Fly-Girl 50.00
17 A:Fly-Girl 50.00
18 A:Fly-Girl 50.00
19 A:Fly-Girl 50.00
20 O:Fly-Girl 55.00
21 A:Fly-Girl 40.00
22 A:Fly-Girl 40.00
23 A:Fly-Girl,Jaguar 40.00
24 A:Fly-Girl 40.00
25 A:Fly-Girl 40.00
26 A:Fly-Girl,Black Hood. 40.00
27 A:Fly-Girl,Black Hood. 40.00
28 A:Black Hood. 40.00
29 A:Fly-Girl,Black Hood. 40.00
30 A:Fly-Girl,R:Comet. 50.00
31 A:Black Hood, Shield, Comet. . 55.00
Becomes:

FLYMAN

ADVENTURES OF THE JAGUAR
Archie Publications/ Radio Comics 1961–63
1 I:Ralph Hardy/Jaguar 175.00
2 10 cent cover 100.00
3 Last 10 cent cover 75.00
4 A:Cat-Girl 50.00
5 A:Cat-Girl 50.00
6 A:Cat-Girl 40.00
7 . . . . 35.00
8 . . . . 35.00
9 . . . . 35.00
10 . . . . 35.00
11 . . . . 35.00
12 A:Black Hood. 35.00
13 A:Cat-Girl,A:Black Hood. 35.00
14 A:Black Hood. 35.00
15 V:Human Octopus,last issue . . 30.00

ADVENTURES OF YOUNG DR. MASTERS
Archie Comics 1964
1 . . . . 25.00
2 . . . . 15.00

ADVENTUROUS UNCLE SCROOGE McDUCK
Gladstone Oct. 1997
1 . . . . 1.95
2 Don Rosa, A Little Something
Special 1.95
3 The Black Widow 1.95

AETERNUS
Brick Comics
1 thru 3 . . . . @2.95

AGAINST BLACKSHARD
Sirius Comics Aug., 1986
1 3-D. 2.25

AGENT: AMERICA
Awesome Entertainment 1997
1 RLe 2.50
2 RLe,JSb,JLb,F:Supreme,
   V:Smash 2.50

AIR FIGHTERS, SGT. STRIKE SPECIAL
Eclipse 1988
1 A:Airboy,Valkyrie. 1.95

AIR WAR STORIES
Dell Publishing Co. 1964
1 . . . . 50.00
2 . . . . 40.00
3 thru 8 . . . . @30.00

AIRBOY
Eclipse 1986–89
1 TT/TY,D:Golden Age Airboy
   O:New Airboy. 3.25
2 TT/TY,I:Marisa,R:SkyWolf 2.25
3 A:The Heap 2.50
4 A:Misery. 2.50
5 DSt(c),R:Valkyrie 4.00
6 R:Iron Ace,I:Marlene. 3.00
7 PG(c), ... 2.50
8 FH/TT(c). 2.50
9 R:Flying Fool, Riot, O'Hara
   Cocky, Judge & Turtle 1.75
10 I:Manic,D:Cocky, Judge & Turtle 1.50
11 O:Birdie 1.50
12 R:Flying Fool. 1.50
13 I:New Bald Eagle. 1.50
14 A:Sky Wolf, Iron Ace 1.50
15 A:Ku Klux Klan 1.50
16 D:Manic,A:Ku Klux Klan. 1.50
17 A:HarryS.Truman,Misery 1.75
18 A:Gold.Age Black Angel. 1.75
19 A:Gold.Age Rats 1.75
20 Rat storyline 1.75
21 I:Lester Mansfield (rel. of
   Gold.Age Rackman), Artic
   Deathzone #1. . . . . 1.75
22 DSp,Artic Deathzone #2 . . . . . 1.75
23 A:Gold.Age Black Angle, Artic
   Deathzone #3. . . . . 1.75
24 A: Heap. 1.75
25 TY,I:Manure Man,A:Heap. 1.50
26 R:Flying Dutchman 1.50
27 A:Iron Ace, Heap. 1.50
28 A:Heap 1.50
29 . . . . 1.50
30 A:Iron Ace; Sky Wolf story 1.50
31 A:Valkyrie; Sky Wolf story 1.75
32 Hostage Virus, ... 1.75
33 DSp,SkyWolf sty,A:Sgt.Strike. . . 1.75
34 DSp,A:La Lupina 1.75
35 DSp,A:La Lupina, Sky Wolf . . . 1.75
36 . . . . 1.75
37 DSp. 1.75
38 CI, Heap story 1.75
39 CI, Heap story 1.75
40 CI, Heap story 1.75
41 V:Steel Fox, Golden Age rep.
   O:Valkyrie. 1.75
42 A:Rackman 1.95
43 Sky Wolf sty, A:Flying Fool. . . . 1.95
44 A:Rackman 1.95
45 . . . . 1.95
46 EC,Airboy Diary #1 . . . . 1.95
47 EC,Airboy Diary #2 . . . . 1.95
48 EC,Airboy Diary #3 . . . . 1.95
49 EC,Airboy Diary #4 . . . . 1.95
50 AKu/NKu,double-size. 3.95
Spec. Meets the Prowler. 1.95
Spec. Mr. Monster 1.75

Spec. Vs Airmaidens 1.95

AIRMAIDENS SPECIAL
Eclipse Comics 1987
1 A:Valkyrie. 1.75

AKEMI
Brainstorm Comics 1997
1 . . . . 2.95

ALADDIN
Walt Disney
Prestige. Movie Adapt. 4.95

ALAN MOORE'S AWESOME ADVENTURES
Awesome Entertainment 1999
1 AMo. 2.50
1a alternate AxR cover 6.95
Spec. Awesome Universe Handbook. . .
2.95
Spec.A alternate AxR cover 2.95

ALARMING ADVENTURES
Harvey Publications 1962–63
1 AW,RC,JSe 70.00
2 AW,BP,RC,JSe 50.00
3 JSe 50.00

ALARMING TALES
Harvey Publications 1957–58
1 JK,JK(c) 150.00
2 JK,JK(c) 120.00
3 JK 75.00
4 JK,BP. 70.00
5 JK,AW 90.00
6 JK 60.00

ALBEDO, VOL. 3
Antartic Press 1994–95
Vol. 1 and II, See B&W
1 thru 4 Various Artists. . . . . @2.95

ALBINO SPIDER OF DAJETTE
Verotik 1998
0 by Glenn Danzig
   & Wayne Robertson 2.95
0a alternate cover 5.00

ALIAS
Now Comics 1990
1 . . . . 2.00
2 thru 5 . . . . @1.75

ALIAS: STORMFRONT
Now Comics
1 . . . . 1.75
2 . . . . 1.75

ALIEN ENCOUNTERS
Eclipse Comics 1985–87
1 . . . . 3.50
2 . . . . 3.00
3 "I Shot the Last Martian". 3.00
4 JBo(c) 2.00
5 RCo,"Night of the Monkey" 2.00
6 "Now You See It,""Freefall" 2.00
7 . . . . 2.00
8 TY,"Take One Capsule Every

Alien Encounters #1
© Eclipse

   Million Years,M.Monroe(c) 2.75
9 The Conquered 2.00
10 . . . . 2.00
11 TT,"Old Soldiers" 2.00
12 "What A Relief,""Eyes of
   the Sibyl" 2.00
13 GN,"The Light at the End" 2.00
14 JRy,GN,TL,RT,"Still born". 2.00

ALIEN TERROR
Eclipse 1986
3-D #1 "Standard Procedure" 2.00

ALIEN WORLDS
Pacific 1982
1 AW,VM,NR 4.00
2 DSt. 3.50
3 . . . . 3.00
4 DSt(i) 3.00
5 . . . . 3.00
6 . . . . 3.00
7 . . . . 3.00
3-D #1 AAd,DSt 5.50
           Eclipse 1985
8 AW 2.50
9 . . . . 2.50

[CAPTAIN JOHNER AND] ALIENS, THE
Gold Key 1967
1 Rep. Magnus Robot Fighter . . . 12.50

ALISTER THE SLAYER
Midnight Press 1995
1 I:Alister The Slayer. 2.50
2 V:Lady Hate 2.50
3 JQ&JP(c) V:Subterranean
   Vampire Bikers. 2.50

ALL AMERICAN SPORTS
Charlton 1967
1 . . . . 25.00

ALL HALLOWS EVE
Innovation 1991
1 . . . . 4.95

ALLEY OOP
Dell Publishing Co. 1962–63
1 ....50.00
2 ....45.00

ALLEY OOP ADVENTURES
Antarctic Press 1998
1 ....2.95
2 ....2.95
3 I:Granny Green. 2.95
TPB 11.00

ALLIES
Awesome Entertainment 1999
1 RLe,AMo 2.50
1a alternate RLe cover 6.95

ALPHA KORPS
Diversity Comics 1996
1 I:Alpha Korps 3.00
1 signed 4.95
2 "The Price of Freedom," pt.2. ...2.50
2 signed 4.95
3 "The Price of Freedom," pt.3. ...2.50
3 signed 4.95
4 "The Price of Freedom", pt.4. ...2.50

ALPHA WAVE
Darkline 1987
1 ....1.75

ALTER EGO
First 1986
1 RTs, Ron Harris 1.75
2 ....1.50
3 ....1.50
4 ....1.25

ALVIN (& THE CHIPMUNKS)
Dell Publishing Co. 1962–73
1 ....100.00
2 ....65.00
3 ....50.00
4 thru 10 ....@45.00
11 thru 20 ....@35.00
21 thru 28 ....@30.00
1 Alvin for President & his pals in Merry Christmas with Clyde Crashcup & Leonardo. 25.00

AMAZING CHAN & THE CHAN CLAN
Gold Key 1973
1 ....25.00
2 ....15.00
3 and 4 ....@12.00

AMAZING HEROES SWIMSUIT ANNUALS
Fantagraphics 1990–93
1990 Spec. A:Dawn 25.00
1990 2nd printing 15.00
1991 A: Dawn. 20.00
1992 A: Dawn. 20.00
1993 A: Dawn. 20.00

AMAZON, THE
Comico 1989
1 ....1.95
2 ....1.95
3 end mini-series. 1.95

AMERICAN FLAGG
First 1983–88
1 HC,I:American Flagg, Hard Times, pt.1 ....3.50
2 HC,Hard Times,pt.2 ....2.75
3 HC,Hard Times,pt.3 ....2.75
4 HC,Southern Comfort,pt.1. .....2.75
5 HC,Southern Comfort,pt.2. .....2.75
6 HC,Southern Comfort,pt.3. .....2.75
7 HC,State of the Union,pt.1 .....2.50
8 HC,State of the Union,pt.2 .....2.50
9 HC,State of the Union,pt.3 .....2.50
10 HC,Solidarity-For Now,pt.1 I:Luthor Ironheart 2.50
11 HC,Solidarity-For Now,pt.2.....2.50

American Flagg #3
© First

12 HC,Solidarity-For Now,pt.3. ....2.50
13 HC 2.25
14 PB. 2.25
15 HC,American Flagg A Complete story,pt.1 ....2.25
16 HC,Complete Story,pt.2 ....2.00
17 HC,Complete Story,pt.3 ....2.00
18 HC,Complete Story,pt.4 ....2.00
19 HC,Bullets & Ballots, pt.1.....2.00
20 HC,LSn,Bullets & Ballots,pt.2. ..2.00
21 AMo,HC,LSn,Bull&Ballots,pt.3 .2.00
22 AMo,HC,LSn,Bull&Ballots,pt.4 .2.00
23 AMo,HC,LSn,England Swings, pt.1 ....2.00
24 AMo,HC,England Swings,pt.2 ..2.00
25 AMo,HC,England Swings,pt.3 ..2.00
26 AMO,HC,England Swings,pt.4 ..2.00
27 AMo with Raul the Cat. 2.00
28 BWg 1.50
29 JSon 1.50
30 JSon 1.50
31 JSon,O:Bob Violence. 1.50
32 JSon,A:Bob Violence. 1.50
33 A:Bob Violence 1.50
34 A:Bob Violence 1.50
35 A:Bob Violence 1.50
36 A:Bob Violence 1.50
37 A:Bob Violence 1.50
38 New Direction 1.50
39 JSon,A:Bob Violence. 1.50
40 A:Bob Violence 1.50
41 ....1.50
42 F:Luther Ironheart 1.50
43 ....1.50
44 ....1.50
45 ....1.50
46 PS. 1.75
47 PS. 1.75
48 PS. 1.75
49 ....1.75
50 HC,last issue. 1.75
Special #1 HC,I:Time2 ....2.50
See Also: Howard Chaykin's American Flagg

AMERICOMICS
AC Comics 1983
1 GP(c),O:Shade. 3.00
2 ....2.00
3 Blue Beetle. 2.00
4 O:Dragonfly 2.00
5 and 6 ....@1.75
Spec.#1 Capt.Atom,BlueBeetle. ...1.50

AMERICAN WOMAN
Antarctic Press 1998
1 by Richard Stockton & Brian Denham. 2.95
2 ....2.95
2a deluxe 5.95

ANDROMEDA
Andromeda
1 I:Andromeda. 2.50
2 Andromeda vs. Elite Force 2.50

ANGEL FIRE
Crusade Comics 1997
1 BiT, from Shi #12, BiT(c). 2.95
1a with Roberto Flores cover. 2.95
1b with photo cover 2.95
2 F:Shi 2.95
3 F:Shi, concl. 2.95

ANIMAL MYSTIC: WATER WARS
Sirius 1996
1 (of 6) DOe 4.00
2 thru 6 DOe ....@3.00

ANNE McCAFFREY'S THE UNICORN GIRL
Big Entertainment 1997
GN F:Acorna 22.00

ANYTHING GOES
Fantagraphics 1986
1 GK,FlamingCarrot,Savage 3.50
2 S:AnM,JK,JSt,SK 3.50
3 DS,NA(c),A:Cerebus. 3.00
4 ....2.50
5 A:TMNTurtles. 5.00
6 ....2.00

APE NATION
Adventure Comics 1991
1 Aliens land on Planet of the Apes 3.00
2 General Ollo. 3.00
3 V:Gen.Ollo,Danada. 2.50
4 D:Danada. 2.50

APOLLO SMILE
Eagle Wing 1998
1 When the Levee Breaks 2.95
2 When the Levee Breaks, pt.2 . . . 2.95
3 When the Levee Breaks, pt.3 . . . 2.95

ARACHNAPHOBIA
Walt Disney 1990
1 Movie Adapt 5.95
1a Newsstand 2.95

ARACHNID FOUNDATION
Quantum Comics 1998
1 . . . . 2.95

ARAKNIS
Mushroom Comics 1995–96
1 I:Araknis, Shades of Evil pt.1 . . . 3.50
2 Shades of Evil pt.2 . . . . 3.50
3 with pin-ups 2.50
4 . . . . 2.50

ARAKNIS
Mushroom Comics April 1996
0 Michael & Mario Ortiz 3.00
0 signed 4.00
1 . . . . 2.50
1 special edition 10.00
Mystic Comics
2 thru 6 . . . . @2.50

ARAKNIS: RETRIBUTION
Morning Star Productions 1997
1 (of 4) by Michael & Mario Ortiz . . 2.50
1 signed 10.00
2 thru 4 . . . . @2.50

ARAKNIS: SHADES OF EVIL
Morning Star Productions
1 thru 4 . . . . @2.50

ARCHANGELS: THE SAGA
Eternal Studios
1 I:Cameron 2.50
2 V:Demons 2.50
3 . . . . 2.75
4 . . . . 2.75
5 . . . . 2.50
6 . . . . 2.50
7 . . . . 3.50

ARCHIE
Archie Publications
1 thru 300 see Golden Age
301 thru 400 . . . . @3.50
401 thru 449 . . . . @3.00
450 thru 467 . . . . @3.00
468 thru 477 . . . . @2.00
478 thru 489 . . . . @1.75
Archie's Christmas Stocking #4 . . . . 2.00
Archie's Christmas Stocking #5 . . . . 2.00
Archie's Christmas Stocking #6 . . . . 2.25
Archie's Spring Break Spec.1 . . . . . 2.00
Archie's Spring Break Spec.2 . . . . . 2.00
Archie's Spring Break Spec.3 . . . . . 2.25
Archie's Spring Break Spec.4 (1999)2.25
Archie's Vacation Spec.#4 . . . . . . 2.00
Archie's Vacation Spec.#5 . . . . . . 2.00
Archie's Vacation Spec.#6 . . . . . . 2.25
Archie's Vacation Spec.#7 . . . . . . 2.25

ARCHIE AMERICANA SERIES
Archie Comics
TPB Best of the Forties 10.95
TPB Best of the Fifties 8.95
TPB Best of the Sixties 9.95
TPB Best of the Seventies 9.95

ARCHIE AND FRIENDS
Archie Publications 1992—98
1 thru 10 . . . . @1.50
11 thru 20 . . . . @1.50
20 thru 26 . . . . @1.50
27 thru 37 . . . . @1.75

ARCHIE AND ME
Archie Publications 1964–87
1 . . . . 150.00
2 . . . . 75.00
3 . . . . 50.00
4 . . . . 40.00
5 . . . . 40.00
6 thru 10 . . . . @30.00
11 thru 20 . . . . @10.00
21 thru 100 . . . . @5.00
101 thru 162 . . . . @2.00

ARCHIE AS PUREHEART THE POWERFUL
Archie Publications 1966–67
1 superhero parody 70.00
2 . . . . 50.00
3 thru 6 Captain Pureheart . . . . @30.00

Archie at Riverdale High #55
© *Archie Publications*

ARCHIE AT RIVERDALE HIGH
Archie Publications 1972
1 . . . . 65.00
2 . . . . 30.00
3 . . . . 15.00
4 . . . . 10.00
5 . . . . 10.00
6 thru 10 . . . . @3.00
11 thru 114 . . . . @2.00

ARCHIE COMICS DIGEST
Archie Comics Digest 1973
1 . . . . 50.00

2 . . . . 30.00
3 . . . . 12.00
4 . . . . 7.00
5 thru 10 . . . . @3.00
11 thru 88 . . . . @2.00

ARCHIE MEETS THE PUNISHER
Archie/Marvel 1994
1-shot crossover, same contents
as Punisher meets Archie 3.00

ARCHIE'S MADHOUSE
Archie Publications 1959–69
1 . . . . 225.00
2 . . . . 135.00
3 thru 5 . . . . @90.00
6 thru 10 . . . . @50.00
11 thru 16 . . . . @40.00
17 thru 21 . . . . @20.00
22 . . . . 50.00
23 thru 30 . . . . @15.00
31 thru 40 . . . . @5.00
41 thru 66 . . . . @2.00

ARCHIE'S PAL JUGHEAD SEE: JUGHEAD

ARCHIE'S SUPERHERO MAGAZINE
Archie Publications
1 JSm/SK,Rept.Double of
Capt.Strong #1,FLy,Black Hood 1.20
2 GM,NA/DG,AMc,I:'70's Black
Hood, Superhero rept. 2.00

ARCHIE'S TV LAUGH-OUT
Archie Publications 1969–86
1 . . . . 50.00
2 . . . . 25.00
3 . . . . 12.00
4 . . . . 12.00
5 . . . . 12.00
6 thru 10 . . . . @4.00
11 thru 106 . . . . @2.00

ARCHIE 3000
Archie Publications
May, 1989–July, 1991
1 thru 16 . . . . 1.00

ARENA, THE
Alchemy
1 . . . . 1.00
2 . . . . 1.00

ARIANE & BLUEBEARD
Eclipse 1988
Spec. CR 3.95

ARISTOKITTENS, THE
Gold Key 1971–75
1 Disney 25.00
2 thru 9 . . . . @15.00

ARMAGEDDON FACTOR
AC Comics
1 Sentinels of Justice 1.95
2 . . . . 1.95

ARMOR
Continuity 1985
1 TGr,NA,A:Silver Streak,
silver logo 5.00
1a 2nd printing,red logo 2.50
2 TGr,NA(c) 2.50
3 TGr,NA(c) 2.50
4 TGr,NA(c) 2.50
5 BS,NA(c) 2.50
6 TVE,NA(c) 2.50
7 NA(c) 2.50
8 FS,NA(c) 2.50
9 FS,NA&KN(c) 2.50
10 FS,NA&KN(c) 2.50
11 SDr(i),KN(c) 2.50
12 KN(c) 2.50
13 NA(c),direct sales 2.50
14 KN(c), newsstand 2.50

[2nd Series]
1 V:Hellbender,Trading Card 2.50

[3rd Series, Deathwatch 2000]
1 Deathwatch 2000 pt.3,w/card . . . 4.00
2 Deathwatch 2000 pt.9,w/card . . . 2.50
3 Deathwatch 2000 pt.15,w/card . . 2.50
4 . . . . 2.50
5 Rise of Magic 2.50
6 Rise of Magic 2.50

ARMORED TROOPER VOTOMS
CPM Comics
1 TEl 2.95
2 TEl 2.95
3 TEl 2.95
4 TEl 2.95
GN Supreme Survivor 16.95

ARMY ATTACK
Charlton 1964
1 SG 35.00
2 SG 15.00
3 SG 10.00
4 thru 47 . . . . @10.00

ARMY WAR HEROES
Charlton 1963–70
1 . . . . 35.00
2 . . . . 15.00
3 thru 21 . . . . @15.00
22 GS,O&I:Iron Corporal 20.00
23 thru 38 . . . . @10.00

ART OF ZEN INTER-GALACTIC NINJA
Entity Comics 1994
1 Various artists 2.95

ARTESIA
Sirius 1999
1 (of 6) by Mark Smylie 2.95
2 thru 6 . . . . @2.95

ASH
Event Comics
1 JQ,JP,Fire and Crossfire,pt.1 . . 12.00
1a David Finch/Batt(c) 3.00
1b omnichrome commemorative . 14.95
1c omnichrom signed & numbered 29.95
2 JQ,JP,Fire and Crossfire,pt.2 . . . 7.00
2a David Finch/Batt (c) 3.00
3 JQ,JP,Secret of Origin 4.50
4 I:Actor 3.00
5 I:New Character 3.00

6 V:Gabriel 3.00
0 Red Laser ed., Current Ash (c) . 20.00
0 Red Laser ed., Future Ash (c) . . 20.00
TPB rep. #1–#5 . . . . 14.95
TPB Vol. 1, JQ,JP,sgn. lim 34.95

ASH: CINDER AND SMOKE
Event Comics 1997
1 MWa,BAu,HuR,JP 2.95
1a autographed virgin JQ cover . . 19.95
1b signed limited edition 29.95
2 HuR(c) 2.95
2 JQ(c) 2.95
3 (of 6) JQ&JP(c) 2.95
3 variant JP&HuR(c) 2.95
4 (of 6) JQ&JP(c) 2.95
4 variant JP&HuR(c) 2.95
5 (of 6) JQ&JP(c) 2.95
5 variant JP&HuR(c) 2.95
6 (of 6) JQ&JP(c) 2.95
6 variant JP&HuR(c) 2.95

ASH FILES, THE
Event Comics 1997
1 JQ,JP 2.95
1 signed, limited 19.95

ASH: FIRE AND CROSSFIRE
Event Comics 1998
1 (of 5) JQ,JP 2.95
1a signed & numbered 24.95
2 . . . . 2.95

ASH: THE FIRE WITHIN
Event Comics
2 JQ,JP 2.95
3 JQ,JP, Ash Rooftop cover 2.95
3a JQ,JP, Ash Firefighter cover . . . 2.95

ASH/22 BRIDES
Event Comics 1996
1 FaN,HuR,JP 2.95

ASSASSIN, INC.
Solson
1 thru 4 . . . . @1.95

ASTER
Entity Comics 1995
0 O:Aster the Celestial Knight 4.50
1 I:Celestial Knight 5.00
1b 2nd printing 3.00
2 . . . . 3.50
3 V:Tolmek 3.25
3a Variant cover 7.00
4 Final Issue 3.00
TPB Rep.#1–#4 + pin-up gallery . . 12.95

ASTER THE LAST CELESTIAL KNIGHT
Entity Comics 1995
1 R:Aster Chromium Cover 2.50
1a Clear Chromium Edition 4.00
1b Holo Chrome Edition 5.00
2 World Defender 2.50

ASTRO BOY
Gold Key Aug., 1965
1 I:Astro Boy 300.00

Astro Boy #1
© Gold Key Comics

ASTRO BOY
Now
Prev. Original Astro Boy
18 . . . . 1.75
19 . . . . 1.75
20 . . . . 1.75

ASYLUM
Pendragon 1995
1 . . . . 2.95
2 . . . . 2.95
3 three stories 2.95

ASYLUM
Maximum Press Dec. 1995
1 Warchild, Beanworld, Avengelyne,
Battlestar Galactica 3.00
2 I:Deathkiss 3.00
3 . . . . 3.00
4 RLd,A:Cybrid 3.00
5 I:Black Seed 3.00
6 R:Steve Austin & Jaime
Sommers 3.00
7 RLe,F:Bloodwulf 3.00
8 RLd 3.00
9 RLd 3.00
10 . . . . 3.00
11 . . . . 3.00
12 MMy,F:Blindside 3.00
13 . . . . 3.00

ATOM ANT
Gold Key Jan., 1966
1 . . . . 75.00

ATOM-AGE COMBAT
Fago Magazines 1958–59
1 . . . . 165.00
2 . . . . 140.00
3 . . . . 120.00

ATOMIK ANGELS
Crusade Entertainment 1996
1 BiT 2.95
1 variant cover (1:25) 5.00
2 BiT 2.95
3 BiT 2.95
4 BiT, conclusion 2.95

ATOMIC RABBIT
Charlton Comics 1955–58
1	150.00
2	50.00
3 thru 10	@30.00
11	50.00

Becomes:

ATOMIC BUNNY
12	75.00
13 thru 18	@35.00
19 Dec., 1959.	35.00

AUTHORITY, THE
Wildstorm/DC 1999
1 WEl(s),BHi,PNe	2.50
2 WEl(s),BHi,PNe,V:Kaizen Gamorra.	2.50
3 WEl(s),BHi,PNe,destruction	2.50
4 WEl(s),BHi,PNe,save L.A.	2.50
5 WEl(s),BHi,PNe,Swiftships,pt.1	2.50
6 WEl(s),BHi,PNe	2.50

AVENGEBLADE
Maximum Press 1996
1 RLe	3.00
2 RLe	3.00

AVENGELYNE
Maximum Press 1995
1 RLd,I:Avengelyne Dir ed.	8.00
1a Newstand Edition	4.00
1b Holochrome Edition	5.00
1 gold edition.	6.00
2 V:B'Lial.	4.00
3 I:Magogi.	4.00
3 variant cover, pin-up	5.00
TPB rep. #1–#3	9.95

Regular Series April 1996
0 RLd,O:Avengelyne	3.00
1 RLd,BNa,F:Devlin.	3.00
1 variant photo cover	3.00
2 I:Darkchylde.	10.00
2a variant photo cover	11.00
3	3.00
4 A:Cybrid.	3.00
5 A:Cybrid,	3.00
6 RLd,F:Divinity	3.00
7 RLd,F:Divinity	3.00
8 RLd,	3.00
9 RLd,	3.00
10 BNa,"The Possession," pt.1	3.00
11 BNa,"The Possession," pt.2	3.00
12 BNa,"The Possession," pt.3	3.00
13 BNa,"The Possession," pt.4	3.00
14 A:Bloodwulf	3.00
15 A:Glory, Prophet	3.00
Swimsuit Edition	3.50
Swimsuit book, American Entertainment exclusive	7.50

AVENGELYNE
Awesome Entertainment 1999
Prelude	2.50
1 RLe,RNa	2.50
1a, b & c variant covers	2.50
2 RLe,	2.50
3	2.50
Spec. Swimsuit 1999	3.00

AVENGELYNE: ARMAGEDDON
Maximum Press 1996–97
1 (of 3) RLd.	3.00
2 RLd,	3.00
3 BNa,ScC, finale	3.00

AVENGELYNE BIBLE: REVELATIONS
Maximum Press
one-shot RLd,	3.50

AVENGELYNE: DEADLY SINS
Maximum Press 1996
1 RLd (c).	3.00
1 photo (c).	3.00
2 RLd(c)	3.00

AVENGELYNE/GLORY
Maximum Press 1995
1 V:B'Lial.	3.95
1a variant cover.	5.00
Swimsuit Spec. #1	2.95

AVENGELYNE/GLORY: THE GODYSSEY
Maximum Press 1996
1 RLd,BNa	3.00
2 thru 5 RLd.	@3.00

Avengelyne Power #2
© Maximum Press

AVENGELYNE/POWER
Maximum Press 1995–96
1 RLd,V:Hollywood	3.00
1 variant cover.	3.50
2 RLd(c)	3.00
3	3.00
3a photo (c).	3.00

AVENGELYNE/PROPHET
Maximum Press April 1996
1 RLd,BNa,MD2	3.00

AVENGELYNE/ WARRIOR NUN AREALA
Maximum Press 1997
Spec.	3.00

AVENGELYNE/ WARRIOR NUN AREALA II THE NAZARENE AFFAIR
Awesome Entertainment 1997
one-shot?	3.00

AVENGERS, THE
Gold Key Nov., 1968
1	250.00

AWESOME HOLIDAY SPECIAL
Awesome Entertainment 1997
Spec. #1	2.50

AWESOME SPRING '99 TOURBOOK
Awesome Entertainment 1999
1	5.00

AXA
Eclipse 1987
1 "Axa the Adopted"	1.75
2	1.75

AXEL PRESSBUTTON
Eclipse 1984
1 BB(c),Origin	1.75
2	1.75
3 thru 4	@1.75

Becomes:

PRESSBUTTON

AXION
Icon Creations
1 I:Obsidian.	2.50

AXIS ALPHA
Axis Comics
1 LSn,I:BEASTIES,Dethgrip, Shelter,W	2.75

AZ
Comico
1	3.00
2	2.25

AZTEC ACE
Eclipse 1984
1 NR(i),I:AztecAce.	3.50
2 NR(i)	3.50
3 NR(i)	3.00
4 NR(i)	3.00
5 NR(i)	3.00
6 NR(i)	3.00
7 NR(i)	3.00
8 NR(i)	3.00
9 NR(i)	3.00
10 NR(i)	2.00
11	3.50
12	2.50
13	2.50
14	2.50
15 F:Bridget	2.50

BABES OF BROADWAY
Broadway 1996
1	2.95

BABY HUEY, THE BABY GIANT
Harvey Publications 1956–80
1	350.00
2	175.00
3	125.00
4	100.00
5	100.00
6 thru 10	@50.00
11 thru 20	@30.00
21 thru 40	@25.00
41 thru 60	@15.00
61 thru 79	@10.00
80	10.00
81 thru 95	@5.00
96 Giant size	6.00
97 Giant size	6.00
98	2.50
99	2.50

BABY HUEY AND PAPA
Harvey Publications 1962–68
1	150.00
2	75.00
3	50.00
4	50.00
5	50.00
6	20.00
7	20.00
8	20.00
9	20.00
10	20.00
11 thru 20	@5.00
21 thru 33	@3.50

BABY HUEY DUCKLAND
Harvey Publications 1962–66
1	100.00
2	50.00
3	50.00
4	50.00
5	50.00
6 thru 14	@15.00
15	15.00

BACHELOR FATHER
Dell Publishing Co. 1962
1	85.00
2	65.00

BACK TO THE FUTURE
Harvey 1991
1 Chicago 1927	1.25
2 Cretaceous Period	1.25
3 World War I	1.25
4 Doc Retires	1.25

BAD BOY
Oni Press 1997
GN Frank Miller & Simon Bisley	4.95

BAD COMPANY
Quality 1988
1 thru 19	@1.50

BADGER
Capital 1983
1 JBt,I:Badger,Ham,Daisy Yak,Yeti.	3.00
2 JBt,I:Riley,A:YakYeti	3.00
3 JBt,O:Badger,Ham	3.00
4 JBt,A'Ham	3.00

First 1984–91
5 BR,DruidTree Pt1	2.50

Badger #4
© Capital Comics

6 BR,DruidTree Pt2	2.50
7 BR,I:Wonktendonk,Lord Weterlackus	2.50
8 BR,V:Demon	2.50
9 BR,I:Connie,WOatesCbra	2.50
10 BR,A:Wonktendonk, I:Hodag Meldrum	2.50
11 BR,V:Hodag,L.W'lackus	2.50
12 BR,V:Hodag,L.W'lackus	2.50
13 BR,A:L.W'lakus,Clonezone, Judah	2.50
14 BR,I:HerbNg	2.50
15 BR,I:Wombat,JMoranIbob	2.50
16 BR,A:Yak,Yeti	2.50
17 JBt,I:Lamont	3.00
18 BR,I:SpudsGroganA:Cbra	2.50
19 BR,I:Senator1,ClZone	2.50
20 BR,Billionaire'sPicnic	2.50
21 BR,I&O:Phantom	2.50
22 BR,I:Dr.Buick Riviera	2.50
23 I:BobDobb,A:Yeti	2.50
24 BR,A:Riley	2.50
25 BR,I:Killdozer	2.50
26 BR,I:RoachWranger	2.50
27 BR,O:RoachWranger	2.50
28 BR,A:Yeti	2.50
29 A:Clonezone,C:GrimJack	2.50
30 BR,I:Dorgan	2.00
31 BR,I:HopLingSung	2.00
32 BR,D:Dorgan,HopLingSng	2.00
33 RLm/AN,I:KidKang	3.00
34 RLm,I:Count Kohler	3.00
35 RLm,I:Count Kohler	3.00
36 RLm,V:Dire Wolf	3.00
37 AMe,A:Lamont	2.50
38 Animal Band	2.00
39 I:Buddy McBride	2.00
40 RLm,I:Sister Twyster	3.50
41 RLm,D:Sister Twyster	3.50
42 RLm,A:Paul Bunyan	3.50
43 RLm,V:Vampires	3.50
44 RLm,V:Vampires	3.50
45 RLm,V:Dr.Buick Riviera	3.50
46 RLm,V:Lort Weterlackus	3.50
47 RLm,Hmds.Sacr.BloodI	3.50
48 RLm,Hmds.Sacr.BloodII	3.50
49 RLm,TRoof off SuckerI	3.50
50 RLm,TRoof off SuckerII	5.00
51 RLm,V:Demon	3.00
52 TV,Tinku	4.00
53 TV,I:Shaza,Badass	4.00
54 TV,D:Shaza	4.00
55 I:Morris Myer	2.00
56 I:Dominance	2.00

57 A:KKang,V:L.W'lackus	2.00
58 A:Lamont,W'bat,V:SpudsJack	2.00
59 Bad Art Issue	2.00
60 I:ChisumBros	2.25
61 V:ChismBros	2.00
62 I:Shanks	2.00
63 V:Shanks	2.00
64 A:Mavis Sykes	2.25
65 A:BruceLee	2.25
66 I:Joe Nappleseed	2.25
67 Babysitting	2.25
68 V:GiantFoot	2.25
69 O:Mavis	2.25
70 BR:Klaus(last monthly)	2.25
Graphic Nov.BR,I:Mazis Sykes,D:Hodag	10.00
Badger Bedlam	4.95

BADGER GOES BERSERK
First 1989
1 I:Larry,Jessie	4.00
2 MZ,V:Larry,Jessie	3.50
3 JBt/MZ,V:Larry,Jessie	3.00
4 JBt/MZ,V:Larry,Jessie	3.00

BAD GIRLS OF BLACKOUT
Blackout Comics 1995
0	3.50
1 I:Ms. Cyanide, Ice	3.50
Ann.#1 Hari Kari, Lady Vampire	3.50
Ann.#1 Commemorative ed.	9.95

BADROCK/WOLVERINE
Awesome Entertainment 1997
Spec. #1 JV,CYp,V:Sauron,48pg	4.95

BAKER STREET
1	3.00
2	2.50

BALLAD OF HALO JONES
Quality 1987
1 IG Alan Moore story	2.00
1a IG rep	2.00
2 thru 12	@1.25

BAMM BAMM & PEBBLES FLINTSTONE
Gold Key Oct., 1964
1	75.00

BARBARIANS, THE
Atlas June, 1975
1 O: Andrax,F:Iron Jaw	1.75

BARBIE & KEN
Dell Publishing Co. May-July, 1962
1	400.00
2	300.00
3	300.00
4	300.00
5	325.00

THE BARBIE TWINS ADVENTURES
Topps 1995
1 I:Shane, Sia	2.50

COLOR PUB.

BARBI TWINS ADVENTURES
Studio Chikara 1998
Color Spec. The Roswell Incident . . 3.95

BARNEY AND BETTY RUBBLE
Charlton Comics 1973–76
1 . . . . 50.00
2 . . . . 20.00
3 . . . . 20.00
4 . . . . 20.00
5 . . . . 20.00
6 thru 10 . . . . @15.00
11 thru 23 . . . . @10.00

BARRY M. GOLDWATER
Dell Publishing Co. March, 1965
1 . . . . 35.00

BART-MAN
Bongo 1993
1 Foil(c),I:Bart-Man 4.00
2 I:Penalizer 2.25
3 When Bongos Collide,pt.3, with card 2.25
4 Crime-Time,pt.1 . . . . 2.25
5 Bad Guys Strike Back. 2.25

BART SIMPSONS TREEHOUSE OF HORROR
Bongo Comics 1995
1 Bart People 2.95
2 thru 4 . . . . @2.95

BART SIMPSON'S TREEHOUSE OF TERROR
Bongo Comics 1995
One-shot 2.50

BASEBALL
Kitchen Sink 1991
1 WE (c) reprint of 1949 orig.. . . . 3.95
2 Ray Gotto (c), w/4 BB cards 2.95

BAT, THE
Adventure
1 R:The Bat,inspiration for Batman says Bob Kane. 2.50

BATTLEBOOKS
Battlebooks Inc. 1999
all BTi(c)
Bubba-Busters Battlebook 5.00
Captain America Battlebook
 Blue print, signed edition 10.00
Colossus Battlebook. 4.00
Daredevil Battlebook BTi(c) 4.00
Daredevil Battlebook JQ&JP(c). . . . 4.00
Darkchylde A Battlebook. 4.00
Darkchylde B Battlebook. 4.00
The Darkness Battlebook 4.00
Dr. Doom Battlebook 4.00
Elektra Battlebook 4.00
 Blue print, signed edition 12.95
Elektra Battlebook, revised 4.00
Gambit Battlebook. 4.00
Green Goblin Battlebook. 4.00
Iron Man Battlebook
 Blue print, signed edition 12.95

Blue print, signed edition 12.95
The Incredible Hulk Battlebook 4.00
 Blue print, signed edition 12.95
Magneto Battlebook 4.00
President Clinton Battlebook. 5.00
Rogue Battlebook. 4.00
 Blue print, signed edition 12.95
Sabretooth Battlebook 4.00
Shi: The Spirit of Benkei Battlebook 4.00
 Blue print, signed edition 10.00
Spider-Man Battlebook
 Blue print, signed edition 12.95
Storm Battlebook 4.00
The Thing Battlebook 4.00
Tomoe: Fan's of Fury Battlebook. . . 4.00
Vampirella Hell on Earth Battlebook 4.00
White Queen Battlebook. 4.00
Witchblade Battlebook 4.00
Wolverine Battlebook 4.00
Wolverine with Bone Claws Battlebook
 Blue print, signed edition 12.95

BATTLE FORCE
Blackthorne 1987
1 and 2 . . . . @1.50
3 . . . . 1.75

BATTLE OF THE PLANETS
Gold Key June, 1979
1 TV Cartoon. 20.00
2 . . . . 15.00
3 . . . . 15.00
4 . . . . 15.00
5 . . . . 15.00
Whitman
6 . . . . 7.00
7 thru 10 . . . . 7.00

BATTLESTAR GALACTICA
Maximum Press 1995
1 Finds Earth. 2.50
2 Council of Twelve 2.50
3 R:Adama 2.50
4 Pyramid Secrets 2.50
TPB series rep.. . . . . 12.95
Spec. Ed. Painted Book (1997). . . . 3.00
Battlestar Galactica: The Compendium #1 rep. from Asylum. 3.00

BATTLESTAR GALACTICA
Realm Press 1997
1 by Chris Scalf. 3.00
1a variant cover. 3.00
2 Law of Volhad. 3.00
3 Prison of Souls, pt.1 . . . . 3.00
3a alternate cover 3.00
4 Prison of Souls, pt.2 . . . . 3.00
5 . . . . 3.00
6 A Path of Darkness, pt.1. . . . . . . 3.00
7 A Path of Darkness, pt.2. . . . . . . 3.00
7a photo (c). 3.00
7b signed and numbered. 6.00
8 Centurion Prime 3.00
Spec.#1 20 Yahren Reunion 5.00
Spec.#1 No Memory of Earth 3.00
Spec.#2 Centurion Prime 3.00
Spec. 1999 Tourbook 3.00
Spec. 1999 Tourbook con. ed. 7.00
Spec. 1999 Tourbook sign. 30.00
TPB New Beginnings, rep. #1–#4 . 14.00

Battlestar Galactica, Apollo's Journey #2 © Maximum Press

BATTLESTAR GALACTICA APOLLO'S JOURNEY
Maximum Press April 1996
1 story by Richard Hatch 2.95
2 . . . . 2.50
3 . . . . 2.50

BATTLESTAR GALACTICA THE ENEMY WITHIN
Maximum Press Feb. 1996
1 . . . . 3.00
2 . . . . 2.50
3 . . . . 2.50

BATTLESTAR GALACTICA JOURNEY'S END
Maximum Press 1996
1 (of 4) RLd 3.00
2 RLd 3.00
3 RLd, the end of Galactica? 3.00
4 RLd, conclusion 3.00

BATTLESTAR GALACTICA SEARCH FOR SANCTUARY
Realm Press 1998
1 (of 4) 3.00
2 Path of Darkness 3.00
3 tensions grow 3.00
4 . . . . 3.00

BATTLESTAR GALACTICA SEASON THREE
Real Press 1999
1 . . . . 3.00
1a alternate JaL(c) 5.00
2 . . . . 3.00
2a alternate cover 5.00
3 Fire in the Sky 3.00
3a alternate cover 5.00

BATTLESTAR GALACTICA STARBUCK
Maximum Press 1997
1 (of 3) RLd. 2.50

2 RLd 2.95
3 RLd, the end of Galactica? 2.95

BATTLETECH
Blackthorne 1987
1 . . . . 1.50
2 . . . . 1.50
3 . . . . 1.50
4 . . . . 1.75
5 . . . . 1.75
6 . . . . 1.75
(Changed to Black & White)
1 3-D 2.50
2 3-D 2.50

BEAGLE BOYS, THE
Gold Key 1964–79
1 . . . . 40.00
2 thru 5 . . . . @30.00
6 thru 10 . . . . @20.00
11 thru 20 . . . . @15.00
21 thru 46 . . . . @10.00
47 . . . . 10.00

BEANIE THE MEANIE
Fargo Publications 1958
1 thru 3 . . . . @30.00

B.E.A.S.T.I.E.S.
Axis Comics
1 JS(a&s),I:Beasties 2.25

THE BEATLES, LIFE STORY
Dell Publishing Co. 1964
1 . . . . 500.00

BEAUTY AND THE BEAST
Innovation
1 From TV series 2.50
1a Deluxe 3.95
2 . . . . 2.50
3 . . . . 2.50
4 Siege 2.50
5 Siege 2.50
6 Halloween 2.50
7 . . . . 2.50

BEAUTY AND THE BEAST PORTRAIT OF LOVE
First 1989–90
1 WP,TV tie in 12.00
2 . . . . 8.00
Book II:Night of Beauty 5.95

BEAUTY AND THE BEAST
Walt Disney 1992
Movie adapt.(Prestige) 4.95
Movie adapt.(newsstand) 2.50
mini-series
1 Bewitched 1.50
2 Elsewhere 1.50
3 A:Catherine 2.50

BEDLAM!
Eclipse 1985
1 SBi,RV,reprint horror 1.75
2 SBi,RV,reprint horror 1.75

BEETLE BAILEY
Harvey 1992
1 F:Mort Walker's B.Bailey 1.95
2 Beetle builds a bridge 1.25
3 thru 12 . . . . 1.25

BEETLEJUICE
Harvey 1991
1 EC,"This is your lice" 2.00
Holiday Special #1 . . . . 1.25

BEN CASEY
Dell Publishing Co.
June-July, 1962
1 Ph(c) 65.00
2 Ph(c) 40.00
3 Ph(c) 30.00
4 Drug, Ph(c) 35.00
5 Ph(c) 30.00
6 thru 10 Ph(c) . . . . @30.00

BERNI WRIGHTSON MASTER OF THE MACABRE
Pacific
1 BWr 5.25
2 BWr 3.75
3 BWr 3.50
4 BWr 3.50
Eclipse 1984
5 BWr 3.50

BEST FROM BOY'S LIFE
Gilberton Company Oct., 1957
1 . . . . 80.00
2 . . . . 50.00
3 . . . . 40.00
4 LbC 60.00
5 . . . . 40.00

BEST OF DONALD DUCK & UNCLE SCROOGE
Gold Key 1964–67
1 . . . . 75.00
2 . . . . 70.00

BEST OF DONALD DUCK
Gold Key Nov., 1965
1 . . . . 75.00

BEST OF BUGS BUNNY
Gold Key 1966–68
1 Both Giants 35.00
2 . . . . 25.00

BEST OF DENNIS THE MENACE, THE
Hallden/Fawcett Publ.
Summer, 1959
1 . . . . 35.00
2 thru 5 Spring, 1961 . . . . 20.00

BETTA: TIME WARRIOR
Immortal Comics 1997
1 (of 3)Beginnings's End,pt.1 . . . . 2.95
2 The Beginnings's End,pt.2 . . . . . 2.95

BETTI COZMO
Antarctic Press 1999
1 (of 3) 3.00
2 . . . . 3.00
3 Raygun For Hire 3.00

BETTY
Archie Publications 1992
1 thru 39 . . . . @1.50
40 thru 57 . . . . @1.50
58 thru 79 . . . . @1.75

Betty and Me #3
© *Archie Publications*

BETTY AND ME
Archie Publications 1965–92
1 . . . . 100.00
2 . . . . 50.00
3 . . . . 30.00
4 . . . . 30.00
5 . . . . 30.00
6 thru 10 . . . . @15.00
11 thru 30 . . . . @8.00
31 thru 50 . . . . @4.00
51 thru 55 . . . . @3.00
56 thru 199 . . . . @2.00
200 . . . . 2.00

BETTY AND VERONICA
Archie Publications June, 1987
1 thru 100 . . . . @1.50
101 thru 104 . . . . @1.50
105 thru 119 . . . . @1.50
120 thru 141 . . . . @1.75
Summer Fun Special #5 . . . . 2.25
Summer Fun Special #6 . . . . 2.25

BETTY & VERONICA SPECTACULAR
1 thru 27 . . . . @1.50
28 thru 38 . . . . @1.75

BETTY BOOP'S SUNDAY BEST
Kitchen Sink 1998
TPB Complete Color Comics,
   1934–36, new printing 19.95
HC Complete Color Comics,
   1934–36, new printing 34.95

COLOR PUB.

BEVERLY HILLBILLYS
Dell Publishing Co.
April-June, 1963

1 Ph(c)		150.00
2 Ph(c)		80.00
3 Ph(c)		50.00
4		30.00
5		50.00
6		50.00
7		50.00
8 Ph(c)		50.00
9 Ph(c)		50.00
10 Ph(c)		50.00
11 Ph(c)		50.00
12 Ph(c)		50.00
13 Ph(c)		50.00
14 Ph(c)		50.00
15		30.00
16		30.00
17 Ph(c)		30.00
18 Ph(c)		30.00
19 Ph(c)		30.00
20 Ph(c)		30.00
21 Ph(c)		30.00

BEWITCHED
Dell Publishing Co.
April-June, 1965

1		150.00
2		85.00
3 Ph(c)		60.00
4 Ph(c)		60.00
5 Ph(c)		60.00
6 Ph(c)		60.00
7 Ph(c)		60.00
8 Ph(c)		60.00
9 Ph(c)		60.00
10 Ph(c)		60.00
11 Ph(c)		60.00
12 Ph(c)		60.00
13 Ph(c)		60.00
14		40.00

BEYOND THE GRAVE
Charlton Comics 1975–84

1 SD,TS(c),P(c)		30.00
2 thru 5		@20.00
6 thru 17		@15.00

BIG BANG
Caliber Press

0 Whole Timeline inc.		2.95
1		1.95
2		1.95
3		1.95
4 25 years after #3		1.95

BIG VALLEY, THE
Dell Publishing Co. June, 1966

1 Ph(c)		50.00
2		25.00
3		25.00
4		25.00
5		25.00
6		25.00

BILL BLACK'S FUN COMICS
AC Comics

1 Cpt.Paragon,B&W		2.50
2 and 3 B&W		@2.25
4 Color		2.25

BILL THE GALACTIC HERO
Topps

1 thru 3 Harry Harrison adapt.		@4.95

BILLY NGUYEN
Caliber

1		2.50

BILLY THE KID
Charlton Publ. Co. 1957–83

9		50.00
10		30.00
11		25.00
12		20.00
13 AW,AT		30.00
14		20.00
15 AW,O:Billy the Kid		30.00
16 AW		30.00
17		20.00
18		20.00

Billy the Kid #148
© Charlton Comics

19		20.00
20		30.00
21		30.00
22		30.00
23		10.00
24		30.00
25 JSe		30.00
26 JSe		30.00
27		10.00
28		10.00
29		10.00
30		10.00
31 thru 40		@8.00
41 thru 60		@6.00
61 thru 80		@3.00
81 thru 153		@2.00

BIONEERS
Mirage/Next

1 New Heroes		2.75
2		2.75
3 All-out War		2.75

BIONIC WOMAN, THE
Charlton

1 Oct, 1977, TV show adapt.		10.00
2		5.00

3		5.00
4		5.00
5		5.00

BIONIX
Maximum Press 1996

1 (of 3) RLd,F:Steve Austin & Jaime Sommers		3.00
2 RLd,		3.00

BIZARRE 3-D ZONE
Blackthorne

1		2.50

[ORIGINAL] BLACK CAT

1 Reprints		2.00
2 MA(c) rep.		2.00
3 rep.		2.00

BLACK DIAMOND
AC Comics

1 Colt B..U. story		3.00
2 PG(c)		2.00
3 PG(c)		2.00
4 PG(c)		2.00
5 PG(c)		2.00

BLACK ENCHANTRESS
Heroic Publishing

1 and 2 Date Rape issues		@1.95

BLACK FLAG
Maximum Press

1 Dan Fraga		3.00
2 I:New Character		2.50
3 V:Network, I:Glitz		2.50
4 V:Glitz, Network		2.50
5 I:Jammers		2.50
6 I:Alphabots		2.50

BLACK FURY
Charlton Comics May, 1955

1		45.00
2		20.00
3 thru 15		@8.00
16 SD		35.00
17 SD		35.00
18 SD		35.00
19 and 20		@5.00
21 thru 30		@3.00
31 thru 56		@3.00
57 March-April, 1966		3.00

BLACK HOLE, THE
Whitman 1980

1 & 2 movie adaptation		@1.50
3 & 4 new stories		@1.50

BLACK HOOD
Archie Publications

1 ATh,GM,DW		1.00
2 ATh,DSp,A:Fox.		1.00
3 ATh,GM		1.00

BLACK JACK
Charlton Comics 1957–59

20		55.00
21		20.00
22		30.00
23 AW,AT		35.00
24 SD		30.00
25 SD		30.00

COLOR PUB.

26 SD.	30.00
27	15.00
28 SD.	30.00
29	12.00
30	12.00

BLACKJACK:
BLOOD & HONOR
Dark Angel 1997

1 by Alex Simmons,JoB, 1930s Adventure, Hildebrandts(c)	2.95
2 KeL,	2.95
3 Tim Cheng disappears	2.95
4	2.95

BLACK PHANTOM
AC Comics

1 F:Red Mask	2.50
2 F:Red Mask	2.50

BLACK RAVEN
Mad Monkey Press 1996

1 Blueprints pt.1	2.95
2 Blueprints pt.2	2.95
3 V:Temple Assassins	2.95
4 Blueprints pt.4	2.95
GN#1 Blueprints	6.95
GN#2 Blueprints	4.95

BLACK TERROR
Eclipse 1989–90

1	3.95
2	3.95
3	4.95

BLACK WEB
Inks Comics

1 thru 3 V:Seeker.	@2.50

BLACKBALL COMICS
Blackball Comics

1 KG,A:Trencher	3.25

BLAST-OFF
Harvey Publications Oct., 1965

1 JK,AW	45.00

Blazing Six-Guns #1
© Skywald Comics

BLAZING COMBAT
Warren Publishing Co. 1965–66

1 FF(c)	90.00
2 FF(c)	20.00
3 and 4 FF(c).	@15.00

BLAZING SIX-GUNS
Skywald Comics 1971

1 F: Red Mask, Sundance Kid	15.00
2 Jesse James	10.00

BLONDIE
See Golden Age Section

BLOOD & ROSES
Sky Comics

1 I:Blood,Rose.	2.75

BLOOD SWORD
Jademan 1988

1	3.00
2	2.50
3 thru 5	@2.00
6 thru 9	@1.75
10 thru 21	@2.50
22 LW	1.95
23 LW,D:Poisonkiller.	1.95
24 LW,A:Hero	1.95
25	1.95
26	1.95
27	1.95
28 V:DevilHeart	1.95
29	1.95
30 A:Purgatory	1.95
31	1.95
32 V:Mummy	1.95
33 V:Mummy	1.95
34	1.95
35	1.95
36 A:King Rat.	1.95
37	1.95
38 Kim Hung in Danger	1.95
39 Masked Men to the Rescue	1.95
40	1.95
41	1.95
42	1.95
43 A:Russell School Pack.	1.95
44 FirefoxV:Tyrant of Venom.	1.95
45 A:Yuen Mo.	1.95
46 V:Cannibal.	2.50
47	1.95
48 A:Clairvoyant Assassin	1.95
49 Prophecy of Hero's fate	1.95
50 D:Poison Entity	1.95
51	1.95
52 Hero vs.Cannibal.	1.95
53 Hero vs.Cannibal.	1.95

BLOOD SWORD DYNASTY
Jademan 1989

1	2.25
2 thru 6	@1.50
7 thru 14 MB	@1.95
15 thru 18 MB	@1.25
19 Kim & Zeo Escape the Crips	1.25
20 Skeleton Executioners	1.25
21 Kim,Seeto.	1.25
22 Infinite Wounded	1.25
23 Kim vs. Ask me not	1.25
24	1.25
25	1.25
26 V:Fiery Bird	1.25
27 A:Hero, Shou, Fiery Bird	1.25
28 Hero vs. Fiery Bird.	1.25
29	1.25

30	1.25
31 V:Devil Child	1.25
32	1.25
33	1.25
34	1.25
35 Hero's ancestry	1.25
36 Hero & son in danger.	1.25
37 A:Hell Clan,D:North Pole	1.25
38 Fiery Hawk Vs.Inf.Seeto	1.25
39 Hero vs.Infinite seeto	1.25
40 Kim Hung vs.Inf.Seeto.	1.25

BLOODBATH
Samson Comics

1 I:Alien,V:Starguile	2.50

BLOODCHILDE
Millenium

0 O:Bloodchilde	2.95
1 Neil Gaiman, Vampires	2.95
1 signed (lim. to 500).	4.95
2 Neil Gaiman, Vampires	2.95
3 Neil Gaiman, Vampires.	2.95
4	2.95
5 Talk Show Host	2.95

BLOODFIRE
Lightning Comics

0 O:Bloodfire	3.00
1 JZy(s),JJn, red foil	5.00
1a Platinum foil Ed.	5.00
1b B&W Promo Ed. Silver ink	4.00
1c B&W Promo Ed. Gold ink	6.00
2 JZy(s),JJn,O:Bloodfire	4.00
3 JZy(s),JJn,I:Dreadwolf, Judgement Day,Overthrow	3.00
4 JZy(s),JJn,A:Dreadwolf,	3.00
5 JZy(s),JJn,I:Bloodstorm, w/card	3.00
6 SZ(s),TLw,V:Storman	3.00
7 SZ(s),TLw,A:Pres.Clinton	3.00
8 SZ(s),TLw,O:Prodigal	3.00
9 SZ(s),TLw,I:Prodigal (in Costume)	3.00
10 SZ(s),TLw,B:Rampage,I:Thorpe.	3.00
11	2.95
12	2.95

BLOODFIRE/HELLINA
Lightning Comics

1 V:Slaughterhouse	3.00
1a Nude Version	9.95

BLOODLORE
Brave New Worlds

1 Dreamweavers	1.95
2 A Blow to the Crown.	1.95

BLOODSCENT
Comico

1 GC.	2.00

BLUE BEETLE
Charlton Comics June, 1964
{1st S.A. Series}

1 O:Dan Garrett/BlueBeetle	135.00
2	75.00
3 V:Mr.Thunderbolt	80.00
4 V:Praying Mantis Man.	50.00
5 V:Red Knight	50.00

(2nd S.A. Series) July 1965
Previously: UNUSUAL TALES

50 V:Scorpion.	50.00
51 V:Mentor	50.00
52 V:Magno.	50.00

*(side margin)* COLOR PUB.

53 V:Praying Mantis Man 50.00
54 V:Eye of Horus 50.00
Becomes:

GHOSTLY TALES
(3rd S.A. Series) 1967
1 SD,I:Question 75.00
2 SD,O:TedKord,D:DanGarrett . . . 35.00
3 SD,I:Madmen,A:Question 25.00
4 SD,A:Question 25.00
5 SD,VicSage(Question) app.
   in Blue Beetle Story 25.00

BLUE BULLETEER
AC Comics
1 . . . . 2.25

BLUE PHANTOM, THE
Dell Publishing Co.
June-Aug., 1962
1 . . . . 65.00

BLUE RIBBON
Archie Publications
1 JK,AV,O:Fly rep. 1.50
2 TVe,Mr.Justice 1.50
3 EB/TD,O:Steel Sterling 1.50
4 . . . . 1.00
5 S&K,Shield rep. 1.00
6 DAy/TD,Fox 1.00
7 TD,Fox 1.00
8 NA,GM,Blackhood 1.00
9 thru 11 . . . . @1.00
12 SD,ThunderAgents 1.00
13 Thunderbunny 1.00
14 Web & Jaguar 1.00

BOLD ADVENTURE
Pacific
1 . . . . 2.00
2 . . . . 1.50
3 JSe 1.50

BOLT & STARFORCE
AC Comics
1 . . . . 1.75
Bolt Special #1 . . . . 1.50

BOMBAST
Topps
1 V:Savage Dragon,Trading Card . 3.25

BONANZA
Dell Publishing Co.
June-Aug., 1960
1 . . . . 200.00
2 . . . . 100.00
3 thru 10 . . . . @75.00
11 thru 20 . . . . @50.00
21 thru 37 . . . . @40.00

BORIS KARLOFF
TALES OF MYSTERY
Gold Key 1963–80
1 (Thriller) 85.00
2 (Thriller) 60.00
3 thru 8 . . . . @30.00
9 WW 40.00
10 . . . . 25.00
11 AW,JO 35.00
12 AT,AMc,JO 30.00
13 & 14 . . . . @25.00
15 RC,GE 25.00

Boris Karloff Tales of Mystery
© Gold Key Comics

16 thru 20 . . . . @25.00
21 JJ,Screaming Skull 40.00
22 thru 50 . . . . @20.00
51 thru 74 . . . . @15.00
75 thru 97 . . . . @10.00

BOZO
Innovation
1 1950's reprint stories 6.95

BOZO THE CLOWN
Blackthorne
1 3-D 2.50
2 3-D 2.50

BRADY BUNCH, THE
Dell Publishing Co. Feb., 1970
1 . . . . 100.00
2 . . . . 75.00

BRAIN BOY
Dell Publishing Co.
April-June, 1962
1 . . . . 100.00
2 . . . . 60.00
3 . . . . 50.00
4 . . . . 50.00
5 . . . . 50.00
6 . . . . 50.00

BREEDING GROUND
Samson Comics
1 I:Mazit, Zero 2.50

BRENDA LEE STORY, THE
Dell Publishing Co. Sept., 1962
1 . . . . 65.00

BRENDA STARR
REPORTER
Dell Publishing Co. Oct., 1963
1 . . . . 150.00

BRIAN BOLLAND'S
BLACK BOOK
Eclipse 1985
1 BB 2.50

BRAM STOKER'S
BURIAL OF THE RATS
Roger Corman's Comics 1995
1 thru 3 film adaptation . . . . . . @2.50

BRIDES IN LOVE
Charlton Comics 1956–65
1 . . . . 35.00
2 . . . . 15.00
3 thru 10 . . . . @10.00
11 thru 30 . . . . @5.00
31 thru 44 . . . . @3.00
45 . . . . 3.00

BRUTE, THE
Atlas Feb.–July 1975
1 thru 3 . . . . @15.00

BUCK ROGERS
Gold Key 1964
1 P(c) 55.00
2 AMc,FBe,P(c),movie adapt 15.00
3 AMc,FBe,P(c),movie adapt 15.00
4 FBe,P(c) 15.00
5 AMc,P(c) 10.00
6 AMc,P(c) 10.00
Whitman
7 thru 9 AMc,P(c) . . . . @8.00
10 and 11 AMc,P(c) . . . . @4.00
12 and 13 P(c) 3.00
14 thru 16 . . . . 3.00

BUCK ROGERS
TSR 1990–91
1 thru 3 O:Buck Rogers . . . . . . @2.95
4 thru 6 Black Barney . . . . @2.95
7 thru 10 The Martian Wars . . . . @2.95

BUCKY O'HARE
Continuity
1 MGo 2.75
2 & 3 . . . . @2.00

BUFFALO BILL JR.
Dell Publishing Co. 1956
1 . . . . 50.00
2 . . . . 30.00
3 . . . . 30.00
4 . . . . 30.00
5 . . . . 30.00
6 . . . . 30.00
7 . . . . 25.00
8 . . . . 25.00
9 . . . . 25.00
10 . . . . 25.00
11 thru 13 . . . . @25.00

BUGGED-OUT
ADVENTURES OF
RALFY ROACH
Bugged Out Comics
1 I: Ralfy Roach 2.95

BULLWINKLE
Gold Key 1962
1 Bullwinkle & Rocky 200.00
2 . . . . 125.00
3 thru 5 . . . . @60.00
6 and 7, rep. . . . . @50.00
8 thru 11 . . . . 60.00
12 rep. 35.00

COLOR PUB.

13 and 14 . . . . @40.00
15 thru 19 . . . . @35.00
20 thru 24, rep. . . . . @15.00
25 . . . . 25.00

BULLWINKLE
Charlton Comics July, 1970
1 . . . . 35.00
Becomes:

BULLWINKLE AND ROCKY
Charlton Comics 1970–71
2 thru 7 . . . . @25.00

BULLWINKLE & ROCKY
Eclipse
3-D 15.00

BULLWINKLE FOR PRESIDENT
Blackthorne
1 3-D Special 2.50

BURKE'S LAW
Dell Publishing Co. 1964
1 from TV Show 50.00
2 . . . . 35.00
3 . . . . 35.00

Butch Cassidy #1
© Skywald Comics

BUTCH CASSIDY
Skywald Comics 1971
1 . . . . 15.00
2 & 3 . . . . 12.00

CABBOT: BLOODHUNTER
Maximum Press 1997
1 thru 4 RV . . . . @2.50

CADILLACS & DINOSAURS
Kitchen Sink
1 Rep. from Xenozoic Tales in 3-D. 6.00
Topps
BLOOD & BONES
1 thru 3 rep. Xenozoic Tales,
all covers . . . . @2.50

MAN-EATER
1 thru 3, all covers 2.50
THE WILD ONES
1 thru 3, all covers 2.50

CAGES
Tundra
1 DMc 14.00
2 DMc 11.00
3 DMc 7.50
4 DMc 7.50
5 thru 7 DMc 5.00

CAIN
Harris
1 B:DQ(s),I:Cain,Frenzy. 5.00
2 BSz(c),HBk,V:Mortatira 3.25

CAIN'S HUNDRED
Dell Publishing Co.
May-July, 1962
1 . . . . 25.00
2 . . . . 20.00

CALIFORNIA RAISINS
Blackthorne
1 thru 4 3-D . . . . @2.50
5 3-D,O:Calif.Raisins 2.50
6 thru 8 3-D . . . . @2.50

CALVIN & THE COLONEL
Dell Publishing Co.
April-June, 1962
1 . . . . 75.00
2 . . . . 50.00

CAP'N QUICK & FOOZLE
Eclipse 1984–85
1 . . . . 2.00
2 and 3 . . . . @2.50

CAPT. ELECTRON
Brick Computers Inc.
1 . . . . 2.00
2 . . . . 2.25

CAPTAIN ATOM
See: STRANGE
SUSPENSE STORIES

CAPTAIN CANUCK
Comely Comix 1975–81
1 I:Blue Fox. 15.00
2 I:Red Coat 10.00
3 I:Heather 10.00
4 thru 14 . . . . 7.00
Summer Spec. #1. . . . . 7.00

CAPTAIN GLORY
Topps
1 A:Bombast,Night Glider,
Trading Card 3.25

CAPTAIN GRAVITY
Penny Farthing Press 1998
1 by Steve Vrattos
& Keith Martin 2.75

2 No one escapes the
Law of Gravity 2.75
3 . . . . 2.75
4 . . . . 2.75

CAPTAIN HARLOCK: FALL OF THE EMPIRE
Eternity
1 R:Captain Harlock 2.50
2 V:Tadashi 2.50
3 Bomb on the Arcadia 2.50
4 Final issue 2.50

CAPTAIN MARVEL
M. F. Enterprises April, 1966
1 . . . . 25.00
2 . . . . 20.00
3 Fights The Bat 15.00
4 . . . . 15.00
5 Captain Marvel Presents the
Terrible Five 12.00

CAPTAIN NAUTICUS
Entity 1994
1 V:Fathom 2.95
2 V:Fathom's Henchman 2.95
3 Surf's Up 1.95

CAPTAIN NICE
Gold Key Nov., 1967
1 Ph(c) 50.00

CAPTAIN PARAGON
Americomics
1 thru 4 . . . . @2.00

CAPTAIN POWER
Continuity
1a NA,TVtie-in(direct sale). 2.00
1b NA,TVtie-in(newsstand) 2.00
2 NA 2.00

CAPTAIN STERN
Kitchen Sink Press
1 BWr,R:Captain Stern 5.25
2 BWr,Running Out of Time 4.95

CAPTAIN THUNDER AND BLUE BOLT
Hero Graphics
1 I:Capt.Thunder & Paul Fremont . 1.95
2 Paul becomes Blue Bolt 1.95
3 O:Capt.Thunder 1.95
4 V:Iguana Boys 1.95
5 V:Ian Shriver, in Scotland 1.95
6 V:Krakatoa 1.95
7 V:Krakatoa 1.95
8 A:Sparkplug (from League
of Champions) 1.95
9 A:Sparkplug 1.95
10 A:Sparkplug. 1.95

CAPTAIN VENTURE & THE LAND BENEATH THE SEA
Gold Key Oct., 1968
1 . . . . 50.00
2 . . . . 40.00

Captain Victory and the Galactic Rangers #3 © Pacific Comics

CAPTAIN VICTORY AND THE GALACTIC RANGERS
Pacific 1982
1 JK	2.00
2 JK	1.50
3 JK,BU:NA,I:Ms.Mystic	1.75
4 JK	1.00
5 JK	1.00
6 JK,SD	1.00
7 thru 13 JK	@1.00
Spec.#1 JK	1.50

CAR 54, WHERE ARE YOU?
Dell Publishing Co.
March-May, 1962
1 Ph(c)	75.00
2 thru 7 Ph(c)	@40.00

CARCA JOU RENAISSANCE
1 and 2	@1.50

CARNOSAUR CARNAGE
Atomeka
TPB	4.95

CAROLINE KENNEDY
Charlton Comics 1961
1	100.00

CASEY JONES & RAPHAEL
Mirage
1 Family War	2.75
2 Johnny Woo Woo	2.75
3 V:Johnny Woo Woo	2.75
4 9mm Raphael	2.75

CASPER ENCHANTED TALES
Harvey
1 short stories	1.25

CASPER THE FRIENDLY GHOST
Blackthorne
1 3-D	2.50

CASPER & FRIENDS
Harvey
1 thru 4	@1.00
5 short stories, cont	1.25

CASPER GHOSTLAND
Harvey
1 short stories	1.25

CASPER'S GHOSTLAND
Harvey Publications
Winter, 1958-59
1	125.00
2	50.00
3 thru 10	@30.00
11 thru 20	@20.00
21 thru 40	@10.00
41 thru 61	@8.00
62 thru 77	@5.00
78 thru 97	@3.00
98 Dec., 1979	3.00

CASPER THE FRIENDLY GHOST
Harvey 1990–91
Prev: The Friendly Ghost Casper
254 thru 260	@1.00

[Second Series] 1991–94
1 thru 14	@1.25
15 thru 28	@1.50

CATSEYE
Awesome/Hyperwerks 1999
0 KIA,BNa,O:Catseye	2.95

CAT TALES
Eternity
1 3-D	1.95

CAULDRON
Real Comics 1995
1 Movie Style Comic	2.95
1a Variat cover	2.95

CAVE GIRL
AC Comics
1	2.95

CAVE KIDS
Gold Key 1963
1	50.00
2	30.00
3	30.00
4	30.00
5	30.00
6	20.00
7 A:Pebbles & Bamm Bamm	30.00
8 thru 10	15.00
11 thru 16	15.00

CHAINS OF CHAOS
Harris
1 Vampirella, Rook	5.00
2 V:Chaoschild	3.25
3 Final issue	3.25

CHAMPIONS
Eclipse 1986–87
1 I:Flare,League of Champions Foxbat, Dr.Arcane	15.00
2 I:Dark Malice	15.00
3 I:Lady Arcane	10.00
4 O:Dark Malice	15.00
5 O:Flare	8.00
6 D:Giant Demonmaster	8.00

[New Series]
Hero Graphics
1 EL,I:Madame Synn,Galloping Galooper	5.00
2 I:Fat Man, Black Enchantress	2.25
3 I:Sparkplug&Icicle,O:Flare	2.25
4 I:Exo-Skeleton Man	2.25
5 A:Foxbat	2.25
6 I:Mechanon, C:Foxbat	1.95
7 A:Mechanon,J:Sparkplug,Icicle	1.95
8 O:Foxbat	1.95
9 Flare #0 (Flare preview)	1.95
10 Olympus Saga #1	1.95
11 Olympus Saga #2	1.95
12 Olympus Saga #3	1.95
Ann.#1 O:Giant & DarkMalice	2.75
Ann.#2	3.95

CHAMPIONS CLASSIC
Hero Graphics
1 GP(c),Rep.1st champions series	1.00

CHAOS BIBLE
Chaos! Comics
1 Character Profiles	3.50

CHAOS! GALLERY
Chaos! Comics 1997
1	2.95

CHAOS! NIGHTMARE THEATER
Chaos! Comics 1997
1 (of 4) BWr(c)	2.50
2 BWr(c)	2.50
3 BWr(c)	2.50
4 BWr(c)	2.50

CHAOS QUARTERLY
Harris Comics 1995
1 F:Lady Death	4.95
1a Premium Edition	10.95
1b Signed,limited edition	20.00

CHAPEL
Awesome Entertainment 1997
1 BNa, from Spawn,Youngblood	2.95

CHARLEMAGNE
Defiant
1 JiS(s),From Hero	2.00
2 JiS(s),I:Charles Smith	2.75
3 JiS(s),A:War Dancer	2.75
4 DGC(s),V:Dark Powers	2.75
5 Schism prequel	2.75
6 V:Wardancer	2.75
7 R:To Vietnam	2.75

CHARLIE CHAN
Dell Publ. Co., Oct.-Dec., 1965
1	35.00
2	20.00

Charlton Bullseye #3
© Charlton Comics

CHARLTON BULLSEYE
Charlton 1981–82
1 Blue Beetle, I:Rocket Rabbit.... 3.50
2 Capt. Catnip; Nell the Horse.... 2.50
3 Grundar 2.50
4 Vanguards 2.50
5 Warhund 2.50
6 Thunder-bunny........... 2.50
7 Captain Atom 2.50
8 weird stories............. 2.50
9 .... 2.50
10 .... 2.50
Spec. #1................. 2.00
Spec. #2 Atomic Mouse 2.00

CHARLTON SPORT LIBRARY
Charlton 1970
1 Professional Football 25.00

CHASSIS
Millenium/Expand 1995
1 I:Chassis McBain, Aero Run.... 2.95
1 2nd printing 2.95
1 chrome cover.............. 9.95
2 .... 2.95
2a with racing card 4.95
2b Amanda Conner cover 2.95
2c Amanda Conner cover, signed . 9.95
2d foil cover, signed......... 7.95
[Vol. 2] Hurricane Comics 1998
0 by Joshua Dysart & Wm.O'Neill . 2.95
0a variant cover............ 2.95
1 .... 2.95
2 .... 2.95
3 .... 2.95

CHASTITY LUST FOR LIFE
Chaos! Comics 1999
1 (of 4) PNu 2.95
1a alternate cover........... 6.95
1b alternate cover, signed 20.00
1c premium edition 10.00
2 V:Hemlock............... 2.95
3 .... 2.95

CHASTITY ROCKED
Chaos! Comics 1998
1 (of 4) PNu 2.95

1a & 1b variant covers......... 2.95
2 V:Jade 2.95
3 V:Jade 2.95
4 conclusion 2.95
Chastity/Cremator Preview
Book, B&W 5.00

CHASTITY: THEATRE OF PAIN
Chaos! Comics 1997
1 (of 3) BnP, ... 6.00
1a premium edition 15.00
2 .... 3.00
3 .... 3.00
3a premium edition 15.00
TPB rep.#1–#3, Sketchbook..... 9.95

CHEAP SHODDY ROBOT TOYS
Eclipse
1 A:Ronald Reagan 1.75

CHECKMATE
Gold Key Oct., 1962
1 Ph(c) 45.00
2 Ph(c) 30.00

CHEMICAL MAN
1 .... 1.75

CHERYL BLOSSOM
Archie Comics April 1996
1 "Love Showdown".......... 1.50
2 "Inn Big Trouble".......... 1.50
3 "Home Um-Improvement" 1.50
4 "Radio Daze" 1.50
5 "Cheryl in the Morning" 1.50
6 "What a Disaster" 1.50
7 "Educating Cheryl" 1.50
8 "Masquerade Madness" 1.50
9 "Tis the Season"........... 1.75
10 "Who's That Girl", pt.1 ...... 1.75
11 "Who's That Girl", pt.2 ...... 1.75
12 "Stop the Presses".......... 1.75
13 .... 1.75
14 "Cheers to You" 1.75
15 "Cheryl's Beach Bash, pt.1 ... 1.75
16 "Lights, Camera, Action," pt.2.. 1.75
17 "Cheryl-Mania". 1.75
18 "Strike A Pose!" 1.75
19 "Chill Out" 1.75
20 "Cinderblossom" 1.75
21 "Sugar World" 1.75
22 "Big In Japan" 1.75
23 Cheryl & Betty friends? 1.75
24 .... 1.75
25 "Creature Feature on
Party Beach" 1.75
26 "Take The Mummy and Run" ... 1.75
27 "It's A Maze Thing" 1.75

CHERYL BLOSSOM GOES HOLLYWOOD
Archie Comics 1996
1 (of 3) by Dan Parent &
Bill Golliher............. 1.50
2 and 3 .... @1.50

CHEYENNE
Dell Publishing Co. Oct., 1956
1 Ph(c) all 150.00
2 .... 75.00
3 .... 50.00
4 thru 12 .... @40.00

13 thru 25 .... @35.00

CHEYENNE KID
(see WILD FRONTIER)

CHI-CHIAN
Sirius 1997
1 (of 6) by Voltaire........... 2.95
2 thru 6 .... @2.95

CHILD'S PLAY 2
Innovation
1 Movie Adapt Pt 1 .... 2.50
2 Adapt Pt 2 .... 2.50
3 Adapt Pt 3 .... 2.50

CHILD'S PLAY 3
Innovation
1 Movie Adapt Pt 1 .... 2.50
2 Movie Adapt Pt.2 .... 2.50

CHILD'S PLAY: THE SERIES
Innovation
1 Chucky's Back 2.50
2 Straight Jacket Blues 2.50
3 M.A.R.K.E.D. 2.50
4 Chucky in Toys 4 You........ 2.50
5 Chucky in Hollywood 2.50

CHILDREN OF FIRE
Fantagor
1 thru 3 RCo .... @2.00

Chilling Adventures in Sorcery #2
© Archie Publications

CHILLING ADVENTURES IN SORCERY AS TOLD BY SABRINA
Archie 1972–74
1 .... 15.00
2 .... 10.00
3 thru 5 .... @8.00

CHIP 'N DALE
Dell Publishing 1955–66
4 .... 50.00

5 thru 10	@45.00
11 thru 30	@35.00

Gold Key 1967

1 reprints	20.00
2 thru 10	@10.00
11 thru 20	@5.00
21 thru 83	@2.50

CHIP 'N DALE RESCUE RANGERS
Walt Disney 1990

1 Rescue Rangers to the Rescue, pt.1	3.50
2 Rescue Rangers to the Rescue, pt.2	3.00
3 thru 7	@2.50
8 Coast to Coast Pt 1	2.00
9 Coast to Coast Pt 2	2.00
10 Coast to Coast Pt 3	2.00
11 Coast to Coast Pt 4	2.00
12 "Showdown at Hoedown"	1.75
13 Raining Cats & Dogs	1.75
14 "Cobra Kadabra"	1.75
15 I:Techno-Rats,WaspPatrol Fearless Frogs Pt.1	1.75
16 A:Techno-Rats,WaspPatrol, Fearless Frogs Pt.2	1.75
17 "For the Love of Cheese"	1.75
18 "Ghastly Goat of Quiver Moore, Pt.1	1.50

CHOO CHOO CHARLIE
Gold Key Dec., 1969

1	50.00

CHOPPER: EARTH, WIND, AND FIRE
Fleetway

1 F:Chopper	2.95

CHOSEN, THE
Click Comics 1995

1 I:The Chosen	2.50
2 I:Herman Cortez	2.50

CHRISTIAN
Maximum Press 1996

1 and 2 (of 3) RLd	@2.95

CHRISTMAS PARADE
Gladstone

1 GiantEdition	4.00
2	3.50

CHRISTMAS SPIRIT, THE
Kitchen Sink

TPB Will Eisner art	15.00

CHROMA-TICK SPECIAL EDITION
New England Press

1 Rep.Tick#1,new stories	4.00
2 Rep.Tick#2,new stories	5.00
3 thru 8 Reps.& new stories	@3.50

CHROME
Hot Comics

1 Machine Man	3.50
2 thru 4	@2.00

CHROME WARRIORS IN A '59 CHEVY
Black Out Comics 1998

0	2.95
0a Nude cover	9.95
0b deluxe nude edition	14.95
1 Rob Roman & Tommy Castillo	2.95
1a nude cover	9.95
1b deluxe nude edition	14.95

CHROMIUM MAN, THE
Triumphant Comics

0 Blue Logo	6.00
0 Regular	2.50
1 I:Chromium Man,Mr.Death	3.50
2 I:Prince Vandal	3.00
3 I:Candi,Breaker,Coil	2.50
4 JnR(s),AdP,Unleashed	2.50
5 JnR(s),AdP,Unleashed	2.50
6 JnR(s),Courier,pt.1	2.50
7 JnR(s),Courier,pt.2	2.50
8 JnR(s),Chromium finds peace	2.50
9 V:Tarsak	2.50
10	2.50
11 Prince Vandal #8	2.50
12 Prince Vandal #9	2.50
13 V:Realm	2.50
14 A:Light	2.50
15	2.50

CHROMIUM MAN: VIOLENT PAST
Triumphant Comics

1 thru 4 JnR(s)	@2.50

Chronicles of Corum #3
© First

CHRONICLES OF CORUM
First 1987–88

1 Michael Moorcock adapt.	2.25
2 thru 12	@2.00

CICERO'S CAT
Dell Publishing Co.
July-Aug., 1959

1	25.00
2	20.00

CIMMARON STRIP
Dell Publishing Co. Jan., 1968

1	45.00

CITY PERILOUS
Broadway Comics

1 GI,"I Remember the Future," pt. #1	2.95
2 GI,"I Remember the Future," pt. #2	2.95

Becomes:

KNIGHTS ON BROADWAY

3 GI,"I Remember the Future," pt. #3	2.95
4 GI,"I Remember the Future," pt. #4	2.95
5 GI,"I Remember the Future," part #5	2.95

CLASSICS ILLUSTRATED
See Also:CLASSICS ILLUSTRATED SECTION

CLASSICS ILLUSTRATED
First

1 GW,The Raven	3.75
2 RG,Great Expectations	3.75
3 KB,Thru the Looking Glass	3.75
4 BSz,Moby Dick	3.75
5 SG,TM,KE, Hamlet	3.75
6 PCr,JT, Scarlet Letter	3.75
7 DSp,Count of Monte Cristo	3.75
8 Dr.Jekyll & Mr.Hyde	3.75
9 MP,Tom Sawyer	3.75
10 Call of the Wild	3.75
11 Rip Van Winkle	3.75
12 Dr. Moreau	3.75
13 Wuthering Heights	3.75
14 Fall of House of Usher	3.75
15 Gift of the Magi	3.75
16 A: Christmas Carol	3.75
17 Treasure Island	3.75
18 The Devils Dictionary	3.95
19 The Secret Agent	3.95
20 The Invisible Man	3.95
21 Cyrano de Bergerac	3.95
22 The Jungle Book	3.95
23 Swiss Family Robinson	3.95
24 Rime of Ancient Mariner	3.95
25 Ivanhoe	3.95
26 Aesop's Fables	3.95
27 The Jungle	3.95

CLAUS
Draco 1997

1 by John Kennedy Bowden & Corinne Y. Guichardon	2.95
2 thru 4	@3.25

CLIVE BARKER'S DREAD
Eclipse

Graphic Album	7.95

CLIVE BARKER'S TAPPING THE VEIN
Eclipse

1	13.00
2	8.50
3	8.50
4	8.50
5 inc."How Spoilers Breed"	8.50

CLYDE CRASHCUP
Dell Publishing Co.
Aug.-Oct., 1963
1	65.00
2	50.00
3 thru 5	@50.00

COBALT 60
Innovation
1 reprints	4.95

COBALT BLUE
Innovation
Spec.#1	1.95
Spec.#2	1.95
1 and 2	@1.95

CODENAME: DANGER
Lodestone
1 RB/BMc,I:Makor	2.50
2 KB,I:Capt.Energy	2.00
3 PS/RB	1.50
4 PG	1.50

CODE NAME: DOUBLE IMPACT
High Impact 1997
1 RCl	3.00
1 variant cover	10.00
1 signed holofoil cover	14.95

CODENAME: STRIKEFORCE
Spectrum
1	1.00

COLLECTOR'S DRACULA
Millennium
1	4.25

COLOSSAL SHOW, THE
Gold Key Oct., 1969
1	35.00

COLOUR OF MAGIC
Innovation
1 Terry Pratchet novel adapt	3.00
2 "The Sending of Eight"	2.50
3 "Lure of the Worm"	2.50
4 final issue	2.50

COLT .45
Dell Publishing Co. 1958
1 Ph(c) all	95.00
2	50.00
3	50.00
4	50.00
5	50.00
6 ATh	65.00
7	50.00
8	50.00
9	50.00

COLT SPECIAL
AC Comics
1	1.75
2	1.75
3	1.75

COMBAT
Dell Publishing Co. 1961
1 SG	50.00
2 SG	25.00
3 SG	25.00
4 JFK cover, Story 2-D	35.00
5 SG	20.00
6 SG	15.00
7 SG	15.00
8 SG	15.00
9 SG	15.00
10 SG	15.00
11 thru 27 SG	@10.00
28 thru 40 SG	@7.00

COMET
Red Circle/Archie Publications
1 Cl,O:Comet	1.00
2 Cl,D:Hangman	1.00

COMET, THE
Red Circle 1983
1 Alex Nino	1.50

COMIC ALBUM
Dell Publishing Co. 1958
March-May, 1958
1 Donald Duck	75.00
2 Bugs Bunny	30.00
3 Donald Duck	50.00
4 Tom & Jerry	30.00
5 Woody Woodpecker	30.00
6 Bugs Bunny	30.00
7 Popeye	35.00
8 Tom & Jerry	30.00
9 Woody Woodpecker	30.00
10 Bugs Bunny	30.00
11 Popeye	35.00
12 Tom & Jerry	25.00
13 Woody Woodpecker	25.00
14 Bugs Bunny	25.00
15 Popeye	35.00
16 Flintstones	60.00
17 Space Mouse	30.00
18 3 Stooges,Ph(c)	75.00

COMICO X-MAS SPECIAL
Comico
1 SR/AW/DSt(c)	1.50

COMIX INTERNATIONAL
Warren Magazines July, 1974
1	35.00
2 WW,BW	25.00
3	10.00
4 RC	10.00
5 Spring, 1977	5.00

COMMANDER BATTLE AND HIS ATOMIC SUB
#20 3-D	2.50

COMMANDOSAURS
1	3.50

CONSTRUCT
Mirage
1 I:Constructs	2.75
2 F:Sect.Eight, Armor	2.75
3 O:Constructs	2.75
4 Fist-O-God	2.75

CORBEN SPECIAL
Pacific
1 RCo	1.75

CORUM: THE BULL & THE SPEAR
First
1 thru 4 Michael Moorcock adapt.	@1.95

COSMONEERS SPECIAL
1	1.95

COUGAR, THE
Atlas Apr.–July 1975
1 & 2	@10.00

COURTSHIP OF EDDIE'S FATHER
Dell Publishing Co. 1970
1 Ph(c)	30.00
2 Ph(c)	20.00

Coven #1
© *Awesome Entertainment*

COVEN
Awesome Entertainment 1997
1 IaC,JLb,JSb,V:The Pentad	15.00
1a variant covers	15.00
2 IaC,JLb,Who is Spellcaster?	8.00
3 IaC,JLb,V:The Pentad	6.00
4 IaC,JLb,Pentad, concl.	4.00
5 IaC,JLb,	4.00
5 gold foil cover	10.00
6 IaC,JLb,Mardi Gras madness	3.00
6 gold foil edition	10.00
7 IaC,JLb,V:Babylon	2.50
8 IaC,JLb,F:Thor, the God of Thunder	2.50
9 IaC,JLb,	2.50
Coll.Ed. #1, rep. #1–#2, new IaC(c)	4.95
Fan Appreciation #1, rep. #1, new cover	2.50
Coven/Menace S.D.Con preview book	5.00

VOL 2
1 IaC,JLb	2.50
1a,b & c variant covers	2.50
1d chrome edition	15.00
1e gold foil cover	10.00

2 IaC,JLb,V:Supreme 2.50
3 IaC,JLb, Long Flight Home 2.50
4 IaC,JLb 2.50

COVEN 13
No Mercy Comics 1997
1 by Rikki Rockett & Matt Busch . . 2.50
2 . . . . 2.50
3 . . . . 2.50
4 . . . . 2.50

COVEN/RE:GEX
Awesome Entertainment 1999
1 (of 2) RLe,JLb,IaC 2.50
1a alternate IaC cover 6.95
2 JLb, conclusion. 2.50

COVEN: DARK ORIGINS
Awesome Entertainment 1999
1 . . . . 2.50
1a & b variant covers. 2.50

COVER GIRL
1 . . . . 1.95

COWBOY IN AFRICA
Gold Key March, 1968
1 Chuck Conners,Ph(c) 25.00

CRACKED
Major Magazines Feb.-Mar. 1958
1 AW. 125.00
2 . . . . 50.00
3 thru 6 . . . . @30.00
7 thru 10 . . . . @20.00
11 thru 20 . . . . @15.00
21 thru 30 . . . . @10.00
31 thru 60 . . . . @4.00
61 thru 252 . . . . @3.00

[THE INCREDIBLE] CRASH DUMMIES
Harvey 1993
1 thru 3, from the toy series . . . . @1.50

CRAZYMAN
Continuity
[1st Series]
1 Embossed(c),NA/RT(i),
. . . . O:Crazyman
6.00
2 NA/BB(c) 2.50
3 DBa,V:Terrorists 2.50
[2nd Series]
1 Die Cut(c). 2.50
2 thru 3 . . . . 2.50
4 In Demon World 2.50

CREATURE
Antarctic Press Oct. 1997
1 (of 2) by Don Walker & Jason
Maranto 2.95
2 concl. 2.95

CREED/TEENAGE MUTANT NINJA TURTLES
Lightning Comics April 1996
1 . . . . 3.00
1 variant cover. 3.00

1 platinum edition B&W 9.95

CREED: CRANIAL DISORDER
Lightning Comics
1 (of 3) 3.00
1a variant cover, *Previews*
exclusive 3.00
1b Platinum edition 9.00
1c Platinum edition, autographed 16.00
2 . . . . 3.00
2a variant cover. 3.00

CREMATOR: HELL'S GUARDIAN
Chaos! Comics 1998
1 (of 5) LJi 2.95
2 . . . . 2.95
3 V:Asteroth 2.95
4 . . . . 2.95
5 . . . . 2.95

CRIME MACHINE
Skywald Publications Feb., 1971
1 . . . . 20.00
2 . . . . 15.00

CRIME SUSPENSE STORIES
Russ Cochran
1 Rep. C.S.S. #1 (1950) 1.75
2 Rep. C.S.S. 1.75
3 Rep. C.S.S. 1.75
4 thru 6 Rep. C.S.S. 2.00
7 Rep. C.S.S. 2.00
8 thru 15 Rep. 2.00
Gemstone
16 thru 27 EC comics reprint. . . . @2.50
Ann.#1, rep. #1–#5. . . . . 8.95
Ann.#2, rep. #6–#10 . . . . 8.95
Ann.#3, rep. #11–#15 . . . . 9.95
Ann.#4, rep. #16–#19 . . . . 10.50
Ann.#5, rep. #20–#23 . . . . 10.95
Ann.#6 rebinding #24–#27 . . . . . 10.95

CRIMSON NUN
Antarctic Press 1997
1 (of 4) 2.95
2 . . . . 2.95
3 . . . . 2.95
4 concl 2.95

CRIMSON PLAGUE
Event Comics
1 GP,F:DiNA: Simmons 2.95
2 GP, ... 2.95

CROSSFIRE
Eclipse 1984–86
1 DSp 3.00
2 DSp 2.50
3 DSp 1.50
4 DSp 1.50
5 DSp 1.50
6 DSp 1.50
7 DSp 2.50
8 DSp 2.50
9 DSp 1.75
10 DSp. 1.75
11 DSp. 1.75
12 DSp,DSt(c),M.Monroe cover
& story 2.50

Crossfire #1
© Eclipse

13 DSp. 1.75
14 DSp. 1.75
15 DSp,O:Crossfire 1.75
16 DSp,"The Comedy Place" 1.75
17 DSp,"Comedy Place" Pt.2 . . . . . 1.75

CROSSFIRE & RAINBOW
Eclipse 1986
1 DSp,V:Marx Brothers 1.75
2 DSp,PG(c),V:Marx Brothers 1.50
3 DSp,HC(c),A:Witness 1.50
4 DSp,DSt(c),"This Isn't Elvis" 3.50

CROSSROADS
First
1 Sable,Whisper 4.00
2 Sable,Badger 4.00
3 JSon,JAl,Badger/Luther Ironheart 4.00
4 Grimjack/Judah Macabee 4.00
5 LM,Grimjack/Dreadstar/Nexus . . 4.00

CROW, THE: CITY OF ANGELS
Kitchen Sink
1 thru 3 movie adaptation. . . . . @2.95
1 thru 3 movie adaptation,
photo covers. . . . . @2.95
TPB The Crow, The Movie, new
printing. 18.95

CRYBABY
Event Comics 1999
1 GrL,SLo 2.95

CRYING FREEMAN III
Viz
1 A:Dark Eyes,Oshu 6.00
2 A:Dark Eyes, V:Oshu 5.25
3 Freeman vs. Oshu 5.25
4 Freeman Defeated 5.25
5 Freeman clones, A:Nitta 5.25
6 V:Nitta 5.25
7 . . . . 4.95
8 . . . . 4.95
9 . . . . 4.95

CRYING FREEMAN IV
Viz
1 B:The Pomegranate	4.95
2	2.75
3	2.75
4	2.75
5 thru 7	@2.75
8 E:The Pomegranate	2.75

[2nd Series]
1 The Festival	2.50

CRYPT OF DAWN
Sirius 1996
1 JLi	2.95

CRYPTIC WRITINGS OF MEGADETH
Chaos! Comics 1997
1 BnP	2.95
1a Tour Edition, leather	25.00
1b Tour Edition, deluxe	50.00
2 BnP	2.95
3 BnP	2.95
4 BnP	2.95
TPB	12.95

CYBER CITY: PART ONE
CPM Comics 1995
1 I:Oedo City	2.95
2 Sengoku	2.95

CYBER CITY: PART TWO
CPM Comics 1995
1 Based on Animated Movie	2.95

CYBERCRUSH: ROBOTS IN REVOLT
Fleetway/Quality
1 inc.Robo-Hunter,Ro-Busters	1.95
2 and 3	@1.95
4 and 5 V:Terraneks	@1.95

Cyberfrog #2
© Harris

CYBERFROG
Harris 1995
0 O:Cyberfrog	2.95
0 AAd(c), signed	19.95
0 Alternate AAd(c)	9.95

1	2.00
1a Signed,numbered	24.95
1b Ultra Violent Cover	49.95
2	2.95
3	2.95
4	2.95
4a alternate cover, signed & numbered (#300)	29.95

CYBERFROG: RESERVOIR FROG
Harris
1 Preview Ashcan, signed & numbered	24.95
1 EL(c),V:the Swarm, Mr. Skorpeone	2.95
1 Signed & numbered (#250)	19.95
2	2.95
1 & 2 Signed & numbered, in binder (#250)	39.95

CYBERHOOD
Entity Comics 1995
1 R:Cyberhood	2.50
1a with PC Game	6.95

CYBERPUNK
Innovation
1	1.95
2	1.95
Book 2,#1	2.25
Book 2,#2	2.25

CYBERPUNK: THE SERAPHIM FILES
Innovation 1990
1	2.50
2	2.50

CYBERPUNX
Maximum Press 1997
1 MHw,	2.50

CYBERRAD
Continuity
1 NA layouts,I:Cyberran.	3.00
2 NA I/o.	2.50
3 NA I/o.	2.50
4 NA I/o.	2.50
5 NA I/o Glow in the Dark cov	5.00
6 NA I/o,Pullout poster.	2.50
7 NA I/o,See-thru(c).	2.50

[2nd Series]
1 Hologram cover	2.00
2 NA(c),"The Disassembled Man"	2.00

[3rd Series]
1 Holo.(c),just say no.	3.50

[4th Series, Deathwatch 2000]
1 Deathwatch 2000 pt.8,w/card	2.50
2 Deathwatch 2000 pt. w/card	2.50

CYBRID
Maximum Press 1995
1 F:Cybrid, I:The Clan	2.95

CYBRID
Maximum Press 1997
0 RLd, 48pg	3.50
1 MsM,BNa	3.00
2 MsM,BNa	3.00

CYNDER
Immortelle Studios
1 thru 3: see B&W
Ann. #1	2.95

Series II 1997
1 A:Nira X	2.95

CYNDER/NIRA X
Immortelle Studios 1996
1 x-over.	2.95
1 variant cover.	3.00
1 gold edition.	10.00

DAEMONSTORM
Caliber 1997
1 TM(c),JMt.	3.95
1 signed	3.95
1 gold edition.	19.95

DAEMONSTORM: DEADWORLD
Caliber
one-shot	3.95

DAEMONSTORM: OZ
Caliber 1997
1	3.95

DAGAR THE INVINCIBLE
Gold Key 1972–82
1 O:Daggar;I:Villians Olstellon & Scorpio	20.00
2	15.00
3 I:Graylon	10.00
4	10.00
5	10.00
6 1st Dark Gods story	5.00
7	5.00
8	5.00
9	5.00
10	5.00
11 thru 19	@3.00

DAI KAMIKAZE
Now 1987–88
1 Speed Racer	7.00
1a 2nd printing	1.50
2	2.00
3	1.50
4	1.50
5	1.50
6 thru 12	@1.75

DAKTARI
Dell Publishing Co. July, 1967
1	25.00
2	15.00
3	15.00
4	15.00

DALGODA
Fantagraphics
1	3.50
2 KN,I:Grinwood'Daughter	3.00
3 KN	2.50
4 thru 8	@2.25

DALKIEL: THE PROPHECY
Verotik 1998
1-shot, prequel to Satanika	3.95

All comics prices listed are for *Near Mint* condition.

DANGER
Charlton Comics June, 1955
12 . . . . 50.00
13 . . . . 35.00
14 . . . . 35.00
Becomes:

JIM BOWIE
15 . . . . 25.00
16 . . . . 12.00
17 . . . . 12.00
18 . . . . 12.00
19 April, 1957. . . . . 12.00

DANGER RANGER
Checker Comics 1998
1 I:Kirby Jackson, BSz(c). 1.95
2 . . . . 1.95

DANIEL BOONE
Gold Key 1965–69
1 . . . . 75.00
2 thru 5 . . . . @30.00
6 thru 14 . . . . @20.00
15 . . . . 15.00

DANNY BLAZE
Charlton Comics Aug., 1955
1 . . . . 45.00
2 . . . . 35.00
Becomes:

NATURE BOY
3 JB,O:Blue Beetle 135.00
4 . . . . 100.00
5 Feb., 1957 . . . . 85.00

DARE
Fantagraphics
1 F:Dan Dare 2.75
2 F:Dan Dare 2.75
3 F:Dan Dare 2.50
4 F:Dan Dare 2.50

Dare the Impossible #1
© Fleetway Quality

DARE THE IMPOSSIBLE
Fleetway/Quality
1 DGb,rep.Dan Dare from 2000AD 1.95
2 DGb, Dare on Waterworld. 1.95
3 DGb. 1.95
4 DGb. 1.95

5 DGb,"The Garden of Eden" 1.95
6 DGb 1.95
7 DGb,V:Deadly Primitives. 1.95
8 DGb,The Doomsday Machine. . . 1.95
9 thru 14 DGb . . . . @1.95

DARK, THE
Continum 1992
1 LSn(c),MBr,V:Futura. 4.00
2 LSn,Shot by Futura. 3.00
3 MBr,Dark has amnesia 3.00
4 GT(c),MBr,O:The Dark 3.00
Convention Book 1992 MBr,GP,
  MFm,MMi,VS,LSn,TV. 5.00
Convention Book 1993 MBr,PC,
  ECh,BS,BWi,GP(c),Foil(c), ... 4.00
Aug. House
1 BS(c),Red Foil(c), ... 3.00
1a BS(c),newstand ed. 3.00
1b BS(c),Blue foil. 3.00
2 . . . . 3.00
3 BS(c),Foil(c), ... 3.00
4 GP(c),Foil(c),w/cards 3.00
5 thru 9 . . . . @2.50
[2nd Series]
1 Dark Regains Memory 3.00
1a Signed, Foil Cover 2.75
2 War on Crime. 2.75
3 Geoffery Stockton 2.50
4 I:First Monster 2.50

DARK ADVENTURES
1 thru 3 . . . . @1.75

DARK CHYLDE
Maximum Press June 1996
1 RQu. 16.00
1 American Entertainment edition 15.00
1 variant cover. 15.00
2 RQu. 12.00
2 variant cover. 14.00
3 RQu. 10.00
3 variant cover. 12.00
4 RQu. 5.00
5 RQu,"No One Here Gets Out
  Alive" 12.00
Spec. Dark Chylde/Avengelyne RLd,
  RQu,I:Witch Tower 3.00
Spec. Dark Chylde/Glory RQu, . . . 3.00

DARK DOMINION
Defiant
1 SD,I:Michael Alexander 3.25
2 LWn(s),SLi(i), ... 2.75
3 LWn(s),SLi(i), ... 2.75
4 LWn(s),B:Hoxhunt 3.00
5 LWn(s),I:Puritan,Judah 2.75
6 LWn(s),I:Lurk 2.75
7 LWn(s),V:Glimmer 2.75
8 LWn(s),V:Glimmer 2.50
9 LWn(s)V:Puritan 2.50
10 LWn(s),Schism Prequel 2.50
11 LWn(s), X-Over 2.50
12 LWn(s), V:Chasm. 2.50

DARK ONE'S THIRD EYE
Sirius April 1996
one-shot Vol. 1 DOe. 4.95
Vol. 2 DOe 4.95

DARK SHADOWS
Gold Key March, 1969
1 W/Poster,Ph(c) 250.00
2 Ph(c) 100.00
3 W/Poster,Ph(c) 125.00

4 thru 7,Ph(c). . . . . @75.00
8 thru 10 . . . . @60.00
11 thru 20 . . . . @50.00
21 thru 35 . . . . @40.00

DARK SHADOWS
Innovation
1 Based on 1990's TV series. 3.50
2 O:Victoria Winters. 2.50
3 Barnabus Imprisoned 2.50
4 V: Redmond Swann 2.75
[2nd Series]
1 A:Nathan 2.75
2 thru 4 . . . . 2.75
Dark Shadows:Resurrected 15.95

DARK SIDE
Maximum Press 1997
1 RLd,RQu 3.00

DARKSHRINE
Antarctic Press 1999
1 by Shelby Robertson 3.00
1a deluxe 6.00
2 16-page 2.50

DARK TOWN
Mad Monkey Press
1 (of 13) 3.95
2 thru 7 . . . . @3.95

DARKLON THE MYSTIC
Pacific
1 JSn 1.50

DARKWING DUCK
Walt Disney
1 I:Darkwing Duck. 1.75
2 V:Taurus Bulba. 1.75
3 "Fowl Play" 1.75
4 "End o/t beginning,"final issue. . . 1.75

DARKWOOD
Aircel
1 thru 5 . . . . @2.00

DAUGHTERS OF TIME
3-D
1 I:Kris,Cori,Lhana 3.95

FRONTIER FIGHTER
Charlton Comics Aug., 1955
1 . . . . 50.00
2 . . . . 25.00
Becomes:

DAVY CROCKETT
3 thru 7 . . . . @20.00
8 Jan., 1957 . . . . 15.00
Becomes:

KID MONTANA
9 . . . . 20.00
10 . . . . 9.00
11 . . . . 6.00
12 . . . . 6.00
13 . . . . 14.00
14 thru 20 . . . . @6.00
21 thru 35 . . . . @3.50
36 thru 49. . . . . @2.00
50 March, 1965 . . . . 2.00

DAWN
Sirius 1995–97
½ Wizard mail-in	15.00
½ variant	25.00
1 JLi,R:Dawn	12.00
1a white trash edition	40.00
1b black light edition	35.00
1c look sharp edition	45.00
2 JLi, Trip to Hell	10.00
2 variant cover	36.00
3 JLi	9.00
3 limited edition	40.00
4 JLi,"The Gauntlet"	5.00
4a variant cover	30.00
5 JLi,"Everybody Dies"	4.00
5a variant cover	20.00
6 (of 6) JLi	6.00
6a variant cover	15.00
TPB Lucifer's Halo	20.00
TPB Tears of Dawn	18.00

DAWN: THE RETURN OF THE GODDESS
Sirius 1999
1 (of 4) JLi	2.95
1a limited, signed	20.00
2 A:Marinen	2.95
2a limited, signed	20.00

DAZEY'S DIARY
Dell Publishing Co.
June-Aug., 1962
1	30.00

DEAD BOYS: DEATH'S EMBRACE
London Night 1996
1 EHr	3.00
1 platinum edition	6.00

DEADFORCE
Antarctic Press 1999
1 (of 3) by Roy Burdine	3.00
2	3.00
3	3.00

DEAD KING
Chaos! Comics 1997
1 (of 4) Burnt, pt.1, F:Homicide	2.95
2 Burnt, pt.2	2.95
3 Burnt, pt.3	2.95
4 Burnt, pt.4, concl.	2.95
TPB Dead King Burnt	12.95

DEAMON DREAMS
Pacific
1	1.50
2	1.50

DEAR NANCY PARKER
Gold Key 1963
1 P(c)	20.00
2 P(c)	15.00

DEATHDEALER
Verotika 1995
1 FF(c), I:Deathdealer	15.00
2 thru 4 FF(c)	@12.00

DEATH OF HARI KARI
Blackout Comics 1997
0	2.95
0 super Sexy Kari Cover	9.95
0 3-D super Sexy Kari Cover	14.95

DEATHRACE 2020
Roger Corman Cosmic Comics
1 Pat Mills, Tony Skinner	2.50
2 V:Spyda, Sawmill Jones	2.50
3 O:Frankenstein	2.50
4 Deathrace cont.	2.50
5 F:Death Racers, D:Alchoholic	2.50
6 V:Indestructiman	2.50
7 Smallville Mall	2.50

DEATH OF LADY VAMPRE
Blackout Comics 1995
1 V:Baraclaw	2.95
1 Commemorative Issue	9.95

DEATH RATTLE
Kitchen Sink 1985–88
1 thru 7	@2.00
8 I:Xenozoic Tales	5.00
9 thru 18	@2.00

DECOY
Penny Farthing Press 1999
1 (of 4)	2.75
2	2.75
3	2.75
4	2.75

DEFENDERS, THE
Dell Publishing Co.
Sept.-Nov., 1962
1	45.00
2	30.00

DEFIANT: ORIGIN OF A UNIVERSE
Defiant
1 Giveaway	1.50

DEITY
Hyperwerks Sept. 1997
0	3.00
1 KIA	5.00
1a Director's Cut	3.00
2 thru 6 KIA	@3.00
TPB rep. #1–#3	7.95
TPB rep. #4–#6	7.95

VOL II Awesome/Hyperworks 1998
1 KIA,BNa, F:Jamie	2.95
1a Limited edition	7.95
1b Silver Foil edition	12.95
1c Gold Edition	19.95
2 KIA,BNa, A:Diamond Diaz	2.95
3 KIA,BNa, The Soul Crusher	2.95
4 KIA,BNa, A:Ogden	2.95
5 KLa,BNa,V:Ma'Shiva	2.95
6 KIA,BNa	2.95

DEITY II: CATSEYE
Hyperwerks 1998
1 KIA,BNa,F:Digby	2.95
2 KIA,BNa,A:II	2.95
3 KIA,BNa,F:Catseye	2.95
4 KIA,BNa,conclusion	2.95

DELIVERER
Zion Comics
1 thru 3	1.95
4 F:Gabriel	1.95
5 V:Division	1.95

DEMONIC TOYS
Eternity
1 Based on 1992 movie	2.50
2 thru 4	2.50

DEMONIQUE
London Night 1996
0 Manga	3.00
0a nude cover variant	10.00
0a nude cover variant, signed	8.00
1 EHr	3.00
1a nude cover	6.00
1a nude cover, signed	8.00
2 (of 2)	3.00
2a nude cover	6.00

DEN
Fantagor
1 thru 10 RCo	@2.00

DEN SAGA
Tundra/Fantagor
1 RCo,O:Den begins	4.95

*Dennis the Menace and His Friends
#16 © Fawcett*

DENNIS THE MENACE
Fawcett 1960-61
Fun Book #1	50.00
And his Pal Joey #1	30.00
And his Dog Ruff #1	30.00
Television Special #1	40.00
Triple Feature #1	40.00
Television Special #2	25.00

DENNIS THE MENACE AND HIS FRIENDS
[VARIOUS SUBTITLES]
Fawcett 1969–1980
1 thru 10 rep.	@10.00
11 thru 20 rep.	@8.00
21 thru 46 rep.	@4.00

DENNIS THE MENACE GIANTS
[VARIOUS SUBTITLES]
Fawcett 1955–69
N# Vacation Special 125.00
N# Christmas 100.00
2 thru 10 . . . . 85.00
11 thru 20 . . . . 50.00
21 thru 30 . . . . 35.00
31 thru 40 . . . . 20.00
41 thru 75 . . . . 15.00
Becomes:

DENNIS THE MENACE BONUS MAGAZINE
[VARIOUS SUBTITLES]
Fawcett 1970–79
76 thru 100 . . . . @4.00
101 thru 120 . . . . @3.00
121 thru 185 . . . . @2.00
186 thru 196 Big Bonus Series . . @2.00
Becomes:

DENNIS THE MENACE
Fawcett 1979–80
#16 Fun Fest 3.00
#17 Fun Fest 3.00
#10 Big Bonus Series 3.00
#11 Big Bonus Series 3.00

DEPUTY DAWG
Gold Key Aug., 1965
1 . . . . 120.00

DER VANDALE
Innervision 1998
1 (of 3) 2.50
2 (of 3) 2.50
3 (of 3) 2.50
3 variant cover 2.50

Destroyer Duck #3
© Eclipse

DESTROYER DUCK
Eclipse 1982–84
1 JK,AA,SA,I:Groo. 12.00
2 JK,AA,Starling 1.50
3 thru 5 JK . . . . @1.50
6 thru 7 JK . . . . @2.00

DESTRUCTOR, THE
Atlas Feb.–Aug. 1975
1 thru 4 . . . . @15.00

DETECTIVES, INC.
Eclipse 1985
1 MR,rep.GraphicNovel 3.00
2 MR 2.25
[2nd Series]
1 GC,"A Terror of Dying Dreams" . . 2.50
2 GC 2.25
3 GC,"Cut to the Bone" 1.50

DETONATOR
Chaos! Comics 1994–95
1 I:Detonator 2.95
2 V:Messiah & Mindbender 2.75

DEVIL KIDS STARRING HOT STUFF
Harvey Publications 1962–81
1 . . . . 80.00
2 . . . . 40.00
3 thru 10 . . . . @20.00
11 thru 20 . . . . @15.00
21 thru 30 . . . . @10.00
31 thru 40 . . . . @7.00
41 thru 50 68 pgs. . . . . @7.00
51 thru 55 62 pgs. . . . . @5.00
56 thru 70 . . . . @3.00
71 thru 100 . . . . @2.00
101 thru 106 . . . . @1.00
107 . . . . 1.00

DEVILMAN
Verotika 1995
1 Go Nagi 2.95
1a San Diego Con Gatefold edition 4.95
2 F:Devilman 2.95
3 Through History 2.95
4 French Revolution 2.95
5 Custer's Last Stand 2.95

DEVLIN
Maximum Press 1996
1 A:Avengelyne,3-part mini-series . 2.50
2 (of 3) RLd,BNa,A:Avengelyne . . . 2.50

DICK TRACY
1 3-D 2.50

DICK TRACY: BIG CITY BLUES
1 Mini Series 3.95
2 Mini Series 5.95
3 Mini Series 5.95

DINO ISLAND
Mirage
1 thru 2 . . . . 2.75

DINOSAUR REX
Upshot/Fantagraphics 1987
1 thru 3 by Jan Strand & Henry Mayo. . @2.00

DINOSAURS
Walt Disney
1 Citizen Robbie(From TV) 2.95

DINOSAURS ATTACK
Eclipse
1 HT,Based on Topps cards 3.50
2 and 3 HT,Based on cards . . . . @3.50

DISNEY ADVENTURES
Walt Disney
1 . . . . 2.75
2 . . . . 2.50
3 thru 6 . . . . @2.25
7 Joe Montana 2.25
8 Bronson Pinchot 2.25
9 Hulk Hogan 2.25
10 Mayim Bialik 2.25
11 . . . . 2.25
12 Monsters 2.25
13 A:Darkwing Duck (inc. work
  by DW) 2.25
14 inc. "Big Top, Big Shot" 1.95
15 . . . . 1.95
16 inc."Turnabout is Fowl Play" . . . 1.95
17 inc."Kitty Kat Kaper" 1.95
18 Kitty Kat Kaper 1.95
19 The Voice of Wisdom 1.95
20 thru 28 . . . . @1.95

DISNEY COLOSSAL COMICS COLLECTION
Walt Disney
1 inc.DuckTales, Chip'n'Dale 2.25
2 inc.Tailspin,Duck Tales 1.95
3 inc.Duck Tales 1.95
4 O:Darkwing Duck 1.95
5 Tailspin,Duck Tales 1.95
6 Darkwing Duck,Goofy 1.95
7 inc.Darkwing Duck.Goofy 1.95
8 inc.Little Mermaid 1.95
9 inc.Duck Tales 1.95

DISNEY COMICS IN 3-D
Walt Disney
1 . . . . 2.95

DISNEY COMICS SPEC: DONALD & SCROOGE
1 inc."Return to Xanadu" 8.95

DISNEYLAND BIRTHDAY PARTY
Gladstone
1 . . . . 6.00

DIVER DAN
Dell Publishing Co.
Feb.-April, 1962
1 . . . . 45.00
2 . . . . 30.00

DIVINE INTERVENTION
Wildstorm/DC 1999
1 . . . . 2.50
Wildcats, pt.2, JLe,SLo,RiB 2.50
Gen13, pt.3, JLe,SLo,RiB 2.50

DIVINE MADNESS
Dark Moon
1 Human Flesh Artist 2.50
2 . . . . 2.50
3 Ancient Cult 2.50

DNAgents #20
© Eclipse

DNAGENTS
Eclipse 1983–85

1 O:DNAgents	4.00
2	3.00
3	2.50
4	2.50
5	2.50
6	2.50
7	2.50
8	2.50
9 DSp	2.50
10	2.00
11	2.00
12	2.50
13	2.00
14	2.00
15	2.50
16	2.50
17 thru 21	@2.00
22	1.75
23	1.75
24 DSt(c)	1.75
25	1.75

See also: NEW DNAGENTS

DO YOU BELIEVE IN NIGHTMARES?
St. John Publishing Co. 1957–58

1 SD	250.00
2 DAy	160.00

DOBER-MAN

1	2.50

DOC SAVAGE
Millenium

1 V:Russians	2.50

DOC SAVAGE, THE MAN OF BRONZE
Millenium

1 Monarch of Armageddon,pt.1	3.00
2 Monarch of Armageddon,pt.2	2.75
3 Monarch of Armageddon,pt.3	2.75
4 Monarch of Armageddon,pt.4	2.75

DOC SAVAGE: THE DEVIL'S THOUGHTS
Millenium

1 V:Hanoi Shan	2.50
2 V:Hanoi Shan	2.50
3 Final issue	2.50

DOC SAVAGE: DOOM DYNASTY
Millenium

1 and 2	@2.50

DOC SAVAGE: MANUAL OF BRONZE
Millenium

1 Fact File	2.50

DOC SAVAGE: REPEL
Innovation

1 DvD(c)	2.50

DOCTOR BOOGIE
Media Arts

1 and 2	@1.75

DOCTOR CHAOS
Triumphant Comics 1993

1 JnR(s),I:Doctor Chaos	2.50
2 JnR(s),	2.50
3 JnR(s),The Coming of the Cry,pt.1,I:Cry	2.50
4 JnR(s),The Coming of the Cry,pt.2,b:Ky'Li	2.50
5 JnR(s),E:Coming of the Cry,pt.3,V:Cry	2.50
6 Recovery	2.50
7 w/coupon	2.50
8 w/coupon	2.50
9 V:Mirth	2.50
10 Co. X #3	2.50
11 Co. X #4	2.50
12 A:Charlotte	2.50

DOCTOR SOLAR MAN OF THE ATOM
Gold Key

1 BF,I:Dr. Solar	300.00
2 BF,I:Prof.Harbinger	110.00
3 BF,The Hidden Hands	75.00
4 BF,The Deadly Sea	75.00
5 BF,I:Dr.Solar in costume	75.00
6 FBe,I:Nuro	50.00
7 FBe,Vanishing Oceans	50.00
8 FBe,Thought Controller	50.00
9 FBe,Transivac The Energy Consuming Computer	50.00
10 FBe,The Sun Giant	50.00
11 FBe,V:Nuro	35.00
12 FBe,The Mystery of the Vanishing Silver	35.00
13 FBe,Meteor from 100 Mill.BC	35.00
14 FBe,Solar's Midas Touch	35.00
15 FBe O:Dr.Solar	45.00
16 FBe,V:Nuro	35.00
17 FBe,The Fatal Foe	35.00
18 FBe,The Mind Master	35.00
19 FBe,SolarV:Solar	35.00
20 AMc,Atomic Nightmares	35.00
21 AMc,Challenge from Outer Space	25.00
22 AMc,Nuro,I:King Cybernoid	25.00
23 AMc,A:King Cybernoid	25.00
24 EC,The Deadly Trio	25.00
25 EC,The Lost Dimension	25.00
26 EC,When Dimensions Collide	25.00
27 (1969) The Ladder to Mars	25.00
28 (1981),1 pg AMc,The Dome of Mystery	12.00
29 DSp,FBe,Magnus	12.00
30 DSp,FBe,Magnus	12.00

DOGHEAD
Tundra

1 Al Columbia,"Poster Child"	4.95

DOGS OF WAR
Defiant

1 F:Shooter,Ironhead	2.75
2	2.50
3 Mouse Deserts	2.50
4 Schism Prequel	2.50
5 X-over	2.50
6 Aftermath	2.50

DOLLMAN
Eternity

1 Movie adapt. sequel	2.50
2 V:Sprug & Braindead Gang	2.50
3 Toni Costa Kidnapped	2.50
4	2.50

DONALD DUCK
Dell/Gold Key Dec. 1962

85 thru 97	35.00
98 rep. #46 CB	35.00
99	25.00
100	22.00
101	20.00
102 A:Super Goog	20.00
103 thru 111	@20.00
112 I:Moby Duck	20.00
113 thru 133	@20.00
134 CB rep.	20.00
135 CB rep.	20.00
136 thru 156	@18.00
157 CB rep.	15.00
158 thru 163	@12.00
164 CB rep.	12.00
165 thru 216	@5.00

Whitman

217	5.00
218	5.00
219 CB rep.	5.00
220 thru 245	@5.00

Gladstone

246 CB,Gilded Man	15.00
247 CB	10.00
248 CB,Forbidden Valley	10.00
249 CB	10.00
250 CB,Pirate Gold	15.00
251 CB,Donald's Best Xmas	4.00
252 CB,Trail o/t Unicorn	4.00
253 CB	3.50
254 CB, in old Calif.	7.00
255 CB	3.50
256 CB,Volcano Valley	3.50
257 CB,Forest Fire	4.00
258 thru 260 CB	@3.00
261 thru 266 CB	@2.50
267 thru 277 CB	@2.00
278 CB	4.00
279 CB	4.00
280 thru 298 CB rep.	@1.50
299 "Life Guard Daze"	1.50
300 "Donald's 300th Triumph" 48pg	2.25
301 "The Gold Finder"	1.95
302 "Monkey Business"	1.95
303 "The Cantankerous Cat"	1.95
304 "Donald Duck Rants about Ants"	1.95

COLOR PUB.

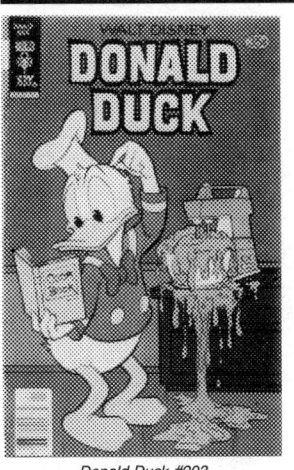

Donald Duck #203
© Gold Key Comics

305 "Mockingbird Ridge"	1.95
306 "Worst Class Mail"	1.95
307 "Going to Sea"	1.95
308 "Worst Class Mail"	1.95

DONALD DUCK ADVENTURES
Gladstone

1 CB,Jungle Hi-Jinks	5.00
2 CB,Dangerous Disquise	4.00
3 CB,Lost in the Andes	5.00
4 CB,Frozen Gold	4.00
5 Rosa Art	3.50
6	2.50
7	2.50
8 Rosa	3.50
9	2.50
10	2.50
11	2.50
12 Giant size,Rosa	3.50
13 Rosa(c)	2.50
14	3.00
15 CB	2.00
16	2.00
17	2.00
18	2.00
19	4.00
20 Giant size	4.00
21 thru 30	@2.95
31 thru 40	@1.50
41 "Bruce McDuck"	1.50
42 "The Saga of Sourdough Sam"	1.50
43 "The Lost Charts of Columbus"	1.50
44 "The Kitchy-Kaw Diamond"	1.95
45 "The Red Duck"	1.95
46	1.95
47 "Trick or Treat"	1.95
48 "The Saphead Factor"	1.95

DONALD DUCK ADVENTURES
Walt Disney 1990

1 Don Rosa, "The Money Pit"	5.00
2	3.00
3	2.50
4	2.50
5	2.50
6	2.50
7	2.00
8	2.00
9	2.00

10 "Run-Down Runner"	2.00
11 "Whats for Lunch-Supper"	2.00
12 "Head of Rama Putra"	2.00
13 "JustAHumble,BumblingDuck"	2.00
14 "DayGladstonesLuckRanOut"	1.75
15 "A Tuft Luck Tale"	1.75
16 "Magica's Missin'Magic"	1.75
17 "Secret of Atlantis"	1.75
18 "Crocodile Donald"	1.75
19 "Not So Silent Service"	1.75
20 "Ghost of Kamikaze Ridge"	1.50
21 "The Golden Christmas Tree"	1.50
22 "The Master Landscapist"	1.50
23 "The Lost Peg Leg Mine"	1.50
24 "On Stolen Time"	1.50
25 Sense of Humor	1.50
26 Race to the South Seas	1.50
27 Nap in Nature	1.50
28 Olympic Tryout	1.50
29 rep.March of Comics#20	1.50
30 A:The Vikings	1.50
31 The Sobbing Serpent of Loch McDuck	1.50
32 It Was No Occident	1.50
33 Crazy Christmas on Bear Mountain	1.50
34 Sup.Snooper Strikes Again	1.50
35 CB rep.	1.50
36 CB rep.	1.50
37 CB rep.	1.50

DONALD DUCK ALBUM
Dell Publishing Co.
May-July, 1959

1 CB(c)	50.00
2	30.00

DONATELLO
Mirage

1	10.00

DONNA MIA
Dark Fantasy Prod. 1995

1 I:Donna Mia	4.00
1a Deluxe Edition	5.00
1 signed & numbered (100 copies)	8.95
2	3.00

DOOMSDAY + 1
Charlton 1975–79

1 JBy,JBy(c)	15.00
2 JBy(c),P(c)	10.00
3 JBy,JBy(c),P(c)	7.00
4 JBy(c),P(c),I:Lok.	7.00
5 and 6 JBy,JBy(c),P(c)	@7.00
7 thru 12 JBy,JBy(c),rep	3.00

DOOMSDAY SQUAD
Fantagraphics

1 rep. JBy	2.00
2 rep. JBy	2.00
3 rep. SS,A:Usagi Yojimbo	4.00
4 thru 7, rep. JBy	@2.00

DOUBLE DARE ADVENTURES
Harvey Publications

1 I:B-man,Glowing Gladiator, Magicmaster	22.00
2 AW/RC rep. A:B-Man,Glowing Gladiator, Magicmaster	17.00

DOUBLE IMPACT
High Impact Studios 1995–96

1 RCI,I:China & Jazz, chrome(c)	7.00
1 holographic rainbow (c) with certificate	15.00
1 rainbow (c), no certificate	10.00
1 chromium variant (c)	8.00
2 RCI,V:Castillo	3.00
2a signed, with certificate	4.00
2b nude cover	8.00
2c China Exposed edition	8.00
2d signed by China	10.00
3 China on cover	5.00
3a Jazzler on cover	3.00
3b Nikki on cover	3.00
3c "Blondage"	6.00
4 F:Mordred, The Rattler	2.95
4a "Phoenix" variant (c)	6.00
5 RCI	3.00
5a nude cover	6.00
6 "Buttshots"	4.00
6a Jazz (c)	3.00
6a signed	6.00
7 I:Nikki Blade	3.00
8	3.00
8a variant (c)	4.00
Gold edition, Lingerie special	3.00

Volume 2 1996–97

0 RCI	3.00
0a nude cover	8.00
1 RCI.	3.00
1a deluxe edition	4.00
1b prism foil (c)	5.00
1cgold foil (c).	5.00
2 RCI.	3.00
2a Swedish Erotica cover	8.00
2b Swedish Erotica cover, signed	12.00
3	2.95
3a special edition RCI(c)	8.00
3b Photo nude cover	12.00

DOUBLE IMPACT: ALIVE
ABC Studios 1999

1 RCI,F:China & Jazz	3.00
1a deluxe	8.00

DOUBLE IMPACT/ HELLINA
High Impact 1996

1-shot RCI.	3.00
1a nude cover	9.95
1b Gold edition, nude cover	9.95
1c Spec. nude cover, signed	14.95

DOUBLE IMPACT/ LETHAL STRYKE: DOUBLE STRIKE
High Impact/London Night 1996

1-shot RCI	3.00
1a nude cover	9.95

DOUBLE IMPACT SUICIDE RUN
High Impact

1 RCI.	3.00
1 gold edition.	10.00
1 platinum edition	20.00
2	3.00
2a Suicide Cover	10.00
2b Photo Nude cover	14.95

DOUBLE IMPACT: 2069
ABC Studios 1999

1 RCI,Independent Day	3.00

COLOR PUB.

1a premium edition	5.00
1b Sexy China ed.	5.00
1c Nude cover	10.00

DOUBLE LIFE OF PRIVATE STRONG
Archie Publications

1 JSm,JK,I:Lancelot Strong/Shield The Fly	450.00
2 JSm,JK,GT A:Fly	300.00

DR. KILDARE
Dell Publishing Co.
April–June, 1962

1	60.00
2	40.00
3	40.00
4	40.00
5	40.00
6	40.00
7	40.00
8	40.00
9	40.00

DRACULA
Dell Publishing Co. Nov., 1966

2 O:Dracula	30.00
3	20.00
4	20.00
6	15.00
7	12.00
8	12.00

DRACULA
Topps

1 MMi,Movie adaptation (trading cards in each issue)	5.00
1a Red Foil Logo.	12.00
1b 2nd Print.	2.95
2 MMi,Movie adapt.contd.	4.00
3 MMi,Movie adapt.contd.	4.00
4 MMi,Movie adapt.concludes	4.00
TPB Collected Album	13.95

DRACULA CHRONICLES
Topps

1 True Story of Dracula	2.50
2 RTs,rep. Vlad #2.	2.50
3 RTs,rep. Vlad #3.	2.50

DRACULA VS. ZORRO
Topps

1 DMg(s),TY,Black(c),	3.25
2 DMg(s),TY,w/Zorro #0.	2.95
TPB	5.95

DRACULA: VLAD THE IMPALER
Topps

1 EM,I:Vlad Dracua, w/cards	5.00
1a Red Foil	10.00
2 EM, w/cards	3.25

DRAGONCHIANG
Eclipse

1 TT	2.95

DRAGONFLIGHT
Eclipse 1991

1 Anne McCaffrey adapt.	4.95
2 novel adapt	4.95
3 novel adapt	4.95

DRAGONFLY
AC Comics

1	3.50
2 and 3	@2.00
4 thru 8	@1.75

DRAGONFORCE
Aircel

1 DK	6.00
2 thru 7 DK	@4.00
8 thru 12	@4.00
13	2.00

DRAGONRING
Aircel 1987–88, Vol. 2

1	3.50
2 O:Dragonring	2.50
3 thru 15	@2.00
See also: B&W	

DRAKKON WARS, THE
Realm Press

0 by Richard Hatch & Chris Scalf.	3.00
1	3.00

Dreadstar #51
© First

DREADSTAR
First

27 JSn,from Epic,traitor	2.50
28 JSn	2.25
29 JSn,V:Lord Papal.	2.25
30 JSn,D:Lord Papal.	2.25
31 JSn,I:The Power	2.25
32 JSn	2.25
33	2.25
34 LM/VM,A:Malchek	2.25
35 LM/VM.	2.25
36 LM/VM.	2.25
37 LM/VM,A:Last Laugh	2.25
38 LM/VM.	2.25
39 AMc,Crossroads tie-in	2.25
40 LM/VM.	2.25
41 AMe	2.25
42 JSn,AMe,B.U.Pawns begins	2.25
43 JSn,AMe,Pawns,pt.2	2.25
44 JSn,AMe,Pawns,pt.3	2.25
45 JSn,AMe,Pawns,pt.4	2.25
46 JSn,AMe,Pawns,pt.5	2.25
47 JSn,AMe,Pawns,pt.6	2.25
48 JSn,AMe,Pawns,pt.7	2.25
49 JSn,AMe,Pawns,pt.8	2.25

50 JSn,AMe,Pawns,pt.9 prestige	4.25
51 PDd,Woj,Pawns,pt.10, Paladox epic begins.	2.25
52 AMe	2.25
53 AMe,"Messing with Peoples Minds"	2.25
54 JSn,AMe,Pawns ends	2.25
55 AMe,I:Iron Angel	2.25
56 AME,A:Iron Angel	2.25
57 A:Iron Angel	2.25
58 A:Iron Angel	2.25
59 A:Iron Angel	2.25
60 AMe,Paladox epic ends	2.25
61 AME,A:Iron Angel	2.25
62 O:Dreadstar,I:Youngscuz	2.25
63 AMe,A:Youngscuz	2.25
64 AMe,A:Youngscuz	2.25

DREDD RULES
Fleetway/Quality

1 SBs(c),JBy,Prev.unpubl. in USA	5.00
2 inc."Eldster Ninja Mud Wrestling Vigilantes"	3.50
3 inc."That Sweet Stuff".	3.50
4 Our Man in Hondo City	3.50
5	3.25
6 BKi,DBw.	3.25
7 "Banana City".	3.25
8 "Over the Top"	3.25
9 "Shooting Match".	3.25
10 SBs,inc.Mega-City primer	3.25
11 SBs,Legend/Johnny Biker	3.25
12 SBs,Rock on Tommy Who	3.25
13 BMy,The Ballad of Toad McFarlane	3.25
14 thru 15.	@3.25
16 A:Russians	3.25
17 F:Young Giant	3.25
18 F:Jonny Cool.	2.95
19 V:Hunter's Club .	2.95

DRIFT MARLO
Dell Publishing Co.
May–July, 1962

1	25.00
2	20.00

DRUG WARS
Pioneer

1	1.95
2	1.95
3	1.95

DRUNKEN FIST
Jademan

1	3.25
2	2.50
3	2.00
4	1.75
5	1.75
6 thru 9	@1.75
10 thru 27	@1.95
28 D:Mack	1.95
29	1.95
30	1.95
31	1.95
32 Wong Mo-Gei vs.Swordsman	1.95
33 Mo-Gei commits suicide.	1.95
34	1.95
35	1.95
36 D:Fire Oak.	1.95
37 Iron Law Kills Elephant-Man	1.95
38 A:Wayne Chan	1.95
39 D:Wayne Chan	1.95
40 D:Toro Yamamoto	1.95
41 Lord Algol vs. Ghing Mob.	1.95
42	1.95

43 D:Yamamoto,Swordsman in USA	1.95
44 "Cool Hand Wong"	1.95
45 "Black Cult Rising"	1.95
46	1.95
47	1.95
48 Evil Child	1.95
49 I:Hurricane Child	1.95
50 Lord Algol vs.Diabol.Ent.	1.95
51 F:Flying Thunder	1.95
52 Madcap vs.Yama	1.95
53 Swordsman vs.Catman	1.95

DUCKMAN
Topps

1 USA Cartoon	2.50
2 XXX Files	2.50
3 I:King Chicken	2.50
4 V:Toys	2.50
5 F:Cornfed	2.50
6 Star Trek Parody	2.50
7 rep. 1990 B&W 1st app., now in color	2.50

DUCKMAN: THE MOB FROG SAGA
Topps

1 I:Mob Frog	2.50
2 D:Mob Frog	2.50
3 In the Name of the Duck	2.50

DUCK TALES
Gladstone

1 CB(r)I:LaunchpadMcQuck	6.00
2 CB(r)	4.00
3	4.00
4 CB(r)	4.00
5 thru 11	@4.00
12	5.00
13	5.00

DUCK TALES
Walt Disney

1	4.00
2	2.50
3	2.25
4	2.25
5 Scrooges'Quest	2.25
6 Scrooges'Quest	2.00
7 Return to Duckburg	2.00
8	2.00
9 7 Sojourns of Scrooge	2.00
10 Moon of Gold	2.00
11 Once & Future Warlock	2.00
12 Lost Beyond the MilkyWay	2.00
13 The Doomed of Sarras	2.00
14 Planet Blues	2.00
15 The Odyssey Ends	2.00
16 The Great Chase	2.00
17 Duck in Time Pt.1	2.00
18 Duck in Time Pt.2	2.00
19 Bail Out	2.00

DUDLEY DO-RIGHT
Charlton Comics 1970–71

1	50.00
2 thru 7	@30.00

DUNC & LOO
Dell Publishing Co.
Oct.-Dec., 1961

1	65.00
2	50.00
3 thru 8	@30.00

COLOR PUB.

DWIGHT D. EISENHOWER
Dell Publishing Co. Dec., 1969

1	35.00

DYNAMO
Tower Comics Aug., 1966

1 WW,MSy,RC,SD,I:Andor	45.00
2 WW,DA,GT,MSy,Weed solo story A:Iron Maiden	35.00
3 WW,GT,Weed solo story, A:Iron Maiden	35.00
4 WW,DA,A:Iron Maiden, June, 1967	35.00

DYNAMO JOE
First 1986–87

1	3.00
2	2.00
3 thru 14	@1.50
Spec.#1	1.25

EARLY DAYS OF SOUTHERN KNIGHTS
Vol. 2 Graphic Novel | 5.00

EARTH 4
Continuity
[1st Series, Deathwatch 2000]

1 Deathwatch 2000 Pt.6,w/card	2.50
2 Deathwatch 2000 Pt.11,w/card	2.50
3 V:Hellbenders, w/card	2.50

[2nd Series]

1 WMc,	2.50
2	2.50
3	2.50

EAST MEETS WEST
Innovation

1	2.50
2	2.50
3	2.50

EBONY WARRIOR
Africa Rising

1 I:Ebony Warrior	1.95

ECHO OF FUTUREPAST
Continuity

1 NA,MGo,I:Bucky O'Hare, Frankenstein	4.00
2 NA,MGo,A:Bucky O'Hare, Dracula, Werewolf	3.50
3 NA,MGo,A:Bucky	3.50
4 NA,MGo,A:Bucky	3.50
5 NA,MGo,A:Drawla&Bucky	3.50
6 Ath,B:Torpedo	3.50
7 ATh	3.50
8 Ath,	3.25
9 Ath,Last issue	3.25

ECLIPSE GRAPHIC NOVELS
Eclipse

1 Axa	7.00
2 MR,I Am Coyote	7.00
3 DSt,Rocketeer	10.00
3a hard cover	40.00
4 Silver Heels	9.00
4a hard cover	40.00
5 Sisterhood of Steel	10.00
6 Zorro in Old Calif.	8.00

ECLIPSE MONTHLY
Eclipse

1 SD,DW,I:Static&Rio	2.00
2 GC,DW	2.00
3 thru 8 DW	@1.50
9 DW	1.75
10 DW	1.75

EDGE OF CHAOS
Pacific

1 GM	2.00
2 GM	2.00
3 GM	2.00

87th PRECINCT
Dell Publishing Co.
April-June, 1962

1 BK	75.00
2	60.00

Elementals #20
© Comico

ELEMENTALS
Comico 1984–88

1 BWg,I:Destroyers	5.00
2 BWg	3.00
3 BWg	3.00
4 BWg	2.50
5 BWg	2.50
6 BWg	2.00
7 BWg	2.00
8 BWg	2.00
9 BWg	2.00
10 BWg	2.00
11 BWg	1.50
12 BWg	1.50
13 thru 22	@1.50
23 thru 29	@1.75
Spec.#1	1.75
Spec.#2	1.95

[Second Series] 1989–94

1	2.25
2 thru 4	@1.95
5 thru 28	@2.50
Spec.#1 Lingerie special	2.95
GN The Natural Order, rep.	9.95
GN Death & Resurrection	12.95

[Third Series] 1995

1 R:Elementals, polybagged with Chrysalis promo card	2.50
2 R:Original Monolith, polybagged with Chrysalis promo card	2.50

3A Destroy the Shadowspear 2.50
3B variant cover 2.50
4 Memoirs,pt.1 .... 2.95
5 Memoirs,pt.2 .... 2.95
GN Ghost of a Chance 5.95
Spec. "Babes," photo multimedia
   bikini special. 3.95
Spec. Hot Bikini Valentine. 3.95
Spec. All New Summer Special ... 4.95
Spec.#1 Lingerie Metalite 3.95

ELEMENTALS:
HOW THE WAR WAS ONE
Comico 1996
1 thru 4 .... @2.95

ELEMENTALS: THE
VAMPIRE'S REVENGE
Comico 1996–97
1 thru 4 .... @2.95

ELEMENTALS VS.
THE CHARNEL PRIESTS
Comico 1996
Spec. 1 (of 2) 2.95
2 .... 2.95

ELEVEN OR ONE
Sirius 1995
1 JLi 5.00

ELFLORD
Aircel 1986–88
Volume 1: See B&W
Volume II
1 .... 3.50
2 .... 2.50
3 thru 20 .... @2.00
21 double size 4.95
22 thru 24 .... @2.00
Spec.#1 .... 2.00
25 thru 32, see B&W

ELFQUEST
Warp Graphics 1998
TPB 20th Anniv. Special 8.95
HC Bedtime Stories,RPi, 128pg... 19.95
TPB Scores, WPi, best of Elfquest
   stories 19.95

ELFQUEST: BLOOD OF
TEN CHIEFS
Warp Graphics 1993–95
1 WP. 2.50
2 WP. 2.25
3 WP,B:Swift Spear pt. 1 .... 2.25
4 WP,B:Swift Spear pt. 2 .... 2.25
5 V:Dinosaurs 2.25
6 Snowbeast 2.25
7 .... 2.25
8 Spirit Quest 2.25
9 Shadow Shifter. 2.25
10 Spheres pt. 1. .... 2.25
11 Spheres pt. 2. .... 2.25
12 .... 2.25
13 Forest 2.25
14 F:Mantricker 2.25
15 F:Bearclaw 2.25
16 Scar Vs. Bearclaw 2.50
17 F:Eldolil,"Howl for Eldolil". 2.50
18 F:Finder. 2.50
19 F:Cutter & Skywise 2.50

20 final issue 2.50

ELFQUEST:
HIDDEN YEARS
Warp Graphics
1 WP 3.00
2 WP, w/coupon promo.......... 2.75
3 WP, w/coupon promo.Cont.sty.
   previewed in Harbinger#11 .... 3.25
4 WP,w/coupon 2.50
5 WP,O:Skywise 2.50
6 WP,F:Timmain 2.50
7 F:Timmain 2.50
8 Daughter's Day. 2.50
9 WP(s),Enemy Face 2.50
9 1/2 WP,JBy,Holiday Spec...... 3.50
10 thru 14 WP. .... @2.50
15 WP Wolfrider Tribe Splits 3.50
16 thru 18 WP 2.25
19 Mousehunt 2.25
20 F:Recognition 2.25
21 F:Teir, Messenger 2.50
22 F:Embu, Making a Point. 2.50
23 Not Wolf And Teir 2.50
24 Magic Menace. 2.50
25 B&W Wolfrider's Death 2.25
26 thru 29 B&W finale......... @2.25

ELFQUEST: JINK
Warp Graphics 1994–96
1 Future 3.00
2 Future 2.25
3 Neverending Story 2.25
4 Neverending Story 2.25
5 V:True Sons, Hide and Seek. .. 2.50
6 V:Truth Holder, Should Auld
   Acquaintance 2.50
7 F:Black Snakes 2.50
8 B&W V:Black Snakes 2.25
9 thru 12 .... 2.50

ELFQUEST:
NEW BLOOD
Warp Graphics 1992–96
1 JBy,artists try Elfquest 5.00
2 Barry Blair story 3.50
3 thru 5 .... @2.50
6 thru 24 .... @2.25
25 Forevergreen pt. 13......... 2.25
26 V:Humans 2.25

Elfquest: New Blood #17
© Warp Graphics

27 V:Door. 2.25
28 I:Windkin, Triompe and Defeat. . 2.50
29 F:Windkin 2.50
30 V:Door. 2.50
31 F:The Wanderer 2.50
32 B&W Sorrow's End 2.25
33 thru 35 B&W 2.25
Summer Spec.1993 .... 4.25

ELFQUEST: THE REBELS
Warp Graphics 1994–96
1 Aliens, set several hundred
   years in future 2.75
2 Escape. 2.50
3 He That Goes. 2.25
4 Reasons. 2.25
5 V:Skyward 2.50
6 F:Shimmer, The Edge. 2.50
7 .... 2.50
8 Squatters & Defenders 2.50
9 B&W Brother vs. Brother 2.25
10 thru 12 .... @2.50

ELFQUEST: SHARDS
Warp Graphics 1994–96
1 Division 2.25
2 thru 5 .... @2.25
6 F:Two-Edge 2.25
7 F:Shuma 2.25
8 WP,Turnabout,pt.1 .... 2.25
9 WP,Turnabout,pt.2,V:Djun 2.50
10 Revelations,pt.1. .... 2.50
11 V:Humans 2.50
12 B&W F:High One Timmain..... 2.25
13 thru 16 B&W finale......... @2.25

ELFQUEST:
WAVE DANCERS
Warp Graphics 1993–96
1 Foil enhanced. 3.25
2 thru 6 .... @2.25
Spec. #1. .... 3.00

ELIMINATOR
COLOR SPECIAL
Eternity 1991
1 DDo(c) set in the future 2.95

ELRIC
Pacific 1983–84
1 CR. 4.00
2 CR. 3.00
3 thru 6 CR .... @2.50

ELRIC
Topps April 1996
0 NGa,CPR, "One Life," based on
   Michael Moorcock character. .. 2.95

ELRIC, BANE OF
THE BLACK SWORD
First 1988–89
1 Michael Moorcock adapt. 1.75
2 .... 1.75
3 thru 5 .... @1.95

ELRIC, SAILOR ON
THE SEAS OF FATE
First 1985–86
1 Michael Moorcock adapt. 4.00
2 .... 3.00
3 thru 7 .... @2.00

ELRIC–VANISHING TOWER
First 1987–88
1 Michael Moorcock adapt. 2.50
2 thru 6 . . . . @2.00

ELRIC, WEIRD OF THE WHITE WOLF
First 1986–87
1 Michael Moorcock adapt. 3.00
2 thru 5 . . . . @2.00
Graphic Novel CR 7.00

E-MAN
Charlton Comics 1973–75
1 JSon,O:E-Man 20.00
2 SD 8.00
3 . . . . 8.00
4 SD 8.00
5 SD,Miss Liberty Belle 6.00
6 JBy,Rog 2000 . . . . 8.00
7 JBy,Rog 2000 . . . . 8.00
8 J:Nova 10.00
9 JBy,Rog 2000 . . . . 8.00
10 JBy,Rog 2000 . . . . 8.00

E-MAN
First
1 JSon,O:E-Man & Nova, A:Rog 2000, 1 pg. JBy 1.75
2 JSon,I:F-Men (X-Men satire) 1-page Mike Mist. 1.25
3 JSon, V:F-Men 1.25
4 JSon,Michael Mauser solo 1.25
5 JSon,I:Psychobabbler,A:Omaha, The Cat Dancer 1.25
6 JSon,O:E-Man,V:Feeder 1.25
7 JSon,V:Feeder 1.25
8 JSon,V:HotWax,A:CuteyBunny . . 1.25
9 JSon,I:Tyger Lili 1.25
10 JSon,O:Nova Kane pt.1 . . . . . . 1.25
11 JSon,O:Nova Kane pt.2 . . . . . . 1.25
12 JSon,A:Tyger Lili 1.25
13 JSon,V:Warp'sPrinceChaos 1.25
14 JSon,V:Randarr 1.25
15 JSon,V:Samuel Boar 1.25
16 JSon,V:Samuel Boar 1.25
17 JSon,"Smeltquest" satire 1.25
18 JSon,"Rosemary..& Time" 1.25
19 JSon, "Hoodoo Blues" 1.25
20 JSon,A:Donald Duke 1.25
21 JSon,A:B-Team,(satire) 1.25
22 JSon,A:Teddy Q. 1.25
23 JSon,A:TygerLili,B-Team 1.25
24 JSon,O:Michael Mauser. 1.25
25 JSon,last issue 1.25
Spec. #1. . . . . 2.75

E-MAN
Comico 1990
1 JSon 2.75
2 and 3 JSon . . . . @2.50

E-MAN
Alpha Productions 1993
1 JSon 2.75

EMERGENCY
Charlton Comics 1976
1 JSon(c),JBy 20.00
2 JSon. 12.00
3 Thru 4 . . . . 10.00

ENCHANTED: THE AWAKENING
Sirius 1998
1 by Robert Chang 2.95
2 . . . . 2.95
3 conclusion 2.95

ENGIN
Samson Comics
1 I:The Mesh. 2.50

ENSIGN O'TOOLE
Dell Publishing Co.
Aug.-Oct., 1962
1 . . . . 30.00
2 . . . . 20.00

EPSILON WAVE
Independent
1 . . . . 3.00
2 . . . . 2.50
3 . . . . 2.25
4 . . . . 2.00
Elite Comics
5 thru 10 . . . . @2.00

ESC.(ESCAPE)
Comico 1996
1 SPr. 2.95
2 SPr. 2.95
3 SPr. 2.95
4 SPr. 2.95
TPB SPr Rep. #1–#4 . . . . 14.95

ESC: NO EXIT
Comico 1997
1 . . . . 2.95
1 medallion edition 9.95
2 . . . . 2.95

ESPERS
Eclipse
1 I:ESPers. 2.00
2 JBo(c),V:Terrorists 1.50
3 V:Terrorists. 1.50
4 Beirut 1.75
5 "The Liquidators" 1.75
6 V:Benito Giovanetti. 1.75

ESPIONAGE
Dell Publishing Co.
May-July, 1964
1 . . . . 25.00
2 . . . . 20.00

ETERNITY SMITH
Hero
1 . . . . 1.50
2 . . . . 1.50
3 . . . . 1.50
4 Knightshade solo 1.50
5 Knightshade solo 1.50
6 . . . . 1.50
7 . . . . 1.95
8 I:Indigo 1.95
9 A:Walter Koenig 1.95
10 . . . . 1.95
Heroic Publishing
1 Man Vs. Machine 1.95
2 Man Vs. Machine 1.95

EVA THE IMP
Red Top Comic/Decker 1957
1 . . . . 20.00
2 . . . . 15.00

Evangeline #2
© Comico

EVANGELINE
Comico 1984
1 Guns of Mars 4.00
2 . . . . 3.00
Lodestone
1 . . . . 2.50
2 . . . . 2.50
First
1 . . . . 3.00
2 thru 9 . . . . @1.75
10 . . . . 1.95
11 . . . . 1.95
12 . . . . 1.95

EVERYTHING'S ARCHIE
Archie Publications May, 1969
1 . . . . 55.00
2 . . . . 25.00
3 thru 5 . . . . @15.00
6 thru 10 . . . . @10.00
11 thru 20 . . . . @5.00
21 thru 40 . . . . @3.00
41 thru 134 . . . . @3.00

EVIL ERNIE
Eternity 1991–92
See: B&W

EVIL ERNIE (THE SERIES)
Chaos! Comics 1998
1 V:Purgatori 2.95
2 Search for Chastity, A:Savior . . . 2.95
3 V:Purgatori 2.95
4 return to New Jersey 2.95
5 two beings 2.95
6 heart of America. 2.95
7 Unholy Nights. 2.95
8 Trauma,pt.1 . . . . 2.95
9 Trauma,pt.2 . . . . 2.95
10 Trauma,pt.3 . . . . 2.95

COLOR PUB.

EVIL ERNIE: DEPRAVED
Chaos! Comics 1999
1 (of 3)	2.95
1a premium edition	10.00
2	2.95
3	2.95

EVIL ERNIE: DESTROYER
Chaos! Comics 1997
Prev.#1	2.95
1 (of 9) BnP	2.95
2 BnP	2.95
3 to Atlanta	2.95
4 siege of Atlanta	2.95
5	2.95
6 Nuclear launch codes	2.95
7 Nuclear attack	2.95
8 Nuclear attack continues	2.95
9 New forms of living dead, concl.	2.95

EVIL ERNIE: REVENGE
Chaos! Comics 1994–95
1 SHu,BnP,A:LadyDeath,glow(c)	10.00
1a limited, glow-in-the-dark (c)	25.00
1a Commemorative edition	20.00
2 SHu, BnP,Loses Smiley	8.00
3 SHu,BnP,V:Dr. Price	7.00
4 SHu,BnP,Final Issue	7.00
TPB Rep. #1-#4	12.95
TPB Revenge #2, signed	20.00

EVIL ERNIE: STRAIGHT TO HELL
Chaos! Comics 1995–96
1 Rampage in Hell, coffin(c)	5.00
1 limited, chromium edition	25.00
2 Cremator	4.00
3	4.00
3a Chastity (c)	22.00
4 and 5	@4.00
Ashcan	1.50
Spec.	25.00

EVIL ERNIE: THE RESURRECTION
Chaos! Comics 1993–94
1 R:Evil Ernie	20.00
1a gold edition	50.00
2 Enhanced Cover	14.00
3 "Massive Mayhem" Lady Death poster	14.00
4 final issue, extra pages	14.00
TPB Rep. #1-#4	14.95

EVIL ERNIE VS. THE MOVIE MONSTERS
Chaos! Comics
1 one-shot	3.00
1 omega edition	5.00
1 premium edition, signed	20.00

EVIL ERNIE VS. THE SUPER-HEROES
Chaos! Comics 1995
1 one-shot	3.50
1a foil (c)	30.00
1b limited	20.00
Spec. #2 by Hart Fisher & Steve Butler	2.95
Spec. #2, Premium edition	10.00

EVIL ERNIE'S BADDEST BATTLES
Chaos! Comics 1996
1-shot, imaginary battles	2.00

EXECUTIONER
Innovation 1993
1 Don Pendleton(s),F:Mack Bolan	3.95
1a Collector's Gold Ed.	2.95
1b Tyvek cover	3.95
2 War against Mafia	2.75
3 War against Mafia,pt.3	2.75

EXEMPLARS
1 and 2	@1.95

EXODUS, THE
Conquest Comics
1 V:Aliens	2.50

Exo-Squad #0
© Topps Comics

EXO-SQUAD
Topps 1994
[Mini-Series]
0	1.00
1 From Animated Series	2.50
2 F:Nara Burns	2.50
3 V:Neo-Sapiens	2.50

EXPLORERS
Explorer Press 1995
1 I:Explorers	2.95
2 The Cellar	2.95

EXTREME VIOLET
Blackout Comics
0 I:Violet	2.95
1 V:Drug Lords	2.95
Becomes:	

EXTREMES OF VIOLET
2 A:Matt Chaney	2.95
Commemorative Issue, 5000c.	9.95

EXTINCTIONERS
Vision Comics 1998
1 by Shawntae Howard & Malcolm Earle	3.95
2	3.95

EYE OF THE STORM
Rival Productions
1 I:Killian, Recon, Finesse, Stray	2.95
2 Conspiracy	2.95
3 3-D Comic Background	2.95
4 F:Recon	2.95
5 Sinclair & Rott	2.95

FALCON, THE
Aircel
Spec. #1	2.00

FAMILY AFFAIR
Gold Key Feb., 1970
1 W/Poster,Ph(c)	50.00
2	25.00
3 Ph(c)	25.00
4 Ph(c)	25.00

FAMILY MATTER
Kitchen Sink 1998
GN by Will Eisner	15.95
HC	24.95

FAMOUS INDIAN TRIBES
Dell Publishing Co. July-Sept., 1962
1	20.00
2	10.00

FANG
Sirius
1 V:Vampires, I:Fang	4.00
2 5	3.25
3 V:The Master	2.95

FANTASTIC VOYAGES OF SINBAD, THE
Gold Key Oct., 1965
1 Ph(c)	30.00
2 June, 1967	20.00

FANTASY FEATURES
AC
1	1.75
2	1.75

FASHION IN ACTION
Eclipse
Summer Special #1	1.75
Winter Special #1	2.00

FAT ALBERT
Gold Key 1974–79
1	15.00
2	10.00
3 thru 10	@10.00
11 thru 29	@8.00

FATALE
Broadway 1995
1 thru 6 JJo, "Inherit the Earth," pt.5	@2.95
7 Fatale now Queen of the World	2.95
8 "Crown of Thorns", pt.2	2.95
9 "Crown of Thorns", pt.3	2.95
TPB Inherit the Earth	14.95
HC Inherit the Earth	75.00

COLOR PUB.

FATE'S FIVE
Innervision 1998
1 (of 4) 2.50
1 variant cover 2.50
2 (of 4) 2.50
3 (of 4) 2.50

FATHOM
Comico 1987
1 thru 3 From Elementals...... @2.50

FATMAN, THE HUMAN FLYING SAUCER
Lightning Comics April, 1967
1 CCB,O:Fatman & Tin Man 45.00
2 CCB 30.00
3 CCB,(Scarce)............. 45.00

FAUST: BOOK OF M
Avatar Press 1999
1 (of 3) DQ,TV............... 3.95
1a signed, leather cover 20.00
2 .... 3.95

FAZE ONE
AC Comics
1 .... 1.75

FAZE ONE FAZERS
AC Comics
1 .... 5.00
2 .... 3.00
3 .... 2.00
4 thru 6 .... @1.75

FEARBOOK
Eclipse
1 SBi,RV,"A Dead Ringer" 1.75

FELIX THE CAT
Harvey
1 thru 4.................... 1.25
5 thru 7 .... 1.50

FELIX THE CAT: THE MOVIE
Felix Comics 1998
1-shot, issued a mere 10 years after movie............... 3.95

FELIX'S NEPHEWS INKY & DINKY
Harvey Publications Sept., 1957
1 .... 50.00
2 thru 7 .... @20.00

FEM 5
Entity 1995
1 thru 4 five-part series .... @2.95
1 signed & numbered 12.95

FEMFORCE
AC Comics
1 O:Femforce 7.00
2 A:Captain Paragon........... 3.50
3 "Skin Game"............... 3.00
4 "Skin Game".............. 3.00
5 Back in the Past............ 3.00
6 EL,Back in the Past 3.00

Felix's Nephews Inky & Dinky #7
© Harvey

7 HB,O:Captain Paragon........ 3.00
8 V:Shade................. 3.00
9 V:Dr.Rivits 3.00
10 V:Dr.Rivits 3.00
11 D:Haunted Horsemen 3.00
12 V:Dr.Rivits 3.00
13 V:She-Cat 3.00
14 V:Alizarin Crimson.......... 3.00
15 V:Alizarin Crimson.......... 3.00
16 thru 56 See Black & White Pub.
57 V:Goat God.............. 2.75
58 I:New Sentinels 2.75
59 I:Paragon............... 2.75
60 V:Sentinels 2.75
61 F:Tara 2.75
62 V:Valkyra............... 2.75
63 I:Rayda 2.75
64 thru 67................. @2.75
68 "Spellbound" 2.75
69 "She-Cat Possessed"........ 2.75
70 "Island Out of Time"......... 2.75
71 .... 2.75
72 w/Sentinels of Justice 4.00
72a no extras 3.00
73 w/Compact Comic 4.00
73a Regular edition 3.00
74 Daughter of Darkness 4.00
74a Regular edition 3.00
75 Gorby Poster............. 5.00
75a Regular edition 3.00
76 Daughters pt. 3, polybagged with Compact Comic 4.00
76a no bag or comic 3.00
77 V:Sea Monster............ 3.00
78 V:Gorgana, bagged with comic . 5.00
78a no bag or comic 3.00
79 V:Iron Jaw, polybagged with Index............... 5.00
79a no bag or index 3.00
80 polybagged with Index....... 6.00
80a F:Mr. Brimstone, Rad....... 3.00
81 polybagged with Index....... 6.00
81a Valentines Day Spec........ 3.00
82 polybagged with index....... 6.00
82a F:Ms. Victory 3.00
83 F:Paragon............... 3.00
84 The Death of Joan Wayne polybagged with index #4B.... 6.00
84a no bag or index 3.00
85 Synn vs. Narett, polybagged with card 5.00
85a no bag or card 3.00
86 polybagged with index #5 ..... 5.00
86a unbagged, no suplements 3.00
87 Pandemonium in Paradise,

polybagged with plate....... 10.00
87a unbagged, no plate 3.00
88 F:Garganta, polybagged with index #6................ 6.00
88a unbagged, no index........ 3.00
89 polybagged with index 6.00
89a unbagged, no index........ 3.00
90 polybagged with index 6.00
90a unbagged, no index........ 3.00
91 polybagged with index 6.00
91a unbagged, no index........ 3.00
92 polybagged with index 6.00
92a unbagged, no index........ 3.00
Spec.#1 .... 1.50
Untold Origin Spec #1 .... 4.95

FEMFORCE: UP CLOSE
AC Comics
1 F:Stardust 2.75
2 F:Stardust 2.75
3 .... 2.75
4 .... 2.75
5 with Sticker............... 3.95
5a Regular Edition............ 2.95
6 with Sticker............... 3.95
6a Regular Edition............ 2.95
7 with Sticker............... 3.95
7a Regular Edition............ 2.95
8 with Sticker............... 3.95
8a Regular Edition............ 2.95
9 thru 11 .... @2.95

FENRY
Raven Publications
1 .... 6.95
1a Platinum Ed.............. 15.00

FIGHT THE ENEMY
Tower Comics Aug., 1966
1 BV,Lucky 7 .... 30.00
2 AMc 20.00
3 WW,AMc 20.00

FIGHTING AMERICAN
Harvey
1 SK,Rep Fighting American from 1950's 17.50

FIGHTING AMERICAN
Awesome Entertainment
1 .... 4.00
1a variant (c)................ 4.00
1b Platinum (c) 15.00
2 .... 3.00
Coll.Ed.#1 rep.#1–#2 .... 4.95
Spec.#1 Fighting American: Cold War RLe,JLb................. 2.50

FIGHTING AMERICAN: DOGS OF WAR
Awesome Entertainment 1998
1 JSn,SPa,F:John Flagg 2.50
1a Tour Edition, RLe cover 5.00
1b Tour Edition, signed 14.00
2 JSn,SPa,other super-soldiers ... 2.50
2a variant cover.............. 2.50
3 A:Crimson Dragon 2.50
4 Who is No Name? 2.50
Spec.'98 Con preview,b&w,16-page 5.00

FIGHTING AMERICAN: RULES OF THE GAME
Awesome Entertainment 1997
1 JLb..................... 3.00

2 JLb........................ 2.50
3 JLb, Baby Buzz Bomber....... 2.50

FIRST ADVENTURES
First
1 thru 5 .... @1.25

FIRST GRAPHIC NOVELS
First
1 JBi,Beowolf 8.00
1a 2nd Printing 7.00
2 TT,Time Beavers 6.00
3 HC,American Flag Hard Times . 12.00
4 Nexus,SR. 8.00
5 Elric,CR 15.00
6 Enchanted Apples of Oz...... 6.00
7 Secret Island of Oz.......... 8.00
8 HC,Time 2 .... 28.00
9 TMNT 20.00
10 TMNT II................... 18.00
11 Sailor on the Sea 15.00
12 HC,American Flagg 12.00
13 Ice Ring................. 8.00
14 TMNT III 14.00
15 Hex Breaker 8.00
16 Forgotten Forest 9.00
17 Mazinger 9.00
18 TMNT IV 13.00
19 O;Nexus 8.00
20 American Flagg 12.00

1st FOLIO
Pacific
1 Joe Kubert School 1.50

FISH POLICE
Comico
Vol 2 #6 thru #15 rep......... @2.50
Vol 2 #16 rep............... 3.00
Vol 2 #17 rep.,AuA 3.00
1 Color Special (July 1987) 3.50

FITCH IN TIME
1 and 2 .... @1.50

FLAMEHEAD
JNCO Comics 1998
1 I:Flamehead.............. 2.00
2 .... 2.00
3 .... 2.00
4 .... 2.00
5 .... 2.00

FLARE
Hero Graphics
1 I:Darkon&Prof.Pomegranite 4.00
2 Blonde Bombshell,A:Galooper .. 3.00
3 I:Sky Marshall............. 3.00
Ann.#1 .... 4.50
[2nd Series]
1 A:Galloping Galooper......... 3.00
2 A:Lady Arcane 3.00
3 I:Britannia................. 3.00
4 A:Indigo 2.50
5 R:Eternity Smith,O:Die Kriegerin. 3.95
6 I:Tigress................. 3.50
7 V:The Enemies............. 3.95
8 Morrigan Wars#4,A:Icicle Dragon 3.50
9 Morrigan Wars Pt.7 (B&W) 3.50

FLARE ADVENTURES
Hero Graphics
1 rep...................... 2.95
2 flipbook w/Champions Classics .. 2.95
3 flipbook w/Champions Classics .. 2.95
Becomes: B&W

FLASH GORDON
Gold Key June, 1965
1 .... 15.00

Flash Gordon #3
© King Comics

FLASH GORDON
King 1966–69
1 AW,DH,A:Mandrake 35.00
1a Comp. Army giveaway ... 50.00
2 FBe,A:Mandrake,R:Ming ... 25.00
3 RE,"Lost in the Land of
   The Lizardmen" 30.00
4 AW,B:Secret Agent X-9...... 32.00
5 AW..................... 32.00
6 RC,On the Lost Continent
   of Mongo 30.00
7 MR, rep. "In the Human Forest" 30.00
8 RC,JAp................... 30.00
9 AR,rep.................. 35.00
10 AR,rep................. 35.00
11 RC.................... 25.00
Charlton 1969–70
12 RC.................... 25.00
13 JJ 20.00
14 .... 20.00
15 .... 20.00
16 .... 20.00
17 Brick Bradford story........ 20.00
18 MK,"Attack of the Locust Men". 20.00
Gold Key Oct.-Nov 1975
19 Flash returns to Mongo 6.00
20 thru 30 .... @5.00
31 thru 37 AW movie adapt..... @3.00

FLATLINE COMICS
Flatline Comics
1 Three stories River Prarie...... 2.50

FLAXEN: ALTER EGO
Caliber
1 V:Dark Flaxen.............. 2.95

FLESH AND BONES
Fantagraphics
1 Moore.................... 2.50
2 thru 4 Moore............. @2.00

FLINTSTONES
Harvey
1 .... 1.25
2 Romeo and Juliet 1.25

FLINTSTONES
Archie 1995
1 thru 10 .... @1.50
11 thru 14 .... @1.50
15 "Frankenstone's Monster" ... 1.50
20 "An Heir-Raising Tale"....... 1.50
21 "King Fred The Last" 1.50
22 "Something Gruesome This
   Way Comes" 1.50

FLINTSTONES, THE
Dell Publishing Co.
Nov.-Dec., 1961
#1 *see Dell Giant*
2 .... 100.00
3 .... 75.00
4 .... 75.00
5 and 6 .... @60.00
Gold Key
7 .... 60.00
8 A:Mr.& Mrs J. Evil Scientists ... 50.00
9 A:Mr.& Mrs.J. Evil Scientists ... 50.00
10 A:Mr.& Mrs.J. Evil Scientists ... 50.00
11 I:Pebbles 60.00
12 "The Too-Old Cowhand"..... 40.00
13 thru 15................. @40.00
16 I:Bamm-Bamm........... 50.00
17 thru 20 .... @40.00
21 thru 23 .... @25.00
24 I:Gruesomes 28.00
25 thru 29 .... @22.00
30 "Dude Ranch Roundup".... 22.00
31 Christmas(c) 22.00
32 .... 20.00
33 A:Dracula & Frankenstein .. 22.00
34 I:The Great Gazoo.......... 30.00
35 .... 20.00
36 "The Man Called Flintstone".. 20.00
37 thru 40 .... @20.00
41 thru 60 .... @16.00

FLINTSTONES, THE
Charlton Comics 1970
1 .... 50.00
2 .... 30.00
3 thru 7 .... @20.00
8 .... 25.00
9 .... 20.00
10 .... 20.00
11 thru 20 .... @15.00
21 thru 50 .... @12.00

FLINTSTONES IN 3-D
Blackthorne
1 thru 5 .... @2.50

FLIPPER
Gold Key April, 1966
1 Ph(c) from TV series........ 40.00
2 and 3 Ph(c)............. @25.00

FLY IN MY EYE
EXPOSED
Eclipse
1 JJo(c),"Our Visitor" 4.95

FLY, THE
Archie Publications
1 JSn,A:Mr.Justice. 1.25
2 thru 9 RB,SD . . . . @1.00

FLYING SAUCERS
Dell April, 1967
1 . . . . 25.00
2 thru 5 . . . . 15.00

FLYMAN
Archie Publications
{Prev: Adventures of the Fly}
31 I:Shield (Bill Higgins), A:Comet,
   Black Hood. 35.00
32 I:Mighty Crusaders. 30.00
33 A:Mighty Crusaders, R:Hangman
   Wizard 30.00
34 MSy,A:Black Hood,Shield,Comet Shi
eld back-up story begins. 20.00
35 O:Black Hood 20.00
36 O:Web,A:Hangman in Shield
   strip 20.00
37 . . . . A:Shield
20.00
38 A:Web 18.00
39 A:Steel Sterling 17.00

FOES
Ram Comics
1 TheMaster's Game. 1.95
2 TheMaster's Game #2 . . . . 1.95

FOODANG
Aug. House
1 I:Foodang. 1.95
1a Signed, Foil cover. 2.50
2 I:Maude 2.50
3 V:Undead Clown Man. 2.50
4 V:Executioner. 2.50

FOOTSOLDIERS
Maximum Press 1996
1 KJo,PhH, ... 2.75

FORBIDDEN PLANET
Innovation 1992
1 Movie Adapt. 2.50
2 Movie adapt.contd. 2.50
3 Movie adapt.contd. 2.50
4 Movie adapt.concl. 2.50
GN rep.#1–#4 (1997) 8.95

FORCE OF THE
BUDDHA'S PALM
Jademan
1 . . . . 3.00
2 . . . . 2.25
3 thru 10 . . . . @1.75
11 thru 24. . . . . @1.95
25 V:Maskman 1.95
26 V:Maskman 1.95
27 A:SmilingDemon 1.95
28 Maskman v 10 Demons. 1.95
29 Giant Bat. 1.95
30 . . . . 1.95
31 . . . . 1.95

---

32 "White Crane Villa" 1.95
33 Devilito defeats White Crane
   & Giant Bat 1.95
34 Samsun vs. Devilito. 1.95
35 Samsun vs. Devilito. 1.95
36 Samsun vs. Devilito. 1.95
37 D:Galacial Moon 1.95
38 Persian Elders, Iron Boy 1.95
39 V:Mad Gen.,White Crane,
   Iron Boy 1.95
40 D:Heaven & Earth Elders. 1.95
41 thru 43. . . . . @1.95
44 D:White Crane. 1.95
45 V:Iron Boy 1.95
46 thru 48. . . . . @1.95
49 Iron Boy vs Sainted Jade. 1.95
50 Iron Boy & The Holy Blaze. . . . 1.95
51 D:Aquarius 1.95
52 V:Son o/t Gemini Lord 1.95
53 Nine Continent's return to
   full powers 1.95

4-D MONKEY
1 thru 3 . . . . @1.80

FOREVER WAR, THE
NBM
GN Vol. 1 Joe Haldeman adapt. . . . 8.95
GN Vol. 2 Joe Haldeman adapt. . . . 8.95
GN Vol. 3 Joe Haldeman adapt. . . . 8.95

FRANK
Nemesis
1 thru 4 DGc(s),GgP 2.50

FRANK FRAZETTA
FANTASY ILLUSTRATED
Frank Frazetta 1998
1 . . . . 6.00
1a variant cover 6.00
3 . . . . 6.00
3 Neil Gaiman signed & numbered. . . .
24.95
3 Daniel signed & numbered 19.95
4 thru 8 . . . . @6.00

FRANK FRAZETTA
DEATH DEALER
Verotik 1997
1 thru 4 by Glenn Danzig . . . . . @6.95

FRANK IN THE RIVER
Tundra
1 Avery/Jones style cartoons. 2.95

FRANK MERRIWELL
AT YALE
Charlton Comics 1955–56
1 . . . . 30.00
2 thru 4 . . . . @20.00

FRANKENSTEIN
Dell Publishing Co. 1964
1 . . . . 50.00
2 . . . . 30.00
3 and 4 . . . . @20.00

FRANKENSTEIN
Caliber
Novel Adaptation 2.95

FRANKENSTEIN
DRACULA WAR
Topps
1 Frank Vs. Drac. 2.50
2 F:Saint Germaine 2.50
3 Frank Vs. Drac. 2.50

FREDDY
Dell Publishing Co. 1963
1 . . . . 20.00
2 and 3 . . . . @10.00

FREDDY'S DEAD
3-D. 2.50
1 GN, Movie Adapt 6.95

FREDDY'S DEAD:
THE FINAL NIGHTMARE
Innovation
1 Movie adaption, Pt.1. . . . . 2.50
2 Movie adaption, Pt.2. . . . . 2.50

FRIDAY FOSTER
Dell Publishing Co. Oct., 1972
1 . . . . 22.00

Friendly Ghost Casper #146
© Harvey

FRIENDLY GHOST
CASPER, THE
Harvey Publications 1958
1 . . . . 250.00
2 . . . . 125.00
3 thru 10 . . . . @60.00
11 thru 20 . . . . @40.00
21 thru 30. . . . . @30.00
31 thru 50 . . . . @25.00
51 thru 100 . . . . @15.00
101 thru 159 . . . . @7.00
160 thru 163 52 pgs. . . . . @5.00
164 thru 253 . . . . @3.00
Becomes:

CASPER
THE FRIENDLY GHOST

All comics prices listed are for *Near Mint* condition.

FRIGHT NIGHT
Now
1 thru 22 . . . . @1.75

FRIGHT NIGHT
Now
1 Dracula,w/3-D Glasses 2.95

FRIGHT NIGHT II
Now
Movie Adaptation 3.95

FRISKY ANIMALS
ON PARADE
Ajax-Farrell Publ. Sept., 1957
1 LbC(c) 75.00
2 . . . . 30.00
3 LbC(c) 50.00

FROGMEN, THE
Dell Publishing Co. 1962
1 GE,Ph(c) 75.00
2 GE,FF 50.00
3 GE,FF 50.00
4 . . . . 25.00
5 ATh 30.00
6 thru 11 . . . . @20.00

FROM HERE TO INSANITY
Charlton Comics Feb., 1955
8 . . . . 120.00
9 . . . . 100.00
10 SD(c) 150.00
11 JK 175.00
12 JK 175.00
3-1 . . . . 250.00

FRONTLINE COMBAT
EC Comics 1995
1 thru 4 rep. . . . . @2.00
Gemstone
5 thru 13 rep. . . . . @2.50
14 WW(c) 2.50
15 . . . . 2.50
"Annuals"
TPB Vol. 1 rebinding of #1–#5 . . . 10.95
TPB Vol. 2 rebinding of #6–#10 . . 12.95
TPB Vol. 3 rebinding of #11–#15 . . 13.50

F-TROOP
Dell Publishing Co. 1966
1 Ph(c) 100.00
2 thru 7 Ph(c) . . . . @60.00

FUN-IN
Gold Key 1970–74
1 . . . . 55.00
2 thru 6 . . . . @30.00
7 thru 10 . . . . @15.00
11 thru 15 . . . . @10.00

FUNKY PHANTOM
Gold Key 1972–75
1 . . . . 45.00
2 thru 5 . . . . @25.00
6 thru 13 . . . . @15.00

FUTURIANS
Lodestone
1 DC,I:Dr.Zeus 1.00

---

2 DC,I:MsMercury 1.00
3 DC 1.00
Eternity Graphic Novel, DC, Rep.
+new material. 9.95

GALL FORCE:
ETERNAL STORY
CPM
1 F:Solnoids 2.95
2 V:Paranoid 2.95
3 . . . . 2.95
4 Implant Secrets 2.95

GALLANT MEN, THE
Gold Key Oct., 1963
1 RsM 20.00

GALLEGHER
BOY REPORTER
Gold Key May, 1965
1 . . . . 22.00

GARRISON
Zion Comics
1 I:Wage, Garrison 2.50

GARRISON'S GORRILLAS
Dell Publishing Co. Jan., 1968
1 Ph(c) 40.00
2 thru 5 Ph(c). . . . . @20.00

GASP!
American Comics Group
March, 1967
1 . . . . 25.00
2 thru 4, Aug. 1967 . . . . @15.00

G-8 & BATTLE ACES
1 based on '40's pulp characters . . 3.00

GENE RODDENBERRY'S
LOST UNIVERSE
Teckno-Comics 1994
0 I:Sensua. 2.50
1 Gene Roddenberry's. 2.50
2 Grange Discovered. 2.25
3 Secrets Revealed 1.95
4 F:Penultra 1.95
5 I:New Alien Race 1.95
6 Two Doctor Granges. 1.95
7 F:Alaa Chi Tskare. 1.95

GENE RODDENBERRY'S
XANDER IN
LOST UNIVERSE
Teckno-Comics 1995
1 V:Black Ghost. 2.25
2 V:Walker. 2.25
3 V:Lady Sensua. 2.25
4 thru 7 . . . . @2.25
8 F:Lady Sensua. 2.25
[Mini-Series] Teckno-Comics
1995
1 RoR,F:L.Nimoy's Primortals 2.25

GENSAGA:
ANCIENT WARRIOR
Entity Comics 1995
1 I:Gensaga 2.50

Gene Roddenberry's Lost Universe #6
© Teckno Comics

1a with Computer Games 2.50
2 V:Dinosaurs 2.50
3 V:Lord Abyss 2.50

GENTLE BEN
Dell Publishing Co. Feb., 1968
1 Ph(c) 30.00
2 . . . . 20.00
3 thru 5 . . . . @18.00

GEORGE OF THE JUNGLE
Gold Key Feb., 1969
1 From animated TV show. 100.00
2 . . . . 75.00

GE ROUGE
Verotik 1997
1 by Glenn Danzig & Calvin Irving . 2.95
2 and 3 . . . . @2.95
Biz:GE Rouge #½ SBs 2.95

GET SMART
Dell Publishing Co. June, 1966
1 Ph(c) all 100.00
2 SD 75.00
3 SD 60.00
4 thru 8 . . . . @50.00

[FILMATION'S]
GHOSTBUSTERS
First 1987
1 thru 4 . . . . @1.50

GHOST BUSTERS II
Now
1 thru 3 Mini-series . . . . @1.95

GHOST STORIES
Dell Publishing Co.
Sept.-Nov., 1962
1 . . . . 50.00
2 . . . . 25.00
3 thru 10 . . . . @20.00
11 . . . . 15.00
12 thru 19 . . . . @10.00
20 . . . . 15.00
21 thru 33 . . . . @10.00

COLOR PUB.

34 rep. 10.00		
35 rep. 15.00		
36 rep. 10.00		
37 rep. 10.00		

Ash Can. .75

G.I. R.A.M.B.O.T.
Wonder Color 1987
1 thru 3 . . . . @2.00

G.I. ROBOT
Eternity
1 . . . . 1.80

GIRL FROM U.N.C.L.E.
Gold Key, Jan., 1967
1 "The Fatal Accidents Affair". . . 100.00
2 "The Kid Commandos Caper" . . 50.00
3 "The Captain Kidd Affair" 50.00
4 "One-Way Tourist Affair" 50.00
5 "The harem-Scarem Affair" 50.00

GLOBAL FORCE
Silverline
1 thru 4 . . . . @1.95

GLORY
Maximum Press 1996
1–15 see Image
16 JDy 2.50
17 JDy 2.50
18 JDy 2.50
19 JDy,A:Demeter, Silverfall 2.50
20 JDy,A:Silverfall. 2.50
21 JDy 2.50
22 JDy 2.50
23 A:Prophet 2.50
TPB Vol. 2, rep. 16.95
TPB Glory/Angela RLd,JDy. 16.95

Awesome Entertainment 1999
0 AMo. 2.50
0a & b alternate covers 2.50

GLORY/CELESTINE: DARK ANGEL
Maximum Press 1996
1 & 2 See: Image
3 (of 3) JDy 2.50

G-MAN
Conquest Comics
1 I:Richard Glenn 2.50

GOBLIN LORD, THE
Goblin Studios 1996
1 (of 6) sci-fi/fantasy 2.50
2 signed & numbered 9.95
3 . . . . 2.50
3a signed & numbered 9.95
4 thru 6 . . . . @2.50

GO-GO
Charlton Comics June, 1966
1 Miss Bikini Luv 40.00
2 Beatles. 50.00
3 Blooperman 20.00
4 . . . . 20.00
5 . . . . 15.00
6 JAp 20.00
7 . . . . 20.00
8 JAp 20.00
9 Ph(c),Oct., 1965 . . . . 20.00

Ghostly Tales #169
© Charlton Comics

GHOSTLY TALES
Charlton 1966
Previously: Blue Beetle
55 I&O Dr. Graves 15.00
56 thru 70. . . . . @8.00
71 thru 169 . . . . @6.00

GIANT COMICS
Charlton Comics Summer, 1957
1 A:Atomic Mouse,Hoppy. 150.00
2 A:Atomic Mouse 100.00
3 . . . . 100.00

GIDGET
Dell Publishing Co. April, 1966
1 Ph(c),Sally Field 100.00
2 Ph(c),Sally Field 75.00

GIFT, THE
First
Holiday Special. 6.00

G.I. JOE 3-D
Blackthorne
1 . . . . 3.00
2 thru 5 . . . . @2.50
Ann. #1 . . . . 2.50

GIL THORPE
Dell Publishing Co. 1963
1 . . . . 35.00

GINGER FOX
Comico
1 thru 4 . . . . @1.75

GIN-RYU
Believe In Yourself
1 F:Japanese Sword 2.75
2 Identity Revealed 2.75
3 . . . . 2.75
4 Manhunt For Gin-Ryu 2.75

GODS FOR HIRE
Hot Comics
1 thru 7 . . . . @1.75

GOLDEN COMICS DIGEST
Gold Key 1969–76
1 Tom & Jerry,Woody Woodpecker,
  Bugs Bunny 20.00
2 Hanna-Barbera, TV Fun
  Favorites 25.00
3 Tom & Jerry, Woody
  Woodpecker. 10.00
4 Tarzan 20.00
5 Tom & Jerry, Woody
  Woodpecker, Bugs Bunny. . . . 10.00
6 Bugs Bunny 10.00
7 Hanna-Barbera, TV Fun
  Favorites 12.00
8 Tom & Jerry, Woody
  Woodpecker, Bugs Bunny. 8.00
9 Tarzan 15.00
10 Bugs Bunny. 8.00
11 Hanna-Barbera, TV Fun
  Favorites 8.00
12 Tom & Jerry,Bugs Bunny 8.00
13 Tom & Jerry. 8.00
14 Bugs Bunny, Fun Packed
  Funnies 8.00
15 Tom & Jerry, Woody
  Woodpecker, Bugs Bunny. 8.00
16 Woody Woodpecker. 8.00
17 Bugs Bunny. 8.00
18 Tom & Jerry, ... 8.00
19 Little Lulu. 15.00
20 Woody Woodpecker 8.00
21 Bugs Bunny Showtime. 8.00
22 Tom & Jerry Winter Wingding. . . 8.00
23 Little Lulu & Tubby Fun Fling . . 14.00
24 Woody Woodpecker Fun
  Festival 8.00
25 Tom & Jerry. 8.00
26 Bugs Bunny Halloween Hulla-
  Boo-Loo,Dr. Spektor article. . . . 8.00
27 Little Lulu & Tubby in Hawaii . . 12.00
28 Tom & Jerry. 8.00
29 Little Lulu & Tubby. 12.00
30 Bugs Bunny Vacation Funni. . . . 8.00
31 Turk, Son of Stone. 15.00
32 Woody Woodpecker Summer
  Fun 8.00
33 Little Lulu & Tubby Halloween
  Fun 12.00
34 Bugs Bunny Winter Funnies. . . . 8.00
35 Tom & Jerry Snowtime Funtime . 8.00
36 Little Lulu & Her Friends 14.00
37 WoodyWoodpecker County Fair. 8.00
38 The Pink Panter. 8.00
39 Bugs Bunny Summer Fun 8.00
40 Little Lulu. 15.00
41 Tom & Jerry Winter Carnival . . . 8.00
42 Bugs Bunny. 8.00
43 Little Lulu in Paris 14.00
44 Woody Woodpecker Family Fun
  Festival 8.00
45 The Pink Panther. 8.00
46 Little Lulu & Tubby. 12.00
47 Bugs Bunny. 8.00
48 The Lone Ranger. 8.00

GOLD DIGGER
Antarctic Press 1999
VOL 2
1 by Fred Perry, F:Gina Diggers . . 2.50
2 . . . . 2.50

All comics prices listed are for *Near Mint* condition.

COLOR PUB.

GOLD DIGGER BETA
Antarctic Press 1998
Spec. 0 by Ben Dunn, Special
  Origin Issue, 24pg 1.95
1A bu Fred Perry, John Pound (c) . 2.95
1B Jeff Henderson (c) 2.95
2 and 3 . . . . @2.95

GOLDEN PICTURE STORY BOOK
Racine Press (Western)
Dec., 1961
1 Huckleberry Hound 150.00
2 Yogi Bear 150.00
3 Babes In Toy Land 225.00
4 Walt Disney 150.00

GOLDEN WARRIOR
Industrial Design
1 by Eric Bansen & RB 2.95
2 and 3 . . . . @2.95

GOMER PYLE
Gold Key July, 1966
1 Ph(c) from TV show 75.00
2 and 3 . . . . @50.00

GOOD GUYS
Defiant
1 JiS(s),I:Good Guys 3.75
2 JiS(s),V:Mulchmorg 3.25
3 V:Chasm 2.75
4 Seduction of the Innocent 3.25
5 I:Truc 2.75
6 A:Charlemagne 2.75
7 JiS(s),V:Scourge 2.50
8 thru 11 . . . . @2.50

GOOFY ADVENTURES
Walt Disney 1990
1 "Balboa de Goofy" 2.50
2 . . . . 2.00
3 thru 9 . . . . @1.75
10 Samurai 1.75
11 Goofis Khan 1.75
12 "Arizona Goof" Pt. 1 . . . . 1.75
13 "Arizona Goof" Pt. 2 . . . . 1.75
14 "Goofylution" 1.75
15 "Super Goof Vs.Cold Ray" 1.75
16 "Sheerluck Holmes" 1.50
17 GC,TP,"Tomb of Goofula" 1.50

GOOP, THE
JNCO Comics 1998
1 . . . . 2.00
2 . . . . 2.00
3 . . . . 2.00
4 . . . . 2.00

GORGO
Charlton Comics 1961–65
1 SD 175.00
2 SD,SD(c) 100.00
3 SD,SD(c) 65.00
4 SD(c) 50.00
5 thru 10 . . . . @50.00
11 . . . . 30.00
12 . . . . 20.00
13 thru 15 . . . . @30.00
16 SD 30.00
17 thru 23 . . . . @20.00

GORGO'S REVENGE
Charlton Comics 1962
1 . . . . 45.00
Becomes:

THE RETURN OF GORGO
2 . . . . 30.00
3 . . . . 30.00

G.O.T.H.
Verotik 1995
1 thru 3 mini-series . . . . @2.95
TPB SBi, rep. of series 9.95

THE GOTHIC SCROLLS, DRAYVEN
Davdez Arts 1997
1 16pg 1.50
1a limited edition, new cover 2.95
2 and 3 . . . . @2.50
4 V:Lucifer 2.50
GN 12.95

GRATEFUL DEAD COMIX
Kitchen Sink
1 TT,inc.DireWolf(large format) . . . 5.50
2 TT,inc.Jack Straw 4.95
3 TT,inc. Sugaree 4.95
4 TT,inc. Sugaree 4.95
5 TT,Uncle John's Band 4.95
6 TT,Eagle Mall #1 . . . . 4.95

GREASE MONKEY
Kitchen Sink 1997
1 by Tim Elred 3.50
2 by Tim Elred 3.50

GREAT AMERICAN WESTERN
AC Comics
1 . . . . 1.75
2 . . . . 2.95
3 . . . . 2.95
4 . . . . 3.50

GREAT EXPLOITS
Decker Publ./Red Top
Oct., 1957
91 BK 65.00

GREEN HORNET, THE
Gold Key Feb., 1967
1 Bruce Lee,Ph(c) 175.00
2 Ph(c) 125.00
3 Ph(c) 125.00

GREEN HORNET
Now
1 O:40's Green Hornet 10.00
1a 2nd Printing 4.00
2 O:60's Green Hornet 6.00
3 thru 5 . . . . @4.00
6 . . . . 3.00
7 BSz(c),I:New Kato 3.00
8 thru 12 . . . . @3.50
13 V:Ecoterrorists 3.50
14 V:Ecoterrorists 3.50
Spec.#1 . . . . 2.50
Spec.#2 . . . . 2.25

[2nd Series]
1 V:Johnny Dollar Pt.1 . . . . 2.25

2 V:Johnny Dollar Pt.2 . . . . 2.25
3 V:Johnny Dollar Pt.3 . . . . 2.25
4 V:Ex-Con/Politician 1.95
5 V:Ex-Con/Politician 1.95
6 Arkansas Vigilante 1.95
7 thru 9 The Beast . . . . @1.95
10 Green Hornet-prey 1.95
11 F:Crimson Wasp 1.95
12 Crimson Wasp/Johnny Dollar
  Pt.1,polybagged w/Button 2.50
13 TD(i),Wasp/Dollar Pt.2 . . . . . . 2.50
14 TD(i),Wasp/Dollar Pt.3 . . . . . . 2.50
15 TD(i),Secondsight 1.95
16 A:Commissioner Hamiliton 1.95
17 V:Gunslinger 1.95
18 V:Sister-Hood 1.95
19 V:Jewel Thief 1.95
20 F:Paul's Friend 1.95
21 V:Brick Arcade 1.95
22 V:Animal Testers, with Hologravure c
  ard 2.95
23 with Hologravure card 1.95
24 thru 25 Karate Wars . . . . @1.95
26 B:City under Siege 1.95
27 with Hologravure card 1.95
28 V:Gangs 1.95
29 V:Gangs 1.95
30 thru 37 . . . . @1.95
38 R:Mei Li 2.50

Green Hornet #31
© Now

39 Crimson Wasp 2.50
40 . . . . 2.50
41 . . . . 2.50
42 Baby Killer 2.50
43 Wedding Disasters 2.50
44 F:Amy Hamilton 2.50
45 Plane Hijacking 2.50
46 Airport Terrorists 2.50
Ann.#1 The Blue & the Green 2.50
1993 Ann 2.95

Bonus Books
TPB rep. Now comics #1–#12,
  296pg 10.00
TPB deluxe rep. Now comics
  #1–#12, 296pg 19.95
HC rep. #1–#12 . . . . 10.00

GREEN HORNET: DARK TOMORROW
Now
1 thru 3 Hornet Vs Kato . . . . . . @2.50

GREEN HORNET: SOLITARY SENTINAL
Now
1 Strike Force 2.50
2 thru 3 . . . . 2.50

GREENHAVEN
Aircel
1 . . . . 3.00
2 . . . . 2.50
3 . . . . 2.00

GRENDEL
Comico 1986–91
1 . . . . 8.00
1a 2nd printing 2.00
2 . . . . 5.00
3 thru 6 . . . . @4.00
7 MW 4.00
8 thru 12 . . . . @4.00
13 KSy(c) 3.00
14 KSy(c) 3.00
15 KSy(c) 3.00
16 Mage 5.00
17 thru 19 . . . . @4.00
20 thru 32 . . . . @3.00
33 . . . . 3.50
34 thru 36 . . . . @3.00
37 . . . . 5.00
38 . . . . 9.00
39 . . . . 8.00
40 . . . . 15.00

GREYLORE
Sirius 1985–86
1 thru 5 . . . . @2.00

GRIMJACK
First 1984–91
1 TT Teenage suicide story 3.00
2 TT A:Munden's Bar. 2.50
3 TT A:Munden's Bar. 2.00
4 TT A:Munden's Bar. 2.00
5 TT,JSon,A:Munden's Bar 2.00
6 TT,SR,A:Munden's Bar 2.00
7 TT,A:Munden's Bar. 2.00
8 TT,A:Munden's Bar. 2.00
9 TT "My Sins Remembered". 2.00
10 TT,JOy,A:Munden's Bar 2.00
11 TT,A:Munden's Bar 1.75
12 TT,A:Munden'sBar 1.75
13 TT,A:Munden'sBar 1.75
14 TT,A:Munden'sBar 1.75
15 TT,A:Munden'sBar 1.75
16 TT,A:Munden'sBar 1.75
17 TT,A:Munden'sBar 1.75
18 TT,A:Munden'sBar 1.75
19 TT,A:Munden'sBar 1.75
20 TT,A:Munden'sBar 1.75
21 TS,A:Munden's Bar 1.75
22 A:Munden's Bar. 1.75
23 TS,A:Munden's Bar 1.75
24 PS,TT,rep.Starslayer10-11 . . . 1.75
25 TS,A:Munden's Bar 1.75
26 1st color TMNTurtles 10.00
27 TS,A:Munden's Bar 1.50
28 TS,A:Munden's Bar 1.50
29 A:Munden's Bar. 1.50
30 A:Munden's Bar. 1.50
31 A:Munden's Bar. 1.50
32 A:Spook 1.50
33 JSon,Munden'sBar
    Christmas Tale 1.50
34 V:Spook. 1.50
35 A:Munden's Bar. 1.50
36 3rd Anniv.IssueD:Grimjack. . . . 2.50

37 A:Munden's Bar 1.50
38 A:Munden's Bar 1.50
39 R.Grimjack 1.50
40 . . . . 1.75
41 "Weeping Bride". 1.75
42 "Hardball" 1.75
43 "Beneath the Surface" 1.75
44 Shadow Wars 1.75
45 Shadow Wars 1.75
46 Shadow Wars 1.75
47 Shadow Wars,A:EddyCurrent. . . 1.75
48 Shadow Wars 1.75
49 Shadow Wars 1.75
50 V:Dancer,ShadowWars ends . . . 1.75
51 Crossroads tie-in,
    A:Judah Macabee 2.00
52 . . . . 2.00
53 Time Story. 2.00
54 . . . . 2.50
55 FH. 2.00
56 FH. 2.00
57 FH. 2.00
58 FH. 2.00
59 FH. 2.00
60 FH,Reunion Pt.1 . . . . 2.00
61 FH,Reunion Pt.2 . . . . 2.00
62 FH,Reunion Pt.3 . . . . 2.00
63 FH,A:Justice Drok 2.00
64 FH,O:Multiverse. 2.00
65 FH. 2.00
66 FH(c),Demon Wars Pt.1. . . . . . 2.00
67 FH(c),Demon Wars Pt.2. . . . . . 2.00
68 Demon Wars Pt.3 . . . . 2.00
69 Demon Wars Pt.4 . . . . 2.00
70 FH,I:Youngblood 2.00
71 FH,A:Youngblood. 2.00
72 . . . . 2.00
73 FH(c). 2.00
74 FH(c). 2.00
75 FH,TS,V:The Major 2.00
76 FH,A:Youngblood. 2.00
77 FH,A:Youngblood. 2.25
78 . . . . 2.25
79 FH,Family Business #1 . . . . 2.25
80 FH,Family Business #2 . . . . 2.25
81 FH,Family Business #3 . . . . 2.25

GRIMJACK CASEFILE
First 1990
1 thru 5 rep. . . . . @1.95

GRIMM'S GHOST STORIES
Gold Key/Whitman 1972–82
1 . . . . 25.00
2 . . . . 10.00
3 . . . . 10.00
4 . . . . 10.00
5 AW 12.00
6 . . . . 8.00
7 . . . . 8.00
8 AW 12.00
9 . . . . 8.00
10 . . . . 8.00
11 thru 16 . . . . @7.00
17 RC. 10.00
18 thru 60 . . . . @7.00

GROO
Pacific
1 SA,I:Sage,Taranto. 22.00
2 SA,A:Sage 12.00
3 SA,C:Taranto 10.00
4 SA,C:Sage 9.00
5 SA,I:Ahax 9.00
6 SA,I:Gratic 9.00
7 SA,I:Chakaal 9.00
8 SA,A:Chakaal. 9.00

Groo Vol.2 #6
© *Pacific*

Eclipse
Spec.#1 SA,O:Groo,rep Destroyer
    Duck #1 . . . . 23.00

GROUND ZERO
1 . . . . 1.35

GROUP LARUE
Innovation
1 . . . . 1.95
2 . . . . 1.95
3 . . . . 1.95

GUILLOTIN
ABC 1997
1 JQ(c) 3.00
1a RCl(c). 6.00
1b gold cover, polybagged with
    trading card 10.00
2 . . . . 3.00
2a Serpent (c) 6.00
2b Cold Series (c) 6.00

GULLIVER'S TRAVELS
Dell Publishing Co.
Sept.-Nov., 1965
1 . . . . 40.00
2 and 3 . . . . @30.00

GUMBY
Comico
1 AAd,Summer Fun Special. 5.00
2 AAd,Winter Fun Special 3.50

GUMBY IN 3-D
Spec.#1 . . . . 4.00
2 thru 7 . . . . @2.50

GUNSMOKE
Dell Publishing Co. Feb., 1956
1 J.Arness Ph(c) all 135.00
2 . . . . 65.00
3 . . . . 65.00
4 . . . . 65.00
5 . . . . 65.00
6 . . . . 50.00
7 . . . . 50.00
8 . . . . 60.00

COLOR PUB.

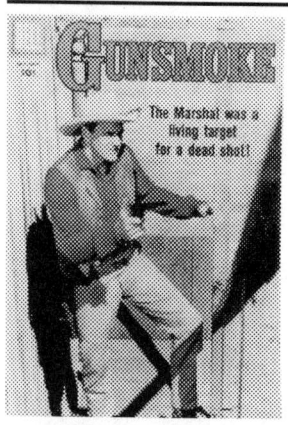

Gunsmoke © Dell Publishing Co.

9	60.00
10 AW,RC	65.00
11	60.00
12 AW	65.00
13 thru 27	@50.00

GUY WITH A GUN:
A ZOMBIE NIGHTMARE
Alpha Productions
1 V:Gracel, Zombies 2.75

HALL OF FAME
J.C. Productions
1 WW,GK,ThunderAgents 1.00
2 WW,GK,ThunderAgents 1.00
3 WW,Thunder Agents. 1.00

HALLOWEEN HORROR
Eclipse 1987
1 . . . . 1.75

HALO:
AN ANGEL'S STORY
Sirius April 1996
1 thru 3 by Chris Knowles . . . . . @2.95
TPB rep. #1–#3 . . . . 12.95

HAMMER OF GOD
First
1 thru 4 . . . . @1.95
Deluxe #1"Sword of Justice Bk#1" . 4.95
Deluxe #2"Sword of Justice Bk#2" . 4.95

HAMSTER VICE
10 . . . . 2.00
3-D #1 . . . . 2.50

HAND OF FATE
Eclipse
1 I:Artemus Fate 1.75
2 F:Artemis & Alexis 2.00
3 Mystery & Suspense. 2.00

HANDS OF THE DRAGON
Atlas June 1975
1 . . . . 15.00

HANNA-BARBERA
ALL-STARS
Archie 1995
1 thru 5 . . . . 1.50

HANNA-BARBERA
BAND WAGON
Gold Key 1962–63
1 . . . . 135.00
2 . . . . 75.00
3 . . . . 60.00

HANNA-BARBERA
PARADE
Charlton Comics 1971–72
1 . . . . 70.00
2 thru 10 . . . . @40.00

HANNA-BARBERA
PRESENTS
Archie 1995
1 thru 15 . . . . @1.50

HANNA-BARBERA
SUPER TV HEROES
Gold Key April, 1968
1 B:Birdman,Herculiods,Moby Dick,
Young Samson & Goliath 150.00
2 . . . . 100.00
3 thru 7 Oct. 1969 . . . . @90.00

HARDY BOYS, THE
Gold Key April, 1970
1 . . . . 20.00
2 thru 4 . . . . @12.00

HARI KARI
Blackout Comics 1995
0 I:Hari Kari. 2.95
1 . . . . 2.95
1a commemorative, variant(c) . . . 10.00
Specials & 1-shots
1 The Beginning, O:Kari (1996) . . . 2.95
1a The Beginning, commemorative,
signed 9.95
1 Bloodshed (1996). 3.00
1a Bloodshed, deluxe, variant(c) . . 10.00
1 Live & Untamed! (1996) 2.95
1 Rebirth (1996) 2.95
0 The Silence of Evil (1996). 2.95
0 The Silence of Evil, limited,
foil stamped 12.95
½ The Diary of Kari Sun (1997) . . . 2.95
½ The Diary of Kari Sun, deluxe . . 9.95
0 Life or Death (1997) 2.95
0a Life or Death, super sexy
parody edition. 12.95
1 Passion & Death (1997) 2.95
1 Passion & Death, photo(c) 9.95
1 Possessed by Evil (1997) 2.95
1 Resurrection (1997) 2.95
1 Resurrection, nude(c) edition . . . 9.95

HARLEM GLOBTROTTERS
Gold Key April, 1972
1 . . . . 25.00
2 thru 12, Jan. 1975. . . . . @15.00

HARLEY RIDER
1 GM,FS 2.00

HARRIERS
Entity 1995
1 I:Macedon Arsenal, Cardinal. . . . 2.95
1a with Video Game 6.95
2 . . . . 2.50
3 V:Kr'llyn 2.50

HARSH REALM
Harris
1 thru 6 JHi(s), ... @2.95

HARVEY HITS
Harvey Publications 1957–67
1	The Phantom	250.00
2	Rags Rabbit	25.00
3	Richie Rich	750.00
4	Little Dot's Uncles	100.00
5	Stevie Mazie's Boy Friend	15.00
6	JK(c),BP,The Phantom	175.00
7	Wendy the Witch	150.00
8	Sad Sack's Army Life	40.00
9	Richie Rich's Golden Deeds	350.00
10	Little Lotta	75.00
11	Little Audrey Summer Fun	50.00
12	The Phantom	150.00
13	Little Dot's Uncles	50.00
14	Herman & Katnip	20.00
15	The Phantom	135.00
16	Wendy the Witch	60.00
17	Sad Sack's Army Life	30.00
18	Buzzy & the Crow	20.00
19	Little Audrey	30.00
20	Casper & Spooky	40.00
21	Wendy the Witch	30.00
22	Sad Sack's Army Life	22.00
23	Wendy the Witch	30.00
24	Little Dot's Uncles	45.00
25	Herman & Katnip	15.00
26	The Phantom	125.00
27	Wendy the Good Little Witch	25.00
28	Sad Sack's Army Life	15.00
29	Harvey-Toon	20.00
30	Wendy the Witch	20.00
31	Herman & Katnip	10.00
32	Sad Sack's Army Life	15.00
33	Wendy the Witch	25.00
34	Harvey-Toon	15.00
35	Funday Funnies	10.00
36	The Phantom	125.00
37	Casper & Nightmare	14.00
38	Harvey-Toon	12.00
39	Sad Sack's Army Life	10.00
40	Funday Funnies	10.00
41	Herman & Katnip	10.00
42	Harvey-Toon	10.00
43	Sad Sack's Army Life	10.00
44	The Phantom	100.00
45	Casper & Nightmare	12.00
46	Harvey-Toon	10.00
47	Sad Sack's Army Life	10.00
48	The Phantom	100.00
49	Stumbo the Giant	50.00
50	Harvey-Toon	10.00
51	Sad Sack's Army Life	10.00
52	Casper & Nightmare	15.00
53	Harvey-Toons	10.00
54	Stumbo the Giant	25.00
55	Sad Sack's Army Life	10.00
56	Casper & Nightmare	12.00
57	Stumbo the Giant	25.00
58	Sad Sack's Army Life	10.00
59	Casper & Nightmare	12.00
60	Stumbo the Giant	25.00
61	Sad Sack's Army Life	10.00
62	Casper & Nightmare	12.00
63	Stumbo the Giant	22.00
64	Sad Sack's Army Life	10.00
65	Casper & Nightmare	10.00
66	Stumbo the Giant	22.00

67 Sad Sack's Army Life. 10.00		
68 Casper & Nightmare 10.00		
69 Stumbo the Giant. 22.00		
70 Sad Sack's Army Life 10.00		
71 Casper & Nightmare 10.00		
72 Stumbo the Giant. 22.00		
73 Little Sad Sack 10.00		
74 Sad Sack's Muttsy 10.00		
75 Casper & Nightmare 10.00		
76 Little Sad Sack 10.00		
77 Sad Sack's Muttsy 10.00		
78 Stumbo the Giant. 20.00		
79 Little Sad Sack 10.00		
80 Sad Sack's Muttsy 10.00		
81 Little Sad Sack 10.00		
82 Sad Sack's Muttsy 10.00		
83 Little Sad Sack 10.00		
84 Sad Sack's Muttsy 10.00		
85 Gabby Gob 10.00		
86 G.I. Juniors 10.00		
87 Sad Sack's Muttsy 10.00		
88 Stumbo the Giant. 20.00		
89 Sad Sack's Muttsy 8.00		
90 Gabby Goo 8.00		
91 G.I. Juniors 8.00		
92 Sad Sack's Muttsy 8.00		
93 Sadie Sack 8.00		
94 Gabby Goo 8.00		
95 G.I. Juniors 8.00		
96 Sad Sack's Muttsy 8.00		
97 Gabby Goo 8.00		
98 G.I. Juniors 8.00		
99 Sad Sack's Muttsy 8.00		
100 Gabby Goo 8.00		
101 G.I. Juniors 6.00		
102 Sad Sack's Muttsy 6.00		
103 Gabby Goo 6.00		
104 G.I. Juniors 6.00		
105 Sad Sack's Muttsy 6.00		
106 Gabby Goo 6.00		
107 G.I. Juniors 6.00		
108 Sad Sack's Muttsy 6.00		
109 Gabby Goo 6.00		
110 G.I. Juniors 6.00		
111 Sad Sack's Muttsy 6.00		
112 G.I. Juniors 6.00		
113 Sad Sack's Muttsy 6.00		
114 G.I. Juniors 6.00		
115 Sad Sack's Muttsy 6.00		
116 G.I. Juniors 6.00		
117 Sad Sack's Muttsy 6.00		
118 G.I. Juniors 6.00		
119 Sad Sack's Muttsy 6.00		
120 G.I. Juniors 6.00		
121 Sad Sack's Muttsy 6.00		
122 G.I. Juniors 6.00		

HATE
Fantagraphics
1 thru 15, see B&W
16 thru 29. . . . . @2.95
30 48pg. 3.95
TPB Hey, Buddy, rep. #1–#5. . . . 12.95
TPB Buddy the Dreamer, rep.
  #6–#10. . . . . 12.95
TPB Fun with Buddy and Lisa. . . . 12.95
TPB Buddy Go Home. 16.95
TPB Buddy's Got Three Moms . . . 16.95

HAUNTED
Charlton 1971–75
1 . . . . 20.00
2 . . . . 10.00
3 thru 5 . . . . @10.00
6 thru 10 . . . . @7.00
11 thru 20 . . . . @7.00

Haunted #55
© Charlton Comics

HAUNT OF FEAR
Gladstone
1 EC Rep. H of F #17,WS#28 . . . . 3.00
2 EC Rep. H of F #5,WS #29. . . . . 2.50

HAUNT OF FEAR
Russ Cochran 1991
1 EC Rep. H of F #15 . . . . 1.50
2 thru 5 EC Rep. H of F . . . . @1.50
Second Series 1992
1 EC Rep. H of F #14,WS#13 . . . . 2.25
2 EC Rep. H of F #18,WF#14 . . . . 2.00
3 EC Rep. H of F #19,WF#18 . . . . 2.00
4 EC Rep. H of F #16,WF#15 . . . . 2.00
5 EC Rep. H of F #5,WF#22 . . . . . 2.00
6 EC Rep. H of F. 2.00
7 EC Rep. H of F. 2.00
8 thru 15 Rep. . . . . @2.00
Gemstone
16 thru 28 EC comics reprint. . . . @2.50
"Annuals"
TPB Vol. 1 rebinding of #1–#5 . . . 8.95
TPB Vol. 2 rebinding of #6–#10 . . 8.95
TPB Vol. 3 rebinding of #11–#15. . 8.95
TPB Vol. 4 rebinding of #16–#20. . 12.95
TPB Vol. 5 rebinding of #21–#25. . 13.50
TPB Vol. 6 rebinding of #26–#28 . . 8.95

HAVE GUN, WILL TRAVEL
Dell Publishing Co. Aug., 1958
1 Richard Boone Ph(c) all 165.00
2 . . . . 100.00
3 . . . . 100.00
4 thru 14 . . . . @75.00

HAWKMOON,
COUNT BRASS
First
1 Michael Moorcock adapt. 1.95
2 . . . . 1.95
3 . . . . 1.95
4 . . . . 1.95

HAWKMOON
JEWEL IN THE SKULL
First
1 Michael Moorcock adapt. 3.00
2 . . . . 2.50

3 . . . . 2.00	
4 . . . . 2.00	

HAWKMOON,
MAD GOD'S AMULET
First
1 Michael Moorcock adapt. 2.00
2 . . . . 1.75
3 . . . . 1.75
4 . . . . 1.75

HAWKMOON,
SWORD OF THE DAWN
First
1 Michael Moorcock adapt. 2.00
2 thru 4 . . . . @1.75

HAWKMOON,
THE RUNESTAFF
First
1 Michael Moorcock adapt. 2.00
2 . . . . 2.00
3 . . . . 1.95
4 . . . . 1.95

HEADMAN
Innovation
1 . . . . 2.50
2 . . . . 2.50

HEARTSTOPPER
Millenium
1 V:Demons 2.95
2 V:Demons 2.95
3 F:Hellfire. 2.95

HEAVY METAL
MONSTERS
3-D-Zone
1 w/3-D glasses. 3.95

HECTOR HEATHCOTE
Gold Key March, 1964
1 . . . . 45.00

HELLINA
See Also *B&W*

HELLINA/
DOUBLE IMPACT
Lightning 1996
1-shot JCy(c). 3.00
1-shot variant (c) 3.00
1-shot nude cover 9.95
1-shot platinum edition, nude cover 9.95
1-shot spec. nude cover, signed. . 12.00

HELLINA:
HEART OF THORNS
Lightning Comics 1996
1 . . . . 3.00
1 nude cover editions 10.00
1 autographed edition 10.00
2 . . . . 3.00
2 variant cover. 3.00
2 platinum edition 5.95
2 nude cover editions 10.00

COLOR PUB.

HELLINA: HELLBORN
Lightning 1997
1 . . . . 2.95
1 autographed edition 9.95

HELLINA/NIRA X: ANGEL OF DEATH
Lightning 1996
1A cover A 3.00
1B cover B 3.00
1C Platinum cover. 9.00
1D signed 9.00

HELLINA/NIRA X: CYBERANGEL
Lightning
1 autographed edition 9.95

HERBIE
American Comics Group
April-May, 1964
1 . . . . 165.00
2 . . . . 75.00
3 . . . . 70.00
4 . . . . 70.00
5 A:Beatles,Dean Martin, Frank
   Sinatra. 100.00
6 . . . . 60.00
7 . . . . 60.00
8 O:Fat Fury 70.00
9 . . . . 60.00
10 . . . . 60.00
11 . . . . 40.00
12 . . . . 40.00
13 . . . . 40.00
14 A:Nemesis,Magic Man 40.00
15 thru 22 . . . . @40.00
23 Feb., 1967. . . . . 40.00

HERCULES
Charlton Comics Oct., 1967
1 . . . . 25.00
2 thru 7 . . . . @15.00
8 scarce 25.00
9 thru 13 Sept. 1969 . . . . 15.00

HERCULES: THE LEGENDARY JOURNEYS
Topps 1996
1 & 2. @3.00
3 RTs,JBt,SeM,The Shaper,pt.1 . . . 5.00
3a Xena Ph(c). 15.00
4 RTs,JBt,SeM,The Shaper,pt.2 . . . 5.00
5 RTs,JBt,SeM,The Shaper,pt.3 . . . 5.00

HERE COMES THE BIG PEOPLE
Event Comics 1997
1 ACo&JP(c) 2.95
1b JfD(c). 2.95
1c JQ&JP alternate (c) 9.95
1d JQ&JP alternate (c) signed . . . 29.95

HERO ALLIANCE
Wonder Color Comics 1987
1 . . . . 2.00
Innovation 1989–91
1 RLm,BS(c),R:HeroAlliance 6.00
2 RLm,BS(c),V:Rage 5.00
3 RLm,A:Stargrazers 4.00
4 . . . . 3.00

Hero Alliance #14
© Innovation

5 RLm(c). 2.50
6 BS(c),RLm pin-up. 3.25
7 V:Magnetron. 2.50
8 I:Vector. 2.50
9 BS(c),V:Apostate 2.50
10 A:Sentry 2.25
11 . . . . 2.25
12 I:Bombshell 2.25
13 V:Bombshell 2.25
14 Kris Solo Story. 2.25
15 JLA Parody Issue 2.25
16 V:Sepulchre. 2.25
17 O:Victor,I&D:Misty. 2.25
Annual #1 PS,BS,RLm 3.00
Spec.#1 Hero Alliance update. . . . 2.50
Spec.Hero Alliance & Justice Machine:
   Identity Crises 2.50

HERO ALLIANCE: THE END OF THE GOLDEN AGE
Pied Piper 1986
1 Bart Sears/Ron Lim 20.00
1a signed 25.00
1b 2nd printing 2.50
2 . . . . 12.00
3 . . . . 3.00
Graphic Novel 10.00
Innovation 1989
1 RLm 5.00
1A 2nd printing 2.50
2 RLm. 4.00
3 RLm. 3.00

HERO ALLIANCE QUARTERLY
Innovation
1 Hero Alliance stories. 2.75
2 inc."Girl Happy" 2.75
3 inc."Child Engagement" 2.75
4 . . . . 2.75

HI-SCHOOL ROMANCE DATE BOOK
Harvey Publications Nov., 1962
1 BP 18.00
2 . . . . 8.00
3 March, 1963 . . . . 8.00

HIGH CHAPPARAL
Gold Key Aug., 1968
1 . . . . 40.00

HIGH SCHOOL CONFIDENTIAL DIARY
Charlton Comics June, 1960
1 . . . . 20.00
2 thru 11 . . . . @10.00
Becomes:
CONFIDENTIAL DIARY
12 . . . . 10.00
13 thru 17 March, 1963. . . . . . . @8.00

HIGH VOLTAGE
Blackout 1996
0 . . . . 2.95

HILLBILLY COMICS
Charlton Comics Aug., 1955
1 . . . . 25.00
2 thru 4 July 1956 . . . . @12.00

HIS NAME IS ROG... ROG 2000
A Plus Comics
1 . . . . 1.75

HOBBIT, THE
Eclipse
1 . . . . 8.00
1a 2ndPrinting. 6.00
2 . . . . 7.00
2a 2ndPrinting. 5.00
3 . . . . 6.00

HOGAN'S HEROES
Dell Publishing Co. June, 1966
1 Ph(c) 80.00
2 Ph(c) 50.00
3 JD,Ph(c). 50.00
4 thru 8 Ph(c) . . . . @35.00
8 and 9 . . . . @35.00

HONEY WEST
Gold Key Sept., 1966
1 . . . . 120.00

HONEYMOONERS
Lodestone
1 . . . . 4.00
5 Mag.. 2.50
Triad [2nd Series]
1 "They Know What They Like" . . . 3.00
2 "The Life You Save" 2.50
3 X-mas special,inc.Art Carney
   interview. 3.50
4 "In the Pink" 3.00
5 "Bang, Zoom, To the Moon" . . . 2.00
6 "Everyone Needs a Hero" inc.
   Will Eisner interview 2.00
7 . . . . 2.00
8 . . . . 2.00
9 Jack Davis(c). 4.50
10 thru 13 . . . . @2.00

HONG KONG
Blackout Comics 1996
0 A:Hari Kari 2.95
0 limited commemorative edition . . 9.95

HOT COMICS PREMIERE
Hot Comics
1 F:Thunderkill, Jacknife 1.95

HOT ROD RACERS
Charlton Comics Dec., 1964
1 . . . . 75.00
2 thru 5 . . . . @50.00
6 thru 15 July 1967 . . . . @30.00

HOT STUFF,
THE LITTLE DEVIL
Harvey Publications Oct., 1967
1 . . . . 175.00
2 1st Stumbo the Giant 100.00
3 thru 5 . . . . @75.00
6 thru 10 . . . . @50.00
11 thru 20 . . . . @30.00
21 thru 40 . . . . @20.00
41 thru 60 . . . . @10.00
61 thru 100 . . . . @5.00
101 thru 105 . . . . @4.00
106 thru 112 52 pg Giants . . . . . @5.00
113 thru 172 . . . . @2.00

HOT STUFF SIZZLERS
Harvey Publications July, 1960
1 B:68 pgs. 90.00
2 thru 5 . . . . @50.00
6 thru 10 . . . . @30.00
11 thru 20 . . . . @25.00
21 thru 30 . . . . @20.00
31 thru 44 . . . . @10.00
45 E:68 pgs 8.00
46 thru 50 . . . . @6.00
51 thru 59 . . . . @5.00

HOTSHOTS
1 thru 4 . . . . @1.95

HOTSPUR
Eclipse
1 RT(i),I:Josef Quist 1.75
2 RT(i),Amulet of Kothique Stolen . 1.75
3 RT(i),Curse of the SexGoddess . 1.75

HOWARD CHAYKIN'S
AMERICAN FLAGG!
First
1 thru 9 . . . . @1.75
10 thru 12 . . . . @1.95

H.P.LOVECRAFT'S
CTHULHU
Millenium
1 I:Miskatonic Project,V:Mi-Go 2.50
2 Arkham, trading cards. 2.50

HUCK & YOGI JAMBOREE
Dell Publishing Co.
March, 1961
1 . . . . 100.00

HUCKLEBERRY HOUND
Charlton Nov., 1970
1 . . . . 25.00
2 thru 7 . . . . @15.00
3 Jan., 1972 . . . . 16.00

HUCKLEBERRY HOUND
Dell Publishing Co.
May-July, 1959
1 . . . . 100.00
2 . . . . 75.00
3 thru 7 . . . . @60.00
8 thru 10 . . . . @50.00
11 thru 17 . . . . @35.00
Gold Key
18 Chuckleberry Tales 60.00
19 Chuckleberry Tales 50.00
20 Chuckleberry Tales 40.00
21 thru 30 . . . . @20.00
31 thru 43 . . . . @10.00

HUEY, DEWEY & LOUIE
JUNIOR WOODCHUCKS
Gold Key Aug., 1966
1 . . . . 50.00
2 thru 5 . . . . @30.00
6 thru 17 . . . . @25.00
18 . . . . 15.00

Hot Stuff, The Little Devil #66
© Harvey Publications

19 thru 25 . . . . @18.00
26 thru 30 . . . . @15.00
31 thru 57 . . . . @15.00
58 . . . . 12.00
59 . . . . 12.00
60 thru 80 . . . . @8.00
81 1984 . . . . 8.00

HYBRIDS
Continuity
1 . . . . 2.50

HYBRIDS
Continuity
0 Deathwatch 2000 prologue 5.00
1 Deathwatch 2000 pt.4,w/card . . 2.50
2 Deathwatch 2000 pt.13,w/card . 2.50
3 Deathwatch 2000 w/card 2.50
4 A:Valeria. 2.50
5 O:Valeria 2.50

HYBRIDS: ORIGIN
Continuity
1 thru 5 . . . . 2.50

HYDE-25
Harris
1 New Drug. 2.95

I DREAM OF JEANNIE
Dell Publishing Co. April, 1965
1 Ph(c),B.Eden 125.00
2 Ph(c),B.Eden 110.00

I SPY
Gold Key Aug., 1966
1 Bill Cosby Ph(c) 250.00
2 Ph(c) 150.00
3 thru 4 AMc,Ph(c) . . . . @125.00
5 thru 6 Ph(c) Sept.1968 . . . . @125.00

I'M DICKENS –
HE'S FENSTER
Dell Publishing Co.
May-July, 1963
1 Ph(c) 50.00
2 Ph(c) 35.00

I-BOTS
Big Comics 1996
1 F:Lady Justice 2.25
2 thru 4 . . . . @2.25
5 StG(s),PB. 2.25
6 StG(s),PB. 2.25
7 PB,"Rebirth," pt.1, triptych (c) . . . 2.25
8 PB,"Rebirth," pt.2, triptych (c) . . . 2.25
9 PB,"Rebirth," pt.3, Original I
    Bots return, triptych (c) 2.25

ICICLE
Hero Graphics
1 A:Flare,Lady Arcane,
    V:Eraserhead. 4.95

IMP
1 . . . . 2.25

IMPACT
Gemstone 1999
1 EC Comic reprint 2.50
2 thru 5 . . . . @2.50
Annual #1 rep. #1–#5 . . . . 13.50
HC 20.00

INMATES:
PRISONERS OF SOCIETY
Delta Comics 1997
1 (of 4) 2.95
2 thru 4 . . . . @2.95

INNER CIRCLE
Mushroom Comics 1995
1.1 I:Point Blank 2.50
1.2 V:Deathcom. 2.50
1.3 V:Deathcom. 2.50
1.4 V:Deathcom. 2.50

INNOCENTS
Radical Comics 1995
1 I:Innocent. 2.50

INNOVATORS
Dark Moon
1 I:Innovator, LeoShan. 2.50

2 O:Mr. Void	2.50
3 I:Quill	2.50

INSANE CLOWN POSSE
Chaos Comics 1999

1	2.95
Spec. The Amazing Jeckel Brothers	2.95

INTERVIEW WITH A VAMPIRE
Innovation

1 based on novel,preq.to Vampire Chronicles	3.50
2	3.00
3 Death & Betrayal	3.00
4	3.00
5 D:Lestat	2.50
6 Transylvania Revelation	2.50
7 Louis & Claudia in Paris	2.50
8 thru 10	@2.50
11	2.50

INTERVIEW WITH A VAMPIRE
Innovation

1 based on novel, preq. to Vampire Chronicles	3.50
2	3.00
3 Death & Betrayal	3.00
4	3.00
5 D:Lestat	2.50
6 Transylvania Revelation	2.50
7 Louis & Claudia in Paris	2.50

INTIMATE
Charlton Comics Dec., 1957

1 thru 3	@20.00

Becomes:
TEEN-AGE LOVE

4	10.00
5 thru 9	@8.00
10 thru 35	@6.00
36 thru 96	@5.00

INTRUDER
TSR 1990–91

1 thru 4	@2.95
5 thru 8 The Next Dimension	@2.95

INVADERS FROM HOME
Piranha Press 1990

1 thru 6	@2.50

INVADERS, THE
Gold Key Oct., 1967

1 Ph(c),DSp.	100.00
2 Ph(c),DSp.	75.00
3 Ph(c),DSp.	75.00
4 Ph(c),DSp.	75.00

INVINCIBLE FOUR OF KUNG FU & NINJA
Victory

1	2.75
2 and 3	@2.50
4	1.80
5 thru 11	@2.00

IO
Invictus Studios

1 I:IO	2.25

2	2.25
3 V:Major Damage	2.25

IRON HORSE
Dell Publishing Co. March, 1967

1	25.00
2	25.00

Iron Jaw #3
© Atlas Comics

IRONJAW
Atlas Jan.–July , 1975

1 NA(c),MSy	10.00
2 NA(c)	8.00
3	8.00
4 O:IronJaw	8.00

IRON MARSHAL
Jademan

1	2.00
2	1.75
3	1.75
4	1.75
5	1.75
6 V:Bloody Duke	1.75
7	1.75
8	1.75
9 The Unicorn Sword	1.75
10 The Great Thor	1.75
11 A:Exterminator	1.75
12 Bloddy Duke vs. Exterminator	1.75
13 Secret of Unicorn Supreme	1.75
14 A:The Great Thor	1.75
15 A:The Great Thor	1.75
16 V:Tienway Champ	1.75
17 thru 20	1.75
21 Bloody Duke wounded	1.75
22 A:Great Thor	1.75
23	1.75
24	1.75
25	1.75
26 Iron Marshal Betrayed	1.75
27 thru 30	@1.75

IRREGULARS, THE: BATTLETECH Miniseries
Blackthorne

1	1.75
2	1.75
3 B&W	1.75

IRUKASHI
1	1.75

ISAAC ASIMOV'S I-BOTS
Tekno-Comix 1995

1 I:I-Bots	1.95
2 O:I-Bots	1.95
3 V:Black OP.	2.25

IT! TERROR FROM BEYOND SPACE
Millenium

1	2.50
2	2.50

IT'S ABOUT TIME
Gold Key Jan., 1967

1 Ph(c)	40.00

ITCHY & SCRATCHY
Bongo Comics

1 DaC(s),	2.25
2 DaC(s),	2.25

IVANHOE
Dell Publishing Co. July-Sept., 1963

1	30.00

JACK
Med Systems Company

1 Anubis in the 90's	2.95
2 Modern Society	2.95

JACK HUNTER
Blackthorne

1	1.25
2	1.25
3	1.25

JACKIE CHAN'S SPARTAN X
Topps 1997

1 "The Armor of Heaven," pt.1	2.95
2 "The Armor of Heaven," pt.2	2.95
3 (of 6)	2.95

JADEMAN COLLECTION
1	4.50
2	3.00
3	2.50
4	2.50
5	2.50

JADEMAN KUNG FU SPECIAL
1 I:Oriental Heroes, Blood Sword, Drunken Fist	5.00

JAGUAR GOD
Verotika 1995

1 Frazetta, I:Jaquar God	2.95
2 V:Yi-Cha	2.95
3 V:Yi-Cha	2.95
4 V:Yi-Cha	2.95
5 AOI	2.95
6 LSh,AOI	2.95
7 LSh,AOI	2.95
8 AOI	2.95
Spec.#1 Return to X'ibala,RCo	4.95

JAKE TRASH
Aircel
1 thru 3 . . . . @2.00

JAMES BOND 007
Eclipse
1 MGr,PerfectBound 5.50
2 MGr 5.00
3 MGr,end series 5.00
GN Licence to Kill, MGr l/o 8.00

JAMES BOND: GOLDENEYE
Topps 1995
1 Movie adaptation 2.95
2 thru 3 Movie adaptation . . . . . . @2.95

JAM SPECIAL
Comico
1 . . . . 2.50

JASON GOES TO HELL
Topps
1 Movie adapt.,w/3 cards 3.25
2 Movie adapt.,w/3 cards 3.25
3 Movie adapt.,w/3 cards 3.25

JASON VS. LEATHERFACE
Topps 1995
1 Jason Meets Leatherface 2.95
2 SBi(c) Leatherface's family 2.95
3 SBi(c),conclusion 2.95

JAVERTZ
Firstlight
1 New Series 2.95
2 thru 5 Pieces of an Icon 2.95

JET DREAM
Gold Key June, 1968
1 . . . . 35.00

JETSONS, THE
Gold Key Jan., 1963
1 . . . . 200.00
2 . . . . 125.00
3 thru 10 . . . . @100.00
11 thru 20 . . . . @65.00
21 thru 36 Oct. 1970 . . . . @50.00

JETSONS, THE
Charlton Comics Nov., 1970
1 from Hanna-Barbera TV show . . 65.00
2 . . . . 40.00
3 thru 10 . . . . @25.00
11 thru 20 Dec. 1973 . . . . @20.00

JETSONS, THE
Harvey Comics 1991–92
1 thru 5 . . . . @1.95

JETSONS, THE
Archie 1995
1 thru 17 . . . . @1.50

JEZEBEL JADE
Comico
1 AKu,A:Race Bannon 2.00

---

2 AKu 2.00
3 AKu 2.00

JIGSAW
Harvey Publications Sept., 1966
1 . . . . 6.00
2 . . . . 3.50

JIMBO
Bongo Comics
1 R:Jimbo 2.95
2 thru 4 . . . . @2.95

JIMMY CORRIGAN
Fantagraphics
1 Chris Ware 3.95

J. N. WILLIAMSON'S MASQUES
Innovation
1 TV,From horror anthology 4.95
2 Olivia(c) inc.Better Than One . . . 4.95

JOHN BOLTON, HALLS OF HORROR
Eclipse
1 JBo 1.75
2 JBo 1.75

JOHN F. KENNEDY LIFE STORY
(WITH 2 REPRINTS)
Dell Publishing Co.
Aug.-Oct., 1964
1 . . . . 50.00
2 . . . . 35.00
3 . . . . 35.00

JOHN JAKES MULLKON EMPIRE
Tekno Comix 1995
1 I:Mulkons 2.25
2 O:Mulkons 1.95
3 D:Company Man 1.95
4 Disposal Problems 1.95

John Jakes Mulkon Empire #6
© Tekno Comics

---

5 F:Granny 1.95
6 Where's Karma 2.25

JOHN LAW
Eclipse 1983
1 WE 2.00

JOHNNY GAMBIT
1 . . . . 1.75

JOHNNY JASON TEEN REPORTER
Dell Publishing Co. 1962
1 . . . . 25.00
2 . . . . 20.00

JOHNNY NEMO
Eclipse 1985–86
1 I:Johnny Nemo 2.00
2 . . . . 2.00
3 F:Sindy Shade 2.50

JOHN STEELE SECRET AGENT
Gold Key Dec., 1964
1 . . . . 100.00

JONNY QUEST
Gold Key Dec., 1964
1 TV show 350.00

JONNY QUEST
Comico June, 1986
1 DW,SR,A:Dr.Zin 4.50
2 WP/JSon,O:RaceBannon 3.50
3 DSt(c) 3.00
4 TY/AW,DSt(i) 2.50
5 DSt(c)A:JezebelJade 2.50
6 AKu 2.00
7 . . . . 2.00
8 KSy 2.00
9 MA 2.00
10 King Richard III 2.00
11 JSon,BSz(c) 1.50
12 DSp 1.50
12 DSp 1.50
13 CI 1.50
14 . . . . 1.50
15 thru 31 . . . . @1.75
Spec.#1 . . . . 1.75
Spec.#2 . . . . 1.75

JONNY QUEST CLASSICS
Comico
1 DW 2.00
2 DW,O:Hadji 2.00
3 DW 2.00

JON SABLE
First
1 MGr,A:President 4.50
2 MGr,Alcohol Issue 3.50
3 MGr,O:Jon Sable 3.00
4 MGr,O:Jon Sable 3.00
5 MGr,O:Jon Sable 3.00
6 MGr,O:Jon Sable 3.00
7 MGr,The Target 2.50
8 MGr,Nuclear Energy 2.50
9 MGr,Nuclear Energy 2.50
10 MGr,Triptych 2.50
11 MGr,I:Maggie 2.50

Jon Sable #14
© First

12 MGr,Vietnam	2.50
13 MGr,Vietnam	2.50
14 MGr,East Germany	2.50
15 MGr,Nicaragua	2.50
16 MGr,A:Maggie	2.50
17 MGr,1984 Olympics	2.50
18 MGr,1984 Olympics	2.50
19 MGr,,The Widow	2.50
20 MGr,The Rookie	2.50
21 MGr,Africa	2.25
22 MGr,V:Sparrow	2.25
23 MGr,V:Sparrow	2.25
24 MGr,V:Sparrow	2.25
25 MGr,Shatter	3.00
26 MGr,Shatter	3.00
27 MGr,Shatter	3.00
28 MGr,Shatter	3.00
29 MGr,Shatter	3.00
30 MGr,Shatter	2.25
31 MGr,Nicaragua	2.00
32 MGr,Nicaragua	2.00
33 MGr,SA,Leprechauns	2.25
34 MGr,Indians	2.00
35 MGr,Indians	2.00
36 MGr,Africa	2.00
37 MGr,Africa	2.00
38 MGr,Africa	2.00
39 MGr,Africa	2.00
40 MGr,1st Case	2.00
41 MGr,1st Case	2.00
42 MGr,V:Sparrow	2.00
43 MGr,V:Sparrow	2.00
44 Hard Way	2.00
45 Hard Way II	2.00
46 MM,The Tower pt.1	2.00
47 MM,The Tower pt.2	2.00
48 MM,Prince Charles	2.00
49 MM,Prince Charles	2.00
50 A:Maggie the Cat	2.00
51 Jon Sable,babysitter pt.1	2.00
52 Jon Sable,babysitter pt.2	2.00
53 MGr.	2.00
54 Jacklight pt.1	2.00
55 Jacklight pt.2	2.00
56 Jacklight pt.3	2.00

JOSIE
Archie Publications Feb., 1963

1	100.00
2	50.00
3	25.00
4	20.00
5	25.00

6 thru 10	@15.00
11 thru 20	@12.00
21 thru 30	@7.00
31 thru 40	@5.00
41 thru 54	@4.00
55 thru 74	@2.00
75 thru 105	@1.00
106 Oct., 1962	1.00

JUDGE COLT
Gold Key Oct., 1969

1	15.00
2	10.00
3	10.00
4 Sept., 1980	10.00

JUDGE DREDD
Eagle 1983

1 BB,I:Judge Death(in USA)	15.00
2 BB(c&a),The Oxygen Board	12.00
3 BB(c),Judge Dredd Lives	10.00
4 BB(c),V:Perps	10.00
5 BB(c),V:Perps	8.00
6 BB(c),V:Perps	8.00
7 BB(c),V:Perps	8.00
8 BB(c),V:Perps	8.00
9 BB(c),V:Perps	8.00
10 BB(c),V:Perps	8.00
11 BB(c)	5.00
12 BB(c)	5.00
13 BB(c), The Day the Law Died, pt.5	5.00
14 BB(c),Dredd vs. Dredd	5.00
15 BB(c)	5.00
16 BB(c)	5.00
17 BB(c)	5.00
18 BB(c)	5.00
19 BB(c)	5.00
20 BB(c)	5.00
21 BB(c)	5.00
22 BB(c),V:Perps	4.00
23 BB(c),V:Perps	4.00
24 BB(c),V:Perps	4.00
25 BB(c),V:Perps	4.00
26 BB(c),V:Perps	4.00
27 BB(c),V:Perps	4.00
28 A:Judge Anderson,V:Megaman	5.00
29 A:Monty, the guinea pig	4.00
30 V:Perps	4.00
31 Destiny's Angel, Pt. 1.	4.00
32 Destiny's Angel, Pt. 2.	4.00
33 V:League of Fatties	4.00
34 V:Executioner	4.00

JUDGE DREDD
Quality

1 Cry of the Werewolf Pt.1	7.00
2 Cry of the Werewolf Pt.2	5.00
3 Anti-smoking	4.00
4 Wreckers	4.00
5 Highwayman	4.00
6	3.00
7	3.00
8	3.00
9	3.00
10	3.00
11	3.00
12 Starborn Thing, Pt.1.	3.00
13 Starborn Thing, Pt.2.	3.00
14 BB, V:50 foot woman	3.00
15 City of the Damned Pt.1.	3.00
16 City of the Damned Pt.2.	3.00
17 City of the Damned conc.	3.00
18 V:Mean Machine Angel	3.00
19 Dredd Angel	3.00
20 V:Perps	3.00
21 V:Perps	3.00
22/23 Booby Trap	3.00

Judge Dredd #2
© Quality

24 Junk food fiasco	3.00
25/26 V:Perps	3.00
27 V:Perps	3.00
28 Dredd Syndrome	3.00
29 V:Perps	3.00
30 V:Perps	3.00
31 Hunt Pudge Dempsey's killer	3.00
32 V:Mutated Sewer Alligator	3.00
33 V:Perps	3.00
34 V:Executioner	3.00
35 V:Shojan	3.00
36 V:Shojan	3.00
37 V:Perps	3.00
38 V:Perps	3.00
39 V:Perps	3.00
40 V:Perps	3.00
41 V:Perps	3.00
42 V:Perps	3.00
43 V:Perps	3.00
44 V:Perps	3.00
45 V:DNA Man	2.50
46 Genie lamp sty	2.50
47 V:Perps	2.50
48 Murder in Mega-City One.	2.50
49 V:Perps	2.50
50 V:Perps	2.50
51 V:Perps	2.50
52 V:Perps	2.50
53 V:Perps	2.50
54 V:Perps	2.50
55 V:Perps	2.50
56 inc.JudgeDredd Postcards	2.50
57 V:Perps	2.50
58 V:370lb Maniac	2.50
59 V:Perps	2.50
60 Social Misfit	2.50
61 V:Perps	2.50
Becomes:	

JUDGE DREDD CLASSICS

62	2.50
63 Mutants from the Radlands	2.50
64	2.50
65	2.50
66 Wit and wisdom of Dredd.	2.50
67 V:Otto Sump	2.50
68 V:Otto Sump	2.50
69	2.50
70 Dinosaurs in Mega City 1.	2.50
71	2.50
72 Pirates o/t Black Atlantic	2.50
73	2.50
74	2.50
75	2.50
76 Diary of a Mad Citizen	3.00

COLOR PUB.

TPB:Democracy Now 10.95	
TPB:Rapture. 12.95	
Judge Dredd Special #1 . . . . 2.50	
GN Bad Science. 7.95	
GN Hall of Justice. 7.95	
GN Metal Fatigue. 7.95	

JUDGE DREDD: AMERICA
Fleetway
1 I:America 3.50

JUDGE DREDD: JUDGE CHILD QUEST
Eagle
1 thru 3 . . . . @3.00	
4 BB(c) 3.00	
5 . . . . 3.00	

JUDGE DREDD'S CRIME FILE
Eagle 1984
1 Ron Smith, "The Perp Runners" . 2.50	
2 thru 6 . . . . @2.50	

Quality (Prestige format)
1 A:Rogue Trooper 6.50	
2 IG,V:Fatties, Energy Vampires & Super Fleas 5.95	
3 Battles foes from dead A:Judge Anderson 5.95	

JUDGE DREDD'S EARLY CASES
Eagle
1 Robot Wars, Pt.1 . . . . 4.00	
2 Robot Wars, Pt.2 . . . . 3.00	
3 V:Perps 3.00	
4 IG, Judge Giant 3.00	
5 V:Perps 3.00	
6 V:Judge killing car Elvis 3.00	

JUDGE DREDD'S HARDCASE PAPERS
Fleetway/Quality
1 V:The Tarantula 7.50	
2 Junkies & Psychos 6.50	
3 Crime Call Vid. Show 6.50	
4 "Real Coffee",A:Johnny Alpha. . . 6.50	

JUDGE DREDD: THE MEGAZINE
Fleetway/Quality 1991
1 Midnite's Children Pt.1 A:Chopper, Young Death 5.25	
2 Midnite's Children Pt.2 . . . . 4.95	
3 . . . . 4.95	
23 thru 34 . . . . @3.95	
35 thru 43 . . . . @5.25	
44 thru 45 . . . . @6.95	

Egmont Fleetway Limited
46 thru 57 . . . . @6.95

JUDGE PARKER
Argo Feb., 1956
1 . . . . 25.00	
2 . . . . 15.00	

JUDGMENT DAY
Lightning Comics
1 B:JZy(s),KIK,V:Razorr,Rift,

Nightmare, red prism(c) 5.00	
1a Gold Prism(c) 5.00	
1b Purple Prism(c). 7.00	
1c Misprint,Red Prism(c), Bloodfire Credits inside 8.00	
1d Misprint,Gold Prism(c), Bloodfire Credits inside 8.00	
1e Misprint,Green Prism(c), Bloodfire Credits inside. 8.00	
1f B&W promo ed. Gold ink 5.00	
1g B&W promo ed. platinum ed. . . 7.00	
2 TLw,I:War Party,BU:Perg, w/Perg card 4.00	
3 ErP,O:X-Treme 3.25	
4 ErP,In Hell 3.25	
5 TLw,In Hell 3.25	
6 TLw,I:Red Front,O:Salurio. 3.25	
7 O:Safeguard. 3.25	
8 . . . . 2.95	
9 . . . . 2.95	
10 . . . . 2.95	

JUDGMENT DAY
Maximum Press 1997
Alpha AMo(s) 2.50	
Alpha variant cover 2.50	
Omega AMo(s). 2.50	
Omega variant cover 2.50	
Final Judgment AMo(s). 2.50	
Final Judgment variant cover 2.50	

JUDOMASTER
Charlton Comics
(Special War Series #4) I:Judomaster . . 15.00	
89 FMc,War stories begin 7.00	
89 (90) FMc,A:Thunderbolt 6.00	
91 FMc,DG,A:Sarge Steel 6.00	
92 FMc,DG,A:Sarge Steel 6.00	
93 FMc,DG,I:Tiger 6.00	
94 FMc,DG,A:Sarge Steel 6.00	
95 FMc,DG,A:Sarge Steel 5.00	
96 FMc,DG,A:Sarge Steel 5.00	
97 FMc,A:Sarge Steel. 4.00	
98 FMc,A:Sarge Steel. 4.00	

JUGHEAD
Archie Publications
Dec., 1965–June, 1987
127 thru 130 . . . . @12.00	
131 thru 150 . . . . @10.00	

Jughead #199
© Archie Publications

151 thru 160 . . . . @8.00	
161 thru 352. . . . . 1.50	

JUGHEAD
Archie Publications
[2nd Series] Aug., 1987
1 thru 45 . . . . @1.25
Becomes:

ARCHIE'S PAL JUGHEAD
June, 1993
46 thru 50. . . . . @1.25	
51 thru 70 . . . . @1.50	
71 thru 99 . . . . @1.50	
100 A Storm Over Uniforms, x-over (Betty #57, Archie #467). 1.50	
101 thru 122 . . . . @1.75	

JUGHEAD AS CAPTAIN HERO
Archie Publications Oct., 1966
1 . . . . 35.00	
2 . . . . 20.00	
3 thru 7 . . . . @15.00	

JUGHEAD'S FANTASY
Archie Publications Aug., 1960
1 . . . . 80.00	
2 . . . . 60.00	
3 . . . . 45.00	

JUGHEAD'S JOKES
Archie Publications Aug., 1967
1 . . . . 26.00	
2 . . . . 14.00	
3 thru 5 . . . . @7.00	
6 thru 10 . . . . @5.00	
11 thru 30 . . . . @2.00	
31 thru 77 . . . . @1.00	
78 Sept., 1982 . . . . 1.00	

JUGHEAD WITH ARCHIE DIGEST
Archie Publications March, 1974
1 . . . . 15.00	
2 . . . . 8.00	
3 thru 10 . . . . @5.00	
11 thru 91 . . . . @3.00	
130 thru 138 . . . . @3.00	
139 thru 144 . . . . @3.00	
145 thru 152 . . . . @2.00	

JUNGLE ADVENTURES
Skywald March–June 1971
1 F:Zangar,Jo-Jo,Blue Gorilla. . . . 20.00	
2 F:Sheena, Jo-Jo,Zangar 15.00	
3 F:Zangar,Jo-Jo,White Princess . 10.00	

JUNGLE BOOK, THE
NBM 1997
TPB by P. Craig Russell,
Kipling adapt. 16.95

JUNGLE COMICS
Blackthorne
1 DSt(c). 2.00	
2 . . . . 2.00	
3 . . . . 2.00	

COLOR PUB.

JUNGLE TALES OF TARZAN
Charlton Comics Dec., 1964
1 . . . . 50.00
2 . . . . 30.00
3 . . . . 30.00
4 July, 1965 . . . . 30.00

JUNGLE WAR STORIES
Dell Publishing Co.
July-Sept., 1962
1 P(c) all 25.00
2 . . . . 10.00
3 . . . . 10.00
4 . . . . 10.00
5 . . . . 10.00
6 . . . . 10.00
7 . . . . 10.00
8 . . . . 10.00
9 . . . . 10.00
10 . . . . 10.00
11 . . . . 10.00
Becomes:

GUERRILLA WAR
12 thru 14 . . . . @10.00

JUNIOR WOODCHUCKS
Walt Disney
1 CB,"Bubbleweight Champ" 2.00
2 CB,"Swamp of no Return". 2.00
3 "Rescue Run-Around". 2.00
4 "Cave Caper" 2.00

JURASSIC PARK
Topps
1 Movie Adapt.,w/card 5.00
1a Newsstand Ed. 4.00
2 Movie Adapt.,w/card 3.25
2a Newsstand Ed. 2.75
3 Movie Adapt.,w/card 3.25
3a Newsstand Ed. 2.75
4 Movie Adapt.,w/card 3.25
4a Newsstand Ed. 2.75
Ann.#1 Death Lizards 3.95

JURASSIC PARK: ADVENTURES
Topps
1 thru 10 reprints titles . . . . @1.95

JURASSIC PARK: RAPTOR
Topps
1 SE w/Zorro #0 ashcan & cards . . 3.25
2 w/3 cards. 2.95

JURASSIC PARK: RAPTORS ATTACK
Topps
1 SEt(s), ... 2.75
2 SEt(s), ... 2.75
3 SEt(s), ... 2.75
4 SEt(s), ... 2.75

JURASSIC PARK: RAPTOR HIJACK
Topps
1 SEt(s), ... 2.50
2 SEt(s), ... 2.50
3 SEt(s), ... 2.50
4 SEt(s), ... 2.50

[JURASSIC PARK:] THE LOST WORLD
Topps 1997
1 (of 4) movie adapt 2.95
2 thru 4 . . . . @2.95

JUSTICE MACHINE
Noble Comics 1981–85
1 JBy(c) Mag size,B&W 30.00
2 MGu,Mag size,B&W 16.00
3 MGu,Mag size,B&W 10.00
4 MGu,Bluecobalt 8.00
5 MGu. 7.00

Texas Comics
Ann.#1:BWG,I:Elementals,
   A: Thunder Agents 5.00

Justice Machine #3
© Comico

JUSTICE MACHINE
[Featuring the Elementals]
Comico 1986
1 thru 4 . . . . @2.50

JUSTICE MACHINE
Comico 1987–89
1 MGu. 2.50
2 MGu. 2.00
3 thru 14 MGu . . . . @1.50
15 thru 27 MGu . . . . @1.75
28 MGu 1.95
29 MGu,IW. 1.95
Ann.#1 . . . . 2.50
SummerSpectacular 1 . . . . 2.75
MINI SERIES 1990
1 thru 4 F:Elementals. . . . . @1.95
Innovation 1990
1 . . . . 1.95
2 thru 4 The Ragnarok Portfilio. . @1.95
5 thru 7 Demon trilogy . . . . @1.95

JUSTICE MACHINE: CHIMERA CONSPIRACY
Millenium
1 AH,R&N:Justice Machine,
   wraparound cover. 2.50

JUST MARRIED
Charlton Comics Jan., 1958
1 . . . . 35.00
2 . . . . 20.00
3 thru 10 . . . . @15.00
11 thru 30 . . . . @10.00
31 thru 113 . . . . @8.00
114 Dec., 1976. . . . . 8.00

KABOOM
Awesome Entertainment 1997
1 JLb,JMs,. 5.00
1a variant (c)s 6.00
2 JLb,JMs,. 3.00
3 JLb,JMs,. 4.00
4 JLb,JMs,Kaboom the
   Barbarian,pt.1 (of 3) 2.50
5 JLb,JMs,Barbarian,pt.2 . . . . . . 2.50
6 JLb,JMs,Barbarian,pt.3 . . . . . . 2.50
VOL II
1 (of 3) 2.50
2 JLe,JLb,F:Kyra 2.50
3 JLe,JLb, conclusion 2.50

KABUKI
Caliber Press
1 Color Gallery,32 paintings 3.00
1-shot Color Special, inc.
   pin-up gallery 3.00
1-shot Fear the Reaper (1994). . . 7.00

KABUKI: SKIN DEEP
Caliber
1 DMk. 2.95
2 DMk(c) 2.95
2 AxR(c) 2.95
3 Origin issue 2.95
4 . . . . 2.95

KATO OF THE GREEN HORNET
Now
1 BA,1st Kato solo story 2.50
2 BA,Kato in China contd. 2.50
3 Kato in China contd 2.50
4 Final Issue 2.50

KATO II
Now
1 VM,JSh,A:Karthage 2.50
2 VM,JSh,V:Karthage 2.50
3 VM,JSh,V:Karthage 2.50

KATY KEENE FASHION BOOK MAGAZINE
Archie Publications
1955
1 . . . . 375.00
2 . . . . 200.00
3 thru 10 not published
11 thru 18 . . . . @150.00
19 . . . . 125.00
20 . . . . 125.00
21 . . . . 125.00
22 . . . . 125.00
23 Winter 1958-59 . . . . 125.00

KATY KEENE PINUP PARADE
Archie Publications
1955
1 . . . . 375.00

Katy Keene Fashion Book #22
© Archie Publications

2	200.00
3	175.00
4	175.00
5	175.00
6	150.00
7	150.00
8	150.00
9	150.00
10	150.00
11 Story on comics	200.00
12	150.00
13	150.00
14	150.00
15 Sept., 1961	300.00

KELLY GREEN
Eclipse

1 SDr,O:Kelly Green	2.50
2 SDr,"One,Two,Three"	2.00
3 SDr,"Million Dollar Hit"	2.00
4 SDr,Rare	4.00

KELVIN MACE
Vortex

1	6.50
1a 2nd printing	1.75
2	4.00

KID DEATH & FLUFFY
Event Comics 1997

Spec.#1 Halloween Spec. John
  Cebollero(c) 2.95
Spec.#1a Halloween Spec. JQ(c) .. 2.95

KILLER TALES
Eclipse 1985

1 Tim Truman 1.75

KING COMICS PRESENTS
King Comics

1 I:Rick Dees, Angel Lopez 1.95

KING LEONARDO AND HIS SHORT SUBJECTS
Dell Publishing Co.
Nov.-Jan., 1961-62

1	125.00
2	100.00
3	100.00

4	100.00

KING LOUIE & MOWGLI
Gold Key May, 1968

1	30.00

KING OF DIAMONDS
Dell Publishing Co.
July-Sept., 1962

1 Ph(c)	40.00

KIT KARTER
Dell Publishing Co.
May-July, 1962

1	25.00

KNIGHTS OF THE ROUND TABLE
Dell Publishing Co.
Nov.-Jan., 1963-4

1 P(c)	35.00

KNUCKLES
Archie Comics

4 Lost Paradise	1.50
5	1.50
6 "Lost Paradise"	1.50
7 "Dark Vengeance"	1.50
8 "The Gauntlet"	1.50
9 x-over Sonic #56	1.75
10 "The Forgotten Tribe"	1.75
11 Sonic x-over	1.75
12 Sonic x-over	1.75
13 The Chaotix.	1.75
14 "A Tenuous Grip on Reality"	1.75
15 "The Chaotix Caper" concl.	1.75
16 "Reunions"	1.75
17 "The Guardian Who Failed"	1.75
18 "Debt of Honor"	1.75
19 "Whatever Happened to Queen Alicia"	1.75
20 "Once Upon A Time In Mobotropolis"	1.75
21 "The Many Facets of the Truth"	1.75
22 JV,"You Say You Want A Revolution"	1.75
23 JV,HMo,	1.75
24 JV,HMo "Primary Night"	1.75
25 "Childhood's End"	1.75
26 "The First Date"	1.75
27 "Who Wrote The Book Of Love, Anyway?"	1.75
28 The First Date, pt.3	1.75
29 "My Special Friend"	1.75
30 "King of the Hill," pt.1	1.75

KNUCKLES: THE DARK LEGION
Archie Comics 1997

1	1.50
2	1.50
3 (of 3)	1.50

KOL MANIQUE RENAISSANCE

1	1.50
2	1.50

KOMAH
Anubis Press

1 Urban Decay Title 2.75

KOMBAT
Random Comics

1 (of 2) by Marcu Marshall
  & Pablo Villalobos 2.95
2 concl 2.95

KONA
Dell Publishing Co.
Feb.-April, 1962

1 P(c) all,SG	50.00
2 SG	25.00
3 SG	25.00
4 SG,B:Anak	25.00
5 SG	25.00
6 SG	25.00
7 SG	25.00
8 SG	25.00
9 SG	25.00
10 SG	25.00
11 SG	20.00
12 SG	20.00
13 SG	20.00
14 SG	20.00
15 SG	20.00
16 SG	20.00
17 SG	20.00
18 SG	20.00
19 SG	20.00
20 SG	20.00
21 SG	20.00

KONGA
Charlton Comics 1960–65

1 SD,DG(c), movie adapt.	235.00
2 DG(c)	125.00
3 SD	100.00
4 SD	100.00
5 SD	100.00
6 thru 15 SD	@70.00
16 thru 23	@50.00

KONGA'S REVENGE
Charlton Comics

2 Summer, 1962	30.00
3 SD,Fall, 1964	40.00
1 Dec., 1968	17.00

KOOKIE
Dell Publishing Co.
Feb.-April, 1962

1	60.00
2	50.00

KORAK, SON OF TARZAN
Gold Key Jan., 1964

1	60.00
2 thru 11	@30.00
12 thru 21	@20.00
22 thru 30	@10.00
31 thru 40	@8.00
41 thru 44	@5.00
45 Jan., 1972	5.00
Continued by DC	

KRUSTY COMICS
Bongo Comics

1 Rise and Fall of Krustyland	2.25
2 Rise and Fall of Krustyland	2.25
3 Rise and Fall of Krustyland	2.25

COLOR PUB.

KULL IN 3-D
Blackthorne
1	2.50
2	2.50
3	2.50

KUNG FU & NINJA
1	1.80
2	1.80
3	1.80
4	1.80

LAD: A DOG
Dell Publishing Co. 1961
1	30.00
2	25.00

LADY ARCANE
Hero Graphics
1 A: Flare,BU:O:Giant	4.95
2 thru 3	2.95

LADY DEATH
Chaos! Comics
1 BnP, A:Evil Ernie	50.00
1a signed gold foil	70.00
2 BnP	30.00
3 BnP	16.00
HC Foil Stamped Rep. #1-#3	24.95
TPB Rep. #1-#3	6.95
TPB The Reckoning	12.95
TPB The Reckoning, revised, BnP,Shu	12.95

Specials & 1-shots
1 Swimsuit Edition	12.00
1a Velvet Edition	30.00
1 reprint with 8-page pin-up gallery	2.95
1 Lady Death in Lingerie, various artists	5.00
1 Lady Death & the Women of Chaos! Gallery, pin-ups (1996)	2.25
1-shot Dragon Wars (1998)	2.95
1-shotA Dragon Wars, Premium Ed, Sketchbook cover	15.00
1-shot Retribution (1998)	2.95
1-shotA Retribution (1998) variant cover	2.95
1-shotB Retribution, premium ed.	10.00

LADY DEATH
Chaos! Comics 1998
½ signed, limited	30.00
1	3.00
1a signed, limited	20.00
2 R:Lady Demon	3.00
3 V:Levithia	3.00
4 V:Pagan	3.00
5 The Harrowing, pt.1	3.00
6 V:Uriel	3.00
7 V:Moloch	3.00
8 time to sieze Hell	3.00
9 world scythe of the covenant	3.00
10 Goddess War,pt.2 x-over	3.00
11 V:Cremator	3.00
12 Unholy Nights	3.00
13 MD2,DQ,Inferno, pt.1.	3.00
13a signed	19.95
14 MD2,DQ,Inferno, pt.2.	2.95
15 MD2,DQ,Inferno, pt.3.	2.95
15a variant cover	6.00
16 MD2,DQ,Inferno, pt.4.	2.95
Swimsuit Spec.#1, signed	20.00

LADY DEATH: BETWEEN HEAVEN & HELL
Chaos! Comics
1 V:Purgatori	6.00
1a Limited Edition 5,000c.	30.00
1b premium velvet cover, signed	50.00
2 Lives As Hope	4.00
3 V:Purgatori	4.00
4 final issue	4.00
TPB	12.95

Lady Death The Crucible #4
© Chaos Comics

LADY DEATH: THE CRUCIBLE
Chaos! Comics 1996
1 (of 6) BnP,SHu,	3.50
1 leather limited edition	18.00
2 BnP,SHu,	3.50
3 BnP,SHu,	3.50
4 BnP,SHu,	3.50
5 BnP,SHu,	3.50
6 BnP,SHu,V:Genocide,concl.	2.95

LADY DEATH: DEATH BECOMES HER
Chaos! Comics 1997
0 follows the *Crucible*, leads to *Wicked Ways*	2.95

LADY DEATH: THE ODYSSEY
Chaos! Comics 1996
Sneak Peek Preview	1.50
1 embossed cover	8.00
1 SHu(c) premium edition	22.00
2	4.00
3	4.00
4	4.00
4a variant cover	20.00
Micro Premium Preview Book	15.00
TPB	9.95

LADY DEATH: THE RAPTURE
Chaos! Comics 1999
1 (of 4) BnP,V:Father Orbec.	2.95
1a dynamic forces cover	6.95
1b dynamic forces, signed	19.95
1c premium edition	10.00

2 Heaven vs. Hell	2.95
3 V:Asteroth	2.95
4 BnP	2.95

LADY DEATH/ VAMPIRELLA: DARK HEARTS
Chaos!/Harris 1999
Spec. x-over, 40-page.	3.50
Spec. Premium Edition	10.00

LADY PENDRAGON
Maximum Press 1996
1 mini-series	2.50
2	2.50
3 (of 3) MD2	2.50

LADY RAWHIDE
Topps 1995
1 All New Solo series	5.00
2 It Can't Happen Here,pt.2	3.50
3	3.00
4	3.00
5 conclusion	3.00
Spec.#1 Rep. Zorro #2-#3	6.50

LADY RAWHIDE
Topps
Mini-Series
1 DMG	4.00
1a DMG,signed, numbered	9.95
2 DMG	2.95
3 DMG	2.95
4 DMG, EM, "Intimate Wounds".	2.95
5 DMG, EM.	2.95
6 DMG	2.95
7 DMG	2.95
TPB	10.95

LADY RAWHIDE: OTHER PEOPLE'S BLOOD
Topps 1996
Mini-Series
1 DMG,EM,"A Slice of Breast".	2.95

LADY VAMPRE
Blackout 1995
0 B&W	3.50
1	3.00

LANCELOT STRONG, THE SHIELD
Red Circle 1983
1 A:Steel Sterling.	3.50
2 A:Steel Sterling.	2.00
3 AN/EB,D:Lancelot Strong	2.00

LAND BEFORE TIME, THE
Kitchen Sink 1998
1-shot 3-D Adventure	3.95

LARS OF MARS
Eclipse 1987
1 3-D MA.	2.50

LASER ERASER & PRESSBUTTON
Eclipse 1985–87
1 GL,R:Laser Eraser	1.75

2 GL 1.75
3 GL,CK,"Tsultrine" 1.75
4 MC,"Death". 1.75
5 MC,JRy,"Gates of Hell" 95
6 "Corsairs of Illunium" 95
3-D#1 MC,GL(c),"Triple Cross" 1.50

LASH LARUE WESTERN
AC Comics
1 . . . . 3.50
Annual 2.95

LAST OF THE
VIKING HEROES
Genesis West
1 JK 4.00
2 JK 3.50
3 . . . . 3.00
4 . . . . 2.50
5A sexy cover 3.00
5B mild cover 2.50
6 . . . . 2.50
7 AA(c) 3.50
8 . . . . 2.25
9 Great Battle of Nidhogger. 2.50
10 "Death Among the Heroes" 2.50
Summer Spec.#1 FF,JK 3.50
Summer Spec.#2 . . . . 3.00
Summer Spec.#3,A:TMNT 2.50

LAUGH
Archie 1987–91
1 thru 29 . . . . @1.00

LAUREL AND HARDY
Dell Publishing Co. Oct., 1962
1 . . . . 55.00
2 . . . . 40.00
3 . . . . 40.00
4 . . . . 40.00

LAUREL & HARDY
Gold Key Jan., 1967
1 . . . . 50.00
2 Oct., 1967 . . . . 35.00

LAWMAN
Dell Publishing Co. Feb., 1959
1 Ph(c) all 125.00
2 . . . . 75.00
3 ATh 80.00
4 . . . . 50.00
5 . . . . 50.00
6 . . . . 50.00
7 . . . . 50.00
8 thru 11 . . . . @50.00

LAW AND ORDER
Maximum Press 1995
1 MMy,D:Law,I:New Law, Order. . . 2.50
2 V:Max Spur 2.50
3 V:Law's Murderer 2.50

LAW OF DREDD
Quality
1 V:Perps 5.00
2 BB,Lunar Olympics. 4.00
3 BB,V:Judge Death 3.00
4 V:Father Earth 3.00
5 Cursed Earth 3.00
6 V:Perps 3.00
7 V:Perps 3.00

Law and Order #1
© *Maximum Press*

Fleetway
8 Blockmania. 3.00
9 BB,DGi,Framed for murders 3.00
10 BB,Day the Law Died Pt.1 . . . . . 2.50
11 BB,Day the Law Died Pt.2 . . . . . 2.50
12 BB,V:Judge Cal 2.50
13 V:Judge Caligula 2.50
14 BB, V:Perps. 2.50
15 Under investigation 2.50
16 V:Alien Mercenary 2.50
17 thru 24 . . . . @2.50
25 Ugly Clinic. 2.50
26 Judge Dredd & Gavel? 2.50
27 Cycles,Lunatics & Graffiti
   Guerillas. 2.50
28 Cadet Training Mission 2.50
29 "Guinea Pig that changed the world .
2.50
30 Meka-City,V:Robot 2.50
31 Iso-Block 666. . . . . 2.50
32 Missing Game Show Hosts 2.50
33 League of Fatties,final issue . . . 3.00

LAZARUS
CHURCHYARD
Tundra
1 From UK Blast anthology 4.50
2 Goodnight Ladies 4.50

LEAGUE OF
CHAMPIONS
Hero Graphics
{Cont. from Champions #12}
1 Olympus Saga #4 . . . . 2.95
2 Olympus Saga #5,O:Malice 2.95
3 Olympus Saga ends 2.95

LEAGUE OF EXTRA-
ORDINARY GENTLEMEN
Wildstorm/DC 1999
America's Best Comics
1 (of 6) AMo(s),KON 3.00
2 AMo(s),KON. 3.00
3 AMo(s),KON. 3.00
4 AMo(s),KON. 3.00
GN Collected Edition 6.00

LEATHERFACE
North Star
1 thru 3 . . . . @2.75

LEGACY
Majestic
0 platinum 12.50
1 I:Legacy 2.25
2 . . . . 2.25

LEGACY
Antarctic Press 1999
1 by Fred Perry 3.00

LEGEND OF CUSTER, THE
Dell Publishing Co. Jan., 1968
1 Ph(c) 25.00

LEGEND OF
SLEEPY HOLLOW
Tundra
One shot.BHa,W.Irving adapt.. . . . . 6.95

LEGEND OF
THE ELFLORD
Davdez Arts 1998
1 by Barry Blair & Colin Chan 2.95
2 . . . . 2.50
3 . . . . 2.95
4 . . . . 2.95
GN Vol. 1 112-page 11.95

LEGENDS OF
JESSE JAMES, THE
Gold Key Feb., 1966
1 . . . . 30.00

LEGENDS OF LUXURA
Comic Cavalcade 1998
Commemorative #1 by Kirk Lindo . . 5.95
Commemorative #1a deluxe 14.95

LEGENDS OF NASCAR
Vortex
1 HT,Bill Eliott ($1.50 cover Price)
   15,000 copies. ñ25.00
1a ($2.00 cover price) 45,000
   copies ñ8.00
1b 3rd pr., 80,000 copies. 5.00
2 Richard Petty 5.00
3 Ken Schroder 3.50
4 Bob Alison 3.00
5 Bill Elliott 2.50
6 Jr. Johnson. 2.50
7 Sterling Marlin 2.25
8 Benny Parsons. 2.00
9 Rusty Wallace 2.00

LEGENDS OF THE
STARGRAZERS
Innovation
1 thru 5 . . . . @1.95

LEJENTIA
1 . . . . 1.95
2 . . . . 2.25

LEMONADE KID
AC Comics
1 . . . . 2.50

LEONARD NIMOY'S
PRIMORTALS
Teckno-Comics 1994
1 I:Primortals. 5.50
2 Zeerus Reveals Himself 4.00
3 Contact 2.50
4 Message Deciphered 2.25
5 Place & Time Announced 2.25
6 Zeerus Arrives on Earth 2.25
7 Zeerus Recieved 2.25
8 Hyperspace Escape 2.25
9 Pristar Lands on Earth 1.95
10 V:U.S. Army. 1.95
11 V:U.S. Army. 1.95
12 V:Zeerus 2.25
13 thru 15 . . . . @2.25
Big Entertainment April 1996
0 SEa,MKb 2.25
1 . . . . 2.25
2 KWo,ANi 2.25
3 KWo,ANi 2.25
4 KWo,ANi 2.25
5 KWo,ANi 2.25
6 KWo,"Scorched Earth," concl. . . . 2.25
7 PB,KWo&ANi(c),Zeerus & Narab
   together again 2.25

LEONARDO
Mirage
1 TMNT Character 5.00

LEOPARD
Millenium
1 I:Leopard 2.95
1a Gold Cover. 3.95
2 O:Leopard,V:Razor's Edge 2.95

LETHAL STRYKE
London Night Studios 1995
1 F:Stryke 3.00
1a commemorative (1999) 5.95
2 O:Stryke 3.00
Ann. #1 EHr 3.00
Ann. #1 platinum edition 10.00

LETHAL STRIKE/
DOUBLE IMPACT:
LETHAL IMPACT
London Night April 1996
1 by Jude Millien 3.00
1 limited 5.00
1 nude edition 6.00

LIBERTY PROJECT, THE
Eclipse 1987–88
1 I:Liberty Project 2.50
2 . . . . 1.75
3 V:Silver City Wranglers. 1.75
4 . . . . 1.75
5 . . . . 1.75
6 F:Cimarron,"Misery and Gin". . . . 1.75
7 I:Menace 1.75
8 V:Savage 1.75

LIDSVILLE
Gold Key Oct., 1972
1 . . . . 20.00
2 . . . . 10.00

---

3 and 4 . . . . @10.00
5 Oct., 1973 . . . . 10.00

LIEUTENANT, THE
Dell Publishing Co.
April-June, 1962
1 Ph(c) 35.00

LIFE & ADVENTURES
OF SANTA CLAUS
Tundra
GN MP,L.Frank Baum adapt. 24.95

LIFE IN HELL
Blackthorne
1 3-D. 2.50

LIFE WITH ARCHIE
Archie Publications Sept., 1958
1 . . . . 250.00
2 . . . . 125.00
3 . . . . 75.00
4 . . . . 75.00
5 . . . . 75.00
6 . . . . 40.00
7 . . . . 40.00
8 . . . . 40.00
9 . . . . 40.00
10 . . . . 40.00
11 thru 20 . . . . @25.00
21 thru 30 . . . . @20.00
31 thru 40 . . . . @15.00
41 . . . . 7.00
42 B:Pureheart. 5.00
43 . . . . 5.00
44 . . . . 5.00
45 . . . . 5.00
46 O:Pureheart. 15.00
47 thru 59 . . . . @3.50
60 thru 100 . . . . @2.50
101 thru 285 . . . . @1.00

LIGHT FANTASTIC, THE
Innovation
1 Terry Pratchett adapt. 2.50
2 Adaptation continues 2.50
3 Adaptation continues 2.50
4 Adapt.conclusion 2.50

LIGHTNING COMICS
PRESENTS
Lightning Comics
1 B&W Promo Ed. 3.50
1a B&W Promo Ed. Platinum. 3.50
1b B&W Promo Ed. Gold. 3.50

LILLITH:
DEMON PRINCESS
Antarctic Press 1996
1 (of 3) from Warrior Nun Areala . . 2.95
1a Commemorative Edition (1999) . 5.95
2 and 3 . . . . @2.95

LINCOLN-16
Skarwood Productions
1 GI. 2.95
2 GI. 2.95
3 GI. 2.95

LINDA LARK
Dell Publishing Co.
Oct.-Dec., 1961
1 . . . . 25.00
2 . . . . 15.00
3 . . . . 15.00
4 . . . . 15.00
5 . . . . 15.00
6 . . . . 15.00
7 . . . . 15.00
8 . . . . 15.00

LINUS, THE
LIONHEARTED
Gold Key Sept., 1965
1 . . . . 100.00

LIONHEART
Awesome Entertainment 1999
1 IaC,JLb, from *The Coven* 2.50
2 IaC,MLb 2.50
2a variant cover. 2.50
2b variant IaC cover 6.95

LIPPY THE LION AND
HARDY HAR HAR
Gold Key March, 1963
1 . . . . 100.00

LISA COMICS
Bongo Comics
1 F:Lisa Simpson 2.25

LITTLE AMBROSE
Archie Publications Sept., 1958
1 . . . . 100.00

LITTLE ARCHIE
Archie Publications
1956
1 . . . . 300.00
2 . . . . 150.00
3 . . . . 100.00
4 . . . . 100.00
5 . . . . 100.00
6 thru 10 . . . . @75.00

Little Archie #137
© Archie Publications

COLOR PUB.

11 thru 20	@40.00
21 thru 30	@25.00
31 thru 40	@15.00
41 thru 60	@10.00
61 thru 80	@5.00
81 thru 100	@3.00
101 thru 180	@2.00

LITTLE ARCHIE MYSTERY
Archie Publications May, 1963

1	100.00
2 Oct., 1963	50.00

LITTLE AUDREY & MELVIN
Harvey Publications May, 1962

1	80.00
2 thru 5	@30.00
6 thru 10	@25.00
11 thru 20	@20.00
21 thru 40	@10.00
41 thru 50	@7.00
51 thru 53 52 pgs Giant size	@7.00
54 thru 60	@10.00
61 Dec., 1973	8.00

LITTLE AUDREY TV FUNTIME
Harvey Publications Sept., 1962

1 A:Richie Rich	60.00
2 same	30.00
3 same	20.00
4	20.00
5	20.00
6 thru 10	@10.00
11 thru 20	@7.00
21 thru 32	@5.00
33 Oct., 1971	5.00

LITTLE DOT DOTLAND
Harvey Publications July, 1962

1	100.00
2	40.00
3	35.00
4	30.00
5	30.00
6 thru 10	@25.00
11 thru 20	@15.00
21 thru 50	@5.00
51 thru 60	@3.00
61 Dec., 1973	3.00

LITTLE DOT'S UNCLES & AUNTS
Harvey Enterprises Oct., 1961

1	90.00
2	50.00
3	40.00
4	30.00
5	30.00
6 thru 10	@25.00
11 thru 20	@22.00
21 thru 40	@15.00
41 thru 51	@7.00
52 April, 1974	7.00

LITTLE LOTTA
Harvey Publications Nov., 1955

1 B:Richie Rich and Little Lotta	250.00
2	150.00
3	120.00
4	70.00
5	70.00

6	50.00
7	50.00
8	50.00
9	50.00
10	50.00
11 thru 20	@30.00
21 thru 40	@20.00
41 thru 60	@15.00
61 thru 80	@7.00
81 thru 99	@5.00
100 thru 103 52 pgs	@3.00
104 thru 120	@2.00
121 May, 1976	2.00

LITTLE LOTTA FOODLAND
Harvey Publications Sept., 1963

1 68 pgs	90.00
2	50.00
3	35.00
4	20.00
5	20.00
6 thru 10	@15.00
11 thru 20	@10.00
21 thru 26	@7.50
27	5.00
28	5.00
29 Oct., 1972	5.00

LITTLE MERMAID
Walt Disney

1 based on movie	1.75
2 "Serpent Teen"	1.50
3 "Guppy Love"	1.50
4	1.50

LITTLE MONSTERS, THE
Gold Key Nov., 1964

1	45.00
2	25.00
3 thru 10	@15.00
11 thru 20	@10.00
21 thru 43	@10.00
44 Feb., 1978	10.00

LITTLE MONSTERS
Now

1 thru 6	@1.75

Little Monsters © Gold Key Comics

LITTLE REDBIRDS

1	2.50
2 thru 4	@2.50

LITTLE SAD SACK
Harvey Publications Oct., 1964

1 Richie Rich(c)	30.00
2	10.00
3	10.00
4	10.00
5	10.00
6 thru 19 Nov. 1967	@10.00

LITTLE STOOGES, THE
Gold Key Sept., 1972

1	25.00
2	12.00
3	12.00
4	12.00
5	12.00
6 and 7 March, 1974	@12.00

LLOYD LLEWELLYN

1	2.00

LOBO
Dell Publishing Co. Dec., 1965

1	25.00
2	20.00

LOCKE
Blackthorne

1 PO.Jones	1.75
2 TD	2.25
3	1.25
4	1.25
5	1.25

LONE RANGER, THE
Gold Key Sept., 1964

1	50.00
2	25.00
3	20.00
4	20.00
5	20.00
6 thru 10	@15.00
11 thru 18	@15.00
18 thru 27	@12.00
28 March, 1977	12.00

LONE RANGER AND TONTO, THE
Topps 1994

1 JLd,TT,RM,The Last Battle	2.50
2 JLd,TT,RM	2.50
3 JLd,TT,RM, O:Lone Ranger	2.50
4 JLd,TT,RM, It Crawls	2.50
TPB rep. #1–#4	9.95

LOOKERS
Avatar

Combo Spec. 16pg	3.00
Combo Spec. nude cover, 16pg	5.00

LOST HEROES
Davdez Arts 1998

0 by Rob Prior, lost SF heroes	2.95
1 thru 5	@2.50
6	2.95
GN 5/6 56-page	7.95

LOST IN SPACE
Innovation
{based on TV series}
1 O:Jupiter II Project 3.00
2 "Cavern of IdyllicSummersLost" . 2.75
2a Special Edition 2.50
3 Do Not Go Gently into that Good
    Night',Bill Mumy script 2.50
4 "People are Strange" 2.50
5 The Perils of Penelope 2.50
6 Time Warp 2.50
7 thru 9 . . . . @2.50
10 inc.Afterthought 2.50
11 F:Judy Robinson 2.50
12 . . . . 2.95
Project Krell 2.50
Ann.#1 (1991) 2.95
Ann.#2 (1992) 2.95
1Spec.#1 & #2 rep. Seduction of
    the Innocent . . . . @2.50
GN Strangers among Strangers . . . 6.00
1-shot Project Robinson, follows
    story in issue #12 (1993) 2.50
Becomes:

LOST IN SPACE:
VOYAGE TO THE
BOTTOM OF THE SOUL
Innovation 1993–94
13 . . . . 2.95
14 thru 18 . . . . @2.50

LOST PLANET
Eclipse 1987–88
1 BHa,I:Tyler FLynn 2.00
2 BHa,R:Amelia Earhart 1.75
3 BHa 1.25
4 BHa,"Devil's Eye" 1.25
5 BHa,A:Amelia Earhart 2.00
6 . . . . 2.00

LOVECRAFT
Adventure Comics
1 "The Lurking Fear" adapt 2.95
2 Beyond the Wall of Sleep 2.95
3 . . . . 2.95
4 . . . . 2.95

LOVE DIARY
Charlton Comics July, 1958
1 . . . . 40.00
2 . . . . 25.00
3 . . . . 20.00
4 . . . . 20.00
5 . . . . 15.00
6 . . . . 20.00
7 thru 10 . . . . @15.00
11 thru 15 . . . . @7.00
16 thru 20 . . . . @7.00
21 thru 40 . . . . @4.00
41 thru 101 . . . . @3.00
102 Dec., 1976 . . . . 3.00

LOVE SHOWDOWN
COLLECTION
Archie Comics 1997
TPB x-over rep. Archie #429 (pt.1),
    Betty #19 (pt.2), Betty & Veronica
    #82, (pt.3), Veronica #39 (pt.4)
    Return of Cheryl Blossom 4.95

LUCIFER'S HAMMER
Innovation 1993–94
1 thru 6 Larry Niven & Jerry

Pournelle novel adaptation . . @2.50

LUCY SHOW, THE
Gold Key June, 1963
1 Ph(c) 150.00
2 Ph(c) 75.00
3 thru 5 . . . . @60.00

LUDWIG VON DRAKE
Dell Publishing Co.
Nov.-Dec., 1961
1 . . . . 75.00
2 thru 4 . . . . @50.00

LUFTWAFFE 1946
Antarctic Press 1998
1 color special, by Ted Namura . . . 2.95

LUGER
Eclipse 1986–87
1 TY,I:Luger,mini-series 2.00
2 TY 1.75
3 TY,BHa,V:Sharks 1.75

LUNATIC
1 and 2 . . . . @1.75

LUNATIC FRINGE
Innovation
1 . . . . 1.95
2 . . . . 1.75

LUNATIC FRINGE
Innovation
1 . . . . 1.75

LUXURA
Comic Cavalcade 1998
Commemorative #1 by Kirk Lindo . . 5.95
Commemorative #1a deluxe 14.95

LUXURA COLLECTION
Brainstorm
Commemorative edition, red foil
    cover, 48pg. 10.00

Lynch Mob #1
© Chaos Comics

LYNCH MOB
Chaos! Comics
1 GCa(c), I:Mother Mayhem 3.00
2 Lynch Mob Loses 2.50
3 1994 Time Trip 2.50
3a Gold cover 3.00
4 Mother Mayhem at UN 2.50

LYNDON B. JOHNSON
Dell Publishing Co. March,
1965
1 Ph(c) 25.00

M
Eclipse 1990–91
1 thru 4 JMu 4.95

M.D.
Gemstone 1999
1 (of 5) New Direction 2.50
2 . . . . 2.50

MACROSS
Comico
1 . . . . 12.00
Becomes:

ROBOTECH, THE
MACROSS SAGA

MAD FOLLIES
E.C. Comics
1963
(N#) 275.00
2 1964 . . . . 200.00
3 1965 . . . . 150.00
4 1966 . . . . 165.00
5 1967 . . . . 125.00
6 & 7 1968 and 1969 . . . . @100.00

MAD HOUSE
Red Circle 1974–82
95 thru 97 Horror stories . . . . . @10.00
98 thru 130 Humor stories . . . . . @5.00
Annual #8 thru #11 . . . . @6.00

MADMAN
Tundra 1992
1 . . . . 15.00
2 . . . . 15.00
3 . . . . 10.00

MADMAN ADVENTURES
Tundra 1992
1 R & N:Madman 10.00
2 . . . . 8.00
3 . . . . 8.00

MADRAVEN
HALLOWEEN SPECIAL
Hamilton Comics 1995
1 Song of the Silkies 2.95

MAD SPECIAL
E.C. Publications, Inc.
Fall, 1970
1 . . . . 75.00
2 . . . . 50.00
3 . . . . 35.00
4 thru 8 . . . . @35.00

9 thru 13	@30.00
14	20.00
15	25.00
16	20.00
17	20.00
18	22.00
19 thru 21	@22.00
22 thru 31	@10.00
32	12.00
33 thru 58	@8.00

MAGE
Comico
1 MWg,I:Kevin Matchstick	20.00
2 MWg,I:Edsel	10.00
3 MWg,V:Umbra Sprite	8.00
4 MWg,V:Umbra Sprite	8.00
5 MWg,I:Sean (Spook)	8.00
6 MWg,Grendel begins	22.00
7 MWg,Grendel	10.00
8 MWg,Grendel	6.00
9 MWg,Grendel	6.00
10 MWg,Grendel,Styx.	6.00
11 MWg,Grendel,Styx.	6.00
12 MWg,D:Sean,Grendel	6.00
13 MWg,D:Edsel,Grendel	6.00
14 MWg,Grendel,O:Kevin	6.00
15 MWg,D:Umbra Sprite.	12.00

MAGEBOOK
Comico
1 rep. Mage #1-4.	8.95
2 rep. Mage #5-8.	8.95

MAGIC FLUTE
Eclipse 1989
1 CR	4.95

MAGILLA GORILLA
Gold Key May, 1964
1	75.00
2 thru 10 Dec. 1968	@60.00

MAGILLA GORILLA
Charlton Comics Nov., 1970
1	50.00
2 thru 5	@25.00

MAGNUS:
ROBOT FIGHTER
Gold Key Feb., 1963
1 RM,I:Magnus,Teeja,A-1, I&B:Capt.Johner&aliens	250.00
2 RM,I:Sen.Zeremiah Clane.	125.00
3 RM,I:Xyrkol.	125.00
4 RM,I:Mekamn,Elzy	75.00
5 RM,The Immortal One	75.00
6 RM,I:Talpa	70.00
7 RM,I:Malev-6,ViXyrkol	85.00
8 RM,I:Outsiders(Chet, Horio, Toun, Malf)	70.00
9 RM, I:Madmot.	70.00
10 RM,Mysterious Octo-Rob.	70.00
11 RM,I:Danae,Neo-Animals.	50.00
12 RM,The Volcano Makers	50.00
13 RM,I:Dr Lazlo Noel	55.00
14 RM,The Monster Robs.	50.00
15 RM,I:Mogul Radur	50.00
16 RM,I:Gophs	50.00
17 RM,I:Zypex	50.00
18 RM,I:V'ril Trent.	50.00
19 RM,Fear Unlimited.	50.00
20 RM,I:Bunda the Great	50.00
21 RM, Space Spectre	50.00
22 Rep. #1	35.00

Magnus Robot Fighter #26
© Gold Key Comics

23 DSp,Mission Disaster	35.00
24 Pied Piper of North Am	35.00
25 The Micro Giants	35.00
26 The Venomous Vaper	35.00
27 Panic in Pacifica	35.00
28 Threats from the Depths	35.00
29 Rep. #7	16.00
30 Rep. #15	16.00
31 Rep. #14	16.00
32 Rep. #2	16.00
33 Rep. #21	16.00
34 Rep. #13	16.00
35 Rep. #6	16.00
36 Rep. #8	16.00
37 Rep. #11	16.00
38 Rep. #12	16.00
39 Rep. #16	16.00
40 Rep. #17	16.00
41 Rep. #18	16.00
42 Rep. #19	16.00
43 Rep. #20	16.00
44 Rep. #23	16.00
45 Rep. #24	16.00
46 Rep. #25	16.00

MAJOR DAMAGE
Invictus Studios
1 I:Major Damage	2.25
2 V:Godkin	2.25
3 First Contact Conclusion.	2.25

MAKABRE
Apocalypse
1 Gangsters	3.95

MALICE
Heroic Publishing
1 I:Queen of the Dead	1.95

MANDRAKE
THE MAGICIAN
King Comics 1966
1	50.00
2	30.00
3	30.00
4 A:Girl Phantom	30.00
5 Cape Cod Caper	30.00
6	30.00
7 O:Lothar	30.00
8	35.00

9 A:Brick Bradford	30.00
10 A:Rip Kirby	35.00

MAN FROM PLANET X
Planet X Prod.
1	3.00

MAN FROM U.N.C.L.E.
Gold Key Feb., 1965
1 "The Explosive Affair"	150.00
2 "The Forthur Cookie Affair"	100.00
3 "The Deadly Devices Affair"	60.00
4 "The Rip Van Solo Affair"	60.00
5 "Ten Little Uncles Affair"	60.00
6 "The Three Blind Mice Affair"	60.00
7 "The Pixilated Puzzle Affair" I:Jet Dream (back-up begins)	65.00
8 "The Floating People Affair"	60.00
9 "Spirit of St.Louis Affair"	60.00
10 "The Trojan Horse Affair"	60.00
11 "Three-Story Giant Affair"	50.00
12 "Dead Man's Diary Affair".	50.00
13 "The Flying Clowns Affair"	50.00
14 "Great Brain Drain Affair".	50.00
15 "The Animal Agents Affair".	50.00
16 "Instant Disaster Affair"	50.00
17 "The Deadly Visions Affair".	50.00
18 "The Alien Affair"	50.00
19 "Knight in Shining Armor Affair"	50.00
20 "Deep Freeze Affair"	50.00
21 rep. #10	40.00
22 rep. #7	40.00

MAN FROM U.N.C.L.E.
Entertainment
1 thru 11	1.50

MAN FROM U.N.C.L.E.
Millennium
1 The Birds of Prey Affair,pt.1	2.95
2 The Birds of Prey Affair,pt.2	2.95

MANGA SHI 2000
Crusade Entertainment 1997
1 (of 3) BiT, "Final Jihad" flip-book Shi: Heaven and Earth.	2.95
2 BiT, flip-book Tomoe: Unforgettable Fire preview	2.95
3 BiT, conclusion.	2.95

MANGLE TANGLE
TALES
Innovation
1	2.95

MANIFEST DESTINY
1	1.95

MAN IN BLACK
Harvey Publications Sept., 1957
1 BP	100.00
2 BP	75.00
3 BP	75.00
4 BP, March, 1958	75.00

MANIK
Millenium/Expand (1995)
1 I:Macedon, Arsenal,Cardinal.	2.95

MANKIND
Chaos! Comics 1999
1-shot StG.	2.95

All comics prices listed are for *Near Mint* condition.

1-shotA photo cover 2.95
1-shotB variant cover. 6.95
1-shotC variant cover, signed. . . . 60.00

MAN OF WAR
Eclipse 1987–88
1 thru 3 . . . . @1.75

MARK RAND'S SKY TECHNOLOGIES INC.
Red Mercenary 1995
1 I:Jae,Elliot,Firnn 2.95

MARKSMAN, THE
Hero Graphics
1 O:Marksman, Pt.#1. . . . . 1.95
2 O:Marksman, Pt.#2. . . . . 1.95
3 O:Marksman ends.I:Basilisk 1.95
4 A:Flare. 1.95
5 I:Radar,Sonar. 1.95
Ann. #1, A:Champions 1.95

MARRIED... WITH CHILDREN
Now
1 . . . . 6.00
1a 2nd printing 2.00
2 . . . . 4.00
3 . . . . 3.00
4 . . . . 2.50
5 . . . . 2.50
6 . . . . 2.00
7 . . . . 2.50

[2nd Series]
1 Peg-Host of Radio Show 2.25
2 The Bundy Invention. 1.95
3 Psychodad,(photo cover) 1.95
4 Mother-In-Law,(photo cover) 1.95
5 Bundy the Crusader 1.95
6 Bundy J: The Order of the
   Mighty Warthog 1.95
7 Kelly the VJ 1.95
Spec. 1.95
3-D Spec. 2.50

MARRIED WITH CHILDREN: DYSFUNCTIONAL FAMILY
Now
1 I:The Bundies. 2.50
2 TV Appearance 2.50
3 Morally Pure Bundys 2.50

MARRIED WITH CHILDREN: FLASHBACK SPECIAL
Now
1 Peg and Al's first date. 1.95
2 and 3 . . . . @1.95

MARRIED WITH CHILDREN: KELLY BUNDY SPECIAL
Now
1 with poster 1.95
2 and 3 with poster . . . . @1.95

MARRIED... WITH CHILDREN: QUANTUM QUARTET
Now
1 thru 4 Fantastic Four parody . . @1.95
Fall 1994 Spec., flip book 1.95

MARRIED WITH CHILDREN 2099
Mirage
1 thru 3 Cable Parody . . . . @2.50

MARS
First
1 thru 12 . . . . @1.25

Mars Attacks #2
© *Topps Comics*

MARS ATTACKS
Topps
1 KG(s). 6.00
2 . . . . 4.00
3 thru 6 KG(s). 4.00

[Series 2] 1995
1 Counterstrike 3.50
2 Counterstrike,pt.2 . . . . 2.95
3 Counterstrike,pt.3 . . . . 2.95
4 Counterstrike,pt.4 Convictions . . 2.95
5 Counterstrike concl. 2.95
6 "Rescue of Janice Brown,"pt.1 . . 2.95
7 "Rescue of Janice Brown,"pt.2 . . 2.95
8 . . . . 2.95
Spec. Baseball 3.00

MARS ATTACKS HIGH SCHOOL
Topps 1997
Spec. #1 (of 2) BSz(c) 2.95
Spec. #2. . . . . 2.95

MARS ATTACKS THE SAVAGE DRAGON
Topps
1 . . . . 3.00
2 . . . . 3.00
3 . . . . 3.00
4 (of 4) 3.00

MARSHALL LAW: HATEFUL DEAD
Apocalypse
1 "Rise of the Zombies" 5.95

MARTIANS!!! IN 3-D
1 . . . . 2.00

MARY WORTH
ARGO March, 1956
1 . . . . 45.00

MASKED MAN
Eclipse 1985–88
1 . . . . 3.00
2 . . . . 2.00
3 . . . . 2.00
4 . . . . 2.00
5 . . . . 2.00
6 V:Roxie Lamada 2.00
7 . . . . 2.00
8 "Roxy" 1.75
9 W:Dick and Maggie 1.75
10 . . . . 2.00

MASTERWORK SERIES
Seagate DC
1 FFrep.DC,ShiningKnight. 1.50
2 FFrep.DC,ShiningKnight. 1.50
3 BWr,Horror DC rep. 1.50

MAVERICK
Dell Publishing Co. April, 1958
1 Ph(c) all 300.00
2 Ph(c) 125.00
3 Ph(c) 125.00
4 Ph(c) 125.00
5 Ph(c) 125.00
6 thru 15 Ph(c) . . . . @85.00

MAVERICK MARSHALL
Charlton Comics Nov., 1958
1 . . . . 30.00
2 . . . . 20.00
3 . . . . 20.00
4 . . . . 20.00
5 . . . . 20.00
6 . . . . 20.00
7 May, 1960 . . . . 20.00

MAVERICKS
Dagger
1 PuD,RkL, I:Mavericks 2.50
2 PuD,RkL. 2.50

MAXIMORTAL
King Hell/Tundra
1 RV,A:True-Man. 4.50
2 Crack in the New World 4.25
3 RV,Secret of the Manhattan
   Project revealed 4.25
4 . . . . 4.25
5 A:True Man 3.25
6 A:El Guano. 3.25
Kitchen Sink 1997
HC Book 1: Cheek, Chin, Knuckle
   or Knee 35.00

MAYA
Gold Key March, 1968
1 . . . . 25.00

MAZE AGENCY
Comico
1 O:Maze Agency 3.00
2 thru 6 . . . . @2.50
7 . . . . 2.75
8 thru 11 . . . . @1.95
12 . . . . 2.50
13 thru 15 . . . . @1.95
16 thru 23 . . . . @2.50
Spec. #1 . . . . 2.75

McHALE'S NAVY
Dell Publishing Co.
May-July, 1963
1 Ph(c) from TV show 65.00
2 Ph(c) 45.00
3 Ph(c) 45.00

McKEEVER & THE COLONEL
Dell Publishing Co.
Feb.-April, 1963
1 Ph(c) 60.00
2 Ph(c) 40.00
3 Ph(c) 40.00

M.D. GEIST
CPM
1 Cartoon Adaptation. 2.95
2 J:Army 2.95
3 V:Final Terminator 2.95

MECHANICS
Fantagraphics
1 HB,rep.Love & Rockets 3.00
2 HB,rep.Love & Rockets 2.50
3 HB,rep.Love & Rockets 2.50

MEDIA STARR
Innovation
1 thru 3 . . . . @1.95

MEGALITH
Continuity
1 MT 6.00
2 MT 4.00
3 MT, Painted issue 2.50
4 NA,TVE 2.50
5 NA,TVE 2.50
6 MN 2.50
7 MN 2.50
8 . . . . 2.50
9 SDr(i) 2.50
10 . . . . 2.50
[2nd Series, Deathwatch 2000]
0 Deathwatch 2000 prologue 5.00
1 Deathwatch 2000 Pt.5,w/card . . . 2.50
2 Deathwatch 2000 Pt.10,w/card . . 2.50
3 pt.16,Indestructible(c),w/card . . 2.50
4 and 5 Rise of Magic . . . . @2.50
6 and 7 . . . . @2.50

MEGATON
1 . . . . 1.50
Entity Comics
Holiday Spec. w/card 2.95

MEGATON EXPLOSION
1 RLd,AMe,I:Youngblood preview 25.00

MEGATON MAN
Kitchen Sink
1 Don Simpson art, I:Megaton Man 6.00
1a rep. B&W 2.00
2 . . . . 4.00
3 and 4 . . . . @3.00
5 . . . . 2.50
6 Border Worlds 2.50
7 Border Worlds 2.50
8 Border Worlds 2.50
9 Border Worlds 2.50
10 final issue, 1986 . . . . 2.50

MELTING POT
Kitchen Sink
1 . . . . 4.00
2 and 3 . . . . @2.95
4 . . . . 3.50
TPB KEa,SBs, rep. 19.95
HC signed, numbered. 50.00

MELVIN MONSTER
Dell Publishing Co.
April-June, 1965
1 . . . . 125.00
2 thru 10 . . . . @75.00

Memories #1
© Epic

[Katshuiro Otomo's] MEMORIES
Epic 1992
1 . . . . 2.50

MEN FROM EARTH
Future Fun
1 based on Matt Mason toy 6.50

MENACE
Awesome Entertainment 1998
1 by Jada Pinkett & Don Fraga . . . 2.50
1a signed 20.00
2 . . . . 2.50
3 . . . . 2.50

MERCENARY
NBM
The Voyage 10.95
The Black Globe. 9.95
The Fortress. 9.95

MERCHANTS OF DEATH
Eclipse 1988
1 King's Castle, The Hero 3.50
2 King's Castle,Soldiers of Fortune 3.50
3 Ransom, Soldier of Fortune 3.50
4 ATh(c),Ransom, Men o/t Legion . 3.50
5 Ransom,New York City Blues . . . 3.50

MERLIN REALM
Blackthorne
1 3-D. 2.50

META 4
First 1990
1 IG. 3.95
2 IG. 2.25
3 IG/JSon,final monthly 2.25

METAL MILITIA
Entity Comics 1995
1 I:Metal Militia 2.50
1a with Video Game 6.95
2 ICO 2.50
3 F:Detective Calahan 2.50
Ashcan 2.50

MICHAELANGELO
Mirage
1 TMNT Character 15.00

MICKEY & DONALD
Gladstone
1 1449 Firestone 8.00
2 . . . . 4.00
3 Man of Tomorrow 3.00
4 thru 15 . . . . @2.50
16 giant-size. 2.50
17 . . . . 3.00
18 . . . . 4.00
Becomes:
DONALD AND MICKEY
19 thru 26 . . . . @1.50

MICKEY MANTLE COMICS
Magnum
1 JSt,Rise to Big Leagues 1.75

MICKEY MOUSE
Gladstone
219 FG,Seven Ghosts 6.00
220 FG,Seven Ghosts 7.00
221 FG,Seven Ghosts 7.00
222 FG,Editor in Grief. 5.00
223 FG,Editor in Grief. 4.00
224 FG,Crazy Crime Wave 3.00
225 FG,Crazy Crime Wave 3.00
226 FG,Captive Castaways 3.00
227 FG,Captive Castaways 3.00
228 FG,Captive Castaways 3.00
229 FG,Bat Bandit 3.00
230 FG,Bat Bandit 3.00
231 FG,Bobo the Elephant 2.50
232 FG,Bobo the Elephant 2.50
233 FG,Pirate Submarine 2.50
234 FG,Pirate Submarine 2.50
235 FG,Photo Racer. 2.50
236 FG,Photo Racer. 2.50
237 FG,Race for Riches 2.50
238 FG,Race for Riches 2.50
239 FG,Race for Riches 2.50
240 FG,March of Comics 2.50
241 FG. 4.00
242 FG. 2.50
243 FG. 2.50

COLOR PUB.

244 FG,60th Anniv	5.00
245 FG	2.25
245 FG	2.25
246 FG	2.25
247 FG	2.25
248 FG	2.25
249 FG	5.00
250 FG	2.25
251 FG	2.25
252 FG	2.25
253 FG	2.25
254 FG	2.25
255 FG	4.00
256 FG	4.00

MICKEY MOUSE
Walt Disney 1990

1 "The Phantom Gondolier"	3.50
2	3.00
3	2.50
4	2.50
5	2.50
6	2.00
7 Phantom Blot	2.00
8 Phantom Blot	2.00
9	2.00
10 Sky Adventure	2.00
11 When Mouston Freezes Over.	2.00
12 Hail & Farewell	2.00
13 "What's Shakin'"	2.00
14 Mouseton,Eagle-Landing	2.00
15 "Lost Palace of Kashi"	2.00
16 "Scoundrels in Space"	2.00
17 "Sound of Blunder" Pt.1	1.75
18 "Sound of Blunder" Pt.2	1.75
19 50th Ann. Fantasia Celebration Sorcerer's Apprentice adapt	1.50

MICKEY SPILLANE'S MIKE DANGER
Tekno Comix 1995

1 I:Mike Danger	2.25
2 Underside of the City	1.95
3 Judicial System	1.95
4 Mike's First Job	1.95
5 Old New York	1.95
6 Sin Syndicate Leader	2.25
7 thru 11	@2.25

Big Entertainment 1996

1	2.25
2	2.25
3 MCn,PGr,TBe,EB	2.25
4	2.25
5 "Time Heels"	2.25
6 TBe,"Paradox Rule"	2.25
7 TBe,"Red Menace," pt.1	2.25
8 TBe,"Red Menace," pt.2	2.25
9 TBe,"Red Menace," pt.3	2.25
10 TBe,"Red Menace," concl.	2.25

MICROBOTS, THE
Gold Key Dec., 1971

1	20.00

MIDNIGHT EYE: GOKU PRIVATE INVESTIGATOR
Viz

1 A.D. 2014: Tokyo city	5.25
2 V:Hakuryu,A:Yoko	4.95
3 A:Ryoko,Search for Ryu	4.95
4 Goku vs. Ryu	4.95
5 Leilah Abducted	4.95
6 Lisa's I.D. discovered	4.95

COLOR PUB.

MIGHTY COMICS
{Prev: Flyman}

40 A:Web	12.00
41 A:Shield, Black Hood	10.00
42 A:Black Hood	10.00
43 A:Shield, Black Hood,Web	9.00
44 A:Black Hood, Steel Sterling Shield	9.00
45 Shield-Black Hood team-up O:Web	9.00
46 A:Steel Sterling, Black Hood, Web	9.00
47 A:Black Hood & Mr.Justice	9.00
48 A:Shield & Hangman	9.00
49 Steel Sterling-Black Hood team-up, A:Fox	9.00

Mighty Crusaders #4
© Red Circle

[ALL NEW ADVENTURES OF] THE MIGHTY CRUSADERS
Red Circle
[1st Series] 1983

1 O:Shield (Joe Higgins & Bill Higgins)	25.00
2 MSy,O:Comet	20.00
3 O:Fly-Man	15.00
4 A:Fireball,Jaguar,Web,Fox, Blackjack Hangman & more Golden Age Archie Heroes	18.00
5 I:Ultra-Men&TerrificThree	15.00

Archie Publications

6 V:Maestro,A:Steel Sterling	12.00
7 O:Fly-Girl,A:Steel Sterling	12.00

[2nd Series]

1 RB,R:Joe Higgins & Lancelot Strong as the SHIELD, Mighty Crusaders, A:Mr.Midnight	1.50
2 RB,V:Brain Emperor & Eterno	1.50
3 RB,I:Darkling	1.50
4 DAy,TD	1.50
5	1.00
6 DAy,TD,Shield	1.00
7	1.00
8	1.00
9 Trial of the Shield	1.00
10	1.00
11 DAy,D:Gold Age Black Hood, I: Riot Squad, series based on toy lines	1.00
12 DAy,I:She-Fox	1.00
13 Last issue	1.00

MIGHTY HERCULES, THE
Gold Key July, 1963

1	150.00
2	125.00

MIGHTY MORPHIN POWER RANGERS
Hamilton 1994–95

1 From TV Series	2.75
2 Switcheroo	2.50
3	2.25
4 F:White Ranger	1.95
5 F:Pink Ranger	1.95
6 V:Garganturon	1.95
TPB Re. #1-#6 photo (c).	9.95

[Series 2] 1995

1 Unstoppable Force	1.95
2 V:Mechanical Octopus	1.95
3	1.95
4 Lost Ranger	1.95

[Series 3] 1995

1 O:Green Ranger	1.95
2 O:Green Ranger	1.95
3 I:New Megazords	1.95

MIGHTY MOUSE
Spotlight 1987

1 FMc,PC(c)	1.50
2 FMc,CS(c)	1.50
1 Holiday Special	1.75

MIGHTY MUTANIMALS
Archie Publications
[Mini-Series]

1 Cont.from TMNT Adventures#19, A:Raphael, Man Ray, Leather-head, Mondo Gecko,Deadman, Wingnut & Screwloose	1.25
2 V:Mr.Null,Malinga,Soul and Bean and the Malignoid Army	1.25
3 Alien Invasion help off, Raphael returns to Earth	1.25
4 "Days of Future Past"	1.25
5 "Into the Sun"	1.25
6 V:Null & 4 Horsemen Pt#2	1.25
7 Jaws of Doom	1.50
Spec.#1 rep. all #1-3 +SBi pin-ups	2.95

MIGHTY MUTANIMALS
Archie

1 Quest for Jagwar's Mother	1.25
2 V:Snake Eyes	1.25
3	1.25
4 "Days of Future Past"	1.25
5 "Into the Sun"	1.25
6 V:Null & 4 Horsemen Pt#2	1.25
7 Jaws of Doom	1.50

MIGHTY SAMSON
Gold Key 1964–82

1 O:Mighty Samson	75.00
2	40.00
3	40.00
4	40.00
5	40.00
6 thru 10	@30.00
11 thru 20	@25.00
21 thru 32	@20.00

MIKE GRELL'S SABLE
First

1 thru 8 rep.	@1.75
9	1.75
10 Triptych	1.75

MIKE SHAYNE PRIVATE EYE
Dell Publishing Co.
Nov.-Jan., 1961-62
1	35.00
2	20.00
3	20.00

MILLENNIUM INDEX
Independent Comics 1988
1	2.00
2	2.00

MILTON THE MONSTER & FEARLESS FLY
Gold Key May, 1966
1	100.00

MIRACLEMAN
Eclipse 1985–94
1 R:Miracleman	5.00
2 AD,Moore,V:Kid Miracleman	4.00
3 AD,Moore,V:Big Ben.	4.00
4 AD,Moore,R:Dr.Gargunza	4.00
5 AD,Moore,O:Miracleman.	4.00
6 Moore,V:Miracledog, D:Evelyn Cream	4.00
7 Moore,D:Dr.Gargunza.	4.00
8 Moore.	4.00
9 RV,Moore,Birth of Miraclebaby	4.50
10 JRy,RV,Moore	4.00
11 JTo,Moore,Book III, I:Miraclewoman	5.00
12 thru 14 Moore	5.00
15 Moore	30.00
16	5.00
17 thru 23	@4.00
24 BWS(c),NGa(s),	4.00
25 thru 28	@2.95
3-D Special #1	2.75

Graphic Albums
HC Book 1 A Dream of Flying	29.95
TPB Book 1 A Dream of Flying	9.95
HC Book 2 The Red Kings Syndrome	30.95
TPB Book 2 The Red Kings Syndrome	9.95
HC Book 3 Olympus	30.95
TPB Book 3 Olympus	12.00

MIRACLEMAN APOCRYPHA
Eclipse 1991–92
1 inc."Rascal Prince"	2.50
2 Miracleman, Family Stories	2.50
3	2.50

MIRACLEMAN FAMILY
Eclipse 1988
1 British Rep.,A:Kid Miracleman	1.95
2 Alan Moore (s)	1.95

MIRACLE SQUAD, THE
Upshot/Fantagraphics 1986
1 Hollywood 30's	2.00
2 thru 4	@2.00

MISS FURY
Adventure Comics
1 O:Cat Suit	2.50
2 Miss Fury impersonator	2.50
3 A:Three Miss Fury's	2.50

4 conclusion	2.50

MISSION IMPOSSIBLE
Dell Publishing Co. May, 1967
1 Ph(c)	100.00
2 Ph(c)	75.00
3 Ph(c)	60.00
4 Ph(c)	60.00
5 Ph(c)	60.00

MISSIONS IN TIBET
Dimension Comics 1995
1 I:New Series	2.50
2 F:Orlando,Ting,Alex	2.50
3 Two Worlds Collide	2.50
4 V:Sada	2.50

MISS PEACH
(& SPECIAL ISSUES)
Dell Publishing Co. 1963
1	75.00

MR. AND MRS. J. EVIL SCIENTIST
Gold Key Nov., 1963
1	100.00
2	50.00
3	50.00
4	50.00

MR. JIGSAW
Spec. #1	1.75

MR. MAJESTIC
Wildstorm/DC 1999
1 JoC,A:Desmond	2.50
1a variant cover.	3.00
2 JoC,time gone berserk	2.50

MR. MONSTER
Eclipse 1985–87
1 I:Mr. Monster	9.00
2 DSt(c).	5.00
3 V:Dr. NoZone	3.50
4 "Trapped in Dimension X"	3.00
5 V:Flesh-eating Amoebo	3.00
6 KG,SD,reprints	3.00
7	3.00
8 V:Monster in the Atomic Telling Machine	3.00
9 V:Giant Clams	3.00
10 R:Dr.No Zone, 3-D	2.00

MR. MONSTER ATTACKS
Tundra
1 DGb,SK,short stories	4.25
2 SK,short stories cont.	4.25
3 DGb,last issue	4.25

MR. MONSTER SUPERDUPER SPECIAL
Eclipse 1986–87
1	2.50
2	2.00
3	2.00
4	2.00
5	2.00
6	2.00
Hi-Voltage Super Science	2.00
3-D Spec. Hi-Octane Horror,JKu,	

"Touch of Death" reprint	1.75
Triple Treat	3.95

MR. MONSTER TRUE CRIME
Eclipse
1	1.75
2	1.75
3-D Spec. #1	2.00

MR. MUSCLES
Charlton Comics 1956
22	40.00
23	35.00

MR. MYSTIC
Eclipse
1	2.00
2	2.00
3	2.00

MR. T AND THE T FORCE
Now
1 NA,R:Mr.T,V:Street Gangs	2.50
1a Gold Ed.	10.00
2 NA,V:Demons.	2.25
3 NBy,w/card.	2.25
4 NBy,In Urban America	2.25
5 thru 10, with card	@2.25

MISTER X
Vortex
1 HB	8.00
2 HB	5.00
3 HB	3.50
4 HB	3.00
5	3.00
6 thru 10	@2.50
11 thru 13	@2.00
14	2.25

MOD SQUAD
Dell Publishing Co. 1969–71
1	55.00
2	30.00
3	30.00
4 thru 8	@30.00

Mod Squad #1
© Dell Publishing Co.

MOD WHEELS
Gold Key 1971–76
1 . . . . 20.00
2 thru 18 . . . . @10.00
19 . . . . 8.00

MONKEE'S, THE
Dell Publishing Co. 1967
1 Ph(c) 100.00
2 Ph(c) 60.00
3 Ph(c) 60.00
4 Ph(c) 60.00
5 . . . . 50.00
6 Ph(c) 60.00
7 Ph(c) 60.00
8 and 9 . . . . @50.00
10 Ph(c) 60.00
11 thru 17 . . . . 40.00

MONOLITH
Comico
1 From Elementals 2.50
2 "Seven Levels of Hell" 2.50
3 "Fugue and Variation" 2.50
4 "Fugue and Variation" 2.50

MONROE'S, THE
Dell Publishing Co. April, 1967
1 Ph(c) 25.00

MONSTER MASSACRE
Atomeka
1 SBs, DBr,DGb 8.50
1a Black Edition 35.00

MOONWALKER IN 3-D
Blackthorne
1 thru 3 . . . . @2.50

MORBID ANGEL
London Night
½ Angel's Tear, signed 10.00
1 Commemorative (1999) 5.95

MORBID ANGEL: PENANCE
London Night
Revised Color Spec., double size . . 4.00

MORE THAN MORTAL
Liar Comics 1997
1 . . . . 2.95
1a 2nd printing 2.95
2 Derdre vs. the Host 2.95
2a variant painted cover 5.95
3 MS(c) 2.95
4 concl. 2.95
TPB rep. #1–#4 . . . . 14.95

MORE THAN MORTAL: SAGAS
Liar Comics 1998
1 by Sharon Scott & Romano
   Molenaar 2.95
1a variant Tim Vigil(c) 2.95
1b variant JLi(c) 9.95
2 . . . . 2.95
3 conclusion 2.95

MORE THAN MORTAL: TRUTHS AND LEGENDS
Liar Comics 1998
1 by Sharon Scott, Steve Firchow,
   Mark Prudeaux, O:Witchfinder . 3.00
1a signed 9.95
2 . . . . 3.00
3 . . . . 3.00
4 . . . . 3.00
5 . . . . 3.00
5a variant cover (1:4) 3.00
6 . . . . 3.00

Morlock 2001, #1
© *Atlas Comics*

MORLOCK 2001
Atlas Feb.–July 1975
1 thru 3 F:Midnight Men . . . . . . @10.00

MORNINGSTAR
Spec. #1 . . . . 2.50

MORRIGAN
Sirius 1997
1 by Lorenzo Bartoli & Saverio
   Tenuta 2.95
2 and 3 . . . . @2.95
GN rep. #1–#3 . . . . 9.95

MOTORBIKE PUPPIES
Dark Zulu Lies
1 I:Motorbike Puppies 2.50

MOVIE COMICS
Gold Key/Whitman Oct., 1962
Alice in Wonderland 35.00
Aristocats 75.00
Bambi 1 . . . . 35.00
Bambi 2 . . . . 25.00
Beneath the Planet of the Apes . . 75.00
Big Red 25.00
Blackbeard's Ghost 25.00
Buck Rogers Giant Movie Edition . 22.00
Bullwhip Griffin 35.00
Captain Sinbad 50.00
Chitty, Chitty Bang Bang 75.00
Cinderella 30.00
Darby O'Gill & the Little People . . 50.00
Dumbo 30.00
Emil & the Detectives 30.00
Escapade in Florence 85.00

Fall of the Roman Empire 35.00
Fantastic Voyage 50.00
55 Days at Peking 30.00
Fighting Prince of Donegal 25.00
First Men of the Moon 30.00
Gay Purr-ee 45.00
Gnome Mobile 30.00
Goodbye, Mr. Chips 30.00
Happiest Millionaire 30.00
Hey There, It's Yogi Bear 60.00
Horse Without a Head 25.00
How the West Was Won 35.00
In Search of the Castaways 75.00
Jungle Book, The 55.00
Kidnapped 30.00
King Kong 30.00
King Kong N# 25.00
Lady and the Tramp 30.00
Lady and the Tramp 1 . . . . 50.00
Lady and the Tramp 2 . . . . 20.00
Legend of Lobo, The 25.00
Lt. Robin Crusoe 25.00
Lion, The 25.00
Lord Jim 25.00
Love Bug, The 25.00
Mary Poppins 45.00
Mary Poppins 1 . . . . 65.00
McLintock 125.00
Merlin Jones as the Monkey's
   Uncle 45.00
Miracle of the White Stallions . . . 30.00
Misadventures of Merlin Jones . . 50.00
Moon-Spinners, The 75.00
Mutiny on the Bounty 30.00
Nikki, Wild Dog of the North 25.00
Old Yeller 25.00
One Hundred & One Dalmations . 25.00
Peter Pan 1 . . . . 30.00
Peter Pan 2 . . . . 25.00
P.T. 109 . . . . 45.00
Rio Conchos 40.00
Robin Hood 25.00
Shaggy Dog & the Absent-Minded
   Professor 50.00
Snow White & the Seven Dwarfs . 25.00
Son of Flubber 25.00
Summer Magic 75.00
Swiss Family Robinson 25.00
Sword in the Stone 60.00
That Darn Cat 50.00
Those Magnificent Men in Their
   Flying Machines 30.00
Three Stooges in Orbt 90.00
Tiger Walks, A 40.00
Toby Tyler 25.00
Treasure Island 25.00
20,000 Leagues Under the Sea . . 25.00
Wonderful Adventures of
   Pinocchio 25.00
X, the Man with the X-Ray Eyes . 70.00
Yellow Submarine 250.00

MS. MYSTIC
Pacific
1 NA,Origin 8.00
2 NA,Origin,I:Urth 4 . . . . 6.00

Continuity
1 NA,Origin rep. 2.00
2 NA,Origin,I:Urth 4 rep 2.00
3 NA,New material 2.00
4 TSh 2.00
5 DT 2.00
6 . . . . 2.00
7 . . . . 2.00
8 CH/Sdr,B:Love Story 2.00
9 DB 2.00
9a Newsstand(c) 2.00

[3rd Series]
1 O:Ms.Mystic 2.50
2 A:Hybrid 2.50

COLOR PUB.

3	2.50
4	2.50

[4th Series, Deathwatch 2000]

1 Deathwatch 2000 pt.8,w/card	2.50
2 Deathwatch 2000 w/card	2.50
3 Indestructible cover, w/card	2.50

MS. TREE'S THRILLING
DETECTIVE ADVENTURES
Eclipse 1983

1 Miller pin up	4.00
2	2.50
3	2.00

Becomes:

MS. TREE
1984–89

4 thru 6	@2.00
7	2.50
8	8.00
9	2.00

Aardvark–Vanaheim

10	2.00

Renegade

1 3-D	2.00

MS. VICTORY
GOLDEN ANNIVERSARY
AC Comics

1 Ms.Victory celebration	5.00

MS. VICTORY SPECIAL
AC Comics

1	1.75

MUMMY, OR RAMSES
THE DAMNED, THE
Millenium 1992

1 Anne Rice Adapt.	5.00
2 JM,"Mummy in Mayfair"	3.75
3 JM	3.25
4 JM, To Egypt	3.00
5 JM"The Mummy's Hand"	2.50
6 JM 20th Century Egypt	2.50
7 JM,More Ramses Past Revealed	2.50
8 JM,Hunt for Cleopatra	2.50
9 JM,Cleopatra's Wrath contd	2.50
10 JM,Subteranian World	2.50
11 JM	2.50

MUMMY ARCHIVES
Millenium

1.JM,Features,articles	2.50

MUNDEN'S BAR
ANNUAL
First

1 BB,JOy,JSn,SR	2.95

MUNSTERS, THE
Gold Key 1965–68

1	225.00
2	100.00
3 thru 5	@75.00
6 thru 16	@70.00

MUPPET BABIES
Harvey

1 Return of Muppet Babies	1.25

MUTANTS & MISFITS
Silverline

1 thru 4	@1.95

MY FAVORITE MARTIAN
Gold Key 1964–66

1	150.00
2	75.00
3 thru 9	@60.00

MY LITTLE MARGIE
Charlton Comics 1954–65

1 Ph(c)	175.00
2 Ph(c)	100.00
3	50.00
4	50.00
5	50.00
6	50.00
7	50.00
8	50.00
9	45.00
10	30.00

Ms. Tree, Thrilling Detective Adventures #3 © Eclipse

11	15.00
12	15.00
13	30.00
14 thru 19	@25.00
20	50.00
21 thru 35	@15.00
36 thru 53	@10.00
54 Beatles (c)	100.00

MYSTERIES OF
UNEXPLORED WORLDS/
SON OF VULCAN
Charlton Comics 1956

1	250.00
2	75.00
3	175.00
4 SD	200.00
5 SD,SD(c)	175.00
6 SD	175.00
7	175.00
8 SD	175.00
9 SD	175.00
10 SD,SD(c)	175.00
11 SD,SD(c)	175.00
12	125.00
13 thru 18	@35.00
19 SD(c)	80.00

20	30.00
21 thru 24 SD	@125.00
25	20.00
26 SD	90.00
27 thru 30	@20.00
31 thru 45	@15.00
46 I:Son ofVulcan,Dr.Kong(1965)	20.00
47 V:King Midas	12.00
48 V:Captain Tuska	12.00

Becomes:

SON OF VULCAN

49 DC redesigns costume	6.00
50 V:Dr.Kong	5.00

MYSTERIOUS SUSPENSE
Charlton 1968

1 SD,F:Question	55.00

MYSTERY COMICS
DIGEST
Gold Key March, 1972–75

1 WW	35.00
2 WW	30.00
3	20.00
4 Ripleys Believe It or Not	15.00
5 Boris Karloff	15.00
6 Twilight Zone	10.00
7 thru 20	@15.00
21 thru 26	@12.00

MYSTIC EDGE
Antarctic Press 1998

1 by Ryan Kinnaird, F:Risa & Symattra	2.95

MYSTIC ISLE

1	1.95

NANCY & SLUGGO
Dell Publishing Co. 1957

146 B:Peanuts	40.00
147	25.00
148	25.00
149	25.00
150 thru 161	25.00
162 thru 165	35.00
166 thru 176 A:OONA	40.00
177 thru 180	35.00
181 thru 187	20.00

NATIONAL VELVET
Dell Publishing Co.
May-July, 1961

1 Ph(c)	45.00
2 Ph(c)	40.00

NEAT STUFF
Fantagraphics

1	4.50
2	3.00
3 thru 5	@2.50
6	2.25
7	2.25

NECROPOLIS
Fleetway

1 SBs(c),CE,A:Dark Judges/ Sisters Of Death	2.95
2	2.95
3 thru 9	@2.95

COLOR PUB.

NEIL GAIMAN'S
LADY JUSTICE
Tekno Comix (1995)

1 I:Lady Justice	2.50
1a	6.00
2 V:Blood Pirate	1.95
3 V:Blood Pirate	1.95
4 New Story Arc	1.95
5 Street Gang War	1.95
6 Street Gang War	2.25
7 thru 11	@2.25

Big Entertainment April 1996

1 thru 4	@2.25
5 DIB(s)	2.25
6 DIB(s),"Woman About Town," pt.1	2.25
7 DIB(s),"Woman About Town," pt.2	2.25
8 DIB(s),"Woman About Town," pt.3	2.25

NEIL GAIMAN'S
MR. HERO
THE NEWMATIC MAN
Tekno-Comics 1994

1 I:Mr. Hero, Tecknophage	2.50
2 A:Tecknophage	2.25
3 I:Adam Kaine	1.95
4 I:New Body	1.95
5 Earthquake	1.95
6 I:New Character	1.95
7 I:Deadbolt, Bloodboil	1.95
8 V:Avatar	1.95
9 in London	1.95
10 V:Demon	1.95
11 V:Monster	1.95
12 The Great Goward	2.25
13 thru 17	@2.25

NEIL GAIMAN'S
PHAGE
Tekno-Comics 1996

1	2.25

NEIL GAIMAN'S PHAGE:
SHADOW DEATH
Big Entertainment

1 thru 4	@2.25
5 O:Orlando Holmes,A:Lady Messalina	2.25
6 conclusion	2.25

NEIL GAIMAN'S
TECKNOPHAGE
Teckno-Comics 1995

1 I:Kalighoul, Tom Vietch	1.95
1a Steel Edition	3.95
2 F:Mayor of New Yorick	1.95
3 Phange Building	1.95
4 Horde eevils	1.95
5 Middle Management	1.95
6 Escape from Phange	1.95
7 Mecca	2.25

NEIL GAIMAN'S
WHEEL OF WORLDS
Teckno-Comics 1995

0 Deluxe Edition w/Posters	2.95
0a I:Lady Justice	1.95
1	3.25

NEMESIS THE
WARLOCK
Eagle

1	2.00
2 thru 8	@1.50

New Adventures of Felix #1
© Felix Comics

NEW ADVENTURES OF
FELIX THE CAT
Felix Comics,Inc

1 New stories	2.25
2 "The Magic Paint Brush"	2.25

NEW ADVENTURES
OF PINNOCCIO
Dell Publishing Co. 1962

1	75.00
2 and 3	@60.00

NEW ADVENTURES OF
SPEED RACER
Now

0 Premiere, 3-D cover	1.95
1 thru 11	@1.95

NEW AMERICA
Eclipse 1987–88

1 A:Scout	1.75
2 A:Scout	1.75
3 A:Roman Catholic Pope	1.75
4 A:Scout	1.75

NEW BREED
Pied Piper

1	2.75
2	2.25

NEW CHAMPIONS

1 and 2	@2.95

NEW DNAGENTS, THE
Eclipse 1985–87

1 R:DNAgents	1.50
2 F:Tank	1.00
3 Repopulating the World	1.00
4 Major Catastrophe for Earth	1.00
5 "Last Place on Earth"	1.00

6 JOy(c),"Postscript"	1.00
7 V:Venimus	1.00
8 DSp,V:Venimus	1.00
9 V:Venimus,I:New Wave.	1.00
10 I:New Airboy	1.00
11 Summer Fun Issue	1.25
12 V:Worm	1.25
13 EL,F:Tank	1.25
14 EL,Nudity,"Grounded"	1.25
15 thru 17	@1.25
3-D #1	2.50

NEW JUSTICE MACHINE
Innovation

1 and 2	@1.95
2	1.95

NEW KABOOM
Awesome Entertainment 1999

1 RLe,JLb	2.50

NEWMEN
Maximum Press
1–22 see Image

23 ErS,CSp,AG,"Anthem," pt.3	2.50
24 ErS,CSp,AG,"Anthem," pt.4	2.50
25 ErS,CSp,AG,"Anthem," pt.5	2.50

NEW ORLEANS SAINTS

1 Playoff season(football team)	6.00

NEW STATESMEN
Fleetway

1	4.50
2 thru 5	@3.95

NEWSTRALIA
Innovation

1 and 2	@1.75
3	1.95

NEW TERRYTOONS
Dell Publishing Co. 1960–61

1	55.00
2 thru 8	@30.00

Gold Key 1962

1 F:Heckle & Jeckle	75.00
2	60.00
3 thru 10	@20.00
11 thru 20	@15.00
21 thru 30	@7.00
31 thru 40	@5.00
41 thru 54	@3.00

NEW WAVE, THE
Eclipse 1986–87

1 Error Pages	2.00
1a Correction	1.50
2	1.00
3 "Space Station Called Hell"	1.00
4 Birth of Megabyte	1.00
5 PG(c),O:Avalon	1.50
6 O:Megabyte	1.50
7 Avalon disappears	1.00
8 V:Heap,V:Druids	1.00
9	1.00
10 V:Heap Team	1.00
11	1.50
12	1.50
13 V:Volunteers	1.50
14 1/3 issue	2.00

COLOR PUB.

NEW WAVE vs. THE VOLUNTEERS
Eclipse
1 3-D,V:Volunteers 2.50
2 3-D,V:Volunteers 2.50

NEXT MAN
Comico 1985
1 I&O:Next Man. 2.50
2 . . . . 1.75
3 . . . . 1.75
4 . . . . 1.50
5 . . . . 1.50

NEXT NEXUS
First
1 SR 1.95
2 SR 1.95
3 SR 1.95
4 SR 1.95

Nexus #2
© Capital

NEXUS
Capital
1 SR,I:Judah Maccabee 5.00
2 SR,Origin,V:Bellows 4.00
3 SR,Sundra Captive. 4.00
4 SR,V:Ziggurat. 4.00
5 SR,"I'm Bored!". 4.00
6 SR,A:Badger,TrialogueTrilogy#1 . 4.00
First
7 SR,A:Badger,TrialogueTrilogy#2 . 4.00
8 SR,A:Badger,TrialogueTrilogy#3 . 3.00
9 SR,Teen Angel 2.50
10 SR,BWg,Talking Heads 2.00
11 SR,V:Clausius. 2.00
12 SR,V:The Old General 2.00
13 SR,Sundra Peale solo 2.00
14 SR,A:Clonezone,Hilariator 2.00
15 SR,A:Clonezone 2.00
16 SR,A:Clonezone 2.00
17 Judah vs. Jacque,the Anvil . . . 2.00
18 SR,A:Clonezone 2.00
19 SR,A:Clonezone 2.00
20 SR,A:Clonezone 2.00
21 SR,A:Clonezone 2.00
22 KG,A:Badger. 2.00
23 SR,A:Clonezone 2.00
24 SR,A:Clonezone 2.00
25 SR,A:Clonezone 2.00
26 SR,A:Clonezone 2.00

27 SR,A:Clonezone 2.00
28 MMi. 2.00
29 A:Kreed & Sinclair 2.00
30 JL,C:Badger 2.50
31 Judah solo story 2.00
32 JG,Judah solo story 2.00
33 SR,A:Kreed & Sinclair 2.00
34 SR,Judah solo story. 2.00
35 SR,Judah solo story. 2.00
36 SR. 2.00
37 PS 2.00
38 . . . . 2.00
39 SR, The Boom Search. 2.00
40 SR. 2.00
41 SR. 2.00
42 SR,Bowl-Shaped world 2.00
43 PS 2.00
44 PS 2.00
45 SR,A:Badger Pt.1 . . . . 2.00
46 SR,A:Badger Pt.2 . . . . 2.00
47 SR,A:Badger Pt.3 . . . . 2.00
48 SR,A:Badger Pt.4 . . . . 2.00
49 SR,A:Badger Pt.5 . . . . 2.00
50 SF,double size,A:Badger Pt.6
   Crossroads tie-in 3.50
51 PS 2.00
52 PS 2.00
53 PS 2.00
54 PS 2.00
55 PS 2.00
56 . . . . 2.00
57 AH. 2.00
58 Sr,I:Stanislaus Korivitsky
   as Nexus 2.00
59 SR. 2.00
60 SR. 2.00
61 . . . . 2.00
62 . . . . 2.00
63 V:Elvonic Order 2.00
64 V:Elvonic Order 2.00
65 V:Elvonic Order 2.00
66 V:Elvonic Order 2.00
67 V:Elvonic Order 2.00
68 LM. 2.00
69 . . . . 2.00
70 . . . . 2.00
71 V:Bad Brains 2.00
72 V:Renegade heads 2.00
73 Horatio returns to Ylum 2.00
74 Horatio vs. Stan. 2.00
75 Horatio vs. Stan. 2.00
76 . . . . 2.25
77 . . . . 2.25
78 O:Nexus,Nexus Files Pt#1 . . . . 2.25
79 Nexus Files Pt#2 . . . . 2.25
80 Nexus.Files Pt#3,last iss. 2.25

NEXUS LEGENDS
First
1 thru 13 rep.Nexus . . . . @1.50
14 rep.Nexus 1.75
15 rep.Nexus 1.75
16 rep.Nexus 1.75
17 rep.Nexus 1.75
18 rep.Nexus 1.95
19 rep.Nexus 1.95
20 SR,Sanctuary 1.95
21 thru 23 SR . . . . @1.95

NICK HOLIDAY
Argo May, 1956
1 Strip reprints. 40.00

NICKI SHADOW
Relentless Comics
1 by Eric Burnham & Ted Naifeh . . 2.50
2 Killing Zone, pt.2. . . . . 2.50
3 Killing Zone, pt.3. . . . . 2.50

4 Killing Zone, concl. 2.50

NIGHT GLIDER
Topps
1 V:Bombast,C:Captain Glory, Trading
Card. 3.25

NIGHTMARE
Innovation
1 . . . . 2.50

NIGHTMARE AND CASPER
Harvey Publications 1963
1 . . . . 50.00
2 . . . . 30.00
3 . . . . 30.00
4 . . . . 30.00
5 . . . . 30.00
Becomes:

CASPER AND NIGHTMARE
6 B:68 pgs. 15.00
7 . . . . 7.00
8 . . . . 7.00
9 . . . . 7.00
10 . . . . 7.00
11 thru 20 . . . . @3.50
21 thru 30. . . . . @2.50
31 . . . . 2.50
32 E:68 pgs 2.50
33 thru 45. . . . . @2.00
46 Aug., 1974. . . . . 2.00

NIGHTMARE ON ELM STREET
Blackthorne
1 3-D. 2.50
2 3-D. 2.50
3 3-D. 2.50

NIGHTMARES ON ELM STREET
Innovation
1 Yours Truly, Freddy Krueger Pt.1 3.00
2 Yours Truly ,Freddy Krueger Pt.2 2.50
3 Loose Ends Pt.1,Return to
   Springwood 2.50
4 Loose Ends Pt 2 . . . . 2.50
5 & 6 . . . . @2.50

NIGHTMARES
Eclipse 1985
1 . . . . 2.50
2 . . . . 2.00

NIGHT MUSIC
Eclipse 1984–88
1 . . . . 2.50
2 . . . . 2.50
3 CR, Jungle Bear. 3.00
4 Pelias & Melisande. 2.00
5 Pelias. 2.00
6 same as Salome #1
7 same as Red Dog #1
Graphic Novel 8.00

NIGHTS INTO DREAMS
Archie Comics 1997
1 based on Sega game 1.75
2 thru 6 . . . . 1.75

NIGHTSHADE
No Mercy Comics 1997
1 by Mark Williams 2.50
2 and 3 . . . . @2.50

NIGHT TRIBES
Wildstorm/DC 1999
1-shot Night Tribes unite. 5.00

NIGHTVEIL
AC Comics
1 . . . . 3.50
2 . . . . 2.50
3 . . . . 2.25
4 . . . . 2.25
5 . . . . 2.25
6 . . . . 1.75
7 . . . . 1.75
Spec.#1 . . . . 1.95

NIGHT WALKER
Fleetway
1 thru 2 . . . . 2.95

NIGHTWOLF
1 . . . . 1.75
2 . . . . 1.75

9 LIVES OF FELIX
Harvey
1 thru 4 . . . . @1.25

NINE LIVES TO LIVE
Fantagraphics
HC 9"x12" Felix the Cat strips,
  by Otto Messmer 40.00

Ninja High School #8
© *Eternity*

NINJA HIGH SCHOOL
Eternity
1 Reps.orig.N.H.S.in color 1.95
2 thru 13 reprints . . . . @1.95

NINJA HIGH SCHOOL VERSION 2
Antarctic Press 1999
1 by Ben Dunn 2.50

2 . . . . 2.50

NINJA HIGH SCHOOL FEATURING SPEED RACER
Eternity 1993
1B 2.95
2B 2.95

NINJA STAR
1 . . . . 1.95

NIRA X: ANIM
Entity Comics 1997
1 BMs 2.95
1a deluxe, foil cover 3.50
2 BMs 2.95
2a deluxe, foil cover 3.50
Swimsuit #0 . . . . 2.75
Swimsuit #0 Manga (c) 2.75

NIRA X: CYBERANGEL
Entity 1994
1 From pages of Zen 2.95
1a 2nd printing 2.75
2 V:Parradox 2.50
3 In Hydro-Dams 2.50
4 final issue 2.50
4a with computer game 6.95
Ashcan 2.50
TPB Birth of an Angel. 12.95
[Series 2] 1995
1 R:Nira X 3.75
1a Clear Chromium Edition 8.00
1b Holo-Chrome edition. 10.00
2 Alien Invasion. 2.50
3 Mecha New York 2.50
4 Final Issue 2.50
[Series 3] 1996
0 . . . . 2.75
0a signed & numbered 8.00
1 . . . . 2.50
1a gold edition, signed & numb. . . 5.00
2 . . . . 2.50
3 . . . . 3.00

NIRA X/CYNDER: ENDANGERED SPECIES
Entity Comics 1996
1 . . . . 3.00
1a gold ink enhanced, bagged. . . 13.00

NOID IN 3-D
Blackthorne
1 thru 3 . . . . @2.50

NOMAN
Tower Comics 1966
1 GK,OW,WW,AW 75.00
2 OW,WW,A:Dynamo 50.00

NOOGIE KOOTCH: SECRET AGENT MAN
Hobo Comics
1 I:Noogie Kootch 2.75
2 F:Celutron CIty 2.75

NOSFERATU: PLAGUE OF TERROR
Millenium
1 I:Orlock 2.50
2 19th Century India,A:Sir W.
  Longsword 2.50
3 WWI/WWII to Viet Nam 2.50
4 O:Orlock,V:Longsword,conc. . . . 2.50

NO TIME FOR SERGEANTS
Dell Publishing Co. July, 1958
1 Ph(c) 50.00
2 Ph(c) 40.00
3 Ph(c) 40.00

NOVA HUNTER
Ryal Comics
1 thru 3 . . . . @2.50
4 Climax 2.50
5 Death and Betrayal. 2.50

NUBIAN KNIGHT
Samson Comics
1 I:Shandai 2.50

NURSES, THE
Gold Key April, 1963
1 . . . . 30.00
2 . . . . 20.00
3 . . . . 20.00

NYOKA, JUNGLE GIRL
Charlton Comics 1955–57
14 . . . . 50.00
15 . . . . 30.00
16 . . . . 30.00
17 . . . . 30.00
18 . . . . 30.00
19 . . . . 30.00
20 . . . . 30.00
21 . . . . 30.00
22 . . . . 30.00

NYOKA, THE JUNGLE GIRL
AC Comics
1 and 2 . . . . @1.95

OBLIVION
Comico 1995
1 R:The Elementals. 2.50
2 I:Thunderboy, Lilith 2.50
3 I:Fen, Ferril. 2.50
4 War 2.95
5 The Unholy Trilogy 2.95

OCCULT FILES OF DR. SPEKTOR
Gold Key April, 1973
1 I:Lakot 25.00
2 thru 5 . . . . 12.00
6 thru 10 . . . . 10.00
11 I:Spertor as Werewolf. 10.00
12 and 13. . . . . 8.00
14 A:Dr. Solar. 25.00
15 thru 24. . . . . 8.00
Whitman
25 rep 2.00

COLOR PUB.

O.G. WHIZ
Gold Key 1971–79
1	60.00
2	35.00
3	25.00
4	25.00
5	25.00
6	25.00
7	8.00
8	8.00
9	8.00
10	8.00
11	8.00

OINK: BLOOD AND CIRCUS
Kitchen Sink 1997
1 (of 4) by John Mueller	4.95
2	4.95
3	4.95
4 conclusion	4.95

O'MALLEY AND THE ALLEY CATS
Gold Key 1971–74
1	25.00
2 thru 9	@20.00

OMEGA 7
Omega 7
1 V:Exterminator X	3.95
½ by Alonzo L. Washington	3.95
0	3.00

OMEGA ELITE
Blackthorne
1	1.50
2	1.50

OMEGA SAGA, THE
Southpaw Publishing 1998
0 by Mike Gerardo & Chris Navetta	3.00
1 Episode One, pt.1	3.00
2 Episode One, pt.2	3.00
Axess Comics
3 by Mike Gerardo, Heroes (c).	3.00
3b Villains (c)	3.00

OMEN, THE
Chaos! Comics
Preview Book, BnP.	1.50
1 by PNu & Justiniano	2.95
2	2.95
3	2.95
4	2.95
5 concl.	2.95
1-shot The Omen Vexed.	2.95
TPB The Omen	12.95

OMNI MEN
Blackthorne
1	1.25
2	1.25

ON A PALE HORSE
Innovation
1 Piers Anthony adapt	4.95
2 "Magician", I:Kronos.	4.95
3	4.95
4 VV,	4.95
5	4.95
6	4.95

ONE-ARM SWORDSMAN
1	2.95
2	2.95
3	2.75
4	1.80
5	1.80
6 thru 8	@1.80
9 thru 11	@2.00

ORBIT
Eclipse 1990
1 DSt(c).	3.95
2	3.95
3	4.95

ORIENTAL HEROES
Jademan
1	2.50
2	2.00
3 thru 13	@1.50
14 thru 27	@1.95
28 V:Skeleton Secretary	1.95
29 Barbarian vs.Lone Kwoon	1.95
30 Barbarian vs.Lone Kwoon	1.95
31 SkeletonSecretaryUprisng	1.95
32 Uprising Continues	1.95
33 Jupiter Kills His Brother	1.95
34 Skeleton Sec. Suicide	1.95
35 Red Sect Vs. Global Cult	1.95
36 A:Tiger	1.95
37 Old Supreme	1.95
38 Tiger vs. 4 Hitmen	1.95
39 D:Infinite White, V:Red Sect.	1.95
40 The Golden Buddha Temple.	1.95
41 thru 43.	1.95
44 SilverChime rescue	1.95
45 Global Cult Battle.	1.95
46 thru 48	@1.95
49 F:GoldDragon/SilverChime	1.95
50 Return to Global Cult	1.95
51 Gang Of Three Vs.White Beau & Lone Kwoon-Tin	1.95
52 Global Cult vs Red Sect.	1.95
53 Global Cult vs.Red Sect.	1.95

ORIGINAL ASTRO BOY
Now
1 KSy	3.00
2 thru 5 KSy.	@2.00
6 thru 17 KSy	@1.75

Original Astro Boy #6
© Now

ORIGINAL DICK TRACY
Gladestone
1 rep.V:Mrs.Pruneface	1.95
2 rep.V:Influence	1.95
3 rep.V:TheMole	1.95
4 rep.V:ItchyOliver	1.95
5 rep.V:Shoulders	2.00

ORIGINAL E-MAN
First
{rep. Charlton stories}
1 JSon,O:E-Man & Nova	1.75
2 JSon,V:Battery,SamuelBoar	1.75
3 JSon,"City in the Sand".	1.75
4 JSon,A:Brain from Sirius.	1.75
5 JSon,V:T.V. Man	1.75
6 JSon,I:Teddy Q.	1.75
7 JSon,Vamfire	1.75

ORIGINAL SHIELD
ABC
1 DAy/TD,O:Shield	1.00
2 DAy,O:Dusty.	.75
3 DAy	.75
4 DAy	.75

ORIGIN OF THE DEFIANT UNIVERSE
Defiant
1 O:Defiant Characters	1.50

OUTBREED 999
Blackout Comics
1 thru 4	@2.95
5 Search For Daige	2.95

OUTCASTS
1	1.25

OUTER LIMITS, THE
Dell Publishing Co.
Jan.-March, 1964
1 P(c)	125.00
2 P(c)	65.00
3 P(c)	50.00
4 P(c)	50.00
5 P(c)	50.00
6 P(c)	50.00
7 P(c)	50.00
8 P(c)	50.00
9 P(c)	50.00
10 P(c)	50.00
11 thru 18 P(c)	40.00

OUTLAWS OF THE WEST
Charlton Comics 1956–80
11	40.00
12	20.00
13	20.00
14 Giant	25.00
15	20.00
16	20.00
17	20.00
18 SD.	50.00
19	15.00
20	15.00
21 thru 30	@10.00
31 thru 50	@6.00
51 thru 70	@4.00
71 thru 88	@3.00

OUT OF THIS WORLD
Charlton Comics 1956–59

1	175.00
2	100.00
3 SD	200.00
4 SD	200.00
5 SD	200.00
6 SD	200.00
7 SD,SD(c)	200.00
8 SD	175.00
9 SD	175.00
10 SD	175.00
11 SD	175.00
12 SD	175.00
13 thru 15	@60.00
16	165.00

OUTPOSTS
Blackthorne

1 thru 6	@1.25

OWL, THE
Gold Key April, 1967

1	30.00
2 April, 1968	20.00

Pacific Presents #1
© Pacific Comics

PACIFIC PRESENTS
Pacific 1992

1 DSt,Rocketeer,(3rd App.)	16.00
2 DSt,Rocketeer,(4th App.)	14.00
3 SD,I:Vanity	2.50
4 and 5	@2.00

P.A.C.
Artifacts Inc

1 I:P.A.C.	1.95

PAINKILLER JANE
Event Comics 1997

1 JQ(c)	2.95
1 RL(c)	2.95
1 Red foil logo, signed	24.95
2 JQ&JP(c)	2.95
2 JP&RL(c)	2.95
3 JQ&JP(c)	2.95
3a JP&RL(c)	2.95
4 JQ&JP(c) A Too Bright Place For Dying	2.95
4a RL&JP(c)	2.95

5 JQ&JP(c) Purgatory Station—Next Stop Hell	2.95
5a RL&JP(c)	2.95
6 RL&JP(c) Blood Harvest	2.95
6a BSz&JP(c)	2.95
7 Jane in the Jungle, pt.1,BiT&JP(c)	2.95
7a RL&JP(c)	2.95
Spec.#0 O:Painkiller Jane,48-page	3.95
Spec.#0A signed	40.00
Spec. Painkiller Jane/Hellboy Ancient Laughter (1998)	2.95
Spec. Painkiller Jane/Hellboy, signed	30.00
Spec. Painkiller Jane/The Darkness, signed, limited edition, JQ(c)	29.95

PAINKILLER JANE/DARKCHYLDE
Event Comics 1998

1 BAu,RQu	2.95
1a signed & numbered	40.00
1b Omnichrome edition	14.95
1c Omnichrome, signed	40.00
1d Dynamic Forces cover	6.95

PAINKILLER JANE VS. THE DARKNESS: STRIPPER
Event Comics 1997

1 GEn,JP,x-over, Amanda Connor cover	2.95
1a Greg & Tim Hildebrandt	2.95
1b MS(c)	2.95
1c JQ(c)	2.95

PALADIN ALPHA
Firstlight

1 I:Paladin Alpha	2.95
2 V:Hellfire Triger	2.95

PANDEMONIUM: DELIVERANCE
Chaos! Comics 1998

1-shot by Jesse Leon McCann & Jack Jadson	2.95

PANIC
Gemstone 1997

1 thru 11 EC Comics reprint	@2.50

"Annuals"

TPB Vol. 1 rebinding #1–#4	10.50
TPB Vol. 2 rebinding #5–#8	10.95

PANTHA
Harris Comics 1997

1 (of 2) MT	3.50
1 Marylin Monroe MT alt.cov.	9.95

PARADAX
Eclipes

1	2.25

PARADIGM
Gauntlet

1 A:Predator	2.95

PARAGON DARK APOCALYPSE
AC 1993

1 thru 4, Fem Force crossover	2.95

PARANOIA
Adventure Comics

1 (based on video game)"Clone1"	3.25
2 King-R-Thr-2	2.95
3 R:Happy Jack,V:N3F	2.95
4 V:The Computer	2.95
5 V:The Computer	2.95
6 V:Lance-R-Lot,last issue	2.95

PARTRIDGE FAMILY, THE
Charlton Comics 1971–73

1	50.00
2 thru 4	@25.00
5 Summer Special	30.00
6 thru 21	@25.00

PASSOVER
Maximum Press

1 (of 2) BNa	3.00
2 BNa,A:Avengelyne	3.00

PATHWAYS TO FANTASY
Pacific

1 BS,JJ art	3.00

PAT SAVAGE: WOMAN OF BRONZE
Millenium

1 F:Doc Savage's cousin	2.50

PEACEMAKER
Charlton

1 A:Fightin' 5	5.00
2 A:Fightin' 5	3.00
3 A:Fightin' 5	3.00
4 O:Peacemaker,A:Fightin' 5	4.00
5 A:Fightin' 5	2.50

PEANUTS
Dell Publishing Co. 1958

1	125.00
2	100.00
3	100.00
4	75.00
5	50.00
6	50.00
7	50.00
8	50.00
9	50.00
10	50.00
11	50.00
12	50.00
13	50.00

PEANUTS
Gold Key May, 1963

1	100.00
2 thru 4	75.00

PEBBLES & BAMM BAMM
Charlton Comics 1972–76

1	50.00
2 thru 10	@25.00

11 thru 36 . . . . @20.00

PEBBLES FLINTSTONE
Gold Key Sept., 1963
1 "A Chip off the old block" 100.00

PELLESTAR
1 . . . . 1.75

PERG
Lightning Comics
1 Glow in the dark(c),JS(c),
  B:JZy(s),KIK,I:Perg. 3.75
1a Platinum Ed. 5.00
1b Gold Ed. 7.00
1 gold edition, glow-in-the-dark
  flip cover 30.00
2 KIK,O:Perg. 3.25
2a Platinum Ed. 5.00
3 Flip Book (c), ... 3.25
3a Platinum Ed 5.00
4 TLw,I:Hellina. 9.00
4a Platinum Ed 5.00
5 A:Hellina. 3.25
6 PIA,A:Hellina 3.25
6 nude cover 9.00
7 . . . . 3.00
8 V:Police 3.00

PERRY MASON MYSTERY MAGAZINE
Dell Publishing Co. 1964
1 . . . . 40.00
2 Ray Burr Ph(c) 30.00

PETER PAN: RETURN TO NEVERNEVER LAND
1 Peter in Mass. 2.50
2 V:Tiger Lily 2.50

PETER POTAMUS
Gold Key Jan., 1965
1 . . . . 100.00

PETTICOAT JUNCTION
Dell Publishing Co. 1964
1 Ph(c) 75.00
2 Ph(c) 50.00
3 Ph(c) 50.00
4 . . . . 50.00
5 Ph(c) 50.00

PHANTOM, THE
Gold Key 1962
1 RsM 150.00
2 B:King, Queen & Jack. 75.00
3 . . . . 50.00
4 . . . . 50.00
5 . . . . 50.00
6 . . . . 50.00
7 "The Super Apes". 50.00
8 . . . . 50.00
9 . . . . 50.00
10 "The Sleeping Giant" 50.00
11 E:King,Queen and Jack 40.00
12 B:Track Hunter 40.00
13 . . . . 40.00
14 "The Historian". 40.00
15 . . . . 40.00
16 . . . . 40.00
17 "Samaris" 40.00
King Comics Sept. 1966
18 "The Treasure of the Skull

Cave;"BU:Flash Gordon 50.00
19 "The Astronaut & the Pirates". . 30.00
20 A:GirlPhantom,E:FlashGordon. 30.00
21 BU:Mandrake. 30.00
22 "Secret of Magic Mountain" . . . 30.00
23 . . . . 30.00
24 A:Girl Phantom 30.00
25 . . . . 30.00
26 . . . . 30.00
27 . . . . 30.00
28 . . . . 30.00
29. . . . . 30.00
Charlton Comics 1969–77
30 . . . . 20.00
31 JAp,"Phantom of Shang-Ri-La" 20.00
32 JAp,"The Pharaoh Phantom" . . 20.00
33 . . . . 20.00
34 . . . . 20.00
35 . . . . 20.00
36 . . . . 20.00
37 . . . . 20.00
38 . . . . 20.00
39 . . . . 20.00
40 "The Ritual" 20.00

Phantom #44
© Charlton Comics

41 . . . . 15.00
42 . . . . 15.00
43 . . . . 15.00
44 "To Right A Wrong" 15.00
45 . . . . 15.00
46 I:Piranha 20.00
47 "The False Skull Cave" 15.00
48 . . . . 15.00
49 . . . . 15.00
50 . . . . 15.00
51 "A Broken Vow" 15.00
52 . . . . 15.00
53 . . . . 15.00
54 . . . . 15.00
55 . . . . 15.00
56 . . . . 15.00
57 NightmareMedicine in Bengali . 15.00
58 . . . . 15.00
59 . . . . 15.00
60 . . . . 15.00
61 "A Dead Man's Promise" 15.00
62 . . . . 15.00
63 . . . . 15.00
64 "Duel With Death" 15.00
65 . . . . 15.00
66 "Goldbeard the Pirate" 15.00
67 "Triumph of Evil" 15.00
68 . . . . 15.00
69 . . . . 15.00

70 . . . . 15.00
71 . . . . 10.00
72 "Man in the Shadows" 10.00
73 . . . . 10.00
74 . . . . 10.00

PHANTOM
Wolf Publishing 1992
1 Drug Runners. 2.25
2 Mystery Child of the Sea. 2.25
3 inc.feature pages on
  Phantom/Merchandise 2.25
4 TV Jungle Crime Buster 2.25
5 Castle Vacula-Transylvania. . . . 2.25
6 The Old West 2.25
7 Sercet of Colussus 2.75
8 Temple of the Sun God. 2.75

PHANTOM BOLT, THE
Gold Key 1964–66
1 . . . . 50.00
2 . . . . 30.00
3 . . . . 20.00
4 . . . . 20.00
5 . . . . 20.00
6 . . . . 20.00
7 . . . . 20.00

PHANTOM FORCE
Genesis West 1994
Previously: Image
0 JK/JLe(c) 2.75
3 thru 10 . . . . @2.50

PHAZE
Eclipse 1988
1 BSz(c),Takes place in future 2.25
2 PG(c),V:The Pentagon 1.95
3 Schwieger Vs. Mammoth 1.95

PHOENIX
Atlas 1975
1 thru 4 . . . . @5.00

PINK PANTHER, THE
Gold Key April, 1971
1 . . . . 45.00
2 thru 10 . . . . @25.00
11 thru 30 . . . . @15.00
31 thru 60 . . . . @10.00
61 thru 10.00

PINOCCHIO
1 . . . . 1.50

PIRACY
Gemstone 1998
1 EC comics reprint. 2.50
2 thru 7 EC comics reprints . . . @2.50
"Annuals"
TPB Vol. 1 rebinding #1–#4 . . . . 10.50
TPB Vol. 2 rebinding #5–#7 . . . . . 7.95

PIRATE CORP.
Eternity
1 thru 5 . . . . @1.95

P.I.'S, THE
First
1 JSon,Ms.Tree,M Mauser. 1.50
2 JSon,Ms.Tree,M Mauser. 1.25
3 JSon,Ms.Tree,M Mauser. 1.25

PITT
Full Bleed Studios
1 thru 9, see Image
10 thru 14 DK . . . . @2.50
14a variant cover 7.00
15 DK. 2.50
16 DK, Ugly Americans, pt.1 . . . . . 2.50
17 DK, Ugly Americans, pt.2 . . . . . 2.50
18 DK, Ugly Americans, pt.3, concl. 2.50
19 by Brian Dawson 2.95
20 DK, Urgral Thul 2.50
TPB Vol. 1, rep. ½ &#1–#4 . . . . . 10.95
TPB Vol. 2, rep. #5–#9 . . . . 11.95
Spec. In the Blood 2.50

PITT CREW
Full Bleed Studios 1998
1 Monster 2.50
2 F:Rai-Kee 2.50
3 Tyrants 2.50
4 The Slayer 2.50

PLANETARY
Wildstorm/DC 1999
1 WEI 2.50
2 WEI 2.50
3 WEI 2.50
4 WEI 2.50
5 WEI 2.50
6 WEI 2.50

PLANET COMICS
Blackthorne
1 DSt(c) 2.00
2 thru 4 . . . . @2.00

PLANET OF VAMPIRES
Atlas Feb.–July 1975
1 thru 3 . . . . @5.00

POGZ N SLAMMER
Blackout Comics 1995
1 I:Pogz N Slammer 1.95
2 Contact Other Schools 1.95

POISON ELVES
Sirius Entertainment 1998
Color Special #1 by Drew Hayes . . 2.95
Color Spec.#1 limited 9.95

POIZON
London Night Studios 1995
0 . . . . 3.00
0 signed gothchik edition 15.00
½ O:Poizon 3.00
½a Commemorative (1999) 5.95
1 . . . . 3.00
1a Necro-Nude edition 5.95
1b Photo Nude Edition signed . . . 10.00
1c signed 10.00
2 EHr 3.00

POIZON: CADILLACS AND GREEN TOMATOES
London Night 1997
2 . . . . 3.00
2a deluxe nude cover 6.00
3 . . . . 3.00
6 deluxe 6.00

POIZON: DEMON HUNTER
London Night 1998
1 . . . . 3.00
1 Green Death edition 14.95

POIZON: LOST CHILD
London Night Studios 1996
0 . . . . 3.00
1 mini series 3.00
1a Necro-Nude variant cover 5.95
1 signed 10.00
1 Green Death edition 14.95
2 thru 3 . . . . @3.00

POPEYE
Gold Key 1962
1-65 See Golden Age Section
66 . . . . 75.00
67 . . . . 50.00
68 thru 80 . . . . @20.00

Popeye #84
© King Comics

King Comics 1966
81 thru 92 . . . . @15.00
Charlton 1969
94 thru 99 . . @12.50
100 . . . . 15.00
101 thru 138 . . . . @12.50
Gold Key 1978
139 thru 143 . . . . @6.00
144 50th Aniv. Spec. 7.50
155 . . . . @6.00
Whitman
156 thru 159 . . . . @4.00
162 thru 171 . . . . @4.00

POPEYE
Harvey Comics 1993–94
1 thru 7 . . . . @1.50
Summer Spec.#1 . . . . 2.25

POPEYE SPECIAL
Ocean 1987–88
1 . . . . 1.75
2 . . . . 2.00

POWER FACTOR
Wonder Color Comics 1986
1 . . . . 4.00
2 & 3 . . . . @3.00

POWER FACTOR
Innovation
1 thru 4 . . . . @2.25

POWERKNIGHTS
Amara 1995
P I:Powerknights 1.50

POWER RANGERS ZEO/YOUNGBLOOD
Maximum Press 1997
1 TNu,NRd 3.00

POWERS THAT BE
Broadway Comics
Preview Editions Sept. 1995
1 thru 3 B&W . . . . @2.50
Regular Series Nov. 1995
1 JiS,I:Fatale, Star Seed 3.00
2 thru 4 . . . . @2.95
5 "It's the End of the World As We Know It" pt.1 . . . . 2.95
6 "It's the End of the World As We Know It" pt.2 . . . . 2.95
Becomes:

STAR SEED
7 "It's the End of the World As We Know It" pt.3 . . . . 2.95
8 "It's the End of the World As We Know It" pt.4 . . . . 2.95
9 "It's the End of the World As We Know It" pt.5 . . . . 2.95
10 JiS(s),JRs,"It's the End of the World As We Know It" pt6 . . . . . 2.95
11 JiS(s),JRs,"It's the End of the World As We Know It" pt7 . . . . . 2.95

PRESSBUTTON
Eclipse
(see Axel Pressbutton)
5 and 6 . . . . @1.75

PRIEST
Maximum Press 1996
1 RLd, F:Michael O'Bannon 3.00
2 RLd,BNa, ... 3.00
3 RLd 3.00

PRIMAL RAGE
Sirius 1996
1 TAr,from video game 2.95
1 foil cover, limited edition 2.95
2 TAr,DOe(c) 2.95

PRIMER
Comico 1982–84
1 . . . . 10.00
2 I:Grendel 85.00
3 . . . . 5.00
4 C:Maxx 7.00
5 I:Maxx 30.00
6 I:Evangelyne 14.00
[Volume 2] 1996
1 F:Lady Bathory 2.95

PRIMUS
Charlton Comics 1972
1 . . . . 10.00
2 thru 5 . . . . @10.00
6 thru 7 . . . . @8.00

PRINCESS SALLY
Archie Comics
1 thru 3 Sonic tie-in . . . . @

PRINCE VANDAL
Triumphant
1 JnR(s), ... 2.50
2 JnR(s), ... 2.50
3 JnR(s),ShG,I:Claire,V:Nicket,
  Vandal goes to Boviden 2.50
4 JnR(s),ShG,Game's End. 2.50
5 JnR(s),ShG,The Sickness, the
  rat appears. 2.50
6 JnR(s),ShG,B:Gothic 2.50

Priority: White Heat #1
© AC Comics

PRIORITY: WHITE HEAT
AC Comics 1986
1 thru 2 miniseries . . . . @1.75

PRISON SHIP
1 . . . . 1.75

PRIVATEERS
Vanguard Graphics
1 . . . . 1.50
2 . . . . 1.50

PROFESSIONAL: GOGOL 13
Viz
1 . . . . 4.95
2 and 3 . . . . @4.95

PROFESSOR OM
Innovation
1 I:Rock Warrior 2.50
2 Samurai Drama 2.50

PROJECT A-KO 0
Antarctic Press 1994
0 digest size 5.00
Continued by Malibu

PROJECT A-KO 2
CPM 1995
Previously Malibu
1 Space Saga 2.95
2 Space Saga 2.95
3 Queen Margarita 2.95

PROJECT A-KO: VERSUS THE UNIVERSE
CPM 1995
1 Based on Animation 2.95
2 strange magician 3.00
3 . . . . 3.00
4 (of 5) TEI 2.95

PROMETHEA
Wildstorm/DC 1999
America's Best Comics
1 AMo(s),F:Sophie Bangs,40-page 3.50
2 AMo(s),Judgment of Solomon. . . 3.00
3 AMo(s),Misty Magic Land 3.00

PROPHECY
Immortelle Studios 1998
1 by Hawk, Lovalle, & Wong,
  F:Cynder & War Dragon 2.95
2 . . . . 2.95

PROPHECY OF THE SOUL SORCERER
Arcane Comics 1999
1 (of 4) by Eric Dean Seaton 2.95
2 . . . . 2.95
3 . . . . 2.95
4 . . . . 2.95

PROPHET/CABLE
Maximum 1997
1 (of 2) RLd x-over 3.50
2 RLd x-over,A:Domino, Kirby,
  Blaquesmith 3.50

PROWLER
Eclipse 1987
1 I:Prowler. 1.75
2 GN,A:Original Prowler 1.75
3 GN 1.75
4 GN 1.75
5 GN, adaption of "Vampire Bat" . . 1.75
6 w/flexi-disk record. 1.75

PROWLER IN "WHITE ZOMBIE", THE
Eclipse 1988
1 . . . . 1.75

PRUDENCE AND CAUTION
Defiant
1 CCI(s), ... 3.25
1a Spanish Version 3.25
2 CCI(s), ... 2.50
2a Spanish Version 2.50
3 CCI(s), ... 2.50
3a Spanish Version 2.50
4 CCI(s), ... 2.50
4a Spanish Version 2.50
5 CCI(s), ... 2.50
5a Spanish Version 2.50

PSYCHO
Innovation
1 Hitchcock movie adapt 2.50
2 continued 2.50
3 continued 2.50

PSYCHOANALYSIS
Gemstone 1999
1 (of 4) 2.50
HC 20.00

PSYCHOBLAST
First
1 thru 9 . . . . @1.75

PUBLIC DEFENDER IN ACTION
Charlton Comics 1957
7 . . . . 60.00
8 and 9 . . . . @40.00
10 thru 12, ... @40.00

PUDGE PIG
Charlton Comics Sept., 1958
1 . . . . 16.00
2 . . . . 15.00

PUPPET MASTER
Eternity
1 Movie Adapt.Andre Toulon 2.50
2 Puppets Protecting Diary 2.50
3 R:Andre Toulon. 2.50
4 . . . . 2.50

PUPPET MASTER: CHILDREN OF THE PUPPET MASTER
Eternity
1 Killer Puppets on the loose 2.50
2 concl. 2.50

PURGATORI
Chaos! Comics
1-shot prelude 3.00
1-shot signed, limited + print 25.00

PURGATORI
Chaos! Comics 1998
1 DQ from slave to Goddess? 2.95
2 Goddess War,pt.1, x-over 2.95
3 Goddess War, epilog 2.95
4 Unholy Nights. 2.95
5 V:Karmilla. 2.95
6 . . . . 2.95
7 V:Dracula 2.95

PURGATORI: THE DRACULA GAMBIT
Chaos! Comics 1997
1 DQ & Brian LeBlanc 3.00
1a signed 20.00
Sketchbook, b&w 3.50

PURGATORI: GODDESS RISING
Chaos! Comics 1999
1 (of 4) MD2 . . . . 2.95
1a premium edition 10.00

2 .... 2.95
3 .... 2.95

PURGATORI:
THE VAMPIRES MYTH
Chaos! Comics
1 (of 3) 4.00
1-shot limited chromium edition . . 19.95
2 BnP,JBa 3.00
3 BnP,JBa, final issue 3.00
TPB with CD................. 30.00
TPB 12.95
Micro Premium Preview Book.... 15.00

QUANTUM LEAP
Innovation
{based on TV series}
1 1968 Memphis 3.50
1a Special Edition 2.50
2 Ohio 1962,"Freedom of the
Press"........................ 3.00
3 1958 "The $50,000 Quest" 3.00
4 "Small Miracles" 2.50
5 .... 2.50
6 .... 2.50
7 Golf Pro,School Bus Driver..... 2.50
8 1958,Bank Robber 2.50
9 NY 1969,Gay Rights.......... 2.50
10 1960s' Stand-up Comic 2.50
11 1959,Dr.(LSD experiments) 2.50
12 .... 2.50

QUEEN OF THE
DAMNED
Innovation
1 Anne Rice Adapt."On the Road
to the Vampire Lestat" 3.50
2 Adapt. continued 2.50
3 The Devils Minion............ 2.50
4 Adapt.continued 2.50
5 Adapt.continued 2.50
6 Adapt.continued 2.50
7 Adapt.continued 2.50
8 Adapt.continued 2.50

QUICK-DRAW McGRAW
Charlton Comics 1970–72
1 TV Animated Cartoon........ 45.00
2 .... 30.00
3 .... 30.00
4 thru 8 .... @30.00

Q-UNIT
Harris
1 I:Q-Unit,w/card 3.25

RACE FOR THE MOON
Harvey Publications 1958
1 BP 100.00
2 JK,AW,JK/AW(c).......... 175.00
3 JK,AW,JK/AW(c) 200.00

RACER-X
Now
Premire Special 5.00
1 thru 3 .... @2.50
4 thru 11 .... @1.75
[2nd Series]
1 thru 10 .... @1.75

RACK & PAIN
Chaos! Comics
3 (of 4) BnP,LJi,. 2.95
4 BnP,LJi, final issue 2.95

RACK & PAIN: KILLERS
Chaos! Comics
1 (of 4) JaL(c) 2.95
2 BnP,LJi,JaL(c) 2.95

RADICAL DREAMER
Blackball
0 .... 2.00
1 thru 5 V:Jorge Futran .... @2.50

RADIOACTIVE MAN
Bongo
1 I:Radioactive Man........... 4.00
1 80pg offered again 3.25
88 V:Lava Man............... 2.00
212 V:Hypno Head............ 2.00
412 V:Dr. Crab 2.25
679 with card 2.25
1000 Final issue.............. 2.25

RAEL
Eclipse
Vol 1....................... 6.95

RAGAMUFFINS
Eclipse 1985
1 .... 3.00

RALPH SNART
ADVENTURES
Now
[Volumes 1 & 2]
see B&W
9 and 10, color 2.50
[Volume 3]
1 .... 4.00
2 thru 10 .... @3.00
11 thru 21 .... @2.00
22 thru 26................. @1.75
TPB 9.95
[Volume 4]
1 thru 3, with 1 of 2 trading cards. . 2.50

Ralph Snart Vol. 5 #5 © Now

[Volume 5]
1 thru 5, with 1 of 2 trading cards. . 2.50
3-D Spec.#1 with 3-D glasses and
12 trading cards 3.50

RAMAR OF THE JUNGLE
Toby Press 1954
1 Ph(c), John Hall 150.00
Charlton
2 .... 100.00
3 .... 100.00
4 .... 100.00
5 Sept., 1956............... 100.00

RAMPANT
Manifest Destiny Comics
1/2 Various Artists 2.50

RANDOM 5
Amara Inc. 1995
1 I:Random 5 .... 1.50

RANGO
Dell Publishing Co. Aug., 1967
1 Tim Conway Ph(c) 35.00

RANMA 1/2
Viz 1992
1 I:Ranma................. 50.00
2 I:Upperclassmen Kuno 25.00
3 F:Upperclassmen Kuno 20.00
4 Confusion................. 5.00
5 A:Ryoga.................. 5.00
6 Ryoga plots revenge......... 9.00
7 Conclusion 5.00
[Part 2]
1 .... 8.00
2 .... 5.00
3 thru 7 .... @4.00
8 .... 5.00
9 .... 6.00
10 and 11................... 3.00
continued, see Other Pub. B&W

RAPHAEL
Mirage
1 TMNTurtle characters 15.00

RARE BREED
Dark Moon Productions 1995
1 V:Anarchy................. 2.50
2 V:Anarchy................. 2.50

RAT BASTARD
Crucial Comics 1997
1 by The Huja Brothers 1.95
2 .... 1.95
3 .... 1.95
4 (of 4) 1.95
5 .... 1.95
5 .... 1.95
6 .... 1.95

RAT PATROL, THE
Dell Publishing Co.,
March, 1967
1 Ph(c) 75.00
2 .... 50.00
3 thru 6 Ph(c)............. @40.00

RAVEN
Renaissance Comics
1 I:Raven 2.50
2 V:Macallister. 2.50
3 thru 5 . . . . @2.50
6 V:Nightmare Creatures 2.75

RAVENING
Avatar 1998
½ Busch (c) F:Ravyn & Glyph 3.00
½a Meadows(c). 3.00
½b nude cover 6.00
½c nude leather cover 30.00
½d Sketched Edition 85.00
½e Blood Red Foil, signed. 10.00

RAVENS AND RAINBOWS
Pacific
1 . . . . 1.50

RAY BRADBURY CHRONICLES
Byron Press
1 short stories 10.00
2 short stories 10.00
3 short stories 10.00

RAY BRADBURY COMICS
Topps 1993–94
1 thru 5 w/Trading Card. 3.25
Spec.#1 The Illustrated Man 3.00
Spec. Trilogy of Terror 2.50
Spec. The Martian Chronicles. . . . 3.00

R.A.Z.E.
Firstlight
1 I:R.A.Z.E., Secret Weapon 2.95
2 V:Exterminators 2.95

RAZOR
London Night Studios
0 . . . . 15.00
0a second printing. 3.00
1 I:Razor. 15.00
1a second printing. 3.00
2 . . . . 10.00
2a limited ed., red & blue. 20.00
2b platinum ed. 25.00
3 . . . . 9.00
3a with poster 18.00
4 . . . . 4.00
4a with poster 15.00
5 . . . . 9.00
5a platinum ed. 22.00
6 . . . . 7.00
7 . . . . 5.00
8 . . . . 3.00
9 . . . . 3.00
10 . . . . 3.00
11 & 12 B&W . . . . @3.00
Ann.#1 I:Shi 25.00
Ann.#2 O:Razor B&W 35.00
Becomes:

RAZOR UNCUT
see B&W
Volume 2 1996
1 DQ, ... 3.00
1 holochrome edition 8.00
2 DQ 3.00
2 holochrome edition 5.00
3 . . . . 3.00
4 . . . . 3.00

5 . . . . 3.00
6 . . . . 3.00
7 . . . . 3.00

RAZOR AND SHI SPECIAL
London Night Studios 1994
1 Rep. Razor Ann.#1 + new art . . . 5.00
1a platinum version 12.00

RAZOR ARCHIVES
London Night
1 & 2 see B&W
3 rep. Razor #10–12 . . . . 7.00

RAZOR BURN
London Night Studios 1994
1 V:Styke. 3.00
1a signed 5.00
2 Searching for Styke 3.00
2a Platinum. 8.00
3 Stryke's War. 3.00
4 D:Razor, bagged 3.00
5 Epilogue. 3.00

RAZOR: CRY NO MORE
London Night Studios 1995
1-shot 3.00
1a variant 4.00
1b Commemorative (1999) 5.95

RAZOR/MORBID ANGEL: SOUL SEARCH
London Night
1 (of 3) 3.00
1 platinum edition 5.00
1 Chromium edition 8.00
2 . . . . 3.00
3 . . . . 3.00

RAZOR/POISON/ AREALA WARRIOR NUN: LITTLE BAD ANGELS
London Night 1999
Spec. x-over Raxor cover 3.95
Spec.A Poison cover 3.95
Spec.B Areala cover. 3.95

RAZOR: THE SUFFERING
London Night Studios 1994
1 . . . . 4.00
1a Director's cut 3.00
1b signed, limited 12.00
2 . . . . 3.00
2a Director's cut 2.50
3 final chapter 3.00

RAZOR: TORTURE
London Night Studios 1995
0 Razor back from dead 4.00
0a signed edition. 8.00
1 . . . . 3.00
1a Commemorative (1999) 5.95
2 . . . . 3.00
3 EHr 3.00
4 . . . . 3.00
5 alt. cover, signed 4.00
6 alt. cover, signed 4.00
7 . . . . 3.00

Razor Torture #5
© London Night

RAZOR SWIMSUIT SPECIAL
London Night Studios 1995
1 pin-ups 3.00
1a platinum version 8.00
1b commemorative edition. 4.00

RAZOR/WARRIOR NUN AREALA: DARK MENACE
London Night 1999
Spec. x-over 3.95
Spec.A x-over, variant cover 3.95

RAZOR/ WARRIOR NUN AREALA: FAITH
London Night
1 by Jude Millien 3.00
1a variant cover. 4.00

REAL GHOSTBUSTERS
Now
1 KSy(c) 4.50
2 thru 7 . . . . @2.50
8 thru 24 . . . . @1.75

[2nd Series]
1 Halloween Special 1.75
Ann. 3-D w/glasses & pinups 2.95

REALITY CHECK
Sirius 1996
1 by Tavicat 2.95
2 thru 8 . . . . @2.95
9 Nonesuch Nonsense, pt.1 . . . . 2.95
10 Nonesuch Nonsense, pt.2 . . . . 2.95
11 Nonesuch Nonsense, pt.3 . . . . 2.95
12 Nonesuch Nonsense, pt.4 . . . . 2.95
TPB Vol. 1 . . . . 17.95

REAL WAR STORIES
Eclipse 1987–91
1 BB 3.00
1a 2nd printing 1.50
2 . . . . 4.95

COLOR PUB.

RE-ANIMATOR
Adventure Comics
1 movie adaption 2.95
2 movie adaption 2.95

RE-ANIMATOR
Adventure
1 Prequel to Orig movie 2.50

RE-ANIMATOR: DAWN OF THE RE-ANIMATOR
Adventure
1 Prequel to movie 2.50
2 . . . . 2.50
3 . . . . 2.50
4 V:Erich Metler. 2.50

RE-ANIMATOR: TALES OF HERBERT WEST
Adventure Comics
1 H.P.Lovecraft stories. 4.95

RED DOG
Eclipse 1988
1 CR,Mowgli "Jungle Book" story . . 2.00

RED DRAGON
Comico 1995
1 SBs,I:Red Dragon. 2.50
2 How Soon is Nau? 2.95

REDEEMERS
Antarctic Press 1997
1 (of 5) by Herb Mallette
   & Patrick Blain 2.95
2 . . . . 2.95

RED HEAT
1 3-D. 2.50

RED SONJA in 3-D
Blackthorne
1 thru 3 . . . . @2.50

REESE'S PIECES
Eclipse 1985
1 reprint from Web of Horror 1.50
2 reprint from Web of Horror 1.50

RE: GEX
Awesome Entertainment 1998
0 RLe,. 2.50
0a Red Foil variant 5.00
1 RLe,JLb 2.50
1a Platinum cover 9.00
1b Red Foil cover 18.00
1c Variant RL cover. 4.00
2 RLe,JLb 2.50
3 RLe,A:The Coven,V:Youngblood. 2.50
Con Spec. '98. . . . . 5.00
Orlando Megacon ashcan. 10.00
Orlando Megacon ashcan, signed. 20.00

REGGIE
Archie Publications 1963–65
15 . . . . 50.00
16 . . . . 40.00
17 . . . . 40.00
18 . . . . 40.00
Becomes:

REGGIE AND ME
Archie Publications 1966–80
19 . . . . 30.00
20 thru 23 . . . . @20.00
24 thru 40 . . . . @8.00
41 thru 126 . . . . @3.00

REGGIE'S WISE GUY JOKES
Archie Publications April, 1968
1 . . . . 35.00
2 . . . . 15.00
3 . . . . 15.00
4 . . . . 15.00
5 . . . . 10.00
6 . . . . 10.00
7 . . . . 10.00
8 . . . . 10.00
9 . . . . 10.00
10 . . . . 10.00
11 thru 60, Jan. 1982 . . . . @4.00

REIVERS
Enigma
1 thru 3 Rock 'n' Roll. 2.95

REPTILICUS
Charlton Comics Aug., 1961
1 . . . . 125.00
2 . . . . 75.00
Becomes:

REPTISAURUS
3 . . . . 50.00
4 . . . . 40.00
5 . . . . 40.00
6 . . . . 40.00
7 . . . . 40.00
8 Summer, 1963 . . . . 40.00

RETURN OF KONGA, THE
Charlton Comics 1962
N# 40.00

RETURN OF MEGATON MAN
Kitchen Sink
1 Don Simpson art (1988) 2.00
2 Don Simpson art. 2.00
3 Don Simpson art. 2.00

RETURN TO JURASSIC PARK
Topps 1995
1 R:Jurassic Park 2.50
2 V:Blosyn Team, Army 2.50
3 The Hunted 2.50
4 Army 2.50
5 Heirs to the Thunder,pt.1 . . . . . 2.95
6 Heirs to the Thunder,pt.2 . . . . . 2.95
7 Inquiring Minds,pt.1 . . . . 2.95
8 Photo Finish, concl. 2.95
9 Jurassic Jam issue 2.95

REVENGE OF THE PROWLER
Eclipse 1988
1 GN,R:Prowler. 1.75
2 GN,A:Fighting Devil Dogs with
   Flexi-Disk. 2.50
3 GN,A:Devil Dogs 1.75
4 GN,V:Pirahna 1.75

REVENGERS
Continuity
1 NA,O:Megalith,I:Crazyman 5.50
2 NA,Megalith meets Armor & Silver Str
eak,Origin Revengers#1 . . . . 2.50
3 NA/NR,Origin Revengers #2. . . . 2.50
4 NA,Origin Revengers #3. . . . . . 2.50
5 NA,Origin Revengers #4. . . . . . 2.50
6 I:Hybrids. 3.00
Spec. #1 F:Hybrids. 4.95

RIBIT
Comico
1 FT,Mini-series. 1.95
2 FT,Mini-series. 1.95
3 FT,Mini-series. 1.95
4 FT,Mini-series. 1.95

Richie Rich #80
© Harvey Publications

RICHIE RICH
Harvey Publications 1960–91
1 . . . . 1,500.00
2 . . . . 500.00
3 . . . . 300.00
4 . . . . 300.00
5 . . . . 300.00
6 . . . . 175.00
7 . . . . 175.00
8 . . . . 175.00
9 . . . . 175.00
10 . . . . 175.00
11 thru 20 . . . . @100.00
21 thru 40 . . . . @75.00
41 thru 60 . . . . @50.00
61 thru 80 . . . . @20.00
81 thru 99 . . . . @10.00
100 . . . . 15.00
101 thru 111 . . . . @7.00
112 thru 116 52 pg Giants . . . . . . @8.00
117 thru 120 . . . . @6.00
121 thru 140 . . . . @4.00
141 thru 160 . . . . @3.00
161 thru 180 . . . . @2.00
181 thru 254 . . . . @1.00

RICHIE RICH
Harvey 1991
1 thru 15 . . . . @3.00
16 thru 28 . . . . @2.00

RICHIE RICH
BANK BOOKS
Harvey 1972–82

1	40.00
2 thru 5	@25.00
6 thru 10	@15.00
11 thru 20	@10.00
21 thru 30	@7.00
31 thru 40	@5.00
41 thru 59	@4.00

RICHIE RICH
BILLIONS
Harvey 1974–82

1	25.00
2 thru 5	@15.00
6 thru 10	@10.00
11 thru 20	@7.00
21 thru 30	@4.00
31 thru 48	@3.00

RICHIE RICH
DIAMONDS
Harvey 1972–82

1	50.00
2 thru 5	@20.00
6 thru 10	@15.00
11 thru 20	@10.00
21 thru 30	@4.00
31 thru 59	@3.00

RICHIE RICH
DOLLARS & CENTS
Harvey Publications 1963–82

1	165.00
2	75.00
3 thru 5	@50.00
6 thru 10	@30.00
11 thru 20	@25.00
21 thru 30	@15.00
31 thru 43	@10.00
44 thru 60	@7.00
61 thru 70	@4.00
71 thru 109	@3.00

RICHIE RICH
FORTUNES
Harvey 1971–82

1	50.00
2 thru 5	@25.00
6 thru 10	@15.00
11 thru 20	@7.00
21 thru 30	@4.00
31 thru 63	@3.00

RICHIE RICH
GEMS
Harvey 1974–82

1	20.00
2 thru 5	@12.00
6 thru 10	@8.00
11 thru 20	@7.00
21 thru 30	@4.00
31 thru 43	@3.00

RICHIE RICH
JACKPOTS
Harvey 1974–82

1	50.00
2 thru 5	@15.00
6 thru 10	@10.00
11 thru 20	@7.00

Richie Rich Jackpots #29
© Harvey Publications

21 thru 30	@4.00
31 thru 58	@3.00

RICHIE RICH MILLIONS
Harvey Publications 1961–82

1	200.00
2	100.00
3 thru 10	@75.00
11 thru 20	@50.00
21 thru 30	@30.00
31 thru 48	@15.00
49 thru 60	@12.00
61 thru 64	@7.00
65 thru 74	@6.00
75 thru 94	@5.00
95 thru 113	@4.00

RICHIE RICH
MONEY WORLD
Harvey 1972–82

1	50.00
2 thru 5	@20.00
6 thru 10	@12.00
11 thru 20	@6.00
21 thru 30	@4.00
31 thru 59	@3.00

RICHIE RICH
PROFITS
Harvey 1974–82

1	30.00
2 thru 5	@15.00
6 thru 10	@10.00
11 thru 20	@7.00
21 thru 30	@4.00
31 thru 47	@3.00

RICHIE RICH
RICHES
Harvey 1972–82

1	50.00
2 thru 5	@15.00
6 thru 10	@10.00
11 thru 20	@7.00
21 thru 30	@4.00
31 thru 59	@3.00

RICHIE RICH
SUCCESS STORIES
Harvey Publications 1964–82

1	175.00
2 thru 5	@75.00
6 thru 10	@50.00
11 thru 30	@35.00
31 thru 38	@25.00
39 thru 55	@12.00
56 thru 66	@7.00
67 thru 105	@4.00

RICHIE RICH
VAULT OF MYSTERY
Harvey 1974–82

1	25.00
2 thru 5	@12.00
6 thru 10	@7.00
11 thru 20	@4.00
21 thru 30	@4.00
31 thru 47	@3.00

RICHIE RICH
ZILLIONS
Harvey 1976–82

1	25.00
2 thru 5	@15.00
6 thru 10	@8.00
11 thru 20	@4.00
21 thru 33	@3.00

RIFLEMAN, THE
Dell Publishing Co. 1959

1 Chuck Connors Ph(c) all	250.00
2	125.00
3 ATh	100.00
4	85.00
5	85.00
6 ATh	110.00
7	85.00
8	85.00
9	85.00
10	85.00
11	75.00
12	75.00
13	75.00
14	75.00
15	75.00
16	75.00
17	75.00
18	75.00
19	75.00
20	75.00

RIOT GEAR
Triumphant

1 JnR(s),I:Riot Gear	2.50
2 JnR(s),I:Rabin	2.50
3 JnR(s),I:Surzar	2.50
4 JnR(s),D:Captain Tich	2.50
5 JnR(s),reactions	2.50
6 JnR(s),Tich avenged	2.50
7 JnR(s),Information Age	2.50
8 JnR(s),	2.50

RIOT GEAR:
VIOLENT PAST
Triumphant

1 and 2	@2.50

R.I.P.
TSR 1990–91

1 thru 4	@2.95

5 thru 8 Brasher, Avenger of the
Dead . . . . @2.95

RIPLEY'S BELIEVE IT OR NOT!
Gold Key 1967–80
4 Ph(c),AMc 40.00
5 GE,JJ 25.00
6 AMc 25.00
7 . . . . 15.00
8 . . . . 25.00
9 . . . . 15.00
10 GE. 25.00
11 . . . . 10.00
12 . . . . 10.00
13 . . . . 10.00
14 . . . . 10.00
15 GE. 12.00
16 . . . . 10.00
17 . . . . 10.00
18 . . . . 10.00
19 . . . . 10.00
20 . . . . 10.00
21 thru 30 . . . . @8.00
31 thru 38 . . . . @5.00
39 RC 6.00
40 thru 50 . . . . @5.00
51 thru 94 . . . . @4.00

RISK
Maximum Press 1995
1 V:Furious 2.50

ROB
Awesome Entertainment 1999
1 RLe 2.50

ROBERT E. HOWARD'S
Cross Plains Comics 1999
GN Marchers of Valhalla 6.95
GN Wolfshead 6.95
GN Worms of the Earth 9.95

ROBIN HOOD
Eclipse 1991
1 TT,Historically accurate series. . . 2.75
2 and 3 TT . . . . @2.75

ROBO HUNTER
Eagle
1 . . . . 1.50
2 thru 5 . . . . @1.00

ROBOTECH
Antarctic Press 1997
1 by Fred Perry & BDn 2.95
2 . . . . 2.95
3 . . . . 2.95
4 Rolling Thunder, pt.1 . . . . 2.95
5 Rolling Thunder, pt.2 . . . . 2.95
6 Rolling Thunder, pt.3 . . . . 2.95
7 Rolling Thunder, pt.4 . . . . 2.95
8 Variants, pt.1 . . . . 2.95
9 Variants, pt.2 . . . . 2.95
10 Variants, pt.3 . . . . 2.95
11 Variants, pt.4 . . . . 2.95
TPB Megastorm by Fred Perry
& Ben Dunn 7.95
Spec.1-shot Robotech: Final Fire . . 2.95
Spec.1-shot Robotech: Class
Reunion 2.95

ROBOTECH: GENESIS
The Legend of Zor
Eternity
1 O:Robotech w/cards 2.95
1a Limited Edition,extra pages with card
s #1 & #2 . . . . 5.95
2 thru 6, each with cards . . . . . @2.50

ROBOTECH IN 3-D
Comico
1 . . . . 2.50

Robotech, The Macross Saga #7
© Comico

ROBOTECH, THE MACROSS SAGA
Comico 1985–89
(formerly Macross)
2 . . . . 5.00
3 . . . . 4.00
4 . . . . 3.00
5 . . . . 2.50
6 J:Rick Hunter 2.50
7 V:Zentraedi 2.00
8 A:Rick Hunter 2.00
9 V:Zentraedi 2.00
10 "Blind Game" 2.00
11 V:Zentraedi 2.00
12 V:Zentraedi 2.00
13 V:Zentraedi 2.00
14 "Gloval's Reports" 2.00
15 V:Zentraedi 2.00
16 V:Zentraedi 2.00
17 V:Zentraedi 2.00
18 D:Roy Fokker 2.00
19 V:Khyron 2.00
20 V:Zentraedi 2.00
21 "A New Dawn" 2.00
22 V:Zentraedi 2.00
23 "Reckless" 2.00
24 HB,V:Zentraedi 2.00
25 "Wedding Bells" 2.00
26 "The Messenger" 2.00
27 "Force of Arms" 2.00
28 "Reconstruction Blues" 2.00
29 "Robotech Masters" 2.00
30 "Viva Miriya" 2.00
31 "Khyron's Revenge" 2.00
32 "Broken Heart" 2.00
33 "A Rainy Night" 2.00
34 "Private Time" 2.00
35 "Season's Greetings" 2.00
36 last issue 2.00

Graphic Novel #1 . . . . 6.00

ROBOTECH MASTERS
Comico 1985–88
1 . . . . 4.00
2 . . . . 3.00
3 Space Station Liberty 3.00
4 V:Bioroids 2.50
5 V:Flagship 2.50
6 "Prelude to Battle" 2.50
7 "The Trap" 2.50
8 F:Dana Sterling 2.50
9 "Star Dust" 2.50
10 V:Zor 2.50
11 A:De Ja Vu 2.00
12 2OR 2.00
13 . . . . 2.00
14 "Clone Chamber,"V:Zor 2.00
15 "Love Song" 2.00
16 V:General Emerson 2.00
17 "Mind Games" 2.00
18 "Dana in Wonderland" 2.00
19 . . . . 2.00
20 A:Zor,Musica 2.00
21 "Final Nightmare" 2.00
22 "The Invid Connection" 2.00
23 "Catastrophe," final issue 2.00

Robotech, The New Generation #2
© Comico

ROBOTECH: THE NEW GENERATION
Comico 1985–88
1 . . . . 4.00
2 "The Lost City" 3.00
3 V:Yellow Dancer 3.00
4 A:Yellow Dancer 3.00
5 SK(i),A:Yellow Dancer. 2.50
6 F:Rook Bartley 2.50
7 "Paper Hero" 2.00
8 . . . . 2.00
9 KSy,"The Genesis Pit" 2.00
10 V:The Invid 2.00
11 F:Scott Bernard 2.00
12 V:The Invid 2.00
13 V:The Invid 2.00
14 "Annie"s Wedding" 2.00
15 "Seperate Ways" 2.00
16 "Metamorphosis" 2.00
17 "Midnight Sun" 2.00
18 . . . . 2.00
19 . . . . 2.00
20 "Birthday Blues" 2.00
21 "Hired Gun" 2.00

22 "The Big Apple" 2.00
23 Robotech Wars 2.00
24 Robotech Wars 2.00
25 V:Invid, last issue. 2.00

ROBOTECH SPECIAL DANA"S STORY
Eclipse
1 . . . . 5.00

ROBOTECH II: THE SENTINELS
Eternity
Swimsuit Spec.#1 . . . . 2.95

ROCK & ROLL
Revolutionary
Prev: Black & White
15 Poison. 3.50
16 Van Halen 1.95
17 Madonna 2.50
18 AliceCooper. 1.95
19 Public Enemy, 2 Live Crew 2.50
20 Queensryche 1.95
21 Prince 1.95
22 AC/DC. 1.95
23 Living Color 1.95
24 Anthrax 1.95
25 Z.Z.Top 2.50
26 Doors 2.50
27 Doors 2.50
28 Ozzy Osbourne 2.50
29 The Cure 2.50
30 . . . . 2.50
31 Vanilla Ice 2.50
32 Frank Zappa 2.50
33 Guns n" Roses 2.50
34 The Black Crowes 2.50
35 R.E.M. 2.50
36 Michael Jackson 2.50
37 Ice T 2.50
38 Rod Stewart 2.50
39 . . . . 2.50
40 N.W.A./Ice Cube 2.50
41 Paula Abdul. 2.50
42 Metallica II 2.50
43 Guns "N" Roses. 2.50
44 Scorpions 2.50
45 Greatful Dead 3.00
46 Grateful Dead 3.00
47 Grateful Dead 3.00
48 (now b/w),Queen 2.50
49 Rush 2.50
50 Bob Dylan Pt.1 . . . . 2.50
51 Bob Dylan Pt.2 . . . . 2.50
52 Bob Dylan Pt.3 . . . . 2.50
53 Bruce Springsteen 2.50
54 U2 Pt.1 . . . . 2.50
55 U2 Pt.2 . . . . 2.50
56 thru 72 . . . . @2.50

ROCK 'N' ROLL HIGH SCHOOL
Cosmic Comics 1995
1 Sequel to the movie 2.50

ROCKETEER
Walt Disney
1 DSt(c)RH,MovieAdaptation 7.00
Newsstand Version. 3.25

ROCKETEER ADVENTURE MAGAZINE
Comico
1 DSt,MK,Rocketeer(6thApp.) . . . 10.00
2 DSt,MK,Rocketeer(7thApp.) 8.00

ROCKETEER SPECIAL
Eclipse 1984
1 DSt, Rocketeer(5th App.) 18.00

ROCKET MAN: KING OF THE ROCKET MEN
Innovation
1 thru 4 Adapts movie series . . . @2.50

ROCKET RANGER
Adventure Comics
1 Based on computer game 2.95

ROCKMEEZ
Jzink Comics
1 I:Rockmeez,V:Pyrites 2.50
2 V:Pyrites,Silv.Embos.(c) 2.50

ROCKY HORROR PICTURE SHOW
Calibre/Tome
1 . . . . 6.00
1a 2nd printing 3.25
2 . . . . 3.50
3 "The Conclusion" 3.25
Rocky Horror Collection reps. 4.95

ROG 2000
Pacific
1 One-Shot, JBy 2.00

ROGER RABBIT
Walt Disney 1990
1 I:Rick Flint, "The Trouble
   with Toons". 5.50
2 . . . . 3.50
3 . . . . 2.50
4 . . . . 2.50
5 . . . . 2.50
6 thru 9 . . . . @2.50

Roger Rabbit #1
© Walt Disney

---

10 "Tuned-in-toons" 2.50
11 "Who Framed Rick Flint" 2.00
12 "Somebunny to Love 2.00
13 "Honey,I Stink with Kids 2.00
14 "Who Fired Jessica Rabbit" 2.00
15 "The Great Toon Detective" 2.00
16 "See you later Aviator". 2.00
17 Flying Saucers over Toontown . . 2.00
18 "I Have Seen the Future" 2.00

ROGER RABBIT'S TOONTOWN
Walt Disney
1 Baby Herman,Jessica stories . . . 2.00
2 "Pre-Hysterical Roger" 1.75
3 "Lumberjack of tomorrow". 1.75
4 "The Longest Daze" 1.75

ROGUE TROOPER
Fleetway/Quality
1 thru 5 . . . . @1.00
6 . . . . 1.50
7 thru 21 . . . . @1.25
22/23 . . . . 1.50
24 . . . . 1.50
25/26 . . . . 1.50
27 thru 35 . . . . @1.50
36 . . . . 1.95
37 . . . . 1.95
38 thru 40 . . . . @1.50
41 thru 43 . . . . @1.75

ROGUE TROOPER: THE FINAL WARRIOR
Fleetway
1 RS,Golden Rebellion,pt 1 . . . . . . 2.95
2 thru 3 . . . . 2.95
4 "Saharan Ice-Belt War 2.95

ROMAN HOLIDAYS, THE
Gold Key 1973
1 . . . . 35.00
2 . . . . 25.00
3 . . . . 25.00
4 . . . . 25.00

ROOK, THE
Harris Comics 1995
0 O:Rook. 2.95
1 N:Rook. 2.95
2 I:Coffin 2.95
3 The Spider Obsidian 2.95

ROOM 222
Dell Publishing Co. Jan. 1970
1 . . . . 45.00
2 . . . . 30.00
3 Drug. 35.00
4 Ph(c) 30.00

ROSWELL
Bongo Comics 1996
1 by Bill Morrison,"The Story of the
Century". 2.95
2 "The Untold Story" 2.95
3 "The Untold Story," concl. 2.95
4 V:Mutato. 2.95
5 . . . . 2.95
6 time-traveling comic collector . . . 2.95
TPB Roswell Walks Among Us . . . 12.95

COLOR PUB.

ROY ROGERS WESTERN CLASSICS
AC Comics
1	2.95
2	2.95
3	2.95
4	3.95

RUFF AND READY
Dell Publishing Co. Sept., 1958
1	150.00
2	100.00
3	100.00
4	75.00
5	75.00
6	75.00
7	75.00
8	75.00
9	75.00
10 thru 12	@75.00

RUN, BUDDY, RUN
Gold Key June, 1967
1	25.00

RUST
Now
1	4.00
2	3.00
3 thru 11	@2.00
12 I:Terminator	10.00
13 thru 15	@1.75

[Volume 2]
1 thru 10	@1.75

Sable #12
© First

SABLE
First 1988–90
1 AIDS story	1.75
2 Sable in Iran	1.75
3 Pentathelon	1.75
4	1.75
5 DCw,V:Tong Gangs	1.75
6 In Atlantic City	1.75
7 V:EnvironmentalTerrorists	1.75
8 In Argentina	1.95
9 In Kenya Pt.1	1.95
10 In Kenya Pt.2	1.95
11 Jon Sable bodyguard	1.95
12 In Cambodia Pt.1	1.95

13 In Cambodia Pt.2	1.95
14 Christmas story	1.95
15 A:Ted Koppel	1.95
16 Sable as "B.B.Flemm" rev.	1.95
17 Turning point issue	1.95
18 Richard Rockwell(i)	1.95
19 A:Maggie the Cat.	1.95
20 A:Gary Adler	1.95
21 Richard Rockwell(i)	1.95
22 A:Eden Kendall	1.95
23 TV cover	1.95
24 TV cover	1.95
25 TV cover	1.95
26 TV cover	1.95
27	1.95
28 last issue	1.95

SABRE
Eclipse 1982–85
1 PG	2.50
2 PG	3.00
3 thru 14	@2.00

SABRINA, THE TEENAGE WITCH
Archie Publications 1971–83
1	100.00
2	50.00
3	30.00
4	30.00
5	30.00
6 thru 10	@25.00
11 thru 20	@5.00
21 thru 77	@4.00

SABRINA THE TEENAGE WITCH
Archie Comics 1996
one-shot photo cover	1.50
1 photo cover	1.50
2 "Trouble in Time"	1.50
3 photo cover	1.50
4 photo cover	1.50
5 "Driver's License"	1.50
6 "Treasure Troubles"	1.50
7 "The Sculpture Switch"	1.50
8 "The Cable Girl" photo (c)	1.50
9 "Farewell Feline"	1.50
10 "No Brain, No Pain"	1.75
11 "Mirror, Mirror"	1.75
12 ""	1.75
13 "Kin You Believe It"	1.75
14 "Too Much Magic"	1.75
15 "Wedding or Not"	1.75
16 How does your garden grow?	1.75
17 F:Josie & The Pussycats	1.75
18 photo (c)	1.75
19 photo (c)	1.75
20 thru 27 photo (c)	@1.75
28 A:Sonic The Hedgehog	1.75
29 thru 31 photo (c)	@1.75
Halloween Spooktacular #1	2.00
Halloween Spooktacular #2	2.00
Holiday Spectacular #3	2.00

SAD SACK AND THE SARGE
Harvey Publications 1957–82
1	135.00
2	50.00
3 thru 10	@40.00
11 thru 20	@25.00
21 thru 40	@15.00
41 thru 50	@12.00
51 thru 90	@5.00

91 thru 96 52 pg Giants	@6.00
97 thru 155	@3.00

SAD SACK'S ARMY LIFE
Harvey Publications 1963–76
1	50.00
2 thru 10	@25.00
11 thru 20	@15.00
21 thru 30	@12.00
31 thru 50	@5.00
51 thru 61	@4.00

SAD SACK'S FUNNY FRIENDS
Harvey Publications 1955–69
1	85.00
2 thru 10	@40.00
11 thru 20	@18.00
21 thru 30	@10.00
31 thru 40	@8.00
41 thru 75	@5.00

SAD SACK in 3-D
Blackthorne
1 and 2	@2.50

SAFETY-BELT MAN ALL HELL
Sirius 1996
1	2.95
2	2.95
3	2.95
4 Linsner back (c)	4.00
5	2.95

SALOME
Eclipse 1987
1 CR	2.00

SAM AND MAX, FREE-LANCE POLICE SPECIAL
Comico 1987–89
1	2.75

SAM SLADE ROBOHUNTER
Quality 1986–89
1	1.00
2	1.00
3 Filby Case	1.00
4	1.00
5	1.00
6 Bax the Burner,Moore	1.00
7	1.00
8 thru 21	@1.25
22/23	1.50
24	1.50
25/26	1.50
27 thru 33	@1.50

SAMSONS
Samsons Comics
1/2 Various Artists	2.50

SAMURAI
Eclipse
1	2.00
2	2.00
3 thru 5	@2.00

    All comics prices listed are for *Near Mint* condition.

SAMUREE
Continuity 1993–94
1 NA,A:Revengers	2.00
2 A:Revengers	2.00
3 NA,A:Revengers	2.00
4 A:Revengers	2.00
5 BSz(c),A:Revengers	2.00
6 A:Revengers	2.00
7	2.00
8 Drug story	2.00
9 Drug story	2.00

[2nd Series]
1 thru 3 Rise of Magic	2.50

SARGE STEEL/ SECRET AGENT
Charlton 1964–66
1 DG,I:SargeSteel & IvanChung	25.00
2 DG,I:Werner Von Hess	15.00
3 DG,V:Smiling Skull	15.00
4 DG,V:Lynx	15.00
5 FMc,V:Ivan Chung	15.00
6 FMc,A:Judomaster	15.00
7 DG	15.00
8 V:Talon	15.00

Becomes:
SECRET AGENT
9 DG,A:The Lynx	12.00
10 DG,JAp,A:Tiffany Sinn	12.00

SATANIKA
Verotik 1995
0	5.00
1 New ongoing series	6.00
2 Femininity	3.50
3	3.00
4	3.00
5	3.00
6 thru 10	@2.95
10a Wingbird variant cover	5.00
11 SBi,final issue	3.95
1-shot Satanika X (adult)	5.00

SATANIKA VS. SHILENE
Verotik April 1996
1-shot	9.95

SATAN'S SIX
Topps 1993
1 F:Satan's Six,w/3 cards	3.25
2 V:Kalazarr,w/3 cards	2.95
3 w/3 cards	2.95
4 w/3 cards	2.95

SATURDAY KNIGHTS
Hot
1	1.50
2 thru 4	@1.50

SAURAUS FAMILY
Blackthorne
1 3-D	2.00

SAVAGE COMBAT TALES
Atlas Feb.–July, 1975
1 F:Sgt Strykers Death Squad	10.00
2 ATh,A:Warhawk	8.00
3 final issue	8.00

SAVAGE DRAGON/ TEENAGE MUTANT NINJA TURLES CROSSOVER
Mirage
1 EL(s)	2.75

SAVED BY THE BELL
Harvey
1 based on TV series	1.25

SCARLET CRUSH
Awesome Entertainment 1998
1 by John Stinsman	2.50
2	2.50
3 Icaria's decision	2.50
4 Nirasawa arrives	2.50

SCARY TALES
Charlton 1975
1	15.00
2 thru 11	@10.00
12 thru 46	@5.00

SCAVENGERS
Quality 1988–89
1 thru 7	@1.25
8 thru 14	@1.50

SCAVENGERS
Triumphant Comics 1993–94
0 Fso(c),JnR(s),	2.50
0a "Free Copy"	2.50
0b Red Logo	2.50
1 JnR(s),I:Scavengers,Ximos, C:Doctor Chaos	2.50
1a 2nd Printing	2.50
2 JnR(s),	2.50
3 JnR(s),I:Lurok	2.50
4 JnR(s),	2.50
5 Fso(c),JnR(s),D:Jack Hanal	2.50
6 JnR(s),	2.50
7 JnR(s),I:Zion	2.50
8 JnR(s),Nativity	2.50
9 JnR(s),The Challenge	2.50
10 JnR(s),Snowblind	2.50

SCHISM
Defiant
1 thru 4 Defiant's x-over	3.25

SCIENCE COMIC BOOK
Nature Publishing House 1997
TPB Earth Adventures by James Laurie	8.95
TPB Car Adventure by James Laurie	8.95
TPB Volcano Adventures by Stu Duval	8.95
TPB World of Dinosaurs, by Paul Xu and James Passmore	8.95
TPB Beyond the Star, by James Passmore	8.95
TPB Weather Genie, by James Laurie	8.95
TPB Rain Forest Adventure by James Passmore	8.95
TPB Wildlife Adventure by Stu Duval	8.95

SCION
1 and 2	@2.00

SCI-TECH
Wildstorm/DC 1999
1 (of 4) BCi,Ebe,	2.50
2 BCi,EBe,	2.50

Scooby Doo, Where Are You #5
© Gold Key Comics

SCOOBY DOO
Gold Key 1970–75
1	75.00
2	50.00
3	50.00
4	50.00
5	50.00
6	40.00
7	40.00
8	40.00
9	40.00
10	40.00
11 thru 20	@25.00
21 thru 30	@20.00

SCOOBY DOO
Charlton Comics 1975–76
1	35.00
2	20.00
3	20.00
4	20.00
5	20.00
6	15.00
7	15.00
8	15.00
9	15.00
10	15.00
11	15.00

SCOOBY DOO
Archie 1995
1 thru 10	@2.00
11 thru 13	@2.00
14 "The Balloon Busters"	2.00
15 "On the Boardwalk in Atlantic City"	2.00
16 "The Ghost of Central Park"	2.00
19 "Electric Monster"	2.00
20 "The Legend of Spooky Doo"	2.00
21 "Monster Park After Dark"	2.00

SCORCHED EARTH
Tundra 1991
1 Earth 2025,I:Dr.EliotGodwin	3.50
2 Hunt for Eliot	2.95

COLOR PUB.

3 Mystical Transformation 2.95

SCORPION, THE
Atlas 1975
1 HC, bondage cover. 5.00
2 HC,BWi,MK 4.00
3 . . . . 3.00

SCORPION CORP.
Dagger 1993
1 PuD,JRI,CH, ... 2.75
2 PuD,JRI,CH,V:Victor Kyner 2.75
3 PuD,BIH,V:Victor Kyner 2.75

SCORPIO ROSE
Eclipse 1983
1 MR/TP,I:Dr.Orient 2.00
2 MR/TP 2.00

SCOUT
Eclipse 1985–87
1 TT,I:Scout,Fash.In Action 6.00
2 TT,V:Buffalo Monster 3.00
3 TT,V:President Grail 2.50
4 TT,V:President Grail 2.50
5 TT,"Killin' Floor" 2.50
6 TT,V:President Grail 2.50
7 TT,TY,Rosanna's Diary 2.50
8 TT,TY 2.50
9 TT,TY,A:Airboy 2.50
10 TT,TY,I:Proj.Mountain Fire 2.00
11 TT,FH,V:Rangers 2.00
12 TT,FH,"Me and the Devil" 2.00
13 TT,FH,Monday:Eliminator. 2.00
14 TT,FH,Monday:Eliminator. 2.00
15 TT,FH,Monday:Eliminator. 2.00
16 TT,3-D issue,F:Santana 2.00
17 TT,A:Beanworld 2.00
18 TT,FH,V:Lex Lucifer 2.00
19 TT,w/Record,V:Lex Lucifer 3.00
20 TT,A:Monday:Eliminator 2.00
21 TT,A:Monday:Eliminator 1.75
22 TT,A:Swords of Texas 1.75
23 TT,A:Swords of Texas 1.75
24 TT,last Issue 1.75

SCOUT: WAR SHAMAN
Eclipse 1988–89
1 TT,R:Scout (now a father) 2.25
2 TT,I:Redwire 1.95
3 TT,V:Atuma Yuma. 1.95
4 TT,"Rollin' on the River" 1.95
5 TT,Hopi Katchina dieties 1.95
6 TT,Scout vs. Rosa Winter 1.95
7 TT,R:Redwire 1.95
8 TT,R:Beau LaDuke 1.95
9 TT,V:Doodyists 1.95
10 TT,TY,V:Redwire 1.95
11 TT,V:Redwire 1.95
12 TT,V:Snow Leopards 1.95
13 TT,F:Beau LaDuke 1.95
14 TT,V:Redwire 1.95
15 TT,V:Redwire 1.95
16 TT,"Wall of Death,"last issue . . . 1.95

SEADRAGON
Elite 1986–87
1 . . . . 3.00
1a 2nd printing 1.75
2 . . . . 2.00
3 . . . . 2.00
4 . . . . 2.00
5 thru 8 . . . . @1.75

SEA HUNT
Dell Publishing Co. 1958
1 L.BridgesPh(c) all 125.00
2 . . . . 100.00
3 ATh. 110.00
4 RsM 100.00
5 RsM 100.00
6 RsM 100.00
7 . . . . 90.00
8 RsM 100.00
9 RsM 100.00
10 RsM 100.00
11 RsM 100.00
12 . . . . 100.00
13 RsM. 100.00

SEAQUEST
Nemesis 1994
1 HC(c),DGC,KP,AA,Based on
   TV Show 2.50

SEBASTIAN
Walt Disney
1 From Little Mermaid 1.50
2 "While da Crab's Away" 1.50

Secret Agent #9
© Gold Key Comics

SECRET AGENT
Gold Key Nov., 1966
1 . . . . 120.00
2 . . . . 75.00

SECRET CITY SAGA
Topps 1993
0 JK 3.25
0 Gold Ed. 15.00
0 Red 10.00
1 w/3 cards 3.25
2 w/3 cards 3.25
3 w/3 cards 3.25
4 w/3 cards 3.25

SECRET SQUIRREL
Gold Key Oct., 1966
1 . . . . 50.00

SEDUCTION OF THE INNOCENT
Eclipse 1985–86
1 ATh,"Hanged by the Neck" reps. . 2.50
2 . . . . 2.25
3 ATh,"The Crushed Gardenia" . . . 2.00
4 ATh,NC,"World's Apart". 2.00
5 ATh,"The Phantom Ship" 2.00
6 ATh,RA,"Hands of Don Jose" . . . 2.00
3-D #1 DSt(c). 2.25
3-D #2 ATh,MB,BWr,"Man Who Was
   Always on Time". 2.00

SEEKER
Sky Comics 1995
1 JMt(s),I:Seeker 2.50

SENSEI
First
1 Mini-Series 2.75
2 . . . . 2.75
3 . . . . 2.75
4 . . . . 2.75

SENTINELS OF JUSTICE
AC Comics
1 Capt.Paragon 1.75
2 . . . . 1.75
3 . . . . 1.75
4 . . . . 1.75
5 . . . . 1.75
6 . . . . 1.75
7 . . . . 1.75

SENTRY: SPECIAL
Innovation 1991
1 . . . . 2.75

SERAPHIM
Innovation 1990
1 and 2 . . . . @2.50

SERINA
Antarctic 1996
1 . . . . 2.95

SERPENTINA
Lightning 1997
1 . . . . 3.00
1a variant cover 3.00

SEVEN SISTERS
Zephyr Comics 1997
1 by Curley, Cruickshank & Garcia. 2.95
2 . . . . 2.95
3 . . . . 2.95
4 . . . . 2.95

77 SUNSET STRIP
Dell Publishing Co.
Jan.-March, 1960
1 Ph(c) 125.00
2 Ph(c),RsM 135.00

SHADE SPECIAL
AC Comics
1 . . . . 1.50

SHADOW, THE
Archie Comics 1964–65

1	50.00
2	35.00
3	35.00
4	35.00
5	35.00
6 and 8	@30.00

SHADOW COMICS
1 Guardians of Justice &
The O-Force............. 1.50

SHADOW OF THE TORTURER, THE
Innovation 1991
1 thru 6 Gene Wolfe adapt. .... @1.95

SHADOW RAVEN
Poc-It Comics
1 I:Shadow Raven............ 2.95

SHADOW STATE
Preview Editions
1 and 2 B&W................ 2.50
Broadway 1995
1 thru 4 F:BloodS.C.R.E.A.M.... @2.50
5 JiS, "Image Isn't Everything,"
concl.................... 2.50
6 "Anger of Lovers" pt.1........ 2.50
7 "Anger of Lovers" pt.2........ 2.95

SHAFT
Maximum Press 1997
1 RLd 2.50

SHAIANA
Entity 1995
1 R:Shaiana from Aster........ 3.75
1a clear chromium........... 8.00
1b Holochrome 10.00
2 Guardians of Earth.......... 2.50

SHANGHAI BREEZE
1 .... 1.75

SHAOLIN
Black Tiger Press
1 I:Tiger.................... 2.95
2 I:Crane................... 2.95

SHATTER
First 1985–88

1	3.00
2	2.50
3	2.50
4 and 5	@2.00
6 thru 14	@1.75
Spec. #1 Computer Comic	5.00
#1a 2nd Printing	2.00

SHE-DEVILS ON WHEELS
Aircel
1 V:Man-Eaters.............. 2.95
2 V:Man-Eaters.............. 2.95
3 V:Man-Eaters.............. 2.95

SHEENA: QUEEN OF THE JUNGLE
London Night
0 by Gabriel Cain & Wilson 3.00
0a Zebra Edition 5.00
0b Leopard Edition............ 5.00
0c Alligator Edition............ 5.00

SHEENA: QUEEN OF THE JUNGLE: BOUND
London Night
1 (of 4) by Everette Hartsoe & Art
Wetherell 3.00
1 ministry ed................ 5.00
1 Leather retro edition 15.00

SHERIFF OF TOMBSTONE
Charlton Comics 1958–61
1 AW,JSe 50.00
2 .... 30.00
3 thru 10 .... @20.00
11 thru 17 .... @20.00

Shi #4 © Crusade

SHI
Crusade Comics
1 BiT,HMo,I:Shi 20.00
2 BiT....................... 8.00
2 BiT, reissue, new cover........ 2.95
3 BiT....................... 5.00
4 BiT....................... 4.00
5 V:Arashi 3.00
5a variant cover.............. 8.00
6 V:Tomoe.................. 3.00
7 V:Nara Warriors 3.00
8 New costume 3.00
9 thru 11 .... @3.00
12 "Way of the Warrior" concl, flip-
book Angel Fire............. 3.00
TPB Vol. 1 revised rep.JuB(c)... 14.95
TPB Vol. 2, rep. Shi #5–#8 ..... 14.95
TPB rep. Shi #9–#12 & Shi vs.
Tomoe 17.95
TPB Shi:Way of the Warrior ... 12.95
Shi/Cyblade Spec.#1 Battle of the
Independents 4.00
Spec.#1a variant cover......... 6.00

SHI: THE SERIES
Crusade Entertainment 1997
1 sequel to *Shi: Heaven and Earth*,
F:Tomoe................... 2.95
2 Unforgettable Fire, concl. 2.95
3 A Rock and a Hard Place, pt.1 .. 2.95
4 A Rock and a Hard Place, pt.2 .. 2.95
5 A Rock and a Hard Place, pt.3 .. 2.95
6 .... 2.95
7 Photographer's lucky picture ... 2.95
8 V:Gemini Dawn twins 2.95
9 Bad Blood, pt.1 .... 2.95
9a variant BTi(c) 2.95
9b variant Ahn (c) 2.95
9c variant Kevin Lau (c) 2.95
10 Bad Blood, pt.2 .... 2.95
10a variant BTi(c) 2.95
10b variant Ahn (c) 2.95
10c variant Kevin Lau (c) 2.95
11 Bad Blood, pt.3 .... 2.95
12 The Dark Crusade, pt.1 (of 8) . 2.95
13 The Dark Crusade, pt.2 (of 8) . 2.95
14 The Dark Crusade, pt.3 (of 8) . 2.95
15 The Dark Crusade, pt.4 (of 8) . 2.95
16 The Dark Crusade, pt.5 (of 8) . 2.95
1-shot The Essential Dark Crusade. 2.95
1-shot Shi:Five Year Celebration... 5.00
1-shotA,B,C,&D variant covers 5.00

SHI: ART OF WAR TOUR BOOK
Crusade Entertainment
Wizard Chicago Con (c) 5.95

SHI: BLACK WHITE & RED
Crusade Entertainment
1 Night of the Rat, pt.1 .... 2.95
2 Night of the Rat, pt.2 .... 2.95
Coll. Ed. rep. #1–#2 .... 6.95

SHI/CYBLADE
Crusade
Spec.#1 The Battle for
Independents...Endgame 2.95

SHI: EAST WIND RAIN
Crusade Entertainment 1997
1 BiT,MSo, fully painted........ 3.50
2 BiT, concl.................. 3.50

SHI: HEAVEN AND EARTH
Crusade Entertainment 1997
1 (of 3) BiT 2.95
1 variant cover............... 2.95
2 BiT....................... 2.95
3 BiT....................... 2.95
4 BiT....................... 2.95
TPB rep. #1–#4 .... 15.95

SHI: MASQUERADE
Crusade Entertainment 1997
1 by Christopher Golden 3.50

SHI: NIGHTSTALKERS
Crusade Entertainment 1997
1-shot by Christopher Golden &
VMk,F:T.C.B. 3.50

SHI: REKISHI
Crusade Entertainment 1997
1 (of 2) BiT 2.95
2 BiT, conclusion 2.95
Coll.Ed. Shi:Reshiki, sourcebook,

COLOR PUB.

MS(c) 4.95

SHI/VAMPIRELLA
Crusade 1997
1 WEI, ... 2.95

SHI VS. TOMOE
Crusade April 1996
Spec. #1 BiT, double size 3.95

SHI-SENRYAKU
Crusade 1995
1 BiT,R:Shi 3.00
1a variant cover. 6.00
1 (of 3) 2nd edition 2.50
2 BiT,Arts of Warfare 3.00
2 2nd edition 2.50
3 BiT 3.00
3 2nd edition 2.50
HC Rep.#1-#2 . . . . 24.95
TPB Rep.#1-#2. . . . . 12.95

Shock SuspenStories #1
© Russ Cochran

SHOCK SUSPENSE STORIES
Russ Cochran Press 1992
1 reps.horror stories 1.50
2 inc.Kickback. 1.50
3 thru 4 . . . . @2.00
5 thru 7 reps.horror stories 2.00
8 reps.horror stories 2.00
Gemstone
18 EC comics reprint 2.50
TPB Vol. 1 rebinding of #1–#5 . . . 8.95
TPB Vol. 2 rebinding of #5–#10 . . 9.95
TPB Vol. 3 rebinding of #11–#15. . 8.95
TPB Vol. 4 rebinding of #16–#20 . . 9.95

SHOCK THE MONKEY
Millenium/Expand 1995
1 Shock therapy 2.95

SHOGUNAUT
Firstlight
1 I:Shogunaut 2.95
2 V:Teckno Terror 2.95

SHOOTING STARS
1 . . . . 2.50

SHOTGUN MARY
Antarctic Press 1995
1 I:Shotgun Mary. 2.95
1a with CD Soundtrack 8.95
1b Red Foil cover 8.00
2 . . . . 2.95
Spec. Shooting Gallery. 2.95
Spec. Deviltown. 2.95
Spec. Deviltown, commem. (1999) . 5.95

SHOTGUN MARY
Antarctic Press
1 by Herb Mallette & Kelsey
    Shannon 2.95
2 Early Days, pt.2 . . . . 2.95
3 Early Days, pt.3 . . . . 2.95

SHOTGUN MARY: BLOOD LORE
Antarctic Press 1997
1 (of 4) by Herb Mallette
    & Neil Googe 2.95
2 . . . . 2.95
3 . . . . 2.95
4 concl. 2.95

SHOTGUN MARY: SON OF THE BEAST, DAUGHTER OF LIGHT
Antarctic Press 1997
1 by Miljenko Horvatic
    & Esad T. Ribic. 2.95

SIEGEL & SHUSTER
Eclipse 1984–85
1 . . . . 1.50
2 . . . . 1.75

SILENT MOBIUS
Viz 1991–92
1 Katsumi 5.75
2 Katsumi vs. Spirit 5.25
3 Katsumi trapped within entity . . . 4.95
4 Nami vs. Dragon. 4.95
5 Kiddy vs. Wire 4.95
6 Search for Wire 4.95
GN 14.95

SILENT MOBIUS II
Viz
1 AMP Officers vs. Entities cont. . . 4.95
2 Entities in Amp H.Q. 4.95
3 V:Entity. 4.95
4 The Esper Weapon. 4.95
5 Last issue. 4.95

SILENT MOBIUS III
Viz
1 F:Lebia/computer network. 2.75
2 Lebia/computer link cont. 2.75
3 Lebia in danger 2.75
4 Return to Consciousness 2.75
5 Conclusion 2.75

SILVERBACK
Comico 1989–90
1 thru 3 . . . . @2.50

SILVER CROSS
Antarctic Press 1997
1 (of 3) by Ben Dunn. 2.95

2 . . . . 2.95

SILVERHEELS
Pacific 1983–84
1 . . . . 2.00
2 and 3 . . . . @1.50

SILVER STAR
Pacific 1983–84
1 JK 1.00
2 JK 1.00
3 JK 1.00
4 JK 1.00
5 JK 1.00
6 JK 1.00

SILVER STAR
Topps
1 w/Cards 2.95

SILVER STORM
1 . . . . 2.25
2 . . . . 1.95
3 . . . . 1.95
4 . . . . 1.95

SIMPSONS COMICS
Bongo Comics 1993
1 Colossal Homer 3.00
2 A:Sideshow Bob. 2.00
3 F:Bart. 2.00
4 F:Bart. 2.25
5 A:Itchy & Scratchy 2.25
6 F:Lisa. 2.25
7 Circus in Town 2.25
8 Mr. Burns Voyage. 2.25
9 Autobiographies 2.25
10 Tales of the Kwik-E-Mart 2.25
11 Ned Flanders Public Enemy. . . . 2.25
12 In the Blodome 2.25
13 F:Bart & Millhouse 2.25
14 Homer owns beer company 2.25
15 Waltons parody 2.25
16 thru 18 . . . . @2.25
19 thru 23. . . . . @2.25
24 . . . . 2.25
25 . . . . 2.25
26 Bart: action hero! 2.25
27 . . . . 2.25
28 Krusty the Clown, tax protest . . . 2.25
29 Captain Slamtastic. 2.25
30 Montgomery Burns clones
    Smithers. 2.25
31 Radioactive Homer 2.25
32 F:Lisa and her sax. 3.00
33 Reality on the blink 2.25
34 C. Montgomery Burns
    International Games. 2.25
35 20 kids 2.25
36 Three geeks computer company 2.25
37 Grampa Abe Simpson 2.25
38 chemically-engineered donuts . . 2.25
39 People vs. Homer Simpson
    and the Comic Book Guy 2.25
40 F:Krusty the Clown 2.50
41 Krusty Fun Factory 2.50
42 . . . . 2.50
43 Urban legends. 2.50
44 substitute teachers. 2.50
TPB Rep.#1-#4. . . . . 10.00
TPB Wing Ding, 120pg. 11.95
TPB Simpsons Comics on Parade
    (1998). 11.95
TPB Simpsons Comics Big
    Bonanza. 11.95
Comic Spectacular,Vol.1 Rep. . . . 10.00
Comic Spectacular,Vol.2 Rep. . . . 10.00

COLOR PUB.

SIMPSONS COMICS & STORIES
Welsh Publishing 1993
1 with poster 4.00
1a without poster 2.50
Bongo Comics 1998
1 F:Bartman, Itchy & Scratchy 2.95

SINTHIA
Lightning 1997
1A by Joseph Adam, Daughter
of Lucifer 3.00
1B 3.00
1c Platinum Edition 9.95
1d Autographed Edition 9.95
2 Sisters of Darkness 2.95
2a variant cover 2.95
3 Wagner(c) 2.95
3a variant Abrams cover 2.95
3b deluxe variant cover 9.95
4 Wagner(c) 2.95
4a variant John Cleary cover 2.95

SISTERS OF MERCY
No Mercy Comics
TPB rep. #1–#5 . . . . 14.95
Vol 2
1 by Mark Williams & Rikki Rockett 2.50
2 . . . . 2.50
3 . . . . 2.50

SISTERS OF MERCY: PARADISE LOST
London Night
by Ricki Rockett & Mark Williams
2 . . . . 2.50
3 . . . . 2.50
4 . . . . 2.50

SISTERS OF MERCY: WHEN RAZORS CRY CRIMSON TEARS
No Mercy Comics
1 . . . . 2.50

SIX MILLION DOLLAR MAN, THE
Charlton June 1976
1 JSon,Lee Majors Ph(c) 15.00
2 NA(c),JSon,Ph(c) 12.00
3 Ph(c) 12.00
4 Ph(c) 8.00
5 Ph(c) 8.00
6 Ph(c) 8.00
7 Ph(c) 8.00
8 Ph(c) 8.00
9 Ph(c) 8.00

666: MARK OF THE BEAST
Fleetway/Quality
1 I:Fludd, BU:Wolfie Smith 1.95
2 thru 18 . . . . @1.95

SIX STRING SAMURAI
Awesome Entertainment 1998
1 RLe 2.95

666 The Mark of the Beast #3
© Fleetway/Quality

SKATEMAN
Pacific 1983
1 NA 1.50

SKY WOLF
Eclipse 1988
1 V:Baron Von Tundra 1.75
2 TL,V:Baron Von Tundra 1.75
3 TL,cont. in Airboy #41 . . . . 1.75

SLAINE THE BERSERKER
Quality 1987–89
1 thru 14 . . . . @1.25
15/16 . . . . 1.50
17 . . . . 1.50
18/19 . . . . 1.50
20 thru 28 . . . . @1.50
Becomes:
SLAINE THE KING
26 . . . . 1.50

SLAINE
Fleetway
1 thru 4 SBs,From 2000 AD . . . . @4.95

SLAINE THE HORNED GOD
Egmont Fleetway 1998
1 (of 3) Pat Millagan & SBs, 68pg.. 7.00
2 (of 3) Pat Millagan & SBs, 68pg.. 7.00
3 68-page, conclusion 7.00

SLIMER
Now 1989
1 . . . . 2.50
2 thru 15 . . . . @1.75
Becomes:
SLIMER & REAL GHOSTBUSTERS
16 thru 18 . . . . @1.75

SMILEY
Chaos! Comics 1998
1 the Psychotic Button 2.95

Spec. Smiley Anti-Holiday Spec.. . . 2.95
Spec. Smiley Psychotic Button's
Spring Break Road Trip 2.95
Spec. Whacky Wrestling Spec.. . . . 2.95

SNAGGLEPUSS
Gold Key 1962–63
1 . . . . 75.00
2 . . . . 60.00
3 . . . . 60.00
4 . . . . 60.00

SNOOPER AND BLABBER DETECTIVES
Gold Key 1962–63
1 . . . . 60.00
2 . . . . 50.00
3 . . . . 50.00

SNOW WHITE & SEVEN DWARVES GOLDEN ANNIVERSARY
Gladstone
1 w/poster & stickers 24.00

SO DARK THE ROSE
CFD 1995
1 Fully Painted 2.95

SOJOURN
Dreamer Comics 1998
1 by Jim Somerville, Stranger @WP
Listing:
& Stranger, pt.1 . . . . 2.95

2 Stranger & Stranger, pt.2 . . . . . 2.95
3 Malice in Wonderland 2.95
4 A Game of Conscience, pt.1 . . . 2.95
5 A Game of Conscience, pt.2 . . . 2.10
6 A Game of Conscience, pt.3 . . . 3.15
7 A Game of Conscience, pt.4 . . . 3.15
8 The Hunt 3.15
9 The Hunt, pt.2 . . . . 3.15
10 The Hunt, Bloodied 3.15

SOLDIERS OF FREEDOM
Americomics 1987
1 . . . . 1.75
2 . . . . 1.95

SOLOMON KANE
Blackthorne
1 3-D Special 2.50
2 3-D Special 2.50
1 thru 4 . . . . @2.50

SOMERSET HOLMES
Pacific 1983–84
1 BA,AW,I:Cliff Hanger &
Somerset Holmes 2.50
2 thru 4 BA,AW . . . . @2.00
Eclipse 1984
5 BA,AW 2.00
6 BA 2.00

SONG OF THE CID
Calibre/Tome
1 Story of El Cid 2.95
2 Story of El Cid concl. 2.95

COLOR PUB.

COLOR PUB.

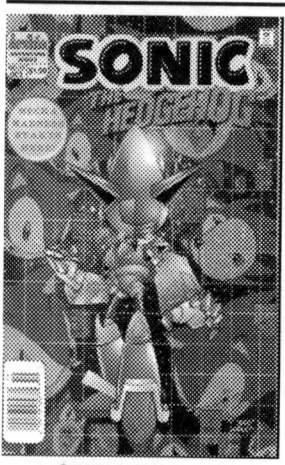

Sonic the Hedgehog #39
© Archie Publications

SONIC THE HEDGEHOG
Archie Publications 1993
1 A:Mobius,V:Robotnik 35.00
2 . . . . 25.00
3 thru 6 . . . . @14.00
7 thru 10 . . . . @10.00
11 thru 30 . . . . @7.00
31 thru 39 . . . . @6.00
40 thru 54 . . . . 5.00
55 . . . . 3.00
56 x-over with Knuckles #9 . . . . . . 3.00
57 . . . . 3.00
58 x-over with Knuckles #11 . . . . . 2.00
59 R:Horizont-Al and Verti-Cal 2.00
60 Arsenal of the Iron King 2.00
61 Downunda 2.00
62 in Sand Dalvador 2.00
63 . . . . 2.00
64 "The Naugus Trilogy" pt.1 . . . . 2.00
65 "The Naugus Trilogy" pt.2 . . . . 2.00
66 "The Naugus Trilogy" pt.3 . . . . 2.00
67 "Tomb Raiders" 1.75
68 "The Year 'O The Hog". 1.75
69 "A Day in the Life" 1.75
70 "Saving Nate Morgan" 1.75
71 All-Backwards Issye. 1.75
72 "I, Robotnik". 1.75
73 "The Truth Is Out There" 1.75
74 "Don't Call It A Comeback". . . . 1.75
75 "A Am The Eggman" 1.75
76 "Business As Usual" 1.75
GN Sonic Firsts, rep.#1/4
   ashcan,#3,#4,#13. . . . . 4.95
Sonic Live Spec.#1. . . . . 2.00

SONIC QUEST:
THE DEATH EGG SAGA
Archie Comics
1 (of 3) by Mike Gallagher & MaG,
   cont. from Sonic the Hedgehog
   #41 . . . . 1.50
2 and 3 . . . . @1.50

SONIC THE HEDGEHOG
PRESENTS
KNUCKLES CHASTIC
Archie Comics 1995
1 I:New Heroes 2.00
Sonic Versus Knuckles Battle Royal
   Spec.#1 . . . . 2.00

SONIC THE HEDGEHOG
PRESENTS TAILS
Archie Comics 1995
1 F:Tails 1.50
2 F:Tails 1.50

SONIC'S FRIENDLY
NEMESIS: KNUCKLES
Archie 1996
1 . . . . 1.50

SONIC SUPER SPECIAL
Archie Comics 1997
1 Brave New World 2.00
3 Sonic Firsts 2.00
4 The Return of the King 2.25
5 Sonic Kids 2.25
6 Expanded Sonic #50, 48pg. . . . 2.25
7 F:Shadowhawk, The Maxx,
   Savage Dragon 2.25
8 four stories, 48-page. 2.25
9 R:Sonic Kids. 2.25
10 Some Enchantra Evening 2.25

SON OF MUTANT WORLD
Fantagor 1990
1 BA 2.00
2 . . . . 2.00

SOJOURN
Dreamer Comics
1 by Jim Somerville, Stranger &
   Stranger, pt.1 . . . . 2.95
2 Stranger & Stranger, pt.2 . . . . . 2.95
3 Malice in Wonderland 2.95
4 A Game of Conscience, pt.1 . . . 2.95

SOULMAN
Quantum Comics 1998
1 . . . . 2.95
2 . . . . 2.95
3 16-page 2.95
4 16-page 2.95
5 24-page 2.95

SOULQUEST
Innovation 1989
1 BA 3.95

SOUPY SALES
COMIC BOOK
Archie Publications 1965
1 . . . . 75.00

SPACE ADVENTURES
Charlton 1967–79, Volume 3
1 (#60) O&I:Paul Mann & The
   Saucers From the Future 35.00
2 thru 8 (1968–69) . . . . @20.00
9 thru 13 (1978–79) . . . . @10.00

SPACE:
ABOVE AND BEYOND
Topps 1995
1 thru 3 TV pilot adaptation . . . . @2.95

SPACE:
ABOVE AND BEYOND—
THE GAUNTLET
Topps 1996
1 . . . . 2.95
2 (of 2) 2.95

SPACE ARK
AC Comics 1985–87
1 . . . . 3.00
2 . . . . 2.00

SPACE FAMILY
ROBINSON
Gold Key Dec., 1962–69
1 DSp 250.00
2 . . . . 125.00
3 . . . . 75.00
4 . . . . 75.00
5 . . . . 75.00
6 B:Captain Venture 75.00
7 . . . . 75.00
8 . . . . 75.00
9 . . . . 75.00
10 . . . . 75.00
11 thru 20 . . . . @50.00
21 thru 36 . . . . @25.00

SPACE GHOST
Gold Key March, 1967
1 . . . . 300.00

SPACE GHOST
Comico 1987
1 SR,V:Robot Master. 6.00

SPACE GIANTS, THE
Pyramid Comics 1997
0 . . . . 1.00
0a deluxe 2.25
1 . . . . 1.00
3 by Jeff Newman 1.00

SPACE MAN
Dell Publishing Co. 1962–72
1 . . . . 75.00
2 . . . . 40.00
3 . . . . 40.00
4 . . . . 30.00
5 . . . . 30.00
6 . . . . 30.00
7 . . . . 30.00
8 . . . . 30.00
9 . . . . 30.00
10 . . . . 30.00

SPACE: 1999
Charlton 1975–76
1 . . . . 10.00
2 JSon,"Survival". 8.00
3 JBy,"Bring Them Back Alive" . . . 7.00
4 JBy. 7.00
5 JBy. 7.00
6 JBy. 7.00
7 . . . . 7.00
8 B&W 7.00

SPACE: 1999
A Plus Comics
1 GM,JBy 2.50

All comics prices listed are for *Near Mint* condition.

SPACE USAGI
Mirage 1993
1 thru 3 From TMNT .... @2.75

SPACE WAR
Charlton Comics Oct., 1959
1 .... 125.00
2 .... 65.00
3 .... 60.00
4 SD,SD(c) 125.00
5 SD,SD(c) 125.00
6 SD 125.00
7 .... 30.00
8 SD,SD(c) 125.00
9 .... 35.00
10 SD,SD(c) 125.00
11 .... 35.00
12 .... 35.00
13 thru 15 .... @35.00
16 thru 27 .... @30.00
Becomes:

FIGHTIN' FIVE
28 SD,SD(c) 35.00
29 SD,SD(c) 35.00
30 SD,SD(c) 40.00
31 SD,SD(c) 40.00
32 .... 5.00
33 SD,SD(c) 40.00
34 Sd,SD(c) 40.00

SPECTRUM COMICS PRESENTS
Spectrum
1 I:Survivors 3.50

SPEED RACER
Now 1987–90
1 .... 3.50
1a 2nd printing 1.50
2 thru 33 .... @2.00
34 thru 38 .... @1.75
Spec. #1 .... 2.50
#1 2nd printing 1.75
Spec. #2. .... 3.50
Classics, Vol #2 .... 3.95
Classics, Vol #3 .... 3.95
[2nd Series]
1 R:Speed Racer. 1.95
2 .... 1.95
3 V:Giant Crab 1.95
4 .... 1.95
5 Racer-X 1.95
6 .... 1.95
7 .... 1.95

SPEED RACER
Wildstorm/DC 1999
1 Demon on Wheels 2.50

SPELLBINDERS
Quality 1986–88
1 Nemesis the Warlock 1.25
2 Nemesis the Warlock 1.25
3 Nemesis the Warlock 1.25
4 Nemesis the Warlock 1.25
5 Nemesis the Warlock 1.25
6 Nemesis the Warlock 1.25
7 Nemesis the Warlock 1.25
8 Nemesis the Warlock 1.25
9 Nemesis the Warlock 1.25
1O Nemesis the Warlock 1.25
11 Nemesis the Warlock 1.25

S.P.I.C.E.
Awesome Entertainment 1998
1 RLe,JLb,F:Kaboom. 2.50

SPIDER
Eclipse 1991
1 TT,"Blood Dance" 7.00
2 TT,"Blood Mark" 6.00
3 TT,The Spider Unmasked 5.50

SPIDER: REIGN OF THE VAMPIRE KING
Eclipse 1992
1 TT,I:Legion of Vermin 5.25
2 thru 4 TT. .... @2.50

SPIDERFEMME
Personality
1 Rep. parody 2.50

SPIDER-MAN/BADROCK
Maximum Press
1 (of 2) DJu,MMy x-over 3.00
2 DJu,DaF x-over 3.00

SPIRAL PATH
Eclipse 1986
1 V:Tairngir 1.75
2 V:King Artuk 1.75

SPIRIT
Harvey 1966
1 WE,O:Spirit 60.00
2 WE,O:The Octopus. 50.00

SPIRIT, THE
Kitchen Sink 1983–92
1 WE(c) (1983) 5.25
2 WE(c). 4.25
3 WE(c) (1984) 4.00
4 WE(c) 4.00
5 WE(c) 3.00
6 WE(c) 3.00
7 WE(c) 3.00
8 thru 11 WE(c) (1985) color 3.00
See: B&W section

Spirit #6
© Kitchen Sink

SPIRIT, THE: THE NEW ADVENTURES
Kitchen Sink 1997
1 AMo,DGb. 3.95
2 Eisner/Stout cover 3.50
2a Eisner/Schultz cover. 3.50
3 AMo,Last Night I Dreamed of Dr. Cobra. 3.50
4 Dr. Broca von Bitelbaum. ... 3.50
5 Cursed Beauty 3.50
6 Swami Vashti Bubu. 3.50
7 Central City 3.50
8 by Joe Lansdale. 3.50
9 .... 3.50
10 CAd,BRa. 3.50

SPOOKY HAUNTED HOUSE
Harvey Publications 1972–75
1 .... 30.00
2 .... 15.00
3 thru 5 .... @15.00
6 thru 10 .... @7.00
11 thru 15 .... @4.00

SPOOKY SPOOKTOWN
Harvey Publications 1966–76
1 B:Casper,Spooky,68 pgs. 150.00
2 .... 75.00
3 .... 50.00
4 .... 50.00
5 .... 50.00
6 thru 10 .... @35.00
11 thru 20 .... @25.00
21 thru 30 .... @25.00
31 thru 39 E:68 pgs. .... @20.00
40 thru 45 .... @4.00
46 thru 66 .... @3.00

SPYMAN
1 GT,JSo,1st prof work, I:Spyman 50.00
2 DAy,JSo,V:Cyclops. 30.00
3 .... 30.00

SQUALOR
First 1989
1 .... 2.75
2 .... 2.75
3 .... 2.75

STAINLESS STEEL RAT
Eagle 1986
1 Harry Harrison adapt. 2.25
2 thru 6 .... @1.50

STAR BLAZERS
Comico 1989
1 .... 3.00
2 .... 1.75
3 .... 1.75
4 .... 1.75
[2nd Series]
1 .... 1.95
2 .... 1.95
3 thru 5 .... @2.50

STARBLAZERS
Argo Press 1995
0 Battleship Yamato. 2.95
1 F:Dereck Wildstar. 2.95
2 After the Comet War. 2.95
3 .... 2.95
4 TEI. 2.95

COLOR PUB.

5	2.95
6	2.95
7 Icarus, pt.2	2.95
8	2.95
9	2.95
10	2.95
11	2.95
12 Nova captured	2.95

STARFORCE SIX SPECIAL
AC Comics

1	1.50

STARGATE
Entity Comics 1996

1	2.95
2	2.95
3	2.95
4 (of 4)	2.95
4a deluxe limited edition	3.50

STARGATE: DOOMSDAY WORLD
Entity Comics 1996

1 new crew explores 2nd StarGate	2.95
1 prism-foil edition	3.50
2	2.95
3	2.95
3 deluxe	3.50

STARGODS
Antarctic Press 1998

1 by Zachary, Clark & Beaty	2.95
1a deluxe	5.95
2 The Golden Bow	2.95
2a deluxe, with poster	5.95
Spec. Stargods Visions	2.95

STARLIGHT

1	1.95

STAR MASTERS
AC Comics

1	1.50

STAR REACH CLASSICS
Eclipse 1984

1 JSn,NA(r)	2.00
2 AN	2.00
3 HC	2.00
4 FB(r)	2.00
5	2.00
6	2.00

STAR SEED
See: POWERS THAT BE

STARSLAYER
Pacific 1982–83

1 MGr,O:Starslayer	3.00
2 MGr,DSt,I:Rocketeer	12.00
3 DSt,MGr,A:Rocketeer(2ndApp.)	8.00
4 MGr,Baraka Kuhr	2.00
5 MGr,SA,A:Groo	10.00
6 MGr.conclusion story	2.00

First

7 MGr layouts	2.00
8 MGr layouts, MG	1.50
9 MGr layouts, MG	2.25
10 TT,MG,I:Grimjack	4.00

Starslayer #7
© First

11 TT,MG,A:Grimjack	2.00
12 TT,MG,A:Grimjack	2.00
13 TT,MG,A:Grimjack	2.00
14 TT,A:Grimjack	2.00
15 TT,A:Grimjack	2.00
16 TT,A:Grimjack	2.00
17 TT,A:Grimjack	2.00
18 TT,Grimjack x-over	2.00
19 TT,TS,A:Black Flame	1.25
20 TT,TS,A:Black Flame	1.25
21 TT,TS,A:Black Flame	1.25
22 TT,TS,A:Black Flame	1.25
23 TT,TS,A:Black Flame	1.25
24 TT,TS,A:Black Flame	1.25
25 TS,A:Black Flame	1.25
26 TS,Black Flame full story	1.25
27 A:Black Flame	1.25
28 A:Black Flame	1.25
29 TS,A:Black Flame	1.25
30 TS,A:Black Flame	1.25
31 2nd Anniversary Issue	1.25
32 TS,A:Black Flame	1.25
33 TS,A:Black Flame	1.25
34 last issue	1.25
Graphic Novel	9.95

STAR TREK
Gold Key 1967–79

1 Planet of No Return	500.00
2 Devil's Isle of Space	300.00
3 Invasion of City Builders	200.00
4 Peril of Planet Quick Change	200.00
5 Ghost Planet	200.00
6 When Planets Collide	165.00
7 Voodoo Planet	175.00
8 Youth Trap	150.00
9 Legacy of Lazarus	150.00
10 Sceptre of the Sun	100.00
11 Brain Shockers	100.00
12 Flight of the Buccaneer	90.00
13 Dark Traveler	80.00
14 Enterprise Mutiny	80.00
15 Museum a/t End of Time	80.00
16 Day of the Inquisitors	80.00
17 Cosmic Cavemen	80.00
18 The Hijacked Planet	80.00
19 The Haunted Asteroid	80.00
20 A World Gone Mad	80.00
21 The Mummies of Heitus VII	65.00
22 Siege in Superspace	65.00
23 Child's Play	65.00
24 The Trial of Capt. Kirk	65.00
25 Dwarf Planet	65.00

26 The Perfect Dream	65.00
27 Ice Journey	65.00
28 The Mimicking Menace	65.00
29 rep. Star Trek #1	65.00
30 Death of a Star	50.00
31 "The Final Truth"	50.00
32 "The Animal People"	50.00
33 "The Choice"	50.00
34 "The Psychocrystals"	50.00
35 rep. Star Trek #4	50.00
36 "A Bomb in Time"	50.00
37 rep. Star Trek #5	35.00
38 "One of our Captains is Missing"	35.00
39 "Prophet of Peace"	35.00
40 AMc,Furlough to Fury, A: Barbara McCoy	35.00
41 AMc,The Evictors	35.00
42 "World Against Time"	35.00
43 "World Beneath the Waves"	35.00
44 "Prince Traitor"	35.00
45 rep. Star Trek #7	35.00
46 "Mr. Oracle"	35.00
47 AMc,"This Tree Bears Bitter Fruit"	35.00
48 AMc,Murder on Enterprise	35.00
49 AMc,"A Warp in Space"	35.00
50 AMc,"The Planet of No Life"	35.00
51 AMc,DestinationAnnihilation6	30.00
52 AMc,"And A Child Shall Lead Them"	30.00
53 AMc,"What Fools..Mortals Be"	30.00
54 AMc,"Sport of Knaves"	30.00
55 AMc,A World Against Itself	30.00
56 AMc,No Time Like The Past, A:Guardian of Forever	30.00
57 AMc,"Spore of the Devil"	30.00
58 AMc,"Brain Damaged Planet"	30.00
59 AMc,"To Err is Vulcan"	30.00
60 AMc,"The Empire Man"	30.00
61 AMc,"Operation Con Game"	30.00

STAR WARS IN 3-D
Blackthorne

1 thru 7	@2.50

STARWOLVES: JUPITER RUN

1	1.95

S.T.A.T.
Majestic 1993

1 FdS(s),PhH,I:S.T.A.T.	2.50

STEALTH SQUAD
Petra Comics 1993

1 I:Stealth Squad	2.50

STEED & MRS PEEL
Eclipse 1990

1 IG,The Golden Game	4.95
2 IG,The Golden Game	4.95
3 IG,The Golden Game	4.95

STEEL CLAW
Quality

1 H:Ken Bulmer	1.25
2	1.00
3	1.00
4	1.00

STEEL STERLING
Archie Publications 1984
(formerly LANCELOT STRONG)
4 EB	1.00
5 EB	1.00
6 EB	1.00
7 EB	1.00

STEVE CANYON 3-D
Kitchen Sink 1986
Milton Caniff & Peter Poplaski(c),
w/glasses (1985) 2.00

STEVE ZODIAC
& THE FIREBALL XL-5
Gold Key Jan., 1964
1 .... 100.00

STING OF THE
GREEN HORNET
Now 1992
1 Polybagged w/trading card	2.75
2 inc.Full color poster	2.75
3 inc.Full color poster	2.75

STINGER
1 .... 1.75

STITCH
Samsons Comics
1 I:Stitch................... 2.50

STORMQUEST
Caliber 1994
1 I:Stormquest.	1.95
2 Time Stone.	1.95
3 BU:Seeker.	1.95
4 F:Shalimar.	1.95
5 Reunion.	1.95
6 V:Samuroids.	1.95

STRANGE DAYS
Eclipse 1984–85
1	3.50
2	2.50
3	1.50

Strange Suspense Stories/Captain Atom #3 © Charlton Comics

STRANGE SUSPENSE
STORIES/
CAPTAIN ATOM
Charlton Comics
75 SD,O:CaptainAtom,1960Rep..	125.00
76 SD, Capt.Atom,1960Rep.	75.00
77 SD, Capt.Atom,1960Rep.	75.00

Becomes:
CAPTAIN ATOM
Charlton Comics 1965–67
78 SD, new stories begin	100.00
79 SD,I:Dr.Spectro	65.00
80 SD.	65.00
81 SD,V:Dr.Spectro	65.00
82 SD,I:Nightshade,Ghost	65.00
83 SD,I:Ted Kord/Blue Beetle	45.00
84 SD,N:Captain Atom	40.00
85 SD,A:Blue Beetle,I:Punch & Jewelee	40.00
86 SD,A:Ghost, Blue Beetle	40.00
87 SD,JAp,A:Nightshade	40.00
88 SD/FMc,JAp,A:Nightshade.	40.00
89 SD/FMc,JAp,A:Nightshade, Ghost, last issue Dec.1967.	40.00

STRAW MEN
Innovation
1 & 2 .... @1.95

STREET FIGHTER
Ocean 1986–87
1 thru 3 .... @1.75

STREET SHARKS
Archie Comics 1995
1 & 2 Based on Cartoons...... @1.50

STRIKE!
Eclipse 1988
1 TL,RT,I&O:New Strike.	1.75
2 TL,RT.	1.25
3 TL,RT.	1.25
4 TL,RT,V:Renegade CIA Agents.	1.25
5 TL,RT,V:Alien Bugs.	1.25
6 TL,RT,"Legacy of the Lost"	1.75
Spec. #1 Strike vs. Sgt. Strike TL,RT,"The Man"	1.95

Strike #1 © Eclipse

STRIKER
Viz
1 thru 2 .... 2.75

STRIKEFORCE AMERICA
Comico 1995
1 ScC,SK(c),I:StrikeforceAmerica	2.50
2 V:Superior-prisoner.	2.95
3 Breakout, pt.2.	2.95

[Volume 2] 1995
1 ScC,polybagged with Chrysalis
promo card. 2.95

STRONG MAN
AC Comics
1 .... 2.95

STRONTIUM DOG
Eagle 1985
1	1.50
2	1.25
3	1.25
4	1.25
5	1.25
6	1.25

Quality
7	1.25
8	1.25
9	1.25
10	1.25
11	1.25
12	1.25
13	1.25
14	1.25
15/16	1.50
17	1.50
18/19	1.50
20 thru 29	@1.50

[2nd Series]
1 .... 1.25

Quality
Spec.#1 .... 1.50

STRYKE
London Night Studios 1995
0 I:Stryke.	5.00
1	4.00

STUMBO THE GIANT
Blackthorne
1 3-D. 2.50

STUMBO TINYTOWN
Harvey Publications 1963–66
1	110.00
2	60.00
3	40.00
4	40.00
5	40.00
6 thru 13	@25.00

STUPID HEROES
Next
1 PeL(s),w/ 2 card-strip	2.75
2	2.75
3 F:Cinder.	2.75

STURM THE TROOPER
1	1.95
2	1.95
3	1.95

SUBSPECIES
Eternity 1991
1 Movie Adaptation 3.00
2 Movie Adaptation 2.50
3 Movie Adaptation 2.50
4 Movie Adaptation 2.50

SUN GLASSES AFTER DARK
Verotik 1995
1 . . . . 2.95
2 and 3 . . . . @2.95
4 thru 6 . . . . @3.95
½ prequel, San Diego Con ed.. . . . 2.95

SUN-RUNNERS
Pacific 1984
1 . . . . 2.50
2 . . . . 2.00
3 . . . . 2.00
Eclipse 1984–86
4 . . . . 2.00
5 . . . . 2.00
6 "Sins of the Father" 1.75
7 "Dark Side of Mark Dancer" 1.75
Summer Special #1 . . . . 1.75

SUNSET CARSON
AC Comics
1 Based on Cowboy Star. 5.00

SUPERBABES: FEMFORCE
AC Comics
1 Various Artists 5.00

SUPER CAR
Gold Key 1962–63
1 . . . . 225.00
2 . . . . 100.00
3 . . . . 100.00
4 . . . . 175.00

SUPERCOPS
Now 1990
1 thru 4 . . . . @1.75

SUPER COPS, THE
Red Circle 1974
1 . . . . 3.00

SUPER GOOF
Gold Key 1965–82
1 . . . . 25.00
2 thru 10 . . . . @15.00
11 thru 20 . . . . @10.00
21 thru 30 . . . . @8.00
31 thru 74 . . . . @5.00

SUPER HEROES VERSUS SUPERVILLIANS
Archie Publications July, 1966
1 A:Flyman,Black Hood,The Web,
The Shield 50.00

SUPERHUMAN SAMURAI SYBER SQUAD
Hamilton Comics 1995
0 Based on TV Show. 2.95

SUPERNAUT
Anarchy 1997
1 (of 3) 3.00
1 gold logo 6.00
2 by Rob Hand, Hand of Doom . . . 3.00
2a gold logo 6.00

SUPREME
Maximum Press
#1–#43 see Image
44 AMo, JoB, A:Glory 3.00
45 AMo, JoB, A:Glory 3.00
46 AMo,Suprema 3.00
47 AMo 3.00
48 AMo 2.50
49 AMo 2.50
50 double size 3.95
51 . . . . 3.50
52A AMo, Book 1 . . . . 3.50
52B AMo, Book 2, continuation. . . . 3.50
53 AMo,CSp,AG,V:Omniman 3.00
54 AMo,CSp,AG,Ballad of Judy
Jordan 3.00
55 AMo,CSp,AG,Silence At
Gettysburg 3.00
56 AMo,CSp,AG,Reflections,pt.1 . . 3.00
57 AMo,CSp,AG,Reflections,pt.2 . . 3.00
58 AMo,CSp,AG,A World of
His Own 3.00
59 AMo,CSp,AG,Professor Night of
the Prism World 3.00
60 AMo,CSp,AG,F:Radar in Puppy
Love. 3.00
61 AMo,CSp,AG,Meet Mr. Meteor. . 3.00
Coll.Ed.#1, rep.#1–#2 . . . . 4.95
Coll.Ed.#2, rep.. . . . . 4.95
Coll.Ed.#3 rep. #45–#46, AMo . . . 4.95
TPB Supreme Madness 14.95
HC Supreme Madness 40.00
TPB rep. #41–#46, AMo 14.95

SUPREME: THE RETURN
Awesome Entertainment 1999
1 AMo,CSp,AG 3.00
1a variant AxR cover. 6.95
2 AMo,JSn, ... 3.00
3 . . . . 3.00
4 . . . . 3.00

Surge #3
© Eclipse

SURGE
Eclipse 1984
1 A:DNAgents 3.00
2 A:DNAgents 2.00
3 A:DNAgents 3.00
4 A:DNAgents 3.00

SURROGATE SAVIOR
Hot Brazer Comic Pub.
1 I:Ralph 2.50
2 Baggage. 2.50

SURVIVORS
Spectrum
1 Mag. size 5.00
2 . . . . 3.50
3 The Old One 2.50
4 . . . . 2.50

SURVIVORS
Fantagraphics
1 thru 3 . . . . @2.50

SUSPIRA: THE GREAT WORKING
Chaos! Comics 1997
1 (of 4) PNa 2.95
2 PNa 2.95
3 PNa 2.95
4 PNa 2.95
HC signed, limited 20.00

SWORDS OF TEXAS
Eclipse 1987
1 FH,New America 2.00
2 FH,V:Baja Badlands 1.75
3 FH,TY(c),V:Dogs of Danger 1.75
4 FH,V:Samurai Master 1.75

SYMBOLS OF JUSTICE
High Impact Studios
1 I:Granger,Justice,Rayven 2.95
2 V:Devil's Brigade 2.95

SYPHONS
Now 1994
1 . . . . 1.50
2 thru 7 . . . . @1.50

SYPHONS: COUNTDOWN
Now
1 F:Brigade 2.95
2 Led By Cross 2.95
3 Blown Cover. 2.95
1995 Ann. Doomsday Device 2.95

SYPHONS: THE STARGATE STRATAGEM
Now
1 thru 3 . . . . @2.95

TALES CALCULATED TO DRIVE YOU BATS
Archie Publications 1961–62
1 . . . . 100.00
2 . . . . 75.00
3 thru 6 . . . . @50.00

TALES FROM THE CRYPT
Gladstone 1990–91
1 E.C.rep.AW/FF,GS 5.00
2 rep. 4.00
3 rep. 3.50
4 rep. 3.00
5 rep.TFTC #45. . . . . 3.00
6 rep.TFTC #42. . . . . 3.00

TALES FROM THE CRYPT
Russ Cochran Publ 1992
1 rep. TFTC #31,CSS#12 . . . . . . 2.75
2 rep. TFTC #34,CSS#15 . . . . . . 2.50
3 rep. TFTC, CSS 2.50
4 rep. TFTC #43,CSS#18 . . . . . . 2.50
5 rep. TFTC,CSS#23. . . . . 2.00

[2nd Series]
1 rep.horror stories 2.00
2 inc.The Maestro's Hand 2.00
3 thru 6 . . . . @2.00
7 thru 8 . . . . @2.00

Gemstone
16 thru 29 EC comics reprint. . . . @2.50
"Annuals"
TPB Vol. 1 rebinding of #1–#5 . . . 8.95
TPB Vol. 2 rebinding of #5–#10 . . . 8.95
TPB Vol. 3 rebinding of #11–#15. . . 8.95
TPB Vol. 4 rebinding of #16–#20. . 12.95
TPB Vol. 5 rebinding #21–#24 . . . 13.95

TALES OF EVIL
Atlas Comics 1975
1 . . . . 5.00

TALES OF TERROR
Eclipse 1985–87
1 . . . . 3.00
2 "Claustrophobia". 2.00
3 GM,"Eyes in the Darkness". 2.00
4 TT,TY,JBo(c),"The Slasher". . . . 2.00
5 "Back Forty,""Shoe Button Eyes" 2.00
6 "Good Neighbors". 2.00
7 SBi,JBo,SK(i),"Video" 2.00
8 HB,"Revenant,""Food for Thought". . . 2.00
9 . . . . 2.00
10 . . . . 2.00
11 TT,JBo(c),"Black Cullen". 2.00
12 JBo,FH,"Last of the Vampires" . . 2.00
13 . . . . 2.00

TALES OF THE GREEN BERET
Dell Publishing Co. Jan., 1967
1 SG. 30.00
2 thru 4 . . . . @20.00
5 . . . . 15.00

TALES OF THE GREEN HORNET
Now 1990
1 NA(c),O:Green Hornet Pt.1 . . . . 3.00
2 O:Green Hornet Pt.2. . . . . 2.50
3 Gun Metal Green 2.50
4 Targets. 1.95

TALES OF THE MYSTERIOUS TRAVELER
Charlton Comics Aug., 1956
1 DG. 325.00

2 SD 300.00
3 SD,SD(c) 300.00
4 SD,SD(c) 325.00
5 SD,SD(c) 325.00
6 SD,SD(c) 325.00
7 SD 275.00
8 SD 275.00
9 SD 275.00
10 SD,SD(c) 300.00
11 SD,SD(c) 300.00
12 . . . . 125.00
13 . . . . 125.00
14 (1985) 3.00
15 (1985) 3.00

TALES OF THE SUN RUNNERS
Sirius Comics 1986
1 . . . . 1.50
2 and 3 . . . . @2.00

TALESPIN
Walt Disney 1991
(Reg.-Series)
1 "Sky-Raker" Pt.1. . . . . 2.50
2 "Sky-Raker" Pt.2. . . . . 2.00
3 "Idiots Abroad" 1.75
4 "Contractual Desperation". 1.75
5 "The Oldman & the Sea Duck" . . 1.75
6 "F'reeze a Jolly Good Fellow" . . . 1.75

TALESPIN
Walt Disney 1991
[Mini-Series]
1 Take-off Pt.1. . . . . 3.00
2 Take-off Pt 2. . . . . 3.00
3 Take-off Pt 3,Khan Job 2.00
4 Take-off pt 4 . . . . 2.00

TAOLAND
Severe Reality Productions
4 1st full color issue. 5.95
5 48pg. 5.95

TAOLAND ADVENTURES
Antarctic Press 1999
1 by Jeff Amano 3.00
2 . . . . 3.00

TARGET AIRBOY
Eclipse 1988
1 SK,A:Clint. 1.95

TARGITT
Atlas March–July 1975
1 thru 3 . . . . @5.00

TARZAN OF THE APES
Gold Key 1962–72
prev. Dell (see Golden Age)
132 . . . . 25.00
133 . . . . 20.00
134 . . . . 20.00
135 . . . . 20.00
136 . . . . 20.00
137 . . . . 20.00
138 . . . . 20.00
139 I:Korak. 22.00
140 . . . . 20.00
141 . . . . 20.00
142 . . . . 20.00
143 . . . . 20.00

144 . . . . 20.00
145 . . . . 20.00
146 . . . . 20.00
147 . . . . 20.00
148 . . . . 20.00
149 . . . . 20.00
150 . . . . 20.00
151 . . . . 20.00
152 . . . . 20.00
153 . . . . 20.00
154 . . . . 20.00
155 O:Tarzan 25.00
156 . . . . 15.00
157 Banlu, Dog o/t Arande, Pt.1 . . 15.00
158 Banlu, Dog o/t Arande, Pt.2 . . 15.00
159 Banlu, Dog o/t Arande, Pt.3 . . 15.00
160 . . . . 15.00
161 . . . . 15.00
162 TV photo (c). 18.00
163 . . . . 15.00
164 . . . . 15.00
165 TV photo (c) 20.00
166 . . . . 15.00
167 . . . . 15.00
168 TV photo (c). 20.00
169 A:Leopard Girl 15.00

Tarzan of the Apes #193
© Gold Key Comics

170 . . . . 15.00
171 TV photo (c). 20.00
172 . . . . 10.00
173 . . . . 10.00
174 . . . . 10.00
175 . . . . 10.00
176 . . . . 10.00
177 . . . . 10.00
178 O:Tarzan, rep. #155. . . . . 10.00
179 A:Leopard Girl 10.00
180 . . . . 10.00
181 . . . . 10.00
182 . . . . 10.00
183 Down Trails of Terror 10.00
184 . . . . 10.00
185 . . . . 10.00
186 . . . . 10.00
187 . . . . 10.00
188 . . . . 10.00
189 . . . . 10.00
190 . . . . 10.00
191 . . . . 10.00
192 Tarzan and the Foreign Legion
    adaptation 10.00
193 "Escape From Sumatra". 10.00
194 thru 199 . . . . @10.00

COLOR PUB.

200 .... 15.00	31 thru 58 .... @4.00	32 A:Sumo Wrestler Tatoo 1.25
201 thru 205 .... @10.00	59 May, 1973 .... 4.00	33 The Karma of Katmandu 1.25
206 last issue 10.00		34 Search For Charlie Llama 1.25
Continued by DC; see also Marvel	**TEENAGE MUTANT**	35 .... 1.25
	NINJA TURTLES	36 V:Shredder 1.25
TARZAN IN COLOR	**First**	37 V:Shredder 1.25
NBM 1997	1 .... 6.00	38 V:Null & 4 Horsemen Pt.1 ..... 1.25
TPB Vol. 1, 1931–1933, by	2 .... 4.50	39 V:Null & 4 Horseman Pt.3 ..... 1.25
Hal Foster 24.95	Graphic Novel........ 17.00	40 1492,A:The Other 1.25
TPB Vol. 2, 1933–1935, by		41 And Deliver us from Evil 1.25
Hal Foster 24.95	**TEENAGE MUTANT**	42 Time Tripping Trilogy #1...... 1.25
TPB Vol. 3, 1935–1937, by	**NINJA TURTLES**	43 thru 51 .... @1.25
Hal Foster 24.95	**Archie**	52 thru 54 .... @1.50
	(From T.V. Series)	55 thru 57 Terracide ...... @1.50
TASK FORCE ALPHA	1 O:TMNT,April O'Neil,Shredder	58 thru 70.......... @1.50
Alpha Productions	Krang 6.00	1990 Movie adapt(direct) 5.50
1 Forged in Fire....... 3.50	2 V:Shredder,O:Bebop &	1990 Movie adapt(newsstand) ... 2.50
	Rocksteady 4.00	1991 TMNT meet Archie........ 2.50
TASMANIAN DEVIL &	3 V:Shredder & Krang 3.00	1991 Movie Adapt II 2.50
HIS TASTY FRIENDS		Spec.#2 Ghost of 13 Mile Island ... 2.50
Gold Key Nov., 1962	**TEENAGE MUTANT**	Spec.#3 Night of the Monsterex ... 2.50
1 .... 125.00	**NINJA TURTLES**	TMNT Mutant Universe Sourcebook 1.95
	Mirage 1993	
TASTEE-FREEZ COMICS	1 A:Casey Jones........ 3.00	
Harvey Comics 1957	2 JmL(a&s) 3.00	
1 Little Dot......... 40.00	3 thru 8 .... @2.75	
2 Rags Rabbit........ 20.00	9 V:Baxter Bot......... 2.75	
3 Casper.......... 30.00	10 Mr. Braunze........ 2.75	
4 Sad Sack........ 20.00	11 V:Raphael........ 2.75	
5 Mazie.......... 20.00	12 V:Darpa........ 2.75	
6 Dick Tracy 35.00	13 J:Triceraton........ 2.75	
TEAM ANARCHY	**TEENAGE MUTANT NINJA**	*Teenage Mutant Ninja Turtles/Flaming*
Anarchy 1993	**TURTLES ADVENTURES**	*Carrot #4 © Mirage/Dark Horse*
1 I:Team Anarchy 2.75	**Archie 1988 [2nd Series]**	
2 thru 3 .... 2.75	1 Shredder,Bebop,Rocksteady	
4 PuD,MaS,I:Primal........ 2.75	return to earth 5.00	**TEENAGE MUTANT**
	2 I:Baxter Stockman 3.00	**NINJA TURTLES/**
TEAM YANKEE	3 "Three Fragments" #1........ 3.00	**FLAMING CARROT**
First 1989	4 "Three Fragments" #2........ 2.50	**Mirage/Dark Horse**
1 Harold Coyle novel adapt...... 1.95	5 Original adventures begin,	1 JmL 3.00
2 thru 6 .... @1.95	I:Man Ray 2.50	2 thru 3 JmL 3.00
Trade Paperback 12.95	6 I:Leatherhead,Mary Bones ... 2.50	4 JmL 3.00
	7 I:Cuddley the Cowlick; Inter-	
T.E.C.H. BOYZ	Galactic wrestling league 2.50	**TMNT PRESENTS:**
HYPERACTIVE	8 I:Wingnut & Screwloose 2.00	**APRIL O'NEIL**
Dynasty Comics	9 I:Chameleon.......... 2.00	**Archie**
1 I:T.E.C.H. Boyz........... 2.95	10 I:Scumbug, Wyrm 2.00	1 A:Chien Khan,Vid Vicious 1.25
2 Man vs. Nature........ 2.95	11 I:Rat King & Sons of Silence;	2 V:White Ninja,A:V.Vicious 1.25
	Krang returns to earth 2.00	3 V:Vhien Khan,concl......... 1.25
TEEN-AGE CONFIDENTIAL	12 Final Conflict #1, A:Leatherhead	
CONFESSIONS	Wingnut,Screwloose,Trap, I:Malinga	**TMNT: THE MALTESE**
Charlton Comics 1960–64	2.00	**TURTLE**
1 .... 30.00	13 Final Conflict #2 .... 2.00	**Mirage**
2 thru 5 .... @20.00	14 Turtles go to Brazil;I:Jagwar	Spec. F:Raphael Detective....... 2.95
6 thru 10 .... @15.00	Dreadman 2.00	
11 thru 22 .... @10.00	15 I:Mr. Null 1.50	**TMNT PRESENTS:**
	16 I&D:Bubbla,the Glubbab 1.50	**DONATELLO AND**
TEENAGE HOTRODDERS	17 Cap'n Mossback 1.25	**LEATHERHEAD**
Charlton Comics April, 1963	18 'Man Who Sold World' 1.25	1 thru 2 .... @1.25
1 .... 45.00	19 I: Mighty Mutanimals 1.25	
2 thru 5 .... @30.00	20 V:Supersoldier,War.Dragon ... 1.25	
6 thru 10 .... @25.00	21 V:Vid Vicious 1.25	
11 thru 23 .... @15.00	22 GC,Donatello captured 1.50	
24 .... 8.00	23 V:Krang,I:Slash,Belly Bomb ... 1.50	
Becomes:	24 V:Krang........... 1.50	
TOP ELIMINATOR	25 .... 1.50	
25 thru 29.......... @5.00	26 I:T'Pau & Keeper....... 1.50	
Becomes:	27 I:Nevermore,Nocturno&Hallocat. 1.50	
DRAG 'N' WHEELS	28 Turtle go to Spain, I:Nindar &	
30 .... 6.00	Chein Klan............. 1.50	
	29 Warrior Dragon captured 1.50	
	30 TMNT/Fox Mutant Ninjara	
	team-up 1.25	
	31 TMNT/Ninjara team-up cont.... 1.25	

TMNT PRESENTS: MERDUDE VS. RAY FILLET
Archie 1993
1 thru 3 . . . . 1.25

TMNT: APRIL O'NEIL THE MAY EAST SAGA
Archie
1 A:TMNT 1.25

TMNT: YEAR OF THE TURTLE
Archie Comics 1995
1 All New Era 1.50

[JACK KIRBY'S] TEENAGENTS
Topps
[Mini-Series]
1 WS,AH,w/3 cards 2.95
2 NV,w/3 cards 2.95
3 NV,w/3 cards 2.95
4 NV,w/3 leftover? cards 2.95

TEEN CONFESSIONS
Charlton Comics 1959–76
1 . . . . 50.00
2 . . . . 25.00
3 . . . . 15.00
4 . . . . 15.00
5 . . . . 15.00
6 . . . . 15.00
7 . . . . 15.00
8 . . . . 15.00
9 . . . . 15.00
10 . . . . 15.00
11 thru 30 . . . . @12.00
31 Beatles cover 40.00
32 thru 36 . . . . @10.00
37 Beatles cover,Fan Club story . . 35.00
38 thru 97 . . . . @6.00

TEEN SECRET DIARY
Charlton Comics 1959–61
1 . . . . 25.00
2 . . . . 20.00
3 . . . . 10.00
4 . . . . 10.00
5 . . . . 10.00
6 . . . . 10.00
7 . . . . 10.00
8 . . . . 10.00
9 . . . . 10.00
10 . . . . 10.00
11 . . . . 10.00

TEKKEN 2
Knightstone 1997
1 (of 4) Tekken Saga, pt.3 . . . . . . 2.95
2 . . . . 2.95
2a photo cover 2.95
3 . . . . 2.95
3a photo cover 2.95

TEKKEN SAGA
Knightstone 1997
1 (of 8) 3.95
2 . . . . 2.95
3 . . . . 2.95
4 Paul vs. Kazuya 2.95

---

5 Paul a prisoner 2.95
Nightstone Unlimited & Tekken ½ . . 2.95

TENSE SUSPENSE
Fargo Publications 1958–59
1 . . . . 50.00
2 . . . . 45.00

TERMINATOR, THE
Now 1988–89
1 . . . . 10.00
2 . . . . 5.00
3 . . . . 4.00
4 . . . . 3.50
5 . . . . 3.50
6 . . . . 3.50
7 . . . . 3.50
8 . . . . 3.50
9 . . . . 3.50
10 . . . . 3.50
11 . . . . 3.50
12 I:JohnConnor($1.75,cov,dbl.sz) . 3.50
13 . . . . 3.50
14 . . . . 3.50
15 . . . . 3.50
16 . . . . 3.50
17 . . . . 3.50
Spec. #1 . . . . 3.50

TERMINATOR: ALL MY FUTURES PAST
Now 1990
1 Painted Art 3.00
2 Painted Art 3.00

TERMINATOR: THE BURNING EARTH
Now 1990
1 . . . . 7.00
2 . . . . 6.00
3 . . . . 6.00
4 . . . . 10.00
5 . . . . 10.00

TERRAFORMERS
Wonder Comics 1987
1 . . . . 1.00
2 . . . . 1.00
3 . . . . 1.00
4 . . . . 1.00

TERRANAUTS
Fantasy General 1986
1 . . . . 1.75
2 . . . . 1.75

TESS
1 . . . . 1.95

TEXAS RANGERS IN ACTION
Charlton Comics 1956–70
5 . . . . 40.00
6 . . . . 25.00
7 . . . . 25.00
8 . . . . 25.00
9 . . . . 25.00
10 . . . . 25.00
11 . . . . 40.00
12 . . . . 15.00
13 . . . . 35.00
14 thru 20 . . . . @15.00
21 thru 30 . . . . @10.00

Texas Rangers in Action
© Charlton Comics

31 thru 59 . . . . @5.00
60 B:Riley's Rangers 6.00
61 thru 79 . . . . @3.00

THAT WILKIN BOY
Archie Publications Jan., 1969
1 . . . . 25.00
2 . . . . 15.00
3 . . . . 15.00
4 . . . . 15.00
5 . . . . 15.00
6 . . . . 15.00
7 . . . . 15.00
8 . . . . 15.00
9 . . . . 15.00
10 . . . . 15.00
11 thru 20 . . . . @6.00
21 thru 26 E:Giant size . . . . @5.00
27 thru 52 . . . . @5.00

THESPIAN
Dark Moon
1 I:Thespian 2.50
2 V:Lemming 2.50
3 Lord of Manhattan 2.50

THING: COLD FEAR
1 R:Thing 3.00
2 . . . . 2.75

THIRD WORLD WAR
Fleetway 1990–91
1 HamburgerLady 2.50
2 . . . . 2.50
3 The Killing Yields 2.50
4 . . . . 2.50
5 . . . . 2.50
6 . . . . 2.50

13: ASSASSIN
TSR 1990–91
1 thru 4 from game . . . . @2.95
5 thru 8 The Search for Maggie Darr . . . . @2.95

THOSE ANNOYING POST BROTHERS
Vortex
1 . . . . 1.75
2 . . . . 1.75

3	1.75
4	1.75
5	1.75
6	1.75

3-D ZONE PRESENTS
Renegade 1987–89

1 L.B.Cole(c)	2.00
2	2.00
3	2.00
4	2.00
5	2.00
12 3-D Presidents	2.50
13 Flash Gordon	2.50
14 Tyranostar	2.50
15 Tyranostar	2.50
16 SpaceVixen	2.50

3-D ZONE - 3 DEMENTIA

15	2.50

THREE FACES OF GNATMAN

1	1.75

THREE STOOGES
Dell Publishing Co.
Oct.-Dec., 1959

6 Ph(c),B:Prof. Putter	100.00
7 Ph(c)	100.00
8 Ph(c)	100.00
9 Ph(c)	100.00

Gold Key 1962

10 Ph(c)	100.00
11 Ph(c)	75.00
12 Ph(c)	75.00
13 Ph(c)	75.00
14 Ph(c)	75.00
15 Ph(c)	90.00
16 Ph(c),E:Prof. Putter	75.00
17 Ph(c),B:Little Monsters	75.00
18 Ph(c)	75.00
19 Ph(c)	75.00
20 Ph(c)	75.00
21 Ph(c)	75.00
22 Ph(c),Movie Scenes	75.00
23 Ph(c)	60.00
24 Ph(c)	60.00
25 Ph(c)	60.00
26 Ph(c)	60.00
27 Ph(c)	60.00
28 Ph(c)	60.00
29 Ph(c)	60.00
30 Ph(c)	60.00
31 Ph(c)	50.00
32 Ph(c)	50.00
33 Ph(c)	50.00
34 Ph(c)	50.00
35 Ph(c)	50.00
36 Ph(c)	50.00
37 Ph(c)	50.00
38 Ph(c)	50.00
39 Ph(c)	50.00
40 Ph(c)	50.00
41 Ph(c)	50.00
42 Ph(c)	50.00
43 Ph(c)	50.00
44 Ph(c)	50.00
45 Ph(c)	50.00
46 Ph(c)	50.00
47 Ph(c)	50.00
48 Ph(c)	50.00
49 Ph(c)	50.00
50 Ph(c)	50.00
51	40.00
52 Ph(c)	50.00
53 Ph(c)	50.00
54 Ph(c)	50.00
55 Ph(c)	50.00

THREE STOOGES 3-D
Eclipse 1991

1 thru 3 reprints from 1953	@2.50
4 reprints from 1953	3.50

THRILLING SCIENCE TALES
AC Comics 1989

1	3.50

THRILLOGY
Pacific 1984

1	1.50

THRILL-O-RAMA
Harvey Publications 1965–66

1 A:Man in Black(Fate),DW,AW	40.00
2 AW,A:Pirana,I:Clawfang, The Barbarian	25.00
3 A:Pirana, Fate	20.00

THUNDER AGENTS
Tower 1965–69

1 WW,RC,GK,MSy,GT,I:Thunder Agents,IronMaiden,Warlord	150.00
2 WW,MSy,D:Egghead	100.00
3 WW,DA,MSy,V:Warlords	60.00
4 WW,MSy,RC,I:Lightning	60.00
5 WW,RC,GK,MSy	60.00
6 WW,SD,MSy,I:Warp Wizard	40.00
7 WW,MSy,SD,D:Menthor	40.00
8 WW,MSy,GT,DA,I:Raven	40.00
9 OW,WW,MSy,A:Andor	40.00
10 WW,MSy,OW,A:Andor	40.00
11 WW,DA,MSy	25.00
12 SD,WW,MSy	25.00
13 WW,OW,A:Undersea Agent	25.00
14 SD,WW,GK,N:Raven,A:Andor	25.00
15 WW,OW,GT,A:Andor	25.00
16 SD,GK,A:Andor	20.00
17 WW,OW,GT	20.00
18 SD,OW,RC	20.00
19 GT,I:Ghost	20.00
20 WW,RC,MSy,all reprints	10.00

T.H.U.N.D.E.R. AGENTS
J.C. Productions 1983

1 MA,Centerfold	2.00
2 I:Vulcan	2.00

T.H.U.N.D.E.R. AGENTS
Maximum 1995

1 and 2	@2.95

THUNDERBOLT
Charlton Comics 1966–67

1 PAM,O:Thuderbolt	25.00
Prev: Son of Vulcan	
51 PAM,V:Evila	15.00
52 PAM,V:Gore the Monster	10.00
53 PAM,V:The Tong	10.00
54 PAM,I:Sentinels	10.00
55 PAM,V:Sentinels	10.00
56 PAM,A:Sentinels	10.00
57 A:Sentinels	10.00
58 PAM,A:Sentinels	10.00
59 PAM,A:Sentinels	10.00
60 PAM,JAp,I:Prankster	15.00

Thunderbolt #1
© Charlton Comics

TIGER GIRL
Gold Key Sept., 1968

1	35.00

TIGER-MAN
Atlas April–Sept. 1975

1 thru 3	@6.00

TIME TUNNEL, THE
Gold Key Feb., 1967

1 from TV show	55.00
2	45.00

TIME TWISTERS
Quality 1987–89

1 Alan Moore ser.	1.25
2 Alan Moore ser.	1.25
3 Alan Moore ser.	1.25
4 Alan Moore ser.	1.25
5	1.25
6 Alan Moore ser.	1.25
7 Alan Moore ser.	1.25
8	1.25
9	1.25
10	1.25
11	1.25
12	1.25
13 thru 21	@1.50

TIME 2

1 Graphic Novel	8.00

TIPPY'S FRIENDS GO-GO & ANIMAL
Tower Comics 1966–69

1	40.00
2	20.00
3	20.00
4	20.00
5	20.00
6	20.00
7	20.00
8 Beatles on cover & back	75.00
9 thru 15	@20.00

TIPPY TEEN
Tower Comics Nov., 1965–70

1	40.00

2 thru 27 . . . . @20.00

TO DIE FOR
1 3-D. 2.50

TOM MIX WESTERN
AC Comics 1988
1 . . . . 2.95

TOMMY & THE MONSTERS
1 . . . . 2.00

TOM TERRIFIC!
Pines Comics
Summer, 1957
1 . . . . 150.00
2 . . . . 100.00
3 . . . . 100.00
4 . . . . 100.00
5 . . . . 100.00
6 Fall, 1958 . . . . 100.00

TOMMI-GUNN
London Night 1997
0 . . . . 3.00
0 nude cover 6.00
½ 3.00
½a photo nude edition 10.00
1 signed 15.00
1a, chromium, elite edition 19.95
2 . . . . 3.00
2 photo nude edition 6.00
3 . . . . 3.00
3 photo nude edition 6.00

TOMMI-GUNN: KILLER'S LUST
London Night 1997
1 . . . . 3.00
1 Japanese Chromium edition . . . 12.00
2 . . . . 3.00
2 photo nude edition 6.00
2 photo nude edition, signed 15.00

TOMOE
Crusade Entertainment 1996
0 BiT, ... 3.00
1 BiT,Fan Appreciation Edition 3.00
2 . . . . 3.00
TPB rep. 13.95

TOMOE/WITCHBLADE: FIRE SERMON
Crusade Entertainment 1996
1 . . . . 5.00
1a Gold foil 10.00

TOMOE: UNFORGETTABLE FIRE
Crusade Entertainment 1997
1 (of 3) 2.95

TOMORROW STORIES
Wildstorm/DC 1999
America's Best Comics
1 AMo,AxR(c) anthology 3.50
1a AxR(c),variant cover 3.50

TOM STRONG
Wildstorm/DC 1999
America's Best Comics
1 AMo(s),CSp,40-page 3.50
2 AMo(s),CSp,Millennium City 3.00
3 AMo(s),CSp,Millennium City 3.00
4 AMo,CSp,AAd,Berlin in WW2 . . . 3.00
5 AMo,JOy,CSp,Memories of
    Pangea 3.00

TOOL AND DIE
Samson Comics
1 Autographed. 4.95
1a Blue Edition 9.95

Top Cat #19
© Charlton Comics

TOP CAT
Charlton Comics 1970–73
1 . . . . 50.00
2 thru 10 . . . . @25.00
11 thru 20 . . . . @20.00

TOP TEN
Wildstorm/DC 1999
America's Best Comics
1 AMo(s),GeH,40-page 3.50
2 AMo(s),GeH 3.00

TOR IN 3-D
Eclipse 1986
1 JKu 3.00
1a B&W limited 100 sign 5.00
2 JKu 3.00

TORI-SHI-KITA
Relative Burn
1 Hunter Prey 2.50

TORMENTRESS: MISTRESS OF HELL
Blackout Comics 1977
0 . . . . 2.95
0a nude variant 9.95

TOTAL ECLIPSE
Eclipse 1988–89
1 BHa,BSz(c),A:Airboy,Skywolf . . . 3.95
2 BHa,BSz(c),A:New Wave, Liberty
    Project 3.95

3 BHa,BSz(c),A:Scout,Ms.Tree . . . 3.95
4 BHa,BSz(c),A:Miracleman,
    Prowler 3.95
5 BHa,BSz(c),A:Miracleman, Aztec
    Ace 3.95

TOTAL ECLIPSE, THE SERAPHIM OBJECTIVE
Eclipse 1988
1 tie-in Total Eclipse #2 . . . . 1.95

Total War #1
© Gold Key Comics

TOTAL WAR
Gold Key July, 1965
1 . . . . 50.00
2 . . . . 50.00
Becomes:
M.A.R.S. PATROL
3 WW 50.00
4 . . . . 25.00
5 . . . . 25.00
6 . . . . 25.00
7 . . . . 25.00
8 . . . . 25.00
9 . . . . 25.00
10 . . . . 25.00

TOY BOY
Continuity 1986–91
1 NA.I&O:Toy Boy,A:Megalith 2.00
2 TVE 2.00
3 TVE 2.00
4 TVE 2.00
5 TVE 2.00
6 TVE 2.00
7 MG. 2.00

TRANCERS: THE ADVEN-TURES OF JACK DETH
Eternity
1 I:Jack Deth 2.50
2 A:Whistler, final issue 2.50

TRANSFORMERS
1 Robotics. 1.50
2 . . . . 2.00
3 . . . . 2.50

COLOR PUB.

COLOR PUB.

TRANSFORMERS in 3-D
Blackthorne
1 thru 5 . . . . @2.50

TRAVEL OF JAMIE McPHEETERS, THE
Gold Key Dec., 1963
1 Kurt Russell 35.00

TRAVELLER
Maximum Press 1996
1 (of 3) RLd,MHw, ... 3.00

TRIBE
Axis Comics 1993–94
1 see Image Comics section
2 TJn(s),LSn,V:Alex. 2.25
3 TJn(s),LSn, ... 1.95
Good Comics 1996
0 TJn,LSn 2.95
1 TJn,LSn,Choice and
Responsibility 2.95
2 TJn,LSn,Choice and
Responsibility 2.95

TROLL LORDS
Comico 1989–90
Spec. #1 . . . . 1.75
1 . . . . 1.75
2 and 3 . . . . @1.75
4 . . . . 2.50

TROUBLE WITH GIRLS
Comico 1987–88
1 . . . . 3.00
2 . . . . 2.50
3 . . . . 2.50
4 . . . . 1.95

TRUE LOVE
Eclipse 1986
1 ATh,NC,DSt(c),reprints 2.00
2 ATh,NC,BA(c),reprints 1.50

TRUE ROMANCE
Pyramid Comics 1997
1 . . . . 1.00
1a deluxe 2.25
2 . . . . 1.00
3 . . . . 1.00
4 . . . . 1.00

TUFF GHOSTS STARRING SPOOKY
Harvey Publications 1962–72
1 . . . . 75.00
2 . . . . 40.00
3 . . . . 40.00
4 . . . . 40.00
5 . . . . 40.00
6 . . . . 30.00
7 . . . . 30.00
8 . . . . 30.00
9 . . . . 30.00
10 . . . . 30.00
11 thru 20 . . . . @15.00
21 thru 30 . . . . @10.00
31 thru 39 . . . . @7.00
40 thru 42 52 pg. Giants . . . . . . @7.00
43 . . . . 7.00

TUROK: SON OF STONE
Gold Key 1962
1 thru 29 see Golden Age
30 . . . . 65.00
31 thru 40 . . . . @50.00
41 thru 50 . . . . @40.00
51 thru 60 . . . . @30.00
61 thru 75 . . . . @25.00
76 thru 91 . . . . @20.00
Whitman
92 thru 130 . . . . @7.00
Giant #1 . . . . 100.00

TURTLE SOUP
Millenium 1991
1 Book 1, short stories 2.50
2 thru 4 . . . . 2.50

TV CASPER & COMPANY
Harvey Publications 1963–74
1 B:68 pg. Giants 75.00
2 . . . . 50.00
3 . . . . 50.00
4 . . . . 50.00
5 . . . . 50.00
6 . . . . 35.00
7 . . . . 35.00
8 . . . . 35.00
9 . . . . 35.00
10 . . . . @35.00
11 thru 20 . . . . @20.00
21 thru 31 E:68 pg. Giants . . . . @15.00
32 thru 46 . . . . @10.00

TWEETY AND SYLVESTER
Gold Key 1963–84
1 . . . . 35.00
2 thru 10 . . . . @15.00
11 thru 30 . . . . @10.00
31 thru 121 . . . . @6.00

22 BRIDES
Event 1996
1 . . . . 3.00
2 . . . . 3.00
2a variant (c) 4.00

Twilight Avenger #1
© Elite

3 . . . . 3.00
3a variant (c) 4.00
4 . . . . 3.00

TWILIGHT AVENGER
Elite 1986
1 thru 4 . . . . @1.75

TWILIGHT MAN
First 1989
1 Mini-Series 2.75
2 Mini-Series 2.75
3 Mini-Series 2.75
4 Mini-Series 2.75

TWILIGHT ZONE, THE
Gold Key
March-May, 1961
1 RC,FF,GE,P(c) all 120.00
2 . . . . 75.00
3 ATh,MSy 55.00
4 ATh 55.00
5 . . . . 50.00
6 . . . . 50.00
7 . . . . 50.00
8 . . . . 50.00
9 ATh 60.00
10 . . . . 50.00
11 . . . . 50.00
12 AW 50.00
13 AW,RC,FBe,AMc 40.00
14 RC,JO,RC,AT 40.00
15 RC,JO 40.00
16 . . . . 25.00
17 . . . . 25.00
18 . . . . 25.00
19 JO 25.00
20 . . . . 20.00
21 RC. 25.00
22 JO 25.00
23 JO 25.00
24 . . . . 20.00
25 GE,RC,ATh 20.00
26 RC,GE. 20.00
27 GE. 20.00
28 . . . . 15.00
29 . . . . 15.00
30 . . . . 15.00
31 . . . . 15.00
32 GE. 20.00
33 . . . . 15.00
34 . . . . 15.00
35 . . . . 15.00
36 . . . . 15.00
37 . . . . 15.00
38 . . . . 15.00
39 WMc 15.00
40 . . . . 12.00
41 . . . . 12.00
42 . . . . 12.00
43 RC. 15.00
44 . . . . 12.00
45 . . . . 12.00
46 . . . . 12.00
47 . . . . 12.00
48 . . . . 12.00
49 . . . . 12.00
50 FBe,WS. 12.00
51 AW 15.00
52 . . . . 12.00
53 . . . . 12.00
54 . . . . 12.00
55 . . . . 12.00
56 . . . . 12.00
57 FBe 12.00
58 . . . . 12.00
59 FBe,AMc 15.00
60 . . . . 10.00

All comics prices listed are for *Near Mint* condition.

61	10.00
62	10.00
63	10.00
64	10.00
65	10.00
66	10.00
67	10.00
68	10.00
69	10.00
70	10.00
71 rep	8.00
72	10.00
73 rep	8.00
74	10.00
75	10.00
76	10.00
77 FBe	12.00
78 FBe,AMc,The Missing Mirage	12.00
79 rep	8.00
80 FBe,AMc	12.00
81	10.00
82 AMc	12.00
83 FBe,WS	12.00
84 FBe,AMc	12.00
85	10.00
86 rep	8.00
87 thru 91	@10.00

TWILIGHT ZONE
Now 1990

1 NA,BSz(c)	8.00
1a 2nd printing Prestige +Harlan Ellison sty	6.00

[Volume 2]

#1 "The Big Dry" (direct)	2.50
#1a Newsstand	1.95
2 "Blind Alley"	1.95
3 Extraterrestrial	1.95
4 The Mysterious Biker	1.95
5 Queen of the Void	1.95
6 Insecticide	1.95
7 The Outcasts,Ghost Horse	1.95
8 Colonists on Alcor	1.95
9 Dirty Lyle's House of Fun (3-D Holo)	2.95
10 Stairway to Heaven,Key to Paradise	1.95
11 TD(i),Partial Recall	1.95
3-D Spec	2.50
Ann. #1	2.75

[Volume 3]

1 thru 2	2.50

Twisted Tales #5
© Pacific Comics

TWISTED TALES
Pacific 1982–84

1 RCo. "Infected"	3.50
2	2.00
3	2.00
4	2.00
5	2.00
6	2.00
7	2.00
8	2.00

Eclipse

9	2.00
10 GM,BWr	2.00

TWISTED TALES OF BRUCE JONES
Eclipse 1982–84

1	2.00
2	2.00
3	2.00
4	2.00

TWISTER
Harris

1 inc.Special newspaper/poster, and trading cards	2.95

TWO FISTED TALES
Russ Cochran 1992

1 JSe,HK,WW,JCr,reps	1.50
2 Reps inc.War Story	1.50
3 rep	1.50
4 thru 6 rep	2.00
7 thru 8 rep	2.00

Gemstone

17 thru 24 EC comics reprints	@2.50

"Annuals"

TPB Vol.#4 reprint #16–#20	12.95
TPB Vol. 2 rebinding of #5–#10	9.95
TPB Vol. 3 rebinding of #11–#15	10.95
TPB Vol. 4 rebinding	10.95
TPB Vol. 5 rebinding	10.95

2000 A.D. MONTHLY
Eagle 1985

1 A:JudgeDredd	4.00
2 A:JudgeDredd	30.00
3 A:JudgeDredd	1.25
4 A:JudgeDredd	1.25
5	1.25
6	1.25

[2nd Series]

1	1.25
2	1.25
3	1.25
4	1.25

Quality

5	1.25
6	1.25
7 thru 27	@1.25
28/29	1.50
30	1.50
31/32	1.50
33	1.50
34	1.50
35	1.50
36	1.50
37	1.50
Becomes:	

2000 A.D. SHOWCASE

38	1.50
39	1.50
40	1.50
41	1.50
42	1.95

43	1.95
44	1.95
45	1.95
46	1.50
47	1.75
48 thru 54	@1.75
TPB:Killing Time	12.95

TZU THE REAPER
Murim Studios 1997

1 by Gary Cohn & C.S. Chun	2.95
2	2.95
3	2.95
4	2.95
5	2.95

TZU: SPIRITS OF DEATH
Murim Studios 1997

1	2.95

UFO & Outer Space #17
© Gold Key Comics

UFO FLYING SAUCERS
Gold Key Oct. 1968

1	30.00
2	20.00
3 thru 13	@10.00
Becomes:	

UFO & OUTER SPACE
Gold Key June 1978

14 thru 25	@5.00

ULTRAMAN
Nemesis 1994

1 EC,O:Ultraman	2.25
2	2.50
3	2.50
4 V:Blue Ultraman	2.50

ULTRAMAN
Harvey/Ultracomics 1993

1 with 1 of 3 cards	2.50
2 with 1 of 3 cards & virgin cover	2.50
3 with 1 of 3 cards & virgin cover	2.50

UNCLE SCROOGE
Dell/Gold Key Dec. 1962

40	125.00
41	100.00
42	100.00

COLOR PUB.

43	100.00	247	2.50
44	100.00	248	2.50
45	100.00	249	2.50
46 Lost Beneath the Sea	100.00	250 CB	3.50
47	100.00	251	2.50
48	100.00	252 "No Room For Human Error"	2.50
49 Loony Lunar Gold Rush	100.00	253 Fab.Philosophers Stone	2.50
50 Rug Riders in the Sky	100.00	254 The Filling Station	2.50
51 How Green Was my Lettuce	90.00	255 The Flying Dutchman	2.50
52 Great Wig Mystery	90.00	256 CB,"Status Seeker"	2.50
53 Interplanetary Postman	90.00	257 "Coffee,Louie or Me"	2.50
54 Billion-Dollar Safari!	90.00	258 CB,"Swamp of no return"	2.50
55 McDuck of Arabia	90.00	259 "The only way to Go"	2.50
56 Mystery of the Ghost		260 The Waves Above, The	
Town Railroad	90.00	Gold Below	2.50
57 Swamp of No Return	90.00	261 Rosa,"Return to Zanadu" Pt.1	2.50
58 Giant Robot Robbers	90.00	262 Rosa,"Return to Zanadu" Pt.2	2.50
59 North of the Yukon	90.00	263 Rosa,"Treasure Under Glass"	2.50
60 Phantom of Notre Duck	90.00	264 Snobs Club	2.25
61 So Far and No Safari	75.00	265 CB,Ten Cent Valentine	2.25
62 Queen of the Wild Dog Pack	75.00	266 The Money Ocean,Pt.1	2.25
63 House of Haunts!	75.00	267 The Money Ocean,Pt 2	2.25
64 Treasure of Marco Polo!	75.00	268 CB,Rosa,Island in the Sky	2.00
65 Micro-Ducks from OuterSpace	75.00		
66 Heedless Horseman	75.00		
67 CB rep.	75.00		
68 Hall of the Mermaid Queen!	75.00		
69 Cattle King!	75.00		
70 CB,The Doom Diamond!	75.00		
71	60.00		
72 CB rep.	75.00		
73 CB rep.	75.00		
74 thru 110	@50.00		
111 thru 148	@30.00		
149	20.00		
150 thru 168	@15.00		
169 thru 173	@10.00		

Whitman

174 thru 182	@8.00
183 thru 200	@6.00
201 thru 209	@5.00

Gladstone

210 CB	15.00
211 CB,Prize of Pizzaro	15.00
212 CB,city-golden roofs	15.00
213 CB,city-golden roofs	15.00
214 CB	15.00
215 CB, a cold bargain	15.00
216 CB	15.00
217 CB,7 cities of Cibola	15.00
218 CB	15.00
219 Don Rosa,Son of Sun	25.00
220 CB,Don Rosa	5.00
221 CB,A:BeagleBoys	3.00
222 CB,Mysterious Island	3.00
223 CB	3.00
224 CB,Rosa,Cash Flow	6.00
225 CB	3.00
226 CB,Rosa	4.00
227 CB,Rosa	4.00
228 CB	3.00
229 CB	3.00
230 CB	5.00
231 CB,Rosa(c)	3.00
232 CB	3.00
233 CB	3.00
234 CB	3.00
235 Rosa	3.50
236 CB	3.00
237 CB	3.00
238 CB	3.00
239 CB	3.00
240 CB	3.00
241 CB,giant	5.00
242 CB,giant	4.00

Walt Disney 1990

243 CB,"Pie in the Sky"	3.50
244	2.50
245	2.50
246	2.50

Uncle Scrooge #252
© Walt Disney

269 The Flowers	2.25
270 V:Magica DeSpell	2.25
271 The Secret o/t Stone	2.25
272 Canute The Brute's Battle Axe	2.25
273 CB,Uncle Scrooge-Ghost	2.00
274 CB,Hall of the Mermaid Queen	2.00
275 CB,Rosa,Christmas Cheers,inc.	
D.Rosa centerspread	2.50
276 Rosa, thru 277	@2.25
278 thru 280	@2.25

Gladstone

281 Rosa	5.00
282 thru 284	2.50
285 Rosa, Life & Times	10.00
286 thru 293 Rosa, Life & Times	@5.00
294 thru 299	@1.50
300 Rosa & Barks	3.00
301 "Statuesque Spendthrifts"	1.50
302	1.50
303 "Rocks to Riches"	1.50
304 "My Private Eye"	1.95
305 "The Vigilante of Pizen Bluff"	1.95
306	1.95
307 "Temper Temper"	1.95
308 "Revenge of the Witch"	1.95
Prestige format, 64pg.	
309 "Whadalottajargon"	6.95
310 "The Sign of the Triple	
Distelfink"	6.95
311 "The Last Lord of Eldorado"	6.95

312 "The Hands of Zeus"	6.95
313 "The Fantastic River Race"	6.95
314	6.95
315 "The Flying Scot," pt.1	6.95
316 "The Flying Scot," pt.2	6.95
317 "Pawns of the Lamp Garou"	6.95
318 "Cowboy Captain of Cutty Sark"	6.95
319 "The Horse Radish Story"	6.95
320 "The Mysterious Stone Ray"	6.95
321 "The Giant Robot Robbers"	6.95
322 "Secret of the Lost	
Dutchman's Mine"	6.95

UNCLE SCROOGE ADVENTURES
Gladstone

1 CB,McDuck of Arabia	9.00
2 translated from Danish	5.00
3 translated from Danish	5.00
4 CB	5.00
5 Rosa	5.00
6 CB	3.50
7 CB	3.00
8 CB	3.00
9 Rosa	3.50
10 CB	3.00
11 CB	3.00
12 CB	3.00
13 CB	3.00
14 Rosa	3.50
15 CB	3.00
16 CB	3.00
17 CB	3.00
18 CB	3.00
19 CB,Rosa(c)	3.50
20 CB,giant	4.00
21 CB,giant	4.00
22 Rosa(c)	5.00
23 CB,giant	4.00
24 thru 26	@2.00
27 Rosa,O:Jr. Woodchuck	4.00
28 giant	3.00
29	1.50
30 giant	4.00
31 thru 32	@3.00
33 Barks	4.00
34 thru 40	@3.00
41	2.00
42 "The Dragon's Amulet"	2.00
43 "Queen of the Wild Dog Pack"	2.00
44	2.00
45 "The Secret of the Duckburg	
Triangle"	2.00
46 "The Tides Turn"	2.25
47 "The Menehune Mystery"	2.25
48 "The Tenth Avatar"	2.25
49 "Dead-Eye Duck"	2.25
50 CB,"The Secret of Atlantis"	2.50
51	1.95
52 The Black Diamond	1.95
53 Secret of the Incas	1.95
54 Secret of the Incas, pt.2	1.95

UNCLE SCROOGE ADVENTURES
Gladstone 1997–98
Don Rosa Specials

Spec.#1 (of 4)	10.95
Spec.#2 thru #4	@9.95
Van Horn Specials	
Spec.#1	9.95
Spec.#2	9.95
Spec.#3	9.95
Spec.#4	9.95

COLOR PUB.

UNCLE SCROOGE ADVENTURES IN COLOR
Gladstone
Carl Barks reprints
1 thru 32	@8.95
33 thru 35	@9.95
36 32pg.	8.95
37 thru 53	@9.95
54 Hall of the Mermaid Queen	9.95
55 The Doom Diamond	9.95
56 two adventures	9.95

UNCLE SCROOGE & DONALD DUCK
Gold Key
1 rep.	75.00

UNCLE SCROOGE AND DONALD DUCK
Gladstone Oct. 1997
1	1.95
2 Christmas stories	1.95
3 Back to Long Ago	1.95
TPB Vol. 1	9.95
TPB Vol. 2	9.95
TPB Vol. 3	9.95
TPB Vol. 4	9.95

UNCLE SCROOGE GOES TO DISNEYLAND
Gladstone 1985
1 CB,etc. 100pp.	11.00

UNDERDOG
Charlton July, 1970
1 Planet Zot	70.00
2 Simon Sez/The Molemen	40.00
3 Whisler's Father	40.00
4 The Witch of Pycoon	40.00
5 The Snowmen	40.00
6 The Big Shrink	40.00
7 The Marbleheads	40.00
8 The Phoney Booths	40.00
9 Tin Man Alley	40.00
10 Be My Valentine (Jan. 1972)	40.00

UNDERDOG
Gold Key March, 1975
1 The Big Boom	50.00
2 The Sock Singer Caper	25.00
3 The Ice Cream Scream	25.00
4	25.00
5	25.00
6 Head in a Cloud	25.00
7 The Cosmic Canine	25.00
8	25.00
9	25.00
10 Bouble Trouble Gum	25.00
11 The Private Life of Shoeshine Boy	15.00
12 The Deadly Fist of Fingers	15.00
13	15.00
14 Shrink Shrank Shrunk	15.00
15 Polluter Palooka	15.00
16 The Soda Jerk	15.00
17 Flee For Your Life	15.00
18 Rain Rain Go Away...Okay	15.00
19 Journey To the Center of the Earth	15.00
20 The Six Million Dollar Dog	15.00
21 Smell of Success	15.00
22 Antlers Away	15.00
23 Wedding Bells In Outer Space (Feb.,1979)	15.00

Underdog #1
© Spotlight

UNDERDOG
Spotlight 1987
1 FMc,PC(c),The Eredicator	1.50
2 FMc,CS(c), Prisoner of Love/ The Return of Fearo	1.50

UNDERDOG IN 3-D
Blackthorne
1 Wanted Dead or Alive	2.50

UNDERSEA AGENT
Tower 1966–97
1 F:Davy Jones,UnderseaAgent	60.00
2 thru 4	@40.00
5 O&I:Merman	45.00
6 GK,WW(c)	45.00

UNDERTAKER
Chaos! Comics 1999
Preview BSt, WWF character	2.50
Preview, photo (c)	2.50
1 Prophecy of the Dead	2.95
1a photo cover	2.95
1b premium edition	10.00
1c Death Chrome cover	14.95
1d Death Chrome cover, signed	19.95
2 V:Embalmer & Paul Bearer	2.95
3 O:Undertaker	2.95
4 Kane	2.95
5 Jezebel	2.95
6	2.95
2a thru 6a photo covers	@2.95
TPB Prophecy of the Dead, rep.#1–#4	12.95

UNEARTHLY SPECTACULARS
1 DW,AT,I:Tiger Boy	20.00
2 WW,AW,GK,I:Earthman,Miracles, Inc. A:Clawfang,TigerBoy	35.00
3 RC,AW,JO,A:Miracles,Inc.	30.00

U.N. FORCE
Gauntlet Comics
0 BDC(s)	2.95
1 B:BDC(s),I:U.N.Force	2.95
2 O:Indigo	2.95
3	2.95

4 A:Predator	2.95
5 B:Critial Mass	2.95

U.N. FORCE FILES
Gauntlet Comics
1 KP(c),F:Hunter Seeker, Lotus	2.95

UNION OF JUSTICE
Quantum Comics 1998
1 by David Watkins & Steve Kurth	2.95
2	2.95
3 A:Golden Age Union	2.95

UNIVERSAL SOLDIER
Now 1992
1 Based on Movie,Holo.(c)	2.75
2 Luc & Ronnie on the run from UniSols	2.50
2a Photo cover	1.95
3 Photo(c)	1.95

UNKNOWN WORLDS OF FRANK BRUNNER
Eclipse 1985
1 and 2 FB	@2.50

UNLEASHED!
Triumphant
0 JnR(s),I:Skyfire	2.50
1 JnR(s),	2.50

UNLV
1 Championship season (basketball based on college team)	3.00

UNTAMED LOVE
1 FF	2.00

UNUSUAL TALES
Charlton Comics 1955–65
1	175.00
2	100.00
3 thru 5	@65.00
6 SD,SD(c)	165.00
7 SD,SD(c)	165.00
8 SD,SD(c)	165.00
9 SD,SD(c)	175.00
10 SD,SD(c)	165.00
11 SD	165.00
12 SD	120.00
13	60.00
14 SD	120.00
15 SD,SD(c)	135.00
16 thru 20	@50.00
21	35.00
22 SD	90.00
23	35.00
24	35.00
25 SD	85.00
26 SD	85.00
27 SD	85.00
28	35.00
29 SD	85.00
30 thru 49	@35.00

URI-ON
1 and 2	@1.50

URTH 4
Continuity 1990
1 TVE,NA(c)	2.00
2 TVE,NA	2.00
3 TVE,NA	2.00

COLOR PUB.

4 NA,Last issue. 2.00

USAGI YOJIMBO
Mirage 1993
1 A:TMNT 3.00
2 . . . . 3.00
3 . . . . 3.00
4 thru 16 . . . . @3.00
17 . . . . 8.00

VALERIA THE SHE BAT
Continuity 1993
1 NA,I:Valeria 20.00
2 thru 4. . . . . [NOT RELEASED]
5 Rise of Magic 2.50

VALHALLA
Antarctic Press 1999
1 BDn set in 1939 . . . . 3.00

VALKYRIE
Eclipse 1988
1 PG,I:Steelfox,C:Airboy, Sky Wolf. 3.00
2 PG,O:New Black Angel. 2.50
3 PG 2.50

[2nd Series]
1 BA,V:Eurasian Slavers 2.00
2 BA,V:Cowgirl 2.00
3 BA,V:Cowgirl 2.00

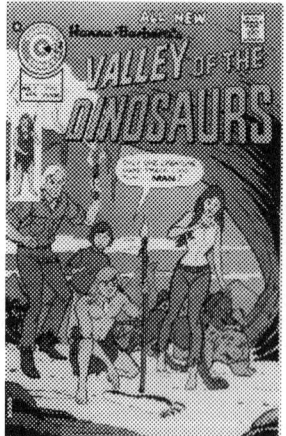

Valley of the Dinosaurs #1
© Charlton Comics

VALLEY OF
THE DINOSAURS
Charlton 1975
1 Hanna-Barbera TV adapt. 3.00
2 thru 11 . . . . @2.00

VALOR
Gemstone 1998
1 EC comics reprint. 2.50
2 . . . . 2.50
3 AW, The Cloak of Command. . . . 2.50
4 WW(c) 2.50
5 final issue. 3.50
HC. 20.00
Annual
TPB Vol. 1 rebinding of series. . . . 13.50

VAMPEROTICA
Brainstorm
1–16 see B&W
17 . . . . 3.00
17a signed 5.00
17 Holochrome cover 65.00
18 Blood of the Damned (color) . . . 3.00
18a Blood of the Damned,
    nude cover. 4.00
18b signed 5.00
18c nude cover, signed. 10.00
19 "Hunter's Blood". 3.00
19a deluxe 3.00
20 "Vampire Quest" 3.00
20a nude edition. 4.00
21 hunting & feeding. 3.00
21a nude edition. 4.00
21b nude luxury edition. 10.00
21c nude deluxe luxury edition . . . 15.00
22 . . . . 3.00
22a nude edition. 4.00
TPB Red Reign, rep. 12.95

VAMPEROTICA LINGERIE
Comic Cavalcade 1998
Commemorative #1 by Kirk Lindo . . 5.95
Commemorative #1a deluxe 14.95

VAMPIRE LESTAT
Innovation 1990–91
1 Anne Rice Adapt. 26.00
1a 2nd printing 4.00
1b 3rd printing 2.50
2 . . . . 13.00
2a 2nd printing 4.00
2b 3rd printing 2.50
3 . . . . 10.00
3a 2nd printing 2.50
4 . . . . 8.00
4a 2nd printing 2.50
5 . . . . 7.00
6 . . . . 5.00
7 . . . . 5.00
8 . . . . 5.00
9 scarce 8.00
9a 2nd Printing 3.00
10 . . . . 5.00
11 "Those Who Must Be Kept" . . . 4.00
12 conclusion 4.00
Vampire Companion #1 . . . . 4.00
Vampire Companion #2 (preview
    "Interview With The Vampire" . . 3.00
Vampire Companion #3 . . . . 3.00
GN rep.#1-#12 (Innovation) 24.95
GN rep.#1-#12 (Ballantine) 25.00

VAMPIRELLA
Warren Publishing Co. 1969–83
1 NA,FF(c),I:Vampirella 400.00
2 B:Amazonia 125.00
3 Very scarce 300.00
4 . . . . 100.00
5 FF(c) 100.00
6 . . . . 100.00
7 FF(c) 120.00
8 B:horror 100.00
9 BWS,BV(c),WW 110.00
10 No Vampirella,WW. 30.00
11 TS,FF(c)O&I Pendragon. 50.00
12 WW 50.00
13 . . . . 40.00
14 . . . . 40.00
15 . . . . 40.00
16 . . . . 40.00
17 B:Tomb of the Gods 40.00
18 . . . . 40.00
19 WW,1973 Annual. 50.00

20 thru 25 . . . . @40.00
26 . . . . 35.00
27 1974 Annual 40.00
28 thru 30 . . . . @35.00
31 FF(c) 40.00
32 thru 36 . . . . @30.00
37 1975 Annual 40.00
38 . . . . 30.00
39 . . . . 30.00
40 . . . . 30.00
41 thru 45 . . . . @25.00
46 O:Vampirella 30.00
47 thru 99 . . . . @25.00
100 Double Size 35.00
101 thru 110 . . . . @20.00
111 Giant Edition 30.00
112 . . . . 25.00

VAMPIRELLA
Harris 1992
0 Dracula Wars 5.00
0a Blue version 40.00
1 V:Forces of Chaos, w/coupon for
    DSt poster 30.00
1a 2nd printing 15.00
2 AH(c) 20.00
3 A:Dracula 8.00
4 A:Dracula 5.00
5 . . . . 5.00
TPB The Dracula War signed &
    numbered. 39.95

Harris Comics 1996
0 gold foil signed & numbered . . . 30.00
1 Commemorative Edition 3.00
1a Commemorative Edition,
    sgn & num.. . . . . 17.00
25th Anniv. Spec., FF(c) 5.95
25th Anniv. Spec., lim. 6.95
25th Anniv. Spec., lim., signed, . . . 49.95
Spec. Death of Vampirella,
    memorial, chromium cover . . . . . .
Spec. Death of Vampirella,
    memorial, chromium cover,
    signed 29.95

VAMPIRELLA
Harris Comics 1997
1 (of 3) Ascending Evil, pt.1 . . . . . 2.95
1 ultra-violent cover 2.95
1 JaL(c) 9.95
1 signed & numbered 19.95
2 Ascending Evil, pt.2 . . . . 2.95

Vampirella #12
© Harris Comics

COLOR PUB.

2a JaL(c)................... 9.95
3 Ascending Evil, pt.3.......... 2.95
3a JaL(c)................... 9.95
4 Holy War, pt.1............... 2.95
4a Crimson edition, Joe Linsner (c) 2.95
5 Holy War, pt.2............... 2.95
6 Holy War, pt.3............... 2.95
7 Queen's Gambit, pt.1.......... 2.95
7a variant cover, signed....... 29.95
7b chromium Edition.......... 10.95
8 Queen's Gambit, pt.2.......... 2.95
8a San Diego Con variant cover .. 9.95
9 Queen's Gambit, pt.3, concl..... 2.95
10 Hell on Earth, pt.1 (of 3) V:Nyx . 2.95
10a signed and numbered...... 19.95
10b variant JaL cover........... 9.95
10c Holoplaid Chromium Ed. ... 19.95
11 Hell on Earth, pt.2 .... 2.95
12 Hell on Earth, pt.3,
    New costume............... 2.95
12a variant cover, new costume ... 2.95
12b chromium cover........... 10.95
13 World's End,pt.1 .... 2.95
13a variant cover 2.95
13b Pantha cover.............. 9.95
14 World's End,pt.2 .... 2.95
14a variant cover 2.95
15 World's End,pt.3 .... 2.95
15a variant cover 2.95
16 Pantha #1 .... 2.95
16a Pantha photo cover 2.95
17 Pantha #2 .... 2.95
17a Phantha photo cover 2.95
18 Rebirth, pt.1,JaL(c) 2.95
18a alternate cover, signed & num. 29.95
Ashcan, Ascending Evil, b&w, 16pg. 1.50
Ashcan, Ascending Evil, b&w,
    signed, limited 24.95
Ashcan, Queen's Gambit, 16 pg.
    b&w 6.00
Ashcan, Queen's Gambit, 16 pg.
    b&w, signed & numbered ... 24.95
Ashcan World's End, b&w 16pg.... 6.00
Ashcan Rebirth preview,b&w 16-pg. 6.00
Vampirella, Queen's Gambit #1
    special edition, alternate (c) .. 9.95
    Chromium Edition......... 10.95
Vampirella/Lady Death Limited
    Preview Ashcan B&W........ 6.00
TPB Ascending Evil 7.50
Spec.#0 A:Lady Death,B.U.:Pantha 2.95
Spec.#0a Pantha(c)............. 2.95
Spec.#0b Vampirella(c)......... 9.95
Spec.#0c Vampirella(c), signed. . . 29.95
Spec.#0d Pantha(c)............. 9.95

VAMPIRELLA/CAIN
Harris 1996
1-shot flipbook, 72-pages....... 6.95

VAMPIRELLA/DRACULA:
THE CENTENNIAL
Harris 1997
1-shot Vampirella/Dracula & Pantha
    Showcase, 16pg........... 1.50
1 48pg..................... 4.95

VAMPIRELLA/
LADY DEATH
Harris/Chaos! 1999
1 x-over.................... 3.50
1a Valentine ed. 9.95
1b signed and numbered....... 20.00
1c gold edition............... 29.95
1d penciled edition........... 10.00

VAMPIRELLA/
PAINKILLER JANE
Harris 1998
1 foil JQ(c) 3.50
1a signed & numbered........ 39.95
1b alternate RL&JP(c).......... 9.95
1c alternate RL&JP(c) signed &
    numbered................ 29.95
1d Gold Edition 24.95
Ashcan Preview, signed &
    numbered................ 29.95

VAMPIRELLA/
SHADOWHAWK:
CREATURES OF
THE NIGHT
Harris/Image 1995
1 Book One................. 5.50

Vampirella/Shi #1
© Harris

VAMPIRELLA/SHI
Harris
Ash-Can #1, limited, 16pg........ 4.00
1 .... 2.95
1a Chromium Edition.......... 8.00
1b signed & numbered........ 19.95
1c penciled cover 9.95
1c penciled cover, signed
    and numbered 29.95

VAMPIRELLA/WETWORKS
Harris 1997
1 StG,SSh,image x-over 2.95
1 signed & numbered 17.95
1b Sean Shaw & Kevin Nowlan (c) 9.95

VAMPIRELLA:
BLOOD LUST
Harris 1997
1 (of 2) JeR & JJu 3.95
2 JJu(c)................... 3.95
Book 1, JJu(c) Virgin edition 10.95
Book 2, JJu(c) Virgin edition 10.95
HC leather-bound 95.00
HC 40.00

VAMPIRELLA CLASSIC
Harris Comics 1995
1 Dark Angel................ 3.50
2 V:Demogorgon............. 3.25
3 V:Were Beast.............. 3.25
4 R:Papa Voodoo 3.25
5 .... 3.00

VAMPIRELLA:
CROSSOVER GALLERY
Harris 1997
1 art gallery................ 2.95
1a signed and numbered...... 19.95
1b chromium edition 10.00
1c Painkiller Jane JQ(c),signed . . 29.95
1d Holochrome cover.......... 20.00

VAMPIRELLA: DEATH
AND DESTRUCTION
Harris
1 limited preview ash can 5.00
1a limited preview ash can, signed
    & numbered 25.00
1b "The Dying of the Light" 3.00
1c signed & numbered......... 3.00
1d satin edition 30.00
1e satin edition, signed & numb. . 60.00
1f Lim. Ed., Mark Beachum (c) .. 9.95
2 "The Nature of the Beast"..... 3.00
3 (of 3) TSg,ACo,JP,JJu(c),Mistress
    Nyx kills Vampi............ 2.95
TPB 14.95

VAMPIRELLA LIVES
Harris
1 Linen Edition 8.00
1a Censored Photo cover edition. . 8.00
2 Vengeance edition 3.00
2 Model photo edition 3.00
2 alternate edition, AH(c)...... 10.00
2 alternate edition, AH(c) signed . 10.00
3 WEl(s),ACo,JP,Graveyard edition,
    JSC(c)................... 3.00
3 WEl(s),ACo,JP,Model photo
    edition 3.00

VAMPIRELLA
OF DRAKULON
Harris Comics 1996
1 V:assassin 3.00
1a alternate MiB(c) 9.95
2 Dracula returns............ 3.00
2a signed & numbered 8.00
3 thru 5 .... @3.00

VAMPIRELLA
PINUP SPECIAL
Harris Comics 1995
1 Various Artists 3.50

VAMPIRELLA:
SAD WINGS OF DESTIMY
Harris
1 DQ(s),JJu(c)............... 4.00
1 signed & numbered (#1,500)... 5.00
Gold Emblem Seal Edition 4.00
Gold Emblem Seal Edition, signed 25.00

VAMPIRELLA STRIKES
Harris Comics 1995
1 The Prize,pt.1.............. 3.00
1a limited, signed & numbered. . . 10.00

COLOR PUB.

1b full moon background	3.50
2 V:Dante Corp.,A:Passion	3.00
3 V:subway stalker	3.00
4 IEd,RN "Soul Food"	3.00
5 DQ,RN,F:Eudaemon	3.00
5 signed & numbered, (200)	10.00
6	3.00
6 signed, alternate cover	10.00
6 signed & numbered	12.00
7 silver special flip book	3.00
Ann. #1 new cover	10.00
Ann. #1 new cover, signed & numbered	25.00

VAMPIRELLA
VS. EUDAEMON
Harris 1996

1	10.00
1 signed & numbered	25.00

VAMPIRELLA
VS. HEMORRHAGE
Harris 1997

1 IEd,MIB	3.50
1 signed & numbered	15.00
1 Linen edition, signed & numb.	30.00
1 MIB alternate cover	9.95
2 IEd,MIB	3.50
3 (of 3) IEd,MIB	3.50

VAMPIRELLA VS. PANTHA
Harris 1997

Showcase #1 preview	2.00
1 MMr,MT, MT(c) Vampirella vs. Pantha	3.50
1 MMr,MT, MT(c) Pantha vs. Vampirella	3.50
1 MT(c) Vampirella vs. Pantha, signed	19.95
1 MT(c) Pantha vs. Vampirella, signed	19.95
1a MMr,MT, MT(c)	9.95
1a MMr,MT, MT(c) signed & numbered	29.95

VAMPRESS LUXURA, THE
Brainstorm 1996

1	3.00
1a gold edition	10.00
2	2.95
2a gold foil	10.00

VANGUARD

1	1.50

VANGUARD
ILLUSTRATED
Pacific 1983

1	1.50
2 DSt(c)	1.50
3 thru 5 SR	@1.50
6 GI	1.50
7 GE,I:Mr.Monster	6.00

VANITY
Pacific 1984

1 and 2	@1.50

VAULT OF HORROR
Gladstone 1990–91

1 Rep.GS,WW	5.00
2 Rep.VoH #27 & HoF #18	3.00
3 Rep.VoH #13 & HoF #22	3.00

Vanguard Illustrated #4
© Pacific Comics

4 Rep.VoH #23 & HoF #13	2.50
5 Rep.VoH #19 & HoF #5	2.50
6 Rep.VoH #32 & WF #6	2.50
7 Rep.VoH #26 & WS #7	2.50

VAULT OF HORROR
Russ Cochran Publ. 1991–92

1 Rep.VoH #28 & WS #18	2.25
2 Rep.VoH #33 & WS #20	2.25
3 Rep.VoH #26 & WS #7	2.25
4 Rep.VoH #35 & WS #15	2.00
4 Rep.VoH #18 & WS #11	2.00
5 Rep.VoH #18 & WS #11	2.00

2nd Series

1 thru 7 Rep.VoH	@1.50
8	2.00

Gemstone

17 thru 29 EC comics reprints	@2.50

"Annuals"

TPB Vol. 1 rebinding of #1–#5	8.95
TPB Vol. 2 rebinding of #6–#10	8.95
TPB Vol. 3 rebinding of #11–#15	10.95
TPB Vol. 4 rebinding of #16–#20	12.95
TPB Vol. 5 rebinding #21–#25	13.50

VECTOR
Now 1986

1	2.50
2 thru 5	@1.75

VEGAS KNIGHTS
Pioneer 1989

1	1.95
2	1.95
3	1.95

VENGEANCE OF
VAMPIRELLA
Harris 1994

1 Hemmorage	7.00
1a Gold Edition	10.00
1 gold edition, signed, numbered	25.00
2 Dervish	3.00
3 On the Hunt	3.00
4 Teenage Vampires	3.00
5 Teenage Vampires	3.00
6	3.00
7	3.00
8 bagged w/card	3.00

9	3.00
10 Bad Jack Rising	3.00
11 Pits of Hell, w/card	3.00
12 V:Passion	3.00
13 V:Passion	3.00
14 Prelude to the Walk,pt.2	3.00
14a Buzz	5.00
15 The Mystery Walk,pt.1	3.25
15a Buzz	5.00
16 The Mystery Walk,pt.2	3.25
16a Buzz	5.00
17 The Mystery Walk,pt.3	3.25
17a Buzz	5.00
18 The Mystery Walk,pt.4	3.00
18a Buzz	5.00
19 The Mystery Walk,pt.5	3.00
19a Buzz	5.00
20 Mystery Walk epilog	3.00
21 thru 24	@3.00
25 "The End"	3.00
25 variant cover, signed & numbered	8.00
25 signed & numbered (2,500)	8.00
25 gold edition, signed & numb.	20.00
25 alternate cover, signed by Jae Lee & numbered (#1,500)	15.00
Mini-comic gold foil, signed	20.00
TPB 1-3 Bloodshed	6.95

VENTURE
AC Comics 1986

1	2.00
2 thru 4	@1.75

VERONICA
Archie Publications April, 1989

1 thru 50	@1.50
51 thru 71	@1.50
72 thru 93	@1.75

VEROTIKA
Verotika 1995

1 thru 3 Jae Lee, Frazetta	@2.95
4 thru 9	@2.95

VEROTIK ILLUSTRATED
Verotik 1997

1 48pg.	6.95
2	6.95
3	6.95
3a alternate cover	6.95
3 variant cover	10.00

VEROTIK ROGUES
GALLERY OF VILLAINS
Verotik 1998

1-shot	3.95

VESPERS
Mars Media Group

1 Tony Caputo	2.50
2 I:Dark Side	2.50

VIC FLINT
Argo Publ. Feb., 1956

1	40.00
2	30.00

VICKI
Atlas Feb.–Aug. 1975

1 Rep.	8.00
2 thru 4	@5.00

COLOR PUB.

VICTORIAN
Penny Farthing Press 1999
1	2.95
2	2.95
3	2.95
4	2.95
5	2.95
6	2.95

Villians & Vigilantes #2
© Eclipse

VILLAINS & VIGILANTES
Eclipse 1986–87
1 A:Crusaders,Shadowman	2.00
2 A:Condor	2.00
3 V:Crushers	2.00
4 V:Crushers	2.00

VIOLENT CASES
Tundra
1 20's Chicago	11.00

VIRGINIAN, THE
Gold Key June, 1963
1	50.00

VIRTEX
Oktomica Entertainment 1998
0 16-page	1.50
1 V:Ripnun	2.50
2 V:Ripnun	2.50
3 alternate endings	2.50
4 Night of the Ninjella,pt.1	2.50
5 Night of the Ninjella,pt.2	2.95
6 All My Sins Remembered	2.95

VOLTRON
Solson 1985
1 TV tie-in	2.00
2	1.50
3	1.50

VORTEX
Vortex 1982–88
1 Peter Hsu art	22.00
2 Mister X on cover	9.00
3	5.00
4	4.00
5	3.00
6 thru 8	@3.00

9 thru 13	@1.75

VORTEX
Comico 1991
1 SBt,from Elementals	2.50
2 SBt,	2.50

VORTEX:
THE SECOND COMING
Entity 1996
1 (of 6)	2.95
1a variant cover	2.95
2	2.95

VOYAGE TO THE DEEP
Dell Publishing Co.
Sept.-Nov., 1962
1 P(c)	45.00
2 P(c)	30.00
3 P(c)	30.00
4 P(c)	30.00

WACKY ADVENTURES
OF CRACKY
Gold Key 1972–75
1	12.00
2 thru 11	@8.00
12	5.00

WACKY WITCH
Gold Key 1971–75
1	20.00
2	10.00
3 thru 20	@6.00
21	4.00

WAGON TRAIN
Gold Key Jan.–Oct., 1964
1	60.00
2	40.00
3	40.00
4	40.00

WALLY
Gold Key 1962–63
1	30.00
2	20.00
3	20.00
4	20.00

WALLY WOOD'S
THUNDER AGENTS
Delux 1984–86
1 GP,KG,DC,SD,I:New Menth	3.00
2 GP,KG,DC,SD,"The Raven"	2.50
3 KG,DC,SD	2.00
4 GP,KG,RB,DA	2.00
5 JOy,KG,A:CodenamDangr	2.00

WALT DISNEY
ANNUALS
Walt Disney's Autumn Adventure	4.00
Walt Disney's Holiday Parade #1	3.50
Walt Disney's Spring Fever	3.25
Walt Disney's Summer Fun	3.25
Walt Disney's Holiday Parade #2	3.25

WALT DISNEY'S
AUTUMN ADVENTURE
1 Rep. CB	4.00

WALT DISNEY'S
COMICS AND STORIES
Dell/ Gold Key 1962
264 CB;Von Drake & Gearloose	30.00
265 CB; Von Drake & Gearloose	30.00
266 CB; Von Drake & Gearloose	30.00
267 CB; Von Drake & Gearloose	30.00
268 CB; Von Drake & Gearloose	30.00
269 CB; Von Drake & Gearloose	30.00
270 CB; Von Drake & Gearloose	30.00
271 CB; Von Drake & Gearloose	30.00
272 CB; Von Drake & Gearloose	30.00
273 CB; Von Drake & Gearloose	30.00
274 CB; Von Drake & Gearloose	30.00
275 CB	25.00
276 CB	25.00
277 CB	25.00
278 CB	25.00
279 CB	25.00
280 CB	25.00
281 CB	25.00
282 CB	25.00
283 CB	25.00
284	15.00
285	15.00
286 CB	25.00
287	15.00
288 CB	20.00
289 CB	20.00
290	15.00
291 CB	20.00
292 CB	20.00
293 CB; Grandma Duck's Farm Friends	20.00
294 CB	20.00
295	15.00
296	15.00
297 CB; Gyro Gearloose	20.00
298 CB; Daisy Duck's Dairy	20.00
299 CB rep	20.00
300 CB rep	20.00
301 CB rep	20.00
302 CB rep	20.00
303 CB rep	20.00
304 CB rep	20.00
305 CB rep. Gyro Gearloose	20.00
306 CB rep	20.00
307 CB rep	20.00
308 CB	20.00
309 CB	20.00
310 CB	20.00
311 CB	20.00
312 CB	20.00
313 thru 327	@15.00
328 CB rep	20.00
329	12.00
330	12.00
331	12.00
332	12.00
333	12.00
334	12.00
335 CB rep	15.00
336	12.00
337	12.00
338	12.00
339	12.00
340	12.00
341	12.00
342 CB rep	15.00
343 CB rep	15.00
344 CB rep	15.00
345 CB rep	15.00
346 CB rep	15.00
347 CB rep	15.00
348 CB rep	15.00
349 CB rep	15.00
350 CB rep	15.00
351 CB rep. with poster	20.00
351a CB rep. without poster	15.00
352 CB rep. with poster12	20.00

352a CB rep. without poster	15.00
353 CB rep. with poster	20.00
353a CB rep. without poster	15.00
354 CB rep. with poster	20.00
354a CB rep. without poster	15.00
355 CB rep. with poster	20.00
355a CB rep. without poster	15.00
356 CB rep. with poster	20.00
356a CB rep. without poster	15.00
357 CB rep. with poster	20.00
357a CB rep. without poster	15.00
358 CB rep. with poster	20.00
358a CB rep. without poster	15.00
359 CB rep. with poster	20.00
359a CB rep. without poster	15.00
360 CB rep. with poster	20.00
360a CB rep. without poster	15.00
361 thru 400 CB rep.	@15.00
401 thru 409 CB rep.	@12.00
410 CB rep. Annette Funichello . .	12.00
411 thru 429 CB rep.	@12.00
430.	8.00
431 CB rep.	10.00
432 CB rep.	10.00
433.	8.00
434 CB rep.	10.00
435 CB rep.	10.00
436 CB rep.	10.00
437.	5.00
438.	5.00
439 CB rep.	8.00
440 CB rep.	8.00
441.	5.00
442 CB rep.	8.00
443 CB rep.	8.00
444.	5.00
445.	5.00
446 thru 465 CB rep.	@8.00
466	8.00
467 thru 473 CB rep.	@8.00

Whitman

474 thru 493 CB rep.	@6.00
494 CB rep. Uncle Scrooge	7.00
495 thru 505 CB rep.	@6.00
506.	5.00
507 CB rep.	6.00
508 CB rep.	6.00
509 CB rep.	6.00
510 CB rep.	6.00

Gladstone

511 translation of Dutch	22.00
512 translation of Dutch	15.00
513 translation of Dutch	15.00
514 translation of Dutch	8.00
515 translation of Dutch	8.00
516 translation of Dutch	8.00
517 translation of Dutch	3.50
518 translation of Dutch	3.50
519 CB, Donald Duck	3.50
520 translation of Dutch, Rosa . .	7.00
521 Walt Kelly	3.00
522 CB, WK, nephews	3.00
523 Rosa, Donald Duck.	7.00
524 Rosa, Donald Duck.	7.00
525 translation of Dutch	3.00
526 Rosa, Donald Duck.	7.00
527 CB.	3.00
528 Rosa, Donald Duck.	5.00
529 CB.	3.00
530 Rosa, Donald Duck.	5.00
531 WK(c), Rosa, CB	5.00
532 CB.	2.50
533 CB.	2.50
534 CB.	2.50
535 CB.	2.50
536 CB.	2.50
537 CB.	2.50
538 CB.	2.50
539 CB.	2.50
540 CB new art	3.50

541 double-size, WK(c)	3.00
542 CB.	5.00
543 CB, WK(c)	2.50
544 CB, WK(c)	2.50
545 CB.	2.50
546 CB, WK, giant	4.00
547 CB, WK, Rosa, giant	4.50

Walt Disney 1990

548 CB, WK, "Home is the Hero" . . .	3.00
549 CB, ...	2.50
550 CB, prev. unpub. story!	3.50
551	2.25
552	2.25
553	2.25
554	2.25
555	2.25
556	2.25
557	2.25
558 "Donald's Fix-it Shop"	2.25
559 "Bugs"	2.25
560 CB, April Fools Story	2.00
561 CB, Donald the "Flipist"	2.00

Walt Disney's Comics and Stories
#446 © Gold Key Comics

562 CB, "3 Dirty Little Ducks"	2.00
563 CB, "Donald Camping"	2.00
564 CB, "Dirk the Dinosaur".	2.00
565 CB, Donald Duck, Truant Officer .	2.00
566 CB, "Will O' the Wisp"	2.00
567 CB, "Turkey Shoot"	2.00
568 CB, "A Christmas Eve Story" . . .	2.00
569 CB, New Years Resolutions . . .	2.00
570 CB, Donald the Mailman + Poster . . . 2.00	
571 CB, "Atom Bomb"	4.50
572 CB, April Fools	2.00
573 TV Quiz Show	2.00
574 Pinnochio, 64 pgs	3.50
575 Olympic Torch Bearer, Li'l Bad Wolf, 64 pgs.	3.50
576 giant	3.50
577 A: Truant Officers, 64 pgs.	3.50
578 CB, Old Quacky Manor	2.00
579 CB, Turkey Hunt	2.00
580 CB, The Wise Little Red Hen, 64 page-Sunday page format. . . .	3.50
581 CB, Duck Lake	2.00
582 giant	3.50
583 giant	3.50
584	1.75
585 CB, giant	3.00

Gladstone

586	2.00

587 thru 600	@2.00
601 thru 605 prestige format	@5.95
606 "Winging It"	6.95
607 "Number 401"	6.95
608 "Sleepless in Duckburg".	6.95
609.	6.95
610 "Treasures Untold".	6.95
611 "Romance at a Glance"	6.95
612 "The Sod Couple"	6.95
613 "Another Fine Mess"	6.95
614 "Airheads"	6.95
615 "Backyard Battlers"	6.95
616.	6.95
617 "Tree's A Crowd"	6.95
618 "A Dolt from the Blue"	6.95
619 "Queen of the Ant Farm"	6.95
620 "Caught in the Cold Rush" . . .	6.95
621 "Room and Bored"	6.95
622 ""	6.95
623 "All Quacked Up"	6.95
624 "Their Loaded Forebear"	6.95
625 "Mummery's the Word".	6.95
626 "A Real Gone Guy"	6.95
627 "To Bee or Not to Bee".	6.95
628 "Officer for a Day"	6.95
629 "The Ghost Train"	6.95
630 two Donald Duck stories	6.95
631 "Music Hath Charms".	6.95
632 "A Day in a Duck's Life"	6.95
633 All Donald issue.	6.95
634 "The Runaway Train".	6.95
635 "Volcano Valley".	6.95
636 "Mission to Codfish Cove" . . .	6.95
637 "Pizen Springs Dude Ranch" .	6.95

WALT DISNEY COMICS DIGEST
Gold Key 1968–76
[All done by Carl Barks]

1 Rep, Uncle Scrooge.	40.00
2	25.00
3	25.00
4	25.00
5	45.00
6	20.00
7	20.00
8	20.00
9	20.00
10	20.00
11	20.00
12	20.00
13	20.00
14	10.00
15	10.00
16 rep. Donald Duck #26	20.00
17	15.00
18	15.00
19	15.00
20	15.00
21	18.00
22	18.00
23	18.00
24	18.00
25	18.00
26	18.00
27	18.00
28	18.00
29	18.00
30	18.00
31	18.00
32	8.00
33	18.00
34 rep. Four Color #318	15.00
35	15.00
36	15.00
37	15.00
38 rep. Disneyland #1	15.00
39	15.00
40	10.00

COLOR PUB.

41	8.00
42	8.00
43	8.00
44 Rep. Four Color #29 & others	25.00
45	6.00
46 CB	8.00
47	6.00
48	6.00
49	6.00
50 CB	8.00
51 rep.Four Color #71	12.00
52 CB	8.00
53	6.00
54	6.00
55	6.00
56 CB,rep. Uncle Scrooge #32	10.00
57 CB	8.00

WALT DISNEY SHOWCASE
Gold Key 1970–80

1 Boatniks (photo cover)	20.00
2 Moby Duck	10.00
3 Bongo & Lumpjaw	8.00
4 Pluto	10.00
5 $1,000,000 Duck (photo cover)	15.00
6 Bedknobs & Broomsticks	12.00
7 Pluto	10.00
8 Daisy & Donald	10.00
9 101 Dalmatians rep	14.00
10 Napoleon & Samantha	12.00
11 Moby Duck rep	7.00
12 Dumbo rep	8.00
13 Pluto rep	8.00
14 World's Greatest Athlete	12.00
15 3 Little Pigs rep	12.00
16 Aristocats rep	12.00
17 Mary Poppins rep	12.00
18 Gyro Gearloose rep	12.00
19 That Darn Cat rep	12.00
20 Pluto rep	10.00
21 Li'l Bad Wolf & 3 Little Pigs	7.00
22 Unbirthday Party rep	10.00
23 Pluto rep	10.00
24 Herbie Rides Again rep	8.00
25 Old Yeller rep	8.00
26 Lt. Robin Crusoe USN rep	7.00
27 Island at the Top of the World	7.00
28 Brer Rabbit, Bucky Bug rep	10.00
29 Escape to Witch Mountain	8.00
30 Magica De Spell rep	15.00
31 Bambi rep	12.00
32 Spin & Marty rep	10.00
33 Pluto rep	10.00
34 Paul Revere's Ride rep	7.00
35 Goofy rep	7.00
36 Peter Pan rep	7.00
37 Tinker Bell & Jiminy Cricket rep	7.00
38 Mickey & the Sleuth, Pt. 1	8.00
39 Mickey & the Sleuth, Pt. 2	8.00
40 The Rescuers	8.00
41 Herbie Goes to Monte Carlo	10.00
42 Mickey & the Sleuth	7.00
43 Pete's Dragon	10.00
44 Return From Witch Mountain & In Search of the Castaways	12.00
45 The Jungle Book rep	12.00
46 The Cat From Outer Space	7.00
47 Mickey Mouse Surprise Party	8.00
48 The Wonderful Adventures of Pinocchio	7.00
49 North Avenue Irregulars; Zorro	7.00
50 Bedknobs & Broomsticks rep	6.00
51 101 Dalmatians	6.00
52 Unidentified Flying Oddball	6.00
53 The Scarecrow	6.00
54 The Black Hole	6.00

WALT DISNEY COMICS IN COLOR
Gladstone 1998

TPB Vol. 1	9.95
TPB Vol. 2	9.95
TPB Vol. 3	9.95
TPB Vol. 4	9.95

WALT KELLY'S CHRISTMAS CLASSICS
Eclipse 1987

1	2.00

WALT KELLY'S SPRINGTIME TALES
Eclipse 1988

1	2.50

WARCAT SPECIAL
Entity Press 1995

1 I:Warcat	2.95

WARCHILD
Maximum Press 1995

1 I:Sword, Stone	3.50
2 I:Morganna Lefay	3.00
3 V: The Black Knight	2.50
4 Rescue Merlyn	2.50

[2nd Series]

1	2.50

WAR DANCER
Defiant 1994

1 B:JiS(s),I:Ahrq Tsolmec	2.75
2 I:Massakur	2.75
3 V:Massakur	2.75
4 JiS(s),A:Nudge	3.25

WARHAWKS
TSR 1990–91

1 thru 6 from game	@2.95
7 thru 10 The Battle of Britain	@2.95

WARHAWKS 2050
TSR

1 Pt.1	2.95

WAR HEROES
Charlton Comics 1963–67

1	25.00
2 thru 10	@15.00
11 thru 27	@12.00

WARLASH
CFD

1 Project Hardfire	2.95

WARMASTER

1 and 2	@3.95

WARP
First, March, 1983

1 FB,JSon,I:Lord Cumulus & Prince Chaos, play adapt pt.1	2.00
2 FB,SD,play adapt pt.2	1.50
3 FB,SD,play adapt pt.3	1.50
4 FB,SD,I:Xander,play pt.4	1.50
5 FB, play adapt pt.5	1.50
6 FB/MG, play adapt pt.6	1.50

Warp #2
© First

7 FB/MG, play adapt pt.7	1.50
8 FB/MG,BWg,play adapt pt.8	1.25
9 FB/MG,BWg,play adapt conc	1.25
10 JBi/MG, BWg, Second Saga, I:Outrider	1.25
11 JBi/MG,A:Outrider	1.25
12 JBi/MG,A:Outrider	1.25
13 JBi/MG,A:Outrider	1.25
14 JBi/MG,A:Outrider	1.25
15 JBi/MG/BWg	1.25
16 BWg/MG,A:Outrider	1.25
17 JBi/MG,A:Outrider	1.25
18 JBi/MG,A:Outrider&Sargon	1.25
19 MG,last issue	1.25
Spec. #1 HC,O:Chaos	1.50
Spec. #2 MS/MG,V:Ylem	1.50
Spec. #3	1.50

WARRIOR NUN AREALA
Antartic Press 1995

1 V:Lilith	4.00
1a limited edition	7.00
2 V:Lilith	3.00
3 V:Hellmaster	3.00
3 silver edition	12.00
TPB Rep.#1-#3	9.95

BOOK II: RITUALS 1996

1 Land of Rising Sun	2.95
1 Red edition	12.00
1 signed	9.95
2 I:Cheetah	2.95
3 Iraq, 1989	2.95
4	2.95
5 Rituals,pt.5	2.95
6	2.95
Spec. Warrior Nun Portraits	3.95
Spec. Warrior Nun Portraits Commemorative Edition (1999)	5.95
TPB Rituals	15.95

BOOK III 1997

1 The Hammer & the Holocaust	2.95
2 Hammer & the Holocaust,pt.2	2.95
3 Hammer & the Holocaust,pt.3	2.95
4 Holy Man, Holy Terror,pt.1	2.95
5 Holy Man, Holy Terror,pt.2	2.95
6 by Barry Lyga & Ben Dunn	2.95
TPB Vol. 1	9.95
TPB Vol. 1 reprint	9.95
HC Vol. 2, lim. to 1,000 copies	29.95
Spec. Warrior Nun Areala/Glory by Ben Dunn	2.95
Spec. poster edition	5.95

Spec. Warrior Nun Areala vs. Razor,
  BDn,JWf x-over 3.95
Spec.Warrior Nun Areala vs. Razor
  commemorative (1999) 5.95
Spec.Warrior Nun Areala/Avengelyne
  comm. edition (1999) 5.95

VOL 3
1 F:Sister Shannon Masters 2.50
2 . . . . 2.50

Warrior Nun Areala: Scorpio Rose
#4 © Antarctic

WARRIOR NUN AREALA:
SCORPIO ROSE
Antarctic Press 1996
1 SEt & BDn 2.95
1a commemorative (1999) 5.95
2 thru 4 (of 4) . . . . @2.95

WARRIOR NUN DEI:
AFTERTIME
Antarctic Press 1997
1 (of 3) by Patrick Thornton 2.95
1 Commemorative edition (1999) . . 5.95
2 . . . . 2.95
3 . . . . 3.00

WARRIOR NUN: FRENZY
Antarctic Press 1998
1 (of 2) by Miki Horvatic
  & Esad T. Ribic. 2.95
2 . . . . 2.95

WARRIOR NUN:
RESURRECTION
Antarctic Press 1998
1 by Ben Dunn 2.95
1a deluxe 5.95
2 quest for lost God Armor. 3.00
3 . . . . 3.00

WARRIORS OF PLASM
Defiant 1993–95
1 JiS(s),DL,A:Lorca 3.25
2 JiS(s),DL,Sedition Agenda 3.25
3 JiS(s),DL,Sedition Agenda 3.25
4 JiS(s),DL,Sedition Agenda 3.25
5 JiS(s),B:The Demons of
  Darkedge. 2.75
6 JiS(s),The Demons of

Darkedge,pt.2. . . . . 2.75
7 JiS(s),DL, ... 2.75
8 JiS(s),DL,40pages 3.00
9 JiS(s),LWn(s),DL,40pages 3.00
10 DL, ... 2.50
GN Home for the Holidays 5.95

WARRIOR'S WAY
Bench Press Studios 1998
1 . . . . 3.00
2 . . . . 3.00
3 . . . . 3.00
4 . . . . 3.00
5 . . . . 3.00
6 V:Technoborgs 3.00
7 . . . . 3.00

WART AND THE
WIZARD
Gold Key Feb., 1964
1 . . . . 40.00

WAVE WARRIORS
1 . . . . 2.00
2 . . . . 2.00

WAXWORK in 3-D
Blackthorne
1 . . . . 2.50

WAYFARERS
Eternity
1 . . . . 1.80
2 . . . . 1.80

WEAPON ZERO
See: Image

WEASEL GUY
WITCHBLADE
Hyperwerks 1998
1-shot by Steve Succellato 3.00
1a variant Jeff Matsuda(c) 5.00
1b variant Karl Altstoeter(c) 8.00

WEB-MAN
Argosy
1 flip book with Time Warrior 2.50

WEB OF HORROR
Major Magazines Dec., 1969
1 JJ(c),Ph(c),BWr 85.00
2 JJ(c),Ph(c),BWr 60.00
3 BWr,April, 1970 . . . . 60.00

WEDDING OF POPEYE
AND OLIVE, THE
Ocean Comics 1999
1 PDa, ... 2.75
1a signed, numbered. 15.95
Spec. Sketch edition. 40.00

WEIRD FANTASY
Russ Cochran 1992
1 Reps 2.00
2 Reps.inc.The Black Arts 2.00
3 thru 4 rep. . . . . @2.00
5 thru 7 rep. 2.50
8 . . . . 2.50

Gemstone
9 thru 22 EC comics reprint . . . . @2.50
"Annuals"
TPB Vol. #1 rebinding of #1–#5 . . . 8.95
TPB Vol. #2 rebinding of #6–#10 . . 9.95
TPB Vol. #3 rebinding of #11–#14. . 8.95
TPB Vol. #4 rebinding of #15–#18. . 9.95
TPB Vol. #5 rebinding of #19–#22. 10.50

Weird Science #15
© Gemstone

WEIRD SCIENCE
Gladstone 1990–91
1 Rep. #22 + Fantasy #1 . . . . 4.00
2 Rep. #16 + Fantasy #17 . . . . . . 3.50
3 Rep. #9 + Fantasy #14. . . . . . . 3.50
4 Rep. #27 + Fantasy #11 . . . . . . 2.00
Russ Cochran/Gemstone 1992
1 thru 21 EC comics reprint . . . . @2.50
"Annuals"
TPB Vol. #1 rebinding of #1–#5 . . . 8.95
TPB Vol. #2 rebinding of #6–#10 . . 9.95
TPB Vol. #3 rebinding of #11–#15. . 8.95
TPB Vol. #4 rebinding of #16–#18. . 9.95
TPB Vol. #5 rebinding of #19–#22. 10.50

WEIRD
SCIENCE–FANTASY
Russ Cochran/Gemstone 1992
1 Rep. W.S.F. #23 (1954) 2.00
2 Rep. Flying Saucer Invasion. . . . 2.00
3 Rep. 2.00
4 thru 6 Rep. 2.00
7 rep #29. . . . . 2.00
8 . . . . 2.00
Gemstone
"Annuals"
TPB Vol. #1 rebinding of #1–#5 . . . 8.95
TPB Vol. #2 rebinding of #6–#10 . . 12.95

WEIRD SUSPENSE
Atlas Feb.–July 1975
1 thru 3 F:Tarantula . . . . @12.00

WEIRD TALES
ILLUSTRATED
Millenium 1992
1 KJo,JBo,PCr,short stories 4.95

WENDY
Blackthorne
1 3-D...................... 2.50

WENDY, THE GOOD LITTLE WITCH
Harvey Publications 1960–76
1 .... 150.00
2 .... 75.00
3 .... 50.00
4 .... 50.00
5 .... 50.00
6 .... 40.00
7 .... 40.00
8 .... 40.00
9 .... 40.00
10 .... 40.00
11 thru 20 .... @25.00
21 thru 30 .... @15.00
31 thru 50 .... @10.00
51 thru 69 .... @7.00
70 thru 74 52 pg Giants ...... @4.00
75 thru 93 .... @4.00

WENDY WITCH WORLD
Harvey Publications 1961–74
1 .... 90.00
2 .... 40.00
3 .... 40.00
4 .... 40.00
5 .... 40.00
6 .... 25.00
7 .... 25.00
8 .... 25.00
9 .... 25.00
10 .... 25.00
11 thru 20 .... @20.00
21 thru 30 .... @10.00
31 thru 39 .... @7.00
40 thru 50 .... @4.00
51 thru 53 .... @4.00

WEREWOLF
Blackthorne
1 3-D...................... 3.50

WESTERN ACTION
Atlas Feb. 1975
1 F:Kid Cody,Comanche Kid 1.00

WESTWYND
Westwynd 1995
1 I:Sable,Shiva,Outcast,Tojo 2.50

WHAM
1 .... 1.75

WHISPER
Capital 1983–84
1 MG(c)................... 10.00
2 .... 8.00
First
1 .... 2.50
2 .... 2.00
3 .... 2.00
4 .... 1.50
5 .... 1.50
6 thru 12 .... @1.25
13 thru 19................ @1.75
20 O:Whisper............... 1.95
21 thru 26................ @1.95
27 Ghost Dance #2 .... 1.95
28 Ghost Dance #3 .... 1.95
29 thru 37................ @1.95

Whisper #2
© *Capital*

Spec. #1.................... 4.00

WHITE FANG
Walt Disney 1990
1 Movie Adapt. 5.95

WHITE TRASH
Tundra
1 I:Elvis & Dean............. 3.95
2 Trip to Las Vegas contd...... 3.95
3 V:Purple Heart Brigade........ 3.95

WHODUNNIT
Eclipse 1986–87
1 DSp,A:Jay Endicott.......... 2.00
2 DSp,"Who Slew Kangaroo?".... 2.00
3 DSp,"Who Offed Henry Croft"... 2.00

WIDOW MADE IN BRITAIN
N Studio
1 I:Widow 2.60
2 F:Widow.................. 2.60
3 Rampage 2.60
4 In Jail 2.60

WIDOW METAL GYPSIES
London Night Studios 1995
1 I:Emma Drew 3.00
2 Father Love 3.00
3 Final issue 3.00

WILD ANIMALS
Pacific 1982
1 .... 1.50

WILD BILL PECOS
AC Comics 1989
1 .... 3.50

WILDCATS
Wildstorm/DC 1999
Previously from Image
VOLUME 2
1 SLo,TC, ... 2.50
1a variant cover.............. 2.50
1b variant cover.............. 2.50

1c variant cover.............. 2.50
1d variant cover.............. 2.50
1e variant cover.............. 2.50
2 SLo,TC................... 2.50
3 SLo,TC,F:Grifter........... 2.50
4 SLo,TC,.................. 2.50
TPB WildC.A.T.S.: Compendium.. 10.00
TPB WildC.A.T.S.: Homecomming 20.00

WILDFIRE
Zion Comics
1 thru 3 V:Mr. Reeves .... @1.95
4 Lord D'Rune............... 1.95

WILD FRONTIER
Charlton Comics Oct., 1955
1 Davy Crockett.............. 60.00
2 same 35.00
3 same 35.00
4 same 35.00
5 same 35.00
6 same 35.00
7 O:Cheyenne Kid 35.00
Becomes:

CHEYENNE KID
8 .... 25.00
9 .... 15.00
10 .... 45.00
11 .... 45.00
12 .... 45.00
13 .... 30.00
14 .... 30.00
15 .... 15.00
16 .... 15.00
17 .... 15.00
18 .... 30.00
19 .... 15.00
20 .... 18.00
21 .... 18.00
22 .... 18.00
23 .... 8.00
24 .... 8.00
25 .... 15.00
26 .... 10.00
27 .... 8.00
28 .... 8.00
29 .... 8.00
30 .... 10.00
31 thru 59................ @3.00
60 thru 98................ @2.00
99 Nov., 1973.............. 2.00

WILD TIMES
Wildstorm/DC 1999
Deathblow 2.50
DV8 .... 2.50
Gen13 .... 2.50
Grifter.................... 2.50
Wetworks.................. 2.50

WILD WEST C.O.W.-BOYS OF MOO MESA
Archie 1992–93
1 Based on TV cartoon 1.25
2 Cody kidnapped............ 1.25
3 Law of the Year Parade,
  last issue 1.25
(Regular series)
1 Valley o/t Thunder Lizard 1.25
2 Plains, Trains & Dirty Deals 1.25

WILD WESTERN ACTION
Skywald 1971
1 thru 3 .... @8.00

WILD WILD WEST
Gold Key 1966–69
1 TV show tie-in. 135.00
2 . . . . 125.00
3 . . . . 90.00
4 . . . . 90.00
5 . . . . 90.00
6 . . . . 90.00
7 . . . . 90.00

WILD WILD WEST
Millenium 1990–91
1 . . . . 2.95
2 thru 4 . . . . @2.95

WILL EISNER'S
3-D CLASSICS
Kitchen Sink
WE art, w/glasses (1985) 2.00

WIN A PRIZE COMICS
Charlton Comics Feb., 1955
1 S&K,Edgar Allen adapt. 400.00
2 S&K 300.00
Becomes:

TIMMY THE
TIMID GHOST
3 . . . . 30.00
4 . . . . 20.00
5 . . . . 20.00
6 . . . . 10.00
7 . . . . 10.00
8 . . . . 10.00
9 . . . . 10.00
10 . . . . 10.00
11 . . . . 20.00
12 . . . . 20.00
13 thru 20 . . . . @5.00
21 thru 44 . . . . @4.00
45 1966 . . . . 2.00

WINDRAGE
1 and 2 . . . . @1.25

WINTERWORLD
Eclipse 1987–88
1 JZ,I:Scully, Wynn 1.75
2 JZ,V:Slave Farmers 1.75
3 JZ,V:Slave Farmers 1.75

WIREHEADS
Fleetway
1 . . . . 2.95

WISP
Oktomica Entertainment 1999
1 All Along the Watchtower,pt.1 . . . 2.50
2 All Along the Watchtower,pt.2 . . . 2.50
3 All Along the Watchtower,pt.3 . . . 2.95
4 The Acheron Protocol 2.95

WITCHBLADE
See Image

WITCHING HOUR, THE
Millenium/Comico
1 Anne Rice adaptation 2.50
2 thru 5 . . . . 2.50

Woody Woodpecker #1
© Harvey Publications

WOODY WOODPECKER
Harvey 1991–93
1 thru 5 . . . . 1.25

WORLD OF ARCHIE
Archie 1994
1 thru 21 . . . . @1.50

WORLD OF WOOD
Eclipse 1986–87
1 WW 1.75
2 WW,DSt(i) 1.75
3 WW 1.75
4 WW 1.75

WORLD WAR II: 1946
Antarctic Press 1999
1 by Ted Nomura 2.50
2 Born to Die 2.50

WULF THE BARBARIAN
Atlas Feb.–Sept., 1975
1 O:Wulf 10.00
2 NA,I:Berithe The Swordsman . . . 8.00
3 & 4 . . . . @5.00

WYATT EARP
Dell Publishing Co. Nov., 1957
1 . . . . 150.00
2 . . . . 100.00
3 . . . . 75.00
4 . . . . 60.00
5 . . . . 60.00
6 . . . . 60.00
7 . . . . 60.00
8 . . . . 60.00
9 . . . . 60.00
10 . . . . 60.00
11 . . . . 50.00
12 . . . . 50.00
13 . . . . 50.00

XANADU
Eclipse 1988
1 . . . . 2.00

XENYA
Sanctuary Press 1994
1 Hildebrandt Brothers 4.00
2 . . . . 3.25
3 . . . . 3.25
4 conclusion, Homecoming 2.95

XENA:
WARRIOR PRINCESS
Topps 1997
1 RTs,Revenge of the Gorgons,
   pt.1 . . . . 5.00
1a photo (c) 8.00
2 (of 2) rescue of Gabrielle 4.00
TPB 9.95
[VOL 2]
0 AaL Temple of the Dragon God. . 3.00
1 (of 3) Joxer, Warrior Prince, pt.1 . 5.00
1a deluxe 8.00
2 Joxer, Warrior Prince, pt.2 . . . . . 4.00
2a photo (c) 4.00
TPB rep. #0–#2 . . . . 9.95

XENA:
WARRIOR PRINCESS:
BLOOD LINES
Topps 1997
1 (of 3) ALo 3.00
1a photo (c) 3.00
2 (of 3) ALo 3.00
2a photo (c) 3.00

XENA:
WARRIOR PRINCESS:
CALLISTO
Topps 1997
1 (of 3) RTs, ... 3.00
1a photo (c) 3.00
2 (of 3) RTs, ... 3.00
2a photo (c) 3.00
3 (of 3) RTs, ... 3.00
3a photo (c) 3.00

XENA:
WARRIOR PRINCESS:
ORPHEUS
Topps 1998
1 (of 3) 3.00
1a photo (c) 3.00
2 (of 3) 3.00
2a photo (c) 3.00
3 (of 3) 3.00
3a photo (c) 3.00

XENA:
WARRIOR PRINCESS:
THE ORIGINAL OLYMPICS
Topps 1998
1 (of 3) 3.00
1a photo cover 3.00
2 F:Hercules 3.00
2a photo cover 3.00
3 . . . . 3.00
3a photo cover 3.00

XENA:
WARRIOR PRINCESS:
THE WEDDING OF XENA
& HERCULES
Topps 1998
1-shot. 3.00
1-shot photo (c) 3.00

XENA,
WARRIOR PRINCESS:
THE WRATH OF HERA
Topps 1998
1 (of 2) 3.00
1a photo cover edition 3.00
2 conclusion 3.00
2a photo cover edition 3.00

XENA:
WARRIOR PRINCESS:
XENA AND THE
DRAGON'S TEETH
Topps 1997
1 (of 3) RTs, ... 3.00
1a photo (c). 3.00
2 (of 3) RTs, ... 3.00
2a photo (c). 3.00
3 (of 3) RTs, ... 3.00
3a photo (c). 3.00

XENO MAN
1 . . . . 1.75

XENOTECH
Mirage 1993–94
1 I:Xenotech 2.75
2 . . . . 2.75
3 w/2 card strip 2.75

X-FILES
Topps 1994–97
1 From Fox TV Series 50.00
1a Newstand 40.00
2 Aliens Killing Witnesses 30.00
3 The Return 20.00
4 Firebird,pt.1 . . . . 15.00
5 Firebird,pt.2 . . . . 10.00
6 Firebird,pt.3 . . . . 8.00
7 Trepanning Opera 7.00
8 Silent Cities of the Mind,pt.1 . . . . 6.00
9 Silent Cities of the Mind,pt.2 . . . . 5.00
10 Feeling of Unreality,pt.1 . . . . . . 5.00
11 Fealing of Unreality,pt.2 . . . . . . 5.00
12 Fealing of Unreality,pt.3 . . . . . . 5.00
13 A Boy and His Saucer 5.00
14 . . . . 4.00
15 Home of the Brave. 4.00
16 Home of the Brave,pt.2 . . . . . . 3.50
17 DgM,CAd. 3.50
18 thru 21 . . . . @3.50
22 JRz,CAd,"The Kanishibari". . . . 3.00
23 JRz,CAd,"Donor" 3.00
24 JRz, "Silver Lining" 3.00
25 JRz,CAd,"Remote Control,"pt.1 . 3.00
26 JRz,CAd,"Remote Control,"pt.2 . 3.00
27 JRz,CAd,"Remote Control,"pt.3 . 3.00
28 JRz,"Be Prepared," pt.1,
    V:Windigo. 3.00
29 JRz,"Be Prepared," pt.2 . . . . . . 3.00
30 JRz,"Surrounded," pt.1. . . . . . . 3.00
31 JRz,"Surrounded," pt.2 (of 2) . . . 3.00
32 . . . . 3.00
33 widows on San Francisco 2.95

X-Files #20
© Topps Comics

33 variant photo (c) 2.95
34 Project HAARP 2.95
35 Near Death Experience 2.95
36 Near Death Experience, pt.2 . . . 2.95
37 JRz,The Face of Extinction 2.95
38 JRz, ... 2.95
39 JRz, Widow's Peak 2.95
40 Devil's Advocate 2.95
40a photo cover 2.95
41 Severed. 2.95
41a photo cover 2.95
Ann.#1 Hollow Eve 5.00
Ann.#2 E.L.F.S. 4.50
Spec.#1 Rep. #1-#3 . . . . 6.00
Spec.#2 Rep. #4-#6 Firebird 5.00
Spec.#3 Rep. #7-#9 . . . . 5.00
Spec.#4 Rep. 5.00
TPB Vol. 2 . . . . 19.95
GN Afterflight 5.95
GN Official Movie Adapt. (1998) . . . 5.95

X-FILES DIGEST
Topps 1995
1 All New Series, 96pg. 3.50
2 and 3 . . . . 3.50

X-FILES, THE:
GROUND ZERO
Topps 1997
1 (of 4) based on novel 2.95
2 . . . . 2.95
3 . . . . 2.95
4 . . . . 2.95

X-FILES, THE:
SEASON ONE
Topps
1 RTs,JVF(c) "Deep Throat" 4.95
Deep Throat, variant (c) 7.50
2 RTs,JVF(c) "Squeeze" 3.95
Squeeze, RTs, JVF(c). 4.95
3 RTs,SSc,"Conduit" 3.95
Conduit, RTs. 4.95
4 RTs,"The Jersey Devil" 3.95
5 RTs,"Shadows" 3.95
Shadows JVF(c) 4.95
6 "Fire" 3.95
Fire 4.95
7 RTs,JVF,"Ice" 3.95
Ice 4.95

8 RTs,"Space" 3.95
Space JVF(c) 4.95
Spec. Pilot Episode RTs,JVF
  new JVF(c). 4.95
Beyond the Sea JVF(c). 4.95

XIMOS: VIOLENT PAST
Triumphant 1994
1 JnR(s) 2.50
2 JnR(s) 2.50

XL
1 . . . . 1.25

XXXENA:
WARRIOR PORNSTAR VS.
BUSTY THE VAMPIRE
MURDERER
Blatant Comics 1998
1 parody 2.95
2 nude cover 9.95

YAKKY DOODLE
& CHOPPER
Gold Key Dec., 1962
1 . . . . 50.00

YEAH!
Homage/DC 1999
1 GHe 3.00

YIN FEI
Leung's Publications 1988–90
5 . . . . 1.80
6 thru 11 . . . . @2.00

YOGI BEAR
Dell Feb.-March, 1962
#1 thru #6, See Dell Four Color
7 thru 9 . . . . 75.00
Gold Key
10 . . . . 75.00
11 Jellystone Follies 50.00
12 . . . . 35.00
13 Surprise Party 75.00
14 thru 19 . . . . @35.00
20 thru 29 . . . . @20.00
30 thru 42 . . . . @15.00

YOGI BEAR
Charlton Comics 1970–76
1 . . . . 35.00
2 thru 10 . . . . @25.00
11 thru 35 . . . . 15.00

YOGI BEAR
Archie Comics 1997
1 . . . . 1.50

YOSEMITE SAM
Gold Key/Whitman 1970–84
1 . . . . 25.00
2 thru 10 . . . . @15.00
11 thru 40 . . . . @10.00
41 thru 81 . . . . @7.00

COLOR PUB.

YOUNGBLOOD
Maximum Press/Extreme
Volume 2 1996
Vol. 1 & Vol. 2 #1–#10,
see Image
11 RLd,RCz,. 2.50
12 Rle, V:Lord Dredd,A:New
  Man,double size 3.50
13 RLd,RCz,F:Die-Hard 2.50
14 RLd,RCz,. 2.50
Super Spec.#1 ErS,CSp,AG 3.00
TPB Youngblood, rep. orig.
  Youngblood #1–#5 . . . . 16.95
TPB Baptism of Fire rep.
  Youngblood #6–#8, #10 & Team
  Youngblood #9–#11 . . . . 16.95

YOUNGBLOOD
Awesome Entertainment 1998
1 AMo,SSr. 2.50
1a variant covers, 7 different 2.50
2 AMo,SSr,Baptism of Fire. 2.50
3 AMo,SSr,V:Professor Night 2.50
4 AMo,SSr,Young Guns 2.50
5 AMo,SSr,Young Guns 2.50

YOUNGBLOOD CLASSICS
Image/Extreme Sept. 1996
1 RLd,ErS,rewritten & redrawn,
  new cover 2.25
2 RLd,ErS,rewritten & redrawn,
  new cover 2.25
3 RLd,ErS,rewritten & redrawn,
  new cover 2.25

YOUNGBLOOD/X-FORCE
Awesome Entertainment 1998
1-shot, 48pg. 4.95

ZAANAN
Mainstream Comics
1 The Collectio,I:Zaanan 2.50

ZEN INTERGALACTIC NINJA
Archie 1992
1 Rumble in the Rain Forest
  prequel,inc.poster 1.25
2 Rumble in Rain Forest #1 . . . . . . 1.25
3 Rumble in Rain Forest #2 . . . . . . 1.25
Entity Comics 1994
0 Chromium (c),JaL(c) 4.00
1 Joe Orbeta 2.50
1a Platinum Edition 20.00
2 Deluxe Edition w/card. 4.95
3 V:Rawhead. 3.00
4 thru 7 . . . . 3.25
GN A Fire Upon The Earth 12.95
[2nd Series]
1 Joe Orbeta 4.95
2 . . . . 4.95
3 thru 5 . . . . @2.50
Zen Comics 1998
Commemorative Ed. #1 . . . . 5.95

ZEN/NIRA X: HELLSPACE
Zen Comics
1 . . . . 2.95

ZEN: NOVELLA
Eternity Comics
1 thru 8 . . . . 2.95

ZEN SPECIALS
Eternity
Spring#1 V:Lord Contaminous 2.50
April Fools#1 parody issue 2.50
Color Spec.#0 . . . . 3.50

ZEN: WARRIOR
Eternity Comics 1994
1 vicious video game. 3.00

ZENITH PHASE II
Fleetway
1 thru 2 . . . . 1.95

ZERO PATROL
Continuity 1984–90
1 EM,NA,O&I:Megalith. 2.50
2 EM,NA 1.95
3 EM,NA,I:Shaman 1.95
4 EM,NA 1.95
5 EM 1.95
6 thru 8 EM . . . . @2.00

ZERO TOLERANCE
First 1990–91
1 TV 3.50
2 TV 3.00
3 TV 2.25
4 TV 2.25

ZOONIVERSE
Eclipse 1986–87
1 I:Kren Patrol,wrap-around(c) 1.25
2 . . . . 1.25
3 . . . . 1.25
4 V:Wedge City 1.25
5 Spak vs. Agent Ty-rote 1.25
6 last issue 1.25

ZORRO
Dell Publ. Co. 1959–61
1 thru 8, see Dell 4-Color
8 . . . . 100.00
9 . . . . 85.00
10 . . . . 85.00
11 . . . . 85.00
12 ATh 100.00
13 . . . . 75.00
14 . . . . 75.00
15 . . . . 75.00

ZORRO
Gold Key 1966–68
1 Rep. 75.00
2 Rep. 50.00
3 Rep. 50.00
4 Rep. 50.00
5 Rep. 50.00
6 Rep. 50.00
7 Rep. 50.00
8 Rep. 50.00
9 Rep. 50.00

ZORRO
Topps Nov., 1993
0 BSf(c),DMG(s), came bagged
  with Jurassic Park Raptor #1 and
  Teenagents #4 . . . . 4.00
1 DMG(s),V:Machete 3.00
2 DMG(s) 5.00
3 DMG(s) I:Lady Rawhide 15.00
4 MGr(c),DMG(s),V:Moonstalker . . 2.50
5 MGr,DMG(s),V:Moonstalker 2.50
6 A:Lady Rawhide 8.00
7 A:Lady Rawhide 7.00
8 MGr(c),DMG(s). 3.00
9 A:Lady Rawhide 4.00
10 A:Lady Rawhide 4.50
11 A:Lady Rawhide. 8.00

Zot #9
© Eclipse

ZOT!
Eclipse 1984–85
1 by Scott McCloud 7.00
2 . . . . 3.00
3 Art and Soul 3.00
4 Assault on Castle Dekko. 3.00
5 Sirius Business. 3.00
6 Its always darkest. 2.00
7 Common Ground 2.50
8 Through the Door 2.00
9 Gorilla Warfare 2.50
10 T.K.O. The Final Round 2.00
10a B&W 6.00
10b 2nd printing 2.50
Original Zot! Book 1 . . . . 9.95
Book One TPB 24.95
(Changed to B & W)

ZOT!
Kitchen Sink
Book One TPB 24.95
Book One HC signed & numbered 55.00

B&W COMICS

A1
Atomeka Press 1989–92
1 BWs,A:Flaming Carrot,Mr.X.... 10.00
2 BWs...................... 9.75
3 .... 9.75
4 .... 5.95
5 .... 6.95
6a 4.95

AARDWOLF
Aardwolf 1994
1 DC,GM(c)................. 2.95
1a Certificate ed. signed 12.00
2 World Toughest Milkman....... 2.95
3 R.Block(s),O:Aardwolf........ 2.95

A.B.C. WARRIORS
Fleetway/Quality
1 thru 8 .... @1.95

ABSOLUTE ZERO
Antarctic Press 1995
1 .... 2.95
2 Rooftop,Athena 2.95
3 Stan Sakai 3.50
4 3-D Man and Kirby 2.95
5 & 6 Super Powers.......... @2.95

AC ANNUAL
Aircel 1990
1 .... 3.95
2 Based on 1940's heroes....... 5.00
3 F:GoldenAge Heroes 3.50
4 F:Sentinels of Justice 3.95

ACE COMICS PRESENTS
Ace 1987
1 thru 7 .... @1.75

ACES
Eclipse 1988
1 thru 5, mag. size.......... @2.95

ACHILLES STORM
Brainstorm 1997
1 by Sandra Chang 2.95
1a nude cover 2.95

ACHILLES STORM: DARK SECRET
Brainstorm 1997
1 by Sandra Chang 2.95
1 nude cover edition 3.95
2 .... 2.95
2a nude cover edition 2.95
2 luxury edition 5.00

ACME
Fandom House
1 thru 9 .... @1.95

ACOLYTE CHRONICLES
Azure Press 1995
1 I:Korath 2.95

---

2 V:Korath................. 2.95

A COP CALLED TRACY
ACG Comics 1998
1 by Chester Gould 2.95
2 thru 8 .... @2.95

ACTION FORCE
Lightning 1987
1 .... 1.75

ACTION GIRL COMICS
Slave Labor Graphics 1994
1 thru 7 .... @2.75
1 thru 7, later printings .... @2.75
8 thru 12 .... @2.95
13 Halloween issue 2.95
14 F:Elizabeth Lavin........... 2.95
15 .... 2.95
16 GoGo Gang, pt.1........... 2.75
17 GoGo Gang, pt.2........... 2.75
18 Blue Monday 2.95

ADAM AND EVE A.D.
Bam
1 .... 3.00
2 thru 10 .... @1.50

Addam Omega #1
© Antarctic Press

ADDAM OMEGA
Antarctic Press 1997
1 (of 4) by Bill Hughes 2.95
2 thru 4 .... @2.95

ADOLESCENT RADIOACTIVE BLACK-BELT HAMSTERS
Eclipse
1 I:Bruce,Chuck,Jackie,Clint 2.50
1a 2nd printing 2.00
2 A parody of a parody 2.00
3 I:Bad Gerbil 2.00

---

4 A:Heap (3-D),Abusement Park .. 1.50
5 Abusement Park #2 .... 1.50
6 SK,Abusement Park #3 .... 2.00
7 SK,V:Toe-Jam Monsters 2.00
8 SK 2.00
9 All-Jam last issue 2.00
[2nd Series]
Parody Press
1 .... 2.50
2 Hamsters Go Hollywood....... 2.50

ADVENTURES INTO THE UNKNOWN
A Plus Comics 1990
1 AW,WW, rep. classic horror 2.95
2 AW..................... 2.95
3 AW..................... 2.95
Halloween Spec. reps. Charlton &
   American Comics GroupHorror. 2.50
ACG Comics 1997
1 FF,AW, Charlton comics reprint.. 2.95

ADVENTURERS
Aircel/Adventure Publ.
0 Origin Issue 2.50
1 with Skeleton 5.00
1a Revised cover............. 3.00
1b 2nd printing 2.00
2 Peter Hsu (c) 2.50
3 Peter Hsu (c) 2.50
4 Peter Hsu (c) 2.00
5 Peter Hsu (c) 2.00
6 Peter Hsu (c) 2.00
7 thru 9 .... @2.00

ADVENTURERS BOOK II
Adventure Publ.
0 O:Man Gods............... 1.95
1 .... 1.95
2 thru 9 .... @1.95

ADVENTURERS BOOK III
1A Lim.(c)Ian McCaig 2.25
1B Reg.(c)Mitch Foust.......... 2.25
2 thru 6 .... @2.25

ADVENTURES OF CHRISSY CLAWS, THE
Heroic 1991
1 thru 2 .... @3.25

ADVENTURES OF CHUK THE BARBARIC
White Wolf
1 & 2 .... @1.25

ADVENTURES OF LUTHER ARKWRIGHT
Valkyrie Press 1987–89
1 thru 9 .... @2.25
See Also: Dark Horse section

All comics prices listed are for *Near Mint* condition.

ADVENTURES OF MR. PYRIDINE
Fantagraphics
1 .... 2.25

ADVENTURES OF THE AEROBIC DUO
Lost Cause Productions
1 thru 3 .... @2.25
4 Gopher Quest............. 2.25
5 V:Stupid Guy 2.25

ADVENTURES OF THEOWN
Pyramid 1986
1 thru 3, Limited series .... @1.75

AESOP'S FABLES
Fantagraphics
1 Selection of Fables........... 2.25
2 Selection of Fables........... 2.25
3 inc. Boy who cried wolf....... 2.25

AETOS THE EAGLE
Ground Zero Aug. 1997
1 (of 3) by Dan Parsons........ 3.00
2 .... 3.00
3 concl..................... 3.00

AETOS 2: CHILDREN OF THE GRAVES
Orphan Underground 1995
1 A:Nightmare............... 2.50

Agent Unknown #3
© Renegade

AGENT UNKNOWN
Renegade 1987
1 thru 3 .... @2.00

AGE OF HEROES, THE
Halloween Comics 1996
1 JHI....................... 2.95
1A signed 2.95
2 JHI....................... 2.95
2A signed 2.95

AGONY ACRES
AA2 Entertainment
1 thru 3 .... @2.50
4 and 5 .... @2.95

AIRCEL
1 Graphic Novel year 1 .... 6.95

AIRFIGHTERS CLASSICS
Eclipse
1 O:Airboy,rep.Air Fighters#2..... 3.00
2 rep.Old Airboy appearances 3.00
3 thru 6 .... @3.95

AIRMEN
Mansion Comics
1 I:Airmen 2.50

AIRWAVES
Caliber 1990
1 Radio Security 2.50
2 A:Paisley,Ganja 2.50
3 Formation of Rebel Alliance 2.50
4 Big Annie,pt. 1 .... 2.50
5 Big Annie,pt 2.............. 2.50

AKIKO
Sirius 1996
1 MCi 6.50
2 MCi 4.00
3 thru 17 MCi............... @3.00
18 Alia Rellapor, concl........... 3.00
19 new story, pt.1............ 3.00
20 F:Mr. Beeba............... 3.00
21 On the Road 3.00
22 .... 3.00
23 space station Fognon-6 .... 3.00
24 escape spaceship 3.00
25 Done in One, 32pg.......... 3.00
26 reunited on planet Smoo 3.00
27 MCi,Bornstone's Elixir, pt.2 .... 2.50
28 MCi,Bornstone's Elixir, pt.3 .... 2.50
29 MCi,Bornstone's Elixir, pt.4 .... 2.50
30 MCi,Bornstone's Elixir, pt.5 .... 2.50
31 MCi,Bornstone's Elixir, concl.... 2.50
32 MCi,On Planet Earth, pt.1 ..... 2.50
33 MCi,On Planet Earth, pt.2 ..... 2.50
34 MCi,On Planet Earth, pt.3 .... 2.50
35 Moonshopping, pt.1 .... 2.50
TPB Vol. 1 rep. #1–#6 .... 14.95
HC Vol. 1 .... 20.00
TPB Vol. 2 rep. #8–#13......... 11.95
TPB Vol. 3 .... 11.95
GN Akiko on the Planet Smoo ... 14.95
Spec. Akiko on the Planet Smoo... 3.50

ALBEDO
Thoughts & Images
0 white cover, yellow drawing table
   Blade Runner............ 25.00
0a white(c) 15.00
0b blue(c),1st ptg........... 12.00
0c blue(c),2nd ptg 10.00
0d blue(c),3rd ptg 5.00
0e Photo(c),4th ptg.,inc. extra
   pages.................. 3.00
1 SS,I:Nilson Groundthumper,
   dull red cover 7.00
1a bright red cover 6.00
2 SS,I:Usagi Yojimbo.......... 5.00
3 SS,Erma, Usagi 4.00
4 SS,Usagi 6.00
5 Nelson Groundthumper........ 5.00
6 Erma, High Orbit............ 4.00
7 .... 2.00

8 Erna Feldna 2.00
9 High Orbit,Harvest Venture..... 2.00
10 thru 14 .... @2.00

ALBEDO VOL. II
Antarctic Press 1991–93
1 New Erma Story............. 2.50
2 E.D.F. HQ................. 2.50
3 Birth of Erma's Child.......... 2.50
4 Non action issue............ 2.50
5 The Outworlds 2.50
6 War preparations 2.50
7 Ekosiak in Anarchy.......... 2.50
8 EDF High Command 2.50
Spec. Color 3.00

VOL. III
1 .... 3.50

ALIEN ENCOUNTERS
Fantagor
1 .... 1.25

ALIEN FIRE
Kitchen Sink Press 1987
1 Eric Vincent art.............. 3.50
2 Eric Vincent art............. 2.50
3 Eric Vincent art............. 2.00

ALIEN NATION: A BREED APART
Adventure Comics 1990
1 Friar Kaddish 3.00
2 .... 2.50
3 The 'Vampires' Busted 2.50
4 Final Issue 2.50

ALIEN NATION: THE FIRSTCOMERS
Adventure Comics 1991
1 New Mini-series 2.50
2 Assassin.................. 2.50
3 Search for Saucer 2.50
4 Final Issue 2.50

ALIEN NATION: THE PUBLIC ENEMY
Adventure Comics 1991
1 'Before the Fall' 2.50
2 Earth & Wehlnistrata.......... 2.50
3 Killer on the Loose 2.50

ALIEN NATION: THE SKIN TRADE
Adventure Comics 1991
1 'Case of the Missing Milksop' ... 2.50
2 'To Live And Die in L.A' 2.50
3 A:Dr. Jekyll................ 2.50
4 D.Methoraphan Exposed 2.50

ALIEN NATION: THE SPARTANS
Adventure Comics
1 JT/DPo,Yellow wrap 4.00
1a JT/DPo,Green wrap 4.00
1b JT/DPo,Pink wrap.......... 4.00
1c JT/DPo,blue wrap 4.00
1d LTD collectors problem 7.00
2 JT,A:Ruth Lawrence 2.50
3 JT/SM,Spartians............ 2.50
4 JT/SM,conclusion 2.50

ALL-PRO SPORTS
All Pro Sports
1 Unauthorized Bio-Bo Jackson . . . 2.50
2 Unauthorized Bio-Joe Montana . . 2.50

ALLURA AND THE CYBERANGELS
Avatar Press 1998
Spec.#1 by Bill Maus 3.95
Spec.#1 nude cover 6.00

ALLY
Ally Winsor Productions 1995
1 I&O: Ally. 2.95
2 and 3 . . . . @2.95

ALTERNATE HEROES
Prelude Graphics
1 and 2 . . . . @1.95

AMAZING COMICS
PREMIERES
1 thru 9 . . . . @1.95

AMAZING CYNICALMAN
Eclipse
1 . . . . 1.50

AMAZON WOMAN
Fantaco
Christmas Spec. 4.95
Beach Party 5.95
Amazing Colossal Amazon
    Woman #1 . . . . 7.95
Amazing Colossal Amazon Album 12.95
Jungle Annual #1 . . . . 5.95
Jungle Album 9.95
TPB Amazon Woman: The Art of
    Tom Simonton 9.95
TPB Amazon Woman, deluxe 19.95
Spec. Invaders of Terror 5.95
TPB Book One by Tom Simonton . 14.95
TPB Book Two The Curse of the
    Amazon 14.95
HC, limited 50.00
HC, limited, signed, numbered . . . 75.00
1-shot Attack of the Amazon Girls,
    cont. nudity 4.95

AMAZONS GONZANGAS: BAD GIRLS OF THE JUNGLE
Academy Comics 1995
0 Rites of passage(Jason Waltrip) . 3.50

AMERICAN ANNIHILATOR
Night Realm Publishing
0 V:Synthetic Assassin 1.85

AMERICAN SPLENDOR
Harvey Bekar 1976–90
1 thru 15 . . . . @3.25
Tundra 1991
16 . . . . 3.95

AMERICAN WOMAN
Antarctic Press 1998
1 by Brian Denham & Richard
    Stockton. 2.95

AMUSING STORIES
Blackthorne
1 thru 3 . . . . @2.00

ANATOMIC BOMBS
Brainstorm 1998
1 Angelissa, by Mike James 2.95
1a Angelissa, nude cover edition . . 3.95
1 Bad Tabitha, by Mike James. . . . 2.95
1a Bad Tabitha, photo cover edition 3.95

ANGEL GIRL
Angel Entertainment 1997
0 by David Campiti & Al Rio. 2.95
1 by David Campiti & Richard
    Fraga. 2.95
1 deluxe 5.95
1 Virgin nude cover 5.00
1 Nude Manga cover 5.00
1 Nude Platinum cover 8.00
Spec. #1 Angels Illustrated Swimsuit
    Special. 5.00
Spec. #1 Swimsuit Special, Nude
    Oily Angels (c) 5.00
1-shot Against All Evil. 2.95
1-shot Against All Evil, nude cover . 2.95
1-shot Before the Wings 2.95
1-shot Before the Wings, nude
    cover A 2.95
1-shot Before the Wings, nude
    cover B 2.95
1-shot Demonworld, by Ellis Bell &
    Mark Kuettner 2.95
1-shot Doomsday, by Ellis Bell &
    Mark Kuettner 3.00

ANGEL GIRL: HEAVEN SENT
Angel Entertainment 1997
0 by David Campiti & Al Rio. 2.95
0 Virgin nude. 5.00
0 nude platinum cover 12.00
1 . . . . 3.00
1 nude Michelle in Hell cover. 4.00

ANGEL OF DEATH
Innovation
1 thru 4 . . . . @2.25

Animal Mystic #3
© Sirius

ANIMAL MYSTIC
Cry For Dawn/Sirus 1993–95
1 DOe 32.00
1a variant, signed 42.00
1b 2nd printing, new (c) 7.00
2 I:Klor 30.00
2a 2nd printing, new (c) 6.00
3 . . . . 12.00
3a 2nd printing 5.00
4 last issue 4.00
4a special 15.00
TPB DOe 14.95

ANIMAL MYSTIC: KLOR
Sirius 1999
1 (of 3) DOe 2.95
2 DOe 2.95

ANIMERICA
Viz Comics
1 F:Bubble Gum Crisis 2.95
2 F:Bubble Gum Crisis 2.95
3 F:Bubble Gum Crisis 2.95

ANIMERICA EXTRA
Viz Communications 1998
VOL 1
1 & 2. . . . . @4.95
VOL 2, 1998
1 thru 9 . . . . @4.95

ANTARES CIRCLE
Antarctic Press
1 . . . . 1.75
2 . . . . 1.75

ANUBIS
Unicorn Books
1 I:Anubis 2.50
2 F:Anubis. 2.50
3 . . . . 2.50
Didactic Chocolate Press
3 by Scott Berwanger 2.75
4 thru 6 . . . . @2.75
Adventure Comics
7 "Sandy's Plight" 2.75
8 . . . . 2.95

A-OK
Antarctic Press
1 Ninja H.S. spin-off series 2.50
2 F:Paul,Moniko,James 2.50
3 Confrontation 2.50
4 . . . . 2.50

APATHY KAT
Entity 1995
1 . . . . 2.75
1 signed, numbered. 9.95
1 2nd printing 2.75
2 . . . . 2.75
2 2nd printing 2.75
3 & 4 . . . . 2.75
TPB Kollection #1. . . . . 7.95

APE CITY
Adventure Comics
1 Monkey Business 3.00
2 thru 4 . . . . @2.50

APPARITION, THE
Caliber
1 thru 4 . . . . @2.95
5 "Black Clouds" 2.95

Appleseed, Book 3 #3
© Eclipse

APPLESEED
Eclipse
1 MSh,rep. Japanese comic 9.00
2 MSh,arrival in Olympus City 6.00
3 MSh,Olympus City politics 5.00
4 MSh,V:Director 5.00
5 MSh,Deunan vs. Chiffon 5.00
Book Two
1 MSh,AAd(c),Olympus City 4.00
2 MSh,AAd(c),Hitomi vs.EswatUnit 3.50
3 MSh,AAd(c),Deunan vs.Gaia . . . 3.50
4 MSh,AAd(c),V:Robot Spiders . . . 3.50
5 MSh,AAd(c),Hitome vs.Gaia 3.50
Book Three
1 MSh,Brigreos vs.Biodroid 5.00
2 MSh,V:Cuban Navy 3.50
3 MSh,'Benandanti' 3.50
4 MSh,V:Renegade biodroid 3.50
5 MSh 3.50
Book Four 1990
1 MSh,V:Munma Terrorists 3.50
2 MSh,V:Drug-crazed Munma 3.50
3 Msh,V:Munma Drug Addicts 3.50
4 MSh,Deunan vs. Pani 3.50

ARAMIS WEEKLY
1 mini-series 1.95
2 . . . . 1.95
3 . . . . 1.95

AREA 88
Eclipse
1 I:Shin Kazama 3.00
1a 2nd printing 1.50
2 Dangerous Mission 2.00
2a 2nd printing 1.50
3 O:Shin,Paris '78 . . . . 2.00
4 thru 8 . . . . @2.00
9 thru 39 . . . . @1.50
40 . . . . 1.75
41 . . . . 1.75
42 . . . . 2.00

ARGONAUTS
Eternity
1 thru 5 . . . . @1.95

ARGOSY
Caliber
1 'Walker' vs. Myth Beasts 2.50

ARIK KHAN
A Plus Comics
1 I:Arik Khan 2.50
2 . . . . 2.50
ACG Comics 1998
1 by Frank Reyes, heroic fantasy . 2.95

ARISTOCRATIC EXTRA-TERRESTRIAL TIME-TRAVELING THIEVES
Fictioneer Books
1 V:IRS 3.00
2 V:Realty 1.75
3 V:MDM 1.75
4 thru 12 . . . . @1.75

ARIZONA: A SIMPLE HORROR
London Night/ EH Productions 1998
1 (of 3) by Joe Kennedy &
Jerry Beck 3.00
1a nude cover 6.00
2 double sized 3.00
2a nude cover 6.00
3 . . . . 3.00
3a nude cover 6.00
1-shot Wild at Heart, signed
alternate cover 10.00

A.R.M.
Adventure Comics 1990
1 Larry Niven adapt. Death by
Ecstasy,pt.1 . . . . 2.50
2 Death by Ecstasy,pt.2 . . . . 2.50
3 Death by Ecstasy,pt.3 . . . . 2.50

ARROW SPOTLIGHT
Arrow Comics 1998–99
Advendures of Simone & Ajax . . . 2.95
Allison Chains 2.95
Descendants of Toshin 2.95
Max Velocity, by Jack Snider 2.95
Red Vengeance, by Chris Kemple . 2.95
Talonback 2.95

ASHEN VICTOR
Viz Communications 1998
1 (of 4) by Yukito Kishiro 2.95
2 thru 4 concl. . . . . @2.95
TPB 14.95

ASHES
Caliber 1990–91
1 thru 6 . . . . @2.50

ASHLEY DUST
Knight Press 1995
1 thru 3 . . . . @2.50
4 V:Allister Crowley 2.50
5 Metaphysical Adventure 2.50

ASRIAL VS. CHEETAH
Antarctic Press 1995–96
1 & 2 Ninja High School Gold
Digger x-over . . . . @2.95

ASSASSINETTE
Pocket Change Comics
1 thru 3 . . . . @2.50
4 Psychic Realm 2.50
5 V:Nemesis 2.50
6 The Second Coming,pt.2 . . . . . . 2.50
7 The Second Coming,pt.3 . . . . . . 2.50
8 V:Crazy Actor 2.50
9 . . . . 2.50
10 final issue. 2.50
Spec. Assassinette Returns 2.50
Spec. Assassinette Violated 2.50
Deluxe Assassinette Violated 4.25

ASSASSINETTE: HARDCORE
Pocket Change Comics
1 By Shadow Slasher Team. 2.50
2 V:Bolero 2.50

ASTOUNDING SPACE THRILLS
Day One Comics 1998
1 by Steve Conley, The Codex
Reckoning, pt.1 . . . . 2.95
2 Bros. Hildebrandt (c). 2.95
3 Aspects of Iron 2.95
4 The Robot Murders. 2.95

ASTRONAUTS IN TROUBLE: LIVE FROM THE MOON
Gun Dog Comics 1999
1 (of 5) 2.95
2 thru 5 . . . . @2.95

ATHENA
A.M. Works
7 thru 14 by Dean Hsieh . . . . . . @2.95
TPB Vol. 1 . . . . 14.95
TPB Vol. 2 . . . . 15.95

ATOMIC COMICS
1 . . . . 1.50
Becomes:

MARK I

ATOMIC MAN
1 . . . . 3.00
2 . . . . 2.00
3 . . . . 1.75

ATOMIC MOUSE
A Plus Comics 1990
1 A:Atomic Bunny 2.50

ATOMIC OVERDRIVE
Caliber
1 by Dave Darrigo & PGr 2.95
2 1950s Sci-Fi,Horror,Humor 2.95
3 . . . . 2.95

A TRAVELLER'S TALE
Antarctic Press
1 I:Goshin the Traveller 2.50
2 . . . . 2.50

ATOMIC CITY TALES
Kitchen Sink
1 thru 4 by Jay Stephens . . . . . . @3.50
TPB Vol. 1 Go Power 12.95
TPB Vol. 1 signed & numbered . . . 20.95

ATTACK OF THE MUTANT MONSTERS
A Plus Comics
1 SD,rep.Gorgo(Kegor) 2.50

AUGUST
Arrow Comics 1998
1 by Scott Rosema 2.95
2 thru 4 . . . . @2.95

AUTUMN
Caliber Press 1995
1 I:James Turell 2.95
GN 7"x10" 12.95

Avalon #3
© Harrier

AVALON
Harrier, 1987
1 thru 3 . . . . 1.50

AVANT GUARD
Day 1 Comics
1 thru 4 F:Feedback 2.50

AVATARS
Avatar Press 1998
1 (of 2) by Gregory & Holaso 3.95
1a nude cover 6.00
2 F:Pandora & Atlas 3.50
2a nude cover 6.00

AV IN 3D
Aardvark–Vanaheim
1 Color,A:FlamingCarot 6.00

AVELON
Kenzer & Company 1998
1 . . . . 2.95
2 thru 5 . . . . @2.95
6 thru 8 Legacy of Thrain . . . . . . @2.95

AVENUE X
Innovation
1 Based on NY radio drama 2.50
Purple Spiral
3 signed & numbered 3.00

AWAKENING COMICS
Awakening Comics 1997
1 by Steve Peters 3.50
2 . . . . 3.50
3 . . . . 2.95
4 . . . . 2.95
Awakening Comics 1999
1 by Steve Peters 3.50

AWESOME COMICS
1 thru 3 . . . . @2.00

AWESOME
Awesome Entertainment
1 anthology, partial color 2.95

AXED FILES, THE
Entity Comics
1 X-Files Parody 2.50
1 3rd printing, parody 2.75

B-MOVIE PRESENTS
B-Movie Comics
1 . . . . 1.70
2 . . . . 1.70
3 Tasma, Queen of the Jungle . . . 1.70
4 . . . . 1.70

BABES OF AREA 51
Blatant Comics 1997
1 . . . . 2.95
1a Nude Alien Autopsy cover 9.95
1b Nude Roswell Crash cover 9.95

BABY ANGEL X
Brainstorm 1996
1 . . . . 2.95
2 . . . . 2.95
3 gold edition 5.00
3a signed edition 10.00

BABY ANGEL X: SCORCHED EARTH
Brainstorm 1997
1 by Scott Harrison 2.95
1a nude cover 2.95
2 . . . . 2.95
2a nude cover 2.95

BABYLON CRUSH
Boneyard Press
1 I:Babylon Crush 2.95
2 V:A Gang 2.95
3 V:Mafiaso Brothers 2.95
4 & 5 . . . . @2.95
CFD
6 & 7 . . . . @3.95

Boneyard 1998
1-shot Buddha, F:Lesbian dominatrix
vigilante 4.95
Spec. Babylon Bondage Christmas . 2.95
Spec. Bondage nude (c) 3.95
Spec. Girlfriends 2.95
Spec. Girlfriends, nude (c) 3.95
Spec. The Last Shepherd 2.95
Spec. The Last Shepherd, nude(c) . 4.95

BAD APPLES
High Impact Jan. 1997
1 . . . . 2.95
1 Bad Candies cover 9.95
2 . . . . 2.95
2 deluxe 15.00
3 by Billy Patton 2.95
3 deluxe adult cover 10.00
ABC Studios 1999
VOL 2
1 RCI 3.00
1a deluxe variant 8.00
1b adult manga 8.00
2 . . . . 3.00
2 nude manga ed 8.00
VOL 3
1 by Greg Narvasa 3.00
1a manga nude cover 8.00
1b gold manga 10.00

BAD APPLES: HIGH EXPECTATIONS
ABC Studios 1999
1 . . . . 3.00
1a Beach Fun (c) 8.00

BAKER STREET
(Prev. color)
Caliber
3 . . . . 3.25
4 . . . . 1.95
5 Children of the Night Pt.1 . . . . . 1.95
6 Children of the Night Pt.2 . . . . . 1.95
7 thru 10 Children of the Night
pt.3–pt.6 . . . . @2.50

BAKER ST.: GRAPHITTI
Caliber
1 `Elemenary, My Dear' 2.50

BALANCE OF POWER
MU Press 1990–91
1 thru 4 . . . . @2.50

BANDY MAN, THE
Caliber 1996
1 SPr,CAd 2.95
2 SPr,CAd,JIT 2.95
3 SPr,CAd,JIT, conclusion 2.95
HC 96pg 19.95
HC Deluxe 39.95

BAOH
Viz 1990
1 thru 8 . . . . @2.95
GN V:Juda Laboratory 14.95

BARABBAS
Slave Labor
1 . . . . 4.50
2 thru 4 . . . . @1.50

BARBARIANS
ACG Comics
1 by Jeff Jones, Mike Kaluta,
Wayne Howard. 2.95
2 WW 2.95

BARBARIC TALES
Pyramid
1 . . . . 3.00
2 and 3 . . . . @1.70

BASEBALL SUPERSTARS
Revolutionary
1 Nolan Ryan 2.50

Battle Angel Alita, Part Eight, #5
© Viz

BATTLE ANGEL ALITA
Viz 1992
1 I:Daisuka,Alita 8.00
2 Alita becomes warrior 6.00
3 A:Daiuke,V:Cyborg 4.00
4 Alita/Cyborg,A:Makaku 4.00
5 The Bounty Hunters Bar 4.00
6 Confrontation 4.00
7 Underground Sewers,A:Fang . . . 3.00
8 & 9 . . . . @2.75
Part Two 1993
1 V:Zapan 3.00
2 V:Zapan 3.00
3 F:Ido 2.75
4 thru 7 V:Zapan . . . . @2.75
TPB Killing Angel 15.95
Part Three 1993
1 thru 5 . . . . @2.75
6 . . . . 5.00
7 thru 13 . . . . @2.75
Part Four 1994
1 thru 7 . . . . @2.75
Part Five 1995
1 thru 6 . . . . @2.75
7 . . . . 2.95
Part Six 1995–96
1 thru 8 YuK. . . . . @2.95
TPB Angel of Chaos. 15.95
Part Seven Oct. 1996
1 thru 8 YuK. . . . . @2.95
Part Eight 1997
1 thru 9 YuK. . . . . @2.95
TPB Vol. 2 Tears of an Agnel 15.95
TPB Vol. 4 Angel of Victory. 15.95

TPB Vol. 5 . . . . 15.95
TPB Vol. 6 Angel of Death 15.95
TPB Vol. 7 Angel of Chaos 15.95
TPB Vol. 8 Fallen Angel 15.95
TPB Vol. 9 Angel's Ascension. . . . 16.95

BATTLE ARMOR
Eternity
1 thru 4 . . . . @1.95

BATTLE BEASTS
Blackthorne
1 thru 4 . . . . @1.50

BATTLEGROUND EARTH
Best Comics 1996
1 . . . . 2.50
2 . . . . 2.50
3 "Destiny Quest: The Vengeance"
concl. 2.50
4 V:Conjura 2.50
5 "The Pit of Black Death" 2.50

BATTLETECH
(Prev. Color)
7 thru 12 . . . . @1.75
Ann.#1 . . . . 4.50

BATTRON
NEC
1 WWII story 2.75
2 WWII contd. 2.75

BEAST WARRIOR
OF SHAOLIN
1 thru 5 . . . . @1.95

THE BEATLES
EXPERIENCE
Revolutionary
1 Beatles 1960's 3.00
2 Beatles 1964-1966 . . . . 2.50
3 . . . . 2.50
4 Abbey Road, Let it be. 2.50
5 The Solo Years. 2.50
6 Paul McCartney & Wings 2.50
7 The Murder of John Lennon . . . 2.50
8 To 1992, final issue. 2.50

BECK AND CAUL
Gauntlet
1 I:Beck and Caul 2.95
2 thru 6 . . . . @2.95
Ann.#1 A Single Step 3.50

BERZERKER
Gauntlet (Caliber)
1 thru 6 . . . . @2.95

BEST OF THE WEST
AC Comics 1998
1 F:Durango Kid 4.95
2 F:The Haunted Horseman 4.95
3 F:The Haunted Horseman 4.95
4 F:Roy Rogers, 44-page 5.95
5 F:Durango Kid 5.95
6 F:Durango Kid 5.95

BETHANY THE VAMPFIRE
Brainstorm Dec. 1997
0 O:Bethany 2.95
0a nude cover 3.95
1 by Holly Galightly 2.95
1 luxury edition 5.00
2 . . . . 2.95
2a nude cover 3.95
3 . . . . 2.95
3a nude cover 3.95
3b Photo cover 3.95

BEYOND MARS
Blackthorne
1 thru 5 . . . . @2.00

BIG BLACK KISS
Vortex
3 HC some color 3.75

BIG NUMBERS
1 BSz 6.00
2 BSz 5.50

BILL THE BULL
Boneyard Press
1 I:Bill the Bull. 2.95
2 & 3 For Hire . . . . @2.95

BILLY DOGMA
Millennium April 1997
1 by Dean Haspiel. 2.95
1 signed print edition 4.95
2 . . . . 2.95
3 . . . . 2.95
4 They Found A Sawed-Off in
My Afro 2.95

BILLY NGUYEN
PRIVATE EYE
Caliber 1990
1 . . . . 2.00
1a 2nd Printing 2.00
2 thru 6 . . . . @2.00

BIO-BOOSTER
ARMOR GUYVER
Viz
Part II
1 thru 3 F:Sho . . . . @2.75
4 V:Enzyme II 2.75
5 Sho VS Enzyme II 2.75
6 Final Issue 2.75
Part III
1 Sho Unconscious 2.75
2 V:Zoanoids 2.75
3 F:Murahani. 2.75
4 . . . . 2.75
5 . . . . 2.75
6 V:Commando Guyver 2.75
7 Sho to the rescue 2.75
Part Four
1 thru 7 . . . . @2.95
Part Five
1 thru 7 . . . . @2.95
Part Six Dec. 1996
1 thru 6 by Yoshiki Takaya . . . . . @2.95
TPB Vol. 1 . . . . 15.95
TPB Vol. 2 Revenge of Chronos . 15.95
TPB Vol. 4 Escape From Chronos 15.95
TPB Vol. 5 Guyver Reborn 15.95
TPB Vol. 6 Heart of Chronos. . . . 15.95

    All comics prices listed are for *Near Mint* condition.

TPB Vol. 7 Armageddon 15.95

BIZARRE HEROES
Kitchen Sink 1990
1 DSs, parody 2.50
Fiasco Comics
1 DSs, reprint 2.95

[Original] BLACK CAT
4 rep. 2.00
5 A:Ted Parrish 2.00
6 50th Anniv. Issue 2.00
7 rep. 2.00

BLACKENED
Enigma
1 V:Killing Machine 2.95
2 V:Killing Machine 2.95
3 Flaming Altar 2.95

BLACK KISS
Vortex
1 HC,Adult. 7.00
1a 2nd printing 4.00
1b 3rd printing. 1.25
2 HC 6.00
2a 2nd printing 3.00
3 HC 5.00
4 HC 4.00
5 & 6 HC . . . . @2.00
7 thru 12 HC . . . . @1.50

Blaskmask #3
© Eastern Comics

BLACKMASK
Eastern Comics
1 thru 6 . . . . @1.75

BLACK MIST
Caliber Core 1998
1 by James Pruett & Mike Perkins,
  Blood of Kali, pt.1 . . . . 2.95
1a variant MV(c) 2.95
1b variant Jordan Raskin(c) 2.95
1c variant GyD(c) 2.95
1d premium edition, signed 9.95
2 thru 5 Blood of Kali,pt.2–pt.5 . . @2.95
Spec. Dawn of Armageddon, Blood
  of Kali, pt.6 & pt.7, 48-page . . . 3.95

BLACK SCORPION
Special Studio 1991
1 Knight of Justice 2.75
2 A Game for Old Men 2.75
3 Blackmailer's Auction 2.75

BLACKTHORNE 3 in 1
1 and 2 . . . . @2.00

BLACK ZEPPLIN
Renegade
1 . . . . 2.50
2 thru 6 . . . . @2.00

BLADE OF SHURIKEN
Eternity
1 thru 8 . . . . @1.95

BLAIR WITCH PROJECT
Oni Press 1999
Spec. Movie adapt. 2.95

BLANDMAN
Eclipse
1 Sandman parody 2.50

BLIND FEAR
Eternity
1 thru 4 . . . . @1.95

BLONDE AVENGER: DANGEROUS CONCLUSIONS
Brainstorm 1997
1 V:Victor Von Fuchs 2.95
1a photo deluxe cover 3.95
2 . . . . 2.95
2a photo deluxe cover 3.95

BLOOD & ROSES ADVENTURES
Knight Press
1 F:Time Agents 2.95
2 F:Time Agents 2.95
3 Search for Time Agents 2.95
4 Time Adventures 2.95

BLOOD 'N' GUTS
Aircel 1990
1 thru 3 . . . . @2.50

BLOODBROTHERS
Eternity
1 thru 4 . . . . @1.95

BLOOD IS THE HARVEST
Eclipse 1992
1 I:Nikita,Milo. 4.50
2 V:M'Raud D:Nikita? 2.50
3 Milo captured 2.50
4 F:Nikita/Milo 2.50

BLOOD JUNKIES
Eternity
1 Vampires on Capitol Hill 2.50
2 final issue 2.50

BLOODLETTING
Fantaco
1 A Shilling for a Redcoat 2.95
2 . . . . 2.95
3 Flee 2.95
4 thru 10 (of 11) by Chynna
  Clugston, ... @3.95

BLOOD OF DRACULA
Apple 1987–90
1 thru 7 . . . . @1.75
8 thru 14 . . . . @1.95
15 +Record&Mask 3.50
16 . . . . 1.95
17 thru 20 . . . . @2.25

BLOOD OF INNOCENT
Warp Graphics
1 thru 4 . . . . @2.50

BLOODSHED
Damage
1 Little Brother. 2.95
1a Commemorative issue 4.00
1 Encore edition, gold foil(c) 3.50
2 Little Brother. 2.95
3 O:Bloodshed 2.95
3 "The Wastelands," cont. 3.50
4 The City 3.50
5 the end is near 3.50
6 . . . . 3.50
7 Lies, concl. 3.50
"M" 3.50
"M" deluxe 5.00
Spec. Lunatics Fringe. 3.50
Spec. Lies Epilogue, final issue . . 3.50
Spec. Chris Mass #1 . . . . 3.50
Spec. Requiem. 3.50

BLOODWING
Eternity
1 thru 5 . . . . @1.95

BLUDGEON
Aardwolf 1997
1 by JPi & David Chylsetk 2.95
2 "Alise in Wonderland" 2.95
3 "Seeing Red" 2.95

BOGIE MAN: CHINATOON
Atomeka
1 I:Francis Claine 2.95
2 F:Bogie Man. 2.95
3 thr 4 F:Bogie Man. 2.95

BOGIE MAN: MANHATTEN PROJECT
Apocalypse
1-Shot. D.Quale Assassination Plot 3.95

BONAFIDE
Bonafide Productions
1 F:Doxie 'th Mutt 3.50
2 F:Doxie 'th Mutt 3.50
3 F:Doxie 'th Mutt 3.50

BONE
Cartoon Books 1991
1 I:Bone 90.00
1a 2nd printing 10.00
1b 3rd Printing. 8.00
1c 4th printing 3.00

B & W PUB.

1d thru 1f 5th-7th printing . . . . . @3.00
2 . . . . 50.00
2a 2nd printing 7.00
2b thru 2e 3rd-6th printing . . . . @3.00
3 . . . . 35.00
3a 2nd printing 5.00
3b thru 3d 3rd-5th printing . . . . @3.00
4 . . . . 25.00
4a thru 4c 2nd-4th printing . . . . @3.00
5 . . . . 20.00
5a thru 5c 2nd-4th printing . . . . @3.00
6 . . . . 15.00
6a thru 6c 2nd-4th printing . . . . @3.00
7 . . . . 10.00
7a,7b 2nd,3rd printing . . . . @3.00
8 . . . . 9.00
8a,8b 2nd,3rd printing . . . . @3.00
9 . . . . 8.00
9a 2nd printing 3.00
10 . . . . 6.00
11 . . . . 3.00
12 . . . . 3.00
13 . . . . 3.00
14 thru 17 . . . . @3.25
18 V:Bar owner. 3.25

Bone #19
© Cartoon Books

19 F:Phoney Bone 3.25
20 Dragonslayer Phoney Bone 3.25
21 thru 27, *see Image*
21 thru 27 reprints. . . . . @2.95
28 "Rockjaw: Master of the
    Eastern Border" 3.00
29 . . . . 3.00
30 . . . . 3.00
31 . . . . 3.00
32 Bartleby the Rat Creature Cub
    saga, concl. 3.00
33 Phoney's fate. 3.00
34 Kingdok Slayer 2.95
35 return of Gran'ma Ben 2.95
36 Return of Rockjaw 2.95
37 Extravaganza Issue 2.95
PB rep.#1-4 . . . . 14.00
TPB Vol. 1 Rep.1-#6. . . . . 12.95
TPB Vol. 2 Rep.#7-#12. . . . . 12.95
TPB Vol. 3 Eyes of the Storm . . 16.95
HC Vol. 3 . . . . 24.95
TPB Vol.4 Dragonslayer 16.95
HC Vol. 4 . . . . 24.95
TPB Vol. 5 Rock Jaw: Master of the
    Eastern Border. 14.95
HC Vol. 5 . . . . 22.95
TPB Vol. 6 Old Man's Cave 17.95
TPB Bone Reader 9.95

BONESHAKER
Caliber Press
1 Suicidal Wrestler 3.50

BOOK, THE
DreamSmith Studios 1998
1 epic fantasy 72pg. 3.50
2 . . . . 3.50
3 . . . . 3.95
4 . . . . 3.95
5 . . . . 4.00
6 . . . . 4.00
7 . . . . 4.00
Ashcan Preview, 24-page 3.50
Ashcan Preview, GP(c) 10.00
Handbook, 32-page 1.95

BOOK OF BALLADS AND SAGAS
Green Man Press
1 False Knight in the Road 2.95
2 thru 5 . . . . 3.00
5 . . . . 3.50

BOOK OF THE TAROT
Caliber Tome Press 1998
1 History/Development o/t Tarot. . . 3.95
1 64pg. 4.95
1 signed 4.95

BOOKS OF LORE
Peregrine
Spec.#1 fantasy anthology 2.95
Spec.#2 . . . . 2.95
Spec.#3 . . . . 2.95

BOOKS OF LORE: THE KAYNIN GAMBIT
Peregrine 1998
0 by Kevin Tucker
    & David Napoliello 2.95
1 (of 4) 2.95
1a Xavier (c) 2.95
2 thru 4 . . . . @2.95

BOONDOGGLE
Knight Press 1995
1 Waffle War 2.95
2 Waffle War 2.95
3 Waffle War 2.95

BOONDOGGLE
Caliber Tapestry 1997
Spec. 2.95
Spec., signed 2.95
1 thru 3 . . . . @2.95
4 At Wo's. 2.95

BORDER WORLDS
Kitchen Sink
1 adult. 2.00
2 thru 7 . . . . @2.00
Spec.#1 Border Worlds: Marooned . 2.00

BORIS' ADVENTURE MAGAZINE
Nicotat
1 and 2 . . . . @2.00
3 thru 6 . . . . @2.95

BORIS THE BEAR
Nikotat
1–12: See Dark Horse section
13 thru 29 . . . . @2.00
30 thru 34 . . . . @2.50

BORN TO KILL
Aircel 1991
1 thru 3 . . . . @2.50

BOSTON BOMBERS
Caliber
1 . . . . 1.95
2 . . . . 2.50
Spec.#1 . . . . 3.95
*Note: other issues are flipbooks with:
Oz #17; The Searchers #5; Raven
Chronicles #12; & LegendLore #6*

BOUNTY
Caliber 1991
1 `Bounty,'' Navarro' Pt.1 . . . . 2.50
2 `Bounty,'' Navarro' Pt.2 . . . . 2.50
3 `Bounty,'' Navarro' Pt.3 . . . . 2.50

BOX OFFICE POISON
Antarctic Press 1996
1 by Alex Robinson 9.00
2 . . . . 6.00
3 thru 5 . . . . @4.00
6 thru 10 . . . . @3.00
11 thru 15 . . . . @3.00
TPB 160-page 14.95
Big Super Spec.#1 . . . . 4.95

BRAT PACK
King Hell Publications
1 . . . . 6.00
1a 2nd printing 3.00
2 thru 5 . . . . @4.00
Brat Pack Collection 13.00

BRATPACK/MAXIMORTAL
King Hell
Super Spec.#1 RV 3.00
Super Spec.#2 RV 3.00

BREAKNECK BLVD
Slave Labor Graphics 1995–96
1 thru 3 Jhonen Vasques art . . . @2.95
4 by Timothy Markin 2.95
5 . . . . 2.95
6 . . . . 2.95

BRENDA STARR, ACE REPORTER
ACG Comics 1998
1 by Dale Messick, Charlton reprint 3.00
2 . . . . 2.95
Spec.#1 Pin-ups,rep. from 40s
    and 50s (1998). 2.95

BRILLIANT BOY
Circus Comics 1997
1 . . . . 2.95
2 Drake, pt.1 (of 5) 2.95
3 Drake, pt.2 . . . . 2.50
4 Drake, pt.3 . . . . 2.50
5 Drake, pt.4 . . . . 2.50
6 Drake, pt.5 . . . . 2.50
7 The Great Thunder, pt. 1 (of 6) . . 2.50
8 The Great Thunder, pt. 2 . . . . . . 2.50

B & W PUB.

Broid #2
© Eternity

BROID
Eternity
1 thru 4 . . . . @2.25

BROKEN HALO: IS THERE NOTHING SACRED
Broken Halos Comics 1998
1 by Donald J. Vigil & Tim Vigil . . . 2.95
1a nude cover 4.95
2 . . . . 2.95
2a nude cover 4.95
3 . . . . 2.95
3a Adult edition, nude cover 5.95
Ashcan, limited ed. 16-page 6.95
TPB Vol. 1 by Joe & Tim Vigil,
   limited ed. 9.95

BROKEN HEROES
Sirius 1998
1 by Fillbach Bros 2.50
2 The Neon Graveyard 2.50
3 Rocket Man 2.50
4 thru 12 final issue . . . . @2.50

BRONX
Eternity 1991
1 A.Saichann Short Stories 2.50
2 to 3 . . . . @2.50

Aircel
Reprint 2.95

BROTHER MAN
New City Comics
1 . . . . 5.00
1a 2.00
2 thru 7 . . . . @2.00

BRUCE JONES: OUTER EDGE
Innovation
1 All reprints 2.00

BRUCE JONES: RAZORS EDGE
Innovation
1 All reprints 2.50

---

2 D:Grimm, Gritty 2.50

BRU-HEAD
Schism Comics
1 Blockhead 2.95
1a 2nd printing 2.75
2 Blockhead 2.95
Vol 1 Bru-Hed's Bunnies, Baddies
   & Buddies (1998) 2.50
Vol 1 Bru-Hed's Guide to Gettin'
   Girls Now 2.50

BUCE-N-GAR
RAK
1 . . . . 1.75
2 . . . . 1.75
3 . . . . 1.75

BUCK GODOT
Palliard Press
1 I:Buck Godot 2.95

BUCK GODOT: ZAP GUN FOR HIRE
Studio Foglio
1 thru 7 . . . . @2.95
7 by Phil Foglio & Barb Kaalberg . . 2.95
8 finale 3.50

BUFFALO WINGS
Antarctic Press
1 and 2 . . . . @2.50

BUG
Planet X Productions
1 . . . . 1.50
2 . . . . 1.50

BULLET CROW
Eclipse
1 & 2 . . . . @2.00

BULWARK
Millenium 1995
1 I:Bulwark 2.95
2 O:Bulwark 2.95

BUSHIDO
Eternity
1 thru 6 . . . . @1.95

BUZZ
Kitchen Sink
1 Mark Landman (c) (1990) 2.95
2 Mark Landman (c) 2.95
3 Mark Landman (c) (1991) 2.95

CABLE TV
Parody Press
1 Cable Satire 2.50

CADILLACS AND DINOSAURS
Kitchen Sink
3-D comic. 3.95

CALIBER CORE
Caliber 1998
0 48pg. 2.95
1 gestalt cover. 2.95
1a Rain People cover 2.95
1b Spiral cover 2.95
2 F:Al-Haquat 2.95

CALIBER PRESENTS
(Prev. High Caliber)
1 TV,I:Crow 50.00
2 Deadworld 7.00
3 Realm 3.00
4 Baker Street 3.00
5 TV,Heart of Darkness,
   Fugitive 2.50
6 TV,Heart of Darkness,
   Fugitive 2.50
7 TV,Heart of Darkness,
   Dragonfeast 2.50
8 TV,Cuda,Fugitive 2.50
9 Baker Street,Sting Inc. 2.00
10 Fugitive, The Edge 2.50
11 Ashes,Random Thoughts. 2.50
12 Fugitive,Random Thoughts 2.50
13 Random Thoughts,Synergist . . . 2.50
14 Random Thoughts,Fugitive 2.50
15 Fringe, F:The Crow 4.00
16 Fugitive, The Verdict 3.50
17 Deadworld, The Verdict 3.50
18 Orlak,The Verdict. 3.50
19 Taken Under,Go-Man. 3.50
20 The Verdict,Go-Man. 3.50
21 The Verdict,Go-Man 3.50
22 The Verdict,Go-Man. 3.50
23 Go-Man,Heat Seeker. 3.50
24 Heat Seeker,MacktheKnife. 3.50
Christmas Spec A:Crow,Deadworld
   Realm,Baker Street 10.00
Summer Spec. inc. the Silencers,
   Swords of Shar-Pei (preludes) . 3.95
1-Shot 2.50
1-shot Hybrid 2.50

CALIBER SPOTLIGHT
Caliber
1 F:Kabuki,Oz 2.95

CALIBRATIONS
Caliber
1 WEI,MCy,"Atmospherics," pt.1. . . 2.95
2 WEI,MCy,"Atmospherics," pt.2. . . 2.95
3 WEI,MCy,"Atmospherics," pt.3. . . 2.95
4 WEI,MCy,"Atmospherics," pt.4. . . 2.95
5 WEI,MCy,"Atmospherics," concl. . 2.95

CALIFORNIA GIRLS
Eclipse
1 thru 8 . . . . @2.00

CALIGARI 2050
1 Gothic Horror 2.25
2 Gothic Horror 2.25

CAMELOT ETERNAL
Caliber 1990
1 . . . . 3.00
2 . . . . 2.50
3 . . . . 2.50
4 Launcelot & Guinevere 2.50
5 Mordred Escapes 2.50
6 MorganLeFay returns from dead. 2.50
7 Revenge of Morgan 2.50
8 Launcelot flees Camelot 2.50

CAPTAIN CANUCK REBORN
Semple Comics 1995–96
1 thru 3 by Richard Comely .... @2.50

Captain Confederacy #6
© Steel Dragon

CAPT. CONFEDERACY
Steel Dragon 1985–88
1 adult.	6.00
2	2.50
3	2.00
4	2.00
4a	1.50
5 thru 8	@2.00
9 thru 11	@1.75
12	1.95

CAPT. ELECTRON
Brick Computers Inc.
1	2.00
2	2.25

CAPTAIN HARLOCK
Eternity
1	3.00
1a 2nd printing	2.50
2	2.50
3	2.50
4 thru 13	@1.95
Christmas special	2.50
Spec.#1 The Machine People	2.50

CAPTAIN HARLOCK DEATHSHADOW RISING
Eternity 1991
1	2.75
2	2.50
3	2.25
4 Harlock/Nevich Truce	2.25
5 Reunited with Arcadia Crew	2.25
6	2.95

[ADVENTURES OF] CAPTAIN JACK
Fantagraphics
1	4.00
2 & 3	@2.50
4 thru 12	@2.00

CAPTAIN KOALA
Koala Comics 1997
1	2.95
2 thru 7	@2.50

CAPTAIN STERNN: RUNNING OUT OF TIME
Kitchen Sink
1 BWr(c) (1993).	4.95
2 BWr(c)	4.95
3 BWr(c) (1994).	4.95
4 BWr(c)	4.95

CAPTAIN THUNDER AND BLUE BOLT
Hero Graphics
1 New stories	3.50
2 Hard Targets.	3.50

CARTOON HISTORY OF THE UNIVERSE
Rip Off Press
1 Gonick art.	2.50
2 Sticks & Stones	2.50
3 River Realms	2.50
4 Old Testament	2.50
5 Brains & Bronze	2.50
6 These Athenians	2.50
7 All about Athens	2.50

CASES OF SHERLOCK HOLMES
Renegade
1 thru 18	@2.00
19	2.25

CASTLE WAITING
Olio 1997
1 by Linda Medley	10.00
2	5.00
1a 2nd printing	3.00
2a 2nd printing	3.00
3 Labors of Love	3.00
4 birth of Lady Jain's baby	3.00
5	3.00
6 City Mouse, Country Mouse, pt.1	3.00
7 City Mouse, Country Mouse, pt.2	3.00
8	3.00
Spec. The Curse of Brambly Hedge (1996)	3.00
Spec. Curse of Brambly Hedge, revised 1998, 96-page	9.00

CAT & MOUSE
Aircel 1989–92
1	4.00
2	3.00
3 thru 8	@2.25
9 Cat Reveals Identity	2.25
10 Tooth & Nail.	2.25
11 Tooth & Nail.	2.25
12 Tooth & Nail, Demon	2.25
13 'Good Times, Bad Times'.	2.25
14 Mouse Alone	2.25
15 Champion ID revealed	2.25
16 Jerry Critically Ill	2.25
17 Kunoichi vs. Tooth	2.25
18 Search for Organ Donor.	2.25
Graphic Novel	9.95

CAT CLAW
Eternity 1990
1 O:Cat Claw.	2.75
1a 2nd printing	2.50
2 thru 9	@2.50

CATFIGHT
Lightning Comics
1 V:Prince Nightmare.	4.00
1a Gold Edition	6.00
Spec.#1 Dream Warrior, V:The Slasher	2.75
Spec.#1 Dream intoAction,A:Creed.	3.00
Spec.#1a signed and numbered	8.00
Spec.#1b nude cover edition.	8.00
Spec.#1 Escape From Limbo	2.75
Spec.#1a variant cover (1996)	2.75
Spec.#1b platinum cover	5.95
Spec.#1c nude cover	8.00
Spec.#1d variant nude cover	8.00
Spec.#1 Sweet Revenge (1997)	2.95
Spec.#1a variant cover.	2.95
Spec.#1b nude cover	8.00
Spec.#1c nude variant cover.	8.00

CAT-MAN RETRO COMIC
AC Comics
0 by Bill Black & Mark Heike	5.95
1 thru 3	@5.95
Ashcan #1 I:Catman & Kitten.	5.95

CAVEWOMAN
Bacement/Caliber 1994–95
1	70.00
1 by Budd Root 2nd printing	4.00
1 3rd printing, new cover.	3.00
2	40.00
2a 2nd printing	3.00
2 3rd printing, new cover.	3.00
3	35.00
4	35.00
5 Cavewoman vs. Klyde, Round Two.	25.00
6	25.00

CAVEWOMAN: RAIN
Caliber 1996
1 by Budd Root	7.00
1a 2nd printing	3.00
2	5.00
2a 2nd printing	3.00
3	4.00
3a 2nd edition, new cover	3.00
4	4.00
4a 2nd edition, new cover	3.00
5	3.50
5 2nd edition, new cover	3.00
6 thru 8	@3.00

CAVEWOMAN: MISSING LINK
Basement Comics 1997
1 (of 4)	2.95
2 thru 4	@2.95
TPB 96-page	19.95

CAVEWOMAN: PANGAEAN SEA
Basement Comics 1999
1	4.95
Prologue.	2.95

CECIL KUNKLE
Darkline Comics 1987
1 . . . . 1.50

CELESTIAL MECHANICS
Innovation
1 thru 3 . . . . @2.25

CEMENT SHOOZ
Horse Feathers 1991
1 with color pin-up 2.50

CENOTAPH:
CYBER GODDESS
Northstar
1 I:Cenotaph 3.95

CEREBUS
Aardvark–Vanaheim
0 . . . . 3.00
0a Gold Ed. 10.00
1 B:DS(s&a),I:Cerebus 300.00
1a Counterfeit 50.00
2 DS,V:Succubus 75.00
3 DS,I:Red Sophia. 70.00
4 DS,I:Elrod. 50.00
5 DS,A:The Pigts. 40.00
6 DS,I:Jaka 40.00
7 DS,R:Elrod 30.00
8 DS,A:Conniptins 30.00
9 DS,I&V:K'cor. 30.00
10 DS,R:Red Sophia 30.00
11 DS,I:The Cockroach. 30.00
12 DS,R:Elrod 30.00
13 DS,I:Necross. 25.00
14 DS,V:Shadow Crawler 25.00
15 DS,V: Shadow Crawler 25.00
16 DS, at the Masque. 20.00
17 DS,"Champion" 20.00
18 DS,Fluroc 20.00
19 DS,I:Perce & Greet-a 20.00
20 DS,Mind Game 20.00
21 DS,A:CaptCockroach,rare 35.00
22 DS,D:Elrod 15.00
23 DS,DuFort's school 10.00
24 DS,IR:Prof.Clarmont 10.00
25 DS,A:Woman-thing 10.00
26 DS,High Society 10.00
27 DS,Kidnapping of an Avrdvark . 10.00
28 DS,Mind Game!! 10.00
29 DS,Reprocussions 10.00
30 DS,Debts. 8.00
31 DS,Chasing Cootie 8.00
32 DS. 8.00
33 DS,DS,Friction. 5.00
34 DS,Three Days Before. 5.00
35 thru 50 DS . . . . @5.00
51 DS,(scarce) 17.00
52 DS. 5.00
53 DS,C:Wolveroach 7.00
54 DS,I:Wolveroach 9.00
55 DS,A:Wolveroach 8.00
56 DS,A:Wolveroach 8.00
57 DS. 5.00
58 DS. 5.00
59 DS,Memories Pt.V 5.00
60 DS,more vignettes 5.00
61 DS,A:Flaming Carrot 6.00
62 DS,A:Flaming Carrot 6.00
63 DS,Mind Game VI 5.00
64 DS,Never Pray for Change 5.00
65 DS,Papal Speech 5.00
66 DS,Thrill of Agony 5.00
67 thru 70 DS . . . . @5.00
71 thru 74 DS . . . . @4.00
75 DS,Terrible Analogies 4.00

76 DS,D:Weisshaupt 4.00
77 DS,Surreal daydream 4.00
78 DS,Surreal daydream 4.00
79 DS,Spinning Straw. 4.00
80 DS,V:Stone Tarim 4.00
81 DS,A:Sacred Wars Roach 4.00
82 DS,A:Tarim 3.50
83 DS,A:Michele. 3.50
84 DS,Weisshaupt's Letter 3.50
85 DS,A:Mick Jagger 3.50
86 DS,A:Mick Jagger 3.50
87 DS,Tower Climb. 3.50
88 DS,D:Stone Tarim 3.50
89 DS,A:Cute Elf 3.50
90 DS,Anti-Apartheid(c) 3.50
91 DS. 3.50
92 DS,A:Bill & Seth 3.50
93 DS,Astoria in Prison. 3.50
94 DS,Rape of Astoria 3.50
95 DS,Sophia-Astoria Dream 3.50
96 DS,Astoria in Prison. 3.50

Cerebus #47
© Aardvark–Vanaheim

97 DS,Escape Planned. 3.50
98 DS,Astoria's Trial 3.50
99 DS,Sorcery in Court. 3.50
100 DS,A:Cirin 3.50
101 DS,The Gold Sphere 3.00
102 DS,The Final Ascension. 3.00
103 DS,On the Tower. 3.00
104 DS,A:Flaming Carrot 3.00
105 DS,V:Fred & Ethel. 3.00
106 DS,D:Fred & Ethel. 3.00
107 DS,Judge on the Moon 3.00
108 DS,All History 3.00
109 DS,O:Universe. 3.00
110 DS,More Universe 3.00
111 DS,Cerebus' Fate. 3.00
112 DS,Memories. 3.00
113 DS,Memories. 3.00
114 DS,I:Rick nash. 3.00
115 DS,I:Pud Withers 3.00
116 DS,Rick Meets Cerebus. 3.00
117 DS,Young Jaka Injured. 3.00
118 DS,Cerebus Apologizes 3.00
119 DS,Jaka Opens Door 3.00
120 DS,I:Oscar. 3.00
121 DS,Women Explained 3.00
122 DS,Iest History. 3.00
123 DS,Each One's Dream. 3.00
124 DS. 3.00
125 DS,C:Lord Julius 3.00
126 DS,R:Old Vet'ran 2.50
127 DS,Jaka Dances 2.50
128 DS,L:Cerebus as Fred 2.50
129 DS,Jaka's Story 2.50

130 DS,D:Pud Withers 2.50
131 DS,Jaka Imprisoned. 4.00
132 DS,A:Nurse 4.00
133 DS,I:Mrs. Thatcher. 4.00
134 DS,Dancing Debate 4.00
135 DS,Jaka Signs. 4.00
136 DS,L:Rick 4.00
137 DS,Like-a-Looks 4.00
138 DS,Maids'Gossip. 4.00
139 A:Misogynist-roach 4.00
140 I:Old Oscar 4.00
141 A:Cerebus 4.00
142 C:Mick Jagger 4.00
143 DS,Oscars Forboding 4.00
144 DS,I:Doris 4.00
145 thru 146 DS . . . . @4.00
147 Neil Gaiman, DS 7.00
148 thru 150 DS 3.00
151 DS,B:Mothers & Daughters,
  Book 1: Flight pt.1 . . . . 4.00
151a 2nd printing 2.50
152 DS,Flight pt.2. . . . . 4.00
152a 2nd printing 2.50
153 DS,Flight pt.3. . . . . 4.00
153a 2nd printing 2.50
154 DS,Flight pt.4. . . . . 4.00
155 DS,Flight pt.5. . . . . 4.00
156 DS,Flight pt.6. . . . . 3.00
157 DS,Flight pt.7. . . . . 3.00
158 DS,Flight pt.8. . . . . 3.00
159 DS,Flight pt.9. . . . . 3.00
160 DS,Flight pt.10. . . . . 3.00
161 DS,Flight pt.11, Bone story . . . 8.00
162 DS,E:M&D,Bk.1:Flight pt.12 . . 3.00
163 DS,B:Mothers & Daughters
  Book 2: Women pt.1 . . . . 2.75
164 DS,Women pt.2,inc. Tour
  Momentos 2.50
165 thru 174 Women pt.3–12 . . @2.50
175 DS,B:Mothers & Daughters,
  Book 3: Reads pt.1. . . . . 2.50
175 thru 186 Reads pt.1–12 . . . @2.50
187 DS,B:Mothers & Daughters,
  Book 4:Minds pt.1 . . . . 2.50
188 thru 199 Minds pt.5–13. . . . @2.25
200 . . . . 2.50
201 thru 219 Guys pt.1 to pt.19. . @2.25
220 thru 231 Rick's Story, pt.1
  to pt.12. . . . . @2.25
232 thru 245 Going Home,pt.1–14 @2.25
Spec.#1 Cerebus Companion 3.95
TPBs
Vol.1 Cerebus, rep.#1–#25 . . . . . 25.00
Vol.2 High Society, rep.#26–#50 . . 25.00
Vol.3 Church & State I,
  rep.#52–#85. . . . . 30.00
Vol.4 Church & State II,
  rep.#86–#111 . . . . 30.00
Vol.5 Jaka'sStory,rep.#114–#136. . 25.00
Vol.6 Melmoth, rep.#139–#150 . . . 17.00
Vol.7, Flight, rep.#151–#162 . . . . . 17.00
Vol.8 Women, rep.#163–#174. . . . 17.00
Vol.9 Reads, rep.#175–#186. . . . . 17.00
Vol.9 Reads, 2nd printing 15.00
Vol.9 Reads, signed & numb. 28.00
Vol.10 Minds, rep.#187–#199 . . . 16.00
Vol.11 Guys rep.#201–#219 . . . . . 30.00
Vol.11, 2nd printing 20.00
Vol. 12 Rick's Story. 17.00
Vol. 12 signed. 25.00

CEREBUS
CHURCH & STATE
Aardvark–Vanaheim
1 DS rep #51. . . . . 2.25
2 thru 30 DS rep #52–#80 . . . . . @2.00

CEREBUS HIGH SOCIETY
Aardvark–Vanaheim
1 thru 14 DS (biweekly) . . . . . . @1.70
15 thru 24 DS rep. . . . . @2.00
25 DS rep. #50, final. 2.00

CEREBUSJAM
Aardvark–Vanaheim
1 MA,BHa,TA,WE,A:Spirit 15.00

CEREBUS REPRINTS
Aardvark–Vanaheim
1A thru 28A DS rep . . . . @1.25
See also: Church & State
See also: Swords of Cerebus

CHAINSAW VIGILANTE
New England Press
1 Tick Spinoff 3.25

CHAMPION, THE
Special Studio 1991
1 . . . . 2.50

CHAMPION OF KITARA: DUM DUM & DRAGONS
MU Press
1 Dragons Secret 2.95
2 Dragons Secret 2.95
3 Dragons Secret 2.95

CHARLIE CHAN
Eternity
1 thru 4 . . . . @1.95
5 and 6 . . . . @2.25

CHASER PLATOON
Aircel 1990–91
1 Interstellar War. 2.25
2 Ambush 2.25
3 New Weapon 2.25
4 Saringer Battle Robot 2.25
5 Behind Enemy Lines. 2.25
6 Operation Youthtest 2.25

CHESTY SANCHEZ
Antarctic Press 1995
1 & 2. @2.95
Giant Size Spec. #1 (1999). 6.00

CHIBI-POP MANGA
Chibi-Pop (1998)
2 thru 6 64-page . . . . @3.95
VOL 2
1 72-page 3.95

CHINA & JAZZ
ABC Comics 1999
1 RCI. 3.00
1a nude cover. 8.00
1b nude manga ed. 8.00
VOL. 2
1 (of 3) RCI 3.00
1a nude cover. 8.00

CHINA & JAZZ CODE NAME DOUBLE IMPACT
High Impact Oct. 1996
1 . . . . 3.00
1a nude cover. 9.95
2 . . . . 2.95
2a nude RCI(c) cover. 9.95

CHINA & JAZZ: TRIGGER HAPPY
ABC Comics 1998
1 (of 4) by Clayton Henry 3.00
1a Jazz Bikini cover. 3.95
1b China Bikini cover. 3.95
1c gold variant cover 5.95
2 . . . . 3.00
2a Playtoy edition 5.95
2b Mercenary edition. 5.95
2c Gold edition 5.95
Spec. Trigger Happy Special 3.00
Spec.A manga cover 8.00
Spec.B nude manga cover 8.00
Spec. China & Jazz 3.00
Spec. Nude cover A or B. . . . . . . @8.00

CHIRALITY
CPM Manga Comics 1997
6 by Satoshi Urushihara, SS(c) . . . 2.95
7 final battle for Shiori's life 2.95
8 . . . . 2.95
9 Adam transformed into
  duplicate Carol. 2.95
10 . . . . 2.95
11. . . . . 2.95
12 V:Adam 2.95
13 toward Alaska 2.95
14 reach Gaia. 2.95
15 Carol and Shiori. 2.95
16 . . . . 2.95
17 descend into Gaia 2.95
18 final issue 2.95
Spec. Gallery, pin-up book 3.95
GN Book One rep. #1–#4 . . . . 9.95
GN Book Two rep. #4–#8 . . . . 9.95
GN Book Three rep. #8–#12. . . . . 15.95

CHIRALITY: TO THE PROMISED LAND
CPM Comics 1997
1 by Satoshi Urushihara 2.95
2 thru 4 . . . . @2.95

CHIRON
Annurel Studio Graphics
1 . . . . 2.50
1a 2nd printing 2.50
2 Transported to Doran 2.50
3 Transported to Doran 2.50
3a Gold Edition 4.00

CHRONOS CARNIVAL
Fleetway
1 reps. 200 AD stories 7.95

CIRCLE WEAVE, THE
Indigo Bean Productions 1995
1 Apprentice to a God 2.00
2 Apprentice to a God,pt.2. . . . . . 2.00
3 Apprentice to a God,pt.3. . . . . . 2.00
4 Apprentice to a God,pt.4. . . . . . 2.00
5 Apprentice to a God,pt.5. . . . . . 2.50

CLAN APIS
Active Synapse 1998
1 (of 5) by Jay Hosler, F:Bees 2.95
2 F:Nyuki, Zambur. 2.95
3 . . . . 2.95
4 . . . . 2.95
5 conclusion 2.95

CLANDE, INC.
Domain Publishing
1 I:Sam Davidson, Jeremy Clande. 2.95
2 V:Dias 2.95

CLERKS: THE COMIC BOOK
Oni Press 1998
1 by Kevin Smith & Jim Mahfood . . 2.95
Spec. The Lost Scene 2.95
Holiday Special. 2.95

CLIFFHANGER COMICS
AC Comics
1 rep. 2.50
2 rep. 2.50

CLINT THE HAMSTER
Eclipse
1 . . . . 2.50
2 . . . . 1.50

COBRA
Viz 1990–91
1 thru 6 . . . . @2.95
7 . . . . 3.25
8 V:SnowHawks 3.25
9 Zados. 3.25
10 thru 12 . . . . @3.25

COLD BLOODED CHAMELEON COMMANDOS
Blackthorne 1986
1 . . . . 2.00
2 . . . . 1.50
3 . . . . 1.50
4 . . . . 1.75

Cold Blooded Chameleon Commandos #3 © Blackthorne

5 .... 1.75
6 .... 2.00
7 .... 2.00

COLD EDEN
Legacy 1995
1 Last City on Earth............ 2.35
2 V:Mutant Hunting Pack........ 2.35
3 D6 Tower.................. 2.35

COLE BLACK
1 Vol.I........................ 15.00
2 Vol.I........................ 10.00
3 Vol.I........................ 10.00
4 Vol.I........................ 10.00
5 Vol.I........................ 12.00
1 Vol.II....................... 3.50
2 Vol.II....................... 2.00
3 Vol.II....................... 1.50

COLONEL KILGORE
Special Studios
1 WWII stories................ 2.50
2 Command Performance 2.50

COLT
K-Z Comics
1 .... 4.00
2 pin-up by Laird............. 6.00
2 pin-up by Henbeck.......... 2.00
3 thru 5 .... @1.00

COMICS EXPRESS
1 thru 4 .... @2.95
5 thru 11 .... @3.95

COMING OF APHRODITE
Hero Graphics
1 Aphrodite/modern day 3.95

COMMAND REVIEW
Thoughts & Images
1 rep. Albedo #1-4............ 6.00
2 rep. Albedo #5-8............ 4.00
3 rep. Albedo #9-13........... 4.00

CONDOM-MAN
Aaaahh!! Comics
1 I:Condom Man.............. 3.50
2 F:Condom Man.............. 3.50
3 V:Alien Army 3.50
4 Brother bought back to life ... 3.50
5 O:Condom-Man (Chris Swafford) 3.50

CONQUEROR
Harrier 1984–86
1 .... 3.50
2 thru 4 .... @2.00
5 thru 9 .... @1.75

CONQUEROR UNIVERSE
Harrier
1 .... 2.75

CONSPIRACY COMICS
Revolutionary
1 Marilyn Monroe 2.50
2 Who Killed JFK 2.50
3 Who Killed RFK 2.50

CONSTELLATION GRAPHICS
STG
1 thru 4 .... @1.50

CONSTRUCT
Caliber "New Worlds"
1 (of 6) PJe,LDu, sci-fi,48pg ... 3.95
2 PJe,LDu.................... 2.95
3 PJe,LDu.................... 2.95
4 PJe,LDu.................... 2.95
5 PJe,LDu.................... 2.95
6 PJe,LDu, conclusion......... 2.95

CORMAC MAC ART
1 thru 4 R.E.Howard adapt..... @1.95

CORTO MALTESE: BALLAD OF THE SALT SEA
NBM 1997
1 by Hugo Pratt............... 2.95
1 a 2nd printing 2.95
2 by Hugo Pratt............... 2.95
3 Escondida 2.95
4 .... 2.95
5 .... 2.95
6 .... 2.95
7 final issue 2.95
TPB by Hugo Pratt, "In Siberia".. 10.95
TPB "Fable of Venice"......... 10.95
TPB "Banana Conga" 8.95
TPB "Voodoo for the President" .. 8.95
TPB "Midwinter's Morning" 8.95
TPB "In Africa"............... 8.95

Cosmic Heroes #7
© Eternity

COSMIC HEROES
Eternity
1 Buck Rogers rep............. 1.95
2 thru 6 Buck Rogers rep...... @1.95
7 thru 9 Buck Rogers rep...... @2.25
10 .... 3.50
11 .... 3.95

COUNTER PARTS
Tundra
1 thru 3 .... @2.95

COVENTRY
Fantagraphics Oct. 1996
1 BWg, "The Frogs of God" 3.95
2 BWg, "Thirteen Dead Guys
   Named Bob" 3.95
3 BWg....................... 3.95
4 .... 3.95

CRAY BABY ADVENTURES, THE
Electric Milk 1997
1 by Art Baltazar............. 3.00
TV Comics 1997
1 2nd printing 3.00
2 .... 3.00
4 Captain Camel............. 3.00
5 .... 3.00
Advent.Spec.San Diego Con
   lim. ed................... 5.00
TPB Vol. 1 rep. #1–#5 .... 14.95

CRAY BABY ADVENTURES: WRATH OF THE PEDDIDLERS
TV Comics 1998
1 (of 3) by Art Baltazar 3.00
2 .... 3.00
3 concl. 3.00

CREED
Hall of Heroes 1994
1 TKn,I:Mark Farley........... 30.00
1A Wizard Ace edition rep. 20.00
2 TKn,Camping.............. 35.00

CREED
Lightning Comics 1995
1-shot TKn retelling of #1&#2 .... 2.75
See also: Color

CREED THE VOID
TPB Collected edition.......... 5.95
TPB Deluxe 9.95

CREED/TEENAGE MUTANT NINJA TURTLES
Lightning Comics 1996
1 TKn(c) 3.00
2 TKn(c) 3.00
1 Gold Collector's Edition....... 5.95
1 Platinum Edition 9.95

CREED: CRANIAL DISORDER
Lightning Comics
1 .... 3.00
1A Previews variant cover....... 3.00
1B Platinum Edition........... 6.00
1C signed platinum edition...... 8.00
2 .... 3.00
2b variant cover............. 2.95
3 .... 2.95
3b variant cover............. 2.95
3c limited edition 9.95

CREED: THE GOOD SHIP & THE NEW JOURNEY HOME
Lightning Comics
1 .... 2.95

1a variant cover 2.95
1b limited edition 9.95

CREED: USE YOUR DELUSION
Avatar Press 1998
1 (of 2) by Trent Kaniuga 3.00
1 white leather 30.00
2 . . . . 3.00
2 deluxe 4.95
GN rep. #1–#2 . . . . 3.95

CRIME BUSTER
AC Comics
0 from FemForce 2.95
1 Rep. From Boys Illustrated 3.95

CRIME CLASSICS
Eternity
1 thru 11 rep Shadow comicstrip @1.95
12 . . . . 2.25

CRIMSON DREAMS
Crimson
1 thru 11 . . . . @2.00

CRIMSON NUN
Antarctic Press 1997
1 (of 4) 2.95

CRITTERS
Fantagraphics Books 1986–90
1 SS,Usagi Yojimbo,Cutey 5.00
2 Captain Jack,Birthright 4.00
3 SS,Usagi Yojimbo,Gnuff 4.00
4 Gnuff,Birthright 3.00
5 Birthright 3.00
6 SS,Usagi Yojimbo,Birthright 3.00
7 SS,Usagi Yojimbo,Jack Bunny . . 3.00
8 SK,Animal Graffiti,Lizards 2.50
9 Animal Graffiti 2.50
10 SS,Usagi Yojimbo 3.00
11 SS,Usagi Yojimbo, ... 3.00
12 Birthright II 2.00
13 Birthright II,Gnuff 2.00
14 SS,Usagi Yojimbo,BirthrightII . . 2.50
15 Birthright II,CareBears 2.00
16 SS,Groundthumper,Gnuff 2.00
17 Birthright II,Lionheart 2.00
18 Dragon's 2.00
19 Gnuff,Dragon's 2.00
20 Gnuff 2.00
21 Gnuff 2.00
22 Watchdogs,Gnuff 2.00
23 Flexi-Disc,X-Mas Issue 4.00
24 Angst,Lizards,Gnuff 2.00
25 Lionheart,SBi,Gnuff 2.00
26 Angst,Gnuff 2.00
27 SS,Ground Thumper 2.00
28 Blue Beagle,Lionheart 2.00
29 Lionheart,Gnuff 2.00
30 Radical Dog,Gnuff 2.00
31 SBi,Gnuffs,Lizards 2.00
32 Lizards,Big Sneeze 2.00
33 Gnuff,Angst,Big Sneeze 2.00
34 Blue Beagle vs. Robohop 2.00
35 Lionheart,Fission Chicken 2.00
36 Blue Beagle,Fission Chicken . . . 2.00
37 Fission Chicken 2.00
38 SS,double size,Usagi Yojimbo . . 2.75
39 Fission Chicken 2.00
40 Gnuff 2.00
41 Duck'Bill Platypus 2.00
42 Glass Onion 2.00
43 Lionheart 2.00

44 Watchdogs 2.00
45 Ambrose the Frog 2.00
46 Lionheart 2.00
47 Birthright 2.00
48 Birthright 2.00
49 Birthright 2.00
50 SS,Neil the Horse, UsagiYojimbo 5.00
Spec.1 Albedo,rep+new 10pgStory . 2.00

CROSSFIRE
Eclipse
18 thru 26 DSp . . . . @2.00

CROW, THE
Caliber
1 . . . . 30.00
1a 2nd Printing 4.00
1b 3rd Printing 3.00
2 . . . . 22.00
2a 2nd Printing 4.00
2b 3rd Printing 3.00
3 . . . . 20.00
3a 2nd Printing 3.00
4 . . . . 20.00
Tundra
1 reps. Crow #1, #2 . . . . 15.00
2 . . . . 8.00
3 . . . . 10.00
TPB 20.00

CROW, THE
Kitchen Sink
TPB Flesh & Blood Collection 10.95
TPB The Crow Collection,
  7th printing 224pg. 15.95
HC Author's Edition 280-page 35.00
HC signed and numbered 60.00

CROW, THE: DEAD TIME
Kitchen Sink
1 . . . . 5.00
2 . . . . 4.00
3 . . . . 3.00
TPB Collection rep. 10.95

CROW, THE: DEMON IN DISGUISE
Kitchen Sink 1997
1 (of 4) by John J. Miller &
  Dean Ormston 2.95
2 . . . . 2.95
3 . . . . 2.95

CROW, THE: FLESH AND BLOOD
Kitchen Sink 1996
1 thru 3 . . . . @2.95
TPB rep. 96-page 10.95
HC signed & numbered 50.00

CROW, THE: WAKING NIGHTMARES
Kitchen Sink Jan. 1997
1 PhH 2.95
2 thru 4 PhH . . . . @2.95

CROW, THE: WILD JUSTICE
Kitchen Sink
1 thru 3 . . . . @2.95

Crow/Razor: Kill the Pain #0
© London Night

CROW/RAZOR: KILL THE PAIN
London Night 1998
1 (of 3) JOb,EHr, ... 3.00
1b EHr & Jerry Beck, Director's
  Cut, 40pg 5.00
1c black leather, signed
  & numbered 29.95
1d Ministry of Night (c) 5.00
2 . . . . 3.00
2a Ministry of Night (c) 5.00
3 . . . . 3.00
3a Ministry of Night (c) 5.00
4 . . . . 3.00
4a Ministry of Night (c) 6.00
4b Leather edition 15.00
4c Leather edition, signed 15.00
Spec. Finale 3.00
Spec. Finale, Ministry (c) 5.00
0 . . . . 3.00
0a Ministry (c) 5.00
0b Red Velvet Elite 20.00
1-shotA Tour Book, cover A 5.00
1-shotB Tour Book, cover B 5.00
1-shotC Tour Book, cover C 5.00
1-shotD Tour Book, ministry edition. 5.00
1-shotE Tour Book, limited black
  leather 15.00
1-shotF Tour Book, signed 18.00
Spec. Nocturnal Masque 48-page . . 5.95
TPB Kill The Pain, 150-page 15.95
HC Kill The Pain, Sketch
  limited signed ed 50.00

EH! Productions 1999
Spec. The Lost Chapter 4.95
Spec. The Lost Chapter,
  Elite Fan Ed. 6.00

CROW OF THE BEAR CLAN
Blackthorne
1 . . . . 2.25
2 thru 6 . . . . @1.75

CRUSADERS
Guild
1 Southern Knights 10.00

All comics prices listed are for *Near Mint* condition.

B & W PUB.

CRY FOR DAWN
Cry For Dawn 1989–90
1	155.00
1a 2nd Printing	70.00
1b 3rd Printing.	65.00
2	100.00
2a 2nd Printing	25.00
3	65.00
4	50.00
5	40.00
6	40.00
7 Corporate Ladder,Rock A Bye Baby	30.00
8 Decay,This is the Enemy	25.00
9	25.00
1-shot Subtle Violents,F:Ryder	3.00

CRYING FREEMAN
Viz 1989
1	4.00
2	3.50
3 thru 5	@3.50
6 thru 8	@3.00

CRYING FREEMAN II
Viz 1990–91
1	4.00
2	3.50
3	3.50
4 thru 6	@3.00
7 V:Bugnug	3.00
8 Emu & The Samurai Sword	3.00
9 Final Issue	3.00

CRYING FREEMAN III
Viz 1991
1 thru 10	@4.00

CRYING FREEMAN IV
Viz 1992
1 thru 3	@4.00
4 thru 8	@2.75

CRY FREEMAN V
Viz 1993
1 Return to Japan	4.00
2 A:Tateoka-assassin.	4.00
3	4.00
4 A:Bagwana.	4.00
5 V:Tsunaike	4.00
6 V:Aido Family	4.00
7 V:Tsunaike	4.00
GN:Taste of Revenge	14.95

CRYPT OF DAWN
Sirius 1996
1 JLi(c)	6.00
1 variant cover.	12.00
2 JLi(c)	3.50
3	3.00
4 JLi(c)	3.00
5 JLi(c)	2.95
6 Vanguard of Comics	2.95

CRYSTAL BREEZE
High Impact 1996
1 thru 3	@2.95
1 thru 3a nude covers	@10.00
Spec.#1 Crystal Breeze Unleashed.	3.00
Spec.#1a nude cover	14.95
Spec.#1 Crystal Breeze Revenge.	2.95
Spec.#1a adult photo cover	10.00
Spec.#1b gold edition cover	10.00

CUDA
Rebel Studios
1 I:Cuda,Zora,V:Shanga Bai	2.00
CUDA B.C. (Rebel Studios) signed	12.95

Avatar Press 1998
1 (of 4) by Tim & Joe Vigil	3.50
1a Gore cover.	3.95
1b Lether cover.	25.00
1c nude cover.	6.00
1d signed	15.00
1e Royal Blue edition.	75.00
2	3.50
2a Gore cover.	3.95
2b nude cover.	6.00
3	3.50
3a Gore cover.	6.00
3b nude cover.	6.00
4	3.50
4a Gore cover.	6.00
4b nude cover.	6.00

CULTURAL JET LAG
Fantagraphics
1	2.50

CUTEY BUNNY
1	8.00
2 thru 4	@4.00

Eclipse
5	3.00

CUTIE HONEY
Ironcat 1997
1 crime fighting android	2.95
2	2.95
3 Wonderful Mask	2.95
4 thru 6	@2.95

VOL 2 CUTIE HONEY '90 1998
1 Sorayama cover.	2.95
2 thru 6	@2.95

CYBER 7
Eclipse
1	2.50
2 thru 5	@2.00

Book 2: Rockland 1990
1 thru 7	@2.00
8 thru 10	@2.50

Cyber 7, Book Two, #7
© Eclipse

CYBERFROG
Hall of Heroes
1 I:Cyberfrog.	5.00
1a 2nd printing	2.50
2 V:Ben Riley	4.00
2a 2nd printing	2.50

CYBERFROG
Harris Jan. 1997
1 3rd Anniv. Special.	3.00
1a Walt Simonson(c).	6.00
1b signed & numbered.	10.00
2	3.50
2a variant cover.	4.00
3	3.50
4	3.50
4a signed	10.00
Ashcan Cyberfrog: Amphibionix	6.00

CYBERFROG VS CREED
Harris 1997
1	3.50
1 Creed vs. Cyberfrog, alternate edition	9.95

CYBERZONE
Jet Black Graphics
1 thru 5 Never-never Land.	2.50

CYCLOPS
Blackthorne
1 Mini-series	1.95
2	1.95
3	1.95

CYGNUS X-1
Twisted Pearl Press
1 V:Yag'Nost	2.50
2 F:Rex and Bounty Hunters	2.50

CYNDER
Immortelle Studios
1 I:Cynder.	5.00
2	3.00
3 conclusion	2.50

Second Series
1 thru 3	3.00

CYNDER/HELLINA
Immortelle Studios
Spec. 1 x-over	3.00

DAIKAZU
1	5.00
1a 2nd Printing	1.50
2	3.00
2a 2nd Printing	1.50
3	3.00
3a 2nd Printing	1.50
4 thru 7	@1.50
8	1.75

DA'KOTA
Millennium Jan. 1997
1 by Pavlet & Petersen	2.95
1 signed	4.95
1 foil edition.	9.95
2	2.95
2 foil edition.	4.95
3 foil deluxe edition	6.95
3	2.95
3a variant cover.	2.95

Spec.#1 Orig.Art Edition 9.95

DAMONSTREIK
Imperial Comics
1 I:Damonstreik. 1.95
2 V:Sonix. 1.95
3 V:Sonix. 1.95
4 J:Ohm 1.95
5 V:Drakkus. 1.95

DANGEROUS TIMES
1 MK. 2.50
2 MA(c) 2.00
2a 2nd printing 1.75
3 MR(c) 1.95
3a 2nd printing 1.95
4 GP(c) 1.95

DAN TURNER
HOLLYWOOD DETECTIVE
Eternity 1991
1 `Darkstar of Death' 2.50
Spec.#1 Dan Turner, Homicide
  Hunch, Dan Turner Framed . . . 2.50
Spec.#1 Dan Turner, The Star
  Chamber, Death of Folly
  Hempstead. 2.50

DARK ANGEL
Boneyard 1997
1 by Hart Fisher &
  James Helkowski 1.95
2 . . . . 1.95
3 by Hart Fisher & John Cassaday 1.95
4 The Quiet Demon 1.95
Spec.#1 Dark Angel/Bill the Bull,
  48-page (1998). 4.95
Spec. 1999 . . . . 4.95

DARK ANGEL
CPM Manga 1999
1 by Kia Asamiya 2.95
2 . . . . 2.95
3 . . . . 2.95
4 . . . . 2.95

DARK ASSASSIN
1 thru 3 . . . . @1.50
Vol. 2
1 thru 5 . . . . @2.00

DARK CITY ANGEL
Freak Pit Productions
1 I:Lt.Michelle Constello. 3.50
2 . . . . 3.50
3 Sex Doll is Prime Suspect 3.50

DARK FANTASIES
Dark Fantasy 1994–97
0 Donna Mia foil (c) 8.00
0 Destiny Angel foil (c). 7.50
0 photo or nude (c)s. . . . . @6.00
1 Jli (c) 9.00
1a test print Jli (c) 12.00
1 2nd printing 3.95
1 signed & numbered 7.95
2 Kevin J. Taylor Girl (c) 3.50
2a foil stamped 3.50
3 JOb Crow (c) 4.00
3a foil stamped 3.50
4 . . . . 2.95
4a foil stamped 3.50
5 . . . . 2.95
5a foil stamped 3.50

Dark Fantasies #6
© Dark Fantasy

6 Angel Destiny 2.95
6a foil stamped 3.50
7 . . . . 2.95
7a foil stamped 3.50
8 . . . . 2.95
8 Blue cover 3.50
8 Red cover. 3.50
8 deluxe foil-enhanced. 3.95
9 Destiny Angel (c) 3.95
9a Destiny Angel, red foil (c) 3.95
9b Horror (c) 3.50
9c Horror, red foil (c) 3.95
10 . . . . 3.50
10a red foil (c) 3.95
Spec.#1 Summers Eve Pin-up 2.95
Spec.#1 foil-stamped 3.50

DARK FORCE
Omega 7
1 A:Dark Force 2.00

DARK FRINGE
Brainstorm 1996
1 . . . . 2.95

DARK FRINGE:
SPIRITS OF THE DEAD
Brainstorm 1997
1 by Eman Torre & John Kisse. . . . 2.95
2 concl. 2.95

DARK ISLAND
Davdez Arts 1998
1 by Barry Blair & Colin Chan 2.50
2 thru 4 . . . . @2.50

DARK LORD
RAK
1 thru 3 . . . . @1.75

DARK MANGA
London Night
1 Featuring Demonique 4.95
1 nude cover 6.00

DARK MUSE
Dark Muse Productions
1 with mini-comic. 3.50
1a with mini-comic. 5.00
2 . . . . 3.95
3 F:Coffin Joe 3.95

DARK OZ
Arrow Comics 1997
1 (of 5) by Griffith, Kerr & Bryan. . . 2.75
2 . . . . 2.75
3 . . . . 2.75
4 . . . . 2.75
5 . . . . 2.75
Spec. Bill Bryan's Oz Collection . . . 2.95

DARK REGIONS
1 . . . . 2.50
2 . . . . 2.50
3 Scarce 3.00
4 and 5 . . . . @1.50

DARK STAR
1 I:Ran 2.25
2 thru 3 . . . . @2.25

DARK VISIONS
Pyramid
1 I:Wasteland Man. 1.70
2 thru 4 . . . . @1.70

DARK WOLF
Eternity
1 and 2 . . . . @1.95
Volume 2
1 thru 14 . . . . @1.95
Ann. #1 . . . . 2.25

DARQUE RAZOR
London Night 1996
½ by Dan Membeila & Albert Holaso,
  Dark Birth. 2.25
½ necro-embossed edition. 10.00
1 . . . . 3.00
1a nude cover 10.00
2 . . . . 3.00
3 . . . . 3.00

DAYS OF DARKNESS
Apple
1 From Pearl Harbor
  to Midway. 2.75
2 Pearl Harbor Attack,cont. 2.75
3 Japanese Juggernaut 2.75
4 Bataan Peninsula 2.75
GN 14.95

DEADBEATS
Claypool Comics 1993
1 thru 13 . . . . @2.50
14 New Ways to Dream 2.50
15 thru 25. . . . . @2.50
26 by Richard Howell & Ricardo
  Villagran, The Southland
  Family Saga. 2.50
27 Christine transformed into
  Predator. 2.50
28 . . . . 2.50
29 forbidden antiquities. 2.50
30 V:Dracula 2.50
31 Reconstructing Deadbeats. . . . 2.50
32 New generation of Deadbeats . . 2.50
33 Quiet Night in Fear City 2.50
34 Dagger of Deliverance 2.50

35 Deadbeats of Danger Street . . . 2.50
36 By His Majesty's Request 2.50
37 Carnival of Goals. 2.50
TPB Rep. #1–#6. . . . . 12.95

DEADKILLER
Caliber
1 Rep Deadworld 19 thru 21 . . . . . 2.95

DEADTALES
Caliber
1 'When a Body Meets a Body' . . . 2.95

DEADTIME STORIES
1 AAd,WS 1.75

DEADWORLD
Arrow
1 Arrow Pyb 5.00
2 . . . . 4.00
3 V:King Zombie 3.50
4 V:King Zombie 3.50
5 Team Rests 3.50
6 V:King Zombie 3.50
7 F:KZ & Deake, Graphic(c). 3.50
7a Tame cover. 2.00
8 V:Living Corpse, Graphic(c) 2.50
8a Tame cover. 2.00
9 V:Sadistic Punks, Graphic(c). . . 2.50
9a Tame cover. 2.00
10 V:King Zombie, Graphic(c). . . . 2.50
10a Tame cover 2.00
11 V:King Zombie, Graphic(c) 3.00
11a Tame cover 2.50
12 I:Percy, Graphic(c). 3.00
12a Tame cover 2.50
13 V:King Zombie, Graphic(c). . . . 3.00
13a Tame cover 2.50
14 V:Voodoo Cult,Graphic(c). 3.00
14a Tame cover 2.50
15 Zombie stories,Graphic(c) 3.00
15a Tame cover 2.50
16 V:`Civilized' Community 2.50
17 V:King Zombie. 2.50
18 V:King Zombie. 2.50
19 V:Grakken 2.50
20 V:King Zombie. 2.50
21 Dead Killer. 2.50
22 L:Dan & Joey. 2.50
23 V:King Zombie. 2.50
24 . . . . 2.50
25 (R:Vince Locke). 2.50
26 . . . . 2.50

Caliber
1 thru 11 . . . . @2.95
12 thru 14 Death Call . . . . @2.95
15 Death Call pt. 6 . . . . 2.95
Spec. Deadworld Archives, rep. . . . 2.50
Spec. Bits & Pieces, rep.
    Caliber Presents #2&#8 . . . . . . 1.60
Spec. To Kill A King,R:Deadkiller . . 2.95

DEATH ANGEL
Lightning 1997
1 by J. Cleary & Anderson. 2.95
1 variant cover. 2.95
1 limited edition A 9.95
1 limited edition B 9.95

DEATH OF ANGEL GIRL
Angel Entertainment 1997
1 by Ellis Bell & Cam Forrest,
    F:Michelle 2.95
1A Deluxe Erotic Nude cover. 3.95
1B Deluxe Erotic Nude cover. . . . 15.00

DEATH OF BLOODFIRE
Lightning
1 . . . . 3.00
1a variant cover. 3.00

DEATHDREAMS OF DRACULA
Apple
1 Selection of short stories 2.50
2 short stories 2.50
3 Inc. Rep. BWr,`Breathless' 2.50
4 short stories 2.50

DEATH HUNT
Eternity
1 . . . . 1.95
2 . . . . 1.95

DEATHMARK
Lightning Comics
1 O:War Party 2.75

DEATH RATTLE
Kitchen Sink
(Prev. Color)
4 . . . . 3.00
5 . . . . 2.50
6 Steve Bissette(c) 2.00
7 Ed Gein 2.00
8 I:Xenozoic Tales 10.00
9 BW,rep. 2.00
10 AW,rep. 2.00
11 thru 15 . . . . @2.00
16 BW,Spacehawk 2.00
17 Rand Holmes(c) 2.00
18 FMc. 2.00

DEATH'S HEAD
Crystal
1 thru 3 . . . . @1.95

DEATHWORLD
Adventure Comics 1990
1 Harry Harrison adapt. 2.50
2 thru 4 . . . . @2.50
BOOK II 1991
1 Harry Harrison adapt. 2.50
2 thru 4 . . . . @2.50
BOOK III 1991
1 H.Harrison adapt.,colonization . . 2.50
2 Attack on the Lowlands. 2.50
3 Attack on the Lowlands contd. . . 2.50
4 last issue 2.50

DEE VEE
Dee Vee Feb. 1997
1 ECa, F:Alex 2.95
2 ECa 2.95
3 ECa 2.95
4 thru 12 . . . . @2.95
Spec. #1 Life is Cheap 2.95

DEFENSELESS DEAD
Adventure Comics 1991
1 Larry Niven adapt. A:Gil 2.50
2 A:Organlegger 2.50
3 A:Organlegger 2.50

DELTA TENN
1 thru 11 . . . . @1.50

Defenceless Dead #3
© Adventure

DEMON BABY
SQP/666 Comics Jan. 1997
1 by Rich Larson, seq. to Hell
    on Heels 2.95
1a deluxe 9.95
2 . . . . 2.95
2a deluxe 9.95
3 . . . . 2.95
3a deluxe 9.95
GN Hell on Heels 9.95
GN Hell on Heels, deluxe 19.95

DEMON BITCH
Forbidden 1997–98
1-shot 2.95
    Nude cover 2.95
Spec.#1 DemonBitch vs.AngelGirl . 2.95
    Nude cover 4.00
Spec.#1 Demon Bitch: Devilspawn, by
    Angela Benoit & Nirut Chaswan 3.00
    Nude cover 3.00
Spec.#1 Demon Bitch: Hellslave,
    Free on Earth cover 3.00
    Nude Hellslave cover 3.00
Spec.#1 Demon Bitch: Tales of
    the Damned 2.95
    Nude cover 4.00

DEMONGATE
Sirius 1996–97
1 thru 12 by Bao Lin Hum &
    Colin Chan . . . . @2.50

DEMON GUN
Crusade Entertainment
1 thru 3 GCh,KtH . . . . @2.95

DEMON HUNTER
Aircel
1 thru 4 . . . . @1.95

DEMON HUNTER
Davdez Arts 1998
1 by Barry Blair & Colin Chan 2.50
2 F:Hunter Gordon 2.50
3 . . . . 2.50

DEMONIQUE
London Night 1997
½ by SKy Owens, A:Anvil 3.00
½a nude cover 6.00
1 by Membeila & Owens 3.00
1a nude cover variant 8.00
2 F:Viper 3.00
3 Mayhem 3.00
4 Final issue 3.00

DEMONIQUE:
ANGEL OF NIGHT
London Night 1997
1 (of 3) by Skylar Owens 3.00
1a nude cover variant 6.00
2 . . . . 3.00
2a nude cover variant 6.00
3 final issue 3.00
3a nude cover variant 6.00

DEMON'S TAILS
Adventure
1 . . . . 2.50
2 A:Champion 2.50
3 V:Champion 2.50
4 V:Champion 2.50

DEMON WARRIOR
1 thru 12 . . . . @1.50
13 and 14 . . . . @1.75

DENIZENS OF
DEEP CITY
Jabberwocky
1 thru 8 . . . . @2.00

DERRECK WAYNE'S
STRAPPED
Gothic Images
1 Confrontational Factor 2.25
2 Confrontational Factor 2.25

Descending Angels #1
© Millenium

DESCENDING ANGELS
Millenium 1995
1 I:3 Angels 2.00
2 F:Jim Johnson 2.95
3 F:Jim Johnson 2.95

DESERT PEACH
Thoughts & Images
1 thru 4 . . . . @2.00

DESTINY ANGEL
Dark Fantasy Productions 1996
1 (of 3) 3.95
1 2nd printing 3.95
1a deluxe 4.50
2 "Sunless Garden" 3.50
2a foil cover 3.95
2b photo cover 3.95

DESTROY
Eclipse
1 Large Size 4.95
2 Small Size,3-D 4.95

DETECTIVE, THE
Caliber 1998
1 by Gerard Goffaux 2.95
2 . . . . 2.95
3 Clutches of the Past 2.95

DEVIL JACK
Doom Theatre 1995
1 I:Devil Jack 2.95
1a Directors Cut 2.95
2 V:Belegosi 2.95
3 . . . . 3.00

DEVIL'S WORKSHOP
Blue Comet Press 1995
1 Iron Cupcakes 2.95

DICK DANGER
Olsen Comics 1998
1 by W.W. Olsen 2.95
2 F:Red Olga 2.95
3 The Angel Murder 2.95
4 Is Hitler Still Alive? 2.95
5 Nikita, The Cat Girl 2.95

DICK TRACY
CRIMEBUSTER
ACG Comics 1998
1 by Max Allan Collins
   & Dick Locher 2.95
2 thru 7 . . . . @2.95

DICK TRACY MAGAZINE
1 V:Little Face Finnyo 3.95

DICK TRACY MONTHLY
Blackthorne
1 thru 25 . . . . @2.00

DICK TRACY:
THE EARLY YEARS
5 and 6 . . . . @2.95
7 and 8 . . . . @3.50

DICK TRACY WEEKLY
26 thru 108 . . . . @2.00
Unprinted Stories #3 . . . . 2.95
1 3-D Special 3.00
Spec. #1 . . . . 2.95
Spec. #2 . . . . 2.95
Spec. #3 . . . . 2.95

DICKS
Caliber 1997
1 (of 4),GEn,JMC, ... 2.95
2 GEn,JMC 2.95
3 GEn,JMC 2.95
4 concl. 2.95
TPB GEn,JMC 12.95

DIGITAL DRAGON
Peregrine Entertainment 1999
1 by Bryan Heyboer 2.95
2 . . . . 2.95
3 . . . . 2.95
4 . . . . 2.95

DILLINGER
Rip Off Press
1 Outlaw Dillinger 2.50

DIM-WITTED DARRYL
Slave Labor Graphics 1998
1 by Michael Bresnahan 2.95
2 thru 5 . . . . @2.95

DINOSAURS
Caliber
1 History of Dinosaurs 3.00

DINOSAURS FOR HIRE
Eternity
1 . . . . 3.00
1a Rep. 1.95
2 thru 9 . . . . @1.95
Fall Classic #1 . . . . 2.25

Malibu
#1 3-D special 3.50

DIRECTORY TO A NON-
EXISTENT UNIVERSE
Eclipse
1 . . . . 1.95

DIRTY PAIR
1 . . . . 10.00
2 . . . . 8.00
3 . . . . 7.00
4 end mini-series 7.00

Eclipse
reprint 1-3 . . . . 5.00
Vol 2 #1 thru 5 . . . . @5.00

DIRTY PAIR:
PLAGUE OF ANGELS
Eclipse 1990
1 thru 5 . . . . @5.00

DIRTY PAIR:
SIM EARTH
Eclipse
1 thru 4 . . . . 4.00

DISCIPLES
Caliber Core 1998
1 Climate of fear 2.95
2 . . . . 2.95

A DISTANT SOIL
Warp Graphics
1 A:Panda Khan 10.00

2	5.00
3	4.00
4	3.00
5	3.00
6 thru 9	@3.00

Aria Press

1 F:Seasons of Spring	6.00
1a-2nd to 4th printing	2.50
2	5.00
3	3.00
4	3.00
5 thru 8	2.50
9 thru 11 Knights of the Angel	@2.50
12 thru 14	@3.00
GN Knights of the Angel, deluxe	15.95
GN Immigrant Song rep.#1–#3	6.95

DITKOS WORLD: STATIC
Renegade

1 thru 3 SD	@1.70

DOCTOR
Ironcat 1997

1 (of 5) by Bang Ippongi	2.95
2	2.95
4	2.95
5 Pay Back in the City of Santa La Paz	2.95
6 final issue	2.95

DR. GORPON
Eternity 1991

1 I:Dr.Gorpon,V:Demon	2.25
2 A:Doofus,V:ChocolateBunny	2.50
3 D:Dr.Gorpon	2.50

DR. RADIUM
Silverline

1	3.00
2	2.00
3 and 4	@1.50

DR. RADIUM: MAN OF SCIENCE
Slave Labor

1 And Baby makes 2, BU: Dr. Radiums' Grim Future	2.50

DOC WEIRD'S THRILL BOOK

1 AW	1.75
2	1.75
3	1.75

DOCTOR WEIRD
Caliber Press

1 V:Charnogg	2.50
2 V:Charnogg	2.50

DODEKAIN
Antarctic Press

1 and 2 by Masayuki Fujihara	@2.95
3 Rampage Vs. Zogerians	2.95
4 V:Zogerians	2.95
5 F:Takuma	2.95
6 Dan vs. Takuma	2.75
7 V:Okizon	2.75
8 V:Okizon	2.95

DOGAROO
Blackthorne 1988

1	2.00

Dogs of War #3
© Crusade Entertainment

DOGS O'WAR, THE
Crusade Entertainment 1996–97

1 thru 3 (of 3)	@2.95

DOLLS
Sirius 1998

1-shot science fiction	2.95

DOMINION
Eclipse

1	3.00
2 thru 6	@2.00

DOMINO CHANCE
Chance

1 1,000 printed	10.00
1a 2nd printing	3.50
2 thru 6	@3.00
7 I:Gizmo	7.00
8 A:Gizmo	11.00
9	2.50

[2nd Series]

1	3.00
2 and 3	@1.95

DONATELLO
Mirage

1 A: Turtles	12.00

DONNA MIA
Avatar Press 1997

0 by Tevlin Utz	3.00
0a nude cover	4.95
0b leather cover	15.00
0c signed	8.00
1	3.95
1a signed	8.00
1b Royal Blue edition	50.00
2	3.95
2a deluxe	4.50
3 (of 3)	3.00
3a deluxe	10.00
Giant Size #1	3.00
Giant Size #1 nude	4.95
Giant Size #1 leather cover	15.00
Giant Size #1 signed	8.00
Giant Size #2	3.95

Giant Size #2 Deluxe	10.00
TPB rep. #0–#3 & Giant Size #1–#2	15.95
HC rep. #0–#3 & Giant Size #1–#2 deluxe	39.95
HC rep. #0–#3 & Giant Size #1–#2 with original sketch	150.00
Spec. Infinity	3.00
Spec. Infinity, nude cover	4.95
Spec. Infinity, Leather cover	25.00
Spec.#1 Pin-up (1997)	3.00
Spec.#1a nude cover	4.95

DON SIMPSON'S BIZARRE HEROES
Fiasco Comics

0 thru 7	2.95
8 V:Darkcease	2.95
9 R:Yan Man	2.95
10 F:Mainstreamers	2.95
11 Search for Megaton Man	2.95
12	2.95
13 House of Megaton Man	2.95
14 Cec Vs. Dark Cease	2.95
TPB Apocalypse Affiliation	12.95

DOOMSDAY + 1
ACG Comics 1998

1 by JBn rep. Charlton	2.95
2 A Faceless Foe	2.95
3	2.95
4 The Hidden Enemy	2.95
5 Rule of Fear	2.95
6	2.95
7 NA(c), final issue	2.95

DOUBLE EDGE DOUBLE
Double Edge

1 thru 3	3.50
4 Heroes Inc. Rep.#1–#2	2.95

DOUBLE IMPACT
High Impact Studios 1995–96

1 I: China & Jazz	5.00
1a Chromium (c) variant, signed	6.00
1b Rainbow (c) w/certificate	15.00
1c Rainbow (c) w/o certificate	10.00
2 Castilo's Crime	3.00
2a nude cover variant	10.00
2b silver version	10.00
2c signed, w/certificate	5.00
3	5.00
3a Bondage (c)	15.00
4	5.00
4a Phoenix (c)	15.00
5	5.00
5a nude cover	15.00
6 China cover	3.00
6a Jazz cover	3.00
6b signed China or Jazz(c)	15.00
6c bondage(c)	10.00
7 & 8	@3.00
8a variant (c)	8.00

2nd Series 1996–97

0	3.00
0a nude (c)	10.00
1	3.00
1a chromium (c)	4.00
1b Chromium variant edition	14.95
1c Christmas (c)	10.00
2	3.00
2a Sweedish Erotica(c)	10.00
Spec.#1 Double Impact/Lethal Strike: Double Strike, x-over	3.00
Nude RCl(c) cover	9.95
Spec.#1 Double Impact/Nikki Blade:	

Hard Core x-over (1997) 2.95
Platinum variant RCl(c). 10.00
Gold Metal variant RCl(c) 20.00
Spec.#1 Raising Hell, RCl,RkB 2.95
Spec.#1 Raising Hell, nude art(c) . 10.00
Spec.#1 Raising Hell,nude
photo(c) 15.00

ABC Comics 1998

1 encore 3.00
1a encore, Chicago cover 6.00
1b encore, San Diego nude cover . 6.00
Spec. Double Impact/Luxura (1998) 3.00
Spec. nude collectors edition 5.95
Spec. Vampeurotica edition. 5.95
Bikini Spec. 3.00
Bikini Spec. nude covers 6.00
Christmas Spec.. . . . . 3.00
Christmas Spec., gold foil 10.00
Christmas Spec., nude cover 8.00
Coll.#1 . . . . 3.00
Coll.#1a x-mas 8.00
Coll.#1b nude cover 8.00
Coll.#1c nude gold foil 10.00
Spring Spec.#1. . . . . 3.00
Spring Spec.#1a manga cover 8.00
Spring Spec.#1b nude manga cover 8.00
Spring Spec.#1c nude photo cover . 8.00
Summer Bikini Spec. 1999 . . . . . . 3.00
Summer Bikini Spec. 1999 nude(c). 8.00

DOUBLE IMPACT ALIVE
ABC Comics 1999

1 (of 3) Double Impact Alive 2000 . 3.00
1a Double Impact Alive 2000,
gold foil ed. 8.00
1b Red Leather 15.00
2 RCl. 3.00
2a Manga cover 8.00
2b Nude cover. 8.00
2c silver embossed foil 10.00

DOUBLE IMPACT:
ASSASSINS FOR HIRE
High Impact April 1997

1 RCl,RkB 3.00
1 nude art cover 10.00
1 nude photo cover 15.00
2 . . . . 3.00
2 gold nude cover 10.00
2 signed nude cover 15.00

ABC Comics 1998

1 . . . . 3.00
1a gold nude RCl cover. 10.00
1b gold nude RCl cover, signed. . 15.00

DOUBLE IMPACT:
FROM THE ASHES
ABC Comics 1998

1 (of 2) RCl 3.00
1B variant Swedish Erotika cover B 5.95
1C variant Swedish Erotika cover C 5.95
2 RCl. 3.00
2A variant cover A. 5.95
2B variant cover B. 5.95

DOUBLE IMPACT:
HOT SHOTS
ABC Studios 1999

1 RCl. 3.00
1a adult covers 8.00
1b gold medal edition, nude (c) . . 10.00
2 . . . . 3.00
2a adult covers 8.00

DOUBLE IMPACT MERCS
ABC Comics 1999

1 (of 3) RCl 3.00
1a deluxe 8.00

DOUBLE IMPACT:
ONE STEP BEYOND
ABC Comics 1998

1 (of 2) RCl 3.00
1a Leather cover 20.00
1b nude cover 6.00

DOUBLE IMPACT RAW
ABC Comics 1997

1 (of 3) RCl, adult 3.00
1a adult variant (c). 8.00
1b Star photo (c) 10.00
1A Wraparound cover A 5.95
1B Wraparound cover B 5.95
2 . . . . 2.95
2a nude cover 5.95
3 concl.. . . . . 2.95
3A Variant cover A. 5.95
3B Variant live model nude cover B 5.95

VOL. 2

1 (of 3) adult material 3.00
1a silver nude cover 6.00
1b nude platinum cover 6.00

DOUBLE IMPACT
SUICIDE RUN
ABC Comics 1998

1 (of 2) RCl 3.00
1a nude variant (c) 6.00
1b Nude live model (c). 6.00
1b Leather cover 15.00
2 adult material 3.00
2a nude cover A 8.00
2b nude cover B 8.00
Collected edition. 3.00
Collected, gold foil 10.00
Collected, Manga nude (c) 8.00

DOUBLE IMPACT 2069
ABC Comics 1999

1 Virgin Encore Edition 3.00
1a Deluxe Erotica edition. 8.00

DRACULA

1 . . . . 3.75
1a 2nd printing 2.50
2 thru 4 . . . . @2.50

DRACULA IN HELL
Apple

1 O:Dracula. 2.50
2 O:Dracula contd. 2.50

DRACULA: SUICIDE CLUB
Adventure

1 I:Suicide Club in UK 2.50
2 Dracula/Suicide Club cont. 2.50
3 Club raid,A:Insp.Harrison 2.50
4 Vision of Miss Fortune 2.50

DRACULA: THE LADY
IN THE TOMB
Eternity

1 . . . . 2.50

DRACULA'S
COZY COFFIN
Draculina Publishing 1995

1 thru 4 Halloween issue 2.95

DRAGONBALL
**Viz Communications March
1998**

1 (of 12) by Akira Toriyama 5.00
2 thru 4 . . . . @4.00
5 thru 12 . . . . @3.00

PART TWO 1999

1 (of 15) by Akira Toriyama 25.00
2 thru 4 . . . . @4.00
5 thru 9 . . . . @3.00

DRAGONBALL Z
**Viz Communications March
1998**

1 (of 9) by Akira Toriyama 2.95
2 thru 9 . . . . @2.95

PART TWO 1998

1 (of 14) by Akira Toriyama 2.95
2 thru 9 . . . . @2.95

DRAGONFORCE
Aircel
(Prev. Color)

8 thru 13 DK . . . . @2.50

DRAGONFORCE
CHRONICLES
Aircel

Vol. 1 thru Vol. 5 rep. . . . . @2.95

DRAGONMIST
Raised Brow Publications

1 I:Dragonmist. 2.75
2 F:Assassin 2.75

DRAGON OF THE VALKYR

1 . . . . 1.75
2 thru 4 . . . . @2.00

DRAGON QUEST

1 TV 15.00
2 TV 7.50
3 TV 6.50

DRAGONRING
[1st Series]

1 B.Blair,rare 110.00

Aircel

1 . . . . 3.50
2 . . . . 2.00
3 thru 6 . . . . @1.75
See Also Color Comics

DRAGON WARS
Ironcat 1998

1 by Ryukihei 2.95
2 thru 11 . . . . @2.95

DRAGON WEEKLY

1 Southern Knights 1.75
2 and 3 . . . . @1.75

DREAD OF NIGHT
Hamilton
1 Horror story collection 3.95
2 Json, inc.`Genocide' 3.95

DREAM ANGEL
AND ANGEL GIRL
Angel Entertainment 1998
1 . . . . 2.95
1a nude delicious Dream Angel (c) 4.00
1b nude anxious Angel Girl (c) 4.00

DREAM ANGEL:
THE QUANTUM DREAMER
Angel Entertainment 1997
0 Nude Manga cover 5.00
1 by Mort Castle & Adriana Melo . . 2.95
1 Virgin nude cover 5.00
1 Nude Platinum cover 15.00
2 . . . . 2.95
2 Virgin nude cover 5.00
2 Nude Platinum cover 15.00

DREAM ANGEL:
WORLD WITHOUT END
Angel Entertainment 1998
1 Dream world cover 3.00
1 nude nightmare cover 3.00

DREAMGIRL
Angel Entertainment 1996
0 by David Campitti & Al Rio 2.95
0 Virgin Nude cover 5.00
0 Lost in Heaven nude cover 7.00
0 platinum edition, nude cover 8.00
1 . . . . 2.95
1 deluxe 5.95
1 Manga cover 5.00
1 Nude Manga cover 5.00

DREAMERY
Eclipse
1 thru 13 . . . . @2.00

DREAMLANDS
Caliber "New Worlds" 1996
1 . . . . 2.95
2 flip book with Boston Bombers #3 2.95

DREAMTIME
Blind Rat
1 Young Deserter 2.95
2 Gypsy Trouble 2.50

DREAMWALKER
Caliber Tapestry 1997
1 . . . . 2.95
2 . . . . 2.95
3 . . . . 2.95
4 . . . . 2.95
5 by Jenni Gregory, 2nd story arc . . 2.95
6 2nd story arc, concl 2.95

DREAMWALKER:
CAROUSEL
Avatar 1998
0 . . . . 3.00
1 by Jenni Gregory 3.00
2 conclusion 3.00

DREAMWALKER:
SUMMER RAIN
Avatar 1999
1 by Jenni Gregory 3.00

DREAMWOLVES
Dramenon Studios
1 . . . . 3.00
2 . . . . 3.00
3 F:Desiree 3.00
4 V:Venefica 3.00
5 V:Venefica 3.00
6 R:Carnifax 3.00
7 . . . . 3.00
8 F:Wendy Bascum 3.00

DRIFTERS
Infinity Graphics 1986
1 . . . . 1.75

DRYWALL AND OSWALD
SHOW, THE
Fireman Press 1998
1 by Mandy Carter,Trent Kaniuga . 2.95

DUNGEONEERS
1 thru 8 . . . . @1.50

Eagle #2
© Crystal Publications

EAGLE
Crystal, 1986
1 . . . . 3.00
1a signed & limited 5.00
2 thru 5 . . . . @2.75
6 thru 11 . . . . @2.25
12 . . . . 2.50
13 thru 17 . . . . @2.00

Apple
18 thru 26 . . . . @1.95

EAGLE: DARK MIRROR
Comic Zone
1 A:Eagle, inc reps 2.75
2 In Japan, V:Lord Kagami 2.75
3 . . . . 2.95
4 . . . . 2.95

EAGLES DARE
Aager Comics
1 thru 4 . . . . 1.95
5 V:Dragon 1.95

EARTH LORE: LEGEND
OF BEK LARSON
Eternity
1 . . . . 1.80

EARTH LORE: REIGN
OF DRAGON LORD
1 . . . . 1.80
2 . . . . 1.75

EARTH WAR
Newcomers Publishing 1995
1 and 2 from Newcomers Illus. . . . 2.95

EARTH: YEAR ZERO
Eclipse
1 thru 4 . . . . @2.00

EAT-MAN
Viz Communications 1997
1 (of 6) by Akihito Yoshitami 2.95
2 thru 6 . . . . @2.95
Vol.1 Full Course Meal,rep.Pt.1 . . . 15.95
PART TWO Feb. 1998
1 (of 5) by Akihito Yoshitami 2.95
2 (of 5) 3.50
3 thru 5 . . . . @3.25
TPB Vol. 2 Second Course 15.95

EB'NN THE RAVEN
Now
1 . . . . 5.00
2 . . . . 3.00
3 . . . . 2.50
4 . . . . 2.00
5 thru 9 . . . . @1.50

EBONIX-FILES, THE
Blatant Comics 1998
1A TV parody, cover A 3.95
1B TV parody, cover B 3.95
1c Nude Agent Sculky cover 9.95
1d Nude Agents in Bed cover 9.95

EDDIE CAMPELL'S
BACCHUS
Eddie Campell Comics 1995
1 V:Telchines 2.95
1 2nd printing 2.95
2 thru 10 V:Telchines 2.95
11 thru 26 ECa . . . . @2.95
27 thru 37 ECa . . . . @2.95
38 thru 46 . . . . @2.95
GN Collected Bacchus, Vol. 1 . . . . 9.95
GN Collected Bacchus, Vol. 2 . . . . 9.95
GN Collected Bacchus, Vol. 3,
  Doing the Islands 17.95
GN Collected Bacchus, Vol. 4,
  One Man Show 8.50
GN Collected Bacchus, Vol. 5
  Earth, Air Water & Fire 9.95
GN Collected Bacchus, Vol. 9,
  King Bacchus 12.95

EDDY CURRENT
1 thru 12 . . . . @2.00

EDGAR ALLAN POE
Tell Tale Heart 1.95
Pit & Pendulum 1.95
Masque of the Red Death 1.95
Murder in the Rue Morgue 1.95

EDGE
1 . . . . 3.00
Vol 2 #1 thru #3 . . . . @3.00
Vol 2 #4 thru #6 . . . . @2.00

EIGHTBALL
Fantagraphics
1 . . . . 10.00
1a 2nd to 6th printing. 3.00
2 . . . . 7.00
2a 2nd to 5th printing. 3.00
3 . . . . 6.00
3a 2nd to 4th printing. 3.00
4 . . . . 5.00
4a 2nd to 4th printing. 3.00
5 . . . . 5.00
5 3rd printing 3.50
6 thru 10 . . . . @4.00
11 A:Ghost World 3.50
12 F:Ghost World 3.25
13 thru 17 . . . . @3.00
18 . . . . 4.00
19 . . . . 3.95
20 . . . . 3.95
TPB Orgy Bound, rep. from #7–#14. . . .
14.95
TPB Lout Rampage 14.95
TPB Pussey 8.95
HC Caricature. 29.95

ELECTRIC BALLET
Caliber
1 Revisionist History of Industrial
Revolution 2.50

ELFLORD
[1st Series]
1 all rare 50.00
2 . . . . 35.00
3 . . . . 30.00
4 . . . . 25.00
5 . . . . 25.00
6 . . . . 40.00
7 . . . . 40.00
8 . . . . 40.00
9 thru 15 . . . . @30.00

ELFLORD
Aircel 1986
1 I:Hawk 5.00
1a 2nd printing 3.50
2 . . . . 3.00
2a 2nd printing 2.00
3 V:Doran 3.00
4 V:Doran 3.00
5 V:Doran 2.00
6 V:Nendo 2.00
Compilation Book 4.95
(Vol 2, #1 to #24, see Color)
25 thru 31 . . . . @1.95
32 . . . . 2.50

ELFLORD
Warp Graphics Jan. 1997
1 (of 4) by Barry Blair & Colin Chan 2.95
2 . . . . 2.95
3 . . . . 2.95
4 . . . . 2.95

ELFLORD: ALL THE LONELY PLACES
Warp Graphics Aug. 1997
1 (of 4)Barry Blair & Colin Chan. . . 2.95
Becomes:

HAWK AND WINDBLADE: ALL THE LONELY PLACES
2 (of 2) 2.95

ELFLORD CHRONICLES
Aircel 1990
1 (of 12) thru 8 rep B.Blair . . . . . @2.50

ELFLORD CUTS LOOSE
Warp Graphics Sept. 1997
1 by Barry Blair and Colin Chan. . . 2.95
2 F:Hawk Erik-san 2.95
3 . . . . 2.95
4 all out attack. 2.95
5 north to safety 2.95
6 homward 2.95
7 back to Greenhaven 2.95
8 Greenhaven Siege 2.95
9 Felines, Nothing More Than
Felines 2.95

ELFLORD: HAWK
China Winds 1998
1-shot by Barry Blair and
Colin Chan 3.50

ELFLORE: THE HIGH SEAS
Raw Comics
4 by Barry Blair (500 copies) 4.95

ELFQUEST
Warp Graphics 1979–85
1 WP. 40.00
1a WP,2nd printing 12.00
1b WP,3rd printing 5.00
1c WP,4th printing (1989) 4.00
2 WP. 20.00
2a WP,2nd printing 4.00
2b WP,3rd printing 3.00
2c WP,4th printing (1989) 2.50

Elfquest #2
© Warp Graphics

3 WP. 15.00
3a WP,2nd printing 4.00
3b WP,3rd printing 3.00
3c WP,4th printing (1989) 2.50
4 WP. 15.00
4a WP,2nd printing 4.00
4b WP,3rd printing 3.00
4c WP,4th printing (1989) 2.50
5 WP. 15.00
5a WP,2nd printing 4.00
5b WP,3rd printing 3.00
6 WP. 15.00
6a WP,2nd printing 4.00
6b WP,3rd printing 3.00
7 WP. 12.00
7a WP,2nd printing 3.00
8 WP. 12.00
8a WP,2nd printing 3.00
9 WP. 12.00
9a WP,2nd printing 3.00
10 thru 15 . . . . @8.00
16 WP,I:DistantSoil. 8.00
17 thru 21 WP. . . . . @8.00
TPB Gatherum 19.95

ELFQUEST
Warp Graphics
4 thru 14 ed. RPi 4.95
15 . . . . 4.95
16 What if Cutter never
became chief 4.95
17 F:Fire-Eye 4.95
18 Dreamtime, concl. 4.95
19 Wolfrider begins 4.95
20 . . . . 4.95
21 20th anniv. 4.95
22 F:Wolfrider 4.95
23 F:WaveDancers 4.95
24 F:Wolfrider. 4.95
25 F:Wolfrider. 4.95
26 Wild Hunt 4.95
27 . . . . 4.95
28 F:Ember & Teir 4.95
29 three new stories 4.95
30 new stories 4.95
31 new stories 4.95
32 Wild Hunt, pt.1, 24-page 2.95
33 Wild Hunt, pt.2. . . . . 2.95
34 Wild Hunt, pt.3. . . . . 2.95
35 Wild Hunt, pt.4. . . . . 2.95
READERS COLLECTIONS
TPB Vol.1 Fire & Flight 11.95
TPB Vol.2 The Forbidden Grove . . 11.95
TPB Vol.3 Captives of
Blue Mountain 11.95
TPB Vol.4 Quest's End 11.95
TPB Vol.5 Siege at Blue Mountain 11.95
TPB Vol.6 Secret of Two-Edge . . . 11.95
TPB Vol.7 Cry From Beyond 11.95
TPB Vol.8 Kings of the
Broken Wheel 11.95
TPB Vol.8A Dreamtime 11.95
TPB Vol.11A Huntress 11.95
TPB Vol.11B Ascent 12.95
TPB Vol.12 Ascent 12.95
TPB Vol.12A Reunion 12.95
TPB Vol.13A Rebels 11.95
TPB Vol.13B Junk. 11.95
TPB Vol.14A Skyward Shadow . . . 11.95
TPB Vol.14A Mindcoil 11.95
TPB Vol. 15 Forevergreen 12.95
HC Vol.1 thru Vol.8 . . . . @19.95
HC Beadtime Stories, 128-page . . 19.95
HC The Big Elfquest Gatherum. . . 19.95
HC New Blood 19.95
TPB The Rebels, 176-page. 11.95
GN Shards 13.95
GN Legacy (Hidden Years #16–#22) . . .
11.95
GN A Gift of Her Own. 16.95

HC Wolfrider's Guide to the World
of Elfquest 19.95
TPB Wolfrider's Guide, revised . . . 16.95
Spec. Metamorphosis, WP,
RPi (1996) 2.95
Spec. Elfquest: Wolfrider 2.95

ELFQUEST: KAHVI
Warp Graphics 1995
1 thru 6 I:Kahvi . . . . @2.25

ELFQUEST: KINGS OF
THE BROKEN WHEEL
Warp Graphics 1990–92
1 WP. 2.25
2 thru 9 WP . . . . @2.25

ELFQUEST: SEIGE
AT BLUE MOUNTAIN
**Warp Graphics/Apple
Comics, 1987–88**
1 WP,JSo. 11.00
1a 2nd printing 3.00
2 WP. 6.00
2a 2nd printing 3.00
3 WP. 5.00
3a 2nd printing 2.00
4 thru 8 WP . . . . @5.00

ELFQUEST: TWO SPEAR
Warp Graphics 1995
1 thru 3 (of 5) Two-Spears past . @2.25

ELFQUEST: WORLDPOOL
Warp Graphics
Spec.#1 (of 2). 2.95
Spec.#2 (of 2). 2.95

ELFTHING
Eclipse
1 . . . . 3.00

ELFTREK
Dimension
1 Elfquest's Star Trek parody. 2.00
2 . . . . 1.75

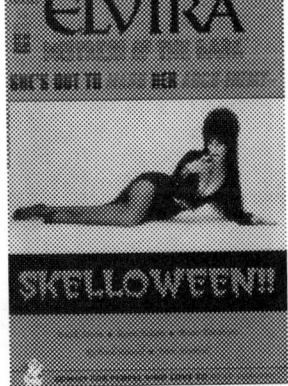
Elvira, Mystress of the Dark #57
© Claypool Comics

ELF WARRIOR
1 . . . . 3.00
2 . . . . 2.50
3 thru 5 . . . . @1.95

ELIMINATOR
Eternity
1 'Drugs in the Future' 2.50
2 . . . . 2.50

ELVIRA, MISTRESS
OF THE DARK
Claypool Comics
1 thru 35 . . . . @2.50
36 thru 74 photo covers . . . . . . @2.50
75 Mistress of the Jungle,pt.1 . . . 2.50
76 Mistress of the Jungle,pt.2 . . . 2.50
TPB Elvira, Mistress of the Dark . . 12.95

ELVIRA
Eclipse
1 Rosalind Wyck 2.50

EMBRACE
London Night
1 NC17 edition, EHr, signed. 10.00

EMBRACE:
HUNGER OF THE FLESH
London Night 1997
1 DQ,last of the original
vampire race 3.00
1a DQ,deluxe 6.00
1b signed by Kevin West 15.00
2 DQ. 3.00
2a DQ,deluxe 6.00
3 by Dan Membiela & Kevin
West, concl. 3.00
3a nude cover edition 6.00

EMERALDAS
Eternity 1990
1 thru 4 . . . . @2.25

EMMA DAVENPORT
Lohamn Hill Press
1 I:Emma Davenport 2.75
2 . . . . 2.75
3 O:Hammerin Jim 2.75
4 Cookie Woofer War 2.75

EMPIRE
Eternity
1 thru 4 . . . . @1.95

EMPTY ZONE
Sirius 1998
1 by Jason Alexander 2.95
1a limited edition 5.00
2 . . . . 2.50
3 . . . . 2.50
4 . . . . 2.50
TPB 11.95

VOL. 2 TRANSMISSIONS 1999
1 by Jason Alexander 2.95
2 . . . . 2.95

ENCHANTED
Sirius 1997
1 (of 3) by Robert Chang. 2.95

2 . . . . 2.95
3 concl. 2.95

ENCHANTED VALLEY
Blackthorne
1 . . . . 1.75
2 . . . . 1.75

ENCHANTER
Eclipse
1 thru 3 . . . . @2.00

ENCHANTER:
APOCALYPSE
WIND NOVELLA
Entity
1 Foil Enhanced Cover 2.95

ENFORCERS
Dark Visions Publishing 1995
0 From Anthology Title. 2.50

ENTITY
Avatar
½ Nira X cover 5.95
½ Snowman cover. 10.95
½ Nira X silver cover 10.95
½ Snowman silver cover 15.95

ENTROPY TALES
1 . . . . 2.00
2 Domino Chance 1.50
3 thru 5 . . . . @1.50

EPSILON WAVE
Elite
1 . . . . 3.00
2 . . . . 2.00
3 thru 5 . . . . @1.60

EQUINE THE UNCIVILIZED
Graphspress
1 . . . . 4.00
2 . . . . 2.50
3 thru 6 . . . . @2.00

Equinox Chronicles #1
© Innovation

EQUINOX CHRONICLES
Innovation
1 I:Team Equinox, Black Avatar . . . 2.25
2 Black Avatar Plans US conquest. 2.25

ERADICATORS
Greater Mercury 1990–91
1 RLm (1st Work) 5.00
1a 2nd printing 1.50
2 . . . . 2.50
3 Vigil 2.00
4 thru 8 . . . . @1.50

ERIC PRESTON IS
THE FLAME
B-Movie Comics
1 Son of G.A.Flame 95

ESCAPE TO THE STARS
Visionary
1 thru 7 . . . . @1.25
[2nd Series]
1 . . . . 1.25
2 . . . . 1.25

ESCAPE VELOCITY
Escape Velocity Press
1 and 2 . . . . @1.50

ESMERALDAS
Eternity
1 thru 4 . . . . 2.25

ESPERS
Halloween Comics April 1996
1 JHI, R:ESPers 2.95
1 JHI,signed 2.95
2 JHI,signed 2.95
3 JHI, ... 2.95
3 JHI,signed 2.95
4 thru 6 JHI, conclusion . . . . . . @2.95
Volume 2
1 "Undertow" 2.95
2 . . . . 2.95

EVENT PRESENTS
THE ASH UNIVERSE
Event Comics 1998
1-shot JQ,JP, 48pg 2.95

EVIL ERNIE
Eternity 1991–92
1 SHu,BnP,I&O:Evil Ernie,
   Lady Death 75.00
1a Spec. 1992 reprint, 16 extra
   pages 50.00
2 Death & Revival of Ernie, A:Lady
   Death, 1st (c) 60.00
3 Psycho Plague, A:Lady Death. . 55.00
4 A:Lady Death 50.00
5 A:Lady Death 50.00
TPB rep #1-5 . . . . 10.95

EVIL ERNIE
Chaos! Comics
1 thru 5 reprints . . . . @2.50
Spec. Youth Gone Wild, die-cut
   cover, Director's cut 5.00
TPB Youth Gone Wild 9.95

Chaos! Comics 1996
1 encore presentation 2.50
2 thru 5 encore presentation 1.95

EXIT
Caliber 1995
1 I:New series 2.95
2 thru 4 "The Traitors," pt.2–pt.4 . . 2.95
Epilogue 2.95
GN rep. 320 pages 19.95
GN rep. 160 pages 14.95

Ex-Mutants #4
© Amazing Comics

EX-MUTANTS
Amazing Comics 1986
1 AC/RLm 5.00
1a 2nd printing 2.00
2 and 3 . . . . @3.00
EC
4 and 5 . . . . @2.00
6 PP 1.95
7 . . . . 1.95
8 . . . . 1.95
Ann. #1 . . . . 1.95
Pin-Up Spec. #1 . . . . 1.95

EX-MUTANTS:
THE SHATTERED
EARTH CHRONICLES
Eternity
1 thru 3 . . . . @1.95
4 RLd(c) 2.75
5 RLd(c) 2.75
6 thru 14 . . . . @1.95
Winter Special #1 . . . . 1.95

EXPLORERS
Caliber Tapestry 1997
1 . . . . 2.95
2 . . . . 2.95
3 "Nahuatl" 2.95
4 "The Sky is Falling" 2.95

EXTREMELY SILLY
Antarctic Press
1 . . . . 4.00
1 Vol. II 1.25
2 Vol. II 1.25

EYE OF MONGOMBO
Fantagraphics Books 1990–91
1 . . . . 3.00
2 thru 7 . . . . @2.00

FAITH
Lightning Comics 1997
1 (of 2) 2.95
1a variant cover 2.95
1b Limited, cover A 9.95
1c Limited, cover B 9.95
1d signed & numbered 9.95
1 encore edition 2.95
1a encore, cover B 2.95
1b deluxe encore edition, cover A . 9.95
1c deluxe encore edition, cover B . 9.95

FANG: TESTAMENT
Sirius 1997
1 by Kevin J. Taylor 2.50
2 . . . . 2.50
3 . . . . 2.50
4 (of 4) 2.50

FANGS OF THE WIDOW
Ground Zero
1 I:Emma 2.50
London Night Studios 1995
1 O:The Widow 3.00
1a platinum edition 5.00
2 Body Count 3.00
3 Emma Revealed 3.00
Ground Zero
7 thru 9 "Metal Gypsies," pt.#1–#3. 3.00
10 thru 13 rep. Widow: Bound by
   Blood #1–#4 + additional
   material 3.50
14 "Search and Destroy" pt.1 . . . . . 3.00
15 "Search and Destroy" pt.2 . . . . . 3.00
Ann. #1 Search and Destroy 5.95

FANTASCI
Warp Graphics-Apple
1 . . . . 2.50
2 and 3 . . . . @2.00
4 . . . . 4.00
5 thru 8 . . . . @1.75
9 `Apple Turnover' 1.75

FANTASTIC ADVENTURES
1 thru 5 . . . . @1.75

FANTASTIC FABLES
Silver Wolf
1 and 2 . . . . @1.50

FANTASTIC PANIC
Antarctic 1993–94
1 thru 8 Ganbear . . . . @2.75
[Volume 2]
1 thru 4 . . . . @2.75
4 thru 9 . . . . @2.95
10 concl. 3.50

FANTASTIC WORLDS
Flashback Comics
1 Space Opera 2.95
2 F:Attu, Captain Courage 2.95

FANTASY QUARTERLY
1 1978 1st Elfquest 65.00

FART WARS:
SPECIAL EDITION
Entity Comics 1997
1 Star Wars trilogy parody,A:Nira X	2.75
1a Empire Attacks Back cover....	2.75
1b Return of the One-Eye cover	2.75

FAR WEST
Antarctic Press 1998
1 (of 4) by Richard Moore	2.95
2	3.00
3	3.00
4	3.00

FASTLANE ILLUSTRATED
Fastlane Studios
1 Super Powers & Hot Rods	2.50

FATALIS
Caliber Core 1998
1 by Mark Chadbourn & Vince Danks	2.95
1a signed & numbered	6.95
2	2.95

Fat Ninja #5
© Silver Wolf

FAT NINJA
Silver Wolf Comics 1985–86
1	2.50
2 Vigil	2.50
3 thru 8	@1.50

FAUST
North Star
1 Vigil	42.00
1a Vigil,2nd Printing.	5.00
1b Vigil,3rd Printing	2.00
1c Tour Edition	30.00
2 Vigil	32.00
2a Vigil,2nd Printing.	3.00
2b Vigil,3rd Printing	2.50
3 Vigil	18.00
3a Vigil,2nd Printing.	2.50
4 Vigil	15.00
5 Vigil	9.00
6 Vigil	9.00
Rebel Studios
7 Vigil	5.00
8 TV	3.50

9 TV,Love of the Damned	3.50
10 E:DQ(s),TV,Love o/t Damned.	3.50
VOL. II
1 TV,Love of the Damned	2.50

FAUST PREMIERE
North Star
1 Vigil	45.00

FAUST/777: THE WRATH
Avatar Press 1998
0 by David Quinn & Tim Vigil, Darkness in Collision x-over	3.00
0a wrap	3.95
0b nude cover	6.00
0c leather cover.	25.00
0d Royal Blue edition.	75.00
0e Platinum edition	15.95
1 (of 4)	3.50
1a nude cover.	6.00
2 Darkness in Collision,pt.3	3.50
2a nude cover.	6.00
3	3.50
3a nude cover.	6.00
4	3.50
4a nude cover.	6.00

FELIX THE CAT B&W
Felix Comics 1997
1 inc. Felix's Cafe	1.95
2 Crusin' for a Brusin'	1.95
3 Ah Choo.	1.95
4 inc. Spaced Out	1.95
5 Holiday/Winter issue.	1.95
6 The Felix Force	2.25
7 A Rash of Trash	2.25

FEM FANTASTIQUE
AC Comics
1	1.95

FEM FORCE
AC Comics
1 thru 15 See Color	
16 I:Thunder Fox	3.00
17 F:She-Cat,Ms.Victory, giant	3.00
18 double size	3.00
19	3.00
20 V:RipJaw, Black Commando	3.00
21 V:Dr.Pretorius	3.00
22 V:Dr.Pretorius	3.00
23 V:Rad	3.00
24 A:Teen Femforce	3.00
25 V:Madame Boa	3.00
26 V:Black Shroud	3.00
27 V:Black Shroud	3.00
28 A:Arsenio Hall	3.00
29 V:Black Shroud	3.00
30 V:Garganta	3.00
31 I:Kronon Captain Paragon	3.00
32 V:Garganta	3.00
33 Personal Lives of team	3.00
34 V:Black Shroud	2.75
35 V:Black Shroud	2.75
36 giant,V:Dragonfly,Shade.	2.75
37 A:Blue Bulleteer,She-Cat	2.75
38 V:Lady Luger.	2.75
39 F:She-Cat	2.75
40 V:Sehkmet.	2.75
41 V:Captain Paragon	2.75
42 V:Alizarin Crimson	2.75
43 V:Glamazons of Galaxy G	2.75
44 V:Lady Luger,F:Garganta.	2.75
45 Nightveil Rescued	2.75
46 V:Lady Luger.	2.75
47 V:Alizarin Crimson	2.75

48	2.75
49 I:New Msw.Victory	2.75
50 Ms.Victory Vs.Rad,flexi-disc.	2.95
51	2.75
52 V:Claw & Clawites	2.75
53 I:Bulldog Deni,V:(Dick Briefer's)Frightenstein.	2.75
54 The Orb of Bliss.	2.75
55 R:Nightveil.	2.75
56 V:Alizarin Crimson	2.75
57 thru 92 See Color	
93 "Shattered Memories," pt.2	3.00
93a deluxe	5.90
94 "Shattered Memories," pt.3	3.00
94a deluxe	5.90
95	3.00
95a deluxe	5.90
96	3.00
96a deluxe	5.90
97	3.00
98 deluxe	5.90
98	3.00
98 deluxe	5.90
99	3.00
99 deluxe	5.90
100 Anniv. issue, with poster	6.90
100A signed, with poster.	12.00
100B no poster, not signed	4.00

THE YESTERDAY SYNDROME
101 Pt.1	4.95
102 Pt.2	4.95
103 Pt.3	4.95

RETURN FROM THE ASHES
104 pt.1 Firebeam, 44pg.	4.95
105 pt. 2	4.95
106 pt. 3 concl.	4.95

DARKGODS: RAMPAGE
107 Darkgods: Rampage, pt.1	4.95
108 Darkgods: Rampage, pt.2	4.95
109 Darkgods: Rampage, pt.3	5.95
Spec.#1 FemForce Timelines, O:Femforce (1995).	2.95
Spec.#1 FemForce:Frightbook, Horror tales by Briefer, Ayers, Powell.	2.95
Untold Origin of FemForce	4.95
GN The Capricorn Chronicles.	12.50
GN FemForce: Timestorm	9.95
GN, FemForce: Timestorm, deluxe	14.95
TPB Origins	12.95
TPB Origins, signed	13.95
Secret Files of Femforce, deluxe.	4.95

FEMFORCE SPECIAL
AC Comics 1999
1 Femforce Special: Rayda– The Cyberian Connection.	2.95
1a Variant cover.	2.95
1b Variant cover, signed	9.95
2	2.95
3 conclusion	3.95

FEVER, THE
Dark Vision Publishing
1 O:The Fever.	2.50
2 Fever's Father	2.50

FIFTIES TERROR
Eternity
1 thru 6	@1.95

FINAL CYCLE
Sirius
Graphic Novel	4.00
1 thru 4	@1.50

B & W PUB.

FINDER
Lightspeed Comics Nov. 1996
1 thru 5 by Carla Speed McNeil . @2.95
6 thru 14 . . . . @2.95
TPB Vol. 1 Sin Eater. 15.95

FINDER FOOTNOTES
Lightspeed Press
2 . . . . 6.00
3 . . . . 6.00
4 . . . . 6.00

FIRE TEAM
Aircel 1990
1 thru 3 by Don Lomax. . . . . . . @2.50
4 V:Vietnamese Gangs. 2.50
5 Cam in Vietnam 2.50
6 . . . . 2.50

FISH POLICE
Fishwrap Productions Dec. 1985
1 1st printing 7.00
1a 2nd printing 3.00
2 . . . . 5.00
3 thru 5 . . . . @4.00
Comico Publ.
6 thru 12 . . . . @3.50
13 thru 17 see Color issues
Apple Publ.
18 thru 24. . . . . @2.50

FISH SHTICKS
Apple
1 and 2 . . . . @2.75
3 and 4 . . . . @2.50

FIST OF GOD
Eternity
1 thru 4 . . . . @1.95

Fist of the North Star #7
© Viz Select

FIST OF THE NORTH STAR
Viz Select
1 thru 3 . . . . @3.25
4 . . . . 1.95
5 . . . . 3.25

6 . . . . 2.95
7 . . . . 2.95
TPB Vol. 2 Night of the Jackal, rep.16.95
Part Three
1 thru 5 by Buronson
& Tetsuo Hara. . . . . @2.95
Part Four Dec. 1996
1 thru 7 . . . . @2.95
TPB Volume 2: Southern Cross . . 16.95

FLAG FIGHTERS
Ironcat 1997
1 by Masaomi Kanzaki 2.95
2 Student Flagger, pt.1 . . . . 2.95
3 Student Flagger, pt.2 . . . . 2.95
4 Student Flagger, pt.3 . . . . 2.95
5 . . . . 2.95
6 Death Window 2.95
7 F:Murasame 2.95

FLAMING CARROT
Aardvark–Vanaheim
1 1981 Killian Barracks 65.00
1a 1984. . . . . 35.00
2 . . . . 30.00
3 . . . . 30.00
4 thru 6 . . . . @25.00
Renegade
7 . . . . 18.00
8 . . . . 12.00
9 . . . . 10.00
10 . . . . 10.00
11 . . . . 6.00
12 . . . . 6.00
13 thru 15 . . . . @5.00
15a variant without cover price . . . 10.00
16 and 17 . . . . @5.00
See: Dark Horse

FLARE
Hero Graphics
1 thru 8 . . . . @3.95
9 F:Sparkplug 3.95
10 thru 12. . . . . 2.95

FLARE ADVENTURES
Hero Graphics
1 Rep 1st issue Flare 1.00
Becomes:
FLARE ADVENTURES/ CHAMPIONS CLASSICS
2 thru 15 . . . . @3.95

FLARE VS. TIGRESS
Hero Graphics
1 and 2 . . . . @3.50

FORBIDDEN KINGDOM
1 thru 11 . . . . @1.95

FORBIDDEN VAMPIRE TALES
Forbidden 1997
0 . . . . 2.95
0A Erotic nude cover. 3.95
0b Erotic nude cover 3.95
1 sexy vampire 2.95
1a nude cover 3.95
1b photo nude cover 3.95
2 . . . . 2.95
2A Dulexe erotic nude cover A . . . 3.95
2b Deluxe erotic nude cover B. . . . 3.95
3 . . . . 2.95

3a nude cover 2.95
4 . . . . 2.95
4a erotic nude cover 2.95
5 . . . . 2.95
5a erotic nude cover 2.95
6 . . . . 3.00
6a Forbidden Embrace nude cover 4.00
7 Bloodlust and Bust cover 3.00
7a Nude Kissing the Countess(c) . 3.00
Spec.#1 Vault of Innocents 2.95
Spec.#1 Vault of Innocents, nude(c) 4.00

FORBIDDEN WORLDS
ACG 1996
1 SD,JAp,rep. 2.50

FORCE 10
Crow Comics
0 Ash Can Preview 75
1 I:Force 10. . . . . 2.50
2 Children of the Revolution,pt#2. . 2.50
3 Against all Odds 2.50

FORETERNITY
Antarctic Press 1997
1 by Rod Espinoza 2.95
2 . . . . 2.95
3 . . . . 2.95

FOREVER WARRIORS
Aardwolf 1996
1 (of 3) RTs,RB 2.95
2 RTs,RB. 2.95
3 RTs,RB, concl. 2.95

FOREVER WARRIORS
CFD 1997
1 RB,RTs. 2.95
2 RB,RTs,KN 2.95
3 RB,RTs, finale 2.95

FORTY WINKS
Oddjobs Limited 1997
1 (of 4) by Sneed & Peters 2.95
2 Everything Right is Wrong Again. 2.95
3 Where Your Eyes Don't Go. . . . 2.95
4 There Might be Giants 2.95
Peregrine Entertainment 1998
Christmas Spec. 2.95
TV Party Spec. 2.95
Spec.#1 The Fabled Pirate Queen
of the South China Sea (1999) . 2.95

FOX COMICS
1 Spec. 2.95
25 . . . . 2.95
26 . . . . 3.50

FRANKENSTEIN
Eternity
1 . . . . 1.95
2 . . . . 1.95
3 . . . . 1.95

FRANKIES FRIGHTMARES
1 Celebrates Frank 60th Anniv. . . . 1.95

FRANK THE UNICORN
Fish Warp
1 thru 7 . . . . @2.00

FREAK-OUT ON INFANT EARTHS
1 Don Chin 1.75
2 Don Chin 1.75

FREAKS
Monster Comics
1 Movie adapt 2.50
2 Movie adapt.cont. 2.50
3 thru 4 Movie adapt. 2.50

FRED THE POSSESSED FLOWER
Happy Predator 1998
1 The Plant Behind the Scenes . . . 2.95
2 . . . . 2.95
3 Interview with a Demon 2.95
4 The People vs. Hell 2.95
5 . . . . 2.95
6 The Origin of Fred 2.95

FRENCH ICE
Renegade Press
1 thru 15 . . . . @2.00

FRIENDS
1 thru 5 . . . . @2.00

FRIGHT
Eternity
1 thru 13 . . . . @1.95

FRINGE
Caliber
1 thru 7 . . . . @2.50

FROM BEYOND
Studio Insidio
1 Short stories-horror. 2.25
2 inc.Clara Mutilares 2.50
3 inc.The Experiment. 2.50
4 inc.Positive Feedback. 2.50

FROM HELL
Tundra
1 . . . . 18.00
1a 2nd printing 8.00
2 . . . . 10.00
Kitchen Sink
Volume Three
1 AMo,ECa 9.00
2 AMo,ECa 5.00
2a 2nd printing 6.00
3 . . . . 5.00
3a 2nd printing 6.00
4 . . . . 6.00
4 new printing 5.00
5 . . . . 6.00
5 new printing 5.00
6 . . . . 5.00
7 . . . . 5.00
8 . . . . 5.00
8 AMo,ECa,new printing 5.00
9 AMo,ECa 5.00
9 new printing 5.00
10 AMo,ECa. 5.00
10 new printing. 5.00
Spec. Dance of the Gull Catchers . . 4.95

FROM THE DARKNESS
Adventure Comics 1990
1 JBa 30.00
2 . . . . 35.00
3 and 4 . . . . @15.00

FROM THE DARKNESS II BLOODVOWS
Cry For Dawn
1 R:Ray Thorn,Desnoires 15.00
2 V:Desnoires 10.00
3 . . . . 10.00

FROM THE VOID
1 1st B.Blair,1982 . . . . 75.00

FROST
1 Heart of Darkness 1.95

FROST: THE DYING BREED
Caliber
1 thru 3 Vietnam Flashbacks . . . @2.95

F–III BANDIT
Antarctic Press
1 F:Akira, Yoohoo 2.95
2 F:Yukio. 2.95
3 F:Were-Women 2.95
4 . . . . 2.95
5 Romeo & Juliet story 2.95
6 thru 8 . . . . @2.95

FUGITOID
Mirage
1 TMNT Tie-in 12.00

FULL METAL FICTION
London Night Feb. 1997
1 EHr 4.00
1a Nun with a Gun edition 10.00
1b dark room edition cover 4.00
2 . . . . 4.00
2a signed 10.00
3 "Hellborne" concl. 4.00
4 . . . . 4.00
5 EHr 4.00
6 . . . . 4.00
7 . . . . 4.00
8 . . . . 4.00

FURRLOUGH
Antarctic Press 1991
1 Funny Animal Military stories . . . 3.00
2 thru 10 . . . . @2.50
11 thru 20 . . . . @2.75
21 thru 33 . . . . @2.75
34 . . . . 2.95
35 48pg 4.00
36 thru 40 . . . . @2.95
41 thru 51 . . . . @2.95
Best of Furlough, Vol.1 . . . . 4.95
Best of Furlough, Vol.2 . . . . 4.95
Radio Comix
52 "Ninjara," pt.4. . . . . 2.95
53 "Bronze Age" 2.95
54 "Heebas" 2.95
55 "Star Run" cont. 2.95
56 "Tobias Wah: Vampire Hunter". . 2.95
57 "Star Run" 2.95
58 F:Heebas. 2.95
59 Sixth anniv., 48pg 3.95

Furrlough #71
© Radio Comix

60 F:Tobias Wah: Vampire Hunter" . 2.95
61 "" 2.95
62 F:Tobias Wah 2.95
63 F:Full Knight Gear 2.95
64 F:The Wild. 2.95
65 F:Full Knight Gear 2.95
66 F:Tobias Wah: Vampire Hunter. . 2.95
67 F:Full Knight Gear 2.95
68 inc. "Misty the Mouse" 2.95
69 inc. "Full Knight Gear" 2.95
70 inc. "Cross of the Dolls" 2.95
71 inc. "Bronze Age". 2.95
72 inc. "The Judgment". 2.95
73 inc. "Dragon Heaven". 2.95
74 inc. "Chronicles of Athras" 2.95
75 inc. "Dragon Heaven". 2.95
76 inc. "China Kate and
   the Frisco Force" 2.95
77 inc. "Gama Duck". 2.95
78 inc. "Siberia" 2.95
79 . . . . 2.95
80 inc. "Siberia" 2.95

FURY
Aircel
1 thru 3 . . . . @1.70

FURY OF HELLINA, THE
Lightning Comics 1995
1 V:Luciver 3.50
1a limited & signed 10.00
1b platinum 10.00

FUSION
Eclipse
1 . . . . 2.50
2 thru 17 . . . . @2.00

FUTABA-KUN CHANGE
Ironcat 1998
1 by Hiroshi Aro. 2.95
2 thru 6 . . . . @2.95
GN Vol. 1 . . . . 15.95
VOL 2
1 . . . . 2.95
2 thru 6 . . . . @2.95
VOL 3 1999
1 . . . . 2.95
2 . . . . 2.95

B & W PUB.

FUTURAMA
Slave Labor
1 thru 4 . . . . @1.75

FUTURETECH
Mushroom Comics
1 Automotive Hi-Tech 3.50
2 Cyber Trucks 3.50

FUTURIANS
Aardwolf 1995
0 DC R:Futurians, sequal to
  Lodestone color series 2.95
0 second printing, DC 2.95

GAIJIN
Caliber 1990
1-shot, 64pg. 3.50
1 thru 3 . . . . @1.95

GALAXION
Helikon 1997
1 by Tara Jenkins, science fiction. . 2.75
2 . . . . 2.75
3 . . . . 2.75
4 Choices 2.75
5 . . . . 2.75
6 Communication 2.75
7 Song of Hiawatha 2.75
8 Persuasion 2.75
9 Deal with the Devil 2.75
10 . . . . 2.75
11 . . . . 2.75
Spec. #1, 16pg. 1.00
GN Vol 1 . . . . 15.95
Spec. Flip Book Galaxion
  & Amy Unbound. 2.75

GATEKEEPER
GK Publishing
1 . . . . 2.50
2 and 3 . . . . @2.95

GATES OF THE NIGHT
Jademan
1 thru 4 . . . . @3.50

GATEWAY TO HORROR
1 BW. 1.75

GEAR
Fireman Press 1998
1 (of 6) by Douglas TenNaple 2.95
2 thru 6 . . . . @2.95
TPB 14.95

GEISHA
Oni Press 1998
1 (of 4) by Andi Watson. 2.95
2 . . . . 2.95
3 . . . . 2.95
4 . . . . 2.95
TPB by Andi Watson 9.95

GEMS OF THE SAMURAI
Newcomers Publishing
1 I:Master Samurai 2.95

GENOCYBER
Viz
1 I:Genocyber 2.75

---

2 . . . . 2.75
3 ToT. 2.75
4 ToT. 2.75
5 ToT. 2.75

GEOBREEDERS
CPM Manga 1999
1 by Akhiro Ito. 2.95
2 thru 6 . . . . @2.95

GERIATRIC GANGRENE
JUJITSU GERBILS
Planet X Productions
1 . . . . 2.50
2 . . . . 1.50

GHOSTS OF DRACULA
Eternity
1 A:Dracula & Houdini 2.50
2 A:Sherlock Holmes. 2.50
3 A:Houdini 2.50
4 Count Dracula's Castle 2.50
5 Houdini, Van Helsing, Dracula
  team-up 2.50

GI GOVERNMENT ISSUED
Paranoid Press
1 thru 7 F:Mac, Jack . . . . @2.00

GIDEON HAWK
Big Shot Comics
1 I:Gideon Hawk, Max 9471. . . . . 2.00
2 The Jewel of Shamboli,pt.2. . . . 2.00
3 The Jewel of Shamboli,pt.3. . . . 2.00
2 The Jewel of Shamboli,pt.4. . . . 2.50
3 The Jewel of Shamboli,pt.5. . . . 2.50

GIZMO
Chance
1 . . . . 7.50
Mirage
1 . . . . 5.50
2 . . . . 2.50
3 . . . . 2.00
4 thru 7 . . . . @1.50

GIZMO & THE FUGITOID
1 and 2 . . . . @1.75

GNATRAT
Prelude
1 . . . . 5.00
2 Early Years. 2.00

GNATRAT: THE MOVIE
1 . . . . 2.25

GOBBLEDYGOOK
Mirage
1 1st series, Rare 200.00
2 1st series, Rare 150.00
1 TMNT series reprint 5.00

GOJIN
Antarctic Press 1995
1 F:Terran Defense Force 2.95
2 F:Terran Defense Force 2.95
3 V:Alien Monster 2.95
4 Aliens Bone 2.95
5 thru 8 . . . . @2.95

Gold Digger #14
© Antarctic

GOLD DIGGER
Antarctic Press
[Limited Series]
1 Geena & Cheetah in Peru. 8.00
2 Adventures contd. 6.00
3 Adventures contd 6.00
4 Adventures contd 5.00
GN Rep. #1–#4 + new material. . . 9.95
[Volume 2]
1 by Fred Perry . . . . @10.00
2 Fred Perry 8.00
3 Fred Perry 8.00
4 Fred Perry 6.00
5 misnumbered as #0 . . . . 5.00
6 thru 8 by Fred Perry . . . . @4.00
9 and 10 by Fred Perry . . . . . . @3.50
11 thru 27 by Fred Perry . . . . . @3.00
28 and 29 by Fred Perry . . . . . @2.75
30 . . . . 3.00
31 . . . . 3.00
32 Time Warp Part One 3.00
33 . . . . 3.00
34 . . . . 3.00
35 Time Warp Part Seven. 3.00
36 . . . . 3.00
37 . . . . 2.95
38 V:Dynasty of Evil 2.95
39 . . . . 2.95
40 Wedding day 2.95
41 Gold Digger Beta. 2.95
42 . . . . 2.95
43 Beta Phase phenomenon. 2.95
44 Beta tool 2.95
45 F:Priestess Tanya 2.95
46 Agent M. 2.95
47 Old Dirty Bastard 3.00
48 . . . . 3.00
49 The Library of Time 3.00
50 . . . . 3.00
50a deluxe 6.00
Ann. 1995, 48pg. 3.95
Ann. 1996. . . . . 3.95
Ann. 1997. . . . . 3.95
Ann. 1998. . . . . 3.95
Best of Gold Digger Ann. Vol. 1 . . 3.00
Collected Gold Digger,Vol.1 . . . . . 9.95
Collected Gold Digger,Vol.2 . . . . . 9.95
Collected Gold Digger,Vol.3 . . . . . 9.95
Collected Gold Digger,Vol.4 . . . . . 9.95
Collected Gold Digger,Vol.5 . . . . . 9.95
Collected Gold Digger,Vol.6 . . . . 10.95
Collected Gold Digger,Vol.7 . . . . 10.95
Collected Gold Digger,Vol.8 . . . . 10.95

Mangazine Spec. #1 . . . . 3.00

GOLD DIGGER/ NINJA HIGH SCHOOL
Antarctic Press 1998
Spec. Asrial vs. Cheetah Compilation,
x-over rep. 4.95
Spec. Science Fair Compilation,
x-over rep. 4.95

GOLDEN AGE GREATS
AC Comics 1995
Vol.#1 thru #6 40s and 50s . . . . . @9.95
Vol. 7 Best of the West 9.95
Vol. 8 F:Phantom Lady, Miss Victory 9.95
Vol. 9 Fabulous Femmes of Fiction
House 9.95
Vol. 11 Roy Rogers & The Silver
Screen Cowboys 11.95
Vol. 12 Thrilling Science Fiction . . . 9.95
Vol. 13 . . . . 9.95
Vol. 14 The Comic Book Jungle . . 11.95

GOLDEN-AGE MEN OF MYSTERY
AC Comics
5 . . . . 6.95
7 . . . . 5.95
8 . . . . 5.95
9 . . . . 5.95
10 Masked comic book
heroes, 52 pg. 6.95
11 rep. Cat-Man comics 6.95
12 Espionage, WE 6.95
13 F:Daredevil vs. The Claw 6.95
14 F:Commando Yank 6.95
15 F:Captain 3-D 6.95
16 F:Mr. Scarlet, Airboy 6.95
17 F:Stuntman 6.95

GOLDEN WARRIOR ICZER ONE
Antartic 1994
1 thru 5 . . . . @2.95

GOLDWYN 3-D
Blackthorne
1 . . . . 2.00

GO-MAN
1 thru 4 . . . . @1.50
Graphic Novel `N' 9.95

GOOD GIRL COMICS
AC
1 F:Tara Fremont 3.95

GOOD GIRLS
Fantagraphics
1 adult 2.00
2 thru 4 . . . . @2.00

GOON, THE
Avatar Press 1999
1 by Eric Powell 3.00
2 . . . . 3.00
3 . . . . 3.00

GORE SHRIEK
Fantagor
1 . . . . 2.50

Good Girls #1
© Fantagraphics

2 and 3 . . . . @1.50
4 +Mars Attacks 2.95
5 . . . . 2.95
6 . . . . 3.50
Vol 2 #1 . . . . 2.50

GOTHESS: DARK ECSTASY
SCC Entertainment 1997
1 (of 3) 2.95
2 . . . . 2.95
2a nude Kristen edition 9.95
2b nude Gothess edition 9.95
3 . . . . 2.95
3a nude vampire slayer edition . . . 9.95
3b nude halloween edition 9.95

GRAPHIC STORY MONTHLY
1 thru 5 . . . . @2.95

GRAPHIQUE MUSIQUE
Slave Labor 1989–90
1 . . . . 45.00
2 . . . . 40.00
3 . . . . 35.00

GRAVE TALES
Hamilton
1 JSon,GM, mag. size 3.95
2 JSon,GM,short stories 3.95
3 JSon,GM, inc.`Stake Out' 3.95

GREMLIN TROUBLE
Anti-Ballistic Pixelation
1 & 2 Airstrike on Gremlin Home @2.95
1 new printing 2.95
3 thru 5 . . . . @2.95
6 "Fun with Electricity" 2.95
7 "Cypher in Fairyland" 2.95
8 . . . . 2.95
9 F:Candy Tsai 2.95
10 The Tuberians are coming 2.95
11 V:X-the-Unmentionable 2.95
12 preemptive strike on Site X . . . 2.95
13 Gremlin-Goblin war 2.95
14 . . . . 2.95
15 Battle of 5 Armies 2.95

16 . . . . 2.95
17 kidnapped to Fairyland 2.95
18 . . . . 2.95
19 The Sky Stone 2.95
TPB Vol.1 . . . . 14.95

GRENDEL
Comico
1 MW,Rare 75.00
2 MW,Rare 60.00
3 MW,Rare 55.00

GREY
Viz Select
Book 1 . . . . 5.00
Book 2 scarce 5.50
Book 3 . . . . 3.00
Book 4 . . . . 3.00
Book 5 . . . . 3.00
Book 6 thru Book 9 . . . . @2.50

GREYMATTER
Alaffinity Studios
1 thru 14 by Marcus Harwell . . . @2.95

GRIFFIN, THE
Slave Labor
1 . . . . 1.75
1a 2nd printing 1.75
2 thru 4 . . . . @1.75
5 . . . . 1.95
Amaze Ink 1997
1 by DVa & Phil Allora 2.95
2 by DVa & Paul Way 2.95

GRIPS
Silver Wolf
1 Vigil 20.00
2 Vigil 16.00
3 Vigil 11.00
4 Vigil 9.00
Vol 1 #1 rep 2.50
Volume 2
1 . . . . 2.50
2 . . . . 2.50
3 thru 6 . . . . @2.00
7 . . . . 2.25
8 . . . . 2.25
9 thru 12 . . . . @2.50

GROUND POUND
1 John Pound art 2.00

GROUND ZERO
Eternity
1 Science Fiction mini-series 2.50
2 Alien Invasion Aftermath 2.50

GUERRILA GROUNDHOG
Eclipse
1 . . . . 1.50
2 . . . . 1.50

GUILLOTINE
Silver Wolf
1 and 2 . . . . @1.50

GUILLOTIN
High Impact 1997
Preview JQ,RCI 5.00

ABC Studios 1999
Spec. Ed. 3.00
Spec. Ed. Serpent Ed. 8.00

GUN CRISIS
Ironcat 1998
1 (of 3) by Masoami Kanzaki 2.95
2 . . . . 2.95
3 . . . . 2.95

GUN FURY
Aircel
1 thru 10 . . . . @1.95

GUN FURY RETURNS
Aircel
1 . . . . 2.95
2 . . . . 2.95
3 V:The Yes Men. 2.25
4 . . . . 2.25

GUNNER
Gun Dog Comics 1999
1 by Eric Yonge. 2.95
2 thru 6 . . . . @2.95

GUNS OF SHAR-PEI
Caliber
1 The Good,the Bad & the Deadly . 2.95

GUTWALLOW
Numbskull Press 1998
1 by Dan Berger 2.95
2 thru 7 The Gingerbread Man . . @2.95

GYRE
Abaculus 1997
1 by Martin Shipp & Marc Laming . 2.95
2 . . . . 2.95
3 Soul Keeper, pt.3 . . . . 2.95
4 . . . . 2.95
5 . . . . 2.95
6 . . . . 2.95
Spec. Edition 56-page 4.50

HADES
Domain Publishing 1995
1 F:Civil War Officer 3.00

HALL OF HEROES
Hall of Heroes 1993
1 I:Dead Bolt. 16.00
2 and 3 . . . . @4.50
Ashcan, 8-page 5.95
Halloween Horror Special 2.50
Halloween Horror Special '98 . . . . 2.50

HALL OF HEROES PRESENTS
Hall of Heroes 1996–97
0 by Doug Brammer & Matt Roach,
  "Slingers" by Matt Martin 2.50
1 . . . . 2.50
1a signed & numbered 4.00
2 "The Last Days" 2.50
3 "The Power of the Golem" 2.50
4 F:Turaxx the Trobbit 2.50
5 . . . . 2.50

HALLOWIENERS
Mirage
1 . . . . 1.50
2 . . . . 1.50

HALO BROTHERS
Fantagraphics
Special #1 . . . . 2.25

HAMMER GIRL
Brainstorm April 1996
1 dinosaur, sci-fi adventure 2.95
2 . . . . 2.95
2a deluxe 5.00

HAMSTER VICE
Blackthorne
1 . . . . 3.50
2 . . . . 2.50
3 thru 11 . . . . @2.00
New Series
Eternity
1 and 2 . . . . @1.95

HANGED MAN
Caliber Feb. 1998
1 (of 2) by AIG & Arthur Ranson . . 2.95
2 (of 2) 2.95
TPB 5.95

HARD ROCK COMICS
Revolutionary
1 Metallica-The Early Years 2.50

HARI KARI
Blackout 1995
1 . . . . 3.00
1a platinum 10.00
1-shot Possessed by Evil(1997) . . . 2.95
1-shot Hari Kari Goes Hollywood
  (1997) 2.95
  Nude edition. 9.95
  Deluxe 14.95
Spec #1 Sexy Summer Rampage,
  gallery issue (1997) 2.95
  Deluxe, super sexy cover 9.95
1-shot Cry of Darkness (1998) . . . 2.95
  Variant photo ultra sexy ed. . . 9.95
1-shot The Last Stand (1998) 2.95
  Ultra sexy edition 9.95
  Deluxe 14.95

HARI KARI MANGA
Blackout Comics 1998
Spec. 0 Sex, Thugs & Rock 'n' Roll 2.95
  Nude cover 9.95
1-shot Manga Adventures (1997) . 2.95
1-shot Deadly Exposure, by Rob
  Roman & Nigel Tully. 2.95
  Nude cover 9.95
  Deluxe 14.95
1-shot Deadtime Stories, by Rob
  Roman & Nigel Tully. 2.95
  Nude cover 9.95
  Deluxe edition 14.95
1-shot Manga To Die For 2.95
  nude cover. 9.95
  Deluxe 14.95
1-shot Running From Poison 2.95
  nude cover. 9.95

HARPY: PRIZE OF THE OVERLORD
Ground Zero
1 (of 6) 3.00
2 thru 6 . . . . @3.00
1-shot Harpy Preview, prequel 3.00
Peregrine 1998
TPB rep. #1–#6 . . . . 14.95
Spec. Harpy Pin-up Book 2.95

HARTE OF HARKNESS
Eternity
1 I:Dennis Harte,Vampire
  private-eye. 2.50
2 V:Satan's Blitz St.Gang. 2.50
3 Jack Grissom/Vampire 2.50
4 V:Jack Grissom, conc. 2.50

HARVY FLIP BOOK
Blackthorne
1 . . . . 2.00
2 . . . . 2.00
3 . . . . 2.00

HATE
Fantagraphics
1 . . . . 20.00
2 . . . . 15.00
3 . . . . 12.00
4 . . . . 10.00
5 . . . . 10.00
6 . . . . 10.00
7 . . . . 9.00
8 thru 10 . . . . 8.00
11 and 12 . . . . 5.00
1a to 12a reprints. . . . . @2.50
13 thru 15. . . . . 4.00
Hate Jamboree, 64-page 3.95

HAVOC, INC.
Radio Comix 1998
1 by Mark Barnard & Terrie Smith . 2.95
2 . . . . 2.95
3 . . . . 2.95
4 . . . . 2.95
5 . . . . 2.95
6 . . . . 2.95

HEAD, THE
1 Old Airboy (1966). 2.00

HEAVY METAL MONSTERS
Revolutionary
1 `Up in Flames' 2.25

HE IS JUST A RAT
Exclaim Bound Comics
1 & 2 V:Jimmy and Billy Bob 2.75

HELLGIRL
Knight Press
1 I:Jazzmine Grayce 2.95
1-shot Demonseed II, Bob Hickey &
  Bill Nichols (1997) 2.95
1-shot Demonsong, Bob Hickey &
  Bill Nichols (1997) 2.95
1-shot Purgatory (1997). 2.95

HELLINA
Lightning Comics 1994
1-shot I&O:Hellina	5.00
Commemorative	10.00
Nude cover	8.00
1996 rep. gold	5.00
1996 rep nude (c)	8.00
Spec. Hellina: Genesis with poster	
(1996)	3.00
Platinum edition	4.00
Nude cover	5.00
Platinum nude edition	8.00
Spec. Hellina: In the Flesh (1997)	
two diff. mild covers	@3.00
Nude covers, 2 diff.	@5.00
Spec. Hellina: Naked Desire (1997)	2.95
Cover B	2.95
Signed,	2.95
Nude cover A	5.00
Nude cover B	5.00
Spec. Hellina: Taking Back the Night	
(1995) V:Michael Naynar	3.00
Nude cover	5.00
Spec. Hellina: Wicket Ways (1995)	
A:Perg	2.75
Nude cover	5.00
Encore editions	3.00
Encore variant (c)	3.00
Encore, nude cover	5.00
Encore, nude variant (c)	5.00
Spec. Hellina: X-Mas in Hell (1996)	
two different covers	3.00
Platinum edition	5.00
Nude cover	5.00
Nude variant cover	5.00
Nude platinum edition	15.00
Spec. Hellina: The Relic	3.00
Variant cover	3.00
Nude cover	5.00
Variant nude cover	5.00
Spec. 1997 Pin-up	3.50
1997 Pin-up, cover B	3.50
1997 Pin-up, cover A, nude	5.00
1997 Pin-up, cover B, nude	5.00
X-Over Hellina/Catfight (1995)	
V:Prince of Sommia	2.75
Gold	4.00
Nude cover	4.00
Encore edition, mild covers,	
2 different	2.95
Encore, nude covers, 2 diff.	5.00
X-Over Hellina/Cynder (1997) covA	2.95
Cover B	2.95
Nude cover A	5.00
Nude cover B	5.00
Spec Hellina #1 Skybolt Toyz	
lim. ed. (1997)	1.50
TPB rep. Hellina appearances	8.95
TPB rep. one-shots.	12.95

HELLINA: HEART OF THORNS
Lightning Comics
1 (of 2)	3.00
1a nude cover	5.00
1b autographed	5.00
2	2.75
2a variant cover	2.75
2b platinum edition	5.95
2c nude cover	5.00
2d variant nude cover	5.00
2e platinum nude edition	12.00

HELLINA: HELL'S ANGEL
Lightning Comics Oct. 1996
1	2.75
1a platinum edition	8.00
1a platinum edition, signed	10.00

1b nude cover	5.00
1c nude platinum edition	15.00
2	2.75
2a platinum edition	8.00
2b nude cover	5.00
2c nude platinum edition	15.00
1 encore edition, cover A	2.95
1a encore edition, cover B	2.95
1b deluxe encore edition, cover A	5.00
1c deluxe encore edition, cover B	5.00

HELLINA: KISS OF DEATH
Lightning Comics 1995
1-shot A:Perg	4.00
1-shot nude cover	5.00
1-shot gold edition	10.00
1-shot Encore editions	3.00
1-shot Encore, nude cover	5.00
Lightning Feb. 1997
1A	2.95
1B variant cover	2.95
1A nude cover	5.00
1B nude cover	5.00
1 encore, signed & numbered	5.00

HELSING
Caliber Core March 1998
1W by Gary Reed & Low,	
Wozniak(c)	2.95
1L Loudon (c)	2.95
1 variant cover	8.95
1 premium, signed	9.95
2	2.95
3	2.95
4 Secrets and Lies	2.95
Spec. Dawn of Armageddon, Secrets	
& Lies, concl. 48-page	3.95

HELTER SKELTER
Antarctic Press 1997
0 by Mike Harris & Duc Tran	2.95
1 (of 4)	2.95
2 thru 6	@2.95

HEPCATS
Double Diamond
1	20.00
2	15.00
3 Snow Blind	15.00
4 thru 9	@10.00

Hepcats #6
© Antarctic Press

10 thru 13	@3.50
14 Chapter 12	3.00
15 Snowblind Chp. 13	2.75
Antarctic Press
1 by Martin Wagner	3.00
2 "Trial by Intimacy"	3.00
3 Snowblind, pt.1	3.00
4 Snowblind, pt.2	3.00
5 Snowblind, pt.3	3.00
6 Snowblind, pt.4	3.00
7 Snowblind, pt.5 Intrusion	2.95
8 Snowblind, pt.6 Super Heroes	2.95
9 Snowblind, pt.7 Kevin & Kathryn	2.95
10 Snowblind, pt.8 Exorcism,	
Prelude	2.95
11 Snowblind, pt.10 Exorcism(a)	2.95
12 Snowblind, pt.10 Exorcism(b)	2.95
13 Snowbling, pt.11 It's a Garden	
of Eden.	3.50
TPB Collected Hepcats	14.95

HERCULES
A Plus Comics
1 Hercules Saga	2.50

HERCULES PROJECT
Monster Comics 1991
1 Origin issue,V:Mutants	1.95

HEROES
Blackbird
1	6.00
2	3.00
3	2.25
4 comic size	2.00
5 thru 7	@2.00

HEROES FROM WORDSMITH
Special Studios
1 WWI,F:Hunter Hawke	2.50

HEROES INCORPORATED
Double Edge Publishing
1 I:Heroes, Inc.	2.95
2 Betrayal	2.95

HEROIC TALES
Lone Star Press 1997
1 by Robb Phipps & Bill Williams	2.50
2 Steel of a Soldier's Heart, pt.2	2.50
3 Steel of a Soldier's Heart, pt.3	2.50
4	2.50
5	2.50
6 The Belles of Freedom, prequel	2.50
7 The Children of Atlas, pt.1	2.50
8 by Bill Williams & Jeff Parker,	
I:Atlas	2.50

HEROINES, INC.
1 thru 5	@1.75

HERO SANDWICH
Slave Labor
1 thru 4	@1.50
5 thru 8	@1.75
9	1.95
Graphic Novel	7.95

HEY MISTER
Insomnia Comics
1	2.50

Hero Sandwich #1
© Slave Labor

2 . . . . 2.50

Top Shelf
3 by Pete Sickman-Garner. 2.95
4 . . . . 2.95
TPB After School Special 4.95
Spec. Behind the Green Door. 2.95
TPB Celebrity Roast 144-page 9.95

HIGH CALIBER
1 . . . . 4.00
2 . . . . 3.00
3 and 4 . . . . @2.50
Becomes:

CALIBER PRESENTS

HIGH CALIBER
Caliber 1997
1 64pg. 4.00
1 signed edition. 4.00
2 64pg. 4.00
3 48pg. 4.00
4 . . . . 4.00

HIGH SCHOOL AGENT
Sun Comics
1 I:Kosuke Kanamori 2.50
2 Treasure Hunt at North Pole . . . 2.50
3 and 4 . . . . @2.50

HIGH SHINING BRASS
Apple
1 thru 4 . . . . @2.75

HIGH SOCIETY
Aardvark–Vanaheim
1 DS,Cerebus 25.00

HILLY ROSE'S
SPACE ADVENTURES
Astro Comics 1995
1 confronts Steeltrap 8.00
1 2nd & 3rd pr. by B.C. Boyer 3.00
2 . . . . 5.00
2 2nd & 3rd printing. 3.00
3 . . . . 3.50
3 2nd printing 3.00
4 thru 9 . . . . @3.00

TPB Vol.1 Rocket Reporter. 12.95

HIT THE BEACH
Antarctic 1993
1 . . . . 2.95
1a deluxe edition 5.00
2 & 3 . . . . @2.95

HITOMI AND
HER GIRL COMMANDOS
Antarctic Press 1992
1 Shadowhunter,from Ninja HS . . . 2.50
2 Synaptic Transducer. 2.50
3 Shadowhunter in S.America 2.50
4 V:Mr.Akuma,last issue 2.50
[Series II]
1 thru 10 . . . . @2.75

HOLLYWOOD'S
GOLDEN ERA 1930S
A-List Comics 1999
1 (of 3) 2.95
2 . . . . 2.95
3 . . . . 2.95

HOLO BROTHERS, THE
Monster Comics
1 thru 10 . . . . @1.95
Fantagraphics
Spec.#1 . . . . 2.25
TPB The Curse of the Bloated Toad 4.95

HOLY KNIGHT
Pocket Change Comics
1 thru 3 . . . . @2.50
4 V:His Past 2.50
5 V:Souljoiner 2.50
6 V:Demon Priest 2.50
7 Silent Scream,pt.2 . . . . 2.50
8 "Dragon Quest," pt.1. . . . . 2.50
9 "Dragon Quest," pt.2. . . . . 2.50
10 "Dragon Quest," pt.3 . . . . 2.50
11 "Dragon Quest," pt.4 . . . . 2.50

HONK
Fantagraphics
1 Don Martin 2.75
2 . . . . 2.75
3 . . . . 2.75

HONOR AMONG THIEVES
Gateway Grapnics, 1987
1 and 2 . . . . @1.50

HOON
Eenieweenie Comics
1 I:Hoon 2.50
2 Calazone Disaster 2.50
3 Reality Check. 2.50
4 thru 8 . . . . @2.50

HOON, THE
Caliber Tapestry 1996
1 . . . . 2.95
2 . . . . 2.95
3 . . . . 2.95

HOROBI
Viz
1 . . . . 4.00

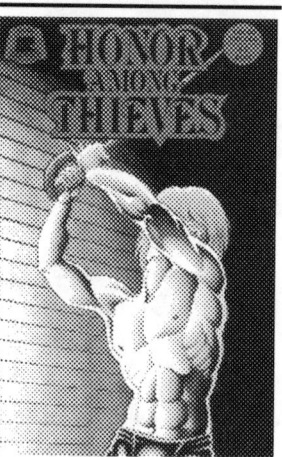

Honor Among Thieves #2
© Gateway

2 thru 8 . . . . @3.75
Book 2 1990–91
1 by Yoshihisa Tagami. 3.50
2 D:Okado,Shoko Kidnapped. 4.25
3 Madoka Attacks Zen. 4.25
4 D:Abbess Mitsuko. 4.25
5 Catharsis!. 4.25
6 Shuichi Vs. Zen. 4.25
7 Shuichi vs. Zen, conc. 4.25

HORROR IN THE DARK
Fantagor
1 RCo,Inc.Blood Birth 2.00
2 RCo,Inc.Bath of Blood 2.00
3 RCo. 2.00
4 RCo,Inc.Tales o/tBlackDiamond . 2.00

HORROR SHOW
Caliber
1 GD,1977-80 reprint horror 3.50

HOUSE OF
FRIGHTENSTEIN
AC Comics
1 . . . . 2.95

HOUSE OF HORROR
AC Comics
1 . . . . 2.50

HOWL
Eternity
1 & 2 . . . . @2.25

HOW TO DRAW TEENAGE
MUTANT NINJA TURTLES
Solson
1 Lighter cover 15.00
1a Dark cover 5.00

H.P. LOVECRAFT'S
THE DREAM-QUEST
OF UNKNOWN KADATH
Mock Man Press 1997
1 (of 5) by Jason Thompson 2.95

1 2nd printing 2.95
2 thru 5 . . . . @2.95

HUGO
Fantagraphics
1 . . . . 4.00
2 . . . . 2.00
3 . . . . 2.00
4 . . . . 2.00

HUMAN GARGOYLES
Eternity
Book one 1.95
Book two 1.95
Book three 1.95
Book four 1.95

HUMAN HEAD
Caliber
1 Alice in Flames. 2.50

HUNT AND
THE HUNTED, THE
Newcomers Publishing
1 I:Aramis Thiron 2.95
2 V:Werewolves 2.95
3 Rio De Janero 2.95
4 F:Aramis Thiron 2.95

HURRICANE GIRLS
Antarctic Press 1995
1 & 2 Tale of Dinon . . . . @3.50
3 thru 7 seven part series. . . . . . @2.95

HUZZAH
1 I:Albedo'sErmaFelna. 60.00

HY-BREED
Division Publishing
1 thru 3 F:Cen Intel . . . . @2.25
4 thru 9 . . . . @2.50

HYPER DOLLS
Ironcat Manga 1998
1 by Shinpei Itoh, F:Miyu & Maika . 2.95
2 thru 6 . . . . @2.95

VOL 2
1 . . . . 2.95
2 thru 6 . . . . @2.95

I.F.S. ZONE
1 thru 6 . . . . @1.25

I AM LEGEND
Eclipse
1 Novel Adaptation 5.95
2 Novel Adaptation cont'd 5.95
3 Novel Adaptation cont'd 5.95

ICARUS
1 thru 9 . . . . @1.70

ICON DEVIL
1 . . . . 2.00
2 . . . . 2.00
2nd Series
1 thru 5 . . . . @1.85

ILIAD
Amaze Ink 1997
1 by Darren Brady & Alex Ogle . . . 2.95
2 . . . . 2.95
3 . . . . 2.95
4 . . . . 2.95
5 . . . . 2.95
6 . . . . 2.95
7 . . . . 2.95

ILIAD II
1 . . . . 3.00
1a 2nd cover variation 3.00
2 . . . . 2.00
3 . . . . 2.00
4 . . . . 1.70

ILLUMINATUS
1 . . . . 2.00
2 . . . . 2.50
3 . . . . 2.50

INFERNO
Caliber Press
1 I:City of Inferno. 2.95
2 Search for Identity 2.95
3 V:Malatesta 2.95
4 by MCy and Michael Gaydos . . . 2.95
5 . . . . 2.95

INTERZONE
Brainstorm Comics
1 w/4 cards 2.50
2 w/4 cards 2.50

INU YASHA
Viz Communications Jan. 1997
1 thru 5 (of 10) by Rumiko
  Takahashi . . . . @2.95
PART TWO:
A FEUDAL FAIRY TALE
1 (of 9) by Rumiko Takahashi 2.95
2 (of 9) 2.95
6 . . . . 2.95
7 . . . . 2.95
8 . . . . 3.25
11 thru 15 (of 15) . . . . @3.25
TPB 15.95
TPB Vol. 2 . . . . 15.95
PART THREE 1999
1 (of 7) thru 5 . . . . @3.25
TPB Vol. 3 . . . . 15.95
TPB Vol. 4 . . . . 15.95

INVADERS FROM MARS
Eternity
1 . . . . 2.50
2 . . . . 2.50
3 . . . . 2.50
BOOK II 1991
1 Sequel to '50's SF classic. 2.50
2 Pact of Tsukus/Humans 2.50
3 Last issue. 2.50

INVASION '55
Apple
1 . . . . 2.25
2 . . . . 2.25
3 . . . . 2.25

INVISIBLE PEOPLE
Kitchen Sink
1 WE,I:Peacus Pleatnik 2.95
2 WE,The Power 2.95
3 WE,Final issue 2.95
HC GN by Will Eisner 24.95

ISMET
1 Cartoon Dog. 12.00
2 . . . . 5.00
3 Rare. 5.00
4 . . . . 5.00

IT'S SCIENCE
WITH DR. RADIUM
1 thru 7 . . . . @1.50
8 . . . . 1.75
9 . . . . 1.95
Spec #1 . . . . 2.95

Jackaroo #1
© Eternity

JACKAROO
Eternity, 1990
1 GCh. 2.25
2 GCh. 2.25
3 GCh. 2.25

JACK HUNTER
Blackthorne
1 . . . . 3.50
2 . . . . 3.50
3 . . . . 3.50

JACK OF NINES
1 . . . . 1.25
2 thru 4 . . . . @1.50
5 . . . . 2.00

JACK THE RIPPER
1 thru 4 . . . . @2.25

JAM, THE
Slave Labor
1 . . . . 2.00
2 . . . . 2.00
3 thru 5 . . . . @2.25
Dark Horse
6 thru 8 . . . . 2.50

Caliber
9 . . . . 2.95
9 signed edition 2.95
10 It's a Kafka Thing 2.95
11 thru 14 . . . . @2.95
15 "The Kinetic," pt.3 . . . . 2.95

JAM SPECIAL, THE
Matrix
1 . . . . 2.50

JAMES O'BARR TASTY BITES
ACG Comics 1999
1 . . . . 2.95
1a signed 9.95

JASON AND THE ARGONAUTS
Caliber
1 thru 5 . . . . @2.50

JAY & SILENT BOB
Oni Press 1998
1 (of 4) by Kevin Smith & Duncan
   Fregedo 2.95
2 . . . . 2.95
3 . . . . 2.95
4 . . . . 2.95

JAZZ
High Impact
1 Gold variant edition RCl(c) 9.95

JAZZ: SOLITAIRE
ABC Comics 1998
1 (of 4) by Jose Varese 3.00
1a photo cover 5.95
1b nude variant (c) 5.95
2 . . . . 3.00
2a Variant Exotika (c) 5.95
2b Variant Naughty (c) 5.95
3 . . . . 3.00
3a Variant Kaspar nude (c) 5.95
3b Variant Jazz nude (c) 5.95
Collected Ed. 4.95

JAZZ: SUPERSTAR
ABC Comics 1998
1 (of 3) by Jose Varese 3.00
1a JQ cover 6.00
1b Jazz nude variant (c) 10.00

JAZZ AGE CHRONICLES
1 thru 6 . . . . @1.50
7 . . . . 2.50

JCP FEATURES
1 1st MT;S&K,NA/DG rep.
   A:T.H.U.N.D.E.R.Agents,
   TheFly, Black Hood Mag.Size . . 4.50

JEREMIAH: BIRDS OF PREY
Adventure Comics
1 I: Jeremiah,A:Kurdy 2.50
2 conclusion 2.50

JEREMIAH: FIST FULL OF SAND
Adventure Comics
1 A:Captain Kenney 2.50
2 conclusion 2.50

JEREMIAH: THE HEIRS
Adventure Comics 1991
1 Nathanial Bancroft estate 2.50
2 conclusion 2.50

JERRY IGERS FAMOUS FEATURES
Blackthorne
1 . . . . 3.00
2 thru 4 . . . . @2.00
Pacific
5 thru 8 . . . . @2.00

JIM
Fantagraphics 1987–90
1 . . . . 20.00
2 . . . . 15.00
3 and 4 . . . . @10.00
Second Series 1994
1 . . . . 4.00
1a 2nd printing 3.00
2 . . . . 3.50
2a 2nd printing 3.00
3 thru 5 . . . . @3.00

J. O'BARR's THE CROW
Kitchen Sink 1998
0 F:Eric Draven, 48-page 3.50
1 . . . . 3.50
2 Demon in Disguise 3.50

JOE PSYCHO & MOO FROG
Goblin Studios
1 Fanatics Edition 2.50
1 Fanatics signed and numbered
   Edition 9.95
2 . . . . 2.50
2 signed & numbered 9.95
3 . . . . 2.50
4 . . . . 2.50
4B San Diego con cover 4.95
5 . . . . 2.50
Spec. Psychosis Abnormalis 2.50

JOE SINN
Caliber
1 I:Joe Sinn,Nikki 2.95
2 . . . . 2.95

JOHNNY ATOMIC
Eternity
1 I:Johnny A.Tomick 2.50
2 Project X-contingency plan 2.50
3 . . . . 2.50

JOHNNY DARK
Double Edge
1 V:Biker Gang 2.95

JOHNNY THE HOMICIDAL MANIAC
Slave Labor 1996
1 by Jhonen Vasquez 45.00

1 3rd printing 4.00
1 signed, limited 9.00
2 . . . . 20.00
2 3rd printing 3.00
3 . . . . 12.00
3 3rd printing 3.00
4 . . . . 5.00
4 2nd & 3rd printing 3.00
5 . . . . 4.00
5 2nd printing 3.00
6 . . . . 3.00
7 . . . . 3.00
TPB 19.95
HC 29.95
TPB Director's Cut 19.95

JOURNEY
Aardvark–Vanaheim
1 . . . . 13.00
2 . . . . 9.00
3 . . . . 8.00
4 . . . . 5.00
5 thru 7 . . . . @3.00
8 thru 14 . . . . @2.50
Fantagraphics
15 . . . . 2.50
16 thru 28 . . . . @2.00

JR. JACKALOPE
1 orange cover,1981 . . . . 8.00
1a Yellow cover,1981 . . . . 15.00
2 . . . . 8.00

JULIE'S JOURNEY/ GRAVITY
Paper Live Studios 1998
1 by David Keye 2.50
2 thru 6 . . . . @2.50

JUNGLE COMICS
Blackthorne
4 thru 6 . . . . @2.00

JUNGLE COMICS
A-List Comics
1 reprint of golden age 2.95
2 . . . . 2.95
3 . . . . 2.95
4 . . . . 2.95
5 . . . . 2.95
6 . . . . 2.95
TPB Book of Jungle Comics
   Covers, 1940–54 . . . . 7.95

JUNGLE GIRLS
AC Comics
1 incGold.Age reps. 1.95
2 . . . . 1.95
3 Greed,A:Tara 2.75
4 CaveGirl 2.75
5 Camilla 2.75
6 TigerGirl 2.75
7 CaveGirl 2.75
8 Sheena Queen o/t Jungle 2.95
9 Wild Girl,Tiger Girl,Sheena 2.95
10 F:Tara,Cave Girl,Nyoka 2.95
11 F:Sheena,Tiger Girl,Nyoka 2.95
12 F:Sheena,Camilla,Tig.Girl 2.95
13 F:Tara, Tiger Girl 2.95

JURASSIC JANE
London Night 1997
1 by Sky Owens, F:Tira, elf
   princess of Atlantis 3.00

1 deluxe nude edition 6.00	
1 deluxe nude edition, signed . . . 10.00	
2 . . . . 3.00	
2 deluxe 6.00	
3 . . . . 3.00	
3 deluxe 6.00	
4 EHr, Sky Owens 3.00	
4 nude cover edition 6.00	
5 by Preston Owens 3.00	
5 nude cover edition 6.00	
6 by Sky Owens 3.00	
6 nude cover edition 6.00	
7 by Sky Owens 3.00	
7 nude cover edition 6.00	
Coll. Ed. 5.00	
Coll. Ed. nude EHr(c) 7.00	

JUSTICE
Newcomers Publishing 1995
1 I:Judiciary Urban Strike Team . . . 2.95

JUSTY
1 thru 9 . . . . @1.75

KABUKI: CIRCLE OF BLOOD
Caliber Press
1 R:Kabuki 7.00	
2 Kabuki Goes Rogue 5.00	
3 V:Noh Agents 5.00	
4 V:Noh Agents 3.50	
5 V:Kai 3.00	
6 . . . . 3.00	
TPB Rep.#1–#6. . . . . 16.95	
TPB 2nd printing. 16.95	
HC DAv,rep.#1–#6 272pg. 100.00	
TPB deluxe, signed, etc. 24.95	
TPB Compilation 7.95	

KABUKI: DANCE OF DEATH
London Night Studios
1 1st Full series 5.00

KABUKI: MASKS OF THE NOH
Caliber April 1996
1A JQ(c) 3.00	
1B Mays/Mack(c). 3.00	
1C Buzz(c) 3.00	
2 . . . . 3.00	
3 DMk 3.00	
4 epilog 3.00	

KAFKA
1 thru 5 . . . . @2.00
The Execution Spec. 2.25

KAMUI
Eclipse
1 Sanpei Shirato Art 4.00	
1a 2nd printing 2.50	
2 Mystery of Hanbie 3.00	
2a 2nd printing 1.50	
3 V:Ichijiro 2.00	
3a 2nd printing 1.50	
4 thru 15 . . . . @1.50	
16 thru 19 . . . . @1.95	
20 thru 37 . . . . @1.50	

KAOS MOON
Caliber 1996
1 by DdB 3.50

1a 2nd edition 3.00	
2 . . . . 3.50	
2a 2nd edition, new cover 3.00	
3 . . . . 3.00	
4 Anubian Nights, Chapter 2 . . . . 3.00	
GN Full Circle, rep #1–#2 . . . . . . 5.95	

KAPTAIN KEEN
1 thru 3 . . . . @1.75	
4 and 5 . . . . @1.50	
6 and 7 . . . . @1.75	

KATMANDU
Antarctic Press
1 thru 3 . . . . @2.75
4 & 5 Woman of Honor 2.75
6 F:Laska 2.75

Med Systems
7 and 8 . . . . @1.95

Vision Comics
9 "When Warriors Die," pt.3(of 3) . . 1.95	
10 "The Curse of the Blood," pt.1 . . 2.50	
11 "The Curse of the Blood," pt.2 . . 2.50	
12 "The Curse of the Blood," concl . 2.95	
13 "The Search For Magic," pt.1 . . . 2.95	

Shanda Fantasy Arts
14 "The Search For Magic," pt.2 . . 2.95	
15 "The Search For Magic," pt.3 . . 2.95	
16 "Ceremonies," pt.1 (of 3) 2.95	
17 . . . . 2.95	
22 . . . . 2.95	

KEIF LLAMA
1 thru 6 . . . . @2.00

KELLEY BELLE, POLICE DETECTIVE
Newcomers Publishing
1 Debut issue 2.95	
2 Case of the Jeweled Scarab 2.95	
3 Case o/t Jeweled Scarab,pt.2 . . . 2.95	
TPB #1. 8.95	

KID CANNIBAL
Eternity
1 I:Kid Cannibal 2.50	
2 Hunt for Kid Cannibal 2.50	
3 A:Janice 2.50	
4 final issue 2.50	

KI-GORR THE KILLER
AC
1 I:Ki-Gorr, Rae 2.95

KIKU SAN
Aircel
1 thru 6 . . . . @1.95

KILLING STROKE
Eternity 1991
1 British horror tales 2.50	
2 inc.'Blood calls to Blood'. 2.50	
3 and 4 . . . . @2.50	

KILROY
Caliber Core 1998
1C by Joe Pruett & Feliciano	
Zecchin, John Cassaday(c) . . 2.95	
1P JoP (c). 2.95	
1a premium edition 9.95	
2 . . . . 2.95	
3 . . . . 2.95	

---

4 O:Kilroy 2.95	
Spec. Dawn of Armageddon,	
x-over, 48-page 3.95	

KILROY IS HERE
Caliber Press 1995
1 Kilroy Rescues Infant 2.95	
2 Reflections,pt.2. . . . . 2.95	
3 Reflections,pt.3. . . . . 2.95	
4 Lincoln Memorial 2.95	
5 thru 8 . . . . @2.95	
9 and 10 . . . . @2.95	
11 WEI,RPc,"Screen" 2.95	
12 Khymer Rouge 2.95	
Spec. Kilroy: Daemonstorm (1997) . 2.95	

KIMBER, PRINCE OF FELONS
Antarctic Press
1 I:Kimber 2.50
2 V:Lord Tyrex 2.50

KINGDOM OF THE WICKED
Caliber 1996
1 IEd. 2.95	
2 IEd. 2.95	
3 IEd. 2.95	
4 IEd. 2.95	
HC rep. #1–#4 . . . . 49.95	
TPB rep. #1–#4 . . . . 12.95	

King Kong #1
© Monster Comics

KING KONG
Monster Comics 1991
1 thru 6 . . . . @2.50

KINGS IN DISGUISE
1 thru 5 . . . . @2.00	
6 end Mini-series 2.00	

KING ZOMBIE
Caliber 1998
1L by Tom Sniegoski & Jacen	
Burroughs, VcL(c) 2.95	
1M Meadows (c) 2.95	
2 . . . . 2.95	
3 . . . . 2.95	

B & W PUB.

KIRBY KING OF THE SERIALS
Blackthorne
1	2.00
2	2.00
3	2.00
4	2.00

KITZ 'N' KATZ
1	3.50

Eclipse
2	2.00
3	1.50
4 and 5	@2.00

KLOWN SHOCK
North Star
1 Horror Stories	2.75

KNEWTS OF THE ROUND TABLE
Pan Entertainment 1998
1	2.50
2 thru 6	@2.50

KNIGHTMARE
Antartic Press
1	2.75
2	2.75
3 Wedding Knight pt.1	2.75
4 Wedding Knight pt.2	2.75
5 F:Dream Shadow	2.75
6 V:Razorblast	2.75

KNIGHT MASTERS
1 thru 7	@1.50

KNIGHTS OF THE DINNER TABLE
Kenzer & Company
4 Have Dice Will Travel	2.95
5 Master of the Game	2.95
6 on the high seas	2.95
7 Lord of Steam	2.95
8 A:magic cow	2.95
9 To Dice for Sister Sara	2.95
16 thru 18	2.95
19 Heroes of the Hack League	2.95
20 Hack in Space	2.95
21 Home is Where You Hang Yer Dice Bag	2.95
22 Opportunity Knocks	2.95
23 Dice Follies	2.95
24 Hackzilla	2.95
25 Secrets of the Hackfiles	2.95
26 The Mask of El Ravager	2.95
27 Hackburger Hill	2.95
28 Hoody Freakin' Hoo	2.95
29 Bad Moon Risin'	2.95
30 No Honor	2.95
31 Don't Fear the Reaper	2.95
32 Tales From Hawg Wallers	2.95
33 Wild, Wild Hack	2.95
34 Of Dice & Men	2.95
TPB Vol. 1 Bundle of Trouble	9.95
TPB Vol. 2 Bundle of Trouble	9.95
TPB Vol. 3 Bundle of Trouble	9.95
TPB Tales From the Vault	9.95

KNIGHTS OF THE DINNER TABLE/FAANS
Six-Handed Press 1999
X-over Spec.	2.95

KNIGHT WATCHMAN
Caliber Press
1 Graveyard pt. 1	2.95
2 Graveyard pt. 2	2.95

KOMODO & THE DEFIANTS
1 thru 6	@1.50

KORVUS
Human Monster Press 1997
1 by Mick Fernette	2.95
2	2.95
Arrow Comics 1998
3	2.95
VOL 2
1	2.95
2	2.95

KUNG FU WARRIORS
(Prev. ROBOWARRIORS)
CFW
12	1.95
13 thru 19	@2.25

KUNOICHI
Lightning Comics 1996
1 2 diff. mild covers	3.00
1 platinum edition	5.95
1 autographed edition	9.95

KYRA
Elsewhere 1989
1 thru 5 by Robin Ator	@1.75
TPB rep #1–#5 + pin-ups	6.95

L.A. RAPTOR
Morbid Graphics
1 Velocaraptor loose	2.95

LABOR FORCE
Blackthorne
1 thru 4	@1.50
5 thru 8	@1.75

LA COSA NOSTROID
Fireman Press 1997
1 by Don Harmon & Rob Schrab	2.95
2 by Don Harmon & Edvis	2.95
3	2.95
4	2.95
5	2.95
6 x-over madness	2.95
7	2.95
8	2.95
9	2.95
10 final issue of Volume 1	2.95

LACUNAE
CFD Producitons 1995
1 thru 4 F:Monkey Boys	2.50
5 thru 10	@2.50
11 HMo	2.50
12 HMo	2.50

LADIES OF LONDON NIGHT
London Night 1997
Fall Special	5.00
Nude Heather Parkhurst (c)	7.00

Nude Gloria Gilbert (c)	7.00
Winter Special	5.00
Winter Wonderland Edition	7.00
Spring 98 Special	5.00
Nude Gloria Ann (c)	7.00
Nude Wendy Leigh (c)	7.00
Spotlight: Devon Michaels	3.95
Devon Michaels nude (c)	6.00

LADY ARCANE
Heroic Publishing
1 thru 3	@3.50

LADY CRIME
AC Comics
1 Bob Powell reprints	2.75

Lady Vampre #0
© *Blackout Comics*

LADY VAMPRE
Blackout Comics 1996
0 (1995)	2.75
1 flip-book	2.95
0 Immortal No More (1998)	2.95
0a nude cover	9.95
Spec.#1 In the Flesh (1996)	2.95
Spec.#1a photo sexy cover	9.95

LADY VAMPRE RETURNS
Blackout Comics 1998
1 by Rob Roman & Kirk Manley	2.95
1a nude cover	9.95
1b Deluxe edition	14.95

LAFFIN GAS
Blackthorne
1	2.50
2 thru 12	@2.00

LANCE STANTON WAYWARD WARRIOR
1 and 2	@1.50

LANDER
Mermaid Producions
1 Power of the Dollar,pt.1	2.25
2 Power of the Dollar,pt.2	2.25
3 Power of the Dollar,pt.3	2.25
Vol. 2
1 "By Whose Authority," pt.1	2.75

2 "By Whose Authority," pt.2 . . . . . 2.75

LAND OF OZ
Arrow Comics 1998
1 by Gary Bishop & Bill Bryan 2.95
2 . . . . 2.95
3 . . . . 2.95
4 . . . . 2.95
5 . . . . 2.95
6 . . . . 2.95

LAST DITCH
Edge Press
1 CCa(s),THa,. 2.50

LAST GENERATION
Black Tie Studios
1 . . . . 6.00
2 . . . . 4.00
3 . . . . 2.25
4 . . . . 2.25
5 . . . . 2.25
Book One Rep.. . . . . 6.95

LAST KISS, THE
Eclipse
Spec. 3.95

LATIGO KID WESTERN
AC Comics
1 . . . . 1.95

LAUREL & HARDY
1 3-D.. 2.50

LEAGUE OF CHAMPIONS
Hero Comics
(cont. from Innovation L.of C. #3)
1 GP,F:Sparkplug,Icestar. 3.50
2 GP(i),F:Marksman,Flare,Icicle. . . 3.50
3 . . . . 3.50
4 F:Sparkplug,League 3.50
5 Morrigan Wars Pt.#1. . . . . 3.50
6 Morrigan Wars Pt.#3. . . . . 3.50
7 Morrigan Wars Pt.#6. . . . . 3.50
8 Morrigan Wars Conclusion 3.50
9 A:Gargoyle. 3.50
10 A:Rose 3.50
11 thru 12. . . . . 3.95
13 V:Malice 3.95
14 V:Olympians 3.95
15 V:Olympians 2.95

LE FEMME VAMPRIQUE
Brainstorm 1997
1 . . . . 3.50
1a nude edition 5.00

LEGENDLORE
Caliber "New Worlds"
1 JMt signed 2.95
3 JMt.. 2.95
4 JMt 2.95
5 JMt.. 2.95
6 flip book w/Boston Bombers #4 . 2.95
7 JMt.. 2.95
8 JMt.. 2.95
TPB Tainted Soul, rep. #1–#4 . . . . 12.95
TPB In Misery's Shadow,
    Rep. #5–#7 . . . . 9.95

LEGENDLORE: REALM WARS
Caliber "New Worlds"
1 by Joe Martin & Philip Xavier,
    Fawn cover by Xavier. 2.95
1a Falla cover by Boller. 2.95
1b signed 2.95
2 . . . . 2.95
3 . . . . 2.95
4 concl. 2.95

LEGENDLORE: WRATH OF THE DRAGON
Caliber Fantasy 1998
1 by JMt & Philip Xavier. 2.95
1 variant Philip Xavier(c) 2.95
2 . . . . 2.95
3 . . . . 2.95
4 . . . . 2.95
5 Prisoner set free. 2.95
Spec. Handbook. 3.95
1-shot Legendlore: Slave of Fate
    by JMt & Philip Xavier 2.95
1-shot The Wind Spirits, 48-page . . 3.95
Giant Size Spec. 48-page. 3.95

LEGENDS OF CAMELOT
Caliber Fantasy 1999
Excalibur 2.95
Quest For Honor. 2.95
Merlin. 2.95
The Enchanted Lady 2.95
Sir Balin & The Dolorous Stroke . . . 2.95

LEGEND OF LEMNEAR
CPM Manga 1997
1 . . . . 2.95
2 thru 17 . . . . @2.95
18 final issue 2.95
TPB Vol 1, 160-page 15.95

LEGENDS OF LUXURA
Brainstorm 1996
1 platinum edition 5.00
2 gold edition. 5.00
3 . . . . 2.95
TPB #1. . . . . 12.95

Legends of Luxura #3
© Brainstorm

LEGION ANTHOLOGY
Limelight 1997
1 four stories. 2.95
2 . . . . 2.95
3 F:Binary Angel 2.95
4 . . . . 2.95
5 Binary Angel. 2.95

LEGION X-I
1 McKinney. 5.00
2 McKinney,rare 15.00
Volume 2
1 thru 4 . . . . @2.00

LEGION X-2
Vol 2 #1 . . . . 2.00
Vol 2 #2 . . . . 2.00
Vol 2 #3 . . . . 2.00
Vol 2 #4 . . . . 2.00

LENORE
Slave Labor 1998
1 by Roman Dirge 2.95
2 . . . . 2.95
3 . . . . 2.95
4 . . . . 2.95
5 . . . . 2.95
6 . . . . 2.95
TPB 11.95

LENSMAN
Eternity 1990
1 E.E.`Doc' Smith adapt. 2.25
2 . . . . 2.25
3 . . . . 2.25
4 . . . . 2.25
5 On Radelix 2.25
6 . . . . 2.25
Collectors Spec #1, 56 pgs. 3.95
TPB Birth of a Lensman, rep. 5.95
TPB Secret of the Lens, rep.. . . . . 5.95

LENSMAN: GALACTIC PATROL
Eternity 1990
1 thru 7 E.E. `Doc' Smith adapt.. . @2.25

LENSMAN: WAR OF THE GALAXIES
Eternity 1990
1 thru 7 . . . . @2.25

LEONARDO
1 TMNT. 13.00

LETHAL LADIES OF BRAINSTORM
Brainstorm 1997
1 F:Luxura, Vampfire, etc. 2.95
1 nude cover edition 3.95
1 luxury edition 5.00

LETHAL STRIKE ARCHIVES
London Night 1997
1 rep. Razor #7, #10 & Uncut
    #19–#21. . . . . 3.00
1 nude cover edition 10.00
TPB Lethal Strike (1998). 12.95

LETHAL STRIKE: SHADOW VIPER
London Night 1998
1 (of 2) from Razor: Torture #4. . . . 3.00
1 nude cover. 6.00
1 leather 15.00

LETHARGIC LAD ADVENTURES
Crusade Entertainment 1997
1 by Greg Hyland 2.95
2 . . . . 2.95
Becomes:

LETHARGIC LAD
TV Comics 1997
3 by Greg Hyland 2.95
4 . . . . 2.95
5 . . . . 2.95
TPB Big Book of Lethargic Lad. . . 15.95
Lethargic Comics
6 by Greg Hyland 2.95
7 thru 11 . . . . @2.95

LEVEL X
Caliber 1997
1 . . . . 2.95
2 32pg. 2.95
3 48pg 3.95

LEVEL X: THE NEXT REALITY
Caliber 1997
1 (of 2) by Dan Harbison & Randy
  Buccini, 64pg 3.95
2 48pg. 3.95

LIBBY ELLIS
1 . . . . 1.95
2 . . . . 1.95
Eternity
1 thru 4 . . . . @1.95

LIBERATOR
Eternity
1 thru 6 . . . . @1.95

L.I.F.E. BRIGADE
Blue Comet
1 A:Dr. Death 1.50
1a 2nd printing 1.50
2 . . . . 1.50

LIFEQUEST
Caliber Dec. 1997
1 by Matt Vanderpol 2.95
2 . . . . 2.95
3 . . . . 2.95
4 . . . . 2.95
5 . . . . 2.95
6 . . . . 2.95

LIVINGSTONE MOUNTAIN
Adventure Comics 1991
1 I:Scat,Dragon Rax 2.50
2 Scat & Rax Create Monsters . . . 2.50
3 Rax rescue attempt 2.50
4 Final issue 2.50

LLOYD LLEWELLYN
Fantagraphics
1 Mag Size 4.00
2 Mag Size 2.25
3 Mag Size 2.25
4 Mag Size 2.25
5 Mag Size 2.25
6 Mag Size 2.25
7 Regular Size. 2.25

LOCO VS. PULVERINE
Eclipse
1 Parody 2.50

LODOSS WAR: THE GREY WITCH
CPM Manga 1998
1 by Ryo Mizuno & Yoshihiko Ochi 2.95
2 by Ryo Mizuno & Akikiro Yamada 2.95
3 thru 10 . . . . @2.95

LODOSS WAR: THE LADY OF PHARIS
CPM Manga 1999
1 by Ryo Mizuno & Akihiro Yamada 2.95
2 . . . . 2.95
3 . . . . 2.95
4 . . . . 2.95
5 . . . . 2.95

Logan's Run #3
© Adventure Comics

LOGAN'S RUN
Adventure Comics 1990
1 thru 6 Novel adapt. . . . . @2.50

LOGAN'S WORLD
Adventure Comics 1991
1 Seq. to Logan's Run 2.50
2 thru 6 . . . . @2.50

LONER
Fleetway
1 Pt. 1 of 7 . . . . 1.95
2 Pt. 2 . . . . 1.95
3 Pt. 3 . . . . 1.95
4 Pt. 4 . . . . 1.95
5 Pt. 5 . . . . 1.95
6 Pt. 6 . . . . 1.95

LONE WOLF & CUB
First
1 FM(c) 7.00
1a 2nd printing 2.50
1b 3rd printing 1.50
2 . . . . 4.00
2a 2nd printing 2.00
3 . . . . 3.50
4 thru 10 . . . . @3.00
11 thru 17 . . . . @2.75
18 thru 25 . . . . @2.50
26 thru 36 . . . . @2.95
37 and 38 . . . . @3.25
39 120 Page 5.95
40 . . . . 3.25
41 MP(c), 60 page 3.95
42 MP(c) 3.25
43 MP(c) 3.25
44 MP(c) 3.25
45 MP(c) 3.25

LOOKERS
Avatar Press 1997
1 . . . . 3.00
1 deluxe 5.00
1 signed 15.00
2 . . . . 3.00
2 Deluxe cover 10.00
Spec. #1 . . . . 3.00
Spec. #1, nude cover 4.95
Spec. #1 signed 10.00
Spec. Allure of the Serpent (1999) . 3.50
Spec. Allure of the Serpent,nude(c) 6.00
Spec. Slaves of Anubis (1998) . . . 3.50
Spec. Slaves of Anubis,nude(c) . . 6.00

LORD OF THE DEAD
Conquest
1 R.E.Howard adapt. 2.95

LORI LOVECRAFT
Caliber 1997
1 MV, 48pg 3.95
1a signed 3.95
1-shot The Dark Lady (1997) 2.95
1-shot Repression (1998) 2.95
Spec. The Big Comeback (1998) . . 2.95

LOST, THE
Caliber
1 . . . . 3.00
1a special ed. 7.00
1b signed 3.00
2 thru 4 . . . . @3.00

LOST ANGEL
Caliber
1 . . . . 3.50

LOST CONTINENT
Eclipse 1990
1 thru 5, Manga . . . . @3.50

LOST STORIES
Creative Frontiers 1998
1 . . . . 2.95
2 . . . . 2.95
3 . . . . 2.95
4 The Big Horn Bruhaha 2.95
5 Strike Force O'Shea, pt.1 . . . . . 2.95
6 Strike Force O'Shea, pt.2 . . . . . 2.95
7 Gnome for a Day 2.95
8 A Vampire Too Far 2.95
9 The Undertroll Saga, pt.1 . . . . . 2.95

LOST WORLD, THE
Millennium 1996
1 & 2 Arthur Conan Doyle adapt. @2.95

LOTHAR
Powerhouse Graphics
1 I:Lothar,Galactic Bounty Hunter . 2.50
2 I:Nightcap. 2.50

LOVE AND ROCKETS
Fantagraphics Books 1982–96
1 HB,B&W cover, adult 60.00
1a HB,Color cover. 30.00
1b 2nd printing 4.00
2 HB 25.00
3 HB 15.00
4 HB 15.00
5 HB 15.00
6 HB 7.00
7 HB 8.00
8 HB 8.00
9 HB 7.00
10 HB. 7.00
11 HB. 5.00
12 HB. 5.00
13 HB. 5.00
14 HB. 5.00
15 HB. 5.00
16 thru 21 HB . . . . @3.00
22 thru 39 HB . . . . @3.00
40 thru 50 . . . . @3.00
Bonanza rep. 3.00
TPB Vol 9 Flies on the Ceiling,
  2nd printing 16.95
HC Vol 10 Love & Rockets X . . 35.00
HC Vol 10 deluxe 39.95
TPB Vol 10 . . . . 11.95
HC Vol 11 Wigwam Bam. 35.00
HC Vol 11 deluxe 39.95
TPB Vol 11 . . . . 14.95
HC Vol 12 Poison River 35.00
HC Vol 12 deluxe 39.95
TPB Vol 12 . . . . 16.95
HC Vol 13 Chester Square 34.95
TPB Vol 14 Luba Conquers the
  World 14.95
HC Vol 14 Luba Conquers the World. . .
34.95
HC Vol 14 , signed 39.95
TPB Vol 15 . . . . 14.95
HC Vol 15 . . . . 34.95
HC Vol 15 , signed 39.95

LUFTWAFFE 1946
Antarctic Press
1 (of 4) by Ted Namura & BDn. . . . 2.95
2 Luftsturm, pt.2 thru 4. . . . . . . @2.95
3 . . . . 2.95
4 . . . . 2.95
5 new weapons 2.95
6 Projekt Saucer, pt.1 . . . . 2.95
7 Projekt Saucer, pt.2 . . . . 2.95
8 Projekt Saucer, pt.3 . . . . 2.95
9 Projekt Saucer, pt.4 . . . . 2.95
10 Projekt Saucer, pt.5 . . . . 2.95
11 Projekt Saucer, epilogue 2.95
12 Richthofen's Flying Circus, pt.1 . 2.95
13 Richthofen's Flying Circus, pt.2 . 2.95
14 Jagdeschwader,pt.2 . . . . 2.95
15 Jagdeschwader, pt.3 . . . . 3.00
16 Jagdeschwader, pt.4 . . . . 3.00
17 Jagdeschwader, pt.5 . . . . 3.00
18 Schweinfurt 3.00
Tech Manual Vol. 1 . . . . 3.95
Tech Manual Vol. 2. . . . . 4.00
Spec. #1 Triebflugel 2.95
Spec.#1 World War II: 1946 . . . . . 3.95
Ann. #1 prototype artwork. 2.95

Luftwaffe 1946 #5
© Antarctic Press

TPB Vol.1, rep.mini-series #1–#4 . 10.95
TPB Vol.2, rep. #1–#5. . . . . 10.95
TPB Vol. 3, rep. 10.95

LUM*URESEI YATSURA
1 Art by Rumiko Takahashi 2.95
2 . . . . 2.95
3 . . . . 2.95
4 . . . . 2.95
5 . . . . 3.25
6 thru 8 . . . . @2.95

LUNAR DONUT
Cosmic Lunchbox Comics
1 thru 4 by Keelan Parham
  & Ted Tucker . . . . @2.95
Lunar Donut
5 . . . . 2.95
6 Powdered Sugar. 2.95

LUXURA
Brainstorm 1996
Convention Book 2. . . . . 2.95
Ann.#1 48pg (1998) 3.95
Ann.#1a nude cover 3.95

LUXURA & VAMPFIRE
Brainstorm 1997
1 by Fauve 2.95
1a nude cover 3.95

LUXURA/BABY ANGEL X
Brainstorm 1996
Spec. x-over. 2.95
Spec. deluxe 5.00
Luxury edition 10.00
Deluxe luxury edition 15.00

LUXURA LEATHER
Brainstorm
Platinum edition 5.00
Signed edition. 10.00

LUXURA/WIDOW:
BLOOD LUST
Brainstorm
Omega x-over pt.2 concl. 2.95

Omega Fusion cover 5.00
Luxury edition 10.00
Deluxe luxury edition 15.00
See: Widow/Luxura for pt.1

LYNX: AN ELFLORD TALE
Peregrin 1999
1 by Barry Blair 2.95
2 by Barry Blair & Colin Chan 2.95
3 . . . . 2.95
4 . . . . 2.95

MACH 1
Fleetway
1 I:John Probe-Secret Agent 1.95

MACKENZIE QUEEN
1 thru 5 . . . . @3.75

MACROSS II
Viz
1 Macross Saga sequel. 2.75
2 A:Ishtar 2.75
3 F:Reporter Hibiki,Ishtar. 2.75
4 V:Feff,The Marduk 2.75
5 . . . . 2.75
6 . . . . 2.75
7 Sylvie Confesses 2.75
8 F:Ishtar. 2.75
9 V:Marduk Fleet. 2.75
10 . . . . 2.75

MACROSS II: THE
MICRON CONSPIRACY
Viz 1994
1 Manga 2.75

MAD DOGS
Eclipse 1992
1 I:Mad Dogs(Cops) 2.50
2 V:Chinatown Hood. 2.50
3 . . . . 2.50

MAD RACCOONS
MU Press 1991
1 thru 7 by Cathy Hill, Angst of
  an Artist . . . . @2.95

MAELSTROM
Aircel
1 thru 5 . . . . @1.70
6 thru 13 . . . . @1.50

MAGGOTS
1 JSon, mag size. 3.95
2 JSon, mag size. 3.95
3 GM/JSon,inc.`Some Kinda
  Beautiful' 3.95

MAGICAL MATES
Antarctic Press 1995
1 & 2 Manga, by Mio Odagi . . . . @2.95
3 thru 8 (of 8). . . . . @2.95

MAGUS
Caliber Core May 1998
1L by Gary Reed & Craig Brasfield,
  VcL(c) 2.95
1D GyD(c). 2.95
1 premium edition, signed 9.95
2 Magus secrets 2.95

---

3 Lilith & Beezlebub. 2.95
1-shot Magus: The Forever King. . . 2.95
Spec. Dawn of Armageddon,
   x-over, 48-page 2.95

MAI, THE PSYCHIC GIRL
Eclipse
1 I:Mai,Alliance of 13 Sages 3.75
1a 2nd printing 2.00
2 V:Wisdom Alliance 2.00
2a 2nd printing 1.50
3 V:Kaieda,I:Ojii-San 2.00
4 . . . . 2.00
5 thru 19 . . . . @1.75
20 thru 28 . . . . @1.50

MAISON IKKOKU
Viz
1 thru 7 . . . . 2.95
[Part Two]
1 thru 6 . . . . 2.95
[Part Three]
1 thru 6 . . . . 2.95
[Part Four]
1 thru 6 F:Kyoko 2.95
7 thru 10 . . . . @2.95
[Part Six] Aug. 1996
1 thru 11 by Rumiko Takahashi . @3.50
[Part Seven] July 1997
1 thru 8 by Rumiko Takahashi . . @3.25
9 thru 13 . . . . @3.50
[Part Eight] Aug. 1998
1 (of 8) 3.25
2 . . . . 3.50
3 thru 8 . . . . @3.25
[Part Nine] 1999
1 (of 10) thru 5 . . . . @3.25
TPB Vol. 4 Good Housekeeping . . 15.95
TPB Vol. 5 Empty Nest 15.95
TPB Vol. 6 Bedside Manners 15.95
TPB Vol. 7 Intensive Care. 15.95
TPB Vol. 8 Domestic Dispute 16.95
TPB Vol. 10 Dogged Pursuit 17.95
TPB Vol. 11 Student Affairs. 16.95
TPB Vol. 12 The Hounds of War . . 16.95

MAN EATING COW
1 Spin-off from the Tick 3.25
2 O:Mr.Krinkles,A:Lt.Valentine . . . 2.75
3 Final issue 2.75
Bonanza #1, 128pg 4.95
Bonanza #2, 100pg. 4.95

MAN-ELF
3 A:Jerry Cornelius 2.25

MANDRAKE
1 . . . . 3.95
2 . . . . 3.95
3 . . . . 3.95
Ultimate Mandrake 14.95

MANDRAKE MONTHLY
1 . . . . 3.95
2 . . . . 3.95
3 . . . . 4.95
4 . . . . 4.95
5 . . . . 4.95
6 . . . . 6.95
Special #1 . . . . 6.95

MAN FROM U.N.C.L.E.
Entertainment Publ.
1 `Number One with a Bullet Affair. 2.50

2 `Number One with a Bullet Affair. 2.00
3 `The E-I-E-I-O Affair'. 1.50
4 `The E-I-E-I-O Affair,' concl. 1.50
5 `The Wasp Affair' 1.50
6 `Lost City of THRUSH Affair'. . . . 1.50
7 `The Wildwater Affair' 1.50
8 `The Wilder West Affair' 1.50
9 `The Cahadian Lightning Affair'. . 1.75
10 `The Turncoat Affair' 1.75
11 `Craters of the Moon Affair' 1.75

MANGA MONTHLY
0 . . . . 3.00

MANGA VIZION
Viz
1 thru 8 Ogre Slayer 4.95

MANGAZINE
Antartic Press
1 newsprint cover 7.00
1a reprint. 3.00
2 . . . . 5.00
3 . . . . 4.00
4 . . . . 2.00
5 . . . . 1.50
New Series
1 . . . . 3.00
2 . . . . 3.00
3 . . . . 1.75
4 . . . . 1.75
5 thru 7 . . . . @1.95
8 thru 13 . . . . @2.25
14 New Format. 2.95
15 . . . . 2.95
16 . . . . 2.95
17 . . . . 2.95

MANIMAL
1 EC,rep. 1.70

Man of Rust #1B
© Blackthorne

MAN OF RUST
Blackthorne 1986
1 Cover A 1.50
1 Cover B 1.50

MANSLAUGHTER
Brainstorm 1996
1 . . . . 2.95

1a gold foil edition 5.00

MANTUS FILES
Eternity
1 Sidney Williams novel adapt. . . . 2.50
2 Vampiric Figures. 2.50
3 Securas' Mansion. 2.50
4 A:Secarus 2.50

MARCANE
Eclipse
1 Book 1,JMu 5.95

MARK I
(Prev.: Atomic Comics)
2 . . . . 1.50

MARQUIS, THE
Caliber 1997
1 GyD 3.00
1 spec. double gatefold cover 7.00
2 Marquis cover by Vincent Locke . 3.00
2a Marquis view of world GyD(c) . . 3.00
3 . . . . 3.00
Spec. The Marquis, Gallery of
   Hell, GyD 3.95
Spec. The Marquis: Les Preludes, GyD
   prelude edition (1996). 2.95
Spce.A Les Preludes, signed 2.95

MASKED WARRIOR X
Antarctic Press April 1996
1 (of 6) by Masayuki Fujihara. . . . 3.50
2 . . . . 2.95
3 The Girls of Olympus," pt.2. . . . . 2.95
4 "Protect the Silver Fortress" 2.95

MASQUERADE
Eclipse
1 . . . . 1.50
2 . . . . 1.95
3 . . . . 1.95

MATAAK
K-Blamm 1995
1 I:Mataak 2.50
2 Spirit of Peace 2.50

MATT CHAMPION
1 EC 2.00
2 EC 2.00

MAVIS
Exhibit A 1998
1 BLs, F:Wolff & Byrd's secretary. . 2.95
2 . . . . 2.95

MAX OF REGULATORS
1 . . . . 5.00
2 . . . . 3.50
3 . . . . 3.50
4 . . . . 3.50

MAXWELL MOUSE FOLLIES
1 Large format (1981) 5.00
1a Comic Size(1986). 3.00
2 thru 6 . . . . @2.00

MAYHEM
1 thru 6 . . . . @2.50

MAZE AGENCY
Caliber 1997
1 "The Death of Justice Girl"
  reprint series 2.95
1a signed 2.95
2 stranded in a monastery, Gene
  Gonzales(c) 2.95
2a Adam Hughes (c) 2.95
3G The Two Wrong Rhoades,
  Gonzales(c) 2.95
3H Adam Hughes(c) 2.95

MEASLES
Fantagraphics 1998
1 by Gilbert Hernandez 2.95
2 . . . . 2.95
3 . . . . 2.95
4 . . . . 2.95

MECHANOIDS
Caliber 1991
1 . . . . 2.50
2 thru 5 . . . . @3.50

MECHARIDER: THE REGULAR SERIES
Castle
1 thru 3 F:Winter 2.95
Spec.#1 Limited Edition 2.95

MEGATON
Megaton
1 JG(c),EL(1stProWork),GD,MG,
  A:Ultragirl,Vanguard 8.00
2 EL,JG(pin-up),A:Vanguard 8.00
3 MG,AMe,JG,EL,I:Savage Dragon . . . 13.00
4 AMe,EL,2nd A:Savage Dragon
  (inc.EL profile) 9.00
5 AMe,RLd(inside front cover) 3.00
6 AMe,JG(inside back cover),
  EL(Back cover) 3.00
7 AMe 3.00
8 RLd,I:Youngblood(Preview). . . . 18.00

MEGATON MAN
1 . . . . 2.00

MEGATON MAN MEETS THE UNCATEGORIZABLE X-THEMS
Jabberwocky
1 . . . . 2.00

MEGATON MAN VS. FORBIDDEN FRANKENSTEIN
Fiasco Comics April 1996
1 by Don Simpson & Anton Drek . . 2.95

MELISSA MOORE: BODYGUARD
Draculina Publishing 1995
1 thru 3 V:Machine Gun Eddie . . @2.95

MEN IN BLACK
Aircel 1991
1 by Lowell Cunningham & Sandy
  Carruthers, basis of Movie . . . 50.00

Men in Black #1
© Aircel

2 . . . . 30.00
3 F:Jay, Arbiter Doran 25.00
(Book II) 1991
1 . . . . 20.00
2 thru 3 . . . . @10.00

MEN IN BLACK: THE ROBORG INCIDENT
Castle
1 thru 3 . . . . @2.95

MEMORY MAN
Emergency Stop Press 1995
1 thru 2 Some of the Space Man . . 2.95

MERCEDES
Angus Publishing
8 thru 15 by Mike Friedland
  & Grant Fuhst. . . . . @2.95
TPB Vol. 2 . . . . 10.95
TPB Vol. 3, rep. The Wicked
  from #11–#15 . . . . 10.95
VOL. 4
1 thru 4 . . . . @2.95
VOL. 5 1997
1 . . . . 2.95
2 . . . . 2.95
3 . . . . 2.95
Spec. Senseless Acts of
  Beauty (1998) 2.95

MERCHANTS OF DEATH
Eclipse
1 thru 5 . . . . @1.95

MERCY
Avatar Press Dec. 1997
0 O:Mercy 3.00
0a nude cover 6.00
0b leather cover. 30.00
1 (of 2) by Bill Maus 3.00
1 nude cover 4.95
1 leather cover 25.00
1 signed 10.00

MERLIN
Adventure Comics Dec. 1990
1 BMC,Merlin's Visions 2.50
2 V:Warlord Carados 2.50
3 . . . . 2.50
4 Ninevah 2.50
5 D:Hagus. 2.50
6 Final Issue 2.50
[2nd Series]
1 Journey of Rhiannon & Tryon . . . 2.50
2 Conclusion 2.50

MERMAID'S GAZE
Viz
1 thru 3 V:Shingo. 2.75
4 final issue. 2.75
TPB 15.95

Metacops #1
© Monster Comics

METACOPS
Monster Comics
1 and 2 . . . . @1.95

METAL GUARDIAN FAUST
Viz Communications March 1997
1 thru 5 (of 8) by Tetsuo Ueyama @2.95
6 thru 8 . . . . @2.95
TPV Vol. 1 . . . . 16.95

METROPOLIS
Caliber 1997
0 movie adaptation, series
  prequel,48pg 3.95
1 The Last Fredersen, pt.1 . . . . . . 2.95
2 The Last Fredersen, pt.2 . . . . . . 2.95
3 The Last Fredersen, pt.3 . . . . . . 2.95

METAPHYSIQUE
Eclipse
1 NB,Short Stories. 2.50
2 NB,Short Stories. 2.50

MIAMI MICE
Rip Off Press
1 1st printing 3.00
1a 2nd printing 2.00
3 . . . . 2.00
4 Record,A:TMNT 3.00

MICHELANGELO
Mirage
1 TMNT................. 17.00
1a 2nd Printing 4.50

Micra #1
© Fictioneer

MICRA
Fictioneer
1 .... 4.00
2 and 3 .... @3.00
4 .... 2.00
5 thru 7 .... @1.75
8 .... 2.25

MIDNIGHT
Blackthorne
1 thru 4 .... @1.75

MIDNIGHT PANTHER
CPM Comics 1997
1 Manga, translated........... 2.95
2 .... 2.95
3 .... 2.95
4 .... 2.95
5 .... 2.95
6 Den of Scoundrels 2.95
7 The Sleeping Town......... 2.95
8 to Reincarnation City 2.95
9 O:Midnight Panthers........ 2.95
10 .... 2.95
11 .... 2.95
12 .... 2.95
TPB Sex, Death and Rock 'n' Roll.
  rep #1–#6............. 15.95
TPB Book 2: Feline Fanatics,
  rep.#7–#12........... 15.95
Spec. Breaking Up is Hard to Do .. 2.95

MIDNIGHT PANTHER:
FEUDAL FANTASY
CPM Manga 1998
1 by Yu Asagiri 2.95
2 thru 5 .... @2.95
TPB Book 4: Feudal Fantasy 15.95

MIDNIGHT PANTHER:
SCHOOL DAZE
CPM Comics 1998
1 (of 5) by Yu Asagiri.......... 2.95

2 thru 5 .... @2.95
TPB Book 3: School Daze 15.95

MIDNITE SKULKER
1 thru 7 .... @1.75

MIGHTY GUY
C&T
1 thru 6 .... @1.50
Summer Fun Spec #1 .... 2.50

MIGHTY MITES
Continum
1 I:X-Mites................. 1.95
2 .... 1.95

MIGHTY MOUSE
ADVENTURE MAGAZINE
1 .... 2.00

MIGHTY TINY
1 thru 4 .... @1.75
5 .... 2.50
Mouse Marines Collection rep..... 7.50

MILK & CHEESE
Slave Labor 1991–97
1 EDo, Milk Products gone bad . 100.00
1a 2nd thru 7th printing 3.50
2 .... 50.00
2a 2nd thru 4th printing 10.00
3 .... 30.00
3a 2nd thru 4th printing 10.00
4 .... 20.00
4a 2nd & 3rd printing......... 3.00
5 .... 20.00
5a 2nd & 3rd printing......... 3.00
6 .... 15.00
6a 2nd printing 2.75
Other #1................. 2.75
Third #1................. 2.75
Fourth #1................ 2.75
First #2................. 2.75
Six Six Six #1............. 2.75
Six Six Six 2nd printing, EDo ... 2.75
Latest Thing 2.95
TPB Fun with Milk & Cheese, rep.
  1st 4 issues 11.95

MINIMUM WAGE
Fantagraphics
Vol. 1, new printing............ 9.95
Vol. 2
5 by Bob Fingerman 2.95
6 .... 2.95
7 .... 2.95
8 .... 2.95
9 Artsy Fartsy 2.95
10 .... 2.95
TPB Vol. 2, rep. #1–#5 .... 12.95

MIRACLE SQUAD
BLOOD & DUST
Apple
1 thru 3 .... @1.95

MISTER BLANK
Amaze Ink 1997
0 by Chris Hicks 1.75
0a 2nd printing 1.75
1 F:Sam Smith 2.95
2 thru 11 .... @2.95

MISTER X
Vortex, Vol 2
1 thru 11 .... @2.00

MITES
1 .... 2.50
1a 1.90
2B 1.80
3 and 4 .... @1.80

MOBILE POLICE
PATLABOR
Viz Communications
1 (of 12) by Masami Yuki........ 2.95
PART TWO
1 by Masami Yuki 2.95
2 thru 6 .... @2.95
TPB Vol. 1 .... 15.95
TPB Vol. 2 Basic Training....... 15.95

MOBILE SUIT
GUNDAM 0079
Viz Communications 1999
1 (of 8) by Kazhisa Kondo ..... @2.95
2 thru 6 .... @2.95

MODERN PULP
Special Studio
1 Rep.from January Midnight..... 2.75

MOEBIUS COMICS
Caliber 1996
1 Moe.................... 2.95
2 Moe 2.95
3 Moe 2.95
4 Moe,MP 2.95
5 Moe,SL 2.95
6 Moe 2.95

MOGOBI DESERT RATS
Midnight Comics
1 I&O:Desert Rats 'Waste of the
  World'................ 2.25

MONNGA
Daikaiyu Enterprises 1995
1 & 2 Titanic Omega 3.95

MONOGRAPHS
Coppervale 1997
1 by James Owen 2.95
2 Bob Phantom 2.95
3 Sidekick Wanted—Benefits
  Available 2.95
4 thru 6 .... 2.95

MONSTER BOY
Monster Comics
1 A:Monster Boy 2.25

MONSTER FRAT HOUSE
Eternity
1 .... 2.25

MONSTER POSSE
Adventure
1 thru 3.................. 2.50

MONSTERS ATTACK
1 GM,JSe 2.00
2 GC. 1.75
3 ATh,GC 1.50

MONSTERS FROM OUTER SPACE
Adventure 1992
1 thru 3 . . . . @2.50

MORBID ANGEL: DESPERATE ANGELS
London Night 1998
0 EHr, & Jude Millien 3.00
0A Powell(c) 5.00
0B Powell(c) 5.00

MORBID ANGEL: PENANCE
London Night Studios 1995
1 I:Brandon Watts 4.00

MORBID ANGEL: TO HELL AND BACK
London Night Oct. 1996
1 (of 3) EHr, ... 4.00
2 and 3 . . . . @3.00

MORNING GLORY
Radio Comix 1998
1 by Loran Gayton & Michael Vega 2.95
2 thru 6 . . . . @2.95

MORTAL COIL
Mermaid
1 thru 3 . . . . @2.25
4 F:Red-Line,Gift. 2.25
5 Pin-Up Issue. 2.25

MORTAR MAN
Marshall Comics
1 I:Mortar Man. 1.95
2 thru 3 . . . . @1.95

MOSAIC
Oktober Black Press
1 F:Halo,Daeva 2.25
2 "Gun Metal Gray" 2.50
3 . . . . 2.50
4 Elf(c) 2.50
5 Wisps. 2.50

MOSAIC
Sirius 1999
1 by Kyle Hotz. 2.95
2 thru 5 conclusion. . . . . @2.95

MOUNTAIN WORLD
Newcomers Press 1995
1 I:Jeremiah Rainshadow 2.95

MR. BEAT ADVENTURES
Moordam Comics Jan. 1997
1 . . . . 2.95
1 deluxe 5.00
Spec. House of Burning Jazz Love . 2.95
Spec. deluxe 5.00
Two-Fisted Atomic Action
    Super Spec. 2.95

Two-Fisted Atomic Action
    Super Spec., deluxe 10.00
Two-Fisted Atomic Action
    Super Spec., mega deluxe . . . 20.00
Spec. Mr. Beat: Superstar. 3.00
Spec. Mr. Beat: Superstar, deluxe. 10.00
Ann.#1 Babes and Bongos 2.95

MR. FIXITT
Apple
1 and 2 . . . . @1.95

MR. MYSTIC
Eclipse
1 Will Eisner 2.50

MR. NIGHTMARE'S WONDERFUL WORLD
Moonstone 1995
1 thru 3 Dreams So Real,
    pt.1–pt.3 . . . . @2.95

MS. CHRIST
Draculina Publishing 1995
1 I:Ms. Christ. 2.95

Ms Tree #44
© Renegade

MS. TREE
Aardvark–Vanaheim
1-10 see Other Pub. (color)
11 thru 18 . . . . @2.00
Renegade
19 thru 49. . . . . @2.00
50 . . . . 4.50
1 3-D Classic. 2.95

MUMMY, THE
Monster Comics
1 A:Dr.Clarke,Prof.Belmore 1.95
2 Mummy's Curse 1.95
3 A:Carloph 1.95
4 V:Carloph, conc. 1.95

MUMMY'S CURSE
Aircel 1990
1 thru 4 B.Blair. . . . . @2.25

MUNSTERS, THE
TV Comics 1998
1 photo (c). 3.00
1a variant (c). 8.00
2 Beverly Owen(c). 3.00
2 Pat Priest (c) 3.00
2 Pat Priest (c) signed 19.95
3 . . . . 3.00
3a Celebrity autograph edition . . 22.95
4 . . . . 3.00
4a variant photo (c) 3.00
4b variant (c) celebrity autograph
    edition 22.95
5 Herman photo (c) 3.00
5 Grandpa photo (c) 3.00
Spec. Comic Con edition 9.95
Celebrity Autograph Edition: Butch
    Patrick 22.95
TPB Vol 1, rep. #1–#4 . . . . 10.95
Spec.#1 Herman/Grandpa (c). . . . 3.00
Spec.#1a Grandpa (c) 3.00
Halloween Spec. Munsters 1313. . . 3.00
Golden Age Adventure Spec.A(c) . . 3.00
Golden Age Adventure Spec.B(c) . . 3.00

MUNSTERS CLASSICS
TV Comics
0 The Fregosi Emerald 3.00
0 variant (c). 7.95

MURCIELAGA: SHE-BAT
Hero Graphics
1 Daerick Gross reps. 1.50
2 Reps. contd 2.95

MURDER
Renegade 1986
1 SD 1.70
2 CI(c). 1.70
3 SD 1.70

MURDER (2nd series)
1 . . . . 2.00

MURDER CAN BE FUN
Slave Labor
1 thru 6 . . . . @2.95
2 2nd printing 2.95
7 . . . . 2.95
8 . . . . 2.95
9 Seedy Side of Sex 2.95
10 We Love Sports. 2.95
11 . . . . 2.95
12 Amusement Park Terror. 2.95

MUTANT ZONE
Aircel
1 Future story 2.50
2 F.B.I. Drone Exterminators 2.50
3 conclusion 2.50

MYSTERY MAN
Slave Labor
1 thru 5 . . . . @1.75

MYTH ADVENTURES
Warp Graphics
1 Mag size 1.50
2 thru 4 . . . . @1.50
5 Comic size 1.50
6 thru 11 . . . . @1.50
12 . . . . 1.75

All comics prices listed are for *Near Mint* condition.   **CVA Page 643**

MYTH CONCEPTIONS
Apple
1	1.75
2	1.75
3 thru 8	@1.95

MYTHOGRAPHY
Bardic Press 1966
1 F:Poison Elves	3.95
2 fantasy stories	3.95
3 fantasy stories, inc. Elfquest	3.95
4	4.25
5 72pg.	4.25
6 F:Anubis Squadron 72pg.	3.95
7 80 pg.	4.25
8 72 pg.	4.25

MYTHOS
Wonder Comix
1 and 2	@1.50

NATURE OF THE BEAST
Caliber
1 thru 3 'The Beast'	@2.95

NAUGHTY BITS
Fantagraphics
20	2.95
21 I:Bitchy Butch	2.95
22	2.95
23 O:Bitchy Butch	2.95
24	2.95
25 by Roberta Gregory	2.95
26	2.95
27	2.95
28	2.95
29	2.95
TPB Vol. 4: Bitchy's School Daze	9.95
TPB Vol. 5: Bitchy Butch	9.95

NAUSICAA OF THE VALLEY OF WIND
Viz Select
Book One	4.50
Book Two	5.50
Book Three	4.00
Book Four	3.00
Book Five	2.50

Book Six	2.95
Book Seven	2.95

[Part 2]
#1 thru #4	@2.95

[Part 3]
#1 thru #3	@2.95
TPB Vol. 4	17.95

NAZRAT
Imperial 1986
1	2.50
2 thru 6	@2.00

NECROSCOPE
Caliber 1997
1 Brian Lumley adapt.	2.95
1 signed	2.95
2	2.95
3	2.95
4	2.95

NEGATIVE BURN
Caliber
1 I:Matrix 7, Flaming Carrot	5.00
2	3.50
3 Bone preview	12.00
4 thru 12 various stories	@3.25
13 Strangers in Paradise	10.00
14 thru 18 various stories	@3.50
19 Flaming Carrot	5.00
20 In the Park	3.25
21 Trollords	3.00
22 Father the Dryad	3.00
23 I:The Creep	3.00
24 The Factor	3.00
25 The Factor	4.00
26 Very Vicki	3.00
27 Nancy Kate	3.00
28 Favorite Song	4.00
29 thru 33	4.00
34 Kaos Moon	7.00
35 thru 38	@4.00
39 "Iron Empires," pt. 4	4.00
40 "Suzi Romaine"	4.00
41 "Iron Empires," cont.	4.00
42	4.00
43 "Iron Empires," concl.	4.00
44 "Skeleton Key"	4.00
45 "Divine Winds"	4.00
46 "A Bullet For Me"	4.00
47	4.00
48 special 80 page issue	5.00
49 special 80 page issue	5.00
50 96pg, final issue	6.95
TPB Best of Year One	9.95
TPB Best of Year Two	9.95

NEIL THE HORSE
Aardvark–Vanaheim
1 Art:Arn Sara	5.00
1a 2nd printing	2.00
2	3.00
3	4.00
4	3.00
5 Video Warriors	2.00
6 Video Warriors	2.00
7 Video Warriors	2.00
8 Outer Space	2.00
9 Conan	2.00
10	2.00

Renegade
11 Fred Astair	1.70
12	1.70
13	1.70
14 Special	3.00
15	1.70

NEMESIS THE WARLOCK
Fleetway
1 thru 16	@1.95

NEON CITY
Innovation
1	2.25

NEON GENESIS EVANGELION
Viz Communication 1997
1 (of 6) by Gainax & Yoshiyuki Sadamoto	3.25
1 special collectors edition	2.95
2 thru 6	@2.95
2 thru 6 special collectors ed.	@2.95
TPB Vol. 1	16.50
TPB Vol. 1 special collectors ed.	16.50

BOOK TWO March 1998
1 (of 5) by Yoshiyuki Sadamoto	2.95
1 special collectors edition	2.95
2 thru 5	@2.95
2 thru 5 special collectors ed.	@2.95
TPB Book 2	15.95
TPB Book 2, collector ed.	15.95

BOOK THREE
1 thru 6 by Yoshiyuki Sadamoto	@2.95
1a thru 6a Collectors edition	@2.95
GN Vol. 3 Evangelion	15.95
GN Vol. 3 Evangelion, coll. ed.	15.95

BOOK FOUR 1999
1 thru 7 by Yoshiyuki Sadamoto	@2.95
1a thru 7a special collectors ed.	@2.95

NERVOUS REX
1	3.00
1a 2nd printing	2.00
2	3.00
3	3.00
4	2.50
5 thru 10	@2.00
GraphicNovel	3.50

NEW ADVENTURES OF TERRY & THE PIRATES
ACG Comics 1998
1 by Bros. Hildebrandt	2.95
2	2.95
3	2.95
4	2.95
5	2.95
6	2.95

NEWCOMERS ILLUSTRATED
Newcomers Publishing
1 thru 5 various artists	@2.95
6 Science Fiction	2.95
7 thru 8	@2.95
9 Shocking Machines	2.95
10	2.95
11 Hitman	2.95
12 final issue	2.95

NEW ERADICATORS
Vol 2 #1 NewBeginnings	2.00
Vol 2 #2 NewBeginnings	2.00
Vol 2 #3 NewFriends	2.00

NEW FRONTIERS
1 CS(c)	3.00
1a 2nd Printing	1.75

NEW FRONTIERS
Evolution
1 A:Action Master, Green Ghost . . 1.95

NEW HERO COMICS
Pierce
1 and 2 . . . . @1.00

NEW HORIZONS
Shanda Fantasy Arts Jan. 1997
1 . . . . 4.95
2 . . . . 4.50
3 . . . . 4.50
4 . . . . 4.50
5 . . . . 4.50
6 . . . . 4.95

NEW HUMANS
Eternity
1 . . . . 1.80
2 thru 15 . . . . @1.95
Ann. #1 . . . . 2.95

NEW HUMANS
1 Shattered Earth Chronicles. 1.95

NEW PULP
ADVENTURES SPECIAL
Dunewadd Comics
1 I:Kawala. 2.50

NEW REALITY
1 thru 6 . . . . @1.25

NEWSTRALIA
Innovation
(Prev. Color)
4 . . . . 2.25
5 . . . . 2.25

NEW TRIUMPH
Matrix Graphics
1 F:Northguard 3.00
1a 2nd printing 1.75
2 thru 4 . . . . @1.50

New Triumph #3
© Matrix

NEW VAMPIRE MIYU
Ironcat 1997
1 by Narumi Kakinouchi 2.95
2 . . . . 2.95
3 . . . . 2.95
4 . . . . 2.95
5 . . . . 2.95
6 . . . . 2.95
7 The Past Lies Beyond a Door,
    finale 2.95
GN rep. #1–#7 . . . . 17.95
Vol. 2 1998
1 by Narumi Kakinouchi 2.95
2 thru 6 . . . . @2.95
Vol. 3 1998
1 . . . . 2.95
2 thru 7 . . . . @2.95
Vol. 4
1 by Narumi Kakinouchi 2.95
2 . . . . 2.95
3 . . . . 2.95
4 . . . . 2.95

NEW WORLD DISORDER
Millenium 1995
1 I:King Skin Gang 2.95

NEW WORLD ORDER
Blazer Studios
1 thru 8 . . . . @2.50

NEW YORK CITY
OUTLAWS
1 thru 5 . . . . @2.50

NEW YORK, YEAR ZERO
Eclipse
1 thru 4 . . . . @2.00

NEXUS
Capital
1 SR,I:Nexus,large size 15.00
2 SR,Mag size. 10.00
3 SR,Mag size. 6.00

NIGHT
Amaze Ink 1995
0 V:The Prince 1.50

NIGHT ANGEL
Substance Comics 1995
1 I:Night Angel. 2.95

NIGHT CRY
CFD Productions 1995
1 Evil Ernie & Razor story 10.00
1 signed 12.00
2 . . . . 6.00
3 . . . . 5.00
4 . . . . 4.00
4a platinum (c) 6.00
5 . . . . 4.00
6 . . . . 2.75
6a signed 8.00

NIGHT LIFE
Caliber
1 thru 7 . . . . @1.50

NIGHT MASTER
1 Vigil 5.50
2 Vigil 2.50
3 . . . . 1.50

NIGHT OF THE
LIVING DEAD
Fantaco
0 prelude 1.75
1 based on cult classic movie 4.95
2 Movie adapt,continued 4.95
3 Movie adapt,conclusion 4.95
5 . . . . 5.95
TPB Official Complete story, rep. . 24.95
TPB London, Clive Barker's story . 14.95

NIGHT'S CHILDREN
Fantaco
1 . . . . 3.50
2 and 3 . . . . @3.50

NIGHT'S CHILDREN
Millenium 1995
1 The Ripper, Klaus Wulfe. 3.95
Spec. High Noon (1996) 2.95
Spec. The Churchyard (1997). . . . 3.25

NIGHT'S CHILDREN:
THE VAMPIRE
Millenium 1995
1 F:Klaus Wulfe. 2.95
2 F:Klaus Wulfe. 2.95

NIGHT STREETS
Arrow
1 . . . . 2.50
2 thru 4 . . . . @1.50

NIGHTVISION
London Night Nov. 1996
1 DQ,KHt, All About Eve 3.00
1 signed 12.95
1a erotica edition. 10.00

NIGHT WARRIORS:
DARKSTALKERS'
REVENGE
Viz Communications 1998
1 (of 6) by Run Ishida 2.95
2 . . . . 3.25
3 thru 6 . . . . @2.95

NIGHT ZERO
Fleetway
1 thru 4 . . . . @1.95

NIKKI BLADE
High Impact 1997
0 . . . . 2.95
0a deluxe adult cover 10.00
0b gold edition variant cover 14.95
Spec.#0 Nikki Blade: Forever Nikki
    (1997) MIB(c). 2.95
    Deluxe RCI(c). 10.00
ABC Comics 1998
Spec. Nikki Blade: Blades of Death
    (1998) by RCI & Clayton Henry. 3.00
    Puzzle variant A cover 5.95
    Puzzle variant B cover 5.95
    Puzzle variant C cover 5.95

B & W PUB

Spec. Nikki Blade: Revenge 3.00
RCI nude cover 5.95
Clayton Henry nude variant (c) . 5.95

NINJA
Eternity

1 . . . . 3.00
2 thru 6 . . . . @1.80
7 thru 13 . . . . @1.95

NINJA ELITE

1 thru 5 . . . . @1.50
6 thru 8 . . . . @1.95

NINJA FUNNIES
Eternity

1 and 2 . . . . @1.80
3 thru 5 . . . . @1.95

NINJA HIGH SCHOOL
Eternity

1 . . . . 1.75
2 thru 4 . . . . @1.50
5 thru 22 . . . . @1.95
23 Zardon Assassin 2.25
24 . . . . 2.25
25 Return of the Zetramen 2.25
26 Stanley the Demon 2.25
27 Return of the Zetramen 2.25
28 Threat of the super computer. . . 2.25
29 V:Super Computer. 2.25
30 I:Akaru. 2.25
31 Jeremy V:Akaru. 2.25
32 thru 34 V:Giant Monsters Pt.1
thru Pt. 3 . . . . @2.50
35 thru 43 . . . . @2.50
44 Combat Cheerleaders 2.75
45 Cheerleader Competition 2.75
46 Monsters From Space 2.75
47 . . . . 2.75
48 F:Jeremy Feeple 2.75
49 thru 51 . . . . @2.95
52 thru 57 Time Warp, pt.4–pt.8 . @2.95
58 Zardon ambassador, BU:BDn . . 2.95
59 Akaru overwhelmed. 2.95
60 to the Himalayas 2.95
61 ancient Himalayan temple 2.95
62 Hillbilly girl. 2.95
63 F:Tetsuo Rivalsan 2.95
64 Jeremy Feeple: Saboteur?. . . . 2.95
65 Quagmire Trial of the Century . . 2.95
66 . . . . 2.95
67 F:Eolata. 3.00
68 F:Akaru & Asrial 3.00
69 Guri-Guri Island. 3.00
70 Mad Bomber in Space 2.50
Special #1 . . . . 2.95
Special #2 . . . . 2.95
Special #3 . . . . 2.95
Special #3 1/2 . . . . 2.25
Ann. 1989. . . . . 2.95
Ann.#3 . . . . 3.95
TPB Vol. 1 rep. #1–3 . . . . 12.00
TPB Vol. 1, new edition. 14.95
TPB Vol. 2 rep. #4–7 . . . . 12.00
TPB Vol. 3 rep. #8–11. . . . . 9.00
TPB Vol. 3, rep. #8–#11 . . . . . . 10.95
TPB Vol. 4 rep. #12–15 . . . . 8.00
TPB Vol. 4, rep. #12–#15 . . . . . 10.95
TPB Vol. 5 rep. #16–18 . . . . 7.95
TPB Vol. 6 rep. #19–21 . . . . 7.95
TPB Vol. 7 rep. #22–24 . . . . 7.95
TPB Vol. 7, rep. #22–#24 The Ides
of May 10.95
TPB Vol. 8 rep. #25–27 . . . . 7.95
TPB Vol. 9 rep. #28–31. . . . . . . 10.95
TPB Vol. 9, rep. #28–#31 Long
Distance Bottle. 10.95

TPB Vol. 10 rep. #32–35. . . . . . 10.95
TPB Vol. 11 rep. #36–39. . . . . . 10.95
TPB Vol. 11, rep. #36–#39 Shades
of Grey. 10.95
TPB Vol. 12 . . . . 10.95
TPB Vol. 15 three stories 7.95
Yearbook 1994 . . . . 4.00
Yearbook 1995 . . . . 3.95
Yearbook 1996 . . . . 3.95
Yearbook 1997, cover A 3.95
Yearbook 1997, cover B 3.95
Yearbook 1998, cover A 2.95
Yearbook 1998, cover B 2.95
Spec. Girls of Ninja High School
(1997) 3.95
Spec. Girls of Ninja High School
1998 cover A 2.95
1998 cover B 2.95
Spec. 1999 . . . . 3.00
Spotlight #4 Rod Espinosa 3.00
Summer Spec.#1 . . . . 3.00

NINJA HIGH SCHOOL GIRLS
Antarctic Press

0 . . . . 2.75
1 and 2 rep. . . . . @2.75
3 thru 5 rep. 3.95
Yearbook 3.95

NINJA HIGH SCHOOL PERFECT MEMORY
Antarctic Press

1 thru 2, 96pg . . . . @4.95

NINJA HIGH SCHOOL SMALL BODIES
Antarctic Press

1 "Monopolize" 2.50
2 Omegadon Cannon 2.75
3 Omegadon Cannon 2.75
3a deluxe 4.50
4 Omegadon Cannon 2.75
5 Wrong Order 2.75
6 Chicken Rage. 2.95
7 . . . . 2.95

NIRA X: CYBERANGEL
Entity Comics April 1996

1 . . . . 5.00
1a deluxe 8.00
2 BMs 4.00
3 and 4 BMs . . . . @3.00
4a with PC Game 8.00
Ann.#1 BMs flip-cover. 2.75

2nd Mini Series 1995

1 . . . . 4.00
1a 2nd printing 2.50
2 thru 4 . . . . @2.50

3rd Mini Series 1995–96

1 . . . . 2.50
1a Gold(c). 5.00
2 . . . . 2.50
3 . . . . 3.00

Regular Series

1 . . . . 2.75
1a with game. 7.00
2 thru 4 . . . . @2.75
4a with game. 7.00
Spec. Nira X:Headwave, encore
special toy edition. 2.50
Encore special toy edition, signed
& numbered 12.95
Spec. Nira X:Memoirs (1997) BMs . 2.75
Deluxe 3.50

NIRA X/HELLINA: HEAVEN & HELL
Entity Comics

1 San Diego Con edition, BMs 5.00
1a foil. 3.00

Nira X: Exodus #1
© Avatar

NIRA X: EXODUS
Avatar 1997

0 (of 2) BMs 3.00
0a Nude cover. 4.95
0b Leather cover 25.00
0 signed 10.00
1 (of 2) 3.00
1a nude cover. 4.95
1b leather cover. 25.00
1 signed 10.00
2 . . . . 3.00
2 nude cover 4.95
Spec. Shoot First 3.00
Spec. Shoot First, nude cover. . . . 4.95
Spec. Summer Splash 4.95
Spec. Summer Splash, nude cover. 6.00

NIRA X: HISTORY
Avatar Press 1999

1 (of 2) by Bill Maus 3.50
1a nude cover. 6.00
2 . . . . 3.50
2a nude cover 6.00

NIRA X: SOUL SKURGE
Entity Oct. 1996

1 (of 3) BMs, A:Vortex 2.75
2 BMs, ... 2.75
3 . . . . 2.75

NO GUTS, NO GLORY
Fantaco

1-shot, K.Eastman's 1st solo
work since TMNT. 2.95

NOMADS OF ANTIQUITY

1 thru 6 . . . . @1.50

NO NEED FOR TENCHI
Viz Comics
PART ONE

1 thru 7 (of 7). . . . . @2.95

PART TWO Nov. 1996
1 thru 7 by Hitoshi Okuda . . . . . . @2.95
TPB Sword Play 15.95

PART THREE 1997
1 (of 6) by Hitoshi Okuda 2.95
2 . . . . 2.95
3 thru 6 . . . . @2.95
TPB Magical Girl Pretty Sammy . . 15.95

PART FOUR Dec. 1997
1 (of 6) by Hitoshi Okuda 2.95
2 thru 6 . . . . @2.95
TPB Vol. 4 Samurai Space Opera. 15.95

PART FIVE 1998
1 (of 6) 2.95
2 thru 6 . . . . @2.95
TPB Vol. 5 Unreal Genius 15.95

PART SIX 1998
1 (of 6) 2.95
2 thru 6 . . . . @2.95

PART SEVEN 1999
1 (of 6) 2.95
2 thru 5 . . . . @2.95

NORMAL MAN
Aardvark–Vanaheim
1 . . . . 4.00
2 thru 9 . . . . @2.50
Renegade
10 thru 19 . . . . @1.70

NOVA GIRLS
MN Design 1998
1 The Immortality Quest, pt.1 . . . . . 1.95
1a JJu (c) 2.95
1b photo (c) 3.95
1 variant Starship Discover #0(c) . . 3.95
1 variant Phazer #0 cover 3.95
2 The Immortality Quest, pt.2 . . . . . 1.95
2a deluxe 2.95
3 The Immortality Quest, pt.3 . . . . . 1.95
3a deluxe 2.95
Space 34–24–34 Gold Seal 10th
   Anniv. Edition 74.95

NOWHERESVILLE
Caliber March 1996
1 thru 3 by MRc . . . . @2.95
Spec. The History of Cool 2.95

NYOKA THE JUNGLE GIRL
AC Comics
3 . . . . 2.25
4 . . . . 2.25
5 . . . . 2.50

OFFERINGS
Cry For Dawn
1 Sword & Sorcery stories 7.00
2 and 3 . . . . @6.00

OFFICIAL BUZ SAWYER
1 . . . . 2.00
2 . . . . 2.00
3 . . . . 2.00
4 . . . . 1.50
5 . . . . 2.00
6 . . . . 2.00

OFFICIAL HOW TO DRAW G.I. JOE
Blackthorne
1 thru 5 . . . . @2.00

OFFICIAL HOW TO DRAW ROBOTECH
Blackthorne
1 thru 11 . . . . @2.00
12 . . . . 2.95
13 thru 16 . . . . @2.00

OFFICIAL HOW TO DRAW TRANSFORMERS
Blackthorne
1 thru 7 . . . . @2.00

OFFICIAL JOHNNY HAZARD
1 thru 3 . . . . @2.00
4 . . . . 1.50
5 . . . . 2.00

OFFICIAL JUNGLE JIM
1 thru 5 AR,rep. . . . . @2.00
6 AR,rep. 1.50
7 thru 10 AR,rep. . . . . @2.00
11 thru 20 AR,rep. . . . . @2.50
Ann.#1 . . . . 2.00
Giant Size 3.95

OFFICIAL MANDRAKE
1 thru 5 . . . . @2.00
6 . . . . 1.50
7 thru 10 . . . . @2.00
11 . . . . 2.50
12 . . . . 2.00
13 thru 17 . . . . @2.50
Ann. #1 . . . . 3.95
King Size #1 . . . . 3.95
Giant Size #1 . . . . 3.95

OFFICIAL MODESTY BLAISE
Pioneer 1988
1 thru 4 . . . . @2.00

Official Modesty Blaise #1
© Pioneer

5 . . . . 1.50
6 thru 14 . . . . @2.00
Ann. #1 . . . . 3.95
King Size #1 . . . . 3.95

OFFICIAL PRINCE VALIANT
1 Hal Foster,rep. 2.00
2 Hal Foster,rep. 2.00
3 Hal Foster,rep. 2.00
4 Hal Foster,rep. 2.00
5 Hal Foster,rep. 2.00
6 Hal Foster,rep. 2.00
7 . . . . 1.50
8 thru 14 . . . . @2.00
15 thru 24 . . . . @2.50
Ann. #1 . . . . 3.95
King Size #1 . . . . 3.95

OFFICIAL RIP KIRBY
1 thru 3 AR . . . . @2.00
4 AR 1.50
5 and 6 AR . . . . @2.00

OFFICIAL SECRET AGENT
Pioneer
1 thru 5 AW rep . . . . @2.00
6 AW 1.50
7 thru 9 AW . . . . @2.00

OF MIND AND SOUL
Rage Comics 1997
0 . . . . 2.95
0a nude cover edition 6.50
1 . . . . 2.50
1 nude photo cover 6.50
2 . . . . 2.50
2 nude cover 6.50
3 . . . . 1.50
Spec. Standing on a Beach 2.50
Spec. Soul'd Out` 2.95
Spec. A Day in Hell 2.95
Spec. 1-shot 1.50
Spec. 1-shot nude cover 6.00

OHM'S LAW
Imperial Comics
1 thru 2 . . . . @1.95
3 V:Men in Black 1.95
4 A:Damonstriek 1.95
5 F:Tryst 1.95

OKTOBERFEST
Now & Then
1 (1976) Dave Sim 20.00

OMEGA
North Star
1 1st pr by Rebel,rare 80.00
1a Vigil(Yellow Cov.) 27.00
2 . . . . 2.00

OMEN
North Star
1 . . . . 8.00
1a 2nd printing 2.00
2 thru 4 . . . . @3.50

OMICRON
1 and 2 . . . . @2.25
3 . . . . 2.50

ONE SHOT WESTERN
Calibur
1-shot F:Savage Sisters, Tornpath
Outlaw 2.50

ONI DOUBLE FEATURE
Oni Press 1997
1 F:Secret Broadcast 15.00
1a 2nd printing 3.00
2 F:Car Crash on the 405 . . . . . . 3.00
3 F:Troy Nixey 3.00
4 F:A River in Egypt 3.00
5 F:Fan Girl From Hell 3.00
6 inc. NGa Only the End of the
World, pt.1 . . . . 3.00
7 inc. NGa Only the End of the
World, pt.2 . . . . 3.00
8 inc. NGa Only the End of the
World, pt.3 . . . . 3.00
9 thru 13 . . . . @3.00

ONIGAMI
Antarctic Press 1998
1 (of 3) by Michael Lacombe, sequel
to Winter Jade storyline from
Warrior Nun: Black and White. . 2.95
2 . . . . 2.95
3 concl. 2.95

OPEN SEASON
Renegade
1 thru 7 . . . . @2.00

OPTIC NERVE
Adrian Tomine 1990
1 thru 5, mini-comic 18.00
6 . . . . 7.00
7 . . . . 5.00

OPTIC NERVE
Drawn & Quarterly 1995
1 Summer Job 7.00
1a 2nd printing 3.00
2 . . . . 5.00
3 and 4 . . . . @3.00
5 and 6 . . . . @2.95
TPB 32 Stories 9.95
HC Sleepwalk and Other Stories,
limited 29.95

ORACLE PRESENTS
1 thru 4 . . . . @1.50

ORBIT
Eclipse
1 and 2 . . . . @3.95
3 . . . . 4.95

ORIGINAL TOM CORBET
Eternity 1990
1 thru 10 rep. newspaper strips . @2.95

ORLAK: FLESH & STEEL
Caliber
1 '1991 A.D.' 2.50

ORLAK REDUX
Caliber 1991
1 rep. Caliber Presents,64pg. . . . 3.95

Original Tom Corbett #2
© Eternity

OUTLANDER
1 . . . . 4.50
2 . . . . 3.00
3 thru 5 . . . . @2.50
6 and 7 . . . . @1.95
8 . . . . 2.25

OUTLAW OVERDRIVE
Blue Comet Press
1 Red Edition I:Deathrow 2.95
1a Black Edition 2.95
1b Blue Edition 2.95

OZ
Imperial Comics
1 Land of Oz Gone Mad 12.00
2 Land of Oz Gone Mad 10.00
3 Land of Oz Gone Mad 6.00
4 Tin Woodsmen 6.00
5 F:Pumkinhead 6.00
6 Emerald City 6.00
7 V:Bane Wolves 4.00
8 V:Nome Hordes 4.00
9 Freedom Fighters Vs. Heroes . 4.00
10 thru 15 . . . . @4.00
16 . . . . 3.50
Spec.#1 . . . . 6.00
Spec. Scarecrow #1 . . . . 3.00
Spec. Lion #1 . . . . 3.00
Spec. Tin Man #1 . . . . 3.00
Spec. Freedom Fighters #1 . . . 3.00
TPB Rep. #1-#4 . . . . 14.95
Caliber "New Worlds"
17 by Ralph Griffith, Stuart Kerr &
Tim Holtrop 3.50
18 . . . . 3.00
19 . . . . 3.00
20 . . . . 3.00
21 "Witches War" pt.1 (of 5) 3.00
22 . . . . 2.95
GN Heroes of Oz 14.95

OZ: ROMANCE IN RAGS
Caliber 1996
1 thru 3 Bill Bryan . . . . @2.95

OZ SQUAD
Patchwork Press
1 thru 6 . . . . @2.95
7 Time Train Destroyed 2.95

8 Old West 2.75

OZ: STRAW AND SORCERY
Caliber "New Worlds" 1997
1 thru 3 . . . . @2.95

PAKKINS' LAND
Caliber Tapestry 1996
1 . . . . 6.00
1a signed edition 3.00
1a second edition, new cover . . . 3.00
2 . . . . 4.00
2a second edition, new cover . . . 3.00
3 . . . . 3.00
3 2nd edition, new cover 3.00
4 thru 6 . . . . @3.00
GN Book One: Paul's Adventure . . 9.95

PAKKINS' LAND: FORGOTTEN DREAMS
Caliber March 1998
1 by Gary & Rhoda Shipman 2.95
2 thru 5 . . . . @2.95

PAKKINS' LAND: QUEST FOR KINGS
Caliber 1997
1G by Gary & Rhoda Shipman,
Shipman(c) 2.95
1J by Gary & Rhoda Shipman,
JSi(c) 2.95
2 . . . . 2.95
3 Rahsha's city 2.95
4 . . . . 2.95
5 . . . . 2.95

PALANTINE
Gryphon Rampant 1995
1 thru 5 V:Master of Basilisk 2.50

PANDA KHAN
1 thru 4 . . . . @2.00

PANDORA
Brainstorm 1996
1 (of 2) 3.00
1a nude cover 5.00

PANDORA
Avatar Press 1997
0 . . . . 3.00
0 nude cover 4.95
1 signed 15.00
2 (of 2) 3.00
2 deluxe 10.00
X-over Pandora/Rancor: Devil Inside
(1998) signed 15.00
Rick Lyon nude (c) 6.00
Haley (c) 5.00
X-over Pandora/Razor (1999) 3.50
Nude cover 6.00
Leather cover, signed 20.00
X-over Pandora/Shotgun Mary:
Demon Nation (1998) 3.00
Deluxe 4.95
Leather 30.00
Royal Blue edition 75.00
X-over Pandora/Widow (1997) 3.95
Nude cover 4.95
Leather cover 25.00
Spec. Arachnophobia 3.50
Nude cover 6.00

Nude Bloodbath cover 6.00
Spec. Pandora Special (1997) 3.00
Nude cover 4.95
Leather cover 25.00
Avatar convention cover edition. . . .
15.00
Spec. Pandora Pin-up (1997) 3.00
Nude cover 4.95
Signed 20.00
Spec. Nudes (1997) 3.50
Nude Lyon cover 6.00
Nude Meadows cover. 6.00

PANDORA'S CHEST
Avatar Press 1999
1 (of 3) 2.75
1a nude cover 6.00

PANDORA: DEMONOGRAPHY
Avatar Press 1997
1 . . . . 3.00
1 nude cover 5.00
2 (of 3) 3.00
2 nude cover 4.95
3 (of 3) 3.00
3 nude cover 4.95

PANDORA DEVILS ADVOCATE
Avatar Press 1999
1 (of 3) 3.50
1a nude cover 6.00
2 . . . . 3.50
2a nude cover 6.00
3 . . . . 3.50
3a nude cover 6.00

PANDORA: PANDEMONIUM
Avatar Press 1997
1 Pandora goes to Hell 3.00
1 nude cover 4.95
1 leather cover 25.00
1 signed 10.00
2 (of 3) 3.00
2 nude cover 4.95

PANTHEON
Lone Star Press 1998
1 (of 12) 2.95
2 Welcome to the Machine 2.95
3 V:Death Boy. 2.95
4 F:Tangeroa. 2.95
5 Under Pressure 2.95
6 All-villain issue 2.95
Spec. Ancient History (1999) 3.50

PAPER CUTS
1 E Starzer-1982 . . . . 17.50
2 and 3 . . . . @2.50

PARTICLE DREAMS
Fantagraphics
1 . . . . 3.00
2 thru 6 . . . . @2.25

PARTNERS IN PANDEMONIUM
Caliber
1 `Hell on Earth' 2.50
2 Sheldon&Murphy become mortal 2.50

3 A:Abra Cadaver 2.50

PARTS OF A HOLE
Caliber 1991
1 Short Stories 2.50

PARTS UNKNOWN
Eclipse
1 I:Spurr,V:Aliens. 2.50
2 Aliens on Earth cont. 2.50

PARTS UNKNOWN: DARK INTENTIONS
Knight Press
0 . . . . 2.95
1 I:Prelude to limited Series. 2.95
2 V:Luggnar. 2.95
3 V:Luggnar. 2.95
4 . . . . 2.95
1-shot, Handbook, The Roswell
Agenda 2.95
Super-Ann. #1 . . . . 3.95

PATTY CAKE
Caliber Tapestry 1996
1 by Scott Roberts. 2.95
2 . . . . 2.95
3 . . . . 2.95
4 . . . . 2.95
Christmas special 3.95

PATTY-CAKE & FRIENDS
Slave Labor 1997
1 by Scott Roberts 2.95
2 thru 15 . . . . @2.95
Halloween Spec. 3.95

PAUL THE SAMURAI
New England Comics 1991
1 thru 3 . . . . @2.75
Bonanza #2 100pg. 4.95
GN Collected 8.95

PENDULUM
Adventure
1 Big Hand,Little Hand. 2.50
2 The Immortality Formula. 2.50
3 . . . . 2.50

PENNY CENTURY
Fantagraphics 1997
1 by Jaime Hernandez. 2.95
2 . . . . 2.95
3 . . . . 2.95
4 . . . . 2.95
5 . . . . 2.95
6 The Frog Mouth 2.95

PENTACLE: SIGN OF 5
Eternity
1 . . . . 2.25
2 Det.Sandler,H.Smitts 2.25
3 Det.Sandler => New Warlock . . . 2.25
4 5 warlocks Vs. Kaji 2.50

PETE THE P.O.'D POSTAL WORKER
Sharkbait Press 1998
1 by Marcus Pierce & Pete
Garcia, Route 666 . . . . 2.95
2 prison mail 2.95

3 To Aliens with Love. 2.95
4 Special Delivery to
Conad the Alien 2.95
5 England Vacation 2.95
6 Benedict Postman 2.95
7 Postman on Elm Street. 2.95
8 Postman on Elm Street. 2.95
9 Pete Meets Jerry Ringer. 2.95
10 Y2K Express 2.95

PHANTOM
1 thru 3 . . . . @5.95
4 and 5 . . . . @6.95

Phantom of Fear City #12
© Claypool

PHANTOM OF FEAR CITY
Claypool 1994–95
1 thru 12 . . . . 2.50

PHANTOM OF THE OPERA
Eternity
1 . . . . 1.95

PHASE ONE
Victory
1 . . . . 3.00
2 . . . . 2.00
3 thru 5 . . . . @1.50

PHIGMENTS
Eternity
1 . . . . 5.00
2 . . . . 2.00
3 . . . . 1.95

PHONEY PAGES
Renegade
1 and 2 . . . . @1.70

PINEAPPLE ARMY
1 thru 10 . . . . @1.75

PINK FLOYD EXPERIENCE
Revolutionary
1 based on rock group 2.50
2 Dark Side of the Moon 2.50
3 Dark Side of the Moon, Wish you

were here............... 2.50
4 The Wall.................. 2.50
5 A Momentary lapse of reason... 2.50

PIRATE CORPS!
Eternity
6 and 7 .... @1.95
Spec. #1 .... 1.95

PIRANHA! IS LOOSE
Special Studio
1 Drug Runners,F:Piranha....... 2.95
2 Expedition into Terror 2.95

PIXI JUNKET
Viz
1 thru 6 .... @2.75

P.J. WARLOCK
Eclipse
1 thru 3 .... @2.00

PLANET COMICS
Blackthorne
(Prev. Color)
4 and 5 .... @2.00

PLANET COMICS
A-List Comics 1997
1 by Lance Hampton & Ras
Leonardo 2.50
2 rep. from 1940 .... 2.95
3 .... 2.95
5 .... 2.95
6 .... 2.95
TPB Book of Planet Comics
Covers, 1949–54 .... 7.95

PLANET OF TERROR
1 BW..................... 1.75

Planet of the Apes #1
© Adventure Comics

PLANET OF THE APES
Adventure Comics 1990
1 WD,collect.ed. 7.00
1 2 covers.................. 5.00
1a 2nd printing............. 2.50
1b 3rd printing............. 2.25

2 .... 3.00
3 .... 2.75
4 .... 2.75
5 D:Alexander?............. 2.75
6 Welcome to Ape City 2.75
7 .... 2.75
8 Christmas Story 2.50
9 Swamp Ape Village 2.50
10 Swamp Apes in Forbidden City . 2.50
11 Ape War continues.......... 2.50
12 W.Alexander/Coure 2.50
13 Planet of Apes/Alien Nation/ Ape
City x-over 2.50
14 Countdown to Zero Pt.1...... 2.50
15 Countdown to Zero Pt.2...... 2.50
16 Countdown to Zero Pt.3...... 2.50
17 Countdown to Zero Pt.4...... 2.50
18 Ape City (after Ape Nation mini-
series.................. 2.50
19 1991 'Conquest..' tie-in 2.50
20 Return of the Ape Riders 2.50
21 The Terror Beneath,Pt.1....... 2.50
22 The Terror Beneath,Pt.2....... 2.50
23 The Terror Beneath,Pt.3....... 2.50
Ann #1,'Day on Planet o/t Apes'... 3.50
Lim.Ed. #1 .... 5.00

PLANET OF THE APES: BLOOD OF THE APES
Adventure Comics
1 A:Tonus the Butcher.......... 3.00
2 Valia/Taylorite Connection...... 2.50
3 Ape Army in Phis 2.50
4 .... 2.50

PLANET OF THE APES: FORBIDDEN ZONE
Adventure
1 Battle for the Planet o/t Apes &
Planet o/t Apes tie-in 2.50
2 A:Juilus 2.50

PLANET OF THE APES: SINS OF THE FATHER
Adventure Comics
1 Conquest Tie-in 2.50

PLANET OF THE APES URCHAKS' FOLLY
Adventure Comics
1 .... 3.00
2 .... 2.50
3 'The Taylorites'............. 2.50
4 Conclusion 2.50

PLANET 29
Caliber
1 A Future Snarl Tale 2.50
2 A:Biff,Squakman............ 2.50

PLANET-X
Eternity 1991
1 three horror stories.......... 2.50

PLAN 9 FROM OUTER SPACE
Eternity
1 .... 2.50
2 and 3 .... @2.25

PLASMA BABY
Caliber
1 'Strange New World'......... 2.50

PLASTIC LITTLE
CPM Comics 1997
1 (of 5) Manga, by Satoshi
Urushihara R:Captain Tita 2.95
2 F:Joshua Balboa 2.95
3 .... 2.95
4 .... 2.95
5 concl. 2.95
TPB Captain's Log, rep. #1–#5 ... 15.95

PLASTRON CAFE
Mirage
1 RV,inc.North by Downeast 2.25

POE
Cheese Comics
1 by Jason Asala, reoffer........ 2.00
2 .... 2.00
3 "The System of Doctor Tarr and
Professor Fether".......... 2.00
4 thru 6 .... @2.00
Sirius/Dog Star
10 by Jason Asala, Small Town, pt.3 2.50
TPB Vol. 1 .... 14.95
VOL 2
1 by Jason Asala............. 2.50
2 House of Usher, pt.1 (of 4) 2.50
3 House of Usher, pt.2......... 2.50
4 House of Usher, pt.3......... 2.50
5 House of Usher, pt.4......... 2.50
6 .... 2.50
7 .... 2.50
8 Small Town............... 2.50
9 Small Town, pt.2........... 2.50
10 Small Town, pt.3 .... 2.50
11 Gold & Lead, pt.1.......... 2.50
12 Gold and Lead, pt.2......... 2.50
13 F:Pluto the cat............ 2.50
14 A:Mad Meg Mayflower....... 2.50
15 Airship................. 2.50
16 path of next demon 2.50
17 22 one-page stories......... 2.50
18 Airship................. 2.50

POINT BLANK
Eclipse
1 thru 5 .... @2.95

POISON ELVES
Mulehide Graphics 1993–95
Previously: I, Lusipher
8 DHa(c&a)................ 35.00
9 DHa 30.00
10 DHa................... 30.00
11 DHa, comic size........... 25.00
12 DHa................... 25.00
13 DHa................... 25.00
14 and 15 DHa .... @25.00
15a 2nd printing 7.00
16 and 17 DHa .... @20.00
17a 2nd printing 6.00
18 DHa.................. 12.00
19 DHa.................. 12.00
20 DHa.................. 12.00
2nd Series, Sirius 1995–97
1 F:Lusipher 10.00
2 V:Assassins Guild........... 5.00
3 Sanctuary, pt.3 .... 5.00
4 Sanctuary, pt.4............ 6.00
5 Sanctuary, pt.5............ 5.00
6 I:Lester Gran 5.00

Poison Elves #11
© Sirius

7 thru 24 . . . . @4.00
25 DHa. 3.00
26 DHa. 2.50
27 DHa,. 2.50
28 DHa,F:Lusiphur 2.50
29 DHa,. 2.50
30 DHa,F:Vido 2.50
31 DHa. 2.50
32 DHa, Cassandra is dead 2.50
33 DHa, temporary truce 2.50
34 DHa, Lusiphur's feminine side . . 2.50
35 DHa, Purple Marauder reappears. . .
2.50
36 DHa, Lusiphur tracked down . . . 2.50
37 DHa, questionable hlep 2.50
38 DHa. 2.50
39 DHa. 2.50
40 DHa, Sanctuary, concl. 2.50
41 DHa, on to Amrahly'nn. 2.50
42 DHa, Just in Town
for the Night,pt.1. . . . . 2.50
43 DHa, Town for the Night, pt.2 . . . 2.50
44 DHa, Town for the Night, pt.3 . . . 2.50
45 DHa, Petunia. 2.50
46 DHa, High Price of
Unemployment. 2.50
47 The Fairy and the Imp 2.50
48 South for the Winter,pt.1 . . . . . . 2.50
TPB Vol. 1 Requiem for an Elf . . . 14.95
TPB Vol. 2 Traumatic Dogs. 14.95
TPB Vol. 3 Desert of the Third Sin 14.95
TPB Vol. 4 Patrons, 48pg 4.95
TPB Vol. 5 rep. 272-page 14.95

POIZON: DEMON HUNTER
London Night 1998
1 . . . . 3.00
1a nude cover edition 6.00
2 . . . . 3.00
2a deluxe 6.00
3 . . . . 3.00
3a nude cover edition 6.00
4 double sized finale 3.00
4a nude cover edition 6.00

POKEMON: ELECTRIC
PIKACHU BOOGALOO
Viz Communications 1999
1 (of 4) by Toshihiro Ono, 48-page. 3.50
2 . . . . 2.95

POKEMON:
PIKACHU SHOCKS BACK
Viz Communications 1999
1 (of 4) by Toshihiro Ono 3.50
2 . . . . 3.50
3 . . . . 3.50
4. . . . . 3.25

POKEMON:
THE ELECTRIC
TALE OF PIKACHU
Viz Communications 1998
1 (of 4) by Toshiro Ono 14.00
1a 2nd printing 3.50
2 . . . . 7.00
2a 2nd printing 3.50
3 . . . . 4.00
4 . . . . 3.50
GN The Electric Tale of Pikachu . . 12.95

POOT
Fantagraphics 1997
1 by Walt Holcombe 2.95
2 Swollen Holler, pt.2. . . . . 2.95
3 sex issue 2.95
4 final issue, 40-page 3.95

POPCORN
Discovery 1993
1 . . . . 3.95

PORT
Silver Wolf
1 . . . . 1.50
2 . . . . 1.50

PORTIA PRINZ
Eclipse
1 thru 5 . . . . @2.00

POST BROTHERS
@WP Heading 1:Rip
Off Press
15 thru 18. . . . . @2.00
19 and 20 . . . . @2.50

POWER COMICS
1 Smart-Early Ardvaark 25.00
1a 2nd printing 8.00
2 I:Cobalt Blue. 10.00
3 and 4 . . . . @3.00
5 . . . . 4.00

POWER COMICS
Eclipse
1 BB,DGb,Powerbolt 2.00
2 BB,DGb 2.00
3 BB,DGb 2.00

PRACTICE IN PAIN
Dramemon Studios
1 I:Queen of the Dead 3.00

PREMIERE
Diversity Comics 1995
1 F:Kolmec The Savage 2.75

PRETEEN DIRTY GENE
KUNG FU KANGAROOS
Blackthorne 1986
1 and 2 . . . . @1.50

PRETTY CITY ROXX
Mars Press
1 I:Roxx. 3.50

PREY
Monster Comics
1 I:Prey,A:Andrina 2.25
2 V:Andrina 2.25
3 conclusion 2.25

PRICE, THE
1 Dreadstar mag. size 20.00

PRIMITIVES
Spartive Studios 1995
1 thru 3 On the Moon. . . . . @2.50

PRIME CUTS
Fantagraphics
1 adult. 3.50
2 thru 6 . . . . @3.50
7 thru 12 . . . . @3.95

PRIMER
Comico
1 . . . . 10.00
2 MW,I:Grendel 100.00
3 . . . . 5.00
4 . . . . 8.00
5 SK(1st work),I:Maxx 29.00
6 IN,Evangeline. 14.00

PRIME SLIME TALES
Mirage
1 . . . . 5.00
2 . . . . 2.50
3 thru 6 . . . . @1.50

PRINCE VALIANT
1 thru 4 . . . . @4.95
Spec #1 . . . . 6.95

PRINCE VALIANT
MONTHLY
1 thru 6 . . . . @3.95
6 . . . . 4.95
7 . . . . 4.95
8 . . . . 4.95
9 . . . . 6.95

PRIVATE EYES
Eternity
1 Saint rep. 1.95
2 . . . . 1.95
3 . . . . 1.95
4 . . . . 1.95
5 . . . . 1.95

PSI–JUDGE ANDERSON
1 thru 15 . . . . @1.95

PSYCHOMAN
Revolutionary
1 I:Psychoman 2.50

PULP
Viz Communications 1997
1 Manga anthology magazine 5.95
2 thru 5 .... @5.95
VOL TWO
#1 thru #12 .... @5.95
VOL THREE
#1 thru #9 .... @5.95

PULP FICTION
A-List Comics 1997
1 thru 2 rep. of golden age..... @2.50
3 .... 2.95
4 .... 2.95
5 .... 2.95
6 .... 2.95
7 .... 2.95
Spec. Art of Pulp Fiction........ 2.95

PUMA BLUES
Aardvark–Vanaheim
1 10,000 printed 4.50
1a 2nd printing 2.00
2 .... 3.00
3 .... 2.00
4 thru 19 .... @1.70
20 Special 2.25
Mirage
21 thru 24............... @1.70
25 .... 2.50
26 thru 28............... @1.75

QUACK
Star Reach
1 .... 2.00
2 .... 2.00
3 .... 2.00
4 Dave Sim................. 3.00
5 Dave Sim................. 3.00
6 .... 2.00

QUANTUM MECHANICS
Avatar 1999
1 (of 2) by Barry Gregory &
Jacen Burrows............ 3.50
1a wraparound cover.......... 3.95
2 conclusion 3.50
2a wraparound cover.......... 3.95

QUEST PRESENTS
Quest
1 JD 1.75
2 JD 1.75
3 JD 1.75

QUICKEN FORBIDDEN
Cryptic Press 1998
1 .... 2.95
2 .... 2.95
3 .... 2.95
4 .... 2.95
5 .... 2.95
6 Trial Separation,pt.1 .... 2.95
7 Trial Separation,pt.2 .... 2.95
8 Trial Separation, concl........ 2.95
TPB 152-page 14.95

RABID MONKEY
D.B.I. Comics Jan. 1997
1 thru 4 by Joel Steudler ...... @2.25
5 thru 7 .... @2.25
8 thru 13 .... @2.50
#1–#5 Autographed pack....... 12.00

Dreamriders Workshop 1998
Vol. 2
1 .... 2.95

RADICAL DREAMER
Mark's Giant Economy Sized Comics
1 thru 3 F:Max Wrighter........ 3.00
4 is Max the Devil? 3.00
VOL 2 1998
1 (of 6) by Mark Wheatley, sci-fi. . . 2.95

RADIO BOY
Eclipse
1 .... 2.00

RAGMOP
Planet Lucy Press
1 by Rob Walton, 3rd. printing 3.10
2 thru 8 reoffer.............. @2.75
8 .... 2.75
9 .... 2.75
10 .... 2.75
VOL 2 (1997)
3 by Rob Walton 2.95
4 O-ring saga, pt. 2 (of 3) 2.95

RAGNAROK
Sun Comics
1 I:Ragnarok Guy,Honey 2.50
2 The Melder Foundation........ 2.50
3 Guy/Honey mission contd. 2.50
4 I:Big Gossage.............. 2.50

RAIKA
Sun Comics
1 thru 12 .... @2.50

RAISING HELL
ABC Comics 1997
1 .... 2.95
1a gold series, 2 extra pages..... 3.00
1b nude Jazz gold series....... 10.00
2 RCI,F:China & Jazz 2.95
2 live nude model cover........ 14.95
3 conclusion, A:Wild Things..... 2.95
3 Baby Cheeks edition........ 10.00
3 Baby Cheeks Gold Edition 14.95

RALPH SNART
Now
1 .... 5.00
2 .... 4.00
3 .... 4.00
[Volume 2]
1 .... 3.00
2 thru 8 .... @1.50
Trade Paperback 2.95

RAMBO
Blackthorne
1 thru 5 .... @2.00

RAMBO III
Blackthorne
1 .... 2.00

RAMM
Megaton Comics 1987
1 and 2 .... @1.50

Ramm #2
© Megaton Comics

RANMA 1/2
Viz 1993
Parts 1 & 2, see color
[Part 3] 1993–94
1 thru 13 .... 3.00
[Part 4] 1995
1 thru 11 .... 3.00
[Part 5] 1996
1 thru 9 .... 3.00
10 thru 12................. @3.00
[Part Six] Dec. 1996
1 thru 8 (of 14)............. @3.00
9 thru 14 .... @3.00
TPB Vol. 6 .... 15.95
TPB Vol. 7 .... 15.95
TPB Vol. 8 .... 15.95
TPB Vol. 9 .... 15.95
TPB Vol. 10 rep. Part Six, 1st half. 15.95
TPB Vol. 11 rep. Part Six, 2nd half 15.95
[Part Seven] Feb. 1998
1 (of 14)................. @2.95
2 thru 14 .... @2.95
TPB Vol. 12 .... 15.95
TPB Vol. 13 .... 15.95
[Part Eight] 1999
1 (of 13) thru 5 .... @2.95

RAPHAEL
1 TMNT................... 17.50
1a 2nd printing 7.50

RAPTUS
High Impact
1 .... 3.00
1 2nd printing, new cover........ 3.00
2 .... 3.00
3 .... 3.00

RAPTUS: DEAD OF NIGHT
High Impact
1 .... 2.95
2 .... 2.95
3 .... 3.00

RAT FINK
World of Fandom
```
1 ......................... 2.50
2 ......................... 2.50
```

RAVAGER
Kosmic Comic 1997
```
0 Ashcan.................... 1.50
1 The First Coming ........... 3.55
2 ......................... 3.55
3 ......................... 3.55
4 by Kirk Patrick & Babak
   Homayoun ............... 3.55
5 ......................... 3.55
6 by Kirk Patrick & Romel Cruz ... 3.55
```

RAVEN CHRONICLES
Caliber Press
```
1 ......................... 2.95
1a Special Edition ............ 5.95
2 Landing Zone ............... 2.95
3 The Rain People............. 2.95
4 The Healer................. 2.95
5 thru 9 .................. @2.95
```
Caliber "New Worlds"
```
10 by Scott Andrews, Laurence
    Campbell & Tim Perkins ...... 2.95
11 "The Ghost of Alanzo Mann" ... 2.95
12 "The Compensators" flip book
    with Boston Bombers #1...... 2.95
13 48pg, bagged with back issue .. 3.95
14 ........................ 2.95
15 ........................ 2.95
16 inc. Black Mist ............ 2.95
Spec. Heart of the Dragon ...... 2.95
HC ...................... 19.95
GN 192pg rep............... 16.95
```

RAVENING, THE
Avatar Press 1997
```
0 Trevlin Utz (c)............. 3.95
0 Matt Martin (c) ............. 3.95
0 Matt Haley (c)............. 3.95
0 nude cover ................ 6.00
0 leather cover ............. 25.00
0 signed ................... 15.00
1 ......................... 3.00
1 nude cover................ 4.95
1 leather cover ............. 25.00
1 Avatar con cover edition ...... 15.00
2 (of 2) ................... 3.00
2 nude cover................ 4.95
Spec. Secrets of the Ravening .... 2.75
Spec.A Secrets, nude(c)........ 6.00
```

RAW CITY
Dramenon Studios
```
1 I:Dya,Gino ................ 3.00
2 V:Crucifier ................ 3.00
3 The Siren's Past............ 3.00
```

RAW MEDIA MAGS.
Reb
```
1 TV,SK,short stories ......... 5.00
```

RAZOR
London Night
```
6 signed ................... 25.00
10 signed .................. 15.00
TPB The Suffering, rep. #1–#3 .. 12.95
GN Let Us Prey, rep. of Razor/Wild
    Child, 80pg.............. 5.00
X-over Razor/Embrace: The
    Spawning (1997) .......... 3.00
```

```
Carmen Electra photo (c) ..... 3.00
Carmen Electra photo embossed
   (c), signed .............. 19.00
Spec. Razor: Switchblade
   Symphony, Tour Book, limited
   black leather............. 15.00
```

RAZOR: ARCHIVES
London Night 1997
```
1 EHr, rep #1–#4.............. 5.00
1a signed ................. 15.00
2 EHr, rep #5–#8.............. 5.00
3 EHr, rep #9–#15............. 5.00
4 EHr, rep #16–#17........... 5.00
```

RAZOR/DARK ANGEL:
THE FINAL NAIL
Boneyard/London Night
```
1 X-over (Boneyard Press) ...... 4.00
2 X-over concl.(London Night) .... 3.00
```

RAZOR:
THE DARKEST NIGHT
London Night 1998
```
1 ......................... 4.95
1a white velvet ............. 25.00
2 velvet edition ............. 10.00
```
EH! Productions 1999
```
1 ......................... 4.95
1a Velvet Edition, signed ...... 30.00
2 ......................... 4.95
3 ......................... 4.95
3a Fan ed.................. 6.00
```

RAZOR: GOTHIC
London Night 1998
```
1 (of 4) by EHr and Scott Wilson .. 3.00
1 nude photo cover ........... 6.00
1 leather .................. 15.00
2 EHr ..................... 3.00
2a Graphic/violent cover ....... 6.00
2b Gothic/leather cover ........ 15.00
```
EH! Productions
```
3 ......................... 3.00
3a Elite Fan ed.............. 5.00
4 ......................... 3.00
4a Elite Fan ed.............. 5.00
```

RAZOR: TORTURE
London Night
```
0 chromium signed ........... 12.00
1 platinum signed ............ 12.00
```

RAZOR UNCUT
London Night Studios
Prev. RAZOR (Ind. Color)
```
13 ........................ 3.00
14 V:Child Killer ............. 3.00
15 Questions About Father....... 3.00
16 Nicole's Life,pt.1 .......... 3.00
17 Nicole's Life,pt.2 .......... 3.00
18 ........................ 3.00
19 & 20 Kiss from a Rose ...... @3.00
21 "Kiss From a Rose," pt.3 ..... 3.00
22 thru 24 ............... @3.00
25 mild cover I:Knyfe .......... 3.00
25a nude photo cover.......... 4.00
25b signed ............... 12.95
26 ........................ 3.00
27 A:Sade, pt.1 ............. 3.00
28 A:Sade, pt.2 ............. 3.00
29 ........................ 3.00
30 ........................ 3.00
```

```
31 "Strength by Numbers"........ 3.00
32 double sized .............. 3.50
32a signed nude edition ........ 6.00
33 "Let Us Prey," pt.2 .......... 3.00
34 "Let Us Prey," pt.4 (of 4) ..... 3.00
35 Let the battle begin ......... 3.00
36 all-out war for Queen City ..... 3.00
37 "After the Fall" pt.1.......... 3.00
38 "After the Fall," pt.2 ......... 3.00
39 "Money For Hire"............ 3.00
40 "Father's Bane," pt.1 ........ 3.00
40 nude cover ............... 5.00
41 "Father's Bane," pt.2 ........ 3.00
42 "Father's Bane," pt.3........ 3.00
43 "Father's Bane," pt.4 ........ 3.00
44 Razor finds abandoned child ... 3.00
45 An American Tragedy, pt.1 (of 5) 3.00
```

Razor Uncut #23
© London Night

```
45a commemmorative edition, EHr. 5.00
46 An American Tragedy, pt.2..... 3.00
47 An American Tragedy, pt.3..... 3.00
48 An American Tragedy, pt.4..... 3.00
49 An American Tragedy, pt.5..... 3.00
50 back in Asylum, Tony Daniel (c). 3.00
50a Michael Bair (c) ........... 5.00
50b Stephen Sandoval (c) ...... 5.00
50c Blood Red Velvet EHr (c) .... 25.00
Spec. Deep Cuts (1997) 5th Anniv.
   rep. #6,#13–#15, 80 pg ...... 5.00
   Nude cover............... 10.00
```
EH! Productions 1999
```
51 ........................ 3.00
51a Nude cover .............. 5.00
```

RAZORGUTS
Monster Comics 1992
```
1 thru 4.................... 2.25
```

RAZOR'S EDGE
London Night 1999
```
1 ......................... 4.95
1a Arizona (c) ............... 4.95
1b Dorian nude (c)............ 4.95
1c Nude Chrissy Mountjoy (c) .... 6.00
2 Razorblaze (c) ............. 4.95
2a Battle Girl (c) ............ 6.00
2b Nightvixen (c) ............ 4.95
2c nude cover ............... 6.00
0 Razor/Stryke (c) ............ 4.95
0a Nude Razor photo (c)........ 6.00
0b Night Vixen (c) ........... 4.95
0c Nude Stryke photo (c)........ 6.00
```

B & W PUB. (vertical side tab)

REACTOMAN
B-Movie Comics
1 . . . . 1.50
1a signed,numbered 2.75
2 thru 4 . . . . @1.50
collection 4.95

REAGAN'S RAIDERS
1 thru 6 . . . . @2.50

REALM
Arrow
1 Fantasy 7.50
2 . . . . 4.00
3 . . . . 3.00
4 TV,Deadworld. 21.00
5 I:L.Kazan 2.00
6 thru 13 . . . . @1.50
14 thru 18. . . . . @1.95
19 . . . . 2.50

REAL STUFF
Fantagraphic
1 thru 12. . . . . 2.50

REAPER
Newcomers Publishing
1 V:The Chinde. 2.95
2 . . . . 2.95
3 conclusion 2.95

REBELLION
Daikaiyu Enterprises 1995
1 I:Rebellion 2.50

RED DIARY
Caliber 1998
1 (of 4) F:Marilyn, JFK, Hoover, CIA . . .
3.95
1a deluxe 6.95
2 . . . . 3.95
3 (of 4) 3.95
1 (signed). 3.95
4 . . . . 3.95
HC Red Diaries 19.95
HC deluxe 39.95

RED FOX
Harrier
1 scarce 6.00
1a 2nd printing 2.50
2 rare 5.00
3 . . . . 3.00
4 I:White Fox. 3.00
5 I:Red Snail 3.00
6 . . . . 1.75
7 Wbolton 1.75
8 . . . . 1.75
9 Demosblurth. 1.75

RED & STUMPY
Parody Press
1 Ren & Stimpy parody 2.95

REDLAW
Caliber
1 Preview Killer of Crows. 2.50

RE:GEX: BLACK & WHITE
Awesome Entertainment 1999
1 RLe,JLb 2.95

Reid Fleming #3
© *Eclipse*

REID FLEMING
Blackbird-Eclipse
1 David Boswell,I:Reid Fleming . . 10.00
1a 2nd printing 5.50
1b 3rd–5th printing. . . . . @2.50

Volume 2
#1 Rogues to Riches Pt.1. . . . . . . 6.00
#2 Rogues to Riches Pt.2. . . . . . . 4.00
#2a Later printings 2.50
#3 Rogues to Riches Pt.3. . . . . . . 3.00
#3a Later printings 2.50
#4 Rogues to Riches Pt.4. . . . . . . 3.00
#5 Rogues to Riches Pt.5. . . . . . . 2.50

REID FLEMING, WORLD'S TOUGHEST MILKMAN
Deep-Sea Comics
3 "Rogue to Riches," pt.2,4th pr . . 2.95
4 "Rogue to Riches," pt.3,3rd pr . . 2.95
5 "Rogue to Riches," pt.4,2nd pr . . 2.95
6 "Rogue to Riches," pt.5,2nd pr . . 2.95
7 "Another Dawn,"Pt.1 . . . . 2.95
8 "Another Dawn,"Pt.2 . . . . 2.95
9 "Another Dawn,"Pt.3 . . . . 2.95
TPB Rogue to Riches rep. 13.95
Spec#1 Origins (1998) 3.00

REIVERS
Enigma
1 thru 2 Ch'tocc in Space. 2.95

RENEGADES OF JUSTICE
Blue Masque
1 I:Monarch,Bloodshadow 2.50
2 Madfire. 2.50
3 Television Chronicles 2.50
4 R:Karen Styles. 2.50

RENFIELD
Caliber
GN Conclusion of series. 8.95
HC by Gary Reed & Galen
Showman. 19.95
HC Deluxe 39.95

REPENTANCE
Advantage Graphics 1995
1 I:Repentance 1.95

REPLACEMENT GOD
Amaze Ink 1995
1 Child in The Land of Man 6.00
1a 2nd & 3rd printing 3.00
2 Eye of Knute 4.00
3 & 4 "Bravery" . . . . @3.50
5 thru 7 . . . . @3.00
8 Fairie, book one, concl.. . . . . . . 2.95
TPB rep. #1–#8 . . . . 19.95

REPLACEMENT GOD & OTHER STORIES
Handicraft Guild
Previously published by Image
6 by Zander Cannon, 80pg 6.95

RETALIATOR
Eclipse
1 I&O:Retaliator. 2.50
2 O:Retaliator cont. 2.50

RETIEF
Adventure 1990
1 thru 6 Keith Laumer adapt. . . . @2.00
[New Series]
1 thru 6 . . . . @2.25
Spec.#1 Retief:Garbage Invasion . . 2.50
Spec.#1 Retief:The Giant Killer,
V:Giant Dinosaur 2.50
Spec.#1 Grime & Punishment,
Planet Slunch. 2.50

RETIEF OF THE CDT
1 Keith Laumer Novel Adapt. 2.00
2 . . . . 2.00

RETIEF AND THE WARLORDS
Adventure Comics
1 Keith Laumer Novel Adapt. 2.50
2 Haterakans. 2.50
3 Retief Arrested for Treason. . . . 2.50
4 Final Battle (last issue) 2.50

RETIEF: DIPLOMATIC IMMUNITY
Adventure Comics
1 Groaci Invasion. 2.50
2 Groaci story cont. 2.50

RETRO-DEAD
Blazer Unlimited
1 Dimensional Rift. 2.95
2 by Dan Reed 2.95

RETROGRADE
Eternity
1 thru 4 . . . . @1.95

RETURN OF HAPPY THE CLOWN
Caliber Press
1 & 2 V:Oni 2.95

RETURN OF LUM, THE
Viz Comics
PART THREE
3 thru 11 by Rumiko Takahashi . @2.95
TPB Trouble Times Ten, rep. pt. 2

B & W PUB.

& Pt.3 #1 . . . . 15.95
TPB Creature Features 15.95

PART FOUR*URUSEI YATSURA
1 thru 11 by Rumiko Takahashi . @2.95
TPB Vol. 5 Feudal Furor 15.95
TPB Vol. 6 Creature Features 15.95
TPB Vol. 7 For Better or Curse . . . 15.95
TPB Vol. 8 Ran Attacks 15.95

RETURN OF THE SKYMAN
Ace Comics
1 SD 1.75

REVOLVER
Renegade
1 SD 1.70
2 thru 6 . . . . @1.70
Ann. #1 . . . . 2.00

REVOLVING DOORS
Blackthorne
1 . . . . 1.75
2 . . . . 1.75
3 . . . . 1.75
Graphic Novel 3.95

RHUDIPRRT
PRINCE OF FUR
MU Press 1990–91
1 thru 6 . . . . @2.00

RICK RAYGUN
1 . . . . 2.00
2 thru 8 . . . . @1.75

RIO KID
Eternity
1 I:Rio Kid 2.50
2 V:Blow Torch Killer 2.50
3 . . . . 2.50

RION 2990
Rion
1 . . . . 2.75
2 . . . . 1.50

RIOT
Viz 1995
1 F:Riot,Axel 2.75
2 & 3 . . . . 2.75
4 final issue 2.75
TPB Rep. 15.95

RIOT ACT TWO
Viz Comics
1 thru 7 . . . . @2.95
TPB rep. 15.95

RIP IN TIME
Fantagor
1 RCo,Limited series 3.00
2 RCo 2.00
3 RCo 2.00
4 RCo 2.00
5 RCo,Last 2.00

RIPLASH:
SWEET VENGEANCE
Pocket Change Comics
1 O:Riplash 2.95

ROACHMILL
1 . . . . 5.50
2 . . . . 3.00
3 . . . . 3.00
4 . . . . 3.00
See: Dark Horse

ROBIN HOOD
1 thru 4 . . . . @2.25

ROBO DEFENSE TEAM
MECHA RIDER
Castle Comics
1 I:RDT Mecha Rider 2.95
2 Identity of Outlaw 2.95

R.O.B.O.T.
BATTALION 2050
Eclipse
1 . . . . 2.00

ROBO WARRIORS
CFW
1 thru 11 . . . . @1.95
Becomes:
KUNG FU WARRIORS

ROBOTECH
Eternity
1-shot Untold Stories 2.50
Academy Comics 1995–96
0 Robotech Information 2.50
Spec. Robotech: Macross Tempest
F:Roy Fokker, Tempest (1995) . 2.95
Spec. Robotech: Mech Angel,
I:Mech Angel (1995) 2.95
Spec. Robotech: The Misfits, from
Sothern Cross transferred to
Africa 2.95
Spec. #1 & #2 Robotech The Movie,
Benny R. Powell & Chi . . . . @2.95
Spec. Robotech Romance 2.95
Spec. Robotech: Sentinels Star Runners
Carpenter's Journey (1996) . . . 2.95
GN The Threadbard Heart 9.95
Antarctic Press 1998
Ann. #1 . . . . 2.95
Spec.#1 Robotech: Escape (1998) . 2.95

ROBOTECH:
ACADEMY BLUES
Academy Comics
0 Classroom Blues 3.50
1 F:Lisa 2.95
2 Bomb at the Academy 2.95
3 Roy's Drinking Buddy 2.95

ROBOTECH: AFTERMATH
Academy Comics
1 thru 10 R:Bruce Lewis . . . . . . @2.95
11 Zentradi Traitor 2.95
12 and 13 . . . . @2.95

ROBOTECH: CLONE
Academy Comics
1 Dialect of Duality 2.95
2 V:Monte Yarrow 2.95
3 Ressurection 2.95
4 Ressurection 2.95
5 F:Bibi Ava. 2.95

ROBOTECH:
COVERT OPS
Antarctic Press 1998
1 (of 2) by Greg Lane 2.95
2 . . . . 2.95

Robotech Invid War #8
© Eternity

ROBOTECH: INVID WAR
Eternity 1993
1 No Man's Land 2.50
2 V:Defoliators 2.50
3 V:The Invid,Reflex Point 2.50
4 V:The Invid 2.50
5 Moonbase Aluce II 2.50
6 Moonbase-Zentraedi plot 2.50
7 Zentraedi plot contd. 2.50
8 A:Lancer 2.50
9 A:Johnathan Wolfe 2.50
10 . . . . 2.50
11 F:Rand 2.50
12 thru 15 . . . . 2.50

ROBOTECH: INVID
WAR AFTERMATH
Eternity
1 thru 6 F:Rand 2.75

ROBOTECH: MORDECAI
Academy Comics
1 . . . . 2.95
2 Annie meets her clone 2.95

ROBOTECH:
RETURN TO MACROSS
Eternity 1993
1 thru 5 . . . . 2.50
Academy Comics
1 thru 17 Roy Fokker 2.75
18 F:The Faithful 2.75
19 F:Lisa 2.75
20 F:Lisa 2.75
21 V:Killer Robot 2.95
22 War of the Believers 2.95
23 War of the Believers,pt.2 . . . . . 2.95
24 War of the Believers,pt.3 . . . . . 2.95
25 War of the Believers,pt.4 . . . . . 2.95
26 thru 30 . . . . @2.95
31 What is the Federalist Plan? . . . 2.95
32 thru 34 . . . . @2.95

35 Typhoon threatens Macross
    Island. 2.95
36 . . . . 2.95
37 round up of Federalist Agents . . 2.95

ROBOTECH: SENTINELS: RUBICON
Antarctic Press 1998
1 (of 7) 2.95
2 Shadows of the Past. 2.95

ROBOTECH II THE SENTINELS
Eternity
1 . . . . 3.50
1a 2nd printing 1.95
2 . . . . 3.00
2a 2nd printing 1.95
3 . . . . 2.00
3a 2nd printing 1.95
4 thru 16 . . . . @1.95
Book 2
1 thru 12 . . . . @2.25
13 thru 20. . . . . @2.25
Wedding Special #1 . . . . 1.95
Wedding Special #2 . . . . 1.95
Robotech II Handbook 2.50
Book Three
1 thru 8 V:Invid 2.50
Book Four
Academy Comics Dec. 1995
1 by Jason Waltrip. 2.95
2 thru 4 F:Tesla . . . . @2.75
5 JWp,JWt,interior of Haydon IV . . 2.95
6 thru 8 . . . . @2.95
9 JWp,JWt,Breetai, Wolf & Vince
    return to Tirol 2.95
10 JWp,JWt,Ark Angel attacked by
    The Black Death Destroyers. . . 2.95
11 JWp,JWt,Tirol, Wolff, Vince &
    Breetai on trial for treason 2.95
12 JWp,JWt,Dr. Lang exposes
    General Edwards' evil designs . 2.95
13 F:Tesla 2.75
14 V:Invid 2.75
15 . . . . 2.75
16 . . . . 2.75
17 V:Invid Mechas 2.75
18 F:"HIN" 2.95
19 V:Invid. 2.95
20 Final Aplp. Invid Regiss 2.95
21 Predator and Prey 2.95
22 A Clockwork Planet 2.95
Halloween Special JWp,JWt, ... 2.95

ROBOTECH II: THE SENTINELS: CYBERPIRATES
Eternity 1991
1 The Hard Wired Coffin 2.25
2 thru 4 . . . . @2.25

ROBOTECH II: THE SENTINELS: THE MALCONTENT UPRISING
Eternity
1 thru 12 . . . . @1.95

ROBOTECH: VERMILION
Antarctic Press 1997
1 (of 4) by Duc Tran 2.95

Robotech Vermillion #1
© Antarctic

2 Why did Hiro die?. 2.95
3 . . . . 2.95
4 . . . . 2.95

ROBOTECH: WARRIORS
Academy Comics
1 F:Breetai 2.95
2 F:Mirya. 2.95
3 F:Mirya. 2.95
GN The Terror Maker 9.95

ROBOTECH: WINGS OF GIBRALTAR
Antarctic Press 1998
1 (of 2) by Lee Duhig. 2.95
2 . . . . 2.95

ROCK & ROLL COMICS
Revolutionary
1 Guns & Roses 6.00
1a 2nd printing 3.50
1b 3rd printing 2.00
1c 4th-7th printing 2.00
2 Metalica 5.00
2a 2nd printing 3.00
2b 3rd-5th printing 2.00
3 Bon Jovi 3.50
4 Motley Crue 4.00
5 Def Leppard 2.50
6 RollingStones. 5.00
6a 2nd-4th printing 2.00
7 The Who 3.50
7a 2nd-3rd printing 2.00
9 Kiss 6.00
9a 2nd-3rd Printing 2.00
10 Warrant/Whitesnake 2.50
10a 2nd Printing 2.00
11 Aerosmith 2.00
12 New Kids on Block. 4.00
12a 2nd Printing. 2.00
13 LedZeppelin. 3.00
14 Sex Pistols 2.00
See Independent Color

ROCKET RANGERS
Adventure
1 . . . . 2.95
2 . . . . 2.95
3 . . . . 2.95

ROCKIN ROLLIN MINER ANTS
Fate Comics
1 As seen in TMNT #40 . . . . 2.25
1a Gold Variant copy 7.50
2 Elephant Hunting, A:Scorn,Blister . . . 2.25
3 V:Scorn, Inc.,K.Eastman Ant
    pin-up. 2.25
4 Animal Experiments,V:Loboto . . 2.25

ROLLING STONES: THE SIXTIES
Personality
1 Regular Version 2.95
1a Deluxe Version,w/cards 6.95

ROSE
Hero Graphics
1 From The Champions. 3.50
2 A:Huntsman 3.50
3 thru 5 . . . . @2.95

ROSE AND GUNN
London Night
1 . . . . 3.00
1a nude cover 6.00
1b signed 10.00
2 . . . . 3.00
3 . . . . 3.00

ROSE AND GUNN: RECKONING
London Night
1 (of 2) 3.00

Rose 'N Gun Creator's Choice #1
© Bishop

ROSE 'N GUNN
Bishop Pres 1995
1 Deadly Duo 5.00
2 V:Marilyn Monroe 3.00
3 Presidential Affairs 3.00
4 Without Each Other 3.00
5 V:Red. 3.00
6 & 7 . . . . @3.00
Creator's Choice Rep. #1 . . . . 2.95
Creator's Choice Rep. #2 . . . . 2.95
Creator's Choice Rep. #3 . . . . 2.95

B & W PUB.

ROVERS
Eternity
1 thru 7 . . . . @1.95

RUBES REVIVED
Fish Warp
1 . . . . 2.00
2 and 3 . . . . @2.00

RUK BUD WEBSTER
Fish Warp
1 thru 3 . . . . @1.70

SADE
Bishop Press
0 B:Adventures of Sade. 3.00
1 . . . . 3.00
1a variant 6.00
2 . . . . 3.00

SADE
London Night
1 . . . . 3.00
1a nude cover 7.00
2 thru 5 . . . . @3.00

SADE SPECIAL
Bishop Press
1 V:Razor 5.00
1a signed 7.00

SADE/ROSE AND GUNN
London Night Nov. 1996
1 Confederate Mist 3.00

SADE: TESTAMENTS OF PAIN
London Night Jan. 1997
1 (of 2) 3.00

SAGA OF THE MAN-ELF
1 thru 5 . . . . @2.25

SAGE
Fantaco 1995
1 O:Sage. 4.95

SAILOR MOON
Mixx Entertainment 1998
1 by Naoko Tekeuchi 2.95
2 thru 11 . . . . @2.95
Novel A Scout is Born. 5.00
Novel The Power of Love 5.00
Novel 3: Mercury Rising 5.00

SAILOR MOON SUPER S
Mixx Entertainment 1999
1 (of 18) 192-page. 9.95
2 Pocket Mixx 9.95
3 Pocket Mixx 9.95
4 Pocket Mixx 9.95

SAINT
Kick Ass Comics
1 & 2 V:Cerran 2.50

SAINT GERMAINE
Caliber "Core" 1997
0 O:St. Germaine 3.95
1 VcL, two immortals, St. Germain
  cover 2.95
1 Lilith cover 2.95
2 VcL 2.95
3 VcL 2.95
3a signed 2.95
4 VcL 2.95
5 The Kilroy Mandate, VcL(c) 2.95
5a Meyer (c) 2.95
6 Kilroy Mandate 2.95
8 Ghost Dance 2.95
8 The Man in the Iron Mask. 2.95
10 The Tragedy of Falstaff 2.95
11 by Gary Reed & James Lyle. . . . 2.95
GN Shadows Fall, rep. #1–#4. . . . 14.95
Spec. Casanova's Lament, 48-page 3.95
Spec. Restoration, VcL. 3.95

SAINT GERMAINE: PRIOR ECHOES
Caliber "Core" 1998
1 (of 4) by Gary Reed 2.95
2 . . . . 2.95
3 . . . . 2.95

SALIMBA
Blackthorne
1 . . . . 3.50

SAMURAI (1st series)
1 . . . . 60.00
2 . . . . 30.00
3 . . . . 30.00
4 . . . . 30.00
5 . . . . 30.00

SAMURAI
Aircel
1 rare 6.00
1a 2nd printing 3.00
1b 3rd printing. 2.00
2 . . . . 5.00
2a 2nd printing 2.50
3 . . . . 3.00
4 . . . . 3.00
5 thru 12 . . . . @2.00
13 DK (1st art) 4.00
14 thru 16 DK . . . . @4.00
17 thru 22 . . . . @2.00

[3rd series]
#1 thru 3 . . . . @1.70
#4 thru 7. . . . . @1.95
Compilation Book 4.95

SAMURAI
Warp Graphics 1997
1 by Barry Blair & Colin Chan 2.95
2 . . . . 2.95
3 . . . . 2.95
4 . . . . 2.95

SAMURAI FUNNIES
Solson
1 thru 3 . . . . @2.00

SAMURAI PENGUIN
Solson
1 . . . . 3.00
2 I:Dr.Radium 2.00
3 . . . . 2.00

4 . . . . 1.50
5 FC 1.50
6 color. 2.25
7 . . . . 2.25
8 . . . . 1.75
9 . . . . 1.75

SAMURAI 7
Gauntlet Comics
1 I: Samurai 7 . . . . 2.50

SAMURAI, SON OF DEATH
Eclipse
1 . . . . 3.95
1a 2nd printing 3.95

SANCTUARY
Viz
1 World of Yakuza 5.00
2 thru 4 . . . . @5.00
5 thru 9 . . . . @5.00

[Part Two] 1993–94
1 thru 9 . . . . @5.00

[Part Three] 199–95
1 thru 8 . . . . @3.50

[Part Four] 1995–96
1 thru 7 . . . . @3.50

[Part Five] 1996
7 thru 13 by Sho Fumimura &
  Ryoichi Ikegami . . . . @3.50
GN rep. ½ of part 4 & ½ part 5 . . . 16.95
GN Vol. 5 . . . . 17.95
GN Vol. 6 . . . . 17.95
GN Vol. 9 . . . . 16.95

SANTA CLAWS
Eternity
1 `Deck the Mall with Blood
  and Corpses' 2.95

SAVAGE HENRY
Vortex
1 thru 13 . . . . @1.75

Rip Off Press
14 thru 15. . . . . @2.00
16 thru 24. . . . . @2.50

SCARAMOUCH
Innovation
1 . . . . 2.50

SCARLET IN GASLIGHT
1 A:SherlockHolmes 4.00
2 . . . . 3.00
3 & 4 . . . . @2.50

SCARLET SCORPION/ DARKSIDE
AC Comics
1 & 2 Flipbooks 3.50

SCARLET THUNDER
Amaze Ink
1 thru 3 . . . . @2.50

SCIMIDAR
Eternity
1 . . . . 4.00

1a 2nd Printing 2.50
2 and 3 . . . . @3.00
4 HotCover 3.50
4A MildCover. 3.00

SCORN
SCC Entertainment 1996
Lingerie Spec. 2.95
Lingerie Spec. deluxe 9.95
Super Spec.#1 rep. Deadly
  Rebellion, Headwave, Fabric
  of the Mind. 4.95
X-over Scorn/Ardy: Alien Influence
  (1997) by Rob Potchak & Timothy
  Johnson 3.95
  Bill Maus (c). 3.95
  Deluxe gold 9.95
X-over Scorn/Dracula: The Vampire's
  Blood (1997) 3.95
  Dracula cover 3.95
  Scorn cover 3.95
  Nude cover 9.95
Spec.#1A Scorn; Dead or Alive
  (1997) Mike Morales(c). 3.95
  Andrea Seri(c) 3.95
Spec.# Scorn:Deadly Rebellion. . . . 3.95
  Birthday Suit cover 9.95
  Celebrity photo cover 9.95
Spec.#1 Scorb: Fractured (1997)
  Fear cover 3.95
  Rage cover 3.95
  Nude cover 9.95
Spec: Scorn: Heatwave (1997) by
  Chris Crosby & Mike Morales . . 3.95
  Nude cover 9.95
Spec. Scorn: Hostage 3.95
  Nude cover 9.95
Spec. Scorn: Naked Truth (1997) . . 3.95
  Nude cover 9.95

SCOUT HANDBOOK
Eclipse
1 . . . . 1.75

SCRATCH
Outside
1 . . . . 3.00
2 . . . . 2.00
3 . . . . 1.75
4 . . . . 1.75

SCRIMIDAR
CFD Productions 1995
1 I:Bloody Mary 2.75

SCUD: DISPOSABLE ASSASSIN
Fireman Press
1 I:Scud. 16.00
1a 3rd printing. 3.50
2 . . . . 8.00
3 . . . . 6.00
4 thru 6 F:Scud . . . . @5.00
7 Lupine Thoughts. 4.00
8 Scud Looks for His Arm 4.00
9 Scud Looks for His Arm 4.00
10 thru 16 by Rob Schrab . . . . . . @3.00
17 . . . . 3.00
18 . . . . 3.00
19 . . . . 3.00
20 Horse series, concl. 3.00
TPB Rep.#1–#4. . . . . 12.95
TPB Programmed for Damage,
  rep.#5–#9. . . . . 14.95
TPB Solid Gold Bomb. 17.95

Scud: Disposable Assassin #3
© Fireman Press

SCUD: TALES FROM THE VENDING MACHINE
Fireman Press 1998
1 . . . . 2.50
2 . . . . 2.50
3 . . . . 2.50
4 . . . . 2.50
5 . . . . 2.50

SEARCHERS
Caliber "New Worlds"
1A Red cover, signed 3.00
1B Blue cover, signed 3.00
3 . . . . 3.00
4 . . . . 3.00
5 flip book with Boston Bombers . . 3.00

SEARCHERS: APOSTLE OF MERCY
Caliber 1997
1 (of 2) 3.95
2 . . . . 3.95

Vol 2
1 . . . . 2.95
2 . . . . 2.95
3 (of 3) 48pg 3.95

SECRET FILES
Angel Entertainment 1996
0 gold edition. 8.00
0 nude cover 10.00
0 commemorative edition. 2.95
0 nude commemorative edition . . . 5.00
1 . . . . 2.95
1 spooky silver foil edition 5.95
1 nude signed 10.00
2 . . . . 2.95
2 deluxe 5.95
2 nude cover A 10.00
2 nude cover B 10.00
Spec. Secret Files vs. Vampire Girls:
  The Vampire Effece (1997) . . . 2.95
  Erotic nude cover. 2.95
Pin-up Book Secret Files: Erotic
  Experiments (1997) 2.95
  Erotic nude cover A 2.95
  Erotic nude cover B 2.95
Spec.#1 Secret Files: F.B.I.
  Conspiracy (1997)F:Sabrina

& Susanna Sorenson 2.95
Nude cover 2.95

SECRET FILES: THE STRANGE CASE
Angel Entertainment 1996
0 by David Campitti & Al Rio 2.95
0 Virgin nude cover 5.00
0 Slimy Wet Twins nude cover. . . . 7.00
0 nude manga cover 5.00
0 nude platinum cover 15.00
1 by David Campiti & Al Rio. 2.95
1 Virgin nude cover 5.00
1 nude manga cover 5.00
1 nude platinum cover 15.00

SECTION 8
Noir Press 1995
1 Anthology series. 2.50
2 thru 6 . . . . @2.50
7 "Retribution," pt.1 . . . . 2.50
8 "Retribution," pt.2 . . . . 2.50
9 . . . . 2.50
10 "Chance" 2.50

SEEKER
Caliber "Core" 1998
1M by Gary Reed & Chris
  Massarotto, Meadows(c) 2.95
1W David Williams(c) 2.95
1a variant Greg Louden (c) 2.95
1 premium, signed. 9.95
2 . . . . 2.95
3 . . . . 2.95
4 . . . . 2.95
5 Gestalt vs. LeAnn Heywood . . . 2.95
Spec. Dawn of Armageddon,
  x-over, 48-page 3.95

SENTINEL
1 . . . . 1.95
2 thru 4 . . . . @1.95

SERAPHIN
Newcomers Press 1995
1 I:Roy Torres 2.95

777: THE WRATH
Avatar Press 1998
1 (of 3) by David Quinn & Tim Vigil 3.00
1a wraparound cover 3.50
1b nude cover 6.00
1c leather cover 6.00
1d royal blue foil logo. 75.00
1e signed 15.00
1f foil platinum edition 16.95
2 . . . . 3.00
2 nude cover. 6.00
3 concl. 3.00
3 nude cover. 6.00
TPB 777:The Wrath/Faust Fearbook . . . 15.95

SHADES OF GRAY COMICS AND STORIES
Caliber Tapestry 1996
1 . . . . 2.95
2 . . . . 2.95
3 . . . . 2.95
4 . . . . 2.95
Super Summer Spec. rep. 3.95

SHADOW CROSS
Darkside Comics 1995
1 I:Shadow Cross 4.95
2 thru 7 . . . . @2.50

SHADOWALKER
Aircel
1 thru 4 . . . . @1.70

SHADOW SLASHER
Pocket Change Comics
1 I:Shadow Slasher 2.50
2 V:Riplash 2.50
3 F:Matt Baker. 2.50
4 Evolution 2.50
5 F:Riplash 2.50
6 Next Victim. 2.50
7 What Can Kill Him 2.50
8 . . . . 2.50
9 final issue. 2.50

SHANDA [THE PANDA]
Antarctic Press
1 thru 11 . . . . @2.75
12 thru 14. . . . . @2.95
Med Systems
15 and 16 . . . . @1.95
Vision Comics
17 by Mike Curtis & Michelle Light . 1.95
18 "Rocky Horror Picture Show" . . . 1.95
19 "Shine on Me, Cajun Moon" 2.50
20 falling in love 2.50
22 Bright Eyes 2.95
Shanda Fantasy
23 Sweet Young Things 2.95
24 graduation night. 2.95
25 48-page. 4.95

SHANGHAIED
Eternity
1 & 2 . . . . @1.80
3 & 4 . . . . @1.95

SHARDS
Acension Comics
1 I:Silver, Raptor, Ripple 2.50
2 F:Anomoly 2.50

SHATTERED EARTH
Eternity 1988–89
1 thru 9 . . . . @1.95

SHATTERPOINT
Eternity 1990
1 thru 4 Broid miniseries . . . . . . @2.25

SHEBA
Sirius Dogstar 1997
VOL 2
1 by Walter S. Crane IV. 2.50
2 . . . . 2.50
3 . . . . 2.50
4 . . . . 2.50
Sick Mind Press
5 . . . . 2.95
6 . . . . 2.95
7 . . . . 2.95

SHE-CAT
AC Comics
1 thru 4 . . . . @2.50

SHE-DEVILS ON WHEELS
Aircel
1 thru 3. . . . . 2.95

SHERLOCK HOLMES
Eternity
1 thru 22 . . . . @1.95

SHERLOCK HOLMES
Caliber/Tome Press 1997
1-shot Dr. Jekyll and Mr. Holmes by
Steve Jones & Seppo Makinen. 2.95
1-shot Return of the Devil. 3.95
1-shot Return of the Devil, signed. . 3.95
GN Adventure of the Opera Ghost . 6.95
TPB Case of Blind Fear 12.95
TPB Scarlet in Gaslight. 12.95
TPB Sussex Vampire 12.95

SHERLOCK HOLMES CASEBOOK
Eternity
1 and 2 . . . . @2.25

SHERLOCK HOLMES: CHRONICLES OF CRIME AND MYSTERY
Northstar
1 `The Speckled Band' 2.25

SHERLOCK HOLMES: HOUND OF THE BASKERVILLES
Caliber/Tome Press Dec. 1997
1 (of 3) by Martin Powell & PO . . . 2.95

SHERLOCK HOLMES: MARK OF THE BEAST
Caliber/Tome Press 1997
1 (of 3) by Martin Powell
& Seppo Makinen. 2.95
2 . . . . 2.95
GN 12.95

SHERLOCK HOLMES MYSTERIES
Moonstone 1997
1-shot by Joe Gentile & Richard
Gulick. 2.95

SHERLOCK HOLMES OF THE '30's
Eternity
1 thru 7 . . . . @2.95

SHERLOCK HOLMES READER
Caliber "Tome Press" 1998
1 Curse of the Beast 3.95
2 The Loch Ness Horror 3.95
3 The Loch Ness Horror 3.95

Sherlock Holmes Return of the Devil #2
© Adventure

SHERLOCK HOLMES: RETURN OF THE DEVIL
Adventure
1 V:Moriarty. 2.50
2 V:Moriarty. 2.50

SHERLOCK JUNIOR
Eternity
1 Rep.NewspaperStrips. 1.95
2 Rep.NewspaperStrips. 1.95
3 Rep.NewspaperStrips. 1.95

SHI: BLACK, WHITE, AND RED
Crusade Entertainment 1998
1 by Tom Sniegoski & J.G. Jones . 2.95
Spec. San Diego (Con) Art of War
Tour Book 1998 . . . . 9.95

SHI/DAREDEVIL BANZAI
Crusade Entertainment 1998
Spec. Lim. Ed. 10.00

SHI: KAIDAN
Crusade Entertainment
1 macabre. 2.95
1 signed & numbered 19.95

SHIELA TRENT VAMPIRE HUNTER
Draculina Publishing
1 O:Sheild Trent 2.50

SHIP OF FOOLS
Caliber 1996
1 signed edition. 3.00
2 "Dante's Compass" 3.00
3 The Great Escape begins 3.00
4 MiA 3.00
5 MiA 3.00
Spec. #1, Bon Voyage, Go to Hell,
Mama Hades 3.95
continued: See Image Comics

SHOCK THE MONKEY
Millenium
1 & 2 Entering the Psychotic Mind . 3.95

SHRED
CFW
1 thru 10 . . . . @2.25

SHRIEK
1 . . . . 4.95
2 . . . . 4.95
3 . . . . 7.95

Shuriken #6
© Victory

SHURIKEN
Victory 1986
1 Reggi Byers 6.00
1a 2nd printing 1.50
2 . . . . 3.00
3 . . . . 2.00
4 . . . . 1.75
5 thru 13 . . . . @1.50
Graphic Nov. Reggie Byers 8.00

SHURIKEN
Eternity 1991
1 Shuriken vs. Slate 2.50
2 Neutralizer, Meguomo 2.50
3 R:Slate 2.50
4 Morgan's Bodyguard Serrate . . . 2.50
5 Slate as Shuriken & Megumo . . . 2.50
6 Hunt for Bionauts, final issue . . . 2.50

SHURIKEN: COLD STEEL
1 . . . . 1.95
2 . . . . 1.95
3 thru 6 . . . . @1.95

SHURIKEN TEAM-UP
1 thru 3 . . . . @1.95

SIEGEL & SHUSTER
2 . . . . 1.70

SILBUSTER
Antarctic Press
1 thru 10 . . . . 3.50

---

11 I:Kizuki Sister. 3.50
12 thru 14 . . . . @3.50
15 . . . . 3.95
16 thru 19 . . . . @3.50
TPB Rep. #1-#4 . . . . 10.95
TPB Vol.2 . . . . 10.95

SILENT INVASION
Renegade
1 . . . . 4.00
2 thru 12, final issue . . . . @3.00

SILENT INVASION
Caliber
4 Red Shadows, pt.1 . . . . 3.00
5 Red Shadows, pt.2 . . . . 3.00

SILENT INVASION: ABDUCTIONS
Caliber 1998
1 by Larry Hancock & Michael
   Cherkos 2.95

SILVER STORM
Aircel 1990
1 thru 4 . . . . 2.25

SIMON/KIRBY READER
1 . . . . 1.75

SINBAD
1 . . . . 2.25
2 . . . . 2.25
3 . . . . 2.25
4 . . . . 2.25

SINBAD: HOUSE OF GOD
Adventure Comics
1 Caliph's Wife Kidnapped 2.50
2 Magical Genie 2.50
3 Escape From Madhi 2.50
4 A:Genie 2.50

SINNAMON
Catfish Comics 1995
1 remastered 2.75
1a remastered deluxe 3.75
6 thru 8 . . . . @2.75
Mythic Comics
9 "Ashes to Ashes—The Pyre-Anna
   Saga," pt.2 . . . . 2.75
10 "Twas Beauty Bashed
   The Beast" 2.75
11 . . . . 2.75
12 M.G.Delaney (c) 2.75
12 Poliwko (c) 2.75
Archives #1 . . . . 2.75

SISTER ARMAGEDDON
Dramenon Studios
1 & 2 Nun with a Gun 2.50
3 Mother Superior 2.50
4 V:Apoligon 2.95

SKELETON KEY
Amaze Ink 1995
1 1 I:Skeleton Key 1.50
1 2nd printing 1.75
2 F:Tansin 1.50
3 V:Japanese Burglar 1.50
4 V:Closet Monster 1.50
5 thru 10 . . . . @1.75

---

11 . . . . 1.75
12 . . . . 1.75
14 by Andi Watson 1.75
15 "The Celestial Calendar" 1.75
16 thru 30 . . . . @1.75
Spec. 4.95
TPB Vol. 1, Threshold rep.#1–#6 . 11.95
TPB Vol.2 Celestial Calendar,
   rep.#7–#18 . . . . 19.95
TPB Vol. 3, rep. #19–#24 . . . . . . 12.95
TPB Vol. 4, Cats & Dogs, rep.
   #25–#30 . . . . 12.95
Spec.Skeleton Key/Sugar Kat 2.95

VOL 2
1 (of 4) 2.95
2 . . . . 2.95
3 . . . . 2.95
4 conclusion 2.95

SKIN 13
Entity/Parody 1995
1/2a Grungie/Spider-Man 2.50
1/2b Heavy Metal 2.50
1/2c Gen-Et Jackson 2.50

SKUNK, THE
Entity Comics April 1997
#Uno 2.75
5 BMs 2.75
6 BMs 2.75
Collection #1 rep. #1–#3 . . . . 4.95
Collection #1a signed & numbered . 9.95
Collection #2 rep. #4–#6 . . . . 4.95

SKUNK/FOODANG
FOODANG/SKUNK
Entity Comics
Spec. 1 BMs, BMs(c) 2.75
Spec. 1a BMs, Mike Duggan(c) . . . 2.75

SKYNN & BONES: DEADLY ANGELS
Brainstorm April 1996
1 . . . . 2.95

SKYNN & BONES: FLESH FOR FANTASY
Brainstorm 1997
1 erotic missions 2.95
1a nude cover 2.95
2 erotic missions 2.95
2a nude cover 2.95
Spec. #1 Dare to Bare 3.00
Spec. #1 Dare to Bare, nude cover. 4.00

SLACK
Legacy Comics
1 Slacker Anthology 2.50
2 Loser 2.50

SLAUGHTERHOUSE
Caliber
1 Bizarre medical Operations 2.95
2 House of Death 2.95
3 House of Death 2.95
4 Dead Killer vs. Mosaic 2.95

SMITH BROWN JONES: ALIEN ACCOUNTANT
Slave Labor 1998
1 by Jon Hastings 2.95
2 . . . . 2.95

B & W PUB.

3 . . . . 2.95	1c Royal Blue edition. 75.00
4 . . . . 2.95	2 concl. 3.00
Spec.#1 Halloween Special 2.95	2a Sudden Death variant cover . . . 4.95

SNAKE, THE
Special Studio 1991

1 . . . . 3.50

SNARF
Kitchen Sink

1 thru 10 . . . . @2.00	
10 (c)BE. 2.00	
11 thru 13 . . . . @2.00	

SNOWMAN
Hall of Heroes 1996

1 . . . . 20.00	
1a variant (c) 25.00	
1 3rd printing 2.75	
1 San Diego Con. ed. 5.00	
2 . . . . 10.00	
2a 2nd printing 2.75	
2b variant (c) 12.00	
3 . . . . 6.00	
3a variant (c) 9.00	

SNOWMAN
Avatar Press 1997

0 by Matt Martin, O:Snowman 3.00	
0a Frozen Fear extra-bloody 4.95	
0b Leather cover 25.00	
0c signed. 10.00	
Spec.#1 Snowman 1944. . . . . 3.95	
Spec.#1 Snowman 1944, deluxe. . . 4.95	
Spec.#1 Snowman 1944, signed. . 10.00	
1-shot Flurries, Glynn (c) 4.95	
1-shotA Flurries, Snowman (c) 4.95	

SNOWMAN:
DEAD & DYING
Avatar Press 1997

1 (of 3) by Matt Martin 3.00	
1 deluxe 4.95	
1 signed 10.00	
2 . . . . 3.00	
2 deluxe 4.95	
3 by Matt Martin 3.00	
3 Frozen Fear 4.95	
3 White Velvet 25.00	

SNOWMAN:
HORROR SHOW
Avatar Press 1998

1 by Matt Martin 3.00	
1a Frozen Fear (c). 4.95	
1b Leather cover 30.00	
1 deluxe 4.95	

SNOWMAN: 1994
Entity Oct. 1996

1 flip cover #0, by Matt Martin,	
O:Snowman 3.00	
1 signed, numbered. 8.00	
3 . . . . 2.75	
3 deluxe, variant, foil cover 3.50	
4 . . . . 2.75	
4 deluxe, variant, foil cover 3.50	

SNOWMAN2
Avatar Press 1997

1 (of 2) Snowman vs. Snowman . . 3.00	
1a Face-off cover 4.95	
1b Leather cover 30.00	

SOB: SPECIAL
OPERATIONS BRANCH
Promethean Studios 1994

1 I:SOB. 2.50

SOCKETEER
Kardia

Rocketeer parody 2.25

SOLD OUT
Fantagor

1 & 2 . . . . @1.75

SOLO EX-MUTANTS
Eternity

1 thru 6 . . . . @1.95

SONG OF THE SIRENS
Millennium

Earth 2.95	
Earth, signed print edition 6.95	
Fire 2.95	
Fire, signed print edition 9.95	
Wind 2.95	
Wind collectors edition 4.95	
Wind with trading card 4.95	
Secrets, Lies, & Videotape Pin-Up	
Special. 2.95	
Secrets, Lies, & Videotape Pin-Up	
Special, foil logo. 5.95	
Secrets, Lies, & Videotape Pin-Up	
Special, deluxe. 9.95	

SOUL
Samson Comics

1 thru 3 F:Sabbeth . . . . @2.50

SOULFIRE
Aircel

1 mini-series 1.70	
2 . . . . 1.70	
3 . . . . 1.70	

SOULSEARCHERS
AND CO.
Claypool 1993–98

1 thru 10 Peter David(s) . . . . @3.00	
11 thru 20 . . . . @2.50	
21 thru 24. . . . . @2.50	
25 ACo&SL(c) 2.50	
26 O:Soulsearchers, pt.1 . . . . 2.50	
27 O:Soulsearchers, pt.2 . . . . 2.50	
28 O:Soulsearchers, pt.3 . . . . 2.50	
29 O:Soulsearchers, pt.4 . . . . 2.50	
30 . . . . 2.50	
31 The Mystery of the Lighthouse	
Pirate Treasure 2.50	
32 thru 36. . . . . 2.50	
TPB 12.95	

SOUTHERN KNIGHTS
1 See Crusaders

2 . . . . 8.00	
3 and 4 . . . . @5.00	
5 thru 7 . . . . @4.00	

Fictioneer

8 thru 11 . . . . @2.50	
12 thru 33 . . . . @2.00	

Southern Knights #18
© Fictioneer

34 . . . . 2.25	
35 The Morrigan Wars Pt.#2. . . . . 3.50	
36 Morrigan Wars Pt.#5 . . . . 3.50	
37 Hell ina Handbasket. 2.50	
Ann. #1 . . . . 2.50	
DreadHalloweenSpec #1 . . . . 2.25	
Primer #1 . . . . 2.25	

SOUTHERN SQUADRON
Aircel

1 thru 4 . . . . @2.25

Eternity

1 I:SQUAD 2.50	
2 . . . . 2.25	
3 . . . . 2.25	
4 . . . . 2.25	

SOUTHERN SQUADRON
FREEDOM OF INFO. ACT.
Eternity

1 F.F.#1 Parody/Tribute cov. 2.50	
2 A:Waitangi Rangers 2.50	
3 . . . . 2.50	

SPACE ARK
Apple

1 . . . . 2.75	
2 . . . . 2.50	
3 . . . . 1.75	
4 . . . . 1.75	
5 . . . . 1.75	

SPACE BEAVER
Ten-Buck Comics

1 . . . . 2.50	
2 . . . . 1.50	
3 O&I:Stinger. 1.50	
4 A:Stinger 1.50	
5 . . . . 1.50	
6 O:Rodent 1.50	
7 thru 12 . . . . @1.50	

SPACED

1 I:Zip; 800 printed 40.00	
2 . . . . 25.00	
3 I:Dark Teddy. 15.00	
4 . . . . 15.00	
5 and 6 . . . . @5.00	

B & W PUB.

7 and 8 . . . . @2.00

Eclipse

9 . . . . 1.75
10 . . . . 1.75
11 thru 13 . . . . @1.50

SPACE PATROL
Adventure

1 thru 3 . . . . 2.50

SPACE USAGI
Mirage Studios

1 Stan Sakai,Future Usagi 2.00
2 Stan Sakai,Future Usagi 2.00
3 Stan Sakai.Future Usagi 2.00

SPACE WOLF
Antarctic Press

1 From Albedo,by Dan Flahive 2.50

SPANDEX TIGHTS
Lost Cause Prod. Jan. 1997
Vol.2

1 . . . . 2.50
2 prelude to Space Opera 2.95
6 . . . . 2.95
Spec. Vs. Mighty Awful Sour
 Rangers, signed 2.95

SPANDEX TIGHTS PRESENTS: SPACE OPERA
Lost Cause Productions 1997

Part 1 by Bryan J.L. Glass & Bob
 Dix, parody 2.95
Part 1, signed, Star Wars parody . . 2.95
Part 2 "Star Bored", pt.2 . . . . 2.95
Part 3 . . . . 2.95

THE GIRLS OF '95
1 The Good, Bad and Deadly,
 signed (1997) 3.95

WIN A DREAM DATE WITH SPANDEX-GIRL
1 (of 3) (1998) 2.95
2 . . . . 2.95
3 . . . . 2.95

SPANDEX TIGHTS: THE LOST ISSUES
Lost Cause Productions

1 (of 4) 2.95
2 . . . . 2.95
3 . . . . 2.95
4 concl. 2.95

SPARKPLUG
Hero Graphics

1 From League of Champions 2.95

SPARKPLUG SPECIAL
Heroic Publishing

1 V:Overman 2.50

SPARROW
Millenium

1 I:Sparrow 2.95
2 . . . . 2.95

---

3 Valley of Fire 2.50

SPEED RACER

1 . . . . 3.00
1a 2nd Printing 1.50

SPENCER SPOOK
A.C.E. Comics

1 and 2 . . . . @.95
3 thru 8 . . . . @1.75

SPICY TALES

1 thru 13 . . . . @1.95
14 thru 20 . . . . @2.25
Special #2 . . . . 2.25

SPIDER KISS

1 Harlan Ellison 3.95

SPINELESS MAN
Parody Press

1 Spider-Man 2099 spoof 2.50

Spirit #82
© *Kitchen Sink*

SPIRIT, THE
Kitchen Sink

Note: #1 to #11 are in color

12 thru 86 WE,rep (1986–92) . . . @2.00
GN The Spirit Casebook 16.95
GN The Spirit Jam, 50 artists in
 48-page (1998) 5.95

SPIRIT, THE: THE ORIGIN YEARS
Kitchen Sink 1997

1 F:The Origin of the Spirit 3.00
2 F:The Black Queen's Army 3.00
3 F:Palyachi,The Killer Clown 3.00
4 F:The Return of the Orang 3.00
5 WE 3.00
6 WE,Kiss of Death 3.00
7 F:The Kidnapping of Ebony 3.00
8 F:Christmas Spirit of 1940 . . . . . 3.00
9 WE 3.00
10 F:The Substitute Spirits 3.00

SPIRITS
Mindwalker 1995

1 thru 3 Silver City 2.95
4 Caleb Escapes Zeus 2.95

SPITTING IMAGE
Eclipse

1 Marvel & Image parody 2.50

SQUEE
Slave Labor 1997

1 by Jhonen Vasquez 6.00
1a 2nd printing 3.00
2 . . . . 3.00
3 . . . . 3.00
4 . . . . 3.00
TPB 15.95
HC 29.95

STAIN
Fathom Press 1998

1 Byler (c) 3.00
1a Vigil (c) 3.00
1b limited edition 7.95
2 . . . . 3.00
2a Vigil (c) 3.00
3 . . . . 3.00
3a Vigil (c) 3.00
4 . . . . 3.00
4a Vigil (c) 3.00
5 King cover 3.00
5a Ang cover 3.00
6 . . . . 3.00
7 . . . . 3.00
7a nude cover 3.95

STAINLESS STEEL ARMIDILLO
Antarctic Press

1 I:Saisni, Tania Badan 2.95
2 V:Mirage 2.95
3 V:Mirage 2.95
4 Spirit of Gaia 2.95
5 V:Giant 2.95
6 finale 2.95

STAR BLEECH THE GENERATION GAP
Parody Press

1 Parody 3.95

STARCHILD
Taliesin Press 1992–97

0 . . . . 35.00
1 . . . . 50.00
1a 2nd printing 4.00
2 . . . . 50.00
2a 2nd printing 4.00
3 . . . . 15.00
4 . . . . 7.00
5 . . . . 5.00
6 . . . . 5.00
7 . . . . 5.00
8 . . . . 5.00
9 . . . . 5.00
10 thru 13 . . . . 5.00
14 . . . . 3.00

Coppervale

TPB Coll. Ed. Awakenings, rep.
 #1–#12 . . . . 20.00
HC 35.00

STARCHILD: CROSSROADS
Coppervale
1 thru 4, reoffer, by James Owen @2.95
TPB Coll. Ed.112 pg. 12.00
HC Coll.Ed. 20.00
Conoisseurs Edition 100.00

STARCHILD MYTHOPOLIS
Coppervale 1997
6 (of 14) Fisher King, concl. 2.95

STARGATE: THE NEW ADVENTURES COLLECTION
Entity 1997
1 rep. Underworld; One Nation
  Under Ra 5.95
1a photo cover 4.95

Stargate: One Nation Under Ra #1
© Entity

STARGATE: ONE NATION UNDER RA
Entity March 1997
1 . . . . 2.75
1a deluxe 3.50

STARGATE: REBELLION
Entity 1997
1 (of 3) from novel, sequel to movie2.75
1 deluxe 3.50
2 . . . . 2.75
2 deluxe 3.50
3 (of 3) 2.75
3 foil cover 3.50
GN rep. 80 pg. 7.95
GN photo (c) 7.95

STARGATE: UNDERWORLD
Entity April 1997
1 . . . . 2.75
1a deluxe 3.50

STARK FUTURE
Aircel
1 . . . . 2.50

2 thru 7 . . . . @1.75
8 . . . . 2.00
9 thru 14 . . . . @1.70

STAR RANGERS
1 thru 3 . . . . @3.00
4 . . . . 1.95
BOOK II
1 . . . . 1.95
2 . . . . 1.95

STAR REACH
Taliesin Press
1 HC,I:CodyStarbuck. 8.00
2 DG,JSn 2.00
3 FB 2.00
4 HC 2.00
5 JSon 2.00
6 GD,Elric 2.00
7 DS 2.00
8 CR,KSy 2.00
9 KSy 2.00
10 KSy 2.00
11 GD 2.00
12 MN,SL 2.00
13 SL,KSy 2.00
14 . . . . 2.00
15 . . . . 2.00
16 . . . . 2.00
17 . . . . 2.00
18 . . . . 2.00

STARLIGHT AGENCY
Antartic Press
1 I:Starlight Agency 1.95
2 Anderson Kidnapped 1.95
3 . . . . 1.50

STATIC
1 SD 1.50
2 SD 1.50
3 SD 1.50

STEALTH FORCE
1 thru 8 . . . . @.95

STEALTH SQUAD
Petra Comics
0 O:Stealth Squad 2.50
1 I:Stealth Squad. 2.50
2 I:New Member 2.50
Volume II
1 F:Solar Blade 2.50
2 American Ranger Vs.Jericho . . . 2.50

STEELE DESTINES
Nightscapes
1 & 2 I:One Eyed Stranger. 2.95
3 Kidnapped by Aliens. 2.95

STERN WHEELER
Spotlight
1 JA 1.75

STEVE CANYON
Kitchen Sink
1 thru 14 . . . . @5.00
3-D Spec. #1 . . . . 6.00

STEVEN
Kitchen Sink
1 . . . . 4.00

1a 2ndPrinting. 2.95
2 . . . . 4.00
3 . . . . 2.95
4 and 5 . . . . @3.50
TPB The Best of Steven by Doug
  Allen (1998) 12.95

STICKBOY
Revolutionary
1 . . . . 2.00
2 thru 5 . . . . @2.50

STIG'S INFERNO
Vortex
1 . . . . 6.00
2 . . . . 3.50
3 . . . . 3.00
4 . . . . 3.00
5 . . . . 2.00
Eclipse
6 . . . . 1.75
7 . . . . 1.75

STINZ
Fantagraphics
1 . . . . 4.00
2 . . . . 4.00
3 . . . . 4.00
4 . . . . 4.00
[2nd series]
Brave New Words
1 thru 3 . . . . 2.50

STORMBRINGER
Taliesin Press
1 thru 3 . . . . @2.00

STORMWATCHER
Eclipse
1 thru 4 . . . . @2.00

STRANGE BEHAVIOR
Twilite Tone Press
1 LSn,MBr,Short Stories 2.95

STRANGE BREW
Aardvark–Vanaheim
1 . . . . 5.00

STRANGEHAVEN
Abiogenesis Press
1 Surrealistic Comic. 2.95
2 Secret Brotherhood 2.95
3 thru 10 by Gary S. Millidge . . . @2.95
11 . . . . 2.95
12 . . . . 2.95
TPB Arcadia, rep. #1–#6. . . . . . . 14.95

STRANGE SPORTS STORIES
Adventure 1992
1 w/2 card strip 2.50
2 The Pick-Up Game,w/cards 2.50
3 Spinning Wheels,w/cards 2.50
4 thru 6 w/cards. . . . . @2.50

STRANGE WEATHER LATELY
Metaphrog 1997
1 . . . . 3.50

2 thru 4	@3.50
5 thru 10	@3.00
TPB Vol. 1 rep. #1–#5	9.95
HC Vol. 1 signed & numbered	40.00
TPB Vol. 2	9.95
HC Vol. 2	35.95

STRANGE WORLDS
1	3.95
2 thru 4	@3.95

Strangers in Paradise #11
© Abstract

STRANGES IN PARADISE
Antarctic Press 1993–94
1 by Terry Moore, I:Katchoo	75.00
1a 2nd printing	15.00
1b 3rd printing	5.00
2	50.00
3	34.00

Abstract Studio
1 TMr, Gold Logo edition	20.00
1a 2nd printing	5.00
2 and 3, Gold Logo edition	@10.00
4	5.00
5 R:Mrs. Parker	6.00
6	5.00
7 Darcey Uses Francine	5.00
8 thru 13 TMr	@4.00
HC Complete Strangers In Paradise, Book One	29.95

VOL. 2
1 TMr, Gold Logo edition, I Dream of You	3.00
2 thru 13 gold logo	@3.00
TPB I Dream of You	16.95

VOL III
1 thru 8 See Image	
9 TMr,Detective Walsh returns	2.75
10	2.75
11	2.75
12	2.75
13 High School, pt.1 (of 3)	2.75
14 High School, pt.2	2.75
15 High School, pt.3	2.75
16A Francine/Katchoo Princess Warrior (c)	2.75
16B Tambi Princess Warrior (c)	2.75
17	2.75
18 Francine & Datchoo	2.75
19 Lifesize nude of Francine	2.75
20 Night at the Opera	2.75
21 All not well in paradise	2.75
22 The Big Rift	2.75

23 Katchoo moves out	2.75
24 steamy affairs	2.75
25 All Beach, All the Time	2.75
26	2.75
TPB Vol.4 Love Me Tender	12.95
TPB Vol.5 Immortal Enemies, rep. #6–#12	12.95
TPB Vol. 6 High School	8.95
Spec. #93268 Songs & Lyrics	2.75

STRANGELOVE
Entity Comics 1995
1 I:Strangelove	2.50
2 V:Hyper Bullies	2.50
3 I:Bogie	2.50

STRATA
Renegade 1986
1	3.00
2	2.50
3	1.70
4	1.70
5	1.70
6	2.00

STRAW MEN
1 thru 5	@1.95
6 thru 8	@2.25

STRAY BULLETS
El Capitan
1	22.00
1a 2nd & 3rd printing	4.00
2	15.00
2a 2nd printing	3.50
3	12.00
4	10.00
5 Dysfunctional Family	5.00
6 F:Amy Racecar	4.50
7 Virginias Freedom	4.50
8 DL,"Lucky to Have Her"	3.00
9 DL,"26 Guys Named Nick"	3.00
10 DL,"Here Comes the Circus"	3.00
11 DL,"How to Cheer Up Your Best Friend"	3.00
12 DL, People Will be Hurt	3.00
13 DL "Selling Candy"	3.00
14 DL,The Killers arrive,48pg	3.50
15 Sex and Violence	3.00
16	3.00
17 While Ricky Fish Was Sleeping	3.00
18 Sex and Violence, pt.2	3.00
19 Young and sexy	3.00
20 Motel	3.00
TPB Vol. 1	11.95
TPB Vol. 2	11.95
HC Vol. 2 Somewhere Out West	34.95

STREET FIGHTER
Ocean Comics
1 thru 4 limited series	@1.75

STREET HEROES 2005
Eternity
1 thru 3	@1.95

STREET MUSIC
Fantagraphics
1	2.75
2	2.75
3	2.95
4	2.95
5	2.50
6	3.95

STREET POET RAY
Fantagraphics
1	2.50
2	2.00
3	2.95
4	2.95

STREET WOLF
1 limited series	2.00
2 and 3	@2.00
Graphic Novel	6.95

STRIKER: SECRET OF THE BERSERKER
Viz
1 & 2 V:The Berserker	2.75
3 F:Yu and Maia	2.75

STRIKER: THE ARMORED WARRIOR
Viz
1 Overture	2.75
2 V:Child Esper	2.75
3 Professor taken hostage	2.75
GN Vol.1 The Armored Warrior	16.95
GN Vol.2 Forest of No Return	15.95

STYGMATA YEARBOOK
Entity
1 V:The Rodent	2.95
TPB Dragon Prophet	6.95

SUBTLE VIOLENTS
CFD Productions 1991
1 Linsner (c&a)	39.00
1a San Diego Con	100.00

SUGAR RAY FINHEAD
Wolf Press
1 I&O Sugar Ray Finhead	2.50
2 I:Bessie & Big-Foot Benny the Pit Bull Man	2.95
3 thru 7 Mardi Gras	@2.95
9 & 10	@2.95

SULTRY TEENAGE SUPER-FOXES
Solson
1 thru 4 RB,Woj	@2.00

SUPERMODELS IN THE RAINFOREST
Sirius 1998
1 (of 3)	2.95
2 and 3	@2.95

SUPERSWINE
Caliber
1 Parody, I:Superswine	2.50

SURVIVALIST CHRONICLES
Survival Art
1	6.50
2	6.50
3 I:Bessie & Big Foot Benny	1.95

SWAN
Little Idylls
1 thru 3 Ghost of Lord Kaaren 2.95
4 V:Slake. 2.95

SWEET CHILDE
BATTLE BOOK
Advantage Graphics 1995
1 I:Tasha Radcliffe 2.50

SWEET CHILDE:
LOST CONFESSIONS
Anarchy Bridgeworks 1997
1 F:Tasha Radcliffe 2.95

SWEET LUCY
Brainstorm Comics
1 with 4 cards 2.50
2 . . . . 2.50

SWERVE
Amaze Ink Dec. 1995
1 thru 3 by Kyle Hunter . . . . @1.75

SWIFTSURE
Harrier Comics
1 . . . . 2.00
2 . . . . 2.00
3 thru 8 . . . . @1.75
9 . . . . 9.00
9a 2nd printing 1.75
10 . . . . 1.75
11 . . . . 1.95

SWITCH B.L.A.Z.E.
MANGA
London Night 1999
0 . . . . 3.50
0a nude Japanese cover 6.00
½ Con special 4.95
½ Con special, Japanese (c) 6.00
1 . . . . 3.50
1a Elite fan ed. 6.00
1b Anime cell ed. 19.95

SWORD OF VALOR
A Plus Comics
1 JAp,rep.Thane of Bagarth 2.50
2 JAp/MK rep 2.50

SWORDS AND SCIENCE
Pyramid
1 thru 3 . . . . @1.70

SWORDS OF CEREBUS
Aardvark–Vanaheim
1 rep. Cerebus 1-4 . . . . 18.00
1a reprint editions 10.00
2 rep. Cerebus 5-8 . . . . 12.00
2a reprint editions 8.00
3 rep. Cerebus 9-12. . . . . 12.00
3a reprint editions 8.00
4 rep. Cerebus 13-16. . . . . 12.00
4a reprint editions 8.00
5 rep. Cerebus 17-20. . . . . 12.00
5a reprint editions 8.00
6 rep. Cerebus 21-25. . . . . 12.00
6a reprint editions 8.00

SWORDS OF SHAR-PAI
Caliber 1991
1 Mutant Ninja Dog 2.50
2 Shar-Pei. 2.50
3 Final issue 2.50

SWORDS OF VALORS:
ROBIN HOOD
A Plus Comics
1 rep. of Charlton comics. 2.50

SYSTEM SEVEN
Arrow
1 thru 4 . . . . @1.50

TAKEN UNDER
COMPENDIUM
Caliber
1 rep. Cal Presents #19-#22 . . . . 2.95

TALES FROM
DIMENSION X
Edge Publishing 1995
1 Dinosaur Mansion. 3.95

TALES FROM
THE ANIVERSE
Arrow
1 7,400 printed 10.00
2 . . . . 4.00
3 10,000 printed 2.50
4 . . . . 2.50

[2nd series]
Massive Comics Group
1 thru 3 . . . . 1.50

TALES FROM THE EDGE
Vanguard
5 . . . . 2.95
5 signed 5.95
6 . . . . 2.95
7 . . . . 2.95
7 signed 5.95
8 . . . . 2.95
8 signed 5.95
9 . . . . 2.95
10 . . . . 2.95
10 signed 5.95
11 F:Sacred Monkeys. 2.95
12 spec.F:Steranko 4.00
12 signed, limited 15.00
13 F:Steranko. 2.95
14 . . . . 2.95
15 Sienkiewicz special 4.00
Spec. Nightstand Chillers Benefit
  Edition 4.95
Spec. Nightstand Chillers, signed . 10.00
Spec. Sienkiewicz Special 10.00

TALES FROM THE HEART
1 thru 5 . . . . @1.75
6 . . . . 1.95
7 . . . . 1.95

TALES OF BEANWORLD
Eclipse
1 . . . . 10.00
2 . . . . 4.00
3 . . . . 2.50
4 I:Beanish 1.50
5 thru 20 . . . . @2.00

TALES OF TEENAGE
MUTANT NINJA TURTLES
1 . . . . 13.00
1B 2nd printing 3.00
2 . . . . 8.00
3 . . . . 5.00
4 . . . . 5.00
5 . . . . 5.00
6 thru 9 . . . . @4.00

TALES OF THE FEHNRIK
Antarctic Press
1 I:Lady Zeista. 2.95

TALES OF
THE JACKALOPE
BF
1 . . . . 5.00
2 . . . . 3.00
3 and 4 . . . . @2.50
5 thru 9 . . . . @2.00

TALES OF THE
NINJA WARRIORS
CFW
1 thru 14 . . . . @1.95
15 thru 19 . . . . @2.25

TALES OF THE PLAGUE
Eclipse
1 RCo 4.00

Tales Too Terrible to Tell #4
© New England Comics

TALES TOO TERRIBLE
TO TELL
1 thru 6 Pre-code horror stories . @3.50

TALL TAILS
Vision Comics March 1998
1 Earth Shaking. 2.95
1a Anime Blast cover. 2.95
1b Spell Warrior cover. 2.95
1c nude variant cover 3.95
1d signed 4.95
2 Fire Quest, Pt.1 . . . . 2.95
2a nude variant cover 3.95
3 Fire Quest, Pt.2 . . . . 2.95
4 Pain and Compromises,pt.1 . . . 2.95

B & W PUB.

5 . . . . 2.95
6 Trail Blazing, pt.1 . . . . 2.95
7 Trail Blazing, pt.2 . . . . 2.95
8 When It Almost Happened 2.95
GN Vol. 1 . . . . 8.95

TANTALIZING STORIES
Tundra
1 F:Frank & Montgomery Wart. . . . 2.25
2 Frank & Mont.stories cont. 2.25

TAOLAND
Sunitek
1 V:The Crocodile Warlord. 1.50
2 & 3 I:New Enemy 3.25

TASK FORCE ALPHA
Academy Comics
1 I:Task Force Alpha 3.50

TEAM NIPPON
Aircel
1 thru 7 . . . . @1.95

TECHNOPHILIA
Brainstorm Comics
1 with 4 cards 2.50

Teenage Mutant Ninja Turtles #38
© Mirage

TEENAGE MUTANT NINJA TURTLES*
Mirage Studios
*Counterfeits Exist - Beware
1 I:Turtles 350.00
1a 2nd printing 50.00
1b 3rd printing 25.00
1c 4th printing 15.00
1d 5th printing 4.00
2 . . . . 80.00
2a 2nd printing 18.00
2b 3rd printing 4.00
3 . . . . 25.00
3a 2nd printing 3.50
3b Special printing,rare 75.00
4 . . . . 10.00
4a 2nd printing 3.50
5 A:Fugitoid. 8.00
5a 2nd printing 3.50
6 A:Fugitoid. 7.00

6a 2nd printing 2.50
7 A:Fugitoid. 8.00
7a 2nd printing 2.50
8 A:Cerebus 10.00
9 . . . . 7.00
10 V:Shredder 7.00
11 A:Casey Jones 6.00
12 thru 18 . . . . @6.00
19 Return to NY 4.00
20 Return to NY 4.00
21 Return to NY,D:Shredder 4.00
22 thru 32 . . . . @4.00
33 color, Corben 3.50
34 Toytle Anxiety 3.50
35 Souls Withering 3.50
36 Souls Wake 3.50
37 Twilight of the Rings 3.50
38 Spaced Out Pt.1, A:President
   Bush 3.50
39 Spaced Out Pt.2 . . . . 3.50
40 Spaced Out concl.,I:Rockin'
   Rollin' Miner Ants (B.U. story). . 2.00
41 Turtle Dreams issue. 2.00
42 Juliets Revenge. 2.00
43 Halls of Lost Legends 2.00
44 V:Ninjas. 2.00
45 A:Leatherhead. 2.00
46 V:Samurai Dinosaur. 2.00
47 Space Usagi. 2.00
48 Shades of Grey Part 1 . . . . 2.00
49 Shades of Grey Part 2 . . . . 2.00
50 Eastman/Laird,new direction,
   inc.TM,EL,WS pin-ups 2.00
51 City at War #2 . . . . 2.00
52 City at War #3 . . . . 2.25
53 City at War #4 . . . . 2.25
54 City at War #5 . . . . 2.25
55 thru 65 . . . . @2.25
1990 Movie adaptation 6.50
Spec. The Haunted Pizza 2.25
Volume 2
1 thru 8 . . . . 2.75
9 V:Baxter Bot. 2.75
10 Mr. Braunze. 2.75
11 F:Raphael 2.75
12 V:DARPA. 2.75
13 J:Triceraton 2.75

TMNT TRAINING MANUAL
1 . . . . 5.00
2 thru 5 . . . . @3.00

TEMPEST COMICS PRESENTS
Academy Comics
1 I:Steeple, Nemesis 2.50

TERROR ON THE PLANET OF THE APES
Adventure Comics 1991
1 MP,collectors edition. 2.50
2 MP, the Forbidden Zone 2.50
3 . . . . 2.50

TERROR TALES
Eternity
1 Short stories. 2.50

TERRY AND THE PIRATES
ACG Comics 1998
1 by Georges Wunder, Charlton
   reprint 3.00
2 . . . . 2.95
3 . . . . 2.95

TEX BENSON
Metro Comics
1 thru 3 . . . . @2.00

39 SCREAMS
1 thru 6 . . . . @2.00

THEY WERE 11
Viz
1 Galactic University 2.75
2 The Accident 2.75
3 Virus 2.75
4 V:Virus. 2.75

THIEVES AND KINGS
I Box 1994–97
1 F:Ruebel The Intrepid. 9.00
1a 2nd printing 2.50
2 . . . . 6.00
2a 2nd printing 2.50
3 . . . . 5.00
3a 2nd printing 2.50
4 . . . . 4.00
5 . . . . 4.00
6 V:Shadow Lady 4.00
7 V:Shadow Lady 2.50
8 thru 18 by Mark Oakley. . . . . @2.50
19 thru 24 . . . . @2.35
25 thru 28 . . . . @2.50
TPB Vol. 1: The Red Book,
   rep.#1–#6. . . . . 12.00
TPB Vol. 1: 2nd printing 13.50
TPB Vol. 2: The Green Book. . . . 14.00
TPB Vol. 2: 2nd printing 16.50
TPB Vol. 3: The Blue Book 16.50

THORR SUERD OR SWORD OF THOR
1 . . . . 3.00
1a 2nd printing 2.00
2 . . . . 1.75
3 . . . . 1.50

THREAT
1 . . . . 5.00
2 . . . . 3.00
3 and 4 . . . . @2.00
5 thru 10 . . . . @2.25

3 X 3 EYES
Innovation
1 Labyrinth o/t DemonsEyePt.1 . . . 2.25
2 Labyrinth o/t DemonsEyePt.2 . . . 2.25
3 Labyrinth o/t DemonsEyePt.3 . . . 2.25
4 Labyrinth o/t DemonsEyePt.4 . . . 2.25
5 Labyrinth o/t DemonsEye conc. . 2.25

THREE GEEKS, THE
3 Finger Prints 1997
1 by Rich Koslowski, Going
   to the Con, pt.1 . . . . 2.50
2 Going to the Con, pt.2 . . . . 2.50
3 Going to the Con, pt.3 (of 3) 2.50
4 . . . . 2.50
5 five more geeks 2.50
6 F:Allen 2.50
7 . . . . 2.50
8 48-page 3.50
9 24-page 2.50
10 Happy Birthday Allen 2.50
10a variant cover 3.50
11 Happy Birthday Allen, pt.2 . . . . 2.50
TPB 8.95

All comics prices listed are for *Near Mint* condition.

B & W PUB.

THREE MUSKETEERS
1	1.95
2	1.95
3	1.95

THREE ROCKETEERS
Eclipse
1 JK,AW,rep.	2.00
2 JK,AW,rep.	2.00

THRESHOLD
Avatar Press 1998
1 Snowman cover	4.50
1a Tales of the Cyberangels cover.	4.50
1b Tales of the Cyberangels, nude cover	6.00
1c Furies cover	4.50
1d Furies, nude cover	6.00
1e Fuzzie Dice cover	4.50
2 Snowman cover	4.95
2a Tales of the Cyberangels cover	4.95
2b Tales of the Cyberangels, nude cover	6.00
2c Furies cover	4.95
2d Furies, nude cover	6.00
2e Pandora cover	4.95
3 Ravening (c).	4.95
3a Ravening Nude (c)	6.00
3b Tales of the Cyberangels (c)	4.95
3c Calico (c)	4.95
3d Pandora (c)	4.95
3e Pandora nude (c)	6.00
4 Donna Mia (c).	4.95
4a Dona Mia nude (c)	6.00
4b Lookers (c).	4.95
4c Lookers nude (c).	6.00
4d Black Reign (c).	4.95
4e Journeymen (c)	4.95
5 Black Reign (c).	4.95
5a Journeymen (c)	4.95
5b Midnight Doyle (c).	4.95
5c Midnight Doyle nude (c)	6.00
5d Widow (c).	4.95
5e Widow nude (c)	6.00
6 Luna cover	4.95
6a Pandora (c)	4.95
6b Onyx (c)	4.95
6c Onyx nude (c).	6.00
7 Darkness in Collision, Cavewoman(c).	4.95
7a Ravening (c).	4.95
7b 777 Wrath (c)	4.95
7c 777 Wrath nude (c).	6.00
8 Vigil/Cuda (c)	4.95
8a Lookers (c).	4.95
8b Cyberangels (c)	4.95
8c Cyberangels nude (c)	6.00
9 August (c).	4.95
9a Cyberangels (c)	4.95
9b Donna Mia (c).	4.95
9c Donna Mia nude (c)	6.00
10 Calico (c).	4.95
10a Cyberangels (c)	4.95
10b Pandora (c)	4.95
10c Pandor nude (c).	6.00
11 Scythe (c)	4.95
11a Twilight (c).	4.95
11b Wicked (c).	4.95
11c Maelstrom Nude (c)	6.00
12 Snowman (c).	4.95
12a Pandora (c).	4.95
12b Midnight Doyle (c).	4.95
12c Midnight Doyle nude (c).	6.00
13 Snowman (c).	4.95
13a Pandora (c).	4.95
13b Harpy (c).	4.95
13c Pandor nude (c).	6.00
14 Kaos Moon (c).	4.95
14a Ravening (c)	4.95

14b Calico (c).	4.95
14c Ravening nude (c)	6.00
15 Luna (c).	4.95
15a Avatars (c)	4.95
15b Ravening (c)	4.95
15c Ravening nude (c)	6.00
16 Scythe (c)	4.95
16a Avatars (c).	4.95
16b Cimmerian (c)	4.95
16c Maelstrom nude (c)	6.00
17 Cimmerian (c)	4.95
17a Harpy (c).	4.95
17b Nightvision (c)	4.95
17c Cimmerian nude (c)	6.00
18 Nightvision (c).	4.95
18a Harpy (c).	4.95
18b Furies (c).	4.95
18c Furies nude (c)	6.00
19 Pandora (c).	4.95
19a Wilde Knight (c).	4.95
19b Furies (c).	4.95
19c Furies nude (c)	6.00

THRESHOLD OF REALTY
1 5,000 printed	2.50
2 thru 4	@2.00

THRILLKILL
Caliber
1 rep. Caliber Presents #1–#4	2.50

THUNDERBIRD
Newcomers Publishing
1 & 2 2 Stories.	@2.95
3	2.95
4 I:Mercer	2.95
5 R:Raven.	2.95
6 & 7	2.95
8 final issue	3.50
Ann.#1 The Great Escape	3.50

THUNDER BUNNY
1 O:Thunder Bunny	2.50
2 VO:Dr.Fog	2.00
3 I:GoldenMan.	1.75
4 V:Keeper	1.75
5 I:Moon Mess.	1.75
6 V:Mr.Endall.	1.75
7 VI:Dr.Fog	1.75
8	1.75
9 VS:Gen. Agents	1.75
10 thru 12	@1.75

THUNDER MACE
1 Proto type-blue & red very rare:1,000 printed	15.00
1a four color cover.	3.00
2 thru 5	@1.75
6	2.00
7	2.00
Graphic Novel, rep.1-4	5.00

TICK
New England Comics
1 BEd	55.00
1a 2nd printing	35.00
1b 3rd printing	6.00
1c 4th printing	2.50
2 BEd	50.00
2a 2nd printing	25.00
2b 3rd printing	4.00
2c 4th printing	2.50
3 BEd	18.00
3a 2nd printing	2.50
4 BEd	12.00
4a 2nd printing	2.50

Tick #7
© *New England Comics*

5 BEd	12.00
6 BEd	11.00
7 BEd,A:Chairface Chippendale.	11.00
8 BEd	10.00
8a Spec.No Logo edition	20.00
9 BEd,A:Chainsaw Vigilante, Red Eye.	5.00
10 BEd	5.00
11 thru 12 BEd	4.00
9 thru 12, new printings	2.95
Spec. Ed. #1, I:Tick	45.00
Spec. Ed. #2, 2nd App. Tick	40.00
Spec. #1 Reprise edition.	5.95
TPB Omnibus #1 rep. #1–#6.	17.95
TPB Omnibus #2 BEd,fifth printing	14.95
TPB Omnibus #3 BEd.	10.95
TPB Omnibus #4 BEd.	10.95
The Tick Big Yule Log Special 1998	3.50
The Tick Big Yule Log Special 1999	3.50
Big Giant Summer Special #1, The Sidekicks are Revolting	3.50
Big Summer Annual #1.	3.50
TPB Tick Bonanza #3.	4.95
TPB Tick Bonanza #4.	4.95
Spec.#1 Back to School	3.50

TICK AND ARTHUR, THE
New England Comics 1999
1 by Sean Wang & Mike Baker	3.50
2 Return of the Thorn,pt.2	3.50
3 Return of the Thorn,pt.3	3.50
4 Tick & Arthur meet Flea & Doyle.	3.50

TICK, THE: BIG BLUE DESTINY
New England Comics 1997
1 by Eli Stone, Keen edition.	3.00
1 Wicked Keen edition.	5.00
2A cover A	3.00
3B cover B	3.00
3	3.50
4	3.50
5 The Chrysalis Crisis	3.50

TICK: GIANT CIRCUS OF THE MIGHTY
New England Press
1 A-O	3.00
2 P-Z.	3.00
3	3.00

TICK, THE: HEROES OF THE CITY
New England Comics 1999
1 three stories 3.50
2 . . . . 3.50
3 . . . . 3.50
4 . . . . 3.50

TICK: KARMA TORNADO
New England Press
1 . . . . 4.00
1 2nd printing 3.00
2 . . . . 3.50
2 2nd printing 3.00
3 thru 9 . . . . 3.50
3 thru 9 2nd printings. 3.00
TPB #1 second edition 13.95

TICK, THE: LUNY BIN
New England Comics 1998
1 (of 3) by Eli Stone, Back to
   the Luny Bin. 3.50
2 To the Rescue 3.50
3 Six Eyes in Tears 3.50
Preview Special, 32pg 1.50
TPB Luny Bin Trilogy 120-page . . 4.95

TICK OMNIBUS
New England Press
1 1 to 6 Rep. 14.95

TICK'S BACK, THE
New England Comics
0 by Eli Stone, V:Toy DeForce 3.00

TIGERS OF TERRA
Mind-Visions
1 6,000 printed 4.50
1a Signed & Num. 14.00
2 . . . . 2.00
2a Signed & Num. 11.00
5 thru 7 . . . . @3.50
8 thru 10 . . . . @3.75
Antarctic
11 and 12 . . . . @3.95
[Vol. 2]
0 thru 14 . . . . @2.75
15 Totenkopf Police,pt.2 . . . . 2.75
16 Battleship Arizona,pt.3. . . . . . . 2.75
17 thru 22 . . . . @2.95
23 "Trouble with Tigers" pt.3 . . . . . 2.95
24 48pg 10th Anniv. 3.95
25 "Battle for Terra" pt.1 . . . . 2.95
TPB Book Two. 9.95
TPB Book Three. 9.95
TPB Book Four. 9.95

TIGRESS
Hero Graphics
3 A:Lady Arcane 2.95
4 inc. B.U. Mudpie. 2.95

TIGER-X
Eternity
Special #1 . . . . 2.50
Spec. #1a 2nd printing 2.25
1 thru 3 . . . . @1.95
Book II
1 thru 4 . . . . @1.95

TIME DRIFTERS
Innovation
1 . . . . 2.25
2 . . . . 2.25
3 . . . . 2.25

TIME GATES
Double Edge
1 SF series,The Egg #1. . . . . 1.95
2 The Egg #2 . . . . 1.95
3 Spirit of the Dragon #1 . . . . 1.95
4 Spirit of the Dragon #2 . . . . 1.95
4a Var.cover 1.95

TIME JUMP WAR
Apple
1 thru 3 . . . . @1.95

TIME MACHINE
1 thru 3 . . . . @2.50

TIME WARRIORS
Fantasy General
1 rep.Alpha Track #1 . . . . 1.50
1a Bi-Weekly. 75
2 75
3 75

TITANESS
Draculina Publishing 1995
1 I:Titaness,Tomboy. 2.95

TO BE ANNOUNCED
1 thru 6 . . . . @1.50

TOM CORBETT SPACE CADET
Eternity
1 . . . . 2.00
2 . . . . 2.00
3 . . . . 2.25
4 . . . . 2.25

TOM CORBETT II
1 . . . . 2.25
2 . . . . 2.25
3 . . . . 2.25
4 . . . . 2.25

TOM MIX HOLIDAY ALBUM
Amazing Comics
1 . . . . 3.50

TOM MIX WESTERN
AC Comics
1 . . . . 2.50
2 . . . . 2.50

TOMMI GUNN: KILLERS LUST
London Night Jan. 1997
1 . . . . 3.00
1a nude cover. 6.00
1 photo cover 6.00
3 nude cover, signed. 12.00
Ann. #1 . . . . 3.00
Ann. #1a nude cover edition 3.00

TOMMY & THE MONSTERS
1 thru 3 . . . . @1.95

TOMORROW MAN
Antarctic
1 R:Tommorrow Man 2.95
Spec.#1 48 pages 3.95

Too Much Coffee Man? #3
© Adhesive Comics

TOO MUCH COFFEE MAN
Adhesive Comics 1995
1 F:Too Much Coffee Man 19.00
1a 2nd printing 5.00
2 Wheeler (s&a). 11.00
3 Wheeler (s&a) 6.00
4 In love 5.00
5 thru 7 . . . . @4.00
8 . . . . 3.00

TORG
Adventure
1 Based on Role Playing Game. . . 2.50
2 thru 3 Based on Game . . . . . . @2.50

TOR JOHNSON: HOLLYWOOD STAR
Monster Comics
1 Biographical story 2.50

TORRID AFFAIRS
1 . . . . 2.25
2 . . . . 2.25
3 thru 5, 60 pages . . . . @2.95

TOTALLY ALIEN
1 . . . . 17.00
2 . . . . 12.00
3 . . . . 8.00

TOUGH GUYS AND WILD WOMEN
Eternity
1 . . . . 2.25
2 . . . . 2.25

TRACKER
Blackthorne
1	2.00
2	1.75
3	2.00
4	2.00

TRANSIT
1	2.00
2 thru 6	@1.75

TRICKSTER
KING MONKEY
1 thru 5	@1.75

TRIDENT
1 thru 7	@3.50
8	4.50

TRIMUVERATE
Mermaid Productions
1 I:Trimverate	2.25
2 & 3 Team captured	2.25
4 V:Ord,Ael	2.25

Troll Lords #1, 2nd printing
© Tru Studios

TROLLORDS
Tru Studios 1986
1 1st printing	6.00
1a 2nd printing	2.00
2	3.00
3	2.00
4 thru 15	@1.50
#1 special	1.75

TROLLORDS
Apple Comics 1989–90
1 thru 6	@2.50

TROLLORDS
Caliber Tapestry 1996
1 and 2	@2.95

TROLLORDS:
DEATH & KISSES
1	1.95
2 thru 5	@2.25

TROUBLE SHOOTERS
Nightwolf
1 I:Trouble Shooters	2.50
2 V:Ifrit,Djin,Ghul	2.50
3 V:Morgath	2.50

TROUBLE WITH GIRLS
Eternity 1989–91
1	3.00
2	2.50
3 thru 14	@1.95
15 thru 21	@2.25
22 Lester's Origin	2.25
Ann. #1	2.95
Graphic Novel	7.95
Graphic Novel #2	7.95
Xmas special 'World of Girls'	2.95

NEW SERIES
1 thru 4 see color	
5 thru 11	@1.95

TROUBLE WITH TIGERS
Antarctic Press
1 NinjaHighSchool/Tigers x-over	2.00
2	2.00

TRUE CRIME
Eclipse
1 thru 2	2.95

TRUFAN ADVENTURES THEATRE
1	8.00
2 3-D issue	5.00

TURTLE SOUP
1 A:TMNT	6.00

TURTLES TEACH KARATE
Solson
1	4.00
2	3.50

TWILIGHT AVENGER
Eternity
1 thru 18	@1.95

Miracle Studios
Spec. Twilight Avenger Super Summer Special	2.75

TWILIGHT X QUARTERLY
Antarctic Press
1 thru 3 by Joseph Wright	@2.95
4 Celebration	2.95

TWIST
Kitchen Sink
1	1.95
2 and 3	@2.00

TWISTED TANTRUMS OF THE PURPLE SNIT
Blackthorne 1986
1	2.50
2	2.00

2001 NIGHTS
Viz 1990–91
1 by Yukinobu Hoshino	5.00

Twisted Tantrums of the Purple Snit #2
© Blackthorne

2	4.00
3 thru 5	@3.75
6 thru 10	@4.25

TYRANNY REX
Fleetway
GN reps. from 2000A.D.	7.95

ULTIMATE STRIKE
London Night 1996
1	2.00
1 holochrome edition	15.00
1a nude commemorative edition	5.00
2	2.00
3	2.00
4	2.00
4 Photo nude cover	5.00
5	2.00
5 Photo nude cover	5.00
6 sequel to Strike #0	2.00
6 limited nude cover	5.00
7 by Kevin Hill, "Stryke: Year One" concl.	2.00
7 limited nude cover	5.00
8 Year One,	2.00
8a nude cover	5.00
9 Year One, cont.	2.00
9a Nude cover	5.00
10	2.00
10a Nude cover	5.00
11	2.00
11a Nude cover	5.00
12	2.00
12a Nude cover	5.00

ULTRA KLUTZ
Onward Comics
1	2.50
2 thru 18	@1.50
19 thru 24	@1.75
25 thru 30	@2.00

Bad Habit
TBP Book One, rep. #1–#23	29.95

UNCANNY MAN-FROG
Mad Dog
1 and 2	@1.75

B & W PUB.

UNCENSORED MOUSE
Eternity
1 Mickey Mouse 10.00
2 Mickey Mouse. 11.00

UNFORGIVEN, THE
Trinity Comics Ministries
Mission of Tranquility
1 thru 6 V:Dormian Grath. 1.95
7 I:Faith. 1.95

UNICORN ISLE
Genesis West
1 . . . . 2.50
2 . . . . 1.50
3 . . . . 1.50
Apple
4 thru 6 . . . . @1.75

UNLEASHED
Caliber Press
1 F:Carson Davis. 2.95
2 V:North Harbor Crime. 2.95

UNSUPERVISED EXISTENCE
1 . . . . 2.00
2 and 3 . . . . @2.50

UNTOUCHABLES
1 thru 20 . . . . @.75

UNTOUCHABLES
Caliber 1997
1K by Joe Pruett & John Kissee,
MK(c). 2.95
1S by Joe Pruett & John Kissee,
Showman (c) 2.95
2 . . . . 2.95
3 MK (c) 2.95
4 MK (c) 2.95
HC New Beginning 19.95
Spec. The High Society Killer (1998)3.95

USAGI YOJIMBO
Fantagraphics 1987
1 SS 10.00
1a 2nd printing 5.00
2 SS,Samurai 8.00
3 SS,Samurai,A:Croakers 6.00
4 SS 5.00
5 thru 7 SS . . . . @5.00
8 SS,A Mother's Love 5.00
8a 2nd printing 3.00
9 SS 5.00
10 SS,A:Turtles 5.00
10a 2nd printing 3.00
11 thru 18 SS . . . . @4.00
19 SS,Frost & Fire,A:Nelson
Groundthumper 4.00
20 thru 21 SS . . . . @4.00
22 SS,A:Panda Khan 4.00
23 SS,V:Ninja Bats. 4.00
24 SS 4.00
25 SS,A:Lionheart 4.00
26 SS,Gambling 4.00
27 SS. 4.00
28 thru 31 SS,Circles pt.1–4 . . . @4.00
32 . . . . 4.00
33 SS,Ritual Murder. 4.00
34 thru 37 . . . . @4.00
Spec.#1 SS,SummerSpec, C:Groo 45.00
TPB Vol 4, rep. 16.95
TPB Vol 6, rep., new printing 12.95

TPB Vol 7, Gen's Story 16.95
Radio Comix
Vol. 1 The Art of Usagi Yojimbo . . . 3.95

VALENTINO
Renegade
1 . . . . 1.70
2 and 3 . . . . @2.00

VALOR THUNDERSTAR
1 and 2 . . . . @1.75

VAMPEROTICA
Brainstorm Comics
1 I:Luxura 10.00
1a 2nd & 3rd printing 3.00
2 . . . . 8.00
2 2nd printing 3.00
3 . . . . 4.00
4 I:Blood Hunterq 4.00
5 Deadshot 4.00
6 Deadshot 4.00
7 Baptism 4.00
8 Pains,Peepers 4.00
9 thru 11 . . . . @4.00
12 thru 16 . . . . @3.00
17 thru 22 see: color
20 signed 5.00
20 nude cover, signed 5.00
21 nude cover, signed 5.00
23 . . . . 3.00
23a nude edition 3.00
23 encore edition 2.95
23a encore edition, nude cover . . . 3.95
24 . . . . 3.00
24a nude cover 3.00
25 . . . . 3.00
25a deluxe, nude cover 3.00
26 . . . . 3.00
26a nude cover 3.00
26a nude cover 3.95
27 . . . . 3.00
27 Nude Luxury edition. 5.00
28 A:China & Jazz 3.00
28a nude cover 3.00
28 Nude Luxury edition. 5.00
28 Nude Luxury edition, signed. . . . 5.00
29 mild cover 3.00
30 Legends of Luxura x-over, concl. 2.95
30a nude cover 3.95
31 V:Red Militia 2.95
31a nude cover 3.95
32 . . . . 2.95
32a nude cover 3.95
33 by Kirk Lindo 2.95
33a nude cover 3.95
34 V:Pontius Vanthor 2.95
34a nude cover edition 5.00
34b luxury edition 5.00
35 . . . . 2.95
35a nude cover 5.00
36 I:Countess Vladimira 2.95
36a nude cover edition 3.95
36a photo cover edition 3.95
37 . . . . 2.95
37 nude cover 2.95
37 statue cover. 2.95
38 . . . . 2.95
38 nude cover 3.95
38 nude luxury edition 5.00
39 Death From Above, pt.1 . . . . . . 2.95
39a nude cover 3.95
39b nude embrace cover 3.95
40 Death From Above, pt.2 . . . . . . 2.95
40a nude cover 3.95
40a nude embrace cover 3.95
41 . . . . 3.00
41a nude cover 4.00

42 Hostile Seduction. 3.00
42a nude cover 4.00
43 Harvest 3.00
43a nude cover 4.00
44 F:Luxura 3.00
44a nude cover 4.00
45 The Kindred Kill 3.00
45a nude cover 4.00
45b photo cover 4.00
46 Murder Most Foul 3.00
46a nude cover 4.00
47 Camelot. 3.00
47a nude cover 4.00
48 Reflections Over Blood 3.00
48a nude cover 4.00
49 Love's Story. 3.00
49a nude cover 4.00
50 final issue, 48-page 5.00
50a nude cover 5.00
50b commemmorative edition, Julie
Strain photo (c) 7.00
50c commemm. signed. 10.00
Commemorative Edition 2.95
Lingerie Special #1 . . . . 2.95
Spec. Lingerie, encore edition. . . . 2.95
Spec. Lingerie, deluxe 3.95
Spec. Swimsuit, encore edition . . . 2.95
Spec. Swimsuit, deluxe nude cover. 3.95
Gallery #1. . . . . 4.95
Gallery #1 nude cover 5.95
Bondage Spec. #1 . . . . 2.95
Bondage Spec. #1, nude cover. . . . 3.95
Bondage Spec. #1, manga 3.95
Ann. #1 Encore 3.00
Ann. #1 Encore, nude cover 4.00
Spec. #2 Dare to Bare 3.00
Spec. #2 Dare to Bare, nude cover. 4.00
Spec. #4 Encore Edition, new(c). . . 2.95
Spec. #4a Encore Edition, nude(c) . 2.95
Spec. #5 Encore Edition 2.95
Spec. #5a Encore Edition, nude(c) . 3.95
Spec.#1 Vamperotica Presents:
Countess Vladimira (1998) 3.00
Nude cover edition 4.00

VAMPEROTICA: BLOOD OF JAPAN
Brainstorm 1999
1 . . . . 3.00
1a nude cover 4.00

VAMPEROTICA: DIVIDE & CONQUER
Brainstorm 1999
1 V:The Juicious Edicts 3.00
1a nude cover 4.00
2 conclusion 3.00
2a nude cover 4.00

VAMPEROTICA MANGA
Brainstorm 1998
1 . . . . 2.95
1a nude cover 3.95
1b nude embrace cover 3.95
2 . . . . 3.00
2a nude cover 4.00

VAMPEROTICA TALES
Brainstorm 1998
1 . . . . 2.95
1a nude cover edition 3.95
1 nude luxury edition 5.00
2 . . . . 2.95
2a nude cover 3.95
2b nude embrace cover 3.95
3 . . . . 3.00

B & W PUB.

3a nude cover 4.00
4 Veiled Threat 3.00
4a nude cover 4.00
5 A Night of Wine and Roses. 3.00
5a nude cover 4.00

VAMPFIRE
Brainstorm 1996
1 . . . . 2.95
1a nude cover 3.95
1 commemorative photo cover . . . 10.00
2 . . . . 2.95
2a nude cover 5.00
2 signed 5.00
2 nude, signed. 5.00
Pin-Up Spec. 2.95
Pin-Up Spec. deluxe. 3.95
Tour Book #1 . . . . 2.95
Tour Book #1 nude cover 2.95

VAMPFIRE: EROTIC ECHO
Brainstorm 1997
1 by Fauve 2.95
1a nude cover 2.95
1b photo cover 3.00
2 . . . . 2.95
2a nude cover 2.95
2b photo cover 2.95

VAMPFIRE: NECROMANTIQUE
Brainstorm 1997
1 by Holly Golightly 2.95
1a nude edition 3.95
1b luxury edition, virgin cover 5.00
1c luxury edition, signed 15.00
1d regular, signed 8.00
1e nude cover, signed 10.00
2 by Fauve 2.95
2a nude edition 3.95

VAMPIRE BITES
Brainstorm
2 . . . . 2.95
2a nude cover 2.95

VAMPIRE CONFESSIONS
Brainstorm 1998
1 . . . . 3.00
1a nude cover 4.00

VAMPIRE GIRLS: CALIFORNIA 1969
Angel Entertainment 1996
0 nude cover, signed 5.95
1 blood red foil deluxe edition 5.95
2 . . . . 2.95
2 deluxe 5.95
2 nude cover A 10.00
2 nude cover B 10.00
TPB 5.00

VAMPIRE GIRLS: NEW YORK 1979
Angel Entertainment 1996
0 . . . . 2.95
0 virgin nude cover 5.00
0 nude platinum cover 15.00
0 gold edition. 8.00
1 . . . . 2.95
1 virgin nude cover 5.00
1 nude platinum cover 15.00

VAMPIRE GIRLS EROTIQUE
Angel Entertainment 1996
1 . . . . 2.95
1 nude cover 2.95
2 . . . . 2.95
2 erotic nude cover A 2.95
2 deluxe nude cover B 2.95
3 . . . . 2.95
3 nude cover 2.95
4 . . . . 2.95
4 erotic nude cover 2.95
5 . . . . 2.95
5 erotic nude kissing Candaze
   cover 4.00
6 . . . . 2.95
6 nude cover 2.95
7 Bloodsucker cover 3.00
7 nude gettin lunch cover 3.00
Spec. Gravedigger (1996) by
   Alexandra Scott & Bill Wylie . . . 3.00
   Nude Alexandra cover 3.00
   Nude Candice and Simone cover . .
3.00
Spec. Paris 1968 (1997) by
   Alexandra Scott & Dean Burnett 2.95
   Nude cover 4.00
Spec. Titanic 1912 (1998) by
   Alexandra Scott & Dean Burnett 2.95
   Nude cover 4.00

VAMPIRE GIRLS: BUBBLEGUM & BLOOD
Angel Entertainment 1996
1 . . . . 2.95
1 deluxe edition. 5.95
1 nude cover 10.00
2 . . . . 2.95
2 deluxe edition 5.95
2 nude cover 10.00

VAMPIRE GIRLS EROTIQUE: GRAVEDIGGER
Angel Entertainment 1996
1 by Alexandra Scott & Bill Wylie. . 3.00
1a Nude Alexandra cover 3.00
1b Nude Candice and Simone(c). . 3.00

VAMPIRE GIRLS VS. ANGEL GIRL
Angel Entertainment 1997
1 . . . . 2.95
1a erotic nude cover 3.95
1b deluxe nude cover 3.95

VAMPIRELLA
Harris
1 DC,SL,Summer Nights,48page . . 3.95

VAMPIRELLA
Silver Anniversary Collection
Harris 1996
0 Vampirella of Darkulon, EM 3.00
1 good girl edition 2.50
1a bad girl edition 2.50
2 good girl edition 2.50
2a bad girl edition 2.50
3 good girl edition 2.50
3a bad girl edition. 2.50
4 Silkie(c) 2.50
4a MBc(c) 2.50

VAMPIRELLA HELL ON EARTH
Harris 1999
Leather Ashcan 14.95
Leather Ashcan, signed 29.95

Vampirella: Morning in America #3
© Harris/Dark Horse

VAMPIRELLA: MORNING IN AMERICA
Harris/Dark Horse 1991–92
Book 1 thru 4 . . . . 7.00
Book 2 thru 4 . . . . @5.00
TPB 25.00

VAMPIRELLA/ PAINKILLER JANE
Harris 1998
Ashcan, preview. 6.00

VAMPIRELLA RETRO
Harris 1998
1 (of 3) rep. Warren stories 2.50
2 (of 3) rep. Warren stories 2.50
3 (of 3) rep. Warren stories 2.50

VAMPIRELLA 2999 A.D.
Harris Comics 1998
Manga Ashcan. 7.95
Manga Ashcan, leather edition . . . 14.95

VAMPIRELLA 3000 A.D.
Harris Comics 1999
Manga Ashcan. 7.95
Manga Ashcan, leather edition . . . 14.95

VAMPIRELLA VS. HEMORRHAGE
Harris
1 Limited Preview Ashcan 5.00

VAMPIRE MIYU
Antarctica Press
1 l:Vampire Princess Miyu 2.95
2 thru 5 . . . . @3.95
6 48pg. 4.95

VAMPIRE'S TATTOO
London Night 1997
1 (of 2) by Art Wetherell. 3.00
1 deluxe edition, nude cover 6.00
2 . . . . 3.00
2 deluxe edition, nude cover 6.00
1b nude cover edition, signed . . . 10.00
3 . . . . 3.00
3a nude cover. 6.00

VAMPIRE ZONE, THE
Brainstorm 1998
1 . . . . 2.95
1a nude cover. 3.95

VAMPORNRELLA
Forbidden 1997
1 parody 2.95
1 erotic nude cover A 2.95
1 erotic nude cover B 2.95

VAMPYRES
Eternity
1 thru 4 . . . . @2.25

VANGUARD: OUTPOST EARTH
1 and 2 . . . . @2.00

VAULT OF DOOMNATION
B-Movie Comics
1 . . . . 1.70

VENGEANCE OF DREADWOLF
Lightning Comics
1 O:Dreadwolf. 2.75

VERDICT
Eternity
1 thru 4 . . . . @1.95

VEROTIKA
Verotika 1995–97
1 Magical Times 15.00
2 . . . . 8.00
3 . . . . 5.00
4 thru 6 . . . . @4.00
7 thru 15 . . . . @3.00

VERY VICKY
Meet Danny Ocean
1 . . . . 3.50
1a 2nd printing 3.00

VERY VICKY: CALLING ALL HILLBILLIES
Meet Danny Ocean 1995
1 Pea Pickin Patty. 2.50

VIC & BLOOD
Renegade
1 and 2 RCo,Ellison. . . . . @2.00

VICKY VALENTINE
Renegade
1 thru 4 . . . . @1.70

VICTIMS
Silver Wolf
1 & 2 . . . . @1.50

VICTIMS
Eternity
1 thru 5 . . . . @1.95

VIDEO CLASSICS
1 Mighty Mouse. 3.50
2 Mighty Mouse. 3.50

VIETNAM JOURNAL
Apple Comics
1 . . . . 5.00
1a 2nd printing 3.00
2 . . . . 3.00
3 thru 5 . . . . @2.50
6 thru 13 . . . . @2.00
14 thru 16. . . . . @2.25

VIGIL: DESERT FOXES
Millenium
1 & 2 F:Grace Kimble 3.95

VIGIL: FALL
FROM GRACE
Innovation
1 'State of Grace' 2.75
2 The Graceland Hunt. 2.50

VINSON WATSON'S RAGE
Trinity Visuals
1 I:Rena Helen 3.00

VINSON WATSON'S SWEET CHILDE
Advantage Graphics
Vol. 2
1 F:Spyder 1.95

VIRGIN: SLUMBER
Entity 1997
1 BMs. 2.75
1 deluxe 3.50

VIRGIN: SURROUNDED
Entity 1997
1 BMs. 2.75
1 deluxe 3.50

VIRGIN: TILL DEATH DO US PART
Entity April 1997
1 BMs. 2.75
1 deluxe 3.50

VISIONS
Vision Publication 1979–83
1 I:Flaming Carrot 125.00
2 Flaming Carrot 30.00
3 Flaming Carrot 20.00
4 Flaming Carrot 30.00

VISUAL ASSAULT OMNIBUS
Visual Assault Comics 1995
1 thru 4 O:Dimensioner 3.00

VIXEN
Meteor Comics
1 & 2 Battle of the Vixens 2.95

VORTEX
Hall of Heroes
1 . . . . 20.00
1a commemorative 5.00
2 . . . . 12.00
3 thru 5 . . . . @3.50
6 V:The Reverend 3.00

VORTEX SPECIAL: CYBERSIN
Avatar Press 1997
1 by Matt Martin & Bil Maus. 3.00
1 nude cover. 4.95
1 velvet cover 25.00
1 signed 10.00

VORTEX: DR. KILBOURN
Entity March 1997
1 by Matt Martin 2.75
1a deluxe 3.50

VORTEX: INTO THE DARK
Entity 1997
1 . . . . 2.75
1 deluxe 3.50

Vox #1
© Apple Comics

VOX
Apple
1 JBy(c). 1.95
2 and 3 . . . . @1.95
4 and 5 . . . . @2.25

WABBIT WAMPAGE
Amazing Comics 1987
1 . . . . 2.00

WACKY SQUIRREL
1 thru 4 . . . . @1.75
Summer Fun Special #1 . . . . 2.00
Christmas Special #1 . . . . 1.75

WALKING DEAD
Aircel
1 thru 4 . . . . @2.25
Zombie Spec. 1 . . . . 2.25

WALK THROUGH OCTOBER
Caliber
1 I:Mr. Balloon 2.95
2 . . . . 2.95
3 All Hallow's Eve 2.95

WALT THE WILDCAT
Motion Comics 1995
1 I:Walt the Wildcat 2.50

Wandering Star #17
© Sirius

WANDERING STAR
Pen & Ink
1 I:Casandra Andrews 25.00
1a 2nd & 3rd printing 3.00
2 . . . . 8.00
3 . . . . 5.00
4 . . . . 4.00
5 . . . . 4.00
6 . . . . 2.50
7 . . . . 2.50
8 and 9 F:Casandra Andrews 2.75
10 R:Mekron. 2.75
11 . . . . 2.75
Sirius 1995–97
12 thru 20 TWo . . . . @2.50
21 TWo, final issue 2.50
TPB Vol. 1 rep. #1–#7 . . . . 14.95
TPB Vol. 2 . . . . 14.95
TPB Vol. 3 168-page 14.95

WAR
A Plus Comics
1 . . . . 2.50

WARCAT
Alliance Comics
1 thru 7 A:Ebonia 2.50

WARD: A BULLET SERIES
Liar Comics
1 Foresight,pt.1 . . . . 2.50
2 Foresight,pt.2 . . . . 2.50
3 Foresight,pt.3 . . . . 2.50

WARLACE
K-Blamm 1995
1 I:Warlace 2.95

WARLOCK 5
Aircel
1 . . . . 6.00
2 . . . . 5.00
3 . . . . 6.00
4 . . . . 5.00
5 . . . . 5.00
6 thru 11 . . . . @4.00
12 . . . . 3.50
13 . . . . 3.50
14 thru 16 . . . . @2.00
17 . . . . 1.70
18 . . . . 1.75
19 thru 22 . . . . @1.95
Book 2 #1 thru #7 . . . . @2.00

WARLOCK 5
Sirius 1997
1 (of 4) by Barry Blair & Colin Chan 2.50
2 . . . . 2.50
3 . . . . 2.50
4 finale 2.50

WARLOCKS
Aircel
1 thru 3 . . . . @1.70
4 thru 12 . . . . @1.95
Spec #1 Rep. 2.25

WAR OF THE WORLDS
Eternity
1 TV tie-in 1.95
2 thru 6 . . . . @1.95

WAR OF THE WORLDS, THE
Caliber "New Worlds" 1996
1 from H.G. Wells 2.95
1a signed 2.95
2 war for Kansas City 2.95
3 Haven & The Hellweed 2.95
4 . . . . 2.95
5 . . . . 2.95
TPB rep. #1–#5 . . . . 14.95

WAR OF THE WORLDS: THE MEMPHIS FRONT
Arrow Comics 1998
1 (of 5) by Randy Zimmerman
  & Richard Gulick 2.95
Spec.#1 signed & numbered. 2.95
2 . . . . 2.95
3 . . . . 2.95
4 . . . . 2.95

WAR PARTY VS. DEATHMARK
Lightning Comics
1 War Party vs. Deathmark 2.75

War of the Worlds #1
© Caliber

WARP WALKING
Caliber
1 `Quick and the Dead' 2.50

WARRIOR NUN: BLACK AND WHITE
Antarctic Press 1997
1 . . . . 3.00
2 . . . . 3.00
3 . . . . 3.00
4 Winter Jade, pt.1 F:Ninja Nun . . . 3.00
5 Winter Jade, pt.2 . . . . 3.00
6 Winter Jade, pt.3 . . . . 3.00
7 . . . . 3.00
8 . . . . 3.00
9 Return of the Redeemers 3.00
10 Return of Lillith 3.00
11 The Redeemers, cont. 3.00
12 The Redeemers, cont. 3.00
13 I:Sister Trinity 2.95
14 Redeemers saga again 2.95
15 F:Sister Trinity 2.95
16 F:Sister Trinity 2.95
17 Showdown. 3.00
18 Reaction 3.00
19 Carnivale. 3.00
20 Twilight Earth. 3.00
21 Lost Souls of Blue
  Moon Mountain 2.50
Spec. Warrior Nun Areala/Razor:
  Revenge 3.00
Spec.A Revenge, deluxe 6.00

WARRIORS
1 . . . . 2.50
2 thru 7 . . . . @1.95

WARZONE
Entity
1 I:Bella & Supra 2.95
2 F:Bladeback, Alloy, Granite. 2.95
3 F:Bladeback 2.95

WATCHDOG
Hammerhead Comics
1 I:Watchdog 2.95

B & W PUB.

WEASEL PATROL
Eclipse
Spec. #1. 2.00

WEBWITCH
Avatar Press 1997
0 by Raff Ienco 3.00
0 nude cover. 5.00
1 (of 2) signed 10.00
1 (of 2) 3.00
1 nude cover. 5.00
2 (of 2) 3.00
2 nude cover. 4.95
Boxed Set, all rare editions 35.00

WEBWITCH:
PRELUDE TO WAR
Avatar Press 1998
1 by Raff Jenco 3.00
1a nude cover. 6.00
1b Leather cover 30.00

WEBWITCH: WAR
Avatar Press 1998
1 (of 2) by Bill Maus 3.00
1a nude cover. 6.00
1b Leather cover 30.00
2 conclusion 3.00
2a nude cover. 6.00

WEIRDFALL
Antarctic Press 1995
1 I:Weirdfall. 2.75
2 O:Weirdfall 2.75
3 . . . . 2.75

WEIRD ROMANCE
Eclipse
1 . . . . 2.00

WEIRDSVILLE
Blindwolf Studios 1997
1 . . . . 2.95
1 2nd printing 2.95
2 . . . . 2.95
2 2nd printing 2.95
3 . . . . 2.95
3 2nd printing 2.95
4 . . . . 2.95
5 . . . . 2.95
6 The Usual Weirdoes, concl. . . . 2.95
7 . . . . 2.95
8 An American Werewolf in
  Weirdsville, pt.1 (of 2). 2.95
9 An American Werewolf in
  Weirdsville, pt.2 . . . . 2.95

WEIRDSVILLE/CRYBABY:
HEY YOU TWO
Blindwolf Studios 1999
1 . . . . 2.95

WEREWOLF
Blackthorne 1988–89
1 TV tie-in 2.00
2 thru 7 . . . . @2.00

WHAT IS THE FACE?
A.C.E. Comics
1 SD/FMc,I:New Face 1.95
2 SD/FMc 1.95

3 SD 1.75

WHISPERS & SHADOWS
1 8 1/2 x 11 . . . . 2.00
1a Regular size 1.50
2 8 1/2 x 11 . . . . 1.50
3 8 1/2 x 11 . . . . 1.50
4 thru 9 . . . . @1.50

White Devil #6
© Eternity

WHITE DEVIL
Eternity
1 thru 6 adult. 2.50

WHITEOUT
Oni Press 1998
1 (of 4) by Greg Rucka &
  Steve Leiber. 2.95
2 . . . . 2.95
3 . . . . 2.95
4 conclusion 2.95
TPB 128-page 10.95

WHITE RAVEN
Visionary Publications
1 Government Intrigue. 2.95
2 . . . . 2.95
3 Mystery Man Gets Wheels 2.95
4 Facility 2.95
5 V:Douglas. 2.95
6 . . . . 2.95
7 . . . . 2.95

WHITLEY STRIEBER'S
BEYOND COMMUNION
Caliber Sept. 1997
1 UFO Odyssey 2.95
1 signed 2.95
1 special edition, signed
  by Strieber 6.95
1a 2nd printing 2.95
2 . . . . 2.95
3 . . . . 2.95
4 . . . . 2.95

WICKED
Millenium
1 thru 4 . . . . 2.50

WICKED:
THE RECKONING
Millenium
1 R:Wicked 2.95
2 F:Rachel Blackstone. 2.95

WIDOW
Ground Zero 1996
Cinegraphic Spec.#1: Daughter
  of Darkness 4.00

WIDOW/LUXURA:
BLOOD LUST
Ground Zero 1996
Alpha x-over, pt.1 . . . . 3.50
see Luxura/Widow for pt. 2

WIDOW:
BOUND BY BLOOD
Ground Zero 1996
1 thru 5 by Mike Wolfer . . . . @3.50

WIDOW: PROGENY
Ground Zero April 1997
1 by Mike Wolfer & Karl Moline . . . 3.00
2 (of 3) 3.00
3 concl. 3.00

WIDOW:
THE COMPLETE WORKS
Ground Zero 1996
Vol.1 Flesh and Blood. 10.95
Vol.1 deluxe 16.95
Vol.2 Kill Me Again 10.95
Vol.2 deluxe 16.95
Vol.3 Metal Gypsies 10.95
Vol.3 deluxe 16.95

WIDOW
Avatar Press 1997
0 by Mike Wolfer 3.95
0a nude cover. 6.00
0b Black leather cover 25.00
0 signed 10.00

WIDOW: THE ORIGIN
Avatar Press 1997
1 (of 3) by Mike Wolfer 3.95
1a nude cover. 6.00
1a leather cover. 25.00
2 (of 3) 3.00
2 nude cover. 4.95

WILD, THE
1 and 2 . . . . @1.50
3 thru 7 . . . . @1.75

WILD KNIGHTS
Eternity
1 thru 10 . . . . @1.95
Shattered Earth Chron. #1 . . . . . . 1.95

WILDMAN
1 and 2 . . . . @1.50
3 thru 6 . . . . @1.85

WILD THINGZ
ABC Comics 1998
0 RCl & Armando Huerta 3.00

Classics Illustrated

Classics Illus.

[Issued As Classic Comics]
001-THE THREE MUSKETEERS
By Alexandre Dumas

10/41 (---) MKd,MKd(c),
Original,10› (c) Price 4,500.00
05/43 (10) MKd,MKd(c),
No(c)Price; rep 250.00
11/43 (15) MKd,MKd(c),Long
Island Independent Ed;. 175.00
6/44 (18/20) MKd,MKd(c),
Sunrise Times Edition;rep. . . 125.00
7/44 (21) MKd,MKd(c),Richmond
Courrier Edition;rep. 110.00
6/46 (28) MKd,MKd(c);rep. 90.00
4/47 (36) MKd,MKd(c),
New ClLogo;rep 40.00
6/49 (60) MKd,MKd(c),Cl Logo;rep 25.00
10/49 (64) MKd,MK(c),Cl Logo;rep 25.00
12/50 (78) MKd,MKd(c),15›(c)
Price; Cl Logo;rep 18.00
03/52 (93) MKd,MKd(c),
Cl Logo;rep 16.00
11/53 (114) Cl Logo;rep 12.00
09/56 (134) MKd,MKd(c),New
P(c),Cl Logo,64 pgs;rep 12.00
03/58 (143) MKd,MKd(c),P(c),
Cl Logo,64 pgs;rep 11.00
05/59 (150) GE&RC New Art,
P(c),ClLogo;rep 11.00
03/61 (149) GE&RC,P(c),
Cl Logo;rep 7.00
62-63 (167) GE&RC,P(c),
Cl Logo;rep 7.00
04/64 (167) GE&RC,P(c),
Cl Logo;rep 7.00
01/65 (167) GE&RC,P(c),
Cl Logo;rep 7.00
03/66 (167) GE&RC,P(c),
Cl Logo;rep 7.00
11/67 (166) GE&RC,P(c),
Cl Logo;rep 7.00
Sp/69 (166) GE&RC,P(c),25›(c)
Price,ClLogo, Rigid(c);rep. 7.00

Cl #1, The Three Musketeers
© Gilberton Publications

Sp/71 (169) GE&RC,P(c),
Cl Logo,Rigid(c);rep 7.00

002-IVANHOE
By Sir Walter Scott

1941 (---) EA,MKd(c),Original. . 1,900.00
05/43 (1) EA,MKd(c),word "Presents"
Removed From(c);rep. 225.00
11/43 (15) EA,MKd(c),Long Island
Independent Edition;rep 150.00
06/44 (18/20) EA,MKd(c),Sunrise
Times Edition;rep 125.00
07/44 (21) EA,MKd(c),Richmond
Courrier Edition;rep. 110.00
06/46 (28) EA,MKd(c),rep. 90.00
07/47 (36) EA,MKd(c),New
Cl Logo; rep. 50.00
06/49 (60) EA,MKd(c),Cl Logo;rep 30.00
10/49 (64) EA,MKd(c),Cl Logo;rep 25.00
12/50 (78) EA,MKd(c),15›(c)
Price; Cl Logo;rep 18.00
11/51 (89) EA,MKd(c),Cl Logo;rep 16.00
04/53 (106) EA,MKd(c),Cl
Logo;rep. 14.00
07/54 (121) EA,MKd(c),Cl
Logo;rep. 12.00
01/57 (136) NN New Art,New
P(c),Cl Logo;rep. 14.00
01/58 (142) NN,P(c),Cl Logo;rep . . 7.00
11/59 (153) NN,P(c),Cl Logo;rep. . . 7.00
03/61 (149) NN,P(c),Cl Logo;rep . . . 7.00
62/63 (167) NN,P(c),Cl Logo;rep . . 5.00
05/64 (167) NN,P(c),Cl Logo;rep . . . 7.00
01/65 (167) NN,P(c),Cl Logo;rep . . . 7.00
03/66 (167) NN,P(c),Cl Logo;rep . . . 7.00
09/67 (166) NN,P(c),Cl Logo;rep . . . 7.00
1968 (166) NN,P(c),Cl Logo;rep . . . 7.00
Wr/69 (169) NN,P(c),Cl
Logo Rigid(c);rep 7.00
Wr/71 (169) NN,P(c),Cl
Logo,Rigid(c);rep 7.00

003-THE COUNT OF MONTE CRISTO
By Alexandre Dumas

03/42 (---) ASm,ASm(c),Original1,200.00
05/43 (10) ASm,ASm(c);rep 200.00
11/43 (15) ASm,ASm(c),Long Island
Independent Edition;rep 150.00
06/44 (18/20) ASm,ASm(c),
Sunrise Times Edition;rep. . . 135.00
06/44 (20) ASm,ASm(c),Sunrise
Times Edition;rep 125.00
07/44 (21) ASm,ASm(c),Richmond
Courrier Edition;rep. 110.00
06/46 (28) ASm,ASm(c);rep 100.00
04/47 (36) ASm,ASm(c),New
Cl Logo; rep 50.00
06/49 (60) ASm,ASm(c),Cl
Logo;rep. 35.00
08/49 (62) ASm,ASm(c),Cl
Logo;rep. 45.00
05/50 (71) ASm,ASm(c),Cl
Logo;rep. 25.00
09/51 (87) ASm,ASm(c),15›(c)
Price, Cl Logo;rep 18.00
11/53 (113) ASm,ASm(c),
Cl Logo; rep. 15.00
11/56 (---) LC New Art,New
P(c),Cl Logo;rep 15.00
03/58 (135) LC,P(c),Cl Logo;rep. . . 7.00
11/59 (153) LC,P(c),Cl Logo;rep . . . 7.00

03/61 (161) LC,P(c),Cl Logo;rep. . . 7.00
62/63 (167) LC,P(c),Cl Logo;rep . . . 7.00
07/64 (167) LC,P(c),Cl Logo;rep. . . 7.00
07/65 (167) LC,P(c),Cl Logo;rep. . . 7.00
07/66 (167) LC,P(c),Cl Logo;rep. . . 7.00
1968 (166) LC,P(c),25›(c)
Price, Cl Logo;rep 7.00
Wn/69 (169) LC,P(c),Cl Logo,
Rigid(c);rep 7.00

004-THE LAST OF THE MOHICANS
By James Fenimore Cooper

08/42 (---) RR,RR(c),Original . . 1,000.00
06/43 (12) RR,RR(c),Price
Balloon Deleted;rep 200.00
11/43 (15) RR,RR(c),Long Island
Independent Edition;rep 175.00
06/44 (20) RR,RR(c),Long Island
Independent Edition;rep 150.00
07/44 (21) RR,RR(c),Queens
Home News Edition;rep 125.00
06/46 (28) RR,RR(c);rep. 100.00
04/47 (36) RR,RR(c),New
Cl Logo; rep. 50.00
06/49 (60) RR,RR(c),Cl Logo;rep . 35.00
10/49 (64) RR,RR(c),Cl Logo;rep . 25.00
12/50 (78) RR,RR(c),15›(c)
Price,Cl Logo rep 20.00
11/51 (89) RR,RR(c),Cl Logo;rep . 18.00
03/54 (117) RR,RR(c),Cl Logo;rep 15.00
11/56 (135) RR,New P(c),
Cl Logo; rep. 15.00
11/57 (141) RR,P(c),Cl Logo;rep . 16.00
05/59 (150) JSe&StA New Art;
P(c), Cl Logo; rep 15.00
03/61 (161) JSe&StA,P(c),Cl
Logo; rep 7.00
62/63 (167) JSe&StA,P(c),Cl
Logo; rep 7.00
06/64 (167) JSe&StA,P(c),Cl
Logo; rep 7.00
08/65 (167) JSe&StA,P(c),Cl
Logo; rep 7.00
08/66 (167) JSe&StA,P(c),Cl
Logo; rep 7.00

CC #4, The Last of the Mohicans
© Gilberton Publications

1967 **(166)** JSe&StA,P(c),25›(c)
Price, CI Logo;rep 7.00
Sp/69 **(169)** JSe&StA,P(c),CI
Logo, Rigid(c);rep. 7.00

005-MOBY DICK
By Herman Melville
09/42 **(---)** LZ,LZ(c),Original . . . 1,300.00
05/43 **(10)** LZ,LZ(c),Conray Products
Edition, No(c)Price;rep 225.00
11/43 **(15)** LZ,LZ(c),Long Island
Independent Edition;rep 175.00
06/44 **(18/20)** LZ,LZ(c),Sunrise
Times Edition;rep 150.00
07/44 **(20)** LZ,LZ(c),Sunrise
Times Edition;rep 135.00
07/44 **(21)** LZ,LZ(c),Sunrise
Times Edition;rep 125.00
06/46 **(28)** LZ,LZ(c);rep. 100.00
04/47 **(36)** LZ,LZ(c),New CI
Logo;rep. 60.00
06/49 **(60)** LZ,LZ(c),CI Logo;rep . 35.00
08/49 **(62)** LZ,LZ(c),CI Logo;rep . 40.00
05/50 **(71)** LZ,LZ(c),CI Logo;rep . 25.00
09/51 **(87)** LZ,LZ(c),15›(c)
Price, CI Logo;rep 20.00
04/54 **(118)** LZ,LZ(c),CI Logo;rep . 15.00
03/56 **(131)** NN New Art,New
P(c), CI Logo;rep 15.00
05/57 **(138)** NN,P(c),CI Logo;rep . . 7.00
01/59 **(148)** NN,P(c),CI Logo;rep . . 7.00
09/60 **(158)** NN,P(c),CI Logo;rep . . 7.00
62/63 **(167)** NN,P(c),CI Logo;rep . . 7.00
06/64 **(167)** NN,P(c),CI Logo;rep . . 7.00
07/65 **(167)** NN,P(c),CI Logo;rep . . 7.00
03/66 **(167)** NN,P(c),CI Logo;rep . . 7.00
09/67 **(166)** NN,P(c),CI Logo;rep . . 7.00
Wn/69 **(166)** NN,P(c),25›(c) Price,
CI Logo, Rigid(c);rep 12.00
Wn/71 **(169)** NN,P(c),CI Logo;rep . 12.00

006-A TALE OF TWO CITIES
By Charles Dickens
11/42 **(---)** StM,StM(c),Original . 1,000.00
09/43 **(14)** StM,StM(c),No(c)
Price; rep 200.00
03/44 **(18)** StM,StM(c),Long Island
Independent Edition;rep 150.00
06/44 **(20)** StM,StM(c),Sunrise
Times Edition;rep 135.00
06/46 **(28)** StM,StM(c);rep. 90.00
09/48 **(51)** StM,StM(c),New CI
Logo; rep 50.00
10/49 **(64)** StM,StM(c),CI
Logo;rep. 30.00
12/50 **(78)** StM,StM(c),15›(c)
Price, CI Logo; rep 20.00
11/51 **(89)** StM,StM(c),CI Logo;rep 18.00
03/54 **(117)** StM,StM(c),CI
Logo;rep. 15.00
05/56 **(132)** JO New Art,New
P(c), CI Logo;rep 18.00
09/57 **(140)** JO,P(c),CI Logo;rep . . . 7.00
11/57 **(147)** JO,P(c),CI Logo;rep . . . 7.00
09/59 **(152)** JO,P(c),CI Logo;rep . 125.00
11/59 **(153)** JO,P(c),CI Logo;rep . . . 7.00
03/61 **(149)** JO,P(c),CI Logo;rep . . . 7.00
62/63 **(167)** JO,P(c),CI Logo;rep . . . 7.00
06/64 **(167)** JO,P(c),CI Logo;rep . . . 7.00
08/65 **(167)** JO,P(c),CI Logo;rep . . . 7.00
05/67 **(166)** JO,P(c),CI Logo;rep . . . 7.00
Fl/68 **(166)** JO,NN New P(c),
25›(c)Price,CI Logo;rep 15.00
Sr/70 **(169)** JO,NN P(c),CI
Logo, Rigid(c);rep. 15.00

CI #7, Robin Hood
© Gilberton Publications

007-ROBIN HOOD
By Howard Pyle
12/42 **(---)** LZ,LZ(c),Original 800.00
06/43 **(12)** LZ,LZ(c),P.D.C.
on(c) Deleted;rep 200.00
03/44 **(18)** LZ,LZ(c),Long Island
Independent Edition;rep 150.00
06/44 **(20)** LZ,LZ(c),Nassau
Bulletin Edition;rep 135.00
10/44 **(22)** LZ,LZ(c),Queens
City Times Edition;rep. 125.00
06/46 **(28)** LZ,LZ(c),rep. 90.00
09/48 **(51)** LZ,LZ(c),New CI
Logo;rep. 45.00
06/49 **(60)** LZ,LZ(c),CI Logo;rep . . 25.00
10/49 **(64)** LZ,LZ(c),CI Logo;rep . . 20.00
12/50 **(78)** LZ,LZ(c),CI Logo;rep . . 20.00
07/52 **(97)** LZ,LZ(c),CI Logo;rep . . 18.00
03/53 **(106)** LZ,LZ(c),CI Logo;rep . 15.00
07/54 **(121)** LZ,LZ(c),CI Logo;rep . 15.00
11/55 **(129)** LZ,New P(c),
CI Logo;rep 15.00
01/57 **(136)** JkS New Art,P(c);rep . 7.00
03/58 **(143)** JkS,P(c),CI Logo;rep . 7.00
11/59 **(153)** JkS,P(c),CI Logo;rep . 7.00
10/61 **(164)** JkS,P(c),CI Logo;rep . 7.00
62/63 **(167)** JkS,P(c),CI Logo;rep . 7.00
06/64 **(167)** JkS,P(c),CI Logo;rep . 8.00
05/65 **(167)** JkS,P(c),CI Logo;rep . 7.00
07/66 **(167)** JkS,P(c),CI Logo;rep . 7.00
12/67 **(166)** JkS,P(c),CI Logo;rep . 8.00
Sr/69 **(169)** JkS,P(c),CI
Logo, Rigid(c);rep. 7.00

008-ARABIAN KNIGHTS
By Antoine Galland
03/43 **(---)** LCh,LCh(c),Original. 1,400.00
09/43 **(14)** LCh,LCh(c);rep. 500.00
01/44 **(17)** LCh,LCh(c),Long Island
Independent Edition;rep 550.00
06/44 **(20)** LCh,LCh(c),Nassau
Bulletin Edition,64 pgs;rep . . 400.00
06/46 **(28)** LCh,LCh(c);rep 250.00
09/48 **(51)** LCh,LCh(c),New CI
Logo; rep 250.00
10/49 **(64)** LCh,LCh(c),CI
Logo;rep. 200.00
12/50 **(78)** LCh,LCh(c),CI
Logo;rep. 160.00
10/61 **(164)** ChB New Art,P(c),
CI Logo;rep 135.00

009-LES MISERABLES
By Victor Hugo
03/43 **(---)** RLv,RLv(c),Original . . 750.00
09/43 **(14)** RLv,RLv(c);rep. 200.00
03/44 **(18)** RLv,RLv(c),Nassau
Bulletin Edition;rep. 160.00
06/44 **(20)** RLv,RLv(c),Richmond
Courier Edition;rep. 150.00
06/46 **(28)** RLv,RLv(c);rep 125.00
09/48 **(51)** RLv,RLv(c),New CI
Logo; rep 50.00
05/50 **(71)** RLv,RLv(c),CI
Logo;rep 40.00
09/51 **(87)** RLv,RLv(c),CI Logo,
15›(c)Price;rep 35.00
03/61 **(161)** NN New Art,GMc
New P(c), CI Logo;rep 30.00
09/63 **(167)** NN,GMc P(c),CI
Logo; rep 25.00
12/65 **(167)** NN,GMc P(c),CI
Logo; rep 25.00
1968 **(166)** NN,GMc P(c),25›(c)
Price, CI Logo;rep 25.00

010-ROBINSON CRUSOE
By Daniel Defoe
04/43 **(---)** StM,StM(c),Original . . 650.00
09/43 **(14)** StM,StM(c);rep. 225.00
03/44 **(18)** StM,StM(c),Nassau Bulletin
Ed.,'Bill of Rights'Pge.64;rep. 175.00
06/44 **(20)** StM,StM(c),Queens
Home News Edition;rep 150.00
??/45 **(23)** StM,StM(c);rep. 100.00
06/46 **(28)** StM,StM(c);rep. 100.00
09/48 **(51)** StM,StM(c),New CI
Logo; rep 45.00
10/49 **(64)** StM,StM(c),CI Logo;rep 30.00
12/50 **(78)** StM,StM(c),15›(c)
Price, CI Logo;rep 25.00
07/52 **(97)** StM,StM(c),CI Logo;rep 20.00
12/53 **(114)** StM,StM(c),CI
Logo;rep. 20.00
01/56 **(130)** StM,New P(c),CI
Logo; rep 20.00
09/57 **(140)** SmC New Art,P(c),
CI Logo; rep. 15.00
11/59 **(153)** SmC,P(c),CI Logo;rep . 7.00
10/61 **(164)** SmC,P(c),CI Logo;rep . 7.00
62/63 **(167)** SmC,P(c),CI Logo;rep . 9.00
07/64 **(167)** SmC,P(c),CI Logo;rep 10.00
05/65 **(167)** SmC,P(c),CI Logo;rep . 7.00
06/66 **(167)** SmC,P(c),CI Logo;rep . 9.00
Fl/68 **(166)** SmC,P(c),CI Logo,
25›(c)Price;rep 8.00
1968 **(166)** SmC,P(c),CI Logo,No
Twin Circle Ad;rep 7.00
Sr/70 **(169)** SmC,P(c),CI Logo,
Rigid(c);rep 7.00

011-DON QUIXOTE
By Miguel de Cervantes Saavedra
05/43 **(---)** LZ,LZ(c),Original 700.00
03/44 **(18)** LZ,LZ(c),Nassau
Bulletin Edition;rep 200.00
07/44 **(21)** LZ,LZ(c),Queens
Home News Edition;rep 150.00
06/46 **(28)** LZ,LZ(c);rep. 100.00
08/53 **(110)** LZ,TO New P(c),New
CI Logo;rep 25.00
05/60 **(156)** LZ,TO P(c),Pages
Reduced to 48,CI Logo;rep. . . 15.00
1962 **(165)** LZ,TO P(c),CI Logo;rep 10.00
01/64 **(167)** LZ,TO P(c),CI
Logo;rep. 10.00
11/65 **(167)** LZ,TO P(c),CI
Logo;rep. 10.00
1968 **(166)** LZ,TO P(c),CI Logo,
25›(c)Price;rep 20.00

012-RIP VAN WINKLE & THE HEADLESS HORSEMAN
By Washington Irving
06/43 (----) RLv,RLv(c),Original . . 700.00
11/43 **(15)** RLv,RLv(c),Long Island
  Independent Edition;rep 180.00
06/44 **(20)** RLv,RLv(c),Long Island
  Independent Edition;rep 150.00
10/44 **(22)** RLv,RLv(c),Queens
  City Times Edition;rep. 135.00
06/46 **(28)** RLv,RLv(c);rep. 100.00
06/49 **(60)** RLv,RLv(c),New CI
  Logo;rep. 40.00
08/49 **(62)** RLv,RLv(c),CI
  Logo;rep. 30.00
05/50 **(71)** RLv,RLv(c),CI
  Logo;rep. 25.00
11/51 **(89)** RLv,RLv(c),15›(c)
  Price, CI Logo;rep 15.00
04/54 **(118)** RLv,RLv(c),CI
  Logo;rep. 15.00
05/56 **(132)** RLv,New P(c),
  CI Logo; rep 18.00
05/59 **(150)** NN New Art;P(c),
  CI Logo; rep 18.00
09/60 **(158)** NN,P(c),CI Logo;rep . . 7.00
62/63 **(167)** NN,P(c),CI Logo;rep . . 7.00
12/63 **(167)** NN,P(c),CI Logo;rep . . 7.00
04/65 **(167)** NN,P(c),CI Logo;rep . . 8.00
04/66 **(167)** NN,P(c),CI Logo;rep . . 7.00
1969 **(166)** NN,P(c),CI Logo,
  25›(c)Price,Rigid(c);rep. 12.00
Sr/70 **(169)** NN,P(c),CI Logo,
  Rigid(c);rep 12.00

013-DR. JEKYLL AND MR.HYDE
By Robert Louis Stevenson
08/43 (---) AdH,AdH(c),Original 1,000.00
11/43 **(15)** AdH,AdH(c),Long Island
  Independent Edition;rep 250.00
06/44 **(20)** AdH,AdH(c),Long Island
  Independent Edition;rep 175.00
06/46 **(28)** AdH,AdH(c),No(c)
  Price; rep 125.00
06/49 **(60)** AdH,HcK New(c),New CI
  Logo,Pgs.reduced to 48;rep . . 40.00
08/49 **(62)** AdH,HcK(c),CI
  Logo;rep. 35.00
05/50 **(71)** AdH,HcK(c),CI
  Logo;rep. 25.00
09/51 **(87)** AdH,HcK(c),Erroneous
Return
  of Original Date,CI Logo;rep . . 20.00
10/53 **(112)** LC New Art,New
  P(c),CI Logo;rep 20.00
11/59 **(153)** LC,P(c),CI Logo;rep . . 7.00
03/61 **(161)** LC,P(c),CI Logo;rep . . . 7.00
62/63 **(167)** LC,P(c),CI Logo;rep . . . 7.00
08/64 **(167)** LC,P(c),CI Logo;rep . . . 7.00
11/65 **(167)** LC,P(c),CI Logo;rep . . . 7.00
1968 **(166)** LC,P(c),CI Logo,
  25›(c)Price;rep 8.00
Wr/69 **(169)** LC,P(c),CI Logo,
  Rigid(c);rep 7.00

014-WESTWARD HO!
By Charles Kingsley
09/43 (---) ASm,ASm(c),Original1,600.00
11/43 **(15)** ASm,ASm(c),Long Island
  Independent Edition;rep 550.00
07/44 **(21)** ASm,ASm(c);rep 400.00
06/46 **(28)** ASm,ASm(c),No(c)
  Price; rep 300.00
11/48 **(53)** ASm,ASm(c),Pages reduced
  to 48, New CI Logo;rep. 275.00

015-UNCLE TOM'S CABIN
By Harriet Beecher Stowe
11/43 (---) RLv,RLv(c),Original. . . 650.00
11/43 **(15)** RLv,RLv(c),Blank
  Price Circle, Long Island
  Independent Ed.;rep 200.00
07/44 **(21)** RLv,RLv(c),Nassau
  Bulliten Edition;rep 150.00
06/46 **(28)** RLv,RLv(c),No(c)
  Price; rep 100.00
11/48 **(53)** RLv,RLv(c),Pages Reduced
  to 48, New CI Logo;rep. 40.00
05/50 **(71)** RLv,RLv(c),CI Logo;rep 30.00
11/51 **(89)** RLv,RLv(c),15›(c)
  Price, CI Logo;rep 30.00
03/54 **(117)** RLv,New P(c),CI
  Logo, Lettering Changes;rep. . 15.00
09/55 **(128)** RLv,P(c),"Picture
  Progress"Promotion,CI
  Logo;rep. 12.00
03/57 **(137)** RLv,P(c),CI Logo;rep . . 7.00
09/58 **(146)** RLv,P(c),CI Logo;rep . . 7.00
01/60 **(154)** RLv,P(c),CI Logo;rep . . 7.00
03/61 **(161)** RLv,P(c),CI Logo;rep . . 7.00
62/63 **(167)** RLv,P(c),CI Logo;rep . . 7.00
06/64 **(167)** RLv,P(c),CI Logo;rep . . 7.00
05/65 **(167)** RLv,P(c),CI Logo;rep . . 7.00
05/67 **(166)** RLv,P(c),CI Logo;rep . . 7.00
Wr/69 **(166)** RLv,P(c),CI
  Logo, Rigid(c);rep. 12.00
Sr/70 **(169)** RLv,P(c),CI
  Logo, Rigid(c);rep. 12.00

016-GULLIVER'S TRAVELS
By Johnathan Swift
12/43 (----) LCh,LCh(c),Original. . 600.00
06/44 **(18/20)** LCh,LCh(c),Queen's
  Home News Edition,No(c)Price;
  rep 175.00
10/44 **(22)** LCh,LCh(c),Queen's
  Home News Editon;rep 135.00
06/46 **(28)** LCh,LCh(c);rep 100.00
06/49 **(60)** LCh,LCh(c),Pgs. Reduced
  To 48, New CI Logo;rep 40.00
08/49 **(62)** LCh,LCh(c),CI Logo;rep 25.00
10/49 **(64)** LCh,LCh(c),CI Logo;rep 25.00
12/50 **(78)** LCh,LCh(c),15›(c)
  Price, CI Logo;rep 15.00
11/51 **(89)** LCh,LCh(c),CI Logo;rep 15.00
03/60 **(155)** LCh,New P(c),CI
  Logo; rep 7.00
1962 **(165)** LCh,P(c),CI Logo;rep . . 7.00
05/64 **(167)** LCh,P(c),CI Logo;rep . . 7.00
11/65 **(167)** LCh,P(c),CI Logo;rep . . 7.00
1968 **(166)** LCh,P(c),CI Logo,
  25›(c)Price;rep 7.00
Wr/69 **(169)** LCh,P(c),CI
  Logo, Rigid(c);rep. 7.00

017-THE DEERSLAYER
By James Fenimore Cooper
01/44 (----) LZ,LZ(c),Original 550.00
03/44 **(18)** LZ,LZ(c),No(c)Price;
  rep 175.00
10/44 **(22)** LZ,LZ(c),Queen's
  City Times Edition;rep 150.00
06/46 **(28)** LZ,LZ(c);rep. 100.00
06/49 **(60)** LZ,LZ(c),Pgs. Reduced
  to 48,New CI Logo;rep 40.00
10/49 **(64)** LZ,LZ(c),CI Logo;rep . . 25.00
07/51 **(85)** LZ,LZ(c),15›(c)
  Price, CI Logo;rep 20.00
04/54 **(118)** LZ,LZ(c),CI Logo;rep . 18.00
05/56 **(132)** LZ,LZ(c),CI Logo;rep . 15.00
11/66 **(167)** LZ,LZ(c),CI Logo;rep . 15.00
1968 **(166)** LZ,StA New P(c),CI
  Logo, 25›(c)Price;rep 20.00
Sg/71 **(169)** LZ,StA P(c),CI Logo,

Rigid(c), Letters From Parents
and Educators;rep 15.00

CI #18, The Hunchback of Notre Dame
© Gilberton Publications

018-THE HUNCHBACK OF NOTRE DAME
By Victor Hugo
03/44 (---) ASm,ASm(c),Original
  Gilberton Edition. 700.00
03/44 (---) ASm,ASm(c),Original
  Island Publications Edition . . 600.00
06/44 **(18/20)** ASm,ASm(c),Queens
  Home News Edition;rep 200.00
10/44 **(22)** ASm,ASm(c),Queens
  City Times Edition;rep. 150.00
06/46 **(28)** ASm,ASm(c);rep 125.00
06/49 **(60)** ASm,HcK New(c)8 Pgs.
  Deleted, New CI Logo;rep . . . 40.00
08/49 **(62)** ASm,HcK(c),CI
  Logo;rep. 25.00
12/50 **(78)** ASm,HcK(c),15›(c)
  Price; CI Logo;rep 20.00
11/51 **(89)** ASm,HcK(c),CI
  Logo;rep. 15.00
04/54 **(118)** ASm,HcK(c),CI
  Logo;rep. 25.00
09/57 **(140)** ASm,New P(c),CI
  Logo; rep 20.00
09/58 **(146)** ASm,P(c),CI Logo;rep 20.00
09/60 **(158)** GE&RC New Art,GMc
  New P(c),CI Logo;rep 8.00
1962 **(165)** GE&RC,GMc P(c),CI
  Logo; rep 8.00
09/63 **(167)** GE&RC,GMc P(c),CI
  Logo; rep 8.00
10/64 **(167)** GE&RC,GMc P(c),CI
  Logo; rep 7.00
04/66 **(167)** GE&RC,GMc P(c),CI
  Logo; rep 7.00
1968 **(166)** GE&RC,GMc P(c),CI
  Logo, 25›(c)Price;rep 7.00
Sr/70 **(169)** GE&RC,GMc P(c),CI
  Logo, Rigid(c);rep. 7.00

019-HUCKLEBERRY FINN
By Mark Twain
04/44 (---) LZ,LZ(c),Original
  Gilberton Edition. 450.00
04/44 (---) LZ,LZ(c),Original Island
  Publications Company Edition475.00
03/44 **(18)** LZ,LZ(c),Nassau
  Bulliten Editon;rep 200.00
10/44 **(22)** LZ,LZ(c),Queens City

Times Edition;rep 150.00
06/46 **(28)** LZ,LZ(c);rep. 100.00
06/49 **(60)** LZ,LZ(c),New CI Logo,
Pgs.Reduced to 48;rep. 35.00
08/49 **(62)** LZ,LZ(c),CI Logo;rep . . 25.00
12/50 **(78)** LZ,LZ(c),CI Logo;rep . . 20.00
11/51 **(89)** LZ,LZ(c),CI Logo;rep . . 18.00
03/54 **(117)** LZ,LZ(c),CI Logo;rep . 18.00
03/56 **(131)** FrG New Art,New
P(c), CI Logo; rep6.00
09/57 **(140)** FrG,P(c),CI Logo;rep . . 7.00
05/59 **(150)** FrG,P(c),CI Logo;rep . . 7.00
09/60 **(158)** FrG,P(c),CI Logo;rep . . 7.00
1962 **(165)** FrG,P(c),CI Logo;rep . . 7.00
62/63 **(167)** FrG,P(c),CI Logo;rep . . 7.00
06/64 **(167)** FrG,P(c),CI Logo;rep . . 7.00
06/65 **(167)** FrG,P(c),CI Logo;rep . . 7.00
10/65 **(167)** FrG,P(c),CI Logo;rep . . 7.00
09/67 **(166)** FrG,P(c),CI Logo;rep . . 7.00
Wr/69 **(166)** FrG,P(c),CI Logo,
25›(c)Price, Rigid(c);rep 7.00
Sr/70 **(169)** FrG,P(c),CI Logo,
Rigid(c);rep 7.00

020-THE CORSICAN BROTHERS
By Alexandre Dumas
06/44 **(---)** ASm,ASm(c),Original
Gilberton Edition. 425.00
06/44 **(---)** ASm,ASm(c),Original
Courier Edition 400.00
06/44 **(---)** ASm,ASm(c),Original Long
Island Independent Edition . . 400.00
10/44 **(22)** ASm,ASm(c),Queens
City Times Edition;rep. 175.00
06/46 **(28)** ASm,ASm(c);rep 150.00
06/49 **(60)** ASm,ASm(c),No(c)Price,
New CI Logo,Pgs. Reduced
to 48;rep. 125.00
08/49 **(62)** ASm,ASm(c),CI
Logo;rep. 115.00
12/50 **(78)** ASm,ASm(c),15›(c)
Price, CI Logo;rep 100.00
07/52 **(97)** ASm,ASm(c),CI
Logo;rep. 90.00

021-FAMOUS MYSTERIES
By Sir Arthur Conan Doyle
Guy de Maupassant
& Edgar Allan Poe
07/44 **(---)** ASm,AdH,LZ,ASm(c),
Original Gilberton Edition . . . 800.00
07/44 **(---)** ASm,AdH,LZ,ASm(c),
Original Island Publications
Edition; No Date or Indicia . . 825.00
07/44 **(---)** ASm,AdH,LZ,ASm(c),
Original Richmond Courier
Edition 700.00
10/44 **(22)** ASm,AdH,LZ,ASm(c),
Nassau Bulliten Edition;rep. . 275.00
09/46 **(30)** ASm,AdH,LZ,ASm(c);
rep 225.00
08/49 **(62)** ASm,AdH,LZ,ASm(c),
New CI Logo;rep 185.00
04/50 **(70)** ASm,AdH,LZ,ASm(c),
CI Logo;rep 175.00
07/51 **(85)** ASm,AdH,LZ,ASm(c),
15›(c) Price,CI Logo;rep . . . 150.00
12/53 **(114)** ASm,AdH,LZ,New
P(c), CI Logo;rep 150.00

022-THE PATHFINDER
By James Fenimore Cooper
10/44 **(---)** LZ,LZ(c),Original
Gilberton Edition. 400.00
10/44 **(---)** LZ,LZ(c),Original
Island Publications Edition;. . 300.00

10/44 **(---)** LZ,LZ(c),Original
Queens County Times Edition300.00
09/46 **(30)** LZ,LZ(c),No(c)
Price;rep. 100.00
06/49 **(60)** LZ,LZ(c),New CI Logo,
Pgs.Reduced To 48;rep 35.00
08/49 **(62)** LZ,LZ(c),CI Logo;rep . . 28.00
04/50 **(70)** LZ,LZ(c),CI Logo;rep . . 25.00
07/51 **(85)** LZ,LZ(c),15›(c)
Price, CI Logo;rep 20.00
04/54 **(118)** LZ,LZ(c),CI Logo;rep . 15.00
05/56 **(132)** LZ,LZ(c),CI Logo;rep . 15.00
09/58 **(146)** LZ,LZ(c),CI Logo;rep . 25.00
11/63 **(167)** LZ,NN New P(c),CI
Logo; rep 20.00
12/65 **(167)** LZ,NN P(c),CI
Logo;rep. 20.00
08/67 **(166)** LZ,NN P(c),CI
Logo;rep. 20.00

023-OLIVER TWIST
By Charles Dickens
(First Classic produced by the Iger shop)
07/45 **(---)** AdH,AdH(c),Original. . 350.00
09/46 **(30)** AdH,AdH(c),Price
Circle is Blank;rep 250.00
06/49 **(60)** AdH,AdH(c),Pgs. Reduced
To 48, New CI Logo;rep 35.00
08/49 **(62)** AdH,AdH(c),CI
Logo;rep. 25.00
05/50 **(71)** AdH,AdH(c),CI
Logo;rep 25.00
07/51 **(85)** AdH,AdH(c),15›(c)
Price CI Logo;rep 20.00
04/52 **(94)** AdH,AdH(c),CI
Logo;rep. 20.00
04/54 **(118)** AdH,AdH(c),CI
Logo;rep. 15.00
01/57 **(136)** AdH,New P(c),CI
Logo; rep 15.00
05/59 **(150)** AdH,P(c),CI Logo;rep. 12.00
1961 **(164)** AdH,P(c),CI Logo;rep . 12.00
10/61 **(164)** GE&RC New Art,P(c),
CI Logo;rep 20.00
62/63 **(167)** GE&RC,P(c),CI
Logo; rep 6.00
08/64 **(167)** GE&RC,P(c),CI
Logo; rep 6.00
12/65 **(167)** GE&RC,P(c),
CI Logo;rep 6.00
1968 **(166)** GE&RC,P(c),CI
Logo, 25›(c)Price;rep 6.00
Wr/69 **(169)** GE&RC,P(c),CI
Logo, Rigid(c);rep. 6.00

024-A CONNECTICUT YANKEE IN KING ARTHUR'S COURT
By Mark Twain
09/45 **(---)** JH,JH(c),Original 300.00
09/46 **(30)** JH,JH(c),Price Circle
Blank;rep 100.00
06/49 **(60)** JH,JH(c),8 Pages
Deleted,New CI Logo;rep 30.00
08/49 **(62)** JH,JH(c),CI Logo;rep . . 28.00
05/50 **(71)** JH,JH(c),CI Logo;rep . . 20.00
09/51 **(87)** JH,JH(c),15›(c) Price
CI Logo; rep 18.00
07/54 **(121)** JH,JH(c),CI Logo;rep . 15.00
09/57 **(140)** JkS New Art,New
P(c),CI Logo; rep 15.00
11/59 **(153)** JkS,P(c),CI Logo;rep . . 7.00
1961 **(164)** JkS,P(c),CI Logo;rep. . . 7.00
62/63 **(167)** JkS,P(c),CI Logo;rep . . 7.00
07/64 **(167)** JkS,P(c),CI Logo;rep . . 7.00
06/66 **(167)** JkS,P(c),CI Logo;rep . . 7.00
1968 **(166)** JkS,P(c),CI logo,

CI #24, A Connecticut Yankee in King
Arthur's Court © Gilberton Publications

25›(c)Price;rep 7.00
Sg/71 **(169)** JkS,P(c),CI Logo,
Rigid(c);rep 7.00

025-TWO YEARS BEFORE THE MAST
By Richard Henry Dana Jr.
10/45 **(---)** RWb,DvH,Original; . . . 300.00
09/46 **(30)** RWb,DvH,Price Circle
Blank;rep 100.00
06/49 **(60)** RWb,DvH,8 Pages
Deleted,New CI Logo;rep 35.00
08/49 **(62)** RWb,DvH,CI Logo;rep . 30.00
05/50 **(71)** RWb,DvH,CI Logo;rep . 20.00
07/51 **(85)** RWb,DvH,15›(c) Price
CI Logo;rep 15.00
12/53 **(114)** RWb,DvH,CI Logo;rep 15.00
05/60 **(156)** RWb,DvH,New P(c),CI
Logo,
3 Pgs. Replaced By Fillers;rep 15.00
12/63 **(167)** RWb,DvH,P(c),CI
Logo; rep 7.00
12/65 **(167)** RWb,DvH,P(c),CI
Logo; rep 7.00
09/67 **(166)** RWb,DvH,P(c),CI
Logo; rep 7.00
Wr/69 **(169)** RWb,DvH,P(c),25›(c)
Price, CI Logo,Rigid(c);rep 7.00

026-FRANKENSTEIN
By Mary Wollstonecraft Shelley
12/45 **(---)** RWb&ABr,RWb
& ABr(c), Original 800.00
09/46 **(30)** RWb&ABr,RWb &ABr(c),
Price Circle Blank;rep 225.00
06/49 **(60)** RWb&ABr,RWb&ABr(c),
New CI Logo;rep 65.00
08/49 **(62)** RWb&ABr,RWb
& ABr(c), CI Logo;rep 100.00
05/50 **(71)** RWb&ABr,RWb
& ABr(c), CI Logo;rep 45.00
04/51 **(82)** RWb&ABr,RWb &ABr(c),
15›(c) Price,CI Logo;rep 30.00
03/54 **(117)** RWb&ABr,RWb
& ABr(c),CI Logo;rep 20.00
09/58 **(146)** RWb&ABr,NS
New P(c), CI Logo; rep. 20.00
11/59 **(153)** RWb&ABr,NS
P(c),CI Logo; rep. 35.00
01/61 **(160)** RWb&ABr,NS
P(c),CI Logo; rep 8.00

165 **(1962)** RWb&ABr,NS P(c),
CI Logo; rep 8.00
62/63 **(167)** RWb&ABr,NS P(c),
CI Logo; rep 7.00
06/64 **(167)** RWb&ABr,NS P(c),
CI logo; rep 7.00
06/65 **(167)** RWb&ABr,NS P(c),
CI Logo; rep 7.00
10/65 **(167)** RWb&ABr,NS P(c),
CI Logo; rep 7.00
09/67 **(166)** RWb&ABr,NS P(c),
CI Logo; rep 7.00
Fl/69 **(169)** RWb&ABr,NS P(c),25›(c)
Price,CI Logo,Rigid(c);rep. 7.00
Sg/71 **(169)** RWb&ABr,NS P(c),
CI Logo, Rigid(c);rep 7.00

027-THE ADVENTURES
MARCO POLO
By Marco Polo & Donn Byrne
04/46 **(----)** HFI,HFI(c);Original. . 350.00
09/46 **(30)** HFI,HFI(c);rep 100.00
04/50 **(70)** HFI,HFI(c),8 Pages Deleted,
No(c) Price,New CI Logo;rep . 30.00
09/51 **(87)** HFI,HFI(c),15›(c)
Price,CI Logo;rep 20.00
03/54 **(117)** HFI,HFI(c),CILogo;rep 15.00
01/60 **(154)** HFI,New P(c),CI
Logo;rep. 15.00
1962 **(165)** HFI,P(c),CI Logo;rep. . . 7.00
04/64 **(167)** HFI,P(c),CI Logo;rep . . 7.00
06/66 **(167)** HFI,P(c),CI Logo;rep . . 7.00
Sg/69 **(169)** HFI,P(c),CI Logo,
25›(c)Price,Rigid(c);rep. 7.00

028-MICHAEL STROGOFF
By Jules Verne
06/46 **(---)** AdH,AdH(c),Original. . 350.00
09/48 **(51)** AdH,AdH(c),8 Pages
Deleted,New CI Logo;rep . . . 100.00
01/54 **(115)** AdH,New P(c),CI
Logo; rep 25.00
03/60 **(155)** AdH,P(c),CI Logo;rep. 12.00
11/63 **(167)** AdH,P(c),CI Logo;rep. 12.00
07/66 **(167)** AdH,P(c),CI Logo;rep. 12.00
Sr/69 **(169)**AdH,NN,NewP(c),25›(c)
Price, CI Logo,Rigid(c);rep . . . 15.00

029-THE PRINCE
AND THE PAUPER
By Mark Twain
07/46 **(---)** AdH,AdH(c),Original. . 500.00
06/49 **(60)** AdH,New HcK(c),New CI
Logo,8 Pages Deleted;rep . . . 35.00
08/49 **(62)** AdH,HcK(c),CILogo;rep 30.00
05/50 **(71)** AdH,HcK(c),CILogo;rep 25.00
03/52 **(93)** AdH,HcK(c),CILogo;rep 20.00
12/53 **(114)** AdH,HcK(c),CI
Logo;rep. 15.00
09/55 **(128)** AdH,New P(c),CI
Logo; rep 15.00
05/57 **(138)** AdH,P(c),CI Logo;rep. . 7.00
05/59 **(150)** AdH,P(c),CI Logo;rep. . 7.00
1961 **(164)** AdH,P(c),CI Logo;rep . . 7.00
62/63 **(167)** AdH,P(c),CI Logo;rep. . 7.00
07/64 **(167)** AdH,P(c),CI Logo;rep . . 7.00
11/65 **(167)** AdH,P(c),CI Logo;rep. . 7.00
1968 **(166)** AdH,P(c),CI Logo,
25›(c)Price;rep. 7.00
Sr/70 **(169)** AdH,P(c),CI Logo,
Rigid(c);rep 7.00

030-THE MOONSTONE
By William Wilkie Collins
09/46 **(---)** DRi,DRi(c),Original. . . 350.00
06/49 **(60)** DRi,DRi(c),8 Pages
Deleted,New CI Logo;rep 40.00
04/50 **(70)** DRi,DRi(c),CI Logo;rep 35.00
03/60 **(155)** DRi,LbC New P(c),
CI Logo;rep 45.00
1962 **(165)** DRi,LbC P(c),CI Logo;
rep 20.00
01/64 **(167)** DRi,LbC P(c),CI Logo;
rep 18.00
09/65 **(167)** DRi,LbC P(c),CI Logo;
rep 10.00
1968 **(166)** DRi,LbC P(c),CI Logo,
25›(c)Price;rep 8.00

CI #31, The Black Arrow
© *Gilberton Publications*

031-THE BLACK ARROW
By Robert Louis Stevenson
10/46 **(---)** AdH,AdH(c),Original. . 275.00
09/48 **(51)** AdH,AdH(c),8 Pages
Deleted,New CI Logo;rep 35.00
10/49 **(64)** AdH,AdH(c),CI
Logo;rep. 20.00
09/51 **(87)** AdH,AdH(c),15›(c)
Price;CI Logo;rep 17.00
06/53 **(108)** AdH,AdH(c),CI
Logo;rep. 15.00
03/55 **(125)** AdH,AdH(c),CI
Logo;rep. 14.00
03/56 **(131)** AdH,New P(c),CI
Logo; rep 12.00
09/57 **(140)** AdH,P(c),CI Logo;rep. . 7.00
01/59 **(148)** AdH,P(c),CI Logo;rep. . 7.00
03/61 **(161)** AdH,P(c),CI Logo;rep. . 7.00
62/63 **(167)** AdH,P(c),CI Logo;rep. . 7.00
07/64 **(167)** AdH,P(c),CI logo;rep . . 7.00
11/65 **(167)** AdH,P(c),CI Logo;rep. . 7.00
1968 **(166)** AdH,P(c),CI Logo,
25›(c)Price;rep 7.00

032-LORNA DOONE
By Richard Doddridge
Blackmore
12/46 **(---)** MB,MB(c),Original . . . 300.00
10/49 **(53/64)** MB,MB(c),8 Pages
Deleted,New CI Logo;rep 40.00
07/51 **(85)** MB,MB(c),15›(c)
Price, CI Logo;rep 30.00
04/54 **(118)** MB,MB(c),CI Logo;rep 20.00
05/57 **(138)** MB,New P(c); Old(c)
Becomes New Splash Pge.,CI
Logo;rep. 20.00
05/59 **(150)** MB,P(c),CI Logo;rep . . 9.00
1962 **(165)** MB,P(c),CI Logo;rep . . 9.00
01/64 **(167)** MB,P(c),CI Logo;rep . . 9.00

11/65 **(167)** MB,P(c),CI Logo;rep . . 9.00
1968 **(166)** MB,New P(c),CI Logo;
rep 18.00

033-THE ADVENTURES
OF SHERLOCK HOLMES
By Sir Arthur Conan Doyle
01/47 **(---)** LZ,HcK(c),Original. . 1,000.00
11/48 **(53)** LZ,HcK(c),"A Study in
Scarlet"
Deleted,New CI Logo;rep . . . 350.00
05/50 **(71)** LZ,HcK(c),CI Logo;rep 275.00
11/51 **(89)** LZ,HcK(c),15›(c)
Price,CI Logo;rep 225.00

034-MYSTERIOUS ISLAND
By Jules Verne
Last Classic Comic
02/47 **(---)** RWb&DvH,Original. . . 350.00
06/49 **(60)** RWb&DvH,8 Pages
Deleted,New CI Logo;rep 35.00
08/49 **(62)** RWb&DvH,CI Logo;rep 25.00
05/50 **(71)** RWb&DvH,CI Logo;rep 40.00
12/50 **(78)** RWb&DvH,15›(c) Price,
CI Logo;rep 20.00
02/52 **(92)** RWb&DvH,CI Logo;rep 20.00
03/54 **(117)** RWb&DvH,CI Logo;
rep 20.00
09/57 **(140)** RWb&DvH,New P(c),
CI Logo;rep 20.00
05/60 **(156)** RWb&DvH,P(c),CI
Logo;rep. 7.00
10/63 **(167)** RWb&DvH,P(c),CI
Logo;rep. 7.00
05/64 **(167)** RWb&DvH,P(c),CI
Logo;rep. 7.00
06/66 **(167)** RWb&DvH,P(c),CI
logo;rep 7.00
1968 **(166)** RWb&DvH,P(c),CI Logo,
25›(c)Price;rep 7.00

035-LAST DAYS
OF POMPEII
By Lord Edward Bulwer Lytton
First Classics Illustrated
03/47 **(---)** HcK,HcK(c),Original . . 350.00
03/61 **(161)** JK,New P(c),
15›(c)Price;rep 30.00
01/64 **(167)** JK,P(c);rep. 16.00
07/66 **(167)** JK,P(c);rep. 16.00
Sg/70 **(169)** JK,P(c),25›(c)
Price, Rigid(c);rep. 17.00

036-TYPEE
By Herman Melville
04/47 **(---)** EzW,EzW(c),Original . 175.00
10/49 **(64)** EzW,EzW(c),No(c)price,
8 pages deleted;rep 40.00
03/60 **(155)** EzW,GMc New
P(c);rep 15.00
09/63 **(167)** EzW,GMc P(c);rep . . . 10.00
07/65 **(167)** EzW,GMc P(c);rep. . . 10.00
Sr/69 **(169)** EzW,GMc P(c),25›(c)
Price, Rigid(c);rep. 10.00

037-THE PIONEERS
By James Fenimore Cooper
05/47 **(37)** RP,RP(c),Original. . . . 135.00
08/49 **(62)** RP,RP(c),8 Pages
Deleted;rep 30.00
04/50 **(70)** RP,RP(c);rep 25.00
02/52 **(92)** RP,RP(c),15›(c)price;
rep 25.00
04/54 **(118)** RP,RP(c);rep 20.00
03/56 **(131)** RP,RP(c);rep 20.00

Classics Illus.

05/56 **(132)** RP,RP(c);rep 20.00
11/59 **(153)** RP,RP(c);rep 15.00
05/64 **(167)** RP,RP(c);rep 15.00
06/66 **(167)** RP,RP(c);rep 15.00
1968 **(166)** RP,TO New P(c),
25›(c)Price;rep 25.00

038-ADVENTURES OF CELLINI
By Benvenuto Cellini
06/47 **(---)** AgF,AgF(c),Original . . 250.00
1961 **(164)** NN New Art,New P(c);
rep 20.00
12/63 **(167)** NN,P(c);rep 10.00
07/66 **(167)** NN,P(c);rep 10.00
Sg/70 **(169)** NN,P(c),25›(c)
Price, Rigid(c);rep. 12.00

039-JANE EYRE
By Charlotte Bronte
07/47 **(---)** HyG,HyG(c),Original. . 225.00
06/49 **(60)** HyG,HyG(c),No(c)Price,
8 pages deleted;rep 35.00
08/49 **(62)** HyG,HyG(c);rep. 30.00
05/50 **(71)** HyG,HyG(c);rep 25.00
02/52 **(92)** HyG,HyG(c),15›(c)
Price; rep 20.00
04/54 **(118)** HyG,HyG(c);rep 20.00
01/58 **(142)** HyG,New P(c);rep . . 20.00
01/60 **(154)** HyG,P(c);rep 20.00
1962 **(165)** HjK New Art,P(c);rep. . 20.00
12/63 **(167)** HjK,P(c);rep 20.00
04/65 **(167)** HjK,P(c);rep 20.00
08/66 **(167)** HjK,P(c);rep. 20.00
1968 **(166)** HjK,NN New P(c);rep . 40.00

040-MYSTERIES
**(The Pit & the Pendulum,
The Adventures of Hans Pfall,
Fall of the House of Usher)
By Edgar Allan Poe**
08/47 **(---)** HcK,AgF,HyG,HcK(c),
Original 525.00
08/49 **(62)** HcK,AgF,HyG,HcK(c),
8 Pages deleted;rep 225.00
09/50 **(75)** HcK,AgF,HyG,
HcK(c);rep 200.00
02/52 **(92)** HcK,AgF,HyG,HcK(c)
15›(c) Price;rep. 150.00

041-TWENTY YEARS AFTER
By Alexandre Dumas
09/47 **(---)** RBu,RBu(c),Original . . 400.00
08/49 **(62)** RBu,HcK New(c),No(c)
Price, 8 Pages Deleted;rep. . . 35.00
12/50 **(78)** RBu,HcK(c),15›(c)
Price; rep 25.00
05/60 **(156)** RBu,DgR New P(c);
rep 20.00
12/63 **(167)** RBu,DgR P(c);rep . . . 10.00
11/66 **(167)** RBu,DgR P(c);rep . . . 10.00
Sg/70 **(169)** RBu,DgR P(c),25›(c)
Price, Rigid(c);rep. 10.00

042-SWISS FAMILY ROBINSON
By Johann Wyss
10/47 **(42)** HcK,HcK(c),Original . . 175.00
08/49 **(62)** HcK,HcK(c),No(c)price,
8 Pages Deleted,Not Every Issue
Has 'Gift Box' Ad;rep 35.00
09/50 **(75)** HcK,HcK(c);rep 20.00
03/52 **(93)** HcK,HcK(c);rep 20.00

03/54 **(117)** HcK,HcK(c);rep 15.00
03/56 **(131)** HcK,New P(c);rep . . . 15.00
03/57 **(137)** HcK,P(c);rep 15.00
11/57 **(141)** HcK,P(c);rep 15.00
09/59 **(152)** NN New art,P(c);rep. . 15.00
09/60 **(158)** NN,P(c);rep 8.00
12/63 **(165)** NN,P(c);rep 15.00
12/63 **(167)** NN,P(c);rep 7.00
04/65 **(167)** NN,P(c);rep 7.00
05/66 **(167)** NN,P(c);rep 7.00
11/67 **(166)** NN,P(c);rep 6.00
Sg/69 **(169)** NN,P(c);rep. 6.00

043-GREAT EXPECTATIONS
By Charles Dickens
11/47 **(---)** HcK,HcK(c),Original . . 700.00
08/49 **(62)** HcK,HcK(c),No(c)price;
8 pages deleted;rep 450.00

044-MYSTERIES OF PARIS
By Eugene Sue
12/47 **(44)** HcK,HcK(c),Original . . 575.00
08/47 **(62)** HcK,HcK(c),No(c)Price,
8 Pages Deleted,Not Every Issue
Has'Gift Box'Ad;rep 225.00
12/50 **(78)** HcK,HcK(c),15›(c)
Price; rep 200.00

045-TOM BROWN'S SCHOOL DAYS
By Thomas Hughes
01/48 **(44)** HFl,HFl(c),Original,
1st 48 Pge. Issue 125.00
10/49 **(64)** HFl,HFl(c),No(c)
Price;rep 40.00
03/61 **(161)** JTg New Art,GMc
New P(c);rep 15.00
02/64 **(167)** JTg,GMc P(c);rep. . . . 12.00
08/66 **(167)** JTg,GMc P(c);rep. . . . 12.00
1968 **(166)** JTg,GMc P(c),
25›(c)Price;rep 12.00

046-KIDNAPPED
By Robert Louis Stevenson
04/48 **(47)** RWb,RWb(c),Original. 100.00
08/49 **(62)** RWb,RWb(c),Red Circle
Either Blank or With 10›;rep . . 62.00
12/50 **(78)** RWb,RWb(c),15›(c)
Price; rep 25.00
09/51 **(87)** RWb,RWb(c);rep 20.00
04/54 **(118)** RWb,RWb(c);rep 15.00
03/56 **(131)** RWb,New P(c);rep. . . 15.00
09/57 **(140)** RWb,P(c);rep 7.00
05/59 **(150)** RWb,P(c);rep 7.00
05/60 **(156)** RWb,P(c);rep 7.00
1961 **(164)** RWb,P(c),Reduced Pge.
Wdth;rep 7.00
62/63 **(167)** RWb,P(c);rep 7.00
03/64 **(167)** RWb,P(c);rep 7.00
06/65 **(167)** RWb,P(c);rep 7.00
12/65 **(167)** RWb,P(c);rep 7.00
09/67 **(167)** RWb,P(c);rep 7.00
Wr/69 **(166)** RWb,P(c),25›(c)
Price, Rigid(c);rep. 7.00
Sr/70 **(169)** RWb,P(c),Rigid(c);rep . 7.00

047-TWENTY THOUSAND LEAGUES UNDER THE SEA
By Jules Verne
05/58 **(47)** HcK,HcK(c),Original . . 100.00
10/49 **(64)** HcK,HcK(c),No(c)

Price; rep 30.00
12/50 **(78)** HcK,HcK(c),15›(c)
Price; rep 25.00
04/52 **(94)** HcK,HcK(c);rep 25.00
04/54 **(118)** HcK,HcK(c);rep 20.00
09/55 **(128)** HcK,New P(c);rep . . . 15.00
07/56 **(133)** HcK,P(c);rep 15.00
09/57 **(140)** HcK,P(c);rep 7.00
01/59 **(148)** HcK,P(c);rep 7.00
05/60 **(156)** HcK,P(c);rep 7.00
62/63 **(165)** HcK,P(c);rep 7.00
05/48 **(167)** HcK,P(c);rep 7.00
03/64 **(167)** HcK,P(c);rep 7.00
08/65 **(167)** HcK,P(c);rep 7.00
10/66 **(167)** HcK,P(c);rep 7.00
1968 **(166)** HcK,NN New P(c),
25›(c)Price;rep 12.00
Sg/70 **(169)** HcK,NN P(c),
Rigid(c);rep 12.00

048-DAVID COPPERFIELD
By Charles Dickens
06/48 **(47)** HcK,HcK(c),Original. . 100.00
10/49 **(64)** HcK,HcK(c),Price Circle
Replaced By Image of Boy
Reading;rep 30.00
09/51 **(87)** HcK,HcK(c),15›(c)
Price; rep 25.00
07/54 **(121)** HcK,New P(c);rep . . . 15.00
10/56 **(130)** HcK,P(c);rep 8.00
09/57 **(140)** HcK,P(c);rep 8.00
01/59 **(148)** HcK,P(c);rep 8.00
05/60 **(156)** HcK,P(c);rep 8.00
62/63 **(167)** HcK,P(c);rep 7.00
04/64 **(167)** HcK,P(c);rep 7.00
06/65 **(167)** HcK,P(c);rep 7.00
05/67 **(166)** HcK,P(c);rep 7.00
R/67 **(166)** HcK,P(c);rep. 11.00
Sg/69 **(169)** HcK,P(c),25›(c)
Price, Rigid(c);rep. 7.00
Wr/69 **(169)** HcK,P(c),Rigid(c);rep. . 7.00

049-ALICE IN WONDERLAND
By Lewis Carroll
07/48 **(47)** AB,AB(c),Original. . . . 150.00
10/49 **(64)** AB,AB(c),No(c)Price;
rep 40.00
07/51 **(85)** AB,AB(c),15›(c)Price;
rep 30.00
03/60 **(155)** AB,New P(c);rep 30.00
1962 **(165)** AB,P(c);rep. 25.00
03/64 **(167)** AB,P(c);rep. 20.00
06/66 **(167)** AB,P(c);rep 20.00
Fl/68 **(166)** AB,TO New P(c),25›(c)
Price, New Soft(c);rep 30.00
Fl/68 **(166)** AB,P(c),Both Soft &
Rigid(c)s;rep. 50.00

050-ADVENTURES OF TOM SAWYER
By Mark Twain
08/48 **(51)** ARu,ARu(c),Original. . 125.00
09/48 **(51)** ARu,ARu(c),Original. . 130.00
10/49 **(64)** ARu,ARu(c),No(c)
Price; rep 25.00
12/50 **(78)** ARu,ARu(c),15›(c)
Price; rep 20.00
04/52 **(94)** ARu,ARu(c);rep 20.00
12/53 **(114)** ARu,ARu(c);rep 15.00
03/54 **(117)** ARu,ARu(c);rep 15.00
05/56 **(132)** ARu,ARu(c);rep 15.00
09/57 **(140)** ARu,New P(c);rep . . . 10.00
05/59 **(150)** ARu,P(c);rep 15.00
10/61 **(164)** New Art,P(c);rep 7.00
62/63 **(167)** P(c);rep 7.00

All comics prices listed are for *Near Mint* condition.

01/65 **(167)** P(c);rep 7.00
05/66 **(167)** P(c);rep 7.00
12/67 **(166)** P(c);rep 7.00
Fl/69 **(169)** P(c),25›(c) Price,
Rigid(c);rep 7.00
Wr/71 **(169)** P(c);rep 7.00

051-THE SPY
By James Fenimore Cooper
09/48 **(51)** AdH,AdH(c),Original,
Maroon(c) 100.00
09/48 **(51)** AdH,AdH(c),Original,
Violet(c) 100.00
11/51 **(89)** AdH,AdH(c),15›(c)
Price; rep 25.00
07/54 **(121)** AdH,AdH(c);rep 20.00
07/57 **(139)** AdH,New P(c);rep . . . 15.00
05/60 **(156)** AdH,P(c);rep 7.00
11/63 **(167)** AdH,P(c);rep 7.00
07/66 **(167)** AdH,P(c);rep 7.00
Wr/69 **(166)** AdH,P(c),25›(c)Price,
Both Soft & Rigid(c)s;rep 20.00

052-THE HOUSE OF SEVEN GABLES
By Nathaniel Hawthorne
10/48 **(53)** HyG,HyG(c),Original . 100.00
11/51 **(89)** HyG,HyG(c),15›(c)
Price; rep 25.00
07/54 **(121)** HyG,HyG(c);rep 20.00
01/58 **(142)** GWb New Art,New
P(c); rep 15.00
05/60 **(156)** GWb,P(c);rep 7.00
1962 **(165)** GWb,P(c);rep 7.00
05/64 **(167)** GWb,P(c);rep 7.00
03/66 **(167)** GWb,P(c);rep 7.00
1968 **(166)** GWb,P(c),25›(c)
Price; rep 7.00
Sg/70 **(169)** GWb,P(c),Rigid(c);rep . 7.00

053-A CHRISTMAS CAROL
By Charles Dickens
11/48 **(53)** HcK,HcK(c),Original . . 150.00

054-MAN IN THE IRON MASK
By Alexandre Dumas
12/48 **(55)** AgF,HcK(c),Original . . 100.00
03/52 **(93)** AgF,HcK(c),15›(c)
Price; rep 25.00
09/53 **(111)** AgF,HcK(c);rep 35.00
01/58 **(142)** KBa New Art,New
P(c); rep 15.00
01/60 **(154)** KBa,P(c);rep 7.00
1962 **(165)** KBa,P(c);rep 7.00
05/64 **(167)** KBa,P(c);rep 7.00
04/66 **(167)** KBa,P(c);rep 7.00
Wr/69 **(166)** KBa,P(c),25›(c)
Price, Rigid(c);rep 7.00

055-SILAS MARINER
By George Eliot
01/49 **(55)** AdH,HcK(c),Original . . 100.00
09/50 **(75)** AdH,HcK(c),Price Circle
Blank,'Coming next'Ad(not
usually in reps.);rep 30.00
07/52 **(97)** AdH,HcK(c);rep 20.00
07/54 **(121)** AdH,New P(c);rep . . . 15.00
01/56 **(130)** AdH,P(c);rep 7.00
09/57 **(140)** AdH,P(c);rep 7.00
01/60 **(154)** AdH,P(c);rep 7.00
1962 **(165)** AdH,P(c);rep 7.00
05/64 **(167)** AdH,P(c);rep 7.00
06/65 **(167)** AdH,P(c);rep 7.00

05/67 **(166)** AdH,P(c);rep 7.00
Wr/69 **(166)** AdH,P(c),25›(c) Price,
Rigid(c);rep,Soft & Stiff 16.00

056-THE TOILERS OF THE SEA
By Victor Hugo
02/49 **(55)** AgF,AgF(c),Original . . 175.00
01/62 **(165)** AT New Art,New
P(c); rep 30.00
03/64 **(167)** AT,P(c);rep. 20.00
10/66 **(167)** AT,P(c);rep. 20.00

057-THE SONG OF HIAWATHA
By Henry Wadsworth Longfellow
03/49 **(55)** AB,AB(c),Original. . . . 100.00
09/50 **(75)** AB,AB(c),No(c)price,'
Coming Next'Ad(not usually
found in reps.);rep 30.00
04/52 **(94)** AB,AB(c),15›(c)
Price;rep 20.00
04/54 **(118)** AB,AB(c);rep 20.00
09/56 **(134)** AB,New P(c);rep . . . 15.00
07/57 **(139)** AB,P(c);rep 7.00
01/60 **(154)** AB,P(c);rep 7.00
62/63 **(167)** AB,P(c),Erroneosly
Has Original Date;rep 7.00
09/64 **(167)** AB,P(c);rep 7.00
10/65 **(167)** AB,P(c);rep 7.00
Fl/68 **(166)** AB,P(c),25›(c) Price;rep 7.00

CI #58 The Prairie
© Gilberton Publications

058-THE PRAIRIE
By James Fenimore Cooper
04/49 **(60)** RP,RP(c),Original. . . . 100.00
08/49 **(62)** RP,RP(c);rep 45.00
12/50 **(78)** RP,RP(c),15›(c) Price
In Double Circle;rep 25.00
12/53 **(114)** RP,RP(c);rep 20.00
03/56 **(131)** RP,RP(c);rep 15.00
05/56 **(132)** RP,RP(c);rep 15.00
09/58 **(146)** RP,New P(c);rep 15.00
03/60 **(155)** RP,P(c);rep 8.00
05/64 **(167)** RP,P(c);rep 7.00
04/66 **(167)** RP,P(c);rep 7.00
Sr/69 **(169)** RP,P(c),25›(c)
Price; Rigid(c);rep 7.00

059-WUTHERING HEIGHTS
By Emily Bronte
05/49 **(60)** HcK,HcK(c),Original . . 125.00
07/51 **(85)** HcK,HcK(c),15›(c)
Price; rep 35.00
05/60 **(156)** HcK,GB New P(c);rep 20.00
01/64 **(167)** HcK,GB P(c);rep 10.00
10/66 **(167)** HcK,GB P(c);rep 10.00
Sr/69 **(169)** HcK,GBP(c),25›(c)
Price, Rigid(c);rep. 9.00

060-BLACK BEAUTY
By Anna Sewell
06/49 **(62)** AgF,AgF(c),Original . . 100.00
08/49 **(62)** AgF,AgF(c);rep. 125.00
07/51 **(85)** AgF,AgF(c),15›(c) Price;
rep 25.00
09/60 **(158)** LbC&NN&StA New
Art, LbC New P(c);rep 25.00
02/64 **(167)** LbC&NN&StA,LbC
P(c); rep 20.00
03/66 **(167)** LbC&NN&StA,LbC
P(c); rep 20.00
03/66 **(167)** LbC&NN&StA,LbC
P(c), 'Open Book'Blank;rep. . . 50.00
1968 **(166)** LbC&NN&StA,AIM New
P(c) 25›(c) Price;rep 35.00

061-THE WOMAN IN WHITE
By William Wilke Collins
07/49 **(62)** AB,AB(c),Original,
Maroon & Violet(c)s 110.00
05/60 **(156)** AB,DgR New P(c);rep 25.00
01/64 **(167)** AB,DgR P(c);rep 20.00
1968 **(166)** AB,DgR P(c),
25›(c)Price;rep 20.00

062-WESTERN STORIES
(The Luck of Roaring Camp & The Outcasts of Poker Flat)
By Bret Harte
08/49 **(62)** HcK,HcK(c),Original . . 100.00
11/51 **(89)** HcK,HcK(c),15›(c)
Price; rep 25.00
07/54 **(121)** HcK,HcK(c);rep 20.00
03/57 **(137)** HcK,New P(c);rep . . . 15.00
09/59 **(152)** HcK,P(c);rep 8.00
10/63 **(167)** HcK,P(c);rep 8.00
06/64 **(167)** HcK,P(c);rep 7.00
11/66 **(167)** HcK,P(c);rep 7.00
1968 **(166)** HcK,TO New P(c),
25› Price;rep 20.00

063-THE MAN WITHOUT A COUNTRY
By Edward Everett Hale
09/49 **(62)** HcK,HcK(c),Original . . 100.00
12/50 **(78)** HcK,HcK(c),15›(c)Price
In Double Circles;rep 25.00
05/60 **(156)** HcK,GMc New P(c);
rep 22.00
01/62 **(165)** AT New Art,GMc P(c),
Added Text Pages;rep 12.00
03/64 **(167)** AT,GMc P(c);rep 7.00
08/66 **(167)** AT,GMc P(c);rep 7.00
Sr/69 **(169)** AT,GMc P(c),25›(c)
Price, Rigid(c);rep. 7.00

064-TREASURE ISLAND
By Robert Louis Stevenson
10/49 **(62)** AB,AB(c),Original. . . . 90.00
04/51 **(82)** AB,AB(c),15›(c)
Price;rep 25.00

03/54 **(117)** AB,AB(c);rep 17.00
03/56 **(131)** AB,New P(c);rep 14.00
05/57 **(138)** AB,P(c);rep 7.00
09/58 **(146)** AB,P(c);rep 7.00
09/60 **(158)** AB,P(c);rep 7.00
1962 **(165)** AB,P(c);rep. 7.00
62/63 **(167)** AB,P(c);rep 7.00
06/64 **(167)** AB,P(c);rep 7.00
12/65 **(167)** AB,P(c);rep 7.00
10/67 **(166)** AB,P(c);rep 11.00
10/67 **(166)** AB,P(c),GRIT Ad
  Stapled In Book;rep 64.00
Sg/69 **(169)** AB,P(c),25›(c)
  Price, Rigid(c);rep. 7.00

065-BENJAMIN FRANKLIN
By Benjamin Franklin
11/49 **(64)** AB,RtH,GS(Iger Shop),
  HcK(c),Original. 100.00
03/56 **(131)** AB,RtH,GS(Iger Shop),
  New P(c) ;rep 20.00
01/60 **(154)** AB,RtH,GS(Iger Shop),
  P(c);rep 8.00
02/64 **(167)** AB,RtH,GS(Iger Shop),
  P(c);rep 8.00
04/66 **(166)** AB,RtH,GS(Iger Shop),
  P(c);rep 8.00
Fl/69 **(169)** AB,RtH,GS(Iger Shop),
  P(c), 25›(c)Price,Rigid(c);rep . 10.00

066-THE CLOISTER AND THE HEARTH
By Charles Reade
12/49 **(67)** HcK,HcK(c),Original . . 225.00

067-THE SCOTTISH CHIEFS
By Jane Porter
01/50 **(67)** AB,AB(c),Original. . . . 100.00
07/51 **(85)** AB,AB(c),15›(c)
  Price;rep 25.00
04/54 **(118)** AB,AB(c);rep 20.00
01/57 **(136)** AB,New P(c);rep . . . 15.00
01/60 **(154)** AB,P(c);rep 12.00
11/63 **(167)** AB,P(c);rep 12.00
08/65 **(167)** AB,P(c);rep 12.00

068-JULIUS CEASAR
By William Shakespeare
02/50 **(70)** HcK,HcK(c),Original. . . 90.00
07/51 **(85)** HcK,HcK(c),15›(c)
  Price; rep 25.00
06/53 **(108)** HcK,New P(c);rep 20.00
05/60 **(156)** HcK,LbC New P(c);rep25.00
1962 **(165)** GE&RC New Art,
  LbC P(c);rep. 25.00
02/64 **(167)** GE&RC,LbC P(c);rep. . 7.00
10/65 **(167)** GE&RC,LbC P(c),Tarzan
  Books Inside(c);rep 7.00
1967 **(166)** GE&RC,LbC P(c);rep . 7.00
Wr/69 **(169)** GE&RC,LbC P(c),
  Rigid(c);rep 7.00

069-AROUND THE WORLD IN 80 DAYS
By Jules Verne
03/50 **(70)** HcK,HcK(c),Original. . . 90.00
09/51 **(87)** HcK,HcK(c),15›(c)
  Price; rep 25.00
03/55 **(125)** HcK,HcK(c);rep 20.00
01/57 **(136)** HcK,New P(c);rep . . . 15.00
09/58 **(146)** HcK,P(c);rep 8.00
09/59 **(152)** HcK,P(c);rep 8.00
1961 **(164)** HcK,P(c);rep 8.00
62/63 **(167)** HcK,P(c);rep 7.00

07/64 **(167)** HcK,P(c);rep 7.00
11/65 **(167)** HcK,P(c);rep 7.00
07/67 **(166)** HcK,P(c);rep 7.00
Sg/69 **(169)** HcK,P(c),25›(c)
  Price, Rigid(c);rep. 7.00

070-THE PILOT
By James Fenimore Cooper
04/50 **(71)** AB,AB(c),Original. 75.00
10/50 **(75)** AB,AB(c),15›(c)
  Price;rep 25.00
02/52 **(92)** AB,AB(c);rep 20.00
03/55 **(125)** AB,AB(c);rep 20.00
05/60 **(156)** AB,GMc New P(c);rep 15.00
02/64 **(167)** AB,GMc P(c);rep 15.00
05/66 **(167)** AB,GMc P(c);rep 12.00

071-THE MAN WHO LAUGHS
By Victor Hugo
05/50 **(71)** AB,AB(c),Original. 125.00
01/62 **(165)** NN,NN New P(c);rep . 70.00
04/64 **(167)** NN,NN P(c);rep 65.00

072-THE OREGON TRAIL
By Francis Parkman
06/50 **(73)** HcK,HcK (c),Original . . 75.00
11/51 **(89)** HcK,HcK (c),15›(c)
  Price; rep 25.00
07/54 **(121)** HcK,HcK (c);rep. 20.00
03/56 **(131)** HcK,New P(c);rep . . . 15.00
09/57 **(140)** HcK,P(c);rep 8.00
05/59 **(150)** HcK,P(c);rep 7.00
01/61 **(164)** HcK,P(c);rep 7.00
62/63 **(167)** HcK,P(c);rep 7.00
08/64 **(167)** HcK,P(c);rep 7.00
10/65 **(167)** HcK,P(c);rep 7.00
1968 **(166)** HcK,P(c),25›(c)Price;rep 7.00

073-THE BLACK TULIP
By Alexandre Dumas
07/50 **(75)** AB,AB(c),Original. . . . 275.00

074-MR. MIDSHIPMAN EASY
By Captain Frederick Marryat
08/50 **(75)** BbL,Original. 275.00

075-THE LADY OF THE LAKE
By Sir Walter Scott
09/50 **(75)** HcK,HcK(c),Original. . . 80.00
07/51 **(85)** HcK,HcK(c),15›(c)
  Price; rep 25.00
04/54 **(118)** HcK,HcK(c);rep 20.00
07/57 **(139)** HcK,New P(c);rep . . . 15.00
01/60 **(154)** HcK,P(c);rep 7.00
1962 **(165)** HcK,P(c);rep. 7.00
04/64 **(167)** HcK,P(c);rep 7.00
05/66 **(167)** HcK,P(c);rep 7.00
Sg/69 **(169)** HcK,P(c),25›(c)
  Price, Rigid(c);rep. 7.00

076-THE PRISONER OF ZENDA
By Anthony Hope Hawkins
10/50 **(75)** HcK,HcK(c),Original. . . 75.00
07/51 **(85)** HcK,HcK(c),15›(c) Price;
  rep 25.00
09/53 **(111)** HcK,HcK(c),rep 20.00
09/55 **(128)** HcK,New P(c);rep . . . 15.00
09/59 **(152)** HcK,P(c);rep 9.00
1962 **(165)** HcK,P(c);rep. 7.00

04/64 **(167)** HcK,P(c);rep 7.00
09/66 **(167)** HcK,P(c);rep 7.00
Fl/69 **(169)** HcK,P(c),25›(c) Price,
  Rigid(c);rep 7.00

077-THE ILLIAD
By Homer
11/50 **(78)** AB,AB(c),Original. 80.00
09/51 **(87)** AB,AB(c),15›(c)
  Price;rep 25.00
07/54 **(121)** AB,AB(c);rep 20.00
07/57 **(139)** AB,New P(c);rep 15.00
05/59 **(150)** AB,P(c);rep 9.00
1962 **(165)** AB,P(c);rep. 7.00
10/63 **(167)** AB,P(c);rep. 7.00
07/64 **(167)** AB,P(c);rep. 7.00
05/66 **(167)** AB,P(c);rep. 7.00
1968 **(166)** AB,P(c),25›(c)Price;rep . 7.00

078-JOAN OF ARC
By Frederick Shiller
12/50 **(78)** HcK,HcK(c),Original. . . 70.00
09/51 **(87)** HcK,HcK(c),15›(c)
  Price; rep 25.00
11/53 **(113)** HcK,HcK(c);rep 20.00
09/55 **(128)** HcK,New P(c);rep . . . 15.00
09/57 **(140)** HcK,P(c);rep 7.00
05/59 **(150)** HcK,P(c);rep 7.00
11/60 **(159)** HcK,P(c);rep 7.00
62/63 **(167)** HcK,P(c);rep 7.00
12/63 **(167)** HcK,P(c);rep 7.00
06/65 **(167)** HcK,P(c);rep 7.00
06/67 **(166)** HcK,P(c);rep 7.00
Wr/69 **(166)** HcK,TO New P(c),
  25›(c)Price, Rigid(c);rep 20.00

079-CYRANO DE BERGERAC
By Edmond Rostand
01/51 **(78)** AB,AB(c),Original,Movie
  Promo Inside Front(c) 75.00
07/51 **(85)** AB,AB(c),15›(c)
  Price;rep 25.00
04/54 **(118)** AB,AB(c);rep 20.00
07/56 **(133)** AB,New P(c);rep 20.00
05/60 **(156)** AB,P(c);rep 15.00
08/64 **(167)** AB,P(c);rep 15.00

080-WHITE FANG
By Jack London
(Last Line Drawn (c)
02/51 **(79)** AB,AB(c),Original. 75.00
09/51 **(87)** AB,AB(c);rep 25.00
03/55 **(125)** AB,AB(c);rep 20.00
05/56 **(132)** AB,New P(c);rep 20.00
09/57 **(140)** AB,P(c);rep 9.00
11/59 **(153)** AB,P(c);rep 9.00
62/63 **(167)** AB,P(c);rep. 7.00
09/64 **(167)** AB,P(c);rep. 7.00
07/65 **(167)** AB,P(c);rep. 7.00
06/67 **(166)** AB,P(c);rep. 7.00
Fl/69 **(169)** AB,P(c),25›(c)
  Price, Rigid(c);rep. 7.00

081-THE ODYSSEY
By Homer
(P(c)s From Now on)
03/51 **(82)** HyG,AB P(c),Original. . 75.00
08/64 **(167)** HyG,AB P(c);rep 15.00
10/66 **(167)** HyG,AB P(c);rep 15.00
Sg/69 **(169)** HyG,TyT New P(c),
  Rigid(c);rep 15.00

082-THE MASTER OF BALLANTRAE
By Robert Louis Stevenson
04/51 (82) LDr,AB P(c),Original. . . 50.00
08/64 (167) LDr,AB P(c);rep 18.00
Fl/68 (166) LDr,Syk New P(c),
Rigid(c);rep 20.00

083-THE JUNGLE BOOK
By Rudyard Kipling
05/51 (85) WmB&AB,AB P(c),
Original 40.00
08/53 (110) WmB&AB,AB P(c);rep . 8.00
03/55 (125) WmB&AB,AB P(c);rep . 8.00
05/56 (134) WmB&AB,AB P(c);rep . 8.00
01/58 (142) WmB&AB,AB P(c);rep . 8.00
05/59 (150) WmB&AB,AB P(c);rep . 7.00
11/60 (159) WmB&AB,AB P(c);rep . 7.00
62/63 (167) WmB&AB,AB P(c);rep . 7.00
03/65 (167) WmB&AB,AB P(c);rep . 7.00
11/65 (167) WmB&AB,AB P(c);rep . 7.00
05/66 (167) WmB&AB,AB P(c);rep . 7.00
1968 (166) NN Art,NN New P(c),
Rigid(c);rep 18.00

084-THE GOLD BUG & OTHER STORIES
(The Gold Bug-The Telltale HeartThe Cask of Amontillado)
By Edgar Allan Poe
06/51 (85) AB,RP,JLv,AB P(c),
Original 100.00
07/64 (167) AB,RP,JLv,AB P(c);rep 75.00

085-THE SEA WOLF
By Jack London
08/51 (85) AB,AB P(c),Original . . . 35.00
07/54 (121) AB,AB P(c);rep 8.00
05/56 (132) AB,AB P(c);rep 8.00
11/57 (141) AB,AB P(c);rep 8.00
03/61 (161) AB,AB P(c);rep 7.00
02/64 (167) AB,AB P(c);rep 7.00
11/65 (167) AB,AB P(c);rep 7.00
Fl/69 (169) AB,AB P(c),25›(c)
Price, Rigid(c);rep 7.00

086-UNDER TWO FLAGS
By Oiuda
08/51 (87) MDb,AB P(c),Original. . 30.00
03/54 (117) MDb,AB P(c);rep 10.00
07/57 (139) MDb,AB P(c);rep 10.00
09/60 (158) MDb,AB P(c);rep 7.00
02/64 (167) MDb,AB P(c);rep 7.00
08/66 (167) MDb,AB P(c);rep 7.00
Sr/69 (169) MDb,AB P(c),25›(c)
Price, Rigid(c);rep 7.00

087-A MIDSUMMER NIGHTS DREAM
By William Shakespeare
09/51 (87) AB,AB P(c),Original . . . 30.00
03/61 (161) AB,AB P(c);rep 9.00
04/64 (167) AB,AB P(c);rep 7.00
05/66 (167) AB,AB P(c);rep 7.00
Sr/69 (169) AB,AB P(c),25›(c)
Price; rep 7.00

088-MEN OF IRON
By Howard Pyle
10/51 (89) HD,LDr,GS,Original . . . 35.00
01/60 (154) HD,LDr,GS,P(c);rep . . 9.00
01/64 (167) HD,LDr,GS,P(c);rep . . 7.00
1968 (166) HD,LDr,GS,P(c),

25›(c)Price;rep 7.00

089-CRIME AND PUNISHMENT
By Fedor Dostoevsky
11/51 (89) RP,AB P(c),Original . . . 40.00
09/59 (152) RP,AB P(c);rep. 10.00
04/64 (167) RP,AB P(c);rep 7.00
05/66 (167) RP,AB P(c);rep 7.00
Fl/69 (169) RP,AB P(c),25›(c)
Price, Rigid(c);rep. 7.00

090-GREEN MANSIONS
By William Henry Hudson
12/51 (89) AB,AB P(c),Original. . . 35.00
01/59 (148) AB,New LbC P(c);rep. 15.00
1962 (165) AB,LbC P(c);rep 7.00
04/64 (167) AB,LbC P(c);rep 7.00
09/66 (167) AB,LbC P(c);rep. 7.00
Sr/69 (169) AB,LbC P(c),25›(c)
Price, Rigid(c);rep. 7.00

091-THE CALL OF THE WILD
By Jack London
01/52 (92) MDb,P(c),Original 35.00
10/53 (112) MDb,P(c);rep 10.00
03/55(125)MDb,P(c),'PictureProgress'
Onn. Back(c);rep 10.00
09/56 (134) MDb,P(c);rep 10.00
03/58 (143) MDb,P(c);rep 7.00
1962 (165) MDb,P(c);rep 7.00
1962 (167) MDb,P(c);rep 7.00
04/65 (167) MDb,P(c);rep 7.00
03/66 (167) MDb,P(c);rep 7.00
03/66 (167) MDb,P(c),Record
Edition;rep 7.00
11/67 (166) MDb,P(c);rep 7.00
Sg/70 (169) MDb,P(c),25›(c)
Price, Rigid(c);rep. 7.00

092-THE COURTSHIP OF MILES STANDISH
By Henry Wadsworth Longfellow
02/52 (92) AB,AB P(c),Original . . . 30.00
1962 (165) AB,AB P(c);rep 9.00
03/64 (167) AB,AB P(c);rep 9.00
05/67 (166) AB,AB P(c);rep 9.00
Wr/69 (169) AB,AB P(c),25›(c)
Price, Rigid(c);rep. 9.00

093-PUDD'NHEAD WILSON
By Mark Twain
03/52 (94) HcK,HcK P(c),Original . 35.00
1962 (165) HcK,New P(c);rep 15.00
03/64 (167) HcK,GMc P(c);rep . . 12.00
1968 (166) HcK,GMc P(c),25›(c)
Price, Soft(c);rep 12.00

094-DAVID BALFOUR
By Robert Louis Stevenson
04/52 (94) RP,P(c),Original 35.00
05/64 (167) RP,P(c);rep 15.00
1968 (166) RP,P(c),25›(c)Price;rep 15.00

095-ALL QUIET ON THE WESTERN FRONT
By Erich Maria Remarque
05/52 (96) MDb,P(c),Original . . . 100.00
05/52 (99) MDb,P(c),Original 60.00

10/64 (167) MDb,P(c);rep 20.00
11/66 (167) MDb,P(c);rep 20.00

CI Daniel Boon#
© Gilberton Publications

096-DANIEL BOONE
By John Bakeless
06/52 (97) AB,P(c),Original. 30.00
03/54 (117) AB,P(c);rep 8.00
09/55 (128) AB,P(c);rep 8.00
05/56 (132) AB,P(c);rep 8.00
----- (134) AB,P(c),'Story of
Jesus'on Back(c);rep 8.00
09/60 (158) AB,P(c);rep 8.00
01/64 (167) AB,P(c);rep 8.00
05/65 (167) AB,P(c);rep 8.00
11/66 (167) AB,P(c);rep 8.00
Wr/69 (166) AB,P(c),25›(c)
Price, Rigid(c);rep. 12.00

097-KING SOLOMON'S MINES
By H. Rider Haggard
07/52 (96) HcK,P(c),Original 30.00
04/54 (118) HcK,P(c);rep 10.00
03/56 (131) HcK,P(c);rep 10.00
09/51 (141) HcK,P(c);rep 10.00
09/60 (158) HcK,P(c);rep 7.00
02/64 (167) HcK,P(c);rep 7.00
09/65 (167) HcK,P(c);rep 7.00
Sr/69 (169) HcK,P(c),25›(c)
Price; Rigid(c);rep. 8.00

098-THE RED BADGE OF COURAGE
By Stephen Crane
08/52 (98) MDb,GS,P(c),Original . 32.00
04/54 (118) MDb,GS,P(c);rep . . . 10.00
05/56 (132) MDb,GS,P(c);rep . . . 10.00
01/58 (142) MDb,GS,P(c);rep . . . 10.00
09/59 (152) MDb,GS,P(c);rep 7.00
03/61 (161) MDb,GS,P(c);rep 7.00
62/63 (167) MDb,GS,P(c),Erronously
Has Original Date;rep 7.00
09/64 (167) MDb,GS,P(c);rep 7.00
10/65 (167) MDb,GS,P(c);rep 7.00
1968 (166) MDb,GS,P(c),25›(c)
Price, Rigid(c);rep. 15.00

099-HAMLET
By William Shakespeare
09/52 (98) AB,P(c),Original. 35.00

07/54 **(121)** AB,P(c);rep 10.00
11/57 **(141)** AB,P(c);rep 10.00
09/60 **(158)** AB,P(c);rep 7.00
62/63 **(167)** AB,P(c),Erroneusly
　　Has Original Date;rep 7.00
07/65 **(167)** AB,P(c);rep 7.00
04/67 **(166)** AB,P(c);rep 7.00
Sg/69 **(169)** AB,EdM New P(c),
　　25›(c)Price, Rigid(c);rep 15.00

100-MUTINY ON THE BOUNTY
By Charrles Nordhoff
10/52 **(100)** MsW,HcK P(c),Original30.00
03/54 **(117)** MsW,HcK P(c);rep . . . 10.00
05/56 **(132)** MsW,HcK P(c);rep . . . 10.00
01/58 **(142)** MsW,HcK P(c);rep . . . 10.00
03/60 **(155)** MsW,HcK P(c);rep 7.00
62/63 **(167)** MsW,HcK P(c),Erroneusly
　　Has Original Date;rep 7.00
05/64 **(167)** MsW,HcK P(c);rep . . . 7.00
03/66 **(167)** MsW,HcK P(c),N#
　　or Price;rep 10.00
Sg/70 **(169)** MsW,HcK P(c),
　　Rigid(c); rep 4.00

101-WILLIAM TELL
By Frederick Schiller
11/52 **(101)** MDb,HcK P(c),Original30.00
04/54 **(118)** MDb,HcK P(c);rep . . . 10.00
11/57 **(141)** MDb,HcK P(c);rep . . . 10.00
09/60 **(158)** MDb,HcK P(c);rep 7.00
62/63 **(167)** MDb,HcK P(c),Erroneusly
　　Has Original Date;rep 7.00
11/64 **(167)** MDb,HcK P(c);rep 7.00
04/67 **(166)** MDb,HcK P(c);rep 7.00
Wr/69 **(169)** MDb,HcK P(c)25›(c)
　　Price, Rigid(c);rep 7.00

102-THE WHITE COMPANY
By Sir Arthur Conan Doyle
12/52 **(101)** AB,P(c),Original 65.00
1962 **(165)** AB,P(c);rep 25.00
04/64 **(167)** AB,P(c);rep 25.00

103-MEN AGAINST THE SEA
By Charles Nordhoff
01/53 **(104)** RP,HcK P(c),Original . 35.00
12/53 **(114)** RP,HcK P(c);rep 20.00
03/56 **(131)** RP,New P(c);rep 15.00
03/59 **(149)** RP,P(c);rep 15.00
09/60 **(158)** RP,P(c);rep 25.00
03/64 **(167)** RP,P(c);rep 15.00

104-BRING 'EM BACK ALIVE
By Frank Buck & Edward Anthony
02/53 **(105)** HcK,HcK P(c)Original. 30.00
04/54 **(118)** HcK,HcK P(c);rep. . . . 10.00
07/56 **(133)** HcK,HcK P(c);rep 9.00
05/59 **(150)** HcK,HcK P(c);rep 7.00
09/60 **(158)** HcK,HcK P(c);rep 7.00
10/63 **(167)** HcK,HcK P(c);rep 7.00
09/65 **(167)** HcK,HcK P(c);rep 7.00
Wr/69 **(169)** HcK,HcK P(c),25›(c)
　　Price, Rigid(c);rep 7.00

105-FROM THE EARTH TO THE MOON
By Jules Verne
03/53 **(106)** AB,P(c),Original 30.00
04/54 **(118)** AB,P(c);rep 8.00
03/56 **(132)** AB,P(c);rep 8.00
11/57 **(141)** AB,P(c);rep 8.00
09/58 **(146)** AB,P(c);rep 8.00
05/60 **(156)** AB,P(c);rep 8.00
62/63 **(167)** AB,P(c),Erroneusly
　　Has Original Date;rep 7.00
05/64 **(167)** AB,P(c);rep 7.00
05/65 **(167)** AB,P(c);rep 7.00
10/67 **(166)** AB,P(c);rep 7.00
Sr/69 **(169)** AB,P(c),25›(c)
　　Price, Rigid(c);rep. 7.00
Sg/71 **(169)** AB,P(c);rep 7.00

106-BUFFALO BILL
By William F. Cody
04/53 **(107)** MDb,P(c),Original . . . 30.00
04/54 **(118)** MDb,P(c);rep 9.00
03/56 **(132)** MDb,P(c);rep 9.00
01/58 **(142)** MDb,P(c);rep 9.00
03/61 **(161)** MDb,P(c);rep 7.00
03/64 **(167)** MDb,P(c);rep 7.00
07/67 **(166)** MDb,P(c);rep 7.00
Fl/69 **(169)** MDb,P(c),Rigid(c);rep . . 7.00

107-KING OF THE KHYBER RIFLES
By Talbot Mundy
05/53 **(108)** SMz,P(c),Original 30.00
04/54 **(118)** SMz,P(c);rep 9.00
09/58 **(146)** SMz,P(c);rep 9.00
09/60 **(158)** SMz,P(c);rep 7.00
62/63 **(167)** SMz,P(c),Erroreunsly
　　Has Original Date;rep 7.00
62/63 **(167)** SMz,P(c);rep 7.00
10/66 **(167)** SMz,P(c);rep 7.00

108-KNIGHTS OF THE ROUND TABLE
By Howard Pyle?
06/53 **(108)** AB,P(c),Original 35.00
06/53 **(109)** AB,P(c),Original 42.00
03/54 **(117)** AB,P(c);rep 9.00
11/59 **(153)** AB,P(c);rep 7.00
1962 **(165)** AB,P(c);rep 7.00
04/64 **(167)** AB,P(c);rep 7.00
04/67 **(166)** AB,P(c);rep 7.00

109-PITCAIRN'S ISLAND
By Charles Nordhoff
07/53 **(110)** RP,P(c),Original 35.00
1962 **(165)** RP,P(c);rep 11.00
03/64 **(167)** RP,P(c);rep 11.00
06/67 **(166)** RP,P(c);rep 11.00

110-A STUDY IN SCARLET
By Sir Arthur Conan Doyle
08/53 **(111)** SMz,P(c),Original . . . 100.00
1962 **(165)** SMz,P(c);rep. 75.00

111-THE TALISMAN
By Sir Walter Scott
09/53 **(112)** HcK,HcK P(c),Original 40.00
1962 **(165)** HcK,HcK P(c);rep 8.00
05/64 **(167)** HcK,HcK P(c);rep 8.00
Fl/68 **(166)** HcK,HcK P(c),
　　25›(c)Price;rep 8.00

CI #109, Pitcairn's Island
© Gilberton Publications

112-ADVENTURES OF KIT CARSON
By John S. C. Abbott
10/53 **(113)** RP,P(c),Original 40.00
11/55 **(129)** RP,P(c);rep 8.00
11/57 **(141)** RP,P(c);rep 8.00
09/59 **(152)** RP,P(c);rep 7.00
03/61 **(161)** RP,P(c);rep 7.00
62/63 **(167)** RP,P(c);rep 7.00
02/65 **(167)** RP,P(c);rep 7.00
05/66 **(167)** RP,P(c);rep 7.00
Wr/69 **(166)** RP,EdM New P(c),
　　25›(c)Price, Rigid(c);rep 12.00

113-THE FORTY-FIVE GUARDSMEN
By Alexandre Dumas
11/53 **(114)** MDb,P(c),Original 60.00
07/67 **(166)** MDb,P(c);rep 30.00

114-THE RED ROVER
By James Fenimore Cooper
12/53 **(115)** PrC,JP P(c),Original . . 60.00
07/67 **(166)** PrC,JP P(c);rep 30.00

115-HOW I FOUND LIVINGSTONE
By Sir Henry Stanley
01/54 **(116)** SF&ST,P(c),Original . . 65.00
01/67 **(167)** SF&ST,P(c);rep 40.00

116-THE BOTTLE IMP
By Robert Louis Stevenson
02/54 **(117)** LC,P(c),Original 70.00
01/67 **(167)** LC,P(c);rep 40.00

117-CAPTAINS COURAGEOUS
By Rudyard Kipling
03/54 **(118)** PrC,P(c),Original 60.00
02/67 **(167)** PrC,P(c);rep. 22.00
Fl/69 **(169)** PrC,P(c),25›(c)
　　Price, Rigid(c);rep. 20.00

118-ROB ROY
By Sir Walter Scott
04/54 (119) RP,WIP,P(c),Original. . 70.00
02/67 (167) RP,WIP,P(c);rep 40.00

119-SOLDERS OF FORTUNE
By Richard Harding Davis
05/54 (120) KS,P(c),Original 50.00
03/67 (166) KS,P(c);rep 22.00
Sg/70 (169) KS,P(c),25›(c)
Price, Rigid(c);rep. 20.00

120-THE HURRICANE
By Charles Nordhoff
1954 (121) LC,LC P(c),Original. . . 50.00
03/67 (166) LC,LC P(c);rep. 30.00

121-WILD BILL HICKOCK
Author Unknown
07/54 (122) MI,ST,P(c),Original. . . 25.00
05/56 (132) MI,ST,P(c);rep 9.00
11/57 (141) MI,ST,P(c);rep 9.00
01/60 (154) MI,ST,P(c);rep 9.00
62/63 (167) MI,ST,P(c);rep 7.00
08/64 (167) MI,ST,P(c);rep 7.00
04/67 (166) MI,ST,P(c);rep 7.00
Wr/69 (169) MI,ST,P(c),Rigid(c);rep 7.00

122-THE MUTINEERS
By Charles Boardman Hawes
09/54 (123) PrC,P(c),Original 35.00
01/57 (136) PrC,P(c);rep. 9.00
09/58 (146) PrC,P(c);rep. 9.00
09/60 (158) PrC,P(c);rep. 7.00
11/63 (167) PrC,P(c);rep. 7.00
03/65 (167) PrC,P(c);rep. 7.00
08/67 (166) PrC,P(c);rep. 7.00

123-FANG AND CLAW
By Frank Buck
11/54 (124) LnS,P(c),Original 35.00
07/56 (133) LnS,P(c);rep 9.00
03/58 (143) LnS,P(c);rep 9.00
01/60 (154) LnS,P(c);rep 7.00
62/63 (167) LnS,P(c),Erroneously
Has Original Date;rep 7.00
09/65 (167) LnS,P(c);rep 7.00

124-THE WAR OF THE WORLDS
By H. G. Wells
01/55 (125) LC,LC P(c),Original . . 50.00
03/56 (131) LC,LC P(c);rep. 10.00
11/57 (141) LC,LC P(c);rep. 10.00
01/59 (148) LC,LC P(c);rep. 10.00
05/60 (156) LC,LC P(c);rep. 12.00
1962 (165) LC,LC P(c);rep 10.00
62/63 (167) LC,LC P(c);rep. 10.00
11/64 (167) LC,LC P(c);rep. 10.00
11/65 (167) LC,LC P(c);rep. 10.00
1968 (166) LC,LC P(c),25›(c)
Price; rep 10.00
Sr/70 (169) LC,LC P(c),Rigid(c);rep
. . . . 10.00

125-THE OX BOW INCIDENT
By Walter Van Tilberg Clark
03/55 (---) NN,P(c),Original. 25.00
03/58 (143) NN,P(c);rep 8.00

CI #125, The Ox-Boy Incident
© Gilberton Publications

09/59 (152) NN,P(c);rep 8.00
03/61 (149) NN,P(c);rep 8.00
62/63 (167) NN,P(c);rep 7.00
11/64 (167) NN,P(c);rep 7.00
04/67 (166) NN,P(c);rep 7.00
r/69 (169) NN,P(c),25›(c)
Price, Rigid(c);rep. 7.00

126-THE DOWNFALL
By Emile Zola
05/55 (---) LC,LC P(c),Original,'
Picture Progress'Replaces
Reorder List 35.00
08/64 (167) LC,LC P(c);rep. 12.00
1968 (166) LC,LC P(c),25›(c)
Price;rep 12.00

127-THE KING OF THE MOUNTAINS
By Edmond About
07/55 (128) NN,P(c),Original. 35.00
06/64 (167) NN,P(c);rep 12.00
Fl/68 (166) NN,P(c),25›(c)Price;rep 12.00

128-MACBETH
By William Shakespeare
09/55 (128) AB,P(c),Original 35.00
03/58 (143) AB,P(c);rep 9.00
09/60 (158) AB,P(c);rep 9.00
62/63 (167) AB,P(c);rep 7.00
06/64 (167) AB,P(c);rep 7.00
04/67 (166) AB,P(c);rep 7.00
1968 (166) AB,P(c),25›(c)Price;rep . 7.00
Sg/70 (169) AB,P(c),Rigid(c);rep. . . 7.00

129-DAVY CROCKETT
Author Unknown
11/55 (129) LC,P(c),Original 100.00
09/66 (167) LC,P(c);rep 75.00

130-CAESAR'S CONQUESTS
By Julius Caesar
01/56 (130) JO,P(c),Original 40.00
01/58 (142) JO,P(c);rep 9.00
09/59 (152) JO,P(c);rep 9.00
03/61 (149) JO,P(c);rep 9.00
62/63 (167) JO,P(c);rep 7.00
10/64 (167) JO,P(c);rep 7.00

04/66 (167) JO,P(c);rep 7.00

131-THE COVERED WAGON
By Emerson Hough
03/56 (131) NN,P(c),Original. 25.00
03/58 (143) NN,P(c);rep 8.00
09/59 (152) NN,P(c);rep 8.00
09/60 (158) NN,P(c);rep 8.00
62/63 (167) NN,P(c);rep 7.00
11/64 (167) NN,P(c);rep 7.00
04/66 (167) NN,P(c);rep 7.00
Wr/69 (169) NN,P(c),25›(c)
Price, Rigid(c);rep. 7.00

132-THE DARK FRIGATE
By Charles Boardman Hawes
05/56 (132) EW&RWb,P(c),Original. . . .
35.00
05/59 (150) EW&RWb,P(c);rep . . . 12.00
01/64 (167) EW&RWb,P(c);rep . . . 12.00
05/67 (166) EW&RWb,P(c);rep . . . 12.00

133-THE TIME MACHINE
By H. G. Wells
07/56 (132) LC,P(c),Original 45.00
01/58 (142) LC,P(c);rep 12.00
09/59 (152) LC,P(c);rep 12.00
09/60 (158) LC,P(c);rep 12.00
62/63 (167) LC,P(c);rep 12.00
06/64 (167) LC,P(c);rep 15.00
03/66 (167) LC,P(c);rep 12.00
03/66 (167) LC,P(c),N# Or Price;
rep 12.00
12/67 (166) LC,P(c);rep 12.00
Wr/71 (169) LC,P(c),25›(c)
Price, Rigid(c);rep. 12.00

134-ROMEO AND JULIET
By William Shakespeare
09/56 (134) GE,P(c),Original. 30.00
03/61 (161) GE,P(c);rep 9.00
09/63 (167) GE,P(c);rep 7.00
05/65 (167) GE,P(c);rep 7.00
06/67 (166) GE,P(c);rep 7.00
Wr/69 (166) GE,EdM New P(c),
25›(c)Price, Rigid(c);rep 22.00

135-WATERLOO
**By Emile Erckmann &
Alexandre Chatrian**
11/56 (135) Grl,AB P(c),Original . . 35.00
11/59 (153) Grl,AB P(c);rep 9.00
62/63 (167) Grl,AB P(c);rep 7.00
09/64 (167) Grl,AB P(c);rep 7.00
1968 (166) Grl,AB P(c),25›(c)
Price; rep 7.00

136-LORD JIM
By Joseph Conrad
01/57 (136) GE,P(c),Original. 35.00
62/63 (165) GE,P(c);rep 7.00
03/64 (167) GE,P(c);rep 7.00
09/66 (167) GE,P(c);rep 7.00
Sr/69 (169) GE,P(c),25›(c)
Price, Rigid(c);rep. 7.00

137-THE LITTLE SAVAGE
By Captain Frederick Marryat
03/57 (136) GE,P(c),Original 35.00
01/59 (148) GE,P(c);rep 8.00
05/60 (156) GE,P(c);rep 8.00

62/63 **(167)** GE,P(c);rep 7.00
10/64 **(167)** GE,P(c);rep 7.00
08/67 **(166)** GE,P(c);rep 7.00
Sg/70 **(169)** GE,P(c),25ᐟ(c)
  Price, Rigid(c);rep. 7.00

138-A JOURNEY TO THE CENTER OF THE EARTH
By Jules Verne
05/57 **(136)** NN,P(c),Original. 45.00
09/58 **(146)** NN,P(c);rep 8.00
05/60 **(156)** NN,P(c);rep 8.00
09/60 **(158)** NN,P(c);rep 8.00
62/63 **(167)** NN,P(c);rep 8.00
06/64 **(167)** NN,P(c);rep 9.00
04/66 **(167)** NN,P(c);rep 9.00
1968 **(166)** NN,P(c),25ᐟ(c)Price;rep. 7.00

139-IN THE REIGN OF TERROR
By George Alfred Henty
07/57 **(139)** GE,P(c),Original. 25.00
01/60 **(154)** GE,P(c);rep 10.00
62/63 **(167)** GE,P(c),Erroneusly
  Has Original Date;rep. 7.00
07/64 **(167)** GE,P(c);rep 10.00
1968 **(166)** GE,P(c),25ᐟ(c)Price;rep. 7.00

140-ON JUNGLE TRAILS
By Frank Buck
09/57 **(140)** NN,P(c),Original. 25.00
05/59 **(150)** NN,P(c);rep 8.00
01/61 **(160)** NN,P(c);rep 8.00
09/63 **(167)** NN,P(c);rep 7.00
09/65 **(167)** NN,P(c);rep 7.00

141-CASTLE DANGEROUS
By Sir Walter Scott
11/57 **(141)** StC,P(c),Original 42.00
09/59 **(152)** STC,P(c);rep 9.00
62/63 **(167)** StC,P(c);rep. 7.00
07/67 **(166)** StC,P(c);rep. 7.00

142-ABRAHAM LINCOLN
By Benjamin Thomas
01/58 **(142)** NN,P(c),Original. 40.00
01/60 **(154)** NN,P(c);rep 8.00
09/60 **(158)** NN,P(c);rep 8.00
10/63 **(167)** NN,P(c);rep 7.00
07/65 **(167)** NN,P(c);rep 7.00
11/67 **(166)** NN,P(c);rep 7.00
Fl/69 **(169)** NN,P(c),25ᐟ(c) Price,
  Rigid(c);rep 7.00

143-KIM
By Rudyard Kipling
03/58 **(143)** JO,P(c)Original 30.00
62/63 **(165)** JO,P(c);rep 7.00
11/63 **(167)** JO,P(c);rep 7.00
08/65 **(167)** JO,P(c);rep 7.00
Wr/69 **(169)** JO,P(c),25ᐟ(c) Price,
  Rigid(c);rep 7.00

144-THE FIRST MEN IN THE MOON
By H. G. Wells
05/58 **(143)** GWb,AW,AT,RKr,GMC
  P(c), Original 35.00
11/59 **(153)** GWb,AW,AT,RKr,GMC
  P(c); rep. 8.00
03/61 **(161)** GWb,AW,AT,RKr,GMC
  P(c); rep. 7.00

62/63 **(167)** GWb,AW,AT,RKr,GMC
  P(c); rep. 7.00
12/65 **(167)** GWb,AW,AT,RKr,GMC
  P(c); rep. 7.00
Fl/68 **(166)** GWb,AW,AT,RKr,GMC
  P(c),25ᐟ(c) Price,Rigid(c);rep . . 7.00
Wr/69 **(169)** GWb,AW,AT,RKr,GMC
  P(c), Rigid(c);rep 18.00

145-THE CRISIS
by Winston Churchill
07/58 **(143)** GE,P(c),Original. 35.00
05/60 **(156)** GE,P(c);rep 9.00
10/63 **(167)** GE,P(c);rep 7.00
03/65 **(167)** GE,P(c);rep 7.00
1968 **(166)** GE,P(c),25ᐟ(c)Price;rep. 7.00

146-WITH FIRE AND SWORD
By Henryk Sienkiewicz
09/58 **(143)** GWb,P(c),Original . . . 40.00
05/60 **(156)** GWb,P(c);rep. 12.00
11/63 **(167)** GWb,P(c);rep. 12.00
03/65 **(167)** GWb,P(c);rep. 12.00

147-BEN-HUR
By Lew Wallace
11/58 **(147)** JO,P(c),Original 35.00
11/59 **(153)** JO,P(c);rep 40.00
09/60 **(158)** JO,P(c);rep 7.00
62/63 **(167)** JO,P(c),Has the
  Original Date;rep 7.00
----- **(167)** JO,P(c);rep 7.00
02/65 **(167)** JO,P(c);rep 7.00
09/66 **(167)** JO,P(c);rep 7.00
Fl/68 **(166)** JO,P(c),25ᐟ(c)Price,
  Both Rigid & Soft (c)s;rep. . . . 35.00

148-THE BUCKANEER
By Lyle Saxon
01/59 **(148)** GE&RJ,NS P(c),orig. . 30.00
----- **(568)** GE&RJ,NS P(c),Juniors
  List Only;rep. 10.00
62/63 **(167)** GE&RJ,NS P(c);rep . . . 7.00
09/65 **(167)** GE&RJ,NS P(c);rep . . . 7.00
Sr/69 **(169)** GE&RJ,NS P(c),25ᐟ(c)
  Price, Rigid(c);rep. 7.00

149-OFF ON A COMET
By Jules Verne
03/59 **(149)** GMc,P(c),Original . . . 35.00
03/60 **(155)** GMc,P(c);rep. 9.00
03/61 **(149)** GMc,P(c);rep. 9.00
12/63 **(167)** GMc,P(c);rep. 7.00
02/65 **(167)** GMc,P(c);rep. 7.00
10/66 **(167)** GMc,P(c);rep. 7.00
Fl/68 **(166)** GMc,EdM New P(c),
  25ᐟ(c)Price;rep 20.00

150-THE VIRGINIAN
By Owen Winster
05/59 **(150)** NN,DrG P(c),Original . 40.00
1961 **(164)** NN,DrG P(c);rep 20.00
62/63 **(167)** NN,DrG P(c);rep 25.00
12/65 **(167)** NN,DrG P(c);rep 20.00

151-WON BY THE SWORD
By George Alfred Henty
07/59 **(150)** JTg,P(c),Original 40.00
1961 **(164)** JTg,P(c);rep 15.00
10/63 **(167)** JTg,P(c);rep 15.00
1963 **(167)** JTg,P(c);rep 15.00
07/67 **(166)** JTg,P(c);rep 15.00

CI #149, Off on a Comet
© Gilberton Publications

152-WILD ANIMALS I HAVE KNOWN
By Ernest Thompson Seton
09/59 **(152)** LbC,LbC P(c),Original 45.00
03/61 **(149)** LbC,LbC P(c),P(c);rep . 8.00
09/63 **(167)** LbC,LbC P(c);rep. 7.00
08/65 **(167)** LbC,LbC P(c);rep. 7.00
fl/69 **(169)** LbC,LbC P(c),25ᐟ(c)
  Price, Rigid(c);rep. 7.00

153-THE INVISIBLE MAN
By H. G. Wells
11/59 **(153)** NN,GB P(c),Original. . 45.00
03/61 **(149)** NN,GB P(c);rep 9.00
62/63 **(167)** NN,GB P(c);rep 7.00
02/65 **(167)** NN,GB P(c);rep 7.00
09/66 **(167)** NN,GB P(c);rep 7.00
Wr/69 **(166)** NN,GB P(c),25ᐟ(c)
  Price, Rigid(c);rep. 7.00
Sg/71 **(169)** NN,GB P(c),Rigid(c),
  Words Spelling'Invisible Man'
  Are' Solid'Not'Invisible';rep 7.00

154-THE CONSPIRACY OF PONTIAC
By Francis Parkman
01/60 **(154)** GMc,GMc P(c),
  Original 45.00
11/63 **(167)** GMc,GMc P(c);rep . . . 18.00
07/64 **(167)** GMc,GMc P(c);rep. . . 18.00
12/67 **(166)** GMc,GMc P(c);rep. . . 18.00

155-THE LION OF THE NORTH
By George Alfred Henty
03/60 **(154)** NN,GMc P(c),Original 42.00
01/64 **(167)** NN,GMc P(c);rep 15.00
1967 **(166)** NN,GMc P(c),25ᐟ(c)
  Price; rep 12.00

156-THE CONQUEST OF MEXICO
By Bernal Diaz Del Castillo
05/60 **(156)** BPr,BPr P(c),Original . 40.00
01/64 **(167)** BPr,BPr P(c);rep 12.00
08/67 **(166)** BPr,BPr P(c);rep 12.00
Sg/70 **(169)** BPr,BPr P(c),25ᐟ(c)
  Price; Rigid(c);rep. 10.00

Classics Illus.

157-LIVES OF THE HUNTED
By Ernest Thompson Seton
07/60 **(156)** NN,LbC P(c),Original . 45.00
02/64 **(167)** NN,LbC P(c);rep 16.00
10/67 **(166)** NN,LbC P(c);rep 16.00

158-THE CONSPIRATORS
By Alexandre Dumas
09/60 **(156)** GMc,GMc P(c),
  Original 42.00
07/64 **(167)** GMc,GMc P(c);rep... 16.00
10/67 **(166)** GMc,GMc P(c);rep... 16.00

159-THE OCTOPUS
By Frank Norris
11/60 **(159)** GM&GE,LbC P(c),
  Original 42.00
02/64 **(160)** GM&GE,LbC P(c);rep 16.00
166 **(1967)** GM&GE,LbC P(c),25·(c)
  Price;rep 16.00

160-THE FOOD OF THE GODS
By H.G. Wells
01/61 **(159)** TyT,GMc P(c),Original 45.00
01/61 **(160)** TyT,GMc P(c),Original;
  Same Except For the HRN#.. 40.00
01/64 **(167)** TyT,GMc P(c);rep.... 16.00
06/67 **(166)** TyT,GMc P(c);rep.... 16.00

161-CLEOPATRA
By H. Rider Haggard
03/61 **(161)** NN,Pch P(c),Original . 45.00
01/64 **(167)** NN,Pch P(c);rep..... 20.00
08/67 **(166)** NN,Pch P(c);rep..... 20.00

162-ROBUR THE CONQUEROR
By Jules Verne
05/61 **(162)** GM&DPn,CJ P(c),
  Original 45.00
07/64 **(167)** GM&DPn,CJ P(c);rep. 16.00
08/67 **(166)** GM&DPn,CJ P(c);rep. 16.00

163-MASTER OF THE WORLD
By Jules Verne
07/61 **(163)** GM,P(c),Original 40.00
01/65 **(167)** GM,P(c);rep........ 16.00
1968 **(166)** GM,P(c),25·(c)
  Price;rep 16.00

164-THE COSSACK CHIEF
By Nicolai Gogol
1961 **(164)** SyM,P(c),Original 40.00
04/65 **(167)** SyM,P(c);rep....... 16.00
Fl/68 **(166)** SyM,P(c),25·(c)
  Price;rep 16.00

165-THE QUEEN'S NECKLACE
by Alexandre Dumas
01/62 **(164)** GM,P(c),Original 40.00
04/65 **(167)** GM,P(c);rep........ 16.00
Fl/68 **(166)** GM,P(c),25·(c)
  Price;rep 16.00

166-TIGERS AND TRAITORS
By Jules Verne
05/62 **(165)** NN,P(c),Original..... 80.00
02/64 **(167)** NN,P(c);rep........ 30.00
11/66 **(167)** NN,P(c);rep........ 30.00

167-FAUST
By Johann Wolfgang von Goethe
08/62 **(165)** NN,NN P(c),Original. 110.00
02/64 **(167)** NN,NN P(c);rep..... 50.00
06/67 **(166)** NN,NN P(c);rep..... 50.00

168-IN FREEDOM'S CAUSE
By George Alfred Henty
Wr/69 **(169)** GE&RC,P(c),
  Original, Rigid (c) 130.00

169-NEGRO AMERICANS THE EARLY YEARS
AUTHOR UNKNOWN
Sg/69 **(166)** NN,NN P(c),
  Original, Rigid(c). 100.00
Sg/69 **(169)** NN,NN P(c),
  Rigid; rep 60.00
See Also:
Independent Color Listings

CLASSICS ILLUSTRATED GIANTS
An Illustrated Library of Great
Adventure Stories
 -(reps. of Issues 6,7,8,10) . 1,200.00
An Illustrated Library of Exciting
Mystery Stories
 -(reps. of Issues 30,21,
  40,13) 1,300.00
An Illustrated Library of Great
Indian Stories
 -(reps. of Issues 4,17,22,
  37) 1,200.00

CLASSICS ILLUSTRATED JUNIOR
501-Snow White and the
  Seven Dwarves 75.00
502-The Ugly Duckling 50.00
503-Cinderella 30.00
504-The Pied Piper........... 20.00
505-The Sleeping Beauty 20.00
506-The Three Little Pigs 20.00
507-Jack and the Beanstalk 20.00
508-Goldilocks and the Three
  Bears 20.00
509-Beauty and the Beast 20.00
510-Little Red Riding Hood..... 20.00
511-Puss-N-Boots........... 20.00
512-Rumpelstilskin 20.00
513-Pinnochio 35.00
514-The Steadfast Tin Soldier.... 45.00
515-Johnny Appleseed........ 20.00
516-Alladin and His Lamp...... 25.00
517-The Emperor's New Clothes . 20.00
518-The Golden Goose 20.00
519-Paul Bunyan 20.00
520-Thumbelina 28.00
521-King of the golden River..... 20.00
522-The Nightingale 15.00
523-The Gallant Tailor 15.00
524-The Wild Swans.......... 15.00
525-The Little Mermaid........ 22.00
526-The Frog Prince.......... 20.00

527-The Golden-Haired Giant.... 15.00
528-The Penny Prince 15.00
529-The Magic Servants....... 15.00
530-The Golden Bird 15.00
531-Rapunzel............... 20.00
532-The Dancing Princesses 16.00
533-The Magic Fountain....... 16.00
534-The Golden Touch....... 16.00
535-The Wizard of Oz......... 35.00
536-The Chimney Sweep 20.00
537-The Three Faires......... 20.00
538-Silly Hans 20.00
539-The Enchanted Fish....... 30.00
540-The Tinder-Box 30.00
541-Snow White and Rose Red .. 20.00
542-The Donkey's Tail 20.00
543-The House in the Woods 18.00
544-The Golden Fleece 35.00
545-The Glass Mountain....... 22.00
546-The Elves and the Shoemaker 20.00
547-The Wishing Table........ 20.00
548-The Magic Pitcher 15.00
549-Simple Kate............. 15.00
550-The Singing Donkey 15.00
551-The Queen Bee......... 15.00
552-The Three Little Dwarves.... 20.00
553-King Thrushbeard 15.00
554-The Enchanted Deer 15.00
555-The Three Golden Apples ... 15.00
556-The Elf Mound........... 15.00
557-Silly Willy.............. 30.00
558-The Magic Dish 30.00
559-The Japanese Lantern..... 35.00
560-The Doll Princess 35.00
561-Hans Humdrum 20.00
562-The Enchanted Pony 35.00
563-The Wishing Well......... 15.00
564-The Salt Mountain 15.00
565-The Silly Princess 15.00
566-Clumsy Hans............ 15.00
567-The Bearskin Soldier 15.00
568-The Happy Hedgehog 15.00
569-The Three Giants......... 15.00
570-The Pearl Princess 15.00
571-How Fire Came to the Indians 22.00
572-The Drummer Boy 22.00
573-The Crystal Ball.......... 22.00
574-Brightboots 18.00
575-The Fearless Prince....... 22.00
576-The Princess Who Saw
  Everything 32.00
577-The Runaway Dumpling..... 40.00

CLASSICS ILLLUSTRATED SPECIAL ISSUE
N# United Nations 250.00
129-The Story of Jesus........ 65.00
132A-The Story of America...... 45.00
135A-The Ten Commandments... 50.00
138A-Adventures in Science..... 40.00
141A-The Rough Rider........ 45.00
144A-Blazing the Trails........ 40.00
147A-Crossing the Rockies...... 50.00
150A-Royal Canadian Police 45.00
153A-Men, Guns, and Cattle..... 45.00
156A-The Atomic Age......... 45.00
159A-Rockets, Jets and Missles... 45.00
162A-War Between the States .. 100.00
165A-To the Stars........... 50.00
166A-World War II 75.00
167A-Prehistoric World........ 80.00

AMAZING DOPE TALES
Greg Shaw
1 Untrimmed black and white pages,
  out of order;artist unknown . . 110.00
2 Trimmed and proper pages. . . . 95.00

AMERICAN SPLENDOR
Harvey Pekar May, 1976
1 B:Harvey Pekar Stories,
  HP,RCr,GDu,GBu 20.00
2 HP,RCr,GDu,GBu 10.00
3 HP,RCr,GDu,GBu 10.00
4 HP,RCr,GDu,GBu 8.00
5 HP,RCr,GDu,GBu 8.00
6 HP,RCr,GDu,GBu,GSh 7.00
7 HP,GSh,GDu,GBu 5.00
8 HP,GSh,GDu,GBu 3.00
9 and 10 HP,GSh,GDu,GBu. . . . @3.00
11 . . . . 3.00
12 . . . . 4.50
13 thru 19. . . . . @3.50
20 E:Harvey Pekar Stories 4.00

ANTHOLOGY OF SLOW DEATH
Wingnut Press/Last Gasp
1 140 pgs, RCr,RCo, GiS, DSh,
  Harlan Ellison VB,RTu 37.00

APEX TREASURY OF UNDERGROUND COMICS, THE
Links Books Inc. Oct.,1974
1 . . . . 40.00

APEX TREASURY OF UNDERGROUND COMICS –BEST OF BIJOU FUNNIES
Quick Fox 1981
1 Paperback,comix,various artists 21.00

ARCADE THE COMICS REVUE
Print Mint Inc. Spring, 1975
1 ASp,BG,RCr,SRo,SCW. 16.50
2 ASp,BG,RCr,SRo 12.00
3 ASp,BG,RCr,RW,SCW 8.50
4 ASp,BG,RCr,WBu,RW,SCW . . . 8.50
5 thru 7 ASp,BG,SRo,RW,SCW . @7.50

BABYFAT
Comix World/Clay Geerdes 1978
1 B:8pg news parodies, one page
  comix by various artists 4.50
2 thru 9 same . . . . @3.00
10 thru 26 same . . . . @2.00

BATTLE OF THE TITANS
University of Illinois SF Society 1972
1 Sci-Fi;VB,JGa 50.00

BEST BUY COMICS
Last Gasp Eco-Funnies
1 Rep Whole Earth Review;RCr. . . 3.50

BEST OF BIJOU FUNNIES, THE
Links Books Inc. 1975
1 164 pgs,paperback 235.00

BEST OF RIP-OFF PRESS
Rip Off Press Inc. 1973
1 132 pgs paperback,SCW,
  RCr,SRo,RW 25.00
2 100 pgs,GS,FT 27.50
3 100 pgs,FS. 10.75
4 132 pgs,GiS,DSh 13.00

BIG ASS
Rip Off Press 1969–71
1 28 pgs,RCr. 80.00
2 RCr 50.00

BIJOU FUNNIES
Bijou Publishing Empire 1968
1 B:JLy,editor;RCr,GS SW 285.00
2 RCr,GS,SW 110.00
3 RCr,SWi,JsG 60.00
4 SWi,JsG 30.00
5 SWi,JsG. 33.50
6 E:JLy,editor,SWi,RCr,JsG 27.00
7 and 8 . . . . @26.00

BINKY BROWN MEETS THE HOLY VIRGIN MARY
Last Gasp Eco-Funnies March, 1972
N# Autobiography about Growing up
  w/a Catholic Neurosis,JsG. . . 22.50
2nd Printing:only text in
  bottom left panel. 12.00

BIZARRE SEX
Kitchen Sink Komix May, 1972
1 B:DKi,editor,various
  artists 27.00
2 . . . . 22.00
3 . . . . 16.00
4 thru 6 . . . . @11.00
7 . . . . 4.00
8 . . . . 3.50
9 Omaha the Cat Dancer,RW . . . 16.50

Bizarre Sex #10
© Kitchen Sink

10 inc.Omaha the Cat
  Dancer,RW. 12.50

BLACK LAUGHTER
Black Laughter Pub. Co, Nov. 1972
1 James Dixon art 64.00

BLOOD FROM A STONE (GUIDE TO TAX REFORM)
New York Public Interest Research Group Inc. 1977
1 Tax reform proposals 8.50

BOBBY LONDON RETROSPECTIVE AND ART PORTFOLIO
Cartoonist Representatives
1 . . . . 19.50

BOBMAN AND TEDDY
Parrallax Comic Books Inc 1966
1 RFK & Ted Kennedy's struggle to
  control Democratic party. 35.50

BODE'S CARTOON CONCERT
Dell Sept., 1973
1 132 pgs; VB 27.50

BOGEYMAN COMICS
San Fransisco Comic Book Co., 1969
1 Horror,RHa. 55.00
2 Horror,RHa . . . .
42.00@WP Heading 1:The Company &
Sons
3 . . . . 31.00

BUFFALO RAG/THE DEAD CONCERT COMIX
Kenny Laramey Dec. 1973
1 Alice in Wonderland parody . . . 55.00

CAPTAIN GUTS
The Print Mint 1969
1 Super patriotV:Counter
  culture 26.50
2 V:Black Panthers 19.00
3 V:Dope Smugglers 19.00

CAPTAIN STICKY
Captain Sticky 1974–75
1 Super lawyer V:SocialInjustice . 17.50

CARTOON HISTORY OF THE UNIVERSE
Rip Off Press Sept., 1978
1 Evolution of Everything;
  B:Larry Gonick 6.50
2 Sticks and Stones 6.50
3 River Realms-Sumer & Egypt . 6.50
4 Part of the Old Testament 4.50
5 Brains and Bronze 4.50
6 Who are these Athenians 3.75

Underground

CASCADE COMIX MONTHLY
Everyman Studios March, 1978
1 Interviews,articles about
comix & comix artists 6.50
2 and 3 same . . . . @6.50
4 thru 11 . . . . @3.00
12 thru 23 . . . . @2.25

CHECKERED DEMON
Last Gasp July, 1977
1 SCW 13.00
2 SCW 8.50
3 SCW 6.50

CHEECH WIZARD
Office of Student Publications, Syracuse U 1967
n/n VB 120.00

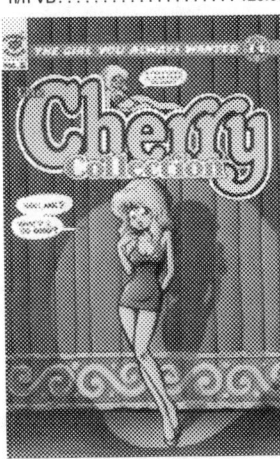

Cherry Collection TPB #2
© Kitchen Sink

CHERRY
Kitchen Sink
1 by Larry Welz 7.50
2 . . . . 6.00
3 thru 5 . . . . @5.00
6 thru 10 . . . . @4.00
11 thru 15 . . . . @3.50
TPB Cherry Collection #1 . . . . 15.00
TPB Cherry Collection #2 . . . . 15.00
TPB Cherry Collection #3 . . . . . . 12.95
Cherry's Jubilee #1 thru #4 . . . . . @3.00

CHICAGO MIRROR
Jay Lynch/Mirror Publishing Empire Autumn, 1967
1 B:Bijou Funnies 45.00
2 same 35.00
3 same 115.00

COLLECTED CHEECH WIZARD, THE
Company & Sons 1972
n/n VB 55.00

COLLECTED TRASHMAN #1, THE
Fat City & The Red Mountain Tribe Productions
n/n SRo 32.50

COMICS & COMIX
October, 1975
1 . . . . 12.00

COMIX BOOK
Magazine Management Co. Oct., 1974
1 . . . . Compilation for newsstand
distribution 14.50
2 and 3 . . . . @9.00
Kitchen Sink Enterprises
4 . . . . 14.50
5 . . . . 8.50

COMIX COLLECTOR, THE
Archival Press Inc. Dec., 1979
1 Fanzine 5.00
2 & 3 Fanzine . . . . @4.00

COMMIES FROM MARS
Kitchen Sink March, 1973
1 TB 32.50
Last Gasp
2 thru 5 TB . . . . @9.50

COMPLETE FRITZ THE CAT
Belier Press 1978
n/n RCr,SRo,DSh 55.00

CONSPIRACY CAPERS
The Conspiracy 1969
1 . . . .
Benefit Legal Defense of the
Chicago-8 . . . . 79.00

DAN O'NEIL'S COMICS & STORIES
Company & Sons, VOL.1
1 B:Dan O'Neill 45.00
2 & 3 . . . . @30.00
1971 VOL.2
1 . . . . 6.50
2 and E:Dan O'Neil . . . . @4.50

DAS KAMPF
Vaughn Bode May, 1963
N# 100 Loose pgs. 750.00
2nd Printing 52pgs.-produced by
Walter Bachner&Bagginer,1977 9.50

DEADBONE EROTICA
Bantam Books Inc. April, 1971
n/n 132 pgs VB 45.00

DEADCENTER CLEAVAGE
April, 1971
1 14 pgs 40.00

DEATH RATTLE
Kitchen Sink June, 1972
1 RCo,TB 25.00
2 TB 20.00
3 TB 16.00

DESPAIR
The Print Mint 1969
1 RCr 33.00

DIRTY DUCK BOOK, THE
Company & Sons March, 1972
1 Bobby London 25.00

DISNEY RAPES THE 1st AMENDMENT
Dan O'Neil 1974
1 Benefit Air Pirates V:Disney
Law suit; Dan O'Neill 8.50

DOPE COMIX
Kitchen Sink Feb., 1978
1 Drugs comix;various artists 7.50
2 same 5.75
3 & 4 LSD issue . . . . @4.00
5 Omaha the Cat Dancer, RW . . . 10.00

DOPIN DAN
Last Gasp Eco-Funnies April, 1972
1 TR 12.00
2 and 3 TR . . . . @8.50
4 Todays Army,TR 7.50

DR. ATOMIC
Last Gasp Eco-Funnies Sept., 1972
1 B:Larry S. Todd 12.00
2 and 3 . . . . @10.00
4 . . . . 7.50
5 E:Larry S. Todd 4.75

DR. ATOMIC'S MARIJUANA MULTIPLIER
Kistone Press 1974
1 How to grow great pot 7.50

DRAWINGS BY S. CLAY WILSON
San Francisco Graphics
1 28 pgs 185.00

DYING DOLPHIN
The Print Mint 1970
n/n 14.50

EBON
San Francisco Comic Book Company
1 Comix version; RCr 25.00
1 Tabloid version 18.00

EL PERFECTO COMICS
The Print Mint 1973
N# Benefit Timothy Leary 27.00
2nd Printing-1975 . . . . 4.00

ETERNAL TRUTH
Sunday Funnies Comic Corp
1 Christian Comix 19.50

EVERMUCH WAVE
Atlantis Distributors
1 Nunzio the Narc; Adventures
    of God 60.00

The Fabulous Furry Freak Brothers #9
© Rip Off Press

FABULOUS FURRY FREAK BROTHERS, THE
COLLECTED ADVENTURES OF
Rip Off Press #1 Feb., 1971
1 GiS 75.00
FURTHER ADVENTURES OF
Rip Off Press #2
1 GiS,DSh 47.50
A YEAR PASSES LIKE NOTHING WITH
Rip Off Press #3
1 GiS. 17.00
BROTHER CAN YOU SPARE $.75 FOR
Rip Off Press #4
1 GiS,DSh 12.00
FABULOUS FURRY FREAK BROTHERS, THE
Rip Off Press #5
1 GiS,DSh 9.50
SIX SNAPPY SOCKERS FROM THE ARCHIVES OF
Rip Off Press #6
1 GiS 5.25

FANTAGOR
1970
1 (Corben), fanzine 100.00
1a (Last Gasp) 22.00
2 & 3 . . . . @20.00
4 . . . .
30.00

THE ADVENTURES OF FAT FREDDY'S CAT,
Rip Off Press Feb., 1977
1 . . . . 14.00
2 . . . . 4.50
3 . . . . 6.00
4 . . . . 5.00
5 & 6 . . . . @2.50

FEDS 'N' HEADS
Gilbert Shelton/Print Mint 1968
N# l:Fabulous Furry Freak Bros.;
    Has no `Print Mint' Address
    24 pgs. 350.00
2nd printing, 28 pgs. 55.00
3rd printing, May, 1969 . . . . 45.00
4th printing, Says `Forth
    Printing' 17.50
5th-12th printings . . . . @8.00
13th printing 6.50
14th printing 4.75

FELCH
Keith Green
1 RW,SCW,RCr 40.00

FEVER PITCH
Kitchen Sink Enterprises July, 1976
1 RCo 20.00
Jabberwocky Graphix
2 250 signed & numbered 14.50
3 400 signed & numbered 13.50
4 . . . . 8.50

50'S FUNNIES
Kitchen Sink Enterprises 1980
1 Larry Shell, editor,various
    artists 5.00

FLAMING CARROT
Kilian Barracks Free Press 1981
1 Bob Budden,various artists 10.00

FLASH THEATRE
Oogle Productions 1970
1 44 pgs 37.50

FLESHAPOIDS FROM EARTH
Popular Culture Dec., 1974
1 36 pgs 33.00

THE COMPLETE FOO!
Bijou Publishing Sept., 1980
1 RCr, Charles Crumb, r:Crumb
    brothers fanzines 40.00

FRITZ BUGS OUT
Ballentine Books 1972
n/n RCr 60.50

FRITZ THE CAT
Ballentine Books 1969
n/n RCr. 120.00

FRITZ THE NO-GOOD
Ballentine Books 1972
n/n RCr 50.00

FRITZ: SECRET AGENT FOR THE CIA
Ballentine Books 1972
n/n RCr 45.00

FUNNY AMINALS
Apex Novelties/Don Donahue 1972
1 RCr 60.00

GAY COMIX
Kitchen Sink Sept., 1981
1 36 pgs 7.50
2 36 pgs 5.00

GEN OF HIROSHIMA
Educomics/Leonard Rifas Jan., 1980
1 Antiwar comix by Hiroshima
    survivor Keiji Nakawaza 9.50
2 same 6.50

GHOST MOTHER COMICS
John "Mad" Peck 1969
1 SCw,JsG 47.50

GIMMEABREAK COMIX
Rhuta Press Feb., 1971
2 . . . .
48 pgs, #0 & #1 were advertised,but . .
may not have been printed 95.00

GIRLS & BOYS
Lynda J. Barry 1980
1 B:12 pgs with every other page
    blank, all Barry art 8.00
2 thru 10 same. . . . . @6.50
11 thru 20 same . . . . @4.50
20 thru 25 same . . . . @3.50

GOD NOSE
Jack Jackson/ Rip Off Press 1964
N# 42 pgs. 995.00
2nd printing,Pinkish(c);44p. 60.00
3rd printing,Blue Border(c) 30.00
4th printing,Red Border(c) 15.00

GOTHIC BLIMP WORKS LTD.
East Village Other/ Peter Leggieri 1969
1 VB,Editor,various artists 185.00
2 same 145.00
3 KDe,editor 135.00
4 KDe,editor 130.00
5 thru 7 KDe,editor. . . . . @125.00
8 various artists 185.00

GREASER COMICS
Half-Ass Press Sept. 1971
1 28 pgs, George DiCaprio 17.50
Rip Off Press July 1972
2 George DiCaprio. 10.00

GRIM WIT
Last Gasp 1972
1 RCo 35.00
2 RCo 25.00

HAROLD HEAD, THE COLLECTED ADVENTURES OF
Georgia Straight 1972
1 . . . . 45.00
2 . . . . 10.00

HARRY CHESS THAT MAN FROM A.U.N.T.I.E.
The Uncensored Adventures
Trojan Book Service 1966
N# 1st Comix By & For Gay
Community 100.00

HEAR THE SOUND OF MY FEET WALKING....
Glide Urban Center 1969
1 Dan O'Neill, 128 pgs 65.00

HISTORY OF UNDERGROUND COMIX
Straight Arrow Books 1974
1 Book by Mark James Estren about
Underground Comix 30.00

HOMEGROWN FUNNIES
Kitchen Sink 1971
1 RCr 45.00

HONKYTONK SUE, THE QUEEN OF COUNTRY SWING
Bob Boze Bell Feb., 1979
1 BBB 7.00
2 & 3 BBB . . . . @5.00

IKE LIVES
Warm Neck Funnies 1973
1 20 pgs,Mark Fisher 10.00

INSECT FEAR
Last Gasp 1970
1 SRo,GiS,RHa,JsG 75.00
Print Mint 1970–72
2 . . . . 30.00
3 . . . . 20.00

IT AIN'T ME BABE
Last Gasp Eco-Funnies July. 1970
n/n First all women comix
Womens Liberation theme . . . 32.50

JAPANESE MONSTER
Carol Lay July, 1979
1 8pgs, Carol Lay 5.00

JESUS LOVES YOU
Zondervan Books/Craig Yoe

1972
1 Christian, RCr 29.50

THE NEW ADVENTURES OF JESUS
Rip Off Press Nov., 1971
1 44 pgs, FSt. 50.00

JIZ
Apex Novelty 1969
1 36 pgs; RCr, SRo, VMo, SCW; hand
trimmed and unevenly stapled 45.00

JUNKWAFFEL
The Print Mint 1971
1 VB 30.00
2 and 3 VB . . . . @25.00
4 VB,JJ 18.00

KANNED KORN KOMIX
Canned Heat Fan Club 1969
1 20pgs. 8.00

KAPTAIN AMERIKA KOMIX
Brief Candle Comix March 1970
1 anti U.S. involvement in Laos. . . 27.50

KING BEE
Apex/Don Donahue & Kerry Clark 1969
1 RCr,SCW 120.00

KURTZMAN COMIX
Kitchen Sink Sept., 1976
1 HK,RCr,GiS,DKi,WE 20.00

LAUGH IN THE DARK
Last Gasp
n/n KDe,RHa,SRo,SCW 14.00

LENNY OF LAVEDO
Sunbury Productions/Print Mint 1965
N# Green(c);1st Joel Beck-a . . . 545.00
2nd printing, Orange(c) 390.00
3rd printing, White(c) 195.00

THE MACHINES
Office of Student Publications Syracuse University 1967
1 VB 125.00

THE MAN
Office of Student Publications Syracuse University 1966
1 VB 155.00

MAGGOTZINE
Charles Schneider May, 1981
1 Various Artists,conceptual
maggot stuff 3.50

MANTICORE
Joe Kubert School of Cartooning & Graphic Arts Inc.

Autumn, 1976
1 Fanzine,various artists 7.50

MEAN BITCH THRILLS
The Print Mint 1971
1 SRO. 7.00

MICKEY RAT
Los Angeles Comic Book Co. May, 1972
1 Robert Armstrong 32.50
2 same 29.00
3 same 9.50

MOM'S HOMEMADE COMICS
Kitchen Sink June 1969
1 DKi, RCr. 125.00
The Print Mint
2 DKi. 35.00
Kitchen Sink Enterprises
3 DKi,RCr 17.00

MONDAY FUNNIES, THE
Monday Funnies 1977
1 8pgs,various artists 6.50
2 16pgs,various artists 9.00
3 16pgs,various artists 6.50
4 16pgs,various artists 5.50

MONDAY FUNNIES, THE
Passtime Publ. July–Aug., 1980
1 thru 8 Marc L.Reed . . . . @4.00

MOUSE LIBERATION FRONT
COMMUNIQUE #2 August, 1979
1 SRo, SCW, VMo,DKi; Disney's sues
Dan O'Neil's Air Pirates 9.50

MOONCHILD COMICS
Nicola Cuti 1968
0 Nicola Cuti 27.00
2 Nicola Cuti 27.00
3 Nicola Cuti 75.00

MOONDOG
The Print Mint March, 1970
1 All George Metzer. 11.00
2 same 6.50
3 and 4 same. . . . . @3.75

MORE ADVENTURES OF FAT FREDDY'S CAT
Rip Off Press Jan., 1981
1 GiS. 14.00

MOTOR CITY COMICS
Rip Off Press April, 1969
1 RCr 165.00
2 RCr 125.00

MR. NATURAL
San Fransisco Comic Book Co. August, 1970
1 RCr 100.00
2 RCr 50.00

Omaha, The Cat Dancer #1
© Reed Waller

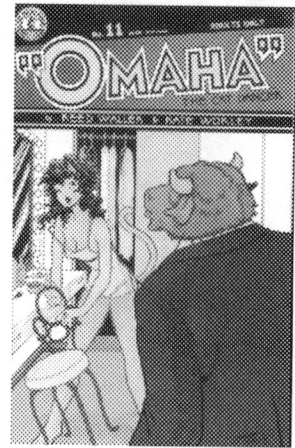

Omaha, The Cat Dancer #11
© Reed Waller

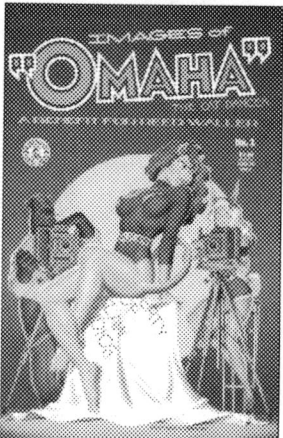

Images of Omaha, Book 1
© Reed Waller

Kitchen Sink
3 RCr, (B&W) 20.00

**NARD 'N' PAT,
JAYZEY LYNCH'S**
Cartoonists Cooperative Press
March, 1974
1 Jay Lynch. 7.00
2 Jay Lynch. 4.50
Kitchen Sink Press 1972
3 . . . . 10.00

NEVERWHERE
Ariel Inc. Feb., 1978
1 RCo 17.50

NICKEL LIBRARY
Gary Arlington
1 1 pg heavy stock colored
   paper, Reed Crandall 5.00
2 Kim Deitch 1.50
3 Harrison Cady 1.50
4 Frank Frazetta 4.00
5 Will Eisner 4.00
6 Justin Green. 1.50
7 C.C. Beck 4.00
8 Wally Wood 4.00
9 Winsor McCay 1.50
10 Jim Osborne 1.50
11 Don Towley. 1.50
12 Frank Frazetta. 4.00
13 Will Eisner. 4.00
14 Bill Griffith 1.50
15 George Herriman. 1.50
16 Cliff Sterrett. 1.50
17 George Herriman. 1.50
18 Rory Hayes & Simon Deitch. . . . 1.50
19 Disney Studios 2.00
20 Alex Toth 2.00
21 Will Eisner 2.00
22 Jack Davis. 3.00
23 Alex Toth 2.00
24 Michele Brand 1.50
25 Roger Brand 1.50
26 Arnold Roth 1.50
27 Murphy Anderson 2.00
28 Wally Wood 3.00
29 Jack Kirby 4.00
30 Harvey Kurtzman. 3.00
31 Jay Kinney. 1.50

32 Bill Plimpton 1.50
33 . . . . 1.50
34 Charles Dallas. 1.50
35 thru 39 . . . . @1.50
40 Bill Edwards 1.50
41 Larry S. Todd. 1.50
42 Charles Dallas. 1.50
43 Jim Osborne 1.50
43 1/2 Larry S. Todd. 1.50
44 Jack Jackson. 1.50
45 Rick Griffin. 1.50
46 Justin Green 1.50
47 and 48 Larry S. Todd . . . . . . @1.50
49 Charles Dallas. 1.50
50 Robert Crumb 3.00
51 Wally Wood 3.00
52 Charles Dallas. 3.00
53 and 54 Larry S. Todd . . . . . . @1.50
55 Charles Dallas. 1.50
56 Jim Chase. 1.50
57 Charles Dallas. 1.50
58 Larry S. Todd. 1.50
59 Dave Geiser 1.50
60 Charles Dallas. 1.50

**ODD WORLD OF
RICHARD CORBEN**
Warren Publishing 1977
1 84pgs paperback 20.00

O.K. COMICS
Kitchen Sink June, 1972
1 and 2 Bruce Walthers . . . . . . @7.00

O.K. COMICS
O.K. Comic Company 1972
1 Tabloid with comix, articles,
   reviews, nudie cuties photos. . 27.50
2 thru 18 . . . . @18.75

**OMAHA
THE CAT DANCER**
Steel Dragon Press, 1984
1 RW,F:Omaha, Shelly, Chuck. . . 10.00
Kitchen Sink, 1986
1 RW. 9.00
2 RW 8.00
3 thru 5 . . . . 7.00
6 thru 10 . . . . 6.00

11 thru 20 . . . . 5.00
Spec.#0, 25th Anniv. Classic. . . . 15.00
Images of Omaha, RW benefit 8.00
Images No. 2 . . . . 7.00
TPB Collected Omaha #1, rep. . . . 15.00
TPB Collected Omaha #2, rep. . . . 13.00
TPB Collected Omaha #3, rep. . . . 13.00
TPB Collected Omaha #4, rep. . . . 13.00
TPB Collected Omaha #5, rep. . . . 13.00
Vol. 2, Fantagraphics, 1994
1 . . . . 5.00
2 . . . . 5.00

ORACLE COMIX
Thru Black Holes
Comix Productions Oct., 1980
1 and 2 Michael Roden . . . . . . @2.50

PENGUINS IN BONDAGE
Sorcerer Studio/
Wayne Gibson July, 1981
1 8pgs,Wayne Gibson 2.75

PHANTOM LADY
Randy Crawford June, 1978
1 Sex funnies 4.50

PHUCKED UP FUNNIES
Suny Binghamton 1969
1 ASp;insert bound in yearbook . 400.00

PINK FLOYD, THE
October, 1974
1 sold at concerts 27.50

PLASTIC MAN
Randy Crawford May, 1977
1 Sex funnies,RandyCrawford 4.00

PORK
Co-op Press May, 1974
1 SCW. 11.00

PORTFOLIO OF UNDERGROUND ART
Schanes & Schanes 1980
1 SRo,SCW,VMo,RW and many others
13 loose sheets in folder, 32pg
book, 1200 signed & numb. . . . 75.00

POWERMAN AND POWER MOWER SAFETY
Frank Burgmeir, Co.
Outdoor Power Equipment
1 VB; educational comic about power
mower safety 185.00

PROMETHIAN ENTERPRISES
Promethian Enterprises Memorial Day, 1969
1 B:Jim Vadeboncuor editor 72.00
2 same 60.00
3 thru 5 . . . . @25.00

PURE ART QUARTERLY
John A. Adams July, 1976
1 16pgs, All John A.Adams 8.50
2 thru 5 same . . . . @8.50
6 thru 10 same. . . . . @5.00
11 thru 14 same . . . . @3.50

QUAGMIRE COMICS
Kitchen Sink Summer, 1970
1 DKi,Peter Poplaski 11.00

RAW
Raw Books 1980
1 36pgs,10pgs insert 310.00
2 36pgs,20pgs insert 185.00
3 52pgs,16pgs insert 155.00
4 44pgs,32pgs insert,Flexi
disk record 125.00

R. CRUMB'S COMICS AND STORIES
Rip Off Press 1969
1 RCr 90.00

RAWARARAWAR
Rip Off Press 1969
1 GSh. 55.00

RED SONJA & CONAN "HOT AND DRY"
Randy Crawford May, 1977
1 Sex funnies,Randy Crawford . . . 3.50

REID FLEMING WORLD'S TOUGHEST MILKMAN
David E. Boswell Dec., 1980
1 . . . . 6.00

RIP OFF COMIX
Rip Off Press April, 1977
1 GiS,FSt,JsG,DSh 17.50
2 thru 5 GiS,FSt. . . . . @6.00
6 thru 10 . . . . @4.25

ROWLF
Rip Off Press July, 1971
1 RCo 55.00

RUBBER DUCK TALES
The Print Mint March, 1971
1 Michael J Becker 12.00
2 Michael J Becker 11.00

S. CLAY WILSON TWENTY DRAWINGS
Abington Book Shop Inc. 1967
N# (a),Cowboy(c) 460.00
(b),Pirate(c) 460.00
(c),Motorcyclist(c) 460.00
(d),Demon(c) 460.00
(e),Deluxe with all 4
variations on same(c) with
Gold Embossed
Lettering 675.00

SAN FRANCISCO COMIC BOOK
San Francisco Comic Book Co. Jan.-Feb., 1970
1 . . . . 120.00
2 . . . . 20.00
3 . . . . 17.50
4 thru 6 . . . . @12.00

SAVAGE HUMOR
The Print Mint 1973
1 . . . . 4.00

SAY WHAT?
Loring Park Shelter Community Cartooning Workshop April, 1979
1 B:Charles T. Smith,editor,
various artists 7.00
2 thru 6 same . . . . @6.50

SCHIZOPHRENIA, CHEECH WIZARD
Last Gasp Eco-Funnies Jan., 1974
1 VB 30.00

SEX AND AFFECTION
C.P. Family Publishers 1974
1 Sex Education for Children 5.50

SHORT ORDER COMIX
Head Press/Family Fun 1973
1 50 cents,36pgs. 8.50
2 75 cents,44pgs. 2.25

SKULL COMICS
Last Gasp March, 1970
1 Horror,RHa 47.00
2 GiS,DSh,RCo 25.50
3 RCo,DSh,RCo 14.00
4 DSh,Lovecraft issue 14.00
5 SRo,RCo,Lovecraft issue 14.00
6 RCo,Herman Hesse 14.00

SLOW DEATH FUNNIES
Last Gasp April 1970
1 Ecological Awarness & Red
Border on (c) 47.00
2nd-4th Printings White
Border(c) 10.00
2 Silver(c);1st edition' 34 pgs. . . . 85.00
2b Non Silver(c);Says 1st
Edition, 34 pgs 20.00
2nd Amorphia Ad on pg 34 . . . . . . 6.75
3rd Yellow Skull on (c) 5.00
4th `Mind Candy For the Masses'
Ad on pg. 34 . . . . 5.00
5th $1.00(c) price 3.50
3 thru 5 . . . . @12.00
6 thru 10 . . . . @4.50

SMILE
Kitchen Sink Summer, 1970
1 Jim Mitchell 13.50
2 Jim Mitchell 12.00
3 Jim Mitchell 11.00

SNARF
Kitchen Sink Feb., 1972
1 DKi,editor,various artists 24.50
2 thru 5 same . . . . @15.00
6 thru 9 same . . . . @6.50

SNATCH COMICS
Apex Novelties 1968
1 . . . . RCr,SCW
295.00
2 . . . . RCr,SCW
150.00
3 RCr,SCW,RW 75.00

SNATCH SAMPLER
Keith Green 1979
n/n RCr,SCw,RW,RHa 32.00

SPACE INVADERS COMICS, DON CHIN'S
Comix World/Clay Geerdes April, 1972
1 8pgs 4.00

SPASM!
Last Gasp Eco-Funnies April, 1973
1 JJ 15.00

STONED PICTURE PARADE
San Francisco Comic Book Co., 1975
1 RCr,SRo,SCW,WE 20.00

SUBVERT COMICS
Rip Off Press Nov., 1970
1 SRo 25.00
2 SRo 20.00
3 SRo 12.00

TALES OF SEX & DEATH
Print Mint 1971
1 JsG,KDe.RHa,SRo 32.50
2 JsG,KDe.RHa,SRo 19.50

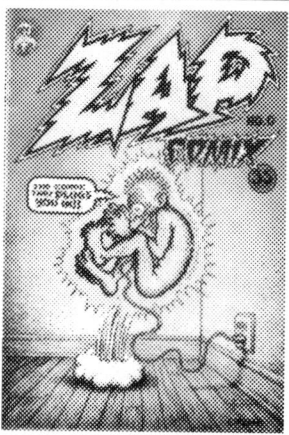

Zap #0 © Apex Novelties

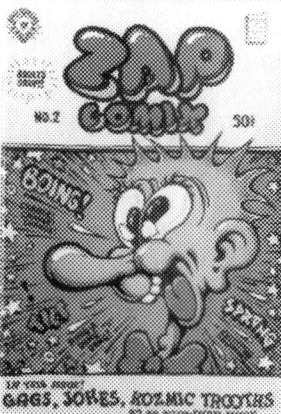

Zap #2 © Apex Novelties

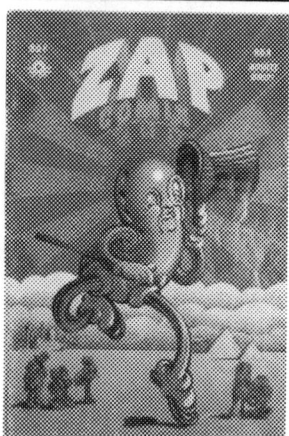

Zap #4 © Apex Novelties

THRILLING MURDER COMICS
San Francisco Comic Book Co., 1971
1 SCW,KDe,RCr,SRo,Jim Arlington,editor 24.50

2 (TWO)
Keith Green Feb., 1975
1 SCW 7.00

VAMPIRELLA
Randy Crawford June, 1978
1 Sex Funnies 3.50

VAUGHN BODE THE PORTFOLIO
Northern Comfort Com. 1976
1 VB,16pgs 125.00

VAUGHN BODE PORTFOLIO #1
Vaughn Bode Productions 1978
1 VB,10 pgs 35.00

VAUGHN BODE'S CHEECH WIZARD, THE COLLECTED ADVENTURES OF THE CARTOON MESSIAH
Northern Comfort Com. 1976
1 VB,88pgs 55.00

VAUGHN BODE'S DEADBONE, THE FIRST TESTAMENT OF CHEECH WIZARD
Northern Comfort Com. 1975
1 VB 65.00

VIETNAM
N# 20pgs. Role of Blacks in the War,TG Lewis 125.00

WEIRDO
Last Gasp Eco-Funnies March, 1981
1 thru 3 RCr . . . . @10.00

WEIRDO, THE
Rodney Schroeter Oct., 1977
1 B:Rodney Schroezer,1pg 4.50
2 88pgs 4.50
3 44pgs 4.50

WIMMEN'S COMIX
Last Gasp Eco-Funnies Nov., 1972
1 All women artists&comix 10.75
2 thru 3 same . . . . @10.00
4 thru 7 same . . . . @6.75

WONDER WART-HOG AND THE NURDS OF NOVEMBER
Rip Off Press Sept., 1980
1 GiS 15.00

WONDER WART-HOG, CAPTAIN CRUD & OTHER SUPER STUFF
Fawcett Publications 1967
1 GiS,VB 22.00

YELLOW DOG
The Print Mint May, 1968
1 4pgs,RCr 30.00
2 and 3 8pgs,RCr . . . . @25.00
4 8pgs,RCr,SCW 25.00
5 8pgs,RCr,SCW,KDe 25.00
6 thru 12 . . . . @25.00
13/14 52pgs RCr,Jay Lynch 12.00

15 Don Scheneker,editor 59.00
16 . . . . 55.00
17 thru 24 . . . . @15.00

YOUNG AND LUSTLESS
San Francisco Comic Book Co., 1972
1 BG 15.50

YOUNG LUST
Company & Sons Oct., 1970
1 BG,ASp 27.00
2 BG 15.00
3 BG,JsG,RCr,ASp 12.00
4 KDe,BG,SRo 10.50
5 BG,SRo 7.50
6 SRo,KDe 5.50

YOW
Last Gasp April, 1978
1 BG 5.75
2 BG 4.75
Becomes:

ZIPPY
3 BG 6.50

ZAP COMIX
Apex Novelties Oct., 1967
0 RCr 335.00
1 RCr 325.00
2 RCr,SCW 100.00
3 RCr,SCW,VMo,SRo 55.00
4 VMo,RW,RCr,SCW.SRo,GiS . . . 55.00
5 RW,GiS,RCr,SCW,SRo 50.00
6 RW,GiS,RCr,SCW,SRo 25.00
7 RW,GiS,RCr,SCW,SRo 18.50
8 RW,GiS,RCr,SCW,SRo 10.00
9 RW,GiS,RCr,SCW,SRo 12.00

Underground

BIBLIOGRAPHY

Daniels, Les. *Comix: A History of Comic Books in America.* New York, NY: Bonanza Books, 1971.

Gerber, Ernst. *The Photo Journal Guide to Comic Books.* Minden, NV: Gerber Publishing, 1989. Vols. 1 & 2.

Gerber, Ernst. *The Photo Journal Guide to Marvel Comics.* Minden, NV: Gerber Publishing, 1991. Vols. 3 & 4.

Goulart, Ron. *The Adventurous Decade.* New Rochelle, NY: Arlington House, 1975.

Goulart, Ron. *The Encyclopedia of American Comics.* New York, NY. Facts on File Publications, 1990.

Goulart, Ron. *Over 50 Years of American Comic Books.* Lincolnwood, IL: Mallard Press, 1991.

Hegenburger, John. *Collectors Guide to Comic Books.* Radnor, PA: Wallace Homestead Book Company, 1990.

Kennedy, Jay. *The Official Underground and Newave Price Guide.* Cambridge, MA: Boatner Norton Press, 1982.

Malan, Dan. *The Complete Guide to Classics Collectibles.* St. Louis, MO: Malan Classical Enterprises, 1991.

O'Neil, Dennis. *Secret Origins of DC Super Heroes.* New York, NY: Warner Books, 1976.

Overstreet, Robert. *The Overstreet Comic Book Price Guide (28th Edition).* New York, NY. Avon Books, 1998

Rovin, Jeff. *The Encyclopedia of Super Heroes.* New York, NY: Facts on File Publications, 1985.

Rovin, Jeff. *The Encyclopedia of Super Villians.* New York, NY: Facts on File Publications, 1987.

Thompson, Don & Maggie. 7he *Golden Age of Comics, Summer 1982.* Tainpa, FL: New Media Publishing, 1982.

CVA GRADING GUIDE

Grading comics is an objective art. This grading guide outlines the many conditions you should look for when purchasing comics, from the highest grade and top condition to the lowest collectible grade and condition. Your own comics will fall into one of these categories. A more complete description and our comments on comics grades can be found inside. We would like to point out, however, that no reader or advertiser is required to follow this or any other standard. All prices in Comics Values Annual are for comics in Near Mint condition. Happy collecting!

Mint: Perfect, pristine, devoid of any trace of wear or printing or handling flaws. Covers must be fully lustrous with sharply pointed corners. No color fading. Must be well centered. Many "rack" comics are not "Mint" even when new.

Near Mint: Almost perfect with virtually no wear. No significant printing flaws. Covers must be essentially lustrous with sharp corners. Spine is a tight as new. In older comics, minimal color fading is acceptable, as is slight aging of the paper. Most price guides, including CVA, quote prices in this grade.

Very Fine: Well preserved, still pleasing in appearance. Small signs of wear, most particularly around the staples. Most luster is readily visible. Corners may no longer be sharp, but are not rounded. Typical of a comic read only a few times and then properly stored.

Fine: Clean, presentable, with noticeable signs of wear. Some white may show through enamel around staples, and moderate rounding of corners. No tape or writing damage. Book still lies flat.

Very Good: A well worn reading copy with some minor damage such as creasing, small tears or cover flaking. Some discoloration may be evident, with obvious wear around the staples. Little luster remains, and some rolling of the spine may be seen when comic is laid flat on the table.

Good: A fully intact comic with very heavy wear. Tears, cover creases and flaking, and rolled spine will all be evident. No tape repairs present. Only very scarce or valuable issues are collected in this state.

The adjoining price table shows the prices for the other collectible grades which correspond to any "near mint" price given in this book.

Mint	Near Mint	Very Fine	Fine	Very Good
$6,000	$5,000	$3,500	$2,000	$1,000
4,800	4,000	2,800	1,600	800
3,600	3,000	2,100	1,200	600
2,400	2,000	1,400	800	400
1,800	1,500	1,050	600	300
1,200	1,000	700	400	200
1,080	900	630	360	180
960	800	560	320	160
900	750	525	300	150
840	700	490	280	140
780	650	455	260	130
720	600	420	240	120
660	550	385	220	110
600	500	350	200	100
570	475	332	190	95
540	450	315	180	90
510	425	297	170	85
480	400	280	160	80
450	375	262	150	75
420	350	245	140	70
390	325	227	130	65
360	300	210	120	60
330	275	192	110	55
300	250	175	100	50
270	225	157	90	45
240	200	140	80	40
210	175	122	70	35
180	150	105	60	30
150	125	87	50	25
120	100	70	40	20
114	95	66	38	19
108	90	63	36	18
102	85	59	32	17
96	80	56	32	16
90	75	52	30	15
84	70	49	28	14
78	65	45	26	13
72	60	42	24	12
66	55	38	22	11
60	50	35	2	10
54	45	31	18	9
48	40	28	16	8
42	35	24	14	7
36	30	21	12	6
30	25	17	10	5
24	20	14	8	4
22	18	12	7	4
21	17	11	7	4
18	15	10	6	3
17	14	9	5	3
16	13	9	5	3
15	12	8	5	2
14	11	7	4	2
12	10	7	4	2
11	9	6	4	2
10	8	5	3	1
9	7	5	3	1
7	6	4	3	1
6	5	4	2	1
5	4	3	2	0
4	3	2	1	0
3	2	2	0	0
2	1	0	0	0